CARSWELL

CASES AND MATERIALS ON THE LAW OF TORTS

TENTH EDITION

by

ROBERT M. SOLOMON

Professor Emeritus of Law
Distinguished University Professor
Western University

MITCHELL McINNES

Professor of Law
University of Alberta

ERIKA CHAMBERLAIN

Dean and Professor of Law
Western University

STEPHEN G.A. PITEL

Professor of Law
Western University

THOMSON REUTERS®

A cataloguing record for this publication is available from Library and Archives Canada

ISBN 978-0-7798-9137-5

Printed in the United States by Thomson Reuters

 THOMSON REUTERS®

THOMSON REUTERS CANADA, A DIVISION OF THOMSON REUTERS CANADA LIMITED

One Corporate Plaza
2075 Kennedy Road
Toronto, Ontario
M1T 3V4

Customer Support
1-416-609-3800 (Toronto & International)
1-800-387-5164 (Toll Free Canada & U.S.)
Fax 1-416-298-5082 (Toronto)
Fax 1-877-750-9041 (Toll Free Canada Only)
Email CustomerSupport.LegalTaxCanada@TR.com

This book is dedicated to
the memory of
MYER RALPH SOLOMON

Preface

In writing this book, now in its tenth edition, we have three goals in mind. First, we want to help students understand the principles and policies of Canadian tort law. Second, through the use of notes, questions and problems, we want to challenge students' understanding of the materials and assist them in developing their analytical, critical and organizational skills. The notes and questions also serve as a convenient reference to related cases, articles and scholarly writing from Canada and abroad. Third, by presenting the jurisprudence within a broader intellectual context, we want students to appreciate the legal, social and philosophical issues upon which tort law is currently based and which will likely drive its future development.

Although we have written this book with introductory courses in mind, we have included sufficient detail and nuance to make it also appropriate for advanced courses. To that end, some of the notes, questions and problems are straightforward while others are quite complex. The book addresses every major area of Canadian tort law. It is designed to accommodate a wide variety of academic interests, teaching styles and pedagogical approaches. While topics are presented in a logical sequence, each chapter is capable of standing alone. This allows instructors to teach the chapters in an order which fits their own approach to the subject. We have used cases and materials from across Canada and, where appropriate, from abroad.

Readers familiar with previous editions of this book will notice that many features have been retained. They will also notice some important changes. We have added excerpts from recent Supreme Court of Canada decisions on negligent misrepresentation, reasonable foreseeability, and recovery for psychiatric harm. We have expanded the discussion of tort actions for various types of invasion of privacy, including the use of drones and the non-consensual recording and distribution of intimate images, and have added new sections on the nature of damage in negligence and on losses beyond the scope of the risk. We have also updated the discussion of waivers and exclusion clauses, defamation cases decided pursuant to anti-SLAPP legislation, the illegality defence, nuisance, conspiracy, the unlawful means tort, and *Charter* damages. Finally, throughout the book we have added many recent cases and articles to the notes, included some new review problems and, to keep the book to a manageable length, removed some of the more dated or obscure references.

Most of the changes have been necessitated by judicial developments, as both the Supreme Court of Canada and the provincial appellate courts have remained active in the field of tort law. This edition also analyzes several new decisions from other Commonwealth countries.

The tenth edition was prepared by the founding author, Professor Emeritus Robert Solomon, and by Professors Mitchell McInnes, Erika Chamberlain and Stephen Pitel. Western Law students Winnie Hu, Don Roberto, Lyrica Roche, Armin Sohrevardi, and Andrew Willcox did a fine job collecting and organizing materials, verifying references, and assisting in the editing process. Those of us at Western University thank our Faculty for providing research and administrative support. For the most part we have stated the law as of December 2018 although the production process has allowed for some consideration of developments early in 2019.

Professors Solomon, Chamberlain and Pitel are members of Western University's Tort Law Research Group and they are grateful to their colleagues for raising many tort law issues for discussion and consideration since the previous edition. Suggestions for the eleventh edition are welcome from all users of the book.

We remain grateful to Carswell, our publisher, for its support and encouragement. In particular, we would like to thank Melissa Vieira and Patti Bayley-Thompson for supervising the preparation of this edition.

Table of Contents

CHAPTER 1   AN INTRODUCTION TO THE LAW OF TORTS 1
1. **Tort Law Defined** 1
    Notes 2
2. **Tort and Contract** 3
    Notes 5
    Review Problem 5
3. **A Brief History of Tort Law** 6
    Notes 8
4. **Trespass and Case: A Brief Review of the Case Law** 9
    Scott v. Shepherd 9
    Notes and Questions 12
    Leame v. Bray 13
    Williams v. Holland 13
    Notes and Questions 14
    Holmes v. Mather 14
    Notes and Questions 16
    Cook v. Lewis 16
    Notes and Questions 17
5. **The Bases for Imposing Liability in Tort** 18
    (a) Absolute Liability 18
    (b) Strict Liability 18
    (c) Negligence 19
    (d) Intention 19
    (e) No Liability 19
6. **The Functions of Tort Law** 20
    (a) Compensation 21
    (b) Appeasement and Vindication 21
    (c) Punishment 22
    (d) Deterrence 22
    (e) Market Deterrence 22
    (f) Justice 23
    Notes and Questions 23
7. **The Rights Theory of Tort Law** 25
    Notes and Questions 27

CHAPTER 2   THE BASIC CONCEPTS OF REMEDIES IN
INTENTIONAL TORTS 29
1. **Introduction** 29
2. **Judicial and Extrajudicial Remedies** 29
    Notes 30
3. **Classifications of Damages** 31
    Note 32
4. **Nominal Damages** 32
    The Mediana 32
    Notes and Questions 33
5. **Compensatory Damages** 34

    (a) Assessing Damages for Pecuniary Losses 34
    The Mediana... 34
    Notes and Questions... 35
    (b) Assessing Damages for Non-Pecuniary Losses 36
    Review Problem... 36
  6. **Aggravated Damages**... 37
    Notes and Questions... 37
  7. **Punitive Damages**.. 38
    Notes and Questions... 39
    B.(P.) v. B.(W.) 39
    Notes and Questions... 41
    (a) The Principles in *Whiten v. Pilot* 43
    Notes and Questions... 44
  8. **Disgorgement Damages** 45
    (a) True Restitution for Unjust Enrichment 46
    (b) "Restitution" for "Unjust Enrichment" 47
    Notes and Questions... 47
    Penarth Dock Engineering Co. Ltd. v. Pounds............... 47
    Notes and Questions... 48
    Review Problem... 49

CHAPTER 3 INTENTIONAL INTERFERENCE WITH THE
    PERSON.. 51
  1. **Introduction** 51
  2. **Basic Principles of Liability** 51
    (a) Volition 51
    Smith v. Stone... 52
    Notes and Questions... 52
    (b) Intent 52
      (i) Imputed (Constructive) Intent........................... 53
      (ii) Transferred Intent.. 53
    Notes and Questions... 53
  3. **Related Issues: Motive, Mistake and Accident** 55
    (a) Motive.. 55
    Notes... 55
      (i) Duress... 55
      Gilbert v. Stone 55
      Notes and Questions... 56
      (ii) Provocation 57
      Miska v. Sivec.. 57
      Notes and Questions... 58
    (b) Mistake 59
    Hodgkinson v. Martin.. 59
    Ranson v. Kitner 60
    Notes and Questions... 60
    (c) Accident 61
    Review Problems 61
    (d) The Liability of Children and Those with a Mental
      Illness 62

Notes and Questions...62
4. **Battery** 63
Notes and Questions...64
Bettel v. Yim...64
Notes and Questions...67
5. **Assault**..70
Notes and Questions...70
Holcombe v. Whitaker..71
Police v. Greaves...72
Notes and Questions...73
Review Problems 75
6. **False Imprisonment** 75
Bird v. Jones 75
Notes and Questions...77
(a) False Arrest...78
Campbell v. S.S. Kresge Co...79
Notes and Questions...80
(b) Consensual Restraint...82
Herd v. Weardale Steel, Coal and Coke Co. Ltd. 82
Notes and Questions...84
Review Problem...84
7. **Malicious Prosecution**...84
Nelles v. Ontario 85
Notes and Questions...88
(a) The Tort of Abuse of Process 92
Notes and Questions...93
Review Problem...93
8. **Intentional Infliction of Nervous Shock (Mental
Distress, Psychiatric Harm)** 94
Wilkinson v. Downton..94
Notes and Questions...96
Radovskis v. Tomm 96
Samms v. Eccles...97
Notes and Questions...99
(a) Broadening of Liability..100
Notes and Questions..100
(b) The Innominate Intentional Tort 103
Notes and Questions..103
Review Problems 104
9. **Invasion of Privacy**...105
(a) Introduction 105
Motherwell v. Motherwell...105
Notes and Questions..107
(b) The American Common Law Privacy Actions 108
Notes and Questions..108
(c) Emerging Common Law Privacy Actions in
Canada...109
Notes and Questions..109

(d) Established Common Law Tort Actions in
   Canada 113
Jones v. Tsige 113
Notes and Questions 115
(e) The Statutory Protection of Privacy 117
Notes and Questions 118
(f) The Provincial Privacy Statutes 118
Hollinsworth v. BCTV 118
Notes and Questions 120
Review Problem 121
(g) Breach of Confidence 121
Notes and Questions 122
Review Problem 123
10. **Discrimination** 124
Seneca College of Applied Arts & Technology v.
Bhadauria 124
Notes and Questions 126

CHAPTER 4   INTENTIONAL INTERFERENCE WITH
              CHATTELS 129
1. **Introduction** 129
2. **The Development of the Actions** 129
   (a) Trespass 129
   (b) Detinue 130
   (c) Trover and Conversion 131
   Notes and Questions 133
3. **Trespass to Chattels** 135
   Fouldes v. Willoughby 135
   Notes and Questions 137
4. **Conversion** 139
   (a) General Principles 139
   MacKenzie v. Scotia Lumber Co. 139
   Notes and Questions 141
   Review Problems 148
   (b) Conversion of Cheques and Other Unusual
       Chattels 149
   373409 Alberta Ltd. (Receiver of) v. Bank of
   Montreal 149
   Notes and Questions 152
   (c) Remedies for Conversion 158
   Aitken v. Gardiner 158
   Notes and Questions 160
5. **Detinue** 165
   Gen. & Finance Facilities Ltd. v. Cooks Cars
   (Romford) Ltd. 165
   Aitken v. Gardiner 167
   Notes and Questions 168
6. **Recaption and Replevin** 171
   (a) Recaption 171

(b) Replevin 171
Notes and Questions.. 173
Review Problems 174

CHAPTER 5   INTENTIONAL INTERFERENCE WITH REAL
            PROPERTY.. 177
            1. **Trespass to Land**.. 177
            Entick v. Carrington.. 177
            Turner v. Thorne 177
            Notes and Questions.. 179
            Review Problems 182
            Harrison v. Carswell.. 182
            Notes and Questions.. 186
            2. **Trespass and Nuisance**...................................... 189
            Kerr v. Revelstoke Bldg. Materials Ltd. 190
            Notes and Questions.. 191
            Review Problem... 193
            3. **Trespass to Airspace and Subsoil** 194
            (a) Trespass to Airspace.. 194
            Bernstein v. Skyviews & General Ltd.............................. 194
            Notes and Questions.. 196
            (b) Trespass to Subsoil 197
            Notes and Questions.. 198
            Review Problems 198

CHAPTER 6   THE DEFENCE OF CONSENT 201
            1. **Introduction to the Defences** 201
            2. **General Principles of Consent** 201
            (a) Introduction 201
            Notes and Questions.. 202
            (b) Implied Consent 202
            Wright v. McLean 202
            Notes and Questions.. 204
            (c) Exceeding Consent... 204
            Agar v. Canning 204
            Notes and Questions.. 205
            Review Problems 208
            (d) Competency to Consent.. 208
            3. **Factors Vitiating Consent: Fraud, Mistake, Duress,**
            and Public Policy 209
            (a) Introduction 209
            (b) Fraud (Deceit).. 209
            Notes and Questions.. 210
            Review Problems 212
            (c) Mistake 212
            Notes and Questions.. 212
            Review Problems 213
            (d) Duress (Coercion)... 213
            Latter v. Braddell 213

Notes and Questions.. 216
(e) Public Policy... 217
Notes and Questions.. 218
Review Problems 219
4. **Consent to Criminal or Immoral Acts**............................ 220
Notes and Questions.. 220
5. **Consent to Treatment, Counselling and Care** 222
(a) General Principles of Consent................................ 222
Notes and Questions.. 222
(b) Exceptions to the Common Law Principles of
Consent 223
Marshall v. Curry.. 224
Malette v. Shulman 226
Notes and Questions.. 228
(c) The Burden of Proof and Consent Forms.............. 230
Notes and Questions.. 231
(d) Competency to Consent..................................... 231
(i) Minors.. 231
C. v. Wren 232
Notes and Questions.................................... 234
Review Problem... 235
(ii) Adults 236
Notes and Questions.................................... 236
(e) Substitute Consent to Treatment.......................... 238
Notes and Questions.. 238
(f) Informed Consent: Battery or Negligence? 242
Note 242
Review Problem.. 242
CHAPTER 7 DEFENCES RELATED TO THE PROTECTION OF
PERSON AND PROPERTY 245
1. **Introduction** 245
2. **Self-Defence**.. 245
Wackett v. Calder 245
Notes and Questions.. 247
3. **Defence of Third Parties**...................................... 251
Gambriell v. Caparelli... 251
Notes and Questions.. 253
4. **Discipline** 254
R. v. Dupperon... 254
Notes and Questions.. 256
5. **Defence of Real Property** 259
MacDonald v. Hees.. 259
Notes and Questions.. 261
Bird v. Holbrook 263
Notes and Questions.. 264
6. **Defence and Recaption of Chattels**............................ 264
Notes and Questions.. 265
Review Problem.. 266

7. **Public and Private Necessity** 266
   (a) Public Necessity 266
   Surocco v. Geary 266
   Notes and Questions 268
   (b) Private Necessity 270
   Vincent v. Lake Erie Tpt. Co. 270
   Notes and Questions 273
8. **Apportionment of Fault in Intentional Torts** 274
   Notes and Questions 275
   Review Problems 277

CHAPTER 8   THE DEFENCE OF LEGAL AUTHORITY 279
1. **Introduction** 279
   Notes and Questions 280
2. **The *Canadian Charter of Rights and Freedoms*** 281
   (a) Liability Under Section 24(1) 282
   (b) The Impact of Section 52 on the Defence of
       Legal Authority 283
   Notes and Questions 283
3. **Authority and Privilege to Arrest Without a Warrant** 285
   (a) Introduction 285
   Notes 286
   (b) A Peace Officer's Power to Arrest without a
       Warrant 286
   Notes and Questions 287
   (c) Privilege or Justification Under the
       Criminal Code 288
   Notes and Questions 289
   (d) A Private Citizen's Authority and Privilege to
       Arrest without a Warrant 290
   Notes and Questions 291
4. **Rights and Obligations in the Arrest Process** 294
   (a) Reasons for the Arrest 294
   Koechlin v. Waugh and Hamilton 294
   Notes and Questions 297
   (b) The Use of Reasonable Force 299
   Notes and Questions 299
5. **The Common Law Power to Search Pursuant to a
   Lawful Arrest** 301
   R. v. Caslake 301
   Notes and Questions 303
6. **A Peace Officer's Common Law Power of Entry to
   Search for a Wanted Person** 308
   Eccles v. Bourque 308
   Notes and Questions 311
   Review Problems 314

CHAPTER 9   INTRODUCTION TO THE LAW OF NEGLIGENCE ... 317
1. **Negligence: Defining Terms** 317

2. **The Historical Development of Negligence**.................... 317
    Notes and Questions... 319
3. **The Elements of a Negligence Action** 320
    (a) Introduction 320
        (i) Duty of Care 321
        (ii) The Standard of Care and its Breach............... 321
        (iii) Causation 321
        (iv) Remoteness of Damages 321
        (v) Actual Loss 321
        (vi) Defences 322
    Notes and Questions... 322
    (b) Negligence: A Case Illustration............................ 322
    Dunsmore v. Deshield 323
    Notes and Questions... 325

CHAPTER 10 THE DUTY OF CARE 327
1. **Evolution of the Duty of Care Test** 327
    (a) The Classical Approach 327
    (b) The General Duty of Care Test 328
    M'Alister (or Donoghue) v. Stevenson 328
    Notes and Questions... 332
    (c) The Development of the Modern Law of Duty...... 334
    Notes and Questions... 336
    (d) *Anns* and the Supreme Court of Canada 337
    Cooper v. Hobart 338
    Notes and Questions... 343
    (e) Developments Since *Cooper v. Hobart*................... 345
    Notes and Questions... 348
2. **Reasonable Foreseeability** 349
    (a) Foreseeable Risk of Injury................................... 350
    Moule v. N.B. Elec. Power Comm. 350
    Amos v. N.B. Elec. Power Comm................................. 351
    Rankin (Rankin's Garage & Sales) v. J.J...................... 354
    Notes and Questions... 357
    (b) Foreseeable Plaintiff 359
    Palsgraf v. Long Island Ry. Co................................... 359
    Notes and Questions... 362

CHAPTER 11 SPECIAL DUTIES OF CARE: AFFIRMATIVE
    ACTION.. 367
1. **Introduction to Special Duties of Care** 367
2. **Introduction to Duties of Affirmative Action**.................. 367
    Notes and Questions... 368
3. **The Duty to Rescue**... 370
    Osterlind v. Hill 370
    Notes and Questions... 371
    Matthews v. MacLaren; Horsley v. MacLaren 373
    Notes and Questions... 378
    Good Samaritan Act, 2001 (Ontario) 382

Review Problems 382
4. **The Duty to Control the Conduct of Others** 383
    (a) Liability for the Intoxicated 383
    Crocker v. Sundance Northwest Resorts Ltd. 383
    Notes and Questions.. 387
    (b) Other Duty to Control Situations 393
    Notes and Questions.. 393
    (c) The Duty to Prevent Crime and Protect Others 398
    Jane Doe v. Metropolitan Toronto (Municipality)
    Commissioners of Police 398
    Notes and Questions.. 401
    Review Problems 409
5. **The Duty to Perform Gratuitous Undertakings** 410
    Notes and Questions.. 410
    Smith v. Rae 412
    Zelenko v. Gimbel Bros., Inc. 412
    Soulsby v. Toronto 413
    Notes and Questions.. 414
    Review Problems 416

CHAPTER 12   SPECIAL DUTIES OF CARE: MISCELLANEOUS
              CATEGORIES... 417
1. **Introduction**.. 417
2. **The Duty of Care Owed to Rescuers** 417
    Horsley v. MacLaren... 418
    Notes and Questions.. 422
    Review Problems 427
3. **Duties Owed to the Unborn** 427
    (a) Pre-Conception Wrongs.. 427
    Notes and Questions.. 428
    (b) Wrongful Birth and Wrongful Life 430
    Bovingdon (Litigation Guardian of) v. Hergott 430
    Notes and Questions.. 435
    (c) Wrongful Pregnancy 437
    Notes and Questions.. 439
    (d) Pre-Natal Injuries 442
    Notes and Questions.. 444
4. **Psychiatric Harm** 448
    (a) Introduction 448
    Notes and Questions.. 449
    (b) Commonwealth Developments............................... 451
    Alcock v. Chief Constable of South Yorkshire Police 453
    Notes and Questions.. 458
    (c) The Canadian Position 461
    Saadati v. Moorhead 462
    Notes and Questions.. 467
    Review Problem... 469
5. **A Health Professional's Duty to Inform** 469
    Haughian v. Paine... 470

Notes and Questions... 472
Review Problem... 476
6. **A Manufacturer's and Supplier's Duty to Warn**............ 477
Hollis v. Dow Corning Corp. 477
Notes and Questions... 483
Review Problems 490
7. **Duty of Care Owed by a Barrister** 490
Demarco v. Ungaro 491
Notes and Questions... 493

CHAPTER 13 SPECIAL DUTIES OF CARE: NEGLIGENT
MISREPRESENTATION... 497
1. **Introduction** 497
Notes and Questions... 499
2. **Negligent Misrepresentation Causing Pure Economic**
Loss... 505
Deloitte & Touche v. Livent Inc. 505
Notes and Questions... 518
R. v. Imperial Tobacco Canada Ltd. 521
Notes and Questions... 527
3. **Negligent Misrepresentation and Contract** 527
(a) Concurrent Liability in Tort and Contract............. 528
BG Checo International Ltd. v. B.C. Hydro
& Power Authority 528
Notes and Questions... 534
(b) Pre-Contractual Misrepresentations 535
Queen v. Cognos Inc... 535
Notes and Questions... 539
Review Problem... 541

CHAPTER 14 SPECIAL DUTIES OF CARE: RECOVERY OF PURE
ECONOMIC LOSS IN NEGLIGENCE 543
1. **Introduction** 543
Notes and Questions... 544
2. **New Categories of Pure Economic Loss** 544
Martel Building Ltd. v. Canada 545
Notes and Questions... 549
3. **Negligent Performance of a Service**.............................. 554
B.D.C. Ltd. v. Hofstrand Farms Ltd. 554
James v. British Columbia 556
Notes and Questions... 557
4. **Negligent Supply of Shoddy Goods or Structures**........... 559
Winnipeg Condominium Corp. No. 36 v. Bird
Construction Co. 559
Notes and Questions... 565
Review Problems 570
5. **Relational Economic Loss**.. 572
Bow Valley Husky (Bermuda) Ltd. v. Saint John
Shipbuilding Ltd... 572

Notes and Questions 579

CHAPTER 15   THE STANDARD OF CARE 583

1. **Introduction** 583
2. **The Common Law Standard of Care: The Reasonable Person Test** 585
   Arland v. Taylor 585
   Notes and Questions 586
3. **Factors Considered in Determining Breach of the Standard of Care** 588
   (a) Probability and Severity of the Harm 589
   Bolton v. Stone 589
   Paris v. Stepney Borough Council 591
   Notes and Questions 594
   (b) Cost of Risk Avoidance 596
   Vaughn v. Halifax-Dartmouth Bridge Comm. 596
   Law Estate v. Simice 597
   Notes and Questions 598
   (c) Social Utility 600
   Watt v. Hertfordshire County Council 600
   Notes and Questions 601
4. **An Economic Analysis of the Standard of Care** 602
   United States v. Carroll Towing Co. 602
   Notes and Questions 603
5. **Special Standards of Care** 606
   (a) The Standard of Care Expected of the Disabled 606
   Fiala v. Cechmanek 606
   Notes and Questions 611
   (b) The Standard of Care Expected of Children 613
   Joyal v. Barsby 613
   Notes and Questions 615
   (c) The Standard of Care Expected of Professionals 617
   White v. Turner 617
   Notes and Questions 619
6. **Degrees of Negligence** 625
   Notes and Questions 626
7. **Custom** 627
   ter Neuzen v. Korn 627
   Notes and Questions 630
   Review Problems 633

CHAPTER 16   CAUSATION 635

1. **Introduction** 635
2. **The But-For Test** 636
   Kauffman v. Toronto Transit Commission 636
   Barnett v. Chelsea & Kensington Hospital Management Committee 637
   Notes and Questions 638
3. **Established Exceptions to the But-For Test** 640

(a) The Multiple Negligent Defendants Rule 641
(b) The Learned Intermediary Rule 641
(c) Informed Consent 641
Notes and Questions 642
4. **Recent Attempts to Modify the But-For Test** 643
(a) Materially Increased Risk of Injury Test 643
Snell v. Farrell 644
Notes and Questions 648
(b) Material Contribution to Injury Text 652
Notes and Questions 653
Clements v. Clements 654
Notes and Questions 658
(c) Proportionate Cause and Loss of Chance 659
Notes and Questions 660
Review Problem 661
5. **Multiple Causes** 661
Notes and Questions 662
(a) Independent Insufficient Causes 664
Athey v. Leonati 664
Nowlan v. Brunswick Construction Ltee 667
Notes and Questions 667
(b) Independent Sufficient Causes 669
Lambton v. Mellish 669
Notes and Questions 670
Review Problems 671
6. **Issues in Assessing the Plaintiff's Loss** 671
(a) Successive Causes of Parallel Injury 671
Penner v. Mitchell 672
Notes and Questions 673
(b) Devaluing the Plaintiff's Loss 674
Dillon v. Twin State Gas and Elec. Co. 674
Notes and Questions 675
Review Problems 676

CHAPTER 17   REMOTENESS 679
1. **Introduction** 679
2. **Directness Versus Foreseeability** 680
(a) The Directness Test 680
Notes and Questions 680
(b) The Foreseeability Test 681
The Wagon Mound (No. 1); Overseas Tankship
(U.K.) Ltd. v. Morts Dock & Engineering Co. 681
Notes and Questions 683
Review Problems 685
3. **Modifications to the Foreseeability Test** 685
(a) The Kind of Injury 685
Hughes v. Lord Advocate 685
Notes and Questions 687
(b) The Thin-Skulled Plaintiff Rule 689

Smith v. Leech Brain & Co. 689
Marconato v. Franklin 690
Notes and Questions 691
(c) The Possibility of Injury 695
The Wagon Mound (No. 2); Overseas Tankship
(U.K.) Ltd. v. Miller Steamship Co. Pty 695
Notes and Questions 698
Assiniboine South School Division, No. 3 v. Greater
Winnipeg Gas Co. 698
Notes and Questions 701
Mustapha v. Culligan of Canada Ltd. 702
Notes and Questions 704
4. **Intervening Causes** 705
Bradford v. Kanellos 706
Notes and Questions 708
Price v. Milawski 710
Notes and Questions 711
Hewson v. Red Deer 713
Notes and Questions 715
5. **Beyond the Scope of the Risk** 717
Deloitte & Touche v. Livent (Receiver of) 718
Notes and Questions 718
Review Problems 719

CHAPTER 18   THE ASSESSMENT OF DAMAGES 721
1. **Introduction** 721
(a) The Purposes of Damage Awards in Negligence 721
Notes and Questions 722
(b) The Existence of Damage 724
Notes and Questions 725
(c) Preliminary Issues 726
Notes and Questions 727
2. **Damages for Personal Injuries** 731
(a) Introduction 731
Andrews v. Grand & Toy Alberta Ltd. 732
Notes and Questions 733
(b) Pecuniary Loss: Future Care 736
Andrews v. Grand & Toy Alberta Ltd. 736
Notes and Questions 740
(c) Pecuniary Loss: Lost Earning Capacity 743
Andrews v. Grand & Toy Alberta Ltd. 743
Notes and Questions 744
(d) Considerations Relevant to Both Heads of
Pecuniary Loss 749
Andrews v. Grand & Toy Alberta Ltd. 749
Notes and Questions 751
(e) Non-Pecuniary Loss 752
Andrews v. Grand & Toy Alberta Ltd. 752
Notes and Questions 754

(f) Other Categories of Loss 757
3. **Survival of Actions and Dependants' Claims** 758
(a) Survival of Actions 758
Survival of Actions Act (Alberta) 758
Trustee Act (Ontario) 759
(b) Fatal Accidents Legislation 759
Fatal Injuries Act (Nova Scotia) 760
Family Law Act (Ontario) 761
Notes and Questions 761
    (i) The Death of the Family Provider 763
    Keizer v. Hanna 763
    Notes and Questions 767
    (ii) The Death of a Dependant Family Member 768
    Notes and Questions 768
4. **Damages for Property Loss** 770
(a) The Assessment of the Damage to the Property
     Itself 770
(b) The Assessment of Economic Losses Consequent
     on the Damage to the Property 771
(c) The Plaintiff's Obligation to Mitigate 772
Notes and Questions 772
5. **Collateral Benefits** 775
(a) The Doctrine of Subrogation 777
Notes and Questions 777
Review Problems 779

CHAPTER 19   DEFENCES IN NEGLIGENCE 783
1. **Introduction** 783
2. **Contributory Negligence** 783
(a) The Development of the Defence 783
Notes and Questions 784
(b) Conduct Constituting Contributory Negligence 785
Walls v. Mussens Ltd. 785
Notes and Questions 787
Gagnon v. Beaulieu 790
Notes and Questions 793
(c) Apportionment of Loss 794
Negligence Act (Ontario) 794
Notes and Questions 795
Mortimer v. Cameron 798
Notes and Questions 801
Review Problem 803
3. **Voluntary Assumption of Risk** 803
Dube v. Labar 804
Notes and Questions 807
4. **Participation in a Criminal or Immoral Act** 810
Hall v. Hebert 810
Notes and Questions 814
5. **Inevitable Accident** 817

	Rintoul v. X-Ray and Radium Indust. Ltd.	817
	Notes and Questions	819
	Review Problem	820
CHAPTER 20	PROOF OF NEGLIGENCE	821
	1. The Burden of Proof in a Negligence Action	821
	Wakelin v. London & South Western Ry. Co.	822
	Notes and Questions	825
	2. Exceptions to the General Principles Governing the Burden of Proof	827
	(a) Statutes and Shifting Burdens of Proof	827
	MacDonald v. Woodard	827
	Notes and Questions	828
	(b) Directly Caused Injury: Unintended Trespass	829
	Dahlberg v. Naydiuk	829
	Notes and Questions	831
	(c) Multiple Negligent Defendants	831
	Cook v. Lewis	831
	Clements v. Clements	833
	Notes and Questions	834
	3. *Res Ipsa Loquitur*	840
	Fontaine v. British Columbia (Official Administrator)	841
	Notes and Questions	844
	Review Problems	846
CHAPTER 21	THE TORT LIABILITY OF PUBLIC AUTHORITIES	847
	1. Introduction	847
	2. Special Rules for Public Authorities	848
	(a) Legislative and Judicial Functions	848
	Bradley v. Fisher	849
	Notes and Questions	850
	(b) Crown Immunity	854
	Notes and Questions	854
	(c) Limitation Periods and Special Procedures	857
	Notes	857
	3. The Negligence Liability of Public Authorities	858
	(a) Introduction	858
	Just v. British Columbia	859
	Notes and Questions	866
	(b) The Effect of *Cooper v. Hobart*	869
	Notes and Questions	871
	R. v. Imperial Tobacco Canada Ltd.	872
	Notes and Questions	876
	4. Misfeasance in a Public Office	877
	(a) Introduction	877
	Roncarelli v. Duplessis	877
	Notes and Questions	879
	(b) Modern Developments	880

		Odhavji Estate v. Woodhouse	880
		Notes and Questions	887
	5.	**Other Torts**	889
		Notes and Questions	890
		Review Problems	891

CHAPTER 22		STATUTORY PROVISIONS AND TORT LIABILITY	893
	1.	**Introduction**	893
		Note	894
	2.	**Express Statutory Causes of Action**	894
		Trespass to Property Act (Ontario)	894
		Competition Act (Canada)	895
		Notes and Questions	896
		Trachsler v. Halton	896
		Notes and Questions	897
		Review Problem	899
	3.	**The Use of Statutes in Common Law Negligence**	901
		R. in Right of Can. v. Sask. Wheat Pool	901
		Notes and Questions	907
		(a) Breach of Statutory Duty and Common Law Standard of Care	912
		Ryan v. Victoria (City)	912
		Marshall v. Annapolis County School Board	915
		Notes and Questions	917
	4.	**A Note on the *Canadian Charter of Rights and Freedoms***	918
		Canadian Charter of Rights and Freedoms	918
		Notes	921
		Vancouver (City) v. Ward	923
		Notes and Questions	927
		Review Problems	930

CHAPTER 23		OCCUPIERS' LIABILITY	931
	1.	**Introduction**	931
	2.	**The Common Law Principles of Occupiers' Liability**	933
		(a) Who is an Occupier?	933
		Palmer v. St. John	933
		Notes and Questions	935
		(b) Categories of Entrants and Corresponding Duties	936
		(i) Contractual Entrants	936
		Finigan v. Calgary	936
		Notes and Questions	938
		(ii) Invitees and Licensees	939
		McErlean v. Sarel	939
		Notes and Questions	942
		(iii) Trespassers	944
		Veinot v. Kerr-Addison Mines Ltd.	944

Notes and Questions.. 948
3. **The Provincial Occupiers' Liability Statutes**................. 948
  (a) Introduction 948
  (b) Ontario *Occupiers' Liability Act*........................... 949
  Occupiers' Liability Act (Ontario) 949
  Notes and Questions.. 952
  Waldick v. Malcolm 960
  Notes and Questions.. 964
  Review Problem.. 964

CHAPTER 24 NUISANCE.. 967
1. **Introduction** 967
  Note.. 968
2. **Private Nuisance** 968
  *340909 Ont. Ltd. v. Huron Steel Products (Windsor)
  Ltd.* 968
  Notes and Questions.. 972
  *Antrim Truck Centre Ltd. v. Ontario
  (Transportation)* 977
  Notes and Questions.. 982
  Hollywood Silver Fox Farm Ltd. v. Emmett................. 983
  Notes and Questions.. 985
  (a) Defence of Statutory Authority..................... 986
  Tock v. St. John's Metropolitan Area Board 986
  Notes and Questions.. 990
3. **Public Nuisance**.. 994
  A.-G. Ont. v. Orange Productions Ltd....................... 995
  Hickey v. Electricity Reduction Co. 997
  Notes and Questions.. 999
4. **Remedies**.. 1002
  Mendez v. Palazzi 1002
  Notes and Questions.. 1004
  Miller v. Jackson.. 1005
  Notes and Questions.. 1010
  *Spur Industries Inc. v. Del E. Webb
  Development Co.* 1011
  Notes and Questions.. 1013
  Review Problem.. 1017

CHAPTER 25 STRICT AND VICARIOUS LIABILITY..................... 1019
1. **Introduction** 1019
  (a) Strict Liability 1019
  (b) Vicarious Liability 1020
  Notes and Questions.. 1020
2. **Strict Liability for Escape of Dangerous Substances:**
  Rylands v. Fletcher.. 1021
  (a) Introduction 1021
  Rylands v. Fletcher.. 1021
  Notes and Questions.. 1023

(b) Escape 1026
Read v. J. Lyons & Co. 1026
Notes and Questions.. 1029
(c) Non-Natural Use.. 1030
Gertsen v. Municipality of Metropolitan Toronto 1030
Notes and Questions.. 1032
(d) Defences to the Rule in *Rylands v. Fletcher*.......... 1033
     (i) Consent 1033
     (ii) Common Benefit.............................. 1033
     (iii) Default of the Plaintiff................... 1034
     (iv) Act of God................................. 1034
     (v) Act of a Stranger......................... 1034
     (vi) Statutory Authority 1034
(e) Comparative Perspectives on
     Rylands v. Fletcher 1035
Notes and Questions.. 1037
3. **Strict Liability for Animals**...................................... 1037
(a) Dangerous Animals 1038
Cowles v. Balac.. 1038
Notes and Questions.. 1042
(b) Cattle Trespass 1047
Acker v. Kerr 1047
Notes and Questions.. 1048
4. **Products Liability: Negligence or Strict Liability?**........ 1049
Notes and Questions.. 1050
5. **Vicarious Liability**.. 1051
(a) Statutory Vicarious Liability............................... 1051
Notes and Questions.. 1052
(b) Principal-Agent Relationship 1054
T.G. Bright & Co. v. Kerr 1054
Notes and Questions.. 1055
(c) Master-Servant Relationship............................ 1057
Bazley v. Curry 1058
Notes and Questions.. 1064
(d) Independent Contractors 1073
671122 Ontario Ltd. v. Sagaz Industries Canada Inc.. .. 1073
Notes and Questions.. 1079
(e) Non-Delegable Duties.................................... 1080
Notes and Questions.. 1082
Review Problem... 1084

CHAPTER 26   BUSINESS TORTS.. 1087
1. **Introduction** 1087
2. **Deceit (Fraud)**... 1088
Derry v. Peek.. 1088
Bruno Appliance and Furniture Inc. v. Hryniak 1091
Notes and Questions.. 1093
3. **Passing Off**.. 1100
Ciba-Geigy Canada Ltd. v. Apotex Inc..................... 1100

Notes and Questions... 1104
4. **Intimidation** 1109
Central Can. Potash v. Govt. of Sask......................... 1110
Notes and Questions... 1112
5. **Conspiracy** 1114
Posluns v. Toronto Stock Exchange 1115
Notes and Questions... 1116
6. **Interference with Contractual Relations**...................... 1124
Lumley v. Gye.. 1125
Notes and Questions... 1127
7. **The Unlawful Means Tort** 1133
A.I. Enterprises Ltd. v. Bram Enterprises Ltd.............. 1134
Notes and Questions... 1141
Review Problem... 1145

CHAPTER 27 DEFAMATION.. 1147
1. **Introduction** 1147
Notes and Questions... 1148
2. **Elements of a Defamation Action**.............................. 1151
(a) Defamatory Material 1151
Sim v. Stretch 1152
Notes and Questions... 1154
(b) Reference to the Plaintiff.................................... 1158
Knuppfer v. London Express Newspaper, Ltd. 1158
Notes and Questions... 1159
(c) Publication 1160
Notes and Questions... 1161
3. **Defences** 1164
(a) Justification 1164
Williams v. Reason... 1165
Notes and Questions... 1167
(b) Absolute Privilege.. 1168
    (i) Executive Officers....................................... 1169
    Dowson v. The Queen.................................... 1169
    (ii) Parliamentary Privilege 1172
    (iii) Judicial Proceedings.................................... 1172
    Hung v. Gardiner... 1172
    Notes and Questions....................................... 1176
(c) Qualified Privilege 1178
Hill v. Church of Scientology 1180
Notes and Questions... 1184
(d) Fair Comment... 1185
WIC Radio Ltd. v. Simpson.................................. 1186
Notes and Questions... 1195
(e) Responsible Communication on Matters of
    Public Interest 1198
Grant v. Torstar Corp. 1199
Notes and Questions... 1208
(f) Consent.. 1209

Jones v. Brooks 1209
Notes and Questions... 1211
4. **Remedies**.. 1212
   (a) Injunction.. 1212
   (b) Damages.. 1213
Hill v. Church of Scientology 1213
Notes and Questions... 1222
Review Question.. 1223

CHAPTER 28   TORT LAW: THEORIES, CRITICISMS AND
ALTERNATIVES 1225
1. **Introduction**.. 1225
2. **Theoretical Criticism of Tort Law**............................ 1225
   (a) Introduction 1225
Notes... 1226
   (b) Deterrence 1226
Notes and Questions... 1228
   (c) Compensation.. 1230
Notes and Questions... 1232
   (d) Theories of Tort Law Based on Concepts of
Justice 1233
Notes and Questions... 1236
   (e) Feminist Perspectives 1240
Notes and Questions... 1241
3. **The No-Fault Alternatives** 1243
   (a) Introduction 1243
   (b) No-Fault Accident Compensation in New
Zealand 1244
Notes and Questions... 1245
   (c) Workers' Compensation... 1248
Notes and Questions... 1248
   (d) No-Fault Automobile Insurance in Canada 1249
Notes and Questions... 1250
Review Problem... 1253

Table of Cases

1043 Bloor Street Inc. v. Vilhena   501
10565 Nfld. Inc. v. Canada (Attorney
General)   1024
1083994 Ontario Inc. v. Kotsopoulos   143
1316223 Ontario Inc. (c.o.b. 1,000,000
Comix) v. Giancoulas   173
1318777 Ontario Ltd. v. 1004847 Ontario
Inc.   1094
1522491 Ontario Inc. v. Stewart, Esten
Professional Corporation   1177
1631370 Ontario Inc. v. 805352 Ontario
Inc.   986
1670002 Ontario Ltd. (c.o.b. Canadian
Professional Recruiters) v. Redtree
Contract Carriers Ltd.   1127
1688782 Ontario Inc. v. Maple Leaf Foods
Inc.   348, 552
1694879 Ontario Inc. v. Krilavicius   143
1704604 Ontario Ltd. v. Pointes Protection
Association   1150
1746646 Alberta Inc. v. Aman Carrier
Ltd.   1072
2105582 Ontario Ltd. (c.o.b. Performance
Plus Golf Academy) v. 375445 Ontario
Ltd. (c.o.b. Hydeaway Golf Club)   164
2105582 Ontario Ltd. v. 375445 Ontario
Ltd.   143
2249659 Ontario Ltd. v. Sparkasse
Siegen   539
270233 Ontario Ltd. v. Weall & Cullen
Nurseries Ltd.   977
321665 Alberta Ltd. v. Mobil Oil Canada
Ltd.   1122
**340909 Ont. Ltd. v. Huron Steel Products
(Windsor) Ltd.   968**
3464920 Canada Ltd. v. Strother   1069
347671 B.C. Ltd. v. Heenan Blaikie   500
369413 Alberta Ltd. v. Pocklington   1127,
1131
**373409 Alberta Ltd. (Receiver of) v. Bank
of Montreal   149**, 153
384238 Ontario Ltd. v. The Queen in Right
of Can.   137
4 Eng Ltd. v. Harper   1097
410784 Ontario Ltd. v. Little Zinger Inc.
(c.o.b. Corktown Esso)   1128
469238 B.C. Ltd. (c.o.b. Lawrence Heights)
v. Okanagan Aggregates Ltd. (c.o.b.
Motoplex Speedway and Event
Park)   1004

495793 Ontario Ltd. (Central Auto Parts)
v. Barclay   624, 625
644036 Alberta Ltd. v. 625494 Alberta
Ltd.   622
66295 Manitoba Ltd. v. Imperial Oil
Ltd.   568
**671122 Ontario Ltd. v. Sagaz Industries
Canada Inc.   1073**, 1119
783783 Alberta Ltd. v. Canada (Attorney
General)   348
790668 Ontario Inc. v. D'Andrea
Management Inc.   1118
A (A Minor) v. A Health & Social Services
Trust   429
A. & B. Sound Ltd. v. Future Shop
Ltd.   1132, 1142
A.(D.A.) v. B.(D.K.)   38
A.C. v. Manitoba (Director of Child and
Family Services)   234
A.C.B. v. Thomson Medical Pte. Ltd.   430
A.G. B.C. v. Couillard   1000
A.G. Can. v. Diamond Waterproofing Ltd;
Pillar Const. v. Defence Const. (1951)
Ltd.   1033
A.G. Man. v. Adventure Flights Centre
Ltd.   1000
A.G. Man. v. Campbell   196, 985
A.G. N.S. v. Beaver   999, 1004
A.G. Ont. v. Fatehi   774
A.G. Ont. v. Keller   787, 828
**A.-G. Ont. v. Orange Productions
Ltd.   995**
A.-G. v. Bastow   997
A.-G. v. Cole & Son   995
A.-G. v. Corke   995
A.G. v. Nissan   269
A.-G. v. P.Y.A. Quarries, Ltd.   995
A.-G. v. Stone   995
**A.I. Enterprises Ltd. v. Bram Enterprises
Ltd.**   1130, **1134**
A.J.W. v. B.W.   1184
A.K. v. Kennedy   218
A.L. v. Ontario (Minister of Community
and Social Services)   868
A.M., R. v.   308
A.T.-B. v. Mah   755, 756
A.U.P.E. v. Edmonton Sun   1159
Abbott (Next Friend of) v. Jarocki   208
Abbott v. Gerges   674
Abbott v. Kasza   716

ABC v. Whillock 103
Abel v. McDonald 1094
Abel, R. v. 292
Abraham v. The Advocate Co. 1159
Abramowitz v. Lee 1097
Aces System Development v. Yenty Lily 170
Acker v. Kerr 1047
Ackerman v. Wascana Centre Authority 943
Ackley v. Audette 785
Adair (Litigation Administrator of) v. Hamilton Health Sciences Corp. 620
Adam v. Ward 1178, 1180
Adamiec, R. v. 204
Adams v. Borrel 344, 867
Adams v. Taylor 621
Adan v. Davis 231
Adventure Tours Inc. v. St. John's Port Authority 887
Agar v. Canning 204, 205
Agar v. Weber 952
Agouman v. Leigh Day 535, 695
Agribrands Purina Canada Inc. v. Kasamekas 1119
Agricultural Development Corp. of Saskatchewan v. Vigro Seed & Supply Ltd. 173
Ahmed v. Stefaniu 63, 394
Ahmed-Kadir, R. v. 307
Air Canada v. M & L Travel Ltd. 1124
Air Canada v. West Jet 143
Air Nova v. Messier-Dowty Ltd. 809
Airedale Hospital Trustees v. Bland 369
Aitken v. Gardiner 158, 167
Aitkin Agencies Ltd. v. Richardson 148
Akeelah v. Clow 674
Akenzua v. Secretary of State for the Home Department 403, 889
Alaffe v. Kennedy 768
Al-Amiri, R. v. 312
Albarquez v. Ontario 344
Albert v. Lavin 249, 298
Alberta (Minister of Public Works, Supply and Services) v. Nilsson 883
Alberta Wheat Pool v. Northwest Pile Driving Ltd. 798
Alcan Gove Pty Ltd v. Zabic 651, 724
Alcoa Minerals of Jamaica v. Broderick 693
Alcock v. Chief Constable of South Yorkshire Police 341, **453**
Alcorn v. Mitchell 64

Aldana v. March 620
Aldridge v. Van Patter 1023, 1029
Aleksic v. Canada (Attorney General) 856
Alexander, R. v. 52
Alexandrou v. Oxford 403
Alexson (T.L.), R. v. 313
Alfarano v. Regina 1032
Allan v. Saskatoon 898
Allarco Entertainment 2008 Inc. v. Rogers Communications Inc. 908
Allard v. Manahan 487
Allen (Next friend of) v. University Hospitals Board 584
Allen v. Chadwick 807
Allen v. Flood 20, 1087, 1088, 1112, 1114, 1118, 1127
Allen v. Head (C.) Ltd. 80
Allen v. Hounga 222
Allen v. Lucas 807
Allenby v. H 1246
Alleslev-Krofchak v. Valcom Ltd. 1130, 1139, 1142
Alliance & Leicester Building Society v. Edgestop Ltd. 789
Allis-Chalmers, Rumely Ltd. v. Forbes Equipment Ltd. 173
Allison v. Rank City Wall Can. Ltd. 406, 935, 958
Allsop v. Allsop 95, 96
All-Up Consulting Enterprises Inc. v. Dalrymple 504
Al's Steak House & Tavern Inc. v. Deloitte & Touche 853
Alton v. Lower Mainland Motocross Club 810
Amaca Pty Limited v. Latz; Latz v Amaca Pty Limited 746
Amar Cloth House Ltd. v. LA Van & Co. 694
Amato v. Walsh 1177
Amertek Inc. v. Canadian Commercial Inc. 1098
Amin (Litigation Guardian of) v. Klironomos 485
Amos v. N.B. Elec. Power Comm. 351
Anderson v. Excel Collection Services Ltd. 449
Anderson v. Greene 620
Anderson v. Lawrence 539
Anderson v. Ottawa (City) 127
Anderson v. Queen Elizabeth II Health Sciences Centre 473, 620

Anderson v. Skender 192
Anderson v. Wilson 449, 450
Andre Gravelle v. Ontario 90
Andrews v. Grand & Toy Alberta Ltd.
  36, 729, 731, **732**, **736**, **743**, **749**, **752**, 766,
  1214
Andrews v. R A. Douglas 973
Angelopoulos v. Machen 828
Angerer v. Cuthbert 192, 1004
Angers v. Mutual Reserve Fund Life
  Assn. 1092
Angle v. LaPierre 1184
Anglehart v. Canada 888
Annand v. The Merchant's Bank 148
Anns v. Merton London Borough
  Council 334, 506, 522, 546, 554, 574,
  811, 862, 864, 865, 866, 867
Antell v. Simons 688
Antrim Truck Centre Ltd. v. Ontario
  (Transportation) 192, **977**
Apex Mountain Resort Ltd. v. British
  Columbia 520
Apotex Inc. v. Canada 889
Arce (Guardian ad litem of) v. Simon
  Fraser Health Region 740
Archer v. Brown 1099
Argyll v. Argyll 122
Ari v. Insurance Corp. of British
  Columbia 910
Ari v. Insurance Corporation of British
  Columbia 120
Arif v. Li 960
Aristorenas v. Comcare Health Services
  621
Arkwright v. Newbould 1089
Arland v. Taylor 585
Armak Chemicals Ltd. v. Canadian
  National Railway Co. 774
Armes v. Nottinghamshire County
  Council 1072
Armory v. Delamirie 147, 163
Armstrong v. Langley (City) 999
Arnault v. Prince Albert (City) Police
  Commissioners 1043
Arndt v. Ruskin Slo Pitch Assn. 809
Arndt v. Smith 436, 475, 642
Arneil v. Paterson 668
Arnold v. Cartwright Estate 460
Arnold v. Teno 731, 745, 766, 1214, 1232
Arnott v. College of Physicians and
  Surgeons (Sask) 1159
Arora v. Whirlpool Canada LP 566, 569
Arsenovski v. Bodin 42

Arthur J.S. Hall & Co. v. Simons 491,
  494
Arthur v. Anker 263
Asamera Oil Corp. v. Sea Oil & Gen.
  Corp. 162
Asante-Mensah, R. v. 189, 249, 299
Ashby v. White 124, 126, 877, 881, 909,
  998
Ashcroft v. Dhaliwal 779
Ashland Dry Goods Co. v. Wages 82
Ashley v. Chief Constable of Sussex
  Police 64, 250
Assiniboine South School Division, No. 3 v.
  Greater Winnipeg Gas Co. 698
Astley v. Verdun 1212
Atcheson v. College of Physicians and
  Surgeons (Alta.) 1132
Athans v. Canadian Adventure Camps
  117, 1108
Athey v. Leonati 652, **664**, 674, 693, 712,
  728, 730
Atkinson v. Newcastle & Gateshead
  Waterworks Co. 902
Atlantic Aviation Ltd. v. N.S. Light &
  Power Co. 194
Atlantic Leasing Ltd. v. Newfoundland
  867
Atlantic Lottery Corporation Inc.-Société
  des lotteries de l'Atlantique v. Babstock
  726
Attis v. Canada (Minister of Health) 344,
  489
Attorney General v. Blake 47
Attorney General v. Guardian Newspapers
  (No. 2) 45
Attwells & Anor v. Jackson Lalic Lawyers
  Pty Ltd 494
Aubry v. Éditions Vice-Versa 113
Augustine v. Lopes 474
Augustus v. Gosset 724
Ault v. Canada (Attorney General) 504
Austin v. 3M Canada Ltd. 484, 488
Austin v. Dowling 81
Austin v. Lynch 1157
Austin v. Rescon Construction (1984)
  Ltd. 197
Authorson v. Canada 856
Auto Concrete Curb Ltd. v. South Nation
  River Conservation Authority 502, 623
Auton (Guardian ad litem of) v. British
  Columbia (Attorney General) 599
Avco Financial Services Realty Ltd. v.
  Norman 503, 789

Avender v. Western Canadian Timber
Products Ltd. 181
AvePoint Inc. v. Power Tools Inc. 1156
Awan v. Levant 1196, 1223
AXA Insurance Singapore Pte. Ltd. v.
Chandran s/o Natesan 107
Ayana v. Skin Klinic 620
Ayangma v. Prince Edward Island 127
B. Cusano Contracting Inc. v. Bank of
Montreal 520
B.(A.) v. J.(I.) 41
B.(D.) v. Children's Aid Society of Durham
(Region) 407, 624
B.(D.C.) v. Arkin 63
B.(E.) v. Order of the Oblates of Mary
Immaculate in the Province of British
Columbia 1068
B.(K.), R. v. 207
B.(K.L.) v. British Columbia 1067, 1083
B.(M.) v. British Columbia 1067
B.(P.) v. B.(W.) 39
B.(R.) v. Children's Aid Society of
Metropolitan Toronto 235
B.(T.B.), R. v. 207
B.C. Elec. Ry. Co. v. Loach 784
B.C. Electric Ry. Co. v. Clarke 728
B.D.C. Ltd. v. Hofstrand Farms Ltd. 337,
554
B.M. (Litigation Guardian of) v. R.M.
624
B.M. v. British Columbia (Attorney
General) 401
B.P.B. v. M.M.B. 668
B.S.A. Investors Ltd. v. DSB 653
Babcock v. Carr; Babcock v. Archibald
1132
Babiuk v. Trann 253
Bachalo v. Robson 728
Badenach v. Calvert 558
Bafaro v. Dowd 584
Baglow v. Smith 1156
Bagnell v. Taser International, Inc. 871
Bain v. Black & Decker Canada (1989)
Inc. 450, 704
Bain v. Calgary Board of Education 395
Baird v. British Columbia 133
Bajkov v. Canil 616, 788
Baker Estate v. Poucette 768
Baker v. Bolton 759
Baker v. Market Harborough; Wallace v.
Richards 836
Baker v. Quantum Clothing Group Ltd.
589, 632

Baker v. Willoughby 672
Baldwin v. Daubney 520, 521
Balkos v. Cook 762
Ball v. Imperial Oil Limited 649
Ball v. Manthorpe 262
Ballina Shire Council v. Ringland 1203
Balmain Hotel Group L.P. v. 1547648
Ontario Ltd. 1011
Banerjee v. K Mart Canada Ltd. 291
Banfai v. Formula Fun Centre Inc. 1004
Bank of British Columbia v. Canadian
Broadcasting Corporation 1167
Bank of Montreal v. Tortora 1119
Bank of N.S. v. Gaudreau 1132
Bank of Nova Scotia v. Black River
Logging Inc. 1131
Bank of Nova Scotia v. Gaudreau 1127
Banks v. Bliefernich 91
Banks v. Globe & Mail Ltd. 1179
Bannister, R. v. 588
Bannon v. Thunder Bay (City) 584, 858
Banyasz v. K Mart Canada Ltd. 292
Baptiste, R. v. 256
Barber v. Vrozos 1142
Barclay v. Penberthy 581, 759
Barker v. Barker 63
Barker v. Corus (UK) plc 650
Barker v. Montfort Hospital 621, 653
Barkway v. South Wales Transport Co.
840
Barltrop v. Canadian Broadcasting
Corp. 1189
Barnard v. Carnegie 358
Barnes v. Carter 1159
Barnett v. Chelsea & Kensington Hospital
Management Committee 414, **637**
Barnett v. Collection Service Co. 98
Barratt v. District of North Vancouver
860, 866
Barreiro v. Arana 1054
Barrett v. Enfield London Borough
Council 874
Barrett v. Ministry of Defence 390
Barrick Gold Corp. v. Lopehandia 1212,
1222
Barron v. Barron 820
Bartin Pipe & Piling Supply Ltd. v. Epscan
Industries Ltd. 145
Bartlett et al. v. Weiche Apartments Ltd.
940
Bartlett v. Children's Hospital Corp. 840
Bartlett v. Corner Brook (City) 993

Barton v. Nova Scotia (Attorney General) 625

Barton v. Weaver 835

Bartoszek v. Ontario (Consent and Capacity Board) 237

Bérubé v. Ontario Court of Justice 852

Barwin v. IKO Industries Ltd. 567

Basra v. Gill 820

Bastien v. Ottawa Hospital (General Campus) 449

Bateman v. Doiron 598

Battrum v. British Columbia 223

Baud Corp., N.V. v. Brook 169

Bauder v. Wilson 283

Baumeister v. Drake 389

Baurose v. Hart 729

Baxter & Co. v. Jones 410, 411, 414

Bazley v. Curry 1057, **1058**, 1073

BBMB Finance (Hong Kong) Ltd. v. Eda Holdings Ltd. 162

BC Civil Liberties Association v. University of Victoria 187

Beare, R. v.; R. v. Higgins 301

Beatty v. Waterloo (Regional Municipality) 967

Beaudesert Shire Council v. Smith 104

Beaulieu c. Bourgouin 81

Beaulieu v. Sutherland 449

Beaulne v. Ricketts 1096

Beausoleil v. Soeurs de la Charité de la Providence 237

Bechard v. Haliburton Estate 362, 460

Beck Estate v. Johnston, Meier Insurance Agencies Ltd. 623

Beckford v. R. 249

Bedard (Next Friend of) v. Martyn 779

Beebe v. Robb 519

Beecham v. Henderson 663

Beecham v. Hughes 449

Behrens v. Bertram Mills Circus 1043

Beldycki Estate v. Jaipargas 660

Beljanski (Guardian ad litem of) v. Smithwick 767, 815

Belknap v. Meakes 648

Bell Canada v. Cope (Sarnia) Ltd. 275, 796, 831

Bell Telephone Co. v. The Mar-Tirenno 270

Bellan v. Curtis 889

Bellini Custom Cabinetry Ltd. v. Delight Textiles Ltd. 188, 197, 208

Belyea v. Hammond 757

Belzile v. Dumais 689, 701

Benarr v. Kettering Health Authority 440

Benavides v. Insurance Corp. of British Columbia 846

Benhaim v. St-Germain 639, 648, 660, 826, 835

Bennett v. Kailua Estates Ltd. 964

Bennett v. Stupich 1157

Benning v. Wong 1035

Benoit v. Farrell Estate 867

Benstead v. Murphy 746

Bentley (Litigation Guardian of) v. Maplewood Seniors Care Society 237, 241

Berardinelli v. Ontario Housing Corp. 858

Berendsen v. Ontario 596, 858

Berezowski v. Edmonton 899

Bergauer-Free, R. v. 304

Bergen v. Guliker 300, 624

Bergen v. Guliker Estate 602

Berkoff v. Burchill 1157

Bernard v. Attorney General of Jamaica 1073

Bernstein v. Poon 1157

Bernstein v. Skyviews & General Ltd. **194**

Bernstein v. Stoytcheva-Todorova 92

Berntt v. Vancouver (City) 275, 300, 301, 796

Berry v. Pulley 1119, 1121

Berthiaume c. Cinéma Guzzo inc. (Cinéma Méga-plex Marché central 18) 284

Bertuzzi, R. v. 206

Beshada v. Johns-Manville Products Corp. 486

Bessell v. Wilson 304

Best v. Weatherall 1155

Bettel v. Yim 64

Better v. Williams 499

Betts v. Sanderson Estate 392, 807

Beutler v. Beutler, Adams v. Beutler 400

Bevilacqua v. Altenkirk 440

Beyond Bears Inc. v. Woodley 164

Bezusko v. Waterfall 473

BG Checo International Ltd. v. B.C. Hydro and Power Authority 528, 536, 537

BGM Holdings Ltd. (c.o.b. Birchwood Chevrolet Buick GMC) v. Jim Gauthier Chev Cadillac Ltd. (c.o.b. Jim Gauthier Chevrolet Cadillac) 1108

Bianco v. Fromow 770

Bici v. Ministry of Defence 54

Bielitski v. Obadiak 54, 96

Biffa Waste Services Ltd. v.
  Maschinenfabrik Ernst Hese GmbH
  1080
Bifolchi v. Sherar   747
Big Point Club v. Lozon   197
Bigcharles v. Dawson Creek & District
  Health Care Society   649
Bigcharles v. Merkel   262
Bigstone v. St. Pierre   120
Bijeau v. Pelletier   415
Bingley v. Morrison Fuels   595, 599
Birch Builders v. Esquimalt (Township)
  851
Birchard v. Alberta Securities
  Commission   496
Bird v. Fort Francis   133
Bird v. Holbrook   263
Bird v. Jones   75, 103
Biron, R. v.   287, 291
Bisoukis v. Brampton (City)   857
Bitton v. Jakovljevic   1098
Bjornson v. McDonald   770
Black v. Chrétien   855
Black v. New York, New Haven &
  Hartford Railroad   370
Blacklaws v. 470433 Alberta Ltd.   552
Blackwater v. Plint   41, 69, 668, 693, 797,
  1066, 1068, 1083
Blackwood v. Butler   819
Blades v. Higgs   265
Blair, R. v.   262
Blair's Plumbing & Heating Ltd. v.
  McGraw   773
Blake v. Attorney General   1133
Blake v. Barnard   73
Blake v. Kensche   935
Blanco-Arriba v. British Columbia   127
Blatz v. Impact Energy Inc.   1025
Blessing v. United States   861
Bliss v. Hall   1008
Block v. Martin   712
Bloor Italian Gifts Ltd. v. Dixon   623
Blyh v. Fladgate   1055
Blyth v. Birmingham Waterworks Co.
  585, 590
Bocardo SA v. Star Energy UK Onshore
  Ltd.   198
Bodley v. Reynolds   160
Body Corporate No. 207624 (Spencer on
  Byron) v. North Shore City Council
  569
Boehringer v. Montalto   198
Bogoroch v. Toronto (City)   953

Bogue, R. v.   249
Bohn, R. v.   298
Bohun v. Sennewald   653
Bolam v. Friern Hospital Management
  Committee   632
Boland v. Globe and Mail Ltd.   1197
Bolduc and Bird v. R.   210
Bollinger v. Costa Brava Wine Co.   1107
Bollman v. Soenen   475, 476
Bolton v. Forest Pest Management
  Institute   1000, 1004
Bolton v. Stone   589, 696, 697
Boma Manufacturing Ltd. v. C.I.B.C.
  796
Boma Manufacturing Ltd. v. Canadian
  Imperial Bank of Commerce   150, 153,
  275
Boma Manufacturing, Teva Canada Ltd. v.
  TD Canada Trust   153, 155
Bongiardina v. York (Regional
  Municipality)   953
Bongiardina v. York Regional
  Municipality   943
Bonham v. Pure Water Association   1157
Boomer v. Atlantic Cement Co.   1014
Boomer v. Penn   612
Boomhour v. Durham (Regional
  Municipality) Police Service   625
Boon v. Mann   640, 659, 660
Booth et al. v. St. Catharines et al.   714
Booth v. B.C.T.V. Broadcasting Systems
  1159
Booyink, R. v.   187
Borden Chemical Co. (Canada) v. J.G.
  Beukers Ltd.   163
Border Enterprises Ltd. v. Beazer East
  Inc.   93, 501
Bosard v. Davey   474
Boss v. Robert Simpson Eastern Ltd.   712
Botiuk v. Toronto Free Press Publications
  Ltd.   1155, 1162, 1184
Bottom v. Ont. Leaf Tobacco Co.   1014
Bottomley v. Todmorden Cricket Club
  1080
Bou Malhab v. Diffusion Metromedia
  CMR Inc.   1159
Bouchard Estate v. Chalifoux   829
Boucher v. Wal-Mart Canada Corp.   43,
  44, 102
Boudreau v. Bank of Montreal   411
Boudreau v. Benaiah   468, 494
Boulay v. Charbonneau   620
Boulay v. Rousselle   784

Boulet c. Entreprises M. Canada (Abitibi) Ltée   261

Bourden v. Alloway   11

Bourgoin v. Leamington (Municipality)   713

Bourgoin v. Ministry of Agriculture, Fisheries and Food   889

Bourhill v. Young   454, 464

Boutcher v. Stewart   820

Boutin v. Boutin   180

Bovingdon (Litigation Guardian of) v. Hergott   430, 473, 742

Bow Valley Husky (Bermuda) Ltd. v. Saint John Shipbuilding Ltd.   341, 487, 506, 522, **572**, 784, 797

Bowen Contracting Ltd. v. B.C. Log Spill Recovery Co-operative Assn.   33

Bowes v. Edmonton (City)   867

Bowles v. Wilton   1045

Boyachyk v. Dukes   1174

Boychuk v. Northwest Territories Housing Corp.   1114

Boyd Knight v. Purdue   519

Boyd v. Edington   621, 731

Boyd v. Harris   756

Boys v. Star Printing and Publishing Co.   1197

BPE Solicitors v. Hughes-Holland (in substitution for Gabriel)   718

Bracken v. Fort Erie (Town)   187

Bradford Corp. v. Pickles   984, 986

Bradford et al. v. Kanellos et al.   706, 710

Bradford-Smart v. West Sussex County Council   395

Bradley v. Fisher   849

Bradley v. Groves   668

Bradshaw Construction Ltd. v. Bank of Nova Scotia   155

Brady v. Schatzel   70

Brae Centre Ltd. v. 1044807 Alberta Ltd.   1128, 1131

Branco v. American Home Assurance Co.   38, 44

Brandeis Goldschmidt & Co. v. Western Transport Ltd.   141

Brannon v. Airtours plc   392

Brant Avenue Manor Limited Partnership v. Transmerica Life Insurance Co. of Canada   155

Brauer v. New York Cent. & H.R.R. Co.   716

Braun v. Peszko (c.o.b. Roe & Co.)   801

Bray v. Palmer   835

Breeden, R. v.   187

Breen v. Saunders   283

Brennan, R. v.   290

Bresatz v. Przibilla   743

Brett-Young Seeds Ltd. v. K.B.A. Consultants Inc.   567

Brezack, R. v.   307

Brian v. Mador   729

Briante (Litigation Guardian of) v. Vancouver Island Health Authority (c.o.b. Royal Jubilee Hospital)   621

Briante (Litigation guardian of) v. Vancouver Island Health Authority   63, 621

Briante v. Vancouver Island Health Authority   660

Bridge v. Dalton   249

Bridge v. Jo   425, 426

Bridges Brothers Ltd. v. Forest Protection Ltd.   199

Briffet v. Gander & District Hospital Board   621

Briggs v. Laviolette   292

Brimelow v. Casson   1132

Brisson v. Brisson   727

Bristol & West of England Bk. v. Midland R. Co.   168

British Columbia (Attorney General) v. Insurance Corporation of British Columbia   602, 1070

British Columbia (Workers' Compensation Appeal Tribunal) v. Fraser Health Authority   649, 826

British Columbia (Workers' Compensation Board) v. Flanagan Enterprises (Nevada) Inc   489

British Columbia Automobile Assn. v. O.P.E.I.U. Local 378   1106

British Columbia Public School Employers' Assn. v. British Columbia Teachers' Federation   187

British Columbia Recreation and Parks Assn. v. Zakharia   1106, 1108

British Columbia v. Canadian Forest Products Ltd.   659, 774, 911

British Columbia v. Imperial Tobacco Canada Ltd.   1117

British Columbia v. R.B.O. Architecture Inc.   500

British Columbia v. Zastowny   221, 717, 815

British Railways Board v. Herrington   932, 944

British Telecommunications Plc. v. One in a Million Ltd. 1106

Brito (Guardian ad litem of) v. Wooley 475

Broadfoot v. Ontario (Minister of Transportation and Communication) 389

Brock v. Anderson 473

Brodeur (Litigation Guardian of) v. Provincial Health Services Authority (c.o.b. British Columbia Women's Hospital and Health Center) 620

Brookfield Multiplex Ltd. v. Owners Corporation Strata Plan 61288 568

Brooks v. Canadian Pacific Railway Ltd. 362, 468

Brooks v. Commissioner of Police for the Metropolis 403

Broome v. Prince Edward Island 69, 1067

Brown (Next Friend of) v. University of Alberta Hospital 407, 620

Brown and Brown v. B. & F. Theatres Ltd. 937

Brown v. Baugh 301

Brown v. British Columbia (Minister of Transportation and Highways) 867

Brown v. Cole 796

Brown v. Dunsmuir 814

Brown v. Mack 1161

Brown v. Wilson 248

Brown, R. v. 286

Browne, R. v. 426

Browning v. War Office 654

Brownlie v. Campbell 1089

Bruce Estate v. Toderovich 450

Bruce v. Coliseum Management Ltd. 59

Bruce v. Dyer 71, 249

Brumer v. Gunn 622

Bruno Appliance And Furniture Inc. v. Hryniak 1091

Brushett v. Cowan 231, 712

Bryan v. Maloney 568

Bryson v. Canada (Attorney General) 758

Buchan v. Ortho Pharmaceutical (Can.) Ltd. 472, 487

Buckland v. Guildford Gas Light & Coke Co. 351, 353

Buckley and T.T.C. v. Smith Transport Ltd. 610

Buckley v. John Allen & Ford (Oxford), Ltd. 764

Buckley v. Smith Transport Ltd. 612

Buehl v. Polar Star Enterprises Inc. 392

Burbank v. Bolton 602

Burbank v. R.T.B. 917

Burdett v. Eidse 728

Burke v. Watson & Barnard (A Firm) 558

Burke, R. c. 286, 288

Burke, R. v. 312

Burmah Oil Co. v. Lord Advocate 269

Burman's Beauty Supplies Ltd. v. Kempster 501

Burnett Estate v. St. Jude Medical, Inc. 450

Burnie Port Authority v. General Jones Pty. Ltd. 1036, 1083

Burrell v. Metropolitan Entertainment Group 348, 910

Burrowes v. Lock 1089

Burrows v. Burke 1099

Buteikis v. Adams 691

Buthmann v. Balzer 568

Butler (Litigation Representative of) v. Ma-Me-O Beach (Summer Village) 953

Butler v. Egg Board 162

Butler v. Southam Inc. 1159

Butler v. Standard Telephones & Cables, Ltd. 1003

Butterfield v. Forrester 784

Byciuk v. Hollingsworth 473, 475

Byrne v. Boadle 840

Byrne v. Deane 1159

C. v. Wren 232, 234

C.(C.), R. v. 206

C.(D.) v. Newfoundland (Minister of Social Services) 407

C.(L.) v. Pinhas 235

C.A.L. No. 14 Pty Ltd. v. Motor Accidents Insurance Board; C.A.L. No. 14 Pty Ltd. v. Scott 393

C.C.B. v. I.B. 41

C.E.S. v. Superclinics (Australia) Pty. Ltd. 440

C.M.G. v. D.W.S. 240

C.N.R. Co. v. Sask. Wheat Pool 689

C.N.R. v. Bakty 425

C.R.F. Holdings Ltd. v. Fundy Chemical Int. Ltd. 1094, 1098

C.S. (Next friend of) v. Miller 616

Cachay v. Nemeth 64, 247, 253

Cadbury Schweppes Inc. v. FBI Foods Ltd. 47, 122, 893

Cairns v. John Fairfax & Sons Ltd. 1151

Caissie v. Assels   180
Calgary (City) v. Thomas   612
Calliou Estate (Trustee of) v. Calliou   388
Calveley v. Chief Constable of
  Merseyside   889
Calvert v. Law Soc. of Upper Can.   495,
  853
Calvert v. William Hill Credit Ltd.   398
Camaso Estate v. Egan   299, 623
Cambridge Water Co. Ltd. v. Eastern
  Counties Leather plc   973, 1024, 1035
Cameron v. Morang   137
Campbell v. Bruce (County)   955
Campbell v. Calgary Power Ltd.   358
Campbell v. Dominion Breweries Ltd.
  162
Campbell v. Gordon   907
Campbell v. Hudyma   297, 298
Campbell v. Jones   1179
Campbell v. MGN Ltd.   113
Campbell v. Royal Bank of Canada   941,
  959
Campbell v. S.S. Kresge Co.   79
Campbell v. Spottiswoode   1198
Campomar v. Nike   1107
Can v. Calgary Police Service   79
Can. Gen. Elec. Co. v. Pickford & Black
  Ltd.   362
Can. Pac. Ltd. v. Gill   777
Can. Western Nat. Gas Co. v. Pathfinder
  Surveys Ltd.   775, 797
Cana International Distributing Inc. (c.o.b.
  Sexy Living) v. Standard Innovation
  Corp.   1109
Canada (A.G.) v. Ottawa Carleton (City)
  990
Canada (Attorney General) v. Clorey
  773
Canada (Attorney General) v. Connolly
  610
Canada (Attorney General) v.
  Livingstone   581
Canada (Attorney General) v. Walsh   392
Canada (House of Commons) v. Vaid
  850
Canada Cement LaFarge Ltd. v. B.C.
  Lightweight Aggregate Ltd.   1114, 1119
Canada Metal Co. Ltd. v. Canadian
  Broadcasting Corporation   1212
Canada Post v. G3 Worldwide (Canada)
  Inc.   911
Canada Safeway Ltd. v. Manitoba Food &
  Commercial Workers, Local 832   104

Canada v. Saskatchewan Wheat Pool
  127
Canadian Aero Service Ltd. v. O'Malley
  47
Canadian Assn. of Regulated Importers v.
  Canada (A.G.)   922
Canadian Foundation for Children, Youth
  and the Law v. Canada (Attorney
  General)   258
Canadian Imperial Bank of Commerce v.
  Green   521
Canadian National Railway Co. v. Norsk
  Pacific Steamship Co.   340, 506, 522,
  572, 574, 579
Canadian National Railway Co. v.
  Vincent   913
Canadian Newspapers Co. v. Canada
  (Attorney General)   1182
Canadian Pacific Ltd. v. Gill   627
Canadian Pacific Ltd. v. Paul   188
Canadian Tire Bank v. Roach   107
Canadian Training and Development
  Group v. Air Canada   1120
Candler v. Crane, Christmas & Co.   498
Candlewood Navigation Corporation Ltd.
  v. Mitsui O.S.K. Lines Ltd. (The Mineral
  Transporter)   336
Canson Enterprises Ltd. v. Boughton &
  Co.   3, 1094
Cant v. Cant   101, 104
Canterbury v. Spence   471
Cantile v. Canadian Heating Products Inc.
  (c.o.b. Montigo Canada)   488
Cantlie v. Canadian Heating Products
  Inc.   1050
Canus Fisheries Ltd. v. Canada (Customs
  & Revenue Agency)   888
Caparo Industries plc v Dickman   335,
  336, 344, 508, 553
Capelet v. Brookfield Homes (Ontario)
  Limited   704, 705
Car & General Ins. Corp. Ltd v. Seymour
  et al.   805
Cardinal v. Loo   829
Cardwell v. Perthen   569
Carere v. Cressman   621
Carlson v. Steeves   473
Carmichael v. Kwon   758
Caron Estate v. Paneak Estate   763
Carr v. Edmonton (City) Police   82
Carr v. Ottawa Police Services Board   82
Carrie v. Tolkien   1212

Carrière v. Bd. of Gravelbourg School Dist. No. 2244 of Sask. 938
Carriss v. Buxton 937
Carroll 298
Carroll v. Chicken Palace Ltd. 612
Carr-Saunders v. Dick McNeil Associates Ltd. 1005
Carson v. Thunder Bay 204, 808
Carstairs v. Taylor 1033
Carter v. B.C. Federation of Foster Parents Assn. 1163
Carter v. Canada (Attorney General) 229
Casey v. Automobiles Renault Canada Ltd. 90
Caslake, R. v. 301
Casses v. Canadian Broadcasting Corporation 1167
Castle v. Ontario 402
Côté, R. v. 313
Catalyst Capital Group Inc. v. Veritas Investment Research Corp. 1120
Catalyst Pulp and Paper Sales Inc. v. Universal Paper Export Co. 1098
Catholic Child Welfare Society v. Various Claimants 1072
Cattanach v. Melchior 438, 439
Cattell v. Great Plains Leaseholds Ltd. 1010
Cattle v. Stockton Waterworks Co. 543, 579, 1027
Caxton Publishing Co. v. Sutherland Publishing Co. 159
Cejvan v. Blue Mountain Resorts Limited 809
Cempel v. Harrison Hot Springs Hotel Ltd. 801
Central & Eastern Trust v. Rafuse 529, 530
Central B.C. Planers Ltd. v. Hocker 499, 500
Central Can. Potash v. Govt. of Sask. 1110, 1112
Central Trust Co. v. Rafuse 622
Century 21 Canada Ltd. Partnership v. Rogers Communications Inc. 138
Chadwick v. British Railways Commission 460
Chae v. Min 801, 803
Chaisson v. Hebert 615
Chalifoux v. Alberta Health Sciences 230
Chélin c. Gill 1197
Chamberlain v. Canadian Physiotherapy Association 810

Chamberlains v. Lai 494
Chamberland v. Fleming 802
Champigny v. Ste-Marie 621
Chan, R. v. 250
Chand v. Sabo Brothers Realty Ltd. 499
Chandra v. Canadian Broadcasting Corp. 115
Chang v. Feng 748
Channel Seven Adelaide Pty. Ltd. v. Manock 1192, 1197
Chaoulli v. Québec (Attorney General) 599
Chapeskie v. Canadian Imperial Bank of Commerce 503
Chapman v. 3M Canada Inc. 127
Chapman v. Hearse 425
Chappel v. Hart 475, 642
Chappell v. Baratti 772
Charing Cross Electric Co. v. Hydraulic Power Co. 1026
Charles, R. v. 301
Charrington v. Simons & Co. Ltd. 197
Chartier v. Att. Gen. (Que.) 286
Chasczewski Estate v. 528089 Ontario Inc. 584
Chasse v. Evenson 621
Chaster (Guardian ad litem of) v. LeBlanc 622, 640
Chatha v. Uppal 91
Chatterton v. Secretary of State for India in Council 1169
Cheevers v. Van Norden 627
Chehil, R. v. 308
Chen, R. v. 82, 291
Cherneskey v. Armadale Publishers Ltd. (1974), 53 D.L.R. (3d) 79 (Sask. C.A.) 796
Cherneskey v. Armadale Publishers Ltd., [1979] 1 S.C.R. 1067 1157, 1180, 1186, 1195
Chernetz v. Eagle Copters Ltd. 742
Cherrey v. Steinke 807
Cherry (Guardian ad litem of) v. Borsman 621
Cherry v. Borsman 439
Cherry v. Ivey 92
Chesher v. Monaghan 736
Chessie v. J.D. Irvine Ltd. 1001
Chester v. Afshar 642
Cheticamp Fisheries Co-operative Ltd. v. Canada 1132
Cheung (Litigation Guardian of) v. Toyota Canada Inc. 839

Chidley-Hill v. Daw   1184
Child and Family Services of Central
  Manitoba v. Lavallee   229
Childs v. Desormeaux   346, 358, 369, 389,
  522
Chilton v. Carrington   167
Chin v. Venning   17
Chmiliar v. Chmiliar   235
Cho Ki Yau Trust (Trustees of) v. Yau
  Estate   142
Choc v. Hudbay Minerals Inc.   701
Chopra v. T. Eaton Co.   82
Chow (Litigation Guardian of) v. Wellesley
  Hospital   620
Chow v. Hiscock   42, 662
Chow-Hidasi v. Hidasi   820, 839, 844
Chretien v. Jensen   392
Chrispen v. Kalinowski   891
Christian Medical and Dental Society of
  Canada v. College of Physicians and
  Surgeons of Ontario   230
Christie v. Davey   985
Christie v. Leachinsky   295
Christie v. Westcom Radio Group Ltd.
  1198
Chrysanthis v. Rutkowska   1032
Chu v. Dawson   973, 1032
Chubak, R. v.   304
CIA Inspection Inc. v. Dan Lawrie
  Insurance Brokers   411
Ciarlariello v. Schacter   238
Ciba-Geigy Canada Ltd. v. Apotex
  Inc.   1100
Cimolai v. Hall   1176
Cinapri v. Guettler   1172
Cinar Corporation v. Robinson   42
Cinous, R. v.   249
City of Brandon v. Farley   941
City of Ft. Smith v. Western Hide & Fur
  Co.   1013
City of Kamloops v. Nielsen   862, 864,
  866
Claiborne Industries Ltd. v. National Bank
  of Canada   42
Claiborne Industries v. National Bank of
  Canada   1122
Claiter v. Rose   793
Clark v. Canada   102, 127, 395
Clark v. D.A. Hargreaves Insurance Ltd.
  623
Clark v. Hunka   90
Clark v. Orr   168
Clark v. Scotiabank   450, 552

Clark, R. v.   262
Clarke v. Penny   731
Clarke v. Stewart   1160
Claxton v. Grandy   818
Clay v. Roberts   1154
Clayton v. LeRoy   169
Clayton, R. v.   281
Cleary v. Hansen   423
Clement v. Leslies Storage Ltd.   767
Clements v. Clements   641, 643, 654, 833
Cleveland (Litigation Guardian of) v.
  Hamilton Health Sciences Corp.
  (Henderson General Division)   621
CLG & Ors v. Chief Constable of
  Merseyside Police   404
Cliche c. Baie-James (Commission
  scolaire)   396
Cloud v. Canada   856
Cloutier v. Langlois   302
Club Cruise Entertainment & Travelling
  Services Europe BV v. Department for
  Transport (The Van Gogh)   142
Clunis v. Camden & Islington Health
  Authority   815
Clyke v. Clyke   425
CN & Anor v. Poole Borough Council
  406
Coady v. Burton Canada Co.   485
Coburn v. Wilkie   237
Cochran v. Hunter   61
Cock v. Windsor   954
Codner v. Gosse   52, 820
Cody v. Leonard   729
Coe Estate v. Tennant   768
Coffyne v. Silver Lake Regional Park
  Authority   932
Coggs v. Bernard   410
Cohen v. Lion Products Co.   98
Cojocaru v. British Columbia Women's
  Hospital and Health Centre   446
Colangelo v. Mississauga (City)   857, 922
Colborne Capital Corp. v. 542775 Alberta
  Ltd.   1132
Colby v. Schmidt   206
Cold River Resources LLC v. 1279514
  Ontario Inc.   520
Cole v. Lockhart   1072
Cole v. South Tweed Heads Rugby League
  Football Club Limited   392
Coleiro v. Premier Fitness Clubs (Erin
  Mills) Inc.   958
Coleman v. MacLennan   1197
Colet, R. v.   249, 312

Colistro v. Tbaytel   1066

College of Dental Surgeons (Saskatchewan) v. Thorvaldson   1130

Collins v. Renison   260

Collins, R. v.   307

Color Your World Corp. v. Canadian Broadcasting Corp.   1155, 1193

Colour Quest Ltd. v. Total Downstream U.K. plc   973, 999

Comeau v. Laliberte   789

Comeau v. Saint John Regional Hospital   631

Comeau's Sea Foods Ltd. v. Canada (Minister of Fisheries & Oceans)   867

Cominco Ltd. v. Westinghouse Can. Ltd.   485

Commissioner of Police of the Metropolis v. DSD & Anor   404

Committee for the Commonwealth of Canada v. Canada   187

Conarken Group Ltd. v. Network Rail Infrastructure Ltd.   694

Condominium Corp. No. 0321365 v. 970365 Alberta Ltd.   347, 541

Conklin v. Smith   728

Connery v. Gov't. of Man.   685

Connolly v. Royal Bank   500

Conrad v. Crawford   807

Conseil pour la protection des maladies c. Fédération des médecins specialists (Québec)   380

Constantine v. Imperial London Hotels, Ltd.   124

Consumers Distributing Co. v. Seiko Time Canada Ltd.   1102

Conversions By Vantasy Ltd. v. General Motors of Canada Ltd.   501, 541

Conway v. O'Brien   605

Cook v. Cook   616

Cook v. Lewis   8, **16**, 65, 641, 652, 662, 829, 830, **831**, 835, 838

Cook v. S.   468

Cook v. The Insurance Corporation of British Columbia   120

Cooper v. Blackwell   810

Cooper v. Flood   473

Cooper v. Hobart   337, **338**, 343, **345**, 349, 367, 368, 417, 425, 493, 499, 506, 522, 545, 869

Co-operators Insurance Association v. Kearney   1077

Coopersmith c. Air Canada   381

Cope v. Sharpe   268

Copeland v. Hamilton (City)   809

Coquitlam School District No. 43 v. Clement   63

Coquitlam School District No. 43 v. D.(T.W.)   397

Cormack v. Mara (Township)   957

Cormier v. Nova Scotia   852

Cormier v. Saint John (City)   297

Cornell, R. v.   298, 312

Corothers v. Slobodian   423, 425

Corr v. IBC Vehicles Ltd.   692, 713, 789

Correct Building Corp. v. Lehman   1141

Correia v. Canac Kitchens   102, 1128, 1130, 1139, 1144

Corrie v. Gilbert   728

Costa v. Wimalasekera   540

Costello v. Blakeson   692

Costello v. Calgary (City)   180, 188

Costello v. Chief Constable of Derbyshire Constabulary   133

Cote, R. v.   709

Cotic v. Gray   358

Couch v. McCann; Ferguson v. McCann   935

Couch v. Steel   902

Coueslan v. Canadian Mini-Warehouse Properties Ltd. (c.o.b. Public Storage Canadian)   406

Coughlin v. Kuntz   472, 476, 724

Couillard v. Waschulewski Estate   713

Council of Civil Service Unions v. Minister for the Civil Service   856

County of Parkland No. 31 v. Stetar; County of Parkland No. 31 v. Woodrow   415

Courchene v. Marlborough Hotel Co.   1164

Courdin v. Meyers   756

Courneyea, R. v.   52

Cousins v. Wilson   179

Coventry v. Lawrence   974, 993, 1015

Cowan v. Hydro One Networks Inc.   640

Coward v. Baddeley   64

Cowles v. Balac   276, 797, 809, 825, **1038**, 1042

Cox v. Fleming   449, 459

Cox v. Ministry of Justice   1072

Cox. v. Coulson   937

Cragg v. Tone   380, 402

Craig v. McCreath   169

Cramaso LLP v. Ogilvie-Grant, Earl of Seafield   500

Crawford (Litigation Guardian of) v. Penney 620

Crawford Adjusters v. Sagicor General Insurance (Cayman) Ltd. 90

Crawford v. Halifax 612

Creative Salmon Company Ltd. v. Staniford 1197

Cresswell v. Sirl 265

Crew v. Nicholson 829

Crimeni v. Chandra 748

Crinson v. Toronto (City) 626

Crits v. Sylvester 619

Crocker v. Sundance Northwest Resorts Ltd. 358, **383**, 803, 807, 808, 1042

Crofter Hand Woven Harris Tweed Co. v. Veitch 1122, 1132

Cronk v. F.W. Woolworth Co. 291

Crookes v. Wikimedia Foundation Inc. 1163

Crosby v. Curry 1048

Crossan v. Gillis 663

Crossman v. R. 891

Crouch v. Snell 116

Crowe v. Noon 288

Crown West Steel Fabricators v. Capri Insurance Services Ltd. 504, 797

Cruise Connections Canada v. Cancellieri 123, 156

Cudmore v. Home Chec Canada Ltd. 809

Cuerrier, R. v. 210

Culzean Inventions Ltd. v. Midwestern Broom Co. 1119

Cunningham v. Wheeler 776

Cunningham, R. v. 301

Curll v. Robin Hood Multifoods Ltd. 468

Curran v. Northern Ireland Co-ownership Housing Assoc. Ltd. 336

Currie v. Blundell 473

Curry v. Vancouver (City) 495

Custer, R. v. 312

Customs and Excise Commissioners v. Barclays Bank plc. 552

Cuthbertson v. Rasouli 230

D. & F. Estates Ltd. v. Church Commissioners for England 336

D. v. East Berkshire Community NHS Trust 407

D.(C.) v. Canada (Attorney General) 344

D.(D.R.) v. G.(S.E.) 1097

D.(P.A.) v. H.(A.E.) 692

D.N. v. Oak Bay (District) 624

D&F Estates Ltd. v. Church Commissioners for England 565, 568

Dabous v. Zuliani 623

D'Addario v. Smith 1178

Dagenais v. Canadian Broadcasting Corp. 1187

D'Agnone v. D'Agnone 1118

Dahlberg v. Naydiuk 66, 197, **829**

Dahler v. Bruvold 1033

Dairy Queen Canada Inc. v. M.Y. Sundae Inc. (c.o.b. DQ Grill and Chill) 1107

Daishowa Inc. v. Friends of the Lubicon 1114, 1118, 1133

Daishowa-Marubeni International Ltd. v. Toshiba International Corp. 1050

Dale v. Munthali 620

Dale v. Veda Advantage Information Services and Solutions Limited 552

Dale's Trad'N Post v. Rhodes 1160

Dallison v. Caffery 301, 307

D'Almeida v. Barron 237

Dalton v. Angus 1081

D'Amato v. Badger 572, 580

Daniells v. McLellan 115

Daniels v. Thompson 723

Danku v. Town of Fort Frances 1034

Dann, R. v. 301

Dao v. Sabatino 615

D'Aoust v. Lindsay 362

Darbishire v. Warren 772, 773

Darling v. Attorney-General 1083

Das v. George Weston Ltd. 416, 1037, 1083

Davenport v. Miller 101

Davey v. Harrow Corp. 1003

Davey v. Victoria General Hospital 447

David v. Toronto Transit Comm. 712

Davidson v. British Columbia 588

Davidson v. Chief Constable of North Wales 81

Davidson v. Connaught Laboratories 486

Davidson v. Toronto Blue Jays Baseball Ltd. 188

Davies & Davies Ltd. v. Kott 1178

Davies v. Gabel Estate 621

Davies v. Mann 784

Davies v. Taylor 728

Davis v. Anderson 793

Davis v. McArthur 110, 120

Davis v. Radcliffe 345

Davis v. Shields 793

Davis v. Sutton 192

Day v. Chaleur Developments Ltd. 935

Day v. Doerksen 742

Day v. Toronto Transportation
Commission 623, 845

DC Thomson & Co. Ltd. v. Deakin 1129

De Gurse v. Henry 829

De Jetley Marks v. Greenwood (Lord) et
al. 1116

de Montigny v. Brossard (Succession) 45

De Vos v. Robertson 598

Deacon v. Canada (A.G.) 217

Deakins v. Aarsen 1053

Deavitt v. Greenly 1032

Debot, R. v. 307

Decock v. Alberta 851, 1066

Dedman, R. v. 281

Dee Trading Co. Pty. Ltd. v. Baldwin
134

Dee v. Telegraph Media Group Ltd.
1157

DeFerrari v. Neville 473

Defosse v. Wilde 59, 253

Degennaro v. Oakville Trafalgar Memorial
Hospital 692

Dehekker v. Anderson-Penno 475

Delacroix v. Thevenot 1161

Delancey v. Dale & Co. Ltd. 90

Delaney v. Cascade River Holidays Ltd.
808

Delaney v. Pickett 816

Delaware Mansions Ltd. v. Westminster
City Council 976

Dellwo v. Pearson 615

**Deloitte & Touche v. Livent (Receiver
of)** 221, 346, 348, **505**, 554, 570, 623,
640, 684, **718**, 814, 817

Delong, R. v. 312

Demarco v. Ungaro 491

Dendekker v. F.W. Woolworth Co. 291

Dennis v. Ministry of Defence 975, 992

Dennis v. Ontario Lottery and Gaming
Corp. 398, 911

Dennis v. Southam Co. 1157

Dennison v. Sanderson 33

Dentec Safety Specialists Inc. v. Degil
Safety Products (1989) Inc., 2014 ONSC
2449 (Div. Ct.) 1107

Dentec Safety Specialists Inc. v. Degil
Safety Products (1989) Inc., 2012 ONSC
4721 1106

Depue v. Flateau 272, 274

Deraps v. Coia 519

Dering v. Uris 33

Deros v. McCauley 704, 705

Derry v. Peek 498, **1088**, 1092, 1093,
1094, 1095

Des Brisay v. Canadian Government
Merchant Marine Ltd. 584

Des Champs v. Conseil des Écoles séparées
catholiques de langue française de
Prescott-Russell 858

Desando v. Canadian Transit Co. 982

Desanti v. Gray 958

Desautels v. Katimavik 589

Deshane v. Deere & Co. 488

DeShaney v. Winnebago County
Department of Social Services 405

Design Services Ltd. v. Canada 344, 526,
550

Desjardins v. Arcadian Restaurants Ltd.
954

Devenish Nutrition Ltd. v. Sanofi-Aventis
SA (France) 911

Devji v. Burnaby (District) 459, 703

Devlin v. Smith 333

Devoe v. Long 265

Devon Lumber Co. v. MacNeill 192, 986

Deyo v. Kingston Speedway Ltd. 1029

Dhalla v. Jodrey 619

Diageo Canada Inc. v. Heaven Hill
Distilleries Inc. 1108

Diaz v. Tossa 81

Dickey v. McCaul 149

Didow v. Alberta Power Ltd. 197

Dietelbach v. British Columbia (Public
Trustee) 468

Dilello v. Montgomery 756

Dill v. Excel Packing Company 1012

Dillon v. LeRoux 620

Dillon v. O'Brien and Davis 304, 307

**Dillon v. Twin State Gas and Elec.
Co. 674**

Dixon v. British Columbia Snowmobile
Federation 809

Djoufo c. Mailloux 1160

Dobbs v. Mayer 52, 612, 819

Dobson (Litigation Guardian of) v.
Dobson 20, 434, 442, 921

Dodd Properties (Kent) Ltd. v. Canterbury
C.C. 34, 771

Doe d. Rochester v. Bridges 902

Doe v. London Free Press, a Division of
Sun Media (Toronto) Corp. 704

Doe v. N.D. 116, 122

Doern v. Phillips Estate 300, 625, 829

Doiron v. Brideau 807

Doiron v. Orr   439
Dokuchia v. Domansch   1029
Dolphin Delivery Ltd. v. R.W.D.S.U.,
   Local 580   283
Dom. Securities Ames Ltd. v. Deep   623
Dom. Securities Ltd. v. Glazerman   162
Dominion Chain Co. v. Eastern
   Construction Co.   529
Donaldson v. John Doe   347, 388
Donnelly v. Jackman   64
Donoghue v. Stevenson   8, 319, 328, 334,
   335, 338, 339, 340, 454, 478, 498, 811, 948,
   1028, 1049
Dorschell v. Cambridge (City)   626
Dorset Yacht Co. v. Home Office   867
D'Orta-Ekenaike v. Victoria Legal Aid
   494
Doucet-Boudreau v. Nova Scotia (Minister
   of Education)   31, 282, 924
Doucette v. Parent   192
Doughty v. Turner Mfg. Co.   687
Douglas College v. Douglas/Kwantlen
   Faculty Assoc   921
Douglas v. Hello! Ltd.   113, 156
Douglas v. Kinger (Litigation Guardian
   of)   1072
Douglas v. Tucker   1181
Dowler v. Bravender   1040, 1041
Dowson v. The Queen   1169
Dr. X v. Everson   621
Drader v. Abbotsford (City)   993
Drady v. Canada (Minister of Health)
   489
Drager v. Lojstrup   1005
Drainville v. Vilchez   91
Draper v. Trist   1107
Dredger Liesbosch v. S.S. Edison
   (Owners)   771
Dredger Liesbosch v. Steamship Edison
   693
Driskell v. Dangerfield   853, 1118
Drouillard v. Cogeco Cable Inc.   1127,
   1139, 1142
Dryden v. Campbell Estate   389, 391
Dryden v. Johnson Matthey   724
D'Souza v. D.P.P.   313
Dubai Aluminium Co. Ltd. v. Salaam
   1072
Dube (Litigation Guardian of) v. Penlon
   Ltd.   449
Dube v. Labar   804
Duce v. Rourke   680, 716
Ducharme v. Davies   789

Dudeck v. Brown   1033
Dudek v. Li   712
Dudley v. Victor Lynn Lines Inc.   414
Dudley, R. v.   268
Dufault v. Excelsior Mortgage Corp.
   425, 958
Duffy, R. v.   251, 253
Duggan v. Newfoundland   855
Duke v. Puts   1177
Dulieu v. White & Sons   452, 689
Dulude v. Canada   284
Dumbell v. Roberts   286
Duncalf v. Capital Health Authority   621
Duncan Estate v. Baddeley   761
Duncan v. Cammell Laird & Co. Ltd.
   934
Dunlap v. Philadelphia Newspapers Inc.
   1167
Dunlea v. Attorney-General   924
Dunn v. Birmingham Canal Co.   1034
Dunn v. Dominion Atlantic Railway Co.
   262, 385
Dunsmore v. Deshield   323
Dunster v. Abbott   932
Dupperon, R. v.   254
Dupuis v. New Regina Trading Co. Ltd.
   420
Durakovic v. Guzman   1157
Dura-Lite Heat Transfer Products Ltd. v.
   CEDA Environmental Services (c.o.b.
   Wasteco Environmental Services Ltd.)
   484
Durling v. Sunrise Propane Energy Group
   Inc.   954
Dushynski v. Rumsey   692
Dutton v. Bognor Regis United Building
   Co.   501
Duval v. O'Beirne   1151
Duval v. Seguin   442
Duwyn v. Kaprielian   450
Dwyer v. Staunton   269, 273
Dyck v. Laidlaw   808
Dyck v. Manitoba Snowmobile Assn.
   Inc.   531, 808
Dyke v. British Columbia Amateur
   Softball Assn.   798
Dynasty Furniture Manufacturing Ltd. v.
   Toronto-Dominion Bank   910
E. Hulton & Co. v. Jones   1157
E.(D.) (Guardian ad litem of) v. British
   Columbia   68, 240
E.(Mrs.) v. Eve   238, 240
E.W. Scripps Co. v. Cholmondelay   1159

E.W.B. Venootschap. v. J. Townend & Sons (Hull) Ltd. 1107
Eady v. Tenderenda 621
Earl v. Wilhelm 411
East Crest Oil Co. v. R. 180
East Suffolk Rivers Catchment Bd. v. Kent 426
Eastern & South African Telegraph Co. v. Cape Town Tramways Cos. 984
eBay v. Bidder's Edge Inc. 138
Eccles v. Bourque 280, **308**
Economical Insurance Co. v. Fairview Assessment Centre Inc. 1120
Economou v. De Freitas 1208
Edgar v. Richmond (Township) 587
Edgeworth Construction Ltd. v. N. D. Lea& Associates Ltd. 511, 554
Ediger (Guardian ad litem of) v. Johnston 446
Ediger v. Johnston 638, 659
Edmonton (City) v. Lovat Tunnel Equipment Inc. 566
Edmonton Journal v. Alberta (Attorney General) 1182, 1183
Edwards v. Law Society of Upper Canada 345
Edwards v. Lee's Administrators 45, 198
Eid v. Dumas 805, 807
El Dali v Panjalingam 845
Elder, Dempster& Co. v. Paterson, Zochonis & Co. 532
Elderkin v. Merrill Lynch, Royal Securities Ltd. 499, 500
Eldridge v. British Columbia (Attorney General) 599
Elfassy v. Sylben Invts. Ltd. 1033
Eli Lilly & Co. v. Novopharm Ltd. 1107
Eliopolous v. Ontario (Minister of Health & Long Term Care) 524, 870
El-Khodr v. Lackie 775
Elkow v. Sana 1185
Elliot v. Chiarelli 623
Elliott and Elliott v. Amphitheatre Ltd. 204
Elliott v. Canadian Broadcasting Corp. 1120, 1159
Elliott v. Insurance Crime Prevention Bureau 1177
Ellis v. Fallios-Guthierrez 58, 208, 248, 253
Ellis v. Stenning 166
Ellis, R. v. 281, 304, 307
Ellone v. Mesa 58

Elloway v. Boomars 691
Elmardy v. Toronto Police Services Board 79, 281, 284, 298, 928
Emeh v. Kensington and Chelsea and Westminster Area Health Authority 439
Emerald Const. Co. v. Lowthian 1130
Emerson v. Insurance Corporation of British Columbia 426
Emmonds v. Makarewicz 632
Endean v. Canadian Red Cross Society 839
Engel v. Kam-Ppelle Holdings Ltd. 713, 729, 747
Engemoen Holdings Ltd. v. 100 Mile House 198
England v. Crowley 142
Engler v. Rossignol 627
Enterprises Sibeca Inc. v. Frelighsburg (Municipality) 851
Entick v. Carrington **177**, 285
Enviro-Tex Products Ltd. v. Fibrex Insulations Inc. 1133
Epstein v. Cressey Development Corp. 198
Erickson and Hathaway, R. v. 297
Erie Ry. Co. v. Stewart 415
Erison v. Higgins 840
Ernst v. Alberta Energy Regulator 922
Erven Warnink B.V. v. J. Townend & Sons (Hull) Ltd. 1101
Esanda Finance Corp. v. Peat Marwick Hungerfords (Reg) 519
Esser v. Brown 552
Esso Petroleum Co. v. Mardon 534
Estabrooks v. New Brunswick Real Estate Association 90
Estate of Sinthasamphone v. City of Milwaukee 405
Evans v. Bank of Nova Scotia 115
Evans v. MacMicking 1098
Evans v. Queanbeyan City Council 650
Everett v. Griffiths 853
Eyres v. Gillis & Warren Ltd. 586
F.(K.) v. White 69
F.(P.) v. Ontario 112
Facilities Subsector Bargaining Assn. v. B.C.N.U. 115
Fairchild v. Glenhaven Funeral Services Ltd. 649, 836
Faircrest v. Buchanan 959
Fairhurst v. Anglo American PLC 1117
Falkenham v. Zwicker 685

Fanjoy v. Gaston 938
Fardon v. Harcourt-Rivington 696
Farish v. National Trust Co. 499
Farkas v. Sunnybrook and Women's College Health Sciences Centre 450
Farrant v. Laktin 668
Farrell v. Canadian Broadcasting Corporation 1222
Farrell v. Sutton and Wandsworth Health Authority 459
Fearon, R. v. 304
Federal Sugar Refining Co. v. United States Sugar Equalization Bd. 1133
Federic v. Perpetual Investments Ltd. 1033
Feener v. McKenzie 829
Feeney, R. v. 307, 312
Feist v. Gordon 473
Feldstein v. 364 Northern Development Corp. 501, 540
Feltham v. Terry 137
Fenn v. Peterborough 747, 755
Fennell, R. v. 252
Ferenczy v. MCI Medical Clinics 111
Ferguson v. Hamilton Civic Hospitals 237
Ferguson, R. v. 922
Ferland v. Keith 411
Fernandes v. Araujo 1052, 1053
Fernandes v. Penncorp Life Insurance Co. 38
Ferri v. Root 91
Ferrier v. Hubbert 389
Fiala v. Cechmanek 52, **606**
Fidler v. Sun Life Assurance Co. of Canada 37, 38, 44
Figueiras v. Toronto (Police Services Board) 281
Fillier v. Whittom 797
Fillingham v. ABC Corp. (c.o.b. as Big White Ski Resort Ltd.) 810
Fillion v. New Brunswick International Paper Co. 998
Fillipowich v. Nahachewsky 206
Findley v. Driver 789
Fine's Flowers Ltd. v. General Accident Assurance Co. 411, 499, 559
Finigan v. Calgary 936
Finlayson v GMAC Leaseco Ltd. 1053
Finney v. Barreau du Québec 496
Finnigan v. Sandiford 312, 313
Fiorillo v. Krispy Kreme Doughnuts Inc. 500, 1095

First Choice Outfitters Ltd. v. Neilly 1141
First National Properties v. McMinn 888
Fisher v. Knibbe 722
Fisher v. Prince 165
Fitkin (Litigation Administrator of) v. Latimer 389
Fitzpatrick v. Durham Regional Police Services Board 90
Fitzpatrick v. Orwin 100
Flame Bar-B-Q Ltd. v. Hoar 92
Flanagan v. Houlihan 393
Fleming v. Atkinson 1044, 1048
Fleming v. Fleming 1097
Fleming v. Ontario 299, 301
Fletcher v. Autocare & Transporters, Ltd. 739
Fletcher v. Bealey 1003
Fletcher v. Collins 280, 288
Fletcher v. M.P.I.C. 499
Fletcher v. Manitoba Public Insurance Co. 411
Flock v. Beattie 853
Flood v. Times Newspapers Ltd. 1208, 1212
Floyd and Barker 849
Fobel v. Dean 746
Fogden v. Wade 73
Foley v. Imperial Oil Ltd. 952, 954
Folland v. Reardon 494, 622
Fontaine v. British Columbia (Official Administrator) 841
Fontaine, R. v. 52
Fontenelle v. Canada (Attorney General) 624
Foran v. Tatangello 852
Forde v. Skinner 64
Forde, R. v. 248
Foreman v. Chambers 122
Foreman v. Foster 727
Forest v. Kirkland 928
Forsberg v. Naidoo 620
Fortey (Guardian ad litem of) v. Canada (Attorney General) 789
Fortier v. Kapeller 180
Fouldes v. Willoughby 135
Fournier v. Wiens 674
Fowler v. Lanning 830
Fowler v. Schneider National Carriers Ltd. 803
Fowlow v. Southlake Regional Health Centre 649

Fragomeni v. Greater Sudbury Police Service, 928
Frame v. Smith 101, 1123
France v. Gaudet 160
Francis v. Cockrell 937
Francis v. Dingman 1094
Francis v. I.P.C.F. Properties Inc. 932
Frank v. Legate 1143
Franklin Supply Co. v. Midco Supply Co. 1132
Fraser Jewellers v. Dominion Electric 809
Fraser v. Berkeley 57
Fraser v. Board of School Trustees of School District No. 72 (Campbell River) 623
Fraser v. Board of Trustees of Central United Church 1127
Fraser v. Westminer Canada Ltd. 552
Fraser-Reid v. Droumtsekas 562
Frawley v. Asselstine 769
Frazer v. Haukioja 704
Fredette v. Wiebe 440
Free Trade Medical Network Inc. v. RBC Travel Insurance Co. 122
Freedman v. Cooper 192
Freeman v. Harrington 172
Freeman v. Perlman 1094
Freeman v. Sutter 441, 559
Freeman-Maloy v. Marsden 887, 889
Freer (Guardian ad litem of) v. Okanagan/Skaha School District No. 67 397
French v. Harbour Grace (Town) 798
Frenchay Healthcare National Health Service Trust v. S. 241
Frey v. Fedoruk 280, 289
Froom v. Butcher 791, 793
Fullerton (Guardian ad litem of) v. Delair 778
Fullowka v. Royal Oak Ventures Inc. 348, 405, 460, 523, 653, 662, 717, 872, 943, 1070
Funk Estate v. Clapp 393
Funk v. Clapp 709
Funnell v. Canadian Pacific Railway 275
G.(A.) v. British Columbia (Superintendent of Family & Child Services) 407
G.(E.D.) v. Hammer 69, 1067, 1083
G.(H.R.) v. L.(M.S.) 122
G.(R.) v. Christison 407
G.A. v. McGregor 406
G.C. v. Ontario (Attorney General) 89
Gaca v. Pirelli General plc. 778

Gadhri v. 0760815 B.C. Ltd. 93
Gagne v. St. Regis Paper Co. 358
Gagnier v. Canadian Forest Products Ltd. 1000
Gagnon v. Beaulieu 790
Gala Homes Inc. v. Flisar 1176
Gala v. Preston 811, 814
Galantiuk v. Regina 775
Galaske v. O'Donnell 358, 584, 789, 793, 917
Galea v. Wal-Mart Canada Corp. 42
Galka v. Stankiewicz 358, 808, 955
Gallant v. Brake-Patten 475
Gallant v. Central Credit Union Ltd. 500
Gallant v. Fanshawe College of Applied Arts and Technology 809
Gallant v. Thames Valley District School Board 394
Galloway v. Telegraph Group Ltd. 1206
Gambriell v. Caparelli 65, 251
Gamracy v. R. 297
Garcia-Guiterrez, R. v. 307
Gardiner v. MacDonald Estate 588
Gardner v. Canada (Attorney General) 91
Garland v. Rowsell 762
Garratt v. Orillia Power Distribution Corp. 631
Garrett v. Attorney General 882, 889
Garrioch v. Tessman 1053
Garry v. Sherritt Gordon Mines Ltd. 1130
Garry v. St. Eloi 1121
Gartside v. Sheffield, Young & Ellis 558
Gaudet v. Sullivan 206
Gaudreault c. Drapeau 380
Gaunt v. Fynney 984, 985
Gaur v. Datta 1142
Gauthier & Co. 844
Gauvin v. Clark 621
Gay v. New Brunswick (Regional Health Authority 7) 450
Gazette Printing Co. v. Shallow 1181, 1183
Geld v. Dehavilland Aircraft of Can. Ltd. 774
Gemco Equipment Ltd. v. Westen 1069
Gen. & Finance Facilities Ltd. v. Cooks Cars (Romford) Ltd. 162, 165
Gendron v. Doug C. Thompson Ltd. (c.o.b. Thompson Fuels) 485
General Baking Co. v. Gorman 1103

General Motors Acceptance Corp. of Canada v. Fulton Insurance Agencies Ltd.   499

General Motors of Canada Ltd. v. Johnson   584

Genik v. Ewanylo   794

Geophysical Service Inc. v. Canada (Attorney General)   1144

George v. Beaubien   851

George v. Eagle Air Services Ltd.   845

George v. Larkin   625

George v. Newfoundland and Labrador   876, 1000

George v. Skivington   332, 333

Georgian Glen Development v. Barrie (City)   887

Gerelus v. Lim   473

Geremia v. Nielsen Estate   449

Gerling Global General Insurance Co. v. Siskind, Cromarty, Ivey & Dowler   796

German v. Major   495

Gershman v. Manitoba (Vegetable Producers' Marketing Board)   887, 890, 1114

Gertsen v. Municipality of Metropolitan Toronto   498, 1023, **1030**, 1035

Gervais v. Richard   762

Ghiassi v. Singh   639, 660

Giacomelli Estate v. Canada (Attorney General)   284

Giannone v. Weinberg   742

Gibbons v. Duffell   1170, 1177

Gibbons v. Port Hope & District Hospital   447

Gibbs v. Jalbert   1185

Gibson v. Sun   1005

Giesbrecht v. Canada Life Assurance Co.   502, 541

Giffels Associates Ltd v. Eastern Const. Co.   797

Gifford v. Dent   194

Gilberds v. Sobey   475

Gilbert v. Giffin   1054

Gilbert v. Showerman   1012

Gilbert v. Stone   55

Gill v. A&P Fruit Growers Ltd.   956

Gilles E. Néron Communication Marketing Inc. v. Chambre des notaires du Québec   1147

Gillick v. West Norfolk & Wisbech Area Health Authority et al.   232

Gilson v. Kerrier District Council   1034

Gittani Stone Pty Ltd v. Pavkovic   717

Giuliani v. Halton (Regional Municipality)   898

Gladue v. Alberta (Attorney General)   163

Glamorgan Coal Co. v. South Wales Miner's Federation   1131

Glanville v. Sutton   1043

Glanzer v. Shepard   508, 518

Glasgow Corporation v. Muir et al.   585

Globalnet Management Solutions Inc. v. Cornerstone CBS Building Solutions Ltd.   567

Globe & Mail Ltd. v. Boland   1179

Gloster v. Toronto Electric Light Co.   596

Gnanasegaram v. Allianz Insurance Co. of Canada   127

Gobin (Guardian ad litem of) v. British Columbia   867

Godfrey v. Sony Corp.   1142

Godin v. Wilson Laboratories Inc.   488

Godoy, R. v.   312

Golden Capital Securities Ltd. v. Holmes   1117, 1119

Golden, R. v.   305

Goldhawke v. Harder   712

Goldman v. Hargrave   976, 1034

Golub, R. v.   307, 312

Gonzales, R. v.   304, 308

Goodman v. Viljoen   446, 649, 660

Good-Wear Treaders v. D. & B. Holdings Ltd.   489

Goodwin (Litigation Guardian of) v. Olupona   624

Goodwin v. Becker   469

Goodwin v. McCully   630

Goodwin v. Pine Point Park   1001

Goodwyn v. Cheveley   1049

Google Inc. v. Duffy   1163

Gootson v. R.   52, 612

Gordelli Management Ltd. v. Turk   501

Gordon v. Denison   304

Gordon v. Greig   731, 751

Gordon v. Harper   134

Gordon v. Moen   519

Gordon v. Wallace   612

Gormick v. Amenta   668

Gottardo Properties (Dome) Inc. v. Toronto (City)   358

Gould Estate v. Stoddart Publishing Co.   117

Goulet c. Gazette (The)   113

Governor of Brockhill Prison, R. v., Ex Parte Evans (No. 2) 78

Governors of the Peabody Donation Fund v. Sir Lindsay Parkinson & Co. 336

Goyal v. Niagara College of Applied Arts and Technology 552

Graham v. 7 Eleven Canada Inc. 953

Graham v. Bonnycastle 558

Graham v. Hodgkinson 820

Graham v. K.D. Morris & Sons Pty. Ltd. 197

Graham v. MacMillan 449

Graham v. Persyko 587

Graham v. Picot Gorman and A.E.S. Consultants Ltd. 623

Graham v. Purdy 1209

Graham v. Rourke 692, 747

Graham v. Saville 104, 210, 1096

Grand Beach Management Co. v. Manitoba 982

Grand Financial Management Inc. v. Solemio Transportation Inc. 1132, 1141

Grand Restaurants of Canada Ltd. v. Toronto (City) 503, 789

Granite Power Corp. v. Ontario 888

Grant v. Torstar Corp. 1179, 1198, **1199**, 1208

Grant v. Winnipeg Regional Health Authority 122

Grant, R. v. 281

Gratton-Masuy Environmental Technologies Inc. v. Ontario 855

Gray v. Cotic 692, 713

Gray v. Gill 729

Gray v. Macklin 794

Gray v. Thames Trains Ltd. 221, 815, 816

Great Atlantic & Pacific Tea Co. v. Roch 98

Greatorex v. Greatorex 451

Green v. Goddard 260

Green v. Lawrence 299

Green v. Minnes 1167

Green, R. v. 206

Greenhalgh v. Douro-Dummer (Township) 600

Greening v. Wilkinson 160

Greenock Corp. v. Caledonian Railway Co. 1034

Greenwood v. Bennett 164, 266

Greeven v. Blackcomb Skiing Enterprises Ltd. 809

Greffe, R. v. 305

Gregory v. Insurance Corporation of British Columbia 757

Gregory v. Portsmouth City Council 90

Grenier v. Southam Inc. 1200

Grenon v. Canada Revenue Agency 93

Grimmer v. Carleton Road Industries Assn. 1161, 1211

Gringmuth v. North Vancouver (District) 858

Grise v. Rankin et al. 819

Grochowich v. Okanagan University College 959

Groom v. Selby 439

Gros v. Victoria General Hospital 587

Gross v. Great-West Life Assurance Co. 501, 511

Gross v. Wright 208

Grove Services Ltd. v. Lenhart Agencies Ltd. 415

Groves v. Morton 472

Grue v. McLellan 716

Grzywacz v. Vanderheide 459

Gu (Litigation Guardian of) v. Friesen 616

Guay v. Sun Publishing Co. 97, 468

Guergis v. Novak 856, 1122, 1177

Guiliani v. Halton 899

Guillaume v. Toronto (City) 974

Guimond v. Laberge 212

Gujra v Roath 816

Gulati v. MGN Ltd. 110

Gunning, R. v. 262

Gurniak v. Nordquist 775

Gutowski v. Clayton 1177, 1179

Guy v. Trizec Equities Ltd. 777

GWK Ltd. v. Dunlop Rubber Co. Ltd. 1129

Gwynne v. Dominion Stores Ltd. 932

H.(D.) v. Kline 407

H.(M.) v. Bederman 406

H.(R.) v. Hunter 436

H.(V.A.) v. Lynch 504

H.G. v. Shamrock School Division No. 38 257

H.L. v. Canada (Attorney General) 584, 717, 776, 815

H.L. v. Canada 1067

H.R.C. Tool & Die Mfg. Ltd. v. Naderi 122

Ha, R. v. 286

Haag v. Marshall 648

Haaretz.com v. Goldhar 1150

Haberstock, R. v. 256

Hackshaw v. Shaw   17, 262
Hadley v. Baxendale   694
Hagan v. Drover   1157
Hagblom v. Henderson   622
Haggarty v. Desmarais   389
Haggerty Estate v. Rogers   402
Haglof, R. v.   313
Hague v. Billings   388, 663
Hague v. Deputy Governor of Parkhurst
  Prison   78
Haig v. Bamford   500, 507, 623
Haile v. Johns   728
Halcrow, R. v.   256
Hale v. Jennings Brothers   1034
Haley v. London Electric Board   364, 612
Haley v. Richardson; McCrae v.
  Richardson   793
Haliburton (County) v. Gillespie   953
Halifax Building Society v. Thomas   1098
Halkyard v. Mathew   474
Hall (Litigation Guardian of) v. Kellar
  445
Hall v. Bennett Estate   558
Hall v. Hebert   220, 392, 802, **810**
Hall v. Smith   1055
Hall-Chem Inc. v. Vulcan Packaging Inc.
  1117
Halliwell v. Lazarus   623
Halprin v. The Sun Publishing Company
  Ltd.   1160
Hambourg v. T. Eaton Co. Ltd.   940
Hambrook v. Stokes Brothers   452, 455
Hamel et al. v. Prather et al.   754
Hamilton Health Sciences Corp. v. D.H.
  235, 239
Hamilton v. 1214125 Ontario Ltd.   502
Hamilton v. Callaway   535
Hamilton v. Kember   391
Hamilton v. Papakura District Council
  1036
Hamlin v. Invercargill City Council   569
Hamlyn v. Houston & Co.   1055
Hammer v. Kemmis   1120
Hammond v. DeWolfe   581
Hammond v. Wabana (Town)   601
Hamstra (Guardian ad litem of) v. British
  Columbia Rugby Union   730
Handcock v. Baker   292, 312
Hanes v. Kennedy   70
Hanisch v. Canada   81
Hanke v. Resurfice Corp.   643, 652
Hansen v. Sulyma   388, 801, 802
Hansen v. Tilley   1209

Hanson et al. v. City of St. John et al.
  940
Hanson v. St. John Horticultural Assn.
  808
Hanson v. Wayne's Café Ltd.   77
Hôpital Notre-Dame de l'Espérance v.
  Laurent   1076
Harbour Equipment v. Canadian National
  Railway Co.   165
Harbour Radio Pty Ltd. v. Trad   1178
Harbutt's Plasticine v. Wayne Tank &
  Pump Co.   773
Harder v. Brown   218
Hardisty v. 851791 N.W.T. Ltd.   1069
Hare & Grolier Society v. Better Business
  Bureau   1167
Harela v. Powell   622
Harker v. Birkbeck   10
Harland v. Fancsati   1096
Harms, R. v.   210
Harpe v. Lefebvre   663
Harrington (Public Trustee of) v.
  Pappachristos   853
Harris v. Digital Pulse Pty. Ltd.   3
Harris v. GlaxoSmithKline Inc.   93, 1118
Harris v. Nashville Trust Co.   1161
Harrison v. Carswell   33, **182**, 269, 930
Harrison v. Fallis   558
Harrison v. University of British
  Columbia   187
Harrison, R. v.   304
Harriton v. Stephens   436
Hartjes v. Carmen   474
Hartlen v. Chaddock   207
Hartman v. Fisette   797
Harvey v. New Brunswick (Attorney
  General)   850
Hasenclever v. Hoskins   99, 107
Hashem and Hashem v. N.S. Power
  Corp.   196
Hashemi-Sabet Estate v. Mazzulla   500
Haskett v. Equifax Canada Inc.   521, 552
Haskett v. Univ. of Western Ont.   935
Hastings, R. v.   296
Hatton v. Webb   67
Haughian v. Paine   470
Hauk Estate v. Hudson   692
Haward v. Bankes   10
Hawkins v. McGee   36
Hawkins v. Ontario (Attorney General)
  91
Hawley v. Bapoo   88, 853
Hay (or Bourhill) v. Young   362, 450, 699

Hay v. Platinum Equities Inc.   117

Hayduk v. Pidoborozny   1053

Haynes v. Nfld. Telephone Co.   179, 198

Hayter v. Bezanson   204, 808

Hayward v. Thompson   1159

Healey v. Lakeridge Health Corporation 449, 450, 704

Hearndon v. Rondeau   728

Heaslip Estate v. Mansfield Ski Club Inc. 523, 871

Heath v. Weist-Barron School of Television (Canada) Ltd.   117

Heaven v. Pender   318, 329, 330, 332

Heckert v. 5470 Investments Ltd.   120

Hedley Byrne & Co. v. Heller & Partners Ltd.   334, 335, 341, 410, 497, 498, 499, 500, 501, 502, 503, 556, 1099, 1128

Heeney v. Best   630, 788

Hefferman v. Elizabeth Irving Service Centre   773

Heffron v. Imperial Parking Co.   147

Hegarty v. Shine   210, 220

Heighington v. Ontario   99, 449, 724

Heil v. Rankin   757

Heinicke v. Cooper Rankin Ltd.   552, 566

Hellenius v. Lees   840

Heller v. Martens   793, 801

Helmy v. Helmy   1122

Hembruff v. Ontario (Municipal Employees Retirement Board)   520

Hempler v. Todd   392

Henderson v. Dorset Healthcare University NHS Foundation Trust   815

Hendrick v. De Marsh   498, 624, 709

Hendricks v. R.   415

Henly v. Mayor of Lyme   882

Henry Thorne & Co. v. Sandow   1104

Henry v. British Columbia (Attorney General), 2015 SCC 24   31, 89, 284, 891, 927, 928

Henry v. British Columbia (Attorney General), 2016 BCSC 1038   31, 33, 89, 284

Herbert (Litigation Guardian of) v. Brantford (City)   956

Hercules Managements Ltd. v. Ernst & Young   505, 506, 522, 575

Herd v. Weardale Steel, Coal and Coke Co. Ltd.   82

Herman v. Graves   58, 249

Hermiz v. Canada   888

Hern v. Nichols   1054

Herring v. England (Ministry of Defence)   747

Hertfordshire Police v. Van Colle   404

Heward v. Eli Lilly & Co.   483

Hewson v. Red Deer   713

Heydary Hamilton P.C. v. Muhammad 1131, 1161

Hibberd v. William Osler Health Centre 748

Hickey v. Electricity Reduction Co.   997

Hicks v. Faulkner   85

Higgins Estate v. Arseneau   761

Higgins v. William Inglis & Sons Pty. Ltd.   1044

High Parklane Consulting Inc. v. Royal Group Technologies Ltd.   101

Hilderman v. Rattray   829

Hill v. British Columbia   78

Hill v. Chief Constable of West Yorkshire   336, 402

Hill v. Church of Scientology   39, 43, 755, 922, 1147, 1149, 1179, **1180, 1213**

Hill v. Hamilton Wentworth Regional Police Services Board   89, 347, 522, 623, 625

Hill v. Hurst   601

Hill v. Intact Insurance Co.   959

Hill v. Van Erp   344, 558

Hill v. Victoria Hospital Corp.   475

Hills v. Bridgeview Little League Association   396

Himmelman v. Nova Const. Co.   1035

Hinse v. Canada (Attorney General)   284, 856

Hinz v. Berry   449, 452, 464

Hiscoe, R. v.   304

Hislop v. Canada (Attorney General) 283, 284

Hneihen (Litigation guardian of) v. Centre for Addiction and Mental Health   928

Hoang v. Trieu   779

Hoare v. McAlpine   1034

Hockley v. Riley   41, 407

Hodgkinson v. Martin   59

Hodgson v. Canadian Newspapers Co. 1155, 1196, 1198

Hoffman v. Monsanto Canada Inc.   180

Hofstrand Farms Ltd. v. B.D.C. Ltd. 623

Hogarth v. Rocky Mountain Slate Inc. 502

Hogstead (Litigation Guardian of) v. Spiers   835

Holan Estate v. Stanton Regional Health Board 394

Holcombe v. Whitaker 71

Holderness v. Goslin 1034

Hole v. Sittingbourne & Sheerness Railway Co. 1083

Holinaty v. Hawkins 1033, 1034

Holland v. Saskatchewan 588, 871, 910

Hollebone v. Barnard 275, 796

Hollett v. Coca-Cola Ltd. 406, 716

Hollins v. Fowler 141, 144

Hollinsworth v. BCTV 118

Hollis v. Dow Corning Corp. 477, 641, 1050

Hollywood Silver Fox Farm Ltd. v. Emmett 983

Holmes (Litigation guardian of) v. Edmunds 957

Holmes v. Mather 14

Holt v. Rother 820

Holt v. Sun Publishing Co. Ltd. 1196

Holtby v. Brigham & Cowan (Hull) Ltd. 650, 837

Holtslag v. Alberta 871

Home Office v. Dorset Yacht Co. 334, 393, 873

Homer v. Comeau 829

Homsi v. Homsi 451

Honan v. Gerhold 1054

Honda Canada Inc. v. Keays 127

Honeywill & Stein Ltd. v. Larkin Bros. 1079

Hongkong Bank of Canada v. Richardson Greenshields of Canada Ltd. 729

Honing v. Phinney 535

Hooey v. Mancini 392

Hooiveld v. Van Biert 691

Hook v. Cunard SS. Co. 259

Hooper v. Rogers 1004

Hopkins v. Kay 115

Hopp v. Lepp 224, 227, 242, 470, 471, 472, 641

Horne v. New Glasgow (Town) 452

Hornick v. Kochinsky 728

Horrocks v. Lowe 1180

Horseshoe Bay Retirement Society v. S.I.F. Development Corp. 181

Horsford v. Bird (Antigua and Barbuda) 181

Horsley v. MacLaren 127, 379, **418**, 602, 908

Horton v. Tim Donut Ltd. 117, 1108

Hosking v. Runting 113

Host v. Bassett 835

Houle v. S.S. Kresge Co. 943

Hounga v. Allen 815, 816

Houseman v. Coulson 1157

Housen v. Nikolaisen 358, 584

Howard v. Furness Houlder Argentine Lines, Ltd. 1026

Howarth v. The Queen 853

Howes v. Crosby 729

Hryniak v. Mauldin 1093

HSBC Bank Canada v. 1100336 Alberta Ltd. (c.o.b. Incredible Electronics Wholesale) 1120

Huang v. Fraser Hillary's Ltd. 180, 967, 1024, 1032

Hub Excavating Ltd. v. Orca Estates Ltd. 502

Hubley v. Hubley Estate 554

Hudson v. Brantford Police Services Board 290

Hudson v. Riverdale Colony of Hutterian Brethren 1033

Hudson's Bay Co. v. White 188

Huggins, R. v. 10, 1046

Hughes 689

Hughes Estate v. Hughes 504

Hughes v. Lord Advocate 685, 699

Hughes v. Sunbeam Corp. (Canada) 558, 567

Hundley v. Punnett 844

Hung v. Gardiner 1172, 1176

Hunt (Litigation Guardian of) v. Sutton Group Incentive Realty Inc. 390, 825

Hunt Oil Co. of Canada Ltd. v. Galleon Energy Inc. 93

Hunt v. Carey Canada Inc. 649, 1120

Hunt v. Sutton Group 391

Hunter and New England Local Health District v. McKenna 394

Hunter v. Briere 684, 784, 797

Hunter v. Canary Wharf Ltd. 107, 975

Hunter v. Chandler 1209

Hunter v. Manning 691

Hunter, R. v. 312

Hurley v. Eddingfield 414

Hurley v. Moore 59

Hussack v. Chilliwack School District No. 33 395, 623, 704, 713, 747

Hussain v. Lancaster City Council 976

Hutchings v. Dow 668

Hutchings v. Nevin 612, 789

Hutchinson, R. v. 210

Huth v. Huth 1161

Hutscal v. I.A.C. Ltd.   161
Hutterly v. Imperial Oil Ltd.   425
Hymas v. Ogden   167
Hynes v. Hynes   1004
I.H.V. (Re)   230
I.W. Holdsworth Ltd. v. Assoc.
  Newspapers Ltd.   1155
Iannarella v. Corbett   844
IBM Canada Limited v. Waterman   779
Imbree v. McNeilly   616
Imperial Tobacco Canada Ltd., R. v.
  344, 348, 489, **521**, 859, **872**, 876
In re A.C.   447
In re Corby Group Litigation   1001
In Re F (Mental Patient: Sterilization)
  239
In re Polemis   681
In Thrifty-Tel, Inc. v. Bezenek   138
Indermaur v. Dames   936, 937, 940
Indian Head Credit Union Ltd. v. A. Hosie
  & Co.   623
Indian Towing Co.   862
Indust. Teletype Electronics Corp. v.
  Montreal   775
Indutech Canada Ltd. v. Gibbs Pipe
  Distributors Ltd.   47
Inform Cycle Ltd. v. Rebound Inc.   38,
  1107
Ingles v. Tutkaluk Construction Ltd.
  798, 867, 869
Ingram v. Lowe   396
Innes v. Kotylak   993
Innes v. Wylie   68, 70
Insurance Corp. of British Columbia v.
  Mandzuk   742
Int. Brotherhood of Teamsters v.
  Therien   1112
International Sausage House Ltd. v.
  Hammer Estate   1142
Intrawest Corp. v. No. 2002 Taurus
  Ventures Ltd.   540
Inverugie Investments Ltd. v. Hackett
  35, 36
Iqbal v. Prison Officers Association   78
Ireland, R. v.   74
Irvine v Smith   395
Irvington Holdings Ltd. v. Black   144
Irwin Toy Ltd. v. Québec (Attorney
  General)   1201
Isaac Estate v. Matuszynska   627
Ismail v. Treats Inc.   500, 541
Israel James Hussey   262

ITO — International Terminal Operators
  Ltd. v. Miida Electronics Inc.   808
iTrade Finance Holdings Inc. v. Webworx
  Inc.   1098
Ivall v. Aguiar   1025
Iversen v. Purser   392
Ivic v. Lakovic   1065
J.(L.A.) v. J.(H.)   407
J.(M.I.) v. Grieve   68, 78
J.A., R. v.   219
J.A.T., R. v.   211
J.C. Kerkhoff & Sons Contracting Ltd. v.
  XL Ironworks Co.   1113
J.M. v. W.B.   798
J.M.G., R. v.   257
J.P. v. British Columbia (Children and
  Family Development)   624
J.T. Stratford & Son v. Lindley   1112
Jack Cewe Ltd. v. Jorgenson   777
Jack v. Tekavec   957
Jackman, R. v.   308
Jackpine, R. v.   306
Jacks v. Davis   622
Jackson v. Kelowna General Hospital
  653
Jackson v. Millar   754, 840
Jackson v. Murray   802
Jacobi v. Griffiths   1066
Jacobsen v. Nike Canada Ltd.   390
Jaensch v. Coffey   456
Jalava v. Webster   33
Jaman Estate v. Hussain   1065
Jameel v. Wall Street Journal Europe
  SPRL   1208
James Street Hardware and Furniture Co.
  v. Spizziri   771, 773
James v. British Columbia   556
Jamieson Laboratories Ltd. v. Reckitt
  Benckiser LLC   1108
Jamieson v. Whistler Mountain Resort
  Limited Partnership   810
Jane Doe 464533 v. D.(N.)   116, 122
Jane Doe 72511 v. Morgan   116
**Jane Doe v. Metropolitan Toronto
  (Municipality) Commissioners of Police
  398**, 890
Janiak v. Ippolito   660, 713, 728
Janigan v. Taylor   1098
Jans v. Ducks Unlimited Canada   1079
Janvier, R. v.   287
Janzen v. Janzen   241
Jarbeau v. McLean   495, 660, 771
Jarvis v. Treberg   757

Jarvis v. Williams   170
Jarvis, R. v.   115
Jebson v. Ministry of Defence   392, 689
Jeffrey v. Commodore Cabaret Ltd.   958
Jema International Food Products Inc. v.
  Scholle Canada Ltd.   488
Jennings, R. v.   898
Jens v. Mannix Co. Ltd.   773
Jensen v. Fit City Health Centre Inc.
  810, 960
Jetivia S.A. v. Bilta (UK) Limited   817
Jevco Insurance Co. v. Pacific Assessment
  Centre Inc.   1120
Jews for Jesus v. Brodsky   1107
Jill Fishing Ltd. v. Koranda Management
  Inc.   1215
Jinks v. Cardwell   394
Jobidon, R. v.   207, 219
Jobling v. Associated Dairies Ltd.   674
Joe v. Paradis   807
Johansson v. General Motors of Canada
  Ltd.   632, 844
Johar v. Kucy   91
John A. Ford & Associates Inc. (c.o.b.
  Training Services) v. Keegan   1109
John Bead Corp. v. Soni   221, 814
John Campbell Law Corp. v. Strata Plan
  1350   1032
John Doe v. Bennett   407, 1068
John Doe v. Fifield   1068
John Lewis & Co. v. Tims   292, 301
John Maryon Int. Ltd. v. N.B. Telephone
  Co.   775
John v. Flynn   390, 391
John v. Kim   1196
Johnson v. BFI Canada Inc.   1131
Johnson v. British Columbia Hydro and
  Power Authority   188
Johnson v. Canada (Minister of National
  Revenue)   1079
Johnson v. Leigh   310
Johnson v. Milton (Town)   789
Johnson v. Royal Can. Legion Grandview
  Branch No. 179   218
Johnson v. Webb   808, 958
Johnston Estate v. Johnston   558
Johnston v. Day   716
Johnston v. NEI International Combustion
  Limited; Rothwell v. Chemical and
  Insulating Company Limited   651
Johnston v. Re/max Real Estate
  (Edmonton) Ltd.   499
Jolley v. Sutton London B.C.   688, 709

Jones (Guardian ad litem of) v. Rostvig
  437
Jones Masonry Ltd. v. Defence
  Construction (1951) Ltd.   551
Jones v. Bennett   1184, 1196
Jones v. Brooks   1209
Jones v. Dowle   166, 168
Jones v. Niklaus   803
Jones v. Richard   933
Jones v. Swansea City Council   889
Jones v. Tsige   113
Jones v. Wabigwan   684, 685
Jones, R. v.   304
Jordan House Ltd. v. Menow   127, 262,
  384, 807
Joseph Brant Memorial Hospital v.
  Koziol   621, 648, 834
Joshi v. Wooley   439
Joslyn v. Berryman; Wentworth Shire
  Council v. Berryman   807
Joudrey v. Swissair Transport Company
  426
Joule Ltd. v. Poole   147
Joy v. Newell (t/a Copper Room)   392
Joyal v. Barsby   613
Joyce v. O'Brien   816
Jozwiak v. Sadek   1159
JSC BTA Bank v. Khrapunov   1088,
  1116, 1119, 1121
Juelle v. Trudeau   149
Junior Books Ltd. v. Veitchi   567
Just v. British Columbia   337, 341, 856,
  859, 872
K. (K.) v. G. (K.W.)   69
K.(F.) c. K.(H.)   41
K.(K.) v. G.(K.W.)   37, 41, 407
K.(M.J.) v. M.(J.D.)   974
K.(W.) v. Pornbacher   692
K.L. v 1163957799 Quebec Inc.   127
K.L.B. v. British Columbia   69
K.M. v. Marson   757
K.R. Thompson Engineering Ltd. v.
  Webster Industries Ltd.   156
K.S. (Litigation Representative of) v.
  Willox   621
Kahlon (Litigation Guardian of) v.
  Vancouver Coastal Health Authority
  740, 789
Kakavas v. Crown Melbourne Limited
  398
Kalish v. Rosenbaum   622
Kallstrom v. Yip   668
Kamin v. Kawartha Dairy Ltd.   954

Kamloops (City) v. Nielsen   337, 546, 568, 574, 811

Kamloops-Cariboo Regional Immigrants Society v. Herman   1116

Kang-Brown, R. v.   308

Kaplan v. Canada Safeway Ltd.   932

Kaptor Financial Inc. v. Alexander   1141

Karagozlu v. Commissioner of Police of the Metropolis   889

Karn v. Sturgeon   956

Karogiannis v. Poulus   291

Karpenko v. Paroian, Courey, Cohen & Houston   494

Kassian Estate v. Canada (Attorney General)   300, 1067

Katzman v. Yaeck   712

Kauffman v. Toronto Transit Commission   636

Kavanagh v. Akhtar   692

Kealey v. Berezowski   439, 441

Keats v. Pearce   440

Keays v. Honda Canada Inc.   43

Keeble v. Hickeringill   1087

Keegstra, R. v.   1201

Keep v. Quallman   61

Keeping v. Canada (Minister of Fisheries and Oceans)   867

Keith Plumbing & Heating Co. v. Newport City Club Ltd.   502

Keith v. Abraham   621

Keizer v. Hanna   750, **763**

Kelemen v. El-Homeira   1095

Kelly v. Lundgard   500, 631

Kelsen v. Imperial Tobacco Co. (of Great Britain and Ireland) Ltd.   194, 197

Kempf v. Nguyen   204, 627, 809

Kendrew v. McDonald's Restaurants of Canada Ltd.   468

Kenlin v. Gardiner   298

Kennaway v. Thompson   1011

Kennedy v. Coe   371

Kennedy v. Hughes Drug (1969) Inc.   685

Kennedy v. London (City)   956

Kennedy v. Waterloo (County) Board of Education   954

Kent (Litigation Guardian of) v. Laverdiere   1045

Kent v. Dom. Steel & Coal Corp. Ltd.   973

Kent v. East Suffolk Rivers Catchment Board   864, 866

Kent v. Griffiths   380

Kent v. Martin   1117

Kent v. Postmedia Network Inc.   1162

Kerlenmar Holdings Ltd. v. Matsqui (District)   977

Kern v. Steele   729

Kerr v. Fleming Financial Corp.   162

Kerr v. Revelstoke Bldg. Materials Ltd.   190

Kessel v. Van Rikkoort   155

Ketler v. Nova Scotia (Attorney General)   639

Kettlewell v. Refuge Assurance Co.   1098

Kevington Building Corp. v. Lee   772

Keyland Development Corp. v. Rocky View (Municipal District No. 44)   1118

Keys v. Mistahia Regional Health Authority   446

Khaira v. Nelson   1095

Khalil v. Barakat   1155

Khalil v. R.   910

Khan v. El Al Israel Airlines   84

Khan v. Vernon Jubilee Hospital   539

Khanna v. Royal College of Dental Surgeons (Ontario)   90

Khorasandjian v. Bush   107, 974

Killip's Television Service Ltd. v. Stony Plain (Town)   601

Kim v. Lin   758

Kim v. Thammavong   389

King Lofts Toronto I Ltd. v. Emmons   622, 624

King v. Fanklin   259

King v. Leith   163

King v. Philcox   458

King v. Phillips   362, 699

Kingsbridge Development Inc. v. Hanson Needler Corp.   197

Kinsella v. Club "7" Ltd.   169

Kirby v. Amalgamated Income Ltd. Partnership   1072

Kirby v. Canadian Tire   488

Kirkbi AG v. Ritvik Holdings Inc.   1105, 1106

Kirkham v. Chief Constable of Greater Manchester Police   221

Kitchen v. Royal Air Forces Association   660

Kitchener (City of) v. Robe & Clothing Co.   1083

Klein v. American Medical Systems, Inc.   871

Klein v. Stiller   959

Kleinsasser v. Alexander   1071

Knife (Litigation Guardian of) v.
   Charles   449
Knodell v. New Westminster (City)   868
Knuppfer v. London Express Newspaper,
   Ltd.   1158
Knutson v. Farr   756
Kobi's Auto Ltd. v. 5174245 Manitoba
   Ltd.   144
Koechlin v. Waugh and Hamilton   294
Kohn v. Globerman   82
Kokanee Mortgage M.I.C. Ltd. v Burrell
   503
Kolosov v. Lowe's Companies Inc.   286
Kondis v. State Transport Authority
   1083
Koopman v. Fehr   793
Koperdak v. Wiesblatt   955
Kopka et ux. v. Bell Telephone Co. of
   Pennsylvania   178
Koszulap, R. v.   301
Kotai v. Queen of the North (The)   449
Koubi v. Mazda Canada Inc.   49
Kozak v. Funk   728
Kraft (Next friend of) v. Oshawa General
   Hospital   722
Kralik v. Mount Seymour Resorts Ltd.
   748
Kralj v. Murray   585
Krangle (Guardian ad litem of) v. Brisco
   436, 741, 776
Krawchuk v. Scherbak   501, 539, 540,
   623, 624
Krieger v. Law Society of Alberta   89,
   853
Kripps v. Touche Ross & Co.   498, 500
Kroeker v. Jansen   746
Kroeker v. Krebs   143
Krouse v. Chrysler Canada Ltd.   117,
   1108
Krznaric v. Chevrette   891
Ksiazek v. Newport Leasing Ltd.   729
Kuddus v. Chief Constable of
   Leicestershire Constabulary   889, 1113
Kuhl v. Zurich Financial Services Australia
   Ltd.   600
Kurdina v. Gratzer   624
Kuru v. State of New South Wales   313
Kuwait Airways Corp. v. Iraqi Airways
   Co.   161
L.(A.) v. Ontario (Minister of Community
   & Social Services)   888
L.(J.) v. Canada (Attorney General)   395
L.R. v. Bromley Estate   1083

Labrador School Board v. R.P.   63
Labrecque v. Saskatchewan Wheat Pool
   485
Lacroix (Litigation Guardian of) v.
   Dominique   431, 437
Lacroix v. R.   196
Laface v. Williams   388
Laferrière v. Lawson   660
Laflamme v. Groupe TDL Ltée   485
Lafleur v. Maryniuk   392
Lagden v. O'Connor   694, 772
Lahaie v. Canada (Attorney General)
   284
Lai v. Gill   769
Lajeunesse v. Janssens   1054
Lajoie v. Kelly   127
Lakefield (Village) v. Black   520
Lakeview Gardens Ltd. v. Regina (City)
   1010
Lam v. Sorochan Estate   693
Lamb v. London Borough of Camden
   716
Lambert v. Lastoplex Chemicals Co.
   478, 485
Lambert v. Thomson   1160
Lambton v. Mellish   669
Lamine v. Dorrell   163
Lampert v. Simpson Sears Ltd.   943
Lan v. Wu   747
Landry v. Patterson   58
Landry, R. v.   312
Lane v. Holloway   207, 217
Lang v. Burch   297
Lang v. Giraudo   1098
Langridge v. Levy   95, 333
Lapchuk v. Saskatchewan   1122
Lapensee v. Ottawa Day Nursery Inc.
   397
Lapierre v. A.G. (Que.)   270, 486
LaPlante (Guardian ad litem of) v.
   LaPlante   397, 616
Lapointe v. Hôpital Le Gardeur   587, 628
Larche v. Ontario   394
Lareau v. La Compagnie d'Imprimerie de
   la Minerve   1155
Larizza v. Royal Bank of Canada   115
Larsen v. Wilson   712
LaSalle Extension University v. Fogarty
   98
Latimer, R. v.   268
Latin v. Hospital for Sick Children   620
Létourneau v. JTI-MacDonald Corp   488
Latter v. Braddell   213, 216

Laudon v. Roberts 779

Laugher v. Pointer 1069

Lauritzan v. Barstead 688

Lauzon v. Auger 69

Lavallee, R. v. 249

Lavender v. Miller Bernstein LLP 552

Lavigne v. O.P.S.E.U. 921

Laviolette v. C.N.R. 616, 788, 807

Law Estate v. Simice 597

Law Society (British Columbia) v. Canada
  Domain Name Exchange Corp. 1106

Lawrence v. Finch 1157

Lawrence v. Peel Regional Police Force
  625

Lawrence v. Prince Rupert (City) 798

Lawson v. Burns 1216

Lawson v. Wellesley Hospital 63

Layden v. Cope 619

Layton, R. v. 187

LBP Holdings Ltd. v. Hycroft Mining
  Corporation 552

Le Lievre v. Gould 318, 329, 330, 519

Le Soleil Hospitality Inc. v. Louie 1119

Leake v. Loveday 147

Leaman v. Rea 835, 838

Leame v. Bray 13

LeBar v. Canada 78

LeBlanc v. Canada 889

Lebrun v. High-Low Foods Ltd. 81

LeClerc v. Westfair Foods Ltd. 757

Leddicote v. Nova Scotia (Attorney
  General) 748

Lee (Guardian ad litem of) v. Barker 788

Lee Tat Development Pte. Ltd. v.
  Management Corporation Strata Title
  Plan No. 301 92, 93

Lee v. Dawson 755, 756

Lee v. O'Farrell 789

Lee v. Shalom Branch No. 178 Building
  Society 192

Leech v. Leader Publishing Co. 1197

Leenen v. Canadian Broadcasting Corp.
  1196, 1200

Leerdam v. Noori 889

Lehnert v. Nelson 391

Lehnert v. Stein 805, 806

Lei, R. v. 265

Leigh v. Cole 304

Leigh and Sullivan Ltd. v. Aliakmon
  Shipping Co. 336

Leighton v. Best 206

Leishman (Legal Guardian of) v.
  Hoechsmann et al. 394

Leitch, R. v. 298

Lem v. Barotto Sports Ltd. 487

Leon v. Tu 621, 632

Leroux v. Canada (Revenue Agency) 908

Les Laboratoires Servier v. Apotex Inc.
  816

Leslie v. Ball 491, 492

Letang v. Cooper 17, 137, 830

Letnik v. Metropolitan Toronto
  (Municipality) 648

Leung v. Campbell 473

Leung v. Shanks 122

Levesque v. Day & Ross Ltd. 819

Levesque v. Wedge 627

Levita v. Crew 206, 810

Lewis (Guardian ad litem of) v. British
  Columbia 867, 958, 1080

Lewis v. Chief Constable 297

Lewis v. Daily Telegraph 1154

Lewis v. Oeming 1040, 1041, 1043, 1044

Lewis v. Prince Edward Island 867

Lewis v. Todd 751, 767, 788

Lewvest Ltd. v. Scotia Towers Ltd. 197

Liboiron v. Majola 1177

Lichtenstein v. Bathurst Towers Inc. 397

Lickoch v. Madu 1001, 1033

Liebig v. Guelph General Hospital 349,
  446

Ligate v. Abick 751

Lim v. Titov 198

Lincoln v. Daniels 1173, 1174, 1177

Lindal v. Lindal 754

Lindon v. Hooper 137

Lines v. Gordon 735, 744

Lion v. Money 769

Lipiec v. Borsa 112

Lipischak v. DeWolf 974

Lippa v. Colletta 623, 624, 810

Lippiatt v. South Gloucestershire
  Council 976

Lister v. Hesley Hall Ltd. 1072, 1073

Lister v. Romford Ice & Cold Storage
  Co. 1057, 1071

Little v. Ottawa (City) 853

Littleford v. Loanex Financial Services
  173

Liu v. Bipinchandra 729

Liu v. Sung 1118, 1122

Livingstone v. Rawyards Coal Co. 34

Lloyd v. Grace, Smith & Co. 1055, 1060

Lloyd, R. v. 997

Lloydminster Credit Union Ltd. v. 324007
  Alberta Ltd. 134

Indermaur v. Dames   937

Loan v. MacLean   1157

Lodge v. Fraser Health Authority   468

Loewen, R. v.   286, 304

Lofstrom v. Hydamaka   1045

Logan Lake (Dist.) v. Rivtow Industries
Ltd.   568

London Artists, Ltd. v. Littler   1204

London Borough of Southwark v.
Williams   269

London Computer Operators Training
Ltd. v. British Broadcasting
Corporation   1167

London Drugs Ltd. v. Kuehne & Nagel
International Ltd.   1058, 1061

London Graving Dock Co. Ltd. v.
Horton   940

London Passenger Transport Board v.
Upson   902, 918

Loney v. Burtch   208

Long v. Gardner   59

Long v. R.   144

Long v. Toronto Ry. Co.   784

Longley v. Canada   889

Longley v. M.N.R.   887

Longmeid v. Holliday   333

Lonrho Ltd. v. Shell Petroleum Co. (No.
2)   1121

Lonrho plc. v. Tebbit   853

Loop v. Litchfield   333

Lord (Litigation Guardian of) v.
Downer   762

Lord v. McGregor   111

Lorenz v. Winnipeg (City)   358

Los Angeles Salad Co. v Canadian Food
Inspection Agency   348

Losee v. Clute   333

Lougheed v. Canadian Broadcasting
Corporation   1156

Louie v. Lastman (No. 2)   101

Lovely v. Kamloops (City)   599, 623, 959

Low v. Pfizer Canada Inc.   1141, 1142

Lowe v. Guarantee Co. of North
America   521, 552, 853

Lowe v. The Guarantee Company of North
America   871

Lowns v. Woods   380

Lowry v. Cdn. Mountain Holidays Ltd.
632

Loychuk v. Cougar Mountain Adventures
Ltd.   809

Lucas v. Antoniak   793

Lucas, R. v.   1202

Lumba v. Secretary of State for the Home
Department   78

Lumley v. Gye   1125, 1127, 1129, 1130,
1131, 1133

Lumley v. Wagner   1127

Lumsden v. Barry Cordage Ltd.   487

Lund v. Black Press Group Ltd.   1157

Lunenburg (County) District School Board
v. Piercey   395

Lynch v. Knight   94

Lynch v. Lynch   445

Lyne v. McClarty   621, 693

Lyon v. Village of Shelburne   1035

Lyons, R. v.   262

Lysko v. Braley   1128, 1133

Lyth v. Dagg   218, 407

M. Hasegawa & Co. v. Pepsi Bottling
Group (Canada) Co.   566, 568

M. v. Sinclair   845

M.(A.) v. Matthews   91

M.(B.) (Litigation Guardian of) v.
M.(R.)   407

M.(J.) v. Toronto Board of Education
236

M.(J.), R. v.   207

M.(K.) v. M.(H.)   69

M.(M.) v. K.(K.)   217

M.(M.R.), R. v.   257, 280, 308

M.A., R. v.   257

M.B. v. 2014052 Ontario Ltd. (Deluxe
Windows of Canada)   668

M.B. v. British Columbia   748, 776

M.C. Mehta v. Union of India   1037

M.S. v. Baker   441

M.V. Polar Star v. Arsenault   143

M.Y. v. Boutros   441

Mabior, R. v.   210, 212

MacAlpine v. H.(T.)   853

Macartney v. Warner   761, 762

MacCabe v. Westlock Roman Catholic
Separate School District No. 110   395,
397, 623, 747

MacDonald (Guardian ad litem of) v.
Neufeld   742

MacDonald (Litigation Guardian of) v.
Goertz   709

MacDonald Estate v. Martin   625

MacDonald v. Alderson   740

MacDonald v. Goertz   654

Macdonald v. Hees   259

Macdonald v. Mail Printing Co.   1155

MacDonald v. Mitchell   1053

MacDonald v. Sebastian   68, 724

Macdonald v. Woodard 827
MacDonald, R. v. 281
Macdonell v. Robinson 1194
Mack v. Canada (Attorney General) 589, 856
MacKay Estate v. Smith 761
MacKay v. Buelow 107
MacKay v. MacLellan 797
MacKay v. Starbucks Corp. 953
MacKay, R. v. 312
MacKeigan v. Hickman 853
MacKenzie v. John Doe 468
Mackenzie v. Scotia Lumber Co. 139
Mackey (Litigation Guardian of) v. British Columbia (Provincial Capital Commission) 745, 801
Mackin v. New Brunswick (Minister of Justice) 283, 923
MacKinnon v. Ellis 1048
MacLean v. Liquor Lic. Bd. of Ontario 855
MacLean v. MacDonald 761
Maclenan v. Segar 937, 938
MacMillan v. Hincks 249
MacNeil v. Bryan 731
Macooh, R. v. 313
MacPherson v. Buick Motor Company 333
Maddison, R. v. 257
Mader v. MacPhee 1054
Madge v. Meyer 793
Magill v. Magill 1096
Magnusson v. Bd. of Nipawin School Unit No. 61 of Sask. 397
Maguire v. Padt 425
Mahal v. Young 68, 71, 104
Mahe v. Boulianne 803
Maher v. K Mart Can. Ltd. 80
Mainland Sawmills Ltd. v. I.W.A.- Canada 74, 100, 107, 662
Mainstream Properties Limited (Appellants) v. Young 156, 1132
Mainville v. Ottawa Board of Education 397
Majrowski v. Guy's & St. Thomas' N.H.S. Trust 1064, 1066
Maki, R. v. 206
Makow v. Winnipeg Sun 1168
Malat v. Bjornson (No. 2) 867
Malette v. Shulman 64, **226**, 228
Malinowski v. Schneider 475
M'Alister (or Donoghue) v. Stevenson 318, **328**, 682

Malleck v. Baum 621
Mallet v. New Brunswick 127
Mallett v. McMonagle 749
Mallory v. Werkmann Estate 663
Malott, R. v. 250
Malton v. Attia 625
Mammoliti v. Niagara Regional Police Service 283, 928
Manary v. Strban 622
Mandeville v. Manufacturers Life Insurance Co. 348, 544, 552
Mandrake Management Consultants Ltd. v. Toronto Transit Commission 990
Mangal v. William Osler Health Centre 639
Mangat, R. v. 301
Manina Investments Ltd. v. Regatta Investments Ltd. 155
Manitoba Métis Federation Inc. v. Canada (Attorney General) 858
Manitoba Sausage Manufacturing Ltd. v. Winnipeg (City) 498
Manitoba v. Air Canada 196
Mann v. Balaban 248
Mann v. Canadian Tire Corp. 82, 293
Mann v. Kendall 826
Mann v. O'Neill 1177
Mann v. Saulnier 192
Mann, R. v. 281
Manoukian c. Procureur général du Canada 38
Mansfield v. Weetabix 612
Mantella v. Mantella 495
Mantini v. Smyth Lyons LLP (No. 2) 1155
Manufacturers Life Insurance Co. v. Pitblado & Hoskin 520
Marakah, R. v. 304
Marcoccia (Litigation Guardian of) v. Gill 731, 742, 802
Marconato v. Franklin 690
Marcotte c. Société TVA Inc. 1156
Marcoux v. Bouchard 473
Marcq v. Christie Manson & Woods Ltd. (trading as Christie's) 146
Mariani v. Lemstra 540, 566
Mark Fishing Company Ltd. v. United Fishermen and Allied Workers Union 1130
Market Investigations, Ltd. v. Minister of Social Security 1077
Marks v. Campbell 829
Marley v. Kains 1156

Marlin Investments Inc. v. Moldovan 623

Marrinan v. Vibart 1176

Marsh v. Keating 163

Marshall (Litigation Guardian of) v. Annapolis (County) District School Board 62, 788, **915**

Marshall v. Curry 224

Martel Building Ltd. v. Canada 528, **545**

Martin v. America International Assurance Life Co. 424

Martin v. Benson 33

Martin v. Findlay 475

Martin v. Inglis 473

Martin v. Lavigne 974, 986

Martin v. Listowel Memorial Hospital 798

Martin v. Martin 662

Martin v. Mineral Springs Hospital 447

Martin v. Murray Estate 835

Martin v. Reynolds Metal Co. 193

Martin v. Watson 91

Marynowsky v. Stuartburn (District) 33

Mason v. Morrow's Moving & Storage Ltd. 411

Mason v. Peters 762, 768, 769

Mason v. Westside Cemeteries Ltd. 449, 772

Masters v. Fox 1198

Matharu v. Nam 808

Matheson v. CIBC World Markets Inc./ Marches Mondiaux CIBC Inc. 502

Matheson v. Smiley 228

Mathison v. Hofer 449

Mathura v. Scarborough General Hospital 648

Mattel Inc. v. 3894207 Canada Inc. 1106

Matthews v. MacLaren; Horsley v. MacLaren 373, 416, 653

Mattis v. Pollock 1065

Maughan v. University of British Columbia 853

Maunsell v. Lethbridge Northern Irrigation District 188

Mawe v. Pigott 1155

Maxey v. Can. Perm. Trust Co. 411

Maxwell Properties Ltd. v. Mosaik Property Management Ltd. 197

Mayfair Ltd. v. Pears 181

Mayne v. Kidd 164, 266

Maynes v. Galicz 1040, 1043, 1044

Mayrand v. Cronier 852

Mazzucco v. Herer 779

McAllister v. Calgary (City) 958

McAlpine v. Bercow 1156

McArdle Estate v. Cox 584

McBain v. Laurentian Hospital 231

MCC Proceeds Ltd. v. Lehman Bros. (Europe) 158

McC v. Mullan 851

McCallum v Kent (District) 993

McCarty v. Pheasant Run Inc. 605

McClelland v. Stewart 345

McCombe v. Read et al. 1003

McConnell, R. v. 250

McCulloch v. Murray 625

McCullough v. Riffert 558, 622

McDermott v. Ramadanovic Estate 768

McDonald v. Doe 844

McDonald v. National Grid Electricity Transmission plc 907

McDonald, R. v. 208

McDonic v. Hetherington 1055

McDougall v. Black & Decker Canada Inc. 839

McEllistrum v. Etches 614, 615

McErlean v. Sarel 615, **939**

McEvoy v. Capital Motors 789

McFarlane v. Tayside Health Board (Scotland) 439

McGarrigle v. Dalhousie University 1184

McGeough v. Don Enterprises Ltd. 943

McGhee v. National Coal Board 643, 836

McGillivray v. Kimber 878

McGinlay v. British Railway Bd. 807

McGinty v. Cook 938, 958

McGivney v. Rustico Summer Haven 938

McGowan v. Bank of Nova Scotia 347

McGrath v. Dawkins 1163

McHale v. Watson 17

McHugh v. Okai-Koi 816

Mcihael 404

McIntosh v. Bell 818

McIntosh, R. v. 249

McIntyre v. Docherty 757

McIntyre v. Grigg 45, 388, 723, 755

McIntyre v. MacKnight 59

McIntyre v. Sawatsky 627

McIver v. McIntyre 1054

McKay v. Essex Area Health Authority 435

McKay, R. v. 249, 262

McKee (Guardian ad litem of) v. McCoy
616
McKee v. Dumas   1069
McKee v. Malenfant   784
McKerr v. CML Healthcare Inc.   620
McKew v. Holland & Hannen & Cubitts
(Scotland) Ltd.   454, 712
McKinney v. University of Guelph   921
McLachlan v. Canadian Imperial Bank of
Commerce   155
McLaren v. McLaren Estate   616, 741
McLean v. 366543 B.C. Ltd.   248
McLean v. Danicic   100
McLean v. Knox   796, 807
McLean v. Law Society of British
Columbia   1116
McLean v. Parmar   746, 748
McLellan v. Melanson   170
McLeod v. Palardy   778
McLintock v. Alidina   621
McLorie v. Oxford   307
McLoughlin v. Arbor Memorial Services
Inc.   449
McLoughlin v. Kutasy   1178, 1180
McLoughlin v. O'Brian   452, 454, 455,
457, 464
McMaster v. R.   887
McMillan v. Rural Municipality of
Thompson   1251
McMullin v. F.W. Woolworth Co.   468
McNeil v. Brewers Retail Inc.   90
McNeill v. Frankenfield   1043, 1044
McNichol v. Grandy   1161
McNulty v. Edmonton (City)   801
McPherson v. Daniels   1164
McQuillan v. Wong   1043
McRae v. British Norwegian Whaling Co.
Ltd.   997
McSorley, R. v.   206
McTaggart v. Commonwealth Hospitality
Ltd.   938
McTaggart v. Ontario   284
McTavish v. MacGillivray   746
McVea (Guardian ad litem of) v. T.B.
769
Meady v. Greyhound Canada
Transportation Corp.   599, 624
Mears v. London & South Western Ry.
Co.   134
Mee v. Gardiner   181
Meehan v. Good   623
Meier v. Klotz   1164, 1168
Meier v. Rose   558, 622

Meister v. Coyle   622
Mellanby v. Chappie   958
Mellenthin, R. v.   308
Melnychuk v. Moore   829
Meloche v. Bezaire   1045
Meloche v. Hotel Dieu Grace Hospital
648
Mendelssohn v. Normand Ltd.   534
Mendez v. Palazzi   192, **1002**
Menear v. Miguna   1162
Menna v. Guglietti   411
Mennie v. Blake   171
Meraw v. Curl Estate   392
Mercer v. Gray   711
Mercer v. South Eastern & Chatham Ry.
Co.'s Managing Committee   415, 711
Merchant Law Group v. Canada (Revenue
Agency)   887
Merivale v. Carson   1191
Merkur Island Shipping Corp. v.
Laughton   1130
Merlo v. Canada   395
Merricks v. Nott-Bower   1177
Merrifield v. Canada (Attorney General)
101, 102, 107
Mersey Docks and Harbour Board v.
Coggins & Griffiths (Liverpool) Ltd.
1069
Messina, R. v.   286
Mete v. Mississauga   626
Metro-North Commuter Railroad Co. v.
Buckley   758
Metropolitan Conference Centre Inc. v.
Hunter   1109
Meyer Estate v. Rogers   224, 472, 473
Meyer v. Parker   423
Meyers (Next friend of) v. Moscovitz   622
Miazga v. Kvello Estate   88, 89, 495
Michael v. Chief Constable of South Wales
Police   403
Michalak v. Governors of Dalhousie
College and University   395
Michaud v. Dupuis   396
Michaud v. Tardif   808
Middleton v. Fowler   1064
Middleton v. Humphries   1003
Midgley v. Nguyen   668
Midwest Properties Ltd. v. Thordarson
44, 1005
Migliore v. Gerard   396
Miguna v. Toronto (City) Police Services
Board   889
Mikolic v. Tanguay   775

Miles v. Judges   620

Milgaard v. Kujawa   495, 853

Miller Dredging Ltd. v. Dorothy Mackenzie (The)   775

Miller v. Associated Newspapers Ltd. 1206

Miller v. Brian Ross Motorsports Corp. 35

Miller v. Decker   805

Miller v. Jackson   193, 594, 973, **1005**, 1013, 1016

Miller v. Miller   344, 817

Miller v. Wolbaum   601, 787

Millette v. Kalogeropoulos   898

Milliken v. Rowe   758

Milne v. Coast Mountain Bus Co.   826

Milne v. Saltspring Island Rod and Gun Club   1004

Milne v. St. Joseph's Health Centre   620, 731

Milner v. Manufacturers Life Insurance Co.   111, 120

Mineault v. Kamloops (City)   1032

Minister Administering the Environmental Planning and Assessment Act 1979 v. San Sebastien Pty. Ltd.   357, 683

Mintuck v. Valley River Band No. 63A 1109

Mintz v. Hamilton Radial Electric Railway   1001

Mirhadizadeh v. Ontario   857, 922

Mirsoltani v. Canadian Memorian Chiropractic College   953

Mirvahedy v. Henley   1046

Misir v. Baichulall   68

Miska v. Sivec   57

Misko v. John Doe   730

Mitchell et al. v. C.N.R. Co.   940

Mitchell v. Glasgow City Council   406

Mitchell v. John Heine and Son Ltd.   86

Mitchell v. McDonald   237

Mitchell v. Times Printing and Publishing Company Limited (No. 2)   1196

Mochinski v. Trendline Industries Ltd. 1083

Moffett v. Downing   1044

Mogul S.S. Co. v. McGregor, Gow & Co.   1122

Mohamed v. Banville   826

Mohamud v. Wm. Morris Supermarkets plc   1072

Mohl v. University of British Columbia 115

Mohsina v. Ornstein   231

Moisan v. Loftus   605

Molnar v. Coates   394

Moloney v. Parry Sound (Town)   956

Molson Canada v. Oland Breweries Ltd. 1106

Monahan v. Nelson   727

Monkman v. Singh   701

Monks v. ING Insurance Co. of Canada 668

Monney, R. v.   304

Montaron v. Wagner   231

Monteith v. N.B. Command, Royal Can. Legion   943

Montgomery v. Lanarkshire Health Board   472, 642

Montgomery v. Thompson   1105

Montréal (City of) v. Biondi   43

Montréal (Ville) c. Lonardi   663

Montreal Tramways Co. v. Léveillé   442

Montreal v. Montreal Locomotive Works Ltd.   1076

Moody v. Toronto (City)   953

Moore Stephens v. Stone Rolls Limited 816

Moore v. Brown   745

Moore v. Fanning   406, 601, 716, 788, 829

Moore v. R.   298

Moores v. Fish, Food and Allied Workers Union   47

Moores v. Salter   1157

Moorgate Mercantile Co. Ltd. v. Finch 149

Moran v. Wyeth-Ayerst Canada Inc. (c.o.b. Cyanamid Crop Protection)   487

Morash v. Lockhart & Ritchie Ltd.   415

More v. Bauer Nike Hockey Inc.   558

Morel v. Bryden   729

Moretto v. Nicolini-Femia   1045

Morgan v. Galbraith   748

Morgan v. Khyatt   1003

Morgan v. Loyacomo   64

Morier v. Rivard   852

Morland-Jones v. Taerk   112

Morris v. Baily   1044

Morris v. Beardmore   312, 313

Morris v. Johnson   1150

Morrish v. Murrey   310

Morrison v. Fishwick   148

Morrison v. Hooper   397

Morrow v. Hôpital Royal Victoria   218

Morse v. Cott Beverages West Ltd.   1051

Mortimer v. Cameron   798, 867
Morton v. William Dixon   593
Moseley-Williams v. Hansler Industries
   Ltd.   1177
Moskal v. Costco Wholesale Corp.   959
Moskaleva v. Laurie   729
Moss v. Ferguson   632, 715
Mostyn v. Fabrigas   879
Motherwell v. Motherwell   105, 974
Motkoski Holdings Ltd. v. Yellowhead
   (County)   541
Moule v. N.B. Electric Power Com'n   350,
   353
Moulton Contracting Ltd. v. British
   Columbia   1130
Mount Isa Mines Ltd. v. Pusey   448
Mowatt c. Québec (Procureur Général)
   392
Mraiche Investment Corp. v. McLennan
   Ross LLP   1119
Mraz v. Herman   625
Mudford v. Smith   1222
Mugford v. Weber   1053
Muir v. Alberta   240, 589
Muirhead v. Timber Bros. Sand & Gravel
   Ltd.   974
Mullen v. Barr & Co.   332
Mullins v. Levy   82
Mummery v. Olsson   441
Municipal Spraying & Contracting Ltd. v.
   J. Harris & Sons. Ltd.   773
Munir v. Jackson   473
Munn & Co. v. The Motor Vessel Sir John
   Crosbie   274
Munro v. Canada   495
Munro v. Porthkerry Park Holiday Estates
   Ltd.   392
Munro v. Toronto Sun Publishing Corp.
   1198
Munro v. Willmott   168
Munshaw Colour Service Ltd. v.
   Vancouver   358
Murkute v. Owners Condominium Plan
   8210034   959
Murphy v. Brentwood District Council
   335, 565, 568, 573, 579
Murphy v. LaMarsh   1157, 1196
Murphy v. Little Memphis Cabaret Inc.
   958
Murphy v. Little Memphis Cabaret Ltd.
   392
Murphy v. St. Catharines Gen. Hosp.
   484

Murray v. Bitango   953
Murray v. McMurchy   228
Murray v. Ministry of Defence   78
Murray v. TDL Group Ltd.   1079
Murray v. Toth   132
Musselman v. 875667 Ontario Inc. (c.o.b.
   Cities Bistro)   957
Mustafic v. Smith   63, 394, 621
Mustapha v. Culligan of Canada Ltd.
   100, 346, 448, 449, 450, 461, **702**, 845
Mutual Life & Citizens' Assurance Co. v.
   Evatt   501
Mutungih v. Bokun   164
My Kinda Town Ltd. v. Soll   1107
Mychajluk v. Kolisnyk   1157
Myers v. Blackman   1109
Myers v. Canadian Broadcasting
   Corporation   1196
Myers v. Graham   1043
Myers v. Haroldson   42
Myers v. Peel County Board of
   Education   395, 397, 616, 623, 788
Myles-Leger Ltd. (Trustee of) v. 755165
   Ontario Inc.   496
Myran v. R.   188
N.B. Telephone Co. v. Wright   772
N.C. c. F.T.   41
Nagy v. Canada   81
Naidu v. Mann   729
Nan v. BlackPine Manufacturing Ltd.
   773
Nanaimo-Ladysmith School District No.
   68 v. Dean (Litigation guardian of)   63
Nantel v. Parisien   181
Nasogalauk, R. v.   299
Nason v. Nunes   844
National Bank of Greece S.A. v. Pinios
   Shipping Co. (No. 1)   534
National Coal Board v. J.E. Evans & Co.
   (Cardiff) Ltd.   138
National Crane Services Inc. v. AON Reed
   Stenhouse   411, 559
National Hockey League v. Pepsi Cola
   Ltd.   1106
National Trust Co. v. Wong Aviation
   Ltd.   645
Nattrass v. Weber   589, 632
Nazerali v. Mitchell   1167
NBD Bank, Canada v. Dofasco Inc.   520
Neate v. Harding   137
Neff v. Patry   90
Neil v. Equifax Canada Inc.   552
Neil v. Lodge   632

Neill v. New South Wales Fresh Food & Ice Pty. Ltd.   599

Neill v. Vancouver Police Department   171

Nelitz v. Dyck   219

Nelles v. Ontario   **85**, 495, 852, 928

Nelson v. Welsh   723

Nelson v. Whetmore   140, 141

Nelson, R. v.   250

Nespolon v. Alford   362, 616

Neto v. Klukach   237

Netupsky v. Craig   1180

Network Rail Infrastructure Ltd. v. Handy   694

Neufeld v. Foster   388

Neufeld v. Landry   787

Neuman v. Parkland County   867

Nevill v. Fine Art & General Insurance Co   1153

New Brunswick Broadcasting Co. v. Nova Scotia (Speaker of the House of Assembly)   850, 921

New South Wales v. Fahy   358

New South Wales v. Lepore   1073, 1083

New York Times Co. v. Sullivan   1148, 1149, 1193

Newcastle (Town) v. Mattatall   662

Newell v. Towns   829

Newfoundland Light and Power Co. v. Furlong Estate   844

Newman v. Halstead   41, 1157

Newman v. Terdik   1053

Newton v. Newton   358

Ng Chun Pui v. Lee Chuen Tat   840

Niblock v. Pacific National Exhibition   391

Nice v. Calgary (City)   846

Nice v. John Doe   798, 829

Nichol v. MacKay   59

Nicholls v. Richmond (Township)   1128

Nichols v. Marsland   1034

Nichols v. Wal-Mart Canada Corp.   293

Nicholson v. John Deere Ltd.   485

Nickell v. City of Windsor   932

Niedermeyer v. Charlton   809

Nielsen v. Kaufmann   762, 769

Nieman v. Kroeker   567

Niemela v. Malamas   1163

Nightingale v. Mazerall   770

Nilsson Bros. Inc. v. McNamara Estate   144

Nippa v. C.H. Lewis (Lucan) Ltd.   1004

Nissen v. Durham Regional Police Services Board   123

Nitsopoulos v. Wong   112

Nixon v. MacIver   535

No. 1 Collision Repair & Painting (1982) Ltd. v. Insurance Corp. of British Columbia   1136

Nolan v. Toronto (Metropolitan) Police Force   127

Nolet, R. v.   304

Non-Marine Underwriters, Lloyd's of London v. Scalera   68, 202

Norberg v. Wynrib   39, 217, 221

Nord-Deutsche Versicherungs-Gesellschaft, R. v.   415

Norman v. Great Western Railway Co.   940

Norman v. Soule   92

Normart Management Ltd. v. West Hill Redevelopment Co.   1120

North Shore City Council v. Body Corporate 188529 (Sunset Terraces)   569

North Sydney Associates v. United Dominion Industries Ltd.   566

North Vancouver School District No. 44 v. Jubran   396

Northern Territory of Australia v. Mengel   104, 882, 889

Northwest Organics v. Maguire   1150

Northwestern Mut. Ins. Co. v. J.T. O'Bryan & Co.   411

Northwestern Utilities Ltd. v. London Guarantee & Accident Co.   1026, 1034

Nor-Video Services Ltd. v. Ontario Hydro   975, 986

Nova Scotia (Attorney General) v. Carvery   69, 1066

Nowlan v. Brunswick Construction Ltee.   664, **667**

Nowsco Well Service Ltd. v. Canadian Propane Gas & Oil Ltd.   648

Oakley v. Lyster   142

Oates v. Morgan   757

OBG Ltd. v. Allan   122, 155, 156, 1120, 1129, 1133

O'Bonsawin v. Paradis   231

O'Connell (Litigation Guardian of) v. Yung   740, 757

O'Connor v. Waldron   1174

O'Connor v. Wambera   631

O'Connor, R. v.   93

Ocsko v. Cypress Bowl Recreations Ltd. 809

Odhavji Estate v. Woodhouse 346, 872, **880**, 910

O'Dwyer v. Ontario Racing Commission 887, 890

O'Fallon v. Inecto Rapid (Can.) Ltd. 487

Ogal, R. v. 246

Ogg-Moss, R. v. 255, 258

O'Grady v. Brown 447

Ogwo v. Taylor 424, 685

O'Hara v. Belanger 745, 767

Okanagan Exteriors Inc. v. Perth Developments Inc. 406, 717

Oke v. Weide Transport 371, 709

Olar v. Laurentian University 500

Oleschak Estate v. Wilganowski 767

Olinski v. Johnson 964

Oliveira v. Zareh 142

Oliver (Guardian ad litem of) v. Ellison 446

Oliver v. Miles 833

Olsen v. Olsen 41

O'Malley v. O'Callaghan 1161

OMV Petrom SA v. Glencore International AG 1098

O'Neil v. Van Horne 276

O'Neill v. Esquire Hotels Ltd. 1033

Oniel v. Metropolitan Toronto Police Force 89

Ontario (Attorney General) v. Crompton 322

OPO v. MLA 101

Orbanski, R. v.; R. v. Elias 281

Organ v. Newfoundland and Labrador (Minister of Social Services) 852

O'Rourke v. Schacht 898

Osman v. 629256 Ontario Ltd. 769

Osman v. Ferguson 403

Osman v. United Kingdom 403

Osterlind v. Hill 370, 379

Ottawa Community Housing Corp. v. Foustanellas 42

Ottosen v. Kasper 616

Oughton v. Seppings 137

Outaouais Synergest Inc. v. Lang Michener LLP 623

Overseas Tankship (U.K.) Ltd. v. Miller S.S. Co. Pty. 702, 991

Overseas Tankship (U.K.) v. Morts Dock & Engineering Co. (The Wagon Mound) 690, 702

Oyagi v. Grossman 391

Oz Optics Ltd. v. Timbercon, Inc. 539

P Perl (Exporters) Ltd. v. Camden London Borough Council 717

P.(K.) v. Desrochers 92

P.(N.I.) v. B.(R.) 1066

P.(P.) v. D.(D.) 1096

P.(S.T.), R. v. 287

P.P. v. D.D. 211

Pac. Blasting Ltd. v. D.J. Byrne Const. Ltd. 772

Pac. Elevators Ltd. v. C.P.R. Co. 773

Pacific Associates Inc. v. Baxter 534

Page v. Smith 460

Paice, R. v. 207, 217, 248

Pajot v. Commonwealth Holiday Inns of Can. Ltd. 943

Palmer v. N.S. Forest Indust. 1004

Palmer v. St. John 933

Palsgraf v. Long Island Ry. Co. 359680, 1062, 1234

Paniccia Estate v. Toal 729

Pannett v. McGuinness & Co. Ltd. 945

Papadimitropoulos v. R. 210

Papineau v. Dorman 729

Papp v. Leclerc 712

Paquette (Litigation guardian of) v. School District No. 36 (Surrey) 801

Paquette c. Fédération (La) cie d'assurances du Canada 389

Paquette v. Desrochers 92

Paquette v. Surrey School District No. 36 955

Paramount Pictures Corp. v. Howley 1106

Paris v. Stepney Borough Council 591

Park v. B & B Electronics Ltd. 484

Park v. Park 237

Park v. Targonski 729

Park, R. v. 257

Parkhurst v. Forster 10

Parkinson v. St. James and Seacroft University Hospital NHS Trust 439, 1243

Parkland No. 31 v. Stetar 899

Parlett v. Robinson 1200

Parmley v. Parmley 213, 228

Parna v. G. & S. Properties Ltd. 1092

Parypa v. Wickware 729

Pasley v. Freeman 94, 95, 1099

Pasternack v. Poulton 793

Patching v. Howarth 1157

Pate Estate v. Galway-Cavendish and Harvey (Township) 44, 90

Patel (Respondent) v. Mirza (Appellant) 222
Patel v. Mirza 816
Patel v. Seth 115
Pétel, R. v. 249
Patenaude c. Roy 601
Paton Estate v. Ontario Lottery and Gaming Corporation (Fallsview Casino Resort and OLG Casino Brantford) 347, 398
Patrick, R. v. 281, 304
Patrong v. Banks 402
Patry v. General Motors Acceptance Corp. of Canada Ltd. 146
Pat's Off-Road Transport v. Campbell 123
Patten v. Silberschein 716
Pattison v. Prince Edward Region Conservation Authority 1033
Pauluik v. Paraiso 712
Paur (Committee of) v. Providence Health Care 63, 620
Pawlaczyk v. Dong 143
Pawlak v. Doucette 1054
Paxton v. Ramji 344, 429, 435
Payne v. Maple Leaf Gardens Ltd. 204, 808
Payton v. New York; Riddick v. New York 313
PD Management Ltd. v. Chemposite Inc. 541
Peak Innovations Inc. v. Pacific Rim Brackets Ltd. 1177
Pearson v. Black 1071
Pelletier v. Ontario 746
Pelletier v. Stewart 587
Pelucco, R. v. 304
Pemberton v. Southwark London Borough Council 975
Pembina County Water Resource District v. Manitoba 1144
Pembina Resources Ltd. v. ULS International Inc. 773
Penarth Dock Engineering Co. Ltd. v. Pounds 47
Penfolds Wines Proprietary Ltd. v. Elliott 138, 141
Penner v. Mitchell 672
Penney v. Gosse 180
Penney v. John Doe 407
Penny v. Bolen 237
People Recycling Inc. v. Vancouver (City) 1144

Percy v. Glasgow Corp. 1055
Pereira v. Hamilton Township Farmers' Mutual Fire Insurance Co. 44
Perez v. Galambos 625
Performance Industries Ltd. v. Sylvan Lake Golf & Tennis Club Ltd. 1098
Perilli v. Marlow 616
Perka, R. v. 270
Perren v. Lalari 748
Perrin v. Blake 798
Perry v. Fried 297
Perry v. Kendricks Transport Ltd. 1023
Perry v. Truefitt 1101
Persaud v. Telus Corp. 1128
Perth Insurance Co. v. Osler Rehabilitation Centre Inc. 1120
Peruvian Guano Co. v. Dreyfus Brothers & Co. 164, 266
Pesonen v. Melnyk 691
Pete v. Axworthy 867
Peter Ballantyne Cree Nation v. Canada (Attorney General) 179
Peters v. Prince of Wales Theatre (Birmingham) Ltd. 1033
Peters v. The Queen 182
Peterson v. Windsor (City) 944
Petkovic (Litigation Guardian of) v. Olupona 437
Pett v. Pett 745
Philip v. Whitecourt General Hospital 449
Phillip v. Bablitz 709, 712
Phillips v. Brittania Hygienic Laundry Co. 819
Phillips v. Calif. Standard Co. 193
Pia Grillo c. Google inc. 112
Pick v. 1180475 Alberta Ltd. (c.o.b. Queen of Tarts) 1107
Picka v. Porter 388
Pickard v. Smith 1081
Pickering v. Rudd 195
Piercey (Guardian ad litem of) v. Lunenburg (County) District School Board 397
Pierre (Next Friend of) v. Marshall 621
Pilieci v. Lockett 257
Pilliterri v. Nor. Const. Co. 993
Pilon v. Janveaux 795, 807
Pilotte v. Gilbert, Wright & Kirby Barristers and Solicitors 622
Pinard v. Coderre 1102
Pinch (Guardian ad litem of) v. Morwood 621, 660

Pintar, R. v.   249

Piper v. Mitsubishi Heavy Industries
  Ltd.   459

Piresferreira v. Ayotte   101

Pisani v. Pearce   746

Pittman Estate v. Bain   224, 472, 621

Pitts v. Hunt   811, 814

Pizza Pizza Ltd. v. Toronto Star
  Newspapers Ltd.   1167

Pizzolon v. Pedrosa   388, 663

Place Concorde East Limited Partnership
  v. Shelter Corp. of Canada Ltd.   170

Planned Parenthood Newfoundland/
  Labrador v. Fedorik   1157

Plas-Tex Canada Ltd. v. Dow Chemical of
  Canada Ltd.   570

Platinum Equity Funding Inc. v.
  Reingold   1099

Player Estate v. Janssen-Ortho Inc.   1050

Ploof v. Putnam   272, 274

Poirier v. Aubrey   728, 757

Poirier v. Canada (Minister of Veterans
  Affairs)   921

Poirier v. Wal-Mart Canada Corp.   1108

Poirier, R. v.   301, 305

Poissant v. Robalo   358

Poitras v. Goulet   797

Police Complaints Commissioner v.
  Dunlop   407

Police v. Greaves   72

Polly Peck (Holdings) plc v. Trelford
  1167

Pololos v. Cinnamon-Lopez   668

Polsinelli v. Marzilli   1107

Pontes, R. v.   308

Ponting v. Noakes   1034

Poole v. Ragen   110

Pope v. R.G.C. Management Inc.   615

Pope v. Route 66 Clothing Inc.   964

Popovich v. Lobay (No. 2)   1162

Posluns v. Toronto Stock Exchange   1115,
  1127

Potechin v. Yashin   1130

Potter v. Rowe   1129

Potts v. Heutink   868

Potvin v. Stipetic   808

Poulin, R. v.   256

Pound v. Nakonechny   622

Pound v. Scott   1197

Poupart v. Lafortune   280, 289

Powder Mountain Resorts Ltd. v. British
  Columbia   888

Power, R. v.   299

Pozdzik (Next friend of) v. Wilson   446

Pratt & Goldsmith v. Pratt   468

Precision Remodeling Ltd. v. Soskin,
  Soskin & Potasky LLP   494

Prefontaine v. Gosman   852

Premakumaran v. Canada   520

Prentice v. Sault Ste. Marie   1001

Prentzas v. Rivera   1053

Prescott v. Connell   425

Pressler v. Lethbridge   1156, 1197

Preston v. Canadian Legion of British
  Empire Service League, Kingsway Branch
  No. 175   943

Preston v. Chow   621

Prete v. Ontario   853, 857

Prevost (Committee of) v. Vetter   389,
  391

Price v. Chicoutimi Pulp Co.   1165, 1186,
  1196

Price v. Garcha   692

Price v. Kelday   625

Price v. Milawski   710

Price Waterhouse v. Kwan   519

Pridgen v. Boston Housing Authority
  379

Priestman v. Colangelo   280, 289, 601,
  787

Prim8 Group Inc. v. Tisi   1119, 1131

Prime v. Fraser Valley Foods Ltd.   825

Prince Alfred College Inc. v. A.D.C.
  1073

Print N' Promotion (Canada) Ltd. v.
  Kovachis   1128

Prinzo v. Baycrest Centre for Geriatric
  Care   100

Pritchard v. Van Nes   1005

Procea Products Ltd. v. Evans & Sons
  Ltd.   1107

Project 360 Investments Ltd. (c.o.b. Sound
  Emporium Nightclub) v. Toronto Police
  Services Board   402

Pro-Sys Consultants Ltd. v. Microsoft
  Corporation   1114, 1116, 1117

Proulx v. Québec (A.G.)   88, 853

Provost v. Bolton   406, 602, 716

Prud'homme v. Prud'homme   1179

Puddister v. Wells   1157

Pugh v. London, Brighton and South
  Coast Ry. Co.   95

Pugsley v. Rahbar   1054

Purdy v. Woznesensky   54, 96

Pursell v. Horn   64

Puyenbroek, R. v.   313

Pyke v. TriGro Enterprises Ltd. 192, 992
Pyper v. Crausen 188
Q. v. Minto Management Ltd. 406
Qualcast (Wolverhampton) Ltd. v. Haynes 639
Quan v. Cusson 1208
Queen v. Cognos Inc. 499, 501, 528, **535**
Queen's University at Kingston v. Oliver Twist Domains Inc. 1107
Queenstown Lakes District Council v. Charterhall Trustees Ltd. 569
Queensway Tank Lines Ltd. v. Moise 905
Quenneville v. Robert Bosch GmbH 569
Quinn v. Leathem 1127
R. in Right of Can. v. Sask. Wheat Pool 894, **901**
R. in Right of Ont. v. Schenck; R. in Right of Ont. v. Rokeby 892
R.(L.) v. Nyp 112, 624
R.C. v. McDougall 826
R.C., R. v. 306
R.D. v. G.S. 692
R.F. Fry & Associates (Pacific) Ltd. v. Reimer 162
R.H. Willis and Son v. Br. Car Auctions Ltd. 144
R.W.D.S.U., Local 580 v. Dolphin Delivery Ltd. 920, 921
Racine v. C.J.R.C. Radio Capitale Ltée 1108
Racz v. Home Office 889
Radke v. S.(M.) (Litigation Guardian of) 602
Radovici v. Toronto Police Services Board 79
Radovskis v. Tomm 96
Rahal v. Rahal 46
Rahemtulla v. Vanfed Credit Union 100, 107, 127
Rahman v. Arearose Ltd. 712
Rain Coast Water Corp. v. British Columbia 527, 1143
Rainbow Industrial Caterers Ltd. v. Canadian National Railway 504, 529
Rainham Chemical Works, Ltd. (in Liquidation) et al. v. Belvedere Fish Guano Co., Ltd. 1031
Rajan v. Hudon 668
Rajkhowa v. Watson 1174
Raju v. Kumar 1096
Ralston Purina of Can. Ltd. v. Whittaker 161

Ramdath v. George Brown College of Applied Arts and Technology 500
Ramsay v. Saskatchewan 91, 495
Randall (Litigation Guardian of) v. Lakeridge Health Oshawa 584
Ranieri v. Nagari 237
Rankin (Rankin's Garage & Sales) v. J.J. 221, **354**, 406, 716, 814
Ranson v. Kitner 60
Rattray v. Daniels 986
Ratych v. Bloomer 776
Raworth v. Stratford (City) Police Services Board 625
Ray , R. v. 249
Rayner v. Knickle 740
Raypath Resources Ltd. v. Toronto Dominion Bank 500
Raywalt Construction Co. v. Bencic 662
Re (a child by her mother and litigation friend LE) and others v. Calderdale & Huddersfield NHS Foundation Trust 460
Re A (Children) (Conjoined Twins: Surgical Separation) 240, 268
Re B (a minor) (wardship: sterilization) 238
Re B (Consent to Treatment: Capacity) 228
Re BCE Inc. 910
Re C (Adult: Refusal of Medical Treatment) 228, 237
Re Dueck 234
Re Indian Residential Schools 407
Re K. and Public Trustee 238
Re K.(L.D.) 235
Re Kostiuk 158
Re M.(J.) 229, 241
Re Matthews' Claim 375
Re Polemis 680, 681, 698
Re Polemis and Furness, Withy & Co. 680
Re Royal Can. Legion Branch 177 852
Re Scarth 166
Re W (a minor) 235
Re White 259
Re Yoner 852
Reaburn v. Langen 1209
Reach M.D. Inc. v. Pharmaceutical Manufacturers Association of Canada 1139
Reach MD Inc. v. Pharmaceutical Manufacturers Association of Canada 1142

Read v. Coker 73

Read v. J. Lyons & Co. 1023, **1026**, 1031

Reckitt & Colman Products Ltd. v. Borden Inc. 1101

Red Chris Development Co. v. Quock 1109

Reed v. Maley 99

Reekie v. Messervey 757

Rees v. Canada (Royal Canadian Mounted Police) 395

Rees v. Darlington Memorial NHS Trust 439, 442

Reese v. Coleman (No. 1) 362

Reeve v. Palmer 166

Reeves v. Metropolitan Police Commissioner 789

Refco Futures (Canada) Ltd. v. SYB Holdings Corp. 623

Reference re Broome v. Prince Edward Island 348, 871

Regina v. Walker 1076

Reibl v. Hughes 224, 242, 469, 471, 641

Reid v. Maloney 231

Reid v. Webster 90

Reidy v. McLeod 762

Reilly, R. v. 250

Rekken Estate v. Health Region No. 1 763

Remo Imports Ltd. v. Jaguar Cars Ltd. 1106

Remtulla v. Zeldin 472

Rendall v. Ewart 406

Renken v. Harvey Aluminum (Inc.) 973

Resolute Forest Products Inc. v. 2471256 Canada Inc. (c.o.b. Greenpeace Canada) 1143

Revill v. Newbery 262

Rewcastle v. Sieben 793

Reyes v. Esbin 143

Reynen v. Antonenko 304

Reynen v. Canada 853

Reynolds v. Clarke 10, 11

Reynolds v. Times Newspapers Ltd. 1192, 1208

Rhodes v. Canadian National Railway 468

Rhodes v. OPO 54

Rhora v. Ontario 394

Rice v. Connolly 298

Richard v. C.N.R. 639, 684

Richard v. Synak 172

Richards v. Lothian 1032, 1034

Richardson v. Sanayhie 389

Rickards v. Lothian 1030

Rideau Falls Generating Partnership v. Ottawa (City) 991

Rigby v. Chief Constable of Northamptonshire 269, 312

Rinas v. Regina (City) 917

Ring v. Canada (Attorney General) 758

Rintoul v. X-Ray and Radium Indust. Ltd. 817

Rioux v. Smith 41

Risk v. Zeller's Ltd. 1160

Ristimaki v. Cooper 494

Rivtow Marine Ltd. v. Washington Iron Works 341, 478, 485, 560

Rizzi v. Mavros 803

Roach v. Long 90

Robb Estate v. Canadian Red Cross Society 839, 844

Robb Estate v. St. Joseph's Health Care Centre 839

Roberge v. R. 787

Robert Addie & Sons (Collieries), Ltd. v. Dumbreck 944

Roberts v. 964639 Ontario Ltd. 388

Roberts v. Morana 425, 755

Roberts v. Wyatt 149

Robertson v. Stang 406

Robin Hood Management Ltd. (c.o.b. Merriman & Co.) v. Gelmich 1109

Robinson (Litigation Guardian of) v. Bud's Bar Inc. (c.o.b. Bud's Bar and Lounge) 796

Robinson v. 1390709 Alberta Ltd. (c.o.b. Chopped Leaf) 959

Robinson v. Balmain New Ferry Co. 77, 84

Robinson v. Chief Constable of West Yorkshire Police 403

Robinson v. Kilvert 984

Robinson v. Post Office 712

Robinson v. Williams Estate 807

Robitaille v. Vancouver Hockey Club Ltd. 44, 722

Robson v. Ashworth 394

Robson v. Chrysler Canada Ltd. 498

Robson v. Law Society of Upper Canada 90

Rodgers v. Maw 137

Rodriguez v. British Columbia (Attorney General) 229

Roe v. Dabbs 440

Roe v. Leone 409

Roe v. Minister of Health 322, 589, 834

Roehl v. Houlahan   1113
Rogacki v. Belz   1196
Rogers Cable TV Ltd. v. 373041 Ontario Ltd.   1132
Rogers v. Faught   345
Rollin v. Baker   621
Rollinson v. R.   163, 284, 771
Rolof v. Morris   473
Rolon v. Bell   1178
Roman Corp. v. Hudson's Bay Oil & Gas Co.   850, 1133
Roncarelli v. Duplessis   877, 882
Roncato v. Caverly   502
Rondel v. Worsley   491, 492, 494
Rookes v. Barnard   37, 39, 56, 1111, 1113
Roper v. Harper   212
Rose et al. v. Miles   999
Rose v. Fishery Products International Ltd.   169
Rosenberg v. Percival   642
Rosenburg v. Grand River Conservation Authority   999
Rosenthal v. Alderton & Sons, Ltd.   166, 167
Rosewell v. Prior   10
Ross (Litigation Guardian of) v. Vidnes   358
Ross v. British Columbia Lottery Corp.   398
Ross v. Canada (Attorney General)   69
Ross v. Caunters   557, 558
Ross v. New Brunswick Teachers' Assn.   1188, 1197
Ross v. United States   405, 414
Ross v. Vidnes   1042
Roth v. Roth   107, 1113
Rothfield v. Manolakos   337
Rothwell v. Chemical & Insulating Co. Ltd.   451, 724
Rothwell v. Raes   486, 632
Rousseau, R. v.   304
Rowe v. Bobell Express Ltd.   746
Rowe v. Brown   762
Rowland's Transport Ltd. v. Nasby Sales & Services Ltd.   724
Rowlands v. Wright   624
Rowley v. Secretary of State for Department of Work and Pensions   553
Roy c. Toxi-Co-Gîtes inc.   394
Roy v. 1216393 Ontario Inc.   1099
Roy v. Thiessen   566

Royal Aquarium and Summer & Winter Garden Society Ltd. v. Parkinson   1172, 1176
Royal Bank of Canada v. Intercon Security Ltd.   1066
Royal Bank of Canada v. W. Got & Associates Electric Ltd.   155, 163
Royal Bank v. Holoboff   1120
Royal Bank v. Wilton   1128
Rozenhart v. Skier's Sport Shop (Edmonton) Ltd.   487, 488, 498
Rozon v. Patenaude   1048
Rubin v. Ross   1177, 1185
Ruckheim v. Robinson   1048
Rumley v. British Columbia   407, 717
Rumsey v. R.   59, 723
Rupert v. Toth   621
Rushmer v. Polsue & Afieri Ltd.   971
Russell Transport Ltd. v. Ontario Malleable Iron Co.   993
Russell v. Edwards   391
Russell v. Esson (M.F.) & Sons Ltd.   713
Russo v. Ontario Jockey Club   186
Rutman v. Rabinowitz   1163
Ruzic, R. v.   56
RVB Managements Ltd. v. Rocky Mountain House (Town)   908
Ryan v. Auclair   298
Ryan v. Hickson   615
Ryan v. St. John's (City)   134
Ryan v. Victoria (City)   337, 587, 802, 909, **912**, 990
Ryan, R. v.   249, 250
Rybachuk v. Dyrland   1177
Ryder Truck Rental v. Walker   172
Rydzik v. Edwards   898
Rylands v. Fletcher   18, 892, 986, 987, 1019, **1021**, 1023, 1024, 1025, 1026, 1027, 1030, **1033**, 1035, 1036, 1037, 1038, 1043, 1044, 1049, 1081
S. (K.) (Litigation representative of) v. Willox   649
S. Bransfield Ltd. v. Fletcher   663
S. Maclise Enterprises Inc. v. Union Securities Ltd.   499, 503, 623, 789
S.(F.) v. H.(C.)   1097
S.(J.) v. Clement   393
S.A.B., R. v.   306
Saadati v. Moorhead   101, 448, 449, **462**, 511, 705, 725
Sable Offshore Energy Inc. v. Ameron International Corp.   569
Sabo v. Canada (Attorney General)   170

Saccardo v. Hamilton   712, 1034
Saccone v. Fandrakis   425
Saccone v. Orr   110
Sachs v. Miklos   160, 162, 166
Sacks v. Ross   639, 659, 660, 835
Sadhu Singh Hamdard Trust v. Navsun
 Holdings Ltd.   1105
Saeed, R. v.   306
Sagman v. Politi   1222
Said (Husain) v. Said   211
Saif Ali v. Sidney Mitchell & Co. (a firm) et
 al.   493
Saik'uz First Nation v. Rio Tinto Alcan
 Inc.   976
Saint-Jacques v. Canada (Solicitor
 General)   78
Salame v. Sutherland   728
Saltpetre's Case   267, 269
Sam v. Ministry of Public Safety &
 Solicitor General   1043
Samaroo v. Canada Revenue Agency   42
Samms v. Eccles 97
Sammut v. Islington Golf Club Ltd.   1010
San Miguel Brewing International Ltd. v.
 Molson Canada 2005   1105
Sanders v. Janze   730
Sanderson, R. v.   313
Sandhar v. Rolston   712
Sandhu (Litigation Guardian of) v.
 Wellington Place Apartments   731, 742,
 755, 769
Sandu v. Fairmont Hotels Inc.   1167
Sankreacha v. Cameron J. and Beach Sales
 Ltd.   1109
Sansome v. Rubens   624
Sant v. Jack Andrews Kirkfield Pharmach
 Ltd.   450
Sar Petroleum Inc. v. Peace Hills Trust
 Co.   1127
Saskatchewan (Attorney General) v.
 Pritchard   289
Saskatchewan Power Corp. v. Wolf   1001
Saskatchewan v. Eacom Timber Corp.
 890, 1130
Saskatchewan Wheat Pool, R. v.   870
Saskatoon (City) v. Smith   868
Satara Farms Inc. v. Parrish &
 Heimbecker, Ltd. (c.o.b. New-Life
 Feeds)   449
Saulnier v. Diamond   498
Saumur (Litigation Guardian of) v.
 Antoniak   788

Saunders v. Randolph Hotel Co. Ltd.
 1155
Saunders v. Smith   195
Sauve v. Provost   944
Savage v. Boies   98
Savage v. Wilby   1079
Savard v. Urbano   807
Savino v. Shelestowsky   107
Sayers v. Harlow Urban Dist. Council
 423, 425
Scaffidi-Argentina v. Tega Homes
 Developments Inc.   771
Scandinavia Belting Co. v. Asbestos &
 Rubber Works of America, Inc.   1103
Scarff v. Wilson   741
Scelfo v. Rutgers University   1159
Sceptre Resources Ltd. v. Deloitte Haskins
 & Sells   623
Schacht v. The Queen in right of the
 Province of Ontario   399
Schachter v. Canada   923
Schact v. R.   400
Schell v. Truba   297
Schellenberg v. Tunnel Holdings Pty.
 Ltd.   845
Schenck v. R.; Rokeby v. R.   193, 994,
 1032, 1035
Schentag v. Gauthier   170
Schiavo ex rel. Schindler v. Schiavo   241
Schieber v. City of Philadelphia   405
Schlink v. Blackburn   362
Schmidt v. Sharpe   388
Schnarr v. Blue Mountain Resorts Ltd.
 810, 960
Schneider v. St. Clair Region Conservation
 Authority   956
Schnurr v. Insurance Corp. of British
 Columbia   693
School Div. of Assiniboine South (No. 3) v.
 Hoffer   917
Schouten v. Rideau (Township)   601
Schroeder v. DJO Canada, Inc.   485
Schroth v. Innes   1054
Schrump v. Koot   728
Schubert v. Sterling Trusts Corp.   1023,
 1034
Schultz v. Miki   1065
Schulz v. Leeside Dev. Ltd.   395, 488
Schwartz v. Canada   358
Schweizer v. Central Hospital   213
Scoates v. Dermott   668
Scobie v. Wing   772
Scopelliti, R. v.   249

Scory v. Krannitz   1150
Scott (c.o.b. Oldfield Orchard) v.
  Filipovic   158
Scott v. Fulton   1193
Scott v. London and St. Katherine Docks
  Co.   840
Scott v. McAlpine   148
Scott v. R.   307
Scott v. Shepherd   9, 54
Scullion v. Bank of Scotland plc (trading as
  Colleys)   521
Scurfield v. Cariboo Helicopter Skiing
  Ltd.   808
Sea Shepherd UK (Appellant) v Fish &
  Fish Limited (Respondent)   662
Seaboard Life Insurance Co. v. Babich
  581
Sealand of Pac. Ltd. v. Robert C. McHaffe
  Ltd.   500
Sealand of the Pacific v. Robert C.
  McHaffie Ltd.   1094
Searle v. Wallbank   1048
Second Cup Ltd. v. Eftoda   1222
Secretary of State for Foreign and
  Commonwealth Affairs, R. v., ex parte
  Everett   856
Secretary, Department of Health and
  Community Services v. J.W.B.   239
Sedleigh-Denfield v. O'Callaghan   976,
  1006
Seede v. Cameo Inc.   762
Segal v. Derrick Golf and Winter Club
  193
Selig v. Mansfield   1112
Semayne's Case   309
**Seneca College of Applied Arts Technology
  v. Bhadauria   124**, 909, 930
Senger v. Lachman   828
Sentinel Self-Storage Corp. v. Dyregrov
  566
Seraphim v. Sterling Newspapers Ltd.
  1157
Serhan v. Johnson & Johnson   570
Sevenoaks District Council v. Pattullo &
  Vinson Ltd.   1005
Seyom v. Toronto Transit Commission
  846
Shackleton v. Knittle   394, 685
Shakoor v. Situ   621
Shamac Country Inns Ltd. v. Sandy's
  Oilfield Hauling Ltd.   1072
Shanklin Pier Ltd. v. Detel Products Ltd.
  534

Shannon v. Westman (Litigation Guardian
  of)   397
Shantry v. Thompson   621
Shavluk v. Green Party of Canada   1185
Shaw v. Berman   117
Shaw v. Gorter   58
Shaw v. Lewis   1121
Shaw v. Roemer   793
Shearman v. Folland   729
Shelfer v. London Electric Lighting Co.
  1002, 1004
Shell UK Limited v. Total UK Limited
  581
Sheridan v. Ontario   90, 91
Sherrin v. Haggerty   273
Shiffman v. Order of St. John   1023
Shilson v. Northern Ont. Light & Power
  Co.   596
Shkwarchuk v. Hansen   794
Shobridge v. Thomas   724
Shoker, R. v.   217
Shorter v. Surrey and Sussex Healthcare
  NHS Trust   450
Shreddfast Inc. v. Oak Point Alignment
  Ltd.   173
Shultz v. Miki   406
Shute v. Premier Trust Co.   632
Siametis v. Trojan Horse (Burlington)
  Inc.   1098
Sibley v. Sibley   134
Sickel Estate v. Gordy   1079
Sidaway v. Bethlem Royal Hospital
  Governors   471
Sidhu Estate v. Bains   1095
Sidhu v. Hiebert   389
Siemens v. Pfizer C. & G. Inc   487
Sienkiewicz v. Greif (UK) Ltd.   650
Sigouin (Guardian ad litem of) v. Wong
  619
Siksika Nation v. Crowchief   1142
Silkin v. Beaverbrook Newspapers Ltd.
  1185
Silver v. IMAX Corp.   521
Sim v. Stretch   1152
Simans v. Burnaby (City)   148
Simmons v. Yeager Properties Inc.   803,
  954, 959
Simms v. Butt   680
Simms v. Foyer Wales Home   1157
Simpson v. Geswein   69, 249
Simpson v. Mair   1205
Sinclair v. Dines   748
Sinclair v. Woodward's Store Ltd.   80

Sinclaire v. Boulton   474
Sindell v. Abbott Laboratories   446, 651, 659, 837
Singer Manufacturing Co. v. Loog   1101
Singh v. Ali   133, 170
Singh v. Trump   501, 539
Singleton v. Morris   844
Singleton v. Williamson   1048
Sirois v. Gustafson   71
Sirros v. Moore   851
Skelding (Guardian ad litem of) v. Skelding   769
Skelton v. Collins   753
Skelton v. London and North Western R.W. Co.   413
Skinner v. Guo   798
Skropnik v. B.C. Rail Ltd.   956
Skyward Resources Ltd. v. Cessna Aircraft Co.   772
Slaferek v. TCG International Inc.   964
Slater v. Baker   10
Slim v. Daily Telegraph Ltd.   1156
Smart v. Sears Canada Inc.   292
Smart v. Simpson Sears Ltd.   81
Smith Brothers Excavating Windsor Ltd. v. Camion Equipment & Leasing Inc. (Trustee of)   1024
Smith New Court Ltd. v. Scrimgeour Vickers   1098
Smith v. B.C. (A.G.)   393, 587, 623, 709
Smith v. British Columbia   163, 170
Smith v. Chadwick   1089, 1095
Smith v. Chief Constable of Sussex Police   403
Smith v. Collett   745
Smith v. Cross   1184
Smith v. Eric S. Bush (a firm)   623
Smith v. Inco Ltd.   192, 725, 1024
Smith v. Jones   409
Smith v. Landstar Properties Inc.   535
Smith v. Leech Brain & Co. Ltd.   **689**, 690
Smith v. Littlewoods Organisation Ltd.   407, 689, 717
Smith v. National Money Mart Co.   1117
Smith v. Ont. & Minnesota Power Co.   1034
Smith v. Ontario (Attorney General)   88
Smith v. Rae   412
Smith v. Rusk   93
Smith v. Scott   1034
Smith v. Shade   674
Smith v. Stone   52

Smith v. Tucker   425, 426
Smith v. Union of Icelandic Fish Producers Ltd.   540
Smith v. Widdicombe   1033
Smithson v. Saskem Chemicals Ltd.   489
Smorag v. Nadeau Estate   394
Smythe v. Reardon   210
Snell v. Farrell   643, **644**, 835, 836, 954, 1092
Snushall v. Fulsang   793, 801, 802
Soboczynski v. Beauchamp   501, 540
Sodd Corp. v. Tessis   500
Solloway v. McLaughlin   159, 162
Solomon v. Ali   474
Somwar v. McDonald's Restaurants of Canada Ltd.   109
Sonnenberger v. Creamer   775
Soomre (Litigation guardian of) v. P.A. Ramey Enterprises Ltd.   957
Sopinka (Litigation Guardian of) v. Sopinka   99
Sorensen v. Kaye Holdings Ltd.   1094
Soulsby v. Toronto   413
Sound Stage Entertainment v. Burns   796
South Australia Asset Management Corp. v. York Montague Ltd.   504, 718
Southam v. Smout   310
Southern Pacific Co. v. Jensen   183
Southern Portland Cement Ltd. v. Cooper   945
Souto v. Anderson   728
Spagnolo v. Margesson's Sports Ltd.   406, 716
Sparks v. Thompson   801
Spasic Estate v. Imperial Tobacco Ltd.   839
Spectra Architectural Group Ltd. v. Eldred Sollows Consulting Ltd.   1131
Spencer v. Wincanton Holdings Ltd.   712
Spiewak v. 251268 Ont. Ltd.   623
Spiller v. Joseph   1186, 1197
Sportelli v. MacLeod   171
Spring v. Guardian Assurance plc   1185
Sprung Instant Structures Ltd. v. Royal Bank of Canada   170
Spur Industries Inc. v. Del E. Webb Development Co.   973, **1011**
Squib Case: Scott v. Shepherd   708
Squittieri v. De Santis   63
Ssenyonga, R. v.   210
St. George, R. v.   70
St. George's Healthcare NHS Trust v. S.   446

St. John (City) v. Donald 1083

St. John's (City) v. Lake 990

St. Lawrence Cement Inc. v. Barrette 974

St. Lawrence Seaway Management Corporation v. BBC Lena (Vessel) 580

St. Lewis v. Rancourt 1212

St. Louis v. R. 839

St. Pierre v. Ontario 974

Stacey v. Anglican Church of Canada (Diocesan Synod of Eastern Newfoundland & Labrador) 942

Stafford v. Motomochi 729

Stamp v. R. in Right of Ontario 835

Standard Chartered Bank v. Pakistan National Shipping Corp. (Nos. 2 and 4) 1094, 1100

Stanley v. Powell 16, 17

Stansbie v. Troman 716

Stapley v. Hejslet 757

Stapley v. London, Brighton, and South Coast R.W. Co. 413

Starbucks (H.K.) Ltd. v. British Sky Broadcasting Group Plc 1104, 1105

Stark v. Auerbach 1172, 1176

Starson v. Swayze 236

State Farm Mutual Automobile Insurance Co. v. Canada (Privacy Commissioner) 111

State of N.S.W. v. Kable 78

State of South Australia v. Lampard-Trevorrow 889

Statler v. Ray Mfg. Co. 333

Steadman v Lambton (County) 193

Steadman v. Erickson Gold Mining Corp. 193

Steagald v. U.S. 313

Steel v. NRAM Ltd. 502

Steenblok v. Funk 728

Stefanyk v. Steven 957

Steiman v. Steiman 162

Stein v. Gonzales 999

Stein v. Kathy K (The Ship) 802

Steinebach (Litigation Guardian of) v. Fraser Health Authority 620, 756

Steinebach (Litigation Guardian of) v. O'Brien 660

Steinebach v. O'Brien 638

Steinkrauss v. Afridi 762

Ste-Marie c. Placements J.P.M. Marquis 111

Stephens v. Corcoran 208

Stephens v. Myers 71, 74

Stephenson v. Waite Tileman 702

Sterling Trusts Corp. v. Postma 905

Stevens v. Brodribb Sawmilling Co. Ltd. 1080

Stevens v. Rockport Granite Co. 1013

Stevenson Estate v. Siewert 161

Stevenson Jordan and Harrison, Ltd. v. Macdonald 1076

Stevenson v. Clearview Riverside Resort 379, 381

Steward v. Berezan 748

Stewart v. Gustafson 263

Stewart v. Pettie 358, 388, 909

Stewart v. Traders Trust Co. 212

Stiles v. Hatfield 473

Stillman, R. v. 306

Stocker v. Stocker 1155

Stockford v. Johnston Estate 440

Stoke-on-Trent City Council v. W. & J. Wass Ltd. 33, 1005

Stokes v. Carlson 52

Storrey, R. v. 286, 301

Stovin v. Wise 369, 868, 874

Strachan (Guardian ad litem of) v. Reynolds 727

Stradiotto v. BMO Nesbitt Burns 623

Strand Electric and Engineering Co. Ltd. v. Brisford Entertainments Ltd. 48, 170

Strand Theatre Ltd. v. Prince Albert (City) 982

Strand v. Emerging Equities Inc. 501

Stratford (J.T.) & Son Ltd. v. Lindley 1130

Street v. Ontario Racing Commission 347, 871

Stricken v. Stewart 621

Strickland v. St. John's 612

Stringer v. Ashley 955

Strohmaier v. British Columbia (Attorney General) 908

Strom (Litigation Guardian of) v. White 1045

Strudwick v. Applied Consumer & Clinical Evaluation Inc. 102

Stuart v. Kirkland-Veenstra 394

Stuart v. R. in Right of Can. 935

Sturges v. Bridgman 971, 993, 1008, 1009, 1014

Suite v. Cooke 439

Sullivan v. Moody 344

Sullivan, R. v. 447

Sulz v. British Columbia (Minister of Public Safety and Solicitor General) 127

Sulz v. Canada (A.G.)   102, 395
Summers v. Tice   833
Sumner v. Colborne   954
Sun Life Assurance Co. of Canada v. Dalrymple   1181, 1187
Sun Rype Products Ltd. v. Archer Daniels Midland Company   1117
Sunrise Co. v. Lake Winnipeg (The)   674
Superintendent of Belchertown State School v. Saikewicz   241
Super-Save Enterprises Ltd. v. 249513 B.C. Ltd. (c.o.b. Mike's Auto Towing)   1128
Surocco v. Geary   266
Surujdeo v. Melady   639, 659
Susan Heyes Inc. (Hazel & Co.) v. South Coast B.C. Transportation Authority   991
Susan Heyes Inc. v. Vancouver (City)   999
Sussman v. Eales   1173, 1176
Sutherland Shire Council v. Heyman   336, 553, 868
Sutherland v. Canada (A.G.)   991, 999
Swaile v. Zurdayk   180
Swales v. Cox   313
Swami v. Lo   692, 713
Swan, R. v.   258
Sweeney v. Boylan Nominees Pty. Ltd.   1073
Sweeney v. Coote   1117
Sweet, R. v.   257, 280
Sweiss v. Alberta Health Services   229
Swick Nominees Pty. Ltd. v. Leroi International Inc. (No. 2)   518
Swift Current (City) v. Saskatchewan Power Corp.   887, 1143
Swinamer v. Nova Scotia (Attorney General)   341, 867
Swinney v. Chief Constable of the Northumbria Police   404
Syl Apps Secure Treatment Centre v. D.(B.)   347, 407, 871
Symington v. Halifax (Regional Municipality)   90
Syms v. Warren   1211
Szalatnay-Stacho v. Fink   1170
Szarfer v. Chodos   122
Szecsodi v. MGM Resorts International   1141
T. (J.) c. Barber   122
T.G. Bright & Co. v. Kerr   1054
T.L.C. v. Vancouver (City)   1043
T.S. v. Adey   437

T.W.N.A. v. Canada (Ministry of Indian Affairs)   41
T.W.N.A. v. Clarke   693, 1066
Taaffe v. Downes   849
Taller (Guardian ad litem of) v. Goldenshtein   1046
Tame v. New South Wales; Annetts v. Australian Stations Pty. Ltd.   458, 703
Tanner v. Norys   409
Tarasoff v. Regents of the University of California   408
Taraviras v. Lovig   729
Tarleton v. M'Gawley   1135
Tataquason v. Saskatoon (City) Board of Police Commissioners   1043
Tétard c. R.   313
Taylor v. A. Novo (U.K.) Ltd.   460
Taylor v. Allard   392, 957
Taylor v. Asody   801
Taylor v. Canada (Attorney General)   730
Taylor v. Despard   1180
Taylor v. King   358
Taylor v. Morrison   621
Taylor v. Weston Bakeries Ltd.   468
Taylor v. Whitehead   269
Te Mata Properties Limited v. Hastings District Council   569
Teamsters Local Union 987 v. O'Holloran   1184
Teavana Corp. v. Teayama Inc.   1105
Teichner v. Bellan   1210
Telnikoff v. Matusevitch   1192
Temilini v. Ontario Provincial Police (Commissioner)   90
Temple v. Hallem   808
Tenning v. Manitoba   127
Teolis v. Moscatelli   206
ter Neuzen v. Korn   619, **627**, 631, 727, 755
Terastream Networks Inc. v. Grossholz   173
Tercon Contractors Ltd. v. British Columbia (Ministry of Transportation and Highways)   539, 808, 960
The Catalyst Capital Group v. Moyse   123
The Catholic Child Welfare Society v. The Institute of the Brothers of the Christian Schools   1069, 1080
The Children's Aid Society of Ottawa-Carleton v. M.C.   241

The Lancashire Wagon Co. Ltd. v. Fitzhugh   149

The Maersk Colombo   773

The Mediana   25, 32, 34, 36, 722

The Owners, Strata Plan LMS 3851 v. Homer Street Development Limited Partnership   504, 719

The Quartz Hill Consolidated Gold Mining Co. v. Eyre   92

The Queen v. Jennings   750

The Queen v. Levy Brothers Co.   1060

The Schwan   818, 819

The Wagon Mound (No. 1); Overseas Tankship (U.K.) Ltd. v. Morts Dock & Engineering Co.   681

The Wagon Mound (No. 2); Overseas Tankship (U.K.) Ltd. v. Miller Steamship Co. Pty.   695

The Winkfield   148

Theakston v. Bowley   730

Theater v. Richardson   1157

Thermo King Corp. v. Provincial. Bank of Can.   1132

Thibault v. Fewer   472

Thiele v. Rod Service (Ottawa) Ltd.   716

Thiessen v. Mutual Life Assurance Co. of Canada   1079

Thomas Management Ltd. v. Alberta (Minister of Environmental Protection)   38

Thomas v. Hamilton (City) Board of Education   616

Thompson v. James Fowler Senior High School   397

Thompson v. Thompson   173

Thompson v. Toorenburgh   712

Thompson v. Webber   92

Thompson, R. v.   211, 212

Thomson v. Herman   1167

Thomson v. Lambert   1162

Thorne v. Deas   410

Thornton (Next friend of) v. Prince George School District No. 57   731

Thornton v. Board of School Trustees of School District No. 57 (Prince George)   1214

Thornton v. Prince George Board of Education   766

Thorson v. A.G. Can.   999

Three Rivers District Council v. Bank of England (No. 3)   882, 888

Tibbetts v. Murphy   775, 778

Tiglao v. Sleightholm   475

Tillander v. Gosselin   62

Timberwolf Log Trading Ltd. v. British Columbia (Ministry of Forests, Mines and Lands)   889

Timmermans v. Buelow   104

To v. Toronto (City) Board of Education   769

Tock v. St. John's Metropolitan Area Board   978, **986**, 1032, 1036

Toews (Guardian ad litem of) v. Weisner   61, 213

Tomizza v. Fraser   713

Tomlinson v. Congleton Borough Council   955

Tompkins Hardware Ltd. v. North West Flying Services Ltd.   797

Toneguzzo-Norvell (Guardian ad litem of) v. Burnaby Hospital   358, 746, 747

Tong v. Bedwell   406, 716

Toogood v. Spryring   1178

Torgeson v. Schultz   333

Toronto Dominion Bank v. Forsythe   501

Toronto Railway Co. v. Toms   464

Toronto Ry. Co. v. Grinstead   680

Toronto-Dominion Bank v. Forsythe   504, 520

Torquay Hotel Co. v. Cousins   1130

Torrance v. Alberta   851

Toshi Enterprises Ltd. v. Coffee Time Donuts Inc.   1079

Total Network SL v. Revenue and Customs Commissioners   1120, 1143

Tottrup v. Lund   867, 1066

Townsend v. Kroppmanns   742, 752

Towson v. Bergman   735

Toy v. Argenti   423, 425

Trachsler v. Halton   896

Tracy v. Atkins   500

Tran v. Financial Debt Recovery Ltd.   1142

Tran v. Kerr   625, 815

Transco plc v. Stockport Metropolitan Borough Council   1023, 1029, 1036

Trapp v. Mackie   1176

Traquair v. National Arts Centre Corp.   959

Treaty Group Inc. (c.o.b. as Leather Treaty) v. Drake International Inc.   500

Tremain v. Pike   687

Tremblay c. Cie d'assurance Standard Life   111

Tremblay v. Campbell   1222

Tremblay v. McLauchlan   473

Tremblay v. Ottawa Police Service Board 89, 286

Trends Holdings Ltd. (Trustee of) v. Tilson   796

Trevison v. Springman   688

Tridan Developments Ltd. v. Shell Canada Products Ltd.   774

Trillium Motor World Ltd. v. Cassels Brock & Blackwell LLP   624

Trillium Power Wind Corporation v. Ontario (National Resources)   888, 892

Trizec Equities Ltd. v. Ellis-Don Management Services Ltd.   623

Trkulja v. Google LLC   1160

Tronrud v. French   742

Trotter-Brons (Litigation Guardian of) v. Corrigan   762

Trueman v. The King; Dewan v. The King   897

Truong v. Saskatoon (City)   938

"Truth" (N.Z.) Ltd. v. Holloway   1207

Tsaoussis (Litigation Guardian of) v. Baetz   733

Tse Wai Chun Paul v. Albert Cheng   1198

Tubervell v. Savadge   73

Tucker (Public Trustee of) v. Asleson 663, 747

Tucker v. Cadillac Fairview Corporation Limited   189

Tudor Inn Reception Hall (1992) Ltd. v. Merzat Industries Ltd.   488, 1051

Turcotte v. Lewis   388

Turenne v. Chung   728

Turner v. Bederman   473

Turner v. Delta Shelf Co. Ltd.   977

Turner v. Thorne   177, 213

Turton v. Hanson   79, 281

Tutton v. A.D. Walter Ltd.   362

Twan v. Hudson's Bay Company   81

U.A.W. v. Johnson Controls   428

U.F.C.W., Local 1252 v. Cashin   1142

U.S. v. Caltex (Philippines) Inc.   269

U.S. v. Holmes   268

Uber BV v. Howarth   1112

Udale v. Bloomsbury Area Health Authority   439

Uhrovic v. Masjhuri   743

Ultramares Corp. v. Touche   497, 508, 555, 562

Unident v. DeLong   1128

Uni-Jet Industrial Pipe Ltd. v. Canada (Attorney General)   883, 889

Unisys Canada Inc. v. Imperial Optical Co.   142

United Airlines Inc. v. Cooperstock   1107

United Australia Ltd. v. Barclay's Bank Ltd.   46, 163

United Project Consultants Pte. Ltd. v. Leong Kwok Onn   553

United Services Funds (Trustees of) v. Richard Greenshields of Can. Ltd. 1095

United States v. Carroll Towing Co.   602

United States v. Gaubert   874

United States v. Muniz   861

Univ. Hospital Bd. v. Lepine; Monckton v. Lepine   394

Universal Environmental Services Inc. v. West Newfoundland Regional Appeal Board   855

Universe Tankship Inc. of Monrovia v. I.T.W.F.   1113

Université Laval v. Carriere   416

University of Regina v. Pettick   568, 729

Unruh (Guardian ad litem of) v. Webber 808

Urbanski v. Patel   362, 424, 426

Urbanson v. Western Canadian Place Ltd.   960

V.K. Mason Construction Ltd. v. Bank of Nova Scotia   500

Valentine, R. v.   287, 304

Valiquette c. Gazette (The)   112

Valley Salvage Ltd. v. Molson Brewery B.C. Ltd.   1121

Van Burgsteden v. Long   158

Van de Perre v. Edwards   358

Van Dyke v. Grey Bruce Regional Health Centre   475

Van Mol (Guardian ad litem of) v. Ashmore   472

Vana v. Tosta   770

Vancouver (City) v. Ward   31, 33, 282, 306, 890, **923**

Vancouver Community College v. Vancouver Career College (Burnaby) Inc.   1107

Vancouver Gen. Hosp. v. McDaniel   632

Vancouver General Hospital v. Fraser Estate   620

Vancouver General Hospital v. Stoffman 921

Vander Zalm v. Times Publishers   1196

Vanderkooy v. Vanderkooy   1184

Vanek v. Great Atlantic & Pacific Co. of
  Canada   450, 703
Vanvalkenburg v. Northern Navigation
  Co.   375, 378
Varcoe v. Sterling   623, 917
Vasey v. Wosk's Ltd   1065
Vaughan v. Menlove   608
**Vaughn v. Halifax-Dartmouth Bridge
  Comm.   596**
Vaughn v. Kelowna Speedometer Ltd.
  958
Veert Landscaping Inc. v. Ranger
  Insurance Brokers Ltd.   623
Veinot v. Kerr-Addison Mines Ltd.   944
Veinot v. Veinot   249, 262
Vellacott v. Saskatoon Starphoenix Group
  Inc.   1209
Vellino v. Chief Constable of Greater
  Manchester Police   815
Verchere v. Greenpeace Canada Ltd.
  1132
Vernon v. Bosley (No. 1)   458
Viasystems (Tyneside) Ltd. v. Thermal
  Transfer (Northern) Ltd.   1069
Victorian Railways Commissioner v.
  Coultas   95, 96, 451
Videan v. British Transport Commission
  418, 420, 422
Videto v. Kennedy   470, 474
Vienneau Assur. Ltée v. Roy   415
Vigna v. Levant   1209
Vigoren v. Nystuen   803
Villemure v. L'Hôpital Notre-Dame   394
Villing v. Husseni   748
Vincent v. Abu-Bakare   748
Vincent v. Blake Cassels & Graydon
  LLP   558
Vincent v. Lake Erie Tpt. Co.   270
Visanji v. Eaton   623, 845
Visscher v. Triple Broek Holdings Ltd.
  143
VitaPharm Canada Ltd. v. F. Hoffmann-
  LaRoche Ltd.   1117
Vizetelly v. Mudie's Select Library Ltd.
  1162
Vlchek v. Koshel   44, 485, 723
Vogel v. Canadian Broadcasting
  Corporation   1156, 1198
Vorvis v. Insurance Corp. of British
  Columbia   37, 45, 722
Vowles v. Evans   396
W. v. A.   1155
W. v. Essex County Council   459

W.(A.), R. v.   208
Wackett v. Calder   245
Waddell v. Hemerson   405
Wade v. Ball   491, 493
Wade v. C.N.R.   948, 1232
Wade v. Hoyt   493
Wade v. Martin   207, 218
Wagner v. Int. Ry. Co.   422, 423
Wainwright v. Home Office   96, 99, 109
Wakelam v. Johnson & Johnson   49
**Wakelin v. London & South Western Ry.
  Co.   822**
Wakley v. Cooke   1164
Walden v. Mitchell   1155
Waldick v. Malcolm   932, 948, 954, 959,
  960
Waldman's Fish Co. v. Anderson Ins.
  Ltd.   623
Walford (Litigation Guardian of) v.
  Jacuzzi Canada Inc.   500
Walford v. Jacuzzi Canada Ltd.   485, 489
Walker (Litigation Guardian of) v. Region
  2 Hospital Corp.   235
Walker Estate v. York-Finch General
  Hospital   631, 652, 1050
Walker v. CFTO Ltd.   1213, 1219, 1221
Walker v. Coates   625
Walker v. Ontario   88
Walker v. Ritchie   747, 751, 757, 775
Wallace v. Berrigan   794
Wallace v. United Grain Growers Ltd.
  102
Wallbridge v Brunning   1057
Waller v. James; Waller v. Hoolahan   436
Walls v. Mussens Ltd.   785
Walmsley v. Humenick   829
Walsh Energy Inc. v. Better Business
  Bureau of Ottawa-Hull Incorporated
  1197
Walt Disney Productions v. Fantasyland
  Hotel Inc.   1106
Walt Disney Productions v. Triple Five
  Corp.   1106
Walters (Litigation Guardian of) v.
  Ontario   624, 868
Walters v. North Glamorgan NHS Trust
  459
Walters v. W.H. Smith & Son Ltd.   292
Wandsworth Board of Works v. United
  Telephone Co. Ltd.   195
Wandy v. River Valley Ventures Inc.   392
Wang v. British Columbia Medical
  Association   1179

Wang v. Shao   1099

Ward v. Cannock Chase Dist. Council   716

Ward v. James   753

Ward v. Lewis   1120

Ward v. Magna International Inc.   986, 1004

Wardak v. Froom   391

Ware's Taxi Ltd. v. Gilliham   599

Warman v. Grosvenor   74

Warren v. Green   1157

Warren v. Henlys, Ltd.   1060

Warren v. King   753

Waterloo Warehousing & Storage Ltd. v. Swenco Mfg. Ltd.   773

Waters v. Bains   41

Waters v. Commissioner of Police for the Metropolis   395

Waters v. Metropolitan Police Commissioner   1241

Waters v. Michie   1120

Watkins v. Olafson   734, 741

Watkins v. Secretary of State for the Home Department   888

Watson v. Bank of America Corp.   1124, 1142

Watson v. Longsdon   1178

Watson v. M'Ewan, Watson v. Jones   1176

Watt v. Hertfordshire County Council   600

Watters v. White   437

Watts v. Klaemt   110

Weare, R. v.   265

Weaver v. Ball   1156

Weaver v. Corcoran   1117

Weaver v. Pollock   757

Webb v. Birkett   622

Webber v. Crawford   794

Webster v. Edmonton (City) Police Services   286

Webster v. Low   192

Wechsel v. Stutz   494

Weenen v. Biadi   1005, 1032

WeGo Kayaking Ltd. v. Sewid   1198

Wegren v. Prince Albert (City)   868

Weiner v. Zoratti   685

Weingerl v. Seo   1066

Weisbeck v. Regina (City)   763

Weiss v. Solomon   476

Welbridge Holdings Ltd. v. Greater Winnipeg   848, 851, 867

Welch, R. v.   219

Wellesley Hospital v. Lawson   394

Wellesley Partners LLP v. Withers LLP   535, 695

Wellington v. Ontario   347

Wells v. Parsons   789

Wells v. Sears   1179

Wenden v. Trikha   394, 409, 607, 621

Wenger SA v. Travel Way Group International Inc.   1107

Wennhak v. Morgan   1161

Wentzell v. Veinot   265

Werbeniuk v. Maynard   406, 709, 716

Wernikowski v. Kirkland, Murphy & Ain   494

Wessell v. Kinsmen Club of Sault Ste. Marie Ont. Inc.   762

West Bromwich Albion Football Club Ltd. v. El-Safty   559

West Coast Finance Ltd. v. Gunderson, Stokes, Walton & Co.   1098

Westbroek v. Brizuela   758

Western Ontario Natural Gas Co. Ltd. v. Aikens   1117

Westfair Foods Ltd. v. Lippens Inc.   1119

Westlake v. The Queen in Right of the Province of Ontario   855

Wetmore, R. v.   257

Whaley v. Cartusiano   63

Wheaton, R. v.   257

Wheeler v. Muri   624

Wheeler v. Somerfield   1157

Whelan v. Parsons & Sons Transportation Ltd.   599

Whighton v. Integrity Inspections Inc.   500, 540

Whitaker, R. v.   887

White Distribution Ltd. v. Goring   163

White v. Blackmore   808

White v. Chief Constable of South Yorkshire   424, 450, 453, 460, 703

White v. Colliers Macaulay Nicholls Inc.   502

White v. Johnston   202

White v. Jones   26, 411, 490, 557, 558

White v. Turner   617, 1095

White v. Withers LLP   142

Whiteley Ltd. v. Hilt   167

Whiten v. Pilot Insurance Co.   43, 164, 721, 1005, 1114, 1133

Whitfield v. Whitfield   41

Whitfield, R. v.   280

Whittingham v. Crease & Co.   411, 490, 557, 558

Whitwham v. Westminster Brymbo Coal and Coke Company 48

Whynot (Stafford), R. v. 250

WIC Radio Ltd. v. Simpson 1156, **1186**

Wiche v. Ontario 90

Wickberg v. Patterson 797

Wickline v. California 599

Wicks Estate v. Harnett 143

Wicks v. State Rail Authority of New South Wales; Sheehan v. State Rail Authority of New South Wales 458

Wicks v. State Rail Authority of New South Wales 460

Widdowson v. Newgate Meat Corp. 841

Widdrington Estate v. Wightman 520

Wiebe Door Services Ltd. v. M.N.R. 1076

Wiebe v. Canada (Attorney General) 394

Wiebe v. Gunderson 775

Wieland v. Cyril Lord Carpets Ltd. 712

Wight v. Pickering Automobiles Inc. 839

Wilcox v. Johnston 622

Wilcox v. Police 186, 269

Wildwood Mall Ltd. v. Stevens 186

Wiley v. Tymar Management Inc. 953

Wilhelm v. Hickson 558

Wilhelmson v. Dumma 741, 755, 757, 758

Wilk v. Arbour 710, 1045

Wilkinson v. Downton 9, **94**, 107, 127

Willers v. Joyce 90

William Leitch & Co. v. Leydon 137

William v. Kelowna (City) 640

Williams (Respondent) v. The Bermuda Hospitals Board (appellant) (Bermuda) 653

Williams v. Attorney General of Canada 1066

Williams v. Canada (Attorney General) 347, 871

Williams v. Holland 13

Williams v. Mulgrave (Town) 179

Williams v. New Brunswick 393

Williams v. Ontario 344

Williams v. Peel River Land & Mineral Co. Ltd. 170

Williams v. Polgar 519

Williams v. Reason 1164, **1165**

Williams v. Richard 389

Williams v. St. John (City) 689

Williams v. Toronto (City) 348, 519

Williams, R. v. 210

Willis v. Halifax (Regional Municipality) 974

Willows v. Williams 1160

Wills v. Doe 713

Wills v. Saunders 620

Wilmington Gen. Hosp. v. Manlove 415

Wilsher v. Essex Area Health Authority 644, 645, 836

Wilson v. Bobbie 59, 276

Wilson v. Brett 625

Wilson v. Honda Canada Financial Inc. 748

Wilson v. Lind 723

Wilson v. Lombank Ltd. 147

Wilson v. Martinello 735

Wilson v. New Brighton Panelbeaters Ltd. 144

Wilson v. Pringle 64

Wilson v. Servier Canada Inc. 758

Wilson v. Swanson 587

Wilson v. Williams 1177

Wince v. Ball 391

Windrem v. Hamill 1048

Windsor Energy Inc. v. Northrup 1109

Windsor v. Canadian Pacific Railway Ltd. 1024

Winnipeg Child & Family Services (Northwest Area) v. G.(D.F.) 446

Winnipeg Condominium Corporation No. 36 v. Bird Construction Co. 559, 577

Winnipeg Elec. Ry. Co. v. Can. Nor. Ry. 680

Winnipeg Electric Co. v. Geel 828

Wint, R. v. 304

Winterbottom v. Wright 333

Winters v. Haldimand (County) 955

Wipfli v. Britten 99, 778

Wise v. Abbott Laboratories Ltd. 649, 837

Wise, R. v. 308

Witman v. Johnson 1044

Woelk v. Halvorson 729

Woestenburg v. Kamloops (City) 851

Wolf v. Ontario (Attorney General) 1120

Wolkowski, R. v. 313

Wong (Litigation Guardian of) v. Lok's Martial Arts Centre Inc. 808

Wong (Litigation Guardian of) v. Towns 757

Wong v. Grant Mitchell Law Corporation 622

Wong v. Rashidi 179

Wood v. Jaffer 1197

Wood v. Kennedy 89
Wood v. Ward 955
Woodhouse v. Snow Valley Resorts (1987) Ltd. 960
Woodland v. Swimming Teachers Association 1083
Woolcock Street Investments Pty. Ltd. v. C.D.G. Pty. Ltd. 568
Woollerton and Wilson Ltd. v. Richard Costain Ltd. 197
Wormald v. Chiarot 785, 793
Wormald v. Cole 1049
Wotta v. Haliburton Oil Well Cementing Co. 835
Wright Estate v. Davidson 692, 713
Wright v. McCrea 715
Wright v. McLean 202
Wright v. Wilson 77
Wrightman, R. v. 298
Wu v. Vancouver (City) 910
Wuttunee v. Merck Frosst Canada Ltd. 68, 504
Wyant v. Crouse 181
Wynberg v. Daley 499, 502
Wynberg v. Ontario 867
Wyong Shire Council v. Shirt 358
X (Minors) v. Bedfordshire County Council 868
X v. Bedfordshire County Council 874
X. v. Everson 82
XY, LLC v. Canadian Topsires Selection Inc. 42, 44, 47, 48, 122, 1117
Yarmouth v. France 805
Yates v. Lansing 849
Ybarra v. Spangard 834
Yearworth v. North Bristol NHS Trust 772
Yelic v. Gimli (Town) 942
Yellow Submarine Deli Inc. v. A.G.F. Hospitality Associates Inc. 1128
Yepremian v. Scarborough Gen. Hosp. 734

Ycung (Guardian ad litem of) v. Au 1052
Yin v. Lewin 727
York v. Alderney Consultants Ltd. 500
York v. Okanagan Broadcasters Ltd. 1168
Young v. Bella 407, 553, 623, 755, 1185
Young v. Borzoni 100
Young v. Green 1040
Young v. Toronto Star Newspapers Ltd. 1201
Your Response Ltd. v. Datateam Business Media Ltd. 157
Youssef (Litigation guardian of) v. Misselbrook 954
Yu v. Yu 459
Yuan v. Farstad 790
Yuen Kun Yeu v. A.G. of Hong Kong 336, 339, 345, 511
Z v. United Kingdom 403
Zaccardo c. Chartis Insurance Co. of Canada 206
Zacharias v. Leys 693
Zall v. Zall 1212, 1222
Zambri v. Grammelhofer 181
Zanetti v. Bonniehon Enterprises Ltd. 1176
Zapf v. Muckalt 808
Zary v. Canada Housing and Mortgage Corp. 959
Zavaglia v. Maq Holdings Ltd. 957
Zbarsky v. Lukashuk 974
Zelenko v. Gimbel Bros., Inc. 412
Zervobeakos v. Zervobeakos 425, 787
Zhou v. Wang 1095
Zidaric v. Toshiba of Canada Ltd. 566
Zinck v. Strickland and Blake 218
Zsoldos v. Canadian Pacific Railway Co. 632, 785, 959
Zurich Insurance PLC UK Branch v. International Energy Group Ltd. 837

1

AN INTRODUCTION
TO THE LAW OF TORTS

1. Tort Law Defined
2. Tort and Contract
3. A Brief History of Tort Law
4. Trespass and Case: A Brief Review of the Case Law
5. The Bases for Imposing Liability in Tort
6. The Functions of Tort Law
7. The Rights Theory of Tort Law

1. Tort Law Defined

Tort law is difficult to define. The word itself is not commonly used outside of the legal community. It is derived from the Latin word "torquere," which means twisted or crooked. Tort law therefore is concerned with things that have gone wrong, or, to use more technical language, with the *breach of obligations*. It is important to realize, however, that our legal system recognizes various types of wrongdoing, and that only some of those fall within tort law.

At the most general level, a distinction must be drawn between *public wrongs* and *private wrongs*. Public wrongs are addressed through *criminal law*. A crime is committed when a person breaches an obligation that was owed to society as a whole. Because crime is a public matter, action is taken by the Crown (the government) rather than the individual victim (if there is one). That fact is reflected in the *style of cause* (*i.e.* the name of the case). The Crown appears as *Rex* or *Regina* (which is Latin for King or Queen) in order to prosecute the *accused*: *R. v. Smith*. Likewise, because the primary goals of criminal law are concerned with the protection of society, a successful prosecution, in which the accused is found *guilty*, usually results in some form of punishment, such as imprisonment. Even if the offender is ordered to pay a fine, the money usually benefits the Crown rather than the victim.

Tort law, in contrast, is concerned with private wrongs. The wrongdoer breached an obligation that was owed to an individual, rather than to society as a whole. Consequently, the victim of the wrong (the *plaintiff*) personally takes action against the party in breach (the *defendant*), and the style of cause takes the form of *Smith v. Jones*. Likewise, because a tort is a private matter, successful litigation, in which the defendant is held *liable*, usually results in a remedy that reflects the manner in which the breach affected the parties. For instance, if a benefit is acquired as a result of a wrong, the court may order the defendant to *disgorge* that enrichment to the plaintiff (as when a thief earns a profit by using a stolen car as a taxi). Typically, however, the focus falls upon the plaintiff's loss, rather than the defendant's gain. The appropriate remedy therefore requires the defendant to *compensate* the plaintiff (as when a person wrongfully suffers an injury that entails medical expenses or lost income). Although the plaintiff occasionally is entitled to recover the very thing that was lost (as when a thief steals a family heirloom), compensation usually takes the form of monetary *damages*. Remedies are considered in greater detail in Chapters 2 and 18.

To this point, tort law generally has been discussed in terms of the rights and remedies associated with legal relationships between private parties. That definition, however, is too broad. First, it is necessary to emphasize that since tort law is concerned with wrongdoing, it does not govern situations of true *strict liability*, which do not presume breach of obligation. (As explained later in this chapter, a different conception of "strict liability," which *does* involve the breach of an obligation, *is* part of tort law.) For instance, the law of *unjust enrichment* applies if, in the absence of any juristic reason, the defendant receives a benefit from the plaintiff. That may be true even if the defendant was entirely unaware, and wholly innocent, of the impugned transfer (as when a company mistakenly pays money into the defendant's bank account, rather than its own). The claimant nevertheless is entitled to *restitution* from the recipient.

Moreover, even within the broad category of private wrongdoing, some situations fall outside of tort law. Most obviously, although a breach of contract is a private wrong, it is governed by the law of contract rather than the law of tort. (The next section further considers the relationship between tort and contract.) The category of "torts" is also usually defined to exclude wrongs that originally developed in the *courts of equity*. That practice has become difficult to defend as a matter of principle, but it may be defended on purely practical grounds. Tort law is a large subject. The addition of equitable wrongs would contribute substantially to its size. Moreover, if equitable wrongs were included, it would be difficult to justify the exclusion of still more categories of private wrongdoing. That would be true, for instance, of the various causes of action that protect intellectual property rights: breach of patent, breach of copyright, and so on. Accordingly, while this book is confined to the forms of private wrongdoing that traditionally have been characterized as torts, it is important to remember that obligations and liabilities often arise in other ways as well.

NOTES

1. Although a distinction is now drawn between public wrongs and private wrongs, criminal law and tort law share a common heritage that predates the Norman Conquest of England. See generally Holdsworth, *A History of English Law*, vol. 2 (1932) at 43-54; Malone, "Ruminations on the Role of Fault in the History of the Common Law of Torts" (1970) 31 La. L. Rev. 1; and Hall, "Interrelations of Criminal Law and Torts" (1943) 43 Columbia L. Rev. 753 and 967.

2. A strong argument for subsuming equitable wrongs within the law of tort is made by Birks, "Civil Wrongs: A New World" in *Butterworths Lectures 1990-91* (1992) at 55-112.

3. On the importance of legal taxonomy, see Birks, "This Heap of Good Learning: The Jurist in the Common Law Tradition" in Markesinis, ed., *Law Making, Law Finding and Law Shaping: The Diverse Influences* (1997) at 113-38; and Birks, "Equity in the Modern Law: An Exercise in Taxonomy" (1996) 26 U.W.A.L. Rev. 1.

4. The *Judicature Acts* of the 19th century undoubtedly fused the *administration* of law and equity. There is a debate, however, as to whether Parliament also intended *substantive fusion*. Some commentators, especially in Australia, argue that while law and equity are now administered in a single set of courts, they retain their historical characteristics and therefore remain fundamentally different in outlook and operation: Meagher, Heydon & Leeming, eds., *Meagher, Gummow and Lehane's Equity: Doctrines and Remedies*, 5th ed. (2014); and *Harris v. Digital Pulse Pty. Ltd.* (2003), 56 N.S.W.L.R. 298 (C.A.). Other commentators, however, insist that it is unhelpful, if not irrational, to maintain two perspectives in a single system: Burrows, "We Do This At Common Law But That In Equity" (2002) 22 O.J.L.S. 1; and Birks, "Annual Miegunyah Lecture: Equity, Conscience, and Unjust Enrichment" (1999) 23 Melbourne U.L. Rev. 1.

5. While Canadian courts demonstrate relatively little interest in the fusion debate, the Supreme Court of Canada has suggested that, in some circumstances at least, different principles apply depending upon whether the plaintiff's allegation of wrongdoing lies in equity rather than law: *Canson Enterprises Ltd. v. Boughton & Co.*, [1991] 3 S.C.R. 534.

2. Tort and Contract

Although it is important to distinguish tort law from other areas of law, the facts of life do not always fall neatly into place. A single set of facts may support several different analyses. For instance, the same events may support both a claim in tort law and a prosecution in criminal law. If one person physically attacks another, the victim may recover damages in tort law and the perpetrator may be punished for the crime. Likewise, a single set of events may support several claims in tort law. A security guard who grabs a customer wrongly thought to be a shoplifter may be liable in tort for both false imprisonment and battery. Arguably the most significant overlap occurs between tort and contract. A professional person (such as a lawyer or an accountant) who acts carelessly may be held responsible for breach of contract or the tort of negligence. As a general rule, a plaintiff is entitled to simultaneously sue for several causes of action, but if successful on several grounds, the claimant must normally *elect* between the options. The courts will not allow *double recovery* for the same loss.

Because of the significance of the overlap between tort and contract, it is necessary to say more about the relationship between those two areas of law.

- *Structure*: Both tort and contract involve *primary* and *secondary* obligations. Primary obligations tell people how they ought to act. For instance, the tort of battery says, "Do not touch another person in an offensive way" and the law of contract says, "Keep your promises." Secondary obligations are remedial. They tell people how they must act after primary obligations have been broken. In most cases, the defendant is told, "Because you wrongfully hurt the plaintiff, you must pay compensation." That is true whether the case involves a tort or a contract.

- *Source of Primary Obligations*: Despite sharing the same basic structure, tort and contract differ in several important respects. The first pertains to the source of the primary obligations. Obligations in tort are imposed by law on the basis of circumstance. A motorist, for instance, owes a duty of care to a nearby pedestrian even if the motorist never agreed to take care and even if (remarkably) the motorist is unaware of that duty. In contrast, contractual obligations are generally created by the parties. If contractual parties are required to act in certain ways, it is because they voluntarily agreed to do so.

- *Privity*: Because contractual obligations are voluntarily created by the parties, their enforcement is subject to the doctrine of *privity*. As a general rule, only the parties to an agreement can sue or be sued if that agreement is broken. That means, for instance, that an outsider cannot sue for breach of contract, even if the breach caused that person to suffer substantial harm. In contrast, because tort obligations are imposed by law, they apply even if the parties otherwise are complete strangers.

- *Enforcement*: Primary obligations are generally enforced by means of secondary obligations. A party that commits a tort or fails to fulfil a contractual undertaking is normally compelled to pay damages to the victim. Exceptionally, however, the law may insist on the performance of a primary obligation. Rather than dealing with the consequences of a wrong, a court may insist that things be done right. Suppose, for instance, that the defendant agreed to sell a family heirloom to the plaintiff. Because no amount of money would allow the plaintiff to obtain a substitute for the heirloom — it is one of a kind after all — a judge may issue an order for *specific performance* that requires the defendant to transfer the item for the price. Something similar may happen in tort. Suppose, for instance, that a pair of homeowners subject their neighbour to a terrible nuisance. In addition to awarding damages for past losses, a judge may issue an *injunction* that prohibits the tortfeasors from continuing to annoy their neighbours in the future. Although the performance of a primary obligation is almost always superior to damages for breach, those two forms of *specific enforcement* are limited to exceptional circumstances.

- *Compensation*: The vast majority of claimants in tort and contract actions seek compensatory damages. Once again, however, the underlying obligations result in an important distinction. Suppose that the defendant persuaded the plaintiff to purchase a business opportunity for $100,000 by fraudulently saying that the venture would earn $150,000. The plaintiff discovers the truth of the matter only after paying the purchase price. It may be possible to sue for the tort of deceit or for breach of contract. The measure of relief will be different in each instance. Tort obligations are imposed in order to prevent harm and protect an existing state of affairs. Torts, in other words, are events that *should not* happen. Compensation in tort law consequently looks *backward*. It monetarily puts the plaintiff back into the position that would have been enjoyed if the wrong had never occurred. The plaintiff in this case would therefore receive damages of $100,000. Going back in time, that is what was lost. In contrast, contracts are based on promises, and promises pertain to events that *should* happen in the future. Compensation in contract consequently (usually) looks *forward*. It monetarily puts the plaintiff into the position that would have been enjoyed once the agreement had been properly performed. The plaintiff in this case would therefore be entitled to receive $150,000. Looking ahead in time, that is what the claimant expected to receive. Of course, if both actions are successful, the plaintiff will elect to receive damages in contract rather than in tort.

NOTES

1. Although the orthodox model continues to reflect the general distinction between tort and contract, the line between these two areas of law has become increasingly blurred. Contractual obligations are not invariably created by the parties. In many situations, they are imposed upon the parties by operation of law. The *Sale of Goods Act*, R.S.O. 1990, c. S.1, for instance, automatically inserts a large number of terms into contracts for the sale of goods. That is true even if the parties did not consider the matter. Some commentators regard such developments as the "death of contract," in the sense that contractual obligations are not exclusively a function of the parties' volition. See Gilmore, *The Death of Contract* (1974); Atiyah, *The Rise and Fall of Freedom of Contract* (1979); and Blom, "Fictions and Frictions on the Interface Between Tort and Contract" in Burns, ed., *Donoghue v. Stevenson: The Modern Law of Negligence* (1991) at 139.

2. Likewise, while many tort obligations are imposed without regard to volition, others arise only if a person voluntarily enters into a relationship or agrees to undertake certain acts. The decision to own a parcel of land, for instance, automatically imports obligations involving occupiers' liability and nuisance. Other examples will be seen throughout this book.

REVIEW PROBLEM

Angus, a consumer advocate, was conducting a speaking tour criticizing the safety standards of a new Canadian subcompact automobile. The car, which had been hailed as the key to the future of the Canadian automobile industry, was supposed to reverse the trend of falling sales and high unemployment. Several days before his appearance in Windsor, Angus received threatening phone calls. As a precaution he hired Joseph, a local private detective, who agreed to serve as his bodyguard during his speech.

Just before the end of the speech, a man jumped onto the stage shouting, "Canadian jobs first!" and flailed at Angus. Joseph ran off to call the police, but offered no direct assistance. Angus' secretary, Doris, who was an expert in the martial arts, also failed to come to his assistance. The assailant, an unemployed auto worker named Victor, was eventually restrained by two members of the audience, but not before he had severely beaten Angus.

1. As you are probably aware, Victor's attack on Angus is a violation of Canadian criminal law. Who is responsible for bringing charges against Victor, gathering the evidence, and conducting and paying for the prosecution? What role will Angus play at the criminal trial? What private and social benefits result from the criminal prosecution?

2. Victor's attack on Angus also constitutes the intentional tort of battery. Contrast the events involved in bringing a tort claim against Victor with the criminal process. What general distinctions between criminal and tort law emerge?

3. Angus and Joseph are in a contractual relationship. What legal wrong has Joseph done to Angus? What is the public interest in enforcing contractual obligations?

4. Angus also wants to sue Doris, whose legal wrong, if any, was a failure to come to Angus' aid. Distinguish Angus' legal relationship with Doris from his legal relationship with Joseph.

5. A failure to act is referred to as a nonfeasance. In tort law, it has always been more difficult to establish liability for a nonfeasance than for a misfeasance, which is a wrongful positive act. Can you explain why? Provided that a defendant has agreed to act, he or she will generally be held liable in contract for the failure to do so. Why should nonfeasance be more readily actionable in contract than in tort?

6. Should Doris be held liable in tort if she knew of the threats against Angus and promised to protect him? Would your answer be different if: (a) Angus had relied on her assurances and told Doris that he had dismissed Joseph; or (b) Doris was unaware that Angus had dismissed Joseph?

3. A Brief History of Tort Law

The history of tort law is not the evolution of a single idea, but rather the history of how a residual category of civil wrongs came to be formed. The story begins with the separation of public and private wrongs, and continues with the emergence of tort (and other discrete heads of liability) from a general body of civil wrongs.

In Anglo-Saxon England, the primary object of the law was to prevent blood feuds among the clans. There were few divisions in the law, and no distinction was drawn between crimes and torts. The appeasement of the clan's pride and the symbolism of public adjudication were the law's main goals. The wrongdoer paid a *bot* to the other clan for appeasement and a *wite* to the King for having breached the peace. Gradually, as political power became centralized in the King, a distinction between public and private wrongs developed. By the 11th century, the *appeal of felony*, a criminal action that could not be amended by private payment, was recognized. Paralleling this development was a breakdown in the agreed scale of the *bot* among the clans. As a result, there was no legal mechanism for making a private claim for damages.

After the Norman Conquest, there were further attempts to centralize and unify legal authority. In order to consolidate power and avoid the inconvenience that the diverse local laws created for tax collectors and judicial officers, William the Conqueror and his successors sought to impose a uniform set of laws throughout England. Greatly advanced by Henry II, this set of laws came to be known as the *common law*. A central feature of the common law was the writ system — a system that became dominated by an intense concern with procedural formality.

The writs themselves were standardized pleadings issued by the Chancery clerks on behalf of the King, stating that a defendant had committed certain unlawful acts. In order to commence an action in the King's common law courts, a plaintiff had to allege facts that would bring the case within the standard form of the writ. No matter how obviously wrongful the defendant's conduct, no action would lie if it was not governed by an existing writ.

At first, access to the King's courts was limited to suits concerning violent acts — those done with force of arms and against the King's peace (*vi et armis et contra pacem regis*). Causes of action now recognized as torts were grouped into a family of writs called *trespass*. It included actions for assault, battery, trespass to land, and the taking of goods.

The most important factor in the history of tort law after 1200 was jurisdiction, not policy. To meet the demand for access to the King's courts and to expand the King's jurisdiction, it was necessary to broaden the types of wrongs that could be heard. However, this had to be accomplished without increasing the limited number of writs. The solution, as in much of the common law's history, was "a pack of lies": see Langbein, "The Later History of Restitution" in Cornish *et al.*, eds., *Restitution: Past, Present & Future* (1998) at 57. Plaintiffs would plead trespass *vi et armis et contra pacem regis* even if no force or breach of the peace was involved, and the clerks would honour this fiction to assume jurisdiction. For example, if the defendant refused to return goods in storage, the plaintiff would plead that the defendant took them *vi et armis et contra pacem regis* in order to have the case tried in the King's courts.

Although the King's courts eventually assumed jurisdiction over most civil wrongs and the *vi et armis* allegation became unnecessary in the 1300s, the writ system remained. A second writ, called *trespass on the case*, emerged. Its origins are a matter of dispute. The pleadings in an action on the case raised special circumstances which made the act wrongful, whereas in the original trespass action a general plea would suffice.

Before the 19th century, what we would now call actions in tort were not frequently litigated. It appears that most conflicts over intentional and unintentional wrongs were resolved extra-legally. However, the advent in England of more densely populated, impersonal, and technologically-advanced communities after 1800 gave rise to increased levels of tort litigation. Just as lawyers for plaintiffs attempted to extend the scope of liability in the writs of trespass and case, so too lawyers for defendants attempted to terminate litigation on procedural grounds. In this context, the longstanding, but conceptually awkward, distinction between trespass and case assumed even more significance. The cases excerpted in the fourth section of this chapter illustrate how the common law judges gradually developed new theories of liability for these torts.

The core normative principle in tort law in the 19th century was the idea of fault or moral blameworthiness. In this era, judges came to agree that, with rare exceptions, liability in tort required proof that the plaintiff's loss had been caused by some wrongdoing of the defendant. For instance, liability in trespass would be established when the plaintiff proved that the defendant had intentionally interfered with his or her rights to security of the person or property. Liability on the case would lie when the plaintiff proved that an actual loss to person or property had been caused by the defendant's carelessness. Although in recent years the "fault-based" conception of liability has been blurred in some types of cases, it continues to underscore most of the contemporary torts of intent and negligence.

After 50 years of debate, the writ system in England was abolished by the *Judicature Acts* in the 1870s. Similar legislation soon followed in other common law jurisdictions, including Canada. It no longer was necessary for a litigant to fit the claim within an existing writ. Instead, the plaintiff pleaded the facts of the case, and if these facts justified relief under any recognized cause of action, the courts would grant that relief. Nevertheless, the break with the old forms of actions was neither sharp nor complete. As F.W. Maitland famously observed, "The forms of action we have buried, but they rule us from their graves": *Equity — A Course of Lectures* (1939) at vi.

For example, the intentional torts derived from trespass *vi et armis* have remained strictly defined, typically require proof of direct injury, and have developed little over the years. As *Cook v. Lewis*, [1951] S.C.R. 830, extracted below, illustrates, plaintiffs still benefit if they can prove that they were directly injured.

It was not until the end of the 19th century that academics and lawyers began to speak of torts as a distinct branch of law. Initially, the search for a theoretical basis for tort law centred on the issue of whether there was a general principle of tort liability. J. Salmond argued that tort law was merely a patchwork of distinct causes of action, each protecting different interests and based on separate principles of liability. On that view, the law of torts essentially was a finite set of independent rules, and the courts were not free to recognize new heads of liability. In contrast, writers such as F. Pollock contended that the law of torts was based upon the single unifying principle that all harms were tortious unless they could be justified. On that view, courts were free to recognize new torts.

The debate over the existence of a general theory of tort liability was not limited to academics. The courts, confronted with new claims in the growing area of negligence, also had to decide whether to expand tort liability and, if so, upon what principles. In *Donoghue v. Stevenson*, [1932] A.C. 562 at 580 (H.L.), Lord Atkin suggested that, at least in the tort of negligence, the courts were prepared to expand the scope of recovery and recognize a general theory of liability:

> At present I content myself with pointing out that in English law there must be, and is, some general conception of relations giving rise to a duty of care, of which the particular cases found in the books are but instances. The liability for negligence, whether you style it such or treat it as in other systems as a species of "culpa," is no doubt based upon a general public sentiment of moral wrongdoing for which the offender must pay.

The debate continues today. The increased role of government in all facets of life, the growth of social welfare and social services, the proliferation of liability insurance, and the rapid pace of technological change all continue to influence the development of tort law. Depending upon the legal, social, economic, and philosophical circumstances that prevail in a given time and place, the scope of liability may expand or contract. For instance, as explained in Chapters 9 and 10, the elements of the tort of negligence (the most important of modern torts) occasionally are reformulated or re-phrased, as courts in Canada, England, and Australia attempt to strike an appropriate balance between competing interests. As conditions change, so too does the plaintiff's burden of proof. If the judiciary fears that liability is stifling innovation or creating an insurance crisis, it may narrow the defendant's duty of care. If, in contrast, the courts are concerned that industries are improperly profiting at the expense of injured consumers, they may loosen the reins.

NOTES

1. Anglo-Saxon law was characterized by very strict ideas of causation. The issue of fault was largely ignored and an actor was held liable for even the most remote consequences of his or her actions. It was common, in fact, for offending animals and even inanimate objects which had been the instruments of harm to be destroyed merely because they were part of the causal chain. On the history of Anglo-Saxon law see Winfield, "The Myth of Absolute Liability" (1926) 42 L.Q.R. 37; Baker, *An*

Introduction to English Legal History, 3d ed. (1990) at 1-43; and Pollock & Maitland, *History of English Law Before the Time of Edward I*, 2d ed., vol. 1 (1898) at 1-63. See also Arnold, "Accident, Mistake, and Rules of Liability in the Fourteenth Century Law of Torts" (1979) 128 U. Pa. L. Rev. 361.

2. On the origins of the writ of trespass *vi et armis* see Ames, *Lectures On Legal History* (1886-87) at 41-60; Maitland, *Forms of Actions* (1904) at 48-50; Woodbine, "The Origin of the Action of Trespass" (1924) 33 Yale L.J. 799 & (1925) 34 Yale L.J. 343; and Milsom, *Historical Foundations of the Common Law*, 2d ed. (1981) at 283-313. See also Fifoot, *History and Sources of the Common Law* (1952) at 44-65.

3. For a history of the writ of trespass on the case see Landon, "The Action on the Case and the Statute of Westminster II" (1936) 52 L.Q.R. 68; Dix, "The Origins of the Action of Trespass on the Case" (1937) 46 Yale L.J. 1142; Kiralfy, *The Action on the Case* (1951); and Milsom, *supra*.

4. It is debatable whether fault first assumed significance in the 19th century or whether the absence of fault had long provided a valid defence that was simply not apparent from the writ system. See Malone, "Ruminations on the Role of Fault in the History of the Common Law of Torts" (1970) 31 La. L. Rev. 1.

5. Largely as a result of frequent usage, most of the actions in trespass and some of the actions in trespass on the case acquired specific names (*e.g.* battery, assault). As a category, these are known as the nominate, or named, actions. There are other torts, innominate actions, that have not been named.

6. With the enactment of the *Judicature Acts*, the plaintiff no longer had to fit the claim into an existing writ. However, these statutes did not address whether the courts could create new tort actions to deal with situations that had not been covered by the writs. In *Wilkinson v. Downton*, [1897] 2 Q.B. 57, discussed in Chapter 3, the court created a new innominate action for intentional, indirectly caused physical injury. This filled some of the gaps left by the established nominate torts. Although it is now generally accepted that courts may recognize new causes of action, plaintiffs have had considerable difficulty establishing new intentional tort claims. In contrast, the scope of liability in negligence has increased dramatically.

4. Trespass and Case: A Brief Review of the Case Law

SCOTT v. SHEPHERD
[1558-1774] All E.R. 296

[The defendant threw a lighted squib, or firecracker, into a crowded marketplace. The squib landed on a stall that was operated by Yates. In order to prevent injury to himself or Yates, or to Yates' goods, Willis picked up the squib and threw it. The squib then landed on a stall operated by Ryal. In order to save himself and his goods, Ryal picked it up and threw it toward another part of the market. The squib struck the plaintiff in the face, exploded, and put out one of his eyes. The plaintiff sued the defendant for trespass and assault.

At the trial before Nares, J., the jury found a verdict for the plaintiff with £100 damages, subject to the opinion of the court on a case. The question for the opinion of the court was whether this action was maintainable.]

NARES, J.:—I am of opinion that trespass would well lie in the present case. The natural and probable consequence of the act done by the defendant was injury to somebody, and, therefore, the act was illegal at common law. The throwing of squibs has by 9 Will. 3, c. 7 [*Fireworks Act, 1697*: repealed], been since made a nuisance. Being, therefore, unlawful, the defendant was liable to answer for the consequences, be the injury mediate or immediate. YEAR BOOK 21 Hen. 7, 28, is express that malus animus is not necessary to constitute a trespass. . . . The principle I go on is what is laid down in *Reynolds v. Clarke* [(1725), 93 E.R. 747], that if the act in the first instance be unlawful, trespass will lie. Wherever, therefore, an act is unlawful at first, trespass will lie for the consequences of it. So, in Y.B. 12 Hen. 4, fo. 3, pl. 4, trespass lay for stopping a sewer with earth so as to overflow the plaintiff's land. In Y.B. 26 Hen. 8, 8, for going on the plaintiff's land to take the boughs off which had fallen thereon in lopping. . . . I do not think it necessary, to maintain trespass, that the defendant should personally touch the plaintiff; if he does it by a mean it is sufficient. Qui facit per aliud facit per se. He is the person who, in the present case, gave the mischievous faculty to the squib. That mischievous faculty remained in it until the explosion. No new power of doing mischief was communicated to it by Willis or Ryal. It is like the case of a mad ox turned loose in a crowd. The person who turns him loose is answerable in trespass for whatever mischief he may do. The intermediate acts of Willis and Ryal will not purge the original tort in the defendant. But he who does the first wrong is answerable for all the consequential damages: so held in *R. v. Huggins* [(1730), 92 E.R. 518]; *Parkhurst v. Forster* [(1698), 87 E.R. 746]; *Rosewell v. Prior* [(1701), 90 E.R. 1175]. And it was declared by this court, in *Slater v. Baker* (1767), 2 Wils. K.B. 359, that they would not look with eagle's eyes to see whether the evidence applies exactly or not to the case; but if the plaintiff has obtained a verdict for such damages as he deserves, they will establish it if possible.

BLACKSTONE, J. (dissenting):—I am of opinion that an action of trespass does not lie for the plaintiff against the defendant on this Case. I take the settled distinction to be that, where the injury is immediate, an action of trespass will lie; where it is only consequential, it must be an action on the Case: *Reynolds v. Clarke* [*supra*]; *Haward v. Bankes* [(1760), 97 E.R. 740]; *Harker v. Birkbeck* [(1764), 97 E.R. 978]. The lawfulness or unlawfulness of the original act is not the criterion, although something of that sort is put into Lord Raymond's mouth in *Reynolds v. Clarke* [*supra*], where it can only mean that if the act then in question, of erecting a spout, had been in itself unlawful, trespass might have lain; but as it was a lawful act (on the defendant's own ground) and the injury to the plaintiff only consequential, it must be an action on the case. But this cannot be the general rule, for it is held by the court in the same case that if I throw a log of timber into the highway (which is an unlawful act) and another man tumbles over it and is hurt, an action on the case only lies, it being a consequential damage; but if in throwing it I hit another man, he may bring trespass because it is an immediate wrong. Trespass may sometimes lie for the consequences of a lawful act. If in lopping my own trees a bough accidentally falls on my neighbour's ground and I go thereon to fetch it, trespass lies. This is the case cited from Y.B. 6 Edw. 4, fo. 7, pl. 18. But then the entry is of itself an immediate wrong. And case will sometimes lie for the consequence of an unlawful act. If by false imprisonment I have a special damage, as if I forfeit my recognisance thereby, I shall have an action on the case: per Powell, J., in *Bourden v. Alloway* [(1708), 88 E.R. 975]. Yet here the original act was unlawful, and in the nature of trespass. So that lawful or unlawful is quite out of the case.

The solid distinction is between direct or immediate injuries on the one hand and mediate or consequential on the other, and trespass never lay for the latter. If this be so, the only question will be whether the injury which the plaintiff suffered was immediate, or consequential only; and I hold it to be the latter. The original act was, as against Yates, a trespass; not as against Ryal or the plaintiff. The tortious act was complete when the squib lay at rest on Yates's stall. He, or any bystander, had, I allow, a right to protect themselves by removing the squib, but should have taken care to do it in such a manner as not to endanger others. But the defendant, I think, is not answerable in an action of trespass and assault for the mischief done by the squib in the new motion impressed on it, and the new direction given it, by either Willis or Ryal, who both were free agents and acted on their own judgment. This distinguishes it from the cases put of turning loose a wild beast or a madman. They are only instruments in the hand of the first agent. Nor is it like diverting the course of an enraged ox, or of a stone thrown, or an arrow glancing against a tree; because there the original motion, the vis impressa, is continued, though diverted. Here the instrument of mischief was at rest until a new impetus and a new direction are given it, not once only, but by two successive rational agents. But it is said that the act is not complete, nor the squib at rest, until after it is spent or exploded. It certainly has a power of doing fresh mischief, and so has a stone that has been thrown against my windows and now lies still. Yet if any person gives that stone a new motion and does further mischief with it, trespass will not lie for that against the original thrower. No doubt but Yates may maintain trespass against the defendant. And, according to the doctrine contended for, so may Ryal and the plaintiff. Three actions for one single act! nay, it may be extended in infinitum. If a man tosses a football into the street and, after being kicked about by one hundred people, it at last breaks a tradesman's windows, shall he have trespass against the man who first produced it? Surely only against the man who gave it that mischievous direction. But it is said, if the plaintiff has no action against the defendant, against whom must be seek his remedy? I give no opinion whether case would lie against the defendant for the consequential damage; though, as at present advised, I think that on the circumstances, it would. But I think that, in strictness of law, trespass would lie against Ryal, the immediate actor in this unhappy business. Both he and Willis have exceeded the bounds of self-defence and not used sufficient circumspection in removing the danger from themselves. The throwing it across the market-house instead of brushing it down, or throwing it out of the open sides into the street (if it was not meant to continue the sport, as it is called), was at least an unnecessary and incautious act. Not even menaces from others are sufficient to justify a trespass against a third person, much less a fear of danger to either his goods or his person; nothing but inevitable necessity . . . .

It is said by Lord Raymond, and very justly, in *Reynolds v. Clarke* [*supra*]: "We must keep up the boundaries of actions, otherwise we shall introduce the utmost confusion." As I, therefore, think no immediate injury passed from the defendant to the plaintiff (and without such immediate injury no action of trespass can be maintained), I am of opinion that in this action judgment ought to be for the defendant.

GOULD, J.:—I am of the same opinion with Nares, J., that this action is well maintainable. The whole difficulty lies in the form of the action and not in the substance of the remedy. The line is very nice between case and trespass on these occasions. I am persuaded that there are many instances wherein both or either will lie. I agree with Nares, J., that, wherever a man does an unlawful act, he is answerable for all the consequences; and trespass will lie against him, if the consequence be in nature of trespass. But, exclusive of this, I think that the defendant may be considered in the same view as if he himself had personally thrown the squib in the plaintiff's face. The terror impressed on Willis and Ryal excited self-defence and deprived them of the power of recollection. What they did was, therefore, the inevitable consequence of the defendant's unlawful act. Had the squib been thrown into a coach full of company, the person throwing it out again would not have been answerable for the consequences. What Willis and Ryal did was by necessity, and the defendant imposed that necessity on them.

DE GREY, C.J.:—This case is one of those wherein the line drawn by the law between actions on the case and actions of trespass is very nice and delicate. Trespass is an injury accompanied with force, for which an action of trespass vi et armis lies against the person from whom it is received. The question here is whether the injury received by the plaintiff arises from the force of the original act of the defendant, or from a new force by a third person. I agree with Blackstone, J., as to the principles he has laid down but not in his application of those principles to the present case. The real question certainly does not turn on the lawfulness or unlawfulness of the original act; for actions of trespass will lie for legal acts when they become trespasses by accident, as in the cases cited of cutting thorns, lopping of a tree, shooting at a mark, defending oneself by a stick which strikes another behind, etc. They may also not lie for the consequences even of illegal acts, as that of casting a log in the highway, etc. But the true question is whether the injury is the direct and immediate act of the defendant; and I am of opinion that in this case it is.

. . .

I look on all that was done subsequent to the original throwing as a continuation of the first force and first act which will continue until the squib was spent by bursting. I think that any innocent person removing the danger from himself to another is justifiable; the blame lights on the first thrower. The new direction and new force flow out of the first force, and are not a new trespass. The writ in the REGISTER, 95 a, for trespass in maliciously cutting down a head of water which thereupon flowed down to and overwhelmed another's pond shows that the immediate act need not be instantaneous, but that a chain of effects connected together will be sufficient. It has been urged that the intervention of a free agent will make a difference; but I do not consider Willis and Ryal as free agents in the present case, but acting under a compulsive necessity for their own safety and self-preservation. On these reasons I concur with Gould and Nares, JJ., that the present action is maintainable.

Judgment for plaintiff.

NOTES AND QUESTIONS

1. In reference to Blackstone J. and his judgment in *Scott*, Lord Denning stated in *What's Next in the Law* (1982) at 18: "like many learned men, he was not a great

judge. He was too technical. He was one of four judges in an important case of those days called *Scott v. Shepherd.* . . . He had a technical point about the difference in ancient learning between an action of trespass and an action on the case." Do you agree with Lord Denning that Blackstone J. was simply arguing a technical point?

2. In *Scott,* did the court require that intent or negligence be established? If not, on what issue was liability based?

3. Could the court have concluded that the action should have been framed in trespass on the case and nonsuited the plaintiff? As we have already seen, the plaintiff had to predict in advance whether the action properly lay in trespass *vi et armis* or trespass on the case. As *Scott* illustrates, it was not always possible to make such predictions with any assurance.

LEAME v. BRAY
(1803), 102 E.R. 724 (K.B.)

[The plaintiff sued the defendant in trespass. It was alleged that the defendant drove his horse-drawn carriage "with force and arms" into the plaintiff's carriage, that the plaintiff's horses panicked, and that the plaintiff fractured his collarbone when he jumped from his carriage in order to save his own life.]

It appeared in evidence at the trial before Lord Ellenborough C.J. at the last sittings at Westminster, that the accident described in the declaration happened in a dark night, owing to the defendant driving his carriage on the wrong side of the road, and the parties not being able to see each other; and that if the defendant had kept his right side there was ample room for the carriages to have passed without injury. But it did not appear that blame was imputable to the defendant in any other respect as to the manner of his driving. It was therefore objected for the defendant, that the injury having happened from negligence, and not wilfully, the proper remedy was by an action on the case and not of trespass *vi et armis*; and the plaintiff was thereupon nonsuited.

. . .

LORD ELLENBOROUGH C.J.:—The true criterion seems to be whether the plaintiff received an injury by force from the defendant. If the injurious act be the immediate result of the force originally applied by the defendant, and the plaintiff be injured by it, it is the subject of an action of trespass vi et armis by all the cases both ancient and modern. It is immaterial whether the injury be wilful or not.

. . . [H]ere the defendant himself was present, and used the ordinary means of impelling the horse forward, and from that the injury happened. And therefore there being an immediate injury from an immediate act of force by the defendant, the proper remedy is trespass; and wilfulness is not necessary to constitute trespass.

[Grose, Lawrence and LeBlanc JJ. concurred.]

WILLIAMS v. HOLLAND
(1833), 131 E.R. 848 (C.P.)

[The plaintiff owned a carriage that was carrying his son, who was also his servant. The defendant owned and operated another carriage. It was alleged that the defendant "so carelessly, unskilfully, and improperly drove, governed, and directed" his carriage that it collided with the plaintiff's. It was further alleged that, as a result of the defendant's "carelessness, negligence, unskilfulness, and improper conduct," the plaintiff's carriage was "crushed, broke to pieces, and damaged," and the plaintiff's son was injured, with the result that the plaintiff was deprived of his services and "put to expense for doctor's bills."]

. . .

TINDAL C.J.:—. . .The declaration, in this case, states the ground of action to be an injury occasioned by the carelessness and negligence of the Defendant in driving his own gig; and that such carelessness and negligence is, strictly and properly in itself, the subject of an action on the case, would appear, if any authority were wanting, from Com. Dig. tit. Action upon the Case for Negligence; and the jury have found in the very terms of the declaration, that the jury was so occasioned. Under such a form of action, therefore, and with such a finding by the jury, the present objection ought not to prevail, unless some positive and inflexible rule of law, or some authority too strong to be overcome, is brought forward in its support. If such are to be found, they must, undoubtedly, be adhered to; for settled forms of action, adapted to different grievances, contribute much to the certain administration of justice.

But upon examining the cases cited in argument, both in support of, and in answer to, the objection, we cannot find one in which it is distinctly held, that the present form of action is not maintainable under the circumstances of this case.

. . .

Where the injury is occasioned by the carelessness and negligence of the Defendant, the Plaintiff is at liberty to bring an action on the case, notwithstanding the act is immediate, so long as it is not a wilful act; and, upon the authority of that case, we think the present form of action maintainable to recover damages for the injury.

NOTES AND QUESTIONS

1. Why was the plaintiff nonsuited at trial in *Leame*? Why did Lord Ellenborough disagree? What is the *ratio* of the case and what distinction is made between trespass and case?

2. The great significance of *Williams* was that it gave a plaintiff a choice between trespass and case when there was a direct, negligent act. For a detailed consideration of this case see Prichard, "Trespass, Case and the Rule in *Williams v. Holland*" [1964] C.L.J. 234.

3. The immediate result of *Williams* was a marked increase in the number of actions brought in case. Nevertheless, it was still necessary for the plaintiff to frame the action in either trespass or case. It was not until the *Common Law Procedure Act*, 1852 (15 & 16 Vict.), c. 76, that a plaintiff was able to join the two actions. See generally Winfield, "Trespass and Negligence" (1933) 49 L.Q.R. 359.

HOLMES v. MATHER
(1875), L.R. 10 Exch. 261

[The defendant and his servant were driving a horse cart on the highway when the horses became unmanageable. The servant attempted to guide the runaway horses, but with limited success. While turning a corner, the servant led the horses into the plaintiff's path, knocking him down and injuring him. The plaintiff sued in negligence and trespass. The jury found that there was no negligence.]

BRAMWELL B.:—. . .The driver is absolutely free from all blame in the matter; not only does he not do anything wrong, but he endeavours to do what is the best to be done under the circumstances. The misfortune happens through the horses being so startled by the barking of a dog that they run away with the groom and the defendant, who is sitting beside him. Now, if the plaintiff under such circumstances can bring an action, I really cannot see why she could not bring an action because a splash of mud, in the ordinary course of driving, was thrown upon her dress or got into her eye and so injured it. It seems manifest that, under such circumstances, she could not maintain an action. For the convenience of mankind in carrying on the affairs of life, people as they go along roads must expect, or put up with, such mischief as reasonable care on the part of others cannot avoid. I think the present action not to be maintainable.

That is the general view of the case. Now I will put it a little more specifically, and address myself to the argument of Mr. Herschell. Here, he says, if the driver had done nothing, there is no reason to suppose this mischief would have happened to the woman, but he did give the horses a pull, or inclination, in the direction of the plaintiff — he drove them there. It is true that he endeavoured to drive them further away from the place by getting them to turn to the right, but he did not succeed in doing that. The argument, therefore, is, if he had not given that impulse or direction to them, they would not have come where the plaintiff was. Now, it seems to me that argument is not tenable, and I think one can deal with it in this way. Here, as in almost all cases, you must look at the immediate act that did the mischief, at what the driver was doing before the mischief happened, and not to what he was doing next before what he was then doing. If you looked to the last act but one, you might as well argue that if the driver had not started on that morning, or had not turned down that particular street, this mischief would not have happened.

I think the proper answer is, You cannot complain of me unless I was immediately doing the act which did the mischief to you. Now the driver was not doing that. What I take to be the case is this: he did not guide the horses upon the plaintiff; he guided them away from her, in another direction; but they ran away with him, upon her, in spite of his effort to take them away from where she was. It is not the case where a person has to make a choice of two evils, and singles the plaintiff out, and drives to the spot where she is standing. That is not the case at all. The driver was endeavouring to guide them indeed, but he was taken there in spite of himself. I think the observation made by my Brother Pollock during the argument is irresistible, that if Mr. Herschell's contention is right, it would come to this: if I am being run away with, and I sit quiet and let the horses run wherever they think fit, clearly I am not liable, because it is they, and not I, who guide them; but if I unfortunately do my best to avoid injury to myself and other persons, then it may be said that it is my act of guiding them that brings them to the place where the accident happens. Surely it is impossible.

As to the cases cited, most of them are really decisions on the form of action, whether case or trespass. The result of them is this, and it is intelligible enough: if the act that does an injury is an act of direct force vi et armis, trespass is the proper remedy (if there is any remedy) where the act is wrongful, either as being wilful or as being the result of negligence. Where the act is not wrongful for either of these reasons, no action is maintainable, though trespass would be the proper form of action if it were wrongful. That is the effect of the decisions.

[Cleasby and Pollock BB. concurred.]

NOTES AND QUESTIONS

1. How does Bramwell B. distinguish this case from one in which the defendant has to choose between two evils? Is the distinction meaningful?

2. What is the *ratio*? What is the impact of *Holmes* on the elements of a trespass action?

3. In *Stanley v. Powell*, [1891] 1 Q.B. 86, the principle in *Holmes* was reaffirmed and extended to accidents other than those that occurred on the highway.

COOK v. LEWIS
[1952] 1 D.L.R. 1 (S.C.C.)

CARTWRIGHT J.:—. . . On the 11th of September, 1948, the plaintiff was hunting with his brother John Lewis and one Dennis Fitzgerald in the vicinity of Quinsam Lake on Vancouver Island. It was the opening day of the hunting season for blue grouse and deer and it was said that the country in which they were hunting was full of hunters. The defendants, accompanied by John Wagstaff, then sixteen years of age, were hunting grouse together. They were using a dog which belonged to Akenhead. They had agreed to divide their bag evenly.

It is said that Cook, Akenhead and Wagstaff were proceeding approximately in line, Cook being on the left, Akenhead in the centre and Wagstaff to the right. The dog, which was some little distance ahead of them, came to a point and at about that moment Fitzgerald, who had come into view on Cook's left, called out a warning and pointed towards a clump of trees which was ahead of Cook and Akenhead and in which at that moment the plaintiff was. Cook heard Fitzgerald's call but did not hear what he said. He thought that Fitzgerald was pointing at the dog and was calling attention to the fact that the dog was on point. Akenhead states that he did not hear Fitzgerald's call. Momentarily after this, a covey of some four or five grouse flew up a short distance in front of the dog. Akenhead says that he fired at the bird which was farthest to the right, leaving the other birds to Cook. Cook says that he fired at a bird straight ahead of him. They appear to have fired almost simultaneously. Immediately afterwards there was a scream from the clump of trees, mentioned above, and the plaintiff appeared. He had received several shot in his face, one of which caused the loss of an eye.

. . .

It was the theory of the plaintiff that either Cook or Akenhead or both of them had shot him and that each was liable even if only one of them had fired the shot which struck him. The theory of the defendant Cook was that he had fired only one shot and had fired in such a direction that it was quite impossible that any shot from his gun could have struck the plaintiff. He also stated that there had been a third shot fired almost simultaneously with those fired by himself and Akenhead and suggested that an unidentified third person had fired the shot which injured the plaintiff. His counsel disclaimed before the jury any suggestion that Akenhead had shot the plaintiff.

Akenhead's position at the trial was that he had fired to the right, that he could not have shot the plaintiff and that if it was either of them it was Cook and not he who had done so.

. . .

With the greatest respect, I think that the learned trial judge did not charge the jury correctly in regard to the onus of proof of negligence. While it is true that the plaintiff expressly pleaded negligence on the part of the defendants he also pleaded that he was shot by them and in my opinion the action under the old form of pleading would properly have been one of trespass and not of case. In my view, the cases collected and discussed by Denman J. in *Stanley v. Powell*, [[1891] 1 Q.B. 86] established the rule (which is subject to an exception in the case of highway accidents with which we are not concerned in the case at bar) that where a plaintiff is injured by force applied directly to him by the defendant his case is made by proving this fact and the onus falls upon the defendant to prove "that such trespass was utterly without his fault." In my opinion *Stanley v. Powell* rightly decides that the defendant in such an action is entitled to judgment if he satisfies the onus of establishing the absence of both intention and negligence on his part.

. . .

[The judgment of Estey, Cartwright and Fauteux JJ. was delivered by Cartwright J. Rand J. gave a separate concurring judgment, and Locke J. dissented on a different issue.]

NOTES AND QUESTIONS

1. According to *Cook*, why is this an action in trespass and not case? What are the advantages of suing in trespass? What is the practical significance of this advantage in cases such as *Cook*? Does the distinction between directly and indirectly-caused harms warrant maintaining these advantages?

2. In *Letang v. Cooper*, [1965] 1 Q.B. 232 (C.A.), the court rejected the approach in *Cook*. Rather, it required a plaintiff to bring the action in negligence even if he or she had been directly injured, unless the defendant had acted intentionally. For a discussion of the Australian position see *McHale v. Watson* (1964), 111 C.L.R. 384 (H.C.A.); *Chin v. Venning* (1975), 49 A.L.J.R. 378 (H.C.); and *Hackshaw v. Shaw* (1985), 59 A.L.J.R. 156 (H.C.).

3. Even in Canada, the rule in *Cook* has been widely criticized. See Wright, "Res Ipsa Loquitur" in Linden, ed., *Studies in Canadian Tort Law* (1968) 41 at 42-45; and Sharp, "Negligent Trespass in Canada: A Persistent Source of Embarrassment" (1978) 1 Adv. Q. 311. But see Sullivan, "Trespass to the Person in Canada: A Defence of the Traditional Approach" (1987) 19 Ottawa L. Rev. 533. See also Fridman, "Trespass or Negligence?" (1971) 9 Alta. L. Rev. 250; and Trindade, "The Burden of Proof in Actions for Negligent Trespass in Canada" (1971) 49 Can. Bar Rev. 612.

5. The Bases for Imposing Liability in Tort

As we have seen, early tort law was dominated by the procedural formalities of the writ system and its focus on directly and indirectly caused injury. It was only in the last half of the 19th century that fault in the form of intent or negligence was established as a prerequisite to liability in most areas of tort law. With the *Judicature Acts* and the abolition of the writ system, fault in various forms emerged as a central organizing principle of tort law. Generally, modern tort law is divided into four categories of actions: (1) intentional torts, (2) negligence, (3) strict liability, and (4) a residual group of actions, such as defamation, which are based on unique principles of liability.

Those categories, along with other considerations, inform the basic structure of this book. The current section provides an introduction to the four categories by stepping back and discussing the full range of liability rules — including one that falls outside of tort law. That discussion begins with a diagram that identifies the possibilities.

The Bases of Tort Liability

Absolute Liability ——— Strict Liability ——— Negligence ——— Intentional Torts

(a) ABSOLUTE LIABILITY

Under a rule of absolute liability, the defendant is held liable for simply engaging in proscribed behaviour and thereby causing the plaintiff to suffer a loss. The plaintiff is not required to prove that the defendant's conduct was intentional or negligent. It is enough that the prohibited act caused the loss. The defendant, moreover, is not entitled to plead exculpatory defences.

Canadian law does not contain any torts of absolute liability, but that concept does provide a useful model against which others can be compared.

(b) STRICT LIABILITY

"Strict liability" is an ambiguous phrase. As previously explained, it sometimes refers to a cause of action that does not require proof that the defendant breached an obligation. Liability in unjust enrichment is strict in that sense. As long as there was no juristic reason for the benefit that the defendant received from the plaintiff, liability for restitution will arise even if the defendant was entirely innocent in the transfer.

In contrast, "strict liability" in the tort context means that while an obligation *was* breached, the defendant did not do so intentionally or carelessly. In that sense, strict liability is similar to the concept of absolute liability. The two concepts differ, however, in that a strict liability regime allows the defendant to plead some defences. For instance, as discussed in Chapter 25, the tort of *Rylands v. Fletcher* (1868), [1861-73] All E.R. Rep. 1 (H.L.) imposes strict liability if, as a result of the defendant's non-natural use of land, something escapes from that property and injures the plaintiff. The plaintiff's right to relief does not depend upon proof that the defendant intentionally or negligently did wrong. Damages nevertheless will be denied if, for instance, (1) the escape was caused by either a third party or an act of God against which the defendant could not have guarded, or (2) if the plaintiff's loss was the inevitable result of the defendant's performance of a statutorily authorized activity.

Strict liability is more prevalent in the United States than in Canada. In many American jurisdictions, for instance, manufacturers are held strictly liable for injuries caused by defective products. The plaintiff must prove that the product in question was somehow defective when it left the manufacturer, but does not have to prove that that defect resulted from the manufacturer's intentional or negligent breach. In contrast, the Canadian plaintiff must show either intentional or negligent wrongdoing on the part of the manufacturer. In Canada, strict liability tends to be confined to discrete circumstances, such as *Rylands v. Fletcher* and harm inflicted by dangerous animals.

The doctrine of *vicarious liability* is said to constitute an important form of strict liability. That doctrine allows a court to hold one person responsible for a tort committed by another. That most often occurs under the rule of *respondeat superior*. An employer may be legally responsible for torts committed by an employee. In that event, the plaintiff is entitled to recover damages from either the employee or the employer. The employer's liability is said to be strict because it does not require proof that the employer carelessly or intentionally breached an obligation.

(c) NEGLIGENCE

Negligence consists of a failure to take reasonable care to prevent foreseeable harm to another person. The difference between negligence and strict liability is well illustrated in the context of products liability. In negligence, the plaintiff has to prove that the defendant failed to take reasonable care to prevent the defect that caused the harm. In contrast, under a strict liability regime, the plaintiff merely has to prove that the defect caused the harm. It should be noted that, in some situations of negligence, the burden of proof may be shifted onto the defendant, thereby providing the plaintiff with some of the benefits of strict liability. This possibility is discussed in Chapter 20.

(d) INTENTION

Liability for intentionally-inflicted harm is, like negligence, based on fault. In most cases, the plaintiff must prove actual subjective intent on the part of the defendant. There are several legal principles that help the plaintiff to do so, however. For example, under the doctrine of imputed intent (discussed in Chapter 3), the law ascribes the requisite intention to the defendant if the plaintiff's loss was certain or substantially certain to follow from the defendant's act. Moreover, in Canada, if the plaintiff proves that an injury was caused directly, the burden of proof shifts to the defendant to disprove intent and negligence. Although this rule arises in some negligence cases, it is more relevant in intentional torts.

(e) NO LIABILITY

Finally, it is important to appreciate that some types of harm simply are not recognized under any rule of tort liability, even if the person who caused the harm did so intentionally or carelessly. Despite the existence of a causal connection between the defendant's conduct and the plaintiff's injury, the type of conduct or the type of harm may lie outside the scope of tort law. *Allen v. Flood*, [1898] A.C. 1 (H.L.) stands for the proposition that, as long as it otherwise acts lawfully, a business will not be liable for financially ruining a competitor, even if it does so intentionally or maliciously. The court in that instance was anxious to encourage competition in the marketplace. More recently, the Supreme Court of Canada held that while a child who is born with injuries sustained *in utero* generally is entitled to hold the perpetrator liable in negligence, no action lies if the injury was caused by the *mother's* careless actions during pregnancy. The court was unwilling to impose any duty of care that might interfere with a pregnant woman's freedom of action: *Dobson (Litigation Guardian of) v. Dobson*, [1999] 2 S.C.R. 753.

6. The Functions of Tort Law

Tort law did not develop from a co-ordinated attempt to achieve specific social goals. The common law process is highly decentralized and modern tort law is a patchwork of judicial decisions and statutory provisions. As the preceding section illustrates, much of tort law has been shaped by procedural concerns rather than policy. Granted, modern legislators and judges do occasionally tailor the law to achieve particular social goals on a case-by-case basis. It nevertheless remains impossible to reduce tort law as a whole to any single principle.

Every judicial decision, legal principle, or set of legal rules favours certain interests over others. The law is not objective or value free. It is a social institution that serves social functions. It therefore is important to raise certain questions with respect to every relevant social concern. Which principles and rules does tort law currently endorse? Which principles and rules *should* it endorse? What mischief does tort law seek to prevent or what benefit does it seek to promote? Can those goals be better served by other legal or non-legal means? To ask such questions is to take *a functional approach* to tort law. It obviously is impossible in this book to resolve all of the debates raised by such an approach. At this point, it is sufficient to focus attention on the social concerns that underlie tort law and to provide the tools required for a functional approach to tort law.

Some of the uncertainty regarding the functions of tort law stems from a failure to delineate various potential perspectives. If one focuses on the litigants' objectives, the goals of tort law will be narrowly defined in terms of the expectations of those parties who have a financial stake in the exercise. And indeed, the parties' motivations certainly are important insofar as they determine the issues that are brought to court. Nevertheless, such a narrow focus overlooks some of the broader social functions of tort law.

Unfortunately, when we adopt a broader focus, the debate regarding tort law's functions becomes largely speculative. There is little empirical evidence on the impact of tort law. That is hardly surprising, given the serious methodological difficulties involved in distinguishing the effects of tort law from the effects of other legal and social forces. Furthermore, tort law is inherently limited in its ability to modify behaviour. Although the prospect of litigation may influence some people, tort law primarily operates through awards of damages. Liability is apt to have little effect on defendants who are impecunious, insured, or otherwise able to avoid the financial burden of being held responsible. Even more clearly, many potential tort claims are never litigated. A potential claimant may be unable to identify and locate the tortfeasor. Alternatively, a potential claimant may be unaware of the relevant laws, may not be able to afford to hire a lawyer, or may refrain from suing for non-legal reasons (*e.g.* a desire to maintain harmonious relations with a valued customer).

The ability of tort law to affect behaviour is also limited by the fact that tort is simply one of many legal and non-legal mechanisms of social control. The role that tort law plays in a particular instance will reflect a broad range of factors, including the crime rate, the effectiveness of the criminal justice system, the existence and enforcement of health and safety standards, the scope of the social welfare system, and the availability of state-funded universal health care. Debates regarding the functions of tort law often mask unstated assumptions about these other issues.

The remainder of this section summarizes some of the most commonly cited functions of tort law. You should read this material critically. It is important to assess the empirical basis upon which the various propositions are stated, and to consider the relevance of each purported function to modern Canadian society.

(a) COMPENSATION

From the plaintiff's point of view, compensation, in the sense of reparation for loss, is the most important function of tort law. Society also has a legitimate interest in minimizing the disruptions accompanying an injury by ensuring that the aggrieved party receives compensation. Unfortunately, the current system of tort law has many failings in that respect. First, it provides compensation to a relatively small number of accident victims and then only in very limited circumstances. Second, the accident victim must make a substantial financial investment to initiate the process (*e.g.* by hiring a lawyer). Third, the plaintiff must prove fault, not need, and will recover only if "fortunate" enough to have been injured by a tortfeasor with assets or insurance. Finally, it is generally accepted and clearly documented that tort law is an extremely inefficient mechanism for providing compensation. These failings are further discussed in Chapter 28.

(b) APPEASEMENT AND VINDICATION

A successful tort action may vindicate the plaintiff's position and condemn the defendant's conduct. In the context of incestuous sexual assault, for instance, claimants often are motivated far more by the hope that the tortfeasor will be officially condemned than by the prospect of financial damages (especially against impecunious defendants). It is for such reasons that *nominal damages* are available in response to some torts. Even though the plaintiff suffered little or no loss as a result of the tort, the court may order the defendant to pay a small amount (such as $10) as symbolic recognition of the wrong. However, given the cost and inconvenience of litigation, as well as the possibility of an unfavourable award of *costs* against the claimant, few plaintiffs sue for nominal damages.

(c) PUNISHMENT

As previously explained, criminal and tort law share a common heritage. Although criminal law is most often associated with punishing wrongdoers, tort law has retained traces of its early punitive elements. For example, punitive damages are available to sanction high-handed, vicious, or otherwise outrageous conduct. As tort law has become increasingly dominated by negligence, however, the importance of punishment has declined. As well, most of the morally blameworthy conduct that warrants punishment in tort law also constitutes a federal or provincial offence. It is arguable that the issue of punishment in such circumstances should be left to the criminal justice system.

(d) DETERRENCE

Punishment is different than deterrence. Punishment looks backward at the wrongful act and attempts to mete out a sanction that reflects the wrong. Deterrence, in contrast, is concerned with discouraging the defendant (*specific deterrence*) and others (*general deterrence*) from repeating a wrong. Deterrence and punishment are, of course, closely related insofar as any punishment is capable of deterring. The penalty necessary to achieve optimum deterrence, however, may be quite different from that necessary to achieve just punishment.

In order to be an effective deterrent, tort law must clearly define the undesirable conduct and then provide sufficient inducements for discouraging it. Deterrence works best when the defendant is aware of both the required legal standard and the sanctions for its breach. Tort law therefore has a greater deterrent impact on premeditated conduct than on spontaneous careless behaviour. Even when the conduct is planned, however, the potential damage award must be sufficient to change the defendant's behaviour. The law will have a limited impact if a tortfeasor believes that it is cheaper to pay the various costs associated with liability (*e.g.* damages and adverse publicity) than to alter a course of conduct. If the criminal justice system is any indication, there is little reason for optimism about the deterrent impact of tort law.

(e) MARKET DETERRENCE

Some academics, particularly economists, view tort law as a system of *loss allocation. Market deterrence* is an important goal of allocating the costs of accidents. The basic idea is the costs of accidents ought to be incorporated into the price of the activities that generate them. A good example is the rule in most American states that holds manufacturers strictly liable for injuries caused by their defective products. Manufacturers increase their prices to cover their potential liability costs. As prices rise, fewer products are sold and fewer product-related injuries occur. To the extent that a product continues to be purchased at the higher price, economists would say that consumers have demonstrated that they believe that the benefits of the product exceed the cost of the accidents it generates. According to economists, this allocation of accident costs through the market enables society to experience the "optimum" number of accidents. Notice, however, that this theory assumes that damages accurately reflect losses, that all meritorious claims are successfully litigated, and that manufacturers and other well-financed defendants cannot avoid tort liability by securing favourable legislation or threatening to bankrupt potential claimants.

The term "loss allocation" has also been used to describe several other possibly inconsistent schemes. First, R. Posner, an American judge and scholar, argues that an actor should be held liable in negligence whenever the cost of harm exceeds what it would have cost to prevent it. The defendant's fault lies in squandering scarce social resources. Posner's loss allocation system therefore furthers the goal of *efficiency*. Second, the term "loss allocation" sometimes is used to describe a *loss spreading* function, whereby a loss is imposed on the party who is best able to distribute it over time and among a large number of people. Others speak of the *deep pocket* approach to loss distribution, whereby tort law is used to allocate losses to those parties who are best able to bear them. However, even if the courts had sufficient information and expertise to make the correct allocative decision, many argue that it is inappropriate to use tort law as a system to redistribute wealth.

(f) JUSTICE

In recent years, legal philosophers have begun to study tort law. Having found the traditional explanations unsatisfactory, they have focused on the theories of *justice* underlying tort law. Some tort doctrines can be explained in terms of *retributive justice*. Other tort principles apparently are designed to achieve *distributive justice* by ensuring that wealth is properly distributed within society. However, most legal philosophers view tort law in terms of *corrective justice*. Corrective justice accepts the existing distribution of wealth and is concerned with correcting improper deviations from that pattern by annulling "wrongful" gains and compensating "wrongful" losses. The classification of a gain or loss as "wrongful" may be made with reference to several different principles. Depending upon the particular principle, what constitutes a "wrong" may be defined in terms of the actor's conduct, the victim's loss, or a combination of these factors. Corrective justice is discussed further in Chapter 28.

NOTES AND QUESTIONS

1. On the aims of tort law, see generally Wright, "The Province and Function of the Law of Torts" in Linden, ed., *Studies in Canadian Tort Law* (1968) 1; Cane, *Atiyah's Accidents, Compensation and the Law*, 7th ed. (2006), ch. 17; Linden *et al.*, *Canadian Tort Law*, 11th ed. (2018), ch. 1; and England, "The System Builders: A Critical Appraisal of Modern Tort Theory" (1980) 10 J. Legal Stud. 27. See also Saks, "Do We Really Know Anything About the Behavior of the Tort Litigation System — And Why Not?" (1992) 140 U. Pa. L. Rev. 1147, which casts doubt on our ability to accurately analyze the tort system.

2. Although compensation often is said to be the primary purpose of tort law, the evidence indicates that other systems may achieve the same goal more efficiently. For instance, a study conducted in connection with Québec's no-fault automobile insurance scheme found that while the scheme allocates 88¢ of every dollar to compensation, traditional tort schemes spend 64¢ of every dollar on compensation and require the rest for administrative costs. The same report indicated that while the no-fault scheme on average provides compensation within 22 days of the receipt of a

claim, tort claimants regularly are required to wait two to ten years: SAAQ, *Québec's Automobile Insurance Plan* (2001) at 6-11.

3. Even assuming that compensation is an appropriate social goal, the relative effectiveness of tort law in achieving it is questionable. See generally Sugarman, "Doing Away with Tort Law" (1985) 73 Cal. L. Rev. 558; Arlen, "Compensation Systems and Efficient Deterrence" (1993) 52 Md .L. Rev. 1093; Schwarz, "Reality in the Economic Analysis of Tort Law: Does Tort Law Really Deter?" (1994) 42 U.C.L.A.L. Rev. 377; Cane, *The Anatomy of Tort Law* (1997) at 217-225; and Osborne, *Report of Inquiry into Motor Vehicle Accident Compensation in Ontario* (1988).

4. The importance of appeasement in Anglo-Saxon law is illustrated in Malone, "Ruminations on the Role of Fault in the History of the Common Law of Torts" (1970) 31 La. L. Rev. 1 at 2:

> This same demand for appeasement of the sense of honor was manifested in non-fatal injuries. Here the amount of the tariff to be paid was determined to a large extent by the public shame that attended the wound. According to the laws of Ethelbert: "If the bruise be black in a part not covered by the clothes, let bot be made with thirty scaetts. If it be covered by the clothes, let bot be made for each with twenty scaetts." Pound refers to a provision of Howell the Good, King of the Welsh, to the effect that a scar on the face is worth six score pence, whereas the permanent loss of both joints of the thumb (an injury that would virtually disable the hand) brought only seventy-six pence and a half-penny.

5. Linden argued that tort law can act as an *ombudsman*. A private law proceeding may focus public attention on systemic wrongdoing that might otherwise not be detected or prosecuted by the state. The adverse publicity generated by such proceedings may provide a powerful deterrent and motivate the government to take corrective action. Can you suggest a situation in which tort law has served or might serve this function? See Linden, "Reconsidering Tort Law as Ombudsman" in Steel and Rogers-Magnet, eds., *Issues in Tort Law* (1983) 1.

6. Assume that just punishment for a wrong is a fine of $100 and that the perceived conviction rate is 1 in 100. How large must the penalty be in order to actually deter the wrong? Would the imposition of that penalty be unjust? Explain your answer.

7. What do economists mean by the "optimum" number of accidents? Why is the optimum number of accidents not zero? See England, "Law and Economics in American Tort Cases: A Critical Assessment of the Theory's Impact on Courts" (1991) 41 U.T.L.J. 359.

8. For a discussion of the deterrent function of tort law, see Calabresi, *The Cost of Accidents* (1970); Dewees & Trebilcock, "The Efficacy of the Tort System and Its Alternatives: A Review of Empirical Evidence" (1992) 30 Osgoode Hall L.J. 57; Posner, "A Theory of Negligence" (1972) 1 J. Legal Stud. 29; Brown, "Deterrence in Tort and No-Fault: The New Zealand Experience" (1985) 73 Cal. L. Rev. 976; Viscusi, "Toward a Diminished Role for Tort Liability: Social Insurance, Government Regulation, and Contemporary Risks to Health and Safety" (1989) 6 Yale J. on Reg.

65; and Komesar, "Injuries and Institutions: Tort Reform, Tort Theory, and Beyond" (1990) 65 N.Y.U.L. Rev. 23.

9. For a discussion of the loss allocation function of tort law, see Coase, "The Problem of Social Costs" (1960) 3 J.L. & Econ. 1; Calabresi; "Some Thoughts on Risk Distribution and the Law of Torts" (1961) 70 Yale L.J. 449; and Posner, *supra*.

10. For a philosophical analysis of the functions of tort law, see Fletcher, "Fairness and Utility in Tort Theory" (1972) 85 Harv. L.J. 537; Englard, *The Philosophy of Tort Law* (1993); Epstein, "A Theory of Strict Liability" (1973) 2 J. Legal Stud. 151; Steiner, "Economics, Morality and the Law of Torts" (1976) 26 U.T.L.J. 227; and Coleman, *Risks and Wrongs* (1992).

7. The Rights Theory of Tort Law

The preceding section canvassed the various functions served by tort law. On that view, tort law is instrumental. It exists for the purpose of *repairing* losses, *punishing* wrongful acts, *deterring* future misconduct, promoting *economic efficiency*, and so on. Broadly speaking, those models present tort law as either a *compensatory* mechanism that provides relief from losses, perhaps as part of a loss-spreading scheme, or a *regulatory* regime that is aimed at shaping social behaviour. Recent years, however, have seen the rise of *rights theory*. Instead of being employed as a means to an end, tort law is viewed in terms of rights. The parties are joined in a private relationship of correlative rights and obligations. A tort consists of the defendant's failure to honour an obligation and the concomitant breach of the plaintiff's right. Liability is imposed not in the aim of fulfilling some extraneous goal (such as alleviating the plaintiff's financial burden or penalizing the defendant's transgression) but rather as vindication of the parties' moral relationship. Simply stated, tort law is concerned with the recognition, enforcement, and redress of individual rights.

This description of rights theory is potentially misleading insofar as it may suggest that the development is unique to tort law. In fact, rights-based analysis cuts across the whole of private law: contract, property, unjust enrichment, trusts, and so on. Tort law nevertheless dominates, in part because the subject traditionally was thought to best illustrate instrumental analysis and in part because the violation and vindication of rights arguably is most dramatic within the tort context.

A simple example helps to illustrate the idea. The plaintiff owns a horse and, as a result, enjoys the right to determine the use of the animal. The defendant is subject to a corresponding obligation. In breach of that obligation, the defendant rides the horse to work each day that the plaintiff is away on vacation. The plaintiff returns home, discovers the facts, and sues for the tort of conversion. The defendant resists the claim by saying, "You have no grounds for complaint. You have suffered no loss. Indeed, the horse is better as a result of the exercise." The courts have imposed liability in such circumstances (*The Mediana*, [1900] A.C. 113 (H.L.)), but such decisions are controversial. If, as many commentators traditionally believed, tort law serves a compensatory function, how can the court award anything more than nominal damages? For the rights theorist, however, substantial damages are entirely appropriate. The defendant breached an obligation owed to the plaintiff. Regardless of any financial loss, damages are available for the purpose of vindicating the plaintiff's primary right. Monetary relief acts as a substitute for that right. The quantum of recovery reflects the value of the right itself — not the external consequences of the event (the horse, after all, was none the worse for wear).

While the literature contains many variations on the same theme, rights theory generally is marked by certain characteristics. One defining feature already has been explained. Rights theory is *non-instrumentalist*. It maintains that private law does not exist to promote external goals, such as compensation or deterrence. Other features are equally prominent. The theory is *structuralist*. Rights are not merely incidents or contingent elements of a larger enterprise. They instead underlie and inform the entire subject. Tort law cannot be understood apart from rights. Rights theory is *formalist*. Twentieth century legal theory was dominated by the realist belief that judicial decision-making invariably is influenced by "extra-legal" considerations. In one famous phrase, "Justice is what the judge ate for breakfast." Disputes turn less on precedent and principles — more on personality and policy. Rights theorists, in contrast, maintain that rules must govern. The outcome of any particular case is determined by the existence and enforcement of individual rights. Finally, rights theory is *individualist*. Running alongside realism in 20th century legal theory were various forms of *communalistic* analysis. Private law was conceived as part of a broader project aimed at reforming or improving society as a whole. Depending upon one's personal perspective, tort law ought to help to eliminate sexual inequality, or secure a more equitable distribution of resources, or move assets to their highest use, or protect the environment. Litigation between private parties provided the occasion for changing the world. Rights theory, however, focusses squarely on the plaintiff and the defendant. And while the cumulative effect of liability certainly extends farther, the rules reflect the narrow relationship between the parties.

Although rights theorists share a set of fundamental beliefs, there are several species in the genus. Three strands of thought predominate. *Analytical* rights theorists seek to understand the nature of rights and explain the ensuing implications. Within tort law, for instance, a distinction may be drawn between legal rights and strictly moral rights, and between a right that another person refrain from harmful acts (such as a right not to be intentionally imperiled) and a right to receive some benefit (as a duty to rescue would entail). *Interpretive* rights theorists aim to provide a coherent account of the existing law. For example, by peeling away obfuscating labels, by disproving competing models, and by viewing past decisions from the preferred perspective, tort scholars may demonstrate that rights provide the best explanation for the law of nuisance or the liability that attaches to lawful means conspiracy. Finally, *normative* rights theorists take the exercise a step farther by arguing that the law *ought to* develop by reference to rights and obligations. For example, it is arguable that the courts have erred in allowing a would-be beneficiary to recover damages from a solicitor if the lawyer's careless failure to properly advise the testator caused the testamentary gift to fail: *White v. Jones*, [1995] 2 A.C. 207 (H.L.). In such circumstances, the argument runs, rights are properly owed by the solicitor to the testator alone, so that the ostensible beneficiary has no basis for an action.

Accepting that disputes in tort law ought to be resolved by reference to rights, it remains necessary to explain the nature and origins of such rights. There is no easy answer. Given the theory's fundamental premise, it is clear that rights cannot exist simply as a matter of policy. It is not enough for a court to say that the community would be improved through the recognition of a right and a correlative obligation. More positively, rights theorists generally believe that legal rights must reflect interpersonal moral rights. R. Stevens, for example, maintains that legal rights consist of those moral rights that have been selected by the courts for enforcement: Stevens, *Torts and Rights* (2007) at 330. E. Weinrib, in contrast, derives legal rights and obligations from the philosophy of Immanuel Kant: Weinrib, *The Idea of Private Law* (1995) at 19.

NOTES AND QUESTIONS

1. Rights theory literature is large and growing. For introductions to the area, see Stevens, *Torts and Rights* (2007); Nolan & Robertson, "Rights and Private Law" in Nolan & Robertson, eds., *Rights and Private Law* (2010), ch. 1; and McBride, "Rights and the Basis of Tort Law" in Nolan & Robertson, *supra*, ch. 12. That same collection also contains articles dealing with rights-based analysis of specific topics in tort and other areas of private law. See also Beever, *A Theory of Tort Liability* (2016).

Not everyone agrees, of course. A number of commentators have questioned, critiqued, and occasionally rejected the rights theory: Zipursky, "Coming Down to Earth: Why Rights-Based Theories of Tort Can and Must Address Cost-Based Proposals for Damages Reform" (2006) 55 DePaul L. Rev. 469; Murphy, "Rights, Reductionism and Tort Law" (2008) 28 O.J.L.S. 393; and Goudkamp & Murphy, "The Failure of Universal Theories of Tort Law" (2016) 22 Leg. Theory 1.

The rights theory of tort law is discussed elsewhere in this book in connection with specific torts.

2. Does the rights theory of tort law appeal to you? What are its strengths and weaknesses? Should tort law evolve in accordance with rights theory? Is it plausible to say that courts in the past employed the substance, but not the form, of rights-based analysis? Are judges and lawyers inclined, by nature or training, to conceive of disputes in terms of the recognition, violation and vindication of rights? Is there a danger of selectively reading past decisions to fit with modern theory?

Should Canadian society support a system of tort law that is not designed for the purpose of repairing financial losses, or spreading the cost of accidents, or punishing misconduct, or deterring potential tortfeasors? Given the fundamental importance of tort law, and its notorious expense, do you agree with Weinrib, *The Idea of Private Law* (1995) at 8, that "the sole purpose of private law is to be private law"?

3. The rights theory of tort has a number of competitors. Others are examined in Chapter 28.

2

THE BASIC CONCEPTS OF REMEDIES
IN INTENTIONAL TORTS

1. Introduction
2. Judicial and Extrajudicial Remedies
3. Classifications of Damages
4. Nominal Damages
5. Compensatory Damages
6. Aggravated Damages
7. Punitive Damages
8. Disgorgement Damages

1. Introduction

In a tort action, the plaintiff must first establish the elements of the tort in issue. Even after the plaintiff has proven the elements of the tort, the defendant will not necessarily be held liable. If the defendant can establish a defence, he or she will be absolved of liability. Thus, it is only after the plaintiff has proven the commission of the tort and the defendant has failed to establish a defence that the issue of an appropriate remedy arises. Therefore, issues relating to remedies are usually addressed last.

There are, however, two reasons for introducing the general concepts of remedies before examining the torts and defences. First, it is important to emphasize that establishing liability is a means to an end. The plaintiff is ultimately seeking a remedy for the wrong caused by the defendant. The nature of the available remedy will influence the plaintiff's decision to bring an action. Second, on a more practical level, many of the cases in the following chapters raise issues that cannot be appreciated without some understanding of remedies, particularly damages.

2. Judicial and Extrajudicial Remedies

There are two broad categories of remedies: judicial and extrajudicial. There are four types of judicial remedies in tort law, the first and most important of which is an award of damages. An award of damages is available across the range of tort actions. Contrary to what some people may believe, an award of damages does not result in the immediate transfer of money from the defendant to the plaintiff. Rather, it merely grants the plaintiff a legal right to a specific sum. In order to collect the award, the plaintiff may have to pursue creditors' remedies, such as the seizure and sale of assets, which are entirely independent of tort law.

The second type of judicial remedy is an injunction. An injunction is a court order that directs a party to do or refrain from doing certain things. There are many types of injunctions. For instance, a court may impose a prohibitive injunction that forbids the defendant from doing something (*e.g.* committing a trespass by walking across the plaintiff's lawn) or a mandatory injunction that compels the defendant to do something (*e.g.* tear down a billboard that he or she wrongfully built on the plaintiff's land). Injunctions have a number of unique features. A person who ignores an injunction may be held in contempt of court and, in an extreme case, imprisoned. Unlike damage awards, injunctions were granted by courts of equity and not by common law courts. Equitable remedies were available only if the common law remedies were inadequate. Moreover, equitable remedies were discretionary. While a successful plaintiff was generally entitled to compensatory damages as of right, the court had discretion to grant injunctive relief. As a result of the merging of the common law and equitable courts, Canadian courts have authority to grant both legal and equitable remedies. Nevertheless, equitable relief generally remains discretionary and dependent upon whether a damage award would provide adequate relief.

The other two types of judicial remedies are declarations and orders of specific restitution. Declarations are formal statements or decisions of a court that are usually issued to resolve a dispute or an issue of legal rights. An order of specific restitution directs a party to restore a pre-existing condition or return an object. Like injunctions, these remedies are granted in limited circumstances and are sought in relatively few tort actions.

The *Canadian Charter of Rights and Freedoms*, Part I of the *Constitution Act, 1982*, being Schedule B of the *Canada Act 1982* (U.K.), 1982, c. 11 adds another dimension to judicial remedies in some intentional torts cases. Section 24(1) of the *Charter* provides that a person whose *Charter* rights have been infringed or denied may apply to a court of competent jurisdiction to seek whatever remedy the court considers just and appropriate in the circumstances. While s. 24(1) only provides the right to seek a remedy for *Charter* breaches, many of the *Charter* cases involve conduct that also constitutes an intentional tort. Unlike in a common law tort action, an aggrieved plaintiff who is making a claim under s. 24(1) is not entitled to any remedy, let alone a damage award. For example, a court might conclude that it is not just and appropriate to provide a remedy under s. 24(1) if the *Charter* breach was minor, the government officials acted in good faith, or the plaintiff's interests can be adequately protected under existing common law tort principles.

A more detailed discussion of s. 24(1) is provided in Chapter 8. For current purposes, it is sufficient to note that a court may, among other things, issue a declaration or award compensatory, aggravated and punitive damages under s. 24(1).

Extrajudicial remedies (also called self-help remedies), such as recapture of chattels, re-entry onto land and abatement of nuisance, are also applicable in a small number of cases. These remedies will be discussed when they arise in relation to individual torts.

NOTES

1. For a comprehensive review of the Canadian law of damages, see Waddams, *The Law of Damages*, looseleaf (2017) (consulted July 2018).

2. Although frequent reference is made to the general rule that an injunction will only be granted when a damage award would be inadequate, the Canadian courts appear to be adopting a more flexible approach. For a comprehensive analysis of injunctions, see generally Sharpe, *Injunctions and Specific Performance*, looseleaf

(2017) (consulted July 2018); and Berryman, *The Law of Equitable Remedies*, 2d ed. (2013).

3. For a discussion of s. 24(1), see *Doucet-Boudreau v. Nova Scotia (Minister of Education)*, 2003 SCC 62; and *Vancouver (City) v. Ward*, 2010 SCC 27. In *Henry v. British Columbia (Attorney General)*, 2015 SCC 24, the plaintiff sued the province and others, seeking damages for being wrongfully convicted and imprisoned for almost 27 years. While the majority and minority agreed that the plaintiff could sue under s. 24(1) for prosecutorial abuse, they disagreed on the threshold test for such claims. The plaintiff was subsequently awarded over $8 million, of which $7.5 million was awarded to serve the "vindication and deterrence functions" of s. 24(1): *Henry v. British Columbia (Attorney General)*, 2016 BCSC 1038.

4. For a discussion of the extrajudicial remedies, see Heuston & Buckley, *Salmond and Heuston on the Law of Torts*, 21st ed. (1996) at 572-78; and Sinel, "De-Ciphering Self-Help" (2017) 67 U.T.L.J. 31.

3. Classifications of Damages

Academics, practitioners and judges have classified damage awards according to various criteria, such as the nature of the plaintiff's loss, the way in which the loss is calculated and proven, and the purpose for which the award is made. Since the criteria are unrelated, the corresponding classification systems are not mutually exclusive. The task of mastering the terminology of damages is further complicated by disagreements on the definition of some of the terms.

Perhaps the simplest way to analyze damages is to divide the plaintiff's claims into pecuniary (monetary) and non-pecuniary (non-monetary) losses. Pecuniary losses are those that can be calculated in dollars and cents, such as lost earnings, medical bills and repair costs. In contrast, non-pecuniary losses, such as pain, humiliation and disfigurement, have no monetary equivalent and thus cannot be subject to exact calculation.

In the pleadings of a cause of action, the plaintiff's losses are generally classified as either special or general damages. Special damages are those that can be exactly quantified at the time of trial, whereas general damages are those that are incapable of such quantification. The plaintiff is required to strictly plead and prove special damages, but not general damages because of their speculative nature.

Although both of these classification systems can be applied to damages arising from any torts case, they are most frequently associated with complex damage claims. Since such claims arise most commonly in negligence actions, further discussion of these classification systems will be deferred until Chapter 18.

In intentional torts, damages are most frequently classified according to the purpose for which they are awarded or the function that they are intended to serve. From that perspective, there are four basic categories of damages: nominal (token), compensatory, punitive (retributive, vindictive or exemplary), and disgorgement (gain-based).

NOTE

1. Although the terms "special" and "general" damages have several distinct meanings, we have used the definitions that are most relevant to the issue of pleadings. See Edelman, *McGregor on Damages*, 20th ed. (2018) at 20-24; and Burrows, "Damages" in Jones *et al.*, eds., *Clerk & Lindsell on Torts*, 22d ed. (2018) 1985 at 1988-89. For a discussion of pecuniary and non-pecuniary losses, see Burrows, *ibid.* at 1997-98.

4. Nominal Damages

Nominal damages are awarded in a small sum (*e.g.* $50) to redress a violation of a legal right that the law deems worthy of protection even in the absence of actual harm. For example, a defendant who steps onto the plaintiff's property causing no harm to the land will be held liable in trespass for nominal damages. The award of nominal damages vindicates the plaintiff's legal right to exclusive possession. Had the defendant crushed several flowers, the plaintiff could have been awarded compensatory damages to redress his or her actual losses. Although the size of the nominal damage award in the first case would be similar to the compensatory damage award in the second, it is important to emphasize that the distinction between these awards is based on the purpose for which they are given, not their amounts. Unfortunately, the term nominal damages is not always used consistently, and some judges have used it to refer to a small award of compensatory damages.

According to the traditional view, nominal damages are only awarded for torts that are actionable *per se*; that is, actionable without proof of loss. The intentional torts derived from the writ of trespass *vi et armis*, such as battery and trespass to land, are actionable *per se*. However, the intentional torts derived from trespass on the case, such as malicious prosecution and torts based on negligence, are not actionable *per se*. Rather, the plaintiff must establish actual damages as an essential element of these causes of action. If the plaintiff fails to establish loss in these cases, he or she has no cause of action and the issue of damages does not arise.

THE MEDIANA
[1900] A.C. 113 (H.L.)

EARL OF HALSBURY: . . . And, my Lords, here I wish, with reference to what has been suggested at the bar, to remark upon the difference between damages and nominal damages. "Nominal damages" is a technical phrase which means that you have negatived anything like real damage, but that you are affirming by your nominal damages that there is an infraction of a legal right which, though it gives you no right to any real damages at all, yet gives you a right to the verdict or judgment because your legal right has been infringed. But the term "nominal damages" does not mean small damages. The extent to which a person has a right to recover what is called by the compendious phrase damages, but may be also represented as compensation for the use of something that belongs to him, depends upon a variety of circumstances, and it certainly does not in the smallest degree suggest that because they are small they are necessarily nominal damages.

NOTES AND QUESTIONS

1. In *Bowen Contracting Ltd. v. B.C. Log Spill Recovery Co-operative Assn.*, 2009 BCCA 457, the defendant inadvertently trespassed, without causing any damage, on a portion of the plaintiff's private road that was not posted as private property. At trial, the plaintiff was awarded $1 in nominal damages, and its punitive damage claim was dismissed. The trial judgment was upheld on appeal.

2. In contrast to the traditional view, it has been suggested that nominal damages may be awarded in tort claims that require proof of loss. For example, while the tort of nuisance is premised upon loss, nominal damages may be available if, in the circumstances of a particular case, loss is presumed. See *Stoke-on-Trent City Council v. W. & J. Wass Ltd.*, [1988] 1 W.L.R. 1406 (C.A.). Likewise, nominal damages are sometimes awarded if damage is shown, but the amount is not sufficiently established. See *Marynowsky v. Stuartburn (District)* (1994), 97 Man. R. (2d) 60 (C.A.); and *Jalava v. Webster*, 2017 BCCA 378. What purpose would such an award serve?

3. In a small number of cases, courts have awarded "vindicatory" damages to redress violations of the plaintiff's autonomy, privacy and human rights, in the absence of any injury, loss or damage. However, in contrast to traditional nominal damage awards, these awards may be substantial, thereby emphasizing the importance of the legal right in issue. See *Vancouver (City) v. Ward*, 2010 SCC 27; *Henry v. British Columbia (Attorney General)*, 2016 BCSC 1038; Varuhas, "The Concept of 'Vindication' in the Law of Torts: Rights, Interests and Damages" (2014) 34(2) Oxford J. of Leg. Stud. 253; and Edelman, "Vindicatory Damages" in Barker, Fairweather & Grantham, eds., *Private Law in the 21st Century* (2017) 343.

4. A judge may award a trifling sum as contemptuous or derisory damages to express his or her disapproval of the plaintiff's claim, despite its technical validity. In *Dering v. Uris*, [1964] 2 All E.R. 660 (Q.B.), the plaintiff was awarded one halfpenny in damages for the defendant's defamatory comments overstating the extent of the plaintiff's collaboration with the Nazis in a concentration camp. See also *Martin v. Benson*, [1927] 1 K.B. 771; and *Dennison v. Sanderson*, [1946] O.R. 601 (C.A.). Explain the difference between nominal and contemptuous damages.

5. Another mechanism the courts may use to show their disapproval of a plaintiff's claim is an award of costs. Costs are generally awarded to the successful party. However, the court has discretion to deny costs to a successful plaintiff, or perhaps even award costs against him or her if it feels that the claim was a frivolous attempt at "empty vindication." See Laskin C.J.'s dissent in *Harrison v. Carswell*, [1976] 2 S.C.R. 200.

6. Given the social and private costs of civil litigation, does an action for nominal damages serve a worthwhile purpose for society or the plaintiff? Does your answer depend on whether the case involves personal security, real property or personal property?

7. For a discussion of nominal damages, see Edelman, *McGregor on Damages*, 20th ed. (2018) at 406-13; and Waddams, *The Law of Damages*, looseleaf (2017) (consulted July 2018), ch. 10.

5. Compensatory Damages

Most tort actions are brought to obtain financial redress for actual loss. The general principle for assessing compensatory damages was stated by Donaldson L.J. in *Dodd Properties (Kent) Ltd. v. Canterbury C.C.*, [1980] 1 All E.R. 928 at 938 (C.A.): "The general object underlying the rules for the assessment of damages is, so far as is possible by means of a monetary award, to place the plaintiff in the position which he would have occupied if he had not suffered the wrong complained of, be that wrong a tort or a breach of contract."

In *Livingstone v. Rawyards Coal Co.* (1880), 5 App. Cas. 25 at 39 (H.L.), Lord Blackburn stated that the compensatory measure of damages in tort law is: "that sum of money which will put the party who has been injured, or who has suffered, in the same position as he would have been in if he had not sustained the wrong for which he is now getting his compensation or reparation." This principle is sometimes referred to as "*restitutio in integrum.*"

Despite its apparent simplicity, this principle may be difficult to apply in specific situations. The following two subsections examine the types of challenges that may arise in calculating compensatory damages.

(a) ASSESSING DAMAGES FOR PECUNIARY LOSSES

Some claims involve complex damage calculations based on speculative factors stretching far into the future. A young person rendered a paraplegic may have an almost normal life expectancy, and thus may claim compensatory damages for lost earnings, future medical care, personal assistance services and other support for the next 50 years. In other situations, the challenge may be assigning a value to a particular loss. For example, how should compensatory damages be assessed for the loss of a unique work of art or a prized family heirloom? Similarly, what is the appropriate measure of damages for the defendant's wrongful use of the plaintiff's property that would have otherwise sat idle? *The Mediana*, which was discussed earlier in connection with nominal damages, addresses this last issue.

THE MEDIANA
[1900] A.C. 113 (H.L.)

EARL OF HALSBURY: . . . Supposing a person took away a chair out of my room and kept it for twelve months, could anybody say you had a right to diminish the damages by shewing that I did not usually sit in that chair, or that there were plenty of other chairs in the room? The proposition so nakedly stated appears to me to be absurd; but a jury have very often a very difficult task to perform in ascertaining what should be the amount of damages of that sort. I know very well that as a matter of common sense what an arbitrator or a jury very often do is to take a perfectly artificial hypothesis and say, "Well, if you wanted to hire a chair, what would you have to give for it for the period"; and in that way they come to a rough sort of conclusion as to what damages ought to be paid for the unjust and unlawful withdrawal of it from the owner. Here, as I say, the broad principle seems to me to be quite independent of the particular use the plaintiffs were going to make of the thing that was taken, except — and this I think has been the fallacy running through the arguments at the bar — when you are endeavouring to establish the specific loss of profit, or of something that you otherwise would have got which the law recognises as special damage. In that case you must shew it, and by precise evidence, so much so that in the old system of pleading you could not recover damages unless you had made a specific allegation in your pleading so as to give the persons responsible for making good the loss an opportunity of inquiring into it before they came into court. But when we are speaking of general damages no such principle applies at all, and the jury might give whatever they thought would be the proper equivalent for the unlawful withdrawal of the subject-matter then in question. It seems to me that that broad principle comprehends within it many other things. There is no doubt in many cases a jury would say there really has been no damage at all: "We will give the plaintiffs a trifling amount" — not nominal damages, be it observed, but a trifling amount; in other cases it would be more serious.

NOTES AND QUESTIONS

1. Do you agree that the plaintiff suffered a loss in the example of the appropriated chair? If so, what was lost? What if the defendant had ridden the plaintiff's horse without the plaintiff's consent, and the horse benefitted from the exercise?

2. In the example of the appropriated chair, damages are said to be "at large" because the jury has considerable latitude in quantifying them. The award is not limited to the pecuniary losses that the plaintiff has specifically pleaded and proven. The Earl of Halsbury indicated that, depending on the facts of the case, the jury could award a trifling sum as compensatory damages. Distinguish such an award from an award of nominal damages.

3. The issue raised by the appropriated chair example occasionally arises in connection with trespass to land. In such circumstances, the plaintiff is entitled to "mesne profits" (pronounced "mean" profits) equal to the reasonable rental value of the property. In *Inverugie Investments Ltd. v. Hackett*, [1995] 1 W.L.R. 713 (P.C.), the plaintiff purchased the leasehold to 30 units in a hotel, which the defendant wrongfully occupied for 20 years and tried to rent out to third parties. When the plaintiff claimed compensation, the defendant presented evidence that the average occupancy rate was only 35-40%. The Privy Council largely rejected that evidence, stating that the quantification of damages was not concerned with the plaintiff's actual loss, nor with the profit made by the defendant. Instead, compensatory damages were assessed in terms of the reasonable rental value of the property. Lord Lloyd explained: "If a man hires a concrete mixer, he must pay for the daily hire, even though he may not in the event have been able to use the mixer because of rain. So also must the trespasser who takes the mixer without the owner's consent. He must pay the going rate, even though in the event he has derived no benefit from the use of the mixer." Consequently, damages in *Inverugie* were calculated on the basis of the wholesale rate paid by tour operators, which accounted for seasonal variations in room rates.

4. In *Miller v. Brian Ross Motorsports Corp.*, 2017 BCCA 166, the plaintiff was awarded $15,000 at trial for the nine-month loss of the use of his Ferrari resulting from the defendant's negligence. The plaintiff appealed because the award was

assessed on the basis of how frequently he would have used the car, and not the cost of renting a comparable vehicle. The Court of Appeal upheld the trial judge's flexible approach, stating that the rental cost is only one means of assessing compensatory damages "for the loss of enjoyment of property held for pleasure." Does this decision adequately compensate the plaintiff for the loss of his ability to use his property as he sees fit? The approach in *Miller* is inconsistent with that in *The Mediana* and *Inverugie*. Which approach better advances the underlying goal of compensatory damage awards?

(b) ASSESSING DAMAGES FOR NON-PECUNIARY LOSSES

A different challenge arises when a court is asked to award damages for non-pecuniary losses, which by definition have no monetary equivalent. How should compensatory damages be assessed for the humiliation arising from being slapped in the face or for having to endure severe pain? Clearly, there is a loss, but how can seemingly immeasurable values, such as one's public standing or quality of life, be expressed in dollars? Dickson J. addressed this issue in *Andrews v. Grand & Toy Alberta Ltd.*, [1978] 2 S.C.R. 229 at 260-61:

> Andrews used to be a healthy young man, athletically active and socially congenial. Now he is a cripple, deprived of many of life's pleasures and subjected to pain and disability. For this, he is entitled to compensation. But the problem here is qualitatively different from that of pecuniary losses. There is no medium of exchange for happiness. There is no market for expectation of life. The monetary evaluation of non-pecuniary losses is a philosophical and policy exercise more than a legal or logical one. The award must be fair and reasonable, fairness being gauged by earlier decisions; but the award must also of necessity be arbitrary or conventional.

Although challenges in assessing compensatory damages arise in intentional torts cases, they are more common in negligence actions. Consequently, a detailed examination of compensatory damages is left to Chapter 18.

REVIEW PROBLEM

The palm of the plaintiff's hand was severely disfigured by scar tissue. The defendant doctor had a special interest in experimental skin grafting and induced the plaintiff to undergo an operation by stating that he would guarantee to make the hand 100% perfect. The plaintiff agreed, and the doctor grafted skin from the plaintiff's chest to his hand. Unfortunately, the operation was unsuccessful. Not only did considerable scar tissue remain, but hair began to grow on the plaintiff's palm.

This fact situation is based on *Hawkins v. McGee*, 146 A. 641 (N.H. 1929). The court held that the doctor's statement constituted a binding contractual promise to give the plaintiff a perfect hand and that the doctor was strictly liable in contract for breaching this warranty. Assume that a parallel situation arose in tort. For example, if the doctor had made the statement knowing it to be false and there was no contractual relationship between the parties, the plaintiff could have brought an action for the tort of deceit. The following questions illustrate the quantification of compensatory damages in tort and several differences between tort and contract law.

(a) What damages would you award in tort to compensate the plaintiff for having to live the rest of his life with a scarred and hairy hand? Should this calculation be based on the judge's objective assessment of this disability or on the plaintiff's subjective view?

(b) Applying the principles in *Dodd Properties*, calculate the plaintiff's compensatory damages in deceit. For the purpose of this calculation, assume that the hand had been worth $50 before the operation, $25 after the operation, and that it would have been worth $100 had the operation succeeded.

(c) As stated above, the court in *Hawkins* considered the doctor's statement about making the hand perfect to be a contractual warranty. Based on the previously stated values of the hand, what should the plaintiff's compensatory damage award be in contract? If you have calculated correctly, you will have concluded that the plaintiff's compensatory damages are not the same in tort and contract. Can you reconcile this result with the statement in *Dodd Properties* about the purpose of compensatory damages?

(d) Assume that the plaintiff had lost $100 in wages when he missed work to undergo the operation. Based on the values of the hand stated above, calculate the plaintiff's compensatory damages in tort and contract.

6. Aggravated Damages

Although some Canadian courts had used the terms as synonyms, it is now well established that aggravated damages are distinct from punitive damages. Aggravated damages are defined as a form of compensatory damages that are awarded to compensate the plaintiff for additional injuries to dignity and similar feelings arising from the defendant's reprehensible conduct. In principle, aggravated damages are predicated on two requirements. First, given that aggravated damages are compensatory, plaintiffs must establish that they suffered additional injuries to their feelings. Second, the defendant's conduct must be highly offensive or particularly repugnant, and not simply tortious. However, if the defendant's cconduct is viewed as sufficiently offensive, as in many intentional tort claims, some courts simply assume that it caused additional injuries to the plaintiff's feelings.

NOTES AND QUESTIONS

1. In *Rookes v. Barnard*, [1964] 1 All E.R. 367 (H.L.), the court defined aggravated damages in terms of injuries to the plaintiff's "proper feelings of dignity or pride" arising from the defendant's malice or manner of committing the wrong. The Supreme Court of Canada adopted a similar definition in *Vorvis v. Insurance Corp. of British Columbia*, [1989] 1 S.C.R. 1085. See also *Fidler v. Sun Life Assurance Co. of Canada*, 2006 SCC 30.

2. Given that aggravated damages are intended to compensate the plaintiff for injuries to his or her feelings, should they be based on a subjective standard?

3. Can meaningful distinctions be made between the injured feelings that normally arise from being the victim of a tort and the additional emotional injuries stemming from the defendant's reprehensible conduct? See *K.(K.) v. G.(K.W.)* (2008),

90 O.R. (3d) 481 (C.A.), where the trial court held that compensation for the defendant's aggravating conduct should be included in the general damage award without attempting to assess a specific amount for aggravated damages. The Court of Appeal reduced the trial judge's award for loss of earnings, but did not discuss whether aggravating factors should be included in the general damage award without separate assessment. See also *A.(D.A.) v. B.(D.K.)* (1995), 27 C.C.L.T. (2d) 256 (Ont. Gen. Div.).

4. In *Thomas Management Ltd. v. Alberta (Minister of Environmental Protection)* 2006 ABCA 303, the court ruled that a closely held, family-owned corporation could not recover aggravated damages for the mental anguish that its shareholders might suffer. See also *Inform Cycle Ltd. v. Rebound Inc.*, 2008 ABQB 369, in which the corporate plaintiff was denied aggravated damages because it could not suffer mental distress or hurt feelings, but was awarded $5,000 in punitive damages. The defendant knowingly registered a misleading domain name that was almost identical to the plaintiff's and then directed customers looking for the plaintiff's website to a pornographic website instead.

5. In *Fidler, supra* at paras. 52-53, the court distinguished between aggravated damages "which arise out of aggravating circumstances" and "mental distress damages" which "arise out of the contractual breach itself." The court stated that "mental distress damages" are independent of any aggravating circumstances and are based solely on the parties' contractual expectations. Explain in your own words the difference between aggravated and mental distress damages. Is this distinction helpful? See also *Fernandes v. Penncorp Life Insurance Co.*, 2014 ONCA 615 at paras. 1 and 85-103; and *Branco v. American Home Assurance Co.*, 2015 SKCA 71 at paras. 134-42.

6. In Québec, plaintiffs may be awarded "moral damages" if they can establish that they have suffered psychological or emotional harm. In contrast to claims for aggravated damages, plaintiffs may recover "moral damages" without having to establish that they suffered additional emotional harm or that the defendant's conduct was particularly repugnant or offensive. Moreover, these awards may be very substantial. See for example *Manoukian c. Procureur général du Canada*, 2018 QCCS 30.

7. For a general discussion of aggravated damages, see Murphy, "The Nature and Domain of Aggravated Damages" [2010] C.L.J. 353.

7. Punitive Damages

The issue of punitive damages has generated considerable judicial and academic attention. Much of the discussion has stemmed from disagreements about the proper role of such awards in tort law. Traditionally, the Canadian courts limited punitive damages to situations in which a defendant's reprehensible conduct warranted punishment. More recently, the courts have recognized that such awards may serve a dual function, providing punishment and/or deterrence. However, a damage award addressing one of these goals may differ significantly from an award focusing on the other.

Punishment looks backwards to condemn the defendant's actions, whereas deterrence looks forward to discourage the defendant and others from committing such wrongs. Since it is generally thought that punishment must be proportionate to the wrongdoing, damages based on punishment will be quantified primarily with reference to the defendant's moral blameworthiness. In contrast, damages based on deterrence will be quantified in terms of the financial disincentive required to discourage future wrongdoing.

In *Rookes v. Barnard*, [1964] 1 All E.R. 367 (H.L.), the court limited punitive damages to three categories of cases: oppressive, arbitrary or unconstitutional conduct by government officials; conduct calculated to make a profit in excess of the likely compensatory damage award; and situations in which such awards were expressly authorized by statute. Even within these categories, punitive damages were to be awarded with restraint, the plaintiff must be the victim of the tort, and the financial means of the parties must be considered. Finally, punitive damages are awarded if, and only if, an award of compensatory and aggravated damages is insufficient to adequately punish the defendant, denounce the conduct and deter a repetition.

The Canadian courts rejected limiting punitive damages to these three categories of cases and award punitive damages far more frequently than their English counterparts. Nevertheless, punitive damage awards are relatively uncommon in Canada.

NOTES AND QUESTIONS

1. For a discussion of the deterrence function of punitive damages in torts, see *Norberg v. Wynrib*, [1992] 2 S.C.R. 226; and *Hill v. Church of Scientology*, [1995] 2 S.C.R. 1130.

2. A common argument for strictly limiting punitive damages is that they constitute a quasi-criminal fine imposed in a civil proceeding in which the defendant is denied the evidentiary and procedural safeguards of a criminal trial. Do you find this argument compelling? See Jeffries, "A Comment on the Constitutionality of Punitive Damages" (1986) 72 Va. L. Rev. 139.

B.(P.) v. B.(W.)
(1992), 11 O.R. (3d) 161 (Gen. Div.)

[The plaintiff was sexually assaulted from the age of 5 until she was almost 18 by the defendant, her father. There were other violent incidents and threats, and the defendant raped the plaintiff when she was 20. The defendant pleaded guilty to criminal charges of incest, but two additional charges related to the rape were stayed. He was sentenced to 5½ years imprisonment on the incest conviction.

The plaintiff sued the defendant for assault and battery. The defendant did not defend the action, and the case proceeded on the issue of damages. The plaintiff's doctor testified that the plaintiff was the most traumatized sexual assault victim he had ever seen. He stated that she was left emotionally and socially dysfunctional, and that it was highly unlikely that she would ever be able to function in normal relationships.]

CUNNINGHAM J.: . . .

Non-pecuniary general damages

There can be no doubt that the repugnant and reprehensible conduct of the defendant towards his daughter has severely affected her life. Abuse by fathers has to have a far more negative impact upon children than any other form of abuse. More particularly, a very special relationship exists between fathers and daughters and when that trusting, loving relationship is violated, the results can be catastrophic. They certainly were here. This plaintiff has been, in the words of Dr. Bartashunas, as severely psychologically damaged as anyone he has seen, not only in his practice but in the literature. Not only was there a total breach of trust involved here but also a very significant element of fear. Violence permeated this entire family unit and during her tender years, while being subjected to regular sexual abuse by her father, she often witnessed her mother being beaten by the defendant and indeed had been subjected to his physical violence herself. By the time the plaintiff reached her mid-teens, she began to experience great difficulty coping with her life. She suffered blackouts and before she was brought to the attention of Dr. Bartashunas, she had been through neurological and CAT scan examinations, all of which proved negative.

This case is clearly the most serious I have seen in my review of Canadian authorities. As the plaintiff described in her evidence, it is worse than being murdered. It is something that she has had to live with for a very long time and probably will have to live with every day for the rest of her life. Her great fear, because she recognizes her difficulty in forming meaningful relationships, is that she will grow old alone.

Accordingly, for her non-pecuniary general damages the plaintiff will have the sum of $100,000. [The judge listed a number of cases that he had considered.] . . . In my view, the closest to our case is *Brandner v. Brandner*, where a father sexually abused his daughter, almost continuously from six to fifteen leaving her severely traumatized. In that case, the professional witnesses described it as being one of the worst cases of a sexually damaged person ever encountered, a person who would need continual psychotherapy. In fact, most of the difficulties suffered by the plaintiff in that case are very similar to the difficulties being experienced by this plaintiff. Feelings of vulnerability, victimization and profound shame with the attendant lack of self-esteem and self-worth are the results in both cases. In *Brandner*, De Graves J. awarded the sum of $100,000 for psychological trauma and $50,000 for aggravated damages. I intend to deal with aggravated damages separately.

Aggravated damages

Aggravated damages are awarded in cases where, because of the defendant's conduct, the measure of damages is increased. In my view, aggravated damages are not punitive damages which I will deal with later in these reasons. Aggravated damages may be taken into account in the overall assessment of non-pecuniary general damages but in certain circumstances, may be dealt with separately and in addition to general damages where the facts so warrant. This, in my view, is one of those situations. The assaults in this case occurred over a period of many years on a little girl who loved and trusted her father. It was not until she was about 10 years of age that she realized, through interaction with her peers at school, something was wrong with her relationship with her father. This defendant, even during periods of access while the plaintiff was living with her mother, continued his predatory and disgraceful conduct on a young girl approaching adolescence. Even worse, after obtaining custody of the plaintiff in her early teens, he continued his disgusting conduct. Never have I seen a situation where a person in authority has taken such advantage of another and accordingly, I assess aggravated damages at $75,000 for this gross breach of trust. Had it not been for this pattern of abuse, I have no doubt this young woman would today be functioning at a much higher level.

. . .

Punitive damages

In my view, it is clear law that where tortious acts are also crimes and the conduct has already been sanctioned, to award punitive damages in a civil lawsuit would amount of [*sic*] double jeopardy: *B.(A.) v. J.(I.)* [(1991), 81 Alta. L.R. (2d) 84 (Q.B.)]; *Rioux v. Smith* (1983), 48 B.C.L.R. 126 (C.A.).

In the present case, as I indicated early on, only part of the defendant's conduct was criminally sanctioned. The defendant pleaded guilty to having committed incest upon his daughter between the years 1976 and 1987. From my reading of the proceedings in the criminal court, although there was some brief mention of the 1989 occurrence, the full details of that sexual assault were not documented. The plaintiff has testified that on that occasion she was raped by her father at a time when she was in a particularly vulnerable state. The recitation of the facts in the criminal court indicated that the defendant fondled the plaintiff's breasts and rubbed his penis against her vagina suggesting to her that, despite the fact she was having her menstrual period, it would be a good time to have sex. What the recitation of the facts did not disclose, however, was the fact of the rape. I am satisfied that this conduct in 1989, was not sanctioned. Accordingly, the plaintiff will have punitive damages against the defendant in the amount of $50,000.

NOTES AND QUESTIONS

1. What factors did the judge consider in awarding aggravated damages and punitive damages? Do you agree with the judge's analyses and the amount of these awards? Damage awards in incest cases have increased since *B.(P.)*. See for example *Waters v. Bains*, 2008 BCSC 823; and *C.C.B. v. I.B.*, 2009 BCSC 1425.

2. Aggravated and punitive damage awards are common in sexual assault cases. See for example *T.W.N.A. v. Canada (Ministry of Indian Affairs)*, 2003 BCCA 670; *Blackwater v. Plint*, 2005 SCC 58; and *N.C. c. F.T.*, 2018 QCCS 3939. Punitive damages have also been awarded against people who have falsely accused others of such conduct. See for example *Newman v. Halstead*, 2006 BCSC 65; *K.(F.) c. K.(H.)*, 2016 QCCS 6065; and *Whitfield v. Whitfield*, 2016 ONCA 581.

3. The courts have declined to award punitive damages against: a defendant who sexually abused his younger brother when they were both underage; and a woman who failed to take steps to prevent her husband from continuing to sexually abuse their daughter over a seven-year period. See respectively *Olsen v. Olsen*, 2006 BCSC 560; and *K.(K.) v. G.(K.W.)*, 2008 ONCA 489. See also *Hockley v. Riley*, 2007 ONCA 804.

4. Does the fact that the criminal justice system is overburdened justify expanding the role of punitive damages in torts, particularly in cases of deliberate and repeated

wrongdoing? See Englard, "The System Builders: A Critical Appraisal of Modern American Tort Theory" (1980) 9 J. Legal Stud. 27.

5. Can punitive damages play an important role in publicly condemning unacceptable behaviour and acknowledging the plaintiff's injuries? Sexual abuse victims occasionally sue in tort, not to recover damages but to obtain official vindication of their grievances. See *Myers v. Haroldson* (1989), 76 Sask. R. 27 (Q.B.).

However, in *Chow v. Hiscock* (2005), 41 C.C.L.T. (3d) 155 (B.C.S.C.), the court declined to award punitive damages against three young gang members who viciously assaulted the plaintiff. The judge stated that since the defendants were unlikely to pay even a small fraction of the almost $6 million of compensatory damages, awarding punitive damages was unnecessary because it would be purely symbolic. Do you agree with the judge's reasoning?

6. In *XY, LLC v. Canadian Topsires Selection Inc.*, 2016 BCSC 1095, the plaintiff was awarded damages of almost $270 million against a large group of defendants and damages of $60 million against two individual defendants. The court accepted that the large group and individual defendants had engaged in "a fraud of epic proportions" that more than warranted punishment and denunciation, and awarded the plaintiff a $500,000 punitive damage award. The court stated that the punitive damages would send a clear message and serve a deterrent function. Do you agree?

7. While punitive damage awards have become more common in Canada, they remain exceptional and tend to be modest in size. However, there have been a relatively small number of very large punitive damage awards in Canada. In addition to the cases involving the bad-faith denial of insurance benefits, which will be discussed shortly, see *Claiborne Industries Ltd. v. National Bank of Canada* (1989), 69 O.R. (2d) 65 (C.A.) (almost $1,500,000 in punitive damages awarded against a bank that assisted one customer in defrauding another); *Cinar Corporation v. Robinson*, 2013 SCC 73 ($500,000 in punitive damages for copyright infringement); *Ottawa Community Housing Corp. v. Foustanellas*, 2015 ONCA 276 ($250,000 in punitive damages for fraud); *Arsenovski v. Bodin*, 2016 BCSC 359 ($350,000 in punitive damages for wrongfully referring the plaintiff's insurance claim for criminal prosecution); *Galea v. Wal-Mart Canada Corp.*, 2017 ONSC 245 ($500,000 in punitive damages and $250,000 in "moral damages" for wrongful dismissal); and *Samaroo v. Canada Revenue Agency*, 2018 BCSC 324 ($750,000 in punitive damages and $600,000 in aggravated damages for malicious prosecution).

8. In *Cinar, supra*, at para. 134, the Supreme Court of Canada stated that an appellate court may only interfere with a trial judge's assessment of punitive damages if there was an error in law or the amount was not rationally connected to the purposes for which the damages were awarded, namely prevention, deterrence and denunciation. Are the individual goals of prevention, deterrence and denunciation precise enough to ensure consistency in awarding punitive damages? For example, how does the goal of prevention differ from the goal of deterrence? Should it be up to the trial judge to decide on the goal or goals of a punitive damage award? As indicated, the size of a punitive damage award addressing one of these goals may differ significantly from an award focusing on another.

9. For examples of large punitive damage awards being negated or significantly reduced on appeal, see *Keays v. Honda Canada Inc.*, 2008 SCC 39 ($500,000 punitive damage award reduced to $100,000 by the Ontario Court of Appeal and then negated by the Supreme Court of Canada); *Montréal (City of) v. Biondi*, 2013 QCCA 404 ($2,000,000 punitive damage award negated); and *Boucher v. Wal-Mart Canada Corp.*, 2014 ONCA 419 ($1,000,000 punitive damage award against Wal-Mart reduced to $100,000, and $150,000 punitive damage award against a Wal-Mart supervisor reduced to $10,000).

10. In *Hill v. Church of Scientology*, [1995] 2 S.C.R. 1130, the defendants held a press conference during which they alleged that the plaintiff, a Crown attorney, had misled a judge and intentionally breached an order sealing certain documents. The statements were untrue and the Crown Attorney was awarded $300,000 in compensatory damages, $500,000 in aggravated damages and $800,000 in punitive damages for being publicly defamed. Can you reconcile these compensatory, aggravated and punitive damage awards with those in *B.(P.)*?

(a) THE PRINCIPLES IN *WHITEN v. PILOT*

The principles governing punitive damages were reviewed in *Whiten v. Pilot Insurance Co.*, [2002] 1 S.C.R. 595. The defendant insurer refused to pay the plaintiffs' claim when their house was destroyed by fire. The defendant alleged that the plaintiffs intentionally burned down their own house, despite the conclusion of the fire chief and the defendant's own adjuster, expert engineer and investigators that the fire was accidental. When its adjuster strongly recommended paying the claim, the defendant replaced the adjuster. Counsel for the defendant pressured his own experts to conclude that the fire was caused by arson and provided them with misleading information. The defendant asserted the arson defence throughout the four-week trial. In the end result, the court restored the jury's $1,000,000 punitive damage award against the defendant. Although the claim arose from breach of contract, Binnie J. comprehensively reviewed punitive damage awards in both torts and contracts. Binnie J.'s conclusions are summarized below.

(i) Unlike in the United Kingdom, punitive damages in Canada are not limited to specific categories of cases, but rather can be awarded in any type of case to punish the defendant, deter the defendant and others, denounce the defendant's conduct, or strip the defendant of profits that his or her outrageous conduct generated in excess of the likely compensatory damage award.

(ii) Characterizing the defendant's misconduct as malicious, high-handed or oppressive is not helpful in setting the amount of punitive damages. However, it is clear that only very serious misconduct warrants punishment, deterrence or denunciation and thus punitive damages.

(iii) Punitive damages are most likely to be awarded in intentional torts, but they may also be awarded in nuisance, negligence and other tort actions, as well as in contracts.

(iv) The fact that the defendant has been punished criminally does not preclude a punitive damage award, but rather is only one factor to be considered by the courts.

(v) Punitive damages should be awarded with restraint and then only if an award of compensatory damages, including aggravated damages, is insufficient to accomplish the specific goal of the contemplated punitive damage award.

(vi) There should be no fixed ratios between compensatory and punitive damages, nor should the latter be subject to a cap. Rather, the size of the punitive damage award should be based on the underlying goal and should be the lowest sum necessary to accomplish that end.

(vii) Juries should be informed of the functions of punitive damages and the factors that govern both the award and the assessment of the amount.

(viii) Appellate courts are entitled to intervene if the punitive damage award exceeds the outer bounds of a rational and measured response to the facts of the case.

(ix) Under s. 24(1) of the *Charter*, the court may grant whatever remedy it deems appropriate for a violation of a person's *Charter* rights, including compensatory, aggravated and punitive damages.

NOTES AND QUESTIONS

1. Can you reconcile the punitive damage award in *Whiten* with that in *B.(P.)*? What public benefit results from the Whitens receiving a $1,000,000 windfall in excess of their compensatory damage award? See Buller, "*Whiten v. Pilot*: Controlling Jury Awards of Punitive Damages" (2003) 36 U.B.C. L. Rev. 357.

2. For cases illustrating the need to consider compensatory and aggravated damages in determining whether to award punitive damages, see *Pate Estate v. Galway-Cavendish and Harvey (Township)*, 2013 ONCA 669; *Boucher v. Wal-Mart Canada Corp.*, 2014 ONCA 419; and *XY, LLC v. Canadian Topsires Selection Inc.*, 2016 BCSC 1095.

3. The bad-faith denial of insurance benefits has resulted in several very large punitive damage awards at trial, some of which were reduced or negated on appeal. See *Pereira v. Hamilton Township Farmers' Mutual Fire Insurance Co.* (2006), 209 OAC 127 (C.A.) ($2,500,000 punitive damage award reversed because it was "grossly excessive" and "irrational"); *Fidler v. Sun Life Assurance Co. of Canada*, 2006 SCC 30 ($100,000 punitive damage award reversed because the denial of benefits was not done in bad faith); and *Branco v. American Home Assurance Co.*, 2015 SKCA 71 ($4.5 million punitive damage award reduced to $675,000 because it was excessive).

4. As noted in *Whiten*, punitive damages are rarely awarded in negligence cases because they typically involve careless behaviour and not intentional wrongdoing. However, exceptions exist. In *Robitaille v. Vancouver Hockey Club Ltd.* (1981), 30 B.C.L.R. 286 (C.A.), the plaintiff was told by management that his injury was "all in his head," and he was pressured to continue playing. As a result, the plaintiff suffered a permanent and disabling injury. In awarding $35,000 in punitive damages, the court held that the team's conduct had been "arrogant and high-handed." For a punitive damage award in a products liability case and in a nuisance and negligence case, see respectively *Vlchek v. Koshel* (1988), 30 B.C.L.R. (2d) 97 (S.C.), aff'd (1988), 32 B.C.L.R. (2d) xxxi (C.A.), and *Midwest Properties Ltd. v. Thordarson*, 2015 ONCA 819.

5. In *McIntyre v. Grigg* (2006), 83 O.R. (3d) 161 (C.A.), the court reduced the $100,000 punitive damage award against an impaired driver to $20,000. The driver, whose blood-alcohol level was more than 2½ times the limit in the *Criminal Code*, R.S.C. 1985, c. C-46, s. 253(1)(b), drove through a stop sign, sheared off a lamp post and struck the plaintiff. Should punitive damages be awarded in such cases?

6. In *de Montigny v. Brossard (Succession)*, 2010 SCC 51, the court awarded punitive damages under the Québec *Charter* against the estate of a man who killed his wife and two children before killing himself. The court stated that the award served the purposes of denunciation and affirmation of the importance of the right to life. Since the murderer's estate was insolvent, a symbolic sum of $10,000 in punitive damages was awarded to be shared among the successors of the three victims. Are punitive damages necessary or appropriate in such cases to denounce conduct that is clearly abhorrent? Did the punitive damage award in this case trivialize the deceased's conduct?

7. Should a wrongdoer be subject to both criminal penalties and quasi-criminal civil sanctions for the same act? What factors should be considered in resolving this issue? Note that a criminal conviction has no impact on the plaintiff's compensatory and aggravated damage award in a related tort action.

8. In *Vorvis v. Insurance Corp. of British Columbia*, [1989] 1 S.C.R. 1085, the court said that punitive damages could only be awarded if the defendant's conduct was of a "harsh, vindictive, reprehensible and malicious nature." Other courts described the requisite wrongdoing in terms of "contemptuous," "evil" or "callous" behaviour. Do you agree with Binnie J.'s comments in *Whiten* that such characterizations are unhelpful in determining whether to award punitive damages?

9. For a discussion of punitive damages, see Beaulac, "A Comparative Look at Punitive Damages in Canada" in Beaulac, Pitel & Schulz, eds., *The Joy of Torts* (2003) 351; and Waddams, *The Law of Damages*, looseleaf (2017) (consulted July 2018), ch. 11.

8. Disgorgement Damages

Once the plaintiff establishes that the defendant is liable in tort, the court typically assesses damages in terms of the amount of money required to compensate the plaintiff for his or her loss. However, in certain situations, the appropriate remedy is not compensation but rather disgorgement of the defendant's profit. Disgorgement shifts the focus from the plaintiff's loss to the defendant's gain, compelling the defendant to give up the benefits obtained from his or her tortious conduct. Disgorgement is consistent with the principle that people should not profit from their own wrongdoing: *Attorney General v. Guardian Newspapers (No. 2)*, [1990] 1 A.C. 109 at 286 (H.L.).

In *Edwards v. Lee's Administrators* (1936), 96 S.W.2d 1028 (Ky. C.A.), the defendant operated a profitable cave touring business from an entrance located on his own property. A significant portion of the cave was under the plaintiff's property, but there was no entrance on his land to the cave, which was 360 feet below the surface. The plaintiff sued in trespass to land, seeking an accounting for a share of the profits and an injunction to prevent future trespassing. The court held that the defendant was a trespasser and granted an accounting and an injunction. Given that the plaintiff had no access to the cave and his land had not been adversely affected by the defendant's cave touring business, he suffered no tangible loss requiring compensation. However, the court stated that it is unjust to allow a tortfeasor to escape liability and profit from his or her wrongdoing. Consequently, the court held that the appropriate "basis of recovery" was "profits received, rather than damages sustained" and ordered the defendant to pay the plaintiff a percentage of his profits.

A tort may result in both a loss for the plaintiff and a gain for the defendant. In that event, the plaintiff is entitled to seek both compensatory and disgorgement damages, but ultimately must choose one remedy: *United Australia Ltd. v. Barclay's Bank Ltd.*, [1941] A.C. 1 (H.L.); and *Rahal v. Rahal*, [1932] 3 D.L.R. 259 (B.C.C.A.). The defendant is not required to pay both compensatory and disgorgement damages.

While, as *Edwards* illustrates, disgorgement can provide a valuable form of redress, the law is not as clear as might be hoped. First, the courts have not determined which causes of action support disgorgement. The proprietary torts (trespass to land, trespass to goods, conversion, and detinue) undoubtedly allow the plaintiff to choose between compensatory and disgorgement damages. As explained in later chapters, the same is true for several other torts, such as deceit and passing off. In contrast, disgorgement has never been awarded for battery, false imprisonment or the other intentional torts that protect physical autonomy. Granted, disgorgement claims will rarely arise in such cases. Most importantly, it remains to be seen whether disgorgement damages will be awarded in negligence cases.

Second, Canadian courts often analyze cases not in terms of disgorgement, but rather "restitution" for "unjust enrichment," thereby generating considerable confusion. Depending on the context, the terms "restitution" and "unjust enrichment" mean very different things.

(a) TRUE RESTITUTION FOR UNJUST ENRICHMENT

Unjust enrichment is an independent cause of action. It is neither a type of tort, nor a category of contract. It is an independent claim that deals exclusively with unjustified transfers of benefits involving the plaintiff and the defendant. Assume that the plaintiff intends to deposit $5,000 in his or her own bank account, but due to an innocent mistake, puts the money in the defendant's account instead. Although the defendant has done nothing wrong, the plaintiff is entitled to recover in unjust enrichment. A cause of action in unjust enrichment consists of three elements: (i) an enrichment to the defendant; (ii) a corresponding deprivation to the plaintiff; and (iii) an absence of a juristic reason for the enrichment. This last element requires the plaintiff to establish that the defendant did not receive the enrichment as a gift, pursuant to a contract, or as a result of a judgment, other legal disposition or performance of an obligation. If the plaintiff establishes these three elements, the defendant must make restitution, a word that means "to give back." Restitution is appropriate because the remedy is limited to returning the benefit that moved between the parties. The plaintiff cannot get back more than what he or she lost, and the defendant cannot give back more than he or she gained.

(b) "RESTITUTION" FOR "UNJUST ENRICHMENT"

The quotation marks in this heading indicate that the words are being used incorrectly. *Edwards* provides an example. A Canadian court would be apt to say that the defendant was ordered to provide "restitution" because his cave touring business "unjustly enriched" him at the plaintiff's expense. However, the purpose of the damage award in *Edwards* was not to reverse an unjustified transfer of a benefit from the plaintiff to the defendant. Rather, damages were awarded to strip the defendant of his wrongful gain in trespassing on the plaintiff's land. The cause of action was not unjust enrichment, but rather the tort of trespass to land. The remedy was not true restitution, but rather disgorgement. The plaintiff never suffered a loss and thus cannot "get back" what he never gave up. The defendant was ordered to give up the profits that he received from the tourists as a result of trespassing on the plaintiff's property. As in most instances, the award of disgorgement damages in *Edwards* resulted in a windfall to the plaintiff in that he received a benefit that he would not have obtained in the ordinary course of events.

NOTES AND QUESTIONS

1. For the distinction between disgorgement of wrongful gains and restitution for unjust enrichment, see McInnes, "The Measure of Restitution" (2002) 52 U.T.L.J. 163 at 185-86; and McInnes, *The Canadian Law of Unjust Enrichment and Restitution* (2014) at 3-16.

2. For a discussion of the torts in which disgorgement damages are available, see Jones, ed., *Goff and Jones: The Law of Restitution*, 7th ed. (2007) 801-26; and Rotherham, "Gain-Based Relief in Tort after *Attorney General v. Blake*" (2010) 126 L.Q.R. 102. Should compensatory and disgorgement damages be available in all torts? What arguments can be made in support of, and in opposition to, permitting plaintiffs to claim both types of damages in all tort claims?

3. Disgorgement damages are not confined to torts. They may be awarded to strip away profits that were obtained from any civil wrongdoing. Disgorgement is available for all equitable wrongs, including breach of fiduciary duty and breach of confidence. See for example *Canadian Aero Service Ltd. v. O'Malley* (1973), 40 D.L.R. (3d) 371 (S.C.C.); *Cadbury Schweppes Inc. v. FBI Foods Ltd.* (1999), 167 D.L.R. (4th) 577 (S.C.C.); *XY, LLC v. Canadian Topsires Selection Inc.*, 2016 BCSC 1095; and *Moores v. Fish, Food and Allied Workers Union*, 2017 NLCA 38. Disgorgement damages have also been awarded for "exceptional" breaches of contract: *Attorney General v. Blake*, [2001] 1 A.C. 268 (H.L.); and *Indutech Canada Ltd. v. Gibbs Pipe Distributors Ltd.*, 2011 ABQB 38 at para. 507, aff'd 2013 ABCA 111.

PENARTH DOCK ENGINEERING CO. LTD. v. POUNDS
[1963] 1 Lloyds' Rep. 359 (Q.B.)

[The plaintiff sold a floating pontoon to the defendant. The defendant agreed to remove the pontoon from the premises that the plaintiff rented from the British Transport Commission by August 9, 1962. However, the defendant did not remove the pontoon until March 25, 1963, and thus committed a trespass to the plaintiff's land. The evidence at trial indicated that the plaintiff suffered no loss as a result of the tort. Accordingly, the plaintiff sought disgorgement of the defendant's gain rather than compensation for its own loss.]

LORD DENNING M.R.: . . . The question which remains is, what are the damages? True it is that the Penarth company themselves would not seem to have suffered any damage to speak of. They have not to pay any extra rent to the British Transport Commission. The dock is no use to them; they would not have made any money out of it. But, nevertheless, in a case of this kind, as I read the law, starting with *Whitwham v. Westminster Brymbo Coal and Coke Company*, [1896] 2 Ch. 538, on which I commented myself in the case of *Strand Electric and Engineering Company, Ltd. v. Brisford Entertainments Ltd.*, [1952] 2 Q.B. 246, at pp. 253 to 254, the test of the measure of damages is not what the plaintiffs have lost, but what benefit the defendant obtained by having the use of the berth; and he has been a trespasser, in my judgment, since Aug. 9, 1962. What benefit has the defendant obtained by having the use of it for this time? If he had moved it elsewhere, he would have had to pay [rent] for a berth for a dock of this kind. . . . [The] damages are to be assessed in accordance with the law as I have stated it at the rate of £32 5s. a week for a period commencing from Aug. 9, 1962, which I would let run to Mar. 25, 1963, because the dock has now been removed. I do not know what that sum will come to, but that can be a matter of calculation.

NOTES AND QUESTIONS

1. As in *Edwards* and *Penarth*, should plaintiffs in tort actions be permitted to claim disgorgement damages even when this results in a windfall?

2. It is difficult to find cases in which the courts have clearly awarded disgorgement damages. This stems from the fact that lawyers seldom recognize the possibility of claiming disgorgement and the fact that a single award may be described as constituting either compensatory or disgorgement damages. For example, *Strand Electric and Engineering Co. Ltd. v. Brisford Entertainments Ltd.*, [1952] 2 Q.B. 246 (C.A.) is frequently cited as a disgorgement case. The defendant company failed to return the plaintiff's electrical equipment after the rental agreement expired, thereby incurring liability in the tort of detinue. Denning L.J. held the defendant liable for the amount that it gained by not returning the equipment. On that view, the remedy was disgorgement. The other two members of the court awarded the same amount, but did so on the basis that the plaintiff had lost a rental fee when the defendant kept its equipment without payment. On that view, the relief was compensatory.

Similarly, in Sharpe & Waddams, "Damages for Lost Opportunity to Bargain" (1982) 2 O.J.L.S. 290, the authors argue that *Penarth* can be explained in a manner that is entirely consistent with the compensatory theory of damages. They suggest that the plaintiff suffered a real loss, namely the opportunity to rent the dock to the defendant. Do you agree that the plaintiff in *Penarth* suffered a compensable loss? See also McInnes, "Account of Profits for Common Law Wrongs" in Degeling & Edelman, eds., *Equity in Commercial Law* (2005) 405.

3. In *XY, LLC v. Canadian Topsires Selection Inc.*, 2016 BCSC 1095, the court upheld the plaintiff's claim for "disgorgement of profits on the basis of unjust enrichment," holding one group of defendants liable for almost $270 million based on

the profits that they made from wrongfully using the plaintiff's confidential information. Would it have been more accurate to characterize the plaintiff's claim as a breach of confidence action in which disgorgement damages were sought?

4. Disgorgement is the subject of misunderstanding on other grounds. First, such relief is often said to be "equitable." However, the historical basis of disgorgement lies primarily in the ancient common law writ of *indebitatus assumpsit*. See Baker, *An Introduction to English Legal History*, 4th ed. (2002) at 343-48. Second, Canadian courts continue to discuss disgorgement in terms of "waiver of tort." See for example *Koubi v. Mazda Canada Inc.*, 2012 BCCA 310; and *Wakelam v. Johnson & Johnson*, 2014 BCCA 36. The phrase "waiver of tort" is misleading because the plaintiff does not waive the tort in the sense of ignoring or excusing it. Rather, in some tort actions, the plaintiff may choose either compensatory damages for his or her wrongfully inflicted loss or disgorgement damages based on the defendant's wrongful gain. See Birks, "The Law of Restitution at the End of an Epoch" (1999) 28 U.W.A.L. Rev. 13 at 49-54.

5. A single incident may support more than one cause of action, and a single cause of action may support more than one measure of relief. Assume that: (i) John committed the tort of deceit by tricking Mary into paying him $20,000; (ii) a third party, who hated Mary, paid John $10,000 to defraud Mary; and (iii) the fraud resulted in Mary losing $5,000, in addition to the $20,000 that she gave to John. Assuming that Mary and John are the only parties before the court, what actions can Mary successfully bring and what damages can she claim?

REVIEW PROBLEM

What damages would be awarded in the following fact situations?

(a) The defendant strikes John and breaks his jaw. The defendant is a known bully with previous criminal convictions for assault. No criminal charge is pending in this case.

(b) The same bully strikes John and breaks his jaw at an office party, attended by John's wife, friends and fellow workers. The defendant ridicules John while administering the beating.

(c) The bully strikes John and breaks his jaw at the office party, but is unaware that John is in the company of family and friends. The defendant is silent throughout the incident and bears John no personal malice.

(d) The bully is hired for $5,000 to beat John. Compensatory damages, other than aggravated damages, are $2,000.

3

INTENTIONAL INTERFERENCE
WITH THE PERSON

1. Introduction
2. Basic Principles of Liability
3. Related Issues: Motive, Mistake and Accident
4. Battery
5. Assault
6. False Imprisonment
7. Malicious Prosecution
8. Intentional Infliction of Nervous Shock (Mental Distress, Psychiatric Harm)
9. Invasion of Privacy
10. Discrimination

1. Introduction

This chapter begins with the intentional torts that protect an individual's physical integrity. Most of these causes of action, namely battery, assault and false imprisonment, were derived from the writ of trespass *vi et armis*, and therefore were characterized by direct interference with the person. These actions have remained largely unchanged over the years. The chapter also considers malicious prosecution and the intentional infliction of nervous shock. These torts are also premised on the defendant's intention. However, in contrast to the traditional intentional torts, they are derived from the action on the case and therefore involve indirect interference with the person. Invasion of privacy and discrimination, the remaining intentional torts discussed in this chapter, focus on personal interests other than physical integrity. Although the Canadian courts have recognized a common law tort action for the invasion of privacy in specific categories of cases, the existence of a tort action for discrimination remains a matter of ongoing debate.

2. Basic Principles of Liability

Generally, a defendant can only be held liable for an intentional tort if his or her conduct is both voluntary and intentional. Before turning to the specific elements of the intentional torts, it is important to define these two concepts and to distinguish them from the related concepts of motive, mistake and accident. This task is complicated by the fact that many of these terms have a unique legal meaning.

(a) VOLITION

The first issue to address in an intentional tort action is whether the defendant's act that gave rise to the tort was voluntary. In general, a defendant's act is voluntary if it is directed by his or her conscious mind.

SMITH v. STONE
(1647), 82 E.R. 533 (K.B.)

Smith brought an action of trespasse against Stone . . . the defendant pleads this special plea in justification, viz. that he was carried upon the land of the plaintiff by force, and violence of others, and was not there voluntarily, which is the same trespasse, for which the plaintiff brings his action. The plaintiff demurs to this plea: in this case Roll Iustice said, that it is the trespasse of the party that carried the defendant upon the land, and not the trespasse of the defendant: as he that drives my cattel into another mans land is the trespassor against him, and not I who am owner of the cattell.

NOTES AND QUESTIONS

1. Would the defendant's act have been voluntary if (a) he had been chased onto the plaintiff's land by a swarm of bees, or (b) he had entered the plaintiff's land to prevent a child from drowning? Would an individual who instinctively grabs the arm of another person while falling have acted voluntarily?

2. In *Stokes v. Carlson*, 240 S.W.2d 132 (Mo. S.C. 1951), the judge defined involuntary actions to include reflex reactions, convulsive movements and movements during sleep and unconsciousness. Is a person who is acting in a state of automatism acting voluntarily? See *R. v. Fontaine*, [2004] 1 S.C.R. 702; *R. v. Courneyea*, 2013 CACM 3; *R. v. Alexander*, 2015 BCCA 484; and Smith, "Automatism — A Defence to Negligence?" (1980) 130 New L.J. 1111.

3. The issue of volition is seldom addressed in the case law. In intentional torts, this issue will most likely arise in relation to children and those with a mental illness. The most comprehensive discussion of volition is provided in negligence cases involving drivers who claim to have been rendered unconscious by sudden illness. See for example *Gootson v. R.*, [1948] D.L.R. 33 (S.C.C.) (epileptic seizure); *Dobbs v. Mayer* (1985), 32 C.C.L.T. 191 (Ont. Div. Ct.) (heart attack); *Fiala v. Cechmanek* (1999), 246 A.R. 120 (Q.B.), aff'd (2001), 281 A.R. 248 (C.A.) (manic episode); and *Codner v. Gosse* (2003), 227 Nfld. & P.E.I.R. 132 (N.L.S.C. (T.D.)) (blackout).

(b) INTENT

In tort law, the term "intent" is used to refer to an individual's desire to bring about the consequences of his or her act, rather than his or her desire to do the physical act itself. If the defendant fires at a crow but the bullet misses and hits a cow, the shooting of the cow is unintentional because the result was not desired. The fact that the defendant desired to pull the trigger is not relevant to the issue of intent to shoot the cow. A single act may bring about several consequences, only some of which may be intentional and only one of which may be relevant to the tort claim in question. For example, assume that Frank, believing that he is alone in a secluded forest, shoots at a tin can and hits it, but the bullet ricochets and strikes the plaintiff. The consequence of hitting the tin can is intentional because Frank desired the bullet to strike that object. However, if the plaintiff sues Frank for the intentional tort of battery, the relevant issue is whether Frank desired to cause an offensive or harmful physical contact with the plaintiff. Since the shooting of the plaintiff was unintentional, the intentional tort claim would fail.

The issue is whether the defendant desired to bring about the specific consequence that gave rise to the tort in question. The defendant's intent need not be hostile or otherwise blameworthy. For example, a defendant who, at great personal risk, saves a child's life by pushing the child out of the path of a car has the requisite intent for battery. The fact that the defendant had intent does not mean that he or she will be liable — intent is only one element of an intentional tort. One must then analyze the other elements of the action, as well as the defences.

However, the fact that the defendant did not desire to bring about the consequence giving rise to the tort may not always resolve the intent issue. As discussed below, the plaintiff may establish intent under the doctrines of imputed and transferred intent.

(i) *Imputed (Constructive) Intent*

The concept of intent also encompasses situations in which the defendant did not desire the consequences to occur, but they were certain or substantially certain to result from his or her act. Thus, a defendant who plants a powerful bomb in the outer office of his boss will likely be held liable to the nearby staff who are injured in the ensuing explosion. Although the defendant may not have wished to injure the staff, the intent to do so will be imputed to him or her if the injuries to the staff were certain or substantially certain to follow from planting the bomb.

(ii) *Transferred Intent*

The doctrine of transferred intent provides another basis for imposing liability on a defendant for the unintended consequences of his or her act. It is invoked when a defendant intends to commit an intentional tort against one party, but unintentionally commits an intentional tort against the plaintiff. The doctrine also applies if the defendant intends to commit one type of intentional tort against the plaintiff, but unintentionally commits another. In essence, the defendant's wrongful intent regarding the first tort is transferred to the second tort to permit recovery. Traditionally, transferred intent was restricted to directly caused injuries involving hurling, casting and shooting. It was also limited to the intentional torts derived from the writ of trespass *vi et armis*, namely battery, assault, false imprisonment, trespass to chattels, and trespass to land. The Canadian courts have not addressed whether these historical limits on the doctrine should be maintained.

NOTES AND QUESTIONS

1. What is the rationale for the doctrine of imputed intent? American authorities have defined imputed intent in terms of the actor's own belief in the certainty or substantial certainty of the consequences. See The American Law Institute, *Restatement Third, Torts: Liability for Physical and Emotional Harm* (2010) vol. 1 at §1 comment (c); and *Garratt v. Dailey*, 279 P.2d 1091 (Wash. S.C. 1955). What problems, if any, arise in adopting this subjective definition of imputed intent?

2. In *Bielitski v. Obadiak* (1922), 65 D.L.R. 627 (Sask. C.A.) and *Purdy v. Woznesensky*, [1937] 2 W.W.R. 116 (Sask. C.A.), the court applied an extremely broad test of imputed intent, based in part on the criminal law presumption that individuals intend the natural and probable consequences of their acts. What is the practical effect of this presumption? For a critique of the presumption in intentional torts, see Atrens, "Intentional Interference with the Person" in Linden, ed., *Studies in Canadian Tort Law* (1968) 378 at 381-82. But see Epstein, "Intentional Harm" (1975) 4 J. Legal Stud. 391.

In *Rhodes v. OPO*, [2015] UKSC 32, the court stated at para. 81 that imputing intent based on a rule of law (*i.e.* individuals are presumed to intend the natural and probable consequences of their acts) "is a vestige of a previous age and has no proper role in the modern law of tort." While the court rejected imputing intent as a matter of law, it approved of "inferring" intent based on the facts. Would the court agree with "inferring" intent when the consequences giving rise to the tort were certain or substantially certain to result from the defendant's act?

3. What is the rationale for the doctrine of transferred intent? Historical factors aside, should it still be limited to torts derived from trespass *vi et armis* and situations involving hurling, casting and shooting? See Prosser, "Transferred Intent" (1967) 45 Tex. L. Rev. 650; and Reynolds, "Transferred Intent: Should Its 'Curious Survival' Continue?" (1997) 50 Okla. L. Rev. 529.

4. In *Bici v. Ministry of Defence*, [2004] EWHC 786 (Q.B.), the court transferred the defendants' intent to commit a battery against Farhi Bici, the deceased, to the battery that they unintentionally committed in shooting Mohammed Bici. However, the court rejected Skender Bici's assault claim based on transferred intent because the defendants did not intend to commit an assault against Farhi Bici.

One author criticized *Bici*, arguing that the doctrine of transferred intent should have no place whatsoever in the law of torts: Beever, "Transferred malice in tort law?" (2009) 29 L.S. 400. Another author stated that intent can be transferred within trespasses to the person (*i.e.* battery, assault and false imprisonment) and within trespasses to property (*i.e.* trespass to land or trespass to chattels). However, the author argued that intent should not be transferred between these two categories of trespass because the intent to interfere with a person is fundamentally different from the intent to interfere with property: Kutner, "The Prosser Myth of Transferred Intent" (2016) 91 Ind. L.J. 1105.

Would you favour abolishing the doctrine of transferred intent in intentional torts? If not, should the types of intentional torts to which the doctrine applies be limited?

5. Give an example in which: (a) both transferred and imputed intent would apply; (b) only transferred intent would apply; and (c) only imputed intent would apply. See *Scott v. Shepherd* (1773), 96 E.R. 525 (K.B.), an extract of which appears in Chapter 1.

6. For a discussion of intent and its role in intentional torts, see Oliphant, "The Structure of the Intentional Torts" in Neyers, Chamberlain & Pitel, eds., *Emerging Issues in Tort Law* (2007) 509; and Simons & Cardi, "Restating the Intentional Torts to Persons: Seeing the Forest and the Trees" (2018) 10 J. Tort Law 343.

3. Related Issues: Motive, Mistake and Accident

(a) MOTIVE

The concept of intent refers to the actor's desire to bring about a particular consequence, not his or her motive or reason for wanting that result to occur. A friend who moves your car to prevent it from being impounded, a practical joker who moves it on April Fools' Day, and a thief who steals it all have the intent to commit trespass to chattels, but their motives obviously differ. The plaintiff must prove that the defendant's conduct was intentional, but does not have to establish that the defendant's motive was blameworthy. Unlike intent, motive is generally not an element of the cause of action. Thus, in the example above, all three defendants have committed the tort of trespass to chattels, even though their motives ranged from altruism to greed. The concept of motive is extremely broad, encompassing the full range of factors that induce human behaviour. The following discussions of duress and provocation should be viewed as illustrations of the courts' response to motive.

NOTES

1. Motive is an element of some of the intentional torts derived from the writ of trespass on the case. For example, in order to establish the tort of malicious prosecution, the plaintiff must prove, among other things, that the defendant acted maliciously or for some other improper purpose.

2. A praiseworthy motive is not a defence *per se*, although it may be an element of a valid defence. For example, to invoke the defence of public necessity, a defendant must establish that he or she was acting to protect the public interest from an impending harm.

3. As indicated in Chapter 2, there are several ways in which the parties' motives may be taken into account in assessing damages. The defendant's highly blameworthy motive may provide grounds for awarding aggravated or punitive damages. It may also influence the size of the general damage award, because the trier of fact has considerable discretion in setting this figure. In some provinces, the fact that the plaintiff provoked the defendant may reduce the size of the compensatory damage award that the plaintiff would have otherwise received. Similarly, the court may express its disapproval of a vexatious plaintiff by awarding only contemptuous damages.

(i) *Duress*

GILBERT v. STONE
(1648), 82 E.R. 539 (K.B.)

Demurrer upon a plea in trespasse. Gilbert brought an action of trespasse quare clausum fregit [trespass to land], and taking of a gelding, against Stone. The defendant pleads that he for fear of his life, and wounding of twelve armed men, who threatened to kill him if he did not the fact [sic], went into the house of the plaintiff, and took the gelding. The plaintiff demurred to this plea; Roll Iustice, This is no plea to justifie the defendant; for I may not do a trespasse to one for fear of threatnings of another, for by this means the party injured shall have no satisfaction, for he cannot have it of the party that threatned. Therefore let the plaintiff have his judgement.

NOTES AND QUESTIONS

1. Analyze the issues of volition, intent and motive in *Gilbert*. Distinguish this case from *Smith v. Stone*, an excerpt from which appears at the beginning of this chapter. Is the defendant's conduct in *Gilbert* any more morally blameworthy than that in *Smith*? Can you suggest another rationale for the different results in these two cases?

2. The fact that the defendant acted under duress will not negate his or her volition or intent, nor serve as a defence. However, as will be discussed in Chapter 6, duress may negate the plaintiff's consent and thereby prevent the defendant from relying on this defence. Duress is also a factor that the courts may consider in assessing damages. It has been suggested that duress should be recognized as a defence, in keeping with the principle of no liability without fault: Howarth, "Defences to Intentional Torts" in Sappideen & Vines, eds., *Fleming's The Law of Torts*, 10th ed. (2011) 87 at 112-13. Outline the competing interests at stake in resolving this issue.

3. Although Stone has no defence in reference to Gilbert, he would have a valid claim in assault against the armed men. As well, the conduct of the armed men would now give rise to an action for intimidation. In *Rookes v. Barnard*, [1964] A.C. 1129 (H.L.), the court defined intimidation as coercing a person, by unlawful threats, into doing something or refraining from doing something that he or she has a right to do.

4. Is it appropriate that compulsion (duress) is a defence in criminal law, but not tort law? Under s. 17 of the *Criminal Code*, R.S.C. 1985, c. C-46, the defence of compulsion is limited to threats of immediate physical injury. Moreover, the defence cannot be raised by an accused charged with treason, murder or other serious crimes of violence. It should be noted that the Supreme Court of Canada struck down the requirement in s. 17 that the accused be subject to an immediate threat by a person who was present because those limits violated s. 7 of the *Canadian Charter of Rights and Freedoms*, Part I of the *Constitution Act, 1982*, being Schedule B to the *Canada Act 1982* (U.K.), 1982, c. 11: *R. v. Ruzic*, [2001] 1 S.C.R. 687.

5. If duress were recognized as a defence in intentional torts, how would you define it? Should the defence be unavailable, as in s. 17 of the *Criminal Code*, if the defendant causes serious physical harm? Should the defendant be able to raise the defence when threatened with: (a) immediate and serious physical harm; (b) the destruction of his or her home; (c) being the victim of any federal criminal offence; or (d) being the victim of any illegal act?

(ii) *Provocation*

MISKA v. SIVEC
(1959), 18 D.L.R. (2d) 363 (Ont. C.A.)

[Miska sued for injuries that he sustained when Sivec intentionally shot him. Sivec claimed that he was acting in self-defence. Sivec testified that: Miska had cut him off and blocked his car on the road; Miska emerged from the car and threatened him with a knife and an iron bar; he fled 200 yards to his own house with Miska in hot pursuit; when he reached his house, he retrieved his shotgun and fired two warning shots; and Miska was injured after he moved into the line of fire. Miska denied that version of events. There was evidence of previous bad blood between the parties.

The jury found in Miska's favour and Sivec appealed. Sivec argued that the trial judge had misdirected the jury on the burden of proof in self-defence and had failed to instruct the jury to take provocation into account when assessing the damages.]

MORDEN J.A.: [delivering the judgment of the court]
. . . In my opinion, Wells J. properly directed the jury on the burden of proof, and the first ground of appeal fails.

The defendant's second ground of appeal was that the learned trial Judge failed and when requested by counsel for the defendant refused to charge the jury on the effect of provocation in mitigation of damages. There is no doubt that where there is evidence of provocation the jury should be instructed to consider it in assessing damages for assault. In this connection, Mr. Goodman submitted that the bad feeling and other incidents between the parties, going back over a period of eight or nine months, should be considered evidence of provocation.

The conduct of the plaintiff to be capable of being considered provocation must have been such as to cause the defendant to lose his power of self-control and must have occurred at the time of or shortly before the assault. In *Fraser v. Berkeley* (1836), 7 Car. & P. 621, three days after the plaintiff published a libel on the defendant and his family, the defendant beat the plaintiff with a heavy whip and his fists and in the action for damages for assault evidence of this libel was given. Lord Abinger C.B. in charging the jury said at p. 624: "The law I think would be an unwise law, if it did not make allowance for human infirmities; and if a person commit violence at a time when he is smarting under immediate provocation, that is a matter of mitigation."

. . .

In deciding in this case whether there was evidence of provocation, incidents occurring between the parties prior to the night of the assault are not to be considered. They were not immediate and by the night in question, if available at all to the defendant, could only be available to show provocation if it were asserted that the effect of the immediate provocative acts upon the defendant's mind was enhanced by those previous incidents being recalled to him and thereby inflaming his passion. There is no such evidence directly or by way of inference to be drawn from the defendant's testimony. A careful perusal of the defendant's evidence of the occurrences on the fateful evening does not disclose any insulting or abusive conduct or language on the part of the plaintiff, nor any sudden passion, lack of self-control or even any annoyance on the defendant's part. His evidence was that the plaintiff had blocked his car and approached him armed with an iron bar and a knife.

The defendant then beat a successful retreat back to his house which was about 200 yards away. After he entered the house his wife locked the door and he loaded his shotgun and went upstairs. At this point his wife went to the telephone to notify the police. The defendant took up his position at an open window on the second story from which he fired without any warning at the plaintiff. He did not say that at that time he was annoyed or provoked. His conduct was careful and deliberate and belied the existence of any sudden and uncontrolled passion. In my opinion, there was no evidence of provocation to be left to the jury and the learned trial Judge was correct in refusing to do so.

On both grounds the appeal fails and must be dismissed with costs.

NOTES AND QUESTIONS

1. How did Morden J.A. define provocation? Do you find his application of this definition to the facts convincing? Why did Morden J.A. not consider the previous incidents between the parties as evidence of provocation?

2. In *Miska*, the court appears to use a subjective test that focuses on whether the defendant lost his or her power of self-control. Nevertheless, the test is usually phrased objectively, in terms of whether the plaintiff's conduct caused the defendant, as a reasonable person, to lose his or her power of self-control. Should the defendant's claim of provocation be denied if his or her loss of self-control was reasonable, but the retaliatory behaviour was out of proportion to the plaintiff's provocative behaviour?

3. The courts generally confine provocation to situations in which the provocative act occurs at the time of, or immediately before, the alleged tort. In *Miska*, the court noted that prior incidents between the parties can be considered if they trigger or enhance the defendant's loss of self-control stemming from the immediate provocative act. See *Ellone v. Mesa*, 1997 CarswellOnt 1938 (Gen. Div.) (WL Can).

4. Research indicates that sudden outbursts of rude, threatening and violent behaviour are not uncommon on Canadian roads. A 2003 study of Ontario drivers found that almost half had been cursed, shouted at or subjected to rude gestures in the past year, and that 7.2% were threatened with personal injury or damage to their vehicles: Smart *et al.*, "Road Rage Experience and Behaviour: Vehicle, Exposure, and Driver Factors" (2004) 5 Traffic Injury Prevention 343. Should the poor or discourteous driving of another motorist ever be viewed as a sufficient basis for establishing provocation? See *Herman v. Graves* (1998), 217 A.R. 275 (Q.B.).

5. Initially, the Canadian courts considered provocation a factor that could reduce compensatory damages, and preclude or reduce punitive damages. However, in *Shaw v. Gorter* (1977), 77 D.L.R. (3d) 50 (Ont. C.A.), the court held that provocation was only relevant in regard to punitive damages. In reaching this decision, the court erroneously stated that there were no Canadian cases directly on point. *Shaw* was followed with considerable reservations in *Landry v. Patterson* (1978), 93 D.L.R. (3d) 345 (Ont. C.A.), which indicated that the Supreme Court of Canada should resolve the issue. This has not occurred and *Shaw* continues to be followed in Ontario: *Ellis v. Fallios-Guthierrez*, 2012 ONSC 1670. What legal and policy arguments would you make if *Landry* had been appealed to the Supreme Court?

6. In most other provinces, provocation continues to be a factor that may be taken into account to reduce compensatory damages. See for example *Nichol v. MacKay* (1999), 180 N.S.R. (2d) 76 (C.A.); *Hurley v. Moore* (1993), 112 Nfld. & P.E.I.R. 40 (Nfld. C.A.); *Defosse v. Wilde*, [1999] 4 W.W.R. 205 (Sask. Q.B.); *Bruce v. Coliseum Management Ltd.* (1998), 165 D.L.R. (4th) 472 (B.C.C.A.); *Wilson v. Bobbie* (2006), 394 A.R. 118 (Q.B.); and *McIntyre v. MacKnight*, 2017 NBQB 24.

7. Consistent with other Ontario cases, the court in *Ellis, supra* stated that while provocation could not reduce compensatory damages, it could preclude or reduce both aggravated and punitive damages. Is it appropriate for provocation to be considered in assessing aggravated damages but not compensatory damages?

8. It has been argued that a plaintiff's provocative act may constitute contributory negligence and thus give rise to apportionment of damages under the provincial negligence acts. If this argument is accepted, the plaintiff's compensatory and other damages would be reduced by a specified percentage to reflect his or her contributory negligence. See generally *Long v. Gardner* (1983), 144 D.L.R. (3d) 73 (Ont. H.C.); and *Rumsey v. R.*, [1984] 5 W.W.R. 585 (F.C.T.D.).

9. Unlike duress, provocation is not a defence in criminal law. Rather, under s. 232(1) of the *Criminal Code*, provocation may result in reducing a murder charge to manslaughter. However, s. 232(2) strictly defines provocation, requiring that the victim's conduct must have, among other things, constituted an indictable offence.

(b) MISTAKE

In tort law, a mistake occurs when defendants intend the consequences of their acts, but those consequences have a different factual or legal significance than that contemplated. Since mistake, by definition, has no effect on the issue of intent, it is not relevant in establishing the elements of a cause of action. Moreover, neither a mistake of fact nor a mistake of law is recognized *per se* as a defence to intentional tort liability.

HODGKINSON v. MARTIN
[1929] 1 D.L.R. 367 (B.C.C.A.)

MARTIN J.A.: This is an action for trespass to the person and in view of certain unusual incidents I have carefully read the whole appeal book in addition to those portions cited by counsel with the result that it was, in my opinion, open to the Judge below, upon the sharply conflicting evidence to take the view that the defendant, being the deputy minister of industries and industrial commissioner, laid his hands upon the plaintiff and wrongfully put him out of the office premises in question without using any more force than was necessary to effect that object, and that the act was unlawful and therefore a trespass, and that it was done in the sincerely mistaken belief that the defendant was justified in the protection of the interests of the Crown in doing so in order to retain access to the premises which had been in his possession through his servants for 10 days beforehand, and also that his intention in preserving such right of access was not to exclude the custodian in bankruptcy from the premises but to insure their common access thereto.

. . .

It then becomes a question of the amount of damages to be awarded, upon said facts and the appellant submits that the sum of $500 assessed below is excessive and can only be supported on the basis of exemplary damages which are foreign to the case. This, in my opinion, is the proper view to take of the matter which has been made too much of because while the sincere yet mistaken belief of the defendant in the propriety of his illegal action is no excuse therefor yet it is a mitigation of his liability which must be taken into consideration where not the slightest injury has been occasioned to the plaintiff's person, clothing or reputation. It is truly said in that high authority, Salmond on the Law of Torts, 7th ed., p. 145, that: — "Exemplary damages . . . are given only in cases of conscious wrongdoing in contumelious disregard of another's rights." See Clerk & Lindsell on Torts, 7th ed., p. 140.

It is with reluctance that I feel compelled to interfere in the assessment of damages but having no doubt that nominal damages will amply compensate the plaintiff for the trespass it is my duty to give effect to my opinion by awarding the sum of $10 . . .

RANSON v. KITNER
31 Ill.App. 241 (1889)

CONGER J.: This was an action brought by appellee against appellants to recover the value of a dog killed by appellants, and a judgment rendered for $50.

The defense was that appellants were hunting for wolves, that appellee's dog had a striking resemblance to a wolf, that they in good faith believed it to be one, and killed it as such.

Many points are made, and a lengthy argument filed to show that error in the trial below was committed, but we are inclined to think that no material error occurred to the prejudice of appellants.

The jury held them liable for the value of the dog, and we do not see how they could have done otherwise under the evidence. Appellants are clearly liable for the damages caused by their mistake, notwithstanding they were acting in good faith.

We see no reason for interfering with the conclusion reached by the jury, and the judgment will be affirmed.

NOTES AND QUESTIONS

1. Are *Hodgkinson* and *Ranson* cases of mistake of fact or mistake of law? Can you suggest another example of each type of mistake?

2. What legal impact did the defendant's mistake have in *Hodgkinson* and *Ranson*? What did the judge mean in *Hodgkinson* when he said that the defendant's sincere but mistaken belief "is a mitigation of his liability"? Do you agree with the judge's use of the term "nominal damages" in *Hodgkinson*?

3. Would an individual be liable in intentional torts if he or she shot at a wolf, but the bullet ricocheted and hit a neighbour's dog? Compare this situation to that in *Ranson*.

4. What arguments would you make for recognizing a general defence of mistake? Would your answer depend on whether it was a mistake of law or fact?

5. The impact of a mistake of fact on the validity of the defences varies. Thus, a defendant who strikes the plaintiff in a reasonable but mistaken belief that the latter is about to attack him or her may successfully plead self-defence. See *Keep v. Quallman*, 32 N.W. 233 (Wisc. S.C. 1887).

In contrast, a defendant's honest but mistaken belief that the plaintiff consented provides no defence in tort law if the plaintiff did not in fact consent. See for example *Toews (Guardian ad litem of) v. Weisner* (2001), 3 C.C.L.T. (3d) 293 (B.C.S.C.); and *Cochran v. Hunter*, 2004 BCSC 1263. For a general discussion of why mistake invalidates some defences but not others, see Keeton *et al.*, *Prosser and Keeton on the Law of Torts*, 5th ed. (1984) at 110-12.

(c) ACCIDENT

In early English common law, accident was limited to cases in which the defendant could prove that the tort occurred utterly without fault on his or her part. As the principle of no liability without fault became increasingly entrenched in intentional torts, the definition of accident was broadened. The term "accident" is now used to refer to any situation in which the defendant unintentionally and without negligence injured the plaintiff. By definition, a defendant cannot be held liable in intentional torts or negligence for injuries caused by accident. It is the absence of intent that distinguishes accident from mistake.

REVIEW PROBLEMS

Analyze Mary's conduct in the following situations:

1. John shouted insults at Mary through an open window. In response, Mary threw a rock at John but missed, smashing a neighbour's window. The neighbour sues Mary.

2. Fred insulted Mary for several days. Later that week, Mary spotted Fred standing at the window and threw a rock at him. Unknown to Mary, Fred's window was closed. The rock broke the window, but missed Fred. Fred sues Mary for the broken window.

3. Mary attempted to get Bill's attention by gently throwing a few small pebbles at his window. Unfortunately, one of the pebbles cracked the window. Bill sues Mary for the cracked window.

4. As Mary was leaving work, she picked up what she thought was her wallet. In fact, it belonged to Ralph. On her way home, Mary was grabbed by a thief armed with a gun, who ordered Mary to hand over her wallet. Mary turned over Ralph's wallet, believing it to be her own. Analyze Mary's conduct: (a) when she initially picked up Ralph's wallet; and (b) when she handed it to the thief.

(d) THE LIABILITY OF CHILDREN AND THOSE WITH A MENTAL ILLNESS

Rather than applying the accepted tests of volition and intent in intentional torts cases involving children and those with a mental illness, the Canadian courts have tended to rely on the first part of the defence of mental disorder in s. 16(1) of the *Criminal Code* (referred to as the defence of insanity prior to 1992). Thus, the issue is often framed in terms of whether the defendant was capable of "appreciating the nature and quality" of his or her act. The courts have not explained why they have adopted this test or how it relates to volition and intent.

Parents and teachers are not vicariously liable at common law for the torts committed by children under their care. Rather, those supervising children can only be held liable if they are a party to a child's wrongful conduct or they negligently fail to monitor or control the child. Although several provinces have enacted "parental responsibility" statutes, the legislation limits the liability of parents to situations in which they have been negligent in supervising their children.

Similarly, individuals who are treating or supervising patients with a mental illness are not held vicariously liable for their patients' conduct. Under both the common law and the mental health statutes, doctors, nurses and other staff can only be held liable if they are a party to the patient's wrongful act or if they are negligent in treating, supervising or releasing the patient.

NOTES AND QUESTIONS

1. In *Tillander v. Gosselin*, [1967] 1 O.R. 203 (H.C.), aff'd (1967), 61 D.L.R. (2d) 192 (Ont. C.A.), the court held that a child just under the age of three could not be held liable in battery because he did not have "the mental ability to appreciate or know the real nature of the act he was performing." The defendant child had pulled an infant out of her carriage and dragged her 100 feet. Would the result have been the same if the standard tests of volition and intent had been applied? Is the test used in *Tillander* easier to apply than the standard tests? The child was also absolved of liability in negligence because he lacked sufficient judgment to exercise reasonable care. See also *Marshall (Litigation Guardian of) v. Annapolis (County) District School Board*, 2011 NSCA 13, rev'd on other grounds, 2012 SCC 27, which dealt with whether the four-year-old plaintiff could be held to have been contributorily negligent.

2. Section 13 of the *Criminal Code* provides that no child under 12 can be convicted of a criminal offence. Would you favour a statutory provision to govern a child's liability in tort? If so, what is an appropriate age threshold? If not, what is the justification for adopting different principles for criminal and tortious liability?

3. While the Ontario, Manitoba and British Columbia parental responsibility statutes impose the burden on parents to prove that they have acted reasonably in supervising their children, the legislation is otherwise far narrower in scope than the common law. Liability is limited to property damage that the child has intentionally caused, and damages cannot exceed $25,000 in Ontario and $10,000 in Manitoba and British Columbia. See *Parental Responsibility Act, 2000*, S.O. 2000, c. 4; *The Parental Responsibility Act*, C.C.S.M. c. P8; and *Parental Responsibility Act*, S.B.C. 2001, c. 45.

This legislation has considerable political appeal, and several other provinces have contemplated introducing such statutes. What are the arguments for and against such legislation? See Adjin-Tetty, "Significance and Consequences of Parental Responsibility Legislation" in Beauluc, Pitel & Schulz, eds., *The Joy of Torts* (2003) 221.

4. Some large retail chain stores send letters to the parents of children who have been caught shoplifting. The letters typically inform the parents that they are legally responsible for the child's conduct and offer to settle the matter if the parents pay several hundred dollars to cover the store's alleged costs. Is there any common law or statutory basis for the claim that the parents are civilly liable for these costs? See generally *B.(D.C.) v. Arkin*, [1996] 8 W.W.R. 100 (Man. Q.B.).

5. Although the parental responsibility statutes do not impose vicarious liability on parents, some of the education statutes do. For example in *Coquitlam School District No. 43 v. Clement* (1999), 170 D.L.R. (4th) 107 (B.C.C.A.), the parents of a pupil were held liable under s. 10 of the *School Act*, S.B.C. 1989, c. 61 for $3 million in damages resulting from the fire that their son had intentionally started. See also *Nanaimo-Ladysmith School District No. 68 v. Dean (Litigation guardian of)*, 2015 BCSC 11. In reference to Newfoundland and Labrador, see *Schools Act, 1997*, SNL 1997, c. S-12.2, s. 21; and *Labrador School Board v. R.P.* (2003), 229 Nfld. & P.E.I.R. 105 (N.L.S.C. (T.D.)).

6. The defendant in *Squittieri v. De Santis* (1976), 15 O.R. (2d) 416 (H.C.) was found not guilty by reason of insanity at his criminal trial. Although he appreciated the nature and quality of his act in stabbing Squittieri, he did not know that it was wrong. In holding the defendant liable in battery, the court stated that the issue in a civil action is whether the defendant was capable of understanding the nature and quality of his or her actions. Does this test relate to volition, intent or both issues? Why is knowing that your conduct is wrong relevant in criminal law, but not tort law? See also *Whaley v. Cartusiano* (1987), 72 O.R. (2d) 523 (H.C.J.), aff'd (1990), 72 O.R. (2d) 523 (C.A.).

7. For a discussion of the liability of psychiatrists, nurses and others in supervising and treating psychiatric patients, see *Lawson v. Wellesley Hospital* (1975), 61 D.L.R. (3d) 445 (Ont. C.A.), aff'd on other grounds [1978] 1 S.C.R. 893; *Mustafic v. Smith* (1988), 55 Man. R. (2d) 188 (C.A.); *Ahmed v. Stefaniu* (2006), 216 O.A.C. 323 (C.A.); *Paur (Committee of) v. Providence Health Care*, 2017 BCCA 161; *Briante (Litigation guardian of) v. Vancouver Island Health Authority*, 2017 BCCA 148; and *Barker v. Barker*, 2017 ONSC 3397, varied 2018 ONCA 255.

4. Battery

The tort of battery may be defined as the direct and intentional bringing about of a physically harmful or socially offensive physical contact with the person of another. While the defendant must have intent to bring about a physical contact, he or she need not have the intent to harm or offend the plaintiff. Aside from commonly accepted practices, such as gently tapping a person on the shoulder to get his or her attention, any direct and intentional physical contact may give rise to battery. Thus, the tort prohibits a broad range of physical interferences with the person, including for example: spitting in someone's face (*Alcorn v. Mitchell*, 63 Ill. 553 (S.C. 1872)); pouring water on someone (*Pursell v. Horn* (1838), 112 E.R. 966 (K.B.)); and cutting someone's hair (*Forde v. Skinner* (1830), 172 E.R. 687 (N.P.)). A defendant may also be held liable in battery for direct and intentional physical interferences with anything that the plaintiff is carrying, wearing or riding on: *Morgan v. Loyacomo*, 1 So.2d 510 (Miss. S.C. 1941).

A plaintiff may recover in battery even if he or she has suffered no physical harm or injury. Indeed, in *Malette v. Shulman* (1990), 72 O.R. (2d) 417 (C.A.), a doctor was held liable for $20,000 in battery for administering blood transfusions to the plaintiff, a Jehovah's Witness, who otherwise would likely have died. A plaintiff need not be aware of the physical contact when it occurred to recover. Thus, a woman kissed in her sleep would have a battery claim against her assailant. In Canada, the plaintiff is not required to prove that he or she did not consent, as the absence of consent is not an element of the tort of battery. Rather, consent is an affirmative defence that the defendant must assert and prove.

NOTES AND QUESTIONS

1. Should commonly accepted practices be excused because they do not involve socially offensive conduct or because they are justified by implied consent? Is there any meaningful difference between these two approaches? See *Coward v. Baddeley* (1859), 157 E.R. 927 (Ex. Div.); and *Donnelly v. Jackman*, [1970] 1 All E.R. 987 (Q.B.). See also *Wilson v. Pringle*, [1987] Q.B. 237 (C.A.), in which the court indicated that ordinary school horseplay might constitute an accepted social practice.

Should the perspective of the plaintiff, defendant or society be adopted in defining what constitutes an accepted social practice? Would the practice of a hostess who greeted guests at her party with a kiss subject her to liability in battery? How would you analyze a case in which a woman interpreted a male associate's affectionate greeting as a sexual assault and struck him, claiming that she was acting in self-defence? See *Cachay v. Nemeth* (1972), 28 D.L.R. (3d) 603 (Sask. Q.B.).

2. Damage awards in battery reflect societal concerns with protecting dignity. Consequently, a plaintiff who is slapped in the face or touched in a sexually inappropriate manner will likely receive a far larger damage award than a plaintiff who suffered greater physical pain and injury when punched in the arm by a friend in horseplay.

In *Ashley v. Chief Constable of Sussex Police*, [2008] 1 A.C. 962 (H.L.), the battery claim was allowed to proceed even though the police admitted liability in negligence in killing the deceased. The court reasoned that the battery action could serve a legitimate vindicatory purpose despite having no effect on the damage award.

BETTEL v. YIM
(1978), 88 D.L.R. (3d) 543 (Ont. Co. Ct.)

BORINS CO. CT. J.: In this action the infant plaintiff, Howard Bettel, seeks damages for assault. His father, Murray Bettel, seeks special damages in the amount of $1,113. . . .

The facts

The events giving rise to this action took place on May 22, 1976, in a variety store owned and operated by the defendant, Ki Yim, situated in a small commercial plaza located in Metropolitan Toronto.

. . .

The defendant testified that the plaintiff, together with six or seven other boys, entered the store and went to the area of the pin-ball machines. Some of the boys were playing with a toy football and toy guns and the defendant told them to leave his store. Half of the boys, including the plaintiff, left and went outside. The defendant saw the plaintiff lighting matches and throwing them into the store. On the first occasion the plaintiff entered the store and retrieved a burning match. The second match that was thrown into the store burned itself out. Then the plaintiff re-entered the store, proceeded toward the pin-ball machines and said "What's the smell?" The defendant smelled nothing, but after 20 or 30 seconds he saw flames coming from the bag of charcoal and proceeded to remove the bag from the store unassisted by the plaintiff who remained inside. The defendant did not see [who had] thrown the match which started the fire.

As the defendant returned to the store he saw the plaintiff walking toward the door. He grabbed the plaintiff by the arm as he did not want the plaintiff to leave. The plaintiff denied that he set the fire. The plaintiff did not try to leave. He stood where he was. Because the plaintiff denied setting the fire the defendant grabbed him firmly by the collar with both hands and began shaking him. His purpose in doing so was to obtain a confession from the plaintiff before he called the police. The plaintiff's constant denials had made the defendant unhappy. He shook the plaintiff two or three times and then his head came down and struck the plaintiff's nose. He relaxed his hold on the plaintiff who fell to the ground. The defendant obtained some kleenex for the plaintiff, who was bleeding from the nose, and helped him to his feet. The defendant then telephoned the police.

In explaining the incident the defendant said: "I shook him maybe three times and my head and his nose accidentally hit; I didn't intend to hit him." In cross-examination he stated that he did not mean to hit the plaintiff with his head and that is why he said it was an accident.

. . .

The law

The plaintiff has framed his action in assault. Properly speaking the action should have been framed in battery which is the intentional infliction upon the body of another of a harmful or offensive contact. However, in Canada it would appear that the distinction between assault and battery has been blurred and when one speaks of an assault, it may include a battery: *Gambriell v. Caparelli* (1974), 7 O.R. (2d) 205, 54 D.L.R. (3d) 661. It is on the basis that this is an action framed in battery that I approach the facts in this case.

It would appear to be well established in this country (although not necessarily warmly received), following the dictum of Cartwright, J. (as he then was), in *Cook v. Lewis*, [1951] S.C.R. 830 at p. 839, [1952] 1 D.L.R. 1 at p. 15, that once the plaintiff proves that he was injured by the direct act of the defendant, the defendant is entitled to judgment only "if he satisfies the onus of establishing the absence of both intention and negligence on his part": *Dahlberg v. Naydiuk* (1969), 10 D.L.R. (3d) 319, 72 W.W.R. 210 (Man. C.A.), *per* Dickson, J.A. (as he then was), at pp. 328-9. On the defendant's evidence, his act in grabbing the plaintiff with both his hands and shaking him constituted the intentional tort of battery. It is obvious that he desired to bring about an offensive or harmful contact with the plaintiff for the purpose of extracting a confession from him. Viewed as such, the defendant's own evidence proves, rather than disproves, the element of intent in so far as this aspect of his physical contact with the plaintiff is concerned. Indeed, the defendant's admitted purpose in grabbing and shaking the plaintiff does not fit into any of the accepted defences to the tort of battery — consent, self-defence, defence of property, necessity and legal authority: Fleming, *Law of Torts*, 5th ed. (1977), p. 74 *et seq.* . . .

That there is no liability for accidental harm is central to the submission of defence counsel who argues that the shaking of the plaintiff by the defendant and the striking of the plaintiff by the defendant's head must be regarded as separate and distinct incidents. While he concedes that the defendant intentionally grabbed and shook the plaintiff, he submits that the contact with the head was unintentional. I have, of course, accepted the defendant's evidence in this regard. This, in my view, gives rise to the important question: Can an intentional wrongdoer be held liable for consequences which he did not intend? Another way of stating the problem is to ask whether the doctrine of foreseeability as found in the law of negligence is applicable to the law of intentional torts? Should an intentional wrongdoer be liable only for the reasonably foreseeable consequences of his intentional application of force or should he bear responsibility for all the consequences which flow from his intentional act?

To approach this issue one must first examine what interests the law seeks to protect. A thorough discussion of the history of the old actions of trespass and case is found in Prosser, *Law of Torts*, 4th ed. (1971), p. 28 *et seq.* Terms such as battery, assault and false imprisonment, which were varieties of trespass, have come to be associated with intent. The old action on the case has emerged as the separate tort of negligence. Today it is recognized that there should be no liability for pure accident, and that for there to be liability the defendant must be found at fault, in the sense of being chargeable with a wrongful intent, or with negligence. Thus, "with rare exceptions, actions for injuries to the person, or to tangible property, now require proof of an intent to inflict them, or of failure to exercise proper care": Prosser, *supra*, p. 30.

In discussing battery Fleming writes, *supra*, pp. 23-4:

> Of the various forms of trespass to the person the most common is the tort known as battery, which is committed by intentionally bringing about a harmful or offensive contact with the person of another. The action, therefore, serves the dual purpose of affording protection to the individual not only against bodily harm but also against any interference with his person which is offensive to a reasonable sense of honour and dignity. The insult involved in being touched without consent has been traditionally regarded as sufficient to warrant redress, even though the interference is only trivial and not attended with actual physical harm. "The least touching of another in anger is a battery", and so is such offensive and insulting behaviour as spitting in another man's face, cutting his hair or kissing a woman. The element of personal indignity is given additional recognition in the award of aggravated damages to compensate for any outrage to the plaintiff's feelings . . .

. . .

Battery is an intentional wrong: the offensive contact must have been intended or known to be substantially certain to result. On the other hand, it is not necessary that the actor intended to inflict bodily harm, since we have seen that the legal injury is complete without it. Indeed it may be sufficient that he intended only to frighten but in a manner fraught with serious risk of bodily contact or harm. [Footnotes omitted]

. . .

It is my respectful view that the weight of opinion is that the concept of foreseeability as defined by the law of negligence is a concept that ought not to be imported into the field of intentional torts. While strong policy reasons favour determining the other limits of liability where conduct falls below an acceptable standard, the same reasons do not apply to deliberate conduct, even though the ultimate result in terms of harm caused to plaintiff is not what was intended by the defendant. In the law of intentional torts, it is the dignitary interest, the right of the plaintiff to insist that the defendant keep his hands to himself, that the law has for centuries sought to protect. In doing so, the morality of the defendant's conduct, characterized as "unlawful", has predominated the thinking of the Courts and is reflected in academic discussions. The logical test is whether the defendant was guilty of deliberate, intentional and unlawful violence or threats of violence. If he was, and a more serious harm befalls the plaintiff than was intended by the defendant, the defendant, and not the innocent plaintiff, must bear the responsibility for the unintended result. If physical contact was intended, the fact that its magnitude exceeded all reasonable or intended expectations should make no difference. To hold otherwise, in my opinion, would unduly narrow recovery where one deliberately invades the bodily interests of another with the result that the totally innocent plaintiff would be deprived of full recovery for the totality of the injuries suffered as a result of the deliberate invasion of his bodily interests. To import negligence concepts into the field of intentional torts would be to ignore the essential difference between the intentional infliction of harm and the unintentional infliction of harm resulting from a failure to adhere to a reasonable standard of care and would result in bonusing the deliberate wrongdoer who strikes the plaintiff more forcefully than intended. . . .

I have, therefore, reached the conclusion that the defendant must bear the responsibility for the injury suffered by the plaintiff. The defendant intentionally grabbed the plaintiff and shook him. This constituted a battery. While he was shaking the plaintiff, the defendant's head came into contact with the plaintiff's nose and injured it. This was the end result of a brief chain of events set in motion by the defendant. Subjectively, the defendant did not intend to strike the plaintiff's nose. Legally, because it was the result of the defendant's intentional interference with the plaintiff, responsibility for the injury which it caused must fall on the defendant.

NOTES AND QUESTIONS

1. How did Borins J. define battery? Identify the act of the defendant that gave rise to this tort. Why was the burden of disproving intent and negligence imposed on the defendant? Would the result have been the same if the burden of proving these issues had been on the plaintiff? See *Hatton v. Webb* (1977), 81 D.L.R. (3d) 377 (Alta. Dist. Ct.).

2. Are Borins J.'s reasons for holding individuals liable for all the consequences of their intentional acts compelling? Would it have made a difference if he had limited recovery to foreseeable losses? See also *Mahal v. Young* (1986), 36 C.C.L.T. 143 (B.C.S.C.), a case in which the defendant was held liable for the plaintiff's unforeseeable depressive reaction.

3. Could the defendant have successfully argued provocation? If so, what effect would it have had on the damage award? Given the facts of *Bettel*, would you advocate that provocation be taken into account to reduce compensatory damages?

4. In keeping with its historical origins, a battery can only be committed when the defendant undertakes a positive act that causes a physical contact. For example, blocking another's path will not constitute a battery, although it may give rise to liability in false imprisonment. See *Innes v. Wylie* (1844), 174 E.R. 800 (Q.B.). But see *MacDonald v. Sebastian* (1987), 81 N.S.R. (2d) 189 (S.C. (T.D.)), in which the defendant landlord was held liable in battery for failing to inform the plaintiff that the water supply was contaminated with arsenic. See also *Wuttunee v. Merck Frosst Canada Ltd.*, 2008 SKQB 78.

5. Battery was traditionally confined to directly caused injury cases. Consequently, if the plaintiff was indirectly injured by having his or her food poisoned or a trap set in his or her path, the plaintiff could not sue in battery. Many Commonwealth authors continue to treat directness as an essential element of battery. See for example Sullivan, "Trespass to the Person in Canada: A Defence of the Traditional Approach" (1987) 19 Ottawa L. Rev. 533; Barker *et al.*, *The Law of Torts in Australia*, 5th ed. (2011) at 36-37; and Peel & Goudkamp, *Winfield and Jolowicz on Tort*, 19th ed. (2014) at 58-59. In contrast, American authorities have broadened the tort of battery to include intentional conduct that indirectly causes physical harm: Dobbs, Hayden & Bublick, *The Law of Torts*, 2d ed. (2011) vol. 1 at 82.

In *Non-Marine Underwriters, Lloyd's of London v. Scalera*, [2000] 1 S.C.R. 551, the court stated that the plaintiff must establish a direct physical interference to sue in battery. It then stated that an interference is direct if it is "the immediate consequence of a force" that the defendant set in motion. See also *E.(D.) (Guardian ad litem of) v. British Columbia* (2005), 37 B.C.L.R. (4th) 89 (C.A.). Would poisoning the plaintiff's food or setting a trap in his or her path satisfy the Supreme Court of Canada's directness requirement? In both *J.(M.I.) v. Grieve*, 1996 CarswellBC 260 (S.C.) (WL Can) and *Misir v. Baichulall*, 2012 ONSC 893, the defendant was held liable in battery for putting drugs in the plaintiff's drink.

As a matter of public policy, should the tort of battery be limited to directly caused harm?

6. The term "negligent battery" has sometimes been used to refer to a situation in which a negligent hunter, golfer or other defendant directly injures the plaintiff. Consistent with the writ system's distinction between directly and indirectly caused injury, the Canadian courts have held that once a direct injury is established, the burden of proof shifts to the defendant to disprove both intent and negligence. These cases typically do not involve intent, but rather whether the defendant breached the standard of care in negligence. Consequently, we discuss these cases in Chapter 20 as an exception to the general principles governing the burden of proof in negligence.

7. A defendant's conduct will often give rise to both a criminal charge of assault and a civil action in battery. In *Simpson v. Geswein* (1995), 25 C.C.L.T. (2d) 49 (Man. Q.B.), the certificate of conviction and the judge's reasons in the criminal trial were admissible in the subsequent civil action arising from the same event. The certificate and reasons were not to be regarded as conclusive proof, but as strong *prima facie* evidence. Should a defendant in a civil proceeding be allowed to introduce into evidence the fact that the police did not lay criminal charges or dropped the criminal charges against him or her? Should a defendant's acquittal be admissible as strong *prima facie* proof in a subsequent civil action? See *F.(K.) v. White* (2001), 53 O.R. (3d) 391 (C.A.).

8. The number of childhood sexual abuse claims has increased dramatically. Many of the claims involved conduct that occurred 10, 20 or 30 years ago and were initiated long after the general limitation period had expired: *Blackwater v. Plint*, [2005] 3 S.C.R. 3; *K. (K.) v. G. (K.W.)* (2006), 40 C.C.L.T. (3d) 139 (Ont. S.C.J.), aff'd in part, (2008), 56 C.C.L.T. (3d) 165 (C.A.); and *Lauzon v. Auger* (2010), 73 C.C.L.T. (3d) 265 (C.S. Qc.), varied 2012 QCCA 27. Limitation periods are set by statute and establish the time within which a plaintiff must commence an action. The courts have held that the limitation period in childhood abuse cases will only begin to run once the plaintiff becomes aware of the wrongful conduct and its harmful consequences, and is psychologically capable of seeking legal redress: *M.(K.) v. M.(H.)*, [1992] 3 S.C.R. 6.

Some limitation statutes now exclude sexual assault and other categories of cases involving vulnerable complainants. For example, Ontario recently eliminated the limitation period in all sexual assault cases, other sexual misconduct or assault cases involving complainants who were under 18 years of age, and all assault cases committed in intimate relationships: *Limitations Act, 2002*, S.O. 2002, c. 24, Sch. B, s. 16(1)(h), (h.1) and (h.2). See also *Limitation Act*, S.B.C. 2012, c. 13, s. 3(j).

9. Aside from the limitation issue, claims against alleged child abusers generally involve straightforward battery actions. However, claims against the Crown and government agencies that have a supervisory or funding role in education, residential care, adoption, and other aspects of child welfare have been based on vicarious liability, negligence, the *parens patriae* doctrine, fiduciary duties, and non-delegable duties. See for example *G.(E.D.) v. Hammer*, [2003] 2 S.C.R. 459; *K.L.B. v. British Columbia*, [2003] 2 S.C.R. 403; *Broome v. Prince Edward Island*, [2010] 1 S.C.R. 360; *Nova Scotia (Attorney General) v. Carvery*, 2016 NSCA 21; and *Ross v. Canada (Attorney General)*, 2018 SKCA 12.

10. Proposals have been made to alter the scope of the battery action. For example, it has been argued that exposing a person to a poorly understood or potentially dangerous chemical should give rise to a *prima facie* claim in battery. The claim would fail if the defendant could prove that he or she had obtained the plaintiff's implicit or explicit informed consent to the exposure. How would this battery action differ from the accepted definition of battery? See Collins & McLeod-Kilmurray, "Toxic battery: A tort for our time?" (2008) 16 Tort L. Rev. 131; Mogyoros, "Deconstructing Directness in Canada: A Critical Evaluation of the Role of Directness in the Tort of Battery" (2013) 21 Tort L. Rev. 24; *MacDonald, supra*; and *Wuttunee, supra*.

In contrast, it has been argued that state-sponsored torture should be hived off from battery and made a new intentional tort. See Larocque, "The tort of torture" (2009) 17 Tort L. Rev. 158. What are the benefits and drawbacks to such a proposal? Could an equally compelling case be made for recognizing new intentional torts for child abuse, domestic violence and sexual battery?

11. It has also been suggested that a well-funded government compensation program be created for victims of domestic violence to replace battery and other intentional tort actions. See Kelly, "Private Law Responses to Domestic Violence: The Intersection of Family Law and Tort" in Rodgers, Ruparelia & Bélanger-Hardy, eds., *Critical Torts* (2009) at 321. Do the issues posed by domestic violence warrant creating a special government compensation fund separate from the compensation fund that is available to victims of other violent crimes?

5. Assault

The tort of assault can be defined as the intentional creation in the mind of another of a reasonable apprehension of immediate physical contact. It has been stated that conditional threats, future threats and words alone without some overt act cannot constitute assault. However, Canadian courts have reconsidered these limitations and increasingly focus instead on the impression created in the plaintiff's mind.

NOTES AND QUESTIONS

1. The defendant threw a chair at B, who ducked, as did C, D and E, the three people standing behind B. The chair hit F and G, who were standing nearby. F saw the chair coming but could not get out of the way, and G had his back turned. Which parties would have an action in assault against the defendant, and which would have an action in battery?

2. Can a police officer who is standing passively in a doorway and blocking the plaintiff's path be held liable in assault? If the plaintiff continued walking towards the motionless officer, making a collision inevitable, would the officer have a cause of action in assault? See *Innes v. Wylie* (1844), 174 E.R. 800 (Q.B.).

3. Would a 50-kilogram, unarmed man be held liable in assault for threatening to hit a 100-kilogram boxer who viewed the threat with arrogant indifference? If so, what interests would be served by the tort? See *Brady v. Schatzel*, [1911] St. R. Qd. 206 (S.C.).

4. A defendant who has the apparent intent and ability to make contact with the plaintiff can be held liable even if he or she has no actual intent or ability to carry out the battery. For example, as a practical joke, the staff of Club Med in Cancun staged a very realistic bus hijacking. Two guests held at gunpoint for 30 minutes sued, claiming $1,000,000 each in assault and false imprisonment. See "Practical joke victims seek their last laughs in court" *Ontario Lawyers Weekly* (5 April 1985) 14. See also *R. v. St. George* (1840), 173 E.R. 921 (N.P.); and *Hanes v. Kennedy*, [1941] S.C.R. 384.

5. Traditionally, damage awards for assault unaccompanied by battery were small. See *Stephens v. Myers* (1830), 172 E.R. 735 (C.P.), where the plaintiff was awarded one shilling. However, in *Mahal v. Young* (1986), 36 C.C.L.T. 143 (B.C.S.C.), the plaintiff was awarded $6,000 for an assault arising from the defendant's unprovoked threat to kill him. The defendant had previously kicked the plaintiff in the shin, and the parties worked together in circumstances in which the defendant could readily carry out the threat. The plaintiff suffered from severe depression following the threat and missed several months of work. See also *Sirois v. Gustafson*, [2003] 3 W.W.R. 110 (Sask. Q.B.).

6. If the assault is a prelude to a battery, the court may ignore or only superficially discuss the assault and may not consider it in assessing damages. Nevertheless, the occurrence of an assault may colour the court's interpretation of the subsequent events. The fact that the defendant was assaulted may provide grounds for raising the defences of consent and self-defence, or provide a basis for claiming provocation. See *Bruce v. Dyer* (1966), 58 D.L.R. (2d) 211 (Ont. H.C.), aff'd (1967), 8 D.L.R. (3d) 592 (Ont. C.A.).

7. It is not uncommon for the courts to conflate the torts of assault and battery. In Canada, this misuse of the terms may be largely due to how the federal criminal offence of assault is defined. Under s. 265(1)(a) and (b) of the *Criminal Code*, the crime of assault includes the intentional application of force to another (which is comparable to the tort of battery) and a threat of imminent physical contact (which is comparable to the tort of assault).

HOLCOMBE v. WHITAKER
318 So.2d 289 (Ala. S.C. 1975)

SHORES J.: . . . The next issue argued by defendant [a doctor] concerns the assault count. The plaintiff claimed that the defendant committed an assault when in June of 1971, she went to see him and tried to get him to get an annulment, he said "If you take me to court, I will kill you."; and again in October, 1971, after she had filed the instant suit on September 29, 1971, when he went to her apartment and beat on the door, tried to pry it open, and said again, "If you take me to court, I will kill you." (The complaint was amended to include this act.) The defendant claims this in no way can constitute an assault, because it was merely a conditional threat of violence and because no overt act was involved. . . .

While words standing alone cannot constitute an assault, they may give meaning to an act and both, taken together, may constitute an assault. Prosser, supra (2nd Ed. 1955). In addition, words may negative an act in a manner that apprehension in such a case would be unreasonable. "On the other hand, a show of force accompanied by an unlawful or unjustifiable demand, compliance with which will avert the threatened battery, is an assault." 1 Harper & James, The Law of Torts, page 223 (1956). ". . . the defendant is not free to compel the plaintiff to buy his safety by compliance with a condition which there is no legal right to impose." Prosser, supra, page 40 (4th Ed. 1971). It is obvious that the defendant in the instant case had no right to impose the condition he did on the plaintiff; and we cannot say that this condition explained away his threat to harm her.

The defendant says his conduct cannot constitute an assault because there was no overt action taken by him. The evidence from the plaintiff was that the defendant was pounding on her door making every effort to get into the apartment, and threatening to kill her if she persisted in "taking him to court." We cannot say, as a matter of law, that this was not sufficient to arouse an apprehension of harm or offensive conduct. We think it was a jury question, as was the question of whether the defendant had the apparent ability to effectuate the threatened act.

. . .

According to the testimony offered on behalf of the plaintiff, the doctor succeeded in his efforts to frighten the plaintiff. She was fearful enough to ask friends to stay with her at night; never left the apartment alone after the threats on her life; had her brother-in-law nail the windows closed after the break-in of her apartment; and told one of her friends that she was afraid there might be poison in her coffee. We believe this testimony was relevant under the circumstances of this case. The defendant threatened to kill the plaintiff if she did something she had a legal right to do. We think the evidence of what occurred subsequent to his threats and emanating from them was relevant to the issues being tried.

POLICE v. GREAVES
[1964] N.Z.L.R. 295 (C.A.)

The facts were these — a Mrs. Tolley who occupied with her children a State house situate in Kowhai Street, Naenae, called on the police for help after she had been attacked by the respondent who also resided in the house. It appears that he was somewhat inebriated. When two policemen arrived, the respondent came to the door with a carving knife in his right hand poised at waist height and pointed towards the leading constable, and said, "Don't you bloody move. You come a . . . step closer and you will get this straight through your — guts." The leading constable continued, "The defendant was in a maniacal mood . . . and was not prepared to listen to any reasoning at all. He said, . . . 'Get off this — property before you get this in your guts.'"

The constables, faced with this threat, withdrew to obtain further assistance.

The appellant was convicted of assault in the Magistrate's Court but the conviction was quashed in the Supreme Court on the ground that the threat made by the appellant was a conditional one and did not constitute an assault.

The prosecutor appealed by special leave to the Court of Appeal.

. . .

NORTH P.: . . . In our opinion, if the other conditions of the definition were met — as they undoubtedly were — there is no reason why a conditional threat should not constitute an assault. A threat in its very nature usually provides the person threatened with an alternative, unpleasant though it may often be. It is only necessary to recall the oft repeated threat of the highwayman, "Your money or your life" to see that if a pistol be pointed at the victim it would be idle to say that there was not a threat to apply force to the person of another in circumstances in which the person making the threat had, or at least caused the other to believe on reasonable grounds that he had, present ability to effect his purpose, and therefore that an assault had been committed. On the facts of the present case it was enough that the menacing attitude of the respondent caused the police officers to retire. . . . The present case is to be distinguished from such cases as *Tubervell v. Savadge* (1669) 1 Mod. 3; 86 E.R. 684, where the person from whom the threat came made it clear that he had no present intention of carrying out his threat. In that case the words used were, "Were it not assize . . . time" he would tell more of his mind.

With all respect for the view of the learned Judge, we do not think that *Read v. Coker* (1853) 13 C.B. 850; 138 E.R. 1437 which was relied on by the prosecution is distinguishable from the present case. There the plaintiff being in the defendant's workshop and refusing to quit when desired, was surrounded by the defendant's servants, who tucked up their sleeves and aprons and threatened to break his neck if he did not go out. It was argued that this did not constitute an assault, but the Court was clearly of opinion that it did, Jervis C.J. saying, "If anything short of actual striking will in law constitute an assault, . . . the facts here clearly show that the defendant was guilty of an assault. . . . There was a threat of violence exhibiting an intention to assault and . . . a present ability to carry the threat into execution" (*ibid.*, 860; 1441). There is not the slightest suggestion in the argument or in the judgment that the fact that the plaintiff was offered an alternative prevented the threat from constituting an assault. Again, in *Blake v. Barnard* (1840) 9 Car. & P. 626; 173 E.R. 985, the report of Lord Abinger's summing up to the jury makes no point of the fact that the cocked pistol presented at the defendant's head was accompanied by the statement that "if Blake was not quiet he would blow his brains . . . out." We can see no difference in principle between a demand that the person threatened should retire and a demand that he should not proceed further on his lawful occasions. The policemen were present here on their lawful occasions and their entry was barred; that in our opinion was sufficient. But in any event — though nothing was made of this either in the Court below or before us — it would appear that in fact both kinds of threats were made.

NOTES AND QUESTIONS

1. In *Holcombe*, the judge indicated that words alone, without some overt act, cannot give rise to assault. Do you think the judge would have held the defendant liable in assault if he had threatened to kill the plaintiff without beating on her door and trying to pry it open?

2. The principle that words alone cannot give rise to assault has been accepted in cases of insulting or abusive language. However, it has been criticized where the words were intended to cause, and in fact caused, a reasonable apprehension of imminent physical contact. As indicated in Dobbs, Hayden & Bublick, *The Law of Torts*, 2d ed. (2011) at 100, "in one sense there is no such thing as a 'words alone' case; all words occur in a social context and that context may reinforce and add substance to the verbal threat. The apparent reality of the threat, not its form, is what counts." See also Handford, "Tort Liability for Threatening or Insulting Words" (1976) 54 Can. Bar Rev. 563; and Howarth, "Trespass and Intentional Interference with the Person" in Sappideen & Vines, eds., *Fleming's The Law of Torts*, 10th ed. (2011) 23 at 35.

3. In *Fogden v. Wade*, [1945] N.Z.L.R. 724 (S.C.), the accused was convicted of criminal assault when he approached a woman and, while he was close enough to touch her, stated: "Don't go in yet, you've got time for a quick one." The woman

screamed, and the accused ran off without touching her. Would the accused's conduct have constituted an assault in tort law?

4. How did the court in *Greaves* distinguish *Tubervell*? Given that the essence of assault is the impression created in the plaintiff's mind, is this distinction valid? On what basis, if any, would you distinguish *Tubervell* and *Holcombe*?

5. In *Greaves*, the court also distinguished between conditional threats that require the plaintiff to take immediate action to avoid the threat and those that do not. In contrast, *Mainland Sawmills Ltd. v. I.W.A.-Canada*, 2006 BCSC 1195 rejected this distinction. Among other things, the defendants in *Mainland* confronted three workers and physically threatened them if they attempted to enter the workplace. Since the workers were not required to take action to avoid the threat, the defendants argued that there could be no assault. The court stated that the defendants were not absolved of liability for assault simply because the workers could avoid the threatened harm by forgoing their right to enter the workplace. Is the approach in *Greaves* preferable to that in *Mainland*?

6. How was the decision in *Greaves* influenced by the fact that the officers had a legal duty to apprehend the defendant? If the defendant made the same threat to a door-to-door salesperson, would the salesperson have an action in assault? See The American Law Institute, *Restatement, Second, Torts* (1965) vol. 1 at §30.

7. Traditionally, a future threat only constituted an assault if it was capable of being carried out immediately. See for example *Stephens v. Myers* (1830), 172 E.R. 735 (C.P.). However, the courts have relaxed the immediacy requirement, focusing instead on the threat's impact on the plaintiff.

At what point in the following scenario should the immediacy requirement be met? The defendant, who lives eight hours away, calls and threatens to come over and beat up the plaintiff. The defendant calls, indicates that he is two hours away and repeats the threat. The defendant calls indicating that he is across the street from the plaintiff's apartment. The defendant knocks on the plaintiff's door.

8. In *R. v. Ireland*, [1997] 1 All E.R. 112 (C.A.), the defendant made numerous telephone calls to three women but remained silent when they answered. The Court of Appeal held that he was guilty of criminal assault, stating that the material act was the making of the calls and that it was irrelevant whether words or silence ensued. In either event, the nature of the calls was such that they were likely to cause the victims to apprehend immediate and unlawful violence. The court also stated that it was irrelevant that there was no immediate proximity between the accused and the victims because fear could be instilled over the telephone. Should Canadian courts adopt these principles in tort claims for assault?

9. The trend towards broadening the tort of assault is reflected in *Warman v. Grosvenor* (2008), 92 O.R. (3d) 663 (S.C.J.). The defendant posted 14 threatening and defamatory messages on the internet over a two-year period that, among other things, called on the public to harass and physically assault the plaintiff. The defendant provided the plaintiff's home address and phone number, referred to the plaintiff as a "dead Jew walkin'" and stated that he had a gun and bullets with the plaintiff's name

on them. The defendant also sent more than 60 emails to the plaintiff of a similar nature. The plaintiff sued and the defendant was held liable in defamation and assault.

10. Even if the defendant's conduct falls short of assault, it may give rise to liability for other torts, such as intentional infliction of nervous shock, invasion of privacy, defamation, or intimidation. The criminal law also prohibits a broad range of offensive, obscene and racist conduct. See for example the *Criminal Code*, s. 264 (criminal harassment), s. 264.1 (uttering threats), ss. 298-301 (defamatory libel), ss. 318-320 (hate propaganda), s. 346 (extortion), and s. 372 (indecent or harassing telephone calls and letters).

REVIEW PROBLEMS

1. George drove to a gas station and asked Ralph, the attendant, to fill up his car. Ralph was distracted by some other customers and did not return for five minutes. George became increasingly angry and called Ralph an incompetent fool. Ralph, who was ten metres away, threatened to beat George's brains in if he did not apologize immediately. George approached Ralph, punched him in the head once and walked away. Ralph picked up a wrench and threw it at George, who ducked. The wrench struck Tom, who was walking on the sidewalk eight metres in front of the station. Ralph has sought your advice on the assault and battery actions that he may bring, and the assault and battery actions that may be brought against him.

2. The defendant attempted to rob a bank with an unloaded shotgun. When a police officer rushed in, the defendant threatened to shoot Stella, a teller, if the officer came any closer. Stella, who was standing three metres from the defendant, fainted when she heard the threat, fell to the floor and fractured her skull. Stella and the officer wish to know whether they would succeed in an assault action.

6. False Imprisonment

Originally designed to provide a remedy for wrongful incarceration, the tort of false imprisonment now encompasses most situations in which an individual's movement is intentionally restrained. The restraint of movement must be total even if only momentary. The restraint may be imposed by barriers, other physical means, an implicit or explicit threat of force, or an implicit or explicit assertion of legal authority. Although often discussed as an element of the tort, the courts treat the issue of whether the imprisonment was lawfully justified (*i.e.* not false) as a defence that the defendant must assert and prove.

BIRD v. JONES
(1845), 115 E.R. 668 (Q.B.)

COLERIDGE J. . . . [T]he plaintiff, being in a public highway [Hammersmith Bridge] and desirous of passing along it, in a particular direction, is prevented from doing so by the orders of the defendant, and that the defendant's agents for the purpose are policemen, from whom, indeed, no unnecessary violence was to be anticipated, or such as they believed unlawful, yet who might be expected to execute such commands as they deemed lawful with all necessary force, however resisted. But, although thus obstructed, the plaintiff was at liberty to move his person and go in any other direction, at his free will and pleasure: and no actual force or restraint on his person was used, unless the obstruction before mentioned amounts to so much.

. . .

And I am of opinion that there was no imprisonment. To call it so appears to me to confound partial obstruction and disturbance with total obstruction and detention. A prison may have its boundary large or narrow, visible and tangible, or, though real, still in the conception only; it may itself be moveable or fixed: but a boundary it must have; and that boundary the party imprisoned must be prevented from passing; he must be prevented from leaving that place, within the ambit of which the party imprisoning would confine him, except by prison-breach. Some confusion seems to me to arise from confounding imprisonment of the body with mere loss of freedom: it is one part of the definition of freedom to be able to go whithersoever one pleases; but imprisonment is something more than the mere loss of this power; it includes the notion of restraint within some limits defined by a will or power exterior to our own.

. . .

PATTESON J. . . . I have no doubt that, in general, if one man compels another to stay in any given place against his will, he imprisons that other just as much as if he locked him up in a room: and I agree that it is not necessary, in order to constitute an imprisonment, that a man's person should be touched. I agree, also, that the compelling a man to go in a given direction against his will may amount to imprisonment. But I cannot bring my mind to the conclusion that, if one man merely obstructs the passage of another in a particular direction, whether by threat of personal violence or otherwise, leaving him at liberty to stay where he is or to go in any other direction if he pleases, he can be said thereby to imprison him. He does him wrong, undoubtedly, if there was a right to pass in that direction, and would be liable to an action on the case for obstructing the passage, or of assault, if, on the party persisting in going in that direction, he touched his person, or so threatened him as to amount to an assault. But imprisonment is, as I apprehend, a total restraint of the liberty of the person, for however short a time, and not a partial obstruction of his will, whatever inconvenience it may bring on him. The quality of the act cannot, however, depend on the right of the opposite party. If it be an imprisonment to prevent a man passing along the public highway, it must be equally so to prevent him passing further along a field into which he has broken by a clear act of trespass.

. . .

LORD DENMAN C.J. [dissenting] . . . A company unlawfully obstructed a public way for their own profit, extorting money from passengers, and hiring policemen to effect this purpose. The plaintiff, wishing to exercise his right of way, is stopped by force, and ordered to move in a direction which he wished not to take. He is told at the same time that a force is at hand ready to compel his submission. That proceeding appears to me equivalent to being pulled by the collar out of the one line and into the other.

. . .

I had no idea that any person in these times supposed any particular boundary to be necessary to constitute imprisonment, or that the restraint of a man's person from doing what he desires ceases to be an imprisonment because he may find some means of escape.

It is said that the party here was at liberty to go in another direction. I am not sure that in fact he was, because the same unlawful power which prevented him from taking one course might, in case of acquiescence, have refused him any other. But this liberty to do something else does not appear to me to affect the question of imprisonment. As long as I am prevented from doing what I have a right to do, of what importance is it that I am permitted to do something else? How does the imposition of an unlawful condition shew that I am not restrained? If I am locked in a room, am I not imprisoned because I might effect my escape through a window, or because I might find an exit dangerous or inconvenient to myself, as by wading through water or by taking a route so circuitous that my necessary affairs would suffer by delay?

. . .

It is said that, if any damage arises from such obstruction, a special action on the case may be brought. Must I then sue out a new writ stating that the defendant employed direct force to prevent my going where my business called me, whereby I sustained loss? And, if I do, is it certain that I shall not be told that I have misconceived my remedy, for all flows from the false imprisonment, and that should have been subject of an action of trespass and assault? For the jury properly found that the whole of the defendant's conduct was continuous: it commenced in illegality; and the plaintiff did right to resist it as an outrageous violation of the liberty of the subject from the very first.

NOTES AND QUESTIONS

1. Although the law is settled, do you prefer the majority or minority view of false imprisonment? What problems, if any, would arise from adopting the minority definition?

2. Would it have made any difference to the majority if the plaintiff had been on an urgent business trip that could not have been delayed without serious financial loss? Should it make any difference if the defendant's purpose in obstructing the bridge was praiseworthy?

3. Since false imprisonment will not lie in the absence of a total restraint, the court may have to determine if there was a reasonable means of escape known to the plaintiff. Clearly, the plaintiff need not risk physical injury in attempting to escape. Less certain, however, is the amount of inconvenience that the plaintiff will be expected to endure in attempting to free him or herself. See *Robinson v. Balmain New Ferry Co.*, [1910] A.C. 295 (P.C.); and *Hanson v. Wayne's Café Ltd.* (1990), 84 Sask. R. 220 (Q.B.). But see *Wright v. Wilson* (1699), 91 E.R. 1394 (N.P.), in which the defendant was not held liable in false imprisonment even though the plaintiff could only escape by trespassing on a third party's property.

4. Alan, Barb and Carol were about to leave the 115th-floor observation deck of the C.N. Tower when they were informed that the elevator service was being discontinued for 30 minutes to permit publicity photos to be taken. All three refused to use the stairs, the only other exit. They now wish to know whether they can maintain a false imprisonment action against C.N. Alan is 30, Barb is 23 and 5 months pregnant, and Carol is 68.

5. Initially, a plaintiff had to establish that he or she was conscious of the imprisonment at the time that it occurred. This requirement no longer applies in the United Kingdom and Canada: *J.(M.I.) v. Grieve*, 1996 CarswellBC 260 (S.C.) (WL Can); and *Murray v. Ministry of Defence*, [1988] 1 W.L.R. 692 (H.L.). In the United States, a plaintiff may now succeed if he or she was aware of the imprisonment when it occurred or was harmed by it: Dobbs, Hayden & Bublick, *The Law of Torts*, 2d ed. (2011) vol. 1 at 104. Is the United Kingdom and Canadian position preferable to the American position?

6. Prisoners who are detained after they should have been released may recover in false imprisonment. See for example *LeBar v. Canada*, [1989] 1 F.C. 603 (C.A.). In *R. v. Governor of Brockhill Prison, Ex Parte Evans (No. 2)*, [2001] 2 A.C. 19 (H.L.), the court permitted recovery even though the defendant had used the then-accepted sentence calculation approach, which was only later found to be incorrect. Do you agree with the result in *Brockhill Prison*? Is the decision consistent with the principles governing the impact of mistake on intentional tort liability? See generally *Lumba v. Secretary of State for the Home Department*, [2011] UKSC 12; and *State of N.S.W. v. Kable*, [2013] HCA 26.

7. Should a lawfully detained prisoner who is improperly held in segregation, improperly transferred to another institution or held in intolerable conditions be entitled to recover in false imprisonment? In *Hague v. Deputy Governor of Parkhurst Prison*, [1991] 3 All E.R. 733 (H.L.), the court held that prisoners held in such circumstances may have a public remedy and a private action in negligence, but not a false imprisonment action. The court stated that the defendant's conduct affected the conditions of confinement and not the prisoner's liberty. See also *Iqbal v. Prison Officers Association*, [2010] 2 W.L.R. 1054; and Varuhas, "False Imprisonment of Prisoners: Lawful Authority, Omissions and Damages" [2010] C.L.J. 438.

Canadian courts have taken the opposite approach. See *Saint-Jacques v. Canada (Solicitor General)* (1991), 45 F.T.R. 1 (T.D.) (prisoner awarded damages for being wrongfully placed in solitary confinement); and *Hill v. British Columbia* (1997), 38 C.C.L.T. (2d) 182 (B.C.C.A.) (prisoner awarded damages for being wrongly placed in segregation, a "prison within a prison," depriving him of the liberty enjoyed by other prisoners).

Do you agree with the English courts that false imprisonment is not the appropriate remedy for addressing the conditions of imprisonment within the prison system? Would different considerations apply regarding the improper cancellation of day parole?

(a) FALSE ARREST

The terms "false imprisonment" and "false arrest" are often used interchangeably. However, false arrest refers to only one category of false imprisonment actions, namely those in which a total restraint of movement is brought about by an implicit or explicit assertion of legal authority. Peace officers and others may inadvertently commit a "false arrest" when stopping or questioning an individual, even though they have no intention of arresting him or her.

The number of "false arrest" and malicious prosecution actions has sharply increased in Canada. As will be discussed in Chapter 8, the Canadian courts have become far more concerned about civil liberties with the advent of the *Charter*. While many pre-*Charter* cases reflected an undue deference to law enforcement officials, many recent cases impose demanding standards on the police and prosecutors.

Even relatively straightforward false imprisonment cases may now result in a multitude of common law tort and *Charter* claims. For example, in *Can v. Calgary Police Service*, 2012 ABQB 340, the plaintiff's arrest generated claims for assault, battery, false imprisonment, wrongful arrest, intentional infliction of emotional distress, malicious prosecution, negligent investigation, and breach of his *Charter* rights. See also *Radovici v. Toronto Police Services Board* (2007), 86 O.R. (3d) 691 (S.C.J.); *Elmardy v. Toronto Police Services Board*, 2015 ONSC 2952; and *Turton v. Hanson*, 2018 ABCA 84.

CAMPBELL v. S.S. KRESGE CO.
(1976), 74 D.L.R. (3d) 717 (N.S.S.C. (T.D.))

HART J.: On December 14, 1974, about 6 p.m., the plaintiff went to the K-Mart store of the corporate defendant at Dartmouth to do some pre-Christmas shopping. She took a cart and placed a hockey stick and one or two other articles in the cart and then tried to get the attention of one of the clerks at a counter at the back of the store to make a further purchase. She says that she waited about five minutes while the two clerks discussed their own personal affairs, and decided to wait no longer. She left the cart with the several items in it and proceeded out the main door of the shop.

The defendant, Gary Williamson, was a full-time member of the Dartmouth Police Force with the rank of corporal, who was employed by S.S. Kresge Company Limited as a security officer during his off-duty hours. His chief responsibility for the defendant was the protection of the defendant's property and the catching of shoplifters.

In the early evening of December 14th, while Corporal Williamson was on floor duty in the store, a lady asked him if he was a police officer. He confirmed that he was, and she advised him that she thought she had seen the plaintiff put something in her coat pocket. Corporal Williamson then observed the plaintiff and noticed that she had abandoned her shopping cart and was leaving the store. He followed her outside and confronted her in the parking lot. He showed her his police badge and said that he had reason to believe that she had something that did not belong to her and asked that she come into the store to his office to avoid embarrassment to them both. The plaintiff was upset but went into the store and started towards the back of the store with Corporal Williamson following behind. When she reached the location of the jewellery counter she stopped and demanded to know what it was all about before she went any further. She offered her purse to Corporal Williamson claiming that there was nothing in it that belonged to the store and offered to be searched. At this point Corporal Williamson, not now being able to see the woman who had given him the information, told the plaintiff that he was merely trying to get the facts and that she was free to go. Mrs. Campbell then left the store.

The plaintiff says that she was very upset by this encounter and drove to her mother-in-law's house where she told what had happened. She then returned to the store and spoke to the manager. From this office she proceeded to Mr. Williamson's office to speak with him. They met in the store and she asked if there was a private place where they could talk. He indicated that the security office would be suitable and they went there. The plaintiff then asked why Corporal Williamson had stopped her, and he advised that a woman, who he was not able to identify, had told him that she had put something on her person. He said that he felt this combined with her leaving of the articles in the store cart made him suspicious and that he wanted to get the facts.

In his evidence Corporal Williamson says that he followed the same procedure with Mrs. Campbell that he would have followed if he were certain that a shopper had something on her person taken from the store. He indicates that he probably would have let her go if she had refused to come inside with him, but I am satisfied that the plaintiff being confronted by a member of the police force and being invited inside to avoid embarrassment would have felt that she was obligated to follow the request. It was only when the plaintiff rebelled inside the store and the police officer realized that his source of information was no longer there, and the plaintiff had offered her purse to be searched, that he told her she was free to go.

I am satisfied from the evidence as a whole that the plaintiff was imprisoned by Corporal Williamson, acting in his capacity as agent for the corporate defendant, from the time she was confronted outside the store until the time she was told that she was free to go. In the mind of Corporal Williamson he was not arresting her but merely taking her in in order to get a statement of the facts, but he was using the force of his position as a police officer to take her in a direction that she did not wish to go. She was not consenting to accompany Corporal Williamson, but was going with him out of fear of the consequences should she refuse. If, as Corporal Williamson said, he was not going to arrest her and there was no one present to observe what was going on, then there could have been no "embarrassment" to be avoided and they could easily have had their discussion in the parking lot. The impression he was giving, however, was that she should accompany him or else there might be a scene which would be embarrassing to her. It was the practice of Corporal Williamson to physically detain those suspects whom he believed to have stolen goods on their person, and there is nothing to indicate that he would not have followed the usual procedure had the plaintiff refused to accompany him. He did not know when he was outside the store that his informant would not be present when he returned with the suspect.

[The court then rejected the defence of legal authority and discussed damages.]

The plaintiff alleges that she was greatly upset by this experience and suggests that she was additionally embarrassed that it took place in the presence of many members of the public. I am satisfied from the evidence, however, that the matter was handled discreetly by Corporal Williamson and, although there were shoppers in the vicinity, that no scene was created which would have brought her in disrepute. The damages which she suffered therefore are limited to her personal inconvenience and upset arising from the incident, and I assess these damages in the amount of $500.

NOTES AND QUESTIONS

1. At what point did the officer imprison the plaintiff? In terms of the criminal law, did the officer intend to, or in fact, arrest the plaintiff? Why did the plaintiff submit to the officer's assertion of authority? How would you distinguish between a situation in which a suspect reluctantly co-operates and one in which a suspect submits against his or her will? See *Sinclair v. Woodward's Store Ltd.*, [1942] 2 D.L.R. 395 (B.C.S.C.); *Allen v. Head (C.) Ltd.* (1985), 54 Nfld. & P.E.I.R. 108 (Nfld. S.C.); and *Maher v. K Mart Can. Ltd.* (1990), 84 Nfld. & P.E.I.R. 271 (Nfld. T.D.).

Even if a plaintiff willingly goes with a store's security officers, they can be held liable in false imprisonment for subsequently detaining the plaintiff. See *Smart v. Simpson Sears Ltd.* (1984), 51 Nfld. & P.E.I.R. 215 (Nfld. Dist. Ct.), aff'd (1987), 64 Nfld. & P.E.I.R. 187 (Nfld. C.A.); and *Twan v. Hudson's Bay Company* (2008), 93 O.R. (3d) 582 (Div. Ct.).

2. An individual may be held liable in false imprisonment not only for restraining the plaintiff, but also for ordering another person to do so. For example, if a store manager shouts, "Stop that man, he's a thief!" and a police officer does so, both are responsible for the imprisonment. However, if the manager merely provides information to the officer, who assesses it and decides to make an arrest, the officer alone is responsible. It may be difficult to distinguish between these situations. If an individual makes the statement "I think that man has my wallet," is he giving an implicit order to arrest or merely providing information? Had the informant in *Campbell* been identified, could she have been held liable in false imprisonment? See *Lebrun v. High-Low Foods Ltd.* (1968), 69 D.L.R. (2d) 433 (B.C.S.C.); *Davidson v. Chief Constable of North Wales*, [1994] 2 All E.R. 597 (C.A.); *Hanisch v. Canada* (2004), 35 B.C.L.R. (4th) 33 (C.A.); and *Diaz v. Tossa*, 2017 ONSC 54.

3. A defendant who swears an information before a judge cannot be held liable in false imprisonment if the judge issues a warrant pursuant to which the plaintiff is arrested. Judges are deemed to exercise independent decision-making authority. Thus, the plaintiff's arrest is viewed as being brought about by the judge, not the defendant. See *Austin v. Dowling* (1870), L.R. 5 C.P. 534. As discussed shortly, it is the tort of malicious prosecution that provides redress for the wrongful initiation of criminal charges.

As a matter of public policy, should private citizens and police remain liable in false imprisonment if they intentionally or negligently misled a judge in swearing an information that subsequently resulted in the issuance of warrant and the plaintiff's arrest?

4. Why was the store held vicariously liable for the officer's conduct in *Campbell*? Should the police force have been held vicariously liable as well?

5. Was the damage award in *Campbell* appropriate? Large damage awards are now routinely made in false imprisonment actions, particularly in cases involving intimate search or physical force. In *Nagy v. Canada*, 2006 ABCA 227, the plaintiff was strip-searched, arrested and taken to the hospital for a cavity search after arriving at the Edmonton Airport. She sued for battery, unlawful search and false imprisonment. At trial, the doctor who conducted the cavity search and the supervising police officer were held liable for $150,000 in general damages. The officer was held liable for an additional $30,000 in general damages for the strip search and initial imprisonment, and $50,000 in punitive damages. The damage awards were upheld on appeal.

In *Beaulieu c. Bourgouin* (2007), 51 C.C.L.T. (3d) 33 (C.S. Qc.), varied 2008 QCCA 1652, the plaintiff was awarded almost $2.2 million in general damages, $150,000 in moral damages and $75,000 in punitive damages after being threatened, handcuffed and assaulted by an armed and masked member of a Québec police swat team who suspected that he was a robber. The large award was based on the court's conclusion that the fright, distress and mental anguish the plaintiff suffered would prevent him from regaining gainful employment. The Court of Appeal sent the case back to the lower court solely to resolve issues related to interest and "additional indemnity." See also *Carr v. Ottawa Police Services Board*, 2017 ONSC 4331.

6. In *Ashland Dry Goods Co. v. Wages*, 195 S.W.2d 312 (Ky. C.A. 1946), the judge held that the defendant's seizure of the plaintiff's purse and the statement that she could not leave with the goods until they were wrapped amounted to an imprisonment. Would parents be able to recover in false imprisonment if they remained with one of their children who had been detained? See *Carr v. Edmonton (City) Police* (1992), 97 D.L.R. (4th) 651 (Alta. Q.B.).

7. Even a shoplifter apprehended in the act by a storekeeper will be able to establish the elements of a false imprisonment action: volition, intent and a total restraint of movement. Once the shoplifter proves that the tort has been committed, the storekeeper will be held liable unless he or she can establish a defence. The outcome of the criminal proceedings against the shoplifter may be relevant to, but not necessarily determinative of, whether the storekeeper can successfully assert the defence of legal authority. The impact of a suspect's guilt on the defence of legal authority is discussed in Chapter 8.

8. Advise a store detective on how to approach a suspected thief or disruptive customer without committing false imprisonment. See generally *Chopra v. T. Eaton Co.* (1999), 240 A.R. 201 (Q.B.); *Twan, supra*; *R. v. Chen*, 2010 ONCJ 641; and *Mann v. Canadian Tire Corp.*, 2016 ONSC 4926. Note that the *Citizen's Arrest and Self-defence Act*, S.C. 2012, c. 9, altered private citizens' authority to protect property and make arrests under the *Criminal Code*.

9. Although most false imprisonment claims involve the police and private security, the issue can arise under the civil commitment provisions of the provincial mental health legislation. See for example *Kohn v. Globerman*, [1986] 4 W.W.R. 1 (Man. C.A.); *Mullins v. Levy* (2009), 88 B.C.L.R. (4th) 306 (C.A.); and *X. v. Everson*, 2013 ONSC 6134.

(b) CONSENSUAL RESTRAINT

HERD v. WEARDALE STEEL, COAL AND COKE CO. LTD.
[1915] A.C. 67 (H.L.)

The appellant was employed as a hewer at the Thornley Colliery in the county of Durham. The respondents the Weardale Steel, Coal and Coke Company were the proprietors of the colliery, the respondent Curry was the manager, and the respondent Turner was an overman employed at the colliery.

The appellant brought an action against the respondents for damages for false imprisonment. By his statement of claim he alleged that on May 30, 1911, the respondents wrongfully prevented him from using the cage, which was the only means of egress from the mine, whereby he was imprisoned in the mine till 1:30 p.m. The respondents denied the alleged false imprisonment and justified their refusal to raise the appellant on the ground that he had been guilty of a breach of contract in refusing to do some work which he was ordered to do.

. . .

VISCOUNT HALDANE L.C.: My Lords, by the law of this country no man can be restrained of his liberty without authority in law. That is a proposition the maintenance of which is of great importance; but at the same time it is a proposition which must be read in relation to other propositions which are equally important. If a man chooses to go into a dangerous place at the bottom of a quarry or the bottom of a mine, from which by the nature of physical circumstances he cannot escape, it does not follow from the proposition I have enunciated about liberty that he can compel the owner to bring him up out of it. The owner may or may not be under a duty arising from circumstances, on broad grounds the neglect of which may possibly involve him in a criminal charge or a civil liability. It is unnecessary to discuss the conditions and circumstances which might bring about such a result, because they have, in the view I take, nothing to do with false imprisonment.

My Lords, there is another proposition which has to be borne in mind, and that is the application of the maxim volenti non fit injuria. If a man gets into an express train and the doors are locked pending its arrival at its destination, he is not entitled, merely because the train has been stopped by signal, to call for the doors to be opened to let him out. He has entered the train on the terms that he is to be conveyed to a certain station without the opportunity of getting out before that, and he must abide by the terms on which he has entered the train. So when a man goes down a mine, from which access to the surface does not exist in the absence of special facilities given on the part of the owner of the mine, he is only entitled to the use of these facilities (subject possibly to the exceptional circumstances to which I have alluded) on the terms on which he has entered. . . . So, my Lords, it is not false imprisonment to hold a man to the conditions he has accepted when he goes down a mine.

. . .

Now, my Lords, in the present case what happened was this. The usage of the mine — a usage which I think must be taken to have been notified — was that the workman was to be brought up at the end of his shift. In this case the workman refused to work; it may have been for good reasons or it may have been for bad, — I do not think that question concerns us. He said that the work he had been ordered to do was of a kind that was dangerous, and he threw down his tools and claimed to come up to the surface. The manager, or at any rate the person responsible for the control of the cage, said: "No, you have chosen to come at a time which is not your proper time, and although there is the cage standing empty we will not bring you up in it," and the workman was in consequence under the necessity of remaining at the bottom of the shaft for about twenty minutes. There was no refusal to bring him up at the ordinary time which was in his bargain; but there was a refusal, — and I am quite ready to assume that the motive of it was to punish him, I will assume it for the sake of argument, for having refused to go on with his work — by refusing to bring him up at the moment when he claimed to come. Did that amount to false imprisonment? In my opinion it did not. No statutory right under the Coal Mines Regulation Act, 1887, avails him, for the reason which I have already spoken of. Nor had he any right in contract. His right in contract was to come up at the end of his shift. Was he then falsely imprisoned? There were facilities, but they were facilities which, in accordance with the conditions that he had accepted by going down, were not available to him until the end of his shift, at any rate as of right.

. . .

[W]hat we are concerned with at the moment is this and this simply: that no conditions existed which enabled the miner in this case to claim the right which he asserted, and that there was nothing which comes within the definition well known in the law of England which amounts to false imprisonment.

NOTES AND QUESTIONS

1. *Herd* was preceded by *Robinson v. Balmain New Ferry Co.*, [1910] A.C. 295 (P.C.). In that case, the plaintiff paid a penny in order to take the ferry, but changed his mind on learning that it was not leaving for 20 minutes. The plaintiff refused to pay an additional penny to exit and was detained on the wharf for a short time before he was able to escape. The court denied the plaintiff's false imprisonment claim, stating that the parties had not contemplated this possibility and thus there was no agreement on the issue. The court held that the defendants were permitted to impose a reasonable condition for exiting, which in their view included charging an additional penny. Did the plaintiff consent in advance to this restraint on his freedom of movement? If not, why would the "reasonableness" of the exit fee be relevant?

2. In *Herd*, did the plaintiff consent unconditionally to go into the mine and remain there until the shift ended? If not, what impact should that have had on the plaintiff's false imprisonment claim? See Amos, "A Note On Contractual Restraint of Liberty" (1928) 44 L.Q.R. 464; and *Khan v. El Al Israel Airlines* (1991), 4 O.R. (3d) 502 (Gen. Div.).

3. To what extent was this decision affected by the then prevailing views of labour and management relations? Would the case be decided differently today?

4. Comprehensive occupational safety standards are now imposed by both federal and provincial legislation. For example, the *Occupational Health and Safety Act*, R.S.O. 1990, c. O.1, s. 43(3) allows employees to refuse to work in unsafe conditions.

REVIEW PROBLEM

Outside the entrance of his store, the defendant posted a large sign that read: "The management reserves the right to inspect all unsealed packages and shopping bags." The plaintiff, who is blind, entered the store with her seeing-eye dog. After learning that the store did not carry what she wanted, the plaintiff attempted to leave. The defendant politely explained that she could not leave until her shopping bag was inspected. The plaintiff refused to permit the search and was detained until the police arrived and resolved the issue. Will the plaintiff succeed in false imprisonment against the store? Would the outcome be different if the plaintiff were illiterate, rather than blind? Which party has the burden of proving consent?

7. Malicious Prosecution

Both false imprisonment and malicious prosecution provide redress for unjustified interference with individual freedom and the embarrassment, injury to reputation and other losses that flow from it. Malicious prosecution, however, is derived from trespass on the case. Consequently, it is concerned with indirect interferences, namely those that result from the improper initiation of criminal proceedings against an individual. Moreover, malicious prosecution is not actionable *per se*; rather, the plaintiff must establish that he or she has suffered loss or harm.

There has recently been a great deal of litigation on the elements of malicious prosecution, the proceedings to which it applies and alternative causes of action.

NELLES v. ONTARIO
[1989] 2 S.C.R. 170

[The plaintiff was charged with first degree murder in the deaths of four babies at the Hospital for Sick Children in Toronto. After a lengthy and extremely well-publicized preliminary hearing, all charges were dropped against Nelles because of a lack of evidence. She sued several police officers, the Ontario Attorney General and the Crown attorney for false imprisonment, malicious prosecution, negligence, and violation of her *Charter* rights.

The following excerpt addresses the elements of the tort of malicious prosecution and whether the common law should continue to grant the Attorney General and Crown attorneys absolute immunity from civil liability in discharging their prosecutorial duties.]

LAMER J. (DICKSON C.J.C. and WILSON J. concurring):

. . .

2. *The Tort of Malicious Prosecution*

There are four necessary elements which must be proved for a plaintiff to succeed in an action for malicious prosecution:

a) the proceedings must have been initiated by the defendant;
b) the proceedings must have terminated in favour of the plaintiff;
c) the absence of reasonable and probable cause;
d) malice, or a primary purpose other than that of carrying the law into effect.
(See J.G. Fleming, *The Law of Torts* (5th ed. 1977), at p. 598.)

The first two elements are straightforward and largely speak for themselves. The latter two elements require explicit discussion. Reasonable and probable cause has been defined as "an honest belief in the guilt of the accused based upon a full conviction, founded on reasonable grounds, of the existence of a state of circumstances, which, assuming them to be true, would reasonably lead any ordinarily prudent and cautious man, placed in the position of the accuser, to the conclusion that the person charged was probably guilty of the crime imputed" (*Hicks v. Faulkner* (1878), 8 Q.B.D. 167, at p. 171, Hawkins J.)

This test contains both a subjective and objective element. There must be both actual belief on the part of the prosecutor and that belief must be reasonable in the circumstances. The existence of reasonable and probable cause is a matter for the judge to decide as opposed to the jury.

The required element of malice is for all intents, the equivalent of "improper purpose." It has according to Fleming, a "wider meaning than spite, ill-will or a spirit of vengeance, and includes any other improper purpose, such as to gain a private collateral advantage" (Fleming, op. cit., at p. 609). To succeed in an action for malicious prosecution against the Attorney General or Crown Attorney, the plaintiff would have to prove both the absence of reasonable and probable cause in commencing the prosecution *and* malice in the form of a deliberate and improper use of the office of the Attorney General or Crown Attorney, a use inconsistent with the status of "minister of justice." In my view this burden on the plaintiff amounts to a requirement that the Attorney General or Crown Attorney perpetrated a fraud on the process of criminal justice and in doing so has perverted or abused his office and the process of criminal justice. In fact, in some cases this would seem to amount to criminal conduct. (See for example breach of trust, s. 122, conspiracy re: false prosecution s. 465(1)(b), obstructing justice s. 139(2) and (3) of the *Criminal Code*, R.S.C., 1985, c. C-46.)

Further, it should be noted that in many, if not all cases of malicious prosecution by an Attorney General or Crown Attorney, there will have been an infringement of an accused's rights as guaranteed by ss. 7 and 11 of the *Canadian Charter of Rights and Freedoms*.

By way of summary then, a plaintiff bringing a claim for malicious prosecution has no easy task. Not only does the plaintiff have the notoriously difficult task of establishing a negative, that is the absence of reasonable and probable cause, but he is held to a very high standard of proof to avoid a non-suit or directed verdict (see Fleming, op. cit., at p. 606, and *Mitchell v. John Heine and Son Ltd.* (1938), 38 S.R. (N.S.W.) 466, at pp. 469-71). Professor Fleming has gone so far as to conclude that there are built-in devices particular to the tort of malicious prosecution to dissuade civil suits (at p. 606):

> The disfavour with which the law has traditionally viewed the action for malicious prosecution is most clearly revealed by the hedging devices with which it has been surrounded in order to deter this kind of litigation and protect private citizens who discharge their public duty of prosecuting those reasonably suspected of crime.

3. *Policy Considerations*

In light of what I have said regarding the role of the prosecutor in Canada, and the tort of malicious prosecution, it now is necessary to assess the policy rationales. I would begin by noting that even those decisions that have come out firmly in favour of absolute immunity have described the rule as "troubling", a "startling proposition", "strained and difficult to sustain". . . .

It is said by those in favour of absolute immunity that the rule encourages public trust and confidence in the impartiality of prosecutors. However, it seems to me that public confidence in the office of a public prosecutor suffers greatly when the person who is in a position of knowledge in respect of the constitutional and legal impact of his conduct is shielded from civil liability when he abuses the process through a malicious prosecution. The existence of an absolute immunity strikes at the very principle of equality under the law and is especially alarming when the wrong has been committed by a person who should be held to the highest standards of conduct in exercising a public trust.

. . .

Regard must also be had for the victim of the malicious prosecution. The fundamental flaw with an absolute immunity for prosecutors is that the wrongdoer cannot be held accountable by the victim through the legal process. As I have stated earlier, the plaintiff in a malicious prosecution suit bears a formidable burden of proof and in those cases where a case can be made out, the plaintiff's *Charter* rights may have been infringed as well. Granting an absolute immunity to prosecutors is akin to granting a license to subvert individual rights. Not only does absolute immunity negate a private right of action, but in addition, it seems to me, it may be that it would effectively bar the seeking of a remedy pursuant to s. 24(1) of the *Charter*. . .

It is also said in favour of absolute immunity that anything less would act as a "chilling effect" on the Crown Attorney's exercise of discretion. It should be noted that what is at issue here is not the exercise of a prosecutor's discretion within the proper sphere of prosecutorial activity as defined by his role as a "minister of justice." Rather, in cases of malicious prosecution we are dealing with allegations of misuse and abuse of the criminal process and of the office of the Crown Attorney. We are not dealing with merely second-guessing a Crown Attorney's judgment in the prosecution of a case but rather with the deliberate and malicious use of the office for ends that are improper and inconsistent with the traditional prosecutorial function.

Therefore it seems to me that the "chilling effect" argument is largely speculative and assumes that many suits for malicious prosecution will arise from disgruntled persons who have been prosecuted but not convicted of an offence. I am of the view that this "flood-gates" argument ignores the fact that one element of the tort of malicious prosecution requires a demonstration of improper motive or purpose; errors in the exercise of discretion and judgment are not actionable. Furthermore, there exist built-in deterrents on bringing a claim for malicious prosecution. As I have noted, the burden on the plaintiff is onerous and strict. . . . Finally, the potential that costs will be awarded to the defendant if an unmeritorious claim is brought acts as financial deterrent to meritless claims. Therefore, ample mechanisms exist within the system to ensure that frivolous claims are not brought. In fact, the difficulty in proving a claim for malicious prosecution itself acts as a deterrent. This high threshold of liability is evidenced by the small number of malicious prosecution suits brought against police officers each year. In addition, since 1966, the province of Québec permits suits against the Attorney General and Crown prosecutors without any evidence of a flood of claims. Therefore, I find unpersuasive the claim that absolute immunity is necessary to prevent a flood of litigation.

As for alternative remedies available to persons who have been maliciously prosecuted, none seem to adequately redress the wrong done to the plaintiff. The use of the criminal process against a prosecutor who in the course of a malicious prosecution has committed an offence under the *Criminal Code*, addresses itself mainly to the vindication of a public wrong not the affirmation of a private right of action. . . . I do however pause to note that many cases of genuine malicious prosecution will also be offences under the *Criminal Code*, and it seems rather odd if not incongruous for reparation to be possible through a probation order but not through a private right of action.

Further, the use of professional disciplinary proceedings, while serving to some extent as punishment and deterrence, do not address the central issue of making the victim whole again. And as has already been noted, it is quite discomforting to realize that the existence of absolute immunity may bar a person whose *Charter* rights have been infringed from applying to a competent court for a just and appropriate remedy in the form of damages.

NOTES AND QUESTIONS

1. Based on *Nelles*, define the elements of a malicious prosecution action. Although not discussed by the court, the plaintiff must also prove that he or she has suffered loss or damage. In *Nelles*, the court suggested that the rigorous requirements of malicious prosecution would limit the proliferation of claims, but this has not been the case.

2. Explain the subjective and objective elements of the "reasonable and probable cause" requirement. Based on *Nelles*, must there be reasonable grounds to believe that the accused committed the offence or that he or she will be convicted?

In *Miazga v. Kvello Estate*, [2009] 3 S.C.R. 339, the court stated that a subjective/ objective test of reasonable grounds is appropriate in actions between private parties, but it should not apply to Crown prosecutors. They have a duty to act solely in the public interest and should not permit their personal views of the case to interfere with their public duty. Consequently, the reasonable grounds test for Crown prosecutors should be based on an objective assessment of whether there were reasonable grounds to initiate and continue the prosecution. Are prosecutors now held to a less or more rigorous test of reasonable grounds than private parties? Should this test apply to actions against the police, who also discharge a public duty?

3. How did the court define the element of malice or improper purpose? Would it be improper to charge a suspect with 12 similar break and enters, if there was currently only evidence linking the suspect to: (a) 4 of these offences; or (b) 10 of these offences? According to *Nelles*, must there be an element of subjective ill-will or malice?

4. What arguments were made in support of maintaining the common law absolute immunity rule? On what basis did the court reject these arguments? What additional policy issues did the court raise in opposition to the immunity rule? Would these same arguments justify denying absolute immunity to judges and quasi-judicial decision makers? Not surprisingly, the Canadian courts have consistently reaffirmed that judges and other quasi-judicial decision makers are subject to immunity at common law.

5. Section 5(6) of the *Proceedings Against the Crown Act*, R.S.O. 1990, c. P.27 grants the Crown statutory immunity for the conduct of the Attorney General and Crown prosecutors in discharging or purportedly discharging their prosecutorial functions. What is the impact of *Nelles* and s. 5(6) on the personal liability of the Attorney General and Crown prosecutors? See *Walker v. Ontario* (1997), 40 C.C.L.T. (2d) 197 (Ont. Gen. Div.); *Hawley v. Bapoo* (2005), 76 O.R. (3d) 649 (S.C.J.), rev'd (2007), 227 O.A.C. 81 (C.A.); and *Smith v. Ontario (Attorney General)*, 2018 ONSC 993.

6. While both the majority and the dissent in *Proulx v. Québec (A.G.)*, [2001] 3 S.C.R. 9 purportedly applied *Nelles*, they disagreed on whether the plaintiff could establish malice. The fact situation was complicated. Essentially, the majority was willing to infer malice against the prosecutor from the lack of reasonable and probable grounds, coupled with the prosecutor's hiring of a former police officer who was at that time being sued by the accused for defamation. The dissent held that there was insufficient evidence to establish that the prosecutor had subjectively acted with a malicious or improper intent.

See also Harris, "Innocent Albertan got $2.2M payout" *Calgary Sun* (4 October 2006). In this case, a man spent seven years in prison for a rape that he did not commit. It was later revealed that the complainant had sex with the investigating officer on several occasions and with a witness who testified against the accused at trial.

7. In *Oniel v. Metropolitan Toronto Police Force* (2001), 195 D.L.R. (4th) 59 (Ont. C.A.), the court stated that malice could be inferred from the lack of reasonable and probable cause in appropriate cases. Specifically, an officer's failure to make adequate inquiries before continuing a prosecution could amount to malice. See also *Wood v. Kennedy* (1998), 165 D.L.R. (4th) 542 (Ont. Gen. Div.). The Supreme Court of Canada resolved this issue in *Miazga, supra*, stating at para. 80 that a lack of reasonable and probable grounds due to inexperience, incompetence, negligence, gross negligence, or even recklessness does not constitute malice. A lack of reasonable grounds and malice "must not be conflated."

8. The Canadian courts have held that it is only the core elements of prosecutorial discretion that are immune from the tort of malicious prosecution, and these have been defined to include the decision to prosecute, enter a stay of proceedings, accept a plea to a lesser charge, or withdraw from proceedings: *Krieger v. Law Society of Alberta*, 2002 SCC 65; *Miazga, supra*; and *G.C. v. Ontario (Attorney General)*, 2014 ONSC 455.

9. In *Henry v. British Columbia (Attorney General)*, 2015 SCC 24, the plaintiff sued the province and others in negligence, malicious prosecution, misfeasance in public office, abuse of process, and breach of his ss. 7 and 11(d) rights for being wrongfully convicted and imprisoned for almost 27 years. The court stated that malicious prosecution did not provide redress for police and prosecutorial misconduct that fell short of malice. Although the court unanimously held that proof of malice was not required to recover damages for *Charter* breaches, there was disagreement on the threshold test for such claims. According to the majority, the Crown should only be held liable for intentionally withholding information when it knew or ought to have known that the information was material and that its nondisclosure would likely impinge the accused's *Charter* right to make full answer and defence. The minority stated that any breach of the Crown's constitutional disclosure obligation should give rise to *Charter* damages if such an award is appropriate and just, and serves the purpose of compensation, deterrence and/or vindication. Would the test laid out by the minority assist lower courts in determining which *Charter* breaches warrant damages?

The Supreme Court allowed the plaintiff to amend his pleadings to include a claim for *Charter* damages. In the subsequent trial, the plaintiff was awarded over $8 million, of which $7.5 million was awarded to serve the "vindication and deterrence functions" of s. 24(1): *Henry v. British Columbia (Attorney General)*, 2016 BCSC 1038. See also *Tremblay v. Ottawa Police Service Board*, 2016 ONSC 4185, rev'd 2018 ONCA 497.

10. In *Hill v. Hamilton Wentworth Regional Police Services Board*, [2007] 3 S.C.R. 129, the court created a less stringent alternative to suing the police in malicious prosecution by recognizing an action for negligent police investigation. In contrast, most Commonwealth jurisdictions have held that, given their public duty, the police cannot owe a duty of care to individual suspects in conducting investigations. See

Chamberlain, "Negligent Investigation: The End of Malicious Prosecution in Canada?" (2008) 124 L.Q.R. 205.

11. Police officers have begun bringing malicious prosecution actions against individuals who had them charged with criminal offences. See *Wiche v. Ontario* (2001), 9 C.C.L.T. (3d) 72 (Ont. S.C.J.); *Fitzpatrick v. Durham Regional Police Services Board* (2005), 76 O.R. (3d) 290 (S.C.J.); and *Sheridan v. Ontario*, 2015 ONCA 303. What factors do you think contributed to this trend?

12. In *Reid v. Webster* (1966), 59 D.L.R. (2d) 189 at paras. 56 and 57 (P.E.I.S.C.), the court defined criminal proceedings broadly. It held that a municipal by-law prosecution can give rise to a malicious prosecution action if the by-law provides for imprisonment for failing to pay the fine, the prosecution affects the plaintiff's trade, and the publicity creates an aura of scandal. See also *Delancey v. Dale & Co. Ltd.* (1959), 20 D.L.R. (2d) 12 (N.S.S.C.) (arrest as a potential absconding debtor).

13. The courts in several provinces have held that the wrongful initiation of disciplinary proceedings against healthcare and other self-regulated professionals can give rise to a malicious prosecution action. See for example *Khanna v. Royal College of Dental Surgeons (Ontario)* (2000), 47 O.R. (3d) 95 (C.A.) (dentist); *Roach v. Long* (2002), 161 O.A.C. 218 (C.A.) and *Robson v. Law Society of Upper Canada*, 2016 ONSC 5579 (lawyers); *Symington v. Halifax (Regional Municipality)*, 2013 NSCA 152 (police officer); and *Clark v. Hunka*, 2017, ABCA 346 (chartered accountant). But see *Estabrooks v. New Brunswick Real Estate Association*, 2014 NBCA 48, in which the majority reached the opposite conclusion, based largely on concerns about extending malicious prosecution to civil proceedings. As a matter of policy, which approach is preferable? See Marin, "The uncertain scope of malicious prosecution: Insights from Canada" (2016) 24(2) Tort L. Rev. 80.

A 5:4 majority in *Willers v. Joyce*, [2016] UKSC 43 held that the "malicious prosecution of civil proceedings" was actionable. The split decision in *Willers* reflects the conflicting views in the earlier cases: *Gregory v. Portsmouth City Council*, [2000] UKHL 3; and *Crawford Adjusters v. Sagicor General Insurance (Cayman) Ltd.*, [2013] UKPC 17.

14. A defendant cannot be held liable in malicious prosecution for merely providing information to the police or testifying in court. Rather, the defendant must be the driving force in the initiation or prosecution of the action. In most cases, this requirement is met by laying the criminal charge. See *Casey v. Automobiles Renault Canada Ltd.*, [1965] S.C.R. 607; *Temilini v. Ontario Provincial Police (Commissioner)* (1990), 73 O.R. (2d) 664 (C.A.); and *Andre Gravelle v. Ontario*, 2012 ONSC 5149.

However, a defendant may also be responsible for initiating the proceedings if he or she lied to the police or wrongfully pressured them to lay the charges. In *McNeil v. Brewers Retail Inc.*, 2008 ONCA 405, the defendant failed to draw the attention of the police to exculpatory portions of a videotape that it handed over to them. In upholding the plaintiff's $2 million damage award for malicious prosecution, the Court of Appeal stated that it was open to the jury to find that the defendant knowingly withheld exculpatory information that the police would not likely find and that, but for this omission, the police would not have charged the plaintiff. See also *Neff v. Patry*, 2008 BCSC 163; and *Pate Estate v. Galway-Cavendish and Harvey (Township)*, 2012 ONSC 6740, aff'd 2013 ONCA 669.

In *Martin v. Watson*, [1996] 1 A.C. 74 (H.L.), the court stated that individuals who do not lay a criminal charge may only be held liable in malicious prosecution if: (i) they falsely and maliciously give the police information that the accused committed a crime and offer to testify, making it clear that they want the accused prosecuted; and (ii) the facts are only available to them, such that the police cannot exercise independent judgment in the matter. See also *Drainville v. Vilchez*, 2014 ONSC 4060; and *Chatha v. Uppal*, 2018 BCSC 6. How do the tests in *McNeil* and *Martin* differ?

15. A defendant can be held liable in malicious prosecution not only for the wrongful initiation of a criminal charge, but also for its wrongful continuation. See *Oniel, supra; Neff, supra;* and *Hawkins v. Ontario (Attorney General)* (2010), 98 O.R. (3d) 321 (S.C.J.), additional reasons 2010 ONSC 1753. What impact would this principle have on a police officer who laid four charges of theft, but learned prior to trial that the accused could not have been responsible for two of the thefts?

16. In *Casey, supra*, the majority held that the defendant had initiated criminal proceedings by laying a criminal charge before a magistrate who was competent to deal with the matter, even though the defendant withdrew the charge before the magistrate took any action. The court further held that the subsequent withdrawal of the charge amounted to a termination of the proceedings in the plaintiff's favour. See also *Ferri v. Root* (2007), 219 O.A.C. 340 (C.A.).

17. In *M.(A.) v. Matthews* (2003), 20 C.C.L.T. (3d) 54 (Alta. Q.B.), it was held that a malicious prosecution claim cannot be commenced until the criminal proceedings on which it is based have been completed. See also *Johar v. Kucy*, 2009 BCSC 648; and *Gardner v. Canada (Attorney General)*, 2013 ONCA 423.

18. In *Banks v. Bliefernich* (1988), 44 C.C.L.T. 144 (B.C.S.C.), it was held that despite pleading guilty to one criminal offence, the stay of proceedings on two other charges constituted a termination in the plaintiff's favour. Moreover, the court stated that the withdrawal of a more serious charge in exchange for a guilty plea to a lesser included offence would also constitute a termination in the plaintiff's favour.

In contrast, the court in *Ramsay v. Saskatchewan* (2004), 234 Sask. R. 172 (Q.B.) held that the dropping of a more serious charge in exchange for a guilty plea to a lesser charge does not constitute a termination in the plaintiff's favour. The court in *Ramsay* indicated that *Banks* should be limited to its facts and noted that it was decided prior to *Nelles*. Is *Banks* or *Ramsay* preferable in regard to: (a) lesser included offences; (b) pleas relating to different offences arising from a single incident; and (c) pleas relating to a series of criminal offences occurring at different times, such as six break and enter offences that were committed over a three-month period?

In *Sheridan v. Ontario*, 2015 ONCA 303, the plaintiff sued several parties for malicious prosecution, among other things, after the criminal charges against him were dismissed. The lower court held that since a peace bond had been imposed on the plaintiff in the criminal proceedings, those proceedings had not terminated in his favour. Consequently, the plaintiff's malicious prosecution claims were struck. The Court of Appeal upheld the lower court decision. Do you agree with the Court of Appeal decision and is it consistent with *Ramsay*?

19. Although malicious prosecution initially provided redress for the wrongful initiation of certain civil actions, it was until recently limited almost exclusively to

penal and quasi-penal matters. The wrongful initiation of bankruptcy and winding-up proceedings is the most notable exception. See *The Quartz Hill Consolidated Gold Mining Co. v. Eyre* (1883), 11 Q.B.D. 674 (C.A.); *Flame Bar-B-Q Ltd. v. Hoar* (1979), 106 D.L.R. (3d) 438 (N.B.C.A.); and *Cherry v. Ivey* (1982), 37 O.R. (2d) 361 (H.C.). See also *Norman v. Soule* (1991), 7 C.C.L.T. (2d) 16 (B.C.S.C.), *Bernstein v. Stoytcheva-Todorova* (2007), 44 C.C.L.T. (3d) 181 (B.C.S.C.) and *Lee Tat Development Pte. Ltd. v. Management Corporation Strata Title Plan No. 301*, [2018] SGCA 50, which suggest that these limited exceptions are not likely to be extended to other types of civil litigation.

20. It has been suggested that there may be a tort for malicious failure to prosecute. In *Paquette v. Desrochers* (2000), 52 O.R. (3d) 742 at 749 (S.C.J.), McKinnon J. said: "One can contemplate a situation where, as a result of proven malice, an accused is not prosecuted for a vicious attack upon a victim. Subsequently, the same individual viciously attacks the same victim, once again occasioning severe bodily harm. Surely, if malice can be proved, the failure to prosecute may well be alleged as a cause giving rise to the subsequent damage." In a later stage of the litigation, the Court of Appeal expressly refused to comment on the malicious failure to prosecute: *P.(K.) v. Desrochers* (2001), 9 C.C.L.T. (3d) 317 (Ont. C.A.). But see *Thompson v. Webber* (2010), 75 C.C.L.T. (3d) 183 (B.C.C.A.), in which the court rejected the plaintiff's negligence claim against the police for failing to charge his estranged wife with assaulting their children. Should a tort for malicious or negligent failure to prosecute be recognized? What are the arguments for and against such a tort?

21. The litigation relating to police and prosecutorial practices has become increasingly complex, particularly in Ontario. As in *Desrochers*, the malicious prosecution issue may be novel, or accompanied by a raft of other claims. In this latter regard, see *Bernstein, supra*, which included claims for malicious prosecution, abuse of process, conspiracy, intentional interference with economic relations, defamation, restitution, unjust enrichment, and breach of various statutes. See also *Khanna, supra*.

(a) THE TORT OF ABUSE OF PROCESS

Until recently, it was generally accepted that there was no tort remedy for the misuse of civil proceedings. However, courts in some provinces, including Alberta, British Columbia, Saskatchewan, and Ontario, have recognized a common law tort action for abuse of process. It is increasingly common for plaintiffs to bolster their pleadings by adding an abuse of process allegation to a long list of other tort claims. Many of these abuse of process claims are struck out prior to trial and relatively few are successful.

Unlike malicious prosecution, abuse of process is not primarily concerned with the wrongful initiation of proceedings. Rather, it focuses on the misuse of civil proceedings for a collateral or illicit purpose other than the resolution of the claim. Traditionally, the plaintiff had to prove that: (i) the defendant brought a civil action; (ii) the defendant did so for some extrinsic purpose; (iii) the defendant undertook or threatened to undertake some overt act other than the litigation itself in order to further the improper purpose; and (iv) the plaintiff consequently suffered a loss.

In contrast to the tort of malicious prosecution, the plaintiff does not have to prove that the earlier proceedings terminated in his or her favour, or that the defendant lacked reasonable and probable grounds for engaging in the earlier proceedings. Although the tort of abuse of process appears easier to establish than malicious prosecution, it is often difficult to prove that the defendant undertook an overt act independent of the litigation itself. See *Hunt Oil Co. of Canada Ltd. v. Galleon Energy Inc.*, 2010 ABQB 212; *Harris v. GlaxoSmithKline Inc.*, 2010 ONCA 872; and *Grenon v. Canada Revenue Agency*, 2017 ABCA 96. However, the courts in British Columbia have in effect done away with the requirement for an overt act other than initiating the litigation: *Border Enterprises Ltd. v. Beazer East Inc.* (2002), 216 D.L.R. (4th) 107 (B.C.C.A.); *Smith v. Rusk*, 2009 BCCA 96; and *Gadhri v. 0760815 B.C. Ltd.*, 2017 BCCA 31.

NOTES AND QUESTIONS

1. The term "abuse of process" arises in three distinct contexts. First, as discussed above, the term "abuse of process" may be used to refer to a common law tort action. Second, the term is also used in reference to the civil courts' discretionary authority to stay proceedings to prevent the re-litigation of issues that a court has already resolved. Third, as stated in *R. v. O'Connor*, [1995] 4 S.C.R. 411 at para. 59, the criminal courts have discretionary authority to stay proceedings "where compelling an accused to stand trial would violate those fundamental principles of justice which underlie the community's sense of fair play and decency. . ."

2. Does the tort of abuse of process serve any useful purpose? In *Lee Tat Development Pte. Ltd. v. Management Corporation Strata Title Plan No. 301*, [2018] SGCA 50, the court refused to recognize a tort of abuse of process because it would undermine the principle of finality. Do you agree with the court in *Lee Tat*?

3. See Irvine, "The Resurrection of Tortious Abuse of Process" (1989) 47 C.C.L.T. 217; and Perell, "Tort Claims for Abuse of Process" (2007) 33 Adv. Q. 193.

REVIEW PROBLEM

Vincent was browsing in the Super Mart. The store detective, Steven, became suspicious because Vincent spent 15 minutes at the cosmetic counter and had a bottle of deodorant sticking out of his shopping bag. When Vincent left without paying for the deodorant, Steven ran after him and tapped him on the shoulder. When Vincent turned around, Steven politely asked him to come to the manager's office. Vincent, who neither spoke nor understood English, smiled and accompanied Steven. John, the store manager, listened to Steven's explanation and called the police. After several minutes, Vincent became nervous and stated in Italian that he was leaving. John told him in Italian that he had to remain, and Steven pushed him towards a chair. Vincent finally realized that he was being arrested, but he had no idea why.

John explained the situation in English to the officers and told them that he was going to press charges. The officers took Vincent into custody and seized his shopping bag as evidence. Once at the station, the desk sergeant explained to Vincent in Italian the reason for his arrest. Vincent replied that there was a receipt in his shopping bag to prove that the deodorant had been purchased at another store. The desk sergeant said that he would look into the matter. The sergeant thought Vincent might be an illegal immigrant and decided to lay the theft charge as a means of holding him until his immigration status could be determined. Vincent was charged with theft, brought before a judge and released on a promise to appear. When the desk sergeant learned later in the day that Vincent was a lawful visitor he looked into the shopping bag for the first time. Upon finding the receipt, he called the prosecutor to withdraw the charge.

Vincent has sought your legal advice. He wishes to know what tort actions he can bring against the various parties, the bases for such actions and their likelihood of success.

8. Intentional Infliction of Nervous Shock (Mental Distress, Psychiatric Harm)

Prior to *Wilkinson v. Downton*, [1897] 2 Q.B. 57, nervous shock was not recoverable unless it was consequent upon some physical injury that the plaintiff suffered. The courts' attitude to nervous shock was summarized by Wensleydale L.J. in *Lynch v. Knight* (1861), 11 E.R. 854 at 863 (H.L.): "Mental pain or anxiety the law cannot value, and does not pretend to redress, when the unlawful act complained of causes that alone; though where a material damage occurs, and is connected with it, it is impossible a jury, in estimating it, should altogether overlook the feelings of the party interested."

As our understanding of what is now often called "mental distress" or "psychiatric harm" increased, the courts became less skeptical of such claims. The strict limits in *Wilkinson* have been eased, the scope of recovery has increased, albeit in a piecemeal fashion, and the terminology has changed.

WILKINSON v. DOWNTON
[1897] 2 Q.B. 57

WRIGHT J.: In this case the defendant, in the execution of what he seems to have regarded as a practical joke, represented to the plaintiff that he was charged by her husband with a message to her to the effect that her husband was smashed up in an accident, and was lying at The Elms at Leytonstone with both legs broken, and that she was to go at once in a cab with two pillows to fetch him home. All this was false. The effect of the statement on the plaintiff was a violent shock to her nervous system, producing vomiting and other more serious and permanent physical consequences at one time threatening her reason, and entailing weeks of suffering and incapacity to her as well as expense to her husband for medical attendance. These consequences were not in any way the result of previous ill-health or weakness of constitution; nor was there any evidence of predisposition to nervous shock or any other idiosyncrasy.

In addition to these matters of substance there is a small claim for 1*s*. 10½*d.* for the cost of railway fares of persons sent by the plaintiff to Leytonstone in obedience to the pretended message. As to this 1*s* 10½*d.* expended in railway fares on the faith of the defendant's statement, I think the case is clearly within the decision in *Pasley v. Freeman* [(1789), 100 E.R. 450 (K.B.)]. The statement was a misrepresentation intended to be acted on to the damage of the plaintiff.

The real question is as to the [£]100, the greatest part of which is given as compensation for the female plaintiff's illness and suffering. It was argued for her that she is entitled to recover this as being damage caused by fraud, and therefore within the doctrine established by *Pasley v. Freeman* [*supra*] and *Langridge v. Levy* [(1837), 150 E.R. 863 (Ex. Ct.)]. I am not sure that this would not be an extension of that doctrine, the real ground of which appears to be that a person who makes a false statement intended to be acted on must make good the damage naturally resulting from its being acted on. Here there is no injuria of that kind. I think, however, that the verdict may be supported upon another ground. The defendant has, as I assume for the moment, wilfully done an act calculated to cause physical harm to the plaintiff — that is to say, to infringe her legal right to personal safety, and has in fact thereby caused physical harm to her. That proposition without more appears to me to state a good cause of action, there being no justification alleged for the act. This wilful injuria is in law malicious, although no malicious purpose to cause the harm which was caused nor any motive of spite is imputed to the defendant.

It remains to consider whether the assumptions involved in the proposition are made out. One question is whether the defendant's act was so plainly calculated to produce some effect of the kind which was produced that an intention to produce it ought to be imputed to the defendant, regard being had to the fact that the effect was produced on a person proved to be in an ordinary state of health and mind. I think that it was. It is difficult to imagine that such a statement, made suddenly and with apparent seriousness, could fail to produce grave effects under the circumstances upon any but an exceptionally indifferent person, and therefore an intention to produce such an effect must be imputed, and it is no answer in law to say that more harm was done than was anticipated, for that is commonly the case with all wrongs. The other question is whether the effect was, to use the ordinary phrase, too remote to be in law regarded as a consequence for which the defendant is answerable. . . . It is, however, necessary to consider two authorities which are supposed to have laid down that illness through mental shock is a too remote or unnatural consequence of an injuria to entitle the plaintiff to recover in a case where damage is a necessary part of the cause of action. One is the case of *Victorian Railways Commissioners v. Coultas* [(1888), 13 A.C. 222 (P.C.)], where it was held in the Privy Council that illness which was the effect of shock caused by fright was too remote a consequence of a negligent act which caused the fright, there being no physical harm immediately caused. That decision was treated in the Court of Appeal in *Pugh v. London, Brighton and South Coast Ry. Co.* [[1896] 2 Q.B. 248] as open to question. . . . Nor is it altogether in point, for there was not in that case any element of wilful wrong; nor perhaps was the illness so direct and natural a consequence of the defendant's conduct as in this case. On these grounds it seems to me that the case of *Victorian Railways Commissioners v. Coultas* [*supra*] is not an authority on which this case ought to be decided.

A more serious difficulty is the decision in *Allsop v. Allsop* [(1860), 157 E.R. 1292 (Ex. Ct.)] . . . . In that case it was held by Pollock C.B., Martin, Bramwell, and Wilde BB., that illness caused by a slanderous imputation of unchastity in the case of a married woman did not constitute such special damage as would sustain an action for such a slander. That case, however, appears to have been decided on the ground that in all the innumerable actions for slander there were no precedents for alleging illness to be sufficient special damage, and that it would be of evil consequence to treat it as sufficient, because such a rule might lead to an infinity of trumpery or groundless actions. Neither of these reasons is applicable to the present case. Nor could such a rule be adopted as of general application without results which it would be difficult or impossible to defend. Suppose that a person is in a precarious and dangerous condition, and another person tells him that his physician has said that he has but a day to live. In such a case, if death ensued from the shock caused by the false statement, I cannot doubt that at this day the case might be one of criminal homicide, or that if a serious aggravation of illness ensued damages might be recovered. I think, however, that it must be admitted that the present case is without precedent. . . .

There must be judgment for the plaintiff for [£]100 1s. 10½.

NOTES AND QUESTIONS

1. What was the basis on which the plaintiff recovered the cost of her railway ticket? While she also recovered a larger amount for nervous shock, why was that award not based on the same cause of action?

2. How did Wright J. define the principles governing the intentional infliction of nervous shock? Do you agree with the way he applied these principles to the facts? Why was he not bound by *Victorian Railways Commissioners v. Coultas* and *Allsop v. Allsop*? How did Wright J. address the types of concerns raised by Lord Wensleydale in *Lynch*?

3. Did Wright J. consider nervous shock to be an independent cause of action or merely an indirect means of causing physical injury? What is the practical significance of such a distinction?

4. In *Purdy v. Woznesensky*, [1937] 2 W.W.R. 116 (Sask. C.A.), the female plaintiff suffered nervous shock when the defendant punched her husband in the head, knocking him unconscious. The judge held that the defendant should have foreseen that by causing the plaintiff to witness the attack, he would probably upset her nervous system. Consequently, the judge imputed this intent to the defendant. In *Bielitski v. Obadiak* (1922), 65 D.L.R. 627 (Sask. C.A.), the defendant started a rumour that the plaintiff's son had hanged himself. After being retold several times, the rumour reached the plaintiff, who suffered serious nervous shock and became physically ill. Noting the defendant's failure to explain his conduct, the majority imputed intent to him. Haultain C.J.S. dissented, holding that the plaintiff's injury was not intentionally inflicted, nor the natural, probable or necessary consequence of the defendant's act. Was the doctrine of imputed intent correctly applied in *Wilkinson*, *Purdy* and *Bielitski*? Why did the court not apply the doctrine of transferred intent?

5. In *Wainwright v. Home Office*, [2004] 2 A.C. 406 at paras. 37-40 (H.L.), Lord Hoffmann indicated that *Wilkinson* was a negligence case, which Wright J. characterized as an intentional tort case in order to avoid having to deny the plaintiff's claim pursuant to the then-binding authority of *Victorian Railways Commissioners*. Would you agree with this analysis of *Wilkinson*?

RADOVSKIS v. TOMM
(1957), 9 D.L.R. (2d) 751 (Man. Q.B.)

WILLIAMS C.J.Q.B.:—On August 28, 1956, the infant plaintiff, 5½ years old Anda Radovskis, was raped by the defendant who was convicted of the offence and is presently serving a lengthy sentence in the Penitentiary.

This action is brought by the child suing by her father Robert Radovskis as next friend to recover damages for the trespass to her person; by the father to recover hospital and medical expenses, loss of wages, and for "worry and inconvenience"; and by the child's mother to recover damages for nervous shock alleged to have been sustained by the mother.

. . .

No medical evidence was offered and the mother did not give evidence. Her husband did say that his wife had not good nerves before and that since they had been bad.

But that is not sufficient to support a claim for damages. In *Guay v. Sun Publishing Co.*, *supra*, Estey J., after discussing the medical evidence before the Court, said (p. 589 D.L.R., p. 238 S.C.R.): "Moreover, it is important to keep in mind what must be proved in order that damages may be recovered, as stated in Pollock on Torts, 15th ed., pp. 37-8, as follows: 'A state of mind such as fear or acute grief is not in itself capable of assessment as measurable temporal damage. But visible and provable illness may be the natural consequence of violent emotion, and may furnish a ground of action against a person whose wrongful act or want of due care produced that emotion. . . . In every case the question is whether the shock and the illness were in fact natural or direct consequences of the wrongful act or default; if they were, the illness, not the shock, furnishes the measurable damage, and there is no more difficulty in assessing it than in assessing damages for bodily injuries of any kind.'"

In this case there was no visible and provable illness within the meaning of this quotation. The mother's action is dismissed without costs.

SAMMS v. ECCLES
358 P.2d 344 (Utah S.C. 1961)

CROCKETT J.: Plaintiff Marcia G. Samms sought to recover damages from David Eccles for injury resulting from severe emotional distress she claims to have suffered because he persistently annoyed her with indecent proposals.

. . .

Plaintiff alleged that she is a respectable married woman; that she has never encouraged the defendant's attentions in any way but has repulsed them; that all during the time from May to December, 1957, the defendant repeatedly and persistently called her by phone at various hours including late at night, soliciting her to have illicit sexual relations with him; and that on one occasion came to her residence in connection with such a solicitation and made an indecent exposure of his person. She charges that she regarded his proposals as insulting, indecent and obscene; that her feelings were deeply wounded; and that as a result thereof she suffered great anxiety and fear for her personal safety and severe emotional distress for which she asks $1,500 as actual, and a like amount as punitive, damages.

. . .

Due to the highly subjective and volatile nature of emotional distress and the variability of its causations, the courts have historically been wary of dangers in opening the door to recovery therefor. This is partly because such claims may easily be fabricated: or as sometimes stated, are easy to assert and hard to defend against. They have, therefore, been reluctant to allow such a right of action unless the emotional distress was suffered as a result of some other overt tort. Nevertheless, recognizing the reality of such injuries and the injustice of permitting them to go unrequited, in many cases courts have strained to find the other tort as a peg upon which to hang the right of recovery.

Some of these have been unrealistic, or even flimsy. For instance, a technical battery was found where an insurance adjuster derisively tossed a coin on the bed of a woman who was in a hospital with a heart condition, and because of this tort she was allowed to recover for distress caused by his other attempts at intimidation in accusing her of goldbricking and attempting to defraud his company; courts have also dealt with trespass where hotel employees have invaded rooms occupied by married couples and imputed to them immoral conduct; and other similar torts have been used as a basis for such recovery. But a realistic analysis of many of these cases will show that the recognized tort is but incidental and that the real basis of recovery is the outraged feelings and emotional distress resulting from some aggravated conduct of the defendant. The lengths to which courts have gone to find a basis for allowing such recoveries serves to emphasize their realization that justice demands that grossly wrong conduct which causes such an injury to another should be held accountable.

In recent years courts have shown an increasing awareness of the necessity and justice of forthrightly recognizing the true basis for allowing recovery for such wrongs and of getting rid of the shibboleth that another tort peg is necessary to that purpose. Examples are: *Great Atlantic & Pacific Tea Co. v. Roch*, injuries caused by shock where a grocery man included a dead rat in a package as a joke; *Savage v. Boies*, distress caused by false representation that plaintiff's child had been injured in an automobile accident; *Cohen v. Lion Products Co.*, distress to plaintiff's husband resulted from mandatory orders and charges of failure made to him as an employee by defendant's officers.

In *LaSalle Extension University v. Fogarty*, upon defendant's refusal to pay plaintiff's demand, plaintiff sent threatening letters to the defendant, and to his neighbors and employer, for the purpose of harassing him into paying their claim, against which it ultimately proved he had a good defense. Recovery was allowed on his counterclaim for emotional distress thus wrongfully caused him. The court cited the Iowa case of *Barnett v. Collection Service Co.* and quoted the rule which has come to be widely recognized that: "where the act is willful or malicious, as distinguished from being merely negligent, that recovery may be had for mental pain, though no physical injury results."

A case closely analogous to the instant one where such recovery was allowed is the recently decided one of *Mitran v. Williamson*. It holds that a complaint alleging that the defendant had repeatedly solicited plaintiff to have illicit intercourse and had sent obscene photographs of himself to her stated a cause of action.

. . .

Our study of the authorities, and of the arguments advanced, convinces us that, conceding such a cause of action may not be based upon mere negligence, the best considered view recognizes an action for severe emotional distress, though not accompanied by bodily impact or physical injury, where the defendant intentionally engaged in some conduct toward the plaintiff, (a) with the purpose of inflicting emotional distress, or, (b) where any reasonable person would have known that such would result; and his actions are of such a nature as to be considered outrageous and intolerable in that they offend against the generally accepted standards of decency and morality. This test seems to be a more realistic safeguard against false claims than to insist upon finding some other attendant tort, which may be of minor character, or fictional.

It is further to be observed that the argument against allowing such an action because groundless charges may be made is not a good reason for denying recovery. If the right to recover for injury resulting from the wrongful conduct could be defeated whenever such dangers exist, many of the grievances the law deals with would be eliminated. That some claims may be spurious should not compel those who administer justice to shut their eyes to serious wrongs and let them go without being brought to account. It is the function of courts and juries to determine whether claims are valid or false. This responsibility should not be shunned merely because the task may be difficult to perform.

We quite agree with the idea that under usual circumstances the solicitation to sexual intercourse would not be actionable even though it may be offensive to the offeree. It seems to be a custom of long standing and one which in all likelihood will continue. The assumption is usually indulged that most solicitations occur under such conditions as to fall within the well-known phrase of Chief Justice Magruder that, "there is no harm in asking." The Supreme Court of Kentucky in *Reed v. Maley* pertinently observed that an action will not lie in favor of a woman against a man who, without trespass or assault, makes such a request; and that the reverse is also true: that a man would have no right of action against a woman for such a solicitation.

But the situations just described, where tolerance for the conduct referred to is indulged, are clearly distinguishable from the aggravated circumstances the plaintiff claims existed here. Even though her complaint may not flawlessly state such a cause of action, the facts were sufficiently disclosed that the case she proposes to prove could be found to fall within the requirements hereinabove discussed. Therefore, the trial court erred in dismissing the action.

NOTES AND QUESTIONS

1. Why did the mother's claim fail in *Radovskis*? Is the judge suggesting that grief and mental distress are not worthy of compensation or that they are incapable of assessment in the absence of physical injury? Would these factors justify denying recovery for grief or mental distress?

2. Traditionally, the Canadian and English courts required the plaintiff to prove either actual physical harm or some serious psychological illness to recover for nervous shock. For example in *Heighington v. Ontario* (1987), 60 O.R. (2d) 641 (H.C.), aff'd (1989), 69 O.R. (2d) 484 (C.A.), the court stated that damages were recoverable in nervous shock for recognizable psychiatric disorders, but not for stress, strain, upset, or anxiety. See also *Wipfli v. Britten* (1982), 22 C.C.L.T. 104 (B.C.S.C.); *Hasenclever v. Hoskins* (1988), 47 C.C.L.T. 225 (Ont. Div. Ct.); *Sopinka (Litigation Guardian of) v. Sopinka* (2001), 55 O.R. (3d) 529 (S.C.J.); and *Wainwright v. Home Office*, [2004] 2 A.C. 406 at para. 47 (H.L.).

3. According to *Samms*, what must the plaintiff establish to succeed in an action for the intentional infliction of emotional distress? How does this tort action differ from the one in *Wilkinson*? Based on the principles in *Samms*, would the mother in *Radovskis* have recovered? For a thoughtful discussion of the differences between the

Canadian and American approach, see *Mainland Sawmills Ltd. v. I.W.A.-Canada*, 2006 BCSC 1195.

(a) BROADENING OF LIABILITY

The Canadian courts have expanded recovery for the intentional infliction of nervous shock. This has resulted from either generously interpreting the facts to meet the traditional requirements of the tort or by rephrasing these requirements in broader terms. In *Rahemtulla v. Vanfed Credit Union* (1984), 29 C.C.L.T. 78 (B.C.S.C.), a woman who was accused of theft and summarily fired was awarded $5,000 for the intentional infliction of nervous shock. McLachlin J. stated that the requirement in *Wilkinson* that the defendant's act must be plainly calculated to cause harm would be met if the defendant's conduct was flagrant or outrageous, and the defendant acted in reckless disregard to possible harm or if it was foreseeable that profound distress would ensue. Moreover, while McLachlin J. quoted *Radovskis* for the principle that visible and provable illness was required, she stated that the absence of expert medical evidence was not fatal to the claim. McLachlin J. acknowledged that the plaintiff's other problems, including the discovery of a tumour in her chest, might have contributed to her distress, but stated at para. 33 that: "the most significant cause of her depression and continuing unhappiness" was the defendant's conduct and its effect on her employment prospects.

In *Prinzo v. Baycrest Centre for Geriatric Care* (2002), 60 O.R. (3d) 474 (C.A.), the plaintiff had worked for 17 years in a beauty shop. She missed work for several months because of a mental illness. During that time, her employer announced that her position was being eliminated for financial reasons and accused her of malingering. There was no financial need to eliminate the plaintiff's position and she was not malingering. As a result of the defendant's conduct, the plaintiff's fragile health deteriorated. The plaintiff sued on several grounds including the intentional infliction of mental suffering. Relying on *Rahemtulla*, the Court of Appeal stated that the defendant's conduct must be flagrant and outrageous, calculated to produce harm, and result in visible provable injury. The court upheld the $15,000 award of general damages but overturned the $5,000 punitive damage award.

NOTES AND QUESTIONS

1. In *Mustapha v. Culligan of Canada Ltd.*, 2008 SCC 27, a negligent infliction of "mental injury" case, McLachlin C.J. stated at para. 9 "The law does not recognize upset, disgust, anxiety, agitation or other mental states that fall short of injury. I would not purport to define compensable injury exhaustively, except to say that it must be serious and prolonged and rise above the ordinary annoyances, anxieties and fears that people living in society routinely, if sometimes reluctantly, accept." Is McLachlin J.'s approach in *Rahemtulla* consistent with her statement in *Mustapha*?

2. In what ways do *Rahemtulla* and *Pinzo* differ from the principles in *Wilkinson*? The general approach in those two cases has been widely followed. See for example *Young v. Borzoni* (2007), 64 B.C.L.R. (4th) 157 (C.A.); *McLean v. Danicic* (2009), 95 O.R. (3d) 570 (S.C.J.); and *Fitzpatrick v. Orwin*, 2012 ONSC 3492, aff'd 2014 ONCA 124.

But see *High Parklane Consulting Inc. v. Royal Group Technologies Ltd.* (2007), 44 C.C.L.T. (3d) 169 (Ont. S.C.J.); and *Piresferreira v. Ayotte* (2010), 263 O.A.C. 347 (C.A.). In the latter case, it was stated that the court must find that the defendant had a subjective intent to harm the plaintiff or that such an intent can be imputed. A defendant's reckless disregard for the plaintiff's emotional well-being does not satisfy this intent requirement. Can you reconcile the analysis of intent in *Piresferreira* with that in *Rahemtulla* and *Prinzo*?

3. In *Saadati v. Moorhead*, 2017 SCC 28, the plaintiff sued for psychological injuries, including personality changes and cognitive difficulties, following a traffic collision. However, the plaintiff failed to adduce expert evidence that he suffered a recognized psychiatric illness. The court allowed the claim, stating at para. 2: "Just as recovery for *physical* injury is not, as a matter of law, conditioned upon a claimant adducing diagnostic evidence in support, recovery for *mental* injury does not require proof of a recognizable psychiatric illness. This and other mechanisms by which some courts have historically sought to control recovery for mental injury are, in my respectful view, premised upon dubious perceptions of psychiatry and of mental illness in general, which Canadian tort law should repudiate." Do you agree that no distinction should be drawn between claims for physical and psychological injuries? What impact, if any, will *Saadati* have on claims for the intentional infliction of nervous shock?

4. In *Cant v. Cant* (1984), 49 O.R. (2d) 25 (Co. Ct.), the court entertained a claim for intentional infliction of nervous shock arising out of a custody battle over a child. However, in *Frame v. Smith*, [1987] 2 S.C.R. 99, the court stated that it would be inappropriate to permit common law tort actions in child custody and separation disputes given the comprehensive legislative schemes in place for dealing with these issues. Wilson J., who dissented on a different issue, specifically said that intentional infliction of nervous shock claims should not be available in family law because they would provide arbitrary coverage and encourage vindictive litigation. See also *Davenport v. Miller* (1990), 108 N.B.R. (2d) 336 (Q.B.); and *Louie v. Lastman (No. 2)* (2001), 54 O.R. (3d) 301 (S.C.J.), aff'd on other grounds (2002), 61 O.R. (3d) 459 (C.A.). Do you prefer the approach in *Frame* to that in *Cant*? See Cole, "Intentional Infliction of Emotional Distress Among Family Members" (1984) 61 Denver L. Rev. 553.

In *OPO v. MLA*, [2014] EWCA Civ 1277, rev'd [2015] UKSC 32, an injunction was sought on the plaintiff's behalf preventing his father from publishing a semi-autobiographical book containing graphic descriptions of the abuse that the father had suffered and the father's acts of self-harm. The evidence suggested that the book's publication would cause the plaintiff, a pre-teen with various cognitive disabilities, significant psychological harm. The injunction was refused on the basis that the plaintiff would not have a viable claim for the intentional infliction of nervous shock under *Wilkinson* if the book were published. Do you agree? What policy factors would you raise in support of, or in opposition to, the decision?

5. There has been a tendency to sue for intentional infliction of nervous shock in conjunction with harassment and other actions, particularly in wrongful dismissal and other employment-related cases. For example, in *Merrifield v. Canada (Attorney General)*, 2017 ONSC 1333, the plaintiff sued his employer and supervisors for the

intentional infliction of mental suffering, harassment, *Charter* breaches, breach of the employment contract, abuse of public office, and breach of fiduciary duty. Ten years after the litigation began, Merrifield's claims for the intentional infliction of nervous shock and harassment were upheld and he was awarded $100,000 in general damages, $41,000 in special damages and $825,000 in costs.

In overturning the trial judgment, the Ontario Court of Appeal called for a more carefully reasoned and incremental approach to recognizing new intentional torts, stating at para. 105: "the trial judge erred in concluding that the tort of harassment exists in Ontario and we are not persuaded that the tort should be recognized." The Court of Appeal also held that the trial judge erred in concluding that the intentional infliction of nervous shock claim was made out on the facts. Merrifield's employer and supervisors were awarded costs on the appeal, cross-appeal and trial. *Merrifield v. Canada (Attorney General)*, 2019 ONCA 205.

Given the current scope of the torts of assault and intentional infliction of nervous shock, is there any reason to recognize an independent action for harassment? As we have seen and will discuss later in this chapter, even relatively simple intentional torts cases often generate a proliferation of overlapping and novel claims. What impact will or should the Court of Appeal decision in *Merrifield* have on this trend?

Even though the trial judgment was overturned, it is worth noting that Merrifield's costs as of the end of the trial were almost six times greater than the damage award. The case has taken 12 years to resolve and it is not clear if Merrifield will seek leave to appeal to the Supreme Court of Canada

6. In *Wallace v. United Grain Growers Ltd.*, [1997] 3 S.C.R. 701, the court stated that damages for mental distress cannot be awarded in wrongful dismissal cases simply because the employer acted in bad faith or unfairly. Rather, in order to recover mental distress damages, the employee must establish that the employer's conduct amounted to a separate actionable wrong in tort or contract.

Nevertheless, mental distress claims are commonplace in wrongful dismissal and workplace "harassment" suits and the damage awards may be substantial. In *Boucher v. Wal-Mart Canada Corp.*, 2014 ONCA 419, the plaintiff who had a very good employment record with Wal-Mart for nine years was subject to an unrelenting six-month campaign of demoralizing, profane and demeaning conduct to force her resignation. The plaintiff's supervisor initiated the campaign after the plaintiff refused his demand that she falsify a food safety record. The plaintiff quit and sued her supervisor and Wal-Mart for constructive dismissal. The plaintiff was awarded $100,000 in compensatory damages for the intentional infliction of "mental suffering," the equivalent of 20 weeks' salary, $200,000 in aggravated damages, and a total of $110,000 in punitive damages. See also *Clark v. Canada*, [1994] 3 F.C. 323 (T.D.); *Sulz v. Canada (A.G.)* (2006), 54 B.C.L.R. (4th) 328 (S.C.), aff'd (2006), 60 B.C.L.R. (4th) 43 (C.A.); *Correia v. Canac Kitchens* (2008), 91 O.R. (3d) 353 (C.A.); *Piresferreira, supra*; and *Strudwick v. Applied Consumer & Clinical Evaluation Inc.*, 2016 ONCA 520.

7. Do the concerns about the multiplicity of actions and vindictive litigation expressed in *Frame, supra* regarding family law apply equally to employment-related litigation?

8. In *ABC v. Whillock*, [2015] EWHC 268 (Q.B.), the vice-principal of a special needs school emotionally manipulated a vulnerable student into sending him explicit sexual emails and pictures, and subsequently sexually abused her. After the relationship was discovered and the vice-principal was arrested, the student attempted suicide more than once, injured herself and suffered severe emotional distress which included heart palpitations, panic attacks and shortness of breath. The court indicated that the "sexual grooming" and emotional manipulation of the student would give rise to liability for the intentional infliction of nervous shock even in the absence of any physical contact. Should sexual grooming and emotional manipulation give rise to potential liability in relationships among peers?

9. For a discussion of the intentional infliction of nervous shock, see Réaume, "The Role of Intention in the Tort in *Wilkinson* v *Downton*" in Neyers, Chamberlain & Pitel, eds., *Emerging Issues in Tort Law* (2007) 533; Slade, "Intentional Infliction of Mental Suffering: Reconsidering the Test for Liability" (2008) 34 Adv. Q. 322; Handford, "*Wilkinson* v *Downton*: Pathways to the Future?" (2012) 20 Tort L. Rev. 145; Gray, "*Wilkinson* v *Downton*: New work for an old tort to do?" (2015) 23 Tort L. Rev. 127; and Liew, "The Rule in *Wilkinson* v *Downton*: Conduct, Intention, and Justifiability" (2015) 78 M.L.R. 349.

10. Should the Canadian courts abandon their purported allegiance to *Wilkinson* and adopt a broader common law tort for the intentional infliction of emotional distress based on the American approach?

(b) THE INNOMINATE INTENTIONAL TORT

Several Commonwealth authors have viewed *Wilkinson* as establishing an innominate intentional tort claim for all unjustified, intentionally inflicted bodily injuries — nervous shock being but one example. The other illustrations cited include intentionally infecting someone with a disease, setting a trap in someone's path, poisoning someone's food, and removing essential medicine from an incapacitated patient. Although such intentional conduct is morally blameworthy and likely to cause serious injury, it does not come within the traditional definition of the nominate intentional torts. Thus, the innominate action provides a convenient mechanism for redressing such claims without disturbing accepted principles.

NOTES AND QUESTIONS

1. An "innominate tort" is a tort that has not been specifically named. In contrast, nominate torts have specific names, such as "battery," "assault" and "false imprisonment."

2. It is difficult to determine the scope of the innominate intentional tort action. For example, does it apply solely to bodily injury or does it also include other interferences with physical autonomy? If accepted, would the innominate intentional tort action have provided a remedy in *Bird v. Jones*, included above in the section on false imprisonment? Could it be invoked in cases of sexual harassment that did not involve assault, battery or intentional infliction of nervous shock? See Howarth,

"Trespass and Intentional Interference with the Person" in Sappideen & Vines, eds., *Fleming's The Law of Torts*, 10th ed. (2011) 23 at 44-46.

3. In the United States, the courts have tended to deal with indirect injury cases by relaxing the requirements of directness in the nominate actions. This approach eliminates the need for an innominate intentional tort action and permits the intentional infliction of nervous shock to be recognized as an independent tort that is not tied to proof of physical injury. Nevertheless, there is support in the American case law for a *"prima facie* tort" doctrine, a principle that appears to be broader, but otherwise comparable to, the innominate intentional tort action. As one author noted:

> The prima facie tort is generally defined as the "infliction of intentional harm, resulting in damages, without excuse or justification, by an act or series of acts which would otherwise be lawful." The specific applications of this definition vary greatly based on the manner in which courts interpret these elements. These divergencies in interpretation lead courts to apply the prima facie tort in inconsistent ways: Shapiro, "The Prima Facie Tort Doctrine: Acknowledging the Need for Judicial Scrutiny of Malice" (1983) 63 Boston U.L. Rev. 1101 at 1101.

4. The High Court of Australia recognized a related cause of action in *Beaudesert Shire Council v. Smith* (1966), 120 C.L.R. 145 (H.C.A.). The court stated at page 156 that: "independently of trespass, negligence or nuisance but by an action for damages upon the case, a person who suffers harm or loss as the inevitable consequence of the unlawful, intentional and positive acts of another is entitled to damages from that other." However, the High Court subsequently ruled that this principle was unsound and should not be followed: *Northern Territory of Australia v. Mengel* (1995), 185 C.L.R. 307 (H.C.A.). See Mullany, *"Beaudesert* Buried" (1995) 111 L.Q.R. 583; and Cane, "The Inexorable Advance of Negligence" (1995) 3 Torts L.J. 205.

5. The Canadian position is difficult to assess because of the dearth of academic and judicial discussion. See Atrens, "Intentional Interference with the Person" in Linden, ed., *Studies in Canadian Tort Law* (1968) 378 at 397-401; *Graham v. Saville*, [1945] O.R. 301 at 310-11 (C.A.); *Canada Safeway Ltd. v. Manitoba Food & Commercial Workers, Local 832* (1983), 25 C.C.L.T. 1 (Man. C.A.); and *Cant v. Cant* (1984), 49 O.R. (2d) 25 (Co. Ct.).

6. Although the innominate intentional tort action, the *prima facie* tort doctrine and *Beaudesert* create distinct causes of action, they all reflect a concern with the inflexibility of the intentional torts. Based on the intentional tort actions discussed in this chapter, is this a legitimate concern? Can you suggest alternative mechanisms for dealing with this concern? As we shall see, at least some Canadian courts have responded to this situation by attempting to create new nominate intentional tort actions.

REVIEW PROBLEMS

1. The torts of assault and the intentional infliction of nervous shock both involve the apprehension created in the mind of the plaintiff. Provide an example of conduct that would give rise to both actions. See *Timmermans v. Buelow* (1984), 38 C.C.L.T. 136 (Ont. H.C.); and *Mahal v. Young* (1986), 36 C.C.L.T. 143 (B.C.S.C.).

2. Jones, a professional boxer, was incensed by a story that had been written about him by Smith, a local sports writer. Jones called Smith and told him to retract the story "or else." While Jones was not a particularly good boxer, he was widely known for his temper and long criminal record for unprovoked assaults. Smith was scared. When he explained to his wife what had happened, she fainted and hit her head on the floor, suffering a concussion. As Smith was preparing to take his wife to the hospital, Jones called again and indicated that he was coming over to "discuss these matters." Smith, who had a weak heart, suffered a minor heart attack brought on by the severe emotional strain of the boxer's threats coupled with his wife's injuries. Mr. and Mrs. Smith survived the incident and now wish to sue Jones. Your initial investigation has revealed that Jones was unaware of Smith's weak heart.

9. Invasion of Privacy

(a) INTRODUCTION

In Canada, privacy interests are protected in a piecemeal fashion by a myriad of civil actions and statutory provisions. The nominate intentional torts were not designed to redress invasions of privacy and only incidentally protect these interests. For example, homeowners will succeed in trespass to land against someone who has planted a listening device on their property, but not against an individual who intercepts their conversations without entering their land. Similar illustrations can be cited involving assault, intentional infliction of nervous shock, defamation, and intimidation. Shortcomings in the existing remedies have prompted consideration of both common law tort actions for invasion of privacy and the enactment of various types of privacy legislation.

MOTHERWELL v. MOTHERWELL
(1976), 73 D.L.R. (3d) 62 (Alta. S.C. (A.D.))

[The defendant, who suffered from a paranoid condition and was mentally unstable, continually harassed the plaintiffs (her brother, sister-in-law and father), making false accusations by way of telephone and mail. After the defendant refused their repeated requests to cease, the plaintiffs sued her for, *inter alia*, invasion of privacy and nuisance, claiming nominal damages and an injunction. The plaintiffs won at trial and the defendant appealed. The defendant argued that "no action lies with the plaintiffs . . . to restrain her lawful communications" with them.]

CLEMENT J.A.: . . . The arguments in appeal advanced by the appellant draw a distinction between nuisance and invasion of privacy. It is said that invasion of privacy does not come within the principle of private nuisance, and that it is a species of activity not recognized as remedial by the common law. It is urged that the common law does not have within itself the resources to recognize invasion of privacy as either included in an existing category or as a new category of nuisance, and that it has lost its original power, by which indeed it created itself, to note new ills arising in a growing and changing society and pragmatically to establish a principle to meet the need for control and remedy; and then by categories to develop the principle as the interests of justice make themselves sufficiently apparent. . . .

The rule of stare decisis operates, as it seems to me, to regulate the application of precedents to cases which can be said to fall within a category. When the circumstances of a case do not appear to bring it fairly within an established category, they may lie sufficiently within the concept of a principle that consideration of a new category is warranted. The scope of a category may in time be broadened by a trend in precedents which reflect judicial considerations going beyond the disciplines of *stare decisis*. Those same considerations, arising from adequately demonstrated social need of a continuing nature, may lead, when necessary to maintain social justice, to a new category or the review of a principle. . . .

[The court discussed the law of private nuisance at length and made particular reference to the three categories of nuisance recognized in *Clerk & Lindsell on Torts*, 13th ed. (1969) at 781. The third category — the undue interference with a neighbour in the comfortable and convenient enjoyment of his land — was the most germane to the case at bar.]

I think that the interests of our developing jurisprudence would be better served by approaching invasion of privacy by abuse of the telephone system as a new category [of private nuisance], rather than seeking by rationalization to enlarge the third category recognized by *Clerk & Lindsell*. We are dealing with a new factor. Heretofore the matters of complaint have reached the plaintiff's premises by natural means; sound through the air waves, pollution in many forms carried by air currents, vibrations through the earth, and the like. Here, the matters complained of arise within the premises through the use by the appellant of communication agencies in the nature of public utilities available to everyone, which the plaintiffs have caused to serve their premises. They are non-selective in the sense that so long as they are employed by the plaintiffs they have no control over the incoming communications. Nevertheless there are differences between the two agencies of telephone and mail and it does not necessarily follow from their similarities that both should be accepted into a new category.

The telephone system is so much the part of the daily life of society that many look on it as a necessity. Its use is certainly taken as a right at least in a social sense. It virtually makes neighbours not only of the persons close at hand, but those in distant places, other cities, other countries. It is a system provided for rational and reasonable communication between people, and its abuse by invasion of privacy is a matter of general interest. . . . It is essential to the operation of such a system that a call from someone be signalled to the intended receiver by sound such as the ringing of a bell. The receiver cannot know who is calling him until he answers. Calls must be answered if the system is to work. There are not many who would assert that protection against invasion of privacy by telephone would be a judicial idiosyncrasy. Further than that, the people of this Province through the Legislature have expressed a public interest in the proper use of the system in enacting s. 31 of the *Alberta Government Telephones Act*.

In *Clerk & Lindsell*, p. 785, para. 1396, this is said: "A nuisance of this kind, to be actionable, must be such as to be a real interference with the comfort or convenience of living according to the standards of the average man." This statement is amply supported by authority and I take it to be applicable to invasion of privacy. . . .

[Clement J.A. concluded that the respondents had valid claims in private nuisance for the invasion of their privacy through the abuse of the telephone system. He upheld the trial judge's award of nominal damages and the granting of an injunction against further calls. The harassing and offensive mail did not constitute a nuisance because it did not result in a substantial and unreasonable interference with the plaintiffs' use and enjoyment of their property.]

NOTES AND QUESTIONS

1. What was the basis of the decision in *Motherwell?* What factors did Clement J.A. consider in deciding to extend common law protection in nuisance? Would repeated threatening emails to the plaintiff's home computer constitute a private nuisance? For a critique of *Motherwell*, see *Hunter v. Canary Wharf Ltd.*, [1997] 2 All E.R. 426 (H.L.).

2. What remedies did the plaintiffs seek in *Motherwell?* Why did they not claim compensatory damages? Should that have been fatal to their claim? See *Hasenclever v. Hoskins* (1988), 47 C.C.L.T. 225 (Ont. Div. Ct.), in which the inadequacies in pleading damages resulted in the dismissal of a claim similar to that in *Motherwell*.

3. The number of "harassment" claims has increased. Like *Motherwell*, some involve offensive phone calls and mail, but others include direct verbal confrontations, threats and stalking. In some cases, the defendant's motion to strike out the harassment claim was denied, while in others the court held that such conduct might give rise to a common law tort action for harassment or the invasion of privacy. See generally *Roth v. Roth* (1991), 4 O.R. (3d) 740 (Gen. Div.); *MacKay v. Buelow* (1995), 24 C.C.L.T. (2d) 184 (Ont. Gen. Div.); *Canadian Tire Bank v. Roach*, 2006 BCPC 120; and *Savino v. Shelestowsky*, 2013 ONSC 4394.

4. In *Mainland Sawmills Ltd. v. I.W.A.-Canada*, 2006 BCSC 1195, the court noted that the Canadian authorities were split on whether a common law tort action for harassment existed. Without resolving the issue, the court stated that if such a tort existed, the plaintiff would have to establish that: the defendant's conduct was outrageous; the defendant intended to cause emotional distress or acted in reckless disregard as to this possibility; and the plaintiff suffered severe or extreme emotional distress as a result. The court then dismissed the plaintiffs' claims for harassment because they did not suffer extreme or severe emotional distress. How do the elements of harassment in *Mainland* differ from those of intentional infliction of nervous shock in: (a) *Wilkinson v. Downton*, [1897] 2 Q.B. 57; and (b) *Rahemtulla v. Vanfed Credit Union* (1984), 29 C.C.C.T. 78 (B.C.S.C.)?

5. As noted earlier, the Ontario Court of Appeal recently held that the tort of harassment did not exist in Ontario and doubted that the tort should be recognized: *Merrifield v. Canada (Attorney General)*, 2019 ONCA 205. In contrast to *Merrifield*, *Mainland*, *supra* takes a more positive position on the recognition of a tort of harassment. Which approach is preferable?

6. The English courts recognized a common law tort for a range of harassing and threatening conduct in 1993, only to reject it four years later once statutory protection from harassment was enacted. See *Khorasandjian v. Bush*, [1993] Q.B. 727 (C.A.); and *Hunter, supra*. See also *AXA Insurance Singapore Pte. Ltd. v. Chandran s/o Natesan*, [2013] SGHC 158, in which the court dismissed the plaintiff's harassment claim,

stating that Parliament rather than a court was the appropriate forum for addressing the complex issues that such claims raise.

7. For a discussion of the protection provided by the existing nominate torts, see Burns, "Privacy and the Common Law: A Tangled Skein Unravelling?" in Gibson, ed., *Aspects of Privacy Law* (1980) 21; Irvine, "The Invasion of Privacy in Ontario: A 1983 Survey" [1983] L.S.U.C. Special Lectures 25; and Fenrich, "Common Law Protection of Individual Rights in Personal Information" (1996) 65 Fordham L. Rev. 951.

(b) THE AMERICAN COMMON LAW PRIVACY ACTIONS

One of the challenging issues in recognizing a common law tort for the invasion of privacy is defining the concept. The broader the definition of privacy, the more it conflicts with other interests, such as freedom of speech, movement and association. These problems have led some authors to question the value of privacy as a legal concept. Rather than attempting to formulate a single broad definition of privacy, most American states recognize four categories of cases that may give rise to common law tort action for the invasion of privacy. These four categories were first formulated by W. Prosser in "Privacy" (1960) 48 Cal. L.R. 383 and later adopted by The American Law Institute in the *Restatement, Second, Torts* (1977) vol. 3 at §652A-E. The Institute set out the following general principles:

(1) One who invades the right of privacy of another is subject to liability for the resulting harm to the interests of the other.

(2) The right of privacy is invaded by:

(a) unreasonable intrusion upon the seclusion of another, as stated in §652B (i.e., intentionally intruding, physically or otherwise, upon the solitude or seclusion of another or his private affairs or concerns, if the intrusion would be highly offensive to a reasonable person); or
(b) appropriation of the other's name or likeness, as stated in §652C; or
(c) uunreasonable publicity given to the other's private life, as stated in §652D; (i.e., giving publicity to a matter concerning the private life of another if the matter publicized is of a kind that would be highly offensive to a reasonable person and is not of legitimate concern to the public); or
(d) publicity that unreasonably places the other in a false light before the public, as stated in §652E (i.e., giving publicity to a matter concerning another that places the other before the public in a false light, if the false light in which the other was placed would be highly offensive to a reasonable person, and the actor had knowledge of or acted in reckless disregard as to the falsity of the publicized matter and the false light in which the other would be placed).

NOTES AND QUESTIONS

1. For a searing criticism of the concept of privacy, see Wacks, "The Poverty of 'Privacy'" (1980) 96 L.Q.R. 73. In his conclusion he states at page 88:

"Privacy" has grown into a large and unwieldy concept. Synonymous with autonomy, it has colonised traditional liberties, become entangled with confidentiality, secrecy, defamation, property, and the storage of information. It would be unreasonable to expect a notion so complex as "privacy" not to spill into regions with which it is closely related, but this process has resulted in the dilution of "privacy" itself, diminishing the prospect of its own protection as well as the protection of the related interests.

Is Wacks opposed to protecting the specific interests that fall within the rubric of privacy or to the lumping of all of these matters into privacy?

2. The American Law Institute, *Restatement, Second, Torts* (1977) vol. 3 at §652A comment c indicates that additional privacy interests may be recognized as warranting recognition. What additional privacy interests, if any, warrant recognition as an independent category of common law privacy protection?

3. For a review of the American law see Bezanson, "The Right to Privacy Revisited: Privacy, News, and Social Change, 1890-1990" (1992) 80 Cal. L. Rev. 1133; Richards & Solove, "Prosser's Privacy Law: A Mixed Legacy" (2010) 98:6 Cal. L. Rev. 1887; and Dobbs, Hayden & Bublick, *The Law of Torts*, 2d ed. (2011) vol. 3 at 351-84. Would you agree with Dobbs, Hayden & Bublick who state at 354 that the four categories overlap and create problems of interpretation?

(c) EMERGING COMMON LAW PRIVACY ACTIONS IN CANADA

The common law principles of privacy have evolved piecemeal in Canada, providing redress for some particularly troubling and easily defined categories of privacy cases. While the Canadian courts are moving toward recognizing additional categories of privacy claims, the exact state of the law in these areas cannot be determined with certainty. Several of the relevant cases simply involve unsuccessful pretrial motions to strike out the plaintiff's privacy claims. In other cases, the court's comments on privacy are made in passing or phrased in equivocal terms. Some courts have awarded global damages for a plaintiff's overlapping claims in assault, intentional infliction of nervous shock, malicious prosecution, harassment, and invasion of privacy without providing much analysis. Finally, rapidly changing technology and its abuse has and will continue to pose new privacy and confidentiality issues. The tentative nature of the current common law tort of privacy is aptly reflected in *Somwar v. McDonald's Restaurants of Canada Ltd.* (2006), 79 O.R. (3d) 172 at 180 (S.C.J.), in which the court concluded that "it is not settled law in Ontario that there is no tort of invasion of privacy."

NOTES AND QUESTIONS

1. The Australian and New Zealand courts, like their Canadian counterparts, have recognized a common law tort action for invasion of privacy in various categories of cases. See Barker *et al.*, *The Law of Torts in Australia*, 5th ed. (2011) at 390-416. In contrast, the English courts have refused to recognize tort of privacy. According to the House of Lords in *Wainwright v. Home Office*, [2004] 2 A.C. 406 (H.L.), the creation of a tort of privacy requires a comprehensive approach that can only be provided by legislation. However, the English courts have provided redress for phone hacking and other intentional misuses of private information. See generally

Jones, "Principles of Liability in Tort" 1 at 23-25 and Carty, "Breach of Confidence and Privacy" 1931 in Jones *et al.*, eds., *Clerk & Lindsell on Torts*, 22nd ed. (2018).

2. The Canadian courts have not yet resolved whether watching and following a person in public or questioning a person's friends or neighbours constitutes a common law tort for the invasion of privacy. Should there be any limits on such behaviour? Should it make a difference if the person watching is a police officer, private detective, devoted fan, newspaper photographer, or curious member of the public?

See *Poole v. Ragen*, [1958] O.W.N. 77 (H.C.) (damages awarded for private nuisance for being repeatedly followed by the police); and *Davis v. McArthur* (1971), 17 D.L.R. (3d) 760 (B.C.C.A.) (provincial privacy act claim for being followed over a seven-month period by private investigator dismissed).

3. In *Saccone v. Orr* (1981), 19 C.C.L.T. 37 (Ont. Co. Ct.), the defendant secretly tape-recorded his telephone call with the plaintiff. When the plaintiff learned about the tape, he warned the defendant not to use it, but the defendant denied its existence. The defendant subsequently played the tape at a municipal council meeting in an effort to clear himself of certain allegations. The local newspaper printed the tape's content, to the embarrassment of the plaintiff. The judge summarized the facts and stated at page 46: "Certainly, for want of a better description as to what happened, this is an invasion of privacy, and despite the very able argument of defendant's counsel that no such action exists, I have come to the conclusion that the plaintiff must be given some right of recovery for what the defendant has in this case done."

Was it the unauthorized recording, the unauthorized playing of the tape or both, that constituted the invasion of privacy? Would the judge have reached the same conclusion had the defendant made and revealed detailed written notes of the call without the plaintiff's knowledge? Unless the plaintiff demanded and received assurances of confidentiality, why should he assume that the defendant would keep their conversation private?

4. Should different considerations apply when a person who is not a party to a telephone call secretly tapes, scans or otherwise intercepts the call? In *Watts v. Klaemt*, 2007 BCSC 662, the defendant was subject to ongoing insults, taunts and verbal threats by one of his neighbours. The defendant surreptitiously intercepted and recorded the neighbour's cordless telephone calls for about a year, including those between the neighbour and the plaintiff. In two of the intercepted calls, the plaintiff wrongfully disclosed confidential workplace information. The defendant then shared these two calls with the plaintiff's employer, which resulted in the plaintiff being fired for breach of trust. The defendant was held liable for $30,000 in general damages and $5,000 in punitive damages for breaching the provincial privacy act.

5. In *Gulati v. MGN Ltd.*, [2016] 3 All E.R. 799 (C.A.), the defendant newspaper publishers repeatedly hacked the plaintiffs' cell phones over a period of years and used the information in various published articles. The court framed the defendants' liability in terms of the "misuse of private information," and awarded the plaintiffs damages for the wrongful accessing of their private communications (*i.e.* the hacking itself), the disclosure of their private information in the published articles and the accompanying distress. The damage awarded to the eight plaintiffs ranged from £72,500 to £260,250. Does the term "misuse of private information" appropriately

characterize the defendants' wrongful conduct? See Wright, *Tort Law and Human Rights*, 2d ed. (2017) at 269-306.

6. In *Ste-Marie c. Placements J.P.M. Marquis* (2005), 31 C.C.L.T. (3d) 167 (Qc. C.A.), an employer secretly wire-tapped phone lines that an employee used at work. The employer gave the police a tape of the employee's conversation with a known safecracker. The employee was arrested but never charged, and was fired. The employee sued for invasion of privacy, claiming breaches of his rights under the *Civil Code of Québec*, S.Q. 1991, c. 64 and the Québec *Charter of Human Rights and Freedoms*, C.Q.L.R., c. C-12. In dismissing the action, the court stated that employees have a diminished expectation of privacy, as their rights must be reconciled with their contractual and other duties to their employer. In contrast to *Saccone, supra* the Québec Court of Appeal stated that the fact that the conversation was taped rather than overheard changed nothing, given its content and relationship to the employee's duties.

7. In *Milner v. Manufacturers Life Insurance Co.* (2005), 36 C.C.L.T. (3d) 232 (B.C.S.C.), the defendant believed that the plaintiff's application for long-term disability benefits was based on false claims. The defendant arranged for video surveillance of the plaintiff, which incidentally captured members of her family. The plaintiff claimed damages for breach of privacy under the *Privacy Act*, R.S.B.C. 1996, c. 373. In dismissing the claim, the court stated that the defendant had a legitimate interest in conducting video surveillance, given the nature of the plaintiff's claim and her questionable credibility.

In *Tremblay c. Cie d'assurance Standard Life*, 2008 QCCS 2488, aff'd 2010 QCCA 932, a medical re-examination of the plaintiff raised doubts about the extent of his injuries. The defendant arranged to have the plaintiff secretly video-taped over a three-day period on five separate occasions in the span of about a year. During one of these sessions, the defendant's investigator mistakenly video-taped the plaintiff's brother engaged in very active tasks. Based on that mistake, the defendant cut off the plaintiff's disability benefits, but resumed them once the plaintiff brought this error to its attention. The plaintiff sued for invasion of his privacy and damage to his reputation in being treated as a liar. The court held that the defendant had not acted reasonably in ordering the surveillance and awarded the plaintiff compensatory damages and $100,000 in punitive damages. Do you agree with the court that the defendant acted unreasonably in the circumstances? Should insurance companies have to meet a minimum threshold to justify arranging surveillance of potential claimants? If so, how would you define that threshold?

For other cases involving the use of video surveillance in defence of personal injury claims, see *Ferenczy v. MCI Medical Clinics* (2004), 70 O.R. (3d) 277 (S.C.J.); and *State Farm Mutual Automobile Insurance Co. v. Canada (Privacy Commissioner)*, 2010 FC 736.

8. In *Lord v. McGregor* (2000), 50 C.C.L.T. (2d) 206 (B.C.S.C.), the plaintiff's disruptive behaviour during earlier visits with his son, a prisoner, resulted in the plaintiff being barred from the penitentiary. Nevertheless, the plaintiff informed the prison officials that he was going to visit his son and notified the media. The plaintiff's visit, including his altercation with the staff, was video-taped and a copy was released to a television station that broadcasted it. The video was taken in a public reception

area in which there were signs informing visitors of the possibility of being video-taped. The plaintiff brought various claims, including a common law action for the invasion of privacy. In dismissing the claim, the judge stated that the emerging academic discussion and case law did not support a common law right to privacy on the facts.

In what circumstances, if any, should video-taping of an individual in public give rise to a common law tort action for the invasion of privacy? Should the defendant's motive or the fact that the plaintiff was informed be considered in determining if the video-taping gives rise to a common law privacy action? Should security cameras in banks, stores or high-risk crime areas be treated differently than the targeted surveillance of a specific individual?

9. In *Lipiec v. Borsa* (1996), 31 C.C.L.T. (2d) 294 (Ont. Gen. Div.), the defendants became obsessed with their neighbour's landscaping. Out of spite, the defendants removed a fence separating the properties and installed a surveillance camera that continuously monitored the plaintiffs' backyard. The plaintiffs sued and recovered for invasion of privacy. While expressing reluctance to impose liability for the surveillance alone, the judge quoted Fleming, *The Law of Torts*, 8th ed. (1992) at 604 for the proposition that "there is considerable authority which could support redress against overlooking or spying on the premises of others for the sole purpose of causing annoyance." Would liability have been warranted if the defendants had installed the camera partially for security purposes? See also *Morland-Jones v. Taerk*, 2014 ONSC 3061.

10. As discussed in Chapter 5, the advent of drones raises issues regarding nuisance, trespass to land and the invasion of privacy. In regard to privacy, what limits should be placed on the public and private use of drones, particularly if they are equipped with video cameras? What are the privacy implications, if any, of public access to Google Streetsview? See *Pia Grillo c. Google inc.*, 2014 QCCQ 9394, in which the plaintiff recovered damages for the invasion of privacy when an embarrassing picture of her was captured by Google Steetview.

11. Increasingly, the Canadian courts have accepted that unwanted media attention may constitute an actionable invasion of privacy. See for example *F.(P.) v. Ontario* (1989), 47 C.C.L.T. 231 (Ont. Dt. Ct.) (young offender's picture published in local newspaper); *R.(L.) v. Nyp* (1995), 25 C.C.L.T. (2d) 309 (Ont. Gen. Div.) (media disclosing that undercover police officer was sexually assaulted); and *Valiquette c. Gazette (The)* (1991), 8 C.C.L.T. (2d) 302 (Qc. S.C.), rev'd in part, [1997] R.J.Q. 30 (C.A.) (media disclosing that a teacher had AIDS).

In *Nitsopoulos v. Wong* (2008), 60 C.C.L.T. (3d) 318 (Ont. S.C.J.), the defendant reporter pretended to be a maid to gather information for a series of newspaper articles. Based on this deception, the defendant was allowed into the plaintiffs' home. Twenty-two months after the articles were published in the Globe and Mail, the plaintiffs sued for invasion of privacy and deceit. In rejecting the defendants' motion to strike the claims, the court emphasized that the defendants knowingly deceived the plaintiffs in order to gather information about their private lives.

Would *F.(P.)*, *R.(L.)*, *Valiquette*, and *Nitsopoulos* give rise to a common law tort action pursuant to The American Law Institute, *Restatement, Second, Torts* (1977) vol. 3 at §652D for unreasonable publicity given to the private life of another?

12. In *Aubry v. Éditions Vice-Versa*, [1998] 1 S.C.R. 591, a photographer took a picture of a young woman sitting on the steps of a building in Montreal. When the photograph was subsequently published in an arts magazine, the young woman sued the photographer and the magazine, claiming invasion of privacy. A majority of the court upheld the lower court's $2,000 damage award under Québec's *Civil Code*. The majority stated that a balance had to be struck in each case between the individual's right to privacy and the right to freedom of expression under the Québec *Charter of Human Rights and Freedoms*. The plaintiff's right prevailed in this case, partially because the photographer could have asked for permission to take her picture and because she was identifiable from the published picture. See also *Goulet c. Gazette (The)*, 2012 QCCA 1085.

Assuming a person is in public, should taking a picture of his or her face give rise to a common law privacy action if the person's consent is not obtained and the picture is: (a) used for commercial purposes; or (b) not used for commercial purposes? Should the same principles apply to drawing a picture of the person's face? See also *Douglas v. Hello! Ltd.*, [2001] 2 All E.R. 289 (C.A.); *Campbell v. MGN Ltd.*, [2004] 2 All E.R. 995 (H.L.); and *Hosking v. Runting*, [2005] 1 N.Z.L.R. 1 (C.A.).

13. In the absence of comprehensive privacy legislation, the patchwork of common law cases will continue. For example, in *Somwar*, *supra* the court refused to strike out the plaintiff's invasion of privacy claim that undertaking a credit check without the subject's consent gave rise to a common law tort action for the invasion of privacy.

14. The common law tort action for the invasion of privacy and related liability issues have resulted in a flood of recent articles. For example, a search for scholarly articles in Canada since 2010 generated over 160 references. While some of the articles focused on the emerging and established common law tort actions for the invasion of privacy, others dealt with narrowly defined issues and esoteric topics.

(d) ESTABLISHED COMMON LAW TORT ACTIONS IN CANADA

JONES v. TSIGE
2012 ONCA 32

SHARPE J.A.: . . . In July 2009, the appellant, Sandra Jones, discovered that the respondent, Winnie Tsige, had been surreptitiously looking at Jones' banking records. Tsige and Jones did not know each other despite the fact that they both worked for the same bank and Tsige had formed a common-law relationship with Jones' former husband. As a bank employee, Tsige had full access to Jones' banking information and, contrary to the bank's policy, looked into Jones' banking records at least 174 times over a period of four years.

The central issue on this appeal is whether the motion judge erred by granting summary judgment and dismissing Jones' claim for damages on the ground that Ontario law does not recognize the tort of breach of privacy.

[Sharpe J.A. noted that while aspects of privacy had long been protected by existing causes of action, the recognition of a distinct cause of action for invasion of privacy remained uncertain. He then discussed the four categories of common law privacy actions that were first set out by Prosser and later adopted by The American Law Institute.]

· · ·

The tort that is most relevant to this case, the tort of "intrusion upon seclusion", is described by the Restatement, at § 652B as:

> One who intentionally intrudes, physically or otherwise, upon the seclusion of another or his private affairs or concerns, is subject to liability to the other for invasion of his privacy, if the invasion would be highly offensive to a reasonable person.

The comment section of the Restatement elaborates this proposition and explains that the tort includes physical intrusions into private places as well as listening or looking, with or without mechanical aids, into the plaintiff's private affairs. Of particular relevance to this appeal, is the observation that other non-physical forms of investigation or examination into private concerns may be actionable. These include opening private and personal mail or examining a private bank account, "even though there is no publication or other use of any kind" of the information obtained.

If Jones has a right of action, it falls into Prosser's first category of intrusion upon seclusion. While I will make some reference to the fourth category of appropriation of the plaintiff's name or likeness in my discussion below, I will focus primarily on intrusion upon seclusion. I do so for two reasons. First, I accept Prosser's insight that the general right to privacy embraces four distinct torts, each with its own considerations and rules, and that confusion may result from a failure to maintain appropriate analytic distinctions between the categories. Second, as a court of law, we should restrict ourselves to the particular issues posed by the facts of the case before us and not attempt to decide more than is strictly necessary to decide that case. A cause of action of any wider breadth would not only over-reach what is necessary to resolve this case, but could also amount to an unmanageable legal proposition that would, as Prosser warned, breed confusion and uncertainty.

[Sharpe J.A. provided a lengthy review of the common law and statutory protection of privacy in Canada and elsewhere. Citing Prosser as authority, Sharpe J.A. stated that to make out a claim for intrusion on seclusion, a plaintiff had to establish that: (i) the intrusion was unauthorized; (ii) the intrusion was highly offensive to a reasonable person; (iii) the matter intruded upon was private; and (iv) the intrusion caused anguish and suffering. He then reviewed the damage awards in several different types of Canadian privacy cases.]

It is my view that in this case, Tsige committed the tort of intrusion upon seclusion when she repeatedly examined the private bank records of Jones. These acts satisfy the elements laid out above: the intrusion was intentional, it amounted to an unlawful invasion of Jones' private affairs, it would be viewed as highly offensive to the reasonable person and caused distress, humiliation or anguish.

In determining damages, there are a number of factors to consider. Favouring a higher award is the fact that Tsige's actions were deliberate and repeated and arose from a complex web of domestic arrangements likely to provoke strong feelings and animosity. Jones was understandably very upset by the intrusion into her private financial affairs. On the other hand, Jones suffered no public embarrassment or harm to her health, welfare, social, business or financial position and Tsige has apologized for her conduct and made genuine attempts to make amends. On balance, I would place this case at the mid-point of the range I have identified and award damages in the amount of $10,000. Tsige's intrusion upon Jones' seclusion, this case does not, in my view, exhibit any exceptional quality calling for an award of aggravated or punitive damages.

NOTES AND QUESTIONS

1. Did Sharpe J.A. implicitly recognize the four categories of privacy actions adopted by The American Law Institute as giving rise to distinct common law tort actions in Ontario? Do you agree that Tsige's conduct caused Jones anguish and suffering?

2. Sharpe J.A. rejected the defendant's argument that recognizing a common law tort action for invasion of privacy would interfere with the "carefully crafted" Ontario and federal privacy statutes. In contrast, the court in *Facilities Subsector Bargaining Assn. v. B.C.N.U.*, 2009 BCSC 1562 and *Mohl v. University of British Columbia*, 2009 BCCA 249 held that the provincial privacy legislation precluded the recognition of a common law tort claim.

3. *Jones* was applied in *Hopkins v. Kay*, 2014 ONSC 321, aff'd 2015 ONCA 112 (280 patient records wrongfully accessed); *Evans v. Bank of Nova Scotia*, 2014 ONSC 2135 (clients' financial data stolen by bank employee); and *Daniells v. McLellan*, 2017 ONSC 3466 (14 hospital employees improperly accessed the records of 5,804 patients). For cases in which *Jones* did not apply, see *Chandra v. Canadian Broadcasting Corp.*, 2016 ONCA 448; and *Larizza v. Royal Bank of Canada*, 2018 ONCA 632.

4. *Jones* has generated numerous articles. See for example Hunt, "Privacy in the Common Law: A Critical Appraisal of the Ontario Court of Appeal's Decision in *Jones v. Tsige*" (2012) 37 Queen's L.J. 665; Phillips, "The Changing Dimensions of Privacy in the Workplace: Legal Rights and Labour Realities" (2015) 18 C.L.E.L.J. 467; Chamberlain, "Snooping: How Should Damages be Assessed for Harmless Breaches of Privacy?" in Barker, Fairweather & Grantham, eds., *Private Law in the 21st Century* (2017) 389; and Hartshorne, "The need for an intrusion upon seclusion privacy tort within English law" (2017) 46 C.L.W.R. 287.

5. An increasing number of common law tort claims for invasion of privacy will be brought for the surreptitious recording of individuals in intimate or personal settings. For example, in *Patel v. Seth*, 2016 ONSC 6964, the defendant, who hid a video camera in the master bedroom, was held liable for $15,000 for invading his wife's privacy.

In 2005, the federal government enacted the criminal offence of voyeurism in response to public concerns about secretly spying on others and hacking into their computers and cell phones for sexual purposes: *Criminal Code*, s. 162(1). See also *R. v. Jarvis*, 2019 SCC 10.

6. The highly publicized suicide of Rehtaeh Parsons and other young people following cyberbullying have generated federal and provincial legislation. Parsons committed suicide 17 months after photographs of her were taken without her consent while being sexually assaulted by four boys. Parsons, who was 15 years old at the time of the assault, had become extremely intoxicated and reportedly passed out.

Shortly after Parsons' death, Nova Scotia enacted the *Cyber-safety Act*, S.N.S. 2013, c. 2, which permits "victims" to sue their harassers for damages and obtain a court order prohibiting any further such conduct. The Act defined cyberbullying extremely broadly to include any electronic communication that was intended or reasonably expected to cause distress or harm to another person's "emotional well-being, self-esteem or reputation." The Act was struck down for violating the right to freedom of expression under s. 2(b) and the right to life, liberty and security of the person under s. 7 of the *Canadian Charter of Rights and Freedoms. Crouch v. Snell*, 2015 NSSC 340. The province subsequently enacted more narrowly defined cyberbullying legislation: Bill No. 27, *Intimate Images and Cyber-protection Act*, 1st Sess., 63rd General Assembly, Nova Scotia, 2017. For examples of similar provincial legislation, see *Protecting Victims of Non-Consensual Distribution of Intimate Images Act*, R.S.A. 2017, c. P-26.9; and *The Intimate Image Protection Act*, S.M. 2015, c. 42.

Following Parsons' suicide, the federal government made it a criminal offence to transmit, distribute or make available an intimate image (*i.e.* a visual recording) of another person, knowing that the person did not consent or being reckless as to whether he or she consented. The offence is limited to circumstances in which there was a reasonable expectation of privacy when the recording was made and the person depicted retained that expectation when the offence was committed. *Criminal Code*, s. 162.1.

7. Even if the plaintiff consents to being photographed or video-taped in intimate circumstances, its subsequent unauthorized sharing or distribution may give rise to tort liability on several bases. In *Jane Doe 464533 v. D.(N.)*, 2016 ONSC 541, the 18-year-old plaintiff reluctantly sent her boyfriend an intimate video of herself based on assurances that he alone would view it. He reportedly posted the video on a pornographic website that day and shared it with some friends who were acquaintances of the plaintiff. The plaintiff, who was emotionally devastated and humiliated, sued. In addition to granting an injunction, the court awarded the plaintiff a total of $100,000 in damages, which included awards for aggravated and punitive damages.

As well as liability based on breach of confidence and the intentional infliction of nervous shock, the defendant was held liable for the tort of invasion of privacy. The court stated that there were both established and developing legal grounds for imposing liability on the basis of invasion of privacy. After discussing the *Jones* case and intrusion on seclusion at length, the courts stated that the facts in *Jane Doe* more closely fell within the "public disclosure of private embarrassing facts." This category of privacy cases involves disclosure of private aspects of another's life, which would be highly offensive to a reasonable person and of no legitimate concern to the public. The court held that any reasonable person would find the defendant's conduct to be highly offensive and serve no legitimate public interest. See Khoday, "Resisting Revenge Pornography: When Victims Strike Back" (2016) 25 C.C.L.T. (4th) 45.

This default judgment was set aside. If the plaintiff wishes to proceed, the case will have to be relitigated in its entirety: *Doe v. N.D.*, 2016 ONSC 4920. See however *Jane Doe 72511 v. Morgan*, 2018 ONSC 6607, in which the defendant was held liable for $50,000 in general damages, $25,000 in aggravated damages and $25,000 in punitive damages for posting a sexually explicit video of the plaintiff on a pornographic website without her consent or knowledge.

8. The Canadian courts have also recognized a common law tort action for the appropriation of personality for the unauthorized use of a person's name or likeness. However, as the following cases indicate, the action is not viewed as a privacy claim but rather as an intentional economic tort. See *Krouse v. Chrysler Canada Ltd.* (1973), 1 O.R. (2d) 225 (C.A.); *Athans v. Canadian Adventure Camps* (1977), 80 D.L.R. (3d) 583 (Ont. H.C.); *Heath v. Weist-Barron School of Television (Canada) Ltd.* (1981), 34 O.R. (2d) 126 (H.C.). See also Howell, "The Common Law Appropriation of Personality Tort" (1986) 2 I.P.J. 149; and Abramovitch, "Misappropriation of Personality" (2000) 33 C.B.L.J. 230.

9. In *Gould Estate v. Stoddart Publishing Co.* (1996), 31 C.C.L.T. (2d) 224 (Ont. Gen. Div.), aff'd on other grounds (1998), 39 O.R. (3d) 545 (C.A.), the defendant journalist interviewed and photographed Glenn Gould in 1956, before Gould became famous. Forty years later, the defendant published a book after Gould's death containing some of those photographs and transcripts of their conversations. Gould's estate sued unsuccessfully for the appropriation of personality. The court stated that it had to balance the individual's privacy interests and the public's interests in freedom of expression and dissemination of newsworthy information. It held that appropriation of personality is limited to the use of a celebrity's name or image to sell the defendant's products. Consequently, the tort does not extend to situations in which the celebrity is the subject of the work itself, as in a biography. See also *Shaw v. Berman* (1997), 144 D.L.R. (4th) 484 (Ont. Gen. Div.), aff'd (1998), 167 D.L.R. (4th) 576 (Ont. C.A.); *Horton v. Tim Donut Ltd.* (1997), 104 O.A.C. 234 (C.A.); *Hay v. Platinum Equities Inc.*, 2012 ABQB 204; and Collins, "Age of the Living Dead: Personality Rights of Deceased Celebrities" (2002) 39 Alta. L. Rev. 914.

(e) THE STATUTORY PROTECTION OF PRIVACY

Although the term "privacy" is not used in the *Charter*, this interest underlies many of the guarantees in ss. 2 and 7-15. If an individual's *Charter* rights have been violated and that violation cannot be justified under s. 1, the individual may apply to a court of competent jurisdiction under s. 24(1) for a remedy. The courts have broad discretion to grant whatever remedy they deem appropriate in the circumstances, including substantial awards of compensatory, aggravated and punitive damages. However, it should be noted that the *Charter* is limited by s. 32 to federal and provincial laws and governmental actions.

Existing federal and provincial legislation also protects a broad range of privacy interests. For example, those convicted of the unauthorized electronic interception of private communications under the *Criminal Code*, ss.183-196 may be imprisoned for up to five years and ordered to pay the aggrieved party $5,000 in punitive damages. As well as cyber-bullying and voyeurism, the *Criminal Code* prohibits obscene, racist, threatening, stalking, and other behaviour that may infringe on an individual's privacy. There are two federal privacy statutes that directly govern the collection, use and disclosure of information in specified circumstances: *Privacy Act*, R.S.C. 1985, c. P-21; and *Personal Information Protection and Electronics Documents Act*, S.C. 2000, c. 5.

There has been a dramatic increase in the number and scope of the provincial and territorial statutes governing the collection, use and disclosure of personal information. Typically, this includes legislation regulating provincial, territorial and municipal government records and the information practices of a broad range of institutions, agencies and individuals, such as public schools, credit reporting agencies, commercial data banks, and health, counselling and care professionals. Individuals are often governed by a complex patchwork of statutory record-keeping, confidentiality and disclosure provisions.

NOTES AND QUESTIONS

1. For the *Charter*'s impact on the tort of invasion of privacy, see Craig, "Invasion of Privacy and *Charter* Values: The Common-Law Tort Awakens" (1997) 42 McGill L.J. 355.

2. The federal *Privacy Act*, R.S.C. 1985, c. P-21 governs the personal information practices of almost all federal government departments, institutions and agencies. More recently, the federal government enacted the *Personal Information Protection and Electronics Documents Act*, S.C. 2000, c. 5, which applies to the collection, use and disclosure of "personal information" by the private sector "in the course of commercial activity." The statute generally applies to both federal and provincial custodians of records, unless the province has enacted comparable commercial data protection legislation.

3. Many provinces have enacted complex health information protection legislation. This legislation applies in addition to the statutory record-keeping, confidentiality, disclosure, and access provisions in the public hospitals, mental health, regulated health professions, and other acts. In addition to these statutory provisions, health and counselling professionals owe parallel common law, equitable and ethical obligations to their patients. Fortunately, the key requirements of these overlapping provisions are very similar, and agencies can develop a single set of information policies that simultaneously meet all of their legal obligations.

(f) THE PROVINCIAL PRIVACY STATUTES

The most specific statutory protection of privacy is provided by the British Columbia, Manitoba, Newfoundland and Labrador, Nova Scotia, and Saskatchewan privacy statutes.

HOLLINSWORTH v. BCTV
[1999] 6 W.W.R. 54 (B.C.C.A.)

LAMBERT J.A. (orally): . . . In 1984 the plaintiff, Mr. Hollinsworth, began to go bald. He started wearing a toupee but he was not content with his appearance. Two years later, in 1986, Mr. Hollinsworth entered into a contract with Look International Enterprises (1983) Incorporated and underwent tunnel graft surgery so that a hairpiece could be attached to his head. Dr. Williams performed the surgery. Mr. Hollinsworth signed a release and consent [that allowed the procedure to be filmed for instructional purposes only.]

Eric Cable, a camera person for BCTV, filmed the operation at the request of Dr. Williams and Look International. Mr. Cable recorded the procedure under a freelance contract entered into with Dr. Williams or Look International or both. He did not do it for his regular employer, BCTV.

The videotape was made for medical instructional purposes only. Dr. Williams knew that. Look International knew that. And Mr. Hollinsworth only consented to that.

Dr. Williams gave the video to Look International after he received it from Mr. Cable following the operation and the filming.

. . .

[S]even years later, BCTV decided to do a five minute feature on baldness after the 6:00 . . . news one night. Ms. Aylesworth was assigned to the task by BCTV and Mr. Cable was assigned as her cameraman. . . . Mr. Cable mentioned to Ms. Aylesworth that Dr. Williams did tunnel graft surgery for baldness; that Mr. Cable himself had photographed the procedure; and that there was a videotape.

Mr. Cable and Ms. Aylesworth went to Dr. Williams' office and interviewed him. He was willing or eager to give them the tape. He phoned Mr. van Samang at Look International, found out that the tape was there, and suggested to Ms. Aylesworth and Mr. Cable that they go over to see Mr. van Samang. Dr. Williams said nothing to Mr. Cable or Ms. Aylesworth about confidentiality in relation to his patient, Mr. Hollinsworth.

Mr. van Samang gave Ms. Aylesworth the videotape of the 1986 operation on Mr. Hollinsworth. Ms. Aylesworth was concerned about doctor/patient confidentiality and asked whether the patient in the operation had consented to this use of the videotape. Mr. van Samang assured Ms. Aylesworth that BCTV could use the videotape and that the patient had consented to that. Mr. van Samang also told Ms. Aylesworth that he did not know the current whereabouts of the patient.

. . .

[A]fter the 6:00 . . . news one night, BCTV broadcast the feature on baldness. Part of the videotape on Mr. Hollinsworth was shown, including an unmistakable likeness of his full face. He was easily identifiable by his family and by his friends. His full face appeared on the screen for about three seconds.

[The plaintiff sued BCTV, Look International, Mr. van Samang and others for defamation, breach of confidentiality and breach of the provincial *Privacy Act*, R.S.B.C. 1996, c. 373. The trial judge dismissed the actions against BCTV, but awarded the plaintiff $15,000 on his claims against Look International and Mr. van Samang. The plaintiff appealed the dismissal of the claims against BCTV and the damage award.

Lambert J.A. confirmed that BCTV could not be held liable in defamation because it had not made a false statement. Nor was BCTV liable for breach of confidence as there was no evidence that it knew or ought to have known that the videotape was confidential. Lambert J.A. then considered the privacy claim under the statute.]

The claim based on an allegation of a statutory tort under the *Privacy Act* rests on the terms of the Act itself. Section 1, which establishes the tort, reads in this way:

Violation of privacy actionable

1 (1) It is tort, actionable without proof of damage, for a person, *wilfully* and *without a claim of right*, to violate the privacy of another.

(2) The nature and degree of privacy to which a person is entitled in a situation or in relation to a matter is that which is reasonable in the circumstances, giving due regard to the lawful interests of others.

(3) In determining whether the act or conduct of a person is a violation of another's privacy, regard must be given to the nature, incidence and occasion of the act or conduct and to any domestic or other relationship between the parties.

(4) Without limiting subsections (1) to (3), privacy may be violated by eavesdropping or surveillance, whether or not accomplished by trespass. [emphasis added]

I turn first to the word "willfully." In my opinion the word "wilfully" does not apply broadly to any intentional act that has the effect of violating privacy but more narrowly to an intention to do an act which the person doing the act knew or should have known would violate the privacy of another person. That was not established in this case.

I move now to the phrase, "without a claim of right." I adopt the meaning given by Mr. Justice Seaton to that very phrase, "without a claim of right" in *Davis v. McArthur* (1969), 10 D.L.R. (3d) 250 (B.C.S.C.):

. . . an honest belief in a state of facts which, if it existed, would be a legal justification or excuse . . .

It is unnecessary in this case to decide whether the honest belief must be a reasonable one. Here, on the evidence, the belief was both honest and reasonable. I would not accede to this claim under the *Privacy Act*. It is not necessary for me to consider the exceptions under the Act.

In my opinion, the award of $15,000 damages against Mr. van Samang and Look International was neither too high nor too low. I would not vary it. It follows that I would dismiss the appeal.

NOTES AND QUESTIONS

1. Why was the plaintiff in *Hollinsworth* successful against Look International and Mr. van Samang, but not against BCTV? See also *Bigstone v. St. Pierre*, 2011 SKCA 34; *Cook v. The Insurance Corporation of British Columbia*, 2014 BCSC 1289; and *Ari v. Insurance Corporation of British Columbia*, 2015 BCCA 468.

2. In *Heckert v. 5470 Investments Ltd.* (2008), 62 C.C.L.T. (3d) 249 (B.C.S.C.), the plaintiff was awarded $3,500 for the breach of her rights under the provincial privacy statute. The court stated that while legitimate security concerns warranted installing video cameras in the hallway of the apartment building, it was not necessary to train the camera on the plaintiff's door and record close-up images of every person entering or leaving. The defendant acknowledged that she viewed the plaintiff as an undesirable tenant who was engaging in illicit activities and that she wanted to evict the plaintiff. Do you agree with *Heckert*? See Osborne, "Home Alone: Privacy, Personal Residences and the British Columbia Privacy Act" (2009), 64 C.C.L.T. (3d) 3; and *Milner v. Manufacturers Life Insurance Co.* (2005), 36 C.C.L.T. (3d) 232 (B.C.S.C.).

REVIEW PROBLEM

John Smith and Mary Jones had been partners in a lucrative business that Mary founded. Their working relationship deteriorated as the business grew. Despite Mary's efforts to resolve their differences amicably, John refused. Finally, Mary left the business and initiated what was likely to be a successful million-dollar action. Mary offered to settle on fair terms but John refused, offering her only a small fraction of what she would likely recover.

John then set about to pressure her into settling on his terms. He hired private detectives to follow Mary in public and collect information on her new business. John directed the detectives to take pictures of anyone with whom Mary met and to question all of her friends, relatives, neighbours, business associates, and acquaintances. John realized that these interviews were unlikely to yield much useful information for the litigation, but he thought that they would increase the emotional pressures on Mary to settle. John told the detectives not to initiate any verbal contact with Mary, enter her property, interfere with her freedom of movement, or physically intimidate her.

Mary became aware of the detectives' activities almost immediately, and her friends and associates complained to her about being approached by the detectives. Although John did not contact Mary, his lawyer called her repeatedly. The lawyer demanded information related to the litigation and the return of all company property, including any documents, business records and even stationery supplies. The lawyer also sent Mary a barrage of complex, time-limited settlement offers, all of which proved to be woefully inadequate. The lawyer's correspondence was so threatening and upsetting that Mary had to stop reading it.

As John expected, these tactics began to take their toll on Mary. Her migraine headaches increased in frequency and duration, she could not sleep and she became increasingly reluctant to leave her house. Mary called John and told him that his conduct was making her sick. John showed no remorse, stating that he would "call off the dogs" if she settled on his terms.

This was the last straw. In addition to pursuing her original claim, Mary now wishes to sue John for his conduct and that of his detectives and lawyer in attempting to pressure her into settling on his terms. Your senior partner has asked you to address the following two issues and to assume for these purposes that John was legally responsible for the conduct of his detectives and lawyer:

(a) Would the detectives' conduct give rise to a common law tort action for the invasion of privacy?
(b) Would John's conduct, coupled with that of his detectives and lawyer, give rise to an action for the intentional infliction of nervous shock?

(g) BREACH OF CONFIDENCE

As discussed above, claims for "intrusion on seclusion" address the wrongful accessing of confidential information. In contrast, the tort action for breach of confidence provides a remedy for the wrongful use and/or disclosure of confidential information.

Breach of confidence has been used to protect sensitive business information and, more recently, personal information. In *LAC Minerals Ltd. v. International Corona*

Resources Ltd., [1989] 2 S.C.R. 574, the defendant used confidential information it received from the plaintiff to acquire for itself a gold mine that they had discussed developing as a joint venture. The defendant was held liable for breaching confidentiality and its fiduciary duty. The court stated that recovery for breach of confidence requires the plaintiff to establish that: (i) the information was confidential in nature; (ii) it was disclosed in circumstances creating an obligation of confidentiality; and (iii) its unauthorized use was detrimental to the confider. The same principles apply in regard to third parties to whom confidential information is sent.

In *Cadbury Schweppes Inc. v. FBI Foods Ltd.*, [1999] 1 S.C.R. 142, the defendant had wrongfully used the plaintiff's secret formula for Clamato juice to create a similar beverage. The court stated that breach of confidence was a hybrid action drawing on both common law and equitable principles, which gave judges broad discretion in formulating damages. The plaintiff was awarded damages based on the profits that it lost as a result of the defendant's breach of confidence.

In *XY, LLC v. Canadian Topsires Selection Inc.*, 2016 BCSC 1095, the plaintiff was awarded almost $270 million in damages against a large group of defendants and $60 million against two individual defendants for their misuse of its technology and intellectual property, based on breach of confidence, civil conspiracy and unjust enrichment. See also *H.R.C. Tool & Die Mfg. Ltd. v. Naderi*, 2016 ABCA 334 (misuse of confidential client list).

The wrongful use of confidential personal information can also give rise to liability for breach of confidence. For example, in *Szarfer v. Chodos* (1986), 27 D.L.R. (4th) 388 (Ont. H.C.), aff'd (1988), 54 D.L.R. (4th) 383 (Ont. C.A.), a lawyer was held liable for breaching his fiduciary duty by misusing confidential information about his client's marital problems to have an affair with the client's wife. See also *Leung v. Shanks*, 2013 ONSC 4943, in which a nurse at a fertility clinic had a sexual relationship with the husband of a couple who were patients.

Until recently, there were few tort claims for the wrongful disclosure of confidential personal information. In *Argyll v. Argyll*, [1965] 1 All E.R. 611 (Ch. D.), the court stated that a spouse's disclosure of personal communications made during marriage may be actionable. In *G.(H.R.) v. L.(M.S.)* (2007), 75 B.C.L.R. (4th) 141 (S.C.), the plaintiff sued her former husband for disclosing that she had been a sex trade worker. While her defamation action succeeded, her confidentiality claim was dismissed but only because the confidence they shared had already been disclosed to the public through information published on websites. Even though the default judgment in *Jane Doe 464533 v. D.(N.)*, 2016 ONSC 541 was set aside, the sharing or distribution of intimate images of an individual without their consent will likely give rise to a successful breach of confidence claim. See *Doe v. N.D.*, 2016 ONSC 4920.

Given the heightened sensitivity about the privacy of personal health information, there will likely be increasing claims for the wrongful disclosure of confidential patient information. See *Grant v. Winnipeg Regional Health Authority*, 2015 MBCA 44; and *T. (J.) c. Barber*, 2016 QCCA 1194.

NOTES AND QUESTIONS

1. For additional cases on breach of confidence concerning business information, see *Free Trade Medical Network Inc. v. RBC Travel Insurance Co.* (2006), 215 O.A.C. 230 (C.A.); *Foreman v. Chambers* (2007), 69 B.C.L.R. (4th) 17 (C.A.); *OBG Ltd. v. Allan*,

[2008] 1 A.C. 1 (H.L.); *Pat's Off-Road Transport v. Campbell* (2010), 75 C.C.L.T. (3d) 300 (Alta. Q.B.); *Cruise Connections Canada v. Cancellieri*, 2013 BCSC 1; and *The Catalyst Capital Group v. Moyse*, 2018 ONCA 283.

2. Would the plaintiff in *Argyll* have had a remedy under the privacy principles in The American Law Institute, *Restatement, Second, Torts* (1977) vol. 3 at §652A-E?

3. In *Nissen v. Durham Regional Police Services Board*, 2017 ONCA 10, the plaintiff made a video-taped statement about her neighbour's son to the police after being promised anonymity. The son was arrested and charged several days later. Without making any attempt to protect the plaintiff's identity, the videotape was given to the Crown, who in turn gave a copy to the accused. The accused's father harassed and physically threatened the plaintiff and her family to the point that they were forced to move. The court analyzed the case in terms of informant privilege and awarded the plaintiff and her family $460,000 in damages for the officers' breach of their duty to protect her anonymity. What distinguishes this claim from the common law tort action for breach of confidence?

4. Since the English courts do not recognize a common law tort for the invasion of privacy, they have used actions for "breach of confidence" and "misuse use of private information" to protect sensitive personal information. These cases typically involve detailed discussions of the need to balance the plaintiff's privacy interests against freedom of expression. See generally Jones, "Chapter 1: Principles of Liability in Tort" 1 at 23-25 and Carty, "Breach of Confidence and Privacy" 1931 in Jones *et al.*, eds., *Clerk & Lindsell on Torts*, 22nd ed. (2018), ch. 27.

REVIEW PROBLEM

Phillip and Sarah had been going out for five years and had talked about getting engaged. Phillip suddenly broke off the relationship without warning or any explanation. Sarah later learned that Phillip had been seeing someone else during the last three months of their relationship. Sarah's initial upset turned to anger.

About three months after their break-up, Phillip and Sarah happened to be at the same party. Phillip was shy, said nothing and tried to avoid Sarah. In contrast, Sarah was seething with anger toward Phillip and began making inappropriate comments. During their relationship, Phillip had shared with Sarah sensitive details of his childhood and troubled youth. These included the fact that Phillip was raised in a provincial orphanage and was convicted of a series of break and enters as a young adult. Phillip's convictions had been reported in the local newspaper at the time, but that was over a decade ago. In addition to proclaiming that Phillip had cheated on her and was dishonest, Sarah began disclosing the sensitive details of Phillip's life in a loud voice that could be readily heard by anyone in the vicinity.

Phillip left the party as quickly as possible. He had worked hard to get an education, succeed at work, establish a network of friends, and leave his past behind. Phillip felt that Sarah had dragged him back to his horrible childhood and youth, and had undermined his years of struggle to make something of himself.

Analyze whether Phillip would have a cause of action against Sarah for: (a) invasion of privacy; and (b) breach of confidence.

10. Discrimination

SENECA COLLEGE OF APPLIED ARTS & TECHNOLOGY v. BHADAURIA
(1979), 105 D.L.R. (3d) 707 (Ont. C.A.), rev'd [1981] 2 S.C.R. 181

WILSON J.A.: [For the Court of Appeal] — The plaintiff in this case complains that she has been discriminated against by the defendant on the ground of her ethnic origin. She makes the following allegations in her statement of claim. She is a highly educated East Indian woman holding a Bachelor of Arts, Master of Arts, and Doctorate of Philosophy in Mathematics. She is also qualified to teach in the Province of Ontario and has seven years' teaching experience. From June of 1974 to May of 1978, she applied for 10 openings on the teaching staff of the defendant college. All of these openings were advertised in the Toronto press. The plaintiff was not granted an interview for any of them although she had the requisite qualifications. She alleges that this was because of her ethnic origin.

The plaintiff, instead of filing a complaint under the *Ontario Human Rights Code*, R.S.O. 1970, c. 318, as amended, issued a writ claiming damages for discrimination and for breach of s. 4 of the Code. In her statement of claim she identifies the nature of her damages. She alleges that she has been deprived of the opportunity to join the defendant's teaching staff and to earn her livelihood as a teacher and that she has suffered mental distress, frustration and loss of dignity and self-esteem.

Section 4(1) of the Code reads as follows:

4(1) No person shall,

(a) refuse to refer or to recruit any person for employment;
(b) dismiss or refuse to employ or to continue to employ any person;

. . .

because of race, creed, colour, age, sex, marital status, nationality, ancestry, or place of origin of such person or employee.

Counsel for the defendant concedes that the conduct alleged against it in the statement of claim falls within cls. (a) and (b) above.

. . .

The judgment of Mr. Justice Birkett in *Constantine v. Imperial London Hotels, Ltd.*, [1944] 2 All E.R. 171, is also instructive in this area. In that case the manageress of the defendant hotel, in what was alleged to be a contemptuous and insulting manner, had refused the plaintiff a room because of his colour. He was, however, able to obtain accommodation quite readily at another hotel owned by the defendant. Accordingly, he suffered no special damage. No claim for defamation or slander was made and the learned trial Judge held on the pleadings that the plaintiff's action was an action on the case for the defendant's refusal to accommodate him in the hotel of his choice without any just cause or excuse. The gist of the action on the case, however, is special damage and in this case the plaintiff was unable to prove special damage.

The judgment is a significant one because the learned Judge applied the celebrated principle of *Ashby v. White et al.* (1703), 2 Ld. Raym. 938, 92 E.R. 126, enunciated by Chief Justice Holt at p. 953, as follows:

If the plaintiff has a right, he must of necessity have a means to vindicate and maintain it, and a remedy if he is injured in the exercise or enjoyment of it; and indeed it is a vain thing to imagine a right without a remedy; for want of right and want of remedy are reciprocal.

Mr. Justice Birkett found that a common law right of the plaintiff was violated in this case. The defendant was an innkeeper under a duty to receive and house the plaintiff. The action was maintainable without proof of special damage because, as Chief Justice Holt had made plain, the injury itself imported damage. He awarded the plaintiff nominal damages in the amount of five guineas.

. . .

Against this background of authorities, we are called on to decide the matter now on appeal before us, namely, assuming that the plaintiff can prove the allegations set forth in her statement of claim, do they give rise to a cause of action at common law and, if they do not, do they give rise to a civil cause of action under the *Ontario Human Rights Code*?

In my view, they give rise to a cause of action at common law. While no authority cited to us has recognized a tort of discrimination, none has repudiated such a tort. The matter is accordingly *res integra* before us.

Prosser in his text, *Handbook of the Law of Torts*, 4th ed. (1971), at pp. 3-4, states:

The law of torts is anything but static, and the limits of its development are never set. When it becomes clear that the plaintiff's interests are entitled to legal protection against the conduct of the defendant, the mere fact that the claim is novel will not of itself operate as a bar to the remedy.

I think there can be no doubt that the interests of persons of different ethnic origins are entitled to the protection of the law. The preamble to the *Ontario Human Rights Code* reads as follows:

WHEREAS recognition of the inherent dignity and the equal and inalienable rights of all members of the human family is the foundation of freedom, justice and peace in the world and is in accord with the Universal Declaration of Human Rights as proclaimed by the United Nations;

AND WHEREAS it is public policy in Ontario that every person is free and equal in dignity and rights without regard to race, creed, colour, sex, marital status, nationality, ancestry or place of origin;

AND WHEREAS these principles have been confirmed in Ontario by a number of enactments of the Legislature;

AND WHEREAS it is desirable to enact a measure to codify and extend such enactments and to simplify their administration;

Therefore, Her Majesty, by and with the advice and consent of the Legislative Assembly of the Province of Ontario, enacts as follows:

I regard the preamble to the Code as evidencing what is now, and probably has been for some considerable time, the public policy of this Province respecting fundamental human rights. If we accept that "every person is free and equal in dignity and rights without regard to race, creed, colour, sex, marital status, nationality, ancestry or place of origin", as we do, then it is appropriate that these rights receive the full protection of the common law. The plaintiff has a right not to be discriminated against because of her ethnic origin and alleges that she has been injured in the exercise or enjoyment of it. If she can establish that, then the common law must, on the principle of *Ashby v. White et al., supra,* afford her a remedy.

I do not regard the Code as in any way impeding the appropriate development of the common law in this important area. While the fundamental human right we are concerned with is recognized by the Code, it was not created by it. Nor does the Code, in my view, contain any expression of legislative intention to exclude the common law remedy. Rather the reverse since s. 14*a* [enacted 1974, c. 73, s. 5] appears to make the appointment of a board of inquiry to look into a complaint made under the Code a matter of ministerial discretion.

It is unnecessary, in view of the finding that a cause of action exists at common law, to determine whether or not the Code gives rise to a civil cause of action.

I would allow the appeal and set aside the order of Callaghan, J. The defendant shall have 20 days from the date of the order herein to file its statement of defence. The appellant shall have her costs both here and below in the cause.

[The decision was then appealed to the Supreme Court of Canada. Chief Justice Laskin wrote the decision of the court.]

THE CHIEF JUSTICE: . . . The view taken by the Ontario Court of Appeal is a bold one and may be commended as an attempt to advance the common law. In my opinion, however, this is foreclosed by the legislative initiative which overtook the existing common law in Ontario and established a different regime which does not exclude the courts but rather makes them part of the enforcement machinery under the Code.

For the foregoing reasons, I would hold that not only does the Code foreclose any civil action based directly upon a breach thereof but it also excludes any common law action based on an invocation of the public policy expressed in the Code. The Code itself has laid out the procedures for vindication of that public policy, procedures which the plaintiff respondent did not see fit to use.

NOTES AND QUESTIONS

1. What factors did Wilson J.A. consider in recognizing a common law tort of discrimination? How did she use the remarks of Holt C.J., who was dissenting in *Ashby v. White*, and the Ontario *Human Rights Code*?

2. Laskin C.J. distinguished *Ashby* as a case in which a remedy was granted for an independent pre-existing right and suggested that Wilson J.A. had relied on *Ashby* to create the right. Do you agree with Laskin C.J.?

3. The Commission responsible for enforcing the *Human Rights Code* has broad discretion in deciding whether to initiate an investigation, convene a hearing or take a matter to court. Given the Commission's control over the proceedings and the complainant's subordinate role, is there any reason why the *Code* proceedings and a common law tort action for discrimination should not co-exist?

4. Laskin C.J.'s judgment is difficult to reconcile with the Canadian courts' approach to the relationship between common law causes of action and statutes. There is ample support for Wilson J.A.'s use of a statute in deciding to recognize a common law tort action. Indeed, Laskin C.J. did the same thing in the landmark cases of *Horsley v. MacLaren*, [1972] S.C.R. 441 and *Jordan House Ltd. v. Menow*, [1974] S.C.R. 239. See also *Canada v. Saskatchewan Wheat Pool*, [1983] 1 S.C.R. 205. Is there something unique about a common law tort action for discrimination that would justify departing from the general trend?

5. Would Bhadauria have had a cause of action against the College based on (a) *Wilkinson v. Downton*, [1897] 2 Q.B. 57; or (b) *Rahemtulla v. Vanfed Credit Union* (1984), 29 C.C.L.T. 78 (B.C.S.C.), discussed above in the section on intentional infliction of nervous shock?

6. *Bhadauria* has been applied to cases involving the human rights legislation in other provinces. See *Tenning v. Manitoba* (1983), 4 D.L.R. (4th) 418 (Man. C.A.); *Mallet v. New Brunswick* (1982), 43 N.B.R. (2d) 309 (Q.B.), aff'd (1983), 47 N.B.R. (2d) 234 (C.A.); *Ayangma v. Prince Edward Island* (1998), 168 Nfld. & P.E.I.R. 1 (P.E.I.S.C. (T.D.)); and *Blanco-Arriba v. British Columbia* (2001), 96 B.C.L.R. (3d) 183 (S.C.).

7. Some courts have sidestepped *Bhadauria* and provided redress for discriminatory conduct on the basis of wrongful dismissal or the intentional infliction of nervous shock. See *Gnanasegaram v. Allianz Insurance Co. of Canada* (2005), 251 D.L.R. (4th) 340 (Ont. C.A.) and *Honda Canada Inc. v. Keays*, [2008] 2 S.C.R. 362 (wrongful dismissal); and *Clark v. Canada* (1994), 20 C.C.L.T. (2d) 241 (F.C.T.D.) and *Nolan v. Toronto (Metropolitan) Police Force*, [1996] O.J. No. 1764 (Gen. Div.) (QL) (intentional infliction of nervous shock).

8. In *Lajoie v. Kelly*, [1997] 3 W.W.R. 181 (Man. Q.B.) and *Sulz v. British Columbia (Minister of Public Safety and Solicitor General)* (2006), 60 B.C.L.R. (4th) 43 (C.A.), the court stated that the human rights legislation did not prevent recovering in a common law tort action for sexual harassment. In contrast, *Bhadauria* was relied on to strike out harassment claims in *Chapman v. 3M Canada Inc.* (1995), 24 C.C.L.T. (2d) 304 (Ont. Gen. Div.), aff'd (1997), 37 C.C.L.T. (2d) 319 (Ont. C.A.), *Anderson v. Ottawa (City)* (2005), 255 D.L.R. (4th) 223 (Ont. S.C.J.), and *K.L. v 1163957799 Quebec Inc.*, 2015 ONSC 2417. See also Demeyere, "Common Law Actions for Sexual Harassment: The Jurisdiction Question Revisited" (2003) 28 Queen's L.J. 637.

9. Can *Bhadauria* be justified on either doctrinal or policy grounds? See generally Radnoff & Foy, "The Tort of Discrimination" (2002) 26 Adv. Q. 309; and McLaren, "The Intentional Torts to the Person Revived?: Protecting Autonomy, Dignity and Emotional Welfare in a Pluralistic Society" in Beauluc, Pitel & Schulz, eds., *The Joy of Torts* (2003) 67.

10. Section 15 of the *Charter* grants individuals the right to equal protection and benefit of the law without discrimination and, in particular, discrimination based on race, national or ethnic origin, colour, religion, sex, age, or mental or physical disability. If the *Charter* applies, individuals may seek a remedy under s. 24(1) if their equality rights under s. 15 have been violated. See Braun, "Adverse Effect Discrimination: Proving the *Prima Facie* Case" (2005) 11 Rev. Const. Stud. 119.

11. Should the courts or the legislature extend protection against invasions of privacy, breach of confidence, discrimination, sexual harassment, and other similar intentional interferences with the person?

INTENTIONAL INTERFERENCE WITH CHATTELS

1. Introduction
2. The Development of the Actions
3. Trespass to Chattels
4. Conversion
5. Detinue
6. Recaption and Replevin

1. Introduction

The modern law governing intentional interference with chattels is the product of a tangled history in which pleadings and procedure preceded the development of substantive principles. Moreover, the origins of this body of law are not contained exclusively within the realm of torts, but rather lie at the intersection of tort, property, contract, and unjust enrichment.

This chapter begins with a short history of the tort actions governing intentional interference with chattels. We then discuss the three major modern actions — *trespass to chattels, conversion* and *detinue* — before concluding with a brief explanation of *replevin* and *recaption*.

As you read through this chapter, ask yourself whether the existing rules satisfactorily serve the needs of modern society. There is growing belief in the need for statutory reform. Although English legislation simplified some of the rules thirty years ago, through the *Torts (Interference with Goods) Act 1977*, considerable confusion and difficulty remain in that country. The problems are, of course, even greater in Canada, where the traditional rules continue to apply.

2. The Development of the Actions

The common law recognized three ways in which a person could be deprived of chattels and it developed an action for each. *Trespass* was designed for cases of wrongful *taking, detinue* for cases of wrongful *detention,* and *trover* for cases of wrongful *disposal.* Trespass and detinue remain actionable today. Trover, in contrast, was superseded by *conversion.* As the most modern action, conversion avoids many of the procedural defects that undermine the other two. It therefore is by far the most popular of the proprietary torts.

(a) TRESPASS

The predecessor of the modern action for trespass to chattels — trespass *de bonis asportatis* — emerged in the 13th century. It apparently was an attempt to overcome difficulties affecting the recovery of property under the criminal actions of theft and larceny. Although trespass *de bonis asportatis* initially could be invoked only if goods were taken or destroyed, it later expanded to cover cases of mere damage or interference. In any event, the tort required proof that (1) the defendant's interference was direct and forceful, and (2) the affected goods were in the claimant's possession.

With the abolition of the writ system during the 19th century, intent generally became a prerequisite to liability. The modern tort of trespass to goods therefore now provides a remedy for any direct and intentional interference with chattels in the possession of another. As explained below, however, claimants generally prefer to sue for conversion, rather than trespass, whenever possible.

(b) DETINUE

The origins of the modern action for detinue lie in the *praecipe* writs. Such writs took the form of a command to either do right or provide an explanation to the King's justices. Consequently, in contrast to trespass, the *praecipe* writs were designed to secure compliance with a right, rather than to remedy the breach of a right. The *praecipe* writs took several forms depending upon the circumstances. For instance, a person might be compelled to surrender a piece of land, pay a debt, or (in the case of detinue) return a chattel.

The gist of detinue was that the defendant was wrongfully withholding a chattel to which the plaintiff had a right of immediate possession. The law recognized two possibilities. Detinue *sur bailment* governed those cases in which the defendant had acquired possession of the chattel through bailment. Detinue *sur trover* dealt with cases in which the defendant either found the chattel or acquired possession through some means other than bailment. Bailment occurs when the owner or possessor of a chattel (the bailor) temporarily transfers possession to another person (the bailee) with an expectation that the chattel will be returned at some future time. In common language, bailment refers to the lending of a thing.

Detinue *sur bailment* evolved into a strict action. Once the plaintiff established a bailment and an immediate right to possession, the defendant was required to return the chattel or, if unable to do so, pay its full market value. The fact that the bailee no longer had possession of the item did not provide a defence. Significantly, however, detinue *sur bailment* was not available if the bailee had returned the property in damaged condition. In that situation, the bailor's only claim was in trespass.

Detinue *sur trover* was available in situations not involving bailment. It therefore was used against a finder, a thief, or even an innocent "purchaser" who had acquired possession of the chattel without knowledge of the claimant's underlying rights. However, the action was subject to three major limitations.

- *Chain of Possession*: Possession had to be established in an unbroken chain between the claimant and the defendant. Each link of the chain could be challenged.

- *Continuing Possession*: Liability presumed that the defendant remained in possession of the chattel. Detinue therefore was not available if the defendant had lost, sold, or destroyed the goods. Similarly, it was exhausted once the chattel was returned to the claimant, even if the goods had been damaged.

- *Wager of Law*: Most significantly, a claim in detinue could be defended through the process known as *wager of law*. The defendant could avoid liability by swearing an oath attesting to his or her innocence and by presenting the requisite number of *compurgators* ("oath helpers") who swore not to the facts, but rather to the purity of the defendant's oath. Whatever its initial merits as a method for finding facts, wager of law deteriorated as society gradually placed greater weight on Earthly matters than on fear of God. Indeed, the situation eventually degenerated to the point where professional compurgators were available for hire! Although wager of law increasingly fell into disrepute, it was not officially abolished until 1833.

(c) TROVER AND CONVERSION

The deficiencies of the various *praecipe* writs led to the emergence of more effective actions. Detinue therefore was supplanted by the action in trespass on the case *sur trover*, or, more simply, the action in trover. The gist of trover was the defendant's wrongful appropriation of the claimant's chattel. The wording of the writ required an allegation that the plaintiff had lost lawful possession of the item, and that the defendant had found it and taken possession. By the end of the 16th century, however, the allegations of losing and finding were obligatory, but non-traversable. The plaintiff continued to assert them, but the court refused to hear argument on point, and the defendant could not escape liability by disproving the allegations of loss and finding. The dispute therefore focused on the central issue as to whether the defendant, by some positive act, had converted the goods, thereby depriving the plaintiff of possession.

The scope of trover, or "conversion" as the action came to be called, was expanded in another way as well. The simplest way of protecting a proprietary interest in a chattel is through a *vindicatio*. If you have possession of my personal property, I simply point to the item in your hands, prove my superior title, and say, "Give it back!" Most law students are surprised to learn, however, that that option is available only in special circumstances. *Equitable* title is protected by a *vindicatio*. Consequently, if property that is held on trust for the plaintiff improperly falls into the defendant's hands, then the plaintiff has a right to recover it *in specie*. In contrast, *legal* title is not protected by a *vindicatio*. If the defendant improperly takes possession of an asset to which the plaintiff holds only legal title, the claimant has no right to prove the superior title and enforce a right of return. The plaintiff must instead satisfy the elements of some cause of action. That cause of action is usually the tort of conversion.

The tort of conversion (or trover) initially required the plaintiff to prove that the defendant was at fault in misappropriating the chattel. That requirement, however, created an intolerable gap. If the defendant dealt in good faith with the plaintiff's property, liability could not be imposed in conversion. Furthermore, even if the defendant still retained the goods, the lack of a *vindicatio* precluded recovery on the basis of the plaintiff's subsisting property interest. To alleviate that difficulty, the allegation of dishonesty under the tort of conversion became non-traversable. It remained in the pleadings, but the defendant could not dispute it. As a result, liability can now be imposed for an "innocent" conversion: Birks, "Personal Property: Proprietary Rights and Remedies" (2000) 11 King's College L.J. 1. As we shall see, that is true if a rogue steals the plaintiff's chattel and sells it to the defendant, who is entirely unaware of the theft.

Trover was a clear improvement upon detinue: the defendant could not avoid liability through wager of law, by returning the goods in damaged condition, or by showing that they were no longer in his or her possession. The plaintiff enjoyed other benefits as well. Liability potentially extended to any person who dealt with the claimant's chattels, even if they did so reasonably and innocently. And as a species of *trespass on the case*, trover triggered the remedy of damages. The plaintiff generally was entitled to the monetary value of the chattels at the time of the tort. As discussed below, all of this remains true today.

Although conversion is the most commonly encountered proprietary tort, claimants continue to use detinue in certain circumstances.

- *Unintentional Loss by Bailee*: Because conversion presumes that the defendant positively and intentionally exercised dominion over the plaintiff's chattel, it is not available if a lawful bailee loses the plaintiff's property or carelessly allows it to be stolen.

- *Specific Recovery*: Detinue is the appropriate form of action if the claimant seeks recovery of the chattel, rather than damages representing its value.

- *Calculation of Damages*: Even if the claimant is content to receive monetary relief, damages are measured differently in conversion and detinue. The former generally proceeds by reference to market value at the *time of the defendant's final act of conversion*; the latter generally calculates compensation on the basis of the market value *at the date of trial*. Accordingly, where both options exist, conversion usually is preferable in a falling market, whereas detinue is advantageous in a rising market.

Likewise, while conversion is far more common than trespass, the older action remains important. Because the remedy for conversion compels the defendant to pay damages representing the chattel's market value, that tort effectively leads to *a forced sale*. The plaintiff receives the value of the item and, in exchange, the defendant acquires the right to retain the item itself (if it is still in possession). The courts recognize, however, that some forms of interference are insufficient to warrant such a result. In such circumstances, the claimant is confined to a claim in trespass and compensation for losses actually suffered.

NOTES AND QUESTIONS

1. The intentional property torts are based on the concept of possession, rather than ownership: *Murray v. Toth*, 2012 ONSC 5815 at para. 25. Trespass, conversion and, arguably, detinue directly protect the plaintiff's possessory interests. This area of law is not primarily concerned with ownership and title *per se*. The essence of possession appears to be physical custody or control, coupled with the intent to possess. See Palmer, "Possessory Title" in Palmer & McKendrick, eds., *Interests in Goods*, 2d ed. (1998), ch. 3; and Harris, "The Concept of Possession in English Law" in Guest, ed., *Oxford Essays on Jurisprudence* (1961), ch. 4.

The legal concept of possession often proves problematic in the context of wild animals. When does one "possess" a fox in such a manner as will support a proprietary tort? In 1802, Lodowick Post was in hot pursuit of a fox that he intended to kill. Despite knowing that the poor creature was already under attack, Jesse Pierson intervened, killed the fox, and took it. Post sued in trespass, but the court dismissed the claim on the ground that he never enjoyed a proprietary interest. In order to take possession of a wild animal, one must do more than chase — one must either seize or mortally wound (so as to deprive the animal of its natural liberty). This decision is a favourite subject of tort and property scholars: see, *e.g.*, "Symposium: Foxes, Seals, Whales, and the Rule of Capture" (2013) 63 U.T.L.J. 30.

2. The fact that the intentional property torts protect the right to possession, rather than ownership, is highlighted by the remarkable case of *Costello v. Chief Constable of Derbyshire Constabulary*, [2001] 1 W.L.R. 1437 (C.A.). From all outward appearances, the plaintiff was in the business of selling stolen cars. He was found in possession of a vehicle that he had purchased from a friend who had numerous convictions for car theft. That vehicle's registration and engine identification numbers had been rubbed off, and a kit for forging car registration numbers was found in the backseat of the plaintiff's vehicle. The police lawfully seized the car, but were never able to determine its true owner. They nevertheless refused the plaintiff's demand to return the car to him. He then sued in conversion. The Court of Appeal held in his favour. Lightman J. held that, according to orthodox property law principles, the plaintiff, as possessor of the vehicle, had a better right to the car than everyone except the true owner. He further explained that, as a matter of tort law, "possession . . . is entitled to the same legal protection whether or not it has been obtained lawfully or by theft or by other unlawful means." Do you agree with the result of that decision? How else might tort law deal with such situations? See Fox, "Enforcing a Possessory Title to a Stolen Car" [2002] C.L.J. 27. In similar circumstances, however, courts occasionally have invoked the *ex turpi* doctrine in order to deny a "wrongdoer's" claim to property: *Baird v. British Columbia* (1992), 77 C.C.C. (3d) 365 (B.C.C.A.). The defence of *jus tertii*, which may deny liability on the ground that some third party has better rights to the chattel than does the plaintiff, is discussed below. For discussion of the criminal consequences of "stealing" abandoned property, see Hickey, "Stealing Abandoned Goods: Possessory Title in Proceedings for Theft" (2006) 26 L.S. 584.

The principles underlying *Costello* have been applied in Canada as well. In *Bird v. Fort Francis*, [1949] 2 D.L.R. 791 (Ont. C.A.) a boy found a can while trespassing under a building on private property. The can contained $1400 in cash. The police seized the money and when the rightful owner could not be found, the municipality kept the cash for itself. Despite characterizing the boy as a "wrongdoer" of sorts, the court upheld his ensuing claim in conversion. See also *Singh v. Ali*, [1960] A.C. 167 (P.C. Malaya).

3. The fact that the proprietary torts are based on the protection of possession limits the types of "things" that can be the subject of claims. The courts traditionally imposed liability with respect to *choses in possession* but not *choses in action* (such as a debt). As discussed below, however, Canadian courts have begun to adopt a more relaxed approach.

Difficult questions also arise regarding the distinction between personal property and real property. The torts considered in this chapter protect the former, but not the latter. Accordingly, for instance, the tort of conversion may impose liability for acts done to felled timber, but not standing trees. A more common illustration arises from the fact that a household appliance is personal property when it is purchased at a store, but it may be regarded as part of the land if it becomes affixed to the home.

4. The proprietary torts protect possessory rights. The plaintiff consequently must have had a possessory interest at the time of the alleged wrong: *Ryan v. St. John's (City)*, 2017 NLTD(G) 173. The proprietary torts consequently cannot be used by a person who, despite being entitled to possess a chattel in the future, does not have a right to immediate possession. That rule may create hardship. For instance, if a car was damaged while on lease, the lessor of the vehicle would not be entitled to demand compensation from the wrongdoer. To deal with such cases, tort law recognizes an innominate ("unnamed") action for the benefit of owners out of possession and people who hold *reversionary interests* in damaged goods. See *Mears v. London & South Western Ry. Co.* (1862), 142 E.R. 1029 (C.P.); and *Dee Trading Co. Pty. Ltd. v. Baldwin*, [1938] V.L.R. 173.

The rights-based theory of tort law was introduced at the end of Chapter 1. It posits that the proper function of private law is not to serve social purposes (such as compensating losses and deterring misconduct), but rather to enforce and vindicate interpersonal rights. That theory offers a number of insights into the proprietary torts: Green, "Rights and Wrongs: An Introduction to the Wrongful Interference Actions" in Nolan & Robertson, eds., *Rights and Private Law* (2010) at 526-30. Consider the case in which the tortfeasor converts property that was being held on bailment. The bailee, who was in temporary possession of the chattel, obviously suffers a loss. But so too, the bailor, who was out of possession but anticipated recovering the chattel in due course, also is injured in a very real sense. The tort of conversion nevertheless allows an action by the bailee but not the bailor. On a compensatory model of tort law, that proposition is difficult to understand. The picture becomes clear, however, when viewed in terms of rights theory. Trespass and conversion are concerned with immediate rights to possession. The relevant right therefore is held by the bailee and not by the bailor. The same analysis explains why a bailor may be held liable to the bailee if the bailor dispossesses the bailee before the bailment term expires. Regardless of the bailor's own property interest, the act of dispossessing the bailee constitutes an infringement of the right to immediate possession: *Gordon v. Harper* (1796), 101 E.R. 828.

5. In appropriate circumstances, the plaintiff's apparent lack of a right to immediate possession may be overcome by the very facts that constitute the alleged tort. Consider a simple case. If chattels are placed on bailment for a stated period, the bailor normally has no right to sue during that time. Nevertheless, if the bailee breaches the conditions of the bailment by improperly conveying the goods to a third party, the bailment may come to a premature end, the bailor may re-acquire the right to immediate possession, and a proprietary tort may be available: *Sibley v. Sibley* (1871), 8 N.S.R. 325 (C.A.).

6. The defendant's intentional act may be classified as tortious only if it occurs without the plaintiff's consent. The defence of consent, which is discussed at length in Chapter 6, often is applied in connection with the proprietary torts. Accordingly, while the defendant's sale of the plaintiff's chattels might otherwise constitute conversion, liability will be denied if the court is satisfied that the plaintiff effectively assented to the defendant's actions: *Lloydminster Credit Union Ltd. v. 324007 Alberta Ltd.*, 2011 SKCA 93.

7. For a more detailed account of the history of the intentional property torts see Holmes, *The Common Law* (1881) at 77-129 and 165-205; Ames, "The History of Trover" (1897) 11 Harv. L. Rev. 277-89 and 374-86; Fifoot, *History and Sources of the Common Law: Tort and Contract* (1949) at 24-65 and 102-105; Baker, *An Introduction to English Legal History*, 4th ed. (2002) at 390-400; and Milsom, *Historical Foundations of the Common Law*, 2d ed. (1981) at 262-75 and 366-79.

3. Trespass to Chattels

FOULDES v. WILLOUGHBY

(1841), 151 E.R. 1153 (Ex. Ct.)

On the 15th October 1840, the plaintiff had embarked on board the defendant's ferry-boat at Birkenhead, having with him two horses, for the carriage of which he had paid the usual fare. It was alleged that the plaintiff misconducted himself and behaved improperly after he came on board the steam-boat, and when the defendant came on board he told the plaintiff that he would not carry the horses over, and that he must take them on shore. The plaintiff refused to do so, and the defendant took the horses from the plaintiff, who was holding one of them by the bridle, and put them on shore on the landing slip. They were driven to the top of the slip, which was separated by gates from the high road, and turned loose on the road. They were shortly afterwards seen in the stables of an hotel at Birkenhead, kept by the defendant's brother. The plaintiff remained on board the steam-boat, and was conveyed over the river to Liverpool. On the following day the plaintiff sent to the hotel for the horses, but the parties in whose possession they were refused to deliver them up. A message, however, was afterwards sent to him by the hotel-keeper, to the effect that he might have the horses on sending for them and paying for their keep; and that if he did not send for them and pay for their keep, they would be sold to pay the expense of it. The plaintiff then brought the present action. The horses were subsequently sold by auction. The defence set up at the trial was, that the plaintiff had misconducted himself and behaved improperly on board, and that the horses were sent on shore in order to get rid of the plaintiff, by inducing him to follow them. The learned Judge told the jury, that the defendant by taking the horses from the plaintiff and turning them out of the vessel, had been guilty of a conversion, unless they thought the plaintiff's conduct had justified his removal from the steam-boat, and he had refused to go without his horses; and that if they thought the conversion was proved, they might give the plaintiff damages for the full value of the horses. The jury found a verdict for the plaintiff with £40 damages, the value of the horses.

In Easter Term last, a rule was obtained calling upon the plaintiff to shew cause why the verdict should not be set aside on the ground of misdirection.

. . .

LORD ABINGER C.B.:—This is a motion to set aside the verdict on the ground of an alleged misdirection; and I cannot help thinking that if the learned Judge who tried the cause had referred to the long and frequent distinctions which have been taken between such a simple asportation [*i.e.* movement] as will support an action of trespass, and those circumstances which are requisite to establish a conversion, he would not have so directed the jury. It is a proposition familiar to all lawyers, that a simple asportation of a chattel, without any intention of making any further use of it, although it may be sufficient foundation for an action of trespass, is not sufficient to establish a conversion. I had thought that the matter had been fully discussed and this distinction established, by the numerous cases which have occurred on this subject; but, according to the argument put forward by the plaintiff's counsel to-day, a bare asportavit is sufficient foundation to support an action of trover. I entirely dissent from this argument; and therefore I think that the learned Judge was wrong, in telling the jury that the simple fact of putting these horses on shore by the defendant, amounted to a conversion of them to his own use. In my opinion, he should have added to his direction, that it was for them to consider what was the intention of the defendant in so doing. If the object, and whether rightly or wrongfully entertained is immaterial, simply was to induce the plaintiff to go on shore himself, and the defendant, in furtherance of that object, did the act in question, it was not exercising over the horses any right inconsistent with, or adverse to, the rights which the plaintiff had in them. Suppose, instead of the horses, the defendant had put the plaintiff himself on shore, and on being put on shore, the plaintiff had refused to take his horses with him, and the defendant had said he would take them to the other side of the water, and had done so, would that be a conversion? That would be a much more colourable case of a conversion than the present, because, by separating the man from his property, it might, with some appearance of fairness, be said the party was carrying away the horses without any justifiable reason for so doing. Then, having conveyed them across the water, and finding neither the owner nor any one else to receive them, what is he to do with them? Suppose, under those circumstances, the defendant lands them, and leaves them on shore, would that amount to a conversion? The argument of the plaintiff's counsel in this case must go the length of saying that it would. Then, suppose the reply to be, that those circumstances would amount to a conversion, I ask, at what period of time did the conversion take place? Suppose the plaintiff had immediately followed his horses when they were put on shore, and resumed possession of them, would there be a conversion of them in that case? I apprehend, clearly not. It has been argued that, the mere touching and taking them by the bridle would constitute a conversion, but surely that cannot be: if the plaintiff had immediately gone on shore and taken possession of them, there could be no conversion. Then the question, whether this were a conversion or not, cannot depend on the subsequent conduct of the plaintiff in following the horses on shore. Would any man say, that if the facts of this case were, that the plaintiff and defendant had had a controversy as to whether the horses should remain in the boat, and the defendant had said, "If you will not put them on shore, I will do it for you," and in pursuance of that threat, he had taken hold of one of the horses to go ashore with it, an action of trover could be sustained against him? There might, perhaps, in such a case, be ground for maintaining an action of trespass, because the defendant may have had no right to meddle with the horses at all: but it is clear that he did not do so for the purpose of taking them away from the plaintiff, or of exercising any right over them, either for himself or for any other person.

. . .

In order to constitute a conversion, it is necessary either that the party taking the goods should intend some use to be made of them, by himself or by those for whom he acts, or that, owing to his act, the goods are destroyed or consumed, to the prejudice of the lawful owner. As an instance of the latter branch of this definition, suppose, in the present case, the defendant had thrown the horses into the water, whereby they were drowned, that would have amounted to an actual conversion; or as in the case cited in the course of the argument, of a person throwing a piece of paper into the water; for, in these cases, the chattel is changed in quality, or destroyed altogether. But it has never yet been held, that the single act of removal of a chattel, independent of any claim over it, either in favour of the party himself or any one else, amounts to a conversion of the chattel. In the present case, therefore, the simple removal of these horses by the defendant, for a purpose wholly unconnected with any the least denial of the right of the plaintiff to the possession and enjoyment of them, is no conversion of the horses, and consequently the rule for a new trial ought to be made absolute.

NOTES AND QUESTIONS

1. Did the defendant's act of removing the horses from the barge constitute a trespass? If so, what would have been the appropriate measure of damages? Why did this act not amount to a conversion? If the defendant had pushed the horses off the barge in the middle of the crossing and they drowned, what damages would the plaintiff have been entitled to in trespass and conversion?

2. Although plaintiffs rarely do so, there is authority for the proposition that, as an alternative to claiming compensation, the plaintiff may choose to use the action in trespass to goods to receive disgorgement of the defendant's gains. See for example *Oughton v. Seppings* (1830), 109 E.R. 776; *Neate v. Harding* (1851), 155 E.R. 577; *Rodgers v. Maw* (1846), 153 E.R. 924; *Feltham v. Terry* (1773), 98 E.R. 613; and *cf. Lindon v. Hooper* (1776), 98 E.R. 1160. Given the ambiguity of the ancient writs, however, many of those cases alternatively may be explained not in terms of gain-based relief for wrongdoing, but rather as restitution under the cause of action in unjust enrichment: McInnes, *The Canadian Law of Unjust Enrichment and Restitution* (2014), ch. 5.

3. Despite occasional suggestions to the contrary, the better view is that trespass to goods is actionable without proof of loss: *William Leitch & Co. v. Leydon*, [1931] A.C. 90 at 106 (H.L.); and Rogers, *Winfield and Jolowicz on Tort*, 18th ed. (2010) at §17-3; *cf. Letang v. Cooper*, [1964] 2 All E.R. 929 (C.A.) (damage required if interference is unintentional). Given that trespass to land and trespass to the person are actionable *per se*, how could a different rule for trespass to chattels be justified?

In the United States, a distinction is drawn between dispossession and mere interference. Dispossession is considered sufficient damage in itself, whereas interference is not actionable without proof of loss. See American Law Institute, *Restatement (Second) of Torts* (1965) at §218. Do you favour the English or American position?

4. The defendant will not escape liability by proving that the trespass occurred as a result of an honest and reasonable mistake. See for example *Cameron v. Morang* (1978), 32 N.B.R. (2d) 22 (Co. Ct.); and *384238 Ontario Ltd. v. The Queen in Right of Can.* (1983), 8 D.L.R. (4th) 676 (F.C.A.). What arguments can be made in favour of this rule? Should a reasonable and honest mistake be recognized as a defence to trespass to chattels?

In contrast, a proprietary tort may be defeated by an "inevitable accident." The word "inevitable" is something of a misnomer. In this context, it does not mean that the accident was entirely unavoidable. It merely "means an accident not avoidable by taking reasonable precautions": Williams & Hepple, *Foundations of Tort* (1976) at 86. A leading case is *National Coal Board v. J.E. Evans & Co. (Cardiff) Ltd.*, [1951] 2 K.B. 861 at 881. The plaintiffs buried a cable underground without the landowner's consent. Workers hired by the landowner later damaged the cable during excavations. The plaintiffs' demand for compensation failed. Morris L.J. illustrated the doctrine of inevitable accident with an example: "If someone is lawfully digging on his own land and someone else comes and interposes an article between the spade as it is descending and the ground, so that the article is damaged, and damaged without any intention on the part of the person digging, it could not, in my judgment, be said that the latter was guilty of a trespass."

5. The central importance of possession in trespass is illustrated by *Penfolds Wines Proprietary Ltd. v. Elliott* (1946), 74 C.L.R. 204 (H.C.A.). Penfolds, the plaintiff, made wine and sold it in bottles. The plaintiff at all times retained ownership of the bottles, which were embossed with its name. Customers were expected to drink the wine and return the bottles. An action was commenced in connection with two Penfolds bottles that were delivered to the defendant by his brother. The defendant filled the bottles with a different brand of wine and returned them to his brother. The plaintiff sued in trespass, conversion, and detinue. In addressing the trespass issue, Dixon J. said at 224-25:

> I think that it is quite clear that trespass would not lie for anything which the foregoing facts disclose. Trespass is a wrong to possession. But, on the part of the respondent, there was never any invasion of possession. At the time he filled the two bottles his brother left with him, he himself was in possession of them. If the bottles had been out of his own possession and in the possession of some other person, then to lift the bottles up against the will of that person and to fill them with wine would have amounted to trespasses. The reason is that the movement of the bottles and the use of them as receptacles are invasions of the possession of the second person. But they are things which the man possessed of the bottles may do without committing trespass. The respondent came into possession of the bottles without trespass.

6. The world of commerce, of course, has changed considerably since the time of *Penfolds Wines*. Rather than being concerned about its embossed wine bottles, a business today is more likely to be concerned about its online operations. Is the tort of trespass available in such circumstances? American courts believe so. In *eBay v. Bidder's Edge Inc.*, 100 F. Supp.2d 1058 (N.D. Cal. 2000) the plaintiff, a sort of online auctioneer, complained that the defendant "crawled" its website thousands of times a day, extracted data regarding ongoing auctions, and posted that information on its own competing website. The court found that the defendant's unauthorized use of the plaintiff's computer systems constituted an infringement of eBay's possessory interest and hence a trespass to chattels. See also *In Thrifty-Tel, Inc. v. Bezenek*, 46 Cal. App. 4th 1559 (Cal, C.A. 1996). Canadian courts have been less adventurous. *Century 21 Canada Ltd. Partnership v. Rogers Communications Inc.*, 2011 BCSC 1196 involved similar facts. The plaintiff real estate company generated property listings and published the information on a website. On a daily basis, the defendant accessed that website, copied the data, and posted it on its own web pages. While upholding the plaintiff's claims on other grounds, Punnett J. dismissed an allegation of trespass to chattels. On the issue of "whether or not electronic access is 'physical' or whether it

needs to be 'physical' for the tort claim to succeed," he found that "[i]t is not at all clear that Canadian law supports the proposition that electronic access to a computer system is a physical act": at paras. 295-96. Nevertheless, even if Canadian law did mirror the position south of the border, the plaintiff was destined to fail because its website operated on a server that was owned by a third party. However the concept of "possession" is defined, the plaintiff must prove that its own property interests were infringed by the defendant's trespass.

7. Sappideen & Vines, eds., *Fleming's The Law of Torts*, 10th ed. (2011) at 65 lists trustees, personal representatives and franchise owners as exceptions to the general principle that only the person in actual possession is protected in trespass. It also states that a person with a mere right to possession can sue in trespass if his or her servant, bailee at will, or agent had actual possession at the time of the wrong. These exceptions are considered by Rogers, *Winfield and Jolowicz on Tort*, 18th ed. (2010) at §17-17. The author, while acknowledging that these parties can sue in trespass, doubts whether they really are exceptions. What is the significance of this controversy?

4. Conversion

(a) GENERAL PRINCIPLES

MACKENZIE v. SCOTIA LUMBER CO.
(1913), 11 D.L.R. 729 (N.S. S.C.)

RUSSELL J.:—I base my judgment in this case on the learned Judge's findings, as to the facts. The plaintiff was the owner of a raft which had drifted away from its proper, or perhaps improper, moorings, and had become, without any interference of the defendants, attached to two rafts belonging to the defendants, which had also gone adrift, all three rafts being stranded on a ledge called "Stopper Rock," in St. Mary's river, Guysborough.

The defendants sent their servants for their own rafts, not for the rafts of anybody else. The servants, finding all three rafts together, and supposing that all three belonged to the defendants, brought them all to the defendants' mill. I take it that the defendants did not know that the raft was at their mill. It is certain that they did not know that the plaintiff's raft was at their mill, but the statement in this form would be equivocal, for although they did not know that the plaintiff's raft was at their mill, they may have known that this particular raft, which was in fact the plaintiff's raft, was at their mill. And it is upon this *équivoque* that the plaintiff bases his claim, contending that if the defendants, under the mistaken idea that the raft was their own, detained it for ever so short a period, treating it as their own, and exercising a dominion over it as their own property, they are liable for a conversion of the raft, even though the moment they discovered the mistake, they returned it to the proper owner.

. . .

The only evidence I can find of a conversion in this case is that of a possible conversion by the servants of the defendants, who, acting without authority from the defendants, did certainly exercise acts of ownership on behalf of the defendants over the raft, under the mistaken idea that the raft belonged to the defendants. Although this proceeding on the part of the servants was not authorized or acquiesced in by any responsible official of the defendant company, I assume that it was so far within the scope of the servants' duty that the company must answer for the act of their servants if that act was a tort.

We are, therefore, I think, obliged to answer the question whether one who takes the property of another person, mistaking it for his own, but returns it to the owner immediately upon discovery of the mistake, can be held liable for conversion of the property. The case must have occurred a thousand times, but the reason why counsel, who argued the appeal, were unable to cite any authority directly bearing upon the question, is probably that, until this case arose, there never was anybody wrongheaded enough to make such an accident the subject of an action at law.

I have examined all the cases collected by Ames and also the selection of cases on torts made by Mr. Wigmore, and I can find none to answer the simple question whether one who, by mistake, takes up the defendant's umbrella in place of his own, but who discovers his mistake before he has reached the street, and immediately returns it to the owner, is, or is not, liable for a conversion of the umbrella. I suspect that he would, strictly speaking, be legally liable, but if upon tender of the umbrella to the owner, the latter were to accept and resume the ownership, I am quite certain it would be a mistake to give damages for the full value of the umbrella and adjudge the property to the defendant. And that is what has been done, in this case. The defendant returned the raft, in the present case, to the plaintiff immediately upon the discovery of the mistake and the plaintiff resumed the ownership, when he asked for the use of a boat to take the raft up the river. From that moment until the action was brought, the plaintiff and defendant were both treating the property as the property of the plaintiff. I suppose that the right of action, having once arisen, the plaintiff must recover nominal damages, but why he should have the full value of the property which was returned to him and which he accepted back from the defendants, I cannot understand, and I think that the judgment of the learned trial Judge is erroneous in this respect.

. . .

The case of *Nelson v. Whetmore*, from South Carolina, 1 Rich. L. 318 (1 Ames' Cases on Torts 349), is also closely in point, but it was decided in favour of the defendant because he did not know that the plaintiff's slave, whom he engaged as a servant, was property at all, and could not therefore have had the intention of converting the defendant's property: "His treatment of Frank as a servant did not indicate an assertion of property." He did not exercise any act of ownership over the defendant's property, because he did not treat the slave as property at all. In this dearth of authority and absence of any clear answer to the question, I think we must hold that the defendants' servants did convert the plaintiff's property, and as they did it in the course of the employment by the defendant company, the latter must be held liable for conversion. But the plaintiff cannot have the property and the full damages for its conversion at the same time. Whether the defendants would have been liable for the full value of the property if the plaintiff had not accepted it, the defendants being ready and willing and offering to return it, may be an open question, but there can be no such question here, because the property was taken back by the plaintiff when the mistake was discovered.

The appeal should therefore be allowed with costs, and there should be judgment for the plaintiff for nominal damages only.

NOTES AND QUESTIONS

1. Conversion has been defined as "an intentional exercise of control over a chattel which so seriously interferes with the right of another to control it that the intermeddler may justly be required to pay its full value": Sappideen & Vines, eds., *Fleming's The Law of Torts*, 10th ed. (2011) at 66-67. See also the American Law Institute, *Restatement (Second) of Torts* (1965) at §222A; and Prosser, "The Nature of Conversion" (1957) 42 Cornell L.Q. 168 at 173-74. Based on Fleming's approach, deliberate wrongdoing will likely result in a finding of conversion even if the chattel can be returned undamaged. In contrast, innocent intermeddling will not amount to conversion unless the plaintiff suffers considerable damage. Is Fleming's view consistent with either *Fouldes* or *MacKenzie*? If not, would you favour the adoption of Fleming's approach?

Even if it finds liability in conversion, the court may permit the defendant to return the chattel and reduce the damages accordingly, if it considers a forced judicial sale to be unwarranted. Given this discretionary power, how significant is the difference between Fleming's approach and that in *Fouldes* and *MacKenzie*?

2. The modern tort of conversion is derived from the *action on the case*. As a general rule, an action on the case requires proof of loss. For that reason, some authorities have held that conversion is not actionable unless the plaintiff establishes the existence of a loss. See for example Law Reform Commission, *Conversion and Detinue* (1971) (18th Report, Cmn. 4774) at 7; Dugdale & Jones, eds., *Clerk & Lindsell on Torts*, 19th ed. (2006) at 1059; and Tyler & Palmer, *Crossley Vaines' Personal Property*, 5th ed. (1973) at 22. Other authorities, however, hold that, history notwithstanding, the tort of conversion is now actionable *per se*: see for example *Brandeis Goldschmidt & Co. v. Western Transport Ltd.*, [1981] 1 Q.B. 864 (C.A.). As explained in an earlier note, trespass to goods is actionable *per se*. Is there any good reason in modern law for treating conversion and trespass differently?

3. In *MacKenzie*, Russell J. cited *Nelson v. Whetmore*, which suggested that the precise nature of a chattel may be significant in determining whether a conversion has been committed. A similar suggestion appears in *Penfolds Wines Proprietary Ltd. v. Elliott* (1946), 74 C.L.R. 204 at 243 (H.C.A.). The facts *of Penfolds* were explained in the previous section. On this point, Williams J. explained:

> The importance of rights attached to ownership vary according to the nature of the particular property. Bottles are meant to be filled so that to fill the bottle of another person is to deprive him of the use of his property. In the present case the brother purported to place the defendant in possession of the bottles as a bailee for him. If they had been 'clean bottles', although in fact the property of the plaintiff, the defendant might not have been guilty of conversion in filling and returning them to the person from whom he got them, unless the plaintiff had made a claim that they were its bottles and had demanded their return. . . . But the endorsements on the bottles proclaimed that they were the property of the plaintiff. In *Hollins v. Fowler* (1875), L.R. 7 H.L. 757, at p. 766 (U.K. H.L.), Blackburn J. said that: 'In considering whether the act is excused against the true owner it often becomes important to know whether the person, doing what is charged as a conversion, had notice of the plaintiff's title. There are some acts which from their nature are necessarily a conversion, whether there was notice of the plaintiff's title or not. There are others which if done in a *bona-fide* ignorance of the plaintiff's title are excused, though if

done in disregard of a title of which there was notice they would be a conversion.' The use which the defendant made of the bottles with knowledge of the plaintiff's title was . . . 'an interference with the property which would not as against the true owner, be justified, or at least excused, in one who came lawfully into possession of the goods.'

4. The full benefit of a letter or document may be gained by reading, rather than taking. Can the tort of conversion be committed simply by reading? This issue was addressed in *White v. Withers LLP*, [2009] EWCA Civ 1122. In the course of acrimonious divorce proceedings, the defendants (a woman and her solicitor) intercepted and read correspondence sent to the plaintiff. The documents contained both financial and personal information. The Court of Appeal held that, even though the letters were not taken from the plaintiff, the defendants' conduct could trigger liability for wrongful interference with goods under the *Torts (Interference with Goods) Act 1977*. The crucial fact, Ward L.J. explained (at para. 52), was that the husband, as owner of the documents, was entitled to "control who reads his documents or who copies them and keeps them." In England, the statutory action replaced the traditional torts of conversion and trespass to goods. If the same facts occurred in Canada, which tort would be applicable?

5. The tort of conversion normally is committed when the defendant takes physical control of an asset. Is liability possible if the defendant, without actually taking possession of an asset, causes its detention? This issue was addressed in *Club Cruise Entertainment & Travelling Services Europe BV v. Department for Transport (The Van Gogh)*, [2009] 1 All E.R. (Comm.) 955 (Q.B.). The plaintiff operated a cruise ship named *The Van Gogh*. After an outbreak of novovirus (an unpleasant, but generally mild, illness) the plaintiff brought the ship to the port of Harwich for cleaning and sanitation. While the ship was in port, the defendant government agency inspected the vessel, declared it to be unfit, and prohibited the plaintiff from setting sail. That order was lifted two days later after a second inspection was passed. It subsequently was discovered that the initial order had failed to comply with statutory regulations and therefore was a complete nullity. The plaintiff consequently sued the defendant and argued that, since the order was unjustified, the detention of the ship constituted a conversion.

Relying on *England v. Crowley* (1873), L.R. 8 Exch. 126, Flaux J. held that liability may be triggered by the detention of an asset, even if the defendant did not physically take the thing away. The crucial question asks whether or not the defendant seriously interfered with the plaintiff's superior right of possession. However, if the alleged tort did not actually entail physical control of the relevant property, then the court must be satisfied either that the defendant absolutely denied the plaintiff's rights or that the defendant asserted a right that was inconsistent with the plaintiff's rights. Neither proposition was established on the facts of *The Van Gogh*. While the defendant prohibited the ship from leaving port, the plaintiff's rights otherwise were not questioned. See also *Oakley v. Lyster*, [1931] 1 K.B. 148 (C.A.); *Cho Ki Yau Trust (Trustees of) v. Yau Estate* (1999), 29 E.T.R. (2d) 204 (Ont. S.C.J.); and *Unisys Canada Inc. v. Imperial Optical Co.* (1998), 43 C.C.L.T. (2d) 286 (Ont. Gen. Div.).

6. The tort of conversion protects property rights. The plaintiff therefore must demonstrate an interest in the disputed asset. That requirement proved fatal in *Oliveira v. Zareh*, 2015 ONSC 4293. The plaintiffs purchased a house that had belonged to a person who committed suicide. While viewing the house, they saw a

number of expensive chattels (a piano, gym equipment, art work) to which no one laid claim. Those items were not formally subject to the sale, but the plaintiffs expected to simply take possession when the sale closed. By the time that they moved into the house, however, the items had been taken by the defendant real estate agent. The claim for conversion failed because, at the time of the alleged tort, the plaintiffs held only a "a *spes successionis* or an expectancy" of possessing the chattels.

M.V. Polar Star v. Arsenault (1964), 43 D.L.R. (2d) 354 (P.E.I.S.C.) provides a gruesome illustration of how property rights can be for the first time. The plaintiff captured, slaughtered and skinned thousands of baby seals. The skins were left for collection in various locations, but the defendant took hold of them before the plaintiff could return. In the litigation that followed, the court held that while the seal pups in the wild were *ferae naturae* and hence ownerless, the plaintiff acquired absolute title by capturing and killing them. By taking the pelts for himself, the defendant accordingly committed the tort of conversion.

Just as ownership may be acquired over previously un-owned property, so too rights of ownership may be given up through abandonment. Intention is crucial, as demonstrated by *Wicks Estate v. Harnett* (2007), 48 C.C.L.T. (3d) 155 (Ont. S.C.J.). Ben Wicks, a remarkably successful cartoonist, left two bags full of his drawings at his son's house. The son mistakenly left the bags behind when he sold his house and the purchaser, delighted with the unexpected find, asserted ownership over "abandoned" property. The court rejected that argument and imposed liability for conversion. Lederer J. explained that abandonment required both a physical act and an intention to relinquish an interest in the goods. The Wicks family always intended to retain its interest in the cartoons.

Abandonment sometimes is relatively clear. Documents that have been shredded and tossed into a recycling bin are abandoned: *Air Canada v. West Jet* (2004), 72 O.R. (3d) 669 (S.C.J.). The issue is apt to be more contentious in other circumstances. What, for instance, is a landlord to do if a tenant leaves goods behind? As a general rule, the landlord can dispose of the goods that have been abandoned: *Kroeker v. Krebs*, 2018 BCPC 1; *Reyes v. Esbin*, 2016 ONSC 7755; and *Visscher v. Triple Broek Holdings Ltd.* (2006), 40 C.C.L.T. (3d) 351 (Alta. Q.B.). Unfortunately, it may be difficult to determine whether property actually was abandoned. The leading text, Palmer, *Palmer on Bailment*, 3d ed. (2009) at 26-030, explains the general rule:

> [A]bandonment is a defence to conversion provided that a party entitled to do so has renounced possession and the immediate right to possession of the chattels in question. Clear evidence both of intention to abandon and of some physical act of relinquishment will be required and, given the element of strict liability in conversion as contrasted with the need for *mens rea* in crime, it would seem that a mere reasonable belief that abandonment had taken place would not suffice as a defence.

If goods have not been abandoned by the tenant, then they cannot simply be tossed away by the landlord. The landlord must take reasonable steps to allow the former tenant to retrieve them: *1083994 Ontario Inc. v. Kotsopoulos*, 2012 ONCA 143; and *Pawlaczyk v. Dong*, 2017 ONSC 66 (condo purchaser liable for disposing of goods left on premises by vendor; damages partially off-set by purchaser's costs of storage). Similarly, a landlord may incur liability by wrongfully detaining a tenant's goods, under the cloak of distress for rent, without authority: *1694879 Ontario Inc. v. Krilavicius*, 2017 ONSC 2396. Additional complications may arise with respect to fixtures: *2105582 Ontario Ltd. v. 375445 Ontario Ltd.*, 2017 ONCA 980.

7. As *MacKenzie* illustrates, a defendant who makes an innocent and reasonable mistake in handling the plaintiff's chattels may be held liable in conversion. Should such mistakes provide a defence? If so, could you justify recognizing mistake as a defence to conversion, but not to the other intentional torts? In addition to *MacKenzie*, see *Kobi's Auto Ltd. v. 5174245 Manitoba Ltd.*, 2018 MBCA 134; *R.H. Willis and Son v. Br. Car Auctions Ltd.*, [1978] 2 All E.R. 392 (C.A.); *Irvington Holdings Ltd. v. Black* (1987), 58 O.R. (2d) 449 (C.A.); *Wilson v. New Brighton Panelbeaters Ltd.*, [1989] 1 N.Z.L.R. 74 (H.C.); and *Nilsson Bros. Inc. v. McNamara Estate*, [1992] 3 W.W.R. 761 (Alta. C.A.).

Although the liability of "innocent" convertors may seem counterintuitive, the rights-based theory of tort law that was introduced in Chapter 1 provides a possible explanation. That theory states that tort law serves to protect rights and not to fulfill other functions, such as punishing wrongdoers or compensating victims. In that respect, Gardner draws an important "distinction between doing the wrong thing and doing something wrongful": Gardner, "Wrongs and Faults" in Simester, ed., *Appraising Strict Liability* (2005) at 55-56. Even if the defendant did not "do something wrongful" by knowingly converting the plaintiff's property, it remains true that the defendant has "done wrong" by acting in a manner that was inconsistent with the plaintiff's right to immediate possession. The relevant right is not defined in terms of the defendant's awareness. It more broadly is formulated in terms of the plaintiff's right to possession *tout court*. See Green, "Rights and Wrongs: An Introduction to the Wrongful Interference Actions" in Nolan & Robertson, eds., *Rights and Private Law* (2010) at 548-50.

8. There are several exceptions to the rule that an innocent mistake provides no defence to conversion. Two of the more important common law exceptions are the rule governing involuntary bailees and the rule in *Hollins v. Fowler* (1875), L.R. 7 H.L. 757.

An *involuntary bailee* is a person who did not acquire possession by choice. This is true, for instance, when a person receives goods unsolicited through the mail, or when a theatre owner finds a package that a patron left behind. An involuntary bailee will not be held liable in conversion for misdelivering a chattel, provided the act was done with reasonable care and solely for the purpose of returning the item to its rightful owner. The scope of this doctrine remains uncertain and is subject to several complex restrictions. See *Long v. R.* (1922), 63 D.L.R. 134 (Ex. Ct.); Burnett, "Conversion by an Involuntary Bailee" (1976) 76 L.Q.R. 364; Palmer, *Bailment*, 3d ed. (2009) at 705-21; and Tyler & Palmer, *Crossley Vaines' Personal Property*, 5th ed. (1973) at 108-10.

In *Hollins v. Fowler*, Blackburn J. stated at 767:

> [O]ne who deals with goods at the request of the person who has the actual custody of them, in the *bona fide* belief that the custodier is the true owner, should be excused for what he does if the act is of such a nature as would be excused if done by the authority of the person in possession, if he was a finder of the goods, or intrusted with their custody. . . . A warehouseman with whom goods have been deposited is guilty of no conversion by keeping them, or restoring them to the person who deposited them with him, though that person turns out to have had no authority from the true owner.

For a discussion of this principle, see Palmer, *supra* at 219-23; and Rogers, *Winfield and Jolowicz on Tort*, 18th ed. (2010) at §17-24.

9. Conversion cases often involve a dispute between two innocent parties. Assume that some third party purports, without authority, to sell the plaintiff's goods to the defendant. This third party then disappears or is judgment-proof. The law therefore must strike a balance between the two innocent parties. The plaintiff seeks protection of a pre-existing property right under the doctrine of *nemo dat quo non habet* ("one cannot give what one does not have"). If that view prevails, it means that the defendant was unable to acquire title from the third party and therefore converted the plaintiff's property. The defendant, in contrast, seeks protection of a seemingly legitimate commercial transaction under the doctrine of *bona fide* purchase. If that view prevails, it means that, despite the lack of actual authority, the third party was able to pass title to the defendant, and that the defendant's dealings with the item did not constitute conversion of the plaintiff's property.

The tort of conversion generally favours security of title (*nemo dat*) over security of transactions (*bona fide* purchase). In some situations, however, legislation reverses the general rule by favouring the purchaser, rather than the original owner.

One such exception was applied in *Bartin Pipe & Piling Supply Ltd. v. Epscan Industries Ltd.* (2004), 346 A.R. 95 (C.A.). A rogue purchased an oil refinery, and then sold a specific pipe within the refinery to the plaintiff in November. Because the rogue was in the process of dismantling the refinery, it agreed that the plaintiff could collect its new pipe by February. Unfortunately, before the plaintiff could do so, the rogue sold the same pipe to the defendant, who had no reason to suspect anything improper. When the plaintiff eventually discovered that the defendant had removed some of the pipe, it sued in conversion. The defendant sought protection under s. 26(1) of the *Sale of Goods Act*, R.S.A. 2000, c. S-2:

> When a person who has sold goods continues or is in possession of the goods or of the documents of title to the goods, the delivery or transfer by that person or by a mercantile agent acting for that person of the goods or documents of title under any sale, pledge or other disposition thereof, to any person receiving them in good faith and without notice of the previous sale has the same effect as if the person making the delivery or transfer were expressly authorized by the owner of the goods to make it.

The Alberta Court of Appeal agreed and denied liability on the grounds that the defendant (1) had purchased from a "vendor in possession," (2) in good faith, and (3) without being aware of the previous sale to the plaintiff.

Section 26(3) of the same statute likewise provides a defence to a defendant who in good faith purchased goods from a "buyer in possession" (*i.e.* a party who obtained possession, but not title, of goods after agreeing to purchase them from the plaintiff). Similar legislation exists across Canada. See Fridman, *Sale of Goods in Canada*, 6th ed. (2013), ch. 6.

10. As explained in the previous note, the common law generally prefers the doctrine of *nemo dat* to the doctrine of *bona fide* purchase. As a result, a person who honestly and reasonably purports to purchase another's chattel may be held liable for conversion. The general rule is reversed, however, if the chattel in question is money (or, to some extent, a negotiable instrument, such as a cheque). Why is that so? Consider what would happen if a *bona fide* purchase of money (as when a grocer receives $5 in exchange for a bag of carrots) did not ensure clear title. See Fox, "Bona Fide Purchase and the Currency of Money" [1996] C.L.J. 547. For general discussion of exceptions to the *nemo dat* principle, see Ziegel & Duggan, *Commercial and*

Consumer Sales Transactions, 4th ed. (2002), ch. 14; and Goode, *Commercial Law*, 2d ed. (1995), ch. 14.

11. Another form of statutory protection for unwitting convertors appears in the Ontario *Factors Act*, R.S.O. 1990, c. F.1 and in similar statutes in other provinces. Such a statute may apply if an owner provided possession of a chattel to *a factor* or a *mercantile agent* with a view to having the item sold on *consignment*. If a sale occurs on consignment as anticipated, title passes directly from the original owner to the purchaser. The mercantile agent never holds title — it merely enjoys temporary possession of the item for the specified purpose. A difficulty may occur, however, if the mercantile agent exceeds its authority and improperly disposes of the chattel. In that situation, the recipient of the chattel *prima facie* commits a tort by dealing with the plaintiff's property. It nevertheless may enjoy a statutory defence. Section 2(1) of the Ontario *Factors Act*, R.S.O. 1990, c. F.1 (which is typical of the legislation) states:

> Where a mercantile agent is, with the consent of the owner, in possession of goods or of the documents of title to goods, a sale, pledge or other disposition of the goods made by the agent when acting in the ordinary course of business of a mercantile agent is, subject to this Act, as valid as if the agent were expressly authorized by the owner of the goods to make the disposition, if the person taking under it acts in good faith and has not at the time thereof notice that the person making it has not authority to make it.

This provision was applied in *Patry v. General Motors Acceptance Corp. of Canada Ltd.* (2000), 48 O.R. (3d) 370 (C.A.). The plaintiff delivered a boat to X, a dealer in watercraft, on consignment. The boat was treated as part of X's inventory while it was in X's possession. It therefore fell within the terms of a chattel mortgage that X improperly gave to the defendant. When X became bankrupt, the defendant seized the boat and sold it in order to receive payment on X's debt. The plaintiff sued the defendant in conversion. The claim was rejected because (1) X possessed the boat, with the plaintiff's consent, in its capacity as a mercantile agent, and (2) the defendant obtained a chattel mortgage over the boat in good faith. The Court of Appeal for Ontario emphasized that, as long as the defendant acted honestly, it could not be denied protection merely because it failed to investigate true ownership of the boat. The defence would fail only if the defendant refrained from investigating an actual suspicion. The same is true of the "vendor in possession" and "buyer in possession" exceptions that appear in provincial sale of goods statutes.

12. Despite the general rule that an honest and reasonable defendant may be held liable for unwittingly committing a conversion, it sometimes is possible to avoid liability by demonstrating that a purportedly tortious act did not constitute conversion. In *Marcq v. Christie Manson & Woods Ltd. (trading as Christie's)*, [2003] 3 W.L.R. 980 (C.A.), the claimant owned a painting by Jan Steen known as *The Backgammon Players* (1677). The painting was stolen and eventually taken to the defendant's auction house by a third party. The piece failed to sell, however, and the defendant merely returned the piece to the third party. The defendant was not liable in conversion, even though it had intended to sell the painting. The result would have been different, however, if a sale had occurred. The Court of Appeal stressed that liability is based on actions, rather than intentions. It also said that the defendant was

under no duty to the claimant to investigate ownership because there was nothing suspicious in the circumstances.

13. Since conversion is an intentional tort, a carrier or custodian can be held liable in conversion for innocently delivering the plaintiff's chattels to a third party, but not for carelessly losing them. Is this result justified? See *Joule Ltd. v. Poole* (1924), 24 S.R. (N.S.W.) 387 (Dist. C.A.); and *Heffron v. Imperial Parking Co.* (1974), 46 D.L.R. (3d) 642 (Ont. C.A.). It should be noted, however, that the careless defendant in these cases may be liable in detinue and negligence.

14. A person sued in conversion may establish *jus tertii* ("right of a third party") by proving that someone other than the plaintiff has the best right of possession. The gist of that argument is that tort law should protect only the true owner. As a general rule, however, a claim in conversion will not be defeated by *jus tertii*. This rule is justified on the ground that it avoids the complexity that would arise if a court was required to deal with all possible claims to a chattel, rather than merely the dispute between the parties.

An important example occurred in *Armory v. Delamirie* (1722), 93 E.R. 664 (K.B.). A boy found a ring while working as a chimney sweep. He brought it to an apprentice goldsmith. The apprentice removed the stones from the ring on the pretence of weighing them and then returned the empty ring to the boy. The fact that the boy was not the ring's "true owner" did not provide the apprentice with a defence to a claim in conversion. See also *Wilson v. Lombank Ltd.*, [1963] 1 All E.R. 740 (C.A.). See generally Jolly, "The *Jus Tertii* and the Third Man" (1955) 8 Mod. L. Rev. 371; Sappideen & Vines, eds., *Fleming's The Law of Torts*, 10th ed. (2011) at 77-79; and Tyler & Palmer, *Crossley Vaines' Personal Property*, 5th ed. (1973) at 24-25.

15. Notwithstanding the general rule, *jus tertii* may provide a defence in certain circumstances. A distinction must be drawn between two scenarios. If the plaintiff was in possession at the time of the conversion, then the defendant is entitled to raise *jus tertii* only with authority from the true owner. In contrast, if the plaintiff merely had a right to possession, then, according to most authorities, the claimant must establish an absolute title. Assume, for instance, that the plaintiff purchased goods, but temporarily left them in possession of the vendor. The vendor subsequently became bankrupt, and the goods in question were seized and sold. It has been held that the plaintiff does not have an action in conversion against the person who performed the sale: *Leake v. Loveday* (1842), 134 E.R. 399. See Sappideen & Vines, *supra* at 78; and Tyler & Palmer, *supra* at 24-25.

In England, the defence of *jus tertii* is addressed by the *Torts (Interference with Goods) Act 1977*. Sections 7 and 8 of that statute (1) permit the defence of *jus tertii*, (2) require the claimant to identify other parties interested in the property, (3) allow a court to eliminate any rights that may be held by third parties who fail to appear as commanded, and (4) prohibit double recovery in the event that, for instance, a person liable in conversion is sued successfully by both the finder and the true owner of a chattel. A similar approach has been proposed in Canada: Ontario Law Reform Commission, *Study Paper on Wrongful Interference with Goods* (1989), ch. 12.

16. Alleging *jus tertii* generally will not protect a defendant. More surprisingly, full damages may be awarded to a bailee, even though that plaintiff (1) commenced an action in conversion exclusively on the basis of a possessory interest, and (2) is not

liable to account to the bailor. The leading case is *The Winkfield*, [1902] P. 42 (C.A.). The Postmaster-General had possession of mail as a bailee. The defendant negligently caused an accident that resulted in the loss of that mail. The Postmaster-General was entitled to full compensation even though it was not, in turn, liable to the actual owners of the items. What is the rationale for this principle? How does this relate to the issue of who should be permitted to sue in conversion? For more discussion of this case see Welling, *Property in Things in the Common Law System* (1996) at 339-44.

17. Liability is not incurred if, despite taking control of the plaintiff's chattels, the defendant acted with legal authority. In *Simans v. Burnaby (City)* 2014 BCSC 2442, the SPCA seized 52 dogs and 19 cats after the claimants were evicted from their premises for non-payment of rent. Some of the animals were returned when the plaintiffs secured suitable new premises; some were adopted to third parties; some sadly were euthanized. A claim for conversion failed because the defendant acted with legal authority under the *Prevention of Cruelty to Animals Act*, R.S.B.C. 1996, c. 372.

18. The English courts have been unusually active in this area in recent years. Scholarly opinion has kept pace. See generally Douglas, *Liability for Wrongful Interferences with Chattels* (2011); Sheehan, *The Principles of Personal Property Law* (2011), ch. 8; Green & Randall, *The Tort of Conversion* (2009); Green, "Understanding the Wrongful Interference Actions" (2010) 74 Conv. 15; and Hickey, "Wrongs and the Protection of Personal Property" [2011] Conv. 30.

REVIEW PROBLEMS

1. Conversion can be committed in various ways. The essential issue nevertheless is always the same: has the defendant intentionally acted in a way that interferes with the plaintiff's right to possess the goods? As the following examples illustrate, this principle is often difficult to apply.

- *Taking Possession*: If Barry takes Allen's car without his consent, Barry will be liable in conversion. Would Barry be liable in conversion if, in an effort to make room for his own vehicle, he pushed Allen's car three metres without damaging it? See *Aitkin Agencies Ltd. v. Richardson*, [1967] N.Z.L.R. 65 (S.C.).

- *Withholding Possession*: If Mary asks Barry to return her chattels in accordance with their storage contract and Barry refuses, he will be held liable in conversion. If she demands that the chattels be delivered at midnight and he refuses, but promises to deliver them the next morning, he will not be liable in conversion. Can you explain these two results? Would Barry be held liable in conversion if he refused to deliver the chattels without receiving proof that Mary was the true owner? See *Scott v. McAlpine* (1887), 6 U.C.C.P. 302; *Annand v. The Merchant's Bank* (1878), 12 N.S.R. 329 (S.C.); and *Morrison v. Fishwick* (1879), 13 N.S.R. 59 (S.C.).

- *Transferring Possession*: Assume that Allen, acting as an agent for Barry, negotiates to purchase goods from Carol which have been stolen from Diane. Assume as well that Allen delivers them to Barry. In this situation, both Allen and Carol will be liable in conversion. If Barry had negotiated the purchase himself and Allen had only picked up the goods from Carol and delivered them to Barry, then Allen would not be liable in conversion. Can you explain these results? If Allen receives goods from Barry which he had not ordered and he mistakenly returned them to Carol instead of Barry, would Allen be liable in conversion? See *The Lancashire Wagon Co. Ltd. v. Fitzhugh* (1861), 158 E.R. 206 (Ex. Ct.); *Dickey v. McCaul* (1887), 14 O.A.R. 166 (C.A.); *Juelle v. Trudeau* (1968), 7 D.L.R. (3d) 82 (Qc. S.C.); and Lawson, "The Passing of Property and Risk in Sale of Goods" (1949) 65 L.Q.R. 35.

- *Destruction, Damage and Use*: If Allen stores ice in a freezer and Barry intentionally opens the freezer door causing some of the ice to melt, Barry will be liable for conversion of the melted ice. Would he also be liable in conversion for the remaining ice? *See Moorgate Mercantile Co. Ltd. v. Finch*, [1962] 2 All E.R. 467 (C.A.).

- *Asserting Ownership*: Assume Allen has stored some chattels on property which Barry subsequently purchased. If Barry refuses to permit Allen to recover the chattels and Barry then removes some of them, he will be liable in conversion. Would Barry have been liable if he had simply refused to permit Allen to recover the chattels? See *Dickey v. McCaul, supra*.

2. Mark stole a herd of bison from Meena and sold the animals to you for $50,000. Before you paid, you checked the animals and noticed that they were not branded. You also asked Mark about the herd and were convinced by his answer that he owned the animals. Unfortunately, he has disappeared and Meena has sued you for conversion. Although you had acted honestly, you would probably be held liable for conversion. In buying the animals and treating them as your own, you seriously interfered with Meena's rights. Consequently, you probably would have to pay her $50,000, which was the market value of the animals. Notice that while you will be entitled to keep the herd, you have now paid $100,000 for it. You could try to recover $50,000 from Mark, but he has disappeared, as rogues often do. Are the rules for conversion fair? Why is the law of conversion so strict?

3. Pam owns a computer that she rented to Dave for a period of six months. Although Dave paid the full rent at the beginning of the term, Pam realized that she desperately required the computer after only two months. She therefore re-acquired possession of the computer without Dave's consent. In the circumstances, can Dave successfully sue her for conversion? See *Roberts v. Wyatt* (1810), 127 E.R. 180 (C.P.).

(b) CONVERSION OF CHEQUES AND OTHER UNUSUAL CHATTELS

373409 ALBERTA LTD. (RECEIVER OF) v. BANK OF MONTREAL
(2002), 220 D.L.R. (4th) 193 (S.C.C.)

MAJOR J.:—The outcome of this appeal depends on whether the appellant Bank of Montreal (the "Bank") by itself or with others acted in any way to cause financial loss to the respondents. As the appellant Bank acted with proper authority, the answer is no. The appeal is allowed with costs.

I. Facts

The facts are not in dispute. Douglas Lakusta was the sole shareholder and directing mind of both 373409 Alberta Ltd. ("373409") and Legacy Holdings Ltd.

("Legacy"). The events that give rise to this action occurred after 373409 entered into a General Security Agreement with the respondent Province of Alberta Treasury Branches, but before the respondent Ernst & Young Inc. was appointed as 373409's Receiver and Manager.

Lakusta received a cheque payable to 373409 for the sale of an automobile to a *bona fide* customer, Lea Sanderson. Lakusta altered the cheque by adding "/Legacy" so that the payee read "373409 Alberta Ltd./ Legacy." He deposited the altered cheque into Legacy's account at the appellant Bank. The cheque was not endorsed. The Bank credited Legacy's account with the proceeds of the cheque, and the funds were later withdrawn by Lakusta.

373409 subsequently went into liquidation, and its Receiver and Manager brought the present action in conversion against the Bank for having accepted for deposit 373409's unendorsed cheque into Legacy's account. . . .

IV. Analysis
A. The Tort of Conversion

The tort of conversion "involves a wrongful interference with the goods of another, such as taking, using or destroying these goods in a manner inconsistent with the owner's right of possession": *Boma Manufacturing Ltd. v. Canadian Imperial Bank of Commerce*, [(1996), 140 D.L.R. (4th) 463 (S.C.C.)], per Iacobucci J., at para. 31. It has long been recognized that an action in conversion may be brought by the rightful holder of a cheque against a wrongful dispossessor: *Crawford and Falconbridge: Banking and Bills of Exchange* (8th ed. 1986), vol. 2, at p. 1386 . . . The tort is one of strict liability, and although the dispossession must arise as a result of the defendant's intentional act, "it is no defence that the wrongful act was committed in all innocence": *Boma, supra*, at para. 31.

An owner's right of possession includes the right to authorize others to deal with his or her chattel in any manner specified. As a result, dealing with another's chattel in a manner authorized by the rightful owner is consistent with the owner's right of possession, and does not qualify as wrongful interference.

. . .

Boma, supra, presented an entirely different factual basis than the case at bar. There, a bookkeeper committed fraud against the companies she worked for by issuing a series of fraudulent cheques made payable to various individuals. The collecting bank deposited the proceeds of the fraudulent cheques into the bookkeeper's account. Iacobucci J. cited (at para. 36) with approval the following passage from *Crawford and Falconbridge*, at p.1386:

> It has been repeatedly held that a bank converts an instrument by dealing with it under the direction of one not authorized, either by collecting it or, semble (although this has not yet actually been decided) by paying it and in either case, making the proceeds available to someone other than the person rightfully entitled to possession. [Footnotes omitted.]

That means a lending institution's liability in conversion is predicated upon finding both that payment upon the cheque was made to someone other than the rightful holder of the cheque, and that such payment was not authorized by the rightful holder. If either of these criteria is not satisfied, there is no tort. On the facts of *Boma, supra*, Iacobucci J. held, at para. 40, that the bookkeeper's actions were beyond the ambit of authority granted to her by the companies she worked for. As a result, the bank's actions were undertaken without the authority of the companies which were rightfully entitled to the cheques' proceeds, and resulted in the dispossession of those companies' entitlements. Consequently, the bank was held to be prima facie liable in conversion for having deposited the cheques' proceeds into the bookkeeper's account.

. . .

In this appeal, it is acknowledged that the Bank dealt with 373409's cheque in a manner which, if unauthorized, would have created liability in conversion. Before the cheque was brought to the Bank by Lakusta, 373409 was the rightful holder of the cheque and entitled to its proceeds. Lakusta's alteration of the cheque had no effect upon 373409's sole entitlement to it. The deposit of the cheque's proceeds into Legacy's account led to the dispossession of 373409's entitlement. The issue is whether the Bank was authorized by 373409 to deal with the cheque as it did, the result being to deprive 373409 of the cheque's proceeds. If 373409 authorized the Bank to deposit the proceeds of the cheque into Legacy's account, then the Bank's actions cannot be wrongful interference and cannot give rise to liability in conversion because it acted with the authority of the true owner of the cheque.

The respondents' argument turns on their submission that only a proper endorsement of the cheque would have provided the Bank with the authority needed to deal with it. In their submission, Lakusta had to endorse the cheque in accordance with the provisions of the Act. Absent that endorsement, the respondents argue, Lakusta's explicit instructions to the Bank did not constitute authorization to deal with the cheque. The trial judge and the majority of the Alberta Court of Appeal agreed with this analysis. The Court of Appeal stated, at para. 6, that "the Bank cannot argue that Lakusta had authority on behalf of the numbered company without actually obtaining an endorsement to that effect." With respect, that conclusion is wrong as it would remove the possessory rights attached to the ownership of the cheque.

Iacobucci J. stated in *Boma, supra*, at para. 30, that "[a]n individual obtains title to a bill through negotiation." Negotiation, then, refers to the transfer of a bill's title between two parties. As per s. 59(3) of the Act, "[a] bill payable to order is negotiated by the endorsement of the holder." An endorsement, therefore, is the formal mechanism by which the holder of a bill payable to order transfers title in that bill to another party.

The issue in this case, however, is not whether 373409 transferred its title in the cheque to Legacy, but whether the Bank dealt with the cheque on the authority of 373409. As long as the Bank's actions were authorized by 373409, then the criterion of wrongful interference does not arise. An owner's capacity to authorize others to deal with his or her chattel is fundamental to that owner's right of possession. The provisions of the Act do not in any way limit the capacity of a cheque owner to delegate such authority. The rightful owner of any chattel, including a bill of exchange, is capable of authorizing another party to deal with that chattel, notwithstanding the absence of a formal transfer of title.

Consequently, whether 373409 negotiated the cheque and effected a transfer of title to Legacy is not dispositive of whether 373409 authorized the Bank to deal with its cheque as it did. The owner of a cheque is capable of authorizing another party to collect the proceeds of the cheque and transfer those proceeds to a third party. The granting of such authority is not dependent upon a transfer of legal title pursuant to the requirements of the Act.

[A] bank assumes significant risk in accepting an unendorsed third party cheque into a customer's account. An endorsement is the formal mechanism by which a bank is able to verify that it has the authority to deposit a cheque's proceeds into a customer's account. However, where the rightful owner has in fact authorized the bank to deal with the cheque, the lack of endorsement will not negate that authority. [A] bank's . . . assumption of that risk . . . does not by itself constitute conversion . . .

In this case, Lakusta instructed the Bank to deposit the proceeds of the cheque payable to 373409 into Legacy's account. As Lakusta was the sole owner of 373409, he could, as he did, authorize the Bank to deal with 373409's cheque, and the Bank played no role in conversion. To state the obvious, if Lakusta was not acting on behalf of 373409, then the Bank would not have had authorization to deal with the cheque and would be liable in conversion for having dispossessed 373409 of the cheque's proceeds.

There can be no doubt that Lakusta's act of directing the Bank to deposit the proceeds of the cheque into Legacy's account can be attributed to and considered authorized by 373409.

. . .

Here, Lakusta was the sole shareholder, director, and officer of 373409. He was the only person capable of acting as the corporation's directing mind, and he formed the entire "ego" and "personality" of the corporation. In his capacity as sole shareholder and director of the corporation, he had the full capacity to delegate authority to the corporation's agents. He was the sole officer of the corporation, and its only agent. Consequently, any act which he undertook as 373409's agent must be deemed authorized by the corporation. The only conclusion available on the evidence was that Lakusta, *qua* shareholder and director, authorized Lakusta, *qua* officer, to deposit 373409's funds into Legacy's account.

. . .

The impropriety of the corporation's diversion of funds from its creditors does not undermine Lakusta's authority to deal with those funds on behalf of the corporation. The wrongfulness of an officer's act in relation to a third party does not negate that act's attribution to the corporate body. For instance, a corporation may be responsible for the criminal acts of its agents... The key question in determining attribution is whether that agent's action was within the scope of authority delegated to him or her by the corporation. Since Lakusta was acting within the scope of authority granted to him by 373409, his act of instructing the Bank to deposit the cheque's proceeds into Legacy's account must be attributed to the corporation.

373409, through Lakusta, authorized the Bank, as it was entitled to do, to deposit the cheque's proceeds into Legacy's account. As a result, the Bank did not wrongfully interfere with 373409's cheque, as it did not deal with that cheque in a manner inconsistent with 373409's instructions. Consequently, the Bank is not liable in conversion to 373409's Receiver and Manager for the proceeds of the cheque.

NOTES AND QUESTIONS

1. Explain the concepts of "negotiation" and "endorsement." Were these concepts important for the purposes of Major J.'s decision?

2. When will a bank be held liable for conversion of a cheque?

3. Does Major J.'s decision seem fair to you? What would have been the practical implications of holding the defendant liable? Do banks often receive unendorsed cheques? Consider a situation in which an unendorsed cheque is deposited by way of an automated teller. See Rafferty, "Developments in Contract and Tort Law: The 2002-2003 Term" (2003) 22 S.CL.R. (2d) 175.

4. How did Major J. distinguish the facts before him from the facts of *Boma Manufacturing Ltd. v. Canadian Imperial Bank of Commerce*, [1996] 3 S.C.R. 727? For discussion of *Boma*, see Geva, "Conversion of Unissued Cheques and the Fictitious or Non-Existent Payee — *Boma v. CIBC*" (1997) 28 C.B.L.J. 177; and Ogilvie, "*If Boma is Wrong, Is the Bank Always Right?*: *373409 Alberta Ltd. (Receiver of) v. Bank of Montreal*" (2003) 39 C.B.L.J. 138.

Cases involving the alleged conversion of cheques are doubly complicated. In addition to dealing with the rules of tort, courts must take account of the rules that govern negotiable instruments. The *Bills of Exchange Act* is a complex statute: R.S.C. 1985, c. B-4 (the *BEA*). In codifying centuries of case law, it sensitively balances disparate considerations, including commercial certainty and fair allocations of risk. Like *373409 Alberta Ltd.* and *Boma Manufacturing, Teva Canada Ltd. v. TD Canada Trust*, 2017 SCC 51 illustrates the interaction between the tort of conversion and the law of negotiable instruments.

Teva, a large pharmaceutical company, employed Neil McConachie as a finance manager. McConachie was authorized to draw cheques on the company's bank account, but only for the payment of the company's debts. Over the course of four years, McConachie used his position to draw 64 cheques, for a total of about $5,400,000, in favour of six payees. Teva was not genuinely indebted to any of those payees. Four of the payees bore the names of parties that did business with Teva, but were not actually owed money. The other two payees bore names that were very similar to parties that dealt with Teva, but again, were owed nothing.

The cheques were drawn as part of a fraudulent scheme. McConachie arranged for all of them to be deposited into accounts that he controlled, including an account with TD, the defendant bank. Oblivious to the underlying fraud, TD collected payment from Teva's bank and credited McConachie's account. McConachie later withdrew the funds for his own benefit.

After the fraud was discovered, McConachie lost his job, and Teva sued TD for conversion of the cheques. That claim required a determination as to which of two innocent parties — Teva and TD — would bear the financial burden of McConachie's fraud. That task required an examination of the principles and policies that inform the tort of conversion and the *BEA*. The Supreme Court of Canada, by a slim 5:4 majority, held for the claimant.

TD was *prima facie* liable because it dealt with Teva's property (the cheques) without the company's authority. True, TD had received the cheques from McConachie, but he had no authority to draw cheques on Teva's account for his own benefit. TD was consequently liable unless it was protected by a defence.

The availability of a defence depended on the nature of the cheques. There were two possibilities. (1) A cheque is *payable to order* if it is drawn in favour of a specific person. In that event, a collecting bank (like TD) can deal with the cheque only if the instrument has been delivered and *endorsed* by the named payee. (Endorsement is achieved by signing the back of a cheque.) Since none of the named payees actually endorsed any of the cheques, TD would be liable if the instruments were payable to order. (2) A cheque is *payable to bearer* if it does not name a specific payee and consequently is payable to whoever bears (holds) it. A collecting bank can deal with a bearer cheque through simple delivery and without any endorsement. Since TD had taken delivery of the fraudulent instruments, it would not be liable if the cheques were payable to bearer. At first glance, that might not seem possible given that each cheque bore the name of a supposed payee. Under s. 20(5) of the *BEA*, however, a cheque that is payable to "a fictitious or non-existing person" is treated as payable to bearer. TD's liability consequently depended on whether the payees of the 64 cheques were "fictitious or non-existent."

Writing for the majority, Abella J. held that s. 20(5) entails a two-stage test. (1) The first stage is *subjective*. It classifies a payee as *fictitious* if, instead of intending to pay the payee, the drawer (in this case Teva) inserted the payee's name onto the cheque as a mere pretence. In that event, the instrument would be treated as a bearer cheque and the drawer would have no rights against the collecting bank. TD, however, could not prove that the payees were fictitious. Notwithstanding McConachie's fraud, Teva itself never intended the payees to be pretences rather than genuine payees. As a matter of commercial reality, Abella J. held, a large corporation cannot be expected to direct its mind to each individual cheque, but it can be assumed — unless there is persuasive evidence to the contrary — that payees are intended to receive payment. (2) The second stage of the test is *objective*. A cheque is again treated as a bearer cheque if the payee is *non-existent* because it is not — and could not be reasonably mistaken for — a legitimate creditor. The drawer, after all, should be able to detect cheques that are created in favour of parties to whom it could not plausibly be indebted. On the facts, however, Abella J. held that the payees were not non-existent. While they were not actual creditors, they were — or appeared to be — parties to whom Teva might well be indebted. TD consequently was not entitled to use the defence in s. 20(5) of the *BEA*.

Aside from enjoying a long history under the *BEA*, the two-part test, both subjective and objective, appealed to Abella J. on policy grounds. The Act, she said, creates a complex system for the use of negotiable instruments. And the primary beneficiaries of that system, she said, are banks. She accordingly concluded that, as between an innocent drawer and an innocent bank, the burden of fraud within the system should be allocated to the banks. They are best situated to absorb the loss and widely spread the associated costs amongst their customers.

Writing for themselves, as well as McLachlin C.J.C. and Wagner J., Côté and Rowe JJ. delivered a powerful dissent. They too favoured a two-stage test, but they insisted that it should be objective throughout — the parties' intentions should not be relevant. According to the dissent, a payee is (1) *non-existent* if, in fact, it does not exist when the instrument is created, and (2) *fictitious* if, in fact, there is no transaction between the drawer and the payee. *Teva Canada* provided an illustration of each possibility. The two names that McConachie made up were said to be non-existent because no such parties actually existed. The other four payees did exist, but since the cheques pertained to false purchase orders rather than genuine transactions with Teva, they were classified as fictitious. The dissentients accordingly believed that TD was entitled to resist Teva's claim on the basis of the *BEA* defence.

Turning to policy, Côté and Rowe JJ. explained that the *BEA* is based on the principles of negotiability, certainty, and finality. A subjective approach, they said, conflicts with those principles. A test that turns on the drawer's intention cannot be applied by simply looking at the face of an instrument. Moreover, a test that depends on an *ex post facto* determination of objective facts is much easier to apply. And finally, Côté and Rowe JJ. observed that the drawer of a cheque is much better positioned than a bank to detect and prevent fraud of the sort that occurred in *Teva Canada*. How was TD to know that McConachie exceeded his authority by causing Teva to draw cheques for a fraudulent purpose rather that for the payment of legitimate debts? Perhaps s. 20(5) of the *BEA* should be interpreted in a manner that allocates the risk of loss to the drawer.

Of the two approaches presented in the Supreme Court of Canada, which do you prefer? Is your answer a reflection of justice, commercial efficiency, or statutory interpretation? See Ogilvie, "The Tort of Conversion and the Collecting Bank: Teva Canada Ltd v Bank of Nova Scotia" (2014) 91 Can. Bar Rev. 731.

Accepting that Teva and TD were both "innocent" of the fraud, McConachie's scheme could have been detected earlier by a more rigorous system of checks and balances. In a case like *Teva Canada*, should a court allocate the losses in accordance with the parties' relative blameworthiness? Would that approach be compatible with the nature of the liability that arises under the tort of conversion? Abella J. addressed that question at *Boma Manufacturing, Teva Canada Ltd. v. TD Canada Trust*, 2017 SCC 51 at para. 69.

5. The claim in *373409 Alberta Ltd.* pertained to a cheque, which is a *tangible* form of property. Different considerations arise if the plaintiff complains that the defendant wrongfully interfered with an *intangible* piece of property. Conversion traditionally was viewed as protecting the right to possession and it is, of course, impossible to physically possess something that is intangible. For that reason, English courts continue to reject actions in conversion with respect to intangible assets: *OBG Ltd. v. Allan*, [2008] 1 A.C. 1 (H.L.). Canadian courts, in contrast, have imposed liability in such circumstances: *McLachlan v. Canadian Imperial Bank of Commerce* (1987), 13 B.C.L.R. (2d) 300 (S.C.), aff'd (1989), 35 B.C.L.R. (2d) 100 (C.A.); *Bradshaw Construction Ltd. v. Bank of Nova Scotia*, [1993] 1 W.W.R. 596 (B.C.C.A.), additional reasons at (1992), 73 B.C.L.R. (2d) 212 (C.A.); and *Royal Bank of Canada v. W. Got & Associates Electric Ltd.* (1994), 150 A.R. 93 (Q.B.), additional reasons at (1994), 18 Alta. L.R. (3d) 140 (Q.B.), aff'd (1997), 47 C.B.R. (3d) 1 (Alta. C.A.), aff'd on other grounds [1999] 3 S.C.R. 408. Is this a desirable development? See Ricks, "Conversion of Intangible Property: Bursting the Ancient Trover Bottle with New Wine" [1991] B.Y.U.L. Rev. 1681; Tettenborn, "Liability for Interfering with Intangibles: Invalidly Appointed Receivers, Conversion, and the Economic Torts" (2006) 122 L.Q.R. 31; and Goymour & Watterson, "Testing the Boundaries of Conversion: Account-Holders, Intangible Property and Economic Harm" [2012] L.M.C.L.Q. 204.

Difficult questions similarly arise with other forms of personal property. Can liability be imposed for conversion of a "business" as opposed to the physical assets of that business? That question was left unresolved in *Kessel v. Van Rikxoort*, 2012 BCSC 1270. Similarly, Canadian courts have split on the issue of imposing liability for the conversion of the goodwill associated with a business: *Brant Avenue Manor Limited Partnership v. Transmerica Life Insurance Co. of Canada* (2000), 48 O.R. (3d) 363 (S.C.J.); and *Manina Investments Ltd. v. Regatta Investments Ltd.* (1993), 92 Man. R. (2d) 88 (C.A.). The misappropriation of a business's "customer list" was in issue in *Borden*

Chemical Co. (Canada) v. J.G. Beukers Ltd. (1972), 29 D.L.R. (3d) 337 (B.C.S.C.). After finding that the defendant had converted the piece of paper on which that list was written, the court calculated damages not by reference to the paper itself, but rather on the basis of the value of the information that it contained (*i.e.* the price that the defendant would have been willing to pay for the list). See also *Cruise Connections Canada v. Cancellieri*, 2012 BCSC 53. In contrast, it has been said that a business's "secret formula," being intangible, cannot be possessed and consequently cannot be the subject of a conversion claim: *K.R. Thompson Engineering Ltd. v. Webster Industries Ltd.* (1980), 31 N.B.R. (2d) 329 (Q.B.). If damages can be assessed by the value of the information, and not by the value of the paper on which it may be written, should liability depend upon the form in which the defendant acquires that information? Should the tort of conversion protect intangible property? Or should the proprietary torts be confined to possessory interests, leaving intangible assets to be governed by intellectual property law?

6. The House of Lords recently reiterated the orthodox belief that conversion is confined to interference with tangible property: *OBG Ltd. v. Allan; Douglas v. Hello!; Mainstream Properties Ltd. v. Young*, [2008] 1 A.C. 1 (H.L.). The defendants in the first named case improperly acted as receivers of the claimant company. In that ostensible capacity, they liquidated the company's contractual assets. The company subsequently sought relief under the tort of conversion on the basis that the defendants had interfered with its contractual relations. Lord Hoffmann, writing for the majority, emphatically stated (at para. 100) that the "subject matter of conversion or trover must be specific personal property, whether goods or chattels" and said that it would be extraordinary to extend strict liability to people who in good faith, though improperly, had acted as receivers. He also said that since Parliament had examined the area and not taken action, it would be inappropriate, on policy grounds, for the courts to adopt the revisions advocated by the claimant.

In the modern world, much of what people value exists in digitized form. This is true, for instance, of computer software programs. Aside from the physical devices upon which such assets may be impressed, should those digitized assets themselves be protected by the tort of conversion? What are the arguments for and against such protection? See Green, "Can a Digitized Product be the Subject of Conversion?" [2006] L.M.C.L.Q. 568.

7. Although Lord Hoffmann's views carried the day in *OBG*, the case contained two dissents. In a forceful opinion, Lord Nicholls vigorously criticized the artificially narrow scope of conversion. That tort developed largely by way of fictions. The writ originally recited that the plaintiff, having enjoyed possession of goods, lost them, and that the defendant, having found the goods, converted them to his own use. The allegations of finding and losing became non-traversable and fictitious, so that the only issues before the court pertained to the plaintiff's prior possession and the defendant's conversion. By their very nature, however, the underlying allegations made sense only in connection to physical things that can be moved. Chattels can be lost and found, but land cannot. Land consequently cannot be the subject of an action in conversion. Likewise, tangible things like cows can be lost and found, but intangible things like debts cannot. That is why the tort of conversion historically could not apply with respect to choses in action. A chose in action is a thing, such as a debt, that can be enjoyed only though legal action. A chose in possession is a thing, such as a

cow, that can be enjoyed through physical possession. To overcome the fact that choses in action have no physical existence, the courts developed another fiction. While a debt is intangible, a document that records or evidences a debt is tangible. Courts accordingly held that a document that is created to represent a debt or an obligation carries the same value as the underlying debt or obligation. By that means, the tort of conversion applied in connection with contractual rights evidenced in documents like cheques, insurance policies, share certificates and guarantees.

In *OBG*, Lord Nicholls (at paras. 229-33) criticized the artificiality of that rule and argued that the tort of conversion should apply to contractual rights, regardless of documentation:

> [W]hy should this extension of the tort of conversion be confined to cases where the intangible rights are specially recorded in a document? I would like to think that, as a mature legal system, English law has outgrown the need for legal fictions. . . .
>
> Rationally the dividing line cannot be the existence or not of a piece of paper. The existence of a document is essentially irrelevant. Intangible rights can be misappropriated even if they are not recorded in a document.
>
> In principle an intangible right not recorded in writing may merit protection just as much as a right which is recorded in this way.
>
> In practice misappropriation is more likely to occur with a right embodied in a document such as a cheque which passes through several hands in the ordinary course of business. But that is no reason for withholding protection in other cases. This is especially so today when information is increasingly stored and communicated, and transactions are effected, by electronic means.
>
> The better approach today is to discard the fictional significance of a piece of paper. Instead one should seek to identify the common characteristic of the intangible rights in respect of whose misappropriation English law, as a matter of reality, already provides the remedy of conversion. The common characteristic, it seems to me, is that the rights protected in this way are contractual rights. No principled reason is apparent for attempting, for this purpose, to distinguish between different kinds of contractual rights.
>
> The time has surely come to recognise this and, additionally, to recognise that the tort of conversion applies to contractual rights irrespective of whether they are embodied or recorded in writing. . . . This would be a modest but principled extension of the scope of the tort of conversion. It would rid the law of an artificial limitation derived from the limited scope of an enabling legal fiction.

See also Douglas, "Converting Contractual Rights" [2008] L.M.C.L.Q. 129.

8. The House of Lords' decision in *OBG* has generated considerable attention. Much like Lord Nicholls, S. Green believes that the tort of conversion should extend to intangible assets. To deal with the problems associated with the lack of physical existence, she proposes that, instead of distinguishing between corporeal and incorporeal forms of property, the law should distinguish between things that can and cannot be subject to manual control. To that end, she further proposes that the courts should employ the criteria of exclusivity and exhaustivity. The former requires that an asset be amenable to exclusive custody, and the latter requires that it may be exhausted so as to deprive the plaintiff of its value: Green, "To Have and To Hold?: Conversion and Intangible Property" (2008) 71 Mod. L. Rev. 114. That proposal was considered in *Your Response Ltd. v. Datateam Business Media Ltd.*, [2014] EWCA Civ 281. In the course of addressing the specific issue as to whether a common law

possessory lien can be exercised over an electronic database, Moore-Bick L.J. saw considerable merit in Green's argument, but ultimately held that such a development was foreclosed by *OBG*.

9. The tort of conversion applies to chattels, but not land. That proposition was reiterated in *Re Kostiuk* (2002), 215 D.L.R. (4th) 78 (B.C.C.A.). A house was owned by a married couple as tenants in common. Being bankrupt and indebted to the applicant, the husband transferred his interest as a gift to his wife. A court held that the transfer was void as a fraudulent conveyance and that the applicant was entitled to a one-half interest in the property. The house was then sold by court order. Dissatisfied with the distribution of the proceeds from that sale, the applicant sued, *inter alia*, for conversion. The British Columbia Court of Appeal dismissed that claim on the basis that, whereas the applicant's rights pertained to real property, the tort applies only in connection with personal property. The need for a property interest in chattels similarly proved fatal in *Scott (c.o.b. Oldfield Orchard) v. Filipovic*, 2015 BCCA 409. Land was leased for the purpose of growing blueberries. When the lease ended and the landlord removed the plants, the tenant sued for conversion. The court held that the plants were fixtures and not chattels. *Cf. Van Burgsteden v. Long*, 2014 SKCA 115 (parties agreed that adult trees planted on property pending sales would remain chattels).

10. Because conversion is a *legal* cause of action, it cannot be used to remedy interference with an equitable interest in property. See *MCC Proceeds Ltd. v. Lehman Bros. (Europe)*, [1998] 4 All E.R. 657 (C.A.).

11. Most proposals to extend the tort of conversion reflect the changing nature of wealth. Whereas it historically tended to be tied up in physical assets, such as land and cattle, a great deal of wealth now takes the form of intangible assets, such as contractual rights and patents. Such interests arguably should be subject to the rules of conversion. Other suggestions to expand the scope of conversion, however, are more difficult to understand or accept. It has been suggested, for instance, that liability for conversion ought to be imposed upon those who purchase sex from people forced into prostitution: Keren-Paz, "Poetic Justice: Why Sex-Slaves Should Be Allowed to Sue Ignorant Clients in Conversion" (2010) 29 Law & Phil. 307. The author maintains that since "sex-slaves" are treated as chattels, they should be entitled to sue those who interfere with an "owner's" right of dominion. Does that proposal risk legitimizing the deplorable idea that "sex-slaves" are chattels? If liability is to protect involuntary prostitutes, would it be preferable to fashion a new tort?

(c) REMEDIES FOR CONVERSION

AITKEN v. GARDINER
(1956), 4 D.L.R. (2d) 119 (Ont. H.C.)

[The defendants purchased share certificates without knowing that they had been stolen from the plaintiff. By the time the action came to trial, the defendants already had sold some of the certificates. Spence J. held that the defendants were liable in either conversion or the old action of detinue *sur trover*. He ordered the defendants to return the remaining certificates they possessed, and then considered the proper measure of damages for the shares they had sold.

The defendants argued that they were liable only in conversion for the sold certificates and that the proper measure of damages was the value of the certificates when they were converted, rather than their much higher value at the time of the trial. Only the portion of Spence J.'s judgment dealing with the measure of damages in conversion is reproduced below.]

SPENCE J.:—. . . Even if I am in error in concluding that the plaintiff is entitled to assert her claim in an action like the old action of *detinue sur trover*, and is limited to an action for conversion, it is not at all certain that the result of such limitation would be to confine her damages to the small sum of money realized by the defendants upon the sale of these shares. It is true, and it has been stated time after time, that the measure of damages in actions in conversion is *generally* the value of the chattel converted at the time of the conversion.

In 4 C.E.D. (Ont.), 2nd ed., p. 168, it is said: "In an action for conversion the general principle of law, although not an inflexible one, is that the jury can give no more damages than the value of the goods at the time of the conversion."

In *Caxton Publishing Co. v. Sutherland Publishing Co.*, [1939] A.C. 178 at p. 203, Lord Porter said:

> There is no dispute as to the principle on which in general the measure of damages of conversion is calculated. It is the value of the thing converted at the date of the conversion, and this principle was accepted by both sides in the present case.

In *Solloway v. McLaughlin*, [1937] 4 D.L.R. 593 at p. 596, [1938] A.C. 247, Lord Atkin said:

> Their disposal of the deposited shares amounted to nothing short of conversion: and the client on each occasion on which the shares were sold had vested in him a right to damages for conversion which would be measured by the value of the shares at the date of the conversion.

Mayne on Damages, 11th ed., p. 417, explains the latter case further. The defendant stockbroker had converted the plaintiff's shares, but on the closing of the plaintiff's account with him he bought the same number of shares in the same company at a substantially lower price than at the conversion, and tendered these to the plaintiff, who took them without knowledge of the conversion. On discovering this the plaintiff sued for damages and the Court held that the defendants were liable for damages for the conversion and that the measure of damages was the value at the date of the conversion, less the value of the shares bought in replacement at the time when the plaintiff accepted such shares.

In *Salmond on Torts, op. cit.*, p. 348, it is said:

> If, on the other hand, the property increases in value after the date of the conversion, a distinction has to be drawn. If the increase is due to the act of the defendant, the plaintiff has no title to it, and his claim is limited to the original value of the chattel...

> If, however, the subsequent increase in value is not due to the act of the defendant, but would have occurred in any case, even had no conversion been committed, the plaintiff is entitled to recover it as special damage resulting from the conversion, in

addition to the original value of the property converted: as when goods taken or detained have risen in value by reason of the fluctuation of the market.

The author cites *Greening v. Wilkinson* (1825), 1 Car. & P. 625, 171 E.R. 1344, but adds in a footnote that it is different "if the plaintiff knew or ought to have known of the conversion" for in such case "he cannot claim the benefit of the subsequent rise in value: *Sachs v. Miklos*, [1948] 2 K.B. 23."

Salmond continues at p. 349: "In all actions for a conversion the plaintiff may recover, in addition to the value of the property . . . any additional damage which he may have sustained by reason of the conversion which is not too remote." He cites *Bodley v. Reynolds* (1846), 8 Q.B. 779, 115 E.R. 1066, and *France v. Gaudet* (1871), L.R. 6 Q.B. 199.

It would seem that the damage which a plaintiff suffers due to the defendants' inability to deliver certificates which have increased in value from a few cents to $17.50 per share are not damages which are too remote to enter into the calculation of her loss. Mayne is not so definite as is Salmond, and at p. 416 the author remarks: "Where the article has fluctuated in price, it is by no means settled in England whether it is to be estimated at its value at the time of conversion, or at any later time." And at p. 417 he expresses the opinion that an increase in value of goods from a rise in price is a gratuitous and accidental bonus, obtained by the holder of the goods, and that, consequently, if in trover for goods, damages were fixed at the time of their conversion, it might deprive the rightful owner of a profit, but that profit might be one which he never would have acquired, and for which he gave no consideration. Nevertheless, I am of the opinion that a person who owns shares and holds them for subsequent sale is a person who intends to acquire a profit if and when those shares increase in value, and that the conversion of those shares has deprived the plaintiff of an opportunity to obtain the profit which the plaintiff planned to obtain should the shares increase in value, and that the deprivation of the opportunity to obtain that profit is a proper element in considering the loss which the plaintiff suffered by the conversion.

. . .

[Spence J. concluded by giving the defendants the opportunity to return share certificates of the same kind to the plaintiff or pay $35,000 damages, the value of the share certificates at the date of trial. He also indicated, in *obiter dicta*, that the proper date for assessing damages was the trial date and not the judgment date if the values on these dates differed.]

NOTES AND QUESTIONS

1. It generally is said that a successful claimant in conversion is entitled to the market value of the chattel at the *time of the conversion*, whereas a successful claimant in detinue is entitled to the market value of the chattel at the *time of trial*. By way of explanation, it should be noted that an act of conversion is perceived a specific event, whereas the refusal to return a chattel that underlies detinue is viewed as an ongoing event. Given that difference, it often is said that, if an option exists, the plaintiff should sue in detinue in a rising market and in conversion in a falling market. That apparently simple proposition unfortunately is not helpful in fluctuating markets, as is often the case with stocks and other investments. Similar problems arise if judgment is awarded in a foreign currency, the value of which fluctuates between the time of

conversion and the time of trial: see *Stevenson Estate v. Siewert* (2001), 286 A.R. 181 (C.A.). Additional problems also may arise if the plaintiff was subject to an obligation to *mitigate* the losses flowing from the defendant's tort. See Ren, "The Normal Measure of Damages for Tortious Damage to Chattels under English Law" (2015) 23 Tort L. Rev. 148.

2. As *Aitken* illustrates, a plaintiff in a conversion action may be entitled to recover not only the market value of the chattel at the time of the conversion, but also *consequential losses* caused by the conversion. Spence J. appears to adopt J. Salmond's analysis of the circumstances in which the plaintiff can recover for consequential economic losses. What limitations does Salmond impose on such awards? Are they compatible with a plaintiff's obligation to mitigate?

3. In *Kuwait Airways Corp. v. Iraqi Airways Co.*, [2002] 2 W.L.R. 1353 (H.L.), the House of Lords addressed various aspects of the tort of conversion, including the issue of consequential damages. Iraqi forces invaded Kuwait, seized ten aircraft belonging to the plaintiff, moved them to Iraq, and delivered them to the defendant. The Iraqi government, acting through the Revolutionary Command Council, then passed Resolution 369, which transferred property in the aircraft to the defendant. Four of the planes subsequently were destroyed by coalition forces. The other six planes were sent by the defendant to Iran. The plaintiff eventually recovered those planes, but only after paying $20,000,000 in storage fees to the government of Iran. The plaintiff sued the defendant for that amount, plus the revenue that it lost as a result of not being able to use the aircraft during their detention.

As a matter of public law, the defendant enjoyed state immunity with respect to any acts performed prior to the passage of Resolution 369. The defendant's first line of argument therefore was that it could not be held liable for conversion because it received the aircraft during the period covered by state immunity. The House of Lords rejected that argument. It held that, while the defendant had previously come into possession of the aircraft, its actions after Resolution 369 constituted conversion. It had dealt with the aircraft in a manner that was inconsistent with the plaintiff's right of possession (*e.g.* by repainting and insuring the planes) and it had prevented the plaintiff from regaining possession of the aircraft.

On the question of damages, the House of Lords held that the plaintiff was entitled to recover (1) the $20,000,000 that it had paid to the Iranian government to secure the release of the aircraft, and (2) the revenue that it lost during the period of detention. See O'Keefe & Tettenborn, "English Public Policy Internationalised — And Conversion Clarified Too" [2002] C.L.J. 499; and Cane, "Causing Conversion" (2002) 118 L.Q.R. 544.

4. In *Ralston Purina of Can. Ltd. v. Whittaker* (1973), 6 N.B.R. (2d) 443 (C.A.), the defendant seized the plaintiff's pigs and sold them. Had the pigs not been converted, the plaintiff would have kept them until they were heavier and then sold them at a higher price. The court awarded the plaintiff the value of the pigs at the date of conversion, plus an additional amount to compensate him for what the pigs would have been worth had they been fattened.

In *Hutscal v. I.A.C. Ltd.* (1974), 48 D.L.R. (3d) 638 (Y.C.A.), the defendant unlawfully repossessed the plaintiff's house trailer. The plaintiff was awarded the value of the trailer at the date of the conversion, but denied damages for the loss of use of the trailer while it was in the defendant's possession. The court held that the plaintiff otherwise would have received compensation twice for the same loss. Do you agree?

Can you reconcile *Hutscal* and *Ralston*? Are these cases consistent with Salmond's analysis of damage awards in conversion?

5. In *Sachs v. Miklos*, [1948] 1 All E.R. 67 (C.A.), the court suggested that there was no practical difference between the measure of damages in detinue and conversion, because the plaintiff can recover any post-conversion increase in the chattel's value by means of a claim for consequential economic loss.

As we shall discuss, the court in *Gen. & Finance Facilities Ltd. v. Cooks Cars (Romford) Ltd.*, [1963] 2 All E.R. 314 (C.A.), specifically rejected this view, while reaffirming that consequential economic loss was available in certain situations involving conversion. That view similarly was rejected in *Steiman v. Steiman* (1982), 143 D.L.R. (3d) 396 (Man. C.A.). The Manitoba Court of Appeal held that damages in conversion must be calculated on the assumption that the plaintiff mitigated by replacing the chattel as early as reasonably possible. A plaintiff who has replaced a converted chattel will not lose any appreciation in a rising market. If awarded damages for consequential economic loss, the plaintiff would recover appreciation twice: once on the converted chattel and again on the replacement chattel. Do you agree with this analysis? Is *Steiman*, in effect, merely trying to ensure that the victim of a conversion mitigate as soon as possible? Can you reconcile *Steiman, Gen. & Finance* and *Aitken*? See *Dom. Securities Ltd. v. Glazerman* (1984), 29 C.C.L.T. 194 (Man. C.A.); and Irvine, "Annotation" (1984), 29 C.C.L.T. 195. See also *Asamera Oil Corp. v. Sea Oil & Gen. Corp.*, [1979] 1 S.C.R. 633; *R.F. Fry & Associates (Pacific) Ltd. v. Reimer*, [1993] 8 W.W.R. 663 (B.C.C.A.); and Waddams, "Damages for Failure to Return Shares" (1979) 3 C.B.L.J. 398.

6. As a general principle, damages in tort are intended to position the plaintiff as if the wrong had not occurred. They are not intended to create a windfall. The relief that is available in conversion, however, occasionally appears to have exactly that effect. Consider a case in which the defendant converts the plaintiff's chattel at a time when it has a market value of $5000. After the market drops, the defendant purchases a replacement at a cost of only $3000 and delivers that item to the plaintiff. In one sense, the plaintiff has suffered no loss because he or she is in possession of a substitute for the original asset. Nevertheless, while the plaintiff must account for the value of the substitute, damages will be assessed by reference to the market value at the time of the tort: *Solloway v. McLaughlin*, [1938] A.C. 247 (P.C. Can.), rev'g [1937] 4 D.L.R. 593 (S.C.C.); *Butler v. Egg Board* (1966), 114 C.L.R. 185 at 189 (H.C.A.); *BBMB Finance (Hong Kong) Ltd. v. Eda Holdings Ltd.*, [1990] 1 W.L.R. 409 (P.C. H.K.); *Campbell v. Dominion Breweries Ltd.*, [1994] 3 N.Z.L.R. 559 (C.A.); *Kerr v. Fleming Financial Corp.*, [1998] 9 W.W.R. 176 (Man. Q.B.), aff'd (1998), 131 Man. R. (2d) 116 (C.A.); and Tettenborn, "Damages in Conversion — The Exception or the Anomaly" [1995] C.L.J. 128.

The apparent anomaly of such relief may be explained by the rights-based theory of tort law that was introduced in Chapter 1. That theory holds that tort is concerned with the vindication of rights and not with the compensation of loss. The remedial focus therefore does not fall upon the *consequences* of the tort — the extent, if any, to which the plaintiff has financially lost. It instead falls upon the infringement itself —

the value associated with the right that the defendant violated. See Green, "Rights and Wrongs: An Introduction to the Wrongful Interference Actions" in Nolan & Robertson, eds., *Rights and Private Law* (2010) at 535.

How are damages calculated if the value of the converted chattel is unknown? That question arose in *Armory v. Delamirie* (1722), 93 E.R. 664 (K.B.) after a chimney sweep found a ring set with jewels and brought it to a goldsmith for valuation. The goldsmith, however, removed the stones and gave the empty ring back to the boy. Because the defendant's wrongful act prevented a proper assessment of the evidence, the court awarded relief on the assumption that the gems were of "the finest water." That is not to say, however, that every uncertainty will be resolved against the defendant. In most instances, the court is able to reach a decision on the balance of probabilities. In *Smith v. British Columbia*, 2011 BCSC 298, the defendant lost personal property that it had taken from the plaintiff while committing him to jail. In addition to a wallet, a driver's license, and a bus pass, the lost items included some sort of stone set in a ring. The plaintiff, a habitual criminal and welfare fraud, claimed that the stone was expensive Alexandrite, but Gray J. ultimately concluded that it probably was a good quality fake and calculated damages accordingly.

Should damages be available to the extent that a converted chattel held special sentimental or spiritual significance for the plaintiff? That issue was discussed in *Gladue v. Alberta (Attorney General)*, 2011 ABQB 651 after the defendant police department improperly disposed of a blanket that the Aboriginal claimant had received after participating in a sweat lodge ceremony.

7. In *Royal Bank v. W. Got & Associates Electric Ltd.*, [1999] 3 S.C.R. 408, the bank was held liable for $100,000 in punitive damages for its high-handed conversion of the plaintiff's business assets. In *White Distribution Ltd. v. Goring*, 2018 ONSC 2333, $10,000 in punitive damages were added to $170,000 in compensatory damages after a consignee of art work refused to return the plaintiff's paintings. And in *Rollinson v. R.* (1994), 73 F.T.R. 16, customs and RCMP officers were held liable in conversion for compensatory, aggravated, and punitive damages for repeatedly seizing the plaintiff's boat and for "escalating their eight-year mistreatment of the [claimants], from a very bad, stupid beginning." The court awarded the plaintiffs an additional $8,000 under s. 24(1) of the *Canadian Charter of Rights and Freedoms*, Part I of the *Constitution Act, 1982*, being Schedule B to the *Canada Act 1982* (U.K.) 1982, c. 11 for the defendants' violation of their ss. 7, 8, 12 and 15 rights.

8. Although many of the cases are ambiguous, the response to conversion may consist of disgorgement of the defendant's wrongful gain, rather than compensation of the plaintiff's loss. (Canadian courts unfortunately often say "restitution" rather than disgorgement. Restitution, which is limited to benefits that the defendant acquired from the plaintiff, is properly available only in response to the action in unjust enrichment. Disgorgement, which includes benefits that the defendant acquired from a third party as a result of breaching the plaintiff's rights, is available in response to many types of wrongs.) The remedial option generally lies with the plaintiff. See for example *United Australia Ltd. v. Barclays Bank Ltd.*, [1941] A.C. 1 (H.L.); *Borden Chemical Co. (Canada) v. J.G. Beukers Ltd.* (1972), 29 D.L.R. (3d) 337 (B.C.S.C.); *Lamine v. Dorrell* (1705), 92 E.R. 303; *King v. Leith* (1787), 100 E.R. 77; and *Marsh v. Keating* (1834), 131 E.R. 1094.

Canadian courts occasionally conflate disgorgement and punitive damages: *Whiten v. Pilot Insurance Co.*, 2002 SCC 18 at para. 72 ("it is rational to use punitive damages to relieve a wrongdoer of its profit where compensatory damages would amount to nothing more than a licence fee to earn greater profits"). That happened in *2105582 Ontario Ltd. (c.o.b. Performance Plus Golf Academy) v. 375445 Ontario Ltd. (c.o.b. Hydeaway Golf Club)*, 2016 ONSC 3746, varied 2017 ONCA 980. Having leased land from the defendant, the plaintiff brought $200,000 worth of equipment onto the premises so that it could be used as a golf driving range. After the plaintiff fell behind on rent, the defendant resumed possession and, for the next eight years, used the equipment for its own purposes. Since the equipment constituted trade fixtures, which the plaintiff should have been allowed to remove when the lease was terminated, the defendant was liable for conversion. The trial judge awarded $188,033 in compensatory damages, plus $80,000 in exemplary or punitive damages. The latter sum was calculated as $10,000 per year for eight years. The Court of Appeal overturned that part of the award. There was no call for punishment because the defendant had not acted in a malicious or high-handed manner. Moreover, as Juriansz J.A. explained, the trial judge had effectively awarded disgorgement despite the absence of any proof of the extent to which the defendant had actually profited as a result of committing a tort against the claimant.

9. In an action for conversion or detinue, the plaintiff exceptionally may obtain recovery *in specie* (that is, of the specific thing). So too, as discussed at the end of this chapter, the owner may retrieve a chattel by means of recaption. While in possession of the property, however, the defendant may have effected considerable repairs or improvements to the item. When, if ever, should the owner be liable in unjust enrichment to provide restitution to the defendant for the value of such benefits? It has been suggested that while an owner who recovers property with judicial assistance must make restitution, one who resorts to the self-help remedy need not pay for the benefit: *Greenwood v. Bennett*, [1972] 3 All E.R. 586 (C.A.); *Peruvian Guano Co. v. Dreyfus Brothers & Co. Ltd.*, [1892] A.C. 166 (H.L.); cf. *Mayne v. Kidd* (1951), 1 W.W.R. 833 (Sask. C.A.). Is that rule fair? Should a defendant who honestly repairs a chattel enjoy always an independent claim in unjust enrichment?

In *Mutungih v. Bokun* (2006), 40 C.C.L.T. (3d) 313 (Ont. S.C.J.), the defendant spent considerable money repairing a car that had been stolen from the plaintiff. In awarding relief for conversion, the court noted that the defendant had purchased the stolen vehicle from a third party under suspicious circumstances, and therefore refused to make any allowance for the improvements.

The issue of improvements arose in *Beyond Bears Inc. v. Woodley*, 2010 BCSC 358. The parties had a long-standing relationship involving various animals owned by the plaintiff. The defendant provided training and the plaintiff negotiated for the animals to appear in films and television. After several years, the parties had a falling out and the plaintiff sued the defendant, alleging conversion of a raccoon, two coyotes, and three dogs, one of whom — a Golden Retriever named Bud — had starred in a series of highly profitable movies. The defendant denied those allegations and argued, by way of counterclaim, that the plaintiff had been unjustly enriched by the training services. The judge found that some, though not all, of the animals were owned by the plaintiff. Since the defendant had refused to return the relevant animals to the plaintiff, conversion was established and damages *prima facie* were calculated as the cost of replacing the animals at the time of the tort. Consequential damages, for loss of potential profits, were denied for lack of proof. Relief ultimately was refused, however, to the extent that the replacement costs reflected "improvements" attributable to the defendant's services. Indeed, the court held that the plaintiff's unjust enrichment supported not only restitution but a constructive trust in the defendant's favour. The defendant therefore was entitled to retain the animals.

10. Conversion involves a complex, and occasionally difficult, amalgam of tort and property. The proprietary nature of the claim is evidenced by the fact that a judgment in conversion takes priority over the tortfeasor's other personal debts. That proposition becomes tremendously important if the defendant is insolvent. In that situation, tort claimants generally must stand in line with the defendant's other creditors. As a result, they are apt to receive very little, if any, of the money to which they are entitled. In contrast, a successful claimant in conversion enjoys priority and therefore is entitled to receive full payment ahead of most other creditors.

11. The courts at one time allowed the tortfeasor to return the chattel, rather than accept a "forced sale," at least if the goods were undamaged: *Fisher v. Prince* (1762), 97 E.R. 876 (K.B.). Although some modern cases contemplate a judicial power to compel the plaintiff to accept restoration *in specie*, it is not entirely clear when, or if, that power actually exists: *Harbour Equipment v. Canadian National Railway Co.* (1976), 25 N.S.R. (2d) 166 (T.D.); and Sappideen & Vines, eds., *Fleming's The Law of Torts*, 10th ed. (2011) at 84. How did the court resolve this issue in the extract from *MacKenzie v. Scotia Lumber Co.* earlier in this chapter?

On the availability of specific relief generally, see Curwen, "The Remedy in Conversion: Confusing Property and Obligation" (2006) 26 L.S. 570.

5. Detinue

GEN. & FINANCE FACILITIES LTD. v. COOKS CARS (ROMFORD) LTD.
[1963] 1 W.L.R. 644 (C.A.)

DIPLOCK L.J.:—This appeal raises a neat point as to the remedies available to a plaintiff who sues for the wrongful detention of goods. The plaintiffs by a specially endorsed writ claimed "the return of a mobile crane index No. OMF 347 or its value and damages for detaining the same." They pleaded their title to the crane and relied on a demand for its delivery updated May 8, 1961. The prayer included an alternative claim for damages for conversion.

There are important distinctions between a cause of action in conversion and a cause of action in detinue. The former is a single wrongful act and the cause of action accrues at the date of the conversion; the latter is a continuing cause of action which accrues at the date of the wrongful refusal to deliver up the goods and continues until delivery up of the goods or judgment in the action for detinue. It is important to keep this distinction clear, for confusion sometimes arises from the historical derivation of the action of conversion from detinue sur bailment and detinue sur trover; of which one result is that the same facts may constitute both detinue and conversion. Demand for delivery up of the chattel was an essential requirement of an action in detinue and detinue lay only when at the time of the demand for delivery up of the chattel made by the person entitled to possession the defendant was either in actual possession of it or was estopped from denying that he was still in possession. Thus, if there had been an actual bailment of the chattel by the plaintiff to the defendant the latter was estopped from asserting that he had wrongfully delivered the chattel to a third person or had negligently lost it before demand for delivery up and the plaintiff could sue in detinue notwithstanding that the defendant was not in actual possession of the chattel at the time of the demand (see *Jones v. Dowle*, [(1841), 152 E.R. 9]; *Reeve v. Palmer*, [(1858), 141 E.R. 9]). Alternatively the plaintiff could sue in conversion for the actual wrongful delivery of the chattel to the third person, though not for its loss. On the other hand an unqualified refusal to comply with a demand for delivery up of a chattel made by the person entitled to possession may also amount to conversion, but only if the defendant at the time of the refusal was in actual possession of the chattel. If he has wrongfully delivered it to a third person before the date of the demand the prior wrongful delivery constitutes the conversion, not the subsequent refusal to comply with the demand (see *Sachs v. Miklos*, [[1948] 1 All E.R. 67]). But even where, as in the present case, the chattel is in the actual possession of the defendant at the time of the demand to deliver up possession, so that the plaintiff has alternative causes of action in detinue or conversion based on the refusal to comply with that demand, he has a right to elect which cause of action he will pursue (see *Rosenthal v. Alderton & Sons, Ltd.*, [[1946] 1 All E.R. 583]) and the remedies available to him will differ according to his election.

The action in conversion is a purely personal action and results in a judgment for pecuniary damages only. The judgment is for a single sum of which the measure is generally the value of the chattel at the date of the conversion together with any consequential damage flowing from the conversion and not too remote to be recoverable in law. With great respect to the dictum of Lord Goddard, C.J., in *Sachs v. Miklos*, [*supra*], this is not necessarily the same as the measure of damages for detinue, where the same act constitutes detinue as well as conversion, although in many cases this will be so. This dictum was based on the headnote to *Rosenthal v. Alderton*, [*supra*], which, in my view, misrepresents the effect of the last paragraph of the actual judgment. The law is in my view correctly stated in the current edition of *Salmond on Torts* at pp. 287 and 288. A judgment for damages for conversion does not, it is true, divest the plaintiff of his property in the chattel (see the analysis of the cases in *Ellis v. Stenning*, [[1932] All E.R. Rep. 597]). The judgment, however, does not entitle the plaintiff to the assistance of the court or the executive, videlicet the sheriff, in recovering possession of the chattel.

On the other hand the action in detinue partakes of the nature of an action in rem in which the plaintiff seeks specific restitution of his chattel. At common law it resulted in a judgment for delivery up of the chattel or payment of its value as assessed, and for payment of damages for its detention. This, in effect, gave the defendant an option whether to return the chattel or to pay its value, and if the plaintiff wished to insist on specific restitution of the chattel he had to have recourse to Chancery (see *Re Scarth*, [(1874), 10 Ch. App. 234], per Mellish, L.J.). The Common Law Procedure Act, 1854, s. 78, gave the court power to order delivery up of the chattel by the defendant without giving him the option to pay its value as assessed. Such an order was enforceable by execution and if the chattel could not be found distraint could be had on the defendant's lands and goods until he delivered up the specific chattel, or at the option of the plaintiff, distraint could be had of the defendant's goods for the assessed value of the chattel. This, in effect, where the court thought fit to make such an order, gave the plaintiff an option to insist on specific restitution of his chattel if the defendant did not deliver it up voluntarily; but this remedy was not available unless and until the value of the chattel had been assessed (see *Chilton v. Carrington*, [(1855), 139 E.R. 735]). This remedy continues to exist under the modern law, but if the plaintiff does not wish to exercise his option to recover the assessed value of the chattel the assessment of its value is no longer a condition precedent to an order for specific restitution (see *Hymas v. Ogden*, [[1950] 1 K.B. 246]; R.S.C., Ord. 48, r. 1). In addition to an order for specific restitution of the chattel or for payment of its value as assessed the plaintiff was always entitled to damages for wrongful detention of the chattel.

In the result an action in detinue today may result in a judgment in one of three different forms: (i) for the value of the chattel as assessed and damages for its detention; or (ii) for return of the chattel or recovery of its value as assessed and damages for its detention; or (iii) for return of the chattel and damages for its detention. A judgment in the first form is appropriate where the chattel is an ordinary article in commerce, for the court will not normally order specific restitution in such a case, where damages are an adequate remedy (see *Whiteley Ltd. v. Hilt*, [[1918] 2 K.B. 808]). A judgment in this form deprives the defendant of the option which he had under the old common law form of judgment of returning the chattel; but if he has failed to do so by the time of the judgment the plaintiff, if he so elects, is entitled to a judgment in this form as of right (cf. R.S.C., Ord. 13, r. 6). In substance this is the same as the remedy in conversion although the sum recoverable, as I have indicated, may not be the same as damages for conversion, for the cause of action in detinue is a continuing one up to the date of judgment and the value of the chattel is assessed as at that date (see *Rosenthal v. Alderton & Sons, Ltd.*, [*supra*]). A final judgment in such a form is for a single sum of money. A judgment in the second form gives to the defendant the option of returning the chattel, but it also gives to the plaintiff the right to apply to the court to enforce specific restitution of the chattel by writ of delivery, or attachment or sequestration as well as recovering damages for its detention by writ of fieri facias (R.S.C., Ord. 42, r. 6). This is an important right and it is essential to its exercise that the judgment should specify separate amounts for the assessed value of the chattel and for the damages for its detention, for if the plaintiff wishes to proceed by writ of delivery for which he can apply ex parte (Ord. 48, r. 1) he has the option of distraining for the assessed value of the chattel if the chattel itself is not recovered by the sheriff. He would be deprived of this option if the value of the chattel were not separately assessed. A judgment in the third form is unusual but can be given (see *Hymas v. Ogden*, [*supra*]). Under it the only pecuniary sum recoverable is damages for detention of the chattel. Its value need not be assessed and the plaintiff can obtain specific restitution of the chattel only by writ of delivery, attachment, or sequestration. He has no option under the writ of delivery to distrain for the value of the chattel.

AITKEN v. GARDINER
(1956), 4 D.L.R. (2d) 119 (Ont. H.C.)

SPENCE J.: . . . Also, the plaintiff alleges that in order to succeed in an action for detinue he need only prove (1) that the chattel was in the possession of the defendant who refuses to deliver the same, and (2) that, if the defendant on the issuance of the writ no longer had possession of the chattel, he parted with it wrongfully. Counsel for the defendants on the other hand submitted that the action of detinue is restricted to actions based on a bailment by the plaintiff to the defendants.

Clerk & Lindsell on Torts, 11th ed., pp. 441 *et seq.*, points out that the two types of action in detinue are (1) an action in *detinue sur trover*, and the other, an action in *detinue sur bailment*; and the same matter is dealt with in much the same fashion in Potter. Historical Introduction to English Law, 2nd ed., pp. 353 *et seq.* At p. 355 the latter author says: "During the fifteenth century this plea gave rise to a special form of action of Detinue known as *detinue sur trover*, which must be distinguished from the action of Trespass on the Case *sur trover* (shortly called *Trover*), which ultimately took its place . . . This distinction [between *detinue sur trover* and *detinue sur bailment*] represented the recognition of the two forms of wrongful detention: one based upon a purely tortious wrong and the other connected with agreement between the parties."

Salmond on Torts, 11th ed. pp. 317-8, quotes Parke B. in *Jones v. Dowle* (1841), 9 M. & W. 19, 152 E.R. 9, as follows: "'Detinue does not lie against him who never had possession of the chattel, but does lie against him who once had but has improperly parted with the possession of it.'" The author continues: "This being so, it is clear that detinue was available as a remedy for wrongful conversion as well as for wrongful detainer."

The action of detinue declined in popularity because of certain defects — defects which have been largely cured now that, since 1852, the Court has had the option of ordering the actual return of the chattel rather than merely granting damages for it. The fact that the defendants had not possession of the certificate at the time the writ was issued is no answer to an action in detinue so long as they got rid of the possession of the chattel improperly: *Jones v. Dowle, supra,* and *Bristol & West of England Bk. v. Midland R. Co.,* [1891] 2 Q.B. 653.

In *Clark v. Orr* (1854), 11 U.C.Q.B. 436 at p. 437, Robinson C.J. says: "It seems clear, we think, on numerous authorities, that it is not indispensable to shew that the defendant in the action of *detinue* had possession of the goods when the action was brought; if he had possession of them before, that may suffice."

In *Jones v. Dowle, supra,* the Court said: "Detinue does not lie against him who never had possession of the chattel, but it does against him who once had, but has improperly parted with the possession of it."

See also *Munro v. Willmott,* [1948] 2 All E.R. 983.

Was, then, the defendants' parting with the certificates in question in this action an improper parting? I have found that the certificates were stolen and I have come to the opinion that no principle of negotiability gave to the defendants any right which they could assert as against the true owner of the certificates. In these circumstances I am of the opinion that the sale by the defendants of the shares represented by those certificates was, in law, a conversion, and was therefore an improper parting with possession and was a sufficient basis for the present action in detinue.

[Spence J. held that the plaintiff had an option of suing in either detinue or conversion, and went on to assess damages.]

NOTES AND QUESTIONS

1. Do Diplock L.J. in *Gen. & Finance* and Spence J. in *Aitken* agree on when a detinue action will lie against a defendant who no longer is in possession? If not, which view is preferable?

2. Under what circumstances will the plaintiff have the option of suing in either conversion or detinue? When will the plaintiff be limited to only one?

3. Detinue has been abolished in the United Kingdom by s. 8 of the *Torts (Interference with Goods) Act 1977*. For a discussion of the impact of the legislation see Palmer, "The Abolition of Detinue" (1981) 45 Conv. & Prop. Law 62.

4. In *Baud Corp., N.V. v. Brook* (1973), 12 A.R. 311 (C.A.), varied without reference to this point, [1979] 1 S.C.R. 633 (*sub nom. Asamera Oil Corp. v. Sea Oil & General Corp.*), the court held that a formal demand and refusal is not required for detinue if the plaintiff clearly shows that the demand would have been refused. But see Palmer, "Comment" (1975) 53 Can. Bar Rev. 121.

The timing of a demand may be significant. In *Rose v. Fishery Products International Ltd.*, 2016 NLTD(G) 52, aff'd 2018 NLCA 65 it meant the difference between success and failure. The plaintiffs owned a seine (a type of fishing net) that the defendant agreed to store in 1992. The parties routinely did business together and the arrangement was found to be mutually beneficial. Beginning in 2001, the plaintiffs were aware that "there could be a problem with the . . . seine" (at para. 59), but they did not formally demand the return of their chattel until 2003, when they again had need of it. When a claim was eventually commenced in 2008, the defendant argued that the six-year limitation period had lapsed. It accordingly became necessary for the court to determine when the action in detinue arose. After reviewing the authorities, Faour J. explained that "the critical element of detinue appears not to be knowledge that the goods may be missing, but failure to deliver them *upon demand*" (at para. 52). The defence consequently failed because the clock began running in 2003 rather than 2001.

The reasoning in *Rose v. Fishery Products International Ltd.* raises the possibility that a strategic claimant may postpone the commencement of a limitation period by refraining from making a demand. Going further, if the facts support both conversion and detinue, it may be possible for the former to be time-barred even before the clock begins to run on the latter. That is not a desirable situation. The court in *Rose* responded, not entirely convincingly, by saying that the "possibility can be dealt with in an assessment of damages" (at para. 56).

The need for a demand reflects the fact that, as when goods are found, the defendant may have obtained possession innocently. In that situation, it would be unfair to impose liability without first giving the defendant an opportunity to return the goods to the plaintiff.

The tort of detinue occurs when the defendant refuses the plaintiff's demand to restore the goods. That does not mean, however, that a demand must be satisfied immediately. The defendant enjoys a reasonable opportunity to investigate the matter and determine the claimant's right to possession: *Craig v. McCreath*, [1922] 2 W.W.R. 1276 (Sask. Dist. Ct.); *Clayton v. LeRoy*, [1911] 2 K.B. 1031 (C.A.). Detinue consists of a failure to deliver chattels on demand, but not every failure will lead to liability. The refusal must reflect the defendant's refusal to hand over goods on hand, or the defendant's prior wrongful disposition of the goods, or the defendant's failure to satisfy an obligation to safeguard the goods. Those possibilities capture most circumstances, but liability will not lie if the defendant cannot satisfy the plaintiff's demand because, without any fault on the defendant's part, the chattels have been lost, stolen, or destroyed. Consequently, as long as a bailee exercises reasonable care, it will not incur liability despite being unable to restore the goods to a bailor: *Kinsella v. Club "7" Ltd.* (1993), 115 Nfld. & P.E.I.R. 150 (Nfld. T.D.); *Guarantee Co. of North*

America v. Century Services Inc., 2004 ABQB 446; and *Smith v. British Columbia* , 2011 BCSC 298 at para. 33.

5. Although there is disagreement, it appears that where detinue is based on an immediate right to possession, a right of property must be established. Unfortunately, it is not clear what the courts mean by "a right of property" in these cases. See for example *Jarvis v. Williams*, [1955] 1 All E.R. 108 (C.A.); and *Singh v. Ali*, [1960] A.C. 167 (P.C.). It is accepted, however, that the plaintiff does not have to prove title and that the defendant cannot escape liability simply by showing that some third party has a better right to the goods: *Schentag v. Gauthier* (1972), 27 D.L.R. (3d) 710 (Sask. Dist. Ct.). Liability for detinue is triggered by the fact that the plaintiff has a better right to possession than the defendant: *McLellan v. Melanson* (1967), 62 D.L.R. (2d) 40 (N.S.S.C.A.D.).

6. According to *Gen. & Finance*, in what circumstances is a plaintiff entitled to recover a chattel in detinue? Notice that a claimant in detinue never enjoys a *right* to the detained chattel. That option lies with the judge. While a court may give the defendant the option of returning the item or paying damages, it will satisfy the plaintiff's demand for restoration only if the property is unique or special. It will ask, as in a claim for specific performance of a contract of sale, whether damages would constitute an adequate remedy. Monetary relief generally will be sufficient if, given the nature of the chattel, a reasonable replacement could be purchased in the market.

7. Although many of the cases are ambiguous, a plaintiff in detinue may seek disgorgement of the defendant's gain, rather than either specific recovery or compensatory relief. See for example Lord Denning's analysis in *Strand Electric and Engineering Co. v. Brisford Entertainments Ltd.*, [1952] 2 Q.B. 246 (C.A.); *cf. Sprung Instant Structures Ltd. v. Royal Bank of Canada* (2008), 87 Alta. L.R. (4th) 111 (Q.B.); and *Aces System Development v. Yenty Lily*, [2013] SGCA 53.

8. Despite some debate, detinue appears to be actionable *per se*. See *Williams v. Peel River Land & Mineral Co. Ltd.* (1886), 55 L.T. 689 (C.A.); Waddams, *The Law of Damages*, 4th ed. (2004) at 10.10; and *cf.* Tyler & Palmer, *Crossley Vaines' Personal Property*, 5th ed. (1973) at 22. It follows that if the defendant is liable for detinue, but the plaintiff cannot prove any loss, the court will award nominal damages. Unfortunately, the *quantum* of nominal damages remains controversial. There is much to be said for the Ontario Court of Appeal's insistence that nominal damages in principle ought to be restricted to an award of $1: *Place Concorde East Limited Partnership v. Shelter Corp. of Canada Ltd.* (2006), 270 D.L.R. (4th) 181 at 203 (Ont. C.A.). Some judges, however, do not feel so constrained.

The issue arose in *Sabo v. Canada (Attorney General)*, 2013 YKCA 2. The plaintiff found what he believed was a meteorite. He also believed that the item's strange greenish hue indicated that it was host to alien life forms. He accordingly delivered it to the defendant and permitted a government agency to remove a slice, known as an "off-cut," for testing. After finding nothing of interest, the defendant returned the primary item but kept the off-cut. The plaintiff sued on a number of grounds, including detinue. The trial judge declared that the tort had been committed, but refused damages because the plaintiff had failed to prove any loss. On appeal, however, Harris J.A. held the defendant liable for nominal damages of $1000. What is the purpose or function of nominal damages? Is $1000 necessary to fulfill that purpose or function? Would you consider $1000 to be damages in name only?

6. Recaption and Replevin

While property sometimes is recovered *in specie* under an action in detinue, the plaintiff has no *right* to such relief. A dispossessed owner therefore may attempt to retrieve a chattel by other means. This section considers two possibilities: *recaption* and *replevin*.

(a) RECAPTION

Recaption occurs when a dispossessed owner simply takes back the goods. Although the right of recaption may provide an effective solution to an immediate problem, it ought to be exercised with great care. This is true of self-help remedies generally. There often is considerable risk that tempers will flare and that a minor incident will deteriorate into violence. The right of recaption therefore is limited to results that can be achieved without the use of unreasonable force and without a breach of peace. It may be possible to use *some* force, just as it may be permissible to trespass upon land in order to retrieve a chattel. As always, however, reasonableness depends upon the facts of each case.

(b) REPLEVIN

Even if a dispossessed owner cannot retrieve a chattel through recaption, recovery may be possible by means of *replevin*. Unlike trespass, conversion, and detinue, replevin is *not* a tort. (That fact is sometimes overlooked: *Sportelli v. MacLeod*, 2016 ONSC 6915.) It is, rather, a form of interlocutory relief. A successful invocation of replevin involves two steps: "an interim order only for the recovery of property" and a "final order for the return of specific property": *Neill v. Vancouver Police Department*, 2005 BCSC 277 at para. 29.

- *Replevy*: The first stage involves a court order directing an official to seize the disputed property from the defendant and return it to the plaintiff. Although the application normally occurs on notice, the plaintiff may proceed *ex parte* (that is, without notice to the defendant) if there is a risk that the defendant will destroy or dispose of the goods if forewarned. In either event, the plaintiff must provide *security*. That security ensures that, if the matter ultimately is resolved in the defendant's favour, the plaintiff will be able to pay compensation and costs. The initial order also is premised upon the plaintiff's promise to return the goods to the defendant if the court eventually decides in the latter's favour.

- *Action in Replevin*: Having recovered the property, the plaintiff must expeditiously proceed to a full trial for a determination of which party enjoys the better right of possession.

In essence, then, replevin is a means of restoring the *status quo ante*, pending resolution of the matter. That function was explained in *Mennie v. Blake* (1856), 119 E.R. 1078 at 1080 (Q.B.):

[A]s a general rule it is just that a party in the peaceable possession of land or goods should remain undisturbed ... until the right be determined and the possession shewn to be unlawful. But, where, either by distress or merely by a strong hand, the peaceable possession has been disturbed, an exceptional case arises; and it may be just that, even before any determination of the right, the law should interpose to replace the parties in the condition in which they were before the act done, security being taken that the right shall be tried, and the goods be forthcoming to abide the decision.

Although the basic process is well-settled, replevin's precise scope is somewhat contentious. Indeed, it has been said that "no action, either in its foundation or in its practice, has given rise to so many contradictory expositions as that of replevin": *Freeman v. Harrington* (1863), 5 N.S.R. 352 at 354 (S.C.). For the purposes of exposition, it is important to draw a distinction between England and Canada.

The doctrine of replevin originated in England. It initially arose, during the medieval period, to remedy cases in which goods were wrongfully subject to *distress* (that is, cases in which a creditor improperly seized a debtor's chattels in an effort to extract payment). Over the ensuing centuries, the procedure expanded to cover *any* wrongful taking, but it fell out of favour during the 19th century and today it is seldom, if ever, used in England. The primary explanation for that demise was procedural. While replevin continues to be governed by several complex and technical rules, the tort of detinue was substantially improved and streamlined during the 1800s. Most significantly, the *Common Law Procedure Act 1854* empowered judges in detinue to order specific restoration, without allowing defendants the option of paying damages. Dispossessed owners therefore came to prefer detinue over replevin. Detinue was abolished by the *Torts (Interference with Goods) Act 1977*, but that statute also created a judicial discretion to compel "delivery up of any goods" that are the subject of litigation.

Replevin has followed a much different course in Canada. Although it tends to be neglected in textbooks, it is thriving in practice. Its popularity is largely attributable to its expanded scope. While English courts never extended the doctrine beyond wrongful *takings*, Canadian law also allows replevin to be used in cases of wrongful *detention* (even if the defendant obtained possession lawfully). Moreover, the claimant need not necessarily establish a right of absolute ownership. The interlocutory order is available as long as the plaintiff can demonstrate *any* immediate right to possession (a legal, equitable, or statutory right will suffice): Stewart, "Remedies — Replevin — Recovery *In Specie*" (1984) 62 Can. Bar Rev. 418 at 427. Finally, in contrast to most forms of interlocutory relief (*e.g.* mandatory injunctions and orders for interim preservation of property), replevin does not require proof of irreparable harm or demonstrated danger. Instead, the plaintiff simply must show *prima facie* or "substantial grounds" to support the alleged right to possession: *Ryder Truck Rental v. Walker*, [1960] O.W.N. 70 at 71 (Master).

Even in Canada, however, replevin is, by its very nature, limited in some respects. It cannot, for instance, provide compensatory relief (*Richard v. Synak* (2007), 51 C.C.L.T. (3d) 231 (Ont. S.C.J.)) and it obviously is defeated if the defendant no longer has possession of the disputed chattel. Furthermore, because the essence of replevin is a restoration of the *status quo ante*, it presumes that the claimant previously enjoyed possession. Accordingly, while many courts are moving toward a more relaxed approach, relief may be denied if, for instance, a creditor seeks possession of a chattel that the debtor provided as collateral for a loan: *Manitoba Agricultural Credit Corp. v.*

Heaman (1990), 70 D.L.R. (4th) 518 (Man. C.A.); and *cf. Agricultural Development Corp. of Saskatchewan v. Vigro Seed & Supply Ltd.* (1989), 64 D.L.R. (4th) 385 (Sask. C.A.). Because it restores the *status quo ante*, replevin will also be denied if the applicant cannot convince the court that the target property and the property that he previously possessed are one and the same: *1316223 Ontario Inc. (c.o.b. 1,000,000 Comix) v. Giancoulas*, 2018 ONSC 5603. Finally, even if the formal elements are in place, the requirement of security may be prohibitively expensive for individual claimants.

Replevin is well-established and widely used in Canada. In an effort to simplify and clarify the historically complex rules, however, the procedure has been codified: *Terastream Networks Inc. v. Grossholz*, 2018 BCSC 837. The traditional process of replevin generally has been replaced by legislated procedures with inelegant names, such as Ontario's "order for recovery of possession of personal property": *Courts of Justice Act*, R.S.O. 1990, c. C.43, s. 104; and Rules of Civil Procedure, R.R.O. 1990, Reg. 194, R. 44. Finally, although several Canadian jurisdictions previously created *Replevin Acts*, the modern approach (as in Ontario) is to deal with the issue through the rules of court.

NOTES AND QUESTIONS

1. The rules governing a dispossessed owner's ability to recover an asset through self-help are discussed in Hawes, "Recaption of Chattels: The Use of Force Against the Person" (2006) 12 Canterbury L. Rev. 253.

2. Although replevin has fallen into disuse in England, there continues to be debate regarding its formal abolition. In his report to the Chancellor, Beatson recommended retention: *Independent Review of Bailiff Law: A Report to the Lord Chancellor* (2000) at para. 16.16. The Lord Chancellor's Department, however, disagreed and saw "little need" for the "ancient remedy": *Towards Effective Enforcement — A Single Piece of Bailiff Law and a Regulatory Structure for Enforcement* (2001) (Cm. 5096) at para. 4.70.

3. In *Allis-Chalmers, Rumely Ltd. v. Forbes Equipment Ltd.* (1969), 8 D.L.R. (3d) 105 (B.C.S.C.), the plaintiff agreed to supply machinery to the defendant on consignment. After the defendant's alleged default, the plaintiff terminated the agreement and sought recovery of the property under the provincial *Replevin Act*. In granting relief, the court stressed that the interlocutory order does not require a determination of the merits of the competing claims. See also *Shreddfast Inc. v. Oak Point Alignment Ltd.* (2005), 192 Man. R. (2d) 169 (C.A.); *Thompson v. Thompson*, [1947] O.W.N. 393 (H.C.J.); and *Littleford v. Loanex Financial Services* (1986), 28 D.L.R. (4th) 613 (Man. C.A.).

4. Are recaption and replevin consistent with tort law's general attitude regarding the recovery of chattels *in specie*? Is it possible to reconcile replevin with the fact that both law and equity strongly presume in favour of monetary relief?

5. In exchange for an order of replevin, a plaintiff must undertake to expeditiously bring the matter to court for final resolution. Once the plaintiff gains possession, however, the defendant may decide that the issue no longer is worth fighting.

6. Replevin may be used in small, private disputes, as when a neighbour refuses to return a borrowed lawnmower. Significantly, however, the procedure also is attractive to commercial parties. Consider a situation in which a company sells an expensive machine on credit. The customer is entitled to take the equipment away immediately, but will not receive full title until the price is paid in full. Consider further that the customer soon becomes bankrupt and is unable to pay its debts. Although the vendor is entitled to the outstanding purchase price, that debt will be unenforceable in effect. Replevin, in contrast, may provide the vendor with a quick and effective remedy.

7. See generally Fridman *et al.*, *The Law of Torts in Canada*, 3d ed. (2010) at 142-144; Stewart, "Remedies — Replevin — Recovery *In Specie*" (1984) 62 Can. Bar Rev. 418; Simmonds & Stewart, *Study Paper on Wrongful Interference with Goods* (1989) at 40-46; Law Reform Commission of British Columbia, *Report on Replevin* (1978); and Kruse, "Replevin — Repeal or Retain?" (2001) 23 Liverpool L. Rev. 95.

REVIEW PROBLEMS

1. The defendant wrongfully refused to respond to the plaintiff's demand for the return of his shares at a time when they were worth five dollars each. The shares then rose in value to ten dollars, but fell to seven dollars at the date of trial. Can the plaintiff recover ten dollars per share in detinue and in conversion?

2. The defendant took the plaintiff's taxi. Ten days later, the plaintiff demanded its return, while it was still in the defendant's possession. The taxi's value did not change from the date it was taken until the date of trial. Would you suggest suing in conversion or detinue, given that the plaintiff prefers damages to specific restitution?

3. Smith lent his car to Jones to make a return trip to New York City. While in New York, Brown intentionally scratched the car. What action can Smith maintain against Brown? Must Smith wait until Jones returns the scratched car before bringing an action?

Now assume that Smith had agreed with Jones to assume all responsibility for damages while Jones had the car and that Brown stole and destroyed the car in New York. What actions could Jones maintain against Brown? Can Brown raise the agreement between Smith and Jones as a defence? If Brown is held liable to Jones, would Jones be required to compensate Smith?

4. Allan was the owner of an expensive portable TV, but his need to meet pressing debts forced him to sell it. His friend Judy told him that she was interested in buying it, but would like to have it for a week on a trial basis to help her decide. Allan agreed and on Monday evening Judy took the TV, promising either to return it or purchase it by the following Monday.

On Wednesday, Judy took the TV to the beach to watch her favourite programs while tanning. During the late afternoon Judy met a group of friends and went for a walk, carelessly leaving the TV and some clothing behind. While Judy was away, Justin appeared on the scene. Finding the beach deserted and the TV and clothing in danger of being swept away by the advancing tide, Justin took them home for safekeeping. He immediately placed an advertisement in the "lost and found" column of the local newspaper.

Meanwhile, Judy informed Allan of the loss of the TV. On Thursday, Allan spotted Justin' s advertisement. Justin refused to return the TV to Allan, explaining that the TV's owner must also be the owner of the clothing which obviously did not belong to Allan. Judy also noticed Justin's advertisement and visited him on Saturday of the same week. Confronted with proof that Judy was the owner of the clothing, Justin was convinced that the TV also belonged to her and agreed to return it. Justin had lent the TV to Sarah on Friday night so he phoned Sarah and told her that Judy would be coming to pick it up. Judy collected the TV from Sarah, but instead of returning it to Allan, she absconded.

One month later, after failing to find Judy, Allan sued Justin. Allan's TV is now worth 40% more than it was two weeks earlier, due to a shortage of portable television parts. Advise Allan.

5

INTENTIONAL INTERFERENCE WITH REAL PROPERTY

1. Trespass to Land
2. Trespass and Nuisance
3. Trespass to Airspace and Subsoil

1. Trespass to Land

The tort of trespass to land may be defined as the direct and intentional physical intrusion onto the land in the possession of another. The tort is actionable *per se*. Given the central role of land in society, the elements of this action were broadly defined under the writ system. Despite the fundamental changes brought about by urbanization and industrialization in the last 200 years, the elements of this tort remain essentially unchanged.

ENTICK v. CARRINGTON
(1765), 19 State Tr. 1029 (C.P.)

[The defendants, claiming authority under a warrant from the Secretary of State, broke into the plaintiff's house and carried away some papers. The plaintiff sued the defendants in trespass.]

PRATT C.J.C.P.: The great end, for which men entered into society, was to secure their property. That right is preserved sacred and incommunicable in all instances, where it has not been taken away or abridged by some public law for the good of the whole. The cases where this right of property is set aside by positive law, are various. Distresses, executions, forfeitures, taxes, wherein every man by common consent gives up that right, for the sake of justice and the general good. By the laws of England, every invasion of private property, be it ever so minute, is a trespass. No man can set his foot upon my ground without my licence, but he is liable to an action, though the damage be nothing; which is proved by every declaration in trespass, where the defendant is called upon to answer for bruising the grass and even treading upon the soil. If he admits the fact, he is bound to shew by way of justification, that some positive law has empowered or excused him. . . . If no such excuse can be found or produced, the silence of the books is an authority against the defendant, and the plaintiff must have judgment.

TURNER v. THORNE
(1959), 21 D.L.R. (2d) 29 (Ont. H.C.)

MCRUER C.J.H.C.:—This is an action brought to recover damages sustained by the plaintiff on September 5, 1958. The facts are simple. The defendant Robert N. Thorne operates a business known as the Speedit Delivery Service, and the defendant George Thorne was a driver employed by his co-defendant.

The business of the Speedit Delivery Service is to pick up parcels on request for delivery to designated persons. On the day in question a call was received from a customer of the defendant to pick up 14 cartons of material for delivery to the Gas Machinery Co. (Canada) Ltd., Lime Ridge Rd., on the outskirts of the City of Hamilton. . . .

The Gas Machinery Co. (Canada) Ltd. had done business before in a garage in the rear of some private property and the defendant George Thorne had made deliveries to that garage. On the day in question, on arriving at Lime Ridge Rd., Mr. Thorne without further information assumed that the Gas Machinery Co. was located on the plaintiff's property. He went to the plaintiff's house and rapped on the door but got no answer. In fact, both the plaintiff and his wife were at work. Without making further inquiries Mr. Thorne went to the plaintiff's double garage . . . and found it unlocked. . . .

Finding no one at home on the plaintiff's property, Mr. Thorne backed his truck into the driveway and opened the west door and unloaded the cartons which were about 24 ins. long and 9 ins. square, and piled them in the centre of the garage where they would be between the truck and the automobile if the automobile was in the west section of the garage. There is some dispute as to whether the cartons were piled so as to project southerly past the end of the truck. I am satisfied that they were. When the plaintiff came home that evening he and his wife went shopping and returned after dark. The garage was not equipped with any artificial light. For the purpose of opening the west door the plaintiff entered the east door of the garage and walked past the rear of the truck and fell over the cartons which had been deposited in the garage, sustaining serious injuries which were assessed by the jury at $9,626, including out-of-pocket expenses.

. . .

I think the defendant George Thorne is undoubtedly liable in damages. He was a trespasser on the plaintiff's property and it was a trespass to leave the packages in the garage.

. . .

Liability for incidental damage resulting from trespass is most concisely dealt with in the Restatement of the Law of Torts, vol. I, commencing at p. 359. At pp. 375-6 it is stated: "A trespass, actionable under the rule stated in s. 158, may be committed by the continued presence on the land of a structure, chattel or other thing which the actor has tortiously placed thereon, whether or not the actor has the ability to remove it."

A most useful discussion of the relevant law is contained in *Kopka et ux. v. Bell Telephone Co. of Pennsylvania* (1952), 91 Atl. (2d) 232. Although this is a case in the United States Courts I think it accurately states the common law applicable in Ontario. The case arose out of injuries sustained by the owner of land when he fell into a hole dug on his land by servants of the defendant. At p. 235 Mr. Justice Stern, giving the judgment of the Court of Appeal of the State of Pennsylvania, stated:

> Before considering the question of the liability of a trespasser for personal injuries suffered by the possessor of land as an indirect result of the trespass, there are two relevant legal principles to be borne in mind. The first is that the fact that a trespass results from an innocent mistake and, in that sense, is not deliberate or wilful, does not relieve the trespasser of liability therefor or for any of the results thereof.

And on the same page: "The liability of defendant Company for the trespass involved in the digging of the hole on plaintiff's land without his knowledge or consent being thus established, does such liability extend to the personal injuries sustained by him as the result of his falling into the hole? The authorities are clear to the effect that where the complaint is for trespass to land the trespasser becomes liable not only for personal injuries resulting directly and proximately from the trespass but also for those which are indirect and consequential."

At p. 236 the learned Judge quoted from s. 163 of the Restatement of the Law of Torts as follows: " 'So too, he [a trespasser] is liable for any harm to the possessor . . . if such harm is caused by the actor's presence on the land, irrespective of whether it was caused by conduct which, were the actor not a trespasser, would have subjected him to liability.' "

. . .

The plaintiff is therefore entitled to judgment in the sum of $9,626, the damages as assessed by the jury.

NOTES AND QUESTIONS

1. For the purpose of a trespass action, the term "land" includes not only the surface area, but also houses, other structures, trees, and anything else that is affixed to the land. Thus, an individual who threw a ball against a fence that was on a neighbour's side of the boundary line would be liable in trespass.

2. A trespass may be committed by entering the plaintiff's land in person, propelling an object or third person onto the property, or failing to leave after permission to enter has been revoked. A trespass may also be committed by bringing an object onto the plaintiff's land and wrongfully failing to remove it. The doctrine of continuing trespass applies in such situations, allowing the plaintiff to maintain successive actions until the object is removed. Damages are assessed at the date of each action. For a discussion of continuing trespass, see *Haynes v. Nfld. Telephone Co.* (1985), 168 A.P.R. 162 (Nfld. Dist. Ct.); *Cousins v. Wilson*, [1994] 1 N.Z.L.R. 463 (H.C.); and *Wong v. Rashidi*, 2011 BCCA 489.

3. The concept of continuing trespass is important in determining whether a plaintiff's claim is statute-barred under the limitations legislation. In *Williams v. Mulgrave (Town)*, 2000 NSCA 24, the defendant ran a drain across the plaintiff's property. The drain caused flooding, but the plaintiff took no legal action for several years, even after discovering that the defendant had no right to act as it did. The trial judge dismissed the plaintiff's trespass claim as statute-barred because she commenced her claim more than six years after she had discovered the defendant's wrongful conduct. The Nova Scotia Court of Appeal overturned the decision. It held that a new cause of action arose every day that the defendant continued its trespass by leaving its drain on the plaintiff's land. Consequently, while the plaintiff was entitled to damages for only the six years immediately preceding the commencement of her action, her claim was not entirely statute-barred. See also *Peter Ballantyne Cree Nation v. Canada (Attorney General)*, 2016 SKCA 124.

4. In order to maintain a trespass action, the plaintiff is generally required to be in possession of the land at the time of the intrusion. For example, in *Townsview*

Properties Ltd. v. Sun Construction and Equipment Co. Ltd. (1974), 7 O.R. (2d) 666 (C.A.), the plaintiff's trespass action failed because the wrongful excavation occurred before it acquired possession.

5. Those with legal title and tenants with a legal right to land are presumed to possess the entire area. Squatters and others without title or a legal right are viewed as possessing only the land that they actually occupy, enclose or cultivate. Nevertheless, a squatter without title who has possession of land can maintain a trespass action against a subsequent trespasser. As indicated in *Penney v. Gosse* (1974), 6 Nfld. & P.E.I.R. 344 at 346 (Nfld. S.C.), "Any form of possession, so long as it is clear and exclusive and exercised with the intention to possess, is sufficient to support an action for trespass against a wrongdoer. Actual possession is good against all except those who can show a better right of possession in themselves." See also *Swaile v. Zurdayk*, [1924] 2 W.W.R. 555 (Sask. C.A.). In contrast, a person who is merely using land without any possessory interest cannot maintain a trespass action. Why does trespass protect possession, rather than ownership?

Note that possession of Crown land does not provide a sufficient interest to maintain a trespass action. For example, a squatter on Crown land could not bring a trespass action against a subsequent intruder. See *Boutin v. Boutin* (1985), 23 D.L.R. (4th) 286 (Sask. Q.B.); and *Fortier v. Kapeller* (1999), 183 Sask. R. 135 (Prov. Ct.).

6. The doctrine of trespass by relation provides an exception to the possession requirement. The doctrine permits a plaintiff who had only an immediate right to possession when the trespass occurred to sue in trespass for that intrusion once he or she subsequently acquires possession. This result is achieved through a legal fiction that deems the plaintiff to have been in possession from the moment he or she acquired a right to possession. Trespass by relation is most frequently invoked in cases involving vacant land.

7. Trespass to land is limited to direct intrusions onto the land in the possession of another. For example, in *Hoffman v. Monsanto Canada Inc.*, 2007 SKCA 47, the defendant farmers who planted genetically modified seeds in their fields were not held liable in trespass when the seeds "found their way" onto the land of the neighbouring organic farmers. See also *Huang v. Fraser Hillary's Ltd.*, 2017 ONSC 1500, aff'd 2018 ONCA 527.

Similarly, snow thrown onto the plaintiff's land from the defendant's snow blower will give rise to a trespass action, whereas snow blown onto the plaintiff's land by the wind from a snow bank on the defendant's land will not. Nor can a trespass action be brought when roots and limbs of trees grow onto neighbouring property. As will be discussed later in this chapter, some indirect intrusions may give rise to an action in private nuisance.

8. As illustrated by *Entick* and *Turner*, the action for trespass to land is strictly defined and applied. As Rand J. stated in *East Crest Oil Co. v. R.*, [1945] S.C.R. 191 at 195, "If I walk upon my neighbour's land, I am a trespasser even though I believe it to be my own." See also *Costello v. Calgary (City)* (1997), 38 C.C.L.T. (2d) 101 at 112 (Alta. C.A.), where Picard J.A. stated that "a trespass occurs, regardless of consciousness of wrongdoing, if the defendant intends to conduct itself in a certain manner and exercises its volition to do so." See also *Caissie v. Assels*, 2012 NBQB 110.

What is the rationale for holding the defendant's motive to be irrelevant and for refusing to recognize mistake as a defence?

9. Once it is established that the defendant is a trespasser, he or she is liable for all the consequences of the trespass, whether or not they are foreseeable. In addition to *Turner*, see *Wyant v. Crouse*, 86 N.W. 527 (Mich. S.C. 1901) (spread of fire); and *Mee v. Gardiner*, [1949] 3 D.L.R. 852 (B.C.C.A.) ("tramp" spreading skin disease). But see *Mayfair Ltd. v. Pears*, [1987] 1 N.Z.L.R. 459 (C.A.), where the defendant was absolved of liability for the unforeseeable consequences of his trespass. Which position is preferable?

10. A defendant in a trespass action cannot raise the defence of *jus tertii*, claiming that a third party has a better right to possession than the plaintiff, unless that third party authorized the defendant's entry.

11. Trespass to land must be distinguished from ejectment, which is not a tort action but rather a proprietary action for the recovery of land. Unlike trespass, ejectment does not depend on the plaintiff's possession of, or entry onto, the land. The plaintiff may succeed in ejectment by establishing that he or she has a better right to possession than the defendant. However, the defendant may raise the *jus tertii* defence in an ejectment action.

12. In *Horsford v. Bird (Antigua and Barbuda)*, [2006] 1 E.G.L.R. 75 (P.C.), the defendant had a costly boundary wall built that incorporated 455 square feet of the plaintiff's property. The trial judge refused the plaintiff's request for a mandatory injunction to have part of the boundary wall demolished and rebuilt, and awarded the plaintiff $75,000, which included an unspecified amount for aggravated damages. The damage award was eventually appealed to the Privy Council. It agreed with the appeal court that aggravated damages were inappropriate, but rejected the appeal court's valuing of the expropriated property at $13,650 based on the cost of undeveloped land. The Privy Council doubled the appeal court's valuation to reflect the value of the land to the defendant, and also awarded the plaintiff mesne profits for the defendant's use of the 455 square feet prior to trial.

13. The Canadian courts have awarded substantial punitive damages in trespass when the defendant has acted in a high-handed or arrogant fashion. In *Nantel v. Parisien* (1981), 18 C.C.L.T. 79 (Ont. H.C.), a corporate defendant was required to pay $35,000 in punitive damages when its employees, without warning, broke into the plaintiff's business to demolish the building. The plaintiff had a valid lease and lawful possession. In *Horseshoe Bay Retirement Society v. S.I.F. Development Corp.* (1990), 66 D.L.R. (4th) 42 (B.C.S.C.), the court awarded $100,000 in punitive damages against the defendant for cutting down the plaintiff's trees to enhance the value of its development lots. See also *Zambri v. Grammelhofer*, 2009 CarswellOnt 7287 (S.C.J.), aff'd 2010 ONCA 780; and *Avender v. Western Canadian Timber Products Ltd.*, 2018 BCSC 1711.

14. For a more detailed discussion of trespass to land, see Fridman *et al.*, *The Law of Torts in Canada*, 3d ed. (2010) at 29-46; Peel & Goudkamp, *Winfield & Jolowicz on Tort*, 19th ed. (2014) at 427-44; and Dobbs, Hayden & Bublick, *The Law of Torts*, 2d ed. (2011) vol. 1 at 125-60.

REVIEW PROBLEMS

1. Arthur lives in a mansion in one corner of his 500-acre estate. Unknown to him, Bill erected a small shelter on the opposite corner of the estate and lived there for two years. While Bill was away for several days, Carl moved into his shelter. What actions can Bill bring against Carl? What actions can Arthur bring against Carl and Bill?

2. Ned rented his house to Tom for a year. After six months, Ned went to see how Tom was faring, only to find that Tom was on holiday and that a squatter had moved in with some old furniture. The squatter left, but refused to take his furniture with him until he could get resettled. Advise Ned on the actions that he may bring against the squatter.

HARRISON v. CARSWELL
[1976] 2 S.C.R. 200

DICKSON J.:—The respondent, Sophie Carswell, was charged under *The Petty Trespasses Act*, R.S.M. 1970, c. P-50, with four offences (one on each of four days) of unlawfully trespassing upon the premises of the Fairview Corporation Limited, trading under the firm name and style of Polo Park Shopping Centre, located in the City of Winnipeg, after having been requested by the owner not to enter on or come upon the premises. The appellant, Peter Harrison, manager of Polo Park Shopping Centre swore the informations. The charges were dismissed by the Provincial Judge, but on a trial *de novo* in the County Court, Mrs. Carswell was convicted and fined $10 on each of the charges. The convictions were set aside by the Manitoba Court of Appeal . . . and the present appeal followed, by leave of this Court.

With great respect, I am unable to agree with the majority reasons, delivered in the Court of Appeal by Chief Justice Freedman, for I find it difficult, indeed impossible, to make any well-founded distinction between this case and *Peters v. The Queen* (1971), 17 D.L.R. (3d) 128, decided by this Court four years ago in a unanimous decision of the full bench. The constitutional issue raised in *Peters* no longer concerns us; the only other issue was whether the owner of a shopping plaza had sufficient control or possession of the common areas, having regard to the unrestricted invitation to the public to enter upon the premises, as to enable it to invoke the remedy of trespass. The Court decided it did. That case and the present case came to us on much the same facts, picketing within a shopping centre in connection with a labour dispute.

. . .

The evidence discloses that distribution of pamphlets or leaflets in the mall of Polo Park Shopping Centre or on the parking lot, has never been permitted by the management of the centre and that this prohibition has extended to tenants of the centre. The centre as a matter of policy has not permitted any person to walk in the mall carrying placards. There is nothing in the evidence supporting the view that in the present case the owner of the centre was acting out of caprice or whimsy or *mala fides*. In a comment entitled *Labour Law — Picketing in Shopping Centres*, 43 Can. Bar Rev. 357 at p. 362 (1965), H.W. Arthurs referred to the following as one of the legitimate concerns of the landlord of a shopping centre:

. . . while public authorities may, on behalf of the community, strike a reasonable balance between traffic and picketing on public sidewalks and streets, the shopping centre owner can hardly be expected to make such a choice: he has no authority to speak for the community; to grant picketing or parading privileges to all would invite chaos, while to do so selectively would invite commercial reprisals. He is thus driven to adopt a highly restrictive approach to granting permission to groups who wish to parade or picket in the shopping centre.

It is urged on behalf of Mrs. Carswell that the right of a person to picket peacefully in support of a lawful strike is of greater social significance than the proprietary rights of an owner of a shopping centre, and that the rights of the owner must yield to those of the picketer. . . .

The submission that this Court should weigh and determine the respective values to society of the right to property and the right to picket raises important and difficult political and socio-economic issues, the resolution of which must, by their very nature, be arbitrary and embody personal economic and social beliefs. It raises also fundamental questions as to the role of this Court under the Canadian constitution. The duty of the Court, as I envisage it, is to proceed in the discharge of its adjudicative function in a reasoned way from principled decision and established concepts. I do not for a moment doubt the power of the Court to act creatively — it has done so on countless occasions; but manifestly one must ask — what are the limits of the judicial function? There are many and varied answers to this question. Holmes J., said in *Southern Pacific Co. v. Jensen* (1917), 244 U.S. 205 at p. 221: "I recognize without hesitation that judges do and must legislate, but they can do it only interstitially; they are confined from molar to molecular actions." Cardozo, *The Nature of the Judicial Process* (1921), p. 141, recognized that the freedom of the Judge is not absolute in this expression of his view:

> This judge, even when he is free, is still not wholly free. He is not to innovate at pleasure. He is not a knight-errant, roaming at will in pursuit of his own ideal of beauty or of goodness. He is to draw his inspiration from consecrated principles.

. . .

Society has long since acknowledged that a public interest is served by permitting union members to bring economic pressure to bear upon their respective employers through peaceful picketing, but the right has been exercisable in some locations and not in others and to the extent that picketing has been permitted on private property the right hitherto has been accorded by statute. For example, s. 87 [since rep. & sub. 1975, c. 33, s. 21] of the *Labour Code of British Columbia Act*, 1973 (B.C.) (2nd Sess.), c. 122, provides that no action lies in respect of picketing permitted under the Act for trespass to real property to which a member of the public ordinarily has access.

Anglo-Canadian jurisprudence has transitionally recognized, as a fundamental freedom, the right of the individual to the enjoyment of property and the right not to be deprived thereof or any interest therein, save by due process of law. The Legislature of Manitoba has declared in *The Petty Trespasses Act* that any person who trespasses upon land, the property of another, upon or through which he has been requested by the owner not to enter, is guilty of an offence. If there is to be any change in this statute law, if A is to be given the right to enter and remain on the land of B against the will of B, it would seem to me that such a change must be made by the enacting institution, the Legislature, which is representative of the people and designed to manifest the political will, and not by this Court.

I would allow the appeal, set aside the judgment of the Court of Appeal for Manitoba and restore the judgment of the County Court Judge.

THE CHIEF JUSTICE [Laskin C.J.] (*dissenting*) . . . An ancient legal concept, trespass, is urged here in all its pristine force by a shopping centre owner in respect of areas of the shopping centre which have been opened by him to public use, and necessarily so because of the commercial character of the enterprise based on tenancies by operators of a variety of businesses. To say in such circumstances that the shopping centre owner may, at his whim, order any member of the public out of the shopping centre on penalty or liability for trespass if he refuses to leave, does not make sense if there is no proper reason in that member's conduct or activity to justify the order to leave.

Trespass in its civil law sense, and in its penal sense too, connotes unjustified invasion of another's possession. Where a dwelling-house is concerned, the privacy associated with that kind of land-holding makes any unjustified or unprivileged entry a trespass, technically so even if no damage occurs. A court, however, would be likely to award only nominal damages for mere unprivileged entry upon another's private premises where no injury occurs, and it is probable that the plaintiff would be ordered to pay costs for seeking empty vindication. If the trespasser refuses to leave when ordered, he could be forcibly removed, but, more likely, the police would be called and the issue would be resolved at that point, or a basis for an action, or for a penal charge would arise. In short, apart from privileged entry, a matter to which I will return in these reasons, there is a significant element of protection of privacy in resort to trespass to exclude or remove persons from private dwellings.

The considerations which underlie the protection of private residences cannot apply to the same degree to a shopping centre in respect of its parking areas, roads and sidewalks. Those amenities are closer in character to public roads and sidewalks than to a private dwelling. All that can be urged from a theoretical point of view to assimilate them to private dwellings is to urge that if property is privately owned, no matter the use to which it is put, trespass is as appropriate in the one case as in the other and it does not matter that possession, the invasion of which is basic to trespass, is recognizable in the one case but not in the other. There is here, on this assimilation, a legal injury albeit no actual injury. This is a use of theory which does not square with economic or social fact under the circumstances of the present case.

What does a shopping centre owner protect, for what invaded interest of his does he seek vindication in ousting members of the public from sidewalks and roadways and parking areas in the shopping centre? There is no challenge to his title and none to his possession nor to his privacy when members of the public use those amenities. Should he be allowed to choose what members of the public come into those areas when they have been opened to all without discrimination? Human rights legislation would prevent him from discriminating on account of race, colour or creed or national origin, but counsel for the appellant would have it that members of the public can otherwise be excluded or ordered to leave by mere whim. It is contended that it is unnecessary that there be a reason that can stand rational assessment. Disapproval of the owner, in assertion of a remote control over the "public" areas of the shopping centre, whether it be disapproval of picketing or disapproval of the wearing of hats or anything equally innocent, may be converted (so it is argued) into a basis of ouster of members of the public. Can the common law be so devoid of reason as to tolerate this kind of whimsy where public areas of a shopping centre are concerned?

. . .

It seems to me that the present case involves a search for an appropriate legal framework for new social facts which show up the inaptness of an old doctrine developed upon a completely different social foundation. The history of trespass indicates that its introduction as a private means of redress was directed to breaches of the peace or to acts likely to provoke such breaches. Its subsequent enlargement beyond these concerns does not mean it must be taken as incapable of further adaptation, but must be applied on what I can only characterize as a level of abstraction which ignores the facts. Neither logic nor experience (to borrow from Holmes' opening sentence in his classic *The Common Law*) supports such a conclusion.

Recognition of the need for balancing the interests of the shopping centre owner with competing interests of members of the public when in or on the public areas of the shopping centre, engaged Courts in the United States a little earlier than it did the Courts in this country. Making every allowance for any constitutional basis upon which Courts there grappled with this problem, their analyses are helpful because they arise out of the same economic and social setting in which the problem arises here. Thus, there is emphasis on unrestricted access to shopping centres from public streets, and on the fact that access by the public is the very reason for the existence of shopping centres; there is the comparison drawn between the public markets of long ago and the shopping centre as a modern market place; there is the appreciation that in the light of the interests involved there can be no solution to their reconciliation by positing a flat all or nothing approach. The cases in the United States . . . appear to me to reject the appellant's proposition that (as his counsel put it) "the issue is trespass, not picketing" because that, in my opinion, involves a predetermination without regard to the issues of fact. . . .

A more appropriate approach . . . is to recognize a continuing privilege in using the areas of the shopping centre provided for public passage subject to limitations arising out of the nature of the activity thereon and to the object pursued thereby, and subject as well to a limitation against material damage. There is analogy in existing conceptions of privilege as an answer to intentional torts, such as trespass.

. . .

I would agree that it does not follow that because unrestricted access is given to members of the public to certain areas of the shopping centre during business hours, those areas are available at all times during those hours and in all circumstances to any kind of peaceful activity by members of the public, regardless of the interest being prompted by that activity and regardless of the numbers of members of the public who are involved. The Court will draw lines here as it does in other branches of the law as may be appropriate in the light of the legal principle and particular facts. In the present case it is the respondent who has been injured rather than the shopping centre owner.

I would dismiss the appeal.

[Martland, Judson, Ritchie, Pigeon, and de Grandpré JJ. concurred with Dickson J., and Spence and Beetz JJ. concurred with Laskin C.J. Note that the order of the reasons for judgment has been reversed.]

NOTES AND QUESTIONS

1. Do you agree with Dickson J. that *Peters* and the statute resolve the issue? Can Laskin C.J.'s judgment be reconciled with *Peters* and the statute?

2. In *Russo v. Ontario Jockey Club* (1987), 62 O.R. (2d) 731 (H.C.), the plaintiff was a skilled bettor who had won a considerable amount of money at the defendant's race tracks. While at Woodbine Race Track, the plaintiff was served with a notice under the provincial trespass act, ordering her to leave and informing her that she would be arrested for trespassing if she returned to any of the defendant's properties. There was no allegation that the plaintiff had engaged in any wrongdoing, and no reason was given for banning her. In dismissing the plaintiff's challenge to the notice, the court stated that the defendant, as a property owner, had an absolute right to deny entry to anyone under both the common law and the applicable trespass legislation.

3. Would Dickson J.'s analysis and conclusion have been the same if the case had been a common law action for trespass, rather than a prosecution under *The Petty Trespasses Act*, R.S.M. 1970, c. P50? In *Wildwood Mall Ltd. v. Stevens*, [1980] 2 W.W.R. 638 (Sask. Q.B.), the court distinguished *Harrison* on the basis that Saskatchewan had no legislation creating a provincial offence of trespassing. The mall owner's claim against the picketing workers was then dismissed because the owner did not have a sufficient possessory interest to exclude all others. Do you agree with the reasoning or the result in *Wildwood*?

4. Would you agree with the statement of Colangelo in "Labour Law: *Harrison v. Carswell*" (1976) 34 U.T. Fac. L. Rev. 236 that Dickson J.'s judgment lacks creativity? What values underlie the judgments of Laskin C.J. and Dickson J.?

5. Is Laskin C.J.'s rationale for modifying the traditional definition of trespass compelling? What impact would Laskin C.J.'s approach have on the provincial offence of trespass and on the common law tort? How does Laskin C.J. suggest that the conflicting interests of plaza owners and picketers be resolved? Can meaningful distinctions be drawn between different types of landowners and picketers?

In *Wilcox v. Police*, [1994] 1 N.Z.L.R. 243 (H.C.), ten anti-abortionists were convicted of trespass for blocking entry to a hospital after they had been told to leave. The defendants sought to justify the trespass on the need to protect the unborn from unlawful abortions. Although the court accepted the honesty of the defendants' beliefs, it convicted them. How would Laskin C.J. have resolved this case?

6. Manitoba amended its trespass legislation shortly after *Harrison*. In general terms, the amendment provides that individuals who peacefully protest outside of premises that are normally open to the public are not guilty of an offence under the Act. See *The Petty Trespasses Act*, R.S.M. 1987, c. P50, s. 4. Should the amendment be viewed as a vindication of Dickson J.'s or Laskin C.J.'s approach? Is it appropriate for the courts or the legislature to resolve the types of value conflicts raised by *Harrison* and *Wilcox*?

7. Section 2 of the *Canadian Charter of Rights and Freedoms*, Part I of the *Constitution Act, 1982*, being Schedule B to the *Canada Act 1982* (U.K.), 1982, c. 11 guarantees a broad range of fundamental freedoms, including freedom of expression,

peaceful assembly and association. However, by virtue of s. 32, the *Charter* does not apply to private persons and associations in a common law tort action.

When the University of Victoria prohibited a student pro-life club from booking outdoor space on campus, the club challenged the decision under s. 2 of the *Charter*. The Court of Appeal held that the *Charter* did not apply to the University's decision because it was unrelated to the exercise of any government policy or program; rather the decision fell within the university's autonomous operational decision-making authority: *BC Civil Liberties Association v. University of Victoria*, 2016 BCCA 162. See also *Harrison v. University of British Columbia*, [1990] 3 S.C.R. 451, in which the majority of the court held that the university's mandatory retirement policies did not come within the purview of the *Charter*.

Nevertheless, since the *Charter* applies to both federal and provincial law, trespass legislation that limits or infringes the rights guaranteed by the *Charter* may be struck down. If the legislation is struck down, there can be no prosecution or statutory cause of action based on such provisions.

8. In *R. v. Layton* (1986), 38 C.C.C. (3d) 550 (Ont. Prov. Ct.), trespass charges against a union organizer who had been distributing material in the public part of a mall were dismissed. The court ruled that the provisions of the trespass act constituted an unjustifiable infringement of the accused's freedom of expression and association under s. 2(b) and (d) of the *Charter*.

See also *British Columbia Public School Employers' Assn. v. British Columbia Teachers' Federation* (2005), 257 D.L.R. (4th) 385 (B.C.C.A.).

9. Bracken, who was protesting outside of the Town Hall, was arrested for trespass after he refused to comply with a trespass notice ordering him to leave. He was subsequently banned from all town property for a year. Bracken was a large man who some people found to be intimidating and who could be "confrontational, loud, agitated, and excitable." Bracken successfully challenged the ban under s. 2(b) of the *Charter*. The Court of Appeal stated at para. 49 that the Town Hall staff's "subjective feelings of disquiet, unease, and even fear, are not in themselves capable of ousting expression categorically from the protection of s. 2(b)": *Bracken v. Fort Erie (Town)*, 2017 ONCA 668.

In *R. v. Breeden*, 2009 BCCA 463, when the accused ignored orders to stop carrying protest signs inside a court and other government buildings, he was charged under the *Trespass Act*. Breeden applied for an order striking down the charges pursuant to s. 2(b) of the *Charter*. In upholding the trespass convictions, the Court of Appeal ruled that carrying protest signs in the foyer of a court and other government buildings did not fall within the scope of free expression under s. 2(b). The court stated at para. 34 that the "discomfiting of staff and members of the public going about necessary business in these places is an unwarranted interference with the proper function of these premises." The court emphasized that the accused was free to protest in the public areas outside of the buildings.

Can you reconcile *Bracken* and *Breeden*? Which decision is preferable? See *Committee for the Commonwealth of Canada v. Canada*, [1991] 1 S.C.R. 139 and *R. v. Booyink*, 2013 ABPC 185, which upheld an individual's right to engage in a political protest at an airport. See also Hamill, "Location Matters: How Nuisance Governs Access to Property for Free Expression" (2014) 47 UBC Law Review 129.

10. *Harrison* raises the issue of the revocability of a licence to enter private property. In *Hudson's Bay Co. v. White* (1997), 32 C.C.L.T. (2d) 163 (Ont. Gen. Div.), the court stated that while the public has an implied licence to enter stores to browse and shop, a person entering to shoplift would not be present for any authorized purpose and thus would be a trespasser.

In *Davidson v. Toronto Blue Jays Baseball Ltd.* (1999), 170 D.L.R. (4th) 559 (Ont. Gen. Div.), the plaintiff was arrested under the *Trespass to Property Act*, R.S.O. 1990, c. T.21 when a dispute arose over whether he had to show his ticket when returning to his seat. The plaintiff sued in false imprisonment. The court held that the plaintiff had a licence to be in the stadium pursuant to the contract for the ticket. An implied term of that licence was that the plaintiff had an obligation to show his ticket when entering the stadium, when initially taking his seat, or when resolving a dispute with another patron over the same seat. Since the court ruled that the plaintiff did not have to show his ticket at any other time, his licence to be present remained valid and he should not have been arrested. Given that the defendant had a financial interest in preventing patrons from occupying more expensive seats than those for which they had paid, should the court have concluded that ticketholders had an implied obligation to show their ticket whenever occupying or claiming a seat?

11. In both *Bellini Custom Cabinetry Ltd. v. Delight Textiles Ltd.* (2007), 47 C.C.L.T. (3d) 165 (Ont. C.A.) and *Pyper v. Crausen* (2008), 37 C.E.L.R. (3d) 257 (Ont. S.C.J.), the plaintiffs acquiesced to the initial trespass, but subsequently sued when the defendants' boundary wall further encroached on their land.

12. For trespass actions involving native land claims, see *Myran v. R.*, [1976] 2 S.C.R. 137; *Johnson v. British Columbia Hydro and Power Authority* (1981), 16 C.C.L.T. 10 (B.C.S.C.); and *Canadian Pacific Ltd. v. Paul*, [1988] 2 S.C.R. 654. While a trespass action may resolve a specific legal dispute, it cannot address the native communities' longstanding grievances concerning land claims and treaty rights.

13. A trespass action may be brought following an invalid expropriation. In *Costello v. Calgary (City)* (1997), 152 D.L.R. (4th) 453 (Alta. C.A.), the City expropriated the plaintiffs' land and took possession of it. The plaintiffs claimed that they had not been given sufficient notice and, after 11 years of litigation, the Supreme Court of Canada held that the expropriation was invalid. The plaintiffs then sued the City in trespass for improperly possessing their land during this 11-year period. Picard J.A. found for the plaintiffs despite the fact that the expropriation would have been valid but for a mere technical error regarding the statutory notice period. See also *Maunsell v. Lethbridge Northern Irrigation District*, [1926] S.C.R. 603; and Todd, *The Law of Expropriation and Compensation in Canada*, 2d ed. (1992) at 29.

14. The plaintiff may have the option of bringing an action under the trespass legislation, rather than a common law action for trespass. For example, the Ontario *Trespass to Property Act, supra*, provides:

> 12(1) Where a person is convicted of an offence under section 2, and a person has suffered damage caused by the person convicted during the commission of the offence, the court shall, on the request of the prosecutor and with the consent of the person who suffered the damage, determine the damages and shall make a judgment for damages against the person convicted in favour of the person who suffered the damage.

(2) Where a prosecution under section 2 is conducted by a private prosecutor, and the defendant is convicted, unless the court is of the opinion that the prosecution was not necessary for the protection of the occupier or the occupier's interests, the court shall determine the actual costs reasonably incurred in conducting the prosecution and, despite section 60 of the *Provincial Offences Act*, shall order those costs to be paid by the defendant to the prosecutor.

(3) A judgment for damages under subsection (1), or an award of costs under subsection (2), shall be in addition to any fine that is imposed under this Act.

(4) A judgment for damages under subsection (1) extinguishes the right of the person in whose favour the judgment is made to bring a civil action for damages against the person convicted arising out of the same facts.

(5) The failure to request or refusal to grant a judgment for damages under subsection (1) does not affect a right to bring a civil action for damages arising out of the same facts.

Similar provisions apply in other provinces. See for example *Trespass Act*, R.S.B.C. 1996, c. 462, s. 11; and *Trespass to Property Act*, R.S.P.E.I. 1988, c. T-6, s. 10.

15. Most trespass legislation gives the police, occupiers or both the right to arrest without a warrant anyone whom they reasonably believe is trespassing. See for example the Ontario *Trespass to Property Act, supra*, s. 9(1); the British Columbia *Trespass Act, supra*, s. 10(2) and (3); and *Petty Trespass Act*, R.S.A. 2000, c. P-11, s. 4. For a discussion of a private citizen's right to use force to arrest without a warrant under the Ontario *Trespass to Property Act*, see *R. v. Asante-Mensah*, [2003] 2 S.C.R. 3; and *Tucker v. Cadillac Fairview Corporation Limited* (2005), 200 O.A.C. 140 (C.A.). The latter case involved "Reverend Brothers" Tucker and Baldasaro soliciting on behalf of the Marijuana Party in the defendant's mall, despite having been previously forbidden to do so. For a discussion of the impact of the trespass legislation, see Parkdale Community Legal Services, "Submissions to the Task Force on the Law Concerning Trespass to Publicly Used Property as it Affects Youth and Minorities" (1997) 35 Osgoode Hall L.J. 819.

16. Section 177 of the *Criminal Code*, R.S.C. 1985, c. C-46 makes it a summary conviction offence to trespass, without a lawful excuse, on another person's land at night near a dwelling. Section 35 gives those in peaceful possession of property broad authority to use force to prevent a trespasser from entering or remaining on their property.

2. Trespass and Nuisance

The law of private nuisance is discussed in detail in Chapter 24. It is introduced at this stage merely to distinguish it from trespass. A private nuisance may be defined as a substantial and unreasonable interference with the use and enjoyment of land in the possession of another. There are several differences between trespass to land and nuisance. First, trespass to land is actionable *per se*, whereas nuisance requires proof of loss. Second, trespass protects possession, whereas nuisance protects the quality of that possession. Third, the law of nuisance is concerned with the effect of the defendant's conduct on the plaintiff's use and enjoyment of the land, and not with the nature of that conduct. Fourth, liability in trespass requires intent, whereas liability in nuisance may be imposed even if the defendant's conduct was neither intentional nor negligent.

KERR v. REVELSTOKE BLDG. MATERIALS LTD.
(1976), 71 D.L.R. (3d) 134 (Alta. S.C.)

SHANNON J.:—In this action the plaintiffs allege trespass, nuisance and negligence. They seek an injunction and damages.

. . .

During his youth Mr. Kerr worked in a general store and later, in 1935, operated a service station and garage at Coleman, Alberta. He and his wife decided that they wanted to build and operate a motel business. . . .

The site selected was chosen for its tranquility and scenic beauty. Looking to the south from the site they had a magnificent view of a river valley in a natural state, except for a railway line, and beyond that foothills and a range of rocky mountains dominated by the Crowsnest Mountain peak.

They used approximately two acres of that parcel for the motel site. The remainder was used for agricultural purposes. On the motel site they built a residence and six motel units which were opened for business in 1951. The business was known as "Chinook Motel." In the summer of 1953 two more units were constructed and opened for business. Two additional units were constructed and opened in the summer of 1955. Mr. Kerr was in charge of construction operations and was assisted by his wife and sons. Some outside assistance was obtained but it was primarily a family project as was the motel operation thereafter.

. . .

The defendant is an Alberta lumber company that has carried on an active business in this Province for many years.

It commenced business across the highway from the Chinook Motel in 1958. A planing mill and small teepee burner went into operation that year. The defendant's loading ramp was approximately 800 ft. from the office door of the motel. A sawmill was moved to the same site and commenced operating in 1968. Chipper and debarker operations were added to the sawmill complex in 1971. Also, other industries, such as Phillips Cables Ltd., Sartoga Processing Co. Ltd. and Petro-Chemicals Ltd. were established in the valley. The operation of the defendant's planing mill and teepee burner in 1958 caused the plaintiffs some concern and disturbance but the situation worsened when the sawmill, chipper and debarker operations were introduced later.

It should be noted that the defendant's decision to bring the chipper and debarker operations to the site in 1971 was influenced to some extent by the fact that it received financial inducements from the federal Government to do so. The Crowsnest Pass area was then designated as a depressed economic area and the Government provided incentives to encourage industry to locate there.

From time to time the plaintiffs complained about smoke, sawdust, dust, fly ash and objectionable noises emanating from the defendant's operations. The defendant tried to ameliorate the situation by enclosing a conveyor belt in 1971, lubricating the conveyer belt with rock-drill oil in 1972, enclosing the planer in 1972-73, enclosing the chipper in 1973, enlarging the garage for warm-up of machinery in 1972 and adding an underfire to the teepee burners to improve their efficiency.

Notwithstanding the foregoing efforts on the part of the defendant the plaintiffs continued to complain and in the fall of 1971 they closed their motel operation and it has never been reopened.

I am satisfied on the evidence that they have established a cause of action founded in trespass. The evidence establishes that their premises were invaded from time to time by smoke, sawdust, fly ash and objectionable sounds. The physical invasion of their premises by sawdust and fly ash was so severe on occasion that it interfered with their use and enjoyment of their property. Actual samples of fly ash were collected and placed in vials by the plaintiff James Runciman Kerr, and were entered in evidence as exhibits.

. . .

I am also convinced by the preponderance of evidence that the plaintiffs are entitled to succeed in nuisance. The fly ash, smoke and dust which assaulted the plaintiff's premises from time to time was serious enough in itself, but the objectionable sounds which emanated from the sawmill operations were such that they constituted a nuisance which was so serious it substantially interfered with the operation of the plaintiff's motel business and with their use and enjoyment of their premises. Also the concern, anxiety and discomfort generated by the situation had a harmful effect on the health of Mrs. Kerr. She became nervous, preoccupied, humourless and irritable and that in turn had a negative effect on her husband and his enjoyment of life. The offensive noises were not constant. They came and went depending upon the state of the lumber market and the resultant activities across the highway at the sawmill.

The intensity and frequency of the objectionable noises increased substantially after the sawmill commenced operating in 1968 and again later in 1971 when the chipper and debarker were added. It is difficult to provide a comprehensive description of the objectionable noises because they were many and varied. Various witnesses, who were guests at the motel, used such adjectives as "squealing, clanking, whining, ear piercing, etc.", to describe them. Another witness referred to the noise as "a high pitched squeal that seemed to go on all night", while another likened the sound to that which is given off by a jet engine. In any event it was so intense at times that it interfered with ordinary conversation in the plaintiff's yard. It also seriously interfered with their rest and sleep and with that of their motel guests because the sawmill carried on its operations at night and during the early morning hours.

. . .

On the facts of this case I am unable to find that the defendant was negligent in its operations. The simple fact is that the two business operations were not compatible.

In these circumstances an injunction would not be an appropriate remedy and that form of relief will not be granted. However, the plaintiffs are entitled to succeed in trespass and nuisance and the appropriate remedy is damages.

. . .

The plaintiffs are awarded judgment against the defendant in the amount of $30,000.

NOTES AND QUESTIONS

1. Which interferences did the judge hold to be trespasses and which did he find to be nuisances? Do you agree with his analysis? Would a different characterization of the interferences have affected the damage award? In *Execotel Hotel Corp. v. E.B. Eddy*

Forest Products Ltd., 1988 WL 875157 (Ont. H.C.), the court held that airborne woodchips and particles settling on the plaintiff's property could not give rise to trespass because there was no direct and intentional intrusion. Is the analysis of this issue in *Execotel* more compelling than the analysis in *Kerr*? See also *Devon Lumber Co. v. MacNeill* (1987), 82 N.B.R. (2d) 319 (C.A.).

2. In *Mann v. Saulnier* (1959), 19 D.L.R. (2d) 130 (N.B.C.A.), snow and frost caused the top of the defendant's fence to encroach on the plaintiff's land by several inches. The court held that this was neither a trespass (because the injury was indirectly caused), nor a nuisance (because no special damages were proven). Can you suggest additional reasons why the trespass claim and the nuisance claim should fail?

3. While roots and limbs growing onto neighbouring property will not give rise to a trespass action, they may constitute a private nuisance if they unreasonably interfere with the neighbour's use and enjoyment of his or her property or constitute a reasonably foreseeable risk of significant harm. Generally speaking, a property owner may trim back limbs and roots on their side of the property line, but cannot enter the neighbouring property to do so. See *Mendez v. Palazzi* (1976), 68 D.L.R. (3d) 582 (Ont. Co. Ct.); *Anderson v. Skender* (1993), 84 B.C.L.R. (2d) 135 (C.A.); *Freedman v. Cooper*, 2015 ONSC 1373; and *Davis v. Sutton*, 2017 ONSC 2277.

4. In *Smith v. Inco Ltd.*, 2011 ONCA 628, Inco's operations dramatically increased the level of nickel particulates in the soil of nearby homeowners and a class action lawsuit in trespass and nuisance was brought on behalf of 7,000 of them. The trespass action failed because the alleged harms were not directly caused. The nuisance claim failed because the homeowners failed to prove that the increased levels of nickel particulates constituted "actual, substantial, physical damage to their properties," interfered with the use of their properties, posed a risk to their health, or decreased the value of their properties.

5. A substantial and unreasonable interference is one that is offensive and inconvenient to a reasonable person. The unreasonableness of the interference is assessed in terms of the plaintiff's use of his or her property, and the relative interests of the defendant and plaintiff. In *Angerer v. Cuthbert*, 2017 YKSC 54, the court issued an injunction preventing the defendant from operating a dog rescue program on her property which housed as many as 80 dogs. The court held that the dogs' barking, which disrupted the sleep of some of the plaintiffs, constituted a nuisance. The court stated that the social utility of the defendant's dog rescue operation did not justify forcing the plaintiffs to bear a disproportionate burden. The trial decision was upheld on appeal: 2018 YKCA 8.

See also *Pyke v. TriGro Enterprises Ltd.* (2001), 55 O.R. (3d) 257 (C.A.); *Webster v. Low* (2009), 74 C.C.L.T. (3d) 154 (Ont. S.C.J.); and *Antrim Truck Centre Ltd. v. Ontario (Transportation)*, 2013 SCC 13. An extract of *Antrim* can be found in Chapter 24.

6. In *Doucette v. Parent* (1996), 31 C.C.L.T. (2d) 190 (Ont. Gen. Div.), the defendant was absolved of liability in nuisance when a tree on her property that showed minimal signs of disease fell on the plaintiff's property. Natural uses of the defendant's land that do not pose a foreseeable risk are unlikely to give rise to a nuisance action. See also *Lee v. Shalom Branch No. 178 Building Society* (2001), 96 B.C.L.R. (3d) 384 (S.C.).

7. Traditionally, trespass to land has been limited to the direct, intentional intrusion of objects that are visible to the naked eye. However, in *Martin v. Reynolds Metal Co.*, 342 P. (2d) 790 (Oregon S.C. 1959), the defendant manufacturer was held liable in trespass because its operations caused invisible fluoride particles to settle on the plaintiff's land, making it unfit for cattle. The judge rejected the argument that the size of the invading object should be a criterion for distinguishing between trespass and nuisance, preferring instead to emphasize the issue of energy and force. As in *Harrison*, the court in *Martin* was faced with the task of applying established legal principles to new situations. Did the court in *Martin* make a compelling argument in favour of altering the traditional principles of trespass to land? For example, should a plaintiff be entitled to recover in trespass to land if the defendant intentionally directs a bright light, high-frequency sound waves or an image onto the plaintiff's property? What impact would the principles in *Martin* have on the distinction between trespass and nuisance?

While the Canadian courts apparently have not addressed the issue, several American courts have imposed liability in trespass for the physical intrusion of invisible particles that have caused harm. See Dobbs, Hayden & Bublick, *The Law of Torts*, 2d ed. (2011) vol. 1 at 138.

8. Traditionally, the courts were more reluctant to grant injunctions in nuisance than in trespass. Why do you think the courts adopted this position? See generally, Sharpe, *Injunctions and Specific Performance*, looseleaf (2017) (consulted July 2018), ch. 4; and Wilde, "Nuisance Law and Damages in Lieu of an Injunction: Challenging the Orthodoxy of the *Shelfer* Criteria" in Pitel, Neyers & Chamberlain, eds., *Tort Law: Challenging Orthodoxy* (2013) 355.

REVIEW PROBLEM

What claims are available to the plaintiff in the following situations?

(a) The defendant's seismographic explosions cause vibrations that damage the plaintiff's well. See *Phillips v. Calif. Standard Co.* (1960), 31 W.W.R. 331 (Alta. S.C.).

(b) Golf balls from the defendant's golf course are hit so frequently onto the plaintiff's land that he is unable to use his backyard. See *Segal v. Derrick Golf and Winter Club* (1977), 76 D.L.R. (3d) 746 (Alta. T.D.). See also *Miller v. Jackson*, [1977] Q.B. 966 (C.A.).

(c) The Transport Ministry's use of salt on the highway results in salt being directly deposited, and a salt spray being indirectly splashed, on the plaintiff's land, which causes substantial damage to his fruit orchard. See *Schenck v. R.; Rokeby v. R.* (1981), 34 O.R. (2d) 591 (H.C.), aff'd (1985), 49 O.R. (2d) 556 (C.A.), aff'd [1987] 2 S.C.R. 289; and *Steadman v Lambton (County)*, 2015 ONSC 101.

(d) The defendant's construction project causes silt to be carried into the plaintiff's reservoir that contains his domestic water supply. See *Steadman v. Erickson Gold Mining Corp.* (1987), 43 D.L.R. (4th) 712 (B.C.S.C.), aff'd (1989), 56 D.L.R. (4th) 577 (B.C.C.A.).

3. Trespass to Airspace and Subsoil

(a) TRESPASS TO AIRSPACE

The elements of this action are essentially the same as those of trespass to land. Traditionally, defendants were held liable in trespass to airspace for any direct and intentional physical intrusion into the airspace above the plaintiff's land. However, the need for unfettered air traffic has resulted in a distinction being drawn between overflights and other types of intrusions. Although the theories concerning overflights vary, they all tend to limit the landowner's rights in order to facilitate air traffic.

In *Atlantic Aviation Ltd. v. N.S. Light & Power Co.* (1965), 55 D.L.R. (2d) 554 (N.S.S.C.), the court indicated that while an overflight at any altitude constitutes a trespass, it will be privileged if it is done for a legitimate purpose, in a reasonable manner, and at a height that does not unreasonably interfere with the possessor's use of his or her land. On the central issue of the case, the court ruled that aviators have no common law right to prevent landowners from putting up buildings or transmission wires that might impede flights in and out of nearby airports.

BERNSTEIN v. SKYVIEWS & GENERAL LTD.
[1978] Q.B. 479

GRIFFITHS J.: . . . By the statement of claim it is alleged that the defendants wrongfully entered the air space above Lord Bernstein's premises in order to take an aerial photograph of his house and were thus guilty of trespass and an actionable invasion of his right to privacy. The defendants admit that they took the aerial photograph but deny that they entered the air space above the premises to do so; they say that the photograph was taken when the aircraft was flying over adjoining land not owned by Lord Bernstein. Alternatively they say that if they did fly over Lord Bernstein's land to take the photograph they had his implied permission to do so . . . .

I turn now to the law. The plaintiff claims that as owner of the land he is also owner of the air space above the land, or at least has the right to exclude any entry into the air space above his land. He relies upon the old Latin maxim, cujus est solum ejus est usque ad coelum et ad inferos ["whomsoever the soil belongs, he owns also to the sky and to the depths"], a colourful phrase often upon the lips of lawyers since it was first coined by Accursius in Bologna in the 13th century. There are a number of cases in which the maxim has been used by English judges, but an examination of those cases shows that they have all been concerned with structures attached to the adjoining land, such as overhanging buildings, signs or telegraph wires, and for their solution it has not been necessary for the judge to cast his eyes towards the heavens; he has been concerned with the rights of the owner in the air space immediately adjacent to the surface of the land.

. . .

In *Gifford v. Dent*, [1926] W.N. 336, Romer J. held that it was a trespass to erect a sign that projected 4 ft. 8 ins. over the plaintiff's forecourt and ordered it to be removed. He invoked the old maxim in his judgment . . .

That decision was followed by McNair J. in *Kelsen v. Imperial Tobacco Co. (of Great Britain and Ireland) Ltd.*, [1957] 2 Q.B. 334, in which he granted a mandatory injunction ordering the defendants to remove a sign which projected only 8 ins. over the plaintiff's property. The plaintiff relies strongly upon this case, and in particular upon the following passage when, after citing the judgment of Romer J. to which I have already referred, McNair J. continued, at p. 345:

> That decision, I think, has been recognised by the textbook writers, and in particular by the late Professor Winfield, as stating the true law. It is not without significance that the legislature in the Air Navigation Act 1920, section 9 (replaced by section 40(1) of the Civil Aviation Act 1949), found it necessary expressly to negative the action of trespass or nuisance arising from the mere fact of an aeroplane passing through the air above the land. It seems to me clearly to indicate that the legislature at least were not taking the same view of the matter as Lord Ellenborough in *Pickering v. Rudd*, but rather taking the view accepted in the later cases, such as the *Wandsworth District* case, subsequently followed by Romer J. in *Gifford v. Dent*. Accordingly, I reach the conclusion that a trespass and not a mere nuisance was created by the invasion of the plaintiff's air-space by this sign.

I very much doubt if in that passage McNair J. was intending to hold that the plaintiff's rights in the air space continued to an unlimited height or "ad coelum" as Mr. Gray submits. The point that the judge was considering was whether the sign was a trespass or a nuisance at the very low level at which it projected. This to my mind is clearly indicated by his reference to *Winfield on Tort*, 6th ed. (1954) in which the text reads, at p. 380: "it is submitted that trespass will be committed by [aircraft] to the air space if they fly so low as to come within the area of ordinary user." The author in that passage is careful to limit the trespass to the height at which it is contemplated an owner might be expected to make use of the air space as a natural incident of the user of his land. If, however, the judge was by his reference to the Civil Aviation Act 1949 and his disapproval of the views of Lord Ellenborough in *Pickering v. Rudd* (1815) 4 Camp. 219, indicating the opinion that the flight of an aircraft at whatever height constituted a trespass at common law, I must respectfully disagree.

I do not wish to cast any doubts upon the correctness of the decision upon its own particular facts. It may be a sound and practical rule to regard any incursion into the air space at a height which may interfere with the ordinary user of the land as a trespass rather than a nuisance. Adjoining owners then know where they stand; they have no right to erect structures overhanging or passing over their neighbours' land and there is no room for argument whether they are thereby causing damage or annoyance to their neighbours about which there may be much room for argument and uncertainty. But wholly different considerations arise when considering the passage of aircraft at a height which in no way affects the user of the land.

There is no direct authority on this question, but as long ago as 1815 Lord Ellenborough in *Pickering v. Rudd* expressed the view that it would not be a trespass to pass over a man's land in a balloon; and in *Saunders v. Smith* (1838) 2 Jur. 491, Shadwell V.-C. said, at p. 492:

> Thus, upon the maxim of law, 'Cujus est solum ejus est usque ad coelum' an injunction might be granted for cutting timber and severing crops; but, suppose a person should apply to restrain an aerial wrong, as by sailing over a person's freehold in a balloon; this surely would be too contemptible to be taken notice of . . . .

I can find no support in authority for the view that a landowner's rights in the air space above his property extend to an unlimited height. In *Wandsworth Board of Works v. United Telephone Co. Ltd.*, 13 Q.B.D. 904 Bowen L.J. described the maxim, usque ad coelum, as a fanciful phrase, to which I would add that if applied literally it is a fanciful notion leading to the absurdity of a trespass at common law being committed by a satellite every time it passes over a suburban garden. The academic writers speak with one voice in rejecting the uncritical and literal application of the maxim . . . I accept their collective approach as correct. The problem is to balance the rights of an owner to enjoy the use of his land against the rights of the general public to take advantage of all that science now offers in the use of air space. This balance is in my judgment best struck in our present society by restricting the rights of an owner in the air space above his land to such height as is necessary for the ordinary use and enjoyment of his land and the structures upon it, and declaring that above that height he has no greater rights in the air space than any other member of the public.

Applying this test to the facts of this case, I find that the defendants' aircraft did not infringe any rights in the plaintiff's air space, and thus no trespass was committed. It was on any view of the evidence flying many hundreds of feet above the ground and it is not suggested that by its mere presence in the air space it caused any interference with any use to which the plaintiff put or might wish to put his land. The plaintiff's complaint is not that the aircraft interfered with the use of his land but that a photograph was taken from it. There is, however, no law against taking a photograph, and the mere taking of a photograph cannot turn an act which is not a trespass into the plaintiff's air space into one that is a trespass. . . .

NOTES AND QUESTIONS

1. How does the court's approach to overflights in *Atlantic Aviation* differ from liability based on private nuisance?

2. In *A.G. Man. v. Campbell* (1985), 32 C.C.L.T. 57 (Man. C.A.), the defendant built a 70-foot tower on his land to obstruct the adjacent airport and to prevent its further development. The plaintiff's claim in nuisance was successful, and an injunction was granted ordering the defendant to dismantle the tower. Can you reconcile this case with the ruling in *Atlantic Aviation* that pilots have no common law right to prevent landowners from undertaking construction that might impede flights in and out of nearby airports? See also *Hashem and Hashem v. N.S. Power Corp.* (1980), 43 N.S.R. (2d) 150 (S.C.), where the defendant's tower and lines, although an unwelcome annoyance to pilots, did not interfere with the safe use of the plaintiff's aerodrome, and thus did not constitute a nuisance.

3. Summarize the principles governing tort liability for overflights based on *Bernstein*. What is the basic difference between *Bernstein* and *Atlantic Aviation*, and why is that difference significant? Which position do you favour?

4. Although the Canadian courts have clearly rejected the *usque ad coelum* maxim, they have not addressed whether *Atlantic* or *Bernstein* should govern overflights. Nevertheless, the Canadian authorities appear to be more consistent with *Bernstein*. See *Lacroix v. R.*, [1954] 4 D.L.R. 470 (Ex. Ct.); and *Manitoba v. Air Canada*, [1980] 2 S.C.R. 303. See generally Dobbs, Hayden & Bublick, *The Law of Torts*, 2d ed. (2011) vol. 1 at 143-45; and Pilsk, "Airport Noise Litigation in the 21st Century: A Survey of Current Issues" (2012) 11 Issues in Aviation Law and Policy 371.

5. As *Bernstein* indicated, it is generally accepted that any direct and intentional intrusion into the airspace within the plaintiff's zone of use, such as shooting across

his or her land, constitutes a trespass. See *Big Point Club v. Lozon*, [1943] 4 D.L.R. 136 (Ont. H.C.); and *Dahlberg v. Naydiuk* (1969), 10 D.L.R. (3d) 319 (Man. C.A.). Similarly, a trespass action will arise from erecting a sign, fence or hydro tower that encroaches on the plaintiff's land. See *Kelsen v. Imperial Tobacco Co. (of Great Britain and Ireland) Ltd.*, [1957] 2 All E.R. 343 (Q.B.); *Didow v. Alberta Power Ltd.* (1988), 88 A.R. 250 (C.A.); and *Bellini Custom Cabinetry Ltd. v. Delight Textiles Ltd.* (2007), 47 C.C.L.T. (3d) 165 (Ont. C.A.). See also Irvine, "Some Thoughts on Trespass to Airspace" (1986), 37 C.C.L.T. 99.

6. At what height would an intentional overflight by a drone constitute an intrusion within a landowner's zone of use, thereby giving rise to a trespass action? Would the size of the drone and whether it carried a camera with a powerful telescopic lens alter your decision? Should it make any difference if the overflight is undertaken by a private citizen for purely recreational purposes, as opposed to the police for surveillance purposes? What impact would these factors have on whether the overflight unreasonably interfered with a landowner's use and enjoyment of his or her property?

Is tort law an appropriate or effective way of regulating the private and state use of drones? See generally McNeal, "Drones and the Future of Aerial Surveillance" (2016) 84 The George Washington Law Review 354; and Farber, "Keep Out! The Efficacy of Trespass, Nuisance and Privacy Torts as Applied to Drones" (2017) 33 Ga. Sta. U.L. Rev. 359.

7. It has been held that the arm of a crane periodically swinging above the plaintiff's land constitutes a trespass. See *Woollerton and Wilson Ltd. v. Richard Costain Ltd.*, [1970] 1 All E.R. 483 (Ch. D.); and *Lewvest Ltd. v. Scotia Towers Ltd.* (1981), 126 D.L.R. (3d) 239 (Nfld. T.D.). However, in *Didow*, *supra*, the court noted that it would be inclined to view overhead cranes as a nuisance.

In *Woollerton*, the judge felt compelled by authority to issue an injunction to restrain the defendant's trespass, but suspended its operation until the project was completed. The judge noted that the plaintiff had stubbornly refused to settle and suggested that such matters should be negotiated by the parties outside of the courts. The decision to suspend the injunction has been questioned. In addition to *Lewvest*, see *Charrington v. Simons & Co. Ltd.*, [1971] 2 All E.R. 588 at 592 (C.A.); *Graham v. K.D. Morris & Sons Pty. Ltd.*, [1974] Qd. R. 1; and *Maxwell Properties Ltd. v. Mosaik Property Management Ltd.*, 2017 NSCA 76. But see *Kingsbridge Development Inc. v. Hanson Needler Corp.* (1990), 71 O.R. (2d) 636 (H.C.). For a review of these issues, see Wilde, "Nuisance Law and Damages in Lieu of an Injunction: Challenging the Orthodoxy of the *Shelfer* Criteria" in Pitel, Neyers & Chamberlain, eds., *Tort Law: Challenging Orthodoxy* (2013) 355.

(b) TRESPASS TO SUBSOIL

Subterranean intrusions raise the same issue as intrusions into airspace; namely, which interferences should be governed by trespass and which by nuisance. In *Austin v. Rescon Construction (1984) Ltd.* (1989), 48 C.C.L.T. 64 (B.C.C.A.), the defendant was held liable in trespass for inserting steel anchor rods beneath the plaintiff's land at three different unidentified depths. Aside from causing temporary vibrations, the insertion of the rods caused no damage to the plaintiff's land, did not interfere with the foundation of the plaintiff's house and did not limit the plaintiff's use of his property. In increasing the punitive damage award to $30,000, the court emphasized that landowners may deny entry for any reason they choose and have no obligation to accommodate a contractor or anyone else wishing to enter. In *Epstein v. Cressey Development Corp.*, [1992] 3 W.W.R. 566 (B.C.C.A.), the defendant was held liable for $45,000 in punitive damages for temporarily inserting anchor rods into the plaintiff's subsoil. Similarly, the defendant in *Bocardo SA v. Star Energy UK Onshore Ltd.*, [2010] UKSC 35 was held liable in trespass for drilling and laying pipeline beneath the plaintiff's property even though it caused no damage or interference.

The court in *Austin* did not address the issue of whether the depth of the intrusion would affect the cause of action. However, in *Boehringer v. Montalto*, 254 N.Y.S. 276 (S.C. 1931), the court held that the existence of a sewer 150 feet underground was not a trespass. The court concluded that a landowner's title to the subsoil extends only to the depth that he or she can reasonably use.

NOTES AND QUESTIONS

1. Can you reconcile *Austin, Epstein* and *Bocardo* with the cases indicating that landowners have no possessory interest in the airspace above their zone of use?

2. Can you reconcile *Austin, Epstein* and *Bocardo* with *Boehringer*? See also *Haynes v. Nfld. Telephone Co.* (1985), 168 A.P.R. 162 (Nfld. Dist. Ct.); *Engemoen Holdings Ltd. v. 100 Mile House*, [1985] 3 W.W.R. 47 (B.C.S.C.); and *Lim v. Titov*, [1998] 5 W.W.R. 495 (Alta. Q.B.).

3. In *Edwards v. Lee's Administrators*, 96 S.W.2d 1028 (Ky. C.A. 1936), the defendant operated a profitable cave touring business from an entrance located on his own property. The plaintiff discovered that one-third of the cave was under his property, but there was no entrance from his land to the cave, which was 360 feet below. The court concluded that the defendant was a trespasser and granted an injunction and an accounting of profits. Pursuant to the accounting, which is an equitable remedy, the plaintiff was awarded a share of the defendant's net proceeds from the cave tours. Do you agree that the defendant was a trespasser? If so, how would you reconcile *Edwards* and *Boehringer*? Could the plaintiff have recovered in nuisance? Had the plaintiff not sought an accounting, what damages would you have awarded for the trespass? It has been suggested that *Edwards* involved neither trespass nor nuisance, and should be viewed as bad law based on a "dog-in-the-manger" approach: Keeton, *Prosser and Keeton on The Law of Torts*, 5th ed. (1984) at 82. Do you agree?

REVIEW PROBLEMS

1. Amy and Bruce own adjoining rural properties. Amy has an orchard and Bruce produces organically grown vegetables for health food stores. On a day when a strong wind was blowing directly onto Bruce's property, Amy sprayed chemicals on her fruit trees. A large quantity of the chemicals drifted onto Bruce's mature vegetables. No apparent damage was done, but Bruce's usual customers refused to purchase the crop because it had come in contact with the spray. As a result, Bruce was forced to sell the vegetables as pig food. The spray also killed the bees on Bruce's

property, interfering with the pollination and production of the new crop. Amy knew that Bruce grew vegetables, but she was unaware that they were sold as organic crops. Bruce now seeks your advice on suing Amy for his losses. See generally *Bridges Brothers Ltd. v. Forest Protection Ltd.* (1976), 14 N.B.R. (2d) 91 (Q.B.).

2. Albert is an experienced private pilot. Early one Sunday morning in February, he and his son rented a plane from his flying club to do some stunts. Although the officer at the club had directed Albert to a particular plane, Albert misunderstood and took a plane of the same model that belonged to Bob, an instructor at the club. The key fit Bob's plane and Albert did not realize his mistake. The plane intended for Albert's use had been cleared for stunt flying, but Bob's had not. The clearance involved a careful check of the plane to ensure that, among other things, nothing would come loose.

Once Albert got over open country, he decided that it was safe to begin. As the plane somersaulted, a tool box came loose and burst through the door of the plane. The box crashed onto a greenhouse some 1,000 meters below, severely damaging it. The cold winter air ruined the valuable orchids that were growing inside. While Albert's son struggled to close the door, Albert rapidly reduced his altitude to bring down the air pressure. He swooped so low over a barn that he frightened a horse, causing it to kick its stall, breaking a back leg. As soon as he could, Albert returned to the airport.

You have been asked to advise Albert on his potential liability.

6

THE DEFENCE OF CONSENT

1. Introduction to the Defences
2. General Principles of Consent
3. Factors Vitiating Consent: Fraud, Mistake, Duress, and Public Policy
4. Consent to Criminal or Immoral Acts
5. Consent to Treatment, Counselling and Care

1. Introduction to the Defences

Even if the plaintiff establishes that the defendant committed an intentional tort, liability may not be imposed. The defendant may be entitled to raise a common law or statutory defence. For analytical purposes, we have divided these defences into three categories: consent; defences related to the protection of person and property; and defences arising from the assertion of legal authority. Consent will be discussed in this chapter and the remaining categories of defences will be discussed in the following two chapters. It is important to appreciate, however, that the defences are not mutually exclusive. For example, assume that the defendant is sued in battery for pushing the plaintiff during a physical confrontation over a disputed fence. Depending on the facts, the defendant may be able to assert defences based on consent, defence of real property and self-defence. If any of these defences succeed, the defendant will be absolved of liability despite having committed the battery.

2. General Principles of Consent

(a) INTRODUCTION

There is considerable older authority for the view that consent is not a defence, but rather a substantive element of the intentional torts, the absence of which the plaintiff must assert and prove on the balance of probabilities. If the plaintiff cannot establish the absence of consent, no tort will have been committed and his or her action will fail. While this remains the prevailing approach in England and New Zealand, authorities in Australia appear to be divided on the issue. In Canada, the courts treat consent as a defence that the defendant must plead and prove.

The issue of consent is linked to the tort in issue. Consequently, the consent issue must be framed narrowly in terms of whether the plaintiff consented to the specific act that gave rise to his or her tort action. The plaintiff may consent explicitly in writing, verbally or by a gesture such as nodding. Consent may also be given implicitly through participation, demeanor or other behaviour.

When a person consents to an act, he or she is generally viewed as consenting to the risks normally inherent in that act. This principle is easy to apply in some cases, but difficult to apply in others. For example, while a football player in a full-contact recreational league will be viewed as implicitly consenting to being tackled, is he or she implicitly consenting to the conduct involved in the typical or foreseeable penalties that occur in such games?

NOTES AND QUESTIONS

1. For the English and New Zealand position on the role of consent in intentional torts, see respectively Peel & Goudkamp, *Winfield & Jolowicz on Tort*, 19th ed. (2014) at 784-86; and Hughes *et al.*, *The Law of Torts in New Zealand*, 4th ed. (2005) at 864-65. While one leading Australian text treats consent as a defence, the New South Wales Court of Appeal subsequently reached the opposite conclusion. See respectively Barker *et al.*, *The Law of Torts in Australia*, 5th ed. (2011) at 36 and 70; and *White v. Johnston*, 2015 NSWCA 18.

2. In *Non-Marine Underwriters, Lloyd's of London v. Scalera*, [2000] 1 S.C.R. 551, the court unanimously agreed that consent is an affirmative defence in "traditional" battery cases. While the majority ruled that this principle applied equally in sexual battery cases, the minority held that the plaintiff should have the burden of proving the absence of consent in such cases. Which approach to consent in sexual battery cases is preferable?

3. In order to establish the defence of consent, the defendant must prove that the plaintiff agreed to the act giving rise to the tort. A plaintiff's failure to physically resist the defendant's conduct falls far short of the affirmative conduct, behaviour or demeanor necessary to establish consent. However, it is more difficult to determine the circumstances in which a failure to object verbally, a failure to withdraw or passivity will be viewed as constituting implied consent. Assume that following a verbal confrontation between two men in a bar, the defendant approaches the plaintiff. Would the plaintiff's conduct in: (a) failing to leave the bar; (b) standing his ground; or (c) standing his ground and staring at the approaching defendant constitute implied consent to a fight? Would your answer be different if the parties were men in their 20s, men in their 60s, or women? Should a woman's failure to turn away from, or voice opposition to, her date who is approaching to kiss her goodnight be viewed as implicitly consenting to being kissed?

(b) IMPLIED CONSENT

WRIGHT v. McLEAN
(1956), 7 D.L.R. (2d) 253 (B.C.S.C.)

MACFARLANE J.: . . . Four boys were playing near a mound of earth thrown up in an excavation incident to the construction of a house on a city lot. They were tossing mud balls or lumps of clay found on the pile of earth there at each other. The infant defendant was passing on his bicycle delivering the afternoon paper around 4:30 p.m. One of these mud balls or lumps came up around the infant defendant and another he says went through the spokes of the wheel of the bicycle he was riding. He was not in a hurry, so he dismounted, pushing his bicycle up against a tree and went over toward a mound of this material which he calls the embankment and said "want a fight?" They continued throwing at each other. There is no exact evidence as to how many of these missiles were thrown or how long. One boy said it continued for probably 5 minutes but he says he quit because he was being pelted too much. It would appear that one boy Ross who admits he threw the lumps at McLean while he was on his bicycle, when asked if he was inviting him to play the game, said "In a way I guess so." He appears to have been the leader of the 3 or 4 boys, originally engaged in this play and he and the infant plaintiff and McLean were throwing at each other when the lump or whatever it was which hit the infant plaintiff was thrown by McLean. . . . [The plaintiff] put his hand to his temple, cried out and fell or sat down. The play stopped immediately. It is agreed by all the boys that the fighting was not carried on in anger and that there was no malice. The infant plaintiff was then 12 years of age; Ross, a little older, and the other two boys on their side a little younger. McLean was 14. It was not the thought of any of them that the injury was serious as it then appeared as no more than a slight scratch and the infant plaintiff went to a party with the two younger boys and both Ross and McLean went about their ways, after having talked and after McLean had expressed his regrets.

. . .

It was not contended that there was any evidence that it was a stone that hit the boy who was injured unless that is to be inferred from the nature of the injuries. McLean quite frankly says that he did not look when he reached down to pick up something to throw, his attention obviously and of necessity being directed to dodging the missiles coming at him, and did not notice just what it was he picked up but threw it in the direction in which they (his opponents) were. He said he would not deliberately pick up a rock or stone and did not intend to do so.

. . .

[The judge then considered the issue of consent and quoted *Pollock on Torts*, 15th ed. (1951) at 112]

"Harm suffered by consent is, within limits to be mentioned, not a cause of civil action." Very briefly, the purport of that paragraph is that in sport where there is no malice, no anger and no mutual ill will, that combatants consent to take the ordinary risks of the sport in which they are engaged. In a note given at the foot of p. 114 in Pollock, there is a reference to an article in the Law Quarterly Review, vol. 6, pp. 111-12. In that article, the author uses this language: "The reasonable view is that the combatants consent to take the ordinary risks of the sport in which they engage, the risks of being struck, kicked, or cuffed, as the case may be, and the pain resulting therefrom; but only while the play is fair, and according to rules, and the blows are given in sport and not maliciously . . . If these tacit conditions of fair play and good temper are not kept the consent is at an end, and the parties are remitted to their rights."

In all the circumstances where it is agreed that there was no ill will and where the evidence shows that the infant defendant was invited to join the game by the others, then I think that no liability arises apart from culpable carelessness. I think it is quite clear that there is no evidence of that in this case.

. . .

I therefore dismiss the action.

NOTES AND QUESTIONS

1. The action in *Wright* was framed in negligence rather than battery. Nevertheless, the principles set out by the court are applicable to intentional torts.

2. To what acts did the plaintiff consent? What risks were inherent in those acts? Would it have made any difference if it were established that: (a) the plaintiff's injuries were caused by a stone; (b) the defendant had been completely indifferent as to whether he was throwing a mud ball or a stone; or (c) the defendant realized he had a stone in his hand but threw it anyway?

3. The judge considered the absence of ill will on the defendant's part to be an important consideration in the outcome of the case. Was this element relevant to the issue of the plaintiff's consent? Provide an example in which the plaintiff's consent would be: (a) negated by the defendant's motive; and (b) unaffected by the defendant's motive.

4. For cases involving implied consent and sports injuries, see *Hayter v. Bezanson*, 2009 NSCA 113; *R. v. Adamiec*, 2013 MBQB 246; and *Kempf v. Nguyen*, 2013 ONSC 1977, rev'd 2015 ONCA 114. See also Yeo, "Accepted Inherent Risks Among Sporting Participants" (2001) 9 Tort L. Rev. 114; and Anderson, "Personal Injury Liability in Sport: Trends" (2008) 16 Tort L. Rev. 95.

5. Do spectators implicitly consent to injuries incidental to attendance at sporting events? In *Elliott and Elliott v. Amphitheatre Ltd.*, [1934] 3 W.W.R. 225 (Man. K.B.), the defendant was absolved of liability for the injuries that the plaintiff suffered when hit by a puck that went into the seats. The court held that as an amateur hockey player, the plaintiff was aware of the risks and the protections customarily provided. Would it have made any difference if: (a) this had been the plaintiff's first visit to the arena and the protective screens were substantially lower than those provided at other rinks; or (b) the plaintiff had been visiting from another country and was completely unaware of the possibility of being hit by a puck? See also *Payne v. Maple Leaf Gardens Ltd.*, [1949] O.R. 26 (C.A.); *Carson v. Thunder Bay* (1985), 52 O.R. (2d) 173 (Dist. Ct.); Horton, "Rethinking Assumption of Risk and Sports Spectators" (2003) 51 U.C.L.A.L. Rev. 339; and Khare, "Foul Ball! The Need to Alter Current Liability Standards for Spectator Injuries at Sporting Events" (2010) 12 Texas Review of Entertainment & Sports Law 91.

(c) EXCEEDING CONSENT

AGAR v. CANNING
(1965), 54 W.W.R. 302 (Man. Q.B.)

BASTIN J.: This is an action by a member of a hockey team against a member of an opposing team, for damages arising out of injuries sustained during the course of a hockey match. . . .

. . . The plaintiff and defendant followed the puck into the south-west corner at the Hartney end of the rink. Defendant body-checked plaintiff, took possession of the puck and started to skate with it, or after it, in the direction of the Killarney goal. Plaintiff attempted to delay defendant by hooking him with his stick and in so doing hit defendant a painful blow on the back of the neck. Defendant thereupon stopped, turned, and holding his stick with both hands, brought it down on plaintiff's face, hitting him with the blade between the nose and right eye. I find that he did this in retaliation for the blow he had received. Plaintiff fell to the ice unconscious and the game terminated at that point.

. . .

Neither counsel has been able to find a reported case in which a claim was made by one player against another for injuries suffered during a hockey game. Since it is common knowledge that such injuries are not infrequent, this supports the conclusion that in the past those engaged in this sport have accepted the risk of injury as a condition of participating. Hockey necessarily involves violent bodily contact and blows from the puck and hockey sticks. A person who engages in this sport must be assumed to accept the risk of accidental harm and to waive any claim he would have apart from the game for trespass to his person in return for enjoying a corresponding immunity with respect to other players. It would be inconsistent with this implied consent to impose a duty on a player to take care for the safety of other players corresponding to the duty which, in the normal situation, gives rise to a claim for negligence. Similarly, the leave and licence will include an unintentional injury resulting from one of the frequent infractions of the rules of the game.

The conduct of a player in the heat of the game is instinctive and unpremeditated and should not be judged by standards suited to polite social intercourse.

But a little reflection will establish that some limit must be placed on a player's immunity from liability. Each case must be decided on its own facts so it is difficult, if not impossible, to decide how the line is to be drawn in every circumstance. But injuries inflicted in circumstances which show a definite resolve to cause serious injury to another, even when there is provocation and in the heat of the game, should not fall within the scope of the implied consent. I have come to the conclusion that the act of the defendant in striking plaintiff in the face with a hockey stick, in retaliation for the blow he received, goes beyond the limit marking exemption from liability.

. . .

Even though provocation was not pleaded, and defendant denied acting on provocation, I have made a finding that defendant acted on provocation so I should take this into account in my assessment of damages.

Special damages amount to $115, consisting of doctor's accounts of $30 and hospital accounts of $85. The medical evidence is that the plaintiff has lost all useful vision of his right eye and has injuries to his nose which will affect his breathing and may require to be corrected by an operation. I allow damages of $250 for pain and suffering and for the injuries to the nose, and $5,500 for the loss of the sight of the right eye. I am reducing these damages by one-third, on the ground that there was great provocation.

[The decision was affirmed on appeal: *Agar v. Canning* (1966), 55 W.W.R. 384 (Man. C.A.).]

NOTES AND QUESTIONS

1. Would any conduct in violation of the rules have exceeded the plaintiff's consent? By breaching the rules himself, did the plaintiff implicitly consent to the risks

inherent in other players violating the rules? Had the defendant only retaliated by tripping the plaintiff, could he have availed himself of the defence of consent?

Predicting when a violation of the rules will be held to exceed a player's consent may be difficult. In *Levita v. Crew*, 2015 ONSC 5316, the plaintiff was hit from behind or the side by the defendant, crashed into the boards and suffered a fractured arm. In dismissing the plaintiff's claim, the court stated at para. 102 that the plaintiff "assumed the inherent risk that such injury could occur even in the non-contact recreational league." In *Zaccardo c. Chartis Insurance Co. of Canada*, 2016 QCCS 398, the defendant checked the plaintiff into the boards from behind with considerable force, which resulted in the plaintiff being rendered a quadriplegic. The judge stated that checking from behind was categorically forbidden by the rules and was not a risk inherent in participating in the full-contact AA Midget league. The injured plaintiff and his family were awarded $8 million in damages. Would the consent issue have been resolved differently had the plaintiff suffered only a minor injury? See also *Colby v. Schmidt* (1986), 37 C.C.L.T. 1 (B.C.S.C.); *Gaudet v. Sullivan* (1992), 128 N.B.R. (2d) 409 (Q.B.); *Leighton v. Best*, 2009 CarswellOnt 2887 (S.C.J.) (WL Can); and Yeo, "Determining Consent in Body Contact Sports" (1998) 6 Tort L. Rev. 199.

2. Traditionally, the Canadian courts were reluctant to convict hockey players of assault when they intentionally injured each other in fights. See for example *R. v. Green*, [1971] 1 O.R. 591 (Prov. Ct.); and *R. v. Maki*, [1970] 3 O.R. 780 (Prov. Ct.). However, the Canadian courts have become somewhat less tolerant of hockey violence.

After losing a fight to Donald Brashear in the first period of an NHL game, Marty McSorley tried several times without success to persuade Brashear to fight again. With three seconds left in the game, McSorley hit Brashear in the head with his stick. Brashear was knocked unconscious and suffered a grand mal seizure and a serious concussion. McSorley was criminally charged. The trial judge held that hockey players implicitly consent to physical contact that is permitted by the rules of the game, as well as to some commonly occurring physical contact that results in penalties. However, he also held that some forms of conduct are "too dangerous for the players to consent to" and that McSorley's conduct fell into this category. McSorley was convicted of assault with a weapon and given an 18-month conditional sentence: *R. v. McSorley*, 2000 BCPC 117. See also *R. v. Bertuzzi* (2004), 26 C.R. (6th) 71 (B.C. Prov. Ct.); *R. v. C.(C.)*, 2009 ONCJ 249; Thiele, "Sports and Torts: Injuring a Fellow Participant Can be Costly" (2000) 23 Adv. Q. 348; and Elvin, "Liability for Negligent Refereeing of a Rugby Match" (2003) 119 L.Q.R. 560.

3. In a fist fight to which both parties consent, one party's use of a knife or other weapon would exceed the other party's consent. See *Teolis v. Moscatelli*, 119 A. 161 (R.I. 1923); and *Fillipowich v. Nahachewsky* (1969), 3 D.L.R. (3d) 544 (Sask. Q.B.).

4. Even if both parties use only their fists, is there a point at which the loser's consent would no longer protect the victor? For example, would the plaintiff's initial consent be exceeded if he was punched while lying on the ground or struggling to get up?

5. How would you analyze consent in a fight if it was obvious from the outset that the plaintiff was no match for the defendant? Although the courts have provided redress in these situations, they have predicated recovery on the defendant's use of

excessive or unnecessary force. Is this rationale compatible with the principles of consent? See *Wade v. Martin*, [1955] 3 D.L.R. 635 (Nfld. S.C.); *Hartlen v. Chaddock* (1957), 11 D.L.R. (2d) 705 (N.S.S.C.); and *Lane v. Holloway*, [1968] Q.B. 379 (C.A.).

6. In *R. v. Jobidon*, [1991] 2 S.C.R. 714, the accused was charged with manslaughter when his fellow combatant died following their consensual fight. The trial judge acquitted the accused because it was a fair fight and the victim's consent had not been exceeded. The Court of Appeal held that the common law concept of consent applies to the *Criminal Code* offence of assault, and that therefore the defence is only available if bodily harm is neither intended nor caused. The court reasoned that this interpretation was consistent with the goals of protecting the public and keeping the peace. The Court of Appeal overturned the acquittal and entered a manslaughter conviction.

The Supreme Court of Canada affirmed the Court of Appeal decision. The majority ruled that in a consensual fight between adults, the combatants' consent is vitiated if they intentionally "apply force causing serious hurt or non-trivial bodily harm." The minority expressly rejected this reasoning and upheld the conviction on the basis that the accused knowingly exceeded the victim's consent by continuing to hit him when he was unconscious.

Was there a compelling public policy basis for invalidating consent in *Jobidon*? Would the court have reached the same decision had the combatant not died? Can you reconcile *Jobidon* with the thousands of bar fights and televised hockey brawls that routinely occur without any criminal charges being brought?

7. *Jobidon* has been criticized on various grounds. For example, the common law concept of consent applied to situations in which physical harm was intended and caused. In any event, why did the court resort to a "common law" concept in interpreting the clear statutory language of s. 265(1)(a) of the *Criminal Code*? That section limits the offence of assault to situations in which force is applied to another without consent. The lack of consent is a substantive element of the criminal offence which the prosecutor must prove beyond a reasonable doubt. In effect, the Supreme Court of Canada created a new criminal offence of assault. See Usprich, "Annotation" (1991), 7 C.R. (4th) 235.

8. The courts have struggled to apply *Jobidon*, particularly in fights involving teenagers. In *R. v. B.(K.)*, 2002 ABPC 56, the accused and another 16-year-old student agreed to a fist fight after school. The fight lasted only a few seconds as the deceased was killed by the accused's first punch. The punch, which was described as a powerful blow, ruptured an artery in the deceased's neck. The court held that, despite punching the deceased in the head with considerable force, the accused lacked the necessary intent to cause bodily harm and found the accused not guilty of manslaughter. Do you agree with the court's application of *Jobidon*? See also *R. v. B.(T.B.)* (1994), 124 Nfld. & P.E.I.R. 328 (P.E.I.C.A.); and *R. v. M.(J.)* (2001), 149 O.A.C. 310 (C.A.).

9. In *R. v. Paice*, [2005] 1 S.C.R. 339, the court narrowed the principles in *Jobidon*, ruling that consent will only be negated if the accused both intends and causes serious bodily harm. In *Paice*, the court refrained from using the term "non-trivial harm," suggesting that *Jobidon* will be limited to incidents involving serious physical injuries. Based on the test in *Paice*, would the deceased's consent to the fight in *B.(K.)*, *supra*

have been negated? Some lower courts remain reluctant to apply *Jobidon* even as modified by *Paice*. See for example *R. v. W.(A.)*, 2012 ONCJ 472.

The challenge in applying *Jobidon* and *Paice* is illustrated by *R. v. McDonald*, 2015 ONCA 791. McDonald put the complainant in a headlock during a consensual fight. The complainant lost consciousness, fell to the floor and suffered serious permanent brain damage. McDonald was convicted of aggravated assault in 2010, but the Ontario Court of Appeal overturned the conviction and ordered a new trial due to problems in the judge's jury instructions regarding consent. McDonald's 2013 conviction in the second trial was overturned on the same grounds. A plea agreement was reached in 2016 during the third trial eight years after the event.

10. Are *Jobidon* and *Paice* consistent with the common law's preference for autonomy? Our law does not prevent individuals from engaging in various high-risk behaviours such as kickboxing, sky-diving and automobile racing.

11. What impact, if any, should *Jobidon* and *Paice* have on the defence of consent in tort law? For an application of *Jobidon* and/or *Paice* in civil cases, see *Loney v. Burtch*, 1989 CarswellOnt 2924 (Dist. Ct.) (WL Can); *Abbott (Next Friend of) v. Jarocki* (1997), 208 A.R. 133 (Prov. Ct.); and *Ellis v. Fallios-Guthierrez*, 2012 ONSC 1670.

12. For a discussion of exceeding consent in trespass to land, see *Gross v. Wright*, [1923] S.C.R. 214; *Stephens v. Corcoran*, [1968] 1 O.R. 49 (H.C.); and *Bellini Custom Cabinetry Ltd. v. Delight Textiles Ltd.* (2007), 47 C.C.L.T. (3d) 165 (Ont. C.A.).

REVIEW PROBLEMS

1. George, a 110-kilogram college football player, rudely pushed his way to the bar. When Bill, a slight middle-aged man, complained George challenged him to a "fist fight outside." After ten minutes of verbal abuse, Bill reluctantly agreed. As Bill approached, George held the door open and bowed, stating: "After you, coward." Seizing this opportunity, Bill kicked George in the head once, knocking him unconscious and ending the fight. What tort liability, if any, has Bill incurred as a result of this altercation? Would your answer differ if George had been less specific about the nature of the fight and had merely said "let's settle this outside?"

2. Steve suffered a broken arm when brought down by a well-executed tackle on the first play of a football game at the local playground. He was caught off guard because he thought they were playing touch football. Although he missed the preliminary discussions, he simply assumed the game was touch football because no one was wearing football equipment, his friends rarely played tackle and he had not been told that it was tackle. Advise Steve on whether his battery claim will be defeated by the defence of consent.

(d) COMPETENCY TO CONSENT

In order for consent to be valid, the person giving the consent must be capable of appreciating the nature and consequences of the act to which it applies. If the person lacks this capacity due to age, physical or mental illness, intoxication, or other factors, the consent will be invalid. The issue of competency to consent addresses a person's ability to understand the information relevant to the act in issue. The fact that the courts or others may view the decision as unreasonable is not necessarily relevant to the issue of competency. This broad test of competency is consistent with the common law's concern with safeguarding autonomy. If a person is competent, the law must uphold his or her right to make both wise and unwise decisions.

It should be noted that some statutes deem certain individuals to lack capacity to give a valid consent for specific purposes. For example, s. 150.1(1), (2) and (2.1) of the *Criminal Code* states that the consent of a person under the age of 16 provides no defence to a sexual assault charge unless: the complainant is 12 or 13 and the accused is less than two years older; or the complainant is 14 or 15 and the accused is less than five years older. Numerous provincial healthcare and counselling statutes also contain statutory age requirements. The issue of competency to consent will be examined in greater detail in the subsection on consent to treatment, counselling and care later in this chapter.

3. Factors Vitiating Consent: Fraud, Mistake, Duress, and Public Policy

(a) INTRODUCTION

Once the defendant establishes that the plaintiff consented to the act giving rise to the tort, the plaintiff may raise factors that vitiate his or her consent. If the consent is vitiated, the defendant will be held liable as if there had been no consent. The Canadian courts have tended to rely on criminal law principles and have narrowly defined these vitiating factors. While a narrow definition of these factors may be appropriate in criminal law, it is questionable whether this is the case in tort law, which focuses primarily on compensation.

(b) FRAUD (DECEIT)

Fraud includes situations in which the defendant: knowingly makes a false statement; makes a statement in total disregard as to its truth; or knowingly creates a misleading impression by omitting relevant information. Most fraud cases involve written or verbal statements. However, in some situations, the defendant's conduct or simple failure to reveal information may also constitute fraud.

The fact that the plaintiff's consent was based on a fraudulently induced belief will not necessarily vitiate the consent. First, it must be established that the defendant was aware of, or responsible for, the plaintiff's misapprehension. Second, the fraud will only negate consent if it relates to the nature and quality of the act, as opposed to a "collateral" matter. In keeping with the criminal law approach, the courts in tort cases have held that a broad range of factors are collateral matters and that fraud regarding these issues will not negate the plaintiff's consent. For example, the courts have held that a man who lies about his marital status or goes through a feigned marriage ceremony in order to induce a woman to have sex with him will be absolved of liability in battery.

The issue of fraud in obtaining consent has arisen most recently in regard to HIV-positive individuals who lie about, or fail to disclose, their HIV status to their sexual partners. The fraud in these cases does not go to the nature of the sexual act, but rather to its potentially harmful consequences. Traditionally, fraud as to the harmful consequences of an act did not negate a person's consent and thus did not give rise to a battery action or a criminal charge for sexual assault: *Hegarty v. Shine* (1878), 4 L.R. Ir. 288 (C.A.); and *R. v. Ssenyonga* (1992), 81 C.C.C. (3d) 257 (Ont. Gen. Div.). It was not until *R. v. Cuerrier*, [1998] 2 S.C.R. 371 that the Supreme Court of Canada rejected this principle.

In *R. v. Mabior*, 2012 SCC 47, the court attempted to clarify the conflicting case law that had developed since *Cuerrier*. The Supreme Court of Canada stated that fraud as to the possible harmful consequences of an act will negate consent if the fraud physically harmed the complainant or exposed him or her to a significant risk of serious bodily harm. According to the court, a significant risk of serious bodily harm would exist if there was a "realistic possibility" of HIV transmission. It also stated that such a possibility would exist unless the accused both had a low viral load and used a condom.

The principles in *Mabior* were applied in the novel case of *R. v. Hutchinson*, 2014 SCC 19. The complainant consented to sexual intercourse but insisted that the accused wear a condom. The accused poked holes in the condom and the complainant became pregnant. The Supreme Court of Canada unanimously upheld the accused's conviction for aggravated sexual assault. The majority held that although the complainant had consented to the physical act, the accused's deception had negated her consent. It reasoned that depriving a woman of the choice to become pregnant or increasing the risk of pregnancy is as serious as a "significant risk of serious bodily harm" and is sufficient to establish fraud vitiating consent. The minority held that since the complainant had not consented to unprotected intercourse, there was no consent to the sexual activity and the accused was guilty of aggravated sexual assault.

NOTES AND QUESTIONS

1. The distinction between fraud as to the nature of the act and fraud as to collateral matters is well established in criminal law. In *R. v. Williams*, [1923] 1 K.B. 340 (C.A.), a singing teacher was convicted of rape for inducing a 16-year-old student to have intercourse under the pretence that it was a therapeutic procedure to improve her voice. The court emphasized that the girl did not know that she was engaging in a sexual act. In *Papadimitropoulos v. R.* (1958), 98 C.L.R. 249 (H.C.A.), the accused was acquitted of rape for having intercourse with an illiterate woman after he had fraudulently convinced her that they had been married. In this case, the woman was aware that she was participating in a sexual act and consented to it. The court held that the fraud went to a collateral matter and thus did not vitiate her consent. See also *R. v. Harms*, [1944] 2 D.L.R. 61 (Sask. C.A.); and *Bolduc and Bird v. R.*, [1967] S.C.R. 677.

2. Similar reasoning has been adopted in civil cases. In *Graham v. Saville*, [1945] O.R. 301 (C.A.) and *Smythe v. Reardon* (1949), 23 A.L.J. 409 (Circ. Ct.), the defendant fraudulently claimed to be a bachelor and induced the plaintiff to marry him. In both cases the plaintiff recovered damages based on the tort of deceit, but presumably could not have recovered in battery. What arguments would you make for treating fraud as to collateral matters differently in tort law than in criminal law? See Fischer, "Fraudulently Induced Consent to Intentional Torts" (1977) 46 Cinn. L. Rev. 71.

3. Whose perspective should be adopted in determining which matters are collateral? Since the defendant has the burden of proving that the plaintiff consented, should the plaintiff's views prevail? See *Said (Husain) v. Said* (1986), 8 B.C.L.R. (2d) 323 (C.A.).

4. Do you agree with *Mabior* that a "realistic possibility" of HIV transmission: (a) is tantamount to a "significant risk of serious bodily harm;" and (b) will arise unless the accused has a low viral load and uses a condom? Prior to *Mabior*, the majority in *Cuerrier* stated that careful condom use alone could reduce the transmission risk to the point where there was no longer a significant risk of serious bodily harm. Similarly, in *R. v. J.A.T.*, 2010 BCSC 766, the court held that the accused's low viral alone resulted in there no longer being a significant risk of serious bodily harm. Despite *Mabior*, the Nova Scotia Court of Appeal has held that no realistic possibility of HIV transmission would arise if the accused wore a condom or had a low viral load. The court also stated that the psychological harm that the complainant may have suffered due to the accused's failure to disclose his HIV status did not vitiate her consent to the sexual activity. See also *R. v. Thompson*, 2018 NSCA 13.

Based on the existing case law, what steps would a sexually active person with hepatitis C (a potentially life-threatening disease that is more readily transmissible than HIV) have to take to avoid criminal liability?

5. Do you prefer the majority or minority analysis of consent in *Hutchinson*? Would the result have been the same had the complainant not become pregnant? Could a male who refused to have unprotected sex because he did not want to become a father succeed in battery against a female who had poked holes in the condom if: (a) she did not become pregnant; or (b) she became pregnant?

In *P.P. v. D.D.*, 2017 ONCA 180, the plaintiff sued the defendant for non-pathological emotional harm on various grounds for being deceived into having "recreational intercourse" and fathering a child contrary to his wishes. He argued that he had only consented to unprotected intercourse based on her repeated assurances that she was using effective birth control and that her deceit in this regard vitiated his consent. The defendant's application to strike the plaintiff's claim was granted on the basis that it disclosed no viable cause of action. The Ontario Court of Appeal subsequently upheld the order. Would the minority in *Hutchinson* have concluded that the plaintiff did not consent to having intercourse with the defendant, given that she was not using effective birth control?

6. Should fraud as to an act's harmful consequences be treated differently in tort and criminal law? Should it negate a plaintiff's consent in torts regardless of: (a) the probability of physical harm; (b) the severity of the potential physical harm; or (c) whether the potential harm was physical, psychological or financial? See generally The American Law Institute, *Restatement of the Law Second: Torts* (1979) vol. 4 at §892(B)(2); Howarth, "Defences to Intentional Torts" in Sappideen & Vines, eds., *Fleming's The Law of Torts*, 10th ed. (2011) 87 at 92-93; and Peel & Goudkamp, *Winfield & Jolowicz on Tort*, 19th ed. (2014) at 785.

7. It should be noted that procuring a feigned marriage and polygamy are offences under ss. 292 and 293 of the *Criminal Code*. In 1985, the *Criminal Code*

offence of communicating a venereal disease, unless one was unaware of the infection, was repealed.

REVIEW PROBLEM

Based on *Mabior*, in which of the following scenarios would Tracy's consent be vitiated? Assume that Luke is aware of his HIV status and his viral load. Answer the same question based on *R. v. Thompson*, 2018 NSCA 13, discussed *supra* in note 4.

(i)   Luke, who has a high viral load, has consensual, protected sex with Tracy without disclosing his HIV status.

(ii) Luke, who has a low viral load, has consensual, unprotected sex with Tracy without disclosing his HIV status.

(iii) Luke, who has a high viral load, has consensual, unprotected sex with Tracy after disclosing his HIV status.

(iv) Luke, who has a high viral load, has consensual, unprotected sex with Tracy without disclosing his HIV status.

(c) MISTAKE

Traditionally, the plaintiff's consent would only be vitiated by mistake if the defendant was responsible for creating the plaintiff's misapprehension and the misapprehension went to the nature or quality of the act. Based on the approach in *R. v. Mabior*, 2012 SCC 47, the plaintiff's consent would also be negated if the misapprehension went to the harmful consequences of the act and the act physically harmed the plaintiff or exposed him or her to a significant risk of serious physical harm. Situations in which the plaintiff consents based on a mistaken belief must be distinguished from those in which the defendant erroneously believes that the plaintiff has consented. In the latter situations, since the plaintiff has not consented to the act giving rise to the tort, the defence of consent is not in issue.

NOTES AND QUESTIONS

1. Explain in your own words the difference between a fraudulently and a mistakenly induced belief. Provide an example of each.

2. There are few cases on the impact of the plaintiff's mistaken belief on the validity of his or her consent. See *Roper v. Harper* (1837), 132 E.R. 696 (C.P.); *Stewart v. Traders Trust Co.*, [1936] 4 D.L.R. 139 (Man. C.A.); and *Guimond v. Laberge* (1956), 4 D.L.R. (2d) 559 (Ont. C.A.).

3. The American Law Institute, *Restatement of the Law Second: Torts* (1979) vol. 4 at §892(B)(2) provides that the defendant's mere knowledge that the plaintiff consented under a mistaken belief vitiates the consent. Dobbs, Hayden & Bublick, *The Law of Torts*, 2d ed. (2011) vol. 1 at 342 states that the plaintiff's consent will be vitiated if the defendant knew or ought to have known that the plaintiff's consent was based on a mistaken belief. Which rule should the courts adopt in these situations? See generally Forbes, "Mistake of Fact with Regard to Defences in Tort Law" (1970) 4

Ottawa L. Rev. 304; and Williams, "Deception, Mistake and Vitiation of the Victim's Consent" (2008) 124 L.Q.R. 132.

4. Several cases clearly establish that the defendant's mistaken belief that the plaintiff consented provides no defence. See *Parmley v. Parmley*, [1945] S.C.R. 635; *Turner v. Thorne* (1959), 21 D.L.R. (2d) 29 (Ont. H.C.); and *Schweizer v. Central Hospital* (1974), 6 O.R. (2d) 606 (H.C.).

In *Toews (Guardian ad litem of) v. Weisner* (2001), 3 C.C.L.T. (3d) 293 (B.C.S.C.), the defendant was a public health nurse providing Hepatitis B vaccinations in schools. The parents of 11-year-old Georgia Toews had not signed the consent form, and Georgia specifically told Weisner that her parents did not want her to be vaccinated. However, Weisner mistakenly believed that Georgia's mother had given verbal consent and vaccinated Georgia. Although no harm resulted and Weisner had a good faith belief that Georgia's mother had consented, she was held liable in battery for $1,000.

REVIEW PROBLEM

Wendy consulted Thinband, a private clinic that performs weight-reducing gastric band surgery. During the consultation, Thinband's general surgeon described the dramatic weight-loss results of the surgery and told Wendy that fewer than 4% of patients suffer significant post-surgical complications. Wendy was given a booklet that outlined the surgery's complications, but it did not indicate the likelihood of experiencing them. Reassured by the low risk of significant complications, Wendy consented to the surgery. During the surgery, Wendy experienced a stomach perforation, which caused a near-fatal infection. Wendy's lawyer researched the surgery and found that it was well known among general surgeons that the likelihood of significant post-surgical complications was approximately 15%, and these risks included stomach perforation. Based on existing Canadian law, which of the following statements are incorrect?

(i) Wendy's consent to treatment may be negated, but only on the basis of mistake.

(ii) Wendy's consent to treatment may be negated, but only on the basis of fraud.

(iii) Wendy's consent to treatment cannot be negated on the basis of either mistake or fraud.

(iv) Wendy's consent to treatment may be negated on the basis of both mistake and fraud.

(d) DURESS (COERCION)

LATTER v. BRADDELL
(1880), 50 L.J.Q.B. 166 (C.P.)

LOPES J.: This was an action of assault which . . . resulted in a verdict for the defendant [doctor]. The learned Judge . . . withdrew the case against Captain and Mrs. Braddell from the jury, holding that there was no evidence against them upon which a jury could reasonably act.

. . .

I think the case against Captain and Mrs. Braddell ought to have been left to the jury. I do not think it was correct to tell the jury that to maintain this action the plaintiff's will must have been overpowered by force or the fear of violence. This I understand was the direction given by the learned Judge to the jury in summing up the case against the defendant [doctor], and I presume this view of the law induced him to withdraw from the jury the case against Captain and Mrs. Braddell.

I will now call attention to the facts. The plaintiff was a housemaid in the service of Captain and Mrs. Braddell. Captain and Mrs. Braddell had been absent from home, and returned on the 23rd of December. From some information given by a charwoman, Mrs. Braddell came to the conclusion that the plaintiff was in the family way. On the 27th of December Mrs. Braddell told the plaintiff to pack up and leave before twelve o'clock, as she was in the family way. This the plaintiff denied. Mrs. Braddell replied, "The doctor will be here directly." (The doctor had been previously sent for unknown to the plaintiff) Mrs. Braddell told the plaintiff to go to her room. The plaintiff cried. Mrs. Braddell forbade her to speak. The plaintiff went to her bedroom. The doctor came and went to the plaintiff's bedroom. The plaintiff cried and said she never had such treatment before. She asked the doctor what he was going to do, and said she did not wish to be examined. The doctor said he was a professional man, and told the plaintiff to take off her dress. The plaintiff said she did not like to do so. The doctor said, "Never mind, it would satisfy Mrs. Braddell and him." The doctor told the plaintiff to take off her petticoat. The plaintiff cried and said she did not like to take off her other things. The doctor said, "You must." The plaintiff took off her stays. The doctor said she must take off her chemise. The plaintiff said she did not like to do so. The doctor said she must, and told her to slip her arms through. The doctor then told her to lie on her back on the bed and to loosen the strings of her drawers. He then pinched her breasts and stomach and sounded it. The plaintiff cried all the time. The doctor, after examining her, said she was all right, and he must speak seriously to Mrs. Braddell about it. The plaintiff then dressed.

. . .

If the plaintiff voluntarily consented, or if, in other words, the assault was committed with her leave and licence, the action is not maintainable; and to justify the ruling of the learned Judge, what was done must have been so unmistakably with the plaintiff's consent that there was no evidence of non-consent upon which a jury could reasonably act. It seems to me there was abundant evidence of non-consent to be left to the jury.

The sending for a doctor by a master or mistress and directing him to examine a female servant, without first apprising her, is, in any circumstances, an arbitrary and high-handed proceeding, and cannot, in my opinion, be justified unless the servant's consent is voluntarily given. A submission to what is done, obtained through a belief that she is bound to obey her master and mistress; or a consent obtained through a fear of evil consequences to arise to herself, induced by her master's or mistress's words or conduct, is not sufficient. In neither case would the consent be voluntarily given: it would be consent in one sense, but a consent to which the will was not a party. The plaintiff's case is stronger. She swears she did not consent. I know not what more a person in the plaintiff's position could do unless she used physical force. She is discharged without a hearing, forbidden to speak, sent to her room, examined by her mistress's doctor alone, no other female being in the room, made to take off all her clothes and lie naked on the bed. She complains of the treatment, cries continuously, objects to the removal of each garment and swears the examination was without her consent. Could it be said, in these circumstances, that her consent was so unmistakably given that her state of mind was not a question for a jury to consider? I cannot adopt the view that the plaintiff consented because she yielded without her will having been overpowered by force or fear of violence. That, as I have said, is not, in my opinion, an accurate definition of consent in a case like this.

I do not understand why, if there was a case against the doctor there was none against Captain and Mrs. Braddell. The doctor was employed to see if the plaintiff was in the family way. The plaintiff does not suggest in her evidence that he did more than was necessary for ascertaining that fact. If this is so, the Braddells are responsible for what was done by the doctor.

It is said there ought to be no new trial as against the doctor. I cannot agree with the definition of consent given by the learned Judge, and I think the withdrawing the case against the Braddells influenced the jury in finding for the doctor. They would naturally think the doctor only did what he was told. The Braddells put him in motion, and it would be hard, when the principals are acquitted, to find the agent guilty.

There should be a rule absolute for a new trial.

LINDLEY J.: I am of opinion that, assuming everything said by the plaintiff in this case to be true, a verdict in her favour against the master and mistress could not be supported in point of law, and that as to them she was properly nonsuited.

. . .

The plaintiff's case cannot be put higher than this, namely, that without consulting her wishes, her mistress ordered her to submit to be examined by a doctor, in order that he might ascertain whether she (the plaintiff) was in the family way, and that she (the plaintiff) complied with that order reluctantly — that is, sobbing and protesting — and because she was told she must, and she did not know what else to do. There was, however, no evidence of any force or violence, nor of any threat of force or violence, nor of any illegal act done or threatened by the mistress beyond what I have stated; nor did the plaintiff in her evidence say that she was in fear of the mistress or of the doctor, or that she was in any way overcome by fear. She said she did not consent to what was done; but the sense in which she used this expression was not explained, and to appreciate it regard must be had to the other facts of the case. The plaintiff had it entirely in her own power physically to comply or not to comply with her mistress's orders, and there was no evidence whatever to shew that anything improper or illegal was threatened to be done if she had not complied. It was suggested that her mistress ordered the examination with a view to see whether she could dismiss her without paying a month's wages. But there was no evidence of any threat to withhold wages, nor of any conversation on the subject of wages, until the plaintiff was paid them on leaving. The question, therefore, is reduced to this: Can the plaintiff, having complied with the orders of her mistress, although reluctantly, maintain this action upon the ground that what was done to her by the doctor was against her will, or might properly be so regarded by a jury? I think not. It is said that the jury ought to have been asked whether the plaintiff in effect gave her mistress leave to have her examined, or whether the plaintiff's will or mind went with what she did. But, in my opinion, such questions inadequately express the grounds on which alone the defendants can be held liable. The plaintiff was not a child; she knew perfectly well what she did and what was being done to her by the doctor. She knew the object with which he examined her, and upon the evidence there is no reason whatever for supposing that any examination would have been made or attempted if she had told the doctor she would not allow herself to be examined. Under these circumstances I am of opinion that there was no evidence of want of consent as distinguished from reluctant obedience or submission to her mistress's orders, and that in the absence of all evidence of coercion, as distinguished from an order which the plaintiff could comply with or not as she chose, the action cannot be maintained.

. . .

I do not, however, wish to be understood as being of opinion that the plaintiff had no cause of complaint against her mistress; but, in my opinion, the real substantial grievance was that the plaintiff accused of being in the family way was ordered to be examined, and when the accusation proved to be unfounded was summarily dismissed without any apology. Whether the mistress could or could not have justified such harsh conduct I cannot say, not having heard her evidence. But, harsh as such conduct apparently was, it does not affect the question on which this action turns. I cannot, however, help thinking that if the conduct of the mistress as regards the manner of dismissal had been more considerate, the impossibility of maintaining this action would be more plainly apparent.

As regards the doctor, who is made a defendant, I am of opinion, for the reasons already given, that there was no misdirection in point of law, and that the verdict in his favour was perfectly correct. His conduct throughout was kind and considerate; and whatever grievance the plaintiff may have against her mistress, she has none whatever against the doctor.

. . .

Rule Discharged.

[The Court of Appeal affirmed Lindley J.'s judgment discharging the rule: *Latter v. Braddell* (1881), 50 L.J.Q.B. 448 (C.A.).]

NOTES AND QUESTIONS

1. Did Lindley J. adequately address the issue of consent before focusing on duress? Did the plaintiff in *Latter* consent to the medical examination?

2. How did Lindley J. define duress? What economic threats, if any, would be included in his definition? Do you agree with his application of this definition to the facts? Answer these questions in reference to Lopes J. Which judgment do you prefer?

3. Under s. 17 of the *Criminal Code*, the concept of compulsion (duress) is defined narrowly in terms of a credible threat of immediate death or bodily harm. Although the American Law Institute rejects this narrow definition of duress for civil law purposes, it does not provide an alternative: *Restatement of the Law Second: Torts* (1979) vol. 4 at §892B, comment on subsection (3). Should the definition of duress differ in tort and criminal law? In Dobbs, Hayden & Bublick, *The Law of Torts*, 2d ed. (2011) vol. 1 at 347-50, the authors adopt a far broader definition of duress, which includes threats of physical harm, crimes or torts. How would you define duress for the purposes of tort law?

4. Should an employee who submits to her employer's sexual demands to keep her job succeed in battery on the basis that her consent was vitiated by duress? Would your answer differ if the employer's threat of dismissal contravened the provincial labour and human rights legislation? Dobbs, Hayden & Bublick, *supra*, at 349-57, indicate that serious abuses of power, such as sexual demands by employers and others in positions of authority, will negate consent or provide an independent basis for tort liability. Is it preferable to expand the definition of duress to encompass these tort claims, treat these claims as providing an independent basis for tort liability or leave it to legislators to enact a statutory remedy?

5. Can policies making treatment a condition of parole be successfully challenged on the basis that the parolee's consent is negated by duress? For a discussion of the *Canadian Charter of Rights and Freedoms,* Part I of the *Constitution Act, 1982,* being Schedule B to the *Canada Act 1982* (U.K.), 1982, c. 11 and other legal implications of such policies, see *Deacon v. Canada (A.G.),* [2007] 2 F.C.R. 607 (C.A.); and *R. v. Shoker,* [2006] 2 S.C.R. 399.

(e) PUBLIC POLICY

The courts have increasingly recognized public policy considerations in negating the defence of consent. For example in *Lane v. Holloway,* [1968] 1 Q.B. 379 (C.A.), the court refused to accept the defence of consent because it was obvious from the outset of the fight that the elderly plaintiff was no match for the young defendant. In *R. v. Paice,* [2005] 1 S.C.R. 339, the Supreme Court of Canada held that an accused cannot raise the defence of consent even in a fair fight if serious physical harm was intended and caused.

Some courts have negated the defence of consent if the defendant exploited his or her position of trust. In *M.(M.) v. K.(K.)* (1989), 38 B.C.L.R. (2d) 273 (C.A.), the defendant was convicted of the federal offence of sexual exploitation for having sex with his 15-year-old foster daughter. The daughter's civil action was dismissed at trial on the basis that she had initiated and consented to the sexual contact. However, the Court of Appeal reversed the trial judgment. The court rejected the defence of consent because it was dependent on the defendant's wrongdoing, which included criminal misconduct, breach of trust and breach of his duty to act in the plaintiff's best interests.

In *Norberg v. Wynrib,* [1992] 2 S.C.R. 226, a doctor offered to supply an addicted patient with prescription narcotics if she submitted to his sexual advances. She reluctantly agreed only after she failed to secure the drugs from another source. After recovering from her addiction, the patient sued the doctor for battery, negligence and breach of fiduciary duty. The trial and appeal courts dismissed the patient's action and found, among other things, that she had given a valid consent to the sexual contact. The Supreme Court of Canada unanimously upheld the patient's appeal, awarding her $20,000 in general damages and $10,000 in punitive damages. LaForest, Gonthier and Cory JJ. held the doctor liable in battery, stating that the parties' unequal bargaining power and the exploitive nature of their relationship made it impossible for the plaintiff to "meaningfully consent." Sopinka J. held that the plaintiff's consent to the defendant's sexual advances was not vitiated in the circumstances. However, he found the defendant liable in negligence for prolonging, rather than treating, the patient's addiction. McLachlin and L'Heureux-Dubé JJ. held the doctor liable for breaching his fiduciary duty to the patient by exploiting his position of power and her vulnerability. In their view, this independent cause of action better captured the doctor's wrongful conduct than either battery or negligence.

NOTES AND QUESTIONS

1. Can you identify an underlying principle that explains the result in *Lane, Paice* and *Norberg*? Do you agree with these decisions?

2. Would the result have been the same in *M.(M.)* if the defendant's conduct had not been illegal, but had merely violated his position of trust? For example, assume that the plaintiff was 18 years old and the defendant was a private music teacher or volunteer basketball coach. See *Lyth v. Dagg* (1988), 46 C.C.L.T. 25 (B.C.S.C.); *Harder v. Brown* (1989), 50 C.C.L.T. 85 (B.C.S.C.); and *A.K. v. Kennedy*, 2002 CarswellOnt 345 (S.C.J.) (WL Can).

3. What do you think the majority meant by the phrase "meaningfully consent" in *Norberg*? Would a person who consents to counselling only because it is a term of his or her probation be able to "meaningfully consent?" Which approach in *Norberg* is preferable?

4. *Norberg* raises the issue of the sexual abuse and exploitation of patients by physicians and other healthcare professionals. Following a particularly egregious case in the late 1980s, the Ontario College of Physicians and Surgeons established a task force which found that sexual abuse of female patients was not infrequent and that patients were largely unsuccessful in obtaining redress. See McPhedran *et al.*, *The Final Report of the Task Force on Sexual Abuse of Patients* (1991).

After the report was released, Ontario enacted legislation requiring all regulated health practitioners to report to the appropriate college any situation in which they reasonably believed that a patient had been sexually abused by any regulated health professional. See *Regulated Health Professions Act, 1991*, S.O. 1991, c. 18, Sch. II, ss. 85.1-85.62. Shortly thereafter, Ontario enacted similar mandatory reporting obligations for social workers and teachers.

5. Can you suggest other cases in which public policy considerations should limit the defendant's ability to rely on the plaintiff's consent as a defence?

6. The courts have not reconciled their public policy analysis with the concept of individual autonomy. Nor have they considered the implications of negating a person's consent on policy grounds in other areas, such as healthcare.

There is considerable case law that accepts the plaintiff's consent at face value. In reference to consensual fights, see *Wade v. Martin*, [1955] 3 D.L.R. 635 (Nfld. S.C.); *Zinck v. Strickland and Blake* (1981), 45 N.S.R. (2d) 451 (S.C.); and *Johnson v. Royal Can. Legion Grandview Branch No. 179* (1988), 26 B.C.L.R. (2d) 124 (C.A.). In contrast to *Norberg*, see *Morrow v. Hôpital Royal Victoria* (1989), 3 C.C.L.T. (2d) 87 (Qc. C.A.), in which a schizophrenic patient's consent to electroshock therapy was upheld, even though she had not been informed that the defendant doctor was being paid by the CIA to conduct brain-washing experiments. The court held that because the patient was herself a doctor who was aware of the risks, her consent was valid.

7. Canadian courts have negated the validity of consent to a range of sexual conduct on public policy grounds. Relying on *R. v. Jobidon*, [1991] 2 S.C.R. 714, the court in *R. v. Welch* (1995), 25 O.R. (3d) 665 (C.A.) stated that individuals cannot consent to harm being imposed upon them except for a "generally approved social purpose." According to the court, inherently degrading or dehumanizing conduct or conduct involving sexual gratification from inflicting pain that results in physical harm cannot be the subject of consent. In *R. v. J.A.*, 2011 SCC 28, the majority held that individuals cannot consent in advance to having sexual acts performed on them when they are unconscious. The dissent stated that the majority decision was wrong on the facts, and unwarranted as a matter of statutory interpretation, past decisions and policy.

Can the accused's convictions in *Welch* and *J.A.* be justified, given that the *Criminal Code*'s sexual assault provisions contain no such limits on the validity of consent? Should the courts be the arbiters of what constitutes a "generally approved social purpose," particularly in regard to criminalizing consensual sexual conduct among adults?

REVIEW PROBLEMS

1. Following a car crash, the plaintiff sought accident benefits from the defendant insurance company and provided supporting documentation. The company refused to process her claim without additional medical evidence. The insurance contract permitted the defendant to ask the plaintiff to submit to a second assessment. Without consulting the plaintiff, the company made an appointment for her with a specialist. The company then wrote the plaintiff, instructing her to attend at the pre-arranged date and time. The letter stated that the plaintiff had to submit to the examination or her claim would be refused. However, the letter did not inform the plaintiff of her contractual right to challenge the need for a second assessment, propose an alternate specialist or reschedule the appointment.

In addition to missing work, rearranging her schedule and organizing transportation, the plaintiff was upset about being physically examined by a male specialist. The plaintiff had not gone to a male physician since childhood. Nevertheless, she believed that she had no choice. She was ushered into an examination room and told to change into a dressing gown. She was never asked for consent, did not receive a consent form to sign and did not verbally consent to the examination. She followed the instructions that she was given, answered the specialist's questions and complied with his directions concerning the examination.

The plaintiff only deferred to the company's demands because she believed that the contract required her to do so. When the plaintiff learned that this was not the case, she approached you for legal advice on whether the insurance company can establish a valid defence of consent regarding the physical examination. The company has conceded that it is legally responsible for the specialist's physical examination. See generally *Nelitz v. Dyck* (2001), 52 O.R. (3d) 458 (C.A.).

2. Although Frank and Mary had dated for several months, Mary was reluctant to become physically involved. Before agreeing to become sexually intimate, she asked Frank: "Is it safe to have intercourse with you?" Frank responded that she had "nothing to worry about." Unknown to Mary, Frank had been diagnosed with herpes, a disease that can be transmitted through direct physical contact with an open

sore. These sores are unsightly and may be painful. If a pregnant woman has an outbreak of genital sores when she goes into labour, she will be advised to have a Caesarean section rather than delivering the baby vaginally. However, the virus is otherwise more of an inconvenience than a significant health risk.

Two years ago, when Frank first noticed a sore in his genital area, he sought medical treatment. Frank was so relieved that it was due to herpes and not HIV that he misunderstood what his doctor told him. Frank honestly, albeit erroneously, believed that once the initial sore went away, he would no longer be capable of infecting others. Frank's doctor had given him a brochure that clearly explained that he could infect others if he had intimate contact during a flare-up, but Frank did not read it.

Frank did not tell Mary of his infection because he thought that he could not infect her and because he was embarrassed. While Frank realized that he had not been forthcoming, he believed that he had answered Mary's questions honestly. When Mary discovered that she had contracted herpes from Frank, she ended the relationship. She now seeks your legal advice about suing Frank in battery.

4. Consent to Criminal or Immoral Acts

In *Hegarty v. Shine* (1878), 4 L.R. Ir. 288 (C.A.), the female plaintiff sued her lover in battery for infecting his or her with a venereal disease. One of the bases on which the court denied her claim was the principle that a person cannot recover in tort law for the consequences of his or her own illegal or immoral conduct. This concept, which is often referred to by the Latin maxim *ex turpi causa non oritur actio*, may provide a complete defence to both intentional torts and negligence. For example, successful combatants who were sued in battery following a consensual fight often asserted both the defences of consent and *ex turpi causa*.

The principle has generated controversy, largely part because the courts failed to clarify its purpose. Consequently, the principle was applied on a case-by-case basis, making the decisions difficult to reconcile. Nevertheless, the trend in Canada had been to narrow the principle based on the type of wrongdoing. For example, some courts had held that it only applied to illegal but not immoral acts; other courts had limited it to federal criminal offences and excluded provincial and municipal offences. Finally, some courts had concluded that *ex turpi causa* only applied to some federal criminal offences.

In *Hall v. Hebert*, [1993] 2 S.C.R. 159, the court rejected this approach, stating that recovery could be denied based on a plaintiff's illegal or immoral acts, but only if doing so was necessary to protect the integrity of the legal system. Having defined the purpose of *ex turpi causa*, the court then discussed the limited circumstances in which the doctrine would apply. More specifically, the court stated that while *ex turpi causa* could be invoked to prevent a plaintiff from profiting financially from his or her illegal or immoral behaviour, it would rarely apply to a plaintiff seeking compensation for actual physical injuries.

NOTES AND QUESTIONS

1. One concern has been that the concept of immorality is too open-ended and will vary both over time and across jurisdictions. For example, *Hegarty* would not be

decided the same way now. In *Kirkham v. Chief Constable of Greater Manchester Police*, [1990] 3 All E.R. 246 (C.A.), the plaintiff's husband committed suicide while in police custody. The court rejected the police department's defence of *ex turpi causa* because suicide was no longer viewed as a "moral affront."

2. It was generally accepted that *ex turpi causa* was limited to cases in which the plaintiff's injuries were a direct result of his or her participation in immoral or illegal conduct. See *Norberg v. Wynrib*, [1992] 2 S.C.R. 226. However, some courts applied the directness concept more narrowly than others, particularly in cases involving young plaintiffs injured in crashes while joy-riding in a stolen vehicle. In *Rankin (Rankin's Garage & Sales) v. J.J.*, 2018 SCC 19, the 15-year-old plaintiff suffered catastrophic injuries while riding in a stolen car. The court, without addressing the directness issue, stated that *ex turpi causa* would not apply because denying the plaintiff recovery was not necessary to preserve the integrity of the legal system.

3. The decision in *Hall* was recently affirmed in *Deloitte & Touche v. Livent Inc.*, 2017 SCC 63 and *Rankin, ibid.* Nevertheless, do you agree with *Hall* that *ex turpi causa* should be limited to preserving the integrity of the legal system? What other purposes could the doctrine serve?

Assuming that the doctrine should be limited to preserving the integrity of the legal system, does it follow that the doctrine would rarely apply to wrongdoing plaintiffs seeking compensation for physical injuries? Can you suggest a situation in which denying a wrongdoing plaintiff recovery for physical injuries would be necessary to preserve the integrity of the legal system?

4. In *John Bead Corp. v. Soni* (2002), 158 O.A.C. 80 (C.A.), the plaintiffs sued the defendants on several grounds including fraud, claiming that they had stolen $1.6 million from the plaintiffs' company. The defendants pleaded *ex turpi causa* on the basis that the plaintiffs had also illegally taken money from the company. The court struck out this defence because the plaintiffs' alleged illegal behaviour was unrelated to their claim against the defendants. The court then gave two examples of situations in which *ex turpi causa* would apply. First, one wrongdoer cannot recover in tort against another for his or her share of their theft or other illegal behaviour. Second, a plaintiff who has been physically injured cannot recover loss of earnings arising from an illegal activity. Thus, a defendant who assaults a forger cannot be held liable for the illegal earnings that the forger lost while his or her hand healed.

5. In *British Columbia v. Zastowny*, [2008] 1 S.C.R. 27, a prison official sexually assaulted the plaintiff, who was an 18-year-old inmate at the time. The plaintiff spent 12 of the next 15 years in prison for various crimes, and there was evidence that being sexually assaulted led to his use of heroin and exacerbated his criminality. The plaintiff sued for the sexual assaults and included a claim for his loss of wages during the 12 years that he was incarcerated. The court held that the *ex turpi causa* defence precludes recovery of lost wages due to the plaintiff's incarceration, except in unique situations such as wrongful conviction. The court stated that permitting recovery would create a conflict between criminal and civil law and compromise the integrity of the justice system. Given the prison official's conduct, do you agree with the court that denying the plaintiff's wage claim in its entirety was necessary to preserve the integrity of the legal system? See also *Gray v. Thames Trains Ltd.*, [2009] 1 A.C. 1339 (H.L.).

6. The *ex turpi causa* defence has generated reams of critical comment. See for example Kostal, "Currents in the Counter-Reformation: Illegality and Duty of Care in Canada and Australia" (1995) 3 Tort L. Rev. 100; Goudkamp, "The Defence of Joint Illegal Enterprise" (2010) 34 Melbourne U.L. Rev. 425; and Yap, "Rethinking the Illegality Defence in Tort Law" (2010) 18 Tort L. Rev. 52.

See also Bogg & Novitz, "Race Discrimination and the Doctrine of Illegality" (2013) 129 L.Q.R. 12 at 13, who state that the doctrine of illegality is "something of a mess in the common law," before describing *Allen v. Hounga*, [2012] EWCA Civ. 609 as setting a new low in the doctrine's chequered legal history. Although the Supreme Court overturned the Court of Appeal decision in *Allen*, [2014] UKSC 47, the subsequent cases have done little to resolve the confusion. See Fisher, "The *ex turpi causa* principle in *Hounga* and *Servier*" (2015) 78 M.L.R. 854; and *Patel (Respondent) v. Mirza (Appellant)*, [2016] UKSC 42.

5. Consent to Treatment, Counselling and Care

(a) GENERAL PRINCIPLES OF CONSENT

As a general rule, healthcare professionals must obtain consent to initiate any physical examination, test, procedure, surgery, or counselling. The consent should be obtained in advance and must relate to the specific procedure or treatment that is undertaken. In order to avoid other potential legal problems, the consent should also address any related issues regarding documentation, confidentiality, reporting, and disclosure of information. If the patient is competent, it is his or her consent alone that is required. The consent of a patient's next-of-kin is only relevant if he or she is incapable of consenting.

To be valid, the consent must be given "voluntarily," in the sense that the patient's decision is the product of his or her conscious mind. Consistent with the law's focus on autonomy, the legal definition of volition is extremely broad. For example, patients who reluctantly consent to treatment because they have been threatened with being fired from their job or with being expelled from school will be held to have "voluntarily" consented.

At common law, the patient's consent had to be based on a full and frank disclosure of the nature of the intervention and its risks. The patient need not understand the technical details of the intervention or the research underlying it. However, practitioners and counsellors are increasingly expected to put the proposed treatment in the broader context of the risks and benefits of its alternatives, including forgoing treatment. A patient may consent explicitly, either in writing or verbally, or implicitly by participation or demeanour. The fact that a patient makes an appointment and comes for treatment provides a measure of implied consent.

Patients may seek treatment and yet expressly limit the scope of their consent. Healthcare professionals may refuse to treat a patient if these limitations render the treatment futile or harmful. However, a patient's express prohibitions cannot be ignored or overridden.

NOTES AND QUESTIONS

1. For a review of the general principles of consent to treatment, see Robertson & Picard, *Legal Liability of Doctors and Hospitals in Canada*, 5th ed. (2017) at 51-152;

and Osborne, "Consent to Treatment" in Irvine, Osborne & Shariff, eds., *Canadian Medical Law*, 4th ed. (2013) 19.

2. The common law principles of consent are increasingly being supplemented by complex, piecemeal legislation. For example, in 1995 Ontario proclaimed in force four statutes relating to consent, counselling and care. The next year, the new provincial government repealed, replaced or significantly amended all four statutes. Although the government media campaign suggested that the legislation consolidated the common law principles, this was not the case. For example, the *Health Care Consent Act, 1996*, S.O. 1996, c. 2, Sch. A increased the information that health professionals must provide to patients, and altered the principles governing emergency treatment and substitute consent. Moreover, the statute's treatment provisions only apply to regulated health practitioners such as doctors and dentists, leaving social workers, addiction counsellors, personal support workers, and other professionals governed by the common law. While the statute defines the term "treatment" broadly, it then excludes a long list of procedures, examinations and circumstances from the definition. Thus, the statute replicates some common law principles but not others, and only applies to some health, counselling and care professionals in certain circumstances.

If nothing else, this legislative flurry succeeded in baffling many practitioners. It should be noted that the courts have largely ignored the legislation in their analysis of tort claims. Can you suggest factors that encouraged the government to introduce and publicize this type of legislation?

3. In *Battrum v. British Columbia* (2009), 70 C.C.L.T. (3d) 164 (B.C.S.C.), the plaintiff called 911 for assistance after she fell off a horse and injured her shoulder. She sued the defendant paramedic in battery for taking her vital signs and stabilizing her shoulder, alleging that he was "abrupt and unsympathetic" and had "behaved like a lout." In dismissing the claim, the court noted that the plaintiff expressly sought first aid and wanted to be taken to the hospital. The defendant's touching of the plaintiff was within the reasonable scope of the treatment that she sought and to which she implicitly consented.

(b) EXCEPTIONS TO THE COMMON LAW PRINCIPLES OF CONSENT

Traditionally, the courts have relaxed the strict requirements of consent in three situations. First, in an unforeseen medical emergency, where it is impossible to obtain the patient's consent, a healthcare professional is allowed to intervene without consent to preserve the patient's health or life. This is the basis upon which emergency room staff and members of the public are permitted to provide treatment or first aid to unconscious accident victims.

The second exception involves patients who have given a general consent to a course of treatment, a treatment plan or an operation. In such situations, a patient will be viewed as implicitly consenting to any subordinate tests and procedures that are necessarily incidental to the agreed course of treatment, treatment plan or operation. However, this implied consent will be negated if the patient expressly objects.

Third, at one time, the Canadian courts held that healthcare professionals had a right to withhold information from a patient if its disclosure would undermine the patient's morale and discourage him or her from having needed treatment or surgery. The "therapeutic privilege to withhold information," as it was called, reflected the paternalistic notions of treatment relationships that existed at the time. In two somewhat conflicting cases, the Supreme Court of Canada cast doubt on the continued existence of the privilege: *Hopp v. Lepp*, [1980] 2 S.C.R. 192 at 208; and *Reibl v. Hughes*, [1980] 2 S.C.R. 880 at 899-90. In keeping with the rise in patients' rights, the subsequent cases have either rejected the privilege altogether or narrowed its scope. See respectively *Meyer Estate v. Rogers* (1991), 2 O.R. (3d) 356 (Gen. Div.); and *Pittman Estate v. Bain* (1994), 112 D.L.R. (4th) 257 (Ont. Gen. Div.).

MARSHALL v. CURRY
[1933] 3 D.L.R. 260 (N.S.S.C.)

CHISHOLM, C.J.:—The plaintiff, a master mariner residing at Clifton in the County of Colchester, brings this action in which he claims $10,000 damages against the defendant who is a surgeon of high standing, practising his profession in the City of Halifax.

The plaintiff in his statement of claim alleges: —

(1) That after being employed to perform and while performing an operation on the plaintiff for the cure of a hernia and while plaintiff was under the influence of an anaesthetic, the defendant without the knowledge or consent of the plaintiff removed the plaintiff's left testicle;

(2) In the alternative, that the defendant was negligent in diagnosing the case and in not informing the plaintiff that it might be necessary in treating the hernia to remove the testicle; and

(3) In the further alternative, that in removing the testicle in the above mentioned circumstances, the defendant committed an assault upon the plaintiff.

The defence, in addition to general denials, is, that the removal of the testicle was a necessary part of the operation for the cure of the hernia; that the necessity for removing the testicle could not have been reasonably ascertained by diagnosis before any operation was begun; that consent to the further operation was implied by plaintiff's request to cure the hernia, and that the plaintiff's claim is barred by the Statute of Limitations.

. . .

The defendant states that plaintiff had asked him in July, 1929, what he thought of this hernia. The defendant replied that there was a reasonable chance of curing it; that he thought it was a case suitable for the ordinary hernia operation: the abdominal muscles were in a reasonably good condition. In the operation the defendant found the muscles very much weaker than he had anticipated. In opening the inguinal canal the testicle appeared and was found grossly diseased; it was enlarged, nodular and softened. In order to cure the hernia it was necessary in defendant's opinion to obliterate the canal completely so as not to leave any space. The defendant deemed it necessary to remove the testicle in order to cure the hernia, and also because it would be a menace to the health and life of the plaintiff to leave it. That, he says, was his best judgment in the circumstances. After the operation the defendant cut the testicle in two and found multiple abscesses in it. The defendant gave, as his opinion that if the testicle had not been removed, it might have become gangrenous, and the pus might be absorbed into the circulation, and a condition of blood-poisoning have set up.

[The Court then considered various authorities which supported the following legal principles.]

1. That in the ordinary case where there is opportunity to obtain the consent of the patient it must be had. A person's body must be held inviolate and immune from invasion by the surgeon's knife, if an operation is not consented to. The rule applies not only to an operation but also to the case of mere examination, and it is pointed out in Taylor's Medical Jurisprudence, p. 59, that although the fact that a visit paid by a private patient to a practitioner implies consent to a certain amount of examination it must not be concluded that such a visit entitles the practitioner to compel an examination more intimate than the patient desires. Such an examination can only be made with the patient's consent; if made without such consent, it is technically an assault.

2. That such consent by the patient may be express or implied. If an operation is forbidden by the patient, consent is not to be implied; and Taylor again says:—"It must be constantly remembered that in this connection silence does not give consent, nor is compliance to be taken as consent."

3. That consent may be implied from the conversation preceding an operation or from the antecedent circumstances. . . .

I am unable to see the force of the opinion, that in cases of emergency, where the patient agrees to a particular operation, and in the prosecution of the operation, a condition is found calling in the patient's interest for a different operation, the patient is said to have made the surgeon his representative to give consent. There is unreality about that view. The idea of appointing such a representation, the necessity for it, the existence of a condition calling for a different operation, are entirely absent from the minds of both patient and surgeon. The will of the patient is not exercised on the point. There is, in reality, no such appointment. I think it is better, instead of resorting to a fiction, to put consent altogether out of the case, where a great emergency which could not be anticipated arises, and to rule that it is the surgeon's duty to act in order to save the life or preserve the health of the patient; and that in the honest execution of that duty he should not be exposed to legal liability. It is, I think, more in conformity with the facts and with reason, to put a surgeon's justification in such cases on the higher ground of duty . . .

. . .

In the case at bar, I find that the defendant after making the incisions on plaintiff's body, discovered conditions which neither party had anticipated, and which the defendant could not reasonably have foreseen, and that in removing the testicle he acted in the interest of his patient and for the protection of his health and possibly his life. The removal I find was in that sense necessary, and it would be unreasonable to postpone the removal to a later date. I come to this conclusion despite the absence of express and possibly of implied assent on the part of the plaintiff.

Action dismissed.

MALETTE v. SHULMAN
(1987), 63 O.R. (2d) 243 (H.C.)

[The plaintiff was seriously injured in a car accident and taken to the hospital where she was treated by Dr. Shulman. A nurse found a card in Mrs. Malette's wallet indicating that she was a Jehovah's Witness and was not to be given blood under any circumstances. Dr. Shulman was told about the card. However, when Mrs. Malette's condition deteriorated, Dr. Shulman, believing that she would otherwise die, started the first of several blood transfusions. When the plaintiff's daughter, Mrs. Bisson, arrived four hours later, she confirmed that her mother was a practicing Jehovah's Witness and ordered the blood transfusions to be stopped. Dr. Shulman only stopped the transfusions after the plaintiff's condition was stabilized. She was transferred to the Toronto General Hospital and made a good recovery. She then sued Dr. Shulman in negligence and battery.]

DONNELLY J.: . . . Dr. Shulman, on being confronted by an unconscious patient in a life threatening situation in whose possession was found a card refusing blood as a Jehovah's Witness, faced a dilemma of dreadful finality. An immediate decision was required, either to follow the instruction given by the card or to administer the blood transfusion which he regarded as medically essential. He squarely faced the fundamental issue of the conflict between the patient's right over her own body and society's interest in preserving life.

Dr. Shulman acknowledged an awareness of the patient's right to make a decision against a certain treatment in favour of alternative treatment and of his ethical obligation to abide by that decision. However, upon considering the validity of the card, he was not reasonably satisfied that it constituted an adequate instruction because there was no evidence that: (1) it represented the plaintiff's current intent; (2) the instruction applied to the present life-threatening circumstances; (3) at the time the plaintiff made the decision and signed the card she was fully informed of risks of refusal of treatment and accordingly that this was a rational and informed decision.

. . .

The "card" was subject to attack by the defence on the basis of its inherent frailties — that it may have been signed because of religious peer pressure, under medical misinformation, not in contemplation of life threatening circumstances, or that it may not represent current instructions.

It was further argued on behalf of Dr. Shulman that the relatives' participation compounds the problem by adding further uncertainties, such as: is the relative the closest relative in blood; speaking for a unanimous consensus amongst the relatives; competent to give lawful consent; capable of understanding the risks, and devoid of self-interest?

Mrs. Bisson's participation has the effect of rendering unlikely these speculative frailties. It confirms the card and signature as her mother's, her mother's current status as a Jehovah's Witness and her mother's wish not to have blood. It raises nothing inconsistent with the card representing the mother's current intent applying to life threatening situations. The card itself presents a clear, concise statement, essentially stating, "As a Jehovah's Witness, I refuse blood." That message is unqualified. It does not exempt life threatening perils. On the face of the card, its message is seen to be rooted in religious conviction. Its obvious purpose as a card is as protection to speak in circumstances where the card carrier cannot (presumably because of illness or injury). There is no basis in evidence to indicate that the card may not represent the current intention and instruction of the card holder.

I therefore find that the card is a written declaration of a valid position which the card carrier may legitimately take in imposing a written restriction on her contract with the doctor. Dr. Shulman's doubt about the validity of the card, although honest, was not rationally founded on the evidence before him. Accordingly, but for the issue of informed refusal, there was no rationally founded basis for the doctor to ignore that restriction.

. . .

The defence contended that the doctrine of informed consent should be extended to informed refusal on the following analysis. Since there is an obligation on the doctor recommending treatment to advise as to the risks, it must logically follow there is a higher duty where the patient proposes a course of action that the doctor believes to be prejudicial. Thus Dr. Shulman was obliged in law to advise the refusing patient of the attendant risks. Only then could he be satisfied that the refusal was based on a proper understanding of risks. There was no opportunity to fulfill his obligation to ensure there was an opportunity for an informed choice and so he was not bound by the refusal of treatment.

No case has been cited supporting this concept of informed refusal of treatment. Accordingly, I proceed without the benefit of authority and rely upon the following analysis. The principle underlying the doctrine of informed consent finds its roots in the patient's well recognized right to self determination of his body. The patient has the right to decide what, if anything, will be done to his body: *Hopp v. Lepp* (1980), 112 D.L.R. (3d) 67, [1980] 2 S.C.R. 192, [1980] 4 W.W.R. 645. The treating doctor avoids liability for battery only with a valid consent. To be valid that consent must be informed. Hence the need for the doctor to explain risks. The doctor is legally and ethically obliged to treat within the confines of that consent. The same liability considerations do not apply to a patient's refusal to accept treatment. In that instance the doctor is not exposed to a claim in battery. The right to refuse treatment is an inherent component of the supremacy of the patient's right over his own body. That right to refuse treatment is not premised on an understanding of the risks of refusal.

However sacred life may be, fair social comment admits that certain aspects of life are properly held to be more important than life itself. Such proud and honourable motivations are long entrenched in society, whether it be for patriotism in war, duty by law enforcement officers, protection of the life of a spouse, son or daughter, death before dishonour, death before loss of liberty, or religious martyrdom. Refusal of medical treatment on religious grounds is such a value.

. . .

The doctrine of informed consent does not extend to informed refusal. The written direction contained in the card was not properly disregarded on the basis that circumstances prohibited verification of that decision as an informed choice. The card constituted a valid restriction of Dr. Shulman's right to treat the patient and the administration of blood by Dr. Shulman did constitute battery.

[The judge awarded the plaintiff $20,000 in general damages for her mental distress. The Court of Appeal affirmed the trial judgment, but decided that it was unnecessary to address the issue of informed refusal. The court concluded that Dr.

Shulman had no reason to doubt the validity of the instructions on the card: *Malette v. Shulman* (1990), 67 D.L.R. (4th) 321 (Ont. C.A.).]

NOTES AND QUESTIONS

1. Based on *Marshall*, what must a doctor establish in order to operate without the plaintiff's consent? Do you agree with the application of these principles to the facts?

In *Murray v. McMurchy*, [1949] 2 D.L.R. 442 (B.C.S.C.), the defendant surgeon tied the plaintiff's fallopian tubes during a Caesarian section when he discovered tumours in the wall of her uterus. The court held that the health hazards posed by the tumours in the event of a subsequent pregnancy did not warrant this drastic action and awarded the plaintiff $3,000 in damages. How would you reconcile *Marshall* and *Murray*? See also *Parmley v. Parmley*, [1945] S.C.R. 635.

2. Could *Malette* have been argued as a case involving an unforeseen medical emergency? Do you agree with the trial judge that a patient's refusal is valid even if it is not premised on an understanding of the risks? Would the decision have been the same if the plaintiff's daughter had not been a Jehovah's Witness and had urged Shulman to start the blood transfusions? For a discussion of a capable individual's broad common law right to refuse life-saving treatment, see *Re C (Adult: Refusal of Medical Treatment)*, [1994] 1 All E.R. 819 (Fam. Div.); and *Re B (Consent to Treatment: Capacity)*, [2002] 2 All E.R. 449 (Fam. Div.).

3. How sure must a healthcare professional be that the patient prefers death to treatment? What should healthcare professionals do if they suspect that a patient who is refusing life-saving treatment is drunk or high, has a concussion, or is in shock?

4. What are the implications of *Malette* for cases of attempted suicide? Would you advise a doctor to pump the stomach of an unconscious patient who had taken a potentially lethal overdose of drugs and left a note explaining why dying was preferable to living? Would the patient's reasons for wanting to die be relevant? What if the doctor was convinced that the patient was in a situational crisis and would want to live if he or she could be kept alive for several days?

In *Matheson v. Smiley*, [1932] 2 D.L.R. 787 (Man. C.A.), the deceased's estate was held liable for the services that a physician provided immediately prior to the deceased's death even though the deceased had shot himself in the head and resisted the physician's efforts to save his life. Would the court reach the same result today?

5. In light of *Malette*, can a competent patient give a binding advance directive not to be resuscitated? See Silberfield, Madigan & Dickens, "Liability Concerns about the Implementation of Advance Directives" (1995) 14 Est. & Tr. J. 240; and Hilder & Shariff, "Chapter 24: Advance Directives" in Irvine, Osborne & Shariff, eds., *Canadian Medical Law*, 4th ed. (2013) 675.

6. Should health professionals be able to put a "do not resuscitate" (DNR) order on a patient's chart when they conclude that resuscitation is futile, harmful or medically inappropriate, despite the patient's objections or those of his or her family? How does a physician's decision not to resuscitate differ from a decision not to operate or initiate other treatment that the physician concludes is futile, harmful or

medically inappropriate? See *Child and Family Services of Central Manitoba v. Lavallee* (1997), 123 Man. R. (2d) 135 (C.A.); *Sweiss v. Alberta Health Services*, 2009 ABQB 691; and *Re M.(J.)*, 2011 CarswellOnt 1084 (C.C.B.) (WL Can).

While various medical organizations had indicated that physicians were entitled to place DNR orders on patients' charts, the approach to this issue is changing. For example, the College of Physicians and Surgeons of Ontario (CPSO) has stated that physicians do not have authority to unilaterally issue a DNR order. Rather, physicians must discuss the issue with the patient or his or her substitute decision maker (SDM) at the first reasonable opportunity. If the patient or SDM refuses to consent, the physician should follow the College's conflict resolution process, which may include applying to the Ontario Consent and Capacity Board. See CPSO, *Planning for and Providing Quality End-of-Life Care* (2015) at 7-8.

7. The Ontario *Health Care Consent Act, 1996*, S.O. 1996, c. 2, Sch. A, s. 21(1)1 provides that all substitute decision makers are bound by any prior known relevant wish expressed by the incapable person when he or she was 16 or older and capable. The wish is binding whether: it is included in a power of attorney or any other written document; it is expressed orally; it applies to a minor procedure or life-saving treatment; or it is based on a rational analysis, religious belief, irrational fear, or whim. Does the legislation strike the right balance between patient autonomy and the state's interest in preserving life? Does it adequately protect incapable patients from overzealous or unscrupulous family members who may have personal, religious, financial, or other reasons to ignore or misstate the patient's prior wishes?

8. A distinction must be drawn between stopping ongoing life-sustaining treatment and actively assisting another person in killing himself or herself. In *Rodriguez v. British Columbia (Attorney General)*, [1993] 3 S.C.R. 519, the plaintiff wanted a doctor to set up a device that she could use to end her own life at a time of her choosing. She had Lou Gehrig's disease (amyotrophic lateral sclerosis) and would gradually lose her ability to eat, speak, move, and breathe without a ventilator. Consequently, she challenged the prohibition against assisted suicide in s. 241 of the *Criminal Code*, claiming that it violated her *Charter* rights. In a 5:4 decision, the court upheld the constitutional validity of s. 241.

In *Carter v. Canada (Attorney General)*, 2015 SCC 5, the Supreme Court of Canada unanimously held that the total ban on physician-assisted suicide in s. 241 violated s. 7 of the *Charter*. Moreover, this total ban could not be justified under s. 1 of the *Charter*, in regard to competent adults with a grievous and irremediable medical condition that caused them enduring suffering. The court gave Parliament one year to amend s. 241 before the ruling came into force.

9. The resulting *Criminal Code* amendments permitted physicians and nurse practitioners in strictly limited circumstances to provide medical aid in dying to competent adults with a "grievous and irremediable medical condition." This term was narrowly defined to include only individuals who have a "serious and incurable illness, disease or disability" that causes them intolerable and "enduring physical or psychological suffering," and whose "natural death has become reasonably foreseeable." The amendments also required physicians and nurse practitioners to follow a detailed protocol, which included obtaining a second independent written opinion as to a patient's eligibility. The legislation expressly stated that healthcare

professionals were not required to provide or assist in providing medical aid in dying (s. 241.2(1) and (2)). The amendments were widely criticized as being too restrictive, particularly the requirement that the patient's natural death must be reasonably foreseeable. The amendments have and will likely continue to generate *Charter* challenges, at least some of which will likely be successful.

For a review of these developments and the Québec medical aid in dying legislation, see Giroux, "Informing the Future of End-of-Life Care in Canada: Lessons from the Quebec Legislative Experience" (2016) 39 Dal. L.J. 431.

Should physicians who are morally opposed to providing medical aid in dying be required to refer patients to physicians who are willing to provide these services? See *Christian Medical and Dental Society of Canada v. College of Physicians and Surgeons of Ontario*, 2018 ONSC 579, in which the court upheld the constitutionality of the College's mandatory referral policies.

10. In *Cuthbertson v. Rasouli*, 2013 SCC 53, the majority broadly interpreted the word "treatment" in the Ontario *Health Care Consent Act, 1996* to include the withdrawal of life support. Consequently, the majority ruled that the patient's consent or that of his or her substitute decision maker was required to discontinue ongoing life support. The two dissenting justices stated that the provision was never intended to include withdrawing life support and that physicians should not be required to provide futile care or care that is inconsistent with accepted medical practice. The physicians wanted to take Rasouli off of life support and provide only palliative care because he was in a persistent vegetative state with no prospect of recovery.

What impact does *Rasouli* have in other provinces? In the absence of a statute requiring consent, should health professionals be required to obtain consent to withdraw life-sustaining treatment that they conclude is futile, harmful or medically inappropriate? See *I.H.V. (Re)*, 2008 ABQB 250; and *Chalifoux v. Alberta Health Sciences*, 2014 ABQB 624.

(c) THE BURDEN OF PROOF AND CONSENT FORMS

Canadian courts have held that health professionals have the burden of proving consent on the balance of probabilities. In the absence of a statute to the contrary, the consent may be given orally or in writing. However, healthcare professionals should not be lulled into a false sense of security by having a signed consent form. The key issue is not whether the patient signed a piece of paper, but rather whether he or she understood the nature of the proposed procedures and their risks, benefits and alternatives. A signed consent form is merely one means of documenting consent. Thus, it should be seen as providing only some evidence, not conclusive proof, of consent.

A signed consent form is only as good as the information it contains and the circumstances in which it is signed. A consent form will be of little value if it: (a) is written in general terms that do not identify the proposed procedure and explain its risks, benefits and alternatives; (b) is too technical for the patient to understand; or (c) is presented to the patient as a mere formality or in circumstances in which there is no opportunity to read it.

NOTES AND QUESTIONS

1. In *Montaron v. Wagner* (1988), 84 A.R. 231 (Q.B.), aff'd (1989), 100 A.R. 194 (C.A.), the plaintiff, who had obvious difficulties understanding English, signed a form that purported to provide his consent to a procedure that was far more radical than that to which he had orally agreed. Since no attempt was made to ensure that he understood the procedure, the court held that the consent form was invalid. Would the result have been the same if the plaintiff's inability to read English had not been obvious? See also *Adan v. Davis* (1998), 43 C.C.L.T. (2d) 262 (Ont. Gen. Div.); and *Reid v. Maloney*, 2011 ABCA 355.

2. In *Brushett v. Cowan* (1990), 83 Nfld. & P.E.I.R. 66 (Nfld. C.A.), the plaintiff consented to a muscle biopsy and signed a form that stated, "I also consent to such further or alternative measures as may be found to be necessary during the course of the operation." In performing the biopsy, the defendant observed an abnormal area of bone and did a bone biopsy. The trial court held that the open-ended wording of the consent form was too general to provide consent for the bone biopsy. In contrast, the Court of Appeal held that the consent form should be interpreted broadly, consistent with the goal of determining the cause of the plaintiff's medical problem. Consequently, it held that the form provided consent for the bone biopsy. Which judgment is preferable? See also *O'Bonsawin v. Paradis* (1993), 15 C.C.L.T. (2d) 188 (Ont. Gen. Div.); *Reid, supra;* and *Mohsina v. Ornstein*, 2012 ONSC 6678.

3. For a discussion of the burden of proof and its relation to consent, see *McBain v. Laurentian Hospital* (1982), 35 C.P.C. 292 (Ont. H.C.); and Osborne, "Chapter 2: Consent to Treatment" in Irvine, Osborne & Shariff, eds., *Canadian Medical Law*, 4th ed. (2013) 19 at 24-26.

(d) COMPETENCY TO CONSENT

To be valid, consent must be given by a patient who is competent to consent. It should be noted that some healthcare statutes frame this issue in terms of capacity to consent. The common law test of competency focuses on the patient's ability to understand the nature of the proposed treatment and its risks, benefits and alternatives, and not on his or her ability to make a reasoned or prudent decision. By defining competency broadly, the common law safeguards the autonomy of the individual. A patient may be competent even if he or she is intoxicated or high, young, rash, immature, frail, developmentally delayed, or involuntarily detained in a psychiatric facility. This test must be applied on a case-by-case basis in terms of the specific risks of the proposed treatment. A patient may be competent to make some treatment decisions, but not others. Similarly, a patient may be competent to make treatment decisions at one point in time, but not at others. If the patient is competent, it is his or her consent alone that is relevant.

(i) *Minors*

While there is no minimum age of consent at common law for medical treatment, almost all of the reported cases involve patients who are at or above the age of puberty. If a young person is able to understand the nature of the proposed procedure and its risks, benefits and alternatives, his or her consent is valid and parental consent is not relevant. Healthcare professionals can encourage a competent youth to involve his or her parents, but they cannot disclose information to the parents without the youth's consent, except in narrowly defined circumstances.

Some courts and statutes have reframed the competency issue in terms of the "mature minor rule" which relies on indicia of independence and maturity as a guide to a youth's competency. This reframing of the competency test does not change the central issue or make it easier to resolve the challenges that often arise in these cases. In addition to competency, some provincial statutes (*e.g.* public hospitals, mental health, child welfare, and tissue donation statutes) may contain minimum age requirements for consent to specified procedures, tests and counselling.

C. v. WREN
(1986), 76 A.R. 115 (C.A.)

KERANS J.A.: [The judge began by emphasizing that the case was not about abortion, foetal rights or the operation of the hospital abortion committee. Rather, the only issue was the competency of the expectant mother to consent to the proposed procedure.]

. . .

A 16-year-old girl became pregnant by her boyfriend while she was living at home. Several weeks later, she abruptly left home and went elsewhere and has since avoided contact with her parents. She also attended on a physician and surgeon with a view to an abortion and has received approval for it by the statutory committee provided under the *Criminal Code*. The urgency of the matter is that a statutory deadline looms.

The suit here is by the parents against the doctor, and not the child. The doctor is not represented but the child has retained counsel and she intervenes.

. . .

The ground of appeal is that the learned chambers judge erred in finding that the expectant mother had given informed consent to the proposed surgical procedure.

The law in Alberta is that a surgeon may proceed with a surgical procedure immune from suits for assault if she or he has informed consent from the patient. That test was applied by the learned trial judge, and he found on the evidence before him that this child was capable of giving informed consent and had done so. Without more, that is an end to the matter.

It is argued before us today that informed consent means consent after consideration of issues like the ethics of abortion and the ethics of obligation by children to parents. It may be, as Lord Fraser has said in *Gillick v. West Norfolk & Wisbech Area Health Authority et al.*, [1985] 3 All E.R. 402, that doctors have an ethical obligation in circumstances like this to discuss issues of that sort with young patients. If so, the doctor would account to the College of Physicians and Surgeons for the performance of that obligation. That is not the issue before us today. Rather, the issue is whether these issues relate to the defence of consent to assault. In our view, they do not.

We agree with the learned chambers judge that no serious suggestion exists on the evidence here of a lack of informed consent. Accordingly, there are no grounds to enjoin the doctor from proceeding because there is no suggestion that there will be an illegal assault.

The real issue here relates to an obvious and painful dispute between parent and child about the appropriateness in non-medical terms of the proposed abortion. We express in that respect our sympathy both to the parents and the child for this unfortunate confrontation.

The real thrust of argument before us was that children should obey their parents and the courts should intervene to prevent others from interfering with parental control of those children who are committed to their custody and control. That is not quite the suit that has been brought here today, but we will deal with the issue. Parental rights (and obligations) clearly do exist and they do not wholly disappear until the age of majority. The modern law, however, is that the courts will exercise increasing restraint in that regard as a child grows to and through adolescence. The law and the development of the law in this respect was analyzed in detail by Lord Scarman in the *Gillick* case. He analyzes the law back to Blackstone and extracts this principle [at 421]:

> The principle is that parental right or power of control of the person and property of his child exists primarily to enable the parent to discharge his duty of maintenance, protection and education until he reaches such an age as to be able to look after himself and make his own decisions.

He then reviews the application of that principle in cases over the past century, especially in the "age of discretion" cases. He says [at 422]:

> The "age of discretion" cases are cases in which a parent or guardian (usually the father) has applied for habeas corpus to secure the return of his child who has left home without his consent. The courts would refuse an order if the child had attained the age of discretion, which came to be regarded as 14 for boys and 16 for girls, and did not wish to return. The principle underlying them was plainly that an order would be refused if the child had sufficient intelligence and understanding to make up his own mind.

He then concludes that the governing rule is [at 423]:

> In the light of the foregoing I would hold that as a matter of law the parental right to determine whether or not their minor child below the age of 16 will have medical treatment terminates if and when the child achieves a sufficient understanding and intelligence to enable him or her to understand fully what is proposed.

We accept that in that context he says that "understand fully" means understand things like obligation to parents as well as medical matters.

What is the application of the principle in this case? We infer from the circumstances detailed in argument here that this expectant mother and her parents had fully discussed the ethical issues involved and, most regrettably, disagreed. We cannot infer from that disagreement that this expectant mother did not have sufficient intelligence and understanding to make up her own mind. Meanwhile, it is conceded that she is a "normal intelligent 16 year old." We infer that she did have sufficient intelligence and understanding to make up her own mind and did so. At her age and level of understanding, the law is that she is to be permitted to do so.

Accordingly, we dismiss the appeal.

NOTES AND QUESTIONS

1. What was the basis for the decision in *C. v. Wren*? Would the court have reached the same decision if C. had been 14 years old and living at home? What impact, if any, would these factors have had on C.'s competency? See Robertson & Picard, *Legal Liability of Doctors and Hospitals in Canada*, 5th ed. (2017) at 100-10; and Osborne, "The Consent of Minors" in Irvine, Osborne & Shariff, eds., *Canadian Medical Law*, 4th ed. (2013) 37.

2. In *Re Dueck* (1999), 176 Sask. R. 152 (Q.B.), a 13-year-old boy refused chemotherapy and surgery, which the paediatric oncologist indicated had a 65% chance of resulting in recovery. The boy believed his father, who told him that God would heal him and that there was a treatment in California and Mexico that had an 85% to 90% cure rate without surgery. This "treatment" was not medically recognized, and there was no evidence that it had any beneficial effect. The psychologist and psychiatrist indicated that the boy had no developmental impairment that would prevent him from being competent. However, the boy was less mature than the average 13-year-old, and his father was a dominating authority figure who made the rules in the house.

The court stated that if the boy was a mature minor (*i.e.* competent), then his wishes would be respected. In making this determination, the court considered the boy's age and maturity, the extent of his dependence on his parents, and the complexity of the treatment. Given the profound influence of the domineering father and his misguided faith in a non-existent cure, the boy was not able to understand the relevant medical information or appreciate the consequences of the proposed treatment. Consequently, the boy was not a mature minor and an order was made extending the Minister's authority to make medical decisions on the boy's behalf.

When the cancer spread to the boy's lungs, further legal proceedings were halted. The parents spent $65,000 taking their son to a Mexican clinic, where he was treated with diet, herbs and multivitamins. Although the clinic had reported that there was no evidence of cancer in the boy's lungs, he died 70 days after returning to Canada.

Do you agree that the boy was not a mature minor? Would the court have reached the same conclusion if the boy, rather than his father, believed in the efficacy of the Mexican clinic's "treatment"?

3. In *A.C. v. Manitoba (Director of Child and Family Services)*, [2009] 2 S.C.R. 181, an almost 15-year-old devout Jehovah's Witness was apprehended as a child in need of protection under *The Child and Family Services Act*, C.C.S.M. c. 80 (*CFSA*) when she refused blood transfusions. A.C. was assessed by three psychiatrists and found to be competent. Nevertheless, the Director of Child and Family Services sought an order under s. 25(8), which authorizes a court to order treatment in an apprehended child's best interests if the child is under the age of 16. Section 2(1) requires all relevant factors to be considered in assessing a child's best interests, including his or her: mental, emotional and physical needs; mental, emotional and physical stage of development; views and preferences; and cultural, linguistic, racial, and religious heritage. The court assumed that A.C. was competent. While the court considered her maturity, strong religious beliefs and clear wish not to receive blood, it concluded that it was in A.C.'s best interests to be given blood transfusions as she was in danger of imminent death or serious injury. A.C.'s appeal ultimately reached the Supreme Court of Canada, primarily on the issue of whether s. 25(8) violated her *Charter* rights under

s. 2(a) (freedom of religion), s. 7 (security of the person) and s. 15 (equal protection and benefit of the law).

The majority of the Supreme Court ruled that if a best interests standard, as in s. 25(8), takes into increasing account the young person's views in accordance with his or her maturity, it will not violate the *Charter*. The dissent ruled that s. 25(8) violated A.C.'s *Charter* rights under s. 2(a) and s. 7, and that these violations could not be justified under s. 1. Once it was established that A.C. was competent to make her own medical decisions, overriding her decision could not be justified regardless of the dire consequences of her choice. Which judgment do you prefer?

The child welfare legislation in Ontario and some other provinces does not include authority to override a competent child's refusal of life-saving treatment. Thus, in these provinces there is no statutory basis for challenging a child's decision in a case like *A.C.* As a matter of policy, should those under the age of 16 be permitted to refuse life-saving treatment? Should a refusal based on religious grounds be treated differently than refusals based on other criteria? For other cases involving Jehovah's Witnesses, youth and blood transfusions, see *Re K.(L.D.)* (1985), 48 R.F.L. (2d) 164 (Ont. Prov. Ct.) (12-year-old); *Walker (Litigation Guardian of) v. Region 2 Hospital Corp.* (1994), 150 N.B.R. (2d) 366 (C.A.) (15-year-old); and *B.(R.) v. Children's Aid Society of Metropolitan Toronto*, [1995] 1 S.C.R. 315 (infant).

4. In *C.(L.) v. Pinhas*, 2002 CarswellOnt 4793 (S.C.J.) (WL Can), the 15-year-old plaintiff was hospitalized for anorexia. The psychiatrists found that she lacked capacity to make decisions about the proposed tube-feeding to which she had objected. The plaintiff challenged the psychiatrists' finding to the Ontario Consent and Capacity Board. According to the psychiatrists, the illness itself prevented the plaintiff from making informed decisions even though she intellectually understood the life-threatening risks of continuing to not eat. The Board concluded that she was not capable, and the plaintiff appealed. The court agreed with the Board that the patient's noncompliance was relevant to capacity in psychiatric disorders such as anorexia, where the patient is intellectually capable of understanding the medical risks of refusing treatment. Do you agree that the plaintiff was not capable? Would the court have reached the same conclusion if the plaintiff had been 20 years old or the case had arisen in Manitoba? See also *Re W (a minor)*, [1992] 4 All E.R. 627 (C.A.) (16-year-old with anorexia); *Chmiliar v. Chmiliar* (2001), 295 A.R. 140 (Q.B.) (10 and 13-year-old children not vaccinated for meningitis and some other diseases); and *Hamilton Health Sciences Corp. v. D.H.*, 2014 ONCJ 603 (11-year-old requiring chemotherapy).

5. As discussed, Canadian courts have negated the plaintiff's otherwise valid consent on various "public policy" grounds. Should a competent child's refusal of life-sustaining treatment be negated on public policy grounds? What would be the justification for overriding a competent minor's medical decision in these circumstances, but not that of a competent adult?

REVIEW PROBLEM

The Children's Aid Society received information that Sara, who is 13, had been sexually abused by her father. When asked, Sara denied the allegations and became very upset. She expressed concern about the impact that such a charge would have on her father and family. Sara's school friends said that Sara is afraid of her father. The

Society has requested that Sara undergo a medical examination at the local Children's Hospital. Both Sara and her parents have refused consent to the examination. Advise the Society as to its potential tort liability if it proceeds with the examination. See *M.(J.) v. Toronto Board of Education* (1987), 59 O.R. (2d) 649 (H.C.).

(ii) *Adults*

The issue of an adult's competency to consent arises most often in cases involving patients who have a mental illness, a developmental disability or dementia. Healthcare professionals must start from the assumption that the patient is competent and assess his or her competency in relation to the specific treatment decision that has to be made.

These principles apply equally to those in custody or under other legal restraints, unless there is express statutory authority to the contrary. For example, the fact that a patient's refusal to consent to treatment may violate his or her probation does not alter the healthcare professional's obligation to abide by the decision.

NOTES AND QUESTIONS

1. In *Starson v. Swayze*, [2003] 1 S.C.R. 722, the patient had been frequently institutionalized. His latest psychiatric admission resulted from being found not criminally responsible by reason of mental disability for making death threats. The patient insisted on being called Professor Starson even though he held no academic position and Starson was not his family name. Starson had numerous delusional beliefs. He talked about running "Starson Corporation" from inside his inpatient unit, insisted that he was on the leading edge of building a starship, claimed to be a world-class skier and arm-wrestler, and asserted that he communicated with extraterrestrial beings. His psychiatrist concluded that he suffered from a bipolar disorder and prescribed anti-psychotic medication.

Starson refused the medication because he believed that similar medication had previously interfered with his research. However, his mother stated that he had only written scientific papers prior to 1998 when he was taking his medication. Although not formally trained, Starson was brilliant, had in the past published extensively, and had been accepted as a peer by some leading physicists. Starson's psychiatrist believed that he lacked capacity to refuse consent to the proposed medication. After Starson threatened to kill his first psychiatrist, a second psychiatrist was called in and he also concluded that Starson was not capable. The Consent and Capacity Board upheld the psychiatrists' findings.

Starson appealed the Board's decision. The court was extremely critical of the Board's reliance on the psychiatrists' recounting of Starson's medical and criminal records without introducing the documents into evidence. The court stated that Starson acknowledged that he had mental health problems and showed understanding of his condition. He made a clear choice to reject the medication because it interfered with the high energy level that he believed was conducive to creative thought. The court concluded that Starson was capable because he understood the relevant information and appreciated the consequences of his decision. The Court of Appeal for Ontario and the majority of the Supreme Court of Canada upheld the trial judgment.

The three dissenting Supreme Court justices held that there was no basis for overturning the Board's finding of incapacity. They stated that there was ample evidence that Starson was in "almost total" denial of his mental illness. This denial was compounded by his inability, because of his delusional state, to understand the information relevant to making a treatment decision. The dissenting justices held that: Starson lacked the ability to appreciate the possible benefits of the proposed medication; he would be unlikely to return to his previous level of functioning without the medication; his condition could deteriorate further; and the lack of treatment would likely prevent his future release.

The Ontario Review Board denied Starson's subsequent application for release and the Court of Appeal upheld that decision. Starson remained untreated and, as predicted, his condition deteriorated. He became floridly psychotic, refusing to eat or drink because he believed that the devil would torture his imaginary son. In 2005, when it became apparent that Starson might die, his treating physician found him to be incapable of refusing treatment. The Board affirmed the decision and Starson was treated with the medication that he had previously refused. His condition improved immediately and he was released in 2007. He had to be readmitted in 2008 after he stopped taking his medication, but was subsequently allowed to return to the community. On July 17, 2014, the Ontario Review Board ordered that Starson be detained at the Centre for Addiction and Mental Health.

Would the courts have reached the same initial conclusion on Starson's capacity had he not been as scientifically accomplished? Is it in the interests of society or mentally-ill patients to detain individuals in psychiatric hospitals without treatment? See Kelly *et al.*, "Treatment Delays for Involuntary Psychiatric Patients Associated with Reviews of Treatment Capacity" (2002) 47 Can. J. Psychiatry 181; and Solomon *et al.*, "Treatment Delayed — Liberty Denied" (2009) 87 Can. Bar Rev. 679.

2. For additional cases on competency and mental health patients, see *Re C (Adult: Refusal of Medical Treatment)*, [1994] 1 All E.R. 819 (Fam. Div.); *Neto v. Klukach* (2004), 12 Admin. L.R. (4th) 101 (Ont. S.C.J.); and *D'Almeida v. Barron* (2010), 103 O.R. (3d) 250 (C.A.); *Coburn v. Wilkie*, 2016 ONCA 876; and *Ranieri v. Nagari*, 2017 ONCA 336.

3. The number of cases involving the capacity of seniors to make personal care and financial decisions has increased. See for example *Bartoszek v. Ontario (Consent and Capacity Board)*, 2002 CarswellOnt 3265 (S.C.J.) (WL Can); *Penny v. Bolen*, 2008 CarswellOnt 5644 (S.C.J.) (WL Can); and *Park v. Park*, 2010 ONSC 2627. Consistent with the other cases, the court in *Park* stated that a person's right to make personal care and property decisions should only be removed in the clearest of cases. See also *Bentley (Litigation Guardian of) v. Maplewood Seniors Care Society*, 2015 BCCA 91; and Wahl, Leclair & Himel, "The Geriatric Patient" in Bloom & Bay, eds., *A Practical Guide to Mental Health, Capacity and Consent Law of Ontario* (1996) 343.

4. The Canadian courts have held that consent given while a patient is sedated or in pain may be invalid. See *Beausoleil v. Soeurs de la Charité de la Providence* (1964), 53 D.L.R. (2d) 65 (Qc. Q.B.); and *Ferguson v. Hamilton Civic Hospitals* (1983), 40 O.R. (2d) 577 (H.C.), aff'd (1985), 50 O.R. (2d) 754 (C.A.). In *Mitchell v. McDonald* (1987), 80 A.R. 16 (Q.B.), the court held that the plaintiff's agonized plea, "For God's sake, stop," in the middle of an injection did not constitute an express withdrawal of

consent, but rather a plea to stop the pain. See also *Ciarlariello v. Schacter*, [1993] 2 S.C.R. 119.

5. In the absence of a statute to the contrary, the fact that a patient is a suspect, prisoner or parolee does not alter the obligation of health professionals to obtain his or her consent. See Somerville, "Refusal of Medical Treatment in 'Captive' Circumstances" (1985) 63 Can. Bar Rev. 59; and Miller, "The US Supreme Court Looks at Voluntariness and Consent" (1994) 17 Int'l J. L. & Psychiatry 239.

(e) SUBSTITUTE CONSENT TO TREATMENT

Some patients, such as young children, are clearly incapable of giving or refusing consent to treatment. The practice in such cases has been for healthcare professionals to obtain substitute consent from the patient's next-of-kin. The courts have upheld the validity of such consent provided the patient was incompetent, the next-of-kin acted in good faith and the decision was in the patient's best interest. While relatively easy to state, these principles may be extremely difficult to apply. While the common law principles of substitute consent have been replaced by statutes in several provinces, much of the legislation replicates the common law.

NOTES AND QUESTIONS

1. For examples of provincial substitute consent statutes, see *Substitute Decisions Act, 1992*, S.O. 1992, c. 30; *The Health Care Directives and Substitute Health Care Decision Makers Act, 2015*, S.S. 2015, c. H-0.002; *Advance Health Care Directives Act*, R.S.N.B. 2016, c. 46; and *The Health Care Directives Act*, C.C.S.M., c. H27.

2. In *E.(Mrs.) v. Eve*, [1986] 2 S.C.R. 388, La Forest J., speaking for the court, held that the non-therapeutic sterilization of a mentally incompetent adult could never be justified as being in a patient's best interests. However, in *Re B (a minor) (wardship: sterilization)*, [1987] 2 All E.R. 206 at 213 (H.L.), Lord Hailsham stated in regard to La Forest J.'s analysis:

> I find, with great respect, his conclusion . . . that the procedure of sterilisation 'should *never* be authorised for non-therapeutic purposes' (my emphasis) totally unconvincing and in startling contradiction to the welfare principle which should be the first and paramount consideration in wardship cases. Moreover, . . . the distinction he purports to draw between 'therapeutic' and 'non-therapeutic' purposes of this operation . . . [is] totally meaningless . . . . To talk of the 'basic right' to reproduce of an individual who is not capable of knowing the causal connection between intercourse and childbirth, the nature of pregnancy, what is involved in delivery, unable to form maternal instincts or to care for a child appears to me wholly to part company with reality.

Which judgment is preferable? See Grubb & Pearl, "Sterilisation and the Courts" (1987), 46 C.L.J. 439; Olesen, "Eve and the Forbidden Fruit: Reflections on a Feminist Methodology" (1994) 3 Dal. J. Leg. Studies 231; and Shariff, "Chapter 15: Issues in Reproductive Choice: Part 2" in Irvine, Osborne & Shariff, eds., *Canadian Medical Law*, 4th ed. (2013) 365 at 366-80.

3. In *Re K. and Public Trustee* (1985), 63 B.C.L.R. 145 (C.A.), the court authorized a hysterectomy on a girl with a severe mental disability who had a phobic aversion to

blood and would otherwise begin menstruation soon. In *E.(Mrs.)*, *supra* the Supreme Court of Canada questioned the decision in *Re K.*, but ultimately distinguished it on the grounds that it did not deal with sterilization for contraceptive purposes. Do you agree? See also *Secretary, Department of Health and Community Services v. J.W.B.* (1992), 175 C.L.R. 218 (H.C.A.); and *In Re F (Mental Patient: Sterilization)*, [1990] 2 A.C. 1 (H.L.).

4. In *E.(Mrs.)*, *supra*, the court emphasized that the interests of others cannot be considered in exercising substitute consent on behalf of incompetent patients. Is the court disadvantaging incompetent individuals by ignoring the critical role of their caregivers? What are the implications of the court's approach for the validity of substitute consent to medical research, tissue and organ donations, and circumcision for religious purposes? See Baylis, Downie & Kenny, "Children and Decisionmaking in Health Research" (1999) 8 Health L. Rev. 3.

5. In *Hamilton Health Sciences Corp. v. D.H.*, 2014 ONCJ 603, the mother of an 11-year-old girl withdrew her from chemotherapy at the Hamilton Health Sciences Centre to pursue an "alternative cancer treatment" in Florida. It was accepted that the girl was not capable of making her own medical decisions and that her mother was her substitute decision maker. The girl's paediatric oncologists testified that she had a 90% to 95% chance of being cured with continued chemotherapy. Moreover, they were not aware of any child surviving this type of leukemia without chemotherapy. When the Children's Aid Society refused to intervene, the Centre applied for a protection order under the *Child and Family Services Act*, declaring the girl to be a child in need of protection and requiring the Society to bring her to a place of safety. The term "child in need of protection" in the Act includes situations in which parents or guardians refuse consent to needed medical treatment for their child.

The Court refused to issue the requested order. It stated that the girl was not in need of protection because her mother was "a caring loving parent" and was acting in accordance with her culture and beliefs as a Six Nations Band member. The Court stated that the mother's decision was protected under s. 35(1) of the *Constitution Act, 1982*, which recognizes and affirms Aboriginal and treaty rights.

When her daughter's cancer returned, the mother decided to resume chemotherapy in "conjunction" with traditional medicine. In an attempt to clarify the initial ruling, the parties made a joint submission recognizing that the child's best interests were paramount and that the aboriginal right to use traditional medicine was one of the factors that had to be considered in making that determination. The parties also agreed that given the collaborative approach, the daughter was not in need of protection. The Court adopted the joint submission as an addendum to the original decision: *Hamilton Health Sciences Corp. v. D.H.*, 2015 ONCJ 229.

There was a similar case in which the court refused to intervene. In that case, an 11-year-old First Nations girl suffering from the same type of leukemia died in January 2015 after her parents stopped chemotherapy and took her to the alternative cancer treatment centre in Florida. In a statement, the family claimed that the girl died as a result of the chemotherapy and not cancer.

Can you reconcile the courts' approach in these two cases with that taken by the courts in cases involving Jehovah's Witnesses who refuse to consent to blood transfusions for their critically-ill children?

6. *D.H.* raises numerous troubling issues. For example, the alternative cancer treatment in Florida was not based on traditional Aboriginal beliefs and there was no basis for believing that it would be of any medical or other benefit. Second, the Supreme Court of Canada unanimously held in *E.(Mrs.)*, *supra*, and other cases, that treatment decisions must be made exclusively in an incapable patient's best interests and that the interests of others are not to be considered. Consequently, the mother's cultural heritage and beliefs were irrelevant in making treatment decisions for the child. Third, the fact that the mother was a "caring loving parent" did not alter the fact that her continued refusal to consent to chemotherapy for her daughter would almost certainly result in the child's death.

7. In contrast to the approach adopted in *D.H.*, see *C.M.G. v. D.W.S.*, 2015 ONSC 2201. In *C.M.G.*, the parents, who had joint custody, disagreed on whether their daughter could go on holiday to Germany without being vaccinated. The mother, who believed in homeopathic medicine and vehemently opposed vaccinations, submitted a detailed affidavit and called two "expert" witnesses. In rejecting this evidence, the judge stated that "I find that the mother and her supporting witnesses are locked in a never-ending spiral of blind acceptance of statements by individuals who claim to be experts in the field in which they are not. . . . Most of the supporting research offered by the mother and her supporters is not valid and does not consider objective facts, research and literature that are thorough and peer reviewed." Relying on the evidence of a leading Canadian expert on infectious diseases and immunization, the judge concluded that vaccination was in the girl's best interests. The judge granted the father's motion for sole authority to make medical decisions on the girl's behalf and ordered that the daughter be vaccinated prior to being taken to Germany.

8. In *Muir v. Alberta* (1996), 179 A.R. 321 (Q.B.), the Alberta government was held liable for almost $750,000 for wrongfully institutionalizing and sterilizing the plaintiff under the provincial "mental defectives" legislation. Among other things, the province was held liable for: failing to follow its own legislation in institutionalizing the plaintiff as a "moron"; failing to undertake a timely social or psychological assessment; ignoring an expert who indicated that the plaintiff's problems stemmed from her chaotic home life and not from mental disability; giving her anti-psychotic medication from time to time even though she had never been diagnosed as being psychotic; and sterilizing her contrary to the statute.

Over 2,900 people had been sterilized under the provincial statute. It had been enacted in 1928 and was not repealed until 1972, well after the eugenics movement had been discredited. British Columbia and at least 15 American states had similar legislation. After a failed attempt to legislatively limit similar claims, Alberta created an $80 million compensation package for approximately 290 individuals. See also *E.(D.) (Guardian ad litem of) v. British Columbia* (2005), 28 C.C.L.T. (3d) 283 (B.C.C.A.).

9. *In Re A (Children) (Conjoined Twins: Surgical Separation)*, [2000] 4 All E.R. 961 (C.A.), Jodie and Mary were born joined at the pelvis. The medical evidence indicated that if they were not separated, both would certainly die within three to six months. The evidence also indicated that if they were separated, Mary would certainly die but Jodie would most likely live. The twins' parents, devout Roman Catholics, refused to consent to the operation on religious grounds. They believed that Jodie and Mary

were equal in God's eyes and that one could not be sacrificed for the other. Nevertheless, the court upheld a declaration authorizing the surgery. Although the paramount consideration was the children's welfare, the court stated that it was entitled to prefer Jodie's interests over Mary's, given the exceptional circumstances. It had to choose "the lesser of two evils." The court also reiterated that, in the case of young children, the parents' wishes are not always determinative. Finally, the court held that while the surgeon's proposed actions would otherwise constitute a crime, namely killing Mary, the defence of necessity would apply.

Do you agree with the court's decision? Assume that conjoined twins who currently share a single kidney will both die if they are not separated and that, if separated, the twin given the kidney will live and the other twin will die. Assume as well that each twin has an equal chance of survival if given the shared kidney. On what basis would you decide in favour of one twin over the other? See Bainham, "Resolving the Unresolvable: The Case of the Conjoined Twins" [2001] C.L.J. 49.

10. In what circumstances, if any, is it appropriate for parents to deny or withhold life-sustaining treatment from a disabled child? See *The Children's Aid Society of Ottawa-Carleton v. M.C.* (2008), 301 D.L.R. (4th) 194 (Ont. S.C.J.); and *Re M.(J.)*, 2011 CarswellOnt 1084 (C.C.B.) (WL Can). See also Griffith, "The Best Interests Standard: A Comparison of the State's Parens Patriae Authority and Judicial Oversight in Best Interests Determinations for Children and Incompetent Patients" (1991) 7 Issues L. & Med. 283; and Shariff, "Chapter 23: Foregoing of Treatment for Neonates and Pre-Adolescents" in Irvine, Osborne & Shariff, eds., *Canadian Medical Law*, 4th ed. (2013) 651.

11. In *Superintendent of Belchertown State School v. Saikewicz*, 370 N.E.2d 417 (Mass. S.C. 1977), the court considered whether a 67-year-old man who was dying of leukaemia should undergo painful chemotherapy to prolong his life. The chemotherapy would not provide a cure, but rather a 30% to 40% chance of a temporary remission, which on average prolonged the life of patients by one year. Saikewicz had an IQ of 10 and could not co-operate with chemotherapy. He was not in any pain and was expected to die relatively painlessly within weeks or months if he was not given chemotherapy. The trial court held that the chemotherapy was not in Saikewicz's best interests and ordered that no treatment be administered. The appeal court affirmed the decision.

Was it in Saikewicz's best interests to be allowed to die without treatment? Do you think the decision would have been the same if the therapy had a 30% to 40% chance of prolonging his life by five years? What are the implications of *Saikewicz* for patients who are in a coma? See generally *Frenchay Healthcare National Health Service Trust v. S.*, [1994] 2 All E.R. 403 (C.A.); *Janzen v. Janzen* (2002), 44 E.T.R. (2d) 217 (Ont. S.C.J.); *Schiavo ex rel. Schindler v. Schiavo*, 544 U.S. 957 (2005); *Bentley (Litigation Guardian of) v. Maplewood Seniors Care Society*, 2015 BCCA 91; and Shariff, "The Mentally Incompetent Adult Patient and the Foregoing of Life-Prolonging Treatment" in Irvine, Osborne & Shariff, eds., *Canadian Medical Law*, 4th ed. (2013) 609.

(f) INFORMED CONSENT: BATTERY OR NEGLIGENCE?

Traditionally, a doctor's failure to obtain a valid consent was viewed as a basis for a battery claim, whether the lack of consent was due to a failure to disclose the risks or misrepresentation. In the late 1950s, the American courts began to analyze some medical consent cases in terms of negligence, asking whether the doctor failed to exercise a reasonable standard of care in advising the patient of the nature of the procedure and its risks. The Canadian courts adopted a similar approach. As in the United States, this development created uncertainty as to the boundary between medical battery and medical negligence.

The Supreme Court of Canada addressed this issue in *Reibl v. Hughes*, [1980] 2 S.C.R. 880 and *Hopp v. Lepp*, [1980] 2 S.C.R. 192. It held that once patients are aware of the general nature of the treatment, they cannot bring a battery claim alleging that they were not informed of the risks. Rather, battery claims are limited to cases in which the patient did not consent at all, the consent was exceeded, or the consent was obtained fraudulently. In all other cases, the plaintiff must bring a negligence claim for failure to disclose the risks. By requiring a plaintiff to frame these actions in negligence, the Supreme Court of Canada has significantly limited the scope of health professionals' potential liability.

NOTE

1. Most provinces have incorporated the concept of informed consent into their healthcare legislation. For example, the *Health Care Consent Act, 1996*, S.O. 1996, c. 2, Sch. A, s. 11(2) makes informed consent a required element of a consent to treatment. See also *Health Care (Consent) and Care Facility (Admissions) Act*, R.S.B.C. 1996, c. 181, s. 6(e). Nevertheless, the courts have not held health practitioners liable in battery when they have failed to obtain an informed consent as required by these statutory provisions. Rather, the courts have continued to apply the restrictive grounds for suing in battery set out in *Reibl* and *Hopp*. See Robertson & Picard, *Legal Liability of Doctors and Hospitals in Canada*, 5th ed. (2017) at 158-61.

REVIEW PROBLEM

A physician has contacted you about a 62-year-old alcoholic patient in the emergency room. The patient, who lives alone, fell down his stairs and lay there for several hours before his daughter found him. The patient has a bad gash that requires stitches, but the physician is more concerned about the patient's alcoholism, which has repeatedly brought him into hospital since his wife died two years ago. The physician wants to admit the patient to the hospital for about a week in order to "sober him up," conduct medical tests and procedures related to his alcoholism, stabilize his deteriorating physical condition, and encourage him to enter an alcohol treatment program.

The patient is still somewhat intoxicated, but fully aware of his surroundings. At his daughter's urging, he has reluctantly agreed to have the gash sutured, sleep over in the hospital, and undergo "any stupid tests you want." However, the patient vehemently denies that he is an alcoholic or that his drinking has caused any problems in his life. If his past behaviour is any indication, the patient will leave the next day as soon as he feels well enough to get a cab and go home.

The patient's daughter has pleaded with the physician to keep her father in the hospital long enough to get him back on his feet and break his cycle of self-destructive behaviour. In the daughter's view, her father's denial of his alcoholism and rapidly deteriorating physical and mental health provide overwhelming proof of his incompetency. She is willing to sign whatever documents are necessary to give substitute consent for her father's hospitalization and treatment.

The physician has sought your advice on two issues. First, is the patient currently competent to consent to his admission to hospital and treatment? Second, would the patient be competent to refuse treatment and leave the hospital tomorrow?

DEFENCES RELATED TO THE PROTECTION OF PERSON AND PROPERTY

1. Introduction
2. Self-Defence
3. Defence of Third Parties
4. Discipline
5. Defence of Real Property
6. Defence and Recaption of Chattels
7. Public and Private Necessity
8. Apportionment of Fault in Intentional Torts

1. Introduction

In the previous chapter, we began an examination of the defences to intentional torts by considering the defence of consent. In this chapter, we consider several defences pertaining to the protection of person and property.

2. Self-Defence

In order to invoke the defence of self-defence, individuals must establish on the balance of probabilities that: (a) they honestly and reasonably believed that they were about to be struck; and (b) the amount of force that they used to protect themselves was reasonable in all of the circumstances. An individual's right to invoke the defence ends once the danger has passed. Self-defence is a complete defence. If the defendant successfully invokes the defence, he or she will be absolved of liability.

WACKETT v. CALDER
(1965), 51 D.L.R. (2d) 598 (B.C.C.A.)

MACLEAN J.A. (dissenting):—The defendant appeals a judgment for damages for an assault following an encounter between the plaintiff and defendant in a beer parlour at Dawson Creek, B.C.

The facts have been found by the learned trial Judge as follows:

The most accurate account of what occurred outside the hotel is to be found in the evidence of the defendant and of his brother, Raymond Calder, both of whom were truthful witnesses. The plaintiff testified untruthfully on so many occasions as to the events that occurred earlier that afternoon and during the evening in question that it is impossible to give any credence to his evidence except where it is corroborated by other credible evidence. Having arrived outside, the plaintiff reiterated his insulting remarks and invited the defendant to engage in a fight. He endeavoured, without much success, to strike both the defendant and his brother. He lurched at them and with his fists pounded them in a rather futile way upon their chests, doing no harm whatever. On one occasion when the plaintiff struck at the defendant, the defendant hit the plaintiff in the face with his fist, knocking the plaintiff to the ground. The plaintiff got up and went for the defendant again. The defendant hit him again and that time the plaintiff "didn't get up so fast." The defendant then returned to the beer parlour, leaving the plaintiff still wanting to fight.

The learned Judge then went on to find that the force used by the defendant was excessive under the circumstances, and finally he concluded:

> The anger of the defendant is easily understood, but it is the policy of the law to discourage violence. Challenges to fight are accepted at some considerable peril, at law. It must have been apparent to the defendant soon after he went outside that the plaintiff's challenge to fight was alcoholic-induced bravado and that, by reason of his intoxication, he was incapable of anything but talk and wild swinging. The defendant could and should have terminated the whole unpleasant episode by returning into the hotel, leaving the authorities to deal with the plaintiff. Instead he delivered two blows to the face of the plaintiff with considerable force — sufficient to knock him down and break a well-protected bone in the cheek. While it is not clear how the plaintiff's wrist got broken, I think it is probable that he must have fallen upon it during the fight.

In my view there is implicit in this judgment a finding that the defendant was not entitled to rely on self-defence — he could have walked away and avoided "the unpleasant episode by returning to the hotel", and secondly, that even if he was entitled to use force to defend himself, he used "excessive force under the circumstances".

I take it that in coming to the latter conclusion the learned Judge was aware of the long line of cases which enunciate the principle that a defendant or accused person when attacked is not required to "measure with complete nicety" the force necessary to repel the attack or apprehended attack: *R. v. Ogal*, [1928] 3 D.L.R. 676, 50 C.C.C. 71, 23 A.L.R. 511, [1928] 2 W.W.R. 465.

In my view the learned Judge's conclusions are supported by the evidence and I would not venture to disturb his judgment.

I would dismiss the appeal.

BULL J.A. [Davey J.A. concurring]: . . . It is clear that what constitutes excessive force beyond what was reasonably necessary under all circumstances depends in each case upon its own facts, and is a matter for the trial Judge, the findings of whom an appellate Court should not lightly question. However, with the greatest deference, it seems apparent that the finding of excessive force was based on conclusions and inferences from evidence which did not wholly support them. Although there was evidence that the respondent was clearly intoxicated, there was no evidence that he was physically incapacitated or unduly uncoordinated, or in any way incapable of doing serious physical damage to others. He was a man of middle age weighing some 192 pounds and the evidence was clear that he was not staggering, but was in a belligerent and obviously dangerous mood. Again, the learned trial Judge, in giving his views as to what the appellant might have done to end the dispute, seems to have overlooked the evidence of both the appellant and his brother, both of whom he found truthful witnesses, that they were turning away to re-enter the hotel when the respondent attacked and struck the appellant the second time and, received, in turn, the appellant's second blow. It seemed clear that it was this second blow which was the most serious and caused the injury to the defendant's face.

As the learned trial Judge weighed the force used on conclusions which were, in part at least, unsupported by the evidence, an appellate Court is justified in reassessing the evidence directed to this issue and is, I submit with deference, in as good a position as the trial Judge so to do.

The only question here was whether the two blows by the appellant were more than reasonably necessary under all the attendant circumstances, and no question of the use of disproportionate force is involved. The appellant was entitled to reject force with force and, under the authorities, not being bound to take a passive defence, is entitled to return blow for blow. He could act in the light of the apparent urgency of the situation, but he could not trespass beyond the reasonable limits thereof. However, it has been long held that an attacked person defending himself and confronted with a provoking situation is not held down to measure with exactitude or nicety the weight or power of his blows.

In this case there is no evidence whatsoever that the two blows given by appellant were vicious. That one at least was forceful is obvious, but the combined effect of both were not sufficient to render the intoxicated respondent "hors de combat". The first blow was insufficient to stop the respondent's attack on the appellant, and, in my respectful opinion, the second more forceful blow was well justified to put an end to the episode.

Accordingly, on the facts as found by the learned trial Judge, excluding only his conclusions as to the quantum or measure of force used, I would allow the appeal and order the action dismissed.

NOTES AND QUESTIONS

1. Was the defendant in danger of physical injury? Must the defendant prove that the plaintiff posed a threat of physical injury, or merely a threat of any socially offensive or physically harmful contact? See *Cachay v. Nemeth* (1972), 28 D.L.R. (3d) 603 (Sask. Q.B.).

2. Is Maclean J.A. suggesting that self-defence cannot be raised by a defendant who ignored an opportunity to walk away from a fight? Would you favour the adoption of this principle?

More than 20 American states have enacted "stand your ground laws" that allow the use of deadly force to defend oneself rather than refusing to fight or walking away. In a 2018 Florida case, when a man was pushed to the ground in a dispute over a parking space, he pulled a gun and killed the deceased who was standing several feet away. The police refused to lay criminal charges based on the state's "stand your ground law" despite the fact that the unarmed man was shot without any warning. The sheriff appears to have assumed that the shooter's immediate resort to deadly force was justified in the circumstances. Jacobs, "'Stand Your Ground' Cited by Florida Sheriff Who Declined to Arrest Suspect in Killing" *The New York Times* (21 July 2018), online: < https://www.nytimes.com/2018/07/21/us/florida-stand-your-ground.html >. After several weeks of protests, the county state attorney charged the shooter with manslaughter. As in this and many other high-profile cases, the shooter was white and the victim was black. See Ackermann *et al.*, "Race, law, and health: Examination of 'Stand Your Ground' and defendant convictions in Florida" (2015) 142 Social Science & Medicine 194.

3.   Similar concerns were raised in two 2018 Canadian cases in which young unarmed indigenous men were shot and killed when confronted on the property of the accused homeowners. In both cases, the deceased was alleged to be in the midst of stealing or rummaging through a vehicle of the homeowner, and in both cases, the homeowner was acquitted. In the first case, the accused argued that the gun he was using to scare away the deceased and his friends misfired. In the second case, the accused acknowledged intentionally shooting the deceased, claiming that he thought the deceased had a weapon and feared for his life and that of his girlfriend. See respectively Richards & Friesen, "Crown says it won't appeal Gerald Stanley acquittal in death of Colten Boushie" *The Globe and Mail* (7 March 2018), online: < https:// www.theglobeandmail.com/news/national/crown-says-it-wont-appeal-colten-boushie-verdict/article 38240566/ >; and Paradkar, "Echoes of Colten Boushie verdict as Hamilton-area man acquitted in shooting death of Indigenous man" *The Star* (27 June 2018), online: < https://www.thestar.com/opinion/star-columnists/2018/06/27/ echoes-of-colten-boushie-verdict-as-hamilton-area-man-acquitted-in-shooting-death-of-unarmed-indigenous-man.html >. Should the fact that the deceased men were apparently committing a property offence have any impact on the defence of self-defence?

4. In *R. v. Forde*, 2011 ONCA 592, the accused testified that the deceased was attacking him with a knife when he killed the deceased in self-defence. The jury rejected the self-defence claim and convicted the accused of manslaughter. He appealed on the basis that the trial judge had erred in permitting the jury to consider his failure to retreat from his home in assessing his self-defence claim. The Court of Appeal agreed and ordered a new trial.

5. As indicated in the previous chapter, the Supreme Court of Canada has limited the defence of consent on policy grounds, holding that combatants in a consensual fight cannot raise the defence if they intended to cause and in fact caused serious bodily harm: *R. v. Paice*, [2005] 1 S.C.R. 339. What impact would *Paice* have had on the defendant's liability in *Wackett*? For a discussion of the interplay between the defence of consent in consensual fights and the defence of self-defence, see *Ellis v. Fallios-Guthierrez*, 2012 ONSC 1670.

6. What impact should the fact that the defendant in *Wackett* did not walk away from the fight have on the issue of whether he was entitled to use any force? Assuming that the defendant was entitled to use force, was the amount of force he used excessive in the circumstances? Can you reconcile the principle that the force used must be reasonable and the principle that a person who is assaulted is not required to measure with "nicety the weight of his blows?" The burden of proof is on defendants to establish that they reasonably believed that they were about to be assaulted and that they used only reasonable force: *Mann v. Balaban*, [1970] S.C.R. 74.

7. In determining whether the force used was excessive, the court should consider the nature of the force used and the circumstances, but not necessarily the resulting injuries. For example in *Brown v. Wilson* (1975), 66 D.L.R. (3d) 295 (B.C.S.C.), the defendant picked up Brown, who was about to hit him, in a "bear hug." In attempting to carry Brown out of the bar, the defendant slipped and Brown fell, hitting his head on the concrete. Although Brown died, the court held that the use of a bear hug was reasonable in the circumstances. See also *McLean v. 366543 B.C. Ltd.*, 1995 CarswellBC

2745 (S.C.) (WL Can), aff'd 1997 CarswellBC 2147 (C.A.) (WL Can); and *MacMillan v. Hincks* (2002), 313 A.R. 150 (Q.B.).

8. Evidence that the defendant was convicted of criminal assault provides strong proof against a plea of self-defence in a related civil action. See *Simpson v. Geswein*, [1995] 6 W.W.R. 233 (Man. Q.B.); *Herman v. Graves* (1998), 217 A.R. 275 (Q.B.); and *Bridge v. Dalton*, 2013 ABQB 312.

9. The criminal courts had adopted a complex "subjective/objective" test in determining whether the accused acted reasonably given his or her perception of the threat. See *Beckford v. R.*, [1987] 3 All E.R. 425 (P.C.); *R. v. Pétel*, [1994] 1 S.C.R. 3; and *R. v. Cinous*, [2002] 2 S.C.R. 3.

10. Prior to the *Citizen's Arrest and Self-defence Act*, S.C. 2012, c. 9, the defences of self-defence and defence of third parties were set out in ss. 34-37 of the *Criminal Code*, R.S.C. 1985, c. C-46, which had been criticized by the courts: *R. v. McIntosh*, [1995] 1 S.C.R. 686; and *R. v. Pintar* (1996), 110 C.C.C. (3d) 402 (Ont. C.A.). These sections limited the use of force that was likely to cause death or grievous bodily harm to situations in which the accused honestly and reasonably believed that such force was necessary to protect him or herself, or a third party from death or grievous bodily harm. See *R. v. Bogue* (1976), 30 C.C.C. (2d) 403 (Ont. C.A.).

Section 34(1)(c) of the *Criminal Code* now provides that the amount of force used must be "reasonable in the circumstances." Section 34(2) states that in applying this test, the court must consider the circumstances of the parties and the act, "including, but not limited to," nine listed factors. It remains to be seen whether the courts will adopt the new *Criminal Code* approach in torts cases.

11. In almost all of the American states, individuals who feel threatened while in their home or on their property may use deadly force against intruders, which is commonly referred to as the "Castle Doctrine." In contrast, the Canadian and English courts do not permit individuals to use deadly force in self-defence merely because an intruder is on their property or an altercation is taking place in their home. See respectively *Veinot v. Veinot* (1977), 22 N.S.R. (2d) 630 (C.A.); *R. v. McKay*, 2009 MBCA 53; and *R. v. Ray*, [2017] EWCA Crim 1391.

12. For a discussion of self-defence in the context of resisting arrest, see *Albert v. Lavin*, [1981] 3 All E.R. 878 (H.L.); *R. v. Colet*, [1981] 1 S.C.R. 2; and *R. v. Asante-Mensah*, 2003 SCC 38.

13. A defendant does not have to wait for the other party to strike the first blow. A defendant who attempts to pre-empt an assault by becoming the aggressor may still invoke self-defence. The plaintiff's reputation for violence or prior violent behaviour can be raised to justify the defendant's decision to strike first. See *R. v. Scopelliti* (1981), 63 C.C.C. (2d) 481 (Ont. C.A.); *R. v. Ryan* (1989), 76 Nfld. & P.E.I.R. 26 (Nfld. C.A.); and *Bruce v. Dyer*, [1966] 2 O.R. 705 (H.C.), aff'd [1970] 1 O.R. 482n (C.A.). These principles are reflected in the new *Criminal Code* self-defence provisions in s. 34(2).

14. A more complex situation arises when the defendant kills a person to end a violent relationship. In *R. v. Lavallee*, [1990] 1 S.C.R. 852, a battered woman shot her

partner in the back of the head as he was leaving the room. He had beaten her frequently. He physically abused and taunted her that night, stating that he would kill her if she did not kill him. A psychiatrist testified at trial about the difficulty that battered women have in escaping abusive relationships and the ongoing terror in their lives. He also stated that in his opinion the accused's shooting of the deceased was a desperate act of a woman who sincerely believed that she would otherwise be killed that night. The accused did not testify. She was acquitted at trial, but the majority of the Manitoba Court of Appeal overturned the acquittal and ordered a new trial based on concerns with the psychiatric evidence.

The Supreme Court of Canada restored the accused's acquittal on the basis of self-defence. It stated that the psychiatrist's testimony was necessary to ensure that the jury understood why the accused was psychologically unable to leave and could assess the reasonableness of her belief that killing him was the only way to save her own life. See also *Pétel, supra*; and *R. v. Malott*, [1998] 1 S.C.R. 123.

In *R. v. Ryan*, 2013 SCC 3, the accused unwittingly hired an undercover RCMP officer to kill her physically abusive husband and was charged with counselling to commit murder. At trial, the accused was acquitted on the basis of duress and the Court of Appeal upheld the decision. The Supreme Court of Canada granted the Crown's appeal, holding that self-defence and the defence of duress were not available in the circumstances. However, the court stayed the criminal proceedings against the accused, stating that it would not be "fair" to subject her to another trial.

15. In *R. v. Whynot (Stafford)* (1983), 61 N.S.R. (2d) 33 (C.A.), a woman shot and killed her common law spouse, who had become drunk and passed out. Although the deceased had a history of violence and had often beaten the accused, the Court of Appeal held that self-defence was not available because "no person has the right in anticipation of an assault that may or may not happen to apply force to prevent the imaginary assault." Can you reconcile *Whynot* and *Lavallee*? What non-legal factors might explain the different results in these cases? To what extent should principles developed in criminal law be used in civil actions?

16. What are the implications of *Lavallee* for a high school student who physically attacks the leader of a gang who has repeatedly assaulted, threatened and harassed him over several months? Assume that the student was not in danger when he acted, but hoped that attacking the gang leader would prevent further bullying by sending the message that he would now retaliate in response to any future threats.

Similarly, can a prison inmate rely on the principles of *Lavallee* to pre-empt a future attack by a fellow inmate? Assume that the inmate had been warned that the victim had planned to knife him or her later that week. Assume as well that there were about 10 serious assaults among inmates each year in the institution, resulting in one or two deaths. See generally *R. v. McConnell*, [1996] 1 S.C.R. 1075; and *R. v. Chan* (2005), 232 N.S.R. (2d) 19 (C.A.).

17. A person who makes a reasonable and *bona fide* mistake of fact in acting in self-defence can still rely on the defence. See *R. v. Reilly*, [1984] 2 S.C.R. 396; *R. v. Nelson* (1992), 8 O.R. (3d) 364 (C.A.); *Ashley v. Chief Constable of Sussex Police*, 2008 UKHL 25; and Giles, "Self-Defence and Mistake: A Way Forward" (1990) 53 M.L.R. 187.

3. Defence of Third Parties

GAMBRIELL v. CAPARELLI
(1974), 54 D.L.R. (3d) 661 (Ont. Co. Ct.)

CARTER CO. CT. J.:

. . .

At about 5:30 in the afternoon of July 17, 1970, Fred Caparelli, then 21 years of age, and the son of the defendant, decided to wash his automobile which he had parked in the said laneway at the rear of the backyard of his residence. While he was getting the garden hose, the plaintiff (then aged 50), whose car was parked at the rear of his lot, decided to go shopping. In backing out of his lot onto the laneway, the rear of his vehicle came into contact with the rear of young Caparelli's vehicle.

Attracted by the noise of the impact, the Caparelli lad came running out and saw a little dent in the bumper of his car. He and the plaintiff began screaming at each other. Caparelli said he was going to call the police, there was further argument, the plaintiff started to get back in his car, Caparelli grabbed the plaintiff, who then hit Caparelli on the face with his fist. The blow was returned, other blows exchanged. The Caparelli boy, in the course of the fight, was backing up towards the rear of the plaintiff's car and fell back against the car. The plaintiff says that the Caparelli boy kicked him in the chest, leaving a heel mark on the skin, but this is not concurred in by the plaintiff's wife, nor did the plaintiff show this alleged mark to the police.

The Caparelli boy states that the plaintiff then put both hands around his neck and held him down and was choking him and that he was having trouble breathing. The plaintiff said that he never touched the boy's throat.

At this juncture, the defendant, a woman of 57 years at the time, the mother of young Caparelli, appeared on the scene, attracted by the screaming. She said she saw the plaintiff holding her son by the neck, that her son was under the plaintiff and that she thought her son was being choked. She said that she yelled — "stop! stop! stop!". She then ran into her garden and got a metal three-pronged garden cultivator tool with a five-foot-long wooden handle. She said she struck the plaintiff with this three times on the shoulder and then on the head. As soon as the plaintiff saw the blood flowing from his head he released the defendant's son.

. . .

In *R. v. Duffy*, [1967] 1 Q.B. 63, one Kathleen Duffy hit a man named Mohammed Akbar in a tavern. Elizabeth Duffy, sister of Kathleen, appeared from the wash-room and saw Kathleen on her knees on the floor fighting with Akbar, who was holding her by the hair. Elizabeth pulled Akbar's hair to pull him off her sister but did not succeed, and when he kicked her on the leg she hit him on the head with a bottle, as a result of which Akbar received severe lacerations to his face, forehead and head. Elizabeth was convicted of unlawful wounding. On appeal to the Court of Criminal Appeal, the Court quashed her conviction, and at p. 67, Edmund Davies, J. (as he then was), reading the judgment of the Court, said:

> Quite apart from any special relations between the person attacked and his rescuer, there is a general liberty even as between strangers to prevent a felony.

. . .

Again in *R. v. Fennell*, [1971] 1 Q.B. 428 at p. 431, Lord Justice Widgery, delivering the judgment of the Court said:

> Where a person honestly and reasonably believes that he or his child is in imminent danger of injury it would be unjust if he were deprived of the right to use reasonable force by way of defence merely because he had made some genuine mistake of fact.

While the cases I have cited all deal with criminal matters, the principles outlined therein are of equal weight in a civil case of this nature.

It would appear therefore that, where a person in intervening to rescue another holds an honest (though mistaken) belief that the other person is in imminent danger of injury, he is justified in using force, provided that such force is reasonable; and the necessity for intervention and the reasonableness of the force employed are questions to be decided by the trier of fact.

Having regard, therefore, to the facts as I have found them and to the law as I understand it, in my opinion, when the defendant appeared on the scene and saw her son at the mercy of the plaintiff, and being of the belief that her son was in imminent danger of injury, she was justified in using force to prevent that injury from occurring.

. . .

The next question is — Was the force she used reasonable in the circumstances? In the witness-box, the defendant impressed me as a woman who, under normal circumstances, would be quite cool and collected. She is a woman of average build, and as I have indicated, of mature years. As her knowledge of English was slight, her evidence was given in Italian and translated by an interpreter. When she saw her son with the plaintiff's hand about his neck, she shouted for the plaintiff to stop, to no avail. Then she ran and seized the nearest implement she could find, which happened to be a cultivator fork. She struck the plaintiff three times on the shoulder, again to no avail, and finally struck him on the head. I think the fact that the plaintiff sustained only lacerations to his head rather than a fractured skull is indicative of the fact that the force she used in striking the plaintiff was not, in the circumstances, excessive.

In my opinion she had little other choice. If the plaintiff could overpower her son, the empty-handed aid of a woman some seven years older than the plaintiff would have availed little. On the evidence, she was alone in the laneway with the exception of the combatants and Mrs. Gambriell, who did nothing to assist. Had she run for aid, her son might well have been beyond recovery before she returned, especially as, speaking Italian, she may have encountered difficulty in summoning aid. While I am loath to excuse violence, there are times, and I think this is one of them, when the violence inflicted by the defendant on the plaintiff and the degree of such violence was justified and not unreasonable in the circumstances. I would therefore dismiss the plaintiff's case.

I should, in the event that I am in error in my disposition of the plaintiff's claim, assess the plaintiff's damages. No special damages were claimed. The doctor's report indicated that there were no resulting effects from the head injury and that the plaintiff had fully recovered. I am not satisfied that the plaintiff received an injury to his chest. Further, in cross-examination, he indicated that, although he had headaches for two months, it did not interfere with his work at all.

I am of the opinion that the plaintiff was the author of his own misfortune. On the evidence, the plaintiff struck the first blow, and in the course of the fight, the Caparelli boy was backing away from the plaintiff and the plaintiff could well have desisted. Under all these circumstances, even had I found for the plaintiff I would not have awarded damages in excess of $1.

I do not, however, think that this is a proper case for costs, and I therefore, as I have said above, dismiss the plaintiff's case, but without costs.

NOTES AND QUESTIONS

1. If the only weapon available to the defendant had been a knife, would she have been justified in stabbing the plaintiff in defence of her son?

2. The judge indicated that he would have awarded the plaintiff only one dollar had his action succeeded. Could such an award have been justified based on the principles of damages in intentional torts?

3. In *Cachay v. Nemeth* (1972), 28 D.L.R. (3d) 603 (Sask. Q.B.), the plaintiff attempted to kiss the defendant's wife on the cheek while at a party. The defendant, who was trained in karate, reacted by striking the plaintiff, fracturing his lower jaw and breaking two teeth. The court rejected the defendant's argument that he acted in defence of his wife because the force used was excessive in the circumstances. Nevertheless, the plaintiff's provocative act was taken into account to reduce damages. Would the result have been the same if: (a) the defendant had not been trained in karate, but had merely struck a lucky blow; or (b) the defendant's wife, untrained in karate, had punched the plaintiff, causing the same injury? See also *Defosse v. Wilde*, [1999] 4 W.W.R. 205 (Sask. Q.B.); and *Ellis v. Fallios-Guthierrez*, 2012 ONSC 1670.

4. In *R. v. Duffy* (1973), 11 C.C.C. (2d) 519 (Ont. C.A.), the court held that the defence of third parties is not limited to protecting relatives or others in some special relationship with the accused. Rather, the defence may be raised by anyone who appears on the scene.

5. In *Babiuk v. Trann* (2005), 248 D.L.R. (4th) 530 (Sask. C.A.), the defendant punched the plaintiff, a member of an opposing rugby team. The plaintiff had just stepped backwards onto the face of one of the defendant's teammates. The court accepted the defendant's evidence that he acted instinctively to prevent the plaintiff from further injuring his teammate, even though the defendant threw the punch after the whistle ended the play. The claim of the plaintiff, whose jaw was broken in two places, was denied. Do you agree that the defendant: (a) was acting in defence of his teammate; and (b) used reasonable force?

6. In some American cases, the defence of third parties had been limited to circumstances in which the person protected had a legal right to invoke the defence of self-defence. Thus, if the third party was a drug trafficker who was unlawfully resisting arrest by an undercover officer, the unwitting intervenor could not raise the defence of a third party. However, the majority of authors have rejected this principle. See for example Howarth, "Defences to Intentional Torts" in Sappideen & Vines, eds., *Fleming's The Law of Torts*, 10th ed. (2011) 87 at 100; and Dobbs, Hayden & Bublick, *The Law of Torts*, 2d ed. (2011) vol. 1 at 252-53.

7. In Canada, an intervenor's right to raise the defence is independent of the legal rights or position of the person being defended. See the *Criminal Code*, s. 27 (the right to use force to prevent the commission of specified offences) and s. 34(1) (the right to use force to protect oneself or others).

4. Discipline

Although attitudes and values have changed dramatically, the common law still recognizes a defence of discipline that parents and guardians can invoke to privilege the use of force in dealing with children. A similar defence to criminal liability exists for parents, guardians and educators in s. 43 of the *Criminal Code*, which provides that:

> Every schoolteacher, parent or person standing in the place of a parent is justified in using force by way of correction toward a pupil or child, as the case may be, who is under his care, if the force does not exceed what is reasonable under the circumstances.

The Canadian courts have largely assumed that s. 43 governs both the criminal and the civil defences of discipline.

R. v. DUPPERON
(1984), 16 C.C.C. (3d) 453 (Sask. C.A.)

BY THE COURT: The appellant was charged that on or about November 19, 1983, at the City of Saskatoon, in the Province of Saskatchewan, he did in committing an assault on Michael James Dupperon cause harm to him contrary to s. 245.1(1)(*b*) of the *Criminal Code* of Canada.

After a trial before a judge of the provincial court he was convicted, fined $400 and placed on probation for 18 months. He appeals against his conviction.

The evidence is that he strapped his 13-year-old son on the bare buttocks with a leather belt approximately 10 times leaving four or five bruises on the boy's left buttock which were blue and in a linear pattern. Each bruise was approximately four inches long and of a width of one-quarter to one-half an inch.

. . . In the morning on the day of the assault, Michael had been caught smoking out behind the house and for this he was "grounded". Later that morning the father, Linda Dupperon (his present wife and step-mother to Michael) and Michael were working at the Bingo Palace where the appellant had a janitorial contract. There, Michael admitted, he was "slacking off and doing things I shouldn't have"; and he also used foul language against his father. For this he was grounded for a whole week. When the appellant, Linda Dupperon and Michael returned home from work both the appellant and his wife later left the house and Michael was alone. It was then that he decided to leave home. He left a note to his father which was not produced but concerning which Michael testified: "I think I told him off. I said I wasn't going to come back to home and shit like that." He packed his clothes, radio and some food and left the house. A short time later, Linda Dupperon arrived home, saw the note and telephoned her husband. The appellant came home and about 15 minutes later the telephone rang. It was a call from Michael, who had been at a friend's home down the street, saying he was coming home.

. . .

From the uncontradicted evidence given by Michael there were ample grounds upon which the appellant could conclude that Michael was deserving of a more severe punishment than he had already meted out to him and I am satisfied that he honestly believed that a strapping was required by way of correction. Given the weight of the evidence adduced in this respect, it was unreasonable for the learned trial judge not to have held that the strapping was for correction. . . .

. . . It is quite clear from both the evidence of Michael and Linda Dupperon that the first strapping consisted of only three or four strokes and that would have been the end of the strapping but for the foul language Michael then employed against his father. This resulted in a further five or six strokes. There is no dispute that the total strapping did not exceed 10 strokes.

. . .

Here the learned trial judge in the course of his judgment said:

Secondly, I do not view it at all appropriate in the circumstances to pull down a 13-year-old boy's pants and flail him with a strap on his bare buttocks to the extent of this case. It is an unnatural manner of dealing out punishment and is not justified in these circumstances and in the manner in which it was administered.

. . .

While it appears from the above exchange and from other passages in the transcript that the learned trial judge may be opposed, in principle, to corporal punishment, that is his privilege and unless he allowed such views to interfere with his determination of whether the force applied was reasonable under the circumstances, it was not an error to express his personal view.

Put in another way, I think most people would be shocked if corporal punishment were employed in an institution such as Kilburn Hall or in any agency of government designed for the protection of abused children.

. . .

There is some anomaly in the fact that corporal punishment of criminals is now prohibited while corporal punishment of children is still permitted. The rationale of s. 43 of the *Criminal Code* has been explained by Dickson J. (as he then was) in the recent judgment of the Supreme Court rendered September 17, 1984, in *Ogg-Moss v. The Queen* [(1984), 11 D.L.R. (4th) 549] . . .

Section 43 authorizes the use of force "by way of correction". As Blackstone noted, such "correction" of a child is countenanced by the law because it is "for the benefit of his education". Section 43 is, in other words, a *justification*. It exculpates a parent, schoolteacher or person standing in the place of a parent who uses force in the correction of a child, because it considers such an action not a wrongful, but a *rightful* one. It follows that unless the force is "by way of correction", that is, for the benefit of the education of the child, the use of force will not be justified.

In this case I have said that, in my opinion, all of the evidence supports the view that the force used was by way of correction and that the learned trial judge ought to have so found. However, when we come to the second question, namely, whether the force used exceeded what was reasonable under the circumstances, I think the evidence fully supports the finding of the trial judge.

. . .

The only matter with which I am concerned here, therefore, is whether the force used exceeded what was reasonable under the circumstances so as to deprive the appellant of the protection afforded by s. 43 of the *Criminal Code*. In determining that question the court will consider, both from an objective and subjective standpoint, such matters as the nature of the offence calling for correction, the age and character of the child and the likely effect of the punishment on this particular child, the degree of gravity of the punishment, the circumstances under which it was inflicted, and the injuries, if any, suffered. If the child suffers injuries which may endanger life, limbs or health or is disfigured that alone would be sufficient to find that the punishment administered was unreasonable under the circumstances.

. . .

In my opinion, the evidence in this case amply supports the finding of the trial judge. Ten strokes of a leather belt on the bare buttocks is a severe beating, particularly under the circumstances in which it was inflicted here on an emotionally disturbed boy. There is, therefore, no basis upon which this court would be justified in reversing that finding.

[The court accepted the appellant's argument that he should only be convicted of assault and not assault causing bodily harm. However, it held that the sentence imposed at trial was still appropriate.]

NOTES AND QUESTIONS

1. What must the defendant establish to invoke the defence of discipline under s. 43?

2. Do you agree that the accused in *Dupperon* used force for the purpose of correction? What was the intended benefit? Should a parent who hits a misbehaving child to punish him or her be able to rely on the defence of discipline?

3. Do you agree that the amount of force used in *Dupperon* was excessive? Would the court have reached the same conclusion if the accused had stopped after the first three or four strokes, or the strapping had not left bruises? Would the majority of Canadians in the early 1980s have supported a criminal conviction in these circumstances?

4. It has been held that s. 43 must be interpreted in light of Canada's prevailing social standards and customs, rather than those of the accused. The courts have consistently held that the accused's cultural background and religious beliefs are irrelevant: *R. v. Baptiste* (1980), 61 C.C.C. (2d) 438 (Ont. Prov. Ct.); *R. v. Halcrow* (1993), 80 C.C.C. (3d) 320 (B.C.C.A.), aff'd [1995] 1 S.C.R. 440; and *R. v. Poulin* (2002), 169 C.C.C. (3d) 378 (P.E.I.S.C.). Do you agree that it is necessary to rely on Canadian social standards and customs in order to interpret s. 43?

5. Section 43 also permits teachers to use force by way of correction. Initially, educators were given broad latitude to use force not just to correct student behaviour, but also to punish students who were thought to have misbehaved. For example in *R. v. Haberstock* (1970), 1 C.C.C. (2d) 433 (Sask. C.A.), a vice-principal was absolved of criminal liability under s. 43 for summarily slapping three boys in the face in the schoolyard because he believed that they had called him names while leaving on the

school bus the preceding Friday. See also *R. v. Wheaton* (1982), 35 Nfld. & P.E.I.R. 520 (Nfld. Prov. Ct.). *Haberstock* would not be decided the same way today.

Nevertheless, educators appear to have some leeway under s. 43. In *R. v. Wetmore* (1996), 172 N.B.R. (2d) 224 (Q.B.), the accused taught a tenth-grade science class in which several students including a 20-year-old were frequently obnoxious and disruptive. The teacher, who held a brown belt in karate, called the troublemakers to the front of the class and indicated that he was going to provide a karate demonstration. He took off his shoes and socks and then threw kicks and punches at the students. Although there was some incidental touching of the students, the physical contact was minimal and no harm was caused. The teacher ended the demonstration, called for a discussion and made the troublemakers aware that their offensive conduct, whether directed at him or their classmates, was not acceptable in his classroom. The teacher was subsequently charged with assault. In acquitting the teacher on the basis of s. 43, the court held that his actions were reasonable in light of the troublemakers' conduct and the need to teach them respect for authority. See also *R. v. Park* (1999), 178 Nfld. & P.E.I.R. 194 (Nfld. S.C. (T.D.)).

6. It is important to distinguish between the narrow defence under s. 43 of the *Criminal Code* and the broad common law and statutory powers of educators to maintain order and discipline in a school and at school-related events. The Canadian courts have held that the power to maintain order and discipline can be invoked to physically restrain a student who is acting out of control, detain and question a student suspected of violating the school rules or the law, control a student's movement in school, and prevent a student from leaving. See for example *R. v. Maddison*, 2009 NSPC 16 (subduing an out-of-control student); *R. v. Sweet*, 1986 CarswellOnt 3452 (Dist. Ct.) (WL Can) (investigating potentially criminal conduct); *H.G. v. Shamrock School Division No. 38*, [1987] 3 W.W.R. 270 (Sask. Q.B.) (restricting movement); and *Pilieci v. Lockett*, 1989 CarswellOnt 2870 (Dist. Ct.) (WL Can) (preventing a student from leaving with his father, contrary to the parents' custody order).

7. In *R. v. J.M.G.* (1986), 56 O.R. (2d) 705 (C.A.), the court held that principals, pursuant to their statutory duty to maintain order and discipline, had a legal obligation to investigate any credible allegation of illicit drug use or other serious violations of the school rules. Moreover, if an educator reasonably believed that a student was in possession of drugs, contraband or evidence of a violation of the school rules or the law, the educator could search the student and the student's belongings and locker without a warrant.

In *R. v. M.(M.R.)*, [1998] 3 S.C.R. 393, the court affirmed these principles, explaining that students are subject to a diminished expectation of privacy.

In both cases, the principal's detention and search of the student was upheld under the *Canadian Charter of Rights and Freedoms*, Part I of the *Constitution Act, 1982*, being Schedule B to the *Canada Act 1982* (U.K.), 1982, c. 11.

8. In *R. v. M.A.*, [2008] 1 S.C.R. 569, the police arrested the accused when drugs were found in his backpack during a warrantless canine search of the school. Despite the principal's earlier open invitation to conduct such a search, a majority of the court characterized it as a police-initiated warrantless search and ruled that it violated s. 8 of the *Charter*. Consequently, the drugs were excluded from evidence and the charges

were dismissed. Would the result have been the same if the principal hired a private dog handler to conduct the search and only notified the police after the drugs were found?

9. In *R. v. Ogg-Moss*, [1984] 2 S.C.R. 173, the court held that a counsellor in a residential facility for developmentally-delayed adults could not invoke s. 43 because the defence was limited to parents, teachers and others standing in the position of a parent in relationship to a child or pupil. The court went on to emphasize that s. 43 was to be narrowly interpreted and applied. The decision reflected growing concerns about child abuse, the recognition of the independent legal rights of children and the hardening of attitudes toward the use of corporal punishment.

10. In *Canadian Foundation for Children, Youth and the Law v. Canada (Attorney General)*, [2004] 1 S.C.R. 76, the appellant argued that s. 43 of the *Criminal Code* violated the *Charter* rights of children. Specifically, the Foundation alleged breaches of s. 7 (the right to life, liberty and security of the person), s. 12 (the prohibition against cruel and unusual treatment or punishment), and s. 15 (the guarantee of equal treatment and benefit of the law). While the court upheld the constitutional validity of s. 43, it went to considerable lengths to narrow the defence.

The court stated at para. 40 that the defence was generally limited to "minor corrective force of a transitory and trifling nature." First, force can only be used for a corrective purpose that is designed to restrain and control a child or express symbolic disapproval. The defence does not apply to force that is used out of anger or simply to punish a child. Second, the child must be capable of understanding why the force is being used and be capable of benefiting from it. Consequently, the defence does not apply to children under the age of two and other children who, because of a disability, are incapable of learning from the incident. Third, s. 43 does not apply to the use of force that harms or could reasonably be expected to harm a child. Nor does the defence apply where children are hit with rulers, belts or other such objects, or if children are hit or slapped in the head. Fourth, s. 43 does not apply to any use of force that is cruel or degrading. Fifth, the defence cannot be invoked to justify corporal punishment of teenagers because research indicates that this only generates harmful or antisocial behaviour. Sixth, while teachers may use reasonable force to remove a child from a classroom or secure compliance with instructions, they cannot use force merely as corporal punishment.

Is the court's analysis consistent with: (a) the statutory language of s. 43; and (b) the Canadian "social standards and customs" that allegedly govern the interpretation of s. 43? In any event, is the court qualified to dictate how parents and guardians should discipline their children? In regard to the sixth point, has the court conflated s. 43 with the common law and statutory powers of educators to maintain order and discipline?

11. In *R. v. Swan* (2008), 58 C.R. (6th) 126 (Ont. S.C.J.), the accused was convicted of assaulting his 15-year-old daughter. She was in the temporary care of a Children's Aid Society, but had been released to be with her parents on a home visit. The Society had obtained a restraining order prohibiting the daughter's boyfriend, who had a history of violence and drug use, from having any contact with her. The parents had previously found drug paraphernalia in their daughter's room and a note from her boyfriend suggesting that she "kill the sluts [her parents] when nobody is

around." On the night in question, the daughter left to meet her boyfriend at a party despite being told that she could not do so. The accused went looking for his daughter. On finding her, he told her that she had to come home. When she refused, the accused physically apprehended her and it was on this basis that he was convicted.

On appeal, the court held that the trial judge had misinterpreted *Canadian Foundation for Children, Youth and the Law, supra,* as precluding the application of s. 43 to teenagers. The court noted that there was no age limit in s. 43 and stated that the Supreme Court of Canada had not intended to prohibit parents from using reasonable force to restrain or control their unruly teenagers. The accused reasonably believed that physically apprehending his daughter was necessary to safeguard her, and he used minimal force in doing so. The accused's appeal was granted and he was acquitted of assault.

Do you agree with the appeal decision? On a broader level, has *Swan* also conflated the narrow defence under s. 43 of the *Criminal Code* with the broader common law powers of parents and others to control children under their charge? See K. Sykes, "Bambi Meets Godzilla: Children's and Parents' Rights in *Canadian Foundation for Children, Youth and the Law v. Canada*" (2006) 51 McGill L.J. 131; Stewart, "Parents, Children, and the Law of Assault" (2009) 32 Dal. L.J. 1; and Ferguson, "Commentary on *Canadian Foundation for Children, Youth and the Law v. Canada (Attorney General)*" in Stalford, Hollingsworth & Gilmore, eds., *Rewriting Children's Rights Judgments* (2017) at 381.

12. Ship captains, pilots and others in similar positions of authority also have a common law right to use physical force to maintain order and discipline. Although this power could be used to punish rebellious crew and passengers at one time, it is probably now limited to maintaining safety and order. See *King v. Fanklin* (1858), 175 E.R. 764 (N.P.); *Hook v. Cunard SS. Co.,* [1953] 1 All E.R. 1021 (Q.B.); and *Re White* (1954), 12 W.W.R. 315 (B.C.C.A.), rev'd on a jurisdictional issue [1956] S.C.R. 154.

Section 2 of the *Criminal Code* defines the term "peace officer" to include pilots in command of aircraft while in flight. Moreover, s. 27.1 of the *Criminal Code*, which was enacted in 2004, gives everyone on an aircraft in flight the right to use as much force as is necessary to prevent the commission of an offence.

5. Defence of Real Property

MACDONALD v. HEES
(1974), 46 D.L.R. (3d) 720 (N.S.S.C.)

COWAN C.J.T.D.:—In this action, the plaintiff claims against the defendant for injury, loss and damage said to have been suffered by the plaintiff as a result of an assault alleged to have been committed on the plaintiff by the defendant.

The injuries suffered by the plaintiff were sustained during the early morning of September 23, 1972, when the defendant forcibly ejected the plaintiff from a motel room at the Peter Pan Motel, New Glasgow, Nova Scotia. The defendant, in his defence, in addition to denying any assault, set up the additional defence that, if he used any force upon the person of the plaintiff he was justified in law and the application of force was due to the unlawful entry of the plaintiff and invasion of the defendant's privacy.

. . .

It is clear that the defendant was in lawful occupation of the motel unit No. 54. That unit had been reserved for his use on the night in question. . . . I find that the defendant had not expressly invited the plaintiff or Boyd to visit him, nor was there any implied invitation to anyone to visit him at the motel unit. However, in my opinion, this is not quite the case of a stranger walking in a motel room without any apparent right. The plaintiff was an officer of the local political party in whose interests the defendant was active that day. The plaintiff wished to introduce Glen Boyd to the defendant, and the circumstances to which I have referred above give some excuse to the plaintiff for his entry to the motel unit occupied by the defendant. The plaintiff was told that there were two units set aside for the defendant's use and, when he went to the area so set aside, it was apparent that the light was on in one of the units, while the other was in darkness. The plaintiff cannot be criticized for his action in knocking on the door of the unit which had the light showing. He then heard someone call from the adjoining unit and assumed, erroneously, that he was being invited to enter that unit.

[The defendant raised both self-defence and defence of property as justifications for his conduct. The judge concluded that there was no basis for claiming self-defence and proceeded to discuss the defence of property.]

With regard to the . . . defence . . . that the defendant was justified in law and that the application of force was due to the unlawful entry of the plaintiff and invasion of the defendant's privacy, it is clear that, as stated in *Salmond, op. cit.*, p. 131:

> It is lawful for any occupier of land, or for any other person with the authority of the occupier, to use a reasonable degree of force in order to prevent a trespasser from entering or to control his movements or to eject him after entry.

It is clear, however, that a trespasser cannot be forcibly repelled or ejected until he has been requested to leave the premises and a reasonable opportunity of doing so peaceably has been afforded him. It is otherwise in the case of a person who enters or seeks to enter by force. In *Green v. Goddard* (1702), 2 Salkeld 641, 91 E.R. 540, it was said that, in such a case:

> . . . I need not request him to be gone, but may lay hands on him immediately, for it is but returning violence with violence; so if one comes forcibly and takes away my goods, I may oppose him without any more ado, for there is no time to make a request.

Even in such a case, however, the amount of force that may be used must not exceed that which is indicated in the old forms of pleading by the phrase *molliter manus imposuit*. It must amount to nothing more than forcible removal and must not include beating, wounding, or other physical injury. *Salmond, op. cit.*, 131, and the case of *Collins v. Renison* (1754), Sayer 138, 96 E.R. 830, there cited. In that case, the plaintiff sued for the assault of throwing him off a ladder. It was held a bad plea that the plaintiff was trespassing and refused, after request, to leave the premises, and that the defendant thereupon [at 139] "gently shook the ladder, which was a low ladder, and gently over-turned it, and gently threw the plaintiff from it upon the ground, thereby doing as little damage as possible to the plaintiff." It was held that such force was not justifiable in defence of the possession of land.

In the present case, I find that there was no forcible entry by the plaintiff of the motel unit occupied by the defendant. I accept the evidence of the plaintiff and of Glen Boyd, to the effect that the plaintiff, thinking that he had been invited to enter the motel unit occupied by the defendant, opened the unlocked, outside combination screen and storm door and merely touched the door-knob of the inside door when it opened. It was obviously unlocked. The plaintiff then entered the motel unit, at the same time telling the defendant who he was. The plaintiff said that he was about to apologize for the intrusion when he realized that the defendant was in bed. Even if there had been forcible entry, the defendant did not request the plaintiff and his companion to leave and give them any reasonable opportunity of doing so, peaceably. . . . Where the evidence of the defendant conflicts with that of the plaintiff and Glen Boyd, I do not accept his evidence but that of the plaintiff and Glen Boyd.

The evidence of Glen Boyd was to the effect that the plaintiff had merely stepped into the room and made the statement referred to above, and that the time which elapsed from the time when he opened the door to the time when he was thrown back out through the inner door and into the storm door, was very short. Glen Boyd said that it was only long enough for the plaintiff to walk in and be thrown back out. He said that the defendant had not asked the plaintiff to leave before he threw him out.

I find that the use of force by the defendant to eject the plaintiff was not justified, in the circumstances, and that, in any event, the force used was excessive. I find that the defendant threw the plaintiff bodily through the inside motel door which was open, and against the closed combination screen and storm door, in such a way that the plaintiff's head hit the lower portion of the glass in the door, causing it to break and causing severe lacerations to the plaintiff's head.

I therefore find that the defence that the application of force was justified in law, in that it was due to the unlawful entry of the plaintiff and invasion of the defendant's privacy, has not been established. It follows, therefore, that the plaintiff is entitled to recovery against the defendant of damages for the injury, loss and damage which he suffered by the reason of the action of the defendant in assaulting him, and throwing him against the closed combination door.

NOTES AND QUESTIONS

1. As indicated in *Hees*, the defence of real property is based on the legal status of the entrant. According to *Hees*, what principles govern the defence as it relates to trespassers and violent intruders?

2. Why did the court reject Hees' argument that he was acting in defence of property? Assume that Hees had been startled out of a heavy sleep by the plaintiff and awoke knowing only that there was an intruder in his room. Would Hees have been privileged to use the element of surprise to overpower the plaintiff without first asking him to leave? If so, what would be the basis of his defence? See *Boulet c. Entreprises M. Canada (Abitibi) Ltée* (1986), 38 C.C.L.T. 271 (C.S. Qc.), aff'd [1989] R.R.A. 795 (C.A. Qc.).

3. There is little Canadian or English authority on whether a defendant's reasonable and *bona fide* mistake of fact as to the status of an entrant will negate the defence of real property. The American courts have generally held that a mistake of fact will not negate the defence of real property. However, this principle does not

apply to an intruder who is entering as of legal right, unless he or she misleads the occupier or is otherwise responsible for the occupier's mistaken belief. See Dobbs, Hayden & Bublick, *The Law of Torts*, 2d ed. (2011) vol. 1 at 258-59.

In what circumstances, if any, should a reasonable and *bona fide* mistake of fact negate the defence of property?

4. The *Citizen's Arrest and Self-defence Act*, S.C. 2012, c. 9 repealed and replaced ss. 38-42 of the *Criminal Code*, which had governed the defence of real and personal property. In general terms, s. 35 of the *Criminal Code* permits individuals in lawful possession of property to act to prevent another person from entering or remaining on their land, or destroying, damaging or taking their property. As well, the act undertaken must be "reasonable in the circumstances."

5. The Canadian courts have held that an occupier may be required to tolerate the presence of a trespasser if ejecting him or her would pose a foreseeable risk of physical injury. See for example *Dunn v. Dominion Atlantic Railway Co.* (1920), 60 S.C.R. 310 and *Jordan House Ltd. v. Menow*, [1974] S.C.R. 239, in which the occupiers were held liable in negligence for ejecting the plaintiffs, who were extremely intoxicated and obviously in a vulnerable situation.

6. The Canadian courts will not permit an occupier to use force that is likely to cause death or serious bodily injury solely for the purpose of ejecting a trespasser who cannot be induced to leave by less violent means. See *Veinot v. Veinot* (1977), 22 N.S.R. (2d) 630 (C.A.); *R. v. Gunning*, [2005] 1 S.C.R. 627; and *R. v. McKay*, 2009 MBCA 53. While an occupier cannot shoot trespassers, he or she may be permitted to threaten them with a loaded gun or other weapon. See *R. v. Blair*, 1987 CarswellBC 1477 (Co. Ct.) (WL Can); and *Revill v. Newbery*, [1996] 1 All E.R. 291 (C.A.).

7. The older cases held that deadly force could be used to repel a violent intruder, prevent being dispossessed or prevent a crime from being committed. See *R. v. Lyons* (1892), 2 C.C.C. 218 (Ont. Co. Ct.); and *Israel James Hussey* (1924), 18 Cr. App. R. 160 (Ct. Crim. App.). However, the more recent cases prohibit the use of deadly force simply to protect property. See *Bigcharles v. Merkel*, [1973] 1 W.W.R. 324 (B.C.S.C.); *Hackshaw v. Shaw* (1984), 56 A.L.R. 417 (H.C.A.); and Dias, "Rural homeowner taken into custody after allegedly shooting suspect" *Global News* (25 February 2018), online: < https://globalnews.ca/news/4046226/rural-homeowner-taken-into-custody-after-allegedly-shooting-suspect/ > .

8. The common law right to eject a trespasser does not necessarily include the right to imprison him or her. See *Ball v. Manthorpe* (1970), 15 D.L.R. (3d) 99 (B.C. Co. Ct.). However, some of the provincial trespass statutes authorize the police and occupiers to arrest, without a warrant, individuals who they have reasonable grounds to believe are trespassing. See for example the *Trespass to Property Act*, R.S.O. 1990, c. T.21, s. 9.

9. The use of reasonable force in defending real property and ejecting trespassers was privileged under ss. 40 and 41 of the *Criminal Code*. See for example *R. v. Clark* (1983), 44 A.R. 141 (C.A.); *R. v. Gunning, supra*; and *R. v. McKay* (2009), *supra*. As indicated, the *Citizen's Arrest and Self-defence Act* repealed these sections, and the defence of property is now governed by s. 35 of the *Criminal Code*. See also s. 177,

which prohibits trespassing at night, without a lawful excuse, on the property of another near a dwelling house and s. 494(2), which authorizes occupants to arrest without warrant anyone they find committing a criminal offence on, or in relation to, their property.

10. At common law, occupiers are entitled to damage or even destroy the property of another if doing so is necessary to protect their own property and the damage done is reasonable in relation to the interest protected. Thus, farmers are privileged to kill a trespassing dog that is attacking their sheep, but would not be privileged to kill a cow that had merely entered their field. In addition, under the principle of "distress damage feasant," occupiers may seize any chattel that is unlawfully on their land and has caused damage, and may detain the chattel until they have been compensated. See *Arthur v. Anker*, [1996] 3 All E.R. 783 (C.A.); *Stewart v. Gustafson* (1998), 171 Sask. R. 27 (Q.B.); and Howarth, "Defences to Intentional Torts" in Sappideen & Vines, eds., *Fleming's The Law of Torts*, 10th ed. (2011) 87 at 100-03.

BIRD v. HOLBROOK
(1828), 130 E.R. 911 (C.P.)

[The defendant possessed a walled garden in which he grew valuable tulips. Because of previous acts of vandalism, the defendant set up a spring gun with trip wires across the garden. No notice of the spring gun was posted. Indeed, the defendant sought to keep its existence a secret "lest the villain should not be detected."

A peahen escaped from a neighbouring house and landed in the garden. The plaintiff, seeing that a servant girl was upset at not being able to recover the bird, offered to help. He climbed the garden wall and called several times for the occupant. After receiving no answer he jumped into the garden to retrieve the hen. The gun discharged, seriously wounding him.]

BEST C.J.: . . . I am reported to have said, expressly, "Humanity requires that the fullest notice possible should be given, and the law of England will not sanction what is inconsistent with humanity."

It has been argued that the law does not compel every line of conduct which humanity or religion may require; but there is no act which Christianity forbids, that the law will not reach: if it were otherwise, Christianity would not be, as it has always been held to be, part of the law of England. I am, therefore, clearly of opinion that he who sets spring guns, without giving notice, is guilty of an inhuman act, and that, if injurious consequences ensue, he is liable to yield to redress to the sufferer. But this case stands on grounds distinct from any that have preceded it. In general, spring guns have been set for the purpose of deterring; the Defendant placed his for the express purpose of doing injury; for, when called on to give notice, he said, "If I give notice, I shall not catch him." He intended, therefore, that the gun should be discharged and that the contents should be lodged in the body of his victim, for he could not be caught in any other way. On these principles the action is clearly maintainable, and particularly on the latter ground.

. . .

BURROUGH J.: . . . [T]he present case is of a worse complexion than those which have preceded it; for if the Defendant had proposed merely to protect his property from thieves, he would have set the spring guns only by night. The Plaintiff was only a trespasser: if the Defendant had been present, he would not have been authorised even in taking him into custody, and no man can do indirectly that which he is forbidden to do directly.

NOTES AND QUESTIONS

1. Best C.J. premised his decision in part on Christian beliefs. Of what relevance are such beliefs in modern Canadian law?

2. In *Bird*, what impact did the defendant's intent have on the defence of real property? The court also discussed the absence of a warning sign. What impact should the presence or absence of a warning sign have on the defence of real property? What other impact would a warning sign have on the defendant's case?

3. Would the defendant have been held liable if his trained dog had attacked the plaintiff, causing equally serious injuries? Would the defendant have been held liable if the plaintiff had been an armed and dangerous felon who was planning to break into the house?

In general terms, the common law did not hold owners of domesticated animals liable for injuries they caused to entrants, unless the owner was negligent or had knowledge of the animal's dangerous propensity. The liability of dog owners is now often governed by provincial legislation, which may make the owner liable even in the absence of negligence or knowledge of the animal's aggressive tendencies. See for example the *Dog Owners' Liability Act*, R.S.O. 1990, c. D.16, s. 2; and *The Animal Liability Act*, C.C.S.M., c. A95, s. 2. For a more detailed discussion of an owner's liability for his or her animals, see Chapter 25: Strict and Vicarious Liability.

4. See generally Hart, "Injuries to Trespassers" (1931) 47 L.Q.R. 92; Palmer, "The Iowa Spring Gun Case: A Study in American Gothic" (1970-71) 56 Iowa L. Rev. 1219; and Dobbs, Hayden & Bublick, *The Law of Torts*, 2d ed. (2011) vol. 1 at 260-66.

Pursuant to s. 247 of the *Criminal Code*, setting a "trap, device or other thing" with the intent to cause death or bodily harm is an indictable offence if that object is likely to cause death or bodily harm to others. Should the use of autonomous security robots to protect private property be governed by the same civil and criminal liability principles as spring guns, traps and other similar mechanical devices? See Joh, "Private Security Robots, Artificial Intelligence, and Deadly Force" (2017) 51 U.C. Davis L. Rev. 569.

6. Defence and Recaption of Chattels

The legal principles governing the defence of real property generally apply to the defence of chattels. In order to invoke this defence, the defendant must be in possession of the chattel, attempting to immediately regain possession, or in hot pursuit of the person who had just taken the chattel. If a person innocently picks up the defendant's chattel, the defendant must request its return before using any force. However, if a person grabs the chattel out of the defendant's hand, the defendant can use force to retrieve it without first making a request for its return. The specific facts of the case will dictate whether the possessor is privileged to use force and whether the force used was reasonable. For example in *Cresswell v. Sirl*, [1948] 1 K.B. 241 (C.A.), the court held that the defendant would be privileged in shooting a dog if he had no other practical means of protecting his livestock from attack.

Except as outlined above, an individual cannot invoke the defence of chattels once dispossessed. He or she may seek to regain possession by court action or may be entitled to resort to the self-help remedy of recaption, which was discussed in Chapter 4: Intentional Interference with Chattels. The remedy of recaption, which is also sometimes called recapture, places the dispossessed owner in the role of a potential aggressor who is attempting to regain possession of the goods from another person. As a result, the remedy has been narrowly defined. It may only be invoked by an individual who has an immediate right to possession, and then only after a request has been made for the chattel's return. Although the authorities are divided, it appears that only peaceful means can be used to recapture a chattel from a person who came into possession lawfully. Thus, an individual could not use force to recapture a chattel from a bailee who refused to return it. The right to use force is limited to circumstances in which an individual who wrongfully gained possession refuses to hand over the chattel after being requested to do so.

There is a common law privilege to enter another person's land to recapture chattels in limited circumstances. If the chattel came onto the land accidentally or was left there by a wrongdoer, the owner could enter the property to retake his or her chattel, provided he or she did not use force or cause a breach of the peace. If the occupier of the land came into possession of the chattel unlawfully, its owner could make a forced entry if his or her request for its return had been denied.

NOTES AND QUESTIONS

1. Many commentators only briefly allude to the defence of chattels, indicating that it parallels the defence of real property. See for example Dobbs, Hayden & Bublick, *The Law of Torts*, 2d ed. (2011) vol.1 at 254-55; and Howarth, "Defences to Intentional Torts" in Sappideen & Vines, eds., *Fleming's The Law of Torts*, 10th ed. (2011) 87 at 100-01.

The use of force in defending chattels was privileged under ss. 38 and 39 of the *Criminal Code*. See for example *R. v. Weare* (1983), 56 N.S.R. (2d) 411 (C.A.); and *R. v. Lei* (1997), 123 Man. R. (2d) 81 (C.A.). The *Citizen's Arrest and Self-defence Act*, S.C. 2012, c. 9 repealed ss. 38 and 39 and consolidated the defence of chattels and the defence of real property in s. 35, which applies to both chattels and real property.

2. For a review of recaption and entry on land, see *Blades v. Higgs* (1861), 142 E.R. 634 (H.L.); *Wentzell v. Veinot*, [1940] 1 D.L.R. 536 (N.S.S.C.); *Devoe v. Long*, [1951] 1 D.L.R. 203 (N.B.C.A.); Fridman *et al.*, *The Law of Torts in Canada*, 3d ed. (2010) at 82; and Barker *et al.*, *The Law of Torts in Australia*, 5th ed. (2011) at 135-37.

3. It appears that a reasonable and *bona fide* mistake of fact will not negate the defence of chattels, but will negate the remedy of recaption of chattels. Do you favour this position? If so, what is the justification for making such a distinction? See generally Dobbs, Hayden & Bublick, *supra* at 275-79.

4. Given the potential for violence, should the remedy of recaption be abolished?

5. It has been suggested that an owner who recaptures a chattel need not pay for any improvements that the other party made to it even if the other party acted in good faith. Conversely, if the owner recovers the chattel through court action, he or she may be required to pay for any such improvements. However, the better view appears to be that the owner may be held liable in an action for unjust enrichment for the value of the improvements in either situation. See *Greenwood v. Bennett*, [1973] Q.B. 195 (C.A.); *Peruvian Guano Co. v. Dreyfus Brothers & Co.*, [1892] A.C. 166 (H.L.); and *Mayne v. Kidd* (1951), 1 W.W.R. 833 (Sask. C.A.).

REVIEW PROBLEM

Al and Bob obtained permission to camp and hunt on the waterfront property of one of their friends. They misunderstood his directions, and beached their canoe and pitched their tent on the wrong property. Al built a fire to keep warm and Bob went for a walk. The owner of the property, Stevens, was hunting nearby when he came across Al and the campsite. Stevens told him to pack up and leave immediately. Al paid little heed. Stevens yelled, "I'm not joking, get off my land or else!" Al poured himself a cup of coffee and replied, "What's your hurry, old man?" Infuriated, Stevens blasted the tent and pointed his shotgun at Al.

Bob heard the shot and ran back as Stevens screamed, "Is there any reason why I shouldn't blow your head off?" Stevens had no intention of shooting Al; he just wanted to scare him. Fearing the worst, Bob picked up a rock and tried to knock the shotgun out of Stevens' hands. Unfortunately, the rock hit Stevens in the head, and he fell to the ground unconscious. The shotgun fell beside him, discharging several pellets into Al's shoulder. Al and Bob became alarmed when Stevens showed no signs of regaining consciousness. They placed Stevens in their canoe and rushed him to the hospital.

Al and Bob have contacted you from the hospital, wanting to know if they can return to Stevens' land and retrieve their camping equipment. They also want your advice about the civil claims that they could bring against Stevens, and the claims that he might bring against them.

7. Public and Private Necessity

(a) PUBLIC NECESSITY

The defence of public necessity allows an individual to intentionally interfere with the property rights of another in order to save lives or to protect the public interest from external threats of nature, such as fires, floods and storms. Public necessity provides a complete defence, privileging both the interference with the plaintiff's legal rights to the property and any damages resulting from it.

SUROCCO v. GEARY
3 Cal. 69 (Cal. S.C. 1853)

MURRAY, C.J.: This was an action, commenced in the court below, to recover damages for blowing up and destroying the plaintiff's house and property, during the fire of the 24th of December, 1849.

. . .

The only question for our consideration is, whether the person who tears down or destroys the house of another, in good faith, and under apparent necessity, during the time of a conflagration, for the purpose of saving the buildings adjacent, and stopping its progress, can be held personally liable in an action by the owner of the property destroyed.

The right to destroy property, to prevent the spread of conflagration, has been traced to the highest law of necessity, and the natural rights of man, independent of society or civil government. "It is referred by moralists and jurists to the same great principle which justifies the exclusive appropriation of a plank in a shipwreck, though the life of another be sacrificed; with the throwing overboard goods in a tempest, for the safety of a vessel; with the trespassing upon the lands of another, to escape death by an enemy. It rests upon the maxim, *Necessitas inducit privilegium quod jura privata* [Necessity provides a privilege for private rights]."

The common law adopts the principles of the natural law, and places the justification of an act otherwise tortious precisely on the same ground of necessity. . . .

This principle has been familiarly recognized by the books from the time of *Saltpetre's Case* (1606), 77 E.R. 1294, and the instances of tearing down houses to prevent conflagration, or to raise bulwarks for the defence of a city, are made use of as illustrations, rather than as abstract cases, in which its exercise is permitted. At such times, the individual rights of property give way to the higher laws of impending necessity.

A house on fire, or those in its immediate vicinity, which serve to communicate the flames, becomes a nuisance, which it is lawful to abate, and the private rights of the individual yield to the considerations of general convenience, and the interests of society. Were it otherwise, one stubborn person might involve a whole city in ruin, by refusing to allow the destruction of a building which would cut off the flames and check the progress of the fire, and that, too, when it was perfectly evident that his building must be consumed.

. . .

The counsel for the respondent has asked, who is to judge of the necessity of the destruction of property?

This must, in some instances, be a difficult matter to determine. The necessity of blowing up a house may not exist, or be as apparent to the owner, whose judgment is clouded by interest, and the hope of saving his property, as to others. In all such cases the conduct of the individual must be regulated by his own judgment as to the exigencies of the case. If a building should be torn down without apparent or actual necessity, the parties concerned would undoubtedly be liable in an action of trespass. But in every case the necessity must be clearly shown. It is true, many cases of hardship may grow out of this rule, and property may often in such cases be destroyed, without necessity, by irresponsible persons, but this difficulty would not be obviated by making the parties responsible in every case, whether the necessity existed or not.

. . .

The evidence in this case clearly establishes the fact, that the blowing up of the house was necessary, as it would have been consumed had it been left standing. The plaintiffs cannot recover for the value of the goods which they might have saved; they were as much subject to the necessities of the occasion as the house in which they were situate; and if in such cases a party was held liable, it would too frequently happen, that the delay caused by the removal of the goods would render the destruction of the house useless.

The court below clearly erred as to the law applicable to the facts of this case. The testimony will not warrant a verdict against the defendant.

NOTES AND QUESTIONS

1. As *Surocco* suggests, a reasonable and good-faith mistake of fact as to the need to invoke the defence of necessity will not negate the defence. See also *Cope v. Sharpe*, [1912] 1 K.B. 496 (C.A.).

What damages would the plaintiff have been awarded had the defence of public necessity failed?

2. In order to invoke the defence of public necessity, the defendant must have acted reasonably in terms of the damages caused relative to the likely public benefit. What limits, if any, should be imposed on the exercise of public necessity in cases where only property is threatened?

3. The defence of public necessity has been limited to cases in which the defendant has interfered with the plaintiff's property interests. Should a defendant be privileged to intentionally inflict minor physical injury on the plaintiff to protect another party from serious personal injury or death? Should the law privilege the intentional sacrifice of one innocent person in order to save many other innocent people? In *R. v. Dudley* (1884), 14 Q.B.D. 273, the defendants, while adrift in a lifeboat, killed and ate a fellow passenger to save their own lives. The defendants were found guilty of murder but were subsequently pardoned. Contrast *Dudley* with *U.S. v. Holmes*, 26 F.Cas. 360 (Penn. Cir. Ct. 1842). See Fuller, "The Case of the Speluncean Explorers" (1949) 62 Harv. L. Rev. 616.

See also *R. v. Latimer*, [2001] 1 S.C.R. 3, in which the accused was convicted of second degree murder and sentenced to the mandatory minimum of life imprisonment without parole eligibility for 10 years for intentionally killing his severely disabled daughter. The court rejected the accused's attempt to justify his conduct on the basis of necessity, namely that she had suffered enough.

4. *Surocco* suggests that an individual would not be held liable for using force to acquire exclusive possession of a plank that can keep only one person afloat. Would throwing a passenger overboard to prevent a lifeboat from sinking be analogous to the plank situation? How do these situations differ from Dudley? What defence might apply in the example with the plank and overloaded lifeboat?

Is the plank case based on the same principle as *Re A (Children) (Conjoined Twins: Surgical Separation)*, [2000] 4 All E.R. 961 (C.A.)? That case, which was discussed in the previous chapter, involved conjoined twins who would both die within months without surgical intervention. The court authorized the separation of the twins even though the surgery would cause the death of one twin in order to give the more viable twin a good chance for long-term survival.

5. The House of Lords and the United States Supreme Court indicated that the government need not compensate people for losses inflicted during wartime operations, presumably because the military is acting under a type of public

necessity. See *Burmah Oil Co. v. Lord Advocate*, [1965] A.C. 75 (H.L.); *U.S. v. Caltex (Philippines) Inc.*, 344 U.S. 149 (1952); and "The Burmah Oil Affair" (1966) 79 Harv. L. Rev. 614. However, the courts differed on whether the intentional destruction of private property to prevent it from falling into enemy hands comes within this principle. Contrary to the American decision, the House of Lords held that the plaintiffs were entitled to damages in such circumstances. Nevertheless, the plaintiffs' victory was short-lived as Parliament immediately enacted legislation that negated the decision. For a discussion of the Crown's right to seize property for purposes of war, see *Saltpetre's Case* (1606), 77 E.R. 1294 (K.B.); and *A.G. v. Nissan*, [1970] A.C. 179 (H.L.).

6. In *Rigby v. Chief Constable of Northamptonshire*, [1985] 2 All E.R. 985 (Q.B.), the police burned down the plaintiff's shop by firing tear gas canisters into the building in an effort to force out a dangerous psychopath. The police were absolved of liability in trespass on the basis of public necessity, although they were held liable in negligence for not having any firefighting equipment available. Should the defence of public necessity extend to law enforcement? This issue has not been addressed by the Canadian courts.

7. The defence of public necessity appears to apply to travellers who are forced to cross adjoining land when the public highway is blocked. See *Taylor v. Whitehead* (1781), 99 E.R. 475 (K.B.); and *Dwyer v. Staunton*, [1947] 4 D.L.R. 393 (Alta. Dist. Ct.).

8. Traditionally, the defence of necessity has been limited to situations in which the imminent threat is posed by some external force of nature. For example, in *London Borough of Southwark v. Williams*, [1971] 2 All E.R. 175 (C.A.), it was held that homeless squatters could not invoke the defence of public necessity to privilege their entry into vacant houses owned by the Council. Denning M.R. explained at 179:

> If homelessness were once admitted as a defence to trespass, no one's house could be safe. Necessity would open a door which no man could shut. It would not only be those in extreme need who would enter. There would be others who would imagine that they were in need, or would invent a need, so as to gain entry. Each man would say his need was greater than the next man's. The plea would be an excuse for all sorts of wrongdoing. So the courts must, for the sake of law and order, take a firm stand. They must refuse to admit the plea of necessity to the hungry and homeless; and trust their distress will be relieved by the charitable and the good.

Contrast Denning M.R.'s comments about privileging trespass to land with those of Laskin C.J. in *Harrison v. Carswell*, [1976] 2 S.C.R. 200 at 210-12. See also *Wilcox v. Police*, [1994] 1 N.Z.L.R. 243 (H.C.), where the court rejected the defence of public necessity asserted by anti-abortion protestors who had blocked the entrance to a hospital.

9. The rationale for absolving an individual of liability when acting under public necessity is clear. However, since the public as a whole benefits, why is the state not required to compensate the party whose property has been sacrificed? What is the justification for imposing the entire burden of public necessity on a single innocent property owner? In maritime law, if part of a cargo is jettisoned to prevent a ship from

sinking, the loss is apportioned among all the ship and cargo owners. Should a similar concept be adopted in public necessity cases?

10. In *Lapierre v. A.G. (Que.)*, [1985] 1 S.C.R. 241, a five-year-old girl was left totally incapacitated after suffering an idiosyncratic reaction to an injection that she received as part of a provincial immunization program. Although such reactions are known to occur, the program as a whole saves lives and reduces illnesses caused by infectious diseases. Neither the manufacturer of the serum nor those who administered the program were negligent. The Supreme Court of Canada dismissed the girl's action, stating that there is no legal principle of necessity that requires damages suffered by individuals for the public benefit to be borne by the community. See Capriolo & Turcot, "Strict Liability for Acts of the State: Liability for Non-Negligent Vaccination" (1985) 13 C.C.L.T. 37.

11. Shortly after the *Lapierre* decision, Québec introduced a provincial vaccine injury compensation program. As of April 1, 2018, 43 of the 271 claims have been accepted and $5.5 million has been paid out in compensation. Québec was the only province with such a program as of that date. As a matter of public policy, should the other jurisdictions enact a similar program?

12. An individual who negligently caused or contributed to the emergency situation will not be allowed to benefit from the defence of public necessity. See *Bell Telephone Co. v. The Mar-Tirenno* (1974), 52 D.L.R. (3d) 702 (F.C.T.D.), aff'd (1976), 71 D.L.R. (3d) 608 (F.C.A.); and *Rigby, supra*.

13. Various statutes grant public officials broad powers to invade private property in emergency situations. For example, the fire department may be empowered to invade private dwellings to extinguish a fire or to prevent it from spreading.

14. In *R. v. Perka*, [1984] 2 S.C.R. 232, the accused was smuggling over 33 tons of marijuana from Colombia to the international waters off Alaska when mechanical problems and bad weather forced him to take refuge in a deserted cove on the British Columbia coast. The accused argued that he had never intended to enter Canadian waters and that he was entitled to raise the common law defence of necessity. The court held that this common law defence was preserved by virtue of s. 8(3) of the *Criminal Code* and ordered a new trial. See Wells, "Necessity and the Common Law" (1985) 5 Oxford J. Legal Stud. 471.

15. For a discussion of the defence of public necessity, see Peel & Goudkamp, *Winfield & Jolowicz on Tort*, 19th ed. (2014) at 796-98; and Dobbs, Hayden & Bublick, *The Law of Torts*, 2d ed. (2011) vol.1 at 365-72.

(b) PRIVATE NECESSITY

VINCENT v. LAKE ERIE TPT. CO.
124 N.W. 221 (Minn. S.C. 1910)

O'BRIEN J.: The steamship Reynolds, owned by the defendant, was for the purpose of discharging her cargo on November 27, 1905, moored to plaintiff's dock in

Duluth. While the unloading of the boat was taking place a storm from the northeast developed, which at about 10 o'clock p.m., when the unloading was completed, had so grown in violence that the wind was then moving at 50 miles per hour and continued to increase during the night. There is some evidence that one, and perhaps two, boats were able to enter the harbor that night, but it is plain that navigation was practically suspended from the hour mentioned until the morning of the 29th, when the storm abated, and during that time no master would have been justified in attempting to navigate his vessel, if he could avoid doing so. After the discharge of the cargo the Reynolds signaled for a tug to tow her from the dock, but none could be obtained because of the severity of the storm. If the lines holding the ship to the dock had been cast off, she would doubtless have drifted away; but, instead, the lines were kept fast, and as soon as one parted or chafed it was replaced, sometimes with a larger one. The vessel lay upon the outside of the dock, her bow to the east, the wind and waves striking her starboard quarter with such force that she was constantly being lifted and thrown against the dock, resulting in its damage, as found by the jury, to the amount of $500.

We are satisfied that the character of the storm was such that it would have been highly imprudent for the master of the Reynolds to have attempted to leave the dock or to have permitted the vessel to drift away from it. One witness testified upon the trial that the vessel could have been warped into a slip, and that, if the attempt to bring the ship into the slip had failed, the worst that could have happened would be that the vessel would have been blown ashore upon a soft and muddy bank. The witness was not present in Duluth at the time of the storm, and while he may have been right in his conclusions, those in charge of the dock and the vessel at the time of the storm were not required to use the highest human intelligence, nor were they required to resort to every possible experiment which could be suggested for the preservation of their property. Nothing more was demanded of them than ordinary prudence and care, and the record in this case fully sustains the contention of the appellant that, in holding the vessel fast to the dock, those in charge of her exercised good judgment and prudent seamanship.

It is claimed by the respondent that it was negligence to moor the boat to an exposed part of the wharf, and to continue in that position after it became apparent that the storm was to be more than usually severe. We do not agree with this position. The part of the wharf where the vessel was moored appears to have been commonly used for that purpose. It was situated within the harbor at Duluth, and must, we think, be considered a proper and safe place, and would undoubtedly have been such during what would be considered a very severe storm. The storm which made it unsafe was one which surpassed in violence any which might have reasonably been anticipated.

The appellant contends . . . that, because its conduct during the storm was rendered necessary by prudence and good seamanship under conditions over which it had no control, it cannot be held liable for any injury resulting to the property of others . . .

The situation was one in which the ordinary rules regulating property rights were suspended by forces beyond human control, and if, without the direct intervention of some act by the one sought to be held liable, the property of another was injured, such injury must be attributed to the act of God, and not to the wrongful act of the person sought to be charged. If during the storm the Reynolds had entered the harbor, and while there had become disabled and been thrown against the plaintiff's dock, the plaintiff would not have recovered. Again, if while attempting to hold fast to the dock the lines had parted, without any negligence, and the vessel carried against some other boat or dock in the harbor, there would be no liability upon her owner. But here those in charge of the vessel deliberately and by their direct efforts held her in such a position that the damage to the dock resulted, and, having thus preserved the ship at the expense of the dock, it seems to us that her owners are responsible to the dock owners to the extent of the injury inflicted.

In *Depue v. Flateau*, 100 Minn. 299, 111 N.W. 1, 8 L.R.A. (N.S.) 485, this court held that where the plaintiff, while lawfully in the defendant's house, became so ill that he was incapable of traveling with safety, the defendants were responsible to him in damages for compelling him to leave the premises. If, however, the owner of the premises had furnished the traveller with proper accommodations and medical attendance, would he have been able to defeat an action brought against him for their reasonable worth?

In *Ploof v. Putnam*, 71 Atl. 188, 20 L.R.A. (N.S.) 152, the Supreme Court of Vermont held that where, under stress of weather, a vessel was without permission moored to a private dock at an island in Lake Champlain owned by the defendant, the plaintiff was not guilty of trespass, and that the defendant was responsible in damages because his representative upon the island unmoored the vessel, permitting it to drift upon the shore, with resultant injuries to it. If, in that case, the vessel had been permitted to remain, and the dock had suffered injury, we believe the shipowner would have been held liable for the injury done.

Theologians hold that a starving man may, without moral guilt, take what is necessary to sustain life; but it could hardly be said that the obligation would not be upon such person to pay the value of the property so taken when he became able to do so. And so public necessity, in times of war or peace, may require the taking of private property for public purposes; but under our system of jurisprudence compensation must be made.

Let us imagine in this case that for the better mooring of the vessel those in charge of her had appropriated a valuable cable lying upon the dock. No matter how justifiable such appropriation might have been, it would not be claimed that, because of the over-whelming necessity of the situation, the owner of the cable could not recover its value.

This is not a case where life or property was menaced by any object or thing belonging to the plaintiff, the destruction of which became necessary to prevent the threatened disaster. Nor is it a case where, because of the act of God, or unavoidable accident, the infliction of the injury was beyond the control of the defendant, but is one where the defendant prudently and advisedly availed itself of the plaintiff's property for the purpose of preserving its own more valuable property, and the plaintiffs are entitled to compensation for the injury done.

LEWIS J.:—I dissent. It was assumed on the trial before the lower court that appellant's liability depended on whether the master of the ship might, in the exercise of reasonable care, have sought a place of safety before the storm made it impossible to leave the dock. The majority opinion assumed that the evidence is conclusive that appellant moored its boat at respondent's dock pursuant to contract, and that the vessel was lawfully in position at the time the additional cables were fastened to the dock, and the reasoning of the opinion is that, because appellant made use of the stronger cables to hold the boat in position, it became liable under the rule that it had voluntarily made use of the property of another for the purpose of saving its own.

In my judgment, if the boat was lawfully in position at the time the storm broke, and the master could not, in the exercise of due care, have left that position without subjecting his vessel to the hazards of the storm, then the damage to the dock, caused by the pounding of the boat, was the result of an inevitable accident. If the master was in the exercise of due care, he was not at fault. The reasoning of the opinion admits that if the ropes, or cables, first attached to the dock had not parted, or if, in the first instance, the master had used the stronger cables, there would be no liability. If the master could not, in the exercise of reasonable care have anticipated the severity of the storm and sought a place of safety before it became impossible, why should he be required to anticipate the severity of the storm, and, in the first instance, use the stronger cables?

I am of the opinion that one who constructs a dock to the navigable line of waters, and enters into contractual relations with the owner of a vessel to moor at the same, takes the risk of damage to his dock by a boat caught there by a storm, which event could not have been avoided in the exercise of due care, and further, that the legal status of the parties in such a case is not changed by renewal of cables to keep the boat from being cast adrift at the mercy of the tempest.

JAGGARD J.: I concur with Lewis, J.

NOTES AND QUESTIONS

1. On what bases did O'Brien J. conclude that: (a) inevitable accident; and (b) public necessity did not apply? What was the basis of Lewis J.'s dissent?

2. The first issue that arises in private necessity, as in public necessity, is whether the defendant is privileged to invade the plaintiff's property interests. As stated in Howarth, "Defences to Intentional Torts" in Sappideen & Vines, eds., *Fleming's The Law of Torts*, 10th ed. (2011) 87 at 110, "If the emergency is sufficiently great and the good it is intended to do is not disproportionate to the harm likely to result, one may trespass upon the land of another to save one's self or one's property."

3. Should public or private necessity apply if the defendant is attempting: (a) to save only his or her own life; (b) to protect his or her own interests, but in doing so advances the public interest (*e.g. Dwyer v. Staunton*, [1947] 4 D.L.R. 393 (Alta. Dist. Ct.)); or (c) to protect the plaintiff's property (*e.g. Sherrin v. Haggerty*, [1953] O.W.N. 962 (Co. Ct.))?

4. As with other self-help remedies, such as recaption of chattels, there is a potential for violence inherent in the assertion of private necessity. Can you justify granting broader powers of entry in private necessity than in recaption of chattels?

5. What is the significance of the imminent peril requirement? How would you distinguish *Vincent* from a case in which a landowner found it impossible to complete a construction project without trespassing on the adjoining property?

6. Once a court decides that the defendant was privileged to enter, it must then determine who should pay for the ensuing damages. As indicated in *Vincent*, private

necessity is generally considered to be a partial or incomplete defence in the United States. In other words, the defendant is permitted to trespass on the plaintiff's land, but must provide compensation for any losses that he or she has inflicted. See Bohlen, "Incomplete Privilege to Inflict Intentional Invasions of Interests of Property and Personality" (1926) 39 Harv. L. Rev. 307; and Dobbs, Hayden & Bublick, *The Law of Torts*, 2d ed. (2011) vol.1 at 362-65.

7. Is it inconsistent to grant defendants a right to trespass, but hold them liable for the damages that result? Why would defendants plead private necessity if they still have to pay for the damage they cause? How would the court in *Vincent* have reacted if the dock owner had unmoored the ship, allowing it to be wrecked in the storm? See *Ploof v. Putnam*, 71 A. 188 (Vt. S.C. 1908); Epstein, "Defenses and Subsequent Pleas in a System of Strict Liability" (1974) 3 J. Legal Stud. 165 at 165-70; and Klimchuk, "Necessity and Restitution" (2001) 7 Legal Theory 59.

8. It is not clear whether private necessity is a complete or partial defence in England and Canada. A complete defence would allow a person to trespass without paying compensation for the losses that he or she inflicted. What arguments would you make in favour of each position? See Sussman, "The Defence of Private Necessity and the Problem of Compensation" (1967) 2 Ottawa L. Rev. 184; Finan & Ritson, "Tortious Necessity: The Privileged Defense" (1992) 26 Akron L. Rev. 1; and Sugarman, "The 'Necessity' Defense And The Failure of Tort Theory: The Case Against Strict Liability For Damages Caused While Exercising Self-Help In An Emergency" (2005) 5 Issues in Legal Scholarship 1.

9. The facts in *Munn & Co. v. The Motor Vessel Sir John Crosbie*, [1967] 1 Ex. C.R. 94 were similar to those in *Vincent*, but *Munn* was pleaded and decided in negligence. In *Munn*, the court expressed a preference for the dissent in *Vincent*.

10. Although there is no right to intentionally injure another person in the assertion of either public or private necessity, physical force can be used to overcome resistance to the exercise of necessity. Given the potential for violence inherent in this principle, should it be limited to public necessity? See The American Law Institute, *Restatement of the Law, Second Torts* (1965) vol. 1 at §196 comment (b) and §197 comment (g). An individual who causes harm or injury in resisting the exercise of public or private necessity can be held civilly liable. See *Depue v. Flateau*, 111 N.W. 1 (Minn. S.C. 1907); and *Ploof, supra*.

11. How do the principles governing private necessity differ from those applicable to motive?

12. Can you justify the fact that the common law recognizes a defence of public and private necessity, but not duress?

8. Apportionment of Fault in Intentional Torts

At common law, the fact that the plaintiff negligently contributed to his or her own injuries provided the defendant with a complete defence to negligence liability. This all-or-nothing approach came to be viewed as inappropriate, for it imposed the entire loss on one of the two negligent parties. Consequently, legislation was introduced in most common law jurisdictions to apportion losses in negligence actions between the defendant and the plaintiff, according to their respective degrees of fault. This is discussed in greater detail in Chapter 19: Defences in Negligence. Generally, the legislation in Canada's common law provinces applies in any case where the damages have been caused by "fault or neglect." Depending on the courts' interpretation of the word "fault," the legislation may apply beyond the bounds of negligence. The question has arisen whether a defendant in an intentional tort action can invoke the apportionment legislation and use the plaintiff's contributory negligence or other wrongful conduct as a partial defence.

Some cases indicate that the apportionment legislation may apply to intentional torts. For example in *Bell Canada v. Cope (Sarnia) Ltd.* (1980), 11 C.C.L.T. 170 (Ont. H.C.), aff'd (1981) 119 D.L.R. (3d) 254 (C.A.), the defendant's damages in trespass to land were reduced by 33% to reflect the plaintiff's contributory negligence. Similarly in *Berntt v. Vancouver (City)*, [1997] 4 W.W.R. 505 (B.C.S.C.), the plaintiff's damages in battery were reduced by 75% under the provincial apportionment legislation to reflect his provocative and irresponsible behaviour as a ringleader of a riot following a hockey game. Although the Court of Appeal ordered a new trial on the issue of liability, it did not question the applicability of the apportionment legislation: *Berntt v. Vancouver (City)* (1999), 46 C.C.L.T. (2d) 139 (B.C.C.A.).

However, in *Boma Manufacturing Ltd. v. Canadian Imperial Bank of Commerce*, [1996] 3 S.C.R. 727, the court stated that as a matter of principle, "contributory negligence would not be available in the context of a strict liability tort . . . While this argument would be available in an action for negligence, the notion of strict liability involved in an action for conversion is *prima facie* antithetical to the concept of contributory negligence." The issue in *Boma* arose in an action for conversion of cheques. It is not clear whether the court intended to exclude other intentional torts from the application of the apportionment legislation.

The issue of apportionment can arise not only between the plaintiff and the defendant, but also among various defendants. That issue is also addressed by statute. For example, the *Negligence Act*, R.S.O. 1990, c. N.1, s. 1 states:

> Where damages have been caused or contributed to by the fault or neglect of two or more persons, the court shall determine the degree in which each of such persons is at fault or negligent, and, where two or more persons are found at fault or negligent, they are jointly and severally liable to the person suffering loss or damage for such fault or negligence, but as between themselves, in the absence of any contract express or implied, each is liable to make contribution and indemnify each other in the degree in which they are respectively found to be at fault or negligent.

NOTES AND QUESTIONS

1. Traditionally, the courts interpreted the words "fault" and "negligent" to be synonyms and excluded intentional torts from the scope of the apportionment legislation. See for example *Hollebone v. Barnard*, [1954] 2 D.L.R. 278 (Ont. H.C.); and *Funnell v. Canadian Pacific Railway*, [1964] 2 O.R. 325 (H.C.).

2. In *Boma*, the court stated that contributory negligence is logically incompatible with strict liability torts. In order to establish contributory negligence, the defendant must prove that the plaintiff acted negligently or in an intentionally wrongful manner and that this conduct caused or contributed to the plaintiff's injuries or losses. Given

the definition of contributory negligence, do you agree with the court's analysis of the relationship between this defence and strict liability torts? Is the court's characterization of conversion as a strict liability tort accurate?

In *Cowles v. Balac* (2006), 83 O.R. (3d) 660 (C.A.), the plaintiffs were attacked by Bengal tigers at the defendant's drive-through safari zoo. In regard to *Boma*, Borins J.A. stated at para. 216: "In my respectful view, in stating contributory negligence is not available in the context of a strict liability tort, Iacobucci J. was not intending to state a general principle. Rather, he was referring to the law of bills of exchange." After a detailed review of the cases and academic views, Borins J.A. concluded that contributory negligence should be a defence to strict liability torts. In *Cowles*, Borins J.A. was in dissent. Since the majority held that the plaintiffs were not contributorily negligent, it did not address the strict liability issue.

3. The apportionment legislation only applies when two or more parties have caused or contributed to the same loss or injury. This issue is often framed in terms of whether the plaintiff's loss or injury is "indivisible." The task of determining whether a series of harms should be treated as resulting in a single collective or indivisible injury is often challenging.

For example, in *O'Neil v. Van Horne* (2002), 59 O.R. (3d) 384 (C.A.), the defendant was being sued for sexually assaulting the plaintiff when she was three years old. The defendant sought to add the plaintiff's parents and former boyfriend as third parties because they had allegedly sexually assaulted the plaintiff later in life. The court refused the defendant's motion, stating that while it was inherently difficult to determine which of the plaintiff's damages were attributable to which assaults, the torts were separate and the damages had to be treated as being divisible. Consequently, in this case there could be no joint and several liability and no apportionment.

4. Some courts have attempted to avoid the impact of applying the traditional intentional tort defences in cases in which both parties were to blame. For example, the limits that the courts have imposed on the *ex turpi causa* defence, discussed in the previous chapter, appear to reflect concern about denying a wrongdoing plaintiff any redress. The complex case law governing consensual fights and factors vitiating consent appears to be based on similar concerns. However, by narrowly defining the traditional defences, the courts impose the entire loss on the defendant despite the plaintiff's at-fault conduct that has contributed to his or her own loss. Is this all-or-nothing approach in intentional torts any more justifiable than the now-discredited all-or-nothing approach to negligence liability? In what other areas of intentional torts would apportionment provisions be appropriate? See generally Crocker, "Apportionment of Liability and the Intentional Torts: The Time is Right for Change" (1982-83) 7 Dal. L.J. 172; and Manchester, "Trespass and Contributory Negligence in Ontario" (1982) 31 I.C.L.Q. 203.

As discussed in Chapter 3, the plaintiff's provocative conduct is taken into account in several provinces to reduce the compensatory damage award that he or she might have otherwise received. For a discussion of the relationship between provocation and contributory negligence in intentional torts, see *Wilson v. Bobbie* (2006), 394 A.R. 118 (Q.B.).

REVIEW PROBLEMS

1. Although Steven loved to bet on football games, he seldom picked winners. As a result, he became indebted to a local bookmaker named Estelle for $35,000. She made it clear that unless he paid at least $18,000 by the end of the week, he would have to "face the music." Steven was frightened. He knew that Estelle was dangerous and strongly suspected that she was responsible for two unknown thugs severely beating his friend, who was also indebted to her.

Gambling debts were not Steven's only problem. Although entirely oblivious to the fact, Steven had become a prime suspect in the armed robbery of his former employer, Mel. When asked who might have a motive for such a crime, Mel readily suggested Steven, saying "He always hated me, especially after I fired him for insolence."

As Steven was drowning his sorrows in a glass of beer at a local bar, he noticed that two men were watching him. They were very big and looked very tough. Steven quickly paid his tab, finished his drink and left. However, as he was walking toward his car, he noticed that the two men had followed him. When he crossed the street, they did likewise. When he quickened his pace, they did so as well. He could hear their approaching footsteps close behind. Finally, fearing for his safety, he turned and sprayed the two men with a canister of mace. They dropped to the ground, screaming in pain. As Steven ran to his car, one of the men shouted, "Stop or we will shoot. We are the police and you are under arrest!" Steven kept running, convinced that the two men were actually Estelle's thugs. Steven then heard a gunshot and felt a searing pain in his leg. As he later learned in the hospital, the two men were indeed undercover police officers. They were following him in connection with their investigation into Mel's robbery.

Steven has come to you for advice. In particular, he wants to know if the police officers can sue him for spraying them with mace, and if so, whether he has any defence. He also wants to know if he can sue the police officer who shot him and, if so, whether the officer has any defence.

2. There had been bad feelings between the Smith and Jones families for years. In a recent incident, nine-year-old Frank Smith was bitten by Mr. Jones' dog, Max. Frank had been playing with a Frisbee in his own backyard when the wind carried it over the fence and into Mr. Jones' backyard. Frank had just received the Frisbee as a birthday present. He knew from past experience that Mr. Jones would probably take at least a week to return it. Frank did not see Max when he peered over the fence and concluded that there was no danger. Although Mr. Jones had previously forbidden Frank from doing so, Frank climbed over the fence to retrieve his Frisbee. When Mr. Jones saw Frank in his yard, he became furious. Wanting to scare the boy, he opened his back door and let Max run out. To Mr. Jones' surprise, Max not only barked at Frank, but also bit him. Once that happened, Mr. Jones intervened and pulled Max away. Discuss the intentional torts that may have been committed by Mr. Jones and Frank. Also discuss the defences that each party might raise.

8

THE DEFENCE OF LEGAL AUTHORITY

1. Introduction
2. The *Canadian Charter of Rights and Freedoms*
3. Authority and Privilege to Arrest Without a Warrant
4. Rights and Obligations in the Arrest Process
5. The Common Law Power to Search Pursuant to a Lawful Arrest
6. A Peace Officer's Common Law Power of Entry to Search for a Wanted Person

1. Introduction

This chapter deals with legal authority as a defence to intentional torts that may be committed during an arrest, search, seizure, or entry. Although most commonly associated with false imprisonment, the defence of legal authority may be raised in response to actions for battery, trespass to chattels, conversion, trespass to land, and other intentional torts. Initially, the defence was based on both civil and criminal cases. Consistent with the common law's concern with autonomy, peace officers and private citizens were given only limited powers to act without a warrant or other prior judicial authorization. In many circumstances, even those who acted on reasonable grounds in asserting legal authority were held liable if they arrested the wrong person, seized the wrong goods or entered the wrong property. The early common law viewed law enforcement as a community responsibility, and relatively few distinctions were drawn between the authority of private citizens and various enforcement officials.

In Canada, these common law principles were largely supplanted by legislation. The statutory provisions greatly expanded the powers of police and others to act without prior judicial approval. Moreover, the courts interpreted these statutory powers very broadly. While this chapter focuses on legal authority under federal criminal law, it is important to appreciate that the police and others are granted broad arrest, entry, search, and seizure powers under various provincial and territorial legislation, including the mental health, child welfare, education, liquor, highway traffic, parks, and trespass statutes.

The framework for analyzing the defence of legal authority is essentially the same, whether it is based on the common law or on provincial, territorial or federal legislation. Three issues must be addressed. First, did the defendant have legal authority to undertake the act that gave rise to the tort in issue? Second, was the defendant legally privileged, that is, protected from both civil and criminal liability in doing the act that gave rise to the tort? Third, did the defendant meet all of the other obligations imposed upon him or her in the process? For example, even if the police were authorized and privileged in making an arrest, they may be held civilly liable if they failed to inform the suspect of the reasons for the arrest or used excessive force.

It is not possible to comprehensively review the defence of legal authority in this chapter even if the discussion is limited to federal criminal law or indeed the *Criminal Code*, R.S.C. 1985, c. C-46. Consequently, we will address four common issues that illustrate how the defence of legal authority operates: (i) authority and privilege to arrest without a warrant; (ii) rights and obligations in the arrest process; (iii) the common law power to search pursuant to a lawful arrest; and (iv) a peace officer's common law power of entry to search for a wanted person.

As many of the older cases discussed in this chapter illustrate, until the 1980s the Canadian courts broadly interpreted police powers and only reluctantly held police civilly liable. With the advent of the *Canadian Charter of Rights and Freedoms*, Part I of the *Constitution Act, 1982*, being Schedule B to the *Canada Act 1982* (U.K.) 1982, c. 11, judicial attitudes towards the police changed dramatically. The courts now routinely second-guess police decisions and hold them to rigorous standards.

NOTES AND QUESTIONS

1. For a discussion of the English common law enforcement powers, see Harris, *Principles of the Criminal Law* (1877) at 303-12; Stephen, *A History of the Criminal Law of England*, vol. 1 (1883) at 184-206; and Hall, "Legal and Social Aspects of Arrest Without a Warrant" (1936) 49 Harv. L. Rev. 566.

2. Provincial and territorial statutes grant teachers, physicians, public health inspectors, and others broad authority that in many circumstances far exceeds that of the police. In regard to educators, see *R. v. Sweet*, 1986 CarswellOnt 3452 (Dist. Ct.) (WL Can); and *R. v. M.(M.R.)*, [1998] 3 S.C.R. 393. The mental health statutes typically authorize physicians to detain mentally ill individuals against their will if they pose a significant risk of serious harm to themselves or others. See for example the *Mental Health Act*, R.S.B.C. 1996, c. 288, s. 22; and *Mental Health Act*, R.S.O. 1990, c. M.7, s. 20(1.1).

3. The Canadian courts' reliance on the *Criminal Code* and other federal criminal statutes to define civil liability raises constitutional issues regarding the division of legislative authority between the federal and provincial governments. While criminal law falls within the exclusive authority of the federal government, "property and civil rights," including tort law, is a provincial matter: the *Constitution Act, 1867 (U.K.)*, 30 & 31 Vict., c. 3, ss. 91(27) and 92(13), reprinted in R.S.C. 1985, App. II, No. 5. For the most part, the Supreme Court of Canada has assumed that the *Criminal Code* provisions govern the defence of legal authority in torts cases. See *Frey v. Fedoruk*, [1950] S.C.R. 517; *Priestman v. Colangelo*, [1959] S.C.R. 615; and *Poupart v. Lafortune*, [1974] S.C.R. 175. Even when the courts stated that the criminal and civil defences of legal authority should be treated as distinct issues, they often failed to squarely address the constitutional question. See *Fletcher v. Collins* (1968), 70 D.L.R. (2d) 183 at 188 (Ont. H.C.); and *Eccles v. Bourque*, [1975] 2 S.C.R. 739 at 742.

What constitutional argument would you make in support of the courts' reliance on the *Criminal Code* in civil cases? Would your argument vary depending on whether the defendant was a peace officer or a private citizen?

4. Reliance on criminal statutes and cases in tort law is also complicated by the fact that the criminal law concept of arrest does not correspond to the tort concept of imprisonment. In *R. v. Whitfield*, [1970] S.C.R. 46 at 48, Judson J. quoted 10 Hals. (3d) 342, stating: "Arrest consists of the actual seizure or touching of a person's body with a view to his detention. The mere pronouncing of words of arrest is not an arrest,

unless the person sought to be arrested submits to the process and goes with the arresting officer."

The Canadian courts have recognized that the police have common law authority to stop vehicles and question drivers about their sobriety, conduct pat-down searches of suspects and establish roadblocks to investigate suspected firearms offences. See *R. v. Dedman*, [1985] 2 S.C.R. 2 and *R. v. Orbanski; R. v. Elias*, 2005 SCC 37 (sobriety checks); *R. v. Mann*, 2004 SCC 52, *R. v. MacDonald*, 2014 SCC 3, *Figueiras v. Toronto (Police Services Board)*, 2015 ONCA 208, *R. v. Patrick*, 2017 BCCA 57, and *Elmardy v. Toronto Police Services Board*, 2017 ONSC 2074 (pat-down and safety searches); and *R. v. Clayton*, 2007 SCC 32 (roadblocks). Those stopped, detained, searched, and questioned are not arrested, and yet they are not free to leave. The scope, duration, limits, and purpose of these "investigatory detention" powers are controversial. See generally *R. v. Grant*, 2009 SCC 32; *R. v. Ellis*, 2016 ONCA 598; and *Turton v. Hanson*, 2018 ABCA 84.

As discussed in Chapter 3, the tort of false imprisonment may be defined as the intentional bringing about of a total restraint of movement of another person. How do the concepts of arrest, investigatory detention and imprisonment differ? What are the legal implications of these differences for the defence of legal authority?

5. Most of the early case law is English, and it is difficult to apply in Canada because crimes are categorized differently in the two jurisdictions. The English common law distinction between felonies and misdemeanors was abandoned in Canada with the enactment of Canada's first *Criminal Code*, S.C. 1892, 55-56 Vict., c. 29. Instead, the *Criminal Code* divides offences into those tried by indictment and those tried by summary conviction. There is also a third category, hybrid offences, in which the prosecutor is given discretion to proceed by either indictment or summary conviction.

2. The *Canadian Charter of Rights and Freedoms*

The *Charter* further complicates the analysis of the defence of legal authority. However, the *Charter*'s application is subject to several limitations. Most significantly for our purposes, s. 32 of the *Charter* limits its application to federal and provincial law, and the conduct of government departments, agencies and officials. Consistent with its goal of protecting the public from improper state action, the *Charter* generally does not apply to the actions of entirely private parties.

Some sections of the *Charter* are specifically designed to protect people who are subject to criminal charges or other state-imposed detention, while other sections have a more general application. Sections 7 to 15 of the *Charter* guarantee a broad range of legal rights, including: the right to be secure against unreasonable search or seizure (s. 8); the right not to be arbitrarily detained or imprisoned (s. 9); and the right to legal counsel upon arrest or detention (s. 10(b)). Section 2 contains broad freedoms, including freedom of expression, assembly and association (s. 2(b), (c) and (d)).

Once an individual establishes that his or her *Charter* rights have been violated, the burden shifts to the government to justify that violation under s. 1. If the government cannot satisfy the requirements of s. 1, the individual may pursue one or more remedies under the *Charter*. Section 24(1) gives judges discretion to grant an aggrieved individual whatever remedy they consider "appropriate and just in the circumstances." Section 24(2), which is primarily relevant in criminal cases, requires judges to exclude evidence obtained in violation of an accused's *Charter* rights if admitting the evidence would "bring the administration of justice into disrepute." Moreover, s. 52 provides that the *Charter* is the supreme law of Canada, and that any law inconsistent with it is of no force or effect to the extent of the inconsistency. These provisions may directly affect civil liability in the following two distinct ways.

(a) LIABILITY UNDER SECTION 24(1)

An individual whose *Charter* rights are violated may seek a remedy under s. 24(1). The individual is not automatically entitled to a damage award under s. 24(1), but only the remedy that the court considers "appropriate and just in the circumstances." Thus, a damage award is simply one of the remedies that a judge may consider granting. In *Doucet-Boudreau v. Nova Scotia (Minister of Education)*, [2003] 3 S.C.R. 3, the court stated that an appropriate and just remedy meaningfully vindicates the claimant's rights and freedoms, employs means that are legitimate within Canada's framework of constitutional democracy, is judicial in nature, and is fair to the party against whom it is made. Given this vague statement, it is not surprising that the controversies regarding s. 24(1) continued.

In *Vancouver (City) v. Ward*, [2010] 2 S.C.R. 28, the court specifically addressed when a damage award would be an appropriate and just remedy. The police initially detained Ward because they suspected, albeit mistakenly, that he might throw a pie at the Prime Minister. When Ward loudly protested and caused a disturbance, he was arrested for breach of the peace, his car was seized, and he was subsequently strip-searched and held in a cell for several hours. The trial judge ruled that the arrest was lawful, but that the seizure of Ward's car and his strip search violated his s. 8 *Charter* rights to freedom from unreasonable search or seizure. Although the police were not found to have acted in bad faith and their conduct was not held to be tortious, Ward was awarded damages under s. 24(1) of $100 for the seizure of his car and $5,000 for being strip-searched. When the Court of Appeal upheld the judgment, it was appealed.

The Supreme Court of Canada established a four-part test for awarding damages under s. 24(1). First, the plaintiff must establish that his or her *Charter* rights have been violated. Second, the damage award must advance *Charter* goals by compensating the plaintiff for a personal loss resulting from the violation, vindicating the breach of the plaintiff's rights or deterring future violations by state actors. Third, the state may attempt to establish that a countervailing factor warrants refraining from awarding *Charter* damages. For example, there may be another *Charter* remedy (such as a declaration or apology) or common law remedy (such as a tort action) that adequately addresses the *Charter* violation. Similarly, the state may argue that an award of *Charter* damages would unduly interfere with good governance. The court stated that it would be inappropriate to award *Charter* damages against officials who had reasonably relied on legislation that was subsequently struck down, because it would discourage government officials from enforcing the current law. Fourth, the amount of the damage award should reflect its purpose (compensation, vindication or deterrence), having regard to the impact of the breach on the plaintiff and the seriousness of the state's conduct.

The Supreme Court of Canada upheld the $5,000 damage award for the strip search because it served the purposes of compensation, vindication and deterrence, strip searches are inherently degrading, the search had a significant impact on the plaintiff's "intangible interests," and the police conduct was serious. However, the court replaced the $100 damage award for seizing the car with a declaration under s. 24(1), because the seizure did not result in loss and the police conduct was not sufficiently serious to warrant vindication or deterrence.

(b) THE IMPACT OF SECTION 52 ON THE DEFENCE OF LEGAL AUTHORITY

As indicated, s. 52 provides that any law that is inconsistent with the *Charter* will be of no force or effect to the extent of the inconsistency. Consequently, the *Charter* may eliminate the legal basis upon which a person would have otherwise been able to establish the defence of legal authority. Assume that a peace officer relies upon a *Criminal Code* provision in arresting a suspect and that provision is struck down under s. 52 in the ensuing criminal trial. If the suspect then sues in false imprisonment, the officer will not be able to establish that the detention was authorized by law and the officer may not be able to establish that he or she was privileged from civil liability.

NOTES AND QUESTIONS

1. Although the *Charter* does not generally apply to the private sector, the Supreme Court of Canada has stated that the "judiciary ought to apply and develop the principles of the common law in a manner consistent with the fundamental values" in the *Charter*: *Dolphin Delivery Ltd. v. R.W.D.S.U., Local 580*, [1986] 2 S.C.R. 573 at 603. As a matter of policy, should *Charter* values, which are primarily designed to regulate and limit state action, be imported into common law principles governing private relations?

2. Initially, the Canadian courts were reluctant to award damages for the *Charter* violation itself, and required the plaintiff to prove actual loss. See *Bauder v. Wilson* (1988), 43 C.R.R. 149 (B.C.S.C.); and *Breen v. Saunders* (1986), 71 N.B.R. (2d) 404 (Q.B.). In contrast, *Ward* indicated that *Charter* violations can be actionable *per se*. What goals would such awards serve? Provide examples of circumstances that would warrant such awards. See also Otis, "Constitutional Liability for the Infringement of Rights Per Se: A Misguided Theory" (1992) 26 U.B.C.L. Rev. 21.

3. In what circumstances should the availability of a tort remedy preclude awarding *Charter* damages, and in what circumstances should both remedies be available?

4. Several courts had ruled that *Charter* damages should not be awarded for violations committed in good faith in the absence of recklessness or oppressive conduct. See for example *Mackin v. New Brunswick (Minister of Justice)*, 2002 SCC 13; *Hislop v. Canada (Attorney General)*, 2007 SCC 10; and *Mammoliti v. Niagara Regional Police Service*, 2007 ONCA 79.

However, in *Ward*, the Supreme Court of Canada upheld the award of *Charter* damages for the strip search even though the police had not acted in bad faith and their conduct had not been tortious. Do you agree that the indignities inherent in the strip search warranted *Charter* damages even though the police had not acted in bad faith?

In *Henry v. British Columbia (Attorney General)*, 2015 SCC 24, the plaintiff sued the province and others seeking damages for being wrongfully convicted and imprisoned for almost 27 years. While the majority and minority agreed that the plaintiff could recover for prosecutorial abuse under s. 24(1) without proof of malice, they disagreed on the threshold test for such claims. The plaintiff was subsequently awarded over $8 million, of which $7.5 million was awarded to serve the "vindication and deterrence functions" of s. 24(1): *Henry v. British Columbia (Attorney General)*, 2016 BCSC 1038.

5. As illustrated by *Henry*, serious *Charter* violations have resulted in substantial damage awards under s. 24(1). In *McTaggart v. Ontario*, 2000 CarswellOnt 4808 (S.C.J.) (WL Can), the investigating officer's intentional withholding of exculpatory evidence from the Crown and defence counsel violated the plaintiff's s. 7 *Charter* rights to life, liberty and security of the person. This violation led to the plaintiff's wrongful conviction as a bank robber, 20 months of incarceration in solitary confinement as a dangerous offender, and profound psychological harm. The plaintiff was awarded $230,000 under s. 24(1), made up of $60,000 in lost income, $150,000 in general damages and $20,000 in punitive damages.

Similarly, in *Rollinson v. R.* (1994), 20 C.C.L.T. (2d) 92 (F.C.T.D.), the plaintiff was awarded $224,000 stemming from a series of unjustified police and customs seizures of his boat. The general damage award included $8,000 specifically for the denial of the plaintiff's *Charter* rights. See also *Elmardy v. Toronto Police Services Board*, 2017 ONSC 2074, in which the police stopped the plaintiff, who was black, without any reasonable suspicion that he was involved in criminal activity. When the plaintiff became verbally hostile, he was punched in the face and subdued. The plaintiff was awarded $50,000 for breach of his ss. 8, 9 and 10(a) and (b) *Charter* rights, $25,000 in punitive damages and $5,000 in general damages.

6. In *Dulude v. Canada* (2000), 1 F.C. 545 (C.A.), the plaintiff, a member of the armed forces, had obtained sick leave from a military physician, but not his commanding officer. Since the plaintiff was technically absent without leave, the commanding officer was acting within his power in ordering the plaintiff's arrest. The military police who arrested and detained Dulude did not use excessive force and he suffered no physical or psychological injury. The plaintiff sued the Department of National Defence for unlawful arrest. The trial judge ruled that the arrest was lawful and dismissed the claim. The plaintiff appealed. The Federal Court of Appeal held that the commanding officer should not have exercised his power to have the plaintiff arrested and thereby breached the plaintiff's s. 9 *Charter* rights. The court characterized the defendant's conduct as a serious breach of the *Charter* and awarded the plaintiff $10,000 under s. 24(1). Do you agree with this characterization of the defendant's conduct? See also *Lahaie v. Canada (Attorney General)* (2010), 101 O.R. (3d) 241 (C.A.).

7. An estate cannot pursue *Charter* remedies for violations of ss. 7 and 15 on a deceased's behalf: *Hislop v. Canada (Attorney General)*, 2007 SCC 10; and *Giacomelli Estate v. Canada (Attorney General)* (2008), 90 O.R. (3d) 669 (C.A.).

8. For a discussion of remedies under the Québec *Charter*, see *Berthiaume c. Cinéma Guzzo inc. (Cinéma Méga-plex Marché central 18)* (2009), 68 C.C.L.T. (3d) 146 (C.S. Qc.); and *Hinse v. Canada (Attorney General)*, 2015 SCC 35.

3. Authority and Privilege to Arrest Without a Warrant

(a) INTRODUCTION

Peace officers and private citizens often raise the defence of legal authority when a suspect whom they have arrested or detained sues them for false imprisonment or battery. In such cases, the defendant has to prove that the specific act that gave rise to the tort action was authorized by the common law or a statute. Traditionally, the common law did not lightly grant such authority. As illustrated by *Entick v. Carrington* (1765), 19 State Tr. 1029 (C.P.), individuals enjoy a right to freedom from state interference unless there is clear legal authority that specifically allows for their restraint. Individuals have no general obligation to stop, identify themselves, answer questions, submit to a search, or otherwise co-operate with the police or others.

Individuals are allowed to use force to physically resist unauthorized police conduct. However, such a course of action carries not only physical but also legal risks. If the police are authorized to arrest or detain an individual, that person is required to submit to the officer's legal authority. An individual who defies or physically resists the lawful exercise of police authority may incur criminal liability for obstructing or assaulting an officer in the execution of his or her duty: *Criminal Code*, ss. 129(a) and 270(1)(a).

While various sections of the *Criminal Code* authorize arrest in specific situations, the most important sources of authority to arrest are found in the general arrest provisions of ss. 494 and 495.

494(1) Any one may arrest without warrant

    (a) a person whom he finds committing an indictable offence; or
    (b) a person who, on reasonable grounds, he believes

        (i) has committed a criminal offence, and
        (ii) is escaping from and freshly pursued by persons who have lawful authority to arrest that person.

(2) The owner or a person in lawful possession of property, or a person authorized by the owner or by a person in lawful possession of property, may arrest a person without a warrant if they find them committing a criminal offence on or in relation to that property and

    (a) they make the arrest at that time; or
    (b) they make the arrest within a reasonable time after the offence is committed and they believe on reasonable grounds that it is not feasible in the circumstances for a peace officer to make the arrest.

[Note that subsections (a) and (b) were added to s. 494(2) in 2013 following the controversy generated by *R. v. Chen*, 2010 ONCJ 641.]

(3) Any one other than a peace officer who arrests a person without warrant shall forthwith deliver the person to a peace officer.

495(1) A peace officer may arrest without warrant

    (a) a person who has committed an indictable offence or who, on reasonable grounds, he believes has committed or is about to commit an indictable offence;

(b) a person whom he finds committing a criminal offence; or

(c) a person in respect of whom he has reasonable grounds to believe that a warrant of arrest or committal, in any form set out in Part XXVIII in relation thereto, is in force within the territorial jurisdiction in which the person is found.

NOTES

1. These seemingly straightforward statutory provisions require careful analysis of several variables, including: (a) the status of the person making the arrest; (b) whether the offence is about to be, is being or has been committed; (c) the category of offence in issue (indictable, hybrid or summary conviction); and (d) whether the person making the arrest needs only reasonable grounds or must prove that the person arrested was actually committing or had actually committed the offence.

2. By virtue of the *Interpretation Act*, R.S.C. 1985, c. I-21, s. 34(1)(a), the term "indictable offence" includes hybrid offences. The *Criminal Code* also uses the term "criminal offence," which includes indictable, hybrid and summary conviction offences.

3. The legality of arrests under ss. 494(1)(b) and 495(1)(a) and (c) often turns on whether there were reasonable grounds to believe that the person arrested committed the offence. The term "reasonable grounds" is typically defined as facts that would create in the mind of a reasonable person a strong and honest belief that the suspect had committed the offence in question. The individual must subjectively believe that the person committed the offence, and that belief must be objectively reasonable. An individual must take into account all of the relevant information in determining whether there are reasonable grounds for the arrest. See *R. v. Storrey*, [1990] 1 S.C.R. 241; *Webster v. Edmonton (City) Police Services* (2007), 69 Alta. L.R. (4th) 205 (C.A.); *R. v. Loewen*, 2011 SCC 21; *R. v. Messina*, 2013 BCCA 499; *Kolosov v. Lowe's Companies Inc.*, 2016 ONCA 973 at paras. 3-10; *Tremblay v. Ottawa Police Services Board*, 2018 ONCA 497 at paras. 81-104; and *R. v. Ha*, 2018 ABCA 233.

Mere suspicion is not sufficient. The fact that a suspect has a prior criminal record, refuses to answer questions or is unhelpful does not, in and of itself, constitute reasonable grounds. See *Dumbell v. Roberts*, [1944] 1 All E.R. 326 (C.A.); *Chartier v. Att. Gen. (Que.)*, [1979] 2 S.C.R. 474; *R. c. Burke*, [2009] 3 S.C.R. 566; and *R. v. Brown*, 2012 ONCA 225.

(b) A PEACE OFFICER'S POWER TO ARREST WITHOUT A WARRANT

Several aspects of peace officers' powers to arrest require elaboration. First, although the public and most commentators talk about "police" powers, s. 495 is framed in terms of a "peace officer." Under s. 2 of the *Criminal Code*, the term "peace officer" is defined to include police officers, sheriffs, mayors, commercial pilots, fishery officers, and others. However, the term does not include private security guards or private detectives. Second, a peace officer is entitled to invoke the powers in both ss. 494 and 495. Third, peace officers are given broader authority to arrest than private citizens. Perhaps most importantly, s. 495(1)(a) authorizes peace officers to arrest anyone whom they have reasonable grounds to believe has committed or is about to commit an indictable offence. Pursuant to this provision, individuals who are innocent of any criminal wrongdoing must nevertheless submit to a peace officer's authority to arrest them.

Fourth, prior to the *Charter*'s enactment, the Supreme Court of Canada had interpreted s. 495(1)(b) very broadly. In *R. v. Biron*, [1976] 2 S.C.R. 56, Constable Maisonneuve arrested Biron for the summary conviction offence of creating a disturbance, and handed him over to Constable Dorion. While being led to the police wagon, Biron struggled with Constable Dorion, causing both of them to fall. As a result, Biron was also charged with resisting a peace officer in the execution of his duty. Following Biron's acquittal on the charge of creating a disturbance, the Québec Court of Appeal acquitted him on the charge of resisting. The court reasoned that since Maisonneuve had not found Biron committing the offence of creating a disturbance, he had no authority to arrest Biron. Thus, Biron was legally entitled to go on his way, Dorion had no legal authority to detain him, and Biron could not be convicted of resisting a peace officer in the execution of his duty.

The Crown appealed Biron's acquittal on the charge of resisting arrest. It argued that the term "finds committing" means both finds committing and apparently finds committing. On that view, since Maisonneuve found Biron apparently committing the offence of causing a disturbance, Biron's initial arrest had been lawful. Consequently, Dorion had lawfully detained Biron and, by struggling with Dorion, Biron committed the offence of resisting.

The majority in the Supreme Court of Canada accepted that argument and restored Biron's conviction. They stated that if the term "finds committing" was interpreted literally, an officer could never know with certainty that an arrest was lawful. The majority reasoned that the validity of an arrest had to be determined in relation to the circumstances that were apparent to the officer at the time of the arrest. In a strongly worded dissent, Laskin C.J. stated that the majority's position needlessly expanded police powers, convicted an innocent person of an offence, violated the principles of statutory interpretation, and was contrary to public policy.

NOTES AND QUESTIONS

1. Why did the Crown in *Biron* not rely on s. 495(1)(a)?

2. As a matter of statutory interpretation, was it appropriate for the majority to hold that the term "finds committing" extends to apparently finds committing? Should the legal consequences of an officer's misapprehension of the facts result in an otherwise innocent individual being convicted of a federal criminal offence?

3. The majority in *Biron* did not define the term "apparently finds committing." In *R. v. P.(S.T.)*, 2009 NSCA 86, the court stated at paras. 20-22 that the officer must be present at the incident, actually observe or detect the commission of the offence and have an objective basis for concluding that an offence is being committed.

In *R. v. Janvier* (2007), 302 Sask. R. 190 (C.A.), the court held that the odour of recently smoked marijuana did not provide the officer with an objective basis for concluding that the accused was apparently committing the offence of possession of marijuana. See also *R. v. Valentine*, 2014 ONCA 147.

4. In *R. c. Burke*, [2009] 3 S.C.R. 566, the accused was arrested under s. 495(1)(c) based on an outstanding warrant that had been issued for his brother whom he resembled. The officer searched the accused pursuant to the arrest and seized a bag of crack cocaine. The accused was taken to the station where it was confirmed that he was not the person sought in the arrest warrant. The accused was charged with possession for the purposes of trafficking. The trial judge ruled that the officer did not have reasonable grounds to arrest the accused under s. 495(1)(c) because he did not investigate the accused's claim of mistaken identity at the scene. The arrest and subsequent search were held to be unlawful, the crack cocaine was excluded and the accused was acquitted of the drug charge. The majority of the Supreme Court of Canada upheld the trial judgment. The dissenting justices stated that the officer was being held to a higher standard than that set out in s. 495(1)(c). The trial judge required the arresting officer to be certain or at least persuaded that the accused was the person named in the warrant, whereas s. 495(1)(c) only required the officer to have reasonable grounds for such a belief.

What role, if any, should an accused's claim of mistaken identity or denial of culpability play in determining if an officer had reasonable grounds under s. 495(1)(c)? Is it appropriate for officers to attempt to resolve such matters at the scene?

The majority decision in *Burke* stands in sharp contrast to the pre-*Charter* cases dealing with arrests pursuant to a warrant. See for example *Fletcher v. Collins* (1968), 70 D.L.R. (2d) 183 (Ont. H.C); and *Crowe v. Noon* (1970), 16 D.L.R. (3d) 22 (Ont. H.C.).

(c) PRIVILEGE OR JUSTIFICATION UNDER THE *CRIMINAL CODE*

As illustrated by *Biron*, authorizing provisions empower individuals to take specified actions and require others to submit to that exercise of power. In contrast, privileging provisions address the related, but distinct, issue of the criminal and civil liability of those exercising legal authority. As indicated, individuals asserting the defence of legal authority generally must prove that their conduct was both authorized and privileged.

Privileging provisions can be found in a number of provincial, territorial and federal statutes. While the *Criminal Code* contains several privileging provisions, the most important are the general privileging provisions of s. 25.

25(1) Every one who is required or authorized by law to do anything in the administration or enforcement of the law

    (a) as a private person,
    (b) as a peace officer or public officer,
    (c) in aid of a peace officer or public officer, or
    (d) by virtue of his office,

is, if he acts on reasonable grounds, justified in doing what he is required or authorized to do and in using as much force as is necessary for that purpose.

[s. 25(2) omitted]

(3) Subject to subsections (4) and (5), a person is not justified for the purposes of subsection (1) in using force that is intended or is likely to cause death or grievous bodily harm unless the person believes on reasonable grounds that it is necessary for the self-preservation of the person or the preservation of any one under that person's protection from death or grievous bodily harm.

(4) A peace officer, and every person lawfully assisting the peace officer, is justified in using force that is intended or is likely to cause death or grievous bodily harm to a person to be arrested, if

(a) the peace officer is proceeding lawfully to arrest, with or without warrant, the person to be arrested;
(b) the offence for which the person is to be arrested is one for which that person may be arrested without warrant;
(c) the person to be arrested takes flight to avoid arrest;
(d) the peace officer or other person using the force believes on reasonable grounds that the force is necessary for the purpose of protecting the peace officer, the person lawfully assisting the peace officer or any other person from imminent or future death or grievous bodily harm; and
(e) the flight cannot be prevented by reasonable means in a less violent manner.

As in the case of the authorizing sections, the Canadian courts broadly interpreted s. 25, at least until the enactment of the *Charter*. First, the Supreme Court of Canada held that the term "justified" in s. 25 means protected from both criminal and civil liability. Unfortunately, the Supreme Court of Canada has not addressed the constitutional basis upon which it concluded that the federal *Criminal Code* could govern tort liability, a matter that falls within the provinces' constitutional authority under property and civil rights. In addition to *Biron*, see *Frey v. Fedoruk*, [1950] S.C.R. 517; *Priestman v. Colangelo*, [1959] S.C.R. 615; and *Poupart v. Lafortune*, [1974] S.C.R. 175.

Second, despite the plain wording of s. 25(1), the Canadian courts held that peace officers may be privileged under this provision even if they are not, in fact, authorized or required by law to do the act giving rise to the tort. For example, in *Biron*, Laskin C.J. stated that a peace officer whose actions were not authorized may nevertheless be privileged under s. 25(1) if he or she made a mistake of fact and acted on reasonable grounds. Indeed, that was one of the reasons why the Chief Justice refused to interpret the term "finds committing" to include apparently finds committing. In his view, since s. 25(1) protected the arresting officer from criminal and civil liability, there was no need to distort the plain meaning of the authorizing provision and criminalize the suspect's refusal to submit to an unlawful arrest. In *Frey*, *supra*, the court held that a person who was not authorized would not be privileged under s. 25(1) if he or she had made a mistake of law. See also *Saskatchewan (Attorney General) v. Pritchard* (1961), 130 C.C.C. 61 (Sask. C.A.).

NOTES AND QUESTIONS

1. As a matter of policy, should peace officers be privileged if their actions, however reasonable, were not authorized? By answering that question in the affirmative, the Canadian courts have placed the hardship of any reasonable mistake of fact on an innocent suspect, rather than on an arresting officer.

2. What must an individual establish under s. 25(3) to be justified in using force that is intended or likely to cause death or grievous bodily harm?

3. What must an individual establish under s. 25(4) to be justified in using force that is intended or likely to cause death or grievous bodily harm?

4. In contrast to *Biron*, the court in *R. v. Brennan* (1989), 75 C.R. (3d) 38 (Ont. C.A.) interpreted the *Criminal Code*'s authorizing and privileging sections narrowly. The accused police officer attempted to stop the driver of a suspected stolen vehicle. A high-speed chase ensued during which the officer drove through a stop sign. The court upheld the officer's conviction for failing to stop at the stop sign. While the officer was authorized to arrest the suspect, he was not authorized to run a stop sign. The court held that since the officer's conduct was not specifically authorized by statute, he was not privileged under s. 25. Do you agree with the court's reasoning?

5. In *Hudson v. Brantford Police Services Board* (2001), 204 D.L.R. (4th) 645 (Ont. C.A.), two police officers went to the plaintiff's house because they reasonably believed that he had failed to remain at the scene of an accident. They did not have an arrest warrant, they were not in hot pursuit, and they did not have the plaintiff's permission to enter his house. Nevertheless, they entered his house, arrested him and took him to the police station. When charges for leaving the scene were later dropped, the plaintiff sued for unlawful arrest. The police officers argued that their actions were privileged under s. 25 of the *Criminal Code*. The court held that, since the officers had no authority to enter the house, they were trespassing and this rendered the subsequent arrest unlawful. It further held that while s. 25 provides protection from civil liability if a defendant acts on a reasonable mistake of fact, it does not apply with respect to a reasonable mistake of law. The officers' mistake in this case pertained to their legal authority to enter the plaintiff's house to arrest him, which was a mistake of law. Since the officers were not privileged under s. 25, the plaintiff's claim was successful.

Should the scope of s. 25 depend on the distinction between mistakes of fact and mistakes of law?

6. See s. 25.1 of the *Criminal Code*, which exempts designated police and public officials from criminal liability in narrowly defined circumstances when they commit what would otherwise be an offence in performing their law enforcement duties. This exercise of state-sponsored criminal activity is subject to detailed notification and reporting obligations: *Criminal Code*, ss. 25.2-25.4.

(d) A PRIVATE CITIZEN'S AUTHORITY AND PRIVILEGE TO ARREST WITHOUT A WARRANT

Since the apprehension of criminals was considered a community responsibility, the early common law drew few distinctions between private citizens and peace officers. It was only in the mid-1800s that the common law began distinguishing between the power and authority of peace officers and private citizens. In Canada, the authority and privilege of peace officers and private citizens to arrest without warrant for criminal law purposes is now set out in federal and provincial statutes. In regard to private citizens, the most important arrest and privileging provisions are ss. 494 and 25 of the *Criminal Code*, respectively.

The potential criminal liability of private citizens who make arrests became a major public issue in *R. v. Chen*, 2010 ONCJ 641. Chen, a grocer, was charged with assault and unlawful confinement for arresting a career thief who had stolen from him earlier in the day. When the thief returned, Chen confronted him. The thief fled, but was chased, subdued and restrained by Chen and two co-workers. The thief acknowledged that he had stolen from the grocer earlier in the day and that he had returned to steal more merchandise. The Crown argued that since the thief was not committing an offence when subdued and arrested, Chen had no authority to arrest him under s. 494. The judge clearly sympathized with Chen, ruling that the thief's return to the store was a continuation of the theft that had begun earlier in the day. Based on this reasoning, Chen and his co-workers were authorized to arrest the thief because he was committing an ongoing offence of theft when subdued and arrested. Following Chen's acquittal, the provincial Attorney General initially stated that he had no regrets about bringing the prosecution, but subsequently reversed his position. When the Attorney General's office announced that it would not appeal, it lavishly praised small business owners as the backbone of the provincial economy, indicating that it would work with the federal government to strengthen the ability of merchants to protect their property.

Shortly after *Chen*, Parliament enacted the *Citizen's Arrest and Self-defence Act*, S.C. 2012, c. 9, which came into force in March 2013. Although the statute fundamentally changed the *Criminal Code*'s self-defence and defence of property provisions, it did not expand the grounds for making a citizen's arrest under s. 494(1) or (2). Rather, if the grounds for making an arrest under s. 494(2) are satisfied, citizens may arrest the suspect either immediately or within a reasonable time after the offence was committed if they reasonably believe that it is not feasible for the police to make the arrest in the circumstances.

As the following notes and questions indicate, the law governing a private citizen's civil liability in making an arrest is perplexing. Among other things, the Canadian courts are divided on whether citizen's arrest is governed by the broad privileging provisions in s. 25 or the far narrower common law principles of privilege. Moreover, while the common law principles have been adopted in most cases, they have typically been modified in various ways.

NOTES AND QUESTIONS

1. Except in limited circumstances, private citizens can only arrest suspects whom they find committing an indictable offence, or a criminal offence on, or in relationship to, their property. The Canadian courts are divided on whether the broad interpretation of the term "finds committing" in *R. v. Biron*, [1976] 2 S.C.R. 56 regarding s. 495(1)(b) applies in s. 494(1)(a) and (2). In *Dendekker v. F.W. Woolworth Co.*, [1975] 3 W.W.R. 429 (Alta. S.C.) and *Cronk v. F.W. Woolworth Co.*, [1986] 3 W.W.R. 139 (Sask. Q.B.), the courts indicated that the term "finds committing" in s. 494 should not be defined to include apparently finds committing. The opposite approach was taken in *Karogiannis v. Poulus*, [1976] 6 W.W.R. 197 (B.C.S.C.) and *Banerjee v. K Mart Canada Ltd.* (1983), 43 Nfld. & P.E.I.R. 252 (Nfld. Dist. Ct.). As a matter of statutory interpretation, which line of cases is more compelling? Can you

suggest any public policy justification for treating the term "finds committing" differently in ss. 494 and 495?

2. Do you agree with the court's interpretation and application of the term "finds committing" in *Chen*? Would you have encouraged the Ontario Attorney General to appeal despite the likely adverse public and media reaction? What impact, if any, did the *Citizen's Arrest and Self-defence Act* have on the definition of the term "finds committing"?

3. In *R. v. Abel* (2008), 291 D.L.R. (4th) 110 (B.C.C.A.), Abel concluded correctly and with good reason that Holl had stolen his rifle. Abel and two accomplices confronted Holl and, following a physical altercation, subdued and restrained him. Holl told them that he had hidden the rifle under the wheelchair ramp at a dentist's office. With Holl in tow, Abel and his accomplices retrieved the rifle. They then dropped off Holl at the police station because they knew that there was an outstanding warrant for his arrest. When the police learned all of the facts, Abel and his accomplices were charged with breaking and entering, assault and other offences. The accused argued that they were authorized to arrest Holl because they found him committing the indictable offence of possession of stolen property. The trial judge ruled that since Holl was not in physical possession of the stolen rifle when the accused subdued and arrested him, s. 494(1)(a) was inapplicable. The judge refused to put this defence to the jury and the accused were convicted. The Court of Appeal upheld the convictions.

Do you agree that the accused in *Abel* did not find Holl apparently committing the offence of possession of stolen property? Can you reconcile *Abel* and *Chen*? Would Abel be authorized to arrest Holl pursuant to the current provisions of s. 494?

4. For a discussion of a private citizen's common law authority, privileges and obligations in the arrest process see *Handcock v. Baker* (1800), 126 E.R. 1270 (H.L.); *Walters v. W.H. Smith & Son Ltd.*, [1914] 1 K.B. 595; and *John Lewis & Co. v. Tims*, [1952] A.C. 676 (H.L.). See also Hall, "Legal and Social Aspects of Arrest Without a Warrant" (1936) 49 Harv. L. Rev. 566; and Spencer, "Citizens Arrest — At Their Peril" [1992] C.L.J. 405.

5. In *Dendekker, Karogiannis* and *Banerjee, supra*, the court indicated that a private citizen's privilege is defined by s. 25 of the *Criminal Code*. However, in *Banyasz v. K Mart Canada Ltd.* (1986), 57 O.R. (2d) 445 (Div. Ct.), *Smart v. Sears Canada Inc.* (1987), 64 Nfld. & P.E.I.R. 187 (Nfld. C.A.), *Cronk, supra*, and *Briggs v. Laviolette* (1994), 21 C.C.L.T. (2d) 105 (B.C.S.C.), a private citizen's privilege was defined in terms of the common law principles.

6. The Supreme Court of Canada has repeatedly held that s. 25 of the *Criminal Code* protects peace officers from both criminal and civil liability. Moreover, the section applies to "every one" who is authorized or required by law to undertake an act. What legal or public policy arguments would you make in support of the position that the common law, rather than s. 25, should govern a private citizen's privilege in civil cases?

7. Most of the Canadian cases that have adopted the common law principles of privilege indicate that private citizens must prove that the crime was in fact committed

by the suspect or a third person, and that they had reasonable grounds to believe that the suspect was the perpetrator. See *Smart, supra; Briggs, supra;* and *Nichols v. Wal-Mart Canada Corp.* (2003), 15 C.C.L.T. (3d) 150 (Ont. S.C.J.).

Even those cases that have held that a private citizen's privilege turns on proof that the suspect committed an offence do not require proof that the suspect was criminally convicted. In a civil case, the defendant need only establish the commission of the crime on a balance of probabilities. See *Cronk, supra.*

8. In *Mann v. Canadian Tire Corp.*, 2016 ONSC 4926, the court reviewed what it called "shopkeeper's privilege" in England, Wales, the United States, and Canada. The court adopted the common law principles of privilege, but stated that they had to be broadened to better protect shopkeepers' property in "today's commercial reality." More specifically, the court stated at para. 45 that a shopkeeper had to meet the following conditions to establish privilege:

1. There must be reasonable and probable grounds to believe that property is being stolen or has been stolen from the shopkeeper's place of business. A security alarm triggered when a person is in the process of leaving the store would be sufficient to provide such grounds.
2. The sole purpose of the detention must be to investigate whether any item is being stolen or has been stolen from the store.
3. The detention must be reasonable and involves inviting the suspect to participate in a search to resolve the issue. The privilege does not bestow a power upon the store owner to search the detainee without consent.
4. The period of detention should be as brief as possible and reasonable attempts to determine whether an item of property is being stolen or has been stolen should proceed expeditiously.
5. If the detained suspect refuses co-operation, the store owner is entitled to detain them using reasonable force whilst summoning the police and until they arrive.

Do you agree that a security alarm provides reasonable and probable grounds to believe that property is being stolen? How does *Mann* differ from authority to arrest and privilege pursuant to: (a) the common law; and (b) the *Criminal Code?* See McInnes & Simpson, "The Shopkeeper's Privilege and Canadian Tort Law" (2018) 56 Alta. L. Rev.29.

9. How should the law balance a shopkeeper's interests in protecting his or her inventory and a customer's autonomy? How would you react if you owned a store and suspected that a shopper was stealing merchandise? What risks are involved in making an arrest and in doing nothing? If you called the police and left the matter to them, is it likely that they would be able to apprehend the suspect in a timely manner? What amendments, if any, would you make to s. 494?

4. Rights and Obligations in the Arrest Process

(a) REASONS FOR THE ARREST

KOECHLIN v. WAUGH AND HAMILTON
(1957), 11 D.L.R. (2d) 447 (Ont. C.A.)

LAIDLAW J.A. (orally):—This is an appeal by the plaintiffs from a judgment pronounced by His Honour Judge Shea, in the County Court of the County of York, on May 21, 1956, dismissing with costs an action brought by the plaintiffs for damages for alleged unlawful arrest and imprisonment.

. . .

On the evening of October 11, 1955, the infant plaintiff, aged about 20 years, and his friend Victor Wassilgew, attended a picture show in the Township of Scarborough. The show ended about midnight. They went to a restaurant for coffee and, afterwards, started to walk on the sidewalk on Kingston Road in the direction of the home of Wassilgew. They were stopped by the defendants, who are police officers of the Township of Scarborough. The police officers were in plain clothes and were in a police cruiser car. The police called the infant plaintiff and his companion to their car and asked for their identification. Wassilgew gave his identification at once and told the police officers that they were on their way home after the show. The infant plaintiff objected to giving his identification unless the police officer, Hamilton, who spoke to him, first identified himself. The defendant Hamilton produced a badge and said he was a police officer, but the infant plaintiff was not satisfied with that identification and requested the name and number of the officer. The officer did not give his name, but his number was on the badge. The infant plaintiff continued to refuse to identify himself, and a scuffle ensued during which the infant plaintiff fell into a deep ditch. Subsequently, force was used by the police officer and other officers who were called to the scene to put the infant plaintiff into a police car. He was not told any reason for his arrest. He was taken to the police station and told that he would be charged with assault of a police officer.

The adult plaintiff stated in evidence that he was informed about 2 o'clock in the morning that his son was in custody; he went to the police station; he asked the Sergeant of Police the reason his son was there in custody; the sergeant told him it was for assaulting a police officer. The adult plaintiff asked the sergeant how it happened and, according to the evidence of the adult plaintiff, the sergeant said "he would not tell me, that I would hear about it the next day in Court about 10 o'clock in the morning." He says he asked the sergeant if he could see his son and was refused permission. It was 9 or 10 o'clock the following evening before the infant plaintiff was released on bail. On November 18th, the charge against the infant plaintiff was heard and was dismissed.

The learned Judge stated in reasons given by him that the police officers stopped the infant plaintiff and his companion because they were sauntering along the street, and because of "their dress." There was in fact nothing distinctive about the dress of the infant plaintiff, but his companion was wearing rubber-soled shoes and a jacket. The learned Judge referred also to the fact that there had been a number of "break-ins" in the neighbourhood a few nights before and that the police had reported that a person wearing rubber-soled shoes was involved in one or more of those break-ins.

After referring to the reasons for stopping the infant plaintiff and his companion and asking for identification, the learned Judge said: "Then, from then on, the actions of Koechlin, and his words, would in my opinion justify the officers in believing that this man either had or was about to commit a crime." Later, he said, referring to Koechlin — "his refusal to cooperate — made the officers still more suspicious and firm in the belief, as I said, that something was wrong."

. . .

A police officer has not in law an unlimited power to arrest a law-abiding citizen. The power given expressly to him by the Criminal Code to arrest without warrant is contained in s. 435 [a predecessor to the current s. 495], but we direct careful attention of the public to the fact that the law empowers a police officer in many cases and under certain circumstances to require a person to account for his presence and to identify himself and to furnish other information, and any person who wrongfully fails to comply with such lawful requirements does so at the risk of arrest and imprisonment. None of these circumstances exist in this case. No unnecessary restriction on his power which results in increased difficulty to a police officer to perform his duties of office should be imposed by the Court. At the same time, the rights and freedom under law from unlawful arrest and imprisonment of an innocent citizen must be fully guarded by the Courts. In this case, the fact that the companion of the infant plaintiff was wearing rubber-soled shoes and a windbreaker and that his dress attracted the attention of the police officers, falls far short of reasonable and probable grounds for believing that the infant plaintiff had committed an indictable offence or was about to commit such an offence. We do not criticize the police officers in any way for asking the infant plaintiff and his companion to identify themselves, but we are satisfied that when the infant plaintiff, who was entirely innocent of any wrongdoing, refused to do so, the police officer has no right to use force to compel him to identify himself. It would have been wise and, indeed, a duty as a good citizen, for the infant plaintiff to have identified himself when asked to do so by the police officers. It is altogether likely that if the infant plaintiff had been courteous and co-operative, the incident giving rise to this action would not have occurred, but that does not in law excuse the defendants for acting as they did in the particular circumstances.

We direct attention to an important fact. The infant plaintiff was not told by either of the police officers any reason for his arrest. The infant plaintiff was entitled to know on what charge or on suspicion of what crime he was seized. He was not required in law to submit to restraint on his freedom unless he knew the reason why that restraint should be imposed. In *Christie v. Leachinsky*, [1947] 1 All E.R. 567, a decision of the House of Lords, Lord Simon, after referring to many authorities, said at pp. 572-3:

These citations . . . seem to me to establish the following propositions:

1. If a policeman arrests without warrant on reasonable suspicion of felony, or of other crime of a sort which does not require a warrant, he must in ordinary circumstances inform the person arrested of the true ground of arrest. He is not entitled to keep the reason to himself or to give a reason which is not the true reason. In other words, a citizen is entitled to know on what charge or on suspicion of what crime he is seized.
2. If the citizen is not so informed, but is nevertheless seized, the policeman, apart from certain exceptions, is liable for false imprisonment.

3. The requirement that the person arrested should be informed of the reason why he is seized naturally does not exist if the circumstances are such that he must know the general nature of the alleged offence for which he is detained.
4. The requirement that he should be so informed does not mean that technical or precise language need be used. The matter is a matter of substance, and turns on the elementary proposition that in this country a person is, *prima facie*, entitled to his freedom and is only required to submit to restraint on his freedom if he knows in substance the reason why it is claimed that this restraint should be imposed.
5. The person arrested cannot complain that he has not been supplied with the above information as and when he should be, if he himself produces the situation which makes it practically impossible to inform him, *e.g.*, by immediate counter-attack or by running away.

There may well be other exceptions to the general rule in addition to those I have indicated, and the above propositions are not intended to constitute a formal or complete code, but to indicate the general principles of our law on a very important matter. These principles equally apply to a private person who arrests on suspicion. If a policeman who entertained a reasonable suspicion that X had committed a felony were at liberty to arrest him and march him off to a police station without giving any explanation of why he was doing this, the *prima facie* right of personal liberty would be gravely infringed. No one, I think, would approve a situation in which, when the person arrested asked for the reason, the policeman replied: 'That has nothing to do with you. Come along with me.' Such a situation may be tolerated under other systems of law, as for instance, in the time of *lettres de cachet* in the eighteenth century in France, or in more recent days when the Gestapo swept people off to confinement under an overriding authority which the executive in this country happily does not in ordinary times possess. This would be quite contrary to our conceptions of individual liberty.

In this case it was held that although the police officers *bona fide* and on reasonable grounds believed the plaintiff had committed an offence, they had not informed him as to why he was being arrested and were, therefore, liable in damages for false imprisonment. In *R. v. Hastings* . . . it was held by the New Brunswick Court of Appeal that a person being unlawfully arrested without a warrant is entitled to resist such unlawful arrest.

There is one further matter that deserves comment. A person who has been arrested should not be held *incommunicado*. We do not find it necessary to find as a fact that the infant plaintiff was denied his right to communicate with his father at the first reasonable opportunity. If, however, the father of the infant plaintiff was refused permission by the Sergeant of Police to see his son at any time before the charge came on for hearing in Court, such practice cannot be justified in this or in any other case. A person in custody should never be denied his right to communicate with his relatives at the earliest reasonable opportunity so that he may avail himself of their advice and assistance. That right ought to be recognized and given effect in all cases, and care should be exercised by police authorities to see that it is not wholly disregarded.

Finally, we are not in accord with the view expressed by the learned trial Judge that the actions of the infant plaintiff in resisting the efforts of the police officers can be regarded as justification for their belief that he "either had or was about to commit a crime." In the particular circumstances he was entitled in law to resist the efforts of the police officers, and they have failed in this case to justify their actions.

It was stated in the course of giving oral reasons for judgment that the Courts would strive diligently to avoid putting any unnecessary obstacle in the way of the detection of crime or the lawful arrest of persons in the proper performance of the duties of a police officer. We repeat an expression of that policy of the Courts. Nothing in these reasons for judgment should be taken as encouragement to any person to resist a police officer in the performance of his duties; on the contrary, it is not only highly desirable, but vitally important, that every person should co-operate to the utmost with police officers for the good of the public and to ensure the preservation of law and order in his community.

In this case the police officers exceeded their powers and infringed the rights of the infant plaintiff without justification. Therefore, the appeal will be allowed with costs. The judgment of the Court below will be set aside and in place thereof there will be judgment for the plaintiffs in the amounts assessed, respectively, for damages suffered by the infant plaintiff and by the adult plaintiff.

NOTES AND QUESTIONS

1. At what point was the plaintiff arrested and on what charge? What authority did the police have to stop and question the plaintiff prior to the arrest? Did the police have any legal authority to use force prior to the arrest?

2. Were the defendants authorized and privileged to arrest the plaintiff in the circumstances? Would they have been held liable even if they had properly informed him of the reasons? What arguments would you have made on Koechlin's behalf for punitive damages?

3. What impact does the failure to inform a suspect of the reasons for the arrest have on the validity of the arrest? Can the suspect simply leave or use physical force to prevent his or her detention? See *Campbell v. Hudyma* (1985), 66 A.R. 222 (C.A.); *Schell v. Truba* (1989), 79 Sask. R. 27 (Q.B.), aff'd (1990), 89 Sask. R. 137 (C.A.); *Cormier v. Saint John (City)* (1994), 153 N.B.R. (2d) 293 (C.A.); and *Lewis v. Chief Constable*, [1991] 1 All E.R. 206 (C.A.).

4. Laidlaw J.A. was very critical of the defendants for holding the plaintiff incommunicado. Should such conduct result in liability even if the arrest was lawful and the suspect was informed of the reasons for his or her arrest? See *Perry v. Fried* (1972), 9 N.S.R. (2d) 545 (S.C.); and *Lang v. Burch* (1982), 140 D.L.R. (3d) 325 (Sask. C.A.).

5. Section 29 of the *Criminal Code* also imposes disclosure requirements on an individual making an arrest. However, s. 29 was interpreted as being less stringent than the parallel common law torts principles. For example, in *Gamracy v. R.*, [1974] S.C.R. 640, the court held that an officer making an arrest pursuant to an outstanding arrest warrant had no obligation to obtain the warrant or ascertain its contents in order to inform the suspect. Upon being informed of the warrant's existence, the suspect was required to defer to the officer's authority. See also *R. v. Erickson and Hathaway* (1977), 5 A.R. 602 (S.C.).

6. In addition to bringing a common law tort action, an individual who is not informed of the reasons for his or her arrest may seek redress under the *Charter*.

Pursuant to s. 10(a) and (b) of the *Charter*, everyone has the right upon arrest or detention to retain and instruct counsel without delay and to be informed of that right, and the right to be informed promptly of the reasons for the arrest or detention. See *Elmardy v. Toronto Police Services Board*, 2015 ONSC 2952.

In *R. v. Wrightman* (2004), 72 O.R. (3d) 187 (Ct. J.), the accused was acquitted of charges for resisting an officer's attempt to arrest him under a warrant. The judge held that under s. 10(b) of the *Charter*, the officer had an obligation to inform the accused of the particulars of the warrant; it was not sufficient to simply advise the accused of the warrant's existence. Consequently, the accused was under no obligation to submit to the arrest. In *R. v. Bohn*, 2000 BCCA 239, the court held that an officer's failure to bring the warrant and produce it on request, without a good reason, constituted a significant breach of s. 8 of the *Charter*. Can you reconcile these cases with *Gamracy, supra*? See also *R. v. Cornell*, 2010 SCC 31.

7. As suggested in *Koechlin*, individuals are generally under no obligation to identify themselves, account for their presence, answer questions, remain on the scene, accompany an officer, or submit to a search. See *R. v. Carroll* (1959), 23 D.L.R. (2d) 271 (Ont. C.A.); *Rice v. Connolly*, [1966] 2 Q.B. 414; *Kenlin v. Gardiner*, [1967] 2 Q.B. 510; *Albert v. Lavin*, [1981] 3 All E.R. 878 (H.L.); and *Campbell v. Hudyma* (1985), 66 A.R. 222 (C.A.). There are, however, many statutory exceptions to this rule. See for example the provincial highway traffic statutes, which typically require drivers to identify themselves. As indicated, police also have common law authority to briefly stop and question suspects for investigatory purposes in some limited circumstances.

8. In *Moore v. R.*, [1979] 1 S.C.R. 195, the majority of the court held that a person who violates a provincial statute may have a positive duty to co-operate with the police. Moore had refused to identify himself to an officer who was attempting to ticket him for riding his bicycle through a red light. The officer then arrested Moore under s. 129 of the *Criminal Code* for obstructing a peace officer in the execution of his duty. The majority reasoned that the officer had a legal duty to enforce the provincial highway traffic statute and that Moore's refusal to identify himself prevented the officer from performing this duty. It was on this basis that the majority upheld Moore's obstruction conviction. The decision in *Moore* has been criticized. See for example Cohen, "The Investigation of Offences and Police Powers" (1981) 13 Ottawa L. Rev. 549 at 551-56. See also *R. v. Leitch* (1992), 18 C.R. (4th) 224 (Alta. Prov. Ct.), rev'd (1993), 13 Alta. L.R. (3d) 97 (Q.B.).

In *Ryan v. Auclair* (1989), 60 D.L.R. (4th) 212 (Qc. C.A.), the police arrested two nuns, who were violating a municipal by-law by distributing religious pamphlets after they refused to identify themselves beyond giving their religious names. When the nuns resisted, the officers used force to overpower them. The Court of Appeal upheld the trial judge's dismissal of the nuns' claim for false imprisonment.

9. Can you reconcile *Moore* and *Ryan, supra* with the cases cited in note 7? In the absence of express statutory authority, should the police have authority to arrest those who refuse to identify themselves in cases involving municipal or provincial offences? Given the courts' increased reluctance to defer to police authority, would *Moore* and *Ryan* be decided the same way now?

(b) THE USE OF REASONABLE FORCE

Both the common law and the *Criminal Code* give those acting pursuant to legal authority broad powers to use force. Nevertheless, as a general rule, suspects must be given an opportunity to submit peacefully before any force is used. If a suspect resists, then as much force as is reasonably necessary may be used to subdue him or her. In assessing whether the force used was reasonable, the courts examine the nature of the force used in the circumstances and not the resulting injuries. A reasonable and *bona fide* mistake of fact as to the need to use force will not defeat the assertion of the right to use force. Provided individuals are acting lawfully, they will not be held liable for using force simply because the suspect is innocent.

As discussed earlier, s. 25(1) privileges those who use reasonable force in doing what they are authorized or required by law to do. Section 25(3) limits the use of force that is intended or likely to cause death or grievous bodily harm to individuals who reasonably believe that such force is necessary to protect themselves or others under their protection from death or grievous bodily harm. Section 25(4) permits peace officers to use force that is intended or likely to cause death or grievous bodily harm to apprehend a fleeing suspect who cannot be stopped in a less violent manner. The offence for which the suspect is sought must be one for which he or she can be arrested without a warrant. Moreover, the officer must have reasonable grounds to believe that such force is necessary to protect him or herself or a third person from imminent or future death or grievous bodily harm.

NOTES AND QUESTIONS

1. In what circumstances would self-defence and the right to use force under s. 25(1), (3) and (4) overlap?

2. In *Green v. Lawrence* (1998), 163 D.L.R. (4th) 115 (Man. C.A.), the plaintiff slipped backwards on the stairs into one of the two arresting officers. One of the officers put the plaintiff in a full-nelson hold with sufficient force to break his neck. The plaintiff, who was rendered a paraplegic, sued the officer in battery. The defendant claimed that the plaintiff had thrust himself backwards and that force was necessary to prevent his escape or subdue him. The court held that there was no reasonable basis for believing that the plaintiff was attempting to escape. In any event, the amount of force used was excessive. The defendant was held liable in battery for the plaintiff's injuries.

For other cases on the use of force, see *R. v. Asante-Mensah*, [2003] 2 S.C.R. 3; *R. v. Nasogaluak*, [2010] 1 S.C.R. 206; *Camaso Estate v. Egan*, 2013 BCCA 6; *R. v. Power*, 2016 SKCA 29; and *Fleming v. Ontario*, 2018 ONCA 160.

3. According to the CBC, 461 people were killed in police encounters from 2000 to 2018, which resulted in criminal charges against 18 officers. Only two of these officers were convicted and both are appealing: Annable & Kubinec, "Criminal consequences for police officers are rare when a civilian dies" *CBC News* (6 April 2018), online: < http://www.cbc.ca/news/canada/manitoba/deadly-force-police-criminal-charges-1.4607134 >. The number of civil suits arising from these fatal police encounters is unknown.

4. The right to use deadly force to prevent the escape of a fleeing suspect is controversial. What arguments, if any, would you make for abolishing the right to use deadly force to apprehend fleeing suspects? The deaths and injuries associated with high-speed chases have resulted in the increased regulation of these police pursuits. See for example *Suspect Apprehension Pursuits*, O.Reg. 266/10. In addition to setting out rules on initiating and continuing high-speed chases, s. 7 of the Regulation specifically prohibits officers from firing at a fleeing vehicle for the sole purpose of attempting to stop it. See *Doern v. Phillips Estate* (1994), 23 C.C.L.T. (2d) 283 (B.C.S.C.); *Kassian Estate v. Canada (Attorney General)*, 2015 ONCA 544; and *Bergen v. Guliker*, 2015 BCCA 283.

5. In addition to s. 25, the *Criminal Code* authorizes the use of force to prevent the commission of certain offences (s. 27), to subdue those committing an offence on an airplane (s. 27.1), to prevent breaches of the peace (s. 30), to suppress riots (s. 32), in self-defence (s. 34), and to defend property (s. 35). The Canadian courts appear to assume that these sections govern both criminal and civil liability.

6. *Berntt v. Vancouver (City)* (1999), 174 D.L.R. (4th) 403 (B.C.C.A.) illustrates the factual analysis undertaken to determine if the amount of force used was reasonable in the circumstances. The plaintiff was one of the ringleaders of 50,000 to 70,000 people who rioted in downtown Vancouver after the Canucks lost game seven of the Stanley Cup. After throwing objects at the police and approaching the police line waving a long screwdriver, the plaintiff was shot in the back with a plastic "baton." After receiving treatment, he rejoined the riot, confronting the officers and swearing. He turned his back to the police to show them the welt caused by the first shot. While he was walking away, he was shot with a second plastic baton. The evidence indicated that although the officer had aimed at the plaintiff's back, the baton hit him in the head.

The plaintiff suffered serious injuries from the second shot and sued for battery and negligence. The trial judge held that only the first shot was justified under s. 32 of the *Criminal Code*, which privileges using force to suppress a riot. The judge reasoned that when the second shot was fired, the police had gained control of the situation, the riot had lessened and the plaintiff posed no immediate threat. Consequently, the second shot was unnecessary and the officer was liable in battery. The officer appealed. The Court of Appeal ordered a new trial on the issue of the second shot. It stated that the reasonableness of the force used had to be assessed in terms of what a reasonable officer at the scene would have believed. The officer need not have been personally endangered to use force under s. 32. If the officer honestly and reasonably believed that firing the second baton was necessary to suppress the riot, he was justified in doing so.

During the retrial, the judge addressed four questions as directed by the Court of Appeal: (i) did the officer believe that the force he was about to use was necessary to suppress the riot; (ii) did the officer believe that the force was not excessive given the apprehended danger from the continuation of the riot; (iii) if the answer to the first question was yes, did the officer have reasonable grounds for that belief; and (iv) if the answer to the second question was yes, did the officer have reasonable grounds for that belief? The trial judge answered all the questions in the defendant's favour. From the officer's perspective, the key to defusing the riot was removing the ringleaders, including the plaintiff, and making an arrest was not feasible in the circumstances.

Moreover, the plaintiff's brandishing of the screwdriver, an edged weapon, made him very dangerous in a crowd. See *Berntt v. Vancouver (City)* (2001), 209 D.L.R. (4th) 494 (B.C.S.C.). See also *Fleming v. Ontario*, 2018 ONCA 160 for a discussion of the common law authority to arrest in order to keep the peace.

7. There are additional rights and obligations in the arrest process. For example, once a private citizen makes an arrest at common law, he or she has to hand over the suspect to the police or a justice as soon as possible. This obligation is now codified in s. 494(3) of the *Criminal Code*, which requires that suspects be handed over "forthwith." In *R. v. Cunningham* (1979), 49 C.C.C. (2d) 390 (Man. Co. Ct.), the court said that forthwith did not mean immediately, but rather as soon as reasonably practicable. Although granted somewhat more leeway to investigate incidents, peace officers were under a similar obligation to bring suspects before a justice without unreasonable delay. See *John Lewis & Co. v. Tims*, [1952] A.C. 676 (H.L.); and *Dallison v. Caffery*, [1965] 1 Q.B. 348 (C.A.). See also the *Criminal Code*, s. 503; and *R. v. Koszulap* (1974), 20 C.C.C. (2d) 193 (Ont. C.A.).

This issue has also arisen under s. 9 of the *Charter*, which guarantees everyone protection from arbitrary detention or imprisonment. In *R. v. Charles* (1987), 36 C.C.C. (3d) 286 (Sask. C.A.), a 36-hour detention before being brought before a justice was held to violate s. 9. In *R. v. Storrey*, [1990] 1 S.C.R. 241, the court held that an 18-hour delay to arrange a line-up did not violate s. 9. See also *R. v. Dann* (2001), 201 N.S.R. (2d) 6 (S.C.); *R. v. Mangat* (2006), 213 O.A.C. 266 (C.A.); and *R. v. Poirier*, 2016 ONCA 582.

8. The *Criminal Code*'s complex pretrial release provisions are set out in ss. 493-515. The police powers to fingerprint and photograph arrested suspects are contained in the *Identification of Criminals Act*, R.S.C. 1985, c. I-1. *See Brown v. Baugh*, [1984] 1 S.C.R. 192; and *R. v. Beare; R. v. Higgins*, [1988] 2 S.C.R. 387.

5. The Common Law Power to Search Pursuant to a Lawful Arrest

R. v. CASLAKE
[1998] 1 S.C.R. 51

[Six hours after the accused was arrested for marijuana possession, his impounded vehicle was subject to an inventory search to safeguard its contents and note its general condition. The vehicle search was conducted without a warrant or the accused's consent. Cash and cocaine were found in the car, and the accused was charged with cocaine possession. The issue before the Supreme Court was whether the vehicle search constituted an unreasonable search or seizure contrary to s. 8 of the *Charter* and whether the cocaine had to be excluded from evidence under s. 24(2). The court noted that for a search or seizure to be reasonable under s. 8 of the *Charter*, it had to be authorized by law.]

LAMER C.J. (Cory, McLachlin and Major JJ. concurring)

. . .

In this case, the Crown is relying on the common law power of search incident to arrest to provide the legal authority for the search. In *Cloutier* [*v. Langlois*, [1990] 1 S.C.R. 158], my colleague L'Heureux-Dubé J. (for a unanimous Court) discussed this power in detail. She held that it is an exception to the ordinary requirements for a reasonable search . . . in that it requires neither a warrant nor independent reasonable and probable grounds. Rather, the right to search arises from the fact of the arrest. This is justifiable because the arrest itself requires reasonable and probable grounds (under s. 494 of the *Code*) or an arrest warrant (under s. 495). However, since the legality of the search is derived from the legality of arrest, if the arrest is later found to be invalid, the search will be also. . . .

She then set out three important limits on the power to search incident to arrest (at p. 186):

1. This power does not impose a duty. The police have some discretion in conducting the search. Where they are satisfied that the law can be effectively and safely applied without a search, the police may see fit not to conduct a search . . .
2. The search must be for a valid objective in pursuit of the ends of criminal justice, such as the discovery of an object that may be a threat to the safety of the police, the accused or the public, or that may facilitate escape or act as evidence against the accused. The purpose of the search must not be unrelated to the objectives of the proper administration of justice, which would be the case for example if the purpose of the search was to intimidate, ridicule or pressure the accused in order to obtain admissions.
3. The search must not be conducted in an abusive fashion and in particular, the use of physical or psychological constraint should be proportionate to the objectives sought and the other circumstances of the situation.

If all three of these conditions are met, and the arrest itself is lawful, the search will be "authorized by law" for the purposes of s. 8 of the *Charter*. In the case at bar there is no allegation that the arrest was unlawful or that the search was abusive. Rather, the problem in this case is that the objective and scope of the search exceeded its permissible limits.

C. The Scope of Search Incident to the Arrest

Since search incident to arrest is a common-law power, there are no readily ascertainable limits on its scope. It is therefore the courts' responsibility to set boundaries which allow the state to pursue its legitimate interests, while vigorously protecting individuals' right to privacy. The scope of search incident to arrest can refer to many different aspects of the search. It can refer to the items seized during the search. In *Stillman*, Cory J. for a majority of this Court held, at para. 42, that bodily samples could not be taken as incident to arrest, as a search so invasive is an "affront to human dignity". It can also refer to the place to be searched. The appellant argues that the power of search incident to arrest does not extend to automobiles. I would reject this position. Automobiles are legitimately the objects of search incident to arrest, as they attract no heightened expectation of privacy that would justify an exemption from the usual common law principles referred to above.

Scope can also refer to temporal limits on the power of search, which are at the core of the case at bar. The appellant suggests that the delay between the search and the arrest (six hours in this case) was too long to make the search "incident" to the arrest. In my opinion, the Court should be reluctant to set a strict limit on the amount of time that can elapse between the time of search and the time of arrest.

In my view, all of the limits on search incident to arrest are derived from the justification for the common law power itself: searches which derive their legal authority from the fact of arrest must be truly incidental to the arrest in question. . . . This means, simply put, that the search is only justifiable if the purpose of the search is related to the purpose of the arrest.

. . .

To be clear, this is not a standard of reasonable and probable grounds, the normal threshold that must be surpassed before a search can be conducted. Here, the only requirement is that there be some reasonable basis for doing what the police officer did.

. . .

As explained above, these limits will be no different for automobiles than for any other place. The right to search a car incident to arrest and the scope of that search will depend on a number of factors, including the basis for the arrest, the location of the motor vehicle in relation to the place of the arrest, and other relevant circumstances.

The temporal limits on search incident to arrest will also be derived from the same principles. There is no need to set a firm deadline on the amount of time that may elapse before the search can no longer said to be incidental to arrest. As a general rule, searches that are truly incidental to arrest will usually occur within a reasonable period of time after the arrest. A substantial delay does not mean that the search is automatically unlawful, but it may cause the court to draw an inference that the search is not sufficiently connected to the arrest. Naturally, the strength of the inference will depend on the length of the delay, and can be defeated by a reasonable explanation for the delay.

[Lamer C.J. held that the vehicle search fell outside of the scope of the common law power to search pursuant to a lawful arrest. He did not view the six-hour delay as determinative, especially given the limited staff in the detachment. Rather, he held that the vehicle search was not truly incidental to the accused's arrest. It was conducted for inventory purposes and not to gather evidence or serve some other legitimate ends of criminal justice. Since the vehicle search was not authorized, it violated s. 8 of the *Charter*. Nevertheless, Lamer C.J. ruled that the evidence was admissible under s. 24(2) and upheld the accused's conviction.

Bastarache J. (L'Heureux-Dubé and Gonthier JJ. concurring) agreed that the six-hour delay did not preclude the vehicle search from being incidental to the arrest. However, he held that, regardless of the officer's subjective belief about the purpose of the search, the officer had a common law power to search the vehicle incidental to the arrest in the circumstances of the case. Since the vehicle search was authorized by common law, there was no violation of the accused's *Charter* rights under s. 8. It was on this basis that the minority upheld the accused's conviction for cocaine possession.]

NOTES AND QUESTIONS

1. Traditionally, the common law right to search pursuant to a lawful arrest was narrowly defined. In order to search the person arrested, the police needed reasonable grounds to believe that he or she was in possession of evidence of the offence or a

weapon. See *Bessell v. Wilson* (1853), 118 E.R. 518 (Q.B.); *Leigh v. Cole* (1853), 6 Cox C.C. 329 (Oxford Circuit Stftd. Assizes); *Dillon v. O'Brien and Davis* (1887), 16 Cox C.C. 245 (Exch.); and *Gordon v. Denison* (1895), 22 O.A.R. 315. See also Wade, "Police Search" (1934) 50 L.Q.R. 354; and Leigh, "Recent Developments in the Law of Search and Seizure" (1970) 33 M.L.R. 268.

2. In *Caslake*, Lamer C.J. stated that the police need some reasonable basis for the search, but do not need reasonable and probable grounds. In *R. v. Chubak*, 2009 ABCA 8, the court held that the officer must have a subjective belief, which is objectively reasonable, that the search will serve the purpose of safety, preservation of evidence or recovery of evidence related to the charge. Can you reconcile these statements in *Caslake* and *Chubak*?

3. Do you agree with the majority or minority in *Caslake* on whether the inventory search of the vehicle was incidental to the accused's arrest?

4. The issue of vehicle searches continues to generate considerable *Charter* litigation. See *R. v. Harrison*, 2009 SCC 34, *R. v. Loewen*, 2011 SCC 21, *R. v. Valentine*, 2014 ONCA 147, and *R. v. Patrick*, 2017 BCCA 57 (vehicle search following arrest); *R. v. Wint* (2009), 93 O.R. (3d) 514 (C.A.) and *R. v. Ellis*, 2016 ONCA 598 (inventory search prior to impoundment under provincial law); *R. v. Nolet*, 2010 SCC 24 and *R. v. Gonzales*, 2017 ONCA 543 (search pursuant to provincial highway traffic legislation); and *R. v. Bergauer-Free* (2009), 255 O.A.C. 233 (C.A.) ("consent" search of vehicle following routine traffic stop).

5. In *R. v. Hiscoe*, 2013 NSCA 48, the police arrested the accused for possession of cocaine for the purposes of trafficking and seized his cellphone which was on the seat of his car. The court stated that seizing the cellphone and examining its recent contents at the scene and shortly thereafter came within the officers' common law right to search pursuant to arrest. However, the subsequent downloading of the cellphone's entire contents one month later was held to exceed the scope of the common law search power and to violate s. 8 of the *Charter*. In what circumstances, if any, would the police have been entitled to search the accused's cellphone if he had been arrested for: (a) impaired driving; (b) assault; or (c) fraud?

In *R. v. Fearon*, 2014 SCC 77, the court stated that searching a suspect's cell phone or similar device pursuant to his or her arrest would not violate s. 8 of the *Charter* if: the arrest was lawful; the search was truly incidental to the arrest (*i.e.* the search had to be performed promptly in order to meet a legitimate law enforcement goal); the nature and extent of the search were tailored to its purpose; and the police made detailed notes on what they searched on the device and how they examined it.

For additional cases on the seizure of electronic communication see *R. v. Pelucco*, 2015 BCCA 370; *R. v. Marakah*, 2017 SCC 59; and *R. v. Jones*, 2017 SCC 60.

6. The common law power to search pursuant to arrest did not extend to intimate physical searches, seizing bodily samples, or undertaking medical or surgical procedures. Nevertheless, the Canadian courts had permitted a broad range of intrusive and intimate searches in drug cases. See for example *Reynen v. Antonenko* (1975), 54 D.L.R. (3d) 124 (Alta. S.C.) (surgical removal of drugs from the suspect's rectum); *R. v. Rousseau*, [1985] R.L. 108 (Qc. C.S.P.) (laxatives and drugs to hasten retrieval of drugs); and *R. v. Monney*, [1999] 1 S.C.R. 652 (detention of suspected

heroin courier in an airport "drug-loo" facility). This lenient attitude regarding searches in drug cases is changing.

In *R. v. Greffe*, [1990] 1 S.C.R. 755, airport customs officials received a tip that the accused was carrying heroin. However, no heroin was found when he was strip-searched. The R.C.M.P. then arrested the accused for unpaid traffic tickets, and arranged for him to be given a rectal search using a sigmoidoscope. Two bags of heroin were recovered. The Crown admitted that the search violated s. 8, but argued that the evidence should not be excluded under s. 24(2). The majority of the court held that subjecting the accused to a rectal search pursuant to an arrest for traffic tickets, without reasonable grounds that he was carrying drugs, constituted a serious violation of s. 8 that required exclusion of the evidence.

As in *Greffe*, the courts now often fail to discuss the scope of the common law authority to search, focusing instead on whether the search was reasonable under s. 8. Would the rectal search have been justifiable if Greffe had been arrested for drug possession? Why did the police not arrest Greffe on this charge?

7. In *R. v. Poirier*, 2016 ONCA 582, the accused was held under a warrant authorizing a "bedpan vigil search" (*i.e.* held in a dry cell and accompanied to a commode until all the drugs in his bowels were eliminated). He was kept for 43 hours before being taken before a justice. He was chained to the bars of his cell above his head using three sets of handcuffs for the first 21 to 22 hours, and was then handcuffed and fitted with oven mitts that that were duct-taped together for about the next 9 hours. At trial, the accused was convicted of possession of three drugs for the purposes of trafficking and simple possession of a fourth drug.

The Court of Appeal stated that in appropriate circumstances the *Criminal Code*'s general search warrant provisions would provide authority for a bedpan vigil search, as would the common law right to search pursuant to a lawful arrest. However, in ordering the accused's acquittal, the Court held that warrant was invalid in that it purported to authorize the accused's indefinite detention until the drugs were excreted, contrary to s. 503 of the *Criminal Code* which requires an accused to be brought before a justice without unreasonable delay and in any event within 24 hours. The Court also held that the way in which the bedpan vigil was conducted violated the accused's rights under ss. 7 and 8 of the *Charter* and that the drug evidence had to be excluded.

8. In *R. v. Golden*, [2001] 3 S.C.R. 679, the police observed the accused making drug sales and lawfully arrested him. After a pat-down search did not result in finding drugs or a weapon, the police decided to strip-search Golden at the top of the restaurant's back stairwell. When Golden resisted, he was taken to a booth in the back of the restaurant, held down, aggressively strip-searched and a package of drugs was removed from his buttocks. Both the majority and the dissent noted that strip searches were inherently degrading and condemned the way in which the strip search was conducted. The majority stated that strip searches can be conducted pursuant to a lawful arrest if the police have reasonable and probable grounds to believe that doing so is necessary to ascertain if the individual has a weapon, ensure the safety of the police, the individual and others, or secure evidence related to the arrest. The majority stated that the lower courts erred in concluding that the strip search was reasonable in the circumstances and consequently erred in admitting the impugned evidence.

The dissent stated that once the police establish that the accused's arrest was lawful, they do not require reasonable and probable grounds for a strip search.

Rather, a strip search will be lawful and reasonable if the police have an objectively valid reason for the arrest, and the search is undertaken for a valid purpose and is not conducted in an abusive fashion. While the dissent agreed that the way in which the strip search was conducted was unreasonable and violated s. 8, they stated that the admission of the drug evidence would not bring the administration of justice into disrepute.

How did the majority and dissent define the grounds for undertaking a strip search and which position better reflects the common law principles governing search pursuant to a lawful arrest? Do you agree with the majority or the dissent on the admissibility of the drug evidence?

9. In *Golden, ibid.* and *Vancouver (City) v. Ward*, [2010] 2 S.C.R. 28, the court indicated that the routine strip search of detainees cannot be justified if they are being held for only a short time in police cells, they are not mingling with the general prison population, and there are no legitimate concerns that they are concealing a weapon. Can you reconcile these comments with the duty of the police to protect all detainees and to prevent contraband from being brought into the facility? Should the fact that Ward was a lawyer at a political event have any impact on how he is processed once arrested and put in a police lockup? For a review of the case law on strip searches, see Fontana & Keeshan, *The Law of Search & Seizure in Canada*, 10th ed. (2017) at 1063-69.

10. In *R. v. Stillman*, [1997] 1 S.C.R. 607, the 17-year-old accused was arrested for the brutal murder of a teenage girl. The accused's lawyer told the police that his client was refusing consent to any tests or to make any statement. Nevertheless, in order to link the accused to bite marks on the deceased and a semen sample that was recovered, the police demanded that the accused provide hair samples, submit to saliva and buccal swabs, and allow dental impressions to be made. Since the *Criminal Code* did not include warrants for searching individuals or seizing bodily samples in 1991 when the offence was committed, the police had to rely on their common law right to search pursuant to arrest. Seven of the Supreme Court justices held that the common law right to search did not extend beyond protecting the arresting officer or seizing evidence that might otherwise be lost. Consequently, they ruled that the police had no authority to seize the hair samples, obtain bodily fluids or take dental impressions. Can you reconcile *Stillman* with the drug cases discussed in note 6 above?

In 1995, Parliament enacted legislation creating a judicial warrant authorizing the taking of hair, saliva and blood samples for DNA testing from those suspected of designated criminal offences. See *Criminal Code*, ss. 487.04-487.092; *R. v. S.A.B.*, [2003] 2 S.C.R. 678; *R. v. R.C.*, 2005 SCC 61; and *R. v. Jackpine*, [2006] 1 S.C.R. 554.

11. In *R. v. Saeed*, 2016 SCC 24, the accused was arrested after a woman was viciously attacked and sexually assaulted. The police felt that there were reasonable and probable grounds to believe that the victim's DNA would still be found on the accused's penis and handcuffed the accused to a wall in a dry cell for 30 to 40 minutes before a penile swab could be undertaken. The accused was permitted to conduct the swab himself in the presence of two male officers who blocked the cell window. The police did not seek a warrant because they believed that they had common law authority to conduct the search pursuant to the accused's arrest. The swab tested positive for the victim's DNA and the accused was convicted. The trial judge and a

majority of the appeal court held that the search violated s. 8 of the *Charter* but ruled that the evidence was admissible.

Seven of the Supreme Court of Canada justices ruled that the penile swab fell within the common law power to search pursuant to a lawful arrest and did not violate s. 8 the *Charter*. The majority distinguished *Stillman* on three grounds. First, a penile swab is not conducted to seize the accused's bodily material, but rather that of the complainant. Second, in some ways the taking of a penile swab is less invasive than taking a dental impression or forcefully seizing the accused's hair or bodily fluids. Third, the complainant's DNA degrades over time, unlike an accused's dental impression or bodily material. According to the majority, "the issue in this case cannot be resolved by a straightforward application of *Stillman*. A penile swab implicates different privacy interests and law enforcement objectives than seizures of an accused's bodily samples and certain impressions."

Do you agree that: (a) the common law right to search pursuant to a lawful search extends to penile swabs; and (b) penile swabs do not violate s. 8 of the *Charter*? Was the majority's attempt to distinguish *Stillman* compelling? Is the majority's analysis in *Saeed* consistent with that in *Poirier* and *Golden, supra*?

12. In the absence of specific statutory authority, there is generally no right to search a suspect until after he or she has been lawfully arrested. However, the Canadian courts have created exceptions in drug enforcement. See *R. v. Brezack* (1949), 96 C.C.C. 97 (Ont. C.A.); and *Scott v. R.* (1975), 61 D.L.R. (3d) 130 (Fed. C.A.), in which the courts upheld the use of "throat-holds." Typically, suspects are grabbed by the throat without warning to prevent them from swallowing any drugs that they may be carrying in their mouth.

Despite the *Charter*, the Canadian courts largely ignored the dangers inherent in throat-holds and upheld their use. In *R. v. Collins*, [1987] 1 S.C.R. 265, the court held that the use of a throat-hold would not constitute an unreasonable search if the officer reasonably believed that the suspect was a "drug handler." Does this test adequately balance the physical integrity of drug suspects and the interests of the state? See also *R. v. Debot*, [1989] 2 S.C.R. 1140; and *R. v. Garcia-Guiterrez* (1991), 65 C.C.C. (3d) 15 (B.C.C.A.).

13. Following a lawful arrest, an officer has a common law right to search not only the suspect and his or her personal effects but also the immediate scene, provided the arrest took place in public or the suspect's premises. It is doubtful whether this search power provides authority for a wholesale search of the suspect's or a third party's home simply because the suspect was apprehended there. See generally *R. v. Feeney*, [1997] 2 S.C.R. 13; *R. v. Golub* (1997), 34 O.R. (3d) 743 (C.A.); *R. v. Ahmed-Kadir*, 2015 BCCA 346; and *R. v. Ellis*, 2016 ONCA 598. Similar doubts have been raised about an officer's right to take a suspect home to search his or her residence. See *Dillon v. O'Brien and Davis* (1887), 16 Cox C.C. 245 (Exch.); *McLorie v. Oxford*, [1982] 3 All E.R. 480 (Q.B.); and Wade, "Police Search" (1934) 50 L.Q.R. 354. But see *Dallison v. Caffery*, [1964] 2 All E.R. 610 (C.A.).

14. For a detailed review of the common law power to search pursuant to arrest, see Fontana & Keeshan, *The Law of Search & Seizure in Canada*, 10th ed. (2017) at 917-24 and 985-92.

15. Various federal and provincial statutes contain broad powers to search suspects which may be invoked independently of the common law power. See for example the *Criminal Code*, ss. 117.02-117.06 (search and seizure of weapons); *Controlled Drugs and Substances Act*, S.C. 1996, c. 19, ss. 11-12 (search and seizure of illicit drugs); and the provincial liquor, parks, highway traffic, hunting, and fishing statutes. However, the post-*Charter* cases have limited these provincial powers to ensure that they are not used as a pretext for a general investigation or a wider unrelated search. See *R. v. Mellenthin*, [1992] 3 S.C.R. 615; and *R. v. Gonzales*, 2017 ONCA 543.

16. The societal interest in conducting a search must be balanced against an individual's reasonable expectation of privacy. However, the nature of that expectation may vary with the circumstances. For example, the Supreme Court of Canada has held that individuals have a diminished expectation of privacy while driving, given that it is a heavily regulated, licensed activity that poses significant risks: *R. v. Wise*, [1992] 1 S.C.R. 527; and *R. v. Pontes*, [1995] 3 S.C.R. 44. Similarly, students are entitled to a diminished expectation of privacy while at school. Consequently, a search that might be impermissible if undertaken by a police officer may be permissible if undertaken by a principal: *R. v. M.(M.R.)*, [1998] 3 S.C.R. 393; and *R. v. A.M.*, 2008 SCC 19.

Should a diminished expectation of privacy apply in regard to the use of "sniffer" dogs? Should the standards vary in regard to: (a) airports, borders, schools, and shopping malls; (b) whether the dog is trained to detect drugs as opposed to explosives; and (c) whether the dog is searching a general area or a specific individual? See *R. v. Kang-Brown*, 2008 SCC 18; and *R. v. A.M., supra.*

The Canadian courts have distinguished between using drug dogs to screen passengers on flights within Canada as opposed to passengers on flights entering Canada. While the use of drug dogs constitutes a search within the meaning of s. 8 in regard to passengers on domestic flights, their use does not constitute a search in regard to passengers entering Canada. See *R. v. Chehil*, 2013 SCC 49; and *R. v. Jackman*, 2016 ONCA 121. Is this distinction compelling?

6. A Peace Officer's Common Law Power of Entry to Search for a Wanted Person

ECCLES v. BOURQUE
[1975] 2 S.C.R. 739

DICKSON J.:—The claim of the appellant, Mr. Eccles, is against the respondents, three constables on the Vancouver Police Force, for damages for trespass alleged to have been committed when the police officers entered the apartment occupied by Mr. Eccles in the City of Vancouver at about 4:00 p.m. on August 12, 1971. The constables were in plain clothes but were armed. The purpose of the entry was to apprehend one Edmund Cheese, also known as Billy Deans, for whom there were three outstanding Montreal warrants. Cheese was not found in the apartment. . . . Mr. Eccles was successful at trial. Mr. Justice Wootton awarded him $300 damages and costs. The Court of Appeal for British Columbia by a majority (Robertson and Taggart JJ.A., with Nemetz, J.A. dissenting) reversed. . . .

There are two issues: (1) Were the respondents authorized by s. 25 of the *Criminal Code* forcibly to enter and search the appellant's apartment pursuant to their right of arrest without warrant under s. 450 [the predecessor to s. 494(1) of the *Criminal Code*] . . . ? (2) If not, were their actions justified on common law principles? On the first issue, s. 450(1)(a) of the *Code* provides that any one may arrest without warrant a person who, on reasonable and probable grounds, he believes has committed a criminal offence. There were reasonable and probable grounds for believing that Cheese had committed a criminal offence and had the respondents found him in the apartment or elsewhere there is no doubt they would have been authorized by s. 450(1)(a) to arrest him. . . .

It is the submission of counsel for the respondents that a person who is by s. 450 authorized to make an arrest is, by s. 25, authorized by law to commit a trespass with or without force in the accomplishment of that arrest, provided he acts on reasonable and probable grounds. I cannot agree with this submission. Section 25 does not have such amplitude. The section merely affords justification to a person for doing what he is required or authorized by law to do in the administration or enforcement of the law, if he acts on reasonable and probable grounds, and for using necessary force for that purpose. The question which must be answered in this case, then, is whether the respondents were required or authorized by law to commit a trespass; and not, as their counsel contends, whether they were required or authorized to make an arrest. If they were authorized by law to commit a trespass, the authority for it must be found in the common law for there is nothing in the *Criminal Code*. The first issue, therefore, depends upon the second issue, *videlicet*, can the trespass be justified on common law principles? For these principles, we go back to vintage common law, to 1604, and *Semayne's Case*, 5 Co. Rep. 91a, 77 E.R. 194, in which the principle, so firmly entrenched in our jurisprudence, that every man's house is his castle, was expressed in these words [at p. 91b]: "That the house of every one is to him as his castle and fortress, as well for his defence against injury and violence, as for his repose . . .". That, then, is the basic principle, as important today as in Biblical times (Deuteronomy 24:10) or in the 17th century. But there are occasions when the interest of a private individual in the security of his house must yield to the public interest, when the public at large has an interest in the process to be executed. The criminal is not immune from arrest in his own home nor in the home of one of his friends. So it is that in *Semayne's Case* a limitation was put on the "castle" concept and the Court resolved that: [at p. 916]

> In all cases when the King is party, the Sheriff (if the doors be not open) may break the party's house, either to arrest him, or to do other execution of the K.'s process, if otherwise he cannot enter. But before he breaks it, he ought to signify the cause of his coming, and to make request to open doors . . .

See also, a century later, to the same effect, Hale, *Pleas of the Crown* (1736), 582; Foster, *Crown Law* (1762), 320. Thus it will be seen that the broad basic principle of sanctity of the home is subject to the exception that upon proper demand the officials of the King may break down doors to arrest. The incidental point was made in *Semayne's Case* that [at p. 93a] "the house of any one is not a castle or privilege but for himself, and shall not extend to protect any person who flies to his house . . ."

The *Criminal Code* empowers a justice, on proper grounds being shown, to issue a warrant authorizing a search for things but there is no power to issue a warrant to search for persons. Counsel for Mr. Eccles advanced the argument that if a fugitive was in the home of a friend a police officer could not enter to arrest him unless the homeowner gave consent. I cannot agree that this properly expresses the position in law. If that be right, a fugitive could obtain permanent sanctuary merely by residing with a friend. I know of no place that gives a criminal fugitive sanctuary from arrest.

In some of the American jurisdictions a distinction is drawn between entering to arrest a fugitive in his own home and entering the home of another person to arrest the fugitive. I am unable to find any Anglo-Canadian authority supporting a distinction of this nature and in principle it seems to me to be wrong. The fact that the premises to be entered are those of a third person may have a bearing in the determination of reasonable and probable cause. There may be less likelihood of a fugitive being in the home of another than in his own home, but otherwise I can see no good reason for distinguishing between the two types of case.

I would wish to make it clear, however, that there is no question of an unrestricted right to enter in search of a fugitive. Entry can be made against the will of the householder only if (a) there are reasonable and probable grounds for the belief that the person sought is within the premises and (b) proper announcement is made prior to entry.

(a) Reasonable and probable grounds

In the case of civil process the rule is that if a sheriff's officer enters the house of A to execute process against the goods of B or to arrest B he enters at his peril and if the goods or B, as the case may be, are not present, he is guilty of trespass. It is said the entry can be justified only by the event: *Johnson v. Leigh* (1815), 6 Taunt. 246, 128 E.R. 1029; *Morrish v. Murrey* (1844), 13 M. & W. 52, 153 E.R. 22; *Southam v. Smout*, [1964] 1 Q.B. 308. But in the execution of criminal process the test is whether there are reasonable and probable grounds for acting. If so, the entry does not become unlawful if the fugitive is not found on the premises. The entry of the police is legal or illegal from the moment of entry and does not change character from the result. . . . If the police officer has reasonable and probable cause to believe that the person named in the warrant for arrest is in the home of a stranger he has the right, after proper demand, to enter the home forcibly, to search and to arrest. In the present case there can be no doubt the police officers believed and in my view had reasonable and probable grounds for believing that Cheese, or Deans as he was known to Mr. Eccles, was in the Eccles apartment. Constable Simmonds had been told by one of his superiors that Eccles was the closest known associate of Cheese. That this information was hearsay does not exclude it from establishing probable cause. Additionally, both Eccles and Cheese had informed Constable Simmonds prior to the entry that Cheese had been staying in the Eccles apartment. On August 12, 1971, the day of the alleged trespass, Cheese had been in the apartment, he had been seen entering and leaving the building and just prior to the impugned entry had been seen to enter the building. Constable Bourque had seen police department bulletins pertaining to both Eccles and to Cheese.

(b) Announcement

Except in exigent circumstances, the police officers must make an announcement prior to entry. There are compelling considerations for this. An unexpected intrusion of a man's property can give rise to violent incidents. It is in the interests of the personal safety of the householder and the police as well as respect for the privacy of the individual that the law requires, prior to entrance for search or arrest, that a police officer identify himself and request admittance. No precise form of words is necessary. . . . The traditional demand was "Open in the name of the King". In the ordinary case police officers, before forcing entry, should give (i) notice of presence by knocking or ringing the doorbell, (ii) notice of authority, by identifying themselves as law enforcement officers and (iii) notice of purpose, by stating a lawful reason for entry. Minimally they should request admission and have admission denied although it is recognized there will be occasions on which, for example, to save someone within the premises from death or injury or to prevent destruction of evidence or if in hot pursuit notice may not be required. Was proper notice given in this case? The police officers gave notice of presence by knocking on the door of the apartment. After a pause it was opened and an officer gave notice of identity by production of his badge and the words "Vancouver City Police". On August 10th, two days before the alleged trespass, Mr. Eccles had been stopped and searched by two of the respondents. One of the respondents had stopped him on two earlier occasions, so the identity of two of the three persons who appeared at the door of the apartment on August 12th could hardly have been a matter of which Mr. Eccles was ignorant. Whether notice of purpose was given is more difficult. Mr. Eccles testified that when the door was opened one man stood there while the other two ran into different rooms without identifying themselves or their purpose. In his evidence-in-chief, Constable Simmonds, after referring to the opening of the door, said:

> I don't recall if Mr. Eccles answered, I don't recall if he said: "What do you want", or something like that, he probably did and Constable Bourque said: "We're looking for a wanted man and we want to search the premises", so forth —

Constable Wise testified, "Constable Bourque told Mr. Eccles that we were looking for a man wanted on a warrant." Constable Bourque said that when the door opened he observed Mr. Eccles standing in the doorway and he, Bourque, entered the apartment. In reply to the question by Mr. Eccles, "What do you want?" Constable Bourque replied, according to his evidence, "I told him that I had reason to believe a man wanted by our department had just entered this apartment." In my view, the police officers, on the facts of this case, discharged the duty which rested upon them to give notice before forcing entry.

I would, accordingly, dismiss the appeal with costs.

MARTLAND J.:—I do not wish to express any view with respect to the application of s. 25(1) of the *Criminal Code* to the circumstances of this case. Subject to this, I agree with the reasons of my brother Dickson and I would dispose of this appeal in the manner which he proposes.

[Laskin C.J. and Judson and Spence JJ. concurred with Dickson J., and Ritchie, Pigeon, Beetz and de Grandpré JJ. concurred with Martland J.]

NOTES AND QUESTIONS

1. According to Dickson J., what is the source of an officer's authority and privilege to make an entry without a search warrant to arrest a wanted person? What is the effect of *Eccles* on the issue of whether s. 25 can be used as an authorizing provision?

2. Did Dickson J. limit this power of entry to cases involving suspects named in an outstanding warrant? Is the power limited to suspects wanted for indictable offences, rather than summary conviction offences? What is the practical significance of these restrictions?

3. What is required in making a proper announcement? Do you agree with Dickson J.'s application of these requirements to the facts in *Eccles*? In what circumstances would Dickson J. permit the police to make an unannounced entry? In contrast to *Eccles*, other courts have held that there is no common law authority to undertake warrantless entries to seize evidence of an offence: *Morris v. Beardmore*, [1980] 2 All E.R. 753 (H.L.); *Finnigan v. Sandiford*, [1981] 2 All E.R. 267 (H.L.); and *R. v. Colet*, [1981] 1 S.C.R. 2. In your opinion, does preventing the possible destruction of evidence outweigh the risk of a violent confrontation? See also *R. v. Hunter*, 2015 BCCA 428.

4. The general principles in *Eccles* were affirmed in *R. v. Landry*, [1986] 1 S.C.R. 145. While the court limited the entry power to persons wanted for indictable offences, it held that the police could also enter if they reasonably believed that an indictable offence was about to be committed. But see LaForest J.'s dissent in *Landry*. The principles in *Landry* apply even if the door of the dwelling is open. See *R. v. Delong* (1989), 31 O.A.C. 339 (C.A.).

5. In *R. v. Feeney*, [1997] 2 S.C.R. 13, the majority stated that s. 8 of the *Charter* limits the common law right to enter in search of a wanted person to situations of hot pursuit and perhaps other exigent circumstances. The four dissenting judges rejected this limitation. In *R. v. Golub* (1997), 34 O.R. (3d) 743 (C.A.), the court interpreted *Feeney* as permitting such warrantless entries in any exceptional circumstances in which the state interest outweighs the general prohibition against warrantless searches of the home.

6. In 1997, Parliament amended the *Criminal Code* to create statutory rights to enter dwellings to arrest a wanted person. The amendments provide for: warrants to enter dwellings to arrest a wanted person; authority to enter without a warrant in exigent circumstances; authority to enter without prior announcement in exigent circumstances; and the issuance of telewarrants if it is impracticable to obtain a regular warrant: *Criminal Code*, ss. 529-529.5. See also the *Controlled Drugs and Substances Act*, S.C. 1996, ss. 11-12.1. These statutory provisions apply in addition to any common law authority an officer may have to make such entries. For applications of these provisions, see *R. v. Cornell*, 2010 SCC 31; *R. v. MacKay*, 2012 ONCA 671; *R. v. Burke*, 2013 ONCA 424; and *R. v. Al-Amiri*, 2015 NLCA 37.

7. Although not well defined, there is a common law right of forced entry to prevent the commission of murder and other felonies, but it is distinct from the right of entry to search for wanted suspects. Aside from the nature of the impending harm, this right appears similar to that granted in cases of public necessity. See *Handcock v. Baker* (1800), 126 E.R. 1270 (C.P.); and *R. v. Custer* (1984), 32 Sask. R. 287 (C.A.). See also *Rigby v. Chief Constable of Northamptonshire*, [1985] 2 All E.R. 985 (Q.B.).

8. In *R. v. Godoy*, [1999] 1 S.C.R. 311, the police received a 911 call from a woman, but the call was disconnected before she could explain the situation. When the

police arrived at the apartment, the woman's husband told them that there was no problem and refused them entry. The police made a forced entry, interviewed the wife and then charged the husband with assault. He resisted arrest and was charged with assaulting the police in the execution of their duty. This charge turned on whether the police entry was lawful. The court ruled that the forced entry was justifiable in the circumstances. The court stated that, if it could be inferred that a caller was or may be in some distress, the police had a common law right to demand entry under their common law "duty to protect life." See also *R. v. Sanderson* (2003), 64 O.R. (3d) 257 (C.A.); *R. v. Wolkowski* (2009), 189 C.R.R. (2d) 312 (Ont. S.C.J.); and *R. v. Alexson (T.L.)*, 2015 MBCA 5.   But see *R. v. Côté*, 2011 SCC 46. See Fontana & Keeshan, *The Law of Search & Seizure in Canada*, 10th ed. (2017) at 904-10.

9. In *Kuru v. State of New South Wales* (2008), 236 C.L.R. 1 (H.C.A.), the police responded to a complaint about a noisy domestic argument. When the police arrived, the door to the flat was open and the plaintiff's fiancée had left. After initially allowing the police to look around and providing a phone number at which his fiancée might be contacted, the plaintiff repeatedly told the police to leave. However, they did not do so. A violent confrontation ensued in which the plaintiff was punched, pepper-sprayed, handcuffed, and taken to the police station in his boxer shorts. In upholding the plaintiff's damage claim against the police, the court stated that the police have no common law power to enter or remain on private property without consent to investigate whether a breach of the peace has occurred or was threatened. Had the fiancée been present, would the police have had authority to remain until: (a) it was determined that she was safe; or (b) they had an opportunity to speak to her in private about what had occurred? Can you reconcile *Kuru* and *Godoy, supra*?

10. The House of Lords and the United States Supreme Court have defined the common law right of entry to search for a wanted person far more narrowly than the Supreme Court of Canada. See *Payton v. New York; Riddick v. New York*, 100 S. Ct. 1371 (U.S. 1980); *Steagald v. U.S.*, 101 S. Ct. 1642 (U.S. 1981); *Morris v. Beardmore, supra*, and *Finnigan v. Sandiford, supra*.

11. The common law authorized the police to enter a dwelling without prior judicial authorization when in hot pursuit of a person who had committed an arrestable offence. The crime, pursuit and arrest had to be continuous, forming a single transaction. See *Swales v. Cox*, [1981] 1 All E.R. 1115 (Q.B.); *D'Souza v. D.P.P.*, [1992] 4 All E.R. 545 (H.L.); *R. v. Haglof* (2000), 149 C.C.C. (3d) 248 (B.C.C.A.); and *Tétard c. R.*, 2010 QCCA 2235. In *R. v. Macooh*, [1993] 2 S.C.R. 802, the court extended this common law doctrine to provincial offences. Do you agree with the Supreme Court of Canada that there is no logical reason to distinguish between federal indictable offences and provincial offences in analyzing hot pursuit?

12. In *R. v. Puyenbroek*, 2007 ONCA 824, the court stated that the common law principles of hot pursuit should be narrowly interpreted and applied in a manner consistent with the 1997 *Criminal Code* amendments, which authorized entry into dwellings. What are the justifications for allowing entry into a dwelling house without a warrant in hot pursuit?

REVIEW PROBLEMS

1. Fifteen members of a local motorcycle gang pulled into John's Service Station and Restaurant. The owner, aware of the gang's reputation for violent crime, called the police. The gang went to the service centre, where one of the cyclists politely asked to borrow a wrench, which the attendant retrieved from the back of the station. Upon her return, the attendant thought that two small cans of lubricating oil were missing from the display, but she did not see anyone take them. Nevertheless, she assumed that one of the gang members had stolen the oil in her brief absence.

When six police officers and their trained dog arrived, the attendant explained that one of the cyclists had stolen some oil, but she had no idea which one it was. Officer Jones approached the gang leader, Steve, and asked him to open his pack. Steve ignored Jones until the dog, on command from Jones, bared its teeth and backed Steve into a corner. In the interim, Jones was informed that no oil had been found in the possession of the other cyclists. He ordered Steve to open his pack. Steve, who was unaware of the attendant's allegation, refused and walked to his motorcycle.

Jones signalled the dog to subdue Steve. It jumped on Steve's back, knocking him to the ground. Just before the dog struck, Jones shouted, "You are under arrest for theft!" Steve was handcuffed and led away to a police car. Although the search of his pack revealed that it was empty, Steve was told that he was under arrest for obstructing a peace officer in the execution of his duty.

The charge against Steve was dropped. He wishes to sue Jones and the attendant in tort and has asked for your advice.

2. Ralph, a former professional football player, owned a small cigar store. Late one night, he heard someone yell: "Help, thief!" As he stepped outside, he saw Gaston running towards him carrying an expensive camera. In hot pursuit, about 30 metres behind, was George. Both were strangers to Ralph, and were unexceptional in size or manner of dress. Gaston turned into a dead-end alley and Ralph, still well ahead of George, joined in the chase. Just as Gaston slowed down at the end of the alley, Ralph tackled him. Gaston attempted to struggle free, but Ralph hauled him to his feet with ease and threw him into a fence with such force that it knocked down an overhanging neon sign. Breathless and badly shaken, Gaston was finally able to scream at Ralph, "I'm not the thief. The guy chasing me tried to grab the camera out of my hand. He's the thief and he is getting away!" When Ralph turned around he saw that George had disappeared, and realized his mistake.

Ralph has sought your legal advice regarding his potential tort liability.

3. John was woken by loud banging on his door on Wednesday at 2:00 a.m. When he opened the door, John was confronted by three uniformed police officers, who stated that they were looking for Bobby Seal. John told them to put their guns away and that only his family were in the house. The officers ran past John, stating that he would be arrested if he tried to stop them. The officers entered the bedrooms with their guns at their sides. After thoroughly searching the house, the officers left without providing any further explanation and without apologizing. John's wife was initially fearful, but this soon turned to anger. The children remained upset and had nightmares for several weeks.

The officers knew that Bobby and John were lifelong friends and that they had been convicted of several robberies nine years ago when they were teenagers. While Bobby had a number of arrests and convictions after that, John had no other arrests.

The police were investigating an armed robbery at a jewellery store that had been committed at 8:00 p.m. on Tuesday evening. The security camera had captured pictures of the thief, who resembled Bobby Seal. The thief was carrying a gun. Since the thief wore a ski mask, it was impossible to make a positive identification.

The staff of the bar in the jewellery store plaza told the police that Bobby and John had lunch together in the bar on the day of the robbery. A car somewhat similar to Bobby Seal's was spotted near the plaza at 7:00 p.m. that night. A usually reliable informant had told the police that he wouldn't be surprised if Bobby had robbed the jewellery store, but he doubted that John would get involved. The informant had also told the police that Seal spent time at John's house, particularly when he was in trouble.

The police had checked Bobby Seal's house and his girlfriend's apartment before coming to John's house. However, Bobby's car was not parked nearby and no one reported seeing the car or Bobby in the vicinity of John's house. Nevertheless, the police were anxious to find Bobby as soon as possible. If he was the robber, they did not want to give him an opportunity to dispose of the jewellery.

John has approached your law firm. Your senior partner wants you to analyze the tort claims that John and his family can bring against the officers for entering and searching their home, and the defence that the police will likely raise.

INTRODUCTION TO THE LAW OF NEGLIGENCE

1. Negligence: Defining Terms
2. The Historical Development of Negligence
3. The Elements of a Negligence Action

1. Negligence: Defining Terms

The term "negligence" is used by tort lawyers in two distinct ways. First, in the broader sense, it refers to a cause of action that constitutes a branch of tort law concerned with liability for careless conduct. As discussed below, that cause of action contains a number of elements. Second, in its narrower sense, the term "negligence" refers to one particular element within that cause of action, namely, whether the defendant's conduct met the standard of care. Because of that ambiguity, it sometimes is difficult to know what a court or commentator means when using the term "negligence." Consequently, it may be better to speak of "negligence" only when referring to the cause of action as a whole, and to use the term "carelessness" when referring to conduct that fails to satisfy the standard of care.

Unlike the intentional torts, the cause of action in negligence has few predetermined boundaries. To a large extent, its scope is as wide or as narrow as the judicial interpretation of its core concept, the duty of care. The threshold issue in every negligence case is whether the defendant was subject to a legal obligation, or "duty," to exercise care with respect to the plaintiff's interests. The approach to that issue has varied from time to time and place to place. Toward the end of the 20th century, Canadian judges, in contrast to their English and Australian counterparts, tended to work from a relatively expansive, plaintiff-friendly perspective. As discussed in the next chapter, however, the current century has seen a shift in this country towards a more conservative attitude. In any event, the breadth and flexibility of the cause of action in negligence has made it the most frequently litigated tort.

2. The Historical Development of Negligence

The modern law of negligence, like that of intentional torts, has its origins in the writ system. Trespass *vi et armis*, the first writ relating to torts, provided strict liability for direct, forceful interferences with person or property. If the plaintiff established a direct injury, the defendant would be held liable unless he or she could prove that the injury occurred utterly without his or her fault. The stringent nature of liability in trespass *vi et armis* grew out of a strong judicial motivation to vindicate the security of the person and property and to deter public disorder.

The writ of trespass on the case developed after trespass *vi et armis,* and provided a remedy for losses that were not directly and forcefully inflicted. Since such incidents were less likely to cause violent confrontations, trespass on the case was never as stringent as trespass *vi et armis*. The plaintiff was required to prove that he or she had suffered actual loss and that the defendant's conduct was either intentional or negligent. A variety of actions on the case were eventually established, including defamation, nuisance, deceit, and negligence.

The first actions on the case involved defendants in public callings, such as apothecaries, surgeons, common carriers, and innkeepers, who were alleged to have breached the standards of customary practice. Outside of these types of relationships, individuals generally were not held accountable simply because, through carelessness, they indirectly injured others.

As illustrated by the cases in Chapter 1, by the early 19th century, the action on the case was also being used by plaintiffs who had been carelessly run down on public roads. So too by plaintiffs who had been injured through the mismanagement of fire or animals. In all of those situations, judges came to recognize legal duties of care in the absence of contract or, indeed, any prior relationship between the parties. As the number of lawsuits involving inadvertent conduct increased, the judges also began to articulate more clearly a "fault" theory of liability. They eventually held that a plaintiff was entitled to relief only if a defendant was at fault, that is, if the defendant failed to conform to the standard of care required in the circumstances. Both the duty of care concept and the fault principle were used by the courts as means of controlling the expansive tendencies of the tort of negligence.

In a series of cases in the mid and late 19th century, plaintiffs' lawyers attempted to extend the concept of the legal duty of care beyond the established categories, but those efforts were largely unsuccessful. Although lawsuits in negligence became commonplace, they were mainly confined to repetitive situations, such as railroad accidents, which were covered by settled precedent. In *Heaven v. Pender* (1883), 11 Q.B.D. 503 (C.A.), Brett M.R. boldly attempted to promulgate a general theory of the legal duty to take care, one that would apply in any circumstances where the actions of one party created a foreseeable risk of harm to another. However, that proposition was flatly rejected both by the other justices in *Heaven* and by judges in subsequent decisions, and was even qualified by Brett M.R. himself in *Le Lievre v. Gould*, [1893] 1 Q.B. 491 (C.A.) (by which time he had become Lord Esher).

The idea of establishing a synthesized and expansive duty of care in negligence found little support in the English courts until the House of Lords revisited the issue in *M'Alister (or Donoghue) v. Stevenson*, [1932] A.C. 562. The plaintiff alleged that she got sick after consuming the remnants of a decomposed snail in the defendant manufacturer's ginger beer. In what is now regarded as a classic speech, Lord Atkin stated at 580:

> At present I content myself with pointing out that in English law there must be, and is, some general conception of relations giving rise to a duty of care, of which the particular cases found in the books are but instances. The liability for negligence, whether you style it such or treat it as in other systems as a species of "culpa," is no doubt based upon a general public sentiment of moral wrongdoing for which the offender must pay. But acts or omissions which any moral code would censure cannot in a practical world be treated so as to give a right to every person injured by them to demand relief. In this way rules of law arise which limit the range of complainants and the extent of their remedy. The rule that you are to love your neighbour becomes in law, you must not injure your neighbour; and the lawyer's question, Who is my neighbour? receives a restricted reply. You must take reasonable care to avoid acts or omissions which you can reasonably foresee would be likely to injure your neighbour.

Who, then, in law is my neighbour? The answer seems to be — persons who are so closely and directly affected by my act that I ought reasonably to have them in contemplation as being so affected when I am directing my mind to the acts or omissions which are called in question.

Donoghue v. Stevenson is the seminal case in modern negligence law because it established a basic framework that could be used for determining when to recognize a duty of care. Despite initial reluctance to adopt a general conception of duty, Lord Atkin's test eventually became widely accepted as governing liability for negligent acts causing physical injury or property damage. There was far greater reluctance, however, to apply the test to those categories of negligence that had previously been subject to restrictive liability rules. These special categories included cases involving a defendant's failure to take affirmative action for the plaintiff's benefit, negligent statements, nervous shock, pure economic loss, and occupiers' liability. During the past 80 years, the courts have gradually, on a piecemeal basis, rejected much of this pre-1932 case law in favour of broader principles more akin to those in *Donoghue*.

NOTES AND QUESTIONS

1. P.H. Winfield identified four areas of the early common law from which the modern negligence action evolved: liability in nuisance; liability based on the control of dangerous things; duties voluntarily undertaken in assumpsit; and the duty cast upon bailees and persons pursuing a common calling. See "The History of Negligence in the Law of Torts" (1926) 42 L.Q.R. 184. See also Wigmore, "Responsibility for Tortious Acts: Its History" (1894) 7 Harv. L. Rev. 315 & 383; Ames, "Law and Morals" (1908) 22 Harv. L. Rev. 97; and Arterburn, "The Origin and First Test of Public Callings" (1926-27) 75 U. Pa. L. Rev. 411.

2. There has been considerable debate over the impact of the Industrial Revolution and the concept of fault on the emergence of negligence as an independent tort action. The orthodox view is perhaps best reflected by C.H.S. Fifoot in *History and Sources of the Common Law* (1949) at 164:

> The prime factor in the ultimate transformation of negligence from a principle of liability in Case to an independent tort was the luxuriant crop of "running down" actions reaped from the commercial prosperity of the late eighteenth and early nineteenth century. Their significance lay rather in their number than in their nature. So long as they could be indulged as the occasional accidents of litigation, they called for no special attention; but when they became a daily occurrence, the judges were forced to recognize a formidable phenomenon which could not be confined, without too gross an artificiality, within the conventional categories.

G.E. White contends that the evolution of negligence in the United States was more complex than the orthodox view suggests. He maintains that the development of negligence was fostered by three 19th century trends: the impulse towards conceptualization among American intellectuals; the collapse of common law writ pleading; and a gradual change in tort cases from those involving parties in "closely defined relations to those involving strangers." Only the last factor is directly related to industrialization and urbanization. See White, *Tort Law In America: An Intellectual History*, expanded ed. (2003). See also Melamed & Westin, "Anti-Intellectual History" (1981) 90 Yale L.J. 1497.

3. Legal historians continue to debate the question of the social and economic impact of the rise of the negligence tort. In his influential book, *The Transformation of American Law, 1780-1860* (1970), M. Horwitz argued that the judicial development and application of fault-based negligence principles delivered crucial subsidies to American industry, especially in the area of work-related accidents. This view has been substantially revised by more recent scholarship emphasizing the diversity — doctrinal, regional, and temporal — of negligence law and its consequences for American history. See generally, Schwartz, "Tort Law and the Economy in Nineteenth Century America: A Reinterpretation" (1981) 90 Yale L.J. 1717; Kaczorowski, "The Common Law Background of Nineteenth Century Tort Law" (1990) 51 Ohio St. L.J. 1127; Bergstrom, *Courting Danger* (1994); Welke, *Recasting American Liberty* (2001); and Witt, *The Accidental Republic* (2004). For an analysis of 20th century tort law in the United States, see Abraham, *The Liability Century: Insurance and Tort Law from the Progressive Era to 9/11* (2008).

For a study of the relationship between negligence law and the rise of industry in England, see Kostal, *Law and English Railway Capitalism 1825-1875* (1995) at 254-321.

4. As late as 1924, J.W. Salmond argued that negligence was not an independent branch of tort law: *Law of Torts*, 6th ed. (1924). Contrast his position with that of Pollock, *The Law of Torts* (1887) at 22; and Winfield, "The History of Negligence in the Law of Torts" (1926) 46 L.Q.R. 184.

5. Relatively little has been published on the historical development of tort law in Canada. But see Risk, "The Last Golden Age: Property and the Allocation of Losses in Ontario in the Nineteenth Century" (1977) 27 U.T.L.J. 199; and Kostal, "Legal Justice, Social Justice: The Social History of Work-Related Accident Law in Ontario, 1880-86" (1988) 6 Law and Hist. Rev. 1.

6. It should be noted that several academics had formulated theories of negligence which were very similar to that eventually articulated by Lord Atkin. See for example, Pollock, *The Law of Torts* (1887) at 353; and Smith, *A Treatise on the Law of Negligence*, 2d ed. (1887) at 1.

3. The Elements of a Negligence Action

(a) INTRODUCTION

Unlike the nominate intentional torts, the various manifestations of the cause of action in negligence all fall within a single conceptual framework, regardless of the precise nature of the defendant's conduct or the plaintiff's loss. That is not to say that exactly the same rules apply in each instance. For example, the liability rules governing psychiatric harm are more restrictive than those governing physical injury. It is correct to say, however, that the basic elements of analysis remain constant.

Unfortunately, while there is broad consensus on that proposition, there is less agreement regarding the manner in which the constituent elements of the claim ought to be named and organized. To a large extent, the incidence of liability should not be affected by the choice of one model over another. Nevertheless, for the sake of consistency and clarity, it is critically important to adopt and adhere to some particular scheme. With that in mind, we have divided the negligence claim into six parts. The plaintiff usually has the burden of proving the first five, while the defendant has the burden of proving the sixth.

(i) *Duty of Care*

The court must decide, as a matter of law, whether the defendant was under any legal obligation to exercise care with respect to the plaintiff's interests in the type of case under consideration. If necessary, the court must also determine the nature and scope of that obligation. Because the duty of care often defines the boundaries of negligence liability, it has historically been the element of negligence most concerned with legal policy.

(ii) *The Standard of Care and its Breach*

Having identified and defined the duty of care, the court must next establish the standard of care required of the defendant. Ordinarily, the defendant is expected to meet the standard of care that would be exercised by a reasonable person in all the circumstances of the case. However, some professionals who have special training or qualifications are expected to meet the standard of their professional colleagues.

The trier of fact will then apply that standard of care to the defendant's conduct to determine whether the defendant breached his or her obligation by acting carelessly (or "negligently").

(iii) *Causation*

Even if the defendant was under a duty of care and breached the standard of care, he or she will not be held liable unless the careless conduct was a cause of the plaintiff's loss. This element of the negligence action is commonly known as cause-in-fact.

(iv) *Remoteness of Damages*

Once it has been established that the defendant carelessly caused the plaintiff's injury, the court must determine whether the relationship between the breach and the injury is too tenuous, or remote, to warrant recovery. In intentional torts, defendants are normally liable for all of the consequences of their wrongful conduct. However, in negligence, liability is generally limited to those losses that were foreseeable consequences of the defendant's negligent act.

(v) *Actual Loss*

Unlike most intentional torts, negligence is not actionable *per se*. The plaintiff must establish that he or she suffered legally-recognized injuries and losses, as well as their nature and extent. Certain losses, such as death and grief, were not recoverable at common law; however, they are generally recoverable under legislation.

(vi) *Defences*

Finally, once the plaintiff has established a *prima facie* claim, the court must address the issue of defences. The plaintiff's damages may be reduced or eliminated on account of his or her own conduct (contributory negligence, voluntary assumption of risk or illegality) or on account of other considerations (inevitable accident). The defendant may also raise general defences, such as lapse of limitation period, that are not peculiar to the action in negligence.

NOTES AND QUESTIONS

1. English authors often divide negligence into three main issues: duty, breach and damages. See for example Heuston & Buckley, *Salmond and Heuston on the Law of Torts*, 21st ed. (1996) at 195-98; and Peel & Goudkamp, *Winfield and Jolowicz on Tort*, 19th ed. (2014) at 78-79. This framework may prove difficult for students because it tends to fuse, rather than isolate, the various issues that must be resolved in a negligence case.

Even more worrying, it has sometimes been suggested that the entire negligence action can be reduced to a single inquiry. In *Roe v. Minister of Health*, [1954] 2 Q.B. 66 at 85 (C.A.), Denning L.J. said that "the three questions, duty, causation, and remoteness, run continually into one another. It seems to me that they are simply three different ways of looking at one and the same problem. . . . Instead of asking three questions, I should have thought that in many cases it would be simpler and better to ask one question: is the consequence within the risk? And to answer it by applying ordinary plain common sense." See also *Ontario (Attorney General) v. Crompton* (1976), 74 D.L.R. (3d) 345 (Ont. H.C.). What does Denning L.J.'s statement say about his view of judging? Would his approach to negligence lead to more or less certainty in the litigation process? Would it make judgments more or less "transparent," in terms of allowing litigants to know why they won or lost?

2. For alternative formulations of the elements of negligence, see The American Law Institute, *Restatement of the Law, Third, Torts: Liability for Physical and Emotional Harm* (2010) § 6; Sappideen & Vines, eds., *Fleming's The Law of Torts*, 10th ed. (2011) at 121-22; and Linden *et al.*, *Canadian Tort Law*, 11th ed. (2018) at 124-26. See also Gibson, "A New Alphabet of Negligence" in Linden, ed., *Studies in Canadian Tort Law* (1968) 189; Smith, *Liability in Negligence* (1984); and Owen, "The Five Elements of Negligence" (2007) 35 Hofstra L. Rev. 1671. The major differences arise primarily in the authors' approaches to the elements of duty and remoteness.

(b) NEGLIGENCE: A CASE ILLUSTRATION

The following case is typical of many negligence decisions, particularly at the trial level. The facts dominate the court's attention, while legal principles are only briefly discussed. Some issues may be analyzed at length, while others are not mentioned or are discussed only briefly. For example, the judge does not analyze the duty of care because the case falls within an established category and the existence of duty is not contentious. In many cases, judges appear to decide whether the plaintiff has a meritorious claim and then set about the task of legally justifying their initial conclusion. This pragmatic, result-oriented approach makes it difficult to identify the legal basis of the decision.

DUNSMORE v. DESHIELD
(1977), 80 D.L.R. (3d) 386 (Sask. Q.B.)

MACPHERSON J.:—The plaintiff was playing touch football when he collided with another player and one lens of his glasses broke and injured his right eye. The defendant Deshield is the optometrist who supplied the glasses, the defendant Imperial Optical (Imperial) manufactured the lenses.

The plaintiff ordered from Deshield a type of lens known as Hardex which is specially treated by Imperial in a hot and cold process to make it more impact-resistant than ordinary glass lenses. The glasses were supplied as Hardex by Imperial to Deshield and in turn to the plaintiff about February 26, 1973, who wore them off and on until the accident on September 7, 1974.

I am satisfied on the balance of probabilities that the lenses were not Hardex.

The plaintiff sues both defendants for damages alleging that if they were Hardex they would not have broken and he would not have been injured. The action against Deshield is in breach of contract or, alternatively, negligence. Against Imperial he claims in negligence.

The plaintiff is now 34 (then 31). He is a highly educated man who occupies a responsible position in the civil service.

Both defendants plead contributory negligence. The burden of establishing this plea is upon them. They must satisfy me that the plaintiff caused or contributed to his loss and injury by playing touch football with his glasses on. If they were to succeed on this point, the defendants had to show that it was, like football, a game of violence and this they failed to do. The plaintiff said it was a non-contact game but on this occasion he collided with another player. It is a running game in which, he admitted, there has been the odd broken wrist or sprained ankle. There was no evidence that the game involved bodily contact except on this occasion.

I cannot take judicial notice of the rules of the game or how it was played on this occasion. I was not told how many were playing.

I cannot find contributory negligence even on the balance of probabilities.

Imperial was negligent in failing to supply Hardex lenses. Its system of supply and manufacture is not flawless as Mr. Most, its manufacturing optician for 35 years, admitted. Sometimes ordinary lenses are delivered as Hardex. The percentage is small, but is impossible to estimate because it is not known how many are tested by the ophthalmologists or optometrists through whose hands they pass to the consumer. Imperial and many of the optical practitioners possess a small machine called a colmiscope (I think) through which a lens is examined and if it is Hardex a characteristic Maltese cross pattern appears in it. The test is easily done. In addition to its failure to temper the lenses, Imperial failed to test them before delivery to Deshield.

Deshield, likewise, did not test them. He now has a colmiscope but probably did not have one at the time of delivery. In my view he had a duty to the plaintiff to test them but instead relied on Imperial, thus accepting or adopting Imperial's negligence.

But negligence is only part of the plaintiff's cause of action. His more difficult hurdle is causation, the causal relationship between the negligence and the injury. The plea of *res ipsa loquitur* does not help the plaintiff. That involves an inference of negligence not causation. The defendant's wrong cannot be the cause of the injury if it would have happened without the wrong. Therefore, the defendants argue quite rightly that the plaintiff must prove that the impact he received, although sufficient to break the ordinary and untempered lens he wore, would probably not have been sufficient to break a Hardex lens.

Imperial is possessed of another machine, one designed to test the hardness of Hardex lenses. It drops a steel ball having a diameter of 5/8 of an inch onto a lens from a height of 50 ins. Any properly tempered Hardex lens is expected to withstand this blow. Only about one such lens is so tested each month in Imperial's laboratory in Regina, probably enough.

I cannot with certainty conclude that the blow of the steel ball on the lens was lighter or harder than the impact which caused the plaintiff's lens to shatter. I had no expert evidence. But the plaintiff's burden is not to show certainty. He has only to show that more probably than not the one which caused the injury was less violent or of less force than the steel ball test.

I feel the plaintiff has met this burden. The steel ball test shows the strength of Hardex lenses and their ability to withstand a direct blow of considerable force. The momentum of the collision between the plaintiff and the other player would be greater but much diffused, I would think, not as concentrated as the steel ball. All of the force of the bodies in collision at the time of the injury would not be on the lens which broke.

There was evidence suggesting that the Hardex lens breaks in a manner different from an ordinary lens. If acceptable, this evidence would be useful to the plaintiff because the injury might have been less severe or trifling, if, in fact, a Hardex lens had broken in the circumstances. But the evidence on the point is not good enough for me to draw that conclusion. Mr. Most broke an ordinary lens and a Hardex lens of identical prescription in the identical manner and brought the pieces to the trial. My unskilled eye could see nothing but similarity in the glass fragments of the two, but Drs. Griffith and Deshield who have considerable experience seemed to expect smaller fragments. Whether this would cause less injury is too speculative for me to judge.

The plaintiff is not the type of young man who might take unnecessary risks. There seems nothing frivolous about him. If he had known that the lenses were not Hardex, he would not have worn them on this occasion. The defendants by their error failed in their duty to protect the plaintiff against the risk of breakage of ordinary lenses. The risk was foreseeable whether or not they knew that he had athletic pastimes.

The defendants are therefore liable.

In the accident, part of the fractured lens entered the plaintiff's right eye. He was taken to hospital where he saw his family doctor who in turn called Dr. Griffith, an ophthalmologist. He found an irregular laceration of the cornea which healed after removal of a number of small fragments of clear glass from the eye.

Over the next year to 18 months the vision in the right eye improved until it stabilized at 20/25. Before the accident it was 20/20 as was (and is) the left eye. The references are to corrected vision because the plaintiff has been nearsighted all his life.

He was just a few days in hospital and six days off work.

Previously he was able to wear soft contact lenses but now because of the irregularity of the corneal surface he finds them uncomfortable, and wears them only when playing hockey or football. His vision in the right eye is now not as good with contacts as with glasses.

Even with glasses the right eye tires earlier which is a material consideration to a man who plans a career in government requiring much reading and other close work. This factor makes the assessment of damages difficult.

I award the plaintiff $7,500 in general damages and special damages in the agreed amount of $646.50.

Each of the defendants has made a claim over against the other for indemnity.

As I view the facts each of the defendants had a duty to the plaintiff to ensure that he got Hardex lenses and avoided the risk consequent upon the breakage of ordinary lenses. I cannot say that the manufacturer had a greater duty than the optometrist or *vice versa,* but the duty is to the plaintiff. What is their duty to one another? Imperial had no promise or undertaking or contract with Deshield that Deshield would test lenses for hardness before delivery to the plaintiff or any other consumer. Mr. Most does not know today which optometrists have colmiscopes and which do not. How, then, can Imperial say that Deshield had a duty to Imperial to apply the Hardex test? Optical practitioners have colmiscopes to protect their patients not Imperial, I would think. Deshield was entitled to rely on Imperial's duty to supply Hardex lenses notwithstanding Deshield's own duty to his patient, the plaintiff.

Therefore I award judgment against the defendants jointly and severally for the sum of $8,146.50 and costs to be taxed.

The defendant Deshield shall have indemnification from Imperial for the entire judgment plus his own costs.

NOTES AND QUESTIONS

1. As is often the case, the judge did not discuss the basis upon which he concluded that the defendants owed the plaintiff a duty of care. Why do you think the judge imposed a duty on the defendants in this situation?

2. Did the judge specifically address the question of the standard of care that the defendants were expected to meet? How did Deshield and Imperial Optical breach the standard of care? If, as the judge suggests, Deshield did not have a colmiscope, why was he held negligent for not testing the lenses? Considering that Imperial Optical is a large company, should it be found negligent every time it delivers the wrong lenses to one of its clients?

3. What did the plaintiff have to prove in order to establish that Deshield and Imperial Optical caused his injury? If the collision between the plaintiff and the other player was violent enough to shatter a normal glass lens, is it not likely that it would have shattered a Hardex lens? How did the judge decide this issue without expert testimony?

4. How did the judge resolve the issue of remoteness of damages?

5. Summarize the plaintiff's material losses. What was the basis upon which the judge determined that $7,500 was an appropriate award of general damages?

6. Why did the judge conclude that the plaintiff was not contributorily negligent? Do you think that this conclusion would have been different if the game had been tackle football?

7. What is the legal effect of finding the defendants jointly and severally liable? Why did Imperial Optical have to indemnify Deshield for the entire judgment? Would the result have been the same if the judge had relieved Deshield of liability and simply found Imperial Optical liable?

10

THE DUTY OF CARE

1. Evolution of the Duty of Care Test
2. Reasonable Foreseeability

1. Evolution of the Duty of Care Test

As discussed in the previous chapter, the core concept within the tort of negligence is the duty of care. Relief is not available unless the court is satisfied that the defendant was under a legal obligation to exercise care with respect to the plaintiff's interests. The materials in this chapter outline the evolution of the duty concept and the current state of duty jurisprudence in Canada.

(a) THE CLASSICAL APPROACH

In the 19th and early 20th centuries, the duty of care was confined to a narrow set of actors and conduct. While the ambit of duty was expanded in isolated cases, the expansion was cautious and piecemeal. Most common law lawyers and judges operated within a fairly rigid set of legal, social and political assumptions about the nature and purpose of negligence law. This set of assumptions may be viewed as the "classical" approach to the duty of care.

The first premise of the classical approach was that legal responsibility for negligence did not flow inexorably from moral responsibility. The classical lawyers respected both precedent and the absence of precedent. If the common law had not established a particular legal duty of care, that was reason enough to doubt its desirability. The conservatism of Victorian judges was driven in part by trust in the wisdom of the common law and in part by a particular vision of social responsibility. In a society committed to individual liberty and self-reliance, legal rights and obligations generally were seen to be a function of voluntary agreements between consenting parties. Legal duties of care imposed by courts, irrespective of individual agreements, did not easily square with these convictions.

The second premise of the classical view was political in nature. As unelected bodies within representative democracies, courts were seen as having a limited role in imposing liability outside the confines of common law precedent. Even if a broader duty of care were required, it was for legislators to enact.

The third premise concerned the theory of legal obligations. Acts were seen to be more culpable than omissions. Consequently, judges drew a distinction between misfeasance and nonfeasance. The courts were much more likely to impose liability if the defendant did something that hurt the plaintiff than if the defendant merely failed to do something that would have helped the plaintiff. For instance, a person would be held responsible for carelessly shooting a stranger, but not for failing to rescue a stranger who had been shot by someone else. Whatever morality might dictate, there was no legal obligation to act as one's "brother's keeper."

Fourth, the classical view rested on assumptions about the value of various interests. Physical injuries to individuals and property were broadly compensable, but emotional harms and loss of commercial profits were not. Physical injuries were seen as more tangible and measurable. The common law also more readily compensated harms caused by deeds than those caused by words. While bankers had a legal duty to prevent their customers' entrusted valuables from being stolen, they had no legal obligation to ensure that their gratuitous financial advice was accurate or sound. Again, the common law focused on what was perceived to be a more concrete and cautious basis for imposing negligence liability.

As we shall see, some of the classical currents are reflected in *Donoghue v. Stevenson*, [1932] A.C. 562 (H.L.), particularly in the dissent of Lord Buckmaster. Even though *Donoghue* marked the beginning of the modern law of negligence, the classical approach to duty — albeit in an altered form — has continued to shape the evolution of the duty of care.

(b) THE GENERAL DUTY OF CARE TEST

M'ALISTER (or DONOGHUE) v. STEVENSON
[1932] A.C. 562 (H.L.)

[The plaintiff's friend purchased a dark, opaque bottle of ginger-beer and gave it to the plaintiff. She drank some before her friend discovered a decomposed snail in the bottle. The plaintiff sued the manufacturer, alleging shock and severe gastroenteritis.]

LORD ATKIN:—My Lords, the sole question for determination in this case is legal: Do the averments made by the pursuer in her pleading, if true, disclose a cause of action? I need not restate the particular facts. The question is whether the manufacturer of an article of drink sold by him to a distributor, in circumstances which prevent the distributor or the ultimate purchaser or consumer from discovering by inspection any defect, is under any legal duty to the ultimate purchaser or consumer to take reasonable care that the article is free from defect likely to cause injury to health. I do not think a more important problem has occupied your Lordships in your judicial capacity: important both because of its bearing on public health and because of the practical test which it applies to the system under which it arises. The case has to be determined in accordance with Scots law; but it has been a matter of agreement between the experienced counsel who argue this case, and it appears to be the basis of the judgments of the learned judges of the Court of Session, that for the purposes of determining this problem the laws of Scotland and England are the same. I speak with little authority on this point, but my research, such as it is, satisfies me that the principles of the law of Scotland on such a question as the present are identical with those of English law; and I discuss the issue on that footing. The law of both countries appears to be that in order to support an action for damages for negligence the complainant has to show that he has been injured by the breach of a duty owed to him in the circumstances by the defendant to take reasonable care to avoid such injury. In the present case we are not concerned with the breach of the duty; if a duty exists, that would be a question of fact which is sufficiently averred and for present purposes must be assumed. We are solely concerned with the question whether, as a matter of law in the circumstances alleged, the defender owed any duty to the pursuer to take care.

It is remarkable how difficult it is to find in the English authorities statements of general application defining the relations between parties that give rise to the duty. The Courts are concerned with the particular relations which come before them in actual litigation, and it is sufficient to say whether the duty exists in those circumstances. The result is that the Courts have been engaged upon an elaborate classification of duties, as they exist in respect of property, whether real or personal, with further divisions as to ownership, occupation or control, and distinctions based on the particular relations of one side or the other, whether manufacturer, salesman or landlord, customer, tenant, stranger, and so on. In this way it can be ascertained at any time whether the law recognizes a duty, but only where the case can be referred to some particular species which has been examined and classified. And yet the duty which is common to all the cases where liability is established must logically be based upon some element common to the cases where it is found to exist. To seek a complete logical definition of the general principle is probably to go beyond the function of the judge, for the more general the definition the more likely it is to omit essentials or to introduce non-essentials. The attempt was made by Brett M.R. in *Heaven v. Pender*, in a definition to which I will later refer. As framed, it was demonstrably too wide, though it appears to me, if properly limited, to be capable of affording a valuable practical guide.

At present I content myself with pointing out that in English law there must be, and is, some general conception of relations giving rise to a duty of care, of which the particular cases found in the books are but instances. The liability for negligence, whether you style it such or treat it as in other systems as a species of "culpa," is no doubt based upon a general public sentiment of moral wrongdoing for which the offender must pay. But acts or omissions which any moral code would censure cannot in a practical world be treated so as to give a right to every person injured by them to demand relief. In this way rules of law arise which limit the range of complainants and the extent of their remedy. The rule that you are to love your neighbour becomes in law, you must not injure your neighbour; and the lawyer's question, Who is my neighbour? receives a restricted reply. You must take reasonable care to avoid acts or omissions which you can reasonably foresee would be likely to injure your neighbour. Who, then, in law is my neighbour? The answer seems to be — persons who are so closely and directly affected by my act that I ought reasonably to have them in contemplation as being so affected when I am directing my mind to the acts or omissions which are called in question. This appears to me to be the doctrine of *Heaven v. Pender* as laid down by Lord Esher (then Brett M.R.) when it is limited by the notion of proximity introduced by Lord Esher himself and A.L. Smith L.J. in *Le Lievre v. Gould*. Lord Esher says:

> That case established that, under certain circumstances, one may owe a duty to another, even though there is no contract between them. If one man is near to another, or is near to the property of another, a duty lies upon him not to do that which may cause a personal injury to that other, or may injure his property.

And A.L. Smith L.J.:

> The decision of *Heaven v. Pender* was founded upon the principle, that a duty to take due care did arise when the person or property of one was in such proximity to the

person or property of another that, if due care was not taken, damage might be done by the one to the other.

I think that this sufficiently states the truth if proximity be not confined to mere physical proximity, but be used, as I think it was intended, to extend to such close and direct relations that the act complained of directly affects a person whom the person alleged to be bound to take care would know would be directly affected by his careless act. That this is the sense in which nearness or "proximity" was intended by Lord Esher is obvious from his own illustration in *Heaven v. Pender* of the application of his doctrine to the sale of goods.

> This (i.e., the rule he just formulated) includes the case of goods, etc., supplied to be used immediately by a particular person or persons, or one of a class of persons, where it would be obvious to the person supplying, if he thought, that the goods would in all probability be used at once by such persons before a reasonable opportunity for discovering any defect which might exist, and where the thing supplied would be of such a nature that a neglect of ordinary care or skill as to its condition or the manner of supplying it would probably cause danger to the person or property of the person for whose use it was supplied, and who was about to use it. It would exclude a case in which the goods are supplied under circumstances in which it would be a chance by whom they would be used or whether they would be used or not, or whether they would be used before there would probably be means of observing any defect, or where the goods would be of such nature that a want of care or skill as to their condition or the manner of supplying them would not probably produce danger of injury to person or property.

I draw particular attention to the fact that Lord Esher emphasizes the necessity of goods having to be "used immediately" and "used at once before a reasonable opportunity of inspection." This is obviously to exclude the possibility of goods having their condition altered by lapse of time, and to call attention to the proximate relationship, which may be too remote where inspection even of the person using, certainly of an intermediate person, may reasonably be interposed. With this necessary qualification of proximate relationship as explained in *Le Lievre v. Gould*, I think the judgment of Lord Esher expresses the law of England; without the qualification, I think the majority of the Court in *Heaven v. Pender* were justified in thinking the principle was expressed in too general terms. There will no doubt arise cases where it will be difficult to determine whether the contemplated relationship is so close that the duty arises. But in the class of cases now before the Court I cannot conceive any difficulty to arise. A manufacturer puts up an article of food in a container which he knows will be opened by the actual consumer. There can be no inspection by any purchaser and no reasonable preliminary inspection by the consumer. Negligently, in the course of preparation, he allows the contents to be mixed with poison. It is said that the law of England and Scotland is that the poisoned consumer has no remedy against the negligent manufacturer. If this were the result of the authorities, I should consider the result a grave defect in the law, and so contrary to principle that I should hesitate long before following any decision to that effect which had not the authority of this House. I would point out that, in the assumed state of the authorities, not only would the consumer have no remedy against the manufacturer, he would have none against any one else, for in the circumstances alleged there would be no evidence of negligence against any one other than the manufacturer; and, except in the case of a consumer who was also a purchaser, no contract and no warranty of fitness, and in the case of the purchase of a specific article under its patent or trade name, which might well be the case in the purchase of some articles of food or drink, no warranty protecting even the purchaser-consumer. There are other instances than of articles of food and drink where goods are sold intended to be used immediately by the consumer, such as many forms of goods sold for cleaning purposes, where the same liability must exist. The doctrine supported by the decision below would not only deny a remedy to the consumer who was injured by consuming bottled beer or chocolates poisoned by the negligence of the manufacturer, but also to the user of what should be a harmless proprietary medicine, an ointment, a soap, a cleaning fluid or cleaning powder. I confine myself to articles of common household use, where every one, including the manufacturer, knows that the articles will be used by other persons than the actual ultimate purchaser — namely, by members of his family and his servants, and in some cases his guests. I do not think so ill of our jurisprudence as to suppose that its principles are so remote from the ordinary needs of civilized society and the ordinary claims it makes upon its members as to deny a legal remedy where there is so obviously a social wrong.

It will be found, I think, on examination that there is no case in which the circumstances have been such as I have just suggested where the liability has been negatived. There are numerous cases, where the relations were much more remote, where the duty has been held not to exist.

. . .

My Lords, if your Lordships accept the view that this pleading discloses a relevant cause of action you will be affirming the proposition that by Scots and English law alike a manufacturer of products, which he sells in such a form as to show that he intends them to reach the ultimate consumer in the form in which they left him with no reasonable possibility of intermediate examination, and with the knowledge that the absence of reasonable care in the preparation or putting up of the products will result in an injury to the consumer's life or property, owes a duty to the consumer to take that reasonable care.

It is a proposition which I venture to say no one in Scotland or England who was not a lawyer would for one moment doubt. It will be an advantage to make it clear that the law in this matter, as in most others, is in accordance with sound common sense. I think that this appeal should be allowed.

LORD BUCKMASTER (dissenting):—. . . The authorities are against the appellant's contention, and, apart from authority, it is difficult to see how any common law proposition can be formulated to support her claim.

The principle contended for must be this: that the manufacturer, or indeed the repairer, of any article, apart entirely from contract, owes a duty to any person by whom the article is lawfully used to see that it has been carefully constructed. All rights in contract must be excluded from consideration of this principle; such contractual rights as may exist in successive steps from the original manufacturer down to the ultimate purchaser are ex hypothesi immaterial. Nor can the doctrine be confined to cases where inspection is difficult or impossible to introduce. This conception is simply to misapply tort doctrine applicable to sale and purchase.

The principle of tort lies completely outside the region where such considerations apply, and the duty, if it exists, must extend to every person who, in lawful circumstances, uses the article made. There can be no special duty attaching to the manufacture of food apart from that implied by contract or imposed by statute. If such a duty exists, it seems to me it must cover the construction of every article, and I cannot see any reason why it should not apply to the construction of a house. If one step, why not fifty? Yet if a house be, as it sometimes is, negligently built, and in consequence of that negligence the ceiling falls and injures the occupier or any one else, no action against the builder exists according to English law, although I believe such a right did exist according to the laws of Babylon. Were such a principle known and recognized, it seems to me impossible, having regard to the numerous cases that must have arisen to persons injured by its disregard, that, with the exception of *George v. Skivington*, no case directly involving the principle has ever succeeded in the Courts, and, were it well known and accepted, much of the discussion of the earlier cases would have been waste of time, and the distinction as to articles dangerous in themselves or known to be dangerous to the vendor would be meaningless.

In *Mullen v. Barr & Co.*, a case indistinguishable from the present excepting upon the ground that a mouse is not a snail, and necessarily adopted by the Second Division in their judgment, Lord Anderson says this:

> In a case like the present, where the goods of the defenders are widely distributed throughout Scotland, it would seem little short of outrageous to make them responsible to members of the public for the condition of the contents of every bottle which issues from their works. It is obvious that, if such responsibility attached to the defenders, they might be called on to meet claims of damages which they could not possibly investigate or answer.

In agreeing, as I do, with the judgment of Lord Anderson, I desire to add that I find it hard to dissent from the emphatic nature of the language with which this judgment is clothed. I am of opinion that this appeal should be dismissed, and I beg to move your Lordships accordingly.

[Lords Macmillan and Thankerton gave concurring speeches and Lord Tomlin gave a dissenting speech. Note that the order of Lord Atkin's and Lord Buckmaster's speeches has been reversed.]

NOTES AND QUESTIONS

1. What role did *Heaven v. Pender* (1883), 11 Q.B.D. 503 (C.A.), play in Lord Atkin's analysis? In his view, what factors justified applying negligence law to products liability?

2. What was the legal basis of Lord Buckmaster's dissent? What considerations did he raise against extending negligence to products liability? Were his concerns about extending negligence to other areas of tort liability justified? Did Lord Atkin adequately address these issues? See Chamberlain, "Lord Buckmaster: The reluctant villain in *Donoghue v. Stevenson*" [2013] 3 Jurid. Rev. 245.

3. How did Lord Atkin define the test for determining when a duty of care would be imposed in a products liability case? Based on his analysis, would negligence law extend to a case in which: (a) the retailer or consumer had an opportunity to inspect the bottle's contents before consumption; (b) the product was simply unpalatable, rather than harmful; or (c) the product was a dangerously defective machine intended solely for industrial use?

4. How did Lord Atkin determine that a duty of care was owed to the plaintiff? Explain what this test means in your own words. If a thirsty waiter drank the ginger beer that Mrs. Donoghue had left in the bottle, would he have been owed a duty of care?

5. What standard of care did Lord Atkin suggest ought to apply? How would the plaintiff prove that the defendant breached the standard in a products liability case? For historical background and analysis of the decision, see Burns, ed., *Donoghue v. Stevenson and the Modern Law of Negligence: The Paisley Papers* (1991); Rodger, "Mrs. Donoghue and Alfenus Varus" (1988) 41 Curr. Legal Probs. 1; Chapman, *The Snail and the Ginger Beer: The Singular Case of Donoghue v. Stevenson* (2010); and [2013] 3 Jurid. Rev., which contains papers presented at an international conference to mark the eightieth anniversary of the decision in *Donoghue v. Stevenson* in May 2012.

6. One major problem in interpreting *Donoghue* is that it deals with many of the most important issues in negligence law. This is compounded by the fact that Lord Atkin discusses several of these issues together in the space of about ten lines. First, as a matter of legal policy, does the law of negligence apply to this type of claim or situation? Second, if negligence law does apply, has the defendant's conduct in this case given rise to a duty of care? Third, does the defendant owe this duty of care to the plaintiff in particular? Although Lord Atkin's duty principles have been used for over 85 years, little progress has been made in reaching a consensus on analyzing their component elements.

7. Prior to *Donoghue,* a lack of contractual privity made it extremely difficult for consumers to sue manufacturers in negligence. See for example *Langridge v. Levy* (1837), 150 E.R. 1458 (Exch.); *Winterbottom v. Wright* (1842), 152 E.R. 402 (Exch.); and *Longmeid v. Holliday* (1851), 155 E.R. 752 (Exch.). But see *George v. Skivington* (1869), L.R. 5 Ex. 1. See also Labatt, "Negligence in Relation to Privity of Contract" (1900) 16 L.Q.R. 168; and Palmer, "Why Privity Entered Tort — An Historical Reexamination of *Winterbottom v. Wright*" (1983) 27 J. Am. Leg. History 85.

8. An exception to the privity requirement was found in cases involving articles that were dangerous *per se*. See Barton, "Liability for Things in the Nineteenth Century" in Guy & Beale, eds., *Law and Social Change in British History* (1984). Why would a different set of rules apply to such products? It was not always simple to classify articles as innocuous or dangerous. For example, the New York Court of Appeals had found the category of imminently dangerous articles to include a scaffold (*Devlin v. Smith*, 89 N.Y. 470 (1882)), bottles of aerated water (*Torgeson v. Schultz*, 192 N.Y. 156 (1908)), and a coffee urn (*Statler v. Ray Mfg. Co.*, 195 N.Y. 478 (1909)), whereas articles not imminently dangerous included a defective balance wheel on a circular saw (*Loop v. Litchfield*, 42 N.Y. 351 (1870)) and a boiler that exploded (*Losee v. Clute*, 51 N.Y. 494 (1873)). Moreover, in the watershed duty case of *MacPherson v. Buick Motor Company*, 217 N.Y. 382 (1916), the majority found that an automobile with a broken wheel was imminently dangerous, but the dissent disagreed.

9. For a historical review of duty, see Winfield, "Duty in Tortious Negligence" (1934) 34 Col. L.R. 41. See also Pollock, "The Snail in the Bottle, and Thereafter" (1933) 49 L.Q.R. 22; Buckland, "The Duty to Take Care" (1935) 51 L.Q.R. 637; Morison, "A Re-examination of the Duty of Care" (1948) 11 Mod. L. Rev. 9;

Fleming, "Remoteness and Duty: The Control Devices in Liability for Negligence" (1953) 31 Can. Bar Rev. 471; Dias, "The Duty Problem in Negligence" [1955] C.L.J. 198; Heuston, *"Donoghue v. Stevenson* in Retrospect" (1957) 20 Mod. L. Rev. 1; Gibson, "A New Alphabet of Negligence" in Linden, ed., *Studies in Canadian Tort Law* (1968) 189; Symmons, "The Duty of Care in Negligence: Recently Expressed Policy Elements — Part I and Part II" (1971) 34 Mod. L. Rev. 394 & 528; Smith, "The Mystery of Duty," in Klar, ed., *Studies in Canadian Tort Law* (1977) 1; Smith & Burns, *"Donoghue v. Stevenson* — The Not So Golden Anniversary" (1982) 46 Mod. L. Rev. 147; Smith, *Liability In Negligence* (1984); and Plunkett, "The Historical Foundations of the Duty of Care" (2015) 41 Monash U.L. Rev. 716.

(c) THE DEVELOPMENT OF THE MODERN LAW OF DUTY

Lord Atkin's formulation of the duty of care concept has not been confined to the area of products liability. It has been used to support the proposition that negligence law potentially extends, with limited exceptions, to any act that causes physical injury (as opposed to other forms of loss). This principle is so deeply entrenched in the law that the courts will often simply assume that negligence law applies. For example, a judge will rarely make more than passing reference to the fact that a driver owes a duty of care to other users of the road, or that surgeons owe a duty of care to their patients.

Initially, however, the courts were reluctant to extend Lord Atkin's test to those special categories of cases in which they previously had refused to recognize a duty or had imposed a limited duty. And while the courts did eventually reject much of the pre-1932 case law in favour of broader principles that were more akin to *Donoghue,* they did so on a category-by-category basis. In that sense, *Donoghue* did not effect a wholesale break with the classical approach.

It was not until the 1960s that appellate courts began to use *Donoghue* to overturn traditional, fundamental assumptions regarding the duty of care. In *Hedley Byrne & Co. v. Heller & Partners Ltd.,* [1964] A.C. 465, the House of Lords held that, in certain situations, a duty of care could be imposed for negligent advice. In *Home Office v. Dorset Yacht Co.,* [1970] A.C. 1004, the House of Lords held that public authorities could be held liable in negligence with respect to their statutory functions and operations. These decisions are important not only as leading cases in specific categories of negligence, but also as examples of the evolving and expanding scope of the duty concept. That trend culminated in Lord Wilberforce's now famous speech in *Anns v. Merton London Borough Council,* [1977] 2 All E.R. 492 at 498 (H.L.):

Through the trilogy of cases in this House, *Donoghue v. Stevenson, Hedley Byrne & Co. Ltd. v. Heller & Partners Ltd.* and *Home Office v. Dorset Yacht Co. Ltd.,* the position has now been reached that in order to establish that a duty of care arises in a particular situation, it is not necessary to bring the facts of that situation within those previous situations in which a duty of care has been held to exist. Rather the question has to be approached in two stages. First one has to ask whether, as between the alleged wrongdoer and the person who has suffered damage there is a sufficient relationship of proximity or neighbourhood such that, in the reasonable contemplation of the former, carelessness on his part may be likely to cause damage to the latter, in which case a prima facie duty of care arises. Secondly, if the first question is answered affirmatively, it is necessary to consider whether there are any considerations which ought to negative, or to reduce or limit the scope of the duty or the class of person to whom it is owed or the damages to which a breach of it may give rise.

Unlike Lord Atkin's speech, this passage does not provide a specific test for determining whether to recognize a duty of care. Rather, it sets out an approach for analyzing existing categories of negligence and for recognizing new categories in novel situations. At the same time, it should be noted that Lord Wilberforce's judgment did not require the general duty principles articulated in *Donoghue v. Stevenson* to be mechanically applied in every case. Indeed, as the House of Lords held in *Anns*, *Hedley Byrne* and *Dorset Yacht*, special circumstances may raise special considerations that justify the formulation of restricted duty principles.

Although the English courts initially embraced the *Anns* approach in a broad range of cases, they began to distance themselves from it by the mid-1980s. After narrowly interpreting *Anns* or ignoring it, the House of Lords decisively overruled it in *Murphy v. Brentwood District Council*, [1991] 1 A.C. 338. *Anns* was criticized as leading to capricious results, providing unworkable tests of liability, unduly expanding the scope of liability, and lacking any foundation in established principle. The leading case in England is now *Caparo Industries plc v. Dickman*, [1990] 2 A.C. 605 (H.L.), in which Lord Bridge offered the following observations.

[S]ince *Anns*'s case a series of decisions of the Privy Council and of your Lordships' House . . . have emphasised the inability of a single general principle to provide a practical test which can be applied to every situation to determine whether a duty of care is owed and, if so, what is its scope. . . . What emerges is that, in addition to the foreseeability of damage, necessary ingredients in any situation giving rise to a duty of care are that there should exist between the party owing the duty and the party to whom it is owed a relationship characterised by the law as one of "proximity" or "neighbourhood" and that the situation should be one in which the court considers it fair, just and reasonable that the law should impose a duty of a given scope upon the one party for the benefit of the other. . . . [T]he concepts of proximity and fairness embodied in these additional ingredients are not susceptible of any such precise definition as would be necessary to give them utility as practical tests, but amount in effect to little more than convenient labels to attach to the features of different specific situations which, on a detailed examination of all the circumstances, the law recognises pragmatically as giving rise to a duty of care of a given scope. Whilst recognising, of course, the importance of the underlying general principles common to the whole field of negligence, I think the law has now moved in the direction of attaching greater significance to the more traditional categorisation of distinct and recognisable situations as guides to the existence, the scope and the limits of the varied duties care which the law imposes.

As a result of *Caparo*, the recognition of a duty of care in England now turns on a three-part test that requires proof that: (i) the plaintiff's loss was a reasonably foreseeable consequence of the defendant's conduct, (ii) there was a sufficiently proximate relationship between the parties, and (iii) it is "fair, just and reasonable" for the court to impose a duty of care in light of the applicable policy considerations. Even more significant than the actual phrasing of that test, however, is the fact that the House of Lords self-consciously distanced itself from the plaintiff-oriented approach of *Anns*.

The experience has been similar elsewhere in the Commonwealth. After an initial honeymoon, *Anns* quickly fell into disfavour in Australia. A leading statement appears in Brennan J.'s judgment in *Sutherland Shire Council v. Heyman* (1985), 157 C.L.R. 424 (H.C.A.):

> It is preferable in my view, that the law should develop novel categories of negligence incrementally and by analogy with established categories, rather than by a massive extension of a prima facie duty of care restrained only by indefinable "considerations which ought to negative, or to reduce or limit the scope of the duty or the class of person to whom it is owed".

The demise of *Anns* outside of Canada reflects a dramatic retreat from the rapid expansion of the duty of care and the spiralling growth in the scope of liability. It also harkens back to the more cautious classical approach.

NOTES AND QUESTIONS

1. In *Anns*, Lord Wilberforce said that a *prima facie* duty of care arises if "there is a sufficient relationship of proximity or neighbourhood such that, in the reasonable contemplation of the [defendant], carelessness on his part may be likely to cause damage to the [plaintiff]." How would you interpret that statement? Specifically, is "proximity" defined entirely in terms of reasonable foreseeability? Or does the first part of the *Anns* test actually consist of two elements: proximity and reasonable foreseeability? See Rodger, "Some Reflections on *Junior Books*" in Birks, ed., *The Frontiers of Liability*, vol. 2 (1994).

2. There were dramatic increases in the scope of negligence liability as the "neighbour principle" in *Donoghue* was applied to new relationships and to many of the special duty of care situations that had previously been governed by more restrictive principles. This led to concern about the adequacy of these principles for resolving modern tort problems. See Linden, "The Good Neighbour on Trial: A Fountain of Sparkling Wisdom" (1983) 17 U.B.C.L. Rev. 67; Smith & Burns, "The Good Neighbour on Trial: Good Neighbours Make Bad Law" (1983) 17 U.B.C.L. Rev. 93; Little, "Erosion of Non-Duty Rules in England, the United States, and Common Law Commonwealth Nations" (1983) 20 Hous. L. Rev. 959; and Chamberlain, "Lord Atkin's Opinion in *Donoghue v. Stevenson*: Perspectives from Biblical Hermeneutics" (2010) 4 Law and Humanities 91.

3. The Commonwealth courts' growing disenchantment *with Anns* can be traced through a series of cases. See for example *Governors of the Peabody Donation Fund v. Sir Lindsay Parkinson & Co.*, [1985] A.C. 210 (H.L.); *Leigh and Sullivan Ltd. v. Aliakmon Shipping Co.*, [1986] A.C. 785 (H.L.); *Candlewood Navigation Corporation Ltd. v. Mitsui O.S.K. Lines Ltd. (The Mineral Transporter)*, [1986] A.C. 1 (P.C.); *Curran v. Northern Ireland Co-ownership Housing Assoc. Ltd.*, [1987] A.C. 17 (H.L.); *Yuen Kun Yeu v. A.G. of Hong Kong*, [1988] A.C. 175 (P.C.); *D. & F. Estates Ltd. v. Church Commissioners for England*, [1989] A.C. 177 (H.L.); *Hill v. Chief Constable of West Yorkshire*, [1989] A.C. 53 (H.L.); and *Caparo Industries v. Dickman*, [1990] 2 A.C. 605 (H.L.).

4. For commentaries on the rise and fall of *Anns*, see McHugh, "Neighbourhood, Proximity and Reliance" in Finn, ed., *Essays on Torts* (1989) 5; Smillie, "The Foundation of the Duty of Care in Negligence" (1989) 15 Monash Univ. L. Rev. 302; Cooke, "An Impossible Distinction" (1991) 107 L.Q.R. 46; Howarth, "Negligence

After *Murphy:* Time to Rethink" [1991] C.L.J. 58; Wallace, "Anns Beyond Repair" (1991) 107 L.Q.R. 228; Markesinis & Deakin, "The Random Element of Their Lordships' Infallible Judgment" (1992) 50 Mod. L. Rev. 619; Stapleton, "In Restraint of Tort" in Birks, ed., *The Frontiers of Liability*, vol. 2 (1994) 83; and Stanton, "Incremental Approaches to the Duty of Care" in Mullany, ed., *Torts in the Nineties* (1997) 34.

See also Witting, "Duty of Care: An Analytical Approach" (2005) 25 O.J.L.S. 33; Howarth, "Many Duties of Care — Or A Duty of Care? Notes from the Underground" (2006) 26 O.J.L.S. 449; and Plunkett, *The Duty of Care in Negligence* (2018).

(d) *ANNS* AND THE SUPREME COURT OF CANADA

The story of *Anns* has been quite different in this country than elsewhere in the Commonwealth. Canadian judges have been, and to some extent continue to be, unusually receptive to Lord Wilberforce's judgment. For many years the leading case was *Kamloops (City) v. Nielsen* (1984), 10 D.L.R. (4th) 641 (S.C.C.). Justice Wilson referred to the English authorities and said (at 662-63) that, in determining whether a duty of care should be recognized, two questions should be asked:

(1) [I]s there a sufficiently close relationship between the parties . . . so that, in the reasonable contemplation of the [defendant], carelessness on its part might cause damage to [the plaintiff]? If so, (2) are there any considerations which ought to negative or limit (a) the scope of the duty and (b) the class of persons to whom it is owed or (c) the damages to which a breach of it may give rise?

See also the Supreme Court of Canada decisions in *B.D.C. Ltd. v. Hofstrand Farms Ltd.* (1986), 26 D.L.R. (4th) 1 (S.C.C.); *Just v. British Columbia* (1989), 64 D.L.R. (4th) 689 (S.C.C.); and *Rothfield v. Manolakos* (1989), 63 D.L.R. (4th) 449 (S.C.C.).

Although it has now been modified by the Supreme Court of Canada, the *Anns/Kamloops* approach was notable for its flexibility and expansiveness. Its first branch merely required the plaintiff to prove reasonable foreseeability of harm, which, as Major J. stated in *Ryan v. Victoria (City)*, [1999] 1 S.C.R. 201, "presents a relatively low threshold." Once that hurdle was cleared, a *prima facie* duty of care was established. The burden then fell to the defendant, under the second branch of the test, to establish why a duty of care should be rejected or limited. This framework made the *Anns/Kamloops* test plaintiff-friendly and inherently expansive, particularly because judges were often less-than-rigorous in their analyses under the second branch.

The *Anns/Kamloops* approach was also characterized by its departure from the traditional, category-by-category evolution of the duty of care in favour of a more general test. This approach tended to downplay the distinctions historically drawn between misfeasance and nonfeasance, deeds and words, physical injury and emotional harm, property damage and economic loss. It also provided a contrast to the more incremental approach favoured by the English and Australian courts by the late 1980s.

In *Cooper v. Hobart*, [2001] 3 S.C.R. 537, the Supreme Court of Canada re-visited and re-stated the *Anns/Kamloops* test. While this restatement addressed some of the concerns raised by *Anns/Kamloops*, it also created new uncertainties of its own. The Canadian courts are still working out the implications of the test outlined in *Cooper*.

COOPER v. HOBART
[2001] 3 S.C.R. 537

[The plaintiff, along with thousands of other people, invested money with Eron Mortgage Corp. Eron was governed by the *Mortgage Brokers Act*, R.S.B.C. 1996, c. 313. That statute allowed the defendant, as Registrar of Mortgage Brokers, to investigate complaints, freeze funds and suspend licences of brokers who had breached their statutory obligations. The defendant did in fact suspend Eron's licence. At that point, the company owed more than $180 million to its investors. Faced with the loss of her investment, the plaintiff sued the defendant for negligence. She claimed that if the defendant had acted more quickly in suspending Eron's licence, she would not have suffered the same magnitude of loss. The defendant brought a motion to strike out the plaintiff's statement of claim on the ground that it did not disclose a cause of action. The issue before the court was whether, in the circumstances, the defendant owed a duty of care to the plaintiff.

At first instance, Tysoe J. applied the standard two-part test and held that a duty of care arose between the parties. At the first stage of analysis, he found that it was reasonably foreseeable that the defendant's carelessness would result in the plaintiff's loss. Consequently, a *prima facie* duty of care existed. At the second stage of analysis, he did not find any factors that would negate or limit that duty. The British Columbia Court of Appeal thought otherwise. Newbury J.A. held that, even if the plaintiff's loss was reasonably foreseeable, there was not a sufficient relationship of proximity between the parties to support a *prima facie* duty of care. She also held that, even if a *prima facie* duty of care arose, various policy considerations under the second branch of the *Anns/Kamloops* test militated against the possibility of liability. The plaintiff appealed to the Supreme Court of Canada.]

MCLACHLIN C.J.C. and MAJOR J.:—The present appeal revisits the *Anns* test . . . and, in particular, highlights and hones the role of policy concerns in determining the scope of liability for negligence.

. . .

Canadian courts have not thus far recognized the duty of care that the appellants allege in this case. The question is therefore whether the law of negligence should be extended to reach this situation. While the particular extension sought is novel, the more general issue of how far the principles of liability for negligence should be extended is a familiar one, and one with which this Court and others have repeatedly grappled since Lord Atkin enunciated the negligence principle in *Donoghue v. Stevenson* . . . almost 70 years ago. That case introduced the principle that a person could be held liable only for reasonably foreseeable harm. But it also anticipated that not all reasonably foreseeable harm might be caught. This posed the issue with which courts still struggle today: to what situations does the law of negligence extend? This case, like so many of its predecessors, may thus be seen as but a gloss on the case of *Donoghue v. Stevenson*.

In *Donoghue v. Stevenson* the House of Lords revolutionized the common law by replacing the old categories of tort recovery with a single comprehensive principle — the negligence principle. Henceforward, liability would lie for negligence in circumstances where a reasonable person would have viewed the harm as foreseeable. However, foreseeability alone was not enough; there must also be a close and direct relationship of proximity or neighbourhood.

But what is proximity? For the most part, lawyers apply the law of negligence on the basis of categories as to which proximity has been recognized in the past. However, as Lord Atkin [*sic*] declared in *Donoghue v. Stevenson*, the categories of negligence are not closed. Where new cases arise, we must search elsewhere for assistance in determining whether, in addition to disclosing foreseeability, the circumstances disclose sufficient proximity to justify the imposition of liability for negligence.

In *Anns* . . . the House of Lords, per Lord Wilberforce, said that a duty of care required a finding of proximity sufficient to create a prima facie duty of care, followed by consideration of whether there were any factors negativing that duty of care. This Court has repeatedly affirmed that approach as appropriate in the Canadian context.

. . .

The House of Lords in *Anns* for the first time expressly recognized the policy component in determining the extension of the negligence principle. However, it left doubt on the precise content of the first and second branches of the new formulation of the negligence principle. This gave rise to debate — debate which the submissions in this case revive. Was the first branch concerned with foreseeability only or foreseeability and proximity? If the latter, was there duplication between policy considerations relevant to proximity at the first stage and the second stage of the test?

To some extent, these concerns are academic. Provided the proper balancing of the factors relevant to a duty of care are considered, it may not matter, so far as a particular case is concerned, at which "stage" it occurs. The underlying question is whether a duty of care should be imposed, taking into account all relevant factors disclosed by the circumstances. *Anns* did not purport to depart from the negligence test of *Donoghue v. Stevenson* but merely sought to elucidate it by explicitly recognizing its policy component.

We continue in the view, repeatedly expressed by this Court, that the *Anns* two-stage test, properly understood, does not involve duplication because different types of policy considerations are involved at the two stages. In our view, *Anns* continues to provide a useful framework in which to approach the question of whether a duty of care should be imposed in a new situation.

Nevertheless, it is important from the point of view of methodology and clarity in the law to be clear on what falls to be considered at each stage of the *Anns* test. In this connection, it is useful to consider the leading English case on that question. The Judicial Committee of the Privy Council held in *Yuen Kun Yeu v. Attorney-General of Hong Kong*, [1988] 1 A.C. 175, that to find a prima facie duty of care at the first stage of the test there must be reasonable foreseeability of the harm plus something more. As will be seen, we agree with this conclusion. The Privy Council went on to opine that *Anns'* second branch, negation for policy reasons, would seldom come into play. If this is read as a suggestion that policy is not important in determining whether the negligence principle should be extended to new situations, we would respectfully differ. . . . [T]he *Donoghue v. Stevenson* foreseeability-negligence test, no matter how it is phrased, conceals a balancing of interests. The quest for the right balance is in reality a quest for prudent policy. The difference in the two positions, if there is one, may turn on how one defines policy; the Privy Council in *Yuen Kun Yeu* appears to regard policy as confined to practical considerations dictating immunity despite a close relationship and foreseeability.

In brief compass, we suggest that at this stage in the evolution of the law, both in Canada and abroad, the *Anns* analysis is best understood as follows. At the first stage of the *Anns* test, two questions arise: (1) was the harm that occurred the reasonably foreseeable consequence of the defendant's act? and (2) are there reasons, notwithstanding the proximity between the parties established in the first part of this test, that tort liability should not be recognized here? The proximity analysis involved at the first stage of the *Anns* test focuses on factors arising from the relationship between the plaintiff and the defendant. These factors include questions of policy, in the broad sense of that word. If foreseeability and proximity are established at the first stage, a prima facie duty of care arises. At the second stage of the *Anns* test, the question still remains whether there are residual policy considerations outside the relationship of the parties that may negative the imposition of a duty of care. It may be, as the Privy Council suggests in *Yuen Kun Yeu*, that such considerations will not often prevail. However, we think it useful expressly to ask, before imposing a new duty of care, whether despite foreseeability and proximity of relationship, there are other policy reasons why the duty should not be imposed.

On the first branch of the *Anns* test, reasonable foreseeability of the harm must be supplemented by proximity. The question is what is meant by proximity. Two things may be said. The first is that "proximity" is generally used in the authorities to characterize the type of relationship in which a duty of care may arise. The second is that sufficiently proximate relationships are identified through the use of categories. The categories are not closed and new categories of negligence may be introduced. But generally, proximity is established by reference to these categories. This provides certainty to the law of negligence, while still permitting it to evolve to meet the needs of new circumstances.

On the first point, it seems clear that the word "proximity" in connection with negligence has from the outset and throughout its history been used to describe the type of relationship in which a duty of care to guard against foreseeable negligence may be imposed. "Proximity" is the term used to describe the "close and direct" relationship that Lord Atkin described as necessary to grounding a duty of care in *Donoghue v. Stevenson.* . . .

Defining the relationship may involve looking at expectations, representations, reliance, and the property or other interests involved. Essentially, these are factors that allow us to evaluate the closeness of the relationship between the plaintiff and the defendant and to determine whether it is just and fair having regard to that relationship to impose a duty of care in law upon the defendant.

The factors which may satisfy the requirement of proximity are diverse and depend on the circumstances of the case. One searches in vain for a single unifying characteristic. As stated by McLachlin J. (as she then was) in *Canadian National Railway Co. v. Norsk Pacific Steamship Co.*, [1992] 1 S.C.R. 1021 at p. 1151, 91 D.L.R. (4th) 289: "Proximity may be usefully viewed, not so much as a test in itself, but as a broad concept which is capable of subsuming different categories of cases involving different factors". . .

What then are the categories in which proximity has been recognized? First, of course, is the situation where the defendant's act foreseeably causes physical harm to the plaintiff or the plaintiff's property. This has been extended to nervous shock (see, for example, *Alcock v. Chief Constable of the South Yorkshire Police*, [1991] 4 All E.R. 907 (H.L.)). Yet other categories are liability for negligent misstatement: *Hedley Byrne & Co. v. Heller & Partners Ltd.*, [1964] A.C. 465 (H.L.), and misfeasance in public office. A duty to warn of the risk of danger has been recognized: *Rivtow Marine Ltd. v. Washington Iron Works*, [1974] S.C.R. 1189, 40 D.L.R. (3d) 530. Again, a municipality has been held to owe a duty to prospective purchasers of real estate to inspect housing developments without negligence: *Anns, supra*; *Kamloops, supra*. Similarly, governmental authorities who have undertaken a policy of road maintenance have been held to owe a duty of care to execute the maintenance in a non-negligent manner: *Just v. British Columbia*, [1989] 2 S.C.R. 1228, 64 D.L.R. (4th) 689; *Swinamer v. Nova Scotia (Attorney General)*, [1994] 1 S.C.R. 445, 112 D.L.R. (4th) 18. Relational economic loss (related to a contract's performance) may give rise to a tort duty of care in certain situations, as where the claimant has a possessory or proprietary interest in the property, the general average cases, and cases where the relationship between the claimant and the property owner constitutes a joint venture: *Norsk, supra*; *Bow Valley Husky (Bermuda) Ltd. v. Saint John Shipbuilding Ltd.*, [1997] 3 S.C.R. 1210, 153 D.L.R. (4th) 385. When a case falls within one of these situations or an analogous one and reasonable foreseeability is established, a prima facie duty of care may be posited.

This brings us to the second stage of the *Anns* test. As the majority of this Court held in *Norsk* . . ., residual policy considerations fall to be considered here. These are not concerned with the relationship between the parties, but with the effect of recognizing a duty of care on other legal obligations, the legal system and society more generally. Does the law already provide a remedy? Would recognition of the duty of care create the spectre of unlimited liability to an unlimited class? Are there other reasons of broad policy that suggest that the duty of care should not be recognized?

. . .

It is at this second stage of the analysis that the distinction between government policy and execution of policy falls to be considered. It is established that government actors are not liable in negligence for policy decisions, but only operational decisions. The basis of this immunity is that policy is the prerogative of the elected Legislature. It is inappropriate for courts to impose liability for the consequences of a particular policy decision. On the other hand, a government actor may be liable in negligence for the manner in which it executes or carries out the policy. In our view, the exclusion of liability for policy decisions is properly regarded as an application of the second stage of the *Anns* test. The exclusion does not relate to the relationship between the parties. Apart from the legal characterization of the government duty as a matter of policy, plaintiffs can and do recover. The exclusion of liability is better viewed as an immunity imposed because of considerations outside the relationship for policy reasons — more precisely, because it is inappropriate for courts to second-guess elected legislators on policy matters.

. . .

The second step of *Anns* generally arises only in cases where the duty of care asserted does not fall within a recognized category of recovery. Where it does, we may be satisfied that there are no overriding policy considerations that would negative the duty of care. In this sense, I agree with the Privy Council in *Yuen Kun Yeu* that the second stage of *Anns* will seldom arise and that questions of liability will be determined primarily by reference to established and analogous categories of recovery. However, where a duty of care in a novel situation is alleged, as here, we believe it necessary to consider both steps of the *Anns* test as discussed above. This ensures that before a duty of care is imposed in a new situation, not only are foreseeability and relational proximity present, but there are no broader considerations that would make imposition of a duty of care unwise.

. . .

VI. Application of the Test

The appellants submit that the Registrar of Mortgage Brokers owed them, as investors with a firm falling under the Registrar's administrative mandate, a duty of care giving rise to liability for negligence and damages for losses that they sustained. The investors allege that the Registrar should have acted earlier to suspend Eron or warn them of Eron's breaches of the Act's requirements, and that their losses are traceable to the Registrar's failure to act more promptly.

The first question is whether the circumstances disclose reasonably foreseeable harm and proximity sufficient to establish a prima facie duty of care. The first inquiry at this stage is whether the case falls within or is analogous to a category of cases in which a duty of care has previously been recognized. The answer to this question is no.

The next question is whether this is a situation in which a new duty of care should be recognized. It may be that the investors can show that it was reasonably foreseeable that the alleged negligence in failing to suspend Eron or issue warnings might result in financial loss to the plaintiffs. However, as discussed, mere foreseeability is not enough to establish a prima facie duty of care. The plaintiffs must also show proximity — that the Registrar was in a close and direct relationship to them making it just to impose a duty of care upon him toward the plaintiffs. In addition to showing foreseeability, the plaintiffs must point to factors arising from the circumstances of the relationship that impose a duty.

In this case, the factors giving rise to proximity, if they exist, must arise from the statute under which the Registrar is appointed. That statute is the only source of his duties, private or public. Apart from that statute, he is in no different position than the ordinary man or woman on the street. If a duty to investors with regulated mortgage brokers is to be found, it must be in the statute.

In this case, the statute does not impose a duty of care on the Registrar to investors with mortgage brokers regulated by the Act. The Registrar's duty is rather to the public as a whole. Indeed, a duty to individual investors would potentially conflict with the Registrar's overarching duty to the public.

. . .

The regulatory scheme governing mortgage brokers provides a general framework to ensure the efficient operation of the mortgage marketplace. The Registrar must balance a myriad of competing interests, ensuring that the public has access to capital through mortgage financing while at the same time instilling public confidence in the system by determining who is "suitable" and whose proposed registration as a broker is "not objectionable". All of the powers or tools conferred by the Act on the Registrar are necessary to undertake this delicate balancing. Even though to some degree the provisions of the Act serve to protect the interests of investors, the overall scheme of the Act mandates that the Registrar's duty of care is not owed to investors exclusively but to the public as a whole.

Accordingly, we agree with the Court of Appeal per Newbury J.A.: even though the Registrar might reasonably have foreseen that losses to investors in Eron would result if he was careless in carrying out his duties under the Act, there was insufficient proximity between the Registrar and the investors to ground a prima facie duty of care. The statute cannot be construed to impose a duty of care on the Registrar specific to investments with mortgage brokers. Such a duty would no doubt come at the expense of other important interests, of efficiency and finally at the expense of public confidence in the system as a whole.

Having found no proximity sufficient to found a duty of care owed by the Registrar to the investors, we need not proceed to the second branch of the *Anns* test and the question of whether there exist policy considerations apart from those considered in determining a relationship of proximity, which would negative a prima facie duty of care, had one been found. However, the matter having been fully argued, it may be useful to comment on those submissions.

In our view, even if a prima facie duty of care had been established under the first branch of the *Anns* test, it would have been negated at the second stage for overriding policy reasons. The decision of whether to suspend a broker involves both policy and quasi-judicial elements. The decision requires the Registrar to balance the public and private interests. The Registrar is not simply carrying out a predetermined government policy, but deciding, as an agent of the executive branch of government, what that policy should be. Moreover, the decision is quasi-judicial. The Registrar must act fairly or judicially in removing a broker's licence. These requirements are inconsistent with a duty of care to investors. Such a duty would undermine these obligations, imposed by the Legislature on the Registrar. Thus even if a prima facie duty of care could be posited, it would be negated by other overriding policy considerations.

The prima facie duty of care is also negated on the basis of the distinction between government policy and the execution of policy. As stated, the Registrar must make difficult discretionary decisions in the area of public policy, decisions which command deference. . . . [T]he decisions made by the Registrar were made within the limits of the powers conferred upon him in the public interest.

Further, the spectre of indeterminate liability would loom large if a duty of care was recognized as between the Registrar and investors in this case. The Act itself imposes no limit and the Registrar has no means of controlling the number of investors or the amount of money invested in the mortgage brokerage system.

Finally, we must consider the impact of a duty of care on the taxpayers, who did not agree to assume the risk of private loss to persons in the situation of the investors. To impose a duty of care in these circumstances would be to effectively create an insurance scheme for investors at great cost to the taxpaying public. There is no indication that the Legislature intended that result.

NOTES AND QUESTIONS

1. Explain the nature of the test that the court articulated in *Cooper v. Hobart.* Did McLachlin C.J.C. and Major J. intend for their test to be applied anew every time that a court is presented with a claim in negligence? Of what relevance are the traditional "categories" of negligence?

2. Prior to *Cooper*, it was commonly said that the first stage of the *Anns/Kamloops* test is generally satisfied by proof of reasonable foreseeability. In *Cooper*,

however, the court said that a *prima facie* duty will arise only if there was reasonable foreseeability of harm *plus* "a close and direct relationship of proximity or neighbourhood." Why did the court stress the need for proximity? How did it define this term? How useful is the Supreme Court of Canada's notion of proximity as a test for establishing new duties of care?

3. The High Court of Australia has been increasingly disparaging of the concept of proximity. In *Miller v. Miller* (2011), 242 C.L.R. 446 (H.C.A.) at para. 60, six judges wrote that "proximity has been discarded from the Australian judicial lexicon" because "it neither states, nor points to, any relevant principle that assists in the resolution of disputed questions about the existence of a duty of care, beyond indicating that something more than foreseeability of damage is necessary." See also *Hill v. Van Erp* (1997), 188 C.L.R. 159 (H.C.A.); and *Sullivan v. Moody* (2001), 207 C.L.R. 562.

4. According to *Cooper*, policy considerations are relevant under both stages of the duty of care analysis. Explain the difference between: (i) the policy considerations that arise in connection with the recognition of a *prima facie* duty of care, and (ii) the policy considerations that arise in connection with the negation or limitation of a *prima facie* duty. Will it always be possible to draw a clear distinction between those two categories? Does the answer to that question really matter? See Robertson, "Policy-based reasoning in duty of care cases" (2013) 33 L.S. 119, distinguishing between considerations based on "interpersonal justice" and those based on "community welfare."

5. What types of policy considerations are sufficient to override a *prima facie* duty of care, keeping in mind that an otherwise deserving plaintiff would thereby be denied recovery? See Sugarman, "A New Approach to Tort Doctrine: Taking the Best From the Civil Law and Common Law of Canada" in Beaulac, Pitel & Schulz, eds., *The Joy of Torts* (2003) 375 at 388. Residual policy considerations that are commonly raised include: the risk of indeterminate liability (*e.g. Attis v. Canada (Minister of Health)*, 2008 ONCA 660; and *Adams v. Borrel*, 2008 NBCA 62); the availability of alternative remedies (*e.g. Albarquez v. Ontario*, 2009 ONCA 374); the non-justiciability of core policy decisions made by the government (*e.g. R. v. Imperial Tobacco Canada Ltd.*, 2011 SCC 42); interference with commercial negotiations (*e.g. Design Services Ltd. v. Canada*, 2008 SCC 22); and potential conflicts with public (*e.g. Williams v. Ontario*, 2009 ONCA 378; and *D.(C.) v. Canada (Attorney General)*, 2014 BCCA 180) or private law duties (*e.g. Paxton v. Ramji*, 2008 ONCA 697).

6. The court in *Cooper* said that *Anns* continues to provide the proper framework for analysis. Is it accurate to say that *Cooper* merely "highlights and hones the role of policy concerns" as initially expressed by *Anns?*

7. What, if anything, is the difference between the test that the Supreme Court of Canada formulated in *Cooper* and the test that the House of Lords formulated in *Caparo v. Dickman?*

8. As compared with *Anns* or *Kamloops,* is *Cooper* more or less favourable to plaintiffs? How do you think this test affects the scope of negligence in Canada?

9. On the same day that it released *Cooper v. Hobart*, the Supreme Court of Canada also delivered judgment in the companion case of *Edwards v. Law Society of Upper Canada* (2001), 206 D.L.R. 211 (S.C.C.). The plaintiff suffered a loss when his lawyer misappropriated funds from his trust account. The plaintiff brought an action in negligence against the defendant, which is the body that regulates lawyers in Ontario. The plaintiff claimed that his loss was caused by the defendant's careless failure to ensure that the lawyer's trust accounts were properly managed. As in *Cooper*, the defendant in *Edwards* brought a motion to strike out the plaintiff's statement of claim on the ground that the circumstances did not support the recognition of a duty of care.

The Supreme Court of Canada affirmed the judgments below and held that the defendant did not owe a duty of care to the plaintiff. Since the facts did not fall within any pre-existing duty category, it was necessary to apply the *Anns/Kamloops* test. The court held that a *prima facie* duty of care did not arise under the first branch of that test because there was insufficient proximity between the parties. In that regard, the court was particularly influenced by: (i) the fact that the plaintiff was not himself a "client" of the lawyer, and (ii) the fact that the legislative scheme under which the defendant operated did not contemplate a private law right of action in the circumstances of the case. The court also held that, even if a *prima facie* duty of care had been established, it would have been negated under the second branch of the test, essentially for the same reasons that would have had effect in *Cooper*. See also *Rogers v. Faught* (2002), 159 O.A.C. 79 (C.A.), as contrasted with *McClelland v. Stewart* (2003), 229 D.L.R. (4th) 342 (B.C.S.C.).

10. On facts similar to *Cooper v. Hobart*, the Privy Council in *Yuen Kun Yeu v. A.G. of Hong Kong*, [1987] 2 All E.R. 705 and the House of Lords in *Davis v. Radcliffe*, [1990] 1 W.L.R. 821 reached the same conclusion as the Supreme Court of Canada.

11. See Pitel, "Negligence: Canada Remakes the *Anns* Test" [2002] C.L.J. 252; Pitel, "A Reformulated *Anns* Test for Canada" (2002) 10 Tort L. Rev. 10; Neyers, "Distilling Duty: The Supreme Court of Canada Amends *Anns*" (2002) 118 L.Q.R. 221; Klar, "Foreseeability, Proximity and Policy" (2002) 25 Adv. Q. 360; and Rafferty, "Developments in Contract and Torts Law: The 2001-2002 Term" (2002) 18 S.C.L.R. 153.

(e) DEVELOPMENTS SINCE *COOPER v. HOBART*

Cooper was intended to clarify the *Anns/Kamloops* test and, in particular, the role of policy considerations in determining the existence and scope of the duty of care. *Cooper* was significant for its affirmation that the first stage of the test involves both foreseeability and proximity. Nevertheless, it left several other questions unanswered, some of which are raised in the notes and questions above. Perhaps most critically, it was not clear whether the approach used in *Cooper* was meant as a general test of duty, or was only to be applied in novel situations. Similarly, the decision in *Cooper* did not explain how the recognized categories of proximate relationships were to be treated under the revised test. Were they exempt from stage one of the test, but still subject to stage two, or did they fall outside the scope of the new test altogether? It was also unclear which party bears the burden of proof in the second stage of the test: the court merely stated that "residual policy considerations fall to be considered here." These unanswered questions have been raised again in subsequent cases.

In *Odhavji Estate v. Woodhouse*, [2003] 3 S.C.R. 263, Iacobucci J., writing for the court, reviewed and summarized the tests from *Anns* and *Cooper*. Iacobucci J. explained at para. 52 that, in order to be successful, the plaintiffs needed to establish "(i) that the harm complained of is a reasonably foreseeable consequence of the alleged breach; (ii) that there is sufficient proximity between the parties that it would not be unjust or unfair to impose a duty of care on the defendants; and (iii) that there exist no policy reasons to negative or otherwise restrict that duty." This restatement appears to suggest that the plaintiffs have the burden of proof throughout the test, which would be contrary to previous jurisprudence on the *Anns/Kamloops* test.

However, in the subsequent decision in *Childs v. Desormeaux*, [2006] 1 S.C.R. 643, McLachlin C.J.C. clarified the appropriate burden of proof at para. 13: "once the plaintiff establishes a *prima facie* duty of care, the evidentiary burden of showing countervailing policy considerations shifts to the defendant, following the general rule that the party asserting a point should be required to establish it." The decision in *Childs* also provided some assistance on the treatment of established categories under the test from *Cooper*. McLachlin C.J.C. wrote at para. 15:

> The Court in *Cooper* introduced the idea that as the case law develops, categories of relationships giving rise to a duty of care may be recognized, making it unnecessary to go through the *Anns* analysis. The reference to categories simply captures the basic notion of precedent: where a case is like another case where a duty has been recognized, one may usually infer that sufficient proximity is present and that if the risk of injury was foreseeable, a *prima facie* duty of care will arise. On the other hand, if a case does not clearly fall within a relationship previously recognized as giving rise to a duty of care, it is necessary to carefully consider whether proximity is established.

The decision in *Childs* suggests that, at the very least, the proximity analysis from stage one of the *Anns/Cooper* test does not apply to established categories. Moreover, the court in *Cooper* commented that the established categories will seldom be subject to policy considerations under stage two of the test. Thus, the combined effect of *Cooper* and *Childs* indicates that the established categories of duty will not be subject to either stage of the *Anns/Cooper* test, which is generally reserved for novel duty situations. This was affirmed in *Mustapha v. Culligan of Canada Ltd.*, [2008] 2 S.C.R. 114, which involved a plaintiff who suffered psychiatric harm after seeing a dead fly in a sealed bottle of water he had purchased for his family. The court found that the case fell into the established category of duty between manufacturer and consumer, and thus declined to discuss the more complex duty questions that often arise in psychiatric harm cases.

More recently, in *Deloitte & Touche v. Livent Inc. (Receiver of)*, 2017 SCC 63, the Supreme Court revisited the relevance of established categories and adopted a more cautious approach. The majority advised that, when faced with a duty situation that is purported to fall within an established category, courts "should be attentive to the particular factors which justified recognizing that prior category in order to determine whether the relationship at issue is, in fact, truly the same as or analogous to that which was previously recognized" (at para. 28). In other words, the established categories should be defined narrowly, based on the specific relationship and actions at issue.

Since *Cooper,* a large percentage of duty cases have been decided at the "proximity" stage of analysis. In particular, where the defendant is a public authority whose duties are grounded in statute, the Canadian courts have generally found that there is insufficient proximity to impose a duty of care. Because the statutes often require the defendant to balance competing interests or to consider the broader public interest, the defendant does not have a sufficiently "close and direct" relationship with any particular individual. See for example *Syl Apps Secure Treatment Centre v. D.(B.),* [2007] 3 S.C.R. 83; *Street v. Ontario Racing Commission* (2008), 88 O.R. (3d) 563 (C.A.); *Williams v. Canada (Attorney General)* (2009), 95 O.R. (3d) 401 (C.A.); and *Wellington v. Ontario,* 2011 ONCA 274. Proximity also plays an important role in actions against defendants who are private actors, perhaps most notably in cases involving pure economic loss. See for example *McGowan v. Bank of Nova Scotia,* 2011 PECA 20 (no proximity between defendant bank and plaintiff shareholders when bank called in a line of credit owed by the corporation); and *Condominium Corp. No. 0321365 v. 970365 Alberta Ltd.,* 2012 ABCA 26 (no proximity between interim financier of condominium project and ultimate purchasers of units); and *Paton Estate v. Ontario Lottery and Gaming Corporation (Fallsview Casino Resort and OLG Casino Brantford),* 2016 ONCA 458 (possible proximate relationship between casino and problem gamblers who are permitted to gamble excessively).

Resort to the second stage of *Anns/Cooper* has been less frequent, and is often a matter of *obiter dicta* after a *prima facie* duty has been rejected due to a lack of proximity. Perhaps the most substantial application of the second stage occurred in *Hill v. Hamilton-Wentworth Regional Police Services Board,* [2007] 3 S.C.R. 129, where the plaintiff was wrongly convicted after an allegedly negligent police investigation. The defendant raised numerous arguments at the second stage of the *Anns/Cooper* test, claiming that imposing a duty of care would interfere with the exercise of discretion during investigations, would have a chilling effect on police behaviour, and would result in a flood of claims by those accused of crimes. The majority of the court considered and rejected each of these residual policy concerns, and cautioned against rejecting a duty of care based on mere speculation. Moreover, the majority also considered the positive implications of imposing a duty of care, particularly that it would raise the standards of police investigations. The decision in *Hill* suggests that defendants will need some evidence to support their claims that imposing a duty of care would have deleterious effects.

As occurred in *Hill,* plaintiffs may raise residual policy considerations that militate in favour of imposing a duty of care. For example, imposing a duty on commercial providers of alcohol discourages them from over-serving patrons and provides an incentive to protect others from the risks that their intoxicated patrons may pose: *Donaldson v. John Doe,* 2009 BCCA 38. However, the plaintiff has no burden of raising such considerations, and they cannot be used to overcome a lack of proximity at stage one of the *Anns/Cooper* analysis. In other words, any residual policy considerations raised by the plaintiff will be merely supportive of the *prima facie* duty that has already been established.

The Canadian courts continue to flesh out the duty framework that was provided in *Cooper.* That said, a general guide to determining whether a duty of care exists can be provided as follows:

(a) As a preliminary matter, is the alleged duty of care within an established category or analogous to an established category? If so, then it will not be necessary to proceed through the *Anns/Cooper* analysis. Proximity is established, and overriding policy considerations will rarely arise. Thus, a duty of care exists. As mentioned in the previous chapter, in cases involving established categories, the duty of care frequently goes unmentioned.

(b) If the case alleges a novel duty of care, was the harm reasonably foreseeable? This is typically not a difficult burden for the plaintiff to meet. However, as discussed in the remainder of this chapter, a duty of care may sometimes be rejected because the harm or the plaintiff was not reasonably foreseeable.

(c) Even if the harm was foreseeable, was there a sufficient relationship of proximity between the parties to make it just and fair to impose a duty of care on the defendant? At this stage, the court will consider policy considerations arising from the relationship between the parties. Factors to consider may include expectations, representations and reliance; the types of interests involved (physical, economic, emotional, etc.); and any statutory or contractual framework. The courts continue to provide guidance on this issue as novel cases arise.

(d) If there was foreseeable harm and a sufficient relationship of proximity, a *prima facie* duty of care exists. Then, according to *Childs*, the evidentiary burden shifts to the defendant to raise any residual policy considerations that might negative or limit the scope of the duty of care. These residual policy considerations pertain to the decision's effects on the legal system or society more generally. For example, is there an alternative remedy available, will a duty of care give rise to indeterminate liability, or does the case involve core policy decisions of the government that should be immune from negligence liability? Presumably, the list of residual policy considerations is only limited by lawyers' imaginations. Nevertheless, given that these policy considerations may deny compensation to an otherwise deserving plaintiff, they should not determine the matter if they are merely speculative.

NOTES AND QUESTIONS

1. For select applications of the *Anns/Cooper* test, see *Fullowka v. Royal Oak Ventures Inc.*, 2010 SCC 5; *Reference re Broome v. Prince Edward Island*, 2010 SCC 11; *783783 Alberta Ltd. v. Canada (Attorney General)*, 2010 ABCA 226; *R. v. Imperial Tobacco Canada Ltd.*, 2011 SCC 42; *Burrell v. Metropolitan Entertainment Group*, 2011 NSCA 108; *Los Angeles Salad Co. v Canadian Food Inspection Agency*, 2013 BCCA 34; *Mandeville v. Manufacturers Life Insurance Co.*, 2014 ONCA 417; *Williams v. Toronto (City)*, 2016 ONCA 666; and *1688782 Ontario Inc. v. Maple Leaf Foods Inc.*, 2018 ONCA 407.

2. How does the decision in *Deloitte & Touche v. Livent (Receiver of)*, *supra*, affect the precedential value of established duty categories?

3. The next four chapters discuss special categories of duty. As mentioned above, the decision in *Childs* suggests that these special categories are not subject to the *Anns/Cooper* test. Instead, they are subject to the more specific rules that have developed to

govern those types of actions in particular. See *e.g. Liebig v. Guelph General Hospital,* 2010 ONCA 450 (prenatal injury); and *Livent, supra* (negligent misstatement). Nevertheless, the decision in *Livent, supra,* suggests that the courts are moving toward an integration of the *Anns/Cooper* test with more specific duty rules.

4. For a review of the impact of *Cooper* and subsequent development of the duty of care in Canada, see Neyers & Gabie, "Canadian Tort Law Since *Cooper v. Hobart:* Part I" (2005) 13 Torts L.J. 302; Neyers & Gabie, "Canadian Tort Law Since *Cooper v. Hobart:* Part II" (2006) 14 Torts L.J. 10; Brown & Brochu, "Once More Unto the Breach: *James v. British Columbia* and Problems with the Duty of Care in Canadian Tort Law" (2008) 45 Alta. L. Rev. 1071; Rafferty & Saunders, "Developments in Tort Law: the 2011-2012 Term" (2012) 59 S.C.L.R. (2d) 313; and Blom, "Do We Really Need the *Anns* Test for Duty of Care in Negligence?" (2016) 53 Alta. L. Rev. 895.

5. There has been considerable debate about the appropriateness of deciding the duty of care by reference to questions of policy. In support of policy-based considerations, see Perry, "Professor Weinrib's Formalism: The Not-So-Empty Sepulchre" (1993) 16 Harv. J.L. & Pub. Pol'y 597; and Stapleton, "Duty of Care Factors: A Selection from the Judicial Menus" in Cane & Stapleton, eds., *The Law of Obligations: Essays in Celebration of John Fleming* (1998). For arguments that policy-based considerations should not be included in duty analyses, see Witting, "Duty of Care: An Analytical Approach" (2005) 25 O.J.L.S. 33; Weinrib, "The Disintegration of Duty" (2006) 31 Adv. Q. 212; Beever, *Rediscovering the Law of Negligence* (2007) at 3-8; and Stevens, *Torts and Rights* (2008) ch. 14. See also Golanski, "A New Look at Duty in Tort Law: Rehabilitating Foreseeability and Related Themes" (2012) 75 Albany L. Rev. 227; Robertson, "Policy-based reasoning in duty of care cases" (2013) 33 L.S. 119; and Plunkett, "Principle and Policy in Private Law Reasoning" [2016] C.L.J. 366.

2. Reasonable Foreseeability

According to *Cooper v. Hobart,* the recognition of a duty of care involves a number of steps. If a case falls within an existing category, either directly or by analogy, then a duty of care will generally apply on the facts. If a case does not fit within an existing or analogous category, then the court must apply the *Anns/Cooper* test. That test involves three main factors: (i) reasonable foreseeability, (ii) proximity, and (iii) residual policy considerations. The first two factors fall under the first branch of the test and are used to identify the existence of a *prima facie* duty of care. The third factor arises under the second branch of the test and is used to negate or limit the *prima facie* duty of care.

The next four chapters, which deal with special categories of duty, focus on what *Cooper v. Hobart* would classify as considerations of proximity and policy. In the remainder of this chapter, we examine the notion of reasonable foreseeability as it pertains to the duty of care.

In the present context, the essential question is whether, at the time of the alleged tort, it was reasonably foreseeable to a person in the defendant's position that carelessness on his or her part could create: (i) a risk of injury, (ii) to the plaintiff or class or persons to which the plaintiff belongs. Although easily stated, the following cases demonstrate that that test is sometimes difficult to apply.

(a) FORESEEABLE RISK OF INJURY

MOULE v. N.B. ELEC. POWER COMM.
(1960), 24 D.L.R. (2d) 305 (S.C.C.)

RITCHIE J.: —. . . At the place where this accident occurred, there was a maple tree which at ground level was some 5 ft. from the pole. This tree really consisted of two intertwined trees and at the height of 33 ft. 6 ins. its trunk was only 3 ft. 2 ins. from the wires; it was cleared of all branches on the side nearest to the wires to a height of about 40 ft. but on the side furthest from the wires there were some branches from about 25 ft. up and there was a crotch in the tree at very nearly the same level as the wires themselves.

A few feet further away from the pole and the wires was a spruce tree which had been cleared of limbs to a height of approximately 13 ft. from the ground but to which some person other than the infant appellant had attached boards which formed a species of ladder so that it was possible for a child to climb up to the lowest remaining branches above which a platform had been constructed going across to the maple tree and just above the platform on the maple tree a board and some straps had been nailed which made it possible to climb up to the lowest remaining branch on the side of that tree which was furthest away from the wires.

About noon on Sunday, September 15, 1957 the infant appellant, who at that time was 10½ years old, had climbed up the spruce tree, crossed on the platform to the maple tree and thence to the crotch of that tree, when he called out to his little friend, Joan Rogers, who came over and who herself climbed up on the platform at which time she says that the appellant "must have been standing in the curve of the tree" and "a little above the wires". The little girl says that she hollered to the boy but got no answer and then saw some smoke coming from where the boy was and she ran for his mother. She and Richard Stewart were the only children who gave evidence except for the appellant himself. They had both been living in the area for 2 or 3 months and neither of them had ever seen any boys climbing the maple tree. The appellant himself says that he had never seen anybody climb as high as he was on the day in question.

The appellant himself does not remember how he got up the tree and in fact says that all he can remember is stepping on a rotten branch. He does, however, admit on cross-examination that he recognized the wires to be dangerous and would not have touched them if he could have avoided them.

. . .

In finding that the respondent "should be held liable for the accident and its consequences" the learned trial Judge said:

> But a tree is much more of an allurement for small boys than a power line pole, and I think it fair to say that it might well be anticipated that they would nail cleats to the tree for climbing purposes. I also think it reasonably foreseeable that a child might slip or fall in his climb and come in contact with a conductor only about 3 feet from the top part of the tree. All of which is not highly probable, but likely enough that where the conductor was such a dangerous source of harm a commensurate degree of care called for removing the tree altogether.

The nature of the boy's injuries make it clear that in falling he not only came "in contact with a conductor about 3 feet from the top part of the tree" but that he did so in such a manner as to bring his body in contact with the tree and the wires at the same time. With the greatest respect for the views of the learned trial Judge, I am nonetheless of the opinion that when this circumstance is considered in conjunction with the presence of the cleats on both trees, the platform between them, the unusual height to which the boy climbed and the fact that he had the misfortune to put his weight on a rotten branch, it discloses a sequence of events which was so fortuitous as to be beyond the range of the foreseeable results which a reasonable man would anticipate as a probable consequence of the presence of the high tension wires, isolated as they were from normal human contact, in the area in question.

Having regard to the proximity of this wooded area to houses occupied by the families of military personnel, it was to be expected that children would play there, and although the respondent was not the owner or the occupier of the land and the pole had been installed by the New Brunswick Telephone Co., the wires were nonetheless a dangerous agency which had been brought into the area by the respondent and it was, therefore, under a duty to take precautions but only against any foreseeable consequence of the presence of that danger which could be said to involve a reasonable probability of causing harm.

That high voltage wires are dangerous goes without saying, and the fact that children are likely to climb trees is certainly a foreseeable circumstance and that it is one to which power companies should give heed in placing their wires so that young climbers will not come unexpectedly on a live wire concealed by the branches of a tree is shown by the case of *Buckland v. Guildford Gas Light & Coke Co.*, [1949] 1 K.B. 410. This does not mean, however, that such a company is necessarily responsible for every accidental contact with its wires by climbing children or that it is deemed to be endowed with prevision of every harmful contingency to which the curiosity, agility and daring of active children may expose them.

In placing the wires 33 ft. 6 ins. from the ground and causing the adjacent trees to be limbed as they were at the place of this accident, I am of opinion that the respondent had taken adequate precautions against such dangers inherent in the presence of the wires as could be reasonably foreseen, and I agree with the learned Judge who, in rendering the decision from which this appeal is taken, has said: "The defendant should not be held guilty of negligence for not having foreseen the possibility of the occurrence of such an unlikely event as happened in this case and provided against it by the removal of the maple tree."

AMOS v. N.B. ELEC. POWER COMM.
(1976), 70 D.L.R. (3d) 741 (S.C.C.)

SPENCE J.:—This is an appeal by leave from the judgment of the Appeal Division of the Supreme Court of New Brunswick pronounced on March 21, 1975. By that judgment, the Appeal Division allowed an appeal from the judgment of Leger, J., given after trial whereby he had allowed the appellants' claim and awarded damages of $36,275.45 and costs.

The infant plaintiff, on July 1, 1970, then nine years old, was visiting his uncle at Kedgwick, New Brunswick, and that afternoon was engaged in play with two other boys Gilbert Le Bourque, age 13, and Leopold Simon, age 10. The uncle's home is located on the edge of a highway and about 25 to 30 ft. therefrom. Along the edge of this highway and within the limits of the highway, the respondent had erected a row of wooden poles carrying various wires, which shall be more particularly described hereafter.

Directly in front of the uncle's house and also on the highway right-of-way, grew a poplar tree. Of course, in July, the tree was in full leaf and made a perfect screen for the series of wires which ran through it. The lowest of those wires was a telephone cable and that cable was 21 ft. above the ground. Some 40 inches farther up was one low voltage line carrying only 110 volts and then some 9 inches to a foot above that two more similar low voltage lines. Above that again, a neutral ground wire and uppermost and 48 inches higher than the neutral ground wire were wires carrying very heavy charges said to be of 7,200 volts. These last three wires were attached to the cross-bar at the top of the pole.

In their play, the three boys devised a contest to determine which one of the three could climb the tree the farthest and the fastest. The plaintiff, although only nine, appears to have been the most agile of the three and he climbed the highest on the tree. He climbed high enough in the tree so that his weight would cause the tree to sway or bend and either the trunk of the tree itself or one of the branches of the tree brushed against these high tension wires. The boy was immediately struck by severe electric shock, knocked unconscious and was actually burning in the tree. A neighbour, at what both Courts below noted was great personal risk, took a chain saw and cut the tree down, so that it fell on the road and the badly injured plaintiff was then taken first to a hospital in nearby St. Quentin and thereafter transferred to a hospital in Montreal.

No issue as to the quantum of damage arose in either the Appeal Division or in this Court, and we are simply concerned with the issue of liability.

In the first place, it may be noted that the power lines and tree were on a public highway and the question of trespass does not arise.

This Court and other Courts have, from time to time, stressed the duty of those who erect electric lines carrying heavy charges to take proper precautions against injury resulting therefrom. . . .

In the present case, the learned trial Judge said [(1974), 9 N.B.R. (2d) 358 at 361]:

> After having considered all of the evidence I have concluded that the tree in combination with the wires constituted an invitation and an allurement for small boys imbued with the natural instinct to climb as high as their strength and energy would permit; that in permitting the power lines to remain without insulation and in failing to maintain the particular tree properly trimmed in proximity to the power lines where the branches or the infant plaintiff could come in contact with them constituted a concealed danger in the nature of a trap for such small infants. The defendant ought reasonably to have foreseen the danger and they must be deemed to have had knowledge of it and ought to have taken the necessary steps to obviate it. Their failure to accomplish this constituted negligence on their part.

With respect, apart from the learned trial Judge's reference to lack of insulation, I agree with him.

Bugold, J.A., giving judgment for the Appeal Division was, in my opinion, ready to accept the law as outlined by the learned trial Judge but was of the opinion that the particular facts in the present case could not result in liability for the respondent because the respondent could not have reasonably foreseen the accident which did occur, and, again, in my opinion, felt that the matter was foreclosed by the decision of this court in *Moule v. N.B. Electric Power Com'n, supra.* . . .

Let us contrast those circumstances and the conduct of the power company in that case with the circumstances of the present case and the conduct of the power company in the present appeal.

The poplar, as noted by the learned trial Judge, is a fast growing tree. The fast growing tree stood directly beneath lines running along the top of the poles and carrying up to 7,200 volts. Yet, the only evidence as to an attempt to keep the tree away from those heavily charged wires was almost casual the inspector of the power company saying it was the practice to trim such trees every four to seven years and so far as he knew the practice had been kept up in reference to this poplar tree. That such practice was indeed insufficient is illustrated by the fact that the accident occurred because it did occur when the tree swayed sufficiently to have the trunk or a branch touch the high tension wires. Those wires were at least 30 ft. above the ground and any contact with those high tension wires could have been avoided by the simple expedient of cutting off the top of the poplar tree. It was left uncut and this heavily leafed tree in mid-summer adequately concealed the presence of the wires from a boy carrying out the perfectly normal play of an active little fellow in climbing the tree.

In *Moule,* in order to get himself injured, the boy had to climb one tree and then cross from it to the maple which had been protected in the fashion I have outlined and then only came in contact with the wire when he stepped on a dead branch and fell. In this appeal, the boy, by climbing what seemed to be a normal poplar tree, caused the tree to bend so that it contacted high tension wires which it should not even have been near. As Ritchie, J., pointed out in *Moule,* that children are likely to climb trees is certainly a foreseeable circumstance. Morris J., said in *Buckland v. Guildford Gas Light & Coke Co.,* [1949] 1 K.B. 410 at p. 419:

> It required no vivid imagination on the part of anyone traversing the route of the wires to appreciate the great peril of having the wires above a tree that could be easily climbed, and whose foliage, being dense in the month of June, would obscure the wires. If anyone did climb the tree he would with every step approach a hidden peril of the direst kind. The facts of the present case show all too dramatically the nature of the peril. It was, in my judgment, easily foreseeable that someone might climb the tree and so might become in close proximity to an unseen deadly peril.

I am of the opinion that those words are particularly applicable to the present appeal.

Although the long series of circumstances which, added together, resulted in the accident in the *Moule* case, could not have been foreseen, I am of the opinion that the accident in the present case was one which could be foreseen and which was almost inevitable when given active boys and a poplar tree running up through and hiding high tension wires, especially when that tree was directly in front of their home.

For these reasons, I am of the opinion that *Moule v. N.B. Electric Power Com'n* does not apply in the present circumstances and that the respondent was liable for the damage caused to the infant plaintiff.

RANKIN (RANKIN'S GARAGE & SALES) v. J.J.
2018 SCC 19

The judgment of McLachlin C.J. and Abella, Moldaver, Karakatsanis, Wagner, Côté and Rowe JJ. was delivered by:

KARAKATSANIS J.:—

I. Background
A. Facts

[3] This case emerges from a tragic set of events. On an evening in July 2006, in the small village of Paisley, Ontario, the plaintiff J. (then 15 years old) and his friend C. (then 16 years old) were at the house of C.'s mother. The boys drank alcohol (some of which was provided by the mother) and smoked marijuana.

[4] Sometime after midnight, the boys left the house to walk around Paisley, with the intention of stealing valuables from unlocked cars. Eventually they made their way to Rankin's Garage & Sales, a car garage located near the main intersection in Paisley that was owned by James Chadwick Rankin. The garage property was not secured, and the boys began walking around the lot checking for unlocked cars. C. found an unlocked Toyota Camry parked behind the garage. He opened the Camry and found its keys in the ashtray. Though he did not have a driver's licence and had never driven a car on the road before, C. decided to steal the car so that he could go and pick up a friend in nearby Walkerton, Ontario. C. told J. to "get in", which he did.

[5] The 16-year-old C. drove the car out of the garage and around Paisley before starting toward Walkerton. On the highway, the car crashed. J. suffered a catastrophic brain injury.

[6] Through his litigation guardian, J. sued Rankin's Garage, his friend C. and his friend's mother for negligence. The issue in this appeal is whether Rankin's Garage owed the plaintiff a duty of care.

. . .

III. The *Anns/Cooper* Test

. . .

Reasonable Foreseeability and Proximity

[21] Since *Donoghue*, the "neighbour principle" has been the cornerstone of the law of negligence. Lord Atkin's famous quote respecting how far a legal neighbourhood extends incorporates the dual concerns of reasonable foreseeability of harm and proximity:

> The rule that you are to love your neighbour becomes in law, you must not injure your neighbour; and the lawyer's question, Who is my neighbour? receives a restricted reply. You must take reasonable care to avoid acts or omissions which you can reasonably foresee would be likely to injure your neighbour. Who, then, in law is my neighbour? The answer seems to be - persons who are so closely and directly affected by my act that I ought reasonably to have them in contemplation as being so affected when I am directing my mind to the acts or omissions which are called in question.

Reasonable foreseeability of harm and proximity operate as crucial limiting principles in the law of negligence. They ensure that liability will only be found when the defendant ought reasonably to have contemplated the type of harm the plaintiff suffered.

[22] The rationale underlying this approach is self-evident. It would simply not be just to impose liability in cases where there was no reason for defendants to have contemplated that their conduct could result in the harm complained of. Through the neighbour principle, the defendant, as creator of an unreasonable risk, is connected to the plaintiff, the party whose endangerment made the risk unreasonable: E. J. Weinrib, "The Disintegration of Duty", in M. S. Madden, ed., *Exploring Tort Law* (2005), 143, at p. 151. The wrongdoing relates to the harm caused. Thus, foreseeability operates as the "fundamental moral glue of tort", shaping the legal obligations we owe to one another, and defining the boundaries of our individual liability: D. G. Owen, "Figuring Foreseeability" (2009), 44 *Wake Forest L. Rev.* 1277, at p. 1278.

. . .

[24] When determining whether reasonable foreseeability is established, the proper question to ask is whether the plaintiff has "offer[ed] facts to persuade the court that the risk of the type of damage that occurred was reasonably foreseeable to the class of plaintiff that was damaged": A. M. Linden and B. Feldthusen, *Canadian Tort Law* (10th ed. 2015), at p. 322 (emphasis added). This approach ensures that the inquiry considers both the defendant who committed the act as well as the plaintiff, whose harm allegedly makes the act wrongful. As Professor Weinrib notes, the duty of care analysis is a search for the connection between the wrong and the injury suffered by the plaintiff: p. 150; see also *Anns*, at pp. 751-52; *Childs*, at para. 25.

[25] The facts of this case highlight the importance of framing the question of whether harm is foreseeable with sufficient analytical rigour to connect the failure to take care to the type of harm caused to persons in the plaintiff's situation. Here, the claim is brought by an individual who was physically injured following the theft of the car from Rankin's Garage. The foreseeability question must therefore be framed in a way that links the impugned act (leaving the vehicle unsecured) to the harm suffered by the plaintiff (physical injury).

[26] Thus, in this context, it is not enough to determine simply whether the theft of the vehicle was reasonably foreseeable. The claim is not brought by the owner of the car for the loss of the property interest in the car; if that were the case, a risk of theft in general would suffice. Characterizing the nature of the risk-taking as the risk of theft does not illuminate why the impugned act is wrongful in this case since creating a risk of theft would not necessarily expose the plaintiff to a risk of physical injury. Instead, further evidence is needed to create a connection between the theft and the unsafe operation of the stolen vehicle. The proper question to be asked in this context is whether the type of harm suffered — personal injury — was reasonably foreseeable to someone in the position of the defendant when considering the security of the vehicles stored at the garage.

. . .

V. Analysis

. . .

A. *Was the Risk of Personal Injury Reasonably Foreseeable in This Case?*

. . .

[Karakatsanis J. reviewed the Ontario Court of Appeal's decision and other jurisprudence, and noted that the evidence in the case suggested that there was a reasonably foreseeable risk of theft in general.]

[45] However, the risk of theft in general does not automatically include the risk of theft by minors. I cannot agree with my colleague's suggestion that because minors are reckless, "minors are no less likely to steal a car than any other individual" and therefore, theft by a minor is reasonably foreseeable (para. 83). The inferential chain of reasoning is too weak — it is not enough to say that it is possible that unsupervised minors would be roaming the lot looking for unlocked vehicles.

[46] The fact that something is *possible* does not mean that it is reasonably foreseeable. Obviously, any harm that has occurred was by definition possible. Thus, for harm to be reasonably foreseeable, a higher threshold than mere possibility must be met: *Childs*, at para. 29. Some evidentiary basis is required before a court can conclude that the risk of theft includes the risk of theft by *minors*. Otherwise theft by a minor would always be foreseeable — even without any evidence to suggest that this risk was more than a mere possibility. This would fundamentally change tort law and could result in a significant expansion of liability.

. . .

[53] Whether or not something is "reasonably foreseeable" is an objective test. The analysis is focussed on whether someone in the defendant's position ought reasonably to have foreseen the harm rather than whether the specific defendant did. Courts should be vigilant in ensuring that the analysis is not clouded by the fact that the event in question actually did occur. The question is properly focussed on whether foreseeability was present *prior* to the incident occurring and not with the aid of 20/20 hindsight: L. N. Klar and C.S.G. Jefferies, *Tort Law* (6th ed. 2017), at p. 212.

[54] I have the same concerns respecting my colleague's reliance on Mr. Rankin's testimony. My colleague suggests that foreseeability is made out here because Mr. Rankin testified that he always locked his vehicles. (This self-serving testimony was rejected by the jury.) In my view, this evidence is not determinative of whether foreseeability was *objectively* present here. Moreover, this testimony only suggests that Mr. Rankin thought that theft, rather than personal injury, was foreseeable.

[55] To summarize, the evidence did not provide specific circumstances to make it reasonably foreseeable that the stolen car might be driven in a way that would cause personal injury. The evidence did not, for example, establish that the risk of theft included the risk of theft by minors. While in this case, it was argued that it was the risk of theft by minors that could make the risk of the unsafe operation of the stolen vehicle foreseeable, had there been other evidence or circumstances making the risk of personal injury reasonably foreseeable, a duty of care would exist.

[56] As was the case in many similar decisions by trial courts, I am not satisfied that the evidence here demonstrates that bodily harm resulting from the theft of the vehicle was reasonably foreseeable. I conclude that the plaintiff did not satisfy the

onus to establish that the defendant ought to have contemplated the risk of personal injury when considering its security practices. The inferential chain of reasoning was too weak to support the establishment of reasonable foreseeability: see *Childs*, at para. 29. For these reasons, the plaintiff has not met his burden of establishing a *prima facie* duty of care owed by Rankin's Garage to him. Reasonable foreseeability could not be established on this record.

Appeal allowed.

[Brown J. (Gascon J. concurring) delivered a dissenting judgement. In their view, the case did not require a full *Anns/Cooper* analysis because the claim fell within the established duty category of foreseeable physical injury. Typically, reasonable foreseeability presents a low hurdle in cases involving physical harm. Further, the dissenting judges opined that minors can be reckless, and thus are just as likely to steal a car as any other individual. Brown J. wrote that the majority's opposite conclusion had "a certain unreality" (at para. 83).]

NOTES AND QUESTIONS

1. Do you agree that *Moule* can be distinguished from *Amos*? Specifically, what facts prompted the court to recognize a duty of care in *Amos*, but not in *Moule*? Would the result in *Amos* have been different if the tree had swayed into the wires as a result of the combined effects of the child's weight and an unusually strong gust of wind?

2. The issue of foreseeability of harm is relevant to three elements of a negligence action: duty, standard of care and remoteness. First, a court will impose a duty of care only if the defendant's conduct created a foreseeable risk of injury to the plaintiff. Second, the probability of injury is one of several factors considered in determining whether the defendant breached the standard of care. Finally, the plaintiff's losses will be held to be too remote if they were not a foreseeable result of the defendant's breach of the standard of care. The courts do not always draw a clear distinction between those three concepts.

3. Identify the foreseeability tests used in the three cases above. What was the legal significance of the courts' findings on these issues? Did the courts address the issue of foreseeability in terms of duty, standard of care or remoteness?

4. The different manifestations of reasonable foreseeability were addressed in the Australian case of *Minister Administering the Environmental Planning and Assessment Act 1979 v. San Sebastien Pty. Ltd.*, [1983] 2 N.S.W.L.R. 268 at 295-96 (C.A.) [emphasis in original]:

> [A] recognition has emerged that the foreseeability inquiry at the duty, breach and remoteness stages raises different issues which progressively decline from the general to the particular. The proximity upon which a *Donoghue* type duty rests depends upon proof that the defendant and plaintiff are so placed in relation to each other that it is reasonably foreseeable as a possibility that careless conduct of *any kind* on the part of the former may result in damage of *some kind* to the person or property of the latter . . . The breach question requires proof that it was reasonably foreseeable as a possibility that *the kind* of carelessness charged against the defendant might cause damage of *some kind* to the plaintiff's person or property. . . The remoteness test is only passed if the plaintiff proves that *the kind* of damage suffered by him was

foreseeable as a possible outcome of the kind of carelessness charged against the defendant.

Since plaintiffs cannot ultimately succeed without satisfying the narrowest manifestation of reasonable foreseeability at the remoteness stage of inquiry, why should they also be required to separately satisfy the broader manifestations of reasonable foreseeability at the stages of standard of care and duty of care? Does it matter that the duty of care is primarily a question of law, while standard of care and, to a lesser extent, remoteness are primarily questions of fact? Who decides questions of fact and who decides questions of law? When can an appellate court overturn a decision on a question of law and when can it overturn a decision on a question of fact? See *Barnard v. Carnegie* (1924), 26 O.W.N. 264 (C.A.); *Cotic v. Gray* (1981), 124 D.L.R. (3d) 641 (Ont. C.A.); *Galaske v. O'Donnell*, [1994] 1 S.C.R. 670; *Toneguzzo-Norvell (Guardian ad litem of) v. Burnaby Hospital*, [1994] 1 S.C.R. 114; *Gottardo Properties (Dome) Inc. v. Toronto (City)* (1998), 162 D.L.R. (4th) 574 (Ont. C.A.); *Schwartz v. Canada*, [1996] 1 S.C.R. 254; *Van de Perre v. Edwards*, [2001] 2 S.C.R. 1014; and *Housen v. Nikolaisen*, [2002] 2 S.C.R. 235.

5. How does the majority decision in *Rankin's Garage* apply the test of reasonable foreseeability? How does it align with the analysis in *San Sebastien, supra*? Do you agree with the majority's conclusion that theft was foreseeable, but not theft by a minor? What populations are most likely to steal unlocked cars from unpatrolled car lots?

6. For additional cases discussing and applying the foreseeability of risk test in duty, see *Munshaw Colour Service Ltd. v. Vancouver* (1962), 33 D.L.R. (2d) 719 (S.C.C.); *Gagne v. St. Regis Paper Co.* (1973), 36 D.L.R. (3d) 301 (S.C.C.); *Crocker v. Sundance Northwest Resorts Ltd.* (1988), 44 C.C.L.T. 225 (S.C.C.); *Campbell v. Calgary Power Ltd.* (1988), 62 Alta. L.R. (2d) 253 (C.A.); *Taylor v. King* (1993), 82 B.C.L.R. (2d) 108 (C.A.); *Lorenz v. Winnipeg (City)*, [1994] 1 W.W.R. 558 (Man. C.A.); *Stewart v. Pettie* (1995), 23 C.C.L.T. (2d) 89 (S.C.C.); *Newton v. Newton* (2003), 17 B.C.L.R. (4th) 1 (C.A.); *Poissant v. Robalo* (2004), 360 A.R. 101 (Q.B.); *Childs v. Desormeaux*, [2006] 1 S.C.R. 643; *Galka v. Stankiewicz*, 2010 CarswellOnt 3346 (S.C.J.) (WL Can), aff'd 2011 ONCA 428; and *Ross (Litigation Guardian of) v. Vidnes*, 2012 SKQB 317.

7. In Goudkamp, "When is a Risk of Injury Foreseeable?" (2008) 124 L.Q.R. 37, the author reviews the High Court of Australia's tests for foreseeability of injury, ranging from injury which is not "far-fetched or fanciful" (*Wyong Shire Council v. Shirt* (1980), 146 C.L.R. 40 (H.C.A.)) to injury which is "significant enough in a practical sense" (*New South Wales v. Fahy* (2007), 81 A.L.J.R. 1021 (H.C.A.)). Does either of these tests provide practical guidance to defendants? What is the relationship between foreseeability of injury and the defendant's fault or blameworthiness? How foreseeable must an injury be before a defendant can be expected to guard against it?

(b) FORESEEABLE PLAINTIFF

PALSGRAF v. LONG ISLAND RY. CO.
248 N.Y. 339 (C.A. 1928)

CARDOZO C.J.:—Plaintiff was standing on a platform of defendant's railroad after buying a ticket to go to Rockaway Beach. A train stopped at the station, bound for another place. Two men ran forward to catch it. One of the men reached the platform of the car without mishap, though the train was already moving. The other man, carrying a package, jumped aboard the car, but seemed unsteady as if about to fall. A guard on the car, who had held the door open, reached forward to help him in, and another guard on the platform pushed him from behind. In this act, the package was dislodged, and fell upon the rails. It was a package of small size, about fifteen inches long, and was covered by a newspaper. In fact it contained fireworks, but there was nothing in its appearance to give notice of its contents. The fireworks when they fell exploded. The shock of the explosion threw down some scales at the other end of the platform many feet away. The scales struck the plaintiff, causing injuries for which she sues.

The conduct of the defendant's guard, if a wrong in its relation to the holder of the package, was not a wrong in its relation to the plaintiff, standing far away. Relatively to her it was not negligence at all. Nothing in the situation gave notice that the falling package had in it the potency of peril to persons thus removed. Negligence is not actionable unless it involves the invasion of a legally protected interest, the violation of a right. "Proof of negligence in the air, so to speak, will not do."

. . .

The plaintiff, as she stood upon the platform of the station, might claim to be protected against intentional invasion of her bodily security. Such invasion is not charged. She might claim to be protected against unintentional invasion by conduct involving in the thought of reasonable men an unreasonable hazard that such invasion would ensue. These, from the point of view of the law, were the bounds of her immunity, with perhaps some rare exceptions, survivals for the most part of ancient forms of liability, where conduct is held to be at the peril of the actor.

. . .

If no hazard was apparent to the eye of ordinary vigilance, an act innocent and harmless, at least to outward seeming, with reference to her, did not take to itself the quality of a tort because it happened to be a wrong, though apparently not one involving the risk of bodily insecurity, with reference to someone else. "In every instance, before negligence can be predicated of a given act, back of the act must be sought and found a duty to the individual complaining, the observance of which would have averted or avoided the injury."

. . .

The argument for the plaintiff is built upon the shifting meanings of such words as "wrong" and "wrongful," and shares their instability. What the plaintiff must show is "a wrong" to herself; i.e., a violation of her own right, and not merely a wrong to someone else, nor conduct "wrongful" because unsocial, but not "a wrong" to any one. We are told that one who drives at reckless speed through a crowded city street is guilty of a negligent act and therefore of a wrongful one, irrespective of the consequences. Negligent the act is, and wrongful in the sense that it is unsocial, but wrongful and unsocial in relation to other travelers, only because the eye of vigilance perceives the risk of damage. If the same act were to be committed on a speedway or race course, it would lose its wrongful quality. The risk reasonably to be perceived defines the duty to be obeyed, and risk imports relation; it is risk to another or to others within the range of apprehension.

. . .

The range of reasonable apprehension is at times a question for the court, and at times, if varying inferences are possible, a question for the jury. Here, by concession, there was nothing in the situation to suggest to the most cautious mind that the parcel wrapped in newspaper would spread wreckage through the station. If the guard had thrown it down knowingly and willfully, he would not have threatened the plaintiff's safety, so far as appearances could warn him. His conduct would not have involved, even then, an unreasonable probability of invasion of her bodily security. Liability can be no greater where the act is inadvertent.

Negligence, like risk, is thus a term of relation. Negligence in the abstract, apart from things related, is surely not a tort, if indeed it is understandable at all.

. . .

Negligence is not a tort unless it results in the commission of a wrong, and the commission of a wrong imports the violation of a right, in this case, we are told, the right to be protected against interference with one's bodily security. But bodily security is protected, not against all forms of interference or aggression, but only against some. One who seeks redress at law does not make out a cause of action by showing without more that there has been damage to his person. If the harm was not willful, he must show that the act as to him had possibilities of danger so many and apparent as to entitle him to be protected against the doing of it though the harm was unintended. Affront to personalty is still the keynote of the wrong.

. . .

The victim does not sue derivatively, or by right of subrogation, to vindicate an interest invaded in the person of another. Thus to view his cause of action is to ignore the fundamental difference between tort and crime. Holland, *Jurisprudence* (12th Ed.) p. 328. He sues for breach of a duty owing to himself.

The law of causation, remote or proximate, is thus foreign to the case before us. The question of liability is always anterior to the question of the measure of the consequences that go with liability. If there is no tort to be redressed, there is no occasion to consider what damage might be recovered if there were a finding of a tort. We may assume, without deciding, that negligence, not at large or in the abstract, but in relation to the plaintiff, would entail liability for any and all consequences, however novel or extraordinary.

. . .

ANDREWS J. (dissenting).:—The result we shall reach depends upon our theory as to the nature of negligence. Is it a relative concept — the breach of some duty owing to a particular person or to particular persons? Or, where there is an act which unreasonably threatens the safety of others, is the doer liable for all its proximate consequences, even where they result in injury to one who would generally be thought to be outside the radius of danger? This is not a mere dispute as to words. We might not believe that to the average mind the dropping of the bundle would seem to involve the probability of harm to the plaintiff standing many feet away whatever might be the case as to the owner or to one so near as to be likely to be struck by its fall. If, however, we adopt the second hypothesis, we have to inquire only as to the relation between cause and effect. We deal in terms of proximate cause, not of negligence.

. . .

But we are told that "there is no negligence unless there is in the particular case a legal duty to take care, and this duty must be one which is owed to the plaintiff himself and not merely to others." Salmond, *Torts* (6th Ed.) 24. This I think too narrow a conception. Where there is the unreasonable act, and some right that may be affected there is negligence whether damage does or does not result. That is immaterial. Should we drive down Broadway at a reckless speed, we are negligent whether we strike an approaching car or miss it by an inch. The act itself is wrongful. It is wrong not only to those who happen to be within the radius of danger, but to all who might have been there — a wrong to the public at large. Such is the language of the street. Such the language of the courts when speaking of contributory negligence. Such again and again their language in speaking of the duty of some defendant and discussing proximate cause in cases where such a discussion is wholly irrelevant on any other theory.

. . .

The proposition is this: Every one owes to the world at large the duty of refraining from those acts that may unreasonably threaten the safety of others. Such an act occurs. Not only is he wronged to whom harm might reasonably be expected to result, but he also who is in fact injured, even if he be outside what would generally be thought the danger zone. There needs be duty due the one complaining, but this is not a duty to a particular individual because as to him harm might be expected. Harm to some one being the natural result of the act, not only that one alone, but all those in fact injured may complain. We have never, I think, held otherwise. Indeed in the *Di Caprio Case* we said that a breach of a general ordinance defining the degree of care to be exercised in one's calling is evidence of negligence as to every one. We did not limit this statement to those who might be expected to be exposed to danger. Unreasonable risk being taken, its consequences are not confined to those who might probably be hurt.

If this be so, we do not have a plaintiff suing by "derivation or succession." Her action is original and primary. Her claim is for a breach of duty to herself — not that she is subrogated to any right of action of the owner of the parcel or of a passenger standing at the scene of the explosion.

. . .

The act upon which defendant's liability rests is knocking an apparently harmless package onto the platform. The act was negligent. For its proximate consequences the defendant is liable. If its contents were broken, to the owner; if it fell upon and crushed a passenger's foot, then to him; if it exploded and injured one in the immediate vicinity, to him also as to A in the illustration. Mrs. Palsgraf was standing some distance away. How far cannot be told from the record — apparently 25 or 30 feet, perhaps less. Except for the explosion, she would not have been injured. We are told by the appellant in his brief, "It cannot be denied that the explosion was the direct cause of the plaintiff's injuries." So it was a substantial factor in producing the result — there was here a natural and continuous sequence — direct connection. The only intervening cause was that, instead of blowing her to the ground, the concussion smashed the weighing machine which in turn fell upon her. There was no remoteness in time, little in space. And surely, given such an explosion as here, it needed no great foresight to predict that the natural result would be to injure one on the platform at no greater distance from its scene than was the plaintiff. Just how no one might be able to predict. Whether by flying fragments, by broken glass, by wreckage of machines or structures no one could say. But injury in some form was most probable.

Under these circumstances I cannot say as a matter of law that the plaintiff's injuries were not the proximate result of the negligence. That is all we have before us. The court refused to so charge. No request was made to submit the matter to the jury as a question of fact, even would that have been proper upon the record before us.

The judgment appealed from should be affirmed, with costs.

POUND, LEHMAN, and KELLOGG, JJ., concur with CARDOZO, C.J.

ANDREWS, J., dissents in opinion in which CRANE and O'BRIEN, JJ., concur.

NOTES AND QUESTIONS

1. How did the majority's analysis of duty differ from that of the dissent? What is the practical significance of this difference?

2. Despite frequent criticism, Cardozo C.J.'s approach has been accepted by the English and Canadian courts. The plaintiff must prove both that the defendant's conduct gave rise to a duty of care and that the duty was owed to him or her. This does not mean that the individual plaintiff must be foreseeable, but rather, that the plaintiff must belong to a class of persons foreseeably at risk. For additional discussions of the foreseeable plaintiff test see *Hay (or Bourhill) v. Young*, [1942] 2 All E.R. 396 (H.L.); *Can. Gen. Elec. Co. v. Pickford & Black Ltd.*, [1971] S.C.R. 41; *Reese v. Coleman (No. 1)*, [1979] 4 W.W.R. 58 (Sask. C.A.); *Tutton v. A.D. Walter Ltd.*, [1985] 3 All E.R. 757 (Q.B.D.); *D'Aoust v. Lindsay* (2000), 253 A.R. 243 (Q.B.); and *Brooks v. Canadian Pacific Railway Ltd.* (2007), 298 Sask. R. 64 (Q.B.). Relatively few claims are dismissed based on the unforeseeability of the plaintiff.

3. The breadth of the foreseeable plaintiff test varies considerably with the type of interest at stake. For example, a very broad test is applied in cases of rescuers, whereas a narrower test is applied in psychiatric harm cases. Contrast *King v. Phillips*, [1953] 1 Q.B. 429 (C.A.) with *Urbanski v. Patel* (1978), 84 D.L.R. (3d) 650 (Man. Q.B.).

By manipulating the foreseeable plaintiff test, the courts have been able to control the ambit of recovery in negligence. See also *Bechard v. Haliburton Estate* (1991), 10 C.C.L.T. (2d) 156 (Ont. C.A.); and *Schlink v. Blackburn* (1993), 18 C.C.L.T. (2d) 173 (B.C.C.A.).

4. In *Nespolon v. Alford* (1998), 40 O.R. (3d) 355 (C.A.), the plaintiff suffered nervous shock after he struck and killed an intoxicated teenager who had fallen on a highway. He sued, *inter alia*, the teenager's estate and two of the teenager's acquaintances, who had accepted him into their car knowing that he was "falling down drunk." Earlier that evening, the acquaintances had assured police that they would safely transport the teenager back to his hometown. At his request, they dropped him off at the roadside, near a house that he recognized as a friend's. The

plaintiff claimed that it was foreseeable that, if the intoxicated teenager were abandoned near a highway, he would stumble onto the road, posing a risk to both himself and others.

The Ontario Court of Appeal dismissed the plaintiff's claim. The majority concluded that it was unforeseeable that dropping the intoxicated teenager off would eventually cause nervous shock to someone in the plaintiff's position. Thus, the acquaintances did not owe the plaintiff a duty of care.

5. Since the majority in *Palsgraf* dismissed the plaintiff's action at the duty stage, only the dissent dealt with the other elements of a negligence action. It should be noted that, at the time *Palsgraf* was decided, the courts in both the United States and England used a directness test of remoteness. Thus, Andrews J. framed the remoteness question in terms of whether the plaintiff's losses were a direct result of the defendant's negligence. Given that directness was the test of remoteness, would Andrews J.'s approach have significantly broadened the scope of recovery? Now that foreseeability is the accepted test of remoteness, is there any practical difference between the majority and dissenting judgments?

6. Smith scathingly criticized the foreseeable plaintiff test in "The Mystery of Duty" in Klar, ed., *Studies in Canadian Tort Law* (1977) 1 at 24:

> [T]he courts have created a doctrine of privity in the law of negligence. It is a privity of fault rather than of contract. The doctrine of privity has raised problems and difficulties in the law of contract. It is a freak, an abortion, in the law of torts. The doctrine of privity confuses questions of risk of harm with problems of remoteness, and the language of duty of care is the vehicle of this confusion.
>
> Judges have said that there is no such thing as negligence in the abstract or in the air, and this is, of course, true. A risk of harm must be a risk to someone in order for it to be a risk of harm or negligence. It is often the case, however, that as a result of negligence persons who are not the prime subjects of the risk are harmed as well. It could be someone whose presence could not be anticipated. It might be a person who suffers a nervous shock as the result of witnessing the main or initial harm, or it might be a rescuer who is injured in trying to prevent the harm. These examples all raise questions of remoteness of damage because the legal issue is whether or not the defendant's liability extends to these persons as well as the persons who were the prime subjects of the risk, or, to rephrase the issue another way, whether the damage suffered by these persons is too remote from the original risk which is the foundation of the finding of negligence. We know that injuries to one person will often result in, or bear a causal connection to, other people. No event stands in a causal isolation. We have to place some limits, however, on just how much of this we are going to require the defendant to compensate.

Smith seems to agree with Andrews J. in viewing the foreseeable plaintiff issue as a practical problem of controlling the extent of the defendant's liability, an issue generally considered under remoteness of damages. However, Cardozo C.J. appears to have had an additional concern, namely, that there be a pre-existing relationship between the parties in order to justify a duty of care. For him, this was a theoretical concern as much as a practical one. Is Cardozo C.J.'s concern justified? For a theoretical justification of the foreseeable plaintiff test, see Dorfman, "Foreseeability as Re-Cognition" (2014) 59 Am. J. Juris. 163.

7. The *American Restatement (Third) of the Law of Torts: Liability for Physical and Emotional Harm* (2010) at §7 (comment j) indicates that questions of foreseeability are not relevant to the duty of care, but only to the question of whether the standard of care has been breached. The purported reasons for this direction are that foreseeability is fact-specific, is therefore not generalizable to categories, and should generally be left to the jury. Moreover, the *Restatement* indicates that questions of duty or no-duty should be based on policy or principle, "without obscuring references to foreseeability."

8. A question sometimes arises regarding the foreseeability of the plaintiff not because of a bizarre concatenation of events, as in *Palsgraf*, but rather because the plaintiff somehow is unusually vulnerable to harm. *Haley v. London Electric Board* (1964), [1965] A.C. 778 (H.L.) is illustrative. The defendant's workmen dug a trench outside the plaintiff's house one morning. They intended to refill it by nightfall. As a safety measure, they surrounded it with a barrier about nine inches in height. The plaintiff, who was blind and used a white cane to find his way about, tripped over the barrier, hit his head and was thereby rendered deaf. He sued in negligence. The defendant denied that it owed a duty of care to him. It argued that it was only obliged to take precautions suitable for able-bodied people and that the barrier that it had used was therefore adequate. Lord Reid rejected that argument, saying that it would mean that "a blind or infirm person who goes out alone goes out at his peril." He then held that the plaintiff's injury did fall within the scope of the reasonable foreseeability test and that the defendant was liable:

> No doubt there are many places open to the public where for one reason or another one would be surprised to see a blind person walking alone, but a city pavement is not one of them; and a residential street cannot be different from any other. The blind people whom we meet must live somewhere, and most of them probably left their homes unaccompanied. It may seem surprising that blind people can avoid ordinary obstacles so well as they do, but we must take account of the facts. There is evidence in this case about the number of blind people in London and it appears from government publications that the proportion in the whole country is near one in five hundred. By no means all are sufficiently skilled or confident to venture out alone, but the number who habitually do so must be very large. I find it quite impossible to say that it is not reasonably foreseeable that a blind person may pass along a particular pavement on a particular day.

> No question can arise in this case of any great difficulty in affording adequate protection for the blind. In considering what is adequate protection again one must have regard to common knowledge. One is entitled to expect of a blind person a high degree of skill and care because none but the most foolhardy would venture to go out alone without having that skill and exercising that care. We know that in fact blind people do safely avoid all ordinary obstacles on pavements; there can be no question of padding lamp posts as was suggested in one case. A moment's reflection, however, shows that a low obstacle in an unusual place is a grave danger; on the other hand it is clear from the evidence in this case and also I think from common knowledge that quite a light fence some two feet high is an adequate warning. There would have been no difficulty in providing a fence here. . . .

> I can see no justification for laying down any hard and fast rule limiting the classes of persons for whom those interfering with a pavement must make provision. It is said that it is impossible to tell what precautions will be adequate to protect all kinds of

infirm pedestrians or that taking such precautions would be unreasonably difficult or expensive. I think that such fears are exaggerated.

Would the court have concluded that the plaintiff was a foreseeable victim of the defendant's carelessness if: (a) only one in 10,000 people in the general population were blind; (b) the barrier was located on a lightly travelled sidewalk that was extremely steep and winding; or (c) the barrier was going to be used for only 20 minutes until a more suitable barrier was delivered?

Given that the *Canadian Charter of Rights and Freedoms*, Part I of the *Constitution Act, 1982*, being Schedule B to the *Canada Act 1982* (U.K.), 1982, c. 11 and both federal and provincial human rights legislation prohibit discrimination on the basis of disability, what assumptions should be made about the foreseeability of disabled people being present in public? What are the implications of holding that a disabled person is not a foreseeable plaintiff?

11

SPECIAL DUTIES OF CARE: AFFIRMATIVE ACTION

1. Introduction to Special Duties of Care
2. Introduction to Duties of Affirmative Action
3. The Duty to Rescue
4. The Duty to Control the Conduct of Others
5. The Duty to Perform Gratuitous Undertakings

1. Introduction to Special Duties of Care

The previous chapter examined the grounds upon which Canadian courts identify duties of care. In *Cooper v. Hobart*, [2001] 3 S.C.R. 537, the Supreme Court of Canada emphasized the role of policy, both in connection with the notion of proximity under the first branch of the *Anns/Cooper* test and in connection with factors that may, under the second branch of the test, negate or limit a *prima facie* duty of care. The court also stressed the need to address policy considerations on a category-by-category basis. Some types of situations raise special concerns regarding either the relationship between the parties or larger societal interests.

This and the next three chapters address policy considerations that arise in various circumstances. This chapter considers the special duties of care applicable in cases of omission. Chapter 12 considers the special duties that may be owed to rescuers, unborn children, and victims of psychiatric harm, as well as those owed by health care professionals, manufacturers and suppliers of potentially dangerous goods, and barristers. Chapters 13 and 14 consider the special duties of care that may arise in connection with negligent statements and pure economic losses. As you read through these chapters, bear *Cooper v. Hobart* in mind. Ask, in each instance, whether the operative policy factors pertain to the parties' relationship or to larger societal interests.

2. Introduction to Duties of Affirmative Action

The common law has traditionally distinguished between misfeasance (positive acts) and nonfeasance (failures to act). As a general rule, the courts have been willing to impose liability for losses caused by the former, but not by the latter. Granted, duties of affirmative action sometimes were recognized, at least in limited form, if the parties shared a "special relationship" or if the defendant had a contractual or statutory obligation to intervene. In most cases, however, the law merely required the defendant to refrain from interfering with the plaintiff's legal interests. Consequently, while a trespasser who innocently entered a neighbour's land, believing it to be his or her own, was held liable, a person who sat idly by and watched a young child drown was immune from liability.

Although various explanations have been provided for the common law's traditional antipathy to duties of affirmative action, many are now of questionable relevance. The early writs did not easily accommodate complaints arising from omissions. And even if they did, the English courts may have been too overburdened with cases of misfeasance to take much interest in nonfeasance:

> [T]he rough and ready law of the . . . garrison society could not spare the manpower in a world of hot blood and quick death, to punish the subtler harms arising by omissions. (Frankel, "Criminal Omissions: A Legal Microcosm" (1965) 11 Wayne L. Rev. 367 at 371)

Moreover, a duty to rescue was thought to sit uneasily with the English character:

> Self direction or personal autonomy is a mark of the English race. The Englishman, as opposed to one of Latin lineage, does not so easily coalesce with the mass. He distinctly wishes to live his own life, make his own contacts, or as he frequently says, "muddle through" in his own way. (Hope, "Officiousness" (1929) 15 Corn. L.Q. 25 at 29)

Likewise, the rise of capitalism and *laissez-faire* ideologies further fostered the belief that "the struggle of selfish individuals automatically produces the common good of all": Rudzinski, "The Duty to rescue: A Comparative Analysis" in Ratcliffe, ed., *The Good Samaritan and the Law* (1981) at 120. During the 20th century, positive duties seemed to some to constitute "an exalted form of socialism": Minor, "Moral Obligations as a Basis of Liability" (1923) 9 Va. L. Rev. 421 at 422. Along similar lines, it was stressed that positive obligations are necessarily more intrusive than negative duties. A person performing a required act cannot simultaneously do anything else. In contrast, a person who is refraining from committing a prohibited act remains free to do everything else. Finally, especially in more recent times, it has been suggested that it is very difficult, as a practical matter, to define the scope of positive obligations. If a general duty to rescue were recognized, it would be necessary, for instance, to determine how much danger and inconvenience a bystander is required to withstand.

As this chapter and the next illustrate, whatever the explanation, the courts still cling to the general principle that there is no liability in negligence for nonfeasance. Beginning in the late 20th century, however, the scope of liability increased noticeably as courts began to recognize various exceptions to that general rule. The end result is a complex patchwork of specialized principles governing individual categories of cases. The general principle has been preserved, but it applies in fewer and fewer circumstances. Further, the full effect of *Cooper v. Hobart* has yet to be determined in this area of the law.

In this chapter, we examine the expansion of positive duties of care in three situations: (i) the duty to rescue, (ii) the duty to control the conduct of third parties, and (iii) the duty to fulfil gratuitous undertakings.

NOTES AND QUESTIONS

1. The distinction between misfeasance and nonfeasance is often difficult to draw. F. Bohlen suggested that the essential difference is that misfeasance involves worsening the plaintiff's position, whereas nonfeasance involves failing to improve

it: "The Moral Duty to Aid Others as a Basis of Tort Liability" (1908) 56 U. Pa. L. Rev. 217 at 220. Although Bohlen's distinction is widely cited and accepted, both courts and academics have continued to find the issue troublesome. See for example E. Weinrib, who describes Bohlen's distinction as "skeletal" and states that its incompleteness undermines its possible usefulness: "The Case for a Duty to Rescue" (1980) 90 Yale L.J. 247 at 251-58. See also Wright, "Negligent 'Acts or Omissions'" (1941) 19 Can. Bar Rev. 465; McNiece & Thornton, "Affirmative Duties in Tort" (1948) 58 Yale L.J. 1272; and Smith, *Liability in Negligence* (1984) at 29-47.

2. The Supreme Court of Canada used the concept of nonfeasance to justify its decision not to impose liability on social hosts for injuries caused by their intoxicated guests in *Childs v. Desormeaux*, [2006] 1 S.C.R. 643. McLachlin C.J.C., writing for the court, characterized the social hosts' actions as a failure to prevent harm from occurring, and found (at para. 39) that there is no duty to prevent harm unless there is a special relationship between the parties: "[The law] permits third parties witnessing risk to decide not to become rescuers or otherwise intervene. It is only when these third parties have a special relationship to the person in danger or a material role in the creation or management of the risk that the law may impinge on autonomy."

3. The House of Lords discussed nonfeasance at some length in *Stovin v. Wise*, [1996] 3 All E.R. 801 (H.L.). Lord Nicholls affirmed the traditional distinction between misfeasance and nonfeasance:

> The distinction is based on a recognition that it is one matter to require a person to take care if he embarks on a course of conduct which may harm others. He must take care not to create a risk of danger. It is another matter to require a person, who is doing nothing, to take positive action to protect others from harm for which he was not responsible, and to hold him liable in damages if he fails to do so. . . .

> There must be some special justification for imposing an obligation of this character. Compulsory altruism needs more justification than an obligation not to create dangers to others when acting for one's own purposes.

4. For a review of liability for nonfeasance, see Little, "Erosion of No-Duty Negligence Rules in England, the United States, and Common Law Commonwealth Nations" (1983) 20 Hous. L. Rev. 959; Markesinis, "Negligence, Nuisance and Affirmative Duties of Action" (1989) 105 L.Q.R. 104; Rowe & Silver, "The Jurisprudence of Action and Inaction in the Law of Tort: Solving the Puzzle of Nonfeasance and Misfeasance from the Fifteenth Through the Twentieth Centuries (1995) 33 Duq. L. Rev. 807; and Benson, "Misfeasance as an Organizing Normative Idea in Private Law" (2010) 60:3 U.T.L.J. 731. See also *Restatement (Third) of Torts: Liability for Physical and Emotional Harm* (2012) at §§37-43; Schwartz & Appel, "Reshaping the Traditional Limits of Affirmative Duties Under the Third Restatement of Torts" (2011) 44 John Marshall L. Rev. 319; and Quill, "Affirmative Duties of Care in the Common Law" (2011) 2 J.E.T.L. 151.

Does the distinction between misfeasance and nonfeasance mask underlying moral judgments? Consider the withdrawal of life-sustaining treatment for terminally ill patients. Is this an act or an omission? See *Airedale Hospital Trustees v. Bland*, [1993] A.C. 789 (H.L.); and Elliott & Ormerod, "Acts and Omissions — A Distinction without a Defence?" (2008) 39 Cambrian L. Rev. 40.

3. The Duty to Rescue

OSTERLIND v. HILL
160 N.E. 301 (Mass. S.C. 1928)

. . .

BRALEY J.:—This is an action of tort, brought by the plaintiff as administrator of the estate of Albert T. Osterlind to recover damages for the conscious suffering and death of his intestate. [The plaintiff] alleges that, on or about July 4, 1925, the defendant was engaged in the business of letting for hire pleasure boats and canoes to be used on Lake Quannapowitt in the town of Wakefield; that it was the duty of the defendant to have a reasonable regard for the safety of the persons to whom he let boats and canoes; that the defendant, in the early morning of July 4, 1925, in willful, wanton, or reckless disregard of the natural and probable consequences, let for hire, to the intestate and one Ryan, a frail and dangerous canoe, well knowing that the intestate and Ryan were then intoxicated, and were then manifestly unfit to go upon the lake in the canoe; that, in consequence of the defendant's willful, wanton, or reckless disregard of his duties, the intestate and Ryan went out in the canoe, which shortly afterwards was overturned and the intestate, after hanging to it for approximately one-half hour, and making loud calls for assistance, which calls the defendant heard and utterly ignored, was obliged to release his hold, and was drowned; that in consequence of the defendant's willful, wanton, or reckless conduct the intestate endured great conscious mental anguish and great conscious physical suffering from suffocation and drowning.

. . .

The declaration must set forth facts which, if proved, establish the breach of a legal duty owed by the defendant to the intestate. . . . The plaintiff relies on *Black v. New York, New Haven & Hartford Railroad*, 193 Mass. 448. . ., as establishing such a duty on the part of the defendant. In that case the jury would have been justified in finding that the plaintiff was "so intoxicated as to be incapable of standing or walking or caring for himself in any way." There was testimony to the effect that, "when he fell, he did not seize hold of anything, his arms were at his side." The defendant's employees placed a helpless man, a man impotent to protect himself, in a dangerous position.

In the case at bar, however, it is alleged in every count of the original and amended declaration that after the canoe was overturned the intestate hung to the canoe for approximately one-half hour and made loud calls for assistance. On the facts stated in the declaration the intestate was not in a helpless condition. He was able to take steps to protect himself. The defendant violated no legal duty in renting the canoe to a man in the condition of the intestate. The allegation appearing in each count of the amended declaration that the intestate was incapacitated to enter into any valid contract states merely a legal conclusion. . . . The allegations, therefore, in the counts of the amended declaration to the effect that the intestate was incapable of exercising any care for his own safety is controlled by the allegations in the same counts that he hung to the side of the canoe for approximately one-half hour, calling for assistance.

In view of the absence of any duty to refrain from renting a canoe to a person in the condition of the intestate, the allegations of involuntary intoxication relating as they do to the issues of contributory negligence become immaterial. The allegations of willful, wanton or reckless conduct also add nothing to the plaintiff's case. The failure of the defendant to respond to the intestate's outcries is immaterial. No legal right of the intestate was infringed. . . . The allegation common to both declarations that the canoe was "frail and dangerous" appears to be a general characterization of canoes. It is not alleged that the canoe was out of repair and unsafe.

It follows that the order sustaining each demurrer is affirmed.

NOTES AND QUESTIONS

1. The plaintiff's action was based on two allegations of negligence, each of which arose from a distinct duty of affirmative action. How would you characterize these duties?

2. The judge suggested that Hill would have been under a duty of care if the deceased had been helpless when he rented the canoe. Why did the fact that the deceased was helpless once the canoe overturned not give rise to a duty to rescue?

3. Would the case have been decided differently if: (a) the deceased had been a young child, (b) the deceased had drowned within arm's length of the dock because Hill refused to throw him a nearby rope, or (c) Hill had canoed out to rescue the deceased but changed his mind when he arrived at the scene?

4. Assuming that a duty to rescue had been imposed on Hill, how would you define the standard of care? Should the defendant be required to take action which might involve: (a) a risk of personal injury, (b) a risk of property damage, or (c) considerable inconvenience?

5. There are several situations in which the common law now imposes a duty to rescue. Defendants have an obligation to intervene if they innocently or negligently create the plaintiff's perilous situation. See *Oke v. Weide Transport* (1963), 41 D.L.R. (2d) 53 (Man. C.A.). So too, as discussed below, if they deny the plaintiff other opportunities for aid, or induce the plaintiff to rely upon them to the plaintiff's detriment. How do these situations differ from that in *Osterlind*?

See also *Kennedy v. Coe*, 2014 BCSC 120, where the court found that the defendant, who had been assigned as the plaintiff's "ski buddy" during a heli-skiing excursion, did not owe a duty to notify tour guides immediately when the plaintiff went missing. The plaintiff fell into a tree well, was buried in snow and suffocated to death. The court reasoned that there was no proximity between the skiers, as the defendant did not create the risk to the plaintiff, undertake to manage the plaintiff's safety, or worsen the plaintiff's position.

6. The debate regarding the duty to rescue typically arises after high-profile, morally repugnant cases. For example, in 1964, it was reported that the tenants of an apartment complex watched idly and listened for forty minutes as Kitty Genovese, who was being attacked in the street below, called for help. She was eventually murdered by her assailant. See Rosenthal, *Thirty-Eight Witnesses: The Kitty Genovese Case* (1999). While the details of that case now appear to have been over-stated, there

is psychological research suggesting that the more bystanders there are in an emergency, the less likely that one of them will respond. For a discussion of such "crowd inertia" or the "bystander effect," see Radcliffe, "A Duty to Rescue: The Good, the Bad and the Indifferent — The Bystander's Dilemma" (1986) 13 Pepp. L. Rev. 2. For a revisionist account of the Genovese case, see Cook, *Kitty Genovese: The Murder, the Bystanders, and the Crime That Changed America* (2014).

Another notorious case occurred in 1997, when a young girl named Sherrice Iverson was raped and killed in the bathroom of a Las Vegas casino. The murderer was criminally convicted, but the greater controversy surrounded the murderer's friend, David Cash, who watched the attack but did nothing to stop his friend or save the dying girl. The Cash case rejuvenated the duty to rescue debate and prompted some states to take legislative action.

However, empirical data suggest that cases of non-rescue are rare — probably only one or two every year in the United States. In fact, the data indicate that confirmed rescues outnumber non-rescues by a ratio of 740:1, and that for every victim who dies due to non-rescue, there are 70 people who die making rescue attempts: Hyman, "Rescue Without Law: An Empirical Perspective on the Duty to Rescue" (2006) 84 Tex. L. Rev. 653. These data suggest that people are generally altruistic (even foolishly so), and will attempt rescue in the absence of any legal obligation to do so. Given this evidence, is a legal duty to rescue necessary? Do one or two heinous cases justify legislative action?

7. Would a legal duty to rescue change the behaviour of those who are currently non-rescuers? There are many reasons why people fail to rescue: although some people may be morally indifferent to suffering, others fail to respond because of common human emotions — shock, fear, panic, loyalty and guilt. Are such people likely to change their behaviour in response to a legal duty to rescue? Would it be fair to hold them liable for the victim's losses? See Volokh, "Duties to Rescue and the Anticooperative Effects of Law" (1999) 88 Geo. L.J. 105. How likely is it that non-rescuers will be prosecuted under so-called Good Samaritan statutes? Are bystanders likely to implicate each other for failing to rescue?

8. There has been a recent movement to introduce bystander training and encourage bystander interventions in situations involving bullying or campus sexual assault. What are the legal and normative implications of such programs? How do they interact with the common law's continued reluctance to impose a duty to intervene? See Swan, "Bystander Interventions" [2015] Wis. L. Rev. 975, which discusses the competing normative influences of bystander intervention programs and the traditional common law.

9. It has been argued that imposing a duty to rescue would downplay the value of heroism in modern society. If heroic acts were to become the legal standard of reasonableness, then the concept of rescuer as hero — someone who inspires hope and provides an ideal to which we can aspire — would be diminished. See Ashton, "Rescuing the Hero: The Ramifications of Expanding the Duty of Rescue on Society and the Law" (2009) 59 Duke L.J. 69. Do you agree? Would imposing a duty of easy rescue reduce our admiration of those who take great risks or make heroic sacrifices in the course of rescue efforts? Does mandating rescue decrease its social value?

10. The increase in so-called "cyber-bullying" has created a new frontier for potential bystander liability. What unique issues are raised by the online environment? Should there be an obligation to inform teachers or other authorities when someone is being threatened online or is likely to harm himself or herself as a result of cyber-bullying? See Benzmiller, "The Cyber-Samaritans: Exploring Criminal Liability for the 'Innocent' Bystanders of Cyberbullying" (2013) 107 Nw. U.L. Rev. 927.

11. In spite of its arguably limited practical impact, the debate over the duty to rescue has generated much scholarship, cutting to the heart of fundamental tort concepts like the relationship between law and morality, the distinction between acts and omissions, and the appropriate boundaries of the tort of negligence. See generally Ratcliffe, ed., *The Good Samaritan and the Law* (1966); Heyman, "Foundations of the Duty to Rescue" (1994) 47 Vand. L. Rev. 673; Sappideen & Vines, eds., *Fleming's The Law of Torts*, 10th ed. (2011) at 165-68; Ziegler, "Nonfeasance and the Duty to Assist: The American *Seinfeld* Syndrome" (2000) 104 Dick. L. Rev. 525; "Good Samaritan Symposium" (2000) 40 Santa Clara L. Rev. 957-1103; Romohr, "A Right/Duty Perspective on the Legal and Philosophical Foundations of the No-Duty-To-Rescue Rule" (2006) 55 Duke L.J. 1025; and Schwartz & Appel, "Reshaping the Traditional Limits of Affirmative Duties Under the Third Restatement of Torts" (2011) 44:2 Marshall L. Rev. 319.

12. What is the difference between imposing a statutory duty to rescue (punishable by fine or imprisonment) and imposing a duty to rescue in tort? Are potential rescuers more likely to be motivated by the risk of a penal sanction or the risk of a substantial damage award if the victim is catastrophically injured? Which sanction seems more appropriate for cases of non-rescue? How would the "victim" of a non-rescue establish causation?

MATTHEWS v. MACLAREN; HORSLEY v. MACLAREN
(1969), 4 D.L.R. (3d) 557 (Ont. H.C.)

LACOURCIÈRE J.:—These two actions under the *Fatal Accidents Act*, R.S.O. 1960, c. 138, were tried together, and involve the claim of the widows and children respectively of the late Roland Edgar Matthews and the late John Albert Horsley, both of whom lost their lives in a tragedy on Lake Ontario on May 7, 1966. The defendant Kenneth MacLaren was at the material time the owner and operator of an Owens, Empress 30-foot six inch cabin cruiser known as the "Ogopogo" powered by two inboard 100 h.p. engines driving two propellors or twin screws. . . .

On the day of the fatal accident, the late Roland Edgar Matthews and the late John Albert Horsley were gratuitous passengers, or invited guests, of the defendant on this boat, which left Port Credit Yacht Club at approximately 6:30 p.m. for the return voyage to Oakville. The weather at that time was starting to cool and a wind, blowing from the north-west created a light chop on Lake Ontario. The "Ogopogo" with the defendant at the helm was proceeding at a speed of 10 to 12 knots; at that time Matthews, who had looked after the bowline on leaving Port Credit, was still sitting on the port side of the foredeck: another passenger, . . . Richard J. Jones, was in the pilot's cockpit and the other four passengers, *i.e.*, Horsley, one Donald Marck, and the two ladies — Mrs. MacLaren and Mrs. Jones — were in the cabin below. Jones observed Matthews get up and proceed towards the stern along the narrow catwalk on the port side of the boat, holding on to the rail, with his back to the water, and topple over backwards at the level of the windscreen. Jones immediately hollered "Roly's overboard" and the rescue operation began.

The defendant threw the boat controls in the neutral position and on leaning back could see Matthews, floating, with head and shoulders out of the water, some 40 or 50 ft. astern to starboard: he reversed the motors and backed towards Matthews, having pinned the control wheel with his stomach and looking over his shoulder using the throttle to manoeuvre and, according to Jones, swerving a bit, until the man in the water disappeared from his view behind the transom. The defendant then shut the engines down completely to drift towards Matthews: meanwhile, Jones had gone to the stern and thrown a life ring which landed some 10 ft. in front of Matthews, and as the boat got closer Donald Marck, also at the stern, was attempting to hook Matthews with a six-foot pikepole. Matthews was still floating — arms outward with his eyes open and staring, apparently unconscious. The motors had been shut down when the stern of the boat got to within four or five feet of Matthews, who could not be hooked when the boat was blown or drifted away a distance of 10 to 20 ft. The defendant MacLaren started the engines and reversed again towards Matthews. Meanwhile, Jones had thrown a second life-jacket which had fallen on top of Matthews or under his nose.

By then some three or four minutes had elapsed since Matthews had fallen overboard and the situation was getting desperate. Horsley from the stern took off his shoes and trousers and yelling "my friend, my friend!" dived in while the boat was moving, and surfaced some 10 ft. away from Matthews. Mrs. Jones then noticed Matthews' body fall forward — face and head in the water: she then courageously jumped in, one foot away, to hold his head up but Matthews had gone under the starboard quarter and could not be helped. Jones, seeing his wife in the water ran up to the defendant and took over the controls without argument, swung the boat around and approached his wife "bow on", getting her on the starboard side. MacLaren and Marck grabbed her arms and pulled her out of the water. MacLaren reassumed the controls and shortly thereafter Horsley was picked up, but could not be resuscitated and was pronounced dead later at Port Credit.

Although the outside temperature had been warm and pleasant in the afternoon, with a temperature of approximately 65°, the water was extremely cold: the only person who survived the immersion, Jean Jones, described how she felt paralysed, as if in a vat of ice cubes. The witness Burtershaw, chief operator of the Waterworks Department of the Oakville Public Utilities, gave evidence that the recorded water temperature at the intake pipe some 2,400 ft. from shore was a constant 39° on that day, with surface temperature probably five degrees higher.

The pathologist, Dr. D. F. Brunsdon, who examined Horsley's body, ascribed the cause of death to cardiac failure resulting from either sudden shock on immersion or from prolonged immersion in cold water. In the latter case, unconsciousness would precede death. It was his opinion after conducting the autopsy that death was probably due to sudden shock as a result of immersion, in which case death would be immediate or extremely quick; the deceased had been perfectly healthy before and there was no evidence of heart or any other disease. The body of Matthews was never recovered and the cause of his death remains undetermined.

Because of the allegation made in both actions (among other items of negligence) that the defendant was operating his motor boat while his ability to do so was impaired by alcohol, I will summarize the events leading up to the tragic occurrence.

The defendant, then a 51-year-old steel salesman, had earlier in the morning one pint of beer with a sandwich at the Oakville Club, later a hamburger and one beer at the Oakville Powerboat Club with Mr. and Mrs. Jones; the outing was improvised, and a case of 24 pints of beer put on board: the defendant and each passenger had one pint of beer on the trip to Port Credit. The arrival of the "Ogopogo" at the Port Credit Club, and the docking process there was described in great detail by various witnesses because of the incident of damage to the stanchion, a vertical member of the stainless steel pulpit, on the stern of the "Stormalong" which was slightly damaged when hit by the bow of the "Ogopogo". I am satisfied that this was a mere mishap caused by the temporary failure of one engine of the "Ogopogo", which can in no way reflect on the ability of the defendant who was at the helm.

The defendant, as captain of the first boat — so he claimed — to dock at the Port Credit Yacht Club that season, arrived in jovial and exuberant mood and ordered champagne for all present. The steward of the yacht club relates that approximately forty people in the club shared four large (32 oz.) bottles of champagne. The MacLaren party was in the club between 3:30 and 6:30. The defendant admits having consumed two glasses of champagne during that period, intermingling freely with the Port Credit members, many of whom were friends. There is no evidence that the defendant had any of the other drinks being ordered and served that afternoon. After the accident, a glass of amber coloured liquid, presumably containing whisky, was found in a glass-holder near the controls of the cockpit. The defendant disclaims any knowledge of its contents and says that it must have been pressed upon him by friends upon leaving the dock of the Port Credit Yacht Club and forgotten and untouched by him.

Liability:
1. *Re Matthews' Claim*

Notwithstanding the allegations pleaded that the defendant failed to ensure the safety of his passengers and particularly of the deceased Matthews by having them wear life-preservers on board, I am satisfied that in the circumstances this does not constitute actionable negligence. The only negligence argued here relates to the defendant's condition and to his conduct following Matthews' fall into the water. The first question therefore is whether there existed a legal duty on the part of the defendant to come to the rescue of a passenger who fell overboard by reason of his own misfortune or carelessness, and without any negligence on the part of the defendant or any person for whom the defendant would be vicariously responsible. This question, strictly a determination of law for the Court and not a question of fact for the jury, was repeatedly answered in the negative in the 19th century decisions (based on the distinction between "misfeasance" and "nonfeasance") illustrated in Ontario by the 1913 decision of the Ontario Court of Appeal in *Vanvalkenburg v. Northern Navigation Co.* (1913), . . . 19 D.L.R. 649. In that case, a seaman employed on a steamboat had fallen overboard by his own carelessness, and drowned: Mulock C.J.Ex., speaking for the Appellate Division said at . . . p. 652 D.L.R.:

> The question then arises whether the defendants were guilty of any actionable negligence in not using all reasonable means in order to rescue the drowning man.

Undoubtedly such is one's moral duty, but what legal duty did the defendants owe to the deceased to rescue him, if possible, from his position of danger, brought about, not by their, but his own, negligence?

And at . . . p. 653 D.L.R.:

His voluntary act in thus putting himself in a position of danger, from the fatal consequences of which, unfortunately, there was no escape except through the defendants' intervention, could not create a legal obligation on the defendants' part to stop the ship or adopt other means to save the deceased.

This decision was followed by an amendment to the *Canada Shipping Act*, R.S.C. 1927, c. 186, enacting [1934, c. 44, s. 519] what is now s. 526 [R.S.C. 1952, c. 29]:

526(1) The master or person in charge of a vessel shall, so far as he can do so without serious danger to his own vessel, her crew and passengers, if any, render assistance to every person, even if that person be a subject of a foreign state at war with her Majesty, who is found at sea and in danger of being lost, and if he fails to do so he is liable to a fine not exceeding one thousand dollars.

The section may not be applicable to or refer to the assistance to a passenger who falls overboard, but the shocking reluctance of the common law to recognize as a legal duty the moral obligation to assist a fellow human being in this predicament has been overcome in cases where a special relation exists, such as that of a carrier to a passenger in peril overboard, by thinly disguising the moral obligation as an "implied contract": See *Prosser on Torts*, 3rd ed., c. 10, p. 336 under the heading "Duty to Aid One in Peril"; *Fleming on Torts*, 2nd ed., p. 166; *Salmond on Torts*, 14th ed., p. 57.

. . .

It is still in the modern law of negligence that, there is no general duty to come to the rescue of a person who finds himself in peril from a source completely unrelated to the defendant, even where little risk or effort would be involved in assisting: thus a person on a dock can with legal impunity ignore the call for help of a drowning person, even refusing to throw a life ring. The law leaves the remedy to a person's conscience.

There is, however, in the words of Fleming, *ibid.*, at p. 148, ". . . strong support for a duty of affirmative care, including aid and rescue, incidental to certain special relations, like that of employer and employee, carrier and passenger, and occupier and his lawful visitors."

Extending the *quasi-contractual* duty of a carrier to his passenger in peril, it seems to me that the relation between the master of a pleasure boat and his invited guest should also require a legal duty to aid and rescue: Parliament reflecting the conscience of the community has seen fit to impose on the master a duty to render assistance to any stranger, including an enemy alien "found at sea and in danger of being lost" (s. 526, *Canada Shipping Act*); the common law can be no less solicitous for the safety of an invited guest and must impose upon the master the duty to attempt a rescue, when this can be done without imperilling the safety of the vessel, her crew and passengers. The common law must keep pace with the demands and expectations of a civilized community, the sense of social obligation, and brand as tortious negligence the failure to help a man overboard in accordance with the universal custom of the sea.

In any event, if the defendant, as he did here, affirmatively undertakes the rescue operation, he is by law regarded as assuming a duty to act, and will thereafter be liable for his negligence: *Prosser on Torts* (1941), pp. 194-5, puts it this way:

> But further, if the defendant attempts to aid him, and takes control of the situation, he is regarded as entering voluntarily into a relation of responsibility, and hence assuming a duty. Thereafter he will be liable for any failure to use reasonable care in dealing with him, until the emergency has ended, and particularly if he abandons him in a position of danger.

Having found a legal duty to rescue, or a voluntary assumption of duty, the next question is, what is the standard of conduct applicable in the performance of such duty? Bearing in mind that the man in the street would not have any knowledge of a sea rescue operation, the test here is: what would the reasonable boat operator do in the circumstances, attributing to such person the reasonable skill and experience required of the master of a cabin cruiser who is responsible for the safety and rescue of his passengers?

Expert witnesses were called on behalf of the plaintiffs to assist the Court in setting out what such ordinary, prudent, reasonable boat operator would have done in the circumstances. . . . These [experts] agree that there are no statutory regulations or guidelines covering the rescue procedure in a "man overboard" situation, and that none is mentioned in the well-known Canadian booklet "Safety Afloat". This situation, according to them, is a common emergency calling for the common sense of every prudent seaman who should be prepared to react quickly and instinctively, so to speak automatically.

The following should be the procedure followed: having ascertained on which side the man fell, the master first turns his boat towards the same side to clear the propellers and leaves the engine in neutral unless the man overboard is astern and in no danger from them. A life ring is cast, and the master then turns around to approach the man against the wind, allowing him to come on the leeward side where passengers or crewmen can grasp him and haul him in at the lowest point of the boat. The maximum time involved would be one to two minutes or slightly more. Both experts emphasized many reasons why the procedure of reversing the engines and backing should never be adopted, unless in a confined area where the boat cannot be turned around: in addition to loss of control and manoeuvrability, there is the impossibility of keeping sight of the man astern when approaching, the danger of the propellers, and complete loss of control, at the mercy of wind and wave, on shutting down the engines. In the opinion of [one of the experts], the bearing down stern first here adopted by the defendant was the sign of an incompetent operator: the average prudent owner of a 30-foot boat according to both experts should be competent in the rescue procedure described, and if not should not undertake to operate his boat. It is the procedure taught to students, and one in fact known by the defendant and practised by him on many previous occasions.

I can only conclude that the defendant's adoption of the wrong procedure in the circumstances was negligent, being a failure to exercise the reasonable care that the ordinary, prudent, reasonable operator would have shown in effecting the "man overboard" rescue. The defendant in his evidence admitted that he made what he described as an error of judgment and did not attempt to justify the rescue procedure adopted.

Detective Sergeant John Brooks. . ., who had ample opportunity to observe the defendant at the yacht club, and at the Police Station after the accident, formed the opinion that MacLaren's ability to drive an automobile or operate a vessel was impaired by alcohol, and he would have recommended the laying of criminal charges to the Crown Attorney. The admitted consumption by the defendant and the necessary inferences from surrounding circumstances, plus the extraordinary conduct of the defendant during the rescue attempt, force me to the conclusion that the defendant was unable to exercise proper judgment in the emergency created because of his excessive consumption of alcohol.

It is trite law that liability does not follow a finding of negligence, even where there exists a legally recognized duty, unless the defendant's conduct is the effective cause of the loss.

. . .

In the present case the burden is on the plaintiff to prove by a preponderance of evidence that the defendant's negligence was the effective cause of Matthews' death. Obviously the defendant is not responsible for Matthews' fall overboard. There is no evidence in the present case that Matthews was ever alive after falling in the water: all witnesses agree that he was motionless and staring. Bearing in mind that Horsley, a younger man than Matthews, in the opinion of the pathologist probably died of shock immediately or shortly after his immersion, it is reasonable to think that Matthews, 16 years older, did not survive longer, and after he hit the water there never was a sign of life or consciousness. It was impossible in the present case to discharge this burden by a pathologist's report; in the case of a missing body, witnesses' evidence of some struggle or sign of life on the part of the deceased during rescue operations would be required. I am reluctantly forced to the conclusion that, on the balance of probabilities, it has not been shown that Matthews' life could have been saved. The defendant's negligence therefore was not the cause of Matthews' death and there can be no liability.

[Lacourcière J.'s discussion of the action arising from Horsley's death is omitted. It was ultimately resolved by the Supreme Court of Canada on different grounds than Matthews' claim. An extract from that decision is in the next chapter.]

NOTES AND QUESTIONS

1. What was the basis on which Lacourcière J. found that MacLaren was under a duty to rescue Matthews? How would you reconcile this result with the decision in *Vanvalkenburg v. Northern Navigation Co.* (1913), 19 D.L.R. 649 (Ont. C.A.)?

2. Why did Lacourcière J. refer to the *Canada Shipping Act*, R.S.C. 1952, c. 29, s. 526(1)?

3. What standard of care was MacLaren required to meet in rescuing Matthews? What factual evidence did Lacourcière J. rely on in concluding that MacLaren breached this standard?

4. Would the result have been different if the burden had been on MacLaren to prove that his negligence did not cause Matthews' death? For a critical analysis of causation in rescue cases, see Benditt, "Liability for Failing to Rescue" (1982) 1 Law & Phil. 391 at 396-400.

5. What is the *ratio decidendi* of Lacourcière J.'s judgment?

6. In the *Horsley* appeal, both the majority and dissent in the Supreme Court of Canada held that *Vanvalkenburg* was no longer good law and that a special relationship giving rise to a common law duty to rescue exists between boat captains and their gratuitous passengers. The majority held that the trial judge erred in finding that MacLaren had breached the standard of care, whereas the dissent agreed with Lacourcière J. on this issue. See *Horsley v. MacLaren* (1971), 22 D.L.R. (3d) 545 (S.C.C.). For a review of this case, see Binchy, "The Good Samaritan at the Crossroads: A Canadian Signpost" (1974) 25 N.I.L.Q. 147.

7. As illustrated by the Supreme Court of Canada's decision, the courts have greatly expanded the common law duty to rescue in recent years by recognizing new special relationships in which they will impose an affirmative duty to act. What characteristics should the courts consider in determining whether to recognize a special relationship — control, reliance, expertise, or some other factor? Should the relationship that existed between the deceased and the defendant in *Osterlind v. Hill* have been considered a special relationship? See *Pridgen v. Boston Housing Authority*, 308 N.E. 2d 467 (S.C. Mass. 1974). On the expansion of situations involving a duty to rescue in the United States, see Groninger, "No Duty to Rescue: Can Americans Really Leave a Victim Lying in the Street? What Is Left of the American Rule, and Will It Survive Unabated?" (1998-99) 26 Pepp. L. Rev. 353.

8. Should a physician, other health professional, or off-duty police officer or firefighter have any special duty to rescue and render aid in an emergency or at the scene of an accident? See McCabe, "Police Officers' Duty to Rescue or Aid: Are They Only Good Samaritans?" (1984) 72 Cal. L. Rev. 661; Picard & Robertson, *Legal Liability of Doctors And Hospitals In Canada*, 5th ed. (2017) at 276-79; Howie, Howie & McMullen, "To Assist or Not Assist: Good Samaritan Considerations for Nurse Practitioners" (2012) 8 J. for Nurse Practitioners 688; and Laur, "Liabilities of Doctors on Aircraft" (2013) 81 Med. Leg. J. 31.

In *Stevenson v. Clearview Riverside Resort*, 2000 CarswellOnt 4888 (S.C.J.) (WL Can), Wilson J. dismissed a claim against an off-duty ambulance attendant for failing to advise civilian rescuers on the proper method of stabilizing the victim of a suspected spinal injury. The plaintiff had dived into shallow water and was floating face down. One of his friends entered the water to turn him over so that he would not drown. She and another friend then pulled the plaintiff from the water, possibly causing further damage to his spine. The defendant off-duty ambulance attendant observed the scene, but did not advise the friends that the plaintiff should have been left in the water once it was clear that he could breathe. Wilson J. concluded that there was no special relationship between an off-duty ambulance attendant and a party requiring assistance. At the time, she was simply a private party who had no duty to assist in the rescue.

9. Should physicians have a special duty to respond to a request for urgent medical assistance from one of their regular patients? The early cases suggest not, but the courts have now recognized that health professionals cannot "abandon a patient." Accordingly, a doctor cannot discontinue care without making adequate arrangements for the patient's ongoing medical treatment. Does this principle address the issue of responding to an urgent request for assistance? See generally *Smith*

v. Rae (1919), 51 D.L.R. 323 (Ont. C.A.); Picard & Robertson, *supra* at 10-13; and Williams, "Medical Samaritans: Is There a Duty to Treat" (2001) 21 O.J.L.S. 393. See also *Conseil pour la protection des maladies c. Fédération des médecins specialists (Québec)*, 2014 QCCA 459.

In *Lowns v. Woods* (1996) Aust. Torts Rep. 81 (N.S.W.C.A.), a doctor was held to owe a duty of care to leave his office and render assistance to the plaintiff, who was suffering a severe and prolonged epileptic seizure several hundred metres away. The court emphasized that legislation in New South Wales imposed a clear ethical obligation on doctors to respond to requests for assistance in emergencies. See Haberfield, "*Lowns v. Woods* and the Duty to Rescue" (1998) 6 Tort L. Rev. 56.

10. In *Kent v. Griffiths*, [2000] 2 W.L.R. 1158 (C.A.), the plaintiff suffered an asthma attack in her home. A call was placed to the English equivalent of 911. The defendant, which operated the ambulance service, indicated that it would provide help immediately. Nevertheless, 40 minutes passed before the ambulance arrived at the plaintiff's home. Because of that unreasonable delay, the plaintiff suffered respiratory arrest. She sued the defendant in negligence. The Court of Appeal cautiously held that a duty of care arose in the circumstances. In reaching that conclusion, it stressed that: (i) the ambulance service was part of the health service, and therefore was more akin to a hospital than to a police or firefighting service, (ii) there was, on the facts, no conflict between the plaintiff's interests and the interests of the larger public, and (iii) there was, on the facts, no question of resource allocation. See also *Cragg v. Tone* (2006), 41 C.C.L.T. (3d) 13 (B.C.S.C.), rev'd (2007), 245 B.C.A.C. 302 (C.A.).

11. Several countries have enacted broad criminal legislation which imposes a general duty on members of the public to stop and render aid in emergency situations. See Rudzinski, "The Duty to Rescue: A Comparative Analysis" in Radcliffe, ed., *The Good Samaritan and the Law* (1966) 91; Codoppi, "Failure to Rescue and the Continental Criminal Law" in Menlowe & McCall Smith, eds., *The Duty to Rescue* (1993) 93; McInnes, "The Question of a Duty to Rescue in Canadian Tort Law: An Answer from France" (1990) 13 Dal. L.J. 85; Vranken, "Duty to Rescue in Civil Law and Common Law" (1998) I.C.L.Q. 934; Tomlinson, "The French Experience with Duty to Rescue: A Dubious Case for Criminal Enforcement" (2000) 20 N.Y.L. Sch. J. Int'l & Comp. L. 451; and Schiff, "Samaritans: Good, Bad and Ugly: A Comparative Law Analysis" (2005) 11 Roger Williams U.L. Rev. 77.

In contrast, the *Criminal Code*, R.S.C. 1985, c. C-46, contains only narrow provisions that require an individual to stop and render aid. First, s. 129(b) requires an individual, unless he or she has a reasonable excuse, to comply with an officer's request for assistance in making an arrest or preserving the peace. Second, except in unusual circumstances, s. 252 requires a driver who is involved in an accident to stop and offer assistance if a person is injured. Some of the provincial highway traffic acts contain comparable provisions. See the Law Reform Commission of Canada, *Omissions, Negligence and Endangering (Working Paper 46)* (1985).

12. Québec's *Charter of Human Rights and Freedoms*, R.S.Q. 1977 c. C-12, s. 2 provides that anyone who is aware of another's peril and is able to assist without risk to himself or herself has a duty to do so. For a successful action to vindicate a breach of this statutory duty, see *Gaudreault c. Drapeau* (1987), 45 C.C.L.T. 202 (C.S. Qc.), where the plaintiff was awarded both compensatory and punitive damages.

13. There are several alternative means of encouraging rescue. Legislation has been enacted in some jurisdictions to provide rescuers with partial immunity from civil proceedings or a statutory right to compensation. See for example the *Volunteer Services Act*, R.S.N.S. 1989, c. 497; the *Compensation for Victims of Crime Act*, R.S.O. 1990, c. C.24, s. 5; *Good Samaritan Act, 2001*, S.O. 2001, c. 2 (excerpted below); and the *Social Action, Responsibility and Heroism Act 2015* (U.K.), c. 3. See also McInnes, "Good Samaritan Statutes: A Summary and Analysis" (1992) 26 U.B.C.L. Rev. 239; and Waisman, "Negligence, Responsibility, and the Clumsy Samaritan: Is there a Fairness Rationale for the Good Samaritan Immunity?" (2013) 29 Ga. St. U.L. Rev 609. In *Stevenson v. Clearview Riverside Resort, supra*, the court applied a version of the "agony of the moment" rule to the friends who pulled the plaintiff out of the water. Given their limited first aid training and the urgent circumstances that they faced, it was not negligent to drag the plaintiff from the water to ensure he was breathing, even if it might cause damage to his spine.

In 2017, Parliament enacted the *Good Samaritan Drug Overdose Act*, S.C. 2017, c. 4, which exempts individuals from criminal prosecution for drug possession where the evidence of such possession was discovered as a result of the individual seeking emergency assistance for a drug overdose to him or herself or another person.

14. In "Waiting for Rescue: An Essay on the Evolution and Incentive Structure of the Law of Affirmative Obligations" (1986) 72 Va. L. Rev. 879, S. Levmore criticizes the existing common law principles because they do not reward those who rescue or punish those who fail to rescue. One author suggests that rewards could be provided by means of restitutionary or salvage awards: McInnes, "Restitution and the Rescue of Life" (1994) 32 Alta. L. Rev. 37; and McInnes, "Life Rescue in Maritime Law" (1994) 25 J. of Maritime L. and Commerce 451. In *Coopersmith c. Air Canada*, 2009 CarswellQue 7235 (C.Q.) (WL Can), the plaintiff was a doctor who was asked to provide medical assistance to a fellow passenger during an international flight. The doctor claimed compensation for his medical services and lost enjoyment of the flight, and was awarded $1,000.

15. For leading articles supporting a legal duty to rescue, see Weinrib, "The Case for a Duty to Rescue" (1980) 90 Yale L.J. 247; Lipkin, "Beyond Good Samaritans and Moral Monsters: An Individualistic Justification of the General Legal Duty to Rescue" (1983) 31 U.C.L.A.L. Rev. 352; Prentice, "Expanding the Duty to Rescue" (1985) 19 Suffolk U.L. Rev. 15; Dingwall & Gillespie, reconsidering the Good Samaritan: A Duty to Rescue?" (2008) 39 Cambrian L. Rev. 26; and Linden, "Toward Tort Liability for Bad Samaritans" (2016) 53:4 Alta. L. Rev. 837.

For a sample of arguments against a duty to rescue, see Epstein, "A Theory of Strict Liability" (1973) 2 J. Legal Stud. 151 at 193-204; Denton, "The Case Against a Duty to Rescue" (1991) 4 C.J.L.J. 101; Franklin & Ploeger, "Of Rescue and Report: Should Tort Law Impose a Duty to Help Endangered Persons or Abused Children?" (2000) 40 Santa Clara L. Rev. 991; Klar & Jefferies, *Tort Law*, 6th ed. (2017) at 230-32; and Scordato, "Understanding the Absence of a Duty to Reasonably Rescue in American Tort Law" (2008) 82 Tul. L. Rev. 1447.

16. Would you favour or oppose the expansion of criminal or civil liability for failure to rescue? What arguments would you make in support of granting rescuers: (a) some form of civil immunity and (b) a statutory right of compensation? Do you think

that the law plays a significant role in encouraging individuals to stop and render aid? Can you suggest additional means of encouraging rescue? See Rosenberg, "The Alternative of Reward and Praise: The Case Against a Duty to Rescue" (1985) 19 Col. J.L. & Soc. Probs. 1. On the behavioural effect of rescue laws, see Brady, "The Duty to Rescue in Tort Law: Implications of Research on Altruism" (1980) 55 Ind. L.J. 551; McInnes, "The Behavioural Implications of Using the Law to Increase the Incidence of Emergency Intervention" (1992) 20 Man. L.J. 656; McInnes, "The Economic Analysis of Rescue Laws" (1992) 21 Man. L.J. 237; Grush, "The Inefficiency of the No-Duty-to-Rescue Rule and a Proposed 'Similar Risk' Alternative" (1998) 146 U. Pa. L. Rev. 881; Kelley, "A Psychological Approach to Understanding the Legal Basis of the No Duty to Rescue Rule" (2000) 14 B.Y.U.J. Pub. L. 271; and Crettez & Deloche, "On the optimality of a duty-to-rescue rule and the cost of wrongful intervention" (2011) Int'l Rev. L. and Econ. 263.

GOOD SAMARITAN ACT, 2001
S.O. 2001, c. 2

Protection from liability

   2. (1) Despite the rules of common law, a person described in subsection (2) who voluntarily and without reasonable expectation of compensation or reward provides the services described in that subsection is not liable for damages that result from the person's negligence in acting or failing to act while providing the services, unless it is established that the damages were caused by the gross negligence of the person.

Persons covered

   (2) Subsection (1) applies to,
   (a)   a health care professional who provides emergency health care services or first aid assistance to a person who is ill, injured or unconscious as a result of an accident or other emergency, if the health care professional does not provide the services or assistance at a hospital or other place having appropriate health care facilities and equipment for that purpose; and
   (b)   an individual, other than a health care professional described in clause (a), who provides emergency first aid assistance to a person who is ill, injured or unconscious as a result of an accident or other emergency, if the individual provides the assistance at the immediate scene of the accident or emergency.

REVIEW PROBLEMS

   1. Analyze whether a duty to rescue will be imposed in the following fact situations:

   (a)   Mike hired a local guide to take him fishing in a canoe. Mike hooked a large carp and stood up in an attempt to land it. The canoe began to rock and Mike, who could not swim, fell into the water.
   (b)   The guide was paddling while Mike fished from the bow. While daydreaming, the guide paddled into a rock, throwing Mike into the water.
   (c)   Mike was clinging to a floating log in the water when the guide paddled to his side and urged him to grab his hand and climb back into the canoe. Releasing

his hold on the log, Mike lunged for the guide's hand, but missed and fell back into the water.

(d) Luke and John were hunting ducks from a row boat in the vicinity when they heard Mike's screams for help. They rowed close to the log and told Mike to stop yelling, because he was scaring away their game.

(e) When the guide realized that he could not rescue Mike with the canoe, he approached some other hunters for help. They agreed and rowed up to Mike as he was slowly slipping from the log. When they came within five feet of Mike, they changed their minds and rowed off in the opposite direction.

4. The Duty to Control the Conduct of Others

This has been one of the most rapidly expanding areas of negligence law during the past 45 years. While it remains true that there is no general duty to control the conduct of another, the courts have recognized a growing number of special relationships in which a duty will be imposed. The duty to control the conduct of intoxicated people, discussed in the next extract, is simply one example.

(a) LIABILITY FOR THE INTOXICATED

CROCKER v. SUNDANCE NORTHWEST RESORTS LTD.
(1988), 51 D.L.R. (4th) 321 (S.C.C.)

WILSON J.:—The principal issue in this appeal is whether the ski resort had a positive duty at law to take certain steps to prevent a visibly intoxicated person from competing in the resort's dangerous "tubing" competition. The resort contends that it had no such duty but, if it did, it adequately discharged it. The appellant Crocker contends that it had such a duty and failed to discharge it.

I. The Facts

The respondent, Sundance Northwest Resorts Ltd. ("Sundance") operates a ski resort. Sundance held a tubing competition in order to promote its resort. This competition involved teams of two people sliding down a mogulled portion of a steep hill in oversized inner tubes. One evening Crocker went skiing at Sundance with a friend. After their skiing they went to a bar at the resort to drink. At the bar a video of the previous year's race was shown. The video showed people being thrown from their inner tubes. Crocker and his friend did not, however, watch much of this video.

Crocker and his friend decided to enter the competition and attempt to win the $200 in prize money. They signed an entry and waiver form and paid the $15 entry fee. The trial Judge found as a fact, however, that Crocker did not read the form and did not appreciate that it was a waiver.

The race was held 2 days later. On the morning of the race Crocker and his friend drank large quantities of their own alcoholic beverages. They also bought alcoholic drinks from the bar at the resort. They were wearing bibs that identified them as "tubing" competitors when they did so.

Crocker and his friend were the winners of their first heat. During the race the two were thrown from their tube and Crocker suffered a cut above his eye. Between the first and second heats Crocker drank two large swallows of brandy offered to him by the driver of a Molson beer van and was sold two more drinks at the bar.

The owner of Sundance, Beals, saw Crocker between the first and second heats. Noting Crocker's condition Beals asked him whether he was in any condition to compete in another heat. Crocker responded that he was. Beals did nothing more to dissuade him.

At the top of the hill Crocker fell down and his inner tube slid down the hill. The competition organizers obtained a new inner tube for him and his friend. Crocker was visibly drunk and Durno, the manager of Sundance, suggested that it would be a good idea if he did not continue in the competition. But Crocker insisted on competing and Durno took no further steps to restrain him.

Crocker and his friend hit a mogul on the way down the hill. The two were flipped out of their inner tube. Crocker injured his neck in the fall and was rendered a quadriplegic. Earlier that afternoon another competitor had been hospitalized for neck injuries sustained during another heat of the race.

Crocker sued Sundance in tort. At trial Sundance was held to be liable for 75 per cent of the damages suffered by Crocker. Crocker was found contributorily negligent.

. . .

III. The Issue

People engage in dangerous sports every day.

In general, when someone is injured in a sporting accident the law does not hold anyone else responsible. The injured person must rely on private insurance and on the public health care system. The broad issue in the present appeal is whether there is something to distinguish the situation here from the run of the mill sports accident. In order to answer this question the Court must address six sub-issues. . . .

1. *Duty of Care*

The common law has generally distinguished between negligent conduct (misfeasance) and failure to take positive steps to protect others from harm (nonfeasance). The early common law was reluctant to recognize affirmative duties to act. Limited exceptions were carved out where the parties were in a special relationship (e.g., parent and child) or where the defendant had a statutory or contractual obligation to intervene. . . .

Canadian Courts have become increasingly willing to expand the number and kind of special relationships to which a positive duty to act attaches.

. . .

[*Jordan House Ltd. v. Menow* (1973), 38 D.L.R. (3d) 105 (S.C.C.)] is the leading Supreme Court authority on the imposition of a duty to take positive action to protect another. In that case the court held that a licensed tavern owed a duty of care to its intoxicated patron, and was liable when that patron was ejected and was struck by a motor vehicle as he stumbled home on a highway. . .

[Laskin J. writing for the majority in *Jordan House*] . . . considered the relationship between the hotel and Menow and concluded that there was a close enough nexus to require the imposition of a duty of care on the hotel. He stated . . . :

The hotel, however, was not in the position of persons in general who see an intoxicated person who appears to be unable to control his steps. It was in an invitor-invitee relationship with Menow as one of its patrons, and it was aware, through its employees, of his intoxicated condition, a condition which, on the findings of the trial judge, it fed in violation of applicable liquor licence and liquor control legislation. There was a probable risk of personal injury to Menow if he was turned out of the hotel to proceed on foot on a much-travelled highway passing in front of the hotel.

. . .

Given the relationship between Menow and the hotel, the hotel operator's knowledge of Menow's propensity to drink and his instruction to his employees not to serve him unless he was accompanied by a responsible person, the fact that Menow was served not only in breach of this instruction but as well in breach of statutory injunctions against serving a patron who was apparently in an intoxicated condition, and the fact that the hotel operator was aware that Menow was intoxicated, the proper conclusion is that the hotel came under a duty to Menow to see that he got home safely by taking him under its charge or putting him under the charge of a responsible person, or to see that he was not turned out alone until he was in a reasonably fit condition to look after himself. There was, in this case, a breach of this duty for which the hotel must respond according to the degree of fault found against it. The harm that ensued was that which was reasonably foreseeable by reason of what the hotel did (in turning Menow out) and failed to do (in not taking preventive measures).

Thus the relationship between the hotel operator and the patron in this case was close enough to justify the imposition of a duty of care. This duty of care required the defendant to take certain positive steps to avert potential calamity.

The general approach taken in *Jordan House* has been applied in a number of cases. Car owners who have permitted or instructed impaired persons to drive their cars have been found liable . . . The common thread running through these cases is that one is under a duty not to place another person in a position where it is foreseeable that that person could suffer injury. The plaintiff's inability to handle the situation in which he or she has been placed — either through youth, intoxication or other incapacity — is an element in determining how foreseeable the injury is. The issue in the present appeal is whether the relationship between Sundance and Crocker gave rise to this kind of duty.

. . .

Sundance set up an inherently dangerous competition in order to promote its resort and improve its financial future. Sundance employees were in charge of the way in which the event was to be conducted. Sundance provided liquor to Crocker during the event and knew of Crocker's inebriated and injured condition before the start of the second heat. Sundance officials were well aware that Crocker's condition heightened the chance of injury. Both Beals and Durno questioned Crocker's ability to continue. It is clearly not open to Sundance to characterize itself as a stranger to Crocker's misfortune. The nexus between Sundance and Crocker is much too close for that. Sundance must accept the responsibility as the promoter of a dangerous sport for taking all reasonable steps to prevent a visibly incapacitated person from participating.

The jurisprudence in this area seems to me to make this conclusion inevitable. When a railway company removes a drunken passenger from one of its trains it owes a duty of care to this passenger to take reasonable steps to see that the passenger does not come to harm: *Dunn v. Dominion Atlantic Railway Co.* [(1920), 52 D.L.R. 149 (S.C.C.)]. Likewise, when a hotel ejects a drunken patron, it owes a duty of care to the patron to take certain steps to ensure that the patron arrives home safely (*Jordan*

House). It would seem a fortiori that when a ski resort establishes a competition in a highly dangerous sport and runs the competition for profit, it owes a duty of care towards visibly intoxicated participants. The risk of calamity in the latter case is even more obvious than in the two preceding cases. I would conclude, therefore, that Sundance was subject to a duty to Crocker to take all reasonable steps to prevent him from entering such a competition. The question that must now be decided is whether Sundance took sufficient steps to discharge that duty.

2. *Standard of Care*

. . .

Numerous steps were open to Sundance to dissuade Crocker from competing. It could, for instance, have disqualified him when it realized he was drunk. This would have been the easiest course to follow. Or it could have tried to prevent him from competing. It certainly did not have to supply him with a fresh tube when he fell down on the slope before the second heat and his tube rolled down to the bottom of the hill! Sundance could have attempted to bring home to Crocker the risk of serious injury in competing while drunk. None of these preventive measures imposed a serious burden on the resort. And yet Sundance did none of them. Sundance officials made mild suggestions that Crocker might not be in any condition to race but this was as far as it went. I agree with the learned trial Judge and with Dubin J.A. dissenting on the Court of Appeal that Sundance failed to meet its standard of care. . . . While it may be acceptable for a ski resort to allow or encourage sober able-bodied individuals to participate in dangerous recreational activities, it is not acceptable for the resort to open its dangerous competitions to persons who are obviously incapacitated. This is, however, what Sundance did when it allowed Crocker to compete. I conclude, therefore, that it failed to meet its standard of care in the circumstances.

3. *Causation*

Sundance strongly urged that, even if it was negligent, its negligence did not cause the injury suffered by Crocker. The argument here is that tubing is inherently dangerous and demands no skill whatsoever. It is thus no more risky to participate in this sport when inebriated than it is to participate in it when sober. Sundance submits, therefore, that Crocker's injury cannot be attributed to his drunkenness. The failure of Sundance to take reasonable steps to prevent Crocker from competing because he was drunk did not cause his injury.

This submission is completely at odds with a finding of fact made at trial.

. . .

4. *Voluntary Assumption of Risk*

The defence of voluntary assumption of risk is based on the moral supposition that no wrong is done to one who consents. By agreeing to assume the risk the plaintiff absolves the defendant of all responsibility for it. . . . Since the volenti defence is a complete bar to recovery and therefore anomalous in an age of apportionment, the Courts have tightly circumscribed its scope. It only applies in situations where the plaintiff has assumed both the physical and the legal risk involved in the activity.

. . .

In the present appeal an attempt could be made to found a volenti defence either on (a) Crocker's voluntary participation in a sport that was obviously dangerous or

(b) the fact that Crocker signed a waiver form 2 days before the competition. I will examine each of these bases in turn.

The first basis can be disposed of in short order. Crocker's participation in the tubing competition could be viewed as an assumption of the physical risks involved. Even this, however, is dubious because of the fact that his mind was clouded by alcohol at the time. It is well-nigh impossible to conclude, however, that he assumed the legal risk involved. Sliding down a hill in an oversized inner tube cannot be viewed as constituting per se a waiver of Crocker's legal rights against Sundance.

The argument that Crocker voluntarily assumed the legal risk of his conduct by signing a combined entry and waiver form is not particularly convincing either. The trial Judge, having heard all the evidence, drew the following conclusion on the issue of the waiver. . . :

> I find that no attempt was made to draw the release provision to Mr. Crocker's attention, that he did not read it, nor in fact, did he know of its existence. Therefore, Sundance had no reasonable grounds for believing that the release truly expressed Mr. Crocker's intention. In fact, in so far as he was signing anything other than an application form, his signing was not his act.

Given this finding of fact, it is difficult to conclude that Crocker voluntarily absolved the resort of legal liability for negligent conduct in permitting him, while intoxicated, to participate in its tubing competition. I would conclude, therefore, that Crocker did not, either by word or conduct, voluntarily assume the legal risk involved in competing. The volenti defence is inapplicable in the present case.

[Wilson J. applied the same analysis to reject the waiver as a contractual defence. She accepted the trial judge's finding that Crocker should be held only 25% contributorily negligent. In the end result, the trial judgment was restored and a new trial was ordered to assess damages.]

NOTES AND QUESTIONS

1. Based on Wilson J.'s judgment, would the Resort have owed Crocker a duty to control his conduct if: (a) he was equally intoxicated, but the Resort had not provided him with any alcohol, or (b) he was sober when allowed to participate in the race? What impact would these factors have on whether the standard of care had been breached?

2. Do you agree with Wilson J.'s analysis of voluntary assumption of risk and contributory negligence? What other steps could the Resort have taken to alert Crocker to the dangers? Would this have changed Wilson J.'s analysis of these issues?

3. *Jordan House*, which is referred to in *Crocker*, generated considerable criticism. In Binchy, "Comment" (1975) 53 Can. Bar Rev. 344, the author was critical of the apportionment of fault, the dismissal of the *volenti* defence and the failure to consider the *ex turpi* defence. See also Scott, "Negligence: Duty of Care" (1974) 6 Ottawa L. Rev. 622. For more recent reviews, see Klar, "Negligence — Reactions Against Alleged Excessive Imposition of Liability — A Turning Point?" (1987) 66 Can. Bar Rev. 159; Solomon, Usprich & Waldock, "Drink, Drive and Sue: Liability for the Intoxicated" (1993) 4 J.M.V.L. 239; McIvor, "Liability in Respect of the Intoxicated" [2001] C.L.J. 109; Dalphond, "Duty of Care and the Supply of Alcohol" in Beaulac,

Pitel & Schulz, eds., *The Joy of Torts* (2002) 97; and Vail, "Host Liquor Liability in Canada" (2009) 36 Adv. Q. 141.

4. The common law duty to control the conduct of the intoxicated person was broadened in a series of cases. In both *Picka v. Porter*, [1980] O.J. No. 252 (C.A.) (QL) and *Schmidt v. Sharpe* (1983), 27 C.C.L.T. 1 (Ont. H.C.), the courts held the alcohol provider liable even though it did not have actual knowledge of the patron's intoxication. In *Hague v. Billings* (1989), 48 C.C.L.T. 192 (H.C.), aff'd (1993), 15 C.C.L.T. (2d) 264 (Ont. C.A.) the Ontario High Court stated that, once the staff realized that Billings was intoxicated and intended to drive, they had a legal duty to take all reasonable steps to stop him. If they failed, they then had a legal duty to call the police. The court also stated that Billings' drinking buddies were equally liable with him for the accident because all three had agreed in advance to go drinking and driving. See *Pizzolon v. Pedrosa* (1988), 46 C.C.L.T. 243 (B.C.S.C.); *Roberts v. 964639 Ontario Ltd.*, [1996] O.J. No. 56 (Gen. Div.) (QL); *Neufeld v. Foster*, 1999 CarswellBC 785 (S.C.) (WL Can); *Laface v. Williams* (2006), 39 C.C.L.T. (3d) 209 (B.C.C.A.); *McIntyre v. Grigg* (2006), 83 O.R. (3d) 161 (C.A.); and *Hansen v. Sulyma*, 2013 BCCA 349.

The duty to control the conduct of intoxicated patrons is not limited to the impaired driving context, but includes other injuries that may be caused by such patrons. For example, in *Donaldson v. John Doe* (2009), 89 B.C.L.R. (4th) 52 (C.A.), the court held that the organizers of an Oktoberfest event owed a duty of care to persons who might be foreseeably injured by intoxicated attendees. The plaintiff in that case suffered facial injuries when an intoxicated man struck him in the face with a souvenir glass that had been distributed to attendees. See also *Turcotte v. Lewis*, 2018 ONCA 359 (concerning liability for a fight that broke out after patrons got off a shuttle service from the defendant bar).

5. The trend toward broadening the scope of alcohol-related liability was somewhat checked by *Stewart v. Pettie*, [1995] 1 S.C.R. 131. While an alcohol provider's duty to prevent foreseeable risks of injury posed by intoxicated patrons was reaffirmed, the Supreme Court of Canada held that serving patrons past the point of intoxication did not, in itself, pose a foreseeable risk. Rather, the court held that there had to be some additional risk factor. Since the intoxicated patron in this case was accompanied by three sober adults, the court held that it was not foreseeable that he would drive. Consequently, the defendant dinner theatre, which had served the intoxicated driver between five and seven double rum and colas, was held not to have breached the standard of care. Given the somewhat convoluted analysis, the unique circumstances, and the fact that the case could have been resolved on the basis of causation, the decision's long-term impact is unclear. See Kostal, "Liability for the Sale of Alcohol: *Stewart v. Pettie*" (1996) 75 Can. Bar Rev. 169.

6. Judicial restraint is also evident in *Calliou Estate (Trustee of) v. Calliou* (2002), 306 A.R. 322 (Q.B.). The defendant hockey team organized and hosted a tournament. In exchange for an entry fee of $350, competing teams were provided with, among other things, beer. A number of people died as a result of an automobile accident that was caused by an intoxicated player. Actions were brought in negligence against the defendant on the basis that it had supplied some of the alcohol that the drunken driver had consumed. The court denied the existence of a duty of care. The judge held that

the facts arose somewhere between the model of a social host and the model of a commercial establishment. He held that, in any event, "the thread running through both the commercial host and the social host cases on the question of duty of care, is a knowledge of a state of intoxication on the part of the guest who drives and injures himself or a third party." On the evidence, however, there is nothing to indicate that the defendant knew, or ought to have known, that the driver was drunk.

7. In *Baumeister v. Drake* (1986), 5 B.C.L.R. (2d) 382 (S.C.), the court applied the liability principles from *Jordan House* to a private social host. The claim against the defendant homeowners was dismissed, but only because they had not provided any alcohol to the intoxicated driver. See also *Broadfoot v. Ontario (Minister of Transportation and Communication)* (1997), 32 O.R. (3d) 361 (Gen. Div.); *Fitkin (Litigation Administrator of) v. Latimer* (1997), 35 O.R. (3d) 464 (C.A.); *Haggarty v. Desmarais* (2000), 5 C.C.L.T. (3d) 38 (B.C.S.C.); *Prevost (Committee of) v. Vetter* (2001), 197 D.L.R. (4th) 292 (B.C.S.C.); and *Dryden v. Campbell Estate* (2001), 11 M.V.R. (4th) 247 (Ont. S.C.J.).

The continued authority of these cases is questionable in light of the Supreme Court of Canada's decision in *Childs v. Desormeaux*, [2006] 1 S.C.R. 643. The defendants hosted a New Year's Eve party at which guests supplied and served their own alcohol. One of the guests was Desmond Desormeaux, who, to the defendants' knowledge, was an alcoholic with several convictions for drunk driving. Although Desormeaux had become obviously and severely intoxicated during the party, the defendants took no steps to dissuade him from driving home. After leaving the defendants' party, Desormeaux caused a crash that left the plaintiff, 18-year-old Zoe Childs, a paraplegic. The plaintiff sued the defendants in negligence.

The trial judge had found that the alleged duty of care owed by social hosts was novel, and applied the *Anns/Cooper* test. He found that a *prima facie* duty of care existed, but was negated for policy reasons. The Court of Appeal for Ontario upheld the result, but on the different basis that there was insufficient proximity on the facts to even establish a *prima facie* duty. The Supreme Court of Canada unanimously agreed. Somewhat curiously, the court decided that allowing guests to become intoxicated in a private residence, and then leave in their vehicles, did not pose a foreseeable risk of harm to other users of the highway. The court also stressed the lack of proximity, distinguishing social hosts from commercial hosts on several bases. First, commercial hosts have a greater ability to monitor alcohol consumption among patrons; second, social hosts are not heavily regulated like those who hold liquor licences; and third, social hosts do not profit from the sale of alcohol. Are these arguments convincing? Would the decision have been different if the hosts actually provided the alcohol to their guests? Or if the plaintiff was also in attendance at the party and was injured by a fellow guest? See *Kim v. Thammavong*, 2007 CarswellOnt 7848 (S.C.J.) (WL Can); *Paquette c. Fédération (La) cie d'assurances du Canada* (2012), 98 C.C.L.T. (3d) 114 (C.S.Q.), aff'd 2014 QCCA 1026; *Ferrier v. Hubbert*, 2015 ONSC 5286; and *Williams v. Richard*, 2018 ONCA 889. In *Sidhu v. Hiebert*, 2011 BCSC 1364, the court noted that *Childs* may be distinguished in situations where the guest's blood-alcohol concentration was so high that his intoxication would be apparent to a casual observer. See also *Richardson v. Sanayhie*, 2010 CarswellOnt 3488 (S.C.J.) (WL Can), which found that a designated driver did not owe a duty of care to prevent his passenger from becoming intoxicated.

See generally Adjin-Tettey, "Social Host Liability: A Logical Extension of Commercial Host Liability?" (2002) 65 Sask. L.R. 515; David, Maroudas & Litchen, "Social Host Liability — A Fresh Approach" (2005) 30 Adv. Q. 457; Kelly, "Before You Host a Party, Read This: Social Host Liability and the Decision in *Childs v. Desormeaux*" (2006) 39 U.B.C.L. Rev. 371; and Malkin & Voon, "Social Hosts' Responsibility for their Intoxicated Guests: Where Courts Fear to Tread" (2007) 15 Torts L.J. 62. For an American perspective, see French, Kaput & Wildman, "Special Project: Social Host Liability for the Negligent Acts of Intoxicated Guests" (1985) 70 Cornell L. Rev. 1958; Sparlin, "Social Host Liability for Guests who Drink and Drive: A Closer Look at the Benefits and the Burdens" (1985-96) 27 Wm. & Mary L. Rev. 583; Dills, "Social host liability for minors and under-age drunk driving accidents" (2010) 29 J. Health Economics 241; and Lewis, "The Legal Implications of BYOB Parties on Social Host Tort Liability" (2015) 48:2 Suffolk U.L. Rev. 487.

8. In some circumstances, the courts have imposed a rigorous duty on employers to control the conduct of employees who may be intoxicated. See *Barrett v. Ministry of Defence*, [1995] 3 All E.R. 87 (C.A.); and *Jacobsen v. Nike Canada Ltd.* (1996), 133 D.L.R. (4th) 377 (B.C.S.C.).

In *Hunt (Litigation Guardian of) v. Sutton Group Incentive Realty Inc.* (2001), 196 D.L.R. (4th) 738 (Ont. S.C.J.), the plaintiff became intoxicated during a Christmas party hosted by the defendant, who was her employer. She attempted to drive herself home from the party. After stopping for two more drinks at a pub, she was severely injured when she lost control of her vehicle on a wintry road. At trial, liability was imposed on both the defendant and the pub (although damages were reduced by 75% on account of the plaintiff's contributory negligence). On the question of a duty of care, the judge said:

> I find that the defendant . . ., as the plaintiff's employer, did . . . owe a duty to the plaintiff, as its employee, to safeguard her from harm. This duty to safeguard her from harm extended beyond the simple duty while she was on his premises. It extended to a duty to make sure that she would not enter into such a state of intoxication while on his premises and on duty so as to interfere with her ability to safely drive home afterwards. This duty was certainly much more evident in the circumstances where the employee was required to travel a substantial distance, at night-time, in the middle of a serious winter storm. [The defendant] ought to have foreseen the dangerous conditions made worse by the intoxicated condition of his employee. He ought to have anticipated the possible harm that could have happened to her and, in fact, taken positive steps to prevent her from driving home.

The Court of Appeal for Ontario ordered a retrial because the trial judge had made several errors, most notably in discharging the jury on the basis that the case was purportedly too complex and had attracted a great deal of publicity: (2002), 215 D.L.R. (4th) 193 (Ont. C.A.). Unfortunately, the appellate court did not squarely address the duty of care issue.

In *John v. Flynn* (2001), 201 D.L.R. (4th) 500 (Ont. C.A.), Shawn Flynn was employed by a company named Eaton Yale. Because he had a severe drinking problem, Flynn had been enrolled in the defendant's "employee assistance program" (EAP) and returned to work under a "last chance agreement" that required him to refrain from drinking on the job. Nevertheless, to the company's knowledge, Flynn continued to abuse alcohol. On the day in question, he drank before reporting to work and during his breaks. At the end of his shift, he drove home without incident, drank more alcohol and then got back into his car. He caused a crash that resulted in injuries to the plaintiffs. The plaintiffs sued Flynn and the defendant company in negligence. The trial judge split responsibility between Flynn and the defendant on a 70%-30% basis. On appeal, the defendant denied that it owed a duty of care to the plaintiff. The Court of Appeal for Ontario agreed. Finlayson J.A. said:

> In my view, the respondents have not established that Eaton Yale owed the Johns a duty of care, which, if breached, could form the foundation of a claim for liability in the circumstances of this case. The fact that Flynn was involved in the EAP . . . and the fact that Eaton Yale was aware that some drinking was occurring on its premises, without more, are not sufficient to establish an expansive duty of care on Eaton Yale to all members of the public who may come into contact with Eaton Yale employees outside the Eaton Yale plant. . . . The trial judge erred in assuming that Eaton Yale, as employer, owed a duty to Flynn, as employee, to protect Flynn from harm, in general, and that this duty of care could be properly extended to hold Eaton Yale liable for all of Flynn's actions following his departure from work. A more thorough examination of the prerequisite issue of duty would have revealed that in the case at bar, there is simply no basis to hold Eaton Yale liable for the loss suffered by the [plaintiffs], given that Eaton Yale was not aware that Flynn was intoxicated on the night in question, did not provide him with alcohol on that night and did not condone his driving while intoxicated, combined with the fact that the accident was not associated with Eaton Yale in any way other than that one of its employees, who had finished his shift for the night, was involved in the crash. The Johns were not within the class of persons to whom a duty of care was owed by Eaton Yale.

What distinction, if any, would you draw between *John v. Flynn* and *Hunt v. Sutton Group*? Should a duty more readily be recognized if alcohol is provided by the employer, rather than by the employee? If a duty of care is recognized as between the employer and the employee, should the employer also necessarily owe a duty of care to anyone injured by the employee?

9. The liquor licence legislation in many jurisdictions, including Manitoba, Nova Scotia, Ontario, and the Northwest Territories, creates a statutory cause of action against those who sell alcohol to a patron past the point of intoxication. Although these provisions differ in scope, they all create a narrower cause of action than that created by the common law. See for example the *Liquor Licence Act*, R.S.O. 1990, c. L.19, s. 39.

10. Courts may be more likely to impose social host liability where the hosts provide alcohol to or facilitate alcohol consumption by minors. See *Wince v. Ball* (1996), 186 A.R. 156 (Q.B.); *Prevost (Committee of) v. Vetter, supra*; and *Dryden v. Campbell Estate, supra*; *Oyagi v. Grossman*, 2007 CarswellOnt 1699 (S.C.J.) (WL Can); *Hamilton v. Kember*, 2008 CarswellOnt 1012 (S.C.J.) (WL Can); and *Wardak v. Froom*, 2017 ONSC 1166. But see the Australian position: *Russell v. Edwards* (2006), 65 N.S.W.L.R. 373 (C.A.).

11. Members of the hospitality industry and private social hosts have long been held liable under principles of occupiers' liability for alcohol-related injuries that occur on their property. See *Lehnert v. Nelson*, [1947] 4 D.L.R. 473 (B.C.S.C.); *Niblock v. Pacific National Exhibition* (1981), 30 B.C.L.R. 20 (S.C.); *Jacobson v. Kinsmen Club of*

Nanaimo (1976), 71 D.L.R. (3d) 227 (B.C.S.C.); *Buehl v. Polar Star Enterprises Inc.* (1989), 72 O.R. (2d) 573 (H.C.); *Murphy v. Little Memphis Cabaret Ltd.*, 1996 CarswellOnt 5170 (Gen. Div.) (WL Can), aff'd (1998), 115 O.A.C. 375 (C.A.); *Iversen v. Purser* (1990), 73 D.L.R. (4th) 33 (B.C.S.C.); *Chretien v. Jensen* (1999), 58 B.C.L.R. (3d) 186 (C.A.); *Taylor v. Allard*, 2010 CarswellOnt 6856 (C.A.) (WL Can); and *Wandy v. River Valley Ventures Inc.*, 2014 SKCA 81.

12. The courts have also held that the owner of a vehicle has a common law duty not to permit an intoxicated person to drive. See *Hempler v. Todd* (1970), 14 D.L.R. (3d) 637 (Man. Q.B.); *Betts v. Sanderson Estate* (1988), 31 B.C.L.R. (2d) 1 (C.A.); and *Hall v. Hebert*, [1993] 2 S.C.R. 159. Should a common law duty of care also be imposed on an owner who lends his or her car to a friend for a week, knowing that the friend has a tendency to drink and drive?

13. Should the police be held civilly liable for failing to detain or otherwise prevent an intoxicated individual from driving? See *Hooey v. Mancini*, [1988] 4 W.W.R. 149 (Man. Q.B.); *Lafleur v. Maryniuk* (1990), 48 B.C.L.R. (2d) 180 (S.C.); *Meraw v. Curl Estate* (1998), 43 C.C.L.T. (2d) 47 (Ont. Gen. Div.); and *Canada (Attorney General) v. Walsh*, 2016 NSCA 60. See also *Mowatt c. Québec (Procureur Général)*, 2011 QCCS 2206, aff'd 2014 QCCA 915, in which police were found liable after they recovered a severely intoxicated man, drove him home, and left him unattended. He subsequently fell and was rendered paraplegic.

14. Given that approximately 40% of all fatal car accidents involve at least one intoxicated driver, and that alcohol is a significant factor in many murders, suicides, drownings, falls, fires, and other serious crimes and accidents, would you favour creating broader common law and statutory duties for those who provide alcohol to others? See Single *et al.*, "Morbidity and Mortality Attributable to Alcohol, Tobacco, and Illicit Drug Use in Canada" (1999) 89 A.J.P.H. 385; Pernanen *et al.*, *Proportions of Crimes Associated with Alcohol and Other Drugs in Canada* (2002); Rehm *et al.*, *The Costs of Substance Abuse in Canada 2002* (2006); Kendall, *Public Health Approach to Alcohol Policy: An Updated Report from the Provincial Health Officer* (2008); Pitel & Solomon, *Estimating the Number and Cost of Impairment-Related Traffic Crashes in Canada: 1999-2010* (2013); and Traffic Injury Research Foundation, *The Alcohol and Drug-Crash Problem in Canada: 2014 Report* (2017).

15. Alcohol-related liability in Canada is generally broader than in other Commonwealth countries, where it is sometimes even difficult to claim against a commercial host. See for example *Munro v. Porthkerry Park Holiday Estates Ltd.* (1984) 81 L.S.G. 1368 (Eng. Q.B.), where an intoxicated patron was ejected from a club at the defendant's cliff-top resort, fell off the cliff and died. His estate's claim against the resort was denied. See also *Joy v. Newell (t/a Copper Room)*, [2000] N.I. 91 (C.A.). But see the English Court of Appeal's decisions in *Brannon v. Airtours plc*, [1999] T.L.R. 73; and *Jebson v. Ministry of Defence*, [2000] 1 W.L.R. 2055, both of which imposed liability on commercial or institutional party organizers after their guests became intoxicated and sustained foreseeable injury. For an overview, see Chamberlain, "Alcohol Provider Liability in Canada and the United Kingdom: Legal and Cultural Influences" (2004) 33 C.L.W.R. 103. The Australian courts have also rejected a duty of care owed by commercial hosts to their patrons, unless there are exceptional circumstances. See *Cole v. South Tweed Heads Rugby League Football Club Limited*

(2004), 217 C.L.R. 469 (H.C.A.); *C.A.L. No. 14 Pty Ltd. v. Motor Accidents Insurance Board; C.A.L. No. 14 Pty Ltd. v. Scott* (2009), 239 C.L.R. 390 (H.C.A.); and *Flanagan v. Houlihan*, [2011] IEHC 105. See also Solomon & Payne, "Alcohol Liability in Canada and Australia: Sell, Serve and be Sued" (1996) 4 Tort L. Rev. 188; Orr & Dale, "Impaired judgments? Alcohol server liability and 'personal responsibility' after *Cole v South Tweed Heads Rugby League Football Club Ltd.*" (2005) 13 Torts L.J. 103; and Kirby, "Of Advocates, Drunks and Other Players: Plain Tales from Australia" (2011) 23 Denning L.J. 47.

16. What liability issues might arise with the decriminalization of the recreational use of cannabis? See Dean, "Through the Haze: Fashioning a Workable Model for Imposing Civil Liability on Marijuana Vendors" (2014) 49:3 Gonz. L. Rev. 611; Fischer *et al.*, "Crude estimates of cannabis-attributable mortality and morbidity in Canada — implications for public health focused intervention priorities" (2016) 38:1 J. Public Health 183; and Berch, "Reefer Madness: How Non-Legalizing States can Revamp Dram Shop Laws to Protect Themselves from Marijuana Spillover from their Legalizing Neighbors" (2017) 58:3 Boston College L. Rev. 863.

(b) OTHER DUTY TO CONTROL SITUATIONS

There are a variety of situations in which one person has the ability to control the actions of another. Generally speaking, that relationship of control is not sufficient to trigger the doctrine of vicarious liability. Consequently, for instance, parents normally are not vicariously liable for torts committed by their children. As discussed in Chapter 3, that is true even in jurisdictions that have enacted "parental responsibility legislation." Parents typically are liable only if, by failing to properly supervise their children, they also failed to fulfill a duty of care that they separately owed to the victims of their children's misconduct.

It is therefore important to understand the situations in which one person will owe a duty of care to another person with respect to the behaviour of a third. The duty of care that arises in connection with the parent and child relationship is the most obvious. A duty similarly may arise in connection with relationships between masters and servants, employers and employees, occupiers and entrants, police/guards and prisoners, and coaches/instructors/supervisors and students.

NOTES AND QUESTIONS

1. For general discussions of the duty to control, see Harper & Kime, "The Duty to Control the Conduct of Another" (1934) 43 Yale L.J. 886; and Hall, "Duty to Protect, Duty to Control and the Duty to Warn" (2003) 82 Can. Bar Rev. 645.

2. A duty of care is imposed on those supervising prisoners to ensure that they do not injure themselves, each other or members of the public. See *Williams v. New Brunswick* (1985), 34 C.C.L.T. 299 (N.B.C.A.) (where a prisoner set a fire that killed 21 inmates in jail); *Funk Estate v. Clapp* (1988), 54 D.L.R. (4th) 512 (B.C.C.A.) (where a prisoner committed suicide); *Smith v. B.C. (A.G.)* (1988), 30 B.C.L.R. (2d) 356 (C.A.) (where one prisoner was beaten by other prisoners in a drunk tank); and *Home Office v. Dorset Yacht Co.*, [1970] A.C. 1004 (H.L.) (where prisoners escaped and damaged the plaintiff's property). See also *S.(J.) v. Clement* (1995), 22 O.R. (3d) 495 (Gen. Div.);

Jerabek c. Accueil Vert-Pré d'Huberdeau (1995), 26 C.C.L.T. (2d) 208 (C.S. Qc.); *Rhora v. Ontario* (2006), 43 C.C.L.T. (3d) 78 (Ont. C.A.); *Wiebe v. Canada (Attorney General)* (2006), 44 C.C.L.T. (3d) 15 (Man. C.A.); and Iftene, Hanson & Manson, "Tort Claims and Canadian Prisoners" (2014) 39 Queen's L.J. 655.

3. Similar principles apply to those responsible for supervising institutionalized mental health patients. See *Univ. Hospital Bd. v. Lepine; Monckton v. Lepine*, [1966] S.C.R. 561; *Villemure v. L'Hôpital Notre-Dame* (1972), [1973] S.C.R. 716; *Wellesley Hospital v. Lawson* (1977), [1978] 1 S.C.R. 893; *Jinks v. Cardwell* (1987), 39 C.C.L.T. 168 (Ont. H.C.), rev'd [1989] O.J. No. 1492 (C.A.) (QL); *Molnar v. Coates* (1991), 5 C.C.L.T. (2d) 236 (B.C.C.A.); and *Roy c. Toxi-Co-Gîtes inc.* (2004), 33 C.C.L.T. (3d) 87 (C.S. Qc.). See also *Shackleton v. Knittle* (1999), 46 C.C.L.T. (2d) 300 (Alta. Q.B.) for a discussion of the duty and standard of care expected of ambulance attendants in transporting patients with mental illnesses. But see *Smorag v. Nadeau Estate* (2008), 61 C.C.L.T. (3d) 305 (Alta. Q.B.), in which the court found that no duty was owed by the guardian of a dependant adult who was living in an extended care facility and who attacked the plaintiff, a staff member. The guardian was not liable for refusing to consent to a recommended increase in the patient's medication, which allegedly would have controlled the patient's violent behaviour.

See *Robson v. Ashworth* (1987), 40 C.C.L.T. 164 (Ont. C.A.); *Mustafic v. Smith* (1988), 55 Man. R. (2d) 188 (C.A.); *Larche v. Ontario* (1990), 75 D.L.R. (4th) 377 (Ont. C.A.); *Wenden v. Trikha* (1991), 8 C.C.L.T. (2d) 138 (Alta. Q.B.), aff'd (1993), 14 C.C.L.T. (2d) 225 (C.A.); *Holan Estate v. Stanton Regional Health Board* (2001), 11 C.C.L.T. (3d) 34 (N.W.T.S.C.); and *Leishman (Legal Guardian of) v. Hoechsmann et al.*, 2016 NWTSC 27, in which health professionals were absolved of liability when non-custodial mentally ill patients were injured, or committed suicide or acts of violence against third parties. But see *Ahmed v. Stefaniu* (2006), 275 D.L.R. (4th) 101 (Ont. C.A.), upholding a jury's decision that a psychiatrist was negligent for changing a patient's status from involuntary to voluntary, after which he left the hospital and ultimately murdered his sister. The duty of care issue was not argued on appeal. See also Simon, "Tort Law: The Duty to Control the Conduct of a Dangerous Person" (1987) 39 U. Fla. L. Rev. 205.

In *Hunter and New England Local Health District v. McKenna*, [2014] HCA 44, a mentally ill man was discharged into the care of a friend so that the friend could drive him to his mother's home (a journey of several days). During the journey, the man killed his friend and himself. The High Court of Australia found that the health authority did not owe a duty of care to the friend because the relevant legislation required that the man be discharged. The court also cited the potential for indeterminate liability.

Should a duty of care be imposed on persons without expertise in psychiatry or psychology? See *Gallant v. Thames Valley District School Board*, 2011 ONSC 869, where the defendant teacher took no action when a student expressed suicidal thoughts in a school essay and later died by suicide. The action by his parents was allowed to proceed. See also Dyer, "Is There a Duty? Limiting College and University Liability for Student Suicide" (2008) 106 Mich. L. Rev. 1379, which discusses two American cases where a duty of care was imposed on non-expert university staff and administrators to prevent student suicide.

In *Stuart v. Kirkland-Veenstra* (2009), 254 A.L.R. 432 (H.C.A.), two police officers came upon a man who was apparently contemplating suicide: he had connected a hose from his exhaust pipe to the interior of his vehicle and was sitting in a parking lot. The officers questioned the man, who indicated he was experiencing marital difficulties and had been thinking of doing "something stupid," but he declined their offers of assistance and removed the hose from his exhaust pipe. The officers believed that the man was acting rationally and was not suffering from a mental illness, and they allowed him to drive away. He committed suicide later that day. In an action commenced by his widow, the High Court of Australia found that the officers did not owe the man a duty of care because they were not in a position to exercise control over him. While the police had legislative power to detain someone they believed to be mentally ill and at risk of suicide, the court found that the officers had not formed that belief in this case. Gummow, Hayne and Heydon JJ. also reasoned that imposing a duty to prevent self-harm would undermine individual autonomy. Do you agree? See Scott, "The Duty of Care Owed by Police to a Person at Risk of Suicide" (2010) 17:1 Psychiatry, Psychology and Law 1.

Finally, in *Irvine v Smith* (2008), 54 C.C.L.T. (3d) 307 (Ont. S.C.J.), the judge held that no duty of care was owed by a practising physician to control his adult son, who was exhibiting erratic behaviour. The son was ultimately struck and killed by the plaintiff's truck, causing the plaintiff to suffer nervous shock. Regardless of his professional expertise, the father did not have a duty to take his son for mental evaluation, and the plaintiff's shock was unforeseeable in any event.

4. An employer may be held personally or vicariously liable if it fails to prevent abuse or harassment in the workplace. See *Clark v. Canada* (1994), 20 C.C.L.T. (2d) 241 (F.C.); *Waters v. Commissioner of Police for the Metropolis*, [2000] 1 W.L.R. 1607 (H.L.); *L.(J.) v. Canada (Attorney General)* (1999), 175 D.L.R. (4th) 559 (B.C.S.C.); *Rees v. Canada (Royal Canadian Mounted Police)* (2004), 239 Nfld. & P.E.I.R. 1 (Nfld. S.C.T.D.), rev'd on jurisdictional grounds (2005), 246 Nfld. & P.E.I.R. 79 (Nfld. C.A.); *Sulz v. Canada (Attorney General)* (2006), 54 B.C.L.R. (4th) 328 (S.C.), aff'd (2006), 60 B.C.L.R. (4th) 43 (C.A.); and *Merlo v. Canada*, 2017 FC 51. See also *Occupational Health and Safety Amendment Act (Violence and Harassment in the Workplace), 2009*, S.O. 2009, c. 23.

5. Coaches, instructors and supervisors may be sued on several grounds, including failure to control the participants and failure to provide adequate warnings, instruction and equipment. See *Schulz v. Leeside Dev. Ltd.*, [1978] 5 W.W.R. 620 (B.C.C.A.); *Myers v. Peel County Board of Education*, [1981] 2 S.C.R. 21; *Michalak v. Governors of Dalhousie College and University* (1983), 133 A.P.R. 374 (N.S.C.A.); *Bain v. Calgary Board of Education* (1993), 18 C.C.L.T. (2d) 249 (Alta. Q.B.); *Lunenburg (County) District School Board v. Piercey* (1998), 41 C.C.L.T. (2d) 60 (N.S.C.A.); *MacCabe v. Westlock Roman Catholic Separate School District No. 110* (2001), 293 A.R. 41 (C.A.); and *Hussack v. Chilliwack School District No. 33* (2009), 97 B.C.L.R. (4th) 330 (S.C.). See also Kelly, "Prospective Liabilities of Sports Supervisors" (1989) 63 Aust. L.J. 669; Davis, "Sports Liability of Coaches and School Districts" [1989] F.I.C.Q. 307; and Noce & von Kaenel, "Individual and Institutional Liability for Injuries Arising from Sports and Athletics" (1996) 63 Def. Counsel J. 517.

In *Bradford-Smart v. West Sussex County Council*, [2002] 1 F.C.R. 425, the English Court of Appeal held that a school may owe a duty of care to protect a student from bullying, not only on school property, but also, in exceptional circumstances, outside the school as well. See Elvin, "The Liability of Schools for Bullying" [2002] C.L.J. 255.

See also *North Vancouver School District No. 44 v. Jubran* (2005), 39 B.C.L.R. (4th) 153 (C.A.); and Kendall & Sidebotham, "Homophobic Bullying in Schools: Is there a Duty of Care?" (2004) 9 Austl. & N.Z.J.L. & Educ. 71. Should school liability also extend to so-called cyber-bullying? See Dwyer & Easteal, "Cyber bullying in Australian schools: The question of negligence and liability" (2013) 38 Alternative L.J. 92; and Jaffe, "From School Yard to Cyberspace: A Review of Bullying Liability" 2014) 40:1 Rutgers Computer & Tech. L.J. 17.

In *Cliche c. Baie-James (Commission scolaire)* (2005), 35 C.C.L.T. (3d) 103 (C.S. Qc.), aff'd 2007 CarswellQue 2091 (C.A.) (WL Can), a municipality was held liable for failing to provide enough lifeguards to supervise a class trip to a municipal pool for 36 kindergarten students. The plaintiff's child was found unconscious in the deep end by a teacher. The child died the following day. Although the teachers were not exempt from the obligation to supervise the children while at the pool, the court found that the municipality took on a duty to ensure the safety of the premises by welcoming the children and teachers into the facility. By failing to provide the required number of lifeguards, the city was at fault.

6. In *Hills v. Bridgeview Little League Association*, 745 N.E.2d 1166 (Ill. 2000), the plaintiff, a little league coach, was severely beaten by coaches from an opposing team. One of those coaches had been yelling and making offensive comments to players and umpires throughout the game. The plaintiff sued the opposing coaches as well as the league for failing to prevent the attack, which was allegedly foreseeable given the coach's continued violent outbursts. The plaintiff also claimed that the umpires and game announcer should have attempted to intervene and end the attack, which lasted for several minutes and included blows with a baseball bat. Although the plaintiff was successful at trial and appeal, his claim was later rejected by the Illinois Supreme Court. The court reasoned that there was no special relationship between the league and the plaintiff. Given what you know of Canadian law, do you think the same result would have been reached in Canada? See D'Amico, "Torts — Negligence in the Protection of Third Parties in Youth Sports Programs" (2002) 12 Seton Hall J. Sport L. 107.

In *Vowles v. Evans*, [2003] W.L.R. 1607 (C.A.), an amateur referee of a rugby match was found to owe a duty of care to players to enforce the rules for their safety. Would a referee also owe a duty of care if his or her failure to enforce the rules caused economic loss to the players, teams, or the league (*e.g.* if a poor decision resulted in a team's elimination from the playoffs)? See Elvin, "Liability for Negligent Refereeing of a Rugby Match" (2003) 119 L.Q.R. 560; and "Don't argue with the ref! — Legal liability for incorrect decisions of sports officials" (2014) 9:1 Austl. & N.Z. Sports L.J. 159.

7. The courts readily acknowledge that children cannot be supervised at all times or prevented from getting into mischief. Nevertheless, if parents, teachers or other supervisors are aware of a child's hazardous activities or permit a child to have unsupervised access to snowmobiles, guns and similar objects, the court will impose a rigorous standard of care.

For a discussion of the parental duty to control, see *Ingram v. Lowe* (1974), 55 D.L.R. (3d) 292 (Alta. C.A.) (where a 9-year-old was allowed to have a pellet gun); *Michaud v. Dupuis* (1977), 20 N.B.R. (2d) 305 (Q.B.) (where an 11-year-old had a propensity to throw rocks); *Migliore v. Gerard* (1987), 61 O.R. (2d) 438 (H.C.) (where children were injured, in part because they were not required to wear seat-belts); and *LaPlante (Guardian ad litem of) v. LaPlante* (1992), 93 D.L.R. (4th) 249 (B.C.S.C.), aff'd (1995), 125 D.L.R. (4th) 596 (B.C.C.A.) (where a 16-year-old with physical and mental impairments was permitted to drive).

For examples of actions against parents under parental responsibility legislation, see *Coquitlam School District No. 43 v. D.(T.W.)* (1999), 64 B.C.L.R. (3d) 199 (C.A.); and *Shannon v. Westman (Litigation Guardian of)* (2002), 12 C.C.L.T. (3d) 46 (Ont. S.C.J.).

8. For a discussion of the liability of school authorities see: *Magnusson v. Bd. of Nipawin School Unit No. 61 of Sask.* (1975), 60 D.L.R. (3d) 572 (Sask. C.A.) and *Mainville v. Ottawa Board of Education* (1990), 75 O.R. (2d) 315 (Prov. Div.) (supervision on school grounds); *Myers v. Peel County Board of Education, supra; Freer (Guardian ad litem of) v. Okanagan/Skaha School District No. 67*, 2002 CarswellBC 2891 (S.C.) (WL Can); and *MacCabe v. Westlock Roman Catholic Separate School District No. 110, supra* (supervision during gymnastics); *Lapensee v. Ottawa Day Nursery Inc.* (1986), 35 C.C.L.T. 129 (Ont. H.C.), varied (1986), 38 C.C.L.T. 113 (Ont. H.C.) (supervision in home care); *Piercey (Guardian ad litem of) v. Lunenburg (County) District School Board, supra* (supervision at adventure camp); and *Thompson v. James Fowler Senior High School*, 2011 ABCA 8.

See also Hoyano, "The Prudent Parent: The Elusive Standard of Care" (1984) 18 U.B.C.L. Rev. 1; MacKay & Dickinson, *Beyond the "Careful Parent": Tort Liability in Education* (1998); and Batzel, "Negligence and the Liability of School Boards and Teachers Towards Students" in Foster & Smith, eds., *Reaching For Reasonableness: The Educator as Lawful Decision-Maker* (1999) 111.

9. Should parents, teachers and others supervising children be held vicariously liable for the torts committed by children under their authority? Are there any reasons for distinguishing this relationship from that of an employer/employee? See Weinstein, "Visiting the Sins of the Child on the Parent: the Legality of Criminal Parental Liability Statutes" (1991) 64 S. Cal. L. Rev. 859; Chapin, "Out of Control? The Uses and Abuses of Parental Liability Laws to Control Juvenile Delinquency in the United States" (1997) 37 Santa Clara L. Rev. 621; Barton, "Reconciling the Burden: Parental Liability for the Tortious Acts of Minors" (2002) 51 Emory L.J. 877; Andrews, "The Justice of Parental Accountability: Hypothetical Disinterested Citizens and Real Victims' Voices in the Debate over Expanded Parental Liability" (2002) 75 Temp. L. Rev. 375; Adjin-Tettey, "Significance and Consequences of Parental Liability Legislation" in Beaulac, Pitel & Schulz, eds., *The Joy of Torts* (2002) 221; Brank, Greene & Hochevar, "Holding Parents Responsible: Is Vicarious Responsibility the Public's Answer to Juvenile Crime?" (2011) 17 Psychol. Pub. Pol'y & L. 507; Bernabe, "Setting Parental Controls: Do Parents Have a Duty to Supervise Their Children's Use of the Internet?" (2014) 31:3 J. Marshall J. Info. Tech. & Privacy L. 309; and Lewis, "The Cost of Raising a Killer — Parental Liability for the Parents of Adult Mass Murderers" (2016) 61:1 Vill. L. Rev. 1.

10. Should adult children owe a duty to control their elderly parents? What policy factors might be raised in support or rejection of such a duty? See *Morrison v. Hooper*, 2010 CarswellOnt 5876 (S.C.J.) (WL Can) (no duty to control an elderly parent who was living independently); and *Lichtenstein v. Bathurst Towers Inc.*, 2014 ONSC 1260

(no duty to assist elderly parent walking to and from her apartment on slippery sidewalk).

11. Should owners of casinos or other gambling facilities owe a duty to control problem gamblers? Should it matter if the gambler, in recognition of his or her addiction, formally requests that he or she be excluded from the casino? What is the basis for the duty of care in these circumstances: vulnerability, control, assumption of responsibility, or gratuitous undertaking? See Mohammed, "Food for Tort: Giving the Casino Some *Consideration*, A Continued Defence of the Gaming Industry" (2009) 27 W.R.L.S.I. 169; Mitchell, "Problem gambling and the law of negligence" (2010) 18 Torts L.J. 1; and Fordham, "Saving us from ourselves — The duty of care in negligence to prevent self-inflicted harm" (2010) 18 Torts L.J. 22. If a duty is owed, what rules of causation should apply, and what kinds of damages should be compensable? See *Calvert v. William Hill Credit Ltd.*, [2009] 2 W.L.R. 1065 (C.A.); *Dennis v. Ontario Lottery and Gaming Corp.*, 2010 ONSC 1332, aff'd 2011 ONSC 7024 (Div. Ct.), aff'd 2013 ONCA 501; *Kakavas v. Crown Melbourne Limited*, [2013] HCA 25; *Ross v. British Columbia Lottery Corp.*, 2014 BCSC 320; and *Paton Estate v. Ontario Lottery and Gaming Corporation (Fallsview Casino Resort and OLG Casino Brantford)*, 2016 ONCA 458.

12. Should gun manufacturers or retailers be held liable in the event that their guns are used criminally? See Eggen & Culhane, "Gun Torts: Defining a Cause of Action for Victims in Suits Against Gun Manufacturers" (2002) 81:1 N.C. L. Rev. 115; Lytton, ed., *Suing the Gun Industry: A Battle at the Crossroads of Gun Control and Mass Torts* (2006); Sugarman, "Tort and Guns" (2017) 10:1 J. Tort Law 3.

(c) THE DUTY TO PREVENT CRIME AND PROTECT OTHERS

The duty to control typically involves situations in which the defendant has direct control over, or supervision of, another. Related issues arise when the defendant has only indirect control or authority, such as the situation with those on probation or out on parole who are living in the community. In other cases, the defendant will simply have an opportunity to prevent or reduce the likelihood of a crime or accident occurring. Several different lines of cases have emerged in this rapidly expanding area of Canadian tort law. The following case illustrates the complex legal and policy issues that must be addressed in these types of cases.

JANE DOE v. METROPOLITAN TORONTO (MUNICIPALITY) COMMISSIONERS OF POLICE
(1998), 160 D.L.R. (4th) 697 (Ont. Gen. Div.).

[The plaintiff sued the police after she was attacked by a serial rapist, Paul Callow, who had raped four other women living in second or third floor apartments in the vicinity. All of the prior attacks had occurred within a one-year period and involved single white women. In each case, the attacker had entered the apartment through the balcony door. The plaintiff's first claim was based on failure to warn. The second claim, based on infringement of rights under the *Canadian Charter of Rights and Freedoms*, Part I of the *Constitution Act, 1982*, being Schedule B to the *Canada Act 1982* (U.K.), 1982, c. 11, has been omitted from this excerpt.]

MACFARLAND J.:—

. . .

Decision Not to Warn

As I have said Sgts. Cameron and Deny determined that this investigation would be "low key" compared to the investigation conducted into [another serial rapist, Dawson Davidson, who was known as] the "Annex Rapist" and no warning would be given to the women they knew to be at risk for fear of displacing the rapist leaving him free to re-offend elsewhere undetected.

I am not persuaded that their professed reason for not warning women is the real reason no warning was issued.

. . .

There was, I find, no "policy" not to issue warnings to potential victims in these cases — clearly warnings had been given in the Dawson Davidson Annex Rapist investigation — warnings which incidentally all defence expert witnesses agreed were appropriate in the circumstances.

I find that the real reason a warning was not given in the circumstances of this case was because Sgts. Cameron and Derry believed that women living in the area would become hysterical and panic and their investigation would thereby be jeopardized. In addition, they were not motivated by any sense of urgency because Callow's attacks were not seen as "violent" as Dawson Davidson's by comparison had been.

I am satisfied on the evidence that a meaningful warning could and should have been given to the women who were at particular risk. That warning could have been by way of a canvass of their apartments, by a media blitz, by holding widely publicized public meetings or any one or combination of these methods. Such warning should have alerted the particular women at risk, and advised them of suggested precautions they might take to protect themselves. The defence experts, with the exception of Mr. Piers, agreed that a warning could have been given without compromising the investigation on the facts of the case.

. . .

I am satisfied on Ms. Doe's evidence that if she had been aware a serial rapist was in her neighbourhood raping women whose apartments he accessed via their balconies she would have taken steps to protect herself and that most probably those steps would have prevented her from being raped.

Section 57 of the *Police Act*, R.S.O. 1980, c. 381 (the governing statute at the time these events occurred) provides:

> 57. . . . members of police forces . . . are charged with the duty of preserving the peace, preventing robberies and other crimes. . .

The police are statutorily obligated to prevent crime and at common law they owe a duty to protect life and property. As Schroeder J.A. stated in *Schacht v. The Queen in right of the Province of Ontario*, [1973] 1 O.R. 221 at 231-2, 30 D.L.R. (3d) 641 (H.C.J.):

> The duties which I would lay upon them stem not only from the relevant statutes to which reference has been made, but from the common law, which recognizes the existence of a broad conventional or customary duty in the established constabulary as an arm of the State to protect the life, limb and property of the subject.

In my view, the police failed utterly in their duty to protect these women and the plaintiff in particular from the serial rapist the police knew to be in their midst by failing to warn so that they may have had the opportunity to take steps to protect themselves.

. . .

Negligence

My task has been rendered less onerous by the very thorough analysis of Henry J. of the issues raised by the pleading in this case . . . when the matter came before him on a motion to strike out the statement of claim and the succinct reasons of Moldaver J. (as he then was) on behalf of the Divisional Court (1990), 74 O.R. (2d) 225, 72 D.L.R. (4th) 580, when the decision of Henry J. went to that Court on appeal.

After citing section 57 of the Police Act, R.S.O. 1980, c. 381, and observing that by virtue thereof the police are charged with the duty of protecting the public from those who would commit or have committed crimes, Moldaver J. (as he then was) goes on . . . as follows:

> Do the pleadings support a private law duty of care by the defendants in this case?

> The plaintiff alleges that the defendants knew of the existence of a serial rapist. It was eminently foreseeable that he would strike again and cause harm to yet another victim. The allegations therefore support foreseeability of risk.

> The plaintiff further alleges that by the time she was raped, the defendants knew or ought to have known that she had become part of a narrow and distinct group of potential victims, sufficient to support a special relationship of proximity. According to the allegations, the defendants knew:

> (1) that the rapist confined his attacks to the Church-Wellesley area of Toronto;
> (2) that the victims all resided in second or third floor apartments;
> (3) that entry in each case was gained through a balcony door; and
> (4) that the victims were all white, single and female.

> Accepting as I must the facts as pleaded, I agree with Henry J. that they do support the requisite knowledge on the part of the police sufficient to establish a private law duty of care. The harm was foreseeable and a special relationship of proximity existed.

> . . .

> On the evidence I find the plaintiff has established a private law duty of care.

. . .

Do the pleadings support a breach of the private law duty of care?

The law is clear that in certain circumstances, the police have a duty to warn citizens of foreseeable harm. See *Schact v. R.*, [1973] 1 O.R. 221, 30 D.L.R. (3d) 641 (C.A.) affd *sub nom. O'Rourke v. Schact*, [1976] 1 S.C.R. 53, 55 D.L.R. (3d) 96, 3 N.R. 453, and *Beutler v. Beutler, Adams v. Beutler* (1983), 26 C.C.L.T. 229 (Ont. H.C.J.). The obvious purpose of the warning is to protect the citizens.

I would add to this by saying that in some circumstances where foreseeable harm and a special relationship of proximity exist, the police might reasonably conclude that a warning ought not to be given. For example, it might be decided that a warning would cause general and unnecessary panic on the part of the public which could lead to greater harm.

It would, however, be improper to suggest that a legitimate decision not to warn would excuse a failure to protect. The duty to protect would still remain. It would simply have to be accomplished by other means.

In this case the plaintiff claims, *inter alia*, that the duty owed to her by the defendants required (1) that she be warned of the impending danger; or (2) in the absence of such a warning, that she be adequately protected. It is alleged that the police did neither.

Instead she claims they made a conscious decision to sacrifice her in order to apprehend the suspect. They decided to use her as "bait". They chose not to warn her due to a stereotypical belief that because she was a woman, she and others like her would become hysterical. This would have "scared off" the attacker, making his capture more difficult.

The evidence establishes that Det. Sgt. Cameron clearly had linked the four rapes which preceded Ms. Doe's by the early days of August in 1986, and he and Det. Sgt. Derry knew that the rapist would continue to attack women until he was stopped. They knew the rapist was attacking single white women living alone in second and third floor apartments with balconies in the Church/Wellesley area of the City of Toronto.

On the evidence I find the plaintiff has established a private law duty of care.

Det. Sgts. Derry and Cameron determined, in the context of their investigation, that no warning would be given to any women — let alone the specific target group they had identified — and among the reasons given for deciding not to warn was their view that women would panic and compromise the investigation. Det. Sgt. Cameron gave this as a reason to Ms. Doe when he interviewed her following her rape and she asked why women had not been warned.

[The plaintiff was awarded $220,000 in damages for her claim in negligence. Although MacFarland J. found that the plaintiff's rights under ss. 7 and 15 of the *Charter* had also been violated, there were no additional damages awarded on that basis.]

NOTES AND QUESTIONS

1. What were the grounds upon which MacFarland J. found that the police owed the plaintiff a duty of care? What factors did the judge consider in determining that the standard of care had been breached?

2. Was the court's analysis of the causation issue in *Doe* convincing? In *B.M. v. British Columbia (Attorney General)* (2004), 31 B.C.L.R. (4th) 61 (C.A.), the plaintiff's claim against police for failure to prevent crime was dismissed for lack of causation. The plaintiff had an abusive marriage. Her husband had been convicted for assaulting her. When she had another violent confrontation with him, she complained to police. Although the police knew of her husband's violent past (he also had convictions for assault causing bodily harm, unlawful confinement, and manslaughter) they did nothing to intervene and told the plaintiff to see a lawyer to get a restraining order and to stay in public places. Seven weeks later, the plaintiff's husband broke into her home with a gun, killed her friend and seriously wounded one of her daughters. The plaintiff suffered post-traumatic stress disorder as a result of the attack. Her claim against the

police was dismissed on the basis that she could not prove causation: human behaviour is unpredictable, and there was no evidence that police intervention would have prevented the violent attack. *Doe* and *B.M.* illustrate some of the difficulties posed by the traditional "but for" test of causation in torts, particularly when predicting what an actor might have done if the defendant had issued a proper warning. For more on causation see Chapter 16.

3. In subsequent claims against the police for failing to prevent violent crimes, the focus has been on the degree of proximity, specifically whether the plaintiff was in a narrow group of potential victims to which the police knew the offender posed a risk of harm. See *Project 360 Investments Ltd. (c.o.b. Sound Emporium Nightclub) v. Toronto Police Services Board*, [2009] O.J. No. 2473 (S.C.J.) (insufficient proximity between police and nightclub where gang member shot a patron). Compare *Patrong v. Banks*, 2015 ONSC 3078, aff'd 2016 ONSC 4200 (Div. Ct.), where Myers J. found a relationship of proximity between police and a young black man who was the victim of a drive-by shooting by a known gang member, Riley. Riley was subject to two court orders prohibiting him from entering Scarborough; nevertheless, surveillance officers did not stop him on the day that he entered Scarborough and shot the plaintiff. Although the plaintiff was not a gang member, Myers J. took a generous reading of *Jane Doe* and found that the plaintiff fit within the narrow class of potential shooting victims. See also *Castle v. Ontario*, 2014 ONSC 3610; and *Haggerty Estate v. Rogers*, 2011 ONSC 5312. For commentary on these cases, see Chamberlain, "To Serve and Protect Whom? Proximity in Cases of Police Failure to Protect" (2016) 53:4 Alta. L. Rev. 977.

4. What are the implications of *Doe* for prison and police officials who learn that a convicted rapist, arsonist, pedophile, or bank robber will be released from prison into a community? What policy considerations do these cases pose that were not relevant to *Doe*? See Davenport, "Convicted paedophiles — disclosure of information after release — police duty to protect public — *R. v. Chief Constable of the North Wales Police and ors ex parte AB and CD*" (1998) 3 J.C.L. 141.

5. In *Cragg v. Tone* (2007), 285 D.L.R. (4th) 754 (B.C.C.A.), the plaintiff sued a police dispatcher for failing to assign sufficient priority to his call. The plaintiff had called a non-emergency police number to report that his car had been vandalized by a man who had previously threatened him. The dispatcher recorded the complaint as damage to a vehicle and did not forward it to an on-duty officer for 20 minutes. A short time later, before police had an opportunity to take a report from the plaintiff, he was attacked at his home by the man who had vandalized his car. The British Columbia Court of Appeal overturned the trial judge's decision that the police dispatcher was liable in negligence. The court held that the attack was unforeseeable and that the dispatcher made a reasonable decision in light of the information she had been given.

6. In *Hill v. Chief Constable of West Yorkshire*, [1989] A.C. 53 (H.L.), the deceased's family sued the police, claiming that, had they acted reasonably, they would have been able to arrest a serial killer before he killed their daughter. The House of Lords struck out the statement of claim, stating that the police owe no duty to victims of crime unless the offender commits the offence while in police custody or after escaping police custody. In particular, the House of Lords was concerned that imposing a duty of care

would be detrimental to the conduct of police investigations and decisions about how to distribute police resources. Moreover, there was insufficient proximity between the police and the deceased: she was one of many potential victims of a yet unidentified killer. Is the narrow scope of the police duty in *Hill* preferable to the broad duty in *Doe*? *Hill* has since been followed to deny police or government liability for the failure to prevent crime. See for example *Alexandrou v. Oxford*, [1993] 4 All E.R. 328 (C.A.) (negligent response to a burglar alarm at the plaintiff's shop); and *Akenzua v. Secretary of State for the Home Department*, [2002] EWCA Civ 1470 (failure to deport a violent criminal who committed further crimes). But see *Robinson v. Chief Constable of West Yorkshire Police*, [2018] UKSC 4 (principles of *Hill* inapplicable to claim by elderly woman who was physically injured during a scuffle when police arrested a suspected drug dealer on a busy shopping street).

7. In *Osman v. Ferguson*, [1993] 4 All E.R. 344 (C.A.), a teacher became obsessed with one of his students and began stalking him. The student's family complained to the police and the parties were interviewed several times. The police did not intervene to protect the student. The teacher subsequently shot and wounded the student and killed the student's father. The student brought a negligence action against the police for failing to protect him in light of the teacher's threatening behaviour. While the Court of Appeal found that there was greater proximity in *Osman* than in *Hill*, in that both the perpetrator and the intended victim were identified, the claim was struck out based on the authority of the policy reasons provided in *Hill*.

However, in *Osman v. United Kingdom* (1998), 29 E.H.R.R. 245, the European Court of Human Rights found that the effectively "blanket immunity" extended to police violated Article 6 of the European Convention on Human Rights, which guarantees access to the courts for the determination of civil rights and obligations. According to the European Court, the plaintiff's claim should not have been struck out at such a preliminary stage. While *Osman v. United Kingdom* had the potential to open wide claims for police and government negligence, its effects were dampened by the subsequent decision in *Z v. United Kingdom* (2002), 34 E.H.R.R. 2. See Gearty, "Unravelling Osman" (2001) 64 M.L.R. 159.

8. The House of Lords reaffirmed its commitment to the principles in *Hill* in three cases. In *Brooks v. Commissioner of Police for the Metropolis*, [2005] 1 W.L.R. 1495 (H.L.), the plaintiff was a victim of a vicious racial attack in which his friend was killed. The House of Lords found that police did not owe the plaintiff a duty of care when they arrived at the scene and showed no concern for his condition. Police stereotyped him as an agitated young black man who could not assist them in capturing the perpetrators. Lord Steyn reasoned that imposing a duty of care would impede the ability of police to perform their functions and would lead to defensive practice. Next, in *Smith v. Chief Constable of Sussex Police* (2008), [2009] 1 A.C. 225 (H.L.), the House of Lords found that no duty of care was owed to protect a man who reported that his estranged partner was making repeated threats on his life. The partner ultimately attacked the plaintiff in his home with a claw hammer, leaving him with a fractured skull and brain damage. Lord Hope explained that imposing a duty of care in the circumstances was not in the interests of the community. Finally, in *Michael v. Chief Constable of South Wales Police*, [2015] UKSC 2, the United Kingdom Supreme Court found that police owed no duty of care to a woman who had called emergency services to report that her ex-partner, who had a history of domestic

violence and had found her having sex with another man, would be returning home imminently to kill her. Lord Toulson found that the operator had not assumed responsibility for the woman's safety by telling her to lock her doors and to keep the phone line open in case police needed to call back. Can these decisions be justified? What community interest is served by denying that police owe a duty of care to victims whose lives are under credible threat from known perpetrators?

9. The English courts are not completely hostile toward claims against police for failure to prevent crime. For example in *Swinney v. Chief Constable of the Northumbria Police*, [1997] Q.B. 464 (C.A.), the Court of Appeal refused to strike out a claim against police for failing to protect an informant. The plaintiff had provided information to the police regarding a suspected police killer, and had requested that the information be kept confidential. The suspect was known to be violent. Nevertheless, the police left the information in an unattended police vehicle, which was broken into by criminals and later came to the attention of the suspect. The suspect subsequently threatened the plaintiff and her family. The Court of Appeal acknowledged that a special relationship of proximity might exist between police and informants, and that the policy considerations employed in *Hill* had to be weighed against other factors such as the need to protect informants and to encourage them to come forward. But see *CLG & Ors v. Chief Constable of Merseyside Police*, [2015] EWCA Civ 836, where the court dismissed a claim by witnesses whose home came under fire by a criminal accused after their address was negligently disclosed in court.

10. British victims may well have a better chance of obtaining relief under human rights legislation than the common law. See for example *Hertfordshire Police v. Van Colle*, [2009] A.C. 225 (H.L.); *Mcihael, supra*, and *Commissioner of Police of the Metropolis v. DSD & Anor*, [2018] UKSC 11, all of which denied claims under common law but allowed similar claims under the *Human Rights Act* 1998 (U.K.) for failing to adequately investigate violent crimes. Nevertheless, damages are discretionary under the human rights legislation and will typically be much lower than in comparable actions in tort. See Nolan, "Negligence and Human Rights Law: The Case for Separate Development" (2013) 76 M.L.R. 286; and Conaghan, "Investigating rape: human rights and police accountability" (2016) 37:1 L.S. 54.

11. For discussions of these issues in Canada and the United Kingdom, see Moroz, "*Jane Doe* and Police Liability for Failure to Apprehend: The Role of the *Anns* Public Policy Principle in Canada and England" (1995) 17 Adv. Q. 261; Childs & Ceyssens, "*Doe v. Metropolitan Toronto Board of Commissioners of Police* and the Status of Public Oversight of the Police in Canada" (1998) 36 Alta. L.R. 1000; Randall, "Sex Discrimination, Accountability of Public Authorities and the Public/Private Divide in Tort Law: An Analysis of *Doe v. Metropolitan Toronto (Municipality) Commissioners of Police*" (2001) 26 Queen's L.J. 451; Hall, "Duty, Causation, and Third Party Perpetrators: The Bonnie Mooney Case" (2005) 50 McGill L.J. 597; Chamberlain, "Negligent Investigation: Tort Law as Police Ombudsman" in Robertson & Tang Hang Wu, eds., *The Goals of Private Law* (2009); Burton, "Failing to Protect: Victims' Rights and Police Liability" (2009) 72 Mod. L. Rev. 283; McIvor, "Getting Defensive About Police Negligence: The *Hill* Principle, The Human Rights Act 1998 and the House of Lords" [2010] C.L.J. 133; Wilberg, "Defensive Practice or Conflict of Duties? Policy Concerns in Public

Authority Negligence Claims" (2010) 126 L.Q.R. 420; Walsh, "Police Liability for a Negligent Failure to Prevent Crime: Enhancing Accountability by Clearing the Public Policy Fog" (2011) 22 King's L.J. 27; Koshan, "State Responsibility for Protection Against Domestic Violence: The Inter-American Commission on Human Rights Decision *Lenehan (Gonzales)* and its Application in Canada" (2012) 30 Windsor Y.B. Access Just. 39; Chamberlain, "Tort Claims for Failure to Protect: Reasons for (Cautious) Optimism Since *Mooney*" (2012) 75 Sask. L.R. 245; Tofaris & Steel, "Negligence Liability for Omissions and the Police" [2016] C.L.J. 128; Shircore, Douglas and Feldthusen, "Bungled Police Emergency Calls and the Problems with Unique Duties of Care" (2017) 68 U.N.B.L.J. 169.

12. American courts are very unlikely to impose liability for police failure to prevent crime. Police or other officials can only be found liable where they worsen the plaintiff's situation by creating the danger, making the plaintiff more vulnerable, or deterring alternative assistance. See for example *DeShaney v. Winnebago County Department of Social Services*, 489 U.S. 189 (1989); *Ross v. United States*, 910 F.2d 1422 (7th Cir. 1990); and *Schieber v. City of Philadelphia*, 156 F.Supp.2d 451 (E.D. Pa. 2001). See Juthani, "Police Treatment of Domestic Violence and Sexual Abuse: Affirmative Duty to Protect vs. Fourth Amendment Privacy" (2003) 59 N.Y.U. Ann. Surv. Am. L. 51. But see *Waddell v. Hemerson*, 329 F.3d 1300 (11th Cir. 2003), which indicated that liability would not be imposed unless the defendant exhibited "deliberate indifference to an extremely great risk of serious injury to someone in the Plaintiffs' position," which rose to the level of "conscience shocking in the constitutional sense."

A particularly horrific case is *Estate of Sinthasamphone v. City of Milwaukee*, 785 F.Supp. 1343 (E.D. Wis. 1992). A 14-year-old Laotian boy was found lying on the street, drugged, naked and bleeding, by two women. Unknown to the women, the boy had escaped from the apartment of serial murderer Jeffrey Dahmer (who had then been convicted of sexual assault but was not as notorious as he later became). The women called the police but, when they arrived, the police refused to listen to them and threatened to arrest them if they tried to assist the boy. When Dahmer came to the scene, the police returned the boy to his custody, allegedly believing that he was Dahmer's sexual partner. On return to the apartment, Dahmer killed the boy. His family sued the police not for failing to protect him, but for preventing others from providing assistance and for delivering him into the hands of someone who was not his legal guardian. Based on this affirmative conduct that worsened the boy's circumstances, the court allowed the claim to proceed to trial.

13. In *Fullowka v. Royal Oak Ventures Inc.*, 2010 SCC 5, a private security firm was held to owe a duty of care toward replacement workers who were hired during a bitter labour dispute. Nine of the workers were killed when a striking miner planted an explosive device in the mine. The explosion was foreseeable because the security firm knew that the striking miners had access to explosives and had made threats against the replacement workers. In addition, a relationship of proximity existed on account of the firm's undertaking to control the striking miners and the replacement workers' reliance on the firm for their safety. The government of the Northwest Territories was also held to have owed a duty of care to the replacement workers. However, both defendants were absolved of liability because they had not breached the standard of care.

14. The courts have also imposed affirmative duties on private citizens to prevent crime. Landlords have been held liable to their tenants for injuries caused by attackers who gained access because of inadequate security. See *Allison v. Rank City Wall Can. Ltd.* (1984), 29 C.C.L.T. 50 (Ont. H.C.); *Q. v. Minto Management Ltd.* (1985), 49 O.R. (2d) 531 (H.C.), aff'd (1986), 57 O.R. (2d) 781 (C.A.); Merril, "Landlord Liability for Crimes Committed By Third Parties Against Tenants on the Premises" (1985) 38 Vand. L. Rev. 431; and Glesner, "Landlords as Cops: Tort, Nuisance and Forfeiture Standards Imposing Liability on Landlords for Crime on the Premises" (1992) 42 Case W. Res. L. Rev. 679. But see *Shultz v. Miki* (2006), 223 B.C.A.C. 248 (C.A.), where the defendant landlord was absolved of liability for the sexual assault committed by his cousin, whom the landlord had hired to perform carpentry work in the plaintiff's apartment.

See also *Rendall v. Ewart* (1989), 38 B.C.L.R. (2d) 1 (C.A.); *H.(M.) v. Bederman* (1995), 27 C.C.L.T. (2d) 152 (Ont. Gen. Div.); *Robertson v. Stang* (1997) 38 C.C.L.T. (2d) 62 (B.C.S.C.); *Coueslan v. Canadian Mini-Warehouse Properties Ltd. (c.o.b. Public Storage Canadian)*, 2000 BCPC 137 (CanLII); and *G.A. v. McGregor* (2003), 347 A.R. 376 (Q.B.).

In *Mitchell v. Glasgow City Council*, [2009] 2 W.L.R. 481 (H.L.), the plaintiff was attacked and killed by a fellow resident of a public housing estate. The man had threatened the plaintiff on numerous occasions over several years, and the defendant local authority was taking steps to evict him from the estate. After a meeting with the local authority where he was informed of his potential eviction, the man violently attacked the plaintiff. The plaintiff's estate claimed that the local authority had a duty to warn the plaintiff about the meeting so that he could take steps to avoid the man afterward. The House of Lords rejected this argument, finding that the local authority had not made any undertaking to protect the plaintiff from his neighbour's criminal acts and that there were broader policy reasons to reject a duty of care. In particular, imposing a duty might lead to defensive practices by landlords or discourage them from taking actions to reduce anti-social behaviour by tenants. Are these policy considerations convincing? See also *CN & Anor v. Poole Borough Council*, [2017] EWCA Civ 2185.

15. Should drivers who leave their keys in their cars be held liable if their vehicles are stolen and involved in car accidents? The answer has largely been fact-specific and turns largely on the question of foreseeability. See *Hollett v. Coca-Cola Ltd.* (1980), 11 C.C.L.T. 281 (B.C.S.C.); *Spagnolo v. Margesson's Sports Ltd.* (1983), 41 O.R. (2d) 65 (C.A.); *Moore v. Fanning* (1987), 60 O.R. (2d) 225 (H.C.); *Werbeniuk v. Maynard* (1994), 93 Man. R. (2d) 318 (Q.B.); *Tong v. Bedwell* (2002), 311 A.R. 174 (Q.B.); and *Provost v. Bolton*, 2017 BCSC 1608. In *Rankin (Rankin's Garage & Sales) v. J.J.*, 2018 SCC 19, the Supreme Court of Canada found that it was not foreseeable to a commercial garage operator that vehicles left unsecured would be stolen by minors and driven in a dangerous manner. Is this compelling? Should commercial enterprises (*e.g.* garages, taxi drivers) be more likely to owe a duty of care than private vehicle owners?

16. In *Okanagan Exteriors Inc. v. Perth Developments Inc.* (2002), 98 B.C.L.R. (3d) 274 (C.A.), the defendant owned an abandoned construction site that neighboured the plaintiff's greenhouse. The defendant knew that its site was frequented by children, transients and alcoholics, and that some of those individuals occasionally set fires. The defendant nevertheless did not take effective steps to control the actions of those third

parties. The plaintiff suffered property damage when a fire that started on the defendant's property spread. The court held that, in the circumstances, the defendant owed a duty of care to the plaintiff. Liability followed. But see *Smith v. Littlewoods Organisation Ltd.*, [1987] 1 All E.R. 710 (H.L.), where a derelict cinema was set on fire by vandals and the fire spread to neighbouring properties. The House of Lords refused to impose liability on the owners of the cinema. *Littlewoods* can be distinguished because the defendants had insufficient knowledge of the presence of trespassers.

17. There has been a flood of cases concerning the duty to protect children from physical and sexual abuse. See *Lyth v. Dagg* (1988), 46 C.C.L.T. 25 (B.C.S.C.) (school); *G.(A.) v. British Columbia (Superintendent of Family & Child Services)* (1989), 38 B.C.L.R. (2d) 215 (C.A.); *J.(L.A.) v. J.(H.)* (1993), 13 O.R. (3d) 306 (Gen. Div.) (claim against mother for failing to protect daughter from father); *Police Complaints Commissioner v. Dunlop* (1995), 26 O.R. (3d) 582 (Gen. Div.) (police officer); *C.(D.) v. Newfoundland (Minister of Social Services)* (1996), 137 Nfld. & P.E.I.R. 206 (Nfld. T.D.) (youth and social workers); *Brown (Next Friend of) v. University of Alberta Hospital* (1997), 197 A.R. 237 (Q.B.) (radiologist); *Hockley v. Riley* (2007), 88 O.R. (3d) 1 (C.A.) (claim against mother for failing to protect daughter from step-father); *K.(K.) v. G.(K.W.)* (2008), 90 O.R. (3d) 481 (C.A.) (claim against mother for failing to protect daughter from father); *H.(D.) v. Kline* (2008), 81 B.C.L.R. (4th) 288 (C.A.) (claim against probation officers and plaintiff's mother for allowing convicted sex offender to have unsupervised access to children, contrary to probation order); and *M.(B.) (Litigation Guardian of) v. M.(R.)* (2009), 64 C.C.L.T. (3d) 210 (B.C.S.C.) (claim against social worker and Crown for failing to protect child from father who had criminal record for child abuse). See Reaume & Van Praagh, "Family Matters: Mothers as Secondary Defendants in Child Sexual Abuse Actions" in Beaulac, Pitel & Schulz, eds., *The Joy of Torts* (2002) 179.

Many of the recent cases deal with abuse suffered years earlier in residential schools or in association with religious orders. See for example *Re Indian Residential Schools* (2000), 183 D.L.R. (4th) 552 (Alta. Q.B.); *Penney v. John Doe* (2002), 215 Nfld. & P.E.I.R. 310 (Nfld. C.A.) (claim against bishop, diocese and others); and *John Doe v. Bennett*, [2004] 1 S.C.R. 436 (claim against diocese).

Children who are physically and sexually abused suffer a broad range of serious psychological and other problems, including an increased likelihood of abusing others. In *Rumley v. British Columbia* (1999), 72 B.C.L.R. (3d) 1 (C.A.), aff'd [2001] 3 S.C.R. 184, the court indicated that claims from "secondary-abuse victims" should not be included in any class actions because they raise difficult issues of duty and foreseeability, as well as plaintiff-specific issues of proximity. On the broader issue, is there any legal or policy reason to limit the claims of "secondary-abuse victims?"

Within the context of child abuse cases, it is important to appreciate that liability may also be imposed in negligence or defamation with respect to unfounded or unwarranted allegations of abuse. See for example, *B.(D.) v. Children's Aid Society of Durham (Region)* (1996), 92 O.A.C. 60 (C.A.); *G.(R.) v. Christison* (1996), 150 Sask. R. 1 (Q.B.); *D. v. East Berkshire Community NHS Trust*, [2005] 2 A.C. 373 (H.L.); and *Young v. Bella*, [2006] 1 S.C.R. 108. But see *Syl Apps Secure Treatment Centre v. D.(B.)*, [2007] 3 S.C.R. 83, where the court found that child welfare authorities owed no duty of care to the family of a child who was suspected to have been abused.

18. What obligations do counsellors, therapists and health professionals have to protect their patients and those endangered by their patients? What impact should the fact that the information was obtained in confidence have on these duties?

In *Tarasoff v. Regents of the University of California*, 17 Cal. Rptr. 3d 425 (U.S. 1976), a patient told his psychologist at the University Hospital that he intended to kill his former girlfriend when she returned from her vacation. The psychologist concluded that the patient was dangerous, and contacted the campus police. The patient was picked up, briefly detained and then released. Neither the woman nor her family was warned of the potential danger. When the woman returned, the patient killed her. The family sued the psychologist for failing to warn. The court acknowledged the psychologist's arguments about the difficulty of predicting dangerousness, but indicated that this was not the issue. The psychologist was not being sued because he had negligently assessed his patient. Rather, he was being sued because he had concluded that the patient was dangerous and yet failed to warn the intended victim. The psychologist argued that there should be no duty to warn because it would necessitate breaching confidentiality. In rejecting this argument, the court emphasized that the confidentiality obligation to the patient ends when the public peril begins. Consequently, the judge rejected the psychologist's request to dismiss the family's claim and sent the case to trial. The psychologist and the University settled out of court before the trial.

19. The dilemma posed by *Tarasoff* is not limited to violent crime. For example, what should a therapist do if an extremely intoxicated patient attempts to leave a treatment session with car keys in hand? Even if the therapist is willing to breach confidence by calling the police, will this do any good? Should the therapist attempt or threaten to physically restrain the patient? What if a patient poses only a risk to him or herself?

Should an addictions counsellor have any legal duty to control the conduct of an alcohol or drug-dependant patient who is currently employed in a safety-sensitive position?

20. *Tarasoff* has generated substantial academic interest in both the legal and treatment communities. See for example Twerski, "Affirmative Duty After *Tarasoff*" (1983) 11 Hofstra L. Rev. 1013; Givelber, Bowers & Blitch, "*Tarasoff*, Myth and Reality: An Empirical Study of Private Law in Action" [1984] Wisc. L. Rev. 433; Bednar, "The Psychotherapist's Calamity: Emerging Trends in the *Tarasoff* Doctrine" [1989] B.Y.U.L. Rev. 261; Egley, "Defining the *Tarasoff* Duty" (1991) 19 J. Psych & Law 19; Rosenhan *et al.*, "Warning Third Parties: The Ripple Effects of *Tarasoff*" (1993) 24 Pac. L.J. 1165; Lake, "Revisiting *Tarasoff*" (1994) 58 Albany L. Rev. 97; Smith, "*Wenden v. Trikha* and Third Party Liability of Doctors and Hospitals: What's Been Happening to *Tarasoff?*" (1995) 4 Health L. Rev. 12; Ferris *et al.*, "Defining the Physician's Duty to Warn: Consensus Statement of Ontario's Medical Expert Panel on Duty to Inform" (1998) 158 C.M.A.J. 1473; Grant, "Psychiatrists Have No Duty to Warn Third Parties of Patient's Threats" (2001) 7 Tex. Wesleyan L. Rev. 157; Van Exan, "The Legal and Ethical Issues Surrounding the Duty to Warn in the Practice of Psychology" (2004) 18 W.R.S.L.I. 123; Ginsberg, "*Tarasoff* at Thirty: Victim's Knowledge Shrinks the Psychotherapist's Duty to Warn and Protect" (2004) 21 J. Contemp. Health L. & Pol'y 1; and Cardi, "A Pluralistic Analysis of the Therapist/ Physician Duty to Warn Third Parties" (2009) 44 Wakeforest L. Rev. 877. See also

Weinstock *et al.*, "No Duty to Warn in California: Now Unambiguously Solely a Duty to Protect" (2014) 42 J. Am. Acad. Psychiatry Law 101, which discusses legislation passed in California in 2013 to clarify that a clinician's obligation is to protect the potential victim. This may be accomplished by warning, but other means of protection may be used if a warning would escalate the danger or otherwise be counterproductive.

21. The issues raised in *Tarasoff* have never been squarely addressed by the Canadian courts, although the decision has been referred to approvingly. See for example *Tanner v. Norys*, [1980] 4 W.W.R. 33 (Alta. C.A.); and *Wenden v. Trikha* (1993), 14 C.C.L.T. (2d) 225 (Alta. C.A.). In *Smith v. Jones* (1999), 169 D.L.R. (4th) 385 (S.C.C.), the *Tarasoff* decision was again referred to approvingly. However, *Smith* did not deal with a therapist's common law duty to warn in negligence. Rather, the majority of the Supreme Court of Canada ruled that a therapist could choose to breach solicitor-client privilege in the public interest to avert a clear risk of imminent death or serious injury to an identifiable person or group. What are the implications of *Smith* in terms of a therapist's duty to warn? See also *Roe v. Leone*, 2012 ONSC 6237, in which the court refused to strike out the action against a health unit and the police for failing to control a man who was HIV-positive and having unprotected sex and failing to warn the female plaintiffs who had intimate relationships with him.

REVIEW PROBLEMS

1. John, the owner of a local variety store, sold one dollar's worth of firecrackers and three packages of matches to Billy, a 10-year-old. Billy was severely burned while he was playing alone with the firecrackers. Would John owe Billy a common law duty of care in these circumstances? How would your analysis differ if: (a) Billy's mother had told John not to sell Billy any firecrackers, (b) Billy had told John that he was taking the firecrackers home to light with his 17-year-old brother, (c) Billy had always appeared to be a polite, well-behaved child, or (d) John had received complaints from some parents about selling their children matches, cigarettes and firecrackers?

2. Mr. Green pulled into a plaza and ran into a store, leaving the engine of the car running and the door unlocked. As he emerged a minute later, he saw a teenager pulling away in his car. He had noticed some teenagers milling about in front of the store, but had thought nothing of it. An hour later, Green was contacted by the police, who informed him that the driver had lost control of the car and had slammed into a bus. The driver of his car and several passengers in the bus were severely injured. Would Mr. Green owe a common law duty of care to the thief or the passengers? Would your answer be different if Mr. Green were a commercial taxi driver?

3. Mandy, a drug addict who is HIV-positive, told her doctor that she had no intention of practising safe sex or informing her partner. The doctor contacted the medical officer of health but did not inform Mandy's partner. Fourteen months later, Mandy's partner tested HIV-positive and now wants to sue the doctor for not warning him of the risk. Did the doctor owe the partner a duty of care? Would it make a difference if: (a) the local medical officer of health had adopted a policy of not contacting sexual partners, (b) Mandy had many sexual partners, or (c) the partner was also one of the doctor's patients?

5. The Duty to Perform Gratuitous Undertakings

In keeping with the distinction between misfeasance and nonfeasance, the common law did not generally require an individual to honour a gratuitous promise. The failure to fulfil such a promise was characterized as a nonfeasance and the remedy, if any, was in contract and not in tort. In the classic case of *Thorne v. Deas* (1809), 4 Johns. 84 (N.Y.), the defendant twice assured the plaintiffs that he would obtain insurance on a boat they jointly owned. Relying on these promises, the plaintiffs did nothing further on the matter. When the boat was wrecked and the plaintiffs learned that it had not been insured, they sued the defendant in tort for their loss. In dismissing their action, the court stated that "by the common law . . . one who undertakes to do an act for another without reward, is not answerable for omitting to do the act, and is only responsible when he attempts to do it, and does it amiss."

Once the defendant begins to perform a gratuitous undertaking, he or she may be held liable in negligence for positively injuring the plaintiff. However, defendants generally are not subject to a common law duty to complete the task itself, or to otherwise act for the plaintiff's benefit. A different rule applies only if the defendant somehow worsened the plaintiff's original position. That may be true, for instance, if the defendant lulled the plaintiff into a false sense of security, denied the plaintiff other opportunities for aid, or put the plaintiff in a more precarious physical position. The courts have held that those principles may apply if the defendant withdrew a gratuitous service that he or she had customarily provided.

Although the rule in *Thorne* has been criticized, it has rarely been rejected — partially because its impact can often be avoided. First, the courts may skirt the issue in *Thorne* by classifying the defendant's conduct as misfeasance, rather than nonfeasance. Second, tort and contract have developed since 1809 to cover many of the situations in which *Thorne* initially denied relief. For example, if the parties are in a contractual relationship, the courts may now invoke the concept of promissory estoppel to enforce some gratuitous promises. Furthermore, liability may be imposed in tort for pure economic losses caused by fraudulent misrepresentations, negligent or innocent misrepresentations made in fiduciary relationships, and negligent misrepresentations made in the special circumstances defined in *Hedley Byrne & Co. v. Heller & Partners Ltd.*, [1964] A.C. 465 (H.L.). A defendant may also be held liable in tort for making a negligent statement that creates a foreseeable risk of physical injury. Recent changes in the common law governing the duties of builders, occupiers, manufacturers, suppliers, and public authorities have further expanded the situations in which the failure to fulfil a gratuitous undertaking may give rise to tort liability. In the end, while the principle in *Thorne* has not been directly rejected, it has been very significantly eroded by the growing number of exceptions to it.

NOTES AND QUESTIONS

1. The principles governing the performance of gratuitous promises appear to have been established in *Coggs v. Bernard* (1703), 92 E.R. 107 (Q.B.), but they were more clearly stated in *Thorne*. One of the first Canadian cases in which these issues were addressed, *Baxter & Co. v. Jones* (1903), 6 O.L.R. 360 (C.A.), cited both *Coggs* and *Thorne* as authority. Thereafter, the Canadian courts have typically cited *Baxter*, rather than either *Coggs* or *Thorne*, in support of these principles.

2. What is the rationale for refusing to impose liability in tort for injuries or losses resulting from a defendant's failure to fulfil a gratuitous promise?

3. It is interesting to contrast *Thorne* with the subsequent cases in which individuals have been held liable for failing to honour a gratuitous promise to obtain insurance. In *Baxter & Co. v. Jones*, *supra*, and *Menna v. Guglietti* (1969), 10 D.L.R. (3d) 132 (Ont. H.C.), the courts characterized the agents' conduct in filling out the application form and taking down information as misfeasance and imposed liability in negligence. See also *Ferland v. Keith* (1958), 15 D.L.R. (2d) 472 (Ont. C.A.) (liability for breach of an independent or collateral contract); *Northwestern Mut. Ins. Co. v. J.T. O'Bryan & Co.* (1974), 51 D.L.R. (3d) 693 (B.C.C.A.) (liability in tort for negligent misrepresentation); *Fine's Flowers Ltd. v. General Accident Assurance Co.* (1977), 81 D.L.R. (3d) 139 (Ont. C.A.) (liability for breach of contract, and liability in tort for negligent misrepresentation and breach of a fiduciary duty); *National Crane Services Inc. v. AON Reed Stenhouse* (2007), 291 Sask. R. 281 (C.A.) (liability for negligence and breach of fiduciary duty); and *CIA Inspection Inc. v. Dan Lawrie Insurance Brokers* (2010), 75 C.C.L.T. (3d) 211 (Ont. S.C.J.) (liability for negligence and breach of fiduciary duty). But see *Mason v. Morrow's Moving & Storage Ltd.* (1978), 5 C.C.L.T. 59 (B.C.C.A.); *Maxey v. Can. Perm. Trust Co.*, [1984] 2 W.W.R. 469 (Man. C.A.); *Fletcher v. Manitoba Public Insurance Co.* (1990), 74 D.L.R. (4th) 636 (S.C.C.); and *Boudreau v. Bank of Montreal*, 2012 ONSC 3965, aff'd 2013 ONCA 211.

4. The rule in *Thorne* also conflicts with a growing body of case law in which defendants have been held liable for economic losses resulting from the negligent performance of, or failure to perform, gratuitous business or professional services. What makes these cases unique is that a duty is imposed even though there is no contractual relationship between the parties and the defendant makes no representation to the plaintiff. A typical case of this kind involves beneficiaries who lose their inheritance due to the negligence of the deceased's lawyer in drafting the will. For the modern law, see *Whittingham v. Crease & Co.* (1978), 6 C.C.L.T. 1 (B.C.S.C.); *White v. Jones*, [1995] 2 A.C. 207 (H.L.); and *Earl v. Wilhelm* (2000), 1 C.C.L.T. (3d) 215 (Sask. C.A.). See also Benson, "Should *White v. Jones* Represent Canadian Law? A Return to First Principles" in Neyers, Chamberlain & Pitel, eds., *Emerging Issues in Tort Law* (2007), ch. 6. This topic is considered further in Chapter 14.

5. The American Law Institute has identified a number of situations in which it favours imposing tort liability for the negligent performance of a gratuitous undertaking. See *Restatement (Third) of Torts: Liability for Physical and Emotional Harm* (2012) at §42. This appears to include the mere failure to perform a gratuitous promise, as long as the defendant induced the plaintiff to rely on the promise and the plaintiff suffered detriment as a result (see comment (f)). The drafters of the *Restatement (Third)* reasoned that, if a promise supported by reliance was sufficient to give rise to promissory estoppel in the law of contract, it could also give rise to liability in tort, at least if it causes personal injury or property damage.

SMITH v. RAE
(1919), 51 D.L.R. 323 (Ont. C.A.)

MIDDLETON J.A.:—The action was brought by a married woman against a practising physician and surgeon residing in the city of Toronto. The plaintiff, expecting confinement, called, with her husband, upon the defendant, who undertook and agreed to attend her.

Upon the facts there can be no doubt that the contract was made with the plaintiff's husband. The confinement, which was expected to take place about the middle of November, did not take place until the 2nd December, 1918. The defendant did not attend the plaintiff, and the child died during delivery. The action is against the defendant for his alleged breach of duty in failing to attend at the time of the confinement.

[The court held that the appellant doctor had not been negligent in failing to attend the birth, given his other responsibilities and the information that he had received.]

Quite apart from this, there is, I think, a serious difficulty in the plaintiff's way. The contract was with the husband. The action is by the wife. She cannot sue on the contract, and her claim must, therefore, be based upon tort. Had there been actual misfeasance in anything done to the plaintiff, she could undoubtedly recover for the tort, but where the action is for damages for failure to attend, then it must be based on a breach of a contract to attend.

ZELENKO v. GIMBEL BROS., INC.
287 N.Y.S. 134 (S.C. 1936)

LAUER J.:—The general proposition of the law is that if a defendant owes a plaintiff no duty, then refusal to act is not negligence. . . . But there are many ways that a defendant's duty to act may arise. Plaintiff's intestate was taken ill in defendant's store. We will assume the defendant owed her no duty at all; the defendant could have let her be and die. But if a defendant undertakes a task, even if under no duty to undertake it, the defendant must not omit to do what an ordinary man would do in performing the task.

Here the defendant undertook to render medical aid to the plaintiff's intestate. Plaintiff says that defendant kept his intestate for six hours in an infirmary without any medical care. If the defendant had left plaintiff's intestate alone, beyond doubt some bystander, who would be influenced more by charity than by legalistic duty, would have summoned an ambulance. Defendant segregated this plaintiff's intestate where such aid could not be given and then left her alone.

The plaintiff is wrong in thinking that the duty of a common carrier of passengers is the same as the duty of this defendant. The common carrier assumes its duty by its contract of carriage. This defendant assumed its duty by meddling in matters with which legalistically it had no concern. The plaintiff is right in arguing that when the duty arose, the same type of neglect is actionable in both cases.

[Affirmed without reasons 287 N.Y.S. 136 (1936).]

SOULSBY v. TORONTO
(1907), 15 O.L.R. 13 (H.C.)

BRITTON J.:—On the 30th October, 1906, the plaintiff was employed as the driver of a baker's delivery wagon, and was delivering bread to customers in the western part of the city. On that day the plaintiff entered High Park, and drove along the road through the park, which leads out of the park, across the tracks of the Grand Trunk Railway and to the Lake Shore road. Within the park and near the railway crossing, the city has erected gates, and during the season when the park is most frequented, the city keeps a watchman at the gate nearest the crossing, keeping it open for users of the road when there is no danger from passing trains, and closing it when trains are approaching this crossing. The statement of claim alleges that the plaintiff on the day mentioned was approaching the crossing along the road in High Park, intending to proceed to the Lake Shore road. When he arrived at the crossing, he found the gate open, and, relying upon that fact as notice to him that no train was approaching, he proceeded to cross the tracks, and while so crossing was struck by a train and seriously injured.

At the close of the evidence, counsel for the defendants asked that the action be dismissed, on the grounds that no actionable negligence had been shewn, and that the plaintiff was guilty of contributory negligence. It was then agreed that the only thing to be left to the jury was the assessment of damages, and that I should dispose of all other questions, subject to the rights of parties to appeal. . . .

The case of *Stapley v. London, Brighton, and South Coast R.W. Co.* (1865), L.R. 1 Ex. 21, was relied upon by the plaintiff. That case is clearly distinguishable. "At the time of the accident, *contrary to the provisions*, by *statute* and by the *defendants' rules*, for the safety of carriage-traffic, the gates on one side of the line were partially open, and there was no gatekeeper." It was held that there was evidence of negligence, inasmuch as by neglecting the required precautions "the defendants might be considered to have intimated that their line might safely be traversed by foot passengers."

It was argued that even if the defendants were not compelled to establish the gate and employ the watchman, having undertaken it, the plaintiff was entitled to rely upon its continuance, at least until notice, actual or constructive, to the contrary.

Skelton v. London and North Western R.W. Co. (1867), L.R. 2 C.P. 631, is against the plaintiff's contention. In that case a railway, consisting of several lines, crossed a public footpath on a level, at a point near a station. On each side of the railway was a gate, as required by statute. The railway company, by way of extra precaution, usually, but not invariably, fastened the gates when a train was approaching. S., wishing to cross the railway, found the gate unfastened, and a coal train standing immediately in front of it. He waited until the coal train had moved off, and then, without looking up or down the line, commenced crossing the railway, and was killed by a passing train. If he had looked up the line, he would have seen the train in time to stop and avoid the accident. It was held that S. contributed to the accident by his negligence, and could not recover. And it was also held by Willes, J., "that the mere failure to perform a self-imposed duty is not actionable negligence; that the omission to fasten the gate did not amount to an invitation to S. to come on the line; and that, therefore, even if S. was not guilty of contributory negligence, the company were not liable."

Here the plaintiff found the gate open, but did not see the watchman. That in itself should have suggested to the plaintiff the possibility at least that the gate was open, not as an intimation that there was no danger, but that the watchman had been withdrawn — that there was no watchman in fact. No inquiry was made. The plaintiff thought the watchman was in his cabin — if so, he was not attending to the gate. The plaintiff knew of the railway, that this road led across it, and he knew of the ordinary danger at any railway crossing, and had these all in mind, so there was nothing to relieve the plaintiff of the duty of taking care and using caution when the crossing was reached, unless that care and caution were unnecessary by the fact of the gate being open.

The plaintiff relied upon *Baxter & Co. v. Jones* (1903), 6 O.L.R. 360, and upon cases cited in Anson on Contracts, 10th ed., p. 98. One case is where a person undertook gratuitously to effect insurance upon another person's house, and, having failed to do so, was held liable. These cases, which are cases of mandate, and nothing of the kind exists here, are said to rest upon this broad ground, as stated by Willes, J., in the *Skelton* case, that if a person undertake to perform a voluntary act, he is liable if he performs it improperly, but not if he neglects to perform it. The charge here is that a watchman employed did not do his duty properly. He was not at the gate at all. He was, as to the plaintiff and the public, when this accident happened, the same as during the night time — or during the rest of the year after October — when withdrawn from the gate.

I do not think the defendants are liable for merely leaving the gate open, as there is not, in my opinion, any duty to keep the gate closed at the time of approaching or passing trains.

NOTES AND QUESTIONS

1. What was the basis upon which the judge resolved the duty issue in *Smith*? Did the doctor deny the plaintiff an opportunity to obtain another doctor by agreeing to attend the birth? Assuming that he had, would this have given rise to a duty to fulfil his promise to attend? See also *Hurley v. Eddingfield*, 59 N.E. 1058 (Ind. 1901). How would the courts resolve this issue now?

2. What was the basis upon which the judge resolved the duty issue in *Zelenko*? If the store's employees had attended to the plaintiff without moving her, but after a few minutes discontinued their efforts, would they have been liable in negligence? Can you reconcile the decision in *Smith* with that in *Zelenko*? Is the decision in *Zelenko* compatible with the principles in *Thorne*? See *Dudley v. Victor Lynn Lines Inc.*, 138 A.2d 53 (N.J. 1958); and *Barnett v. Chelsea & Kensington Hosp. Mgmt. Committee*, [1969] 1 Q.B. 428.

3. In *Ross v. United States*, 910 F.2d 1422 (7th Cir. 1990), the plaintiff's estate claimed against the defendant county for "forcing" its gratuitous services upon him. The deceased was a 12-year-old boy who fell off a deteriorating breakwater and immediately sank below the surface. Several municipal rescue professionals and two civilian scuba divers appeared on the scene and wished to attempt a rescue. However, the municipality had recently made an agreement with the county that rescue efforts on the lake were the responsibility of the county alone. The county's Deputy Sheriff arrived in a patrol boat and informed the would-be rescuers that all rescues were to be

performed by the county. He verbally and physically prevented the would-be rescuers from proceeding, even when they offered to perform the rescue at their own risk. He threatened to arrest them if they persisted. By the time the county divers arrived (some 20-30 minutes later), the boy had died. His estate's claim against the county was allowed to proceed not because the county had failed to rescue him, but because its policy of being the sole provider of rescue services prevented the plaintiff from receiving alternative assistance.

4. What was the basis of the plaintiff's argument in *Soulsby*? Is Britton J. suggesting that an individual can never be held liable for discontinuing a gratuitous service? Do you think that the case would have been decided the same way if the watchman had been present and knew of the train's imminent arrival, but chose not to lower the gate or otherwise warn the plaintiff? Can you distinguish *Soulsby* from *Zelenko*?

5. In *Mercer v. South Eastern & Chatham Ry. Co.'s Managing Committee*, [1922] 2 K.B. 549, the court held that the defendant's regular practice of closing the gate when a train approached constituted a tacit invitation to cross the tracks when the gate was up. The defendant was held liable for the injuries sustained by the plaintiff when he acted upon this invitation and was struck by a train. Can you reconcile *Soulsby* and *Mercer*? What factors would lead to the recognition of a duty of care? Which case is preferable? See also *Erie Ry. Co. v. Stewart*, 40 F.2d 855 (6th Cir. 1930).

6. What must an individual do to notify the public that he or she is withdrawing a gratuitous service? Would it be sufficient for a railroad company to post a sign at the crossing a month before it withdraws its gatekeeper? In such a case, would the company owe a duty of care to an illiterate pedestrian who still expected a gatekeeper to be present at the crossing? Would the company have to post a notice prior to changing a gatekeeper's hours? Do the same principles apply to a municipality that wishes to withdraw a lifeguard from a public beach, a supervisor from a playground or a crossing guard from a school crossing? See generally *Wilmington Gen. Hosp. v. Manlove*, 174 A.2d 135 (Del. 1961); *Hendricks v. R.*, [1970] S.C.R. 237; *R. v. Nord-Deutsche Versicherungs-Gesellschaft*, [1971] S.C.R. 849; and *County of Parkland No. 31 v. Stetar; County of Parkland No. 31 v. Woodrow*, [1975] 2 S.C.R. 884.

7. An insurance company that has previously sent renewal reminders to its clients prior to the expiry of their policies may be under a duty of care in tort to continue this practice until it notifies the policyholders of its contrary intention. See *Morash v. Lockhart & Ritchie Ltd.* (1978), 48 A.P.R. 180 (N.B.C.A.); and *Grove Services Ltd. v. Lenhart Agencies Ltd.* (1979), 10 C.C.L.T. 101 (B.C.S.C.). But see *Vienneau Assur. Ltée v. Roy* (1986), 67 N.B.R. (2d) 16 (C.A.); and *Bijeau v. Pelletier* (1996), 176 N.B.R. (2d) 241 (C.A.).

8. Section 217 of the *Criminal Code* imposes a criminal law duty on an individual who "undertakes to do an act" to complete it, if an omission to do so is or may be dangerous to life. Although the section's origins can be traced to Canada's first *Criminal Code* in 1892, these provisions have generated little comment. Nevertheless, it is interesting to note that one's criminal liability for discontinuing a gratuitous undertaking appears to be far broader than one's civil liability.

9. It has become common for industries and corporations to adopt voluntary codes of conduct as measures of corporate social responsibility. These often involve undertakings not to do business with foreign corporations that have offensive environmental, human rights, or labour practices. Should such voluntary undertakings give rise to potential tort liability? What incentives would such liability create? See Reinschmidt, "The Law of Tort: A Useful Tool to Further Corporate Social Responsibility?" (2013) 34:4 Company L. 103; Conway, "A New Duty of Care? Tort Liability from Voluntary Human Rights Due Diligence in Global Supply" (2015) 40:2 Queen's L.J. 741.

In *Das v. George Weston Ltd.*, 2017 ONSC 4129, aff'd 2018 ONCA 1053, Perell J. refused to certify a class action by workers who were injured in the Rana Plaza collapse in Bangladesh, in which 1130 people died and another 2520 were seriously injured. The workers were attempting to sue Loblaws, which had purchased clothing from a manufacturer whose factory was located in the Plaza, on the basis that the defendant's Corporate Social Responsibility Standards amounted to an undertaking to ensure the structural safety of the buildings in which its business associates operated. Perell J. rejected this contention on several grounds, including the potential for indeterminate liability, the lack of reliance by the plaintiffs, and the unfair distinctions it would create between corporations with and without CSR policies.

10. See generally Seavey, "Reliance Upon Gratuitous Promises or Other Conduct" (1951) 64 Harv. L. Rev. 913; and Gregory, "Gratuitous Undertakings and the Duty of Care" (1951) 1 De Paul L. Rev. 30.

REVIEW PROBLEMS

1. Bill had told John that he would give him a ride to the university to write the LSAT. On the morning of the examination, Bill drove halfway to John's house before he realized that he had left his identification card at home. In his rush and nervousness, Bill forgot about his promise to John. As a result, John missed the last sitting of the LSAT for the next academic year. Discuss whether Bill owed John a duty of care to perform his promise. See *Université Laval v. Carriere* (1987), 38 D.L.R. (4th) 503 (Qc. C.A.).

2. The Vista Credit Card Company had widely advertised that it would provide $100,000 flight insurance free of charge to any cardholder who purchased an airline ticket with the card. The plan was quietly dropped six months after it was initiated, because Vista's market researchers indicated that the free insurance offer was having little impact on sales. Under what circumstances would Vista owe a duty of care to notify a cardholder that it was withdrawing this service?

3. The Marvel Bleach Company marketed its highly toxic household bleach in a childproof jug for ten years. In an attempt to reduce costs, Marvel planned to replace the expensive childproof top with an identical looking, but easy-to-open spout. Since it had never advertised that the jug was childproof, Marvel decided to switch tops without advertising this change. You have been asked to advise Marvel on the potential tort consequences of this decision.

SPECIAL DUTIES OF CARE: MISCELLANEOUS CATEGORIES

1. Introduction
2. The Duty of Care Owed to Rescuers
3. Duties Owed to the Unborn
4. Psychiatric Harm
5. A Health Professional's Duty to Inform
6. A Manufacturer's and Supplier's Duty to Warn
7. Duty of Care Owed by a Barrister

1. Introduction

As explained in Chapter 10, in *Cooper v. Hobart*, [2001] 3 S.C.R. 537, the Supreme Court of Canada established a framework for analyzing novel duties of care. The test in *Cooper* determines the existence of duty based on questions of foreseeability, proximity and policy. However, this general test has not ousted the specific principles that have evolved historically with respect to some particular duties of care. The duties examined in this chapter have specialized analytical frameworks that predate the *Cooper* test and continue to apply.

For the most part, these frameworks involve aspects of foreseeability, proximity and policy, but their principles are more finely-tuned and directed toward particular types of relationships or injuries. For example, the law pertaining to manufacturer's liability depends on the foreseeable risks associated with a product, keeping in mind the intended consumer. In another vein, the availability of recovery for injuries to unborn children involves complex policy arguments about maternal autonomy and the value of life. Thus, the specific duties examined here invoke familiar concepts of duty, but apply them in very specific ways, in accordance with distinct rules that have developed over many decades.

The first part of this chapter examines the special duties of care that may arise in connection with three categories of claimants: (i) rescuers, (ii) unborn children, and (iii) those who suffer psychiatric harm. The second part of this chapter examines the special duties of care that may arise in connection with three categories of defendants: (i) health care professionals who are in a position to inform patients of the risks associated with treatment or care, (ii) manufacturers and suppliers who are in a position to warn consumers of the risks associated with dangerous products, and (iii) barristers.

2. The Duty of Care Owed to Rescuers

In *Matthews v. MacLaren* (1969), 4 D.L.R. (3d) 557 (Ont. H.C.), which was excerpted in the previous chapter, the question was whether MacLaren, as captain of *The Ogopogo*, owed a duty of care to rescue Matthews, a gratuitous passenger who had fallen overboard. That question was answered in the affirmative. In the case that follows, the question is whether MacLaren also owed a duty of care to Horsley, another gratuitous passenger, who died while attempting to rescue Matthews.

HORSLEY v. MACLAREN
(1972), 22 D.L.R. (3d) 545 (S.C.C.)

RITCHIE J.:—I have had the opportunity of reading the reasons for judgment of my brother Laskin and I agree with him that . . . a duty rested upon the respondent MacLaren in his capacity as a host and as the owner and operator of the "Ogopogo", to do the best he could to effect the rescue of one of his guests [Matthews] who had accidentally fallen overboard.

. . .

The duty, if any, owing to the late Mr. Horsley stands on an entirely different footing. If, upon Matthews falling overboard, Horsley had immediately dived to his rescue and lost his life, as he ultimately did upon contact with the icy water, then I can see no conceivable basis on which the respondent could have been held responsible for his death.

There is, however, no suggestion that there was any negligence in the rescue of Horsley and if [MacLaren is to be held liable for Horsley's death] such liability must in my view stem from a finding that the situation of peril brought about by Matthews falling into the water was thereafter, within the next three or four minutes, so aggravated by the negligence of MacLaren in attempting his rescue as to induce Horsley to risk his life by diving in after him.

I think that the best description of the circumstances giving rise to the liability to a second rescuer such as Horsley is contained in the reasons for judgment of Lord Denning, M.R., in *Videan v. British Transport Commission*, [1963] 2 Q.B. 650, where he said, at p. 669:

> It seems to me that, if a person *by his fault* creates a situation of peril, he must answer for it to any person who attempts to rescue the person who is in danger. He owes a duty to such a person above all others. The rescuer may act instinctively out of humanity or deliberately out of courage. But whichever it is, so long as it is not wanton interference, if the rescuer is killed or injured in the attempt, he can recover damages *from the one whose fault has been the cause of it.*

The italics are my own.

In the present case a situation of peril was created when Matthews fell overboard, but it was not created by any fault on the part of MacLaren, and before MacLaren can be found to have been in any way responsible for Horsley's death, it must be found that there was such negligence in his method of rescue as to place Matthews in an apparent position of increased danger subsequent to and distinct from the danger to which he had been initially exposed by his accidental fall. In other words, any duty owing to Horsley must stem from the fact that a new situation of peril was created by MacLaren's negligence which induced Horsley to act as he did . . . .

In assessing MacLaren's conduct in attempting to rescue Matthews, I think it should be recognized that he was not under a duty to do more than take all reasonable steps which would have been likely to effect the rescue of a man who was alive and could take some action to assist himself . . . .

Reconstructing the events from the evidence of those who were actually at the scene, it appears to me that MacLaren was first alerted to Matthews' fall when the body was only about a boat-length and a half behind him. He put the engines momentarily in neutral and as soon as he saw the body he reversed, almost immediately after which Jones threw a life-ring within 10 ft. of the man in the water. . . .

Just before the gust of wind carried the boat to port, Marck had the pike pole within Matthews' reach if he had been able to grab it. . . .

I am satisfied that Matthews' body had been in the water for a little less than two minutes when Marck first had the pike pole within his grasp and a life-jacket thrown by Jones was within six inches of him.

The finding of the learned trial Judge that MacLaren was negligent in the rescue of Matthews is really twofold. On the one hand he finds that there was a failure to comply with the "man overboard" rescue procedure recommended by two experts called for the plaintiff, and on the other hand he concludes that MacLaren "was unable to exercise proper judgment in the emergency created because of his excessive consumption of alcohol." In the course of his reasons for judgment in the Court of Appeal, Mr. Justice Schroeder expressly found that there was nothing in the evidence to support the view that MacLaren was incapable of proper management and control owing to the consumption of liquor, the question was not seriously argued in this Court, and like my brother Laskin, I do not think there is any ground for saying that intoxicants had anything to do with the fatal occurrences. . . .

The procedure recommended by the experts in such circumstances was to bring the boat bow on towards the body and the witness Mumford, who had written a "boating course" for the Canadian Boating Federation and had considerable experience in small boats, testified that "it would take about two minutes to turn the boat around and come back on him and have him along side, and possibly another twenty-five, thirty seconds to get him on the boat". The other expert, Livingstone, took the view that by using the bow-on procedure it would take a maximum of two minutes to effect the rescue. . . .

As I have indicated, the evidence discloses that the boat was first brought to a stop in a maximum of two minutes after the body was sighted and at that time there was not only a life-jacket but a pike pole within Matthews' grasp had he been conscious.

In the present case, however, although the procedure followed by MacLaren was not the most highly recommended one, I do not think that the evidence justifies the finding that any fault of his induced Horsley to risk his life by diving as he did. In this regard I adopt the conclusion reached by Mr. Justice Schroeder in the penultimate paragraph of his reasons for judgment where he says [at 287]:

> . . . if the appellant erred in backing instead of turning the cruiser and proceeding towards Matthews "bow on", the error was one of judgment and not negligence, and in the existing circumstances of emergency ought fairly to be excused.

I think it should be made clear that, in my opinion, the duty to rescue a man who has fallen accidentally overboard is a common law duty, the existence of which is in no way dependent upon the provisions of s. 526(1) of the *Canada Shipping Act*, R.S.C. 1952, c. 29 [now R.S.C. 1985, c. S-9, s. 451].

I should also say that, unlike Jessup, J.A., the failure of Horsley to heed MacLaren's warning to remain in the cockpit or cabin plays no part in my reasoning.

For all these reasons I would dismiss this appeal with costs.

LASKIN J. (dissenting):—. . . In this Court, counsel . . . relied on three alternative bases of liability. There was, first, the submission that in going to the aid of Matthews, as he did, MacLaren came under a duty to carry out the rescue with due care in the circumstances, and his failure to employ standard rescue procedures foreseeably brought Horsley into the picture with the ensuing fatal result. The second basis of liability was doubly found as resting (a) on the common law duty of care of a private carrier to his passengers, involving a duty to come to the aid of a passenger who has accidentally fallen overboard, or (b) on a statutory duty under s. 526(1) of the *Canada Shipping Act*, R.S.C. 1952, c. 29 [now R.S.C. 1985, c. S-9, s. 451], to come to the aid of a passenger who has fallen overboard. There was failure, so the allegation was, to act reasonably in carrying out these duties or either of them, with the foreseeable consequence of Horsley's encounter of danger. The third contention was the broadest, to the effect that where a situation of peril, albeit not brought about originally by the defendant's negligence, arises by reason of the defendant's attempt at rescue, he is liable to a second rescuer for ensuing damage on the ground that the latter's intervention is reasonably foreseeable.

None of the bases of liability advanced by the appellants is strictly within the original principle on which the "rescue" cases were founded. That was the recognition of a duty by a negligent defendant to a rescuer coming to the aid of the person imperilled by the defendant's negligence. The evolution of the law on this subject, originating in the moral approbation of assistance to a person in peril, involved a break with the "mind your own business" philosophy. Legal protection is now afforded to one who risks injury to himself in going to the rescue of another who has been foreseeably exposed to danger by the unreasonable conduct of a third person. The latter is now subject to liability at the suit of the rescuer as well as at the suit of the imperilled person, provided, in the case of the rescuer, that his intervention was not so utterly foolhardy as to be outside of any accountable risk and thus beyond even contributory negligence.

Moreover, the liability to the rescuer, although founded on the concept of duty, is now seen as stemming from an independent and not a derivative duty of the negligent person. As *Fleming on Torts*, 3rd ed. (1965), has put it (at p. 166), the cause of action of the rescuer in arising out of the defendant's negligence, is based "not in its tendency to imperil the person rescued, but in its tendency to induce the rescuer to encounter the danger. Thus viewed, the duty to the rescuer is clearly independent. . . ". This explanation of principle was put forward as early as 1924 by Professor Bohlen (see his *Studies in the Law of Torts*, at p. 569) in recognition of the difficulty of straining the notion of foreseeability to embrace a rescuer of a person imperilled by another's negligence. Under this explanation of the basis of liability, it is immaterial that the imperilled person does not in fact suffer any injury or that, as it turns out, the negligent person was under no liability to him either because the injury was not caused by the negligence or the damage was outside the foreseeable risk of harm to him: *cf. Videan v. British Transport Commission*, [1963] 2 Q.B. 650. It is a further consequence of the recognition of an independent duty that a person who imperils himself by his carelessness may be as fully liable to a rescuer as a third person would be who imperils another. In my opinion, therefore, *Dupuis v. New Regina Trading Co. Ltd.*, [1943] 4

THE DUTY OF CARE OWED TO RESCUERS 421

D.L.R. 275, [1943] 2 W.W.R. 593, ought no longer to be taken as a statement of the common law in Canada in so far as it denies recovery because the rescuer was injured in going to the aid of a person who imperilled himself. . . .

I realize that this statement of the law invites the conclusion that Horsley's estate might succeed against that of Matthews if it was proved that Matthews acted without proper care for his own safety so that Horsley was prompted to come to his rescue. This issue does not, however, have to be canvassed in these proceedings since the estate of Matthews was not joined as a co-defendant. . . .

MacLaren was not a random rescuer. As owner and operator of a boat on which he was carrying invited guests, he was under a legal duty to take reasonable care for their safety. This was a duty which did not depend on the existence of a contract of carriage, nor on whether he was a common carrier or private carrier of passengers. Having brought his guests into a relationship with him as passengers on his boat, albeit as social or gratuitous passengers, he was obliged to exercise reasonable care for their safety. That obligation extends, in my opinion, to rescue from perils of the sea where this is consistent with his duty to see to the safety of his other passengers and with concern for his own safety. The duty exists whether the passenger falls overboard accidentally or by reason of his own carelessness.

. . .

On the view that I take of the issues in this case and, having regard to the facts, the appellants cannot succeed on the first of the alternative submissions on liability if they cannot succeed on the second ground of an existing common law duty of care. Their third contention was not clearly anchored in any original or supervening duty of care and breach of that duty; and, if that be so, I do not see how their counsel's submission on the foreseeability of a second rescuer, even if accepted, can saddle a non-negligent first rescuer with liability either to the rescuee or to a second rescuer. Encouragement by the common law of the rescue of persons in danger would, in my opinion, go beyond reasonable bounds if it involved liability of one rescuer to a succeeding one where the former has not been guilty of any fault which could be said to have induced a second rescue attempt. . . .

The present case is thus reduced to the question of liability on the basis of (1) an alleged breach of a duty of care originating in the relationship of carrier and passenger; (2) whether the breach, if there was one, could be said to have prompted Horsley to go to Matthews' rescue; and (3) whether Horsley's conduct, if not so rash in the circumstances as to be unforeseeable, none the less exhibited want of care so as to make him guilty of contributory negligence.

Whether MacLaren was in breach of his duty of care to Matthews was a question of fact on which the trial Judge's affirmative finding is entitled to considerable weight. That finding was, of course, essential to the further question of a consequential duty to Horsley. Lacourciere J., came to his conclusion of fact on the evidence, after putting to himself the following question: "What would the reasonable boat operator do in the circumstances, attributing to such person the reasonable skill and experience required of the master of a cabin cruiser who is responsible for the safety and rescue of his passengers?" (see 4 D.L.R. (3d) 557 at p. 564. . .). It was the trial Judge's finding that MacLaren, as he himself admitted, had adopted the wrong procedure for rescuing a passenger who had fallen overboard. He knew the proper procedure and had practised it. Coming bow on to effect a rescue was the standard procedure and was taught as such. . . .

I do not see how it can be said that the trial Judge's finding against MacLaren on the issue of breach of duty is untenable. In relation to Horsley's intervention, the finding stands unembarrassed by any question of causation in relation to Matthews. . .

I turn to the question whether the breach of duty to Matthews could properly be regarded in this case as prompting Horsley to attempt a rescue. Like the trial Judge, I am content to adopt and apply analogically on this point the reasoning of Cardozo, J., as he then was, in *Wagner v. International R. Co.* (1921), 133 N.E. 437, and of Lord Denning, M.R., in *Videan v. British Transport Commission, supra.* To use Judge Cardozo's phrase, Horsley's conduct in the circumstances was "within the range of the natural and probable." The fact, moreover, that Horsley's sacrifice was futile is no more a disabling ground here than it was in the *Wagner* case, where the passenger thrown off the train was dead when the plaintiff went to help him, unless it be the case that the rescuer acted wantonly. . .

In responding as he did, and in circumstances where only hindsight made it doubtful that Matthews could be saved, Horsley was not wanton or foolhardy. Like the trial Judge, I do not think that his action passed the point of brave acceptance of a serious risk and became a futile exhibition of recklessness for which there can be no recourse. There is, however, the question whether Horsley was guilty of contributory negligence. This was an alternative plea of the respondent based *inter alia*, on Horsley's failure to put on a life-jacket or secure himself to the boat by a rope or call on the other passengers to stand by, especially in the light of the difficulties of Matthews in the cold water. The trial Judge rejected the contentions of contributory negligence, holding that although "Wearing a life-jacket or securing himself to a lifeline would have been more prudent . . . Horsley's impulsive act without such precautions was the result of the excitement, haste and confusion of the moment, and cannot be said to constitute contributory negligence" (see 4 D.L.R. (3d) at p. 569). In view of its conclusions on the main issue of MacLaren's liability, the Ontario Court of Appeal did not canvass the question of contributory negligence.

The matter is not free from difficulty. About two minutes passed after Matthews had fallen overboard and MacLaren made his first abortive attempt at rescue by proceeding astern. Two life-jackets had been successively thrown towards Matthews without any visible effort on his part to seize them. Then came the second attempt at rescue by backing the boat, and it was in progress when Horsley dived in. Horsley had come on deck at the shout of "Roly's overboard" and was at the stern during MacLaren's first attempt at rescue, and must have been there when the life-jackets were thrown towards Matthews. However, in the concern of the occasion, and having regard to MacLaren's breach of duty, I do not think that Horsley can be charged with contributory negligence in diving to the rescue of Matthews as he did. I point out as well that the evidence does not indicate that the failure to put on a life-jacket or secure himself to a lifeline played any part in Horsley's death.

. . .

[Judson J. and Spence J. concurred with Ritchie J., and Hall J. concurred with Laskin J.]

NOTES AND QUESTIONS

1. Both the majority and dissent in *Horsley* refer to Denning M.R.'s judgment in *Videan v. British Transport Comm.*, [1963] 2 All E.R. 860 (C.A.). In *Videan*, the

stationmaster's young son wandered onto the tracks and the stationmaster attempted to rescue him from an approaching trolley. The driver, who was not keeping a proper lookout, could not stop. The stationmaster was killed and his son was badly injured. The child's claim was dismissed because, as a trespasser, his presence was unforeseeable. Nevertheless, Denning M.R. held that the driver ought to have foreseen that his conduct might create an emergency of some kind. Consequently, the stationmaster's presence as a rescuer was foreseeable and he was owed a duty of care. Is Denning M.R.'s analysis compelling?

2. Cardozo J. had adopted a similar position in *Wagner v. Int. Ry. Co.*, 133 N.E. 437 at 437 (N.Y. 1921). His statement that "danger invites rescue" is now generally accepted. Given this broad test of foreseeability, under what circumstances would a rescuer be denied recovery as an unforeseeable plaintiff? How is the foreseeable plaintiff test applied differently in rescue cases than in other negligence cases? Is this appropriate? See Linden, "Down with Foreseeability! Of Thin Skulls and Rescuers" (1969) 47 Can. Bar Rev. 545 at 558-70; and Smith, "The Mystery of Duty" in Klar, ed., *Studies in Canadian Tort Law* (1977) 1 at 30-32.

3. In *Horsley*, Ritchie J. also quotes Denning M.R.'s statement "if a man by his fault creates a situation of peril, he must answer for it to any person who attempts to rescue the person who is in danger." What does this mean?

According to Ritchie J., what had to be established to prove that MacLaren owed Horsley a duty of care? What is the test for breaching the standard of care? Based on the expert evidence, was MacLaren's use of the reverse, rather than the bow-on method, a causal factor in inducing Horsley's rescue attempt? Why did Ritchie J. dismiss Horsley's claim?

4. What was the basis upon which Laskin J. held that MacLaren owed Horsley a duty of care? How did Laskin J.'s analysis relate to the appellant's three alternative bases of liability? What was the basis upon which Laskin J. concluded that MacLaren breached the standard of care? Do you agree with Laskin J.'s analysis of the causation or contributory negligence issue? Assuming Horsley realized that Matthews was dead, would he have been contributorily negligent in jumping overboard to recover the body?

5. Although the courts have occasionally held rescuers to be contributorily negligent, such findings are rare. Rescuers confronting a sudden emergency are not held to the same standard of care as those acting in less extreme circumstances. See *Sayers v. Harlow Urban Dist. Council*, [1958] 2 All E.R. 342 (C.A.); *Corothers v. Slobodian*, [1975] 2 S.C.R. 633; *Toy v. Argenti*, [1980] 3 W.W.R. 276 (B.C.S.C.); and *Cleary v. Hansen* (1981), 18 C.C.L.T. 147 (Ont. H.C.). See also Binchy, "Torts — Rescuers — Foreseeability — Contributory Negligence" (1974) 52 Can. Bar Rev. 292; and Voechting, "Negligence — Rescuer Doctrine — Liability of a Tortfeasor for Injuries to Rescuers Extended" (1976) 7 Man. L.J. 87.

In *Meyer v. Parker* (1995), 7 B.C.L.R. (3d) 131 (S.C.), aff'd (1996), 21 B.C.L.R. (3d) 33 (C.A.), the plaintiff went to a convenience store after receiving an allegedly "distraught" call from a friend working at the store. On arrival, he found three youths arguing with his friend. After a heated verbal exchange, the plaintiff convinced the youths to leave the store. However, the plaintiff then followed the youths outside and told his friend to lock the store's doors. He was subsequently beaten by the youths and lost his left eye. The plaintiff's attempt to rely on the rescuer doctrine failed because he had left a place of safety and deliberately put himself at risk by confronting the youths outside. The court found that he had not taken reasonable care for his own safety, and his claim was dismissed.

6. The defence of voluntary assumption of risk has been all but eliminated in rescue cases. In *Urbanski v. Patel* (1978), 84 D.L.R. (3d) 650 (Man. Q.B.), the plaintiff donated a kidney to his daughter after the defendant surgeon had negligently removed her only kidney. The plaintiff claimed that the loss of his donated kidney had been caused by the defendant's negligence in injuring his daughter. The court found for the plaintiff, concluding that his act was a reasonably foreseeable result of the defendant's negligence. The defence of voluntary assumption of risk was dismissed with a statement to the effect that the defence is inapplicable where the plaintiff consciously faces a risk in an attempt to rescue another who has been imperilled by the defendant's negligence. In light of *Urbanski*, can you suggest a situation in which a rescuer might be denied recovery on the basis of voluntary assumption of risk? See Robertson, "A New Application of the Rescue Principle" (1980) 96 L.Q.R. 19.

Is the treatment of voluntary assumption of risk in rescue cases consistent with the common law's refusal to impose a duty to rescue (see Chapter 11)? If there is no legal obligation to rescue, then why do the courts not find that rescuers have voluntarily assumed the risks associated with their conduct? Is the decision to risk one's life in a rescue attempt not a conscious assumption of risk? In *Martin v. America International Assurance Life Co.*, [2003] 1 S.C.R. 158 at para. 28, McLachlin C.J. suggested that the favourable treatment of rescuers was justified by the "high redeeming social value" of their conduct.

7. In many jurisdictions in the United States, police officers, firefighters and other professional rescuers are denied recovery from tortfeasors for injuries sustained in their rescue efforts. The "fireman's rule," as it is called, is based in part on voluntary assumption of risk. See generally "Assumption of the Risk and the Fireman's Rule" (1981) 7 Wm. Mitchell L. Rev. 749; Riley, "The Fireman's Rule: Defining its Scope Using the Cost-Spreading Rationale" (1983) 71 Cal. L. Rev. 218; Werner, "*Berko v. Freda*: The Fireman's Rule Burns Police Officers" (1984) 37 Rutgers L. Rev. 195; Palumbo, "Equal Protection and the Fireman's Rule in Ohio" (1987) 38 Case W.L. Rev. 123; and Scholz, "*Rosa v. Dunkin' Donuts*: The Fireman's Rule Revisited" (1992) 44 Rutgers L. Rev. 405; and Casselman, "Re-examining the Firefighter's Rules in Arizona" (2017) 59:1 Ariz. L. Rev. 263. The scope of "professional rescuer" is relatively broad in some jurisdictions. See for example Handley, "Back to the Basics: Restoring Fundamental Tort Principles by Abolishing the Professional Rescuer's Doctrine" (2015) 68:2 Ark. L. Rev. 489, which includes discussion of the rule's expansion to include roadside assistance providers.

In *Ogwo v. Taylor*, [1987] 3 All E.R. 961 (H.L.), the House of Lords stated that the rule had no place in English law. This principle was affirmed in *White v. Chief Constable of South Yorkshire*, [1999] 1 All E.R. 1 (H.L.). In Canada, it also appears that firefighters and other professional rescuers can recover for the injuries they sustain in rescue attempts. What argument would you make in favour of the "fireman's rule?" See Dreiman, "Extending the Fireman's Rule to Great Britain: Protecting British Citizens from Tort Liability for Firefighters' Line-of-Duty Injuries" (1998) 8 Ind. Int'l & Comp. L. Rev. 381.

How should the availability of insurance benefits affect the fireman's rule? Consider (a) the employment benefits of the injured professional rescuer and (b) the liability insurance of a homeowner who negligently sets his or her house on fire? See Heidt, "When Plaintiffs are Premium Planners for Their Injuries: A Fresh Look at the Fireman's Rule" (2007) 82 Ind. L.J. 745. Are the risks associated with professional rescue reflected in the salaries of such professionals? If so, what are the implications for firefighters who are injured during the course of an off-duty rescue? See Berry, "*Espinoza v. Schulenburg*: Arizona Adopts the Rescue Doctrine and Firefighter's Rule" (2007) 49 Ariz. L.R. 171.

8. Since the rescuer's claim is independent of that of the person being rescued, a rescuer may recover for injuries sustained in assisting those who have negligently imperilled themselves. See *Chapman v. Hearse* (1961), 106 C.L.R. 112 (H.C.A.); *Corothers v. Slobodian, supra; C.N.R. v. Bakty* (1977), 18 O.R. (2d) 481 (Co. Ct.); *Roberts v. Morana* (1997), 38 C.C.L.T. (2d) 1 (Ont. Gen. Div.); *Bridge v. Jo* (1998), [1999] 3 W.W.R. 167 (B.C.S.C.); and *Maguire v. Padt*, 2014 ONSC 6099. But see *Clyke v. Clyke* (1987), 80 N.S.R. (2d) 149 (T.D.), aff'd (1988), 83 N.S.R. (2d) 79 (C.A.); and *Smith v. Tucker*, 2007 CarswellBC 709 (S.C.) (WL Can). See also *Dufault v. Excelsior Mortgage Corp.* (2002), 310 A.R. 117 (Q.B.), aff'd (2003), 20 Alta. L.R. (4th) 220 (C.A.), where the plaintiff was injured while trying to protect a night clerk at the defendant's hotel from a gang of aggressive youths. The hotel was found liable for having inadequate security measures in place to protect its night staff. The court found that it was foreseeable that staff might become threatened and that patrons would step in to assist.

9. The general principles governing rescuers also apply to cases in which plaintiffs are injured while attempting to save themselves or their own property. See *Prescott v. Connell* (1893), 22 S.C.R. 147; *Hutterly v. Imperial Oil Ltd.* (1956), 3 D.L.R. (2d) 719 (Ont. H.C.); *Sayers v. Harlow Urban District Council, supra; Zervobeakos v. Zervobeakos* (1969), 8 D.L.R. (3d) 377 (N.S.C.A.); and *Toy v. Argenti, supra.*

A duty of care may be refused, however, if the plaintiff was attempting to protect a purely economic interest. In *Saccone v. Fandrakis* (2002), 11 C.C.L.T. (3d) 151 (B.C.S.C.), the plaintiff saw, from a distance of half a city block, the aftermath of an accident in which his van had been damaged. He ran toward his vehicle because he was concerned that the defendant, who he correctly believed was responsible for the accident, would leave the scene. The plaintiff feared that this would affect his insurance claim. In running to the scene, he slipped and hurt himself. The court applied *Cooper v. Hobart* and held that the defendant did not owe a duty of care with respect to the plaintiff's injuries. While accepting that it "might . . . be reasonably foreseeable that the plaintiff in such a situation would be injured while sprinting . . . to the scene," Catliff J. held that there was insufficient proximity between the parties and, further, that policy considerations militated against the recognition of a duty of care. It was one thing to recognize a duty of care where the plaintiff, pressed by exigency, came to the rescue of person or property; quite another to recognize a duty where, in the absence of an emergency, the plaintiff tried to protect a purely economic interest. Does this decision seem fair to you? How would you have responded to the accident if you had been in the plaintiff's position?

10. One unresolved issue in *Horsley* is whether the general principles governing the discontinuance of a gratuitous undertaking apply to rescue cases. The majority of the Court of Appeal indicated that an individual who has voluntarily begun a rescue attempt is under no duty to continue it unless he or she has worsened the victim's original position. The Court of Appeal cited *East Suffolk Rivers Catchment Bd. v. Kent*, [1941] A.C. 74 (H.L.) as authority, even though that case concerned the liability of public authorities for property damage arising from negligence in exercising their statutory powers. Why did the Supreme Court of Canada not find it necessary to address the gratuitous rescue issue? Laskin J. suggested that *East Suffolk* should not govern liability for the discontinuance of rescue attempts when human lives are at stake. Should there be a duty to continue a voluntary rescue attempt in such circumstances?

11. The courts have taken a relatively broad approach to the definition of "rescuer." See for example *Urbanski v. Patel, supra* (kidney donor); *Bridge v. Jo, supra* (911 caller); and *Emerson v. Insurance Corporation of British Columbia* (2003), 123 A.C.W.S. (3d) 1169 (B.C.S.C.) (woman who helped an elderly couple get out of their car after it left the road). However, in *Joudrey v. Swissair Transport Company* (2004), 225 N.S.R. (2d) 156 (S.C.), the court denied the claim of a member of the armed forces for the psychiatric harm he suffered after attending to the wreckage of Swissair Flight 111, which crashed off the coast of Halifax. Because it quickly became clear that there would be no survivors, the plaintiff was not involved in a "rescue" operation but in a "recovery" operation. The court stressed at para. 35 that, in order to qualify as a "rescuer," the plaintiff "must have been engaged in the process of attempting to save someone who is in danger at the time of the purported rescue." See also *Smith v. Tucker* (2007), 71 B.C.L.R. (4th) 286 (S.C.), where the defendant injured his ankle while assisting the defendant, whose truck had run out of gas and was stuck in an intersection. The court rejected the argument that a duty was owed to him as a rescuer, on account of the fact that neither person nor property was in immediate peril.

For a discussion of the policy considerations behind the generous recovery obtained by rescuers, see Klar, "The Role of Fault and Policy in Negligence Law" (1996) 35 Alta. L. Rev. 24.

12. As indicated in the previous chapter, s. 217 of the *Criminal Code*, R.S.C. 1985, c. C-46, requires an individual who undertakes an act to complete it if an omission to do so is, or may be, dangerous to life. There are few reported cases, but presumably the section should apply to an individual who, having undertaken a voluntary rescue attempt, abandons the victim in a life-threatening situation. Based on this criminal law provision, what argument would you make for recognizing a parallel common law duty in negligence?

In *R. v. Browne* (1997), 33 O.R. (3d) 775 (C.A.), the defendant and the deceased were drug dealers. The deceased swallowed a bag of cocaine in order to avoid detection by police. She was unable to throw up the bag, and began to exhibit symptoms of narcotics poisoning. The defendant told the deceased that he would take her to the hospital. He called a taxi to take her to the hospital but she died shortly after her arrival. At trial, the defendant was convicted of criminal negligence causing death for failing to complete the "undertaking" that he had assumed under s. 217 to take the deceased to the hospital. The trial judge found that calling a taxi, rather than

911, constituted wanton and reckless disregard for the deceased's life. The conviction was reversed by the Court of Appeal for Ontario, which found that the offer to take the deceased to the hospital did not constitute an "undertaking" under s. 217. Abella J.A. (as she then was), speaking for the court, wrote that "[t]he mere expression of words indicating a willingness to do an act cannot trigger the legal duty."

REVIEW PROBLEMS

1. The Apex Corporation was shooting a gangster film in downtown Toronto. One of the scenes depicted two thugs beating a police officer just outside of the Toronto Art Gallery. Apex had obtained permission to film the scene on the Gallery's property, cordoned off the outside area and staged the scene behind the Gallery away from possible intermeddlers. During the middle of the scene, a patron in the Art Gallery burst through a fire door and lunged at the two thugs. He had lost his way in the basement of the Gallery. All he could see through the small window beside the fire door was the officer on the ground being kicked. Believing the officer to be in danger, he opened the fire door, hoping to set off the alarm and scare off the thugs. Unfortunately, in lunging at the thugs, he slipped and broke his leg. You have been asked to advise the patron on his prospects of recovering from the Apex Corporation.

2. Several weeks after he was informed that he had terminal cancer, Mr. Smith decided to commit suicide. However, when he stepped out on the ledge of his fourth floor apartment window, he began to have second thoughts. While he was deliberating, a bystander called the police and fire departments. Within minutes, two emergency rescue teams arrived on the scene. By this time, Smith had changed his mind and had re-entered his apartment. Smith died of natural causes shortly thereafter. Advise the rescue teams who wish to sue Smith's estate for their expenses in coming to the scene.

3. Duties Owed to the Unborn

The courts increasingly are being asked to resolve complex issues surrounding injuries associated with birth. For analytical purposes, it is helpful to divide the cases into discrete categories and to focus on the unique considerations that arise in each. We will consider four such categories: (i) pre-conception wrongs, (ii) wrongful birth and wrongful life, (iii) wrongful pregnancy, and (iv) pre-natal injuries. Within the various categories, claims sometimes are made by a parent or a child or both. It is therefore important to distinguish between the different types of losses that may be involved, including the mother's pain and suffering, the parents' increased financial burdens, and the child's loss of potential earnings. It is also important to consider the legal status of unborn children: the common law does not ascribe the status of "person" until a child is born alive.

In the materials that follow, the text provides a general outline, while further details are presented in the notes.

(a) PRE-CONCEPTION WRONGS

A pre-conception wrong occurs when the defendant carelessly causes a parent to suffer an injury that detrimentally affects a subsequently conceived child. For example, a mother or father may have been exposed to hazardous chemicals that caused injury to her ova or his sperm. That defect is later passed on to a child through conception and becomes manifest upon birth. Aside from very complex problems of causation, these cases often raise policy issues regarding the scope of a defendant's potential liability. It may be necessary to ask, for instance, whether a parent's knowledge of the potential genetic problems has any bearing on the defendant's liability.

Moreover, there is debate regarding what steps a potential defendant may take to avoid harm to the plaintiff's reproductive system. In the American case of *U.A.W. v. Johnson Controls*, 499 U.S. 187 (1991), employees at the defendant's battery factory were exposed to lead levels that posed a risk to foetal health in women planning to have children. Fearing claims for pre-conception harms, the defendant required all women under 70 who worked at the factory to provide medical documentation of their sterility or lose their jobs. The United States Supreme Court ultimately found that this policy was discriminatory against women, and that women should be free to decide whether to expose themselves to the risk. *Johnson Controls* illustrates the delicate balancing of interests involved in protecting the health of potential children against the autonomy rights of their mothers.

NOTES AND QUESTIONS

1. What limits should be placed on recovery for pre-conception torts? Assume that a child suffers injuries during delivery because of his or her mother's misshapen pelvis. Assume as well that the mother's pelvis was misshapen because she was run over by a negligent driver 15 years ago. What claim, if any, should the child have against the driver? What policy objections can be raised concerning such claims? Should those policy concerns be addressed in connection with the duty of care, or at some other stage in the negligence analysis? Should a child have a claim if the behaviour of his or her own parents prior to conception increased the risk that he or she would suffer from certain health conditions? See Wiener, "Transgenerational Tort Liability for Epigenetic Disease" (2011) 13 DePaul J. Health Care L. 319.

2. Should different considerations apply in pre-conception cases involving workplace exposures to hazardous products? Should the employer's obligation be limited to: (a) fully informing all potential employees, (b) complying with workplace health and safety legislation, (c) complying with industry safety norms, or (d) obtaining a waiver of liability from the employees? Should employers be free to deny jobs or limit placements to women of child-bearing age? What other less discriminatory options were available to the employer in *Johnson Controls*? One author has suggested that employers may be able to argue that a discriminatory plan is warranted given the potential for ruinous foetal tort liability. See Grover, "The Employer's Fetal Injury Quandary After *Johnson Controls*" (1992-93) 81 Kentucky L.J. 639.

3. So-called "toxic tort" claims arise out of situations where the defendant has exposed a population to harmful substances, which cause adverse health effects. Should such claims include diseases that may be suffered by the affected individuals' future children? What issues of causation might arise? See Laubach, "Epigenetics and Toxic Torts: How Epidemiological Evidence Informs Causation" (2016) 73:2 Wash. &

Lee L. Rev. 1019; and Putz, "Developing Exposure-Based Preconception Tort Liability: A Scientific Challenge to Traditional Tort Concepts" (2016) 66:2 Cath. U.L. Rev. 475.

4. In *Paxton v. Ramji* (2008), 92 O.R. (3d) 401 (C.A.), the infant plaintiff suffered severe disabilities because her mother took a prescription acne drug prior to the plaintiff's conception and during the ensuing pregnancy. The effects of the drug on a foetus were known to the prescribing doctor, but the mother's partner had had a vasectomy and the doctor did not expect her to become pregnant. The plaintiff claimed that the doctor was negligent in failing to recommend extra birth control to the mother. The Ontario Court of Appeal held that the doctor did not owe a duty of care to a "future" child, that is, a child not yet conceived. While harm to a future child from the prescription drug was foreseeable, policy concerns militated against a finding of proximity. In particular, Feldman J.A. explained that the doctor's sole duty was toward his female patient, and that he must consider only her best interests when providing medical advice. Imposing a duty of care toward a future child might cause doctors to limit the treatment options proposed to women. This would be inconsistent with women's autonomy and privacy rights. According to the court, a doctor's relationship with future children is necessarily indirect, and it is the female patient alone who has the power to make decisions affecting her and any future children she may bear.

5. Advances in genetic testing for babies conceived through in vitro fertilization (IVF) have created the potential for a new branch of liability: pre-implantation wrongs. Some parents may wish to select embryos that carry a particular genetic condition; for example, deaf parents may wish to select for a deaf child. Does such a choice result in a harm to a child who is subsequently born deaf? What if parents wish to select an embryo with Down syndrome, to provide a sibling for another Down syndrome child? See Smolensky, "Creating Children with Disabilities: Parental Tort Liability for Preimplantation Genetic Interventions" (2008) 60 Hastings L.J. 299; and Bosslet, "Parental procreative obligation and the categorization of disease: the case of cystic fibrosis" (2011) 37 J. Med. Ethics 280. See generally Blahuta, "Liability for harms caused in utero: new technologies, new problems" (2017) 21:6 Intl. J.H.R. 759.

What other unique duties might arise in situations where parents can screen embryos for genetic defects or other traits before implantation? Should parents who conceive through IVF have a greater right to compensation on the birth of a disabled child than those who conceive through conventional means (and are thus limited to actions for wrongful birth)? See Wevers, "Prenatal Torts and Pre-implantation Genetic Diagnosis" (2010) 24 Harv. J.L. & Tech. 257; and Scott, "Reconsidering 'Wrongful Life' in England After Thirty Years: Legislative Mistakes and Unjustifiable Anomalies" [2013] C.L.J. 115.

In *A (A Minor) v. A Health & Social Services Trust*, [2010] NIQB 108, parents and their children brought a negligence claim against an IVF service for negligently fertilizing ova with sperm of a different race. The children subsequently suffered emotional upset from the teasing they experienced because their skin was darker than their parents'. Gillen J. denied the existence of a duty of care toward human cells prior to implantation. Moreover, the judge held that being born of a particular race was not an actionable harm, stating that it "would be wrong to allow these children to grow up believing that they suffer from some damage for which they have had to be compensated financially" (at para. 23). What public policy concerns are reflected in this decision? In contrast, see *A.C.B. v. Thomson Medical Pte. Ltd.*, [2017] SGCA 20, where the Singapore Court of Appeal allowed a similar claim on account of the parents' lost "genetic affinity" with their child.

(b) WRONGFUL BIRTH AND WRONGFUL LIFE

A physician may carelessly fail to inform a woman that she faces an unusually high risk of giving birth to a child with a disability, or may negligently perform tests that are designed to detect foetal abnormalities. Because of this negligence or failure to inform, the woman may continue a pregnancy that she otherwise would have terminated. In such circumstances, the defendant physician does not positively cause an injury to the child. Instead, the physician has merely deprived the child's mother of an opportunity to make an informed decision regarding abortion. Nevertheless, the defendant may be faced with a claim by the mother, the child, or both. A claim brought by a parent is said to be for "wrongful birth." A claim brought by a child is said to be for "wrongful life."

The mother's claim is, in large part, based on fairly straightforward principles governing a physician's duty to inform a patient of medical risks. That issue is discussed in greater detail later in this chapter. The child's claim, in contrast, is much more problematic. Its gist is that, but for the defendant's carelessness, the child would not have been born and therefore would not have been required to struggle through life with a disability. In essence, the claim suggests that it would have been better if the child had not been born at all. Not surprisingly, the courts have struggled with questions concerning the sanctity of life and the quantification of damages. These issues, which are canvassed in the case below, remain somewhat unresolved in Canadian law.

BOVINGDON (LITIGATION GUARDIAN OF) v. HERGOTT
(2008), 88 O.R. (3d) 641 (C.A.)

[The defendant doctor prescribed a fertility drug, Clomid, to the plaintiffs' mother. The defendant failed to inform the mother that the drug would increase the chance of multiple pregnancy. The mother became pregnant with the plaintiffs, who were twins. The plaintiffs suffered disabilities due to being born prematurely. The defendant conceded that the drug caused the twin pregnancy, which in turn caused the premature delivery and the ensuing disabilities. The plaintiffs' parents successfully brought an action to recover the costs of raising the disabled children, arguing that the mother would not have taken the fertility drug if properly informed. The plaintiffs also brought a claim for the injuries they suffered on being born disabled, which is discussed in the excerpt below. At trial, the jury had found in the plaintiffs' favour.]

FELDMAN J.A. (for the court):—. . .

Case law on wrongful life

[36] The appellant did not challenge the right of the mother to sue him for damages for the "wrongful birth" of the children, if he was found to be negligent and in breach of the duty of care he owed to her. However, he challenged the right of the twins to claim damages from him to compensate them for being born, that is, for "wrongful life". He raised this issue twice with the trial judge, once before the trial

began with the jury and again following receipt of the jury's verdict. Before the trial, the appellant moved under Rule 21 of the Rules of Civil Procedure, R.R.O. 1990, Reg. 194 for a ruling that, as a matter of law, it was plain and obvious that the claim by the children was a claim for "wrongful life", which courts in Canada have rejected as untenable. Following the verdict, the appellant again asked the trial judge to dismiss the children's claims as disclosing no cause of action. The trial judge ruled that the children had a valid claim against the appellant and that their claim was not a claim for "wrongful life".

[37] The common law world has struggled for the past several decades with the debate over whether a child born with defects or injuries suffered in utero or upon conception can sue a doctor for negligence. In deciding whether to recognize a "wrongful life" claim, the key question is, if a child would not have been born at all without the doctor's negligence, can such a child sue the doctor for the value of the difference between a life burdened with physical or mental defects and no life at all? How can the child be compensated for being born? How can a court give damages that measure the value of no life versus a damaged life? And from a metaphysical point of view, does it make sense to allow such an action, given that if the child had not been born, he or she would not have been able to bring the action at all?

. . .

[39] The leading Canadian case on the issue is the Manitoba Court of Appeal decision in *Lacroix (Litigation Guardian of) v. Dominique* (2001), 202 D.L.R. (4th) 121 (C.A.), where the court divided children's claims into two categories, one that allows a valid claim against a doctor, the other that does not. Only in the first category, where the doctor's negligence caused the damage to the child, will the doctor be liable to the child.

[40] In *Lacroix*, before trying to conceive a child, a mother with epilepsy consulted her doctor about the possible effects of her epilepsy medication on a foetus. The trial judge accepted the parents' evidence that the doctor did not warn them about the risks, and that had they been warned, they would not have had children. Although their first child was unaffected, their second child suffered from retardation caused by the epilepsy drug. Subject to a limitation defence, the parents had a claim against the doctor for damages for "wrongful birth". Because of the doctor's negligence in failing to advise them about the risks of the drug harming an unborn child, the parents conceived and the mother bore the second child. The doctor breached his duty to the parents causing them to suffer damage. The parents could be compensated for the cost associated with the care and treatment of the disabled child.

[41] Turning to the child's claim, the Manitoba Court of Appeal divided cases where a child is born with disabilities into two categories (para. 24):

(i) cases in which the abnormalities have been caused by the wrongful act or omission of another; and
(ii) cases in which, but for the wrongful act or omission, the child would not have been born at all.

[42] In cases in the first category, where the defendant's wrongful act caused the harm, the child has a valid claim. However, in cases in the second category, where the defendant's negligence did not cause the harm to the child but only caused the parents either to proceed to conceive the child, or to bear the child rather than abort, that is an action for wrongful life for which there is no claim in law.

. . .

[48] Having classified infants' claims into two categories, the Manitoba Court of Appeal had to decide into which category the *Lacroix* case fell. The problem was that on the facts, the case could arguably fall into either category. Because it was the epilepsy drug that caused the harm to the child, on one analysis the doctor's negligence caused the harm because he prescribed the drug without warning the parents about its risks. However, the doctor's negligent act did not consist in prescribing the drug, but rather in failing to advise the mother of the risks of getting pregnant while on it. The evidence was that had she been warned of the risks, the mother would have continued taking the drug, which she needed, but she would have avoided pregnancy. The court recognized that the doctor owed the mother a duty to prescribe the epilepsy medication she needed. Furthermore, the risk to a foetus of the mother suffering a seizure while pregnant was greater than the risk of damage that the drug posed to the foetus.

[49] The court concluded that in this situation . . . to impose on the doctor a duty of care to the child would create a conflict with the doctor's duty to the mother to prescribe a drug that she needed. . . .

[50] The court therefore held that the case fell into the second category: but for the doctor's negligence in failing to warn the mother of the risks, the child would not have been born. The negligence was not in prescribing the drug, but in failing to provide the information that the drug was contraindicated if the mother were to become pregnant. Because the case fell into the second category, the court held that it was a case of "wrongful life" and there was no cause of action.

The trial judge's decision

[51] In assessing Dr. Hergott's argument that the twins had no cause of action against him for wrongful life, the trial judge addressed the issue based on the two categories in *Lacroix*. Was this a case where the damage to the children was caused by the doctor's negligence, or was it a case where the doctor's negligence did not cause the damage but caused or permitted the children to be born? To decide the question, the trial judge focused on the causation concession that the appellant had made for the jury — that Clomid caused the twinning, the twinning caused the prematurity, and the prematurity caused the damage to the children. She reasoned that, therefore, Clomid caused the damage and since the doctor had prescribed Clomid without warning the mother of the risks, the doctor had thereby caused the harm to the children. She concluded that the case was a category one case, and therefore not an action for wrongful life.

[52] In coming to this conclusion, the trial judge had to distinguish the result in *Lacroix*. She was satisfied that the facts in this case distinguished it from *Lacroix* because there the mother required the medication for her epilepsy. Furthermore, she stated that *Lacroix* should be narrowly interpreted. The *Lacroix.* court had agreed with *McKay*, *supra*, that wrongful life claims should be barred on policy grounds. The trial judge disagreed with the English Court of Appeal's policy concern in *McKay* that if such claims were not barred, physicians would be encouraged to recommend abortion in order to avoid the risk that a child might be born impaired and that they would thereby be found liable for negligence. She rejected this concern as unfounded, because a woman has the autonomous right to make her own decision about abortion.

Analysis

[53] It is clearly very difficult to articulate a coherent theory of liability of a doctor to an unborn child that is based on a valid legal structure and satisfactorily addresses all the policy concerns that have troubled the courts and academics that have previously considered this issue.

[54] For example, the whole concept of paying compensation to someone born disabled or to their parents is seen by some of those who advocate for the disabled as a negative development that reinforces stereotypical reactions to persons with disabilities. In her article, "The Disabling Impact of Wrongful Birth and Wrongful Life Actions" (2005) 40 Harv. C.R.-C.L.L. Rev. 141 at 195, Professor Wendy F. Hensel concludes that "[o]nly by viewing wrongful birth and life actions as a collective threat facing all individuals with disabilities can tort law avoid endorsing such disabling and disturbing messages." In contrast, other academics and courts take the view that where a child is born with damage resulting from medical negligence, the courts should not be concerned with the conceptual difficulties presented by the "non-existence" issue or with offending those who speak on behalf of persons with disabilities, but should instead focus on achieving full compensation to the family through permitting a combination of actions by the parents and the child: see Dean Stretton, "The Birth Torts: Damages for Wrongful Birth and Wrongful Life" [2005] Deakin Law Review 16 (Australia).

[55] I do not believe that the two-category approach in *Lacroix* provides a coherent theory that can assist courts in making the difficult decision of when a child should be able to recover damages from a doctor for being born with disabilities. The facts in *Lacroix* demonstrate the problem.

[56] The second category is fairly clear. It only includes cases where the damage to the child was not caused in any way by the doctor's negligence. The doctor's failure in these cases consists of improperly performing tests or failing to advise parents of the availability or the results of the tests, thereby preventing the parents from choosing to avoid conceiving a child who could be born with disabilities or the mother from terminating a pregnancy where damage has already occurred.

[57] Cases in the first category, however, are much more difficult to compartmentalize. In those cases, the doctor may have caused or contributed to the damage by prescribing a contraindicated drug or by physically damaging the foetus in utero. . . .

[59] Although Clomid was the first step in the chain of causation that led to the damage, the appellant's negligence did not cause the damage. This was because prescribing Clomid to Mrs. Bovingdon was not contraindicated and was not in itself a negligent act. The preponderance of expert evidence at trial established that prescribing Clomid to a woman in Mrs. Bovingdon's circumstances met the standard of care, as long as Mrs. Bovingdon understood the risks of twinning, prematurity and consequent possible damage. It was her choice to make, although it had to be an informed choice.

[60] In my view, because the doctor did not cause the harm to the twins, the trial judge erred by finding that this case fell into the first category rather than the second category described by *Lacroix*. The fact that the mother in *Lacroix* needed the epilepsy drug does not change the analysis, nor does it distinguish the two cases, especially because the epilepsy drug actually harmed the child in *Lacroix*. Both cases involved

giving the mother full information so that she could choose the course of action she wished to take.

Duty of care

[61] As I stated above, I do not find the two categories described in *Lacroix* particularly useful as a basis for analyzing these claims. I prefer to approach the issue not by using categories such as those set down by *Lacroix*, but rather through the normal analysis of tort liability: duty of care, standard of care, breach and damage. The real question in each case is, did the doctor owe a duty of care to the future child or children under the circumstances? If so, then it becomes appropriate to consider the standard of care, whether the doctor breached the duty, and the correct measure of damages.

[62] The respondents submit that the doctor owed the same duty to the future children that he owed to the mother — the duty to properly inform their mother of the risks associated with Clomid prior to prescribing it to her while she was trying to become pregnant. In their factum, the respondents say that the children's "right was to have a drug-free conception, with a reduced risk of disability, rather than a right not to be born". The trial judge also characterized the appellant as owing a duty to the foetus that is co-extensive with his duty to the mother, even though he could not have disclosed risks to a foetus.

[63] However, when one analyzes this characterization of the duty, it becomes apparent that it does not bear scrutiny. Mrs. Bovingdon came to the appellant in 1992 because she and her new husband wanted to have children, but she could not become pregnant because she was not ovulating. She was also concerned about having a premature birth because she had previously had a miscarriage and a premature pregnancy. The appellant's duty to his patient, the mother, was to help her to become pregnant if possible and to provide her with all the information she needed to decide whether to take fertility medication to assist with the process.

[64] However, once she had the information, it was entirely her choice whether to take Clomid. She was not obliged to act in the best interests of a future child or children or to make the choice they would want. She was not acting as their surrogate making a choice on their behalf. She was entitled to choose to take the risk of having twins. This is similar to a mother's right to choose whether to have an abortion. That is why the Supreme Court protected mothers from any tort liability to an unborn child: see *Dobson (Litigation Guardian of) v. Dobson.* . . .

[65] The right of a mother to choose whether to take Clomid is consistent with the standard of care imposed on the doctor in this case, which was to provide the information his patient needed to make an informed choice, rather than to make the choice for her.

. . .

[67] In fact, the evidence in this case was that most women do elect to take Clomid when fully informed. When the Bovingdons learned that Mrs. Bovingdon was pregnant with twins, Dr. Hergott reassured her and discussed how she should take special precautions during her pregnancy including rest in order to bear the twins as safely as possible. There was no issue in this case of abortion.

[68] Because the doctor's duty with this type of drug is only to provide information sufficient to allow the mother to make an informed choice, it cannot be said that the children have a right to a drug-free birth. Nor can the doctor owe a duty

to the children that is co-extensive with his duty to the mother. To frame the duty in that way is to overlook the fact, as discussed above, that the choice is the mother's; she is entitled to choose to take the drug and risk conceiving twins without considering their interests. If she does, the children have no complaint against her or the doctor.

[69] In contrast, where a drug is contraindicated for a pregnant woman, the standard of care for the doctor may be either not to prescribe the drug or to ensure that the woman is taking all appropriate precautions to prevent pregnancy. That was the standard in *Paxton v. Ramji* . . . where Accutane could be prescribed for acne, but if the patient was a woman, then only if she was not going to become pregnant.

[70] I conclude that in this case, the appellant had no duty of care to the future children not to cause them harm in prescribing Clomid to the mother. The doctor owed a duty of care only to the mother, which duty consisted of ensuring that she possessed knowledge sufficient to make an informed decision whether to take Clomid. This knowledge included the increased risk of conceiving twins arising from the drug, the increased potential for premature birth in a twin pregnancy, and the possible harm to the children that could result from premature birth.

[71] I also believe that a policy analysis supports the conclusion that where the standard of care requires a doctor to give a woman the information to make an informed decision about taking a drug or undergoing a procedure, the doctor cannot owe a co-extensive duty to a future child. Where the standard of care on the doctor is to ensure that the mother's decision is an informed one, a co-extensive duty of care to a future child would create a potential conflict of interest with the duty to the mother. If future children have a right to a drug-free birth, as the respondents suggest, then doctors might decide to deny women the choice of taking Clomid on the basis that providing such choice might be a breach of the doctor's duty to the unborn children. In my view, the policy of ensuring that women's choice of treatment be preserved supports the conclusion that the doctor owed no legal duty to the unborn children in this case.

NOTES AND QUESTIONS

1. Feldman J.A.'s decision is based on the principle that a doctor's duty of care is owed to the (pregnant) woman, not to her unborn children. Why is this principle legally important? When, if ever, would a doctor owe a duty to the unborn children? What policy choices underlie this decision?

For a critique of the decision in *Bovingdon*, see Nelson, "Prenatal Harm and the Duty of Care" (2016) 53:4 Alta. L. Rev. 933.

2. For many years, the leading Commonwealth authority on this topic was *McKay v. Essex Area Health Authority*, [1982] 2 All E.R. 771 (C.A.). The plaintiff contracted measles early in her pregnancy, but the infection was not diagnosed in the blood tests that were done. As a result of the disease, her child was born severely disabled. The mother and child sued the doctor and health authority for failing to treat the infection and for failing to advise the mother of the desirability of an abortion. The court struck out the child's claim as not showing any reasonable cause of action. The child's claim could succeed only if one accepted that the child had a right not to be born. The court stated that such a claim for wrongful life was contrary to public policy as a violation of the sanctity of human life. Do you agree? Moreover, the court stated that it was impossible to assess damages by comparing the value of

non-existence to the value of existence in a disabled state. Is this an appropriate test for assessing the child's losses?

3. The High Court of Australia more recently decided two cases on the issue of wrongful life: *Harriton v. Stephens*, [2006] HCA 15; and *Waller v. James; Waller v. Hoolahan*, [2006] HCA 16. The court affirmed that damages for wrongful life are not available at common law. Among the reasons given by the court were that: it is impossible to compare a life with disabilities to non-existence; broader public policy favoured equal treatment to those with disabilities, and their lives would be devalued by a decision that disabled life is worse than no life at all; and complex decisions of this nature ought to be decided, if at all, by legislators.

For consideration of the policy arguments regarding the recognition of claims for wrongful life, see Stretton, "The Birth Torts: Damages for Wrongful Birth and Wrongful Life" (2005) 10 Deakin L. Rev. 319; Hensel, "The Disabling Impact of Wrongful Birth and Wrongful Life Actions" (2005) 40 Harv. C.R.-C.L.L. Rev. 141; Fordham, "A life less ordinary — The rejection of actions for wrongful life" (2007) 15 Torts L.J. 123; Ellis & McGivern, "The wrongfulness or rightfulness of actions for wrongful life" (2007) 15 Tort L. Rev. 135; Roberts, "What Is The Wrong of Wrongful Disability? From Chance to Choice to Harms to Persons" (2009) 28 Law & Phil 1; Ruda, "'I Didn't Ask to be Born': Wrongful Life from a Comparative Perspective" (2010) 1 J.E.T.L. 204; Houseman, "Wrongful Birth as Negligent Misrepresentation" (2013) 71 U.T. Fac. L. Rev. 9; and Schuster, "Rights Gone Wrong: A Case Against Wrongful Life" (2016) 57:6 Wm. & Mary L. Rev. 2329.

4. These issues are still somewhat unsettled in Canada. In *Arndt v. Smith* (1994), 93 B.C.L.R. (2d) 220 (S.C.), a mother gave birth to a severely disabled child as a result of contracting chicken pox during pregnancy. Although such disabilities rarely result from chicken pox, the physician was found to be negligent for failing to inform the mother of these risks and offer her the option of an abortion. The court commented favourably on the dropping of the child's claim for wrongful life, stating that no viable action could be brought on that basis in British Columbia. The father's claim to recover the costs of supporting the child was dismissed. The court accepted that the mother could claim for the additional expenses of rearing a disabled child, but held that her action failed on the issue of causation. The plaintiff could not prove that a reasonable woman in her position would have had an abortion if informed of the very small risks of serious birth defects. The British Columbia Court of Appeal ordered a new trial on the issue of causation, but the Supreme Court of Canada restored the trial judgment: *Arndt v. Smith* (1995), 6 B.C.L.R. (3d) 201 (C.A.), rev'd [1997] 2 S.C.R. 539.

In *H.(R.) v. Hunter* (1996), 32 C.C.L.T. (2d) 44 (Ont. Gen. Div.), the parents of two disabled children were awarded approximately $3,000,000 for the additional costs they would incur in raising the children. The defendant doctors were held negligent in not referring the mother for additional genetic counselling.

In *Krangle (Guardian ad litem of) v. Brisco* (1997), 55 B.C.L.R. (3d) 23 (S.C.), aff'd on point (2000), 76 B.C.L.R. (3d) 1 (C.A.), rev'd on other grounds [2002] 1 S.C.R. 205, a child was born with Down's Syndrome. The defendant physician had carelessly failed to inform the mother about the availability of an amniocentesis test that would have detected that condition during pregnancy. The evidence indicated that, if so informed, the woman would have had an abortion. The court held that, while the child did not have a cause of action against the physician for wrongful life, the parents were entitled to damages regarding the expenses associated with his care. See also *T.S. v. Adey*, 2017 ONSC 397, where a doctor was found liable for failing to diagnose severe limb abnormalities prior to the 24-week limit on termination of a foetus with a non-lethal abnormality. The parents were not required to "mitigate" their damages by seeking an out-of-country abortion after the 24-week period.

In *Jones (Guardian ad litem of) v. Rostvig* (1999), 44 C.C.L.T. (3d) 313 (B.C.S.C.), the court struck out a wrongful life claim by a child on the basis that it disclosed no cause of action. The court held that, while a physician owes a duty of care to a child regarding pre-natal injuries that become manifest on birth, a physician does not owe a duty of care to a child to provide its mother with information that would lead to an abortion. See also *Lacroix (Litigation Guardian of) v. Dominique* (2001), 156 Man. R. (2d) 262 (C.A.). However, in *Petkovic (Litigation Guardian of) v. Olupona* (2002), 11 C.C.L.T. (3d) 91 (Ont. S.C.J.), aff'd (2002), 30 C.C.L.T. (3d) 266 (Ont. Div. Ct.), the court refused to strike out a similar claim.

In *Watters v. White*, 2012 QCCA 257, the court dismissed a claim against a doctor for failing to inform relatives of an infant who suffered from a debilitating neurological disease that they might also be carriers of the disease. The plaintiff, a second cousin to the initial patient, gave birth to a child who suffered from the disease some thirty years later. The court found that the doctor acted reasonably in assuming that the infant's father would inform other members of his family, and that it would have been a breach of patient confidentiality for the doctor to disclose the patient's condition to a broader range of relatives. See Zawati & Thorogood, "The Physician Who Knew Too Much: A Comment on *Watters v White*" (2014) 21 Health L.J. 1.

5. Presumably, as medical technology improves and more abnormalities become detectable during pregnancy, claims for wrongful birth will increase. Should parents be able to make a claim if the child suffers from a relatively mild disability? What if the child will suffer from a condition that is easily treatable by medication, but the parents do not want the hassle or expense? What if doctors can only predict that the child might, sometime in the future, develop a certain medical condition? What test of causation should be used in such actions? Should the parents have to prove that reasonable parents in their position would decide to terminate the pregnancy? See Sonnenburg, "A Preference for Nonexistence: Wrongful Life and a Proposed Tort of Genetic Malpractice" (1982) 55 S. Cal. L. Rev. 477; Jankowski, "Wrongful Birth and Wrongful Life Actions Arising from Negligent Counselling: The Need for Legislation Supporting Reproductive Choice" (1989) 17 Fordham Urb. L.J. 27; Shapira, "'Wrongful life' lawsuits for faulty genetic counselling: should the impaired newborn be entitled to sue?" (1998) 24 J. Med. Ethics 369; and Pattinson, "Wrongful Life Actions as a Means of Regulating Use of Genetic and Reproductive Technologies" (1999) 7 Health L.J. 19.

(c) WRONGFUL PREGNANCY

The third category is based on general principles of medical negligence. It arises when parents have taken medical steps to prevent pregnancy or childbirth but, due to the negligence of a medical professional, a pregnancy occurs or continues. Suppose, for example, that a physician carelessly performed an abortion with the result that a pregnancy was not terminated. The woman may claim economic loss, pain and suffering, and emotional harm from having to undergo a second abortion. Similarly, if a physician negligently performs a sterilization procedure, the woman may claim damages for having to terminate a pregnancy that she was specifically trying to avoid.

The situation is more complicated, however, if the woman does not terminate the unwanted pregnancy but instead gives birth to the child. Over the years, the courts have responded to these circumstances in different ways. As summarized by Justice Kirby in the Australian case of *Cattanach v. Melchior* (2003), 77 A.L.J.R. 1312 (H.C.A.) at para. 138, the court may decide any of the following:

(1) That no damages may be recovered where the child is born healthy and without disability or impairment;

(2) That damages may be recovered but confined to the immediate damage to the mother (and loss of consortium for the father) together with any expenses and loss of earnings immediately consequential on the pregnancy and delivery but excluding the costs of upkeep until self-reliance of a healthy child;

(3) That damages may be recovered but confined to the foregoing together with any additional costs of rearing a child born with a disability or born to a parent or parents with a disability;

(4) That damages may be recovered in full for the reasonable costs of rearing an unplanned child to the age when that child might be expected to be economically self-reliant, whether the child is "healthy" or "disabled" or "impaired" but with a deduction from the amount of such damages for the joy and benefits received, and the potential economic support derived, from the child; and

(5) That full damages against the tortfeasor for the cost of rearing the child may be allowed, subject to the ordinary limitations of reasonable foreseeability and remoteness, with no discount for joys, benefits and support, leaving restrictions upon such recovery to such limitations as may be enacted by a Parliament with authority to do so.

Traditionally, the Canadian and Commonwealth courts have chosen option (3). Parents who give birth to an unwanted child may claim damages for the expenses associated with the unwanted pregnancy and childbirth, and the mother may claim damages for the related pain and suffering. Further, if the child is disabled, the parents may claim for the extra costs associated with raising a disabled child. However, if the parents give birth to a healthy child, they cannot claim damages for the ordinary costs of raising that child to maturity. The courts have generally adopted the view that a healthy child is a "blessing" and its birth cannot be treated as a legal harm.

More recently, the courts have been more receptive to claims for the expenses of raising a healthy child. Significantly, in *Cattanach* the High Court of Australia rejected earlier authorities and, by a decision of four to three, decided to award damages to a couple for the costs of raising a healthy child. The court was persuaded by the fact that the parents had decided to limit the size of their family and had undergone a sterilization procedure specifically to prevent further pregnancy. Although the unplanned child was welcomed into the family, its birth inevitably led to lifestyle changes and required the parents to forsake other opportunities. The defendant had negligently performed a service, and the unplanned pregnancy was a foreseeable result of that negligence. The High Court decided that there were no longer any convincing policy reasons to grant physicians "immunity" from liability for the foreseeable consequences of their negligence. In the United Kingdom, the House of Lords has affirmed its position that the costs of raising healthy children should not be compensated, but has devised the unique solution of providing a "conventional award" of £15,000 in wrongful pregnancy cases to compensate parents for the violation of their right to choose the size of their family. See *Rees v. Darlington Memorial NHS Trust*, [2004] 1 A.C. 309 (H.L.).

The Canadian courts have also been moving toward greater recovery for the costs of rearing an unplanned child. First, in *Suite v. Cooke* (1993), 15 C.C.L.T. (2d) 15 (Qc. S.C.), aff'd [1995] R.J.Q. No. 2765 (C.A.), the Québec Court of Appeal found that pecuniary damages for the costs of raising a healthy child were recoverable, but also that they had to be set off against the emotional benefits and burdens that the child would bring to its parents. Next, damages for child-rearing costs were awarded without lengthy discussion in *Joshi v. Wooley* (1995), 4 B.C.L.R. (3d) 208 (S.C.), a case that has not been extensively followed. Finally, in a more influential judgment, *Kealey v. Berezowski* (1996), 136 D.L.R. (4th) 708 (Ont. Gen. Div.), Lax J. rejected the argument that claims for child-rearing costs should be universally denied as a matter of public policy. Nevertheless, Lax J. characterized such claims as a form of pure economic loss, and concluded that they could only be recovered where the plaintiffs' primary motivation for wanting to limit the size of their family was financial. This did not apply on the facts of the case, so damages for child-rearing costs were not recoverable. The Canadian law in this area remains unsettled.

NOTES AND QUESTIONS

1. What policy considerations would lead a court to deny claims for the costs of rearing a healthy child? See *Doiron v. Orr* (1978), 20 O.R. (2d) 71 (H.C.J.); *Udale v. Bloomsbury Area Health Authority*, [1983] 2 All E.R. 522 (Q.B.); *McFarlane v. Tayside Health Board (Scotland)*, [1999] 4 All E.R. 961 (H.L.); and *Cattanach v. Melchior* (2003), 77 A.L.J.R. 1312 (H.C.A.). See also Symmons, "Policy Factors in Actions for Wrongful Birth" (1987) 50 Mod. L. Rev. 269; Cameron-Perry, "Return of the burden of the blessing" (1999) 149 N.L.J. 1887; Mason, "Unwanted pregnancy: a case of retroversion?" (2000) 4 Edin. L.R. 191; Weir, "The Unwanted Child" [2000] C.L.J. 238; Elvin, "Are Healthy Children Always a Blessing?" [2002] C.L.J. 516; Hogg, "Damages for Pecuniary Loss in Cases of Wrongful Birth" (2010) 1 J.E.T.L. 156; and Ramsay, "Wrongful Pregnancy and the Offset/Benefits Approach" (2015) 28 C.J.L.J. 129.

2. For cases awarding damages for the costs of rearing a disabled child, see *Emeh v. Kensington and Chelsea and Westminster Area Health Authority*, [1985] 1 Q.B. 1012 (C.A.); *Cherry v. Borsman* (1990), 75 D.L.R. (4th) 668 (B.C.S.C.), varied (1992), 70 B.C.L.R. (2d) 273 (C.A.); and *Parkinson v. St. James and Seacroft University Hospital NHS Trust*, [2002] Q.B. 266 (C.A.). Is there any legal or policy reason for allowing claims for the additional costs of raising a disabled child, but not the general costs of raising a healthy, but unplanned, child? See Kerr, "Indemnity for the Costs of Raising Unwanted Children from Unwanted Pregnancies" (1998) 6 Tort L. Rev. 121.

What principles should apply if an unplanned child is born healthy, but subsequently develops a disability? See *Groom v. Selby*, [2001] E.W.C.A. Civ. 1522, where the plaintiff's baby developed salmonella meningitis a few weeks after birth. The mother's claim for the extra costs of raising a disabled child was allowed.

3. In *Roe v. Dabbs* (2004), 31 B.C.L.R. (4th) 158 (S.C.), Parrett J. surveyed the existing options in wrongful pregnancy cases and found them all to be inadequate. Due to the difficulties in weighing the financial and emotional benefits and burdens of raising a healthy, but unplanned, child, Parrett J. concluded that the damages should be considered as non-pecuniary. The plaintiff in that case was awarded $55,000 in non-pecuniary damages for her distress on discovering that her abortion attempt had failed, and for the limitations on her lifestyle and activities due to the birth of an unplanned child. See also *Fredette v. Wiebe* (1986), 4 B.C.L.R. (2d) 184 (S.C.), where the plaintiff was awarded non-pecuniary damages for the distress caused by having twins as a young, single mother; and *Stockford v. Johnston Estate* (2008), 335 N.B.R. (2d) 74 (Q.B.), where a mother was awarded general damages of $35,000 and future losses of $30,600 after a failed sterilization procedure. The judge in *Stockford* purported to be applying the "offset/benefits" approach to recovery, weighing the costs of raising the healthy child against the financial benefits the mother would receive from the unplanned child's existence. However, the judge refused to offset any emotional benefits that the mother might enjoy. The general damages portion of the award was meant to compensate the mother for undergoing unwanted pregnancy and childbirth and an additional surgical sterilization.

4. What is the legal significance of the parents' choice not to terminate an unplanned pregnancy or put a child up for adoption? Is this a break in the chain of causation, contributory negligence, or a failure to mitigate damages? The courts have typically held that the parents' decision to keep the unplanned child does not affect their claim against a negligent medical professional, since the decision not to abort or put a child up for adoption is reasonable, particularly within the confines of marriage. See *McFarlane, supra.* Nevertheless, in *C.E.S. v. Superclinics (Australia) Pty. Ltd.* (1995), 38 N.S.W.L.R. 47 (C.A.), the court found that the cause of the plaintiff's child-rearing costs was her own decision to keep the unplanned child, and consequently denied her claim. See also *Emeh, supra*, where the trial judge found the mother's decision not to undergo abortion was a *novus actus interveniens*. This decision was reversed on appeal.

Is it fair for a negligent physician to be saddled with all the costs of raising a healthy child that the parents have welcomed into their family? Do the parents receive a windfall in such cases, *i.e.*, they have the emotional benefits of a child, while having its upkeep paid for by a negligent physician? See *Keats v. Pearce* (1984), 48 Nfld. & P.E.I.R. 102 (Nfld. S.C.T.D.). See also Keirse & Schaub, "Self-Determination with a Price Tag: The Legal and Financial Consequences of Wrongful Conception and Wrongful Birth and the Decision of the Parents to Keep the Child" (2010) 1 J.E.T.L. 243.

5. What should be included in the "ordinary costs" of raising a healthy child? These obviously include food and clothing, but what about birthday presents, music lessons, participation in sports, or higher education? If wealthy parents decide to spend more money on their children, should they receive greater compensation for having an unplanned child? See the discussion in *Bevilacqua v. Altenkirk* (2004), 35 B.C.L.R. (4th) 281 (S.C.). See also *Benarr v. Kettering Health Authority*, [1988] N.L.J. 179 (Q.B.), where the judge awarded the costs of private education because that was what the child could expect in that particular family.

6. In *Kealey v. Berezowski* (1996), 136 D.L.R. (4th) 708 (Ont. Gen. Div.), discussed above, Lax J. concluded that child-rearing costs should only be recoverable if the primary motivation for wanting to limit the size of one's family were financial. Are the parents' motives really relevant? Will this tempt plaintiffs to slant their evidence? What about cases where there are mixed reasons for not wanting to become pregnant, or where the father and mother have differing views? See *McFarlane, supra*; and *M.S. v. Baker* (2001), 309 A.R. 1 (Q.B.).

Should courts be more likely to award damages for child-rearing costs if the family's financial resources are already limited? One author has argued that the effects of denying claims for child-rearing costs are disproportionately borne by poor, single mothers: Adjin-Tettey, "Claims for Involuntary Parenthood: Why the Resistance?" in Neyers, Chamberlain & Pitel, eds., *Emerging Issues in Tort Law* (2007). See also *Freeman v. Sutter* (1996), 29 C.C.L.T. (2d) 215 (Man. C.A.), where the court found that no duty of care was owed by a doctor whose negligence caused the birth of a child that the plaintiff father was liable to support.

7. While there has been some willingness to award damages for the costs of raising a healthy child, there are still numerous instances of courts denying such claims. See for example *Mummery v. Olsson*, 2001 CarswellOnt 151 (S.C.J.) (WL Can); *M.Y. v. Boutros* (2002), 313 A.R. 1 (Q.B.); and *Bevilacqua, supra*. Thus, the Canadian law in this area remains unsettled.

8. Is there a legally significant difference between claims for wrongful birth and claims for wrongful pregnancy? In either situation, the parents are left to care for a child who, but for the defendant's negligence, would not exist. Should it matter whether the parents were attempting to avoid pregnancy altogether, or whether they were only attempting to avoid having a disabled child? See Hoyano, "Misconceptions about Wrongful Conception" (2002) 65 Mod. L. Rev. 883; and Mason, "Wrongful Pregnancy, Wrongful Birth and Wrongful Terminology" (2002) 6 Edin. L.R. 46.

9. The decision in *Cattanach* was greeted by political and public disdain, and its effects have been largely abrogated by statute. While the legislation still allows claims for the extra costs associated with raising disabled children, no claims are permitted for the costs of raising healthy children. See the discussion in Hirsch, "Rights and Responsibilities in Wrongful Birth and Wrongful Life Cases" (2006) 29 U.N.S.W.L.J. 233.

10. For general commentary on recent developments in the Commonwealth, see Vranken, "Damages for 'Wrongful Birth': Where to After *Cattanach*?" (2003) 24 Adel. L. Rev. 243; Fordham, "Blessing or Burden? Recent Developments in Actions in Wrongful Conception and Wrongful Birth in the U.K. and Australia" [2004] Sing. J. Legal Stud. 462; Todd, "Wrongful Conception, Wrongful Birth and Wrongful Life" (2005) 27 Syd. L. Rev. 525; Stretton, "Birth Torts: Damages for Wrongful Birth and Wrongful Life" (2005) 10 Deakin L. Rev. 319; Morgan & White, "Everyday Life and the Edges of Existence: Wrongs with No Name or the Wrong Name?" (2006) 29 U.N.S.W.L.J. 239; Priaux, *The Harm Paradox* (2007); Troke, "Wrongful existence claims: the '*McFarlane* Approach', trends in policy and ethics, and the future" (2007) 13 Clinical Risk 187; and Bruce, "A Womb with (An)other View: An Economic Analysis of the Wrongful Birth Doctrine" (2008) 15 J. Legal Econ. 21.

11. Most of the cases address only the costs of rearing unplanned children and treat unwanted pregnancy as a financial harm. Apart from *Rees v. Darlington Memorial NHS Trust*, [2004] 1 A.C. 309 (H.L.), the courts have rarely addressed the harm of the parents' lost autonomy to choose if, when, and with whom to have children. Is the "conventional award" in *Rees* sufficient to account for this loss? Does the general refusal to compensate for lost reproductive freedom discriminate against women? See Feldthusen, "Suppressing Damages in Involuntary Parenthood Actions: Contorting Tort Law, Denying Reproductive Freedom and Discriminating Against Mothers" (2014) 29:1 Can. J. Fam. L. 11. See also Keren-Paz, "Compensating Injury to Autonomy: A Conceptual and Normative Analysis" in Barker, Fairweather & Grantham, eds., *Private Law in the 21st Century* (2017).

(d) PRE-NATAL INJURIES

The final category may be the most significant in terms of frequency of claims. The basic question is whether a child can sue in negligence for injuries sustained *in utero*. The answer to that question begins with the proposition that, unless the child is subsequently born with an injury, no cause of action arises. As indicated above, a foetus is not recognized in Canadian law as a person and therefore has no standing to sue. If, however, the child is subsequently born with a disability, then a claim in negligence may be possible. The courts have long recognized that a person may owe a duty of care to avoid careless actions before birth that may result in a loss upon birth. See *Duval v. Seguin* (1972), 26 D.L.R. (3d) 418 (Ont. H.C.), aff'd (1973), 40 D.L.R. (3d) 666 (Ont. C.A.); and *Montreal Tramways Co. v. Léveillé*, [1933] S.C.R. 456. In *Dobson (Litigation Guardian of) v. Dobson* (1999), 174 D.L.R. (4th) 1 (S.C.C.), however, the Supreme Court of Canada held that a different rule applied with respect to the child's mother.

The facts in *Dobson* were simple. A woman who was 27 weeks pregnant carelessly caused an automobile accident that inflicted damage upon her unborn child. The child was delivered by Caesarean section later the same day with severe and permanent disabilities. By way of a litigation guardian, he subsequently sued his mother in negligence. That action was, in effect, "friendly." Its real purpose was not to recover damages from the mother, but rather from her insurer. Ironically, then, despite being the nominal defendant, the mother was anxious for her son's claim to succeed. Without recourse to insurance benefits, the financial burden associated with his disabilities would fall much more heavily on her personally.

Although the lower courts found in favour of the plaintiff, the Supreme Court of Canada held that liability was impossible because the defendant did not owe a duty of care to her son prior to his birth. Cory J.'s majority decision demonstrates the extent to which policy considerations affect the tort of negligence. He began by assuming that a *prima facie* duty of care arose under the first branch of the then applicable *Anns/Kamloops* test. He found that it was reasonably foreseeable that the mother's carelessness could adversely affect her foetus, and that the relationship between the parties could not possibly have been any closer or more proximate. Under the second branch of the *Anns/Kamloops* test, however, Cory J. found policy considerations that negated the prima facie duty:

> [F]or reasons of public policy, the Court should not impose a duty of care upon a pregnant woman towards her foetus or subsequently born child. To do so would

result in very extensive and unacceptable intrusions into the bodily integrity, privacy and autonomy rights of women.

. . .

The unique relationship between a pregnant woman and her foetus is so very different from the relationship with third parties. Everything the pregnant woman does or fails to do may have a potentially detrimental impact on her foetus. Everything the pregnant woman eats or drinks, and every physical action she takes, may affect the foetus. Indeed, the foetus is entirely dependent upon its mother-to-be. Although the imposition of tort liability on a third party for prenatal negligence advances the interests of both mother and child, it does not significantly impair the right of third parties to control their own lives. In contrast to the third-party defendant, a pregnant woman's every waking and sleeping moment, in essence, her entire existence, is connected to the foetus she may potentially harm. If a mother were to be held liable for prenatal negligence, this could render the most mundane decision taken in the course of her daily life as a pregnant woman subject to the scrutiny of the courts.

. . .

First, the recognition of a duty of care owed by a pregnant woman to her foetus has a very real potential to intrude upon that woman's fundamental rights. Any intervention may create a conflict between a pregnant woman as an autonomous decision-maker and the foetus she carries. Second, the judicial definition of an appropriate standard of care is fraught with insoluble problems due to the difficulty of distinguishing tortious and non-tortious behaviour in the daily life of an expectant woman. Third, certain so-called lifestyle "choices" such as alcoholism and drug addiction may be beyond the control of the pregnant woman, and hence the deterrent value of the imposition of a duty of care may be non-existent. Lastly, the imposition of a duty of care upon a pregnant woman towards her foetus could increase, to an unwarranted degree, the level of external scrutiny focused upon her.

. . .

[Under a general duty of care] a mother could be held liable in tort for . . . the careless performance of household activities — such as preparing meals, carrying loads of laundry, or shovelling. . . .. A mother who injured her foetus in a careless fall, or who had an unreasonable lapse of attention in the home, at work or on the roadways, could potentially be held liable in tort for the damages suffered by her born alive child. The imposition of tort liability in those circumstances would significantly undermine the privacy and autonomy rights of women.

. . .

Moreover, the imposition of tort liability in this context would carry psychological and emotional repercussions for a mother who is sued in tort by her newborn child. To impose tort liability on a mother for an unreasonable lapse of prenatal care could have devastating consequences for the future relationship between the mother and her born alive child. In essence, the judicial recognition of a cause of action for maternal prenatal negligence is an inappropriate response to the pressing social issue of caring for children with special needs. Putting a mother through the trauma of a public trial to determine whether she was at fault for the injury suffered by her child can only add emotional and psychological trauma to an already tragic situation.

. . .

Such litigation would, in all probability, have detrimental consequences, not only for the relationship between mother and child, but also for the relationship between the child and his or her family. Yet, family harmony will be particularly important for the creation of a caring and nurturing environment for the injured child, who will undoubtedly require much loving attention. It seems clear that the well-being of such a child cannot be readily severed from the interests of his or her family. In short, neither the best interests of the injured child, nor those of the remainder of the family, would be served by the judicial recognition of the suggested cause of action.

. . .

The primary purposes of tort law are to provide compensation to the injured and deterrence to the tortfeasor. In the ordinary course of events, the imposition of tort liability on a mother for prenatal negligence would provide neither compensation nor deterrence. The pressing societal issue at the heart of this appeal is the lack of financial support currently available for the care of children with special needs. The imposition of a legal duty of care on a pregnant woman towards her foetus or subsequently born child will not solve this problem. If anything, attempting to address this social problem in a litigious setting would merely exacerbate the pain and trauma of a tragic situation. It may well be that carefully considered legislation could create a fund to compensate children with prenatally inflicted injuries. Alternatively, amendments to the motor vehicle insurance laws could achieve the same result in a more limited context. If, as a society, Canadians believe that children who sustain damages as a result of maternal prenatal negligence should be financially compensated, then the solution should be formulated, after careful study and debate, by the legislature.

In a dissenting opinion, Major J. (Bastarache J. concurring) recognized that it was necessary to mediate a compromise between the child's interest in recovering damages for carelessly inflicted injuries and the mother's interest in being free from unreasonable restraint during pregnancy. He believed, however, that that tension was best resolved by adopting a limited duty of care, rather than by staking a position at either extreme. Like Cory J., he rejected the imposition of a general duty of care upon pregnant women for fear that it would entail judicial scrutiny of "lifestyle choices," such as "smoking, drinking, and dietary and health-care decisions." But, in contrast to the majority, he stressed that those types of policy concerns should not be determinative in circumstances where they do not actually arise. Major J. therefore preferred to impose a duty of care upon a pregnant woman toward her foetus where she already owed a similar duty of care toward other parties. On the facts, the defendant owed a duty of care, while driving, to other motorists. The burdens associated with that obligation would not be increased if it was extended to her unborn child.

NOTES AND QUESTIONS

1. In *Dobson*, Cory J. presented several policy reasons for denying the existence of any duty of care between a pregnant woman and her unborn child. Do you find those reasons persuasive, either individually or collectively?

2. Does the issue of maternal tort liability truly lie beyond judicial competence, such that any solution must be devised by the legislature? If so, should courts similarly refuse to extend the duty of care in other complex situations?

Are there truly insuperable difficulties in formulating a standard of care that would sufficiently respect a woman's autonomy? How do the courts approach the question of breach in other circumstances? Is it realistic to believe that a court would ever find that an expectant mother had breached the standard of care by "preparing meals [or] carrying loads of laundry?"

3. Is it appropriate to refuse recognition of a duty of care for fear of causing tension within the family unit? How did Mrs. Dobson feel about her son's claim? If concerns regarding familial harmony are compelling, should a duty of care similarly be rejected as between a father and an unborn child, or as between a mother and a child that is already alive?

Is it true that "[i]n the ordinary course of events" the recognition of a duty of care "for prenatal negligence would [not] provide compensation"? What evidence did Cory J. have for that proposition? Would a child typically sue its mother unless the real purpose was to secure access to her insurer? In any event, should the courts be influenced by such matters?

4. In *Dobson*, Cory J. suggested that it would be appropriate for the legislators to enact, subject to the provisions of the *Charter*, a statutory cause of action for children who suffer pre-natal injuries caused by their mothers. In Ontario, s. 66 of the *Family Law Act*, R.S.O. 1990, c. F.3, provides that no person is disentitled from recovering damages simply because the injuries were incurred before birth. However, it has been held that s. 66 does not override the maternal immunity outlined in *Dobson*: *Hall (Litigation Guardian of) v. Kellar* (2002) 23 C.C.L.T. (3d) 40 (Ont. S.C.J.). Given Cory J.'s emphasis on women's autonomy rights, would any statutory imposition of maternal tort liability survive a *Charter* challenge?

In 2005, Alberta enacted the *Maternal Tort Liability Act*, S.A. 2005, c. M-75, which creates a limited exception to the common law immunity of mothers that was established in *Dobson*. The Alberta legislation allows born alive children to sue their mothers for injuries suffered *in utero* only if they resulted from the mother's operation of an automobile, and only if the mother was covered by automobile insurance. Does this legislation adequately resolve the problems posed by the decision in *Dobson*? See Ali, "Defining the Standard of Prenatal Care: An Analysis of Judicial and Legislative Responses" (2007) 1 McGill Health Law Publication 69; and Mykitiuk & Scott, "Risky Pregnancy: Liability, Blame, and Insurance in the Governance of Prenatal Harm" (2011) 43 U.B.C.L. Rev. 311.

5. Is it sound public policy to leave a child born with serious preventable disabilities without any common law action against the person who carelessly caused those injuries, just because that person happens to be the child's mother? See Van Praagh & Campbell, "Women and (their) children: wrongs, rights and relationships" (2017) 21:6 Intl. J.H.R. 672.

Australian courts have imposed liability in cases like *Dobson* on the basis that road accident victims should all be compensated and vehicle owners should all contribute, through insurance, to redressing the cost of traffic-related injuries. See *Lynch v. Lynch* (1991), 25 N.S.W.L.R. 411 (C.A.). In *Dobson*, Cory J. rejected this insurance rationale as being an inappropriate basis for making policy decisions. Do you agree?

6. For comments on the implications of *Dobson*, see McInnes, "Pre-Natal Injuries in the Supreme Court of Canada" (2000) 116 L.Q.R. 26; Nelson, "One of These Things is Not Like The Other: Maternal Legal Duties and the Supreme Court of

Canada" (2000) 12 S.C.L.R. 31; Rafferty, "Developments in Contract and Tort: The 1999-2000 Term" (2000) 13 S.C.L.R. 125; and Malkin, "A Mother's Duty of Care to Her Foetus While Driving" (2001) 9 Torts L.J. 109. See also Johnsen, "The Creation of Fetal Rights: Conflicts with Women's Constitutional Rights to Liberty, Privacy, and Equal Protection" (1986) 95 Yale L.J. 599; Kerr, "Pre-Natal Fictions and Post-Partum Actions" (1998) 20 Dal. L.J. 237; Wellington, "Maternal liability for prenatal injury: The preferable approach in Australian law?" (2010) 18 Tort L. Rev. 89; Do & Mapulanga-Hulston, "The Ethical and Legal Conundrum: Should a Mother Owe a Duty of Care to her Unborn Child?" [2013] J. Applied Law and Policy 1; and Grover, "Maternal tort immunity, the born alive rule and the disabled child's right to legal capacity: reconsidering the Supreme Court of Canada judgment in *Dobson v. Dobson*" (2017) 21:6 Intl. J.H.R. 708.

7. Although a pregnant woman does not owe a duty of care to her unborn child, a born alive child can sue other parties for injuries suffered *in utero* and during delivery. Thus, notwithstanding *Dobson*, claims for pre-natal negligence continue to be heard. See for example *Oliver (Guardian ad litem of) v. Ellison*, [2001] 7 W.W.R. 677 (B.C.C.A.); *Keys v. Mistahia Regional Health Authority* (2001), 291 A.R. 97 (Q.B.), aff'd (2002), 320 A.R. 87 (C.A.); *Pozdzik (Next friend of) v. Wilson* (2002), 11 C.C.L.T. (3d) 96 (Alta. Q.B.); *Ediger (Guardian ad litem of) v. Johnston* (2009), 65 C.C.L.T. (3d) 1 (B.C.S.C.), aff'd [2013] 2 S.C.R. 98; *Liebig v. Guelph General Hospital* (2010), 321 D.L.R. (4th) 378 (Ont. C.A.); *Goodman v. Viljoen*, 2012 ONCA 896; and *Cojocaru v. British Columbia Women's Hospital and Health Centre*, 2013 SCC 30. See Ross, "Current and Emerging Issues in Medical Malpractice" (2011) 38 Adv. Q. 233.

8. Pregnancy and the cause of birth defects were largely a mystery to medical professionals for many years, making the causation issue in pre-natal injury cases difficult. See generally Oakley, *The Captured Womb: A History of the medical care of pregnant women* (1984); and McLaren, *Reproductive Rituals* (1984). Concerns regarding pre-natal injuries came to prominence during the 1960s as a result of a worldwide measles epidemic and the litigation stemming from birth defects caused by the drug thalidomide. See Hindell & Simms, *Abortion Law Reformed* (1971); Sarvis & Roman, *The Abortion Controversy*, 2d. ed. (1974); and Sunday Times Insight Team, *Suffer the Children: The Story of Thalidomide* (1979).

Modern advances in the medical sciences have made it easier to prove that drugs, chemicals, radiation, and other substances can cause birth defects. For example, in *Sindell v. Abbott Laboratories*, 607 P.2d 924 (Cal. 1980), a mother's use of a prescription drug, DES, during pregnancy was proven to cause a particular form of deadly cancer in female children a minimum of 10 to 12 years after birth.

9. Are civil claims likely to have any beneficial effect on foetal health? Can you suggest other means of addressing this issue? Should the state have the power to intervene to protect foetal health? Would legislation be any more effective than civil liability? What constitutional arguments would be raised in challenging such laws? How would these challenges be resolved?

Both English and Canadian courts have held that there is no common law authority to impose treatment or restraint upon a pregnant woman for the benefit of a foetus. See *Winnipeg Child & Family Services (Northwest Area) v. G.(D.F.)* (1997), 152 D.L.R. (4th) 193 (S.C.C.); and *St. George's Healthcare NHS Trust v. S.*, [1998] 3 All

E.R. 673 (C.A.). See also Kirman, "Four Dialogues on Fetal Protection" (1993) 2(2) Health L. Rev. 31; and Lemmens, "End of Life Decisions and Pregnant Women: Do Pregnant Women have the Right to Refuse Life Preserving Medical Treatment? A Comparative Study" (2010) 17 Eur. J. Health L. 485.

The issue is much more controversial in the United States, where there have been several high-profile cases of doctors applying to the courts to force pregnant women to undergo caesarean sections or other medical treatments the doctors believe necessary for the health of the foetus. For instance, Angela Carder, who was 25 weeks pregnant, was diagnosed with terminal lung cancer in 1987 and given only weeks to live. Although she agreed to treatments that would improve the survival prospects of her child, she refused consent to an immediate caesarean section. She believed that the foetus was not likely to survive at that age, and that the procedure would likely shorten her own life. Her doctors applied to a court, which ordered that she undergo the caesarean section. The child died within two hours and Angela died two days later. The trial judge's decision on the forced caesarean was reversed by the Court of Appeal in 1990, too late to help Angela. See *In re A.C.*, 573 A.2d 1235 (D.C. App. 1990). For a more thorough discussion of the issue, see Daniels, *At Women's Expense: State Power and the Politics of Fetal Rights* (1993). See also Rahders, "'Natural Incubators': Somatic Support as Reproductive Technology, and the Comparative Constitutional Implications on Cases of Brain Death in the US, Canada, and Ireland" (2016) 27:1 Hastings Women's L.J. 29, which discusses whether women who have been declared "brain dead" should be kept alive artificially until their unborn children become viable.

10. In Canada, damages are not awarded for the death of a foetus; rather, the child must be born alive. See *Davey v. Victoria General Hospital* (1995), 106 Man. R. (2d) 81 (Q.B.); and *Gibbons v. Port Hope & District Hospital* (1998), 44 C.C.L.T. (2d) 198 (Ont. Gen. Div.), rev'd on a different point (1999), 46 C.C.L.T. (2d) 266 (C.A.). This position is consistent with the Supreme Court of Canada's position concerning criminal liability: see *R. v. Sullivan*, [1991] 1 S.C.R. 489.

Some American jurisdictions have modified the "born alive" rule in tort actions, allowing the parents to claim for the loss of companionship and comfort of a foetus that would have, but for the defendant's negligence, been born alive. These jurisdictions recognize the anomaly that a defendant who negligently kills a foetus escapes liability, while a negligent defendant who inflicts less serious injury is held accountable. See *O'Grady v. Brown*, 654 S.W.2d 904 (Mo. S.C. 1983). Should the "born alive" rule be retained in negligence?

In *Martin v. Mineral Springs Hospital* (2001), 283 A.R. 178 (Q.B.), the court affirmed that damages are not recoverable for grief that the parents suffer after the loss of an unborn child. However, the court awarded damages for the extended labour and delivery the plaintiff endured when her foetus died during the birthing process, the clinical depression she suffered afterward, and the two caesarean sections she subsequently underwent for fear that her children would die during vaginal childbirth. Her husband also successfully claimed for loss of consortium.

11. Having now reviewed the law on the various pre-natal torts, what recommendations would you make to a provincial law reform commission on improving and rationalizing this branch of negligence law?

4. Psychiatric Harm

The law relating to the negligent infliction of psychiatric harm (still known to many tort lawyers as "nervous shock") is notoriously confusing. As described below, the common law courts have developed numerous ways to control the scope of liability, with varying degrees of success and coherence. Special rules have evolved regarding, for example, the categories of plaintiffs who can claim for psychiatric harm, the difference between sudden shock and the gradual onset of psychiatric illness, and the distinction between so-called "primary" and "secondary" victims (*i.e.*, those directly involved in an incident and bystanders).

For many years, the Canadian law in this field was governed by a wide range of decisions from the lower and provincial appellate courts. These cases sometimes drew their reasoning from House of Lords decisions, which were themselves heavily criticized as being arbitrary and unprincipled. However, in the decisions of *Mustapha v. Culligan of Canada Ltd.*, 2008 SCC 27 and *Saadati v. Moorhead*, 2017 SCC 28, the Supreme Court of Canada effectively concluded that the ordinary rules of negligence relating to personal injury should also apply to cases of psychiatric harm. While these decisions might seem clear enough on preliminary analysis, they give rise to new questions and uncertainties.

The materials below outline the historical evolution of the law on psychiatric harm in the Commonwealth, including the modern English approach. They also include a summary of the current Canadian position, and an excerpt from the Supreme Court of Canada's decision in *Saadati*. The Supreme Court of Canada's decision in *Mustapha* is excerpted in Chapter 17, as it deals primarily with the issue of remoteness.

(a) INTRODUCTION

In medical terms, the phrase "nervous shock" is an anachronism. It is both overly broad, because it encompasses many different species of psychiatric illness, and inaccurate, because it suggests that a condition must arise in a sudden or "shocking" manner. Nevertheless, the older phrase continues to be heard in the courts, and the requirement of sudden shock has been relatively persistent. The legal meaning of nervous shock has evolved only gradually, and is not as sophisticated or advanced as medical science might allow. The situation is one of "[l]aw marching with medicine, but in the rear and limping a little": See *Mount Isa Mines Ltd. v. Pusey* (1970), 125 C.L.R. 383 at 395 (H.C.A.).

Although the law has slowly become more nuanced and more receptive to the basic idea of recovery for psychiatric injury, there are some respects in which the definition of "nervous shock" has remained constant. It has never encompassed many of the day-to-day emotional upsets (*e.g.* anger, disappointment, frustration, disgust) that are natural incidents of modern life. Nor, more significantly, does the legal concept of nervous shock encompass the feelings of grief and sorrow that inevitably follow upon the death or serious injury of a loved one. At least until *Saadati v. Moorhead, supra*, it was generally accepted that something more, by way of a "recognized psychiatric illness," was required for the purposes of liability. Interestingly, the medical profession has far less confidence in its ability to distinguish psychiatric illness from grief.

The courts traditionally were loath to impose liability for the careless infliction of psychiatric harm. Various reasons were provided in defence of that position. Judges were worried that, as compared with physical illness, psychiatric harm was easy to feign. X-rays can prove the existence of a broken bone, but there (still) is no similarly conclusive test for the existence of a psychiatric illness. The assessment of damages for psychiatric illness was also thought to be particularly difficult. And within the hierarchy of harms, there was a sense that damage to one's psyche was less worthy of protection than damage to one's body. The common law's conception of the "reasonable person" did not include someone who would complain about emotional upset. Perhaps most significantly, however, the courts have always been worried about opening the floodgates of liability. Whereas the agents of physical harm are usually limited in both time and space, the potential triggering mechanisms for psychiatric harm are much more far-ranging. The litigation arising from the Hillsborough disaster, discussed below, is illustrative.

NOTES AND QUESTIONS

1. English and most Canadian courts have defined "nervous shock" narrowly in an attempt to exclude claims for minor emotional upsets. See *Hinz v. Berry*, [1970] 1 All E.R. 1074 (C.A.); *Beaulieu v. Sutherland* (1986), 35 C.C.L.T. 237 (B.C.S.C.); *Heighington v. Ontario* (1987), 60 O.R. (2d) 641 (H.C.), additional reasons at (1987), 41 C.C.L.T. 230 (Ont. H.C.), aff'd (1989), 69 O.R. (2d) 484 (C.A.); *Cox v. Fleming* (1993), 13 C.C.L.T. (2d) 305 (S.C.), aff'd (1995), 15 B.C.L.R. (3d) 201 (C.A.); *Graham v. MacMillan* (2003), 10 B.C.L.R. (4th) 397 (C.A.); *McLoughlin v. Arbor Memorial Services Inc.* (2004), 36 C.C.L.T. (3d) 158 (Ont. S.C.J.); *Anderson v. Excel Collection Services Ltd.* (2005), 260 D.L.R. (4th) 367 (Ont. S.C.J.); *Knife (Litigation Guardian of) v. Charles* (2005), 272 Sask. R. 111 (Q.B.); *Satara Farms Inc. v. Parrish & Heimbecker, Ltd. (c.o.b. New-Life Feeds)* (2006), 280 Sask. R. 44 (Q.B.); *Kotai v. Queen of the North (The)* (2009), 70 C.C.L.T. (3d) 221 (B.C.S.C.); and *Healey v. Lakeridge Health Corporation* (2011), 103 O.R. (3d) 401 (C.A.). But see *Mason v. Westside Cemeteries Ltd.* (1996), 135 D.L.R. (4th) 361 (Ont. Gen. Div.); *Anderson v. Wilson* (1999), 44 O.R. (3d) 673 (C.A.); *Bastien v. Ottawa Hospital (General Campus)* (2001), 56 O.R. (3d) 397 (S.C.J.); and *Philip v. Whitecourt General Hospital* (2004), 359 A.R. 259 (Q.B.).

2. Is it possible to draw a meaningful distinction between psychiatric harm, which is recoverable, and grief and sorrow, which are not recoverable? See *Mathison v. Hofer*, [1984] 3 W.W.R. 343 (Man. Q.B.); *Beecham v. Hughes* (1988), 27 B.C.L.R. (2d) 1 (C.A.); *Cox v. Fleming, supra; Dube (Litigation Guardian of) v. Penlon Ltd.* (1994), 21 C.C.L.T. (2d) 268 (Ont. Gen. Div.); and *Geremia v. Nielsen Estate* (2006), 37 C.C.L.T. (3d) 313 (B.C.S.C.). See also *Mustapha v. Culligan of Canada Ltd.*, [2008] 2 S.C.R. 114 at para. 9, where McLachlin C.J. wrote, "I would not purport to define compensable injury exhaustively, except to say that it must be serious and prolonged and rise above the ordinary annoyances, anxieties and fears that people living in society routinely, if sometimes reluctantly, accept." Return to this question after you have read the excerpt of *Saadati v. Moorhead*, 2017 SCC 28.

Until recently, plaintiffs have been required to prove that the nervous shock manifested itself in some form of physical, psychiatric or psychological disorder. For analysis and criticism of this standard, which was ultimately rejected in *Saadati, supra*, see Mulheron, "Rewriting the Requirement for a 'Recognized Psychiatric Injury' in

Negligence Claims" (2012) 32 O.J.L.S. 77; Bélanger-Hardy, "Reconsidering the 'Recognizable Psychiatric Illness' Requirement in Canadian Negligence Law" (2013) 38 Queen's L.J. 583; Bélanger-Hardy, "Thresholds of Actionable Mental Harm in Negligence: A Policy-Based Analysis" (2013) 36 Dal. L.J. 103; and Orr, "Speaking with different voices: the problems with English law and psychiatric injury" (2016) 36:4 L.S. 547. See also Keating, "When is Emotional Distress Harm?" in Pitel, Neyers & Chamberlain, eds., *Tort Law: Challenging Orthodoxy* (2013) 273; and Schuurman & Sinel, "Matter over Mind: Tort Law's Treatment of Emotional Injury" in Barker, Fairweather & Grantham, eds., *Private Law in the 21st Century* (2017).

3. The courts have also limited recovery for psychiatric harm by requiring claimants to be "of reasonable fortitude and robustness" or "customary phlegm." Hypersensitive individuals are not reasonably foreseeable. See *Hay (or Bourhill) v. Young*, [1942] 2 All E.R. 396 (H.L.); *Duwyn v. Kaprielian* (1978), 22 O.R. (2d) 736 (C.A.); *Vanek v. Great Atlantic & Pacific Co. of Canada* (1999), 48 O.R. (3d) 228 (C.A.); *White v. Chief Constable of South Yorkshire Police*, [1999] 2 A.C. 455 (H.L.); *Mustapha v. Culligan of Canada Ltd.*, *supra*, and *Bain v. Black & Decker Canada (1989) Inc.*, 2009 CarswellOnt 3987 (S.C.J.) (WL Can). But see *Sant v. Jack Andrews Kirkfield Pharmach Ltd.* (2002), 161 Man. R. (2d) 121 (Q.B.), where the court stated that the requirement of reasonable fortitude only applied to claims by bystanders.

In *Clark v. Scotiabank* (2004), 25 C.C.L.T. (3d) 109 (Ont. S.C.J.), the plaintiff suffered depression after he was denied a loan based on a negligent report of his credit status by the defendant. While the court acknowledged that he suffered a recognizable psychiatric illness, it found that a person of reasonable fortitude would not have suffered such illness as the result of an erroneous credit report. Therefore, his illness was not reasonably foreseeable.

Should the plaintiff's profession or other personal characteristics be considered when deciding whether psychiatric harm is foreseeable? For instance, should those who work in emergency services or healthcare be less likely to recover, given that they become "desensitized" to serious injuries? See *Shorter v. Surrey and Sussex Healthcare NHS Trust*, [2015] EWHC 614, where the court held that the plaintiff's own work experience in neurointensive care meant that she would not find it "horrifying" to witness her sister die from an aneurysm. See also Rix & Cory-Wright, "How shocking: compensating secondary victims for psychiatric injury" (2018) 24 B.J. Psych. Advances 110.

4. Should plaintiffs be able to recover for the distress they suffer on being informed that they have been exposed to an infection or disease, even if they never contract it? Are the anxiety of having to undergo testing and fear of future illness sufficient to ground a claim, or would this simply reward hypersensitive individuals? Would claims for mere exposure to disease give rise to indeterminate liability? Would concerns about liability produce a "chilling effect" on the healthcare officials responsible for notifying the public about exposure to disease? See *Anderson v. Wilson* (1999), 44 O.R. (3d) 673 (C.A.); *Farkas v. Sunnybrook and Women's College Health Sciences Centre* (2009), 82 C.P.C. (6th) 222 (Ont. S.C.J.); *Bruce Estate v. Toderovich*, 2010 CarswellAlta 2248 (Q.B.) (WL Can), aff'd 2014 ABCA 44; *Healey v. Lakeridge Health Corporation*, *supra*, and *Gay v. New Brunswick (Regional Health Authority 7)*, 2014 NBCA 10. See also *Burnett Estate v. St. Jude Medical, Inc.*, 2009 BCSC 1651, where the court approved a settlement in a class action by plaintiffs who received an

allegedly defective mechanical heart valve. Only those plaintiffs whose fear and anxiety rose to the level of a recognized psychiatric disorder could make a claim from the relevant fund. For an English perspective, see *Rothwell v. Chemical & Insulating Co. Ltd.*, [2008] 1 A.C. 281 (H.L.) (negligent exposure to asbestos dust caused plaintiff to fear contracting asbestos-related disease); and Jones, "Liability for Future Disease?" (2008) 24 P.N. 13.

5. In *Greatorex v. Greatorex*, [2000] 4 All E.R. 769 (Q.B.), a young man was seriously injured in an automobile accident that he had carelessly caused. Because he was trapped inside his vehicle, firefighters were called to rescue him. One of the firefighters was his father. As a result of the incident, the father suffered a psychiatric disorder. The issue before the court was whether the victim of a self-inflicted injury owed a duty of care to not thereby cause psychiatric harm to a third party. The court answered that question in the negative. It held that recognition of such a duty would impose a significant restraint on a person's freedom of choice, and would open the doors to a particularly undesirable form of intra-familial litigation. See also *Homsi v. Homsi*, [2016] VSC 354.

6. See generally Wheat, *Napier and Wheat's Recovering Damages for Psychiatric Injury*, 2d ed. (2002); Teff, *Causing Psychiatric and Emotional Harm* (2009); and Handford, *Tort Liability for Mental Harm*, 3d ed. (2016).

7. Some writers have argued that the inequitable treatment of psychiatric harm by the common law reflects gendered stereotypes. See Chamallas & Kerber, "Women, Mothers and the Law of Fright: a History" (1990) 88 Mich. L. Rev. 814; Bender, "Feminist (Re)Torts: Thoughts on the Liability Crisis, Mass torts, Power and Responsibilities" [1990] Duke L.J. 848; Handsley, "Mental Injury Occasioned by Harm to Another: a Feminist Critique" (1996) 14 Law & Inequality 391; Welke, *Recasting American Liberty* (2001); Vines, San Roque & Rumble, "Is 'nervous shock' still a feminist issue? The duty of care and psychiatric injury in Australia" (2010) 18 Tort L. Rev. 9; Priaulx, "Endgame: On Negligence and Reparation for Harm" in Richardson & Rackley, eds., *Feminist Perspectives on Tort Law* (2012) 36; Chamallas, "Beneath the Surface of Civil Recourse Theory" (2013) 88 Ind. L.J. 527; and Yakren, "'Wrongful Birth' Claims and the Paradox of Parenting a Child with a Disability" (2018) 87 Fordham L. Rev. 593.

(b) COMMONWEALTH DEVELOPMENTS

Because of the concerns mentioned above, the Commonwealth courts have historically sought to create rules to limit liability. This began with the idea that a plaintiff could not recover unless the psychiatric harm was precipitated by some physical impact. This developed out of *Victorian Railways Commissioner v. Coultas* (1888), 13 App. Cas. 222 (P.C.). The plaintiff suffered severe shock when, as a result of the defendant's carelessness in raising a gate, she was nearly hit by a train. The lower courts imposed liability, but the Privy Council disagreed:

> Damages arising from mere sudden terror unaccompanied by any actual physical injury, but occasioning a nervous or mental shock, cannot . . . be considered a consequence which, in the ordinary course of things, would flow from the negligence of the gatekeeper. . . .

Not only in such a case as the present, but in every case where an accident caused by negligence had given a person a serious nervous shock, there might be a claim for damage on account of mental injury. The difficulty which now often exists in cases of alleged physical injuries of determining whether they were caused by the negligent act would be greatly increased, and a wide field opened for imaginary claims.

Accordingly, for many years the courts held that liability for psychiatric harm was available only if the plaintiff had suffered some physical injury or at least a physical impact. Over time, the artificiality of the so-called "impact rule" became unsustainable. In *Dulieu v. White & Sons*, [1901] 2 K.B. 699 (C.A.), the plaintiff suffered psychiatric harm when the defendant crashed his horse-drawn carriage into the public house in which she was working. She was allowed to recover even though she had not suffered any actual impact, because her psychiatric harm was triggered by "a reasonable fear of immediate personal injury to [herself]." However, *Dulieu* replaced the impact rule with a new restriction on liability: the plaintiff must suffer shock as a result of fear of injury to him or herself. If the plaintiff was not in physical danger, or the plaintiff suffered shock due to fear for injury to someone else, he or she could not recover.

This restriction was also modified, in turn, two decades later. In *Hambrook v. Stokes Brothers* (1924), [1925] 1 K.B. 141 (C.A.), a woman suffered psychiatric harm when she saw a runaway truck speeding down a hill toward the place where she had left her children to walk to school. She rushed to the scene of the crash, and was told that a girl matching her daughter's description had been injured. She suffered psychiatric harm, subsequently gave birth to a stillborn child, and died a few months later. Her husband's claim under fatal accidents legislation was questionable because his wife had not been in any physical danger and she had not feared that she would suffer personal injury. However, rejecting the rule from *Dulieu*, the court held that liability was possible if "the shock was due to a reasonable fear of immediate personal injury either to herself or to her children." See also *Horne v. New Glasgow (Town)* (1953), [1954] 1 D.L.R. 832 (N.S.S.C.); and *Hinz v. Berry*, [1970] 2 Q.B. 40 (C.A.). Nevertheless, the court in *Hambrook* was careful to limit recovery to situations where the shock occurred because of something the claimant "either saw or realized from her own unaided senses, and not from something which someone told her." This created a new limitation on recovery: the plaintiff had to witness the shocking incident with his or her own senses; it was not sufficient if the plaintiff heard about the accident from someone else.

In time, even this limitation was rejected. The high water mark for recovery for psychiatric harm came in *McLoughlin v. O'Brian*, [1982] 2 All E.R. 298 (H.L.). The plaintiff was married with three children. The defendant carelessly caused a traffic accident that killed one of those children and seriously injured the other two, as well as the plaintiff's husband. Having been told of the incident two hours later, the plaintiff went to the hospital where she received details of the tragedy. Thus, the plaintiff's shock was not due to physical impact, fear for her own safety or for the safety of her family, or even her presence at the scene of an accident. Nevertheless, the House of Lords imposed liability largely on the basis that the plaintiff's psychiatric injury was, in all of the circumstances of the case, reasonably foreseeable. Although she was not present at the scene of the accident, she attended to its "aftermath" and saw her injured family with her own eyes. It was foreseeable that a mother in this situation would suffer psychiatric injury.

However, the judges in *McLoughlin* were divided on the need for other limiting factors. Lord Bridge found no reason to continue distinguishing psychiatric injury from physical injury, and argued that reasonable foreseeability would be enough to impose a duty of care. Nevertheless, Lord Wilberforce's leading opinion held that, as a matter of policy, some boundaries on recovery had to be drawn. Lord Wilberforce found (at 422) three considerations to be particularly important: "the class of persons whose claims should be recognised; the proximity of such persons to the accident; and the means by which the shock is caused."

These three criteria were discussed at length in *Alcock v. Chief Constable of South Yorkshire Police*, [1991] 4 All E.R. 907 (H.L.), excerpted below. The case arose out of the Hillsborough disaster of 1989, in which, as a result of police carelessness, a soccer stadium became dangerously overcrowded. As millions watched on television and listened on radio, over 90 fans were crushed to death and many more were seriously injured. Actions were brought by several categories of claimants. *Alcock* involved 16 plaintiffs, representing approximately 150 others, who allegedly suffered psychiatric harm after fearing for the safety of loved ones who were in the Hillsborough Stadium. Some of those plaintiffs were themselves in the stands, others saw the events live on television or heard them live on the radio, and still others saw or heard news reports afterwards. Among the plaintiffs were wives, parents, grandparents, brothers, sisters, uncles, brothers-in-law, fiancés and friends of the (potential) victims. Another case, *White v. Chief Constable of South Yorkshire Police*, [1999] 2 A.C. 455 (H.L.), involved claims by the police officers who were present at the stadium and assisted with the rescue and recovery operation. That case is discussed in the notes and questions that follow.

ALCOCK v. CHIEF CONSTABLE OF SOUTH YORKSHIRE POLICE
[1991] 4 All E.R. 907 (H.L.)

LORD ACKNER:—My Lords, if sympathy alone were to be the determining factor in these claims, then they would never have been contested. It has been stressed throughout the judgments in the courts below and I would emphasise it yet again in your Lordships' House that the human tragedy which occurred on the afternoon of 15 April 1989 at the Hillsborough Stadium when 95 people were killed and more than 400 others received injuries from being crushed necessitating hospital treatment, remains an utterly appalling one.

It is, however, trite law that the defendant, the Chief Constable of South Yorkshire, is not an insurer against psychiatric illness occasioned by the shock sustained by the relatives or friends of those who died or were injured, or were believed to have died or to have been injured. This is, of course, fully recognised by the appellants, the plaintiffs in these actions, whose claims for damages to compensate them for their psychiatric illnesses are based upon the allegation that it was the defendant's negligence, that is to say his breach of his duty of care owed to them as well as to those who died or were injured in controlling the crowds at the stadium, which caused them to suffer their illnesses. The defendant, for the purposes of these actions, has admitted that he owed a duty of care only to those who died or were injured and that he was in breach of only that duty. He has further accepted that each of the plaintiffs has suffered some psychiatric illness. Moreover for the purpose of deciding whether the defendant is liable to pay damages to the plaintiffs in respect of their illnesses, the trial judge, Hidden J., made the assumption that the illnesses were caused by the shocks sustained by the plaintiffs by reason of their awareness of the events at Hillsborough. The defendant has throughout contested liability on the ground that, in all the circumstances, he was not in breach of any duty of care owed to the plaintiffs.

Since the decision of your Lordships' House in *McLoughlin v. O'Brian* [*supra*], if not earlier, it is established law that (1) a claim for damages for psychiatric illness resulting from shock caused by negligence can be made without the necessity of the plaintiff establishing that he was himself injured or was in fear of personal injury; (2) a claim for damages for such illness can be made when the shock results: (a) from death or injury to the plaintiff's spouse or child or the fear of such death or injury and (b) the shock has come about through the sight or hearing of the event, or its immediate aftermath.

To succeed in the present appeals the plaintiffs seek to extend the boundaries of this cause of action by: (1) removing any restrictions on the categories of persons who may sue; (2) extending the means by which the shock is caused, so that it includes viewing the simultaneous broadcast on television of the incident which caused the shock; (3) modifying the present requirement that the aftermath must be "immediate."

A recital of the cases over the last century shows that the extent of the liability for shock-induced psychiatric illness has been greatly expanded. This has largely been due to a better understanding of mental illness and its relation to shock. The extension of the scope of this cause of action sought in these appeals is not on any such ground but, so it is contended, by the application of established legal principles.

. . .

The nature of the cause of action

In *Bourhill v. Young* [1943] A.C. 92, 103, Lord Macmillan said:

in the case of mental shock there are elements of greater subtlety than in the case of an ordinary physical injury and these elements may give rise to debate as to the precise scope of the legal liability.

It is now generally accepted that an analysis of the reported cases of nervous shock establishes that it is a type of claim in a category of its own. Shock is no longer a variant of physical injury but a separate kind of damage. Whatever may be the pattern of the future development of the law in relation to this cause of action, the following propositions illustrate that the application *simpliciter* of the reasonable foreseeability test is, today, far from being operative.

[His Lordship summarized the existing principles of law on nervous shock.]

I do not find it surprising that in this particular area of the tort of negligence, the reasonable foreseeability test is not given a free rein. As Lord Reid said in *McKew v. Holland & Hannen & Cubitts (Scotland) Ltd.* [1969] 3 All E.R. 1621, 1623:

A defender is not liable for a consequence of a kind which is not foreseeable. But it does not follow that he is liable for every consequence which a reasonable man could foresee.

. . .

Although it is a vital step towards the establishment of liability, the satisfaction of the test of reasonable foreseeability does not, in my judgment, *ipso facto* satisfy Lord Atkin's well known neighbourhood principle enunciated in *Donoghue v. Stevenson*

[1932] A.C. 562, 580. For him to have been reasonably in contemplation by a defendant he must be:

> so closely and directly affected by my act that I ought reasonably to have them in contemplation as being so affected when I am directing my mind to the acts or omissions which are called in question.

The requirement contained in the words "so closely and directly affected . . . that" constitutes a control upon the test of reasonable foreseeability of injury. Lord Atkin was at pains to stress, at pp. 580-582, that the formulation of a duty of care, merely in the general terms of reasonable foreseeability, would be too wide unless it were "limited by the notion of proximity" which was embodied in the restriction of the duty of care to one's "neighbour."

The three elements

Because "shock" in its nature is capable of affecting such a wide range of persons, Lord Wilberforce in *McLoughlin v. O'Brian* [*supra*], 422, concluded that there was a real need for the law to place some limitation upon the extent of admissible claims and in this context he considered that there were three elements inherent in any claim. It is common ground that such elements do exist and are required to be considered in connection with all these claims. The fundamental difference in approach is that on behalf of the plaintiffs it is contended that the consideration of these three elements is merely part of the process of deciding whether, as a matter of fact, the reasonable foreseeability test has been satisfied. On behalf of the defendant it is contended that these elements operate as a control or limitation on the mere application of the reasonable foreseeability test. They introduce the requirement of "proximity" as conditioning the duty of care.

The three elements are (1) the class of persons whose claims should be recognised; (2) the proximity of such persons to the accident — in time and space; (3) the means by which the shock has been caused.

I will deal with those three elements seriatim.

(1) The class of persons whose claim should be recognised

When dealing with the possible range of the class of persons who might sue, Lord Wilberforce . . . contrasted the closest of family ties — parent and child and husband and wife — with that of the ordinary bystander. He said that while existing law recognises the claims of the first, it denied that of the second, either on the basis that such persons must be assumed to be possessed with fortitude sufficient to enable them to endure the calamities of modern life, or that defendants cannot be expected to compensate the world at large. He considered that these positions were justified, that other cases involving less close relationships must be very carefully considered, adding, at p. 422:

> The closer the tie (not merely in relationship, but in care) the greater the claim for consideration. The claim, in any case, has to be judged in the light of the other factors, such as proximity to the scene in time and place, and the nature of the accident.

I respectfully share the difficulty expressed by Atkin L.J. in *Hambrook v. Stokes Brothers*. . . — how do you explain why the duty is confined to the case of parent or guardian and child and does not extend to other relations of life also involving intimate associations; and why does it not eventually extend to bystanders? As regards the latter category, while it may be very difficult to envisage a case of a stranger, who is not actively and foreseeably involved in a disaster or its aftermath, other than in the role of rescuer, suffering shock-induced psychiatric injury by the mere observation of apprehended or actual injury of a third person in circumstances that could be considered reasonably foreseeable, I see no reason in principle why he should not, if in the circumstances, a reasonably strong-nerved person would have been so shocked. In the course of argument your Lordships were given, by way of an example, that of a petrol tanker careering out of control into a school in session and bursting into flames. I would not be prepared to rule out a potential claim by a passer-by so shocked by the scene as to suffer psychiatric illness.

As regards claims by those in the close family relationships referred to by Lord Wilberforce, the justification for admitting such claims is the presumption, which I would accept as being rebuttable, that the love and affection normally associated with persons in those relationships is such that a defendant ought reasonably to contemplate that they may be so closely and directly affected by his conduct as to suffer shock resulting in psychiatric illness. While as a generalisation more remote relatives and, *a fortiori*, friends, can reasonably be expected not to suffer illness from the shock, there can well be relatives and friends whose relationship is so close and intimate that their love and affection for the victim is comparable to that of the normal parent, spouse or child of the victim and should for the purpose of this cause of action be so treated. This was the opinion of Stocker L.J. in the instant appeal, *ante*, p. 376E-G, and also that of Nolan L.J. who thus expressed himself, *ante*, pp. 384-385:

> For my part, I would accept at once that no general definition is possible. But I see no difficulty in principle in requiring a defendant to contemplate that the person physically injured or threatened by his negligence may have relatives or friends whose love for him is like that of a normal parent or spouse, and who in consequence may similarly be closely and directly affected by nervous shock . . . . The identification of the particular individuals who come within that category, like that of the parents and spouses themselves, could only be carried out *ex post facto*, and would depend upon evidence of the 'relationship' in the broad sense which gave rise to the love and affection.

. . .

Whether the degree of love and affection in any given relationship, be it that of relative or friend, is such that the defendant, in the light of the plaintiff's proximity to the scene of the accident in time and space and its nature, should reasonably have foreseen the shock-induced psychiatric illness, has to be decided on a case by case basis. As Deane J. observed in *Jaensch v. Coffey*, 155 C.L.R. 549, 601:

> While it must now be accepted that any realistic assessment of the reasonably foreseeable consequences of an accident involving actual or threatened serious bodily injury must, in an appropriate case, include the possibility of injury in the form of nervous shock being sustained by a wide range of persons not physically injured in the accident, the outer limits of reasonable foreseeability of mere psychiatric injury cannot be identified in the abstract or in advance. Much may depend upon the nature of the negligent act or omission, on the gravity or apparent gravity of any actual or apprehended injury and on any expert evidence about the nature and explanation of the particular psychiatric injury which the plaintiff has sustained.

(2) The proximity of the plaintiff to the accident

It is accepted that the proximity to the accident must be close both in time and space. Direct and immediate sight or hearing of the accident is not required. It is reasonably foreseeable that injury by shock can be caused to a plaintiff, not only through the sight or hearing of the event, but of its immediate aftermath.

Only two of the plaintiffs before us were at the ground. However, it is clear from *McLoughlin v. O'Brian.* . . that there may be liability where subsequent identification can be regarded as part of the "immediate aftermath" of the accident. Mr. Alcock identified his brother-in-law in a bad condition in the mortuary at about midnight, that is some eight hours after the accident. This was the earliest of the identification cases. Even if this identification could be described as part of the "aftermath," it could not in my judgment be described as part of the immediate aftermath. McLoughlin's case was described by Lord Wilberforce as being upon the margin of what the process of logical progression from case to case would allow. Mrs. McLoughlin had arrived at the hospital within an hour or so after the accident. Accordingly in the post-accident identification cases before your Lordships there was not sufficient proximity in time and space to the accident.

(3) The means by which the shock is caused

Lord Wilberforce concluded that the shock must come through sight or hearing of the event or its immediate aftermath but specifically left for later consideration whether some equivalent of sight or hearing, *e.g.* through simultaneous television, would suffice: see p. 423. Of course it is common ground that it was clearly foreseeable by the defendant that the scenes at Hillsborough would be broadcast live and that amongst those who would be watching would be parents and spouses and other relatives and friends of those in the pens behind the goal at the Leppings Lane end. However he would also know of the code of ethics which the television authorities televising this event could be expected to follow, namely that they would not show pictures of suffering by recognisable individuals. Had they done so, Mr. Hytner accepted that this would have been a "*novus actus*" breaking the chain of causation between the defendant's alleged breach of duty and the psychiatric illness. As the defendant was reasonably entitled to expect to be the case, there were no such pictures. Although the television pictures certainly gave rise to feelings of the deepest anxiety and distress, in the circumstances of this case the simultaneous television broadcasts of what occurred cannot be equated with the "sight or hearing of the event or its immediate aftermath." Accordingly shocks sustained by reason of these broadcasts cannot found a claim. I agree, however, with Nolan L.J. that simultaneous broadcasts of a disaster cannot in all cases be ruled out as providing the equivalent of the actual sight or hearing of the event or its immediate aftermath. Nolan L.J. gave, *ante*, pp. 386G-387A, an example of a situation where it was reasonable to anticipate that the television cameras, whilst filming and transmitting pictures of a special event of children travelling in a balloon, in which there was media interest, particularly amongst the parents, showed the balloon suddenly bursting into flames. Many other such situations could be imagined where the impact of the simultaneous television pictures would be as great, if not greater, than the actual sight of the accident.

Conclusion

Only one of the plaintiffs, who succeeded before Hidden J., namely Brian Harrison, was at the ground. His relatives who died were his two brothers. The quality of brotherly love is well known to differ widely — from Cain and Abel to David and Jonathan. I assume that Mr. Harrison's relationship with his brothers was not an abnormal one. His claim was not presented upon the basis that there was such a close and intimate relationship between them, as gave rise to that very special bond of affection which would make his shock-induced psychiatric illness reasonably foreseeable by the defendant. Accordingly, the judge did not carry out the requisite close scrutiny of their relationship. Thus there was no evidence to establish the necessary proximity which would make his claim reasonably foreseeable and, subject to the other factors, to which I have referred, a valid one. The other plaintiff who was present at the ground, Robert Alcock, lost a brother-in-law. He was not, in my judgment, reasonably foreseeable as a potential sufferer from shock-induced psychiatric illness, in default of very special facts and none was established. Accordingly their claims must fail, as must those of the other plaintiffs who only learned of the disaster by watching simultaneous television. I, too, would therefore dismiss these appeals.

NOTES AND QUESTIONS

1. How does Lord Ackner define the element of sudden "shock?" Why should claims be limited to those induced by shock, rather than a more gradual onset of psychiatric illness? The High Court of Australia has rejected the requirement of sudden shock: *Tame v. New South Wales; Annetts v. Australian Stations Pty. Ltd.* (2002), 191 A.L.R. 449 (H.C.A.).

However, several states reversed the effects of *Tame/Annetts* through their civil liability legislation, which stipulates that plaintiffs cannot recover for pure psychiatric harm unless they witnessed the event and had a close relationship with the victim. For a summary of the legislation and its effects, see Vines, San Roque & Rumble, "Is 'nervous shock' still a feminist issue? The duty of care and psychiatric injury in Australia" (2010) 18 Tort L. Rev. 9. See also *Wicks v. State Rail Authority of New South Wales; Sheehan v. State Rail Authority of New South Wales*, [2010] HCA 22; *King v. Philcox*, [2015] HCA 19; and Fordham, "Psychiatric Injury, Secondary Victims and the 'Sudden Shock' Requirement" (2014) Sing. J.L.S. 41.

2. How does Lord Ackner define the class of persons whose claims ought to be recognized? How is this related to the concept of foreseeability? What does it mean for claims of bystanders who do not know the accident victims?

3. Why was Brian Harrison's claim denied? How can a plaintiff go about proving close ties of love and affection? If Harrison suffered psychiatric harm due to the tragic death of his brother, does it seem "fair, just and reasonable" to deny his claim because he did not legally prove a sufficiently intimate relationship with his brother?

4. How does Lord Ackner define the scope of "aftermath?" Is this compelling? Plaintiffs who witness the immediate consequences at the scene of a serious accident have generally been allowed to recover for psychiatric harm. For example in *Vernon v. Bosley (No. 1)*, [1997] 1 All E.R. 577 (C.A.), the plaintiff was allowed to recover for the

harm he suffered in witnessing the police attempt to pull the vehicle containing his two drowned children from a fast flowing river.

There are indications that the strict definition of "aftermath" may be relaxed. In *W. v. Essex County Council*, [2000] 2 All E.R. 237 (H.L.), the plaintiffs were parents of four young children. They also accepted foster children into their home. They expressly told the local authority, however, that they were not willing to accept a foster child who posed a risk of sexual abuse. The local authority knowingly disregarded that request and secretly placed into their care a boy of 15 who had been accused of sexual abuse in the past. Once in the home, the boy allegedly assaulted the plaintiffs' children, with the result that the plaintiffs suffered psychiatric illnesses. The defendant's motion to strike the statement of claim was granted at first instance on the ground that the plaintiffs' had not, with their own unaided senses, witnessed the alleged assaults or their immediate aftermath. That decision was affirmed in the Court of Appeal, but reversed in the House of Lords. In the course of judgment, Lord Slynn suggested that:

> . . . the concept of "the immediate aftermath" of the incident has to be assessed in the particular factual situation. I am not persuaded that in a situation like the present the parents must come across the abuser or the abused "immediately" after the sexual incident has terminated. All the incidents here happened in the period of four weeks before the parents learned of them.

The concept of "aftermath" has also been relaxed in cases involving infants who are injured or killed during the birthing process, resulting in psychiatric harm to their mothers. The mother may be unconscious or separated from the baby at the relevant time, and only suffers psychiatric harm on being told of the baby's demise. This has been held to fall within the principle of "aftermath." See *Farrell v. Sutton and Wandsworth Health Authority* (2000), 57 B.M.L.R. 158 (Q.B.); and *Walters v. North Glamorgan NHS Trust*, [2003] Lloyd's Rep. Med. 389 (C.A.). See generally Handford, "Psychiatric injury in breach of a relationship" (2007) 27 L.S. 26. Would the mother in such a case be classified as a primary or a secondary victim?

In some Canadian cases, the plaintiffs have been allowed to recover for the psychiatric harm suffered in seeing their deceased loved ones at the hospital. See *Grzywacz v. Vanderheide*, [1992] O.J. No. 2856 (Gen. Div.) (QL); *Cox v. Fleming* (1995), 15 B.C.L.R. (3d) 201 (C.A.); and *Yu v. Yu* (1999), 48 M.V.R. (3d) 285 (B.C.S.C.). But see *Devji v. Burnaby (District)* (1998), 158 D.L.R. (4th) 747 (B.C.S.C.), aff'd (1999), 70 B.C.L.R. (3d) 42 (C.A.), where recovery was denied because the plaintiffs, who were parents and siblings of the deceased, saw her body in the hospital four hours after the fatal traffic accident occurred.

5. Lord Ackner did not rule out the possibility that a simultaneous television broadcast might constitute the "aftermath" of a traumatic event, thereby giving rise to a successful claim. What if a plaintiff were to suffer shock on viewing subsequent media reports of the event? To what extent does the defendant have control over how the media present their reports? In *Piper v. Mitsubishi Heavy Industries Ltd.*, 2009 CarswellBC 2646 (S.C.) (WL Can), the plaintiff's husband was killed in a plane crash allegedly caused by the negligence of the defendant plane manufacturer. The plaintiff was personally informed of her husband's death, but then watched numerous news broadcasts during which footage of the crash was replayed. She claimed to have suffered psychological trauma as a result of viewing the broadcasts. Her claim was

denied on the basis that it was not reasonably foreseeable that she would suffer shock, and that the broadcasts could not be described as "alarming, horrifying, or shocking" events. Do you find this persuasive? What policy considerations might have informed this decision? See Rajendran, "Told Nervous Shock: Has the Pendulum Swung in Favour of Recovery by Television Viewers?" (2004) 9 Deakin L. Rev. 731.

6. In *White v. Chief Constable of South Yorkshire Police*, [1999] 1 All E.R. 1 (H.L.), the plaintiffs were police officers who witnessed the Hillsborough tragedy firsthand and subsequently developed psychiatric illnesses as a result of being involved in the gruesome events. While addressing the issue of duty of care, Lord Hoffman candidly stated that "in this area, the search for principle was called off in *Alcock*." There was a perceived need to limit the scope of liability, but also recognition that the line-drawing exercise was, perhaps inevitably, arbitrary. On the facts, the court applied the *Alcock* test and denied liability on the ground that the claimants had not shared a close relationship with the victims. In doing so, however, it narrowly, and somewhat unconvincingly, distinguished older authorities that appeared to create special rules for rescuers within the area of psychiatric harm. According to those earlier decisions, a rescuer might be entitled to relief even if he or she had not been exposed to physical danger and even if he or she had not been closely connected to any of the victims. See *Chadwick v. British Railways Commission*, [1967] 2 All E.R. 945 (Q.B.). See also *Bechard v. Haliburton Estate* (1991), 5 O.R. (3d) 512 (C.A.); *Fullowka v. Royal Oak Ventures Inc.*, [2005] 5 W.W.R. 420 (N.W.T.S.C.), rev'd on a different point 2010 SCC 5; *Arnold v. Cartwright Estate* (2007), 76 B.C.L.R. (4th) 351 (S.C.); and *Wicks v. State Rail Authority of New South Wales, supra.*

7. In *Page v. Smith*, [1995] 2 All E.R. 736 (H.L.), the defendant carelessly caused a traffic accident with the plaintiff. No one suffered any physical injury. Nevertheless, as a result of the incident, the plaintiff relapsed into chronic fatigue syndrome, a condition from which he had previously suffered. The court drew a distinction between "primary victims" (*i.e.* people placed in physical danger) and "secondary victims" (*i.e.* people not placed in physical danger). Although the details are complicated in some respects, the general significance of that distinction can be quickly explained. With respect to primary victims, liability for *psychiatric injury* is possible as long as it was reasonably foreseeable that the plaintiff might suffer a *physical injury* as a result of the defendant's carelessness. That is true even if, as in *Page* itself, the foreseeable physical injury never materialized, and even if the psychiatric injury that did materialize was not itself reasonably foreseeable. In contrast, a secondary victim cannot recover for the careless infliction of psychiatric harm unless it was reasonably foreseeable and *Alcock*'s three-part test of proximity is satisfied.

The distinction drawn in *Page v. Smith* between primary and secondary victims has been trenchantly criticized by academics. See especially Hilson, "Nervous Shock and the Categorisation of Victims" (1998) 6 Tort L. Rev. 37; Mullany, "English Psychiatric Injury Law — Chronically Depressing" (1999) 115 L.Q.R. 30; and Bailey & Nolan, "The *Page v. Smith* Saga: A Tale of Inauspicious Origins and Unintended Consequences" [2010] C.L.J. 495. See also *Taylor v. A. Novo (U.K.) Ltd.*, [2013] EWCA Civ 194. Nevertheless, the distinction continues to be applied: *Re (a child by her mother and litigation friend LE) and others v. Calderdale & Huddersfield NHS Foundation Trust*, [2016] EWHC 824 (Q.B.). The authority of the primary/secondary victim distinction in Canada has been doubtful, and it was explicitly rejected by the Court of Appeal for Ontario in *Mustapha v. Culligan of Canada Ltd.* (2006), 84 O.R. (3d) 457 (C.A.), aff'd on other grounds 2008 SCC 27.

8. Recovery for psychiatric harm in Australia is considerably broader than recovery in Canada or England. See generally Vines, "Proximity as Principle or Category: Nervous Shock in Australia and England" (1993) 16 U.N.S.W.L.J. 458; Mullany, "Fear for the Future: Liability for Infliction of Psychiatric Disorder" in Mullany, ed., *Torts in the Nineties* (1997) 101; and Mullany, "Negligently Inflicted Psychiatric Injury and the Means of Communication of Trauma — Should it Matter?" in Mullany & Linden, eds., *Torts Tomorrow: A Tribute to John Fleming* (1998) 162.

However, there is some indication that liability may be contracting as a result of reforms to state legislation on civil liability. See Butler, "*Gifford v Strang* and the new landscape for recovery for psychiatric injury in Australia" (2004) 12 Torts L.J. 108; and Forster & Engel, "Reinforcing historic distinctions between mental and physical injury: the impact of the civil liability reforms" (2012) 19 J.L. & Med. 593.

9. For further commentary on Commonwealth developments in psychiatric harm claims, see Teff, "Liability for Negligently Inflicted Psychiatric Harm: Justification and Boundaries" [1998] C.L.J. 91; Teff, "Liability for Psychiatric Illness: Advancing Cautiously" (1998) M.L.R. 849; Witting, "A Primer on the Modern Law of 'Nervous Shock'" (1998) 22 Melb. U.L. Rev. 62; Belanger-Hardy, "Nervous Shock, Nervous Courts: The *Anns/Kamloops* Test to the Rescue?" (1999) 37 Alta. L. Rev. 553; Mackenzie, "Oh, What a Tangled Web We Weave: Liability in Negligence for Nervous Shock" in Beaulac, Pitel & Schulz, eds., *The Joy of Torts* (2003) 125; Case, "Now you see it, now you don't: Black letter reflections on the legacies of *White v. Chief Constable of South Yorkshire Police*" (2010) 18 Tort L. Rev. 33; and Handford, "Recovery for psychiatric illness in Canada: A tale of two cases" (2011) 19 Tort L. Rev. 1.

(c) THE CANADIAN POSITION

The preceding materials were intended to outline, in general terms, the evolution of the duty of care for psychiatric harm in England and the Commonwealth. The lesson to be drawn from that overview is three-fold: (i) the scope of the duty of care is apt to shift from time to time in response to the judicially perceived need to expand or limit the scope of liability, (ii) there is always some need to impose restrictions on the application of general negligence principles, and (iii) the formulation of such restrictions tends to be, perhaps inevitably, arbitrary.

For many years, it was difficult to gauge the Canadian position on recovery for psychiatric harm, as there were relatively few appellate level decisions. The Supreme Court of Canada's decision in *Mustapha v. Culligan of Canada*, 2008 SCC 27, did little to clarify the area. The plaintiff in *Mustapha* suffered a major personality change after he and his wife saw a dead fly floating in an unopened Culligan water bottle that they had installed in their home. He had difficulty sleeping, became unable to drink water or take long showers, lost interest in sex, and suffered constant abdominal discomfort. The Supreme Court concluded that the case involved the well-established duty owed by manufacturers toward consumers of their products, and thus, did not seriously examine the Commonwealth jurisprudence on the duty of care relating to psychiatric harm. While the court accepted that the plaintiff had suffered a psychiatric illness, it concluded that his reaction was based on his own hypersensitive personality and was so objectively bizarre as to be unforeseeable. Therefore, his damage was too remote to be recoverable.

The decision in *Mustapha* raised many questions. The Supreme Court did not explain why it adopted an approach to psychiatric harm that was out of step with both the Canadian and Commonwealth authorities in the area, which overwhelmingly characterize the scope of recovery for psychiatric harm as a duty issue. Nor did the court explicitly criticize or reject the previous Canadian decisions that analyzed psychiatric harm in terms of the duty of care. This led some to believe that Mustapha might be limited to cases involving manufacturers' liability or so-called hypersensitive plaintiffs. However, in *Saadati v. Moorhead*, excerpted below, the Supreme Court of Canada reaffirmed the approach in *Mustapha* and clarified that the duty of care not to cause foreseeable personal injury included both physical and mental harm. Moreover, there was no need for plaintiffs to prove that their mental harm rose to the level of recognized psychiatric illness.

SAADATI v. MOORHEAD
2017 SCC 28

[The plaintiff was involved in a series of minor motor vehicle collisions and sustained no obvious physical injury. He did, however, suffer personality change and cognitive difficulties. Although there was no medical evidence to support this claim, the trial judge accepted the testimony of the plaintiff's friends and family to this effect, and awarded him $100,000 for non-pecuniary damage. The British Columbia Court of Appeal overturned this decision on the basis that the plaintiff had not proved a medically-recognized psychiatric or psychological condition. The plaintiff appealed.]

BROWN J.:—

. . .

B. Mental Injury

[13] Liability in negligence law is conditioned upon the claimant showing (i) that the defendant owed a duty of care to the claimant to avoid the kind of loss alleged; (ii) that the defendant breached that duty by failing to observe the applicable standard of care; (iii) that the claimant sustained damage; and (iv) that such damage was caused, in fact and in law, by the defendant's breach (Mustapha, at para. 3). At issue here is the third element. As they argued at the Court of Appeal, the respondents say that the trial judge erred by awarding damages for mental injury that did not correspond to a proven, recognized psychiatric illness. More specifically, the Court must answer the narrow question of whether it is strictly necessary, in order to support a finding of legally compensable mental injury, for a claimant to adduce expert evidence or other proof of a recognized psychiatric illness.

[Brown J. reviewed the Commonwealth jurisprudence on recovery for negligently-inflicted psychiatric harm.]

[18] Like the English courts, Canadian courts have occasionally struggled, as Professor Klar has described, "to find words which can clearly explain why, on the basis of arbitrary *policy* choices, certain types of claims seem to be too remote and uncompensable" (L. N. Klar, Tort Law (5th ed. 2012), at p. 505 (emphasis in original)) . . .

[19] This Court has not, however, adopted either the primary/secondary victim distinction, or *McLoughlin v. O'Brian*'s disaggregated proximity analysis. Rather, in *Mustapha*, recoverability of mental injury was viewed (at para. 3) as depending upon the claimant satisfying the criteria applicable to any successful action in negligence — that is, upon the claimant proving a duty of care, a breach, damage, and a legal and factual causal relationship between the breach and the damage. Each of these elements can pose a significant hurdle: not all claimants alleging mental injury will be in a relationship of proximity with defendants necessary to ground a duty of care; not all conduct resulting in mental harm will breach the standard of care; not all mental disturbances will amount to true "damage" qualifiying as mental injury, which is "serious and prolonged" and rises above the ordinary emotional disturbances that will occasionally afflict any member of civil society without violating his or her right to be free of negligently caused mental injury (*Mustapha*, at para. 9); and not all mental injury is caused, in fact or in law, by the defendant's negligent conduct.

[20] Indeed, the claim in *Mustapha* failed on that last element: the claimant's damage was not caused in law by (that is, it was too remote from) the defendant's breach. *Mustapha* thus serves as a salutary reminder that, even where a duty of care, a breach, damage and factual causation are established, there remains the pertinent threshold question of legal causation, or remoteness — that is, whether the occurrence of mental harm in a person of ordinary fortitude was the reasonably foreseeable result of the defendant's negligent conduct (*Mustapha*, at paras. 14-16). And, just as recovery for physical injury will not be possible where injury of that kind was not the foreseeable result of the defendant's negligence, so too will claimants be denied recovery (as the claimant in *Mustapha* was denied recovery) where mental injury could not have been foreseen to result from the defendant's negligence.

[21] It follows that this Court sees the elements of the cause of action of negligence as furnishing principled and sufficient barriers to unmeritorious or trivial claims for negligently caused mental injury. The view that courts should require something more is founded not on legal principle, but on policy — more particularly, on a collection of concerns regarding claims for mental injury . . . founded upon dubious perceptions of, and postures towards, psychiatry and mental illness in general: that mental illness is "subjective" or otherwise easily feigned or exaggerated; and that the law should not provide compensation for "trivial matters" but should foster the growth of "tough hides not easily pierced by emotional responses" (A. M. Linden and B. Feldthusen, *Canadian Tort Law* (10th ed. 2015), at p. 449; R. Mulheron, "Rewriting the Requirement for a 'Recognized Psychiatric Injury' in Negligence Claims" (2012), 32 *Oxford J. Leg. Stud.* 77, at p. 82). The stigma faced by people with mental illness, including that caused by mental injury, is notorious (J. E. Gray, M. Shone and P. F. Liddle, *Canadian Mental Health Law and Policy* (2nd ed. 2008), at pp. 139 and 300-301), often unjustly and unnecessarily impeding their participation, so far as possible, in civil society. While tort law does not exist to abolish misguided prejudices, it should not seek to perpetuate them.

[22] Where, therefore, genuine factual uncertainty arises regarding the worthiness of a claim, this can and should be addressed by robust application of those elements by a trier of fact, rather than by tipping the scales via arbitrary mechanisms (R. Stevens, *Torts and Rights* (2007), at p. 56). Certainly, concerns about "subjective" symptoms or about feigned or exaggerated claims of mental injury are — like most matters of credibility — questions of fact best entrusted to the good sense of triers of

fact, upon whose credibility determinations of liability and even of liberty often rest. In short, such concerns should be resolved by "a vigorous search for the truth, not the abdication of judicial responsibility" (Linden and Feldthusen, at p. 449; see also *Toronto Railway Co. v. Toms* (1911), 44 S.C.R. 268, at p. 276; Stevens, at p. 56).

[23] I add this. As to that first necessary element for recovery (establishing that the defendant owed the claimant a duty of care), it is implicit in the Court's decision in *Mustapha* that Canadian negligence law recognizes that a duty exists at common law to take reasonable care to avoid causing foreseeable mental injury, and that this cause of action protects a right to be free from negligent interference with one's mental health. That right is grounded in the simple truth that a person's mental health — like a person's physical integrity or property, injury to which is also compensable in negligence law — is an essential means by which that person chooses to live life and pursue goals (A. Ripstein, *Private Wrongs* (2016), at pp. 87 and 252-53). And, where mental injury is negligently inflicted, a person's autonomy to make those choices is undeniably impaired, sometimes to an even greater degree than the impairment which follows a serious physical injury (*Bourhill v. Young*, [1943] A.C. 92 (H.L.), at p. 103; *Toronto Railway*, at p. 276). To put the point more starkly, "[t]he loss of our mental health is a more fundamental violation of our sense of self than the loss of a finger" (Stevens, at p. 55).

. . .

(2) *Recognized Psychiatric Illness*

[25] As I have already said, the principal issue presented by this appeal — and, in particular, by the Court of Appeal's conclusion that the appellant's claim failed for lack of expert evidence demonstrating a recognized psychiatric illness — concerns the element of the cause of action of negligence requiring the claimant to show damage. More specifically, it requires the Court to consider what constitutes mental injury, and how it may be proven.

[26] The origins of the putative requirement of showing a recognized psychiatric illness appear to lie in Lord Denning M.R.'s speech in *Hinz v. Berry*, [1970] 2 Q.B. 40 (C.A.), at p. 42:

> In English law no damages are awarded for grief or sorrow caused by a person's death. No damages are to be given for the worry about the children, or for the financial strain or stress, or the difficulties of adjusting to a new life. Damages are, however, recoverable for nervous shock, or, to put it in medical terms, for a recognisable psychiatric illness caused by the breach of duty by the defendant.

This statement has been reiterated, albeit with some variation as to terminology. In *McLoughlin v. O'Brian*, at p. 431, for example, Lord Bridge described this hurdle as requiring "a positive psychiatric illness". It has also been variously referred to as a "genuine", "recognized" or "recognizable" psychiatric illness (Mulheron, at p. 81).

[27] Howsoever the term is phrased, it is far from clear on the text of *Hinz v. Berry* that it was intended to impose upon claimants the burden of showing a positive expert diagnosis. At the very least, it is not obvious that *Hinz v. Berry* sought to download to expert psychiatric witnesses the trier of fact's task of determining whether the claimant sustained mental injury (Teff, at p. 53; Bélanger-Hardy, at pp. 607-11). The respondents' submission, therefore — that, by "recognizable psychiatric illness", it

was intended that mental injury be "recognizable" to a psychiatrically trained expert witness, and not to an ordinary witness — is founded upon a shaky premise.

. . .

[29] In sum — and this is the state of the law which this Court must now evaluate — the law developed by Canadian lower courts (albeit, as I have mentioned, on an unstable premise) requires claimants alleging mental injury to show that such injury has manifested itself to an expert in psychiatry in the form of a clinically diagnosed, recognizable psychiatric illness. This has therefore "place[d] the categories of mental and emotional harm for which damages may be recovered in the hands of psychiatry. Whatever that discipline chooses to identify and name as a psychiatric illness becomes the law's boundaries for damages in this area" (*van Soest*, at p. 205, per Thomas J., dissenting).

[30] Usually, this has been done with reference to what has been said to represent a "considerable degree of international agreement on the classification of mental disorders and their diagnostic criteria", which are contained in the *Diagnostic and Statistical Manual of Mental Disorders* ("DSM"), published by the American Psychiatric Association, and the *International Statistical Classification of Diseases and Related Health Problems* ("ICD"), published by the World Health Organization [citations omitted]. The DSM, now in its 5th edition (2013), stipulates diagnostic criteria for, and classifies, mental disorders, while the ICD, now in its 10th revision (1992), contains statistically based classifications of all diseases (including "mental and behavioural disorders").

[31] Confining compensable mental injury to conditions that are identifiable with reference to these diagnostic tools is, however, inherently suspect as a matter of legal methodology. While, for treatment purposes, an accurate diagnosis is obviously important, a trier of fact adjudicating a claim of mental injury is not concerned with diagnosis, but with symptoms and their effects (Mulheron, at p. 88). Put simply, there is no necessary relationship between reasonably foreseeable mental injury and a diagnostic classification scheme. As Thomas J. observed in *van Soest* (at para. 100), a negligent defendant need only be shown to have foreseen *injury*, and not *a particular psychiatric illness* that comes with its own label. In other words, the trier of fact's inquiry should be directed to the level of harm that the claimant's particular symptoms represent, not to whether a label could be attached to them. Downloading the task of assessing legally recoverable mental injury to the DSM and ICD therefore imports an arbitrary control mechanism upon recovery for mental injury, conditioning recovery not upon any legally principled basis directed to the alleged injury, but upon conformity with a legally irrelevant classification scheme designed to facilitate identification of *particular conditions* (L. Bélanger-Hardy, "Thresholds of Actionable Mental Harm in Negligence: A Policy-Based Analysis" (2013), 36 *Dal. L.J.* 103, at pp. 113-15; Mulheron, at pp. 87-88).

. . .

[35] In short, no cogent basis has been offered to this Court for erecting distinct rules which operate to preclude liability in cases of mental injury, but not in cases of physical injury. Indeed, there is good reason to recognize the law of negligence as already according each of these different forms of personal injury — mental and physical — identical treatment. As the Court observed in *Mustapha* (at para. 8), the distinction between physical and mental injury is "elusive and arguably artificial in the

context of tort". Continuing (and citing *Page v. Smith*, at p. 188), the Court explained that, "[i]n an age when medical knowledge is expanding fast, and psychiatric knowledge with it, it would not be sensible to commit the law to a distinction between physical and psychiatric injury, which may . . . soon be altogether outmoded. Nothing will be gained by treating them as different 'kinds' of personal injury, so as to require the application of different tests in law" (emphasis in original) [other citations omitted]. This is entirely consistent with the Court's longstanding view, expressed over a century ago, by Fitzpatrick C.J. in *Toronto Railway*, at pp. 269-70:

> It would appear somewhat difficult to distinguish between the injury caused to the human frame by the impact and that resulting to the nervous system in consequence of the shock . . . The nature of the mysterious relation which exists between the nervous system and the passive tissues of the human body has been the subject of much learned speculation, but I am not aware that the extent to which the one acts and reacts upon the other has yet been definitely ascertained. . . . I cannot find the line of demarcation between the damage resulting to the human [body] . . . and that which may flow from the disturbance of the nervous system . . . The latter may well be the result of a derangement of the relation existing between the bones, the sinews, the arteries and the nerves. In any event the resultant effect is the same. The victim is incapacitated . . .

Or, as Davies J. (as he then was) added in *Toronto Railways* (at p. 275), "[t]he nervous system is just as much a part of man's physical being as the muscular or other parts". In a similar vein, Lord Macmillan, in *Bourhill v. Young* (at p. 103), said "[t]he distinction between mental shock and bodily injury was never a scientific one, for mental shock is presumably in all cases the result of, or at least accompanied by, some physical disturbance in the sufferer's system."

[36] It follows that requiring claimants who allege one form of personal injury (mental) to prove that their condition meets the threshold of "recognizable psychiatric illness", while not imposing a corresponding requirement upon claimants alleging another form of personal injury (physical) to show that their condition carries a certain classificatory label, is inconsistent with prior statements of this Court, among others. It accords unequal — that is, less — protection to victims of mental injury. And it does so for no principled reason (Beever, at p. 410). I would not endorse it.

[37] None of this is to suggest that mental injury is always as readily demonstrable as physical injury. While allegations of injury to muscular tissue may sometimes pose challenges to triers of fact, many physical conditions such as lacerations and broken bones are objectively verifiable. Mental injury, however, will often not be as readily apparent. Further, and as *Mustapha* makes clear, mental *injury* is not proven by the existence of mere psychological *upset*. While, therefore, tort law protects persons from negligent interference with their mental health, there is no legally cognizable right to happiness. Claimants must, therefore, show much more — that the disturbance suffered by the claimant is "serious and prolonged and rise[s] above the ordinary annoyances, anxieties and fears" that come with living in civil society (*Mustapha*, at para. 9). To be clear, this does not denote distinct legal treatment of mental injury relative to physical injury; rather, it goes to the prior legal question of what constitutes "mental injury". Ultimately, the claimant's task in establishing a mental injury is to show the requisite degree of disturbance (although not, as the respondents say, to show its classification as a recognized psychiatric illness).

[38] Nor should any of this be taken as suggesting that expert evidence cannot assist in determining whether or not a mental injury has been shown. In assessing whether the claimant has succeeded, it will often be important to consider, for example, how seriously the claimant's cognitive functions and participation in daily activities were impaired, the length of such impairment and the nature and effect of any treatment (Mulheron, at p. 109). To the extent that claimants do not adduce relevant expert evidence to assist triers of fact in applying these and any other relevant considerations, they run a risk of being found to have fallen short. As Thomas J. observed in *van Soest* (at para. 103), "[c]ourts can be informed by the expert opinion of modern medical knowledge", "without needing to address the question whether the mental suffering is a recognisable psychiatric illness or not". To be clear, however: while relevant expert evidence will often be helpful in determining whether the claimant has proven a mental injury, it is not required as a matter of law. Where a psychiatric diagnosis is unavailable, it remains open to a trier of fact to find on other evidence adduced by the claimant that he or she has proven on a balance of probabilities the occurrence of mental injury. And, of course, it also remains open to the defendant, in rebutting a claim, to call expert evidence establishing that the accident cannot have caused *any* mental injury, or at least any mental injury known to psychiatry. While, for the reasons I have given, the lack of a diagnosis cannot on its own be dispositive, it is something that the trier of fact can choose to weigh against evidence supporting the existence of a mental injury.

(3) *Application*

[39] The trial judge found that the accident caused the appellant to suffer "psychological injuries, including personality change and cognitive difficulties" (para. 50) such as slowed speech, leading to a deterioration of his close personal relationships with his family and friends. He remarked (at para. 65) that the appellant "was a changed man with his irritability likely reflecting a dark realization that he was not the man he once was". These findings have not been challenged. And, as findings of fact, they are entitled to appellate deference, absent palpable and overriding error (*Housen v. Nikolaisen*, 2002 SCC 33, [2002] 2 S.C.R. 235, at para. 10).

[40] I see no legal error in the trial judge's treatment of the evidence of the appellant's symptoms as supporting a finding of mental injury. Those symptoms fit well within the *Mustapha* parameters of mental injury which I have already recounted. While there was no expert testimony associating them with a condition identified in the DSM or ICD, I reiterate that what matters is substance — meaning, those symptoms — and not the label. And, the evidence accepted by the trial judge clearly showed a serious and prolonged disruption that transcended ordinary emotional upset or distress.

IV. Conclusion and Disposition

[41] I would allow the appeal, with costs in this Court and in the courts below.

NOTES AND QUESTIONS

1. How does Brown J. define the threshold of compensable mental harm? Is it sufficiently distinguishable from grief or sorrow, which are not compensable? See Sinel, "What's your damage? The elimination of the expert-recognised psychiatric illness requirement in the Canadian law of negligence: *Saadati v Moorhead*, [2017] 1

SCR 543" (2017) 24 Torts L.J. 205. Does the elimination of the requirement of recognizable psychiatric illness discard the one helpful, if sometimes troublesome, bright line in this field?

2. Does the decision in *Saadati* adequately address concerns about the scope of liability toward bystanders who suffer from mental injury after witnessing an accident or its aftermath? Are bystanders more or less likely to obtain compensation after *Saadati*?

Prior to *Saadati*, a leading Canadian case on recovery for psychiatric harm in negligence was *Rhodes v. Canadian National Railway* (1990), 50 B.C.L.R. (2d) 273 (C.A.). The plaintiff's son was killed in a train crash negligently caused by the defendant. She heard about the crash on the radio, and travelled from her home on Vancouver Island to Hinton, Alberta to see if her son had been killed. The defendant's employees denied her access to the crash site for eight days. She realized after several days that her son must have been killed, but she never saw his body because it was consumed by fire in the crash. Her claim to recover for her psychiatric injury was denied because it was not a foreseeable consequence of the defendant's negligence. Although she had close ties of love and affection with her son, she had not witnessed the accident or its aftermath with her own unaided senses. Would *Rhodes* be decided the same way today?

3. After you have read Chapter 17, return to this chapter and explain how the test of "ordinary fortitude" is distinguished from the thin-skull principle in remoteness. Why does one principle allow recovery and the other one deny it? What are the implications of the Supreme Court of Canada's decision in *Mustapha* for this distinction?

4. It is not yet clear what evidence will convince triers-of-fact that the plaintiff has suffered mental harm. In *MacKenzie v. John Doe*, 2018 BCSC 104, the judge concluded that the plaintiff, who testified that he suffered from mood irritability following a motor vehicle crash, had not satisfied the burden of proof.

5. Although most cases involve serious automobile, industrial and household accidents, psychiatric harm claims have arisen in a broad range of fact situations. See for example *Curll v. Robin Hood Multifoods Ltd.* (1974), 56 D.L.R. (3d) 129 (N.S.T.D.); *Taylor v. Weston Bakeries Ltd.* (1976), 1 C.C.L.T. 158 (Sask. Dist. Ct.); *Kendrew v. McDonald's Restaurants of Canada Ltd.* (2008), 322 Sask. R. 56 (Q.B.) (involving contaminated food products); *Guay v. Sun Publishing Co.*, [1953] 2 S.C.R. 216 (false newspaper report of husband's and children's deaths); *Cook v. S.*, [1967] 1 All E.R. 299 (C.A.) (solicitor's negligence in divorce proceedings); *Dietelbach v. British Columbia (Public Trustee)* (1973), 37 D.L.R. (3d) 621 (B.C.S.C.); *Pratt & Goldsmith v. Pratt*, [1975] V.R. 378 (S.C.) (involving trauma of adjusting to the injuries of close relatives); *McMullin v. F.W. Woolworth Co.* (1974), 9 N.B.R. (2d) 214 (Q.B.) (diseased turtle infecting plaintiff's children); and *Brooks v. Canadian Pacific Railway Ltd.* (2007), 298 Sask. R. 64 (Q.B.) (plaintiffs evacuated as a precaution after train derailment in area). Except in the food products cases, the courts held that the plaintiffs were not owed a duty of care because psychiatric harm was unforeseeable. But see *Boudreau v. Benaiah* (2000), 46 O.R. (3d) 737 (C.A.) (offender awarded damages for mental distress due to his defence counsellors' negligence in arranging a plea bargain); *Lodge v. Fraser Health Authority* (2009), 91 B.C.L.R. (4th) 44 (C.A.) (widower awarded damages for mental

distress suffered when three rings disappeared from wife's dead body); and *Goodwin v. Becker*, 2013 BCSC 2148 (plaintiff awarded $10,000 in damages for mental distress suffered due to her solicitor's negligence in refinancing her townhouse). Can the principles in *Saadati* explain the results in these cases?

6. Developments in neuroscience point to changes that occur in the brain when an individual suffers mental harm. How should such evidence be treated in negligence cases? Should brain scans replace the former requirement of a recognizable psychiatric illness? See Cassin, "Eggshell Minds and Invisible Injuries: Can Neuroscience Challenge Longstanding Treatment of Tort Injuries?" (2013) 50:3 Hous. L. Rev. 929; Grey, "The Future of Emotional Harm" (2015) 83:5 Fordham L. Rev. 2605; Grey, "Implications of Neuroscience Advances in Tort Law: A General Overview" (2015) 12:2 Ind. Health L. Rev. 671; and Jones & Wagner, "Law and Neuroscience: Progress, Promise, and Pitfalls" in Gazzaniga, Mangun & Poeppel, eds., *The Cognitive Neurosciences*, 6th ed. (2019).

REVIEW PROBLEM

John Smith fell asleep at the wheel of his truck, crashed through a barrier and struck an oncoming car. The driver of the car, Mike Berry, was killed and his wife, Helen, was injured. Although Helen's physical injuries healed quickly, she was unable to cope with the shock of the accident and her husband's death. It was only after 15 months of intensive psychiatric care that Helen was able to return to work and a relatively normal lifestyle. Steven Finch, the other passenger in the Berry car, was uninjured. Unfortunately, David Finch, his father, had been following the Berry car and suffered severe shock on witnessing the collision, as did Mrs. Pewter, an old friend who was travelling in the Finch car. As a result of his attempts to assist the accident victims, Melvin, a bystander, suffered recurring nightmares. The gruesome scene triggered Melvin's memories of a childhood accident in which his younger brother had been killed. As Sarah Berry drove past the scene she recognized the demolished car of her brother, Mike Berry. By the time she stopped and ran back to the scene, all of the accident victims had been taken to the hospital. She fought back her tears long enough to ask one of the officers what had happened. All he was able to tell her was that the accident had been a serious one involving several members of the Berry family. Sarah was overwhelmed and passed out. She was informed of her brother's death when she regained consciousness in the hospital. Lastly, Mike Berry's mother suffered a heart attack when she heard of her son's death in a radio broadcast.

You have been consulted by John Smith for advice concerning his possible liability for the negligent infliction of psychiatric harm.

5. A Health Professional's Duty to Inform

As discussed in Chapter 6, the Supreme Court of Canada decided in *Reibl v. Hughes*, [1980] 2 S.C.R. 880 to limit a doctor's liability in battery to cases in which the patient did not consent at all, the consent was exceeded, or the consent was obtained fraudulently. Once the patient is aware of the general nature of the proposed treatment and consents to it, the doctor's failure to inform will not vitiate the consent and give rise to liability in battery. Rather, the Supreme Court of Canada indicated that the doctor may be held liable in negligence for breaching an affirmative duty to disclose the risks of the proposed treatment. This duty is a special duty of care that arises independently of doctors' general duty to exercise reasonable care in treating patients.

The court focused on the information that a reasonable patient in the plaintiff's position would want. More specifically, the court stated that doctors must disclose all material risks of the proposed treatment. A "material risk" includes a low percentage risk of a serious consequence. In *Reibl*, it was held that a 4% chance of death and a 10% chance of paralysis constituted material risks. A relatively minor consequence of high probability may also constitute a material risk. As well, doctors have an obligation to disclose non-material risks that they know, or ought to know, would be of particular concern to the patient. For example, a doctor may not have to disclose a 5% risk of minor residual stiffness in the shoulder to a patient who is an accountant, but would have to disclose this risk to a patient who is a professional tennis player.

Patients may choose to rely on their doctors' judgment and decide that they do not wish to be informed of the risks. However, the decision not to be fully informed is the patient's to make, and he or she must clearly communicate this to the doctor. All questions must be answered honestly and fully, even if they relate to minor matters or if the answers might be upsetting.

Doctors who do not meet these disclosure requirements will be held to have breached the requisite standard of care. However, patients must also establish that this failure to inform was a cause of their loss. In effect, patients must prove that, had they been adequately informed, they would not have proceeded with the treatment. In *Reibl*, the Supreme Court of Canada rejected the general common law test of causation and adopted a special objective/subjective test of causation. The plaintiff must prove that a reasonable person in the plaintiff's position would have refused the procedure if properly informed.

As the following case and the accompanying notes and questions illustrate, the courts have broadened the duty to inform considerably since it was first established in *Reibl*. The duty is no longer limited to warning patients of the risks of the specific procedure; rather, the doctor is required to provide the patient with sufficient information to make an informed decision. The definition of a material risk has been broadened to include very remote risks of death or serious injury. The courts are far less willing to give doctors discretion to withhold information because doctors believe it will be disconcerting to the patient. Finally, the principles governing the duty to inform now appear to apply to all health professionals and care givers.

HAUGHIAN v. PAINE
(1987), 37 D.L.R. (4th) 624 (Sask. C.A.)

[The plaintiff underwent disc surgery that left him paralyzed. A second operation partially alleviated the paralysis. The plaintiff's action against the defendant surgeon for failing to obtain an informed consent was dismissed at trial. The plaintiff appealed.]

SHERSTOBITOFF J.A.:—[The judge quoted from *Videto v. Kennedy* (1981), 33 O.R. (2d) 497 (C.A.), a summary of the Supreme Court of Canada's conclusions from *Reibl* and *Hopp v. Lepp*, [1980] 2 S.C.R. 192.]

I would add to the principles outlined above a matter which was not under direct consideration in the foregoing cases: In order to enable a patient to give informed consent, a surgeon must also, where the circumstances require it, explain to the patient the consequences of leaving the ailment untreated, and alternative means of treatment and their risks.

. . .

In my respectful view, the trial Judge erred in failing to give any weight, under the aspect of informed consent, to the duty of the respondent in this case to advise the appellant of the consequences of leaving the ailment untreated and the duty to advise of alternate means of treatment. A careful examination of the evidence . . . under the head of negligence indicates that there was no adequate discussion, if any at all, of the consequences of leaving the ailment untreated or of undergoing conservative management, and that the consequences were, at worst, a continuation of pain and discomfort and possible need for surgery in the future. The appellant was not told that the prospect was that the condition might, in a matter of months, very well improve, albeit with the prospect of recurrence from time to time. If the condition deteriorated, surgery was always an option in the future. In the absence of such information having been given to the appellant, he was not in a position to give informed consent.

It makes no difference that the respondent may have been under a misconception that the appellant had had conservative management. If that was the case it was due to the respondent's negligence in failure to take an adequate history, or to consider it.

The other aspect of the informed consent is the failure of the respondent to warn the appellant of the possibility of total paralysis, the risk which in fact materialized. Although no exact statistics were given, a consensus seems to have arisen amongst the neurosurgeons giving evidence that the risk of paralysis in surgery such as under consideration here is not more than one in five hundred. The respondent's practice was not to give any warning if the risk was less than one in one hundred.

. . .

The trial Judge made reference to the similarity of facts in *Hopp v. Lepp* and this case: both involve disc surgery. He commented that the doctor was found not liable in *Hopp v. Lepp* and he told the patient less of the risks than the respondent did in this case. However, a careful reading of *Hopp v. Lepp* does not disclose that any alternative such as conservative management was available in that case. It was certainly not an issue. That is sufficient to distinguish it, on the facts, from this case.

Finally, I touch upon an argument advanced by the respondent. His position is that statistically the risk of paralysis is less than one in five hundred, a risk so insignificant that it could not be considered material. In my respectful view, the issue of materiality cannot be reduced to numbers for all cases. Statistics are but one factor to be taken into account.

In my respectful view, the disclosure made by the respondent was not adequate to enable the appellant to give informed consent. On the principles laid down above which I have quoted from *Hopp v. Lepp, Reibl v. Hughes, Canterbury v. Spence,* and the dissenting opinion of Lord Scarman in *Sidaway v. Bethlem Royal Hospital Governors,* the following deficiencies in disclosure are apparent in this case:

1. A failure to advise adequately, or at all, of the available options of no treatment, or conservative management. While it may have been open to the respondent not to recommend these options by way of treatment, the patient was entitled to be advised that these alternatives were open to him.

2. A failure to advise of the risk of paralysis. Admittedly, the risk was small, but given that alternative non-surgical treatment was available, with lack of risk, a

significant chance of success, and the paucity of evidence that the condition disabled the appellant significantly, disclosure should have been made.

A significant factor is that the trial Judge considered failure to warn of risk of paralysis, and failure to advise of alternatives to surgery, independently of, and in isolation from, each other. These two elements of informed consent have, on the facts of this case, a strong bearing on each other. One cannot make an informed decision to undertake a risk without knowing the alternatives to undergoing the risk.

There is no suggestion here that the respondent withheld the information because of "therapeutic privilege". There was no suggestion that disclosure would have unduly frightened the appellant, caused him psychological harm or deterred him from taking treatment essential to his health. The respondent's position was simply that it was not his practice to warn of this risk.

[Appeal allowed; judgment for the plaintiff.]

NOTES AND QUESTIONS

1. How does *Haughian* expand the principles in *Reibl*? What role did the alternative treatments play in the judge's conclusion in *Haughian* that a 1 in 500 chance of paralysis was a material risk? See also *Coughlin v. Kuntz* (1989), 2 C.C.L.T. (2d) 42 (B.C.C.A.); *Van Mol (Guardian ad litem of) v. Ashmore* (1999), 168 D.L.R. (4th) 637 (Alta. C.A.); *Thibault v. Fewer*, [2002] 1 W.W.R. 204 (Man. Q.B.); *Remtulla v. Zeldin*, 2005 CarswellOnt 4921 (S.C.J.) (WL Can); and *Groves v. Morton* (2006), 44 C.C.L.T. (3d) 108 (Ont. S.C.J.).

2. In *Reibl* and *Haughian*, the courts suggest that a health professional has a limited "therapeutic privilege" to withhold information if its disclosure would unduly frighten or deter the patient. However, in *Hopp v. Lepp*, [1980] 2 S.C.R. 192, the court suggested that the privilege no longer existed. In *Meyer Estate v. Rogers* (1991), 2 O.R. (3d) 356 (Gen. Div.), the judge stated that the doctrine was no longer part of the law. In *Pittman Estate v. Bain* (1994), 112 D.L.R. (4th) 257 (Ont. Gen. Div.), the court acknowledged that the privilege existed, but defined it narrowly (*i.e.*, the doctor may choose how to present the information and what aspects to emphasize). In what circumstances, if any, should the courts recognize a privilege to withhold information? See Côté, "Telling the Truth: Disclosure, Therapeutic Privilege and Intersexuality in Children" (2000) 8 Health L.J. 199; and "To Tell the Truth, the Whole Truth, May Do Patients Harm: The Problem of the Nocebo Effect for Informed Consent" (2012) 12(3) Am. J. Bioeth. 22.

In *Montgomery v. Lanarkshire Health Board*, [2015] UKSC 11, the UK Supreme Court also upheld a very narrow interpretation of therapeutic privilege. The defendant doctor was found liable for failing to inform the plaintiff of the risk of shoulder dystocia if she gave vaginal birth to an unusually large baby. Although the doctor conceded that risk was material, she withheld the information from the plaintiff because she believed that the plaintiff would have insisted on an elective caesarian section.

3. The scope of what constitutes a material risk has been progressively broadened since *Reibl*. See for example *Buchan v. Ortho Pharmaceutical (Canada) Ltd.* (1986), 25 D.L.R. (4th) 658 (Ont. C.A.) (very rare chance of a stroke as a result of taking oral

contraceptives); *Feist v. Gordon* (1989), 67 Alta. L.R. (2d) 283 (Q.B.), aff'd (1990), 76 Alta. L.R. (2d) 234 (C.A.) (1 in 40,000 risk of puncturing eyeball with cortisone treatment); *Rolof v. Morris* (1990), 109 A.R. 128 (Q.B.) (1 in 1,000 risk of an intra-uterine contraceptive device leaving the uterus and requiring surgical removal); *Meyer Estate v. Rogers, supra* (1 in 40,000 to 1 in 100,000 chance of death as a result of a severe reaction to a diagnostic dye); *Leung v. Campbell* (1995), 24 C.C.L.T. (2d) 63 (Ont. Gen. Div.) (rare risk of stroke during neck manipulation by a chiropractor); *Martin v. Inglis*, [2002] 9 W.W.R. 500 (Sask. Q.B.) (a mere possibility of stomach perforation and death from gastric surgery); *Brock v. Anderson* (2003), 20 C.C.L.T. (3d) 70 (B.C.S.C.) (very small likelihood of damaging a major blood vessel which, if it occurred, posed a significant risk of death); *Bovingdon (Litigation Guardian of) v. Hergott* (2008), 88 O.R. (3d) 641 (C.A.) (possibility of having multiple pregnancies when prescribing Clomid); and *Carlson v. Steeves* (2008), 55 C.C.L.T. (3d) 263 (B.C.S.C.) (increased risk of pancreatitis stemming from grossly elevated triglyceride levels). But see *DeFerrari v. Neville* (1998), 42 C.C.L.T. (2d) 327 (Ont. Gen. Div.) (1 in 800,000 chance of permanent numbness arising from dental anaesthetic found not to be a material risk); and *Munir v. Jackson*, 2006 CarswellOnt 2518 (S.C.J.) (WL Can) (3 in 10,000 chance of permanent tracheotomy found not to be a material risk).

4. Disclosing some material risks, while not disclosing others, is insufficient: see *Tremblay v. McLauchlan* (2001), 6 C.C.L.T. (3d) 238 (B.C.C.A.).

5. While healthcare professionals may include a video as part of the process of informing a patient, this does not relieve them of the obligation to ensure that the patient understands the procedure and its risks. See *Byciuk v. Hollingsworth*, 2004 ABQB 370; and *Cooper v. Flood*, 2015 ABQB 567, aff'd without comment on this issue 2016 ABCA 365.

6. A doctor does not have to inform patients that he or she will be assisted by a resident or other treatment professional. It is less clear, however, if a patient must be informed that an intern or resident, rather than the specialist, will be performing the procedure or a major part of it. For example, failing to inform the patient that a resident, as opposed to a fully-qualified specialist, would be performing a cardiac catheterization was held to be a material risk that had to be disclosed in *Currie v. Blundell* (1992), 10 C.C.L.T. (2d) 288 at 290 (Qc. S.C.). But see *Bezusko v. Waterfall* (1997), 45 O.T.C. 241 (Gen. Div.), which reached the opposite conclusion. In what circumstances should a doctor be required to inform a patient that a resident or intern will be involved in the proposed procedure? See also *Marcoux v. Bouchard*, [2001] 2 S.C.R. 726; *Gerelus v. Lim* (2008), 231 Man. R. (2d) 23 (C.A.); and *Cooper v. Flood*, *supra*.

7. Must a health practitioner inform patients that his or her success rate is lower than average? Should the seriousness of the risks involved in the procedure be a factor in resolving this issue? Is the fact that a health professional is being sued for malpractice or investigated by the governing professional body a material risk? See *Turner v. Bederman* (1996), 2 O.T.C. 215 (Gen. Div.), where the court found that there was no duty to disclose the health professional's experience with the procedure or pending lawsuits. See also *Stiles v. Hatfield*, 2003 CarswellOnt 2241 (S.C.J.) (WL Can). But see *Anderson v. Queen Elizabeth II Health Sciences Centre*, 2012 NSSC 360, where

the court found that the plaintiff would not have consented to the medical procedure if he had known of the risk of stroke and the physician's relative inexperience.

8. Is the fact that a doctor or dentist is HIV-positive a material risk that must be disclosed? One difficulty in resolving this issue is the divergent estimates of the risks of infection from doctor to patient. There are only four known cases where HIV-infection has been attributed to a healthcare worker: Johnston, "Professional Competence: The HIV Infected Physician" (online: Royal College of Physicians and Surgeons, Bioethics cases).

In *Halkyard v. Mathew* (1998), 43 C.C.L.T. (2d) 171 (Alta. Q.B.), aff'd (2001), 4 C.C.L.T. (3d) 271 (Alta. C.A.), it was held that practitioners need not disclose personal medical conditions that do not affect their capacity to provide the proposed treatment. The doctor in that case was epileptic. For a discussion of the need to balance the right to make informed consent against the privacy rights of physician and protection from unwarranted discrimination, see Johnson, "Recent Decision: Must Doctors Disclose Their Own Personal Risk Factors? *Halkyard v. Mathew*" (2001) 10 Health L. Rev. 18.

Do you agree with this principle and would it govern an HIV-positive surgeon? See Spielman, "Expanding the boundaries of informed consent: disclosing alcoholism and HIV status to patients" (1992) 93 Am. J. Med. 216; Flanagan, "AIDS-Related Risks in the Health Care Setting: HIV Testing of Health Care Workers and Patients" (1993) 18 Queen's L.J. 71; Canadian Medical Association, "HIV Infection in the Workplace" (1994) 3 Health L. Rev. 27; and DeVille, "Nothing to fear but fear itself: HIV-infected physicians and the law of informed consent" (1994) 22 J. Law Med. Ethics 163.

9. Even if the risks discussed in notes 5 and 6 are held not to be material, should they be viewed as special risks if the patient has expressed concern about them? The Canadian courts have repeatedly held that, if the patient has a particular concern, it is his or her responsibility to raise this with the doctor. See for example, *Videto v. Kennedy* (1981), 125 D.L.R. (3d) 127 (Ont. C.A.) (patient desired minimal scarring so that others would not know she had undergone surgical sterilization); *Augustine v. Lopes*, 1994 CarswellOnt 3969 (Gen. Div.) (WL Can) (patient did not want to stop menstruating because it carried social stigma in her ethnic community); and *Bosard v. Davey* (2005), 191 Man. R. (2d) 254 (Q.B.) (parents failed to inform doctor that they were first cousins, which increased risks of congenital disabilities to their baby). But see *Solomon v. Ali*, 2018 ONSC 3287, where a surgeon was held liable for not fully explaining the risks of wrist surgery to the plaintiff, a former golf pro. See also Siegal, Bonnie & Appelbaum, "Personalized Disclosure by Information-on-Demand: Attending to Patients' Needs in the Informed Consent Process" (2012) 40 J. Law, Medicine & Ethics 359.

10. It has been held that a health professional must answer a patient's questions fully, even if they relate to minor aspects of the procedure. See *Sinclaire v. Boulton* (1985), 33 C.C.L.T. 125 (B.C.S.C.); and *Hartjes v. Carmen* (2003), 20 C.C.L.T. (3d) 31 (Ont. S.C.J.). However, the courts have not defined the range of questions that a health professional must answer.

11. Healthcare professionals must explain the material risks of a proposed treatment in language that the patient can understand. It appears that it is more

important for the patient to understand the substance of the risks than the precise medical terminology. For example, in *Martin v. Findlay* (2008), 432 A.R. 165 (C.A.), the court found that the defendant surgeon had adequately informed the patient of the risks of death, speech impairment and paralysis stemming from surgery to remove a brain tumour, and that it did not matter that the surgeon failed to use the specific term "stroke" in describing the risks. See also *Gilberds v. Sobey*, 2011 ABQB 491 (effective communication of risk includes telling patient the statistical probability of an adverse event); and *Dehekker v. Anderson-Penno*, 2014 ABQB 95 (plaintiff sufficiently informed that laser eye surgery might cause distorted corneal surface and loss of vision, and use of the term "ecstasia" not required).

Related issues may arise if the patient has limited understanding of the English language. The obligation is on the healthcare professional to ensure that the patient understands the risks and alternative remedies available. See for example *Byciuk, supra; Malinowski v. Schneider*, 2012 ABCA 125; and *Tiglao v. Sleightholm*, 2012 ONSC 3092.

12. The preceding questions involve issues that are at least potentially relevant to treatment. Does a health professional have to answer questions that are unrelated to the patient's treatment? For example, are doctors required to answer questions about their religion, position on abortion, or ethnic background?

13. There are numerous situations in tort law in which the plaintiff's claim turns on proving that he or she relied upon the defendant's advice, yet in these cases no special causation test is adopted. Are there any unique factors that warrant adopting a special causation test in cases involving a doctor's duty to inform? Given the test of causation, can a patient ever succeed on the issue of causation in cases of non-elective surgery?

In *Arndt v. Smith* (1997), 35 C.C.L.T. (2d) 233 (S.C.C.), three of the nine justices rejected the objective/subjective test of causation in informed consent cases in favour of the subjective test of causation that generally applies in negligence.

In *Chappel v. Hart* (1998), 156 A.L.R. 517 (H.C.A.), the court held that the subjective test of causation should be applied in medical duty to inform cases. This is consistent with the earlier Australian cases and the position of the English courts. See also McInnes, "Failure to Warn in Medical Negligence — A Cautionary Note From Canada: *Arndt v. Smith*" (1998) 6 Tort L. Rev. 135; and Nelson & Caulfield, "You Can't Get There From Here: A Case Comment on *Arndt v. Smith*" (1998) 32 U.B.C.L. Rev. 353. Nevertheless, the Canadian courts continue to apply the objective/subjective test of causation. See for example *Brito (Guardian ad litem of) v. Wooley* (2003), 16 B.C.L.R. (4th) 220 (C.A.); *Van Dyke v. Grey Bruce Regional Health Centre* (2005), 255 D.L.R. (4th) 397 (Ont. C.A.); *Hill v. Victoria Hospital Corp.*, 2009 ONCA 70; *Gallant v. Brake-Patten*, 2012 NLCA 23; and *Bollman v. Soenen*, 2014 ONCA 36.

Given the difficulties with *Arndt*, and the English and Australian position, should the Canadian courts adopt a subjective test of causation for duty to inform cases?

14. The *Health Care Consent Act, 1996*, S.O. 1996, c. 2, s. 1, provides that, for consent to be valid, it must be "informed." The section then defines "informed" consent in terms very similar to the preceding common law principles. However, the statute is silent on the civil liability consequences of providing treatment without an informed consent. While some might interpret this as meaning that the failure to

obtain informed consent gives rise to an action in battery, the Ontario courts have continued to follow *Reibl, supra*. That is, a less-than-informed consent only gives rise to an action in negligence. See *Bollman v. Soenen*, 2014 ONCA 36.

15. The obligation to inform patients is applied more vigorously in the case of medical research and experimental or unconventional therapies. See for example *Weiss v. Solomon* (1989), 48 C.C.L.T. 280 (S.C. Qc.); and *Coughlin v. Kuntz, supra*. For discussion of this issue, see Côté, "Adequate Protection for the Autonomous Research Subject? The Disclosure of Sources of Funding and Commercialisation in Genetic Research Trials" (2002) 28 Man. L.J. 347. See also Barclay, "Stem-cell experts raise concerns about medical tourism" (2009) 373:9667 The Lancet 883.

16. For an analysis of the effects of the *Reibl* decision on claims based on lack of informed consent, see Robertson, "Informed Consent 20 Years Later" (2003) (unnumbered special ed.) Health L.J. 153. For a general discussion of informed consent, see Picard & Robertson, *Legal Liability of Doctors and Hospitals in Canada*, 5th ed. (2017), ch. 3; Englard, "Informed Consent — The Double-Faced Doctrine" in Mullany & Linden, eds., *Torts Tomorrow: A Tribute to John Fleming* (1998) 152; and Peppin, "Informed Consent" in Downie, Caulfield & Flood, eds., *Canadian Health Law and Policy*, 4th ed. (2011) at 162-94.

17. How should the principles of informed consent be applied to so-called "alternative" medical practitioners, whose treatments might not have undergone rigorous scientific study? See Ries & Fisher, "The Increasing Involvement of Physicians in Complementary and Alternative Medicine: Considerations of Professional Regulation and Patient Safety?" (2013) 39 Queen's L.J. 273. See also Flood, Thomas & Harrison-Wilson, "Cosmetic Surgery Regulation and Regulation Enforcement in Ontario" (2010) 36 Queen's L.J. 31; and Shahvisi, "No Understanding, No Consent: The Case Against Alternative Medicine" (2016) 30:2 Bioethics 69.

REVIEW PROBLEM

Andrew distrusts all doctors and has a morbid fear of hospitals and operations. He was understandably upset when informed that he required an operation to repair a weak blood vessel in his brain. He was told that it was a serious operation and that, without it, he would live only eight to ten years. The general mortality rate for this procedure was 10%, although one surgeon in London, Ontario had a mortality rate of less than 5%. Dr. Baker, Andrew's surgeon, had lost 15% of her patients, but this was due in part to the large number of high-risk patients in her practice. Dr. Baker informed Andrew of the general mortality rate of 10%, but did not mention her own record or that of the very successful surgeon. In addition to the risk of mortality, there was a 5% risk of partial paralysis, and a 1% risk of infection, which is common to all operations. Because of Andrew's general anxiety and the effect that this information might have on his condition, Dr. Baker thought it best not to trouble him with this additional information.

Andrew consented to the operation. Regrettably, the operation left him partially paralyzed, and an infection set in, hindering his recovery. It had been Andrew's lifelong dream to fly a balloon solo across the Atlantic, but this is now impossible. Dr.

Baker knew nothing of the planned flight, which she dismisses as the unreasonable desire of an eccentric personality. Nonetheless, prior to the operation, Andrew had acquired the sponsorship of a major brewery for what Dr. Baker calls "his flight of fantasy." Andrew is in the depths of depression. He now says that, had he known about these other risks, Dr. Baker's personal record and that of the London surgeon, he would have postponed the operation, made his flight and then gone to the surgeon in London. Advise Andrew on suing Dr. Baker for breaching her duty to inform.

6. A Manufacturer's and Supplier's Duty to Warn

HOLLIS v. DOW CORNING CORP.
(1995), 129 D.L.R. (4th) 609 (S.C.C.)

[The plaintiff underwent breast implant surgery in 1983. The implants had been manufactured by the defendant, Dow Corning. After 17 months, one of the implants ruptured and the plaintiff was required to undergo several operations to remove silicone gel and implant coverings. The literature accompanying the product warned of the risk of rupture during surgery, but not of any risks of post-surgical rupturing "from ordinary, non-traumatic, human activities." The plaintiff sued both the surgeon and Dow Corning. At trial, the claim against the surgeon was dismissed because the risk of injury that in fact materialized was not well-known among surgeons at the time or extensively discussed in the literature. However, Dow Corning was held liable on the basis that the implant had been negligently manufactured.

The British Columbia Court of Appeal granted the plaintiff's appeal and ordered a new trial on the surgeon's liability. The court held Dow Corning liable, but not on the basis that the implant had been negligently manufactured. Rather, it was held liable because it had failed to warn of the risks of post-surgery rupture, even though it had received about 50 reports of ruptures by 1983. Dow Corning appealed to the Supreme Court of Canada.]

LA FOREST J. (L'HEUREUX-DUBÉ, GONTHIER, CORY and IACOBUCCI JJ. concurring): —

. . .

The sole issue raised in this appeal is whether the Court of Appeal erred in finding Dow liable to the respondent Ms Hollis for failing adequately to warn the implanting surgeon, Dr. Birch, of the risk of a post-surgical implant rupture inside Ms Hollis' body. The appellant Dow does not contest Bouck J.'s factual finding that Ms Hollis' seven-year surgical ordeal caused her great physical and psychological pain, residual scarring on her breasts, and a loss of past and future income. However, Dow submits that it was not responsible for Ms Hollis' injuries. In support of this submission, Dow argues, first, that the warning it gave Dr. Birch was adequate and sufficient to satisfy its duty to Ms Hollis, and second, that even if it did breach its duty to warn Ms Hollis, this breach was not the proximate cause of her injuries.

For the reasons that follow, it is my view that the Court of Appeal reached the correct conclusion and that the appeal should be dismissed.

. . .

It is well-established in Canadian law that a manufacturer of a product has a duty in tort to warn consumers of dangers inherent in the use of its product of which it has knowledge or ought to have knowledge. This principle was enunciated by Laskin J. (as he then was), for the court, in *Lambert v. Lastoplex Chemicals Co.* (1971), 25 D.L.R. (3d) 121 at pp. 124-5, [1972] S.C.R. 569.

. . .

The duty to warn is a continuing duty, requiring manufacturers to warn not only of dangers known at the time of sale, but also of dangers discovered after the product has been sold and delivered: see *Rivtow Marine Ltd. v. Washington Iron Works* (1973), 40 D.L.R. (3d) 530 at pp. 536-7, [1974] S.C.R. 1189, [1973] 6 W.W.R. 692, *per* Ritchie J. All warnings must be reasonably communicated, and must clearly describe any specific dangers that arise from the ordinary use of the product:

. . .

The rationale for the manufacturer's duty to warn can be traced to the "neighbour principle", which lies at the heart of the law of negligence, and was set down in its classic form by Lord Atkin in *Donoghue v. Stevenson*, [1932] A.C. 562 (H.L.). When manufacturers place products into the flow of commerce, they create a relationship of reliance with consumers, who have far less knowledge than the manufacturers concerning the dangers inherent in the use of the products, and are therefore put at risk if the product is not safe. The duty to warn serves to correct the knowledge imbalance between manufacturers and consumers by alerting consumers to any dangers and allowing them to make informed decisions concerning the safe use of the product.

The nature and scope of the manufacturer's duty to warn varies with the level of danger entailed by the ordinary use of the product. Where significant dangers are entailed by the ordinary use of the product, it will rarely be sufficient for manufacturers to give general warnings concerning those dangers; the warnings must be sufficiently detailed to give the consumer a full indication of each of the specific dangers arising from the use of the product. This was made clear by Laskin J. in *Lambert, supra,* where this court imposed liability on the manufacturer of a fast-drying lacquer sealer who failed to warn of the danger of using the highly explosive product in the vicinity of a furnace pilot light. The manufacturer in *Lambert* had placed three different labels on its containers warning of the danger of inflammability. The plaintiff, an engineer, had read the warnings before he began to lacquer his basement floor and, in accordance with the warnings, had turned down the thermostat to prevent the furnace from turning on. However, he did not turn off the pilot light, which caused the resulting fire and explosion. Laskin J. found the manufacturer liable for failing to provide an adequate warning, deciding that none of the three warnings was sufficient in that none of them warned specifically against leaving pilot lights on near the working area. . . .

In the case of medical products such as the breast implants at issue in this appeal, the standard of care to be met by manufacturers in ensuring that consumers are properly warned is necessarily high. Medical products are often designed for bodily ingestion or implantation, and the risks created by their improper use are obviously substantial. The courts in this country have long recognized that manufacturers of products that are ingested, consumed or otherwise placed in the body, and thereby have a great capacity to cause injury to consumers, are subject to a correspondingly high standard of care under the law of negligence.

. . .

Given the intimate relationship between medical products and the consumer's body, and the resulting risk created to the consumer, there will almost always be a heavy onus on manufacturers of medical products to provide clear, complete and current information concerning the dangers inherent in the ordinary use of their product.

. . .

As a general rule, the duty to warn is owed directly by the manufacturer to the ultimate consumer. However, in exceptional circumstances, a manufacturer may satisfy its informational duty to the consumer by providing a warning to what the American courts have, in recent years, termed a "learned intermediary".

. . .

Generally, the rule is applicable either where a product is highly technical in nature and is intended to be used only under the supervision of experts, or where the nature of the product is such that the consumer will not realistically receive a direct warning from the manufacturer before using the product. In such cases, where an intermediate inspection of the product is anticipated or where a consumer is placing primary reliance on the judgment of a "learned intermediary" and not the manufacturer, a warning to the ultimate consumer may not be necessary and the manufacturer may satisfy its duty to warn the ultimate consumer by warning the learned intermediary of the risks inherent in the use of the product.

However, it is important to keep in mind that the "learned intermediary" rule is merely an exception to the general manufacturer's duty to warn the consumer. The rule operates to discharge the manufacturer's duty not to the learned intermediary, but to the ultimate consumer, who has a right to full and current information about any risks inherent in the ordinary use of the product. Thus, the rule presumes that the intermediary is "learned", that is to say, fully apprised of the risks associated with the use of the product. Accordingly, the manufacturer can only be said to have discharged its duty to the consumer when the intermediary's knowledge approximates that of the manufacturer. To allow manufacturers to claim the benefit of the rule where they have not fully warned the physician would undermine the policy rationale for the duty to warn, which is to ensure that the consumer is fully informed of all risks.

[I]t is my view that the "learned intermediary" rule is applicable in this context, and that Dow was entitled to warn Dr. Birch concerning the risk of rupture without warning Ms Hollis directly. A breast implant is distinct from most manufactured goods in that neither the implant nor its packaging are placed directly into the hands of the ultimate consumer. It is the surgeon, not the consumer, who obtains the implant from the manufacturer and who is therefore in the best position to read any warnings contained in the product packaging.

. . .

Although Bouck J. declined to rule on this issue, a majority of the Court of Appeal found that Dow's warning to Dr. Birch was inadequate. In my view, the Court of Appeal was correct in reaching this conclusion. . . .

It is significant that the only reference in the 1976 and 1979 warnings to a risk of post-surgical rupture was the statement that "abnormal squeezing or trauma" might rupture the implants. There is no reference in these warnings to the possibility of rupture arising from normal squeezing or non-traumatic, everyday activity. This is significant because, in 1985, Dow began warning physicians of the possibility of rupture due to normal, non-traumatic activity in the product insert for the Silastic II implant, a new breast implant developed in the early 1980s with a thicker envelope and greater durability than the earlier Silastic I model. . . .

It is clear from a comparison of the 1985 warning with the earlier warnings that the 1985 warning is far more explicit, both with respect to the potential causes of post-surgical implant rupture and the potential effects. Of particular significance, in my view, is the statement in the 1985 warning that rupture can be caused by "excessive stresses or manipulation as may be experienced during normal living experiences" such as "vigorous exercise, athletics, and intimate physical contact". There is, without question, a substantial difference between "trauma", on the one hand, and the "stresses" and "manipulation" of "everyday living experiences", on the other hand. The difference is that, while the earlier warnings implied that rupture would occur only in extreme cases of violent impact, the 1985 warning made it clear that a patient who received an implant would have to consider altering her lifestyle to avoid rupture. The difference between the 1985 warning and the earlier warnings was significant to a woman in Ms Hollis' position because, subsequent to her surgery, she decided to enrol in a baker's course, which involved regular and heavy upper body movements. While a baker's course may not cause "trauma" to an implant, it would certainly create a risk of "excessive stresses or manipulation". Thus, a more accurate warning could quite reasonably have affected her choice of profession and her resulting exposure to unnecessary risk.

This is not to say, of course, that the standard of care to which Dow must be held for its warning practices in 1983 should be measured according to its knowledge of the risks of implant rupture in 1985. In light of the significant differences between the 1985 warning and the earlier warnings, the crucial next question is whether Dow knew or should have known of the risks referred to in the 1985 warning when Ms Hollis had her implantation surgery in 1983. In my view, there was sufficient evidence adduced at trial to establish that Dow did have such knowledge.

. . .

[I]t is apparent that, by late 1983, Dow had already received between 48 and 61 of the 78 unexplained rupture reports it received before issuing its revised 1985 warning. Counsel for Dow conceded that the nature and quantity of the information available to Dow did not change significantly between late 1983 and early 1985. Thus, although the reports were admitted into evidence at trial for the purpose of establishing their existence and not as to the truth of their contents, the mere fact that Dow had these reports in their possession demonstrates that, in 1983, Dow had notice that ruptures were occurring that were not directly attributable to abnormal squeezing or trauma. Counsel for Dow was unable to explain why it took Dow more than two years to convey the information concerning the unexplained ruptures to either the medical community or the consumers.

A similar lag time can be discerned with respect to Dow's warnings concerning the effects of implant ruptures on the body. The evidence indicates that, prior to 1983, and even as early as 1979, Dow was aware that implant ruptures could cause adverse reactions in the body arising from loose gel. . . .

In my view, Dow had a duty to convey its findings concerning both the "unexplained" rupture phenomenon and the possible harm caused by loose gel inside the body to the medical community much sooner than it did. In light of the fact that implants are surgically placed inside the human body, and that any defects in these products will obviously have a highly injurious effect on the user, the onus on Dow to be forthcoming with information was extremely high throughout the relevant period. Despite this fact, for over six years Dow took no action to express its concerns to the medical community. Given Dow's knowledge of the potential harm caused by loose gel in the body, this lag time is simply unacceptable. The duty to warn is a continuing one and manufacturers of potentially hazardous products have an obligation to keep doctors abreast of developments even if they do not consider those developments to be conclusive. As Robins J.A. noted in *Buchan, supra*, at p. 678:

> . . . where medical evidence exists which tends to show a serious danger inherent in the use of a drug, the manufacturer is not entitled to ignore or discount that information in its warning because it finds it to be unconvincing; the manufacturer is obliged to be forthright and to tell the whole story.

. . .

I conclude, therefore, that the Court of Appeal made no error in ruling that Dow did not discharge its duty to Ms Hollis by properly warning Dr. Birch concerning the risk of post-surgical implant rupture.

2. Did Dow's breach of the duty to warn cause Ms Hollis' injury?

Dow raises two distinct causation issues in this appeal. The first is whether Ms Hollis would have elected to have the operation if she had been properly warned of the risk by Dr. Birch. Dow submits that a reasonable woman in Ms Hollis' position would have consented to the surgery despite the risk and, on this basis, argues that its failure to warn was not the proximate cause of Ms Hollis' injury. The second issue Dow raises is whether Dr. Birch would have warned Ms Hollis if he had been properly warned by Dow of the risk. Dow submits that Ms Hollis had the onus of establishing that Dr. Birch would not have warned Ms Hollis even if fully apprised by Dow of the risk and, once again, argues that its failure to warn cannot be the proximate cause of her injuries. Counsel for Ms Hollis sought to meet the first issue on a factual basis alone. As to the second issue, however, he contested as well the underpinnings of Dow's argument, which as will appear raises more substantial legal issues. I shall accordingly approach the issues on that basis.

(a) Would Ms Hollis have consented to the operation if properly warned of the risk?

(i) *The appropriate test*

In determining whether Ms Hollis would have consented to the operation had she been properly warned by Dr. Birch of the risk of rupture, Prowse J.A. applied the modified objective test developed by this court in *Reibl, supra*, which involved a negligence action by a patient against a surgeon for failing to warn him of the risk of paralysis entailed in elective surgery performed by that surgeon. The test applied by Prowse J.A. was as follows: would a reasonable woman in Ms Hollis' particular circumstances have consented to the surgery if she had known all the material risks? I note, however, that in *Buchan, supra*, at pp. 685-7, Robins J.A. found the *Reibl* test to be inapplicable to products liability cases, and instead applied a subjective test. . . .

As Robins J.A. intimated in *Buchan*, the duty of the doctor is to give the best medical advice and service he or she can give to a particular patient in a specific context. It is by no means coterminous with that of the manufacturer of products used in rendering that service. The manufacturer, on the other hand, can be expected to act in a more self-interested manner. In the case of a manufacturer, therefore, there is a greater likelihood that the value of a product will be overemphasized and the risk underemphasized. It is, therefore, highly desirable from a policy perspective to hold the manufacturer to a strict standard of warning consumers of dangerous side-effects to these products. There is no reason, as in the case of a doctor, to modify the usual approach to causation followed in other tortious actions. Indeed the imbalance of resources and information between the manufacturer and the patient, and even the doctor, weighs in the opposite direction. Moreover, it is important to remember that many product liability cases of this nature will arise in a context where no negligence can be attributed to a doctor. It would appear ill-advised, then, to distort the rule that is appropriate for claims against a manufacturer simply because of an apparent anomaly that results in cases where a doctor is also alleged to have been negligent.

(ii) *The application of the test to the facts of the case at bar*

In my view, there was sufficient evidence adduced at trial to satisfy the subjective *Buchan* test. Ms Hollis testified quite clearly at trial that, had she been properly warned by Dr. Birch of the risk of rupture, she would not have had the surgery.

. . .

The second causation issue raised by *Dow* is whether Dr. Birch would have warned Ms Hollis of the risk of rupture if Dow had properly warned Dr. Birch about that risk. Dow argues that there is no direct causal link between its breach of the duty to warn and Ms Hollis' injury because, in 1983, Dr. Birch was aware of the risk of implant rupture but did not make a habit of warning his patients about that risk. In support of this argument, Dow relies on Dr. Birch's testimony at trial that, in 1983, he was warning only 20% to 30% of his patients of implant rupture, and that, in determining the nature and scope of his warnings to patients, he relied more on the articles he read in medical journals than on manufacturers' warnings.

It is right to say, however, that the trial judge found that in 1983 the average plastic surgeon in British Columbia did not in fact know about the possibility that rupture of Silastic implants could be a factor of any significance. This finding is supported and amplified by the fact that after Dow began circulating its more extensive 1985 warning and knowledge of the risk of rupture in the medical community became more prevalent, Dr. Birch adapted his practice accordingly, and by 1989 he was warning all his patients of the risk of rupture.

I do not propose to enter further into or assess these factors. I say this because, while Dow is correct in submitting that there was some ambiguity at trial concerning Dr. Birch's warning practices in 1983, Dow's argument is based upon the assumption that to succeed in her claim against Dow Ms Hollis must prove that Dr. Birch would have warned her if Dow had properly warned Dr. Birch. I do not think this assumption is well founded. Ms Hollis, it will be remembered, demonstrated that Dow had breached its duty to warn her of the risk of rupture, that she would not have undergone the medical procedure if she had been fully informed of the risks, and that she suffered injury from the rupture. Had Dr. Birch been adequately warned but had not passed on the information to Ms Hollis, Dow would, it is true, have been absolved of liability by virtue of the learned intermediary doctrine. But I fail to see how one can reason from this that, for Dow to be liable, Ms Hollis must now establish that Dr. Birch would have informed her if he had known. To require her to do so would be to ask her to prove a hypothetical situation relating to her doctor's conduct, one, moreover, brought about by Dow's failure to perform its duty. While the legal and persuasive onus in a negligence case generally falls on the plaintiff, I do not see how this can require the plaintiff to prove a hypothetical situation of this kind.

. . .

Simply put, I do not think a manufacturer should be able to escape liability for failing to give a warning it was under a duty to give, by simply presenting evidence tending to establish that even if the doctor had been given the warning, he or she would not have passed it on to the patient, let alone putting an onus on the plaintiff to do so. Adopting such a rule would, in some cases, run the risk of leaving the plaintiff with no compensation for her injuries. She would not be able to recover against a doctor who had not been negligent with respect to the information that he or she *did* have; yet she also would not be able to recover against a manufacturer who, despite having failed in its duty to warn, could escape liability on the basis that, had the doctor been appropriately warned, he or she still would not have passed the information on to the plaintiff. Our tort law should not be held to contemplate such an anomalous result.

. . .

Conclusion

On the basis of the foregoing, it is my view that Dow breached its duty to warn Dr. Birch concerning the risks of post-surgical rupture in the Silastic implant and because of this failure to warn is liable to Ms Hollis for her injuries. Accordingly, I would dismiss the appeal.

[Sopinka J., with McLachlin J. concurring, dissented. Sopinka J. held that the plaintiff was not entitled to succeed unless she could establish that a reasonable person would have refused the implant if properly warned and that her surgeon would have passed the warning on to her if he had been properly informed.]

NOTES AND QUESTIONS

1. Based on *Hollis*, define a manufacturer's duty to inform consumers of the risks inherent in the use of its products. Did the court impose a unique standard of care on manufacturers of pharmaceuticals and medical products? Why might such products give rise to a more onerous standard of care? See also *Heward v. Eli Lilly & Co.* (2007), 47 C.C.L.T. (3d) 114 (Ont. S.C.J.).

2. In what circumstances can a manufacturer rely on the learned intermediary rule? According to *Hollis*, what information must a manufacturer disclose to a learned intermediary to meet its duty to warn? What obligation, if any, does a manufacturer have after it has adequately informed a learned intermediary to ensure that the information is passed on to the consumer?

3. Given Dow Corning's knowledge of the unexplained ruptures and the accompanying risks, was it negligent in continuing to market the implant in 1983? Had

the plaintiff's case proceeded on this basis, would the adequacy of the warning have been relevant?

4. What was La Forest J.'s rationale for adopting the subjective test of causation in *Hollis*? Was it compelling? If it was, is there any justification for continuing to use the special objective/subjective test in cases involving health professionals' duty to inform?

Sopinka J., in dissent, stated that the subjective approach fails to address the inherent unreliability of the plaintiff's "self-serving assertions" or the fact that the plaintiff's opinion is likely to be coloured by the injury he or she has suffered. Is there anything unique about the credibility issues in this area that would warrant special rules of causation? See Black & Klimchuk, "Torts-Negligent Failure to Warn — Learned Intermediary Rule — Causation — Appellate Court Powers — *Hollis v. Dow Corning Corp.*" (1996) 75 Can. Bar Rev. 355; Lewans, "Subjective Tests and Implied Warranties: Prescriptions for *Hollis v. Dow Corning* and *ter Neuzen v. Korn*" (1996) 60 Sask. L. Rev. 209; Boivin, "Factual Causation in the Law of Manufacturer Failure to Warn" (1998) 30 Ottawa L. Rev. 47; McInnes, "Causation in Tort Law: A Decade in the Supreme Court of Canada" (2000) 63 Sask. L. Rev. 445; McInnes, "Common Sense and Constructive Reasoning: Causal Policy in the Supreme Court of Canada" in *Special Lectures of the Law Society of Upper Canada 1998: Personal Injury* (2000) 422; and Black "Decision Causation: Pandora's Tool-Box" in Neyers, Chamberlain & Pitel, eds., *Emerging Issues in Tort Law* (2007).

5. Why did the court reject the defendant's argument that its failure to inform Dr. Birch played no causal role in the plaintiff's injuries, because Dr. Birch would not have informed her in any event? Could it be argued that the defendant's failure to inform Dr. Birch has caused the plaintiff a loss, namely, the opportunity to sue him for failing to obtain an informed consent to the procedure?

6. What assumptions can a manufacturer make about the people who are likely to use its products? What impact should such considerations have on the standard of care and its breach? In *Austin v. 3M Canada Ltd.* (1974), 54 D.L.R. (3d) 656 (Ont. Co. Ct.) the plaintiff, who professed to be an auto-body repairman, was injured by the defendant's grinding disc which disintegrated while being used at 9,200 rpm. No warnings were provided about the speeds at which the discs should be used. However, the court found that any reasonably competent repairman would have known that it was hazardous to use the discs at more than 8,000 rpm. The court held that the defendant was not negligent in failing to warn the plaintiff of this danger. Would the result have been the same if a neighbour, inexperienced in auto-body repair, borrowed an unopened package of discs and suffered injury while using them at an excessive speed? See also *Murphy v. St. Catharines Gen. Hosp.* (1963), 41 D.L.R. (2d) 697 (Ont. H.C.); *Park v. B & B Electronics Ltd.* (2003), 340 A.R. 246 (Q.B.); and *Dura-Lite Heat Transfer Products Ltd. v. CEDA Environmental Services (c.o.b. Wasteco Environmental Services Ltd.)* (2010), 469 A.R. 350 (C.A.). See generally Downs, "Duty to Warn and the Sophisticated User Defense in Products Liability Cases" (1986) 15 U. Balt. L. Rev. 276; and Sungaila & Mayer, "Limiting Manufacturers' Duty to Warn: The Sophisticated User and Purchaser Doctrines" (2009) 76 Def. Counsel J. 196.

The duty to warn is specific to the primary user of the product. Therefore, a manufacturer must be careful not to assume that a risk is obvious in circumstances where a child or young person is likely to be the primary consumer. See *Amin (Litigation Guardian of) v. Klironomos*, [1996] O.J. No. 826 (Gen. Div.) (QL); and *Coady v. Burton Canada Co.*, 2013 NSCA 95.

7. Given that the plaintiff in *Lambert v. Lastoplex Chemicals Co.* (1971), 25 D.L.R. (3d) 121 (S.C.C.), cited in *Hollis*, was aware of the danger of working with the product near an open flame, should he have been held contributorily negligent for not turning off the pilot light? In *Labrecque v. Saskatchewan Wheat Pool* (1980), 110 D.L.R. (3d) 686 (Sask. C.A.), an experienced farmer was held contributorily negligent because he should have been aware of certain dangers, despite the defendant manufacturer's inadequate warning. Can you reconcile *Lastoplex* and *Labrecque*? See also *Laflamme v. Groupe TDL Ltée*, 2014 QCCS 312, in which the plaintiff was found one-third contributorily negligent for taking no actions to cool off the hot soup that she consumed at the defendant's fast food restaurant prior to putting it in her mouth.

8. In *Cominco Ltd. v. Westinghouse Can. Ltd.* (1981), 127 D.L.R. (3d) 544 (B.C.S.C.), varied on other grounds (1983), 147 D.L.R. (3d) 279 (B.C.C.A.), it was held that a manufacturer who hears of a new risk after its product is distributed has a duty to warn users as soon as possible. The plaintiff did not have to prove that the manufacturer had actual knowledge, provided the manufacturer ought to have been aware of the new risk. See also *Rivtow Marine Ltd. v. Washington Iron Works*, [1974] S.C.R. 1189; *Nicholson v. John Deere Ltd.* (1986), 58 O.R. (2d) 53 (H.C.); *Vlchek v. Koshel* (1988), 44 C.C.L.T. 314 (B.C.S.C.); *Walford v. Jacuzzi Canada Ltd.* (2007), 87 O.R. (3d) 281 (C.A.); *Schroeder v. DJO Canada, Inc.*, 2011 SKCA 106; and *Gendron v. Doug C. Thompson Ltd. (c.o.b. Thompson Fuels)*, 2017 ONSC 4009. For an American perspective, see Ross & Prince, "Post-Sale Duties: The Most Expansive Theory in Products Liability" (2009) 74 Brook L. Rev. 963.

9. In *Hollis*, the Supreme Court of Canada indicated that manufacturers have a broad obligation to inform learned intermediaries of new research findings of adverse consequences, even if those findings are speculative or inconclusive. Does this principle create potential problems? At what point would a manufacturer be required to inform learned intermediaries? Would that obligation have arisen after Dow Corning received 20, 10 or 5 reports of unexplained ruptures? Are such isolated, adverse findings of practical use to the learned intermediary? Is there a risk of overloading the intermediaries and consumers with reports of isolated, unanalyzed adverse findings?

10. In recent years, pharmacies have taken on greater responsibility by inquiring about patients' drug allergies, keeping a record of prescriptions, and providing independent summaries of potential side effects. What implications do these actions have for the application of the learned intermediary doctrine? Can a pharmaceutical manufacturer that provides an inadequate warning be absolved of liability because the pharmacy independently provided a sufficient warning? See Garbutt & Hofmann, "Recent Developments in Pharmaceutical Products Liability Law: Failure to Warn, the Learned Intermediary Defense, and Other Issues in the New Millennium" (2003) 58 Food & Drug L.J. 269.

What are the implications of the increase in direct-to-consumer advertising by pharmaceutical companies (*e.g.* on television or via the internet)? Does such advertising weaken the manufacturers' argument that they cannot communicate directly with the consumer? Should a manufacturer who advertises on television be permitted to rely on the learned intermediary doctrine? See Goetz & Growdon, "A Defense of the Learned Intermediary Doctrine" (2008) 63 Food Drug L.J. 421; and Hall, "Regulating Direct-to-Consumer Advertising with Tort Law: Is the Law Finally Catching Up with the Market?" (2009) 31 W. New Eng. L. Rev. 333.

11. In *Beshada v. Johns-Manville Products Corp.*, 447 A.2d 539 (N.J. 1982), the defendant was held liable for failing to warn of asbestos-related illness, despite the medical community's "presumed unawareness" of such risks at the time. The court stated at 549:

> The burden of illness from dangerous products such as asbestos should be placed upon those who profit from its production and, more generally, upon society at large, which reaps the benefits of the various products our economy manufactures. That burden should not be imposed exclusively on the innocent victim. Although victims must in any case suffer the pain involved, they should be spared the burdensome financial consequences of unfit products. At the same time, we believe this position will serve the salutary goals of increasing product safety research and simplifying tort trials. Defendants have argued that it is unreasonable to impose a duty on them to warn of the unknowable. Failure to warn of a risk which one could not have known existed is not unreasonable conduct. But this argument is based on negligence principles. We are not saying what defendants should have done. That is negligence. We are saying that defendants' products were not reasonably safe because they did not have a warning. Without a warning, users of the product were unaware of its hazards and could not protect themselves from injury. We impose strict liability because it is unfair for the distributors of a defective product not to compensate its victims. As between those innocent victims and the distributors, it is the distributors — and the public which consumes their products — which should bear the unforeseen costs of the product.

Is this an appropriate solution to the allocation of losses arising from hazardous products? Is there something unique about manufacturers, as opposed to other defendants, that justifies imposing liability on them in the absence of negligence? Are the courts an appropriate institution for deciding how to allocate such losses? See Berry, "*Beshada v. Johns-Manville Products Corp.*: Revolution — Or Aberration — in Products' Liability Law" (1984) 52 Fordham L. Rev. 786; Boivin, "Negligence, Strict Liability, and Manufacturer Failure to Warn: On Fitting Round Pegs in a Square Hole" (1993) 16 Dal. L.J. 299; and *Hunt v. T&N plc.* (1990), 4 C.C.L.T. (2d) 1 (S.C.C.).

It is interesting to contrast the approach in *Beshada* with that adopted by the Supreme Court of Canada in *Lapierre v. A.G. Que.* (1985), 16 D.L.R. (4th) 554 (S.C.C.). In *Lapierre*, the court refused to impose strict liability on the government for a measles vaccine that caused the infant plaintiff to suffer a severe attack of encephalitis. See also *Davidson v. Connaught Laboratories* (1980), 14 C.C.L.T. 251 (Ont. H.C.); and *Rothwell v. Raes* (1988), 66 O.R. (2d) 449 (H.C.), aff'd (1990), 2 O.R. (3d) 332 (C.A.). *Lapierre* led to the introduction of a provincial compensation system, based on no-fault principles, for those suffering serious injuries as a result of vaccinations in Québec: see now the *Public Health Act*, R.S.Q. c. S-2.2, s. 71. See generally Kutlesa, "Creating a Sustainable Immunization System in Canada — The Case for a Vaccine-Related Injury Compensation Scheme" (2004) 12 Health L.J. 201.

12. A supplier's duty to warn of risks in the use of its products is largely the same as that of a manufacturer. Suppliers are required to warn of risks of which they know or ought to know. See *Allard v. Manahan* (1974), 46 D.L.R. (3d) 614 (B.C.S.C.); *Lem v. Barotto Sports Ltd.* (1976), 69 D.L.R. (3d) 276 (Alta. C.A.); and *Rozenhart v. Skier's Sport Shop (Edmonton) Ltd.* (2002), 12 Alta. L.R. (4th) 263 (Q.B.), aff'd (2004), 28 Alta. L.R. (4th) 44 (C.A.).

Although the courts increasingly require manufacturers to be experts in their field and to undertake research or at least keep current with the scientific, academic and industry literature, suppliers would not be expected to have the same level of expertise. Can you suggest a situation in which the manufacturer would be held liable for failing to warn, but the supplier would not? See also *Buchan v. Ortho Pharmaceutical (Can.) Ltd.* (1986), 35 C.C.L.T. 1 (Ont. C.A.); and *Lumsden v. Barry Cordage Ltd.* (2010), 287 N.S.R. (2d) 175 (S.C.). The courts have extended the duty to warn to installers and repairers. See *Bow Valley Husky (Bermuda) Ltd. v. Saint John Shipbuilding Ltd.* (1997), 153 D.L.R. (4th) 385 (S.C.C.).

13. Should the way in which a supplier markets a product affect its duty or standard of care? Should a greater obligation be imposed on a specialty store that waits on customers than on a department store, self-service shop or mail-order house?

14. To what extent can a manufacturer or supplier discharge its obligation to warn by providing instructions and cautions in printed material accompanying the product? In *Lem v. Barotto Sports Ltd., supra,* the court denied the plaintiff's claim on the assumption that the plaintiff was aware of the warnings in the instruction booklet, even though he had not read it. The product in question, a shotgun shell re-loader, did not appear to be particularly difficult to use, provided the step-by-step instructions were followed. However, in *O'Fallon v. Inecto Rapid (Can.) Ltd.,* [1939] 1 D.L.R. 805 (B.C.S.C.), aff'd [1940] 4 D.L.R. 276 (B.C.C.A.), it was held that the manufacturer should have put a warning on the container of its hair dye because the warning provided in the separate accompanying literature might not come to the user's attention. Can you reconcile these two cases?

15. In determining if consumers have been adequately informed, the courts will examine the totality of the manufacturer's marketing and promotional activities. In addition to the actual warnings provided, the court may consider any countervailing messages, or advertising, marketing or promotional activities. A manufacturer may be held liable, despite providing an adequate warning, if that warning has been obscured or undermined. See *Buchan v. Ortho Pharmaceutical (Can.) Ltd., supra*; *Siemens v. Pfizer C. & G. Inc.* (1988), 51 Man. R. (2d) 252 (C.A.); and *Moran v. Wyeth-Ayerst Canada Inc. (c.o.b. Cyanamid Crop Protection)* (2004), 369 A.R. 145 (Q.B.). See also Klar, "Recent Developments in Canadian Law: Tort Law" (1991) 23 Ottawa L. Rev. 177; and Howells, *Comparative Product Liability* (1993) at 262.

16. Another important issue raised by *Lem v. Barotto Sports Ltd., supra,* is the manufacturer's and supplier's duty to warn of risks arising from the misuse of a product. The court noted:

In respect of such dangers the duty . . . is to give adequate warning, that is to say explicit warning, not only as to such that would arise out of the contemplated proper use of the product, but also as to such that might arise out of reasonably foreseeable fault on the part of the purchaser in its contemplated use . . . The duty . . . grows more exacting with the degree of danger . . . arising from its misuse, and accordingly the reach of foreseeability is extended further as the circumstances may reasonably require . . . . On the other side of the scale, the dangers of use or misuse may be sufficiently apparent or well known to the ordinary prudent person that a warning in respect of them should be taken to be unnecessary in law. An example would be a sharp knife; another, the effect of electricity at high voltage on the human body.

The issue of what constitutes an obvious risk has generated considerable litigation. See *Austin v. 3M Canada Ltd.*, *supra* (grinding disc will shatter at excessive rpm); *Schulz v. Leeside Devs. Ltd.*, [1978] 5 W.W.R. 620 (B.C.C.A.) (dangerous to ride in the bow of a small motor boat); *Kirby v. Canadian Tire* (1989), 57 Man. R. (2d) 207 (Q.B.) (blade on food processor will cut); *Deshane v. Deere & Co.* (1993), 15 O.R. (3d) 225 (C.A.) (forage harvester poses danger to those coming into contact with feed rolls); *Godin v. Wilson Laboratories Inc.* (1994), 145 N.B.R. (2d) 29 (Q.B.) (rat poison will kill rats, which will then begin to smell); *Rozenhart v. Skier's Sport Shop (Edmonton) Ltd.*, *supra* (novice in-line skater is likely to fall); *Tudor Inn Reception Hall (1992) Ltd. v. Merzat Industries Ltd.*, 2006 CarswellOnt 5496 (S.C.J.) (WL Can) (use of explosive rodent killer in confined area likely to cause fire); *Jema International Food Products Inc. v. Scholle Canada Ltd.*, 2013 ONSC 2270 (stacking many heavy cardboard boxes on top of each other might cause contents to rupture); and *Cantile v. Canadian Heating Products Inc. (c.o.b. Montigo Canada)*, 2017 BCSC 286 (glass on front of fireplace will be very hot when in operation).

17. What obligations should tobacco companies have to warn consumers of the dangers of smoking? How should the following facts influence the manufacturer's duty to warn: (a) smoking is by far the largest preventable cause of death and illness in Canada (estimated at more than 40,000 deaths per year), (b) smoking is addictive, (c) most smokers become addicted before the age of 18, (d) the sale of cigarettes to minors is a federal and provincial offence, and (e) evidence indicates that the tobacco manufacturers were aware of the highly addictive and potentially addictive properties of their products for decades and yet publicly denied that smoking was harmful. For a review see Ashley, *The Health Effects of Tobacco Use* (1995).

See also Cunningham, "Tobacco Products Liability in Common Law Canada" (1990) 11 Health Law in Canada 43; and Smith, "'Counterblastes' to Tobacco: Five Decades of North American Tobacco Litigation" (2002) 14 W.R.S.L.I. 1.

Virtually all Canadian provinces have now passed legislation and brought litigation to recover for the healthcare expenditures attributable to tobacco. See for example *Tobacco Damages and Health Care Costs Recovery Act, 2009*, S.O. 2009, c. 13; and *Tobacco Damages and Health Care Costs Recovery Act*, S.B.C. 2000, c. 30. Much of the litigation is ongoing and is tied up in preliminary matters. Smokers have also brought class actions to recover for their illnesses and addictions. In 2015, the Québec Superior Court ordered tobacco companies to pay $15.5 billion to smokers in a class action lawsuit: *Létourneau v. JTI-MacDonald Corp.* (2015) 20 C.C.L.T. (4th) 1 (Q.S.C.). Liability was based on the systematic non-disclosure of the health risks associated with tobacco, in an effort to maximize profits.

18. It should be noted that a manufacturer who complies with federal or provincial warning legislation may still be held liable for failing to adequately inform.

See *Buchan, supra;* Smithson v. Saskem Chemicals Ltd. (1985), 43 Sask. R. 1 (Q.B.); and Waddams, *Products Liability*, 5th ed. (2011) at 60.

19. What is the relevance of a government regulatory scheme that oversees a particular category of products? Should government approval absolve a manufacturer of liability for a defective product? Should the government be liable for approving a defective product? In *Attis v. Canada (Minister of Health)*, 2008 ONCA 660, the plaintiffs were injured when their breast implants leaked or ruptured. They brought a claim against the Minister of Health, who has broad authority over medical products under the *Food and Drugs Act*, R.S.C. 1985, c. C-27 and its regulations, alleging that it was the Minister's duty to protect citizens from medical devices that might cause harm. The Ontario Court of Appeal found that there was insufficient proximity to find a duty of care, particularly because Health Canada made no representations of safety on which the plaintiffs relied. See also *Drady v. Canada (Minister of Health)* (2008), 300 D.L.R. (4th) 443 (Ont. C.A.); *R. v. Imperial Tobacco Canada Ltd.*, [2011] 3 S.C.R. 45; and *British Columbia (Workers' Compensation Board) v. Flanagan Enterprises (Nevada) Inc.*, 2017 BCSC 99.

20. In *Good-Wear Treaders v. D. & B. Holdings Ltd.* (1979), 98 D.L.R. (3d) 59 (N.S.C.A.), the appellant supplier warned a purchaser that the re-treaded tires he wanted were unsuitable for the front wheels of a heavy gravel truck. Although the appellant knew that the purchaser was going to ignore the warning, he completed the sale. One of these tires failed and the truck crossed the centre line, demolishing an oncoming car. The driver of the car and his two children were killed, and his widow sued both the purchaser and supplier. She succeeded at trial. The supplier appealed, claiming that he had not breached his duty. The court indicated that the warnings absolved the supplier of liability to the purchaser, but not to third parties. The supplier should not have sold the tires to someone he knew would misuse them and thereby endanger other users of the road.

Should this obligation extend to cases in which a supplier merely suspects that a purchaser will misuse a product? Must the misuse of a product pose an obvious risk of injury to third parties? Is the *Good-Wear* case based on a supplier's and manufacturer's duty to warn or on an individual's obligation to control the conduct of others?

In *Walford v. Jacuzzi Canada Ltd., supra*, the Ontario Court of Appeal found that a pool supply store owed a duty of care toward the plaintiff, a customer who purchased a used pool slide elsewhere but sought advice from store employees as to whether it was safe to use the slide in her four-foot-deep backyard pool. Having been told that it was "okay" to install the slide, she did. The plaintiff's daughter became a quadriplegic when she used the slide and entered the water head-first. Although instructions printed on the slide advised feet-first entries only, the court explained that head-first entries were a common misuse by pool users. The store was therefore liable for failing to draw the plaintiff's attention to the serious risk of catastrophic injury posed by installing the slide in her pool.

21. For additional academic commentary, see Logie, "Affirmative Action in the Law of Tort: The Case of the Duty to Warn" [1989] C.L.J. 115; Peppin, "Drug/Vaccine Risks: Patient Decision-Making and Harm Reduction in the Pharmaceutical Company Duty to Warn Action" (1991) 70 Can. Bar Rev. 473; Roccamo, "Medical

Implants and Other Health Care Products: Theories of Liability and Modern Trends" (1994) 16 Adv. Q. 421; and Richmond, "Expanding Products Liability: Manufacturers' Post-Sale Duties to Warn, Retrofit and Recall" (1999) 36 Idaho L. Rev. 7. See also American Law Institute, *Restatement of the Law, Third, Torts: Products Liability* (1998).

REVIEW PROBLEMS

1. Acme Company manufactures special gauges and valves with built-in warning devices for use in the chemical industry. Acme sells gauges to distributors, who in turn resell them to chemical companies. In June 1996, Acme discovered that about one-tenth of its K12 valves were defective in that they were prone to emit false warning signals. Acme had stopped making K12 valves in 1990. To the best of Acme's knowledge, its distributors had sold only four valves in 1990 and none in the years since then. Acme was in the midst of a major advertising campaign, focusing on the reliability of its new valves and gauges. Consequently, it was most reluctant to issue a general recall of its K12 valves. It has sought your advice concerning its potential liability if it were to simply ignore this defect in its K12 valves.

2. Mark, an avid amateur repairman, enjoyed fixing his car. When Mark realized that his brakes were becoming worn he decided to replace them. He went to the local Apex Auto Store and purchased a set of very complicated brake drums. The salesman asked Mark if he was having the job done by the Apex service department or whether he was going to take it to another garage. Mark replied that he would install the brakes himself. The salesman asked Mark if he was a certified automobile mechanic. Mark responded that he was not, but that he enjoyed maintaining his own car. This struck the salesman as being odd because these brakes were extremely difficult to install. The salesman knew that it was highly unlikely that anyone other than a certified mechanic could properly install these brakes. Indeed, he knew that many mechanics refused such work and that they referred it to mechanics who specialized in brake work. Nevertheless, the salesman handed the brakes to Mark without another word or providing any warning as to the difficulty of installing them.

Mark went home and installed the brakes. Unfortunately, he had not installed them properly. While driving in busy traffic, the brakes failed and he ran over Mrs. Winter. Mrs. Winter has sought your advice about suing the Apex Auto Store in negligence for the injuries that she has suffered.

7. Duty of Care Owed by a Barrister

The final area for discussion in this chapter concerns the duty of care owed by a barrister. It is important to place this topic into context. A lawyer undoubtedly owes a general obligation to a client to act competently. That is true in both tort and contract. In limited circumstances, a lawyer may also be held liable in negligence to a third party. See *Whittingham v. Crease & Co.* (1978), 88 D.L.R. (3d) 353 (B.C.S.C.); *White v. Jones*, [1995] 2 A.C. 207 (H.L.). The more specific question addressed here pertains to a lawyer's liability to a client for errors made, as a barrister, in the course of litigation. Under the *Anns/Cooper* test, it certainly is reasonably foreseeable that careless litigation may expose a client to loss. Over time, however, Anglo-Canadian courts have vacillated on the significance of policy considerations that are thought to militate against the recognition of a duty of care. Traditionally, Canadian barristers did not enjoy any immunity from liability: see *Leslie v. Ball* (1863), 22 U.C.Q.B. 522; and *Wade v. Ball* (1870), 20 U.C.C.P. 302. As the next extract demonstrates, that continues to be true. By contrast, the House of Lords held in *Rondel v. Worsley*, [1969] 1 A.C. 191 (H.L.) that, in English law, a barrister could not be sued in negligence for the careless handling of a file. However, the House of Lords has since over-ruled *Rondel v. Worsley* and abandoned the concept of "barristers immunity" in *Arthur J.S. Hall & Co. v. Simons*, [2000] 3 W.L.R. 543 (H.L.).

DEMARCO v. UNGARO
(1979), 95 D.L.R. (3d) 385 (Ont. H.C.)

KREVER J.:—In Ontario is a lawyer immune from action at the suit of a client for negligence in the conduct of the client's civil case in Court? That is the important question of substantive law that, to paraphrase Maine weakly, is secreted interstitially by this procedural motion relating to the adequacy of pleadings.

[Krever J. explained that England "has a divided profession" in which "the barrister enters into no contract with the client and is not entitled to sue for his or her fee." In Ontario, in contrast, "lawyers are both barristers and solicitors" and "the lawyer conducting litigation contracts directly with the client and is entitled to sue for his or her fee."]

For my purposes it will be sufficient to summarize the grounds on which it was held in *Rondel v. Worsley* [*supra*] that public policy requires immunity of the barrister. I shall limit myself to four of these grounds.

The first ground related to the duty, which, in interest of proper administration of justice, every counsel must discharge to the Court, a duty which was said to be higher than and, in some cases, in conflict with, the duty owed to the client. . . . Clearly related to the duty owed by a barrister to the Court was the expressed risk that, in the absence of the barrister's immunity, counsel, out of fear of a potential action for negligence by his or her client, would prolong proceedings, contrary to his or her best judgment, in effect, to prevent the client from complaining.

. . .

The second ground was the harm to the public interest that would result for relitigating the original issue in the negligence action against the client's counsel.

. . .

The third consideration related to the obligation of a barrister to accept any client, however difficult, who sought his or her services, an obligation on which the very freedom of the subject was said to depend.

. . .

The final consideration to which I intend to refer is the anomaly that would result from the absence of barristers' immunity in the light of the absolute privilege all participants in a proceeding in Court enjoy with respect to what is said by them in Court.

. . .

I have come to the conclusion that the public interest (another phrase used in the speeches of *Rondel v. Worsley*) in Ontario does not require that our Courts recognize an immunity of a lawyer from action for negligence at the suit of his or her former client by reason of the conduct of a civil case in Court. It has not been, is not now, and should not be, public policy in Ontario to confer exclusively on lawyers engaged in Court work an immunity possessed by no other professional person. Public policy and the public interest do not exist in a vacuum. They must be examined against the background of a host of sociological facts of the society concerned. Nor are they lawyers' values as opposed to the values shared by the rest of the community. In the light of recent developments in the law of professional negligence and the rising incidence of "malpractice" actions against physicians (and especially surgeons who may be thought to be to physicians what barristers are to solicitors), I do not believe that enlightened, non-legally trained members of the community would agree with me if I were to hold that the public interest requires that litigation lawyers be immune from actions for negligence. I emphasize again that I am not concerned with the question whether the conduct complained about amounts to negligence. Indeed, I find it difficult to believe that a decision made by a lawyer in the conduct of a case will be held to be negligence as opposed to a mere error of judgment. But there may be cases in which the error is so egregious that a Court will conclude that it is negligence. The only issue I am addressing is whether the client is entitled to ask a Court to rule upon the matter.

Many of the sociological facts that are related to public policy and the public interest may be judicially noticed. The population of Ontario is approximately eight and a quarter million people. In 1978 there were approximately 12,300 lawyers licensed by the Law Society of Upper Canada to practise law in Ontario. All of them have a right of audience in any Court in Ontario as well as in the Federal Court of Canada and the Supreme Court of Canada. The vast majority of these lawyers are in private practice and, as such, are required to carry liability insurance in respect of negligence in the conduct of their clients' affairs. No distinction is made in this respect between those exclusively involved in litigation and all other lawyers. The current rate of increase in the size of the profession is approximately 1,000 lawyers annually. It is widely recognized that a graduating class of that size places such an enormous strain on the resources of the profession that the articling experience of students-at-law is extremely variable. Only a small percentage of lawyers newly called to the Bar can be expected to have had the advantage of working with or observing experienced and competent counsel. Yet very many of those recently qualified lawyers will be appearing in Court on behalf of clients. To deprive these clients of recourse if their cases are negligently dealt with will not, to most residents of this Province, appear to be consistent with the public interest.

It is with a great sense of deference that I offer a few brief remarks on the grounds and consideration which formed the basis of the public policy as expressed by the House of Lords in *Rondel v. Worsley*. I am only concerned with the applicability of those considerations to Ontario conditions and have no hesitation in accepting them as entirely valid for England. With respect to the duty of counsel to the Court and the risk that, in the absence of immunity, counsel will be tempted to prefer the interest of the client to the duty to the Court and will thereby prolong trials, it is my respectful view that there is no empirical evidence that the risk is so serious that an aggrieved client should be rendered remediless. Between the dates of the decisions in *Leslie v. Ball*, 1863, and *Rondel v. Worsley*, 1967, immunity of counsel was not recognized in Ontario and negligence actions against lawyers respecting their conduct of Court cases did not attain serious proportions. Indeed, apart from the cases I have cited, I know of no case in which a lawyer was sued for negligence by his or her client in the conduct of a case in Court. A very similar argument is advanced in many discussions of the law of professional negligence as it applies to surgeons. Surgeons, it is claimed, are deterred from using their best judgment out of fear that the consequence will be an action by the patient in the event of an unfavourable result. This claim has not given rise to an immunity for surgeons. As to the second ground — the prospect of relitigating an issue already tried, it is my view that the undesirability of that event does not justify the recognition of lawyers' immunity in Ontario. It is not a contingency that does not already exist in our law and seems to me to be inherently involved in the concept of *res judicata* in the recognition that a party, in an action *in personam*, is only precluded from relitigating the same matter against a person who was a party to the earlier action. I can find no fault with the way in which Hagarty, C.J., dealt with this consideration in *Wade v. Ball et al.* (1870), 20 U.C.C.P. 302 at p. 304: "Practically, such a suit as the present may involve the trying over again of *Wade v. Hoyt*. This cannot be avoided." Better that than that the client should be without recourse.

The third consideration related to the obligation of a lawyer to accept any client. Whether that has ever been the universally accepted understanding of a lawyer's duty in Ontario is doubtful. In any event, I do not believe that such a duty exists in the practice of civil litigation and that is the kind of litigation with which I am now concerned. Indeed, as I understand the speech of Lord Diplock in *Saif Ali v. Sidney Mitchell & Co. (a firm) et al.*, [1978] 3 W.L.R. 849, that learned Law Lord was not persuaded of the validity of this ground. . . .

The last consideration to be dealt with is the perceived anomaly related to the absolute privilege enjoyed in respect of anything said in Court by a lawyer. I confess that I am unable to appreciate why it should follow from the existence of that privilege that a lawyer may not be sued by his or her client for the negligent performance of the conduct of the client's case in court. The privilege, a fundamental aspect of the law of slander, is not concerned with relationships among persons. It relates to legal proceedings in open Court. The special relationship of lawyer and client is not involved as it is, of course, when one is considering the law of negligence.

. . .

It may, in conclusion, be of interest, from a comparative point of view that, in the United States, the Courts have not granted immunity to an attorney in the conduct of litigation: "an attorney must exercise reasonable care, skill and knowledge in the conduct of litigation . . . and must be properly diligent in the prosecution of the case" (see 7 C.J.S. pp. 982-4, §146).

To sum up, for the reasons I have given, in Ontario, a lawyer is not immune from action at the suit of a client for negligence in the conduct of the client's civil case in Court. The defendants' motion, in effect, for a determination that a lawyer does enjoy such immunity is, therefore, dismissed with costs to the plaintiff in the cause.

NOTES AND QUESTIONS

1. Analyze Krever J.'s reasons in light of *Cooper v. Hobart*. Would the policy arguments presented in favour of a barrister's immunity fall under the first branch or the second branch of the *Anns/Cooper* test?

2. What role did the early case law play in Krever J.'s analysis?

3. What were the bases upon which Krever J. rejected the House of Lords' policy considerations in *Rondel v. Worsley*, [1969] 1 A.C.. 191 (H.L.)? What considerations did he rely on in concluding that lawyers engaged in litigation ought to owe their clients a duty of care? On balance, would the differences in the legal profession and practice in England and Ontario warrant imposing a duty in one jurisdiction, but not in the other?

4. As indicated in the text above, England finally abolished barristers' immunity in *Arthur J.S. Hall & Co. v. Simons*, [2000] 3 W.L.R. 543 (H.L.). More recently, New Zealand also abolished the immunity in *Chamberlains v. Lai*, [2006] NZSC 70. Australia remains the main Commonwealth holdout, having affirmed barristers' immunity in *D'Orta-Ekenaike v. Victoria Legal Aid* (2005), 214 A.L.R. 92 (H.C.A.), largely based on the need to maintain the integrity of the legal system and the finality of proceedings. See also *Attwells & Anor v. Jackson Lalic Lawyers Pty Ltd.*, [2016] HCA 16, where the court upheld barristers' immunity but ruled that it did not apply to advice about out of court settlements. See Tobin, "An Uncommon Common Law: Barristers' Immunity in New Zealand" (2006) 14 Torts L.J. 224; Werren & Williamson, "Advocates' Immunity: What Makes Australian Lawyers So Special?" (2006) 9 Y.B.N.Z. Juris. 312; Gordon, "Not Yet Dead: *Wright* v *Paton Farrell* and Advocates' Immunity in Scotland" (2007) 70 M.L.R. 458; and Merkin & Steele, "Advocates' immunity: a UK perspective" (2008) 14 N.Z.B.L.Q. 45.

5. Krever J. makes only passing reference to the issues that courts will have to resolve in imposing liability on lawyers engaged in litigation. For example, what effect should a successful action have on the original case? Would it make a difference if the original case were criminal or civil?

6. Given the nature of litigation, it may be difficult for plaintiffs to establish that their lawyers were negligent. In *Karpenko v. Paroian, Courey, Cohen & Houston* (1980), 117 D.L.R. (3d) 383 (Ont. H.C.), the court held that a lawyer could only be found negligent for recommending a settlement of a civil claim prior to trial if he or she made some "egregious error." The judge noted that it was in the public interest to discourage litigation, that lawyers should not be unduly inhibited in encouraging settlements and that the lawyer's decision to recommend acceptance or rejection of a settlement involved various factors. In *Wechsel v. Stutz* (1980), 15 C.C.L.T. 132 (Ont. Co. Ct.), the court rejected the plaintiff's claim that his former lawyer had been negligent in conducting the cross-examination at trial. The judge stated that the method of cross-examination had to be left to the judgment of counsel.

Nevertheless, in *Folland v. Reardon* (2005), 74 O.R. (3d) 688 (C.A.), the "egregious error" standard was rejected by the Court of Appeal for Ontario. Doherty J.A., for the court, commented at para. 41 that the "judgment calls made by lawyers are no more difficult than those made by other professionals." Thus, there was no justification for departing from a standard of reasonableness. See also *Wernikowski v. Kirkland, Murphy & Ain* (1999), 50 O.R. (3d) 124 (C.A.); *Boudreau v. Benaiah* (2000), 46 O.R. (3d) 737 (C.A.); *Ristimaki v. Cooper* (2006), 79 O.R. (3d) 648 (C.A.); and *Precision Remodeling Ltd. v. Soskin, Soskin & Potasky LLP*, 2008 CarswellOnt 3844 (S.C.J.) (WL Can). See also Franks, "A brief history of barristers' liability" (2012) 30:4 Adv. J. 11.

It has been suggested that English judges may show more favouritism toward barristers than toward other professionals when assessing whether their conduct was reasonable: Davies, "Not an Impartial Tribunal? English Courts and Barristers' Negligence" (2010) 13 Leg. Ethics 113.

7. If a plaintiff proves that its lawyer was negligent in conducting a case, what should the plaintiff's damages be? Should the plaintiff be entitled to recover for its loss of the chance to succeed in the original lawsuit? How should this be valued? In *Jarbeau v. McLean*, 2017 ONCA 115, the Ontario Court of Appeal held that, if the plaintiff can prove that it would have been successful in the original lawsuit but for the lawyer's negligence, then the plaintiff should be entitled to recover the damages claimed in that suit.

8. In *German v. Major* (1985), 20 D.L.R. (4th) 703 (Alta. C.A.), the defendant had been the prosecuting attorney in a tax evasion case against the plaintiff. After the acquittal, the plaintiff sued the defendant in negligence for "failure to investigate" and to "take care." The court held that a prosecutor does not owe an accused any duty of care in negligence, except possibly in cases of bad faith. In dismissing the action, the court stated at 718, "If this suit were permitted, every convict could have his case retried in a civil case." Should prosecutors be subject to different liability principles than other counsel in litigation? Did the judge's concern about re-litigation warrant limiting prosecutors' potential liability in negligence? See also *Munro v. Canada* (1993), 110 D.L.R. (4th) 580 (Ont. Div. Ct.), where the court found that, while the Attorney General and Crown attorneys can be subject to liability for malicious prosecution or conspiracy to injure, they remained immune to liability in negligence.

In *Milgaard v. Kujawa*, [1994] 9 W.W.R. 305 (Sask. C.A.), the plaintiff had served 22 years of a life sentence for murder when it was revealed that the prosecutor had failed to disclose information received during the original appeal period that tended to incriminate another person. The Saskatchewan Court of Appeal refused to strike out Milgaard's claim against the prosecutor. The court stated that the allegations, if true, constituted a form of abuse that should not be protected by prosecutorial immunity. See also *Curry v. Vancouver (City)* (1996), 62 A.C.W.S. (3d) 45 (B.C.S.C.); and *Ramsay v. Saskatchewan* (2003), 234 Sask. R. 172 (Q.B.).

See also *Nelles v. Ontario* (1989), 60 D.L.R. (4th) 609 (S.C.C.); *Miazga v. Kvello Estate*, [2009] 3 S.C.R. 339; and the section on malicious prosecution in Chapter 3 for a discussion of the limits of prosecutorial immunity.

9. As indicated in the text above, lawyers do not owe a duty of care to third parties except in special circumstances. In *Mantella v. Mantella* (2006), 80 O.R. (3d) 270 (S.C.J.), a husband and wife had signed a separation agreement, but the wife later challenged the agreement on the basis of undue influence, unconscionability and inadequate financial disclosure. The husband then brought a claim against the lawyer who had provided his wife with independent legal advice on the agreement. The court found that the wife's lawyer owed no duty of care to the husband, commenting that there is insufficient proximity between a party to an agreement and the other party's lawyer. The court also suggested that policy considerations would negative any *prima facie* duty of care, particularly in the highly personalized context of family law litigation.

10. In *Calvert v. Law Society of Upper Canada* (1981), 32 O.R. (2d) 176 (H.C.), it was held that the Law Society could not be held liable for negligently admitting or failing to disbar a lawyer. The court stated that such decisions were quasi-judicial in

nature and could not be reviewed by a court unless it was shown that the Law Society acted maliciously. Is the result in *Calvert* consistent with the policy underlying *Demarco*? See also *Birchard v. Alberta Securities Commission* (1987), 82 A.R. 273 (Q.B.).

The continued authority of *Calvert* may be called into question by the Supreme Court of Canada's decision in *Finney v. Barreau du Québec*, [2004] 2 S.C.R. 17. In that case, the Barreau was found liable under Quebec's *Civil Code* for failing to take disciplinary action against a lawyer after repeated complaints against him. The court found that the Barreau was not entitled to immunity because its utter inaction in the case amounted to bad faith. The court also stated, *obiter*, that the same principle of liability would apply under the common law duty of care. See also *Myles-Leger Ltd. (Trustee of) v. 755165 Ontario Inc.* (2006), 273 D.L.R. (4th) 11 (N.L.S.C. (T.D.)), where the court refused to strike out a claim against the provincial law society for failing to properly supervise a lawyer's trust account, citing *Finney* as authority.

SPECIAL DUTIES OF CARE: NEGLIGENT MISREPRESENTATION

1. Introduction
2. Negligent Misrepresentation Causing Pure Economic Loss
3. Negligent Misrepresentation and Contract

1. Introduction

The preceding chapters focus on the concept of a duty of care as it pertains to physical actions or omissions. This chapter, in contrast, focuses on the duty of care that may arise with respect to written or oral communications. Common examples include inaccurate or incomplete advice or information provided by financial advisers, business consultants, lawyers, stockbrokers and bankers.

Actions differ from statements in several important respects. One difference is that people tend to be more careful about actions. Because the potential for damage is usually more apparent in the case of physical conduct, the need for caution is often relatively clear. In contrast, because the possibility of harm resulting from statements is often less obvious, people are less cautious in their choice of words. Particularly on social occasions, there can be a tendency to speak using loose rather than careful language.

A more significant difference between actions and statements was noted by Lord Pearce in the leading case of *Hedley Byrne & Co. v. Heller & Partners Ltd.*, [1963] 2 All E.R. 575 (H.L.) at 602. He stated: "Words are more volatile than deeds. They travel fast and far afield. They are used without being expended and take effect in combination with innumerable facts and other words." In most instances, physical actions become a spent force shortly after occurrence; unless injury arises immediately and in close physical proximity, it is unlikely to arise at all. In contrast, statements have greater durability and portability. They more easily may cause damage long after and far removed from where they were made. For the same reasons, careless actions tend to trigger injuries only once; careless words, in contrast, may repeatedly inflict harm.

The volatility of words has led to judicial concern that recognition of a duty of care with respect to negligent misrepresentations can lead to "liability in an indeterminate amount for an indeterminate time to an indeterminate class": *Ultramares Corp. v. Touche*, 255 N.Y. 170 (C.A. 1931). A written report, for example, may be republished after many years to an audience that the author never contemplated. Consequently, the desirability of awarding compensation to people who sustain losses as a result of careless statements must be carefully balanced against the desirability of limiting the potential scope of liability. In some circumstances, it may be appropriate to formulate the rules governing negligent misrepresentations more narrowly than the rules governing negligent actions.

In addition, freedom of speech is a core value of our legal system. It is enshrined, as freedom of "thought, belief, opinion and expression" in the *Canadian Charter of Rights and Freedoms*, Part I of the *Constitution Act, 1982*, being Schedule B to the *Canada Act 1982* (U.K.), 1982, c. 11. Imposing liability in tort for statements has the potential to undercut this important value.

To this point, we have focused on a distinction based on the nature of the defendant's carelessness: actions on the one hand and words on the other. However, we must also draw a further distinction based on the nature of the plaintiff's loss: physical injury on the one hand and pure economic loss on the other. The term "physical injury" broadly covers cases in which the plaintiff or the plaintiff's property is damaged or destroyed. The term "pure economic loss" covers cases in which the plaintiff does not sustain any personal injury or property damage but nonetheless suffers an economic loss. A common example arises when the plaintiff loses money on an investment as a result of relying on the defendant's erroneous advice.

It is certainly possible for a negligent misrepresentation to result in physical injury. For example, as Lord Asquith noted in *Candler v. Crane, Christmas & Co.*, [1951] 2 K.B. 164 (C.A.) at 195, a defective marine map could take a heavy toll on property and human life. For the most part, however, the scope of physical injury is naturally limited whether the defendant's carelessness consists of careless words or careless actions. For that reason, while the cases are somewhat ambiguous, the preferred view is that liability for physical injury resulting from careless statements has long fallen under the basic approach articulated in *Donoghue v. Stevenson*, [1932] A.C. 562 (H.L.). In other words, with respect to personal injury and property damage, no substantial distinction is drawn between negligent actions and negligent words. For example, in *Robson v. Chrysler Canada Ltd.* (1962), 32 D.L.R. (2d) 49 (Alta. C.A.) the defendant instructed the plaintiff, a model, to take a step back while on a stage. When she did so, she fell from the stage and sustained physical injury. The court imposed liability on the basis of the defendant's careless advice. See also *Gertsen v. Municipality of Metropolitan Toronto* (1973), 41 D.L.R. (3d) 646 (Ont. H.C.); *Manitoba Sausage Manufacturing Ltd. v. Winnipeg (City)* (1976), 1 C.C.L.T. 221 (Man. C.A.); *Hendrick v. De Marsh* (1984), 6 D.L.R. (4th) 713 (Ont. H.C.); *Kripps v. Touche Ross & Co.* (1992), 94 D.L.R. (4th) 284 (B.C.C.A.); *Rozenhart v. Skier's Sport Shop (Edmonton) Ltd.* (2004), 28 Alta. L.R. (4th) 44 (C.A.); and *Saulnier v. Diamond*, 2015 NSSC 346.

In contrast, the courts have always taken a more restricted view when carelessness causes pure economic loss. This is discussed more generally in Chapter 14. And it is especially true if the carelessness in question consists of a misrepresentation. Traditionally, the law simply refused to recognize a duty of care in such circumstances. Consequently, the defendant was not liable unless the plaintiff was able to prove that the defendant's words amounted to a breach of fiduciary duty, a breach of contract or, as discussed in Chapter 26, deceit under *Derry v. Peek* (1889), 14 A.C. 337 (H.L.): see *Candler v. Crane, Christmas & Co., supra.* However, in 1963 the House of Lords signalled a new approach in *Hedley Byrne & Co. v. Heller & Partners Ltd., supra.*

The plaintiff in *Hedley Byrne*, a firm of advertising agents, wanted to know whether it would be advisable to extend credit to Easipower, a customer. To that end, the plaintiff's bankers asked the defendant, who was Easipower's banker, to provide a credit rating. The defendant was unaware of the plaintiff's identity, but it did know that the inquiry pertained to an advertising contract. The defendant responded by stating that Easipower was "quite good for the arrangements." In reliance on that information, the plaintiff extended credit to Easipower. In time, however, Easipower went into liquidation without having reimbursed the plaintiff for the expenses that it had incurred in connection with the advertising contract. The plaintiff sued the defendant, claiming that it had suffered a pure economic loss as a result of a negligent misrepresentation. The lower courts dismissed the action on the basis that, in light of the precedents on point, no duty of care arose on the facts. The House of Lords ultimately denied liability, but it did so on the basis that the defendant had expressly given its advice "without responsibility." In *obiter dicta*, the court held that, but for the disclaimer, recovery was possible in certain circumstances. Significantly, then, the House of Lords recognized that a duty of care can arise with respect to careless statements that cause pure economic loss.

Although *Hedley Byrne* recognized the possibility of a duty of care, it left many questions and issues unresolved. Since 1963 the courts have struggled to articulate a principled justification for liability and to delineate a satisfactory set of rules. While it is now accepted that careless statements resulting in pure economic loss can trigger liability, the precise circumstances in which they will do so remains somewhat uncertain and controversial. As you read through the cases in this chapter, think about whether the factors that the courts consider in connection with the duty of care for negligent statements fall under the first branch or the second branch of the *Anns/Kamloops* test as interpreted in *Cooper v. Hobart*, [2001] 3 S.C.R. 537.

It is now generally understood that the tort of negligent misrepresentation requires the following five elements: (1) a duty of care based on a special relationship between the plaintiff and defendant, (2) an untrue, inaccurate or misleading statement by the defendant, (3) a lack of care by the defendant in making the statement, (4) reasonable reliance by the plaintiff on the statement and (5) damage suffered by the plaintiff as a result. See *Queen v. Cognos Inc.*, [1993] 1 S.C.R. 87 which is discussed later in this chapter.

In this chapter we will consider the Supreme Court of Canada's leading judgments pertaining to negligent misrepresentations and pure economic loss. We will also consider the issue of "concurrent liability" in tort and contract. Negligent misstatements are frequently made in the context of contractual relationships. When that occurs, the plaintiff may wish to sue in both negligence and contract.

NOTES AND QUESTIONS

1. *Hedley Byrne* has been applied to members of various businesses and professions. See for example *Chand v. Sabo Brothers Realty Ltd.* (1979), 96 D.L.R. (3d) 445 (Alta. C.A.); *Better v. Williams*, [1992] 2 W.W.R. 534 (B.C.C.A.); and *Johnston v. Re/max Real Estate (Edmonton) Ltd.* (2004), 30 Alta. L.R. (4th) 52 (Q.B.) (real estate agent); *Fine's Flowers Ltd. v. General Accident Assurance Co.* (1977), 81 D.L.R. (3d) 139 (Ont. C.A.); *General Motors Acceptance Corp. of Canada v. Fulton Insurance Agencies Ltd.* (1978), 24 N.S.R. (2d) 114 (C.A.); and *Fletcher v. M.P.I.C.*, [1990] 3 S.C.R. 191 (insurance agent); *Farish v. National Trust Co.* (1974), 54 D.L.R. (3d) 426 (B.C.S.C.) (trust company); *Elderkin v. Merrill Lynch, Royal Securities Ltd.* (1977), 80 D.L.R. (3d) 313 (N.S.C.A.); *Wynberg v. Daley*, 2006 CarswellOnt 4533 (Sm. Cl. Ct.) (WL Can); and *S. Maclise Enterprises Inc. v. Union Securities Ltd.* (2009), 17 Alta. L.R. (5th) 201 (C.A.) (investment dealer); *Central B.C. Planers Ltd. v. Hocker* (1970), 10 D.L.R. (3d) 689 (B.C.C.A.), aff'd (1971), 16 D.L.R. (3d) 368n (S.C.C.) (securities salesman); *Bank of*

Montreal v. Young (1969), [1970] S.C.R. 328; *Raypath Resources Ltd. v. Toronto Dominion Bank* (1996), 184 A.R. 125 (C.A.); and *Connolly v. Royal Bank* (2007), 54 C.C.L.T. (3d) 247 (N.S.S.C.) (banker); *Haig v. Bamford* (1976), [1977] 1 S.C.R. 466; and *Kripps v. Touche Ross & Co.* (1997), 33 B.C.L.R. (3d) 254 (C.A.) (accountant); *Tracy v. Atkins* (1979), 105 D.L.R. (3d) 632 (B.C.C.A.); and *347671 B.C. Ltd. v. Heenan Blaikie* (2002), 98 B.C.L.R. (3d) 205 (C.A.) (lawyer); *Sealand of Pac. Ltd. v. Robert C. McHaffe Ltd.* (1974), 51 D.L.R. (3d) 702 (B.C.C.A.); and *British Columbia v. R.B.O. Architecture Inc.* (1994), 94 B.C.L.R. (2d) 96 (C.A.) (architect); *Kelly v. Lundgard* (2001), 202 D.L.R. (4th) 385 (Alta. C.A.) (physician); *Ismail v. Treats Inc.* (2004), 220 N.S.R. (2d) 151 (S.C.) (franchisor); *York v. Alderney Consultants Ltd.* (2000), 187 N.S.R. (2d) 383 (S.C.) (surveyor); *Whighton v. Integrity Inspections Inc.* (2007), 71 Alta. L.R. (4th) 112 (Q.B.) (home inspector); *Olar v. Laurentian University* (2007), 49 C.C.L.T. (3d) 257 (Ont. S.C.J.), aff'd 2008 ONCA 699; and *Ramdath v. George Brown College of Applied Arts and Technology*, 2012 ONSC 6173, aff'd 2013 ONCA 468 (university/college); and *Treaty Group Inc. (c.o.b. as Leather Treaty) v. Drake International Inc.* (2005), 15 B.L.R. (4th) 83 (Ont. S.C.J.), aff'd (2007), 86 O.R. (3d) 366 (C.A.) (placement agency).

2. Following *Hedley Byrne*, Canadian courts typically said that a duty of care could not be imposed with respect to a negligent misrepresentation causing pure economic loss unless a "special relationship" existed between the parties. Does this concept have clear boundaries? For examples of judicial interpretations of the special relationship concept see *Central B.C. Planers Ltd. v. Hocker, supra*; *Elderkin v. Merrill Lynch, Royal Securities Ltd., supra*; *Sodd Corp. v. Tessis* (1977), 79 D.L.R. (3d) 632 (Ont. C.A.); *V.K. Mason Construction Ltd. v. Bank of Nova Scotia*, [1985] 1 S.C.R. 271; *Gallant v. Central Credit Union Ltd.* (1994), 22 C.C.L.T. (2d) 251 (P.E.I.T.D.); and *Fiorillo v. Krispy Kreme Doughnuts Inc.* (2009), 98 O.R. (3d) 103 (S.C.J.). This concept will be further explained in the remaining sections of this chapter.

3. Courts have sometimes considered whether there was a special relationship between the plaintiff and the defendant even in cases involving physical injury rather than pure economic loss. See for example *Hashemi-Sabet Estate v. Mazzulla*, 2016 ONCA 273. In *Walford (Litigation Guardian of) v. Jacuzzi Canada Inc.* (2007), 87 O.R. (3d) 281 (C.A.) the defendant pool store told the plaintiff's mother there would be "no problem" using a ten-foot-long slide with her four-foot-deep pool. The plaintiff used the slide, hit her head on the bottom of the pool and was rendered quadriplegic. The court held that there was a special relationship and held the defendant liable. On the distinction between physical injury and pure economic loss in negligent misrepresentation cases see Klar & Jefferies, *Tort Law*, 6th ed. (2017) at 267-70.

4. Consider a case in which the defendant makes a representation to an individual. Rather than acting on it in his or her individual capacity, the individual creates a limited partnership and then, as its agent, has it act on the representation (by entering into a contract with the defendant). If the limited partnership sues the defendant for negligent misrepresentation, must the claim fail because the representation was not made to the plaintiff and, indeed, the plaintiff did not even exist at the time of the representation? On what legal theory could such a claim succeed? See *Cramaso LLP v. Ogilvie-Grant, Earl of Seafield*, [2014] UKSC 9.

5. A controversial modification to *Hedley Byrne* was suggested by the Privy Council in *Mutual Life & Citizens' Assurance Co. v. Evatt* (1970), [1971] 1 All E.R. 150 (P.C.). The court reviewed the plaintiff's pleadings in which he alleged that he had received negligent financial advice from the defendant, his own insurance company, about the financial affairs of a subsidiary company of the defendant. The Privy Council held that no valid cause of action had been pleaded. Some courts interpreted this decision to mean that a negligent misrepresentation claim could only be maintained against defendants who were in the business or profession of giving the relevant advice. Other courts took the view that being in the business was merely the usual, but not the only, manner of holding out that one was undertaking responsibility for the advice, and that the claim in *Evatt* had failed because the plaintiff had not pleaded any other way in which the defendant had undertaken responsibility.

In *Queen v. Cognos Inc.*, [1993] 1 S.C.R. 87, an extract of which appears below, Iacobucci J. expressly rejected the "restrictive approach" that confined the duty of care to "professionals." While accepting that the defendant's status as a professional adviser provided evidence of a "special relationship," he denied that it was invariably necessary.

6. Two key considerations in the duty of care analysis are the foreseeable and reasonable reliance by the plaintiff on the defendant's statement. The plaintiff has to establish reliance on the statement: see *Soboczynski v. Beauchamp*, 2015 ONCA 282; and *1043 Bloor Street Inc. v Vilhena*, 2018 ONSC 3326. The plaintiff also has to show that it was reasonably foreseeable that he or she would rely on the representation. In *Border Enterprises Ltd. v. Beazer East Inc.* (2002), 216 D.L.R. (4th) 107 (B.C.C.A.) a corporation held a lease over environmentally contaminated land. After a clean-up effort, the government represented to the corporation that the site was clean. The plaintiff bought shares in the corporation. Some time later, the government issued an order requiring the corporation to undertake a further costly clean-up. The plaintiff alleged that it thereby suffered a financial loss as a result of acting in reliance on the government's initial representation. The Court of Appeal held that the plaintiff's claim in negligence should be struck out on the ground that a duty of care did not arise in the circumstances. The plaintiff was not a reasonably foreseeable victim of the defendant's allegedly careless statement. See also *Toronto Dominion Bank v. Forsythe* (2000), 47 O.R. (3d) 321 (C.A.); and *Gross v. Great-West Life Assurance Co.*, [2002] 4 W.W.R. 421 (Alta. C.A.).

7. On the reasonableness of the plaintiff's reliance, see for example *Dutton v. Bognor Regis United Building Co.*, [1972] 1 All E.R. 562 (C.A.); *Burman's Beauty Supplies Ltd. v. Kempster* (1974), 48 D.L.R. (3d) 682 (Ont. Co. Ct.); *Gordelli Management Ltd. v. Turk* (1991), 6 O.R. (3d) 521 (Gen. Div.); *Strand v. Emerging Equities Inc.* (2008), 425 A.R. 314 (C.A.); *Krawchuk v. Scherbak*, 2011 ONCA 352; *Singh v. Trump*, 2016 ONCA 747; and *Feldstein v. 364 Northern Development Corp.*, 2017 BCCA 174.

In *Conversions By Vantasy Ltd. v. General Motors of Canada Ltd.* (2006), 205 Man. R. (2d) 131 (C.A.) the court held that the plaintiff's own knowledge of the defendant's operations and the fact that three years had passed since the statements were made by the defendant's employees meant that it was not reasonable for the plaintiff to have relied on them.

In *Hub Excavating Ltd. v. Orca Estates Ltd.* (2009), 92 B.C.L.R. (4th) 286 (C.A.) at para. 54 the court stated "Reliance is a question of fact as to the plaintiff's state of mind. It will be sufficient for the plaintiff to prove that the misrepresentation was at least one factor that induced him to act to his detriment. Where a misrepresentation was calculated or would naturally tend to induce the plaintiff to act on it, reliance may be inferred." The court held that on the facts of this case, it had not been reasonable for the plaintiff to rely on the defendant's representations.

In *Steel v. NRAM Ltd.*, [2018] UKSC 13 at para. 38 the court held that "[n]o authority has been cited to the court . . . in which it has been held that there was an assumption of responsibility for a careless misrepresentation about a fact wholly within the knowledge of the representee. The explanation is, no doubt, that in such circumstances it is not reasonable for the representee to rely on the representation without checking its accuracy and that it is, by contrast, reasonable for the representor not to foresee that he would do so."

Courts sometimes say that a misrepresentation was not "material" to how the plaintiff acted: see *White v. Colliers Macaulay Nicholls Inc.* (2009), 95 O.R. (3d) 680 (C.A.). Does this address the reasonableness of reliance, causation or some other issue?

If the plaintiff has a reasonable opportunity to verify the information provided by the defendant, and does not take it, should this be considered as negating a special relationship, negating the foreseeability of reliance, or negating the reasonableness of reliance? Or should this just allow the defendant to raise a defence of contributory negligence? See *Hamilton v. 1214125 Ontario Ltd.* (2009), 84 R.P.R. (4th) 25 (Ont. C.A.).

8. The plaintiff in a negligent misrepresentation case may establish a duty of care but fail to prove some other element of the tort. In *Auto Concrete Curb Ltd. v. South Nation River Conservation Authority* (1993), 105 D.L.R. (4th) 382 (S.C.C.) the court found that the defendant engineers owed the plaintiff a duty of care but had not breached the standard of care. See also *Wynberg v. Daley, supra.*

In *Roncato v. Caverly* (1991), 5 O.R. (3d) 714 (C.A.) the court held that the defendant owed the plaintiff a duty of care and breached the standard of care but dismissed the action because the plaintiff failed to prove that the misrepresentation had caused his loss. See also *Giesbrecht v. Canada Life Assurance Co.*, 2013 MBCA 53; *Matheson v. CIBC World Markets Inc./Marches Mondiaux CIBC Inc.*, 2015 NSCA 22; and Handley, "Causation in Misrepresentation" (2015) 131 L.Q.R. 275.

Causation is considered in detail in Chapter 16. For negligent misrepresentation claims the orthodox view is that the plaintiff is required to show that had the representation not been made, he or she would not have suffered the loss. However, some judges have held that the plaintiff must also show that the loss would not have occurred if what was represented had in fact been true. See for example the disagreement between the judges in *Hogarth v. Rocky Mountain Slate Inc.*, 2013 ABCA 57. What is the difference between these approaches? Which do you prefer?

9. Although the disclaimer clause in *Hedley Byrne* was effective, such provisions are interpreted narrowly and, in the event of ambiguity, against their drafter. Consequently, they may not preclude liability.

In *Keith Plumbing & Heating Co. v. Newport City Club Ltd.* (2000), 184 D.L.R. (4th) 75 (B.C.C.A.) the defendant bank was involved in the financing of a development project. The plaintiff contractor, worried about receiving payment on the project, asked the bank if sufficient funds were available. The bank sent a letter that carelessly answered that question in the affirmative. The letter also contained a disclaimer clause stipulating that the information was provided "without any responsibility on the bank and its signing officers." Some time later, the contractor contacted the bank after a payment had been missed under the project. The bank then carelessly gave its oral assurance that sufficient funds were indeed available. The project subsequently collapsed and the contractor was not paid for its work. It sued the bank for negligent misrepresentation. Despite a vigorous dissent by Ryan J.A., the majority of the Court of Appeal held that the disclaimer clause did not apply with respect to the initial written communication because: (i) it "was not well calculated to convey any clear meaning to persons not versed in the mysteries of banking practice," (ii) the plaintiff had no other means by which to check the developer's financial condition, and (iii) in the circumstances, including trade practice, it was reasonable for the plaintiff to rely upon the defendant's statement. Moreover, the disclaimer clause was held to not apply with respect to the second representation that the bank gave orally. What more could the bank have done to disclaim responsibility for its statements? Should it have refused to give any statement at all? If so, would the project have gone ahead?

What is the connection between the requirement of reasonable reliance and a disclaimer clause? If the plaintiff is aware of such a clause, can there ever be reasonable reliance? Does the clause go to negating reliance or is it a form of defence? See *Kokanee Mortgage M.I.C. Ltd. v Burrell*, 2018 BCCA 151.

Disclaimer clauses are discussed in more detail later in this chapter.

10. The courts recognize the defence of contributory negligence, discussed in Chapter 19, in negligent misrepresentation cases. How can the courts base the duty on reliance but then apportion the loss because the reliance was negligent? In *Grand Restaurants of Canada Ltd. v. Toronto (City)* (1981), 32 O.R. (2d) 757 (H.C.), aff'd (1982), 39 O.R. (2d) 752 (C.A.) Trainor J. stated at 775: "there is a distinction at law between reasonable reliance as a necessary prerequisite to ground liability, to constitute the cause of action under *Hedley Byrne*, and reliance in the context of contributory negligence as simply a factor going to the extent of the damage suffered." This approach was confirmed in *Avco Financial Services Realty Ltd. v. Norman* (2003), 64 O.R. (3d) 239 (C.A.). The court held (at 251) that "a finding that the tort of negligent misrepresentation has been made out is not inherently inconsistent with a finding of contributory negligence because the test that underlies each finding is different." It also observed (at 254) that "an approach that allows for the apportionment of fault in cases of negligent misrepresentation is not only consistent with the approach in other negligence cases, it is also consistent with the principle underlying the very concept of contributory negligence. This principle is rooted in a concern to do justice as between the parties." See also *Chapeskie v. Canadian Imperial Bank of Commerce* (2004), 197 B.C.A.C. 22 (C.A.); *S. Maclise Enterprises Inc. v. Union Securities Ltd.*, *supra*; Roth, "Liability for Loose Lips" (1987) 51 Sask. L. Rev. 317 at 325-26; and Feldthusen, *Economic Negligence*, 6th ed. (2012) at 122-25.

11. It is common for a claim in negligent misrepresentation to be pleaded alongside a claim in fraud, deceit or breach of fiduciary duty. In each instance, the plaintiff's complaint is that the defendant was less than accurate and forthright. The courts carefully approach such claims and insist on clear proof under each cause of

action. See *Toronto-Dominion Bank v. Forsythe, supra*; *H.(V.A.) v. Lynch* (2000), [2001] 1 W.W.R. 83 (Alta. C.A.); and *Crown West Steel Fabricators v. Capri Insurance Services Ltd.*, [2002] 8 W.W.R. 18 (B.C.C.A.).

Courts sometimes refer to fraudulent misrepresentation as distinct from negligent misrepresentation. Fraudulent misrepresentation is the tort of deceit by another name. For more on the tort of deceit see Chapter 26.

12. Can religious views provide a defence to a claim for negligent misrepresentation? In *Hughes Estate v. Hughes* (2009), 454 A.R. 190 (C.A.) a 16-year-old Jehovah's Witness was diagnosed with leukemia and on religious grounds she refused blood transfusions. After she died, her father sued the Watch Tower Bible and Tract Society of Canada for having represented that transfusions would not cure her and that they were an experimental rather than an established procedure. Should such a claim be available? The court did not directly address this issue, as it concluded that the patient refused the transfusions not because of any such representations but because of her own religious faith.

13. As is the case with certain other torts, claims for negligent misrepresentation are increasingly being brought as class actions. Examples include class claims on behalf of all purchasers of a particular investment or product. To take a specific example, in *Wuttunee v. Merck Frosst Canada Ltd.* (2009), 324 Sask. R. 210 (C.A.) the plaintiff class alleged that the defendant had misrepresented the efficacy and safety of the drug Vioxx. Does the issue of reliance make it difficult for a court to resolve negligent misrepresentation cases on a class-wide basis?

14. Negligent representation cases can raise difficult issues at the remoteness stage. See in particular the discussion of the *SAAMCO* principle (from *South Australia Asset Management Corp. v. York Montague Ltd.*, [1997] A.C. 191) in *The Owners, Strata Plan LMS 3851 v. Homer Street Development Limited Partnership*, 2016 BCCA 371, additional reasons 2016 BCCA 491. These issues are discussed in more detail in Chapter 17.

15. The measure of damages for negligent misrepresentation aims to put the plaintiff into the position he or she would have been in had the representation not been made. It does not aim to put the plaintiff in the position he or she would have been in had the representation been correct. See *Rainbow Industrial Caterers Ltd. v. Canadian National Railway*, [1991] 3 S.C.R. 3; *Ault v. Canada (Attorney General)*, 2011 ONCA 147 at para. 118; and *All-Up Consulting Enterprises Inc. v. Dalrymple*, 2013 NSSC 46 at paras. 195-98.

16. The rights-based approach to tort law was explained in Chapter 1. What rights are protected by the law on negligent misrepresentation, especially as concerns pure economic loss? How do these rights differ from those protected by other torts? Does a plaintiff have these rights before the defendant makes the representation or do they only arise once the representation is made? See Beever, *Rediscovering the Law of Negligence* (2007), ch. 8.

17. Books on economic loss typically contain extended analysis of negligent misrepresentation. In addition to Feldthusen, *supra*, see Brown, *Pure Economic Loss in Canadian Negligence Law* (2011), ch. 4; and Burns & Blom, *Economic Torts in*

Canada, 2d ed. (2016), ch. 11. See also Barker, Grantham & Swain, eds., *The Law of Misstatements: 50 Years on from Hedley Byrne v. Heller* (2015).

2. Negligent Misrepresentation Causing Pure Economic Loss

DELOITTE & TOUCHE v. LIVENT INC.
2017 SCC 63

[To make it look more successful and attract investment, directors of Livent Inc. manipulated its financial records. Deloitte & Touche was Livent's auditor. It did not uncover the fraud, but in August 1997 it did identify irregularities in the reporting of profit from an asset sale. Deloitte did not resign as auditor. Instead, for the purpose of helping Livent to solicit investment, Deloitte helped prepare, and approved, a press release issued in September 1997 which misrepresented the basis for the reporting of the profit. In October 1997 Deloitte provided a comfort letter in support of an offering of shares for sale to the public. It also prepared Livent's 1997 audit, which it finalized in April 1998. New shareholders later discovered the fraud. A subsequent investigation and re-audit resulted in restated financial reports. Livent filed for insolvency protection in November 1998. It sold its assets and went into receivership in 1999. Livent sued Deloitte in tort and contract.]

The judgment of Karakatsanis, Gascon, Brown and Rowe JJ. was delivered by Gascon and Brown JJ.

I. Introduction

[1] This appeal provides the Court with an opportunity to affirm the analytical framework by which liability may be imposed in cases of negligent misrepresentation or performance of a service by an auditor.

[2] There is substantial agreement between us and the Chief Justice. We agree on the general analytical framework governing negligent misrepresentation claims (Chief Justice's reasons, at paras. 146-47). And we agree that Deloitte & Touche (now Deloitte LLP) should not be liable for its corporate client Livent Inc.'s increase in liquidation deficit which followed Deloitte's provision of negligent services in relation to the solicitation of investment.

[3] We conclude, however, that Deloitte should be liable for the increase in Livent's liquidation deficit which followed the statutory audit. In *Hercules Managements Ltd. v. Ernst & Young*, 1997 CanLII 345 (SCC), [1997] 2 S.C.R. 165, this Court recognized that a statutory audit is prepared to allow shareholders to collectively "supervise management and to take decisions with respect to matters concerning the proper overall administration of the corporatio[n]" which permits "the shareholders, acting as a group, to safeguard the interests of the corporatio[n]" (para. 56 (emphasis deleted)). This describes precisely the function which Livent's shareholders were unable to discharge by reason of Deloitte's negligence. As a consequence, Livent's corporate life was artificially prolonged, resulting in the interim deterioration of its finances. There was a sufficient evidentiary basis for liability based on impaired shareholder supervision. Application of the *Anns/Cooper* framework, coupled with the basis for auditor liability specifically identified by this Court in *Hercules*, would lead us to uphold the trial judge's finding of liability in relation to the negligently prepared statutory audit.

. . .

[6] The trial judge's findings of negligence can be divided into two separate events: (1) Deloitte's approval of a 1997 press release ("Press Release") and provision of a comfort letter ("Comfort Letter"); and (2) Deloitte's preparation and approval of the 1997 clean audit opinion ("1997 Audit"). We would not label all of these documents "audit statements". Indeed, collapsing the distinctions between these documents obfuscates a proper duty of care analysis.

[7] Livent asserts that it detrimentally relied on Deloitte in each of these events, which impaired its ability to oversee its operations. Specifically, Livent says that, had Deloitte been prudent in relation to these representations, Livent's life would not have been artificially extended and that, in turn, it would have suffered less corporate loss (calculated as the increase in the deficit between its liabilities and assets at the time of its liquidation) . . .

. . .

[15] We reiterate that the purpose of the representation is critical. Unlike the Press Release and Comfort Letter (which were intended to inform investors of Livent's financial position), the 1997 Audit was intended to inform Livent of its own financial position for various purposes, including, most importantly, shareholder oversight of management.

III. Analysis

A. Duty of Care

[16] Traditionally, the test from *Anns v. London Borough of Merton*, [1977] 2 All E.R. 492 (H.L.), governed the duty analysis in decisions of this Court addressing claims for pure economic loss (*Hercules*; *Bow Valley Husky (Bermuda) Ltd. v. Saint John Shipbuilding Ltd.*, 1997 CanLII 307 (SCC), [1997] 3 S.C.R. 1210; *Canadian National Railway Co. v. Norsk Pacific Steamship Co.*, 1992 CanLII 105 (SCC), [1992] 1 S.C.R. 1021). Significantly, however, the *Anns* test for establishing tort liability in Canada has since been refined. In *Cooper v. Hobart*, 2001 SCC 79 (CanLII), [2001] 3 S.C.R. 537, this Court provided greater certainty to the law of tort by clarifying the factors which may be considered at each stage of the *Anns* test. While the resulting *Anns/Cooper* framework has yet to be applied by this Court in a case of auditor's negligence, we adopt this statement of La Forest J. for the Court in *Hercules*: ". . . to create a 'pocket' of negligent misrepresentation cases . . . in which the existence of a duty of care is determined differently from other negligence cases would, in my view, be incorrect . . ." (para. 21).

[17] We turn, therefore, to consider the test for establishing tort liability, beginning with this Court's decision in *Hercules*, and the proper application of the general *Anns/Cooper* framework to cases of auditors' liability.

(1) Hercules: The Anns Test

[18] In *Hercules*, this Court recognized a duty owed by an auditor in preparing a statutory audit of its corporate client. While the Court dismissed the plaintiff shareholders' claim for lost personal investments, it consistently maintained that a claim by the corporation itself for its own losses resulting from a negligent statutory audit could have succeeded . . .

[19] The duty analysis in *Hercules* entailed applying the then-current test for recognizing a duty of care in Canadian negligence law: the *Anns* test. . . .

[20] Under the *Anns* test, a *prima facie* duty of care is recognized where a "sufficiently close relationship between the plaintiff and the defendant" exists such that "in the reasonable contemplation of the [defendant], carelessness on its part may cause damage to the [plaintiff]" (*Hercules*, at para. 22 . . .). In other words, where injury to the plaintiff is a reasonably foreseeable consequence of the defendant's negligence, a duty of care would, *prima facie*, arise. This relationship, where present, was labelled one of "proximity" (*ibid.*). In *Hercules*, the Court provided greater particularity to the test of reasonable foreseeability which established proximity under the *Anns* test in the context of claims for pure economic loss arising from negligent misrepresentation or performance of a service. Specifically, it stated that proximity would inhere in a relationship where two criteria are met: (1) that the defendant should reasonably foresee that the plaintiff will rely on his or her representation; and (2) that the plaintiff's reliance would, in the circumstances of the case, be reasonable. The Court explained that considering the plaintiff's reliance within the test for the reasonable foreseeability of injury did not "abandon the basic tenets underlying the [*Anns*] formula" (para. 25). Rather, as the plaintiff's injury in cases of pure economic loss arising from negligent misrepresentation or performance of a service stems from his or her detrimental reliance, the reasonableness of that reliance informs the determination of whether his or her injury is reasonably foreseeable (paras. 25-26). Where, therefore, the *Anns* test was applied to cases of negligent misrepresentation, reasonable foreseeability of injury alone, as arising from reasonable reliance, was sufficient to establish a proximate relationship supporting a *prima facie* duty of care (*Hercules*, at paras. 25 and 27; *Norsk*, at p. 1154; *Bow Valley*, at para. 61).

[21] The *Anns* test thereby set a low threshold at the first stage, imposing duties in relation to a nearly limitless class of persons who might rely on representations for nearly limitless purposes. Indeed, as this Court stated in *Hercules*, "[i]n modern commercial society, the fact that audit reports will be relied on by many different people (e.g., shareholders, creditors, potential takeover bidders, investors, etc.) for a wide variety of purposes will almost always be reasonably foreseeable to auditors themselves" (para. 32). For that reason — that is, because of the low "foreseeability" threshold for establishing a *prima facie* duty of care at the first stage of the *Anns* test — the Court looked to the second stage of the *Anns* test to negate or narrow the duty on the basis of the "policy consideration" of indeterminacy. It was here that the Court looked to the identity of the plaintiffs and the purpose of the audit opinion to deny liability for investment and devaluation losses of individual shareholders (paras. 27-28; see also *Haig v. Bamford*, 1976 CanLII 6 (SCC), [1977] 1 S.C.R. 466). Specifically, the Court found that one of the purposes of a statutory audit — that is, to "allo[w] shareholders, as a group, to supervise management and to take decisions with respect to matters concerning the proper overall administration of the corporatio[n]" (para. 56 (emphasis in original)) — would have permitted the corporate client to recover its own losses at the time of receivership had the claim been brought in the corporation's name. As we will explain, Livent's injury following the 1997 Audit is precisely the type of injury described in *Hercules* as being compensable.

(2) Cooper. Refining the *Anns* Test

[22] While this Court's holding in *Hercules* remains binding authority governing an auditor's duty of care in relation to a statutory audit, the framework by which that duty is imposed has since been refined. In the companion cases of *Cooper* and *Edwards v. Law Society of Upper Canada*, 2001 SCC 80 (CanLII), [2001] 3 S.C.R. 562, this Court revised the *Anns* test by distinguishing more clearly between foreseeability and proximity, and by placing greater emphasis on a more demanding first stage of the two-stage analysis (*Cooper*, at para. 30). While, therefore, we rely on *Hercules* for the general proposition that an auditor may owe its client a duty of care in relation to a particular undertaking, it is the *Anns/Cooper* framework to which we must have reference in identifying a principled basis for imposing liability. And, properly applied, that framework will rarely, if ever, give rise to a *prima facie* duty of care that could result in indeterminate liability. Accordingly, and with great respect for contrary views, there is no reason to resort to the second stage in order to negate all liability in this case.

. . .

[24] In *Cooper*, the Court did not indicate whether proximity or reasonable foreseeability should be assessed first. In cases of negligent misrepresentation or performance of a service, however, proximity will be more usefully considered before foreseeability. What the defendant reasonably foresees as flowing from his or her negligence depends upon the characteristics of his or her relationship with the plaintiff, and specifically, in such cases, the purpose of the defendant's undertaking. That said, both proximity and foreseeability of injury merit further reflection.

(i) Proximity

. . .

[30] In cases of pure economic loss arising from negligent misrepresentation or performance of a service, two factors are determinative in the proximity analysis: the defendant's undertaking and the plaintiff's reliance. Where the defendant undertakes to provide a representation or service in circumstances that invite the plaintiff's reasonable reliance, the defendant becomes obligated to take reasonable care. And, the plaintiff has a right to rely on the defendant's undertaking to do so (W. N. Hohfeld, "Some Fundamental Legal Conceptions as Applied in Judicial Reasoning" (1913), 23 Yale L.J. 16, at pp. 49-50). These corollary rights and obligations create a relationship of proximity (*Haig*, at p. 477; *Caparo Industries plc. v. Dickman*, [1990] 1 All E.R. 568 (H.L.), at pp. 637-38; *Glanzer v. Shepard*, 135 N.E. 275 (N.Y. 1922), at pp. 275-76; *Ultramares Corp. v. Touche*, 174 N.E. 441 (N.Y. 1931), at pp. 445-46; E. J. Weinrib, "The Disintegration of Duty" (2006), 31 Adv. Q. 212, at p. 230).

[31] Rights, like duties, are, however, not limitless. Any reliance on the part of the plaintiff which falls outside of the scope of the defendant's undertaking of responsibility — that is, of the purpose for which the representation was made or the service was undertaken — necessarily falls outside the scope of the proximate relationship and, therefore, of the defendant's duty of care (Weinrib; A. Beever, *Rediscovering the Law of Negligence* (2007), at pp. 293-94). This principle, also referred to as the "end and aim" rule, properly limits liability on the basis that the defendant cannot be liable for a risk of injury against which he did not undertake to protect (*Glanzer*, at pp. 275 and 277; *Ultramares*, at pp. 445-46; *Haig*, at p. 482). By assessing

all relevant factors arising from the relationship between the parties, the proximity analysis not only determines the existence of a relationship of proximity, but also delineates the scope of the rights and duties which flow from that relationship. In short, it furnishes not only a "principled basis upon which to draw the line between those to whom the duty is owed and those to whom it is not" (*Fullowka* [*v. Royal Oak Ventures Inc.*, 2010 SCC 5], at para. 70), but also a principled delineation of the scope of such duty, based upon the purpose for which the defendant undertakes responsibility. As we will explain, these principled limits are essential to determining the type of injury that was a reasonably foreseeable consequence of the defendant's negligence.

(ii) Reasonable Foreseeability

[32] Assessing reasonable foreseeability in the *prima facie* duty of care analysis entails asking whether an injury to the plaintiff was a reasonably foreseeable consequence of the defendant's negligence (*Cooper*, at para. 30).

[33] Broadly speaking, reasonable foreseeability concerns the likelihood of injury arising from the defendant's negligence (*Donoghue*, at p. 580). This inquiry is not amenable to, and does not require, actuarial precision. The jurisprudence gives content, however, to the foreseeability inquiry, providing courts with guidance. In the abstract, a defendant's negligent misrepresentation or performance of a service could potentially give rise to innumerable injuries tangentially cascading from the originally contemplated service. This was so in *Hercules*, where the Court recognized that an auditor's statement could be relied upon by a potentially limitless number of individuals (e.g., shareholders or takeover bidders), for a potentially limitless array of purposes (e.g., investments or takeover bids), any of which could result in various foreseeable injuries.

[34] As we have already observed, however, reasonable foreseeability of injury is no longer the sole consideration at the first stage of the *Anns/Cooper* framework. Since *Cooper*, both reasonable foreseeability and proximity — the latter expressed in *Cooper* as a distinct and more demanding hurdle than reasonable foreseeability — must be proven in order to establish a *prima facie* duty of care. And, in cases of negligent misrepresentation or performance of a service, the proximate relationship — grounded in the defendant's undertaking and the plaintiff's reliance — informs the foreseeability inquiry. Meaning, the purpose underlying that undertaking and that corresponding reliance limits the type of injury which could be reasonably foreseen to result from the defendant's negligence.

[35] As a matter of first principles, it must be borne in mind that an injury to the plaintiff in this sort of case flows from the fact that he or she detrimentally relied on the defendant's undertaking, whether it take the form of a representation or the performance of a service. It follows that an injury to the plaintiff will be reasonably foreseeable if (1) the defendant should have reasonably foreseen that the plaintiff would rely on his or her representation; and (2) such reliance would, in the particular circumstances of the case, be reasonable (*Hercules*, at para. 27). Both the reasonableness and the reasonable foreseeability of the plaintiff's reliance will be determined by the relationship of proximity between the parties; a plaintiff has a right to rely on a defendant to act with reasonable care for the particular purpose of the defendant's undertaking, and his or her reliance on the defendant for that purpose is therefore both reasonable and reasonably foreseeable. But a plaintiff has no right to

rely on a defendant for any other purpose, because such reliance would fall outside the scope of the defendant's undertaking. As such, any consequent injury could not have been reasonably foreseeable.

[36] We add this. Under the *Anns* test, the Court recognized that auditors may owe a *prima facie* duty of care to an innumerable number of parties on the basis of reasonable foreseeability alone (*Hercules*, at para. 32). We acknowledge that the *Anns/ Cooper* framework, when applied to cases of negligent misrepresentation, will give rise to a far narrower scope of reasonably foreseeable injuries and, therefore, a narrower range of *prima facie* duties of care. This is no indictment of the *Anns/Cooper* analysis. Rather, it was the very purpose and effect of this Court's instruction in *Cooper* that "something more" than mere foreseeability is required at the first stage of the *Anns/ Cooper* framework. By requiring examination of the relationship between the parties as we have just discussed, *Cooper* gave Canadian courts a more complete array of legal tools to determine whether it is "just and fair" to impose a *prima facie* duty of care.

(b) Stage Two: Residual Policy Considerations

[37] Where a *prima facie* duty of care is recognized on the basis of proximity and reasonable foreseeability, the analysis advances to stage two of the *Anns/Cooper* framework. Here, the question is whether there are "residual policy considerations" outside the relationship of the parties that may negate the imposition of a duty of care (*Cooper*, at para. 30; *Edwards*, at para. 10; . . .).

[38] By "residual", we mean that such considerations "are not concerned with the relationship between the parties [already considered at stage one], but with the effect of recognizing a duty of care on other legal obligations, the legal system and society more generally" (*Cooper*, at para. 37; see also *Edwards*, at para. 10). To the extent, therefore, that stage one of the *prima facie* duty of care is said to engage "policy" considerations arising from the relationship between the parties — i.e., the recognition that it is sound "policy" to only hold defendants liable for negligence when they are in a proximate relationship with the plaintiff and when the injury suffered was reasonably foreseeable (see *Cooper*, at para. 25) — such "policy" considerations are not revisited at stage two (*ibid.*, at para. 28). Indeed such reconsideration would be both redundant and analytically confusing (*ibid.*, at para. 29).

[39] *Cooper*, and in particular, its strict delineation between "factors arising from the *relationship* between [the parties]" (para. 30 (emphasis in original)) and factors that "are not concerned with the relationship between the parties" (para. 37) has impacted the stage at which certain factors are considered within the *Anns/Cooper* framework. For example, principles that were traditionally considered at the second stage of the *Anns* test in cases of negligent misrepresentation, such as (1) whether the defendant knew the identity of the plaintiff or the class of plaintiffs who would rely on its representation; and (2) whether the reliance losses claimed by the plaintiff stem from the particular transaction in respect of which the statement at issue was made (*Hercules*, at paras. 27 and 40; *Bow Valley*, at paras. 55-56), are no longer considered at the second stage. This is because, as we have explained, these factors arise from the relationship between the parties and are, therefore, properly accounted for under the first stage proximity and reasonable foreseeability analysis.

[40] What, then, remains to be considered at the second stage of the *Anns/Cooper* framework? In *Cooper*, this Court identified factors which are external to the relationship between the parties, including (1) whether the law already provides a

remedy; (2) whether recognition of the duty of care creates "the spectre of unlimited liability to an unlimited class"; and (3) whether there are "other reasons of broad policy that suggest that the duty of care should not be recognized" (para. 37). In this way, the residual policy inquiry is a normative inquiry. It asks whether it would be better, for reasons relating to legal or doctrinal order, or reasons arising from other societal concerns, not to recognize a duty of care in a given case.

[41] The place within the *Anns/Cooper* framework of this policy inquiry is significant. It follows the proximity and foreseeability inquiries. The policy inquiry assesses whether, despite the proximate relationship between the parties, and despite the reasonably foreseeable quality of the plaintiff's injury, the defendant should nonetheless be insulated from liability (*Cooper*, at para. 30; . . .). That it would limit liability in the face of findings of both proximity and reasonable foreseeability makes plain how narrowly it should be relied upon (*Cooper*, at para. 30, citing *Yuen Kun Yeu v. Attorney-General of Hong Kong*, [1988] 1 A.C. 175 (P.C.); *Edgeworth Construction Ltd. v. N. D. Lea & Associates Ltd.*, 1993 CanLII 67 (SCC), [1993] 3 S.C.R. 206, at p. 218). Only in rare cases — such as those concerning decisions of governmental policy (*Cooper*, at paras. 38 and 53) or quasi-judicial bodies (*ibid.*, at para. 52; *Edwards*, at para. 19) — should liability be denied when a defendant's negligence causes reasonably foreseeable injury to a plaintiff with whom he or she shares a close and direct relationship. In light of the above, the stage at which certain factors are considered in the *Anns/Cooper* framework is material.

[42] In this case, the Chief Justice finds that, if it were necessary to proceed to the second stage of the *Anns/Cooper* framework, she would insulate Deloitte from liability based on the residual policy consideration of indeterminacy (para. 166). We concede that indeterminate liability may, in some cases, be a legitimate residual policy consideration (*Cooper*, at paras. 37 and 54; *Hercules*, at para. 31). In our view, however, rarely, if ever, should a concern for indeterminate liability persist after a properly applied proximity and foreseeability analysis (*Saadati* [*v. Moorhead*, 2017 SCC 28], at para. 34; *Fullowka*, at para. 70). Robust application of stage one of the *Anns/Cooper* framework should almost always obviate concerns for indeterminate liability. This follows from an appreciation of what indeterminate liability, as a concept, actually means.

[43] Indeterminate liability is liability of a specific character, not of a specific amount. In particular, indeterminate liability should not be confused with significant liability (*Gross v. Great-West Life Assurance Co.*, 2002 ABCA 37 (CanLII), 299 A.R. 142, at para. 38). Certain activities — like flying commercial aircraft, manufacturing pharmaceutical drugs, or auditing a large corporation — may well give rise to significant liability. But such liability arises from the nature of the defendant's undertakings and of the severe but reasonably foreseeable scale of injury that can result where such undertakings are negligently performed. This explains the significant compensation which these high risk undertakings typically attract. It also explains why contractual disclaimers limiting liability may often be warranted (*Edgeworth*, at p. 220). In contrast, the liability arising from these "high risk" undertakings may only be characterized as "indeterminate" if the scope of such liability is impossible to ascertain (*Black's Law Dictionary* (10th ed. 2014), *sub verbo* "indeterminate"). In other words, liability is truly "indeterminate" if "the accepted sources of law and the accepted methods of working with those sources such as deduction and analogy . . . are insufficient to resolve the question" (M. V. Tushnet, "Defending the Indeterminacy

Thesis", in B. Bix, ed., *Analyzing Law: New Essays in Legal Theory* (1998), 223, at pp. 224-25). More specifically, there are three pertinent aspects to so-called "indeterminacy" in these cases: (1) value indeterminacy ("liability in an indeterminate amount"); (2) temporal indeterminacy ("liability . . . for an indeterminate time"); and (3) claimant indeterminacy ("liability . . . to an indeterminate class"): *Hercules*, at para. 31, citing *Ultramares*, at p. 444. Naturally, when a claim has value, temporal, and claimant indeterminacy, our legal tools are insufficient to resolve the quantum of infinite damages that will flow from such a claim.

[44] All this said, it would be very difficult for liability of an indeterminate character, so understood, to survive a robust analysis of proximity and foreseeability at the first stage of the *Anns/Cooper* framework. In cases of negligent misrepresentation or performance of a service, the requisite proximity analysis will address claimant indeterminacy because the class of claimants is determinate, including only those in respect of whom the defendant undertook to act. Likewise, foreseeability, which is constrained by the purpose of the undertaking in question, should address concerns about value indeterminacy, because the value of damages is limited — that is, determined — by the reasonably foreseeable quality of the injury (*Hercules*, at para. 32). Finally, proximity and foreseeability should both address temporal indeterminacy since the longer the period of time over which injury is said to have occurred, the less likely the defendant undertook to protect against it and the less foreseeable the injury, taken as a whole. Hence Cardozo C.J.'s statement in the oft-cited *Ultramares* decision that a duty which gives rise to indeterminacy "enkindle[s] doubt whether a flaw may not exist in the implication of a duty that exposes to these consequences" (p. 444; see also Weinrib, at p. 231; Beever, at p. 275). In other words, a finding of indeterminate liability at the damages stage strongly suggests that a legal error occurred at the duty stage, since a finding of a *prima facie* duty of indeterminate scope underlies the resulting indeterminate liability.

[45] We would add one final point. Indeterminate liability is a residual policy consideration, nothing more. The presence of indeterminacy need not be dispositive of liability in all cases. To approach the analysis otherwise would transform indeterminate liability from a policy consideration into a policy veto. While indeterminacy may militate against liability, other policy considerations — such as the immense profit margins that "high risk" actors often benefit from, or the extent to which "high risk" actors voluntarily assume the risk of indeterminate liability — may ultimately justify maintaining that liability, despite its indeterminacy (Beever, at p. 293). Even, therefore, in the rare case where indeterminate liability survives the proximity and foreseeability inquiries, it is not automatic that such indeterminacy will necessarily govern (*Fullowka*, at para. 70). Indeed, any so-called "indeterminate liability" which survives stage one of the *Anns/Cooper* framework presumably arises from the risk against which the defendant voluntarily undertook to protect the plaintiff and, therefore, may justly and fairly result in liability.

B. Application

. . .

[47] In summary, at the first stage of the *Anns/Cooper* framework, a duty of care is established where proximity and reasonably foreseeability of injury are found. In our view, Deloitte's undertakings in relation to soliciting investment, and the 1997 Audit,

gave rise to proximate relationships. The purpose of those undertakings, in turn, determines the type of injury that was reasonably foreseeable as a result of Livent's reliance. Livent relied on the 1997 Audit for the purpose it was provided. Thus, a resulting injury was reasonably foreseeable. The same cannot be said, however, in respect of Deloitte's negligent assistance in soliciting investment.

[48] At the second stage of the *Anns/Cooper* framework, residual policy considerations may negate Deloitte's duty of care. But none apply to the negligent provision of the 1997 Audit.

. . .

[55] Here, Livent argues that it detrimentally relied on Deloitte's services and representations to artificially extend the life of the corporation. This reliance is not, however, tied to the solicitation of investment, but was a matter of oversight of management. Phrased in terms of Deloitte's undertaking, during the fall of 1997 Deloitte undertook to assist Livent in soliciting investment, not in oversight of management. Losses related to this undertaking — for example, an inability to solicit investment because of Deloitte's negligence — may be recoverable from Deloitte. But losses outside the scope of this undertaking, including those claimed here relating to a lack of oversight of management extending Livent's solvency, are not recoverable from Deloitte. Simply put, Deloitte never undertook, in preparing the Comfort Letter, to assist Livent's shareholders in overseeing management; it cannot therefore be held liable for failing to take reasonable care to assist such oversight. And, given that Livent had no right to rely on Deloitte's representations for a purpose other than that for which Deloitte undertook to act, Livent's reliance was neither reasonable nor reasonably foreseeable. Consequently, the increase in Livent's liquidation deficit which arose from its reliance on the Press Release and Comfort Letter was not a reasonably foreseeable injury.

. . .

[63] Livent says that the increase in its liquidation deficit was a reasonably foreseeable consequence of Deloitte's negligent audit, because the audit preserved a false financial picture upon which Livent relied to artificially extend its solvency and delay filing for bankruptcy. In other words, if Deloitte had taken reasonable care in auditing Livent, then Livent would have discovered the fraud and avoided the interim deterioration of its assets.

[64] In our view, this type of injury was a reasonably foreseeable consequence of Deloitte's negligent audit. The purpose of the 1997 Audit was, as this Court described in *Hercules*, two-fold: (1) to protect the company from the consequences of undetected errors and wrongdoing; and (2) to provide shareholders with reliable intelligence enabling oversight (para. 48, citing *Caparo*, at p. 583). Those purposes, as we have already described in our discussion of proximity generally, inform the scope of reasonably foreseeable injury. Specifically, at the time Deloitte undertook to provide the 1997 Audit, Livent was entitled to rely on Deloitte to take reasonable care in doing so for these recognized purposes. Livent's reliance on Deloitte for the purpose of overseeing the conduct of management was therefore both reasonable and reasonably foreseeable. And, as Livent's injury arises from its detrimental reliance, the injury linked to that reliance is itself reasonably foreseeable.

[65] It follows that the type of injury Livent suffered here was a reasonably foreseeable consequence of Deloitte's negligence. Through the 1997 Audit, Deloitte

undertook to assist Livent's shareholders in scrutinizing management conduct. By negligently conducting the audit, and impairing Livent's shareholders' ability to oversee management, Deloitte exposed Livent to reasonably foreseeable risks, including "business losses" that would have been avoided with a proper audit. Indeed, the risk of injury flowing from undetected fraud is precisely the type of injury statutory audits seek to avoid.

. . .

[73] The Chief Justice describes the liability sought to be imposed here as "indeterminate" because Livent's reliance purportedly fell outside the scope of Deloitte's undertaking (para. 170). We disagree. To the contrary, value indeterminacy is limited by the purposes for which the audit was prepared, and Livent's reliance fell squarely within that purpose. In *Hercules*, this Court rejected a claim by investors because they might use audit reports for a "collateral or unintended purpose" (para. 38), thereby giving rise to indeterminate liability (since the variety of purposes to which an audit may be put is potentially limitless). But that is not the case here. The 1997 Audit was prepared for the express purpose of oversight of management by Livent's shareholders, and the loss at issue flowed from those shareholders' inability to conduct that oversight. It follows that the purposes underlying the 1997 Audit — of which, as we have explained, there are only two — do not give rise to potential indeterminacy, and by corollary, relate to potential losses that, too, are not indeterminate. This is not a case where, for example, an unknown third-party relied on an audit to launch a takeover bid — a purpose outside the scope of the audit (*Hercules*, at para. 32). Rather, this is a case in which an established purpose of the audit was undermined, and where losses predictably flowed from that failed purpose (*Haig*, at pp. 478-79).

. . .

[75] The lack of indeterminacy here between Deloitte (an auditor) and Livent (its corporate client) is unsurprising given (1) this Court's recognition in *Hercules* that a duty of care exists between an auditor and its corporate client in relation to a statutory audit; and (2) this Court's direction in *Cooper* that the second stage of the *Anns/Cooper* framework need not be considered where a previously recognized proximate relationship exists.

The reasons of McLachlin C.J. and Wagner and Côté JJ. were delivered by . . . The Chief Justice (dissenting in part)

. . .

[152] In this case, three purposes of Livent's audit statements are discernable: (1) to report accurately on Livent's finances and provide it with audit opinions on which it could rely for the purpose of attracting investment; (2) to uncover heretofore undetected errors or wrongdoing by Livent or its personnel for the purpose of enabling Livent itself to correct or otherwise respond to the misfeasance; and (3) to provide audit reports on which Livent's shareholders could rely to supervise the company's management . . .

[153] The scope of Deloitte's duty of care is defined solely by these purposes. Did its negligence prevent Livent from attracting investment? Did its negligence prevent Livent from uncovering undetected wrongdoing for the purpose of allowing Livent to correct the misfeasance? Finally, did its negligence prevent shareholders from

supervising the company's management? Loss that results from inability to attract investment, from inability of Livent to correct undetected wrongdoing, or from inability of the shareholders to exercise their supervisory authority, may fall within the scope of Deloitte's duty of care.

[154] The first possibility is that Deloitte's wrongful act deprived Livent of the ability to attract investment capital. Livent does not rely on this; in fact, Livent attracted a great deal of capital on the strength of Deloitte's statements. Indeed, that is the essence of its complaint — if it had not been able to attract this money, it would not have been able to spend it on new theatre ventures that failed and decreased Livent's worth. The company's assets were not diminished by an inability to attract investment, but by Livent's improvident management of those investments, revealed only on insolvency.

[155] The second possibility is that the wrongful act prevented Livent — the company itself — from detecting misfeasance in the company's management which Livent's officials would have corrected if they had known the true state of affairs. This possibility envisions the situation where a company's management, acting honestly and diligently, is unable to deal with internal misfeasance because the auditors negligently failed to reveal it.

[156] This is not Livent's situation. Livent led no evidence that its management did not know of Drabinsky's and Gottlieb's misfeasance; indeed, it likely could not have done so. Drabinsky and Gottlieb, the fraudsters, were themselves the management. Far from relying on the audited statements as assurance that everything was well with the company, Drabinsky and Gottlieb knew the audit reports were inaccurate. There is no evidence that anyone at a lower level of Livent management would have blown the whistle if Livent's statements had revealed the fraud at an earlier date.

[157] The third possibility is that Deloitte's wrongdoing prevented Livent's shareholders from exercising shareholder supervision in a manner that would have ended the corporation's loss-creating activities at an earlier date. Livent argues (and my colleagues Gascon and Brown JJ. accept) that it relied on Deloitte to produce a report on the basis of which its shareholders could discharge their supervisory function, which all agree was one of the purposes for which the audited statements were prepared. Livent argues, and my colleagues conclude, that all loss that shareholder supervision might have avoided is recoverable — including the decline in the value of the company.

[158] This proposition faces two difficulties. The first is that Livent never proved, nor did the trial judge find, the elements necessary to establish it. The second is a related policy concern: to allow recovery in the absence of the required proof would be to open the door to indeterminate recovery. I will consider each of these difficulties in turn.

[159] First, although the trial judge's reasons refer to Deloitte's duty to Livent's shareholders as established in *Hercules*, the factual basis for liability based on impaired shareholder supervision was lacking. Livent's theory of the case was simply that all loss as a result of improvident investments after the negligent audits was compensable, on a "but for" basis. Livent did not prove and the trial judge did not find that Livent's shareholders relied on Deloitte's negligent audit statements, or that had they received and relied on accurate statements, they would have acted in a way

that would have prevented Livent from carrying on business and diminishing its assets in the period between the issuance of the relevant statements and Livent's insolvency.

. . .

[161] The broad view of the duty of care taken by Livent, and accepted by the trial judge meant that the trial judge failed to consider the parameters of the shareholders' reasonable and foreseeable reliance as required in *Hercules* when defining the scope of the duty of care with respect to losses stemming from impaired shareholder supervision. My colleagues conclude otherwise, noting that the trial judge believed that the shareholders were entitled to rely on Deloitte's negligent audits as an indication of Livent's health. Crucially, however, the trial judge did not ask whether the shareholders had in fact relied on the audits — a critical element to the cause of action. He did not ask whether, if they had relied, this reliance prevented them from taking steps to replace directors or officers or otherwise alter course. He did not ask whether this would have included shutting down Livent on March 31st, 1998 (or at least earlier than when it was shut down in November 1998). Finally, he did not ask whether these actions, had they been taken, would have prevented the losses that Livent built up during the seven-month period in question. If the trial judge had asked these questions, he would have been obliged to answer them in the negative, since Livent offered no proof to support affirmative answers.

. . .

[163] Livent's position and the trial judge's approach collapse the distinction between shareholder decision making, for which an auditor provides information for one purpose — holding management accountable with a view to the best interest of the company — with management decision making, for which the auditor provides information for a different purpose — responding to error and wrongdoing. Conceiving liability in this way creates a misalignment between the scope of the duty of care, the type of loss that is therein contemplated, and the actual elements that must be proven in order to make a successful claim.

[164] The second and related difficulty the shareholder supervision argument faces in this case is that it would lead to unfair allocation of loss and indeterminate liability for auditors' statements, negating the duty of care: *Hercules*, at paras. 36-37.

[165] Livent's position — that Deloitte is liable for all loss without proof of the elements required to advance a case based on impaired shareholder supervision — would result in an unfair allocation of loss as well as indeterminacy of damages. On the shareholder supervision theory advanced by Livent, breach of a duty owed primarily to the collectivity of shareholders (who do not advance a claim) and only derivatively to the corporation, would result in liability for every dollar that Livent spent after the point in time the shareholders became entitled to rely on the statements. The auditor would be the virtual guarantor of everything Livent — not the collectivity of shareholders to which the duty was owed — did thereafter. This would not be a fair allocation of responsibility. The same scenario would raise the spectre of indeterminate liability. Auditors would be unable to reasonably predict when they are providing services to clients what their ultimate liability would be. It would be out of their control. No matter how bad the decisions made by the client thereafter, no matter how complex the web of dealings that led to the ultimate loss — things that cannot be foreseen in advance — the auditor would be liable for the total loss, on the basis that it would not have occurred "but for" the negligent act.

[166] For the foregoing reasons, I conclude that the losses at issue have not been shown to fall within the scope of Deloitte's duty of care. The first step of the *Anns* test is not established. It is unnecessary to go on to ask whether *prima facie* liability is negated by policy considerations unrelated to the relationship between the parties. However, were it necessary to do so, the policy considerations of unfair allocation of loss and indeterminacy would preclude imposing liability on Deloitte.

. . .

[169] Livent's failure to prove that any of the loss it suffered can be attributed to its shareholders' reliance on the negligent 1997 year-end audit report for the purpose of corporate oversight is a sufficient basis on which to allow the appeal in its entirety. But there is further problematic aspect of the shareholder supervision theory on which Livent now seeks to rely. It is one of principle.

[170] As explained above, an auditor that provides a year-end report for the purpose of enabling a company's shareholders to supervise management does not, absent proof, assume responsibility for what the shareholders decide to do with that information. The purpose of an annual audit report is to inform shareholder decision making, not to govern it. The auditor does not underwrite the entire risk associated with the shareholders' exercise of business judgment; it is liable only for exposing shareholders to the risk of the information it has provided being wrong. Even if the whole loss would have been avoided if the auditor had met the standard of care, the company may recover in damages only that part of the loss that may be attributed to the auditor's breach of its duty of care, which is restricted by the purpose or purposes for which it provided its opinion. The auditor is not liable for the indeterminate quantum of loss that the shareholders' course of action (or inaction) may trigger, since determining that course of action is beyond the auditor's undertaking of responsibility, and thus outside the scope of its duty of care. Similarly, loss that cannot be attributed to the auditor's breach will be too remote to recover.

[171] For this reason, the language of lost opportunity is unavailing. In any case concerned with the tortious provision of information, the plaintiff may claim that, had it only known the truth, it would have had the chance to make different choices than it ultimately did. Unless the provider of information has assumed responsibility not only for the information but also for the decision to be informed by it, what the plaintiff would have done differently if it had been provided with different information is immaterial. Rather, the question is the extent to which the loss that in fact resulted may be attributed to the wrongness (i.e., the tortious quality) of the information provided.

[172] On the trial judge's findings, Deloitte never assumed responsibility for any of the decisions — whether of Livent's management or of its shareholders collectively — that may be said to have occasioned Livent's loss. What Livent proved is that it relied on Deloitte's clean opinions to raise funds from third parties, and that it was successful in doing so. Deloitte is not liable to Livent for loss arising from Livent's use of these funds, even if certain of Deloitte's opinions were prepared for the purpose of *attracting* them, because Livent did not prove that Deloitte undertook responsibility for how Livent *spent* them.

NOTES AND QUESTIONS

1. Prior to *Livent, Hercules* was the leading authority on auditor liability for negligent misstatement causing pure economic loss. According to *Hercules*, when was a duty of care imposed on auditors? On what basis was the first branch of the *Anns/ Kamloops* test satisfied? What considerations fell under the second branch of the test?

2. Why did the court in *Livent* change the analysis that had been set out in *Hercules*? What did it change? Summarize the court's approach to negligent misrepresentation. Does *Livent* apply only to auditors or does it apply to all negligent misrepresentation cases? Could it apply even more broadly? See Klar, "Duty of Care for Negligent Misrepresentation – And Beyond?" (2018) 48 Adv. Q. 235.

3. What are the key differences between the majority and the dissent in *Livent*? To what degree do they agree on the relevant legal principles?

4. What policy considerations have courts identified that warrant a restricted duty of care on auditors? Are any of these concerns overstated or misplaced?

5. B. Feldthusen has argued that recognition of a duty of care in misrepresentation cases often improperly allows a plaintiff to "unilaterally appropriate" the services of the defendant in so far as the plaintiff is entitled to compensation if the defendant's negligent statements cause pure economic loss. He therefore argues that recognition of a duty of care should be carefully confined to circumstances in which the defendant voluntarily assumed responsibility toward the plaintiff. On that view, while absence of reasonable reliance may justify the negation of a duty of care, its presence without more cannot justify the imposition of a duty of care: only assumption of responsibility can serve that role. See Feldthusen, "Liability for Pure Economic Loss: Yes, But Why?" (1999) 28 U.W.A.L. Rev. 84; Feldthusen, Economic Negligence, 6th ed. (2012) at 57-62; and Feldthusen, "*Hedley Byrne*: Misused, then Exiled by the Supreme Court of Canada" in Barker, Grantham & Swain, eds., *The Law of Misstatements: 50 Years on from Hedley Byrne v. Heller* (2015), ch. 11. See also Hollyman, "*Hercules Managements* and the Duty of Care in Negligent Misstatement: How Dispensable is Reliance?" (2001) 34 U.B.C.L. Rev. 515; Murphy, "Rethinking Negligent Misrepresentation" (2003) 9 Auckland U.L. Rev. 1283; and Brown, "Assumption of Responsibility and Loss of Bargain in Tort Law" (2006) 29 Dal. L.J. 345.

For a recent Australian case stressing the role of assumption of responsibility see *Swick Nominees Pty. Ltd. v. Leroi International Inc. (No. 2)*, [2015] WASCA 35.

How does the court in *Livent* address this debate? What approach fits best with a rights-based approach to tort law? See Beever, "The Basis of the *Hedley Byrne* Action" in Barker, Grantham & Swain, *supra*.

6. American and Commonwealth courts have used various tests to control the ambit of liability. They have emphasized the defendant's knowledge of the class of potential plaintiffs, knowledge of the contemplated use of the information, or both. However, most of the cases are consistent with a fairly simple rule, derived from *Glanzer v. Shepard*, 135 N.E. 275 at 277 (N.Y.C.A. 1922). In *Glanzer* the court held the defendant liable for losses which he knew or ought to have known were related to the "end and aim" of the transaction giving rise to the misrepresentation. In *Caparo*

Industries plc. v. Dickman, [1990] 2 W.L.R. 358 (H.L.) the House of Lords observed that advice is tendered with a specific purpose in mind and that liability must be restricted to losses incurred in transactions related to that purpose. See also *Esanda Finance Corp. v. Peat Marwick Hungerfords (Reg)* (1997), 142 A.L.R. 750 (H.C.A.); *Boyd Knight v. Purdue*, [1999] 2 N.Z.L.R. 278 (C.A.); and *Price Waterhouse v. Kwan* (1999), [2000] 3 N.Z.L.R. 39 (C.A.).

7. As noted in the introduction to this chapter, in *Ultramares* Cardozo C.J. expressed concern that the application of the ordinary rules of negligence law might expose accountants to "liability in an indeterminate amount for an indeterminate time to an indeterminate class." Generally, the courts have shared Cardozo C.J.'s concern about the indeterminate amount and have regarded indeterminate time and class as indirect indicators of this issue. However, each factor may have independent significance.

The issue of potentially indeterminate time was raised in *Williams v. Polgar*, 215 N.W.2d 149 (S.C. Mich. 1974). An abstract of a land title was negligently issued in 1926. The defect was not discovered until 1959, when the plaintiffs relied upon the abstract to their detriment. The court held that the defendant's duty extended to any successor in title who relied on the abstract. Whereas the limitation period in contract had long expired, the tort period had not begun to run until the plaintiffs discovered the negligence. Does this decision violate the policy underlying statutory limitations periods?

The problem of a potentially indeterminate class raises the issue of whether there is a sufficient relationship between the plaintiff and defendant to warrant imposing liability, regardless of the amount of the potential loss. In *Beebe v. Robb* (1977), 81 D.L.R. (3d) 349 (B.C.S.C.) a boat owner commissioned the defendant, a marine surveyor, to evaluate his boat in order to assist him in obtaining a bank loan. Unknown to the defendant, the owner showed the assessment to the plaintiff, a prospective purchaser, who relied upon it to his detriment. The plaintiff alleged that the defendant had been negligent and sued under the principles in *Hedley Byrne*. Clearly the defendant knew about the amount at risk. Nevertheless, the court held that the relationship between the parties was insufficient to justify recognizing a duty of care. A similar result was reached in *Le Lievre v. Gould*, [1893] 1 Q.B. 491 (C.A.). In *Gordon v. Moen*, [1971] N.Z.L.R. 526 (S.C.), a case virtually identical to *Beebe*, the court held the defendant liable. Which line of cases is preferable?

Explain the difference in *Livent* between the majority's and the dissent's treatment of the issue of indeterminate liability. Which approach do you prefer?

8. *Hercules* was applied in a variety of circumstances. In *Deraps v. Coia* (1999), 179 D.L.R. (4th) 168 (Ont. C.A.) a woman and her gravely ill husband sought advice from a benefits counsellor employed by the husband's trade union. Because of a careless omission by the counsellor, the woman did not realize that, by signing a certain waiver, she would lose all of her benefits when her husband died. She signed the waiver and, when her husband passed away eight months later, learned that she no longer enjoyed any benefits. In affirming the imposition of liability, the Court of Appeal for Ontario held that the failure to divulge information may be just as actionable as the providing of positively misleading advice. See also *Williams v. Toronto (City)*, 2016 ONSC 42, aff'd 2016 ONCA 666 in which the defendant failed to send required notices to the plaintiffs.

See also *Lakefield (Village) v. Black* (1998), 41 O.R. (3d) 741 (C.A.); *NBD Bank, Canada v. Dofasco Inc.* (1999), 46 O.R. (3d) 514 (C.A.); *Toronto-Dominion Bank v. Forsythe* (2000), 47 O.R. (3d) 321 (C.A.); *Apex Mountain Resort Ltd. v. British Columbia* (2001), 6 C.C.L.T. (3d) 157 (B.C.C.A.); *Hembruff v. Ontario (Municipal Employees Retirement Board)* (2005), 78 O.R. (3d) 561 (C.A.); *Cold River Resources LLC v. 1279514 Ontario Inc.* (2009), 49 B.L.R. (4th) 144 (Ont. S.C.J.), aff'd (2010), 70 B.L.R. (4th) 67 (Ont. C.A.); and *Manufacturers Life Insurance Co. v. Pitblado & Hoskin* (2009), 245 Man. R. (2d) 111 (C.A.). For a discussion of the decision in *Hercules*, see Deturbide, "Liability of Auditors — *Hercules Managements Ltd. et al. v. Ernst and Young et al.*" (1998) 77 Can. Bar Rev. 260.

9. In the wake of high-profile corporate and accounting scandals such as those involving Enron, WorldCom and Nortel, the issue of auditor liability has become a very important tort law topic. See for example Khoury, "The Liability of Auditors beyond Their Clients: A Comparative Study" (2001) 46 McGill L.J. 413; Hession, "Auditor Independence and Liability in Canada: Are We Ready for Third Party Liability?" (2003) 36 U.B.C.L. Rev. 575; Trakman & Trainor, "The Rights and Responsibilities of Auditors to Third Parties: A Call for a Principled Approach" (2005) 31 Queen's L. Rev. 148; and Black, Marques & Burnett, "Dragons & Arrows: *Arrowhead* and Limiting Professional Liability to Third Parties" (2013) 53 C.B.L.J. 430.
Livent is an excellent example of auditor liability in the context of a large-scale corporate fraud. See also, under the law of Quebec, *Widdrington Estate v. Wightman*, 2013 QCCA 1187.

10. In *Premakumaran v. Canada* (2006), 270 D.L.R. (4th) 440 (F.C.A.) the plaintiff alleged that the government had negligently misrepresented to potential immigrants the extent to which accountants could get work in Canada. The plaintiff had come to Canada but had been unable to find work as an accountant. On a motion by the defendant for summary judgment, the court dismissed the claim. It held that there was no special relationship of proximity or reliance between the parties, and that the information provided by the government was "merely general material" for potential immigrants to consider. The court also held that it was far from clear that the statements were negligent or that the plaintiff had actually relied on them.

11. In *Baldwin v. Daubney* (2006), 83 O.R. (3d) 308 (C.A.) the plaintiffs wanted to supplement their income but had limited financial resources. They consulted financial advisors, who referred them to a program which allowed them to borrow money to use for investments. The investments decreased significantly in value and the plaintiffs sued both the advisors and the lenders that had loaned them the money. The plaintiffs argued that the providing of the loans was a direct cause of their financial losses. However, the court held that they had no claim against the lenders. The lenders had not provided any advice, only the money. Further, there was no basis for finding a special relationship between the plaintiffs and the lenders.

12. One of the issues *Livent* considers is the intended audience for a statement. This issue arose in *B. Cusano Contracting Inc. v. Bank of Montreal* (2006), 49 B.C.L.R. (4th) 301 (C.A.). The defendant bank provided a representation to a bonding company as to the financial situation of a developer. A contractor relied on the fact that this representation had been provided and contracted with the developer. The

developer ended up unable to pay the contractor more than $1 million and the contractor sued the bank for negligent misrepresentation. The court held the representation was made to the bonding company and was not intended for the contractor. It noted that "No request for an assurance was made directly or indirectly by or on behalf of the [contractor]. The bank officer understood the information was to be used by the bonding company to determine whether to issue a bond and had no reason to believe the [contractor] would receive a copy of the representation or hear about its contents from anyone."

Similarly, in *Scullion v. Bank of Scotland plc (trading as Colleys)*, [2011] EWCA Civ 693 the defendant prepared a property valuation report for a mortgagee. The prospective mortgagor alleged that he relied on the report in deciding to purchase the property. The court emphasized that the mortgagor was buying the property with the intention to rent it as an investment rather than to live in it, and held that the defendant did not owe a duty of care to the mortgagor. The court noted that in the circumstances the reasonable expectation was that the mortgagor would obtain his own valuation.

13. The same set of facts could be analyzed as involving a negligent misrepresentation, the negligent performance of a service, or a more novel way of causing pure economic loss. As a result, it is not always easy to categorize a case. When you read the next chapter, consider how *Haskett v. Equifax Canada Inc.* (2003), 63 O.R. (3d) 577 (C.A.) and *Lowe v. Guarantee Co. of North America* (2005), 80 O.R. (3d) 222 (C.A.) might be analyzed as negligent misrepresentation cases. See also *Baldwin v. Daubney, supra*.

14. Historically it has been difficult for purchasers of publicly-traded securities to sue officers, directors, auditors or others connected to the corporate issuer in negligent misrepresentation for statements made about the corporation. Such statements are often not made directly to specific purchasers or for the purpose of inducing a purchase. Moreover, purchasers often cannot establish reliance, chiefly because they were not even aware of the statement. Some provinces have enacted legislation that makes it easier for purchasers of such securities to bring misrepresentation-based claims. See for example *Securities Act*, R.S.O. 1990, c. S.5, s. 138.3; and *Securities Act*, R.S.B.C. 1996, c. 418, Part 16.1. These statutory claims are typically pursued as class actions: see for example *Silver v. IMAX Corp.*, 2011 ONSC 1035 (Div. Ct.); and *Canadian Imperial Bank of Commerce v. Green*, 2015 SCC 60.

R. v. IMPERIAL TOBACCO CANADA LTD.
2011 SCC 42

[British Columbia sued the defendant tobacco company to recover costs of providing medical treatment to people with tobacco-related illnesses. A class action was also brought against the defendant on behalf of people who had purchased "light" or "mild" cigarettes. The defendant in turn claimed against the federal government for, *inter alia*, negligent misrepresentation. It claimed that Canada had represented that light or mild cigarettes were less harmful. Canada brought a motion to have that claim struck out.]

The judgment of the Court was delivered by THE CHIEF JUSTICE —

. . .

[37] The first question is whether the facts as pleaded bring Canada's relationships with consumers and the tobacco companies within a settled category that gives rise to a duty of care. If they do, a *prima facie* duty of care will be established: see *Childs v. Desormeaux*, 2006 SCC 18 (CanLII), [2006] 1 S.C.R. 643, at para. 15. However, it is important to note that liability for negligent misrepresentation depends on the nature of the relationship between the plaintiff and defendant, as discussed more fully below. The question is not whether negligent misrepresentation is a recognized tort, but whether there is a reasonable prospect that the relationship alleged in the pleadings will give rise to liability for negligent misrepresentation.

[38] In my view, the facts pleaded do not bring either claim within a settled category of negligent misrepresentation. The law of negligent misrepresentation has thus far not recognized liability in the kinds of relationships at issue in these cases. The error of the tobacco companies lies in assuming that the relationships disclosed by the pleadings between Canada and the tobacco companies on the one hand and between Canada and consumers on the other are like other relationships that have been held to give rise to liability for negligent misrepresentation. In fact, they differ in important ways. It is sufficient at this point to note that the tobacco companies have not been able to point to any case where a government has been held liable in negligent misrepresentation for statements made to an industry. To determine whether such a cause of action has a reasonable prospect of success, we must therefore consider whether the general requirements for liability in tort are met, on the test set out by the House of Lords in *Anns v. Merton London Borough Council*, [1978] A.C. 728, and somewhat reformulated but consistently applied by this Court, most notably in *Cooper v. Hobart*, 2001 SCC 79 (CanLII), [2001] 3 S.C.R. 537.

[39] At the first stage of this test, the question is whether the facts disclose a relationship of proximity in which failure to take reasonable care might foreseeably cause loss or harm to the plaintiff. If this is established, a *prima facie* duty of care arises and the analysis proceeds to the second stage, which asks whether there are policy reasons why this *prima facie* duty of care should not be recognized: *Hill v. Hamilton-Wentworth Regional Police Services Board*, 2007 SCC 41 (CanLII), [2007] 3 S.C.R. 129.

. . .

[42] Proximity and foreseeability are heightened concerns in claims for economic loss, such as negligent misrepresentation: see, generally, *Canadian National Railway Co. v. Norsk Pacific Steamship Co.*, 1992 CanLII 105 (SCC), [1992] 1 S.C.R. 1021; *Bow Valley Husky (Bermuda) Ltd. v. Saint John Shipbuilding Ltd.*, 1997 CanLII 307 (SCC), [1997] 3 S.C.R. 1210. In a claim of negligent misrepresentation, both these requirements for a *prima facie* duty of care are established if there was a "special relationship" between the parties: *Hercules Managements Ltd. v. Ernst & Young*, 1997 CanLII 345 (SCC), [1997] 2 S.C.R. 165, at para. 24. In *Hercules Managements*, the Court, *per* La Forest J., held that a special relationship will be established where: (1) the defendant ought reasonably to foresee that the plaintiff will rely on his or her representation; and (2) reliance by the plaintiff would be reasonable in the circumstances of the case (*ibid.*). Where such a relationship is established, the defendant may be liable for losses suffered by the plaintiff as a result of a negligent misstatement.

[43] A complicating factor is the role that legislation should play when determining if a government actor owed a *prima facie* duty of care. Two situations

may be distinguished. The first is the situation where the alleged duty of care is said to arise explicitly or by implication from the statutory scheme. The second is the situation where the duty of care is alleged to arise from interactions between the claimant and the government, and is not negated by the statute.

[44] The argument in the first kind of case is that the statute itself creates a private relationship of proximity giving rise to a *prima facie* duty of care. It may be difficult to find that a statute creates sufficient proximity to give rise to a duty of care. Some statutes may impose duties on state actors with respect to particular claimants. However, more often, statutes are aimed at public goods, like regulating an industry (*Cooper*), or removing children from harmful environments (*Syl Apps*). In such cases, it may be difficult to infer that the legislature intended to create private law tort duties to claimants. This may be even more difficult if the recognition of a private law duty would conflict with the public authority's duty to the public: see, e.g., *Cooper* and *Syl Apps*. As stated in *Syl Apps*, "[w]here an alleged duty of care is found to conflict with an overarching statutory or public duty, this may constitute a compelling policy reason for refusing to find proximity" (at para. 28; see also *Fullowka v. Royal Oak Ventures Inc.*, 2010 SCC 5, [2010] 1 S.C.R. 132 (S.C.C.), at para. 39).

[45] The second situation is where the proximity essential to the private duty of care is alleged to arise from a series of specific interactions between the government and the claimant. The argument in these cases is that the government has, through its conduct, entered into a special relationship with the plaintiff sufficient to establish the necessary proximity for a duty of care. In these cases, the governing statutes are still relevant to the analysis. For instance, if a finding of proximity would conflict with the state's general public duty established by the statute, the court may hold that no proximity arises: *Syl Apps*; see also *Heaslip Estate v. Mansfield Ski Club Inc.*, 2009 ONCA 594 (CanLII), 2009 ONCA 594, 96 O.R. (3d) 401. However, the factor that gives rise to a duty of care in these types of cases is the specific interactions between the government actor and the claimant.

[46] Finally, it is possible to envision a claim where proximity is based both on interactions between the parties and the government's statutory duties.

[47] Since this is a motion to strike, the question before us is simply whether, assuming the facts pleaded to be true, there is any reasonable prospect of successfully establishing proximity, on the basis of a statute or otherwise. On one hand, where the sole basis asserted for proximity is the statute, conflicting public duties may rule out any possibility of proximity being established as a matter of statutory interpretation: *Syl Apps*. On the other, where the asserted basis for proximity is grounded in specific conduct and interactions, ruling a claim out at the proximity stage may be difficult. So long as there is a reasonable prospect that the asserted interactions could, if true, result in a finding of sufficient proximity, and the statute does not exclude that possibility, the matter must be allowed to proceed to trial, subject to any policy considerations that may negate the *prima facie* duty of care at the second stage of the analysis.

[48] As mentioned above, there are two relationships at issue in these claims: the relationship between Canada and consumers (the *Knight* case), and the relationship between Canada and tobacco companies (both cases). The question at this stage is whether there is a *prima facie* duty of care in either or both these relationships. In my view, on the facts pleaded, Canada did not owe a *prima facie* duty of care to consumers, but did owe a *prima facie* duty to the tobacco companies.

[49] The facts pleaded in Imperial's third-party notice in the *Knight* case establish no direct relationship between Canada and the consumers of light cigarettes. The relationship between the two was limited to Canada's statements to the general public that low-tar cigarettes are less hazardous. There were no specific interactions between Canada and the class members. Consequently, a finding of proximity in this relationship must arise from the governing statutes: *Cooper*, at para. 43.

[50] The relevant statutes establish only general duties to the public, and no private law duties to consumers. The *Department of Health Act*, S.C. 1996, c. 8, establishes that the duties of the Minister of Health relate to "the promotion and preservation of the health of the people of Canada": s. 4(1). Similarly, the *Department of Agriculture and Agri-Food Act*, R.S.C. 1985, c. A-9, s. 4, the *Tobacco Act*, S.C. 1997, c. 13, s. 4, and the *Tobacco Products Control Act*, R.S.C. 1985, c. 14 (4th Supp.), s. 3 [rep. 1997, c. 13, s. 64], only establish duties to the general public. These general duties to the public do not give rise to a private law duty of care to particular individuals. To borrow the words of Sharpe J.A. of the Ontario Court of Appeal in *Eliopoulos Estate v. Ontario (Minister of Health and Long-Term Care)* 2006 CanLII 37121 (ON CA), (2006), 276 D.L.R. (4th) 411, "I fail to see how it could be possible to convert any of the Minister's public law discretionary powers, to be exercised in the general public interest, into private law duties owed to specific individuals": para. 17. At the same time, the governing statutes do not foreclose the possibility of recognizing a duty of care to the tobacco companies. Recognizing a duty of care on the government when it makes representations to the tobacco companies about the health attributes of tobacco strains would not conflict with its general duty to protect the health of the public.

[51] Turning to the relationship between Canada and the tobacco companies, at issue in both of the cases before the Court, the tobacco companies contend that a duty of care on Canada arose from the transactions between them and Canada over the years. They allege that Canada went beyond its role as regulator of industry players and entered into a relationship of advising and assisting the companies in reducing harm to their consumers. They hope to show that Canada gave erroneous information and advice, knowing that the companies would rely on it, which they did.

[52] The question is whether these pleadings bring the tobacco companies within the requirements for a special relationship under the law of negligent misrepresentation as set out in *Hercules Managements*. As noted above, a special relationship will be established where (1) the defendant ought reasonably to foresee that the plaintiff will rely on his or her representation, and (2) such reliance would, in the particular circumstances of the case, be reasonable. In the cases at bar, the facts pleaded allege a history of interactions between Canada and the tobacco companies capable of fulfilling these conditions.

[53] What is alleged against Canada is that Health Canada assumed duties separate and apart from its governing statute, including research into and design of tobacco and tobacco products and the promotion of tobacco and tobacco products (third-party statement of claim of Imperial in the *Costs Recovery* case, A.R., vol. II, at p. 66). In addition, it is alleged that Agriculture Canada carried out a programme of cooperation with and support for tobacco growers and cigarette manufacturers including advising cigarette manufacturers of the desirable content of nicotine in tobacco to be used in the manufacture of tobacco products. It is alleged that officials, drawing on their knowledge and expertise in smoking and health matters, provided

both advice and directions to the manufacturers including advice that the tobacco strains designed and developed by officials of Agriculture Canada and sold or licensed to the manufacturers for use in their tobacco products would not increase health risks to consumers or otherwise be harmful to them (*ibid.*, at pp. 109-10). Thus, what is alleged is not simply that broad powers of regulation were brought to bear on the tobacco industry, but that Canada assumed the role of adviser to a finite number of manufacturers and that there were commercial relationships entered into between Canada and the companies based in part on the advice given to the companies by government officials.

[54] What is alleged with respect to Canada's interactions with the manufacturers goes far beyond the sort of statements made by Canada to the public at large. Canada is alleged to have had specific interactions with the manufacturers in contrast to the absence of such specific interactions between Canada and the class members. Whereas the claims in relation to consumers must be founded on a statutory framework establishing very general duties to the public, the claims alleged in relation to the manufacturers are not alleged to arise primarily from such general regulatory duties and powers but from roles undertaken specifically in relation to the manufacturers by Canada apart from its statutory duties, namely its roles as designer, developer, promoter and licensor of tobacco strains. With respect to the issue of reasonable reliance, Canada's regulatory powers over the manufacturers, coupled with its specific advice and its commercial involvement, could be seen as supporting a conclusion that reliance was reasonable in the pleaded circumstance.

[55] The indicia of proximity offered in *Hercules Managements* for a special relationship (direct financial interest; professional skill or knowledge; advice provided in the course of business, deliberately or in response to a specific request) may not be particularly apt in the context of alleged negligent misrepresentations by government. I note, however, that the representations are alleged to have been made in the course of Health Canada's regulatory and other activities, not in the course of casual interaction. They were made specifically to the manufacturers who were subject to Health Canada's regulatory powers and by officials alleged to have special skill, judgment and knowledge.

[56] Before leaving this issue, two final arguments must be considered. First, in the *Costs Recovery* case, Canada submits that there is no *prima facie* duty of care between Canada and the tobacco companies because the potential damages that the tobacco companies may incur under the *CRA* were not foreseeable. It argues that "[i]t was not reasonably foreseeable by Canada that a provincial government might create a wholly new type of civil obligation to reimburse costs incurred by a provincial health care scheme in respect of defined tobacco related wrongs, with unlimited retroactive and prospective reach" (A.F., at para. 36).

[57] In my view, Canada's argument was correctly rejected by the majority of the Court of Appeal. It is not necessary that Canada should have foreseen the precise statutory vehicle that would result in the tobacco companies' liability. All that is required is that it could have foreseen that its negligent misrepresentations would result in a harm of some sort to the tobacco companies: *Hercules Managements*, at paras. 25-26 and 42. On the facts pleaded, it cannot be ruled out that the tobacco companies may succeed in proving that Canada foresaw that the tobacco industry would incur this type of penalty for selling a more hazardous product. As held by Tysoe J.A., it is not necessary that Canada foresee that the liability would extend to

health care costs specifically, or that provinces would create statutory causes of action to recover these costs. Rather, "[i]t is sufficient that Canada could have reasonably foreseen in a general way that the appellants would suffer harm if the light and mild cigarettes were more hazardous to the health of smokers than regular cigarettes" (*Costs Recovery* case, at para. 78).

[58] Second, Canada argues that the relationship in this case does not meet the requirement of reasonable reliance because Canada was not acting in a commercial capacity, but rather as a regulator of an industry. It was therefore not reasonable for the tobacco companies to have relied on Canada as an advisor, it submits. This view was adopted by Hall J.A. in dissent, holding that "it could never have been the perception of the appellants that Canada was taking responsibility for their interests" (*Costs Recovery* case, at para. 51).

[59] In my view, this argument misconceives the reliance necessary for negligent misrepresentation under the test in *Hercules Managements*. When the jurisprudence refers to "reasonable reliance" in the context of negligent misrepresentation, it asks whether it was reasonable for the listener to rely on the speaker's statement as accurate, not whether it was reasonable to believe that the speaker is guaranteeing the accuracy of its statement. It is not plain and obvious that it was unreasonable for the tobacco companies to rely on Canada's statements about the advantages of light or mild cigarettes. In my view, Canada's argument that it was acting as a regulator does not relate to reasonable reliance, although it exposes policy concerns that should be considered at stage two of the *Anns/Cooper* test: *Hercules Managements*, at para. 41.

. . .

[97] Canada submits that allowing the defendants' claims in negligent misrepresentation would result in indeterminate liability, and must therefore be rejected. It submits that Canada had no control over the number of cigarettes being sold. It argues that in cases of economic loss, the courts must limit liability to cases where the third party had a means of controlling the extent of liability.

[98] The tobacco companies respond that Canada faces extensive, but not indeterminate liability. They submit that the scope of Canada's liability to tobacco companies is circumscribed by the tort of negligent misrepresentation. Canada would only be liable to the smokers of light cigarettes and to the tobacco companies.

[99] I agree with Canada that the prospect of indeterminate liability is fatal to the tobacco companies' claims of negligent misrepresentation. Insofar as the claims are based on representations to consumers, Canada had no control over the number of people who smoked light cigarettes. This situation is analogous to *Cooper*, where this Court held that it would have declined to apply a duty of care to the Registrar of Mortgage Brokers in respect of economic losses suffered by investors because "[t]he Act itself imposes no limit and the Registrar has no means of controlling the number of investors or the amount of money invested in the mortgage brokerage system" (para. 54). While this statement was made in *obiter*, the argument is persuasive.

[100] The risk of indeterminate liability is enhanced by the fact that the claims are for pure economic loss. In *Design Services Ltd. v. Canada*, 2008 SCC 22 (CanLII), 2008 SCC 22, [2008] 1 S.C.R. 737, the Court, *per* Rothstein J., held that "in cases of pure economic loss, to paraphrase Cardozo C.J., care must be taken to find that a duty is recognized only in cases where the class of plaintiffs, the time and the amounts are determinate" (para. 62). If Canada owed a duty of care to consumers of light

cigarettes, the potential class of plaintiffs and the amount of liability would be indeterminate.

[101] Insofar as the claims are based on representations to the tobacco companies, they are at first blush more circumscribed. However, this distinction breaks down on analysis. Recognizing a duty of care for representations to the tobacco companies would effectively amount to a duty to consumers, since the quantum of damages owed to the companies in both cases would depend on the number of smokers and the number of cigarettes sold. This is a flow-through claim of negligent misrepresentation, where the tobacco companies are passing along their potential liability to consumers and to the province of British Columbia. In my view, in both cases, these claims should fail because Canada was not in control of the extent of its potential liability.

NOTES AND QUESTIONS

1. What are the key similarities and differences in the analysis of negligent misrepresentation between *Imperial Tobacco* and the subsequent decision in *Livent* (which refers only once to *Imperial Tobacco*, simply to cite it). What is a "settled category" of negligent misrepresentation, referred to in *Imperial Tobacco*? How does this concept affect the analysis? See Klar, "*R. v. Imperial Tobacco Ltd.*: More Restrictions on Public Authority Tort Liability" (2012) 50 Alta. L. Rev. 157 at 159 and 162.

2. How does the court's discussion of the role of statutes compare with that in *Cooper* (in Chapter 10), *Saskatchewan Wheat Pool* (in Chapter 22) and in the cases in Chapter 21 on the liability of public authorities? See also *Rain Coast Water Corp. v. British Columbia*, 2016 BCSC 845.

3. Why did the court find that Canada had a proximate relationship with tobacco manufacturers but not with tobacco consumers?

4. Do you agree with the court's conclusion on indeterminate liability?

5. There has been debate about whether indeterminate liability should be treated as an overriding policy consideration that can negate a *prima facie* duty of care or should instead be considered as part of the analysis of foreseeability, proximity and reasonable reliance. For the latter view see Brown, *Pure Economic Loss in Canadian Negligence Law* (2011) at 303-07. See also Klar, *supra*, at 169. What approach is adopted in *Imperial Tobacco*? What approach is adopted in *Livent*?

6. The court also held that the *prima facie* duty of care was negated because the statements by Canada were protected expressions of government policy. See the extract of the court's analysis, and discussion of the policy-operational distinction more generally, in Chapter 21.

3. Negligent Misrepresentation and Contract

The rules governing liability for negligent misrepresentations are further complicated if the statement arises in a contractual context. Contract is the primary means by which parties allocate benefits, burdens and risks among themselves. For that reason, there traditionally was strong support for the view that if the parties' relationship was governed by contract, tort law should have little, if any, role to play.

This raises the question of *concurrent liability*: can the defendant incur liability in both contract and tort on the basis of the same event? The answer to that question often has considerable practical significance. While there is no possibility of double recovery, the plaintiff may see some advantage to suing in tort rather than contract. For example, the scope of recoverable damages might be larger in tort than in contract.

Assuming that concurrent liability is possible, it becomes necessary to determine the extent to which the terms of a contract may nevertheless oust or negate a duty of care that would otherwise arise in negligence.

The interplay of contract and tort also raises the question of whether negligence principles should be allowed to operate with respect to the period of negotiation that precedes the formation of a contract. This issue can be further subdivided. This chapter concludes with an examination of *Queen v. Cognos Inc.* (1993), 99 D.L.R. (4th) 626 (S.C.C.) in which the Supreme Court of Canada addressed the existence of a duty of care to avoid negligent misrepresentations during pre-contractual negotiations. The next chapter opens with an examination of *Martel Building Ltd. v. Canada* (2000), 193 D.L.R. (4th) 1 (S.C.C.) in which the Supreme Court of Canada addressed several other issues, including the existence of a duty of care to otherwise conduct pre-contractual negotiations in such a way as to avoid inflicting pure economic loss.

(a) CONCURRENT LIABILITY IN TORT AND CONTRACT

BG CHECO INTERNATIONAL LTD. v. B.C. HYDRO & POWER AUTHORITY
(1993), 99 D.L.R. (4th) 577 (S.C.C.)

[Hydro called for tenders for a contract to erect transmission towers and string transmission lines. Checo had a representative inspect the area by helicopter before it submitted a tender. The representative noted that a right-of-way had been partially cleared and also noted evidence of ongoing clearing activity. He assumed that there would be more clearing prior to the commencement of Checo's work. Hydro accepted Checo's tender and the parties entered into a written contract. The tender documents, which were subsequently incorporated into the contract, stated that clearing of the right-of-way would be done by others and formed no part of the work to be performed by Checo. They also stated that it was Checo's responsibility to inform itself of all aspects of the work and that, should any errors appear in the tender documents, or should Checo note any conditions conflicting with the letter or spirit of the tender documents, it was Checo's responsibility to obtain clarification before submitting its tender. The tender documents also provided that Checo would satisfy itself as to all site conditions and the correctness and sufficiency of the tender for the work and the stipulated prices. In fact, no additional clearing of the right-of-way ever took place and the inadequate clearing caused Checo difficulties in completing its work.

Checo sued Hydro for negligent misrepresentation and breach of contract. The evidence at trial indicated that Hydro had contracted the clearing of the right-of-way to another company, and that, to Hydro's knowledge, the work was not done adequately. There was no direct discussion between the representatives of Checo and Hydro concerning this issue. During the trial, Checo amended its statement of claim to include a claim based on fraud. The trial judge found that Hydro had acted fraudulently in its dealings with Checo and awarded damages representing "the total loss suffered by [Checo] as a result of being fraudulently induced to enter into this contract." Hydro appealed to the British Columbia Court of Appeal, which rejected the finding of fraud but found that there had been a negligent misrepresentation which induced Checo to enter into the contract. The Court of Appeal awarded damages for the misrepresentation but reduced the trial judge's damage award and referred the question of breach of contract back to the trial court. Hydro appealed, and Checo cross-appealed, to the Supreme Court of Canada.]

IACOBUCCI J. (dissenting in part) (SOPINKA J. concurring):—The narrow question raised by this appeal is what remedy should be available for pre-contractual representations made during the tendering process. This question also raises a more general and more important issue. . . [C]an a plaintiff who is in a contractual relationship with the defendant sue the defendant in tort if the duty relied upon by the plaintiff in tort is also made a contractual duty by an express term of the contract?

. . .

As a general rule, the existence of a contract between two parties does not preclude the existence of a common law duty of care. Subject to the substantive and procedural differences that exist between an action in contract and an action in tort, both the duty of care and the liability may be concurrent in contract and tort. In such circumstances, it is for the plaintiff to select the cause of action most advantageous to him or her. That was the position adopted by Le Dain J. in *Central & Eastern Trust v. Rafuse* [(1986), 31 D.L.R. (4th) 481 (S.C.C.)].

. . .

In my opinion, the [rule formulated] by Le Dain J. is an appropriate one. If the parties to a contract choose to define a specific duty as an express term of the contract, then the consequences of a breach of that duty ought to be determined by the law of contract, not by tort law. Whether or not an implied term of a contract can define a duty of care in such a way that a plaintiff is confined to a remedy in contract is not at issue in this case. I leave that determination to another day. While the rule articulated by Le Dain J. is a rule of law which does not depend on the presumed or actual intention of the parties, the intention which can be inferred from the fact that the parties have made the duty an express term of the contract provides policy support for the rule. If a duty is an express term of the contract, it can be inferred that the parties wish the law of the contract to govern with respect to that duty. This is of particular significance given that the result of a breach of a contractual duty may be different from that of a breach of a duty in tort. As Wilson J.A. noted in *Dominion Chain Co.* [v. *Eastern Construction Co.* (1976), 68 D.L.R. (3d) 385 (Ont. C.A.)] a plaintiff's substantive rights may be different in contract and in tort (at p. 409):

> His cause of action may arise later in tort resulting in a later expiry of the limitation period. His damage may be greater in quantum and different in kind if he sues in tort. On the other hand his action in contract may survive him or be the subject of a set-off or counterclaim, neither of which would be so if his action were framed in tort.

The fact that damages may be assessed differently in contract from in tort was recently affirmed by this Court in *Rainbow Industrial Caterers Ltd. v. Canadian National Railway Co.*, [1991] 3 S.C.R. 3.

A further policy rationale for the rule advanced by Le Dain J. is that contracts have become, particularly in commercial contexts, increasingly complex. Commercial contracts allocate risks and fix the mutual duties and obligations of the parties. Where there is an express term creating a contractual duty, it is appropriate that the parties be held to the bargain which they have made.

. . .

However, I do not believe that the rule advanced by Le Dain J. that forecloses a claim in tort is absolute in all circumstances. In this respect, I would favour a contextual approach which takes into account the context in which the contract is made, and the position of the parties with respect to one another, in assessing whether a claim in tort is foreclosed by the terms of a contract. The policy reasons in favour of the rule advanced by Le Dain J. are strongest where the contractual context is commercial and the parties are of equal bargaining power. There was no question of unconscionability or inequality of bargaining power in *Central & Eastern Trust v. Rafuse, supra*, as there is no such question in this case. If such issues, or others analogous to them, were to arise, however, a court should be wary not to exclude too rapidly a duty of care in tort on the basis of an express term of the contract, especially if the end result for the plaintiff would be a wrong without a remedy.

. . .

LA FOREST and MCLACHLIN JJ. (L'HEUREUX-DUBÉ and GONTHIER JJ. concurring): — We have had the advantage of reading the reasons of our colleague Justice Iacobucci. We agree with his conclusion that Hydro is liable to Checo for breach of contract. We disagree, however, with his conclusion that the contract precludes Checo from suing in tort. In our view, our colleague's approach would have the effect of eliminating much of the rationalizing thrust behind the movement towards concurrency in tort and contract. Rather than attempting to establish new barriers in tort liability in contractual contexts, the law should move towards the elimination of unjustified differences between the remedial rules applicable to the two actions, thereby reducing the significance of the existence of the two different forms of action and allowing a person who has suffered a wrong full access to all relevant legal remedies.

. . .

[Having concluded that Hydro was liable to Checo for breach of contract, the court went on to discuss the claim in tort.]

The Claim in Tort

The Theory of Concurrency

The first question is whether the contract precludes Checo from suing in tort.

Iacobucci J. concludes that a contract between the parties may preclude the possibility of suing in tort for a given wrong where there is an express term in the contract dealing with the matter. We would phrase the applicable principle somewhat more narrowly. As we see it, the right to sue in tort is not taken away by the contract in such a case, although the contract, by limiting the scope of the tort duty or waiving the right to sue in tort, may limit or negate tort liability.

In our view, the general rule emerging from this Court's decision in *Central & Eastern Trust v. Rafuse*, [1986] 2 S.C.R. 147, is that where a given wrong prima facie supports an action in contract and in tort, the party may sue in either or both, except where the contract indicates that the parties intended to limit or negative the right to sue in tort. This limitation on the general rule of concurrency arises because it is always open to parties to limit or waive the duties which the common law would impose on them for negligence. This principle is of great importance in preserving a sphere of individual liberty and commercial flexibility. Thus if a person wishes to engage in a dangerous sport, the person may stipulate in advance that he or she waives any right of action against the person who operates the sport facility: *Dyck v. Manitoba Snowmobile Assn. Inc.*, [1985] 1 S.C.R. 589. Similarly, if two business firms agree that a particular risk should lie on a party who would not ordinarily bear that risk at common law they may do so. So a plaintiff may sue either in contract or tort, subject to any limit the parties themselves have placed on that right by their contract. The mere fact that the parties have dealt with a matter expressly in their contract does not mean that they intended to exclude the right to sue in tort. It all depends on *how* they have dealt with it.

Viewed thus, the only limit on the right to choose one's action is the principle of primacy of private ordering — the right of individuals to arrange their affairs and assume risks in a different way than would be done by the law of tort. It is only to the extent that this private ordering contradicts the tort duty that the tort duty is diminished. The rule is not that one cannot sue concurrently in contract and tort where the contract limits or contradicts the tort duty. It is rather that the tort duty, a general duty imputed by the law in all the relevant circumstances, must yield to the parties' superior right to arrange their rights and duties in a different way. In so far as the tort duty is not contradicted by the contract, it remains intact and may be sued upon. For example, where the contractual limitation on the tort duty is partial, a tort action founded on the modified duty might lie. The tort duty as modified by the contractual agreement between the parties might be raised in a case where the limitation period for an action for breach of contract has expired but the limitation period for a tort action has not. If one says categorically, as we understand Iacobucci J. to say, that where the contract deals with a matter expressly, the right to sue in tort vanishes altogether, then the latter two possibilities vanish.

This is illustrated by consideration of the three situations that may arise when contract and tort are applied to the same wrong. The first class of case arises where the contract stipulates a more stringent obligation than the general law of tort would impose. In that case, the parties are hardly likely to sue in tort, since they could not recover in tort for the higher contractual duty. The vast majority of commercial transactions fall into this class. The right to sue in tort is not extinguished, however, and may remain important, as where suit in contract is barred by expiry of a limitation period.

The second class of case arises where the contract stipulates a lower duty than that which would be presumed by the law of tort in similar circumstances. This occurs when the parties by their contract indicate their intention that the usual liability imposed by the law of tort is not to bind them. The most common means by which such an intention is indicated is the inclusion of a clause of exemption or exclusion of liability in the contract. Generally, the duty imposed by the law of tort can be nullified only by clear terms. We do not rule out, however, the possibility that cases may arise in which merely inconsistent contract terms could negative or limit a duty in tort, an issue that may be left to a case in which it arises. The issue raises difficult policy considerations, viz., an assessment of the circumstances in which contracting parties should be permitted to agree to contractual duties that would subtract from their general obligations under the law of tort. These important questions are best left to a case in which the proper factual foundation is available, so as to provide an appropriate context for the decision. In the second class of case, as in the first, there is usually little point in suing in tort since the duty in tort and consequently any tort liability is limited by the specific limitation to which the parties have agreed. An exception might arise where the contract does not entirely negate tort liability (e.g., the exemption clause applies only above a certain amount) and the plaintiff wishes to sue in tort to avail itself of a more generous limitation period or some other procedural advantage offered by tort.

The third class of case arises where the duty in contract and the common law duty in tort are co-extensive. In this class of case, like the others, the plaintiff may seek to sue concurrently or alternatively in tort to secure some advantage peculiar to the law of tort, such as a more generous limitation period. The contract may expressly provide for a duty that is the same as that imposed by the common law. Or the contractual duty may be implied. The common calling cases, which have long permitted concurrent actions in contract and tort, generally fall into this class. There is a contract. But the obligation under that contract is typically defined by implied terms, i.e., by the courts. Thus there is no issue of private ordering as opposed to publicly imposed liability. Whether the action is styled in contract or tort, its source is an objective expectation, defined by the courts, of the appropriate obligation and the correlative right.

The case at bar, as we see it, falls into this third category of case. The contract, read as we have proposed, did not negate Hydro's common law duty not to negligently misrepresent that it would have the right-of-way cleared by others. Had Checo known the truth, it would have bid for a higher amount. That duty is not excluded by the contract, which confirmed Hydro's obligation to clear the right-of-way. Accordingly, Checo may sue in tort.

We conclude that actions in contract and tort may be concurrently pursued unless the parties by a valid contractual provision indicate that they intended otherwise. This excludes, of course, cases where the contractual limitation is invalid, as by fraud, mistake or unconscionability. Similarly, a contractual limitation may not apply where the tort is independent of the contract in the sense of falling outside the scope of the contract, as the example given in *Elder, Dempster & Co. v. Paterson, Zochonis & Co.*, [1924] A.C. 522 (H.L.), of the captain of a vessel falling asleep and starting a fire in relation to a claim for cargo damage.

The Express-Implied Distinction

Our colleague asserts that where the parties deal with a matter expressly in their contract, all right to sue in tort is lost. We have suggested, with great respect, that this proposition is unnecessarily Draconian. The converse of this proposition is that implied terms of contracts do not oust tort liability.

Although Iacobucci J. states . . . that he is leaving open the question of "Whether or not an implied term of a contract can define a duty of care in such a way that a plaintiff is confined to a remedy in contract", the distinction between implied and express terms figures in his discussion of the effect of contract terms on tort liability. For example, . . . our colleague states:

The compromise position adopted by Le Dain J. was that any duty arising in tort will be concurrent with duties arising under the contract, *unless the duty which the plaintiff seeks to rely on in tort is also a duty defined by an express term of the contract*. [The emphasis is Iacobucci J.'s.]

It would seem to follow from this statement that concurrent duties in contract and tort would lie where the contract duty is defined by an *implied* term of the contract, but not where the term is express. In these circumstances, it is not amiss to consider the utility of the distinction between express and implied terms of the contract as a basis for determining when a contract term may affect tort liability.

In our view, using the express-implied distinction as a basis for determining whether there is a right to sue in tort poses a number of problems. The law has always treated express and implied contract terms as being equivalent in effect. Breach of an implied term is just as serious as breach of an express term. Moreover, it is difficult to distinguish between them in some cases. Implied terms may arise from custom, for example, or from the conduct of the parties. In some cases words and conduct intermingle. Why should parties who were so certain in their obligations that they did not take the trouble to spell them out find themselves able to sue in tort, while parties who put the same matters in writing cannot?

Nor is it evident to us that if parties to a contract choose to include an express term in the contract dealing with a particular duty relevant to the contract, they intended to oust the availability of tort remedies in respect of that duty. In such cases, the intention may more likely be:

(a) To make it clear that the parties understand particular contractual duties to exist as between them, rather than having the more uncertain situation of not knowing whether a court will imply a particular duty under the contract; and/or
(b) To prevent litigation (for breach of contract) in the event of disputes arising — the more certain the parties' respective rights and obligations (as is usually the case when those rights and obligations are set out in express contractual terms), the more likely it will be that disputes between the parties can be settled.

While the tort duty may be limited by the contractual terms so as to be no broader than the contract duty, there is no reason to suppose that merely by stipulating a duty in the contract, the parties intended to negate all possibility of suing in tort.

Indeed, a little further on in his reasons, our colleague appears to concede that the ouster of recourse to tort law must depend on more than the fact the contract has expressly dealt with the matter. He indicates . . . that whether the parties will be held to have intended to oust tort remedies in favour of contract remedies will depend on the context, including:

(a) whether the contract is commercial or non-commercial;
(b) whether the parties were of equal bargaining power;
(c) whether the court is of the view that to find such an intention will lead to an unjust result in the court action.

Thus the question of whether a concurrent action in tort lies would depend not only on whether the contract expressly deals with the matter, but also on the elastic distinctions between commercial and non-commercial contracts, the court's perception of relative bargaining power, and finally, whether the court sees the result as just or unjust. We do not agree that parties contracting in a commercial context should be presumed to be more desirous of ousting the availability of tort remedies than parties contracting in a non-commercial context. If there are particular commercial relationships in which the parties wish remedies for disputes between them to be in contract only, then they may be expected to indicate this intention by including an express clause in the contract waiving the right to sue in tort. As for equality of bargaining power and the court's view of whether the result would be just or unjust, we fear they would introduce too great a measure of uncertainty. Parties should be able to predict in advance whether their remedies are confined to contract or whether they can sue concurrently in tort and contract. Finally, it seems to us that Iacobucci J.'s test for determining when concurrent liability is precluded will be difficult to apply in situations where the express contractual term does not exactly overlap a tort duty. In the present case, the contractual term was identical to the negligent misrepresentation, but that is not often to be expected.

. . .

Summary

We conclude that neither principle, the authorities nor the needs of contracting parties, support the conclusion that dealing with a matter by an express contract term will, in itself, categorically exclude the right to sue in tort. The parties may by their contract limit the duty one owes to the other or waive the right to sue in tort. But subject to this, the right to sue concurrently in tort and contract remains.

In the case at bar, the contract did not limit the duty of care owed by Hydro to Checo. Nor did Checo waive its common law right to bring such tort actions as might be open to it. It follows that Checo was entitled to claim against Hydro in tort.

NOTES AND QUESTIONS

1. What is meant by the term "concurrency"? Why was it relevant in *BG Checo*?

2. On what point did Iacobucci and Sopinka JJ. dissent from the majority? What policy considerations divided the court? Whose reasoning is the most persuasive?

3. In contract law, an innocent misrepresentation that induces a contract may support rescission but not damages. Alternatively, the court might view the misrepresentation as the basis of a collateral contract, holding that the plaintiff entered into the main contract in return for the promise in the misrepresentation: see *Shanklin Pier Ltd. v. Detel Products Ltd.*, [1951] 2 K.B. 854. Finally, the court may hold that a misrepresentation which induces a contract is a term of the contract: see *Mendelssohn v. Normand Ltd.*, [1970] 1 Q.B. 177 (C.A.); and *Esso Petroleum Co. v. Mardon*, [1976] 2 All E.R. 5 (C.A.).

4. Concurrent liability in negligent misrepresentation and contract was recognized in England in *Esso Petroleum Co. v. Mardon, supra.* However, the English courts have been more sympathetic to the contractual approach reflected in Iacobucci and Sopinka JJ.'s dissent in *BG Checo*: see for example *National Bank of Greece S.A. v. Pinios Shipping Co. (No. 1)* (1988), [1989] 1 All E.R. 213 (C.A.), rev'd on other grounds (1989), [1990] 1 A.C. 637 (H.L.); and *Pacific Associates Inc. v. Baxter*, [1989] 2 All E.R. 159 (C.A.).

5. It has become common in real estate sales for the buyer to insist that the seller complete a disclosure statement about the property. The statement is explicitly incorporated into the agreement of purchase and sale. This then can allow buyers to sue both for breach of contract and for negligent misrepresentation if the property is materially different from what was disclosed. See for example *Nixon v. MacIver*, 2016 BCCA 8; *Honing v. Phinney*, 2018 BCSC 702; and *Hamilton v. Callaway*, 2016 BCCA 189. What must be disclosed depends on the language of the statement used.

6. For an authoritative discussion of damages in tort and contract, see the majority judgment in *BG Checo*. See also *Smith v. Landstar Properties Inc.*, 2011 BCCA 44.

In cases in which the plaintiff claims in both tort and contract, should both areas of law be consistent as to what is and is not recoverable, or is it acceptable for each to reach its own independent conclusion? See the analysis in *Wellesley Partners LLP v. Withers LLP*, [2015] EWCA Civ 1146; *Agouman v. Leigh Day*, [2016] EWHC 1324 at para. 121; and Taylor, "Whither Remoteness? *Wellesley Partners LLP v Withers LLP*" (2016) 79 M.L.R. 678.

7. For commentary on *BG Checo*, see Sim, "Negligent Misrepresentation in a Pre-Contractual Setting" (1993) 15 Adv. Q. 238; and Blom, "Contract and Tort — Negligent Misstatement Inducing Contract — Concurrent Liability — Effect of Contractual Terms" (1994) 73 Can. Bar Rev. 243. See also Fleming, "Tort in a Contractual Matrix" (1995) 33 Osgoode Hall L.J. 661.

For more recent discussion of concurrency see Jackson, "Concurrent Liability: Where Have Things Gone Wrong?" (2015) 23 Tort L. Rev. 3; and Yihan & Yip, "Concurrent Liability in Tort and Contract: An Analysis of Interplay, Intersection and Independence" (2017) 24:2 Torts L.J. 148.

(b) PRE-CONTRACTUAL MISREPRESENTATIONS

QUEEN v. COGNOS INC.
(1993), 99 D.L.R. (4th) 626 (S.C.C.)

[The respondent, a computer software company based in Ottawa, advertised an accounting position. At the time, the appellant was a chartered accountant who held a well-paying and secure position with a company in Calgary. He applied for the position with the respondent and was granted an interview. During the interview, a manager of the company made several representations regarding the nature of the employment opportunity on offer. He further stated that the advertised position was associated with the "Multiview project," a major project that would be developed over a two-year period, and that the prospects for employment after that time were very positive. He did not, however, reveal that funding for the proposed two-year project had not yet been secured.

The appellant accepted the respondent's offer of a contract and moved his family from Calgary to Ottawa. Shortly after the appellant's arrival in April 1983, however, the company decided to substantially reduce the scope of the proposed project. Eighteen months later, the respondent terminated the appellant's employment. The appellant sued the company, alleging that the respondent's manager had made negligent misrepresentations during the job interview and that he had suffered economic loss as a result.]

LA FOREST J. (L'HEUREUX-DUBÉ and GONTHIER JJ. concurring) — Subject to what I said in *BG Checo International Ltd. v. British Columbia Hydro and Power Authority* . . . I agree with Justices Iacobucci and McLachlin, and would dispose of the appeal in the manner proposed by them. Though Iacobucci J. repeats the essence of his analysis in *Checo,* the present case is not one of concurrency at all. It is sufficient for me to say that the tort here was independent of the contract and the liability was not limited by an exclusion clause in the contract.

. . .

[McLachlin J. substantially agreed with Iacobucci J., subject to her position in *BG Checo*.]

IACOBUCCI J. (SOPINKA J. concurring): — . . . Some have suggested that it is inappropriate to extend the application of *Hedley Byrne, supra,* to representations made by an employer to a prospective employee in the course of an interview because it places a heavy burden on employers. As will be apparent from my reasons herein, I disagree in principle with this view.

. . .

The required elements for a successful *Hedley Byrne* claim have been stated in many authorities, sometimes in varying forms. The decisions of this court cited above suggest five general requirements: (1) there must be a duty of care based on a "special relationship" between the representor and the representee; (2) the representation in question must be untrue, inaccurate, or misleading; (3) the representor must have acted negligently in making said misrepresentation; (4) the representee must have relied, in a reasonable manner, on said negligent misrepresentation; and (5) the reliance must have been detrimental to the representee in the sense that damages resulted. In the case at bar, the trial judge found that all elements were present and allowed the appellant's claim.

In particular, [the trial judge] found, as a fact, that the respondent's representative, Mr. Johnston, had misrepresented the nature and existence of the employment opportunity for which the appellant had applied, and that the appellant had relied to his detriment on those misrepresentations. These findings of fact were undisturbed by the Court of Appeal and . . . the respondent does not challenge them before this court. Thus, the second, fourth, and fifth requirements are not in question here.

The only issues before this court deal with the duty of care owed to the appellant in the circumstances of this case and the alleged breach of this duty (*i.e.*, the alleged negligence). The respondent concedes that a "special relationship" existed between itself (through its representative) and the appellant so as to give rise to a duty of care. However, it argues that this duty is negated by a disclaimer contained in the employment contract signed by the appellant more than two weeks after the interview. Furthermore, the respondent argues that any misrepresentations made during the hiring interview were not made in a negligent manner. For reasons that follow, it is my view that both submissions fail.

However, before turning to these issues, I intend to deal with a preliminary matter not directly raised in argument. This appeal was argued before this Court in close proximity to the case *BG Checo International Ltd. v. British Columbia Hydro and Power Authority.* . . . That case involved circumstances somewhat similar to those in the present appeal in that it also dealt with a claim for damages based on an alleged negligent misrepresentation stemming from pre-contractual negotiations. Generally speaking, in *BG Checo* as in the case at bar, it was argued that certain representations made in a pre-contractual setting did not correspond with the post-agreement reality and were made in a negligent manner. In both cases, the defendants relied on the contract signed by the parties subsequent to the alleged negligent misrepresentation in order to bar the plaintiffs' claim in tort. As my conclusion in *BG Checo* is opposite from the one I take herein, I believe it is useful at the outset to explain why this case is clearly distinguishable from *BG Checo*. In doing so, my hope is to clarify some of the confusion which currently exists with respect to pre-contractual negligent misrepresentations.

B. *Preliminary observations on the effect of the employment agreement on this appeal*

There lies, in my view, [a] fundamental difference between the present appeal and *BG Checo, supra*. In the latter case, the alleged pre-contractual misrepresentation had been incorporated verbatim as an express term of the subsequent contract. As such, the common law duty of care relied on by the plaintiff in its tort action was co-extensive with a duty imposed on the defendant in contract by an express term of their agreement. Thus, it was my view that the plaintiff was barred from exercising a concurrent action in tort for the alleged breach of said duty, and this view was reinforced by the commercial context in which the transaction occurred. In the case at bar, however, there is no such concurrency. The employment agreement signed by the appellant . . . does not contain any express contractual obligation co-extensive with the duty of care the respondent is alleged to have breached. The provisions most relevant to this appeal (clauses 13 and 14) contain contractual duties clearly different from, not co-extensive with, the common law duty invoked by the appellant in his tort action.

Had the appellant's action been based on pre-contractual representations concerning the length of his involvement on the Multiview project or his "job security", as characterized by the Court of Appeal, the concurrency question might be resolved differently in light of the termination and reassignment provisions of the contract. However, it is clear that the appellant's claim was *not* that Mr. Johnston negligently misrepresented the amount of time he would be working on Multiview or the conditions under which his employment could be terminated. In other words, he did not argue that the respondent, through its representative, breached a common law duty of care by negligently misrepresenting his security of employment with Cognos. Rather, the appellant argued that Mr. Johnston negligently misrepresented the nature and existence of the employment opportunity being offered. It is the existence, or reality, of the job being interviewed for, not the extent of the appellant's involvement therein, which is at the heart of this tort action. A close reading of the employment agreement reveals that it contains no express provisions dealing with the respondent's obligations with respect to the nature and existence of the Multiview project. Accordingly, the ratio decidendi of my reasons in *BG Checo* is inapplicable to the present appeal. While both cases involve pre-contractual negligent misrepresentations, only *BG Checo* involved an impermissible concurrent liability in tort and contract; an exception to the general rule of concurrency. . . . The case at bar does not involve concurrency at all, let alone an exception thereto.

Having said this, it does not follow that the employment agreement is irrelevant to the disposition of this appeal. As I mentioned earlier, even if the tort claim is not barred altogether by the contract as in *BG Checo*, the duty or liability of the representor in tort may be limited or excluded by a term of the subsequent contract. In this respect, the respondent submits that the Court of Appeal was correct in finding that clauses 13 and 14 of the employment agreement represent a valid disclaimer for the misrepresentations allegedly made during the hiring interview, thereby negating any duty of care. I shall return to this issue [below]. I prefer to deal next with the questions of whether the respondent or its representative owed a duty of care to the appellant during the pre-employment interview and, if so, whether there was a breach of this duty in all the circumstances of this case.

C. *The duty of care owed to the appellant*

The respondent concedes that it itself and its representative, Mr. Johnston, owed a duty of care towards the six job applicants being interviewed, including the appellant, not to make negligent misrepresentations as to Cognos and the nature and permanence of the job being offered. In so doing, it accepts as correct the findings of both the trial judge and the Court of Appeal that there existed between the parties a "special relationship" within the meaning of *Hedley Byrne, supra*.

In my view, this concession is a sensible one. Without a doubt, when all the circumstances of this case are taken into account, the respondent and Mr. Johnston were under an obligation to exercise due diligence throughout the hiring interview with respect to the representations made to the appellant about Cognos and the nature and existence of the employment opportunity.

. . .

It was foreseeable that the appellant would be relying on the information given during the hiring interview in order to make his career decision. It was reasonable for the appellant to rely on said representations. There is nothing before this court that suggests that the respondent was not, at the time of the interview or shortly thereafter, assuming responsibility for what was being represented to the appellant by Mr. Johnston. As noted by the trial judge, Mr. Johnston discussed the . . . project in an unqualified manner, without making any relevant caveats. The alleged disclaimers of responsibility are provisions of a contract signed more than two weeks after the interview. . . [T]hese provisions are not valid disclaimers. They do not negate the duty of care owed to the appellant or prevent it from arising as in *Hedley Byrne*. . . It was foreseeable to the respondent and its representative that the appellant would sustain damages should the representations relied on prove to be false and negligently made. There was, undoubtedly, a relationship of proximity between the parties at all material times. Finally, it is not unreasonable to impose a duty of care in all the circumstances of this case; quite the contrary, it would be unreasonable *not* to impose such a duty. In short, therefore, there existed between the parties a "special relationship" at the time of the interview. The respondent and its representative Mr. Johnston were under a duty of care during the pre-employment interview to exercise reasonable care and diligence in making representations as to the employer and the employment opportunity being offered.

[Iacobucci J. then addressed the issue of standard of care. He held that the applicable standard was the reasonable person test, which does not require a person to guarantee the accuracy of statements but does require a person to exercise such care as is reasonable in the circumstances. On that basis, Iacobucci J. concluded that the trial judge had not erred in holding that the respondent's manager had acted carelessly in making statements during the appellant's job interview.]

NOTES AND QUESTIONS

1. How is the analysis of the duty of care issue in *Queen* different from that in the more recent decision in *Livent*? Why is the additional element of a special relationship required in negligent misrepresentation cases? How is a special relationship identified? For a case with facts raising issues like those in *Queen* see *Khan v. Vernon Jubilee Hospital* (2008), 90 B.C.L.R. (4th) 157 (S.C.).

The five-element test for a negligent misrepresentation claim in *Queen* is frequently cited by the courts, not only in pre-contractual misrepresentation cases but in other contexts as well. B. Feldthusen has criticized the focus on a special relationship, calling it "no real test at all. At best it is merely a conclusory label, and a misleading one at that": see Feldthusen, *Economic Negligence*, 6th ed. (2012) at 47-50.

Many cases have analyzed the tort of negligent misrepresentation by following *Queen* and without mention of either *Hercules* or *Livent*. See for example *Krawchuk v. Scherbak*, 2011 ONCA 352; *Oz Optics Ltd. v. Timbercon, Inc.*, 2011 ONCA 714; *Anderson v. Lawrence*, 2013 NBQB 21; and *2249659 Ontario Ltd. v. Sparkasse Siegen*, 2018 ONCA 371. Should this be cause for concern?

2. What was the difference between the contracts in *Queen* and *BG Checo*?

3. Having failed to attract majority support in *BG Checo*, why did Iacobucci J. persist in his analysis in *Queen*?

4. There are connections between the issue of liability in tort for pre-contractual representations and the scope of the obligations on contracting parties to act in good faith. See Reynolds, "The New Neighbour Principle: Reasonable Expectations, Relationality, and Good Faith in Pre-Contractual Negotiations" (2017) 60:1 Can. Bus. L.J. 94.

5. Contracts frequently contain a term that purports to exclude liability in tort, including for any representations made in negotiating the contract. The leading contract law decision on the interpretation of an exclusion of liability clause is *Tercon Contractors Ltd. v. British Columbia (Ministry of Transportation and Highways)*, 2010 SCC 4. At paras. 121-23 the court identified three key considerations: whether as a matter of interpretation the exclusion clause applies, whether the exclusion clause was unconscionable when the contract was made and whether the court should refuse to enforce the clause because of an overriding public policy. These considerations were applied in *Singh v. Trump*, 2016 ONCA 747 in which the court held that the exclusion clause was unconscionable, "grossly unfair" and "would shock the conscience" if applied.

Similar considerations apply to liability waivers, under which one contracting party waives liability for any negligence by the other contracting party. These are common in high-risk and sporting activities and are discussed in Chapter 19 in the context of the defence of voluntary assumption of risk.

6. Why did the contractual disclaimer clause in *Queen* not have the effect of negating the duty of care in tort law? How does *Queen* differ from *Hedley Byrne* in that respect? If the defendant in *Queen* did not want to be held liable with respect to its pre-contractual statements, how could it have more effectively disclaimed responsibility?

7. There are many cases on whether to give effect to an exclusion of liability clause. See for example *Intrawest Corp. v. No. 2002 Taurus Ventures Ltd.* (2006), 54 B.C.L.R. (4th) 173 (S.C.), rev'd (2007), 64 B.C.L.R. (4th) 8 (C.A.) in which the defendant sought to avoid liability for certain pre-contractual statements. The defendant failed at trial, for three reasons: the contractual disclaimer did not expressly refer to pre-contractual statements, the statements were made well before the contract was signed, and the plaintiff had no opportunity to verify the accuracy of the statements. The clause stated that the contract "is the entire agreement between the parties and there are no other terms, conditions, representations, warranties or collateral agreements, express or implied." On appeal, the court held that the contract's entire agreement clause did preclude claims for negligent misrepresentation. It reached this conclusion even though the wording of the disclaimer did not mention negligence or negligent misrepresentation. The parties to the contract were sophisticated and accordingly were bound by the clause.

Compare *Intrawest Corp.* with *Mariani v. Lemstra* (2004), 246 D.L.R. (4th) 489 (Ont. C.A.) in which the court indicated that an express "entire agreement" clause in a standard-form agreement of purchase and sale, coupled with the buyer's opportunity to inspect the property, would exclude liability for negligent misrepresentation. See in contrast *Whighton v. Integrity Inspections Inc.* (2007), 71 Alta. L.R. (4th) 112 (Q.B.), in which the court held that because the negligent misrepresentations were made outside the scope of the contract the limitation of liability clause did not apply. See also *Feldstein v. 364 Northern Development Corp.*, 2017 BCCA 174.

In some cases the interpretive issue is what constitutes the "entire agreement." For example, courts have held that a "seller property information statement" is part of the agreement of purchase and sale of residential land: *Krawchuk v. Scherbak, supra;* and *Costa v. Wimalasekera*, 2012 ONSC 6056 (Div. Ct.). See also *Soboczynski v. Beauchamp*, 2015 ONCA 282.

8. For more on the relationship between tort and contract, see Blom, "Fictions and Frictions on the Interface Between Tort and Contract" in Burns & Lyon, eds., *Donoghue v. Stevenson and the Modern Law of Negligence* (1991) at 139-90; Blom, "Tort Recovery for Economic Loss and the Intersection Between Tort and Contract" (1996) 54 The Advocate 367; Whittaker, "The Application of the 'Broad Principle of Hedley Byrne' as Between Parties to a Contract" (1997) 17 L.S. 169; Ogilvie, "Entire Agreement Clauses: Neither Riddle nor Enigma" (2008) 87 Can. Bar Rev. 625; and Trukhtanov, "Misrepresentation: Acknowledgement of Non-Reliance as a Defence" (2009) 125 L.Q.R. 648.

9. In *Queen* the court suggested that "only representations of existing facts, and not those relating to future occurrences, can give rise to actionable negligence." See also *Smith v. Union of Icelandic Fish Producers Ltd.* (2005), 238 N.S.R. (2d) 145 (C.A.);

Hembruff v. Ontario (Municipal Employees Retirement Board) (2005), 78 O.R. (3d) 561 (C.A.); *Conversions By Vantasy Ltd. v. General Motors of Canada Ltd.* (2006), 205 Man. R. (2d) 131 (C.A.); *PD Management Ltd. v. Chemposite Inc.* (2006), 58 B.C.L.R. (4th) 197 (C.A.); *Motkoski Holdings Ltd. v. Yellowhead (County)* (2010), 20 Alta. L.R. (5th) 1 (C.A.) at para. 43; *Condominium Corp. No. 0321365 v. 970365 Alberta Ltd.*, 2012 ABCA 26 at para. 90; and *Giesbrecht v. Canada Life Assurance Co.*, 2013 MBCA 53 at para. 101. Should a forecast as to the future, or a prediction of events to come, ever lead to liability for negligent misrepresentation?

In *Ismail v. Treats Inc.* (2004), 220 N.S.R. (2d) 151 (S.C.) the court stated that "while the pro forma [financial] statements are future predictions, they contain the implicit assertion of fact that they are based on actual operational experience. That assertion may form the basis of a misrepresentation claim." Is this reasoning consistent with the above cases?

REVIEW PROBLEM

Alice, a resident of the City, suffered a serious heart attack one morning while walking to work. Two nearby pedestrians wrapped Alice in warm clothing while a third went to call the police on the central emergency number.

The City had just installed a new central switchboard system designed to handle all calls for the police, fire department and ambulance services. Ideally, the calls would be handled by specially trained operators who would prioritize the emergency and dispatch the appropriate service. The pedestrian tried for over an hour to get through on the central emergency number, but to no avail. When he returned to the scene of the accident, he learned that Alice had just died.

A subsequent investigation indicated that the system's shortcomings were due to inferior equipment supplied by Sonar. Experts in the field indicated that the Sonar equipment was notoriously unreliable and that all those knowledgeable about this type of electrical equipment knew it.

The City had hired Panamar to design the new system, and all parties agree that its design was quite satisfactory. Panamar originally recommended that the equipment be purchased from a Japanese company.

After Panamar had completed its contractual obligations and was paid, it kept in touch with the City. Ralph, Panamar's President, had called the appropriate City officials and offered, free of charge, to provide whatever advice he could. The City engineer responsible for implementing the plan took Ralph up on his offer several times and was favourably impressed by his helpful suggestions.

As a result of labour unrest in Japan, the City fell behind schedule in installing the system. Ralph indicated that the City could get exactly the same equipment immediately for the same price from Sonar. When the City engineer mentioned the unreliability of the Sonar equipment, Ralph stated: "I may not be a certified expert, but rumours about Sonar are fuelled by foreign competitors playing on Canadians' sense of inferiority." Despite the trade reports to the contrary, Ralph stated that the Sonar equipment was as reliable as any produced in the world. Ralph had used Sonar's products in several jobs 15 years ago, but he had no experience with the new product lines in question and he failed to mention this to the City. The City ultimately took Ralph's advice and purchased $500,000 worth of Sonar equipment for its new system.

The equipment never functioned properly and complaints began to mount as the system continually broke down. Alice's death was the last straw. The City was forced to take out all the Sonar equipment and replace it at a cost of $600,000.

Discuss Panamar's liability to Alice's estate and to the City in negligent misrepresentation.

SPECIAL DUTIES OF CARE: RECOVERY OF PURE ECONOMIC LOSS IN NEGLIGENCE

1. Introduction
2. New Categories of Pure Economic Loss
3. Negligent Performance of a Service
4. Negligent Supply of Shoddy Goods or Structures
5. Relational Economic Loss

1. Introduction

As indicated in the previous chapter, liability for pure economic loss — economic loss that does not flow from personal injury or property damage — presents considerable difficulties. Most obviously, it raises the risk of indeterminate liability. Moreover, it extends legal protection to interests that most people would agree are less important than the interests protected by liability for personal injury and property damage. The loss of a life and the destruction of a house, for example, warrant more attention than the loss of money. Given the scarcity of judicial resources, it may be less appropriate to use them on the resolution of disputes arising from the loss of money. Finally, it is often more efficient for pure economic losses to be borne by the victim. That party, typically a business entity, is usually better positioned to assess the prospect of such losses and to arrange insurance coverage or other protection beforehand.

Historically, such difficulties were generally resolved on the basis of a broad rule that entirely excluded liability for such losses: see *Cattle v. Stockton Waterworks Co.* (1874), L.R. 10 Q.B. 453. More recently, however, the Supreme Court of Canada has held that recovery is possible in some situations. In a series of decisions it has adopted a taxonomy developed in Feldthusen, *Economic Negligence*, 6th ed. (2012) that classifies pure economic loss claims into five categories:

1. negligent misrepresentation,
2. independent liability of statutory public authorities,
3. negligent performance of a service,
4. negligent supply of shoddy goods or structures, and
5. relational economic loss.

This classification suggests that, while unified by the common theme of pure economic loss, the different categories of cases involve different policy considerations. The reasons for imposing or denying liability in one situation may not properly apply in another situation.

The five categories of pure economic loss cases will be addressed separately. The first category, negligent misrepresentation, is considered in the previous chapter. The second category, liability of statutory public authorities, is considered in Chapter 21. The majority of this chapter will be devoted to (i) the negligent performance of services, (ii) the supply of shoddy goods or structures and (iii) relational economic loss.

NOTES AND QUESTIONS

1. The issue of tort liability for pure economic loss has spawned a large amount of academic comment. For detailed treatment of the topic as a whole see Feldthusen, *supra*; Brown, *Pure Economic Loss in Canadian Negligence Law* (2011); and Burns & Blom, *Economic Torts in Canada*, 2d ed. (2016). See also Feldthusen, "The Recovery of Pure Economic Loss in Canada: Proximity, Justice, Rationality, and Chaos" (1996) 24 Man. L.J. 1; Feldthusen, "Liability for Pure Economic Loss: Yes, But Why?" (1999) 28 U.W.A.L. Rev. 84; Cherniak & How, "Policy and Predictability: Pure Economic Loss in the Supreme Court of Canada" (1999) 31 C.B.L.J. 209; Klar, "Judicial Activism in Private Law" (2001) 80 Can. Bar Rev. 215; Blom, "Tort, Contract and the Allocation of Risk" in Beaulac, Pitel & Schulz, eds., *The Joy of Torts* (2003) 289; Brown, "Still Crazy After All These Years: *Anns, Cooper v. Hobart* and Pure Economic Loss" (2003) 36 U.B.C.L. Rev. 159; Benson, "The Problem with Pure Economic Loss" (2009) 60 South Carolina L. Rev. 823; and Fridman *et al.*, *The Law of Torts in Canada*, 3d ed. (2010), ch. 13.

2. In recent years several scholars have analyzed tort law with a focus on the way in which it protects rights. This approach is discussed in more detail in Chapter 1 and Chapter 28. It has the potential to assist in the analysis of claims for pure economic loss. Consider, in the cases in this area (including in the previous chapter), the extent to which the law would recognize that the plaintiff had a right to be free from the loss caused by the defendant. What is the source of that right? Did it exist independently of the defendant? Was it created by the defendant assuming certain obligations to the plaintiff?

3. A focus on rights can also help to differentiate claims for property loss from claims for pure economic loss. In *Mandeville v. Manufacturers Life Insurance Co.*, 2014 ONCA 417 the plaintiffs were policyholders in the defendant's insurance company. The defendant transferred the plaintiffs' policies to another insurance company and then demutualized, a process which distributed funds to the current policyholders. Because of the earlier transfer the plaintiffs did not share in these funds. Part of their argument was that the defendant had caused them a loss of property, in that before the transfer they had a proprietary right to share in any demutualization of the defendant and they lost this due to the transfer. The court rejected this argument. It held (at para. 136) that the question was whether the plaintiffs "had a legally recognized right or interest in respect of a possible demutualization." It concluded they had no such right or interest: at the most they had the hope that they would benefit on a possible future demutualization. In the absence of a legally recognized right or interest, the claim was only one for pure economic loss.

2. New Categories of Pure Economic Loss

It is important to understand that the categories of recoverable pure economic loss, like the categories of negligence generally, are not closed. It is open for the courts to recognize a duty of care in a new type of situation, outside the five categories mentioned above. In doing so, they will use the *Anns/Cooper* test: see *Cooper v. Hobart*, [2001] 3 S.C.R. 537. As you read through the next case, consider how you would classify the policy factors that influenced Iacobucci and Major JJ. Do they properly fall under the first branch or the second branch of the test?

MARTEL BUILDING LTD. v. CANADA
(2000), 193 D.L.R. (4th) 1 (S.C.C.)

[The plaintiff leased a building to the defendant. When that lease was about to expire, the parties entered into negotiations for a renewal. The defendant led the plaintiff to believe that it would be amenable to renewing the lease on certain terms. However, when the plaintiff formally extended an offer on those terms, the defendant rejected the proposal and issued a call for tenders. In general terms, a call for tenders consists of an invitation to receive contractual offers, on a competitive basis, from several parties — in this case, building owners willing to lease space to the defendant. The defendant eventually accepted a tender from another party and therefore did not renew its lease with the plaintiff.

The plaintiff sued on several grounds. For present purposes, the relevant claim was that the defendant had breached a duty of care to negotiate in such a way as to avoid causing the plaintiff pure economic loss (the loss of the opportunity to renew the original lease). The defendant allegedly did so by, for example, repeatedly delaying matters, breaking appointments, ignoring requests, and failing to put the plaintiff into contact with the appropriate people.]

IACOBUCCI AND MAJOR JJ: This appeal calls for an extension of the tort of negligence to include a duty of care on parties during negotiations, during the preparation of calls for tender and during the evaluation of bids submitted in response to such calls. In each instance the respondent sought damages for pure economic loss.

. . .

Analysis

1. *Given that one owes a duty of care not to harm those who might foreseeably suffer damage, does a duty of care exist to that same group with respect to negotiations? Does the tort of negligence extend to damages for pure economic loss arising out of the conduct of pre-contractual negotiations?*

. . .

The appellant submitted that to extend the tort of negligence into the conduct of commercial negotiations would be an unnecessary and unsound invasion of the market-place. It argued that this case involves business risks inherent in commercial negotiation, risks which should be borne by parties and not be re-allocated through the imposition of a duty of care.

A breach of a duty of care in negotiations would, in this case, result in the loss of an opportunity to negotiate a lease renewal. This is a claim for damages not accompanied by physical injury or property damage. What is left is a claim for pure economic loss. . . .

As a cause of action, claims concerning the recovery of economic loss are identical to any other claim in negligence in that the plaintiff must establish a duty, a breach, damage and causation. Nevertheless, as a result of the common law's historical treatment of economic loss, the threshold question of whether or not to recognize a duty of care receives added scrutiny relative to other claims in negligence.

An historical review of the common law treatment of recovery for economic loss has been undertaken by this Court on several occasions. . . . Rather than re-canvassing the jurisprudential genealogy reviewed in these cases, it is enough to say that the common law traditionally did not allow recovery of economic loss where a plaintiff had suffered neither physical harm nor property damage. . . .

Over time, the traditional rule was reconsidered. . . . [I]t has been recognized that in limited circumstances damages for economic loss absent physical or proprietary harm may be recovered. The circumstances in which such damages have been awarded to date are few. To a large extent, this caution derives from the same policy rationale that supported the traditional approach not to recognize the claim at all. First, economic interests are viewed as less compelling of protection than bodily security or proprietary interests. Second, an unbridled recognition of economic loss raises the spectre of indeterminate liability. Third, economic losses often arise in a commercial context, where they are often an inherent business risk best guarded against by the party on whom they fall through such means as insurance. Finally, allowing the recovery of economic loss through tort has been seen to encourage a multiplicity of inappropriate lawsuits. . . .

[Iacobucci and Major JJ. then referred to the five recognized categories of recovery for pure economic loss.]

The allegation of negligence in the conduct of negotiations does not fall within any of these classifications. Thus, Martel's claim is novel when weighed against the prior jurisprudence of this Court. That by itself should not preclude the claim. The question is whether the numbered categories ought to be enlarged or some other method identified to include a new head of economic loss. To answer this question it is useful to set out a framework for the recognition of new categories such as that advanced by Martel.

. . .

Canadian jurisprudence has consistently applied the flexible two-stage analysis of *Anns v. Merton London Borough Council*, [1978] A.C. 728 (H.L.), originally adopted in *Kamloops [(City) v. Nielsen*, [1984] 2 S.C.R. 2], in determining whether to extend a duty of care in a given case.

. . .

This analysis begins with the oft-repeated question: Was there a sufficiently close relationship between Martel and the Department so that, in the reasonable contemplation of the Department, carelessness on its part might cause damage to a party such as Martel with whom it negotiated?

. . .

So as to infuse the term "proximity" with greater meaning, the courts take into account a variety of factors in ascertaining whether the relationship between two parties gives rise to a prima facie duty of care.

. . .

It may be foreseeable that carelessness on the part of one negotiating party may cause an opposite negotiating party economic loss. Generally, negotiation is undertaken with a view to obtaining mutual economic gain. Given the bilateral nature of most negotiations, such gains are sometimes obtained at the other party's expense. Although negotiations often provide synergistic effects for all concerned, the prospect of causing deprivation by economic loss is implicit in the negotiating environment. The causal relationship in contractual negotiations is usually significant for a finding of proximity. In the circumstances of this appeal, the appellant's pre-existing contractual arrangement with Martel is an impressive indicator of proximity.

Both the pre-existing lease arrangement and the communications between the appellant and respondent here are indicators of proximity. That does not mean that any exchange loosely viewed as a negotiation will necessarily give rise to a proximate relationship. The expression of interest does not automatically create proximity absent some evidence of genuine and mutual contracting intent. We are satisfied that the parties in this appeal evidenced such an intent. The communications between the appellant and Martel disclose a readiness to arrive at an agreement despite the fact one was never reached.

We conclude that the circumstances of this case satisfy the first stage of *Anns* and raise a prima facie duty of care.

. . .

In the wake of a finding of proximity, the second question in *Anns* arises: Are there any policy considerations that serve to negative or limit (a) the scope of the prima facie duty of care (b) the class of persons to whom it is owed or (c) the damages to which a breach of it may give rise?

Notwithstanding our finding of proximity above, there are compelling policy reasons to conclude that one commercial party should not have to be mindful of another commercial party's legitimate interests in an arm's length negotiation.

. . .

The scope of indeterminate liability remains a significant concern underlying any analysis of whether to extend the sphere of recovery for economic loss. In this appeal, however, the inherent nature of negotiations in this case place definable limits on the ultimate extent of liability so that concerns of indeterminacy are not determinative in this appeal.

Here, the class of potential claimants is limited to those persons that the Department directly negotiated with.

. . .

In addition, although the quantum of damages arising out of failed negotiations may be quite high, it is limited by the nature of the transaction being negotiated. . . . Martel's claim is clearly restricted to the loss of an opportunity to conclude a 10-year lease renewal. While there are serious difficulties in valuing a lost opportunity, the extent of the loss has definable limits.

However, simply addressing indeterminacy does not represent the sole hurdle to extending a duty of care.

. . .

In light of the diverse array of factual circumstances that can fall under the moniker of pure economic loss, unique policy considerations may infuse the analysis of any given case. Indeed, notwithstanding the fact that indeterminacy does not rear its head sufficiently in this appeal, there are a number of ancillary policy considerations that necessitate precluding the extension of the tort of negligence into commercial negotiations. Even in the absence of any serious potential for indeterminate liability, these factors are sufficient to deny recovery notwithstanding the finding of proximity. What we have identified as ancillary policy considerations weighing against recovery are defined by the following five illustrations.

First, the very object of negotiation works against recovery. The primary goal of any economically rational actor engaged in commercial negotiation is to achieve the most advantageous financial bargain. As noted above, in the context of bilateral negotiation, such gains are realized at the expense of the other negotiating party. From an economic perspective, some authors describe negotiation as a zero-sum game involving a transference rather than loss of wealth.

. . .

Perhaps following the traditional view that, at least in some circumstances, economic losses are less worthy of protection than physical or proprietary harm, it has been noted that the absence of net harm on a social scale is a factor weighing against the extension of liability for pure economic loss. That is to say, negotiation merely transfers wealth between parties. Although one party may suffer, another often gains. Thus, as an economic whole, society is not worse off.

Second, . . . to extend a duty of care to pre-contractual commercial negotiations could deter socially and economically useful conduct. The encouragement of economically efficient conduct can be a valid concern in favour of the extension of liability for pure economic loss. . . . Equally, in other circumstances, this goal may be a valid rationale against extending liability.

In essence, Martel claims that the appellant was negligent in not providing it with adequate information concerning the appellant's bargaining position or its readiness to conclude a renewal. The appellant's conduct in negotiating with Martel might be construed as "hard bargaining". The Department's agents displayed casual contempt towards Martel and its personnel as illustrated by broken appointments and general disregard of the minimal courtesy Martel could have reasonably expected. However indifferent the agents of the Department appear from the record, that by itself does not create a cause of action. Doubtless, the appellant's ability to assume such a position in relation to Martel was due to its dominant position in the Ottawa leasing market. The foregoing all point to the advantages enjoyed by the Crown, but do not point to liability.

In many if not most commercial negotiations, an advantageous bargaining position is derived from the industrious generation of information not possessed by the opposite party as opposed to its market position as here. Helpful information is often a by-product of one party expending resources on due diligence, research or other information gathering activities. It is apparent that successful negotiating is the product of that kind of industry.

It would defeat the essence of negotiation and hobble the marketplace to extend a duty of care to the conduct of negotiations, and to label a party's failure to disclose its bottom line, its motives or its final position as negligent. Such a conclusion would of necessity force the disclosure of privately acquired information and the dissipation of any competitive advantage derived from it, all of which is incompatible with the activity of negotiating and bargaining.

Third, to impose a duty in the circumstances of this appeal could interject tort law as after-the-fact insurance against failures to act with due diligence or to hedge the risk of failed negotiations through the pursuit of alternative strategies or opportunities. . . .

Notwithstanding Martel's hope that the negotiations would produce a favourable outcome, it could at any point have concluded that the Department was not serious or interested in concluding a renewal of the Martel Building lease, but simply delaying for an undisclosed reason and seeking other potential landlords. While Martel may have suffered from its innocence and optimism, at least some of the responsibility for the delays in communication evident in this appeal can be attributed to it. The retention of self-vigilance is a necessary ingredient of commerce.

Fourth, to extend the tort of negligence into the conduct of commercial negotiations would introduce the courts to a significant regulatory function, scrutinizing the minutiae of pre-contractual conduct. It is undesirable to place further scrutiny upon commercial parties when other causes of action already provide remedies for many forms of conduct. Notably, the doctrines of undue influence, economic duress and unconscionability provide redress against bargains obtained as a result of improper negotiation. As well, negligent misrepresentation, fraud and the tort of deceit cover many aspects of negotiation which do not culminate in an agreement.

A concluding but not conclusive fifth consideration is the extent to which needless litigation should be discouraged. To extend negligence into the conduct of negotiations could encourage a multiplicity of lawsuits. Given the number of negotiations that do not culminate in agreement, the potential for increased litigation in place of allowing market forces to operate seems obvious.

For these reasons we are of the opinion that, in the circumstances of this case, any prima facie duty is significantly outweighed by the deleterious effects that would be occasioned through an extension of a duty of care into the conduct of negotiations. We conclude then that, as a general proposition, no duty of care arises in conducting negotiations. While there may well be a set of circumstances in which a duty of care may be found, it has not yet arisen.

NOTES AND QUESTIONS

1. On what basis did Iacobucci and Major JJ. reject the recognition of a duty of care? Was the plaintiff's loss reasonably foreseeable? Was there a relationship of sufficient proximity between the parties? What policy considerations influenced the court? Do you agree with the court's decision?

2. Within the law of contract, the tendering process involves an interesting series of events. *Martel* was a typical case. By issuing the call for tenders after negotiations with the plaintiff broke down, the defendant did two things. First, it issued an "invitation to treat" that indicated its willingness to receive contractual offers from interested parties. In doing so, the defendant incurred no obligations. It merely indicated that it might, in the future, accept one of the tenders and thereby enter into a new lease with the winning bidder. That lease would constitute what is known as "Contract B." Second, by issuing the call for tenders, the defendant also extended its own offer, to every potential tenderer, to enter into something called "Contract A." The purpose of "Contract A" is to ensure fairness in the tender process. For instance, it would be unfair, or at least disruptive, if, while the defendant was considering the various tenders that it had received, one of the bidders withdrew its offer. Likewise, it would be unfair if the defendant exercised its choice among the various tenders on the basis of some illegitimate or capricious criterion. "Contract A" therefore typically

imposes obligations on both parties to abide by a certain set of rules. A different "Contract A" is created every time that a party submits a tender. Consequently, in *Martel*, there were as many instances of "Contract A" as there were bidders. There was, in contrast, only one "Contract B" and because the defendant had chosen an offer from another tender that contract did not involve the plaintiff.

In *Martel*, the plaintiff's primary claim was that the defendant breached a duty of care pertaining to the negotiation process. That action failed. However, the plaintiff also brought two other claims in negligence that pertained to the tendering process.

First, the plaintiff argued that it had suffered a loss because the defendant had breached a duty of care when it carelessly drafted its call for tenders. In that regard, the plaintiff stressed that it had made certain assumptions based on its prior negotiations with the defendant. The Supreme Court of Canada rejected that argument. It held that there was no duty of care:

> Assuming without deciding that sufficient proximity existed between the parties, any prima facie duty of care would be negated by policy considerations. Indeed, considerations unique to the tendering process nullify any duty of care sought by Martel. First and foremost, we agree with the Department that it would call into question the integrity of the tender process if, by reason of a past relationship with, or special knowledge of, a potential bidder, there could be an enforceable obligation to take the interests of that particular bidder into account. . .

> A party calling for tenders has the discretion to set out its own specifications and requirements. This includes the discretion to change its mind with respect to the terms or preferences that were discussed in the course of non-committal negotiations. Tender requirements are not negotiable. To decide otherwise would in fact force the party making the call for tenders to continue in its negotiations with one potential bidder even after those negotiations have proven unfruitful.

Second, the plaintiff claimed that the defendant had breached a duty of care in tort law by failing to fairly evaluate the bids that it had received. Having previously found that the defendant had not breached any of the contractual obligations that it owed to the plaintiff under "Contract A," the Supreme Court of Canada rejected the negligence argument as well:

> [W]e acknowledge that . . . an action in tort may lie notwithstanding the existence of a contract. . . . However, in the circumstances of this case, regardless of whether there exists a coextensive duty in tort to treat tenderers fairly and equally in evaluating the bids, Martel's tort claim cannot succeed for the same reasons that a contractual claim would fail. The duty of care alleged in tort in the case at bar is the same as the duty which is implied as a term of Contract A; this is not a case where Martel is suing in tort to avail itself of a more generous limitation period, or some other advantage offered only by tort law.

3. For a discussion of *Martel*, see Rafferty, "Developments in Contract and Tort Law: The 2000-2001 Term" (2001) 15 S.C.L.R. (2d) 173; and Wallace, "Tender Call Obligations in Canada" (2001) 117 L.Q.R. 351.

4. In *Martel* the court left open the question of whether someone who issues a call for tenders could owe a duty of care to subcontractors of a bidding contractor. This issue subsequently arose in *Design Services Ltd. v. Canada*, [2008] 1 S.C.R. 737. Public Works launched a tendering process for the construction of a naval reserve building.

A contractor, Olympic Construction Ltd., tendered a bid but Public Works accepted a non-compliant bid. The subcontractors that were part of Olympic's bid could not sue Public Works in contract, having not themselves tendered the bid, and so they sued in tort. The court held that this claim did not fall into any of the five existing categories of pure economic loss and so had to consider whether to create a new category. The court applied the test from *Cooper*, and at the first stage of the analysis the defendant conceded reasonable foreseeability of harm. The court noted several factors that pointed to proximity, including the fact that considerable information about the plaintiffs was included in the bid documents received and reviewed by the defendant. However, the court concluded that a policy consideration negated a finding of sufficient proximity, namely the plaintiffs' ability to take steps to protect themselves. Rather than relying on the contractor's bid, the plaintiffs could have formed a joint venture with the contractor and so been parties to the bid. The court held at para. 56:

> The fact that the appellants had the opportunity to form a joint venture, and thereby be parties to the "Contract A" made between PW and Olympic, is an overriding policy reason that tort liability should not be recognized in these circumstances. Allowing the appellants to sidestep the circumstances they participated in creating and make a claim in tort would be to ignore and circumvent the contractual rights and obligations that were, and were not, intended by PW, Olympic and the appellants. In essence, the appellants are attempting, after the fact, to substitute a claim in tort law for their inability to claim under "Contract A". After all, the obligations the appellants seek to enforce through tort exist only because of "Contract A" to which the appellants are not parties. In my view, the observation of Professor Lewis N. Klar (*Tort Law* (3rd ed. 2003), at p. 201) — that the ordering of commercial relationships is usually in the bailiwick of the law of contract — is particularly apt in this type of case. To conclude that an action in tort is appropriate when commercial parties have deliberately arranged their affairs in contract would be to allow for an unjustifiable encroachment of tort law into the realm of contract.

As a result, the court found a *prima facie* duty of care did not arise. In *obiter dicta*, it went on to hold that broader policy considerations would have negated the duty of care had one arisen. Even though most of the subcontractors were specifically identified in the bid, at least one was not (only its parent company was mentioned), and so "since the class of plaintiffs seems to seep into the lower levels of the corporate structure of the design-build team members, this case has indications of indeterminate liability." The court went on to observe that "Even where subcontractors are named and known by an owner, those subcontractors will have employees and suppliers and perhaps their own subcontractors who also could suffer economic loss. And these suppliers and subcontractors will have their own employees and suppliers who might claim for economic loss due to the wrongful failure of the owner to award the contract to the general contractor upon which they were all dependant. The construction contract context is one in which the indeterminacy of the class of plaintiffs can readily be seen." Do you agree with the court's conclusion on each stage of the duty of care analysis? See Swan & Adamski, "Comment: *Design Services Ltd. v. Canada*" (2008) 47 C.B.L.J. 87; and Osborne, "*Design Services Ltd. v. Canada*: A Cry for a Remedy Unanswered" (2008) 55 C.C.L.T. (3d) 167. See also *Jones Masonry Ltd. v. Defence Construction (1951) Ltd.* (2010), 353 N.B.R. (2d) 359 (C.A.).

5. The Supreme Court of Canada was unwilling to recognize a new category of recoverable pure economic loss in *Martel* and *Design Services*, as were the appellate

courts in *Blacklaws v. 470433 Alberta Ltd.* (2000), 261 A.R. 28 (C.A.); *Fraser v. Westminer Canada Ltd.* (2003), 215 N.S.R. (2d) 377 (C.A.); *Esser v. Brown* (2004), 242 D.L.R. (4th) 112 (B.C.C.A.); *Mandeville v. Manufacturers Life Insurance Co.*, 2014 ONCA 417; and *Lavender v. Miller Bernstein LLP*, 2018 ONCA 729. See also *LBP Holdings Ltd. v. Hycroft Mining Corporation*, 2017 ONSC 6342; and *Goyal v. Niagara College of Applied Arts and Technology*, 2018 ONSC 2768.

However, the prospect has received more favourable treatment in some other cases. In *Haskett v. Equifax Canada Inc.* (2003), 63 O.R. (3d) 577 (C.A.) the plaintiff was discharged from bankruptcy in 1996. Nevertheless, despite being current on all of his debts and annually earning more than $75,000, he was consistently denied commercial credit. He claimed that his poor credit rating was caused by an inaccurate report that the defendant company, a credit reporting agency, had carelessly prepared and made available to potential creditors. The plaintiff sued in negligence for his alleged losses. The defendant brought a motion to strike out the claim on the basis that it did not disclose a cause of action. More specifically, the defendant argued that since the plaintiff's claim pertained to a pure economic loss, and since it did not fit within any of the five existing categories, it must fail. The judge who heard the motion agreed, but that decision was overturned on appeal. The Court of Appeal for Ontario held that the plaintiff's claim should proceed to trial because either (i) the situation fell by analogy into the established category of negligent misrepresentation, or (ii) it was possible for the trial judge to recognize a new category of recoverable pure economic loss. See also *Clark v. Scotiabank* (2004), 25 C.C.L.T. (3d) 109 (Ont. S.C.J.), rev'd 2006 CarswellOnt 8855 (Div. Ct.) (WL Can); and *Neil v. Equifax Canada Inc.* (2005), 271 Sask. R. 160 (Prov. Ct.), rev'd (2006), 277 Sask. R. 275 (Q.B.). For a similar Australian case see *Dale v. Veda Advantage Information Services and Solutions Limited* (2009), 176 F.C.R. 456.

6. Because the court can create new categories, there may be less concern to fit any particular case into an existing category. In *Haskett, supra*, the court only briefly discussed whether the case could fit into the negligent misrepresentation category. In *Lowe v. Guarantee Co. of North America* (2005), 80 O.R. (3d) 222 (C.A.) the plaintiffs were examined by the defendant, a Designated Assessment Centre under Ontario's scheme for no-fault auto accident benefits. The plaintiffs were denied benefits and as a result sued the defendant in negligence. Rather than consider the case as involving the negligent performance of a service, the court relied on the more general test in *Cooper*. Could using the *Cooper* test lead to a breakdown of the categories? Should the categories be maintained? See *Heinicke v. Cooper Rankin Ltd.* (2007), 210 Man. R. (2d) 125 (Q.B.); and *Lavender v. Miller Bernstein LLP, supra*. See also *1688782 Ontario Inc. v. Maple Leaf Foods Inc.*, 2018 ONCA 407, a case of pure economic loss in which the court applied both the general framework in *Cooper* and the specific jurisprudence on negligent misrepresentation (and arguably should have also applied the specific jurisprudence on the supply of shoddy goods).

If a court, using the *Cooper* test, concludes that the defendant was under a duty of care in respect of pure economic loss suffered by the plaintiff, does this amount to creating a new category?

7. In *Customs and Excise Commissioners v. Barclays Bank plc.*, [2007] 1 A.C. 181 (H.L.) the novel issue was whether a third party, such as a bank, that holds the assets of a defendant whose assets have been frozen by court order, and that carelessly

allows the defendant to transfer the assets despite the order, owes a duty of care to the plaintiff who obtained the order. Lord Bingham noted:

> the authorities disclose three tests which have been used in deciding whether a defendant sued as causing pure economic loss to a claimant owed him a duty of care in tort. The first is whether the defendant assumed responsibility for what he said and did vis-à-vis the claimant, or is to be treated by the law as having done so. The second is commonly known as the threefold test: whether loss to the claimant was a reasonably foreseeable consequence of what the defendant did or failed to do; whether the relationship between the parties was one of sufficient proximity; and whether in all the circumstances it is fair, just and reasonable to impose a duty of care on the defendant towards the claimant. . . Third is the incremental test, based on the observation of Brennan J in *Sutherland Shire Council v Heyman* (1985) 60 ALR 1 at 43-44, (1985) 157 CLR 424 at 481, approved by Lord Bridge of Harwich in *Caparo Industries plc v Dickman* [1990] 1 All ER 568 at 576, [1990] 2 AC 605 at 618, that: "It is preferable in my view, that the law should develop novel categories of negligence incrementally and by analogy with established categories, rather than by a massive extension of a prima facie duty of care restrained only by indefinable 'considerations which ought to negative, or to reduce or limit the scope of the duty or the class of person to whom it is owed'."

The House of Lords refused to impose a duty of care. See also *Rowley v. Secretary of State for Department of Work and Pensions*, [2007] 1 W.L.R. 2861 (C.A.). In response to this diversity of tests in English law, in *United Project Consultants Pte. Ltd. v. Leong Kwok Onn*, [2005] 4 S.L.R. 214 (C.A.) the Singapore Court of Appeal stated:

> While the learned authors of *Clerk & Lindsell on Torts* (Sweet & Maxwell, 18th Ed, 2000) may find this approach useful in that each test may be used to check the provisional conclusion reached by the application of the other tests, we found ourselves unable to agree with this state of affairs. The laws of any country must be sufficiently clear and capable of guiding parties in the regulation of their affairs. While a measure of uncertainty will always be present, for that is the consequence of any jurisdiction that founds its laws upon previously decided cases, it would be undesirable for a court to refrain from coming down in favour of any particular test when faced with various alternative approaches. . .

See on this uncertainty Mitchell & Mitchell, "Negligence Liability for Pure Economic Loss" (2005) 121 L.Q.R. 194; and Barker, "Wielding Occam's Razor: Pruning Strategies for Economic Loss" (2006) 26 O.J.L.S. 289.

Consider the extent to which the cases in this chapter make use of one or more of the three tests outlined by Lord Bingham, and consider also whether the Canadian approach is "sufficiently clear." Should there be only one test for recovery of pure economic loss?

8. In *Young v. Bella*, [2006] 1 S.C.R. 108 the plaintiff was negligently reported as a potential child abuser by the defendant university. In finding that the defendant owed the plaintiff a duty of care the court applied the analysis from *Martel* and *Cooper*. However, the plaintiff's claim was for both personal injury and economic loss, and the court did not analyze the case as one about pure economic loss. If the plaintiff had not suffered anxiety, embarrassment, insomnia, paranoia and depression as a result of the allegations against her, and had only suffered economic loss due to an inability to find work, how should the duty issue have been analyzed?

9. If a defendant driver is negligent and is killed as a result, can the defendant's spouse sue for economic loss suffered as a result of the death, such as loss of a share of employment or pension income? What if the spouse was, at the time, a passenger in the car? What if the spouse also suffered physical injuries as a result of the defendant's negligence? See *Hubley v. Hubley Estate*, 2011 PECA 19.

3. Negligent Performance of a Service

The law on liability for pure economic loss caused by the negligent performance of a service closely mirrors the law on liability for negligent misrepresentations (discussed in Chapter 13). That is hardly surprising: in many situations, there is a fine line between services and representations. As one commentator notes, "Advice is a particular form of business service, and in many representation cases the negligence lies in the performance of an underlying service rather than in the representation itself": Feldthusen, "Economic Loss in the Supreme Court of Canada: Yesterday and Tomorrow" (1991) 17 C.B.L.J. 356 at 366. See also Linden *et al.*, *Canadian Tort Law*, 11th ed. (2018) at 406: "Today Feldthusen would collapse the misrepresentation and services categories into one". For an example of a case on the borderline see *Edgeworth Construction Ltd. v. N.D. Lea & Associates Ltd.*, [1993] 3 S.C.R. 206.

Chapter 13 contains a lengthy extract from *Deloitte & Touche v. Livent Inc.*, 2017 SCC 63. While primarily considered a negligent misrepresentation case, much of the majority decision's discussion of the law expressly refers equally to the negligent performance of a service. You should therefore review that extract.

B.D.C. LTD. v. HOFSTRAND FARMS LTD.
(1986), 26 D.L.R. (4th) 1 (S.C.C.)

[The appellant, a courier company, contracted with the Province of British Columbia to deliver, by the next day, an envelope from a government office in Victoria to the Land Registry Office in Prince George. Unknown to the appellant, the envelope contained a Crown grant in favour of the respondent. The respondent was anxious for the grant to be registered before December 31, 1976: if it was not, the respondent would lose the ability to bind a third party to a contract for the sale of certain land. The appellant delivered the envelope late, with the result that the third party refused to complete the contemplated contract with the respondent. The respondent accordingly suffered an economic loss.

The respondent sued the appellant. The trial judge dismissed the claim on the basis that the courier company was unaware of the envelope's contents and was not informed of the need for timely delivery. The Court of Appeal came to the opposite conclusion. The courier company appealed to the Supreme Court of Canada.]

ESTEY J.: . . .
[Estey J. reviewed the two-stage test that Lord Wilberforce developed in *Anns v. Merton London Borough Council*, [1978] A.C. 728, regarding the recognition of a duty of care.]

Despite this expansion of the principles governing tort liability, however, the courts have remained conscious throughout of the need for reasonable limitations. Nowhere is this need more urgent than in cases involving purely economic losses, many of which, in the words of Cardozo C.J. in *Ultramares Corp. v. Touche*, 255 N.Y. 170 (1931), may involve the possibility of liability "in an indeterminate amount for an indeterminate time to an indeterminate class."

There are various ways of circumscribing, in pure economic loss cases, what otherwise might be an unending chain of liability in an incalculable amount. As Lord Pearce said in *Hedley Byrne*, at p. 615:

> How wide the sphere of the duty of care in negligence is to be laid depends ultimately on the courts' assessment of the demands of society for protection from the carelessness of others.

. . .

Application of the two tests laid out in *Anns* is sufficient to dispose of this appeal. The first test to be met is that there be shown to exist a relationship of proximity or neighbourhood "such that in a reasonable contemplation" of the actor, his carelessness may likely damage the plaintiff. The second test, once the first has been met, is whether there are present any circumstances which would negate or reduce (a) the scope of the duty, or (b) the class of persons to whom such a duty is owed, or (c) the damage seen in law to flow from breach of the duty.

. . .

On the facts as revealed by the evidence before the Court in this appeal, the appellant courier had no knowledge of the existence of the respondent, nor, because of the Crown practice of not disclosing the nature of the documents being forwarded, could it reasonably have known of the existence of a class of persons whose interests depended upon timely transmission of the envelope. There was, therefore, no actual or constructive knowledge in the courier that the rights of a third party could in any way be affected by the transmission or lack of transmission of the envelope in question. If a person in the position of the respondent is included in a class considered to be reasonably within the contemplation of the appellant, there is no logical point of breaking off so as to put a reasonable practical limitation on the courier's range of liability. It is a stretching of concept to conclude that anyone who might conceivably be affected by a failure by the Province of British Columbia to register a Crown grant within the calendar year, constitutes a "limited class", the existence of which is known to a courier employed to deliver the Crown grant to a registry office. In the words of Lord Reid in *Hedley Byrne*, *supra*, ". . . it would be going very far to say that [the defendant] owes a duty to every ultimate 'consumer'. . ."

Another aspect of proximity which was stressed in *Hedley Byrne*, *supra*, . . . is reliance by the plaintiff upon the undertaking or representation made by the defendant.

. . .

What was the reliance here by the respondent? There was none. The respondent was, by the time of the appellant's engagement by the Crown, in a position of risk through no act of its own. The situation of risk, in which a delay would be fatal to the respondent's interests, was created by the terms of the respondent's contract with the third party, in conjunction with the Crown's refusal to allow a representative of the respondent to carry the documents to Prince George himself. There was no assumption of risk in reliance upon the appellant's undertaking to deliver the documents. The respondent did not rely on the appellant in any way prior to the creation of this risk. The respondent did not permit the engagement of the appellant or reject the idea of engaging another courier by reason of any representation made by the appellant. Nor was the decision not to use the facilities of the Post Office motivated by any act or statement by the appellant.

In sum, the requirements of proximity contained in the principles enunciated in *Hedley Byrne, supra*, and confirmed in *Anns, supra*, are not met on the facts of this appeal. As I have concluded that the respondent did not come within a limited class in the reasonable contemplation of a person in the position of the appellant, it is unnecessary to proceed to the second stage or test set out by Lord Wilberforce in *Anns, supra*.

JAMES v. BRITISH COLUMBIA
(2005), 38 B.C.L.R. (4th) 263 (C.A.)

[The plaintiff's employer held a tree farm licence from the province of British Columbia which contained a provision that would have prevented the employer's sawmill from being closed by the employer without the approval of the Minister of Forests. On a renewal of the license, the Minister inadvertently omitted the protective clause and the employer later closed the mill. The plaintiff launched a class action against the government, alleging that its negligence had caused him and others similarly situated to suffer a loss of employment income. The government alleged that the claim was unfounded in law.]

ESSON J.A.: . . .

The Crown's submission that the plaintiff cannot succeed without pleading and proving "detrimental reliance" finds support in some cases and some academic writing but, with respect, appears to be based on a misapprehension of the extent of the "new law" propounded in *Hedley Byrne & Co. v. Heller & Partners Ltd.*, [1964] A.C. 465 (U.K. H.L.). Because that case overruled the longstanding rule that there could be no recovery in tort for pure economic loss, and because it was held that detrimental reliance was an essential element of the cause of action, it seems to have been assumed by some that the requirement of proving detrimental reliance applies to all actions seeking recovery of damages for pure economic loss.

That requirement, however, was "old law". It flowed, not from the decision to change the law with respect to claims for pecuniary loss, but from the fact that *Hedley Byrne* was a claim in misrepresentation. In such an action, it was always incumbent upon the plaintiff to plead and prove reliance upon the false representation. With respect to that issue, there is no logical reason to distinguish between fraudulent misrepresentation and negligent misrepresentation. In either case, proof of reliance is essential to establish causation.

On the facts alleged here, the causal relationship established by reliance in a misrepresentation case is arguably covered by the finding of foreseeability and proximity. The essential feature of each concept is the "something more" which the Supreme Court, in *Cooper*, held must be demonstrated in order to establish that the plaintiff and the defendant were in a sufficiently close relationship. . . .

In this case, it would be unrealistic to impose upon the plaintiffs a burden to establish detrimental reliance. That is not their case. However, the facts may demonstrate a different form of reliance. The employees can be said to have relied upon the Minister to exercise reasonable care to retain Clause 7 in the licence unless and until he reached a decision on policy grounds to remove it. That view of the matter can be inferred from the facts alleged. It does not support the view that the law requires these plaintiffs to prove detrimental reliance.

Perhaps the best known cases in the negligent service category are those brought by a disappointed beneficiary. The earliest such case was the decision of Mr. Justice Aikins (later J.A.) in *Whittingham v. Crease & Co.* (1978), 88 D.L.R. (3d) 353. . .

It is regrettable that the decision of Aikins J., which exhibited the thorough and careful reasoning characteristic of the decisions of that learned judge, has been ignored for so long. To return to the present issue, I would adopt his analysis of the relationship between reliance and liability in cases of this kind, which is the clearest exposition of the issue which has come to my attention. I quote from pp. 373-74:

> The facts in the present case differ in one particular and troublesome aspect from those in the general run of cases in which *Hedley Byrne* has been successfully invoked. I have not been referred to a case, nor have I been able to find one, in which the principle of *Hedley Byrne* has been applied where the plaintiff had not acted on the strength of the representation made by the defendant and it was the plaintiff's own act which was the *immediate* cause of the loss.

> In this case the plaintiff has suffered a loss but without his having done anything in reliance on the implied representation made by [the solicitor]. In my opinion there are two reasons, linked to each other, which enable the plaintiff to succeed in this case, notwithstanding that he remained passive and did nothing, relying on [the solicitor's] implied representation. First, it was unnecessary for the plaintiff to act at all on the implied representation in order to attract the loss which he has suffered; second, [the solicitor] could reasonably foresee that if he, in the performance of his duty, failed to see to it that the will was properly witnessed, then that neglect would cause the very loss the plaintiff has suffered, without the plaintiff doing anything at all. Granted that there was an implied duty on the part of [the solicitor] to the plaintiff and that the plaintiff relied on [the solicitor] fulfilling that duty, it seems to me on principle that it is immaterial that the plaintiff himself did nothing in reliance on the implied representation made by [the solicitor] which brought about his loss. This is so because the negligence of the solicitor caused the loss without there having to be any intervening act by the plaintiff to perfect the chain of causation. . . .

In the reasons of Megarry V.-C. in *Ross v. Caunters* [[1979] 3 All E.R. 580 (Ch.)] and in the speeches of the majority in *White v. Jones* [[1995] 2 A.C. 207], the absence of reliance was held not to preclude recovery because its place was taken by the voluntary assumption of responsibility by the solicitor. I agree with the chambers judge that that approach may be properly applicable to the position of the Minister in this case.

NOTES AND QUESTIONS

1. While the court refused to recognize a duty of care in *B.D.C.*, it did outline the situations in which a duty would be recognized with respect to pure economic losses resulting from the careless provision of services. Summarize the relevant rules. See Blom, "Slow Courier in the Supreme Court" (1986) 12 C.B.L.J. 43.

2. As mentioned in *James*, the issue of liability for pure economic loss resulting from negligent services commonly arises in the context of carelessly prepared wills. Although the Supreme Court of Canada has yet to resolve the issue, it is generally accepted that a lawyer may be held liable to an intended beneficiary who is deprived of

a bequest because of the lawyer's negligence. See *Whittingham v. Crease & Co.* (1978), 88 D.L.R. (3d) 353 (B.C.S.C.); *Ross v. Caunters*, [1979] 3 All E.R. 580 (Ch.); *Gartside v. Sheffield, Young & Ellis*, [1983] N.Z.L.R. 37 (C.A.); *White v. Jones*, [1995] 2 A.C. 207 (H.L.); *Hill v. Van Erp* (1997), 142 A.L.R. 687 (H.C.A.); *Wilhelm v. Hickson* (2000), 189 Sask. R. 71 (C.A.); *Hall v. Bennett Estate* (2003), 64 O.R. (3d) 191 (C.A.); *McCullough v. Riffert* (2010), 76 C.C.L.T. (3d) 71 (Ont. S.C.J.); *Meier v. Rose*, 2012 ABQB 82; and *Badenach v. Calvert*, [2016] HCA 18. See also McJannet, "*Wilhelm v. Hickson*: The Canadian Tort Approach to the Disappointed Beneficiary and the Negligent Solicitor" (2001) 64 Sask. L.R. 113; Benson, "Should *White v Jones* Represent Canadian Law: A Return to First Principles" in Neyers, Chamberlain & Pitel, eds., *Emerging Issues in Tort Law* (2007), ch. 6; and Waddams, "Breaches of Contracts and Claims by Third Parties" in Neyers, Chamberlain & Pitel, *ibid.*, ch. 7.

In the absence of any contractual relationship between the lawyer and the intended beneficiary, and perhaps in the absence of any reliance by the latter, is there any convincing reason to impose liability in such circumstances? Should the plaintiff essentially be entitled to the defendant's services without paying for them? See Klar, "Downsizing Torts" in Mullany & Linden, eds., *Torts Tomorrow: A Tribute to John Fleming* (1998), ch. 16. Consider the possible explanatory impact in this area of the rights-based analysis to tort law mentioned in the first section of this chapter.

Should it matter whether the plaintiff is an intended beneficiary under a will negligently prepared by the lawyer or is a beneficiary under an earlier will that is affected by the lawyer's preparation of the newer will? See *Graham v. Bonnycastle* (2004), 36 Alta. L.R. (4th) 203 (C.A.); *Harrison v. Fallis*, 2006 CarswellOnt 3545 (S.C.J.) (WL Can); *Vincent v. Blake Cassels & Graydon LLP*, 2013 ONSC 980; and *Johnston Estate v. Johnston*, 2017 BCCA 59.

3. Is the analysis in *James* consistent with *B.D.C.*? Should the courts adopt an "assumption of responsibility" test rather than focusing on reliance by the plaintiff? See Brown & Brochu, "Once More unto the Breech: *James v. British Columbia* and the Problems with the Duty of Care in Canadian Tort Law" (2008) 45 Alta. L. Rev. 1071.

In *Burke v. Watson & Barnard (A Firm)*, 2016 BCCA 439 the court indicated that in a case in which the plaintiff could not establish reliance, the plaintiff had to establish that the defendant assumed responsibility for the plaintiff's interests in performing the service.

4. To what extent has the analysis of the negligent performance of a service been changed by *Livent*? Should the analysis be the same as that for negligent misrepresentation? If not, what should the differences be?

5. In *Hughes v. Sunbeam Corp. (Canada) Ltd.* (2002), 61 O.R. (3d) 433 (C.A.) the plaintiffs sued the Underwriters' Laboratories of Canada for negligently endorsing a smoke detector. ULC was neither a statutory regulator nor an institution akin to a statutory regulator. It was a private corporation which undertook to examine and certify the safety of products. The Court of Appeal, relying on *Cooper,* reasoned that no duty was owed by ULC to the plaintiffs. The service offered by ULC was meant to provide a benefit to the public as a whole by encouraging manufacturers to ensure that their products met certain standards. Further, the plaintiffs had not paid ULC for the service. Do you agree with this reasoning? See also *More v. Bauer Nike Hockey Inc.*, 2011 BCCA 419 at paras. 53-61.

6. If a doctor negligently fails to perform an abortion and the baby is born, and the biological father is compelled to pay child support to the mother, should the father be able to sue the doctor? Is this a claim for pure economic loss resulting from the negligent performance of a service, or should it be characterized differently? See *Freeman v. Sutter* (1996), 110 Man. R. (2d) 23 (C.A.).

7. If a hockey team refers a player to a doctor for treatment, and the doctor negligently treats the player, can the team sue the doctor for its lost profits? See, in the context of English football, *West Bromwich Albion Football Club Ltd. v. El-Safty*, [2006] EWCA Civ 1299.

8. Many of the cases on the negligent performance of a service involve insurance agents who have failed to arrange the appropriate coverage. See for example *Fine's Flowers Ltd. v. General Accident Assurance Co.* (1977), 81 D.L.R. (3d) 139 (C.A.); and *National Crane Services Inc. v. AON Reed Stenhouse* (2007), 291 Sask. R. 281 (Q.B.).

4. Negligent Supply of Shoddy Goods or Structures

Liability clearly will lie in tort with respect to personal injuries and property damage that the plaintiff suffers as a result of the defendant's supply of shoddy goods or structures. Indeed, the law on products liability is a significant part of negligence law: see Linden *et al.*, *Canadian Tort Law*, 11th ed. (2018), ch. 13. The defendant will also be held liable in breach of contract for pure economic losses that the plaintiff suffers if the plaintiff is able to establish the requisite agreement. Problems arise, however, if the plaintiff suffers pure economic losses as a result of the defendant's carelessness but is unable to establish privity of contract. Historically, such losses were generally not recoverable. The Supreme Court of Canada has since adopted a more liberal approach.

WINNIPEG CONDOMINIUM CORP. NO. 36 v. BIRD CONSTRUCTION CO.
(1995), 121 D.L.R. (4th) 193 (S.C.C.)

[A land developer contracted with the respondent to construct an apartment building. Some years later, the building was converted into a condominium when the appellant became the registered owner of the land and building. In 1982, the appellant's directors became concerned about the masonry work on the exterior of the building. They retained architects and a firm of consulting engineers to inspect the building. The architects and engineers offered the opinion that the building was structurally sound. In 1989, a section of the exterior cladding fell from the ninth storey of the building. The appellant had further inspections undertaken which revealed structural defects in the masonry work. Following these inspections, the entire cladding was replaced at the appellant's expense.

The appellant brought an action in negligence against several parties, including the respondent. The statement of claim alleged inadequacies in design and workmanship, without assigning specific blame to one defendant or another. The respondent moved for summary judgment and to strike out the claim as disclosing no reasonable cause of action. Both motions were dismissed. The respondent appealed to the Manitoba Court of Appeal. The appeal was dismissed with respect to the motion for summary judgment but allowed with respect to the motion to strike out, and the statement of claim was therefore struck out as against the respondent. The appellant appealed to the Supreme Court of Canada.]

LA FOREST J. [for the court] — May a general contractor responsible for the construction of a building be held tortiously liable for negligence to a subsequent purchaser of the building, who is not in contractual privity with the contractor, for the cost of repairing defects in the building arising out of negligence in its construction?

. . .

Analysis

This case gives this Court the opportunity once again to address the question of recoverability in tort for economic loss. In *Norsk, supra*, at p. 1049, I made reference to an article by Professor Feldthusen in which he outlined five different categories of cases where the question of recoverability in tort for economic loss has arisen ("Economic Loss in the Supreme Court of Canada: Yesterday and Tomorrow" (1990-91), 17 C.B.L.J. 356, at pp. 357-58), namely:

1. The Independent Liability of Statutory Public Authorities;
2. Negligent Misrepresentation;
3. Negligent Performance of a Service;
4. Negligent Supply of Shoddy Goods or Structures;
5. Relational Economic Loss.

I stressed in *Norsk* that the question of recoverability for economic loss must be approached with reference to the unique and distinct policy issues raised in each of these categories. That is because ultimately the issues concerning recovery for economic loss are concerned with determining the proper ambit of the law of tort, an exercise that must take account of the various situations where that question may arise. This case raises issues different from that in *Norsk*, which fell within the fifth category. The present case, which involves the alleged negligent construction of a building, falls partially within the fourth category, although subject to an important *caveat*. The negligently supplied structure in this case was not merely shoddy; it was dangerous. In my view, this is important because the degree of danger to persons and other property created by the negligent construction of a building is a cornerstone of the policy analysis that must take place in determining whether the cost of repair of the building is recoverable in tort. As I will attempt to show, a distinction can be drawn on a policy level between "dangerous" defects in buildings and merely "shoddy" construction in buildings and that, at least with respect to dangerous defects, compelling policy reasons exist for the imposition upon contractors of tortious liability for the cost of repair of these defects.

Traditionally, the courts have characterized the costs incurred by a plaintiff in repairing a defective chattel or building as "economic loss" on the grounds that costs of those repairs do not arise from injury to persons or damage to property apart from the defective chattel or building itself; see *Rivtow Marine Ltd. v. Washington Iron Works*, [1974] S.C.R. 1189, at p. 1207. For my part, I would find it more congenial to deal directly with the policy considerations underlying that classification. . . . However, I am content to deal with the issues in the terms in which the arguments were formulated. Adopting this traditional characterization as a convenient starting point for my analysis, I observe that the losses claimed by the Condominium Corporation in the present case fall quite clearly under the category of economic loss. In their statement of claim, the Condominium Corporation claim damages in excess of $1.5 million from the respondent Bird, the subcontractor Kornovski & Keller and the architects Smith Carter, representing the cost of repairing the building subsequent to the collapse of the exterior cladding on May 8, 1989. The Condominium Corporation is not claiming that anyone was injured by the collapsing exterior cladding or that the collapsing cladding damaged any of its other property. Rather, its claim is simply for the cost of repairing the allegedly defective masonry and putting the exterior of the building back into safe working condition.

. . .

In my view, where a contractor (or any other person) is negligent in planning or constructing a building, and where that building is found to contain defects resulting from that negligence which pose a real and substantial danger to the occupants of the building, the reasonable cost of repairing the defects and putting the building back into a non-dangerous state are recoverable in tort by the occupants. The underlying rationale for this conclusion is that a person who participates in the construction of a large and permanent structure which, if negligently constructed, has the capacity to cause serious damage to other persons and property in the community, should be held to a reasonable standard of care.

. . .

Was There a Sufficiently Close Relationship Between the Parties so that, in the Reasonable Contemplation of Bird, Carelessness on its Part Might Cause Damage to a Subsequent Purchaser of the Building such as the Condominium Corporation?

In my view, it is reasonably foreseeable to contractors that, if they design or construct a building negligently and if that building contains latent defects as a result of that negligence, subsequent purchasers of the building may suffer personal injury or damage to other property when those defects manifest themselves. A lack of contractual privity between the contractor and the inhabitants at the time the defect becomes manifest does not make the potential for injury any less foreseeable. Buildings are permanent structures that are commonly inhabited by many different persons over their useful life. By constructing the building negligently, contractors (or any other person responsible for the design and construction of a building) create a foreseeable danger that will threaten not only the original owner, but every inhabitant during the useful life of the building. . . .

In my view, the reasonable likelihood that a defect in a building will cause injury to its inhabitants is also sufficient to ground a contractor's duty in tort to subsequent purchasers of the building for the cost of repairing the defect if that defect is discovered prior to any injury and if it poses a real and substantial danger to the inhabitants of the building. In coming to this conclusion, I adopt the reasoning of Laskin J. in *Rivtow,* which I find highly persuasive. If a contractor can be held liable in tort where he or she constructs a building negligently and, as a result of that negligence, the building causes damage to persons or property, it follows that the contractor should also be held liable in cases where the dangerous defect is discovered and the owner of the building wishes to mitigate the danger by fixing the defect and putting the building back into a non-dangerous state. In both cases, the duty in tort serves to protect the bodily integrity and property interests of the inhabitants of the building . . . .

Apart from the logical force of holding contractors liable for the cost of repair of dangerous defects, there is also a strong underlying policy justification for imposing liability in these cases. . . . Allowing recovery against contractors in tort for the cost of repair of dangerous defects thus serves an important preventative function by encouraging socially responsible behaviour.

This conclusion is borne out by the facts of the present case, which fall squarely within the category of what I would define as a "real and substantial danger" . . . . Had this cladding landed on a person or on other property, it would unquestionably have caused serious injury or damage. Indeed, it was only by chance that the cladding fell in the middle of the night and caused no harm. In this light, I believe that the Condominium Corporation behaved responsibly, and as a reasonable home owner should, in having the building inspected and repaired immediately. Bird should not be insulated from liability simply because the current owner of the building acted quickly to alleviate the danger that Bird itself may well have helped to create . . . .

Given the clear presence of a real and substantial danger in this case, I do not find it necessary to consider whether contractors should also in principle be held to owe a duty to subsequent purchasers for the cost of repairing non-dangerous defects in buildings. . . .

Without entering into this question, I note that the present case is distinguishable on a policy level from cases where the workmanship is merely shoddy or substandard but not dangerously defective. In the latter class of cases, tort law serves to encourage the repair of dangerous defects and thereby to protect the bodily integrity of inhabitants of buildings. By contrast, the former class of cases bring into play the questions of quality of workmanship and fitness for purpose . . .

Are There Any Considerations that Ought to Negate (a) the Scope of the Duty and (b) the Class of Persons to Whom it is Owed or (c) the Damages to which a Breach of it May Give Rise?

There are two primary and interrelated concerns raised by the recognition of a contractor's duty in tort to subsequent purchasers of buildings for the cost of repairing dangerous defects. The first is that warranties respecting quality of construction are primarily contractual in nature and cannot easily be defined or limited in tort. . . .

The second concern is that the recognition of . . . a duty interferes with the doctrine of *caveat emptor* which, as this Court affirmed in *Fraser-Reid v. Droumtsekas,* [[1980] 1 S.C.R. 720 at 723] "has lost little of its pristine force in the sale of land". The doctrine of *caveat emptor* dictates that, in the absence of an express warranty, there is no implied warranty of fitness for human habitation upon the purchase of a house already completed at the time of sale. Huband J.A. of the Manitoba Court of Appeal relied on this doctrine in concluding that no duty in tort could be owed to subsequent purchasers of a building. . .

In my view, these concerns are . . . merely versions of the more general and traditional concern that allowing recovery for economic loss in tort will subject a defendant to what Cardozo C.J. in *Ultramares Corp. v. Touche,* 174 N.E. 441 (N.Y.C.A. 1931), at p. 444, called "liability in an indeterminate amount for an indeterminate time to an indeterminate class." In light of the fact that most buildings have a relatively long useful life, the concern is that a contractor will be subject potentially to an indeterminate amount of liability to an indeterminate number of successive owners over an indeterminate time period. The doctrines of privity of contract and *caveat emptor* provide courts with a useful mechanism for limiting liability in tort. But the problem, as I will now attempt to demonstrate, is that it is difficult to justify the employment of these doctrines in the tort context in any principled manner apart from their utility as mechanisms for limiting liability.

The Concern with Overlap Between Tort and Contract Duties

Turning to the first concern, a duty on the part of contractors to take reasonable care in the construction of buildings can, in my view, be conceptualized in the absence of contract and will not result in indeterminate liability to the contractor. As I mentioned earlier, this Court has recognized that a tort duty can arise concurrently with a contractual duty, so long as that tort duty arises independently of the contractual duty. . . . As I see it, the duty to construct a building according to reasonable standards and without dangerous defects arises independently of the contractual stipulations between the original owner and the contractor because it arises from a duty to create the building safely and not merely according to contractual standards of quality. It must be remembered that we are speaking here of a duty to construct the building according to reasonable standards of safety in such a manner that it does not contain *dangerous* defects. As this duty arises independently of any contract, there is no logical reason for allowing the contractor to rely upon a contract made with the original owner to shield him or her from liability to subsequent purchasers arising from a dangerously constructed building. . . .

The tort duty to construct a building safely is thus a circumscribed duty that is not parasitic upon any contractual duties between the contractor and the original owner. Seen in this way, no serious risk of indeterminate liability arises with respect to this tort duty. In the first place, there is no risk of liability to an indeterminate class because the potential class of claimants is limited to the very persons for whom the building is constructed: the inhabitants of the building. The fact that the class of claimants may include successors in title who have no contractual relationship with the contractors does not, in my view, render the class of potential claimants indeterminate. . . .

Secondly, there is no risk of liability in an indeterminate amount because the amount of liability will always be limited by the reasonable cost of repairing the dangerous defect in the building and restoring that building to a non-dangerous state. Counsel for Bird advanced the argument that the cost of repairs claimed for averting a danger caused by a defect in construction could, in some cases, be disproportionate to the actual damage to persons or property that might be caused if that defect were not repaired. For example, he expressed concern that a given plaintiff could claim thousands of dollars in damage for a defect which, if left unrepaired, would cause only a few dollars damage to that plaintiff's other property. However, in my view, any danger of indeterminacy in damages is averted by the requirement that the defect for which the costs of repair are claimed must constitute a real and substantial danger to the inhabitants of the building, and the fact that the inhabitants of the building can only claim the reasonable cost of repairing the defect and mitigating the danger. The burden of proof will always fall on the plaintiff to demonstrate that there is a serious risk to safety, that the risk was caused by the contractor's negligence, and that the repairs are required to alleviate the risk.

Finally, there is little risk of liability for an indeterminate time because the contractor will only be liable for the cost of repair of dangerous defects during the useful life of the building. Practically speaking, I believe that the period in which the contractor may be exposed to liability for negligence will be much shorter than the full useful life of the building. With the passage of time, it will become increasingly difficult for owners of a building to prove at trial that any deterioration in the building is attributable to the initial negligence of the contractor and not simply to the inevitable wear and tear suffered by every building. . . .

The Caveat Emptor Concern

Turning to the second concern, *caveat emptor* cannot, in my view, serve as a complete shield to tort liability for the contractors of a building. In *Fraser-Reid, supra*, this Court relied on the doctrine of *caveat emptor* in rejecting a claim by a buyer of a house for the recognition of an implied warranty of fitness for human habitation. However, the Court explicitly declined to address the question of whether *caveat emptor* serves to negate a duty in tort. . . . Accordingly, the question remains at large in Canadian law and must be resolved on the level of principle.

In *Fraser-Reid*, Dickson J. (as he then was) observed that the doctrine of *caveat emptor* stems from the *laissez-faire* attitudes of the eighteenth and nineteenth centuries and the notion that purchasers must fend for themselves in seeking protection by express warranty or by independent examination of the premises. . . . The assumption underlying the doctrine is that the purchaser of a building is better placed than the seller or builder to inspect the building and to bear the risk that latent defects will emerge necessitating repair costs. However, in my view, this is an assumption which (if ever valid) is simply not responsive to the realities of the modern housing market. . . . [C]ontractors and builders, because of their knowledge, skill and expertise, are in the best position to ensure the reasonable structural integrity of buildings and their freedom from latent defect. In this respect, the imposition of liability on builders provides an important incentive for care in the construction of buildings and a deterrent against poor workmanship.

My conclusion that a subsequent purchaser is not the best placed to bear the risk of the emergence of latent defects is borne out by the facts of this case. It is significant that, when cracking first appeared in the mortar of the building in 1982, the Condominium Corporation actually hired Smith Carter, the original architect of the building, along with a firm of structural engineers, to assess the condition of the mortar work and exterior cladding. These experts failed to detect the latent defects that appear to have caused the cladding to fall in 1989. Thus, although it is clear that the Condominium Corporation acted with diligence in seeking to detect hidden defects in the building, they were nonetheless unable to detect the defects or to foresee the collapse of the cladding in 1989. This, in my view, illustrates the unreality of the assumption that the purchaser is better placed to detect and bear the risk of hidden defects. For this Court to apply the doctrine of *caveat emptor* to negate Bird's duty in tort would be to apply a rule that has become completely divorced, in this context at least, from its underlying rationale.

Conclusion

I conclude, then, that no adequate policy considerations exist to negate a contractor's duty in tort to subsequent purchasers of a building to take reasonable care in constructing the building, and to ensure that the building does not contain defects that pose foreseeable and substantial danger to the health and safety of the occupants. In my view, the Manitoba Court of Appeal erred in deciding that Bird could not, in principle, be held liable in tort to the Condominium Corporation for the reasonable cost of repairing the defects and putting the building back into a non-dangerous state. These costs are recoverable economic loss under the law of tort in Canada.

NOTES AND QUESTIONS

1. What policy rationale motivated La Forest J.'s decision? Does that rationale outweigh the concerns that traditionally led courts to deny recovery in such cases?

2. Although the plaintiff's primary argument was that it had suffered a pure economic loss, it argued in the alternative that it had suffered property damage. That claim was based on a passage in *D&F Estates Ltd. v. Church Commissioners for England,* [1989] A.C. 177 (H.L.) in which Lord Bridge had suggested that:

> . . .it may well be arguable that in the case of complex structures . . . one element of the structure should be regarded for the purpose of the application of the principles under discussion as distinct from another element, so that damage to one part of the structure caused by a hidden defect in another part may qualify to be treated as damage to "other property".

Along those lines, the plaintiff in *Winnipeg Condominium* claimed that the collapsed cladding was property damage that had been caused by the defendant's negligent installation of metal ties, and since the action pertained to property damage, there was no need for the unusually restrictive approach that applies in cases of pure economic loss.

La Forest J. rejected this argument. As he observed, Lord Bridge had subsequently retreated from his observations in *D&F Estates.* In *Murphy v. Brentwood District Council* (1990), [1991] 1 A.C. 398 (H.L.) he said:

> The reality is that the structural elements in any building form a single indivisible unit of which the different parts are essentially interdependent. To the extent that there is any defect in one part of the structure it must to a greater or lesser degree necessarily affect all other parts of the structure. Therefore any defect in the structure is a defect in the quality of the whole and it is quite artificial, in order to impose a legal liability which the law would not otherwise impose, to treat a defect in an integral structure, so far as it weakens the structure, as a dangerous defect liable to cause damage to 'other property'. A critical distinction must be drawn here between some part of a complex structure which is said to be a 'danger' only because it does not perform its proper function in sustaining the other parts and some distinct item incorporated in the structure which positively malfunctions so as to inflict positive damage on the structure in which it is incorporated. Thus, if a defective central heating boiler explodes and damages a house or a defective electrical installation malfunctions and sets the house on fire, I see no reason to doubt that the owner of the house, if he can prove that the damage was due to the negligence of the boiler manufacturer in the one case or the electrical contractor in the other, can recover damages in tort on *Donoghue v. Stevenson* principles.

> For these reasons the complex structure theory offers no escape from the conclusion that damage to a house itself which is attributable to a defect in the structure of the

house is not recoverable in tort on *Donoghue v. Stevenson* principles, but represents purely economic loss which is only recoverable in contract or in tort by reason of some special relationship of proximity which imposes on the tortfeasor a duty of care to protect against economic loss.

La Forest J. agreed with those observations and added that in "cases involving the recoverability of economic loss in tort, it is preferable for the courts to weigh the relevant policy issues openly." In his view, the "complex structure" theory merely tends to "circumvent and obscure the underlying policy questions."

3. As a general rule, the plaintiff cannot establish the required property damage simply by pointing to the defective product itself. For example, a plaintiff who has purchased an appliance that does not work has not suffered property damage. See for example *Edmonton (City) v. Lovat Tunnel Equipment Inc.* (2000), 279 A.R. 1 (Q.B.); *Zidaric v. Toshiba of Canada Ltd.* (2001), 5 C.C.L.T. (3d) 61 (Ont. S.C.J.); and *Arora v. Whirlpool Canada LP*, 2013 ONCA 657 at para. 73. Consider, in the cases below, how rigidly the courts uphold this general rule.

4. What arguments did La Forest J. consider in *Winnipeg Condominium* with respect to the possible negation of a duty of care? Are you satisfied with his disposition of those arguments?

5. Architects and engineers involved in the construction of defective structures are engaged in performing a service, which could blur the line between these two categories of pure economic loss. However, *Winnipeg Condominium* indicates that the principles it develops regarding defective structures apply not only to contractors (or subcontractors) but also to architects and engineers. See *Heinicke v. Cooper Rankin Ltd.* (2006), 210 Man. R. (2d) 125 (Q.B.).

6. La Forest J. carefully confined his decision to cases in which the defendant's carelessness results in shoddy goods or structures that pose a "real and substantial danger." That rule was applied in *M. Hasegawa & Co. v. Pepsi Bottling Group (Canada) Co.* (2002), 1 B.C.L.R. (4th) 209 (C.A.). The plaintiff purchased bottled glacial water from a third party. The third party had contracted with the defendant to bottle the water. Because the defendant had not sanitized the bottle caps, the water developed "mould floes." Although that problem meant the water could not be sold, it had not caused physical injury or property damage and it did not pose a health risk to potential consumers. The Court of Appeal therefore held that a duty of care did not arise.

7. Questions sometimes arise as to the scope of the "real and substantial danger" requirement. For example in *Roy v. Thiessen* (2005), 257 Sask. R. 239 (C.A.) the defendant argued that the defect in the plaintiff's house had to create an "imminent" danger. The court disagreed, stating: "The policy goal must be to encourage homeowners to make any necessary repairs as soon as possible in order to mitigate potential losses; they should not have to delay such repairs until there is an imminent danger of harm." See also *Sentinel Self-Storage Corp. v. Dyregrov* (2003), 180 Man. R. (2d) 85 (C.A.); *Mariani v. Lemstra* (2004), 246 D.L.R. (4th) 489 (Ont. C.A.); *North Sydney Associates v. United Dominion Industries Ltd.* (2006), 243 N.S.R. (2d) 372 (C.A.);

Vargo v. Hughes, 2013 ABCA 96; *Barwin v. IKO Industries Ltd.*, 2013 ONSC 3054 (Div. Ct.); and *Nieman v. Kroeker*, 2017 BCSC 368.

In *Hughes v. Sunbeam Corp. (Canada)* (2002), 61 O.R. (3d) 433 (C.A.) the plaintiff purchased an allegedly defective smoke alarm manufactured by the defendant. Although the alleged defect had not caused any additional damage, the plaintiff sued in negligence for the recovery of the pure economic loss that he suffered as a result of replacing the unit. At first instance, the defendant succeeded in having the claim struck out on the ground that it did not disclose a cause of action. The motions judge held that since a defective smoke alarm is not dangerous in itself, the case fell outside the scope of the rule formulated in *Winnipeg Condominium*. On appeal, however, the claim was allowed to proceed. Laskin J.A. agreed that "under the current state of the law," the claim "would likely fail." However, he also insisted that on a motion to strike out, "causes of action should not be barred simply because they are novel." He considered (at 443) the possibility that the scope of *Winnipeg Condominium* should be extended:

> A smoke detector that does not detect fires . . . is not itself dangerous, but relying on it is. The occupants are lulled into a false sense of security. . . . Safety justified compensating the owner of the apartment building in *Winnipeg Condominium* to eliminate the dangerously defective cladding. Safety may also justify compensating the owner of a defective smoke alarm to eliminate dangerous reliance on it.

In *Brett-Young Seeds Ltd. v. K.B.A. Consultants Inc.* (2008), 225 Man. R. (2d) 291 (C.A.) the court noted that "Canadian appellate courts have been inconsistent in determining what is required to meet the threshold of 'real and substantial danger'."

8. In *Globalnet Management Solutions Inc. v. Cornerstone CBS Building Solutions Ltd.*, 2018 BCCA 303 the defendant, in constructing a residence for the plaintiff, negligently built the retaining walls. The trial judge found that the walls posed a substantial danger to the occupants of the building. However, the trial judge dismissed the plaintiff's claim because it had sold the property to a related entity before making repairs to the retaining walls. The trial judge held that the repairs, having been made to someone else's property, were therefore voluntary and so the plaintiff could not recover the cost of the repairs.

On appeal, the court reversed. Had there been no sale to the related entity the plaintiff's recovery would have been clear. In the court's view, that sale should not allow the defendant to escape liability for its carelessness. Do you agree? Should the answer be the same for a sale to an unrelated entity?

In the same litigation the related entity also sued the defendant but its claim failed. Why?

9. In *Winnipeg Condominium* La Forest J. expressly refrained from formulating a rule that would be applicable to cases in which the defendant's carelessness does not create a real and substantial danger. Should a duty of care arise if a defect in a building is non-threatening? An early English decision answered this question in the affirmative. In *Junior Books Ltd. v. Veitchi*, [1982] 3 W.L.R. 477 (C.A.) the defendant subcontractor carelessly installed a floor in the plaintiff's building. Although that floor developed cracks, the defect did not pose any danger to person or property. The plaintiff brought an action in negligence to recover costs associated with replacing the floor, which a majority of the House of Lords allowed. Lord Roskill explained that

the defendant knew that the plaintiff relied upon its expertise and described the parties' relationship as being "as close as it could be short of actual privity of contract." However, while *Junior Books* has not been directly overruled, it has been carefully confined to its unique facts in more recent decisions: *D&F Estates Ltd. v. Church Commissioners for England, supra*, and *Murphy v. Brentwood District Council, supra*. The status of *Junior Books* in Canada is uncertain. La Forest J. did not address it in *Winnipeg Condominium*. In *Kamloops v. Neilson*, [1984] 2 S.C.R. 2 at 32 Wilson J. referred to *Junior Books* as representing "a significant step forward." Some lower courts have followed the English decision, while others have confined it to its special facts: *University of Regina v. Pettick* (1986), 38 C.C.L.T. 230 (Sask. Q.B.); *Buthmann v. Balzer*, [1983] 4 W.W.R. 695 (Alta. Q.B.); *Logan Lake (Dist.) v. Rivtow Industries Ltd.* (1990), 71 D.L.R. (4th) 333 (B.C.C.A.); and *M. Hasegawa & Co. v. Pepsi Bottling Group (Canada) Co., supra*.

10. The focus on a dangerous defect in *Winnipeg Condominium* has been criticized by the High Court of Australia. In *Brookfield Multiplex Ltd. v. Owners Corporation Strata Plan 61288*, [2014] HCA 36 three of the seven judges stated (at para. 161):

> More importantly, in point of principle the approach in *Winnipeg Condominium* is driven by the assumption that the cost of repair or diminution in market value of a building is a reflex of the liability for physical damage to person or property which may occur if the defect is not repaired. Quite apart from the haphazard nature of this notion of equivalence of damage, this approach is flawed in that it detaches the duty not to inflict harm from the harm which is the gist of the cause of action.

They also quoted (at para. 162) Lord Oliver's reasoning from *Murphy, supra*, that drawing distinctions based on whether a defect is dangerous is "fallacious" because once the plaintiff is aware of the defect, no personal injury will actually occur unless the plaintiff ignores the danger. The plaintiff, once aware of the defect, could either cease to use the property or incur expenses that allow continued use. Do you understand these criticisms? Do you agree with them?

The High Court of Australia had previously held that a duty of care could be recognized even if the defect caused by the defendant's carelessness is non-threatening: *Bryan v. Maloney* (1995), 182 C.L.R. 609 (H.C.A.). In that case, the defendant built a house for his sister. The property passed through another owner before being acquired by the plaintiff. Six months after the purchase cracks appeared in the walls. The plaintiff then discovered that the house had been built with footings that were inadequate to withstand seasonal changes in the soil. The defect required costly repairs but did not pose any danger. A majority of the High Court affirmed the trial judge's decision in the plaintiff's favour.

Bryan was then narrowed — confined solely to residential housing — by the High Court of Australia in *Woolcock Street Investments Pty. Ltd. v. C.D.G. Pty. Ltd.* (2004), 205 A.L.R. 522 (H.C.A.). For a similar limiting view see *66295 Manitoba Ltd. v. Imperial Oil Ltd.* (2002), 165 Man. R. (2d) 29 (Q.B.). However in *Brookfield Multiplex* some of the judges noted (at para. 135) that "the distinction between purchases of buildings for domestic and commercial purposes is an unstable one." Do you agree?

If the type of neither defect nor building is of central importance, what is? In *Brookfield Multiplex* the High Court of Australia held that the key consideration as to whether a duty of care would be owed in these types of case is whether the subsequent owner of the building was "vulnerable" to the defendant's lack of reasonable care, in the sense that it was unable to protect itself (see paras. 22, 51, 58 and 130-32). The ability to enter into contracts, such as an agreement of purchase and sale, which expressly address the condition of the building strongly negates vulnerability. *Bryan* was explained in *Brookfield Multiplex* on the basis that the court had accepted the plaintiff as having been vulnerable. Is an analysis based on vulnerability better than one based on dangerousness?

11. A series of cases in New Zealand has considered whether a local council is liable for pure economic loss suffered by subsequent building owners as a result of its errors in supervising the construction of the building. In several of these cases, the central distinction drawn by the courts has been between private dwellings and other types of building. A duty of care has been held to be owed to owners of the former but not to owners of the latter. See *Hamlin v. Invercargill City Council*, [1994] 3 N.Z.L.R. 513 (C.A.), aff'd [1996] 1 N.Z.L.R. 513 (P.C.); *Te Mata Properties Limited v. Hastings District Council*, [2009] 1 N.Z.L.R. 460 (C.A.); *Queenstown Lakes District Council v. Charterhall Trustees Ltd.*, [2009] 3 N.Z.L.R. 786 (C.A.); *North Shore City Council v. Body Corporate 188529 (Sunset Terraces)*, [2010] NZSC 158. More recently this distinction has been rejected and the Supreme Court has allowed claims in respect of commercial buildings to proceed: *Body Corporate No. 207624 (Spencer on Byron) v. North Shore City Council*, [2012] NZSC 83.

12. It has been unclear whether Canadian courts will extend recovery to cases involving products with non-dangerous defects. See the analysis of many of the key cases in *Sable Offshore Energy Inc. v. Ameron International Corp.* (2006), 249 N.S.R. (2d) 122 (S.C.), aff'd (2007), 255 N.S.R. (2d) 164 (C.A.). More recently, in *Arora v. Whirlpool Canada LP*, *supra*, the Court of Appeal for Ontario considered a claim in respect of front-load washing machines. The claim was that the machines had been negligently designed so that their use resulted in the growth of mould and mildew. It was accepted that the machines were not dangerous. The court held (at para. 105):

> At its heart, the appellants' claim is that they paid more for their washing machines than they are worth. It is squarely about relative product quality — a matter that, as LaForest J. noted in *Winnipeg Condominium*, is customarily dealt with by contract and not easily defined by tort. In my view, requiring the courts to analyze a myriad of consumer transactions — some involving small outlays of money for goods that quickly depreciate and become redundant — in tort, without the framework of consumer protection legislation, to determine whether the consumer received value for his or her money, would burden an already taxed court system.

The court held that even if a *prima facie* duty of care was made out on the pleaded facts, policy considerations negated recognizing a cause of action in negligence for diminution in value for a defective, non-dangerous consumer product. The purchasers were left to their statutory and contractual remedies, including express, implied or statutory warranties. See also *Quenneville v. Robert Bosch GmbH*, 2017 ONSC 7422 at paras. 49-55.

Do you agree with this reasoning? To what extent does *Arora* resolve the issue for non-dangerous defects in residential housing?

13. To what extent does the analysis in *Winnipeg Condominium* distinguish between latent defects and patent defects? Do the same principles apply to both? On the distinction see *Cardwell v. Perthen* (2007), 68 B.C.L.R. (4th) 117 (C.A.).

14. If the plaintiff had contracted directly with the defendant for the purchase of a house, could the plaintiff choose to sue in tort relying on *Winnipeg Condominium* rather than in contract? Consider the discussion of concurrency in Chapter 13.

15. As noted in *Arora, supra,* claims for economic loss caused by defective products are also governed by legislation in all of the Canadian provinces. Many provinces have statutory warranties of merchantability which cannot be excluded in consumer transactions, and some abolish the privity requirement for claims against the manufacturer. There is also federal and provincial legislation prohibiting false and misleading advertising.

16. Claims involving defective products can be analyzed in different ways. In *Plas-Tex Canada Ltd. v. Dow Chemical of Canada Ltd.* (2004), 357 A.R. 139 (C.A.) the defendant supplied defective resin. The case was analyzed as involving a duty to warn. In *Serhan v. Johnson & Johnson* (2006), 85 O.R. (3d) 665 (Div. Ct.) the defendants manufactured defective blood glucose monitors. A majority of the court considered the claim to be based on "waiver of tort" and allowed it to proceed. Could these cases have been decided using the analysis in *Hughes, supra*?

17. For academic analysis of this category of pure economic loss see Feldthusen, *"Winnipeg Condominium Corp. #36 v. Bird Construction*: Who Needs Contract Anymore?" (1995) 25 C.B.L.J. 143; Rafferty, "Case Comment: *Winnipeg Condominium v. Bird Construction* — Recovery of Purely Economic Loss in the Tort of Negligence: Liability of Builders to Subsequent Purchasers for Construction Defects" (1996) 34 Alta. L. Rev. 472; Neyers, *"Donoghue v. Stevenson* and the Rescue Doctrine: A Public Justification of Recovery in Situations Involving the Negligent Supply of Dangerous Structures" (1999) 49 U.T.L.J. 475; Quill, "Consumer Protection in Respect of Defective Buildings" (2006) 14 Tort L. Rev. 105; Brown, "Assumption of Responsibility and Loss of Bargain in Tort Law" (2006) 29 Dal. L.J. 345; Todd, "Policy Issues in Defective Property Cases" in Neyers, Chamberlain & Pitel, eds., *Emerging Issues in Tort Law* (2007), ch. 8; Partlett, "Defective Structures and Economic Loss in the United States" in Neyers, Chamberlain & Pitel, *ibid.,* ch. 9; Yap, "Pure Economic Loss and Defects in the Law of Negligence" (2009) 17 Tort L. Rev. 80; Todd, "Difficulties with Leaky Building Litigation" (2012) 20 Tort L. Rev. 19; and Green & Davies, "'Pure Economic Loss' and Defective Buildings" in Robertson & Tilbury, eds., *Divergences in Private Law* (2016).

18. The leading cases in this area were decided before *Cooper.* How might the Supreme Court of Canada change the law in light of *Cooper*? Does *Deloitte & Touche v. Livent Inc.*, 2017 SCC 63 (extracted in Chapter 13) offer any suggestions?

REVIEW PROBLEMS

1. In a construction contract between Owner and Contractor, there is a clause which exculpates Contractor from liability for any losses other than repair costs if the work or materials provided under the contract prove to be substandard. There is no similar clause in the subcontract between Contractor and SubContractor. Should SubContractor be held directly liable to Owner in negligence for business losses consequent on SubContractor's installation of faulty materials? Does it matter

whether the defect is dangerous or merely shoddy? Would your conclusion change if the exculpatory clause was in the subcontract but not in the main contract?

2. The plaintiff purchased carpet from the defendant. The carpet began to wear badly after one year. Is the carpet defective? What further information would assist you in your answer? Does this suggest whether negligence or sales law is best suited to deal with claims about shoddy goods?

3. In 2010 Longstreet Inc., a property development corporation, acquired land on the outskirts of London, Ontario. Over the next year Longstreet Inc. built on the land a series of 22 similar three-story buildings. The philosophy behind the project was to create a community in which professionals would both live and work. To that end, each building contained office and work space on the ground floor and accommodation for one family on the upper floors. In each building, Longstreet Inc. used an unusual system of structural support. Vertical pillars made of a specially-engineered rubber were used in the basement to support the main floor. Once installed, these pillars were sheathed in a flexible cladding.

Between 2011 and 2012 Longstreet Inc. sold all 22 of the buildings. Longstreet Inc. sold Building 18 and the land on which it had been built to Nathan Forrest in 2012 for $450,000. Forrest sold it to Gwen Butler in 2015 and Butler sold it to Georgina Meade in 2016 for $490,000. Meade lives in the building with her family and carries on business in the office space as an accountant.

When Building 18 was constructed, ceramic tile, some in intricate patterns, had been used as the flooring in several of the rooms in the office and work space. During the autumn of 2018 many of these tiles cracked, some quite significantly. Meade suspected that this might be caused by a structural problem and so hired John Pemberton to investigate. In January 2019 Pemberton reported that there was a structural problem with Building 18. Pemberton discovered that scientific research had determined, as long ago as 2008, the rubber used in the pillars would shrink if it came into prolonged contact with certain chemicals. One of these chemicals was used extensively in the cladding that had been used to cover the pillars. In Pemberton's opinion, over time the exposure to the cladding had caused the pillars to shrink sufficiently to cause the ceramic tiles in the floor above to break.

The scientific research indicated that once a certain amount of contact with the chemical had occurred, the process could not be stopped and the rubber would, over time, continue to shrink. In Pemberton's view, even if the cladding was immediately removed further shrinkage would occur over the next four to six years before then ceasing. This additional shrinkage would continue to affect the flooring above and could also cause damage to some of the building's internal systems such as the plumbing and HVAC. However, there was no possibility of collapse or more significant damage.

In March 2019 Meade spent $85,000 to replace the pillars with proper supports and $20,000 to replace the tile floors.

Meade has retained you for an opinion on her ability to recover damages in a claim against Longstreet Inc. for negligence. You should assume that using the combination of the rubber pillars and the cladding as Longstreet Inc. did constituted a breach of any applicable standard of care. While your opinion is to be based on the law of Ontario, you should consider the law of other Commonwealth jurisdictions, especially in areas where Ontario law is unsettled or open to evolution.

5. Relational Economic Loss

The most difficult pure economic loss cases are those involving "relational economic losses." That phrase refers to situations in which the defendant, as a result of negligently damaging property belonging to a third party, causes a pure economic loss to the plaintiff with whom the third party had a relationship. Suppose, for example, that a construction company carelessly cuts a power line belonging to a municipality. Clearly, the construction company may be liable for losses sustained by the municipality. However, should the company also be liable to a factory that receives its supply of electricity from the municipality and that was forced to temporarily shut down as a result of the accident? What if the defendant's carelessness caused an entire city to lose power for an hour, a day or a week?

As the potential for "indeterminate liability" is particularly pronounced in such circumstances, the courts have been required to strike a balance between allowing victims to recover compensation for their losses and protecting defendants from the prospect of crushing liability. The courts have also recognized the need to consider the manner in which, from a societal perspective, the costs associated with such accidents should be distributed.

The Supreme Court of Canada has addressed the issue of relational economic loss in three key cases: *Canadian National Railway Co. v. Norsk Pacific Steamship Co.*, [1992] 1 S.C.R. 1021, *D'Amato v. Badger*, [1996] 2 S.C.R. 1071 and *Bow Valley Husky (Bermuda) Ltd. v. Saint John Shipbuilding Ltd.*, [1997] 3 S.C.R. 1210. An extract from the most recent decision is below. The other two cases are discussed in the notes that follow.

BOW VALLEY HUSKY (BERMUDA) LTD. v. SAINT JOHN SHIPBUILDING LTD.
(1997), 153 D.L.R. (4th) 385 (S.C.C.)

[Husky Oil Operations Ltd. ("HOOL") and Bow Valley Industries Ltd. ("BVI") made arrangements to have an off-shore oil drilling rig constructed by Saint John Shipbuilding Limited ("SJSL"). In order to take advantage of government financing, HOOL and BVI incorporated an offshore company, Bow Valley Husky (Bermuda) Ltd. ("BVHB"). Before construction began, ownership of the rig and the construction contract with SJSL were transferred to BVHB. HOOL and BVI entered into contracts with BVHB for the hire of the rig to conduct drilling operations at sites chosen by HOOL and BVI. These contracts provided that HOOL and BVI would continue to pay "day rates" to BVHB even if the rig was out of service.

A heat trace system was required in order to prevent the rig's pipes from freezing during the winter. BVHB directed SJSL to use a system manufactured by Raychem. That system used Thermaclad wrap to keep moisture away from the insulation and heat trace wire. However, a fire broke out on the rig as a result of the flammability of the Thermaclad wrap. The evidence indicated that neither Raychem nor SJSL warned any of the plaintiffs that Thermaclad wrap was flammable under certain circumstances. The evidence also indicated that the fire was caused in part by BVHB's misuse of the heat trace system.

As a result of the fire damage, the rig had to be towed to port for repairs and was out of service for several months. BVHB, HOOL and BVI sued SJSL for breach of contract and negligence and sued Raychem for negligence. BVHB claimed both for the cost of the repairs to the rig and for the revenue lost as a result of the rig being out of service for several months. HOOL and BVI sought to recover economic losses that they suffered during the repair period, including the day rates that they were contractually required to pay to BVHB.

The trial judge reached four important conclusions. First, he found that the defendant SJSL had, *inter alia*, breached a tort law duty to warn of the flammability of Thermaclad wrap. Second, he similarly held that Raychem had breached a tort law duty to warn. Third, he found that BVHB was primarily at fault for the accident because it had carelessly operated the heat tracing system. Responsibility was apportioned 60% to BVHB and 40% to SJSL and Raychem. Fourth, the trial judge ultimately dismissed the plaintiffs' claims on the basis that the case arose from negligence at sea, and therefore was governed by maritime law, in which contributory negligence constitutes a complete defence.

The Court of Appeal allowed an appeal by BVHB, but not by HOOL and BVI. It held that since the loss suffered by HOOL and BVI was purely economic, it was not recoverable. In contrast to the trial judge, however, it held that either (i) the provincial contributory negligence legislation applied on the facts, or (ii) contributory negligence no longer constituted a complete bar to recovery in maritime law. In either event, it held that BVHB was entitled to 40% of its damages from SJSL and Raychem. Further appeals proceeded to the Supreme Court of Canada.]

The reasons of La Forest and McLachlin JJ. were delivered by

MCLACHLIN J. (dissenting in part):

[McLachlin J. held that: (i) SJSL and Raychem owed a duty to warn BVHB of the flammability of Thermaclad wrap, (ii) SJSL's duty of care to BVHB was not negated by the terms of their contract, (iii) a sufficient causal relationship existed between the defendants' failure to warn and the loss sustained by BVHB, (iv) the trial judge's assessment of BVHB's contributory negligence was appropriate, and (v) BVHB's contributory negligence did not constitute a complete bar to recovery.]

. . .

F. *Did SJSL and Raychem Owe BVI and HOOL a Duty to Warn? (Recovery of Contractual Relational Economic Loss)*

(1) The Law

The plaintiffs HOOL and BVI had contracts with BVHB for the use of the rig owned by BVHB. They seek damages for economic loss incurred as a result of the shutdown of the drilling rig during the period it was being repaired. In other words, the plaintiffs HOOL and BVI seek to recover the economic loss they suffered as a result of damage to the property of a third party. This sort of loss is often called "contractual relational economic loss." The issue is whether the loss suffered by HOOL and BVI is recoverable.

The issue arises because common law courts have traditionally regarded many types of contractual relational economic loss as irrecoverable.

. . .

In England the situation is clear — no relational economic loss can ever be recovered: *Murphy v. Brentwood District Council*, [1991] 1 A.C. 398 (H.L.). Although *Murphy* concerned the liability of a public authority for approval of a negligently constructed building, not relational economic loss, the House of Lords stipulated that pure economic loss is recoverable only where there is actual physical damage to property of the plaintiff, thus excluding recovery for relational economic loss. In the civil law jurisdictions of Québec and France, by contrast, the law does not distinguish between loss arising from damage of one's own property and loss arising from damage to the property of another. If civil law judges restrict recovery, it is not as a matter of law, but on the basis of the facts and causal connection. The law in the common law provinces of Canada falls somewhere between these two extremes. While treating recovery in tort of contractual relational economic loss as exceptional, it is accepted in Canadian jurisprudence that there may be cases where it may be recovered.

The foregoing suggests the need for a rule to distinguish between cases where contractual relational economic loss can be recovered and cases where it cannot be recovered. Such a rule, as I wrote in *Canadian National Railway Co. v. Norsk Pacific Steamship Co.*, [1992] 1 S.C.R. 1021, should be morally and economically defensible and provide a logical basis upon which individuals can predicate their conduct and courts can decide future cases. . . . Although this Court attempted to formulate such a rule in *Norsk*, a split decision prevented the emergence of a clear rule. Given the commercial importance of the issue, it is important that the rule be settled. It is therefore necessary for this Court to revisit the issue.

The differences between the reasons of La Forest J. and myself in *Norsk* are of two orders: difference in result and difference in methodology. The difference in result, taken at its narrowest, is a difference in the definition of what constitutes a "joint venture" for the purposes of determining whether recovery for contractual relational economic loss should be allowed. We both agreed that if the plaintiff is in a joint venture with the person whose property is damaged, the plaintiff may claim consequential economic loss related to that property. We parted company because La Forest J. took a stricter view of what constituted a joint venture than I did.

The difference in methodology is not, on close analysis, as great as might be supposed. Broadly put, La Forest J. started from a general exclusionary rule and proceeded to articulate exceptions to that rule where recovery would be permitted. I, by contrast, stressed the two-step test for when recovery would be available, based on the general principles of recovery in tort as set out in *Anns v. Merton London Borough Council*, [1978] A.C. 728 (H.L.), and *Kamloops (City of) v. Nielsen*, [1984] 2 S.C.R. 2: (1) whether the relationship between the plaintiff and defendant was sufficiently proximate to give rise to a *prima facie* duty of care; and (2) whether, if such a *prima facie* duty existed, it was negated for policy reasons and recovery should be denied.

Despite this difference in approach, La Forest J. and I agreed on several important propositions: (1) relational economic loss is recoverable only in special circumstances where the appropriate conditions are met; (2) these circumstances can be defined by reference to categories, which will make the law generally predictable; (3) the categories are not closed. La Forest J. identified the categories of recovery of relational economic loss defined to date as: (1) cases where the claimant has a possessory or proprietary interest in the damaged property; (2) general average cases; and (3) cases where the relationship between the claimant and property owner constitutes a joint venture.

The case at bar does not fall into any of the above three categories. The plaintiffs here had no possessory or proprietary interest in the rig and the case is not one of general averaging. While related contractually, the Court of Appeal correctly held that the plaintiff and the property owner cannot, on any view of the term, be viewed as joint venturers.

However, that is not the end of the matter. The categories of recoverable contractual relational economic loss in tort are not closed. Where a case does not fall within a recognized category the court may go on to consider whether the situation is one where the right to recover contractual relational economic loss should nevertheless be recognized. This is in accordance with *Norsk, per* La Forest J., at p. 1134:

> Thus I do not say that the right to recovery in all cases of contractual relational economic loss depends exclusively on the terms of the contract. Rather, I note that such is the tenor of the exclusionary rule and that *departures from that rule should be justified on defensible policy grounds.* [Emphasis added.]

More particularly, La Forest J. suggested that the general rule against recovery for policy-based reasons might be relaxed where the deterrent effect of potential liability to the property owner is low, or, despite a degree of indeterminate liability, where the claimant's opportunity to allocate the risk by contract is slight, either because of the type of transaction or an inequality of bargaining power. I agreed with La Forest J. that policy considerations relating to increased costs of processing claims and contractual allocation of the risk are important. . . . I concluded that the test for recovery "should be flexible enough to meet the complexities of commercial reality and to permit the recognition of new situations in which liability ought, in justice, to lie as such situations arise" (p. 1166). It thus appears that new categories of recoverable contractual relational economic loss may be recognized where justified by policy considerations and required by justice. At the same time, courts should not assiduously seek new categories; what is required is a clear rule predicting when recovery is available.

More recently, in *Hercules Managements Ltd. v. Ernst & Young*, . . . this Court described the general approach that should be followed in determining when tort recovery for economic loss is appropriate.

. . .

La Forest J. set out the methodology that courts should follow in determining whether a tort action lies for relational economic loss. He held that the two-part methodology of *Anns, supra,* adopted by this Court in *Kamloops, supra,* should be followed: (1) whether a *prima facie* duty of care is owed; and (2) whether that duty, if it exists, is negated or limited by policy considerations. In applying the second step, La Forest J. wrote that while policy considerations will sometimes result in the *prima facie* duty being negated, in certain categories of cases such considerations may give way to other overriding policy considerations.

La Forest J. held that the existence of a relationship of "neighbourhood" or "proximity" distinguishes those circumstances in which the defendant owes a *prima facie* duty of care to the plaintiff from those where no such duty exists. The term "proximity" is a label expressing the fact of a relationship of neighbourhood sufficient to attract a *prima facie* legal duty. Whether the duty arises depends on the nature of the case and its facts. Policy concerns are best dealt with under the second branch of the test. Criteria that in other cases have been used to define the legal test for the duty of care can now be recognized as policy-based ways by which to curtail indeterminate or inappropriate recovery.

. . .

The same approach may be applied to the contractual relational economic loss at stake in the case at bar. The first step is to inquire whether the relationship of neighbourhood or proximity necessary to found a *prima facie* duty of care is present. If so, one moves to the second step of inquiring whether the policy concerns that usually preclude recovery of contractual relational economic loss, such as indeterminacy, are overridden.

(2) Application of the Law

. . .

I return to the question of whether, on the approach articulated in *Hercules*, *supra*, the plaintiffs' claim for contractual relational economic loss is actionable. The Newfoundland Court of Appeal, without the benefit of *Hercules*, essentially followed the two-step process outlined in that case. It held that the defendants owed a *prima facie* duty of care to BVI and HOOL. The duty arose because BVI and HOOL's economic interests could foreseeably have been affected by a failure to warn BVHB of the danger of fire resulting from the use of products supplied by the defendants. The Court of Appeal went on to hold that there should be no recovery for other reasons. It held that it would be totally impractical to warn every person who could foreseeably suffer economic loss arising from the shutdown of the drilling rig. If there was a duty to warn BVI and HOOL, then there would also be a duty to warn other potential investors in the project, such as Mobil Oil Canada Ltd. and Petro Canada, as well as a host of other persons who stood to gain from the uninterrupted operation of the drilling rig, including employees and suppliers of the rig. In these circumstances, in the Court of Appeal's view, the only duty on the defendants was to warn the person in control and possession of the rig of the dangers of fire associated with the use of Thermaclad.

As in *Hercules*, the decision as to whether a *prima facie* duty of care exists requires an investigation into whether the defendant and the plaintiff can be said to be in a relationship of proximity or neighbourhood. Proximity exists on a given set of facts if the defendant may be said to be under an obligation to be mindful of the plaintiff's legitimate interests in conducting his or her affairs. . . . On the facts of this case, I agree with the Court of Appeal that a *prima facie* duty of care arises.

. . .

Where a duty to warn is alleged, the issue is not reliance (there being nothing to rely upon), but whether the defendants ought reasonably to have foreseen that the plaintiffs might suffer loss as a result of use of the product about which the warning should have been made. I have already found that [the defendants owed a duty to warn to BVHB with respect to the flammability of Thermaclad]. The question is, however, whether [that duty] extended as far as HOOL and BVI. The facts establish that this was the case. The defendants knew of the existence of the plaintiffs and others like them and knew or ought to have known that they stood to lose money if the drilling rig was shut down.

The next question is whether this *prima facie* duty of care is negatived by policy considerations. In my view, it is. The most serious problem is that seized on by the Court of Appeal — the problem of indeterminate liability. If the defendants owed a duty to warn the plaintiffs, it is difficult to see why they would not owe a similar duty to a host of other persons who would foreseeably lose money if the rig was shut down as a result of being damaged. Other investors in the project are the most obvious persons who would also be owed a duty, although the list could arguably be extended to additional classes of persons. What has been referred to as the ripple effect is present in this case. A number of investment companies which contracted with HOOL are making claims against it, as has BVI.

No sound reason to permit the plaintiffs to recover while denying recovery to these other persons emerges. To hold otherwise would pose problems for defendants, who would face liability in an indeterminate amount for an indeterminate time to an indeterminate class. It also would pose problems for potential plaintiffs. Which of all the potential plaintiffs can expect and anticipate they will succeed? Why should one type of contractual relationship, that of HOOL, be treated as more worthy than another, e.g., that of the employees on the rig? In this state, what contractual and insurance arrangements should potential plaintiffs make against future loss?

The plaintiffs propose a number of solutions to the problem of indeterminacy. None of them succeeds, in my respectful view. The first proposal is to confine liability to persons whose *identity* was known to the defendants. This is a reversion to the "known plaintiff test. . . . As commentators have pointed out, the fact that the defendant knew the identity of the plaintiff should not in logic or justice determine recovery. On such a test, the notorious would recover, the private would lose. . . . The problem of indeterminate liability cannot be avoided by arbitrary distinctions for which there is no legal or social justification. . . . There must be something which, for policy reasons, permits the court to say this category of person can recover and that category cannot, something which justifies the line being drawn at one point rather than another.

Second, and in a similar vein, the plaintiffs argue that determinacy can be achieved by restricting recovery to the users of the rig, a class which they say is analogous in time and extent to the owners and occupiers of the building in *Winnipeg Condominium Corporation No. 36 v. Bird Construction Co.*, [1995] 1 S.C.R. 85. This argument fails for the same reasons as the known plaintiff test. There is no logical reason for drawing the line at users rather than somewhere else.

Third, the plaintiffs attempt to distinguish themselves from other potential claimants through the concept of reliance. The defendants correctly answer this argument by pointing out that any person who is contractually dependent on a product or a structure owned by another "relies" on the manufacturer or builder to supply a safe product.

Finally, the plaintiffs argue that a finding of a duty to warn negates the spectre of indeterminate liability as the duty to warn does not extend to everyone in any way connected to the manufactured product. This argument begs the question. The duty to warn found to this point is only a *prima facie* duty to warn in accordance with the first requirement of *Anns, supra,* that there be sufficient proximity or neighbourhood to found a duty of care. It is not circumscribed and imports no limits on liability. Considerations of indeterminate liability arise in the second step of the *Anns* analysis. Hence the *prima facie* duty of care, by itself, cannot resolve the problem of indeterminate liability.

The problem of indeterminate liability constitutes a policy consideration tending to negative a duty of care for contractual relational economic loss. However, the courts have recognized positive policy considerations tending to support the imposition of such a duty of care. One of these, discussed by La Forest J. in *Norsk,* is the need to provide additional deterrence against negligence. The potential liability to the owner of the damaged property usually satisfies the goal of encouraging persons to exercise due care not to damage the property. However, situations may arise where this is not the case. In such a case, the additional deterrent of liability to others might be justified. The facts in the case at bar do not support liability to the plaintiffs on this basis. BVHB, the owner of the drilling rig, suffered property damage in excess of five million dollars. This is a significant sum. It is not apparent that increasing the defendants' potential liability would have led to different behaviour and avoidance of the loss.

Another situation which may support imposition of liability for contractual relational economic loss, recognized by La Forest J. in *Norsk*, is the case where the plaintiff's ability to allocate the risk to the property owner by contract is slight, either because of the type of the transaction or inequality of bargaining power. Again, this does not assist the plaintiffs in this case. BVI and HOOL not only had the ability to allocate their risks; they did just that. It cannot be said that BVI and HOOL suffered from inequality of bargaining power with BVHB, the very company they created. Moreover, the record shows they exercised that power. The risk of loss caused by down-time of the rig was specifically allocated under the Drilling Contracts between BVI, HOOL and BVHB. The contracts provided for day rate payments to BVHB and/ or termination rights in the event of lost or diminished use of the rig. The parties also set out in the contracts their liability to each other and made provision for third party claims arising out of rig operations. Finally, the contracts contained provisions related to the purchase and maintenance of insurance.

I conclude that the policy considerations relevant to the case at bar negative the *prima facie* duty of care to BVI and HOOL.

. . .

The judgment of Gonthier, Cory, Iacobucci and Major JJ. was delivered by

IACOBUCCI J.:—I have had the advantage of reading the lucid reasons of my colleague, Justice McLachlin. At the outset, I wish to commend my colleague for her treatment of the approaches taken by her and La Forest J. in [*Norsk*]. In that respect, I simply wish to add one comment regarding the issue of contractual relational economic loss.

I understand my colleague's discussion of this matter to mean that she has adopted the general exclusionary rule and categorical exceptions approach set forth by La Forest J. in *Norsk*. My colleague has found that the circumstances of the present case do not fall within any of the three exceptions identified in that case. She points out that both her reasons and those of La Forest J. in *Norsk* recognize that the categories of recoverable contractual relational economic loss are not closed and that whether or not a new category ought to be created is determined on a case-by-case basis. In that connection, I approve of her analysis of the facts of this case and applaud the approach she has taken to meld her reasoning in *Norsk* with that of La Forest J. in this very difficult area of the law.

[Iacobucci J., however, held that the contract between BVHB and SJSL did, contrary to McLachlin J.'s opinion, negate the duty to warn that SJSL owed to BVHB.

In the final result, HOOL and BVI failed in their actions in negligence. BVHB failed in its negligence action against SJSL, but succeeded against Raychem. Damages against Raychem were, however, reduced to 40% on account of BVHB's contributory negligence.]

NOTES AND QUESTIONS

1. In light of *Bow Valley*, describe the circumstances in which a duty of care will be owed with respect to relational pure economic losses. Why did HOOL and BVI fail in their claims? Why was it unnecessary for BVHB to rely on the law on relational economic loss? For more on *Bow Valley* see Wallace, "Contractual Relational Loss in Canada" (1998) 114 L.Q.R. 370.

2. Do you agree with Justice Iacobucci's explanation of the approach adopted by Justice McLachlin?

3. Traditionally, recovery did not lie for relational pure economic losses. Rather, the courts followed a general exclusionary rule in circumstances in which the plaintiff sustained neither personal injury nor property damage: see *Cattle v. Stockton Waterworks Co.* (1875), L.R. 10 Q.B. 453. As McLachlin J. noted in *Bow Valley*, the general exclusionary approach governs in England: see *Murphy v. Brentwood District Council*, [1991] 1 A.C. 398 (H.L.).

4. In *Canadian National Railway Co. v. Norsk Pacific Steamship Co.*, [1992] 1 S.C.R. 1021 the plaintiff company entered into a contract for the use of a bridge owned by the government. The defendant carelessly damaged that bridge and as a result the plaintiff sustained considerable economic losses due to the disruption of its services. The Supreme Court of Canada allowed the claim, but was split in doing so.

McLachlin J., writing for herself, L'Heureux-Dubé and Cory JJ., rejected the traditional exclusionary rule, preferring instead an incremental approach in which the courts develop, on a case-by-case basis, a list of categories of situations in which a duty may be recognized. She believed that this task was best achieved through the two-stage test formulated in *Anns* and *Kamloops*. At the first stage of that test, she referred to foreseeability and stressed the concept of proximity, which was said to encompass the existence of a relationship between the parties, physical propinquity, assumed or imposed obligations, and close causal connection. At the second stage of the *Anns/Kamloops* test, she considered factors that might negate a *prima facie* duty of care that arose under the first stage. On her analysis, a duty of care was owed by the defendant to the plaintiff in *Norsk*. A *prima facie* duty arose under the first stage of the *Anns/Kamloops* test, largely because, given the close contractual relationship between the plaintiff and the government, those parties essentially were in a "joint venture" with respect to the bridge. Consequently, a sufficient degree of proximity existed between the plaintiff and the defendant. McLachlin J. further held that, in the circumstances, the spectre of indeterminate liability did not arise and that there was no policy reason to negate the existence of a duty of care.

Stevenson J. agreed that a duty of care existed on the facts, but he reached that conclusion on much narrower reasoning. In his view, a duty of care could arise in a case of relational economic loss only with respect to specific individuals that the defendant could have reasonably foreseen would suffer economic losses. All of the other justices expressly rejected this "notorious plaintiff" test.

In a forceful dissent, La Forest J., writing for himself, Sopinka and Iacobucci JJ., held that a general exclusionary rule should apply except where clear policy considerations demand otherwise. Accordingly, in cases of relational economic loss, he would recognize a duty of care only if: (i) the plaintiff held a proprietary or possessory interest in the damaged property, (ii) the concept of general average (a maritime law concept applied for example among various cargo owners to share in paying for cargo thrown overboard in a storm in order to save the rest of the cargo) applied, or (iii) the plaintiff and the owner of the damaged property were parties in a joint venture. On the facts, it was clear that neither the first nor the second exception applied. Moreover, contrary to McLachlin J., he refused to accept that CNR's contractual relationship with the government gave rise to a joint venture with respect to the damaged bridge. Finally, while recognizing that the general exclusionary rule "excludes recovery by people who have undeniably suffered losses as a result of an accident" and "is not attractive in itself," La Forest J. defended it because it reduces the incidence of litigation, relieves the courts of the need to draw fine lines, and efficiently indicates which parties should purchase insurance coverage.

Interestingly, La Forest J. joined McLachlin J.'s opinion in *Bow Valley*. How were the two able to reconcile the differences between them in *Norsk*? Did McLachlin J. limit the seemingly broad concept of proximity that she favoured in the earlier decision? Does her judgment in *Bow Valley* provide greater certainty and predictability than her judgment in *Norsk*? Did La Forest J. agree to open up the general exclusionary rule he previously supported? Which judge's definition of "joint venture" eventually prevailed? See Feldthusen, "Dynamic Change to Maritime Law — Gracious Retreat on Relational Economic Loss" (1998) 6 Tort L. Rev. 164.

For further discussion of the court's judgment in *Norsk*, see Feldthusen & Palmer, "Economic Loss and the Supreme Court of Canada: An Economic Critique of *Norsk Steamship* and *Bird Construction*" (1997) 74 Can. Bar Rev. 427; Mactavish, "Tort Recovery for Economic Loss: Recent Developments" (1993) 21 C.B.L.J. 395; McInnes, "Contractual Relational Economic Loss" [1993] C.L.J. 12; Fleming, "Economic Loss in Canada" (1993) 1 Tort L. Rev. 68; and Waddams, "Further Reflections on Economic Loss" (1994) 2 Tort L. Rev. 116.

For a recent decision with facts similar to *Norsk*, see *St. Lawrence Seaway Management Corporation v. BBC Lena (Vessel)*, 2018 FC 1026. The plaintiff's claim was successful because it fell within the possessory or proprietary interest exception to the general exclusion.

5. For more on general average see Benson, "The Basis and Limits of Tort Recovery for General Average Contribution Economic Loss" (2008) 16 Torts L.J. 1.

6. In *D'Amato v. Badger*, [1996] 2 S.C.R. 1071 a person who owned a 50% share in a company was injured by the defendant's carelessness. As a result of that accident, the injured party was unable to continue performing services for the company, which consequently was required to hire a new employee. Several claims were brought against the defendant, including one by the company for relational economic loss: the company argued that the cost of hiring a new employee constituted a pure economic loss that arose because of the company's relationship with the injured party. That claim was allowed at trial, but rejected by both the British Columbia Court of Appeal and the Supreme Court of Canada. In a unanimous judgment, Major J. refused to choose between the approaches developed by La Forest J. and McLachlin J. in *Norsk*.

He stated that those approaches usually produce the same result, as was true on the facts before him. The claim did not fall within any of the exceptions that La Forest J. recognized with respect to the general exclusionary rule. Likewise, a duty of care did not arise under McLachlin J.'s *Anns/Kamloops* approach because the company's loss was neither foreseeable nor sufficiently proximate to the defendant's act of negligence to warrant recovery. Moreover, even if a *prima facie* duty did arise under the first stage of the *Anns/Kamloops* test, it was negated under the second stage. If a company was allowed to recover pure economic loss arising from the loss of a key shareholder and employee, the problem of indeterminacy would arise.

There is a long history of debate over the recovery of economic losses suffered as a result of personal injuries sustained by a third party. Some of the cases are based on the old common law action *per quod servitium amisit* under which an employer could sue for the loss of services which would have been provided by an employee. See the discussion in Klar & Jefferies, *Tort Law*, 6th ed. (2017) at 320-26. For a recent Australian case involving detailed analysis of both a claim in negligence by an employer whose employees were carelessly injured and the claim of *per quod servitium amisit* see *Barclay v. Penberthy*, [2012] HCA 40. See also *Hammond v. DeWolfe*, 2012 ABQB 684, rev'd 2014 ABCA 81.

7. In the area of relational pure economic loss, as in other areas of pure economic loss, it may sometimes be difficult to determine whether the plaintiff suffered property damage or pure economic loss. Is computer data property? See *Seaboard Life Insurance Co. v. Babich*, [1995] 10 W.W.R. 756 (B.C.S.C.).

8. The courts have been reluctant to expand the situations in which relational pure economic loss is recoverable, making this arguably the most certain of the categories of pure economic loss cases: see Feldthusen, "The *Anns/Cooper* Approach to Duty of Care for Pure Economic Loss: The Emperor has no Clothes" (2003) 18 C.L.R. (3d) 67 at 71; and *Canada (Attorney General) v. Livingstone* (2004), 357 A.R. 3 (C.A.).

R. Brown has argued that the same principles that support the general rule excluding recovery also support allowing recovery in the three limited situations identified by the courts: Brown, "Justifying the Impossibility of Recoverable Relational Economic Loss" (2005) 5 O.U.C.L.J. 155.

9. In *Shell UK Limited v. Total UK Limited*, 2010 EWCA Civ 180 the plaintiff had a contractual right to have fuel transported through certain pipelines owned by other companies. The defendant negligently damaged the pipelines and as a result the plaintiff suffered economic loss. Under the exclusionary approach in England this claim normally would not succeed. However, the companies that owned the pipelines held title to them on trust for the plaintiff and others. This made the plaintiff a beneficial owner of the pipelines. The court held that as a beneficial owner the plaintiff could recover the economic loss as consequential to the physical damage to its property. It stated:

> It should not be legally relevant that the co-owners of the relevant pipelines, for reasons that seemed good to them, decided to vest the legal title to the pipelines in their service companies and enjoy the beneficial ownership rather than the formal legal title. Differing views about the wisdom of the exclusionary rule are widely held but however much one may think that, in general, there should be no duty to mere

contracting parties who suffer economic loss as a result of damage to a third party's property, it would be a triumph of form over substance to deny a remedy to the beneficial owner of that property when the legal owner is a bare trustee for that beneficial owner.

How significant an exception is this to the English exclusionary rule? See Low, "Equitable Title and Economic Loss" (2010) 126 L.Q.R. 507.

15

THE STANDARD OF CARE

1. Introduction
2. The Common Law Standard of Care: The Reasonable Person Test
3. Factors Considered in Determining Breach of the Standard of Care
4. An Economic Analysis of the Standard of Care
5. Special Standards of Care
6. Degrees of Negligence
7. Custom

1. Introduction

Although there is some disagreement concerning the elements of a negligence action and their correct analysis, most judges recognize a distinction between the concepts of duty and standard of care. The duty of care analysis is generally understood to be an inquiry into the existence, nature and scope of the legal relationship between the plaintiff and the defendant. As we have seen, the duty of care concept is the legal foundation of the tort of negligence. It involves a combination of legal and public policy analyses regarding the boundaries of legal responsibility in the particular factual circumstances of a case.

Once it is established that the defendant owed a duty of care to the plaintiff, it then becomes necessary to formulate the standard of care and to determine whether that standard was breached. Broadly stated, the standard of care determines how the defendant should have acted. A breach occurs if he or she acted without the requisite degree of care.

Lawyers and judges occasionally say that a defendant was "negligent" if he or she breached the standard of care. There is a potential problem with that practice. "Negligence" has two meanings: one narrow and one broad. The narrow meaning refers only to the questions of standard and breach. The defendant was "negligent" in that sense as long as he or she acted without sufficient care. The broader meaning of "negligence" refers, in contrast, to the cause of action as a whole. The defendant was "negligent" in that sense only if, in addition to proving a breach of the standard of care, the plaintiff proved the other elements of the tort (such as causation). As noted at the outset of Chapter 9, one way to avoid possible confusion between these two meanings is to confine the term "negligence" to the cause of action as a whole and to use the term "carelessness" to describe the fact that the defendant breached the standard of care.

It is also important to keep the analysis of duty and standard separate. There is a distinction between cases in which the defendant does not owe a duty to the plaintiff and cases in which the defendant does owe the plaintiff a duty but satisfies the applicable standard of care. For discussion of American courts conflating a breach of the standard of care with the existence of a duty of care, see Sugarman, "Misusing the 'No Duty' Doctrine in Tort Decisions: Following the *Restatement (Third) of Torts* Would Yield Better Decisions" (2016) 53 Alta. L. Rev. 913. In the United Kingdom, see Goudkamp, "Breach of Duty: A Disappearing Element of the Cause of Action in Negligence?" [2017] C.L.J. 480 which notes that "cases that would previously have been understood as being breach cases are increasingly being treated as — and only as — duty cases."

The duty of care is a legal issue and it is therefore resolved by the judge. In contrast, the issues of standard of care and breach raise questions of both law and fact. It is for the judge, who resolves questions of law, to formulate the standard of care and determine the factors that need to be considered. It is then for the jury (or judge, if there is no jury) as the trier of fact to apply those factors to the case and to determine whether the defendant met the standard. In other words, it is for the jury to translate the general into the specific. See *Des Brisay v. Canadian Government Merchant Marine Ltd.*, [1941] 2 D.L.R. 209 (S.C.C.); and Sappideen & Vines, eds., *Fleming's The Law of Torts*, 10th ed. (2011) at 123.

The distinction between questions of law and questions of fact sometimes causes confusion: see *Galaske v. O'Donnell* (1994), 112 D.L.R. (4th) 109 (S.C.C.). The distinction is important even if a judge sits alone, rather than with a jury. Although such a judge will answer both types of questions, an appellate court will treat the answers differently. With respect to a question of law, the appellate court is entitled to substitute its view for that of the trial judge so long as it is satisfied that he or she committed an error. In contrast, with respect to a question of fact, an appellate court is entitled to overturn the trial judge only if it is convinced that he or she committed a "palpable and overriding error" or reached a conclusion that could not be supported by the evidence: see *Housen v. Nikolaisen* (2002), 211 D.L.R. (4th) 577 (S.C.C.); *Bannon v. Thunder Bay (City)* (2002), 210 D.L.R. (4th) 62 (S.C.C.); *Allen (Next friend of) v. University Hospitals Board* (2002), 13 C.C.L.T. (3d) 95 (Alta. C.A.); *H.L. v. Canada (Attorney General)*, [2005] 1 S.C.R. 401; and *General Motors of Canada Ltd. v. Johnson*, 2013 ONCA 502 at paras. 50-52.

The issues of standard of care and breach also raise another recurring difficulty. As the cases and notes below illustrate, judges and jurors struggle to reach decisions that are both fair and consistent. The question of carelessness, perhaps inevitably, is quite open-ended. Canadian courts have resisted attempts to reduce the issue to systematic mathematical or economic formulae. In the final analysis, it therefore may be necessary to be content with the vagaries of human judgment.

The question of whether the standard of care has been breached should be resolved by the court before the question of factual causation. See *McArdle Estate v. Cox*, 2003 ABCA 106 at para. 25; *Bafaro v. Dowd* (2010), 260 O.A.C. 70 (C.A.) at paras. 35-37; *Randall (Litigation Guardian of) v. Lakeridge Health Oshawa* (2010), 75 C.C.L.T. (3d) 165 (Ont. C.A.) at paras. 35-36; and *Chasczewski Estate v. 528089 Ontario Inc.*, 2012 ONCA 97 at para. 15.

2. The Common Law Standard of Care: The Reasonable Person Test

ARLAND v. TAYLOR
[1955] 3 D.L.R. 358 (Ont. C.A.)

[The plaintiff was injured in a motor vehicle accident. At trial, the jury held that the defendant had not breached the requisite standard of care. The plaintiff appealed, objecting to the trial judge's charge to the jury.]

LAIDLAW J.A.: . . . The second ground of appeal arises from the following passage, in particular, in the charge to the jury:

> First of all you will consider his [the respondent's] negligence. I suggest that you put yourself in the driver's seat of his car. After you have determined the weather and the conditions that existed, ask yourself — "Would I have done that? Was that reasonable for him to do? What precautions would I have taken that he did not? Would I have gone over that hill at the same speed that he did? Would I have reduced my speed?", especially if you decide that as he approached he could not have seen over that hill.

I extract another passage of the charge in which the learned judge said: ". . . having put yourself in the driver's seat and asked yourself whether he satisfied you under the circumstances, then we go on to the next question . . ." The learned trial judge told the jury in more than one part of his charge that ten of them "set the standard of what is reasonable under a given set of circumstances."

The learned trial judge was in error in those instructions to the jury, and this manner of leaving the case to the jury was the subject of disapproval in *Kralj v. Murray*, [[1954] 1 D.L.R. 781 (Ont. C.A.)]. The standard of care by which a jury is to judge the conduct of parties in a case of the kind under consideration is the care that would have been taken in the circumstances by "a reasonable and prudent man". I shall not attempt to formulate a comprehensive definition of "a reasonable man" of whom we speak so frequently in negligence cases. I simply say he is a mythical creature of the law whose conduct is the standard by which the Courts measure the conduct of all other persons and find it to be proper or improper in particular circumstances as they may exist from time to time. He is not an extraordinary or unusual creature; he is not superhuman; he is not required to display the highest skill of which anyone is capable; he is not a genius who can perform uncommon feats, nor is he possessed of unusual powers of foresight. He is a person of normal intelligence who makes prudence a guide to his conduct. He does nothing that a prudent man would not do and does not omit to do anything a prudent man would do. He acts in accord with general and approved practice. His conduct is guided by considerations which ordinarily regulate the conduct of human affairs. His conduct is the standard "adopted in the community by persons of ordinary intelligence and prudence." See *Blyth v. Birmingham Waterworks Co.* (1856), 11 Exch. 781, 156 E.R. 1047, and Mazengarb, *Negligence on the Highway*, 2nd ed. 1952, p. 15.

In *Glasgow Corporation v. Muir et al.*, [1943] A.C. 448, [1943] 2 All E.R. 44, Lord Macmillan at p. 457 said:

The standard of foresight of the reasonable man is, in one sense, an impersonal test. It eliminates the personal equation and is independent of the idiosyncracies of the particular person whose conduct is in question. Some persons are by nature unduly timorous and imagine every path beset with lions. Others, of more robust temperament, fail to foresee or nonchalantly disregard even the most obvious dangers. The reasonable man is presumed to be free both from over-apprehension and from over-confidence, but there is a sense in which the standard of care of the reasonable man involves in its application a subjective element. It is still left to the judge to decide what, in the circumstances of the particular case, the reasonable man would have had in contemplation, and what, accordingly, the party sought to be made liable ought to have foreseen. Here there is room for diversity of view . . . What to one judge may seem far-fetched may seem to another both natural and probable.

In Mazengarb, *op. cit.*, p. 18, the learned author says:

In fixing responsibility, the law has adopted an external standard of care. It realizes that care is a matter of degree, and therefore it has set a standard which is neither too high nor too low. It seeks safety without at the same time unduly hampering transport and transit. It does not require the highest degree of care of which mankind is capable.

And I quote further from p. 20:

The legal standard of care always remains the same in the sense that it is what a reasonably prudent man would have done in like circumstances. But although this legal standard is fixed and immutable, the factual standard changes from time to time and from place to place.

It will be plain from the statements I have quoted that it is improper for a juryman to judge the conduct of a person in given circumstances by considering, after the event, what he would or would not have done in the circumstances.

In *Eyres v. Gillis & Warren Ltd.*, 48 Man. R. 164 at 170, [1940] 3 W.W.R. 390, [1940] 4 D.L.R. 747, Trueman J.A., delivering the unanimous judgment of the Court of Appeal of Manitoba, referred to the definition of negligence as given by Baron Alderson in *Blyth v. Birmingham Waterworks Co., supra*, and then said:

In determining the standard of duty so defined a Judge must not interpose himself, for, the accident having happened, his point of view may be warped by extraneous or subjective considerations, however much he may think he is free from bias. It is for this reason that a jury must not be instructed by the Judge or counsel to put themselves in the place of a defendant in a negligence action when called upon to pronounce upon his conduct.

. . .

[Although Laidlaw J.A. felt that there had been a misdirection, he held that there was no substantial wrong caused by the misdirection in this case and so dismissed the appeal.]

NOTES AND QUESTIONS

1. What is the common law standard of care? Is the reasonable person test objective, subjective or a combination of both?

2. The degree to which the perception of "reasonable" conduct is influenced by factors such as the trier of fact's sex, race, social class and ethnic background is a subject of debate among academics and lawyers. Assume that A and B were involved in a traffic accident late at night in a dangerous neighbourhood. A's injuries would have been much less severe if B had stopped to provide assistance. B did not do so, however, for fear of being attacked by a third party. If A sues B for negligence, should the content of the standard of care be influenced by the fact that B is a woman and that several other women had recently been attacked in the area? In the same circumstances, would it be reasonable to expect more of a male driver than a female driver if it could be shown that male drivers were generally not at risk of attack? For an introduction to a feminist analysis of the standard of care, see generally Bender, "An Overview of Feminist Torts Scholarship" (1993) 78 Cornell L. Rev. 575. See also Schlanger, "Gender Matters: Teaching a Reasonable Woman Standard in Personal Injury Law" (2001) 45 St. Louis L.J. 769; and Gardner, "The Many Faces of the Reasonable Person" (2015) 131 L.Q.R. 563. For a critical response see Schwartz, "Feminist Approaches to Tort Law" (2001) 2 Theor. Inq. L. 175.

3. As *Arland* indicates, the reasonable person test is not a standard of perfection. A court therefore may draw a distinction between a non-tortious mistake, referred to as an error of judgment, and actionable carelessness: *Lapointe v. Hôpital Le Gardeur*, [1992] 1 S.C.R. 351 at 362-64; and *Wilson v. Swanson*, [1956] S.C.R. 804 at 812. Examples of cases involving errors of judgment are *Graham v. Persyko* (1986), 55 O.R. (2d) 10 (C.A.); *Smith v. B.C. (A.G.)* (1988), 30 B.C.L.R. (2d) 356 (C.A.); *Edgar v. Richmond (Township)* (1991), 6 C.C.L.T. (2d) 241 (B.C.S.C.); *Gros v. Victoria General Hospital* (2000), 151 Man R. (2d) 111 (Q.B.), aff'd (2001), 160 Man. R. (2d) 7 (C.A.); and *Pelletier v. Stewart*, 2005 CarswellAlta 897 (Q.B.) (WL Can).

4. If the prospect of the plaintiff suffering injury is virtually unforeseeable to the reasonable person, should the plaintiff's claim be resolved at the duty stage or the standard of care stage?

5. Why did the Court of Appeal conclude in *Arland* that the trial judge's charge to the jury constituted a misdirection? Why did the court not order a new trial?

6. Although most negligence cases are governed by the reasonable person test, more specific rules have developed in connection with some commonly litigated activities. In a motor vehicle negligence case, for example, it may be helpful to consult the case law to determine whether the type of conduct in issue has previously been held to have breached the standard of care.

7. In *Ryan v. Victoria (City)*, [1999] 1 S.C.R. 201 at 222 the court summarized the standard of care as follows:

> Conduct is negligent if it creates an objectively unreasonable risk of harm. To avoid liability, a person must exercise the standard of care that would be expected of an ordinary, reasonable and prudent person in the same circumstances. The measure of what is reasonable depends on the facts of each case, including the likelihood of a known or foreseeable harm, the gravity of that harm, and the burden or cost which would be incurred to prevent the injury. In addition, one may look to external indicators of reasonable conduct, such as custom, industry practice, and statutory or regulatory standards.

Most of the elements mentioned by the court in *Ryan* are considered in this chapter. The role of statutory standards is considered in Chapter 22. In general, the reasonable person complies with the law. However, a statutory or regulatory violation does not automatically equate with negligence: see *Holland v. Saskatchewan*, [2008] 2 S.C.R. 551. For a recent analysis in the context of regulations relating to clearing snow from roads, see de Vries, "The Rule of Standards: *Giuliani v. Halton* and the Failure of the Minimum Maintenance Standards" (2013) 41 Adv. Q. 407.

8. For examples of an analysis of the common law standard of care from different times over the past century see Seavey, "Negligence — Subjective or Objective" (1927) 41 Harv. L. Rev. 1; James, "The Qualities of the Reasonable Man in Negligence Cases" (1951) 16 Mod. L. Rev. 1; and Green, "The Reasonable Man — Legal Fiction or Psychological Reality?" (1968) 2 Law & Society Rev. 241.

9. For a detailed analysis of problems with the reasonable person standard see Moran, *Rethinking the Reasonable Person* (2003). She argues in her conclusion that "adopting some ideal person as a standard of behaviour creates an almost irresistible opening to endow that imaginary person with all sorts of qualities that are not in fact prudential." See also Horder, "Can the Law Do Without the Reasonable Person?" (2005) 55 U.T.L.J. 253.

10. Is the reasonable person standard appropriate for a defendant with special or above-average skills? For example, in evaluating the defendant's conduct in the context of a car accident, is it relevant that the defendant is a professional racecar driver or has taken several advanced driving courses? See *Davidson v. British Columbia* (1995), 11 B.C.L.R. (3d) 192 (S.C.); Klar & Jefferies, *Tort Law*, 6th ed. (2017) at 402; and Linden *et al.*, *Canadian Tort Law*, 11th ed. (2018) at 178-79. See also *R. v. Bannister*, [2009] EWCA Crim. 1571, a case involving a negligence-based offence. If such special skills were to be taken into account, would they make it more likely or less likely that the defendant would be found liable? See Goudkamp, "Negligence and Defendants with Special Skills" [2010] C.L.J. 8.

In *Gardiner v. MacDonald Estate*, 2016 ONCA 968 the trial judge held that "The requirement that [the defendant] observe the standard of care of a reasonably prudent driver in like circumstances does not preclude a finding that as a professional driver, he should be held to a higher standard." The Court of Appeal found "no error in the trial judge's consideration of [his] status as an experienced bus driver or in her treatment of this fact as relevant to the determination of the applicable standard of care." Are all people who drive for a living "professional" drivers and thus subject to a higher standard of care than drivers generally? Should they be?

3. Factors Considered in Determining Breach of the Standard of Care

Judges consider, or direct the jury to consider, several factors in determining whether the defendant breached the standard of care. The two most important factors are (i) the probability of injury and (ii) the potential severity of injury. Those considerations are balanced against the private and social costs of avoiding the risk and the social utility of the defendant's conduct.

It is important to understand that these various considerations must be assessed at the time of the alleged breach rather than in hindsight. After the fact it may be obvious that the defendant should have acted more carefully. The real question is how a reasonable person in the defendant's circumstances would have acted at the relevant time. *Roe v. Minister of Health*, [1954] 2 All E.R. 131 (C.A.) is illustrative. The defendant ran a hospital. It stored spinal anaesthetic in glass ampoules, which were placed into liquid phenol for the purpose of sterilization. The plaintiff, who had undergone an operation, suffered spastic paraplegia because the anaesthetic that he received had been contaminated by phenol. The contamination occurred because phenol had seeped into the anaesthetic through imperceptibly small cracks in the glass ampoules. The medical community recognized that risk by the time of the trial in 1954. At the time of the plaintiff's operation in 1947, however, the risk was unknown and not reasonably foreseeable. Liability consequently was denied. Denning L.J. stressed that "We must not look at the 1947 accident with 1954 spectacles." See also *Desautels v. Katimavik* (2003), 175 O.A.C. 201 (C.A.); and *Nattrass v. Weber* (2010), 23 Alta. L.R. (5th) 51 (C.A.) at paras. 29-31. If an awareness of a dangerous situation evolves over time, it can be quite difficult to identify when a defendant's failure to take precautions becomes a breach of the standard of care. See, in the context of employees' ongoing exposure to noise in an industrial workplace, the different views expressed by the judges in *Baker v. Quantum Clothing Group Ltd.*, [2011] UKSC 17.

Some situations raise hindsight issues even more dramatically. During the 1950s, a respectable body of medical opinion favoured the sterilization of "mental defectives," a class of people that was broadly defined. Acting on the basis of that view, a province enacted legislation under which it sterilized a woman. The authorizing legislation was repealed during the 1970s and the woman sued for negligence in the 1990s. By that time the practice of sterilization had been thoroughly discredited. Should the province be held liable? Did it breach the standard of care? See, on stronger facts, *Muir v. Alberta* (1996), 132 D.L.R. (4th) 695 (Alta. Q.B.). See also *Mack v. Canada (Attorney General)* (2002), 217 D.L.R. (4th) 583 (Ont. C.A.). For more on the problem of hindsight and how it can affect the standard of care analysis see Rachlinski, "A Positive Psychological Theory of Judging in Hindsight" (1998) 65 U. Chicago L. Rev. 571.

(a) PROBABILITY AND SEVERITY OF THE HARM

BOLTON v. STONE
[1951] A.C. 850 (H.L.)

[The plaintiff was walking on a road adjacent to a cricket ground when she was struck and injured by a ball that had been hit out of the ground.]

LORD REID:—My Lords, it was readily foreseeable that an accident such as befell the respondent might possibly occur during one of the appellants' cricket matches. Balls had been driven into the public road from time to time, and it was obvious that if a person happened to be where a ball fell that person would receive injuries which might or might not be serious. On the other hand, it was plain that the chance of that happening was small. The exact number of times a ball has been driven into the road is not known, but it is not proved that this has happened more than about six times in about thirty years. If I assume that it has happened on the average once in three seasons I shall be doing no injustice to the respondent's case. Then there has to be considered the chance of a person being hit by a ball falling in the road. The road appears to be an ordinary side road giving access to a number of private houses, and there is no evidence to suggest that the traffic on this road is other than what one might expect on such a road. On the whole of that part of the road where a ball could fall there would often be nobody and seldom any great number of people. It follows that the chance of a person ever being struck even in a long period of years was very small.

This case, therefore, raises sharply the question what is the nature and extent of the duty of a person who promotes on his land operations which may cause damage to persons on an adjoining highway. Is it that he must not carry out or permit an operation which he knows or ought to know clearly can cause such damage, however improbable that result may be, or is it that he is only bound to take into account the possibility of such damage if such damage is a likely or probable consequence of what he does or permits, or if the risk of damage is such that a reasonable man, careful of the safety of his neighbour, would regard that risk as material? I do not know of any case where this question has had to be decided or even where it has been fully discussed. Of course there are many cases in which somewhat similar questions have arisen, but, generally speaking, if injury to another person from the defendants' acts is reasonably foreseeable the chance that injury will result is substantial and it does not matter in which way the duty is stated. In such cases I do not think that much assistance is to be got from analysing the language which a judge has used. More assistance is to be got from cases where judges have clearly chosen their language with care in setting out a principle, but even so, statements of the law must be read in light of the facts of the particular case. Nevertheless, making all allowances for this, I do find at least a tendency to base duty rather on the likelihood of damage to others than on its foreseeability alone.

The definition of negligence which has, perhaps, been most often quoted is that of Alderson, B., in *Blyth v. Birmingham Waterworks Co.* [(1856), 11 Ex. 781]. . .:

> Negligence is the omission to do something which a reasonable man, guided upon those considerations which ordinarily regulate the conduct of human affairs, would do, or doing something which a prudent and reasonable man would not do.

I think that reasonable men do, in fact, take into account the degree of risk and do not act on a bare possibility as they would if the risk were more substantial.

. . .

Counsel for the respondent in the present case had to put his case so high as to say that, at least as soon as one ball had been driven into the road in the ordinary course of a match, the appellants could and should have realised that that might happen again, and that, if it did, someone might be injured, and that that was enough to put on the appellants a duty to take steps to prevent such an occurrence. If the true test is foreseeability alone I think that must be so. Once a ball has been driven on to a road without there being anything extraordinary to account for the fact, there is clearly a risk that another will follow and if it does there is clearly a chance, small though it may be, that somebody may be injured. On the theory that it is foreseeability alone that matters it would be irrelevant to consider how often a ball might be expected to land in the road and it would not matter whether the road was the busiest street or the quietest country lane. The only difference between these cases is in the degree of risk. It would take a good deal to make me believe that the law has departed so far from the standards which guide ordinary careful people in ordinary life. In the crowded conditions of modern life even the most careful person cannot avoid creating some risks and accepting others. What a man must not do, and what I think a careful man tries not to do, is to create a risk which is substantial. Of course, there are numerous cases where special circumstances require that a higher standard shall be observed and where that is recognized by the law, but I do not think that this case comes within any such special category. In my judgment, the test to be applied here is whether the risk of damage to a person on the road was so small that a reasonable man in the position of the appellants, considering the matter from the point of view of safety, would have thought it right to refrain from taking steps to prevent the danger. In considering that matter I think that it would be right to take into account, not only how remote is the chance that a person might be struck, but also how serious the consequences are likely to be if a person is struck, but I do not think that it would be right to take into account the difficulty of remedial measures. If cricket cannot be played on a ground without creating a substantial risk, then it should not be played there at all. I think that this is in substance the test which Oliver, J., applied in this case. He considered whether the appellants' ground was large enough to be safe for all practical purposes and held that it was. This is a question, not of law, but of fact and degree. It is not an easy question, and it is one on which opinions may well differ. I can only say that, having given the whole matter repeated and anxious consideration, I find myself unable to decide this question in favour of the respondent. I think, however, that this case is not far from the border-line. If this appeal is allowed, that does not, in my judgment, mean that in every case where cricket has been played on a ground for a number of years without accident or complaint those who organise matches there are safe to go on in reliance on past immunity. I would have reached a different conclusion if I had thought that the risk here had been other than extremely small because I do not think that a reasonable man, considering the matter from the point of view of safety, would or should disregard any risk unless it is extremely small.

. . .

[Lord Reid allowed the appeal. Lords Porter, Normand, Oaksey and Radcliffe delivered separate concurring speeches.]

PARIS v. STEPNEY BOROUGH COUNCIL
[1951] A.C. 367 (H.L.)

LORD OAKSEY:—My Lords, I agree entirely with the opinion just delivered by my noble and learned friend Lord Normand.

The duty of an employer towards his servant is to take reasonable care for the servant's safety in all the circumstances of the case. The fact that the servant has only one eye, if that fact is known to the employer, and that if he loses it he will be blind, is one of the circumstances which must be considered by the employer in determining what precautions if any shall be taken for the servant's safety. The standard of care which the law demands is the care which an ordinarily prudent employer would take in all the circumstances. As the circumstances may vary infinitely it is often impossible to adduce evidence of what care an ordinarily prudent employer would take. In some cases, of course, it is possible to prove that it is the ordinary practice for employers to take or not to take a certain precaution, but in such a case as the present, where a one-eyed man has been injured, it is unlikely that such evidence can be adduced. The court has, therefore, to form its own opinion of what precautions the notional ordinarily prudent employer would take. In the present case the question is whether an ordinarily prudent employer would supply goggles to a one-eyed workman whose job was to knock bolts out of a chassis with a steel hammer while the chassis was elevated on a ramp so that the workman's eye was close to and under the bolt. In my opinion Lynskey, J., was entitled to hold that an ordinarily prudent employer would take that precaution. The question was not whether the precaution ought to have been taken with ordinary two-eyed workmen and it was not necessary, in my opinion, that Lynskey, J., should decide that question — nor did he purport to decide it, although it is true that he stated the question in one sentence too broadly as "whether the employers in adopting this system and not providing or requiring the use of goggles for the workers on this system were taking reasonable care to provide a suitable system of work and to provide a suitable plant."

The risk of splinters of steel breaking off a bolt and injuring a workman's eye or eyes may be and, I think, is slight and it is true that the damage to a two-eyed workman if struck by a splinter in the eye or eyes may be serious, but it is for the judge at the trial to weigh up the risk of injury and the extent of the damage and to decide whether, in all the circumstances, including the fact that the workman was known to be one-eyed and might become a blind man if his eye was struck, an ordinarily prudent employer would supply such a workman with goggles. It is a simple and inexpensive precaution to take to supply goggles, and a one-eyed man would not be likely, as a two-eyed man might be, to refuse to wear the goggles. Lynskey, J., appears to me to have weighed the extent of the risk and of the damage to a one-eyed man and I am of opinion that his judgment should be restored.

. . .

LORD MORTON OF HENRYTON (dissenting):—My Lords, it cannot be doubted that there are occupations in which the possibility of an accident occurring to any workman is extremely remote, while there are other occupations in which there is constant risk of accident to the workmen. Similarly, there are occupations in which, if an accident occurs, it is likely to be of a trivial nature, while there are other occupations in which, if an accident occurs, the results to the workman may well be fatal. Whether one is considering the likelihood of an accident occurring, or the gravity of the consequences if an accident happens, there is in each case a gradually ascending scale between the two extremes which I have already mentioned.

In considering generally the precautions which an employer ought to take for the protection of his workmen it must, in my view, be right to take into account both elements, the likelihood of an accident happening and the gravity of the consequences. I take as an example two occupations in which the risk of an accident taking place is exactly equal; if an accident does occur in the one occupation, the consequences to the workman will be comparatively trivial; if an accident occurs in the other occupation the consequences to the workman will be death or mutilation. Can it be said that the precautions which it is the duty of an employer to take for the safety of his workmen are exactly the same in each of these occupations? My Lords, that is not my view. I think that the more serious the damage which will happen if an accident occurs, the more thorough are the precautions which an employer must take.

If I am right as to this general principle, I think it follows logically that if A and B, who are engaged on the same work, run precisely the same risk of an accident happening, but if the results of an accident will be more serious to A than to B, precautions which are adequate in the case of B may not be adequate in the case of A, and it is a duty of the employer to take such additional precautions for the safety of A as may be reasonable. The duty to take reasonable precautions against injury is one which is owed by the employer to every individual workman.

In the present case it is submitted by counsel for the appellant that although the appellant ran no greater risk of injury than the other workmen engaged in the maintenance work, he ran a risk of greater injury. Counsel points out that an accident to one eye might transform the appellant into a blind man, and this event in fact happened. A similar accident to one of his comrades would transform that comrade into a one-eyed man, a serious consequence indeed but not so serious as the results have been to the appellant.

My Lords, the Court of Appeal thought that the one-eyed condition of the appellant, known to his employers, was wholly irrelevant in determining the question whether the employer did or did not take reasonable precautions to avoid an accident of this kind. I do not agree. Applying the general principle which I have endeavoured to state, I agree with your Lordships and with Lynskey, J., that the condition of the appellant was a relevant fact to be taken into account.

There still remains, however, the question whether the judge rightly came to the conclusion that there was, "so far as this particular plaintiff was concerned, a duty upon the employers to provide goggles and require the use of goggles as part of their system." He thought, as I read his judgment, and as the Court of Appeal read it, that there was no duty upon the employers to provide goggles for two-eyed men who were employed on the same work as the appellant. With this latter view the Court of Appeal agreed, and I take the same view. The evidence given at the trial has already been analysed by my noble and learned friend on the woolsack, and I shall only add that, although Captain Paterson had knowledge of about half-a-dozen eye injuries in the course of thirty-two years' experience, he did not say whether any of them was of a serious nature. The only other eye injury deposed to was that of Mr. Seeley. He was asked by the judge "Were you off work at all with your eye?", and he answered "Oh no". "Just that something got into your eye?" said the judge. "Yes, and I got it out," replied the witness.

My Lords, is it really possible to draw a distinction, on the facts of the present case, between a two-eyed man and a one-eyed man? If the employers were not negligent in failing to provide goggles for two-eyed men doing this work, during all the years prior to this accident, did they become negligent, so far as regards the appellant alone, as from July 22, 1946, when Mr. Boden, their public cleansing officer, became aware for the first time that the appellant had practically no vision in his left eye? The loss of an eye is a most serious injury to any man, and I can only see two alternatives in this case: (a) that the employers were negligent throughout in failing to provide goggles and insist on their use by all men employed in this type of work; or (b) that the risk of an eye injury to any man was so remote that no employer could be found negligent in failing to take these precautions.

My Lords, I think the first alternative must be rejected. Applying the test laid down by Lord Dunedin in *Morton v. William Dixon* [[1909] S.C. 807] already quoted by my noble and learned friend Lord Normand, I cannot find that the provision of goggles "was a thing which was commonly done by other persons in like circumstances." The evidence is conclusive to the contrary. Nor does the evidence support the view that it was "a thing which was so obviously wanted that it would be folly in anyone to neglect to provide it." Although I recognize that the one-eyed condition of the appellant was a factor to be taken into account, I think alternative (b) is correct. I cannot reach the conclusion that a one-eyed man, but not a two-eyed man, has a remedy against the employer for so serious an injury. I think it must be both or neither, and on the facts of the present case I agree with the conclusion of the Court of Appeal, that the evidence does not establish any negligence on the part of the respondents.

I would dismiss the appeal.

[Lords Normand and MacDermott delivered separate concurring speeches. Lord Simonds dissented for reasons similar to those of Lord Morton.]

NOTES AND QUESTIONS

1. In *Bolton* what factors did Lord Reid consider in determining whether the defendant breached the standard of care? Do you think the defendant would have been absolved of liability if: (a) balls were hit out of the club an average of two times a year; (b) the club was surrounded by busy roadways; or (c) the risk factors were the same, but the last time a ball was hit out it seriously injured a pedestrian walking on the quiet street?

2. *Bolton* is often contrasted with *Miller v. Jackson*, [1977] 1 Q.B. 966 (C.A.). In *Miller*, a new subdivision was built on the edge of a cricket ground that had been in operation for many years. Fewer than ten times a year, cricket balls were hit out of the grounds, cleared a protective fence and landed in someone's backyard. The plaintiff, who owned one of the affected houses, sued in negligence and nuisance and asked for both damages and injunctive relief. The defendant admitted that it could not entirely eliminate the possibility of damage unless it stopped holding cricket matches. Lord Denning M.R. held a strong view on the matter:

> In summer time, village cricket is the delight of everyone. Nearly every village has its own cricket field where the young men play and the old men watch. In the village of Lintz in County Durham they have their own ground where they have played these last 70 years. They tend it well. The wicket area is well rolled and mown. . . . The village team plays there on Saturdays and Sundays. . . . Yet now after 70 years a judge of a High Court has ordered that they must not play there any more. He has issued an injunction to stop them. He has done it at the instance of a newcomer who is no lover of cricket. The newcomer has built, or has had built for him, a house on the edge of the cricket green which four years ago was a field where cattle grazed. The animals did not mind the cricket. But now this adjoining field has been turned into a housing estate. The newcomer bought one of the houses on the edge of the cricket ground. . . . Now he complains that when a batsman hits a six, the ball has been known to land in his garden or near his house. His wife got so upset about it that they always go out at weekends. They say that this is intolerable. So they asked the judge to stop the cricket being played, and the judge, much against his will, has felt he must order the cricket to be stopped, with the consequence, I suppose, that the Lintz Cricket Club will disappear. The cricket ground will be turned to some other use. I expect for more houses or a factory. The young men will turn to other things instead of cricket. The whole village will be much the poorer. And all this because of a newcomer who has just bought a house next to the cricket ground.

Lord Denning M.R. referred to *Bolton*, but rejected Lord Reid's suggestion that "If cricket cannot be played on a ground without creating a substantial risk, then it should not be played there at all." While accepting that the defendant was liable if "by a million-to-one chance a cricket ball does go out of the ground and causes damage," he refused to impose an injunction to prevent the games from being played.

In the majority judgment in *Miller*, Lane L.J. agreed with Cumming-Bruce L.J. that the risk of property damage was both foreseeable and foreseen by the defendants. Lane L.J. further decided that the plaintiffs had no obligation "to protect themselves in their own home" from the threat presented by the defendants' activities. While both judges agreed that the defendants were liable in nuisance and negligence, only Lane L.J. was prepared to grant an injunction.

In the end result, the plaintiff was awarded £400 in damages, but was not granted an injunction. Should the factors that Lord Denning M.R. cited in *Miller* be relevant to the formulation of the standard of care?

3. The defendant only needs to take precautions against "reasonably foreseeable" risks. That concept is difficult to define with any precision. There are, however, some well-accepted propositions. A risk may be reasonably foreseeable even if it is not "probable" in the sense of being greater than 50% or more likely than not. An unusual, even remarkable, event may be sufficiently foreseeable in some circumstances. In *Bolton*, for instance, the risk was sufficiently foreseeable even though only a half dozen balls had been hit onto the road in the preceding thirty years. At the same time, however, the defendant need not guard against dangers that are fanciful or far-fetched. In the final analysis, the concept of reasonable foreseeability creates a generous amount of leeway and discretion for the trier of fact. See generally Sappideen & Vines, eds., *Fleming's The Law of Torts*, 10th ed. (2011) at 132-35.

4. In *Bingley v. Morrison Fuels* (2009), 95 O.R. (3d) 191 (C.A.) Stanzel Plumbing decommissioned an oil heating system at the plaintiff's house in 1979. It left the oil tank and the exterior file pipe in place but it tightened the cap on the pipe so it could not be turned by hand and it rotated the pipe downwards towards the ground so that it could not be filled and to indicate the system was inoperative. In 2001 the defendant's employee misread an oil delivery ticket and went to the plaintiff's house. He rotated the pipe upwards, opened the cap with a wrench and delivered a large quantity of oil. The tank had rusted, causing an oil leak and more than one million dollars in damage. The trial judge held that the loss was not reasonably foreseeable by Stanzel Plumbing: it "could not have reasonably foreseen that a delivery of fuel oil that was not authorized by anyone and that was made in the face of many indicators to the contrary would be made into that tightened and down-turned oil fill pipe." However, the Court of Appeal, by majority, reversed this decision. Justice Juriansz held that the trial judge erred in considering "whether a mistaken delivery occasioned by the particular chain of events that unfolded in this case was reasonably foreseeable rather than considering whether, in general, harm from a mistaken delivery of oil to the Bingley residence was reasonably foreseeable." On this more general approach, he held that a mistaken oil delivery was foreseeable. Even on a more specific approach, he held that it was foreseeable that an employee might misread a delivery ticket, might attempt to rotate a fill pipe that had come loose over time, and might use a wrench to open a tight cap. In contrast, the dissent accepted the trial judge's view that "a reasonable person would not have conceived of it as possible that a trained oil delivery

person would make a mistaken oil-fill into a turned down fill-pipe with a tightened cap." Do you agree with the majority or the dissent (and the trial judge) on what is reasonably foreseeable? See also the analysis in *Berendsen v. Ontario* (2009), 47 C.E.L.R. (3d) 25 (Ont. C.A.).

5. Explain the difference between Lord Oaksey's and Lord Morton's assessment of the risk factors in *Paris*. Would Lord Oaksey have reached the same decision if the plaintiff had possessed normal vision? Would Lord Morton have reached the same conclusion if there had been a previous accident involving a worker with two eyes? See also *Shilson v. Northern Ont. Light & Power Co.* (1919), 59 S.C.R. 443 and *Gloster v. Toronto Electric Light Co.* (1906), 38 S.C.R. 27 in which the court considered the probability of children coming into contact with exposed electric wires.

6. Consider the possible practical effect of the decision in *Paris*. If presented with two applicants for a job, one with one eye and one with two eyes, which would an economically rational employer choose? Would the temptation to (improperly) hire the latter be sufficiently negated by the obligations that exist under human rights legislation?

7. Optimism bias is the name for the phenomenon by which people overestimate the likelihood of positive or desirable outcomes and underestimate the likelihood of negative outcomes such as injuries. This can occur in the absence of data about outcomes but can also operate even where reliable data is available, leading people to discount the data. Because assessing the standard of care considers the likelihood of harm, it is important to control for optimism bias. See Luppi & Parisi, "Beyond Liability: Correcting Liability Bias Through Tort Law" (2009) 35 Queen's L.J. 47.

(b) COST OF RISK AVOIDANCE

VAUGHN v. HALIFAX-DARTMOUTH BRIDGE COMM.
(1961), 29 D.L.R. (2d) 523 (N.S.S.C.)

[A bridge operated and maintained by the defendant was painted. Flecks of paint were blown by the wind onto nearby cars. The owner of one of those cars sued in negligence. The defendant argued that it had taken all necessary and proper measures to prevent or to minimize injury to the plaintiff from paint dripping from the bridge, so that it was not careless.]

MACDONALD J.: . . . We must take it that no amount of ordinary care would prevent the dripping paint nor the likelihood of its being carried by the wind varying distances up to some hundreds of feet, to various parts of the dockyard (including the parking lot in question) when the painting operations were carried on in the general area of the bridge adjacent thereto. Thus we may conclude that it was inevitable that paint should fall on the cars in the parking lot in question and during the painting operations in early July. The duty of the defendant was to take all reasonable measures to prevent that result or to minimize damage from falling paint.

The usual horrific argument was made as to the impracticability of any effective steps to do so except at prohibitive cost, particularly because of the large area of affection, say 300-400 ft. of the dockyard north of the bridge to which paint might come from an extent of the bridge 500 ft. long. The answer is that the season of such painting did not exceed a month; and that we are only concerned with precautions in respect of one parking lot relatively close to the bridge. Moreover, no policy was established of warning car owners or the dockyard authorities in advance of painting operations, though the defendant well knew of the danger to them implicit in such operations. On occasion, however, when complaints did come, as they did from time to time, the defendant did bestir itself by advising the Security Officer of the dockyard of painting operations, with the result that certain cars were moved to safer parts of the dockyard. These instances suggest the feasibility of such a practice which if adopted would have obviated damage in this case. Nor can it be said that the defendant could not have asked for permission to post warning signs at the parking lot (or other parts of the dockyard) or communicated *via* press or radio similar warnings of danger from painting expected to be done in the neighbourhood of that lot. If it be said that neglect in this regard was overcome by the provision of a man in the dockyard charged with the duty of wiping fallen paint from the parked cars, the answer is that this method depended upon the wiping operation being done promptly; and that during such a painting season as that in question such provision was clearly inadequate in point of number of men, as is illustrated by the employment of four or more on other occasions. It is notable that precautions in either of these regards would have entailed relatively little expense in view of the shortness of the painting season and would in all probability have prevented or at least minimized the plaintiff's damage.

[Currie J. and Patterson J. also concluded that the defendant was negligent. Ilsley C.J. did not address this issue.]

LAW ESTATE v. SIMICE
(1994), 21 C.C.L.T. (2d) 228 (B.C.S.C.)

[The plaintiff sued the defendant doctors in negligence, claiming that her husband died because of their failure to provide timely, appropriate and skillful emergency care. Among other things, they had not initially taken a CT scan of the patient. The case dramatically raised the issue of the allocation of limited and costly medical resources.]

SPENCER J.: . . . I must observe that throughout this case there were a number of times when doctors testified that they feel constrained by the British Columbia Medical Insurance Plan and by the British Columbia Medical Association standards to restrict their requests for CT scans as diagnostic tools. No doubt such sophisticated equipment is limited and costly to use. No doubt there are budgetary restraints on them. But this is a case where, in my opinion, those constraints worked against the patient's interest by inhibiting the doctors in their judgment of what should be done for him. That is to be deplored. I understand that there are budgetary problems confronting the health care system. I raise it in passing only to point out that there were a number of references to the effect of financial restraint on the treatment of this patient. I respectfully say it is something to be carefully considered by those who are responsible for financing it. I also say that if it comes to a choice between a physician's responsibility to his or her individual patient and his or her responsibility to the medicare system overall, the former must take precedence in a case such as this. The severity of the harm that may occur to the patient who is permitted to go undiagnosed is far greater than the financial harm that will occur to the medicare system if one more CT scan procedure only shows the patient is not suffering from a serious medical condition.

[Several of the doctors who had treated the patient were held liable in negligence.]

NOTES AND QUESTIONS

1. In *Vaughn* what factors did the court consider in determining that the defendant had breached the standard of care? Would the result have been the same if it had been proven that the accident prevention costs exceeded the total damages?

2. Is a patient entitled to the best available, or to merely the most affordable, medical care? Did the court in *Law Estate* apply an appropriate perspective in assessing the physician's reluctance to order a CT scan? If health professionals have no role to play as financial gatekeepers or allocators of scarce resources, who should play these roles? Has the court adequately considered that ordering a CT scan or booking an operation in one case may result in delays or denials of treatment in other cases?

3. In *Bateman v. Doiron* (1991), 8 C.C.L.T. (2d) 284 (N.B.Q.B.), aff'd (1993), 18 C.C.L.T. (2d) 1 (N.B.C.A.) the court accepted that a Moncton hospital had no choice but to grant privileges to general practitioners in order to fully staff its emergency department. The court acknowledged that this practice resulted in physicians with limited skill and experience staffing the emergency room. However, the court stated (at 292) that:

> to suggest that the defendant Moncton Hospital might be reasonably expected by the community to staff its emergency department with physicians qualified as expert in the management of critically ill patients does not meet the test of reality, nor is it a reasonably expected community standard. The non-availability of trained and experienced personnel, to say nothing of the problems of collateral resource allocation, simply makes this standard unrealistic, albeit desirable.

Justice Rice wrote a scathing dissent, criticizing the staffing and administrative practices of the emergency department.

Should hospitals be held liable in negligence because they cannot afford to adequately staff emergency rooms? Are inadequately staffed emergency rooms preferable to no emergency rooms? Can or should a hospital be held liable in negligence for not allocating sufficient resources to its emergency department? What role, if any, should courts play in reviewing resource allocation and other hospital management decisions?

4. How should courts assess the cost of avoidance issues in dealing with limited health resources? Should the same approach be adopted in analyzing other public agencies, such as the police and child welfare departments, that do not have adequate resources to respond to all the demands for service?

5. In *De Vos v. Robertson* (2000), 48 C.C.L.T. (2d) 172 (Ont. S.C.J.) Lofchik J. used language that is almost identical to the extract above from *Law Estate*. He observed that:

> it was suggested that the time pressures involved in day surgery require that the most expedient form of anaesthesia be used so as not to upset the routine of those involved

in the process. No doubt there are budgetary and time constraints involved in scheduling day surgeries such as those undergone by the plaintiff but, in my view, this is a case where those constraints worked against the patient's interest. . . It is difficult in this case to resist the observation that the patient's problems were at least in part related to what might be described as *"production line medicine"* in that the procedures which were followed and the standard of disclosure applied might be considered acceptable in the vast majority of cases being handled, but this patient did not fit the mould. . . [emphasis in original]

The court held that the anaesthetist breached the standard of care. For an American case raising similar considerations see *Wickline v. California*, 228 Cal. Rptr. 661 (Cal. App. 2 Dist. 1986).

6. Cases like *Law Estate* consider these cost issues in the context of a negligence claim brought by an injured plaintiff. Similar considerations can arise in a different context: administrative proceedings brought by members of the public against the government challenging broader health care resource allocation decisions, such as a decision to close a hospital or to discontinue funding for a procedure. See for example *Eldridge v. British Columbia (Attorney General)*, [1997] 3 S.C.R. 624; *Auton (Guardian ad litem of) v. British Columbia (Attorney General)*, [2004] 3 S.C.R. 657; and *Chaoulli v. Québec (Attorney General)*, [2005] 1 S.C.R. 791.

7. As suggested in *Vaughn* and *Law Estate,* the plaintiff must prove that there was a reasonably practicable precaution that the defendant failed to take. In those cases, the precautions were fairly obvious. See also *Ware's Taxi Ltd. v. Gilliham*, [1949] S.C.R. 637. In other situations, however, the issue may be more difficult. In *Neill v. New South Wales Fresh Food & Ice Pty. Ltd.* (1963), 108 C.L.R. 362 (H.C.A.) the defendant employed the plaintiff for the purpose of washing out a large cylindrical tank that it used for transporting milk. The combination of milk residue and soapy water made the tank very slick. The plaintiff was injured when he slipped and fell. At trial, the jury found that the defendant had breached the standard of care. That decision was reversed on appeal, however, because the plaintiff had not adduced sufficient evidence of a practical solution (such as a handrail inside the tank or non-slip boots). Consequently, there was no basis in evidence upon which the jury could find that the defendant had breached the standard of care. See also *Whelan v. Parsons & Sons Transportation Ltd.* (2005), 250 Nfld. & P.E.I.R. 23 (N.L.C.A.); and *Meady v. Greyhound Canada Transportation Corp.*, 2012 ONSC 657 at paras. 217-32, aff'd 2015 ONCA 6.

8. There are many examples of courts explicitly weighing the cost of precautions against the likelihood and gravity of the harm. In *Bingley v. Morrison Fuels* (2009), 95 O.R. (3d) 191 (C.A.), discussed earlier in this chapter, the majority of the Court of Appeal concluded "Combining reasonable foreseeability with the enormous potential harm and the trifling cost of permanently plugging the fill pipe, I conclude that the respondents breached the standard of care." In *Lovely v. Kamloops (City)* (2009), 64 M.P.L.R. (4th) 259 (B.C.S.C.), aff'd (2010), 71 M.P.L.R. (4th) 210 (B.C.C.A.), the plaintiff, while disposing of rubbish at a transfer station, fell and injured his leg so seriously that it had to be amputated. The trial judge concluded that "the installation of guardrails or grab bars [would] be an economic and simple measure [costing

$4,540.82] relative to the capital and operating costs of the Transfer Station." The judge held the city, as operator of the station, had breached its standard of care.

9. Should a rural township be required to post "no exit" or other warning signs on all of its dead-end roads or only on those roads that have a particular hazard at their end such as a cliff or a lake? See *Greenhalgh v. Douro-Dummer (Township)*, 2009 CarswellOnt 7995 (S.C.J.) (WL Can).

10. Plaintiffs frequently point to measures taken by a defendant subsequent to an incident in an effort to establish that the defendant was negligent in not having taken them earlier. In *Kuhl v. Zurich Financial Services Australia Ltd.*, [2011] HCA 11 at para. 94 the majority noted that "the mere fact that one change was recommended after the accident and the other introduced after the accident does not support a conclusion of breach of duty. The significance of these events is only to show what could have been done, not what should have been done." Given that the majority went on to hold the standard of care was breached, is this much of a distinction?

(c) SOCIAL UTILITY

WATT v. HERTFORDSHIRE COUNTY COUNCIL
[1954] 1 W.L.R. 835 (C.A.)

[The plaintiff, a fire fighter, responded to an emergency call requiring the use of a special jack. The jack had been used only once in the last 15 years. The truck that was fitted for carrying the jack was unavailable and consequently the jack was loaded in the rear of another vehicle. When the driver braked suddenly, the jack became dislodged and seriously injured the plaintiff.]

. . .

The plaintiff claimed that the defendants, his employers, were negligent in that they (a) failed to load or secure the jack in such a way that it could not become dislodged; (b) loaded the jack in such a way that they knew or ought to have known it was likely that if the lorry pulled up suddenly the jack would become dislodged and cause injuries to any person riding on the back of the lorry; (c) permitted and/or caused the plaintiff to ride on the back of the lorry on to which the jack had been loaded; (d) caused or permitted the jack to be transported on the lorry which, as the defendants knew or ought to have known, was not provided with clips, straps, or other suitable means to secure it; (e) failed to provide any or any adequate supervision of the loading of the jack on to the lorry; and it was claimed that the plaintiff's accident was due to negligence and that he was entitled to recover damages against the defendants.

. . .

DENNING L.J.:—It is well settled that in measuring due care you must balance the risk against the measures necessary to eliminate the risk. To that proposition there ought to be added this: you must balance the risk against the end to be achieved. If this accident had occurred in a commercial enterprise without any emergency there could be no doubt that the servant would succeed. But the commercial end to make profit is very different from the human end to save life or limb. The saving of life or limb justifies taking considerable risk, and I am glad to say that there have never been wanting in this country men of courage ready to take those risks, notably in the fire service.

In this case the risk involved in sending out the lorry was not so great as to prohibit the attempt to save life. I quite agree that fire engines, ambulances and doctors' cars should not shoot past the traffic lights when they show a red light. That is because the risk is too great to warrant the incurring of the danger. It is always a question of balancing the risk against the end. I agree that this appeal should be dismissed.

[Singleton and Morris L.JJ. gave separate concurring judgments dismissing the fire fighter's claim.]

NOTES AND QUESTIONS

1. In *Watt* would the defendant have been held liable if the emergency call had involved only property damage? Would the case have been decided differently if the plaintiff had been a volunteer? See *Hammond v. Wabana (Town)* (1998), 170 Nfld. & P.E.I.R. 97 (N.L.C.A.); *Killip's Television Service Ltd. v. Stony Plain (Town)* (2000), 257 A.R. 92 (Q.B.); and *Schouten v. Rideau (Township)* (2009), 251 O.A.C. 133 (C.A.) at para. 7.

2. High-speed police chases raise controversial social utility issues. Should the police be subject to a reduced standard of care because they are attempting to apprehend a fleeing suspect? What effect, if any, should the alleged offence have on the assessment of the officer's conduct?

In *Priestman v. Colangelo* (1959), 19 D.L.R. (2d) 1 (S.C.C.) the defendant police officers had attempted several times to stop a suspected car thief. While travelling at high speeds, the officer in the front passenger seat leaned out the window and fired at the rear tire of the suspect's car in an attempt to stop it as it approached a busy intersection. The bullet hit the car frame, ricocheted and struck the driver, rendering him unconscious. The car went out of control, mounted the curb, hit a hydro pole, and struck and killed two pedestrians. The court reasoned that the officers were under an affirmative duty to apprehend suspects and were justified by what is now s. 25(4) of the *Criminal Code*, R.S.C. 1985, c. C-46 in using as much force as was necessary to prevent their escape. Do you think that the officer was careless in shooting at the vehicle? What impact should the fact that the officer was under a statutory duty to apprehend the suspect have on the issues of standard of care and breach? See also *Miller v. Wolbaum* (1986), 47 M.V.R. 162 (Sask. Q.B.); *Moore v. Fanning* (1987), 41 C.C.L.T. 67 (Ont. H.C.); and *Hill v. Hurst* (2001), 203 D.L.R. (4th) 749 (B.C.S.C.).

3. Would a claim based on the facts in *Priestman, supra,* be decided differently now? How have public and judicial attitudes toward policing and the police changed in the past 25 years? See *Patenaude c. Roy* (1994), 26 C.C.L.T. (2d) 237 (Qc. C.A.). In the 1980s most police departments in Canada adopted strict rules to govern both high-speed chases and the use of firearms. For example, a directive of the Ontario Solicitor General limited police pursuits to a "measure of last resort." The directive listed 11 factors to be considered by police, including the seriousness of the offence, the presence of bystanders and traffic, and the age of the fleeing driver. High-speed chases continued to claim the lives of police officers, fleeing suspects and bystanders.

In *Burbank v. Bolton* (2007), 65 B.C.L.R. (4th) 290 (C.A.) an R.C.M.P. constable pursued what turned out to be a 15-year-old unlicensed driver, impaired by methadone, in a stolen car. The driver ran a stop sign and hit another car, killing one person and injuring four others. The victims sued the driver and the constable. The court reviewed the regulations and R.C.M.P. policies governing police pursuit. It held that while the driver was 85% responsible, the constable was 15% responsible. With respect to the latter, the court concluded that the pursuit "should never have started" and that the constable was in breach of the standard of care. Newbury J.A. dissented, concerned that the majority's approach left little room for police pursuit in any circumstances. *Radke v. S.(M.) (Litigation Guardian of)* (2007), 66 B.C.L.R. (4th) 174 (C.A.) is highly similar to *Burbank*, as are *Bergen v. Guliker Estate*, 2014 BCSC 5, rev'd 2015 BCCA 283; and *Provost v. Bolton*, 2017 BCSC 1608. See also the underlying facts of *British Columbia (Attorney General) v. Insurance Corporation of British Columbia*, [2008] 1 S.C.R. 21, in which an officer pursuing a car stolen by a 14-year-old was found to be 10% at fault for a collision in which another driver was killed.

4. Generally the courts only consider the social utility of the defendant's conduct if he or she is a public officer or is employed by a public authority. Should the social utility of a private citizen's conduct also be considered in determining whether he or she acted carelessly? What problems would arise from this approach? How could this apply to the conduct of the rescuers in *Horsley v. MacLaren* (1972), 22 D.L.R. (3d) 545 (S.C.C.), extracts of which are in Chapters 11 and 12? See Griffiths, "The Standard of Care Expected of a First-aid Volunteer" (1990) 53 Mod. L. Rev. 255.

5. Should social utility be a relevant consideration in product liability cases? Consider for example a defendant manufacturer of medical devices, drugs or vaccines. See Mohrbutter, "*Harrington v. Dow Corning Corp.* and Social Utility: Unfit for Their Purpose within Product Liability Negligence Law" (2012) 75 Sask. L. Rev. 269.

6. A. Beever has argued that "allowing considerations of utility to alter the outcomes of cases would violate distributive (as well as commutative) justice": Beever, "Negligence and Utility" (2017) 17 O.U.C.L.J. 85. On this view, utility should not be relevant to the analysis of the standard of care because considerations of the public interest should not affect the private rights of plaintiffs and defendants. Do you agree?

4. An Economic Analysis of the Standard of Care

UNITED STATES v. CARROLL TOWING CO.
159 F.2d 169 (2d Cir. 1947)

L. HAND, Circuit Judge: . . . It appears . . . that there is no general rule to determine when the absence of a bargee or other attendant will make the owner of the barge liable for injuries to other vessels if she breaks away from her mooring. However, in any cases where he would be so liable for injuries to others, obviously he must reduce his damages proportionately, if the injury is to his own barge. It becomes apparent why there can be no such general rule, when we consider the grounds for such a liability. Since there are occasions when every vessel will break from her moorings, and since, if she does, she becomes a menace to those about her; the owner's duty, as in other similar situations, to provide against resulting injuries is a function of three variables: (1) the probability that she will break away; (2) the gravity of the resulting injury, if she does; (3) the burden of adequate precautions. Possibly it serves to bring this notion into relief to state it in algebraic terms: if the probability be called P; the injury, L; and the burden, B; liability depends upon whether B is less than L multiplied by P: i.e., whether B is less than PL. Applied to the situation at bar, the likelihood that a barge will break from her fasts and the damage she will do, vary with the place and time; for example, if a storm threatens, the danger is greater; so it is, if she is in a crowded harbor where moored barges are constantly being shifted about. On the other hand, the barge must not be the bargee's prison, even though he lives aboard; he must go ashore at times. We need not say whether, even in such crowded waters as New York Harbor a bargee must be aboard at night at all; it may be that the custom is otherwise, as Ward, J., supposed in *"The Kathryn B. Guinan. . ."*. . .; and that, if so, the situation is one where custom should control. We leave that question open; but we hold that it is not in all cases a sufficient answer to a bargee's absence without excuse, during working hours, that he has properly made fast his barge to the pier, when he leaves her. In the case at bar the bargee left at five o'clock in the afternoon of January 3rd, and the flotilla broke away at about two o'clock in the afternoon of the following day, twenty-one hours afterwards. The bargee had been away all the time, and we hold that his fabricated story was affirmative evidence that he had no excuse for his absence. At the locus in quo — especially during the short January days and in the full tide of war activity — barges were being constantly "drilled" in and out. Certainly it was not beyond reasonable expectation that, with the inevitable haste and bustle, the work might not be done with adequate care. In such circumstances we hold — and it is all that we do hold — that it was a fair requirement that the Connors Company should have a bargee aboard (unless he had some excuse for his absence), during the working hours of daylight.

Judgment accordingly.

NOTES AND QUESTIONS

1. In Posner, "A Theory of Negligence" (1972) 1 J. Legal Stud. 29 at 32-33 the author (later Judge Posner) revisited "the Hand formula":

> It is time to take a fresh look at the social function of liability for negligent acts. The essential clue, I believe, is provided by Judge Learned Hand's famous formulation of the negligence standard — one of the few attempts to give content to the deceptively simple concept of ordinary care. . . . In a negligence case, Hand said, the judge (or jury) should attempt to measure three things: the magnitude of the loss if an accident occurs; the probability of the accident's occurring; and the burden of taking precautions that would avert it. If the product of the first two terms exceeds the burden of precautions, the failure to take those precautions is negligence. Hand was adumbrating, perhaps unwittingly, an economic meaning of negligence. Discounting (multiplying) the cost of an accident if it occurs by the probability of occurrence yields a measure of economic benefit to be anticipated from incurring the costs necessary to prevent the accident. The cost of prevention is what Hand meant by the burden of taking precautions against the accident. It may be the cost of installing safety equipment or otherwise making the activity safer, or the benefit foregone by curtailing or eliminating the activity. If the cost of safety measures or of curtailment — whichever cost is lower — exceeds the benefit in accident avoidance to be gained by

incurring that cost, society would be better off, in economic terms, to forego accident prevention. A rule making the enterprise liable for the accidents that occur in such cases cannot be justified on the grounds that it will induce the enterprise to increase the safety of its operations. When the cost of accidents is less than the cost of prevention, a rational profit-maximizing enterprise will pay tort judgments to the accident victims rather than incur the larger cost of avoiding liability. Furthermore, overall economic value or welfare would be diminished rather than increased by incurring a higher accident-prevention cost in order to avoid a lower accident cost. If, on the other hand, the benefits in accident avoidance exceed the costs of prevention, society is better off if those costs are incurred and the accident averted, and so in this case the enterprise is made liable, in the expectation that self-interest will lead it to adopt the precautions in order to avoid a greater cost in tort judgments.

One misses any reference to accident avoidance by the victim. If the accident could be prevented by the installation of safety equipment or the curtailment or discontinuance of the underlying activity by the victim at lower cost than any measure taken by the injurer would involve, it would be uneconomical to adopt a rule of liability that placed the burden of accident prevention on the injurer. Although not an explicit part of the Hand formula this qualification. . . is implicit in the administration of the negligence standard.

Perhaps, then, the dominant function of the fault system is to generate rules of liability that if followed will bring about, at least approximately, the efficient — the cost-justified — level of accidents and safety. Under this view, damages are assessed against the defendant as a way of measuring the costs of accidents, and the damages so assessed are paid over to the plaintiff (to be divided with his lawyer) as the price of enlisting their participation in the operation of the system. Because we do not like to see resources squandered, a judgment of negligence has inescapable overtones of moral disapproval, for it implies that there was a cheaper alternative to the accident. Conversely, there is no moral indignation in the case in which the cost of prevention would have exceeded the cost of the accident. Where the measures necessary to avert the accident would have consumed excessive resources, there is no occasion to condemn the defendant for not having taken them.

If indignation has its roots in inefficiency, we do not have to decide whether regulation, or compensation, or retribution, or some mixture of these best describes the dominant purpose of negligence law. In any case, the judgment of liability depends ultimately on a weighing of costs and benefits.

The economic analysis is not without its critics. See for example Sappideen & Vines, eds., *Fleming's The Law of Torts*, 10th ed. (2011) at 139-40 (footnotes omitted):

The negligence concept, with its complex balance just described, has a decidedly utilitarian flavour. Indeed, it has been forcibly argued that the negligence matrix reflects norms of economic efficiency, tending to maximise wealth and minimise costs, by encouraging cost-justified accident prevention while discouraging excessive investment in safety. If the loss caused by a given activity to the actor and his victim is greater than its benefit, the activity should be (and is) discouraged by being labelled negligent and requiring the actor to compensate the victim; if the balance is the other way, the actor may go ahead scot-free. . . .

But negligence cannot be reduced to a purely economic equation or "calculus". . . . True, economic factors are given weight, especially regarding the value of the defendant's activity and the cost of eliminating the risk. But in general, judicial opinions do not make much of the cost factor, and for good reasons. For one thing, our legal tradition in torts has strong roots in an individualistic morality with its focus primarily on interpersonal equity rather than broader social policy. The infusion of economic criteria like insurability, loss distribution and efficient resource allocation has so far remained largely unsystematic, interstitial and controversial. Secondly, the calculus of negligence includes some important non-economic values, like health and life, aesthetics and preservation of nature and natural beauty, environmental factors, free will or autonomy, and privacy, which defy comparison with competing economic values. Negligence is not just a matter of calculating the point at which the cost of injury to victims (that is the damages payable) exceeds that of providing safety precautions. In particular, avoiding harm is commonly considered more important than promoting increased public welfare. In short, the reasonable person is by no means a caricature cold blooded, calculating Economic Man. Lastly, courts remain sceptical of their ability, let alone that of juries, to pursue economic analyses; especially as precise data are rarely available, particularly in personal injury cases, to quantify the relevant factors.

2. What factors did Judge Hand consider in *Carroll Towing Co.* when determining whether the defendant had breached the standard of care? What did he mean by the phrase "the burden of adequate precautions"?

3. Notwithstanding his judgment in *Carroll Towing Co.*, Judge Hand later warned against placing too much emphasis on an "economic" approach: *Conway v. O'Brien*, 111 F.2d 611 at 612 (2d Cir. 1940). He also observed that, in some cases, the cost of avoiding the risk may be very difficult to calculate. See *Moisan v. Loftus*, 178 F.2d 148 (2d Cir. 1949). See also Englard, "The System Builders: A Critical Appraisal of Modern American Tort Theory" (1980) 9 J. Legal Stud. 27 at 54.

Likewise, in *McCarty v. Pheasant Run Inc.*, 826 F.2d 1554 at 1557 (7th Cir. 1987), Judge Posner stated:

> Ordinarily, and here, the parties do give the jury the information required to quantify the variables that the Hand Formula picks outs as relevant. That is why the formula has greater analytic than operational significance. Conceptual as well as factual difficulties in monetizing personal injuries may continue to frustrate efforts to measure expected accident costs with the precision that is possible, in principle at least, in measuring the other side of the equation — the cost or burden of precaution.

What impact do such concerns have on the viability of the cost-benefit approach?

4. Apply the formula suggested by Judge Hand in *Carroll Towing Co.* to the facts of *Paris*. What does the formula indicate?

5. How would Judge Posner determine whether a defendant had breached the standard of care? According to him, what is the purpose of tort law? Would you agree with his assumption that most actors are rational profit-maximizers who are amenable to deterrence? Does Judge Posner use the formula in the same way that Judge Hand does?

6. Are concerns about the economic analysis of tort law warranted? More specifically, does an economic approach exclude non-economic values like health and life? Do such values "defy comparison with competing economic values"? See Veljanovski, "Economic Theorizing About Tort" [1985] Curr. Legal Probs. 117;

Englard, "Law and Economics in American Tort Cases: A Critical Assessment of the Theory's Impact on Courts" (1991) 41 U.T.L.J. 359; and Saks, "Do We Really Know Anything About the Behavior of the Tort Litigation System — And Why Not" (1992) 140 U. Penn. L. Rev. 1147.

7. Many otherwise valid tort claims fail on technical grounds and others are settled for far less than the full loss. Moreover, the law of damages does not permit the plaintiff to recover for certain losses, such as grief, and has limited recovery for other types of injuries, such as psychiatric harm. Consequently, a tortfeasor's accident liability costs may be far less than the actual social costs of his or her conduct. Does Judge Posner's approach adequately address these features of the tort system? See Epstein, "A Theory of Strict Liability" (1973) 2 J. Legal Stud. 151; Grady, "A New Positive Economic Theory of Negligence" (1983) 92 Yale L.J. 799; and Williams, "Second Best: The Soft Underbelly of Deterrence Theory in Tort" (1993) 106 Harv. L. Rev. 932.

8. E. Weinrib has indicated that the Hand formulation may be adopted on moral rather than economic grounds. One must first assume that this test provides a standard that a rational actor would use in deciding whether to take a risk of personal injury or loss. An actor who breaches the standard and injures another is held liable in negligence for imposing upon others a risk which he or she would not have taken. Thus, the Hand test is used to impose liability on those who have acted in a morally impermissible manner in failing to extend equal consideration to others: Weinrib, "Toward a Moral Theory of Negligence Law" (1983) 2 Law and Phil. 37 at 49-52. See also Abel, "A Critique of Torts" (1994) 2 Tort L. Rev. 99; and Weinrib, *The Idea of Private Law* (2012).

5. Special Standards of Care

(a) THE STANDARD OF CARE EXPECTED OF THE DISABLED

FIALA v. CECHMANEK
(2001), 201 D.L.R. (4th) 680 (Alta. C.A.)

WITTMANN J.A.: . . .

Facts

On the morning of March 11, 1995, Robert John MacDonald ("MacDonald") went for a run. During his run, he experienced a severe manic episode, diagnosed later, but never previously, as bipolar disorder, type 1. He believed he was God and had a plan to save the world. Hoping to inform others of his ideas, MacDonald asked several individuals for their telephone or fax numbers.

Still on his run, MacDonald approached a car, which was stopped at an intersection. MacDonald walked around the car and beat on both its driver-side window and roof. While yelling obscenities at Katalin Cechmanek ("Cechmanek"), the owner and operator of the car, he jumped on the car's trunk and roof. He then broke through the sunroof of the car and began choking Cechmanek. Cechmanek involuntarily hit the gas pedal and accelerated into the intersection, striking another car, owned and operated by the appellant Jana Fiala and carrying as a passenger, her daughter, the appellant Lenka Fiala. The Fialas were injured by the collision.

After the collision, MacDonald continued to threaten and yell obscenities at Cechmanek. He also approached the Fialas and shouted sexually explicit statements at 17-year-old Lenka Fiala. Clearly agitated, he flailed his arms wildly, darted back and forth between individuals who had surrounded the accident scene, and ran down the middle of the road. Despite MacDonald's relatively small stature, it took two policemen and two EMS attendants to forcibly restrain him.

. . .

[Wittmann J.A. reviewed the evidence of the psychiatrists who had examined MacDonald and continued.]

Trial Decision

The trial judge was satisfied that MacDonald was in the midst of a severe manic episode at the time of the attack and was not in control of his mind. The trial judge held that MacDonald had no control over his behaviour and was incapable of appreciating either the nature or quality of his actions. . . .

The trial judge determined that MacDonald [had proved] that he had no reason to foresee any danger that he might be on the verge of a manic episode. Without warning or notice, there was a sudden, absolute change in MacDonald's condition and, as a result, MacDonald had no ability to reason or to appreciate his duty of care to others.

The trial judge noted that, unlike the facts of *Wenden v. Trikha* (1991), 116 A.R. 81 (Q.B.), affirmed 135 A.R. 382 (C.A.), where the defendant was aware of his mental illness before causing the collision that injured the plaintiff, MacDonald was not aware of his mental illness before the alleged tort occurred. He had not been warned, as had Mr. Trikha, of the dangers associated with his illness.

Analysis

The action against MacDonald was pleaded in negligence even though his conduct may more easily fit within the legal framework associated with the intentional tort of battery.

While there has been much debate about the liability of the mentally ill in the context of tort law, considerable uncertainty still abounds: see G.B. Robertson, *Mental Disability and the Law in Canada*, 2nd ed. (Toronto: Carswell, 1994) at 239. A review of the opinions expressed on the topic exemplifies the confusion that has plagued this area of the law.

In A.M. Linden, *Canadian Tort Law*, 6th ed. (Toronto: Butterworths, 1997) at 142, the author states:

> Persons suffering from mental illness may not have to comply with the reasonable person standard, the theory being that it is unfair to hold people liable for accidents they are incapable of avoiding. No allowance is made, however, for those who are merely deficient intellectually and therefore cannot live up to the objective standard. Nor is any mercy shown to defendants whose minds are clouded because of drugs or drunkenness. It is only when the inadequacy amounts to a serious mental illness that the excuse is countenanced.

Linden's approach suggests that the objective reasonable person standard is properly relaxed in instances where a defendant's mental illness prevents him or her from meeting the standard of care normally required. Arguably, this position emphasizes the "fault" requirement underlying tort liability.

In contrast, several authors have stated that the compensatory nature of tort law is of paramount concern and, therefore, those suffering from mental illness should not be allowed a lower standard. Robertson states at 240 that the function of negligence law is to compensate the victim rather than punish the wrongdoer.

Those who support holding the mentally ill to the higher objective standard make similar arguments. First, they suggest that when two innocent persons are involved in an accident, the person who caused the accident should be liable for the resulting damage. According to this view, victim compensation is the primary aim of tort law.

Second, they argue that, unlike instances where the defendant is a child or is afflicted with a physical disability, the practical difficulties associated with determining the extent of a person's mental illness and the person's ability to act in a reasonable manner would create such confusion that the courts would be vulnerable to those feigning mental illness for the purpose of avoiding liability. Courts would be unable to draw a line between incapacitating mental illness and variations of temperament.

Third, they submit that holding the severely mentally ill to the higher standard would encourage their caregivers to take adequate precautions, which is especially important in this de-institutionalization era. It is argued that relieving the mentally ill of liability will result in their increased isolation, as community members will avoid contact with them for fear of harm without compensation.

Finally, those who support holding the mentally ill to an objective standard argue that any consideration of a defendant's mental illness will erode the objective standard to such an extent that it will no longer be of consequence. This concern was encapsulated long ago by Chief Justice Tindal in *Vaughan v. Menlove* (1837), 132 E.R. 490 (C.P.) at 493:

> Instead, therefore, of saying that the liability for negligence should be co-extensive with the judgment of each individual, which would be as variable as the length of the foot of each individual, we ought rather to adhere to the rule which requires in all cases a regard to caution such as a man of ordinary prudence would observe.

While some of these arguments appear valid on their face, a closer analysis reveals weakness.

When two "innocent" persons are involved in an accident, presumably the element of fault is absent. Although the term "innocent" may refer to an absence of moral culpability, negligence law is concerned with fault associated with falling below the requisite standard of care in the circumstances. If a person is suffering from a mental illness such that it is impossible to attribute fault to him, holding him liable for his actions would create a strict liability regime. Although compensation of victims of tort is very important, the statement begs the question: what is a tort? For the most part, fault is still an essential element of Canadian tort law. Strict liability has been imposed in only limited areas of tort law such as conversion, defamation, and non-natural use of land that results in an escape of a harmful substance. But strict liability has not been extended to product liability as it has in the United States, nor to cases like this.

In "The Role of Fault and Policy in Negligence Law" (1996), 35 Alta. L. Rev. 24, Professor Klar describes as misguided the recent emphasis on the compensatory role of tort law. At p. 29, he states:

> Negligence law is about wrongdoing. While this is admittedly an imprecise notion, there ought to be an element of moral blame in all conduct which tort law deems as negligent and hence liable for damages. The elements of the negligence action ought to conform and be interpreted by courts according to this notion of fault and the goal of correcting wrongs. Loss distribution by liability insurance, compensating the disabled, deterring wrongful conduct, regulating and educating professionals and industry, or achieving other public policy objectives, although frequently advanced through negligence law, ought to remain as the consequences of the tort action and not be seen as the purposes of the tort action. In this way, society can maintain a strong system of civil justice while recognizing the limitations to a system of civil justice. These limitations and gaps can then be best accommodated by non-tort schemes which are designed to accomplish these other objectives in an efficient and effective manner.

If compensating the injured is the overriding goal of tort law, the legal process becomes rife with fictions leading to the application of legal principles in a results-oriented manner, thereby compromising tort law as a system of corrective justice. According to Professor Klar, tort law should refocus on a system of corrective justice where fault is a key consideration when determining or apportioning liability. Such a system could be supplemented by programs designed to achieve such policy goals as compensation of victims, punishment of wrongdoers, deterrence and accident prevention — programs that would be more efficient than legal process. . . .

The "innocent" victim argument also falters when one considers how tort law has treated children and those who are suddenly physically disabled. Children of tender years are presumed to be incapable of negligence because they lack sufficient judgment to exercise reasonable care. . . . Unless engaging in adult activities, older children are held to a standard of a reasonable child of the same age, intelligence, and experience. . . . With respect to physically disabled defendants, courts routinely inquire into the voluntariness of their actions, whether the onset of the incapacity to control their actions could have been anticipated, and whether the damage could have been avoided. . . .

Given increased understanding of the biological or physiological roots of mental illness, a distinction between those who are suddenly physically incapacitated due to such conditions as epilepsy or diabetic shock and those who are incapacitated as a result of mental illness seems wholly unjustified. Such a distinction risks legitimizing physical illness while reinforcing negative stereotypes concerning mental illness. Concerns about the erosion of the objective reasonable person standard have not prevented courts from taking age or physical disability into consideration. Therefore, such concern should not prevent consideration of a defendant's mental illness.

Nor should the practical difficulties associated with assessing mental illness and the related lack of control of a defendant's behaviour prevent courts from crafting a test for a mental illness defence in tort actions. When this argument was originally made, an assessment of the capacity of a mentally ill defendant may not have been possible. However, there have been significant advancements in the study of mental illness. Courts can hear the testimony of experts with respect to myriad issues that arise in negligence actions. These experts may provide comprehensive and detailed information. . . .

The need to encourage caregivers of the mentally ill to take adequate precautions is not met effectively by imposing liability on the mentally ill. Rather than using tort law to ensure appropriate care, it seems more reasonable to impose liability directly on caregivers for failing in their duties. In any event, those who advocate adopting a strict liability stance in order to encourage caregivers to adequately care for the mentally ill perhaps assume wrongly that caregivers recognize the legal ramifications of a failure to properly execute their duties.

While several writers suggest that allowing the mentally ill a lower standard will reinforce the stereotype that the mentally ill are dangerous and should be isolated . . . the failure to acknowledge the impact of mental illness risks undermining the legitimacy of such disorders. . . . Arguably, an increased understanding of mental illness will allow the public to distinguish between the real risks associated with the integration of the mentally ill and fears that are mired in ignorance. If mentally ill individuals still have the capacity to conform to the objective standard, they will not be relieved of liability. . . . However, holding the mentally ill to the strict objective standard would essentially create a no-fault regime. . . .

Although Canadian courts have acknowledged that some consideration must be given to a defendant's mental illness, the case law offers a wide range of possible tests.

In *Buckley and T.T.C. v. Smith Transport Ltd.*, [1946] O.R. 798, [1946] 4 D.L.R. 721, the Ontario Court of Appeal held that a defendant who, by reason of mental disorder was either incapable of appreciating the duty to take care or incapable of discharging that duty, would not be liable in negligence. Unlike the test used in criminal law, the determination of whether the plaintiff could appreciate the duty of care owed and whether he could discharge that duty would not involve an assessment of whether the defendant could understand that his actions were "wrong". The Court held that a driver suffering from an insane delusion that his truck was being powered by a remote control was not liable for the collision he caused, as his insanity prevented him from discharging his duty. . . .

In *Canada (Attorney General) v. Connolly* (1989), 41 B.C.L.R. (2d) 162, 64 D.L.R. (4th) 84, the British Columbia Supreme Court held that there could be no liability in the absence of foreseeable harm. Therefore, because the defendant's bipolar disorder prevented him from foreseeing the injury that could result from driving his car at a high rate of speed while the plaintiff's arm was pinned inside the car, he could not be held liable. An essential element of the tort of negligence was absent.

. . .

While it could be argued that *Connolly* and *Buckley* apply a subjective standard and ignore the edict that an inability to meet the reasonable person test is no defence, it is clear that they import an exception to the general rule. In light of the exceptions granted to children, and the physically disabled, such an exception is not unreasonable. However, any such exception must be narrowly defined. As noted by Linden, supra: "It is only when the inadequacy amounts to a serious mental illness that the excuse [will be] countenanced."

The case law and academic literature reveal that there has been judicial recognition in Canada of the need to relieve the mentally ill of tort liability in certain circumstances. While the compensation of victims is still a worthy goal, that should not compromise the basic tenets of tort law. To find negligence, the act causing damage must have been voluntary and the defendant must have possessed the capacity to commit the tort. The burden of showing the absence of either falls on the defendant. If the defendant understood the duty of care he owed and was able to discharge that duty, his actions would be voluntary and the requisite capacity would exist.

In order to be relieved of tort liability when a defendant is afflicted suddenly and without warning with a mental illness, that defendant must show either of the following on a balance of probabilities:

(1) As a result of his or her mental illness, the defendant had no capacity to understand or appreciate the duty of care owed at the relevant time; or

(2) As a result of mental illness, the defendant was unable to discharge his duty of care as he had no meaningful control over his actions at the time the relevant conduct fell below the objective standard of care.

This test will not erode the objective reasonable person standard to such a degree that the courts will be imposing a standard "as variable as the length of the foot". It will preserve the notion that a defendant must have acted voluntarily and must have had the capacity to be liable. Fault will still be an essential element of tort law.

On the facts of this case, the expert evidence . . . clearly indicated that MacDonald was afflicted suddenly, and without prior warning, with a condition that left him with no meaningful control of his behaviour and an inability to appreciate the duty of care he owed to Cechmanek and others, including the Fialas. His mental illness was manifestly incapacitating.

Unlike the defendant in *Wenden*. . . MacDonald was unaware of his mental illness until after the accident. He was not driving a vehicle at the time and there was no way he could have foreseen the onset of his manic episode or taken preventative measures to avoid its result. His fault was no greater than Cechmanek's or the Fialas'; there was no fault.

If a strict liability regime is to apply to the acts of the mentally ill, the Legislature must give such direction. If the courts favour the compensatory goal of tort law by treating like any other person those suddenly afflicted with a serious and debilitating mental illness, the historical roots of tort law would be submerged and fault would become irrelevant. The result would be to taunt the tort.

On the facts found by the trial judge, MacDonald has satisfied the onus of showing that not one, but both of the tests to relieve him of tort liability are met.

NOTES AND QUESTIONS

1. Did the court apply a subjective or an objective standard of care in *Fiala?*

2. What arguments did the plaintiff make in favour of adopting a relatively unforgiving standard of care? How did Wittmann J.A. respond to those arguments? Do you agree with his decision?

3. American Law Institute, *Restatement (Third) of the Law of Torts: Physical and Emotional Harm* (2010) at §11(c) states that: "An actor's mental or emotional disability is not considered in determining whether conduct is negligent, unless the actor is a child." The position in England appears to have been similar. In *Roberts v.*

Ramsbottom, [1980] 1 All E.R. 7 (Q.B.), the court held that mental impairment short of automatism would not relieve the defendant from complying with the objective standard of care. Can you reconcile the American and English positions with the principle of no liability without fault? See generally Picher, "The Tortious Liability of the Insane in Canada" (1975) 13 Osgoode Hall L.J. 1983; Coleman, "Mental Abnormality, Personal Responsibility and Tort Liability" in Brody & Englehardt, eds., *Mental Illness: Law and Public Policy* (1980) 107; Splane, "Tort Liability of the Mentally Ill in Negligence Actions" (1983) 93 Yale L.J. 153; and Light, "Rejecting the Logic of Confinement: Care Relationships and the Mentally Disabled under Tort Law" (1999) 109 Yale L.J. 381.

The English position may have changed. In *Mansfield v. Weetabix*, [1998] 1 W.L.R. 1263 (C.A.) a driver's brain functions became impaired when his blood sugar dropped. The court held that he was not liable for the accidents he caused. Leggatt L.J. stated "the standard of care. . . was that which is to be expected of a reasonably competent driver unaware that he is or may be suffering from a condition that impairs his ability to drive." The court noted that to not take into account the driver's condition would be to impose strict liability rather than a negligence standard.

4. The question of who should bear the risks posed by the mentally ill remains a contentious legal and policy issue. See Klar & Jefferies, *Tort Law*, 6th ed. (2017) at 405-07; and Goudkamp, "Insanity as a Tort Defence" (2011) 34 O.J.L.S. 727. For example in *Hutchings v. Nevin* (1992), 9 O.R. (3d) 776 (Gen. Div.) the defendant, who was having psychotic delusions, caused a car accident, injuring his passenger. While acknowledging the general authority of *Buckley v. Smith Transport Ltd.*, [1946] O.R. 798 (C.A.), the plaintiff's counsel argued that Ontario's compulsory automobile insurance legislation had shifted the risk of mentally ill drivers onto the defendant's insurer. The judge rejected this argument and held that the defendant was not liable.

5. It is well established that the physically disabled are required to meet only the standard of care of a reasonable person with a similar disability. This principle is reflected in the case law dealing with the blind. See *Carroll v. Chicken Palace Ltd.*, [1955] 3 D.L.R. 681 (Ont. C.A.); *Haley v. London Electric Board*, [1965] A.C. 778 (H.L.); *Crawford v. Halifax* (1977), 81 D.L.R. (3d) 316 (N.S.S.C.); and *Strickland v. St. John's* (1982), 37 Nfld. & P.E.I.R. 208 (Nfld. Dist. Ct.). See also Lowry, "The Blind and the Law of Tort: The Position of a Blind Person as Plaintiff in Negligence" (1972) 20 Chitty's L.J. 253; ten Broek, "The Right to Live in the World: The Disabled in the Law of Torts" (1966) 54 Cal. L. Rev. 841; and Milani, "Living in the World: A New Look at the Disabled in the Law of Torts" (1999) 48 Cath. U.L. Rev. 323.

6. What standard of care should be expected of automobile drivers who have heart disease or other similar illnesses? What factors should be taken into account to determine whether this standard has been breached? How much weight should the court give to the argument that such people should attempt to live as normally as possible? See *Gootson v. R.*, [1948] 4 D.L.R. 33 (S.C.C.) (epileptic seizure); *Boomer v. Penn* (1965), 52 D.L.R. (2d) 673 (Ont. H.C.) (insulin reaction); *Gordon v. Wallace* (1973), 42 D.L.R. (3d) 342 (Ont. H.C.); and *Dobbs v. Mayer* (1985), 32 C.C.L.T. 191 (Ont. Dist. Ct.) (heart attack); and *Calgary (City) v. Thomas* (1995), 173 A.R. 51 (Prov. Ct.) (low blood sugar). See also Blalock, "Liability of the Unconscious Defendant"

(1970) 6(2) Trial 29; and Smith, "Automatism — A Defence to Negligence?" [1980] New L.J. 1111.

(b) THE STANDARD OF CARE EXPECTED OF CHILDREN

JOYAL v. BARSBY
(1965), 55 D.L.R. (2d) 38 (Man. C.A.)

MILLER C.J.M. (dissenting): . . . The real point to be decided in this appeal is whether the infant was guilty of contributory negligence. Negligence on the part of the defendant is not disputed and is not in issue on this appeal.

. . .

The infant admittedly ran out onto this busy highway into the side of defendant's motor vehicle and suffered grievous injuries. Her home was between this highway and a railway track, and she and two younger brothers had left their home to cross the highway and enter a park on the opposite side. The infant was aged six years and two months, and both her brothers were younger than she. This is a busy highway and the infant, according to the evidence of the father and the evidence of the infant plaintiff, had been thoroughly instructed in the dangers of crossing this highway and the lesson to "Stop, Look, and Listen" had been thoroughly drilled into her by the father and learned by the infant. There is no question that the evidence established that the infant plaintiff was conscious of the traffic danger inherent on this busy highway.

One of the two younger brothers ran across the highway at a time when it appears to have been dangerous to do so, as a big semi-trailer transport truck was approaching from the north. The truck driver sounded a siren ("fog-horn" as it was called in the evidence) to warn either the boy running across the highway or the children generally. Hearing the "fog-horn", the infant plaintiff and her other brother apparently thought better of following the first venturesome brother across, so they stepped back onto the shoulder of the road and stood there about two feet east of the pavement.

A motorist by the name of Despins was about 100 yards ahead of the defendant's motor vehicle, and, seeing the one boy on the west side of the highway as well as the girl and her other brother on the east side of the highway, he took his foot off the accelerator and by doing so decreased his speed to about 35 m.p.h. He apparently was nervous lest the sister and her other brother should follow the first brother across the highway, but he did not apply his brakes and was satisfied to reduce speed by compression. He saw the girl make a motion to cross the road as he approached and was passing her. Presumably this was just about the time the truck horn sounded, which caused the girl to step back onto the shoulder. She and her brother continued to stand motionless on the shoulder about two feet off the hard surface after Despins had passed. Despins and the defendant were both proceeding north on the east side of the highway. Despins said he first saw the children on the side of the road when he was a considerable distance south, so they must have stood motionless for some little while to let traffic pass. The defendant saw the two children on the east side but concluded — and with some cause — that they had realized traffic was on the highway, were waiting for it to pass, and would stay where they were until he passed them. Apparently he was not close enough to see, or in any event did not see, the one boy run across the highway. Nevertheless, he did as Despins did — took his foot off the accelerator and let the compression decrease his speed from 60 m.p.h. to 38 or 40 m.p.h. When the defendant was less than a car length away from her, the infant plaintiff suddenly started to run across the highway from east to west. She took only four or five steps, and then collided with the rear door of the defendant's vehicle. She was apparently struck by the door handle and sustained severe injuries.

. . .

The defendant's counsel accepted the principle that his client was guilty of some negligence but, as intimated above, conducted his appeal on the ground that the infant was guilty of contributory negligence. This involves first of all the question "Could this six-year old infant be guilty of contributory negligence?"

A binding authority is the decision of the Supreme Court of Canada in *McEllistrum v. Etches*, 6 D.L.R. (2d) 1 at pp. 6-7, [1956] S.C.R. 787, where it is stated:

> It should now be laid down that where the age is not such as to make a discussion of contributory negligence absurd, it is a question for the jury in each case whether the infant exercised the care to be expected from a child of like age, intelligence and experience.

. . .

The learned trial Judge said she was not more heedless than other children of her age, intelligence and experience, which expression is analogous to the words used in the *Etches* case, *supra*. The sad fact remains that she was heedless, careless, and negligent, despite her training and traffic experience. It appears to me the learned trial Judge found that, as she was no more heedless than other similar children, she could not be guilty of contributory negligence and consequently was not so guilty.

I think the infant plaintiff was partly responsible for this regrettable accident. She was thoroughly trained on the dangers of the highway, had experience with the traffic thereon, and, without first looking, had suddenly left a place of safety for a place of danger. There was still traffic proceeding along the highway, including the defendant's vehicle, which, had she looked, she could not help seeing and have thus avoided the accident. If contributory negligence cannot be found in an instance such as this, against a child with such training and experience, then it would be rare indeed that this doctrine could be invoked against a child.

. . .

On the undisputed facts, I feel justified in holding that the infant plaintiff's negligence contributed to the accident and that she can properly be adjudged liable for contributory negligence to the extent of 40%.

I would allow the appeal and vary the judgment of the learned trial Judge by charging the plaintiffs with 40% liability. The plaintiffs will therefore recover 60% of the damages rather than the 100% awarded by the trial Judge, but will still have their costs in the Court below.

The defendant is entitled to his costs in this Court.

. . .

FREEDMAN J.A., concurs with MONNIN J.A.

MONNIN J.A.: . . . The learned trial Judge applied this standard to the case at bar in the manner following. He said:

The age of the infant plaintiff was six years and two months and she appeared to me not to be of above average intelligence. Living near a fairly busy highway she would know of the danger from passing cars and admitted that her father had warned her of this danger; but she would have had far less experience than a city child of her age. I believe she acted as a normal child of her age and experience could be expected to act. She was momentarily stopped from crossing the highway by the blare of the truck siren, but this terrifying warning completely absorbed her attention. When the truck had passed she did not think of other traffic but darted forward as both Mr. Despins and the defendant anticipated she might do. In doing this she was not more heedless than any other child of her age, intelligence and experience. I do not consider that she was guilty of contributory negligence. The defendant must be held solely responsible.

The learned trial Judge considered the conduct of the child in the context of the situation which confronted her. This, of course, was the proper thing to do, since negligence is always a want of care in the particular circumstances. The learned trial Judge does not say that this child of six years and two months was incapable of being guilty of contributory negligence. He says that her behaviour in the specific situation should not be categorized as contributorily negligent. Faced with the approach of this large truck with its horn blaring, she riveted her attention upon it. That necessarily made her inattentive, for the moment, to traffic approaching from the other direction. But the learned trial Judge finds that the ordinary child of her age, intelligence and experience would have responded to the situation in the same way. Hence he refused to stamp her conduct with the label of negligence. I am not prepared to say he was wrong.

. . .

The appeal is therefore dismissed with costs. The cross-appeal is also dismissed with costs fixed at $50; the costs on the cross-appeal to be set off against the other costs.

NOTES AND QUESTIONS

1. What is the standard of care expected of a child? Is this test objective or subjective? Do you think the plaintiff in *Joyal* was contributorily negligent? See in comparison *Dao v. Sabatino* (1996), 24 B.C.L.R. (3d) 29 (C.A.). In *McEllistrum v. Etches*, [1956] S.C.R. 787, a case referred to by both the majority and dissent in *Joyal*, the court indicated that there is an age below which a child cannot be held liable in negligence. Can you suggest an appropriate test of capacity for children?

American Law Institute, *Restatement (Third) of the Law of Torts: Physical and Emotional Harm* (2010) at §10(b) provides that "A child less than five years of age is incapable of negligence."

2. A child involved in an adult activity, such as driving a car, snowmobiling or hunting, is required to meet the standard of care expected of a reasonable adult. What is the rationale for imposing a higher standard of care in these situations? See *Ryan v. Hickson* (1974), 55 D.L.R. (3d) 196 (Ont. H.C.); *Dellwo v. Pearson*, 107 N.W.2d 859 (Minn. S.C. 1961); and *McErlean v. Sarel* (1987), 42 C.C.L.T. 78 (Ont. C.A.). But see *Chaisson v. Hebert* (1986), 187 A.P.R. 105 (N.B.Q.B.).

This raises the question of what will be found to be an adult activity. See *Pope v. R.G.C. Management Inc.* (2002), 8 Alta. L.R. (4th) 143 (Q.B.), a case about playing golf.

In *Cook v. Cook* (1986), 162 C.L.R. 376 (H.C.A.) at 384 the High Court of Australia held that when a passenger is teaching a learner driver to drive, "the standard of care which arises from the relationship of pupil and instructor is that which is reasonably to be expected of an unqualified and inexperienced driver in the circumstances." However, this decision was overruled in *Imbree v. McNeilly* (2008), 236 C.L.R. 510 (H.C.A.). The court held that the inexperienced driver's standard of care is the same as any other person's and is not to be qualified by reference to the level of experience of the driver. It rejected the notion that the passenger was owed a lower standard of care than were other users of the road.

3. For other examples of the standard of care expected of children see *Ottosen v. Kasper* (1986), 37 C.C.L.T. 270 (B.C.C.A.); *Laviolette v. C.N.R.* (1987), 40 C.C.L.T. 138 (N.B.C.A.); *Bajkov v. Canil* (1990), 66 D.L.R. (4th) 572 (B.C.C.A.); *Nespolon v. Alford* (1998), 40 O.R. (3d) 355 (C.A.); *Gu (Litigation Guardian of) v. Friesen*, 2013 BCSC 607; and *Perilli v. Marlow*, 2018 BCSC 495. See also Bohlen, "Liability in Tort of Infants and Insane Persons" (1924) 23 Mich. L. Rev. 9; Dunlop, "Torts Relating to Infants" (1966) 5 U.W.O.L. Rev. 116; Alexander, "Tort Liability of Children and Their Parents" in Mendes da Costa, ed., *Studies In Canadian Family Law* (1975) 845; Bagshaw, "Children Through Tort" in Fionda, ed., *Legal Concepts of Childhood* (2001) 127; and Thorpe, "Adolescent Negligence, 'Obvious Risk' and Recent Developments in Neuroscience" (2014) 21 Torts L.J. 195.

4. If the law is prepared to relax the standard of care based on youth, should it also do so based on old age? Why or why not? See Barrett, "Negligence and the Elderly: A Proposal for a Relaxed Standard of Care" (1984) 17 J. Marshall L. Rev. 873. Should such a relaxed standard apply to activities like driving? See *McKee (Guardian ad litem of) v. McCoy* (2001), 9 C.C.L.T. (3d) 294 (B.C.S.C.).

5. Although parents, guardians and others who supervise children are not held vicariously liable when a child commits a tort, they can be held liable if they have carelessly failed to monitor or control the child's conduct. As discussed in Chapter 3, such liability can also be imposed under legislation such as the *Parental Responsibility Act, 2000*, S.O. 2000, c. 4. The courts have defined the requisite standard of care in terms of a "reasonable parent of ordinary prudence." See *Myers v. Peel County Board of Education*, [1981] 2 S.C.R. 21; *Thomas v. Hamilton (City) Board of Education* (1994), 20 O.R. (2d) 598 (C.A.); and *Gu (Litigation Guardian of) v. Friesen*, supra. Is it appropriate to use this parental standard in assessing the behaviour of educators, daycare workers and others who are not parents or guardians?

In *LaPlante (Guardian ad litem of) v. LaPlante* (1995), 26 C.C.L.T. (2d) 32 (B.C.C.A.) the defendant father was held liable in negligence for permitting his 16-year-old son, who had recently obtained his licence, to drive in traffic at highway speeds under icy conditions. The court held that a reasonable parent of ordinary prudence would not have let the son drive in those conditions. See also *McLaren v. McLaren Estate*, 2011 ABCA 299 where the court found the driver's mother's supervision was not negligent.

In *C.S. (Next friend of) v. Miller* (2002), 306 A.R. 289 (Q.B.) a five-year-old child was sexually molested by Miller, a friend of the child's parents, while the two of them were visiting a Boy Scout Camp. The Camp Chief, who was a volunteer, witnessed the sexual assault but took no action to stop it or to prevent any further assaults while the child was at the camp. The child's mother sued the Boy Scouts for the assaults on her daughter. The court held that, even though she was a volunteer, the Camp Chief was liable in negligence. She had willingly and knowingly entered into a relationship of supervisory care and control over the children at the camp. This imposed on the Camp Chief an obligation to take appropriate steps to protect the victim, despite the fact that she was a visitor and not a registered camper and that she was accompanied by Miller, who had parental authority over the victim. The Boy Scouts were vicariously liable for the volunteer Camp Chief's negligence.

(c) THE STANDARD OF CARE EXPECTED OF PROFESSIONALS

At one time, only those involved in a limited number of public callings, such as innkeepers and common carriers, were held to special standards of care. The courts have now developed modified standards of care to govern not only professionals but also most skilled trades and occupations. The following materials focus on medical cases but the courts' approach applies across many professions and trades.

WHITE v. TURNER
(1981), 31 O.R. (2d) 773 (H.C.),
aff'd (1982), 12 D.L.R. (3d) 319 (Ont. C.A.)

[The defendant plastic surgeon performed a breast reduction operation on the plaintiff. The plaintiff suffered several post-operative complications and her breasts were scarred and poorly shaped. The plaintiff sued the defendant, claiming that he had been negligent in performing the operation.]

LINDEN J.:—Needless to say, a mere error in judgment by a professional person is not by itself negligence. The Courts recognize that professionals may make mistakes during the course of their practice, which do not bespeak negligence. Sometimes medical operations do not succeed. Sometimes lawyers lose cases. The mere fact of a poor result does not mean that there has been negligence. In order to succeed in an action against a professional person, a plaintiff must prove, on the balance of probabilities, not only that there has been a bad result, but that this was brought about by negligent conduct.

Before liability can be imposed for the operation itself, therefore, the plaintiff must prove that the defendant performed the surgery in such a way that a reasonable plastic surgeon would consider it to have been less than satisfactory. . . . In other words, unless it is established on a balance of probabilities that this mammoplasty was done in a substandard way by the defendant, he cannot be held liable in negligence.

Plastic surgery is a specialty that has its own standards — standards which are unique to that specialty. If the work of a plastic surgeon falls below the accepted practices of his colleagues, he will be held civilly liable for any damage resulting. But if his work complies with the custom of his confrères he will normally escape civil liability for his conduct, even where the result of the surgery is less than satisfactory.

. . .

[The plaintiff alleged that the defendant had breached the standard of care in three respects. The first two concerned (i) the defendant's choice of "the Strombeck procedure" and (ii) his planning for the operation. Both of those allegations were rejected on the evidence, some of which had been given by two experts, Dr. Birch and Dr. Robertson.]

The third area of complaint is with the actual execution of the surgery. Although Dr. Birch testified that a similar result to this could occur without the plastic surgeon being negligent, I find that the evidence, on the whole, supports a finding that the poor result obtained in the mammoplasty performed on Mrs. White was the result of Dr. Turner's negligent execution of the surgery.

The reason for the bad result here was that insufficient tissue was removed by Dr. Turner. . . .

There were two reasons why Dr. Turner did not remove sufficient tissue, both of which I find were negligence in the circumstances: (1) the operation was done too quickly, and (2) the suturing was started before a proper check was made of whether enough tissue had been removed.

As for the length of time taken to perform the operation, the evidence is clear that the usual time required is between two and four hours. Dr. Birch said that the Strombeck procedure took an average of two and a half hours to do. Dr. Robertson testified that more than three hours is required to perform a Strombeck properly. If he has only a junior intern assisting him, he normally requires about four hours to do a Strombeck. If he has an expert assistant, he can do it properly in three and a half hours. He indicated that, when the doctors on his staff at the Toronto General Hospital booked only three hours operating-room time for a Strombeck, they often could not complete the operation in time and other doctors were kept waiting for the operating-room. Dr. Robertson advised his own staff, therefore, to book four hours operating-room time in order to perform a Strombeck.

I have found on the facts here that Dr. Turner did this Strombeck in approximately one hour, 35 minutes. This was described by Dr. Birch as "very fast". He said that the operation was "very rapidly done". Dr. Turner must have seen no "hitches" to go at that speed, he concluded. Dr. Robertson was less charitable than Dr. Birch. He testified that even Dr. Turner's estimate of two and a half to two and three-quarters hours was a "pretty short" time for the Strombeck operation. Dr. Robertson could not imagine that a Strombeck could be properly done in one hour and 35 minutes. To him, it was "almost incredible" that it could. He thought it would take one hour just to close up. A simple mastectomy took one hour and 35 minutes to do. This mammoplasty by Dr. Turner was a "very rapid operation", he opined. "Detail takes time", he said and, consequently, the necessary attention to detail, which required some stepping back, was not done in this case. "When one is in a hurry, expediency rather than art comes into play", he suggested. In such a short time, thought Dr. Robertson, all the considerations could not be taken into account. The more time that is taken, the less likely is an undesirable result, he said. In the time Dr. Turner took to perform this operation, Dr. Robertson testified that he could not look back. Dr. Robertson concluded by saying that, although he hated to talk that way, he felt he had to: the patient was entitled to expect more than she received on this occasion.

I hold, therefore, that Dr. Turner did this operation too quickly. This resulted in his not removing enough tissue, which in turn caused the incisions to open, leading to the substandard result. This was actionable negligence.

As for the failure to make a check of the amount of tissue removed before closing, Dr. Birch testified that it was standard practice, at the conclusion of the cutting, to tack the flaps of skin together with a few sutures and make a judgment about the bulk of the breast. He said that some doctors do not do any actual stitching at this stage, but that all plastic surgeons put the pieces together and take a look before proceeding to close up. I find on the basis of this evidence that this was the standard practice of plastic surgeons.

There is no evidence that Dr. Turner did this standard check. It is not mentioned in his notes of the operation, but this is not controlling, according to Dr. Birch, who said that he did not usually make any notes about doing the check, although he invariably did it. Dr. Turner did not say that he made such a check. He did not even indicate that he was aware that it was standard practice. Actually, even though Dr. Turner did not do this check, he admitted that, when he went to close up, he actually noticed more tension on the flaps than usual, but he did nothing about it. He explained this by observing that there was always "quite a bit of tension". This extra tension should have served as a warning to him that insufficient tissue had been removed. But he was too much in a hurry to do anything about it. Moreover, Dr. Turner's written report stated that he had removed 800 gr., although, in fact, he had taken out only 705 gr. He was fully aware that the removal of only 705 gr. of tissue was less than the usual amount removed in such cases. Dr. Turner agreed that he probably should have taken out an additional 300 gr. of tissue. Dr. Robertson, in correcting the result, removed about 350 gr. (or three-quarter pound), an additional 50% of tissue, which demonstrates that this was no small error. If Dr. Turner had paused to do a proper check, he would have learned that he had removed only 705 gr., that this was less than usual, and that there was too much tension on the flaps. This would have revealed his error to him and permitted him to take the necessary corrective measures before closing. This, in turn, would have avoided the bad result. I find, therefore, that this failure to do the customary check was actionable negligence.

NOTES AND QUESTIONS

1. What allegations of breach were made against the defendant? How did the court define the standard of care expected of the defendant? Do you agree with the reasoning in *White*?

2. What is the standard of care that should be imposed on doctors to keep up with new drugs, surgical procedures and treatment programs? See *Dhalla v. Jodrey* (1985), 16 D.L.R. (4th) 732 (N.S.C.A.); *Sigouin (Guardian ad litem of) v. Wong* (1991), 10 C.C.L.T. (2d) 236 (B.C.S.C.); and *ter Neuzen v. Korn* (1995), 127 D.L.R. (4th) 577 (S.C.C.).

3. In *ter Neuzen v. Korn, supra,* Justice Sopinka noted that "physicians have a duty to conduct their practice in accordance with the conduct of a prudent and diligent doctor in the same circumstances." See also *Crits v. Sylvester*, [1956] O.R. 132 (C.A.) at 143, aff'd [1956] S.C.R. 991. General practitioners are thus required to exercise the standard of care of a reasonable, competent general practitioner. This includes knowing their limits and when to refer patients to a specialist. In *Layden v. Cope* (1984), 28 C.C.L.T. 140 (Alta. Q.B.) the plaintiff, who had previously suffered from gout, went to two general practitioners in a small town. They both concluded that he had gout and prescribed medication. The doctors continued treating him for gout, even though his condition deteriorated and the hospital nurses expressed concern.

After nine days, the plaintiff was referred to a specialist, who immediately diagnosed cellulitis with possible secondary infection. The plaintiff's condition deteriorated and his leg had to be amputated. In holding the general practitioners liable, the court stated that the standard of care expected of a general practitioner in a small town is not significantly different from that of general practitioners in a city. They should have considered other diagnoses when the plaintiff's condition did not improve and referred him to a specialist much sooner. See also *Dillon v. LeRoux*, [1994] 6 W.W.R. 280 (B.C.C.A.); *Crawford (Litigation Guardian of) v. Penney* (2003), 14 C.C.L.T. (3d) 60 (Ont. S.C.J.), aff'd (2004), 26 C.C.L.T. (3d) 246 (Ont. C.A.); and *Forsberg v. Naidoo*, 2011 ABQB 252 at para. 16.

4. The standard of care expected of an intern is that of a reasonably competent intern in the circumstances. Although interns have completed medical school and passed their licensing examinations, they are not qualified to practice on their own. Rather, interns are required to work under the supervision of a fully qualified doctor. Consequently, the standard of care expected of interns is lower than that required of general practitioners. See *Vancouver General Hospital v. Fraser Estate*, [1952] 2 S.C.R. 36; and *Aldana v. March* (1999), 44 C.C.L.T. (2d) 164 (B.C.S.C.).

In contrast, residents are fully qualified doctors who seek additional training in a specialty. As a result, even a junior resident would be held to the standard of care expected of a general practitioner. A more senior resident would be expected to have advanced skills in his or her specialty consistent with a resident of comparable training but would not be expected to have the skills of a fully qualified specialist. See *Dale v. Munthali* (1978), 21 O.R. (2d) 554 (C.A.); *Boulay v. Charbonneau* (1988), 46 C.C.L.T. 16 (Qc. C.A.); *Wills v. Saunders*, [1989] 2 W.W.R. 715 (Alta. Q.B.); *Brown (Next friend of) v. University of Alberta Hospital* (1997), 197 A.R. 237 (Q.B.); *Miles v. Judges* (1997), 37 C.C.L.T. (2d) 160 (Ont. Gen. Div.); *Chow (Litigation Guardian of) v. Wellesley Hospital*, 1999 CarswellOnt 349 (Gen. Div.) (WL Can); *Adair (Litigation Administrator of) v. Hamilton Health Sciences Corp.* (2005), 32 C.C.L.T. (3d) 283 (Ont. S.C.J.); *Anderson v. Greene*, 2010 ABQB 676; *Anderson v. Queen Elizabeth II Health Sciences Centre*, 2012 NSSC 360; and *Brodeur (Litigation Guardian of) v. Provincial Health Services Authority (c.o.b. British Columbia Women's Hospital and Health Center)*, 2016 BCSC 968. See also Cabaj, "Entering the Abyss: The Resident's Standard of Care" (2011) 19 Health L.J. 189.

On the standard of care for nurses see *Latin v. Hospital for Sick Children*, 2007 CarswellOnt 19 (S.C.J.) (WL Can); *Milne v. St. Joseph's Health Centre* (2009), 69 C.C.L.T. (3d) 208 (Ont. S.C.J.); *Steinebach (Litigation Guardian of) v. Fraser Health Authority*, 2011 BCCA 302; *Brodeur (Litigation Guardian of) v. Provincial Health Services Authority (c.o.b. British Columbia Women's Hospital and Health Center)*, *supra*; and *Paur (Committee of) v. Providence Health Care*, 2017 BCCA 161. On the standard of care for medical technicians see *Ayana v. Skin Klinic* (2009), 68 C.C.L.T. (3d) 21 (Ont. S.C.J.) at 65; and *McKerr v. CML Healthcare Inc.*, 2012 BCSC 1712.

5. The growing volunteer movement, the recognition of the value of peer counselling and efforts to reduce costs have resulted in greater use of non-professionals in various health and care situations. Although these individuals would not be expected to meet a professional standard of care, they would be required to have the skills and training necessary to do their assigned tasks competently. They would also be expected to know their own limits and when they should get

professional assistance. Agencies that use non-professionals are required to adequately screen, train, place and supervise these workers. For example, an agency might be held liable in negligence for using inadequately trained volunteers to staff a suicide crisis line.

On the standard of care expected of a volunteer (as opposed to professional) firefighter, see the notes following *Watt* earlier in this chapter.

6. Individuals may be held to a professional standard of care if they implicitly or explicitly suggest that they have the skills and training of a professional. By holding themselves out as counsellors or therapists, individuals may be seen as explicitly suggesting that they have professional qualifications and training. Indeed, merely offering to provide a particular service, such as marriage counselling, might reasonably create the impression that one has special training and skills.

By the same token, however, a person practising in a secondary or related field will not be held liable simply because he or she failed to satisfy the standard expected in the primary field. For example in *Shakoor v. Situ*, [2000] 4 All E.R. 181 (Q.B.) the court held that a practitioner of traditional Chinese herbal medicine who did not hold himself out as an "orthodox" physician was only required to meet the standard of care appropriate to his "art." A similar analysis has been applied to midwives: *Carere v. Cressman* (2002), 12 C.C.L.T. (3d) 217 (Ont. S.C.J.).

7. For additional examples of medical malpractice see *Preston v. Chow* (2007), 224 Man. R. (2d) 39 (Q.B.); and *Pinch (Guardian ad litem of) v. Morwood*, 2016 BCSC 938, aff'd 2017 BCCA 234 (taking of patient history); *Davies v. Gabel Estate*, [1995] 2 W.W.R. 35 (Sask. Q.B.); *Briffet v. Gander & District Hospital Board* (1996), 29 C.C.L.T. (2d) 251 (Nfld. C.A.); *Stricken v. Stewart* (2005), 367 A.R. 18 (C.A.); *Barker v. Montfort Hospital* (2007), 223 O.A.C. 201 (C.A.); *Taylor v. Morrison* (2006), 41 C.C.L.T. (3d) 79 (Ont. S.C.J.); *Cleveland (Litigation Guardian of) v. Hamilton Health Sciences Corp. (Henderson General Division)*, 2009 CarswellOnt 7853 (S.C.J.) (WL Can); *Duncalf v. Capital Health Authority* (2009), 4 Alta. L.R. (5th) 201 (Q.B.); *Boyd v. Edington*, 2014 ONSC 1130; *K.S. (Litigation Representative of) v. Willox*, 2016 ABQB 483, aff'd 2018 ABCA 271; and *Briante (Litigation Guardian of) v. Vancouver Island Health Authority (c.o.b. Royal Jubilee Hospital)*, 2017 BCCA 148 (diagnosis); *Gauvin v. Clark* (2006), 303 N.B.R. (2d) 326 (C.A.); and *Leon v. Tu*, 2012 BCSC 1600 (pre-operation procedure); *Eady v. Tenderenda*, [1975] 2 S.C.R. 599; *Cherry (Guardian ad litem of) v. Borsman* (1991), 75 D.L.R. (4th) 668 (B.C.S.C.), aff'd (1992), 94 D.L.R. (4th) 487 (B.C.C.A.); *Lyne v. McClarty* (2003), 170 Man. R. (2d) 161 (C.A.); *Chasse v. Evenson* (2006), 59 Alta. L.R. (4th) 159 (Q.B.); and *Malleck v. Baum*, 2013 SKCA 25 (surgical procedure); *Joseph Brant Memorial Hospital v. Koziol*, [1978] 1 S.C.R. 491; *Pittman Estate v. Bain* (1994), 19 C.C.L.T. (2d) 1 (Ont. Gen. Div.); *Aristorenas v. Comcare Health Services* (2006), 83 O.R. (3d) 282 (C.A.); and *Rollin v. Baker* (2010), 266 O.A.C. 221 (C.A.) (post-operative care); *Champigny v. Ste-Marie* (1993), 19 C.C.L.T. (2d) 307 (Qc. S.C.); *Pierre (Next Friend of) v. Marshall*, [1994] 8 W.W.R. 478 (Alta. Q.B.); and *Shantry v. Thompson*, 2015 ONCA 395 (treatment); *Mustafic v. Smith* (1988), 55 Man. R. (2d) 188 (C.A.); *Wenden v. Trikha* (1993), 14 C.C.L.T. (2d) 225 (Alta. C.A.); *Keith v. Abraham*, 2011 ONSC 2; and *Dr. X v. Everson*, 2013 ONSC 6134 (psychiatric care); *Rupert v. Toth* (2006), 38 C.C.L.T. (3d) 261 (Ont. S.C.J.); and *McLintock v. Alidina*, 2011 ONSC 137 (patient management); *Adams v. Taylor*, 2012 ONSC 4208 (record keeping).

See generally Robertson & Picard, *Legal Liability of Doctors and Hospitals in Canada*, 5th ed. (2017).

8. Some hospitals have adopted a practice of expressly identifying a "most responsible physician" for a specific patient. In *Manary v. Strban*, 2013 ONCA 319 the MRP relied on the treatment plan recommended by a respirologist. The respirologist was found to have met the standard of care but the MRP was not. The dissent held these conclusions were "demonstrably incompatible." In contrast, the majority held that this was not inconsistent and that the MRP, in that role, had broader obligations and responsibilities. Which view do you prefer?

9. In *Meyers (Next friend of) v. Moscovitz* (2005), 363 A.R. 262 (C.A.) the court found that the trial judge had erred in defining the standard of care expected of a reasonable doctor in the management of a birth. Instead of framing the standard in terms of the overall management of the birth, the trial judge focussed on a single aspect of the woman's care: the monitoring of her temperature for infection. The court noted that in some situations the breach of a single element of the standard of care could warrant a finding that the standard has been breached but this was not such a case.

10. The current system for resolving allegations of medical malpractice has been roundly criticized by both patients' rights groups and the medical profession. For a discussion of alternatives to the existing fault-based adversarial approach see Sharpe, "Alternatives to the Court Process for Resolving Medical Malpractice Claims" (1981) 26 McGill L.J. 1036; Mitchell & McDiarmid, "Medical Malpractice: A Challenge to Alternative Dispute Resolution" (1988) 3 Can. J.L. & Society 227; Chapman, "Controlling the Costs of Medical Malpractice: An Argument for Strict Hospital Liability" (1990) 28 Osgoode Hall L.J. 523; Abraham & Weiler, "Enterprise Medical Liability and the Evolution of the American Health Care System" (1994) 108 Harv. L. Rev. 381; and Gibson, "Is It Time to Adopt a No-Fault Scheme to Compensate Injured Patients?" (2016) 47 Ottawa L. Rev. 307.

In 2016 the Ontario government commissioned Stephen Goudge, a former judge, to review the civil justice system as it related to medical liability cases and their costs. His report, *Report to Ontario Ministry of Health and Long Term Care re: Medical Liability Review* (2017) was released in April 2018.

11. For a discussion of the standard of care expected of lawyers see *Brumer v. Gunn* (1982), 18 Man. R. (2d) 155 (Q.B.); *Jacks v. Davis* (1982), 141 D.L.R. (3d) 355 (B.C.C.A.); *Pound v. Nakonechny* (1983), 27 C.C.L.T. 146 (Sask. C.A.); *Central Trust Co. v. Rafuse* (1986), 31 D.L.R. (4th) 481 (S.C.C.); *Harela v. Powell* (1998), 163 D.L.R. (4th) 365 (Ont. Gen. Div.); *Wilcox v. Johnston* (2001), 238 N.B.R. (2d) 325 (Q.B.); *Hagblom v. Henderson* (2003), 232 Sask. R. 81 (C.A.); *Folland v. Reardon* (2005), 74 O.R. (3d) 688 (C.A.); *Chaster (Guardian ad litem of) v. LeBlanc* (2009), 95 B.C.L.R. (4th) 299 (C.A.); *Kalish v. Rosenbaum* (2009), 100 O.R. (3d) 169 (S.C.J.); *McCullough v. Riffert* (2010), 76 C.C.L.T. (3d) 71 (Ont. S.C.J.); *Webb v. Birkett*, 2011 ABCA 13; *Meister v. Coyle*, 2011 NSCA 119; *Meier v. Rose*, 2012 ABQB 82; *King Lofts Toronto I Ltd. v. Emmons*, 2013 ONSC 6113, aff'd 2014 ONCA 215; *Wong v. Grant Mitchell Law Corporation*, 2015 MBQB 88; *644036 Alberta Ltd. v. 625494 Alberta Ltd.*, 2016 ABQB 597, varied 2018 ABCA 236; and *Pilotte v. Gilbert, Wright & Kirby Barristers and Solicitors*, 2016 ONSC 494. See also Mahoney, "Lawyers — Negligence — Standard

of Care" (1985) 63 Can. Bar Rev. 221; Dodek & Hoskins, eds., *Canadian Legal Practice — A Guide for the 21st Century* (2009); Klar & Jefferies, *Tort Law*, 6th ed. (2017) at 475-89; Davies, *Solicitors' Negligence and Liability* (2008); and Whaley, "Solicitor's Negligence: Estates and Trust Context" (2016) 45 Adv. Q. 102. On the standard of care for paralegals see *Elliot v. Chiarelli* (2006), 83 O.R. (3d) 226 (S.C.J.).

As the phenomenon of "unbundling" legal services grows — under which a lawyer only performs certain tasks on a client's behalf and leaves it to the client to perform others which previously would also have been done by the lawyer — a failure to clearly delineate who is responsible for what could lead to claims against lawyers. See *Outaouais Synergest Inc. v. Lang Michener LLP*, 2013 ONCA 526. See also *Meehan v. Good*, 2017 ONCA 103.

12. For examples of other special standards of care see: *Dabous v. Zuliani* (1976), 68 D.L.R. (3d) 414 (Ont. C.A.); and *Trizec Equities Ltd. v. Ellis-Don Management Services Ltd.* (1998), [1999] 5 W.W.R. 1 (Alta. Q.B.) (architects); *Auto Concrete Curb Ltd. v. South Nation River Conservation Authority*, [1993] 3 S.C.R. 201; *Lovely v. Kamloops (City)* (2009), 64 M.P.L.R. (4th) 259 (B.C.S.C.), aff'd (2010), 71 M.P.L.R. (4th) 210 (B.C.C.A.); and Rochester, "Professional Engineers: Does a Higher Risk Imply a Higher Standard of Care?" (2000) 50 C.L.R. (2d) 199 (engineers); *Smith v. B.C. (A.G.)* (1988), 30 B.C.L.R. (2d) 356 (C.A.); *Hill v. Hamilton-Wentworth Regional Police Services Board*, [2007] 3 S.C.R. 129; and *Camaso Estate v. Egan*, 2013 BCCA 6 (police officers); *Myers v. Peel County Board of Education*, [1981] 2 S.C.R. 21; *Fraser v. Board of School Trustees of School District No. 72 (Campbell River)* (1988), 54 D.L.R. (4th) 563 (B.C.C.A.); *MacCabe v. Westlock Roman Catholic Separate School District No. 110* (2001), 96 Alta. L.R. 217 (C.A.); *Young v. Bella*, [2006] 1 S.C.R. 108; and *Hussack v. Chilliwack School District No. 33*, 2011 BCCA 258 (teachers); *Day v. Toronto Transportation Commission*, [1940] S.C.R. 433 at 441; *Hofstrand Farms Ltd. v. B.D.C. Ltd.*, [1986] 1 S.C.R. 228; and *Visanji v. Eaton* (2006), 39 C.C.L.T. (3d) 150 (B.C.S.C.) (common carriers); *Dom. Securities Ames Ltd. v. Deep* (1984), 4 O.A.C. 386 (C.A.); *Varcoe v. Sterling* (1992), 7 O.R. (3d) 204 (Gen. Div.), aff'd (1992), 7 O.R. (3d) 204 (C.A.); and *Refco Futures (Canada) Ltd. v. SYB Holdings Corp.* (2004), 23 B.C.L.R. (4th) 309 (C.A.) (stockbrokers); *S. Maclise Enterprises Inc. v. Union Securities Ltd.* (2009), 17 Alta. L.R. (5th) 201 (C.A.) at paras. 17-18; *Stradiotto v. BMO Nesbitt Burns*, 2014 ONSC 3477; and *Marlin Investments Inc. v. Moldovan*, 2014 BCCA 364 (investment advisors); *Spiewak v. 251268 Ont. Ltd.* (1987), 61 O.R. (2d) 655 (H.C.) (real estate agents); *Haig v. Bamford*, [1977] 1 S.C.R. 466; and *Deloitte & Touche v. Livent (Receiver of)*, 2014 ONSC 2176, aff'd 2016 ONCA 11, varied 2017 SCC 63 (auditors); *Sceptre Resources Ltd. v. Deloitte Haskins & Sells* (1988), 64 Alta. L.R. (2d) 48 (Q.B.); and *Bloor Italian Gifts Ltd. v. Dixon* (2000), 2 C.C.L.T. (3d) 73 (Ont. C.A.) (accountants); *Waldman's Fish Co. v. Anderson Ins. Ltd.* (1979), 25 N.B.R. (2d) 482 (C.A.); *Clark v. D.A. Hargreaves Insurance Ltd.* (2007), 78 Alta. L.R. (4th) 302 (Q.B.); *Beck Estate v. Johnston, Meier Insurance Agencies Ltd.* (2010), 85 C.C.L.I. (4th) 228 (B.C.S.C.), aff'd 2011 BCCA 250; and *Veert Landscaping Inc. v. Ranger Insurance Brokers Ltd.*, 2013 MBQB 117 (insurance agents); *Graham v. Picot Gorman and A.E.S. Consultants Ltd.* (1985), 66 N.B.R. (2d) 434 (T.D.); and *Indian Head Credit Union Ltd. v. A. Hosie & Co.* (1992), 103 Sask. R. 213 (Q.B.), aff'd (1994), 120 Sask. R. 73 (C.A.) (real estate appraisers); *Smith v. Eric S. Bush (a firm)*, [1987] 3 All E.R. 179 (C.A.) (land surveyors); *Krawchuk v. Scherbak*, 2011 ONCA 352 (real estate agents); *Halliwell v. Lazarus*, 2011 ONSC 390, varied 2012 ONCA 348; and *Lippa v. Colletta*, 2017 ONSC 1122 (home

inspectors); *R.(L.) v. Nyp* (1995), 25 C.C.L.T. (2d) 309 (Ont. Gen. Div.) (journalists); *Wheeler v. Muri* (1996), 32 C.C.L.T. (2d) 180 (Sask. Q.B.) (veterinarians); *B.(D.) v. Children's Aid Society of Durham (Region)* (1996), 30 C.C.L.T. (2d) 310 (Ont. C.A.); *B.M. (Litigation Guardian of) v. R.M.* (2009), 97 B.C.L.R. (4th) 234 (C.A.); and *J.P. v. British Columbia (Children and Family Development)*, 2017 BCCA 308 (social workers); *Hendrick v. De Marsh* (1984), 6 D.L.R. (4th) 713 (Ont. H.C.), aff'd (1986), 54 O.R. (2d) 185 (C.A.); and *D.N. v. Oak Bay (District)* (2005), 261 D.L.R. (4th) 692 (B.C.S.C.) (probation officers); *Walters (Litigation Guardian of) v. Ontario*, 2015 ONSC 4855, aff'd 2017 ONCA 53; and *Fontenelle v. Canada (Attorney General)*, 2017 ONSC 6604, rev'd 2018 ONCA 475 (prison guards); and Schulz, "Mediator Liability in Canada: An Examination of Emerging American and Canadian Jurisprudence" (2001) 32 Ottawa L. Rev. 269; and Schulz, "Obstacles to Tortious Liability for Mediator Malpractice" in Beaulac, Pitel & Schulz, eds., *The Joy of Torts* (2003) 149 (mediators).

13. For the standard of care expected of professionals generally see Campion, ed., *Professional Liability in Canada* (1994); and Powell, Stewart & Jackson, eds., *Jackson & Powell on Professional Liability*, 8th ed. (2016).

14. In a professional negligence claim the plaintiff is usually required to provide expert evidence on the issue of the standard of care. See for example *Meady v. Greyhound Canada Transportation Corp.*, 2015 ONCA 6 at paras. 34-35; *Krawchuk v. Scherbak, supra*, at paras. 130-36; *Bergen v. Guliker*, 2015 BCCA 283 at paras. 114-31; and *495793 Ontario Ltd. (Central Auto Parts) v. Barclay*, 2016 ONCA 656. In *Kurdina v. Gratzer*, 2010 CarswellOnt 2251 (C.A.) (WL Can) at para. 2 the court noted that "It is well established that to establish a breach of the standard of care to support a claim for medical negligence, a plaintiff is required to lead expert evidence of a physician practising in the same field as the defendant attesting to the defendant's negligence."

In *Rowlands v. Wright* (2009), 250 O.A.C. 394 (C.A.) at para. 21 the court noted that "Although common sense no doubt has a role to play in assessing medical negligence, it plays a limited role 'where a procedure involves difficult or uncertain question of medical treatment or complex, scientific or highly technical matters that are beyond the ordinary experience and understanding of judge or jury.'," quoting from *ter Neuzen, supra*. It held that the trial judge was not entitled, in the face of conflicting medical opinions as to how to proceed, to rely on common sense to find that the surgical techniques used were inadequate. Does this unduly restrict the role of the trial judge?

The general requirement of expert evidence is subject to exceptions. One is for situations about which an ordinary person could be expected to have knowledge. Another is for conduct so flawed that the breach is obvious even without technical knowledge. So some professional negligence cases have held that the issues involved could be decided based on the ordinary knowledge of the jury or judge, such that the absence of expert evidence on the standard of care was not fatal to the claim. See for example *Goodwin (Litigation Guardian of) v. Olupona*, 2013 ONCA 259; *King Lofts Toronto I Ltd. v. Emmons, supra*, at paras. 74-77 (S.C.J.); *Lippa v. Colletta, supra*, at para. 84; *Trillium Motor World Ltd. v. Cassels Brock & Blackwell LLP*, 2017 ONCA 544 at paras. 300-06; and *Sansome v. Rubens*, 2017 NLCA 32 at paras. 88-93. Might this distinction be difficult for courts to draw? How is a non-expert able to know what conduct is egregious?

Is the requirement for expert evidence lessened in cases of lawyers' negligence, given that judges were once lawyers and are presumed to know the law? See *Malton v. Attia*, 2013 ABQB 642, rev'd 2016 ABCA 130; *Tran v. Kerr*, 2014 ABCA 350 at paras. 21-25; and *Mraz v. Herman*, 2016 ABCA 313 at para. 17.

15. Professionals such as lawyers are often subject to codes of ethical conduct. These codes can be relevant to determining the duties owed in a professional relationship and identifying what the professional is required to do or refrain from doing. However, a violation of the provisions of such a code is not automatically a breach of the standard of care: *Perez v. Galambos*, [2009] 3 S.C.R. 247 at para. 29. See also *MacDonald Estate v. Martin*, [1990] 3 S.C.R. 1235 at 1244-45.

16. As the courts develop new duties of care for people with specialized skills, they must also address the standard of care required in these situations. So, for example, in recognizing the tort of negligent investigation which can be committed by police officers, courts have to consider the elements involved in a reasonable, prudent investigation. In *Hill v. Hamilton-Wentworth Regional Police Services Board, supra*, at paras. 67-73 the Supreme Court of Canada held that the standard was that of the "reasonable police officer." See also *Lawrence v. Peel Regional Police Force*, 2009 CarswellOnt 2161 (S.C.J.) (WL Can); *Raworth v. Stratford (City) Police Services Board*, 2012 ONSC 300 at para. 21; *Boomhour v. Durham (Regional Municipality) Police Service*, [2012] O.J. No. 868 (S.C.J.) (QL); *Barton v. Nova Scotia (Attorney General)*, 2015 NSCA 34; *George v. Larkin*, 2016 ONSC 4961 at para. 8; *495793 Ontario Ltd. (Central Auto Parts) v. Barclay, supra*; and *Price v. Kelday*, 2017 ONSC 6494.

6. Degrees of Negligence

The common law generally recognizes one standard of care in negligence: that of a reasonable person. Even the special standards of care focus on what is reasonable to expect of those with recognized disabilities or unique skills, education or training.

However, statutes occasionally restrict the scope of liability to injuries inflicted as a result of "gross negligence." The definition of that concept has always been something of a mystery. Baron Wolfe once described it as ordinary negligence "with the addition of a vituperative epithet": *Wilson v. Brett* (1843), 152 E.R. 737. It has also been sarcastically suggested that the differences between negligence, gross negligence and recklessness equate to the differences between a fool, a damned fool and a God-damned fool: Linden *et al., Canadian Tort Law*, 11th ed. (2018) at 242-44. For our purposes, it may suffice to say that gross negligence requires something less blameworthy than criminal negligence but something worse than ordinary tort negligence. In *McCulloch v. Murray*, [1942] S.C.R. 141 at 145 the Supreme Court of Canada defined gross negligence as involving "a very marked departure from the standards by which responsible and competent people . . . habitually govern themselves." See also *Walker v. Coates*, [1968] S.C.R. 599 at 601; and *Doern v. Phillips Estate* (1994), 2 B.C.L.R. (3d) 349 (S.C.), aff'd (1997), 43 B.C.L.R. (3d) 53 (C.A.).

The idea of gross negligence tends to be confined to two types of statutes. The first concerns the liability of a municipality for injuries caused by snow or ice on sidewalks. Section 44 of the *Municipal Act, 2001*, S.O. 2001, c. 25 is typical. It provides:

(1) The municipality that has jurisdiction over a highway or bridge shall keep it in a state of repair that is reasonable in the circumstances, including the character and location of the highway or bridge.

. . .

(9) Except in case of gross negligence, a municipality is not liable for a personal injury caused by snow or ice on a sidewalk.

For an application of this provision see *Crinson v. Toronto (City)* (2010), 100 O.R. (3d) 366 (C.A.).

The second type of statute concerns the liability of medical professionals who provide medical assistance during emergencies. Section 2 of the *Good Samaritan Act, 2001*, S.O. 2001, c. 2, is typical, providing:

Protection from liability

(1) Despite the rules of common law, a person described in subsection (2) who voluntarily and without reasonable expectation of compensation or reward provides the services described in that subsection is not liable for damages that result from the person's negligence in acting or failing to act while providing the services, unless it is established that the damages were caused by the gross negligence of the person.

Persons covered

(2) Subsection (1) applies to,

(a) a health care professional who provides emergency health care services or first aid assistance to a person who is ill, injured or unconscious as a result of an accident or other emergency, if the health care professional does not provide the services or assistance at a hospital or other place having appropriate health care facilities and equipment for that purpose; and

(b) an individual, other than a health care professional described in clause (a), who provides emergency first aid assistance to a person who is ill, injured or unconscious as a result of an accident or other emergency, if the individual provides the assistance at the immediate scene of the accident or emergency.

A more specialized example is *Sabrina's Law, 2005*, S.O. 2005, c. 7, s. 3(4) which applies to emergency responses to anaphylactic reactions suffered by students in schools.

Beyond these two types, there are other statutes that use this standard of care. For example, it applies to police conduct under the *Police Act*, R.S.B.C. 1996, c. 367, s. 21 and to trustees in bankruptcy and receivers in several sections of the *Environmental Protection Act*, R.S.O. 1990, c. E.19.

NOTES AND QUESTIONS

1. What is the rationale for legislation that protects municipalities from liability in negligence for slippery sidewalks? See *Dorschell v. Cambridge (City)* (1980), 30 O.R. (2d) 714 (C.A.); and *Mete v. Mississauga*, [1984] O.J. No. 1139 (H.C.) (QL).

2. Good Samaritan statutes are intended to encourage emergency intervention by reducing the threat of liability for those who intervene. It is, however, doubtful that

they have much effect. See McInnes, "Good Samaritan Statutes: A Summary and Analysis" (1992) 26 U.B.C.L. Rev. 239. There have been few cases in Canada brought against those who intervened in an emergency situation.

3. The ordinary standard of care requires the defendant to act as the reasonable person would have acted in similar circumstances. In light of this focus on the circumstances, courts recognize the "sudden peril" doctrine under which conduct that normally would be considered careless is exempted from liability if, in the context of an emergency, it nevertheless was reasonable. Reasonable people make reasonable mistakes under pressure: see *Canadian Pacific Ltd. v. Gill* (1973), 37 D.L.R. (3d) 229 (S.C.C.); and *Isaac Estate v. Matuszynska*, 2018 ONCA 177. In light of that doctrine, how low is the standard of care under Good Samaritan legislation?

4. Under what circumstances does Ontario's *Good Samaritan Act, 2001* apply? Should it apply more broadly? Are there situations in which some types of individuals should not be encouraged to intervene?

5. Under a third type of legislation that previously existed in some provinces, a driver of a non-commercial vehicle could be held liable for injuries sustained by a passenger only if an accident was caused by the driver's gross negligence. The courts were generally suspicious of such provisions and often found gross negligence in conduct that looked remarkably like regular negligence. For an excellent example of the problems of interpreting the guest passenger legislation see *Engler v. Rossignol* (1975), 10 O.R. (2d) 721 (C.A.). See also *Levesque v. Wedge* (1977), 13 Nfld. & P.E.I.R. 283 (P.E.I.C.A.); *Cheevers v. Van Norden* (1980), 42 N.S.R. (2d) 337 (T.D.); and *McIntyre v. Sawatsky* (1982), 18 Sask. R. 406 (Q.B.).

Guest passenger statutes were roundly criticized and have now been abolished.

6. Beyond these specific statutes, are there defendants who should benefit from a lower standard of care? Why or why not? See Nolan, "Varying the Standard of Care in Negligence" [2013] C.L.J. 651. To take an example, should those voluntarily participating in sporting events only be required not to be reckless rather than careless? See *Kempf v. Nguyen*, 2013 ONSC 1977, rev'd 2015 ONCA 114.

7. Custom

TER NEUZEN v. KORN
(1995), 127 D.L.R. (4th) 577 (S.C.C.)

[The plaintiff contracted HIV as a result of artificial insemination in January 1985. The risk of such infection was not widely known in North America when the procedure was performed. The defendant doctor was responsible for screening semen donors. Expert evidence established that the physician had adopted standard medical practices in this regard. The jury nevertheless found him liable. One of the issues on appeal was whether it was open to the jury to find that the standard practice itself fell short of the standard of care.]

SOPINKA J.: —

. . .

1. *Standard of care and evidence of standard practice*

It is well-settled that physicians have a duty to conduct their practice in accordance with the conduct of a prudent and diligent doctor in the same circumstances. In the case of a specialist, such as a gynaecologist and obstetrician, the doctor's behaviour must be assessed in light of the conduct of other ordinary specialists, who possess a reasonable level of knowledge, competence and skill expected of professionals in Canada, in that field. A specialist, such as the respondent, who holds himself out as possessing a special degree of skill and knowledge, must exercise the degree of skill of an average specialist in his field.

. . .

It is also particularly important to emphasize, in the context of this case, that the conduct of physicians must be judged in the light of the knowledge that ought to have been reasonably possessed at the time of the alleged act of negligence. . . .

No issue is taken with this proposition which was applied both in the trial judge's charge to the jury and by the Court of Appeal.

The Court of Appeal, after a thorough review of the evidence, held that it was not possible for a jury acting judicially to have found that, in 1985, the respondent ought to have known of the risk. . . . I agree with this finding and can find no basis upon which it can be questioned. Indeed my review of the evidence leads to the same conclusion. The evidence of standard practice . . . was based entirely on the state of knowledge required of the reasonable practitioner in 1985 and it would have been . . . impossible for a jury acting judicially to have found that, given the state of knowledge, the reasonable practitioner ought to either have discontinued [artificial insemination] or warned the patients of the risk. . . .

The appellant, therefore, can only support a favourable finding on this aspect of the case on the basis that the jury was entitled to find that the standard established by the evidence itself departed from that of a prudent and diligent physician and that the respondent, in failing to conform with a higher standard, was guilty of negligence. . . .

It is generally accepted that when a doctor acts in accordance with a recognized and respectable practice of the profession, he or she will not be found to be negligent. This is because courts do not ordinarily have the expertise to tell professionals that they are not behaving appropriately in their field. In a sense, the medical profession as a whole is assumed to have adopted procedures which are in the best interests of patients and are not inherently negligent. As L'Heureux-Dubé J. stated in [*Lapointe v. Hôpital Le Gardeur*, [1992] 1 S.C.R. 351], in the context of the Québec *Civil Code* . . . :

> Given the number of available methods of treatment from which medical professionals must at times choose, and the distinction between error and fault, *a doctor will not be found liable if the diagnosis and treatment given to a patient correspond to those recognized by medical science at the time, even in the face of competing theories.* As expressed more eloquently by André Nadeau in "La responsabilité médicale" (1946), 6 R. du B. 153 at p. 155:

> "[TRANSLATION] The courts do not have jurisdiction to settle scientific disputes or to choose among divergent opinions of physicians on certain subjects. *They may only make a finding of fault where a violation of universally accepted rules of medicine has occurred. The courts should not involve themselves in controversial questions of assessment having to do with diagnosis or the treatment of preference.*"

(Emphasis added.)

In *The Law of Torts*, 7th ed. (Sydney: Law Book Co., 1987), Professor John G. Fleming observed the following with respect to the role of standard practice, at p. 109:

> *Conformity* with general practice, on the other hand, usually dispels a charge of negligence. It tends to show what others in the same "business" considered sufficient, not that the defendant could not have learnt how to avoid the accident by the example of others, that most probably no other practical precautions could have been taken, and that the impact of an adverse judgment (especially in cases involving industry or a profession) will be industry-wide and thus assume the function of a "test case". *Finally, it underlines the need for caution against passing too cavalierly upon the conduct and decision of experts.*
>
> All the same, even a common practice may itself be condemned as negligent *if fraught with obvious risks.*

(Emphasis added.)

With respect to the medical profession in particular, Professor Fleming noted, at p. 110:

> Common practice plays a conspicuous role in medical negligence actions. Conscious at once of the layman's ignorance of medical science and apprehensive of the impact of jury bias on a peculiarly vulnerable profession, courts have resorted to the safeguard of insisting that negligence in diagnosis and treatment (including disclosure of risks) cannot ordinarily be established without the aid of expert testimony or in the teeth of conformity with accepted medical practice. *However there is no categorical rule. Thus an accepted practice is open to censure by a jury (no expert testimony required) at any rate in matters not involving diagnostic or clinical skills, on which an ordinary person may presume to pass judgment sensibly, like omission to inform the patient of risks, failure to remove a sponge, an explosion set off by an admixture of ether vapour and oxygen or injury to a patient's body outside the area of treatment.*

(Emphasis added. Footnotes omitted.)

It is evident from the foregoing passage that while conformity with common practice will generally exonerate physicians of any complaint of negligence, there are certain situations where the standard practice itself may be found to be negligent. However, this will only be where the standard practice is "fraught with obvious risks" such that anyone is capable of finding it negligent, without the necessity of judging matters requiring diagnostic or clinical expertise.

. . .

As was observed in *Lapointe*, courts should not involve themselves in resolving scientific disputes which require the expertise of the profession. Courts and juries do not have the necessary expertise to assess technical matters relating to the diagnosis or treatment of patients. Where a common and accepted course of conduct is adopted based on the specialized and technical expertise of professionals, it is unsatisfactory for a finder of fact to conclude that such a standard was inherently negligent. On the other hand, matters falling within the ordinary common sense of juries can be judged to be negligent. For example, where there are obvious existing alternatives which any reasonable person would utilize in order to avoid risk, one could conclude that the failure to adopt such measures is negligent notwithstanding that it is the prevailing practice among practitioners in that area.

. . .

I conclude from the foregoing that, as a general rule, where a procedure involves difficult or uncertain questions of medical treatment or complex, scientific or highly technical matters that are beyond the ordinary experience and understanding of a judge or jury, it will not be open to find a standard medical practice negligent. On the other hand, as an exception to the general rule, if a standard practice fails to adopt obvious and reasonable precautions which are readily apparent to the ordinary finder of fact, then it is no excuse for a practitioner to claim that he or she was merely conforming to such a negligent common practice.

The question as to whether the trier of fact can find that a standard practice is itself negligent is a question of law to be determined by the trial judge irrespective of the mode of trial. It is, of course, for the jury to determine on the evidence what the standard practice is. If the evidence is conflicting on this issue, the jury will have to resolve the conflict. If, as in this case, the evidence is virtually conclusive, the trial judge should instruct the jury that failure to accept the evidence may very well result in an unreasonable verdict which will be set aside. Moreover, unless the nature of the issue is of a kind to bring it within the exception to the general rule, the jury should be instructed that once they have determined on the evidence what the standard is, the only remaining issue is whether the defendant conformed to the standard. On the other hand, if the case is one coming within the exception so that the jury can fix the standard on the basis of common sense and the ordinary understanding of the jury without the assistance of expert testimony, the trial judge must instruct the jury accordingly.

[The plaintiff had alleged that the defendant breached the standard of care in two respects: (i) with respect to his screening of potential donors for HIV specifically and (ii) with respect to his screening of donors for sexually transmitted infections generally.

The court held that there should not be a new trial on the first allegation. At the time of treatment, the defendant had complied with a standard practice that was beyond the understanding of a lay person and that was not so obviously fraught with danger that it could be declared careless in itself. A properly instructed jury consequently could not find the defendant liable on that basis.

In contrast, the court held that a new trial should be ordered with respect to the second allegation. HIV falls within a more general class of sexually transmitted infections. The defendant might be held liable for the transmission of HIV if he could have been held liable for the transmission of one of those other infections. There was, however, insufficient evidence regarding the existence of a standard practice for the screening for those infections. The matter was consequently sent back to trial to determine whether there was such a practice. If there was not, then the jury could, without relying upon expert evidence, find that the defendant had been careless.]

NOTES AND QUESTIONS

1. The party relying on either compliance with or breach of custom has the burden of proving that such a custom exists. The courts will only accept that an act, approach or pattern of conduct constitutes a custom if it is a well-established and recognized practice that has been widely accepted in a trade, industry or profession. See generally *Heeney v. Best* (1979), 11 C.C.L.T. 66 (Ont. C.A.); *Goodwin v. McCully*

(1989), 101 N.B.R. (2d) 289 (Q.B.(T.D.)); and *Garratt v. Orillia Power Distribution Corp.* (2008), 90 O.R. (3d) 161 (C.A.) at para. 55.

2. Prior to *ter Neuzen* it was generally accepted that compliance with custom provided evidence of reasonableness and breach of custom provided evidence of negligence. How has the decision in *ter Neuzen* changed the impact of compliance with or breach of custom? Is *ter Neuzen* limited to customary practice in highly technical fields?

3. How was the customary practice established in *ter Neuzen*? What was the nature of the dispute over the role of the jury? How did Sopinka J. resolve it? Did Sopinka J. concede too much authority to professionals to dictate the standards of negligence in their fields?

In *ter Neuzen*, the court referred to North American practices in artificial insemination. How should the courts address the standard of care if the Canadian and American medical practices differ? In *Walker Estate v. York-Finch General Hospital* (1999), 169 D.L.R. (4th) 689 (Ont. C.A.), aff'd (2001), 198 D.L.R. (4th) 193 (S.C.C.) the blood-donor screening practices of the Canadian Red Cross were held to be negligent, given the more specific and detailed screening practices in the United States. What concerns, if any, does this reliance on American practices raise?

4. As Sopinka J. noted in *ter Neuzen*, there can be more than one custom or standard practice in areas that are unsettled. In such cases, following one of the competing approaches generally suffices and it is not for the court to determine which of them is more appropriate. As noted in *O'Connor v. Wambera*, 2018 BCSC 886 at para. 111 "if the evidence establishes more than one recognised and accepted body of medical opinion, a physician is not negligent if they adhere to one accepted school of thought."

5. It is important to understand that *ter Neuzen* does not require deference to expert opinion in every medical case. In *Walker Estate v. York-Finch General Hospital* (2001), 198 D.L.R. (4th) 193 (S.C.C.) the plaintiffs contracted HIV as a result of receiving tainted blood through transfusions. In each instance, the donor was a homosexual male. The plaintiffs claimed that the defendant was liable insofar as it had failed to properly screen potential donors for the risk of HIV. In contrast to its American counterpart, which had used a screening procedure that involved very specific information, the defendant's screening procedure was of a much more general nature. Only two experts gave evidence at trial and both agreed that the defendant's approach, while less specific than the American, was adequate and appropriate.

Despite that evidence, the trial judge held that the defendant had breached the standard of care. The Court of Appeal and the Supreme Court of Canada agreed. Major J. explained that "the trial judge was not asked to assess complex or highly scientific matters. Simply, the issue was whether the general health question was sufficient to deter the infected donor from donating blood. The issue is not how an expert would respond to the donor screening questions in the questionnaire, but how a lay person would respond." See also *Comeau v. Saint John Regional Hospital* (2001), 9 C.C.L.T. (3d) 223 (N.B.C.A.); and *Kelly v. Lundgard* (2001), 202 D.L.R. (4th) 385 (Alta. C.A.).

6. In *Nattrass v. Weber* (2010), 23 Alta. L.R. (5th) 51 (C.A.) the majority of the court noted (at para. 35) that "While the *ter Neuzen* exception is well established in law, it must be exceptionally unusual for a sophisticated professional discipline like orthopaedic surgery to routinely follow an unsafe practice which is not only unsafe, but obviously unsafe to even the lay observer." In that case the majority held the trial judge, in condemning the standard practice as negligent, had gone well beyond what an ordinary trier of fact could do without the assistance of experts. The doctors had followed the standard practice and as such they had to be taken to have met the standard of care. In contrast, the dissent held (at para. 74) "that an ordinary person with no particular expertise in the practice of medicine would understand that it would be reasonable and prudent to follow the effects of a medication prescribed to a recovering patient by monitoring blood platelet levels in order to measure, if not the exact levels, a possible decrease in blood platelet counts." Does this difference of opinion raise concerns about applying the test in *ter Neuzen*? See also *Neil v. Lodge*, 2010 NBCA 83.

7. For other judicial discussions of custom see *Vancouver Gen. Hosp. v. McDaniel*, [1934] 4 D.L.R. 593 (P.C.); *Rothwell v. Raes* (1988), 66 O.R. (2d) 449 (H.C.), aff'd (1990), 2 O.R. (3d) 332 (C.A.); *Emmonds v. Makarewicz* (2000), 81 B.C.L.R. (3d) 75 (C.A.); and *Leon v. Tu*, 2012 BCSC 1600 (doctors); *Moss v. Ferguson* (1979), 35 N.S.R. (2d) 181 (S.C.); *Lowry v. Cdn. Mountain Holidays Ltd.* (1987), 40 C.C.L.T. 1 (B.C.C.A.); *Zsoldos v. Canadian Pacific Railway Co.* (2009), 93 O.R. (3d) 321 (C.A.); and *Johansson v. General Motors of Canada Ltd.*, 2012 NSCA 120 (industrial practices); and *Glivar v. Noble* (1985), 8 O.A.C. 60 (C.A.); and *Shute v. Premier Trust Co.* (1993), 35 R.P.R. (2d) 141 (Ont. Gen. Div.) (lawyers).

8. What if a particular defendant has specific reasons to question the efficacy of a customary practice? Can it continue to use and rely on the practice? If not, would it be discouraged from engaging in certain lines of inquiry or research, as it would suffer consequences as a result of being better informed? See *Baker v. Quantum Clothing Group Ltd.*, [2011] UKSC 17 which deals with the impact on employees of ongoing noise in an industrial workplace.

9. Special concerns can arise when a defendant has a monopoly, so that its custom or practice is therefore also the custom or practice for the whole trade, industry or profession. See for example *Zsoldos v. Canadian Pacific Railway Co.*, *supra*, at para. 27.

10. For a discussion of custom see Linden *et al.*, *Canadian Tort Law*, 11th ed. (2018) at 224-35; Mulheron, "Trumping *Bolam*: A Critical Legal Analysis of *Bolitho*'s 'Gloss'" [2010] C.L.J. 609; and American Law Institute, *Restatement (Third) of the Law of Torts: Physical and Emotional Harm* (2010) at §13. In the United Kingdom, reliance by professionals on custom is governed by the *Bolam* test, flowing from *Bolam v. Friern Hospital Management Committee*, [1957] 1 W.L.R. 582.

11. A doctor performs a neurological examination on a patient, using the standard practice. Part of the examination involves the doctor assessing the way the patient walks, watching from a few metres behind the patient. During the walking the patient falls and is injured. The patient wants to sue the doctor. Has the doctor breached the standard of care?

REVIEW PROBLEMS

1. Dr. Carver, a general practitioner, prescribed a strong buffering agent to Mr. Jones to treat his ulcer, despite the fact that some ulcer patients with certain allergies and 2% of ulcer patients without these allergies suffer serious reactions to it. There was another drug that was equally effective with no risk of a serious reaction to it but it was three times more expensive. Since Mr. Jones was poor, Dr. Carver decided to prescribe the buffering agent, and carried out the customary tests used by most general practitioners to verify that Mr. Jones had none of the known allergies. Although Dr. Carver had heard of a new study which indicated ways of predicting whether an ulcer patient would react badly to the buffering agent, he had not had time to read it prior to treating Mr. Jones. Had Carver read the new study, he would have realized that there was a 25% chance that Mr. Jones would react badly to the buffering compound.

Unfortunately, Mr. Jones had a severe reaction to the buffering agent which necessitated his hospitalization. He is seeking your advice about suing Dr. Carver in negligence. Your preliminary investigation revealed that Dr. Carver had three years of special training in internal medicine and therefore should have known a great deal more about ulcers than an average general practitioner.

2. Mr. Smith was crossing an intersection on a green light one quiet Sunday morning when he was struck by an ambulance which was carrying a critically ill man to the emergency ward of a nearby hospital. Although the intersection was level, Mr. Smith's and the ambulance driver's views of each other were blocked by a large truck that had stopped in the right-hand lane for the red light. The ambulance driver had turned on his flashing beacon and loud siren and had slowed down from 100 to 20 kph when he entered the intersection against the red light. Mr. Smith did not see the ambulance's flashing light because of the truck and did not hear the siren because he was deaf. Discuss whether the ambulance driver, Mr. Smith or both were negligent.

16

CAUSATION

1. Introduction
2. The But-For Test
3. Established Exceptions to the But-For Test
4. Recent Attempts to Modify the But-For Test
5. Multiple Causes
6. Issues in Assessing the Plaintiff's Loss

1. Introduction

In some areas of tort law, the reported cases provide a relatively clear statement of the legal principles and guidance on the courts' likely approach. Since causation is not one such area, this chapter contains more background information, case summaries and commentary than most others. Causation may be seen as involving two issues. First, what test of causation governs the situation? The general test of causation in negligence is the but-for test, although it is subject to modifications and exceptions. Second, based on the facts, can the plaintiff prove on the balance of probabilities that the defendant's breach of the standard of care was a cause of his or her loss? This second issue is often referred to as the cause-in-fact test.

Causation is the element of a negligence action that links the defendant's breach of the standard of care to the plaintiff's loss. Consequently, it is important to state with precision the alleged breach of the standard of care and the injury in issue. The plaintiff may have two or more distinct injuries or sets of injuries, each of which must be separately analyzed in terms of causation. For example, assume that defendant A negligently shoots the plaintiff in the arm, defendant B negligently shoots the plaintiff in the leg and the combined blood loss results in the plaintiff's death. The plaintiff has suffered three distinct losses: the bullet wound in the arm caused by A, the bullet wound in the leg caused by B, and death caused by A and B.

In order to facilitate analysis, it is helpful to focus initially on each distinct loss or category of losses suffered by the plaintiff and determine if it is attributable to a single tortfeasor or to two or more tortfeasors. The term "divisible loss" typically refers to a loss that, as a practical matter, can be attributed to the conduct of a single tortfeasor. The term "indivisible loss" refers to a loss that, as a practical matter, can be attributed to the conduct of more than one tortfeasor. If a plaintiff suffers a series of distinct injuries occurring in rapid succession, such as multiple whiplash injuries in a 15-vehicle chain reaction crash, the courts will likely treat the plaintiff's injuries as a single indivisible loss caused by all of the at-fault drivers. In the example in the previous paragraph, the arm wound and leg wound are each divisible injuries, and the plaintiff's death is an indivisible injury.

Some courts and commentators indicate that a divisible loss requires a "single cause" approach and that an indivisible loss requires a "multiple cause" approach. Traditionally, the courts have used a single cause analysis where, in addition to a negligent defendant, there was an absconding tortfeasor, a contributorily negligent plaintiff or an innocent pre-existing or naturally occurring contributory cause. This approach is compatible with the view that a divisible injury should be defined narrowly, as one that is attributable to a single tortfeasor who is before the courts. In some cases, the courts may acknowledge that there was more than one cause but explain that this other cause was not relevant to the tortfeasor's liability.

The plaintiff need not prove that the defendant's negligence was the sole, immediate, direct, or even the most important cause of his or her loss. Rather, the plaintiff only has to establish that the defendant's negligence was a cause. Moreover, the plaintiff is not required to prove causation to the standard of scientific certainty or beyond a reasonable doubt. Instead, the plaintiff need only establish causation on a balance of probabilities. The courts have modified the accepted burden and standard of proof in causation in narrow categories of cases to prevent a perceived unfairness or to achieve a public policy goal. While some courts have provided a compelling or plausible justification for modifying the accepted principles, others have not. In some cases, the courts modified the accepted principles without acknowledging that they were doing so.

Some courts have failed to distinguish between causation and remoteness of damages, an issue that is discussed in the next chapter. Even if the defendant negligently caused the plaintiff's loss, the defendant will not be held liable if that loss is too far removed from, or too remote a consequence of, his or her negligence. Remoteness of damages is a legal issue that governs the extent of the defendant's liability for the losses that he or she has negligently caused. Unlike in intentional torts, defendants in negligence actions are generally held liable for only the foreseeable injuries that they caused. The American courts and some Canadian courts have used the term "proximate cause" as a convenient means of glossing over the distinct issues of causation and remoteness of damages. If a court concludes that a defendant's negligence was not a proximate cause of the plaintiff's loss, does it mean that: the negligence was not a cause; the negligence was a cause but the loss was too remote to be recoverable; or the negligence was not a cause and that, in any event, the loss was too remote?

2. The But-For Test

The standard test of factual causation is the but-for test. If the plaintiff's injury would not have occurred but for the defendant's negligent act, then that act is a cause of the injury. In such circumstances, a court or commentator may state that the defendant's negligence was "causally effective." If the plaintiff's injury would have occurred regardless of the defendant's negligent act, then that act will generally not be held to be a cause.

KAUFFMAN v. TORONTO TRANSIT COMMISSION
(1959), 18 D.L.R. (2d) 204 (Ont. C.A.), aff'd [1960] S.C.R. 251

MORDEN J.A.:—The defendant appeals from the judgment of McLennan J., dated June 3, 1958, upon the findings of a jury, awarding the plaintiff the sum of $25,000 damages for injuries suffered by her following a fall on an escalator in the defendant's St. Clair Ave. subway station. The defendant's counsel on the appeal argued that the jury's findings were against the evidence, were perverse and did not state any ground of actionable negligence for which the defendant could be held liable.

Late in the evening of February 11, 1955, the plaintiff and a friend, a Mrs. Mathewson, after travelling on a northbound subway train alighted at the St. Clair station . . . The plaintiff stepped upon the escalator followed by Mrs. Mathewson. Immediately ahead of the plaintiff was a man and ahead of him two youths. The youths began scuffling and fell back against the man who in turn lost his balance and fell back upon the plaintiff. The plaintiff fell upon the escalator steps with these two or three people on top of her. As a result of her fall and of the continuing movement upwards of the escalator, the plaintiff sustained very severe and permanent injuries. The defendant's appeal against the amount of the damages was abandoned at the hearing of the appeal.

. . .

The jury found the defendant negligent specifically as follows:
"1. The defendant, in acquiring an escalator of radical departure in hand-rail design, did not sufficiently test or cause to be tested by a qualified expert the coefficient of friction and contour of the Peelle Motor Stair Handrail."

. . .

The theory advanced by the plaintiff's counsel to quote his own words was that "in the operation of an escalator, particularly in a public transit system where large crowds are to be expected, if a person near the top falls backward (for whatever reason) against the person behind him, each person will fall against the other knocking him down in much the same fashion as a row of dominoes". But there was a total absence of evidence that the man immediately ahead of the plaintiff or the two reckless and irresponsible youths ahead of him were grasping or attempted to grasp the hand rail before or in the course of the scuffle and consequent falling. Nor was there any evidence that in the circumstances the plaintiff would not have fallen if her hands had been grasping a rubber oval hand rail. In my opinion, there was no evidence to justify a finding that the type of hand rail in use at the St. Clair Ave. station was a contributing cause of the plaintiff's unfortunate and serious accident. It is a fundamental principle that the causal relation between the alleged negligence and the injury must be made out by the evidence and not left to the conjecture of the jury . . . . The first finding of negligence in view of the evidence in this case does not justify a verdict against the defendant.

. . .

The appeal must be allowed and the action dismissed, both with costs, if demanded.

BARNETT v. CHELSEA & KENSINGTON HOSPITAL MANAGEMENT COMMITTEE
[1969] 1 Q.B. 428

[Three men went to the defendant hospital complaining about vomiting for several hours after drinking tea. The nurse on duty called the medical casualty officer, who instructed the nurse to tell them to go home to bed and call their own doctors. One of the men died of arsenic poisoning about five hours later. The judge held that the doctor's dismissal of the deceased's complaints without even seeing or examining him breached the standard of care. The judge then turned to the issue of whether the doctor's negligence was a cause of the man's death.]

NEILD J.: . . . There has been put before me a timetable which I think is of much importance. The deceased attended at the casualty department at five or 10 minutes past eight in the morning. If the casualty officer had got up and dressed and come to see [him] and examined [him] and decided to admit [him], the deceased . . . could not have been in bed in a ward before 11 a.m. I accept Dr. Goulding's evidence that an intravenous drip would not have been set up before 12 noon, and if potassium loss was suspected it could not have been discovered until 12.30 p.m. Dr. Lockett, dealing with this, said: "If [the deceased] had not been treated until after 12 noon the chances of survival were not good."

Without going in detail into the considerable volume of technical evidence which has been put before me, it seems to me to be the case that when death results from arsenical poisoning it is brought about by two conditions; on the one hand dehydration and on the other disturbance of the enzyme processes. If the principal condition is one of enzyme disruption — as I am of the view it was here — then the only method of treatment which is likely to succeed is the use of the specific antidote which is commonly called B.A.L. Dr. Goulding said in the course of his evidence:

> "The only way to deal with this is to use the specific B.A.L. I see no reasonable prospect of the deceased being given B.A.L. before the time at which he died" — and at a later point in his evidence — "I feel that even if fluid loss had been discovered death would have been caused by the enzyme disturbance. Death might have occurred later."

I regard that evidence as very moderate, and it might be a true assessment of the situation to say that there was no chance of B.A.L. being administered before the death of the deceased.

For those reasons, I find that the plaintiff has failed to establish, on the balance of probabilities, that the defendants' negligence caused the death of the deceased.

NOTES AND QUESTIONS

1. Why did the plaintiff's claim in *Kauffman* fail? What kind of evidence should the plaintiff have introduced to support her allegation that the handrail on the escalator played a causal role in her injuries? The plaintiff also argued that the TTC was liable for failing to prevent the boys from fighting. Although the TTC's failure in this regard clearly played a causal role in the plaintiff's injuries, the court rejected her argument. On what basis do you think the court reached this conclusion?

2. Was the result in *Barnett* fair? Given that most patients are at a disadvantage in understanding medical evidence, accessing medical records, obtaining expert witnesses, and financing litigation, should the standard test of causation, the burden of proof and the standard of proof be modified in medical malpractice cases? Are there any other factors that warrant modifying the established principles in malpractice cases?

3. Medical malpractice claims continue to generate a large percentage of the appellate causation cases. See for example *Steinebach v. O'Brien*, 2011 BCCA 302 (nurse's negligent failure to report her findings to the doctor earlier and doctor's negligent initial assessment of the fetus were causes of the baby being born with cerebral palsy); *Ediger v. Johnston*, 2013 SCC 18 (doctor's negligence in undertaking a

forceps delivery without having a surgical team immediately available was a cause of the baby's brain damage and quadriplegia); *Mangal v. William Osler Health Centre*, 2014 ONCA 639 (anaesthetist's negligent failure to promptly inform obstetrician at a critical stage was not a cause of the patient's death); *Benhaim v. St-Germain*, 2016 SCC 48 (physicians' negligent failure to diagnose patient's lung cancer earlier was not a cause of his death); *Sacks v. Ross*, 2017 ONCA 773 (physician's negligence in diagnosing and treating bowel leak was not a cause of plaintiff's septic shock and subsequent injuries); *Surujdeo v. Melady*, 2017 ONCA 41 (physicians' failure to seek out test results and respond more promptly was a cause of the patient's death due to myocarditis); and *Ghiassi v. Singh*, 2018 ONCA 764 (nurse's failure to promptly notify the paediatric resident that the infant plaintiff was jaundiced was a cause of his subsequent development of severe cognitive and physical disabilities). What factors related to the parties and the causation claims contribute to the number of appeals in medical malpractice cases?

4. In *Qualcast (Wolverhampton) Ltd. v. Haynes*, [1959] A.C. 743 (H.L.), an experienced foundry worker was injured when a ladle slipped and splashed molten metal on his left foot. The defendant company had protective spats that, if worn, would have prevented the injury. However, the company had not told or advised the worker to wear the spats, and he had not asked to use them. After recuperating, the worker returned to the job and still did not wear the spats. The House of Lords held that the defendant had not breached the standard of care in providing the worker with protective equipment. Lord Denning stated that the plaintiff's claim would have failed on causation in any event. Do you agree? Would Lord Denning have reached the same conclusion if the worker had framed the allegation of negligence in terms of the defendant's failure to require workers to wear spats?

5. In *Richard v. C.N.R. Co.* (1970), 15 D.L.R. (3d) 732 (P.E.I.S.C.), the plaintiff was asleep in his car aboard a ferry when he was awakened by someone shouting "we're here." Believing that an attendant had made the statement, the plaintiff started his car and backed it off the ferry. Unfortunately, the boat had not yet docked and the car landed in the Gulf of St. Lawrence. The plaintiff sued and alleged, among other things, that the defendant had been negligent in untying the nylon rope across the end of the ferry before it docked. Quoting an earlier case, the court concluded that the "sole, direct, proximate and effective cause" of the accident was the plaintiff's rash act of backing off the boat, contrary to the warning signs and the crew's attempts to stop him. Do you agree that removing the rope was not a cause of the plaintiff's loss? If, as the plaintiff believed, a ferry employee had shouted "we're here," would his act have been a cause of the plaintiff's loss? Would the result have been the same had the plaintiff alleged that the defendant was negligent in failing to provide an adequate restraining barrier?

6. In *Ketler v. Nova Scotia (Attorney General)*, 2016 NSCA 64, the plaintiff was injured when he veered to avoid a deer and drove through a wooden railing on a bridge. The trial judge found that the defendant negligently failed to maintain the wooden bridge to its original construction standard but held that this breach of the standard of care was not a cause of plaintiff's injuries. What would the plaintiff have been required to prove to succeed on this causation issue?

7. *Kauffman, Qualcast, Richard,* and *Ketler* illustrate the importance of carefully analyzing the specific allegations of negligence and their causative role in the plaintiff's alleged losses. For example, only some of the defendant's acts may be negligent and only some of these negligent acts may have played a causal role in the plaintiff's losses. See for example *Deloitte & Touche v. Livent (Receiver of),* 2017 SCC 63.

8. For cases in which the defendant's negligence was not held to be a cause, see *Chaster (Guardian ad litem of) v. LeBlanc* (2007), 51 C.C.L.T. (3d) 131 (B.C.S.C.) (lawyer's negligent preparation for mediation not a cause of plaintiff's agreeing to an unfavourable settlement); *William v. Kelowna (City),* 2012 BCSC 421 (police failure to contact the plaintiff to confirm her identity and the facts before contacting the plaintiff's prospective employer not a cause of the employer's withdrawal of the job offer); *Cowan v. Hydro One Networks Inc.,* 2011 ONSC 6377, aff'd 2014 ONCA 6 (a mild tingling from voltage differences in objects that the plaintiffs' cows might simultaneously come into contact with in the barn (*i.e.* "tingle voltage") not a cause of the herd's poor milk production and other problems); and *Boon v. Mann,* 2016 BCCA 242 (landlord's failure to install smoke detectors not a cause of damages due to delays in escaping fire).

9. The but-for test has generated volumes of criticism and comment. For example, one author stated: "Rather than seek to outline some neutral or pseudo-scientific test for understanding or navigating the black hole of so-called factual causation, I recommend abandoning that irresolvable and hopeless quest": Hutchinson, "Out of the Black Hole: Toward a Fresh Approach to Tort Causation" (2016) 39:2 The Dalhousie Law Journal 561 at 562-63. See also, Epstein, "A Theory of Strict Liability" (1973) 2 J. Legal Stud. 151 at 161.

For a sampling of some of the more recent writing, see Stapleton, "Unnecessary Causes" (2013) 129 L.Q.R. 39; Knutsen, "Coping with Complex Causation Information in Personal Injury Cases" (2013) 41 Advoc. Q. 149; Clarke, "Causation and Liability in Tort Law" (2014) 5 Jurisprudence 217; Hamer, "'Factual causation' and 'scope of liability': What's the difference?" (2014) 77 M.L.R. 155; Green, *Causation in Negligence* (2015); Steel, *Proof of Causation in Tort Law* (2015); and Turton, *Evidential Uncertainty in Causation in Negligence* (2016).

3. Established Exceptions to the But-For Test

Numerous efforts have been made to rework the but-for test of causation with varying degrees of success. The most widely accepted modifications involve limited exceptions that apply to relatively narrow categories of cases. Moreover, each exception addresses a specific perceived unfairness that would result from applying the but-for test. This section briefly reviews three established exceptions to the but-for test: the multiple negligent defendants rule; the learned intermediary rule; and the objective/subjective test in informed consent cases. The first exception is reviewed in greater detail in Chapter 20 and the second two exceptions are discussed in Chapter 12.

(a) THE MULTIPLE NEGLIGENT DEFENDANTS RULE

In *Cook v. Lewis*, [1951] S.C.R. 830, the plaintiff was shot in the face when two negligent hunters fired in his direction at the same time. Each hunter denied that he had fired in the plaintiff's direction, and the plaintiff could not prove on the balance of probabilities which hunter had shot him. If the but-for test were applied, both negligent hunters would be absolved of liability. The court held that the burden of proving causation would shift from the plaintiff to the defendants if the plaintiff could prove that: (i) both defendants were negligent; (ii) one had to have caused his loss; and (iii) it was impossible to prove which defendant caused his loss. Each defendant would be held liable for negligently causing the loss unless he could disprove causation on the balance of probabilities.

In *Cook*, the court indicated that the multiple negligent defendants rule only applied to cases involving two negligent defendants. As will be discussed later in this chapter, United Kingdom courts and some American courts have applied a variation of this principle in limited categories of cases involving more than two negligent defendants. In *Clements v. Clements*, 2012 SCC 32, the court indicated that this principle, albeit framed in different terms, is not limited to cases involving only two negligent defendants.

(b) THE LEARNED INTERMEDIARY RULE

Manufacturers of products that are not directly available to the public, such as prescription drugs, may discharge their duty to inform consumers by adequately disclosing information to a learned intermediary. In *Hollis v. Dow Corning Corp.*, [1995] 4 S.C.R. 634, the plaintiff was injured when one of Dow's breast implants ruptured inside her. Dow, which had negligently failed to inform the plaintiff's surgeon of the risks of a non-traumatic rupture, argued that it had to be absolved of liability on the basis of causation. Dow alleged that the plaintiff could not prove that her doctor would have warned her even if it had adequately informed the doctor.

The court rejected this argument because it would create an anomalous situation in which the negligently injured plaintiff would have no cause of action. Her claim against the doctor would fail because he was not negligent, as he had never been informed of the risks. Her claim against Dow would fail on causation because she could not prove on the balance of probabilities that her doctor would have warned her of the risk even if Dow had adequately informed him. The court stated that Dow could not use the learned intermediary rule to shield itself from claims arising from its own negligence. The court also noted that the plaintiff would not have had the procedure had she been adequately informed of the risks of a non-traumatic rupture. The court exempted cases involving learned intermediaries from the but-for rule and held Dow liable for the plaintiff's injuries.

(c) INFORMED CONSENT

In *Hopp v. Lepp*, [1980] 2 S.C.R. 192 and *Reibl v. Hughes*, [1980] 2 S.C.R. 880, the court held that healthcare professionals have a duty to put patients in a position to make informed decisions about whether to consent to proposed treatment. The court then adopted an objective/subjective test of causation, framed in terms of whether a reasonable person in the plaintiff's position would have consented had he or she been adequately informed. The court rejected the standard subjective test of causation because of concern that disgruntled patients would provide self-serving evidence — namely that they would not have had the proposed treatment had they been adequately informed. The great majority of informed consent cases fail on this pro-defendant test of causation. The court did not explain why the concerns with self-serving evidence in informed consent cases were unique and warranted altering the standard test of causation.

The majority in *Arndt v. Smith*, [1997] 2 S.C.R. 539 defended the objective/subjective approach on the basis that a purely subjective test would: require the court to hypothesize about how the patient would have reacted if properly informed; result in the patient's testimony being coloured by hindsight and bitterness; and leave the causation issue to be determined solely on the patient's testimony as to how he or she would have acted if properly informed. In contrast, the three dissenting justices applied the standard subjective test of causation. Despite the split in *Arndt,* the Canadian courts continue to apply the objective/subjective test in informed consent cases without comment.

NOTES AND QUESTIONS

1. Do you agree with the decision in *Cook*? If so, what is the rationale for modifying the but-for test of causation to permit recovery in *Cook* when other plaintiffs who fall just short of proving causation are denied recovery? What is the justification for limiting the multiple negligent defendants rule to cases involving only two negligent defendants?

2. In *Cook*, the court stated that a plaintiff's claim would fail if he or she could only prove that either defendant A or defendant B had to be the negligent causer. How does this scenario differ from the facts in *Cook*?

3. Do you agree with the court's approach to causation in *Hollis*? Did Dow's failure to inform the doctor result in a potential loss to the plaintiff, namely the opportunity to sue her doctor had he negligently failed to inform her of the risk of a non-traumatic rupture? Explain in your own words the learned intermediary rule.

4. The objective/subjective test of causation in informed consent cases eases the burden on the courts, in that they can deny a patient's claim without having to expressly impugn the patient's credibility or reject his or her testimony. Can you suggest any policy factors that warrant adopting or rejecting the objective/subjective test of causation in duty to inform cases?

Do you find the majority's reasons in *Arndt* compelling? If so, why do the courts continue to apply a subjective test of causation in manufacturer's duty to warn and other cases in which plaintiffs may be required to testify about how they would have reacted had the defendant adequately informed or advised them?

5. The United Kingdom and Australian courts continue to use the subjective test of causation in informed consent cases. See respectively, *Chester v. Afshar*, [2004] 3 W.L.R. 927 (H.L.); *Montgomery v. Lanarkshire Health Board*, [2015] UKSC 11 at paras. 103-04; *Chappel v. Hart* (1998), 195 C.L.R. 232 (H.C.A.); and *Rosenberg v. Percival*, [2001] HCA 18.

6. See generally Burningham, Rachul & Caulfield, "Informed Consent and Patient Comprehension: The Law and the Evidence" (2013) 7 McGill J.L. & Health 123; Osborne, "Informed Consent" in Irvine, Osborne & Shariff, eds., *Canadian Medical Law*, 4th ed. (2013) at 55; and Robertson & Picard, *Legal Liability of Doctors and Hospitals in Canada*, 5th ed. (2017) at 153-265.

4. Recent Attempts to Modify the But-For Test

This section examines three evolving modifications or exceptions to the standard but-for test: the materially increased risk of injury test, the material contribution to injury test, and the proportionate cause and loss of chance test. There is a measure of uncertainty with each of these tests. In the leading Canadian case on the materially increased risk of injury test, the Supreme Court of Canada applied the but-for test, albeit in different words: *Snell v. Farrell*, [1990] 2 S.C.R. 311. The Supreme Court of Canada discussed the need to take a "robust and pragmatic approach" to the facts in these causation cases and, as an aside, suggested that the burden of proving causation could be shifted to the defendant in various circumstances.

As will be discussed, it was never clear how the material contribution to injury test differed from the but-for test or when the material contribution test was to be applied. In *Hanke v. Resurfice Corp.*, [2007] 1 S.C.R. 333 at paras. 21-28 and *Clements v. Clements*, 2012 SCC 32 at paras. 8-16, the Supreme Court of Canada attempted, with some success, to address the confusion it had generated in previous cases. Finally, the proportionate cause and loss of chance tests continue to be raised on a regular basis even though they have yet to be adopted by the Canadian courts.

Although these modified tests have a relatively limited impact on the analysis of causation, students need to be familiar with their basic principles. These tests come in and out of favour, and the attempts to modify the but-for test are unlikely to abate in the foreseeable future.

(a) MATERIALLY INCREASED RISK OF INJURY TEST

Scientific advances have made it possible to establish that events and exposures to substances, even 15 or 20 years ago, can increase the risk that a person will develop a disease or disability. Under the but-for test, the increased risk must be such as to make it more probable than not that the defendant's negligent act was a cause of the plaintiff's loss. Traditionally, if the plaintiff could not prove that the increased risk met the but-for test, his or her claim would fail. Some courts have been willing to abandon the but-for test in these cases.

The discussion begins with *McGhee v. National Coal Board*, [1972] 3 All E.R. 1008 (H.L.). The defendant employed the plaintiff to clean out brick kilns. The working conditions were such that by the end of the day the plaintiff was covered in sweat and dust. In breach of the requisite standard of care, the defendant failed to provide shower facilities at the work site, and the plaintiff was required to cycle home while still filthy. The plaintiff developed dermatitis and sued the defendant. The expert witnesses indicated that the defendant's failure to provide showers materially increased the risk of the plaintiff developing this condition. However, they were unable to say that the absence of showers was more likely than not to have been a cause of the plaintiff's dermatitis. The dermatitis might have arisen innocently. The

House of Lords found for the plaintiff. Lord Reid held that if a defendant's negligence materially increases the risk of a particular kind of injury occurring and that very injury befalls the plaintiff, then the defendant will be deemed to be a cause. Lords Simon, Salmon and Kilbrandon adopted a similar analysis. In contrast, Lord Wilberforce held that in such circumstances the burden of proving causation should shift from the plaintiff to the defendant, who must then disprove causation on a balance of probabilities. Lord Wilberforce limited this principle to cases in which sound policy warranted making an exception to the standard test of causation.

Several Canadian courts adopted *McGhee*, but almost all focused on Lord Wilberforce's minority approach. Moreover, the Canadian courts often applied *McGhee* well beyond the confines of workplace health and safety issues, and rarely referred to any policy considerations that warranted deviating from the accepted principles of causation and proof. The status of *McGhee* was further complicated by *Wilsher v. Essex Area Health Authority*, [1988] A.C. 1074 (H.L.). In this case, the House of Lords "reinterpreted" *McGhee* in a way that essentially overruled it. This was the backdrop against which the Supreme Court of Canada addressed the materially increased risk test in the following case.

SNELL v. FARRELL
[1990] 2 S.C.R. 311

[Dr. Farrell performed a cataract operation on Mrs. Snell. After injecting a local anaesthetic into the retrobulbar muscles behind the eyeball, Dr. Farrell noticed a slight discolouration, which he stated on discovery was due to a very small retrobulbar bleed. However, on further examination, he found no other signs of bleeding. After waiting 30 minutes, he proceeded with the operation. Following the surgery, there was blood in the eye. It cleared nine months later, but the optic nerve had atrophied, resulting in blindness in that eye.

The damage to the optic nerve could have occurred naturally or been the result of continuing the operation. Neither expert witness was willing to state with certainty what caused the plaintiff's blindness or when the damage occurred. The trial judge accepted the expert testimony that Dr. Farrell was negligent in continuing the operation after noticing the discolouration. Relying on *McGhee*, the trial judge concluded that Mrs. Snell had established a *prima facie* case regarding causation and that the burden shifted to Dr. Farrell to disprove causation. Since Dr. Farrell could not discharge this burden, he was held liable. The Court of Appeal dismissed Dr. Farrell's appeal. He then appealed to the Supreme Court of Canada.]

The judgment of the Court was delivered by

SOPINKA J.—. . .

Both the trial judge and the Court of Appeal relied on *McGhee*, which (subject to its re-interpretation in the House of Lords in *Wilsher*) purports to depart from traditional principles in the law of torts that the plaintiff must prove on a balance of probabilities that, but for the tortious conduct of the defendant, the plaintiff would not have sustained the injury complained of. In view of the fact that *McGhee* has been applied by a number of courts in Canada to reverse the ordinary burden of proof with respect to causation, it is important to examine recent developments in the law relating to causation and to determine whether a departure from well-established principles is necessary for the resolution of this appeal.

The traditional approach to causation has come under attack in a number of cases in which there is concern that due to the complexities of proof, the probable victim of tortious conduct will be deprived of relief. This concern is strongest in circumstances in which, on the basis of some percentage of statistical probability, the plaintiff is the likely victim of the combined tortious conduct of a number of defendants, but cannot prove causation against a specific defendant or defendants on the basis of particularized evidence in accordance with traditional principles. The challenge to the traditional approach has manifested itself in cases dealing with non-traumatic injuries such as man-made diseases resulting from the widespread diffusion of chemical products, including product liability cases in which a product which can cause injury is widely manufactured and marketed by a large number of corporations. . . .

Although, to date, these developments have had little impact in other common law countries, it has long been recognized that the allocation of the burden of proof is not immutable. The legal or ultimate burden of proof is determined by the substantive law "upon broad reasons of experience and fairness": 9 *Wigmore on Evidence*, § 2486, at p. 292. In a civil case, the two broad principles are:

1. that the onus is on the party who asserts a proposition, usually the plaintiff;

2. that where the subject matter of the allegation lies particularly within the knowledge of one party, that party may be required to prove it.

This Court has not hesitated to alter the incidence of the ultimate burden of proof when the underlying rationale for its allocation is absent in a particular case: see *National Trust Co. v. Wong Aviation Ltd.*, [1969] S.C.R. 481. This flexibility extends to the issue of causation. . . .

Proof of causation in medical malpractice cases is often difficult for the patient. The physician is usually in a better position to know the cause of the injury than the patient. On the basis of the second basic principle referred to above, there is an argument that the burden of proof should be allocated to the defendant. . . .

This brings me to the *McGhee* case and its influence on subsequent cases, particularly in the medical malpractice field. . . .

. . .

Two theories of causation emerge from an analysis of the speeches of the Lords in this case. The first, firmly espoused by Lord Wilberforce, is that the plaintiff need only prove that the defendant created a risk of harm and that the injury occurred within the area of the risk. The second is that in these circumstances, an inference of causation was warranted in that there is no practical difference between materially contributing to the risk of harm and materially contributing to the harm itself.

The speeches were subjected to a careful examination and interpretation in *Wilsher v. Essex Area Health Authority* . . . by Lord Bridge when some fifteen years later, the House of Lords revisited the issue. The plaintiff claimed damages from the defendant health authority for negligence in medical treatment which resulted in a condition of the eyes leading to blindness. A likely cause of the condition but not a definite one, in the opinion of medical experts, was too much oxygen. The plaintiff proved that for a period of time he was supersaturated with oxygen. A number of different factors other than excessive oxygen could have caused or contributed to the injury. The expert evidence was conflicting. The trial judge applied *McGhee* and held the defendant liable since it had failed to prove that the plaintiff's condition had not resulted from its negligence. The Court of Appeal dismissed the appeal by a majority judgment with the Vice-Chancellor dissenting. The House of Lords allowed the appeal and directed a new trial. Lord Bridge, delivering the unanimous judgment of the court, reaffirmed the principle that the burden of proving causation rested on the plaintiff. Since the trial judge had not made the relevant finding of fact to sort out the conflicting evidence, a new trial was directed on this basis. Lord Bridge interpreted *McGhee* as espousing no new principle. Instead, *McGhee* was explained as promoting a robust and pragmatic approach to the facts to enable an inference of negligence to be drawn even though medical or scientific expertise cannot arrive at a definitive conclusion. . . .

Lord Bridge concluded with a caution at p. 571:

> But, whether we like it or not, the law, which only Parliament can change, requires proof of fault causing damage as the basis of liability in tort. We should do society nothing but disservice if we made the forensic process still more unpredictable and hazardous by distorting the law to accommodate the exigencies of what may seem hard cases.

Canadian cases decided after *McGhee* but before *Wilsher* tended to follow *McGhee* by adopting either the reversal of onus or the inference interpretation. Which interpretation was adopted made no practical difference because even when the latter approach was applied, the creation of the risk by the defendant's breach of duty was deemed to have established a prima facie case, thus shifting the onus to the defendant. . . .

Decisions in Canada after *Wilsher* accept its interpretation of *McGhee*. In the circumstances in which *McGhee* had been previously interpreted to support a reversal of the burden of proof, an inference was now permissible to find causation, notwithstanding that causation was not proved by positive evidence. . . .

The question that this Court must decide is whether the traditional approach to causation is no longer satisfactory in that plaintiffs in malpractice cases are being deprived of compensation because they cannot prove causation where it in fact exists.

. . . If I were convinced that defendants who have a substantial connection to the injury were escaping liability because plaintiffs cannot prove causation under currently applied principles, I would not hesitate to adopt one of [the *McGhee*] alternatives. In my opinion, however, properly applied, the principles relating to causation are adequate to the task. Adoption of either of the proposed alternatives would have the effect of compensating plaintiffs where a substantial connection between the injury and the defendant's conduct is absent. Reversing the burden of proof may be justified where two defendants negligently fire in the direction of the plaintiff and then by their tortious conduct destroy the means of proof at his disposal. In such a case it is clear that the injury was not caused by neutral conduct. It is quite a different matter to compensate a plaintiff by reversing the burden of proof for an injury that may very well be due to factors unconnected to the defendant and not the fault of anyone.

[Sopinka J. then discussed how the liberalization of the recovery principles in the United States contributed to their malpractice crises of the 1970s. He noted that a British Royal Commission specifically rejected the proposal to shift the burden of proof in malpractice cases.]

I am of the opinion that the dissatisfaction with the traditional approach to causation stems to a large extent from its too rigid application by the courts in many cases. Causation need not be determined by scientific precision.

. . .

In many malpractice cases, the facts lie particularly within the knowledge of the defendant. In these circumstances, very little affirmative evidence on the part of the plaintiff will justify the drawing of an inference of causation in the absence of evidence to the contrary. . . .

. . .

The legal or ultimate burden remains with the plaintiff, but in the absence of evidence to the contrary adduced by the defendant, an inference of causation may be drawn although positive or scientific proof of causation has not been adduced. If some evidence to the contrary is adduced by the defendant, the trial judge is entitled to take account of Lord Mansfield's famous precept. This is, I believe, what Lord Bridge had in mind in *Wilsher* when he referred to a "robust and pragmatic approach to the . . . facts" (p. 569).

It is not therefore essential that the medical experts provide a firm opinion supporting the plaintiff's theory of causation. Medical experts ordinarily determine causation in terms of certainties whereas a lesser standard is demanded by the law. . . .

[Sopinka J. stated that part of the problem stems from the reluctance of doctors to express an opinion unless they are 100% certain. The law does not require certainty but rather a balance of probabilities (*i.e.* 51%). It is in this sense that the plaintiff's case need not be based on a firm medical conclusion. Sopinka J. then reviewed the evidence, emphasizing that Dr. Farrell was negligent in continuing the operation and that doing so greatly increased the risk of the plaintiff suffering the very injury that befell her. While the blindness could have resulted from natural causes, Sopinka J. quoted the expert testimony and it indicated that the continuation of the operation was more likely to have been the cause.]

The appellant was present during the operation and was in a better position to observe what occurred. Furthermore, he was able to interpret from a medical standpoint what he saw. In addition, by continuing the operation which has been found to constitute negligence, he made it impossible for the respondent or anyone else to detect the bleeding which is alleged to have caused the injury. In these circumstances, it was open to the trial judge to draw the inference that the injury was caused by the retrobulbar bleeding. There was no evidence to rebut this inference. The fact that testing the eye for hardness did not disclose bleeding is insufficient for this purpose. If there was any rebutting evidence it was weak, and it was open to the trial judge to find causation, applying the principles to which I have referred.

I am confident that had the trial judge not stated that "I cannot go beyond this since neither [expert witness] did and I should not speculate", he would have drawn the necessary inference. In stating the above, he failed to appreciate that it is not essential to have a positive medical opinion to support a finding of causation. Furthermore, it is not speculation but the application of common sense to draw such an inference where, as here, the circumstances, other than a positive medical opinion, permit.

While this Court does not ordinarily make findings of fact, this course is fully justified in this case. First, I am of the opinion that the trial judge either made the necessary finding or would have but for error of law. Second, it would be a disservice to all to send this case back for a new trial when the evidence is not essentially in conflict. I note that in *Wilsher*, the House of Lords refrained from deciding the case only because the evidence of the experts was seriously in conflict. That is not the case here.

In the result, I would dismiss the appeal with costs.

NOTES AND QUESTIONS

1. Prior to *Snell*, *McGhee* generated considerable confusion and debate. See for example *Nowsco Well Service Ltd. v. Canadian Propane Gas & Oil Ltd.* (1981), 122 D.L.R. (3d) 228 (Sask. C.A.); *Letnik v. Metropolitan Toronto (Municipality)*, [1988] 2 F.C. 399 (C.A.); *Haag v. Marshall* (1989), 1 C.C.L.T. (2d) 99 (B.C.C.A.); and *Belknap v. Meakes* (1989), 1 C.C.L.T. (2d) 192 (B.C.C.A.). See also Weinrib, "A Step Forward in Factual Causation" (1975) 38 M.L.R. 518.

2. According to Sopinka J., was Mrs. Snell able to prove on the balance of probabilities that Dr. Farrell's negligence was a cause of her loss? What test of causation was applied? Did *Snell* simply reject *McGhee* and reaffirm the but-for test? To what extent must the defendant's negligence increase the risk of injury for it to be held to be a cause?

3. Sopinka J. stated that the burden of proving causation was not immutable, but could be shifted where reasons of "experience and fairness" make it appropriate to do so. The examples cited included situations in which the evidence of causation lay exclusively in the defendant's hands.

4. Sopinka J. also indicated that it might be appropriate to shift the burden of proof if the negligent conduct of two defendants destroyed the means of proving causation. Unfortunately, Sopinka J. failed to note that the Supreme Court of Canada had explicitly rejected the "obscuring the evidence" rationale for shifting the burden of proof in *Joseph Brant Memorial Hospital v. Koziol*, [1978] 1 S.C.R. 491. Sopinka J. refused to shift the burden of proof to Dr. Farrell, even though his negligence made it impossible to prove causation. Sopinka J. explained that it would be inappropriate to shift the burden of proof for "any injury that may very well be due to factors unconnected to the defendant and not the fault of anyone." What are the implications of this statement?

See also *Benhaim v. St-Germain*, 2016 SCC 48 at para. 69, where the court stated that the trial judge "was not required by law to draw a presumption of fact which was for the defendants to rebut simply because (i) it was impossible to prove causation as a result of the defendants' fault; and (ii) the plaintiff adduced 'some affirmative evidence' that the defendants' fault was linked to the loss."

5. What are the limits of Sopinka J.'s suggestion that, in some circumstances, it may be possible for a trier of fact to rely on common sense pragmatism to fill in an evidentiary void? See *Meloche v. Hotel Dieu Grace Hospital* (1999), 179 D.L.R. (4th) 77 (Ont. C.A.); and *Mathura v. Scarborough General Hospital*, 1999 CarswellOnt 43 (Gen. Div.) (WL Can), aff'd 2000 CarswellOnt 3320 (C.A.) (WL Can). Does Sopinka J.'s suggestion about common sense pragmatism simply permit courts to give the benefit of the doubt to the plaintiff without having to expressly modify the but-for test of

causation? Can the same be said about the "robust and pragmatic approach to the facts"?

6. Even a "robust and pragmatic approach to the facts" may not help the plaintiff. In *Bigcharles v. Dawson Creek & District Health Care Society* (2001), 5 C.C.L.T. (3d) 157 (B.C.C.A.), the plaintiff was in a car crash and taken to the hospital while unconscious. Based on cervical spine x-rays, the plaintiff was removed from immobilizing equipment to a bed, and then turned and moved regularly. When the plaintiff's legs remained unresponsive, thoracic x-rays were taken that revealed a spinal fracture and spinal cord damage. The doctor acknowledged that he was negligent in moving the plaintiff and not taking the thoracic x-rays earlier. However, the doctor claimed that his negligence was irrelevant as the plaintiff's spinal cord injuries were "complete" at the scene of the crash. The plaintiff argued that the doctor's negligence caused or contributed to his paralysis. The trial judge found the conflicting medical evidence to be equally balanced and dismissed the plaintiff's claim because the plaintiff failed to prove causation on the balance of probabilities. The Court of Appeal upheld the trial decision.

See generally *Ball v. Imperial Oil Limited*, 2010 ABCA 111; *Goodman v. Viljoen*, 2012 ONCA 896; *Fowlow v. Southlake Regional Health Centre*, 2014 ONCA 193; *S. (K.) (Litigation representative of) v. Willox*, 2016 ABQB 483; *British Columbia (Workers' Compensation Appeal Tribunal) v. Fraser Health Authority)*, 2016 SCC 25; and *Wise v. Abbott Laboratories, Limited*, 2016 ONSC 7275. See also Tse, "Tests for factual causation: Unravelling the mystery of material contribution, contribution to risk, the robust and pragmatic approach and the inference of causation" (2008) 16 T.L.J. 249 at 256-64; and Brown, "The Possibility of 'Inference Causation': Inferring Cause-in-Fact and the Nature of Legal Fact-Finding" (2010) 55 McGill L.J. 1.

7. In *Fairchild v. Glenhaven Funeral Services Ltd.*, [2002] 3 W.L.R. 89 (H.L.), *McGhee* made a remarkable comeback in an altered guise. In *Fairchild*, the plaintiff contracted mesothelioma, a fatal cancer that is caused by the inhalation of a single fibre of asbestos. The previous and subsequent inhalation of other fibres is causally irrelevant, and the disease may lie dormant for decades after the causative fibre has been inhaled. The plaintiff had been negligently exposed to asbestos by several employers over the years and had no means of proving which employer had exposed him to the single fibre that caused his disease. The House of Lords again reinterpreted Lord Reid's judgment in *McGhee*, relying on it for the proposition "that a breach of duty which materially increased the risk should be treated as if it had materially contributed to the disease." Several judges provided differing analyses, and accordingly the precise scope of *Fairchild* is unclear. However, in the end result, all of the employers were held jointly and severally liable for the plaintiff's mesothelioma.

Is the result in *Fairchild* fair to the defendants? Although negligent, all but one of the defendants were held liable for an injury that they did not cause and to which they did not contribute. Rather than further muddying the causation analysis, should the House of Lords have expressly acknowledged that it was holding employers strictly liable for negligently exposing workers to the risk of a serious industrial disease?

Canadian courts have not yet addressed the causation issues posed by toxic torts cases like *Fairchild*. While *Hunt v. Carey Canada Inc.*, [1990] 2 S.C.R. 959 involved a mesothelioma claim, the judgment did not address the causation issue. Not surprisingly, much academic ink has been spilled over *Fairchild*. See for example

Weir, "Making It More Likely v. Making It Happen" [2002] C.L.J. 519; Stapleton, "Lords a'leaping evidentiary gaps" (2002) 10 Torts L.J. 276; Morgan, "Lost Causes in the House of Lords: *Fairchild v. Glenhaven Funeral Services*" (2003) 66 M.L.R. 277; and Khoury, "Causation and Risk in the Highest Courts of Canada, England and France" (2008) 124 L.Q.R. 103.

8. In *Barker v. Corus (UK) plc*, [2006] 2 A.C. 572 (H.L.), the deceased was exposed to asbestos while employed by two companies and while self-employed. The majority in *Barker* relied on the fact that the deceased's mesothelioma could have resulted from a non-tortious exposure to asbestos to distinguish *Fairchild*. Thus, rather than being held jointly and severally liable, the defendant company in *Barker* was only held liable for its proportionate share of the risk that it created. In Lord Hoffmann's view, this approach "would smooth the roughness of the justice which a rule of joint and several liability creates."

This principle in *Barker* was overturned by a 2006 amendment to the *Compensation Act 2006* that makes tortfeasors in mesothelioma cases jointly and severally liable. For an application of this statute, see *Sienkiewicz v. Greif (UK) Ltd.*, [2011] UKSC 10 and the torrent of commentary it has generated: O'Sullivan, "Mesothelioma and Risk Aired in the Court of Appeal" [2010] C.L.J. 10; Laleng, "Causal responsibility for uncertainty and risk in toxic torts" (2010) 18 Tort L. Rev. 102; McIvor, "The 'Doubles the Risk Test' for Causation and Other Related Judicial Misconceptions about Epidemiology" in Pitel, Neyers & Chamberlain, eds., *Tort Law: Challenging Orthodoxy* (2013) 215; and Wellington, "Beyond single causative agents: The scope of the *Fairchild* exception post-*Sienkiewicz*" (2013) 20 Torts L.J. 208.

9. *Fairchild*, *Barker* and *Sienkiewicz* were considered in *Evans v. Queanbeyan City Council*, [2011] NSWCA 230. Mr. Evans, a heavy smoker who had been exposed to asbestos in the course of employment, died of lung cancer. His estate sued Mr. Evans' employer and the manufacturer of the asbestos products that Mr. Evans had used much of his working life. In dismissing the claim, the court held that a plaintiff must prove on the balance of probabilities that the defendant's negligent act caused or materially contributed to his or her loss. The court rejected the English cases, stating that it is not enough for the plaintiff to simply show that the wrong materially increased the risk of harm where medical science does not permit any further proof.

10. In *Holtby v. Brigham & Cowan (Hull) Ltd.*, [2000] 3 All E.R. 421 (C.A.), the plaintiff developed asbestosis after working as a marine pipe fitter for nearly 40 years. He was negligently exposed to asbestos fibres for approximately 20 years, half of which he worked for the defendant. Unlike mesothelioma, asbestosis results from the cumulative inhalation of fibres and becomes more severe as more fibres are inhaled. The court held the defendant liable, but for only 25% of the plaintiff's losses, reflecting the proportion of time that he had worked for the defendant. Should the plaintiff have been allowed full recovery against the defendant, which could then seek contribution from the other negligent employers? Can you reconcile *Holtby*, *Fairchild* and *Barker*?

See generally Cassels & Jones, "Rethinking Ends and Means in Mass Tort: Probabilistic Causation and Risk-Based Mass Tort Claims After *Fairchild v. Glenhaven Funeral Services*" (2003) 82 Can. Bar Rev. 597; Porat & Stein, "Indeterminate Causation and Apportionment of Damages: An Essay on *Holtby*,

Allen, and *Fairchild*" (2003) 23 O.J.L.S. 667; Hopkins, "Causation and Contributory Negligence" [2005] C.L.J. 546; and Kramer, "Smoothing the Rough Justice of the Fairchild Principle" (2006) 122 L.Q.R. 547.

11. In *Alcan Grove Pty Ltd v. Zabic,* [2015] HCA 33, the plaintiff was exposed to asbestos fibres from 1974 to 1977 while working for the defendant company, but probably did not develop a malignant mesothelial tumor until shortly before 2013 or 2014. A statutory workers compensation system had come into force on January 1, 1987, barring all common law tort claims for any subsequent workplace injuries. In upholding the plaintiff's common law tort claim, the court held that the damage to the plaintiff's mesothelial cells occurring shortly after inhaling the fibres provided the basis for a common law action and that the subsequent development of malignant mesothelioma was part of that accrued cause of action. In the court's words at para. 6: "based upon the expert evidence concerning the pathology of the disease, it could be inferred that the asbestos fibres inhaled between 1974 and 1977 had then or shortly afterwards (and therefore before 1 January 1987) resulted in initial molecular changes to mesothelial cells which ultimately culminated in the malignant mesothelial tumour." Is the decision consistent with the but-for test of causation?

12. In *Johnston v. NEI International Combustion Limited; Rothwell v. Chemical and Insulating Company Limited,* [2007] UKHL 39, employees who developed pleural plaques from asbestos exposure sued their employers for increasing their risks of subsequently developing asbestos-related diseases and for their psychiatric distress about this prospect. As discussed in Chapter 18, the House of Lords dismissed these claims on the basis that merely increasing the risk of future disease and the associated anxiety are not actionable heads of damage. How would you distinguish this case from *Alcan, supra?*

13. In *Sindell v. Abbott Laboratories,* 26 Cal.3d 588 (Sup. Ct. 1980), the plaintiff developed a deadly cancer caused by a drug called DES, which her mother had taken while pregnant. The cancer had a minimum latency period of 10 to 12 years. About 200 pharmaceutical companies had manufactured DES, but there were no significant differences in the brands. The plaintiff sued several of the larger manufacturers. The court held that all of the companies had been negligent in marketing DES because they knew or ought to have known of its risks at that time. Even though the plaintiff could not prove which company had produced the DES that her mother had taken, the court held all of the defendants liable in proportion to their individual market share. Thus, a company that had 20% of the DES market when the plaintiff's mother was pregnant was held liable for 20% of the plaintiff's losses. See also *In re "Agent Orange" Product Liability Litigation,* 597 F.Supp. 740 (N.Y. Dist. Ct. 1984), which involved numerous manufacturers and plaintiffs in a large class action; and Goldberg, "Epidemiological Uncertainty, Causation, and Drug Product Liability" (2014) 59 McGill L.J. 777.

Can you distinguish the causal role of the defendants in *Sindell* from that in *Fairchild, Barker* and *Holtby?* Is the market share approach to liability in *Sindell* preferable to the approach in *Fairchild?*

14. The Canadian courts have not adopted the approaches in *Fairchild, Barker, Holtby,* or *Sindell.* Rather, pursuant to *Snell,* the plaintiff has to prove that the defendant's negligence increased the risk to the extent that the negligence was more

likely than not to have been a cause of the loss in issue. However, as will be discussed, some statements in *Clements v. Clements*, 2012 SCC 32 can be interpreted as consistent with the approach in *Fairchild*.

15. Is the common law the appropriate vehicle for addressing the policy issues that appear to underlie the causation analysis in the preceding cases? Would it be simpler, clearer and more intellectually candid to enact specific workplace, healthcare, products liability, and other legislation to promote well-defined policy priorities?

For example, all of the provinces have enacted legislation making it far easier for them to recover their tobacco-related healthcare costs from tobacco manufacturers. The legislation authorizes the government to sue the tobacco companies to recover its past and likely future costs resulting from "tobacco-related wrongs," permits general epidemiological and statistical data to be admitted to prove causation, and allows the government to claim damages on an aggregate basis. See for example *Tobacco Damages and Health Care Costs Recovery Act*, S.N.B. 2006, c. T-7.5; and *Tobacco Damages and Health Care Costs Recovery Act, 2009*, S.O. 2009, c.13.

(b) MATERIAL CONTRIBUTION TO INJURY TEST

The material contribution to injury test was introduced in *Athey v. Leonati*, [1996] 3 S.C.R. 458 and applied in *Walker Estate v. York Finch General Hospital*, [2001] 1 S.C.R. 647. In neither case did the court clearly explain what the test meant or the circumstances in which it applied. To further confuse matters, the plaintiff could establish causation on the but-for test in both cases. In *Hanke v. Resurfice Corp.*, [2007] 1 S.C.R. 333, the court addressed some of the problems that arose from *Athey* and *Walker*.

In *Hanke*, the Supreme Court of Canada expressly affirmed that the but-for test is the standard causation test for cases involving either a single cause or multiple causes. The material contribution test would only apply if two requirements were met. First, the plaintiff must establish that it is impossible to prove causation based on the but-for test and that this impossibility results from factors beyond the plaintiff's control, such as the current limits of scientific knowledge. Second, the plaintiff must establish that the defendant breached the standard of care and that his or her injuries fell within the scope of the risk created by the defendant's breach. The court stated that resorting to the material contribution test was justified because it would be unfair and unjust in these circumstances to simply deny the plaintiff's claim pursuant to the but-for test. The court refrained from reviewing the jurisprudence and cited two examples that it said demonstrated the requirements for invoking the material contribution test. The first example was drawn from *Cook v. Lewis*, [1951] S.C.R. 830 and the second from *Walker*. However, the court acknowledged that there was no need to resort to the material contribution test in *Walker*.

While *Hanke* reaffirmed the primacy of the but-for test and limited the situations in which the material contribution test applied, it did not explain what the test means. Nor did the court explain why it is unfair and unjust to apply the but-for test when the requirements of the material contribution test are met. Finally, the court's reference to *Cook* and *Walker* as illustrating the material contribution test of injury is troubling. *Cook* is the classic Canadian example of the multiple negligent defendants rule, which constitutes an established and clearly defined exception to the but-for test. Despite the questionable factual analysis in *Walker*, the result in that case is best explained by the but-for test.

The subsequent discussion of the material contribution test did little to clarify its meaning. It was often unclear whether the test was being used to refer to a material contribution to the plaintiff's injury or to a material contribution to the risk of injury. If used in the first sense, the material contribution test duplicates the but-for test. If used in the second sense, the material contribution test duplicates or modifies the materially increased risk test in *Snell*.

NOTES AND QUESTIONS

1. Since the defendant in *Hanke* did not breach the standard of care, there was no need to discuss causation. Why do you think the court addressed this issue?

2. Do you agree that it would be unfair and unjust to deny a plaintiff's claim pursuant to the but-for test of causation if the requirements of the material contribution test are met? If so, why?

3. In *Matthews v. MacLaren; Horsley v. MacLaren*, [1969] 2 O.R. 137 (H.C.) (discussed in Chapter 11 under the duty to rescue), the plaintiffs claimed that the defendant's negligence in attempting to rescue Matthews, who had fallen overboard, was a cause of Matthews' death. Since Matthews' body was never recovered, it was impossible to prove if he died of cardiac failure immediately on falling into the cold water or if he was alive and could have been saved had a proper rescue been undertaken. The plaintiffs' claim was dismissed because they were unable to prove that the defendant's negligent rescue attempt was a cause of Matthews' death. Would *Hanke* apply on these facts? If so, would the result be different?

4. *Hanke* has been considered or followed in numerous cases. See for example *B.S.A. Investors Ltd. v. DSB* (2007), 69 B.C.L.R. (4th) 242 (C.A.); *Jackson v. Kelowna General Hospital* (2007), 66 B.C.L.R. (4th) 138 (C.A.); *Barker v. Montfort Hospital* (2007), 223 O.A.C. 201 (C.A.); *Bohun v. Sennewald* (2008), 77 B.C.L.R. (4th) 85 (C.A.); and *Fullowka v. Royal Oak Ventures Inc.*, 2010 SCC 5. *Hanke* has also generated considerable commentary: Tse, "Tests for factual causation: Unravelling the mystery of material contribution, contribution to risk, the robust and pragmatic approach and the inference of causation" (2008) 16 Torts L.J. 249; Collins & McLeod-Kilmurray, "Material Contribution to Justice? Toxic Causation after *Resurfice Corp. v. Hanke*" (2010) 48 Osgoode Hall L. J. 411; Brown, "Known Unknowns in Cause-in-Fact" (2011) 39 Adv. Q. 37; and Jones, "Reasoning Through Probabilistic Causation in Individual and Aggregate Claims: The Struggle Continues" (2011-2012) 39 Adv. Q. 18.

5. For recent developments in the material contribution test in the United Kingdom, see *Williams (Respondent) v. The Bermuda Hospitals Board (appellant) (Bermuda)*, [2016] UKPC 4; and Bailey, "'Material Contribution' after *Williams v. The Bermuda Hospitals Board*" (2018) 38 L.S. 411.

CLEMENTS v. CLEMENTS
2012 SCC 32

[The defendant was driving his motorcycle in wet weather with the plaintiff (his wife) sitting behind him on the passenger seat. The bike was overloaded by approximately 100 pounds. Unbeknownst to the defendant, a nail had punctured the rear tire. The defendant accelerated to at least 120 km/h in a 100 km/h zone while passing a car. When the nail fell out, the rear tire deflated and the motorcycle wobbled and crashed. The plaintiff sued the defendant to recover for her severe brain injury, alleging that it was caused by the defendant's negligence in driving an overloaded bike at an excessive speed on a wet road. The trial judge found that the defendant's negligence contributed to the plaintiff's injury. However, the judge also ruled that the plaintiff could not satisfy the but-for test of causation through no fault on her part, due to limitations in the crash reconstruction evidence. Consequently, the trial judge applied the material contribution to injury test and held the defendant liable. The defendant appealed. The Court of Appeal set aside the judgment and dismissed the plaintiff's action because she failed to satisfy the but-for test of causation and the material contribution test did not apply on the facts.]

McLACHLIN C.J., for the majority—

. . .

[5] The legal issue is whether the usual "but for" test for causation in a negligence action applies, as the Court of Appeal held, or whether a material contribution approach suffices, as the trial judge held. For the reasons that follow, I conclude that a material contribution test was not applicable in this case. I would return the matter to the trial judge to be dealt with on the correct basis of "but for" causation.

. . .

[14] "But for" causation and liability on the basis of material contribution to risk are two different beasts. "But for" causation is a factual inquiry into what likely happened. The material contribution to risk test removes the requirement of "but for" causation and substitutes proof of material contribution to risk. As set out by Smith J.A. in *MacDonald v. Goertz*, 2009 BCCA 358, 275 B.C.A.C. 68, at para. 17:

> . . . "material contribution" does not signify a test of causation at all; rather it is a policy-driven rule of law designed to permit plaintiffs to recover in such cases despite their failure to prove causation. In such cases, plaintiffs are permitted to "jump the evidentiary gap". . . .

[15] While the cases and scholars have sometimes spoken of "material contribution to the injury" instead of "material contribution to risk", the latter is the more accurate formulation. As will become clearer when we discuss the cases, "material contribution" as a substitute for the usual requirement of "but for" causation only applies where it is impossible to say that a particular defendant's negligent act in fact caused the injury. It imposes liability not because the evidence establishes that the defendant's act caused the injury, but because the act contributed to the risk that injury would occur. . . .

[16] Elimination of proof of causation as an element of negligence is a "radical step that goes against the fundamental principle stated by Diplock, L.J., in *Browning v. War Office*, [1962] 3 All E.R. 1089 (C.A.), at 1094-95: '. . . A defendant in an action in

negligence is not a wrongdoer at large: he is a wrongdoer only in respect of the damage which he actually causes to the plaintiff' ''. . . . For that reason, recourse to a material contribution to risk approach is necessarily rare, and justified only where it is required by fairness and conforms to the principles that ground recovery in tort.

. . .

When Is a Material Contribution to Risk Approach Available?

[33] We have seen that the jurisprudence establishes that while tort liability must generally be founded on proof that "but for" the defendant's negligence the injury would not have occurred, exceptionally proof of factual causation can be replaced by proof of a material contribution to the risk that gave rise to the injury.

[34] In *Resurfice*, this Court summarized the cases as holding that a material contribution approach may be appropriate where it is "impossible" for the plaintiff to prove causation on the "but for" test and where it is clear that the defendant breached its duty of care (acted negligently) in a way that exposed the plaintiff to an unreasonable risk of injury. As a summary of the jurisprudence, this is accurate. However, as a test it is incomplete. A clear picture of when "but for" causation can be replaced by material contribution to risk requires further exploration of what is meant by "impossible to prove" (*Resurfice*, at para. 28) and what substratum of negligence must be shown. I will discuss each of these related concepts in turn.

(a) "*Impossibility*"

[35] The idea running through the jurisprudence that to apply the material contribution approach it must be "impossible" for the plaintiff to prove that the defendant's negligence caused the plaintiff's injury using the "but for" test has produced uncertainty in this case and elsewhere.

[36] Some have suggested that "but for" proof must be logically or conceptually impossible before material contribution to risk is available, arguing that *Cook* and the toxic agent cases show impossibility in this sense. But it is difficult to know what this means. As a matter of pure logic, it is conceivable that ballistics tests could have revealed which shotgun fired the shot that injured Mr. Lewis. It is also conceivable that with further understanding, medical science may someday be able to say which employer supplied the particle of asbestos that caused the plaintiffs in *Barker* to develop mesothelioma. Clearly the impossibility in those examples was related to difficulties with factual proof, not to logical problems inherent in the peculiarities of the case.

[37] However, the option of finding that a material contribution to risk approach is available whenever proof of "but for" causation cannot be made on the facts is equally problematic. First, how does one distinguish between a case of true impossibility of factual proof and a situation where the plaintiff simply fails to meet her burden of establishing "but for" causation on the evidence? Unless one can make a clear distinction, one effectively undermines the requirement that the plaintiff bears the burden of showing that, "but for" the defendant's negligence, she would not have been injured. In any difficult case, the plaintiff would be able to claim impossibility of proof of causation. Such a result would fundamentally change the law of negligence and sever it from its anchor in corrective justice that makes the defendant liable for the consequences, but only the consequences, of his negligent act.

[38] "Scientific impossibility", relied on by the trial judge in this case, is merely a variant of factual impossibility and attracts the same objections. In many cases of causal uncertainty, it is conceivable that with better scientific evidence, causation could be clarified. Scientific uncertainty was referred to in *Resurfice* in the course of explaining the difficulties that have arisen in the cases. However, this should not be read as ousting the "but for" test for causation in negligence actions. The law of negligence has never required scientific proof of causation; to repeat yet again, common sense inferences from the facts may suffice. If scientific evidence of causation is not required, as *Snell* makes plain, it is difficult to see how its absence can be raised as a basis for ousting the usual "but for" test.

[39]   What then are the cases referring to when they say that it must be "impossible" to prove "but for" causation as a precondition to a material contribution to risk approach? The answer emerges from the facts of the cases that have adopted such an approach. Typically, there are a number of tortfeasors. All are at fault, and one or more has in fact caused the plaintiff's injury. The plaintiff would not have been injured "but for" their negligence, viewed globally. However, because each can point the finger at the other, it is impossible for the plaintiff to show on a balance of probabilities that any one of them in fact caused her injury. This is the impossibility of which *Cook* and the multiple-employer mesothelioma cases speak.

(b) *Substratum of Negligence Involving Multiple Possible Tortfeasors*

[40] The cases that have dispensed with the usual requirement of "but for" causation in favour of a less onerous material contribution to risk approach are generally cases where, "but for" the negligent act of one or more of the defendants, the plaintiff would not have been injured. This excludes recovery where the injury "may very well be due to factors unconnected to the defendant and not the fault of anyone": *Snell*, per Sopinka J., at p. 327. The plaintiff effectively has established that the "but for" test, viewed globally, has been met. It is only when it is applied separately to each defendant that the "but for" test breaks down because it cannot be shown which of several negligent defendants actually launched the event that led to the injury. The plaintiff thus has shown negligence and a relationship of duty owed by each defendant, but faces failure on the "but for" test because it is "impossible", in the sense just discussed, to show which act or acts were injurious. In such cases, each defendant who has contributed to the risk of the injury that occurred can be faulted.

[41] In these circumstances, permitting the plaintiff to succeed on a material contribution to risk basis meets the underlying goals of the law of negligence. Compensation for injury is achieved. Fairness is satisfied; the plaintiff has suffered a loss due to negligence, so it is fair that she turns to tort law for compensation. Further, each defendant failed to act with the care necessary to avoid potentially causing the plaintiff's loss, and each may well have in fact caused the plaintiff's loss. Deterrence is also furthered; potential tortfeasors will know that they cannot escape liability by pointing the finger at others. And these goals are furthered in a manner consistent with corrective justice; the deficit in the relationship between the plaintiff and the defendants viewed as a group that would exist if the plaintiff were denied recovery is corrected. The plaintiff has shown that she is in a correlative relationship of doer and sufferer of the same harm with the group of defendants as a whole, if not necessarily with each individual defendant.

[42] The only case to apply a material contribution to risk approach to a single tortfeasor is *Sienkiewicz*. A plaintiff suffering from mesothelioma had only been exposed to asbestos from a single negligent source and on the trial judge's findings, "but for" causation could not be inferred. The United Kingdom Supreme Court took the view that it was bound by precedent to apply a material contribution to risk approach in all mesothelioma cases. Several members of the court in *Sienkiewicz* noted the difficulty with such a result. Lady Hale observed that she found it hard to believe that a defendant "whose wrongful exposure might or might not have led to the disease would be liable in full for the consequences even if it was more likely than not that some other cause was to blame (let alone that it was not more likely than not that he was to blame)" (para. 167). In my view, nothing compels a similar result in Canada, and thus far, although Sopinka J.'s remarks in *Snell* (quoted above at para. 20) do not preclude it, courts in Canada have not applied a material contribution to risk test in a case with a single tortfeasor.

[43] It is important to reaffirm that in the usual case of multiple agents or actors, the traditional "but for" test still applies. The question, as discussed earlier, is whether the plaintiff has shown that the negligence of one or more of the defendants was a necessary cause of the injury. Degrees of fault are reflected in calculations made under contributory negligence legislation. By contrast, the material contribution to risk approach applies where "but for" causation cannot be proven against any of multiple defendants, all negligent in a manner that might have in fact caused the plaintiff's injury, because each can use a "point the finger" strategy to preclude a finding of causation on a balance of probabilities.

[44] This is not to say that new situations will not raise new considerations. I leave for another day, for example, the scenario that might arise in mass toxic tort litigation with multiple plaintiffs, where it is established statistically that the defendant's acts induced an injury on some members of the group, but it is impossible to know which ones.

. . .

Summary

[46] The foregoing discussion leads me to the following conclusions as to the present state of the law in Canada:

(1) As a general rule, a plaintiff cannot succeed unless she shows as a matter of fact that she would not have suffered the loss "but for" the negligent act or acts of the defendant. A trial judge is to take a robust and pragmatic approach to determining if a plaintiff has established that the defendant's negligence caused her loss. Scientific proof of causation is not required.

(2) Exceptionally, a plaintiff may succeed by showing that the defendant's conduct materially contributed to risk of the plaintiff's injury, where (a) the plaintiff has established that her loss would not have occurred "but for" the negligence of two or more tortfeasors, each possibly in fact responsible for the loss; and (b) the plaintiff, through no fault of her own, is unable to show that any one of the possible tortfeasors in fact was the necessary or "but for" cause of her injury, because each can point to one another as the possible "but for" cause of the injury, defeating a finding of causation on a balance of probabilities against anyone.

D. *Application*

[47] The trial judge made two errors.

[48] The first error was to insist on scientific reconstruction evidence as a necessary condition of finding "but for" causation. . . .

[49] As discussed above, the cases consistently hold that scientific precision is not necessary to a conclusion that "but for" causation is established on a balance of probabilities. It follows that the trial judge erred in insisting on scientific precision in the evidence as a condition of finding "but for" causation.

[50] The trial judge's second error was to apply a material contribution to risk test. The special conditions that permit resort to a material contribution approach were not present in this case. This is not a case where we know that the loss would not have occurred "but for" the negligence of two or more possible tortfeasors, but the plaintiff cannot establish on a balance of probabilities which negligent actor or actors caused the injury. This is a simple single-defendant case: the only issue was whether "but for" the defendant's negligent conduct, the injury would have been sustained.

. . .

[53] We cannot be certain what the trial judge would have concluded had he not made the errors I earlier described. All that can be said is that the parties did not receive a trial based on correct legal principles. In my view, the appropriate remedy in these circumstances is an order for a new trial.

[54] I would allow the appeal and order a new trial.

. . .

[LeBel and Rothstein JJ., in dissent, also held that the but-for test of causation applied. However, they held that the plaintiff's claim should be dismissed because the trial judge had already found that the plaintiff could not satisfy the but-for test.]

NOTES AND QUESTIONS

1. Consistent with the earlier cases, *Clements* states that scientific proof is not required to meet the but-for test of causation and calls on the courts to take a "robust and pragmatic approach" to the facts and to draw "common sense inferences." Given this approach, do you think that the plaintiff in *Clements* has satisfied the but-for test of causation?

2. Has *Clements* eliminated the material contribution to injury test by reframing it in terms of material contribution to risk? Based on *Clements*, what must the plaintiff establish in order to rely on the material contribution to risk test? How does this test differ from the multiple negligent defendants rule in *Cook*, the materially increased risk of injury test in *Snell* and the approach in *Fairchild*?

3. Why did the court in *Clements* limit the material contribution to injury test to situations involving more than one tortfeasor?

4. Consistent with *Hanke*, *Clements* stated that it would be unfair and unjust to apply the but-for test and dismiss the plaintiff's claim when the requirements of the material contribution to risk test are met. Were the arguments that McLachlin C.J. made in this regard compelling? Why should the plaintiff's evidentiary problems in

proving causation be treated differently from his or her evidentiary problems in proving duty of care, breach of the standard of care, remoteness or damages?

5. *Clements* indicated that the material contribution to risk test could apply to situations involving more than two negligent defendants and that each would be liable to the plaintiff. Is it just and fair that one of three or more negligent defendants may be held jointly and severally liable for the plaintiff's entire loss when it is more likely than not that he or she played no causal role in the plaintiff's loss?

6. For cases that have considered or followed *Clements*, see *Ediger v. Johnston*, 2013 SCC 18; *Boon v. Mann*, 2016 BCCA 242; *Sacks v. Ross*, 2017 ONCA 773; and *Surujdeo v. Melady*, 2017 ONCA 41.

7. Should *Snell*, *Athey*, *Walker*, *Hanke*, *Clements*, and the scores of cases that they have generated be explicitly jettisoned? In the end result, have these cases altered the traditional but-for test of causation as modified by the multiple negligent defendants rule in *Cook*?

8. For comments on *Clements*, see Chaudhury, "Causation in the Law of Negligence: Where are we now? Where are we going? *Clements v. Clements*; *Ediger v. Johnston*" (2012) 40 Adv. Q. 257; Mangan, "Confusion in Material Contribution" (2012) 91 Can. Bar Rev. 701; Brewer, "The End of Material Contribution to Injury: *Clements v. Clements*" (2014) 42 Adv. Q. 217; and Black, "The Rise and Fall of Plaintiff-Friendly Causation" (2016) 53 Alta. L. Rev. 1013. See also MacKenzie & Wood, "Common-Sense Causation: How a Robust and Pragmatic Application of the 'But For' Test Can Solve the Circular Causation Problem in Cases of Multiple Contributing Tortfeasors" in Archibald, ed., *Annual Review of Litigation, 2018*, (2018) 457.

9. For a summary of the Supreme Court of Canada's analysis of casation in negligence, see *British Columbia v. Canadian Forest Products Ltd.*, 2018 BCCA 124 at para. 135.

(c) PROPORTIONATE CAUSE AND LOSS OF CHANCE

In several of the preceding cases, the major problem appears to be the all-or-nothing approach to losses occurring prior to trial. If there is only a 49% chance that the defendant's negligence was a cause, the plaintiff's claim fails; whereas if there is a 51% chance, the plaintiff's claim succeeds and he or she recovers 100% of the loss. If, as in *Sindell v. Abbott Laboratories*, 26 Cal. 3d 588 (Sup. Ct. 1980), a proportionate approach were adopted, a plaintiff would recover based on a possibility that the defendant was a cause. Therefore, if there was a 30% chance that the defendant's negligence was a cause, the plaintiff would recover 30% of his or her loss from that defendant. As indicated, the Canadian courts have not adopted the proportionate cause approach in *Sindell* to injuries occurring prior to trial.

However, Canadian courts apply a different standard of proof for losses that may occur after trial. If the plaintiff can establish a substantial or reasonable possibility that the defendant's negligence will cause a future loss, the plaintiff can recover a pro-rated percentage of that loss. For example, assume that there is a 40% chance that the defendant's negligence will cause the plaintiff to go blind and that this injury, if it occurs, will result in $100,000 in damages. Pursuant to *Janiak v. Ippolito*, [1985] 1 S.C.R. 146, the plaintiff would be awarded $40,000 (40% of $100,000) for this possibility.

The loss of chance cases typically arise when it is alleged that the defendant's negligence has denied the plaintiff a possibility of avoiding a loss or injury. Assume that, following their son's death, the parents learn that there would have been a 25% chance for a full recovery had the doctor not negligently delayed their son's cancer treatment. The Canadian and English courts have denied recovery in these medical cases because the parents cannot prove on a balance of probabilities that the doctor's negligence was a cause of their son's death. If the doctor's negligence denied their son a 70% chance for a full recovery, the parents would be able to prove on the balance of probabilities that the doctor's negligence was a cause of their son's death.

However, there are limited circumstances in which pro-rated damages have been awarded for a loss of a chance. For example, in *Jarbeau v. McLean*, 2017 ONCA 115, the court stated at para. 20 that "In some cases of solicitor's negligence, where it is practically impossible to determine what would have happened but for the solicitor's negligent conduct, courts have allowed a plaintiff to advance a claim for loss of the chance to recover." In such cases, the court will determine as best it can the value of the loss of chance and award damages accordingly even if the plaintiff's prospects of success were assessed as being below 50%. See generally *Kitchen v. Royal Air Forces Association*, [1958] 2 All ER 241.

NOTES AND QUESTIONS

1. Would you favour abandoning the all-or-nothing approach to losses occurring prior to trial? What problems, if any, would result from adopting a proportionate cause approach? Would this approach necessitate limiting a plaintiff's recovery to 60% for pretrial losses if causation could only be established to that probability?

2. Can you suggest any justification for treating the loss of chance cases differently from other proportionate cause situations? Do these cases pose unique emotional harms?

3. Numerous healthcare cases involve claims that the defendant negligently failed to undertake a particular test or procedure, or negligently failed to act in a timely fashion. Although these cases could be analyzed in terms of a loss of chance, the court will often state that the plaintiff has or has not established causation without using the term loss of chance.

4. For cases in which the loss of chance was held to fall below a balance of probabilities and was not recoverable, see *Laferrière v. Lawson*, [1991] 1 S.C.R. 541; *Boon v. Mann*, 2016 BCCA 242; *Benhaim v. St-Germain*, 2016 SCC 48; *Sacks v. Ross*, 2017 ONCA 773; and *Briante v. Vancouver Island Health Authority*, 2017 BCCA 148. For cases in which the loss of chance was held to exceed a balance of probabilities and was recoverable, see *Steinebach (Litigation Guardian of) v. O'Brien*, 2011 BCCA 302; *Beldycki Estate v. Jaipargas*, 2012 ONCA 537; *Goodman v. Viljoen*, 2012 ONCA 896; *Pinch (Guardian ad litem of) v. Morwood*, 2016 BCSC 938; and *Ghiassi v. Singh*, 2018 ONCA 764.

5. The loss of chance issue has generated controversy particularly in regard to healthcare cases in which the plaintiff cannot prove causation on a balance of probabilities. Nor is it clear why pro-rated damages are awarded in loss of chance cases involving lawyers but not healthcare professionals. See Stapleton, "Loss of the Chance of Cure from Cancer" (2005) 68 M.L.R. 996; Steel, "Rationalising Loss of a Chance in Tort" in Pitel, Neyers & Chamberlain, eds., *Tort Law: Challenging Orthodoxy* (2013) 235; Edelman, "'Loss of a chance'" (2013) 21 Torts L.J. 1; and Brammall & Svonkin, "The Loss of Chance Doctrine in Canadian Law" in Archibald, ed., *Annual Review of Litigation, 2018*, (2018) 325.

6. See Fleming, "Probabilistic Causation in Tort Law" (1989) 68 Can. Bar Rev. 661.

REVIEW PROBLEM

Assume that the incidence of a particular cancer is 6 per 100,000 in the general population, but 10 per 100,000 in populations exposed to PCBs. Assume as well that Helen contracted this type of cancer after the defendant negligently exposed her to PCBs. Finally, assume that PCB-induced cancer cases cannot be distinguished from naturally occurring cancer cases.

(a) Would the principles of causation in *McGhee* (Lord Reid), *McGhee* (Lord Wilberforce), *Snell, Fairchild, Barker, Holtby, Sindell, Hanke*, or *Clements* be applicable to the causation issue in Helen's claim against the defendant?

(b) What result would be reached in Helen's claim based on the principles in the applicable cases?

(c) Answer the preceding questions, this time based on the assumption that the incidence of this cancer is 4 per 100,000 in the general population, and 10 per 100,000 in populations exposed to PCBs.

5. Multiple Causes

The issue of causation becomes more complex when the plaintiff's injuries are brought about by two or more causes. As indicated at the outset of this chapter, it must first be determined if the injuries are divisible. In other words, can the injuries be divided into distinct losses that are each readily attributable to the conduct of a single tortfeasor? If the plaintiff's injuries are divisible, he or she will have a separate cause of action against each tortfeasor and the but-for test of causation, subject to any relevant modification, will apply.

This situation must be distinguished from one in which two or more tortfeasors cause a single indivisible harm. It may be useful to divide these multiple cause cases into two categories: those involving independent insufficient causes and those involving independent sufficient causes. As the following cases illustrate, the but-for test adequately addresses the causation issues posed by independent insufficient causes but produces anomalous results when applied to independent sufficient causes.

Finally, situations in which the defendants are independent tortfeasors must be distinguished from those in which they are joint tortfeasors. An independent tortfeasor is only liable for the injuries that he or she causes. In contrast, a joint tortfeasor is held liable for the torts committed by his or her fellow joint tortfeasors even if he or she did not cause or contribute to the plaintiff's loss.

In *Cook v. Lewis*, [1951] S.C.R. 830, the court recognized three categories of cases in which individuals will be held to be joint tortfeasors: principal and agent relationships (agents committing a tort while acting on behalf of their principals); master and servant relationships (employees committing a tort in the course of employment); and concerted actions or joint ventures (two or more individuals acting in concert to bring about a common end that is illegal, inherently dangerous, or one in which negligence can be anticipated). The issue of whether the defendants are joint or independent tortfeasors should be considered prior to analyzing the other elements of the cause of action. If the defendants are joint tortfeasors, the plaintiff need only prove that one of them was a negligent cause. Thus, the determination that the defendants are joint tortfeasors alters the subsequent analysis of the remaining issues.

NOTES AND QUESTIONS

1. Provide an example in which the defendants will be: (a) both joint tortfeasors and multiple causers; and (b) joint tortfeasors, but not multiple causers.

2. The third category of joint tortfeasor cases recognized in *Cook* has generated considerable judicial attention. For example, in *Newcastle (Town) v. Mattatall* (1987), 78 N.B.R. (2d) 236 (Q.B.), aff'd (1988), 87 N.B.R. (2d) 238 (C.A.), three intoxicated youths broke into the town rink with the intent of stealing whatever they could find. One of the youths negligently caused a fire that resulted in substantial property damage. Although the other two youths were not negligent or with the other youth when he started the fire, all three were held to be joint tortfeasors and were held equally liable. The court stated that the fire was caused in pursuit of the three youths' common wrongful intention. Do you agree? See also *Raywalt Construction Co. v. Bencic* (2005), 386 A.R. 230 (Q.B.).

3. It is not clear how specific the common plan has to be. Is a plan to go bar hopping with rowdy friends who you know to be violent a common plan to engage in violence? There is also uncertainty regarding the level of participation required to make one member of a group a joint tortfeasor with the other members. In *Martin v. Martin* (1996), 176 N.B.R. (2d) 178 (C.A.), one of the Martin brothers beat up the plaintiff, a creditor. The four brothers were held to be joint tortfeasors, even though only one of them attacked the plaintiff and the other three were leaving when the battery occurred. The court stated that the four brothers were trespassers and aggressors who did not go to the plaintiff's property "for a tea party, to wish him well nor to aid him in the construction of his new home." See also *Chow v. Hiscock* (2005), 41 C.C.L.T. (3d) 155 (B.C.S.C.); *Mainland Sawmills Ltd. v. I.W.A.-Canada*, 2006 BCSC 1195; and *Fullowka v. Royal Oak Ventures Inc.*, 2010 SCC 5.

4. In *Sea Shepherd UK (Appellant) v Fish & Fish Limited (Respondent)*, [2015] UKSC 10, it was generally agreed that an individual's mere approval or facilitation of another person's tortious conduct does not provide a sufficient basis for inferring that they have a common plan or design. Even if the parties have a common plan, the individual must undertake an act in furtherance of that plan. While the individual's act need not constitute a significant or essential element of the tort, the individual will

not be held to be a joint tortfeasor if his or her act is trivial. While the principles for determining when parties will be held to be joint tortfeasors was not an issue, their application to the facts divided the courts. The trial judge's decision that the defendants were not joint tortfeasors was unanimously reversed by the Court of Appeal. In a 3:2 decision, the Supreme Court overturned the Court of Appeal decision and upheld the trial judge's conclusion that the parties were not joint tortfeasors. Are the decisions in *Newcastle (Town)*, *supra*, and *Martin*, *supra*, consistent with the principles set out in the *Sea Shepherd UK* case?

5. Should the defendants in the following situations be considered joint tortfeasors?

(a) A was driving a truck towing B's disabled van with B sitting in its driver's seat. While attempting to pass, the plaintiff was forced off the road by A, who had begun a left turn. The plaintiff could not see the truck's turn signal, and the van's signal was not working: *Harpe v. Lefebvre* (1976), 1 C.C.L.T. 331 (Alta. Dist. Ct.).

(b) A and B each threw a handful of sand at a school bus. Some of the sand hit the plaintiff in the eye, but it was impossible to determine whether A or B had thrown that sand: *Beecham v. Henderson*, [1951] 1 D.L.R. 628 (B.C.S.C.).

(c) A, B and C set out together for a night of heavy drinking. They took turns driving to different bars. All three were impaired, but B was driving when he caused a crash and seriously injured the plaintiff. See generally *Crossan v. Gillis* (1979), 30 N.S.R. (2d) 121 (C.A.); *Hague v. Billings* (1989), 68 O.R. (2d) 321 (H.C.); and *Pizzolon v. Pedrosa* (1988), 46 C.C.L.T. 243 (B.C.S.C.).

(d) Three friends were driving their high-performance motorcycles at speeds reaching double and triple the limit while weaving in and out of traffic. One of the cyclists crashed at about 180 km/h, killing himself and seriously injuring the driver of another vehicle: *Mallory v. Werkmann Estate*, 2014 ONSC 971.

6. At common law, there is no apportionment among joint tortfeasors, and the release of one joint tortfeasor extinguishes the plaintiff's right to sue the other joint tortfeasors: *Tucker (Public Trustee of) v. Asleson*, [1993] 6 W.W.R. 45 (B.C.C.A.); and *S. Bransfield Ltd. v. Fletcher*, 2003 NBCA 71. In order to avoid this latter problem, the plaintiff can settle with one joint tortfeasor and agree not to sue him or her, but not provide a release. Since the settlement is not viewed as a release, the plaintiff is free to seek redress from the remaining joint tortfeasors. While legislation now permits apportionment and contribution among joint tortfeasors, it has not eliminated the common law rule about the impact of releasing a joint tortfeasor in all jurisdictions. For examples of legislation displacing the common law rule, see *Courts of Justice Act*, R.S.O. 1990, c. C.43, s. 139(1); *Contributory Negligence Act*, R.S.P.E.I. 1988, c. C-21, s. 7(1)(b); and *The Contributory Negligence Act*, R.S.S. 1978, c. C-31, s. 7.1(1).

7. In *Montréal (Ville) c. Lonardi*, 2018 SCC 29, fans rioted after a hockey game and destroyed or seriously damaged 15 police cars belonging to the city. About 20 rioters were identified and arrested. The city brought separate suits for the damages done to individual vehicles. It claimed that all of the rioters who damaged a specific vehicle should be held "solidarily" liable for the total damages to that vehicle. Based on the *Civil Code*, the trial judge held that the rioters had no clear intention to engage in a common venture and thus could not be held "solidarily" liable. Rather, each rioter was only held liable for the specific damages that he or she caused.

The Court of Appeal upheld the trial judgment as did the majority in the Supreme Court. The majority stated that the rioters lacked a common intention and that there was no causal connection between each rioter's individual acts and the total damages to the vehicles. The dissent stated that the rioters who damaged a given vehicle were jointly participating in a wrongful act and should be held solidarily liable for the total damages done. Which judgment is preferable? What are the implications of this case for the common law principles governing joint tortfeasors?

(a) INDEPENDENT INSUFFICIENT CAUSES

In this category of cases, several factors combine to cause the plaintiff's loss. Each factor is individually necessary as the loss would not have occurred without it. However, no factor is individually sufficient to have caused the loss in the absence of the other factors. In *Athey v. Leonati*, [1996] 3 S.C.R. 458, the plaintiff's injury was caused by a non-culpable factor (his pre-existing back condition) and culpable factors (the defendants' negligent driving). In contrast, *Nowlan v. Brunswick Construction Ltee.* (1972), 5 N.B.R. (2d) 529 (C.A.), aff'd [1975] 2 S.C.R. 523 addresses the causal role of two negligent parties in damaging the plaintiff's house.

ATHEY v. LEONATI
[1996] 3 S.C.R. 458

[The plaintiff, who had a pre-existing back condition, suffered neck and back injuries in two traffic crashes that were negligently caused by the defendants. On his doctor's advice, the plaintiff began an exercise program at Fitness World. One day during warm-up stretches, he felt a "pop" in his back and sustained a herniated disc. The incident resulted in a permanent partial disability that required him to leave his job as an auto worker and take a less demanding job at lower pay. The defendants admitted they were negligent. There was no allegation that the plaintiff was contributorily negligent with respect to the accidents or his participation in the exercise program. The only issue was whether the disc herniation was caused by the injuries sustained in the accidents or whether it was attributable to the appellant's pre-existing back problems. The trial judge accepted that the crashes causally contributed to the onset of the disability but reduced the plaintiff's damages by 75% to reflect the greater causal role played by his pre-existing back condition. The British Columbia Court of Appeal upheld the trial decision, and the plaintiff appealed.]

MAJOR J.—

. . .

It is not now necessary, nor has it ever been, for the plaintiff to establish that the defendant's negligence was the *sole cause* of the injury. There will frequently be a myriad of other background events which were necessary preconditions to the injury occurring. . . . As long as a defendant is *part* of the cause of an injury, the defendant is liable, even though his act alone was not enough to create the injury. There is no basis for a reduction of liability because of the existence of other preconditions: defendants remain liable for all injuries caused or contributed to by their negligence.

. . .

The respondents submitted that apportionment is permitted where the injuries caused by two defendants are divisible (for example, one injuring the plaintiff's foot and the other the plaintiff's arm) . . . . Separation of distinct and divisible injuries is not truly apportionment; it is simply making each defendant liable only for the injury he or she has caused, according to the usual rule. The respondents are correct that separation is also permitted where some of the injuries have tortious causes and some of the injuries have non-tortious causes . . . Again, such cases merely recognize that the defendant is not liable for injuries which were not caused by his or her negligence.

In the present case, there is a single indivisible injury, the disc herniation, so division is neither possible nor appropriate. The disc herniation and its consequences are one injury, and any defendant found to have negligently caused or contributed to the injury will be fully liable for it.

. . .

The Thin Skull and "Crumbling Skull" Doctrines

The respondents argued that the plaintiff was predisposed to disc herniation and that this is therefore a case where the "crumbling skull" rule applies. The "crumbling skull" doctrine is an awkward label for a fairly simple idea. It is named after the well-known "thin skull" rule, which makes the tortfeasor liable for the plaintiff's injuries even if the injuries are unexpectedly severe owing to a pre-existing condition. The tortfeasor must take his or her victim as the tortfeasor finds the victim, and is therefore liable even though the plaintiff's losses are more dramatic than they would be for the average person. [The thin-skull rule is examined in the next chapter, which deals with the issue of remoteness.]

The so-called "crumbling skull" rule simply recognizes that the pre-existing condition was inherent in the plaintiff's "original position". The defendant need not put the plaintiff in a position *better* than his or her original position. The defendant is liable for the injuries caused, even if they are extreme, but need not compensate the plaintiff for any debilitating effects of the pre-existing condition which the plaintiff would have experienced anyway. The defendant is liable for the additional damage but not the pre-existing damage . . . . Likewise, if there is a measurable risk that the pre-existing condition would have detrimentally affected the plaintiff in the future, regardless of the defendant's negligence, then this can be taken into account in reducing the overall award . . . . This is consistent with the general rule that the plaintiff must be returned to the position he would have been in, with all of its attendant risks and shortcomings, and not a better position.

The "crumbling skull" argument is the respondents' strongest submission, but in my view it does not succeed on the facts as found by the trial judge. There was no finding of any measurable risk that the disc herniation would have occurred without the accident, and there was therefore no basis to reduce the award to take into account any such risk.

. . .

Application of Principles to Facts

A matter to be resolved is the identification of the competing causes. Some of the trial judge's comments suggest that the "Fitness World incident" was a possible cause of the herniation. The "Fitness World incident" was not a cause; it was the *effect*. It was the injury. Mere stretching alone was not sufficient to cause disc herniation in the absence of some latent disposition or previous injuries. There was no suggestion that it was negligent of the appellant to attempt to exercise or that he exercised in a negligent manner.

Some latent weakness spontaneously manifested itself during the stretching, and the issue is whether the weakness was because of the accidents or a pre-existing condition. The reasons of the trial judge show that she understood this. She referred to the appellant's poor spinal health, his history of back problems, and to the fact that there had been no herniation or injury to the disc prior to the accidents. The competing causes in this case were the injuries sustained in the accidents and a pre-existing disposition to back problems.

The applicable principles can be summarized as follows. If the injuries sustained in the motor vehicle accidents caused or contributed to the disc herniation, then the defendants are fully liable for the damages flowing from the herniation. The plaintiff must prove causation by meeting the "but for" or material contribution test. Future or hypothetical events can be factored into the calculation of damages according to degrees of probability, but causation of the injury must be determined to be proven or not proven. This has the following ramifications:

1. If the disc herniation would likely have occurred at the same time, without the injuries sustained in the accident, then causation is not proven.

2. If it was necessary to have *both* the accidents *and* the pre-existing back condition for the herniation to occur, then causation is proven, since the herniation would not have occurred but for the accidents. Even if the accidents played a minor role, the defendant would be fully liable because the accidents were still a *necessary* contributing cause.

3. If the accidents alone could have been a sufficient cause, and the pre-existing back condition alone could have been a sufficient cause, then it is unclear which was the cause-in-fact of the disc herniation. The trial judge must determine, on a balance of probabilities, whether the defendant's negligence materially contributed to the injury.

The findings of the trial judge are slightly ambiguous. She awarded only 25 percent of the global damages because she held that the accidents were a "causation factor" of 25 percent. Taken out of context, this could be read as meaning that there was a 25 percent chance that the injury was caused by the accidents, and a 75 percent chance that it was caused by the pre-existing condition. In that case, causation would simply not be proven. However, it is clear from the reasons for judgment that this is not what the trial judge concluded.

The findings of the trial judge indicate that it was necessary to have *both* the pre-existing condition *and* the injuries from the accidents to cause the disc herniation in this case. She made a positive finding that the accidents contributed to the injury, but that the injuries suffered in the two accidents were "not the sole cause" of the herniation. She expressly found that "the herniation was not unrelated to the accidents" and that the accidents "contributed to some degree" to the subsequent herniation. She concluded that the injuries in the accidents "played some causative role, albeit a minor one". These findings indicate that it was the combination of the pre-existing condition and the injuries sustained in the accidents which caused the herniation. Although the accidents played a lesser role than the pre-existing problems, the accidents were nevertheless a necessary ingredient in bringing about the herniation.

The trial judge's conclusion on the evidence was that "[i]n my view, the plaintiff has proven, on a balance of probabilities, that the injuries suffered in the two earlier accidents contributed to some degree to the subsequent disc herniation". She assessed this contribution at 25 percent. This falls outside the *de minimis* range and is therefore a material contribution. . . . This finding of material contribution was sufficient to render the defendant fully liable for the damages flowing from the disc herniation.

[The appeal was allowed, and the plaintiff was entitled to recover 100% of his damages.]

NOWLAN v. BRUNSWICK CONSTRUCTION LTÉE
(1972), 5 N.B.R. (2d) 529 (C.A.), aff'd [1975] 2 S.C.R. 523

[The defendant contractor had been negligent in constructing the plaintiff's house, which suffered extensive rot due to leaks in the structure. However, the defendant argued that no damage would have occurred but for the architect's poor design, which had not provided for proper ventilation.]

LIMERICK, J.A.:

. . .

While structural design particularly in lack of ventilation contributed greatly to the damage occasioned to the building, the poor workmanship of the defendant and poor quality of materials used also contributed.

This is a case of poor design on the part of the architect, as well as poor workmanship and materials contributing to the same damage.

If the design had provided proper ventilation there would have been no dry rot even though leaks occurred due to poor workmanship. Even though the design was poor there would have been no dry rot if the roof had been impervious to water and a proper drain installed and proper vapour barriers and insulation installed and windows had been properly constructed according to the plan.

Where there are concurrent torts, breaches of contract or a breach of contract and a concurrent tort both contributing to the same damage, whether or not the damage would have occurred in the absence of either cause, the liability is a joint and several liability and either party causing or contributing to the damage is liable for the whole damage to the person aggrieved. . . .

The defendant is a concurrent wrongdoer and the fact that the damage might not have occurred but for the poor design of the building does not excuse him from the liability arising out of his poor workmanship and inadequate material supplied by him.

The appeal is allowed. The judgment of the trial Judge is set aside. The plaintiffs, appellants shall have judgment against the defendant for the amount of $36,068.48 determined by the trial Judge and costs of trial and appeal.

[Hughes C.J.N.B. concurred with Limerick J.A., and Bugold J.A. wrote a separate concurring judgment.]

NOTES AND QUESTIONS

1. The plaintiff's pre-existing condition is generally not discussed when analyzing the causal role of the defendant's negligence. Why was it raised in *Athey*?

2. Why did Major J. reject the defendant's arguments on divisible injuries, the crumbling-skull doctrine and causation? See *Farrant v. Laktin*, 2011 BCCA 336 (plaintiff with pre-existing back problems sued for debilitating pain caused by a crash); and *Gormick v. Amenta*, 2013 BCSC 1128, additional reasons 2013 BCSC 1998 (plaintiff with pre-existing back problems sued for back injuries that required surgery following a crash).

3. As in *Athey*, cases involving overlapping injuries occurring in a series of crashes often raise complex evidentiary issues. The trier of fact must determine which of the plaintiff's injuries are divisible and which are indivisible and also assess the plaintiff's condition prior to the initial, second and subsequent crashes. The assessment may be further complicated if the plaintiff has suffered soft tissue injuries, whiplash, pain, or psychological and other injuries that are difficult to verify.

In *Kallstrom v. Yip*, 2016 BCSC 829, the plaintiff was involved in six separate "low impact" crashes in less than four years and claimed that taken together they resulted in ongoing chronic pain, fatigue, headaches, and depression. She argued that she suffered an indivisible injury for which each defendant should be held jointly and severally liable. The defendants claimed that any chronic pain or psychological problems the plaintiff had were largely due to factors in the plaintiff's life unrelated to the crashes and for which they should not be held liable. Although the court stated that the plaintiff "catastrophized" the impact of the crashes and minimized her pre-existing medical and psychosocial problems, it held the defendants jointly and severally liable for almost $750,000. See *Bradley v. Groves* 2010 BCCA 361; *Scoates v. Dermott*, 2012 BCSC 485; and *Rajan v. Hudon*, 2014 BCSC 1678.

4. The preceding evidentiary challenges are not limited to crashes. In *Blackwater v. Plint*, [2005] 3 S.C.R. 3, the court discussed the difficulty of assessing a residential school's liability for sexually abusing the plaintiff, taking into account the impact of the abuse that he had previously suffered at home and the non-sexual abuse he suffered at the residential school which was unrecoverable due to the limitation period. See also *B.P.B. v. M.M.B.* (2009), 97 B.C.L.R. (4th) 73 (C.A.); and *M.B. v. 2014052 Ontario Ltd. (Deluxe Windows of Canada)*, 2012 ONCA 135.

5. As *Athey* illustrates, once the defendant has been found to be a cause of the plaintiff's loss, the defendant will be held liable for the entire loss even if there were other causal factors. See also *Hutchings v. Dow* (2007), 66 B.C.L.R. (4th) 78 (C.A.); *Monks v. ING Insurance Co. of Canada* (2008), 90 O.R. (3d) 689 (C.A.); *Bradley v. Groves* (2010), 8 B.C.L.R. (5th) 247 (C.A.); *Midgley v. Nguyen*, 2013 BCSC 693; and *Pololos v. Cinnamon-Lopez*, 2016 BCSC 81.

6. As indicated earlier, *Hanke* and *Clements* reaffirmed that the but-for test is the standard causation test for both divisible and indivisible injuries, and redefined the material contribution to injury test that Major J. introduced in *Athey*.

7. In *Arneil v. Paterson*, [1931] A.C. 560 (H.L.), several of the plaintiff's sheep were killed and injured when two dogs belonging to the two defendants separately chased, mauled and bit the sheep. The loss was viewed as being indivisible because it was impossible to determine which dog caused which injuries to which sheep. Both dog owners were held liable for the entire loss.

8. As in *Nowlan*, if two or more negligent defendants cause or contribute to an indivisible injury, each defendant will be held jointly and severally liable for the entire loss. The plaintiff may choose to sue each defendant separately for the whole loss or, as is more often the case, may sue the defendants in the same action. If the plaintiff chooses the latter option and is successful, he or she may enforce the judgment against any one of the defendants.

9. At common law, there is no apportionment of fault and contribution among tortfeasors. Thus, a defendant who played a relatively minor role in causing the plaintiff's loss could be held fully liable and yet have no redress against the other tortfeasors who may have been primarily at fault. The provincial negligence statutes now provide that one tortfeasor may obtain contribution from his or her fellow tortfeasors based upon their respective degrees of fault. See for example *Negligence Act*, R.S.O. 1990, c. N.1, ss. 1-2; and *Negligence Act*, R.S.B.C. 1996, c. 333, s. 4. Apportionment issues are discussed in more detail in Chapter 19.

(b) INDEPENDENT SUFFICIENT CAUSES

The previous section considered cases in which the plaintiff's indivisible loss was brought about by several necessary, but individually insufficient, causal factors. This section addresses the more difficult issues posed when the plaintiff's indivisible loss results from two or more sufficient causes. For example, assume that two negligent hunters fire fatal shots that simultaneously strike the plaintiff or that two negligent companies each permit toxins to escape into a river at levels fatal to the plaintiff's cattle. Under the but-for test, each tortfeasor would be absolved of liability because the plaintiff would have suffered the same loss regardless of any individual tortfeasor's negligence. In order to avoid this obvious inequity, the courts have applied a significant or substantial factor test of causation in such situations.

LAMBTON v. MELLISH
[1894] 3 Ch. 163

. . .

The Defendants Mellish and Cox were rival refreshment contractors who catered for visitors and excursionists to the common, and both the Defendants had merry-go-rounds on their premises, and were in the habit of using organs as an accompaniment to the amusements.

It appeared from the evidence that these organs were for three months or more in the summer continuously being played together from 10 or 11 a.m. till 6 or 7 p.m., and that the noise caused by the two organs was "maddening."

The organs used by Mellish had been changed, and it was alleged by him that the organ in use when the motion was made was a small portable hand-organ making comparatively little noise. That used by Cox was a much larger one provided with trumpet stops and emitting sounds which could be heard at the distance of one mile.

The Plaintiff now moved against the Defendant in each action for an injunction restraining him from playing any organs so as to cause a nuisance or injury to the Plaintiff or his family, or other occupiers of the Plaintiff's property.

. . .

CHITTY J.:—

Notwithstanding the conflict of evidence, I am of opinion that the Plaintiff is entitled to the injunction he asks for as against the Defendant in each action.

A man may tolerate a nuisance for a short period. A passer-by or a by-stander would not find any nuisance in these organs; but the case is very different when the noise has to be continuously endured: under such circumstances it is scarcely an exaggeration to term it "maddening", going on, as it does, hour after hour, day after day, and month after month. I consider that the noise made by each Defendant, taken separately, amounts to a nuisance. But I go further. It was said for the Defendant Mellish that two rights cannot make a wrong — by that it was meant that if one man makes a noise not of a kind, duration, or degree sufficient to constitute a nuisance, and another man, not acting in concert with the first, makes a similar noise at the same time, each is responsible only for the noise made by himself, and not also for that made by the other. If the two agreed and acted in combination each would be a wrongdoer. If a man shouts outside a house for most of the day, and another man, who is his rival (for it is to be remembered that these Defendants are rivals), does the same, has the inhabitant of the house no remedy? It is said that that is only so much the worse for the inhabitant. On the ground of common sense it must be the other way. Each of the men is making a noise and each is adding his quantum until the whole constitutes a nuisance. Each hears the other, and is adding to the sum which makes up the nuisance. In my opinion each is separately liable, and I think it would be contrary to good sense, and, indeed, contrary to law, to hold otherwise. It would be contrary to common sense that the inhabitants of the house should be left without remedy at law. . . . The Defendants here are both responsible for the noise as a whole so far as it constitutes a nuisance affecting the Plaintiff, and each must be restrained in respect of his own share in making the noise. I therefore grant an interim injunction in both the actions in the terms of the notices of motion.

NOTES AND QUESTIONS

1. Did the judge in *Lambton* view the case as one involving independent sufficient causes or independent insufficient causes? How did Mellish attempt to characterize the case? Would the result have been different had the judge accepted this characterization?

2. The significant or substantial factor test is also used when an independent sufficient cause and one or more independent insufficient causes bring about an indivisible loss. Depending on the facts, using the but-for test might result in exonerating some or all of the negligent parties. For example, assume that a fatal level of a toxin is 20 units, and that A negligently releases 21 units and B negligently releases 19. Under the but-for test, A would be held liable and B would be exonerated. However, if A was responsible for 21 units, B was responsible for 19 and C was responsible for 17, the but-for test would absolve all three of liability.

3. Some authors have recommended replacing the existing causation tests with the "NESS" test, which has been described as a more complete casual inquiry. A defendant's tortious act would be a cause-in-fact if it was a necessary element of a set of antecedent actual conditions that were sufficient for the occurrence of the plaintiff's loss. Canadian courts have yet to analyze the NESS test in detail. For a discussion of the NESS test see Wright, "Causation in Tort Law" (1985) 73 Cal. L. Rev. 1735; and

Wright, "Acts and Omissions as Positive and Negative Causes" in Neyers, Chamberlain & Pitel, eds., *Emerging Issues in Tort Law* (2007) 287.

REVIEW PROBLEMS

1. Assume that 20 decibels of noise constitute a nuisance and that noises from different sources have a simple cumulative effect. Based on these assumptions, what test of causation would be applied in the following situations?

(a) Allen causes 21 decibels, Barry causes 19 and Carl causes 5.
(b) Allen and Barry each independently cause 21 decibels.
(c) Allen causes 10 decibels, Barry causes 9.9 and Carl causes 0.2.
(d) Allen, Barry and Carl each cause 6 decibels and the plaintiff causes 3.

2. Allan and Bob were showing each other their favourite revolvers in a basement recreation room when they were called upstairs to meet Carol. They left their revolvers on the coffee table and came upstairs. As they talked, Carol's four-year-old son went off to explore the house. He eventually saw the revolvers, was attracted to them and shot himself with Bob's gun. Allan's gun was also loaded, but the child had not touched it. Carol has sued both Bob and Allan in negligence.

(a) Allan has sought your advice about his potential liability.
(b) Answer the same question, but assume that only Allan's gun would have been visible to the boy when he walked down the basement hall and looked into the recreation room.

6. Issues in Assessing the Plaintiff's Loss

(a) SUCCESSIVE CAUSES OF PARALLEL INJURY

This subsection addresses the legal principles governing the liability of the original tortfeasor when the plaintiff suffers a parallel or overlapping injury in a subsequent incident. First, it is well established that once the appeal period ends, the plaintiff's subsequent fate has no impact on the original tortfeasor's liability. For example, assume that the original tortfeasor paid $5 million to provide the plaintiff with 25 years of future care and that the plaintiff was negligently killed in an unrelated crash three years after the first case was settled. The original tortfeasor cannot recoup the unspent funds for the 22 years of future care that was not required.

Second, it is also well established that a tortfeasor's liability will be reduced to reflect the plaintiff's pre-existing injuries or disabilities, whether they were naturally occurring, innocently caused or the result of a preceding tort. For example, assume that a driver negligently kills a 25-year old pedestrian who was terminally ill and had only a two-year life expectancy at that time. In this case, the defendant would only be held liable for the damages attributable to reducing the pedestrian's life expectancy by two years. This approach is consistent with the general principles of compensatory damages and the principle that tortfeasors take the plaintiff as they find him or her.

Third, as the following case illustrates, there is more uncertainty regarding the extent of an original tortfeasor's liability when the plaintiff suffers an independent successive parallel injury prior to trial on the first injury (often referred to as a supervening injury). However, this issue arises relatively infrequently because there is a limited timeframe within which the supervening act must occur. As noted, the plaintiff's subsequent fate becomes irrelevant to the original tortfeasor once the appeal period ends.

PENNER v. MITCHELL
(1978), 10 A.R. 555 (C.A.)

PROWSE J.A.:

. . .

In the present case the trial Judge awarded the respondent special damages for loss of income for a period of thirteen (13) months following the date of the accident which gave rise to the respondent's cause of action. During that 13 month period the respondent would have been unable to work for a period of three months, even if the accident had not occurred, as she suffered from a heart condition which was unrelated to the accident.

The appellant's submission was that the respondent's award of special damages should not have included compensation for loss of wages during that three month period.

. . .

As the respondent relies on obiter dictum in the judgment of Lord Reid, in *Baker v. Willoughby*, [1970] A.C. 467 at 494 . . . (H.L.), I should first consider that case.

There the plaintiff, while crossing a road, sustained injuries to his left leg when he was struck by a motor vehicle operated by the defendant. Shortly before the trial he was shot in the left leg by a robber during the course of robbery. This later injury necessitated the immediate amputation of his left leg. The issue dealt with by Lord Reid was whether the first tortfeasor could call in aid the second tort to reduce the damages he should be made to pay on the ground that the disability the plaintiff suffered in his left leg resulting from the first tort ceased to be an effective cause of further loss after that leg was amputated as a result of the second tort.

[Reid L.J. concluded that original tortfeasors could only take into account a successive culpable parallel injury if it reduced the plaintiff's disability or shortened the period of time that he or she would suffer it.]

. . .

The issue on the present appeal is whether the rule applied in the *Baker* case, which resulted in treating the injury arising from the second event as irrelevant in assessing damages against the first tortfeasor, should be applied in the present case when the second event, the heart problem, arose in non-culpable circumstances. Lord Reid in the *Baker* case suggested that it should. . . .

In the *Andrews* case, in dealing with prospective loss of income and the effect thereon of contingencies of life, Mr. Justice Dickson stated: "It is a general practice to take account of contingencies which might have affected future earnings such as unemployment, illness, accidents and business depression." It will be noted that the nature of the contingencies of unemployment, illness, and business depression is such that a person who suffers a loss as a result of their occurrence does not have a cause of action against a wrongdoer as a consequence thereof. If the word "accident" is given its ordinary meaning, then its occurrence also arises in non-culpable circumstances. In my view the contingencies taken into account in assessing prospective loss of income should only include those that occur in non-culpable circumstances, that is, in circumstances that do not give rise to a cause of action. The rule applied in the *Baker* case should be applied only to those contingencies which arise from culpable circumstances.

My reason for concluding that future contingencies arising in culpable circumstances should not be taken into account in assessing damages such as prospective loss of income, is, because if that were done, the plaintiff would receive less than full compensation from the two wrongdoers. This would follow as there would be a deduction from the first loss because of the contingency that the second culpable event might occur and there would be a deduction from the second claim as the first culpable incident had occurred. The result of both deductions would produce a result the *Baker* case sought to avoid. Such a result would infringe the dominant rule applied in assessing damages as the injured person would then receive less than full compensation for the injuries he had sustained.

On the other hand not to take into account future contingencies arising in non-culpable circumstances would result in an injured person being overcompensated. For example not to make some allowance for early retirement which might arise for any number of reasons including health, non-culpable accidents, technological changes, or business depression, would result in the plaintiff being overcompensated in the event such contingency occurred.

The same reasoning applies if the contingency in fact is realized before trial. For example if the claimant was a carpenter and massive unemployment arose before the date of the trial then, to afford him compensation by way of special damages for loss of income, which he could not have earned, would result in him being overcompensated.

. . .

In conclusion, I am of the opinion that the learned trial Judge erred in awarding the respondent damages for the three month period she was disabled as a result of her heart condition. To include in her award damages for that three month period would result in her being overcompensated for the injuries caused by the appellant and the award would then infringe what I have referred to above as the dominant rule in assessment of damages for personal injuries. To include in the award damages for the three month period would have the result of including in the award a sum she would not have earned even if the motor accident had not occurred.

In the result I would set aside the award of special damages in the sum of $12,000 for loss of income and substitute therefor an award of $9,230.

NOTES AND QUESTIONS

1. In *Baker*, what injuries did the defendant cause, and were they divisible from those caused by the robbers? For what damages would the robbers have been held liable had they had been caught? Based on *Baker*, state the principles that govern the assessment of damages in cases of successive parallel injuries if: (a) both causes are culpable; and (b) the first cause is culpable and the second is innocent.

2. Did Prowse J.A. agree with the *ratio* in *Baker*? What were the bases upon which he disagreed with Lord Reid? Based on *Penner*, state the principles that govern the assessment of damages in cases of successive parallel injuries if: (a) both causes are

culpable; and (b) the first cause is culpable and the second is innocent. See McInnes, "Causation in Tort Law: Back to Basics at the Supreme Court of Canada" (1997) 35 Alta. L. Rev. 1013.

3. For cases considering *Penner*, see *Athey v. Leonati*, [1996] 3 S.C.R. 458; *Smith v. Shade*, [1996] 6 W.W.R. 52 (B.C.C.A.); *Fournier v. Wiens*, 2004 ABQB 430; *Abbott v. Gerges*, 2014 BCSC 1329; and *Akeelah v. Clow*, 2018 ONSC 3410.

4. In *Sunrise Co. v. Lake Winnipeg (The)*, [1991] 1 S.C.R. 3, the defendant's ship negligently caused the plaintiff's ship to run aground, which necessitated 27 days of repairs. In an unrelated incident, the plaintiff's ship sustained damages requiring 14 days of repairs, which were carried out within the 27-day period. Based solely on shipping cases, the majority found the defendant liable for 27 days of lost income. The dissent, based on general negligence principles, found the defendant liable for only 13 days of lost income. Which reasoning do you prefer?

5. The British courts have adopted a similar position to *Penner* in regard to non-culpable supervening causes. However, the House of Lords appears to have left open the issue of whether a culpable supervening cause might also be taken into account to reduce the first tortfeasor's liability. See *Jobling v. Associated Dairies Ltd.*, [1981] 2 All E.R. 752 (H.L.).

(b) DEVALUING THE PLAINTIFF'S LOSS

DILLON v. TWIN STATE GAS AND ELEC. CO.
163 A. 111 (N.H. 1932)

The defendant maintained wires to carry electric current over a public bridge in Berlin. In the construction of the bridge there were two spans of girders on each side between the roadway and footway. In each span the girders at each end sloped upwards towards each other from the floor of the bridge until connected by horizontal girders about nineteen feet above the floor.

The wires were carried above the framework of the bridge between the two rows of girders. To light the footway of the bridge at its center a lamp was hung from a bracket just outside of one of the horizontal girders and crossing over the end of the girder near its connection with a sloping girder. Wires ran from a post obliquely downward to the lamp and crossed the horizontal girder a foot or more above it. The construction of the wire lines over and upon the bridge is termed aerial. The wires were insulated for weather protection but not against contact.

The decedent and other boys had been accustomed for a number of years to play on the bridge in the daytime, habitually climbing the sloping girders to the horizontal ones, on which they walked and sat and from which they sometimes dived into the river. No current passed through the wires in the daytime except by chance.

The decedent, while sitting on a horizontal girder at a point where the wires from the post to the lamp were in front of him or at his side, and while facing outwards from the side of the bridge, leaned over, lost his balance, instinctively threw out his arm, and took hold of one of the wires with his right hand to save himself from falling. The wires happened to be charged with a high voltage current at the time and he was electrocuted.

. . .

ALLEN J.:—The circumstances of the decedent's death give rise to an unusual issue of its cause. In leaning over from the girder and losing his balance he was entitled to no protection from the defendant to keep from falling. Its only liability was in exposing him to the danger of charged wires. If but for the current in the wires he would have fallen down on the floor of the bridge or into the river, he would without doubt have been either killed or seriously injured. Although he died from electrocution, yet, if by reason of his preceding loss of balance he was bound to fall except for the intervention of the current, he either did not have long to live or was to be maimed. In such an outcome of his loss of balance, the defendant deprived him, not of a life of normal expectancy, but of one too short to be given pecuniary allowance, in one alternative, and not of normal, but of limited, earning capacity, in the other.

If it were found that he would have thus fallen with death probably resulting, the defendant would not be liable, unless for conscious suffering found to have been sustained from the shock. In that situation his life or earning capacity had no value. To constitute actionable negligence there must be damage, and damage is limited to those elements the statute prescribes.

If it should be found that but for the current he would have fallen with serious injury, then the loss of life or earning capacity resulting from the electrocution would be measured by its value in such injured condition. Evidence that he would be crippled would be taken into account in the same manner as though he had already been crippled.

His probable future but for the current thus bears on liability as well as damages. Whether the shock from the current threw him back on the girder or whether he would have recovered his balance, with or without the aid of the wire he took hold of, if it had not been charged, are issues of fact, as to which the evidence as it stands may lead to different conclusions.

NOTES AND QUESTIONS

1. Do the facts of *Dillon* materially differ from those in *Penner*? Is there a material difference between the situations in which: (a) a victim would have been killed by one causal factor if he or she had not been killed by another; and (b) a victim was affected by two causal factors, either of which alone would have been sufficient to cause death?

2. What was the cause of the boy's death in *Dillon*? How did the court calculate the value of his loss of life? Is the court's approach consistent with the general principles for assessing damages in tort law?

3. It has been argued that an impending devaluing factor should only be taken into account to reduce the plaintiff's claim if: (a) the impending factor is innocent in nature; and (b) an objective observer would say that, at the time of the defendant's tortious act, the impending factor was certain to come to pass. Thus, in *Dillon*, even if there had been a slight chance that the boy would have fallen into a small, deep pocket of water and escaped injury, the defendant would have been held fully liable for his death. Is it not more appropriate to discount the defendant's liability according to the likelihood of such possibilities? See Peaslee, "Multiple Causation and Damage" (1934) 47 Harv. L. Rev. 1127 at 1138-41; and Keeton *et al.*, *Prosser and Keeton on The Law of Torts*, 5th ed. (1984) at 353-54.

4. Assume that the plaintiff's $100,000 house is situated in the path of a forest fire negligently started by A. Before the flames reach the plaintiff's property, B negligently demolishes the house while cutting down a massive tree. How would you distinguish this case from *Dillon*? What is the cause of the plaintiff's loss and how would you calculate it? It is generally agreed that the plaintiff's loss would not be devalued in this situation. What is the rationale for this position?

REVIEW PROBLEMS

1. Jack and Harvey, two friends from Fairview University, were attending a football game at Midwest University. After the game they, along with about 50 other Fairview students, rushed onto the field and attempted to pull down the goal posts. Jack and Harvey were the first students to jump to the crossbar, and they urged others to do the same. When the crossbar broke, either Jack or Harvey fell onto Lloyd, a member of the student police who was attempting to protect the goal posts. As Lloyd was clutching his broken arm, Clarkson, another Fairview student who had been hanging from the crossbar, fell onto Lloyd, fracturing Lloyd's leg.

Discuss Lloyd's potential causes of action against Jack, Harvey and Clarkson.

2. John designed a cottage consisting of three bedrooms, a kitchen, a bathroom, and a living room. Morris, who had contracted to build the living room, unwittingly used rotten wooden beams. There was no doubt that the living room would collapse within two years and that its collapse would not damage the other rooms. Ralph was the contractor for the bathroom and the three bedrooms. He noticed that the timbers were rotten, but he decided to take a chance in using them. It was clear that the bathroom and bedrooms would suffer the same fate as the living room. Ernie, the landscape contractor, was levelling the grounds after the cottage was completed. While distracted, he drove the bulldozer into the back of the cottage, destroying the bedrooms and the living room. The next day Desmond, John's neighbour, chopped down a tree which unfortunately landed in the middle of the kitchen. Only the bathroom of John's cottage remained standing.

Ralph, Ernie and Desmond concede that they were negligent, but Morris has been absolved of liability. Discuss the liability of Ralph, Ernie and Desmond.

3. The Cruise Drug Company maintained a research laboratory that was developing a treatment for breast cancer. Lila and the other 47 researchers were required to handle toxic chemicals in the course of their research. Six months after beginning her employment at Cruise, Lila became pregnant. In due course, she gave birth to David, who unfortunately was born with a cognitive disability. Although he will be able to live in a home setting, David will require special education and full-time supervision for the rest of his life. It is agreed that David's total damages are $6 million.

At the time that Lila began working for Cruise, the company had known about an American study of a similar research project. That study revealed a greater incidence of birth defects among the children of female employees who worked with such chemicals during pregnancy. The rate of such birth defects is 6% in the general female population, but 9% among female researchers engaged in the American project. Cruise also knew that an elaborate ventilation system would most likely remove the dangerous chemical fumes from the laboratory. The company chose not to install the ventilation system because it found the $400,000 price tag prohibitive. Nor did it bother to inform its employees of the risks because it thought such knowledge would be bad for morale.

Discuss David's possible claim against the Cruise Drug Company.

17

REMOTENESS

1. Introduction
2. Directness Versus Foreseeability
3. Modifications to the Foreseeability Test
4. Intervening Causes
5. Beyond the Scope of the Risk

1. Introduction

Even if the defendant breached the standard of care in a way that caused the plaintiff to suffer a loss, liability will be denied if the connection between the breach and the loss was too remote. Remoteness is a rule of fairness. In some circumstances, the law relieves the defendant of responsibility for an injury that he or she carelessly caused.

The concept can be dramatically illustrated by a passage in Benjamin Franklin's *Poor Richard's Almanac* (1757):

> For the want of a nail the shoe was lost,
> For the want of a shoe the horse was lost,
> For the want of a horse the rider was lost,
> For the want of a rider the battle was lost,
> For the want of a battle the kingdom was lost,
> And all for the want of a horseshoe nail.

If "the want of a nail" was caused by a blacksmith's carelessness, the question would be whether the blacksmith should be held responsible for the loss of the kingdom. Despite the causal connection between the initial breach and the ultimate loss, the answer seems obvious. As a matter of fairness, the blacksmith must not be liable for the loss of the kingdom.

The blacksmith's case is an easy one. Very often, however, the issue of remoteness is far more contentious. As the cases in this chapter reveal, the courts have struggled to develop a test that strikes an appropriate balance between the desirability of holding the defendant responsible for a loss that he or she carelessly inflicted on the plaintiff and the desirability of relieving the defendant of an unreasonable burden.

There is a close relationship between the issues of remoteness and causation. Causation is concerned with the *factual* connection between the defendant's breach and the plaintiff's loss. Remoteness is concerned with the *legal* connection between the defendant's breach and the plaintiff's loss. For that reason, remoteness is sometimes referred to as "legal causation" or "proximate causation."

However, there is an important difference between causation and remoteness. Causation is, for the most part, an exercise in facts and logic. Even if the law is set aside, it remains possible to sensibly ask the question "did the defendant's conduct cause the plaintiff's loss?" In contrast, a question concerning remoteness only makes sense in a legal context. This is because, as Andrews J. explained in *Palsgraf v. Long Island Ry. Co.*, 248 N.Y. 339 at 352 (1928), "This is not logic. It is practical politics." Indeed, the whole purpose of the remoteness principle is to cut off the logical inquiry at some point. Moreover, that cut-off point will necessarily be somewhat arbitrary, because it is based on policy rather than logic.

In that respect, the concept of remoteness is similar to the concept of duty of care. Both are means by which the courts, for practical policy reasons, control the scope of liability. Not surprisingly, in each instance the content of the applicable rule has tended to vary from time to time, and from place to place, as judicial perceptions of societal values have shifted.

2. Directness Versus Foreseeability

(a) THE DIRECTNESS TEST

In *Re Polemis and Furness, Withy & Co.*, [1921] 3 K.B. 560, the Court of Appeal established "directness" as the test for remoteness. The test stated that the plaintiff's loss would not be too remote to be recoverable if it was a direct result of the defendant's carelessness. For the purpose of that test, directness was defined in terms of a close temporal and spatial connection between the defendant's breach and the plaintiff's loss.

In *Re Polemis*, the defendant's servants carelessly dropped a plank into the hold of the plaintiff's ship, which contained a cargo of benzene. The plank struck something and caused a spark that ignited the benzene fumes. The plaintiff's ship was destroyed by the ensuing explosion. The court held that this sequence of events was not reasonably foreseeable. It nevertheless imposed liability on the basis that there was a direct connection between the defendant's breach and the plaintiff's loss.

NOTES AND QUESTIONS

1. Canadian courts applied the directness test prior to and after *Re Polemis*. See *Toronto Ry. Co. v. Grinstead* (1895), 24 S.C.R. 570; *Winnipeg Elec. Ry. Co. v. Can. Nor. Ry.* (1919), 59 S.C.R. 352; *Duce v. Rourke* (1951), 1 W.W.R. (N.S.) 305 (Alta. S.C.); and *Simms v. Butt* (1975), 8 Nfld. & P.E.I.R. 14 (Nfld. C.A.).

2. The directness test was criticized as unworkable, unfair, illogical, overly pro-plaintiff and theoretically unsound. Do you agree? Much of the criticism is based on the fact that the directness test does not relate the degree of the defendant's fault to the extent of his or her liability. See Seavey, "Mr. Justice Cardozo and the Law of Torts" (1939) 52 Harv. L. Rev. 372 at 381-91; Wright, "The Law of Torts: 1923-1947" (1948) 26 Can. Bar Rev. 46 at 56-58; and Goodhart, "The Imaginary Necktie and the Rule in *Re Polemis*" (1952) 68 L.Q.R. 515.

(b) THE FORESEEABILITY TEST

THE WAGON MOUND (NO. 1); OVERSEAS
TANKSHIP (U.K.) LTD. v. MORTS DOCK & ENGINEERING CO.
[1961] A.C. 388 (P.C.)

[The appellants, charterers of the Wagon Mound (a ship), carelessly permitted oil to spill into Sydney Harbour while taking on fuel. The oil, which continued to escape for over a day, was carried by the wind and tide under the respondent's wharf. The respondent's employees were using welding equipment. Some molten metal fell, igniting a rag that was floating on some debris. The burning debris either directly ignited the floating oil or ignited it after first setting the oil-soaked pilings of the wharf ablaze. The respondent's wharf and some of its equipment were severely damaged in the ensuing fire.]

VISCOUNT SIMMONDS:— . . . The trial judge also made the all-important finding, which must be set out in his own words:

> The raison d'être of furnace oil is, of course, that it shall burn, but I find the defendant did not know and could not reasonably be expected to have known that it was capable of being set afire when spread on water.

. . .

One other finding must be mentioned. The judge held that apart from the damage by fire the respondents had suffered some damage from the spillage of oil in that it had got upon their slipways and congealed upon them and interfered with their use of the slips. He said:

> The evidence of this damage is slight and no claim for compensation is made in respect of it. Nevertheless it does establish some damage, which may be insignificant in comparison with the magnitude of the damage by fire, but which nevertheless is damage which, beyond question, was a direct result of the escape of the oil.

It is upon this footing that their Lordships will consider the question whether the appellants are liable for the fire damage.

. . .

It is inevitable that first consideration should be given to the case of *Re Polemis*. . . For it was avowedly in deference to that decision and to decisions of the Court of Appeal that followed it that the Full Court was constrained to decide the present case in favour of the respondents. In doing so Manning J., after a full examination of that case, said:

> To say that the problems, doubts and difficulties which I have expressed above render it difficult for me to apply the decision in *In re Polemis* with any degree of confidence to a particular set of facts would be a grave understatement. I can only express the hope that, if not in this case, then in some other case in the near future, the subject will be pronounced upon by the House of Lords or the Privy Council in terms which, even if beyond my capacity fully to understand, will facilitate, for those placed as I am, its everyday application to current problems.

This cri de coeur would in any case be irresistible, but in the years that have passed since its decision *Polemis* has been so much discussed and qualified that it cannot claim, as counsel for the respondents urged for it, the status of a decision of such long standing that it should not be reviewed.

Enough has been said to show that the authority of *Polemis* has been severely shaken though lip-service has from time to time been paid to it. In their Lordships' opinion it should no longer be regarded as good law. It is not probable that many cases will for that reason have a different result, though it is hoped that the law will be thereby simplified, and that in some cases, at least, palpable injustice will be avoided. For it does not seem consonant with current ideas of justice or morality that for an act of negligence, however slight or venial, which results in some trivial foreseeable damage the actor should be liable for all consequences however unforeseeable and however grave, so long as they can be said to be "direct". It is a principle of civil liability, subject only to qualifications which have no present relevance, that a man must be considered to be responsible for the probable consequences of his act. To demand more of him is too harsh a rule, to demand less is to ignore that civilised order requires the observance of a minimum standard of behaviour.

This concept applied to the slowly developing law of negligence has led to a great variety of expressions which can, as it appears to their Lordships, be harmonised with little difficulty with the single exception of the so-called rule in *Polemis*. For, if it is asked why a man should be responsible for the natural or necessary or probable consequences of his act (or any other similar description of them) the answer is that it is not because they are natural or necessary or probable, but because, since they have this quality, it is judged by the standard of the reasonable man that he ought to have foreseen them. Thus it is that over and over again it has happened that in different judgments in the same case, and sometimes in a single judgment, liability for a consequence has been imposed on the ground that it was reasonably foreseeable or, alternatively, on the ground that it was natural or necessary or probable. The two grounds have been treated as coterminous, and so they largely are. But, where they are not, the question arises to which the wrong answer was given in *Polemis*. For, if some limitation must be imposed upon the consequences for which the negligent actor is to be held responsible — and all are agreed that some limitation there must be — why should that test (reasonable foreseeability) be rejected which, since he is judged by what the reasonable man ought to foresee, corresponds with the common conscience of mankind, and a test (the "direct" consequence) be substituted which leads to nowhere but the never-ending and insoluble problems of causation. "The lawyer," said Sir Frederick Pollock, "cannot afford to adventure himself with philosophers in the logical and metaphysical controversies that beset the idea of cause." Yet this is just what he has most unfortunately done and must continue to do if the rule in *Polemis* is to prevail.

. . .

Their Lordships conclude this part of the case with some general observations. They have been concerned primarily to displace the proposition that unforeseeability is irrelevant if damage is "direct." In doing so they have inevitably insisted that the essential factor in determining liability is whether the damage is of such a kind as the reasonable man should have foreseen. This accords with the general view thus stated by Lord Atkin in *M'Alister (or Donoghue) v. Stevenson* [[1932] A.C. 562 (H.L.)]:

The liability for negligence, whether you style it such or treat it as in other systems as a species of "culpa", is no doubt based upon a general public sentiment of moral wrongdoing for which the offender must pay.

It is a departure from this sovereign principle if liability is made to depend solely on the damage being the "direct" or "natural" consequence of the precedent act. Who knows or can be assumed to know all the processes of nature? But if it would be wrong that a man should be held liable for damage unpredictable by a reasonable man because it was "direct" or "natural", equally it would be wrong that he should escape liability, however "indirect" the damage, if he foresaw or could reasonably foresee the intervening events which led to its being done. . . . Thus foreseeability becomes the effective test.

. . .

Their Lordships will humbly advise Her Majesty that this appeal should be allowed, and the respondents' action so far as it related to damage caused by the negligence of the appellants be dismissed with costs, but that the action so far as it related to damage caused by nuisance should be remitted to the Full Court to be dealt with as that court may think fit. The respondents must pay the costs of the appellants of this appeal and in the courts below.

NOTES AND QUESTIONS

1. Explain the test of remoteness adopted by the court in *Wagon Mound (No. 1)*.

2. Why did the court reject the directness test of remoteness? Are the court's criticisms of this test equally applicable to the foreseeability test? Are the arguments in favour of the foreseeability test persuasive?

3. The concept of reasonable foreseeability is used in connection with three elements of the negligence analysis: duty of care, standard of care and remoteness. Is the test precisely the same in each instance? If so, what purpose is served by the repetition? And if not, how does the test differ as between duty, breach and remoteness?

In attempting to answer these questions, it is worth re-examining (from Chapter 10) how the different manifestations of reasonable foreseeability were addressed in the Australian case of *Minister Administering the Environmental Planning and Assessment Act 1979 v. San Sebastien Pty. Ltd.*, [1983] 2 N.S.W.L.R. 268 at 295-96 (C.A.) (emphasis in original):

> [A] recognition has emerged that the foreseeability inquiry at the duty, breach and remoteness stages raises different issues which progressively decline from the general to the particular. The proximity upon which a *Donoghue* type duty rests depends upon proof that the defendant and plaintiff are so placed in relation to each other that it is reasonably foreseeable as a possibility that careless conduct of *any kind* on the part of the former may result in damage of *some kind* to the person or property of the latter . . . . The breach question requires proof that it was reasonably foreseeable as a possibility that *the kind* of carelessness charged against the defendant might cause damage of *some kind* to the plaintiff's person or property. . . The remoteness test is only passed if the plaintiff proves that *the kind* of damage suffered by him was

foreseeable as. . . [an] outcome of the kind of carelessness charged against the defendant.

Recently in *Deloitte & Touche v. Livent Inc. (Receiver of)*, 2017 SCC 63 at paras. 78-79 the majority decision noted:

> We acknowledge that remoteness, so understood, overlaps conceptually with the reasonable foreseeability analysis conducted in the *prima facie* duty of care analysis ... But the two are distinct: the duty analysis is concerned with *the type of injury* that is reasonably foreseeable as flowing from the defendant's conduct, whereas the remoteness analysis is concerned with the reasonable foreseeability of *the actual injury* suffered by the plaintiff . . . Remoteness, at its core, turns on the reasonable foreseeability of the actual injury suffered by the plaintiff.

Does it help to understand the different uses of foreseeability to think in terms of a funnel, wide at the near end and narrow at the far end, through which the plaintiff's claim must pass?

4. The court in *Wagon Mound (No. 1)* proceeded on the basis that the plaintiff's losses were directly caused but not foreseeable. Do you agree with these assumptions?

5. Like *Polemis,* the decision in *Wagon Mound (No. 1)* generated considerable academic debate. See Fleming, "The Passing of Polemis" (1961) 39 Can. Bar Rev. 489; Gibson, "The Wagon Mound in Canadian Courts" (1963) 2 Osgoode Hall L.J. 416; Smith, "Requiem for Polemis" (1965) 2 U.B.C.L. Rev. 159; and Davies, "The Road From Morocco: *Polemis* through *Donoghue* to No-Fault" (1982) 45 Mod. L. Rev. 534. More recently, R. Stevens has argued that the approach in *Polemis*, properly limited to the direct consequences of the particular violation of the plaintiff's right, is a superior approach to that in *Wagon Mound (No. 1)*: Stevens, *Torts and Rights* (2007) at 152-58.

6. It has been argued that neither directness nor foreseeability provides an appropriate test of remoteness. See Green, "Foreseeability in Negligence Law" (1961) 61 Columbia L. Rev. 1401; Smith, "The Mystery of Duty" in Klar, ed., *Studies in Canadian Tort Law* (1977) 1 at 15; and Rizzo, "The Imputation Theory of Proximate Cause: An Economic Framework" (1981) 15 Ga. L. Rev. 1007. See also Chiu, "A Just and Fair Principle of Compensation? Rethinking the Remoteness of Damage Rule in Wagon Mound" (2004) 12 Tort L. Rev. 147.

7. It is often difficult to determine which test or tests of remoteness the Canadian courts are applying. For example in *Richard v. C.N.R.* (1970), 15 D.L.R. (3d) 732 (P.E.I.S.C.) the judge concluded (at 739) that the plaintiff was "the sole, direct, proximate and effective cause" of his own injuries. See also *Jones v. Wabigwan* (1969), 8 D.L.R. (3d) 424 (Ont. C.A.); and *Hunter v. Briere* (1989), 49 C.C.L.T. 93 (Man. Q.B.).

Most courts in Canada have followed *Wagon Mound (No. 1)*. See McLaren, "Negligence and Remoteness — The Aftermath of Wagon Mound" (1967) 32 Sask. L. Rev. 45; and Linden *et al., Canadian Tort Law*, 11th ed. (2018) at 324-25.

REVIEW PROBLEMS

Analyze the following situations and determine whether the plaintiff's damages are too remote under each of the directness and foreseeability tests.

(a) The defendant negligently drove into a fire hydrant, causing a heavy flow of water which forced open the basement window of the plaintiff's building. The basement was flooded under several feet of water and the plaintiff sued for the damage done to his supplies. See *Weiner v. Zoratti* (1970), 11 D.L.R. (3d) 598 (Man. Q.B.); and *Kennedy v. Hughes Drug (1969) Inc.* (1974), 47 D.L.R. (3d) 277 (P.E.I.S.C.).

(b) The defendant negligently lit his house on fire while using a blowtorch to burn off the paint under the eaves. A fireman suffered burns, despite wearing protective clothing, while attempting to put out the fire. See *Ogwo v. Taylor*, [1987] 3 All E.R. 961 (H.L.).

(c) The defendant negligently drove into the plaintiff's fence causing metal fence staples to be scattered onto the plaintiff's pasture. Several months later, several of the plaintiff's cattle died as a result of ingesting the staples. The plaintiff sued the defendant for the loss of his cattle. See *Falkenham v. Zwicker* (1978), 93 D.L.R. (3d) 289 (N.S.S.C.).

(d) The defendant took the plaintiff's car without consent and the plaintiff chased him in another vehicle. As a result of his negligence, the defendant knocked down a hydro pole and ended up in a field. The plaintiff stopped and ran into the field, where he stepped on a downed, live hydro wire. The plaintiff was severely burned and his leg had to be amputated. He sued the defendant for his personal injuries. See *Jones v. Wabigwan* (1969), 8 D.L.R. (3d) 424 (Ont. C.A.).

(e) The defendant negligently polluted the plaintiff's well, which in turn resulted in damage to his crops. The plaintiff claimed damages for developing a new water supply, for the loss of his crop and for the heart attack he suffered as a result of the strain caused by the incident. See *Connery v. Gov't. of Man.* (1970), 15 D.L.R. (3d) 303 (Man. Q.B.).

(f) The defendant ambulance attendants allowed the plaintiff, a paranoid schizophrenic, to sit in the front seat while being transported to hospital for treatment. The plaintiff suddenly grabbed the steering wheel and caused a serious accident. The plaintiff, who was injured in the crash, sued the defendants in negligence for allowing him to sit in the front seat. See *Shackleton v. Knittle* (1999), 46 C.C.L.T. (2d) 300 (Alta. Q.B.).

3. Modifications to the Foreseeability Test

(a) THE KIND OF INJURY

HUGHES v. LORD ADVOCATE
[1963] A.C. 837 (H.L.)

[The defendant's employees left a paraffin lamp and open manhole unattended. An eight-year-old boy knocked the lamp into the manhole and the vaporized paraffin that escaped from the broken lamp caused an explosion. The boy fell into the manhole and was badly burned.]

LORD REID:—My Lords, I have had an opportunity of reading the speech which my noble and learned friend, Lord Guest, is about to deliver. I agree with him that this appeal should be allowed and I shall only add some general observations. I am satisfied that the Post Office workmen were in fault in leaving this open manhole unattended and it is clear that if they had done as they ought to have done this accident would not have happened. It cannot be said that they owed no duty to the appellant. But it has been held that the appellant cannot recover damages.

It was argued that the appellant cannot recover because the damage which he suffered was of a kind which was not foreseeable. That was not the ground of judgment of the First Division or of the Lord Ordinary and the facts proved do not, in my judgment, support that argument. The appellant's injuries were mainly caused by burns, and it cannot be said that injuries from burns was unforeseeable. As a warning to traffic the workmen had set lighted red lamps around the tent which covered the manhole, and if boys did enter the dark tent it was very likely that they would take one of these lamps with them. If the lamp fell and broke it was not at all unlikely that the boy would be burned and the burns might well be serious. No doubt it was not to be expected that the injuries would be as serious as those which the appellant in fact sustained. But a defender is liable, although the damage may be a good deal greater in extent than was foreseeable.

So we have (first) a duty owed by the workmen, (secondly) the fact that if they had done as they ought to have done there would have been no accident, and (thirdly) the fact that the injuries suffered by the appellant, though perhaps different in degree, did not differ in kind from injuries which might have resulted from an accident of a foreseeable nature. The ground on which this case has been decided against the appellant is that the accident was of an unforeseeable type. Of course, the pursuer has to prove that the defender's fault caused the accident, and there could be a case where the intrusion of a new and unexpected factor could be regarded as the cause of the accident rather than the fault of the defender. But that is not this case. The cause of this accident was a known source of danger, the lamp, but it behaved in an unpredictable way.

The explanation of the accident which has been accepted, and which I would not seek to question, is that, when the lamp fell down the manhole and was broken, some paraffin escaped, and enough was vaporised to create an explosive mixture which was detonated by the naked light of the lamp. The experts agree that no one would have expected that to happen: it was so unlikely as to be unforeseeable. The explosion caused the boy to fall into the manhole: whether his injuries were directly caused by the explosion or aggravated by fire which started in the manhole is not at all clear. The essential step in the respondent's argument is that the explosion was the real cause of the injuries and that the explosion was unforeseeable. He can only escape liability if the damage can be regarded as differing in kind from what was foreseeable.

. . .

This accident was caused by a known source of danger, but caused in a way which could not have been foreseen, and, in my judgment, that affords no defence. I would therefore allow the appeal.

LORD GUEST: . . . Concentration has been placed in the courts below on the explosion which, it was said, could not have been foreseen because it was caused in a unique fashion by the paraffin forming into vapour and being ignited by the naked flame of the wick. But this, in my opinion, is to concentrate on what is really a non-essential element in the dangerous situation created by the allurement. The test might better be put thus: Was the igniting of paraffin outside the lamp by the flame a foreseeable consequence of the breach of duty? In the circumstances, there was a combination of potentially dangerous circumstances against which the Post Office had to protect the appellant. If these formed an allurement to children it might have been foreseen that they would play with the lamp, that it might tip over, that it might be broken, and that when broken the paraffin might spill and be ignited by the flame. All these steps in the chain of causation seem to have been accepted by all the judges in the courts below as foreseeable. But because the explosion was the agent which caused the burning and was unforeseeable, therefore the accident, according to them, was not reasonably foreseeable. In my opinion, this reasoning is fallacious. An explosion is only one way in which burning can be caused. Burning can also be caused by the contact between liquid paraffin and a naked flame. In the one case paraffin vapour and in the other case liquid paraffin is ignited by fire. I cannot see that these are two different types of accident. They are both burning accidents and in both cases the injuries would be burning injuries. Upon this view the explosion was an immaterial event in the chain of causation. It was simply one way in which burning might be caused by the potentially dangerous paraffin lamp. . .

[Lords Jenkins, Morris of Borth-Y-Gest and Pearce gave concurring speeches holding that the damage was not too remote.]

NOTES AND QUESTIONS

1. Explain the test of remoteness that was applied in *Hughes*. Do you agree with how the test was applied to the facts?

2. The impact of the test in *Hughes* depends on how broadly or narrowly one characterizes the kind of injury that the plaintiff has suffered. In *Doughty v. Turner Mfg. Co.*, [1964] 1 Q.B. 518 (C.A.) an employee in a metal treatment plant was injured when an asbestos cover slid into the treatment vat. The cover reacted chemically with the contents of the vat, causing an eruption of molten liquid that burned the employee. The covers had been used for 20 years but this chemical reaction had never been observed. The man sued his employer, arguing that the injury was foreseeable. The court held for the defendant because it characterized the injury as one caused by a chemical reaction that was not foreseeable. Do you agree? Would it have made a difference if the injury had been characterized as a burn? For a criticism of *Doughty* see Dworkin, "Risk and Remoteness — Causation Worse Confounded?" (1964) Mod. L. Rev. 344. See also Linden *et al.*, *Canadian Tort Law*, 11th ed. (2018) at 318-19.

3. The characterization of the plaintiff's injury played a critical role in *Tremain v. Pike*, [1969] 3 All E.R. 1303. The defendant carelessly failed to control the rat population on his farm. The plaintiff, a farmhand on the farm, contracted Weil's disease after coming into contact with rat urine. Liability was denied. The court held that while it was reasonably foreseeable that the defendant's breach might lead to injury through, say, rat *bites*, it was not reasonably foreseeable that rat *urine* would prove problematic. Do you agree with that assessment? If you were inclined to impose liability, could you convincingly set out a description of the relevant risk so as to facilitate recovery?

4. The characterization of the injury also played a critical role in *Jolley v. Sutton London B.C.*, [1998] 1 W.L.R. 1546 (C.A.), rev'd [2000] 1 W.L.R. 1082 (H.L.). A dangerously decrepit boat was located on property under the defendant's authority. The defendant made a decision to remove the boat for safety reasons, but because of administrative dithering failed to perform the task. The plaintiff and his friend, both aged 14, found the boat. They decided to repair it and sail "to Cornwall because that was where the pirates were to be found!" In order to fix the hull, they hoisted the boat up on a car jack. The jack gave way, the boat fell and the plaintiff was rendered paraplegic. The trial judge imposed liability, subject to a reduction of 25% for contributory negligence.

The Court of Appeal reversed that decision on the basis of remoteness. Taking a narrow view of both *Wagon Mound (No. 1)* and *Hughes*, it said that the accident was "of a different type and kind from anything which the council could have reasonably foreseen." According to the Court of Appeal, while it was reasonably foreseeable that children might be hurt while "playing" on the abandoned boat, it was not reasonably foreseeable that they would be hurt while engaged in the "adult activity" of trying to repair it. See O'Sullivan, "Remoteness of Damage in Negligence: A Rotten Structure Collapses" [1999] C.L.J. 12.

On further appeal to the House of Lords, the trial judgment was restored. Lord Steyn characterized the relevant risk as "the collapse of the propped up boat." He also stressed that when considering the foreseeability of risk to children, it is necessary to bear in mind that "play can take the form of mimicking adult behaviour." Likewise, Lord Hoffmann said that it was reasonably foreseeable that children would "meddle with the boat at some risk of physical injury." By phrasing the relevant risk more broadly, the House of Lords imposed liability where the Court of Appeal had not. See Williams, "Remoteness: Some Unexpected Mischief" (2001) 117 L.Q.R. 30.

Do you agree with the Court of Appeal or the House of Lords? Was the plaintiff's injury reasonably foreseeable? If so, are there any policy considerations that would justify denying liability, and if so, how would these change the analysis?

5. In *Lauritzan v. Barstead* (1965), 53 D.L.R. (2d) 267 (Alta. S.C.) the defendant's negligence resulted in his car becoming stuck in the snow during a bad storm on a relatively unused portion of a rural highway. The plaintiff and defendant were forced by the wind and cold to stay in the vehicle for 36 hours. When the weather broke, the plaintiff went for help. The plaintiff was eventually found by a farmer but, as a result of frostbite, parts of both his feet had to be amputated. The plaintiff's wife of 26 years apparently left him because she did not want to live with a disabled man. While the court held that the plaintiff's physical injuries were not too remote, it held that his claim for loss of *consortium* was not a foreseeable kind of injury and denied this claim. Do you agree with the court's analysis? See also *Antell v. Simons*, [1976] 6 W.W.R. 202 (B.C.S.C.).

6. In *Trevison v. Springman*, [1996] 4 W.W.R. 760 (B.C.S.C.) the defendants had been entrusted with the plaintiff's house key. The defendants' son stole the house key and set fire to the plaintiff's house in order to cover up a series of thefts. The court held that losses due to the fire were too remote from the defendants' negligent failure to supervise and control their frequently delinquent son. The defendants were held liable for only the plaintiff's losses due to theft. What argument would you make on behalf of the plaintiff to recover for the arson?

7. For other judicial discussions of the principle in *Hughes* see *Williams v. St. John (City)* (1985), 34 C.C.L.T. 299 (N.B.C.A.); *C.N.R. Co. v. Sask. Wheat Pool*, [1986] 4 W.W.R. 371 (Sask. Q.B.); *Smith v. Littlewoods Organisation Ltd.*, [1987] 1 All E.R. 710 (H.L.); *Belzile v. Dumais* (1986), 69 N.B.R. (2d) 142 (Q.B.); and *Jebson v. Ministry of Defence*, [2000] 1 W.L.R. 2055 (C.A.).

(b) THE THIN-SKULLED PLAINTIFF RULE

SMITH v. LEECH BRAIN & CO.
[1962] 2 Q.B. 405

[The plaintiff's husband was a galvanizer employed by the defendants. The articles to be galvanized were lowered into a tank containing molten metallic zinc and flux. The method used depended on the size of the article. All articles were first dipped in hydrochloric acid and the larger articles were then lowered into the tank, using an overhead crane, by an operator behind a sheet of corrugated iron. On August 15, 1950, the plaintiff's husband was operating the overhead crane, using the corrugated iron sheet supplied, when a piece of molten metal or flux struck and burned his lower lip. The burn was treated at the time and he thought nothing of it. Some time later, the spot where he had been burned began to ulcerate and get larger. His general practitioner sent him to the hospital, where he was diagnosed with cancer. Treatment destroyed the primary growth but the cancer spread. Despite several operations, he died of cancer on October 14, 1953.

Lord Parker C.J. found that the defendants were negligent, that there had been no contributory negligence and that the burn promoted the cancer in tissues which already had a pre-malignant condition as a result of the employee's exposure to tar or tar vapours from 1926 to 1935.]

LORD PARKER, C.J.: I am confronted with the recent decision of the Privy Council in . . . *The Wagon Mound*. But for *The Wagon Mound*, it seems to me perfectly clear that, assuming negligence proved, assuming that the burn caused in whole or in part the cancer and the death, this plaintiff would be entitled to recover.

. . .

For my part, I am quite satisfied that the Judicial Committee in *The Wagon Mound* did not have what I may call, loosely, the "thin skull" cases in mind. It has always been the law of this country that a tortfeasor takes his victim as he finds him. It is unnecessary to do more than refer to the short passage in the decision of Kennedy, J., in *Dulieu v. White & Sons*, [[1901] 2 K.B. 669] where he said:

> If a man is negligently run over or otherwise negligently injured in his body, it is no answer to the sufferer's claim for damages that he would have suffered less injury, or no injury at all, if he had not an unusually thin skull or an unusually weak heart.

. . . But quite apart from those . . . references, as is well known, the work of the courts for years and years has gone on on that basis. There is not a day that goes by where some trial judge does not adopt that principle, that the tortfeasor takes his victim as he finds him. If the Judicial Committee had any intention of making an inroad into that doctrine, I am quite satisfied that they would have said so.

. . .

In those circumstances, it seems to me that this is plainly a case which comes within the old principle. The test is not whether these defendants could reasonably have foreseen that a burn would cause cancer and that Mr. Smith would die. The question is whether these defendants could reasonably foresee the type of injury which he suffered, namely, the burn. What, in the particular case, is the amount of damage which he suffers as a result of that burn, depends on the characteristics and constitution of the victim. Accordingly, I find that the damages which the plaintiff claims are damages for which these defendants are liable.

MARCONATO v. FRANKLIN
[1974] 6 W.W.R. 676 (B.C.S.C.)

[The female plaintiff suffered relatively minor physical injuries in a car accident caused by the defendant's negligence. Following the accident, she developed symptoms of pain and stiffness for which there was no physical explanation. She became depressed, hostile and anxious. Although the psychiatric evidence indicated that she had paranoid tendencies before the accident, she had been "a good homemaker." The accident triggered a major personality change.]

AIKINS J.: . . . I turn to the question of causation. One would not ordinarily anticipate, using reasonable foresight, that a moderate cervical strain with soft tissue damage would give rise to the consequences which followed for Mrs. Marconato. These arose, however, because of her pre-existing personality traits. She had a peculiar susceptibility or vulnerability to suffer much greater consequences from a moderate physical injury than the average person. The consequences for Mrs. Marconato could no more be foreseen than it could be foreseen by a tortfeasor that his victim was thin-skulled and that a minor blow to the head would cause a very serious injury. It is plain enough that the defendant could foresee the probability of physical injury. It is implicit, however, in the principle that a wrongdoer takes his victim as he finds him, that he takes his victim with all the victim's peculiar susceptibilities and vulnerabilities. The consequences of Mrs. Marconato's injuries were unusual but arose involuntarily. Granted her type of personality they arose as night follows day because of the injury and the circumstances in which she found herself because of the injury.

As to the argument that the damage suffered is too remote because not reasonably foreseeable, I refer first to an English case, *Smith v. Leech Brain & Co. Ltd.* . . . In this case the plaintiff widow claimed damages for the death of her husband under the Fatal Accidents Acts. The defendant was the deceased's employer. The deceased suffered a burn on his lip; as a result cancer developed at that site, from which the injured man died some three years later. Remoteness on the ground of lack of foreseeability was argued. I cite two passages from the judgment of Lord Parker C.J. The first is at p. 414:

> For my part, I am quite satisfied that the Judicial Committee in *Overseas Tankship (U.K.) v. Morts Dock & Engineering Co. (The Wagon Mound)* . . . did not have what I may call, loosely, the thin skull cases in mind. It has always been the law of this country that a tortfeasor takes his victim as he finds him.

. . .

The second passage is at p. 415:

The test is not whether these employers could reasonably have foreseen that a burn would cause cancer and that he would die. The question is whether these employers could reasonably foresee the type of injury he suffered, namely, the burn. What, in the particular case, is the amount of damage which he suffers as a result of that burn, depends upon the characteristics and constitution of the victim.

I also refer to the judgment of McIntyre J. (now J.A.) in *Elloway v. Boomars* (1968), 69 D.L.R. (2d) 605 (B.C.). In *Elloway* the plaintiff developed schizophrenia following injury in a motor accident. At p. 606, McIntyre J. said:

> . . . As I understand the law . . . a schizophrenic condition caused by the wrongful conduct of a defendant may be a basis of compensation as may be a schizophrenia caused by the aggravation of a latent condition but always provided that it can be shown that the cause of the condition was the accident.

At p. 607 McIntyre J. said:

> I find the plaintiff's present condition was caused by the accident. He suffered from a pre-existing condition which predisposed him to a schizophrenic illness and the accident, operating upon this predisposition, brought about the full schizophrenic illness and it is therefore a proper basis for compensation.

What I have cited might well be transposed in the present case to go as follows: Mrs. Marconato was predisposed by her personality to suffer the consequences which she did suffer as a result of the modest physical injury caused by the accident and it was that predisposition which brought on the unusual consequences of the injury. The defendant must pay damages for all the consequences of her negligence.

NOTES AND QUESTIONS

1. Explain what is meant by the thin-skulled plaintiff rule. What is the relationship between the foreseeability test of remoteness and the thin-skulled plaintiff rule? See Stiggelbout, "The Scope and Rationale of the Principle that the Defendant 'Takes His Victim as he Finds Him'" (2009) 17 Tort L. Rev. 140.

The thin-skull rule is captured by the phrase "in for a buck, in for a bundle." If it was not reasonably foreseeable that the defendant's carelessness would cause any injury of a particular type, then the plaintiff cannot recover even if, because of a peculiar vulnerability, he or she actually suffered a great deal. However, if it was reasonably foreseeable that the defendant's carelessness would cause *some* injury of a particular type, then the plaintiff can recover in full even if, because of a special vulnerability, he or she suffered to a greater extent than could have been reasonably foreseen.

2. What would have been the result in *Smith* if the deceased had not had a pre-existing susceptibility to cancer but nevertheless developed cancer at the site of the burn and died of the disease? What would have been the result if the burn had increased the deceased's risk of getting cancer and he developed cancer at the site of the burn and died? See *Pesonen v. Melnyk* (1993), 17 C.C.L.T. (2d) 66 (B.C.C.A.); *Hunter v. Manning*, [1993] 5 W.W.R. 738 (Sask. Q.B.); *Hooiveld v. Van Biert*, [1994] 4 W.W.R. 143 (B.C.C.A.); and *Buteikis v. Adams*, [1994] 7 W.W.R. 119 (B.C.S.C.).

3. Sarah negligently closes a door on Andrew's hand, permanently disabling it. Unknown to Sarah, Andrew is a baseball infielder with the Ithaca Rangers who has lost future earnings of $25 million as a result of the injury. Are these losses too remote?

4. According to *Marconato*, what application does the thin-skulled plaintiff rule have to a plaintiff with an "eggshell" personality? Is the damage award in *Marconato* compatible with the argument that there should be some reasonable relationship between the degree of the defendant's fault and the extent of his or her liability? See *Price v. Garcha* (1988), 44 C.C.L.T. 1 (B.C.S.C.), aff'd (1989), 2 C.C.L.T. (2d) 265 (B.C.C.A.); *Graham v. Rourke* (1988), 43 C.C.L.T. 119 (Ont. H.C.), varied on damages (1990), 75 O.R. (2d) 622 (C.A.); and *Dushynski v. Rumsey* (2001), 94 Alta. L.R. (3d) 26 (Q.B.), varied (2003), 16 Alta. L.R. (4th) 237 (C.A.).

5. In *Swami v. Lo*, [1980] 1 W.W.R. 379 (B.C.S.C.) the plaintiff's husband committed suicide 14 months after he had been seriously injured in a car accident caused by the defendant's carelessness. The constant pain forced the husband to give up work and he began to drink heavily. Although the deceased became very depressed, there was no allegation that he was either criminally or civilly insane. The judge concluded that *Smith* did not apply to the facts of the case and dismissed the plaintiff's claim as too remote. Given the serious physical injuries that the husband suffered in the car accident, was it foreseeable that he would suffer emotional injuries of some kind as a result? If such injuries were foreseeable, should damages for the husband's suicide have been recoverable under the kind-of-injury test in *Hughes*? See also *Wright Estate v. Davidson*, [1992] 3 W.W.R. 611 (B.C.C.A.) where the court held that the deceased's suicide following a minor car accident was too remote. Were *Swami* and *Wright Estate* rightly decided?

See *Gray v. Cotic* (1983), 26 C.C.L.T. 163 (S.C.C.) where the plaintiff recovered damages for her husband's suicide following a car accident because he had a pre-existing mental health problem. See also *Costello v. Blakeson*, [1993] 2 W.W.R. 562 (B.C.S.C.); *Hauk Estate v. Hudson* (1997), 50 C.C.L.I. (2d) 159 (Ont. Gen. Div.); and *Corr v. IBC Vehicles Ltd.*, [2008] 1 A.C. 884 (H.L.)

6. As in *Marconato* and *Swami*, a plaintiff may raise the thin-skulled plaintiff rule to establish that an emotional harm stemming from a physical injury is not too remote to be recoverable. See for example *Degennaro v. Oakville Trafalgar Memorial Hospital* (2009), 67 C.C.L.T. (3d) 294 (Ont. S.C.J.). This issue frequently arises in sexual battery cases. See for example *K.(W.) v. Pornbacher* (1997), 34 C.C.L.T. (2d) 174 (B.C.S.C.); *D.(P.A.) v. H.(A.E.)* (1998), [1999] 2 W.W.R. 139 (B.C.S.C.); and *R.D. v. G.S.*, 2011 BCSC 1118. These cases must be distinguished from claims for the negligent infliction of psychiatric harm. As discussed in Chapter 12, these latter claims are not consequent on any physical injury to the plaintiff. Such claims are discussed in more detail in the next section of this chapter.

7. In *Kavanagh v. Akhtar* (1998), 45 N.S.W.L.R. 588 (C.A.) the plaintiff was injured when a heavy box fell on her at the defendant's store. As a result of physical injuries to her left shoulder and arm she was unable to care for her very long hair. Months after the accident she had her hair cut short. Her husband, a devout Muslim, reacted very badly to her decision to cut her hair short, which he perceived "as defiance of his scripturally-based right of control over his wife as well as her defiance of religious injunctions about women cutting their hair without permission of their

husband." He withdrew immediately from her and ultimately the haircut led to the breakdown of the marriage. She sued the defendant for psychiatric injury suffered as a result. Is this injury too remote? What arguments would you make for each party? For an analysis of this and related cases see Black, "Cultural Thin Skulls" (2010) 60 U.N.B.L.J. 186.

8. The thin-skull rule must be distinguished from the "crumbling skull" rule that Major J. discussed in the extract of *Athey v. Leonati* (1996), 140 D.L.R. (4th) 235 (S.C.C.) in the previous chapter.

Although a plaintiff with a thin skull is unusually vulnerable to harm, he or she was not doomed at the outset. By leading a careful life, he or she might have been able to avoid injury. The legal question therefore is whether the defendant should be held responsible for carelessly cracking a skull that, while weak, might otherwise have survived.

The position of a plaintiff with a crumbling skull is significantly different. His or her skull was not only thin, but doomed to damage. The legal question therefore is whether the defendant should be held responsible for hastening the onset of an injury that eventually would have occurred in any event. The answer is that damages are available, but only to the extent that the defendant worsened the plaintiff's condition. If, for instance, the breach caused the plaintiff's skull to crumble two years earlier than expected, then the defendant's liability is limited to that period. On the difference between a thin skull and a crumbling skull see *Lam v. Sorochan Estate* (2000), 259 A.R. 270 (Q.B.); *T.W.N.A. v. Clarke* (2003), 20 C.C.L.T. (3d) 165 (B.C.C.A.); *Zacharias v. Leys* (2005), 36 C.C.L.T. (3d) 93 (B.C.C.A.); *Blackwater v. Plint*, [2005] 3 S.C.R. 3; and *Schnurr v. Insurance Corp. of British Columbia*, 2015 BCSC 1630. For a discussion of the key cases on the crumbling skull rule see *Lyne v. McClarty* (2003), 170 Man. R. (2d) 161 (C.A.).

9. The thin-skull rule can also be contrasted with the "thin wallet" rule. The latter asks whether the defendant should be held liable for damages that were exacerbated by the fact that the plaintiff had limited financial resources and therefore was unusually vulnerable to financial harm.

This question was traditionally answered in the negative. In *Dredger Liesbosch v. Steamship Edison*, [1933] A.C. 449 (H.L.) the plaintiff's ship was sunk and lost due to the defendant's carelessness. The plaintiff was obviously entitled to damages representing the value of its ship. However, it also claimed additional damages. Before the accident, the plaintiff had contractually promised to use the ship to provide certain services to a third party. As a result of the accident, the ship was not available for this purpose. Furthermore, because of the plaintiff's generally strained financial situation, it was unable to buy a replacement ship immediately. Consequently, it was required to rent another ship for the purpose of fulfilling the contractual obligation. The plaintiff claimed that it was entitled to damages representing the additional cost that it incurred as a result of being required to rent the other ship. The House of Lords rejected that claim on the ground that the defendant was not responsible for the plaintiff's impecuniosity. This decision established the proposition that a plaintiff cannot claim additional damages that flow from the fact that it had a "thin wallet" and therefore was unusually susceptible to economic harm.

The modern approach rejects any such blanket rule in favour of a test of reasonable foreseeability. *Alcoa Minerals of Jamaica v. Broderick*, [2000] 3 W.L.R. 23

(P.C.) is illustrative. The defendant committed the tort of nuisance by operating a smelting plant in Jamaica that emitted corrosive materials. Those materials caused substantial damage to the roof of the plaintiff's house. The plaintiff commenced an action in 1989, at which time the cost of repairing the roof was $211,000. In the following years, the Jamaican economy suffered through a recession and inflation increased markedly. By 1994, when the matter was decided at trial, the cost of repairing the plaintiff's roof was $938,000. The trial judge awarded damages in that amount. The defendant eventually appealed to the Privy Council on the ground that the plaintiff was limited, by the decision in *Liesbosch*, to the initial value of its loss. The defendant argued that the plaintiff should have repaired the roof immediately and that the increased cost of repair was due to the plaintiff's own impecuniosity in being unable to afford immediate repairs.

The Privy Council found in favour of the plaintiff and affirmed the trial judge's decision to award damages of $938,000. The court said that there is no absolute rule that requires damages to be assessed at the date of the initial damage. It also said that there is no absolute rule to the effect that the plaintiff cannot recover the full value of a loss that was exacerbated by its own impecuniosity. The availability of damages in such circumstances is determined by an application of the usual test of reasonable foreseeability. On the facts of the case, it was reasonably foreseeable that a person in the plaintiff's position might not be able to afford to immediately repair the damage caused by the defendant's nuisance and that economic factors would render later repairs more costly. See also *Amar Cloth House Ltd. v. LA Van & Co.* (1997), 35 C.C.L.T. (2d) 99 (B.C.S.C.); and *Lagden v. O'Connor*, [2004] 1 All E.R. 277 (H.L.) in which the House of Lords expressly overruled *Liesbosch*.

10. If the plaintiff suffers a pure economic loss — an economic loss that is not consequent on injury to the plaintiff's person or property — then special duty principles are applied. Those principles were discussed at length in Chapter 14. However, if the plaintiff's economic loss results from injuries to his person or property, the issue is dealt with under the remoteness of damages principles.

A recent example is *Conarken Group Ltd. v. Network Rail Infrastructure Ltd.*, [2011] EWCA Civ 644. This test case considered the liability of motorists who negligently crashed into Network Rail's property (tracks, bridges and overhead cables). Network Rail was contractually obliged to compensate other corporations operating passenger rail services for service interruptions caused by damaged infrastructure. At issue was whether Network Rail could recover those payments, which could be considerable, from the negligent motorists. This was not a case of pure economic loss, but rather economic loss consequential on property damage. The Court of Appeal considered this an issue of remoteness and held that these expenses were a foreseeable type of harm when a commercial asset is negligently damaged. See O'Sullivan, "Negligence, Remoteness and Economic Loss — Staying on Track" [2011] C.L.J. 496. Additional issues relating to the recovery of specific losses were subsequently considered in *Network Rail Infrastructure Ltd. v. Handy*, [2015] EWHC 1175.

11. Remoteness is also an important principle of contract law: damages that are too remote from the breach of contract are not recoverable. There is a considerable jurisprudence, flowing from *Hadley v. Baxendale* (1854), 9 E. 341, of how the remoteness principle operates in contract cases. In general the contractual test is somewhat narrower, and so harder for the plaintiff to meet, than the tort test.

In cases in which the plaintiff claims in both tort and contract, should both areas of law be consistent about what is and is not too remote, or is it acceptable for each to reach its own independent conclusion? See the analysis in *Wellesley Partners LLP v. Withers LLP*, [2015] EWCA Civ 1146; *Agouman v. Leigh Day*, [2016] EWHC 1324 at para. 121; and Taylor, "Whither Remoteness? *Wellesley Partners LLP v Withers LLP*" (2016) 79 M.L.R. 678. Concurrent liability in tort and contract is discussed in Chapter 13.

(c) THE POSSIBILITY OF INJURY

THE WAGON MOUND (NO. 2);
OVERSEAS TANKSHIP (U.K.) LTD. v. MILLER STEAMSHIP CO. PTY.
[1967] 1 A.C. 617 (P.C.)

[This case arose from the same incident as the *Wagon Mound (No. 1)*, extracted earlier in this chapter. The plaintiffs in this action, however, were the owners of two boats that were damaged in the harbour fire. At trial the plaintiffs succeeded in nuisance. However, their action in negligence was dismissed because their damages were not reasonably foreseeable and thus too remote to be recoverable. The defendant appealed and the plaintiffs cross-appealed.]

LORD REID: . . . It is now necessary to turn to the respondents' submission that the trial judge was wrong in holding that damage from fire was not reasonably foreseeable. In *Wagon Mound (No. 1)* the finding on which the Board proceeded was that of the trial judge:

> . . . [the appellants] did not know and could not reasonably be expected to have known that [the oil] was capable of being set afire when spread on water.

In the present case the evidence led was substantially different from the evidence led in *Wagon Mound (No. 1)* and the findings of Walsh J., are significantly different. That is not due to there having been any failure by the plaintiffs in *Wagon Mound (No. 1)* in preparing and presenting their case. The plaintiffs there were no doubt embarrassed by a difficulty which does not affect the present plaintiffs. The outbreak of the fire was consequent on the act of the manager of the plaintiffs in *Wagon Mound (No. 1)* in resuming oxy-acetylene welding and cutting while the wharf was surrounded by this oil. So if the plaintiffs in the former case had set out to prove that it was foreseeable by the engineers of the Wagon Mound that this oil could be set alight, they might have had difficulty in parrying the reply that then this must also have been foreseeable by their manager. Then there would have been contributory negligence and at that time contributory negligence was a complete defence in New South Wales.

The crucial finding of Walsh, J., in this case is in finding (v): that the damage was "not reasonably foreseeable by those for whose acts the defendant would be responsible." That is not a primary finding of fact but an inference from the other findings, and it is clear from the learned judge's judgment that in drawing this inference he was to a large extent influenced by his view of the law. The vital parts of the findings of fact which have already been set out in full are (i) that the officers of the Wagon Mound "would regard furnace oil as very difficult to ignite on water" — not that they would regard this as impossible, (ii) that their experience would probably have been "that this had very rarely happened" — not that they would never have heard of a case where it had happened, and (iii) that they would have regarded it as a "possibility, but one which could become an actuality only in very exceptional circumstances" — not, as in *Wagon Mound (No. 1)*, that they could not reasonably be expected to have known that this oil was capable of being set afire when spread on water. The question which must now be determined is whether these differences between the findings in the two cases do or do not lead to different results in law.

In *Wagon Mound (No. 1)* the Board were not concerned with degrees of foreseeability because the finding was that the fire was not foreseeable at all. So Viscount Simonds had no cause to amplify the statement that the "essential factor in determining liability is whether the damage is of such a kind as the reasonable man should have foreseen." Here the findings show, however, that some risk of fire would have been present to the mind of a reasonable man in the shoes of the ship's chief engineer. So the first question must be what is the precise meaning to be attached in this context to the words "foreseeable" and "reasonably foreseeable".

Before *Bolton v. Stone* [[1951] 1 All E.R. 1078], the cases had fallen into two classes: (i) those where, before the event, the risk of its happening would have been regarded as unreal either because the event would have been thought to be physically impossible or because the possibility of its happening would have been regarded as so fantastic or far-fetched that no reasonable man would have paid any attention to it — "a mere possibility which would never occur to the mind of a reasonable man" (per Lord Dunedin in *Fardon v. Harcourt-Rivington* [[1932] All E.R. Rep. 81]) — or (ii) those where there was a real and substantial risk or chance that something like the event which happens might occur and then the reasonable man would have taken the steps necessary to eliminate the risk.

Bolton v. Stone posed a new problem. There a member of a visiting team drove a cricket ball out of the ground on to an unfrequented adjacent public road and it struck and severely injured a lady who happened to be standing in the road. That it might happen that a ball would be driven on to this road could not have been said to be a fantastic or far-fetched possibility: according to the evidence it had happened about six times in twenty-eight years. Moreover it could not have been said to be a far-fetched or fantastic possibility that such a ball would strike someone in the road: people did pass along the road from time to time. So it could not have been said that, on any ordinary meaning of the words, the fact that a ball might strike a person in the road was not foreseeable or reasonably foreseeable. It was plainly foreseeable; but the chance of its happening in the foreseeable future was infinitesimal. A mathematician given the data could have worked out that it was only likely to happen once in so many thousand years. The House of Lords held that the risk was so small that in the circumstances a reasonable man would have been justified in disregarding it and taking no steps to eliminate it.

It does not follow that, no matter what the circumstances may be, it is justifiable to neglect a risk of such a small magnitude. A reasonable man would only neglect such a risk if he had some valid reason for doing so: e.g., that it would involve considerable expense to eliminate the risk. He would weigh the risk against the difficulty of eliminating it. If the activity which caused the injury to Miss Stone had been an unlawful activity there can be little doubt but that *Bolton v. Stone* would have been decided differently. In their Lordships' judgment *Bolton v. Stone* did not alter the general principle that a person must be regarded as negligent if he does not take steps to eliminate a risk which he knows or ought to know is a real risk and not a mere possibility which would never influence the mind of a reasonable man. What that decision did was to recognise and give effect to the qualification that it is justifiable not to take steps to eliminate a real risk if it is small and if the circumstances are such that a reasonable man, careful of the safety of his neighbour, would think it right to neglect it.

In the present case there was no justification whatever for discharging the oil into Sydney Harbour. Not only was it an offence to do so, but also it involved considerable loss financially. If the ship's engineer had thought about the matter there could have been no question of balancing the advantages and disadvantages. From every point of view it was both his duty and his interest to stop the discharge immediately.

It follows that in their Lordships' view the only question is whether a reasonable man having the knowledge and experience to be expected of the chief engineer of the Wagon Mound would have known that there was a real risk of the oil on the water catching fire in some way: if it did, serious damage to ships or other property was not only foreseeable but very likely. Their Lordships do not dissent from the view of the trial judge that the possibilities of damage "must be significant enough in a practical sense to require a reasonable man to guard against them", but they think that he may have misdirected himself in saying

> there does seem to be a real practical difficulty, assuming that some risk of fire damage was foreseeable, but not a high one, in making a factual judgment as to whether this risk was sufficient to attract liability if damage should occur.

In this difficult chapter of the law decisions are not infrequently taken to apply to circumstances far removed from the facts which give rise to them, and it would seem that here too much reliance has been placed on some observations in *Bolton v. Stone* and similar observations in other cases.

In their Lordships' view a properly qualified and alert chief engineer would have realised there was a real risk here, and they do not understand Walsh, J., to deny that; but he appears to have held that, if a real risk can properly be described as remote, it must then be held to be not reasonably foreseeable. That is a possible interpretation of some of the authorities; but this is still an open question and on principle their Lordships cannot accept this view. If a real risk is one which would occur to the mind of a reasonable man in the position of the defendant's servant and which he would not brush aside as far-fetched, and if the criterion is to be what that reasonable man would have done in the circumstances, then surely he would not neglect such a risk if action to eliminate it presented no difficulty, involved no disadvantage and required no expense.

In the present case the evidence shows that the discharge of so much oil on to the water must have taken a considerable time, and a vigilant ship's engineer would have noticed the discharge at an early stage. The findings show that he ought to have known that it is possible to ignite this kind of oil on water, and that the ship's engineer probably ought to have known that this had in fact happened before. The most that can be said to justify inaction is that he would have known that this could only happen in very exceptional circumstances; but that does not mean that a reasonable man would dismiss such risk from his mind and do nothing when it was so easy to prevent it. If it is clear that the reasonable man would have realised or foreseen and prevented the risk, then it must follow that the appellants are liable in damages. The learned judge found this a difficult case: he said that this matter is "one on which different minds would come to different conclusions." Taking a rather different view of the law from that of the learned judge, their Lordships must hold that the respondents are entitled to succeed on this issue.

. . .

NOTES AND QUESTIONS

1. Why was the plaintiff in *Wagon Mound (No. 2)* able to provide evidence that it was foreseeable that the furnace oil would burn when the court in *Wagon Mound (No. 1)* reached the opposite conclusion? How did the court define foreseeability and what did it mean by the term "real risk"? What did the court mean by the term "justified"? Does *Wagon Mound (No. 2)* apply only to those cases in which the defendant's conduct is without social value? If not, can you distinguish between Lord Reid's test of remoteness and the test used to determine whether the standard of care has been breached?

2. What impact does the rule in *Wagon Mound (No. 2)* have on the scope of recovery in negligence? H. Glasbeek contends that *Wagon Mound (No. 2)* has, for "all practical purposes," restored the *Re Polemis* test, "for surely all direct consequences must be regarded as possible if the ordinary man is not required to foresee how they are to eventuate." J. Smith has written that *Wagon Mound (No. 2)* broadened the test of foreseeability of damages from one based upon probability of damages to one based upon a possibility of damages. See Glasbeek, "Wagon Mound II — Re Polemis Revived: Nuisance Revised" (1967) 6 U.W.O.L. Rev. 192 at 200; and Smith, "The Limits of Tort Liability in Canada: Remoteness, Foreseeability and Proximate Cause" in Linden, ed., *Studies in Canadian Tort Law* (1968) 102. Do you agree with Glasbeek's or Smith's assessment of *Wagon Mound (No. 2)*?

ASSINIBOINE SOUTH SCHOOL DIVISION, NO. 3 v. GREATER WINNIPEG GAS CO.
(1971), 21 D.L.R. (3d) 608 (Man. C.A.), aff'd (1973), 40 D.L.R. (3d) 480 (S.C.C.)

DICKSON J.A.:—The facts giving rise to this case lie in a compact compass and are not in dispute. At approximately 12:00 noon, 25th February 1968 a Ski Daddler auto toboggan owned by Ephraim Hoffer and operated by his son Michael Hoffer ran out of control at a speed of approximately 30 m.p.h., over a snowbank and across a parking lot, for some 100 yards, and struck a gas-riser pipe servicing Laidlaw School in Tuxedo, Manitoba. The pipe was fractured below the pressure regulator and shut-off valve, with the result that gas under high pressure escaped and, being lighter than air, rose and entered the boiler room of the school through a fresh-air inlet duct situate in the wall of the school immediately above the gas-riser pipe and beneath a wide overhanging eave. In the boiler room the gas reached an explosive mixture and was ignited by the naked flame of the pilot light, or the flames of the gas furnace. An explosion and fire occurred, causing extensive damage to the school. Deniset J. . . . allowed damages of $50,739.90 to the School Division of Assiniboine South No. 3, owners of the school, against Ephraim Hoffer and Michael Hoffer as well as against the Greater Winnipeg Gas Company. The Gas Company was responsible for the installation of the gas-riser pipe. The damages were apportioned 50 per cent to

Michael Hoffer and Ephraim Hoffer and 50 per cent to the Gas Company. All defendants have appealed.

. . .

[Dickson J.A. explained that Ephraim Hoffer had specially altered the machine to allow his 11-year-old son to start it. These changes required that the machine be started in high gear. The father advised his son to put up the kickstand when starting the machine. The son forgot to do this and the machine got away from him. Dickson J.A. held that it was probable that a young boy would forget to use the kickstand and "almost inevitable that in such event the machine would get out of control and run away." Dickson J.A. concluded that both the father and son had breached the standard of care.]

The second question is whether the damage done by them was reasonably foreseeable and therefore recoverable within the principles stated in [*Wagon Mound (No. 1)*]. This question is not without difficulty. Denning L.J. said in *King v. Phillips*, [1953] 1 Q.B. 429, [1953] 1 All E.R. 617 at 623: "there can be no doubt since *Hay (or Bourhill) v. Young*, [1942] 2 All E.R. 396, that the test of *liability for shock* is foreseeability of *injury by shock*". (The italics are mine.) In *The Wagon Mound (No. 1)* Viscount Simonds substituted the word "fire" for "shock" and indorsed this statement of the law. Liability depends upon whether the damage is of such a kind as a reasonable man should have foreseen.

It might well be argued that damage by impact is to be expected when a machine runs amok but not damage by fire and explosion. Their Lordships in *The Wagon Mound (No. 1)* were clearly of the opinion that the Court of Appeal erred in *Re Polemis and Furness, Withy & Co. Ltd.* . . ., in allowing recovery in respect of damage from fire and explosion which followed the impact of a plank dropped into the hold of a ship.

In *The Wagon Mound (No. 1)* damage to plaintiffs' wharf by oil fouling was foreseeable when defendants carelessly allowed a large quantity of bunkering oil to spill into Morts Bay but damage by fire was unforeseeable and recovery denied. Vital to the decision was the finding of fact that defendants did not know, and could not reasonably have been expected to know, that furnace oil was capable of being set afire when spread on water.

The force of *The Wagon Mound (No. 1)* was somewhat dissipated by *Hughes v. Lord Advocate*, [1963] 1 All E.R. 705, per Lord Jenkins at p. 710:

> It is true that the duty of care expected in cases of this sort is confined to reasonably foreseeable dangers, but it does not necessarily follow that liability is escaped because the danger actually materialising is not identical with the danger reasonably foreseen and guarded against.

One need not envisage "the precise concatenation of circumstances which led up to the accident": p. 712.

In [*Wagon Mound (No. 2)*], the Privy Council, on different findings of fact, reached a conclusion different from that in *The Wagon Mound (No. 1)*. . . Lord Reid said at p. 717:

> The vital parts of the findings of fact which have already been set out in full are (i) that the officers of the Wagon Mound 'would regard furnace oil as very difficult to ignite on water' — not that they would regard this as impossible, (ii) that their

experience would probably have been 'that this had very rarely happened' — not that they would never have heard of a case where it had happened, and (iii) that they would have regarded it as a 'possibility, but one which could become an actuality only in very exceptional circumstances' — not, as in *Wagon Mound (No. 1)*, that they could not reasonably be expected to have known that this oil was capable of being set afire when spread on water.

These words would suggest that recovery may be had, provided the event giving rise to the damage is not regarded as "impossible", and even though it "very rarely happened . . . only in very exceptional circumstances". The test of foreseeability of damage becomes a question of what is possible rather than what is probable.

. . .

It is enough to fix liability if one could foresee in a general way the sort of thing that happened. The extent of the damage and its manner of incidence need not be foreseeable if physical damage of the kind which in fact ensues is foreseeable. In the case at bar I would hold that the damage was of the *type* or *kind* which any reasonable person might foresee. Gas-riser pipes on the outside of Tuxedo buildings are common. Damage to such a pipe is not of a kind that no one could anticipate. When one permits a power toboggan to run at large, or when one fires a rifle blindly down a city street, one must not define narrowly the outer limits of reasonable prevision. The ambit of foreseeable damage is indeed broad.

. . .

Counsel for Michael Hoffer concedes that the boy was negligent and that the type of damage that resulted was reasonably foreseeable by him as by any other rational person. Counsel submits, however, that the causation chain, the first link of which was forged by his failure to put the machine on the kick stand before starting it, ended when the riser pipe had been broken and the gas began to escape. I cannot accept this argument. Since *The Wagon Mound (No. 1)* the "scholastic theories of causation and their ugly and barely intelligent jargon", have taken a back place to foreseeability. It is now settled that foresight is the test both for duty and for remoteness. Accepting that the "chain of causation" can be broken by a "nova causa" or "novus actus interveniens", it is clear that the state of affairs created by the Gas Company several years prior to the accident could not be considered a novus actus. Where a state of affairs has already occurred at the time of the wrongful act, that act is regarded as the cause of the damage in the absence of subsequent intervening factors.

It is manifest that Michael's culpable conduct was a causally relevant factor. His failure to exercise due care was the "cause" of the damage in the proper sense of the term. If one applies the "but for" test it is readily apparent that the plaintiff's harm would not have occurred but for Michael's fault. Michael cannot escape liability for the consequences of that fault merely because other causal factors for which he is not responsible also contributed to the damage which resulted. He was *a* cause, though not the *sole* cause of the harm. His fault was a cause-in-fact.

. . .

I agree with the finding of Deniset J. that Ephraim Hoffer and Michael Hoffer are joint tortfeasors.

Liability of Greater Winnipeg Gas Company Limited

I am also of the opinion that Greater Winnipeg Gas Company Limited is liable to the plaintiff on the ground that the installation of the gas service was negligently constructed in the sense that it was constructed in such place and manner as to make likely the type of damage which ensued. The Gas Company was responsible for the construction of the service line leading from the street, the service riser, and attached equipment and meter. It is difficult to conceive of any person, conscious of the explosive properties of natural gas, designing and installing a service so patently dangerous. Gas escaping from any fracture of the pipe below the regulator would assuredly find its way into the boiler room. The Gas Company ought to have reasonably foreseen damage to the gas-riser pipe. It is true that persons are not bound to take extravagant precautions but they must weigh the probability of injury resulting and the probable seriousness of the injury. Although the probability of the gas-riser pipe being struck by an automobile, a motorcyle or an auto toboggan was not great, the pipe being tucked into the corner of the building, the probable seriousness of any injury was very great. Against this must be weighed the cost and difficulty of the precautions which could have been taken. Protective pipes could have been installed at small cost and little difficulty. The duty to take protective measures increases in direct proportion to the risk. In these circumstances, the Gas Company failed to exercise reasonable care where there was a duty to exercise a high degree of care.

NOTES AND QUESTIONS

1. Do you agree with Dickson J.A.'s interpretation of the various foreseeability tests and his application of them to the facts? Does the test in *Assiniboine* establish an appropriate relationship between the nature of the defendant's negligent act and the scope of his or her liability?

2. *Assiniboine* has been widely followed in Canada. See for example *Belzile v. Dumais* (1986), 69 N.B.R. (2d) 142 (Q.B.); *Monkman v. Singh* (1989), 62 Man. R. (2d) 277 (Q.B.); and *Choc v. Hudbay Minerals Inc.*, 2013 ONSC 1414 at para. 59.

3. Critical of the existing law, A. Linden has suggested that the courts ought to adopt a "new approach" to the issue of the remoteness of damages. In Linden *et al.*, *Canadian Tort Law*, 11th ed. (2018) the authors state at 328:

> It would also be helpful if the courts would approach these remoteness cases with the attitude that a person found to have been negligent should only be relieved of liability if the unusual result of the negligence was truly "freakish", "one in a million", "far-fetched", "fantastic or highly improbable". In other words, there should be an expectation of liability for the results of one's negligent conduct, unless the court is convinced that the harm is so unrelated to the negligent conduct that it would be too harsh to hold an admittedly negligent defendant liable for those consequences in the circumstances. [footnotes omitted]

Would this approach alleviate the difficulties that exist in this area? What new problems, if any, would it create? See also Coval, Smith & Rush, "'Out of the Maze': Towards a 'Clear Understanding' of the Test for Remoteness of Damages in Negligence" (1983) 61 Can. Bar Rev. 561.

4. Should the principles of remoteness be applied in the same way in personal injury and property damage cases? See *Stephenson v. Waite Tileman*, [1973] 1 N.Z.L.R. 152 (C.A.).

MUSTAPHA v. CULLIGAN OF CANADA LTD.
[2008] 2 S.C.R. 114

[1] THE CHIEF JUSTICE [for the court] — The plaintiff, Mr. Mustapha, sues for psychiatric injury sustained as a result of seeing the dead flies in a bottle of water supplied by the defendant, Culligan. In the course of replacing an empty bottle of drinking water with a full one, Mr. Mustapha saw a dead fly and part of another dead fly in the unopened replacement bottle. He became obsessed with the event and its "revolting implications" for the health of his family, which had been consuming water supplied by Culligan for the previous 15 years. The plaintiff developed a major depressive disorder with associated phobia and anxiety. He sued Culligan for damages.

. . .

[As discussed in Chapter 12, the Court of Appeal for Ontario had used special principles in this case to determine the duty of care issue. That approach was consistent with the jurisprudence on the negligent infliction of psychiatric harm. However, the Supreme Court of Canada adopted a different approach. It held that it was well-established that the manufacturer of a consumable good owes a duty of care to the consumer, so Culligan owed Mustapha a duty of care. It did not address psychiatric harm at the duty stage. It also held that Culligan breached the standard of care and that Mustapha had sustained a recognizable psychiatric injury.]

[11] The fourth and final question to address in a negligence claim is whether the defendant's breach caused the plaintiff's harm in fact and in law. The evidence before the trial judge establishes that the defendant's breach of its duty of care in fact caused Mr. Mustapha's psychiatric injury. We are not asked to revisit this conclusion. The remaining question is whether that breach also caused the plaintiff's damage in law or whether it is too remote to warrant recovery.

[12] The remoteness inquiry asks whether "the harm [is] too unrelated to the wrongful conduct to hold the defendant fairly liable" (Linden and Feldthusen, [*Canadian Tort Law*, 8th ed. (2006)] at p. 360). Since *The Wagon Mound (No. 1)*, the principle has been that "it is the foresight of the reasonable man which alone can determine responsibility" (*Overseas Tankship (U.K.) Ltd. v. Morts Dock & Engineering Co.*, [1961] A.C. 388 (P.C.), at p. 424).

[13] Much has been written on how probable or likely a harm needs to be in order to be considered reasonably foreseeable. The parties raise the question of whether a reasonably foreseeable harm is one whose occurrence is *probable* or merely *possible*. In my view, these terms are misleading. Any harm which has actually occurred is "possible"; it is therefore clear that possibility alone does not provide a meaningful standard for the application of reasonable foreseeability. The degree of probability that would satisfy the reasonable foreseeability requirement was described in *The Wagon Mound (No. 2)* as a "real risk", i.e. "one which would occur to the mind of a reasonable man in the position of the defendan[t] . . . and which he would not brush aside as far-fetched" (*Overseas Tankship (U.K.) Ltd. v. Miller Steamship Co. Pty.*, [1967] A.C. 617 (P.C.), at p. 643).

[14] The remoteness inquiry depends not only upon the degree of probability required to meet the reasonable foreseeability requirement, but also upon whether or not the plaintiff is considered objectively or subjectively. One of the questions that arose in this case was whether, in judging whether the personal injury was foreseeable, one looks at a person of "ordinary fortitude" or at a particular plaintiff with his or her particular vulnerabilities. This question may be acute in claims for mental injury, since there is a wide variation in how particular people respond to particular stressors. The law has consistently held — albeit within the duty of care analysis — that the question is what a person of ordinary fortitude would suffer: see *White v. Chief Constable of South Yorkshire Police*, [1998] 3 W.L.R. 1509 (H.L.); *Devji v. Burnaby (District)* (1999), 180 D.L.R. (4th) 205, 1999 BCCA 599; *Vanek* [*v. Great Atlantic & Pacific Co. of Canada* (1999), 48 O.R. (3d) 228 (C.A.)]. As stated in *White*, at p. 1512: "The law expects reasonable fortitude and robustness of its citizens and will not impose liability for the exceptional frailty of certain individuals."

[15] As the Court of Appeal found, at para. 49, the requirement that a mental injury would occur in a person of ordinary fortitude, set out in *Vanek*, at paras. 59-61, is inherent in the notion of foreseeability. This is true whether one considers foreseeability at the remoteness or at the duty of care stage. As stated in *Tame v. New South Wales* (2002), 211 C.L.R. 317, [2002] HCA 35, *per* Gleeson C.J., this "is a way of expressing the idea that there are some people with such a degree of susceptibility to psychiatric injury that it is ordinarily unreasonable to require strangers to have in contemplation the possibility of harm to them, or to expect strangers to take care to avoid such harm" (para. 16). To put it another way, unusual or extreme reactions to events caused by negligence are imaginable but not reasonably foreseeable.

[16] To say this is not to marginalize or penalize those particularly vulnerable to mental injury. It is merely to confirm that the law of tort imposes an obligation to compensate for any harm done on the basis of *reasonable* foresight, not as insurance. The law of negligence seeks to impose a result that is fair to both plaintiffs and defendants, and that is socially useful. In this quest, it draws the line for compensability of damage, not at perfection, but at reasonable foreseeability. Once a plaintiff establishes the foreseeability that a mental injury would occur in a person of ordinary fortitude, by contrast, the defendant must take the plaintiff as it finds him for purposes of damages. As stated in *White*, at p. 1512, focusing on the person of ordinary fortitude for the purposes of determining foreseeability "is not to be confused with the 'eggshell skull' situation, where as a result of a breach of duty the damage inflicted proves to be more serious than expected". Rather, it is a threshold test for establishing compensability of damage at law.

[17] I add this. In those cases where it is proved that the defendant had actual knowledge of the plaintiff's particular sensibilities, the ordinary fortitude requirement need not be applied strictly. If the evidence demonstrates that the defendant knew that the plaintiff was of less than ordinary fortitude, the plaintiff's injury may have been reasonably foreseeable to the defendant. In this case, however, there was no evidence to support a finding that Culligan knew of Mr. Mustapha's particular sensibilities.

[18] It follows that in order to show that the damage suffered is not too remote to be viewed as legally caused by Culligan's negligence, Mr. Mustapha must show that it was foreseeable that a person of ordinary fortitude would suffer serious injury from seeing the flies in the bottle of water he was about to install. This he failed to do. The only evidence was about his own reactions, which were described by the medical

experts as "highly unusual" and "very individual" (C.A. judgment, at para. 52). There is no evidence that a person of ordinary fortitude would have suffered injury from seeing the flies in the bottle; indeed the expert witnesses were not asked this question. Instead of asking whether it was foreseeable that the defendant's conduct would have injured a person of ordinary fortitude, the trial judge applied a subjective standard, taking into account Mr. Mustapha's "previous history" and "particular circumstances" (para. 227), including a number of "cultural factors" such as his unusual concern over cleanliness, and the health and well-being of his family. This was an error. Mr. Mustapha having failed to establish that it was reasonably foreseeable that a person of ordinary fortitude would have suffered personal injury, it follows that his claim must fail.

. . .

NOTES AND QUESTIONS

1. Is the test for remoteness outlined by Chief Justice McLachlin consistent with *Assiniboine*?

2. Is the court's analysis of the duty of care preferable to that of the Court of Appeal for Ontario? Should issues of psychiatric harm be examined at the duty stage or the remoteness stage or both? See *Healey v. Lakeridge Health Corporation* (2011), 103 O.R. (3d) 401 (C.A.); and *Deros v. McCauley*, 2011 BCSC 195. See also Handford, "Recovery of Psychiatric Illness in Canada: A Tale of Two Cases" (2011) 19 Tort L. Rev. 18.

3. Is the court's analysis consistent with the cases in the previous section on the thin-skull rule?

4. *Mustapha* is a case in which the plaintiff suffered only psychiatric injury; he did not suffer physical injury. *Mustapha* has been applied in cases in which the plaintiff suffers not only psychiatric injury but also foreseeable physical injury: see *Bain v. Black & Decker Canada (1989) Inc.*, 2009 CarswellOnt 3002 (S.C.J.) (WL Can); and *Frazer v. Haukioja* (2010), 101 O.R. (3d) 528 (C.A.). But other cases have held that if the plaintiff suffers foreseeable physical injury, consequential psychiatric injury is recoverable even if not foreseeable: *Hussack v. Chilliwack School District No. 33*, 2011 BCCA 258 at para. 74. Which approach is preferable?

5. In *Doe v. London Free Press, a Division of Sun Media (Toronto) Corp.*, 2015 ONSC 4239 at para. 164 the court applied *Mustapha* and held that "it was foreseeable that a person of ordinary strength, courage and resilience would suffer serious psychological injury if their identity was disclosed when protected by a non-publication order." The injuries were therefore not too remote.

In contrast, in *Capelet v. Brookfield Homes (Ontario) Limited*, 2017 ONSC 7283, aff'd 2018 ONCA 742 the plaintiff sued the defendant homebuilder for emotional and psychological injuries resulting from water leakage and mould. The plaintiff was diagnosed with an "Adjustment Disorder with Mixed Anxiety and Depressed Mood" with symptoms including low mood, feelings of sadness, worry, anxiety, insomnia and poor concentration. Both the motions judge and the Court of Appeal held that these were not reasonably foreseeable consequences to a person of ordinary fortitude of faulty home construction and thus the injuries were too remote.

6. What kind of evidence is required to persuade a court that a person of ordinary fortitude would suffer a particular psychiatric injury? See *Deros v. McCauley, supra*, at paras. 29-31; *Capelet v. Brookfield Homes (Ontario) Limited, supra*, at paras. 22-32; and David & La Horey, "Mustapha Revisited: Damages for Psychological Injury; Is the Job Only Half Done?" (2010) 37 Adv. Q. 372.

7. Cases involving psychiatric injury now need to be read in light of *Saadati v. Moorhead*, 2017 SCC 28 (see the extract in Chapter 12). Previously some claims for negligently caused mental harm would have failed at the duty of care stage or for lack of proof of a recognized psychiatric illness. Now that the scope of potential recovery is broader, it is likely that in future cases more emphasis will be placed on the remoteness issue. Indeed, the court notes at para. 20 that "*Mustapha* thus serves as a salutary reminder that, even where a duty of care, a breach, damage and factual causation are established, there remains the pertinent threshold question of legal causation, or remoteness — that is, whether the occurrence of mental harm in a person of ordinary fortitude was the reasonably foreseeable result of the defendant's negligent conduct."

4. Intervening Causes

To this point, we have discussed situations in which the defendant's careless act was the sole cause of the plaintiff's loss. We will now examine cases in which the plaintiff's loss was caused by the defendant's breach and a subsequent intervening act. An intervening act is one that causes the plaintiff's loss after the original defendant's breach has taken effect. For example, assume that a defendant contractor carelessly blocked a sidewalk, forcing pedestrians to walk on the road, and that one of the pedestrians was struck by a careless driver. Both the contractor and the driver caused the plaintiff's injuries. However, should the contractor be relieved of liability for the injuries because of the role of the driver?

Traditionally, the original tortfeasor was relieved of liability because the causal link between his or her breach and the plaintiff's loss was considered to have been severed by the intervening cause. The issue was framed in various ways: some courts talked about the second act breaking the chain of causation and other courts labelled the act as a *novus actus interveniens* ("a new intervening act"). No matter how it was described, the last wrongdoer was held solely responsible for the plaintiff's loss, even if his or her conduct was a relatively minor cause of the injury.

As the courts developed more complex notions of causation, the "last wrongdoer" doctrine was rejected. The courts divided intervening acts into three categories based on their nature and moral blameworthiness. Cases in the first category, intervening acts that were naturally occurring or non-culpable, were generally held not to break the chain of causation. For example, a contractor could not escape liability merely because its shoddy work resulted in property damage following an unusually severe storm. Cases in the second category, negligent intervening acts, were generally held to break the chain of causation, thereby absolving the original tortfeasor of liability. For example, a careless driver would not be held liable if the plaintiff whom he or she injured died in hospital as a result of being negligently given the wrong drug. Cases in the third category of intervening acts, deliberately wrongful or illegal acts, invariably broke the chain of causation unless the original tortfeasor had a specific duty to prevent the act. Thus, a careless driver would not be held liable for the fact that the pedestrian whom he or she ran down was robbed while lying by the side of the road. In contrast, an armed guard who carelessly left his or her truck unlocked would be held liable if a thief stole several bags of money.

In turn, this elaborate categorization has been replaced by a more general principle: the "within the scope of the risk" test. As the following cases illustrate, the application of that test can create difficulties. Some courts analyze the issue in terms of whether the *loss* caused by the intervening act was within the scope of the risk created by the original tortfeasor. Other courts ask whether the *intervening act* itself was within the scope of the risk created by the original tortfeasor. While focusing on the relationship between the plaintiff's specific injuries and the original tortfeasor's careless act is more consistent with the purpose of the remoteness principles, this issue requires further clarification.

BRADFORD v. KANELLOS
(1973), 40 D.L.R. (3d) 578 (S.C.C.)

MARTLAND J.:—On the morning of April 12, 1967, the appellants, who are husband and wife, were customers in the respondents' restaurant, in the City of Kingston. While seated at the counter in the restaurant, a flash fire occurred in the grill used for cooking purposes. The grill was equipped with an automatic fire extinguisher system, of an approved type, which, when it became operative, discharged carbon dioxide on to the heated area to extinguish the fire.

Shortly after the start of the fire the fire extinguisher was activated, manually, and the fire was extinguished almost immediately. The fire was not a cause of concern to the appellants. No damage was done by the fire because the fire was of very short duration and all that burned was grease that had accumulated in the grill and a rag or rags which had been thrown on the fire when it broke out in an effort to extinguish it.

The fire extinguisher made a hissing or popping noise when it operated. This caused an unidentified patron in the restaurant to shout that gas was escaping and that there was going to be an explosion. The result of these words was to cause a panic in the restaurant. While people ran from the restaurant the appellant wife was pushed or fell from her seat at the counter and sustained injury.

The appellants brought action against the respondents, the appellant wife claiming general damages and the appellant husband claiming special damages for expenses incurred as a result of his wife's injuries.

The trial Judge awarded damages in the amounts of $3,582.43 to the appellant husband and $6,400 to the appellant wife. He found there had been negligence involved in the flash fire because the grill had not been cleaned as efficiently as it should have been, and said: "Therefore while the negligence may be small, it pinpoints this as negligence."

He did not find that the fire, in itself, had caused the panic, but ascribed it to the noise caused by the fire extinguisher. He said:

> As the result of this hissing explosive noise, or whatever it was, some rather foolish people in the restaurant called out that it might explode. For this reason it appears that some considerable panic ensued and there was a rushing for the door.

His conclusion was that, while the act of yelling out almost qualified as that of an "idiotic person", the panic could have been foreseen.

By unanimous decision, the Court of Appeal allowed the appeal of the present respondents. Schroeder, J.A., who delivered the judgment of the Court, said. . .:

> The practical and sensible view to be taken of the facts here leads fairly to the conclusion that it should not be held that the person guilty of the original negligence resulting in the flash fire on the grill ought reasonably to have anticipated the subsequent intervening act or acts which were the direct cause of the injuries and damages suffered by the plaintiffs.

From this judgment the present appeal has, with leave, been brought to this Court.

I agree with the decision of the Court of Appeal. The judgment at trial found the respondents to be liable because there had been negligence in failing to clean the grill efficiently, which resulted in the flash fire. But it was to guard against the consequences of a flash fire that the grill was equipped with a fire extinguisher system. This system was described by the Chief of the Kingston Fire Department, who was called as a witness by the appellants, as, not only an approved installation, but one of the best.

This system, when activated, following the flash fire, fulfilled its function and put out the fire. This was accomplished by the application of carbon dioxide on the fire. In so doing, there was a hissing noise and it was on hearing this that one of the customers exclaimed that gas was escaping and that there was danger of an explosion, following which the panic occurred, the appellant wife was injured.

On these facts it is apparent that her injuries resulted from the hysterical conduct of a customer which occurred when the safety appliance properly fulfilled its function. Was that consequence fairly to be regarded as within the risk created by the respondent's negligence in permitting an undue quantity of grease to accumulate on the grill? The Court of Appeal has found that it was not and I agree with that finding.

In my opinion, the appeal should be dismissed with costs.

Judson and Ritchie, JJ., concur with Martland, J.

SPENCE J. (dissenting):—. . . I am of the opinion that in the particular circumstances of this case, "the person guilty of the original negligence ought reasonably to have anticipated such subsequent intervening negligence and to have foreseen that if it occurred the result would be that his negligence would lead to loss or damage." Upon the evidence, the owners and proprietors, the respondents here, did anticipate that such negligence as leaving the grill in a dirty and greasy condition would cause a fire and frequently warned the cook of such fact, and requiring the cook not once but on several occasions to clean up the grill. The grill was midway down the length of the restaurant. There was seating for many patrons to the rear of the grill so that the grill intervened between them and the only entrance or exit at the front of the restaurant and the space between the grill and the other restaurant equipment through which the said patrons would have to pass was narrow.

The proprietors knew of the fire extinguisher and its action. Such action was described by the witness Warren Gibson, the Chief of Police of Kingston, as being a very rapid expansion of carbon dioxide that makes a hissing noise which explodes rather rapidly as it expands.

I am of the opinion that any reasonable person knew that a greasy grill might well take fire and that in such event a CO^2 fire extinguisher is put into action either automatically or manually and that such fire extinguisher makes a hissing and popping sound and he could not fail to anticipate that a panic might well result. The panic did result and on the evidence the whole affair from beginning to end was almost instantaneous. The plaintiff Elizabeth Bradford described it variously in the words "no, it was quick": Again, that she had been watching the fire approximately a minute when the man next to her called out "gas" and that thereupon there was an immediate panic.

. . .

I am not of the opinion that the persons who shouted the warning of what they were certain was an impending explosion were negligent. I am, on the other hand, of the opinion that they acted in a very human and usual way and that their actions, as I have said, were utterly foreseeable and were part of the natural consequence of events leading inevitably to the plaintiff's injury. I here quote and adopt Fleming, *Law of Torts*, 4th ed. (1971), at pp. 192-3:

> Nowadays it is no longer open to serious question that the operation of an intervening force will not ordinarily clear a defendant from further responsibility, if it can fairly be considered a not abnormal incident of the risk created by him — if, as sometimes expressed, it is "part of the ordinary course of things." Nor is there room any longer for any categorical distinction in this regard between forces of nature, like rain or ice, on the one hand, and the action of human beings even when consciously controlled, on the other.

> Least difficult are instances of just normal and reasonable response to the stimulus of the hazard engendered by the defendant's negligence. . . . . A time-honoured illustration is the famous *Squib Case: Scott v. Shepherd* (1773) 2 W.Bl. 892 [[1558-1774] All E.R. 295 (C.P.)], where a wag threw a lighted fire-work into a market whence it was tossed from one stall to another in order to save the wares until it eventually exploded in the plaintiff's face. Yet it was held that *trespass* lay because "all that was done subsequent to the original throwing was a continuation of the first force and first act and continued until the squib was spent by bursting."

Even if the actions of those who called out "gas" and "it is going to explode" were negligent and, as I have said, I do not think it was, then I am of the opinion that the plaintiffs would still have a right of action against the defendants, here respondents, or against such persons or against both.

. . .

For these reasons, I would allow the appeal and restore the judgment at trial. The appellants are entitled to their costs here and in the Court of Appeal.

Laskin, J., concurs with Spence, J.

NOTES AND QUESTIONS

1. Did Martland and Spence JJ. disagree on the test of remoteness governing the original tortfeasor's liability for intervening causes or on its application to the specific facts? Which judgment do you find more compelling? Based on *Bradford*, define the test of remoteness governing the original tortfeasor's liability for intervening causes. Should this same test be applied whether the intervening cause is a naturally occurring phenomenon, the negligent act of a second tortfeasor, a patently reckless act, a deliberate illegal act or the plaintiff's own contributorily negligent act?

2. In *Oke v. Weide Transport Ltd.* (1963), 41 D.L.R. (2d) 53 (Man. C.A.) the defendant knocked down a traffic sign on a gravel strip separating the eastbound and westbound lanes of traffic. The defendant stopped and removed some debris, but was unable to move the sign post, which was left projecting upwards. Although he informed a garage attendant of the incident, the defendant did not contact the police or highway authorities. The next day a driver, while attempting to pass illegally on the gravel strip, was killed when the post came up through the car's floor and pierced his chest. The majority stated that even if the defendant had been careless in not reporting the incident, he could not be held liable because the deceased's intervening act of driving on the gravel strip and its consequences could not have been foreseen. The dissent concluded that the defendant had been negligent and that an accident of some kind was a foreseeable consequence of his failure to report the hazardous situation that he had created. Thus, the defendant should be held liable even though the exact way in which the accident occurred and its severity may not have been foreseeable. Do you agree with the dissenting or the majority analysis of remoteness? Would the case have been resolved the same way if the deceased had been pulling over to fix a flat tire?

3. In subsequent cases the Canadian courts have adopted a broad interpretation of foreseeability. See for example *R. v. Cote* (1974), 51 D.L.R. (3d) 244 (S.C.C.); *Hendrick v. De Marsh* (1984), 6 D.L.R. (4th) 713 (Ont. H.C.), aff'd (1986), 54 O.R. (2d) 185 (C.A.); *Funk v. Clapp* (1986), 68 D.L.R. (4th) 229 (B.C.C.A.); *Smith v. B.C. (A.G.)* (1988), 30 B.C.L.R. (2d) 356 (C.A.); *Werbeniuk v. Maynard*, [1994] 7 W.W.R. 704 (Man. Q.B.); and *Phillip v. Bablitz*, 2011 ABCA 383.

4. A question sometimes arises as to whether the plaintiff's own contributory negligence constitutes an intervening act that severs the chain of causation flowing from the defendant's breach.

The issue arose in *Jolley v. Sutton London B.C.*, [1998] 1 W.L.R. 1546 (C.A.), rev'd [2000] 1 W.L.R. 1082 (H.L.). As explained earlier in this chapter, a dangerously decrepit boat was located on property under the defendant's authority. The defendant made a decision to remove the boat for safety reasons, but because of administrative dithering failed to perform the task. The plaintiff and his friend, both aged 14, found the boat. They decided to repair it. In order to fix the hull, they hoisted the boat up on a car jack. The jack gave way, the boat fell and the plaintiff was rendered paraplegic.

The trial judge imposed liability, subject to a reduction of 25% for contributory negligence. However, a majority in the Court of Appeal held that the plaintiff's losses were too remote because the boys' actions were "unforeseen" and "extraneous." This was a dubious decision. As J. O'Sullivan has noted, the plaintiff's own carelessness generally does not sever the chain of causation unless it satisfies a very high threshold of being unwarranted or extraneous. Ordinary contributory negligence normally just has the effect of reducing the amount of damages: O'Sullivan, "Remoteness of Damage in Negligence: A Rotten Structure Collapses" [1999] C.L.J. 12.

On further appeal, the House of Lords reinstated the trial decision and held that the plaintiff's losses were not too remote and, more specifically, that the boys' conduct did not sever the chain of causation.

See also *MacDonald (Litigation Guardian of) v. Goertz* (2009), 96 B.C.L.R. (4th) 236 (C.A.) in which the court noted that "the *novus actus interveniens* doctrine is applied less stringently in modern times, with our statutory comparative fault regime, than it once was" and Hodgson, "The Law of Intervening Causation and Children" (2011) 19 Tort L. Rev. 149.

5. In *Wilk v. Arbour*, 2017 ONCA 21 the plaintiff agreed to take the defendant's dog for a walk, during which the dog suffered a seizure and fell down an embankment into a ditch. The plaintiff tried to retrieve the dog but also fell into the ditch, colliding with the dog, which then bit her thumb. The plaintiff lost her thumb above the joint. She sued the defendant in negligence. The court held that the plaintiff's attempt to retrieve the dog, which was not in immediate danger, was a voluntary intervening act and so her injuries were too remote.

PRICE v. MILAWSKI
(1977), 82 D.L.R. (3d) 130 (Ont. C.A.)

[The plaintiff injured his right ankle playing soccer and went to the emergency department of a hospital to have it examined. He told the defendant, Dr. Murray, that he heard his ankle crack and thought it was broken. Dr. Murray sent the plaintiff for x-rays but instructed the technicians to x-ray his right foot, not his right ankle. After examining the x-rays, Dr. Murray informed the plaintiff that there was no fracture and that his ankle was only sprained. In fact, the ankle was broken.

After a series of visits to his family doctor, the plaintiff was eventually referred to Dr. Carbin, an orthopaedic surgeon, because the ankle remained painful and swollen. Dr. Carbin telephoned the hospital and discovered that the plaintiff's x-ray results were negative. Despite the plaintiff's complaints, Dr. Carbin did not order new x-rays, even though he had a machine in his office and a technician available to him. He diagnosed the plaintiff's injury as a strained ligament and applied a cast. When the cast was removed four weeks later, the ankle began to swell. Following some further delays, the plaintiff eventually went to another orthopaedic surgeon who took new x-rays and discovered the fractured ankle. As a result of delays in properly treating the fracture, the plaintiff suffered some permanent disabilities.

At trial, both Dr. Murray and Dr. Carbin were found liable in negligence and were held equally at fault for the plaintiff's permanent injury. Both defendants appealed the finding of negligence and the quantum of damages.

On appeal, Arnup J.A., for the court, affirmed that both defendants had been negligent.]

ARNUP J.A.:

. . .

The "foreseeability" argument

As stated in Part III, it was submitted on behalf of Dr. Murray that it was not foreseeable by him that such dire consequences would flow from his initial acts of negligence.

We are concerned here with what one may properly call an intervening act of negligence (*i.e.*, by Dr. Carbin). In *Bradford et al. v. Kanellos et al.*, [1974] 1 S.C.R. 409 at pp. 412-3. . ., the majority, per Martland, J., referring to the hysterical act of a restaurant customer who shouted out "gas!" and that there was going to be an explosion, resulting in a panic which caused injuries to the plaintiff, said:

Was that consequence fairly to be regarded as within the risk created by the respondents' negligence in permitting an undue quantity of grease to accumulate on the grill [in the restaurant]?

A set of facts having some analogy to the present case arose in *Mercer v. Gray*, [1941] O.R. 127, [1941] 3 D.L.R. 564, where it was held that if reasonable care has been used by the plaintiff to employ a competent physician or surgeon to treat personal injuries wrongfully inflicted by a defendant, the results of the treatment are a proper head of damages, even though through an error in treatment, it is unsuccessful.

In *"Wagon Mound" (No. 2), supra*, Lord Reid, referring to cases "based purely on negligence" states. . .:

It has now been established by *The Wagon Mound (No. 1) supra*, and by *Hughes v. Lord Advocate, supra*, that in such cases damages can only be recovered if the injury complained of was not only caused by the alleged negligence but was also an injury of a class or character foreseeable as a possible result of it.

Applying these principles to a case in which there are negligent acts by two persons in succession, I would hold that a person doing a negligent act may, in circumstances lending themselves to that conclusion, be held liable for future damages arising in part from the subsequent negligent act of another, and in part from his own negligence, where such subsequent negligence and consequent damage were reasonably foreseeable as a possible result of his own negligence.

It was reasonably foreseeable by Dr. Murray that once the information generated by his negligent error got into the hospital records, other doctors subsequently treating the plaintiff might well rely on the accuracy of that information, *i.e.*, that the x-ray showed no fracture of the ankle. It was also foreseeable that some doctor might do so without checking, even though to do so in the circumstances might itself be a negligent act. The history is always one factor in a subsequent diagnosis and the consequent treatment. Such a possibility was not a risk which a reasonable man (in the position of Dr. Murray) would brush aside as far-fetched — see *"Wagon Mound" (No. 2)*. . . .

The later negligence of Dr. Carbin compounded the effects of the earlier negligence of Dr. Murray. It did not put a halt to the consequences of the first act and attract liability for all damage from that point forward. In my view the trial Judge was correct in holding that each of the appellants was liable to the plaintiff and that it was not possible to try to apportion the extent to which each was responsible for the plaintiff's subsequent operation and his permanent disability.

NOTES AND QUESTIONS

1. Is there a significant difference between the "foreseeable as possible" test in *Price* and the test in *Bradford*? Had the latter test been applied in *Price* would the result have been the same?

2. Did Arnup J.A. properly interpret and apply *Wagon Mound (No. 2)*? Can you suggest a way of distinguishing *Wagon Mound (No. 2)* and *Price*?

3. Can you distinguish *Price* from *Mercer v. Gray*, [1941] 3 D.L.R. 564 (Ont. C.A.)? See also *Mercer v. South Eastern & Chatham Ry. Co.'s Managing Committee*, [1922] 2 K.B. 549.

4. In *Papp v. Leclerc* (1977), 16 O.R. (2d) 158 (C.A.), a case decided in the same year as *Price*, Lacourcière J.A., for the court, stated at 161:

> Every tortfeasor causing injury to a person placing him in the position of seeking medical or hospital help, must assume the inherent risks of complications, *bona fide* medical error or misadventure, if they are reasonably foreseeable and not too remote . . . It is for the defendant to prove that some new act rendering another person liable has broken the chain of causation. This was not done in the present case. I must, therefore, rule against the appellant on this first contention based on lack of foreseeability and *novus actus*.

Is this statement compatible with the decision in *Price*? Is there any reason to treat an intervening act of medical negligence differently than any other negligent intervening act? See also *Thompson v. Toorenburgh* (1973), 50 D.L.R. (3d) 717 (B.C.C.A.), aff'd [1973] S.C.R. vii; *Robinson v. Post Office*, [1974] 2 All E.R. 737 (C.A.); *David v. Toronto Transit Comm.* (1976), 77 D.L.R. (3d) 717 (Ont. H.C.); *Katzman v. Yaeck* (1982), 37 O.R. (2d) 500 (C.A.); *Rahman v. Arearose Ltd.*, [2001] Q.B. 351 (C.A.); and *Phillip v. Bablitz*, 2011 ABCA 383.

5. In what circumstances should the defendant be held liable for injuries that the plaintiff sustains while recovering? In *Block v. Martin*, [1951] 4 D.L.R. 121 (Alta. S.C.) the defendant negligently ran over the plaintiff, causing a slight fracture of his leg. The plaintiff followed his doctor's orders and continued to walk. Six months after the accident, the plaintiff slipped while fishing and completely fractured his leg. It was held that the original injury was a cause of the second fracture and that the plaintiff's conduct in going fishing was not a *novus actus interveniens*. The defendant was held liable for the plaintiff's entire loss. See also *Boss v. Robert Simpson Eastern Ltd.* (1968), 2 D.L.R. (3d) 114 (N.S.S.C.); *Wieland v. Cyril Lord Carpets Ltd.*, [1969] 3 All E.R. 1006 (Q.B.); *Saccardo v. Hamilton* (1971), 18 D.L.R. (3d) 271 (Ont. H.C.); *Pauluik v. Paraiso*, [1996] 2 W.W.R. 57 (Man. C.A.); *Athey v. Leonati* (1996), 31 C.C.L.T. (2d) 113 (S.C.C.); and *Larsen v. Wilson* (2007), 49 C.C.L.T. (3d) 88 (B.C.S.C.).

6. Should the original tortfeasor be absolved of liability for an injury the plaintiff sustains while recuperating if the plaintiff has been contributorily negligent? The courts have occasionally answered this question in the affirmative. See *McKew v. Holland*, [1969] 3 All E.R. 1621 (H.L.); *Goldhawke v. Harder* (1976), 74 D.L.R. (3d) 721 (B.C.S.C.); *Brushett v. Cowan* (1990), 69 D.L.R. (4th) 743 (Nfld. C.A.); *Dudek v. Li*, [2000] 6 W.W.R. 209 (B.C.C.A.); and *Sandhar v. Rolston*, 2012 BCSC 495 at para. 52. Is there any reason to treat the plaintiff's contributory negligence in these cases differently from any other intervening cause? Is this approach consistent with *Bradford* or *Price*?

In *Spencer v. Wincanton Holdings Ltd.*, [2009] EWCA Civ 1404 the plaintiff suffered a relatively minor injury. However, this injury led to the eventual amputation of the plaintiff's leg. He made a good recovery and was fitted with a prosthesis. Some months later he stopped at a gas station. Rather than attach the prosthesis, which he did not wear while driving, he exited the car on one leg. He tripped and fell, seriously injuring his other leg. The Court of Appeal allowed the plaintiff to recover for the injuries to the other leg from the original tortfeasor, subject to a deduction for contributory negligence.

7. What if it is not the plaintiff's subsequent conduct that is in issue but rather that of the plaintiff's family members? In *Hussack v. Chilliwack School District No. 33*, 2011 BCCA 258 the 13-year-old plaintiff was injured playing field hockey. He subsequently developed a somatoform disorder (a psychiatric illness in which individuals complain of physical symptoms that have no underlying physiological basis and which are presumed to arise from psychological factors). The defendant alleged that this disorder was due to over-protective parenting after the injury by the plaintiff's father and that his conduct was a *novus actus interveniens.* The trial judge held such parenting was a foreseeable consequence of the initial injury and the Court of Appeal upheld that conclusion.

8. Should the original tortfeasor be held liable for the additional losses a plaintiff suffers as a result of failing to undergo a needed operation? What if the operation posed a small risk of death, was very painful or had only a 70% chance of success? Would it make any difference if the plaintiff had a pre-existing fear of surgery? Is it appropriate to deal with this as a question of remoteness, as an issue of mitigation of loss or as contributory negligence? The Supreme Court of Canada addressed these questions in *Janiak v. Ippolito* (1985), 16 D.L.R. (4th) 1 (S.C.C.). See also *Couillard v. Waschulewski Estate* (1988), 44 C.C.L.T. 113 (Alta. Q.B.); *Tomizza v. Fraser* (1990), 71 O.R. (2d) 705 (H.C.); *Wills v. Doe* (1992), 90 D.L.R. (4th) 164 (B.C.S.C.); and *Engel v. Kam-Ppelle Holdings Ltd.*, [1993] 1 S.C.R. 306.

In *Bourgoin v. Leamington (Municipality)* (2006), 39 C.C.L.T. (3d) 41 (Ont. S.C.J.) the plaintiff suffered an ankle injury while walking on an uneven sidewalk. She developed chronic intractable pain, identified as Complex Regional Pain Syndrome. The defendant municipality argued that she had failed to reduce her damages from the pain by refusing to undergo the treatment recommended by her physiatrist, 95% likely to eliminate the pain, which was to have her leg amputated below the knee. How should the court have resolved this issue?

9. Should a negligent defendant who causes a car accident be held liable for the additional costs associated with the negligent repair of the plaintiff's car? See *Russell v. Esson (M.F.) & Sons Ltd.* (1986), 72 N.B.R. (2d) 55 (Q.B.).

10. In what circumstances should the original tortfeasor be held liable for the additional damages that result from the victim's suicide? See *Swami v. Lo*, [1980] 1 W.W.R. 379 (B.C.S.C.); *Gray v. Cotic* (1983), 26 C.C.L.T. 163 (S.C.C.); *Wright Estate v. Davidson* (1992), 88 D.L.R. (4th) 698 (B.C.C.A.); and *Corr v. IBC Vehicles Ltd.*, [2008] 1 A.C. 884 (H.L.). See also Hodgson, "Suicide and the Law of Intervening Causation" (2008) 16 Tort L. Rev. 69.

HEWSON v. RED DEER
(1976), 63 D.L.R. (3d) 168 (Alta. T.D.)

KIRBY J.:. . . The plaintiff claims damages against the City of Red Deer (hereinafter referred to as "the City"), sustained on May 15, 1973, when a tractor owned by the City crashed into the plaintiff's dwelling-house.

The tractor, a "crawler type" weighing approximately 25 tons, was being used to level and stockpile gravel in an open area approximately two and a half city blocks' distance to the south of the Hewson residence. The gravel was brought to the site by trucks from a crushing plant located elsewhere in the City. Loading at the plant was suspended from 12:00 midnight until 1:00 a.m., the last load before this break generally arriving at the stockpile at about 12:15 a.m. The trucks took the loads of gravel up an inclined roadway built for that purpose to the top of the existing pile of gravel which on the day in question had attained a considerable height.

Following the arrival of the last load before the midnight break, Weisenburger, an employee of the City operating the crawler tractor, left the tractor at the top of the stockpile facing in the direction of the inclined roadway and departed from the site in a city truck for coffee and cigarettes. Before leaving, he lowered the blade, adjusted the throttle to idle gear, turned off the ignition but did not remove the key or close and lock the cab to which he had a key.

Weisenburger impressed me as a credible witness and I accept his account as to the precautions he took before leaving the site.

On his return, which he said was about 12:45 a.m. the tractor was gone. He looked for it around the site thinking some fellow employee may have moved it as a joke. Not finding it, he looked for its tracks and found them leading down the inclined roadway and going to the north. In due course he found the tractor crashed into the Hewson residence. The engine was still running and was in high gear. The blade was up. The time at which the crash took place is established by an electric clock in the residence, serviced by wires severed by the tractor. It had stopped at 12:03 a.m.

In the company of police, Weisenburger closely examined the stockpile in the immediate vicinity of where he had left the tractor. Tracks were found indicating that a motor vehicle had turned around on the top of the stockpile. Two footprints consistent with a person having jumped out of the cab of the tractor were found.

I am satisfied and find that the tractor was set in motion by an unknown person, who raised the blade, turned on the ignition and put the engine into high gear causing it to move from the top of the stockpile, down the inclined roadway, across the open space lying to the north, continuing in its course until it crashed into the Hewson residence.

· · ·

It is argued, however, that if there was negligence upon the part of Weisenburger or the City, the damages that occurred were too remote to be attributed to them and that the defence of *novus actus interveniens* is applicable.

[The judge then quoted several cases to the effect that the "defence" was not available if the defendant failed to guard against the very thing that was likely to occur.]

· · ·

The maxim was not considered applicable by the Supreme Court of Canada in *Booth et al. v. St. Catharines et al.*, [1948] 4 D.L.R. 686, [1948] S.C.R. 564. This case involved an action against the city following an accident which occurred in a city park when a number of boys climbed a flagpole to watch a fireworks exhibit — the pole fell, injuring one plaintiff and killing the daughter of the other plaintiffs. A great deal of the case deals with the question of the duty of care owed by a licensor towards licensees on his property, but the other major issue concerns foreseeability and the *novus actus* doctrine.

Kerwin, J., said at p. 690 D.L.R., p. 569 S.C.R.:

The maxim *novus actus interveniens* has no application because while the structure was sufficient for its purpose as a flag tower, in view of the great concourse of people and of the fireworks, the presence of boys upon the tower, even though unauthorized, was the very thing that should have been anticipated.

Rand, J., at p. 693 D.L.R., p. 573 S.C.R., observed:

On the basis of prudent foresight, it must have been anticipated as natural and probable that boys of all ages would climb the tower to get a better view of what was going on.

. . .

In the instant case, however, as has been pointed out, the tractor could be set in motion by any person opening the door of the cab, turning the ignition key and raising the blade. This might have been prevented by taking the elementary precautions of removing the ignition key, engaging the safety lever and locking the cab door, none of which was done.

The stockpile was located in an open field approximately two city blocks from the nearest residential building, two and a half to three city blocks' distance from Red Deer College which was then in session, about 50 ft. from 32nd St. which was surfaced with rough gravel, connecting with a road allowance which in turn intersected with provincial Highway 2.

The stockpile being so located was accessible to persons living in the residences referred to, students and staff at the college and to persons using 32nd St. or the road allowance.

It seems to me that it was reasonably foreseeable that any one of such persons might become aware that the tractor was being left at the stockpile unattended and might be tempted to put it in motion. The elementary precautions referred to above were not taken to prevent this happening. I am of the view, therefore, that the maxim *novus actus interveniens* is not applicable. Accordingly, the plaintiff is entitled to damages against the City.

NOTES AND QUESTIONS

1. Do you agree with Kirby J. that it was reasonably foreseeable that someone would put the bulldozer in motion? Would the result have been the same if: (a) the bulldozer had been parked in a rural, rather than an urban, area, (b) the defendant had taken the keys and the intruder started the bulldozer by hot-wiring it, and (c) the defendant had left for only five minutes? Do you think that Kirby J. would have reached the same conclusion if the intruder had been caught? See *Wright v. McCrea*, [1965] 1 O.R. 300 (C.A.); and *Moss v. Ferguson* (1979), 35 N.S.R. (2d) 181 (S.C.).

2. *Hewson* was reversed on appeal: (1977), 146 D.L.R. (3d) 32 (Alta. S.C.A.D.). The court, in a brief decision, held that there was no evidence to support the conclusion that the bulldozer being put in motion was reasonably foreseeable. It concluded that "no effective steps could have been taken to prevent third parties tampering with the machine if they were of a mind to do so". The court treated the intervention of the intruder as a *novus actus interveniens*.

3. Should a driver who leaves the keys in his or her car be held liable if the car is stolen and the thief negligently causes a car accident? Would the police be able to recover against the driver if they were injured while attempting to catch the car thief? See *Hollett v. Coca-Cola Ltd.* (1980), 37 N.S.R. (2d) 695 (S.C.); *Spagnolo v. Margesson's Sports Ltd.* (1983), 145 D.L.R. (3d) 381 (Ont. C.A.); *Moore v. Fanning* (1987), 60 O.R. (2d) 225 (H.C.); *Werbeniuk v. Maynard*, [1994] 7 W.W.R. 704 (Man. Q.B.); *Johnston v. Day*, 2013 ABQB 512; *Provost v. Bolton*, 2017 BCSC 1608; and *Grue v. McLellan*, 2018 NSSC 69.

In *Tong v. Bedwell*, [2002] 6 W.W.R. 327 (Alta. Q.B.) the defendant was stopped at an intersection. A hoodlum smashed the windshield of his car. The defendant ran after the hoodlum, leaving the keys in his car. He later returned to find that his car had been stolen. Moreover, he later discovered that the thief had crashed his car into the plaintiff's vehicle. The plaintiff sued the defendant in negligence for the cost of repairs. The court held that while it was reasonably foreseeable that the defendant's car would be stolen if he left the keys in it, it was not reasonably foreseeable that the thief would drive in such a manner as to cause damage. In reaching that conclusion, the court stressed that there were apparently no witnesses to the theft, whose presence would have made the thief drive in a nervous or panicky manner. Do you agree with the court's decision? Is it reasonably foreseeable that a car thief will drive without sufficient care? Consider the possible reasons why a thief may steal a car.

In *Rankin (Rankin's Garage & Sales) v. J.J.*, 2018 SCC 19 (see the extract in Chapter 10) the defendant garage carelessly left a car unlocked with the keys in its ashtray. On discovering this, a 16-year-old boy stole the car and the plaintiff, a 15-year-old boy, accompanied him as a passenger. The older boy had never driven on a road before. He crashed the car and the plaintiff suffered a catastrophic brain injury. The trial judge and the Court of Appeal both held the garage liable but the Supreme Court of Canada reversed, holding that the garage did not owe a duty of care to the plaintiff. The majority held at para. 55 that "the evidence did not provide specific circumstances to make it reasonably foreseeable that the stolen car might be driven in a way that would cause personal injury. The evidence did not, for example, establish that the risk of theft included the risk of theft by minors." In contrast, the dissent held there was ample evidence to support the lower courts' conclusions on reasonable foreseeability. That debate aside, is the central legal issue in this case the existence of a duty of care or is the real issue one of remoteness and intervening acts? Does it matter?

4. If a worker leaves without locking the plaintiff's house, should he or she be held liable for losses caused by a subsequent theft? See *Stansbie v. Troman*, [1948] 2 K.B. 48 (C.A.); *Thiele v. Rod Service (Ottawa) Ltd.* (1962), 45 D.L.R. (2d) 503 (Ont. C.A.); and *Ward v. Cannock Chase Dist. Council*, [1985] 3 All E.R. 537 (Ch. Div.).

5. Assume that a defendant driver negligently runs over the plaintiff and that during the ensuing commotion someone steals the plaintiff's wallet. Should the defendant be held liable for the theft? See *Brauer v. New York Cent. & H.R.R. Co.*, 103 A. 166 (N.J.C.A. 1918); *Patten v. Silberschein*, [1936] 3 W.W.R. 169 (B.C.S.C.); *Duce v. Rourke* (1951), 1 W.W.R. (N.S.) 305 (Alta. C.A.); *Abbott v. Kasza* (1974), [1975] 3 W.W.R. 163 (Alta. S.C.), varied [1976] 4 W.W.R. 20 (Alta. C.A.).

6. In *Lamb v. London Borough of Camden*, [1981] 2 All E.R. 408 (C.A.) the three judges agreed that the reasonable foreseeability test is not always appropriate for cases

involving deliberate intervening acts of third parties. They were concerned that the test would extend the defendant's liability "beyond all reason" and lead to "bizarre and ludicrous" results. However, the judges each adopted a different test to govern these situations. But see *P Perl (Exporters) Ltd. v. Camden London Borough Council*, [1983] 3 All E.R. 161 (C.A.); *Smith v. Littlewoods Organisation Ltd.*, [1987] 1 All E.R. 710 (H.L.); and *Okanagan Exteriors Inc. v. Perth Developments Inc.*, [2002] 3 W.W.R. 224 (B.C.C.A.). See also Lee & Merkin, "Human Action as Novus Actus Interveniens" [1981] New L.J. 965; and Highley, "Comment on *P Perl (Exporters) Ltd. v. Camden London Borough Council*" (1985) 43 U.T. Fac. L. Rev. 136.

7. If an employer knows an employee is potentially dangerous but it negligently does not terminate him or her, and the employee then intentionally shoots another employee, should the employer be liable for the injuries? See *Gittani Stone Pty Ltd v. Pavkovic*, [2007] NSWCA 355 which held that the employee's intentional and criminal conduct was not an intervening act.

8. Here we are considering whether the conduct of a third person is an intervening act that renders the subsequent injury too remote. Recall that in Chapter 11 we looked at situations giving rise to a duty to control the conduct of others. How are these areas of law related, particularly on the issue of foreseeability? See Klar & Jefferies, *Tort Law*, 6th ed. (2017) at 570-73; and *Fullowka v. Royal Oak Ventures Inc.*, [2008] 7 W.W.R. 411 (N.W.T.C.A.) at paras. 42-46, aff'd on other grounds 2010 SCC 5.

9. Some studies show that young sexual assault victims are more likely to subsequently commit crimes and spend time in jail. In a claim against the defendant for the sexual assault, can the victim recover for loss of earnings during any time spent in jail? Can the victim establish that the defendant caused those losses? Is the crime, intentionally committed by the victim, a *novus actus*? Even if the victim can clear these hurdles, should the courts as a matter of policy be awarding such damages? See *H.L. v. Canada (Attorney General)*, [2005] 1 S.C.R. 401; and *British Columbia v. Zastowny*, [2008] 1 S.C.R. 27.

10. A difficult remoteness question can arise in cases of secondary child abuse. If studies establish that an abused child is more likely to go on to abuse his or her own children, then should an abusive parent be liable to his or her grandchildren if they are in turn abused? For a factual situation raising similar issues see *Rumley v. British Columbia* (1999), 180 D.L.R. (4th) 639 (B.C.C.A.), aff'd [2001] 3 S.C.R. 184.

5. Beyond the Scope of the Risk

As a matter of common sense, it seems correct that a defendant should not be liable for a plaintiff's injuries if those injuries arise from events outside the scope of the risk created by the defendant's negligent conduct. But it can be quite difficult to determine where, in the overall negligence analysis, to consider this point. We could say that if the injuries are outside the scope of the risk, there is no duty of care in respect of them. We could say that those injuries have been caused by something other than the defendant's carelessness. But arguably this point relates most closely to remoteness.

DELOITTE & TOUCHE v. LIVENT INC. (RECEIVER OF)
2017 SCC 63

[The facts and decision are set out in Chapter 13. This extract is from the majority decision.]

GASCON AND BROWN JJ.

[90] In simple terms, the *SAAMCO* principle denies recovery for pure economic loss where the plaintiff's injury would still have occurred even if the defendant's negligent misrepresentation were factually true. Rephrased as a test, the principle denies liability where an *alternate* cause that is *unrelated* to the defendant's negligence is the true source of the plaintiff's injury. This alternate and unrelated cause explains why the truth of the negligent misstatement has no bearing on the plaintiff's ultimate injury (i.e., because, even with that truth, the injury would have flowed as a result of the alternate cause). Or, framed from the perspective of the duty of care, the defendant could not have undertaken to protect against injuries that would have been caused by alternate and unrelated sources. In *SAAMCO*, the House of Lords explained the principle with the commendably Albertan example of a mountaineer:

> A mountaineer about to undertake a difficult climb is concerned about the fitness of his knee. He goes to a doctor who negligently makes a superficial examination and pronounces the knee fit. The climber goes on the expedition, which he would not have undertaken if the doctor had told him the true state of his knee. He suffers an injury which is an entirely foreseeable consequence of mountaineering but has nothing to do with his knee. [p. 213]

[91] In this example, the doctor's negligent misrepresentation (the positive knee diagnosis) is a cause that is alternate and unrelated to the cause of the mountaineer's injury (a mountaineering accident unrelated to the knee, for example, an avalanche). As a result, even had the doctor's negligent misrepresentation been true (i.e., even if the mountaineer's knee had been fit), the injury would still have occurred, since the fitness of his knee would not have prevented the injury caused by the avalanche. In other words, the doctor could not have undertaken to protect against an avalanche, which is unrelated to his or her diagnosis.

NOTES AND QUESTIONS

1. The *SAAMCO* principle takes its name from *South Australia Asset Management Corp. v. York Montague Ltd.*, [1997] A.C. 191, a decision of the House of Lords. See also *BPE Solicitors v. Hughes-Holland (in substitution for Gabriel)*, [2017] UKSC 21. *Livent* was a negligent misrepresentation case involving pure economic loss and so the analysis refers specifically to that area of law, but the principle is broader. Indeed, the example of the mountaineer's knee can be seen as simply a breach of a doctor's duty in examining a patient. Nevertheless, most cases that apply this analysis are ones in which the defendant affirmatively agreed to assume certain responsibilities rather than cases in which the defendant's responsibilities are imposed by law.

2. Note how the analysis uses language of causation and of duty of care. Yet in the decision this analysis follows immediately after a section on remoteness, suggesting it relates closely to that issue. In contrast, the dissent in *Livent* treats the issue of the scope of the risk as part of the duty of care analysis and not as an issue of remoteness.

It nonetheless observes that "however one looks at the matter — from the perspective of the scope of the duty of care or from the perspective of remoteness — one arrives at the same point": see paras. 139-43.

It has been suggested that "the *SAAMCO* principle adds a different, complementary perspective to those normally considered under the labels 'causation' and 'remoteness'": Thomson, "*SAAMCO* Revisited" [2017] C.L.J. 476 at 477. See also Hamer, "'Factual Causation' and 'Scope of Liability': What's the Difference?" (2014) 77 M.L.R. 155. Lord Hoffmann, who wrote the decision in *SAAMCO*, subsequently wrote extra-judicially that there "is a close link between the nature of the duty and the extent of liability for breach of that duty": Hoffmann, "Causation" (2005) 121 L.Q.R. 592 at 596.

Where do you think the question of injuries claimed to be outside the scope of the risk created by the defendant should be analyzed? Do the cases in the previous section on intervening causes offer any insights? Are there cases in earlier chapters in which a duty of care was denied that you think are better understood as applications of the *SAAMCO* principle?

3. How would you resolve the example of the mountaineer's knee? Should the doctor be liable?

4. In *Livent* the majority held that the *SAAMCO* principle did not preclude recovery. It stated (at para. 92) that "Deloitte's negligence related to a statutory audit, a purpose of which is management oversight by shareholders. That oversight, in turn, informs (or is related to) subsequent business decisions by the corporation. It follows that Livent's trading losses were not an alternate and unrelated cause of Livent's injury. To the contrary, the shareholders' capacity to oversee the conduct of Livent's business was entirely dependent upon the statutory audit preceding that oversight."

5. Applying the *SAAMCO* principle can be difficult, especially when assessing complex financial losses. With that in mind, the *Livent* majority cautioned (at para. 94) that "a full consideration of *SAAMCO*'s application in Canadian law by this Court should await future cases, with greater consideration of the principle by lower courts, more comprehensive submissions by counsel, and critically, with facts more analogous to those in the *SAAMCO* jurisprudence." Thus far only a handful of Canadian decisions even mention *SAAMCO*. One is *The Owners, Strata Plan LMS 3851 v. Homer Street Development Limited Partnership*, 2016 BCCA 371, additional reasons 2016 BCCA 491.

REVIEW PROBLEM

As a child, Mrs. Adams had been overprotected by her parents. Since they considered bicycles to be dangerous, she had never learned to ride one. In an attempt to overcome her fears, Mrs. Adams purchased a bicycle, which she rode to and from work. While riding on a quiet street, Mrs. Adams witnessed a car accident in front of her. Mr. Jones had gone through a stop sign and struck Mr. King's vehicle. Neither the drivers nor their passengers were hurt. However, the accident startled Mrs. Adams, who veered into the curb and fell, striking her head on the pavement. Her physical injuries were relatively minor and her bike was undamaged, but she became increasingly afraid to leave her house except to go shopping and to work. Her family doctor suggested that she enter therapy to deal with her fear of going outside. Through no fault of the therapist, Mrs. Adams had a very unusual and extremely severe reaction to the treatment and has become a complete shut-in. She now refuses to work or to leave the house for any reason. To make matters worse, her husband has left her because he is incapable of dealing with her "paranoia."

After the collision, Mr. King attempted to drive his car to his usual service station. He signalled a left turn at an intersection and stopped for the oncoming traffic. Unfortunately, Mr. King's rear left signal light was no longer working because of the first accident, and his car was struck from behind by Mr. Smith. As a result of this collision, Mr. King's arm was fractured and he had to be taken to hospital in an ambulance. His arm was put in a cast and he was told not to use the arm until the cast came off. Mr. King was still able to run his plumbing store and initially he followed his doctor's orders. However, in a rush to fill a large order for a very important customer, who had already complained about delays, Mr. King tried to assist. As his doctor feared, in attempting to steady a heavy sink with his broken arm, King fractured the bone again. He had to undergo surgery, was hospitalized for four weeks and was prohibited from returning to work for an additional two months.

You have been contacted by Mrs. Adams and Mr. King. Mrs. Adams wishes to sue Mr. Jones for all of her physical injuries, the deterioration in her mental health, her financial losses due to her inability to work, and the break-up of her marriage. Mr. King is seeking damages from both Mr. Jones and Mr. Smith. Your initial investigations have established that Mr. King's car sustained $1,600 worth of damage in the first collision and an additional $4,400 worth of damage in the second collision. Mr. King has informed you that his tool chests worth $1,000 were stolen at the scene of the second accident.

THE ASSESSMENT OF DAMAGES

1. Introduction
2. Damages for Personal Injuries
3. Survival of Actions and Dependants' Claims
4. Damages for Property Loss
5. Collateral Benefits

1. Introduction

In this chapter we examine the legal principles governing the assessment of damages in Canada. While some of these principles apply equally to intentional tort claims and claims in negligence, our focus here, as in the preceding and subsequent chapters, is on negligence. Some general principles are explained in this introduction and more specific principles are discussed in the remaining sections. We examine the principles relating to personal injury claims and analyze some of the more technical rules governing their assessment. This detailed discussion is intended to illustrate the complexities of applying the general principles to specific cases. Space limitations do not permit us to provide a similar analysis of other types of damage claims. The assessment of property damage is only briefly discussed and the assessment of pure economic loss is not discussed at all.

(a) THE PURPOSES OF DAMAGE AWARDS IN NEGLIGENCE

As noted in Chapter 2, damages may be classified according to the purpose for which they are awarded. In this functional classification system, damages are traditionally divided into three categories: nominal, compensatory and punitive.

Nominal damages are generally awarded to vindicate the plaintiff's rights in situations in which he or she has suffered no injuries. Since the plaintiff must establish loss or injury as one of the elements of a negligence claim, nominal damages are not available in negligence actions.

With rare exceptions, negligence actions are brought to recover compensatory damages. In negligence, as in the intentional torts, the purpose of compensatory damages is to put the plaintiff in the position that he or she would have been in had the tort not been committed. As will become apparent in the material below, this principle is easy to understand but often extremely difficult to apply in even moderately complicated personal injury or property damage cases.

Unlike their English counterparts, Canadian courts have not defined punitive damages narrowly or restricted them to specific categories of cases. Rather, Canadian courts have held that punitive damages may be awarded for one of the following four purposes: punishment, deterrence, denunciation and to relieve a wrongdoer of profits made from the wrong: see *Whiten v. Pilot Insurance Co.*, [2002] 1 S.C.R. 595. Canadian courts have accepted that punitive damages can be awarded in those negligence cases in which the defendant has acted with an arrogant, high-handed or blatant disregard for the plaintiff's safety or other interests. However, the courts remain reluctant to award punitive damages in negligence cases. In large measure this is because the vast majority of negligence cases involve simple carelessness and thus punitive damages are rarely appropriate.

As noted in Chapter 2, the courts distinguish between punitive and aggravated damages. The latter are not intended as punishment. They are a type of compensatory damages designed to compensate for intangible injuries like humiliation or distress caused as a result of how the defendant committed the tort. Like punitive damages, these will rarely be appropriate in cases of simple carelessness.

NOTES AND QUESTIONS

1. For a discussion of nominal damages see *The Mediana*, [1900] A.C. 113 (H.L.), which is extracted in Chapter 2, and Waddams, *The Law of Damages*, looseleaf (1991) (consulted June 2018) at 10.10-10.30. In contrast to the orthodox view, Cooper-Stephenson & Adjin-Tettey, *Personal Injury Damages in Canada*, 3d ed. (2018) at 140 states that "where the plaintiff could have provided evidence of quantum but unreasonably omitted to do so, the reward may be nominal damages." See also *Fisher v. Knibbe* (1992), 125 A.R. 219 (C.A.) where the plaintiff was awarded $100 in nominal damages against the defendant solicitor who missed a limitation period. The court awarded nominal damages because the original action would not have succeeded in any event. What purpose is served by such an award?

2. *Robitaille v. Vancouver Hockey Club Ltd.* (1979), 19 B.C.L.R. 158 (S.C.), aff'd (1981), 124 D.L.R. (3d) 228 (B.C.C.A.) is one of the few negligence cases in which punitive damages have been awarded. The trial judge held that the defendant's medical staff had consciously ignored the plaintiff's complaints about a serious injury. As a result, the plaintiff suffered a permanent disabling injury when he was forced to play hockey in an injured condition. The judge characterized the defendant's conduct as "high-handed, arrogant and displaying a reckless disregard for the rights of the plaintiff" and awarded the plaintiff $35,000 in punitive damages. Do you agree with the court's application of punitive damages to the facts? *Robitaille* was approved by the Supreme Court of Canada in *Vorvis v. Insurance Corporation of B.C.*, [1989] 4 W.W.R. 218 (S.C.C.).

3. In *Kraft (Next friend of) v. Oshawa General Hospital*, [1985] O.J. No. 1085 (H.C.) (QL), varied on other grounds [1986] O.J. No. 838 (C.A.) (QL), the plaintiff, a healthy woman, suffered severe brain damage following a cardiac arrest during a relatively safe and simple surgical procedure. The cardiac arrest was precipitated by the failure of the defendant anaesthetist to properly ventilate the plaintiff or monitor her vital signs for a period of at least four minutes. Rather than attending to the plaintiff, the anaesthetist was apparently doing a crossword puzzle that he had clipped to the plaintiff's chart. In dismissing the plaintiff's claim for punitive damages, the judge stated:

> I am unable to find in the defendant's conduct maliciousness, intent to harm, or that disregard of every principle of decency which is the foundation for an award of punitive damages. It is my view that punitive damages should be awarded only on rare occasions and I am not persuaded that they should be awarded in the circumstances of this case.

Do you agree with the court's statement of the circumstances in which punitive damages may be awarded or the application of this principle to the facts? Is the defendant's conduct in this case any less morally blameworthy than the conduct that gives rise to punitive damages in intentional tort cases? Can you reconcile *Kraft* and *Robitaille*? See also *Rumsey v. R.*, [1984] 5 W.W.R. 585 (Fed. T.D.).

4. In *Vlchek v. Koshel* (1988), 44 C.C.L.T. 314 (B.C.S.C.) the plaintiff was seriously injured when she was thrown from an all-terrain vehicle. She sued the manufacturer for failing to recall or redesign the vehicle despite numerous similar accidents. On a motion to determine a question of law, the court concluded that punitive damages could be awarded even if the defendant's act was not directed toward the plaintiff, as long as it was malicious or reckless enough to indicate a complete indifference to the welfare and safety of others.

5. What principles should apply to a defendant who drives while impaired? In both *Nelson v. Welsh* (1985), 70 N.S.R. (2d) 422 (S.C.) and *Wilson v. Lind* (1985), 35 C.C.L.T. 95 (Ont. H.C.) punitive damages were denied because criminal law provides a mechanism for punishing impaired drivers. However, there was no evidence that either driver had been criminally prosecuted. See also Whitehill, "*Taylor v. Superior Court*: Punitive Damages for Nondeliberate Torts: The Drunk Driving Context" (1980) 68 Cal. L. Rev. 911. Can you suggest other types of negligence cases in which punitive damages might be appropriate? When should a criminal conviction, or the possibility of a criminal conviction, preclude punitive damages? See *Daniels v. Thompson*, [1998] 3 N.Z.L.R. 22 (C.A.); and Waters, "Multiple Punishment: The Effect of a Prior Criminal Conviction on an Award of Punitive Damages" (1996) 18 Adv. Q. 34.

6. In *McIntyre v. Grigg* (2006), 83 O.R. (3d) 161 (C.A.) an impaired driver sped through a stop sign and struck a pedestrian. The defendant initially faced criminal charges but these were withdrawn because the police had not advised him of his right to counsel, making key evidence inadmissible. He pled guilty to careless driving and was fined $500. He was sued by the pedestrian who had suffered serious physical and psychological injuries. In addition to compensatory damages, an Ontario jury awarded $100,000 in aggravated damages and $100,000 in punitive damages. The Court of Appeal overturned the award of aggravated damages, holding that the expert medical evidence did not establish that the plaintiff's psychological injuries were increased as a result of the driver's intoxication. As to the punitive damages, it held by a majority that (at para. 57):

> By making the deliberate choice to drink excessively and then drive, Andrew Grigg's misconduct was more than mere negligence. It demonstrated a conscious and reckless disregard for the lives and safety of others. There was evidence he was two to three times over the legal limit for alcohol consumption and was speeding and driving recklessly. In our view, this was sufficient evidence for the jury to find that an award of punitive damages was warranted. . . . Grigg also argued an award of punitive damages would be inappropriate and unnecessary given that [he] had already been punished, *i.e.* a $500 fine for careless driving. In our view, analyzing the principles articulated by the Supreme Court of Canada in *Whiten*, and given the fact that the misconduct in question was much more serious than careless driving, it was open to the jury to find that punitive damages did not amount to double punishment, that

others would not be deterred by the fine imposed on Andrew Grigg, and that punitive damages were appropriate.

However, the court nonetheless reduced the amount of the punitive damages to $20,000. In dissent, Justice R.A. Blair would have overturned the punitive damage award altogether. He stated (at para. 134): "I think there can be no doubt, however, that if punitive damages are found to be available in this case, they will be found to be available — and will be awarded — in many other personal injury or fatal accident cases arising out of alcohol-related motor vehicle accidents." In his view, such awards had to be confined to truly exceptional cases. Do you agree with the majority or the dissent?

7. A few cases have apparently allowed punitive damages for inadvertent negligence. See for example *Rowland's Transport Ltd. v. Nasby Sales & Services Ltd.* (1978), 16 A.R. 192 (S.C. (T.D.)). The better view is that only advertent negligence, such as in *Robitaille, supra*, will support a punitive damage award.

8. For other cases involving punitive damages in negligence see *Heighington v. Ontario* (1987), 60 O.R. (2d) 641 (H.C.), additional reasons (1987), 60 O.R. (2d) 655 (H.C.), aff'd (1989), 69 O.R. (2d) 484 (C.A.); *Coughlin v. Kuntz* (1987), 42 C.C.L.T. 142 (B.C.S.C.), aff'd (1989), 2 C.C.L.T. (2d) 42 (B.C.C.A.); *MacDonald v. Sebastian* (1987), 81 N.S.R. (2d) 189 (S.C.); *Augustus v. Gosset* (1995), 27 C.C.L.T. (2d) 161 (Qc. C.A.), rev'd (1996), 34 C.C.L.T. (2d) 111 (S.C.C.); and *Shobridge v. Thomas* (1999), 47 C.C.L.T. (2d) 73 (B.C.S.C.).

9. What is the purpose of punitive damages? Although Canadian courts often speak of "punishment and deterrence" those goals are not necessarily consistent or mutually compatible. Suggest situations in which an award of punitive damages would be appropriate for one goal but not the other. For a discussion on that point, and for a general overview of punitive damages, see Polinsky & Shavell, "Punitive Damages: An Economic Analysis" (1998) 111 Harv. L. Rev. 869.

(b) THE EXISTENCE OF DAMAGE

As noted in the discussion of nominal damages in the previous section, negligence is not actionable *per se*. The plaintiff must establish damage recognizable by law in order for the claim to succeed. In most claims this is quite straightforward. But in some cases the defendant alleges that what has happened to the plaintiff does not qualify as damage and that the negligence claim must therefore fail.

In *Rothwell v. Chemical & Insulating Co. Ltd.*, [2008] A.C. 281 the defendants carelessly exposed the plaintiffs to asbestos. As a result, the plaintiffs developed pleural plaques, which are areas of fibrous thickening of the pleural membrane surrounding the lungs. The evidence was that the plaques were in no way harmful: they had no impact at all on the plaintiffs' health. The House of Lords held that the plaintiffs' claim failed for lack of actionable damage. See also *Alcan Gove Pty Ltd v. Zabic*, [2015] HCA 33 at para. 17(2).

In *Dryden v. Johnson Matthey*, [2018] UKSC 18 the defendants carelessly exposed the plaintiffs to platinum salts. As a result the plaintiffs developed platinum salt sensitization. This condition meant that with further exposure to platinum salts, they would develop an allergic reaction with physical symptoms such as a running nose and irritated skin. The Court of Appeal held, relying on *Rothwell*, that the physiological change did not amount to damage. However, the United Kingdom Supreme Court reversed. It held that in *Rothwell*, the change to the plaintiffs did not necessitate any change in conduct by the plaintiffs, but in this case the plaintiffs now had to avoid exposure to platinum salts in the future.

NOTES AND QUESTIONS

1. Do you agree with the decisions in *Rothwell* and *Dryden*? Consider that platinum salts are only encountered in highly specialized environments.

2. See Stapleton, "The Gist of Negligence — Part I: Minimum Actionable Damage" (1988) 104 L.Q.R. 213; Turton, "Defining Damage in the House of Lords" (2007) 71 M.L.R. 1009; Voyiakis, "The Great Illusion: Tort Law and Exposure to Danger of Physical Harm" (2009) 72 M.L.R. 909; Nolan, "Damage in the English Law of Negligence" (2013) 4 J. Eur. Tort L. 259; and Nolan, "Rights, Damage and Loss" (2017) 37 O.J.L.S. 255.

3. If a defendant carelessly emits nickel particles into the soil of the plaintiff's land, has the plaintiff suffered damage sufficient to claim in negligence? Suppose the nickel particles are not a health hazard and do not interfere with the plaintiff's use of the land. Would it matter if the land's market value fell due to irrational public concern about nickel particles? See *Smith v. Inco Ltd.*, 2011 ONCA 628 (a nuisance case).

4. As noted in the discussion of duty of care and remoteness in earlier chapters, courts have historically been more cautious awarding damages for mental harm than for physical harm. This has extended to holding, in some cases, that the mental harm alleged by the plaintiff does not rise to the level of actionable damage. It is well-established, for example, that grief and sorrow are not sufficient.

Recently, the Supreme Court of Canada has addressed what is required, as damage, in cases of mental harm. In *Saadati v. Moorhead*, 2017 SCC 28 (see the extract in Chapter 12), the court held that a plaintiff does not need to show a recognized psychiatric illness in order to recover and does not have to provide expert evidence. However, courts will still have to draw lines between what is recognized as actionable damage and what is not (such as grief and sorrow). The court stated (at para. 37) that what constitutes mental injury is a serious and prolonged disturbance that rises above the ordinary annoyances, anxieties and fears that come with living in civil society. For more on how this line can be drawn (and justified) see Sinel, "What's Your Damage?" (2017) 24 Torts L.J. 205. See also Belanger-Hardy, "Thresholds of Actionable Mental Harm in Negligence: A Policy-Based Analysis" (2013) 36 Dal. L.J. 103; and Belanger-Hardy, "Reconsidering the 'Recognizable Psychiatric Illness' Requirement in Canadian Negligence Law" (2013) 38 Queen's L.J. 583.

5. Do cases in which the plaintiff claims for the loss of a chance of receiving some benefit, discussed in Chapter 16, raise the issue of whether actionable damage has been suffered?

6. Should a plaintiff who has not suffered any damage be able to sue in negligence for disgorgement damages — damages measured with reference not to the plaintiff's loss but rather the defendant's gain? As noted in Chapter 2, it is far from clear whether disgorgement damages are available in negligence. If they are, would allowing such a claim be contrary to the notion that negligence is not actionable *per se*? See the extensive analysis of this issue in *Atlantic Lottery Corporation Inc.-Société des lotteries de l'Atlantique v. Babstock*, 2018 NLCA 71. See also Pitel, "Reels, Rows and Restitution: A Comment on *Atlantic Lottery Corporation Inc. v. Babstock*" (2019) 53 C.C.L.T. (4th) 107

(c) PRELIMINARY ISSUES

There are several preliminary issues relating to the assessment of damages that must be addressed before turning to the specific principles governing different types of damage claims. These include the burden and standard of proof in damages, mitigation of damages, the set-off of parallel expenditures, the use of lump sum payments and the roles of juries, judges and appellate courts.

The plaintiff bears the burden of proving the quantum of the damages that are claimed. The standard of proof for losses that have occurred prior to trial is straightforward. The plaintiff must prove the existence and quantum of such losses on the balance of probabilities. If the plaintiff meets this standard, he or she is entitled to recover 100% of the claim; if not, he or she recovers nothing. The standard of proof for losses that may occur after trial is more complicated. There are two possible approaches. An earlier line of authority in Canada employed a balance of probabilities test. If the plaintiff established on the balance of probabilities that a future loss would occur, he or she recovered the entire amount. However, if he or she could not meet this test, the claim was denied. A more recent line of authorities is based on a reasonable or substantial possibility test. Once the plaintiff establishes that there is a substantial or reasonable possibility of injury, he or she is entitled to recover for this loss, but subject to the likelihood of it occurring. Pursuant to this second line of cases, a plaintiff who establishes that there is a 35% chance of suffering blindness in the future is entitled to 35% of the damages for such blindness.

The plaintiff is under an obligation to act reasonably in all of the circumstances of the case to mitigate his or her loss. The defendant has the burden of proving that the plaintiff failed to do so. Edelman, Varuhas & Colton, eds., *McGregor on Damages*, 20th ed. (2017) at 9-003 outlines three related principles of mitigation. First, the plaintiff must take all reasonable steps to avoid or minimize the loss. Second, the plaintiff may recover for losses incurred in taking such reasonable steps. Third, the plaintiff cannot recover for losses that have been successfully avoided, even if he or she was not required to have avoided them under the first rule. These principles are generally applied more rigorously to claims for property damages and business losses than to claims for personal injuries. Although relatively easy to state, these principles are often very difficult to apply in specific fact situations. See also Cooper-Stephenson & Adjin-Tettey, *Personal Injury Damages in Canada*, 3d ed. (2018) at 1309-49.

A defendant is allowed to set-off against the plaintiff's damage claim any parallel expenditures that the plaintiff would have incurred had the tort not been committed. For example, if the plaintiff is claiming the full cost of nursing home care which includes food, the defendant may be permitted to reduce this claim by the amount the plaintiff would have spent anyway on food during this period. As a general rule, set-off is only permitted if the defendant can establish that the two items in issue are truly parallel in nature and that their values are readily calculable.

At common law, damages are awarded in a one-time lump sum to compensate the plaintiff for all the losses he or she has suffered and will likely suffer in the future. Under the lump-sum payment system the trier of fact is forced to speculate on a range of issues including the future condition of the injured plaintiff, the probable increases in health care and nursing costs, and the impact of inflation on the purchasing power of the damage award. If a loss turns out to be far greater or smaller than that calculated at trial, there is no means of re-assessment. The inadequacies of this system have been widely criticized.

In a jury trial, it is the jury's responsibility to assess damages and the law does not allow counsel or the judge to provide much assistance. With respect to *special damages*, that situation creates relatively few difficulties. Special damages consist of pre-trial pecuniary losses such as expenses incurred and income lost prior to trial. Because such damages must be specifically pleaded and proved by the plaintiff on a balance of probabilities, the jury is provided with considerable guidance for the purposes of quantification. In contrast, juries are provided with relatively little guidance with respect to *general damages*. General damages consist of pre-trial non-pecuniary losses and all post-trial losses, such as pain and suffering, future expenses and loss of income. Traditionally, counsel and judges were not permitted to suggest appropriate amounts or to inform jurors of the usual range of non-pecuniary awards. However, that attitude is changing and the courts are increasingly willing to apprise jurors of suitable ranges and rough upper limits: see *ter Neuzen v. Korn*, [1995] 3 S.C.R. 674; and *Foreman v. Foster* (2001), 84 B.C.L.R. (3d) 184 (C.A.). However, see *Brisson v. Brisson* (2002), 11 C.C.L.T. (3d) 197 (B.C.C.A.); and *Yin v. Lewin* (2006), 61 Alta. L.R. (4th) 138 (Q.B.), aff'd (2007), 82 Alta. L.R. (4th) 255 (C.A.).

At common law counsel and the trial judge are precluded from referring the jury to awards that have been made in similar cases, although counsel may refer to such information on appeal. The problems of inconsistency are further heightened by the general rule that appellate courts are not to interfere with a jury's assessment of damages unless there is a clear error in law or the amount is so grossly out of line that it is a "wholly erroneous" estimate of the damages.

NOTES AND QUESTIONS

1. Because of a delay between the trial of an action and the court rendering its judgment, hypothetical future facts may become past actual facts. In assessing damages, the court should adjust its calculations accordingly. In *Monahan v. Nelson* (2000), 186 D.L.R. (4th) 193 (B.C.C.A.) the defendant negligently injured the plaintiff. The trial judge heard evidence about several heads of damage, including loss of future income, cost of future care and future non-pecuniary losses (like pain and suffering). The plaintiff then died, for reasons unrelated to the defendant's tort, before the trial judge rendered judgment. Relying upon the *Estate Administration Act*, R.S.B.C. 1996, c. 122, s. 59, the trial judge nevertheless proceeded to award damages as if the plaintiff were still alive. The British Columbia Court of Appeal reduced the damages, insisting that recovery reflect actual losses to the extent possible. See also *Strachan (Guardian ad litem of) v. Reynolds* (2006), 39 C.C.L.T. (3d) 79 (B.C.S.C.).

2. It can be difficult to distinguish issues pertaining to the existence of liability from those pertaining to the extent of liability. The courts often take different approaches to these issues and use different terminology. For example, is it most appropriate to state that there is no duty to avoid causing grief and sorrow, that grief and sorrow are too remote or that grief and sorrow are not recognized heads of damage?

3. For cases supporting the balance of probabilities test for future losses see *B.C. Electric Ry. Co. v. Clarke*, [1950] 3 D.L.R. 161 (S.C.C.); *Turenne v. Chung* (1962), 36 D.L.R. (2d) 197 (Man. C.A.); *Corrie v. Gilbert*, [1965] S.C.R. 457; and *Conklin v. Smith* (1978), 5 C.C.L.T. 113 (S.C.C.). For cases supporting the reasonable possibility test see *Davies v. Taylor*, [1972] 3 All E.R. 836 (H.L.); *Schrump v. Koot* (1977), 18 O.R. (2d) 337 (C.A.); *Hearndon v. Rondeau* (1984), 29 C.C.L.T. 149 (B.C.C.A.); *Janiak v. Ippolito* (1985), 16 D.L.R. (4th) 1 (S.C.C.); *Steenblok v. Funk*, [1990] 5 W.W.R. 365 (B.C.C.A.); *Bachalo v. Robson* (1998), 129 Man. R. (2d) 1 (C.A.); *Hornick v. Kochinsky* (2005), 22 C.C.L.I. (4th) 29 (Ont. S.C.J.); *Haile v. Johns* (2005), 50 B.C.L.R. (4th) 241 (C.A.); *Poirier v. Aubrey* (2010), 4 B.C.L.R. (5th) 173 (C.A.); *Burdett v. Eidse*, 2011 BCCA 191 at para. 54; and *Salame v. Sutherland*, 2016 BCSC 1610 at para. 114.

Today it is well established that for future losses Canadian courts follow the reasonable possibility test set out in *Janiak v. Ippolito, supra* and in *Athey v. Leonati*, [1996] 3 S.C.R. 458. Can you provide an example in which the result would be the same regardless of which test was used? Provide an example in which the tests would produce different results. Which test is more in keeping with the purpose of compensatory damage awards? For a discussion of these issues see Kirkham, "Proof of Future Loss: Probabilities and Possibilities" (1984) 24 The Advocate 21; Cooper-Stephenson & Adjin-Tettey, *Personal Injury Damages in Canada*, 3d ed. (2018) at 1085-99; and Waddams, *The Law of Damages*, looseleaf (1991) (consulted June 2018) at 13.260-13.370.

4. It may be difficult to determine whether the plaintiff's conduct should be raised under remoteness, contributory negligence, mitigation or all three. Moreover, some courts deal with the question of set-off of parallel expenditures as an issue of mitigation. For a comprehensive review of the principles of mitigation, see Cooper-Stephenson & Adjin-Tettey, *supra*, at 1309-49; and Waddams, *supra*, ch. 15.

5. In *Janiak v. Ippolito, supra*, the defendant negligently caused the plaintiff's serious back injury. The plaintiff was informed that if he had corrective surgery there was a 70 to 75% chance of complete recovery which would allow him to return to work. The chance of a "poor result" was 10%, including a 1% risk of quadriplegia and a 0.1% risk of death. The plaintiff refused to have the operation. The court had to decide if his refusal constituted an unreasonable failure to mitigate. The court held that this issue was to be resolved by the trier of fact and depended upon the risks of surgery, the consequences of refusing surgery, and its potential benefits. The court concluded that the trial judge was correct in finding that the plaintiff unreasonably failed to mitigate his loss by refusing surgery. Do you agree? See also *Souto v. Anderson*, [1996] 5 W.W.R. 394 (B.C.C.A.); and *Kozak v. Funk*, [1996] 1 W.W.R. 79 (Sask. Q.B.).

In *Janiak* the court also stated that a plaintiff's pre-existing fear of surgery does not justify an unreasonable failure to have an operation unless he or she suffers from a psychological infirmity that precludes rational decision-making. Is this proposition consistent with the general principles governing the thin-skulled plaintiff rule? Should these same principles apply if the surgical procedure violates the plaintiff's religious beliefs? Should the same principles apply to recommended psychiatric treatment, even if participation would stigmatize the plaintiff? See *Brian v. Mador* (1985), 32 C.C.L.T. 157 (Ont. C.A.); *Engel v. Kam-Ppelle Holdings Ltd.* (1993), 15 C.C.L.T. (2d) 245 (S.C.C.); and *Gray v. Gill* (1993), 18 C.C.L.T. (2d) 120 (B.C.S.C.). See also Kemp, "Mitigation of Damage — Plaintiff's Refusal to Undergo Operation — Onus of Proof" (1983) 99 L.Q.R. 497; and Ramsay, "The Religious Beliefs of Tort Victims: Religious Thin Skulls or Failures of Mitigation?" (2007) 20 C.J.L.J. 399.

6. For a discussion of mitigation in a personal injury context see *Parypa v. Wickware* (1999), 169 D.L.R. (4th) 661 (B.C.C.A.); *Kern v. Steele* (2003), 220 N.S.R. (2d) 51 (C.A.); *Morel v. Bryden* (2006), 246 N.S.R. (2d) 43 (S.C.); *Naidu v. Mann* (2007), 53 C.C.L.T. (3d) 1 (B.C.S.C.); *Papineau v. Dorman* (2008), 62 C.C.L.T. (3d) 120 (B.C.S.C.); *Ksiazek v. Newport Leasing Ltd.* (2010), 84 C.C.L.I. (4th) 182 (Ont. C.A.); *Paniccia Estate v. Toal*, 2012 ABCA 397; *Liu v. Bipinchandra*, 2016 BCSC 283; and *Park v. Targonski*, 2017 BCCA 134. For a discussion in commercial and property damage situations, see respectively *Hongkong Bank of Canada v. Richardson Greenshields of Canada Ltd.* (1990), 72 D.L.R. (4th) 161 (B.C.C.A.); and *University of Regina v. Pettick* (1991), 77 D.L.R. (4th) 615 (Sask. C.A.).

7. For a discussion of the set-off of parallel expenditures see *Shearman v. Folland*, [1950] 1 All E.R. 976 (C.A.); *Andrews v. Grand & Toy Alberta Ltd.* (1978), 83 D.L.R. (3d) 452 (S.C.C.); and Cooper-Stephenson & Adjin-Tettey, *supra*, at 765-807.

8. For a discussion of the role of the judge and jury see Schroeder, "The Charge to the Jury" in *Special Lectures of the Law Society of Upper Canada 1959* (1959) 311. In *Howes v. Crosby* (1984), 6 D.L.R. (4th) 698 (Ont. C.A.) the court noted that it would not be an error for a trial judge to inform the jury of the Supreme Court of Canada's limits on awards for non-pecuniary loss (discussed below). However, in *Baurose v. Hart* (1990), 44 C.P.C. (2d) 283 (Ont. Gen. Div.) the court stated that the upper limit should only be mentioned in cases of catastrophic injury. In Ontario the *Courts of Justice Act*, R.S.O. 1990, c. C.43, s. 118 now allows the parties and the judge to inform the jury about general damage awards.

9. Although the principles governing an appellate review of a damage award are well established, it is often difficult to reconcile the cases. For a comprehensive review, see Waddams, *supra*, at 13.420-13.480. See also *Cody v. Leonard*, [1996] 4 W.W.R. 96 (B.C.C.A.); *Stafford v. Motomochi*, [1997] 3 W.W.R. 571 (B.C.C.A.); and *Moskaleva v. Laurie* (2009), 94 B.C.L.R. (4th) 58 (C.A.) at paras. 96-130. In *Woelk v. Halvorson*, [1980] 2 S.C.R. 430 at 435 the Supreme Court of Canada noted that "It is well settled that a Court of Appeal should not alter a damage award made at trial merely because, on its view of the evidence, it would have come to a different conclusion. It is only where a Court of Appeal comes to the conclusion that there was no evidence upon which a trial judge could have reached this conclusion, or where he proceeded upon a mistaken or wrong principle, or where the result reached at the trial was wholly erroneous, that a Court of Appeal is entitled to intervene." For an example of an appellate court varying a jury's damage award see *Taraviras v. Lovig*, 2011 BCCA 200.

10. Traditionally, the courts held that the defendant would have grounds for appeal if the jury was informed that the defendant had liability insurance: *Theakston v. Bowley*, [1950] 3 D.L.R. 804 (Ont. C.A.). However, the Supreme Court of Canada has held that there is no absolute rule regarding the effect of disclosing such information to the jury: *Hamstra (Guardian ad litem of) v. British Columbia Rugby Union*, [1997] 1 S.C.R. 1092. Rather, the trial judge should determine whether, in all of the circumstances of the case, the disclosure of such information was prejudicial to the parties. If so, the trial judge should fashion an appropriate solution. The jury might be dismissed, a new trial might be ordered, or the jury might simply be directed to disregard the information in question.

11. Do the rules governing judges, juries and appeals make sense given the complexity of the law of damages? J. Fleming has argued that the inconsistency and apparent arbitrariness of damage awards has more than anything else led to the restricted use of juries in civil actions: Fleming, "Damages For Non-Material Loss" in *Special Lectures of the Law Society of Upper Canada 1973* (1973) 1 at 5-10. Should the assessment of damages be left to the judge in jury cases? If not, how would you modify the existing rules?

12. The recovery of prejudgment and post-judgment interest on the plaintiff's losses raises complex issues that are increasingly governed by legislation. See for example *Courts of Justice Act*, R.S.O. 1990, c. C.43, ss. 127-130. See Bowles & Whelan, "The Law of Interest: Dawn of a New Era?" (1986) 64 Can. Bar Rev. 142; and Waddams, *supra*, at 7.330-7.1000.

13. Causation issues can lead to difficulties in assessing damages. The defendant is only required to compensate the plaintiff for damages that he or she has caused. So in assessing damages courts often have to distinguish between the damages for which the defendant is responsible and the damages resulting from the actions of another tortfeasor, a non-tortious actor or a plaintiff's pre-existing condition. See the discussion of *Athey v. Leonati*, [1996] 3 S.C.R. 458 in Chapter 16. In *Sanders v. Janze* (2009), 70 C.C.L.T. (3d) 290 (B.C.S.C.) the plaintiff, prior to the car accident in respect of which she was suing, had been injured in three car accidents, two workplace incidents and a chiropractic manipulation. This complicated the assessment of her damages. See also the issues raised in *Misko v. John Doe* (2007), 87 O.R. (3d) 517 (C.A.).

14. In cases in which two defendants are liable, the court often has to apportion liability between them. This is done under provincial statutes on apportionment, discussed in more detail in Chapter 19 in the context of the defence of contributory negligence. It is common for both defendants to be jointly and severally liable to the plaintiff, so that the plaintiff can recover 100% of his or her award from either defendant. As between the defendants, the default apportionment is an equal division. If one defendant pays 100% of the award to the plaintiff, that defendant can recover 50% of the award from the other defendant. However, defendants often request that the court apportion liability unequally. If, for example, liability is apportioned 25% to the first defendant and 75% to the second defendant, and the first defendant pays the plaintiff 100% of the award, then the first defendant can recover 75% of the award from the second defendant. See the discussion in *Taylor v. Canada (Attorney General)* (2009), 95 O.R. (3d) 561 (C.A.) at paras. 16-19. There are many cases in which a key

issue is the apportionment of liability as between the defendants. See for example *Milne v. St. Joseph's Health Centre* (2009), 69 C.C.L.T. (3d) 208 (Ont. S.C.J.).

2. Damages for Personal Injuries

(a) INTRODUCTION

Until the late 1970s Canadian courts used a "global approach" in assessing damages which involved selecting a single figure to compensate the plaintiff for all of his or her injuries. The governing principles were very general and meaningful appellate review was difficult. Moreover, there was no effective means of addressing the large variations in awards for apparently similar injuries. The global approach typically resulted in very low damage awards. For example in *Clarke v. Penny* (1975), 10 Nfld. & P.E.I.R. 220 (Nfld. T.D.) a five-year-old girl who sustained severe brain damage was awarded $180,000 for her loss of earning capacity, future care costs, pain and suffering, and loss of enjoyment of life.

In the late 1970s the Supreme Court of Canada rejected the global assessment approach in favour of the separate assessment of each head of recovery that has been established by the plaintiff: *Andrews v. Grand & Toy Alberta Ltd.*, [1978] 2 S.C.R. 229; *Arnold v. Teno*, [1978] 2 S.C.R. 287; and *Thornton (Next friend of) v. Prince George School District No. 57*, [1978] 2 S.C.R. 267. The "trilogy," as those cases came to be known, established a framework for quantifying general damages under the following headings:

    (1) Pecuniary loss

        (a) Future loss
        (b) Lost earning capacity
        (c) Considerations relevant to both heads of pecuniary loss

    (2) Non-pecuniary loss

Perhaps the most striking consequence of the trilogy has been the increase in the size of damage awards. The courts' efforts to rationalize damage assessments have led to inflation adjustments, home care awards, the increasing (grossing up) of future care costs to offset the impact of taxes, and awards to hire professional financial managers. Million-dollar awards, unheard of in Canada before the late 1970s, were commonplace by the mid-1980s. The jury's award in *Sandhu (Litigation Guardian of) v. Wellington Place Apartments* (2008), 234 O.A.C. 200 (C.A.) to a two-year-old plaintiff who suffered a frontal lobe brain injury was almost $14 million. In *Gordon v. Greig* (2007), 46 C.C.L.T. (3d) 212 (Ont. S.C.J.) a car accident left one plaintiff with severe brain injuries and the other plaintiff paraplegic. Both men were in their early twenties. The judge awarded the former over $11 million and the latter over $12 million, the vast majority of which was in each case for the cost of future care. For other examples of sizable damage awards see *Marcoccia (Litigation Guardian of) v. Gill* (2009), 248 O.A.C. 131 (C.A.); *MacNeil v. Bryan* (2009), 81 C.P.C. (6th) 116 (Ont. S.C.J.); and *Boyd v. Edington*, 2014 ONSC 1130.

In this section, we will examine the current Canadian framework for assessing personal injury claims using the relevant portions of Dickson J.'s judgment in *Andrews*. The first excerpt introduces some of the underlying concepts.

ANDREWS v. GRAND & TOY ALBERTA LTD.
(1978), 83 D.L.R. (3d) 452 (S.C.C.)

DICKSON J.—This is a negligence action for personal injury involving a young man rendered a quadriplegic in a traffic accident for which the respondent Anderson and his employer, Grand & Toy Alberta Ltd., have been found partially liable. Leave to appeal to this Court was granted on the question whether the Appellate Division of the Supreme Court of Alberta erred in law in the assessment of damages. At trial Mr. Justice Kirby awarded $1,022,477.48 . . . : the Appellate Division reduced that sum to $516,544.48. . . .

Let me say in introduction what has been said many times before, that no appellate Court is justified in substituting a figure of its own for that awarded at trial simply because it would have awarded a different figure if it had tried the case at first instance. It must be satisfied that a wrong principle of law was applied, or that the overall amount is a wholly erroneous estimate of the damage. . . .

The method of assessing general damages in separate amounts, as has been done in this case, in my opinion, is a sound one. It is the only way in which any meaningful review of the award is possible on appeal and the only way of affording reasonable guidance in future cases. Equally important, it discloses to the litigants and their advisers the components of the overall award, assuring them thereby that each of the various heads of damage going to make up the claim has been given thoughtful consideration.

The subject of damages for personal injury is an area of the law which cries out for legislative reform. The expenditure of time and money in the determination of fault and of damage is prodigal. The disparity resulting from lack of provision for victims who cannot establish fault must be disturbing. When it is determined that compensation is to be made, it is highly irrational to be tied to a lump-sum system and a once-and-for-all award.

The lump-sum award presents problems of great importance. It is subject to inflation, it is subject to fluctuation on investment, income from it is subject to tax. After judgment new needs of the plaintiff arise and the present needs are extinguished; yet, our law of damages knows nothing of periodic payment. The difficulties are greatest where there is a continuing need for intensive and expensive care and a long-term loss of earning capacity. It should be possible to devise some system whereby payments would be subject to periodic review and variation in the light of the continuing needs of the injured person and the cost of meeting those needs. In making this comment I am not unaware of the negative recommendation of the British Law Commission (Law Com. 56 — *Report on Personal Injury Litigation — Assessment of Damages*) following strong opposition from insurance interests and the plaintiffs' bar.

The apparent reliability of assessments provided by modern actuarial practice is largely illusionary, for actuarial science deals with probabilities, not actualities. This is in no way to denigrate a respected profession, but it is obvious that the validity of the answers given by the actuarial witness, as with a computer, depends upon the soundness of the postulates from which he proceeds. Although a useful aid, and a sharper tool than the "multiplier-multiplicand" approach favoured in some jurisdictions, actuarial evidence speaks in terms of group experience. It cannot, and does not purport to, speak as to the individual sufferer. So long as we are tied to lump-sum awards, however, we are tied also to actuarial calculations as the best available means of determining amount.

In spite of these severe difficulties with the present law of personal injury compensation, the positive administrative machinery required for a system of reviewable periodic payments, and the need to hear all interested parties in order to fashion a more enlightened system, both dictate that the appropriate body to act must be the Legislature, rather than the Courts. Until such time as the Legislature acts, the Courts must proceed on established principles to award damages which compensate accident victims with justice and humanity for the losses they may suffer.

I proceed now to a brief recital of the injuries sustained by the appellant James Andrews in the present case. He suffered a fracture with dislocation of the cervical spine between the fifth and sixth cervical vertebrae, causing functional transection of the spinal cord, but leaving some continuity; compound fracture of the left tibia and left humerus; fracture of the left patella. The left radial nerve was damaged. The lesion of the spinal cord left Andrews with paralysis involving most of the upper limbs, spine and lower limbs. He has lost the use of his legs, his trunk, essentially his left arm and most of his right arm. To add to the misery, he does not have normal bladder, bowel and sex functions. He suffers from spasticity in both upper and lower limbs. He has difficulty turning in bed and must be re-positioned every two hours. He needs regular physiotherapy and should have someone in close association with him at all times, such as a trained male orderly. The only functioning muscles of respiration are those of the diaphragm and shoulders. There is much more in the evidence but it need not be recited. Andrews is severely, if not totally disabled. Dr. Weir, a specialist in neurosurgery, said of Andrews' condition that "there is no hope of functional improvement." For the rest of his life he will be dependent on others for dressing, personal hygiene, feeding, and, indeed, for his very survival. But, of utmost important, he is not a vegetable or a piece of cordwood. He is a man of above average intelligence and his mind is unimpaired. He can see, hear and speak as before. He has partial use of his right arm and hand. With the aid of a wheelchair he is mobile. With a specially designed van he can go out in the evening to visit friends, or to the movies, or to a pub. He is taking driving lessons and proving to be an apt pupil. He wants to live as other human beings live. Since May 31, 1974, he has resided in his own apartment with private attendant care. The medical long-term care required is not at a sophisticated level but rather at a practical care level.

Andrews was 21 years of age and unmarried on the date of the accident. On that date he was an apprentice carman employed by the Canadian National Railways in the City of Edmonton.

I turn now to consider assessment of the damages to which Andrews is entitled.

. . .

NOTES AND QUESTIONS

1. What criticisms did Dickson J. make of the fault system and of lump-sum awards? Dickson J. elaborated on his concerns about lump-sum awards in "The Role and Function of Judges" (1980) 14 L.S.U.C. Gazette 138. Although subsequent events may reveal a lump sum to be grossly inadequate, the courts stress the need for finality and refuse to revisit the assessment of damages: *Tsaoussis (Litigation Guardian of) v. Baetz* (1998), 165 D.L.R. (4th) 268 (Ont. C.A.).

2. There are two types of periodic payment schemes. In one, the payment schedule is fixed in advance and cannot be varied to reflect changes in circumstances. In the other, variable periodic payments may be adjusted as circumstances change. Which type of periodic payment scheme best addresses Dickson J.'s concerns?

3. What extra costs would be incurred with variable periodic payments? Are victims more likely to malinger under such a scheme? Is the case for periodic payments paternalistic? The limited research on how plaintiffs fare after receiving lump-sum damage awards has not been encouraging. See Keeton & O'Connell, *Basic Protection for the Traffic Victim* (1965) at 353-54; Fleming, "Damages: Capital or Rent?" (1969) 19 U.T.L.J. 295 at 299-300; Kretzner, "No-Fault Comes to Israel: The Compensation for Victims of Road Accidents Law, 1975" (1976) 11 Isr. L.R. 288 at 306; and Bale, "Encouraging the Hearse Horse Not to Snicker: A Tort Fund Providing Variable Periodic Payments for Pecuniary Loss" in Steel & Rogers-Magnet, eds., *Issues in Tort Law* (1983) 91.

4. Periodic payments are a central feature of the increasing number of structured settlements being reached by parties. Typically, a structured settlement includes a sum for expenses already incurred followed by a series of periodic payments to cover future losses. In most cases the defendant's insurer purchases an annuity designed to generate periodic payments for the plaintiff's life. The payments may, and usually do, vary over the term of the settlement. For example, cost-of-living increases are built into the schedule and balloon payments may be included to meet projected occasional needs such as the cost of a child's university education. Thus, a structured settlement may be tailored to the individual plaintiff's needs. Such settlements protect plaintiffs who might otherwise squander or inefficiently manage the lump-sum award. However, the conditions for variation are established at the time of settlement and no adjustments for unanticipated changes in circumstances are possible.

5. One advantage of a structured settlement is that the periodic payments which are generated are not taxable. Although a lump-sum award is not taxable either, any interest it generates is taxable. This tax savings with structured settlements thus becomes a matter for negotiation, which may be mutually beneficial. The defendant will be able to purchase an annuity for less than the lump sum that would have been awarded, and yet the plaintiff's periodic payments will exceed the after-tax income he or she would have obtained from the interest on the lump sum. See *Yepremian v. Scarborough Gen. Hosp.* (1981), 120 D.L.R. (3d) 341 (Ont. H.C.) in which a judicially approved structured settlement is set out; Weir, *Structured Settlement* (1984); Holland, "Structured Settlements in Injury and Wrongful Death Cases" (1987) 8 Adv. Q. 185; and Watkin, "The New Method of Structuring Settlement Agreements" (1992) 71 Can. Bar Rev. 27.

6. The tax savings in a structured settlement would also occur in a structured judgment. However in *Watkins v. Olafson* (1989), 61 D.L.R. (4th) 577 (S.C.C.) the court held that the courts lacked jurisdiction to impose judgment in a structured form. Canadian legislatures were reluctant to authorize the imposition of structured judgments, although this was recommended by Osborne J. in the *Report of Inquiry into Motor Vehicle Compensation in Ontario* (1988) and by the Law Reform Commission of Saskatchewan in *Proposals for a Structured Judgments Act* (1993). Under the *Insurance (Vehicle) Act*, R.S.B.C. 1996, c. 231, s. 99(1)(a) the court is required to

order periodic payments when the damages in a vehicle action exceed $100,000 and the court considers the payments to be in the plaintiff's best interests. See *Lines v. Gordon* (2009), 90 B.C.L.R. (4th) 203 (C.A.); and *Towson v. Bergman*, 2011 BCCA 273.

7. The *Courts of Justice Act*, R.S.O. 1990, c. C.43, s. 116, provides:

Periodic payment and review of damages

(1) In a proceeding where damages are claimed for personal injuries or under Part V of the *Family Law Act* for loss resulting from the injury to or death of a person, the court,

> (a) if all affected parties consent, may order the defendant to pay all or part of the award for damages periodically on such terms as the court considers just; and
> (b) if the plaintiff requests that an amount be included in the award to offset any liability for income tax on income from the investment of the award, shall order the defendant to pay all or part of the award periodically on such terms as the court considers just.

No order

(2) An order under clause (1) (b) shall not be made if the parties otherwise consent or if the court is of the opinion that the order would not be in the best interests of the plaintiff, having regard to all the circumstances of the case.

Best interests

(3) In considering the best interests of the plaintiff, the court shall take into account,

> (a) whether the defendant has sufficient means to fund an adequate scheme of periodic payments;
> (b) whether the plaintiff has a plan or a method of payment that is better able to meet the interests of the plaintiff than periodic payments by the defendant; and
> (c) whether a scheme of periodic payments is practicable having regard to all the circumstances of the case.

Future review

(4) In an order made under this section, the court may, with the consent of all the affected parties, order that the award be subject to future review and revision in such circumstances and on such terms as the court considers just.

Amount to offset liability for income tax

(5) If the court does not make an order for periodic payment under subsection (1), it shall make an award for damages that shall include an amount to offset liability for income tax on income from investment of the award.

In *Wilson v. Martinello* (1995), 23 O.R. (3d) 417 (C.A.) the court considered an earlier version of s. 116(1)(b). Resolving ambiguities in the "very badly drafted" wording, it held that where a plaintiff seeks a lump-sum award including a gross up, and the defendant proposes a structured award with periodic payments, s. 116 requires the court to impose a structured award unless the plaintiff can prove that it would not be in his or her best interests. In 1996, in accordance with the reasoning in *Wilson*, the legislature amended s. 116(1)(b) to its present form. See also *Chesher v. Monaghan* (2000), 186 D.L.R. (4th) 595 (Ont. C.A.) in which the Court of Appeal rejected the defendant's request for a structured award because it was not in the plaintiff's best interests. In British Columbia see the *Insurance (Vehicle) Act*, R.S.B.C. 1996, c. 231, s. 99(1)(b).

8. Ontario has recently enacted s. 116.1 of the *Courts of Justice Act*. It goes beyond s. 116 to expand the mandatory use of court-ordered periodic payments for future care costs in medical malpractice cases. Why might the legislature have enacted this section?

9. See generally Ontario Law Reform Commission, *Report on Compensation for Personal Injuries and Death* (1987); and Dufays, "Introducing Provisional Damages for Personal Injuries in Canada" (1997) 6 Dal. J. Leg. Stud. 1. For an analysis of the English experience with court-ordered periodic payment awards see Lewis, "Tort Law in Practice: Appearance and Reality in Reforming Periodical Payments of Damages" in Neyers, Chamberlain & Pitel, eds., *Emerging Issues in Tort Law* (2007), ch. 19.

10. Three useful reference works on a wide range of issues relating to personal injury damages are Cooper-Stephenson & Adjin-Tettey, *Personal Injury Damages in Canada*, 3d ed. (2018); Brown, *Damages: Estimating Pecuniary Loss* (2001); and Bruce, Rathje & Weir, *Assessment of Personal Injury Damages*, 5th ed. (2011).

(b) PECUNIARY LOSS: FUTURE CARE

ANDREWS v. GRAND & TOY ALBERTA LTD.
(1978), 83 D.L.R. (3d) 452 (S.C.C.)

DICKSON J.: . . . In theory a claim for the cost of future care is a pecuniary claim for the amount which may reasonably be expected to be expended in putting the injured party in the position he would have been in if he had not sustained the injury. Obviously, a plaintiff who has been gravely and permanently impaired can never be put in the position he would have been in if the tort had not been committed. To this extent, *restitutio in integrum* is not possible. Money is a barren substitute for health and personal happiness, but to the extent, within reason, that money can be used to sustain or improve the mental or physical health of the injured person it may properly form part of a claim.

Contrary to the view expressed in the Appellate Division of Alberta, there is no duty to mitigate, in the sense of being forced to accept less than real loss. There is a duty to be reasonable. There cannot be "complete" or "perfect" compensation. An award must be moderate, and fair to both parties. Clearly, compensation must not be determined on the basis of sympathy, or compassion for the plight of the injured person. What is being sought is compensation not retribution. But, in a case like the present, where both Courts have favoured a home environment, "reasonable" means reasonableness in what is to be provided in that home environment. It does not mean that Andrews must languish in an institution which on all evidence is inappropriate for him.

The reasons for judgment of the Appellate Division embodied three observations which are worthy of brief comment. The first:

> . . . it is the choice of the respondent to live in a home of his own, and from the point of view of advancing a claim for damages, it is a most salutary choice, because it is vastly the most expensive.

I am not entirely certain as to what is meant by this observation. If the import is that the appellant claimed a home life for the sole purpose of inflating his claim, then I think the implication is both unfair and unsupported by evidence. There is no doubt upon the medical and other evidence that a home environment would be salutary to the health of the appellant and productive of good effects. It cannot be unreasonable for a person to want to live in a home of his own.

The next observation:

> Secondly, it should be observed that in many cases, particularly in Alberta where damages have been awarded, the persons injured were going to live with their families. Here, the evidence (in spite of the fact that the respondent's mother advanced a claim for $237 which represented a towing charge for the motor-cycle and parking, taxis and bus fare expended on visits to her son in the hospital for approximately a nine-month period prior to the issue of the statement of claim) is that the respondent and his mother were not close before the accident, and matters proceeded on the footing that the mother's natural love and affection should have no part in Andrews' future. Again, this situation is the most expensive from the point of view of the respondent.

The evidence showed that the mother of the appellant James Andrews was living alone, in a second-floor apartment and that relations between Andrews and his mother were strained at times. This should have no bearing in minimizing Andrews' damages. Even if his mother had been able to look after Andrews in her own home, there is now ample authority for saying that dedicated wives or mothers who choose to devote their lives to looking after infirm husbands or sons are not expected to do so on a gratuitous basis. The second observation is irrelevant.

The third observation was in these words:

> Thirdly, it should be observed that the learned trial Judge has referred with approval to the English authorities which held that full compensation for pecuniary loss must be given. It does not, however, follow that every conceivable expense which a plaintiff may conjure up is a pecuniary loss. On the evidence, then, should this Court consider that Andrews should live in a home of his own for the next 45 years at the expense of the appellant?

I agree that a plaintiff cannot "conjure up" "every conceivable expense". I do not think that a request for home care falls under that rubric.

Each of the three observations seems to look at the matter solely from the point of view of the respondents and the expense to them. An award must be fair to both parties but the ability of the defendant to pay has never been regarded as a relevant consideration in the assessment of damages at common law. The focus should be on the injuries of the innocent party. Fairness to the other party is achieved by assuring that the claims raised against him are legitimate and justifiable.

. . .

With respect to Andrews' disinclination to live in an institution, the Court commented:

He might equally say that he would not live in Alberta, as he did not wish to face old friends, or for any other reasons, and that he wished to live in Switzerland or the Bahamas.

Andrews is not asking for a life in Europe or in the Caribbean. He asks that he be permitted to continue to live in Alberta and to see his old friends, but in his own home or apartment, not in an institution.

The Court then expressed the view that the standard accepted by the trial Judge was the equivalent of supplying a private hospital. The phrase "private hospital" is both pejorative and misleading. It suggests an extravagant standard of care. The standard sought by the appellant is simply practical nursing in the home. The amount Andrews is seeking is, without question, very substantial, but essentially it means providing two orderlies and a housekeeper. The amount is large because the victim is young and because life is long. He has 45 years ahead. That is a long time.

In reducing the monthly payment to $1,000 the Appellate Division purported to apply a "final test" which was expressed in terms of the expenses that reasonably-minded people would incur, assuming sufficient means to bear such expense. It seems to me difficult to conceive of any reasonably-minded person of ample means who would not be ready to incur the expense of home care, rather than institutional care, for himself or for someone in the condition of Andrews for whom he was responsible. No other conclusion is open upon the evidence adduced in this case. If the test enunciated by the Appellate Division is simply a plea for moderation then, of course, no one would question it. If the test was intended to suggest that reasonably-minded people would refuse to bear the expense of home care, there is simply no evidence to support that conclusion.

The Appellate Division, seeking to give some meaning to the test, said that it should be open to consider "standards of society as a whole as they presently exist." As instances of such standards the Court selected the daily allowances provided under the *Workmen's Compensation Act* . . ., and the federal *Pension Act* . . . . The standard of care expected in our society in physical injury cases is an elusive concept. What a Legislature sees fit to provide in the cases of veterans and in the cases of injured workers and the elderly is only of marginal assistance. The standard to be applied to Andrews is not merely "provision", but "compensation", *i.e.*, what is the proper compensation for a person who would have been able to care for himself and live in a home environment if he had not been injured? The answer must surely be home care. If there were severe mental impairment, or in the case of an immobile quadriplegic the results might well be different; but, where the victim is mobile and still in full control of his mental faculties, as Andrews is, it cannot be said that institutionalization in an auxiliary hospital represents proper compensation for his loss. Justice requires something better.

. . .

Is it reasonable for Andrews to ask for $4,135 per month for home care? Part of the difficulty of this case is that 24-hour orderly care was not directly challenged. Counsel never really engaged in consideration of whether, assuming home care, such care could be provided at lesser expense. Counsel wants the Court, rather, to choose between home care and auxiliary hospital care. There are unanimous findings below that home care is better. Although home care is expensive, auxiliary hospital care is so utterly unattractive and so utterly in conflict with the principle of proper compensation that this Court is offered no middle ground.

The basic argument, indeed the only argument, against home care is that the social cost is too high. In these days the cost is distributed through insurance premiums. In this respect, I would adopt what was said by Salmon, L.J., in *Fletcher v. Autocare & Transporters, Ltd.*, [1968] 1 All E.R. 726 at 750, where he stated:

> Today, however, virtually all defendants in accident cases are insured. This certainly does not mean compensation should be extravagant, but there is no reason why it should not be realistic . . . It might result in some moderate increase in premium rates, which none would relish, but of which no-one, in my view, could justly complain. It would be monstrous to keep down premiums by depressing damages below their proper level, i.e., a level which ordinary men would regard as fair — unprejudiced by its impact on their own pockets.

I do not think the area of future care is one in which the argument of the social burden of the expense should be controlling, particularly in a case like the present, where the consequences of acceding to it would be to fail in large measure to compensate the victim for his loss. Greater weight might be given to this consideration where the choice with respect to future care is not so stark as between home care and an auxiliary hospital. Minimizing the social burden of expense may be a factor influencing a choice between acceptable alternatives. It should never compel the choice of the unacceptable.

(ii) *Life expectancy*. At trial, figures were introduced which showed that the life expectancy of 23-year-old persons in general is 50 years. As Chief Justice McGillivray said in the Appellate Division, it would be more useful to use statistics on the expectation of life of quadriplegics. A statistical average is helpful only if the appropriate group is used. At trial, Dr. Weir and Dr. Gingras testified that possibly five years less than normal would be a reasonable expectation of life for a quadriplegic. The Appellate Division accepted this figure. On the evidence I am willing to accept it.

(iii) *Contingencies of life*. The trial Judge did, however, allow a 20% discount for "contingencies and hazards of life". The Appellate Division allowed a further 10% discount. It characterized the trial Judge's discount as being for "life expectancy" or "duration of life", and said that this ignored the contingency of "duration of expense", *i.e.*, that despite any wishes to the contrary, Andrews in the years to come may be obliged to spend a great deal of time in hospital for medical reasons or because of the difficulty of obtaining help. With respect, the Appellate Division appears to have misunderstood what the trial Judge did. The figure of 20% as a discount for contingencies was arrived at first under the heading of "Prospective Loss of Earnings" and then simply transferred to the calculation of "Costs of Future Care". It was not an allowance for a decreased life expectancy, for this had already been taken into account by reducing the normal 50-year expectancy to 45 years. The "contingencies and hazards of life" in the context of future care are distinct. They relate essentially to duration of expense and are different from those which might affect future earnings, such as unemployment, accident, illness. They are not merely to be added to the latter so as to achieve a cumulative result. Thus, so far as the action taken by the Appellate Division is concerned, in my opinion, it was an error to increase by an extra 10% the contingency allowance of the trial Judge.

This whole question of contingencies is fraught with difficulty, for it is in large measure pure speculation. It is a small element of the illogical practice of awarding lump-sum payments for expenses and losses projected to continue over long periods of time. To vary an award by the value of the chance that certain contingencies may occur is to assure either over-compensation or under-compensation, depending on whether or not the event occurs. In light of the considerations I have mentioned, I think it would be reasonable to allow a discount for contingencies in the amount of 20%, in accordance with the decision of the trial Judge.

. . .

(v) *Cost of special equipment.* In addition to his anticipated expenses, Andrews requires an initial capital amount for special equipment. Both Courts below held that $14,200 was an appropriate figure for the cost of this equipment. In my opinion, this assessment is correct in principle, and I would therefore accept it.

. . .

NOTES AND QUESTIONS

1. Why, in Dickson J.'s opinion, is the level of care provided to injured persons under legislation irrelevant in the case of a tort victim? Do you agree?

2. Do you agree with Dickson J. that the plaintiff in *Andrews* should be entitled to be cared for in his own home? What type of evidence must the plaintiff adduce to obtain an award for home care? See *Rayner v. Knickle* (1988), 47 C.C.L.T. 141 (P.E.I.S.C.). The victim's stated preference for home care is not sufficient to justify an award on that basis. See for example *MacDonald v. Alderson* (1982), 20 C.C.L.T. 64 (Man. C.A.). In *Arce (Guardian ad litem of) v. Simon Fraser Health Region* (2003), 17 C.C.L.T. (3d) 97 (B.C.S.C.) the court concluded on the evidence that home care for a 79-year-old medically fragile plaintiff with quadriplegia was not reasonable or medically justifiable.

3. A plaintiff is not entitled to compensation for future care costs simply because it is conceivable that they could be incurred. In *O'Connell (Litigation Guardian of) v. Yung*, 2012 BCCA 57 at paras. 63-70 the Court of Appeal held the trial judge had erred in stating that the cost of future care was payable whether or not the personal care services would be incurred. Rather, the award must be based on what might reasonably be expected to be required.

4. How does the court calculate the duration of the future care period? The insurance industry relies on actuarial tables of "impaired life expectancy" for particular injuries when computing the cost of an annuity for a structured settlement. The courts tend to estimate a longer expectancy period than the tables, which is another factor that makes structured awards less expensive than lump-sum awards. Should the courts use the actuarial tables? What are the limitations of applying actuarial evidence to individual cases? See generally Boyle & Murray, "Assessment of Damages: Economic and Actuarial Evidence" (1981) 19 Osgoode Hall L.J. 1; and Anderson, *Actuarial Evidence*, 2d ed. (1986). For an example of an analysis of a plaintiff's life expectancy see *Kahlon (Litigation Guardian of) v. Vancouver Coastal Health Authority*, 2009 CarswellBC 1824 (S.C.) (WL Can) at para. 294.

5. What is the purpose of the contingency deduction in future care awards? How was the contingency figure determined in *Andrews*? The court seemed to assume that the contingencies would occur at regular intervals, which is unlikely. If Andrews were

to spend the first 20% of his projected lifespan in an institution, thus using less capital than he would if he was at home, he would be over-compensated. However, if he was institutionalized for the last 20% of his life, he would have to spend more of his capital early in his projected lifespan and would be under-compensated.

The same issue arose in *Krangle (Guardian ad litem of) v. Brisco* (1997), 55 B.C.L.R. (3d) 23 (S.C.), rev'd (2000), 76 B.C.L.R. (3d) 1 (C.A.), rev'd [2002] 1 S.C.R. 205. A child was born with Down's syndrome. The defendant physician negligently failed to detect the condition during pregnancy, thereby depriving the mother of the opportunity to abort. The defendant was therefore liable to the parents for the cost of the child's care. The evidence indicated that the boy would leave his parents' home to live in an institution at the age of 19. At the time of trial, the existing legislation provided that, in such circumstances, the state would pay the associated expenses. However, the trial judge also found that there was a 5% chance that by the time the child actually turned 19 the legislation would no longer provide such benefits. The parents therefore were awarded $80,000, representing 5% of the total cost of that future care that they had requested. That sum was either $80,000 too much or 95% too little. If the existing legislative scheme continued to operate throughout the child's adult life, then his parents did not require any money for that cost of care. In contrast, if the legislative scheme was altered so as to shift that cost of care onto the parents of a disabled adult child, then the plaintiffs received 95% less than required.

6. Over time, a provincial government can change the nature of the services provided for free under a health care plan. It could choose to cover a service that was not previously covered or to stop covering a service. Can courts meaningfully factor these possibilities into the contingency analysis? See *McLaren v. McLaren Estate*, 2011 ABCA 299 at para. 34.

7. A contingency deduction works in only one direction, reducing the award. But courts are required to consider both positive and negative contingencies. Each case depends on its facts, but over time more cases have made awards with no deduction or increase, accepting that the contingencies balance out. A contingency increase can be awarded, though it is unusual: see *Wilhelmson v. Dumma*, 2017 BCSC 616 at paras. 412-15 (15% increase).

8. The lump-sum award is quantified on the assumption that the plaintiff will invest the sum prudently and that the income from the self-extinguishing fund will be sufficient to meet the projected care costs. Although the lump sum itself is not taxable, the interest it generates is taxable. Thus, after the trilogy, courts increased the future care award by the estimated future tax liability to ensure that the fund would generate sufficient after-tax income to meet the cost of care. This increase is known as the "gross up." The Supreme Court of Canada has confirmed that it is appropriate to gross up the future care award: see *Watkins v. Olafson* (1989), 61 D.L.R. (4th) 577 (S.C.C.); and *Scarff v. Wilson* (1989), 61 D.L.R. (4th) 749 (S.C.C.).

9. Although the gross up is sound in principle, it is difficult and expensive to estimate future taxation in individual cases. The Ontario Law Reform Commission, *Report on Compensation for Personal Injuries and Death* (1987) at 139-47 has recommended revisions to the tax laws or standardized assumptions to alleviate these difficulties.

10. The amount awarded for gross up is significant. A gross up in excess of 50% of the future care award has been approved by the courts. See for example *Giannone v. Weinberg* (1989), 68 O.R. (2d) 767 (C.A.); *Tronrud v. French* (1991), 84 D.L.R. (4th) 275 (Man. C.A.); and *MacDonald (Guardian ad litem of) v. Neufeld* (1993), 17 C.C.L.T. (2d) 201 (B.C.C.A.). If the gross up is greater than the expected taxes, as some believe is often the case, plaintiffs will not sacrifice the gross up by consenting to a structured judgment. See Feldthusen, "Mandatory Structured Judgments" (1989) 1 C.I.L. Rev. 1.

11. In *Townsend v. Kroppmanns*, [2004] 1 S.C.R. 315 the defendants argued that since the plaintiff intended to spend some of the lump-sum award immediately to buy a house, the gross up should only be on the remaining amount, since only that lesser amount would actually be invested. The court rejected this argument and confirmed that the gross up was on the full lump sum for future care. It stated (at 324) that "In assessing damages, courts do not take into consideration what victims actually do with the award." Relying on *Andrews*, the court noted (at 325) that "The plaintiff is free to do whatever he or she wants with the sum of money awarded." In part this decision was based on concern that reducing the gross up would adversely affect impecunious plaintiffs, who are more likely to have to spend some of the lump sum immediately than are plaintiffs who are able to invest the whole award. Do you agree with this reasoning?

12. It has been held that the plaintiff can recover a sum to enable the him or her to hire a financial manager "if the plaintiff's level of intelligence is such that he is either unable to manage his affairs or lacks the acumen to invest funds awarded for future care so as to produce the requisite rate of return": *Insurance Corp. of British Columbia v. Mandzuk*, [1988] 2 S.C.R. 650 at 651; *Townsend, supra*. See also *Watkins, supra*. How many people do you think have the necessary acumen? Today management fees are frequently awarded but have been denied in some cases. See *Chernetz v. Eagle Copters Ltd.* (2008), 96 Alta. L.R. (4th) 222 (C.A.); and *Day v. Doerksen*, 2016 BCSC 2145.

In the most serious cases the plaintiff's needs in this area will be even greater. In *Sandhu (Litigation Guardian of) v. Wellington Place Apartments* (2008), 234 O.A.C. 200 (C.A.) a two-year-old suffered a severe brain injury. The jury awarded almost $11 million for the cost of future care. The court acknowledged that, in light of the size of the award, the plaintiff would need both a personal guardian, likely a relative, and a corporate guardian. The court awarded the plaintiff $1,795,800 to cover the costs, including legal fees, of these guardians. See also *Marcoccia (Litigation Guardian of) v. Gill*, 2007 CarswellOnt 2087 (S.C.J.) (WL Can).

13. In a typical case the plaintiff claims on his or her own behalf for the cost of future care. In some cases, like *Krangle, supra*, the future care claim is made by the parents of an injured child. Does this raise concerns about double recovery? Are these concerns resolved by the duty of care analysis? In *Krangle* the defendant owed a duty of care to the parents but not to the child. Compare this result with *Bovingdon (Litigation Guardian of) v. Hergott* (2008), 88 O.R. (3d) 641 (C.A.).

14. A detailed analysis of damages for future care can involve considerable mathematical calculation. However, the courts have cautioned against treating this assessment as capable of precision. They frequently mention that the future cannot be predicted and that these awards involve uncertainty and discretion. On an appeal, the

issue is the overall reasonableness of the compensation rather than the accuracy of the underlying calculations. See for example *Uhrovic v. Masjhuri* (2008), 86 B.C.L.R. (4th) 15 (C.A.) at paras. 28-32, citing several of the leading cases on this point.

(c) PECUNIARY LOSS: LOST EARNING CAPACITY

ANDREWS v. GRAND & TOY ALBERTA LTD.
(1978), 83 D.L.R. (3d) 452 (S.C.C.)

DICKSON J: . . . We must now gaze more deeply into the crystal ball. What sort of a career would the accident victim have had? What were his prospects and potential prior to the accident? It is not loss of earnings but, rather, loss of earning capacity for which compensation must be made. . . . A capital asset has been lost: what was its value?

(i) *Level of earnings.* The trial Judge fixed the projected level of earnings of Andrews at $830 per month, which would have been his earnings on January 1, 1973. The Appellate Division raised this to $1,200 per month, a figure between his present salary and the maximum for his type of work of $1,750 per month. Without doubt the value of Andrews' earning capacity over his working life is higher than his earnings at the time of the accident. Although I am inclined to view even that figure as somewhat conservative, I would affirm the holding of the Appellate Division that $1,200 per month represents a reasonable estimate of Andrews' future average level of earnings.

(ii) *Length of working life.* Counsel for the appellants object to the use of 55 rather than 65 as the projected retirement age for Andrews. It is agreed that he could retire on full pension at 55 if he stayed with his present employer, Canadian National Railways. I think it is reasonable to assume that he would, in fact, retire as soon as it was open for him to do so on full pension.

One must then turn to the mortality tables to determine the working life expectancy for the appellant over the period between the ages of 23 and 55. The controversial question immediately arises whether the capitalization of future earning capacity should be based on the expected working life span prior to the accident, or the shortened life expectancy. Does one give credit for the "lost years"? When viewed as the loss of a capital asset consisting of income-earning capacity rather than a loss of income, the answer is apparent; it must be the loss of that capacity which existed prior to the accident. This is the figure which best fulfils the principle of compensating the plaintiff for what he has lost. . . . I would accept . . . that Andrews had a working life expectancy of 30.81 years.

(iii) *Contingencies.* It is a general practice to take account of contingencies which might have affected future earnings, such as unemployment, illness, accidents and business depression. In the *Bisson* case, which also concerned a young quadriplegic, an allowance of 20% was made. There is much support for this view that such a discount for contingencies should be made. . . . There are, however, a number of qualifications which should be made. First, in many respects, these contingencies implicitly are already contained in an assessment of the projected average level of earnings of the injured person, for one must assume that this figure is a projection with respect to the real world of work, vicissitudes and all. Second, not all contingencies are adverse, as the above list would appear to indicate. As is said in *Bresatz v. Przibilla* (1962), 108 C.L.R. 541, in the Australian High Court, at p. 544: "Why count the possible buffets and ignore the rewards of fortune?" Finally, in a modern society there are many public and private schemes which cushion the individual against adverse contingencies. Clearly, the percentage deduction which is proper will depend on the facts of the individual case, particularly the nature of the plaintiff's occupation, but generally it will be small. . . .

In reducing Andrews' award by 20% Mr. Justice Kirby gives no reasons. The Appellate Division also applied a 20% reduction. It seems to me that actuarial evidence could be of great help here. Contingencies are susceptible to more exact calculation than is usually apparent in the cases. . . . In my view, some degree of specificity, supported by the evidence, ought to be forthcoming at trial.

The figure used to take account of contingencies is obviously an arbitrary one. The figure of 20% which was used in the lower Courts (and in many other cases), although not entirely satisfactory, should, I think, be accepted.

. . .

(iv) *Duplication with compensation for loss of future earnings.* It is clear that a plaintiff cannot recover for the expense of providing for basic necessities as part of the cost of future care while still recovering fully for prospective loss of earnings. Without the accident, expenses for such items as food, clothing and accommodation would have been paid for out of earnings. They are not an additional type of expense occasioned by the accident.

When calculating the damage award, however, there are two possible methods of proceeding. One method is to give the injured party an award for future care which makes no deduction in respect of the basic necessities for which he would have had to pay in any event. A deduction must then be made for the cost of such basic necessities when computing the award for loss of prospective earnings, *i.e.*, the award is on the basis of net earnings and not gross earnings. The alternative method is the reverse, *i.e.*, to deduct the cost of basic necessities when computing the award for future care and then to compute the earnings award on the basis of gross earnings.

The trial judge took the first approach, reducing loss of future earnings by 53%. The Appellate Division took the second. In my opinion, the approach of the trial Judge is to be preferred. This is in accordance with the principle which I believe should underlie the whole consideration of damages for personal injuries; that proper future care is the paramount goal of such damages. To determine accurately the needs and costs in respect of future care, basic living expenses should be included. The costs of necessaries when in an infirm state may well be different from those when in a state of health. Thus, while the types of expenses would have been incurred in any event, the level of expenses for the victim may be seen as attributable to the accident. In my opinion, the projected cost of necessities should, therefore, be included in calculating the cost of future care, and a percentage attributable to the necessities of a person in a normal state should be reduced from the award for future earnings.

. . .

NOTES AND QUESTIONS

1. How did Dickson J. determine the base figure that he used to calculate lost earning capacity? How accurate is this approach?

2. In *Lines v. Gordon* (2009), 90 B.C.L.R. (4th) 203 (C.A.) Justice Saunders stated:

There are two major components to an assessment of loss of future earning capacity. One is the general level of earnings thought by the trial judge to be realistically achievable by the plaintiff but for the accident, taking into account the plaintiff's intentions and factors that weigh both in favour of and against that achievement, and the other is the projection of that earning level to the plaintiff's working life, taking into account the positive and negative vagaries of life. From these two major components must be applied an analysis that produces a present value of the loss, adjusted for all appropriate contingencies.

In *Pett v. Pett* (2009), 93 B.C.L.R. (4th) 300 (C.A.) the court applied this approach to a teenager injured at the start of his working career.

3. In *Arnold v. Teno* (1978), 83 D.L.R. (3d) 609 (S.C.C.), in which a four-year-old child was totally disabled, Spence J. arbitrarily selected $7,500 as an "equitable" yearly income for calculating the child's lost earning capacity. He stated that $5,000 was too low because that would relegate the child to poverty and that $10,000, the figure used by the Court of Appeal, was too high. Can such awards be properly made in the absence of actuarial or other expert evidence?

The damages trilogy helped to identify issues, such as future income, that require expert evidence. Lawyers now rely heavily on expert evidence in establishing base figures and contingencies in the calculation of both future care and earning capacity. Unlike in *Teno*, the courts are no longer put in the position of having to make such unsubstantiated estimates.

What types of expert evidence would have been useful in *Teno*? Injured children now fare far better than the plaintiff in *Teno*. See Bruce, "The Calculation of an Infant's Lost Earnings: *Houle v. Calgary*" (1984) 22 Alta. L. Rev. 291; Sutherland, "Predicting a Child's Future Wage Loss" (1984) 42 The Advocate 169; and *O'Hara v. Belanger* (1989), 98 A.R. 86 (Q.B.).

4. In *Smith v. Collett*, [2009] EWCA Civ. 583 the plaintiff was awarded £3,854,328 for lost future earnings. He was injured as an 18-year-old soccer player in the Manchester United system and was deprived of a career in professional soccer. The court had to determine the plaintiff's most likely level of success as a soccer player and how much he accordingly would have earned.

In *Mackey (Litigation Guardian of) v. British Columbia (Provincial Capital Commission)*, 2016 BCSC 1333 the court had to determine whether there was a real and substantial possibility that the plaintiff, who was 17 at the time of his serious injury, would have become an orthopaedic surgeon. The court considered his high school grades and performance as an Eagle Scout. It held that such a possibility was established and awarded over $5,000,000 for lost future earnings. This amount included a discount of 40% to reflect the contingency that he might not actually become an orthopaedic surgeon.

5. Earnings are most often in the form of wages paid to an employee, but an injured plaintiff can lose future earnings in other ways. For example, he or she might be a partner in a firm and entitled to receive a percentage of the firm's profits each year. If he or she cannot work, the firm could be less profitable and that percentage could end up being smaller. This type of situation can complicate the calculations. See *Moore v. Brown* (2010), 10 B.C.L.R. (5th) 1 (C.A.).

An injured plaintiff might also suffer a loss of income as a result of being delayed entry into an occupation, for example by losing a year of education or training. Courts have awarded damages for such a delay: *Pisani v. Pearce*, 2012 BCSC 1118; and *McLean v. Parmar*, 2015 ABQB 62.

If the plaintiff has already retired and is being paid a monthly amount under a pension or annuity until death, and the injury shortens the plaintiff's life expectancy, can the plaintiff recover for future monthly payments that, as a result, now will not be made? Is this a loss of future earnings? Does it depend on the nature of the pension or annuity? See *Amaca Pty Limited v. Latz; Latz v Amaca Pty Limited*, [2018] HCA 22.

6. Earning capacity is also difficult to estimate when the plaintiff is not a member of the paid labour force, as in the cases of students and homemakers. Many believe that the value of homemaking services, usually provided by women, is undervalued by the courts. How should the lost earning capacity of a person who has decided to work in the home be calculated? See *Fobel v. Dean* (1991), 9 C.C.L.T. (2d) 87 (Sask. C.A.); *Benstead v. Murphy* (1994), 22 C.C.L.T. (2d) 271 (Alta. C.A.); *Toneguzzo-Norvell (Guardian ad litem of) v. Burnaby Hospital* (1994), 110 D.L.R. (4th) 289 (S.C.C.); *Kroeker v. Jansen* (1995), 24 C.C.L.T. (2d) 113 (B.C.C.A.); and *McTavish v. MacGillivray*, [2000] 5 W.W.R. 554 (B.C.C.A.). See also Cassels, "Damages for Lost Earning Capacity: Women and Children Last!" (1992) 71 Can. Bar Rev. 445; Fast & Munro, "Toward Eliminating Gender Bias in Personal Injury Awards: Contributions from Family Economics" (1994) 32 Alta. L. Rev. 1; and Brown, "Exposing and Remedying Vexing Problems in Household Claims for Personal Injury and Wrongful Death Cases: An Economist's View" (1998) 19 Adv. Q. 83.

7. If a highly successful lawyer retired at age 40 to pursue a passion for sailing and was then rendered totally unable to work or sail, how should his or her lost earning capacity be calculated? See generally Reaume, "Rethinking Personal Injury Damages: Compensation For Lost Capacities" (1988) 67 Can. Bar Rev. 82.

In *Rowe v. Bobell Express Ltd.* (2005), 39 B.C.L.R. (4th) 185 (C.A.) the 73-year-old plaintiff was seriously injured in a car accident. At the time he was running a company which he predominantly owned, but he was not being paid by it. The court stated at (para. 34) that "Mr. Rowe was neither a wage-earner nor a salaried employee, nor did he receive remuneration for his work in the form of the profits of a closely-held company through which he carried on business. However, it is not disputed that, by reason of his injuries, he was unable to do many things that, but for his injuries, he could have done to earn income." As a postscript to the case, Justice Southin posed the following question: "Suppose a comparatively young man or woman with a private income who devotes his or her considerable time and talents without remuneration to charitable endeavours is so severely injured as to no longer be able to do so? Is it open to the tortfeasor to say to the plaintiff, 'You have suffered and will suffer no financial loss. The loss is that of the charities for whom you worked and would have continued to work. . .'." How would you answer this question?

8. In *Pelletier v. Ontario*, 2013 ONSC 6898 the plaintiff was struck by a police cruiser while cycling. In describing the plaintiff's situation prior to the injury, the trial judge observed that he had a learning disability, ongoing back and neck pain and serious emotional issues and that he was a drug addict who survived on welfare and crime. What issues does this raise for calculating lost future earnings?

9. How does the court estimate the length of time used in calculating the victim's earning capacity? Contrast this to the length of time used to calculate future care awards. What approach should the courts adopt if the plaintiff dies after trial but before an appeal? See *Bifolchi v. Sherar* (1998), 38 O.R. (3d) 772 (C.A.).

10. What is the purpose of the contingency deduction under lost earning capacity? Distinguish it from the contingency deduction under future care. How did the court arrive at the deduction in *Andrews*? Expert evidence now plays a much greater role and often suggests that positive and negative contingencies tend to cancel one another out. Positive contingencies include private and public plans which cushion the impact of unemployment. See *Fenn v. Peterborough* (1979), 104 D.L.R. (3d) 174 (Ont. C.A.), aff'd [1981] 2 S.C.R. 613; *Graham v. Rourke* (1990), 75 O.R. (2d) 622 (C.A.); and *Hussack v. Chilliwack School District No. 33*, 2011 BCCA 258. In *Herring v. England (Ministry of Defence)* (2003), [2004] 1 All E.R. 44 (C.A.) Potter L.J. observed that the courts have historically overestimated negative contingencies in their awards.

11. Explain the problem of potential duplication between the future care and lost earning capacity awards. Outline the two approaches that Dickson J. identifies to address the duplication problem. The *Andrews* approach generally favours the plaintiff, especially when the unadjusted future care award is grossed up. Which approach is more consistent with the basic principle of damage quantification? See Feldthusen, "Duplication in Personal Injury Damage Awards" (1987) 66 Can. Bar Rev. 784.

12. The damages trilogy involved catastrophic injuries. In less serious cases different types of problems may arise, particularly in calculating damages for partial or temporary loss of earning capacity. See for example *Lan v. Wu* (1980), 14 C.C.L.T. 282 (B.C.C.A.); and *Engel v. Kam-Ppelle Holdings Ltd.* (1993), 99 D.L.R. (4th) 401 (S.C.C.). See also Westcott, "Calculating Loss of Opportunity for Career Advancement: Clearing the Clouds in the Crystal Ball" (1983) 4 Adv. Q. 268; and Wunder, "Compensation for the Plaintiff's Competitive Position on the Labour Market Being Compromised: The Concept and the Law" (1984) 28 C.C.L.T. 117.

13. Given that damages are intended to put the plaintiff in the position that he or she would have been in if the tort had not been committed, the measure of relief awarded with respect to lost earning capacity depends upon the plaintiff's pre-accident employment prospects. It has been argued that those prospects are often subject to discriminatory forces. On average, women earn approximately 64% of what men earn. Consequently, if an infant female suffers permanent and disabling injuries, she is apt to receive considerably less in damages than a similarly injured infant male. The same pattern emerges between aboriginal and non-aboriginal plaintiffs and between disabled and non-disabled plaintiffs. In several cases the courts have been asked to disregard the effect of discriminatory societal forces and to assess damages for injured females on the basis of male income statistics. For cases addressing this issue see *(Public Trustee of) v. Asleson*, [1993] 6 W.W.R. 45 (B.C.C.A.); *Toneguzzo-Norvell (Guardian ad litem of) v. Burnaby Hospital, supra; MacCabe v. Westlock Roman Catholic Separate School District No. 110* (1998), 226 A.R. 1 (Q.B.), rev'd [2002] 1 W.W.R. 610 (Alta. C.A.); *Walker v. Ritchie, supra; Steinebach (Litigation Guardian of) v. Fraser*

Health Authority, 2011 BCCA 302; *McLean v. Parmar, supra*, at paras. 99 and 104; and *Crimeni v. Chandra*, 2015 BCCA 131 at paras. 20-24.

Is this approach compatible with the fundamental aim of tort damages? What are the theoretical and practical implications of this approach? See Gibson, "The Gendered Wage Dilemma" in Cooper-Stephenson & Gibson, eds., *Tort Theory* (1993); and McInnes, "The Gendered Earnings Proposal in Tort Law" (1998) 77 Can. Bar Rev. 153. See also Cassels, "(In)Equality and the Law of Tort: Gender, Race and the Assessment of Damages" (1995) 17 Adv. Q. 158; Adjin-Tettey, "Contemporary Approaches to Compensating Female Tort Victims for Incapacity to Work" (2000) 38 Alta. L. Rev. 504; Cooper-Stephenson, "Sliding Doors: Alternative Life Patterns in Personal Injury Damages" in Beaulac, Pitel & Schulz, eds., *The Joy of Torts* (2003) 315; and Adjin-Tettey, "Replicating and Perpetuating Inequalities in Personal Injury Claims Through Female-Specific Contingencies" (2004) 49 McGill L.J. 309. On related issues see Berryman, "Accommodating Ethnic and Cultural Factors in Damages for Personal Injury" (2007) 40 U.B.C.L. Rev. 1.

14. The focus on lost earning capacity rather than lost earnings has led to a debate in the jurisprudence about whether the loss of future earnings should be based on earnings the plaintiff had the potential or theoretical capacity to earn or based on earnings the plaintiff had a "real possibility" of earning: see *Vincent v. Abu-Bakare* (2003), 259 N.B.R. (2d) 66 (C.A.). In *Steward v. Berezan* (2007), 64 B.C.L.R. (4th) 152 (C.A.) the plaintiff was a realtor who had previously worked as a carpenter. After being injured he was no longer able to work as a carpenter and so the trial judge awarded $50,000 for loss of future earnings based on this loss of capacity. The British Columbia Court of Appeal set this award aside on the basis that there was no reasonable likelihood that he would ever have returned to work as a carpenter even without the injuries. In *Vincent* the New Brunswick Court of Appeal indicated that the better approach was to require "proof of a real and substantial possibility of lost earnings" rather than base an award purely on loss of capacity. See also *Leddicote v. Nova Scotia (Attorney General)* (2002), 203 N.S.R. (2d) 271 (C.A.); *M.B. v. British Columbia*, [2003] 2 S.C.R. 477 at paras. 47-50; *Sinclair v. Dines* (2005), 279 N.B.R. (2d) 227 (C.A.); *Chang v. Feng* (2008), 55 C.C.L.T. (3d) 203 (B.C.S.C.) at para. 73; *Kralik v. Mount Seymour Resorts Ltd.* (2008), 78 B.C.L.R. (4th) 313 (C.A.); *Hibberd v. William Osler Health Centre*, 2010 CarswellOnt 2417 (C.A.) (WL Can); and *Morgan v. Galbraith*, 2013 BCCA 305 at para. 24. To what extent are these cases moving back to a focus on actual lost earnings?

Similar tensions also play out in quantifying the lost earning capacity, because courts have indicated that the lost capacity could be valued by either an earnings approach or a capital asset approach. See for example *Perren v. Lalari*, 2010 BCCA 140 at para. 32; *Wilson v. Honda Canada Financial Inc.*, 2013 BCSC 1137 at paras. 147-53; and *Villing v. Husseni*, 2016 BCCA 422 at paras. 17-20.

(d) CONSIDERATIONS RELEVANT TO BOTH HEADS OF PECUNIARY LOSS

ANDREWS v. GRAND & TOY ALBERTA LTD.
(1978), 83 D.L.R. (3d) 452 (S.C.C.)

DICKSON J.: . . . (i) *Capitalization rate: allowance for inflation and the rate of return on investments.* What rate of return should the Court assume the appellant will be able to obtain on his investment of the award? How should the Court recognize future inflation? Together these considerations will determine the discount rate to use in actuarially calculating the lump-sum award.

The approach at trial was to take as a rate of return the rental value of money which might exist during periods of economic stability, and consequently to ignore inflation. This approach is widely referred to as the Lord Diplock approach, as he lent it his support in *Mallett v. McMonagle*, [1970] A.C. 166. Although this method of proceeding has found favour in several jurisdictions in this country and elsewhere, it has an air of unreality. Stable, non-inflationary economic conditions do not exist at present, nor did they exist in the recent past, nor are they to be expected in the foreseeable future. In my opinion, it would be better to proceed from what known factors are available rather than to ignore economic reality. Analytically, the alternate approach to assuming a stable economy is to use existing interest rates and then make an allowance for the long-term expected rate of inflation. At trial the expert actuary, Mr. Grindley, testified as follows:

> Yes, as I mentioned yesterday, I was comfortable with that assumption 5% interest because it produces the same result as for example 8% interest and 3% inflation.
>
> . . .
>
> I would be happy to use either of the following two packages of assumption, either an 8% interest rate combined with provision for amounts which would increase 3% in every year in the future or a 5% interest rate and level amount, level amounts, that is no allowance for inflation.

One thing is abundantly clear; present interest rates should not be used with no allowance for future inflation. To do so would be patently unfair to the plaintiff. It is not, however, the level of inflation in the short term for which allowance must be made, but that predicted over the long term. It is this expectation which is built into present interest rates for long-term investments. It is also this level of inflation which may at present be predicted to operate over the lifetime of the plaintiff to increase the cost of care for him at the level accepted by the Court, and to erode the value of the sum provided for lost earning capacity.

. . .

The approach which I would adopt, therefore, is to use present rates of return on long-term investments and to make some allowance for the effects of future inflation. Once this approach is adopted, the result, in my opinion, is different from the 5% discount figure accepted by the trial Judge. While there was much debate at trial over a difference of a half to one percentage point, I think it is clear from the evidence that high quality long-term investments were available at time of trial at rates of return in excess of 10%. On the other hand, evidence was specifically introduced that the former head of the Economic Council of Canada, Dr. Deutsch, had recently forecast a rate of inflation of 3.5% over the long-term future. These figures must all be viewed flexibly. In my opinion, they indicate that the appropriate discount rate is approximately 7%. I would adopt that figure. It appears to me to be the correct result of the approach I have adopted, *i.e.*, having regard to present investment market conditions and making an appropriate allowance for future inflation. I would, accordingly, vary to 7% the discount rate to be used in calculating the present value of the awards for future care and loss of earnings in this case. The result in future cases will depend upon the evidence adduced in those cases.

(ii) *Allowance for tax*. In *The Queen v. Jennings* [(1966), 57 D.L.R. (2d) 654 (S.C.C.)], this Court held that an award for prospective income should be calculated with no deduction for tax which might have been attracted had it been earned over the working life of the plaintiff. This results from the fact that it is earning capacity and not lost earnings which is the subject of compensation. For the same reason, no consideration should be taken of the amount by which the income from the award will be reduced by payment of taxes on the interest, dividends, or capital gain. A capital sum is appropriate to replace the lost capital asset of earning capacity. Tax on income is irrelevant either to decrease the sum for taxes the victim would have paid on income from his job, or to increase it for taxes he will now have to pay on income from the award.

In contrast with the situation in personal injury cases, awards under the *Fatal Accident Act*, R.S.A. 1970, c. 138, should reflect tax considerations, since they are to compensate dependants for the loss of support payments made by the deceased. These support payments could only come out of take-home pay, and the payments from the award will only be received net of taxes: see the contemporaneous decision of this Court in *Keizer v. Hanna et al.* (1978), 82 D.L.R. (3d) 449.

The impact of taxation upon the income from the capital sum for future care is mitigated by . . . the *Income Tax Act.* . . ., in respect of the deduction of medical expenses, which provides that medical expenses in excess of 3% of the taxpayer's income includes "remuneration for one full-time attendant upon an individual who was a taxpayer . . . in a self-contained domestic establishment in which the cared for person lived." This exemption, I should think, permits a deduction for the payment of one full-time attendant for seven days a week, regardless of whether this attendance is provided by several attendants working over 24-hour periods, or one person working 24-hour shifts seven days a week.

The exact tax burden is extremely difficult to predict, as the rate and coverage of taxes swing with the political winds. What concerns us here is whether some allowance must be made to adjust the amount assessed for future care in light of the reduction from taxation. No such allowance was made by the Courts below. Elaborate calculations were provided by the appellant to give an illusion of accuracy to this aspect of the wholly speculative projection of future costs. Because of the provision made in the *Income Tax Act* and because of the position taken in the Alberta Courts, I would make no allowance for that item. The Legislature might well consider a more generous income tax treatment of cases where a fund is established by judicial decision and the sole purpose of the fund is to provide treatment or care of an accident victim.

One subsidiary point should be affirmed with respect to the determination of the present value of the cost of future care. The calculations should provide for a self-extinguishing sum. To allow a residual capital amount would be to over-compensate the injured person by creating an estate for him. This point was accepted by the lower Courts and not challenged by the parties.

. . .

NOTES AND QUESTIONS

1. What is the purpose of the discount or capitalization rate? A 7% discount rate, as adopted in *Andrews*, means that the lump sum will be quantified on the assumption that if prudently invested it will generate real earnings (net of inflation) of 7% per year.

2. The 7% discount rate was severely criticized. Experience indicates that in the long run the gap between the rate of interest and the rate of inflation will be in the vicinity of 2 to 2.5%. See Feldthusen & McNair, "General Damages in Personal Injury Suits: The Supreme Court's Trilogy" (1978) 28 U.T.L.J. 381; Rea, "Inflation and the Law of Contracts and Torts" (1982) 14 Ottawa L. Rev. 465; and Bale, "Adding Insult to Injury: The Inappropriate Use of Discount Rates to Determine Damage Awards" (1983) 28 McGill L.J. 1015.

For a comparative study of personal injury discount rates across several jurisdictions see Fairgrieve & Gauci, "Briefing Note on the Discount Rate applying to Quantum in Personal Injury Cases: Comparative Perspectives" (2017), a publication of the British Institute of International and Comparative Law.

3. It is now clear that the calculation of the discount rate is a factual issue to be determined in individual cases. In *Lewis v. Todd* (1980), 115 D.L.R. (3d) 257 (S.C.C.) the court indicated that it lacked the authority to "legislate" a fixed discount rate and that even if it had such authority it was not sufficiently certain of the issues to exercise it.

The costs of litigating the appropriate discount rate on a case-by-case basis are substantial and most Canadian jurisdictions have passed legislation to address this problem. See for example the detailed provisions of the Ontario Rules of Civil Procedure, R.R.O. 1990, Reg. 194, R. 53.09. Fixed legislative rates are generally between 2.5 and 3.5%, considerably lower than the rate used in the trilogy.

It is possible for the courts, in some situations, to depart from the legislated discount rate. See *Ligate v. Abick* (1996), 28 O.R. (3d) 1 (C.A.). In *Walker v. Ritchie* (2005), 197 O.A.C. 81 (C.A.), varied (2006), 43 C.C.L.T. (3d) 1 (S.C.C.) the Court of Appeal stated that "evidence called before the trial judge established that the costs of professional services are increasing faster than the rate of inflation, thus justifying the variation to a 1.5% discount rate." In several more recent cases courts have used a lower discount rate (more favourable to the plaintiff) based on expert evidence that health care costs are expected to rise faster than the rate of inflation. See for example *Gordon v. Greig* (2007), 46 C.C.L.T. (3d) 212 (Ont. S.C.J.) at para. 177.

For a legislative summary and discussion, see The Ontario Law Reform Commission, *Report on Compensation for Personal Injuries and Death* (1987) at 218-25.

4. Why does the court not consider the taxes that the plaintiff would have paid in calculating lost earning capacity? This failure to consider taxes would appear to over-compensate the plaintiff. This is offset, albeit not perfectly, by the fact that the

plaintiff will pay tax on the investment earnings from the earning capacity award, which is not grossed up.

5. Why should the calculation of the future care award provide for a self-extinguishing sum? Why is the same not true of the earning capacity head?

6. In *Townsend v. Kroppmanns*, [2004] 1 S.C.R. 315 the defendants argued that because the plaintiff was being awarded the cost of paying a financial manager, a higher discount rate should be used because with professional assistance the plaintiff would achieve a higher rate of return. The court rejected this argument, in part on the basis that to accept it would defeat the point of having the discount rate set by statute or regulation.

(e) NON-PECUNIARY LOSS

ANDREWS v. GRAND & TOY ALBERTA LTD.
(1978), 83 D.L.R. (3d) 452 (S.C.C.)

DICKSON J.: . . . Andrews used to be a healthy young man, athletically active and socially congenial. Now he is a cripple, deprived of many of life's pleasures and subjected to pain and disability. For this, he is entitled to compensation. But the problem here is qualitatively different from that of pecuniary losses. There is no medium of exchange for happiness. There is no market for expectation of life. The monetary evaluation of non-pecuniary losses is a philosophical and policy exercise more than a legal or logical one. The award must be fair and reasonable, fairness being gauged by earlier decisions; but the award must also of necessity be arbitrary or conventional. No money can provide true restitution. Money can provide for proper care: this is the reason that I think the paramount concern of the Courts when awarding damages for personal injuries should be to assure that there will be adequate future care.

However, if the principle of the paramountcy of care is accepted, then it follows that there is more room for the consideration of other policy factors in the assessment of damages for non-pecuniary losses. In particular, this is the area where the social burden of large awards deserves considerable weight. The sheer fact is that there is no objective yardstick for translating non-pecuniary losses, such as pain and suffering and loss of amenities, into monetary terms. This area is open to widely extravagant claims. It is in this area that awards in the United States have soared to dramatically high levels in recent years. Statistically, it is the area where the danger of excessive burden of expense is greatest.

It is also the area where there is the clearest justification for moderation. As one English commentator has suggested, there are three theoretical approaches to the problem of non-pecuniary loss (A.J. Ogus, "Damages for Lost Amenities: For a Foot, a Feeling or a Function?", 35 Mod. L. Rev. 1 (1972)). The first, the "conceptual" approach, treats each faculty as a proprietary asset with an objective value, independent of the individual's own use or enjoyment of it. This was the ancient "bot", or tariff system, which prevailed in the days of King Alfred, when a thumb was worth 30 shillings. Our law has long since thought such a solution unsubtle. The second, the "personal" approach, values the injury in terms of the loss of human happiness by the particular victim. The third, or "functional" approach, accepts the personal premise of the second, but rather than attempting to set a value on lost happiness, it attempts to assess the compensation required to provide the injured person "with reasonable solace for his misfortune." "Solace" in this sense is taken to mean physical arrangements which can make his life more endurable rather than "solace" in the sense of sympathy. To my mind, this last approach has much to commend it, as it provides a rationale as to why money is considered compensation for non-pecuniary losses such as loss of amenities, pain and suffering, and loss of expectation of life. Money is awarded because it will serve a useful function in making up for what has been lost in the only way possible, accepting that what has been lost is incapable of being replaced in any direct way. As Windeyer, J., said in *Skelton v. Collins* [(1966), 115 C.L.R. 94 (H.C.A.)]:

> . . . he is, I do not doubt, entitled to compensation for what he suffers. Money may be compensation for him if having it can give him pleasure or satisfaction. . .But the money is not then a recompense for a loss of something having a money value. It is given as some consolation or solace for the distress that is the consequence of a loss on which no monetary value can be put.

If damages for non-pecuniary loss are viewed from a functional perspective, it is reasonable that large amounts should not be awarded once a person is properly provided for in terms of future care for his injuries and disabilities. The money for future care is to provide physical arrangements for assistance, equipment and facilities directly related to the injuries. Additional money to make life more endurable should then be seen as providing more general physical arrangements above and beyond those relating directly to the injuries. The result is a coordinated and interlocking basis for compensation, and a more rational justification for non-pecuniary loss compensation.

However one may view such awards in a theoretical perspective, the amounts are still largely arbitrary or conventional. As Lord Denning, M.R., said in *Ward v. James*, [1965] 1 All E.R. 563, there is a great need in this area for assessability, uniformity and predictability. In my opinion, this does not mean that the courts should not have regard to the individual situation of the victim. On the contrary, they must do so to determine what has been lost. For example, the loss of a finger would be a greater loss of amenities for an amateur pianist than for a person not engaged in such an activity. Greater compensation would be required to provide things and activities which would function to make up for this loss. But there should be guidelines for the translation into monetary terms of what has been lost. There must be an exchange rate, albeit conventional. In *Warren v. King*, [[1963] 3 All E.R. 521] at p. 528 the following *dictum* of Harman, L.J., appears, which I would adopt, in respect of the assessment of non-pecuniary loss for a living plaintiff:

> It seems to me that the first element in assessing such compensation is not to add up items as loss of pleasures, of earnings, of marriage prospects, of children and so on, but to consider the matter from the other side, what can be done to alleviate the disaster to the victim, what will it cost to enable her to live as tolerably as may be in the circumstances.

Cases like the present enable the Court to establish a rough upper parameter on these awards. It is difficult to conceive of a person of his age losing more than Andrews has lost. Of course, the figures must be viewed flexibly in future cases in recognition of the inevitable differences in injuries, the situation of the victim, and changing economic conditions.

The amounts of such awards should not vary greatly from one part of the country to another. Everyone in Canada, wherever he may reside, is entitled to a more or less equal measure of compensation for similar non-pecuniary loss. Variation should be made for what a particular individual has lost in the way of amenities and enjoyment of life, and for what will function to make up for this loss, but variation should not be made merely for the Province in which he happens to live.

There has been a significant increase in the size of awards under this head in recent years. As Moir, J.A., of the Appellate Division of the Alberta Supreme Court, has warned: "To my mind, damages under the head of loss of amenities will go up and up until they are stabilized by the Supreme Court of Canada": *Hamel et al. v. Prather et al.* (1976), 66 D.L.R. (3d) 109 at p. 127. . . . In my opinion, this time has come.

It is customary to set only one figure for all non-pecuniary loss, including such factors as pain and suffering, loss of amenities, and loss of expectation of life. This is a sound practice. Although these elements are analytically distinct, they overlap and merge at the edges and in practice. To suffer pain is surely to lose an amenity of a happy life at that time. To lose years of one's expectation of life is to lose all amenities for the lost period, and to cause mental pain and suffering in the contemplation of this prospect. These problems, as well as the fact that these losses have the common trait of irreplaceability, favour a composite award for all non-pecuniary losses.

There is an extensive review of authorities in the Court of Appeal judgment in this case as well as in the *Thornton* and *Teno* cases, *supra*, to which I have referred. I need not review these past authorities. What is important is the general picture. It is clear that until very recently damages for non-pecuniary losses, even from very serious injuries such as quadriplegia, were substantially below $100,000. Recently, though, the figures have increased markedly. In *Jackson v. Millar et al.* (1975), 59 D.L.R. (3d) 246 . . . this Court affirmed a figure of $150,000 for non-pecuniary loss in an Ontario case of a paraplegic. However, this was done essentially on the principle of non-interference with awards allowed by provincial Courts of Appeal. The need for a general assessment with respect to damages for non-pecuniary loss, which is now apparent, was not as evident at that time. Even in Ontario, prior to these recent cases, general damages allocable for non-pecuniary loss, such as pain and suffering and loss of amenities, were well below $100,000.

In the present case, $150,000 was awarded at trial, but this amount was reduced to $100,000 by the Appellate Division. In *Thornton* and *Teno* $200,000 was awarded in each case, unchanged in the provincial Courts of Appeal.

I would adopt as the appropriate award in the case of a young adult quadriplegic like Andrews the amount of $100,000. Save in exceptional circumstances, this should be regarded as an upper limit of non-pecuniary loss in cases of this nature.

NOTES AND QUESTIONS

1. What is the purpose of an award for non-pecuniary loss? What are the differences among the three methods of assessing non-pecuniary loss according to the article by A.J. Ogus cited in *Andrews*? Which approach do you prefer? See Klar, "The Assessment of Damages for Non-Pecuniary Losses" (1978) 5 C.C.L.T. 262; and Ritchie, "Non-pecuniary Damages" in *Special Lectures of the Law Society of Upper Canada: Law of Remedies* (1995). In *Lindal v. Lindal* (1981), 129 D.L.R. (3d) 263

(S.C.C.) the court affirmed the functional approach and elaborated on how that approach should be applied. *Lindal* also approved adjusting the $100,000 figure for inflation.

2. The Supreme Court of Canada has indicated that a plaintiff can recover damages in excess of the upper limit if he or she can prove exceptional circumstances in which a larger award is necessary to provide solace. Nevertheless, the courts have very rarely granted such awards. See *Fenn v. Peterborough* (1979), 104 D.L.R. (3d) 174 (Ont. C.A.), aff'd [1981] 2 S.C.R. 613.

3. Adjusted for inflation, by the late 1990s the upper limit was approximately $260,000: see *Roberts v. Morana* (1997), 38 C.C.L.T. (2d) 1 (Ont. Gen. Div.). It had further increased to between $290,000 and $300,000 by 2006: see *Lee v. Dawson* (2006), 51 B.C.L.R. (4th) 221 (C.A.); and *McIntyre v. Grigg* (2006), 83 O.R. (3d) 161 (C.A.). In *Sandhu (Litigation Guardian of) v. Wellington Place Apartments* (2008), 234 O.A.C. 200 (C.A.) the court awarded $311,000 and in *A.T.-B. v. Mah*, 2012 ABQB 777, additional reasons 2013 ABQB 241 the court awarded $350,000 as the maximum. Recently the maximum was stated to be $367,000 in *Wilhelmson v. Dumma*, 2017 BCSC 616.

4. In *ter Neuzen v. Korn*, [1995] 3 S.C.R. 674 the court held that a non-pecuniary award of $460,000 was inappropriate and ordered that the jury in the new trial be instructed on the approximate upper limit for such damages. But in *Hill v. Church of Scientology*, [1995] 2 S.C.R. 1130 the court approved a $300,000 non-pecuniary general damage award in addition to awards of $500,000 in aggravated and $800,000 in punitive damages. The court said that the cap on non-pecuniary awards does not apply to defamation. Is such a distinction justifiable?

In *Young v. Bella*, [2006] 1 S.C.R. 108 a woman who was negligently reported as a suspected sexual abuser of children was awarded $430,000 in non-pecuniary damages by a jury. On appeal the defendants argued that this exceeded the upper limit. The court, drawing on *Hill*, held (at para. 65) that it was "not established why the policy considerations which arise from negligence causing catastrophic personal injuries, in the contexts of accident and medical malpractice, should be extended to cap a jury award in a case such as the present." What is the rationale for the upper limit? Why does it not apply in cases like *Hill* and *Young*?

5. In *Andrews* Dickson J. stated that non-pecuniary loss "is the area where the social burden of large awards deserves considerable weight." Is the justification he provides compelling? Why should this burden fall on the victims of catastrophic personal injuries and not on those who are defamed or those who would otherwise receive punitive damages?

Assume that a homemaker with no intention of joining the paid workforce is badly burned and suffers severe ongoing pain and permanent disfigurement. How would his or her damages be assessed under *Andrews*? Does the so-called functional approach result in an injustice in cases such as these?

6. Prior to *Andrews*, non-pecuniary losses were divided into claims for pain and suffering, loss of amenities and loss of expectation of life. Traditionally, the award for pain and suffering was assessed on a subjective basis, in terms of the actual pain and suffering the plaintiff experienced. The loss of amenities was assessed objectively in terms of how a reasonable person in the plaintiff's position would have valued the loss

of enjoyment of life. Although the courts stated that awards for loss of expectation of life were not simply conventional sums, these awards were limited to several thousand dollars. S. Waddams has suggested that these categories governing non-pecuniary loss may no longer apply because *Andrews* requires a "functional approach": Waddams, *The Law of Damages*, looseleaf (1991) (consulted June 2018) at 3.650-3.690.

See *Knutson v. Farr* (1984), 30 C.C.L.T. 8 (B.C.C.A.) which clearly supports Waddams' view. *Knutson* indicated that the functional approach meant that an unconscious plaintiff was not entitled to compensation under this head. See also Mew, "Comment" (1986) 64 Can. Bar Rev. 562; and Waddams, "Compensation for Non-Pecuniary Loss: Is There a Case for Legislative Intervention?" (1985) 63 Can. Bar Rev. 734.

Should a plaintiff who is unable to appreciate his or her situation after the injuries — for example because he or she is in a coma — receive any non-pecuniary damages? See *Steinebach (Litigation Guardian of) v. Fraser Health Authority*, 2011 BCCA 302.

7. The upper limit has come under increasing scrutiny, particularly in British Columbia. See the critical comments in *Boyd v. Harris* (2004), 24 B.C.L.R. (4th) 155 (C.A.); *Dilello v. Montgomery* (2005), 37 B.C.L.R. (4th) 72 (C.A.); *Courdin v. Meyers* (2005), 37 B.C.L.R. (4th) 222 (C.A.); and *A.T.-B. v. Mah, supra*. In *Dilello*, the Court of Appeal stated that "the attempt by this and other courts to fit juries' damage awards for personal injuries into a grid or tariff system with an upper limit of any amount (that has not been enacted by a legislature) is an unjustified interference with the function of the jury as finders of fact, and a fettering of the proper principles of appellate review." In *Lee v. Dawson, supra*, the jury awarded non-pecuniary damages of $2 million. This was reduced to $292,000 by the trial judge to comply with the cap. The Court of Appeal thought that "the time may have come for the rationalization or conceptual underpinning for having a rough upper limit on non-pecuniary damages to be re-examined" but felt bound to follow *Andrews* as binding authority. The Supreme Court of Canada refused leave to appeal.

See Good, "Non-Pecuniary Damage Awards in Canada — Revisiting the Law and Theory on Caps, Compensation and Awards at Large" (2008) 34 Adv. Q. 389. Even if the cap remains in place, what impact could these sentiments have on the size of awards?

8. Some commentators have argued for the abolition of non-pecuniary damages. See O'Connell & Simon, *Payment for Pain & Suffering: Who Wants What When and Why?* (1972); Fleming, "Damages for Non-Material Loss" in Law Society of Upper Canada, *Special Lectures on New Developments in the Law of Torts* (1973) 1; Ontario Law Reform Commission, *Report on Motor Vehicle Accident Compensation* (1973); Woodhouse, *The Report of the National Committee of Inquiry on Compensation and Rehabilitation in Australia* (1974); and Pearson, *The Report of the Royal Commission on Civil Liability and Compensation for Personal Injury* (1978). See more recently Avraham, "Should Pain-and-Suffering Damages Be Abolished from Tort Law? More Experimental Evidence" (2005) 55 U.T.L.J. 941. One argument for retaining non-pecuniary damages proceeds from what is called the "*ex ante* insurance perspective" which is based on the view that rational people would not insure themselves against non-pecuniary loss because money cannot compensate for such loss. See generally The Ontario Law Reform Commission, *Report on Compensation for Personal Injuries and*

Death (1987) at 79-114 which supports the present law. For the approach in England see *Heil v. Rankin*, [2001] Q.B. 272 (C.A.).

9. There is some debate about whether the cap on non-pecuniary damages includes any amount awarded as aggravated damages. This is rarely in issue in negligence cases because they rarely trigger aggravated damages.

10. Courts have formulated lists of factors to be considered, particularly in cases not at or near the maximum amount, in determining the award for non-pecuniary loss. In *Stapley v. Hejslet* (2006), 221 B.C.A.C. 272 (C.A.) the court identified the following factors: "(a) age of the plaintiff; (b) nature of the injury; (c) severity and duration of pain; (d) disability; (e) emotional suffering; . . . (f) loss or impairment of life; (g) impairment of family, marital and social relationships; (h) impairment of physical and mental abilities; (i) loss of lifestyle; and (j) the plaintiff's stoicism (as a factor that should not, generally speaking, penalize the plaintiff . . .)."
Should old age lead to a lower award, since the plaintiff will suffer for fewer years, or to a higher award, since the impact of the injury will be worse than on a younger person? See *Wong (Litigation Guardian of) v. Towns*, 2015 BCSC 1333 at paras. 86-96; and *Weaver v. Pollock*, 2018 BCSC 531 at paras. 93-105.

11. In Essert, "Tort Law and Happiness" (2010) 36 Queen's L.J. 1 the author considers the argument that people who suffer a serious injury often rebound, after an initial period of unhappiness, to their pre-injury level of happiness. He concludes that even in cases of this sort, a focus on the defendant's violation of the plaintiff's rights means that non-pecuniary damages should still be awarded. Should a plaintiff who adapts to his or her new circumstances receive the same award as one who does not? Does this raise concerns about overcompensation? How does this fit with issues of mitigation?

(f) OTHER CATEGORIES OF LOSS

The courts have been prepared to award damages for losses beyond those discussed thus far in this section. On innovative awards generally see Nolan, "New Forms of Damage in Negligence" (2007) 70 M.L.R. 59. For example, courts have recognized that damages may be available to reflect the fact that an injury has reduced the plaintiff's chances of entering into a financially advantageous "permanent interdependent relationship." See *Reekie v. Messervey* (1989), 59 D.L.R. (4th) 481 (B.C.C.A.); *Belyea v. Hammond* (2000), 231 N.B.R. (2d) 305 (C.A.); *Walker v. Ritchie* (2005), 197 O.A.C. 81 (C.A.), varied (2006), 43 C.C.L.T. (3d) 1 (S.C.C.); *Wilhelmson v. Dumma*, 2017 BCSC 616 (in which $325,000 was awarded); and *K.M. v. Marson*, 2018 ONSC 3493 at para. 677.
The courts have made awards to compensate plaintiffs for a loss of housekeeping capacity, which is distinct from earning capacity: see *LeClerc v. Westfair Foods Ltd.* (1999), 140 Man. R. (2d) 88 (Q.B.), aff'd (2000), 148 Man. R. (2d) 56 (C.A.); *Oates v. Morgan* (2007), 268 Nfld. & P.E.I.R. 1 (N.L.C.A.); *McIntyre v. Docherty* (2009), 97 O.R. (3d) 189 (C.A.); *Jarvis v. Treberg* (2009), 289 Nfld. & P.E.I.R. 167 (N.L.C.A.); *Poirier v. Aubrey* (2010), 4 B.C.L.R. (5th) 173 (C.A.); *Gregory v. Insurance Corporation of British Columbia*, 2011 BCCA 144; *O'Connell (Litigation Guardian of) v. Yung*, 2012

BCCA 57; *Westbroek v. Brizuela*, 2014 BCCA 48; and *Kim v. Lin*, 2018 BCCA 77 in which $250,000 was awarded.

In *Milliken v. Rowe*, 2012 BCCA 490 at para. 47 the dissenting judge was prepared to award damages for loss of caregiving capacity, stating "the loss of the capacity to provide care to one's ill or disabled child, spouse or aging parent is analogous to the loss of housekeeping capacity, which is already recognized as a separate head of damages. While similar in nature, however, it is, in my opinion, important and distinct enough to require a separate category." On the facts the majority found an award on this basis to be too remote. In *Carmichael v. Kwon*, 2016 BCSC 265 the trial judge distinguished *Milliken* and awarded damages of $40,500 for the loss of caregiving capacity because it was not too remote.

In *Wilhelmson v. Dumma, supra*, the plaintiff lost the ability to give birth to a child. She was awarded $100,000 to cover the cost of using surrogates to have two biological children. The defendant argued that it is illegal to pay a surrogate in Canada, but the court based its award on the plaintiff using surrogates in the United States. Do you agree with this award?

Another novel issue is whether a plaintiff who is not presently showing any symptoms of an illness but who, as a result of the defendant's negligence, now has an increased chance of developing the illness in the future can recover medical monitoring costs. This issue has arisen in the context of exposure to asbestos. See *Wilson v. Servier Canada Inc.* (2000), 50 O.R. (3d) 219 (S.C.J.); *Bryson v. Canada (Attorney General)* (2009), 353 N.B.R. (2d) 1 (Q.B.); and *Ring v. Canada (Attorney General)* (2010), 297 Nfld. & P.E.I.R. 86 (N.L.C.A.) at paras. 52-59. In the United States see *Metro-North Commuter Railroad Co. v. Buckley*, 521 U.S. 424 (1997) at 441-44.

3. Survival of Actions and Dependants' Claims

(a) SURVIVAL OF ACTIONS

At common law when an individual died all outstanding or potential causes of action that could have otherwise been brought by or against the deceased were extinguished. Legislation has been enacted in England and all Canadian jurisdictions to nullify this common law rule. The statutes, which vary from jurisdiction to jurisdiction, allow the deceased's estate to maintain legal actions that the deceased could have otherwise brought. Typically, however, the legislation excludes specified causes of action, such as defamation, malicious prosecution and false imprisonment. Most jurisdictions also exclude recovery of certain types of damages, such as non-pecuniary and punitive damages. These statutes also allow actions to be brought against the deceased's estate that could have been brought against the deceased.

The following provisions of the Alberta and Ontario legislation illustrate some common features of the survival of action statutes.

SURVIVAL OF ACTIONS ACT
R.S.A. 2000, c. S-27

2 A cause of action vested in a person who dies after January 1, 1979 survives for the benefit of the person's estate.

3 A cause of action existing against a person who dies after January 1, 1979 survives against the person's estate.

4 If a cause of action for damages suffered by reason of an act or omission would have existed against a person had that person not died at or before the time the damage was suffered, the cause of action is deemed to have existed against the person before the person's death.

5 (1) If a cause of action survives under section 2, only those damages that resulted in actual financial loss to the deceased or the deceased's estate are recoverable.

(2) Without restricting the generality of subsection (1), the following are not recoverable:

    (a)   punitive or exemplary damages;

    (b)   damages for loss of expectation of life, pain and suffering, physical disfigurement or loss of amenities;

    (c)   damages in relation to future earnings, including damages for loss of earning capacity, ability to earn or chance of future earnings.

(3) Subsection (2)(c) applies only to causes of action that arise after the coming into force of this section.

6 If the death of a person was caused by an act or omission that gives rise to a cause of action, the damages shall be calculated without reference to a loss or gain to the person's estate as a result of the person's death, but reasonable expenses of the funeral and the disposal of the body of the deceased may be included in the damages awarded, if the expenses were, or liability for them was, incurred by the estate.

7 A cause of action that survives under this Act and a judgment or order on it or relating to the costs of it is an asset or liability, as the case may be, of the estate to which the cause of action relates.

TRUSTEE ACT
R.S.O. 1990, c. T.23

38(1) Except in cases of libel and slander, the executor or administrator of any deceased person may maintain an action for all torts or injuries to the person or to the property of the deceased in the same manner and with the same rights and remedies as the deceased would, if living, have been entitled to do, and the damages when recovered shall form part of the personal estate of the deceased but if death results from such injuries no damages shall be allowed for the death or for the loss of the expectation of life, but this proviso is not in derogation of any rights conferred by Part V of the *Family Law Act*.

(2) Except in cases of libel and slander, if a deceased person committed or is by law liable for a wrong to another in respect of his or her person or to another person's property, the person wronged may maintain an action against the executor or administrator of the person who committed or is by law liable for the wrong.

(3) An action under this section shall not be brought after the expiration of two years from the death of the deceased.

(b) FATAL ACCIDENTS LEGISLATION

It was established in *Baker v. Bolton* (1808), 1 Camp. 493 (H.L.) that an individual has no common law cause of action for losses that he or she suffers as a result of the death of another person. See for a recent discussion *Barclay v. Penberthy*, [2012] HCA

40. This common law rule has been superseded by fatal accidents legislation which is designed to compensate the deceased's dependants for the losses they suffer as a result of the death. Generally the purpose of this legislation is to put the dependants in the position they would have been in had the victim not been wrongfully killed. Most of the provincial legislation is modelled after the 1846 English legislation, commonly referred to as *Lord Campbell's Act.* The Nova Scotia legislation illustrates many of the common features of the provincial statutes. We have also included the Ontario provision which provides for broader recovery.

FATAL INJURIES ACT
R.S.N.S. 1989, c. 163

Liability. . .

3 Where the death of a person has been caused by such wrongful act, neglect or default of another as would, if death had not ensued, have entitled the person injured to maintain an action and recover damages in respect thereto, in such case, the person who would have been liable if death had not ensued shall be liable to an action of damages, notwithstanding the death of the person injured, and although the death has been caused under such circumstances as amount in law to a crime.

. . .

Damages

5 (1) Every action brought under this Act shall be for the benefit of the spouse, common-law partner, parent or child of such deceased person and the jury may give such damages as they think proportioned to the injury resulting from such death to the persons respectively for whose benefit such action was brought, and the amount so recovered, after deducting the costs not recovered, if any, from the defendant, shall be divided among such persons in such shares as the jury by their verdict find and direct.

(2) In subsection (1), "damages" means pecuniary and non-pecuniary damages and, without restricting the generality of this definition, includes

(a) out-of-pocket expenses reasonably incurred for the benefit of the deceased;

(b) a reasonable allowance for travel expenses incurred in visiting the deceased between the time of the injury and the death;

(c) where, as a result of the injury, a person for whose benefit the action is brought provided nursing, housekeeping or other services for the deceased between the time of the injury and the death, a reasonable allowance for loss of income or the value of the services; and

(d) an amount to compensate for the loss of guidance, care and companionship that a person for whose benefit the action is brought might reasonably have expected to receive from the deceased if the death had not occurred.

(3) In assessing the damage in any action there shall not be taken into account any sum paid or payable on the death of the deceased, whether by way of pension or proceeds of insurance, or any future premiums payable under any contract of assurance or insurance.

(4) In an action brought under this Act where funeral expenses have been incurred by the parties for whose benefit the action is brought, damages may be

awarded for reasonable necessary expenses of the burial of the deceased, including transportation and things supplied and services rendered in connection therewith.

. . .

Apportionment by Judge

9 In all cases where for any reason the compensation is not apportioned among the several persons entitled under this Act, a judge may apportion the same and dispose of the costs of the application and inquiry as he thinks just.

Limitation of Action

10 Not more than one action shall lie for and in respect to the same subject-matter of complaint and every such action shall be commenced within twelve months after the death of the deceased person.

FAMILY LAW ACT
R.S.O. 1990, c. F.3

Dependants' Claim for Damages

61. (1) If a person is injured or killed by the fault or neglect of another under circumstances where the person is entitled to recover damages, or would have been entitled if not killed, the spouse, as defined in Part III (Support Obligations), children, grandchildren, parents, grandparents, brothers and sisters of the person are entitled to recover their pecuniary loss resulting from the injury or death from the person from whom the person injured or killed is entitled to recover or would have been entitled if not killed, and to maintain an action for the purpose in a court of competent jurisdiction.

(2) The damages recoverable in a claim under subsection (1) may include,

(a) actual expenses reasonably incurred for the benefit of the person injured or killed;

(b) actual funeral expenses reasonably incurred;

(c) a reasonable allowance for travel expenses actually incurred in visiting the person during his or her treatment or recovery;

(d) where, as a result of the injury, the claimant provides nursing, housekeeping or other services for the person, a reasonable allowance for loss of income or the value of the services; and

(e) an amount to compensate for the loss of guidance, care and companionship that the claimant might reasonably have expected to receive from the person if the injury or death had not occurred.

NOTES AND QUESTIONS

1. What is the rationale for restricting the applicable actions and kinds of damages under the provincial survival legislation and the provincial fatal accident legislation? For a discussion of this legislation see *Duncan Estate v. Baddeley* (2000), 266 A.R. 323 (C.A.); *Macartney v. Warner* (2000), 46 O.R. (3d) 641 (C.A.); *MacLean v. MacDonald* (2002), 11 C.C.L.T. (3d) 57 (N.S.C.A.); *MacKay Estate v. Smith* (2003), 230 Nfld. & P.E.I.R. 178 (P.E.I.C.A.); and *Higgins Estate v. Arseneau*, 2014 NBCA 65. See also Cooper-Stephenson & Adjin-Tettey, *Personal Injury Damages in Canada*, 3d ed.

(2018) at 1021-53; Brown, "*Duncan v. Baddeley*: Reconciling the 'Lost Years' Deduction with Fatal Accident Cases" (1997) 35 Alta. L. Rev. 1108; and Waddams, *The Law of Damages*, looseleaf (1991) (consulted June 2018), ch. 12. Note that at the time *Duncan* was decided, s. 5 of the Alberta *Survival of Actions Act* had not yet been amended to exclude claims for loss of earning capacity or future earnings.

2. How does the purpose of the survival legislation differ from that of the fatal accidents legislation? What parties are allowed to recover under each type of legislation? Is there a potential for double recovery because of the overlapping benefits? Generally the actions are brought together to reduce this problem: see *Balkos v. Cook* (1990), 75 O.R. (2d) 593 (C.A.). For a discussion of how the two types of legislation might be combined see Waddams, "Damages For Wrongful Death: Has Lord Campbell's Act Outlived Its Usefulness?" (1984) 47 Mod. L. Rev. 437. See also Handford, "Lord Campbell and the Fatal Accidents Act" (2013) 129 L.Q.R. 420.

3. In what specific ways is the scope of the Ontario *Family Law Act* broader than that of the Nova Scotia *Fatal Injuries Act*? How do you suppose Nova Scotia deals with these claims in the absence of a statutory right such as the one in the Ontario statute? What are the advantages of each approach?

4. Dependants' claims under the Ontario *Family Law Act* have generated considerable litigation and controversy. One of the interesting issues is the status of claims brought in respect of, or on behalf of, persons who acquire dependency status by subsequent birth or marriage. The authorities are reviewed in *Garland v. Rowsell* (1990), 73 O.R. (2d) 280 (Dist. Ct.). Consider also the treatment of children who are adopted by close relatives on the death of their parents. Should this reduce or even eliminate their claim? See *Trotter-Brons (Litigation Guardian of) v. Corrigan*, 2016 BCSC 1891.
Another interesting issue is the scope of non-pecuniary damages available under s. 61(2)(e) (compare with s. 5(2)(d) in Nova Scotia). It has been held that a dependant is entitled to damages under s. 61(2)(e) for loss of care, guidance and companionship in cases of both death and injury. See generally *Mason v. Peters* (1982), 39 O.R. (2d) 27 (C.A.); *Wessell v. Kinsmen Club of Sault Ste. Marie Ont. Inc.* (1982), 37 O.R. (2d) 481 (H.C.); *Reidy v. McLeod* (1984), 30 C.C.L.T. 183 (Ont. H.C.); *Gervais v. Richard* (1984), 48 O.R. (2d) 191 (H.C.); *Seede v. Cameo Inc.* (1985), 50 O.R. (2d) 218 (S.C.); and *Nielsen v. Kaufmann* (1986), 54 O.R. (2d) 188 (C.A.). See also *Macartney v. Warner*, *supra*.

5. Grief and sorrow are not recoverable under s. 61(2)(e) of Ontario's *Family Law Act*. However, some other provincial statutes permit a separate award for grief, as opposed to loss of guidance, care and companionship. See for example *Fatal Accidents Act*, S.N.B. 2012, c. 104, s. 10. Grief and sorrow are discussed in van Praagh, "Who Lost What? Relationship and Relational Loss" in Beaulac, Pitel & Schulz, eds., *The Joy of Torts* (2003) 269. See also Field, "In Mourning of Bereavement Damages" (2014) 22 Torts L.J. 95.

6. The Court of Appeal for Ontario has held that s. 61 of the *Family Law Act* precludes dependants from recovering either punitive or aggravated damages: *Lord (Litigation Guardian of) v. Downer* (1999), 179 D.L.R. (4th) 430 (Ont. C.A.). See also *Rowe v. Brown* (2008), 261 N.S.R. (2d) 332 (S.C.). However, in *Steinkrauss v. Afridi*,

2013 ABCA 417 at para. 14, additional reasons 2014 ABCA 14 the court refused to rule out a claim by a dependant for punitive damages, stating "the key question will be whether that egregious conduct was sufficiently connected to the claim of the dependants arising from the death." See also *Rekken Estate v. Health Region No. 1*, 2015 SKCA 36, applied in *Weisbeck v. Regina (City)*, 2018 SKQB 60.

7. The specific wording of the statute is highly important. Under the *Fatal Accidents Act*, R.S.N.W.T. 1988, c. F-3 and the *Trustee Act*, R.S.N.W.T. 1988, c. T-8, s. 31(1), unlike in several provinces, a deceased's estate can claim for both loss of "expectation of life" (a non-pecuniary head of damages compensating for the lost prospect of a predominantly enjoyable life) and loss of future earnings: see *Caron Estate v. Paneak Estate* (2006), 42 C.C.L.T. (3d) 48 (Nu. C.A.).

(i) *The Death of the Family Provider*

KEIZER v. HANNA
[1978] 2 S.C.R. 342

[Mr. Keizer died as a result of the injuries he sustained in an automobile collision. The defendant admitted that the collision was due solely to his negligence.]

DICKSON J.:—I have had the advantage of reading the reasons for judgment prepared by Mr. Justice Spence and Mr. Justice de Grandpré in this appeal. There are two issues: (i) the deductibility of income tax in arriving at an award of damages; (ii) quantum. . . .

[Dickson J. briefly addressed the taxation issue and continued.]

On point (ii), however, "quantum", I have come to a conclusion other than that arrived at by my brother de Grandpré. I would allow the appeal, and like my brother Spence, award the amount of $100,000 claimed in the statement of claim but deduct therefrom the amount of $6,500 insurance benefits already received by the appellant under the accident and death benefits provision found in . . . the deceased's insurance policy. In the result, the award of general damages would amount to $93,500.

The accident in which Mr. Keizer was killed occurred on July 16, 1973. At that date he was 33 years of age with a life expectancy of 38.55 years. He was a tool-room foreman for the Town of Renfrew, capable, conscientious, industrious and in good health. He had been married for nine years to the appellant who, at the date of his death was 27 years of age with a life expectancy of 49.60 years. Mr. and Mrs. Keizer had one child, an infant of six months.

The trial Judge projected average earnings of $15,000 for a working expectancy of 31 years. From this figure he deducted $3,200 for income tax, $1,800 for personal use, and $3,000 for personal support leaving disposable income for dependants in the amount of $7,000. The Judge made a deduction for income tax with which the Court of Appeal agreed and which, in my view, was proper. The Court of Appeal did not question the Judge's finding that the deceased would expend $1,800 for his personal use and $3,000 for his personal support. Thus, as a result, $7,000 would be available as disposable income for dependants. The evidence was that he contributed his pay cheque weekly to his family reserving only nominal sums and odd-job earnings for his own use. Having concluded that $7,000 per year would have been available to the appellant and her child each year, the Judge said. . .:

Actuarial tables filed as ex. 1 herein at 9% and 10% compound interest show the present value of $1 to age 65 for the male as $9.9375 and $9.1381 respectively. I believe a more realistic interest rate would be the approximate amount of 6.5% which would materially inflate these figures; for example, at 4% the factor is 18.66461. One must consider income tax as a reality of modern life and its depreciating impact along with the contingencies hereinbefore alluded to is reflected in my assessment. Under the provisions of the *Fatal Accidents Act* I award the plaintiff the sum of $120,000, of which sum I apportion $17,500 for the infant Mitchel Stephen.

It is difficult, if not impossible, to know what use, if any, the trial Judge made of actuarial tables to which he was referred. It would seem, however, that he proceeded on an exhausting fund basis, with a discount rate of approximately 6.5%. He made an allowance in respect of the income tax which the deceased would have had to pay on his earnings, had he lived, and he further reduced the award by a contingency allowance. He referred to the contingencies which might bear on assessment, as follows:

(a) Possibility of remarriage;
(b) Possibility of widow's death before expiry of joint expectancy period;
(c) Possibility of deceased's dying under other circumstances prior to expiry of said joint expectancy period;
(d) Possibility of deceased husband's retiring before expiry of joint expectancy period;
(e) Acceleration of inheritance to widow — bearing in mind likelihood of increased inheritance in event death had not occurred;
(f) Possibility the infant child may not be a burden to the father or require additional benefits for the full period of his calculated working life.

On the question of prospects of remarriage, the judge adopted the apt comments of Phillimore J. in *Buckley v. John Allen & Ford (Oxford), Ltd.*, [1967] 1 All E.R. 539, including the statement that Judges should act on evidence rather than guesswork and, there being no evidence of any existing interest or attachment, concluded: "I therefore accord no material significance to this prospect by way of deduction." He does not say that he is according no weight to the contingency.

As to the possibility of the early demise of either husband or wife, the Judge said:

All of the evidence indicates excellent health prospects and I rule that relatively little real significance can be attached to this contingency by way of reduction.

Again, it is not a question of refusing to consider a particular contingency. The judge considered the contingency, but decided it merited little significance. I do not think he can be faulted on this account.

With respect to the possibility of acceleration of the inheritance to the appellant, the Judge had this to say:

So far as the acceleration of her inheritance is concerned, I am readily satisfied that the same should have no reducing effect as in these circumstances. I am assured it is more than offset by the substantial loss she has suffered in future realization from this source.

Finally, the possibility that the infant child might not be a burden during his father's working life. On this point, the Judge said that he would give this fact material consideration in considering his award. These are his words:

> Unquestionably, there is the probability that the child Mitchel Stephen would not have been a burden to his father for anything like the 30 years or so of his working expectancy and I give this fact material consideration in considering this award.

The quantum of the award came before the Court of Appeal for Ontario. In that Court, reference was made by Mr. Justice Arnup, for the Court, to the six contingencies to which the trial Judge referred. Mr. Justice Arnup observed that the trial Judge might have added "possibility of incapacity to earn, occasioned by industrial or other accident, or by illness." He then continued. . . :

> Having listed these contingencies, the trial Judge decided he should make no deduction for any of them. In so doing, he erred. A contingency, in the context of damages under the *Fatal Accidents Act*, is obviously an event that may or may not happen. A defendant is entitled to have contingencies taken into account by way of reduction from the result that would be reached if every contingency turned out favourably to the dependants, although due weight must be given in each case to the probability, or otherwise, of the contingent event actually happening.

I have been unable to find in the trial judgment any statement by the trial Judge that he had decided he should not make any deduction for any of the contingencies. The evidence, as I read it, is to the contrary. It is true that the trial Judge might have considered the possibility of the deceased husband becoming unable to earn, but I do not think it can be said that failure to express himself on this point amounts to reversible error. The award of $120,000 exceeded the amount claimed of $100,000 but that does not preclude an award of $100,000.

In making a gross award of $65,000 the Court of Appeal was content with the following cryptic statement:

> In my view, the appropriate award of general damages in all of the circumstances of this case, as disclosed by the evidence, would have been $65,000.

The judgment does not assist us, or the parties, by explaining why $65,000 should be considered to be the appropriate award. From this amount the Court of Appeal deducted the $6,500 to which I have referred and directed that $10,000 be paid into Court for the infant. In the result, the widow would receive from the defendants for her support and maintenance for the next fifty years the sum of $48,500. This, plus $6,500 already received, totals $55,000.

It is, of course, true that a trial Judge must consider contingencies tending to reduce the ultimate award and give those contingencies more or less weight. It is equally true there are contingencies tending to increase the award to which a Judge must give due weight. At the end of the day the only question of importance is whether, in all the circumstances, the final award is fair and adequate. Past experience should make one realize that if there is to be error in the amount of an award it is likely to be one of inadequacy.

In my opinion, in the circumstances of this case, an award of $55,000 to the appellant can only be described as niggardly. The appellant is entitled to an award of such amount as will assure her the comforts and station in life which she would have enjoyed but for the untimely death of her husband. If one is speaking of contingencies, I think it is not unreasonable to give primary attention to the contingencies, and they are many, the occurrence of which would result in making the award, in the light of events, entirely inadequate. An assessment must be neither punitive nor influenced by sentimentality. It is largely an exercise of business judgment. The question is whether a stated amount of capital will provide, during the period in question, having regard to contingencies tending to increase or decrease the award, a monthly sum at least equal to that which might reasonably have been expected during the continued life of the deceased.

The proper method of calculating the amount of a damage award under the *Fatal Accidents Act* is similar to that used in calculating the amount of an award for loss of future earnings, or for future care, in cases of serious personal injury. In each, the Court is faced with the task of determining the present value of a lump sum which, if invested, would provide payments of the appropriate size over a given number of years in the future, extinguishing the fund in the process. This matter has been discussed in detail in the decisions of this Court in *Andrews v. Grand & Toy Alberta Ltd.*; *Thornton v. Prince George Board of Education*; and *Arnold v. Teno*, which are being delivered with the decision in the present case.

The object here is to award a sum which will replace present-day payments of $7,000 per year for a future period of 31 years, with some reduction for contingencies. The trial Judge used a discount rate of 6.5% without explaining this choice except to say that it was a "more realistic" rate than 9% or 10%. As I have said in *Andrews* and *Thornton*, in my opinion the discount rate should be calculated on the basis of present rates of return on long-term investments with an allowance for the effects of future inflation. Evidence on these matters was not introduced at trial in the present case. However, the 6.52% chosen by the Judge can be tested by the fact that present-day investment rates reach about 10.5%, and Dr. Deutsch of the Economic Council of Canada forecasted an inflation rate of about 3.5% over the long-term future. These two figures suggest that an appropriate discount rate is approximately 7%. This is only marginally different from the rate used by the trial Judge. Ignoring, for the moment, the other factors to be taken into consideration, the sum required to produce $7,000 per year for 31 years, payable monthly, discounted at 6.5%, is slightly less than $95,000. The award should be reduced somewhat to account for contingencies although, as I have mentioned, this amount will probably not be large. On the other hand, in order to yield the sum required net of taxes a greater sum would obviously be called for. The resulting amount would not reach the figure of $120,000 which the trial Judge chose. The sum of $100,000, the amount claimed, can be justified, however, with reasonable allowance made for income tax impact and contingency deduction.

I would allow the appeal, set aside the judgment of the Court of Appeal and direct that the appellant recover from the defendants the sum of $93,500. Out of that sum there should be paid to Marilyn E. Keizer the sum of $78,500 and there should be paid into Court to the credit of the infant, Mitchel Stephen Keizer, the sum of $15,000, to be paid out to the said infant when he attains the age of 18 years, or upon further order of a Judge of the County Court of the County of Renfrew. The appellant is also entitled to her award of $1,600 under the provisions of the *Trustee Act*, R.S.O. 1970, c. 470, in respect of funeral expenses and the value of an automobile.

I would allow the appellant her costs at trial against both defendants and her costs in this Court and in the Court of Appeal against the defendant Buch.

[Laskin C.J.C., Martland, Ritchie, Pigeon and Beetz JJ. concurred. Spence J. dissented in part, holding that income tax should not be taken into account in calculating the value of the deceased's support. De Grandpré J., with whom Judson J. agreed, dissented in part, holding that the Supreme Court of Canada ought not to interfere unless it was convinced the Court of Appeal had erred in principle.]

NOTES AND QUESTIONS

1. According to Dickson J., what basic principle should govern the appellant's claim?

2. What is the purpose of reducing the award by the amounts that the deceased would have spent for his own personal use and support? Do these deductions violate the basic principle identified above?

3. What is the "joint expectancy" period and why is it used in fatal accident cases? Is the possibility of the widow's death before the expiry of that period a relevant contingency?

4. What rationale underlies the other contingency deductions in the case? Do you agree with them? Are there other contingencies, positive or negative, which the court should have considered?

5. What adjustment is made in *Keizer* to reflect the income tax the deceased would have paid? Is it appropriate to make such a deduction here but not in the personal injury cases? See *Lewis v. Todd* (1980), 115 D.L.R. (3d) 257 (S.C.C.). Note that awards for pecuniary loss in fatal accident cases are now "grossed up" for the same purpose and in the same manner as in the personal injury cases. See generally *O'Hara v. Belanger*, [1990] 1 W.W.R. 214 (Alta. Q.B.); and *Oleschak Estate v. Wilganowski* (1991), 70 Man. R. (2d) 149 (C.A.). See also Feldthusen & McNair, "General Damages in Personal Injury Suits: The Supreme Court's Trilogy" (1978) 28 U.T.L.J. 381 at 401-03; and Rea, "Inflation, Taxation and Damage Assessment" (1980) 58 Can. Bar Rev. 280.

6. Why is evidence about the deceased's former prospects so important in a fatal accident case? What evidence would you adduce on behalf of a dependant on this issue?

7. In *Beljanski (Guardian ad litem of) v. Smithwick* (2006), 56 B.C.L.R. (4th) 99 (C.A.) the dependant children of a "career criminal" brought a claim when their father was killed negligently. The case raised difficult valuation questions. For reasons discussed in Chapter 19, the court refused to base an award on any illegal income the deceased would have made through criminal activities. The trial judge concluded that the deceased would have provided no care or guidance to his children nor left them any inheritance. The appeal court disagreed, based on the possibility that the deceased might have reformed later in life, and concluded that the children should recover $15,000 each.

8. How would you assess the damages for dependant children if both parents were killed by a negligent tortfeasor? See *Clement v. Leslies Storage Ltd.* (1979), 97

D.L.R. (3d) 667 (Man. C.A.); *McDermott v. Ramadanovic Estate* (1988), 44 C.C.L.T. 249 (B.C.S.C.); and *Coe Estate v. Tennant* (1990), 46 B.C.L.R. (2d) 62 (C.A.).

9. In *Baker Estate v. Poucette*, 2017 ABCA 344 the deceased performed extensive household services but because his living expenditures exceeded his income he was a pecuniary drain on the household. The defendant argued that the award to his family for loss of household services should be reduced by the savings resulting to the household from his death. The court rejected this argument and made no deduction, stating (at para. 26) "that a tortfeasor should receive, in effect, a credit from the widow and children of a deceased owing to an arithmetic gain under a pecuniary head of damages is repugnant and contrary to any principle of fairness." Do you agree?

10. It is impossible to provide a typical example of a fatal accident case because quantification depends heavily on the specific attributes of the deceased and the relevant relationships. For a comprehensive review of the case law, see Klar *et al.*, *Damages and Remedies in Tort* (1995) at 27-122.28 to 27-146.

(ii) *The Death of a Dependant Family Member*

Actions are usually brought under fatal accidents legislation as a result of the death of a family's primary earner. However, the legislation also extends to other family members, so it is possible for a plaintiff to bring an action as a result of an accident that resulted in the death of his or her dependant spouse or child: see *Alaffe v. Kennedy* (1973), 40 D.L.R. (3d) 429 (N.S.T.D.). Since the fatal accidents legislation is generally intended to provide compensation for pecuniary losses only, the measure of relief awarded with respect to the death of such individuals is often considerably less than the measure of relief awarded with respect to the death of a family provider. Another reason for the relatively low value of awards arising from the death of dependant family members may be that the courts continue to substantially undervalue services provided within the home.

NOTES AND QUESTIONS

1. When a young child dies, it is typically very difficult to accurately assess the pecuniary loss suffered by a parent. Not only must the court speculate as to how the child would have fared economically in life, it must also speculate about the extent to which the parent would have benefited from the child's economic fortunes. Is there any way for a parent's lawyer to overcome these difficulties? In this sort of case, what kind of evidence would you present on a parent's behalf? See Sutherland, "Predicting a Child's Future Wage Loss" (1984) 42 The Advocate 169; Bruce, "Measure of Damages for the Wrongful Death of a Child" (1987) 66 Can. Bar Rev. 344; and Smith, Merchant & Killback, "Risible Compensation for the Dead Child" (1996) 7 M.V.L.R. 125.

2. In *Mason v. Peters* (1980), 30 O.R. (2d) 409 (H.C.), aff'd (1982), 39 O.R. (2d) 27 (C.A.) the trial judge awarded the unusually large sum of $45,000 to a disabled, single mother for the death of her 11-year-old son. This exceptional award was the result of the unusually close bond between the mother and her son and the probability that he would have provided her with emotional and financial support throughout her life.

3. Should the damages awarded for the death of a child be reduced to take into account the parents' expenses in rearing the child? In *Mason v. Peters, supra*, Robins J.A. noted that except in rare circumstances the cost of raising and educating children greatly exceeds the pecuniary benefits that they provide to their parents. However, in *Lai v. Gill*, [1980] 1 S.C.R. 431 the court accepted that Chinese traditions encouraging the supporting of one's parents justified a pecuniary award of $25,000 for the parents of a deceased 14-year-old girl. Similar reasoning led at trial to a pecuniary award of $180,000 in *Lion v. Money*, [1994] 8 W.W.R. 463 (B.C.S.C.), rev'd [1996] 4 W.W.R. 263 (B.C.C.A.). This award was reversed on appeal on the grounds that the trial judge failed to consider the contribution that the deceased's older sister would make to the parents' welfare.

4. In *To v. Toronto (City) Board of Education* (2001), 55 O.R. (3d) 641 (C.A.) a 14-year-old boy was killed as a result of the defendant's negligence. He had been an excellent student. Moreover, because neither of his parents spoke English, he had helped them a great deal with their business and personal correspondence. He was described as a "trusted companion and advisor to his father." Finally, his relationship with his sister was described as "almost paternal." The family was devastated by his death. The jury awarded $100,000 to each of his parents and $50,000 to his sister under the *Family Law Act*. The Court of Appeal found that the awards to the parents were higher than usual, but not so inordinately high as to be reversible. The court did, however, reduce the sibling's award by half, partially on the ground that while she had suffered a terrible loss, she was likely to become independent and have a family of her own. See also *Osman v. 629256 Ontario Ltd.*, 2005 CarswellOnt 2728 (S.C.J.) (WL Can) in which the parents of a 16-year-old boy who was stabbed as a result of the defendants' negligence were each awarded $80,000 and his ten siblings were each awarded $20,000. In *Sandhu (Litigation Guardian of) v. Wellington Place Apartments* (2008), 234 O.A.C. 200 (C.A.) the court upheld a *Family Law Act* award of $100,000 to each parent and a sibling in respect of severe injuries to a two-year old child. The court noted the closeness of the plaintiff's family.

5. The assessment of pecuniary losses resulting from the death of a dependant spouse is also very difficult. In *Nielsen v. Kaufmann* (1984), 28 C.C.L.T. 54 (Ont. H.C.) the value of the deceased's household services was valued in "cold commercial terms" at $8,840 a year. This amount was reduced significantly on appeal: (1986), 54 O.R. (2d) 188 (C.A.). See also *Frawley v. Asselstine* (1990), 73 O.R. (2d) 525 (H.C.); and *Skelding (Guardian ad litem of) v. Skelding*, [1994] 9 W.W.R. 538 (B.C.C.A.). Many people believe that the courts have undervalued these services in the past. See Yale, "The Valuation of Household Services in Wrongful Death Actions" (1984) 34 U.T.L.J. 283; Quah, "Compensation for Loss of Household Services" (1986) 24 Osgoode Hall L.J. 467; and Cooper-Stephenson & Adjin-Tettey, *Personal Injury Damages in Canada*, 3d ed. (2018) at 447-50.

More recently, in *McVea (Guardian ad litem of) v. T.B.* (2002), 5 B.C.L.R. (4th) 367 (S.C.) the victim was killed when a 14-year-old driving a stolen car and pursued by police crashed into her. She was the principal provider of household services and child care but also worked outside the home. Her husband and children were awarded $261,000 for loss of past and future support, $207,900 for loss of past and future services, $60,000 for loss of care, guidance and affection, and $20,000 for loss of inheritance.

6. In *Bjornson v. McDonald*, 2005 CarswellBC 1457 (S.C.) (WL Can) both parents of a 38-year-old single mother of three children were killed in a car accident. The plaintiff recovered $125,000 for loss of child care and household services, loss of financial support, and loss of love, guidance and affection. The court accepted the evidence of the close relationship between the plaintiff and her parents, especially since her divorce.

7. Although awards under fatal accidents legislation have generally been limited to pecuniary losses, as in *Vana v. Tosta*, [1968] S.C.R. 71; and *Bianco v. Fromow* (1998), 161 D.L.R. (4th) 765 (B.C.C.A.), some statutes specifically allow awards for grief and anguish. For example, the Alberta *Fatal Accidents Act*, R.S.A. 2000, c. F-8, s. 8(2) allows a claim for "grief and loss of guidance, care and companionship," up to a maximum of $82,000 to a parent or spouse of the deceased and up to $49,000 to a child. The New Brunswick *Fatal Accidents Act*, S.N.B. 2012, c. 104, s. 10 allows recovery for grief suffered by the parents of a deceased minor: see *Nightingale v. Mazerall* (1991), 9 C.C.L.T. (2d) 186 (N.B.C.A.). A similar provision in the Manitoba *Fatal Accidents Act* was repealed: S.M. 2002, c. 13, s. 3.

8. It is impossible to provide a typical example of a dependant's fatal accident case because quantification depends heavily on the specific attributes of the deceased and the relevant relationships. For a comprehensive review of the case law, see Klar *et al.*, *Damages and Remedies in Tort* (1995) at 27-122.28 to 27-146.

4. Damages for Property Loss

The general principles governing the assessment of compensatory damages in personal injury cases apply to claims for damage to property. For analytical purposes, we have divided the discussion of damages for property loss into three issues: the assessment of the damages to the property itself, the assessment of the economic losses consequent on the damage to the property and the plaintiff's obligation to mitigate.

As indicated at the outset of this chapter, to keep it to a manageable length the discussion in this section is brief. Property loss can raise very complex issues and for a fuller discussion of the points made below you should consult a text on the law of damages.

(a) THE ASSESSMENT OF THE DAMAGE TO THE PROPERTY ITSELF

When real or personal property is damaged or destroyed, the plaintiff is "in the first instance entitled to restitution for the loss of its value to him": Sappideen & Vines, eds., *Fleming's The Law of Torts*, 10th ed. (2011) at 296. This principle is often difficult to apply because there are several different ways of assessing the loss in value, including the cost of repair, the cost of replacement and the decrease in the value of the property. The method chosen for assessing the damage may well affect the size of the award.

In a case of damage to a chattel, it is necessary to determine whether the property in question is commonplace or unique. In the former situation, the plaintiff generally receives the lesser of the amount by which the thing has decreased in value, the cost of repair or the cost of replacement. Essentially, the plaintiff is entitled to be restored to his or her former position by the least expensive means possible. In contrast, if the chattel in question is unique or of great sentimental value, the courts recognize that true restoration may require greater expenditure. In that respect, the courts take account of the plaintiff's subjective valuation of property. Consequently, for example, if a family heirloom is damaged by the defendant's carelessness, the plaintiff may be awarded the cost of repair, even if that amount exceeds the market value of a replacement item. Regardless of market value, a replacement item would be an inadequate substitute for the damaged heirloom. See Ren, "The Normal Measure of Damages for Tortious Damage to Chattels under English Law" (2015) 23 Tort L.R. 148.

Similar principles apply in cases involving damage to real property. In general terms, the plaintiff is also entitled to the lesser of the amount by which the thing has decreased in value, the cost of repair or the cost of replacement. However, just as the measure of relief may be higher if a damaged chattel holds special value for the plaintiff, so too the general approach is displaced if the plaintiff uses the land for residential purposes or would find it difficult to relocate a business that is operated on the property. In those situations, the plaintiff is more apt to be awarded the cost of repair. See *James Street Hardware and Furniture Co. v. Spizziri* (1987), 62 O.R. (2d) 385 (C.A.); *Scaffidi-Argentina v. Tega Homes Developments Inc.*, 2016 ONSC 5448; and *Jarbeau v. McLean*, 2017 ONCA 115.

Should the defendant's liability be reduced if repaired or replaced property is more valuable than the original? To deny a deduction would place the plaintiff in a better position than he or she would have been in had the tort not been committed. However, to allow the deduction in effect would force the plaintiff to pay for the unplanned upgrading of his or her chattel or real property. The courts will usually allow for a betterment deduction, which might be reduced to offset the plaintiff's costs (if proven) of doing the upgrade at a time not of his or her choosing.

(b) THE ASSESSMENT OF ECONOMIC LOSSES CONSEQUENT ON THE DAMAGE TO THE PROPERTY

Particularly in the case of business assets, the plaintiff will often suffer economic losses consequent on the damage to his or her property. The principles governing the recovery of consequential economic loss are largely the same as in personal injury and property loss cases. However, the House of Lords originally indicated in *Dredger Liesbosch v. S.S. Edison (Owners)*, [1933] A.C. 448 (H.L.) that these principles should be applied more strictly in claims for property loss. In that case, the defendants negligently destroyed the plaintiffs' vessel, which could have been replaced quickly at a reasonable price if the plaintiffs had possessed the necessary funds. Unfortunately, the plaintiffs were in financial difficulties and were forced to incur far greater costs in replacing their vessel. The defendants were absolved of liability for this additional economic loss, which was attributable to the plaintiffs' impecuniosity.

Liesbosch was frequently criticized by courts. See for example *Dodd Properties (Kent) Ltd. v. Canterbury C.C.*, [1980] 1 All E.R. 928 (C.A.); and *Rollinson v. R.* (1994), 20 C.C.L.T. (2d) 92 (Fed. T.D.). Moreover, as explained in Chapter 17, the Privy Council has now rejected a blanket rule denying recovery of losses attributable to the plaintiff's "thin wallet." Instead, it has stressed that the general principles of foreseeability and remoteness should govern recovery. See *Alcoa Minerals of Jamaica v.*

Broderick, [2000] 3 W.L.R. 23 (P.C.); and *Lagden v. O'Connor*, [2004] 1 A.C. 1067 (H.L.) in which the House of Lords expressly overruled *Liesbosch*.

(c) THE PLAINTIFF'S OBLIGATION TO MITIGATE

It is generally accepted that the principles of mitigation are applied more rigorously in claims for property loss than in claims for personal injury. In property loss cases the courts appear to demand that the plaintiff act reasonably in a business sense. As in so many other areas of damages, the principle is relatively straightforward but is often difficult to apply in specific cases. For example, it may be reasonable to purchase a replacement machine at an inflated price if waiting for a damaged chattel to be repaired would generate even greater consequential economic losses.

NOTES AND QUESTIONS

1. In some situations it is difficult to accurately assess the loss suffered by the plaintiff as a result of loss or damage to property. In *Mason v. Westside Cemeteries Ltd.* (1996), 29 C.C.L.T. (2d) 125 (Ont. Gen. Div.) the defendant carelessly lost the ashes of the plaintiff's deceased parents. The plaintiff had intended to have those ashes buried near his own grave. How would you assess his loss?

In *Yearworth v. North Bristol NHS Trust*, [2009] EWCA Civ. 37 the defendant negligently allowed the plaintiffs' stored frozen sperm, being kept at the plaintiffs' request for their possible future use, to thaw and perish. The defendant argued the sperm was not the plaintiffs' property, but the Court of Appeal disagreed. How should this loss of property be valued? See Hawes, "Property Interests in Body Parts: *Yearworth v North Bristol NHS Trust*" (2010) 73 M.L.R. 130. See also *Lam v. University of British Columbia*, 2015 BCCA 2.

2. In *Darbishire v. Warren*, [1963] 3 All E.R. 310 (C.A.) the defendant negligently damaged the plaintiff's well-maintained used car. Although the car had a market value of only £85, the plaintiff spent £192 repairing it because he felt he could not get a reliable replacement vehicle for less than the cost of repair. The Court of Appeal limited the plaintiff's award to the market value. Harman L.J. stated (at 314): "this was not an irreplaceable article, and, therefore, as the cost of repairs greatly exceeded the value, the car should be treated as a constructive total loss and the measure of damages is its value." Pearson L.J. held that the plaintiff had not acted reasonably in mitigating his loss because he had not made an effort to find a reliable replacement. Although this case is consistent with the general principles, is the result fair to the plaintiff? This case illustrates the problem of assessing damages for certain kinds of property. See also *Pac. Blasting Ltd. v. D.J. Byrne Const. Ltd.*, [1977] 2 W.W.R. 505 (B.C.S.C.); *Chappell v. Baratti* (1984), 30 C.C.L.T. 137 (Ont. S.C.); *Scobie v. Wing* (1992), 63 B.C.L.R. (2d) 76 (C.A.); *Kevington Building Corp. v. Lee* (1998), 36 C.L.R. (2d) 293 (B.C.S.C.); and *Skyward Resources Ltd. v. Cessna Aircraft Co.* (2007), 212 Man. R. (2d) 130 (C.A.).

3. In *N.B. Telephone Co. v. Wright* (1982), 140 D.L.R. (3d) 188 (N.B.Q.B.) the plaintiff was able to replace the vehicle damaged by the defendant with one of its other vehicles which it was not using. Nevertheless, the plaintiff was able to recover the amount it would have cost to rent a replacement. Although this decision is generally

accepted as correct, is the result fair to the defendant? Is it consistent with the basic principles of compensatory damages? For other discussions of damages for loss of use see *Pac. Elevators Ltd. v. C.P.R. Co.* (1973), 41 D.L.R. (3d) 608 (S.C.C.); *Municipal Spraying & Contracting Ltd. v. J. Harris & Sons. Ltd.* (1979), 35 N.S.R. (2d) 237 (S.C.); *Hefferman v. Elizabeth Irving Service Centre* (1980), 29 Nfld. & P.E.I.R. 470 (Nfld. T.D.); *Blair's Plumbing & Heating Ltd. v. McGraw* (1981), 35 N.B.R. (2d) 501 (Q.B.); and *Pembina Resources Ltd. v. ULS International Inc.*, [1990] 1 F.C 666 (T.D.).

4. In *Harbutt's Plasticine v. Wayne Tank & Pump Co.*, [1970] 1 All E.R. 225 (C.A.) the plaintiffs could not repair their old premises and therefore built a new factory. The issue was whether the plaintiffs were entitled to the cost of replacement even though it exceeded the decrease in the value of the old building. Lord Denning stated (at 236):

> The destruction of a building is different from the destruction of a chattel. If a secondhand car is destroyed, the owner only gets its value, because he can go into the market and get another secondhand car to replace it. He cannot charge the other party with the cost of replacing it with a new car. But, when this mill was destroyed the plaintiffs had no choice. They were bound to replace it as soon as they could, not only to keep their business going, but also to mitigate the loss of profit (for which they would be able to charge the defendants). They replaced it in the only possible way, without adding any extras. I think they should be allowed the cost of replacement. True it is they got new for old, but I do not think the wrongdoer can diminish the claim on that account. If they had added extra accommodation or made extra improvements, they would have to give credit. But that is not this case.

Did the plaintiffs have to rebuild to mitigate their loss? Could they have mitigated by choosing another business investment? Does the fact that they did rebuild indicate that they thought a new factory was a wise business investment? If so, should the defendant have to bear the full cost? See also *James Street Hardware and Furniture Co. v. Spizziri, supra; Nan v. BlackPine Manufacturing Ltd.*, [1991] 5 W.W.R. 172 (B.C.C.A.); and *Canada (Attorney General) v. Clorey* (1996), 144 Nfld. & P.E.I.R. 132 (P.E.I.S.C. (T.D.)). See Berryman, "Betterment Before Canadian Common Law Courts" (1993) 72 Can. Bar Rev. 54.

5. In *Waterloo Warehousing & Storage Ltd. v. Swenco Mfg. Ltd.* (1975), 58 D.L.R. (3d) 180 (Ont. H.C.) the plaintiff's building was destroyed in a fire caused by the defendant's negligence. Prior to the fire, the plaintiff had entered into a contract to sell the land and building. Since the purchaser intended to demolish the building and construct an apartment building in its place, the purchase price remained the same after the fire. The court denied the plaintiff's claim for the amount which it would have cost to replace the building.

In *Jens v. Mannix Co. Ltd.* (1978), 89 D.L.R. (3d) 351 (B.C.S.C.), varied (1979), 30 D.L.R. (4th) 260 (B.C.C.A.) a house was effectively destroyed because of the defendant's negligence. The property had recently been zoned for commercial use, resulting in an increase in its resale value regardless of whether there were buildings on the property. However, because the plaintiff reasonably planned to keep living there, and had received planning approval to rebuild, he was entitled to recover the cost of replacing his home.

Can you reconcile *Jens* and *Darbishire v. Warren, supra*? Can you reconcile *Jens* and *Waterloo Warehousing & Storage Ltd.*? See also, as concerns chattels, *The Maersk Colombo*, [2001] 2 Lloyd's Rep. 275 (C.A.).

6. In *Tridan Developments Ltd. v. Shell Canada Products Ltd.* (2002), 57 O.R. (3d) 503 (C.A.) the defendant owned a service station. It negligently allowed 9,000 litres of gas to leak onto the plaintiff's neighbouring property. A clean-up could be performed to one of two standards: "pristine condition" or a condition that would have satisfied guidelines established by the Ministry of the Environment. The former was more expensive by $250,000. The trial judge held that the plaintiff was entitled to the higher amount. The Court of Appeal agreed even though the plaintiff's property would probably never be used for residential purposes. It reasoned that "[w]here a product that may cause mischief escapes to a neighbour's property, there is 'responsibility for all the damage which is the natural consequence of the escape'." The trial judge also awarded: (i) $350,000 for loss of property value due to the stigma of an environmental hazard and (ii) an injunction requiring the defendant to install an environmental barrier between the properties, or, failing that, additional damages of $85,000. The Court of Appeal, however, eliminated the $350,000 award on the basis that there would be no residual stigma if the land was cleaned up to a pristine condition. It further held that while the plaintiff was entitled to $85,000, representing the cost of an environmental barrier, there was no basis for linking that award to injunctive relief. See van Rensburg, "Deconstructing *Tridan*: A Litigator's Perspective" (2004) 15 J. Envtl. L & Prac. 85.

7. In *British Columbia v. Canadian Forest Products Ltd.*, [2004] 2 S.C.R. 74 the defendants were 70% responsible for a negligently caused forest fire. The province had in place a sophisticated timber pricing system that raised its "stumpage" revenues in other forested areas when revenues in one or more areas fell. After the fire the province sued for loss of revenue from trees that, but for the fire, would have been harvested and for loss of trees set aside in environmentally-sensitive areas. The defendants argued that because of the revenue increases from other areas under the pricing system, and because the set-aside trees were never to be harvested, the province had suffered no financial loss. The trial judge agreed with the defendants. The Court of Appeal agreed with respect to the harvestable trees but awarded the province 33% of the commercial value of the set-aside trees. A majority of the Supreme Court of Canada reinstated the decision of the trial judge, while the dissent held that the province should recover for both the harvestable and set-aside trees. The case illustrates several different approaches to calculating damages for property loss. See Elgie & Lintner, "The Supreme Court's *Canfor* Decision: Losing the Battle but Winning the War for Environmental Damages" (2005) 38 U.B.C.L. Rev. 223.

8. For a comprehensive review of the issues raised by *Dredger Liesbosch* see Phillips, "Compensation For Losses Flowing from an Injured Party's Impecuniosity" (1982) 20 Osgoode Hall L.J. 18; Wexler, "The Impecunious Plaintiff: Liesbosch Reconsidered" (1987) 66 Can. Bar Rev. 129; David *et al.*, "Impecuniosity and the Duty to Mitigate: *Dredger Liesbosch (Owners) v. The Edison (Owners)*" (1998) 20 Adv. Q. 366; and Coote "Damages, *The Liesbosch* and Impecuniosity" [2001] C.L.J. 511. Cases like *Geld v. Dehavilland Aircraft of Can. Ltd.*, [1983] 6 W.W.R. 229 (B.C.S.C.); *A.G. Ont. v. Fatehi* (1984), 31 C.C.L.T. 1 (S.C.C.); and *Armak Chemicals Ltd. v. Canadian National Railway Co.* (1991), 3 O.R. (3d) 1 (C.A.) also raise interesting issues relating to economic loss consequent upon damage to property.

9. The principles of contributory negligence and mitigation of loss overlap in some cases. For example in *Indust. Teletype Electronics Corp. v. Montreal* (1976), 10 N.R. 517 (S.C.C.) the plaintiff considered his flood-damaged inventory to be a total loss and claimed damages for the full replacement cost. The plaintiff offered all of the inventory to the defendant, who declined to take it. Beetz J. stated (at 524):

> Finally, according to a defence expert the damages could have been substantially reduced and some new parts still considered as such after the flood, had a cleaning and drying operation that was simple and inexpensive been diligently carried out. The parts exposed to water remained at the risk of appellants who continued to have custody and ownership of them. If this expert's opinion is accurate, surely the offer made by appellants cannot exempt them from mitigating their damages, as would a reasonable man. Indeed, to allow a plaintiff to rid himself of this obligation by means of such an offer, and allow him the replacement value of the merchandise, would be equivalent to treating as an insurer the perpetrator of the damage. I do not believe that this is the state of our law. This aspect of the case is obviously such as to affect the quantum of the damages, but it goes beyond the question of quantum; it concerns the causal relationship between the fault of the city and the loss sustained by appellants. Thus, the claim of the latter could be reduced to the extent that their own negligence after the flood contributed to increase the damage.

Do you agree with Beetz J. that the plaintiff's conduct should be considered as an issue of contributory negligence rather than as a question of mitigation? Does it make any difference which approach is adopted? For other illustrations of mitigation of loss see *Can. Western Natural Gas Co. v. Pathfinder Surveys Ltd* (1980), 21 A.R. 459 (C.A.); *John Maryon Int. Ltd. v. N.B. Telephone Co.* (1982), 24 C.C.L.T. 146 (N.B.C.A.); *Galantiuk v. Regina*, [1984] 6 W.W.R. 262 (Sask. Q.B.); *Miller Dredging Ltd. v. Dorothy Mackenzie (The)* (1994), 119 D.L.R. (4th) 63 (B.C.C.A.); and *Wiebe v. Gunderson* (2004), 32 B.C.L.R. (4th) 230 (C.A.).

5. Collateral Benefits

To this point it has been assumed that the defendant is the plaintiff's sole source of compensation. However in most cases the plaintiff will also receive compensation in various forms from collateral sources such as government health insurance, private insurance or employment benefits. Should the defendant's liability be reduced to reflect the benefit that the plaintiff has received from such collateral sources?

In the absence of a statutory or contractual provision to the contrary, certain types of collateral benefits need not be deducted from the plaintiff's damages. These include private insurance benefits, charitable or benevolent gifts, and pension benefits. However, the deductibility of many other types of collateral benefits is largely governed by statute, including provincial health insurance, workers' compensation and automobile insurance schemes. For examples involving the latter see *Gurniak v. Nordquist*, [2003] 2 S.C.R. 652; *Sonnenberger v. Creamer*, [2009] I.L.R. I-4804 (Ont. S.C.J.); *Mikolic v. Tanguay*, 2016 ONSC 69 (Div. Ct.); *El-Khodr v. Lackie*, 2017 ONCA 716; and *Tibbetts v. Murphy*, 2017 NSCA 35. See also *Walker v. Ritchie* (2005), 197 O.A.C. 81 (C.A.), varied (2006), 43 C.C.L.T. (3d) 1 (S.C.C.). In this area it is vital to consider the specific statutory language, which can differ from context to context and province to province.

In the past courts have held that public welfare benefits like social assistance are not deducted from the damage award. But in *M.B. v. British Columbia*, [2003] 2 S.C.R. 477 the court held that social assistance is intended as a form of wage replacement and is not akin to private charitable donations. In line with the views of several leading tort scholars, and in accordance with a general trend towards deducting collateral benefits, the court held that social assistance payments were to be deducted from the award. See also *Krangle (Guardian ad litem of) v. Brisco*, [2002] 1 S.C.R. 205; *H.L. v. Canada (Attorney General)*, [2005] 1 S.C.R. 401; and Adjin-Tettey, "The Marginalizing Effect of Deductibility of Past Welfare Benefits from Compensation for Personal Injury" in Rodgers, Ruparelia & Belanger-Hardy, eds., *Critical Torts* (2009) at 37.

The issue of collateral benefits has been particularly significant in the context of employee benefits. In normal circumstances, if a plaintiff is required to miss work as a result of injuries sustained through the defendant's negligence, the lost income is compensable. The situation is more complicated if, as often occurs under employment contracts, the employer continues to pay the employee for the lost days. The proper resolution of that situation has been the subject of considerable controversy.

In *Ratych v. Bloomer* (1990), 69 D.L.R. (4th) 25 (S.C.C.) a police officer continued to receive payment from his employer while recuperating. The Supreme Court of Canada held that the defendant was able to deduct those payments from the damages that were payable. The basic facts of *Cunningham v. Wheeler* (1994), 113 D.L.R. (4th) 1 (S.C.C.) were similar. A railway employee continued to receive payment from his employer during a period of convalescence. In contrast to *Ratych*, a majority of the Supreme Court of Canada held that the defendant was not permitted to deduct those payments from the damages that were payable.

As Cory J. explained in *Cunningham*, the difference between the two cases was attributable to the evidence of proof of loss. In *Ratych* the plaintiff failed to prove that he had in any way "paid" for the disability benefits that he received from his employer. Moreover, the evidence indicated that the police officer did not lose any accumulated "sick days" as a result of missing work. In contrast, the plaintiff in *Cunningham* proved that while he did not pay for the disability benefits by way of pay cheque deductions, he and his fellow employees effectively purchased the right to receive such benefits during labour negotiations. The employer had agreed to provide the employees with a global package of benefits — if the employees had not chosen to receive part of that package in the form of disability benefits, they would have received higher hourly wages. On that basis, Cory J. reasoned that the disability benefits in *Cunningham* were indistinguishable from the benefits acquired under private insurance, which are not deductible. He therefore concluded that it would be "unjust to deprive the employees of benefits which, through prudence and thrift, they had purchased for themselves."

Perhaps not surprisingly, McLachlin J., who wrote the judgment in *Ratych*, dissented in *Cunningham*. Whereas the majority in *Cunningham* was concerned primarily with the injustice of allowing the defendant to derive a benefit from the fact that the plaintiff purchased disability protection, McLachlin J.'s reasoning was primarily motivated by the desire to prevent a claimant from enjoying "double recovery" for the same loss. "The watchword," she wrote, "is restoration; what is required to restore the plaintiff to his or her pre-accident position." She accordingly held that employment benefits should be subject to deductibility "except where it is established that a right of subrogation will be exercised."

(a) THE DOCTRINE OF SUBROGATION

The doctrine of subrogation originated in equity, but the right to subrogation may also be created by contract or legislation. At the risk of oversimplification, the effect of subrogation is that a party who has provided an indemnity payment to another is entitled to recover any excess compensation received by that other party for that same loss. For example, assume that a fire insurance company pays the full value of $250,000 for the loss of a negligently destroyed home, and the insured then recovers $250,000 from the tortfeasor. Under the doctrine of subrogation, the insured will be required to refund $250,000 to the insurance company. If the insured is awarded $250,000 but only recovers $100,000 from the tortfeasor, he or she need only refund $100,000 to the insurance company.

Any party who honours a legal obligation to indemnify another has an equitable right to subrogation. Thus if an employer compensates an injured employee under the provisions of a collective bargaining agreement, the employer can seek recovery from the negligent defendant who caused the injury. However, many employers find it too expensive to pursue subrogated claims and some have abandoned the right in their collective agreements, leaving employees free to attempt to obtain double recovery.

Whenever the right of subrogation is enforced, the collateral source rule becomes a matter of indifference to the plaintiff. Anything the plaintiff recovers from the tortfeasor for which he or she has already been indemnified by the collateral source has to be refunded to the collateral source.

NOTES AND QUESTIONS

1. What is the impact of the majority decision in *Cunningham* on the principle established in *Ratych*? Based on the facts, did the plaintiff in *Cunningham* make a sufficient contribution to the benefit to justify not having it deducted from the damage award?

2. If McLachlin J.'s position in *Cunningham* had been the majority rather than the dissent, what impact might there have been on collective bargaining? Do the theoretical justifications provided for the two positions compel a decision one way or the other?

3. As McLachlin J. noted in her dissenting judgment in *Cunningham*, one of the primary justifications for the private insurance exception is that such insurers have a statutory right of subrogation. When the insurer exercises this right, double recovery is avoided. However, as indicated, it may be expensive to exercise this subrogation right and it is frequently abandoned. It has been argued that double recovery could be more effectively prevented by making all collateral benefits deductible from the defendant's liability. See Cooper, "A Collateral Benefits Principle" (1971) 49 Can. Bar Rev. 501. Legislation governing some public benefits has adopted this approach. See as an historical example the *Insurance Act*, R.S.O. 1990, c. 1.8, s. 267(1); and generally Brown & Donnelly, *Insurance Law in Canada*, looseleaf (1999) (consulted June 2018), ch. 13.

4. For a discussion of Canadian pension and unemployment benefits see *Can. Pac. Ltd. v. Gill*, [1973] S.C.R. 654; *Guy v. Trizec Equities Ltd.*, [1979] 2 S.C.R. 756; and *Jack Cewe Ltd. v. Jorgenson*, [1980] 4 W.W.R. 494 (S.C.C.). In *Demers v. B.R. Davidson*

Mining & Development Ltd., 2012 ONCA 384 the plaintiff received pension disability benefits under the Canada Pension Plan and the Hospitals of Ontario Pension Plan. The court held that these benefits were payable to the plaintiff because she met the requisite conditions of the plan and that they were not paid as income replacement. They were akin to private insurance and accordingly did not have to be deducted. In contrast, in *Tibbetts v. Murphy, supra*, the Nova Scotia Court of Appeal distinguished *Demers* and held that Canada Pension Plan disability payments had to be deducted from the award because of the specific statutory provision in the province relating to automobile accidents.

5. The prevailing view is that health benefits received by the plaintiff will not reduce the defendant's liability. For example in *McLeod v. Palardy* (1981), 124 D.L.R. (3d) 506 (Man. C.A.) the court awarded the plaintiff future care costs even though such care was provided free of charge under the provincial health plan. The contrary position was taken in *Wipfli v. Britten* (1984), 29 C.C.L.T. 240 (B.C.C.A.). In reference to cases similar to *McLeod*, Taggart J.A. stated at 270: "I remain unconvinced that they have application to the case of a claimant protected by a universal hospital plan for which he paid nothing in the past (i.e., no premiums or user fee) and is unlikely to be called on to pay anything in the future." Which view is supported by the decision in *Cunningham*?

6. In Ontario, plaintiffs are required to advance a claim against the defendant on behalf of the Ontario Health Insurance Plan for costs already borne by the OHIP in treating the plaintiff. This avoids the OHIP having to bring its own claim against the tortfeasor. See *Health Insurance Act*, R.S.O. 1990, c. H.6, s. 31(1).

7. If the defendant is not permitted to reduce his or her liability to reflect a collateral benefit that has been received by the plaintiff, should the plaintiff be required to return the excess amount to the collateral source? The courts have generally held that the plaintiff is entitled to retain both the damage award and the collateral benefit unless precluded from doing so by contract or statute.

8. In *Gaca v. Pirelli General plc.*, [2004] 3 All E.R. 348 (C.A.) the plaintiff was injured at work and his employers were responsible. They voluntarily paid him an "ill health gratuity." While in general charitable or benevolent gifts are not deductible from a damage award, the court held that this principle should not apply to a gratuity paid by the defendant rather than by others, and deducted the payment from the subsequent damage award.

9. For a detailed discussion of collateral benefits see Cooper-Stephenson & Adjin-Tettey, *Personal Injury Damages in Canada*, 3d ed. (2018), ch. 9. For a detailed discussion of subrogation see Mitchell, *The Law of Subrogation* (1994).

10. Suppose the government establishes an in-home assistance program for tort victims. Suppose also that it has the discretion to stop the assistance if the victim recovers damages from the tortfeasor to cover in-home care. Should the court award the plaintiff the cost of in-home care? See *Fullerton (Guardian ad litem of) v. Delair* (2006), 55 B.C.L.R. (4th) 252 (C.A.).

More generally, how certain does the court need to be that the plaintiff will receive certain benefits from other sources before deducting them from the amount the defendant must pay? See for example *Hoang v. Trieu*, 2012 ONSC 6644.

11. Concerns about double recovery can also arise in a case in which the plaintiff sues two defendants but settles with one of them prior to trial. In assessing the damages payable by the remaining defendant, to what extent should the court consider amounts recovered under the settlement? For example, suppose the plaintiff accepts a settlement of $200,000 from the first defendant. At trial, the plaintiff's damages are assessed at $300,000 and as between the two defendants liability is apportioned equally. Should the plaintiff be allowed to recover $150,000 from the second defendant? See *Ashcroft v. Dhaliwal* (2008), 83 B.C.L.R. (4th) 279 (C.A.); *Laudon v. Roberts* (2009), 249 O.A.C. 72 (C.A.); and *Bedard (Next Friend of) v. Martyn*, 2010 ABCA 3.

12. Recent decisions suggest that courts have been less willing to defer to the fact that the plaintiff has paid, in some way, for the benefit. In *IBM Canada Limited v. Waterman*, 2013 SCC 70 at para. 76 Cromwell J. for a majority of the court set out the following principles:

> (a) There is no single marker to sort which benefits fall within the private insurance exception. (b) One widely accepted factor relates to the nature and purpose of the benefit. The more closely the benefit is, in nature and purpose, an indemnity against the type of loss caused by the defendant's breach, the stronger the case for deduction. The converse is also true. (c) Whether the plaintiff has contributed to the benefit remains a relevant consideration, although the basis for this is debatable. (d) In general, a benefit will not be deducted if it is not an indemnity for the loss caused by the breach and the plaintiff has contributed in order to obtain entitlement to it. (e) There is room in the analysis of the deduction issue for broader policy considerations such as the desirability of equal treatment of those in similar situations, the possibility of providing incentives for socially desirable conduct, and the need for clear rules that are easy to apply.

On these principles, how would *Cunningham* have been decided? In *Mazzucco v. Herer*, 2015 ONSC 7083 at para. 17 the court stated that in *Waterman* "the Supreme Court of Canada has signalled that a new era has begun regarding the private insurance exception." The plaintiff was receiving long-term disability benefits provided by her employer under a collective agreement. The court held that this was no longer determinative. Based on both the indemnity nature of the benefits and on broader policy considerations, the court held the benefits were deductible.

REVIEW PROBLEMS

1. By all appearances, Helen and Bob were the ideal young couple. Prior to marriage, they carefully made future plans. First, Bob would go to law school while Helen worked and supported him; then Helen would go to law school and Bob would support her. Thereafter, they planned to have two children, one right after the other. Helen would take care of the children until they started school. At that time, Helen would join Bob in the law practice.

Things went exactly as planned for the happy young couple until a week before Helen's first-year law school exams, when she was seriously injured in a grease fire at a local restaurant. Her face was badly scarred, and even after three painful operations she remained badly disfigured. Moreover, in spite of the doctor's initial optimism, an operation to restore her sight was unsuccessful and it is now clear that Helen will be permanently blind. Not surprisingly, the accident also caused acute personality changes in Helen. She refuses to have anything whatsoever to do with her family or friends and sits for hours alone in her room playing classical music. After a year, the marriage was ruined. Although Bob still maintains a home for the two of them and provides for Helen's normal needs, he has lost all interest in the marriage.

(a) Assume Helen has a 50% chance of establishing liability and securing damages from the restaurant's liability insurance company within two years. Prepare Helen's claim for general damages in her tort action. Organize and itemize the claims, and indicate the type of evidence that you would adduce to secure the greatest possible award for Helen.

(b) What factors would you consider and what demands would you make if the insurance company were interested in settling Helen's claim before trial?

2. Albert Sweet was injured when his car was struck by a negligently driven Ace Transport truck. Liability is admitted by Ace Transport and the sole issue at trial is the quantum of damages. At the time of the accident, Albert was 23 years old and had just graduated from law school. He was about to start an articling job at an annual salary of $50,000. His pre-accident life expectancy was 52 years but his doctors now estimate he will die within 20 years. Albert suffered brain damage and now has the intellectual capabilities of a five-year-old child.

Between the time of the accident and the trial, Albert and his wife Miriam have been supported by her wealthy parents. The proceeds of a small insurance policy have covered all medical expenses and have paid for a nurse for Albert, but these funds are almost exhausted.

You have been contacted by Miriam to assess the possible damage claim that can be brought on behalf of Albert, her parents and herself against Ace Transport.

3. Mr. and Mrs. Troup were an elderly childless couple. Both were actively engaged in the work force throughout their 40-year marriage. Mr. Troup is a famous medical doctor and Mrs. Troup was a university professor until July 1, 2010. At that time, she was compelled to retire from the university and was granted a pension worth 80% of her salary for the remainder of her life. The individual income of either Mr. or Mrs. Troup had always been sufficient to meet their joint expenditures, and the Troups had pooled their funds, accumulating a sizeable surplus during their married years.

The only significant quarrel in their lengthy marriage involved Mrs. Troup's nephew. Out of a sense of moral duty to her late sister, Mrs. Troup undertook in 2013 to house and support her nephew for four years while he attended university. Mr. Troup disliked the nephew, whom he regarded as a leech.

Upon retiring, Mrs. Troup became a famous author of historical novels. Her second novel, allegedly fiction, recounted a story which closely resembled the life of a leading Canadian politician. On July 1, 2015, her home-town newspaper, *The Press*, carried a story announcing that the politician had started a defamation action based on the book. National sales of Mrs. Troup's books began to increase dramatically in response to the publicity.

Later that day Mrs. Troup was shopping in the city when she walked past a construction site. Unfortunately, the cable securing a load of concrete failed. Some of the blocks fell on Mrs. Troup, causing her severe injuries. The incident also destroyed the $10,000 gold watch that Mrs. Troup was wearing. Mrs. Troup went into a coma and was taken to the intensive care unit at the hospital. Some 80% of her hospital bills were borne by government medical insurance and the remaining 20% were paid by Mrs. Troup's private Blue Cross plan. Mrs. Troup died ten days later without ever regaining consciousness. She was 67. Mr. Troup was named the sole beneficiary and executor under his wife's will. He was also named the sole beneficiary of her $100,000 life insurance policy.

Mr. Troup now seeks your advice with respect to a possible legal action against the construction company that owned and operated the crane. The company has admitted negligence. Based upon the relevant legislation in your province, what damages will flow from the action, to whom will damages be awarded, and how will damages be divided among the possible plaintiffs?

4. Due to the negligence of the defendant, Jeff suffered blunt thoracic aortic injuries. His heart now works at a diminished capacity. Jeff previously worked as a construction worker. He is now only able to do that work half-days due to his weakened heart. Jeff has smoked his whole adult life and has always been considerably overweight. After the injury, Jeff's doctors recommended that he stop smoking and lose 50 pounds. In their view, this would reduce strain on his heart and allow him to work for full days. Jeff has not made any effort to follow his doctors' advice. Jeff lives in Revelstoke, where it is very difficult for him to find half-day employment in the construction industry. Employment data indicates that he would be able to find such employment in a larger centre. Jeff is single and has no relatives in Revelstoke or the surrounding region, but he does not want to live in a larger centre, or to commute to one, and so he has remained in Revelstoke where he is unemployed.

In assessing Jeff's damages for loss of future earnings, would you conclude that he has failed to mitigate his losses based on any of the following: (1) failure to stop smoking, (2) failure to lose weight, (3) failure to commute to new employment and (4) failure to relocate?

DEFENCES IN NEGLIGENCE

1. Introduction
2. Contributory Negligence
3. Voluntary Assumption of Risk
4. Participation in a Criminal or Immoral Act
5. Inevitable Accident

1. Introduction

Even if the plaintiff proves that he or she was negligently injured by the defendant, damages may be reduced or denied on the basis of a defence. The first three defences that we discuss — contributory negligence, voluntary assumption of risk and participation in a criminal or immoral act — pertain to the plaintiff's own behaviour. The fourth defence, inevitable accident, is concerned with the factual circumstances surrounding the defendant's conduct and can be seen as a special denial of negligence.

For each defence, the burden of proof is on the defendant. The defendant may be able to rely on more than one defence.

For detailed recent analysis, see Goudkamp, *Tort Law Defences* (2013); Descheemaeker, "Tort Law Defences: A Defence of Conventionalism" (2014) 77 M.L.R. 493; and Dyson, Goudkamp & Wilmot-Smith, eds., *Defences in Tort* (2015).

2. Contributory Negligence

(a) THE DEVELOPMENT OF THE DEFENCE

At common law the plaintiff traditionally was denied recovery if his or her negligent conduct was a cause of the injury. There was no apportionment of loss between the defendant and plaintiff, even if the plaintiff's negligence was a relatively insignificant cause. To avoid this inequity, the courts developed what became known as the "last clear chance" or "last opportunity" rule. This doctrine permitted the plaintiff to recover, despite his or her contributory negligence, if the defendant had the last clear chance to avoid the accident and negligently failed to take it. While the doctrine clearly benefited the plaintiff, it perpetuated the existing all-or-nothing approach by placing the entire loss on the defendant. With the acceptance of more complex theories of causation and liability the doctrine came under severe criticism. Sappideen & Vines, eds., *Fleming's The Law of Torts*, 10th ed. (2011) states at 320:

> Over the century of its life, the last opportunity doctrine developed into a plastic instrument for allocating the loss to either plaintiff or defendant in accordance with the court's view of whose was the disproportionately greater share of responsibility . . . . The resulting casuistry tended to make the task of appellate review a veritable farce.

Legislation permitting the apportionment of liability was not enacted until well into the 20th century. By allowing the dividing of liability according to the parties' relative degrees of fault, the legislation tempered the harshness of the common law's all-or-nothing approach.

NOTES AND QUESTIONS

1. The courts first dealt with contributory negligence as a question of legal causation rather than as a defence: see *Butterfield v. Forrester* (1809), 103 E.R. 926 (K.B.); and *Davies v. Mann* (1842), 152 E.R. 588 (Exch.). What are the advantages and disadvantages of this approach?

2. Once the courts recognized that there could be more than one legal cause of an accident, was there any justification for continuing to treat contributory negligence as a complete bar to recovery? See Bohlen, "Contributory Negligence" (1908) 21 Harv. L. Rev. 233; Malone, "The Formative Period of Contributory Negligence" (1946) 41 Ill. L. Rev. 151; James, "Contributory Negligence" (1953) 62 Yale L. Rev. 691; and Fleming, "Forward: Comparative Negligence at Last — by Judicial Choice" (1976) 64 Cal. L. Rev. 239.

3. *Davies v. Mann, supra*, was the first case in which the last clear chance doctrine was clearly articulated. For Canadian applications of the doctrine see *Long v. Toronto Ry. Co.* (1914), 50 S.C.R. 224; *B.C. Elec. Ry. Co. v. Loach*, [1916] 1 A.C. 719 (P.C.); *McKee v. Malenfant*, [1954] S.C.R. 651; *Boulay v. Rousselle* (1984), 30 C.C.L.T. 149 (N.B.Q.B.); and *Hunter v. Briere* (1989), 49 C.C.L.T. 93 (Man. Q.B.). See also MacIntyre, "The Rationale of Last Clear Chance" (1940) 18 Can. Bar Rev. 665; Williams, *Joint Torts and Contributory Negligence* (1951) at 223-55; and Casswell, "Avoiding Last Clear Chance" (1990) 69 Can. Bar Rev. 129.

4. In what circumstances did the last clear chance doctrine work to the defendant's advantage? As we shall later discuss, the apportionment legislation did not eliminate the last clear chance doctrine. Following the enactment of apportionment legislation, in what circumstances would the last clear chance doctrine benefit the defendant? See Linden *et al.*, *Canadian Tort Law*, 11th ed. (2018) at 468-69.

5. The unfairness of the common law rule led the Supreme Court of Canada to abolish it even in the absence of contributory negligence legislation. In *Bow Valley Husky (Bermuda) Ltd. v. Saint John Shipbuilding Ltd.* (1997), 153 D.L.R. (4th) 385 (S.C.C.) McLachlin J. held that Newfoundland and Labrador's *Contributory Negligence Act*, R.S.N.L. 1990, c. C-33 did not apply to a claim arising in maritime law. Nevertheless, she held:

> The considerations on which the contributory negligence bar was based no longer comport with the modern view of fairness and justice. Tort law no longer accepts the traditional theory underpinning the contributory negligence bar — that the injured party cannot prove that the tortfeasor "caused" the damage. The contributory negligence bar results in manifest unfairness, particularly where the negligence of the injured party is slight in comparison with the negligence of others. Nor does the contributory negligence bar further the goal of modern tort law of encouraging care

and vigilance. So long as an injured party can be shown to be marginally at fault, a tortfeasor's conduct, no matter how egregious, goes unpunished.

6. A plaintiff will be found contributorily negligent only where his or her negligence caused the accident or contributed to the severity of his or her injury. It is not necessary that the plaintiff's negligence be the only cause. In *Zsoldos v. Canadian Pacific Railway Co.* (2009), 93 O.R. (3d) 321 (C.A.) the plaintiff was injured when his motorcycle struck a train at a rural crossing at night. The defendant argued the plaintiff was contributorily negligent because he was driving while impaired and was driving too fast. The court held that because the collision would have happened whether or not the plaintiff was impaired, the impairment did not amount to contributory negligence. In contrast, the excessive speed did.

In addition to being a factual cause, the plaintiff's carelessness "must relate to the risk that made the actual harm which occurred foreseeable": see *Wormald v. Chiarot*, 2016 BCCA 415 at para. 15; and *Ackley v. Audette*, 2017 BCCA 283 at paras. 24-30. This is in essence a requirement that the harm is not too remote from the plaintiff's own conduct or, put differently, is within the scope of the risk created by the plaintiff's carelessness. For more on these concepts see Chapter 17.

7. Is contributory negligence correctly called a defence? In Goudkamp, "Rethinking Contributory Negligence" in Pitel, Neyers & Chamberlain, eds., *Tort Law: Challenging Orthodoxy* (2013) at 336-38 the author argues that while initially contributory negligence, in its all-or-nothing form, went to the issue of the defendant's liability and so was a defence, with the advent of apportionment contributory negligence became part of the law of remedies. On this view, this topic belongs not in this chapter but rather in Chapter 18.

(b) CONDUCT CONSTITUTING CONTRIBUTORY NEGLIGENCE

Contributory negligence can take many forms. The plaintiff may carelessly enter into a dangerous situation, such as a sober passenger negligently accepting a ride from a drunk driver who later crashes into a wall. The plaintiff may carelessly contribute to the creation of an accident, such as a passenger engaging a driver in horseplay that results in an accident. The plaintiff may carelessly contribute not to the creation of an accident but rather to the resulting harm, such as a passenger negligently failing to wear a seat belt and consequently suffering more severe injuries. The cases in this section provide further illustrations.

WALLS v. MUSSENS LTD.
(1969), 11 D.L.R. (3d) 245 (N.B.C.A.)

HUGHES J.A.:—In the afternoon of January 18, 1968, the defendant Morrison, a serviceman and mechanic in the employ of the defendant Mussens Limited, drove a machine used in logging operations called a timberjack, belonging to one Murdock Hallihan, to the plaintiff's service station premises where he obtained permission to repair the front drive shaft of the timberjack in one of the bays of the service station. Shortly after 6:30 p.m. while Morrison and Hallihan were working on the machine, a propane gas torch being used by Morrison ignited a pool containing gasoline on the floor beneath the machine.

The learned trial Judge found that the gasoline on the floor had leaked from a tube leading from the gas tank to the engine of the timberjack and that the fire was caused by the negligence of Morrison in the use of the propane gas torch while acting in the course of his employment with Mussens Ltd. There is no appeal against these findings.

When the fire started the plaintiff was at home for his evening meal, having left Terry Hambrook, a 17-year-old high school boy employed by him to tend the gas tanks, change tires and do other such work, in charge of the service station. Hambrook, who was in the office talking with two boys, heard someone call out: "Fire — come on out and bring a fire extinguisher" — but, instead of bringing one of the available extinguishers, Hambrook and others including Morrison, Hallihan and probably the two boys attempted to smother the fire by throwing snow on it. Hallihan says he also tried to extinguish it with water from a hose.

When the plaintiff, who was told of the fire by Hambrook, arrived at the service station the flame was about 18 inches in height and two feet in diameter. The plaintiff joined the others in shovelling snow onto the fire but in the excitement of the emergency the five fire extinguishers which were on the premises were not thought of. Morrison testified that when he realized the snow would not smother the fire he ran out of the building, drove his truck to the door, and tried to tow the timberjack from the building but was unable to do so as his truck was too light to move it. The fire spread quickly and the service station and most of the contents were destroyed.

Alpha D. Curl, an expert in the production, design and use theory of fire prevention equipment, expressed an opinion, which the learned trial Judge accepted, that had the available fire extinguishers been used when the plaintiff arrived at the service station the fire could probably have been extinguished. In their defence the defendants alleged that the damage suffered by the plaintiff was caused wholly by the negligence or breach of duty by the plaintiff, his workmen, licensees, servants and agents. The learned trial Judge carefully considered the evidence and found that the failure of the plaintiff to use the fire extinguishers in the prevailing excitement did not constitute contributory negligence even though his failure to do so may have deprived those present of the chance of minimizing the loss, and he held the negligence of Morrison was the sole cause of the plaintiff's damage.

I have read the evidence with respect to the frantic efforts of all concerned, including the plaintiff, to extinguish the fire, and I agree that the conclusions reached by the learned trial Judge are amply supported by the evidence.

No portion of the responsibility for starting the fire can be attributed to the plaintiff. There was no antecedent negligence on his part and he had no part in the repair work which was carried out by Morrison. The emergency was created solely by the negligence of Morrison for whose acts and omissions Mussens Ltd. is vicariously liable. While it may be unfortunate the plaintiff did not have the presence of mind in the emergency to use the fire extinguishers which were available, and notwithstanding his participation in throwing snow on the fire may have aggravated the situation, I think the plaintiff is entitled to invoke the "agony of the moment" rule as an answer to the allegation of contributory negligence made against him.

The Law of Torts, 3rd ed., by J.G. Fleming, contains the following statement at p. 247:

> On the other hand, a person's conduct, in the face of a sudden emergency, cannot be judged from the standpoint of what would have been reasonable behaviour in the

light of hind-knowledge and in a calmer atmosphere conducive to a nice evaluation of alternatives. A certain latitude is allowed when "in the agony of the moment" he seeks to extricate himself from an emergency not created by his own antecedent negligence. The degree of judgment and presence of mind expected of the plaintiff is what would have been reasonable conduct in such a situation, and he will not be adjudged guilty of contributory negligence merely because, as it turns out, he unwittingly took the wrong course.

. . .

The test to be applied in circumstances such as those as in the case at bar is, in my opinion, not whether the plaintiff exercised a careful and prudent judgment in doing what he did, but whether what he did was something an ordinarily prudent man might reasonably have done under the stress of the emergency.

In my opinion it might well have appeared to an ordinarily prudent man in the emergency with which the plaintiff was confronted that shovelling snow on the fire was the most effective way to extinguish it, although in fact it was not, and may actually have tended to spread the fire. It is now apparent that the fire could not have been smothered as it was being fed by gasoline leaking from the fuel line of the timberjack and it is most improbable the plaintiff had any knowledge of that fact until the cause of the fire was investigated. The plaintiff's reaction to the emergency was merely to do what the others were doing and I cannot say that it was something an ordinarily prudent man might not reasonably have done in the circumstances.

In my opinion the appeal on this ground should fail.

NOTES AND QUESTIONS

1. What criteria did the court in *Walls* use in determining whether the plaintiff had breached the standard of care expected of him? Should the test be applied in exactly the same way in assessing the defendant's carelessness and the plaintiff's contributory negligence? See also *Zervobeakos v. Zervobeakos* (1969), 8 D.L.R. (3d) 377 (N.S.C.A.); and *Neufeld v. Landry* (1975), 55 D.L.R. (3d) 296 (Man. C.A.). It has been suggested that while the same principles theoretically apply to both parties, judges and especially juries tend to be more reluctant to find contributory negligence than negligence: Sappideen & Vines, eds., *Fleming's The Law of Torts*, 10th ed. (2011) at 328-29. What factors do you suspect underlie that tendency? See also Goudkamp, "Rethinking Contributory Negligence" in Pitel, Neyers & Chamberlain, eds., *Tort Law: Challenging Orthodoxy* (2013) at 323-27.

2. In *A.G. Ont. v. Keller* (1978), 94 D.L.R. (3d) 632 (Ont. C.A.) the plaintiff was a police officer who was injured in a high-speed chase when his cruiser went out of control and struck a pole. The officer was driving at about 85 miles per hour on icy roads within 100 to 150 feet of the defendant. The court held that the officer was not contributorily negligent because his actions were "no more than was reasonably necessary to carry out his statutory duty." Nevertheless, given the risks involved in high-speed chases, did the officer act reasonably? Should the police officer in *Keller* have been held to a higher standard of care than the average driver? Would the court have found the officer negligent if he had hit a pedestrian? Should that make any difference in analyzing contributory negligence? See *Priestman v. Colangelo*, [1959] S.C.R. 615; *Roberge v. R.* (1983), 147 D.L.R. (3d) 493 (S.C.C.); *Miller v. Wolbaum*

(1986), 47 M.V.R. 162 (Sask. Q.B.); and *Moore v. Fanning* (1987), 41 C.C.L.T. 67 (Ont. H.C.).

3. In *Lewis v. Todd* (1980), 115 D.L.R. (3d) 257 (S.C.C.) a police officer was killed by a driver while investigating a traffic accident. Working alone and ignoring the traffic, Constable Lewis apparently relied on the warnings given by several flashing lights. The Supreme Court of Canada rejected the argument that Lewis was contributorily negligent for not keeping a proper lookout. It stated that his conduct had to be judged according to the standard of care expected of a police officer investigating an accident and not the standard of an ordinary pedestrian. According to *Lewis* and *Keller*, how would you characterize a police officer's standard of care: is it higher or lower than that of the average citizen?

4. In *Heeney v. Best* (1979), 108 D.L.R. (3d) 366 (Ont. C.A.) the plaintiff's chickens died of asphyxiation when the defendant negligently cut off the power supply to the plaintiff's barns. An alarm system that would have warned of a power failure had inexplicably not been plugged in on the night of the incident. Since only 25 to 50% of local poultry farmers had alarm systems, the plaintiff argued that it was the custom not to have an alarm system. Therefore, the plaintiff contended, he could not be found contributorily negligent for having a non-operating alarm. Nevertheless, the plaintiff was found to have been contributorily negligent for failing to take reasonable care of his own property. Would the court have reached the same conclusion if the plaintiff had not installed an alarm system? Should compliance with and breach of a custom have the same effect in establishing contributory negligence as they do in establishing negligence?

Heeney raises the issue of the precautions that an individual must take to protect against the tortious or illegal conduct of others. Should a homeowner be held contributorily negligent for failing to install a fire alarm if its absence contributed to his or her fire losses? Would a homeowner be contributorily negligent for failing to replace an existing fire alarm with a more modern and reliable device? Would a homeowner be held contributorily negligent for not purchasing a burglar alarm and other security devices? Would your answers be affected by the costs of the devices? See also the discussion of the duty to control the conduct of others in Chapter 11.

5. The standard of care imposed in contributory negligence is affected by the age, disabilities and professional training of the plaintiff. For example, a child is required to meet the standard of care of a reasonable child of like age, intelligence and experience. See *Myers v. Peel County Board of Education*, [1981] 2 S.C.R. 21; *Laviolette v. C.N.R.* (1987), 40 C.C.L.T. 138 (N.B.C.A.); *Bajkov v. Canil* (1990), 66 D.L.R. (4th) 572 (B.C.C.A.); *Lee (Guardian ad litem of) v. Barker*, [1992] 5 W.W.R. 256 (B.C.C.A.); and *Saumur (Litigation Guardian of) v. Antoniak*, 2016 ONCA 851. See the discussion of special standards of care in Chapter 15.

In *Marshall (Litigation Guardian of) v. Annapolis (County) District School Board*, 2009 NSSC 378, rev'd 2011 NSCA 13, aff'd 2012 SCC 27 the four-year-old plaintiff had run out onto a road and been struck by a school bus. The trial judge held that it was not open to the jury to consider whether the plaintiff had been contributorily negligent. Because of his young age, the plaintiff was not capable of being negligent. Nonetheless, after the jury found for the defendants the plaintiff appealed on the basis that the trial judge's instructions to the jury had improperly invited it to consider the plaintiff responsible for the collision. The Supreme Court of Canada upheld the instructions and verdict. See also Hodgson, "The Law of Intervening Causation and Children" (2011) 19 Tort L. Rev. 149 which considers the possible contributory negligence of children.

6. By virtue of the doctrine of identification, the common law attributed the negligence of one party to the conduct of another if a special relationship existed between them. Thus at one time the negligence of a child's supervisor or parent was imputed to the child, thereby reducing the child's claim against the negligent defendant. Although this principle has been eliminated in the parent and child relationship, it still applies in certain situations involving (i) a master and servant and (ii) a car owner and driver. See *Ducharme v. Davies*, [1984] 1 W.W.R. 699 (Sask. C.A.); *Alliance & Leicester Building Society v. Edgestop Ltd.*, [1994] 2 All E.R. 38 (Ch.); *Galaske v. O'Donnell* (1994), 112 D.L.R. (4th) 109 (S.C.C.); and Sappideen & Vines, eds., *Fleming's The Law of Torts*, 10th ed. (2011) at 333-34.

7. As with negligence, the issue of contributory negligence turns on the specific facts of the case. For a discussion of contributory negligence see *Wells v. Parsons* (1970), 1 Nfld. & P.E.I.R. 513 (Nfld. C.A.); *Comeau v. Laliberte* (1986), 69 N.B.R. (2d) 87 (Q.B.); *Lee v. O'Farrell* (1988), 43 C.C.L.T. 269 (B.C.S.C.); *McEvoy v. Capital Motors* (1992), 88 D.L.R. (4th) 358 (B.C.C.A.); *Findley v. Driver* (1992), 7 O.R. (3d) 48 (C.A.); *Hutchings v. Nevin* (1992), 12 C.C.L.T. (2d) 259 (Ont. Gen. Div.); *Fortey (Guardian ad litem of) v. Canada (Attorney General)* (1999), 46 C.C.L.T (2d) 271 (B.C.C.A.); *Johnson v. Milton (Town)* (2008), 91 O.R. (3d) 190 (C.A.); and *Kahlon (Litigation Guardian of) v. Vancouver Coastal Health Authority*, 2009 CarswellBC 1824 (S.C.) (WL Can) at para. 223.

For a recent analysis of English decisions see Goudkamp & Nolan, "Contributory Negligence in the Twenty-First Century: An Empirical Study of First Instance Decisions" (2016) 79 M.L.R. 575-622. See also Goudkamp & Nolan, *Contributory Negligence: Principles and Practice* (2018); and Goudkamp & Nolan, *Contributory Negligence in the Twenty-First Century* (2019).

8. As noted in Chapter 13, there is some concern about allowing contributory negligence to be raised as a defence to a claim of negligent misrepresentation, since that cause of action requires the plaintiff's reliance to be reasonable. The courts have generally allowed the defence to be raised: see *Grand Restaurants of Canada Ltd. v. Toronto (City)* (1981), 32 O.R. (2d) 757 (H.C.), aff'd (1982), 39 O.R. (2d) 752 (C.A.); *Avco Financial Services Realty Ltd. v. Norman* (2003), 64 O.R. (3d) 239 (C.A.); and *S. Maclise Enterprises Inc. v. Union Securities Ltd.* (2009), 17 Alta. L.R. (5th) 201 (C.A.) at paras. 36-39.

9. An employee suffers physical and psychological harm as a result of a workplace injury. Several years later, the employee commits suicide. In a claim by the employee's spouse as a dependant of the deceased to recover losses attributable to the suicide, in what circumstances should the defendant employer be able to argue contributory negligence by the deceased? See *Corr v. IBC Vehicles Ltd.*, [2008] 1 A.C. 884 (H.L.) and see also *Reeves v. Metropolitan Police Commissioner*, [2000] 1 A.C. 360 (H.L.).

GAGNON v. BEAULIEU
[1977] 1 W.W.R. 702 (B.C.S.C.)

FULTON J.:—The plaintiff was injured in a collision which took place on 31st August 1974 on Highway 401 near Chilliwack, British Columbia, when a 1972 Vega "Hatchback", owned and driven by the defendant Beaulieu and in which the plaintiff was riding as a front seat passenger, ran into the rear end of a pick-up truck which was stopped at a railroad crossing waiting for a train to pass by. Liability of the defendant driver is admitted — the main issue in this connection is whether or not the plaintiff was wearing a seat belt and, if not, whether this constituted negligence contributing to the nature and extent of his injuries.

The plaintiff suffered vertical lacerations of the right forehead and scalp, a deep horizontal laceration running across the right lower eyelid and upper right cheek and into the right temple. The cheek was fractured and crushed, and the right eye was damaged. The injuries are consistent with the plaintiff having been thrown forward by the impact, striking the windshield and/or dashboard of the car with his forehead and face. The defendant maintains that the plaintiff was not wearing a seat belt apparatus provided for the passenger, consisting of a lap belt and shoulder harness, and that if the plaintiff had been wearing this apparatus, he would not have suffered those head and facial injuries.

. . .

For the plaintiff it was contended that failure to wear a seat belt is not per se negligence, and that it is not negligence in any circumstances if the person concerned is not convinced of the efficacy of seat belts and/or believes that the wearing of a seat belt, including particularly the shoulder strap, may in certain circumstances create the hazard of greater injury or damage than if it were not worn — that if, for instance, the car were to overturn, the wearer might be trapped between the seat and the roof. There was evidence that the plaintiff had this opinion.

. . .

The leading case in British Columbia is *Yuan v. Farstad*, [(1967), 66 D.L.R. (2d) 295 (B.C.S.C.)], a decision of this court.

. . .

What Munroe J. [the judge in *Yuan*] seems to me to have clearly said is this: that in the light of modern-day knowledge of the benefits and reduction of danger of injury flowing from the use of seat belts, an occupant of a motor vehicle in which such apparatus is provided for his use who nevertheless fails to wear it is negligent in that he has failed to take reasonable precautions for his own safety. If in those circumstances he is injured in a collision, and if it is established as a fact that in the circumstances of that collision the wearing of the seat belt provided would have prevented or lessened the injuries he sustained, then his negligence in failing to wear it has contributed to the extent of his injuries and becomes contributory negligence. If, of course, it is not shown in connection with the particular circumstances of the accident in question that the wearing of the seat belt would have prevented or lessened the injuries, then the failure to wear it, while negligent in itself, does not constitute negligence contributing to the injuries or to the extent thereof.

. . .

[O]n the basis of the authorities which I believe to be binding on me, and which, with respect, I believe also to be the logical and sensible application to the situation of facts of which judges, as rational human beings, do have knowledge, I am of opinion that the law in British Columbia on this subject is as follows:

(a) Failure, while travelling in a motor vehicle on a street or highway, to wear a seat belt or any part thereof as provided in a vehicle in accordance with the safety standards from time to time applicable is failure to take a step which a person knows or ought to know to be reasonably necessary for his own safety.

(b) If in such circumstances he suffers injury as the result of the vehicle being involved in an accident, and if it appears from the evidence that if the seat belt had been worn the injuries would have been prevented or the severity thereof lessened, then the failure to wear a seat belt is negligence which has contributed to the nature and extent of those injuries.

(c) In the case of this particular form of contributory negligence, the onus is on the defendant to satisfy the court, in accordance with the usual standard of proof, not only that the seat belt was not worn but also that the injuries would have been prevented or lessened if the seat belt had been worn. The courts should not find the second of these facts merely by inference from the first, even if that has been established.

. . .

Before reviewing the evidence as to the facts of this case to which these propositions apply, I should refer to the argument addressed that people may in fact be unconvinced of the efficacy, or desirability, of wearing seat belts, as was urged on behalf of the plaintiff here. This argument was carefully reviewed by Lord Denning M.R., in the English Court of Appeal, in the recent case of *Froom v. Butcher*, [1975] 3 All E.R. 520. At p. 526 he said:

> Quite a lot of people, however, think differently about seat belts. Some are like Mr. Froom here. They think that they would be less likely to be injured if they were thrown clear than if they were strapped in. They would be wrong. The chances of injury are four times as great. Yet they believe it honestly and firmly. On this account Nield J. thought they should not bear any responsibility. He recognized that such persons are in a minority, but he thought that proper respect should be paid to the minority view. He said:
>
> > ". . . I do not feel that the courts are justified in invading the freedom of choice of the motorist by holding it to be negligence, lack of care or fault to act on an opinion firmly and honestly held and shared by many other sensible people."
>
> I am afraid I do not agree. In determining responsibility, the law eliminates the personal equation. It takes no notice of the views of the particular individual; or of others like him. It requires everyone to exercise all such precautions as a man of ordinary prudence would observe.

. . .

I agree with counsel for the plaintiff that I am not bound by this English case, and need not apply it in the case before me. However, I say at once that I do respectfully agree with the reasoning expressed in that judgment, and consider that it is entirely applicable to the facts established by the evidence before me, which I now review.

The evidence is that the defendant's car was equipped with seat belts consisting of a lap belt and a cross-over shoulder harness on the passenger side, in good working order. The plaintiff does not remember whether he was wearing either part of this equipment: as a result of the blow to his head, his recollection of the circumstances of the accident itself is entirely blank.

. . .

Expert evidence as to the protection afforded by seat belts was given by Mr. A.C. Shiels, director of traffic safety programs for the province of Saskatchewan. Mr. Shiels has done extensive research into the whole question of the protection of occupants of automobiles from injury in accidents, including the measurement of the relative effectiveness of various safety devices and the measurement of the relative severity of collisions and the type and extent of injury which may be expected in collisions of differing degrees of severity as between occupants who wear seat belts with shoulder harnesses and those who do not. His evidence was of considerable help in this regard.

He testified that from the degree of crushing of the front of the car as shown in the photographs Exs. 18 and 19, and from the description of the items in and on the car which were damaged, he rated the severity of the collision as class 2. In a collision of this type he would expect that a passenger in the front seat not wearing any seat belt apparatus would suffer injuries consisting of bumps and bruises, some undetermined degree of head injuries consisting of lacerations, including lacerations to the eyelids and to the face, and possible damage to the eyeball itself. For a passenger wearing properly adjusted seat belt apparatus including the shoulder harness, he said it would be virtually impossible to contact the windshield or dashboard with his head in a collision of this class and that there would probably be minor bruises and tenderness at the points where the restraining harness had taken the load of the body on impact. Here the evidence is that the windshield was struck and shattered; in the opinion of the expert it was struck by a round object such as the head, and the evidence is equally consistent with its having been struck from inside as from outside. The plaintiff received head and facial injuries of the type said to be expected to be incurred in a collision of this type, by a person not wearing a restraining apparatus, and there is no evidence of any marks or bruising on his body such as would be expected if he had been restrained by a lap and/or shoulder belt.

. . .

On the whole of the evidence I am satisfied that the plaintiff knew or ought to have known that the wearing of the seat belt provided, including the shoulder harness, would reduce the possibility of his being injured in a collision, that at the time of this accident he was not wearing the seat belt equipment provided and that, had he been wearing it, and particularly the shoulder harness, his injuries would have been less severe, if not prevented altogether. I consider that the expert, Mr. Shiels, was not merely speculating as to this result, but had a sound basis for his opinion. Applying the law which I have held to be applicable to these circumstances in this province, I find it to have been established that the plaintiff was negligent and that his negligence contributed to the nature and extent of his injuries.

There will be judgment accordingly.

NOTES AND QUESTIONS

1. Why were the plaintiff's beliefs about the safety value of seat belts considered irrelevant? Would the result have been the same if the plaintiff had refused to wear the seat belt because it was physically uncomfortable for him to do so or because he had a morbid fear of being trapped in a burning vehicle which made wearing a seat belt emotionally traumatic? See *Froom v. Butcher*, [1975] 3 All E.R. 520 (C.A.); *Davis v. Anderson* (1980), 15 C.C.L.T. 192 (B.C.C.A.); and *Shaw v. Roemer* (1982), 134 D.L.R. (3d) 590 (N.S.C.A.).

2. Based on *Gagnon*, would a driver and owner of a car be negligent for: (a) failing to equip a car with seat belts, (b) failing to make passengers aware of the presence of seat belts or (c) permitting a passenger to remain in the car without wearing a seat belt? See *Pasternack v. Poulton*, [1973] 2 All E.R. 74 (Q.B.); *Haley v. Richardson; McCrae v. Richardson* (1975), 60 D.L.R. (3d) 480 (N.B.C.A.); *Heller v. Martens*, [2002] 9 W.W.R. 71 (Alta. C.A.); and *Davis v. Shields*, 2010 NSSC 80. In *Galaske v. O'Donnell*, [1994] 1 S.C.R. 670 the court held that the defendant had a duty to ensure that an eight-year-old passenger wore a seat belt. The fact that the boy's father was also a passenger in the car and may have been negligent did not negate the defendant's duty.

3. In *Rewcastle v. Sieben* (2003), 20 Alta. L.R. (4th) 17 (C.A.) the court found that the plaintiff was not contributorily negligent for not wearing a seat belt. The vehicle had four seat belts but the plaintiff was one of six people in the car. The plaintiff asked to sit in the front seat but was refused. She then sat on the lap of a person in the back seat. At the time the plaintiff was 16 years old. It was close to midnight, she was 7.5 km from home, and she had a cell phone and credit card. The car crashed and the plaintiff was killed. The court held that her decision to ride in the car without a seat belt was reasonable. Do you agree?

4. What evidence did the court in *Gagnon* rely on in concluding that the plaintiff's failure to wear his seat belt contributed to his losses? Was the court's approach consistent with the general principles that govern causation? See *Lucas v. Antoniak* (1978), 7 C.C.L.T. 209 (B.C.S.C.), aff'd (1980), 15 C.C.L.T. 195 (B.C.C.A.); and *Snushall v. Fulsang* (2005), 78 O.R. (3d) 142 (C.A.). For examples in which a plaintiff's failure to wear a seat belt was held to be causally irrelevant to his or her injuries see *Koopman v. Fehr* (1993), 81 B.C.L.R. (2d) 145 (C.A.); *Madge v. Meyer*, [2002] 5 W.W.R. 50 (Alta. C.A.); *Claiter v. Rose*, 2004 CarswellBC 59 (S.C.) (WL Can), additional reasons 2005 CarswellBC 287 (S.C.) (WL Can); and *Wormald v. Chiarot*, 2016 BCCA 415.

5. Would a passenger in a boat who failed to wear a life jacket, a motorcyclist or bicyclist who failed to wear a crash helmet, an airline passenger who failed to wear a seat belt, or a hockey player who failed to wear a helmet be treated the same way as someone who failed to wear a seat belt while driving? Is there any justification for treating the seat belt cases differently from other contributory negligence cases?

6. All of the provinces have enacted legislation requiring occupants of motor vehicles to wear seat belts in most situations. See for example the *Highway Traffic Act*, R.S.O. 1990, c. H.8, s. 106. Should the existence of a statutory duty affect the analysis

of the seat belt defence? See *Genik v. Ewanylo* (1980), 12 C.C.L.T. 121 (Man. C.A.); *Shkwarchuk v. Hansen* (1984), 30 C.C.L.T. 121 (Sask. Q.B.); and *Gray v. Macklin* (2000), 4 C.C.L.T. (3d) 13 (Ont. S.C.J.). But see *Webber v. Crawford* (1988), 46 C.C.L.T. 1. (B.C.S.C.); and *Wallace v. Berrigan* (1988), 47 D.L.R. (4th) 752 (N.S.C.A.). See also Wakeling, "Seat Belt Legislation: An End to Cruel and Unusual Punishment" (1977) 42 Sask. L. Rev. 105.

7. Do you think that the court's recognition of the seat belt defence has significantly affected the patterns of seat belt use? Can you suggest alternative means of inducing people to wear seat belts?

8. For an academic discussion of this issue see Hicks, "Seat Belts and Crash Helmets" (1974) 37 Mod. L. Rev. 308; and Slatter, "Seat Belts and Contributory Negligence" (1977) 4 Dal. L.J. 96.

(c) APPORTIONMENT OF LOSS

In 1924 Ontario enacted Canada's first apportionment legislation. Similar legislation was soon enacted by the other common law provinces. Although the form of the legislation varies, there are few substantial differences in the operation of the provincial statutes. The legislation permits the court to divide responsibility for damages between the parties according to their relative degrees of fault.

NEGLIGENCE ACT
R.S.O. 1990, c. N.1

Extent of liability, remedy over

1. Where damages have been caused or contributed to by the fault or neglect of two or more persons, the court shall determine the degree in which each of such persons is at fault or negligent, and, where two or more persons are found at fault or negligent, they are jointly and severally liable to the person suffering loss or damage for such fault or negligence, but as between themselves, in the absence of any contract express or implied, each is liable to make contribution and indemnify each other in the degree in which they are respectively found to be at fault or negligent.

Recovery as between tortfeasors

2. A tortfeasor may recover contribution or indemnity from any other tortfeasor who is, or would if sued have been, liable in respect of the damage to any person suffering damage as a result of a tort by settling with the person suffering such damage, and thereafter commencing or continuing action against such other tortfeasor, in which event the tortfeasor settling the damage shall satisfy the court that the amount of the settlement was reasonable, and in the event that the court finds the amount of the settlement was excessive it may fix the amount at which the claim should have been settled.

Plaintiff guilty of contributory negligence

3. In any action for damages that is founded upon the fault or negligence of the defendant if fault or negligence is found on the part of the plaintiff that contributed to

the damages, the court shall apportion the damages in proportion to the degree of fault or negligence found against the parties respectively.

Where parties to be deemed equally at fault

4. If it is not practicable to determine the respective degree of fault or negligence as between any parties to an action, such parties shall be deemed to be equally at fault or negligent.

Adding parties

5. Wherever it appears that a person not already a party to an action is or may be wholly or partly responsible for the damages claimed, such person may be added as a party defendant to the action upon such terms as are considered just or may be made a third party to the action in the manner prescribed by the rules of court for adding third parties.

Jury to determine degrees of negligence of parties

6. In any action tried with a jury, the degree of fault or negligence of the respective parties is a question of fact for the jury.

When plaintiff may be liable for costs

7. Where the damages are occasioned by the fault or negligence of more than one party, the court has power to direct that the plaintiff shall bear some portion of the costs if the circumstances render this just.

NOTES AND QUESTIONS

1. Alberta, Nova Scotia and New Brunswick deal with apportionment between the plaintiff and defendant in one statute and contribution among tortfeasors in another. The other common law provinces deal with both issues in the same legislation. For a comparison see the Institute of Law Research and Reform, *Contributory Negligence and Concurrent Wrongdoers* (1979) at 2-7. See Cheifetz, *Apportionment of Fault in Tort* (1981), providing a detailed section-by-section analysis of the Ontario legislation followed by a brief reference to the other provincial statutes. See also Ontario Law Reform Commission, *Report on Contribution Among Wrongdoers and Contributory Negligence* (1988); Law Reform Commission of British Columbia, *Report on Apportionment of Costs and Contributory Negligence: Section 3 of the Negligence Act* (1993); and Manitoba Law Reform Commission, *Contributory Fault: The Tortfeasors and Contributory Negligence Act* (2013).

For a historical analysis of Saskatchewan's legislation see Kleefeld, "The *Contributory Negligence Act* at Seventy" (2015) 78 Sask. L. Rev. 31. See also Brown & Yhard, "'The harshness and injustice of the common law rule . . . has frequently been commented on': Debating Contributory Negligence in Canada, 1914-1949" (2013) 36 Dal. L.J. 137.

2. In *Pilon v. Janveaux* (2005), 203 O.A.C. 345 (C.A.), additional reasons (2006), 211 O.A.C. 19 (C.A.) the plaintiff was injured as a passenger in a car driven by an impaired driver. The driver, the owner of the car and the bar where the driver had been drinking all admitted liability for causing the accident. The judge told the jury to determine the plaintiff's degree of contributory negligence but, apparently because of

the admission, not to apportion liability among the defendants. The jury found the plaintiff, who was also intoxicated, 35.5% responsible for accepting a ride from an impaired driver and failing to wear a seat belt. The jury's verdict did not make clear the bar's degree of liability, and in particular did not address its responsibility for the plaintiff's intoxication. The Court of Appeal held that under s. 3 of the *Negligence Act* the court was required to apportion liability, so that the jury's verdict could not stand. It held that "the jury should have been asked to apportion responsibility for the [plaintiff's] damages in four parts: (1) to the driver (and owner) of the vehicle; (2) to the injured passenger for his contributory negligence; (3) to the tavern for over-serving the driver; and (4) to the tavern for over-serving the passenger." Under the fourth of these parts, the Court of Appeal found the bar responsible for 40% of the plaintiff's 35.5% liability, so that the plaintiff was only 21.3% responsible. See also *McLean v. Knox*, 2013 ONCA 357.

3. There is an ongoing debate as to whether the apportionment legislation applies only to negligence or to all torts. The Court of Appeal for Ontario overruled an earlier decision, *Hollebone v. Barnard*, [1954] O.R. 236 (H.C.), and held that "fault" in s. 1 incorporates all intentional wrongdoing "as well as other types of substandard conduct": *Bell Canada v. Cope (Sarnia) Ltd.* (1980), 11 C.C.L.T. 170 (Ont. H.C.), aff'd (1981), 119 D.L.R. (3d) 254 (Ont. C.A.). See also *Brown v. Cole* (1995), 14 B.C.L.R. (3d) 53 (C.A.); *Berntt v. Vancouver (City)*, [1997] 4 W.W.R. 505 (B.C.S.C.), rev'd on other grounds (1999), 46 C.C.L.T. (2d) 139 (B.C.C.A.); and *Gerling Global General Insurance Co. v. Siskind, Cromarty, Ivey & Dowler* (2004), 12 C.C.L.I. (4th) 278 (Ont. S.C.J.). In contrast, the courts of Saskatchewan have held that the comparable provision in that jurisdiction applies only to negligence: *Cherneskey v. Armadale Publishers Ltd.* (1974), 53 D.L.R. (3d) 79 (Sask. C.A.); and *Trends Holdings Ltd. (Trustee of) v. Tilson* (2006), 25 C.B.R. (5th) 239 (Sask. Q.B.). The Court of Appeal has recently confirmed its approach: see *Sound Stage Entertainment v. Burns*, 2019 SKCA 18. In dissent, Justice Jackson interpreted the legislation as including intentional torts.

As a matter of statutory interpretation, which line of analysis do you prefer? In principle, is there any reason to limit contributory negligence and the statutory right to seek contribution to negligence cases? See Kutner, "Contribution Among Tortfeasors: Liability Issues in Contribution Law" (1985) 63 Can. Bar Rev. 1; and Law Reform Commission of British Columbia, *Report on Shared Liability* (1986).

In the context of the tort of battery, does provocation serve the same role as contributory negligence, such that the latter would not need to be considered? See in the English context Goudkamp, "Contributory Negligence and Trespass to the Person" (2011) 127 L.Q.R. 519. For an example see *Robinson (Litigation Guardian of) v. Bud's Bar Inc. (c.o.b. Bud's Bar and Lounge)*, 2015 BCSC 1767.

4. The Supreme Court of Canada has stated "as a matter of principle that contributory negligence would not be available in the context of a strict liability tort. . . . While this argument would be available in an action for negligence, the notion of strict liability involved in an action for conversion is *prima facie* antithetical to the concept of contributory negligence": *Boma Manufacturing Ltd. v. C.I.B.C.* (1996), 140 D.L.R. (4th) 463 (S.C.C.). The issue in *Boma* arose in the context of an action for conversion of cheques. It is not clear whether the court intended to preclude application of apportionment legislation to other strict liability torts as well. Given

that conversion requires intention, would you agree with characterizing the action as involving strict liability?

In *Cowles v. Balac* (2006), 83 O.R. (3d) 660 (C.A.) the plaintiffs were attacked by Bengal tigers at the defendant's drive-through safari zoo. At para. 216 Justice Borins said of *Boma*: "In my respectful view, in stating contributory negligence is not available in the context of a strict liability tort, Iacobucci J. was not intending to state a general principle. Rather, he was referring to the law of bills of exchange." After a detailed review of the cases and academic views, he concluded that contributory negligence should be a defence to strict liability torts. In *Cowles* Justice Borins was in dissent. The majority held that on the facts the plaintiffs were not contributorily negligent and so did not address this issue.

5. Depending on the tort involved, it may not matter whether a provincial apportionment statute applies more broadly than to negligence because the courts have indicated that liability for some torts can be apportioned at common law. See *Bow Valley Husky (Bermuda) Ltd. v. Saint John Shipbuilding Ltd.*, [1997] 3 S.C.R. 1210. In *Blackwater v. Plint*, [2005] 3 S.C.R. 3 the court apportioned liability 75-25% between two defendants who were each vicariously liable for the sexual batteries by a dormitory supervisor at a residential school.

6. It has been suggested that the apportionment legislation encompasses not only torts but other branches of the law as well. See *Giffels Associates Ltd v. Eastern Const. Co.* (1978), 84 D.L.R. (3d) 344 (S.C.C.); *Can. Western Nat. Gas Co. v. Pathfinder Surveys Ltd.* (1980), 12 C.C.L.T. 211 (Alta. C.A.); *Tompkins Hardware Ltd. v. North West Flying Services Ltd.* (1982), 139 D.L.R. (3d) 329 (Ont. H.C.); and *Crown West Steel Fabricators v. Capri Insurance Services Ltd.* (2002), 214 D.L.R. (4th) 577 (B.C.C.A.). See also Weinrib, "Contribution in a Contractual Setting" (1976) 54 Can. Bar Rev. 338; Klar, "Developments in Tort Law: The 1979-80 Term" (1981) 2 S.C.L.R. 325 at 340-54; and Ontario Law Reform Commission, *Report on Contribution Among Wrongdoers and Contributory Negligence* (1988) at 65-83.

For an analysis of whether the legislation in England covers a claim in contract, including when it is advanced concurrently with a claim in tort, see Goudkamp, "The Contributory Negligence Doctrine: Four Commercial Law Problems" [2017] L.M.C.L.Q. 213.

7. The apportionment legislation eliminated the rationale for the last clear chance doctrine. Initially, however, some Canadian courts continued to apply the doctrine, while others interpreted it narrowly or avoided the issue. See Bowker, "Ten More Years Under Contributory Negligence Acts" (1964) 2 U.B.C.L. Rev. 198; and Casswell, "Avoiding Last Clear Chance" (1990) 69 Can. Bar Rev. 129.

See also *Hartman v. Fisette* (1976), 66 D.L.R. (3d) 516 (S.C.C.); *MacKay v. MacLellan* (1976), 1 C.C.L.T. 310 (N.S.C.A.); *Poitras v. Goulet* (1987), 46 Man. R. (2d) 87 (C.A.); *Hunter v. Briere* (1989), 49 C.C.L.T. 93 (Man. Q.B.); *Fillier v. Whittom* (1995), 171 N.B.R. (2d) 92 (C.A.); and *Wickberg v. Patterson*, [1997] 4 W.W.R. 591 (Alta. C.A.).

The Ontario statute, like the legislation in Manitoba, New Brunswick and Nova Scotia, makes no reference to the doctrine, whereas the Alberta, British Columbia and Prince Edward Island statutes have specifically abolished it. Newfoundland and Labrador and Saskatchewan have attempted to define the doctrine's scope in their apportionment legislation. See Fridman *et al., The Law of Torts in Canada,* 3d ed. (2010) at 469-71. For a case applying the doctrine see *French v. Harbour Grace (Town)* (2001), 203 Nfld. & P.E.I.R. 290 (Nfld. S.C. (T.D.)). On the abolition of the doctrine in British Columbia see *Lawrence v. Prince Rupert (City)* (2005), 49 B.C.L.R. (4th) 89 (C.A.) (Esson J.A. dissenting); *Dyke v. British Columbia Amateur Softball Assn.* (2008), 76 B.C.L.R. (4th) 278 (C.A.); and *Skinner v. Guo* (2010), 6 B.C.L.R. (5th) 23 (C.A.).

8. As s. 4 of the Ontario statute indicates, the parties are deemed to be equally negligent if it is impossible or impractical on the evidence to determine their respective degrees of fault. Although the courts try to accurately assess matters, they sometimes have no choice but to use this default position. See *Nice v. John Doe* (2000), 190 D.L.R. (4th) 402 (Alta. C.A.); *Alberta Wheat Pool v. Northwest Pile Driving Ltd.* (2000), 2 C.C.L.T. (3d) 53 (B.C.C.A.). Compare *Martin v. Listowel Memorial Hospital* (2000), 192 D.L.R. (4th) 250 (Ont. C.A.); and *J.M. v. W.B.* (2004), 71 O.R. (3d) 171 (C.A.).

9. The plaintiff's contributory negligence can have an impact on whether multiple defendants are jointly and severally liable to the plaintiff. This depends on the specific language of the applicable provincial statute. See *Ingles v. Tutkaluk Construction Ltd.,* 2000 SCC 12 at paras. 58-59; and *Perrin v. Blake,* 2016 NSSC 88.

MORTIMER v. CAMERON
(1994), 17 O.R. (3d) 1 (C.A.)

ROBINS J.A.:—On the afternoon of July 17, 1987, following an accounting examination, Stephen Mortimer attended a party at the apartment of a classmate, Sandra Hunt. The apartment was on the second floor of a house owned by Stingray Holdings Limited in the City of London. Those present were drinking and relaxing; no one was boisterous or unruly. By all accounts, the mood was convivial but subdued. At some point late in the afternoon, Mortimer engaged John Cameron, another classmate, in friendly conversation while they were standing at the top of a short stairway in the apartment. They had both been drinking beer and Mortimer was "mildly intoxicated". Neither of them was angry or hostile.

While they were "joking around" with one another, Mortimer made a motion so as to indicate that he was going to pour beer on Cameron. This led to some good-natured horseplay. They began to push each other back and forth and, while doing so, moved down the stairs to the interior landing leading to the front door of the apartment. The door was open at the time. When they reached the interior landing, Mortimer, who was moving backwards, tripped over the raised threshold to the apartment and fell backwards. As he did so, he grabbed Cameron and pulled him towards him. Together, they tumbled onto the exterior landing at the top of the enclosed exterior stairway leading to street level, and came in contact with the exterior wall. Even though they hit the wall with "minimal" or "little" force, it gave way and the two of them plunged to the ground 10 feet below.

Fortunately, Cameron was unhurt. Mortimer, however, suffered a devastating injury. His spinal cord was permanently fractured at the C4-5 or neck level. As a result, Mortimer is a complete quadriplegic without any motor function or sensation below the site of the injury.

The issue here is whether the trial judge erred in holding that the plaintiff's injuries were not proximately caused by his own conduct or by the conduct of the defendant Cameron. The conduct in question is the "horseplay" to which I referred earlier. The city and Stingray contend that, by engaging in this kind of conduct, the plaintiff was guilty of contributory negligence and the defendant Cameron was guilty of negligence. Their negligence, it is contended, contributed in some degree to the loss and should have been taken into account in apportioning liability.

. . .

The trial judge specifically found that Cameron breached his duty of care to Mortimer when he pushed Mortimer at the interior landing by the threshold. He also can be taken to have found that Mortimer, in initiating and participating in the horseplay, was in breach of the duty not to harm himself. The trial judge concluded, however, that their conduct did not constitute a proximate cause of Mortimer's injuries and that no liability should attach to them. In his view, the accident was not within the realm of their reasonable foreseeability.

There is no basis for disturbing this conclusion. On the findings made by the trial judge, which are adequately supported by the evidence, the conduct of Mortimer and Cameron cannot be treated as a proximate or effective cause of Mortimer's injuries. It is, of course, true that "but for" the condition created by the horseplay Mortimer and Cameron would not have fallen from the upper landing of the enclosed exterior stairway to the ground below. However, a defendant's negligence is actionable only with respect to harm that is within the scope of the risk that makes the offending conduct actionable. Similarly, a plaintiff's contributory negligence will not limit his recovery unless it is a proximate cause of his injury.

Here, neither Cameron's negligence nor Mortimer's contributory negligence entailed an unreasonable or foreseeable likelihood of the risk or hazard that actually befell Mortimer. It was reasonable for them to assume that what purported and appeared to be a properly constructed wall was in fact a properly constructed wall. In regulating their conduct and having regard for their own safety, they were entitled to rely on the wall providing them reasonable protection. The risk to which they exposed themselves was the risk of being injured by falling down the stairs or onto the exterior landing or by hitting the exterior wall. The risk that materialized was of a different nature. They had no reason to think that the state of the wall was such that it would give way to the modest degree of lateral force that they were found to have applied to it. The risk of falling to the ground through a defectively constructed and unprotected wall was beyond their reasonable contemplation. This risk was not one to which they can be said to have unreasonably exposed themselves or one another. . . .

These parties were not found to have charged the wall with the force of their combined weight, as the city and Stingray have suggested. Had the wall been properly constructed or a 2 x 4 stud properly installed to eliminate the unprotected gap, and the same sequence of events had occurred, on the findings of the trial judge, the wall could have withstood the minimal force that caused the plywood panel to "pop out". The accident that in fact occurred was, in sum, beyond the reasonable contemplation of these parties; it was not within the scope of the risk created by their horseplay, no matter how imprudent that conduct may be considered.

4. The Apportionment of Liability

The issue here is whether the trial judge erred in apportioning liability as between the city and Stingray at 80 per cent and 20 per cent respectively. In the city's submission, this apportionment is inconsistent with the findings upon which the liability of these parties was based and disproportionate to their relative degrees of culpability.

I agree with this submission. In my respectful opinion, the trial judge reached his findings of relative culpability without proper regard to the facts in this case. In particular, he failed to take into account or give proper weight to the specific findings which he made in holding Stingray liable to the plaintiffs.

The city was held responsible for a far larger proportion of liability than Stingray essentially because the trial judge was of the view that its conduct represented "a marked departure" from the applicable standard of care. The marked departure consisted of its "egregious" failure to comply with the Building Code requirements and good building practice and its having permitted a "particularly insidious condition" to be created by failing to provide the protection to be expected of a wall. In apportioning liability, however, the trial judge did not mention the particulars of Stingray's breach of the duty towards the plaintiff. Nor did he provide any reason why, given his findings, this tortfeasor's negligence was comparatively less egregious or less marked a departure from the applicable standard of care than the city's.

Stingray, it will be recalled, had the "primary burden" for maintaining the stairway in a reasonably safe condition. It was under a legal obligation to take reasonable care to see that persons coming onto the premises were safe while on the premises. In breach of that duty, Stingray failed to conduct a reasonable inspection to determine the soundness of this exterior wooden structure and thus permitted the "particularly insidious condition" to which the trial judge referred to be maintained. It failed to have this inspection notwithstanding the obvious deterioration of the structure. The unsafe condition of the upper landing would have been discovered if a proper inspection had been made, and the plainly foreseeable risk of harm would have been eliminated. Furthermore, Stingray's failure to comply with the building by-law in 1985 resulted in "the continuance of the hazardous condition" that would have been discovered had the required permit been obtained.

In my opinion, a substantially greater degree of fault ought to have been attributed to Stingray for its departures from the standard of care exacted by the law. This company was under an "ongoing duty" to properly inspect these premises. The circumstances were such as to require affirmative action on its part as occupier to see that its premises were reasonably safe for persons in the position of the plaintiff. Its failure to discharge this statutory duty over the many years of its ownership of the property constituted a more proximate or current cause of the accident than did the city's negligence.

Following its final inspection, the city had no reason or opportunity to conduct any further inspection of the premises. The negligence of its inspectors in 1972 when the exterior stairway was constructed, in so far as it was concerned, was undiscoverable. While, as I have said, that negligence remained operative notwithstanding the passage of time, the fact is that had Stingray fulfilled its legal duty the risk created by the city's negligence would have been removed. Stingray cannot, and indeed does not, rely on the inspection made years earlier by the city as an excuse for non-compliance with its primary burden to maintain the safety of the premises. Taking into account Stingray's ongoing breach of the duty of care imposed on it by law, I am of the opinion that the apportionment was disproportionate to the respective degrees of culpability of these parties. Stingray should bear a significantly larger share of responsibility than that fixed by the trial judge.

While I appreciate that an appellate court should rarely interfere with a trial judge's apportionment of liability (*Sparks v. Thompson*, [1975] 1 S.C.R. 618, 46 D.L.R. (3d) 225), I am satisfied that there are sufficiently strong and exceptional circumstances here to warrant doing so. In reaching his conclusion as to relative fault, the trial judge failed to have proper regard to the totality of circumstances and the findings upon which he held Stingray liable. In my opinion, the comparative blameworthiness of these tortfeasors is such that liability for this accident should be apportioned 60 per cent against Stingray and 40 per cent against the city.

NOTES AND QUESTIONS

1. The trial judge held that both Mortimer and Cameron were negligent and that their combined negligence was a cause of Mortimer's devastating injuries. Why was Cameron not held liable to Mortimer and why was Mortimer not found contributorily negligent? Why did the Court of Appeal uphold this aspect of the trial judgment? Do you agree with the trial judge's and Court of Appeal's analysis?

2. Would the courts' analysis of these issues have been the same if the horseplay had not been in fun, if Cameron had been a well-insured corporate defendant, or if Mortimer had suffered only a broken leg and several thousand dollars of economic loss?

3. There are many cases in which the courts apportion liability between the plaintiff and the defendant and each turns on its own facts. The Ontario *Negligence Act* indicates that damages are to be apportioned in relation to the parties' respective degrees of fault or negligence. Does this test relate to the parties' relative causal contributions or relative blameworthiness? How does the Court of Appeal resolve this issue? See *Heller v. Martens*, (2002) 303 A.R. 84 (C.A.) in which Fruman J.A. adopted a comparative blameworthiness approach. See also *Snushall v. Fulsang* (2005), 78 O.R. (3d) 142 (C.A.); *Cempel v. Harrison Hot Springs Hotel Ltd.* (1998), 43 B.C.L.R. (3d) 219 (C.A.); *Chae v. Min* (2005), 43 Alta. L.R. (4th) 1 (C.A.); *McNulty v. Edmonton (City)*, 2011 ABQB 297 at para. 125; *Hansen v. Sulyma*, 2013 BCCA 349 at para. 36; *Paquette (Litigation guardian of) v. School District No. 36 (Surrey)*, 2014 BCCA 456 at para. 22; *Mackey (Litigation guardian of) v. British Columbia (Provincial Capital Commission)*, 2016 BCSC 1333 at para. 53; and *Braun v. Peszko (c.o.b. Roe & Co.)*, 2017 SKCA 93 at para. 68.

One concern about allocating based on causation is that doing so can replicate some of the problems in the last clear chance doctrine. See *Braun v. Peszko (c.o.b. Roe & Co.)*, *supra*, at paras. 74-76.

For additional discussion of the appropriate basis for apportionment see Manitoba Law Reform Commission, *Contributory Fault: The Tortfeasors and Contributory Negligence Act* (2013); and Goudkamp & Klar, "Apportionment of Damages for Contributory Negligence: The Causal Potency Criterion" (2016) 53 Alta. L. Rev. 849. See also Barker & Grantham, eds., *Apportionment in Private Law* (2018).

4. In *Mortimer*, on what basis did the Court of Appeal interfere with the trial judge's apportionment of damages? Do you agree with its decision to intervene and its apportionment decision? See also *Taylor v. Asody*, [1975] 2 S.C.R. 414; *Rabideau v.*

Maddocks (1992), 12 O.R. (3d) 83 (Gen. Div.); *Hall v. Hebert* (1993), 101 D.L.R. (4th) 129 (S.C.C.); and *Hansen v. Sulyma, supra.*

In *Ryan v. Victoria (City)* (1999), 168 D.L.R. (4th) 513 (S.C.C.) the plaintiff was injured after the front tire of his motorcycle became caught in a railway track that ran within a city street. The trial judge held the defendant, who was responsible for the street, liable in negligence. However, the British Columbia Court of Appeal held that the plaintiff had been equally responsible for the accident and reduced recovery by 50%. On further appeal, the Supreme Court of Canada disagreed. Major J. stressed that the issue raised a question of fact and wrote:

> In *Stein v. Kathy K (The Ship)* [(1976), 62 D.L.R. (3d) 1], it was held that while findings of fact with regard to the allocation of fault are not immutable, they should not be reversed by an appellate court "unless it can be established that the learned trial judge made some palpable and overriding error which affected his assessment of the facts". The record reveals no such errors by the trial judge, and the Court of Appeal ought not to have interfered with his findings on the issue of contributory negligence. Accordingly, the assessment of liability against the appellant for 50% of his damages is set aside.

Even more deference is paid to a jury's apportionment of damages. The Court of Appeal for Ontario has held that a jury's decision on apportionment can be changed only in "exceptional circumstances": see *Marcoccia (Litigation Guardian of) v. Gill* (2009), 248 O.A.C. 131 (C.A.) at para. 29.

5. The United Kingdom Supreme Court has observed that "[i]t is not possible for a court to arrive at an apportionment which is demonstrably correct. The problem is not merely that the factors which the court is required to consider are incapable of precise measurement. More fundamentally, the blameworthiness of the pursuer and the defender are incommensurable." See *Jackson v. Murray*, [2015] UKSC 5 at para. 27. In this case the plaintiff's contribution was initially held to be 90%. The Court of Appeal reduced this to 70% and a 3-2 majority of the Supreme Court reduced it to 50%. Should we be concerned about how variable the assessment appears to be? How might this concern be addressed?

6. In *Chamberland v. Fleming* (1984), 29 C.C.L.T. 213 (Alta. Q.B.) the court suggested that a rough upper limit of 25% should be established for contributory negligence if the plaintiff's negligence did not cause the incident but merely affected the extent of the loss. Chamberland, a non-swimmer and inexperienced canoeist, drowned when the defendant negligently approached in his motor boat and caused a wave to overturn the canoe. The deceased had declined to wear a life jacket that would have saved his life. Do you agree with the court's apportionment of loss in this case? What test did the court use to apportion the loss? Do you think that it is appropriate to establish fixed apportionment ratios for specific kinds of cases? See Irvine, "Annotation" (1984) 29 C.C.L.T. 213.

7. In *Snushall v. Fulsang, supra,* the trial judge found the plaintiff 35% contributorily negligent for her injuries in a car accident because she had failed to wear her shoulder belt, although she had worn her lap belt. The Court of Appeal reduced this to 5%. It held that "The relationship of the failure to wear a seatbelt to the injuries is different because the accident would have occurred whether or not a seatbelt was worn. . . . The failure to wear a seatbelt may be said to be a 'cause' of the

plaintiff's injuries only in the sense that it contributes to the extent of the injuries suffered." The court held that the range of contributory negligence for failure to wear a seat belt should always be between 5% and 25%, with 25% appropriate in cases where wearing a proper seat belt would have, as a matter of causation, prevented 100% of the injuries. See also *Fowler v. Schneider National Carriers Ltd.* (2001), 193 N.S.R. (2d) 206 (C.A.); *Chae v. Min, supra;* and *Vigoren v. Nystuen* (2006), 279 Sask. R. 1 (C.A.).

8. In some cases, the plaintiff is found more than 50% contributorily negligent: see for example *Jones v. Niklaus* (2008), 240 O.A.C. 43 (C.A.); *Rizzi v. Mavros* (2008), 236 O.A.C. 4 (C.A.); *Mahe v. Boulianne* (2010), 474 A.R. 223 (C.A.); and *Simmons v. Yeager Properties Inc.*, 2013 BCSC 889, rev'd 2014 BCCA 201. Is this consistent with the requirement that the plaintiff must establish but-for causation on a balance of probabilities?

Can a plaintiff be 100% contributorily negligent? What about 0%? Or 99% or 1%? Why or why not? See Goudkamp, "Rethinking Contributory Negligence" in Pitel, Neyers & Chamberlain, eds., *Tort Law: Challenging Orthodoxy* (2013) at 344-50.

REVIEW PROBLEM

Edward, Ralph and Harry operated a window-washing business in Ontario. Ralph was responsible for checking the equipment and setting up the scaffold. Edward and Harry washed the windows. While the scaffold was at the third storey a frayed rope snapped, tilting the scaffold at a sharp angle. Harry was prevented from falling by his safety line. Edward had forgotten to attach his line and fell onto the roof of Bill's new car.

(a) Edward has sued Ralph in negligence. Ralph concedes that he was negligent, but alleges that Edward was contributorily negligent. Discuss Ralph's defence of contributory negligence and the possible apportionment of liability.
(b) Bill has sued both Edward and Ralph in negligence to recover the damages to his car. Advise Edward as to whether he is likely to be held liable to Bill and, if so, to what extent. Assuming that Bill can recover from Edward, what recourse does Edward have against Ralph?

3. Voluntary Assumption of Risk

With the introduction of modern apportionment legislation Canadian courts have become reluctant to apply the defence of voluntary assumption of risk. The reason is not difficult to see. Unlike contributory negligence, which now leads to a reduction in damages, voluntary assumption of risk remains a complete defence. If established, it precludes recovery altogether, notwithstanding the fact that the defendant negligently caused the plaintiff's injury. The inflexibility of such an all-or-nothing approach can easily lead to injustice. Consequently, while the defence is theoretically available in any negligence action, it tends to be confined to certain situations such as those involving participation in sports. Even in those situations it tends to be interpreted narrowly. An excellent illustration was seen in the extract from *Crocker v. Sundance Northwest Resorts Ltd.* (1988), 51 D.L.R. (4th) 321 (S.C.C.) in

Chapter 11. In that case, the defence was rejected even though the event ("tubing") was obviously fraught with danger and even though the plaintiff had signed a waiver.

DUBE v. LABAR
(1986), 27 D.L.R. (4th) 653 (S.C.C.)

ESTEY J:—The appellant (plaintiff) and respondent (defendant), co-workers at a construction site, became acquainted shortly before the car accident giving rise to the action occurred. The night before the accident, the parties had participated in an evening of drinking and partying in Haines Junction, a town close to the construction camp where both lived. The morning of the accident, drinking was resumed early. The parties decided to retrieve the respondent's car, which had become stuck on the way home the night before, and then drive into Haines Junction to retrieve the appellant's eyeglasses and to try to find two young women they had met the previous night. On their arrival in Haines Junction, the appellant and respondent each consumed more alcohol. They left the bar, found the two women, and drove them approximately 50 or 60 miles toward Whitehorse at their request. Having dropped the women off, the parties started back to Haines Junction. The appellant had been driving throughout. The respondent, while a passenger, had apparently been drinking beer in the car. At some point on the return trip, the parties passed two hitchhikers, and decided to stop to pick them up. When the appellant tried to start the car again, he was unable to do so, and the respondent got into the driver's seat and started the car. At about this time, the appellant saw some friends passing in another vehicle, and, when they stopped, went to talk to them. He returned to the car and went to the driver's side, but the respondent was still in the driver's seat. In a short exchange, the respondent said that he was capable of driving. The appellant then got into the car as a passenger.

The accident occurred very shortly thereafter. The respondent, while driving, turned to speak to the hitchhiker sitting in the back seat. As he did so, the car veered to the right. The appellant, according to the testimony of the other hitchhiker who was seated on the front seat between the appellant and the respondent, attempted to grab the wheel and straighten out the car's course. The respondent's attempts at correction resulted, eventually, in the car's overturning on the righthand embankment, causing personal injuries to the appellant. Samples of the respondent's breath later registered at .25 and .24 in tests administered by the police.

At trial, without objection from the parties, only two defences, *volenti non fit injuria* and contributory negligence, were put to the jury. The trial judge, after summarizing the evidence, charged the jury on the *volenti* defence as follows:

> One of the defences of the defendant in this case is the maxim *volenti non fit injuria*. Translated, that means "to one who is willing no harm is done".

> The burden is on the defendant, in each case, to prove that the plaintiff, expressly or by necessary implication, agreed to exempt the defendant from liability for any damage suffered by the plaintiff, occasioned by the defendant's negligence. In every case, the question is whether the plaintiff gave an express or implied consent to accept or assume the risk without compensation. In other words, did the plaintiff really consent to absolve the defendant from his common-law duty of care, saying or implying, in effect, "I am prepared to take the risk of your negligence and if I am injured you will not be legally responsible for my damages." The question is not simply whether the plaintiff knew of the risk but whether the circumstances were such

as necessarily to lead to the conclusion that the whole risk was intentionally incurred by the plaintiff.

. . .

If you find that there is evidence of an initial common design which would, as a matter of common sense, entail the risk of injury, you might think that the appropriate inference may be not that the defendant undertook to exercise due care throughout, but that the plaintiff agreed to take upon himself the obvious risk of harm. The burden lies upon the defendant of proving that the plaintiff, expressly or by necessary implication, agreed to exempt the defendant from liability.

Therefore your test is not simply whether the plaintiff knew of the risk, but whether the circumstances are such as necessarily to lead to the conclusion that the whole risk was voluntarily incurred by the plaintiff.

Immediately after his discussion of the *volenti* defence, the trial judge said:

Having earlier discussed negligence [which was done in an earlier general part of the charge just before *volenti* was discussed], I want to turn to the allied and associated matter of contributory negligence. . . If you are satisfied by a preponderance of evidence that Dube's conduct amounted to a breach of that duty to take reasonable care for his own safety, then you would be justified in ascribing to him a portion of the blame for his injuries . . .

The judge charged the jury that contributory negligence could arise in two ways, "firstly, from the plaintiff's active conduct in grasping the steering wheel . . . secondly, you may find that the plaintiff was negligent about his own safety, when he remained in the vehicle after the defendant took over the driving, knowing what he knew of the defendant's condition at that time".

. . .

[The jury found that the plaintiff had been contributorily negligent and that he voluntarily assumed the risk. On the basis of the latter, they held for the defendant.]

The plaintiff's appeal to this Court was argued on the basis that the defence of *volenti* is inapplicable to a case involving negligence on the highways. This submission is plainly inconsistent with four decisions of this Court: *Car & General Ins. Corp. Ltd v. Seymour et al.* (1956), 2 D.L.R. (2d) 369. . .; *Miller v. Decker* (1957), 9 D.L.R. (2d) 1. . .; *Lehnert v. Stein* (1962), 36 D.L.R. (2d) 159. . ., and *Eid v. Dumas, Hatherly v. Dumas* (1969), 5 D.L.R. (3d) 561. . . . However, while acknowledging that *volenti* is in principle available to a defendant driver, these cases establish that the defence will only be made out in unusual circumstances. The test has been variously described. . . .

Abbott J., dissenting in the *Miller* case [stated]:

[F]or a negligent driver to be completely relieved from liability, the plaintiff must have agreed expressly or by implication to exempt the defendant from liability for damages suffered by the plaintiff and occasioned by the negligence of the defendant during the carrying out of the latter's undertaking. In other words, to constitute a defence there must have been an express or implied bargain between the parties whereby the plaintiff gave up his right of action for negligence. As was pointed out by Kellock J. . . ., the question in each particular case is, in the language of Lindley L.J. in *Yarmouth v. France* (1887), 19 Q.B.D. 647 at p. 660, "not simply whether the plaintiff knew of the risk but whether the circumstances are such as necessarily to lead to the conclusion that the whole risk was voluntarily incurred by the plaintiff".

Finally, in *Lehnert v. Stein, supra,* Cartwright J. held . . . that:

> [W]here a driver of a motor vehicle invokes the maxim *volenti non fit injuria* as a defence to an action for damages for injuries caused by his negligence to a passenger, the burden lies upon the defendant of proving that the plaintiff, expressly or by necessary implication, agreed to exempt the defendant from liability for any damage suffered by the plaintiff occasioned by that negligence, and that, as stated in *Salmond on Torts,* 13th ed., p. 44:
>
>> "The true question in every case is: did the plaintiff give a real consent to the assumption of the risk without compensation; did the consent really absolve the defendant from the duty to take care?"

Thus, *volenti* will arise only where the circumstances are such that it is clear that the plaintiff, knowing of the virtually certain risk of harm, in essence bargained away his right to sue for injuries incurred as a result of any negligence on the defendant's part. The acceptance of risk may be express or may arise by necessary implication from the conduct of the parties, but it will arise, in cases such as the present, only where there can truly be said to be an understanding on the part of both parties that the defendant assumed no responsibility to take due care for the safety of the plaintiff, and that the plaintiff did not expect him to.

Common sense dictates that only rarely will a plaintiff genuinely consent to accept the risk of the defendant's negligence.

. . .

The defence of *volenti* will, furthermore, necessarily be inapplicable in the great majority of drunken driver-willing passenger cases. It requires an awareness of the circumstances and the consequences of action that are rarely present on the facts of such cases at the relevant time.

. . .

Prior to the enactment of legislation allowing for apportionment of damages in cases where the plaintiff's own negligence had contributed to his injuries. . . drawing a distinction between the defences of *volenti* and contributory negligence was unnecessary. Both had the same drastic effect of denying completely compensation to the plaintiff. This is no longer the case. Apportionment permits a sensible distribution of the financial burden of negligent conduct. It is a more flexible and more appropriate response in the great majority of cases in which negligent conduct of the plaintiff is argued to support a *volenti* defence. Thus, it is of great importance to keep the two defences distinct. . . .

. . .

The jury's conclusion that the plaintiff consented to bear the legal risk when he entered the car as passenger, knowing of the defendant's state of impairment, is doubtless one that not every jury would have reached. It does not have the character of unreasonableness, however, that must be apparent on the face of a jury verdict before an appellate court can upset it. . . .

I therefore would dismiss the appeal with costs to the respondent.

MCINTYRE and CHOUINARD JJ. concur with ESTEY J.
[Wilson J. wrote a concurring judgment.]

NOTES AND QUESTIONS

1. How did the court define the elements of voluntary assumption of risk? What policy reasons were given for narrowly interpreting this defence?

2. The courts have been divided on the issue of whether the defence of *volenti* applies to willing passengers of drunk drivers. Estey J. states that the defence will be inapplicable in the great majority of cases.

What do you think prompted the jury to conclude that Dube voluntarily assumed the risk? Based on the factual record, do you agree with its conclusion? Given that Estey J. did not agree with the jury, why did he deny the appeal?

Estey J. suggests that contributory negligence may be the more appropriate defence in these circumstances. Consider the *Motor Accidents Act 1988* (NSW), s. 74(2)(b)(ii) which requires a finding of contributory negligence where the plaintiff is a "voluntary passenger," the driver was impaired by drugs or alcohol, and the plaintiff was, or ought to have been, aware of the impairment: see *Joslyn v. Berryman; Wentworth Shire Council v. Berryman* (2003), 198 A.L.R. 137 (H.C.A.). For analysis of similar legislation in South Australia see *Allen v. Chadwick*, [2015] HCA 47. In Canada see *Pilon v. Janveaux* (2005), 203 O.A.C. 345 (C.A.), additional reasons (2006), 211 O.A.C. 19 (C.A.); *Robinson v. Williams Estate* (2005), 34 C.C.L.T. (3d) 131 (Alta. Q.B.), aff'd (2007), 401 A.R. 262 (C.A.); *Joe v. Paradis* (2008), 77 B.C.L.R. (4th) 347 (C.A.); and *McLean v. Knox*, 2013 ONCA 357.

3. The courts may find that the plaintiff voluntarily assumed the risk if he or she encouraged the defendant to be careless. See *Allen v. Lucas* (1971), 25 D.L.R. (3d) 218 (Sask. C.A.); *Conrad v. Crawford*, [1972] 1 O.R. 134 (H.C.); and *Cherrey v. Steinke* (1980), 13 C.C.L.T. 50 (Man. C.A.). But see *Eid v. Dumas*, [1969] S.C.R. 668; and *Betts v. Sanderson Estate* (1988), 53 D.L.R. (4th) 675 (B.C.C.A.).

4. As a matter of policy, what principles should govern the legal position of a passenger who accepts a ride from an intoxicated driver? What role does the fact that the driver will most likely be insured have on your analysis? See generally Skene, "Voluntary Assumption of Risk and the Gratuitous Passenger" (1974) 1 Dal. L.J. 605; Harpum, "Contributory Negligence Defences for the Drunken Driver" (1977) 40 Mod. L. Rev. 350; and Koressis, "Injured Passenger Actions Against Intoxicated Drivers — Volenti or Contributory Negligence" (1983) 4 Adv. Q. 297.

5. The debate over the scope of voluntary assumption of risk has also arisen in the context of intoxicated patrons of drinking establishments. See *Jordan House Ltd. v. Menow* (1974), 38 D.L.R. (3d) 105 (S.C.C.); and *Crocker v. Sundance Northwest Resorts Ltd.* (1988), 51 D.L.R. (4th) 321 (S.C.C.). See the discussion in Chapter 11.

6. Is there an age below which children lack the capacity to assess the physical risks of injury and to accept legal responsibility for injuries that may befall them? Should the principles of voluntary assumption of risk be applied the same way in cases involving adults and children? See *Savard v. Urbano* (1977), 85 D.L.R. (3d) 33 (Qc. C.A.); *Doiron v. Brideau* (1979), 28 N.B.R. (2d) 520 (C.A.); *McGinlay v. British Railway Bd.*, [1983] 1 W.L.R. 1427 (H.L.); and *Laviolette v. C.N.R.* (1987), 40 C.C.L.T. 138 (N.B.C.A.).

7. To what extent can a parent consent to the risk of injury on behalf of his or her child? In *Wong (Litigation Guardian of) v. Lok's Martial Arts Centre Inc.* (2009), 100 B.C.L.R. (4th) 183 (S.C.) the court held that the parent of a child enrolled in a martial arts program could not waive the child's right to sue in negligence. Part of the court's analysis was based on the provisions of the *Infants Act*, R.S.B.C. 1996, c. 223 which govern contracts made on behalf of children. See Bowal, Brierton & Rollett, "The Law of Infant Waivers: *Wong v. Lok's Martial Arts Centre Inc.*" (2011) 44 U.B.C.L. Rev. 407.

8. What risks should a participant in a sport be held to have voluntarily assumed? Should it matter whether the participant is experienced or a novice? See *Hanson v. St. John Horticultural Assn.*, [1974] S.C.R. 354; *Delaney v. Cascade River Holidays Ltd.* (1983), 24 C.C.L.T. 6 (B.C.C.A.); *Temple v. Hallem*, [1989] 5 W.W.R. 669 (Man. C.A.); *Potvin v. Stipetic* (1989), 50 C.C.L.T. 233 (Qc. C.A.); *Scurfield v. Cariboo Helicopter Skiing Ltd.*, [1993] 3 W.W.R. 418 (B.C.C.A.); *Dyck v. Laidlaw* (2000), 263 A.R. 241 (Q.B.); *Johnson v. Webb* (2002), 162 Man. R. (2d) 48 (Q.B.), aff'd (2002), 170 Man. R. (2d) 58 (C.A.); *Matharu v. Nam* (2006), 57 B.C.L.R. (4th) 374 (S.C.), aff'd (2007), 68 B.C.L.R. (4th) 143 (C.A.); *Galka v. Stankiewicz*, 2010 CarswellOnt 3346 (S.C.J.) (WL Can), aff'd 2011 ONCA 428; and *Michaud v. Tardif*, 2017 NBQB 48. See generally Yeo, "Accepted Inherent Risks Among Sporting Participants" (2001) 9 Tort L. Rev. 114. Some Canadian courts have been unwilling to apply voluntary assumption of risk even in the context of violent sports: see *Unruh (Guardian ad litem of) v. Webber* (1994), 112 D.L.R. (4th) 83 (B.C.C.A.); and *Zapf v. Muckalt* (1995), 26 C.C.L.T. (2d) 61 (B.C.S.C.), varied (1996), 31 C.C.L.T. (2d) 201 (B.C.C.A.).

In *Hayter v. Bezanson* (2009), 284 N.S.R. (2d) 171 (C.A.) at para. 18, the plaintiff did not consent to the risks involved in the defendant's very unusual method of hitting a golf ball. These were not the normal risks associated with the sport as played properly.

9. What risks should a spectator at a sporting event be held to have voluntarily assumed? See *Payne v. Maple Leaf Gardens Ltd.*, [1949] 1 D.L.R. 369 (Ont. C.A.); *White v. Blackmore*, [1972] 2 Q.B. 651 (C.A.); and *Carson v. Thunder Bay* (1985), 52 O.R. (2d) 173 (Dist. Ct.). See generally Kligman, "Tort Liability for Sports Injuries" (1989) 1 C.I.L. Rev. 153.

10. In the cases discussed to this point the defence of voluntary assumption of risk has been established by drawing an inference from the plaintiff's conduct. The defence may also be established by express agreement. The meaning and effect given to such agreements is essentially governed by the law of contract.

The leading contract law decision on the interpretation of an express waiver clause is *Tercon Contractors Ltd. v. British Columbia (Ministry of Transportation and Highways)*, 2010 SCC 4. At paras. 121-23 the court identified three key considerations: whether as a matter of interpretation the exclusion clause applies, whether the exclusion clause was unconscionable when the contract was made, and whether the court should refuse to enforce the clause because of an overriding public policy.

Exclusion clauses are frequently raised as a defence to negligence claims. See *Dyck v. Manitoba Snowmobile Assn.*, [1985] 1 S.C.R. 589; *ITO — International Terminal Operators Ltd. v. Miida Electronics Inc.* (1986), 28 D.L.R. (4th) 641 (S.C.C.); *Crocker v. Sundance Northwest Resorts Ltd.*, *supra*; *London Drugs Ltd. v. Kuehne & Nagel*

International Ltd. (1992), 97 D.L.R. (4th) 261 (S.C.C.); *Ocsko v. Cypress Bowl Recreations Ltd.* (1992), 95 D.L.R. (4th) 701 (B.C.C.A.); *Greeven v. Blackcomb Skiing Enterprises Ltd.* (1994), 22 C.C.L.T. (2d) 265 (B.C.S.C.); *Fraser Jewellers v. Dominion Electric* (1997), 35 C.C.L.T. (2d) 298 (Ont. C.A.); *Air Nova v. Messier-Dowty Ltd.* (2000), 128 O.A.C. 11 (C.A.); *Cudmore v. Home Chec Canada Ltd.* (2000), 174 Man. R. (2d) 30 (Q.B.); *Dixon v. British Columbia Snowmobile Federation* (2003), 180 B.C.A.C. 99 (C.A.); *Cejvan v. Blue Mountain Resorts Limited,* 2008 CarswellOnt 9269 (S.C.J.) (WL Can); *Copeland v. Hamilton (City),* 2009 CarswellOnt 4760 (S.C.J.) (WL Can); *Gallant v. Fanshawe College of Applied Arts and Technology,* 2009 CarswellOnt 5734 (S.C.J.) (WL Can); *Arndt v. Ruskin Slo Pitch Assn.,* 2011 BCSC 1530; and *Kempf v. Nguyen,* 2013 ONSC 1977, rev'd 2015 ONCA 114. See also Neumann, "Disclaimer Clauses and Personal Injury" (1991) 55 Sask. L. Rev. 312; Tomlinson & Machum, "The contractual waiver of liability in ski resort negligence claims" (1997) 15 Can. J. Ins. L. 49; and Gunter, "Waiver of Liability in Recreation Cases" in Archibald, ed., *Annual Review of Civil Litigation, 2017* (2017) 405.

11. In *Cowles v. Balac* (2005), 29 C.C.L.T. (3d) 284 (Ont. S.C.J.), aff'd (2006), 83 O.R. (3d) 660 (C.A.) the plaintiffs were attacked by tigers while driving through the defendant's wildlife park. Signs at the entry to the park stated "All visitors enter the park at their own risk. No responsibility for damage to vehicle or person however caused is accepted." The brochure given to the plaintiffs contained similar language. Should the defence of voluntary assumption of risk have applied?

12. Over the past few decades courts have been reluctant to allow defendants to rely on express waivers. However, in *Loychuk v. Cougar Mountain Adventures Ltd.,* 2012 BCCA 122, aff'g 2011 BCSC 193 the court upheld such a waiver. The plaintiffs were injured in a collision on a zip-line as a result of the defendant's negligence. There was nothing the plaintiffs could have done, short of not participating in the activity, to avoid the collision. The court held that the waiver was not unconscionable or contrary to public policy. The plaintiffs argued that because they had paid for the zip-lining prior to attending at the facility, there was no consideration provided for their signing of the waiver on arrival. The court found that the consideration was being allowed to participate in the activity.

One of the plaintiffs ran a kick-boxing program and as part of doing so she required participants in the program to sign a waiver of liability. They were not allowed to participate unless they did so. The other plaintiff had recently graduated from law school. Do you think these facts affected the analysis?

13. In *Niedermeyer v. Charlton,* 2014 BCCA 165 the plaintiff participated in a zip-line experience operated by the defendant. She was injured by the defendant's negligence not while zip-lining but rather while being transported by bus back to Whistler Village. The court held that the release she had signed, on its wording, covered not only the actual zip-lining but also the transport by bus. Relying on *Loychuk, supra,* the court held that the plaintiff had agreed to the waiver. However, a majority of the court held that the release was contrary to public policy. The defendant was insured under a mandatory statutory automobile insurance regime from which the parties could not contract out. The dissent held that in the absence of an express statutory provision preventing contracting out of the regime, the release was valid. With which position do you agree?

A different issue of interpretation arose in *Cooper v. Blackwell*, 2017 BCSC 1991. A hunter signed a waiver in respect of a trip to hunt grizzly bear in 2013. The hunt was unsuccessful and the defendants offered the hunter a similar trip in 2014 free of charge. No new waiver was signed. On the 2014 trip the hunter was accidentally shot by a guide. The hunter's family sued in negligence. The defendants relied on the waiver on the basis that the 2014 trip was a continuation or extension of the unsuccessful 2013 trip. The court disagreed and held the waiver did not apply beyond the 2013 trip. Do you agree?

14. In *Schnarr v. Blue Mountain Resorts Limited*, 2018 ONCA 313 the plaintiff argued that the express waiver was void because it was contrary to Ontario's consumer protection legislation. The court held that the legislation did not invalidate the waiver and gave it effect. Other recent decisions upholding waivers include *Levita v. Crew*, 2015 ONSC 5316; *Jensen v. Fit City Health Centre Inc.*, 2015 ONSC 6326; *Fillingham v. ABC Corp. (c.o.b. as Big White Ski Resort Ltd.)*, 2017 BCSC 1702; *Alton v. Lower Mainland Motocross Club*, 2017 BCSC 2460; *Jamieson v. Whistler Mountain Resort Limited Partnership*, 2017 BCSC 1001; and *Lippa v. Colletta*, 2017 ONSC 1122. In contrast, in *Chamberlain v. Canadian Physiotherapy Association*, 2015 BCSC 1260 the court interpreted the waiver as not covering claims in negligence and, in the alternative, found it to be contrary to the reasonable expectations of the plaintiff in signing it.

15. For a general discussion of voluntary assumption of risk see Hertz, "Volenti Non Fit Injuria: A Guide" in Klar, ed., *Studies in Canadian Tort Law* (1977) 101 at 119-26; Jaffey, "Volenti Non Fit Injuria" [1985] C.L.J. 87; Simons, "Assumption of Risk and Consent in the Law of Torts: A Theory of Full Preference" (1987) 67 B.U.L. Rev. 213; Sugarman, "Assumption of Risk" (1997) 31 Val. U.L. Rev. 833; and Fridman *et al.*, *The Law of Torts in Canada*, 3d ed. (2010) at 447-61.

4. Participation in a Criminal or Immoral Act

The defence of *ex turpi causa non oritur actio* was raised in Chapter 6 in relation to intentional torts. The application of the principle is essentially the same in negligence. Significantly, like voluntary assumption of risk, and unlike contributory negligence, the *ex turpi* defence does not merely lead to a reduction in damages: it precludes recovery altogether. As a result, it has been narrowly interpreted.

HALL v. HEBERT
(1993), 101 D.L.R. (4th) 129 (S.C.C.)

[The plaintiff and the defendant got "quite and equally drunk" at a party. While driving home, the defendant stalled his "souped-up muscle" car on a steep, unlit gravel road that sharply dropped away on one side. The defendant agreed to allow the plaintiff to drive. The plaintiff attempted a "rolling start" but lost control almost immediately and flipped the vehicle down the embankment. The plaintiff was severely injured and sued the defendant for allowing him to drive in his intoxicated condition.

The major issue on appeal to the Supreme Court of Canada was whether the defendant could raise the defence of *ex turpi causa non oritur actio* to negate the plaintiff's cause of action.]

MCLACHLIN J.: . . . My colleague Cory J. suggests that the defence of *ex turpi causa non oritur actio* should be eliminated. In its place, he suggests that the courts should be granted the power to disallow a plaintiff's claim, on account of the plaintiff's wrongful conduct, by finding that no duty of care arises. This power is to be exercised under the second branch of the test articulated in *Anns v. Merton London Borough Council*, [1978] A.C. 728, as approved and reformulated in this Court in *Kamloops (City) v. Nielsen*, [1984] 2 S.C.R. 2. On this view, the plaintiff's illegal or immoral conduct may constitute a policy reason for holding that the defendant owed the plaintiff no duty of care.

A variant of this approach has been adopted in Australia, *Gala v. Preston* [(1991), 172 C.L.R. 342] and by the English Court of Appeal, *Pitts v. Hunt* [[1991] 1 Q.B. 24]. This view holds that no duty should be postulated where it is either *impossible* or *improper* for the courts to establish a standard of care to govern the conduct in issue. It is recognized that there is no a priori reason in law why a duty cannot subsist between criminals or wrongdoers. However, some cases raise such "special and exceptional" circumstances that a court cannot, or cannot in good conscience, enquire into the standard of care needed to ground the duty of care in a particular situation. Unlike the view espoused by Cory J., the very possibility of a duty arising is not denied; rather the court declines to enter into the question of whether a duty exists.

With great respect, I am not sure that much is gained by replacing the defence of *ex turpi causa non oritur actio* with a judicial discretion to negate, or to refuse to consider, the duty of care. Shifting the analysis to the issue of duty provides no new insight into the fundamental question of when the courts should be entitled to deny recovery in tort to a plaintiff on the ground of the plaintiff's immoral or illegal conduct. Moreover, it introduces a series of new problems. In the end I fear that it would prove more problematic than has the defence of *ex turpi causa non oritur actio*.

I begin by noting that the duty approach, as expressed by Cory J., does not fully capture what we mean when we invoke the principle of *ex turpi causa*. If what I have said above is correct, the *ex turpi causa* principle operates most naturally as a defence because its purpose is to frustrate what would be, had *ex turpi causa* no role, a complete cause of action. Liability for tort arises out of the relationship between the alleged tortfeasor and the injured claimant. The power of the court to deny recovery where it would undermine the coherence of the legal system, on the other hand, represents concerns independent of this relationship. It is important, if only for the purposes of conceptual clarity, that *ex turpi causa* operate, on those rare occasions where its operation is justified, as a defence to frustrate tort claims which could otherwise be fully made out, because this best expresses what is in fact decided. The courts make it clear that the defendant has acted wrongly in negligently causing harm. They also make it clear that responsibility for this wrong is suspended only because concern for the integrity of the legal system trumps the concern that the defendant be responsible.

Donoghue v. Stevenson, [1932] A.C. 562 (H.L.), the source of our modern law of negligence and of the concept of duty upon which it is founded, requires that a person exercise reasonable care toward all his neighbours. It does not say that the duty is owed only to neighbours who have acted morally and legally. Tort, unlike equity which requires that the plaintiff come with clean hands, does not require a plaintiff to have a certain moral character in order to bring an action before the court. The duty of care is owed to *all* persons who may reasonably be foreseen to be injured by the negligent conduct.

Policy concerns unrelated to the legal rules which govern the relationship between the parties to an action have not generally been considered in determining whether a duty [of] care lies. This follows from the fact that the justice which tort law seeks to accomplish is justice between the parties to the particular action; the court acts at the instance of the wronged party to rectify the damage caused by a particular defendant: see Ernest J. Weinrib, "The Special Morality of Tort Law" (1989) 34 McGill L.J. 403, at p. 408.

The relationship between plaintiff and defendant which gives rise to their respective entitlement and liability arises from a duty predicated on foreseeable consequences of harm. This being the concern, the legality or morality of the plaintiff's conduct is an extrinsic consideration. In the rare cases where concerns for the administration of justice require that the extrinsic consideration of the character of the plaintiff's conduct be considered, it seems to me that this is better done by way of defence than by distorting the notion of the duty of care owed by the defendant to the plaintiff.

It can be argued that the Australian rule avoids these doctrinal problems by recognizing that, while a duty of care might otherwise lie, it cannot be raised because the parties, by their conduct, have made it impossible or improper to consider the claim. In other words, that a duty could arise from the relationship between the parties is not denied — [the] plaintiff is simply barred from relying on it. Thus the Australian High Court formally avoids conflict with the principle it has articulated in earlier judgments: that no person becomes a caput lupinum, or an outlaw, in the eyes of the civil law merely because that person was engaged in some unlawful act. . . . On analysis, however, this notion that the courts cannot, in certain circumstances, consider whether a duty of care arises has the practical effect of denying a duty which would otherwise arise, and hence, in substance, of violating the very principle against making certain parties outlaws to which the court seeks to adhere.

Beyond this, a more practical objection can be raised: why is it necessary to take the rather novel step of positing judicial "inability" to investigate the appropriate standard of care, instead of using the concept by which the law has traditionally recognized considerations that prevent otherwise valid claims from succeeding, that is, the concept of a defence to the action?

The law of tort recognizes many types of defence. Some go to the relationship between the parties; for example, the defence of *volenti non fit injuria*, the plaintiff's assumption of risk. But others go to matters unrelated to that relationship. Limitation periods, for example, are raised by way of defence. I see no reason to treat *ex turpi causa* differently. Like a lapsed limitation period, it represents a reason why a cause of action, which might otherwise be fully made out, should not succeed.

The debate is not purely academic. There are practical reasons for finding that it is proper to view *ex turpi causa* as a defence. I mention three. If the *ex turpi causa* principle arises in the course of the investigation into whether there exists a duty of care, the onus will lie on the plaintiff to show why he or she should not be disentitled by way of his or her conduct. It is well established that the plaintiff bears the onus of establishing a valid cause of action; if not, the plaintiff faces non-suit. Thus a plaintiff whose conduct is alleged to be immoral or illegal might be bound to disprove the illegality or immorality in order to proceed with her action and avoid non-suit. On the other hand, if the matter is left as a defence, the onus rests on the defendant. As I have indicated, the power to preclude recovery on the basis of the plaintiff's immoral or illegal conduct is an *exceptional* power, operating in derogation of the general principles of tort applicable to all persons in our society. As such, it seems to me appropriate that the onus of establishing the exceptional circumstances should rest with the defendant. The plaintiff should not be required to *disprove* the existence and relevance of his or her illegal or immoral conduct; rather it should be for the defendant to establish it.

Second, the duty of care approach is an all or nothing approach, and cannot be applied selectively to discreet [*sic*] heads of damage. As discussed above, cases may arise in which a particular damage claim, e.g., for exemplary damages, or for damages for loss of future earnings, might be seen as claim to profit from an illegal act. Another damage claim in the same action, e.g., one for compensation for personal injuries, could not be so regarded. If the *ex turpi causa* principle operates as a defence it is possible to distinguish between such claims. If it operates as a factor negating a duty of care, on the other hand, it is not possible to treat an action in the selective manner that justice seems to require.

Finally, consideration of illegal or immoral conduct at the stage of determining the duty of care raises procedural problems. A plaintiff may sue in both tort and contract. If the approach suggested by Cory J. is adopted, in the contract claim, the plaintiff's illegal or immoral conduct would be raised as a defence to the claim; in the tort, the same conduct would be an element of the enquiry into the duty of care. In other words, in contract the onus would be on the defendant to prove the relevance of the plaintiff's conduct; in tort, the onus would be on the plaintiff to disprove the relevance of the conduct. The resulting confusion would unnecessarily complicate the task of the trial judge and the parties.

These considerations lead me to conclude that the important but limited power of the court to prevent tort recovery on the ground of the plaintiff's illegal or immoral conduct is better viewed as a defence than as a factor going to the existence of a duty of care.

II. Application to These Facts

The doctrine of *ex turpi causa non oritur actio* properly applies in tort where it will be necessary to invoke the doctrine in order to maintain the internal consistency of the law. Most commonly, this concern will arise where a given plaintiff genuinely seeks to profit from his or her illegal conduct, or where the claimed compensation would amount to an evasion of a criminal sanction. This appellant need not be denied recovery since these grounds are not relevant to his claim. The compensation sought by this appellant is for injuries received. This compensation can be reduced to the extent of the appellant's contributory negligence, but cannot be wholly denied by reason of his disreputable or criminal conduct.

[La Forest, L'Heureux-Dubé and Iacobucci JJ. concurred with McLachlin J. Cory J. concurred in the result, but indicated that the defence of *ex turpi causa* should be eliminated. Gonthier J. concurred in the result. While he agreed that *ex turpi causa* had to be limited, he did not accept that it should be limited to the narrow categories that McLachlin J. set out. Sopinka J. agreed that *ex turpi causa* did not apply on the facts but held that the plaintiff's claim should be dismissed because the defendant did not owe the plaintiff any duty of care.]

NOTES AND QUESTIONS

1. The Canadian courts consistently narrowed *ex turpi causa* in a series of often conflicting cases. Few judges liked the defence and they could not agree on the purpose it should serve. This chequered history is discussed in Chapter 6.

2. McLachlin J. stated in *Hall* that the purpose of the *ex turpi causa* doctrine is to protect "the integrity of the legal system." In her view, the plaintiff's illegal or immoral conduct would only rarely be relevant if the plaintiff was seeking compensation for actual physical injuries or losses. She distinguished these claims from those in which the plaintiff was seeking to profit from his or her wrongdoing.

Do you agree with McLachlin J. that the doctrine's goal should be to protect the integrity of the legal system? Assuming that this is an appropriate goal, does it follow that the doctrine would only rarely apply to claims for actual physical injuries?

3. McLachlin J. raised three "practical reasons" why *ex turpi causa* should be treated as a defence and not dealt with at the duty stage. Are these reasons compelling?

In *Rankin (Rankin's Garage & Sales) v. J.J.*, 2018 SCC 19 at para. 63 the Supreme Court of Canada confirmed this approach. It stated:

> The notion that illegal or immoral conduct by the plaintiff precludes the existence of a duty of care has consistently been rejected by this Court . . . Tort law does not seek to punish wrongdoing in the abstract. Rather, private law is corrective and based on compensation for harm that results from the defendant's unreasonable creation of the risk of that harm. If the mere fact of illegal behaviour could eliminate a duty, this would effectively immunize negligent defendants from the consequences of their actions. Seriously injured victims would be entirely denied recovery, even when the defendant bears most of the fault. While illegality can operate as a defence to a tort action in limited circumstances when it is necessary to preserve the integrity of the legal system, this concern does not arise in the circumstances of this case. . . .

See also *Deloitte & Touche v. Livent Inc.*, 2017 SCC 63 at para. 98.

4. All seven justices appear to agree on the goal of the doctrine, the need to limit it and its inapplicability to the facts in *Hall*. What are the implications of the fact that, despite this agreement, there are four judgments?

The complexity of the legal and policy issues generated by the doctrine is reflected by the range of approaches that have been taken by other Commonwealth courts. See *Pitts v. Hunt*, [1990] 3 All E.R. 344 (C.A.); *Gala v. Preston* (1991), 172 C.L.R. 243 (H.C.A.); and *Brown v. Dunsmuir*, [1994] 3 N.Z.L.R. 485 (H.C.). See also the discussion below of some more recent Commonwealth decisions.

5. In *John Bead Corp. v. Soni* (2002), 10 C.C.L.T. (3d) 318 (Ont. C.A.) the court commented on the effect of *Hall*. The plaintiff claimed that the defendant had stolen $1,600,000 from the plaintiff's company. The defendant denied the allegation and further pleaded *ex turpi causa* on the basis that the plaintiff had also illegally taken money from the company. The issue was whether that defence should be struck from the pleadings. The Court of Appeal answered in the affirmative. It held, first, that the defence does not apply merely because the plaintiff was engaged in an illegal activity that was unrelated to the facts underlying the plaintiff's claim. That is true even if both parties were separately engaged in similar forms of illegal activity (like stealing money

from a company). Second, the court offered two examples of when damages will be refused in order to prevent the plaintiff from profiting from his or her own wrongdoing: (i) "where one wrongdoer claims in tort against another for financial loss arising from an illegal activity," and (ii) "where the plaintiff claims as a head of damage suffered in a personal injury claim, loss of earnings from an illegal activity."

How should these principles apply when one person involved in mortgage fraud sues others also involved in the fraud for contribution and indemnity in respect of the amount owing to the bank under the mortgage? See *Tran v. Kerr*, 2014 ABCA 350.

6. What role could or should *ex turpi causa* play in a case in which the plaintiff was illegally present in the jurisdiction when he or she was injured by the defendant? See *Hounga v. Allen*, [2014] UKSC 47, rev'g [2012] EWCA Civ 609.

7. It is generally accepted that the police owe some duty of care to those in their custody after an arrest. In *Vellino v. Chief Constable of Greater Manchester Police*, [2002] 1 W.L.R. 218 (C.A.) the plaintiff was injured while jumping from a window to escape from police custody. The court denied the claim, in part on the basis that in attempting to escape the plaintiff was committing a criminal offence and could not sue for the injuries sustained while doing so. Do you agree with this reasoning? How else might the case have been decided against the plaintiff?

8. In *Beljanski (Guardian ad litem of) v. Smithwick* (2006), 56 B.C.L.R. (4th) 99 (C.A.) the dependant children of a "career criminal" brought a claim when their father was killed negligently. The court relied on *ex turpi causa* in refusing to base any part of the award on any illegal income the deceased would have made through criminal activities. The related issue of whether a plaintiff could recover lost wages for a period of time during which he or she was otherwise unable to work as a result of being incarcerated arose in *British Columbia v. Zastowny*, [2008] 1 S.C.R. 27. The plaintiff successfully sued the defendant for sexual battery. In assessing the plaintiff's loss of income flowing from the battery, the court refused compensation for the significant periods of time he had subsequently spent in jail for various offences. According to Rothstein J., "An award of damages for wages lost while incarcerated would constitute a rebate of the natural consequence of the penalty provided by the criminal law." Allowing recovery would undermine the integrity of the judicial system. See Neudorf, "Case Comment on *British Columbia v. Zastowny*: Shifting Sanctions and Personal Responsibility" (2010) 73 Sask. L. Rev. 131. See also *H.L. v. Canada (Attorney General)*, [2005] 1 S.C.R. 401 at paras. 137, 143 and 344. For a similar position in England see *Gray v. Thames Trains Ltd.*, [2009] 1 A.C. 1339 (H.L.); and *Clunis v. Camden & Islington Health Authority*, [1998] Q.B. 978 (C.A.). These decisions were recently confirmed in *Henderson v. Dorset Healthcare University NHS Foundation Trust*, [2018] EWCA Civ 1841.

9. For academic commentary see MacDoughall, "*Ex Turpi Causa*: Should a Defence Arise from a Base Cause?" (1991) 55 Sask. L. Rev. 1; McInnes, "Ex Turpi Causa and Tort: A Canadian Perspective" [1993] C.L.J. 378; Klar, "Negligence Defences — Ex Turpi Causa Non Oritur Actio — Volenti Non Fit Injuria — The Purpose of Negligent Accident Law: *Hall v. Herbert*" (1993) 72 Can. Bar Rev. 553; Kostal, "Currents in the Counter-Reformation: Illegality and Duty of Care in Canada and Australia" (1995) 3 Tort L. Rev. 100; Fordham, "The Role of Ex Turpi Causa in

Tort Law" [1998] Sing. J.L.S. 238; and Glofcheski, "Plaintiff's Illegality as a Bar to Recovery of Personal Injury Damages" (1999) 19 L.S. 6.

10. In England the Law Commission reviewed the illegality defence: Law Com. No. 320, *The Illegality Defence* (2010). It rejected the establishing of strict rules in this area. It recommended that courts should consider the policy rationales that underlie the defence and apply them to the facts of each case. In the Commission's view, this would make the law more transparent and less arbitrary. How does this proposed approach compare with the approach in Canada? See *Gray v. Thames Trains Ltd., supra*, and *Moore Stephens v. Stone Rolls Limited*, [2009] 1 A.C. 1391 (H.L.). See also Goudkamp, "The Defence of Illegality: *Gray v Thames Trains Ltd*" (2009) 17 Torts L.J. 205; Yap, "Rethinking the Illegality Defence in Tort Law" (2010) 18 Tort L. Rev. 52; and Virgo, "'We Do This in the Criminal Law and That in the Law of Tort': A New Fusion Debate" in Pitel, Neyers & Chamberlain, eds., *Tort Law: Challenging Orthodoxy* (2013) at 104-10.

In *Delaney v. Pickett*, [2011] EWCA Civ 1532 the plaintiff and defendant were together transporting illegal drugs when the defendant driver lost control of the car. The plaintiff sued and the defendant relied on *ex turpi causa*. The Court of Appeal did not apply the defence, holding that the plaintiff's injuries were not caused by his criminal conduct. The illegal conduct was "incidental" to the injuries. See Goudkamp, "The Defence of Illegality in Tort Law: Wither the Rule in Pitts v Hunt?" [2012] C.L.J. 481. This approach emphasizes the role of causation, building on language from Lord Hoffmann in *Gray v. Thames Trains Ltd., supra*, and focuses less on the extent to which illegal conduct in itself negates a duty of care. See also *Joyce v. O'Brien*, [2013] EWCA Civ 546 at paras. 28-29.

However, in *Hounga v. Allen, supra*, while two judges of the United Kingdom Supreme Court held that the illegality defence failed because the connection between the illegal conduct and the tort was not sufficiently close, three of the judges based their decision on the need to consider public policy and downplayed an analysis based on the strength of the connection. See similar tensions about the defence expressed in *Les Laboratoires Servier v. Apotex Inc.*, [2014] UKSC 55.

In *Patel v. Mirza*, [2016] UKSC 4 that same court again considered the defence, this time in response to an unjust enrichment claim. The majority supported a policy-based approach, assessing whether the public interest would be harmed by enforcement of the illegal contract. The relevant factors considered were (a) the underlying purpose of the prohibition, (b) other relevant public policy concerns and (c) whether denial of the claim would be a proportionate response, bearing in mind that punishment was not a concern of the civil courts. In *McHugh v. Okai-Koi*, [2017] EWHC 710 and *Gujra v Roath*, [2018] EWHC 854 the approach in *Patel* was applied to claims in negligence.

There is extensive recent scholarship about the defence of illegality in the United Kingdom. In addition to the articles mentioned above, see Fisher, "The *Ex Turpi Causa* Principle in *Hounga* and *Servier*" (2015) 78 M.L.R. 854; Strauss, "Ex Turpi Causa Oritur Actio?" (2016) 132 L.Q.R. 236; Lim, "*Ex Turpi Causa*: Reformation not Revolution" (2017) 80:5 M.L.R. 927; Erbacher, *Negligence and Illegality* (2017); and Green & Bogg, eds., *Illegality after Patel v Mirza* (2018).

Should the defence be based on causation or on public policy? How different is the approach in the United Kingdom from that in Canada? Which do you prefer and why?

11. In *Miller v. Miller*, [2011] HCA 9 the 16-year-old plaintiff had stolen a car. She was with two other members of her family. Shortly after taking the car they encountered her mother's cousin, who insisted on driving the car. By then others had joined the group and there were nine people in the car. The cousin drove dangerously, lost control of the car and crashed. One passenger was killed and the plaintiff became tetraplegic. The High Court of Australia held that in principle anyone complicit in stealing the car could not recover damages if and when it was driven dangerously causing them to be injured. In the result the plaintiff did recover but only because she has asked twice to be let out of the car, amounting to withdrawal from the joint illegal enterprise. The court noted that causation alone could not be used to determine the scope of *ex turpi causa*.

12. Even in a limited form, should *ex turpi causa* ever be triggered by conduct that is only immoral but not illegal? See Goudkamp, "*Ex Turpi Causa* and Immoral Behaviour in the Tort Context" (2011) 127 L.Q.R. 354. What if the defendant carelessly injures the plaintiff during adulterous coitus?

13. The *ex turpi causa* defence has been raised in cases in which corporations sue former directors of the corporation for their illegal conduct, typically conspiracy or fraud. The defendants allege that the corporation itself was involved in the illegal conduct, since the corporation acts through its directors. The crucial issue becomes one of attribution, an important issue in corporate law, looking at the extent to which the acts of the directors are attributed to the corporation. See *Jetivia S.A. v. Bilta (UK) Limited*, [2015] UKSC 23. Similar issues arose in *Deloitte & Touche v. Livent Inc.*, *supra*, in which the claim was against the corporation's auditors for not detecting the fraud by the directors. In both of these cases, the acts were not attributed to the corporation and so the defence was not made out.

5. Inevitable Accident

RINTOUL v. X-RAY AND RADIUM INDUST. LTD.
[1956] S.C.R. 674

CARTWRIGHT J.:—The facts as deposed to by Ouellette were as follows. On April 13, 1954, at about 8:50 a.m. Ouellette was driving a 1952 Dodge motor vehicle owned by his employer, the respondent X-Ray and Radium Industries Limited, easterly on Wellington Street in the city of Ottawa. He stopped at the intersection of Bayview Avenue for a traffic-light and his service brakes worked properly. From the time that he had left his home up to this point he had applied his service brakes five times and on each occasion they had worked properly. The traffic-light having changed he proceeded across Bayview Avenue and saw that the line of traffic ahead of him was at a standstill. The appellant's car was at the rear of this line of traffic. When Ouellette was about 150 feet away from the appellant's car he took his foot off the accelerator and applied his service brakes. At this moment he was proceeding uphill at a speed of not more than twelve miles per hour; he found that the brakes did not work; the brake pedal went down to the floor of the car without his feeling any braking action; he allowed the pedal to rise and pressed it down again, still without getting any braking action. Thinking that the service brakes had become useless, he applied his hand brakes; at the moment of this application his car was between 50 and 75 feet from that of the appellant. The application of the hand brakes reduced the speed of his car but did not stop it and it was still moving at about 6 miles per hour when it struck the rear of the appellant's vehicle.

. . .

The defence relied on at the trial and before us was pleaded in the Statement of Defence as follows:—

(4) The Defendants allege and the fact is that at the time and place referred to in the Statement of Claim the brakes of the Defendant motor vehicle suddenly and without warning failed and it was in the circumstances impossible for the Defendant driver to avoid the collision.

(5) The Defendants allege and the fact is that they had taken all reasonable and proper precaution in the care of the brakes on the said motor vehicle and plead that the said collision was an inevitable or an unavoidable accident.

There can be no doubt that, generally speaking, when a car, in broad daylight, runs into the rear of another which is stationary on the highway and which has not come to a sudden stop, the fault is in the driving of the moving car, and the driver of such car must satisfy the Court that the collision did not occur as a result of his negligence. The learned trial judge regarded this principle as applicable to the case at bar but was of the view that the unexpected failure of the service brakes placed Ouellette in a situation of emergency in which he acted without negligence and that the collision was the result of an inevitable accident.

The defence of inevitable accident has been discussed in many decisions. A leading case in Ontario is *McIntosh v. Bell* [[1932] O.R. 179 (C.A.)], which was approved by this Court in *Claxton v. Grandy* [[1934] 4 D.L.R. 257 (S.C.C.) at 263]. At page 187 of the report of *McIntosh v. Bell*, Hodgins J.A. adopts the words of Lord Esher M.R. in *The Schwan* [[1892] P. 419 at 429], as follows:

. . . In my opinion, a person relying on inevitable accident must show that something happened over which he had no control, and the effect of which could not have been avoided by the greatest care and skill.

In my view, in the case at bar the respondents have failed to prove two matters both of which were essential to the establishment of the defence of inevitable accident. These matters are (i) that the alleged failure of the service brakes could not have been prevented by the exercise of reasonable care on their part, and (ii) that, assuming that such failure occurred without negligence on the part of the respondents, Ouellette could not, by the exercise of reasonable care, have avoided the collision which he claims was the effect of such failure.

As to the first matter, assuming that the service brakes failed suddenly, the onus resting on the respondents was to show that such failure could not have been prevented by the exercise of reasonable care. In Halsbury, 2nd Edition, Volume 23, page 640, section 901, the learned author says:

Driving with defective apparatus if the defect might reasonably have been discovered . . . (and other matters) . . . are negligent acts which render a defendant liable for injuries of which they are the effective cause.

This passage has been approved by McCardie J. in *Phillips v. Brittania Hygienic Laundry Co.* [[1923] 1 K.B. 539 at 551] and by Hogg J.A. in *Grise v. Rankin et al.* [[1951] O.W.N. 21 (C.A.) at 22], and, in my opinion, correctly states the law.

In the case at bar the respondents have made no attempt to prove that the sudden failure could not have been prevented by reasonable care on their part and particularly by adequate inspection. They called no witness to explain the extraordinary fact that the service brakes which were working properly immediately before and immediately after the accident and passed satisfactorily the test prescribed in the regulations failed momentarily at the time of the accident. Without going so far as to say that such a story appears to be intrinsically impossible, it is clear that its nature was such as to cast upon the defendants the burden of furnishing a clear and satisfactory explanation of so unusual an occurrence.

Furthermore, the respondents have made no attempt to show that the defect, whatever it was, could not reasonably have been discovered. The evidence is that the respondents' car was a 1952 Dodge. There is no evidence: *(a)* as to when it was purchased, or *(b)* whether it was purchased new or second-hand, or *(c)* how far it had been driven, or *(d)* how often, if ever, the service brakes had been inspected, or *(e)* how often, if ever, the hand brakes had been inspected. The only evidence touching the point at all is Ouellette's statement quoted above that there "was work done on the brakes" the day before the accident. There is nothing to indicate whether the brakes referred to in this statement were the service brakes or the hand brakes although in argument it seemed to be assumed that the reference was to the service brakes. No evidence was given as to what instructions were given to the third party, or as to what work was done by him, or as to what report, if any, was made by the third party when the car was delivered, or as to whether the third party was competent to inspect or repair brakes. The onus resting on the respondents in this regard is not discharged by the bald statement that on the day before the accident there was work (unspecified) done on the brakes.

. . .

In my opinion, on the evidence the respondents have not only failed to show that the alleged failure of the service brakes was inevitable, they have also failed to show that after such failure occurred Ouellette could not by the exercise of reasonable care have avoided the collision. It follows that the appeal of the plaintiff should be allowed.

NOTES AND QUESTIONS

1. What must the defendant establish to invoke the defence of inevitable accident? According to Cartwright J. what standard of care is the defendant required to meet? Is this consistent with Lord Esher's statement in *The Schwan*, [1892] P. 419 which Cartwright J. quotes with approval?

2. What is the effect of the defendant's plea of inevitable accident on the burden of proof? Given its impact in Canada, why would the defendant raise the defence?

3. The Canadian courts have generally applied *Rintoul*. The majority of cases involve sudden mechanical failures and other emergency situations. See *Levesque v. Day & Ross Ltd.* (1976), 15 N.B.R. (2d) 500 (C.A.); *Blackwood v. Butler* (1984), 48 Nfld. & P.E.I.R. 110 (Nfld. C.A.); *Dobbs v. Mayer* (1985), 32 C.C.L.T. 191 (Ont. S.C.); *White*

v. Sheaves (1987), 194 A.P.R. 290 (Nfld. S.C.); *Basra v. Gill*, [1995] 2 W.W.R. 213 (B.C.C.A.); and *Chow-Hidasi v. Hidasi*, 2013 BCCA 73.

However, see *Graham v. Hodgkinson* (1983), 40 O.R. (2d) 697 (C.A.); and *Boutcher v. Stewart* (1989), 50 C.C.L.T. 77 (N.B.C.A.) in which it was indicated that inevitable accident was no more than a denial of negligence and that it did not alter either the plaintiff's or the defendant's case.

4. In *Barron v. Barron* (2003), 214 N.S.R. (2d) 76 (S.C.) the defendant was drinking coffee while driving. He had a sudden choking fit and fainted. He had frequently experienced similar choking fits but had never lost consciousness. This time he crashed, injuring the plaintiff passenger. The court stated that it was more difficult to make out the defence of inevitable accident based on factors "internal" to the defendant rather than "external" factors like icy roads or faulty brakes. The court rejected the defence, concluding that given his history the defendant should have refrained from drinking coffee while driving. See also *Codner v. Gosse* (2003), 227 Nfld. & P.E.I.R. 132 (N.L.S.C. (T.D.)); and *Holt v. Rother*, 2013 BCSC 1065.

5. Is there any reason to treat inevitable accident as a defence? See Klar, "Annotation" (1977) 1 C.C.L.T. 273; Smith, "Automatism — A Defence to Negligence?" [1980] New L.J. 1111; Kligman, "Inevitable Accident and the Infirm Driver: What You Don't Know Can Kill You" (1987) 8 Adv. Q. 311; Gilles, "Inevitable Accident in Classical English Tort Law" (1993) 43 Emory L.J. 575; and Currie, "Affirmative defence *redux* or night of the living dead doctrines? Putting 'Inevitable Accident' To Rest" (2003) 16 C.C.L.T. (3d) 171.

REVIEW PROBLEM

David Carling and Randy Jones, two 15-year-old students, had several very strong drinks at David's house while his parents were out of town. Randy suggested that they take Mr. Carling's car for a drive and pick up their girlfriends, Carol and Mary. Although neither Randy nor David had a driver's licence, David agreed to the plan despite his parents' explicit prohibition against driving. Carol agreed to accompany them and asked them to bring along some liquor for her. Mary also agreed to go for a ride, but she was unaware that they had been drinking. Carol knew that the boys had taken the car without consent, but Mary did not.

During the drive, they picked up Louise, who was hitchhiking to work. She soon realized that David was drunk and very tired. She twice asked him to slow down. She thought about getting out of the car, but she was late for work. As a result of his speeding and intoxication, David lost control of the car and hit Mr. Crown's parked car. The car was parked illegally, partially blocking the roadway. Had David not panicked, however, he could easily have avoided the car. Both cars were badly damaged and all the occupants of Mr. Carling's vehicle were injured.

Mr. Crown, Louise, Mary, Carol and Randy have sued David in negligence. You have been retained to research the possible defences that David might raise and their impact on his liability.

20

PROOF OF NEGLIGENCE

1. The Burden of Proof in a Negligence Action
2. Exceptions to the General Principles Governing the Burden of Proof
3. *Res Ipsa Loquitur*

1. The Burden of Proof in a Negligence Action

It is important to distinguish between legal and evidentiary burdens of proof. The legal burden of proof in a civil action is the burden of proving an issue on the balance of probabilities. In other words, after both sides have been heard, the party who bears the legal burden will lose the issue unless he or she has convinced the judge or jury to this requisite degree of certainty. While the balance of probabilities test is clearly less onerous than the criminal standard of proof beyond a reasonable doubt, it is difficult to define precisely. Sappideen & Vines, eds., *Fleming's The Law of Torts*, 10th ed. (2011) at 357 explains the civil standard in the following terms: "the tribunal of fact must feel an actual persuasion of the occurrence or existence of the fact of which proof is required . . . A mere mathematical or statistical probability of barely 51% is not sufficient because it carries no conviction that the case falls (more probably) within the 51 rather than the 49." The plaintiff usually bears the legal burden of proving all of the elements of a negligence action and the defendant has the legal burden of proving any defence.

The legal burden generally remains on the same party throughout the trial. In contrast, the evidentiary burden may shift back and forth between the parties as evidence is introduced during the course of the trial. The evidentiary burden relates to the practical desirability of adducing evidence in support of one's position, and its placement is determined at any particular time by the cumulative weight of the evidence that has been presented. Thus, the plaintiff, who is required to present his or her case first, is subject to two burdens at the outset. First, he or she bears the obligation of ultimately proving the elements of the case on a balance of probabilities. This obligation arises from the legal burden and is assessed at the end of the entire trial. Second, he or she also bears the obligation of adducing sufficient evidence to establish a *prima facie* case. This obligation arises from the evidentiary burden. If, after the plaintiff has presented his or her case, but before the defendant has presented its case, the judge does not believe that the plaintiff's evidence, considered on its own, could possibly support the imposition of liability, the trial will end immediately (sometimes called a nonsuit) and the defendant will not be required to present its case.

In most situations, the plaintiff is able to discharge the evidentiary burden, establish a *prima facie* case and avoid an immediate dismissal. In that situation, the evidentiary burden then shifts to the defendant. The legal burden remains on the plaintiff; the defendant is not required to prove, on a balance of probabilities, that it was not negligent. However, if it wishes to avoid the risk of liability, it should adduce sufficient evidence to rebut the plaintiff's *prima facie* case against it. In other words, the defendant should introduce evidence that prevents the trier of fact from concluding that the plaintiff has established his or her case on a balance of probabilities.

In theory, the plaintiff may fail to discharge the legal burden of proof even though he or she has discharged the evidentiary burden and the defendant has not introduced any evidence. For example, while a judge might refuse to order a dismissal because the evidence at the end of the plaintiff's case, considered on its own, *could* support a finding of negligence, the jury (assuming that there is one) might in the end conclude that on the balance of probabilities it in fact does not do so. Obviously, however, it is advisable for the defendant to present evidence in support of its position.

WAKELIN v. LONDON & SOUTH WESTERN RY. CO.
(1886), 12 A.C. 41 (H.L.)

The action was brought by the administratrix of Henry Wakelin on behalf of herself and her children under Lord Campbell's Act, 9 & 10 Vict. c. 93.

The statement of claim alleged that the defendant's line between Chiswick Station and Chiswick Junction crossed a public footway, and that on the 1st of May 1882 the defendants so negligently and unskilfully drove a train on the line across the footpath and so neglected to take precautions in respect of the train and the crossing that the train struck and killed one Henry Wakelin the plaintiff's husband whilst lawfully on the footpath.

The statement of defence admitted that on that day the plaintiff's husband whilst on or near the footpath was struck by a train of the defendants, and so injured that he died, but denied the alleged negligence; did not admit that the deceased was lawfully crossing the line at the time in question; and alleged that his death was caused by his own negligence and that he might by the exercise of reasonable caution have seen the train approaching and avoided the accident.

Oral evidence was given that from the cottage where the deceased lived it would take about ten minutes to walk to the crossing; that he left his cottage on the evening of the 1st of May after tea, and that he was never seen again till his body was found the same night on the down line near the crossing. There was no evidence as to the circumstances under which he got on to the line. Witnesses for the plaintiff gave evidence (not very intelligible) as to the limited number of yards at which an approaching train could be seen from the crossing, and as to obstructions to the view.

The defendants called no witnesses, and submitted that there was no case. Manisty J. left the case to the jury who returned a verdict for the plaintiff for £800. The Divisional Court (Grove J. Huddleston B. and Hawkins J.) set aside the verdict and entered judgment for the defendants. The Court of Appeal (Brett M.R. Bowen and Fry L.JJ.) on the 16th day of May 1884 affirmed this decision. In the course of his judgment Brett M.R. said that in his opinion the plaintiff in this case was not only bound to give evidence of negligence on the part of the defendants which was a cause of the death of the deceased, but was also bound to give prima facie evidence that the deceased was not guilty of negligence contributing to the accident; and that by reason of the plaintiff having been unable to give any evidence of the circumstances of the accident she had failed in giving evidence of that necessary part of her prima facie case.

From this decision the plaintiff appealed.

. . .

LORD HALSBURY L.C.:—My Lords, it is incumbent upon the plaintiff in this case to establish by proof that her husband's death has been caused by some negligence of the defendants, some negligent act, or some negligent omission, to which the injury complained of in this case, the death of the husband, is attributable. That is the fact to be proved. If that fact is not proved the plaintiff fails, and if in the absence of direct proof the circumstances which are established are equally consistent with the allegation of the plaintiff as with the denial of the defendants, the plaintiff fails, for the very simple reason that the plaintiff is bound to establish the affirmative of the proposition.

. . .

If the simple proposition with which I started is accurate, it is manifest that the plaintiff, who gives evidence of a state of facts which is equally consistent with the wrong of which she complains having been caused by — in this sense that it could not have occurred without — her husband's own negligence as by the negligence of the defendants, does not prove that it was caused by the defendants' negligence. She may indeed establish that the event has occurred through the joint negligence of both, but if that is the state of the evidence the plaintiff fails . . . It is true that the onus of proof may shift from time to time as matter of evidence, but still the question must ultimately arise whether the person who is bound to prove the affirmative of the issue, i.e., in this case the negligent act done, has discharged herself of that burden. I am of opinion that the plaintiff does not do this unless she proves that the defendants have caused the injury in the sense which I have explained.

In this case I am unable to see any evidence of how this unfortunate calamity occurred. One may surmise, and it is but surmise and not evidence, that the unfortunate man was knocked down by a passing train while on the level crossing; but assuming in the plaintiff's favour that fact to be established, is there anything to shew that the train ran over the man rather than that the man ran against the train?

. . .

Again, is there any legal presumption that people are careful and look before them on crossing a railway, or even when they do see the approach of a train that they never cross when the train is dangerously near? And yet if one of these hypotheses were established the plaintiff must fail, while on the other side it would be extremely difficult to lay down as a matter of law that precautions which the legislature has not enjoined should be observed by a railway company in the ordinary conduct of their traffic. Railway companies are permitted to establish their undertakings for the express purpose of running trains at high speed along their lines. Rightly or wrongly the legislature have permitted the railways to cross roadways on a level, and it must be taken that the legislature, wherever they have given that authority, and without requiring special measures of precaution, have left to the railway company the discretion of using their lines in a reasonable and proper fashion. I can understand that circumstances might exist which might call upon the railway company to take unusual precautions, though not prescribed by statute, but the peculiarity about this case is that no one knows what the circumstances were. The body of the deceased man was found in the neighbourhood of the level crossing on the down line, but neither by direct evidence nor by reasonable inference can any conclusion be arrived at as to the circumstances causing his death.

It has been argued before your Lordships that we must take the facts as found by the jury. I do not know what facts the jury are supposed to have found, nor is it, perhaps, very material to inquire, because if they have found that the defendants' negligence caused the death of the plaintiff's husband, they have found it without a fragment of evidence to justify such a finding.

Under these circumstances, I move that the judgment appealed from be affirmed, and the appeal dismissed.

LORD WATSON: . . . It appears to me that in all such cases the liability of the defendant company must rest upon these facts — in the first place that there was some negligent act or omission on the part of the company or their servants which materially contributed to the injury or death complained of, and, in the second place, that there was no contributory negligence on the part of the injured or deceased person. But it does not, in my opinion, necessarily follow that the whole burden of proof is cast upon the plaintiff. That it lies with the plaintiff to prove the first of these propositions does not admit of dispute. Mere allegation or proof that the company was guilty of negligence is altogether irrelevant; they might be guilty of many negligent acts or omissions, which might possibly have occasioned injury to somebody, but had no connection whatever with the injury for which redress is sought, and therefore the plaintiff must allege and prove, not merely that they were negligent, but that their negligence caused or materially contributed to the injury.

I am of opinion that the onus of proving affirmatively that there was contributory negligence on the part of the person injured rests, in the first instance, upon the defendants, and that in the absence of evidence tending to that conclusion, the plaintiff is not bound to prove the negative in order to entitle her to a verdict in her favour . . . .

The difficulty of dealing with the question of onus in cases like the present arises from the fact that in most cases it is well nigh impossible for the plaintiff to lay his evidence before a jury or the Court without disclosing circumstances which either point to or tend to rebut the conclusion that the injured party was guilty of contributory negligence. If the plaintiff's evidence were sufficient to shew that the negligence of the defendants did materially contribute to the injury, and threw no light upon the question of the injured party's negligence, then I should be of opinion that, in the absence of any counter-evidence from the defendants, it ought to be presumed that, in point of fact, there was no such contributory negligence. Even if the plaintiff's evidence did disclose facts and circumstances bearing upon that question, which were neither sufficient per se to prove such contributory negligence, nor to cast the onus of disproving it on the plaintiff, I should remain of the same opinion. Of course a plaintiff who comes into Court with an unfounded action may have to submit to the inconvenience of having his adversary's defence proved by his own witnesses; but that cannot affect the question upon whom the onus lies in the first instance . . . .

In the present case, I think the appellant must fail, because no attempt has been made to bring evidence in support of her allegations up to the point at which the question of contributory negligence becomes material. The evidence appears to me to shew that the injuries which caused the death of Henry Wakelin were occasioned by contact with an engine or a train belonging to the respondents, and I am willing to assume, although I am by no means satisfied, that it has also been proved that they were in certain respects negligent. The evidence goes no further. It affords ample materials for conjecturing that the death may possibly have been occasioned by that negligence, but it furnishes no data from which an inference can be reasonably drawn that as a matter of fact it was so occasioned.

I am accordingly of opinion that the order appealed from must be affirmed.

[Lord Blackburn concurred with Lord Watson, and Lord Fitzgerald concurred in separate reasons.]

NOTES AND QUESTIONS

1. Should the plaintiff's claim have been dismissed before the defendant presented any evidence? If, as Lord Halsbury indicates, there was not a fragment of evidence to justify the jury's finding, what factors induced the jury to find for the plaintiff?

2. Does *Wakelin* add support to those who would abolish civil jury trials? What arguments can be made in favour of jury trials in civil matters? Although civil jury trials have become infrequent in parts of the Commonwealth, they remain important in some Canadian provinces. See Sommers & Firestone, "In Defence of the Civil Jury Trial in Personal Injury Actions" (1987) 7 Adv. Q. 492; and MacIntyre, Manes & McGrenere, "More in Defence of the Civil Jury Trial in Personal Injury Actions" (1987) 8 Adv. Q. 109.

In *Hunt (Litigation Guardian of) v. Sutton Group Incentive Realty Inc.* (2002), 60 O.R. (3d) 665 (C.A.) the court stated that "the right to trial by jury is a substantial right and one which is not to be taken away lightly. The onus is upon a party moving to discharge a jury and that onus must also be substantial." The court held that the trial judge erred in exercising his discretion to discharge the jury on the grounds that the issues in the case were too complex for it to resolve, and ordered a new trial. Compare with *Cowles v. Balac* (2006), 83 O.R. (3d) 660 (C.A.), where the court held that the trial judge had correctly struck out a jury notice on grounds of complexity.

3. What was the basis on which Lord Halsbury dismissed the plaintiff's case? What did Lord Halsbury mean by the following statement: "It is true that the onus of proof may shift from time to time as a matter of evidence, but still the question must ultimately arise whether the person who is bound to prove the affirmative of the issue . . . has discharged herself of that burden"? For a Canadian case on point see *Prime v. Fraser Valley Foods Ltd.*, [1994] 2 W.W.R. 331 (B.C.C.A.).

4. At the time of *Wakelin* contributory negligence was a complete defence to an action in negligence. What effect did this have on the plaintiff's case? Lord Watson clearly disagreed with Brett M.R. as to who bears the burden of proving contributory negligence. With whom would Lord Halsbury agree?

5. Would the result have been the same if the defendant had the legal and evidentiary burden of disproving negligence?

6. For a discussion of the legal and evidentiary burdens of proof see Tapper, *Cross and Tapper on Evidence*, 12th ed. (2010) at 119-72; Sappideen & Vines, eds., *Fleming's The Law of Torts*, 10th ed. (2011) at 355-59; Redmayne, "Standards of Proof in Civil Litigation" (1999) 62 M.L.R. 167; Fridman *et al.*, *The Law of Torts in Canada*, 3d ed. (2010) at 383-84; Wexler, "Legal Proof and Tort Law" (2007) 33 Adv. Q. 296; and Klar & Jefferies, *Tort Law*, 6th ed. (2017) at 677-80.

7. In *Mohamed v. Banville* (2009), 94 O.R. (3d) 709 (S.C.J.) the plaintiff sued the defendant alleging that he had negligently caused a house fire. The defendant was intoxicated and a smoker, and an insurance investigator's opinion was that the fire was most likely caused by careless smoking. However, there was no specific evidence that the defendant was smoking in the house on the evening in question. The judge held that "In this case, just as there is no evidence the fire started due to an electrical fault or arson, there is no evidence it was started by careless smoking, even if the fire originated in the area where Banville fell asleep." The plaintiff's claim failed for lack of proof of negligence. See also *Milne v. Coast Mountain Bus Co.*, 2008 CarswellBC 1413 (Prov. Ct.) (WL Can). Contrast *Mann v. Kendall*, 2012 BCSC 1895.

8. In *R.C. v. McDougall*, [2008] 3 S.C.R. 41 the court confirmed that "there is only one civil standard of proof at common law and that is proof on a balance of probabilities. Of course, context is all important and a judge should not be unmindful, where appropriate, of inherent probabilities or improbabilities or the seriousness of the allegations or consequences. However, these considerations do not change the standard of proof." The court rejected the notion of an intermediate standard of proof, falling somewhere between balance of probabilities and beyond a reasonable doubt (the criminal law standard), to be used in civil cases raising particularly serious issues such as sexual battery.

9. To what extent should a defendant's apology to the plaintiff be evidence of negligence? Because of concerns about this issue, defendants have been very reluctant to apologize or express regret to plaintiffs lest they provide evidence that will be used against them in litigation. To address this concern and facilitate apologies, some provinces have enacted legislation: see for example *Apology Act*, S.B.C. 2006, c. 19; and *Apology Act, 2009*, S.O. 2009, c. 3. These statutes prevent apologies from being used by plaintiffs as evidence of negligence. See Brown, "Apology Legislation: Oiling the Wheels of Tort" (2009) 17 Tort L. Rev. 127.

10. In *Benhaim v. St-Germain*, 2016 SCC 48 at para. 74 the court noted that "[s]tatistical generalizations are not determinative in particular cases". The evidence was that 78% of fortuitously discovered cancers are at stage 1 and that the deceased's cancer had been fortuitously discovered. The court held that this did not in itself require the trier of fact to conclude, on the balance of probabilities, that the deceased's cancer was at stage 1 when discovered. Do you agree? What value are such aggregate statistics to particular situations before the court? The use of statistics as evidence is discussed in more detail later in this chapter. See also *British Columbia (Workers' Compensation Appeal Tribunal) v. Fraser Health Authority*, 2016 SCC 25.

2. Exceptions to the General Principles Governing the Burden of Proof

(a) STATUTES AND SHIFTING BURDENS OF PROOF

MACDONALD v. WOODARD
(1974), 43 D.L.R. (3d) 182 (Ont. Co. Ct.)

MATHESON CO. CT. J.:—The plaintiff, a service station proprietor, was struck while standing in front of the automobile of the defendant Donald Woodard just after the plaintiff had given a boost to Woodard's battery from his own station wagon which had been conveniently positioned nose to nose facing the Woodard automobile.

. . .

What, in the circumstances, does the plaintiff have to establish in order to succeed against the defendant Donald Woodard? Because Angus MacDonald was on his feet, in the process of disengaging the starter cables when the Woodard vehicle crushed him, this is a case where the provisions of s. 133 of the *Highway Traffic Act*, R.S.O. 1970, c. 202, must be considered.

Section 133 reads as follows:

133(1) When loss or damage is sustained by any person by reason of a motor vehicle on a highway, the onus of proof that the loss or damage did not arise through the negligence or improper conduct of the owner or driver of the motor vehicle is upon the owner or driver.

(2) This section does not apply in case of a collision between motor vehicles or between motor vehicles and cars of electric or steam railways or other motor vehicles running only on stationary rails on the highway nor to an action brought by a passenger in a motor vehicle in respect of any injuries sustained by him while a passenger.

. . .

This section was enacted in order to overcome difficulties experienced by plaintiffs in obtaining and presenting sufficient evidence of a motorist's negligence to avoid a non-suit at the close of their case. Knowledge of relevant acts and circumstances leading up to an accident might be in the possession only of the defendant and injustice might result if a plaintiff was unable to overcome the initial obstacle of a *prima facie* case and to avoid having his case determined before all the evidence was before the Court. Hence the introduction of a type of statutory *res ipsa loquitur* doctrine under which the owner or driver is *prima facie* liable for damage caused by his motor vehicle unless he satisfied the Court on a preponderance of evidence that he was not in fact negligent.

A plaintiff must therefore show, in order that the section may apply, that his damages were occasioned by the presence of a motor vehicle on the highway.

This does not mean that before the onus begins to operate, the plaintiff must first prove that the effective cause of the collision was the conduct of the driver; he need only show that the collision — not the conduct of the driver — was the cause of the damage. . . .

The plaintiff has satisfied me that the damage to his knee was occasioned by the presence of the defendant Woodard's motor vehicle on the highway. The onus thus begins to operate. But specifically what is the nature of this statutory onus now upon the defendant Woodard?

The leading authority on the interpretation of this section is *Winnipeg Electric Co. v. Geel*, [1932] 4 D.L.R. 51. . . . In the Supreme Court of Canada, Duff, J., stated. . . :

> The statute creates, as against the owners and drivers of motor vehicles . . . a rebuttable presumption of negligence. The onus of disproving negligence remains throughout the proceedings. If, at the conclusion of the evidence, it is too meagre or too evenly balanced to enable the tribunal to determine this issue, as a question of fact, then, by force of the statute, the plaintiff is entitled to succeed.

This statement was approved by the Privy Council where Lord Wright further said . . .:

> But the onus which the section places on the defendant is not in law a shifting or transitory onus: it cannot be displaced merely by the defendant giving some evidence that he was not negligent, if that evidence however credible is not sufficient reasonably to satisfy the jury that he was not negligent: the burden remains on the defendant until the very end of the case, when the question must be determined whether or not the defendant has sufficiently shown that he did not in fact cause the accident by his negligence.

> It is accordingly upon the whole of the evidence submitted at the trial, including all the circumstances and inferences to be drawn therefrom that the defendant must satisfy the jury that the accident was not in fact caused by his negligence. . . . And once the onus is placed on the defendant it will not be discharged unless he satisfied the Court not merely that the damages were in fact sustained without such negligence. . . . Thus, it is not necessary to find any specific act of negligence against the defendant in order that liability may attach to him, and if any doubt remains on a consideration of all the evidence as to whether or not the defendant was negligent, the plaintiff is entitled to the verdict.

> The plaintiff throughout this trial has remained virtually mute concerning the cause of the accident, allowing the defendants to fight it out between themselves. Indeed with his meagre information he is scarcely in a position to do otherwise.

. . .

In light of the extreme confusion of Donald Woodard's own testimony in so many particulars and areas, and his inability personally or through his witnesses, who gave mechanical evidence, to suggest how this automobile, if properly operated, could "leap" or "lurch" forward at the time in question, I am compelled to find that Woodard has failed to satisfy the onus which s. 133(1) has imposed upon him.

NOTES AND QUESTIONS

1. What must the plaintiff establish in order to invoke s. 133 (now R.S.O. 1990, c. H.8, s. 193(1))? Explain the effect of this section on the burden of proof in a negligence action.

2. What must the defendant prove to discharge the burden of proof placed on him or her? See *Angelopoulos v. Machen* (1992), 7 O.R. (3d) 45 (C.A.); and *Senger v. Lachman* (2008), 235 O.A.C. 280 (C.A.).

3. In *A.G. Ont. v. Keller* (1978), 94 D.L.R. (3d) 632 (Ont. C.A.) a police officer was seriously injured when his car went out of control and struck a pole during a high-

speed chase. The fleeing driver knew he was being pursued and was attempting to escape. At no time did the two vehicles collide. The Court of Appeal held that the reverse onus provision applied to the escaping driver. Do you agree? Would the result have been the same if the provision had not been applied? See also *Marks v. Campbell* (1977), 76 D.L.R. (3d) 715 (N.S.S.C.); *De Gurse v. Henry* (1984), 47 O.R. (2d) 172 (H.C.); *Moore v. Fanning* (1987), 60 O.R. (2d) 225 (H.C.); and *Crew v. Nicholson* (1989), 68 O.R. (2d) 232 (C.A.).

4. For a discussion of comparable provisions in other provincial legislation see *Feener v. McKenzie* (1971), 25 D.L.R. (3d) 283 (S.C.C.); *Homer v. Comeau* (1988), 88 N.S.R. (2d) 295 (S.C.); *Hilderman v. Rattray* (1988), 93 A.R. 217 (Q.B.); *Melnychuk v. Moore* (1989), 57 Man. R. (2d) 174 (C.A.); *Doern v. Phillips Estate*, [1995] 4 W.W.R. 1 (B.C.S.C.); *Nice v. John Doe* (2000), 190 D.L.R. (4th) 402 (Alta. C.A.); *Cardinal v. Loo*, [2003] 5 W.W.R. 719 (Alta. Q.B.), varied (2006), 384 A.R. 200 (C.A.); and *Bouchard Estate v. Chalifoux* (2004), 11 M.V.R. (5th) 288 (Alta. Q.B.).

5. Many other statutory provisions shift the burden of proof in negligence cases. See, on the issue of consent to operate a motor vehicle, *Newell v. Towns* (2008), 266 N.S.R. (2d) 202 (S.C.). See, beyond the context of claims in negligence, *Workers Compensation Act*, R.S.B.C. 1996, c. 492, s. 250(4) which provides that an appeal tribunal hearing an appeal about the compensation of a worker in which the evidence supporting different findings on an issue is evenly weighted "must resolve that issue in a manner that favours the worker."

(b) DIRECTLY CAUSED INJURY: UNINTENDED TRESPASS

DAHLBERG v. NAYDIUK
(1969), 10 D.L.R. (3d) 319 (Man. C.A.)

[The defendant fired at a deer, but missed. The bullet carried 250 to 300 yards and struck the plaintiff, who was working on his farm. The defendant had obtained consent to hunt from the owner of the land on which he was situated but he had not sought the plaintiff's permission to fire over, or hunt on, the farm.]

DICKSON, J.A.:

. . .

Trespass or negligence

Mr. Dahlberg's action was framed both in negligence and in trespass. This gives rise to one of those strange anomalies of the law. It is this. If Mr. Dahlberg relies on negligence the onus rests upon him to prove Mr. Naydiuk was negligent. This follows the normal evidentiary rule that he who asserts must prove. However, if Mr. Dahlberg relies upon trespass, (i) Mr. Naydiuk is entitled to judgment only "if he satisfies the onus of establishing the absence of both intention and negligence on his part" [*Cook v. Lewis*, [1952] 1 D.L.R. 1 (S.C.C.)] that is to say the onus rests upon him to disprove negligence, and (ii) the question arises whether such "negligence" means "a negligent (*i.e.,* careless) trespass or something which would give rise to an action on negligence": Street, *The Law of Torts*, 4th ed., p. 14.

As Clyne, J., said in *Walmsley v. Humenick*, [1954] 2 D.L.R. 232 at p. 244:

It seems to be equally curious that since the passing of the Judicature Acts a situation should arise where on the same facts the plaintiffs' action must fail if it is framed in negligence, but might succeed if it is brought in trespass.

Two English cases, decided since *Cook v. Lewis, supra*, might be mentioned. In *Fowler v. Lanning*, [1959] 1 Q.B. 426 . . ., Diplock, J. (as he then was), in the course of a lengthy judgment, held that the onus of proving negligence, where the trespass is not intentional, lies upon the plaintiff, whether the action be framed in trespass or in negligence. Lord Denning, M.R., took the matter one step further in *Letang v. Cooper*, [1964] 2 All E.R. 929 at p. 932:

> If he does not inflict injury intentionally, but only unintentionally, the plaintiff has no cause of action in trespass. His only cause of action is in negligence, and then only on proof of want of reasonable care.

The late Dean C. A. Wright has referred (Linden, *Studies in Canadian Tort Law*, at p. 44) to "this irrational and unnecessary exception of trespass", expressing the hope that some Canadian Court would "put an end to the possibility of a difference in burden of proof depending solely on the direct or indirect application of the force." If such a change is to be made in the law it must be made by a Court higher than this. In the present case we, as we must, reached our decision in accord with the dictates of *Cook v. Lewis, supra*.

Finding

It remains to apply the principles enunciated above to the facts before us.

The Judge found that Mr. Naydiuk failed in his duty to take care, and I agree. He failed to prove he was not negligent. In my view of the matter he was negligent in two respects:

(1) In firing in the direction of farm buildings.

. . .

(2) In failing to obtain permission from Mr. Dahlberg before hunting his land or firing across his land.

. . .

Hunters must recognize that firing over land without permission of the owner constitutes a trespass to land and if injury to person results, trespass to person. A hunter who fires in the direction in which he knows or ought to know farm buildings are located must accept full responsibility for resultant damage to person or property. It is no answer to say he thought the buildings were unoccupied. There are vast areas of western Canada in which deer abound and where no farming activities are carried on. Even in farming areas there are often hills from which one can fire at game in the valley below without risk of injury to others. If a hunter chooses to hunt in a farming area he must do so in full awareness of the paramount right of the farmer to carry on his lawful occupation without risk of injury from stray bullets.

NOTES AND QUESTIONS

1. Did the plaintiff succeed in negligence or in trespass? Given the evidence adduced at trial, was it possible for the plaintiff to succeed in either cause of action? When will it be advantageous for a plaintiff to plead one cause of action rather than the other?

2. Dickson J.A. felt compelled to follow the Supreme Court of Canada's judgment in *Cook v. Lewis*, [1951] S.C.R. 830 on the question of proof of carelessness in the context of an action in trespass. As seen in the following extract, the judgment in *Cook v. Lewis* also addresses the issue of proof of causation. What must a plaintiff establish in order to invoke the rule in *Cook v. Lewis* as it pertains to proof of negligence? If the bullet fired from Naydiuk's gun hit a tree and ricocheted before striking Dahlberg, would that rule have applied?

3. Explain the impact of the rule in *Cook v. Lewis* on the burden of proof. Do you agree with the way in which the rule was applied in *Dahlberg*?

4. Do you agree with Dickson J.A.'s criticism of the rule? If not, can you suggest a rationale for its continued use? See *Bell Canada v. Cope (Sarnia) Ltd.* (1980), 11 C.C.L.T. 170 (Ont. H.C.), aff'd (1981), 119 D.L.R. (3d) 254 (Ont. C.A.). See also Trindade, "The Burden of Proof in Actions for Negligent Trespass in Canada" (1971) 49 Can. Bar Rev. 612; Sharp, "Negligent Trespass in Canada: A Persistent Source of Embarrassment" (1978) 1 Adv. Q. 311; and Sullivan, "Trespass to the Person in Canada: A Defence of the Traditional Approach" (1987) 19 Ottawa L. Rev. 533.

(c) MULTIPLE NEGLIGENT DEFENDANTS

COOK v. LEWIS
[1952] 1 D.L.R. 1 (S.C.C.)

[The plaintiff, Lewis, was hit in the face by bird-shot when the defendants, Cook and Akenhead, fired simultaneously at different birds which had flown in the plaintiff's direction. The jury found that the plaintiff had been shot by one of the two hunters, but was unable to say which one. It also found that the injuries were not caused by the negligence of either. The Court of Appeal set aside the jury's finding on the negligence issue and ordered a new trial. This judgment was upheld by the Supreme Court of Canada.]

RAND J.:—I agree with the Court of Appeal . . . that the finding of the jury exculpating both defendants from negligence was perverse and it is unnecessary to examine the facts on which that conclusion is based.

There remains the answer that, although shots from one of the two guns struck the respondent, the jury could not determine from which they came. This is open to at least four interpretations: first, believing that only one discharge could have inflicted the injuries, they found it difficult to decide which testimony, whether that of Cook or Akenhead, was to be accepted, the evidence of each, taken at its face, excluding guilt; or that the shots from both guns having been fired so nearly at the same time and to have been aimed so nearly at the same target, it was impossible for them to say which struck the eye: or that they were unable to say whether the situation was either of those two alternatives: or finally, that they were not unanimous on any one or more of these views.

It will be seen that there is one feature common to the first three: having found that either A or B had been the cause of injury to C, the jury declare that C has not satisfied them which of the two it was. It is then a problem in proof and must be considered from that standpoint.

. . .

What, then, the culpable actor has done by his initial negligent act is, first, to have set in motion a dangerous force which embraces the injured person within the scope of its probable mischief; and next, in conjunction with circumstances which he must be held to contemplate, to have made more difficult if not impossible the means of proving the possible damaging results of his own act or the similar results of the act of another. He has violated not only the victim's substantive right to security, but he has also culpably impaired the latter's remedial right of establishing liability. By confusing his act with environmental conditions, he has, in effect, destroyed the victim's power of proof.

The legal consequence of that is, I should say, that the onus is then shifted to the wrongdoer to exculpate himself; it becomes in fact a question of proof between him and the other and innocent member of the alternatives, the burden of which he must bear. The onus attaches to culpability, and if both acts bear that taint, the onus or prima facie transmission of responsibility attaches to both, and the question of the sole responsibility of one is a matter between them.

. . .

The risks arising from these sporting activities by increased numbers of participants and diminishing opportunity for their safe exercise, as the facts here indicate, require appropriate refinement in foresight. Against the private and public interests at stake, is the privilege of the individual to engage in a sport not inherently objectionable. As yet, certainly, the community is not ready to assume the burden of such a mishap. The question is whether a victim is to be told that such a risk, not only in substantive right but in remedy, is one he must assume. When we have reached the point where, as here, shots are considered spent at a distance of between 150 feet and 200 feet and the woods are "full" of hunters, a somewhat stringent regard to conduct seems to me to be obvious. It would be a strange commentary on its concern toward personal safety, that the law, although forbidding the victim any other mode of redress, was powerless to accord him any in its own form of relief. I am unable to assent to the view that there is any such helplessness.

. . .

Assuming, then, that the jury have found one or both of the defendants here negligent, as on the evidence I think they must have, and at the same time have found that the consequences of the two shots, whether from a confusion in time or in area, cannot be segregated, the onus on the guilty person arises. This is a case where each hunter would know of or expect the shooting by the other and the negligent actor has culpably participated in the proof-destroying fact, the multiple shooting and its consequences. No liability will, in any event attach to an innocent act of shooting, but the culpable actor, as against innocence, must bear the burden of exculpation.

These views of the law were not as adequately presented to the jury as I think they should have been.

I would, therefore, dismiss the appeal with costs. The motion to quash for want of jurisdiction is dismissed with costs.

The judgment of Estey, Cartwright and Fauteux JJ. was delivered by

CARTWRIGHT J. . . . It is argued, however, that *Summers v. Tice* [33 Cal.2d 80 (S.C. 1948)] should be followed and that under the principles stated in that judgment the jury might properly have found both Akenhead and Cook liable for the plaintiff's injury if in their view of the evidence both of them fired in the direction of the clump of trees in which the plaintiff in fact was, under such circumstances that the conduct of each constituted a breach of duty to the plaintiff. I have not been able to find any case in the courts of this country, or of England in which consideration has been given to certain propositions of law laid down in *Summers v. Tice*. The underlying reason for the decision appears to me to be found in the following quotation from the case of *Oliver v. Miles* [144 Miss. 852 (S.C. 1926)]:

> . . . We think that . . . each is liable for the resulting injury to the boy, although no one can say definitely who actually shot him. To *hold otherwise would be to exonerate both from liability, although each was negligent, and the injury resulted from such negligence.*

The judgment in *Summers v. Tice* reads in part as follows:

> . . . When we consider the relative position of the parties and the results that would flow if plaintiff was required to pin the injury on one of the defendants only, a requirement that the burden of proof on that subject be shifted to defendants becomes manifest. They are both wrongdoers — both negligent toward plaintiff. They brought about a situation where the negligence of one of them injured the plaintiff, hence, it should rest with them each to absolve himself if he can. The injured party has been placed by defendants in the unfair position of pointing to which defendant caused the harm. If one can escape the other may also and plaintiff is remediless. Ordinarily defendants are in a far better position to offer evidence to determine which one caused the injury. This reasoning has recently found favour in this Court.

I do not think it necessary to decide whether all that was said in *Summers v. Tice* should be accepted as stating the law of British Columbia, but I am of opinion, for the reasons given in that case, that if under the circumstances of the case at bar the jury, having decided that the plaintiff was shot by either Cook or Akenhead, found themselves unable to decide which of the two shot him because in their opinion both shot negligently in his direction, both defendants should have been found liable. I think that the learned trial judge should have sent the jury back to consider the matter further with a direction to the above effect. . . .

CLEMENTS v. CLEMENTS
2012 SCC 36

The judgment of McLachlin C.J. and Deschamps, Fish, Abella, Cromwell, Moldaver and Karakatsanis JJ. was delivered by the Chief Justice . . .

[46] The foregoing discussion leads me to the following conclusions as to the present state of the law in Canada:

(1) As a general rule, a plaintiff cannot succeed unless she shows as a matter of fact that she would not have suffered the loss "but for" the negligent act or acts of the defendant. A trial judge is to take a robust and pragmatic approach to

determining if a plaintiff has established that the defendant's negligence caused her loss. Scientific proof of causation is not required.

(2) Exceptionally, a plaintiff may succeed by showing that the defendant's conduct materially contributed to risk of the plaintiff's injury, where (a) the plaintiff has established that her loss would not have occurred "but for" the negligence of two or more tortfeasors, each possibly in fact responsible for the loss; and (b) the plaintiff, through no fault of her own, is unable to show that any one of the possible tortfeasors in fact was the necessary or "but for" cause of her injury, because each can point to one another as the possible "but for" cause of the injury, defeating a finding of causation on a balance of probabilities against anyone.

. . .

NOTES AND QUESTIONS

1. According to Rand J., what must the plaintiff establish to shift the burden of proof regarding causation to the defendants? Is his analysis dependent on there being more than one defendant? What would the defendants have to establish to discharge the burden of proof cast upon them? Answer these same questions based on Cartwright J.'s judgment.

2. In *Joseph Brant Memorial Hospital v. Koziol* (1976), 12 O.R. (2d) 142 (C.A.), aff'd [1978] 1 S.C.R. 491 a nurse's negligence in failing to maintain adequate records made it impossible to determine the exact circumstances surrounding a patient's death. The Court of Appeal for Ontario, quoting from Rand J.'s judgment, held that the burden of disproving causation should be on the nurse. The Supreme Court of Canada rejected this proposition, noting that the "destruction of evidence" rationale had been adopted by only Rand J. and formed no part of the majority judgment. Was Rand J.'s rationale for shifting the burden of proof any less compelling than that of the majority?

3. As in *Koziol, supra*, a patient is often unable to identify the person responsible for a negligent act that occurs during or immediately after surgery. Some courts have aided such plaintiffs by shifting the burden of proof regarding causation to the defendant doctors. For example in *Ybarra v. Spangard*, 154 P.2d 687 (Cal. S.C. 1944) the court inferred negligence against an entire surgical team of doctors and nurses even though only one of them may have caused the plaintiff's injury.

Denning L.J. adopted a similar position in *Roe v. Min. of Health*, [1954] 2 All E.R. 131 (C.A.) at 136-37:

> Each of these plaintiffs is entitled to say to the hospital: "While I was in your hands something has been done to me which has wrecked my life. Please explain how it has come to pass". . . . I do not think that the hospital authorities and Dr. Graham can both avoid giving an explanation by the simple expedient of each throwing responsibility on the other. If an injured person shows that one or other or both of two persons injured him, but cannot say which of them it was, then he is not defeated altogether. He can call on each of them for an explanation.

Denning L.J. did not elaborate and moved away from this position in subsequent cases. Given the majority judgment in *Cook* and the decision in *Koziol*, is Denning

L.J.'s approach likely to be followed in Canada? See the discussion in *Sacks v. Ross*, 2017 ONCA 773 at paras. 123-32; MacKenzie & Wood, "Common-Sense Causation: How a Robust and Pragmatic Application of the 'But-For' Test Can Solve the Circular Causation Problem in Cases of Multiple Contributing Tortfeasors" in Archibald, ed., *Annual Review of Civil Litigation, 2018* (2018) 457.

4. Do the problems of establishing causation in medical malpractice cases warrant the creation of special rules concerning the burden of proof? If so, how would you state these rules? In *Snell v. Farrell* (1990), 72 D.L.R. (4th) 289 (S.C.C.) the court stated that the burden of proof was not immutable and suggested that where the facts were within the defendant's knowledge and not accessible to the plaintiff, the burden of proof may be shifted. See Roth, "Causation and the Burden of Proof: An Age Old Dilemma and a New Age Approach" (1992) 14 Adv. Q. 70.

In *Benhaim v. St-Germain*, 2016 SCC 48, the court rejected using an approach which would trigger a mandatory adverse inference, presumption or shift in the burden of proof. It noted (at para. 68) that "[s]hifting the consequences of causal uncertainty in this manner risks turning defendant professionals into insurers."

5. *Cook v. Lewis* involved a situation in which each of two defendants acted carelessly but only one actually caused the plaintiff's injury. A different approach may be adopted when the potential causal factors include the defendant's carelessness and the plaintiff's carelessness. In *Leaman v. Rea*, [1954] 4 D.L.R. 423 (N.B.C.A.) there was a collision between two cars, both of which had been driving in the middle of a highway. The trial judge dismissed a claim and counterclaim on the basis that he could not determine on a balance of probabilities how the accident had occurred or which party was at fault. However, the New Brunswick Court of Appeal held that both parties were equally to blame and apportioned the damages accordingly. Would it have made any practical difference to the parties if the Court of Appeal had simply dismissed both claims as the trial judge had done?

The *Leaman* approach is applied in limited circumstances. In *Wotta v. Haliburton Oil Well Cementing Co.*, [1955] S.C.R. 377 the Supreme Court of Canada explained *Leaman* as a case in which the facts supported an inference of carelessness against *both* parties. The court further held that *Leaman* was inapplicable to situations in which *either* the defendant *or* the plaintiff was negligently responsible but the facts did not point to one or both parties as being the probable cause of the accident. In that situation, *neither* party is able to recover any damages. See also *Bray v. Palmer*, [1953] 2 All E.R. 1449 (C.A.); *Barton v. Weaver* (1981), 36 N.B.R. (2d) 483 (C.A.); *Host v. Bassett* (1983), 48 A.L.R. 404 (H.C.A.); *Stamp v. R. in Right of Ontario* (1984), 47 O.R. (2d) 214 (C.A.); and *Hogstead (Litigation Guardian of) v. Spiers*, 2013 BCSC 764, aff'd 2013 BCCA 524. Compare on highly similar facts *Martin v. Murray Estate*, 1995 CarswellOnt 2463 (Gen. Div.) (WL Can) where the court was able to identify, from the totality of the evidence, the lane in which the accident occurred.

Consider the following situation. Two cars collide in circumstances in which one driver or the other, but not both, is carelessly responsible for the accident. Both drivers suffer injuries that render them incapable of remembering the events in question. A passenger who was asleep in one of the cars at the time of the accident sues both drivers for the injuries that he or she sustained in the collision. How would a court resolve the issues of carelessness and causation? Would both drivers be held liable to the passenger? Would both actions fail according to the decision in *Wotta*? See *Baker v. Market Harborough; Wallace v. Richards*, [1953] 1 W.L.R. 1472 (C.A.).

6. As discussed in Chapter 16, English and American courts have at times adopted a broader approach to difficulties in proving causation. In *McGhee v. National Coal Board*, [1972] 3 All E.R. 1008 (H.L.) Lord Wilberforce stated that the burden of proving causation should shift from the plaintiff to the defendant if the defendant's negligence materially increased the risk of injury and that very injury befell the plaintiff. Lord Wilberforce limited his analysis to cases in which it was impossible to determine the cause of the plaintiff's loss and "policy and justice" warranted imposing liability on the defendant as the creator of a risk. In reaching his conclusion, Lord Wilberforce emphasized that this was an industrial disease case involving an employee's claim against his employer. The other members of the court did not accept Lord Wilberforce's suggestion that the burden of proof should be shifted. However, they did find for the plaintiff on the basis that carelessness that materially increases the risk of injury can be taken to have caused or materially contributed to the occurrence of actual injuries that fall within the scope of risk, thereby discharging the plaintiff's burden.

As explained in Chapter 16, *McGhee*'s legacy continues to evolve. In *Wilsher v. Essex Area Health Authority*, [1988] A.C. 1074 (H.L.) Lord Bridge "re-interpreted" *McGhee* to simply mean that, in certain circumstances, the court may take a robust and pragmatic approach to drawing an inference of causation. Likewise, in *Snell v. Farrell, supra*, which appears in Chapter 16, the court reiterated that the plaintiff bears the legal burden of proving causation on a balance of probabilities and held that evidence of conduct that materially increased the risk of injury does not *per se* constitute sufficient proof. However, it also stressed that questions of causation should be resolved on the basis of common sense and recognized that where the facts are particularly within the knowledge of one party, an inference of causation may be drawn on the basis of very little evidence. See Pardy, "Risk, Cause and Toxic Torts: A Theory for a Standard of Proof" (1989) 10 Adv. Q. 277; Fleming, "Probabilistic Causation in Tort Law" (1989) 68 Can. Bar Rev. 661; Fleming, "Probabilistic Causation in Tort Law: A Postscript" (1991) 70 Can. Bar Rev. 136; Yap, "Indeterminate Causes of Personal Injuries and Probabilistic Risk-Based Assessments" (2009) 17 Tort L. Rev. 175; and Jones, "Reasoning Through Probabilistic Causation in Individual and Aggregate Claims: The Struggle Continues" (2011) 39 Adv. Q. 18.

The House of Lords revisited the issue again in *Fairchild v. Glenhaven Funeral Services Ltd.*, [2002] 3 W.L.R. 89 (H.L.). That decision is explained in Chapter 16. While continuing to reject Lord Wilberforce's theory of a reversed burden of proof, it endorsed Lord Reid's suggestion in *McGhee* that there "is no substantial difference between saying that what the [defendants] did materially increased the risk of injury to the [plaintiff] and that what [they] did made a material contribution to his injury." In *Fairchild*, the House of Lords read that statement to mean that "a breach of duty which materially increased the risk should be treated as if it had materially contributed to the disease." See Weir, "Making It More Likely v. Making It Happen" [2002] C.L.J. 519; Stapleton, "'Lords a Leaping' Evidentiary Gaps" (2002) 10 Torts L.J. 276; Woods, "Establishing Causation in Negligence: The House of Lords Speaks Again" (2003) 26 Adv. Q. 471; Stapleton, "Cause-in-Fact and the Scope of Liability for Consequences" (2003) 119 L.Q.R. 388; Morgan, "Lost Causes in the House of Lords:

Fairchild v. Glenhaven Funeral Services" (2003) 66 Mod. L. Rev. 277; Kramer, "Smoothing the Rough Justice of the Fairchild Principle" (2006) 122 L.Q.R. 547; Stapleton, "Mesothelioma and Risk Aired in the Court of Appeal" [2010] C.L.J. 10; and Klar & Jefferies, *Tort Law*, 6th ed. (2017) at 535-39. See also Laleng, "*Sienkiewicz v Greif (UK) Ltd* and *Willmore v Knowsley Metropolitan Borough Council*: A Material Contribution to Uncertainty?" (2011) 74 M.L.R. 777; and Wellington, "Beyond Single Causative Agents: The Scope of the *Fairchild* Exception Post-*Sienkiewicz*" (2013) 20 Torts L.J. 208.

Courts in the United Kingdom "continue to grapple with the consequences of departing from the 'but for' test of causation in order to provide a remedy to those who have contracted mesothelioma as a result of wrongful exposure to asbestos fibres": *Zurich Insurance PLC UK Branch v. International Energy Group Ltd.*, [2015] UKSC 33. In that case two of the judges (at para. 191) described the approach from *Fairchild* as "a sort of juridical version of chaos theory."

7. The issues posed by cases like *McGhee*, *Wilsher*, *Snell* and *Fairchild* are becoming more important. Advances in the medical sciences now make it possible to prove that exposure to toxic chemicals, radiation and other substances may have serious long-term consequences that do not manifest themselves for 20 or 30 years. By the time the plaintiff becomes ill or disabled, he or she may not be able to isolate the impact of this exposure from other possible risk factors. The plaintiff's evidence may take the form of extrapolations from animal studies, epidemiological data and other statistical information. In the past, such evidence was often dismissed as being "speculative." The more recent cases, however, while somewhat inconsistent in approach, indicate greater judicial willingness to overcome evidentiary hurdles, at least in cases where the nature of the defendant's conduct makes it difficult to prove causation. See also *Holtby v. Brigham & Cowan (Hull) Ltd.*, [2000] 3 All E.R. 421 (C.A.). See generally Mulcahy, "Proving Causation in Toxic Tort Litigation" (1983) 11 Hofstra L. Rev. 1299; Brennan, "Causal Chains and Statistical Links" (1989) 73 Cornell L. Rev. 469; and McIvor, "The 'Doubles the Risk' Test for Causation and Other Related Judicial Misconceptions about Epidemiology" in Pitel, Neyers & Chamberlain, eds., *Tort Law: Challenging Orthodoxy* (2013) 215. For a recent decision discussing epidemiology at some length see *Wise v. Abbott Laboratories Ltd.*, 2016 ONSC 7275.

8. In *Sindell v. Abbott Laboratories*, 607 P.2d 924 (Cal. S.C. 1980) the plaintiff was a cancer victim whose mother had taken diethylstilbestrol (DES) during pregnancy. DES was manufactured by approximately 200 pharmaceutical companies but there were no significant differences in the product between manufacturers. The drug had been prescribed to prevent miscarriages but eventually proved ineffective and was found to pose a risk of causing a particular kind of cancer in female children. This cancer was deadly once it manifested itself, but it had a minimum latency period of 10 to 12 years. The plaintiff could prove that her cancer was caused by DES, but she could not establish which company had produced the DES that her mother had taken. The plaintiff sued all of the major manufacturers, arguing that they had been negligent in continuing to market DES when they knew or ought to have known that it was ineffective and carcinogenic. The court found the defendants negligent and held each liable in proportion to its share of the DES market unless it could prove that it had not produced the DES that caused the plaintiff's cancer. The court acknowledged that

there was a 10% chance that the DES in question had been manufactured by one of the approximately 195 smaller producers which had not been sued.

Would the plaintiff have been able to prove causation based on the general principles governing proof in a negligence action? Would the plaintiff have been able to prove causation based on the multiple negligent defendants rule in *Cook v. Lewis*? In *Clements*? Do you agree with the result on the causation issue in *Sindell*? Can you derive a general principle from *Sindell* to deal with similar causation cases? Could this approach be used to establish causation in tobacco litigation?

9. What would have been the result of applying the established principles of apportionment to the defendants in *Sindell*? Do you agree with the court's resolution of the apportionment issue? What changes would have to be made in the apportionment legislation to accommodate the approach in *Sindell*? See Delgado, "Beyond Sindell: Relaxation of Cause-In-Fact Rules for Indeterminate Plaintiffs" (1982) 70 Cal. L. Rev. 880; Black, "Epidemiological Proof in Toxic Tort Litigation" (1984) 52 Fordham L. Rev. 732; Legum, "Increased Risk of Cancer as an Actionable Injury" (1984) 18 Ga. L. Rev. 563; Farber, "Toxic Causation" (1987) 71 Minn. L. Rev. 1219; Goldberg, "Fungible? New Uses for Sindell" (1992) 78 A.B.A.J. 73; Wiechmann, "Standard of Proof for Increased Risk of Disease or Injury" (1994) 61 Defence Counsel J. 59; Laleng, "Causal Responsibility for Uncertainty and Risk in Toxic Torts" (2010) 18 Tort L. Rev. 102; Collins & McLeod-Kilmurray, "Material Contribution to Justice? Toxic Causation after *Resurfice Corp. v. Hanke*" (2010) 48 O.H.L.J. 411; and Goldberg, "Epidemiological Uncertainty, Causation, and Drug Product Liability" (2014) 59 McGill L.J. 777.

10. By way of review, state the manner in which the courts addressed the issue of proof of causation in each of the following cases: (i) *Cook v. Lewis*, (ii) Lord Wilberforce's judgment in *McGhee*, (iii) Lord Reid's judgment in *McGhee*, (iv) *Wilsher*, (v) *Snell*, (vi) *Fairchild*, (vii) *Sindell* and (viii) *Leaman v. Rea*. How do those various approaches relate to the but-for test of causation?

11. *Clements*, discussed in detail in Chapter 16, was not a case about multiple negligent defendants. However, in its review of the law on causation the Supreme Court of Canada discussed *Cook v. Lewis* under the heading "The Material Contribution to Risk Approach" and in summarizing the law (in the extract above) the court (in para. 46(2)) combines aspects of material contribution to risk and the multiple negligent defendants rule. Yet is arguable that the multiple negligent defendants rule formulated in *Cook v. Lewis* is something quite different from the concept of material contribution to risk. Recall that in *McGhee*, a key case on material contribution to risk, there was only one potential tortfeasor (the plaintiff's employer).

Has *Clements* changed the law on cases involving multiple negligent defendants? Has it changed the law on material contribution to risk? You may need to consider material from Chapter 16 to fully answer these questions.

Few (if any) recent Canadian tort law decisions have spawned as much scholarship as *Clements*. See Chaudhury, "Causation in the Law of Negligence: Where Are We Now? Where Are We Going? *Clements v. Clements*; *Ediger v. Johnston*" (2012) 40 Adv. Q. 257; Cheifetz, "Causation in Negligence: Material Contribution and But-For after *Clements*" (2012) 40 Adv. Q. 275; Brewer, "The End of Material Contribution to Injury: *Clements v. Clements*" (2013) 42 Adv. Q. 217; Cheifetz,

"Factual Causation in Negligence After *Clements*" (2013) 41 Adv. Q. 179; Knutsen, "Coping with Complex Causation Information in Personal Injury Cases" (2013) 41 Adv. Q. 149; Brown, "Cause-in-Fact at the Supreme Court of Canada: Developments in Tort Law in 2012-2013" (2014) 64 S.C.L.R. (2d) 327; Mangan, "Confusion in Material Contribution" (2014) 91 Can. Bar Rev. 701; Weinrib, "Causal Uncertainty" (2016) 36 O.J.L.S. 135; Hutchinson, "Out of the Black Hole: Toward a Fresh Approach to Tort Causation" (2016) 39 Dal. L.J. 561; and Black, "The Rise and Fall of Plaintiff-Friendly Causation" (2016) 53 Alta. L. Rev. 1013.

12. Independently of each other and at precisely the same time A, B and C carelessly lean against a car. Their combined force causes the car to roll forward and over a cliff. Each of A, B and C exerted the same amount of force. The force of any two of A, B and C would have been sufficient to cause the car to roll as it did, but the force of any one of them would not have been. Has C caused the damage the car sustained when it crashed at the bottom of the cliff? See American Law Institute, *Restatement (Third) of the Law of Torts: Liability for Physical and Emotional Harm* (2010) at §27 comment (f); and Stapleton, "Unnecessary Causes" (2013) 129 L.Q.R. 39.

13. As discussed in Chapter 16, deviations from the but-for test raise issues about the underlying theories of tort law. But-for causation is central to a corrective justice or rights-based approach to tort law. Proponents of those theories therefore need to explain why it is appropriate to deviate from that test in certain situations. See for example Botterell & Essert, "Normativity, Fairness, and the Problem of Factual Uncertainty" (2009) 47 O.H.L.J. 663; and Steel, "Justifying Exceptions to Proof of Causation in Tort Law" (2015) 78 M.L.R. 729.

14. A plaintiff may find it difficult to adduce proof on the balance of probabilities because the defendant intentionally destroyed evidence. Such destruction is referred to as spoliation. The orthodox approach is for courts to address spoliation, when it is made out, through various procedural and evidentiary rules. For example, the court can invoke a rebuttable presumption that the destroyed evidence was unfavorable to the party who destroyed it: *St. Louis v. R.* (1895), 25 S.C.R. 649; *Robb Estate v. St. Joseph's Health Care Centre* (1998), 43 C.C.L.T. (2d) 296 (Ont. Div. Ct.); and *Endean v. Canadian Red Cross Society* (1998), 157 D.L.R. (4th) 465 (B.C.C.A.). See Jones, "The Spoliation Doctrine and Expert Evidence in Civil Trials" (1998) 32 U.B.C.L. Rev. 293; Wilhoit, "Spoliation of Evidence: The Viability of Four Emerging Torts" (1998) 46 U.C.L.A.L. Rev. 631; and Sommers & Siebert, "Intentional Destruction of Evidence: Why Procedural Remedies are Insufficient" (1999) 78 Can. Bar Rev. 38.

It has also been suggested that spoliation could constitute an independent tort: see for example *Spasic Estate v. Imperial Tobacco Ltd.* (2000), 188 D.L.R. (4th) 577 (Ont. C.A.); *Robb Estate v. Canadian Red Cross Society* (2001), 152 O.A.C. 60 (C.A.); *Cheung (Litigation Guardian of) v. Toyota Canada Inc.* (2003), 29 C.P.C. (5th) 267 (Ont. S.C.J.). The most recent cases continue to leave this question open: *McDougall v. Black & Decker Canada Inc.*, 2008 ABCA 353; *Wight v. Pickering Automobiles Inc.*, 2011 ONSC 7602; and *Chow-Hidasi v. Hidasi*, 2013 BCCA 73. For Australia see Witzleb, "Spoliation of Evidence — A New Tort for Australia?" (2003) 11 Tort L. Rev. 135.

One of the arguments in favour of treating spoliation as a tort is that this would provide the court with a wider array of remedies with which to assist the innocent party. Do you agree? Should spoliation require intentional destruction of evidence or should careless destruction suffice?

3. *Res Ipsa Loquitur*

In some cases, the plaintiff must rely on circumstantial evidence to prove that the defendant injured him or her. The term "circumstantial evidence" is used to refer to evidence from which an inference may be drawn to reach a conclusion. For example, Carol's testimony that she saw Bob shoot Carl is direct evidence that Bob shot Carl. However, Carol's testimony that she found Bob's fingerprints on the murder weapon is circumstantial evidence. It provides a step in the process of logical inference.

Traditionally, Canadian courts used the Latin maxim *res ipsa loquitur* ("the thing speaks for itself") to describe the circumstances in which the occurrence of an accident provided circumstantial evidence that the plaintiff's injury was caused by the defendant's carelessness. For example, in the classic case of *Byrne v. Boadle* (1863), 159 E.R. 299 (Ex.) the plaintiff was walking on a sidewalk when he was struck by a barrel of flour that had fallen from a window of the defendant's warehouse. The court applied the maxim *res ipsa loquitur* to infer that the barrel fell as a result of the defendant's carelessness. In subsequent cases, the maxim was said to consist of the following elements. First, the occurrence must have been one that does not, in the ordinary course of events, happen without carelessness. Otherwise, it would not be possible to draw an inference of *carelessness* against the defendant. Second, the instrumentality of harm must have been under the sole management and control of the defendant or someone for whom the defendant was responsible. Otherwise, it would not be possible to draw an inference of carelessness against the *defendant* as opposed to someone else. Third, there must not have been any direct evidence as to how or why the accident occurred. Otherwise, the court would resolve the legal issues on the basis of that evidence rather than the inferences supported by *res ipsa loquitur*. See *Scott v. London and St. Katherine Docks Co.* (1865), 159 E.R. 665; *Hellenius v. Lees*, [1972] S.C.R. 165; and *Jackson v. Millar*, [1976] 1 S.C.R. 225.

One of the most difficult issues pertaining to *res ipsa loquitur* concerned its effect. There were at least three views. The first approach, which was favoured historically, held that successful invocation of the maxim reversed the legal burden of proof such that the defendant was required to prove on a balance of probabilities that his or her carelessness did not cause the plaintiff's injury. See *Barkway v. South Wales Transport Co.*, [1948] 2 All E.R. 460 (per Lord Asquith); and *Bartlett v. Children's Hospital Corp.* (1983), 40 Nfld. & P.E.I.R. 88 (Nfld. C.A.). The second, more conservative approach held that while successful invocation of the maxim did not reverse the legal burden of proof, it did require the defendant to adduce evidence that was sufficient to raise an inference of proper care that was at least as strong as the inference of negligence that had been raised by the plaintiff. See *Erison v. Higgins* (1974), 4 O.R. (2d) 631 (C.A.); and *Ng Chun Pui v. Lee Chuen Tat*, [1988] R.T.R. 298 (P.C.). The third and most conservative approach held that successful invocation of the maxim merely provided a basis upon which *some* inference of negligence *might* be drawn. On that view, the trier of fact was entitled, but not required, to draw an inference. Moreover, if an inference was drawn, it might or might not be sufficient to tip the balance of probabilities in the plaintiff's favour. For that reason, even if the maxim was applied, the defendant might avoid liability without even attempting to rebut the plaintiff's inference. See *Easson v.*

L.N.E. Rwy. Co., [1944] K.B. 421 (per Du Parq L.J.); and *Widdowson v. Newgate Meat Corp.*, (1997), [1998] P.I.Q.R. P138 (C.A.).

In Canada, the existence and effect of the maxim was clarified in the following case.

FONTAINE v. BRITISH COLUMBIA (OFFICIAL ADMINISTRATOR)
(1997), 156 D.L.R. (4th) 577 (S.C.C.)

[Edwin Fontaine and Larry Loewen went missing during a weekend hunting trip. Three months later their truck was discovered in a river bed at the bottom of a steep embankment. Loewen's body was buckled behind the steering wheel and Fontaine's body was in the passenger seat. There was no direct evidence regarding the events that resulted in their deaths. The circumstantial evidence indicated that that area had been subject to torrential rain on the weekend when they were presumed to have died. A police officer's report also indicated that there was a swale, or dip, in the road where their truck was believed to have left the road. Finally, the physical evidence revealed that the truck left the road with sufficient speed to cut a path through a patch of small trees.

Fontaine's widow brought an action with respect to her husband's death and sought to prove her claim on the basis of the doctrine of *res ipsa loquitur*. She argued that the mere occurrence of the accident sufficiently established that her husband's death was attributable to Loewen's carelessness. The trial judge disagreed on the basis that the widow had not shown that, in the ordinary course of events, the accident would not have occurred without negligence by the driver. The British Columbia Court of Appeal agreed and the widow brought a further appeal to the Supreme Court of Canada.]

MAJOR J.—This appeal provides another opportunity to consider the so-called maxim of *res ipsa loquitur*. What is it? When does it arise? And what effect does its application have?

. . .

Analysis

A. *When does res ipsa loquitur apply?*

[Major J. set out the traditional rules governing the applicability of the maxim.]

. . .

For *res ipsa loquitur* to arise, the circumstances of the occurrence must permit an inference of negligence attributable to the defendant. The strength or weakness of that inference will depend on the factual circumstances of the case. As described in *Canadian Tort Law* (5th ed. 1993), by Allen M. Linden, at p. 233, "[t]here are situations where the facts merely whisper negligence, but there are other circumstances where they shout it aloud."

As the application of *res ipsa loquitur* is highly dependent upon the circumstances proved in evidence, it is not possible to identify in advance the types of situations in which *res ipsa loquitur* will arise. The application of *res ipsa loquitur* in previous decisions may provide some guidance as to when an inference of negligence may be drawn, but it does not serve to establish definitive categories of when *res ipsa loquitur* will apply. It has been held on numerous occasions that evidence of a vehicle leaving the roadway gives rise to an inference of negligence. Whether that will be so in any given case, however, can only be determined after considering the relevant circumstances of the particular case.

B. *Effect of the application of res ipsa loquitur*

As in any negligence case, the plaintiff bears the burden of proving on a balance of probabilities that negligence on the part of the defendant caused the plaintiff's injuries. The invocation of *res ipsa loquitur* does not shift the burden of proof to the defendant. Rather, the effect of the application of *res ipsa loquitur* is as described in *The Law of Evidence in Canada* (1992), by John Sopinka, Sidney N. Lederman and Alan W. Bryant, at p. 81:

> Res ipsa loquitur, correctly understood, means that circumstantial evidence constitutes reasonable evidence of negligence. Accordingly, the plaintiff is able to overcome a motion for a non-suit and the trial judge is required to instruct the jury on the issue of negligence. The jury may, but need not, find negligence: a permissible fact inference. If, at the conclusion of the case, it would be equally reasonable to infer negligence or no negligence, the plaintiff will lose since he or she bears the legal burden on this issue. Under this construction, the maxim is superfluous. It can be treated simply as a case of circumstantial evidence.

Should the trier of fact choose to draw an inference of negligence from the circumstances, that will be a factor in the plaintiff's favour. Whether that will be sufficient for the plaintiff to succeed will depend on the strength of the inference drawn and any explanation offered by the defendant to negate that inference. If the defendant produces a reasonable explanation that is as consistent with no negligence as the *res ipsa loquitur* inference is with negligence, this will effectively neutralize the inference of negligence and the plaintiff's case must fail. Thus, the strength of the explanation that the defendant must provide will vary in accordance with the strength of the inference sought to be drawn by the plaintiff.

The procedural effect of *res ipsa loquitur* was lucidly described by Cecil A. Wright in "Res Ipsa Loquitur" (*Special Lectures of the Law Society of Upper Canada (1955), Evidence*, pp. 103-36), and more recently summarized by Klar in *Tort Law*, [2d ed. (1996)] at pp. 423-24:

> If the plaintiff has no direct or positive evidence which can explain the occurrence and prove that the defendant was negligent, appropriate circumstantial evidence, as defined by the maxim *res ipsa loquitur*, may be introduced. Should the defendant, at this stage of the proceeding, move for a nonsuit, on the basis that the plaintiff's evidence has not even made out a *prima facie* case for it to answer, the practical effect of the maxim will come into play. The court will be required to judge whether a reasonable trier of fact could, from the evidence introduced, find an inference of the defendant's negligence. That is, could a reasonable jury find that on these facts the maxim *res ipsa loquitur* applies? If it could so find, the motion for a nonsuit must be dismissed. If such an inference could not reasonably be made, the motion must be granted. In other words, the maxim, at the least, will get the plaintiff past a nonsuit.
>
> This, however, does not end the matter. What, if anything, must the defendant do at this point? In theory, where the case is being tried by a judge and jury, the defendant still need not do anything. Although the judge has decided that as a matter of law it would not be an error for the trier of fact to find for the plaintiff on the basis of the circumstantial evidence which has been introduced, it is still up to the jury to decide

whether it has been sufficiently persuaded by such evidence. In other words, the judge has decided that as a matter of law, the maxim can apply. Whether as a question of fact it does, is up to the jury. The jury may decide, therefore, that even despite the defendant's failure to call evidence, the circumstantial evidence ought not to be given sufficient weight to discharge the plaintiff's onus. Thus, even if a defendant has decided not to introduce evidence, a trial judge should not, in an action tried by judge and jury, either take the case from the jury and enter judgment for the plaintiff, or direct the jury to return a verdict in favour of the plaintiff. It is up to the trial judge to determine whether the maxim can apply, but up to the jury to decide whether it does apply.

Whatever value *res ipsa loquitur* may have once provided is gone. Various attempts to apply the so-called doctrine have been more confusing than helpful. Its use has been restricted to cases where the facts permitted an inference of negligence and there was no other reasonable explanation for the accident. Given its limited use it is somewhat meaningless to refer to that use as a doctrine of law.

It would appear that the law would be better served if the maxim was treated as expired and no longer used as a separate component in negligence actions. After all, it was nothing more than an attempt to deal with circumstantial evidence. That evidence is more sensibly dealt with by the trier of fact, who should weigh the circumstantial evidence with the direct evidence, if any, to determine whether the plaintiff has established on a balance of probabilities a *prima facie* case of negligence against the defendant. Once the plaintiff has done so, the defendant must present evidence negating that of the plaintiff or necessarily the plaintiff will succeed.

C. *Application to this case*

In this appeal, the trial judge had to consider whether there was direct evidence from which the cause of the accident could be determined, or, failing that, whether there was circumstantial evidence from which it could be inferred that the accident was caused by negligence attributable to Loewen.

The trial judge found that the only potential evidence of negligence on Loewen's part concerned the fact that the vehicle left the roadway and was travelling with sufficient momentum to break a path through some small trees. She concluded that, when taken together with other evidence concerning the road and weather conditions, this was no more than neutral evidence and did not point to any negligence on Loewen's part. That conclusion was not unreasonable in light of the evidence, which at most established that the vehicle was moving in a forward direction at the time of the accident, with no indication that it was travelling at an excessive rate of speed.

. . .

There are a number of reasons why the circumstantial evidence in this case does not discharge the plaintiff's onus. Many of the circumstances of the accident, including the date, time and precise location, are not known. Although this case has proceeded on the basis that the accident likely occurred during the weekend of November 9, 1990, that is only an assumption. There are minimal if any evidentiary foundations from which any inference of negligence could be drawn.

As well, there was evidence before the trial judge that a severe wind and rainstorm was raging at the presumed time of the accident. While it is true that such weather conditions impose a higher standard of care on drivers to take increased precautions, human experience confirms that severe weather conditions are more likely to produce situations where accidents occur and vehicles leave the roadway regardless of the degree of care taken. In these circumstances, it should not be concluded that the accident would ordinarily not have occurred in the absence of negligence.

If an inference of negligence might be drawn in these circumstances, it would be modest. The trial judge found that the defence had succeeded in producing alternative explanations of how the accident may have occurred without negligence on Loewen's part. Most of the explanations offered by the defendants were grounded in the evidence and were adequate to neutralize whatever inference the circumstantial evidence could permit to be drawn. The trial judge's finding was not unreasonable and should not be interfered with on appeal.

. . .

The appellant submitted that an inference of negligence should be drawn whenever a vehicle leaves the roadway in a single-vehicle accident. This bald proposition ignores the fact that whether an inference of negligence can be drawn is highly dependent upon the circumstances of each case: see *Gauthier & Co.* [[1945] S.C.R. 143 at 150]. The position advanced by the appellant would virtually subject the defendant to strict liability in cases such as the present one.

[The appeal was dismissed and the widow's claim was denied.]

NOTES AND QUESTIONS

1. Major J. stated the maxim of *res ipsa loquitur* should be treated as "expired." Has the law been changed in any substantive sense? Consider *Robb Estate v. Canadian Red Cross Society* (2001), 9 C.C.L.T. (3d) 131 (Ont. C.A.); *Hundley v. Punnett* (2003), 15 C.C.L.T. (3d) 215 (B.C.S.C.); *Newfoundland Light and Power Co. v. Furlong Estate* (2005), 247 Nfld. & P.E.I.R. 65 (N.L.C.A.); *Nason v. Nunes* (2008), 82 B.C.L.R. (4th) 1 (C.A.); and *Johansson v. General Motors of Canada Ltd.*, 2012 NSCA 120 at para. 65. See also Fridman *et al.*, *The Law of Torts in Canada*, 3d ed. (2010) at 384-96.

2. If the plaintiff adduces evidence that is sufficient to raise a presumption of negligence against the defendant, what, if anything, must the defendant do to avoid liability? On the traditional approach, if the maxim was invoked, was it ever possible for the defendant to win despite failing to present any evidence at all? Has the answer been changed by *Fontaine*?

3. In *Singleton v. Morris* (2010), 1 B.C.L.R. (5th) 303 (C.A.) the plaintiff's vehicle was stopped at a stop sign when it was hit from behind by the defendant's vehicle. The court held that the fact that this was a rear-end collision allowed the court to infer that the defendant had been negligent. Accordingly, the plaintiff had established a *prima facie* case. However, the defendant presented evidence that there was an oily substance on the road's surface. The court held that this was sufficient to rebut the inference and the plaintiff's claim failed for lack of proof of negligence. The defendant's explanation was "adequate to neutralize whatever inference the circumstantial evidence could permit to be drawn." See for another example *Chow-Hidasi v. Hidasi*, 2013 BCCA 73.

Similarly, in *Iannarella v. Corbett*, 2015 ONCA 110 the court explained that in a rear-end collision the onus is on the driver of the rear car to show that the collision was not the result of his or her carelessness, and in *McDonald v. Doe*, 2015 ONSC 2607 at para. 24 the court stated that "the fact of spinning out of control . . . calls out for an explanation failing which negligence is the evident assumption" and shifted the burden of proof to the defendant.

In *El Dali v Panjalingam*, 2013 ONCA 24 the court held that *Fontaine* was not inconsistent with its decisions holding that in vehicle collision cases a plaintiff who shows that the defendant driver crossed the centre line has established a *prima facie* case of negligence. The defendant then bears the onus of explaining that the collision could not have been avoided by the exercise of reasonable care.

Do these approaches amount to more than the permissible drawing of an inference? Are they different from *res ipsa loquitur*?

4. Regardless of the technical effect of *Fontaine*, will Major J.'s decision lead lower courts to be more or less inclined to draw inferences on the basis of circumstantial evidence? Are there any reasons to lament the expiry of *res ipsa loquitur?*

5. *Res ipsa loquitur* has long been criticized by Canadian commentators and its expiry has been applauded: *M. v. Sinclair* (1980), 15 C.C.L.T. 57 (Ont. H.C.J.); McInnes, "The Death of *Res Ipsa Loquitur* in Canada" (1998) 114 L.Q.R. 547; and Lederman, Bryant & Fuerst, *The Law of Evidence in Canada*, 5th ed. (2018) at 120 and 148. For further criticism of the doctrine see Beever, *Rediscovering the Law of Negligence* (2007) at 447-53.

6. The High Court of Australia refused to abolish *res ipsa loquitur. Schellenberg v. Tunnel Holdings Pty. Ltd.* (2000), 200 C.L.R. 121 (H.C.A.). See McInnes, "Res Ipsa Loquitur in the High Court of Australia: A Missed Opportunity" (2000) 8 Tort L. Rev. 162. See also Witting, "*Res Ipsa Loquitur*: Some Last Words?" (2001) 117 L.Q.R. 392. For a more recent decision of the Judicial Committee of the Privy Council applying *res ispa loquitur* see *George v. Eagle Air Services Ltd.*, [2009] UKPC 21, discussed in Williams, "*Res Ipsa Loquitur* Still Speaks" (2009) 125 L.Q.R. 567.

7. In *Mustapha v. Culligan of Canada Ltd.* (2005), 32 C.C.L.T. (3d) 123 (Ont. S.C.J.), rev'd on other grounds (2006), 84 O.R. (3d) 457 (C.A.), rev'd on other grounds [2008] 2 S.C.R. 114 the plaintiff became ill on seeing a dead fly in a sealed bottle of water. The trial judge stated "where an injurious substance is in the product when it left the manufacturer, there is a presumption of negligence on the part of the manufacturer and a burden upon him to disprove negligence to the satisfaction of the jury. Here that presumption would exist, it was not disproved, and, in fact, the manager indicated that it would be possible for a fly to get into one of the bottles." Can you reconcile this reasoning with the abolition of *res ipsa loquitur*?

8. Benny and Bjorn, who are both smokers, stay in a room at the Wanderers' Inn. They have no guests during the evening. During the evening a fire starts in their room, caused by careless smoking, which seriously damages the Inn and kills Benny and Bjorn. The Inn wants to sue their estates for the damage. Could it prove negligence using the principle of *res ipsa loquitur* or otherwise?

9. In *Visanji v. Eaton* (2006), 39 C.C.L.T. (3d) 150 (B.C.S.C.) the plaintiff slipped and fell on a wet bus floor. As noted in Chapter 15, historically common carriers, like the bus company, were held to a high standard of care: *Day v. Toronto Transportation Commission*, [1940] S.C.R. 433. This sometimes involved shifting the onus of proof on

the standard of care issue to the defendant. In light of the decision in *Fontaine*, the court in *Visanji* stated (at 157) that "Whether the burden upon a public carrier in cases of injury or accident sustained by a passenger can be referred to as the shifting of the burden as in *Day*, or a matter of inferences to be drawn from the evidence once the plaintiff has established a *prima facie* case of negligence against the defendant carrier as articulated in *Fontaine*, it is for the defendant to present evidence to answer, or be found negligent." See also *Nice v. Calgary (City)* (2000), 83 Alta. L.R. (3d) 1 (C.A.).

These decisions seem to leave open a shift in the onus of proof. However in *Benavides v. Insurance Corp. of British Columbia*, 2017 BCCA 15 the court held that "*Fontaine* has clearly overtaken *Day*" (para. 14) and that the fact that a passenger is injured on a public carrier does not, without more, shift the onus of disproving negligence to the defendant. This approach was applied in *Seyom v. Toronto Transit Commission*, 2018 ONSC 6848 at paras. 9-10.

REVIEW PROBLEMS

Analyze the following situations and discuss the burden of proof. Does the abolition of *res ipsa loquitur* affect your answers?

(a) Ann went to a race track to photograph racing cars. She found a secluded spot near a sharp curve. As she was photographing one car, she was hit from behind by another car that had left the track and travelled 100 metres. She regained consciousness in the hospital and remembered nothing about the accident. She has sought your legal advice about suing the driver of the car.

(b) Bill set out from his farm at 8 a.m. An hour later, Bill's body was found in a ditch beside his overturned jeep. The road was flat and straight and the weather was warm and sunny. There were no skid marks, but there were signs that the car had veered off the highway and onto the gravel shoulder twice, before finally leaving the road and overturning in the ditch. A mechanical check of the jeep revealed that all four bolts in the steering mechanism were sheared off. A month earlier, a mechanic had replaced the bolts. Bill's wife has contacted you about suing the mechanic. You have found an expert witness who is willing to testify that the bolts could be sheared off in such a manner if they had been tightened improperly.

(c) Mr. James had surgery performed by Dr. Reed and Dr. Lang. Dr. Reed, who performed the first part of the operation, took longer than anticipated. In order to make up this lost time, the second surgeon, Dr. Lang, took several shortcuts. Both doctors left the operating room several times to consult with lab technicians and radiologists. During these periods, surgical assistants, operating nurses and medical students explored the incision. When the operation was finished, a nurse indicated that all of the sponges were accounted for. Dr. Lang then closed the incision. Mr. James died two days later because a sponge had been left in his abdomen. What legal recourse does the James family have?

(d) Becky has an oil furnace in the basement of her house. It has been regularly serviced by HeatCo for the past eight years. Becky never services, or even touches, the furnace. One week after being serviced the furnace exploded and Becky's house was severely damaged. If it is impossible to determine why the furnace exploded, can Becky sue HeatCo in negligence?

21

THE TORT LIABILITY OF PUBLIC AUTHORITIES

1. Introduction
2. Special Rules for Public Authorities
3. The Negligence Liability of Public Authorities
4. Misfeasance in a Public Office
5. Other Torts

1. Introduction

In the previous chapter, we completed our basic examination of the cause of action in negligence. Before entirely leaving that tort, however, it is necessary to consider various other situations in which the negligence principle plays a significant role, either directly or indirectly. This and the next two chapters therefore address the tort liability of public authorities (Chapter 21), statutory provisions and tort liability (Chapter 22) and occupiers' liability (Chapter 23).

We begin with the tort liability of public authorities. Although most tort actions involve private actors, claims increasingly are being brought against public officials. That is hardly surprising. Government intervention has reached the point where the typical citizen's day-to-day life is profoundly affected by the decisions and operations of public officials. Of course, in public life, as in private life, accidents are inevitable. And when an accident does occur, the victim may well try to affix responsibility to the government. Indeed, in at least one respect, a public authority presents a very attractive target. In comparison to many types of tortfeasors, a public body is relatively more likely to be solvent and capable of satisfying any judgment issued against it.

The fact that judgment will be satisfied from public funds does, however, create controversy. We sometimes fall into the naive belief that public resources, if not infinite, at least are outside the concern of the average citizen. The truth, of course, is that public authority liability affects us all. Money spent satisfying tort judgments must either be drawn away from other uses (*e.g.* health care and education) or generated through higher taxes. Consequently, there are, broadly speaking, two schools of thought. Some commentators insist that public officials should be subject to the same rules as private actors and that, by extension, the financial burden of misadventure should be borne by society as a whole, rather than by individual victims. Other commentators emphasize the tremendous extent to which modern government, by its very nature, is exposed to potential liability, and therefore insist upon special exemptions. As you read through this chapter, ask yourself how the legal system should resolve that debate. Also ask yourself if and when judges should second-guess decisions made by elected officials and their delegates. Is it legitimate for the courts to perform such a task? And even if so, do the courts have sufficient information upon which to pass judgment on social policies?

This chapter is divided into two sections. The first section outlines some special rules that currently exist to protect public authorities from liability. The second section then considers bases upon which public authorities may be held liable in tort. The focus will be on the torts of negligence and misfeasance in a public office, but reference will also be made to other intentional torts and the *Charter*.

2. Special Rules for Public Authorities

(a) LEGISLATIVE AND JUDICIAL FUNCTIONS

The term "public authorities" is very broad. It obviously encompasses governments and elected officials. However, it also encompasses bodies to which many of the day-to-day functions of government are legislatively delegated. Examples include marketing, licensing and professional boards, regulatory agencies, investigatory commissions, prison administrations, police agencies, labour arbitrators, and municipal governments.

In Canada, public authorities, including those who exercise delegated authority, perform a broad range of functions. First, public authorities that are empowered to enact rules or regulations may exercise a *legislative* function. That is clearly true of Parliament, but it is also true of, say, a municipal government when passing a by-law. Second, public authorities that are empowered to resolve disputes may exercise a *judicial* or *quasi-judicial* function. The courts provide the most obvious example, but again, many bodies exercising delegated authority also fall under the same rubric. In some situations, those bodies closely adhere to normal judicial practices by, for example, hearing submissions from counsel and receiving evidence under oath. In other situations, they employ far less formal procedures. An example of a quasi-judicial function occurs when a labour arbitrator interprets labour relations legislation governing a union-management dispute. Finally, public authorities that are empowered to perform administrative acts may exercise *administrative* functions. Administrative functions involve the establishment and application of policies that affect the public. For example, a liquor licensing board performs an administrative function when it decides to prohibit the sale of alcoholic beverages at sporting events.

It is important to appreciate that a given body may be capable of exercising more than one type of function. For example, while a liquor licensing board may commonly perform an administrative function (as explained in the last paragraph), it may also perform a quasi-judicial function. It will do so, for example, if it evaluates a complaint against a tavern owner and decides to revoke the tavern owner's licence.

For analytical purposes, it is necessary to classify the nature of the function being performed, rather than the nature of the body performing it. The distinction between different types of functions is significant because the Supreme Court of Canada has held that public authorities generally cannot be held liable in tort for actions taken in the performance of legislative, judicial or quasi-judicial functions: *Welbridge Holdings Ltd. v. Greater Winnipeg* (1970), 22 D.L.R. (3d) 470 (S.C.C.). Accordingly, the tort liability of public authorities generally arises in the context of administrative actions.

The reasons for those limitations are not difficult to discern. With respect to legislative functions, the courts recognize that, given the theory of separation of powers that lies at the heart of the Canadian constitutional system, it is generally inappropriate for them to pass judgment on decisions reached by elected officials and their delegates. Judges also recognize that, given the limited range of information that is disclosed in the course of adversarial litigation, they are ill-equipped to undertake the sorts of policy analyses that are required in order to properly mediate compromises between competing social interests. Similar reasons underlie the immunity enjoyed by public authorities with respect to the exercise of judicial and quasi-judicial functions.

BRADLEY v. FISHER
80 U.S. 646 (1872)

[The plaintiff was a member of the Bar of the Supreme Court in the District of Columbia, and the defendant was a judge of the Criminal Court in that jurisdiction. As a result of the plaintiff's contemptuous language and conduct, the defendant directed an order striking the plaintiff's name from the roll of attorneys practicing in the Criminal Court. This was subsequently interpreted as also striking the plaintiff from the rolls of the Supreme Court. A judge of the Criminal Court had no jurisdiction to strike an attorney from the rolls of the Supreme Court, and the plaintiff sued to recover the damages he suffered because he was unable to practice in the Supreme Court. The United States Supreme Court held that the defendant was not responsible for that error. The court then went on to consider the defendant's plea of judicial immunity. The judgment of the majority was delivered by Field J.]

FIELD J.:—For it is a general principle of the highest importance to the proper administration of justice that a judicial officer, in exercising the authority vested in him, shall be free to act upon his own convictions, without apprehension of personal consequence to himself. Liability to answer to everyone who might feel himself aggrieved by the action of the judge, would be inconsistent with the possession of this freedom, and would destroy that independence without which no judiciary can be either respectable or useful. As observed by a distinguished English judge, it would establish the weakness of the judicial authority in a degrading responsibility. *Taaffe v. Downes*, 3 Moore, P.C. 41, n.

The principle, therefore, which exempts judges of courts of superior or general authority from liability in a civil action for acts done by them in the exercise of their judicial functions, obtains in all countries where there is any well-ordered system of jurisprudence. It has been the settled doctrine of the English courts for many centuries, and has never been denied, that we are aware of, in the courts of this country.

It has, as Chancellor Kent observes, "a deep root in the common law." *Yates v. Lansing*, 5 Johns, 291.

Nor can this exemption of the judges from civil liability be affected by the motives with which their judicial acts are performed. The purity of their motives cannot in this way be the subject of judicial inquiry. This was adjudged in the case of *Floyd and Barker*, reported by Coke, in 1608 (12 Coke, 25) where it was laid down that the judges of the realm could not be drawn in question for any supposed corruption impeaching the verity of their records, except before the King himself, and it was observed that if they were required to answer otherwise, it would "tend to the scandal and subversion of all justice, and those who are the most sincere, would not be free from continual calumniations."

The truth of this latter observation is manifest to all persons having much experience with judicial proceedings in the superior courts. Controversies involving not merely great pecuniary interests, but the liberty and character of the parties and, consequently, exciting deepest feelings, are being constantly determined in those courts, in which there is a great conflict in the evidence and great doubt as to the law which should govern their decision. It is this class of cases which imposes upon the judge the severest labor, and often creates in his mind a painful sense of responsibility. Yet it is precisely in this class of cases that the losing party feels most keenly the decision against him, and most readily accepts anything but the soundness of the decision in explanation of the action of the judge. Just in proportion to the strength of his convictions of the correctness of his own view of the case is he apt to complain of the judgment against him, and from complaints of the judgment to pass to the ascription of improper motives to the judge. When the controversy involves questions affecting large amounts of property or relates to a matter of general public concern, or touches the interests of numerous parties, the disappointment occasioned by an adverse decision, often finds vent in imputations of this character, and from the imperfection of human nature this is hardly a subject of wonder. If civil actions could be maintained in such cases against the judge, because the losing party should see fit to allege in his complaint that the acts of the judge were done with partiality, or maliciously or corruptly, the protection essential to judicial independence would be entirely swept away. Few persons sufficiently irritated to institute an action against a judge for his judicial acts would hesitate to ascribe any character to the acts which would be essential to the maintenance of the action.

If upon such allegations a judge could be compelled to answer in a civil action for his judicial acts, not only would his office be degraded and his usefulness destroyed, but he would be subjected for his protection to the necessity of preserving a complete record of all the evidence produced before him in every litigated case, and of the authorities cited and arguments presented, in order that he might be able to show to the judge before whom he might be summoned by the losing party — and that judge perhaps one of an inferior jurisdiction — that he had decided as he did with judicial integrity; and the second judge would be subjected to a similar burden, as he in his turn might also be held amenable by the losing party.

NOTES AND QUESTIONS

1. The privileges of legislators are at least partially governed by statutes in all Canadian jurisdictions. See for example *Parliament of Canada Act*, R.S.C. 1985, c. P-1, s. 4; *Legislative Assembly Act*, R.S.O. 1990, c. L.10, s. 37; and *Legislative Assembly Privilege Act*, R.S.B.C. 1996, c. 259, s. 1. See also *Roman Corp. v. Hudson's Bay Oil & Gas Co.* (1973), 36 D.L.R. (3d) 413 (S.C.C.); *Canada (House of Commons) v. Vaid*, [2005] 1 S.C.R. 667; Millar, ed., *May's Parliamentary Practice*, 24th ed. (2011), ch. 5; Chisholm, "Cautionary tales for actions against Cabinet" *Ont. Lawyers Weekly* (8 November 1985) 1; Maingot, *Parliamentary Privilege in Canada*, 2d ed. (1997); Newman, "Parliamentary Privilege, the Canadian Constitution and the Courts" (2008) 39 Ottawa L. Rev. 573; and Chafetz, *Democracy's Privileged Few: Legislative Privilege and Democratic Norms in the British and American Constitutions* (2007). The Supreme Court of Canada has also affirmed the existence of "inherent" Parliamentary privilege: *New Brunswick Broadcasting Co. v. Nova Scotia (Speaker of the House of Assembly)*, [1993] 1 S.C.R. 319; and *Harvey v. New Brunswick (Attorney General)*, [1996] 2 S.C.R. 876. The court suggested that Parliamentary privilege is not subject to the

Charter of Rights and Freedoms, Part I of the *Constitution Act, 1982*, being Schedule B to the *Canada Act 1982 (UK)*, 1982, c. 11, in the same way as "ordinary" laws.

2. The immunity enjoyed by members of legislatures extends only to actions that are directly or indirectly related to legislative activities. Other actions may be the subject of tort liability. See *George v. Beaubien* (1998), 166 D.L.R. (4th) 185 (Ont. Gen. Div.); and *Decock v. Alberta* (2000), 186 D.L.R. (4th) 265 (Alta. C.A.).

3. *Welbridge Holdings Ltd. v. Greater Winnipeg* was reaffirmed by the Supreme Court of Canada in *Enterprises Sibeca Inc. v. Frelighsburg (Municipality)*, [2004] 3 S.C.R. 304. Deschamps J., for the majority, found that a municipality cannot be held liable in negligence for adopting, amending or repealing a by-law, even if such actions cause foreseeable economic loss to landowners. The majority reasoned (at 315) that "[a] municipality has a margin of legitimate error" and will not be liable "for the exercise of its regulatory power if it acts in good faith or if the exercise of this power cannot be characterized as irrational." Deschamps J. was careful, however, to distinguish immunity in a civil action from judicial review of a by-law's validity. See also *Birch Builders v. Esquimalt (Township)* (1992), 66 B.C.L.R. (2d) 208 (C.A.); and *Woestenburg v. Kamloops (City)* (2001), 18 M.P.L.R. (3d) 257 (B.C.S.C.). In *Torrance v. Alberta* (2010), 477 A.R. 343 (C.A.), the Alberta Court of Appeal explained that a government's legislative immunity also applies to claims alleging that the government negligently failed to enact legislation governing a particular matter. The plaintiff in that case alleged that the Alberta government had been negligent by failing to enact child welfare legislation referring to shared parenting or equal rights for both parents.

4. There are relatively few actions brought against judicial officers. The older case law is very complex. See generally Thompson, "Judicial Immunity and the Protection of Justices" (1958) 21 Mod. L. Rev. 517; Rubenstein, "Liability in Tort of Judicial Officers" (1964) 15 U.T.L.J. 317; Brazier, "Judicial Immunity and the Independence of the Judiciary" [1976] Pub. Law 397; Sadler, "Judicial and Quasi-Judicial Immunities: A Remedy Denied" (1982) 13 Melb. U.L. Rev. 508; Rosenberg, "Whatever Happened to Absolute Judicial Immunity?" (1984) 21 Hous. L. Rev. 875; Law, "A Tale of Two Immunities: Judicial and Prosecutorial Immunities in Canada" (1990) 28 Alta. L.R. 468; Gibson, "Monitoring Arbitrary Government Authority: *Charter* Scrutiny of Legislative, Executive and Judicial Privilege" (1998) 61 Sask. L. Rev. 297; and Murphy, "Rethinking tortious immunity for judicial acts" (2013) 33 L.S. 455.

5. There has been a longstanding debate as to whether judicial immunity should be limited to judges of superior courts, extended to judges of any court of record, or applied to all judges and even justices of the peace. In *Sirros v. Moore*, [1974] 3 All E.R. 776 (C.A.), Lord Denning indicated that the immunity rule ought to cover all judges and justices. However, he failed to consider the *Justices Protection Act*, 1848 (11 & 12 Vict.), c. 44 which specifically governs the liability of justices of the peace. Do you agree with Denning L.J. that the immunity granted to judges should not vary according to the level of court? It would now appear that immunity extends to any court of record. See *McC v. Mullan*, [1984] 3 All E.R. 908 (H.L.).

6. Legislation in Canada's common law jurisdictions typically provides for the immunity of judges at all levels, including masters, justices of the peace, and judges of

small claims courts. See for example *Courts of Justice Act*, R.S.O. 1990, c. C-43, s. 82; *Court of Queen's Bench Act*, R.S.A. 2000, c. C-31, s. 14; and *Provincial Court Act*, R.S.B.C. 1996, c. 379, s. 42. See also *Morier v. Rivard*, [1985] 2 S.C.R. 716, where the statutory immunity was extended to commissioners of a provincial commission of inquiry.

7. Legislation regarding judicial immunity typically provides that a judge can only be held liable in tort if the plaintiff can establish that he or she acted maliciously and without reasonable and probable grounds. See for example *Provincial Court Act*, C.C.S.M. c. C275, s. 71. See also *Foran v. Tatangello* (1976), 73 D.L.R. (3d) 126 (Ont. H.C.); *Organ v. Newfoundland and Labrador (Minister of Social Services)* (2007), 266 Nfld. & P.E.I.R. 339 (N.L.T.D.); *Bérubé v. Ontario Court of Justice*, 2010 CarswellOnt 1930 (S.C.J.) (WL Can); *Cormier v. Nova Scotia*, 2015 NSSC 352; and Feldthusen, "Judicial Immunity: In Search of an Appropriate Limiting Formula" (1980) 29 U.N.B.L.J. 73 at 80. However, the limitation regarding malice or absence of reasonable and probable grounds was excluded from the most recent consolidation of Ontario's judicial immunity legislation, suggesting that judges might enjoy immunity even when acting maliciously. Similarly, in *Prefontaine v. Gosman* (2000), 270 A.R. 97 (Q.B.), aff'd (2002), 317 A.R. 160 (C.A.), Jones J. stated at para. 39 that "a judge acting in her or his judicial capacity will not be liable civilly for any actions done in such judicial capacity whether the judge was acting within or outside of her or his jurisdiction, and even if the judge was acting out of hatred, envy or malice, if the judge believed that he or she was acting with jurisdiction and in the course of his or her judicial duties." Is such broad immunity more likely to foster or hinder public confidence in the judicial system? Can a judge who is acting out of hatred truly be said to be acting in his or her "judicial capacity?"

8. The *Criminal Code*, R.S.C. 1985, c. C-46, s. 783, permits a reviewing court, upon quashing a conviction, order or other proceeding of a provincial court judge or justice of the peace, to issue an order protecting the original judge from tort liability. The reviewing court can also issue a "protection order," as it is called, for anyone acting in accordance with the order (*e.g.* a peace officer who has complied with a warrant or held someone in custody). Similar legislation exists in the provinces. In *Mayrand v. Cronier* (1981), 63 C.C.C. (2d) 561 (Qc. C.A.), the Québec Court of Appeal held that, although these orders should not be made automatically, they should generally be made in the absence of malice, misconduct or ulterior motive by the inferior court judge. See also *Re Royal Can. Legion Branch 177* (1964), 48 D.L.R. (2d) 164 (B.C.S.C.); *Re Yoner* (1969), 7 D.L.R. (3d) 185 (B.C.S.C.); and Johnson, "Tort Liability: Search Warrant Quashed: Protection Order Denied: Magistrate Negligent" (1971) 4 Ottawa L. Rev. 627.

9. In *Nelles v. Ont.* (1989), 60 D.L.R. (4th) 609 (S.C.C.), an extract of which appears in Chapter 3, the court held that the Crown was protected by statute from civil claims based on how it discharged its judicial responsibilities. However, it denied immunity to the Attorney General and Crown Attorneys personally. The court reviewed the rationale and authority for judicial as well as prosecutorial immunity. L'Heureux-Dubé J., dissenting in part, objected to personal liability for acts done in the furtherance of public functions. See also *Proulx v. Québec (Attorney General)* (2001), 206 D.L.R. (4th) 1 (S.C.C.); *MacAlpine v. H.(T.)* (1991), 7 C.C.L.T. (2d) 113

(B.C.C.A.); *Prete v. Ontario* (1993), 16 O.R. (3d) 161 (C.A.); *Milgaard v. Kujawa*, [1994] 1 W.W.R. 338 (Sask. Q.B.), aff'd [1994] 9 W.W.R. 305 (C.A.); *Hawley v. Bapoo* (2000), 187 D.L.R. (4th) 533 (Ont. Div. Ct.); *Krieger v. Law Society of Alberta*, [2002] 3 S.C.R. 372; and *Driskell v. Dangerfield* (2007), 217 Man. R. (2d) 124 (Q.B.), varied (2008), 228 Man. R. (2d) 116 (C.A.). Prosecutorial immunity was also extended to the municipal prosecutor in *Little v. Ottawa (City)* (2004), 49 M.P.L.R. (3d) 115 (Ont. S.C.J.). See generally Roach, "The Attorney General and the *Charter* Revisited" (2000) 50 U.T.L.J. 1.

10. In *MacKeigan v. Hickman* (1989), 61 D.L.R. (4th) 688 (S.C.C.), the court affirmed judicial immunity from being compelled to testify about the decision-making process or composition of the court in a particular case. This immunity principle is grounded in constitutional theory about the independence of the judiciary from legislative control. The decision summarized much of the relevant background to the Donald Marshall Inquiry in Nova Scotia.

11. The courts have extended judicial immunity to public authorities other than judges who perform quasi-judicial functions. However, no clear position has emerged to determine which boards, tribunals and officials will be granted immunity. See *Everett v. Griffiths*, [1921] 1 A.C. 631 (H.L.); *Calvert v. Law Soc. of Upper Can.* (1981), 121 D.L.R. (3d) 169 (Ont. H.C.); *Howarth v. The Queen* (1984), 29 C.C.L.T. 157 (F.C.T.D.), aff'd (1985), 13 Admin. L.R. 189 (F.C.A.); *Lonrho plc. v. Tebbit*, [1991] 4 All E.R. 973 (Ch.); *Harrington (Public Trustee of) v. Pappachristos* (1992), 5 Admin. L.R. (2d) 130 (B.C.S.C.), aff'd 75 B.C.L.R. (2d) 121 (S.C.); *Reynen v. Canada* (1993), 70 F.T.R. 158 (T.D.), rev'd (1995), 184 N.R. 350 (Fed. C.A.); *Al's Steak House & Tavern Inc. v. Deloitte & Touche* (1994), 20 O.R. (3d) 673 (Gen. Div.); *Lowe v. Guarantee Co. of North America* (2005), 80 O.R. (3d) 222 (C.A.); and *Maughan v. University of British Columbia*, 2009 CarswellBC 2766 (C.A.) (WL Can). See also Rubinstein, "Liability in Tort of Judicial Officers" (1964) 15 U.T.L.J. 317; Brazier, "Judicial Immunity and the Independence of the Judiciary" [1976] Pub. Law 397; and Sadler, "Judicial and Quasi-Judicial Immunities: A Remedy Denied" (1982) 4 Melb. U.L. Rev. 508.

12. Are the arguments for limiting the liability of judicial officers compelling? Which types of judicial decisions should be immune from liability? Answer these same questions in relation to Attorneys General, crown counsel, and quasi-judicial decision makers.

13. Should judicial immunity also apply to mediators? Does it make a difference if the mediators are legal practitioners? Does it make a difference if mediation is compulsory or optional in the jurisdiction? See generally Schulz, "Mediator Liability in Canada: An Examination of Emerging American and Canadian Jurisprudence" (2000-2001) 32 Ottawa L. Rev. 269. See also Brown, "The Expression of Arbitral Immunity: Is Absolute Immunity a Foregone Conclusion?" (2009) J. Disp. Resol. 225; Brooker, "Mediator immunity: time for evaluation in England and Wales" (2016) 36:3 L.S. 464; and *Flock v. Beattie* (2010), 25 Alta. L.R. (5th) 49 (Q.B.).

(b) CROWN IMMUNITY

Another type of difficulty may arise if the public authority is a Crown agent. At common law, the courts did not have power to sanction the Crown. The guiding principle was that "the King can do no wrong." The only way for citizens to sue the Crown was by petition of right, which did not apply to most tort actions. Thus, the Crown was effectively immune from tort liability. Various reforms were passed over the 19th and early 20th centuries to address this situation, but it was not until 1947 that the British *Crown Proceedings Act* allowed the Crown to be sued in tort as if it were a person. Canada followed suit with the *Crown Liability Act* in 1952. Now part of the *Crown Liability and Proceedings Act*, R.S.C. 1985, c. C-50, the relevant provisions are as follows:

> 3. The Crown is liable for the damages for which, if it were a person, it would be liable
> . . .
>
> > (b) . . . in respect of
> >
> > > (i) a tort committed by a servant of the Crown, or
> > > (ii) a breach of duty attaching to the ownership, occupation, possession or control of property.

Similar legislation exists in every Canadian jurisdiction, most of it based on a model statute prepared by the Conference of Commissioners on Uniformity of Legislation in Canada in 1950. However, the statutes are complex and, in many respects, a trap for the unwary. Still, it remains true today that the Crown is subject to liability only to the extent that it voluntarily submits itself to judicial authority through such legislation.

Not all public authorities are Crown agents — only those over which the Crown exercises a significant degree of actual or potential control are characterized as such. The Crown includes the executive governments of Canada and the provinces, their ministries, departments, corporations and boards, as well as "servants or agents" thereof. The Crown can be sued directly or, as occurs more frequently, vicariously for torts committed by its servants or agents. It is worthwhile to note here that municipalities are not considered to be part of the Crown, but are covered by other legislative provisions.

NOTES AND QUESTIONS

1. For a general discussion of Crown liability, see Hogg, Monahan & Wright, *Liability of the Crown*, 4th ed. (2011). Examples of provincial legislation include: *Proceedings Against the Crown Act*, R.S.O. 1990, c. P.27, s. 5; *Proceedings against the Crown Act*, R.S.N.S. 1989, c. 360, s. 5; and *Crown Proceeding Act*, R.S.B.C. 1996, c. 89, s. 2.

As part of its omnibus budget legislation released in April 2019, the Ontario government proposed a new *Crown Liability and Proceedings Act, 2019*. Among other things, the Act would prohibit tort actions against the Crown for negligence in carrying out its regulatory functions in good faith, and for its policy functions.

2. In some situations, it may be difficult to sue a public authority that does not enjoy the status of either a natural person or a corporation. Marketing boards provide a common example. The enabling legislation may address the issue, but often is silent

on the point. No clear guidelines have yet developed and the courts continue to struggle with the issue. See *MacLean v. Liquor Lic. Bd. of Ontario* (1975), 51 D.L.R. (3d) 64 (Ont. H.C.J.), rev'd in part (1975), 61 D.L.R. (3d) 237 (Ont. Div. Ct.). *MacLean* also dealt with the issue of whether the Board was a Crown agent. See also *Westlake v. The Queen in Right of the Province of Ontario*, [1971] 3 O.R. 533 (H.C.J.), aff'd [1972] 2 O.R. 605 (C.A.), aff'd (1973), 33 D.L.R. (3d) 256 (S.C.C.); *Duggan v. Newfoundland* (1992), 99 Nfld. & P.E.I.R. 56 (Nfld. S.C. (T.D.)); *Universal Environmental Services Inc. v. West Newfoundland Regional Appeal Board*, 2010 CarswellNfld 370 (S.C. (T.D.)) (WL Can); and *Gratton-Masuy Environmental Technologies Inc. v. Ontario* (2010), 101 O.R. (3d) 321 (C.A.).

3. The issue of Crown immunity arose in *Black v. Chrétien* (2001), 199 D.L.R. (4th) 228 (Ont. C.A.). Conrad Black sued the Prime Minister for negligence, abuse of power, and misfeasance in public office. The Prime Minister brought a motion to have the statement of claim struck out on the basis that it did not disclose a cause of action.

Black, a Canadian, wished to receive a peerage from the Queen and to sit in the House of Lords. The Canadian government initially indicated that it would not object to the honour, as long as Black held dual citizenship and did not use his title in Canada. Subsequently, the Prime Minister had a change of heart and announced his opposition. That decision was ostensibly based on the Nickel Resolution, passed by the Canadian Parliament in 1918, which asked the King "to refrain hereafter from conferring any title or honour or titular distinction upon any of your subjects domiciled or ordinarily resident in Canada." Black alleged, however, that the real reason for the Prime Minister's position was personal animosity.

The Court of Appeal for Ontario upheld LeSage C.J.S.C.'s decision that the matter was non-justiciable and that the statement of claim should be struck out. Laskin J.A. found that the issue of honours and titles fell within the scope of the Prime Minister's Crown prerogative, which he defined as "the residue of discretionary or arbitrary authority, which at any given time is legally left in the hands of the Crown" (quoting Dicey, *Introduction to the Study of the Law of the Constitution*, 10th ed. (1959) at 424). Laskin J.A. agreed that the exercise of the Crown prerogative was amenable to challenge under the *Canadian Charter of Rights and Freedoms*, Part I of the *Constitution Act, 1982*, being Schedule B to the *Canada Act 1982* (U.K.), 1982, c. 11, but noted that Black had not made any such argument. Laskin J.A. also held that Crown prerogative is subject to judicial review if it affects the rights or legitimate expectations of an individual. On the facts, however, Black had neither a right to a peerage, nor a reasonable expectation of receiving one. In the final analysis, then, the dispute was purely political. The Court of Appeal consequently saw no basis for a claim in tort:

> Once Prime Minister Chrétien's exercise of the honours prerogative is found to be beyond review by the courts, how the Prime Minister exercised the prerogative is also beyond review. Even if [the Prime Minister's position] was wrong or careless or negligent, even if his motives were questionable, they cannot be challenged by judicial review.

Despite the setback that he suffered in the courts, Black received his peerage after renouncing his Canadian citizenship. He is currently on leave of absence from the House of Lords, where he sits as Lord Black of Crossharbour in spite of fraud convictions in the courts of the United States. For commentary, see Sossin, "The Rule of Law and the Justiciability of Prerogative Powers: A Comment on *Black v. Chrétien*" (2002) 47 McGill L.J. 435.

4. A different manifestation of Crown prerogative arose in *Aleksic v. Canada (Attorney General)* (2002), 215 D.L.R. (4th) 720 (Ont. Div. Ct.). The plaintiffs sued the Attorney General of Canada in tort and for violations of ss. 7 and 15 of the *Charter*. Their claims arose in connection with Canada's participation in NATO's bombing of Yugoslavia. The plaintiffs alleged that the bombing campaign was illegal and that it had caused injury, death and property damage.

The defendant's motion to strike the statement of claim as disclosing no cause of action was granted. The tort claims were held to be non-justiciable because the decision regarding the bombing campaigns was akin to a declaration of war and hence pertained to a purely political matter. Moreover, even if the government's decision was justiciable, it was a matter of policy, rather than operation, and therefore, according to the decision in *Just v. British Columbia* (1989), 64 D.L.R. (4th) 689 (S.C.C.), an extract of which appears below, it did not give rise to a duty of care. The court held that the plaintiffs' *Charter* claims were similarly futile. In theory, those claims were justiciable because the court had an obligation to determine whether the exercise of the Crown prerogative had violated an aggrieved individual's rights and freedoms. On the facts, however, those actions were doomed.

See also *Guergis v. Novak*, 2013 ONCA 449, in which the plaintiff sued the Prime Minister and the Conservative Party of Canada after she was forced to resign from Cabinet, removed from caucus and denied a further candidacy in her riding. The court affirmed that removal from caucus and cabinet were matters of prerogative that were non-justiciable, and that this extended to the manner in which the prerogative was exercised.

5. The courts have drawn a distinction between acts of Crown prerogative that are justiciable and those that are not. Thus, while the courts will not review prerogative actions like entering into treaties, declaring war, and conducting foreign policy, they will review prerogative acts that have the effect of altering a person's rights or obligations, or depriving him or her of certain advantages or benefits: *Council of Civil Service Unions v. Minister for the Civil Service*, [1985] A.C. 374 (H.L.). The issue and revocation of passports, for example, is a matter of Crown prerogative that is subject to judicial review: *R. v. Secretary of State for Foreign and Commonwealth Affairs, ex parte Everett*, [1989] 2 W.L.R. 224 (C.A.). The issue may be more complicated, however, when the refusal to issue a passport is based on reasons of foreign policy or national security. See Chamberlain, "*Abdelrazik*: Tort Liability for Exercise of Prerogative Powers?" (2010) 18 Const. Forum 119.

In *Hinse v. Canada (Attorney General)*, 2015 SCC 35, the court found that the Attorney General was immune from liability for the exercise (or non-exercise) of the prerogative power of mercy (*i.e.* pardon) unless it was done irrationally or in bad faith.

6. It has been suggested that class actions against the Crown are increasingly being used as a substitute for judicial review. Many of these class actions involve historical political decisions, such as the Chinese "head tax" (*Mack v. Canada (Attorney General)* (2002), 60 O.R. (3d) 737 (C.A.)); the failure to pay interest on pensions to disabled veterans (*Authorson v. Canada*, [2003] 2 S.C.R. 40); and the placement of Aboriginal children in residential schools (*Cloud v. Canada* (2005), 73 O.R. (3d) 401 (C.A.)). What issues are posed by class actions for damages in such cases? Is the

relevant wrong a private wrong, a public wrong, both, or neither? What makes the Crown different from other defendants in class action lawsuits? Interestingly, the Crown has the unique ability to legislate its own retroactive immunity to various class actions. See Sossin, "Class Actions Against the Crown: A Substitute for Judicial Review on Administrative Law Grounds?" (2007) 57 U.N.B.L.J. 9; and Jones & Baxter, "The Class Action and Public Authority Liability: 'Preferability' Re-Examined" (2007) 57 U.N.B.L.J. 27.

7. As part of their broad reforms of the tort law system, Australian legislatures expanded the scope of Crown immunity. See Aronson, "Government Liability in Negligence" (2008) 32 Melbourne U.L. Rev. 44.

8. Somewhat controversially, the United Nations enjoys absolute immunity from the jurisdiction of member states' courts. This is justified as being necessary to secure the independence of the U.N. See Hovell, "Due Process in the United Nations" (2016) 110:1 A.J.I.L. 1; and Boon, "The United Nations as Good Samaritan: Immunity and Responsibility" (2015) 16:2 Chi. J. Int'l L. 341.

(c) LIMITATION PERIODS AND SPECIAL PROCEDURES

A tort action against a public authority may be complicated by the existence of special limitation periods. Invariably, these limitation periods are shorter than normal. They may be found not only in enabling legislation, but also in general legislation governing Crown agencies and public authorities. In addition, there may be other limiting provisions, such as a requirement that the public authority be notified prior to receiving a writ, a prohibition on jury trials in actions involving the Crown, or payment of security for costs.

NOTES

1. For a review of limitation periods and other procedural rules applicable in actions against public authorities, see Mew, *The Law of Limitations*, 3d ed. (2016), ch. 17.

2. For examples of legislation imposing special limitation periods or other special procedural rules, see the *Proceedings Against the Crown Act*, R.S.N.L. 1990, c. P-26; *Public Authorities Protection Act*, R.S.O. 1990, c. P.38; and the *Protection of Persons Acting Under Statute Act*, R.S.N.B. 2011, c. 210.

3. Ontario previously had a six month limitation period for actions against public authorities. However, it was replaced with the generally applicable "basic" two year limitation period under the *Limitations Act, 2002*, S.O. 2002, c. 24. See Krishna, ed., *The New Ontario Limitations Regime: Exposition and Analysis* (2005).

4. Special limitation periods and other procedural rules applying to claims against public authorities have been challenged under the *Charter* (usually s. 15). The results have varied. See for example *Colangelo v. Mississauga (City)* (1988), 53 D.L.R. (4th) 145 (Ont. C.A.), in which the relevant case law is reviewed; and *Mirhadizadeh v. Ontario* (1989), 69 O.R. (2d) 422 (C.A.). See also *Prete v. Ontario* (1993), 16 O.R. (3d) 161 (C.A.); *Bisoukis v. Brampton (City)* (1999), 46 O.R. (3d) 417 (C.A.); *B. (K.L.) v.*

British Columbia (1999), 46 C.C.L.T. (2d) 237 (B.C.C.A.), aff'd [2003] S.C.R. 403; and *Manitoba Métis Federation Inc. v. Canada (Attorney General)*, 2013 SCC 14.

5. Although the limitation periods tend to strongly favour public authorities, it sometimes is possible for the plaintiff to obtain relief. *Bannon v. Thunder Bay (City)* (2002), 210 D.L.R. (4th) 62 (S.C.C.) is illustrative. The plaintiff was injured after she slipped on an icy sidewalk. She was required, under s. 284(5) of the *Municipal Act*, R.S.O. 1990, c. M.45, to give the municipality notice of her intention to sue within seven days. She failed to do so. She nevertheless was permitted to pursue her action because her delay in giving notice was attributable to the narcotics that she was prescribed following the accident. The court applied s. 47 of the *Limitations Act*, R.S.O. 1990, c. L.15, which states: "Where a person entitled to bring an action . . . is at the time the cause of action accrues a minor, mental defective, mental incompetent or of unsound mind, the period within which the action may be brought shall be reckoned from the date when such person became of full age or of sound mind."

6. The harsh effect of an abbreviated limitation period was also avoided in *Berendsen v. Ontario* (2001), 204 D.L.R. (4th) 318 (S.C.C.). The Supreme Court of Canada found that the six month limitation period then applicable in Ontario under the *Public Authorities Protection Act, supra*, only applied to "public" duties performed by government authorities. However, operational decisions of a predominantly private nature were subject to the then six year general limitation period under the *Limitations Act*, R.S.O. 1990, c. L.15, s. 45(1)(g). The alleged wrong in *Berendsen* was the disposal of waste asphalt on private property, which was found to be "predominantly private" by the court. See also *Berardinelli v. Ontario Housing Corp.* (1978), [1979] 1 S.C.R. 275; *Des Champs v. Conseil des Écoles séparées catholiques de langue française de Prescott-Russell*, [1999] 3 S.C.R. 281; and *Gringmuth v. North Vancouver (District)* (2002), 98 B.C.L.R. (3d) 116 (C.A.). The limitation period may also be inapplicable in claims seeking a declaration of legislative invalidity: *Manitoba Métis Federation Inc., supra.*

3. The Negligence Liability of Public Authorities

(a) INTRODUCTION

A person aggrieved by the acts or omissions of a public authority may claim relief under several different types of actions, but by far the most common is the tort of negligence. In discussing a public authority's liability in negligence, it is important to distinguish between two issues. The first involves the doctrine of *vicarious liability*. Depending upon the circumstances, an employer may be vicariously liable for the torts of its employee. That is to say, if an employee commits a tort in the course of employment, responsibility may be imposed on the employee personally and on the employer vicariously. The victim may then recover damages from one, the other, or both. That is true even though the employer did not itself do anything wrong. Its responsibility arises merely by virtue of its relationship to the tortfeasor. The justifications for this rule are examined in Chapter 25. Needless to say, public authorities employ a great many people for whom they may be held vicariously liable.

The current discussion focuses on a different issue. The question is not whether a public authority can be held vicariously liable on the basis of an employee's tort, but rather whether it can be held directly liable for its own negligence.

Within that context, it is important to first determine whether the public authority was exercising a *statutory duty* or a *discretionary power*. If the enabling legislation required the public authority to pursue a particular course of action, the authority was exercising a statutory duty. In contrast, if the public authority had discretion, it was exercising a power. Although liability in negligence may arise in either event, the governing principles differ.

In the case of a statutory *duty*, a public authority cannot be held liable for simply doing what it was required to do. Significantly, however, the existence of a duty (as opposed to a power) means that the court may be relatively less circumspect about imposing liability. Since the public authority was *required* to act in a particular manner, the judge need not be concerned about usurping the legislature's decision-making role. Consequently, liability may be imposed if the public authority performed its task *carelessly*, or if it *failed* to perform its duty at all. The courts are more likely to impose liability in situations where the public authority breached a specific statutory duty that it owed to an identifiable person. Duties that are phrased broadly, or are owed to the public at large, are less likely to give rise to liability.

The situation is more complex in a case involving a discretionary *power*, where the public authority had the authority, but not the obligation, to act in a certain way. In that situation, the court must be concerned about substituting its choices for that of the legislature. For many years, the courts analyzed this issue by distinguishing between policy matters and operational matters. The nature of that distinction was explained by the Supreme Court of Canada in *Just v. British Columbia* (1989), 64 D.L.R. (4th) 689 (S.C.C.), which was a turning point for public authority liability in Canada. However, the policy/operational distinction was not straightforward to apply in practice, and was ultimately revisited by the Supreme Court in *R. v. Imperial Tobacco Canada Ltd.*, 2011 SCC 42.

JUST v. BRITISH COLUMBIA
(1989), 64 D.L.R. (4th) 689 (S.C.C.)

The judgment of Dickson C.J. and Wilson, La Forest, L'Heureux-Dubé, Gonthier and Cory JJ. was delivered by

CORY J.:—This appeal puts in issue the approach that should be taken by courts when considering the liability of government agencies in tort actions.

Factual Background

On the morning of January 16, 1982, the appellant and his daughter set out, undoubtedly with high hopes and great expectations, for a day of skiing at Whistler Mountain. As a result of a heavy snow fall they were forced to stop in the northbound line of traffic on Highway 99. While they were waiting for the traffic to move forward a great boulder weighing more than a ton somehow worked loose from the wooded slopes above the highway and came crashing down upon the appellant's car. The impact killed the appellant's daughter and caused him very serious injuries. He then brought this action against the respondent contending that it had negligently failed to maintain the highway properly.

Highway 99 is a major commuter road between Vancouver and the major ski resorts located at Whistler Mountain. The appellant alleged that there had been earlier rock falls near the scene of the tragedy. As well it was said that the climatic conditions of freezing and thawing, coupled with a heavy build-up of snow in the trees and resulting tree damage created a great risk of rock falls. Trees were said to be a well-known factor in levering rocks loose. It was contended that inadequate attention had been given to all these factors by the respondent and that a reasonable inspection would have demonstrated that the rock constituted a danger to users of the highway.

At the time of the accident the Department of Highways had set up a system for inspection and remedial work upon rock slopes particularly along Highway 99. At the apex of the organization was a Mr. Eastman, the regional geotechnical material engineer. He is a specialist in rock slope maintenance and together with another engineer was responsible for inspecting rock slopes and making recommendations regarding their stability.

. . .

Was the Decision of the Rockwork Section as to the Quantity and Quality of Inspections a "Policy" Decision Exempting the Respondent from Liability?

The respondent placed great reliance on the decision of this Court in *Barratt v. District of North Vancouver*, [1980] 2 S.C.R. 418. In the *Barratt* case injury occurred as a result of a pothole on the road. It was established that the City of North Vancouver had a policy of inspecting its roads for potholes every two weeks. Indeed it had inspected the road where the accident occurred one week earlier and found no pothole. It was found that the inspection policy established by the municipality was a reasonable and proper one. However, Justice Martland in giving the reasons for this Court went on to express an opinion that the municipality could not be held negligent for formulating one inspection policy rather than another. He put it this way at pp. 427-28:

> In essence, he [the trial judge] is finding that the Municipality should have instituted a system of continuous inspection to ensure that no possible damage could occur and holds that, in the absence of such a system, if damage occurs, the Municipality must be held liable.

> In my opinion, no such duty existed. The Municipality, a public authority, exercised its power to maintain Marine Drive. It was under no statutory duty to do so. Its method of exercising its power was a matter of policy to be determined by the Municipality itself. If, in the implementation of its policy its servants acted negligently, causing damage, liability could arise, but the Municipality cannot be held to be negligent because it formulated one policy of operation rather than another.

This statement was not necessary to the decision as it had already been determined that the system of inspection established by the municipality was eminently reasonable. Neither was there any serious question raised that there had been any negligence in carrying out the system of inspection. The finding that a reasonable system of inspection had been established and carried out without negligence constituted the basis for the conclusion reached by the Court in that case. With the greatest respect, I am of the view that the portion of the reasons relied on by the respondent went farther than was necessary to the decision or appropriate as a statement of principle. For example, the Court would not have approved as "policy" a system that called for the inspection of the roads in a large urban municipality once every five years. Once a policy to inspect is established then it must be open to a litigant to attack the system as not having been adopted in a *bona fide* exercise of discretion and to demonstrate that in all the circumstances, including budgetary restraints, it is appropriate for a court to make a finding on the issue.

The functions of government and government agencies have multiplied enormously in this century. Often government agencies were and continue to be the best suited entities and indeed the only organizations which could protect the public in the diverse and difficult situations arising in so many fields. They may encompass such matters as the manufacture and distribution of food and drug products, energy production, environmental protection, transportation and tourism, fire prevention and building developments. The increasing complexities of life involve agencies of government in almost every aspect of daily living. Over the passage of time the increased government activities gave rise to incidents that would have led to tortious liability if they had occurred between private citizens. The early governmental immunity from tortious liability became intolerable. This led to the enactment of legislation which in general imposed liability on the Crown for its acts as though it were a person. However, the Crown is not a person and must be free to govern and make true policy decisions without becoming subject to tort liability as a result of those decisions. On the other hand, complete Crown immunity should not be restored by having every government decision designated as one of "policy". Thus the dilemma giving rise to the continuing judicial struggle to differentiate between "policy" and "operation". Particularly difficult decisions will arise in situations where governmental inspections may be expected.

The dividing line between "policy" and "operation" is difficult to fix, yet it is essential that it be done. The need for drawing the line was expressed with great clarity by Becker J. of the United States District Court, in *Blessing v. United States*, 447 F.S. 1160. The case required him to deal with a claim under the *Federal Tort Claims Act*, 28 U.S.C. § 2680 which provides:

> The provisions of this chapter and section 1346(b) of this title shall not apply to —
>
> > (a) Any claim based upon an act or omission of an employee of the Government, exercising due care, in the execution of a statute or regulation, whether or not such statute or regulation be valid, or based upon the exercise or performance or the failure to exercise or perform a discretionary function or duty on the part of a federal agency or an employee of the Government, whether or not the discretion involved be abused.

He wrote at p. 1170:

> Read as a whole and with an eye to discerning a policy behind this provision, it seems to us only to articulate a policy of preventing tort actions from becoming a vehicle for judicial interference with decisionmaking that is properly exercised by other branches of the government and of protecting "the Government from liability that would seriously handicap efficient government operations," *United States v. Muniz*, 374 U.S. 150, 163, 83 S.Ct. 1850, 1858, 10 L.Ed.2d 805 (1963). Statutes, regulations, and discretionary functions, the subject matter of § 2680(a), are, as a rule, manifestations of policy judgments made by the political branches. In our tripartite governmental structure, the courts generally have no substantive part to play in such decisions.

Rather, the judiciary confines itself — or, under laws such as the FTCA's discretionary function exception, is confined — to adjudication of facts based on discernible objective standards of law. In the context of tort actions, with which we are here concerned, these objective standards are notably lacking when the question is not negligence but social wisdom, not due care but political practicability, not reasonableness but economic expediency. Tort law simply furnishes an inadequate crucible for testing the merits of social, political or economic decisions.

The duty of care should apply to a public authority unless there is a valid basis for its exclusion. A true policy decision undertaken by a government agency constitutes such a valid basis for exclusion. What constitutes a policy decision may vary infinitely and may be made at different levels although usually at a high level.

The decisions in *Anns v. Merton London Borough Council* [[1978] A.C. 728 (H.L.)] and *City of Kamloops v. Nielsen* [[1984] 2 S.C.R. 2] indicate that a government agency in reaching a decision pertaining to inspection must act in a reasonable manner which constitutes a *bona fide* exercise of discretion. To do so they must specifically consider whether to inspect and if so, the system of inspection must be a reasonable one in all the circumstances.

For example, at a high level there may be a policy decision made concerning the inspection of lighthouses. If the policy decision is made that there is such a pressing need to maintain air safety by the construction of additional airport facilities with the result that no funds can be made available for lighthouse inspection, then this would constitute a *bona fide* exercise of discretion that would be unassailable. Should then a lighthouse beacon be extinguished as a result of the lack of inspection and a shipwreck ensue no liability can be placed upon the government agency. The result would be the same if a policy decision were made to increase the funds for job retraining and reduce the funds for lighthouse inspection so that a beacon could only be inspected every second year and as a result the light was extinguished. Once again this would constitute the *bona fide* exercise of discretion. Thus a decision either not to inspect at all or to reduce the number of inspections may be an unassailable policy decision. This is so provided it constitutes a reasonable exercise of *bona fide* discretion based, for example, upon the availability of funds.

On the other hand, if a decision is made to inspect lighthouse facilities the system of inspections must be reasonable and they must be made properly. See *Indian Towing Co.*, 350 U.S. 61 (1955). Thus once the policy decision to inspect has been made, the Court may review the scheme of inspection to ensure it is reasonable and has been reasonably carried out in light of all the circumstances, including the availability of funds, to determine whether the government agency has met the requisite standard of care.

At a lower level, government aircraft inspectors checking on the quality of manufactured aircraft parts at a factory may make a policy decision to make a spot check of manufactured items throughout the day as opposed to checking every item manufactured in the course of one hour of the day. Such a choice as to how the inspection was to be undertaken could well be necessitated by the lack of both trained personnel and funds to provide such inspection personnel. In those circumstances the policy decision that a spot check inspection would be made could not be attacked. . . .

Thus a true policy decision may be made at a lower level provided that the government agency establishes that it was a reasonable decision in light of the surrounding circumstances.

The consideration of the duty of care that may be owed must be kept separate and distinct from the consideration of the standard of care that should be maintained by the government agency involved.

Let us assume a case where a duty of care is clearly owed by a governmental agency to an individual that is not exempted either by a statutory provision or because it was a true policy decision. In those circumstances the duty of care owed by the government agency would be the same as that owed by one person to another. Nevertheless the standard of care imposed upon the Crown may not be the same as that owed by an individual. An individual is expected to maintain his or her sidewalk or driveway reasonably, while a government agency such as the respondent may be responsible for the maintenance of hundreds of miles of highway. The frequency and the nature of inspection required of the individual may well be different from that required of the Crown. In each case the frequency and method must be reasonable in light of all the surrounding circumstances. The governmental agency should be entitled to demonstrate that balanced against the nature and quantity of the risk involved, its system of inspection was reasonable in light of all the circumstances including budgetary limits, the personnel and equipment available to it and that it had met the standard duty of care imposed upon it.

It may be convenient at this stage to summarize what I consider to be the principles applicable and the manner of proceeding in cases of this kind. As a general rule, the traditional tort law duty of care will apply to a government agency in the same way that it will apply to an individual. In determining whether a duty of care exists the first question to be resolved is whether the parties are in a relationship of sufficient proximity to warrant the imposition of such a duty. In the case of a government agency, exemption from this imposition of duty may occur as a result of an explicit statutory exemption. Alternatively, the exemption may arise as a result of the nature of the decision made by the government agency. That is, a government agency will be exempt from the imposition of a duty of care in situations which arise from its pure policy decisions.

In determining what constitutes such a policy decision, it should be borne in mind that such decisions are generally made by persons of a high level of authority in the agency, but may also properly be made by persons of a lower level of authority. The characterization of such a decision rests on the nature of the decision and not on the identity of the actors. As a general rule, decisions concerning budgetary allotments for departments or government agencies will be classified as policy decisions. Further, it must be recalled that a policy decision is open to challenge on the basis that it is not made in the *bona fide* exercise of discretion. If after due consideration it is found that a duty of care is owed by the government agency and no exemption by way of statute or policy decision-making is found to exist, a traditional torts analysis ensues and the issue of standard of care required of the government agency must next be considered.

The manner and quality of an inspection system is clearly part of the operational aspect of a governmental activity and falls to be assessed in the consideration of the standard of care issue. At this stage, the requisite standard of care to be applied to the particular operation must be assessed in light of all the surrounding circumstances including, for example, budgetary restraints and the availability of qualified personnel and equipment.

Turning to the case at bar it is now appropriate to . . . determine whether the decision or decisions of the government agency were policy decisions exempting the province from liability. Here what was challenged was the manner in which the inspections were carried out, their frequency or infrequency and how and when trees above the rock cut should have been inspected, and the manner in which the cutting and scaling operations should have been carried out. In short, the public authority had settled on a plan which called upon it to inspect all slopes visually and then conduct further inspections of those slopes where the taking of additional safety measures was warranted. Those matters are all part and parcel of what [may be] described as "the product of administrative direction, expert or professional opinion, technical standards or general standards of care". They were not decisions that could be designated as policy decisions. Rather they were manifestations of the implementation of the policy decision to inspect and were operational in nature. As such, they were subject to review by the Court to determine whether the respondent had been negligent or had satisfied the appropriate standard of care.

At trial the conclusion was reached that the number and frequency of inspections, of scaling and other remedial measures were matters of policy; as a result no findings of fact were made on the issues bearing on the standard of care. Since the matter was one of operation the respondent was not immune from suit and the negligence issue had to be canvassed in its entirety. The appellant was therefore entitled to a finding of fact on these questions and a new trial should be directed to accomplish this.

. . .

SOPINKA J. (dissenting) — My colleague's reasons are based essentially on an attack on the policy of the respondent with respect to the extent and manner of the inspection program. In my opinion, absent evidence that a policy was adopted for some ulterior motive and not for a municipal purpose, it is *not* open to a litigant to attack it, nor is it appropriate for a court to pass upon it. As stated by Lord du Parcq in *Kent v. East Suffolk Rivers Catchment Board*, [1940] 1 K.B. 319, at p. 338:

> . . . it must be remembered that when Parliament has left it to a public authority to decide which of its powers it shall exercise, and when and to what extent it shall exercise them, there would be some inconvenience in submitting to the subsequent decision of a jury, or judge of fact, the question whether the authority had acted reasonably, a question involving the consideration of matters of policy and sometimes the striking of a just balance between the rival claims of efficiency and thrift.

This statement was approved by Lord Wilberforce in *Anns v. Merton London Borough Council* [1978] A.C. 728, at p. 754.

If a court assumes the power to review a policy decision which is made in accordance with the statute, this amounts to a usurpation by the court of a power committed by statute to the designated body. As pointed out by Wilson J. in *City of Kamloops v. Nielsen, supra*, at pp. 9-10:

> It is for the local authority to decide what resources it should make available to carry out its role in supervising and controlling the activities of builders. For example, budgetary considerations may dictate how many inspectors should be hired for this purpose, what their qualifications should be, and how often inspections should be made. He approved the statement of du Parcq L.J. in *Kent v. East Suffolk Rivers Catchment Board* . . . that public authorities have to strike a balance between the claims of efficiency and thrift and whether they get the right balance can only be decided through the ballot box and not in the courts.

In *Anns v. Merton London Borough Council, supra,* Lord Wilberforce was of the opinion that although the exercise by a public authority of discretionary power was not entirely immune from attack, it was open to challenge only if no consideration was given to whether to exercise the power which, there as here, was whether to inspect and the manner of the inspection, *supra,* at p. 755. He did not elaborate as to whether such a challenge could be by way of a claim for damages by a person injured by the failure to inspect. Lord Salmon, however, was of the view that an improper exercise of discretion could only be corrected by *certiorari* or mandamus, and did not give rise to an action for damages, *supra,* at p. 762.

In the following passage, at p. 755, Lord Wilberforce makes it clear that a decision to inspect, and the time, manner and techniques of inspection, may all be within the discretionary power:

> There may be a discretionary element in its exercise — discretionary as to the time and manner of inspection, and the techniques to be used. A plaintiff complaining of negligence must prove, the burden being on him, that action taken was not within the limits of a discretion bona fide exercised, before he can begin to rely upon a common law duty of care. But if he can do this, he should, in principle, be able to sue.

If, as here, the statute creates no duty to inspect at all, but simply confers a power to do so, it follows logically that a decision to inspect and the extent and manner thereof are all discretionary powers of the authority.

It is not suggested here that the respondent failed to consider whether to inspect or the manner of inspections. The trial judge and the Court of Appeal found that a policy decision was made that inspections would be carried out by a crew of men called the Rockwork Section. In view of the fact that the crew had responsibility for the inspection of the slopes of all highways, the extent and manner of the inspection was delegated to the Rockwork Section. While it might be suggested that guidelines for inspection should have been laid down for the guidance of the crew, this would be second guessing the policy decision and not a matter for the Court. The appellant's attack on the conduct of the respondent and its employees is an attack on the manner in which they carried out the inspection and scaling of the mountain. The Rockwork Section had decided it could not closely monitor all slopes at all times. Some slopes would only be visually inspected from the highway. The appellant contended that the slopes above manmade cuts should have been closely inspected and that the trees should have been removed within ten feet of a cut slope. The trial judge made the following important findings concerning the decision of the respondent as to the extent and manner of the inspection program:

> The question in the case at bar is thus whether the failure of the Crown to take the steps which the plaintiff says it should have taken to prevent the rock fall was a matter of policy or operational. In order to answer it, it is necessary to consider the nature of the decisions here in question. The Crown had never established as a matter of policy that all slopes above highways must be inspected for potential rock fall. Nor had it laid out specific guidelines for dealing with problems if danger was perceived. What it had done was to establish a small crew of men (the rock scaling crew) to deal with problems arising on cliff faces throughout the Province. This crew responded to specific requests from various highway districts for inspection and scaling. For the most part, however, it developed and followed its own program. Given that it was responsible for inspection of slopes and appropriate remedial measures for all the highways in the Province, it could not closely monitor all slopes at all times. The slope

here in question was visually inspected from the highway on a number of occasions. However, there had never been scaling or close inspection of the area above the cut because the rock scaling crew did not deem that work to be a priority.

In stating that the authority "must specifically consider whether to inspect and if so the system must be a reasonable one in all the circumstances", my colleague is extending liability beyond what was decided in *Anns v. Merton London Borough Council, Barratt v. District of North Vancouver*, and *City of Kamloops v. Nielsen, supra.* The system would include the time, manner and technique of inspection. On this analysis it is difficult to determine what aspect of a policy decision would be immune from review. All that is left is the decision to inspect. It can hardly be suggested that all the learning that has been expended on the difference between policy and operational was expended to immunize the decision of a public body that something will be done but not the content of what will be done. It seems to me that a decision to inspect rather than not inspect hardly needs protection from review. The concern that has resulted in extending immunity from review in respect of policy decisions is that those entrusted with the exercise of the statutory powers make the decision to expend public resources. It is not engaged by a decision simply to do something. It is the decision as to what is to be done that will entail the taxation of the public purse. Lord Wilberforce underscores this concern when he states, at p. 754:

> Let us examine the Public Health Act 1936 in the light of this. Undoubtedly it lays out a wide area of policy. It is for the local authority, a public and elected body, to decide upon the scale of resources which it can make available in order to carry out its functions under Part II of the Act — how many inspectors, with what expert qualifications, it should recruit, how often inspections are to be made, what tests are to be carried out, must be for its decision. It is no accident that the Act is drafted in terms of functions and powers rather than in terms of positive duty. As was well said, public authorities have to strike a balance between the claims of efficiency and thrift (du Parcq L.J. in *Kent v. East Suffolk Rivers Catchment Board* [1940] 1 K.B. 319, 338): whether they get the balance right can only be decided through the ballot box, not in the courts.

In this case, the extent of the inspection program was delegated to the Rockwork Section. The respondent acted within its statutory discretion in making that decision. It was a decision that inspections should be done and the manner in which they should be done. In order for a private duty to arise, it would have to be shown that the Rockwork Section acted outside its delegated discretion to determine whether to inspect and the manner in which the inspection is to be made.

NOTES AND QUESTIONS

1. What is the purpose of immunizing policy decisions? Do you agree? Why is this purpose not relevant in the operational sphere? Which definition of the operational sphere in *Just* makes better sense if one accepts the purpose of policy immunity?

2. What special consideration does Cory J. extend to public authorities on the question of the standard of care? Why is the standard not the same as for private defendants? At this point, are the courts not usurping the public authorities' decision on how to allocate their budgets? Are courts institutionally competent to make such determinations?

3. A useful illustration of the policy/operational distinction can be found in *Ingles v. Tutkaluk Construction Ltd.*, [2000] 1 S.C.R. 298, which involved a claim of negligent building inspection. The municipality was not obligated to institute a building inspection system, and the decision whether to do so was a matter of policy that was not reviewable by the courts unless made in bad faith. However, once the city had decided to institute an inspection system, the implementation of that system was an operational function that was subject to the standard of reasonable care, *i.e.*, the inspection had to be carried out reasonably.

4. The first articulation of the policy/operational distinction in the Commonwealth came in *Anns v. Merton London Borough Council*, [1978] A.C. 728 (H.L.) which built upon the decision in *Dorset Yacht Co. v. Home Office*, [1970] A.C. 1004 (H.L.). There are many similarities between *Anns* and the decision in *Welbridge Holdings Ltd. v. Greater Winnipeg* (1970), 22 D.L.R. (3d) 470 (S.C.C.), in which the court immunized legislative functions of municipal governments from negligence liability. See also *Comeau's Sea Foods Ltd. v. Canada (Minister of Fisheries & Oceans)* (1997), 142 D.L.R. (4th) 193 (S.C.C.).

5. For a variety of applications of *Just*, see *Lewis v. Prince Edward Island* (1998), 160 Nfld. & P.E.I.R. 183 (P.E.I.C.A.); *Atlantic Leasing Ltd. v. Newfoundland* (1998), 164 Nfld. & P.E.I.R. 119 (Nfld. C.A.); *Tottrup v. Lund* (2000), 255 A.R. 204 (C.A.); *Gobin (Guardian ad litem of) v. British Columbia* (2002), 214 D.L.R. (4th) 328 (B.C.C.A.); *Neuman v. Parkland County* (2004), 355 A.R. 169 (Prov. Ct.); *Bowes v. Edmonton (City)* (2007), 425 A.R. 123 (C.A.); *Wynberg v. Ontario* (2006), 82 O.R. (3d) 561 (C.A.); and *Adams v. Borrel* (2008), 297 D.L.R. (4th) 400 (N.B.C.A.).

6. The distinction between policy and operational functions is notoriously difficult to make. Compare *Just* with *Swinamer v. Nova Scotia (Attorney General)*, [1994] 1 S.C.R. 445. The plaintiff in *Swinamer* was injured when a diseased tree growing along the highway fell onto his truck. The province had instituted a program to identify and remove dangerous trees, and the plaintiff alleged that this program was subject to review by the courts. The trial judge, relying on *Just*, found that the implementation of the program was an operational function, and found the defendant negligent. However, the Supreme Court of Canada concluded that the tree removal program was a matter of policy that could not be reviewed. See also *Brown v. British Columbia (Minister of Transportation and Highways)*, [1994] 1 S.C.R. 420.

7. The following activities have been found to be operational: the failure to erect higher median barriers on a highway in a timely manner (*Malat v. Bjornson (No. 2)* (1978), 6 C.C.L.T. 142 (B.C.S.C.), aff'd (1980), 14 C.C.L.T. 206 (B.C.C.A.)); a municipality's decision to issue a building permit and its failure to identify construction defects (*Mortimer v. Cameron* (1994), 111 D.L.R. (4th) 428 (Ont. C.A.), excerpted in Chapter 19); the Crown's failure to inspect and maintain a highway (*Lewis (Guardian ad litem of) v. British Columbia*, [1997] 3 S.C.R. 1145); the denial of a crabbing licence by the Ministry of Fisheries and Oceans on account of an Officer's negligent measurement of the plaintiff's boat (*Keeping v. Canada (Minister of Fisheries and Oceans)* (2003), 224 Nfld. & P.E.I.R. 234 (N.L.C.A.)); the failure to anticipate "freeze-up" and apply salt to highways in a timely manner (*Benoit v. Farrell Estate* (2004), 27 B.C.L.R. (4th) 226 (C.A.)); the decision to transfer a violent prisoner to a minimum security facility (*Pete v. Axworthy* (2005), 45 B.C.L.R. (4th) 311 (C.A.)); and

the decision to house the plaintiff prison inmate in a cell block with rival gang members (*Walters (Litigation Guardian of) v. Ontario*, 2015 ONSC 4855, aff'd 2017 ONCA 53).

8. The following activities have been found to involve policy decisions: the maintenance of municipal manhole covers (*Wegren v. Prince Albert (City)* (2004), 251 Sask. R. 313 (Prov. Ct.)); the adoption of a particular system for clearing snow and ice from municipal sidewalks (*Knodell v. New Westminster (City)* (2005), 14 M.P.L.R. (4th) 258 (B.C.S.C.)); a municipality's decision not to reduce the speed limit in a school area (*Potts v. Heutink*, 2006 CarswellBC 2702 (S.C.) (WL Can)); the refusal to enter into an agreement with parents to provide for the needs of a special needs child (*A.L. v. Ontario (Minister of Community and Social Services)* (2006), 83 O.R. (3d) 512 (C.A.); and the decision not to inspect electrical connectors unless in receipt of complaints by customers (*Saskatoon (City) v. Smith* (2008), 304 D.L.R. (4th) 577 (Sask. C.A.)). Can any of these be meaningfully distinguished from the operational functions listed in note 7?

9. J.A. Smillie has argued that public authorities should be under a duty of care whenever the same conduct would attract a duty if the defendant were a private citizen. See "Liability of Public Authorities For Negligence" (1985) 23 U.W.O.L. Rev. 213. Can a meaningful analogy be drawn to private conduct leading to the duty of care in *Just*? In contrast, D. Cohen and J.C. Smith emphasize the unique public authority aspects of cases such as *Just*, where the plaintiff's claim rests on the failure to obtain a public benefit. See "Entitlement and the Body Politic: Rethinking Negligence in Public Law" (1986) 64 Can. Bar Rev. 1. B. Feldthusen has argued that there should be total immunity from liability in negligence with respect to the exercise of public discretion. See Feldthusen, "Failure to Confer Discretionary Public Benefits: The Case for Complete Negligence Immunity" (1997) 5 Tort L. Rev. 17. More recently, in *Paradis Honey Ltd. v. Canada*, 2015 FCA 89, Stratas J.A. argued, *obiter dicta*, that negligence law should be abandoned in public authority cases and substituted with more appropriate public law remedies.

10. The policy/operational distinction was endorsed throughout the Commonwealth, but there is considerable divergence in how it is interpreted within and among the different jurisdictions, and it has been undermined to varying extents. See for example *Sutherland Shire Council v. Heyman* (1985), 60 A.L.R. 1 (H.C.A.); *X (Minors) v. Bedfordshire County Council*, [1995] 2 A.C. 633 (H.L.); and *Stovin v. Wise*, [1996] A.C. 923 (H.L.). See also Bailey & Bowman, "The Policy/operational Dichotomy — a Cuckoo in the Nest" [1986] C.L.J. 430; and Deegan, "The Public/ Private Dichotomy and Its Relationship With The Policy/Operational Factors In Negligence Law" (2001) 1 Queensland U. Tech. L. & Just. J. 241.

11. The scholarly literature on the negligence liability of public authorities is voluminous. See for example Klar, "The Supreme Court of Canada: Extending the Tort Liability of Public Authorities" (1990) 28 Alta. L. Rev. 648; Woodall, "Private Law Liability of Public Authorities for Negligent Inspection and Regulation" (1991-1992) 37 McGill L.J. 83; Cohen, "Government Liability for Economic Losses: The Case of Regulatory Failure" (1992) 20 C.B.L.J. 215; Cohen & Finkle, "Crown Liability in Canada: Developing Compensation Policies for Regulatory Failure" (1994) 37 Can. Pub. Admin. 79; Perell, "Negligence Claims Against Public

Authorities" (1994) 16 Adv. Q. 48; Sopinka, "The Liability of Public Authorities: Drawing the Line" (1994) 1 Tort L. Rev. 123; Hilson & Rogers, "*X v Bedfordshire County Council*: Tort Law and Statutory Functions — Probably not the End of the Story" (1995) 3 Torts L.J. 221; Davies, "Common Law Liability of Statutory Authorities" (1997) U.W.A.L. Rev. 21; Brodie, "Public Authorities — Negligence Actions — Control Devices" (1998) 18 L.S. 1; Kneebone, *Tort Liability of Public Authorities* (1998); Doyle & Redwood, "The Common Law Liability of Public Authorities: The Interface Between Public and Private Law" (1999) 7 Tort L. Rev. 30; Bailey & Bowman, "Public Authority Negligence Revisited" [2000] C.L.J. 85; Booth & Squires, *The Negligence Liability of Public Authorities* (2006); Siebrasse, "Liability of Public Authorities and Duties of Affirmative Action" (2007) 57 U.N.B.L.J 88; Feldthusen, *Economic Negligence*, 6th ed. (2012), ch. 6; Aronson, "Government Liability in Negligence" (2008) 32 Melbourne U.L. Rev. 44; and Feldthusen, "Unique Public Duties of Care: Judicial Activism in the Supreme Court of Canada" (2015) 53:4 Alta. L. Rev. 955.

12. As discussed in Chapter 14, tort law often struggles when the plaintiff's injury takes the form of pure economic loss. However, in the context of claims against public authorities, the Supreme Court of Canada draws no distinction between cases involving physical damage and those involving pure economic loss. Accordingly, once a court recognizes a duty of care and formulates the standard of care applicable to a public authority, the defendant is liable for either type of loss. See *Ingles v. Tutkaluk Construction Ltd.*, *supra*, and Brown, "Still Crazy After All These Years: *Anns, Cooper v. Hobart* and Pure Economic Loss" (2003) 36 U.B.C.L. Rev. 159.

(b) THE EFFECT OF *COOPER v. HOBART*

As discussed in Chapter 10, the Supreme Court of Canada reformulated its analysis of the duty of care in *Cooper v. Hobart*, [2001] 3 S.C.R. 537. The decision in *Cooper* has affected negligence analysis relating to public authorities in four main ways.

First, it has become necessary to situate the policy/operational distinction within the framework provided in *Cooper*. Recall that the first stage of the *Cooper* test involves an analysis of (i) whether the harm was foreseeable and (ii) whether there was a proximate relationship between the parties. The second stage involves a consideration of "residual" policy considerations that might serve to negative or limit the scope of the duty of care. Government immunity for "policy" functions falls within this second stage of the *Cooper* analysis. That is, even if harm was foreseeable and the parties were in a relationship of proximity, a court could still decline to find a duty of care because the public authority was exercising its policy or planning functions, rather than an operational function.

Second, the decision in *Cooper* placed greater emphasis on the element of proximity than had previous decisions in Canada. This means that many cases that would previously have been decided on the issue of policy and operational functions may now be decided based on the question of proximity. However, this does not necessarily make the determination any easier: proximity is notoriously difficult to define, and the considerations are similar to those involved in a policy/operational analysis. For instance, if the relevant conduct involved planning, budgetary considerations and a balancing of competing interests at a ministerial level, a court could conclude either that the decision was one of policy or that the plaintiff was not in a sufficiently proximate relationship with the relevant government authority.

Third, since *Cooper*, the interaction of statutory duties and the common law duty of care has become more complex. Recall that in *Cooper* the Supreme Court of Canada examined the *Mortgage Brokers Act*, R.S.B.C. 1996, c. 313, to determine whether the Registrar of Mortgage Brokers owed a common law duty of care to the plaintiffs. The court described the statute as "the only source of [the defendant's] duties, private or public." This approach essentially conflates statutory and common law duties. This is contrary to historical jurisprudence, which suggests that the common law duty of care must be determined independently from statute, and may arise in addition to any statutory duties. The approach in *Cooper* is also, arguably, contrary to the Supreme Court of Canada's decision in *R. v. Saskatchewan Wheat Pool*, [1983] 1 S.C.R. 205, which is excerpted in the next chapter. That case decided that breach of statutory duty is not a nominate tort in Canada: a plaintiff cannot succeed unless there existed a common law duty of care. While the statute may be relevant to the issue of common law duty, it is not determinative. Unfortunately, as thoroughly discussed by L. Klar in "Breach of Statute and Tort Law" in Neyers, Chamberlain & Pitel, eds., *Emerging Issues in Tort Law* (2007), the approach in *Cooper* has been copied and expanded in subsequent cases, such that breach of statutory duty is sometimes equated with breach of a common law duty of care.

In any event, the effect of *Cooper* has been to increase the importance of the statutory framework when deciding whether a public authority owed a duty of care in the circumstances of the case. This is illustrated by *Eliopoulos v. Ontario (Minister of Health & Long Term Care)* (2006), 82 O.R. (3d) 321 (C.A.), where the plaintiff's estate sued the government after he died from complications arising from West Nile Virus. The plaintiff alleged that the province ought to have prevented the outbreak of the virus, relying on the duties and powers contained in Ontario's *Health Protection and Promotion Act*, R.S.O. 1990, c. H.7. Accordingly, the Ontario Court of Appeal based its proximity analysis almost entirely on the provisions of that statute. As Sharpe J.A. explained at para. 17, the statute did not create a relationship of proximity:

> In my view, these important and extensive statutory provisions create discretionary powers that are not capable of creating a private law duty. . . . [N]o doubt there is a general public law duty that requires the Minister to endeavour to promote, safeguard and protect the health of Ontario residents and prevent the spread of infectious diseases. However, a general public law duty of that nature does not give rise to a private law duty sufficient to ground an action in negligence. I fail to see how it could be possible to convert any of the Minister's public law discretionary powers, to be exercised in the general public interest, into private law duties owed to specific individuals.

As this excerpt illustrates, the statutory framework has now become the primary consideration in negligence claims against public authorities. Because many of the relevant statutory provisions are phrased broadly, with the general public interest in mind, it is not surprising that the courts have had problems finding a private duty of care in the statutory language. See Klar, "The Tort Liability of the Crown: Back to *Canada v. Saskatchewan Wheat Pool*" (2007) 32 Adv. Q. 293; and Brown & Brochu, "Once More Unto the Breach: *James v. British Columbia* and Problems with the Duty of Care in Canadian Tort Law" (2008) 45 Alta. L. Rev. 1071.

Finally, on a broader level, the decision in *Cooper* seems to reflect a more restrictive attitude toward public authority liability in Canada. While the 1970s and 1980s can be characterized as an era of expansion for public authority liability, the new millennium can be characterized by a more conservative attitude. The Canadian courts now seem somewhat more reluctant to impose a duty of care on public authorities.

NOTES AND QUESTIONS

1. *Williams v. Canada (Attorney-General)* (2005), 76 O.R. (3d) 763 (S.C.J.), aff'd (2009), 95 O.R. (3d) 401 (C.A.), involved a class action against the Crown in connection with the SARS outbreak in Toronto in 2003. The plaintiff alleged against the federal Crown, *inter alia*, that it had breached its duty to prevent the spread of diseases in Canada, including surveillance, analysis and testing in relation to the monitoring of new diseases. In particular, the plaintiff alleged that the Attorney General had failed to co-ordinate its response to the SARS crisis with the Ontario Ministry of Health and Long-Term Care, failed to translate a Chinese report regarding a flu outbreak in China, and denied the continuation of the outbreak. Cullity J. struck out the claim against the federal Crown because the element of proximity was not satisfied. In particular, there was no "close and direct causal connection" between the alleged omissions and the harms suffered by members of the class, and the relevant statutory duties were framed in terms of the general public. Could Cullity J. have just as easily struck out the claim as being based on government policy decisions? See also *Lowe v. The Guarantee Company of North America* (2005), 80 O.R. (3d) 222 (C.A.); *Klein v. American Medical Systems, Inc.* (2006), 44 C.C.L.T. (3d) 47 (Ont. Div. Ct.); *Syl Apps Secure Treatment Centre v. D.(B.)*, [2007] 3 S.C.R. 83; *Holland v. Saskatchewan*, [2008] 2 S.C.R. 551; *Street v. Ontario Racing Commission* (2008), 88 O.R. (3d) 563 (C.A.); and *Reference re Broome v. Prince Edward Island*, [2010] 1 S.C.R. 360. See also Klar, "*Syl Apps Secure Treatment Centre v. B.D.*: Looking for Proximity within Statutory Provisions" (2007) 86 Can. Bar Rev. 337; Hardcastle, "Government Tort Liability for Negligence in the Health Sector: A Critique of the Canadian Jurisprudence" (2012) 37 Queen's L.J. 525; and Feldthusen, "Simplifying Canadian Negligence Actions Against Public Authorities — Or Maybe Not" (2012) 20 Tort L. Rev. 176.

2. In *Holtslag v. Alberta* (2006), 55 Alta. L.R. (4th) 214 (C.A.), the plaintiffs sued the provincial Director of Building Standards for issuing a product listing authorizing the use of untreated pine shakes on residential homes. The shakes rotted within five years of installation, and the plaintiffs claimed for the costs of replacing their roofs and the decreased value of their homes. The Alberta Court of Appeal rejected the claim on the basis that the plaintiffs lacked proximity with the Director. However, in deciding the issue of proximity, the court made extensive reference to case law on the policy/operational dichotomy. *Holtslag* therefore shows the difficulty separating the two determinations. See also *Bagnell v. Taser International, Inc.* (2006), 44 C.C.L.T. (3d) 293 (B.C.S.C.), aff'd (2008), 80 B.C.L.R. (4th) 255 (C.A.), where both the proximity and policy/operational tests were resolved in the plaintiff's favour.

3. For a post-*Cooper* illustration of when a public authority might owe a duty of care, see *Heaslip Estate v. Mansfield Ski Club Inc.* (2009), 96 O.R. (3d) 401 (C.A.). The

Ontario Court of Appeal refused to strike out a claim against the Medical Air Transport Centre for failing to assign an air ambulance to the plaintiff after he suffered life-threatening injuries in a tobogganing accident. The plaintiff died after being transported to hospital in a land ambulance. The court found that a relationship of proximity could arise as a result of the direct interaction of the parties, and found that the alleged negligence was of an operational character. See also *Odhavji Estate v. Woodhouse*, [2003] 3 S.C.R. 263; *Fullowka v. Royal Oak Ventures Inc.*, 2010 SCC 5; and *Paradis Honey Ltd. v. Canada*, 2015 FCA 89.

R. v. IMPERIAL TOBACCO CANADA LTD.
2011 SCC 42

[During litigation against Imperial Tobacco for the harms caused to smokers and the costs of their health care on the British Columbia government, Imperial Tobacco brought a third-party claim against the Government of Canada. This claim alleged that Canada owed a duty of care to consumers and to tobacco companies, and that Canada was liable for, *inter alia*, negligently misrepresenting the health attributes of so-called "light" or "mild" cigarettes. The Supreme Court of Canada's discussion of the negligent misrepresentation claims is extracted in Chapter 13. The extract below follows that discussion. Note how it addresses the concept of core policy immunity.]

The judgment of the Court was delivered by

McLACHLIN C.J.C.:—

. . .

[60] In sum, I conclude that the claims between the tobacco companies and Canada should not be struck out at the first stage of the analysis. The pleadings, assuming them to be true, disclose a *prima facie* duty of care in negligent misrepresentation. However, the facts as pleaded in the *Knight* case do not show a relationship between Canada and consumers that would give rise to a duty of care. That claim should accordingly be struck at this stage of the analysis.

(2) Stage Two: Conflicting Policy Considerations

. . .

(a) *Government Policy Decisions*

[63] Canada contends that it had a policy of encouraging smokers to consume low-tar cigarettes, and pursuant to this policy, promoted this variety of cigarette and developed strains of low-tar tobacco. Canada argues that statements made pursuant to this policy cannot ground tort liability. It relies on the statement of Cory J. in *Just v. British Columbia*, [1989] 2 S.C.R. 1228, that "[t]rue policy decisions should be exempt from tortious claims so that governments are not restricted in making decisions based upon social, political or economic factors" (p. 1240).

[64] The tobacco companies, for their part, contend that Canada's actions were not matters of policy, but operational acts implementing policy, and therefore, are subject to tort liability. They submit that Canada's argument fails to account for the "facts" as pleaded in the third-party notices, namely that Canada was acting in an operational capacity, and as a participant in the tobacco industry. The tobacco companies also argue that more evidence is required to determine if the government's

actions were operational or pursuant to policy, and that the matter should therefore be permitted to go to trial.

. . .

(iii) What Constitutes a Policy Decision Immune From Judicial Review?

[72] The question of what constitutes a policy decision that is generally protected from negligence liability is a vexed one, upon which much judicial ink has been spilled. There is general agreement in the common law world that government policy decisions are not justiciable and cannot give rise to tort liability. There is also general agreement that governments may attract liability in tort where government agents are negligent in carrying out prescribed duties. The problem is to devise a workable test to distinguish these situations.

[73] The jurisprudence reveals two approaches to the problem, one emphasizing discretion, the other, policy, each with variations. The first approach focuses on the discretionary nature of the impugned conduct. The "discretionary decision" approach was first adopted in *Home Office v. Dorset Yacht Co.*, [1970] 2 W.L.R. 1140 (H.L.). This approach holds that public authorities should be exempt from liability if they are acting within their discretion, unless the challenged decision is irrational.

[74] The second approach emphasizes the "policy" nature of protected state conduct. Policy decisions are conceived of as a subset of discretionary decisions, typically characterized as raising social, economic and political considerations. These are sometimes called "true" or "core" policy decisions. They are exempt from judicial consideration and cannot give rise to liability in tort, provided they are neither irrational nor taken in bad faith. A variant of this is the policy/operational test, in which "true" policy decisions are distinguished from "operational" decisions, which seek to implement or carry out settled policy. To date, the policy/operational approach is the dominant approach in Canada [citations omitted].

[75] To complicate matters, the concepts of discretion and policy overlap and are sometimes used interchangeably. Thus Lord Wilberforce in *Anns* defined policy as a synonym for discretion (p. 754).

[76] There is wide consensus that the law of negligence must account for the unique role of government agencies: *Just*. On the one hand, it is important for public authorities to be liable in general for their negligent conduct in light of the pervasive role that they play in all aspects of society. Exempting all government actions from liability would result in intolerable outcomes. On the other hand, "the Crown is not a person and must be free to govern and make true policy decisions without becoming subject to tort liability as a result of those decisions": *Just*, at p. 1239. The challenge, to repeat, is to fashion a just and workable legal test.

[77] The main difficulty with the "discretion" approach is that it has the potential to create an overbroad exemption for the conduct of government actors. Many decisions can be characterized as to some extent discretionary. For this reason, this approach has sometimes been refined or replaced by tests that narrow the scope of the discretion that confers immunity.

[78] The main difficulty with the policy/operational approach is that courts have found it notoriously difficult to decide whether a particular government decision falls on the policy or operational side of the line. Even low-level state employees may enjoy some discretion related to how much money is in the budget or which of a range of tasks is most important at a particular time. Is the decision of a social worker when to

visit a troubled home, or the decision of a snow-plow operator when to sand an icy road, a policy decision or an operational decision? Depending on the circumstances, it may be argued to be either or both. The policy/operational distinction, while capturing an important element of why some government conduct should generally be shielded from liability, does not work very well as a legal test.

[79] The elusiveness of a workable test to define policy decisions protected from judicial review is captured by the history of the issue in various courts. I begin with the House of Lords. The House initially adopted the view that all discretionary decisions of government are immune, unless they are irrational: *Dorset Yacht*. It then moved on to a two-stage test that asked first whether the decision was discretionary and, if so, rational; and asked second whether it was a core policy decision, in which case it was entirely exempt from judicial scrutiny: *X v. Bedfordshire County Council*, [1995] 3 All E.R. 353. Within a year of adopting this two-stage test, the House abandoned it with a ringing declamation of the policy/operational distinction as unworkable in difficult cases, a point said to be evidenced by the Canadian jurisprudence: *Stovin v. Wise*, [1996] A.C. 923 (H.L.), *per* Lord Hoffmann. In its most recent foray into the subject, the House of Lords affirmed that both the policy/operational distinction and the discretionary decision approach are valuable tools for discerning which government decisions attract tort liability, but held that the final test is a "justiciability" test: *Barrett v. Enfield London Borough Council*, [2001] 2 A.C. 550. The ultimate question on this test is whether the court is institutionally capable of deciding on the question, or "whether the court should accept that it has no role to play" (p. 571). Thus at the end of the long judicial voyage the traveller arrives at a test that essentially restates the question. When should the court hold that a government decision is protected from negligence liability? When the court concludes that the matter is one for the government and not the courts.

[The Chief Justice then reviewed the Australian and American jurisprudence.]

. . .

[84] A review of the jurisprudence provokes the following observations. The first is that a test based simply on the exercise of government discretion is generally now viewed as too broad. Discretion can imbue even routine tasks, like driving a government vehicle. To protect all government acts that involve discretion unless they are irrational simply casts the net of immunity too broadly.

[85] The second observation is that there is considerable support in all jurisdictions reviewed for the view that "true" or "core" policy decisions should be protected from negligence liability. The current Canadian approach holds that only "true" policy decisions should be so protected, as opposed to operational decisions: *Just*. The difficulty in defining such decisions does not detract from the fact that the cases keep coming back to this central insight. Even the most recent "justiciability" test in the U.K. looks to this concept for support in defining what should be viewed as justiciable.

[86] A third observation is that defining a core policy decision negatively as a decision that is not an "operational" decision may not always be helpful as a stand-alone test. It posits a stark dichotomy between two water-tight compartments — policy decisions and operational decisions. In fact, decisions in real life may not fall neatly into one category or the other.

[87] Instead of defining protected policy decisions negatively, as "not operational", the majority in [*United States v. Gaubert*, 499 U.S. 315 (1991)] defines

them positively as discretionary legislative or administrative decisions and conduct that are grounded in social, economic, and political considerations. Generally, policy decisions are made by legislators or officers whose official responsibility requires them to assess and balance public policy considerations. The decision is a considered decision that represents a "policy" in the sense of a general rule or approach, applied to a particular situation. It represents "a course or principle of action adopted or proposed by a government": *New Oxford Dictionary of English* (1998), at p. 1434. When judges are faced with such a course or principle of action adopted by a government, they generally will find the matter to be a policy decision. The weighing of social, economic, and political considerations to arrive at a course or principle of action is the proper role of government, not the courts. For this reason, decisions and conduct based on these considerations cannot ground an action in tort.

[88] Policy, used in this sense, is not the same thing as discretion. Discretion is concerned with whether a particular actor had a choice to act in one way or the other. Policy is a narrow subset of discretionary decisions, covering only those decisions that are based on public policy considerations, like economic, social and political considerations. Policy decisions are always discretionary, in the sense that a different policy could have been chosen. But not all discretionary decisions by government are policy decisions.

[89] While the main focus on the *Gaubert* approach is on the nature of the decision, the role of the person who makes the decision may be of assistance. Did the decision maker have the responsibility of looking at social, economic or political factors and formulating a "course" or "principle" of action with respect to a particular problem facing the government? Without suggesting that the question can be resolved simply by reference to the rank of the actor, there is something to Scalia J.'s observation in *Gaubert* that employees working at the operational level are not usually involved in making policy choices.

[90] I conclude that "core policy" government decisions protected from suit are decisions as to a course or principle of action that are based on public policy considerations, such as economic, social and political factors, provided they are neither irrational nor taken in bad faith. This approach is consistent with the basic thrust of Canadian cases on the issue, although it emphasizes positive features of policy decisions, instead of relying exclusively on the quality of being "non-operational". It is also supported by the insights of emerging jurisprudence here and elsewhere. This said, it does not purport to be a litmus test. Difficult cases may be expected to arise from time to time where it is not easy to decide whether the degree of "policy" involved suffices for protection from negligence liability. A black and white test that will provide a ready and irrefutable answer for every decision in the infinite variety of decisions that government actors may produce is likely chimerical. Nevertheless, most government decisions that represent a course or principle of action based on a balancing of economic, social and political considerations will be readily identifiable.

[91] Applying this approach to motions to strike, we may conclude that where it is "plain and obvious" that an impugned government decision is a policy decision, the claim may properly be struck on the ground that it cannot ground an action in tort. If it is not plain and obvious, the matter must be allowed to go to trial.

(iv) Conclusion on the Policy Argument

[92] As discussed, the question is whether the alleged representations of Canada to the tobacco companies that low-tar cigarettes are less harmful to health are matters of policy, in the sense that they constitute a course or principle of action of the government. If so, the representations cannot ground an action in tort.

[93] The third-party notices plead that Canada made statements to the public (and to the tobacco companies) warning about the hazards of smoking, and asserting that low-tar cigarettes are less harmful than regular cigarettes; that the representations that low-tar cigarettes are less harmful to health were false; and that insofar as consumption caused extra harm to consumers for which the tobacco companies are held liable, Canada is required to indemnify the tobacco companies and/or contribute to their losses.

[94] The third-party notices implicitly accept that in making the alleged representations, Health Canada was acting out of concern for the health of Canadians, pursuant to its policy of encouraging smokers to switch to low-tar cigarettes. They assert, in effect, that Health Canada had a policy to warn the public about the hazardous effects of smoking, and to encourage healthier smoking habits among Canadians. The third-party claims rest on the allegation that Health Canada accepted that some smokers would continue to smoke despite the adverse health effects, and decided that these smokers should be encouraged to smoke lower-tar cigarettes.

[95] In short, the representations on which the third-party claims rely were part and parcel of a government policy to encourage people who continued to smoke to switch to low-tar cigarettes. This was a "true" or "core" policy, in the sense of a course or principle of action that the government adopted. The government's alleged course of action was adopted at the highest level in the Canadian government, and involved social and economic considerations. Canada, on the pleadings, developed this policy out of concern for the health of Canadians and the individual and institutional costs associated with tobacco-related disease. In my view, it is plain and obvious that the alleged representations were matters of government policy, with the result that the tobacco companies' claims against Canada for negligent misrepresentation must be struck out.

NOTES AND QUESTIONS

1. Summarize the court's criticisms of the policy/operational distinction. Does the new test of "core policy" immunity adequately address those criticisms? When, if at all, will it result in a different outcome than the policy/operational test? See *Paradis Honey Ltd. v. Canada*, 2015 FCA 89 at para. 110, where Stratas J.A. opined that, if anything, "*Imperial Tobacco* leaves us more uncertain than ever as to when the policy bar will apply."

2. For commentary on *R. v. Imperial Tobacco*, see Klar, "*R. v. Imperial Tobacco Ltd.*: More Restrictions on Public Authority Tort Liability" (2012) 50 Alta. L. Rev. 157; and Feldthusen, "Public Authority Immunity from Negligence Liability: Uncertain, Unnecessary, and Unjustified" (2014) 92 Can. Bar Rev. 211. See also *George v. Newfoundland and Labrador*, 2016 NLCA 24, where the province's management of the abundant moose population was considered a core policy

decision. The province thus did not owe a duty of care to motorists who were injured or killed in moose-vehicle crashes.

3. In its proposed *Crown Liability and Proceedings Act, 2019*, the Ontario government purported to "codify" the common law on policy immunity and listed a range of activities that should be categorized as policy matters. This included the creation, design, or modification of programs or initiatives, the funding of programs, and the cancellation of programs. It also included "the carrying out of some or all of a program, project or other initiative." Do you agree that this amounts to a codification of the common law?

4. Misfeasance in a Public Office

(a) INTRODUCTION

Another uniquely public tort is misfeasance in a public office, sometimes called abuse of office or abuse of power. This is an intentional tort, and historically involved malicious conduct by a public officer that was directly aimed at a particular individual. For instance, one of its seminal cases, *Ashby v. White* (1703), 92 E.R. 126 (K.B.), involved a claim that an electoral officer had wrongfully denied the plaintiff the right to vote in an effort to prejudice the candidate for whom the plaintiff wished to vote. However, as will be discussed below, the misfeasance tort has now expanded to include conduct that is less obviously malicious or abusive.

For many years, the leading Canadian case on misfeasance in a public office was *Roncarelli v. Duplessis* (1959), 16 D.L.R. (2d) 689 (S.C.C.). *Roncarelli* is an example of a clear abuse of power deliberately intended to injure a particular individual.

RONCARELLI v. DUPLESSIS
(1959), 16 D.L.R. (2d) 689 (S.C.C.)

[The plaintiff was the proprietor of a restaurant in Montreal which had held a liquor licence for 34 years. He was also a member of the Witnesses of Jehovah, a religious sect whose printed works had been provoking considerable social unrest in the primarily Roman Catholic province of Québec. Starting in 1945, the provincial authorities had arrested large numbers of the Witnesses of Jehovah in an effort to end what they considered to be the group's insulting and offensive conduct. The plaintiff had provided bail for approximately 380 Jehovah's Witnesses. Beyond that, the plaintiff had not engaged in behaviour which the provincial government found objectionable.

Mr. Archambault, the Liquor Commissioner, notified Mr. Duplessis, the Attorney General and Premier of Québec, of the plaintiff's conduct. Duplessis, feeling that his position in the provincial government required him to do so, directed Mr. Archambault to refuse to renew the plaintiff's liquor licence. The plaintiff sued Mr. Duplessis for his loss of profits stemming from the government's refusal to renew the restaurant's liquor licence.

The relevant legislation gave Mr. Archambault the sole authority to grant or cancel liquor licences, and specified that the "Commission may cancel any permit at its discretion."

In a six-three judgment, the defendant was held liable, and the plaintiff was awarded approximately $33,000. Mr. Justice Martland, with whom Kerwin C.J. and

Locke J. agreed, wrote one majority judgment. Mr. Justice Rand, with whom Judson J. agreed, wrote another, and Abbott J. wrote a third. Justices Taschereau, Cartwright and Fauteaux wrote separate dissenting judgments. Only a brief excerpt of Rand J.'s judgment is reprinted below.]

RAND J.: . . . The field of licensed occupations and businesses of this nature is steadily becoming of greater concern to citizens generally. It is a matter of vital importance that a public administration that can refuse to allow a person to enter or continue a calling which, in the absence of regulation, would be free and legitimate, should be conducted with complete impartiality and integrity; and that the grounds for refusing or cancelling a permit should unquestionably be such and such only as are incompatible with the purposes envisaged by the statute: the duty of a Commission is to serve those purposes and those only. A decision to deny or cancel such a privilege lies within the "discretion" of the Commission; but that means that decision is to be based upon a weighing of considerations pertinent to the object of the administration.

In public regulation of this sort there is no such thing as absolute and untrammelled "discretion", that is that action can be taken on any ground or for any reason that can be suggested to the mind of the administrator; no legislative Act can, without express language, be taken to contemplate an unlimited arbitrary power, exercisable for any purpose, however capricious or irrelevant, regardless of the nature or purpose of the statute. Fraud and corruption in the Commission may not be mentioned in such statutes but they are always implied as exceptions. "Discretion" necessarily implies good faith in discharging public duty; there is always a perspective within which a statute is intended to operate; and any clear departure from its lines or objects is just as objectionable as fraud or corruption. Could an applicant be refused a permit because he had been born in another Province, or because of the colour of his hair? The ordinary language of the Legislature cannot be so distorted.

To deny or revoke a permit because a citizen exercises an unchallengeable right totally irrelevant to the sale of liquor in a restaurant is equally beyond the scope of the discretion conferred. There was here not only revocation of the existing permit but a declaration of a future, definitive disqualification of the appellant to obtain one: it was to be "forever". This purports to divest his citizenship status of its incident of membership in the class of those of the public to whom such a privilege could be extended. Under the statutory language here, that is not competent to the Commission and a fortiori to the Government or the respondent: McGillivray v. Kimber (1915), 26 D.L.R. 164, 52 S.C.R. 146. There is here an administrative tribunal which, in certain respects, is to act in a judicial manner; and even on the view of the dissenting Justices in McGillivray, there is liability: what could be more malicious than to punish this licensee for having done what he had an absolute right to do in a matter utterly irrelevant to the Alcoholic Liquor Act? Malice in the proper sense is simply acting for a reason or purpose knowingly foreign to the administration, to which was added here the element of intentional punishment by what was virtually vocation outlawry.

It may be difficult if not impossible in cases generally to demonstrate a breach of this public duty in the illegal purpose served; there may be no means, even if proceedings against the Commission were permitted by the Attorney-General, as here they were refused, of compelling the Commission to justify a refusal or revocation or to give reasons for its actions; on these questions I make no observation; but in the case before us that difficulty is not present: the reasons are openly avowed.

The act of the respondent through the instrumentality of the Commission brought about a breach of an implied public statutory duty toward the appellant; it was a gross abuse of legal power expressly intended to punish him for an act wholly irrelevant to the statute, a punishment which inflicted on him, as it was intended to do, the destruction of his economic life as a restaurant keeper within the Province. Whatever may be the immunity of the Commission or its member from an action for damages, there is none in the respondent. He was under no duty in relation to the appellant and his act was an intrusion upon the functions of a statutory body. The injury done by him was a fault engaging liability within the principles of the underlying public law of Québec: *Mostyn v. Fabrigas* (1774), 1 Cowp. 161, 98 E.R. 1021, and under art. 1053 of the *Civil Code*. That, in the presence of expanding administrative regulation of economic activities, such a step and its consequences are to be suffered by the victim without recourse or remedy, that an administration according to law is to be superseded by action dictated by and according to the arbitrary likes, dislikes and irrelevant purposes of public officers acting beyond their duty, would signalize the beginning of disintegration of the rule of law as a fundamental postulate of our constitutional structure. An administration of licences on the highest level of fair and impartial treatment to all may be forced to follow the practice of "first come, first served", which makes the strictest observance of equal responsibility to all of even greater importance; at this stage of developing government it would be a danger of high consequence to tolerate such a departure from good faith in executing the legislative purpose. It should be added, however, that that principle is not, by this language, intended to be extended to ordinary governmental employment: with that we are not here concerned.

It was urged by Mr. Beaulieu that the respondent, as the incumbent of an office of state, so long as he was proceeding in "good faith", was free to act in a matter of this kind virtually as he pleased. The office of Attorney-General traditionally and by statute carries duties that relate to advising the Executive, including here, administrative bodies, enforcing the public law and directing the administration of justice. In any decision of the statutory body in this case, he had no part to play beyond giving advice on legal questions arising. In that role this action should have been limited to advice on the validity of a revocation for such a reason or purpose and what that advice should have been does not seem to me to admit of any doubt. To pass from this limited scope of action to that of bringing about a step by the Commission beyond the bounds prescribed by the Legislature for its exclusive action converted what was done into his personal act.

"Good faith" in this context, applicable both to the respondent and the General Manager, means carrying out the statute according to its intent and for its purpose; it means good faith in acting with a rational appreciation of that intent and purpose and not with an improper intent or for an alien purpose; it does not mean for the purposes of punishing a person for exercising an unchallengeable right; it does not mean arbitrarily and illegally attempting to divest a citizen of an incident of his civil status.

NOTES AND QUESTIONS

1. *Roncarelli* was an action brought under then article 1053 of the Québec Civil Code. How would you have framed this case if it had been brought in a common law jurisdiction? Would the result have been different if the case had been brought in a

common law court? Would any of the common law legislative immunity rules have protected Duplessis?

2. How does Rand J. define malice and good faith?

3. What is the basis for Rand J.'s finding of liability? Is liability predicated on intentional excess of jurisdiction, excess of jurisdiction independent of any intent, improper purpose, or a combination of these factors?

4. Fauteaux and Taschereau JJ. dissented on the basis that Roncarelli had failed to give Duplessis adequate notice in breach of article 88 of the Code of Civil Procedure, which reads: "No public officer or other person fulfilling any public function or duty can be sued for damages by reason of any act done by him in the exercise of his functions . . . unless notice of such action has been given him at least one month before the issue of the writ of summons. . . ." How do you think the majority avoided the effect of this section?

5. Cartwright J. wrote a separate dissenting judgment in *Roncarelli*. He held that the defendant was exercising an administrative discretion which should not be reviewed by the courts. Alternatively, if the defendant was exercising a quasi-judicial function, Cartwright J. argued that he should be protected by judicial immunity. Do you agree that judicial immunity should be extended to those performing quasi-judicial functions? Even if the principles of judicial immunity applied, would they have protected Duplessis given the facts of the case? Is there any justification for absolving public authorities of liability if they abuse their powers?

6. For contemporary commentary on *Roncarelli*, see McKee, "The Public/Private Distinction in *Roncarelli v. Duplessis*" (2010) 55 McGill L.J. 461; and Mullan, "*Roncarelli v. Duplessis* and Damages for Abuse of Power: For What Did it Stand in 1959 and For What Does it Stand in 2009?" (2010) 55 McGill L.J. 587.

(b) MODERN DEVELOPMENTS

The tort of misfeasance in a public office was litigated infrequently during most of the 20th century, largely because of the dominance of negligence during that period. However, there has been a resurgence of the misfeasance tort during the last few decades, and the elements of the tort have been substantially redefined. These developments are discussed in the Supreme Court of Canada's decision in *Odhavji Estate v. Woodhouse*, [2003] 3 S.C.R. 263, which sets out the modern Canadian position.

ODHAVJI ESTATE v. WOODHOUSE
[2003] 3 S.C.R. 263

The judgment of the Court was delivered by

IACOBUCCI J.: . . . On September 26, 1997, Manish Odhavji was fatally shot by officers of the Metropolitan Toronto Police Service while running from his vehicle subsequent to a bank robbery. Within 25 minutes of the shooting, an assistant to Metropolitan Toronto Chief of Police David Boothby (the "Chief") notified the

Special Investigations Unit of the Ministry of the Solicitor General (the "SIU") of the incident.

The SIU is a civilian agency statutorily mandated to conduct independent investigations of police conduct in cases of death or serious injury caused by the police. The SIU began its investigation immediately. It requested that the defendant officers remain segregated, that they make themselves available for same-day interviews, and that they provide their shift notes, on-duty clothing, and blood samples. Under s. 113(9) of the *Police Services Act*, R.S.O. 1990, c. P.15, members of the force are under a statutory obligation to cooperate with members of the SIU in the conduct of the investigation. Under s. 41(1) of the *Police Services Act*, a chief of police is required to ensure that members of the force carry out their duties in accordance with the provisions of the Act.

The estate of Mr. Odhavji and the members of his immediate family (the "plaintiffs") allege that the defendant officers intentionally breached their statutory obligation to cooperate fully with the SIU investigation. In particular, the plaintiffs allege that the defendant officers did not attend for interviews with the SIU until September 30, that they did not comply with the request to remain segregated, and that they failed to comply with the request for shift notes, on-duty clothing, and blood samples in a timely manner — and that when statements were eventually given to the SIU, they were both inaccurate and misleading. In the plaintiffs' statement of claim, the lack of a thorough investigation into the shooting incident has caused the plaintiffs to suffer mental distress, anger, depression and anxiety. The plaintiffs further allege that these damages are consequences that the defendant officers and the Chief knew or ought to have known would result from an inadequate investigation into the shooting incident.

The actions at issue in this appeal are not related to the allegedly wrongful death of Mr. Odhavji, but, rather, to the defendant officers' alleged failure to cooperate with the SIU. It is the plaintiffs' submission that the foregoing facts give rise to an action for misfeasance in a public office against the defendant officers and the Chief, and actions for negligence against the Chief, the Metropolitan Toronto Police Services Board (the "Board") and Her Majesty the Queen in Right of Ontario (the "Province").

· · ·

(1) *The Defining Elements of the Tort*

The origins of the tort of misfeasance in a public office can be traced to *Ashby v. White* (1703), 2 Ld. Raym. 938, 92 E.R. 126, in which Holt C.J. found that a cause of action lay against an elections officer who maliciously and fraudulently deprived Mr. White of the right to vote. Although the defendant possessed the power to deprive certain persons from participating in the election, he did not have the power to do so for an improper purpose. Although the original judgment suggests that he was simply applying the principle *ubi jus ibi remedium*, Holt C.J. produced a revised form of the judgment in which he stated that it was because fraud and malice were proven that the action lay: J. W. Smith, *A Selection of Leading Cases on Various Branches of the Law* (13th ed. 1929), at p. 282. Thus, in its earliest form it is arguable that misfeasance in a public office was limited to circumstances in which a public officer abused a power actually possessed.

Subsequent cases, however, have made clear that the ambit of the tort is not restricted in this manner. In *Roncarelli v. Duplessis*, [1959] S.C.R. 121, this Court found the defendant Premier of Québec liable for directing the manager of the Québec Liquor Commission to revoke the plaintiff's liquor licence. Although Roncarelli was decided at least in part on the basis of the Québec civil law of delictual responsibility, it is widely regarded as having established that misfeasance in a public office is a recognized tort in Canada. . . . In *Roncarelli*, the Premier was authorized to give advice to the Commission in respect of any legal questions that might arise, but had no authority to involve himself in a decision to revoke a particular licence. As Abbott J. observed, at p. 184, Mr. Duplessis "was given no statutory power to interfere in the administration or direction of the Québec Liquor Commission". Martland J. made a similar observation, at p. 158, stating that Mr. Duplessis' conduct involved "the exercise of powers which, in law, he did not possess at all". From this, it is clear that the tort is not restricted to the abuse of a statutory or prerogative power actually held. If that were the case, there would have been no grounds on which to find Mr. Duplessis liable.

This understanding of the tort is consistent with the widespread consensus in other common law jurisdictions that there is a broad range of misconduct that can found an action for misfeasance in a public office. For example, in *Northern Territory of Australia v. Mengel* (1995), 129 A.L.R. 1 (H.C.), Brennan J. wrote as follows, at p. 25:

> The tort is not limited to an abuse of office by exercise of a statutory power. *Henly v. Mayor of Lyme* [(1828), 5 Bing. 91, 130 E.R. 995] was not a case arising from an impugned exercise of a statutory power. It arose from an alleged failure to maintain a sea wall or bank, the maintenance of which was a condition of the grant to the corporation of Lyme of the sea wall or bank and the appurtenant right to tolls. *Any act or omission done or made by a public official in the purported performance of the functions of the office can found an action for misfeasance in public office.* [Emphasis added.] In *Garrett v. Attorney-General*, [1997] 2 N.Z.L.R. 332, the Court of Appeal for New Zealand considered an allegation that a sergeant failed to investigate properly the plaintiff's claim that she had been sexually assaulted by a police constable. Blanchard J. concluded, at p. 344, that the tort can be committed "by an official who acts or omits to act in breach of duty knowing about the breach and also knowing harm or loss is thereby likely to be occasioned to the plaintiff".

The House of Lords reached the same conclusion in *Three Rivers District Council v. Bank of England (No. 3)*, [2000] 2 W.L.R. 1220. In *Three Rivers*, the plaintiffs alleged that officers with the Bank of England improperly issued a licence to the Bank of Credit and Commerce International and then failed to close the bank once it became evident that such action was necessary. Forced to consider whether the tort could apply in the case of omissions, the House of Lords concluded that "the tort can be constituted by an omission by a public officer as well as by acts on his part" *(per* Lord Hutton, at p. 1267). In Australia, New Zealand and the United Kingdom, it is equally clear that the tort of misfeasance is not limited to the unlawful exercise of a statutory or prerogative power actually held.

What then are the essential ingredients of the tort, at least insofar as it is necessary to determine the issues that arise on the pleadings in this case? In *Three Rivers*, the House of Lords held that the tort of misfeasance in a public office can arise in one of two ways, what I shall call Category A and Category B. Category A involves conduct that is specifically intended to injure a person or class of persons. Category B involves a public officer who acts with knowledge both that she or he has no power to do the act complained of and that the act is likely to injure the plaintiff. This understanding of the tort has been endorsed by a number of Canadian courts. . . . It is important, however, to recall that the two categories merely represent two different ways in which a public officer can commit the tort; in each instance, the plaintiff must prove each of the tort's constituent elements. It is thus necessary to consider the elements that are common to each form of the tort.

In my view, there are two such elements. First, the public officer must have engaged in deliberate and unlawful conduct in his or her capacity as a public officer. Second, the public officer must have been aware both that his or her conduct was unlawful and that it was likely to harm the plaintiff. What distinguishes one form of misfeasance in a public office from the other is the manner in which the plaintiff proves each ingredient of the tort. In Category B, the plaintiff must prove the two ingredients of the tort independently of one another. In Category A, the fact that the public officer has acted for the express purpose of harming the plaintiff is sufficient to satisfy each ingredient of the tort, owing to the fact that a public officer does not have the authority to exercise his or her powers for an improper purpose, such as deliberately harming a member of the public. In each instance, the tort involves deliberate disregard of official duty coupled with knowledge that the misconduct is likely to injure the plaintiff.

Insofar as the nature of the misconduct is concerned, the essential question to be determined is not whether the officer has unlawfully exercised a power actually possessed, but whether the alleged misconduct is deliberate and unlawful. As Lord Hobhouse wrote in *Three Rivers*, *supra*, at p. 1269:

> The relevant act (or omission, in the sense described) must be unlawful. This may arise from a straightforward breach of the relevant statutory provisions or from acting in excess of the powers granted or for an improper purpose.

Lord Millett reached a similar conclusion, namely, that a failure to act can amount to misfeasance in a public office, but only in those circumstances in which the public officer is under a legal obligation to act. Lord Hobhouse stated the principle in the following terms, at p. 1269: "If there is a legal duty to act and the decision not to act amounts to an unlawful breach of that legal duty, the omission can amount to misfeasance [in a public office]." . . . So, in the United Kingdom, a failure to act can constitute misfeasance in a public office, but only if the failure to act constitutes a deliberate breach of official duty.

Canadian courts also have made a deliberate unlawful act a focal point of the inquiry. In *Alberta (Minister of Public Works, Supply and Services) v. Nilsson* (1999), 70 Alta. L.R. (3d) 267, 1999 ABQB 440, at para. 108, the Court of Queen's Bench stated that the essential question to be determined is whether there has been deliberate misconduct on the part of a public official. Deliberate misconduct, on this view, consists of: (i) an intentional illegal act; and (ii) an intent to harm an individual or class of individuals. See also *Uni-Jet Industrial Pipe Ltd. v. Canada (Attorney General)* (2001), 156 Man. R. (2d) 14, 2001 MBCA 40, in which Kroft J.A. adopted the same test. In *Powder Mountain Resorts*, *supra*, Newbury J.A. described the tort in similar terms, at para. 7:

... it may, I think, now be accepted that the tort of abuse of public office will be made out in Canada where a public official is shown either to have exercised power for the specific purpose of injuring the plaintiff (i.e., to have acted in "bad faith in the sense of the exercise of public power for an improper or ulterior motive") or to have acted "unlawfully with a mind of reckless indifference to the illegality of his act" and to the probability of injury to the plaintiff. (See Lord Steyn in *Three Rivers*, at [1231].) Thus there remains what in theory at least is a clear line between this tort on the one hand, and what on the other hand may be called negligent excess of power — i.e., an act committed without knowledge of (or *subjective* recklessness as to) its unlawfulness and the probable consequences for the plaintiff. [Emphasis in original.]

Under this view, the ambit of the tort is limited not by the requirement that the defendant must have been engaged in a particular type of unlawful conduct, but by the requirement that the unlawful conduct must have been deliberate and the defendant must have been aware that the unlawful conduct was likely to harm the plaintiff.

As is often the case, there are a number of phrases that might be used to describe the essence of the tort. In *Garrett, supra*, Blanchard J. stated, at p. 350, that "[t]he purpose behind the imposition of this form of tortious liability is to prevent the deliberate injuring of members of the public by deliberate disregard of official duty." In *Three Rivers, supra*, Lord Steyn stated, at p. 1230, that "[t]he rationale of the tort is that in a legal system based on the rule of law executive or administrative power 'may be exercised only for the public good' and not for ulterior and improper purposes." As each passage makes clear, misfeasance in a public office is not directed at a public officer who inadvertently or negligently fails adequately to discharge the obligations of his or her office: see *Three Rivers*, at p. 1273, *per* Lord Millett. Nor is the tort directed at a public officer who fails adequately to discharge the obligations of the office as a consequence of budgetary constraints or other factors beyond his or her control. A public officer who cannot adequately discharge his or her duties because of budgetary constraints has not deliberately disregarded his or her official duties. The tort is not directed at a public officer who is *unable* to discharge his or her obligations because of factors beyond his or her control but, rather, at a public officer who *could* have discharged his or her public obligations, yet wilfully chose to do otherwise.

Another factor that may remove an official's conduct from the scope of the tort of misfeasance in a public office is a conflict with the officer's statutory obligations and his or her constitutionally protected rights, such as the right against self-incrimination. Should such circumstances arise, a public officer's decision not to comply with his or her statutory obligation may not amount to misfeasance in a public office. I need not decide that question here except that it could be argued. A public officer who properly insists on asserting his or her constitutional rights cannot accurately be said to have deliberately disregarded the legal obligations of his or her office. Under this argument, an obligation inconsistent with the officer's constitutional rights is not itself lawful.

As a matter of policy, I do not believe that it is necessary to place any further restrictions on the ambit of the tort. The requirement that the defendant must have been aware that his or her conduct was unlawful reflects the well-established principle that misfeasance in a public office requires an element of "bad faith" or "dishonesty". In a democracy, public officers must retain the authority to make decisions that, where appropriate, are adverse to the interests of certain citizens. Knowledge of harm is thus an insufficient basis on which to conclude that the defendant has acted in bad faith or dishonestly. A public officer may in good faith make a decision that she or he knows to be adverse to interests of certain members of the public. In order for the conduct to fall within the scope of the tort, the officer must deliberately engage in conduct that he or she knows to be inconsistent with the obligations of the office.

The requirement that the defendant must have been aware that his or her unlawful conduct would harm the plaintiff further restricts the ambit of the tort. Liability does not attach to each officer who blatantly disregards his or her official duty, but only to a public officer who, in addition, demonstrates a conscious disregard for the interests of those who will be affected by the misconduct in question. This requirement establishes the required nexus between the parties. Unlawful conduct in the exercise of public functions is a public wrong, but absent some awareness of harm there is no basis on which to conclude that the defendant has breached an obligation that she or he owes to the plaintiff, *as an individual*. And absent the breach of an obligation that the defendant owes to the plaintiff, there can be no liability in tort.

In sum, I believe that the underlying purpose of the tort is to protect each citizen's reasonable expectation that a public officer will not intentionally injure a member of the public through deliberate and unlawful conduct in the exercise of public functions. Once these requirements have been satisfied, it is unclear why the tort would be restricted to a public officer who engaged in the unlawful exercise of a statutory power that she or he actually possesses. If the tort were restricted in this manner, the tort would not extend to a public officer, such as Mr. Duplessis, who intentionally *exceeded* his powers for the express purpose of interfering with a citizen's economic interests. Nor would it extend to a public officer who breached a statutory obligation for the same purpose. But there is no principled reason, in my view, why a public officer who wilfully injures a member of the public through intentional *abuse* of a statutory power would be liable, but not a public officer who wilfully injures a member of the public through an intentional *excess* of power or a deliberate failure to discharge a statutory duty. In each instance, the alleged misconduct is equally inconsistent with the obligation of a public officer not to intentionally injure a member of the public through deliberate and unlawful conduct in the exercise of public functions.

. . .

(2) *Application to the Case at Hand*

As outlined earlier, on a motion to strike on the basis that the statement of claim discloses no reasonable cause of action, the facts are taken as pleaded. Consequently, the primary question that arises on this appeal is whether the statement of claim pleads each of the constituent elements of the tort.

In respect of the first constituent element, namely, unlawful conduct in the exercise of public functions, the statement of claim alleges that the defendant officers did not cooperate with the SIU investigation, but, rather, took positive steps to frustrate the investigation. As described above, police officers are under a statutory obligation to cooperate fully with members of the SIU in the conduct of investigations, pursuant to s. 113(9) of the *Police Services Act*. On the face of it, the decision not to cooperate with an investigation constitutes an unlawful breach of statutory duty. Similarly, the alleged failure of the Chief to ensure that the defendant officers cooperated with the investigation also would seem to constitute an unlawful breach of duty. Under s. 41(1)(b) of the *Police Services Act*, the duties of a chief of police include ensuring that members of the police force carry out their duties in accordance with the Act. A decision not to ensure that police officers cooperate with the SIU is inconsistent with the statutory obligations of the office.

. . .

Insofar as the second requirement is concerned, the statement of claim alleges that the acts and omissions of the defendant officers "represented intentional breaches of their legal duties as police officers". This plainly satisfies the requirement that the officers were aware that the alleged failure to cooperate with the investigation was unlawful. The allegation is not simply that the officers failed to comply with s. 113(9) of the *Police Services Act*, but that the failure to comply was intentional and deliberate. Insofar as the Chief is concerned, the statement of claim alleges as follows:

(i) Chief Boothby, through his legal counsel, was directed by S.I.U. officers to segregate the defendant officers and he deliberately failed to do so;

(ii) Chief Boothby failed to ensure that defendant police officers produced timely and complete notes;

(iii) Chief Boothby failed to ensure that the defendant police officers attended for requested interviews by S.I.U. in a timely manner; and

(iv) Chief Boothby failed to ensure that the defendant police officers gave accurate and complete accounts of the specifics of the shooting incident.

Although the allegation that the Chief *deliberately* failed to segregate the officers satisfies the requirement that the Chief *intentionally* breached his legal obligation to ensure compliance with the *Police Services Act*, the same cannot be said of his alleged failure to ensure that the defendant officers produced timely and complete notes, attended for interviews in a timely manner, and provided accurate and complete accounts of the incident. As above, inadvertence or negligence will not suffice; a mere failure to discharge the obligations of the office cannot constitute misfeasance in a public office. In light of the allegation that the Chief's failure to segregate the officers was deliberate, this is not a sufficient basis on which to strike the pleading. Suffice it to say, the failure to issue orders for the purpose of ensuring that the defendant officers cooperated with the investigation will only constitute misfeasance in a public office if the plaintiffs prove that the Chief deliberately failed to comply with the standard established by s. 41(1)(b) of the *Police Services Act*.

The statement of claim also alleges that the defendant officers and the Chief "knew or ought to have known" that the alleged misconduct would cause the plaintiffs to suffer physically, psychologically and emotionally. Although the allegation that the defendants *knew* that a failure to cooperate with the investigation would injure the plaintiffs satisfies the requirement that the alleged misconduct was likely to injure the plaintiffs, misfeasance in a public office is an intentional tort that requires subjective awareness that harm to the plaintiff is a likely consequence of the alleged misconduct. At the very least, according to a number of cases, the defendant must have been subjectively reckless or wilfully blind as to the possibility that harm was a likely consequence of the alleged misconduct. . . . This, again, is not a sufficient basis on which to strike the pleading. It is clear, however, that the phrase "or ought to have known" must be struck from the statement of claim.

The final factor to be considered is whether the damages that the plaintiffs claim to have suffered as a consequence of the aforementioned misconduct are compensable.

In the defendant officers' submission, the alleged damages are non-compensable. Consequently, it is their submission that even if the plaintiffs could prove the other elements of the tort, it still would be plain and obvious that the actions for misfeasance in a public office must fail.

[Iacobucci J. comments that, while emotional distress alone is not compensable in Canadian tort law, the plaintiffs might be successful if they could prove a recognizable psychiatric illness. He concludes that, at this stage of the proceedings, it is too early to determine whether the plaintiffs could meet this burden. Therefore, it would be premature to strike out their cause of action.]

· · ·

In the final analysis, I would allow the appeal in respect of the actions for misfeasance in a public office. If the facts are taken as pleaded, it is not plain and obvious that the actions for misfeasance in a public office against the defendant officers and the Chief must fail. The plaintiffs may well face an uphill battle, but they should not be deprived of the opportunity to prove each of the constituent elements of the tort.

NOTES AND QUESTIONS

1. Describe the elements of a claim for misfeasance in a public office. How does Iacobucci J. distinguish the two branches of the tort? For a detailed review of the individual elements, see Chamberlain, *Misfeasance in a Public Office* (2016), ch. 4.

2. Misfeasance in a public office can only be claimed against public officers, who have been described as those "who discharge [] any duty in the discharge of which the public are interested, more clearly so if [they are] paid out of a fund provided by the public" (*R. v. Whitaker*, [1914] 3 K.B. 1283 at 1296). This includes those who are not, strictly speaking, employees of the state, such as a University President (*Freeman-Maloy v. Marsden* (2006), 79 O.R. (3d) 401 (C.A.)). It may also include corporate bodies, such as a Crown Corporation (*Swift Current (City) v. Saskatchewan Power Corp.* (2006), 293 Sask. R. 6 (C.A.)) or a municipality (*Georgian Glen Development v. Barrie (City)* (2005), 13 M.P.L.R. (4th) 194 (Ont. S.C.J.)). How would a plaintiff prove that a corporate body was acting with malice? See also *Merchant Law Group v. Canada (Revenue Agency)* (2010), 321 D.L.R. (4th) 301 (F.C.A.); and *Adventure Tours Inc. v. St. John's Port Authority*, 2011 FCA 198.

3. In *Odhavji Estate*, Iacobucci J. described the wrongful act of misfeasance in a public office as deliberately unlawful conduct, and explained that this included deliberate breach of a statutory duty. Other actions that have been found to be deliberately unlawful for the purposes of the tort include: wrongfully inducing a breach of contract (*Gershman v. Manitoba (Vegetable Producers' Marketing Board)* (1976), 69 D.L.R. (3d) 114 (Man. C.A.)); intentionally providing misleading information regarding the legality of a tax avoidance scheme (*Longley v. M.N.R.* (1999), 176 D.L.R. (4th) 445 (B.C.S.C.)); refusing to grant the plaintiff a review of a licensing decision, as required by statute (*O'Dwyer v. Ontario Racing Commission* (2008), 238 O.A.C. 364 (C.A.)); and refusing to provide a prison inmate with proper fitting footwear (*McMaster v. R.* (2008), 336 F.T.R. 92 (F.C.), aff'd (2009), 352 F.T.R. 255 (F.C.)).

888 THE TORT LIABILITY OF PUBLIC AUTHORITIES

However, misfeasance in a public office will not be available against defendants who legitimately exercise discretion or who make decisions based on budgetary constraints or other matters of public interest. See *Powder Mountain Resorts Ltd. v. British Columbia* (2001), 94 B.C.L.R. (3d) 14 (C.A.); *First National Properties v. McMinn* (2001), 198 D.L.R. (4th) 443 (B.C.C.A.); and *L.(A.) v. Ontario (Minister of Community & Social Services)* (2006), 83 O.R. (3d) 512 (C.A.). Nor is the tort available for mere negligence: *Canus Fisheries Ltd. v. Canada (Customs & Revenue Agency)* (2005), 237 N.S.R. (2d) 166 (S.C.); and *Hermiz v. Canada*, 2013 FC 288, rev'd on other grounds 2013 FC 764.

4. Although the tort was historically based on malice that was targeted toward the plaintiff, such flagrant abuse of power is exceedingly rare in the modern state, and most misfeasance claims are based on the second "limb" of the tort. But see *Gershman, supra*, where the defendant marketing board maliciously "black-listed" the plaintiff vegetable wholesaler, whose company had disputed the constitutional validity of the marketing board's enabling legislation. See also *Anglehart v. Canada*, 2016 FC 1159, where the court found that the Minister of Fisheries and Oceans had unjustifiably reduced the total allowable catch of crab in order to pressure the plaintiff crab fishers to enter into a joint project agreement.

In the absence of targeted malice, the plaintiff must show that the defendant knew or was reckless about the unlawfulness of its actions, and knew or was reckless about whether the plaintiff would be harmed by those actions. However, as explained by Iacobucci J. in *Odhavji Estate*, mere objective foreseeability of harm to the plaintiff is not sufficient to establish a blameworthy state of mind.

5. Compare the tort of misfeasance in a public office with the tort of negligence. Which tort is easier to prove? Would the plaintiffs in *Odhavji* have a successful negligence claim against the officers involved in the shooting? Does the relevant section of the *Police Services Act*, R.S.O. 1990, c. P.15, give rise to a duty of care? Are there policy reasons to negate that duty?

See also *Granite Power Corp. v. Ontario* (2004), 72 O.R. (3d) 194 (C.A.); and *Trillium Power Wind Corporation v. Ontario (National Resources)*, 2013 ONCA 683. In both cases, the plaintiffs' negligence claims were struck out due to a lack of proximity and residual policy considerations, but the misfeasance in a public office claims were allowed to proceed. See generally Chamberlain, "What is the Role of Misfeasance in a Public Office in Modern Canadian Tort Law?" (2010) 88 Can. Bar Rev. 579.

6. The leading Commonwealth decision on misfeasance in a public office is *Three Rivers District Council v. Governor and Company of the Bank of England (No. 3)*, [2003] 2 A.C. 1 (H.L.). In Lord Steyn's leading opinion, he sets out the "ingredients" of the tort as follows: (i) public office, (ii) the exercise of power as a public officer, (iii) the state of mind of the defendant, (iv) duty to the plaintiff, (v) causation, and (vi) damages and remoteness. See also *Watkins v. Secretary of State for the Home Department*, [2006] 2 A.C. 395 (H.L.), where the House of Lords stressed that misfeasance in a public office is not actionable *per se*, even for alleged violations of constitutional rights, but that the plaintiff must prove material damage in order to succeed. What was the material damage suffered by the plaintiffs in *Odhavji Estate*?

7. For cases illustrating the modern revival and expansion of misfeasance in a public office in the Commonwealth, see for example *Dunlop v. Woollahra District*

Council (1981), 33 A.L.R. 621 (P.C.); *Bourgoin v. Ministry of Agriculture, Fisheries and Food*, [1986] Q.B. 716 (C.A.); *Calveley v. Chief Constable of Merseyside*, [1989] A.C. 1228 (H.L.); *Jones v. Swansea City Council*, [1989] 3 All E.R. 162 (C.A.), rev'd on other grounds [1990] 3 All E.R. 737 (H.L.); *Racz v. Home Office*, [1994] 2 A.C. 45 (H.L.); *Northern Territory of Australia v. Mengel* (1995), 185 C.L.R. 307 (H.C.A.); *Garrett v. Attorney General*, [1997] 2 N.Z.L.R. 332 (C.A.); *Kuddus v. Chief Constable of Leicestershire Constabulary*, [2001] 2 W.L.R. 1789 (H.L.); *Akenzua v. Secretary of State for the Home Department*, [2003] 1 All E.R. 35 (C.A.); *Watkins, supra*; *Karagozlu v. Commissioner of Police of the Metropolis*, [2007] 2 All E.R. 1055 (C.A.); *Leerdam v. Noori* (2009), 255 A.L.R. 553 (N.S.W.C.A.); and *State of South Australia v. Lampard-Trevorrow*, [2010] SASC 56.

8. Canada has also experienced an increase in claims for misfeasance in a public office. See for example *Longley v. Canada* (2000), 73 B.C.L.R. (3d) 222 (C.A.); *Powder Mountain Resorts, supra*; *First National Properties, supra*; *Uni-Jet Industrial Pipe Ltd v. Canada* (2001), 198 D.L.R. (4th) 577 (Man. C.A.); *LeBlanc v. Canada* (2005), 339 N.R. 244 (F.C.A.); *Freeman-Maloy v. Marsden, supra*; *Bellan v. Curtis* (2007), 219 Man. R. (2d) 175 (Q.B.); *Miguna v. Toronto (City) Police Services Board* (2008), 243 O.A.C. 62 (C.A.); *O'Dwyer, supra*; *McMaster, supra*; *Merchant Law Group, supra*; *Trillium Power, supra*; *Timberwolf Log Trading Ltd. v. British Columbia (Ministry of Forests, Mines and Lands)*, 2013 BCCA 24; and *Apotex Inc. v. Canada*, 2014 FC 1087, varied 2017 FCA 73.

9. The expansion of the misfeasance tort has been accompanied by an expansion in the relevant scholarly literature. See Evans, "Damages for Unlawful Administrative Action: The Remedy for Misfeasance in Public Office" (1982) 31 I.C.L.Q. 640; Sadler, "Liability for Misfeasance in a Public Office" (1992) 14 Syd. L.R. 137; Kneebone, "Misfeasance in a Public Office After Mengel's Case: A 'Special' Tort No More?" (1996) 4 Tort L.R. 111; Allott, "EC Directives and Misfeasance in Public Office" [2001] C.L.J. 4; Irvine, "Misfeasance in Public Office: Reflections on Some Recent Developments" (2001) 9 C.C.L.T. (3d) 26; Bodner, "The *Odhavji* Decision: Old Ghosts and New Confusion in Canadian Courts" (2005) 42 Alta. L. Rev. 1061; Wruck, "The Continuing Evolution of the Tort of Misfeasance in a Public Office" (2008) 41 U.B.C.L. Rev. 69; Chamberlain, "The Need for a 'Standing' Rule in Misfeasance in a Public Office" (2008) 7 O.U.C.L.J. 215; Chamberlain, "Misfeasance in a Public Office: A Justifiable Anomaly to the Rights-Based Approach" in Robertson & Nolan, eds., *Rights and Private Law* (2011); Aronson, "Misfeasance in Public Office: A Very Peculiar Tort" (2011) 35 Melbourne U.L. Rev. 1; Murphy, "Misfeasance in a Public Office: A Tort Law Misfit?" (2012) 32 O.J.L.S. 51; and Chamberlain, "Fiduciary Aspects of Misfeasance in a Public Office" (2014) 39 Queen's L.J. 733; and Nolan, "A Public Law Tort: Understanding Misfeasance in Public Office" in Barker *et al.*, eds., *Private Law and Power* (2017) 177.

5. Other Torts

Although the action in negligence dominates, and the misfeasance tort is expanding, there are still other bases upon which a public authority may be held liable in tort. Most torts apply equally to both private and public actors. That is true, for instance, of intentional torts (*e.g.* false imprisonment and trespass) and nuisance. Nevertheless, it is important to appreciate that differences do occasionally arise.

Perhaps most significantly, a public official is often able to plead the defence of statutory authority. Briefly stated, that defence precludes recovery with respect to a loss that was the inevitable result of the defendant's performance of a statutorily authorized act. This defence is considered in greater detail in Chapter 24.

Some types of claims, however, arise uniquely in connection with public authorities. That is true of *Charter* "torts," which were previously discussed in Chapters 3, 8 and 11, and which will be further examined in the next chapter. By virtue of s. 32, the *Charter* applies only to government and government agencies — not to purely private actors. Moreover, most *Charter* violations are addressed through public law remedies (*e.g.* invalidation of offending legislation). Nevertheless, s. 24(1) entitles the victim of a *Charter* violation to "such remedy as the court considers appropriate and just in the circumstances."

The guiding principles for awarding damages as a remedy for *Charter* violations were discussed by the Supreme Court of Canada in *Vancouver (City) v. Ward*, [2010] 2 S.C.R. 28. The claimant was arrested on the mistaken suspicion that he was about to throw a pie in the face of Prime Minister Jean Chrétien. He was detained at the local police station, where he was subjected to a strip search. This was found to be an unreasonable search under s. 8 of the *Charter,* and he accordingly claimed damages under s. 24(1). The court indicated that *Charter* damages are discretionary and are distinct from private law damages. An award of *Charter* damages should serve the functions of compensating the claimant for any losses, vindicating the claimant's rights and public confidence in the system, and deterring future breaches. The court should also consider countervailing factors that might render an award of damages inappropriate or unjust, including the availability of alternative remedies and any potential interference with good governance. The quantum of the award must be fair to both the claimant and the state. Thus, the court should consider whether a large award (which would divert public funds from other objects) would be unjust from a public perspective. The claimant in *Ward* was ultimately awarded $5,000 for the violation of his s. 8 rights.

NOTES AND QUESTIONS

1. For an example of the application of the intentional economic torts to public authorities, see *Gershman v. Manitoba (Vegetable Producers Marketing Board)* (1976), 69 D.L.R. (3d) 114 (Man. C.A.). See also *O'Dwyer v. Ontario Racing Commission* (2008), 238 O.A.C. 364 (C.A.); and *Saskatchewan v. Eacom Timber Corp.*, 2012 SKQB 226.

2. As discussed in Chapter 11, a leading case on *Charter* torts is *Jane Doe v. Metropolitan Toronto (Municipality) Commissioners of Police* (1998), 39 O.R. (3d) 487 (Gen. Div.). The plaintiff was sexually assaulted by a serial rapist. Although the police knew that the plaintiff was a member of a group of potential victims, they did not warn her of that danger. The plaintiff argued that they used her as "bait" in their attempts to apprehend the perpetrator. The trial judge found that the officers' decision to not issue a warning was based on their belief that, if alerted, potential victims would become "hysterical" and thereby jeopardize the investigation. The plaintiff's action succeeded in both negligence and under the *Charter.* As to the former, the trial judge held that the police officers failed to discharge the duty of care that they owed to the plaintiff. As to the latter, the trial judge held that the police officers' conduct: (i)

violated s. 7 of the *Charter* in so far as it deprived the plaintiff of security of the person, and (ii) violated s. 15 of the *Charter* in so far as it was based on discriminatory stereotypes regarding the behaviour of women. Damages were assessed on the same basis for both negligence and *Charter* violations.

3. In *Henry v. British Columbia (Attorney General)*, 2015 SCC 24, the Supreme Court of Canada found that *Charter* damages may be available if the Crown intentionally withholds disclosure of information where it knows, or would reasonably be expected to know, that the information is material to the defence and that failure to disclose it will likely affect the accused's ability to make a full answer and defence. This threshold is lower than malice, and recognizes that intentional failure to disclose material information is a serious breach of an accused's rights under section 7 of the *Charter*. How can *Henry* be reconciled with the tort of malicious prosecution, which is discussed in Chapter 3?

At trial, the plaintiff was awarded over $8 million, including $7.5 million to serve the vindication and deterrence functions of the *Charter*.

4. Civil liability of public authorities arising from *Charter* violations is increasing. See *Crossman v. R.*, [1984] 1 F.C. 681 (T.D.); *Chrispen v. Kalinowski* (1997), 156 Sask. R. 58 (Q.B.); and *Krznaric v. Chevrette* (1997), 154 D.L.R. (4th) 527 (Ont. Gen. Div.). See also Charney & Hunter, "Tort Lite? — *Vancouver (City) v. Ward* and the Availability of Damages for *Charter* Infringements" (2011) 54 S.C.L.R. (2d) 393.

5. For a discussion of trends in liability for police conduct, see Childs & Ceyssens, "*Doe v. Metropolitan Toronto Board of Commissioners of Police* and the Status of Public Oversight of the Police in Canada" (1998) 36 Alta. L. Rev. 1000. See also Palmer & Steele, "Police Shootings and the Role of Tort" (2008) 71 Mod. L. Rev. 801; Randall, "Private Law, the State and the Duty to Protect: Tort Actions for Police Failures in Gendered Violence Cases" in Rodgers, Ruparelia & Bélanger-Hardy, eds., *Critical Torts* (2009) 343; Chamberlain, "Negligent Investigation: Tort Law as Police Ombudsman" in Robertson & Tang, eds., *The Goals of Private Law* (2009) 283; Walsh, "Police Liability for a Negligent Failure to Prevent Crime: Enhancing Accountability by Clearing the Public Policy Fog" (2011) 22 King's L.J. 27; and Chamberlain, "To Serve and Protect Whom? Proximity in Cases of Police Failure to Protect" (2016) 53:4 Alta. L. Rev. 977.

6. For a survey of public authority liability in a range of civilian, common law, and hybrid jurisdictions, see Oliphant, ed., *The Liability of Public Authorities in Comparative Perspective* (2016).

REVIEW PROBLEMS

1. Harold is a fruit farmer who owns a number of peach and apple orchards in the Niagara peninsula. His orchards are next to a major provincial highway which receives the highest level of winter maintenance from the Works Department. As part of the maintenance program, the Department spreads large quantities of road salt on the highway whenever conditions are icy. The Department does not use sand for this purpose.

Harold can prove that, when the Department's trucks pass his orchard applying road salt, some of the salt bounces onto his land. In addition, when the Department plows the roads, additional quantities of salt mixed with snow are pushed onto his orchards. However, the majority of the salt on his orchards is carried by water when the roadside snowbanks melt.

Over the years, a sufficient quantity of salt has accumulated on Harold's orchards to render a 30-foot strip of his land adjoining the highway useless for fruit production. The peach trees in this strip have withered and died, and the apple trees produce virtually no fruit.

The pertinent legislation is the *Highway Maintenance Act*. There is only one relevant section which reads: "The Provincial Works Department shall maintain all public highways and take all reasonable steps to ensure that motorists may obtain safe passage thereon at any time."

Is Harold likely to succeed in a tort suit against the Department in: (a) trespass, (b) negligence, (c) nuisance, or (d) under the rule in *Rylands v. Fletcher*? First, analyze these issues assuming that the Department is not a Crown agency. Second, analyze these issues assuming that the Department is a Crown agency, governed by the relevant legislation in your province. This problem is based on the case of *R. in Right of Ont. v. Schenck; R. in Right of Ont. v. Rokeby* (1984), 15 D.L.R. (4th) 320 (Ont. C.A.), aff'd [1987] 2 S.C.R. 289.

2. Sustainable Power is an electricity company specializing in renewable sources of energy. Following a government call for proposals, Sustainable Power developed a detailed plan to provide electricity in southwestern Ontario through wind energy. It was declared an "applicant of record" on a proposed project, which meant that it could begin testing for wind power in the relevant area and seek environmental assessments for the project. Relying on this status, Sustainable Power invested approximately $250,000 securing rights to Crown land on which to construct wind turbines and initiating the environmental assessment process. Sustainable Power also obtained private financing to begin construction of wind turbines.

During the next provincial election, the government faced criticism for its electricity policies and residents around Lake Huron protested the construction of wind turbines in their area. In order to appease voters, the government issued a moratorium on all proposed wind energy development projects, including Sustainable Power's. The government was reelected and it continued the moratorium indefinitely.

Sustainable Power has suffered significant financial loss as a result of the moratorium. Can it establish that the provincial government owes it a duty of care in negligence? Would it have a valid claim for misfeasance in a public office? See *Trillium Power Wind Corporation v. Ontario (Natural Resources)*, 2013 ONCA 683.

22

STATUTORY PROVISIONS AND TORT
LIABILITY

1. Introduction
2. Express Statutory Causes of Action
3. The Use of Statutes in Common Law Negligence
4. A Note on the *Canadian Charter of Rights and Freedoms*

1. Introduction

Tort often is said to be a prime example of a "common law" subject. This certainly is true, but in the interests of clarity, it is important to define the operative phrase. There are at least three possibilities.

- *Systems of Law*: At the broadest level, "common law" refers to a *system of law* that was derived from England. In that respect, "common law" can be contrasted with, say, civil law (as applied, for instance, in Québec, Louisiana, and most of Europe), Jewish law, Islamic law, or Aboriginal law. Although every legal system has some means of redressing private wrongs, the body of rules considered in this book comprise a common law subject insofar as it has English roots.

- *Sources of Law*: On a more specific level, within our legal system as a whole, the phrase "common law" can be used, within any given area of law, to denote rules that were created by judges as opposed to legislators. Some subjects are governed almost entirely by legislation. This is true, for instance, of crime and income tax. The *Criminal Code of Canada*, R.S.C. 1985, c. C-46 and the *Income Tax Act*, R.S.C. 1985, c. 1 (5th Supp.) cover pretty much all of the relevant territory. Judges obviously play an interpretive role, but the governing rules are set by Parliament. Tort, in contrast, is very largely a common law subject. For the most part, legislators have left the area to judicial development.

- *Courts of Law*: Finally, at the most specific level, the term "common law" can be used to distinguish the body of rules historically created in the courts of law, as opposed to the courts of equity or chancery. This distinction was explained in Chapter 1. Tort law has always been classified as a common law subject in this respect as well. It may be questioned, however, whether there remain any compelling reasons for treating some species of private wrongs (*e.g.* negligence) separately from others (*e.g.* breach of fiduciary duty) simply because the former originated in one set of courts and the latter in another. Indeed, there are signs that Canadian courts are becoming less interested in pedigree and more interested in substance. See for example *Cadbury Schweppes Inc. v. FBI Foods Ltd.*, [1999] 1 S.C.R. 142, where the court refused to classify the action in breach of confidence as an exclusively equitable wrong.

For the purposes of this chapter, the most important distinction is the second one. Tort law generally is a "common law" subject because most of its rules were developed by judges rather than legislators. There nevertheless are circumstances in which statutory provisions affect the availability of relief in tort law. We already have encountered several examples. In the previous chapter, for instance, we saw that legislated limitation periods often protect public authorities from liability. In this chapter, we examine two other ways in which statutory provisions may be relevant.

- *Statutory Cause of Action*: Legislation may create a statutory cause of action that is distinct from any judicially developed claim. Quite often, such legislation addresses specific aspects of the statutory claim, such as the standard of care and the quantum of relief. In such circumstances, the judiciary's role is interpretive, rather than creative, and tort law is not "common law" at its *source*.
- *Statutes in Common Law Torts*: Even if a particular piece of legislation does not create an independent statutory cause of action, it may affect the court's analysis of the common law (*i.e.* judicially created) claim. For example, a regulatory statute may prohibit a certain type of conduct and impose a fine for non-compliance, but remain silent on the issue of civil liability. A judge nevertheless may decide, as a matter of principle and policy, that the regulatory scheme supports the recognition of a duty of care in negligence. Likewise, in determining the standard of care under the action in negligence, a judge may be influenced by the provisions of a health and safety statute that Parliament drafted with the assistance of expert advice. In either event, it is important to understand that it is the court, rather than the legislature, that bears ultimate responsibility. In other words, notwithstanding judicial reliance upon statute, tort law is, at its source, "common law."

NOTE

1. Until 1983, Canadian courts occasionally used statutes in a third way. Even if a piece of legislation did not expressly create a statutory cause of action, a judge might *infer* such a claim. Unfortunately, despite numerous attempts to establish guidelines for such inferences, the jurisprudence remained confused. In *R. in Right of Can. v. Sask. Wheat Pool* (1983), 143 D.L.R. (3d) 9 (S.C.C.), an extract of which appears below, the Supreme Court of Canada eliminated the problem by declaring that the courts cannot create implied statutory causes of action. See also Fridman *et al.*, *The Law of Torts in Canada*, 3d ed. (2010) at 597-608.

2. Express Statutory Causes of Action

TRESPASS TO PROPERTY ACT
R.S.O. 1990, c. T.21

2. (1) Every person who is not acting under a right or authority conferred by law and who,

    (a) without the express permission of the occupier, the proof of which rests on the defendant,

        (i) enters on premises when entry is prohibited under this Act, or
        (ii) engages in an activity on premises when the activity is prohibited under this Act; or

    (b) does not leave the premises immediately after he or she is directed to do so by the occupier of the premises or a person authorized by the occupier, is guilty of an offence and on conviction is liable to a fine of not more than $2,000.

(2) It is a defence to a charge under subsection (1) in respect of premises that is land that the person charged reasonably believed that he or she had title to or an interest in the land that entitled him or her to do the act complained of.

. . .

12. (1) Where a person is convicted of an offence under section 2, and a person has suffered damage caused by the person convicted during the commission of the offence, the court shall, on the request of the prosecutor and with the consent of the person who suffered the damage, determine the damages and shall make a judgment for damages against the person convicted in favour of the person who suffered the damage, but no judgment shall be for an amount in excess of $1,000.

(2) Where a prosecution under section 2 is conducted by a private prosecutor, and the defendant is convicted, unless the court is of the opinion that the prosecution was not necessary for the protection of the occupier or the occupier's interests, the court shall determine the actual costs reasonably incurred in conducting the prosecution and, despite section 60 of the *Provincial Offences Act*, shall order those costs to be paid by the defendant to the prosecutor.

(3) A judgment for damages under subsection (1), or an award of costs under subsection (2), shall be in addition to any fine that is imposed under this Act.

(4) A judgment for damages under subsection (1) extinguishes the right of the person in whose favour the judgment is made to bring a civil action for damages against the person convicted arising out of the same facts.

(5) The failure to request or refusal to grant a judgment for damages under subsection (1) does not affect a right to bring a civil action for damages arising out of the same facts.

(6) The judgment for damages under subsection (1), and the award for costs under subsection (2), may be filed in the Small Claims Court and shall be deemed to be a judgment or order of that court for the purposes of enforcement.

COMPETITION ACT
R.S.C. 1985, c. C-34

36. (1) Any person who has suffered loss or damage as a result of

(a) conduct that is contrary to any provision of Part VI, or
(b) the failure of any person to comply with an order of the Tribunal or another court under this Act,

may, in any court of competent jurisdiction, sue for and recover from the person who engaged in the conduct or failed to comply with the order an amount equal to the loss or damage proved to have been suffered by him, together with any additional amount that the court may allow not exceeding the full cost to him of any investigation in connection with the matter and of proceedings under this section.

. . .

PART VI
OFFENCES IN RELATION TO COMPETITION

45. (1) Every person commits an offence who, with a competitor of that person with respect to a product, conspires, agrees or arranges

(a) to fix, maintain, increase or control the price for the supply of the product;
(b) to allocate sales, territories, customers or markets for the production or supply of the product; or
(c) to fix, maintain, control, prevent, lessen or eliminate the production or supply of the product.

(2) Every person who commits an offence under subsection (1) is guilty of an indictable offence and liable on conviction to imprisonment for a term not exceeding 14 years or to a fine not exceeding $25 million, or to both.

NOTES AND QUESTIONS

1. Most violations of s. 2(1) of the *Trespass to Property Act* will also give rise to a common law action for trespass to land. What is the rationale for s. 12? Why is the statutory defence in s. 2(2) broader than the common law defence?

2. One purpose of s. 36 of the *Competition Act* is to encourage private citizens to participate in the enforcement of the criminal law in this field. Similar provisions in the United States provide treble damages to successful private litigants. See for example the *Clayton Act*, 15 U.S.C. §26. What other functions are served by s. 36 of the *Competition Act*? Why is private law enforcement necessary or desirable in this field? Is there any reason why the public enforcement agency cannot adequately protect the public interest? Is a private litigant's interest necessarily similar to the public interest? For further consideration of these issues see Pitel, ed., *Litigating Conspiracy* (2006).

3. The statutory action in s. 36 of the *Competition Act* is similar to the common law tort action for conspiracy. If the plaintiff is unsuccessful under s. 36, should it be possible to bring a common law conspiracy action on the same facts?

4. The sections reproduced above are just some of the many statutory provisions that expressly govern civil liability. Such provisions are especially common in statutes concerning government and public enterprises. There is no such thing as a typical provision, and care must be taken to search for and interpret relevant legislation on a case-by-case basis.

TRACHSLER v. HALTON
[1955] O.W.N. 909 (H.C.)

KING J. [orally, after stating the nature of the actions]: . . . The duty of a municipality is to keep its highways in such condition that travellers using them with ordinary care may do so in safety. Section 453(1) of The Municipal Act [now *Municipal Act, 2001*, S.O. 2001, c. 25, s. 44(1) and (2)] to which I have referred says:

> Every highway and every bridge shall be kept in repair by the corporation the council of which has jurisdiction over it, or upon which the duty of repairing it is imposed by this Act, and in case of default the corporation shall, subject to the provisions of *The Negligence Act*, be liable for all damages sustained by any person by reason of such default.

It will be noticed that the word used in the subsection, and used twice, is "default" and not merely failure to repair.

The question whether a highway is in repair is a question of fact. The duty to repair a highway may be described generally as a duty to do all things that may be reasonably necessary in the way of repairs to keep it fit for the lawful traffic over it. Notice of need of repair is not an ingredient of the duty to repair, but it may be a controlling factor in the question whether that duty has been performed.

When a highway is put out of repair without any fault of those whose duty it is to repair it, then that duty is reasonably performed if the repair is made within a reasonable time after they are informed, know or should have acquired knowledge of the need of repair.

In *Trueman v. The King; Dewan v. The King*, [1932] O.R. 703 at 708-9. . ., Riddell J.A. says:

> In cases against a municipality for damages for injury due to a want of repair, the law of this Province has long been settled, and is not disputed. On the occurrence of a want of repair, the municipality is not liable unless, after such occurrence, the municipality has had an opportunity to repair the defect, either by notice or knowledge, or by the lapse of such time as should have enabled it to have discovered the defect.

. . .

The system of inspecting the highways by the defendant County appeared to me to be adequate. No reasonable inspection of the highways could have led to faster action than occurred on this occasion. I do not say, for example, that the police of Trafalgar Township might not have proceeded at once to the place where the upheaval had been reported, but this does not fix any liability upon the defendant County, in my opinion.

It appears to me that by s. 453(1) of The Municipal Act the Legislature aimed at securing for the public reasonably easy and convenient avenues of communication and, as far as might be done by the exercise of corporate diligence, the safety of persons using the highways, but stopped short of providing an accident policy or indemnity against loss without regard to the effort of the corporation to comply with the statute.

On the evidence it appears to me that with respect to any circumstances that might have prevented the accident with which we are concerned, the defendant did all that might be reasonably expected of it in discharge of its duty under The Municipal Act. I believe that the defendant has shown that it was not in default with respect to its obligations imposed by the statute . . .

I do not find, on the evidence, that there is any liability on the defendant municipality.

[King J. dismissed the plaintiffs' actions. A subsequent appeal by one of the plaintiffs was dismissed by the Ontario Court of Appeal: [1955] O.W.N. 912 (C.A.).]

NOTES AND QUESTIONS

1. The terms "statutory duty" and "statutory standard" are used inconsistently. The term "duty," as used in this chapter, refers to the obligation itself. Thus, in *Trachsler* there was a duty keep the highway in a state of repair. The term "standard" refers to the degree of care that the defendant must exercise to meet this duty. What standard of care did King J. impose? Did he simply adopt the common law standard

or did he derive the standard from the statutory language? How should the standard be determined? See also *R. v. Jennings*, [1966] S.C.R. 532; *Allan v. Saskatoon* (1971), 21 D.L.R. (3d) 338 (Sask. C.A.); *Millette v. Kalogeropoulos* (1974), 51 D.L.R. (3d) 244 (S.C.C.); *O'Rourke v. Schacht* (1976), 55 D.L.R. (3d) 96 (S.C.C.); and *Rydzik v. Edwards* (1982), 38 O.R. (2d) 486 (H.C.).

2. The current common law obligation of a municipality is similar to the obligation in *Trachsler*. However, at that time, the courts were reluctant to impose affirmative common law duties on statutory public authorities. Thus, the express statutory duty in the *Municipal Act* may have been the sole basis for bringing the action in *Trachsler*.

3. As in *Trachsler*, a defendant may avoid liability by satisfying a statutory standard. The standard, however, must actually govern the situation at hand. That proposition resolved a dispute that arose under the current version of the same legislation that was involved in *Trachsler*. In *Giuliani v. Halton (Regional Municipality)*, 2011 ONCA 812, the plaintiff was injured in a motor vehicle accident that was caused by icy road conditions. She alleged that the defendant municipality was statutorily liable. The viability of that allegation turned on the precise facts of the case.

On the evening of March 31, weather forecasts indicated that a significant amount of overnight snow was almost certain. Snow in fact began to fall around 4:00 am. By the time of the plaintiff's accident at 7:00 am on April 1, accumulations had reached 2 cm and the road in question had become icy as a result of snow being compacted by traffic. The defendant, unfortunately, did not begin salting operations until 7:15 am. Within that framework, the trial judge found that (1) given the weather forecasts, the defendant could, and should, have begun operations much earlier, between 3:30 and 4:00 am, and (2) if it had done so, the road would not have become icy and the accident involving the plaintiff would not have occurred.

For the purposes of appeal, the defendant municipality conceded that it had breached s. 44 of the *Municipal Act, 2001*, S.O. 2001, c. 25 ("The municipality . . . shall keep [a highway] in a state of repair that is reasonable in the circumstances. . ."). It argued, however, that it enjoyed a complete defence under the *Minimum Maintenance Standards for Municipal Highways*, O.Reg. 239/02 (MMS), which had been introduced in 2002 under the *Municipal Act, 2001*. Section 4 of the MMS would relieve the defendant of responsibility if, "after becoming aware of the fact that the snow accumulation" had reached 5 cm, it deployed its resources within six hours. Similarly, s. 5 of the MMS provides a defence if "after the municipality becomes aware of the fact that a roadway is icy [it] treats the icy roadway within" four hours.

The Ontario Court of Appeal held that neither defence applied on the facts because neither touched upon the actual claim. Section 4 would have been relevant only if snow had accumulated to a depth of at least 5 cm at the time of the plaintiff's accident. Since the accumulation had reached only 2 cm, the section was inapplicable and the associated defence was unavailable. That did not mean, however, that the defendant was entitled to do nothing. It was obliged to act reasonably in the circumstances. Likewise, the gist of the claim was not that the defendant had failed to respond appropriately *after* it had become aware of icy conditions. The plaintiff instead complained that the defendant had failed to act reasonably to *prevent* icy conditions from forming.

Do you agree with the court's interpretation of the standards established by the MMS? What goals were the MMS defences intended to serve? Does the decision in *Giuliani* advance or stymie those goals? See De Vries, "The Rule of Standards: *Giuliani v. Halton* and the Failure of the Minimum Maintenance Standards" (2013) 41 Adv. Q. 407.

4. Some statutes will specifically define the required standard of care. See for example the Alberta *Municipal Government Act*, R.S.A. 2000, c. M-26, s. 532. The predecessor to the current section was discussed in *Parkland No. 31 v. Stetar* (1974), 50 D.L.R. (3d) 376 (S.C.C.); and *Berezowski v. Edmonton* (1986), 45 Alta. L.R. (2d) 247 (C.A.).

REVIEW PROBLEM

Answer the following questions based on one of the civil liability provisions in the *Marine Liability Act*, S.C. 2001, c. 6.

PART 6: LIABILITY AND COMPENSATION FOR POLLUTION
DIVISION 1: CIVIL LIABILITY FOR POLLUTION

Liability for pollution and related costs

77. (1) The owner of a ship is liable

    (a)   for oil pollution damage from the ship;

    (b)   for costs and expenses incurred by

        (i)   the Minister of Fisheries and Oceans,

        (ii)   a response organization within the meaning of section 654 of the *Canada Shipping Act*,

        (iii)   any other person in Canada, or

        (iv)   any person in a state, other than Canada, that is a party to the Civil Liability Convention,

in respect of measures taken to prevent, repair, remedy or minimize oil pollution damage from the ship, including measures taken in anticipation of a discharge of oil from the ship, to the extent that the measures taken and the costs and expenses are reasonable, and for any loss or damage caused by those measures; and

    (c)   for costs and expenses incurred

        (i)   by the Minister of Fisheries and Oceans in respect of measures taken under paragraph 678(1)(a) of the *Canada Shipping Act*, in respect of any monitoring under paragraph 678(1)(b) of that Act or in relation to any direction given under paragraph 678(1)(c) of that Act, or

        (ii)   by any other person in respect of measures the person was directed to take or prohibited from taking under paragraph 678(1)(c) of the *Canada Shipping Act*,

to the extent that the measures taken and the costs and expenses are reasonable, and for any loss or damage caused by those measures.

Liability for environmental damage

(2) If oil pollution damage from a ship results in impairment to the environment, the owner of the ship is liable for the costs of reasonable measures of reinstatement actually undertaken or to be undertaken.

Strict liability subject to certain defences

(3) The owner's liability under subsection (1) does not depend on proof of fault or negligence, but the owner is not liable under that subsection if the owner establishes that the occurrence

- (a) resulted from an act of war, hostilities, civil war or insurrection or from a natural phenomenon of an exceptional, inevitable and irresistible character;
- (b) was wholly caused by an act or omission of a third party with intent to cause damage; or
- (c) was wholly caused by the negligence or other wrongful act of any government or other authority responsible for the maintenance of lights or other navigational aids, in the exercise of that function.

. . .

Limitation period

(6) No action lies in respect of a matter referred to in subsection (1) unless it is commenced

- (a) if pollution damage occurred, before the earlier of

    - (i) three years after the day on which the pollution damage occurred, and
    - (ii) six years after the occurrence that caused the pollution damage or, if the pollution damage was caused by more than one occurrence having the same origin, six years after the first of the occurrences; or

- (b) if no pollution damage occurred, within six years after the occurrence.

. . .

1. Explain the duty of care that is created by s. 77 of the *Marine Liability Act*. Who owes the duty? To whom is the duty owed?

2. Explain the standard of care that applies under the provision. Will a claim be defeated by proof of reasonable care? Assume that a ship owner knew that a disgruntled ex-crew member was planning to damage the ship, but did nothing to stop the attack. According to the terms of s. 77(3), is the ship owner liable for the resulting pollution? Was the damage "wholly caused" by the vandal's intentional act?

3. What losses are compensable under the statutory action contained in s. 77? Assume that, as a result of an oil spill from the defendant's ship, the plaintiff suffered several losses and injuries, as follows: (1) $25,000 already has been spent to eliminate the pollution, (2) at least $10,000 more will be required for the same purpose in the foreseeable future, (3) as a result of coming into contact with the pollutant, the plaintiff suffers from a physical condition that causes great discomfort, but does not

prevent the plaintiff from working, (4) the pollution has destroyed a natural clam bed that the plaintiff regularly harvested for an annual net profit of $15,000, and (5) the pollution has ruined the aesthetic value of the beach attached to the plaintiff's land, thereby diminishing the property's market value by $50,000. How much is the plaintiff entitled to recover from the defendant under section 77?

4. The *Marine Liability Act* was enacted in 2001. Has s. 77 received judicial comment or interpretation? If so, what is the effect of those decisions?

3. The Use of Statutes in Common Law Negligence

The previous section considered legislative provisions that create express statutory causes of action. In such circumstances, a person who suffers a loss as a result of a legislative violation sues on the statute itself: there is no need to resort to a common law tort such as negligence. Very often, however, legislation directs a party to act in a certain way, but does not expressly provide a statutory right of action. An interesting issue arises in that situation. Accepting that the legislation does not create an express statutory right of action, is a court entitled to either (1) infer a statutory action, or (2) treat a legislative breach, in and of itself, as a common law action? Different courts at different times and in different jurisdictions have provided different answers. The modern Canadian position was formulated in the next case.

R. IN RIGHT OF CAN. v. SASK. WHEAT POOL
(1983), 143 D.L.R. (3d) 9 (S.C.C.)

[The Saskatchewan Wheat Pool delivered infested wheat to the Canadian Wheat Board in violation of s. 86(c) of the *Canada Grain Act*, S.C. 1970-71-72, c. 7. The statute made no reference to the issue of civil liability for breach of its provisions. The Board made no claim in common law negligence, but rather sought damages based solely on the Pool's breach of s. 86(c).]

The judgment of the court was delivered by

DICKSON J.:—This case raises the difficult issue of the relation of a breach of a statutory duty to a civil cause of action. Where "A" has breached a statutory duty causing injury to "B", does "B" have a civil cause of action against "A"? If so, is "A's" liability absolute, in the sense that it exists independently of fault, or is "A" free from liability if the failure to perform the duty is through no fault of his?

. . .

III
STATUTORY BREACH GIVING RISE TO A CIVIL CAUSE OF ACTION

(a) *General*

The uncertainty and confusion in relation between breach of statute and a civil cause of action for damages arising from the breach is of long standing. The commentators have little but harsh words for the unhappy state of affairs, but arriving at a solution, from the disarray of cases, is extraordinarily difficult. It is doubtful that any general principle or rationale can be found in the authorities to resolve all of the issues or even those which are transcendent.

There does seem to be general agreement that the breach of a statutory provision which causes damage to an individual should in some way be pertinent to recovery of compensation for the damage. Two very different forces, however, have been acting in opposite directions. In the United States the civil consequences of breach of statute have been subsumed in the law of negligence. On the other hand, we have witnessed in England the painful emergence of a new nominate tort of statutory breach. . . . It is now imperative for this court to choose.

(b) *The English position*

In 1948 in the case of *London Passenger Transport Board v. Upson*, [1949] A.C. 155 . . ., the House of Lords affirmed the existence of a tort of statutory breach distinct from any issue of negligence. The statute prescribes the duty owed to the plaintiff who need only show (i) breach of the statute, and (ii) damage caused by the breach.

Legitimacy for this civil action for breach of statute has been sought in the *Statute of Westminster II*, 1285, 9 Edw. I, c. 50, which provided for a private remedy by action on the case to those affected by the breach of statutory duties. However, "old though it may be, the action upon the statute has rarely been the subject of careful scrutiny in English law, and its precise judicial character remains a thing of some obscurity": Fricke, "The Juridical Nature of the Action upon the Statute", 76 L.Q.R. 240 (1960). As the gap widened between "public" and "private" law with the passing centuries this broad general right of action, enigmatic as it was, became hedged. Where a public law penalty was provided for in the statute a private civil cause of action would not automatically arise. The oft-quoted formulation of this principle was found in *Doe d. Rochester v. Bridges* (1831), 1 B. & Ad. 847 at p. 857, 109 E.R. 1001:

> And where an Act creates an obligation, and enforces the performance in a specified manner, we take it to be a general rule that performance cannot be enforced in any other manner.

Although taken out of context, the dictum served the purpose of limiting the multiplication of suits of dubious value. "With the vast increase in legislative activity of modern times, if the old rule were still law it might lead to unjust, not to say absurd, results in creating liabilities wider than the legislature can possibly have intended" (Winfield & Jolowicz, *Tort*, 11th ed. (1979), at p. 154). By the end of the 19th century, however, the civil action on the statute began to revive as a response to industrial safety legislation. The statement of the doctrine propounded in *Doe d. Rochester v. Bridges* did not enjoy a long period of acceptance. *Couch v. Steel* (1854), 3 El. & Bl. 402, 118 E.R. 1193, marked the beginning of a new era of construction. Lord Campbell C.J., relying on statements in Comyn's Digest, concluded that the injured party has a common law right to maintain an action for special damage arising from the breach of a public duty. *Couch v. Steel* was questioned some twenty years later in *Atkinson v. Newcastle & Gateshead Waterworks Co.* (1877), 2 Ex. D. 441. Lord Cairns L.C., dealing with the matter apart from authority, concluded that the private remedy had been excluded. He expressed "grave doubts" whether the authorities cited by Lord Campbell in *Couch v. Steel* justified the broad general rule there laid down. Lord Cockburn C.J. agreed that the correctness of *Couch v. Steel* was "open to grave doubts", while Brett L.J. entertained the "strongest doubt" as to the correctness of the broad general rule enunciated in *Couch v. Steel*.

As Street puts it "The effect of the leading cases in the nineteenth century (which remain important authorities) however, was to make the cause of action rest on proof that the legislature intended that violation of the right or interest conferred by the statute was to be treated as tortious" (Street, *Law of Torts*, 2nd ed., p. 273). Fricke pointed out (76 L.Q.R., at p. 260) that that doctrine leads to many difficulties. In the first place it is not clear what the *prima facie* rule or presumption should be. Some of the cases suggest that *prima facie* an action is given by the statement of a statutory duty, and that it exists unless it can be said to be taken away by any provisions to be found in the Act. Other authorities suggest the *prima facie* rule is that the specific statement of a certain manner of enforcement excluded any other means of enforcement. Sometimes the courts jump one way, sometimes the other. Fricke concludes (pp. 263-4) that as a matter of pure statutory construction the law went wrong with the decision in 1854 in *Couch v. Steel*: "If one is concerned with the intrinsic question of interpreting the legislative will as reflected within the four corners of a document which made express provision of a fine, but makes no mention of a civil remedy, one is compelled to the conclusion that a civil remedy was not intended."

. . .

This fragmentation of approach has given rise to some theoretical, and some not-so-theoretical, difficulties. The pretence of seeking what has been called a "will o' the wisp", a non-existent intention of Parliament to create a civil cause of action, has been harshly criticized. It is capricious and arbitrary, "judicial legislation" at its very worst.

> Not only does it involve an unnecessary fiction, but it may lead to decisions being made on the basis of insignificant details of phraseology instead of matters of substance. If the question whether a person injured by breach of a statutory obligation is to have a right of action for damages is in truth a question to be decided by the court, let it be acknowledged as such and some useful principles of law developed.

Winfield & Jolowicz, *supra*, at p. 159. It is a "bare faced fiction" at odds with accepted canons of statutory interpretation: "the legislature's silence on the question of civil liability rather points to the conclusion that it either did not have it in mind or deliberately omitted to provide for it" (Fleming, *The Law of Torts*, 5th ed. (1977), at p. 123). Glanville Williams is now of the opinion that the "irresolute course" of the judicial decisions "reflect no credit on our jurisprudence" and with respect, I agree. He writes:

> The failure of the judges to develop a governing attitude means that it is almost impossible to predict, outside the decided authorities, when the courts will regard a civil duty as impliedly created. In effect the judge can do what he likes, and then select one of the conflicting principles stated by his predecessors in order to justify his decision.

"The Effect of Penal Legislation in the Law of Tort", *supra*, at p. 246. . . .

The door to a civil cause of action arising from breach of statute had swung closed at the beginning of the 19th century with the proliferation of written legislation and swung open again, for reasons of policy and convenience, to accommodate the rising incidence of industrial accidents at the end of the 19th century. But the proposition that every statutory breach gave rise to a private right of action was still untenable, as it is today. The courts looked for a screening mechanism which would determine the cases to which an action should be limited.

Various presumptions or guidelines sprang up. "Thus, it has often been tediously repeated that the crucial test is whether the duty created by the statute is owed primarily to the State, and only incidentally to the individual, or vice versa" (Fleming, *supra*, at p. 125). A duty to all the public (ratepayers, for example) does not give rise to a private cause of action whereas a duty to an individual (an injured worker, for example) may. The purpose of the statute must be the protection of a certain "class" of individuals of whom the plaintiff is one and the injury suffered must be of a kind which it was the object of the legislation to prevent. Both requirements have, in the past, been fairly narrowly construed and fairly heavily criticized.

Although "[i]t is doubtful, indeed, if any general principle can be found to explain all the cases on the subject" (*Salmond on Torts*, 7th ed. (1977), at p. 243) several justifications are given for the tort of statutory breach. It provides fixed standards of negligence and replaces the judgment of amateurs (the jury) with that of professionals in highly technical areas. In effect, it provides for absolute liability in fields where this has been found desirable such as industrial safety. Laudable as these effects are, the state of the law remains extremely unsatisfactory.

. . .

(c) *The American position*

Professor Fleming prefers the American approach which has assimilated civil responsibility for statutory breach into the general law of negligence (*The Law of Torts*, *supra*, at p. 124):

> Intellectually more acceptable, because less arcane, is the prevailing American theory which frankly disclaims that the civil action is in any sure sense a creature of the statute, for the simple enough reason that the statute just does not contemplate, much less provide, a civil remedy. Any recovery of damages for injury due to its violation must, therefore, rest on common law principles. But though the penal statute does not create civil liability the court may think it proper to adopt the legislative formulation of a specific standard in place of the unformulated standard of reasonable conduct, in much the same manner as when it rules peremtorily [*sic*] that certain acts or omissions constitute negligence of the law.

There are, however, differing views of the effect of this assimilation: at one end of the spectrum, breach of a statutory duty may constitute negligence *per se* or, at the other, it may merely be evidence of negligence.

. . .

The majority view in the United States has been that statutory breach constitutes negligence *per se* — in certain circumstances (Prosser, *The Law of Torts*, *supra*, at p. 200):

> Once the statute is determined to be applicable — which is to say, once it is interpreted as designed to protect the class of persons in which the plaintiff is included, against the risk of the type of harm which had in fact occurred as a result of its violation — the great majority of the courts hold that an unexcused violation is conclusive on the issue of negligence, and that the court must so direct the jury. The standard of conduct is taken over by the court from that fixed by the legislature, and "jurors have no dispensing power by which to relax it", except in so far as the court

may recognize the possibility of a valid excuse for disobedience of the law. This usually is expressed by saying that the unexcused violation is negligence "per se", or in itself. The effect of such a rule is to stamp the defendant's conduct as negligence, with all of the effects of common law negligence, but with no greater effect.

. . .

The American courts have not broken away from a consideration of the purpose or intent of the legislature; the *Restatement, Torts, Second*, sets out the circumstances in which the court may adopt a legislative enactment as embodying the standard of care applicable in the circumstances:

> 286. When Standards of Conduct Defined by Legislation or Regulations Will be Adopted The court may adopt as the standard of conduct of a reasonable man the requirements of a legislative enactment or an administrative regulation whose purpose is found to be exclusively or in part
>
> (a) to protect a class of persons which includes the one whose interest is invaded, and
> (b) to protect the particular interest which is invaded, and
> (c) to protect that interest against the kind of harm which has resulted, and
> (d) to protect that interest the particular hazard from which the harm results.

The so-called "minority view" in the United States considers breach of a statute to be merely evidence of negligence. There are, however, varying degrees of evidence. Statutory breach may be considered totally irrelevant, merely relevant, or *prima facie* evidence of negligence having the effect of reversing the onus of proof . . .

The major criticism of the negligence *per se* approach has been the inflexible application of the legislature's criminal standard of conduct to a civil case. I agree with this criticism. The defendant in a civil case does not benefit from the technical defences or protection offered by the criminal law; the civil consequences may easily outweigh any penal consequences attaching to the breach of statute; and finally the purposes served by the imposition of criminal as opposed to civil liability are radically different. The compensatory aspect of tort liability has won out over the deterrent and punitive aspect; the perceptible evolution in the use of civil liability as a mechanism of loss shifting to that of loss distribution has only accentuated this change. And so "[t]he doctrine of negligence *per se* is, therefore, not fitted for relentless use, nor is it so used" (Morris, "The Relation of Criminal Statutes to Tort Liability", 46 Harv. L.R. 453 (1932-33), at p. 460). Thus the guidelines in the *Restatement, Torts, Second*.

(d) *The Canadian position*

Professor Linden has said that the "Canadian courts appear to oscillate between the English and American positions without even recognizing this fact": "Comment, *Sterling Trusts Corporation v. Postma*", 45 Can. Bar Rev. 121 (1967), at p. 126. The most widely used approach, however, has been that stated in *Sterling Trusts Corp. v. Postma, supra*. The breach of a statutory provision is "*prima facie* evidence of negligence". There is some difficulty in the terminology used. "*Prima facie* evidence of negligence" in the *Sterling Trusts* case is used seemingly interchangeably with the expression "*prima facie* liable". In a later case in the Ontario Court of Appeal, *Queensway Tank Lines Ltd. v. Moise* (1969), 9 D.L.R. (3d) 30. . ., MacKay J.A. assumes *prima facie* evidence of negligence to be a presumption of negligence with concomitant shift in the onus of proof to the defendant.

The use of breach of statute as evidence of negligence as opposed to recognition of a nominate tort of statutory breach is, as Professor Fleming has put it, more intellectually acceptable. It avoids, to a certain extent, the fictitious hunt for legislative intent to create a civil cause of action which has been so criticized in England. It also avoids the inflexible application of the legislature's criminal standard of conduct to a civil case. Glanville Williams is of the opinion, with which I am in agreement, that where there is no duty of care at common law, breach of non-industrial penal legislation should not affect civil liability unless the statute provides for it. As I have indicated above, industrial legislation historically has enjoyed special consideration. Recognition of the doctrine of absolute liability under some industrial statutes does not justify extension of such doctrine to other fields, particularly when one considers the jejune reasoning supporting the juristic invention.

. . .

Tort law itself has undergone a major transformation in this century with nominate torts being eclipsed by negligence, the closest the common law has come to a general theory of civil responsibility. The concept of duty of care, embodied in the neighbour principle has expanded into areas hitherto untouched by tort law.

One of the main reasons for shifting a loss to a defendant is that he has been at fault, that he has done some act which should be discouraged. There is then good reason for taking money from the defendant as well as a reason for giving it to the plaintiff who has suffered from the fault of the defendant. But there seems little in the way of defensible policy for holding a defendant who breached a statutory duty unwittingly to be negligent and obligated to pay even though not at fault. The legislature has imposed a penalty on a strictly admonitory basis and there seems little justification to add civil liability when such liability would tend to produce liability without fault. The legislature has determined the proper penalty for the defendant's wrong but if tort admonition of liability without fault is to be added, the financial consequences will be measured, not by the amount of the penalty, but by the amount of money which is required to compensate the plaintiff. Minimum fault may subject the defendant to heavy liability. Inconsequential violations should not subject the violator to any civil liability at all but should be left to the criminal courts for enforcement of a fine.

In this case the Board contends that the duty imposed by the Act is absolute, that is to say, the Pool is liable, even in absence of fault, and all that is requisite to prove a breach of duty is to show that the requirements of the statute have not, in fact, been complied with; it is not necessary to show how the failure to comply arose or that the Pool was guilty of any failure to take reasonable care to comply.

The tendency of the law of recent times is to ameliorate the rigours of absolute rules and absolute duty in the sense indicated, as contrary to natural justice. "Sound policy lets losses lie where they fall except where a special reason can be shown for interference": Holmes, *The Common Law*, p. 50. In the case at bar the evidence is that substantially all of the grain entering the terminal of the Pool at Thunder Bay came from agents of the Board. The imposition of heavy financial burden as in this case without fault on the part of the Pool does not incline one to interfere. It is better that the loss lies where it falls, upon the Board.

For all of the above reasons I would be adverse to the recognition in Canada of a nominate tort of statutory breach. Breach of statute, where it has an effect upon civil liability, should be considered in the context of the general law of negligence.

Negligence and its common law duty of care have become pervasive enough to serve the purpose invoked for the existence of the action for statutory breach.

It must not be forgotten that the other elements of tortious responsibility equally apply to situations involving statutory breach, *i.e.*, principles of causation and damages. To be relevant at all, the statutory breach must have caused the damage of which the plaintiff complains. Should this be so, the violation of the statute should be evidence of negligence on the part of the defendant.

. . .

In sum I conclude that:

1. Civil consequences of breach of statute should be subsumed in the law of negligence.

2. The notion of a nominate tort of statutory breach giving a right to recovery merely on proof of breach and damages should be rejected, as should the view that unexcused breach constitutes negligence *per se* giving rise to absolute liability.

3. Proof of statutory breach, causative of damages, may be evidence of negligence.

4. The statutory formulation of the duty may afford a specific, and useful, standard of reasonable conduct.

5. In the case at bar negligence is neither pleaded nor proven. The action must fail. I would dismiss the appeal with costs.

NOTES AND QUESTIONS

1. How did Dickson J. describe the English position on the use of statutes in tort actions? What criticisms does Dickson J. make of that case law? Do you agree with his criticisms? Although Dickson J.'s description of the English position dates from the last quarter of the 20th century, it remains accurate in outline. English courts continue to hold that while the breach of a statutory duty is not tortious *per se*, it can trigger a search for a legislative intention to allow the party in breach to be held liable in tort. That tort is not negligence but rather an independent head of action known as the tort of breach of statutory duty.

Under the English model, the operative question is whether, on the proper construction of a statute, the legislature evinced an intention to confer a private right of action upon a class of persons (of whom the claimant is one) regarding a type of injury that the statute was intended to prevent and that the claimant suffered as a result of the defendant's breach. That broad formulation encompasses a number of other questions: How is the legislature's intention to be ascertained? What is the effect of statutorily-stipulated sanctions? Are all statutes to be treated the same or, for instance, do workplace health and safety statutes receive special treatment? Is liability possible if the defendant breached a statutory duty despite taking every reasonable precaution? Are employers vicariously liable for employees' statutory violations? By what standard is causation determined? And so on. It is not an easy exercise.

Despite long experience with the doctrine, English courts continue to encounter controversies in connection with the tort of breach of statutory duty: *Campbell v. Gordon*, [2016] UKSC 38; and *McDonald v. National Grid Electricity Transmission plc*,

[2014] UKSC 3. Difficult issues sometimes arise because the scope of liability is sensitive to legislative developments: *Enterprise and Regulatory Reform Act 2013*, c. 24, s. 69. One curious example is the *Social Action, Responsibility and Heroism Act 2015*: 2015, c. 3. The Act states that in determining the standard of care under a claim for negligence or breach of statutory duty, a court must have regard to whether the tort "occurred when the person was acting for the benefit of society or any of its members," whether the defendant "demonstrated a predominantly responsible approach towards protecting the safety or other interests of others," and whether the alleged wrong "occurred when the person was acting heroically by intervening in an emergency to assist an individual in danger." Do those provisions make the judicial task any easier? What other purpose might the statute pursue? See Mulheron, "Legislating Dangerously: Bad Samaritans, Good Society, and the *Heroism Act 2015*" (2017) 80 M.L.R. 88; and Goudkamp, "Restating the Common Law? The *Social Action, Responsibility and Heroism Act 2015*" (2017) 37 Leg. Stud. 577.

To what extent, if at all, do the independent tort of breach of statutory duty and the tort of negligence overlap? Identify a situation in which liability would be imposed for one but not the other. Which tort, if either, is more generous to claimants?

For discussion of the English approach, see Rogers, *Winfield and Jolowicz on Tort*, 18th ed. (2010), ch. 7; Stanton, "New Forms of the Tort of Breach of Statutory Duty" (2004) 120 L.Q.R. 324; Matthews, "Negligence and Breach of Statutory Duty" (1984) 4 O.J.L.S. 429; and Foster, "The Merits of a Civil Action for Breach of Statutory Duty" (2011) 33 Sydney L. Rev. 67.

2. What is the majority position in the United States and how has it been modified by the *Restatement (Second) of Torts* (1965) at §288B and §286? What is the American minority position? Which position is preferable and which one does Dickson J. favour?

3. Explain the Canadian approach to the use of statutes prior to *Saskatchewan Wheat Pool*. Summarize the principles of law that now govern the use of statutes based on *Saskatchewan Wheat Pool*. Has Dickson J. adequately dealt with the problems in the English, American, and prior Canadian positions? For a statement of the Canadian position, see also *Leroux v. Canada (Revenue Agency)*, 2012 BCCA 63 at para. 30; *Strohmaier v. British Columbia (Attorney General)*, 2015 BCSC 1189 at para. 40; *Allarco Entertainment 2008 Inc. v. Rogers Communications Inc.*, 2011 ONSC 5623 at para. 202; and *RVB Managements Ltd. v. Rocky Mountain House (Town)*, 2014 ABQB 51 at para. 192.

4. *Saskatchewan Wheat Pool* was not the first Supreme Court of Canada decision to consider the rules that apply at the intersection of statutory obligations and common law torts.

Chapter 11 contains a lengthy extract from *Horsley v. MacLaren*, [1972] S.C.R. 441. A passenger on a pleasure craft had fallen overboard. It was alleged that the operator of the boat, while innocent of the circumstances that caused the victim to fall overboard, tortiously failed to provide an effective rescue. The court was required to determine the significance of a statutory obligation that applied in the context of commercial shipping. Laskin J. offered the following thoughts:

I do not rest the duty to which I would hold MacLaren in this case on s. 526(1) of the *Canada Shipping Act* [R.S.C. 1952, c. 29], even assuming that its terms are broad enough to embrace the facts herein. That provision, a penal one, is as follows:

> 526(1) The master or person in charge of a vessel shall, so far as he can do so without serious danger to his own vessel, her crew and passengers, if any, render assistance to every person, even if that person be a subject of a foreign state at war with Her Majesty, who is found at sea and in danger of being lost, and if he fails to do so he is liable to a fine not exceeding one thousand dollars.

I do not find it necessary in this case to consider whether s. 526(1), taken alone, entails civil consequences for failure to perform a statutory duty; or, even, whether it fixes a standard of conduct upon which the common law may operate to found liability. There is an independent basis for a common law duty of care in the relationship of carrier to passenger, but the legislative declaration of policy in s. 526(1) is a fortifying element in the recognition of that duty, being in harmony with it in a comparable situation.

Writing on behalf of the majority, Ritchie J. agreed that the defendant was under a common law duty to rescue, but held that that duty was "in no way dependent upon the provisions of s. 526(1)." Unlike Laskin J., the majority concluded that the defendant had not breached the common law standard of care.

In *Seneca College of Applied Arts Technology v. Bhadauria* (1979), 27 O.R. (2d) 142 (C.A.), rev'd [1981] 2 S.C.R. 181, Wilson J.A. for the Ontario Court of Appeal stated that the *Ontario Human Rights Code*, R.S.O. 1970, c. 318, expressed "the public policy of this Province respecting fundamental human rights." She then referred to *Ashby v. White* (1703), 92 E.R. 126 (K.B.) in support of the proposition that, if there was a right, there had to be a remedy. It was on this basis that she recognized a new common law tort of discrimination. The Supreme Court of Canada rejected this argument, distinguishing *Ashby* as a case that granted a remedy for a pre-existing right. The court concluded that the *Code*'s remedial provisions were the only remedy available to the plaintiff. Is the Supreme Court of Canada's decision in *Bhadauria* consistent with its decision in *Saskatchewan Wheat Pool*?

5. Dickson J. indicated that industrial safety statutes have been treated differently than other types of legislation. What is the rationale for this practice? What principles of law now govern the use of industrial safety statutes in Canadian tort actions?

6. Since 1983, the Supreme Court of Canada frequently has reiterated the proposition that breach of a statutory duty does not constitute grounds for liability. *Stewart v. Pettie*, [1995] 1 S.C.R. 131 involved a car accident that was caused by the carelessness of a driver who had been served alcohol at the defendant's dinner theatre. Although the defendant may have breached a statute that prohibited the provision of alcohol to intoxicated patrons, Major J. explained that a legislative violation "does not ground liability." The plaintiff was required instead to establish a common law duty of care. The same view was repeated in *Ryan v. Victoria (City)*, [1999] 1 S.C.R. 201. As detailed in an extract that appears below, the plaintiff cyclist claimed that he was injured as a result of the defendant city's failure to follow regulations regarding the placement of railway tracks within a city street. Citing *Saskatchewan Wheat Pool* and *Stewart v. Pettie*, Major J. held that while proof of a statutory breach may provide some evidence of carelessness, it "does not automatically give rise to civil liability."

Holland v. Saskatchewan, [2008] 2 S.C.R. 551 is another application of *Saskatchewan Wheat Pool*. The plaintiff represented approximately 200 farmers who dealt with domesticated cervids (members of the deer family). The farmers were asked to join a federal program aimed at controlling CWD (chronic wasting disease), but they refused to sign a broadly-worded indemnification and release clause. The government accordingly revoked the farmers' CWD-free certification status, which adversely affected the marketability of their cervine products and caused financial loss. The plaintiff secured a judicial declaration to the effect that the impugned clause was beyond the scope of the federal government's legal authority. The government, however, refused to either reinstate the farmers' CWD-free certification or provide compensation for their losses. The plaintiff then commenced a class action, which the government argued should be struck out for failing to disclose a valid cause of action. The plaintiff's claim in negligence was struck out except insofar as it alleged that the defendant negligently failed to implement the judicial declaration regarding the invalidity of the impugned clause. In the course of that decision, McLachlin C.J.C. also referred to *Saskatchewan Wheat Pool* and reiterated the proposition that "mere breach of a statutory duty does not constitute negligence." As she further explained, "[t]he proper remedy for breach of a statutory duty by a public authority . . . is judicial review for invalidity. . . . No parallel action lies in tort."

Holland and *Saskatchewan Wheat Pool* were applied in *Wu v. Vancouver (City)*, 2019 BCCA 23. The plaintiffs purchased a property in a historical part of Vancouver with the intention of demolishing the existing house and building a new one. At that point, the house was not designated as a heritage property and consequently was not protected from destruction. When the plaintiffs applied for a demolition permit, however, the defendant municipality delayed. Eventually, the entire neighbourhood was designated as heritage property, which both prevented destruction of the existing homes and deprived affected property holders of compensation. Having found that the defendant breached its statutory duty to respond to the application in a reasonably competent and timely manner, the trial judge awarded the plaintiffs compensation for their losses: 2017 BCSC 2072. On appeal, however, the British Columbia Court of Appeal held that the trial judge had improperly converted a public law duty into a private law duty by treating the regulatory obligation as a tort law duty of care. As Harris J.A. explained, the proper course of complaint was not negligence, but rather judicial review.

For other applications of *Saskatchewan Wheat Pool*, see *Khalil v. R.* (2009), 64 C.C.L.T. (3d) 199 (F.C.A.) (breach of statutory duty to resolve a convention refugee's application for permanent residence); *Dynasty Furniture Manufacturing Ltd. v. Toronto-Dominion Bank* (2010), 74 C.C.L.T. (3d) 286 (Ont. S.C.J.), aff'd 2010 ONCA 514 (breach of statutory duty regarding detection of banking fraud); *Re BCE Inc.*, [2008] 3 S.C.R. 560 (statutory duty requiring corporate directors and officers to exercise reasonable care, diligence, and skill); *Ari v. Insurance Corp. of British Columbia*, 2013 BCSC 1308, aff'd 2015 BCCA 468 (privacy legislation); and *Burrell v. Metropolitan Entertainment Group*, 2011 NSCA 108 (casino's alleged breach of statutory duty to exclude claimant as gambling addict).

7. It is important to appreciate the limited nature of *Saskatchewan Wheat Pool*. While a legislative violation does not, by itself, trigger civil liability, it also does not preclude civil liability. That proposition appears in *Odhavji Estate v. Woodhouse*, [2003] 3 S.C.R. 263. Contrary to a section of the *Police Services Act*, R.S.O. 1990, c. P.15,

police officers involved in a fatal shooting refused to cooperate in an investigation. The plaintiff sought relief on several grounds, but for present purposes, the importance of the Supreme Court of Canada's unanimous decision lies in its discussion of *Saskatchewan Wheat Pool* (at para. 31):

> [T]he nominate tort of statutory breach does not exist. *Saskatchewan Wheat Pool* states only that it is *insufficient* that the defendant has breached the statute. It does not, however, establish that the breach of a statute cannot give rise to liability if the constituent elements of tortious responsibility have been satisfied. Put a different way, the mere fact that the alleged misconduct also constitutes a breach of statute is insufficient to exempt the officer from civil liability. Just as a public officer who breaches a statute might be liable for negligence, so too might a public officer who breaches a statute be liable for misfeasance in a public office.

Similar reasoning informed the decision in *Canada Post v. G3 Worldwide (Canada) Inc.* (2007), 85 O.R. (3d) 241 (C.A.). Section 14 of the *Canada Post Corporation Act*, R.S.C. 1985, c. C-10, provided Canada Post with the exclusive privilege of collecting and delivering mail within Canada. After the appellant violated that privilege by providing mail service, Canada Post applied for an injunction. The appellant relied upon *Saskatchewan Wheat Pool* to argue that, leaving aside express statutory claims, the breach of a statutory duty cannot have any effect other than providing some evidence of carelessness under the tort of negligence. On that view, Canada Post would be barred from applying for an injunction. The Ontario Court of Appeal, however, rejected that argument. *Saskatchewan Wheat Pool* does not preclude any form of action — it merely states that breach of a statutory duty does not, in itself, trigger liability.

Of course, given the manner in which breach of statutory duty and the tort of negligence intersect, it is not enough to prove a duty of care, a breach of the standard of care, and an injury. The plaintiff must also demonstrate that its loss was caused by the defendant's failure to satisfy the statutory standard: *British Columbia v. Canadian Forest Products Ltd.*, 2018 BCCA 124.

8. Given the Supreme Court of Canada's rejection of implied statutory causes of action, what impact should strict liability in a regulatory statute have on a common law cause of action?

9. Plaintiffs who complain of a breach of statutory duty almost invariably seek compensatory damages. Is it ever possible for a court to award disgorgement of the defendant's ill-gotten gains rather than compensation of the plaintiff's wrongfully-inflicted loss? In theory, disgorgement may be available if the plaintiff, having established all of the elements of a cause of action, asks the judge to focus on the defendant's gain for remedial purposes. In practice, disgorgement tends to be claimed if the plaintiff cannot prove a compensable loss, but can show that the defendant received some benefit as a result of the breach. Given the constituent elements of the tort of negligence, should disgorgement be possible if the plaintiff complains of the defendant's breach of statutory duty? Should disgorgement be possible in England under the tort of breach of statutory duty? Compare the elements of the two torts. See *Devenish Nutrition Ltd. v. Sanofi-Aventis SA (France)*, [2008] EWCA Civ 1086; *cf. Dennis v. Ontario Lottery and Gaming Corp.*, 2010 ONSC 1332 at paras. 167-82, aff'd 2011

ONSC 7024, aff'd 2013 ONCA 501 at paras. 319-30 (disgorgement discussed under obscure and confusing label of "waiver of tort").

10. For a more detailed discussion of *Saskatchewan Wheat Pool*, see Alexander, "Legislation and Civil Liability: Public Policy and 'Equity of the Statute'" (1984) 30 McGill L.J. 1; Fridman, "Civil Liability for Criminal Conduct" (1984) 16 Ottawa L. Rev. 34; Brudner, "Tort — Civil Liability For Breach of Statutory Duty Abolished" (1984) 62 Can. Bar Rev. 668; and Rogers, "Rusty Beetles in the Elevator" [1984] C.L.J. 23.

(a) BREACH OF STATUTORY DUTY AND COMMON LAW STANDARD OF CARE

As the Supreme Court of Canada explained in *Saskatchewan Wheat Pool*, breach of a statutory duty does not, by itself, trigger liability. In the absence of an express statutory cause of action, the plaintiff must instead prove a common law cause of action, such as the tort of negligence. Within the common law action for negligence, however, a statutory duty may provide some evidence of the standard of care that the defendant is expected to meet. Likewise, proof of a statutory breach may provide some evidence of carelessness for the purposes of the tort of negligence. The next two case extracts demonstrate the proper analysis.

RYAN v. VICTORIA (CITY)
(1999), 168 D.L.R. (4th) 513 (S.C.C.)

[The plaintiff was injured after the front wheel of his motorcycle became caught in a "flangeway" that comprised part of a railway track that ran through the city's street. The plaintiff alleged that the railway was negligent in failing to take precautions against such an occurrence. The defendant resisted liability by arguing that it had complied with all of the relevant statutory regulations.

A duty of care was found to exist between the parties. For present purposes, the crucial question was whether the defendant had met its standard of care.]

MAJOR J.: . . .

Standard of Care

Conduct is negligent if it creates an objectively unreasonable risk of harm. To avoid liability, a person must exercise the standard of care that would be expected of an ordinary, reasonable and prudent person in the same circumstances. The measure of what is reasonable depends on the facts of each case, including the likelihood of a known or foreseeable harm, the gravity of that harm, and the burden or cost which would be incurred to prevent the injury. In addition, one may look to external indicators of reasonable conduct, such as custom, industry practice, and statutory or regulatory standards.

Legislative standards are relevant to the common law standard of care, but the two are not necessarily co-extensive. The fact that a statute prescribes or prohibits certain activities may constitute evidence of reasonable conduct in a given situation, but it does not extinguish the underlying obligation of reasonableness. . . . By the same token, mere compliance with a statute does not, in and of itself, preclude a finding of civil liability. . . . Statutory standards can, however, be highly relevant to the assessment of reasonable conduct in a particular case, and in fact may render reasonable an act or omission which would otherwise appear to be negligent. This allows courts to consider the legislative framework in which people and companies must operate, while at the same time recognizing that one cannot avoid the underlying obligation of reasonable care simply by discharging statutory duties.

. . .

Compliance with a statutory standard of care does not abrogate or supersede the obligation to comply with the common law standard of care. The requirements are concurrent, and each carries its own penalty for breach. However, in appropriate circumstances, compliance with statutory standards may entirely satisfy the common law standard of care and thus absolve a defendant of liability in negligence. . . .

This approach is consistent with the holding in *Canadian National Railway Co. v. Vincent*, [1979] 1 S.C.R. 364, 93 D.L.R. (3d) 663. Although *Vincent* arose in the context of Québec civil law, the reasoning of Pratte J. in that case is instructive, particularly since the common law standard of care is analogous to the requirement of reasonable prudence under the *Civil Code*. The facts in *Vincent* were straightforward. A child was struck by a train while riding her bicycle on a railway crossing in a densely populated area. It was undisputed that the railway had complied with all relevant safety measures prescribed by statute and regulations. The issue was whether the railways should have taken additional precautions in the circumstances of the case. Pratte J. stated at pp. 372-73:

> It must be said at the outset that, under the verdict, appellant is not held liable by reason of any breach of the *Railway Act* . . . or of the regulations of the Canadian Transport Commission. The issue is rather whether appellant can be found guilty of negligence under . . . [the *Civil Code*] although it complied with all the special statutory and regulatory provisions to which it is subject. The special provisions governing appellant certainly do not have the effect of exempting it from the ordinary law of civil liability. . . .

Additional support for this view can be found in s. 367(4) of the *Railway Act* which provides:

> 367(4) No inspection under or by the authority of this Act . . . and nothing in this Act . . . and nothing done, ordered, directed, required or provided for, or omitted to be done . . . under or by virtue of this Act . . . shall, except in so far as a compliance with the Act in question or with the order, direction, requirement or provision constitutes a justification for what would otherwise be wrongful, relieve . . . any company of or from, or in any way diminish or affect, any liability or responsibility resting on it by law . . . for anything done or omitted to be done by that company, or for any wrongful act, negligence or default, misfeasance, malfeasance or nonfeasance of that company.

Section 367(4) confirms that compliance with statutory standards does not normally exhaust a railway's obligations under principles of negligence. . . . A railway is presumptively bound by the common law, subject only to those situations where compliance with the statute or regulations provides "a justification for what would otherwise be wrongful". Like any exculpatory provision limiting common law rights, that passage should be narrowly construed. In the absence of a clear indication to the contrary, compliance with statutory standards should not be viewed as excusing a railway's obligation to take whatever precautions are reasonably required in the circumstances.

The weight to be accorded to statutory compliance in the overall assessment of reasonableness depends on the nature of the statute and the circumstances of the case. It should be determined whether the legislative standards are necessarily applicable to the facts of the case. Statutory compliance will have more relevance in "ordinary" cases — i.e. cases clearly within the intended scope of the statute — than in cases involving special or unusual circumstances. . . . It should also be determined whether the legislative standards are specific or general, and whether they allow for discretion in the manner of performance. It is a well-established principle that an action will lie against any party, public or private, "for doing that which the legislature has authorized, if it be done negligently." . . . It follows that a party acting under statutory authority must still take such precautions as are reasonable within the range of that authority to minimize the risks which may result from its actions. See *Tock, supra* (applying similar principles in the nuisance context).

Where a statute authorizes certain activities and strictly defines the manner of performance and the precautions to be taken, it is more likely to be found that compliance with the statute constitutes reasonable care and that no additional measures are required. By contrast, where a statute is general or permits discretion as to the manner of performance, or where unusual circumstances exist which are not clearly within the scope of the statute, mere compliance is unlikely to exhaust the standard of care. This approach strikes an appropriate balance among several important policies, including deference to legislative determinations on matters of railway safety, security for railways which comply with prescribed standards, and protection for those who may be injured as a result of unreasonable choices made by railways in the exercise of official authority.

Application to the Case at Bar

. . .

The standard of care required of the Railways was that of a prudent and reasonable person in the circumstances, having regard to all relevant factors including applicable statutes and regulations. It is undisputed that the Railways complied with certain safety standards prescribed in regulations and Board orders. The question is whether such compliance satisfied the requirement of objective reasonableness in this case and absolved the Railways of liability for the appellant's injury.

At the outset, it should be noted that the location of the Store Street tracks does not, by itself, give rise to liability. The construction of a branch line on an urban street inevitably creates a risk to the public. When a party is specifically authorized to create that risk, compliance with such authority cannot be negligent. There is negligence only if, in the performance of the authorized activity, the party creates a risk that is objectively unreasonable in the circumstances. The construction of the Store Street tracks was authorized by the Board in 1908 on the basis of a detailed plan and profile, and the location of the tracks was reapproved in 1927. Pursuant to s. 223 of the 1906 *Railway Act*, those orders could not have issued unless the Board was "satisfied that the branch line [was] necessary in the public interest or for the purpose of giving increased facilities to business". It cannot be said that it was unreasonable for the Railways to comply with those orders by constructing the tracks in the manner authorized.

The real issue is whether the Railways were negligent with respect to the dimensions of the flangeways on Store Street. In particular, it must be determined whether the Railways acted unreasonably by enlarging the flangeways to a width of nearly four inches in 1982, and by failing to install flange fillers at any time prior to the appellant's accident. This issue has to do with the minimization of risk, and is separate from the Railways' undisputed duty to warn the public of the inevitable hazard created by the tracks.

. . .

(iii) Application of the Common Law Standard of Care

The trial judge correctly held that the Railways were subject to the common law standard of care. In applying that standard, he noted that the Railways have been aware of the risks associated with the flangeways on Store Street for some time. In particular, he found that the Railways knew or should have known of at least three other accidents between 1982 and 1986 which involved the flangeways and two-wheeled vehicles. On the basis of all the evidence adduced, he concluded as follows (at pp. 197-98):

> In the case at bar, the defendant Railways ought to have built the flangeways either at the minimum allowable width or with some form of flange filler. It was not enough to proceed on the basis that so long as their flangeways were durable and did not exceed the maximum regulatory standards . . . their neighbours must endure the consequent injuries arising from their "preferred" construction choice.

> . . .

> Because of the hazard created and the remedial measures available to the defendant Railways, I find the defendant Railways were obliged to take precautions over and above those mandated by statute and regulation. This they failed to do.

> In the result, I find that the defendant Railways were negligent.

The trial judge's conclusion is consistent with the principles stated above. It was a proper exercise of his role as the finder of fact, and it should not have been disturbed by the Court of Appeal. Accordingly, the appeal is allowed with respect to the claim of negligence against the Railways.

[The court ultimately held that the defendant railway *prima facie* was liable for the plaintiff's injuries, and that damages should not be reduced or denied on the basis of any defence (*e.g.* contributory negligence).]

MARSHALL v. ANNAPOLIS COUNTY SCHOOL BOARD
2012 SCC 27

[Four-year-old Johnathan Marshall lived with his family in a house that was situated along a highway. He suffered catastrophic injuries after he ran on to the highway and was struck by a bus that was operated by the defendant school board. The bus was empty except for the driver and was not scheduled to stop at Johnathan's house.

Damages were denied after a jury found that the driver had not acted negligently. The Nova Scotia Court of Appeal ordered a new trial, however, on the ground that the trial judge had mis-instructed the jury with respect to s. 248 of the *Motor Vehicle Act*, R.S.N.S. 1989, c. 293:

(3) Every pedestrian crossing a roadway at any point other than within a marked or unmarked crosswalk, shall yield the right of way to vehicles upon the highway.

(4) This section shall not relieve the driver of the vehicle or the pedestrian from the duty to exercise care.

The Court of Appeal held that while the jury properly had been told that Johnathan could not be held contributorily negligent because of his tender years, the trial judge incorrectly instructed the jury with respect to the preceding provisions. The trial judge had said:

So a pedestrian has the right to cross the highway at a point which is not a regular crossing for pedestrians, but in such a case, a duty is cast upon him to take special care to use greater vigilance and to yield the right of way to vehicles upon the highway. So in a crosswalk, cars stop. If you re not in a crosswalk, then what I just told you applies.

This . . . is for the obvious reason that drivers of motor vehicles know that there're safety zones and crosswalks for the use of pedestrians where they are normally expected to cross. This is not to say however, that if a pedestrian crosses between intersections, a motorist can run him down with impu[nity]. The question is could or should the driver have seen the pedestrian in time to avoid the collision?

The pedestrian on the other hand has a duty to look out for his own safety, and to keep a lookout for approaching vehicles. . . .

Johnathan was four years, four months old. So the standard of care owed to children on a highway is the same as that owed to adults, but there may be circumstances which should put motorists on their guard. . . .

[A driver] has the right to expect that a pedestrian will not act without care. The duty of a pedestrian when using the public street or highway is to use reasonable care at all times for his own safety, and to avoid placing himself in a position from which injury might result. However, he's entitled to assume that motorists will drive according to the law.

The decision was appealed to the Supreme Court of Canada.]

DESCHAMPS J.: . . .

[6] MacDonald C.J.N.S. [of the Court of Appeal] concluded that, in referring to the right-of-way provisions of the *Motor Vehicle Act*, the trial judge improperly invited the jury to treat Johnathan "like an adult". This, according to MacDonald C.J.N.S., would have left the jury "with little choice but to find Johnathan responsible for this accident". . . even though the trial judge had already concluded that Johnathan could not be contributorily negligent because of his young age. In offering guidance for a possible retrial, MacDonald C.J.N.S. recommended expunging the entire passage dealing with the right-of-way provisions of the *Motor Vehicle Act*.

[7] I agree with the appellant that the Court of Appeal failed to appreciate the dual function of statutory right-of-way provisions. Not only do such provisions inform the assessment of whether a pedestrian was contributorily negligent by failing to yield a right of way, they can also help determine whether a driver breached the applicable standard of care in the circumstances. In this case, even though Johnathan's contributory negligence had been ruled out as a matter of law, the

statutory right-of-way provisions continued to inform the standard of care that [the bus driver] owed to all pedestrians. The jury needed to be told that, absent special circumstances, where the driver has the right of way, he or she can reasonably proceed on the assumption that others will follow the rules of the road and yield the right of way to drivers.

[8] I respectfully disagree with the Court of Appeal's conclusion that, in referring to the right-of-way provisions, the trial judge effectively invited the jury to find Johnathan legally responsible for the accident. At the outset of his charge, Pickup J. made it clear that Johnathan's liability was not at issue because of his young age. . . . In no part of the charge did the trial judge instruct the jury to adjudicate on the child's negligence. When the trial judge's instructions on the right-of-way provisions are read in light of the entire charge, it is clear that they served only to delineate the standard of care applicable to [the bus driver]. The jury was invited to consider the conduct of a reasonable pedestrian in assessing whether [the driver] had demonstrated the requisite degree of precaution.

[The court allowed the appeal and restored the decision at trial to deny the plaintiff's claim.]

NOTES AND QUESTIONS

1. Compare the statutory provisions in *Marshall* with those in *Ryan*. In each instance, upon whom did the legislative obligation fall: the plaintiff or the defendant?

2. Identify the legislative goals of the provisions in *Ryan* and in *Marshall*. In each instance, were those goals promoted or impaired by the Supreme Court of Canada's decision?

3. Which institution is better positioned to formulate a standard of care: a court or a legislature? What advantages and disadvantages affect each institution?

4. In light of your responses to the previous question, how should proof of a statutory breach affect the standard of care analysis within the tort of negligence?

5. Explain the relationship between the factors that may influence the issue of contributory negligence and the factors that may influence the issue of the defendant's standard of care. What, if anything, has *Marshall* contributed to your understanding of the tort of negligence?

6. For other examples of statutory obligations that influenced the formulation of the standard of care in negligence, see *Galaske v. O'Donnell* (1994), 112 D.L.R. (4th) 109 (S.C.C.); *Varcoe v. Sterling* (1992), 7 O.R. (3d) 204 (Gen. Div.), aff'd (1992), 10 O.R. (3d) 574 (C.A.); *School Div. of Assiniboine South (No. 3) v. Hoffer* (1971), 21 D.L.R. (3d) 608 (Man. C.A.), aff'd (1973), 40 D.L.R. (3d) 480 (S.C.C.); *Rinas v. Regina (City)* (1983), 26 Sask. R. 132 (Q.B.); and *Burbank v. R.T.B.* (2007), 65 B.C.L.R. (4th) 290 (C.A.).

7. In *Ryan* and *Marshall*, legislative provisions informed the standard of care under the common law tort of negligence. As we saw earlier in this chapter, however, legislation may provide a statutory cause of action. In that instance, the defendant may be held liable despite satisfying the common law standard of care that would

apply in the same situation. *London Passenger Transport Board v. Upson*, [1949] A.C. 155 (H.L.) provides an example. The defendant bus driver struck a pedestrian in a crosswalk. Lord Porter recognized that the defendant had taken all reasonable care, but nevertheless imposed liability because the statute imposed an additional burden. If unable to see if a crosswalk was clear, a driver was statutorily required to proceed at a speed that could allow the vehicle to be stopped before it entered the crosswalk.

8. For further discussion of the relationship between regulatory norms and the standard of care, see Lee, "Safety, Regulation and Tort: Fault in Context" (2011) 74 Mod. L. Rev. 555.

4. A Note on the *Canadian Charter of Rights and Freedoms*

Aside from specific torts statutes, the *Canadian Charter of Rights and Freedoms*, Part I of the *Constitution Act, 1982*, being Schedule B to the *Canada Act 1982* (U.K.), 1982, c. 11, will probably have as great an impact on civil liability as any single piece of federal or provincial legislation. There are two ways in which the *Charter* may affect tort liability. First, an individual whose *Charter* rights have been violated may have an express statutory cause of action under s. 24(1). Second, as part of the supreme law of Canada, the *Charter* may alter some existing common law causes of action and defences. In this section, we set out some of the most relevant *Charter* provisions and briefly illustrate how they may affect civil liability. The role of the *Charter* in tort law was also considered in Chapters 3, 8, 11, and 21.

CANADIAN CHARTER OF RIGHTS AND FREEDOMS
Part I of the Constitution Act, 1982
Schedule B to the *Canada Act 1982* (U.K.), 1982, c. 11

Rights and freedoms in Canada

1. The Canadian Charter of Rights and Freedoms guarantees the rights and freedoms set out in it subject only to such reasonable limits prescribed by law as can be demonstrably justified in a free and democratic society.

Fundamental freedoms

2. Everyone has the following fundamental freedoms:
    (a) freedom of conscience and religion;
    (b) freedom of thought, belief, opinion and expression, including freedom of the press and other media of communication;
    (c) freedom of peaceful assembly; and
    (d) freedom of association.

. . .

Life, liberty and security of person

7. Everyone has the right to life, liberty and security of the person and the right not to be deprived thereof except in accordance with the principles of fundamental justice.

Search or seizure

8. Everyone has the right to be secure against unreasonable search or seizure.

Detention or imprisonment

9. Everyone has the right not to be arbitrarily detained or imprisoned.

Arrest or detention

10. Everyone has the right on arrest or detention
    (a) to be informed promptly of the reasons therefor;
    (b) to retain and instruct counsel without delay and to be informed of that right; and
    (c) to have the validity of the detention determined by way of *habeas corpus* and to be released if the detention is not lawful.

. . .

Equality before and under law and equal protection and benefit of law

15. (1) Every individual is equal before and under the law and has the right to the equal protection and equal benefit of the law without discrimination and, in particular, without discrimination based on race, national or ethnic origin, colour, religion, sex, age or mental or physical disability.

. . .

Enforcement of guaranteed rights and freedoms

24. (1) Anyone whose rights or freedoms, as guaranteed by this Charter, have been infringed or denied may apply to a court of competent jurisdiction to obtain such remedy as the court considers appropriate and just in the circumstances.

. . .

Application of Charter

32. (1) This Charter applies
    (a) to the Parliament and government of Canada in respect of all matters within the authority of Parliament including all matters relating to the Yukon Territory and Northwest Territories; and
    (b) to the legislature and government of each province in respect of all matters within the authority of the legislature of each province.

. . .

Primacy of Constitution of Canada

52. (1) The Constitution of Canada is the supreme law of Canada, and any law that is inconsistent with the provisions of the Constitution is, to the extent of the inconsistency, of no force or effect.

. . .

Section 24(1) creates an express statutory cause of action for individuals whose *Charter* rights have been violated. However, the plaintiff must first establish that the *Charter* applies to the situation. Two points are clear. First, by reason of s. 32(1), the *Charter* applies to federal and provincial laws, governments, and government agencies. Second, the *Charter* does *not* apply to litigation between private citizens. Difficult issues often arise, however, as to whether a particular person or institution fits into the first category. In that regard, the courts have resolved some questions.

- The *Charter* obviously applies to Parliament, provincial and territorial legislatures, and municipalities. It therefore governs statutes, regulations, by-laws, and the like.

- The *Charter* also applies to the actions of government officials, including the police and Crown corporations. However, while the judiciary is sometimes classified as a branch of "government" (very broadly speaking), the Supreme Court of Canada in *R.W.D.S.U., Local 580 v. Dolphin Delivery Ltd.* (1986), 33 D.L.R. (4th) 174 (S.C.C.) rejected the suggestion that all judicial action is caught by the *Charter*. Since all laws must, in the final analysis, be interpreted and applied by judges, that view would intolerably subject *all* laws to *Charter* scrutiny.

- The *Charter* often applies to people, such as government-appointed adjudicators, who derive their power from legislation. In addition, it applies to bodies, such as law societies and colleges of surgeons, that exercise a regulatory power that has been delegated by government.

- Difficulty remains with respect to institutions that are "public" in a broad sense. The courts have said that the critical factor is the extent to which an institution is controlled by the government. Consequently, the *Charter* applies to community colleges, but not to universities. While both types of institution receive government funding, the government has relatively greater say in the day-to-day operations of the former. Universities, in contrast, generally are marked by a greater degree of independence.

- The *Charter* does not apply to private corporations, despite their statutory foundations. Like universities, private corporations are dependent upon government legislation for their existence. Once in existence, however, they take on an independent life of their own, substantially separate from government control.

If the *Charter* applies, the plaintiff must establish that the defendant violated a *Charter* right. Even if the plaintiff succeeds in doing so, relief will be denied under s. 1 if the defendant proves that the infringement was a "reasonable limit prescribed by law that can be demonstrably justified in a free and democratic society." Only unjustified *Charter* violations give an individual a right to seek a remedy under s. 24(1). The court has broad discretion to grant any remedy that it considers appropriate in the circumstances. Although damages, injunctions, and prohibitions have been awarded under s. 24(1), the plaintiff is not entitled to them as of right.

The *Charter* may also affect the existing common law causes of action and defences. Section 52 of the *Charter* provides that the *Charter* is the supreme law of Canada. Any law that is inconsistent with it consequently is, to the extent of the inconsistency, of no force or effect. Since the words "any law" include common law torts principles, the *Charter* may have a significant impact on existing causes of action. For example, an individual's freedoms of peaceful assembly and association in s. 2(c) and (d) may require some modifications in the common law principles governing trespass to Crown land.

The *Charter* can also be used to negate what would otherwise be a valid common law or statutory defence. Assume, for example, that a police officer searched the plaintiff at random pursuant to ss. 10 and 11 of the *Narcotic Control Act*, R.S.C. 1985, c. N-1. Assume as well that the plaintiff sued in battery and that the officer raised the *Narcotic Control Act* in defence. If the plaintiff established that this search power violated s. 8 of the *Charter*, which prohibits unreasonable search or seizure, and could not be justified under s. 1, then this section would be of no force or effect to the extent that it was inconsistent with s. 8. As a result, the officer's search would no longer be authorized by law and the defence of legal authority could fail.

NOTES

1. As to the scope of s. 32(1), see generally Tassé, "Application of the Canadian Charter of Rights and Freedoms" in Beaudoin & Ratushny, eds., *The Canadian Charter of Rights and Freedoms*, 2d ed. (1989) at 65; and Hogg, *Constitutional Law of Canada — Student Edition 2005* (2005), ch. 34.

2. In *R.W.D.S.U., Local 580 v. Dolphin Delivery Ltd.* (1986), 33 D.L.R. (4th) 174 at 198 (S.C.C.), the Supreme Court of Canada held that the *Charter* does not apply to litigation between private citizens. However, the court also stated that "the judiciary ought to apply and develop the principles of the common law in a manner consistent with the fundamental values enshrined in the Constitution. . . . In this sense, then, the *Charter* is far from irrelevant to private litigants whose disputes fall to be decided at common law." This statement generated considerable academic comment. See for example Beloba, "The Charter of Rights and Private Litigation: The Dilemma of *Dolphin Delivery*" in Finkelstein & Rogers, eds., *Charter Issues in Civil Cases* (1988) at 29. See also *Dobson (Litigation Guardian of) v. Dobson* (1999), 174 D.L.R. (4th) 1 (S.C.C.).

3. As noted above, difficult issues may arise if a party argues that the *Charter* applies to agencies and organizations that operate under statutory authority or are funded by a government. See *Lavigne v. O.P.S.E.U.* (1991), 81 D.L.R. (4th) 545 (S.C.C.); and *New Brunswick Broadcasting Co. v. Nova Scotia (Speaker of the House of Assembly)* (1993), 100 D.L.R. (4th) 212 (S.C.C.). It appears that the *Charter* will apply to an agency that is part of government. This determination is based on the form, function, and degree of government control and funding. Non-government agencies may also be subject to the *Charter* depending on the degree to which they are under government control. See *McKinney v. University of Guelph* (1990), 76 D.L.R. (4th) 545 (S.C.C.); *Douglas College v. Douglas/Kwantlen Faculty Assoc* (1990), 77 D.L.R. (4th) 94 (S.C.C.); and *Vancouver General Hospital v. Stoffman* (1990), 76 D.L.R. (4th) 700 (S.C.C.).

4. For a discussion of damages under s. 24(1) of the *Charter*, see Charles, *Understanding Charter Damages: The Judicial Evolution of a Charter Remedy* (2016); McGivney & Woodin, "The Threshold of Fault: Damages Awards Under Section 24(1) of the Charter" (2015) 43 Adv. Q. 510; Okpaluba, "The Development of Charter Damages Jurisprudence in Canada: Guidelines from the Supreme Court of Canada" (2012) 23 Stellenbosch L. Rev. 55; Toprani, "A Tale of Two Section Twenty-fours: Towards a Comprehensive Approach for Charter Remedies" (2012) 70 U. of T. Fac. L. Rev. 141; Pilkington, "Monetary Redress for Charter Infringement" in Sharpe, ed., *Charter Litigation* (1987) 307; Morgan, "Charter Remedies: The Civil Side After the First Five Years" in Finkelstein & Rogers, *supra*, at 47; and Gibson & Gibson, "Enforcement of the Canadian Charter of Rights and Freedoms" in Beaudoin & Ratushny, eds., *The Canadian Charter of Rights and Freedoms*, 2d ed. (1989) 781. See also *Poirier v. Canada (Minister of Veterans Affairs)*, [1989] 3 F.C. 233 (C.A.).

5. For additional discussion of the *Charter*'s impact on common law causes of action and defences see Doody, "Freedom of the Press: The Canadian Charter of Rights and Freedoms, and a New Category of Qualified Privilege" (1983) 61 Can. Bar Rev. 124; Hutchinson & Petter, "Private Rights/Public Wrongs: The Liberal Lie of the Charter" (1988) 38 U.T.L.J. 278; Weinrib, "Constitutional Values and Private Law in Canada" in Friedmann & Barak-Erez, eds., *Human Rights in Private Law* (2002) 43. See also *Hill v. Church of Scientology*, [1995] 2 S.C.R. 1130.

6. The *Charter* may apply to procedural matters. Special limitation periods and other procedural rules applying to claims against public authorities have been challenged under the *Charter*, usually under s. 15. See for example *Colangelo v. Mississauga (City)* (1988), 53 D.L.R. (4th) 283 (Ont. C.A.); *Mirhadizadeh v. Ontario* (1989), 69 O.R. (2d) 422 (C.A.); and *Canadian Assn. of Regulated Importers v. Canada (A.G.)* (1994), 17 Admin. L.R. (2d) 121 (F.C.A.).

7. A controversial limitation on the availability of *Charter* damages was recognized in *Ernst v. Alberta Energy Regulator*, 2017 SCC 1. The action stemmed from the plaintiff's belief that fracking activity had caused methane and other gases to seep into her well and the surrounding groundwater. She buttressed that claim with videos of her tap water being set on fire. She attempted to participate in the complaints process established by the defendant, but felt that the defendant stifled her ability to communicate her concerns. She accordingly sought *Charter* damages on the basis that the defendant had violated her right to freedom of expression, as guaranteed by s. 2(b) of the *Charter*. The defendant brought a motion to strike that claim under s. 43 of the *Energy Resources Conservation Act*, R.S.A. 2000, c. E 10: "No action or proceeding may be brought against the Board . . . in respect of any act or thing done purportedly in pursuance of this Act . . . or a decision, order or direction of the Board." The motions judge and the Alberta Court of Appeal agreed that *Charter* damages were barred by that immunity.

The Supreme Court of Canada was sharply divided. Cromwell J., writing for the plurality, held that the plaintiff's *Charter* claim was subject to the statutory immunity. He feared that "[o]pening the Board to damages claims [would] distract it from its statutory duties, potentially have a chilling effect on its decision making, compromise its impartiality, and open up new and undesirable modes of collateral attack on its decisions": at para. 55. Judicial review was said to be the appropriate remedy. (Abella J., concurring, similarly doubted that damages would be appropriate but did not expressly address the issue.) In dissent, however, McLachlin C.J.C. and Moldaver and Brown JJ., insisted that "*Charter* compliance is itself a foundational principle of good governance": at para. 169.

8. Both sections provide relief from *Charter* violations, but s. 24(1) and s. 52(1) serve different functions. McLachlin C.J.C. drew the distinction in *R. v. Ferguson*, 2008 SCC 6 at para. 35:

> Section 24(1) confers on judges a wide discretion to grant appropriate remedies in response to Charter violations. [It] has generally been seen . . . as providing a case-by-case remedy for unconstitutional acts of government agents operating under lawful schemes whose constitutionality is not challenged. [Section 52(1)] confers no discretion on judges. It simply provides that laws that are inconsistent with the *Charter* are of no force and effect to the extent of the inconsistency.

Because they serve different functions, s. 24(1) and s. 52(1) are not normally applied in combination, but they are not mutually exclusive either. Situations occasionally warrant both a declaration of invalidity and an award of *Charter* damages. Gonthier J. addressed that possibility in *Mackin v. New Brunswick (Minister of Justice)*, 2002 SCC 13 at paras. 78-9. As "a general rule of public law," he said, "courts will not award damages for the harm suffered as a result of the mere enactment or application of a law that is subsequently declared to be unconstitutional." That "limited immunity [is] given to government [as] a means of creating a balance between the protection of constitutional rights and the need for effective government." Were it otherwise, Gonthier J. said, "the effectiveness and efficiency of government action would be excessively constrained." Nevertheless, *Charter* damages will be awarded, in conjunction with a declaration of invalidity, upon proof of "conduct that is clearly wrong, in bad faith or an abuse of power." Cf. *Schachter v. Canada*, [1992] 2 S.C.R. 679.

. . .

Although the *Charter* came into force in 1982, many years passed without authoritative guidance regarding damages for *Charter* violations. That gap has now been filled by the next case.

VANCOUVER (CITY) v. WARD
[2010] 2 S.C.R. 28

[Prime Minister Chretien visited Vancouver in August of 2002 to commemorate the opening of a new gate to the city's Chinatown. City police received a tip that an unidentified man intended to throw a pie at the Prime Minister. The plaintiff, a lawyer in his mid-40s, attended the event, acted in a suspicious manner, and loosely fit a broad description given to the police. The police, mistakenly believing that the plaintiff was the would-be assailant, handcuffed him and took him to a police station. He was subjected to a strip search and held for approximately four and a half hours. His car was impounded for inspection. When the error eventually was discovered, the plaintiff was released and reunited with his vehicle.

The plaintiff sued the province and the city. The trial judge found that these defendants had acted in good faith and were not liable for any common law tort. He also found, however, that the city, by conducting the strip search, and the province, by detaining the vehicle, violated the plaintiff's right under s. 8 of the *Charter* to be free from unreasonable search and seizure. The court accordingly assessed damages under s. 24(1) of the *Charter*. $5000 for the strip search and $100 for the seizure of the car. The British Columbia Court of Appeal agreed. The case was then appealed to the Supreme Court of Canada. Writing for a unanimous panel, McLachlin C.J.C. formulated the rules governing damages for *Charter* violations.]

MCLACHLIN C.J.C.: . . .

[1] The *Canadian Charter of Rights and Freedoms* guarantees the fundamental rights and freedoms of all Canadians and provides remedies for their breach. The first and most important remedy is the nullification of laws that violate the *Charter* under s. 52(1) of the *Constitution Act, 1982*. This is supplemented by s. 24(2), under which evidence obtained in breach of the *Charter* may be excluded if its admission would bring the administration of justice into disrepute, and s. 24(1) — the provision at issue in this case — under which the court is authorized to grant such remedies to

individuals for infringement of *Charter* rights as it "considers appropriate and just in the circumstances." . . .

[3] This appeal raises the question of when damages may be awarded under s. 24(1) of the *Charter*, and what the amount of such damages should be. Although the *Charter* is 28 years old, authority on this question is sparse, inviting a comprehensive analysis of the object of damages for *Charter* breaches and the considerations that guide their award.

[4] I conclude that damages may be awarded for *Charter* breach under s. 24(1) where appropriate and just. The first step in the inquiry is to establish that a *Charter* right has been breached. The second step is to show why damages are a just and appropriate remedy, having regard to whether they would fulfill one or more of the related functions of compensation, vindication of the right, and/or deterrence of future breaches. At the third step, the state has the opportunity to demonstrate, if it can, that countervailing factors defeat the functional considerations that support a damage award and render damages inappropriate or unjust. The final step is to assess the quantum of the damages. . . .

A. *When are Damages Under Section 24(1) Available?* . . .

[20] The general considerations governing what constitutes an appropriate and just remedy under s. 24(1) were set out by Iacobucci and Arbour JJ. in *Doucet-Boudreau v. Nova Scotia (Minister of Education)*, [2003] 3 S.C.R. 3. Briefly, an appropriate and just remedy will: (1) meaningfully vindicate the rights and freedoms of the claimants; (2) employ means that are legitimate within the framework of our constitutional democracy; (3) be a judicial remedy which vindicates the right while invoking the function and powers of a court; and (4) be fair to the party against whom the order is made. . . .

[21] Damages for breach of a claimant's *Charter* rights may meet these conditions. They may meaningfully vindicate the claimant's rights and freedoms. They employ a means well-recognized within our legal framework. They are appropriate to the function and powers of a court. And, depending on the circumstances and the amount awarded, they can be fair not only to the claimant whose rights were breached, but to the state which is required to pay them. I therefore conclude that s. 24(1) is broad enough to include the remedy of damages for *Charter* breach. That said, . . . *Charter* damages are only one remedy amongst others available under s. 24(1), and often other s. 24(1) remedies will be more responsive to the breach.

[22] [I]t should always be borne in mind that these are not private law damages, but the distinct remedy of constitutional damages. As Thomas J. notes in *Dunlea v. Attorney-General*, [2000] 3 N.Z.L.R. 136 . . . an action for public law damages "is not a private law action in the nature of a tort claim for which the state is vicariously liable, but [a distinct] public law action directly against the state for which the state is primarily liable". . . . The nature of the remedy is to require the state (or society writ large) to compensate an individual for breaches of the individual's constitutional rights. An action for public law damages — including constitutional damages — lies against the state and not against individual actors. Actions against individual actors should be pursued in accordance with existing causes of action. However, the underlying policy considerations that are engaged when awarding private law damages against state actors may be relevant when awarding public law damages directly against the state. . . .

(1) *Step One: Proof of a Charter Breach*

[23] Section 24(1) is remedial. The first step, therefore, is to establish a *Charter* breach. This is the wrong on which the claim for damages is based.

(2) *Step Two: Functional Justification of Damages*

[24] A functional approach to damages finds damages to be appropriate and just to the extent that they serve a useful function or purpose. . . .

[25] . . . For damages to be awarded, they must further the general objects of the *Charter*. This reflects itself in three interrelated functions that damages may serve. The function of *compensation,* usually the most prominent function, recognizes that breach of an individual's *Charter* rights may cause personal loss which should be remedied. The function of *vindication* recognizes that *Charter* rights must be maintained, and cannot be allowed to be whittled away by attrition. Finally, the function of *deterrence* recognizes that damages may serve to deter future breaches by state actors. . . .

(4) *Step Three: Countervailing Factors . . .*

[33] [E]ven if the claimant establishes that damages are functionally justified, the state may establish that other considerations render s. 24(1) damages inappropriate or unjust. A complete catalogue of countervailing considerations remains to be developed as the law in this area matures. At this point, however, two considerations are apparent: the existence of alternative remedies and concerns for good governance. . . .

[45] If the claimant establishes breach of his *Charter* rights and shows that an award of damages under s. 24(1) of the *Charter* would serve a functional purpose, having regard to the objects of s. 24(1) damages, and the state fails to negate that the award is "appropriate and just", the final step is to determine the appropriate amount of the damages.

(5) *Step Four: Quantum of Section 24(1) Damages*

[46] The watchword of s. 24(1) is that the remedy must be "appropriate and just." This applies to the amount, or quantum, of damages awarded as much as to the initial question of whether damages are a proper remedy. . . .

[49] In some cases, the *Charter* breach may cause the claimant pecuniary loss. Injuries, physical and psychological, may require medical treatment, with attendant costs. Prolonged detention may result in loss of earnings. *Restitutio in integrum* requires compensation for such financial losses.

[50] In other cases . . . the claimant's losses will be non-pecuniary. Non-pecuniary damages are harder to measure. [T]ort law provides assistance. Pain and suffering are compensable. Absent exceptional circumstances, compensation is fixed at a fairly modest conventional rate, subject to variation for the degree of suffering in the particular case. In extreme cases of catastrophic injury, a higher but still conventionally determined award is given on the basis that it serves the function purpose of providing substitute comforts and pleasures. . . .

[51] When we move from compensation to the objectives of vindication and deterrence, tort law is less useful. Making the appropriate determinations is an exercise in rationality and proportionality. . . .

[52] A principal guide to the determination of quantum is the seriousness of the breach, having regard to the objects of s. 24(1) damages. The seriousness of the breach

must be evaluated with regard to the impact of the breach on the claimant and the seriousness of the state misconduct. . . .

[53] [Section] 24(1) damages must be fair — or "appropriate and just" — to both the claimant and the state. The court must arrive at a quantum that respects this. Large awards and the consequent diversion of public funds may serve little functional purpose in terms of the claimant's needs and may be inappropriate or unjust from the public perspective. In considering what is fair to the claimant and the state, the court may take into account the public interest in good governance, the danger of deterring governments from undertaking beneficial new policies and programs, and the need to avoid diverting large sums of funds from public programs to private interests. . . .

[55] [T]he court must focus on the breach of *Charter* rights as an independent wrong, worthy of compensation in its own right. At the same time, damages under s. 24(1) should not duplicate damages awarded under private law causes of action, such as tort. . . .

[56] A final word on exemplary or punitive damages. . . . [P]ublic law damages, in serving the objects of vindication and deterrence, may assume a punitive aspect. Nevertheless, it is worth noting a general reluctance in the international community to award purely punitive damages. . . .

(6) *Forum and Procedure*

[58] For a tribunal to grant a *Charter* remedy under s. 24(1), it must have the power to decide questions of law and the remedy must be one that the tribunal is authorized to grant. . . . Generally, the appropriate forum for an award of damages under s. 24(1) is a court which has the power to consider *Charter* questions and which by statute or inherent jurisdiction has the power to award damages. Provincial criminal courts are not so empowered. . . .

[59] [T]he claimant may join a s. 24(1) claim with a tort claim. It may be useful to consider the tort claim first, since if it meets the objects of *Charter* damages, recourse to s. 24(1) will be unnecessary. This may add useful context and facilitate the s. 24(1) analysis. This said, it is not essential that the claimant exhaust her remedies in private law before bringing a s. 24(1) claim.

B. *Application to the Facts*

[60] At trial, Justice Tysoe held that the provincial correction officers' strip search and the Vancouver Police Department's vehicle seizure violated Mr. Ward's right to be free from unreasonable search and seizure under s. 8 of the *Charter*. There are thus two distinct claims to consider.

(1) *Damages for the Strip Search* . . .

[64] [T]he need for compensation bulks large. Mr. Ward's injury was serious. He had a constitutional right to be free from unreasonable search and seizure, which was violated in an egregious fashion. Strip searches are inherently humiliating and degrading regardless of the manner in which they are carried out and thus constitute significant injury to an individual's intangible interests. . . .

[66] The impingement on Mr. Ward calls for compensation. Combined with the police conduct, it also engages the objects of vindication of the right and deterrence of future breaches. It follows that compensation is required in this case to functionally fulfill the objects of public law damages. . . .

[68] The state has not established that alternative remedies are available to achieve the objects of compensation, vindication or deterrence with respect to the strip search. Mr. Ward sued the officers for assault, as well as the City and the Province for negligence. These claims were dismissed and their dismissal was not appealed to this Court. While this defeated Mr. Ward's claim in tort, it did not change the fact that his right under s. 8 of the *Charter* to be secure against unreasonable search and seizure was violated. . . .

[73] Considering all the factors, including the appropriate degree of deference to be paid to the trial judge's exercise of remedial discretion, I conclude that the trial judge's $5,000 damage award was appropriate.

(2) *Damages for the Car Seizure* . . .

[75] The trial judge found that the seizure of the car violated Mr. Ward's rights under s. 8 of the *Charter*. This finding is not contested and thus satisfies the first requirement.

[77] The object of compensation is not engaged by the seizure of the car. . . . Mr. Ward did not suffer any injury as a result of the seizure. His car was never searched and, upon his release from lockup, Mr. Ward was driven to the police compound to pick up the vehicle. Nor are the objects of vindication of the right and deterrence of future breaches compelling. While the seizure was wrong, it was not of a serious nature. The police officers did not illegally search the car. . . . When the officers determined that they did not have grounds to obtain the required warrant, the vehicle was made available for pickup.

[78] I conclude that a declaration under s. 24(1) that the vehicle seizure violated Mr. Ward's right to be free from unreasonable search and seizure under s. 8 of the *Charter* adequately serves the need for vindication of the right and deterrence of future improper car seizures.

NOTES AND QUESTIONS

1. Explain the relationship between tort law and *Charter* violations. Against whom is a *Charter* action brought? How do the functions of tort law compare to the functions served by the *Charter*? What differences, if any, distinguish the quantification of damages in tort and damages under s. 24(1) of the *Charter*?

2. Are damages invariably awarded upon proof of a *Charter* violation? What other remedies are available to a court? *Charter* damages are important, symbolically as well as practically. They are also limited. That is true in terms of both the incidence of successful claims and the quantum of awards. The award of $5000 in *Ward* is representative. Are such sums likely to deter? Given the great expense associated with litigating claims under s. 24(1), is the prospect of such awards (even when coupled with costs awards) likely to induce potential claimants to take action?

That is not to deny the possibility of much larger awards. As discussed below, the remarkable facts in *Henry v. British Columbia (Attorney General)*, 2015 SCC 24 entitled the claimant to $7.5 million.

3. Explain the test that McLachlin C.J.C. formulated in *Ward* for the award of *Charter* damages. Does the first stage require proof of fault? What objectives are relevant to the second stage? What types of "countervailing factors" inform the court's

decision at the third stage? Are *Charter* damages necessarily barred if the plaintiff has the option of pursuing an alternative claim in tort? What is meant by "good governance" and why might *Charter* damages be denied on that basis? What principles guide the assessment of damages at the fourth stage? And finally, which party bears the burden of proof at each stage of the test?

To what extent does the test, as formulated in *Ward*, govern every claim for *Charter* damages? You may want to revisit that question after considering the discussion of *Henry v. British Columbia (Attorney General)*, 2015 SCC 24 that appears below.

Notwithstanding the Supreme Court of Canada's view regarding the relevance of fault, lower courts have a surprising tendency to strike out on their own: *Forest v. Kirkland*, 2012 ONSC 429; *Fragomeni v. Greater Sudbury Police Service*, 2015 ONSC 3937; *Hneihen (Litigation guardian of) v. Centre for Addiction and Mental Health*, 2014 ONSC 55; but *cf. Mammoliti v. Niagara Regional Police Service*, 2007 ONCA 79.

For discussion of the *Ward* test, see Charles, *Understanding Charter Damages: The Judicial Evolution of a Charter Remedy* (2016), ch. 6; Charney and Hunter, "Tort Lite? *Vancouver (City) v. Ward* and the Availability of Damages for Charter Infringements" (2011) 54 S.C.L.R. (2d) 393; Safayeni "Improving the Effectiveness of the Constitutional Damages Remedy: *Vancouver (City) v Ward*" (2017) 47 Adv. Q. 121; and Linden, "Charter Damage Claims: New Dawn or Mirage" (2012) 39 Adv. Q. 426.

4. When, if ever, will a court award punitive damages in response to a *Charter* violation? See also *Elmardy v. Toronto Police Services Board*, 2017 ONSC 2074.

5. Which courts are capable of awarding damages for *Charter* violations? How did McLachlin C.J.C. explain the position of provincial courts on that issue?

6. The issue of *Charter* damages arose again in *Henry v. British Columbia (Attorney General)*, 2015 SCC 24. Between 1980 and 1982, a serial rapist victimized several women in Vancouver. Each of the attacks followed the same *modus operandi*. In 1983, Ivan Henry was accused and convicted of ten counts of sexual assault. After being classified as a dangerous offender, he was sentenced to an indefinite period of incarceration. Henry, however, consistently maintained his innocence. That claim gained credence in 2002 when a "cold-case" investigation linked DNA evidence collected at the crime scenes to Donald McRae, whom police had identified as a suspect at the same time that Henry was first accused. In 2008, a specially-appointed prosecutor provided full disclosure of files that the Crown had possessed, but withheld, during Henry's trial. Those files contained crucial exculpatory evidence. In 2009, Henry was permitted to re-open his appeal, and in 2010, the British Columbia Court of Appeal overturned his convictions and acquitted him on all charges. After nearly 27 years in prison, Henry was free.

Henry then sued the Crown for failing to disclose evidence during his criminal trial. As discussed in Chapter 3, the tort of malicious prosecution requires proof that the defendant acted with malice: *Nelles v. Ontario*, [1989] 2 S.C.R. 170. Few plaintiffs can clear that high hurdle. Henry therefore framed his action as a claim for s. 24(1) *Charter* damages arising from the violation of his *Charter* rights under ss. 7 (life, liberty, and security of the person) and 11(d) (presumption of innocence). The question that came before the Supreme Court of Canada concerned the formulation of that claim. In *Ward*, the court had held that *Charter* damages are not generally premised upon fault or intention, but it also recognized that circumstances may demand otherwise. Was *Henry* one such circumstance? Did the claimant have to prove that the prosecutor acted with a culpable frame of mind? If so, was *mala fides* required as with the tort of malicious prosecution? Or would some lesser degree of fault suffice?

The court was divided. The majority, written by Moldaver J., held that while Henry need not prove malice, he had to do more than establish but-for causation. *Charter* damages are available "where the Crown, in breach of its constitutional obligations, causes harm to the accused by intentionally withholding information when it knows, or would reasonably be expected to know, that the information is material to the defence and that the failure to disclose will likely impinge on the accused's ability to make full answer and defence." Though not as demanding as the tort of malicious prosecution, "[t]his represents a high threshold for a successful *Charter* damages claim" (at para. 31). According to Moldaver J., "[i]t is only by keeping liability within strict bounds that we can ensure a reasonable balance between remedying serious rights violations and maintaining the efficient operation of our public prosecution system" (at para. 81). Having weighed the compensation, deterrence, and vindication functions of *Charter* damages against the notion of "good governance," he found that a less stringent requirement would undermine "the ability of prosecutors to discharge their important public duties . . . with adverse consequences for the administration of justice" (at para. 39). More precisely, the majority worried that the "spectre of liability [might] influence the decision-making of prosecutors and make them more 'defensive' in their approach"; cause Crown counsel to be "motivated by fear of civil liability, rather than their sworn duty to fairly and effectively prosecute crime"; and "open up the floodgates of civil liability and force prosecutors to spend undue amounts of time and energy defending their conduct in court instead of performing their duties" (at para. 40).

McLachlin C.J.C. and Karakatsanis J. considered the majority's concerns regarding good governance to be "misplaced. Imposing a fault requirement for *Charter* damages, where the Crown has breached its duty to disclose," they wrote, "is inconsistent with the purpose of s. 24(1) and with the principled framework established in *Vancouver (City) v. Ward*" (at para. 104). They consequently held that the plaintiff should not have to prove malice or even intention: it should be enough for Henry to "establish (1) a breach of his *Charter* rights and (2) that damages constitute an appropriate and just remedy to advance the purposes of compensation, vindication or deterrence. It is for the state to plead countervailing factors, should it choose to do so" (at para. 108).

Which reasons are more persuasive? Given the remarkable facts of *Henry v. British Columbia (Attorney General)* and the tremendous hardship suffered by the plaintiff, should a judge be more concerned with securing justice between the immediate parties or protecting the efficient operation of criminal justice system? Is it possible to adequately respect the interests of both the individual and the community? How does the *Charter* generally strike that balance?

The formulation of a fault element is important. The placement of that element may be relevant as well. MacLachlin C.J.C. preferred for the first stage of the *Ward* test to merely require proof of a *Charter* breach. Discussions of fault, she believed, properly belonged to the assessment of countervailing factors at *Ward*'s third stage. In contrast, Moldaver J.'s majority opinion required proof of fault at the first stage. Is that reformulation of *Ward*'s first stage significant? Does it signal a shift to a more restrictive approach? See Charles, *Understanding Charter Damages, supra*, at 117-20.

Within the context of the Crown's failure to disclose relevant information, how does the tort of malicious prosecution compare with the claim for *Charter* damages? How do you explain the differences between those two causes of action? What purposes and goals are served by each?

The appeal to the Supreme Court of Canada arose from the claimant's application to amend his pleadings with respect to his *Charter* claim. Having been permitted to do so, he returned to trial for a decision on the substance of his action. The trial judge upheld his claim and awarded a little more than $8 million in damages, including $7.5 million reflecting the vindication and deterrence functions of s. 24(1) of the *Charter*. 2016 BCSC 1038 and 2016 BCSC 2082, aff'd 2017 BCCA 420.

For discussion of *Henry*, see Charles, *Understanding Charter Damages, supra*, ch. 7; MacKenzie "Backpedalling on *Charter* Damages: *Henry v British Columbia (Attorney General)*" (2016) 45 Adv. Q. 359; and Cunliffe, "*Henry v. British Columbia*: Still Seeking a Just Approach to Damages for Wrongful Conviction" (2016) 76 S.C.L.R. (2d) 143.

REVIEW PROBLEMS

1. Assume that s. 15(1) of the *Charter* had been in force at the time of *Seneca College of Applied Arts Technology v. Bhadauria* (1981), 124 D.L.R. (3d) 193 (S.C.C.), which was discussed in Chapter 3. What would the plaintiff have had to establish for an express statutory cause of action under the *Charter*? Would the *Charter* have assisted her claim at common law?

2. Assuming that the *Charter* had been in force, what impact would it have had on the majority and dissenting judgments in *Harrison v. Carswell* (1975), 62 D.L.R. (3d) 68 (S.C.C.), which is extracted in Chapter 5?

OCCUPIERS' LIABILITY

1. Introduction
2. The Common Law Principles of Occupiers' Liability
3. The Provincial Occupiers' Liability Statutes

1. Introduction

Occupiers' liability can be a difficult topic. The law has always recognized that an occupier of land owes at least *some obligation* to safeguard at least *some visitors*. The scope of that obligation, however, has varied significantly over time and place.

The early law was simple, but harsh. J. Fleming explained the situation in *The Law of Torts*, 7th ed. (1987) at 417:

> Until well into the midst of the 19th century, the prominent social value attached to landholding defied all serious challenge to the claim by occupiers to untrammelled use and enjoyment of their domain with least subordination to the interests of others. Qualified only by such concern for *neighbours* as was exacted by the law of nuisance and trespass, the landowner was virtually immune to demands for the safety of people who came *upon* his land, except not to injure them wilfully, set traps or use excessive force expelling trespassers. With respect to the condition of the premises, even a lawful visitor entered for all practical purposes at his own risk.

Over time, the law grew increasingly complex as the courts developed a range of rules that were intended to more sensitively address different situations. For that purpose, visitors were placed into four categories, each of which attracted a different standard of care. Although the cases that appear below provide greater detail, it is possible to quickly summarize the essential features of that scheme. Because the standards of care evolved over time, the table on the following page is merely intended to facilitate discussion. It is not intended to provide a authoritative statement of the law.

TYPE OF VISITOR	DESCRIPTION OF VISITOR	OCCUPIER'S STANDARD OF CARE
trespasser	person who does not have permission to be on property (*e.g.* burglar)	refrain from intentionally or recklessly injuring trespasser
licensee	person who has permission to be on property, but whose presence does not benefit occupier (*e.g.* house guest)	take reasonable care to protect licensee from unusual (or, historically, hidden) dangers about which occupier actually knows
invitee	person who has permission to be on property, and whose presence does benefit occupier	take reasonable care to protect invitee from unusual dangers about which occupier knows or

TYPE OF VISITOR	DESCRIPTION OF VISITOR	OCCUPIER'S STANDARD OF CARE
	(*e.g.* restaurant patron)	ought to know
contractual entrant	person who entered contract to use premises, as opposed to receive services (*e.g.* hotel guest, but not restaurant patron)	take reasonable care to ensure that premises are fit for intended purpose

Not surprisingly, this scheme generates numerous difficulties. First, despite recognizing four categories of visitors, the common law scheme occasionally fails to sensitively distinguish between different types of people. Both the violent burglar and the curious child *prima facie* are trespassers. Yet it seems odd, if not offensive, that the occupier's obligation is the same in either instance. For that reason, courts often rely on fictions, such as the doctrine of allurement or the notion of implied licence, to upgrade a child's status from trespasser to licensee, and thereby to increase the standard of care. The results are certainly more palatable, but the reasoning leaves something to be desired: see *British Railways Board v. Herrington*, [1972] A.C. 877 (H.L.).

Second, it sometimes is difficult to determine a visitor's status. Is a person who uses a municipal library or a national park a licensee or an invitee? Does the occupier in each instance receive a sufficient benefit so as to attract the higher standard of care? See *Nickell v. City of Windsor* (1926), 59 O.L.R. 618 (H.C.); and *Coffyne v. Silver Lake Regional Park Authority* (1977), 75 D.L.R. (3d) 300 (Sask. Q.B.). What of a child who accompanies her father into a store? See *Gwynne v. Dominion Stores Ltd.* (1963), 43 D.L.R. (2d) 290 (Man. Q.B.); and *Kaplan v. Canada Safeway Ltd.* (1968), 68 D.L.R. (2d) 627 (Sask. Q.B.).

Third, a visitor's status may change from one moment to the next. If so, it may be difficult to determine the appropriate standard of care. In *Dunster v. Abbott*, [1953] 2 All E.R. 1572 at 1574 (C.A.), Lord Denning posed the following question.

A canvasser who comes onto your premises without your consent is a trespasser. Once he has your consent, he is a licensee. Not until you do business with him is he an invitee. Even when you have done business with him, it seems rather strange that your duty towards him should be different when he comes to your front door than when he goes away. Does he change his colour in the middle of the conversation?

Fourth, questions may arise regarding the proper description of a given danger. Is an icy sidewalk in a Canadian winter an "unusual" or "hidden" risk against which an occupier must protect a licensee or invitee? See *Francis v. I.P.C.F. Properties Inc.* (1993), 136 N.B.R. (2d) 215 (Q.B.); and *Waldick v. Malcolm* (1991), 83 D.L.R. (4th) 114 (S.C.C.).

Fifth, the social conditions that historically supported the common law scheme have changed. The perceived desirability of protecting landowners from liability has diminished as the population has urbanized and as real property has lost its status as the primary source of wealth. The fiercely individualistic conception of Blackacre has given way to a model that more evenly balances rights and obligations. Moreover, attitudes toward public health and safety have grown much more generous.

Sixth, and perhaps most significantly, as modern tort law has come to focus on the action in negligence, the traditional rules governing occupiers' liability appear to be unnecessarily complex and inflexible.

For all of these reasons, the law of occupiers' liability has been subject to extensive revision. New Brunswick has simply replaced it with the general tort of negligence: *Law Reform Act*, S.N.B. 1993, c. L-1.2, s. 2; and *Jones v. Richard* (1998), 207 N.B.R. (2d) 265 (Q.B.), rev'd (2000), 226 N.B.R. (2d) 207 (C.A.). Several other jurisdictions (British Columbia, Alberta, Manitoba, Ontario, Nova Scotia and Prince Edward Island) have abandoned the common law rules in favour of a statutory regime. And while the common law tort of occupiers' liability continues to exist in the remaining jurisdictions, it has been modified so as to eliminate its more egregious defects.

This chapter will address the traditional common law scheme before turning to the statutory alternatives. In each instance, the case extracts and accompanying notes are intended to be illustrative, rather than exhaustive.

2. The Common Law Principles of Occupiers' Liability

(a) WHO IS AN OCCUPIER?

PALMER v. ST. JOHN
(1969), 3 D.L.R. (3d) 649 (N.B.C.A.)

[The plaintiff was injured when her toboggan went over a hump at the bottom of a hill and flew into the air before landing. A city work crew, in an attempt to make the hill safer, had inadvertently created the hump. The plaintiff sued both the Horticultural Association, which was responsible for maintaining the park, and the City. The trial judge held both defendants liable in occupiers' liability and further indicated that the City was vicariously liable for the negligence of its work crew. The defendants appealed.]

HUGHES J.A.: . . . The defendant, the Saint John Horticultural Association, hereinafter referred to as the Association, is a statutory corporation incorporated by 1893 (N.B.), c. 83, for the establishment and maintenance of public gardens and the encouraging of the cultivation of flowers and planting trees in the City of Saint John. Over a period of many years the Association acquired various parcels of land which now comprise Rockwood Park and has developed the Park for the enjoyment of the public. Near the shore of Lily Lake which is within the Park, the Association has constructed and operates a pavilion. In addition the Association maintains in the Park public gardens, greenhouses and camp sites and has developed recreational facilities for boating, swimming, skating, skiing, coasting and tobogganing.

. . .

The toboggan slide has been used by the public every season since being constructed, without supervision by the Association and without any charge to the public for its use.

The City of Saint John, hereinafter referred to as the City, has for many years made annual grants to the Association to be used to provide recreational facilities in the Park for citizens of the City. From time to time the City also assisted the Association by providing services of City work crews and personnel for maintenance and development of the Park, the cost of which was ordinarily charged by the City against the annual grants. There is no evidence that the City did any work on the slide other than snow plowing after 1934 until the autumn of 1965 when . . . a City works crew removed outcroppings of rock, cleared bushes and generally smoothened the hill to make it faster and safer for tobogganing and sliding. On the same occasion the crew placed gravel between the bank, which borders the paved roadway near the foot of the slide, and the edge of the Lake for the purpose of flattening out the slope in that area to make it safer for those using the slide. Again in November or December, 1966, works crews of the City under instructions of the Commissioner of Works placed and levelled fill across about three-quarters of the width of the slide at or near the shoreline of the Lake to lessen the severity of the drop from the bank to the edge of the Lake, in an effort to remove a hazardous condition for those using the slide.

. . .

I shall now turn to the question of the liability of the City to the plaintiffs.

The learned trial Judge has found that the City as well as the Association was an occupier of the sliding hill and held the City liable to the plaintiffs in that capacity. The question who is an occupier has been considered in a number of cases. In *Salmond on Torts*, 11th ed., p. 548, the author states:

> . . . The person responsible for the condition of the premises is he who is in actual occupation or possession of them for the time being, whether he is the owner of them or not. For it is he who has the immediate supervision and control and the power of permitting or prohibiting the entry of other persons. . .

. . .

In *Duncan v. Cammell Laird & Co. Ltd.*, [1943] 2 All E.R. 621 at p. 627, Wrottesley, J., said:

> It seems to me that the importance of establishing that the defendant who invites is the occupier of the premises lies in the fact that with occupation goes control. And the importance of control is that it affords the opportunity to know that the plaintiff is coming on to the premises, to know the premises, and to become aware of dangers whether concealed or not, and to remedy them, or at least to warn those that are invited on to the premises.

The evidence establishes that the City and the Association co-operated closely in efforts to provide recreational facilities at Rockwood Park. As previously stated the City made annual grants to the Association and from time to time used City work crews to perform work and services in the Park. Sometimes the work was performed after consultation with the Park's superintendent, but on other occasions work was done by City crews without consultation with the Association. On one occasion at least the City plowed the snow from the slide at the request of a private citizen. The City was not the owner of the Park at the time of the plaintiffs' accident and did not operate the slide or regulate its use. With all due deference to the learned trial Judge I am unable to agree that the evidence justifies a finding that the City was an occupier of the sliding hill so as to subject it to the duty of an occupier.

[However, Hughes J.A. agreed with the trial judge that the City was vicariously liable for the negligence of its work crew, and he dismissed the City's appeal on this basis.]

NOTES AND QUESTIONS

1. What test did the Court of Appeal use to determine if the City was an occupier of the hill? Do you agree with the court's application of that test to the facts? Assuming that both the City and the Association had been occupiers of the hill, would their liability as occupants necessarily have been the same?

2. In *Couch v. McCann; Ferguson v. McCann* (1977), 77 D.L.R. (3d) 387 (Ont. C.A.), the plaintiffs were injured when the barn floor collapsed at an auction they were attending. They sued Fry, the owner of the property, McCann, the person who had use of the barn, and Phifher and Coughlin, the auctioneers who had been hired by McCann to run the auction. At trial, the action against Fry was dismissed, and the remaining defendants were held liable in occupiers' liability. On appeal, the court held that since the auctioneers had invited the public to attend and had conducted the auction in the barn, they were joint occupants of the barn with McCann. Is this decision compatible with *Palmer*? Based on *Couch*, would a singer hired to perform in a concert hall be an occupier of the facility? Would it make any difference if the singer was responsible for advertising the event or if the singer's salary was based on a percentage of the seat sales? See *Haskett v. Univ. of Western Ont.*, [1955] 3 D.L.R. 234 (Ont. H.C.).

3. An occupier is responsible not only for the land and permanent structures, but also for moveable objects that are situated on the land, such as aircraft, trains, and scaffolding. See Di Castri, *Occupiers' Liability* (1981) at 12-14.

4. In the absence of fraud or contract, a landlord was under no common law duty to ensure that unfurnished premises were safe for tenants and visitors. What is the rationale for imposing fundamentally different obligations on owners and occupiers? It should be noted that the provincial statutes governing landlords and tenants now require landlords to maintain rented premises in a safe and habitable condition. See for example the *Tenant Protection Act*, S.O. 1997, c. 24, s. 24. See also *Allison v. Rank City Wall Can. Ltd.* (1984), 45 O.R. (2d) 141 (H.C.); and *Day v. Chaleur Developments Ltd.* (1985), 63 N.B.R. (2d) 313 (Q.B.).

Landlords also may owe a duty of care to tenants and their invitees under occupiers' liability legislation in certain circumstances. See for example *Stuart v. R. in Right of Can.*, [1988] 6 W.W.R. 211 (F.C.T.D.); and *Blake v. Kensche* (1990), 3 C.C.L.T. (2d) 189 (B.C.S.C.).

(b) CATEGORIES OF ENTRANTS AND CORRESPONDING DUTIES

(i) *Contractual Entrants*

FINIGAN v. CALGARY
(1967), 65 D.L.R. (2d) 626 (Alta. C.A.)

CAIRNS J.A.: . . . The facts are that on May 23, 1966, the appellant accompanied by her husband entered the park and paid an admission fee of 25¢ to view the exhibits there installed. One of the series of exhibits consisted of a group of Indian teepees erected in a grove of trees. There was a pathway about 4 ft. in width cut through the trees to the entrance of one of the teepees. The pathway had been cleared of trees and roots and other debris but there was a root left on the edge of the pathway about 4 ft. from the entrance to the teepee which protruded about 2 ins. above the surface. Directly in front of the entrance in the middle of the pathway and about one foot from it the stump had been left which protruded about 2 ins. above the surrounding surface. The stump had been cut on a bias and the evidence was that it was difficult to see even if at the time in question, namely, 6:00 p.m., the light was good. In making the pathways the instructions were that all protruding root stumps were to be taken out. It is also a fact that the authorities inspected the grounds continuously and were in the habit of cutting down any obstructions which might be dangerous, but they had not noticed the stump prior to the accident.

The appellant walked down the pathway with the intention of entering the teepee and with her view on the entrance. She tripped on the exposed root and fell forward and was not able to recover her balance until she fell on the stump. . . . There is no doubt that it was the stump which caused her injuries.

The learned trial Judge was of the opinion that the case came within the principles governing the liability of an invitor to an invitee as laid down in *Indermaur v. Dames* (1867), L.R. 2 C.P. 311, and subsequent cases to the effect that the invitee using reasonable care for his own safety "is entitled to expect that the occupier shall on his part use reasonable care to prevent damage from unusual danger of which he knows or ought to know" [p. 313]. He therefore dismissed the action and must have been of the opinion, although he does not say so, that there was no unusual danger in all the circumstances.

In my view with great deference I think that the learned trial Judge was wrong in arriving at this decision and that even applying the principle he did he could not come to the conclusion that this was not an unusual danger. The facts are perfectly clear. We have a pathway leading to a teepee and in the middle of the entrance was a two-inch stump which was practically invisible and on which the appellant fell. Surely a person entering the teepee could expect not to encounter such an obstruction. There is no evidence that she was in any way negligent. Had the pathway been properly constructed the stump would not have been left there. In any event it should have been noticed by the respondent in one of the many inspections which were made to ensure the safety of the public.

For these reasons I am of the opinion that the respondents created or suffered to exist an unusual danger of which, if damage arose because of it as it did in this case, they are liable even on the principles enunciated in *Indermaur v. Dames*.

However, completely apart from the principles of the invitee cases it is my view that the respondents are liable on the basis of breach of contract.

Here the appellant paid an admission fee to view the exhibits and thereby entered into a contract with the respondents that she might enjoy those privileges provided she exercised prudence herself without risk of danger so far as reasonable care could make the premises safe. This principle was laid down by Rand, J., in *Brown and Brown v. B. & F. Theatres Ltd.*, [1947] 3 D.L.R. 593. . ., where the learned Judge, in giving the judgment of the Court excepting that of Kellock, J., who came to the same conclusion following *Francis v. Cockrell* (1870), L.R. 5 Q.B. 501, stated at p. 596:

> The case has been treated as raising the ordinary question of the duty owed by a proprietor of premises towards an invitee. I think, however, I should observe that this is not merely a case of such invitation as was present in *Indermaur v. Dames* (1867), L.R. 2 C.P. 311. Here, Mrs. Brown paid a consideration for the privileges of the theatre, including that of making use of the ladies' room. There was a contractual relation between her and the theatre management that exercising prudence herself she might enjoy those privileges without risk of danger so far as reasonable care could make the premises safe. Although the difference in the degree of care called for may not, in the circumstances here, be material, I think it desirable that the distinction between the two bases of responsibility be kept in mind: *Maclenan v. Segar*, [1917] 2 K.B. 325 following *Francis v. Cockrell* (1870), L.R. 5 Q.B. [501]. In *Cox. v. Coulson*, [1916] 2 K.B. 177 at p. 181, Swinfen Eady L.J. said: "The defendant must also be taken to have contracted to take due care that the premises should be reasonably safe for persons using them in the customary manner and with reasonable care", citing *Francis v. Cockrell* [(1870), L.R. 5 Q.B. 184].

. . .

The rule in *Francis v. Cockrell* was approved by Cartwright, J. in giving the majority judgment of the Court in *Carriss v. Buxton*, 13 D.L.R. (2d) 689 at pp. 713-4, [1958] S.C.R. 441, where he stated:

> The rule in *Francis v. Cockrell* is stated as follows in *Winfield on Tort*, 6th ed., p. 672: "Where A enters B's structure under a contract entitling him to do so, *it is an implied term in the contract that the structure shall be reasonably fit for the purpose for which it is intended; but this does not extend to any unknown defect incapable of being discovered by reasonable means.*"

There is no doubt therefore that there is a higher duty owed to a person who enters premises under a contract than that which is owed to an invitee under *Indermaur v. Dames*; as Rand, J., stated, *supra*, it is that anyone may enter "without risk of danger so far as reasonable care could make the premises safe" or at least under *Francis v. Cockrell* there is an implied warranty that the place is reasonably fit for the purposes for which it was intended.

In so far as this case is concerned it is immaterial whether there is a slight difference in the rule as to the liability to a contracting party. There is no doubt under either interpretation of the liability that the respondents did not discharge their obligations to see that the property was either "without risk of danger" or "reasonably fit for the purpose" in permitting the stump in question to obstruct the entrance to the teepee, and they are liable to the appellant in damages for such failure.

. . .

MCDERMID J.A.:— In *Maclenan v. Segar*, [1917] 2 K.B. 325 at p. 333, McCardie, J., in referring to the warranty implied, stated,

> The principle is basic and applies alike to premises and to vehicles. It matters not whether the subject be a race-stand, a theatre, or an inn; whether it be a taxicab, an omnibus, or a railway carriage. The warranty in each case is the same, and for a breach thereof an action will lie.

As the warranty is contractual I would like to reserve the question as to whether it is the same in respect of a park run for the benefit of the public as it would be in cases where the premises are being run to make a profit for the owner. It does seem odd to me that a public authority who is carrying on a park for the benefit and enjoyment of the public and not for profit has a greater duty than a departmental store which has invited the public onto its premises in order that the store may make a profit; however, such may be the case. In the case at bar the point does not have to be decided, for even if the warranty implied was the same, and I think it could not be less, as the duty imposed in respect of an invitee, there was still a breach of it. Subject to the foregoing comment, I concur in the judgment of my brother Cairns.

ALLEN, J.A., concurs with CAIRNS, J.A.

NOTES AND QUESTIONS

1. What duty of care does an occupier owe to contractual entrants? How does that duty differ from the duty owed to invitees? Do you agree with the court's application of these principles in *Finigan*? See also *Carrière v. Bd. of Gravelbourg School Dist. No. 2244 of Sask.* (1977), 79 D.L.R. (3d) 662 (Sask. C.A.); *Fanjoy v. Gaston* (1981), 127 D.L.R. (3d) 163 (N.B.C.A.); and *McGivney v. Rustico Summer Haven* (1986), 197 A.P.R. 358 (P.E.I.C.A.). Compare *Truong v. Saskatoon (City)* (2001), 211 Sask. R. 115 (Q.B.).

2. Is McDermid J.A. suggesting that the courts should consider the occupier's motive in determining the nature of the implied contractual warranty? What are the advantages and disadvantages of such an approach? Should the contractual duty owed to a patron who paid $50 for a ticket to a boxing match be higher than that owed to a patron who paid $3?

3. Why was the City of Calgary held to be an occupier of the park in *Finigan*? Can you reconcile this case and *Palmer*?

4. Among other things, an occupier must protect a contractual entrant from dangers presented by other entrants. In *McGinty v. Cook*, (1989), 6 D.L.R. (4th) 94 (Ont. H.C.), aff'd (1991), 79 D.L.R. (4th) 95 (Ont. C.A.), the defendant occupied a campsite. Because it failed to enforce its own rules regarding "quiet time" at night, the plaintiff was attacked and beaten by a number of other campers. The occupier was held liable for failing to prevent the attack.

An occupier, however, is not liable for every harm that befalls a contractual entrant. In *McTaggart v. Commonwealth Hospitality Ltd.* (1997), 159 Sask. R. 144 (Q.B.), vandals had removed a mirror from a wall and placed it between the inner and outer doors of an elevator. The plaintiff was injured when the door opened. The occupier was relieved of responsibility on the grounds that it had not received any report of rowdy behaviour and it had no reason to suspect the danger.

5. For a more detailed discussion of the duty owed to contractual entrants see Adair, "Occupier's Liability to the Contractual Visitor" (1979) 2 Adv. Q. 320; and Di Castri, *Occupiers' Liability* (1981) at 15-32.

(ii) *Invitees and Licensees*

McERLEAN v. SAREL
(1987), 42 D.L.R. (4th) 577 (Ont. C.A.)

[McErlean, who was almost 15 years old, and a friend were racing trail bikes on an old road in an abandoned gravel pit. McErlean was severely injured when he collided with Sarel, who also was riding a trail bike. At the time of the accident, Sarel was riding on the wrong side of the road and McErlean was emerging from a sharp corner that offered poor visibility.

The City of Brampton owned the gravel pit and planned to develop it as a park. Although City officials knew that trail bike riders used the pit, they made no attempt to stop or warn them. Because the accident occurred before Ontario's legislation was enacted, the dispute was governed by the common law rules. The trial judge attributed 75% of the responsibility to the City, 15% to Sarel and 10% to McErlean based on his contributory negligence. The City's liability was based on its status as an occupier.]

BY THE COURT:—This is an occupier's liability case. The appeal relates both to liability and damages. The occupier of the land at the relevant time was the appellant the Corporation of the City of Brampton. The trial judge found that the respondent Michael McErlean at the time of the accident was a licensee.

. . .

The first question to be asked is whether the respondent, Michael McErlean, was on the appellant's property as a trespasser or a licensee, it being common ground that he was not an invitee. In our opinion, the respondent must be categorized as a licensee and not a trespasser. A licence to enter or remain on property may be given by conduct which manifests consent or permission. Here, it is clear that the appellant made no effort to exclude pedestrians, bikers or others from its property by means of signs (except with respect to swimming) warning not to trespass, by the erection of adequate fencing, by supervision or by any other means. Their entry from time to time onto the lands over an appreciable period was readily ascertainable if not actually known. The owner's failure to object to their presence can reasonably be construed as tacit permission to their entry. Persons who, for instance, took short-cuts across this long-vacant piece of property or who came there to walk their dogs or ride their motorcycles or trail bikes cannot be treated as mere trespassers. The owner's inaction, while not amounting to an invitation to use the property, at least manifested a willingness to permit them entry and indicated its toleration of their presence. In these circumstances, the owner so conducted itself that it cannot be heard to say that it did not give permission. This is not a case in which an occupier unsuccessfully sought to prevent people from trespassing on its lands, nor is this a situation in which precautions against their intrusion would be unduly burdensome or expensive or, based on past experience, likely to be futile. Applying the common law approach, this respondent must, in our opinion, be treated as a licensee (albeit, on the authorities, a "bare licensee" or a "licensee without an interest") and the occupier's liability must be determined on the basis of that relationship. . . .

What then is the duty owed by an occupier of land to a licensee? Traditionally, it has been spoken of as a duty to warn of concealed dangers or traps of which the occupier had actual knowledge: *Hambourg v. T. Eaton Co. Ltd.*, [1935] 3 D.L.R. 305. . . . This is plainly a less stringent duty than the duty owed to an invitee which has long been expressed as a duty to take reasonable care to prevent damage from unusual danger of which the invitor knew or ought to have known: *Indermaur v. Dames* (1866), L.R. 1 C.P. 274; affirmed L.R. 2 C.P. 311. However, in 1974, the Supreme Court of Canada in *Mitchell et al. v. C.N.R. Co.* (1974), 46 D.L.R. (3d) 363. . ., a case involving a nine-year-old infant-licensee, abandoned the traditional requirement that the danger be concealed and held that mere knowledge of likely danger on the part of a licensee falling short of voluntary assumption of risk will not of itself exonerate the occupier. Later that same year, this court in *Bartlett et al. v. Weiche Apartments Ltd.* (1974), 55 D.L.R. (3d) 44, a case involving a three-year-old infant-licensee, thoroughly canvassed the then current law as to an occupier's liability to a licensee. Based on an analysis of the judgments of the Supreme Court of Canada in *Mitchell et al. v. C.N.R. Co.*, *supra*, and in *Hanson et al. v. City of St. John et al.* (1973), 39 D.L.R. (3d) 417, Jessup J.A., speaking for the majority of the court . . . restated the general principle governing the liability of an occupier to a licensee in the following terms:

> It is to take reasonable care to avoid foreseeable risk of harm from any unusual danger on the occupier's premises of which the occupier actually has knowledge or of which he ought to have knowledge because he was aware of the circumstances. The licensee's knowledge of the danger goes only to the questions of contributory negligence or *volenti*.

That test has been applied by this court in other licensor-licensee situations. . . . It represents an accurate statement of the law in effect at the time of this accident, and liability in this case must be determined in accordance with the principles enunciated therein.

Applying this test, an occupier's liability is clearly limited to "unusual dangers" on his property and does not extend to every danger that might be found thereon. Thus, the first and most important question to be asked in this instance is whether at the time and place of the accident there was an "unusual danger" on the occupier's premises which created a foreseeable risk of harm.

Prior to the *Mitchell* case, the term "unusual danger" was applied to the duty owed by an occupier to an invitee, but not to the duty owed a licensee. The latter duty related only to "concealed dangers" or "traps". "Unusual danger" was defined by the House of Lords . . . in *London Graving Dock Co. Ltd. v. Horton*, [1951] A.C. 737 at p. 745, as follows:

> I think *"unusual"* is used in an objective sense and means such danger as is not usually found in carrying out the task or fulfilling the function which the invitee has in hand, though what is unusual will, of course, vary with the reasons for which the invitee enters the premises. Indeed, I do not think Phillimore, L.J., *in Norman v. Great Western Railway Co.*, [1915] 1 K.B. 584, 596, is speaking of individuals as individuals but of

individuals as members of a type, e.g., that class of persons such as stevedores or seamen who are accustomed to negotiate the difficulties which their occupation presents. A tall chimney is not an unusual difficulty for a steeplejack though it would be for a motor mechanic. But I do not think a lofty chimney presents a danger less unusual for the last-named because he is particularly active or untroubled by dizziness.

(Emphasis added.)

This definition has been generally accepted and was specifically adopted by the Supreme Court of Canada in *Campbell v. Royal Bank of Canada* (1963), 43 D.L.R. (2d) 341, and in *City of Brandon v. Farley* (1968), 66 D.L.R. (2d) 289. In light of the fact that *Mitchell* has blurred the distinction between an occupier's duty to an invitee and his or her duty to a licensee, this definition of "unusual danger" can be applied by analogy also to the case of an occupier's duty to a licensee.

An occupier's duty is limited to "unusual dangers" on the theory that he or she is entitled to assume that ordinary reasonable people know and appreciate usual or common dangers and need not, therefore, be warned or otherwise protected against them. No list of dangers that categorically meet this concept of unusualness can be drawn up because, as Fleming points out. . ., "the quality of unusualness depends not only on the character of the danger itself, but also on the nature of the premises on which it is found and the range of experience with which the [entrant] may fairly be credited". In the final analysis, the issue of what is an unusual danger clearly must, like so many issues in the law of torts, depend on the facts and circumstances of the given case.

. . .

With the negligence of the respondent and Sarel established, the question remaining is whether the owner of the land upon which this unfortunate accident occurred bears any responsibility in law for the occurrence. A licensor is patently not a guarantor of a licensee's safety or an insurer against all injuries which may result from the condition of his or her property. As we have said, a licensor's duty at common law is limited to unusual dangers of which he or she was aware, ought to have known existed with respect to the property. The duty does not extend to usual or common dangers which ordinary reasonable persons can be expected to know and appreciate.

Accepting that the curve could be a danger and that the appellant-landowner should have known that its property was being used in the recreational operation of trail bikes, can it be said that this condition constituted an unusual danger? In our opinion, it cannot be so classified. The requisite quality of unusualness is not present in this case, and the circumstances adverted to by the trial judge in his brief reasons do not elevate the condition into one of unusual danger. We are concerned here with a country-type road on undeveloped private property running between a small lake on one side and dense bush on the other that can only be seen as commonplace and not out of the ordinary in this province. The existence and state of the one curve in this road was open to ordinary observation. It had been there for a long time. When travelled with due care and attention and at an appropriate speed, it was not dangerous. The curve had not been the subject of recent change nor the source of prior mishap. It was not concealed or hidden, nor was it unexpected. It could readily be seen at a considerable distance by persons approaching from either direction.

[Liability was apportioned equally between the plaintiff and the defendant Sarel.]

NOTES AND QUESTIONS

1. How have the courts distinguished between invitees and licensees? Why was the plaintiff not held to be a trespasser? Would the plaintiff have been considered a trespasser if the City had posted signs prohibiting entry and fenced the property?

2. What duty of care did an occupier traditionally owe to an invitee? How did the courts define the concept of an "unusual danger?"

3. What duty of care did an occupier owe to a licensee? How did the courts define the concept of "concealed danger or trap?"

4. How have *McErlean* and *Mitchell* (cited in *McErlean*) altered the traditional tests of an occupier's duty to invitees and licensees? Did these cases also change the definition of "unusual danger?"

5. Do you agree with the Court of Appeal's application of the current common law duty to the City's liability?

6. In *McErlean*, the Court of Appeal substantially collapsed the distinction between invitees and licensees. In *Stacey v. Anglican Church of Canada (Diocesan Synod of Eastern Newfoundland & Labrador)* (1999), 182 Nfld. & P.E.I.R. 1 (Nfld. C.A.), the Newfoundland Court of Appeal went even further. The defendant was the occupier of a cemetery. The plaintiff visited the cemetery during regular hours. There were several paths through the property. The plaintiff was injured when she chose instead to walk down an embankment. She had seen several other people doing so, despite a sign that said "do not walk" in the area. The plaintiff sued the defendant for occupiers' liability.

The court held that visitors no longer should be placed into different categories, each of which attracts a different standard of care. Instead, it formulated a new test that applied to all lawful visitors.

> An occupier's duty of care to a lawful visitor to his or her premises is to take such care as in all the circumstances is reasonable to see that the visitor will be reasonably safe in using the premises for the purposes for which he or she is invited or permitted by the occupier to be there or is permitted by law to be there.

Having regard to all of the circumstances, the court refused to impose liability. The defendant acted reasonably in providing various paths through the cemetery. It was not responsible for the plaintiff's decision to walk down an embankment despite a sign prohibiting her from doing so.

7. A more cautious approach can be seen in *Yelic v. Gimli (Town)* (1986), 33 D.L.R. (4th) 248 (Man. C.A.). The incident occurred before Manitoba's legislation was introduced and so the case was governed by the common law rules. Once again, the defendant was the occupier of a cemetery. The plaintiff wanted to visit a grave outside of the regular hours of operation. For that purpose, he climbed over a decorative fence that surrounded the premises. The fence, which was in a state of disrepair, collapsed and the plaintiff was injured. Because the Manitoba legislation had not yet been introduced, he sued the defendant under the common law rules for occupiers' liability.

The trial judge observed that under the common law rules, a licensee must be protected from dangers about which the occupier *actually knew*, while an invitee must be protected from dangers about which the occupier *knew or should have known*. Since the defendant actually knew of the defect and did nothing about it, the trial judge found it unnecessary to determine whether the categories of licensee and invitee should be merged. Liability would arise even on the higher threshold.

The Court of Appeal reversed the trial decision. It agreed in *obiter dicta* that there may still be a difference between licensees and invitees, insofar as the former must prove the occupier's *actual knowledge* whereas the latter may succeed on the basis of *constructive knowledge*. However, it also held that the plaintiff did not fall into either one of those categories. He was, rather, a trespasser and consequently was owed the lower standard of "common humanity" (as discussed in the next section). That standard did not require the repair of a decorative fence in the absence of evidence that the defendant knew that trespassers regularly climbed over the fence.

8. Occupiers also have a duty to protect invitees and licensees from other people who are allowed onto the premises and who pose a foreseeable risk of harm. This issue often arises after an intoxicated patron in a tavern becomes unruly or violent. The occupier may be found liable for failing to take reasonable steps to eject or restrain the patron. See for example *McGeough v. Don Enterprises Ltd.*, [1984] 1 W.W.R. 256 (Sask. Q.B.).

A dramatic illustration of the possibility of liability in such circumstances occurred in *Fullowka v. Royal Oak Ventures Inc.*, 2010 SCC 5, aff'g (2008), 433 A.R. 69 (N.W.T.C.A.), rev'g [2005] 5 W.W.R. 420 (N.W.T.S.C.). The defendant was the occupier of an underground mine that was the subject of a heated labour dispute. As part of that dispute, Warren deliberately planted a bomb in the mine. The explosion killed nine replacement workers. Warren was convicted of nine counts of second degree murder. The victims' families then sued various parties, including the defendant. The N.W.T. Supreme Court held the defendant liable on the basis that, because it was foreseeable that some such incident would occur, it was required to take reasonable steps to protect the deceased. That decision was overturned on appeal.

9. Canadian courts often take a broad view of the concept of "unusual danger." The following have been held to be "unusual dangers": *Houle v. S.S. Kresge Co.* (1974), 55 D.L.R. (3d) 52 (Ont. Dist. Ct.) (potholes in a parking lot); *Pajot v. Commonwealth Holiday Inns of Can. Ltd.* (1978), 86 D.L.R. (3d) 729 (Ont. H.C.) (unmarked glass door); *Lampert v. Simpson Sears Ltd.* (1986), 75 N.B.R. (2d) 128 (C.A.) (water on the floor of a department store); and *Ackerman v. Wascana Centre Authority*, [1998] 2 W.W.R. 678 (Sask. Q.B.), aff'd [1999] 6 W.W.R. 167 (Sask. C.A.) (gaps between planks of a pier). But see *Monteith v. N.B. Command, Royal Can. Legion* (1973), 8 N.B.R. (2d) 438 (Q.B.) (no liability for slip caused by beer on floor of a tavern).

10. In most provinces, occupiers have statutory duties to keep their walkways free of slippery substances and hazardous obstructions. The central issue in these cases is not the legal duty, but rather the standard of care. For the purposes of these statutes, the common law distinction between an invitee and a licensee no longer is important. See *Preston v. Canadian Legion of British Empire Service League, Kingsway Branch No. 175* (1981), 123 D.L.R. (3d) 645 (Alta. C.A.).

In *Bongiardina v. York Regional Municipality* (1999), 46 O.R. (3d) 345 (S.C.J.), aff'd (2000), 49 O.R. (3d) 641 (C.A.) the court held that owners and occupiers of a dwelling adjacent to a municipal sidewalk, who are subject to a snow-clearing by-law, do not owe pedestrians a duty of care because the *Occupiers' Liability Act*, R.S.O. 1990, c. O.2, does not apply. Moreover, the by-law did not relieve the municipality of its duty to pedestrians under the *Municipal Act*, R.S.O. 1990, c. M.45. See also *Peterson v. Windsor (City)* (2006), 27 M.P.L.R. (4th) 129 (Ont. S.C.J.).

11. An occupier is under a positive duty to carry out periodic inspections of premises in order to maintain a reasonable degree of safety: see *Sauve v. Provost* (1990), 71 O.R. (2d) 774 (H.C.)

(iii) *Trespassers*

VEINOT v. KERR-ADDISON MINES LTD.
(1975), 51 D.L.R. (3d) 533 (S.C.C.)

DICKSON J.:—This is an occupiers' liability case. . . .Whether the entrant is a burglar or wandering child or irreproachable wayfarer, the general principles historically applied were those expressed in *Robert Addie & Sons (Collieries), Ltd. v. Dumbreck*, [1929] A.C. 358, by Lord Hailsham, L.C., at p. 365:

> Towards the trespasser the occupier has no duty to take reasonable care for his protection or even to protect him from concealed danger. The trespasser comes on to the premises at his own risk. An occupier is in such a case liable only where the injury is due to some wilful act involving something more than the absence of reasonable care. There must be some act done with deliberate intention of doing harm to the trespasser, or at least some act done with reckless disregard of the presence of the trespasser.

These rules, of course, perpetuated the traditional 19th century concern for the sanctity of landed property. The general principle was that a landowner could do as he wished with his land. He owed no duty to an intruder, however accidental or inadvertent the intrusion, other than to refrain from shooting him or otherwise recklessly and wantonly doing him harm. . . . As could be expected various inventions were employed from time to time to modify and ameliorate the harshness. In some of the cases the landowner's consent was implied or imputed, particularly in "children cases", the status of the intruder being elevated from that of trespasser, which he clearly was, to that of licensee, which he clearly was not. In other cases a generous meaning was given to the phrase "reckless disregard" or a tenuous distinction was drawn between land in a static condition and land upon which an operational activity was being conducted, productive of injury. In time, two distinct, not easy to reconcile, lines of jurisprudence emerged. One perpetuated the letter and spirit of *Addie*'s case . . . . The other gave effect to changing ideas of social responsibility and imposed upon the owner of land duties well beyond those in contemplation in Addie's case. . . .

. . .

In [*British Railways Board v. Herrington*, [1972] A.C. 877 (U.K. H.L.)] their Lordships exhaustively considered the nature of the duty owed by occupiers to trespassers. Lord Reid applied a subjective test. He said (p. 899):

> So it appears to me that an occupier's duty to trespassers must vary according to his knowledge, ability and resources. It has often been said that trespassers must take the

land as they find it. I would rather say that they must take the occupier as they find him.

and later on the same page:

So the question whether an occupier is liable in respect of an accident to a trespasser on his land would depend on whether a conscientious humane man with his knowledge, skill and resources could reasonably have been expected to have done or refrained from doing before the accident something which would have avoided it. If he knew before the accident that there was a substantial probability that trespassers would come I think that most people would regard as culpable failure to give any thought to their safety. He might often reasonably think, weighing the seriousness of the danger and the degree of likelihood of trespassers coming against the burden he would have to incur in preventing their entry or making his premises safe, or curtailing his own activities on his land, that he could not fairly be expected to do anything. But if he could at small trouble and expense take some effective action, again I think that most people would think it inhumane and culpable not to do that. If some such principle is adopted there will no longer be any need to strive to imply a fictitious licence.

The test of common humanity was also applied by Lord Morris of Borth-y-Gest (p. 909):

In my view, while it cannot be said that the railways board owed a common duty of care to the young boy in the present case they did owe to him at least the duty of acting with common humanity towards him.

. . .

Herrington's case was considered by the Court of Appeal of England in *Pannett v. McGuinness & Co. Ltd.*, [1972] 3 W.L.R. 387. The following excerpt from Lord Denning's judgment aptly expresses, in my opinion, the more salient points a Judge should have in mind when considering intrusion upon land [at pp. 390-1]:

The long and short of it is that you have to take into account all the circumstances of the case and see then whether the occupier ought to have done more than he did. (1) You must apply your common sense. You must take into account the gravity and likelihood of the probable injury. Ultra-hazardous activities require a man to be ultracautious in carrying them out. The more dangerous the activity, the more he should take steps to see that no one is injured by it. (2) You must take into account also the character of the intrusion by the trespasser. A wandering child or a straying adult stands in a different position from a poacher or a burglar. You may expect a child when you may not expect a burglar. (3) You must also have regard to the nature of the place where the trespass occurs. An electrified railway line or a warehouse being demolished may require more precautions to be taken than a private house. (4) You must also take into account the knowledge which the defendant has, or ought to have, of the likelihood of trespassers being present. The more likely they are, the more precautions may have to be taken.

In the very recent case of *Southern Portland Cement Ltd. v. Cooper*, [1974] 1 All E.R. 87, the Privy Council considered the duty owed to a trespasser. Their Lordships rejected the argument that an occupier only comes under a duty to potential trespassers if he estimates or ought to estimate that the arrival of one or more trespassers on his land is "extremely likely". In the course of his speech Lord Reid said: "But in their Lordships' judgment it is now necessary to . . . abandon the limitation of extreme likelihood", and later [at p. 98]:

> If the occupier creates the danger when he knows that there is a chance that trespassers will come that way and will not see or realise the danger he may have to do more. There may be difficult cases where the occupier will be hampered in the conduct of his own affairs if he has to take elaborate precautions. But in the present case it would have been easy to prevent the development of the dangerous situation which caused the plaintiff's injuries.

And so we come to the facts of the present case. There is no need to labour them. The plaintiff, 37 years of age, and his wife, on one snowmobile, accompanied by another married couple on another snowmobile, set out from their home for an evening of healthful recreation through woods and across lakes of northern Ontario. They went along well-travelled snowmobile trails, from Larder Lake to Crosby Lake, along a creek to Beaver Lake, to Bear Lake, to a hydro right of way along which were many ski-doo trails, down an old logging road "which was well ski-doo packed", to a wide, hard-packed, well-ploughed road on which they travelled until the plaintiff, Mr. Veinot, on the leading snowmobile, struck a rusty pipe stretched across the road, at face-height, and sustained very serious injuries. The accident occurred on March 16, 1970. Mr. Veinot had owned snowmobiles since 1966. . . . The jury found that Mr. Veinot did not fail to take reasonable care for his own safety.

The pipe which Mr. Veinot struck was two inches in diameter, supported by unpainted posts located off the road, and invisible at night due to the background of trees. The pipe had been erected some 20 years earlier to prevent the movement of unauthorized vehicular traffic to the defendant company's powder magazine not far from the community of Virginiatown. No point can be made of the fact that the pipe had been there for 20 years without accident for the type of accident which occurred in this case could only have occurred after the advent of snowmobiles.

From the evidence there seems no doubt that during the winter there was a great deal of travel on snowmobiles in and around Virginiatown. . . . The defendant company permitted snowmobile traffic along the road as far as the iron pipe. Such traffic normally then turned to the right and continued north along the right of way until the intersecting east-west hydro right of way was reached which in turn led west to the lakes across which Mr. Veinot and his party had travelled. Generally, as I have indicated, the main ski-doo traffic was east of the iron pipe, but the defendant's security officer conceded that on a very few occasions he had seen ski-doo tracks in the winter of 1969-70 on the powder magazine side of the pipe. He did not report these discoveries to the mine manager and he did nothing about it.

The evidence is undisputed that there were "a lot of snowmobile tracks" on the road leading south from the east-west hydro power line to the ploughed road on which the unfortunate accident occurred. The ploughed road "seemed to be well travelled"; looked like a public road; and had no markings to indicate it was not a public road. Mr. Veinot had no idea he was on private property when he drove along the ploughed road and according to his evidence, which was not challenged, he would not have continued along it if he had known it was private property. Upon all of the evidence and following a charge by the trial Judge to which no objection has been, or could be, taken, the jury made certain findings: (1) That Mr. Veinot on the date of the accident was on the defendant's land with the implied permission of the defendant; (2) That his injuries were caused by a concealed or hidden danger or a trap of which the defendant

had knowledge, described by the jury in its answers as "a rusty pipe approximately 2"
in diameter suspended across the travelled portion of the road at a height of
approximately 45 inches from the road"; (3) The defendant failed to take reasonable
care to avoid injury to persons traversing the area, there being no distinguishing
warnings of the location of the pipe across the roadway from either the east or west
approach to the pipe or on the pipe itself; (4) The finding to which I have already
referred, that plaintiff did not fail to take reasonable care for his own safety. At the
close of the evidence presented by the plaintiff a motion was made for a nonsuit. The
motion was renewed after the evidence for the defendant had been heard and again
after the answers of the jury were received. The trial Judge, Houlden, J., dismissed the
motion. He held that the finding of the jury that there was implied permission for the
plaintiff to be on the land of the defendant could be substantiated on the evidence.

. . .

Whether or not there was an implied permission was a question of fact for the
jury. The jury was properly instructed on the law and brought its finding. I do not
think that finding should be disturbed.

. . .

Even if Mr. Veinot is regarded as a trespasser his appeal to this Court should
succeed. If he was a trespasser, the inquiry must be as to whether his presence on the
ploughed road could reasonably have been anticipated for, if so, the company owed
him a duty and that duty was to treat him with ordinary humanity.

Although as a general rule a person is not bound to anticipate the presence of
intruders on private property or to guard them from injury, a duty may arise if the
owner of land knew of, or from all the surrounding circumstances ought reasonably to
have foreseen, the presence of a trespasser. It appears to me that a person of good
sense in the position of the defendant company, possessing the knowledge which its
responsible officers possessed about snowmobiles and the degree of snowmobile travel
in the area, the proclivity for travel by night, the ease by which the ploughed road
could be reached by several old roads leading on to it would have been alerted, on a
moment's reflection, to the probability of someone reaching the ploughed road as Mr.
Veinot did. Stress was laid during argument upon the fact that the plaintiff came in by
way of the back door, as it were, and that such avenue of approach could not
reasonably have been anticipated. I do not agree. Snowmobiles are ubiquitous. They
have an unusual and well-known capacity for travel on and off the beaten path. In an
uncharted Canadian wilderness area, of forest, rivers and lakes, one could reasonably
expect them to go in almost any direction, at least until such time as they reached
indicia of private property. If there was a likelihood that someone would come upon
the ploughed road on a snowmobile at night, and the evidence in my view supports
such a likelihood, then I do not think there can be doubt that the company failed in
the duty it owed to Mr. Veinot to treat him with common humanity. The ploughed
road gave every appearance of being a public road. Mr. Veinot had good reason to
believe that he might freely use it if he wished to do so. Acting on that belief he failed
to see or appreciate the abeyant danger of the rusty pipe. The defendant company in
my opinion erred in permitting the continuance of what should have been recognized
by it as a covert peril, menacing the safety of anyone who came upon the road at night
on a snowmobile. And it would have been so easy to have averted the accident, by
painting the pipe white or by hanging a cloth or a sign from it.

I would allow the appeal, set aside the judgment of the Court of Appeal and restore the judgment of the trial Judge with costs throughout.

NOTES AND QUESTIONS

1. Do you agree with Dickson J. that the plaintiff was a licensee? In light of *Veinot* and the authorities discussed in it, have the courts rendered the concept of implied licence meaningless?

2. Based on *Herrington* (discussed in *Veinot*), define the duty of care that an occupier owes to a trespasser. Identify the various factors that a court should consider in determining whether this duty applies in a given case. How does this test of duty differ from that established in *Donoghue v. Stevenson*, [1932] A.C. 562 (H.L.)? How did the decisions in *Pannett* and *Southern Portland Cement* (both also discussed in *Veinot*) alter the common humanity test established in *Herrington*? Based on these three cases, define an occupier's common law duty of care to a trespasser. What criticisms would you make of this test?

3. Traditionally, the courts have distinguished between passive and active dangers on the defendant's land. An active danger generally has been governed by ordinary principles of negligence, whereas a passive danger, such as that in *Veinot*, generally has been governed by occupiers' liability. This distinction, like so many other aspects of occupiers' liability, has generated controversy and confusion. See for example *Wade v. C.N.R.* (1977), 80 D.L.R. (3d) 214 (S.C.C.); and Gibson, "Torts — Negligence and Occupiers' Liability — Role of Jury — Confusing Words from the Oracle" (1978) 58 Can. Bar Rev. 693.

4. For further discussion of an occupier's common law duty of care to a trespasser see Osborne, *The Law of Torts*, 5th ed. (2015) at 168-69; Innes, "Recent Developments in the Law of Occupiers' Liability to Trespassers" (1975) 24 U.N.B.L.J. 39; and Di Castri, *Occupiers' Liability* (1981) at 123-46.

3. The Provincial Occupiers' Liability Statutes

(a) INTRODUCTION

Because of problems associated with the common law regime, occupiers' liability legislation was enacted in British Columbia (1974), Alberta (1973), Manitoba (1983), Ontario (1980), Nova Scotia (1996) and Prince Edward Island (1984). Although some differences exist, the legislation is much the same from province to province. By way of illustration, we present the Ontario *Occupiers' Liability Act*, R.S.O. 1990, c. O.2 and then consider its application in the leading case of *Waldick v. Malcolm* (1991), 83 D.L.R. (4th) 114 (S.C.C.).

(b) ONTARIO OCCUPIERS' LIABILITY ACT

OCCUPIERS' LIABILITY ACT
R.S.O. 1990, c. O.2

1. In this Act . . .
"occupier" includes,

(a) a person who is in physical possession of premises, or
(b) a person who has responsibility for and control over the condition of premises or the activities there carried on, or control over persons allowed to enter the premises,

despite the fact that there is more than one occupier of the same premises;

. . .

"premises" means lands and structures, or either of them, and includes,

(a) water,
(b) ships and vessels,
(c) trailers and portable structures designed or used for residence, business or shelter,
(d) trains, railway cars, vehicles and aircraft, except while in operation.

Common law duty of care superseded

2. Subject to section 9, this Act applies in place of the rules of the common law that determine the care that the occupier of premises at common law is required to show for the purpose of determining the occupier's liability in law in respect of dangers to persons entering on the premises or the property brought on the premises by those persons.

Occupier's duty

3. (1) An occupier of premises owes a duty to take such care as in all the circumstances of the case is reasonable to see that persons entering on the premises, and the property brought on the premises by those persons are reasonably safe while on the premises.

(2) The duty of care provided for in subsection (1) applies whether the danger is caused by the condition of the premises or by an activity carried on on the premises.

(3) The duty of care provided for in subsection (1) applies except in so far as the occupier of premises is free to and does restrict, modify or exclude the occupier's duty.

Risks willingly assumed

4. (1) The duty of care provided for in subsection 3(1) does not apply in respect of risks willingly assumed by the person who enters on the premises, but in that case the occupier owes a duty to the person to not create a danger with the deliberate intent of doing harm or damage to the person or his or her property and to not act with reckless disregard of the presence of the person or his or her property.

Criminal activity

(2) A person who is on premises with the intention of committing, or in the commission of, a criminal act shall be deemed to have willingly assumed all risks and is subject to the duty of care set out in subsection (1).

Trespass and permitted recreational activity

(3) A person who enters premises described in subsection (4) shall be deemed to have willingly assumed all risks and is subject to the duty of care set out in subsection (1),

    (a) where the entry is prohibited under the Trespass to Property Act;

    (b) where the occupier has posted no notice in respect of entry and has not otherwise expressly permitted entry; or

    (c) where the entry is for the purpose of a recreational activity and,

        (i)   no fee is paid for the entry or activity of the person, other than a benefit or payment received from a government or government agency or a non-profit recreation club or association, and

        (ii) the person is not being provided with living accommodation by the occupier.

    (4) The premises referred to in subsection (3) are,

(a) a rural premises that is,

        (i)   used for agricultural purposes, including land under cultivation, orchards, pastures, woodlots and farm ponds,

        (ii) vacant or undeveloped premises,

        (iii) forested or wilderness premises;

(b) golf courses when not open for playing;

(c) utility rights-of-way and corridors, excluding structures located thereon;

(d) unopened road allowances;

(e) private roads reasonably marked by notice as such; and

(f) recreational trails reasonably marked by notice as such.

Restriction of duty or liability

5. (1) The duty of an occupier under this Act, or the occupier's liability for breach thereof, shall not be restricted or excluded by any contract to which the person to whom the duty is owed is not a party, whether or not the occupier is bound by the contract to permit such person to enter or use the premises.

Extension of liability by contract

(2) A contract shall not by virtue of this Act have the effect, unless it expressly so provides, of making an occupier who has taken reasonable care, liable to any person not a party to the contract, for dangers due to the faulty execution of any work of construction, maintenance or repair, or other like operation by persons other than the occupier, employees of the occupier and persons acting under the occupier's direction and control.

Reasonable steps to inform

(3) Where an occupier is free to restrict, modify or exclude the occupier's duty of care or the occupier's liability for breach thereof, the occupier shall take reasonable steps to bring such restriction, modification or exclusion to the attention of the person to whom the duty is owed.

Liability where independent contractor

6. (1) Where damage to any person or his or her property is caused by the negligence of an independent contractor employed by the occupier, the occupier is not on that account liable if in all the circumstances the occupier had acted reasonably in entrusting the work to the independent contractor, if the occupier had taken such steps, if any, as the occupier reasonably ought in order to be satisfied that the contractor was competent and that the work had been properly done, and if it was reasonable that the work performed by the independent contractor should have been undertaken.

(2) Where there is more than one occupier of premises, any benefit accruing by reason of subsection (1) to the occupier who employed the independent contractor shall accrue to all occupiers of the premises.

(3) Nothing in this section affects any duty of the occupier that is non-delegable at common law or affects any provision in any other Act that provides that an occupier is liable for the negligence of an independent contractor.

Application of ss. 5(1, 2), 6

7. In so far as subsections 5(1) and (2) prevent the duty of care owed by an occupier, or liability for breach thereof, from being restricted or excluded, they apply to contracts entered into both before and after the commencement of this Act, and in so far as section 6 enlarges the duty of care owed by an occupier, or liability for breach thereof, it applies only in respect of contracts entered into after the 8th day of September, 1980.

Obligations of landlord as occupier

8. (1) Where premises are occupied or used by virtue of a tenancy under which the landlord is responsible for the maintenance or repair of the premises, it is the duty of the landlord to show towards any person or the property brought on the premises by those persons, the same duty of care in respect of dangers arising from any failure on the landlord's part in carrying out the landlord's responsibility as is required by this Act to be shown by an occupier of the premises.

(2) For the purposes of this section, a landlord shall not be deemed to have made default in carrying out any obligation to a person unless the landlord's default is such as to be actionable at the suit of the person entitled to possession of the premises.

Definitions

(3) For the purposes of this section, obligations imposed by any enactment by virtue of a tenancy shall be treated as imposed by the tenancy, and "tenancy" includes a statutory tenancy, an implied tenancy and any contract conferring the right of occupation, and "landlord" shall be construed accordingly.

Application of section

(4) This section applies to all tenancies whether created before or after the commencement of this Act.

Preservation of higher obligations

9. (1) Nothing in this Act relieves an occupier of premises in any particular case from any higher liability or any duty to show a higher standard of care that in that case is incumbent on the occupier by virtue of any enactment or rule of law imposing special liability or standards of care on particular classes of persons including, but without restricting the generality of the foregoing, the obligations of,

(a) innkeepers, subject to the Innkeepers Act;
(b) common carriers;
(c) bailees

Employer and employee relationships

(2) Nothing in this Act shall be construed to affect the rights, duties and liabilities resulting from an employer and employee relationship where it exists.

Application of Negligence Act

(3) The Negligence Act applies with respect to causes of action to which this Act applies.

Act binds Crown

10. (1) This Act binds the Crown, subject to the Proceedings Against the Crown Act.

Exception

(2) This Act does not apply to the Crown or to any municipal corporation, where the Crown or the municipal corporation is an occupier of a public highway or a public road.

NOTES AND QUESTIONS

1. How does the approach adopted in the Ontario statute differ from the common law approach? Does the statute require the courts to ignore the fact that different occupiers have different resources at their disposal? Can the courts consider the category of entrant in determining an occupier's liability under the statute? Do you think that the statute is significantly easier to interpret and apply than the common law?

A trial judge obviously commits a reviewable error by applying the common law test of occupiers' liability in those provinces that have enacted legislation: *Agar v. Weber*, 2014 BCCA 297.

That is not to say, however, that judges in jurisdictions with legislation cannot look to cases decided either prior to the enactment of the occupiers' liability statute or in jurisdictions that have retained the common law approach. Caution is required insofar as the common law rules may involve the application of an improper standard of care: *Foley v. Imperial Oil Ltd.*, 2011 BCCA 262 at para. 29. Those cases nevertheless may be a source of useful guidance: *Mirsoltani v. Canadian Memorian Chiropractic College*, 2018 ONSC 5639 at para. 16.

2. Simple ownership of a property will not constitute "occupation" for the purposes of occupiers' liability. In summarizing the definition of "occupier" under both the *Occupiers' Liability Act* and similar statutes, the Ontario Court of Appeal said that there are four ways in which a person may be an "occupier": "(1) be in physical possession of the land, (2) be responsible for and have control over the condition of the land, (3) be responsible for and have control over the activities there carried on, or (4) have control over persons allowed on the land": *Haliburton (County) v. Gillespie*, 2013 ONCA 40 at para. 23. That case involved a 7000 acre parcel of land that was divided into residential units and "common areas." The appellant leased one of the residential units and was entitled to use the common areas. The court held that he was not an "occupier" of the common areas because he did not sufficiently have responsibility for, and control over, the persons allowed to enter or the activities carried on. While he was entitled to bring guests into the common areas, so too were the other 540 people who leased residential units. See also *Wiley v. Tymar Management Inc.*, [1995] 3 W.W.R. 684 (B.C.S.C.); and *Murray v. Bitango*, [1995] 1 W.W.R. 79 (Alta. Q.B.). Based on the ability to control, a public authority may incur responsibility for structures built on or around natural bodies of water, without being classified as an occupier of a natural lake or river itself: *Butler (Litigation Representative of) v. Ma-Me-O Beach (Summer Village)*, 2015 ABQB 364.

Difficult questions can arise at the intersection of different properties. Shopping centres are a case in point. The shops themselves are occupied by the tenant retailers; common areas within the mall are generally occupied by the owner or landlord; public sidewalks leading up to the mall are generally controlled by the municipality. But what happens if the lines are not cleanly drawn? That question arose in *MacKay v. Starbucks Corp.*, 2015 ONSC 4718, aff'd 2017 ONCA 350. A Starbucks franchise was located on the outer edge of a mall. Outside of the café, an enclosed patio abutted a municipally-owned sidewalk. The various elements were configured to funnel pedestrians into Starbucks. The patio was part of the leased premises, but the sidewalk was not. Starbucks nevertheless exercised a fair degree of control over it. Significantly, it instructed its employees to salt and sand not only the patio, but also the part of the municipal sidewalk that was integrated into its patio entrance. As fate would have it, that was the spot on which the plaintiff slipped and fell. Who was the appropriate target of her claim? As the owner of the sidewalk, the municipality was the primary occupier, but special legislation limited its liability to instances of gross negligence: *Municipal Act*, S.O. 2001, c. 25, s. 44(9). Fortunately for the plaintiff, a single property may have more than one occupier: *Bongiardina v. York (Regional Municipality)* (2000), 49 O.R. (3d) 641 at para. 20 (C.A.). The courts consequently were able to hold that Starbucks, by assuming responsibility for de-icing the sidewalk, by integrating the sidewalk into its patio entrance, and by controlling the ingress and egress of customers, qualified as an "occupier" as well. For further discussion of municipal sidewalks and private businesses, see *Moody v. Toronto (City)* (1996), 31 O.R. (3d) 53 (G.D.); *Bogoroch v. Toronto (City)*, [1991] O.J. No. 1032 (G.D.); and *Graham v. 7 Eleven Canada Inc.*, [2003] O.J. No. 544 (S.C.J.).

3. Given the wording of the statute, it obviously "makes no sense" to say that an occupier may be held liable for events that occur on the premises but cause damage to

people who are located elsewhere. A class action claim for occupiers' liability consequently was unable to proceed after an explosion on the defendant's business premises caused damage to 12,000 nearby residents: *Durling v. Sunrise Propane Energy Group Inc.*, 2013 ONSC 5830. See also *Youssef (Litigation guardian of) v. Misselbrook*, 2018 ONSC 6409; and *Sumner v. Colborne*, [2018] EWCA Civ 1006.

4. Canada's occupiers' liability statutes share much in common. As in Ontario, for example, occupiers in Nova Scotia, Manitoba, and British Columbia are subject to a duty to take reasonable care in the circumstances, without formally recognizing different types of occupiers and categories of entrants. See *Occupiers' Liability Act*, R.S.M. 1987, c. O8, s. 3(1); and *Occupiers' Liability Act*, R.S.B.C. 1996, c. 337.

The Alberta statute adopts a similar duty for lawful entrants, but provides a much more restricted duty for adult trespassers. It also contains a third set of principles governing an occupier's duty to trespassing children. See *Occupiers' Liability Act*, R.S.A. 2000, c. O-4, ss. 5, 12 and 13.

The Prince Edward Island statute also adopts a reasonable care test for lawful entrants. However, it restricts the duty for trespassers, criminals, and those engaging in recreational activities. See *Occupiers' Liability Act*, R.S.P.E.I. 1988, c. O-2, ss. 3 and 4.

5. As under the common law rules, the plaintiff must prove not only that an injury occurred on the defendant's premises, but also that the defendant breached the standard of care. Occupiers' liability is not strict: see *Desjardins v. Arcadian Restaurants Ltd.*, 2005 CarswellOnt 7549 (S.C.J.) (WL Can). The law imposes an obligation to act reasonably; it neither demands perfection nor compels an occupier to act as an insurer: *Foley v. Imperial Oil Ltd.*, 2011 BCCA 262 at para. 28; *Waldick v. Malcolm* (1989), 70 O.R. (2d) 717 (C.A.) at para. 20. The plaintiff must also demonstrate that the defendant's breach caused a loss: *Simmons v. Yeager Properties Inc.*, 2014 BCCA 201.

Although the plaintiff bears the burden of proving the elements of the tort, the Ontario Court of Appeal lightened that burden somewhat in *Kamin v. Kawartha Dairy Ltd.* (2006), 79 O.R. (3d) 284 (C.A.). The plaintiff sued after tripping and falling in the defendant's parking lot. Early authority required the claimant to establish, with some precision, the site and source of the accident: *Cock v. Windsor*, [1944] 2 D.L.R. 778 (Ont. H.C.). In *Kamin*, however, the Ontario Court of Appeal explained that modern authorities allowed a trier-of-fact to draw reasonable inferences: *Snell v. Farrell*, [1990] 2 S.C.R. 311. Consequently, although the plaintiff could not establish the specific details of the accident, the court was able to draw favourable inferences from the fact that the defendant's parking lot was in very poor condition generally.

6. Given its special rules, it is important to distinguish occupiers' liability from other heads of liability. In *Kennedy v. Waterloo (County) Board of Education* (1999), 175 D.L.R. (4th) 106 (Ont. C.A.), the plaintiff was a student at the defendant's school. While leaving the premises on his motorcycle, he struck a barrier that the defendant had erected. The trial judge held the defendant could not be held liable because its decision regarding the placement of the barriers fell under the rubric of "policy" rather than "operational." The Court of Appeal reversed that decision. It held that while the distinction between policy and operational decisions was relevant to the common law action in negligence, it did not apply under the *Occupiers' Liability Act*. The appellate

court accordingly imposed liability, but reduced damages by 75% to reflect the plaintiff's own carelessness.

7. Depending upon the circumstances, an occupier may be obliged to protect people from their own foolishness. Because a cherry tree branch that provides access to a school roof is apt to entice seventh-grade students, the school may be liable for failing to prune back the branch: *Paquette v. Surrey School District No. 36*, 2014 BCSC 205, aff'd 2014 BCCA 456. Adults, of course, generally are better able to look after themselves, but what are the legal implications of intoxication? *Stringer v. Ashley* (unreported, 1994, Ont. H.C.J.) provides a controversial illustration. The plaintiff attended a party at the defendant's house. The defendant warned the plaintiff to not dive into the backyard pool from the roof of the house. The plaintiff repeatedly ignored that warning and eventually was rendered paraplegic. The court held that, given the claimant's intoxicated condition, a mere warning was not sufficient. The defendant should have done more (*e.g.* lock doors or remove the plaintiff from the premises). Do you agree with this decision? See Simpson, "The Occupier's Responsibility to Protect Guests From Themselves: *Stringer v. Ashley*" (1995) 16 Adv. Q. 506; and *cf. Tomlinson v. Congleton Borough Council*, [2004] 1 A.C. 46 (H.L.). An occupier, however, need not guard against "unpredictable folly." In *Galka v. Stankiewicz*, 2010 CarswellOnt 3346 (S.C.J.) (WL Can), aff'd 2011 ONCA 428 the plaintiff was injured, on the defendant's premises, when his friend deliberately shot an arrow over his head in an effort to determine the trajectory of previously lost arrows. The plaintiff suffered serious injuries when the arrow entered his brain through his eye. The friend was held responsible, but since the adventure was bizarre and not reasonably foreseeable, the occupier of the premises was relieved of liability.

An occupier is not required to take unreasonable steps to protect a person from a known risk: *Winters v. Haldimand (County)*, 2015 ONCA 98. In *Wood v. Ward* (2009), 12 Alta. L.R. (5th) 52 (C.A.) the plaintiff helped repair the defendant's roof. The plaintiff was experienced in such matters and the risk of falling was obvious. The plaintiff was injured after stepping backwards and falling from the roof. The trial judge dismissed the claim on the ground that it was not reasonably foreseeable that the plaintiff would step off the roof. The Alberta Court of Appeal came to the same result, but on different reasoning. While the risk of falling was reasonably foreseeable, the defendant was not required to take every conceivable precaution to protect the plaintiff from a known danger. Which analysis is preferable?

If a situation raises a range of risks, the occupier must take reasonable steps to ensure that visitors are able to assess the dangers. That was true in *Campbell v. Bruce (County)*, 2015 ONSC 230, aff'd 2016 ONCA 371. The plaintiff was an experienced trail bike rider, but he did not have experience with the type of constructed bike park that the defendant operated. He suffered a broken neck after falling from an obstacle. Despite posting signs warning riders to operate within their skill levels, the defendant was liable. While the activity was inherently dangerous, the defendant did not provide any means for the plaintiff to assess his own ability to manage the types of risks encountered in a bike park.

8. The statute obviously does not render an occupier liable for every injury that occurs on the premises. In *Koperdak v. Wiesblatt*, 2006 CarswellBC 968 (S.C.) (WL Can) the defendant let his house sit empty for several years. To protect the property from damage, he enclosed it with a fence and double-locked the gate. The plaintiff

nevertheless approached the house because she was interested in purchasing it. She was injured after a front stair collapsed and sent her tumbling. The court considered all of the circumstances and denied liability because (1) the defect in the stair was latent and not reasonably known to the defendant, and (2) the defendant clearly had revoked the implied licence for members of the public to approach the house.

9. Section 4(1) of Ontario's statute relieves an occupier of responsibility for "risks willingly assumed by a person who enters the premises." That section was applied in *Karn v. Sturgeon* (2008) 90 C.C.L.T. (3d) 103 (Ont. S.C.J.). The deceased, who was diabetic, suffered cardiac arrest as a result of drinking beer at the defendant's home. The court rejected a claim under the statute because the deceased knew the risks associated with alcohol and diabetes, and because, in the circumstances, the defendant could not reasonably be expected to intercede to protect her friend from himself.

Section 4(1) further that if a person who enters onto premises willing assumes risks, the standard of care is reduced so that the occupier merely must neither "create a danger with the deliberate intent of doing harm or damage to the person or his or her property" nor "act with reckless disregard" for the person or property.

Subsection 4(2) states that all risks are assumed by a person who enters premises in the commission of a criminal act or with the intention of committing a crime. The occupier's standard of care is accordingly reduced. The same is true, under subsection 4(3), if a person enters as a trespasser. At least one commentator has expressed surprise and dismay that an occupier, as opposed to the defendant in a standard negligence claim, enjoys the benefit of the claimant's deemed assumption of risk: Buckley, "Occupiers' Liability in England and Canada" (2018) 35 Common L. World Rev. 197 at p. 215. He does, however, find some solace in the fact that "convenient findings of fact are used to ensure either that 'trespassers' are treated as lawful visitors, or that merely negligent defendants were 'reckless.'"

Subsection 4(3) also states that risks are assumed and the standard of care is reduced if a person enters premises for a recreational activity and does not pay a fee. The legislature's aim is to encourage occupiers to allow their land to be used for recreational purposes: *Schneider v. St. Clair Region Conservation Authority* (2009), 97 O.R. (3d) 81 (C.A.); *Skropnik v. B.C. Rail Ltd.* (2008), 82 B.C.L.R. (4th) 313 (C.A.); *Herbert (Litigation Guardian of) v. Brantford (City)* (2010), 72 M.P.L.R. (4th) 108 (Ont. S.C.J.), aff'd 2012 ONCA 98 (municipal bike trail; defendant recklessly disregarded need for precautions at location known to be dangerous); and *Kennedy v. London (City)* (2009), 58 M.P.L.R. (4th) 244 (Ont. S.C.J.) (municipal bike trail; defendant recklessly placed bollard without posting warning sign). Would the courts have considered the defendants' conduct to be "reckless" in these cases if the statute had not varied the standard of care?

The special provisions regarding recreation apply, however, only if the premises were actually being used for recreational purposes: *Moloney v. Parry Sound (Town)* (2000), 184 D.L.R. (4th) 121 (Ont. C.A.) (accident occurring on part of path used as both fitness trail and roadway; not "recreational trail"); and *Gill v. A&P Fruit Growers Ltd.* (2010), 3 B.C.L.R. (5th) 203 (C.A.) (parties visited blueberry farm to socialize after wedding; premises not used for recreational purpose). See also Alberta Law Reform Institute, *Occupiers' Liability: Recreational Use of Land* (2000).

Although they could be accommodated within the "recreation" provisions in occupiers' liability statutes, some situations are addressed under more specialized legislation. That is true of snowmobilers in Ontario. In 1974, the provincial legislature intervened in an attempt to resolve conflicts between snowmobile operators and occupiers. See the *Motorized Snow Vehicles Act*, R.S.O. 1990, c. M.44; and *Cormack v. Mara (Township)* (1989), 59 D.L.R. (4th) 300 (Ont. C.A.).

Other provinces similarly make allowances for willingly assumed risks and recreational activities: *Occupiers Liability Act*, R.S.B.C. 1996, c. 337, s. 3; *Occupiers' Liability Act*, R.S.A. 2000, c. O-4, s. 6.1 (recreational users), s. 7 (risks willingly accepted); *The Occupiers' Liability Act*, C.C.S.M. c. O8, s. 3; *Occupiers' Liability Act*, S.N.S. 1996, c. 27, ss. 5, 6; and *Occupiers' Liability Act*, R.S.P.E.I. 1988, c. O-2, s. 4.

10. Section 8 of the Ontario's statute imposes a duty of care on a landlord who, by virtue of the lease, is responsible for maintenance and repair of the premises. Except in Alberta, the same is true in other provinces: *Occupiers Liability Act*, R.S.B.C. 1996, c. 337, s. 6; *The Occupiers' Liability Act*, C.C.S.M. c. O8, s. 6; *Occupiers' Liability Act*, S.N.S. 1996, c. 27, s. 9; and *Occupiers' Liability Act*, R.S.P.E.I. 1988, c. O-2, s. 7.

The need for such provisions is illustrated by *Zavaglia v. Maq Holdings Ltd.* (1986), 6 B.C.L.R. (2d) 286 (C.A.). The defendant rented a house to a man named Ruggles. While visiting Ruggles, the plaintiff was injured after he fell in a stairwell that did not have a handrail. Under a common law regime, the action would have failed because landlords were not classified as occupiers. The claimant was fortunate to have the benefit of British Columbia's statute. See also *Jack v. Tekavec*, 2010 BCSC 1773, aff'd 2011 BCCA 464.

Liability was also imposed in *Taylor v. Allard*, 2010 ONCA 596. The defendant landlord built a fire pit in the backyard of a property. The property was then rented to the defendant tenants. The tenants invited the plaintiff to attend a party on the premises. While intoxicated, the plaintiff fell into the fire pit and was badly burned. The trial judge held the plaintiff and the defendant tenants equally responsible and accordingly reduced damages by half. The defendant landlord escaped liability at trial on the basis that he was not an "occupier." While generally upholding the decision below, the Ontario Court of Appeal held that the landlord was jointly and severally liable, alongside the tenants. Contrary to the trial judge's finding, the landlord admitted in the pleadings that he was an occupier. Furthermore, although the rental agreement relieved the landlord of maintenance obligations, the *Landlord and Tenant Act*, R.S.O. 1990, c. L.7, imposed a statutory duty on residential landlords to maintain premises.

A tenant cannot escape liability merely by proving that the lease imposed responsibility upon the landlord for maintenance of part of the premises. A court may find that the tenant failed to take reasonable steps to ensure that the landlord met its contractual obligation: *Soomre (Litigation guardian of) v. P.A. Ramey Enterprises Ltd.*, 2012 ONSC 782; and *cf. Musselman v. 875667 Ontario Inc. (c.o.b. Cities Bistro)*, 2012 ONCA 41.

Because its legislation does not have anything equivalent to s. 8 of Ontario's statute, landlords in Alberta are not at risk of liability merely because they are responsible for maintenance and repairs under tenancy agreements. In that province, landlords are subject to occupiers' liability for injuries incurred on lease premises only if they enjoy "'minute to minute, hour to hour control' of the premises": *Holmes (Litigation guardian of) v. Edmunds*, 2015 ABQB 798 at para. 14, aff'd 2017 ABCA 28 at para. 10. Of course, landlords may also be liable as occupiers of common areas under their control: *cf. Stefanyk v. Steven*, 2018 ABCA 125.

11. Section 10(1) of Ontario's statute states that the Act generally binds the Crown. Significantly, however, subsection 10(2) exempts "the Crown or . . . municipal corporation, where the Crown or the municipal corporation is an occupier of a public highway or a public road." Given the number of roads and road users in Canada, as well as the need to allocate public resources, the risk of liability would otherwise be overwhelming. That type of provision is an invariable feature of occupiers' liability legislation: *Occupiers Liability Act*, R.S.B.C. 1996, c. 337, s. 8(2); *Occupiers' Liability Act*, R.S.A. 2000, c. O-4, s. 4; *The Occupiers' Liability Act*, C.C.S.M. c. O8, s. 8(2); *Occupiers' Liability Act*, S.N.S. 1996, c. 27, ss. 11, 12; and *Occupiers' Liability Act*, R.S.P.E.I. 1988, c. O-2, s. 9(2).

12. An occupier may be held liable not only for the condition of the premises, but also the activities of individuals on the premises: *Allison v. Rank City Wall Can. Ltd.* (1984), 6 D.L.R. (4th) 144 (Ont. H.C.J.) (apartment owner liable for assault in the parkade); *McGinty v. Cook* (1989), 59 D.L.R. (4th) 94 (Ont. H.C.), aff'd (1991), 79 D.L.R. (4th) 95 (Ont. C.A.) (campground operator liable for failing to provide protection against unruly campers); *Mellanby v. Chappie*, 1995 CarswellOnt 5327 (Gen. Div.) (WL Can) (restaurant liable for failing to protect plaintiff from violent patrons); *Jeffrey v. Commodore Cabaret Ltd.* (1996), 13 B.C.L.R. (3d) 149 (S.C.) (plaintiff attacked during "battle of the bands" competition at defendant's cabaret; defendant liable); *Murphy v. Little Memphis Cabaret Inc.* (1998), 167 D.L.R. (4th) 190 (Ont. C.A.) (plaintiff, ejected from tavern after fighting with other patrons, was beaten by other patrons outside; tavern liable); *Dufault v. Excelsior Mortgage Corp.* (2002), 14 Alta. L.R. (4th) 343 (Q.B.), aff'd (2003), 20 Alta. L.R. (4th) 220 (C.A.) ("badly behaved and aggressive youths" assaulted hotel guest; hotel liable); and *McAllister v. Calgary (City)*, 2018 ABQB 480 (plaintiff beaten by thugs at transit facility; city liable because its video surveillance system was deficient and under-staffed).

In appropriate circumstances, however, liability will be denied: *Coleiro v. Premier Fitness Clubs (Erin Mills) Inc.*, 2010 CarswellOnt 5835 (S.C.J.) (WL Can) (health club not liable to protect patron from attack by another); *Johnson v. Webb* (2002), 162 Man. R. (2d) 48 (Q.B.), aff'd (2002), 170 Man. R. (2d) 58 (C.A.) (plaintiff injured after being checked during annual teacher-student hockey game; neither opposing player nor occupier liable); *Desanti v. Gray*, 2011 ABCA 226 (plaintiff and third party both attended defendant's party; third party assaulted plaintiff; defendant not liable because assault occurred after third party and defendant left premises); and *Vaughn v. Kelowna Speedometer Ltd.*, 2011 BCSC 542 (plaintiff beaten by unknown assailants in alley behind defendant's bar; defendant allegedly failed to adequately light alley; no proof of causal connection between alleged breach and injury).

13. Section 6 of Ontario's statute applies if the plaintiff suffered damage, while on the occupier's premises, as a result of the negligence of an independent contractor. The occupier is shielded from liability as long as it reasonably entrusted the work to the contractor, took reasonable steps to ensure that the contractor was competent, and reasonably decided to have the work undertaken. An occupier, however, cannot use that provision to escape responsibility for a non-delegable duty: *Lewis (Guardian ad litem of) v. British Columbia*, [1997] 3 S.C.R. 1145. See also *Occupiers Liability Act*, R.S.B.C. 1996, c. 337, s. 5; *Occupiers' Liability Act*, R.S.A. 2000, c. O-4, s. 11; *The Occupiers' Liability Act*, C.C.S.M. c. O8, s. 5; *Occupiers' Liability Act*, S.N.S. 1996, c. 27, s. 8; *Occupiers' Liability Act*, R.S.P.E.I. 1988, c. O-2, s. 6. See *Heikkila v. Apex Land*

Corp., 2016 ABCA 126; *Murkute v. Owners Condominium Plan 8210034*, 2006 ABCA 315; *Grochowich v. Okanagan University College*, 2004 BCCA 325; *Moskal v. Costco Wholesale Corp.*, 2015 MBCA 108; *Klein v. Stiller*, 2015 ONSC 3705; and *Hill v. Intact Insurance Co.*, 2015 ONSC 6601.

14. The standard of care requires the occupier to act reasonably in light of the circumstances. As in negligence actions, compliance or non-compliance with a statutory standard provides relevant evidence, but it is not determinative: *Zsoldos v. Canadian Pacific Railway Co.* (2007), 46 C.C.L.I. (4th) 294 (Ont. S.C.J.), aff'd (2009), 93 O.R. (3d) 321 (C.A.) (plaintiff injured after colliding with defendant's train; defendant satisfied statutory and regulatory requirements, but nevertheless failed to act reasonably to protect motorists).

So too, as in negligence, the standard of care also makes allowances for the fact that emergencies modify behaviour: *Faircrest v. Buchanan*, 2015 BCSC 657 (volunteer in mental health care facility bumped by nurse rushing to agitated patient).

15. Courts routinely deal with cases in which customers slip and fall as a result of slick surfaces in stores, restaurants, and markets. The mere fact that the plaintiff suffered an injury as a result of a fall is not presumptive evidence of the occupier's carelessness. Moreover, an occupier can avoid liability by proving that it had formulated and implemented a reasonable system for identifying and eliminating risks: *Robinson v. 1390709 Alberta Ltd. (c.o.b. Chopped Leaf)*, 2017 BCCA 175; *Zary v. Canada Housing and Mortgage Corp.*, 2015 BCSC 1145; *Simmons v. Yeager Properties Inc.*, 2014 BCCA 201; *Waldick v. Malcolm* (1989), 70 O.R. (2d) 717 (Ont. C.A.); but *cf. Campbell v. Royal Bank of Canada* (1963), 37 D.L.R. (2d) 275 at para. 16 (Man. C.A.) ("Many a defendant has been able to escape liability for damage suffered by persons coming upon his premises by . . . a reasonable system of supervision and inspection"), rev'd on other grounds 43 D.L.R. (2d) 431 (S.C.C.).

16. Once liability is imposed under the statute, damages are calculated in the usual manner. The plaintiff in *Traquair v. National Arts Centre Corp.*, 2004 CarswellOnt 4165 (S.C.J.) (WL Can) was "a very talented trombone player" with the National Arts Centre Orchestra in Ottawa. He suffered a concussion and mild brain damage after falling from his chair during a rehearsal. The accident occurred because the leg of his chair was caught in a gap on the stage. The court held the defendant liable as an occupier. It held that it was reasonably foreseeable that musicians would adjust their seats while concentrating on either their music or the conductor. The court also held that the "gaps" in question could have been remedied at little cost.

Given his unique profession, the plaintiff received compensation under several heads: (1) $20,560 for past medical expenses because, as common for people in his position, he did not have medical insurance, (2) $44,362 for future medical expenses, (3) $75,000 for general damages — considerably more than usual — because his reduced capacity to attend social functions affected him to an unusual degree, (4) $21,089 for the fact that he no longer could teach at Queen's University, and (5) $424,956 (reduced to reflect his pre-accident prospect of success) for the loss of opportunity to secure a position with a superior orchestra.

As with most torts, damages may be reduced because of the plaintiff's contributory negligence. In *Lovely v. Kamloops (City)* (2010), 71 M.P.L.R. (4th) 210 (B.C.C.A.) the plaintiff was injured as a result of falling from a platform at the defendant's waste station. The defendant was at fault for failing to take reasonable steps to prevent accidents (such as providing hand railings) but the plaintiff also was at fault for failing to take reasonable care for his own safety. Damages accordingly were reduced by 10% due to the claimant's contributory negligence.

17. Canadian courts have various techniques for controlling contractual waivers of liability: *Tercon Contractors Ltd. v. British Columbia (Ministry of Transportation and Highways)*, 2010 SCC 4. A carefully-drawn agreement may nevertheless allow an occupier to limit or avoid liability. That is true whether an allegation of occupiers' liability arises in a common law jurisdiction or a jurisdiction that has statutorily reformed the tort: *Arif v. Li*, 2016 ONSC 4579; *Jensen v. Fit City Health Centre Inc.*, 2015 ONSC 6326; and *Urbanson v. Western Canadian Place Ltd.*, 2016 ABQB 32.

Consumer protection legislation sometimes purports to control or prohibit waivers of liability. Will such a statute deny an occupier the ability to protect itself through an agreement? That question arose in Ontario. Subsection 3(3) of *Occupiers' Liability Act* says that an occupier's duty of care "applies except in so far as the occupier of premises is free to and does restrict, modify or exclude" it. At the same time, however, s. 9 of the *Consumer Protection Act 2002*, S.O. 2002, c. 30 states not only that a supplier of consumer services is "deemed to warrant that the services . . . are of a reasonably acceptable quality," but also that any agreement to "negate or vary . . . any deemed condition or warranty under this Act is void." In a pair of cases, two skiers were injured on the slopes after signing waivers of liability in favour of the facilities' operators: *Schnarr v. Blue Mountain Resorts Ltd.*, 2017 ONSC 114; and *Woodhouse v. Snow Valley Resorts (1987) Ltd.*, 2017 ONSC 222. Despite some differences, the trial judges held that the *CPA* trumped the *OLA* on at least some claims. The Ontario Court of Appeal disagreed: *Schnarr v. Blue Mountain Resorts Ltd.*, 2018 ONCA 313. The occupiers' liability legislation prevailed across the board; it did not matter whether the plaintiff framed the action in negligence, occupiers' liability, or breach of contract. Nordheimer J.A. found that the legislature had not intended to extend the *CPA*'s higher standard of care to occupiers. The *OLA*, he said, was designed as "an exhaustive scheme" for determining the obligations and rights that flow from an occupier's maintenance or care of premises. That regime would be undermined if a claimant could invoke the *CPA*'s "novel contractual duty" and require an occupier to warrant that the premises are of a "reasonably acceptable quality": at para. 60.

WALDICK v. MALCOLM
(1991), 83 D.L.R. (4th) 114 (S.C.C.)

IACOBUCCI J.—The defendants, Marvin and Roberta Malcolm ("the Malcolms"), appeal from a judgment of the Ontario Court of Appeal dismissing their appeal from the judgment at trial finding the Malcolms liable for personal injuries suffered by the plaintiff, Norman Waldick ("Waldick").

The appeal involves the interpretation of the nature and extent of the duty of care under the Ontario *Occupiers' Liability Act*, R.S.O. 1980, c. 322 (the "Act"). In general terms, the Act sets out the duty of care owed by occupiers of premises to persons who come onto those premises and specifies certain exceptions to the prescribed duty of care. As this appeal is the first involving the Act to reach this Court and as several provinces have similar statutory regimes, it is important to clarify the scope of the duties owed by occupiers to their visitors.

Facts

On February 7, 1984, Waldick suffered a fractured skull when he fell on the icy parking area of the rural residential premises near Simcoe, Ontario which were occupied by the Malcolms. Waldick is Mrs. Malcolm's brother. Mrs. Malcolm worked as a hairdresser but she often cut hair at her home for friends and relatives without receiving any remuneration. The property, which consisted of a farmhouse and barn on approximately three acres of land, was owned by the other appellants, Betty Stainback and Harry Hill. The Malcolms rented the premises from them. Since they were not the occupiers of the farmhouse, the action and cross-claim against Stainback and Hill were dismissed on consent in June, 1986.

On the premises was a gravel laneway that ran for about 200 to 300 feet from the road, past the house, and to the barn. Opposite the house, the laneway widened to form a parking area which could accommodate three or four vehicles at any one time. The house had a small wooden porch with two steps. Leading from the steps toward the laneway was a walk made of cement slabs which was about six feet long but which did not reach the laneway. The rest of the distance between the walk and the laneway was grass-covered. The trial judge noted that there was "a perceptible grade downwards from the house to the parking area."

At the time of the injury, the porch and steps of the house had been shovelled and, while the walk and grassy area had also been shovelled, these were still snow-covered. The laneway had not been salted or sanded. The appellant, Roberta Malcolm, testified that she did not consider it necessary or reasonable to do so. She also testified that to her knowledge few of the residents in that rural region, including Waldick, salted or sanded their laneways in winter. Four days before the accident, the region had experienced an ice storm. Waldick was aware that the laneway was "slippery, very icy with a dusting of snow on it" and acknowledged that its condition could be seen without difficulty. Because of the ice, he took exceptional caution in driving up the laneway. He parked about 20 feet from where the gravel laneway met the grassy stretch, and entered the house, walking very carefully because of the ice. Some time later, he went out to his car to get a carton of U.S. cigarettes which he had purchased for his sister. He put on his winter boots, turned on the porch light, and got the cigarettes. As he was walking back to the house, he slipped on the ice, fell backwards in the parking area, and fractured his skull.

Waldick commenced an action in the Supreme Court of Ontario under the Act, alleging negligence on the part of the Malcolms and the owners of the premises; as noted above, the action against the owners was dismissed on consent. The trial judge found the Malcolms liable for the injuries sustained by Waldick and by agreement of the parties deferred the determination of damages.

Malcolms' appeal was dismissed by the Ontario Court of Appeal.

Analysis

1. Did the Court of Appeal of Ontario err in holding that the Malcolms breached the duty of care imposed by s. 3(1) of the Occupiers' Liability Act?

The courts below concluded that, in light of all the circumstances, the Malcolms breached the duty of care owed under s. 3(1) of the Act by doing nothing to render the parking area entrance to their house less slippery. While the Act in no way obliged them to salt or sand "every square inch of their parking area", Austin J. was of the view that doing nothing fell short of the reasonable care requirement. Blair J.A. agreed, noting the duty was limited only to salting or sanding that part of the parking area next to the entrance and adding that it was undeniable that the Malcolms knew this part would be used by visitors like Waldick.

Both Austin J. and Blair J.A. also stressed that sand and salt are not expensive and are readily available.

Counsel for the Malcolms submitted that the lower courts had reduced the statutory words "in all the circumstances of the case" to a consideration of only two factors: *foreseeability* of an accident, and the *costs* of its avoidance. In counsel's view, this was an oversimplified "calculus of negligence" which constituted a reviewable error of law. More specifically, the Malcolms argued that the courts below should also have taken into account "the practices of persons in the same or similar situations as the person whose conduct is being judged", or in other words, local custom. This, it was argued, would inject an element of community standards into the negligence calculus, and would promote behaviour which better accords with the reasonable expectations of community members.

. . . In the instant appeal, the relevant local custom which the courts below allegedly neglected to consider was "not sanding or salting driveways".

I am unable to agree with the Malcolms' submissions for several reasons. First of all, I do not agree with the premise of their argument, viz., that the lower courts failed to consider local custom. In my view, both Austin J. and Blair J.A. gave ample consideration to all the factors which could enter into an assessment of what constitutes reasonable care, including the alleged custom in the rural community involved.

. . .

The mere fact that the alleged custom was not decisive of the negligence issue does not in any way support the conclusion that it was not considered. After all, the statutory duty on occupiers is framed quite generally, as indeed it must be. That duty is to take reasonable care in the circumstances to make the premises safe. That duty does not change but the factors which are relevant to an assessment of what constitutes reasonable care will necessarily be very specific to each fact situation — thus the proviso "such care as *in all circumstances of the case* is reasonable". One such circumstance is whether the nature of the premises is rural or urban. Another is local custom, which Blair J.A. explicitly mentions and I view his reasons as considering and rejecting the alleged custom.

Secondly, there are proof problems that complicate the Malcolms' argument in this regard. Acknowledging that custom can inform the courts' assessment of what is reasonable in any given set of circumstances, it is nevertheless beyond dispute that, in any case where an alleged custom is raised, the "party who relies on either his own compliance with custom or the other person's departure from general practice bears the onus of proof that the custom is in effect.". . . Only in the rarest and most patently obvious of cases will the courts take judicial notice of a custom. . . .

In the case at bar, there is nothing apart from the completely unsupported testimony of the appellant Mrs. Malcolm that tends to prove something that could qualify as custom. . . .

Thirdly, even if there had been adequate evidence in the record of a general local custom of not salting or sanding driveways, I am not of the view that such a custom would necessarily be decisive against a determination of negligence in the case at bar

. . . . [N]o amount of general community compliance will render negligent conduct "reasonable . . . in all the circumstances". . . . If, as the lower courts found, it is unreasonable to do absolutely nothing to one's driveway in the face of clearly treacherous conditions, it matters little that one's neighbours also act unreasonably. Presumably it is exactly this type of generalized negligence that the Act is meant to discourage.

. . .

2. In the event that the Court of Appeal of Ontario was correct that the Malcolms did not meet the duty of care, did Waldick willingly assume the risks of walking over the icy parking area, thus relieving them from liability, pursuant to s. 4(1) of the Act?

At issue under this ground of appeal is the scope of the defence which s. 4(1) offers to occupiers. They will be absolved of liability in those cases where the losses suffered by visitors on their premises come as a result of "risks willingly assumed" by those visitors. As Austin J. and Blair J.A. noted, there are two quite distinct and conflicting trends in the jurisprudence as to the proper interpretation of this term. In essence, they reflect two standards of what assuming a risk means: the first involves merely knowing of the risk that one is running, whereas the second involves not only knowledge of the risk, but also a consent to the legal risk, or in other words, a waiver of legal rights that may arise from the harm or loss that is being risked. The latter standard is captured by the maxim *volenti non fit injuria* (the *volenti* doctrine) whereas the former is sometimes referred to as "*sciens*", or in other words, mere "knowing" as opposed to actually "willing."

Counsel for the Malcolms argued that s. 4(1) should be interpreted as meaning something between mere knowledge and the strict *volenti* approach. He suggested that s. 4(1) would be met where it could be shown that the visitor had a knowledge and appreciation of the danger on the premises.

In my view, the reasons of Blair J.A. on this issue are also an admirably correct statement of the law. I have no doubt that s. 4(1) of the Act was intended to embody and preserve the *volenti* doctrine. This can be seen by looking at the statutory scheme that is imposed by the Act as a whole. It is clear the intention of the Act was to replace, refine and harmonize the common law *duty of care* owed by occupiers of premises to visitors on those premises. That much seems evident from the wording of s. 2 of the Act. . . .

I am of the view that the Act was *not* intended to effect a wholesale displacement of the common law defences to liability, and it is significant that no mention is made of common law defences in s. 2. Reinforcement of this view is found when one asks why this area of law should entail a defence other than *volenti* which is applicable to negligence actions generally. There does not appear to be anything special about occupiers' liability that warrants a departure from the widely accepted *volenti* doctrine.

. . .

The goals of the Act are to promote, and indeed, require where circumstances warrant, positive action on the part of occupiers to make their premises reasonably safe. The occupier may, however, wish to put part of his property "off limits" rather than to make it safe, and in certain circumstances that might be considered reasonable. Where no such effort has been made, as in the case at bar, the exceptions to the statutory duty of care will be few and narrow.

. . .

In my view, the legislature's intention in enacting s. 4(1) of the Act was to carve out a very narrow exception to the class of visitors to whom the occupier's statutory duty of care is owed. This exception shares the same logical basis as the premise that underlies *volenti*, i.e., that no wrong is done to one who consents. By agreeing to assume the risk the plaintiff absolves the defendant of all responsibility for it. Rare may be the case where a visitor who enters on premises will fully know of and accept the risks resulting from the occupier's non-compliance with the statute. To my mind, such an interpretation of s. 4(1) accords best with general principles of statutory interpretation, is more fully consonant with the legislative aims of the Act, and is consistent with tort theory generally.

Both Austin J. and Blair J.A. were of the view that Waldick did not consent to the legal risk or waive any legal rights that might arise from the negligence of the Malcolms. I agree with their disposition of this ground of appeal and conclude that Waldick is not barred from recovery by the operation of s. 4(1) of the Act.

Conclusion

For the foregoing reasons, I would dismiss the appeal with costs.

NOTES AND QUESTIONS

1. How would the case have been decided under the common law rules?

2. Prior to the decision in *Waldick*, there was considerable debate as to whether s. 4(1) of the Ontario statute essentially codified the common law defence of *volenti*. Do you agree with Iacobucci J.'s decision? For further discussion, see Tomlinson, Machum & Lyons, "The Contractual Waiver of Liability in Ski Resort Negligence Claims" (1997) 15 Can. J. Ins. L. 49.

3. For other decisions pertaining to occupiers' liability legislation, see *Olinski v. Johnson* (1997), 32 O.R. (3d) 653 (C.A.); *Slaferek v. TCG International Inc.* (1997), [1998] 3 W.W.R. 600 (Alta. Q.B.); *Pope v. Route 66 Clothing Inc.* (1997), 41 C.C.L.T. (2d) 72 (Ont. Gen. Div.); and *Bennett v. Kailua Estates Ltd.* (1997), 32 C.C.L.T. (2d) 217 (B.C.C.A.).

REVIEW PROBLEM

Florence rented part of an old house from Ranjit. Florence had possession of the ground floor and Ranjit kept possession of the basement apartment, which he used for storage and kept locked at all times. Neither Florence nor Ranjit used the stairs connecting the basement to the first floor. Florence had no reason or right to enter the basement apartment, and Ranjit always used the street entrance to his apartment.

Florence soon became friends with her neighbour, Lilly, although she disliked Lilly's boyfriend, Hugo. Late one night, some three weeks after Florence had moved in, Florence heard a commotion at Lilly's residence and became fearful for her friend's safety. Minutes later, Lilly arrived at Florence's front door. Lilly was crying and confided that Hugo was drunk and had threatened her. Suddenly Hugo arrived at her door and, ignoring Florence's protests, pushed his way into the house. Lilly ran down the stairs to the basement. Hugo followed her. Unfortunately, two steps were missing and both Lilly and Hugo fell. The missing stairs would have been noticed by anyone who was walking normally. Ranjit knew about the missing stairs but he did not bother to inform Florence, because he thought she would never use them.

Analyze the common law duty of care, if any, that Florence and Ranjit owe to Hugo and Lilly. Would they be held liable to Lilly and Hugo under the Ontario *Occupiers' Liability Act*?

NUISANCE

1. Introduction
2. Private Nuisance
3. Public Nuisance
4. Remedies

1. Introduction

In Chapter 5, we briefly compared the actions for private nuisance and trespass to land. In this chapter, we consider private nuisance in more detail. We also examine the private action for public nuisance.

Although the torts of trespass to land and private nuisance are closely related, they also are clearly distinct. Trespass to land provides a remedy for direct and intentional physical intrusions upon another's land. As we saw in Chapter 5, the concept of reasonableness is irrelevant to the inquiry. The tort originally was designed to ensure the inviolability of property rights and it remains true today that liability may be imposed even if the defendant acted with great care and even if the plaintiff suffered little or no harm.

The tort of nuisance is similar to trespass insofar as it was designed to protect the plaintiff's use and enjoyment of land. Consequently, relief may be granted against overhanging branches, seeping sewage, foul odours, barking dogs, bright lights, traffic vibrations, industrial pollution, subsidence of supporting soil, errant golf balls, and even unwanted telephone calls. Significantly, however, not every interference supports a right of action. Liability depends on proof of unreasonableness. The court must weigh the plaintiff's interest in being free from interference against the defendant's interest in carrying on the impugned activity, as well as society's interest in allowing some types of activities. Relief is available only if, having regard to all of the circumstances, the interference was unreasonable.

In that sense, nuisance might seem to have a great deal in common with the tort of negligence, which also relies on a theory of reasonableness. It therefore is important to draw some distinctions. In negligence, the issue of reasonableness pertains primarily to the nature of the defendant's *conduct*. In nuisance, it pertains primarily to the *effect* that the defendant's conduct has on the plaintiff's enjoyment of land. One result of that distinction is that the defendant may be liable in nuisance despite acting reasonably: *Beatty v. Waterloo (Regional Municipality)*, 2011 ONSC 3599. Similarly, while courts elsewhere in the Commonwealth view the issue differently, Canadian judges have held that foreseeability, despite being central to the action in negligence, is not required for the tort of nuisance: *Huang v. Fraser Hillary's Ltd.*, 2018 ONCA 527.

Nuisance and negligence nevertheless do share at least one important feature. Whether it is used to assess the defendant's conduct or the plaintiff's interference, the concept of reasonableness necessarily imports some measure of judicial discretion. The court cannot simply apply clear rules to hard facts. In addition, it must exercise value judgments in striking a sensitive balance, on a case-by-case basis, between competing interests. Not surprisingly, the analysis is often both complex and contentious. Indeed, it has been suggested that "[t]here is no more impenetrable jungle in the entire law than that which surrounds the word 'nuisance'": Keeton *et al.*, *Prosser & Keeton on Torts*, 5th ed. (1984) at 616.

The tort of private nuisance must also be distinguished from the tort of public nuisance. That tort is linked to the criminal law concept of a "common nuisance." In addition to being criminally prosecuted for injuring society's interests, the defendant may be held civilly liable to those members of the community that suffered special injury.

NOTE

1. The law of nuisance receives detailed consideration in several specialist texts: Pun & Hall, *The Law of Nuisance in Canada* (2010); Bilson, *The Canadian Law of Nuisance* (1991); Beever, *The Law of Private Nuisance* (2013); and Buckley, *The Law of Nuisance*, 2d ed. (1996).

2. Private Nuisance

340909 ONT. LTD. v. HURON STEEL PRODUCTS (WINDSOR) LTD.
(1990), 73 O.R. (2d) 641 (H.C.)

[The defendant's stamping plant had been in operation since 1947. In 1977, the plaintiff bought a nearby apartment building. In 1979, the defendant purchased an 880-tonne press and installed it across the street from the plaintiff's apartment building. The plaintiff complained of noise and vibrations. Although a second such press was installed in 1983, efforts were made to reduce noise and vibrations and the second press met Ministry of the Environment guidelines. The plaintiff brought an action for nuisance claiming loss of rental income and loss of the value of the building.]

POTTS J:—. . .

DOES THE PLAINTIFF HAVE A CAUSE OF ACTION IN NUISANCE?

Private nuisance can be defined as an unreasonable interference with the use and enjoyment of land. J.G. Fleming, in *The Law of Torts*, 4th ed. (Sydney: Law Book Co., 1971), states at p. 346 that the court goes through a balancing process to determine whether a nuisance exists or not:

> The paramount problem in the law of nuisance is, therefore, to strike a tolerable balance between conflicting claims of landowners, each invoking the privilege to exploit the resources and enjoy the amenities of his property without undue subordination to the reciprocal interests of the other. Reconciliation has to be achieved by compromise, and the basis for adjustment is reasonable user. Legal intervention is warranted only when an excessive use of property causes inconvenience beyond what other occupiers in the vicinity can be expected to bear, having regard to the prevailing standard of comfort of the time and place. Reasonableness in this context is a two-sided affair. It is viewed not only from the standpoint of the defendant's convenience, but must also take into account the interest of the surrounding occupiers. It is not enough to ask: Is the defendant using his property in

what would be a reasonable manner if he had no neighbour? The question is, Is he using it reasonably, having regard to the fact that he has a neighbour?

Furthermore, each case must be considered in light of the particular facts in question.

. . .

"Unreasonableness" in nuisance law is when the interference in question would not be tolerated by the ordinary occupier. What constitutes "unreasonable" interference is determined by considering a number of factors:

(1) the severity of the interference, having regard to its nature and duration and effect;

(2) the character of the locale;

(3) the utility of the defendant's conduct;

(4) the sensitivity of the use interfered with.

It is not necessary to deal with the sensitivity of the use interfered with, since the plaintiff's use of its property is not an unusually sensitive one. The remaining three factors will be discussed below.

(1) *The severity of the interference, having regard to its nature, duration and effect*
  (a) *Nature of the interference*

The interference must be considered from the plaintiff company's point of view. However, the noise and vibration are allegedly disrupting the use and enjoyment by the tenants. This will ultimately affect the plaintiff as landlord, since the interference could be one reason why a tenant moves out. Therefore, the interference from the tenants' points of view is relevant, since it is *part of the* interference from the plaintiff's point of view.

. . .

Three expert witnesses testified in the area of sound and vibration assessment. I accept . . . that such evidence is helpful to confirm or disprove the evidence of other witnesses.

. . .

Kende made observations and took sound readings of the Huron Steel plant operations in December 1980. He testified that the #1 press was clearly audible and easily identifiable inside and outside the plant. The sound "was not a residential neighbourhood noise" and he "would not want to live with it".

. . .

He recorded an equivalent sound level (leq) of 69 dBA (not impulse) which exceeded the traffic level of 59 dBA and was in violation of the other guidelines the Ministry of the Environment uses.

. . .

Lightstone and Coulter both took impulse and sound and vibration measurements of Huron Steel plant operations. They agree that the impulse sound level at the apartment building is from 70-73 dBAI, with the Prince Road doors closed. Coulter also took indoor readings at the apartment with the window open and recorded about 60 dBAI. The *E.P.A.* guidelines are not meant for indoor readings. However, Lightstone agreed that this reading appears consistent with what he would expect, *i.e.*, 13-14 dBAI lower indoors. It should be mentioned that on cross-examination, Lightstone agreed that impulsive sounds are more intrusive than continuous ones.

Coulter and Lightstone agree that the #1 press is the source of the problem, although other sounds come from the plant as well. The press sound would be more noticeable at night, especially with the windows open, because the ambient levels are lower. Lightstone emphasizes the fact that many of the apartments facing the plant are equipped with air conditioners. The air conditioners, when running, would supposedly negate much of the sound from Huron Steel.

. . .

(b) *Duration*

The Huron Steel plant has been in operation since 1947. According to Mr. Andy Paonessa, who worked at Huron Steel from 1955 to 1978 and as plant manager from 1972, stamping occurred at the plant when he was there.

The number of shifts varied over the years. In 1974 or 1975, it was a three-shift operation, at which time it went to a one-shift, but when Morrison purchased the plant in 1977, it went to three shifts in three months. This continued after the #1 press was installed in 1979.

The major sound and vibration problems seem to occur when the #1 press is blanking heavy gauge material. This presumably would occur when orders had to be filled. Witnesses testified that, although the problem was not continuous, it was fairly regular. The press often operated during the night and on weekends, although there were periods of time when it did not run at all. The situation has continued since 1979, *i.e.*, ten years.

(c) *Effect*

To be successful, the plaintiff must show that the alleged nuisance has caused it damage. As discussed above, at least one of the plaintiff's tenants, Sbrocca, testified that he moved out primarily because of the noise and vibration coming from Huron Steel. Kenney testified that he received other tenant complaints about Huron Steel and that rents had not been increased and standards had been lowered in order to keep the vacancy rate down. Other property owners in the area testified as to the disruption they had experienced from the Huron Steel operations.

Mr. F.R. Jordan was put forward by the plaintiff as an expert in the value of real estate. He testified that he had examined the rent rolls of the plaintiff's apartment building for 1979-1987, in comparison with Canada Mortgage and Housing Corporation (C.M.H.C.) statistics. Based on a capitalized income approach, he concluded that the building lost revenue because of the comparatively high vacancy rate. Jordan stated that there was something abnormal about the property that caused the high vacancy rate and in his report he pointed to the disruptive Huron Steel operations as a probable cause. Jordan also concluded that there had been a loss in value of the building of about $71,000.

. . .

I accept that the effect of the Huron Steel operations has been such as to cause some damage to the plaintiff.

(2) *Character of the locale*

Counsel for the plaintiff contends that technological advances have weakened the application of this type of "defence". Defendant's counsel places much greater emphasis on this aspect. Relatively recent cases continue to hold that this is an important factor and I accept it as such: In *Walker, supra,* Morden J. stated at p. 38 O.R.:

> The law makes it clear that the character of the locality is of importance in determining the standard of comfort which may reasonably be claimed by an occupier of land. "What would be a nuisance in Belgrave Square would not necessarily be so in Bermondsey": *Sturges v. Bridgman* (1879), 11 Ch.D 852 at p. 865.

The Huron Steel plant is bordered by Sandwich Street to the north (approximately), Peter Street to the south, Hill Avenue to the west and Prince Road to the east.

. . .

I find that the character of the locale is one of "mixed use". The area contains apartment buildings, houses, at least one school, and one church, commercial establishments, and factories.

The standard of comfort to be expected varies from area to area, depending on the character of the locale in question. According to Linden, *Canadian Tort Law*, p. 505, the standard to be expected in a predominantly residential area differs from that of an industrial or commercial one. However, "[t]he process of determining the proper standard becomes more difficult when the area is one of mixed or changing use".

. . .

First of all, it is well established that it is no defence to a nuisance action that the plaintiff moved to the nuisance. . . . Secondly, many of the witnesses testifed that although there was some noise coming from the Huron Steel plant prior to 1979, the problems with noise and vibration began when the #1 press was installed. *Rushmer v. Polsue & Afieri Ltd.*, [1906] 1 Ch. 234 (C.A.). . ., stands for the proposition that the addition of a fresh noise may give rise to a nuisance no matter what the character of the locale. In the Court of Appeal decision, Cozens-Hardy L.J. stated at pp. 250-51:

> A resident in such a neighbourhood must put up with a certain amount of noise. The standard of comfort differs according to the situation of the property and the class of people who inhabit it . . . But whatever the standard of comfort in a particular district may be, I think the addition of a fresh noise caused by the defendant's works may be so substantial as to create a legal nuisance. It does not follow that because I live, say, in the manufacturing part of Sheffield I cannot complain if a steam-hammer is introduced next door, and so worked as to render sleep at night almost impossible, although previously to its introduction my house was a reasonably comfortable abode, having regard to the local standard; and it would be no answer to say that the steam-hammer is of the most modern approved pattern and is reasonably worked. In short . . . it is no answer to say that the neighbourhood is noisy, and that the defendant's machinery is of first-class character.

(3) *The utility of the defendant's conduct*

The importance of the defendant's enterprise and its value to the community is a factor in determining if the defendant's conduct is unreasonable. However, this tends to go to the leniency of the remedy, rather than liability itself. Furthermore, the question whether the defendant took all reasonable precautions is relevant as to whether the interference is unreasonable.

Morrison and defendant's counsel mentioned that the Huron Steel plant is important to the community, since it employs about 200 people. Supposedly these jobs would be at risk if Huron Steel were required to make extensive structural changes to the plant to cut the noise and vibration from the #1 press.

. . .

I accept Mr. Morrison's contention that a lot of thought and effort went into the planning, purchase and installation of the #1 press. I also appreciate that the defendant has taken what it considers to be all reasonable and economically practical steps to alleviate the noise and vibration problem. However, the expert evidence indicates that improvements could be made to the building envelope that would ameliorate the situation.

. . .

CONCLUSION ON LIABILITY

The evidence indicates that the defendant's Huron Steel plant operations have caused and continue to cause an unreasonable interference with the plaintiff's use and enjoyment of its property.

. . .

Although this case has certainly not been clear cut, after considering all of the circumstances and factors set out above, I find that on balance of probabilities, the defendant's operations, and the #1 press in particular, do constitute an actionable nuisance.

[The plaintiff was awarded $14,927 for lost rental revenue and $56,500 for the reduction in value of the apartment building. The parties agreed to a remedial course of action and an injunction was granted incorporating the terms of the agreement.]

NOTES AND QUESTIONS

1. What were the plaintiff's allegations of nuisance? The judge considered four criteria in determining whether a nuisance had been committed. Explain in your own words the matters to be considered under each of the criteria. What evidence did the judge consider in assessing each of the criteria? Do you agree with the judge's application of the criteria to the facts? Did the court act controversially when it took the "character of the locale" into account? See Steel, "The Locality Principle in Private Nuisance" [2017] C.L.J. 145; and Hamill, "Location Matters: How Nuisance Governs Access to Property for Free Expression" (2014) 47 U.B.C.L. Rev. 129.

2. Do you think the judge gave equal weight to all four criteria? Should he have done so?

3. Do you think the judge would have resolved this case the same way if:

(a) the #1 press was operating when the apartment building was constructed?

(b) the #1 press operated within Ministry guidelines with occasional violations?

(c) there was another factory on the other side of the apartment building which produced noise and vibrations equal to the #1 press?

(d) the defendant employed 1,000 workers and was the largest single employer in Windsor?

4. The judge in *Huron Steel* stated that a defendant cannot escape liability merely by proving that the plaintiff came to the nuisance. Nevertheless, such evidence can be considered in determining whether the defendant's conduct constituted an unreasonable interference and, hence, a nuisance. See for example the extracts from *Miller v. Jackson*, [1977] Q.B. 966 (C.A.) and *Spur Industries Inc. v. Del E. Webb Development Co.*, 494 P.2d 700 (Ariz. S.C. 1972) that appear later in this chapter.

5. To what extent should economic efficiency determine the issue of reasonableness? If it is cheaper for the plaintiff to avoid the harm than it is for the defendant to adopt an available alternative, is the defendant using its land in a reasonable way? See *Kent v. Dom. Steel & Coal Corp. Ltd.* (1965), 49 D.L.R. (2d) 241 at 246 (Nfld. S.C.); *Renken v. Harvey Aluminum (Inc.)*, 226 F.Supp. 169 (D. Or. 1963); and *Cambridge Water Co. Ltd. v. Eastern Counties Leather plc*, [1994] 2 A.C. 264 (H.L.).

6. A nuisance may occur in a variety of ways. First, the clearest cases occur when the defendant's activity causes *physical damage* to the plaintiff's property. For instance, an industrial plant may emit chemical particles that drift on the wind and ruin the paint on the plaintiff's building, or heavy machinery may cause vibrations that crack the foundations of the plaintiff's house. Second, even if physical damage does not occur, a nuisance may arise if the defendant *impairs the enjoyment* of the plaintiff's property. For instance, a pig farm may cause an unbearable stench to waft over the plaintiff's outdoor café, or an all-night disco may produce a noise that prevents its neighbours from sleeping. Third, and exceptionally, a nuisance may occur even if the defendant's activity is entirely *non-intrusive*. For instance, the defendant's brothel may attract seedy characters into the plaintiff's neighbourhood, or the defendant may install a sewer system that drains water *away* from the plaintiff's land and thereby causes his land to collapse.

Although a nuisance may arise in various ways, the courts are much more likely to find the defendant's interference to be unreasonable if it causes physical damage to the plaintiff's property. Moreover, some courts have said that an interference that falls short of causing material damage must be continuous before it will constitute a nuisance. See for example *Andrews v. R A. Douglas* (1977), 17 N.S.R. (2d) 181 (C.A.); and *Chu v. Dawson* (1984), 31 C.C.L.T. 146 (B.C.C.A.).

7. A private nuisance typically consists of a continuing state of affairs. Going further, in *Colour Quest Ltd. v. Total Downstream U.K. plc*, [2009] 2 Lloyd's Rep 1 (Q.B.), the defendant argued that liability actually requires proof of an ongoing state of affairs. The case arose as a result of a remarkable incident at the Buncefield oil storage depot in England. An enormous vapour cloud, arising from 250,000 litres of leaked petroleum, ignited to create the largest peace-time explosion ever recorded in Europe. Astonishingly, no one was killed, but property damage was extensive and

business losses were substantial. The ensuing litigation contained allegations of private nuisance. In an important preliminary judgment, the court held that a private nuisance could indeed stem from an isolated incident.

The duration of a nuisance may be important in another respect. A right to act in a manner that otherwise would constitute a nuisance may be acquired through *prescription*. That issue arose in *Coventry v. Lawrence*, [2014] UKSC 13. In 1975, the defendant's predecessor in title obtained planning permission to hold car races in an area that was largely devoid of human activity, except for a lone cottage several hundred yards away. The defendant purchased the speedway in 2005. The plaintiffs — most definitely not speedway fans — purchased the cottage in 2006. The plaintiff sued for nuisance; the defendant pleaded prescription. The Supreme Court of the United Kingdom recognized that relief would have been withheld if the plaintiff had allowed the defendant to regularly hold motorcycle races on its land for twenty years. The evidence, however, fell short of showing that the speedway had constituted a nuisance for that entire time. See also *Willis v. Halifax (Regional Municipality)*, 2010 NSCA 76.

8. It is often difficult to predict which interferences will be held to be nuisances. For example, in what circumstances should nuisance protect a landowner's interest in aesthetic scenery? See Noel, "Unaesthetics Sights as Nuisance" (1939) 25 Cornell L. Rev. 1. See also *Muirhead v. Timber Bros. Sand & Gravel Ltd.* (1977), 3 C.C.L.T. 1 (Ont. H.C.); *St. Pierre v. Ontario*, [1987] 1 S.C.R. 906; and *Zbarsky v. Lukashuk*, [1992] 1 W.W.R. 690 (B.C.C.A.).

P. Osborne lists eight factors that commonly affect the determination as to whether the defendant's conduct constitutes a nuisance — *i.e.* an unreasonable interference with the plaintiff's use and enjoyment of land: (1) the *character of the neighbourhood*, (2) the *intensity* of the interference, (3) the *duration* of the interference, (4) the *time* of day and *day* of the week, (5) the *zoning designation* of the neighbourhood, (6) the *utility* of the defendant's conduct, (7) the *nature* of the defendant's conduct, and (8) the *sensitivity* of the plaintiff: Osborne, *The Law of Torts*, 5th ed. (2015) at 398-403.

9. The categories of interests protected by nuisance have expanded to address new uses of property made possible by modern technology. One court, for instance, found that repeated and harassing phone calls constituted a nuisance: *Motherwell v. Motherwell* (1976), 1 A.R. 47 (C.A.). That finding, however, is possible only if the plaintiff suffered a substantial interference with the use and enjoyment of land. The tort is not available for trivial matters: *Martin v. Lavigne*, 2011 BCCA 104. In contrast, a court refused to find a nuisance when the defendant carried on surveillance through the use of vehicles parked near the plaintiff's home: *K.(M.J.) v. M.(J.D.)* (1998), 167 D.L.R. (4th) 334 (Alta. Q.B.). See also *Khorasandjian v. Bush*, [1993] 3 All E.R. 669 (C.A.); and Cooke, "A Development in the Tort of Private Nuisance" (1994) 57 Mod. L. Rev. 289. Furthermore there is no distinct tort of harassment: *Lipischak v. DeWolf*, 2010 ONSC 3449, aff'd 2011 ONCA 634; and *Guillaume v. Toronto (City)*, 2010 ONSC 5045.

10. Liability under the common law tort of private nuisance is strict. "Whether the interference results from intentional, negligent or non-faulty conduct is of no consequence provided that the harm can be characterized as a nuisance": *St. Lawrence Cement Inc. v. Barrette*, [2008] 3 S.C.R. 392 at 431. In contrast, liability in Québec

under Article 976 of the *Civil Code of Québec*, S.Q. 1991, c. 64 traditionally was conceived in terms of fault. That proposition was tested in *St. Lawrence Cement Inc.* From 1955 the defendant operated a cement plant under the authority of a special statute. Aggrieved by the dust, odours and noise associated with the plant, people living in neighbouring areas commenced a class action in 1993. The trial court awarded $15,000,000 in damages because, even though the defendant was not found to be at fault, the plaintiffs had suffered "abnormal annoyances." The Québec Court of Appeal, in contrast, denied that liability for neighbourhood disturbances was no-fault, but imposed liability to the extent that the defendant had failed to honour its legal obligations. On further appeal, however, the Supreme Court of Canada agreed with the reasoning and result in the trial judgment. In doing so, it moved the civilian action closer to the common law tort of nuisance.

11. In *Nor-Video Services Ltd. v. Ontario Hydro* (1978), 84 D.L.R. (3d) 221 (Ont. H.C.), the defendant was held liable in nuisance because the location of its power lines disrupted the plaintiff's television broadcasts. The judge held that watching television was an important incident of ordinary enjoyment of property and an interest worthy of the law's protection and vindication. The defendant's conduct was held to be an unreasonable interference, even though it had acted in good faith in placing its lines in the most economically efficient location.

In *Hunter v. Canary Wharf Ltd.*, [1997] A.C. 655 (H.L.), the House of Lords held that the defendant's lawful construction of an enormous skyscraper, which interfered with the local residents' television reception, did not constitute a private nuisance. The defendant was free to build on its property any structure it wished, provided it did not violate the planning law. The House of Lords distinguished *Nor-Video* on the basis that, in *Hunter*, it was the mere presence of the structure, as opposed to an activity or something emanating from the land, that interfered with the reception.

Is the House of Lords' attempt to distinguish *Nor-Video* compelling? What other legal, economic and social factors might explain the results in these cases? Do you agree with the House of Lords that compliance with planning law should, in effect, immunize property developers from the tort of private nuisance? See generally O'Sullivan, "Nuisance in the House of Lords — Normal Service Resumed" [1997] C.L.J. 483.

12. *Hunter* also raised the issue of who has standing to sue in nuisance. The majority of the House of Lords ruled that only a person with a possessory interest in land can sue in nuisance. Thus, a tenant can sue, but his or her spouse and children cannot. Similarly, a lodger occupying premises under a licence cannot maintain a nuisance action. See Rook, "Private Nuisance — A Proprietary Interest?" (1996) 4 Tort L. Rev. 181; and Cone, "What a Nuisance!" (1997) 113 L.Q.R. 515. But see *Pemberton v. Southwark London Borough Council*, [2000] 3 All E.R. 924 (C.A.); and *Dennis v. Ministry of Defence* [2003] 2 E.G.L.R. 121 (Q.B.).

Standing to sue similarly was an issue in *Pemberton v. Southwark London Borough Council, supra*. The claimant occupied an apartment as a "tolerated trespasser." Although her lease had expired and she had been subject to an order for possession, the landlord chose not to enforce the order or oust the claimant. The premises subsequently were subject to a nuisance committed by the defendant. The Court of Appeal held that the claimant's status as a tolerated trespasser was sufficient to support an action in nuisance.

In *Saik'uz First Nation v. Rio Tinto Alcan Inc.*, 2013 BCSC 2303 the lower court held that members of the Nechako Nations could not maintain a claim in nuisance until their aboriginal title to the land had been formally accepted or established. On appeal, however, Tysoe J.A. found that the right of exclusive possession of the reserve lands supported a claim in private nuisance: 2015 BCCA 154.

13. Even if the defendant did not *create* a nuisance, liability may be imposed for *continuing* a nuisance. This is true if an occupier, despite actual or constructive knowledge of a nuisance, fails to take reasonable steps to abate it. A further question arose in *Delaware Mansions Ltd. v. Westminster City Council*, [2002] A.C. 321 (H.L.). Is relief available if the damage caused by the nuisance already existed *before* the claimant took possession of the adversely affected property? The House of Lords answered in the affirmative. On the facts, Lord Cooke of Thorndon addressed the issue from the perspective of "reasonableness between neighbours." In that respect, he emphasized the continuing nature of the damage and the need for remedial work. It also was significant that the price that the claimant paid for the property had not been reduced to reflect the existing damage. If it had been otherwise, damages would have constituted double recovery for the same loss, and consequently would have been denied. See generally Parker, "A Continued Nuisance" [2002] C.L.J. 260.

14. A typical nuisance case involves a dispute between neighbours. Strictly speaking, however, only the plaintiff needs to have a possessory interest in land. The defendant need not be a neighbour. It is no defence to say, for instance, that an intolerable noise emanates from a vehicle parked on a public street rather than a nightclub located in a nearby building. Unfortunately, courts occasionally fall into error. A notorious example occurred in *Hussain v. Lancaster City Council*, [2000] Q.B. 1 (C.A.). The claimants, who owned a shop on a council estate (a social housing project), were subject to persistent harassment: racial epithets, thrown bricks, smashed windows, intimidating congregations of thugs, and so on. The governing Council was authorized to evict the perpetrators, but aside from issuing idle threats and striking empty poses, it did nothing to end the abuse. The claimants then sued the Council for failing to deal with the problem. That claim was struck out. Labouring under the belief that the tort necessarily involves a dispute between neighbours, the Court of Appeal believed that since the thugs conducted their harassment from the public streets, rather than from their residences, the claim was doomed to fail.

15. Liability in nuisance may be imposed if an occupier (a) knew, or ought to have known, of a hazard created by a third party or by nature, and (b) failed to take reasonable steps to protect neighbouring properties. Relief therefore was available when an occupier failed to abate a nuisance created after a trespasser's unauthorized drainage work caused flooding on the plaintiff's land: *Sedleigh-Denfield v. O'Callaghan*, [1940] A.C. 880 (H.L.). Likewise, while occupiers traditionally enjoyed immunity from an action in nuisance with respect to the natural condition of their property, the scope of liability has been expanded. In *Goldman v. Hargrave*, [1967] 1 A.C. 645 (P.C.) the plaintiff was entitled to compensation after his property was damaged by the spread of a fire that was started by lightning on the defendant's property.

The same principles were applied in *Lippiatt v. South Gloucestershire Council*, [1999] 4 All E.R. 149 (C.A.). The defendant allowed a group of "travellers" to reside on its property for three years. During that time, the travellers frequently trespassed onto the plaintiffs' neighbouring lands, dumping rubbish and excrement, and tethering animals. The court held that, in the circumstances, the defendants could be held liable for the damage done by the travellers who wandered onto the plaintiffs' properties. See also *Turner v. Delta Shelf Co. Ltd.* (1995), 24 C.C.L.T. (2d) 107 (B.C.S.C.); and *270233 Ontario Ltd. v. Weall & Cullen Nurseries Ltd.* (1993), 17 C.C.L.T. (2d) 176 (Ont. Gen. Div.), aff'd (1997), 41 C.C.L.T. (2d) 239 (Ont. C.A.).

16. Although the provincial limitation statutes generally provide that actions expire a fixed number of years (like two or six) after the cause of action arises, in nuisance a new cause of action arises each day the nuisance continues: see *Kerlenmar Holdings Ltd. v. Matsqui (District)* (1991), 81 D.L.R. (4th) 334 (B.C.C.A.).

ANTRIM TRUCK CENTRE LTD. v. ONTARIO (TRANSPORTATION)
2013 SCC 13

[From 1974 until 2004, the appellant operated a service station and restaurant on Highway 17 in Ontario. In 2004, the respondent province opened a new section of Highway 417 that caused traffic to bypass the appellant's premises and effectively put it out of business. The *Expropriations Act*, R.S.O. 1990, c. E-26, entitled the appellant to claim compensation for "injurious affection" if, but for the respondent's statutory authority to operate the new highway, its conduct would have been actionable in private law. The relevant private law action was the tort of nuisance. At first instance, the Ontario Municipal Board upheld the claim and awarded $58,000 for the appellant's loss of business and $335,000 for the lost market value of its land. The Divisional Court agreed, but the Ontario Court of Appeal set aside the Board's decision on the grounds that, in assessing the reasonableness of the respondent's interference with the appellant's use of its land, the Board failed to consider the character of the neighbourhood, the sensitivity of the appellant, and the social utility of the respondent's conduct in providing an essential public service. A further appeal came before the Supreme Court of Canada.]

CROMWELL J.: . . .
[2] The main question on appeal is this: How should we decide whether an interference with the private use and enjoyment of land is unreasonable when it results from construction which serves an important public purpose? The answer, as I see it, is that the reasonableness of the interference must be determined by balancing the competing interests, as it is in all other cases of private nuisance. The balance is appropriately struck by answering the question whether, in all of the circumstances, the individual claimant has shouldered a greater share of the burden of construction than it would be reasonable to expect individuals to bear without compensation. Here, the interference with the appellant's land caused by the construction of the new highway inflicted significant and permanent loss on the appellant; in the circumstances of this case, it was not unreasonable for the Board to conclude that an individual should not be expected to bear such a loss for the greater public good without compensation.

. . .

C. *First Question: What Are the Elements of Private Nuisance?*

[18] The Court of Appeal concluded that a nuisance consists of an interference with the claimant's use or enjoyment of land that is both substantial and unreasonable. In my view, this conclusion is correct.

[19] The elements of a claim in private nuisance have often been expressed in terms of a two-part test of this nature: to support a claim in private nuisance the interference with the owner's use or enjoyment of land must be both *substantial* and *unreasonable*. A substantial interference with property is one that is non-trivial. Where this threshold is met, the inquiry proceeds to the reasonableness analysis, which is concerned with whether the non-trivial interference was also unreasonable in all of the circumstances.

. . .

[21] The two-part approach is . . . analytically sound. Retaining a substantial interference threshold underlines the important point that not every interference, no matter how minor or transitory, is an actionable nuisance; some interferences must be accepted as part of the normal give and take of life. Finally, the threshold requirement of the two-part approach has a practical advantage: it provides a means of screening out weak claims before having to confront the more complex analysis of reasonableness.

. . .

D. *Second Question: How Is Reasonableness Assessed in the Context of Interference Caused by Projects That Further the Public Good?*

[25] The main question here is how reasonableness should be assessed when the activity causing the interference is carried out by a public authority for the greater public good. As in other private nuisance cases, the reasonableness of the interference must be assessed in light of all of the relevant circumstances. The focus of that balancing exercise, however, is on whether the interference is such that it would be unreasonable in all of the circumstances to require the claimant to suffer it without compensation.

[26] In the traditional law of private nuisance, the courts assess, in broad terms, whether the interference is unreasonable by balancing the gravity of the harm against the utility of the defendant's conduct in all of the . . . [S]everal factors . . . have often been referred to in assessing whether a substantial interference is also unreasonable. In relation to the gravity of the harm, the courts have considered factors such as the severity of the interference, the character of the neighbourhood and the sensitivity of the plaintiff. . . . The frequency and duration of an interference may also be relevant in some cases. . . . A number of other factors . . . are relevant to consideration of the utility of the defendant's conduct. The point for now is that these factors are not a checklist; they are simply "[a]mong the criteria employed by the courts in delimiting the ambit of the tort of nuisance": *Tock v. St. John's Metropolitan Area Board*, [1989] 2 S.C.R. 1181 at 1191. . . . Courts and tribunals are not bound to, or limited by, any specific list of factors. Rather, they should consider the substance of the balancing exercise in light of the factors relevant in the particular case.

. . .

[28] [T]here is a distinction between the utility of the conduct, which focuses on its purpose, such as construction of a highway, and the nature of the defendant's

conduct, which focuses on how that purpose is carried out. Generally, the focus in nuisance is on whether the *interference suffered by the claimant* is unreasonable, not on whether *the nature of the defendant's conduct* is unreasonable. . . .

[29] The nature of the defendant's conduct is not, however, an irrelevant consideration. Where the conduct is either malicious or careless, that will be a significant factor in the reasonableness analysis. . . . Moreover, where the defendant can establish that his or her conduct was reasonable, that can be a relevant consideration, particularly in cases where a claim is brought against a public authority. A finding of reasonable conduct will not, however, necessarily preclude a finding of liability. . . .

[30] The . . . utility of the defendant's conduct is especially significant in claims against public authorities. Even where a public authority is involved, however, the utility of its conduct is always considered in light of the other relevant factors in the reasonableness analysis; it is not, by itself, an answer to the reasonableness inquiry. Moreover, in the reasonableness analysis, the severity of the harm and the public utility of the impugned activity are not equally weighted considerations.

. . .

[38] Generally speaking, the acts of a public authority will be of significant utility. If simply put in the balance with the private interest, public utility will generally outweigh even very significant interferences with the claimant's land. That sort of simple balancing of public utility against private harm undercuts the purpose of providing compensation for injurious affection. That purpose is to ensure that individual members of the public do not have to bear a disproportionate share of the cost of procuring the public benefit. This purpose is fulfilled, however, if the focus of the reasonableness analysis is kept on whether it is reasonable for the individual to bear the interference without compensation, not on whether it was reasonable for the statutory authority to undertake the work.

[39] . . . The distinction is thus between, on one hand, interferences that constitute the "give and take" expected of everyone and, on the other, interferences that impose a disproportionate burden on individuals. That . . . is at the heart of the balancing exercise involved in assessing the reasonableness of an interference in light of the utility of the public authority's conduct.

[40] Of course, not every substantial interference arising from a public work will be unreasonable. The reasonableness analysis should favour the public authority where the harm to property interests . . . is such that the harm cannot reasonably be viewed as more than the claimant's fair share of the costs associated with providing a public benefit. This outcome is particularly appropriate where the public authority has made all reasonable efforts to reduce the impact of its works on neighbouring properties.

[41] It is clear . . . that everyone must put up with a certain amount of temporary disruption caused by essential construction.

[42] . . . [T]he duration of the interference is a relevant consideration. Admittedly, duration was not a relevant factor in this case because the injury was permanent. In cases where it is relevant however, it is helpful to consider that some sorts of temporary inconvenience are more obviously part of the normal "give and take" than are more prolonged interferences. While temporary interferences may certainly support a claim in nuisance in some circumstances, interferences that persist for a prolonged period of time will be more likely to attract a remedy. . . .

[43] Another important idea is that the traditional consideration relating to the character of the neighbourhood may be highly relevant in the overall balancing. This point is particularly relevant in cases where a claim is brought against a public authority. . . .

[44] A final point . . . relates to the manner in which the work is carried out. While nuisance focuses mainly on the harm and not on the blameworthiness of the defendant's conduct, the fact that a public work is carried out with "all reasonable regard and care" for the affected citizens is properly part of the reasonableness analysis. . . .

E. *Third Question: Does the Unreasonableness of an Interference Need to Be Considered When That Interference Is Physical or Material?*

[46] The appellant submits that reasonableness does not need to be considered when the interference constitutes "material" or "physical" damage to the land. Reasonableness only needs to be addressed, the submission goes, with respect to other types of interference such as loss of amenities. In this case, the appellant maintains that the damage to its land was "material" and that therefore no reasonableness analysis was necessary. I respectfully disagree. . . .

[47] The distinction between material or physical harms on the one hand and interferences such as loss of amenities on the other has a long history and deep roots . . . . This approach has since been adopted in many Canadian decisions . . . . At the same time, there is appellate authority affirming the need to consider the reasonableness of the interference in every case. . . .

[48] My view is that the reasonableness inquiry should not be short-circuited on the basis of certain categories of interference that are considered self-evidently unreasonable. . . . The sort of balancing inherent in the reasonableness analysis is at the heart of the tort of private nuisance. . . . The legal analysis in a nuisance case is more likely to yield sound results if this essential balancing exercise is carried out explicitly and transparently rather than implicitly by applying a murky distinction.

[49] There are obvious difficulties in making the analysis turn on classifying interferences as constituting material or physical damage. It will not always, or even generally, be a simple matter to distinguish between damage that is "material or physical" and damage that is a simple "loss of amenity". The distinction proposed by the appellant is particularly difficult to apply in cases like this one, where the nuisance is an interference with access to land. The damage to the appellant here could be considered material in the sense that it caused significant financial loss, but it could perhaps also be considered in some sense to be a loss of amenity because there was no harm to the property itself. The property declined in value, but that is also the case in some loss of amenity situations.

[50] While I am not convinced of the usefulness of the distinction between material injury and loss of amenity, I acknowledge that where there is significant and permanent harm caused by an interference, the reasonableness analysis may be very brief. . . . Thus, even though the reasonableness of the interference should be assessed in every case, the court will sometimes quite readily conclude that some types of interferences are unreasonable without having to engage in a lengthy balancing analysis. . .

[51] I therefore conclude that reasonableness is to be assessed in all cases where private nuisance is alleged. Once a claimant passes the threshold test of showing harm

that is substantial in the sense that it is non-trivial, there ought to be an inquiry into whether the interference is unreasonable, regardless of the type of harm involved.

F. *Fourth Question: Did the Court of Appeal Err in Finding That the Board's Application of the Law of Nuisance to the Facts Was Unreasonable?*

[52] I respectfully disagree with the Court of Appeal's approach to the balancing exercise to determine whether the interference was unreasonable. As I see it, there were two errors in its approach.

[53] Having identified the factors noted earlier that are often referred to in carrying out the balancing exercise . . . the Court of Appeal treated them as a mandatory checklist for courts or tribunals considering this issue. It faulted the Board for failing to consider two of the factors. . . . In my respectful view, the Court of Appeal erred in intervening on this ground.

[54] Provided that the Board reasonably carried out the analysis in substance, it was not required to specifically enumerate and refer by name to every factor mentioned in the case law. . . . [T]he factors . . . are simply examples of the sorts of criteria that the courts have articulated as being potentially of assistance in weighing the gravity of the harm with the utility of the defendant's conduct. They do not make up either an exhaustive or an essential list of matters that must be expressly considered in every case. Failure to expressly mention one or more of these factors is not, on its own, a reviewable error.

[55] The Board's task was to determine whether, having regard to all of the circumstances, it was unreasonable to require the appellant to suffer the interference without compensation. . . . Although it did not refer to them by name, the Board took into account the relevant factors in this case. In particular, it considered the extent of the changes to Highway 17, the fact that those changes were considered necessary for public safety, the appellant's knowledge of — and involvement in — the plans to make changes to the highway, and the extent to which the appellant's concerns about the new highway were taken into account by the respondent in its decision making. The Board concluded that the interference resulting from the construction of the highway was serious and would constitute nuisance but for the fact that the work was constructed pursuant to statutory authority. . . .

[56] Similarly . . . the Board did not fail to take account of the utility of the respondent's activity or fail to engage in the required balancing. . . . [T]he Board adverted to the importance of the highway construction. It did not, however, allow that concern to swamp consideration of whether it was reasonable to require the appellant to bear without compensation the burden inflicted on it by the construction. The Board properly understood that the purpose of the statutory compensation scheme for injurious affection was to ensure that individuals do not have to bear a disproportionate burden of damage flowing from interference with the use and enjoyment of land caused by the construction of a public work. It was reasonable for the Board to conclude that in all of the circumstances, the appellant should not be expected to endure permanent interference with the use of its land that caused a significant diminution of its market value in order to serve the greater public good.

[The appeal was allowed and the Board's original decision was restored.]

NOTES AND QUESTIONS

1. According to *Antrim*, what is the test for a private nuisance? What purpose is served by the two-part test that Cromwell J. discussed?

2. *Antrim* states that the issue of reasonableness does not arise unless the plaintiff suffered a substantial injury. A claim in nuisance failed on that basis in *Strand Theatre Ltd. v. Prince Albert (City)*, 2011 SKQB 209, aff'd 2014 SKCA 85. The plaintiff alleged that its groundwater was contaminated by the defendant's landfill. The court, however, found that the toxins were in "such low concentration that they fall well beneath the provincial criteria to be considered harmful contaminants and in concentrations so low that they are in some tests immeasurable."

As demonstrated in *Desando v. Canadian Transit Co.*, 2018 ONSC 1859, the need for a substantial injury may require people to live with decidedly undesirable situations. In anticipation of a new bridge being built between Windsor and Detroit, the defendant purchased and boarded-up 144 houses near the proposed work site. An inability to obtain municipal demolition permits, however, resulted in those houses sitting empty for more than a decade. The owners of neighbouring homes, understandably upset with the eyesore and concerned about vandalism, crime, and breeding vermin, commenced a claim for nuisance. The action was dismissed. The court denied that the claimants had suffered a substantial loss as a result of the defendant's conduct. The neighbourhood had long been deteriorating, in any event, as it transitioned from single-family dwellings to apartment blocks. Being located next to a major bridge, it inevitably was subject to heavy traffic, noise, and pollution. In the circumstances, the loss of use and enjoyment that was attributable to the defendant was not substantial.

3. What is the importance of the various factors (such as the nature of the neighbourhood) that courts traditionally considered in a claim of nuisance? Did the lower courts in *Antrim* properly deal with those factors? Of what significance, if any, is the nature of the defendant's conduct? Is liability more likely if the defendant acted maliciously or carelessly?

4. The courts have recognized two species of nuisance: private nuisance and public nuisance. The latter is considered in more detail later in this chapter. What is the distinction between the two torts? Which type of nuisance was involved in *Antrim*?

5. Does the defendant's character, as either a private party or a public party, determine the type of nuisance that the plaintiff must claim? How, if at all, did the analysis in *Antrim* reflect the fact that the defendant was the Province?

Grand Beach Management Co. v. Manitoba, 2018 MBCA 80 involved a lease that the defendant province had granted to allow the plaintiff to operate a restaurant within a provincial park. Because of complaints arising from alcohol consumed on the premises, the province decided to reduce the restaurant's hours of operation. The plaintiff sued for nuisance; the defendant applied to have the claim struck. The Court of Appeal reversed the motion judge's finding that the action was doomed to fail. Beard J.A. began by recognizing that the existence of a lease does not preclude a tenant from protecting its right of use and enjoyment from a landlord's unreasonable interference. She then observed that the social utility associated with the acts of a public authority are apt to outweigh even significant interferences with an individual claimant's enjoyment of land. She consequently considered it especially important to properly phrase the governing test. The question was not whether it was reasonable for the public authority to undertake the impugned course of conduct, but rather whether it was reasonable to expect the plaintiff to bear the full burden of that conduct without compensation. Quoting *Antrim*, she asked whether the losses flowing from the interference with the claimant's property was "a cost of 'running the system'" that should fall on the community as a whole, or a type of interference that should be accepted by the individual as "a cost of living in an organized society": at para. 40. Seen in that light, it was not obvious that the facts could not sustain a plea of nuisance, and the province's motion to strike was dismissed.

6. If a tort of nuisance is alleged to have arisen in connection with a public authority's provision of an essential public service, how should the law balance the interests of the community and the interests of the individual? Did *Antrim* strike an appropriate balance? Given that the defendant had decided that the new highway configuration was a necessary public service, what, if anything, could it have done to avoid liability to the plaintiff?

7. The rights-based theory was introduced in Chapter 1. That theory insists that liability must be rooted in the violation of rights, rather than the instrumental pursuit of policies like compensation and deterrence. It necessarily follows that liability is impossible if the plaintiff cannot point to a specific right that the defendant has violated. As Neyers explains, that proposition is particularly significant in the context of private nuisance: Neyers & Diacur, "What (Is) A Nuisance?" (2011) 90 Can. Bar Rev. 213. Ownership of land entails certain rights. It endows the title-holder with the right to be free of unwanted intrusions, but it does not carry the right to receive or enjoy some amenity. By analogy, he observes that the right to bodily integrity entails a right to be free of battery, but it does not extend to a right to be rescued. That distinction is critically important in the context of the tort of private nuisance. Cases in which the defendant is responsible for some emanation (such as noise, smells, or vibrations) that intrudes upon the plaintiff's property are easily accommodated with the rights theory. In contrast, Neyers argues, there is no basis for imposing liability if the gist of the action is that the defendant failed to facilitate some benefit that the plaintiff wished to enjoy. Unfortunately, Neyers says, Canadian law fails to appreciate that point. *Antrim* posits a two-part test of private nuisance: substantial interference and unreasonableness. Contrary to the historical precedents, there no longer is any requirement for the plaintiff to establish the existence of a relevant right. Private nuisance is further examined from a rights perspective in Nolan, "A Tort Against Land: Private Nuisance as a Property Tort" in Nolan & Robertson, eds., *Rights and Private Law* (2010), ch. 16; and Wright, "Private Nuisance Law: A Window on Substantive Justice" in Nolan & Robertson, *ibid.*, ch. 17.

HOLLYWOOD SILVER FOX FARM LTD. v. EMMETT
[1936] 2 K.B. 468

[The plaintiff was a breeder of silver foxes. The sign that he had erected to advertise his business annoyed the defendant, who alleged that it was detrimental to his development of a building estate. When the plaintiff refused to move the sign, the defendant threatened to discharge guns near the fox pens during their breeding season in order to interfere with their whelping. When the defendant carried through with this threat, the plaintiff sued in nuisance.]

MACNAGHTEN J.: . . . Mr. Roche, who put the case for the defendant extremely well, argued that if the defendant had sent his son to shoot at the boundary of his land for the purpose of injuring the plaintiff and that if his conduct was malicious because he wanted to harm the plaintiff, nevertheless he had not committed any actionable wrong. The defendant was entitled to shoot on his own land. He might shoot there to keep down rabbits, or he might shoot for his own pleasure and if it pleased him to annoy his neighbour, although his conduct might be considered unneighbourly, he was entitled at law to do so. In the course of his argument, Mr. Roche relied upon the decision of the House of Lords in the case of *Bradford Corpn. v. Pickles* [[1895] A.C. 587]. In that case the Corporation of Bradford sought an injunction to restrain the defendant from sinking a shaft on land which belonged to him because, according to their view, his object in sinking the shaft was to draw away water which would otherwise become the property of the Corporation. Pickles was acting maliciously. His sole object in digging was to do harm to the Corporation. The House of Lords decided, once and for all, that in such a case the motive of the defendant is immaterial.

Mr. Roche contended that in this case the defendant had committed no nuisance at all in the legal sense of this case and he referred to *Robinson v. Kilvert* [(1889), 41 Ch. D. 88]. In that case complaint was made by the appellant that the brown paper which he kept on the ground floor of his premises suffered some damage from heat in the basement below, and it was held by the Court of Appeal that no actionable wrong was being committed by the defendant in that the heating was not of such a character as would interfere with the ordinary use of the rest of the house. He supplemented the argument, based on the consideration of that case, with the observations of Lord Robertson in *Eastern & South African Telegraph Co. v. Cape Town Tramways Cos.*, [[1902] A.C. 381], where Lord Robertson, delivering the judgment of the Privy Council, said, at page 393:

> A man cannot increase the liabilities of his neighbour by applying his own property to special uses, whether for business or pleasure.

It was argued that the keeping of a silver fox farm was not an ordinary use of land in the county of Kent, and what the defendant had done in discharging the bird-scaring cartridges would cause no alarm to the sheep or cattle which are usually to be found on Kentish farms. It was only because Captain Chalmers had brought these highly nervous animals — not natural to this country — that had caused the plaintiffs any loss and if silver foxes were brought to the county of Kent, one could not thereby restrict their neighbours in the matter of shooting. I am not satisfied that there is any substance in that argument. It is a perfectly lawful thing to keep a silver fox farm and I think the fact that the shooting took place intentionally for the purpose of injuring the plaintiffs made it actionable.

The authority for the view that in cases of alleged nuisance by noise, the intention of the person making the noise is not to be disregarded is to be found in the case of *Gaunt v. Fynney* [(1872), 8 Ch. App. 8]. Lord Selborne, L.C., delivered the judgment of the court, and he was dealing there with the question of nuisances, and he said this, at page 12:

A nuisance by noise (supposing malice to be out of the question) is emphatically a question of degree.

It has been observed by high authority that Lord Selborne was always extremely careful in the use of language and that parenthetical statement "supposing malice to be out of the question" clearly indicates what his Lordship thought in the case of alleged nuisance by noise, where the noise was made maliciously. Different considerations would apply to cases where that ingredient was absent. Indeed, the matter is put beyond doubt by the decision of North, J., in *Christie v. Davey* [[1893] 1 Ch. 316]. The plaintiff and the defendant lived side by side in semi-detached houses in Brixton. The plaintiff was a teacher of music and he had a musical family. The result was that throughout clouds of music pervaded his house and were heard in the house of his neighbour. His neighbour did not like music to be heard and after writing rather an unfortunate letter of protest, he took to making noises himself by beating trays and rapping on the wall, and thereupon the music teacher brought an action for an injunction. The action came before North, J., and he delivered judgment in favour of the plaintiff and granted an injunction restraining the defendant from permitting any sounds or noises in his house so as to annoy the plaintiff or the occupiers of his house, and in the course of his judgment he said, at page 326:

> The result is that I think I am bound to interfere for the protection of the plaintiffs. In my opinion the noises which were made in the defendant's house were not of a legitimate kind. They were what, to use the language of Lord Selborne in *Gaunt v. Fynney* [above] "ought to be regarded as excessive and unreasonable." I am satisfied that they were made deliberately and maliciously for the purpose of annoying the plaintiffs. If what has taken place had occurred between two sets of persons, both perfectly innocent, I should have taken an entirely different view of the case. But I am persuaded that what was done by the defendant was done only for the purpose of annoyance, and in my opinion it was not a legitimate use of the defendant's house to use it for the purpose of vexing and annoying his neighbours.

. . .

In my opinion, the authorities to which I have referred support the view that a person who shoots on his own land, or makes other noises on his own land, for the purpose of annoying or injuring his neighbour, does, by the common law, commit the actionable wrong of nuisance for which he is liable in damages at common law and was liable to be restrained by an injunction in a court of equity before the Judicature Act. I think that the plaintiff is entitled to maintain this action and he has established the cause of action which he alleged.

. . .

[The plaintiff was awarded £250 in damages and granted an injunction which was limited to the breeding season.]

NOTES AND QUESTIONS

1. What is the relationship between the defendant's motive and the elements of a nuisance action? How did the court deal with this issue? See *A.G. Man. v. Campbell* (1985), 32 C.C.L.T. 57 (Man. C.A.).

2. In *Hollywood*, would the shooting have constituted a nuisance if it had been carried out for a legitimate purpose, such as destroying rodents on the defendant's land? *See Rattray v. Daniels* (1959), 17 D.L.R. (2d) 134 (Alta. C.A.).

3. How did the court in *Hollywood* deal with the defendant's contention that it could not be held liable due to the principles established in *Bradford Corp. v. Pickles*, [1895] A.C. 587 (H.L.)? Can you reconcile the decisions in *Hollywood* and *Bradford*? For conflicting interpretations of these two cases, see Sappideen & Vines, eds., *Fleming's The Law of Torts*, 10th ed. (2011) at 504-06; and Heuston & Buckley, *Salmond and Heuston on the Law of Torts*, 21st ed. (1996) at 62.

4. It generally is accepted that an individual's ordinarily innocuous conduct will not constitute a nuisance simply because the plaintiff is abnormally sensitive to that conduct. The defendant in *Hollywood* argued that the plaintiff only suffered loss because he had put his land to an extraordinary use that made him abnormally vulnerable to the sound of gun shots. How did the court address this argument? Do you agree with the court's analysis? For a criticism of that analysis, see *Nor-Video Services Ltd. v. Ontario Hydro* (1978), 84 D.L.R. (3d) 221 (Ont. H.C.); *1631370 Ontario Inc. v. 805352 Ontario Inc.*, 2012 ONSC 2271; *Martin v. Lavigne*, 2011 BCCA 104; *Devon Lumber Co. v. MacNeill* (1987), 42 C.C.L.T. 192 (N.B.C.A.); and *Ward v. Magna International Inc.* (1994), 21 C.C.L.T. (2d) 178 (Ont. Gen. Div.).

(a) DEFENCE OF STATUTORY AUTHORITY

TOCK v. ST. JOHN'S METROPOLITAN AREA BOARD
(1989), 64 D.L.R. (4th) 620 (S.C.C.)

LA FOREST J. (Dickson C.J. concurring):—In the early afternoon of October 10, 1981, a day of exceptionally heavy rainfall, the Tocks discovered that a large amount of water had entered their basement. They immediately notified the Board and attempted, in vain, to pump the water out themselves. Two employees of the Board came to inspect the storm sewer in the vicinity and determined that the sewer was blocked. A crew was summoned and by early evening it had located and removed the blockage. Within ten to fifteen minutes of the removal, the water drained from the basement which had, by this time, incurred substantial damage.

. . .

The trial judge, Adams C.J. Dist. Ct., held that the flooding was caused by the blockage and not by the exceptionally heavy rainfall. He went on to dismiss the claim in negligence, holding that the Board had not been negligent in the construction, maintenance or operation of the storm sewer. He did, however, hold that the escape of the water into the Tock's residence constituted a serious interference with their right of enjoyment of their property and, in consequence, allowed the claim in nuisance. In his opinion, the collection and drainage of water from rain or other sources constituted a non-natural user of land within the meaning of the rule in *Rylands v. Fletcher*. In the result, the trial judge awarded the Tocks a total of $13,456.11 in damages.

The Newfoundland Court of Appeal reversed this judgment. Gushue J.A., writing for a unanimous court, held that the rule in *Rylands v. Fletcher* had no application. In his view, the provisioning of an indispensable service such as a water and sewer system could not be held to constitute a non-natural user of land within the meaning of the rule.

On the question of nuisance, Gushue J.A. expressed the view that a claim in nuisance would not lie against a municipal corporation for damage resulting from a service provided under statutory authority if that body could establish that the occurrence complained of was inevitable in the sense that it could not have been avoided by the exercise of all reasonable and available expertise and care in the design, construction and operation of the service. On the facts, he concluded that the Board had satisfied the onus of demonstrating that it had done everything that could reasonably be expected to avoid the occurrence.

. . .

Turning to the question of inevitability, it seems to me that, in strict logic, most nuisances stemming from activities authorized by statute *are* in fact inevitable. Certainly, if one is to judge from the frequency with which storm drain and sewer cases occur in the reports, it would seem a safe conclusion that blockage of such systems is inevitable if one accepts this to mean that it is demonstrably impossible to operate these systems without such occurrences. But what escapes me is why any particular importance should be accorded this fact when weighing a nuisance claim against a statutory authority. The fact that the operation of a given system will inevitably visit random damage on certain unfortunate individuals among the pool of users of the system does not tell us why those individuals should be responsible for paying for that damage.

. . .

I would allow the appeal, set aside the judgment of the Court of Appeal and restore the judgment of the trial judge. The appellants are entitled to their costs throughout.

The judgment of Lamer, Wilson and L'Heureux-Dubé JJ. was delivered by

WILSON J.—I have had the benefit of reading the reasons for judgment of my colleague, Justice La Forest, and, while I agree with his proposed disposition of the appeal, I have reservations about his approach to the law of nuisance as it applies to public bodies acting under statutory authority. The facts are set out in detail by my colleague and I need not repeat them here.

I agree with my colleague's conclusion that the rule in *Rylands v. Fletcher* (1868), L.R. 3 H.L. 330, has no application to this case but that the appellants are entitled to recover from the respondent in nuisance. I agree with him also that the Court of Appeal erred in concluding that if the respondent could show that it had not been negligent, then it could not be liable in nuisance.

I do not, however, share La Forest J.'s view that this Court should, or indeed can, on this appeal virtually abolish the defence of statutory authority for policy reasons and treat municipalities exercising statutory authority in the same way as private individuals. Such a major departure from the current state of the law would, it seems to me, require the intervention of the legislature.

Moreover, I do not favour replacing the existing law in this area with a general test of whether it is reasonable or unreasonable in the circumstances of the case to award compensation. This test may, because of the high degree of judicial subjectivity involved in its application, make life easier for the judges but, in my respectful view, it will do nothing to assist public bodies to make a realistic assessment of their exposure in carrying out their statutory mandate. Nor will it provide much guidance to litigants in deciding whether or not to sue. It is altogether too uncertain. Nor can I, with respect, accept the proposition that a single individual suffering damage from an isolated nuisance should be dealt with differently from a group of people suffering damage from an ongoing nuisance. This seems to me to be quite incompatible with the concept of principled decision-making. Accordingly, while I agree with my colleague in the result he has reached in this case, I prefer to write my own concurring reasons.

I agree that the flooding of the appellants' basement constituted an unreasonable interference with the appellants' use and enjoyment of the property and that, had the parties been two private individuals, it clearly would have been an actionable nuisance. However, since the respondent is a municipality, the law dictates that different considerations apply. The crucial question is whether or not the respondent is able to rely on the defence of statutory authority in the circumstances of this case.

Since the availability of the defence of statutory authority depends on the language of the statute I set out the relevant provisions of *The Municipalities Act*, S.N. 1979, c. 33, on which the respondent must rely:

> 154. (1) The council may, subject to the provisions of *The Department of Consumer Affairs and Environment Act, 1973* and regulations made thereunder, construct, acquire, establish, own and operate
>
>> (a) a public water supply system for the distribution of water within or, with the approval of the Minister, outside of the town,
>> (b) a public sewerage system, either independently of or in conjunction with a public water supply system, for the collection and disposal of sewerage within or, with the approval of the Minister, outside of the town, and
>> (c) a storm drainage system within or, with the approval of the Minister, outside of the town.
>
> (2) For the purposes of subsection (1) the council may
>
>> (a) acquire any waters required for the purpose of providing a sufficient supply of water for the town, and
>> (b) acquire by purchase or expropriation any lands adjacent to such waters to prevent pollution of those waters.
>
> (3) For the purpose of exercising its powers under subsection (1) the council may lay out, excavate, dig, make, build, maintain, repair, and improve all such drains, sewers, and water supply pipes as the council deems necessary.

There is no doubt that these provisions authorize the respondent to construct and continue to operate and maintain the sewage system in question. They are, however, permissive as opposed to mandatory. They confer a power; they do not impose a duty. Is this distinction relevant to the question of the respondent's liability in nuisance?

. . .

The principles to be derived from the . . . authorities would seem to be as follows:

> (a) if the legislation imposes a duty and the nuisance is the inevitable consequence of discharging that duty, then the nuisance is itself authorized and there is no recovery in the absence of negligence;
> (b) if the legislation, although it merely confers an authority, is specific as to the manner or location of doing the thing authorized and the nuisance is the

inevitable consequence of doing the thing authorized in that way or in that location, then likewise the nuisance is itself authorized and there is no recovery absent negligence.

However:

> (c) if the legislation confers an authority and also gives the public body a discretion, not only whether to do the thing authorized or not, but how to do it and in what location, then if it does decide to do the thing authorized, it must do it in a manner and at a location which will avoid the creation of a nuisance. If it does it in a way or at a location which gives rise to a nuisance, it will be liable therefor, whether there is negligence or not.

In other words, in the situations described in (a) and (b) above the inevitability doctrine is a good defence to the public body absent negligence. In situation (c) it is no defence at all and it is unnecessary for the plaintiff to prove negligence in order to recover.

In my view, these principles make a great deal of sense. The inevitability doctrine represents a happy judicial compromise between letting no one who has suffered damage as a consequence of the statutorily authorized activities of public bodies recover and letting everyone so suffering damage recover. Recovery will be allowed unless it is shown that the interference with the plaintiff's rights was permitted by either:

(1) express language in the statute such as a provision specifying that no action for nuisance may be brought for any damage caused. . .; or

(2) by necessary implication from the language of the statute coupled with a factual finding that the damage was the inevitable consequence of what the statute ordered or authorized the public body to do.

. . .

In my view, to the extent that some of the more recent cases are inconsistent with the early principles, they should not be followed. I find no acceptable rationale for the extension of the inevitable consequences doctrine to cases where the public body was perfectly free to exercise its statutory authority without violating private rights. It is only in cases where the public body has no choice as to the way in which or the place where it engages in the nuisance-causing activity that the inevitable consequences doctrine protects it. For only in such cases can it be said that the legislature has authorized any nuisance which is the inevitable consequence of the public body's carrying out its mandate.

. . .

The legislation in this case was purely permissive within the meaning of these cases. It authorized a sewage system to be constructed but did not specify how or where it was to be done. The respondent was accordingly obliged to construct and operate the system in strict conformity with private rights. It did not do so. The defence of statutory authority is not available to it and the appellants are entitled to recover.

SOPINKA J. . . . . The burden of proof with respect to the defence of statutory authority is on the party advancing the defence. It is not an easy one. The courts strain against a conclusion that private rights are intended to be sacrificed for the common good. The defendant must negative that there are alternate methods of carrying out the work. The mere fact that one is considerably less expensive will not avail. If only one method is practically feasible, it must be established that it was practically impossible to avoid the nuisance. It is insufficient for the defendant to negative negligence. The standard is a higher one. While the defence gives rise to some factual difficulties, in view of the allocation of the burden of proof they will be resolved against the defendant.

If we are to depart from this state of the law, so recently confirmed by two decisions of this Court, there should be very strong ground for so doing. Moreover, there should be substantial unanimity. It is apparent from the reasons in this appeal that there is little unanimity as to whether we should retrench, advance or stay the same.

The change proposed by La Forest J. subsumes the defence of statutory authority within the test as to when it is reasonable to compensate the plaintiff. Trial judges will still have to grapple with the elements of the defence of statutory authority but in the context of a test of reasonableness. This will simply add uncertainty to any uncertainty which is said to exist.

Nor do I agree that it is logical or practical to distinguish between public works that are required and those that are permitted. While it was fashionable to require such works in the railway building age, mandatory public works are a feature of a by-gone era.

The disagreement with the result reached in the Court of Appeal is not because the law is defective but because it was incorrectly applied. As La Forest J. points out, the Court of Appeal exonerated the respondent from liability in nuisance on the basis that there was an absence of negligence. In my opinion, the heavier onus which must be discharged was not met in this case. The trial judge so found. I therefore would dispose of the appeal as proposed by my colleagues.

NOTES AND QUESTIONS

1. What is the major premise in each of the three judgments? With which judgment do you most agree?

2. A period of confusion followed *Tock* as lawyers and judges attempted to digest all three opinions. The situation was clarified, however, when the Supreme Court of Canada unanimously adopted Sopinka J.'s view in *Ryan v. Victoria (City)* (1999), 168 D.L.R. (4th) 513 (S.C.C.). Accordingly, the defence of statutory authority applies only if the defendant proves that it was practically impossible to avoid creating a nuisance. See Rafferty, "Tortious Liability of Railways: Defences of Statutory Compliance and Statutory Authority" (1999) 44 C.C.L.T. (2d) 55; and Rafferty, "Developments in Contract and Tort Law: The 1998-1999 Term" (2000) 11 S.C.L.R. 183. For applications of *Tock*, see *St. John's (City) v. Lake* (2000), 192 Nfld. & P.E.I.R. 84 (Nfld. C.A.); *Mandrake Management Consultants Ltd. v. Toronto Transit Commission* (1993), 102 D.L.R. (4th) 12 (Ont. C.A.); and *Canada (A.G.) v. Ottawa Carleton (City)* (1991), 5 O.R. (3d) 11 (C.A.).

3. All of the judges in *Tock* agreed that the tort of nuisance will not be defeated by proof that the defendant neither intentionally nor carelessly caused the plaintiff's injury. In contrast, liability cannot be imposed under the general tort of negligence

unless the defendant breached the standard of care. Why should the defendant be treated differently depending upon whether the plaintiff's injury arises from nuisance rather than negligence? What is so special about an infringement of the plaintiff's enjoyment of land? The courts' attempts to distinguish between the two torts has not always been helpful. See for example *Overseas Tankship (U.K.) Ltd. v. Miller S.S. Co. Pty.*, [1967] 1 A.C. 617 at 639-40 (P.C.). See also Newark, "The Boundaries of Nuisance" (1949) 65 L.Q.R. 480; and Sappideen & Vines, eds., *Fleming's The Law of Torts*, 10th ed. (2011) at 506.

4. A defence of statutory authority may be created not only by a statute, but also by subordinate legislation, such as orders-in-council and regulations. That was true in *Sutherland v. Canada (Attorney General)* (2002), 215 D.L.R. (4th) 1 (B.C.C.A.). The plaintiffs proved that the noise generated by the operation of a new airport runway constituted a nuisance. The British Columbia Court of Appeal nevertheless denied their claim. The noise was the inevitable product of subordinate legislation. The governing statutes authorized an order-in-council which included a lease that required the Vancouver Airport Authority to construct the new runway. That lease stipulated the location and configuration of the runway, and those details had to be satisfied before an airport certificate would be issued.

5. The defence of statutory authority was successfully invoked in *Susan Heyes Inc. (Hazel & Co.) v. South Coast B.C. Transportation Authority*, 2011 BCCA 77. In anticipation of the 2012 Vancouver Winter Olympics, a new subway line was to be built between the airport and the downtown area. Although it initially was suggested that the line would be built underground, the relevant section ultimately was built above ground by "cut and cover" construction. Because its business was located in the affected area, the plaintiff suffered a substantial loss of revenue between 2005 and 2008. The trial judge found a nuisance and awarded damages of $600,000. The British Columbia Court of Appeal, however, held that the defendant was protected by the defence of statutory authority. True, the legislative regime in place did not formally dictate the mode of construction. And true, the plaintiff would not have suffered a similar nuisance if the line had been tunneled underground. Once cost and safety considerations were taken into account, however, cut and cover was the only feasible means of proceeding. The nuisance consequently was the inevitable result of the statutory authority.

In contrast, the defence was rejected in *Rideau Falls Generating Partnership v. Ottawa (City)* (1999), 174 D.L.R. (4th) 160 (Ont. C.A.). Pursuant to a legislative scheme, the defendant operated a system to prevent upstream flooding in the springtime. For that purpose, it broke up river ice and sent it over a set of falls. The plaintiff's property was located at the foot of the falls. It suffered flood damage as a result of the defendant's operations. The court held that the defence of statutory authority was inapplicable because the defendant had "fallen far short of establishing that it was practically impossible to avoid the nuisance."

6. Aside from the defence of *statutory authority*, the plaintiff may also be met by the defence of *statutory immunity*. Legislation may be enacted that expressly exempts certain forms of activity from liability. For instance, the Manitoba *Nuisance Act*, R.S.M. 1987, c. N.120 states:

2. A person who carries on a business and who, in respect of that business, does not violate

(a) any land use control law; or

(b) *The Public Health Act*; or

(c) any regulation under *The Public Health Act* that deals specifically with the carrying on of that class or type of business; or

(d) *The Clean Environment Act*; or

(e) an order of the Clean Environment Commission made under *The Clean Environment Act* in respect of the business; or

(f) any regulation under *The Clean Environment Act* that deals specifically with the carrying on of that class or type of business;

is not liable in nuisance to any person for any odour resulting from the business and shall not be prevented by injunction or other order of a court from carrying on the business because it causes or creates an odour that constitutes a nuisance.

3. Where a plaintiff or claimant in an action or proceeding against a person who carries on a business claims

(a) damages in nuisance for an odour resulting from the business; or

(b) an injunction or other order of a court preventing the carrying on of the business because it causes or creates an odour that constitutes a nuisance;

the onus of proving that the defendant violated any land use control law, or any Act, regulation or order mentioned in clause 2(b), (c), (d), (e) or (f) lies on the plaintiff or claimant.

It has been suggested that this legislation was a response to lobbying by hog farmers: Osborne, *The Law of Torts*, 5th ed. (2015) at 413. See also *Farm Practices Protection Act*, S.M. 1992, c. 41; *Farm Practices Protection (Right to Farm) Act*, R.S.B.C. 1996, c. 131, s. 2; *Farming and Food Protection Act*, S.O. 1998, c. 1, s. 2; and *Pyke v. TriGro Enterprises Ltd.* (2001), 204 D.L.R. (4th) 400 (Ont. C.A.). How does the defence of statutory immunity differ from the defence of statutory authority?

7. The tort of private nuisance may also be met by the defence of *public interest*. That possibility was recognized in *Dennis v. Ministry of Defence*, [2003] 2 E.G.L.R. 121 (Q.B.). The claimant's rural home was located near a property that the military used as a training base for pilots of Harrier jets (also known as "jump jets"). Harrier jets are unique insofar as they are capable of taking off and landing vertically, like a helicopter. Unfortunately for the claimant, the mechanical process required to achieve such feats produced a "particularly fearsome" noise. The flights, which occurred on weekdays, sometimes as late as 11:00 p.m., shook buildings, terrified children, and made conversation and thought impossible. The situation unsurprisingly adversely affected the value of the neighbouring properties. The claimant sought compensation and a declaration of his infringed rights. While the defendant was statutorily protected against injunctive relief, it had developed the practice of respecting such declarations by refraining from the impugned acts. The claimant in this case hoped for such a result.

The defendant resisted liability by arguing that "defence of the realm . . . was a public interest of a different and greater order altogether from commerce and other interests hitherto considered." It further argued that the training of Harrier pilots was essential to the public's interest in a state-of-the-art military. Buckley J. agreed that the circumstances called for special consideration, but denied that public interest was conclusive. He held instead that a determination as to whether a nuisance has been committed requires consideration of all of the facts. He further held that compensation generally is appropriate when the burdens associated with the public interest otherwise would fall heavily on a single person or a small group of individuals.

On the facts, Buckley J. accepted that the public interest demands the training of Harrier pilots and he therefore refused to issue a declaration. He nevertheless held that the defendant's actions constituted a nuisance and awarded £950,000 in damages. The compensatory award was intended to cover past losses and losses expected to accrue until 2012, when the Harrier training program was scheduled to end.

When, if ever, should public interest override a property owner's general right to be free of unreasonable interference? How does Buckley J.'s attitude regarding injunctive (or injunctive-like) relief compare to the courts' usual approach to such remedies? Would it ever be justifiable, for the sake of public interest, to deny both injunctive relief and compensation? See generally Elvin, "The Law of Nuisance and the Human Rights Act" [2003] C.L.J. 546; and Bagshaw, "Private Nuisance and the Defence of the Realm" (2004) 120 L.Q.R. 37.

8. *Coventry v. Lawrence*, [2014] UKSC 13 involved a variation on the themes addressed in these notes. In 1975, a planning authority granted the defendants permission to use their property for car racing for ten years. In 1985, that permission was made permanent. Because the speedway was located in an otherwise isolated area, the defendants heard no complaints until the claimants purchased Fenland, a house located several hundred yards away. When the claimants sued over the noise, the defendants sought protection in the fact that their activities had received planning permission. Lord Neuberger rejected that argument. To begin, a "planning permission . . . does not mean that [a particular] development is lawful. All it means is that a bar to the use imposed by planning law, in the public interest, has been removed": at para. 89. Furthermore, it is "wrong in principle that, through the grant of a planning permission, a planning authority should be able to deprive a property-owner of a right to object to what would otherwise be a nuisance, without providing her with compensation": at para. 90.

9. A claim of nuisance may also be met by a number of other defences. Liability may be precluded if the plaintiff encouraged or clearly consented to the defendant's activities: *McCallum v Kent (District)*, [1943] 3 W.W.R. 489 (B.C.C.A.); *Bartlett v. Corner Brook (City)*, 2003 NLCA 10; and *Innes v. Kotylak*, 2018 SKQB 325. Moreover, while seldom successfully invoked, the defence of contributory negligence may be used to reduce damages. And, of course, under general contract principles, the right to bring a claim for a continuing or repeated nuisance may be barred if the plaintiff and the defendant previously had entered into a settlement of all related claims: *Drader v. Abbotsford (City)*, 2013 BCCA 376.

The defendant may also plead "prescription." After an uninterrupted period of 20 years, the defendant's conduct may become "retrospectively legalised as if it had been authorized by a grant from the owner of the servient land": Sappideen & Vines, eds., *Fleming's The Law of Torts*, 10th ed. (2011) at 517. This defence can be invoked only if (a) the nature of the nuisance remains the same over the period, and (b) the plaintiff was aware of the nuisance. See *Coventry v. Lawrence, supra*; *Sturges v. Bridgman* (1879), 11 Ch. D. 852 (C.A.); *Pilliterri v. Nor. Const. Co.* (1930), 66 O.L.R. 128 (T.D.); *Russell Transport Ltd. v. Ontario Malleable Iron Co.*, [1952] 4 D.L.R. 719

(Ont. H.C.); and *Schenck v. R.; Rokeby v. R.* (1981), 34 O.R. (2d) 595 (H.C.), aff'd [1987] 2 S.C.R. 289.

10. As the preceding cases and notes illustrate, the law of nuisance frequently is used to resolve conflicts between two lawful and socially useful activities. Traditionally, the courts have assumed that the active party has caused the harm. Although the active party's interest in the use of land is considered, the law favours the passive user. That view was challenged by R. Coase in an influential article, "The Problem of Social Cost" (1960) 3 J.L. & Econ. 1. He argued that nuisance raises the issue of *reciprocity*. By preventing the defendant from interfering with the plaintiff's use of land, a court necessarily prevents the defendant from using its land for its desired lawful purpose. Coase argued that unless the law has a more important reason for favouring one party over another, it should resolve the issue in a manner which maximizes scarce social resources. Liability therefore should be imposed on the *cheapest cost avoider* — *i.e.* the party that can avoid the harm at the lowest cost. That calculation will favour the passive user in some cases and the active user in others.

Can Coase's analysis adequately take into account variables such as peace and quiet, clean air, and unpolluted water that have no easily ascertainable economic value? Do the courts have the ability or sufficient evidence to make determinations about the "cheapest cost avoider?" For a critique of Coase's analysis, see Simpson, "*Coase v. Pigou* Re-examined" (1996) 25 J. Legal Stud. 53; Fletcher, "Fairness and Utility in Tort Theory" (1972) 85 Harv. L. Rev. 537; Epstein, "A Theory of Strict Liability" (1973) 2 J. Legal Stud. 151; Gjerdingen, "The Coase Theorem and the Psychology of Common-Law Thought" (1983) 56 S. Cal. L. Rev. 711; and White, "Risk-Utility Analysis and the Learned Hand Formula: A Hand that Helps or a Hand that Hides?" (1990) 32 Ariz. L. Rev. 77.

3. Public Nuisance

The discussion to this point has considered the concept of *private nuisance*. It now is necessary to consider the distinct concept of *public nuisance*. A public nuisance may take one of two forms.

- *Common Interests*: A public nuisance may arise if the defendant's conduct unreasonably interferes with rights, resources, or interests that are common to the entire community. This may be true, for example, if the defendant blocks a public highway, pollutes a river, or operates a bawdy house.

- *Private Interests Combined*: A public nuisance may arise if the defendant's conduct unreasonably interferes, on a large scale, with the use and enjoyment of *private* property. This is true, for example, if the defendant's factory emits noxious fumes that cause damage to every nearby house. In this situation, two options exist. Each affected homeowner may sue individually in *private* nuisance and seek *private* remedies. Alternatively, the interests of the affected homeowners may be joined together in an action for *public* nuisance that seeks *public* remedies. It often is difficult, however, to determine whether the defendant's conduct adversely affects a sufficient number of *private* claimants so as to support a claim of *public* nuisance. The courts generally ask whether the individual claimants constitute a sufficient "class," and it appears that a public claim generally becomes available as membership in the class approaches ten.

Public nuisances usually are addressed through public law. Section 180(2) of the *Criminal Code*, R.S.C. 1985, c. C-46, defines the crime of "common nuisance":

[E]very one commits a common nuisance who does an unlawful act or fails to discharge a legal duty and thereby

(a) endangers the lives, safety, health, property or comfort of the public; or
(b) obstructs the public in the exercise or enjoyment of any right that is common to all the subjects of Her Majesty in Canada.

If the defendant's conduct constitutes a criminal offence, the government may prosecute. The Attorney General, as the representative of the public, may also sue the defendant for damages and an injunction, or may consent to a *relator action* that allows a private citizen to seek relief in the Attorney General's name. The Attorney General has a virtually unfettered discretion in deciding whether to prosecute criminally, sue civilly, or consent to a relator action.

It occasionally is possible for a private person to sue in his or her own name, but only if that person has suffered some special injury, above and beyond the injury experienced by other members of the public. The development of that private action for public nuisance has generated considerable controversy.

In the following section, we focus on two main issues. First, how do the courts distinguish between private and public nuisance? Second, how do the courts determine which plaintiffs will be permitted to maintain private actions for public nuisance?

A.-G. ONT. v. ORANGE PRODUCTIONS LTD.
(1971), 21 D.L.R. (3d) 257 (Ont. H.C.)

[The Attorney-General sought an interim injunction to restrain the defendants from holding an outdoor rock concert, alleging that it would constitute a public nuisance. Evidence was given that there had been acts of trespass to private property, public sexual intercourse, and public consumption of alcohol and illicit drugs at one of the defendant's previous concerts.]

WELLS C.J.H.C.:—The law relating to public nuisance had its flowering in the late 18th Century and the early 19th Century. However, in 1957, a case, *A.-G. v. P.Y.A. Quarries, Ltd.*, [1957] 1 All E.R. 894, arising from the operation of a quarry in Wales, came before the Court of Appeal in England. A very strong Court consisting of Lord Justice Denning (as he then was), Lord Justice Parker (as he then was) and Lord Justice Romer considered the matter at some length. The principal judgment is that of Romer L.J. He went into the matter in great detail taking into account the various historical definitions of public nuisance over at last two centuries. I do not propose to set out this very detailed review he made but he went back to cases in the middle and late 18th Century and came down from the 19th Century up to the time he gave his judgment. . . . But it is of great assistance in dealing with the problem before me. His conclusions are found at p. 902 and are briefly set out as follows:

The expression "the neighbourhood" has been regarded as sufficiently defining the area affected by a public nuisance in other cases also (see, for example, *A.-G. v. Stone* (1895), 60 J.P. 168; *A.-G. v. Cole & Son*, [1901] 1 Ch. 205; and *A.-G. v. Corke*, [1933] Ch. 89). I do not propose to attempt a more precise definition of public nuisance than those which emerge from the textbooks and authorities to which I have referred. It is, however, clear, in my opinion, that any nuisance is "public" which materially affects the reasonable comfort and convenience of life of a class of Her Majesty's subjects. The sphere of nuisance may be described generally as "the neighbourhood"; but the question whether the local community within that sphere comprises a sufficient number of persons to constitute a class of the public is a question of fact in every case. It is not necessary, in my judgment, to prove that every member of the class has been injuriously affected; it is sufficient to show that a representative cross-section of the class has been so affected for an injunction to issue.

. . .

It was, of course, argued by the defendant quarry that this was in effect a private nuisance and that the action should not have been brought by the Attorney-General on behalf of the public generally, and at p. 906 Romer, L.J., made the following pertinent observations:

Some public nuisances (for example, the pollution of rivers) can often be established without the necessity of calling a number of individual complainants as witnesses. In general, however, a public nuisance is proved by the cumulative effect which it is shown to have had on the people living within its sphere of influence. In other words, a normal and legitimate way of proving a public nuisance is to prove a sufficiently large collection of private nuisances. I am therefore of opinion that there was nothing improper or irregular in the statement of claim as originally delivered, or in the reception at the trial of evidence of the local residents' experiences.

It was also evident that, despite the strongly expressed public discontent with the operation of the quarry, the defendants had paid scant attention to the local residents or the representations of the local authorities and that they were slow to adopt the improvements suggested with reference to the escape of dust which was reasonable to the people living around the quarry. All these matters are found in the present case before me.

Before I part with the case I think I should deal with some of the observations of Lord Justice Denning (as he then was). At p. 908 he dealt with the question as to the distinction between public and private nuisance and he expressed himself as follows:

The classic statement of the difference is that a public nuisance affects Her Majesty's subjects generally, whereas a private nuisance only affects particular individuals. But this does not help much. The question: when do a number of individuals become Her Majesty's subjects generally? is as difficult to answer as the question: when does a group of people become a crowd? Everyone has his own views. Even the answer "Two's company, three's a crowd" will not command the assent of those present unless they first agree on "which two". So here I decline to answer the question how many people are necessary to make up Her Majesty's subjects generally. I prefer to look to the reason of the thing and to say that a public nuisance is a nuisance which is so widespread in its range or so indiscriminate in its effect that it would not be reasonable to expect one person to take proceedings on his own responsibility to put a stop to it, but that it should be taken on the responsibility of the community at large. Take the blocking up of a public highway or the non-repair of it; it may be a footpath very little used except by one or two householders; nevertheless the obstruction affects everyone indiscriminately who may wish to walk along it. Take next a landowner who collects pestilential rubbish near a village or permits gypsies with filthy habits to encamp on the edge of a residential neighbourhood. The householders nearest to it suffer the most, but everyone in the neighbourhood suffers too. In such cases the

Attorney-General can take proceedings for an injunction to restrain the nuisance: and when he does so he acts in defence of the public right, not for any sectional interest: see *A.-G. v. Bastow*, [1957] 1 All E.R. 497. When, however, the nuisance is so concentrated that only two or three property owners are affected by it, such as the three attornies in Clifford's Inn, then they ought to take proceedings on their own account to stop it and not expect the community to do it for them; see *R. v. Lloyd* ((1802), 4 Esp. 200) and the precedent in *3 Chitty on Criminal Law* (1826), pp. 664, 665. Applying this test, I am clearly of opinion that the nuisance by stones, vibration and dust in this case was at the date of the writ so widespread in its range and so indiscriminate in its effect that it was a public nuisance.

. . .

In my opinion, the whole festival with the weight of numbers and the noise and dust, was a painful and troublesome experience for all those living in the neighbourhood and was, in fact, a social disaster to those who normally live there. Until proper sanitation has been installed in the park and some limitation put on the numbers attending, I do not think the festival should take place. It is unfair to the neighbourhood. It is actually unfair to those who attend it and it is operated at considerable risk as to health and well-being both of the guests of the park and those who live in the neighbourhood and who are entitled to quiet enjoyment of their property. The pressure on the neighbourhood when these festivals are held is, in my opinion, grossly excessive and is something that should be restrained.

[Interim injunction granted.]

HICKEY v. ELECTRICITY REDUCTION CO.
(1970), 21 D.L.R. (3d) 368 (Nfld. S.C.)

FURLONG C.J.: . . . The defendants by the discharge of poisonous waste from its phosphorus plant at Long Harbour, Placentia Bay, destroyed the fish life of the adjacent waters, and the plaintiffs, as all other fishermen in the area suffered in their livelihood. I have said "all other fishermen", but the resulting pollution created a nuisance to all persons — "all Her Majesty's subjects" — to use Stephen's phrase. It was not a nuisance peculiar to the plaintiffs, nor confined to their use of the waters of Placentia Bay. It was a nuisance committed against the public.

A somewhat similar occurrence happened at a fishing settlement in Labrador, at Little Grady Island, in 1927, when a whaling company erected a factory at Watering Cove on Big Grady Island and polluted the waters adjacent to the premises of a fishing establishment on the former island. In the event an action was taken by the fishery owners against the whaling company. The case was heard in this Court in 1929 by Kent, J., and his judgment has remained unchallenged. He found that amongst other things, that there was serious pollution of the fishing waters from the waste materials of the whale factory. The case is *McRae v. British Norwegian Whaling Co. Ltd.*, [1927-31] Nfld. L.R. 274. After declaring at p. 282 that:

> It is an established principle that the right to fish in the sea and public navigable waters is free and open to all. It is a public right that may be exercised by any of the King's subjects, and for any interference with it the usual remedies to vindicate a public right must be employed.

He proceeded to apply the principle to the facts before him at pp. 283-4:

The plaintiffs in the present action must, therefore, in order to succeed on this cause of complaint, show that the injury inflicted upon them by the acts of the defendants, insofar as they affect the right of fishing in the public navigable waters in the vicinity of Little Grady Island, is, in regard to them, particular direct and substantial, over and above the injury thereby inflicted upon the public in general. It is not enough for the plaintiffs to show that their business is interrupted or interfered with, by the public nuisance, to enable them to maintain a private action against the defendants in respect thereof, for such interruption or interference is not a direct but merely a consequential damage resulting to them from the nuisance. Neither is it an injury peculiar to the plaintiffs themselves, but is suffered by them in common with everyone else whose right to fish in these public waters is affected by the nuisance. The plaintiff's right, as one of the public, to fish may be affected to a greater extent than that of others, but they have no ground of complaint different from anyone else who fishes or intends to fish in these waters. If the nuisance took the form of obstructing the right of the plaintiffs as adjacent land owners, of access from their land to the public navigable waters, the injury would be peculiar to themselves, not because it interrupted their right to fish in common with others in the public waters, but because it interrupted their right of access to these waters, which is an incident to the occupation of property adjacent to the sea and would therefore be an interference with a right peculiar to themselves and distinct from their right as one of the public to fish in the public waters. For these reasons I have come to the conclusion that the plaintiffs have failed to establish their right to maintain a private action in respect of the pollution by the defendants of these public navigable waters.

A somewhat similar situation arose in New Brunswick in 1934 in *Fillion v. New Brunswick International Paper Co.*, [1934] 3 D.L.R. 22, 8 M.P.R. 89. The waste from a paper mill into the Restigouche River in that Province polluted the waters of a bay where the plaintiff, with others, carried on smelt fishing. An action was taken in nuisance against the owners of the paper-mill and that part of the case was dismissed, Baxter, J., saying at p. 26:

> Assuming then, that the defendant's act constituted a public nuisance, and if it is wrongful I do not see how it can be anything else, the plaintiff has suffered differently from the rest of the public only in degree. That is not enough to entitle him to recover. Nearly all of the cases in which this principle has been invoked concern the obstruction of a highway, but *Ashby v. White*, 2 Ld. Raym. 938, at p. 955, 92 E.R. 126, *per* Holt, C.J., and the case of *Williams* in 5 Co. Rep. 72(b), 77 E.R. 163, show that the *ratio decidendi* is that it is inexpedient that there should be multiplicity of actions and that where a nuisance or injury is common to the whole public the remedy is by indictment but that no private right of action exists unless there is a special or particular injury to the plaintiff.

. . .

I think it is clear that the facts, as we have them, can only support the view that there has been pollution of the waters of this area of Placentia Bay which amounts to a public nuisance. If I am right in this view then the law is clear that a private action by the plaintiffs is not sustainable.

Counsel for the plaintiffs, Mr. Robert Wells, argued that when a public nuisance has been created anyone who suffers special damage, that is direct damage has a right of action. I am unable to agree to this rather wide application of Salmond's view that a public nuisance may become a tortious act. I think the right view is that any person who suffers peculiar damage has a right of action, but where the damage is common to all persons of the same class, then a personal right of action is not maintainable. Mr. Wells suggests that the plaintiff's right to outfit for the fishery and their right to fish is a particular right and this right having been interfered with they have a cause of action. This right which they enjoy is a right in common with all Her Majesty's subjects, an interference with which is the whole test of a public nuisance; a right which can only be vindicated by the appropriate means, which is an action by the Attorney-General, either with or without a relator, in the common interest of the public.

Rose et al. v. Miles, [1814-23] All E.R. Rep. 580, which has been cited is not in point, as the judgment of Lord Ellenborough, C.J., clearly shows [at 581], "This is something substantially more injurious to this person, than to the public at large," and Dampier, J., said "The present case admits of this distinction from most other cases, that here the plaintiff was interrupted in the actual enjoyment of the highway." With great respect I hold that view that that judgment was applicable only to the particular facts of that case, and can only support the general proposition that a peculiar and particular damage, distinct from that of the general public, is necessary to sustain an action.

NOTES AND QUESTIONS

1. How do Denning L.J.'s and Romer L.J.'s tests of public nuisance, both cited in *Orange Productions*, differ? Which test is more useful?

2. What is the rationale for the restrictive standing rule in public nuisance? In *Thorson v. A.G. Can.* (1974), 43 D.L.R. (3d) 1 at 10 (S.C.C.), Laskin J. stated that this rule was justified because "there is a clear way in which the public interest can be guarded through the intervention of the Attorney-General who would be sensitive to public complaints about the interference with public rights." Do you agree? See *Rosenburg v. Grand River Conservation Authority* (1975), 69 D.L.R. (3d) 384 (Ont. C.A.); and Estey, "Public Nuisance and Standing to Sue" (1972) 10 Osgoode Hall L.J. 563.

3. It has been held that as long as the requisite elements can be established, a nuisance may be simultaneously private and public. See *Stein v. Gonzales* (1984), 14 D.L.R. (4th) 263 (B.C.S.C.); *Susan Heyes Inc. v. Vancouver (City)* (2009), 94 B.C.L.R. (4th) 352 (S.C.), rev'd 2011 BCCA 77; *Colour Quest Ltd. v. Total Downstream U.K. plc*, [2009] 2 Lloyd's Rep. 1 (Q.B.); and *Armstrong v. Langley (City)* (1992), 94 D.L.R. (4th) 21 (B.C.C.A.). In *Sutherland v. Canada (A.G.)* (2002), 215 D.L.R. (4th) 1 (B.C.C.A.), the defendant was responsible for an airport near a residential area. The court held that the individual plaintiff had suffered a private nuisance and should not be deprived of a personal right of action merely because the defendant's conduct also adversely affected the public generally. Relief nevertheless was denied on the ground that the defendant's actions fell within the scope of the defence of statutory authority.

4. Had the Attorney-General not acted or consented to a relator action in *Orange Productions*, would the individuals in the vicinity have succeeded in private nuisance or in a private action for public nuisance?

5. In *A.G. N.S. v. Beaver* (1984), 31 C.C.L.T. 54 (N.S.S.C.), aff'd (1985), 32 C.C.L.T. 170 (N.S.C.A.), the plaintiff sought an injunction in public nuisance to

prohibit prostitutes from soliciting. The trial judge dismissed the application. He stated that equitable remedies such as injunctions should not be used to suppress criminal conduct, thereby undermining the important procedural safeguards of criminal law. However, a similar action in *A.G. B.C. v. Couillard* (1984), 31 C.C.L.T. 26 (B.C.S.C.) succeeded. Apparently, this injunction resulted in the prostitutes moving to an adjacent area. The Attorney-General of British Columbia declined to bring a subsequent action at the request of this adjacent neighbourhood. When these individuals brought a private action, the court dismissed their claim on the basis that the annoyance amounted to a public nuisance and they had no standing to sue: *Stein v. Gonzales, supra.*

These cases, and the associated academic commentary, demonstrate how difficult it is to define the tort of public nuisance and reconcile the precedents. See Klar, "Recent Developments in Canadian Tort Law" (1985) 17 Ottawa L. Rev. 325 at 386-88; and Cassels, "Prostitution and Public Nuisance: Desperate Measures and the Limits of Civil Adjudication" (1985) 63 Can. Bar Rev. 764.

6. A plaintiff in a private action for public nuisance must have suffered some "special damage" beyond that experienced by the general public. The court in *Hickey* required the plaintiffs to prove that they had suffered harm that was different in *kind* from that suffered by other members of the public. It was not enough that the *same* harm was suffered to a different *degree*. Do you agree with the way the court applied this test to the facts? See also *A.G. Man. v. Adventure Flights Centre Ltd.* (1983), 25 C.C.L.T. 295 (Man. Q.B.); and *Bolton v. Forest Pest Management Institute* (1985), 21 D.L.R. (4th) 242 (B.C.C.A.).

Hickey's view of "special damage" was rejected in *George v. Newfoundland and Labrador*, 2016 NLCA 24. With a view to providing fun and food for hunters, Newfoundland and Labrador introduced moose into the province at the turn of the 19th century. Moose, however, are large animals — an adult male can weigh 700 kilograms — that cause havoc when mixed with automobiles. In 2010 alone, the province experienced 776 MVCs ("moose-vehicle collisions"). A class action was brought against the province on behalf of people killed or injured in MVCs during the decade ending in 2011. The action in nuisance was dismissed on the ground that the defendant did not unreasonably interfere with the public's use of the highways.

> Balancing the serious adverse consequences of MVCs against having moose available for food and hunting, the difficulty and cost of implementing other risk mitigation projects, and the reasonableness of brush clearing and public awareness projects . . . it would be fair, considering all the circumstances, to relieve the tax paying public from the burden of acting as insurer for the indeterminate and unlimited losses which arise from MVCs.

In *dicta*, however, Barry J.A. critically examined the proposition that a private action for a public nuisance requires proof that the plaintiff, as compared with the general public, suffered damage that was different in kind, rather than merely in degree. Finding that rule to be unduly narrow, he preferred to adopt "the more modern view" that imposes liability as long as the plaintiff's loss was different in either kind or degree. See also *Gagnier v. Canadian Forest Products Ltd.* (1990), 51 B.C.L.R. (2d) 218 (S.C.).

7. The Court of Appeal in England recently held that the action for public nuisance may support damages for personal injuries. The claim in *In re Corby Group Litigation*, [2009] 1 Q.B. 335 (C.A.) pertained to birth defects suffered by 18 children who were born between 1986 and 1999. They alleged that their physical injuries were caused by toxic materials that were released into the air when the local council government cleaned up a heavily contaminated plant previously used by British Steel. The defendants argued that the injuries were beyond the scope of the tort because, for the purpose of public nuisance, "the interest of the plaintiff which is invaded is not the interest of bodily security but the interest of liberty to exercise rights over land in the amplest manner." The Court of Appeal agreed that damages for personal injuries are not available for private nuisance, which (at 340) "is a tort based on the interference by one occupier of land with the right in or enjoyment of land by another." In contrast, however, it held that such injuries were compensable in public nuisance. While accepting that the tort of private nuisance was directed to the enjoyment of property rights, Dyson L.J. explained (at 346) that a public nuisance is "an unlawful act or omission which endangers the life, safety, health, property or comfort of the public." He also observed a line of authority that traditionally allowed damages for personal injuries arising from public nuisances. Section 812B(h) of the *Restatement of the Law, Second, Torts* (1979) similarly states that "[u]nlike a private nuisance, a public nuisance does not necessarily involve interference with use and enjoyment."

The law in Canada is different. Both public and private nuisances support compensation for personal injuries: *Mintz v. Hamilton Radial Electric Railway*, [1923] 1 D.L.R. 268 (Ont. C.A.) (public nuisance); *Prentice v. Sault Ste. Marie*, [1928] S.C.R. 309 (public nuisance); and *Saskatchewan Power Corp. v. Wolf* (1992), 97 Sask. R. 295 (C.A.) ("Although essentially [private] nuisance is a wrong committed with respect to land, or proprietary interests in land, there is no doubt that today conduct which causes personal injury, as distinct from inconvenience, discomfort or interference with the enjoyment of land can result in liability in nuisance"), quoting Fridman, *The Law of Torts in Canada*, vol. 1 (1989) at 125.

8. Probably the largest single category of private actions for public nuisance involves plaintiffs injured on public sidewalks, highways, or waterways. F. Newark has identified this development as the major reason for the blurring of the boundaries of nuisance, a subject which is so "intractable to definition and analysis that it immediately betrays its mongrel origins": Newark, "The Boundaries of Nuisance" (1949) 65 L.Q.R. 480. Others are equally critical, stating that the cases have "saddled" the law "with a series of capricious distinctions which are difficult to justify on any rational basis": Sappideen & Vines, eds., *Fleming's The Law of Torts*, 10th ed. (2011) at 489. See also Laskin, "Torts — Nuisance or Negligence — Collisions On Highways With Standing Truck" (1944) 22 Can. Bar Rev. 468.

The Canadian case law reflects these difficulties. See for example *Lickoch v. Madu* (1973), 34 D.L.R. (3d) 569 (Alta. C.A.); *Goodwin v. Pine Point Park* (1974), 54 D.L.R. (3d) 498 (Ont. C.A.); and *Chessie v. J.D. Irvine Ltd.* (1982), 140 D.L.R. (3d) 501 (N.B.C.A.).

9. For a discussion of nuisance in the context of environmental concerns, see Stewart, "Contamination as a Chemical Interference with Land: Where the (Private Nuisance) Truck Should Stop after Antrim" (2015) Tort L. Rev. 98; Palmer, "The Rise of Injunctions: Injunctive Relief and Common Law Environmental Protection"

(2012) 20 Environ. Liab. 238; Kalmakoff, "A Right to Farm: A Survey of Farm Practices Protection Legislation in Canada" (1999) 62 Sask. L. Rev. 225; and Cross, "Does Only the Careless Polluter Pay? A Fresh Look at the Nature of Private Nuisance" (1995) 111 L.Q.R. 445.

10. For a rights-based analysis of the tort of public nuisance, see Neyers, "Divergence and Convergence in the Tort of Public Nuisance" in Tilbury & Robertson, eds., *Divergences in Private Law* (2015) (arguing that the tort exists to protect private rights akin to easements and profits that every subject enjoys over public property). See also Neyers, "Reconceptualising the Tort of Public Nuisance" [2017] 76 C.L.J. 87.

4. Remedies

If the defendant has committed a nuisance, the plaintiff may be entitled to one or more remedies. The most common options, injunctive relief and damages, are discussed in the cases that follow. A third possibility, the self-help remedy of abatement, is discussed in the notes that follow.

Just as the threshold issue of liability requires the court to balance the plaintiff's interests against those of the defendant and the community as a whole, so too a judge may be required to weigh competing interests when fashioning a response to the tort. The choice between damages and an injunction is often quite difficult.

The principles underlying awards of damages were addressed in Chapter 18. For now, it will suffice to say a few words about injunctive relief. An *injunction* is a court order directing a person to act in a particular way. It may be classified according to whether a party is required to engage in, or refrain from, some form of conduct. A *prohibitory* injunction compels the defendant to refrain from a certain act (*e.g.* stop dumping noxious substances into the plaintiff's pond). A *mandatory* injunction, in contrast, compels performance of a certain act (*e.g.* tear down a structure that hangs over the plaintiff's backyard). Alternatively, injunctions can be classified according to their timing and purpose. An *interlocutory* injunction temporarily restrains the defendant pending the plaintiff's attempt to establish a case for a permanent order. A *quia timet* injunction is intended to prevent the defendant from causing an anticipated harm in the first place. A *permanent* injunction is granted by a court, after a full hearing, in resolution of a dispute.

MENDEZ v. PALAZZI
(1976), 68 D.L.R. (3d) 582 (Ont. Co. Ct.)

HOLLINGWORTH CO. CT. J.: . . . The nub of this action is that roots from the poplar trees have allegedly ruined the plaintiffs' lawn, rock-garden and patio, and are allegedly threatening the septic tank, weeping tiles, and indeed the foundation of the plaintiffs' home and have gravely interfered with the enjoyment of their property.

. . .

What are the plaintiffs' remedies? It is necessary to decide whether damages are a proper remedy or whether a mandatory injunction shall issue or perhaps at the very least a *quia timet* injunction. The governing principles are set forth in the judgment of A.L. Smith, L.J., in *Shelfer v. London Electric Lighting Co.*, [1895] 1 Ch. 287 at pp. 322-3:

(1.) If the injury to the plaintiff's legal rights is small,
(2.) And is one which is capable of being estimated in money,
(3.) And is one which can be adequately compensated by a small money payment,
(4.) And the case is one in which it would be oppressive to the defendant to grant an injunction: —

. . .

I would hold in this case that paras. (2), (3) and (4) of A.L. Smith, L.J.'s dicta would be apposite. Is an injunction justified?

A careful review of the Canadian case law reveals no Canadian case in point. There are, however, English and Commonwealth authorities which are pertinent. In *Middleton v. Humphries* (1912), 47 I.L.T. 160, an Irish case before Ross, J., damage was caused to the plaintiff by the roots of a tree. The trial Judge had no trouble granting an injunction restraining the defendants from continuing to permit the injury and also awarded damages. Similarly, in *Butler v. Standard Telephones & Cables, Ltd.*, [1940] 1 K.B. 399, the plaintiff's house was damaged by Lombardy poplar roots burrowing under the house. Damages were awarded as apparently an injunction, although pleaded, was not asked for at trial.

In *McCombe v. Read et al.*, [1955] 2 All E.R. 458, again poplar roots damaged a house. Harman, J., granted damages and an injunction. In *Davey v. Harrow Corp.*, [1957] 2 All E.R. 305, the plaintiff obtained damages and an injunction when the roots "caused subsidence so that his house has been extensively damaged". Finally, in *Morgan v. Khyatt*, [1964] 1 W.L.R. 475, the Board, on Appeal from the Supreme Court of New Zealand, affirmed that Court's decision in granting damages and an injunction when the roots from four pohutukawa trees damaged a concrete wall and drains.

In order for an injunction to issue, as I read the cases, there must be two conditions precedent. First, there must be actual damage; second, that damage must be substantial. In the case at bar there is actual damage to the lawn, as I have found as a fact, but not that degree of substantial damage, for example, damage to the house foundation or the tile beds, to merit issuing a mandatory injunction. To order here a mandatory injunction would, in the words of A.L. Smith, L.J., be "oppressive to the defendant" but should a *quia timet* injunction issue? The principles governing the *quia timet* injunction have been cited by Pearson, J., in the case of *Fletcher v. Bealey* (1884), 28 Ch. D. 688. At p. 698 the learned Judge laid down the two necessary ingredients:

[1] There must, if no actual damage is proved, be proof of *imminent danger*, and [2] there must also be proof that the apprehended damage will, if it comes, be very substantial. [Emphasis added.]

I would say it must be proved damage will be irreparable; if the danger is not proved to be so imminent that no one can doubt that if the remedy is delayed the damage will be suffered, I think it must be shown that, if the damage does occur at any time, it will come in such a way and under such circumstances, that it will be impossible for the plaintiffs to protect themselves against it if relief is denied to them in a *quia timet* injunction.

Here, there was no evidence at all that the roots had reached the tile bed. Although one root shoot was found near the house, there is no probative evidence before me that the basement has settled or has been damaged as a result of root action. Finally, although plaintiffs' counsel argued for a *quia timet* injunction, his pleadings are silent on this matter.

Therefore, a *quia timet* injunction shall not issue.

. . .

[The judge found damages to be the appropriate remedy and awarded the plaintiffs $500 special and general damages.]

NOTES AND QUESTIONS

1. Should the court have refused the injunction? What difference did it make to the plaintiff?

2. *Fletcher*, a case relied upon in *Mendez*, was reinterpreted in *Hooper v. Rogers*, [1975] Ch. 43 (C.A.). In *Hooper*, the court said that the requirement of "imminent danger" merely raised the issue of whether the plaintiff's request for an injunction was premature. Would *Mendez* have been decided differently using this approach?

3. As in *Mendez*, A.L. Smith L.J.'s comments in *Shelfer v. London Electric Lighting Co.*, [1895] 1 Ch. 287 are often cited by English and Canadian judges in determining whether the plaintiff should receive injunctive relief or merely damages. However, as R. Sharpe notes in *Injunctions and Specific Performance*, looseleaf (2007) (consulted December 2014) at paras. 4.60-4.240, the judicial attitudes toward those comments are very different in the two countries. In England, there is a strong presumption in favour of an injunction and judges are often unmoved by hardship to the defendant or the community, even if the plaintiff's loss is relatively small. In contrast, Canadian courts are much more inclined to flexibly balance the benefits and burdens associated with injunctive relief.

If the plaintiff has suffered a substantial injury and if there is no plausible way of accommodating the defendant's activities, then an injunction may be required. That was true in *Angerer v. Cuthbert*, 2018 YKCA 8. The defendant used her property to operate a dog rescue facility that involved as many as 80 animals. Her neighbours found the constant barking to be intolerable. While recognizing the great social utility of the defendant's endeavour, the courts found that the nuisance could not be remedied by damages, and imposed an injunction that prohibited her from having more than two dogs at a time. In a brief coda, Fitch J.A. hoped that his decision would spur the public to adopt the other dogs.

4. For additional Canadian cases involving the granting of injunctions, see *Palmer v. N.S. Forest Indust.* (1983), 2 D.L.R. (4th) 397 (N.S.S.C.); *Bolton v. Forest Pest Management Institute* (1985), 21 D.L.R. (4th) 242 (B.C.C.A.); *Banfai v. Formula Fun Centre Inc.* (1984), 34 C.C.L.T. 171 (Ont. H.C.); *A.G. N.S. v. Beaver* (1985), 32 C.C.L.T. 170 (N.S.C.A.); *Hynes v. Hynes* (1989), 3 R.P.R. (2d) 142 (Nfld. C.A.); *Nippa v. C.H. Lewis (Lucan) Ltd.* (1991), 82 D.L.R. (4th) 417 (Ont. Gen. Div.); *Milne v. Saltspring Island Rod and Gun Club*, 2014 BCSC 1088; and *Ward v. Magna International Inc.* (1994), 21 C.C.L.T. (2d) 178 (Ont. Gen. Div.); and *469238 B.C. Ltd. (c.o.b. Lawrence Heights) v. Okanagan Aggregates Ltd. (c.o.b. Motoplex Speedway and Event Park)*, 2017 BCCA 127.

5. As in other areas of private law, damages are typically *compensatory*. The court aims, within the limits of monetary relief, to place the successful claimant as if the

defendant had not acted wrongfully. Exceptional circumstances may raise other possibilities.

Because the tort of nuisance is generally thought to be actionable only upon proof of loss, nominal damages would appear to be out of the question. That obstacle, however, may be overcome by means of a presumption. In England, for example, a loss is presumed if the defendant operates a market within 6²/₃ miles of a market that the plaintiff is exclusively entitled to hold: *Sevenoaks District Council v. Pattullo & Vinson Ltd.*, [1984] Ch. 211. Accordingly, in the absence of proven loss, the plaintiff may receive nominal damages: *Stoke-on-Trent City Council v. W. & J. Wass Ltd.*, [1988] 1 W.L.R. 1406 at 1415 (C.A.). In theory, nominal damages might also be awarded if the plaintiff establishes the existence of a loss but cannot adequately quantify it.

Many torts offer the successful claimant the option of receiving either compensation or disgorgement. Whereas the former looks to the plaintiff's loss, the latter is calculated by reference to the defendant's gain. Disgorgement is known by various names (account of profits, "restitution," and so on), but it invariably aims to strip away any benefits that the defendant obtained as a result of breaching the plaintiff's rights. Unfortunately, the concept is under-developed and poorly-understood, and the courts have yet to determine which torts support gain-based relief. Nuisance is a case in point. It is possible to find favourable *dicta*: *Carr-Saunders v. Dick McNeil Associates Ltd.*, [1986] 1 W.L.R. 922 (Q.B.). The weight of authority, however, denies the possibility. In *Stoke-on-Trent City Council v. W. & J. Wass Ltd.*, *supra*, at 1415, the Court of Appeal held that gain-based relief "would not only give a right to substantial damages where no loss had been suffered but would revolutionise the tort of nuisance by making it unnecessary to prove loss." So too, it would provide the claimant with "a greater measure of relief than would be justified by the nature of his right": at 1419. Compensation recognizes and protects a property holder's right to enjoy the land free from unreasonable interference. Disgorgement, in contrast, would effectively entitle property holders, regardless of any loss, to prevent others from pursuing profitable courses of conduct. Nuisance has not historically served that purpose.

Finally, in appropriate circumstances, the tort of nuisance may attract punitive damages. Such relief serves to punish, deter, and denounce: *Whiten v. Pilot Insurance Co.*, 2002 SCC 18 at para. 68. Accordingly, the defendants in *Midwest Properties Ltd. v. Thordarson*, 2015 ONCA 819 at para. 122 were subject to punitive damages of $50,000 each after toxic substances buried on their property leaked and contaminated the soil and groundwater on the plaintiff's property. In reaching that conclusion, Hourigan J.A. cited the defendants' "history of non-compliance" with government remediation orders, their "wanton disregard for . . . environmental obligations," their "utter indifference to the environmental condition of its property and surrounding areas," and the fact that their conduct was "clearly driven by profit." See also *Weenen v. Biadi*, 2017 ONCA 533; *Gibson v. Sun*, 2018 BCSC 1277; *Drager v. Lojstrup*, 2016 BCSC 1447; and *Pritchard v. Van Nes*, 2016 BCSC 686.

MILLER v. JACKSON
[1977] Q.B. 966 (C.A.)

[The plaintiffs bought a house in a new subdivision which was adjacent to a small well-established cricket club. They sued the club in nuisance and negligence after several balls had been hit onto their property, causing minor damage to their house and garden. In an effort to prevent injury to the plaintiffs, the club erected a high fence and instructed players to keep their shots down. The club also offered to place a net over the plaintiffs' garden whenever there was a game, to install unbreakable glass windows, to provide shutters, and to pay for any damage. The plaintiffs rejected these offers and sought damages and an injunction. At trial, the plaintiffs succeeded in both nuisance and negligence, and were awarded damages and granted an injunction. The defendant appealed.

An excerpt from this case appears in the notes in Chapter 15. It may be helpful to read that excerpt before reading the following extract, which is limited to the issue of nuisance and the appropriate remedy.]

LORD DENNING M.R.: . . . In our present case, too, nuisance was pleaded as an alternative to negligence. The tort of nuisance in many cases overlaps the tort of negligence. . . . But there is at any rate one important distinction between them. It lies in the nature of the remedy sought. Is it damages? Or an injunction? If the plaintiff seeks a remedy in damages for injury done to him or his property, he can lay his claim either in *negligence* or *nuisance*. But, if he seeks an injunction to stop the playing of cricket altogether, I think he must make his claim in nuisance. The books are full of cases where an injunction has been granted to restrain the continuance of a nuisance. But there is no case, so far as I know, where it has been granted so as to stop a man being negligent. At any rate in a case of this kind, where an occupier of a house or land seeks to restrain his neighbour from doing something on his own land, the only appropriate cause of action, on which to base the remedy of an injunction is nuisance . . . . It is the very essence of a private nuisance that it is the unreasonable use by a man of his land to the detriment of his neighbour. He must have been guilty of the fault, not necessarily of negligence, but of the unreasonable use of the land. . . .

It has often been said in nuisance cases that the rule is *sic utere tuo ut alienum non laedas*. But that is a most misleading maxim. Lord Wright put it in its proper place in *Sedleigh-Denfield v. O'Callaghan*:

> [It] is not only lacking in definiteness but is also inaccurate. An occupier may make in many ways a use of his land which causes damage to the neighbouring landowners, yet be free from liability . . . a useful test is perhaps what is reasonable according to the ordinary usages of mankind living in society, or, more correctly, in a particular society.

I would, therefore, adopt this test: is the use by the cricket club of this ground for playing cricket a reasonable use of it. To my mind it is a most reasonable use. Just consider the circumstances. For over 70 years the game of cricket has been played on this ground to the great benefit of the community as a whole, and to the injury of none. No one could suggest that it was a nuisance to the neighbouring owners simply because an enthusiastic batsman occasionally hit a ball out of the ground for six to the approval of the admiring onlookers. Then I would ask: does it suddenly become a nuisance because one of the neighbours chooses to build a house on the very edge of the ground, in such a position that it may well be struck by the ball on the rare occasion when there is a hit for six? To my mind the answer is plainly No. The building of the house does not convert the playing of cricket into a nuisance when it was not so before. If and insofar as any damage is caused to the house or anyone in it, it is because of the position in which it was built.

. . .

In this case it is our task to balance the right of the cricket club to continue playing on their cricket ground, as against the right of the householder not to be interfered with. On taking the balance, I would give priority to the right of the cricket club to continue playing cricket on the ground, as they have done for the last 70 years. It takes precedence over the right of the newcomer to sit in his garden undisturbed. After all he bought the house four years ago in mid-summer when the cricket season was at its height. He might have guessed that there was a risk that a hit might possibly land on his property. If he finds that he does not like it, he ought, when cricket is played, to sit in the other side of the house or in the front garden, or go out; or take advantage of the offers the club have made to him of fitting unbreakable glass, and so forth. Or, if he does not like that, he ought to sell his house and move elsewhere. I expect there are many who would gladly buy it in order to be near the cricket field and open space. At any rate he ought not to be allowed to stop cricket being played on this ground.

This case is new. It should be approached on principles applicable to modern conditions. There is a contest here between the interests of the public at large and the interest of a private individual. The *public* interest lies in protecting the environment by preserving our playing fields in the face of mounting development, and by enabling our youth to enjoy all the benefits of outdoor games, such as cricket and football. The *private* interest lies in securing the privacy of his home and garden without intrusion or interference by anyone. In deciding between these two conflicting interests, it must be remembered that it is not a question of damages. If by a million to one chance a cricket ball does go out of the ground and cause damage, the cricket club will pay. There is no difficulty on that score. No, it is a question of an injunction. And in our law you will find it repeatedly affirmed that an injunction is a discretionary remedy. In a new situation like this, we have to think afresh as to how discretion should be exercised. On the one hand, Mrs. Miller is a very sensitive lady who has worked herself up into such a state that she exclaimed to the judge:

> I just want to be allowed to live in peace. Have we got to wait until someone is killed before anything can be done?

If she feels like that about it, it is quite plain that, for peace in the future, one or other has to move. Either the cricket club have to move, but goodness knows where. I do not suppose for a moment there is any field in Lintz to which they could move. Or Mrs. Miller must move elsewhere. As between their conflicting interests, I am of opinion that the public interest should prevail over the private interest. The cricket club should not be driven out. In my opinion the right exercise of discretion is to refuse an injunction; and, of course, to refuse damages in lieu of an injunction. Likewise as to the claim for past damages. The club were entitled to use this ground for cricket in the accustomed way. It was not a nuisance, nor was it negligence of them so to run it. Nor was the batsman negligent when he hit the ball for six. All were doing simply what they were entitled to do. So if the club had put it to the test, I would have dismissed the claim for damages also. But as the club very fairly say that they are willing to pay for any damage, I am content that there should be an award of £400 to cover any past or future damage.

. . .

I would allow the appeal, accordingly.

. . .

GEOFFREY LANE L.J.: . . . The only question is whether it is unreasonable. It is a truism to say that this is a matter of degree. What that means is this. A balance has to be maintained between on the one hand the rights of the individual to enjoy his house and garden without the threat of damage and on the other hand the rights of the public in general or a neighbour to engage in lawful pastimes. Difficult questions may sometimes arise when the defendants' activities are offensive to the senses, for example by way of noise. Where, as here, the damage or potential damage is physical the answer is more simple. There is, subject to what appears hereafter, no excuse I can see which exonerates the defendants from liability in nuisance for what they have done and what they threaten to do. It is true no one has yet been physically injured. That is probably due to a great extent to the fact that the householders in Brackenridge desert their gardens whilst cricket is in progress. The danger of injury is obvious and is not slight enough to be disregarded. There is here a real risk of serious injury.

There is, however, one obviously strong point in the defendants' favour. They or their predecessors have been playing cricket on this ground (and no doubt hitting sixes out of it) for 70 years or so. Can someone by building a house on the edge of the field in circumstances where it must have been obvious that balls might be hit over the fence, effectively stop cricket being played? Precedent apart, justice would seem to demand that the plaintiffs should be left to make the most of the site they have elected to occupy with all its obvious advantages and all its equally obvious disadvantages. It is pleasant to have an open space over which to look from your bedroom and sitting room windows, so far as it is possible to see over the concrete wall. Why should you complain of the obvious disadvantages which arise from the particular purpose to which the open space is being put? Put briefly, can the defendants take advantage of the fact that the plaintiffs have put themselves in such a position by coming to occupy a house on the edge of a small cricket field, with the result that what was not a nuisance in the past now becomes a nuisance? If the matter were *res integra*, I confess I should be inclined to find for the defendants. It does not seem just that a long-established activity, in itself innocuous, should be brought to an end because someone chooses to build a house nearby and so turn an innocent pastime into an actionable nuisance. Unfortunately, however, the question is not open. In *Sturges v. Bridgman* this very problem arose. The defendant had carried on a confectionery shop with a noisy pestle and mortar for more than 20 years. Although it was noisy, it was far enough away from neighbouring premises not to cause trouble to anyone, until the plaintiff, who was a physician, built a consulting-room on his own land but immediately adjoining the confectionery shop. The noise and vibrations seriously interfered with the consulting-room and became a nuisance to the physician. The defendant contended that he had acquired the right either at common law or under the Prescription Act 1832 by uninterrupted use for more than 20 years to impose the inconvenience. It was held by the Court of Appeal, affirming the judgment of Jessel MR, that use such as this which was, prior to the construction of the consulting-room, neither preventible nor actionable, could not found a prescriptive right. That decision involved the assumption, which so far as one can discover has never been questioned, that it is no answer to a claim in nuisance for the defendant to show that the plaintiff brought the trouble on his own head by building or coming to live in a house so close to the defendant's premises that he would inevitably be affected by the defendant's activities, where no one had been affected previously. See also *Bliss v. Hall*. It may be that this rule works injustice, it may be that one would decide the matter differently in the absence of authority. But we are bound by the decision in *Sturges v. Bridgman* and it is not for this court as I see it to alter a rule which has stood for so long.

Injunction

Given that the defendants are guilty of both negligence and nuisance, is it a case where the court should in its discretion give relief, or should the plaintiffs be left to their remedy in damages? There is no doubt that if cricket is played damage will be done to the plaintiffs' tiles or windows or both. There is not inconsiderable danger that if they or their son or their guests spend any time in the garden during the weekend afternoons in the summer they may be hit by a cricket ball. So long as this situation exists it seems to be that damages cannot be said to provide an adequate form of relief. Indeed, quite apart from the risk of physical injury, I can see no valid reason why the plaintiffs should have to submit to the inevitable breakage of tiles and/ or windows, even though the defendants have expressed their willingness to carry out any repairs at no cost to the plaintiffs. I would accordingly uphold the grant of the injunction to restrain the defendants from committing nuisance. However, I would postpone the operation of the injunction for 12 months to enable the defendants to look elsewhere for an alternative pitch.

. . .

CUMMING-BRUCE L.J.: . . . So on the facts of this case a court of equity must seek to strike a fair balance between the right of the plaintiffs to have quiet enjoyment of their house and garden without exposure to cricket balls occasionally falling like thunderbolts from the heavens, and the opportunity of the inhabitants of the village in which they live to continue to enjoy the manly sport which constitutes a summer recreation for adults and young persons, including one would hope and I expect the plaintiff's son. It is a relevant circumstance which a court of equity should take into account that the plaintiffs decided to buy a house which in June 1972 when completion took place was obviously on the boundary of a quite small cricket ground where cricket was played at weekends and sometimes on evenings during the working week. They selected a house with the benefit of an open space beside it. In February, when they first saw it, they did not think about the use of this open space. But before completion they must have realized it was the village cricket ground, and that balls would sometimes be knocked from the wicket into their garden, or even against the fabric of the house. If they did not realize it, they should have done. As it turns out, the female plaintiff has developed a somewhat obsessive attitude to the proximity of the cricket field and the cricketers who visit her to seek to recover their balls. The evidence discloses a hostility which goes beyond what is reasonable, although as the learned judge found she is reasonable in her fear that if the family use the garden while a match is in progress they will run the risk of serious injury if a great hit happens to drive a ball up to the skies and down into their garden. It is reasonable to decide that during matches the family must keep out of the garden. The risk of damage to the house can be dealt with in other ways, and is not such as to fortify significantly the case for an injunction stopping play on this ground.

With all respect, in my view the learned judge did not have regard sufficiently to these considerations. He does not appear to have had regard to the interest of the inhabitants of the village as a whole. Had he done so he would in my view have been led to the conclusion that the plaintiffs having accepted the benefit of the open space marching with their land should accept the restrictions on enjoyment of their garden which they may reasonably think necessary. That is the burden which they have to bear in order that the inhabitants of the village may not be deprived of their facilities for an innocent recreation which they have so long enjoyed on this ground. There are here special circumstances which should inhibit a court of equity from granting the injunction claimed.

. . .

[Appeal allowed. Past and future damages assessed at £400.]

NOTES AND QUESTIONS

1. Given that Lord Denning would have denied relief even if the defendants had refused to pay damages, which of the three suggested outcomes in *Miller* is preferable? Which approach maximizes social resources? What other factors should the court consider?

2. A determination as to whether a particular course of action constitutes a nuisance requires a consideration of all of the circumstances. While Canadians play much less cricket than do the English, they occasionally do hit golf balls onto neighbouring properties. Three cases demonstrate the significance of context. In each instance, the plaintiff sued over errant golf balls. In *Sammut v. Islington Golf Club Ltd.* (2005), 16 C.E.L.R. (3d) 66 (Ont. S.C.J.), the plaintiff's backyard was inundated by hundreds of balls, some of which cracked windows, dented stucco walls, and demolished ornamental statues. The court awarded $5,000 for the past nuisance, $9,000 for past damage, and enjoined the defendant from allowing golfers to play the hole in question until sufficient remedial measures were in place. In *Lakeview Gardens Ltd. v. Regina (City)*, [2005] 1 W.W.R. 651 (Sask. C.A.), 10 to 20 balls landed on the plaintiff's property each year. Windows had been smashed four or five times, but no person was ever injured. Given the layout of the defendant's course, the balls had to have been deliberately hit onto the plaintiff's land. The trial court ordered the defendant to employ a "monitor" to prevent future occurrences. The Court of Appeal, however, overturned that decision. Moreover, while allowing compensation of $73 for a broken window, it refused to award an injunction. In reaching that decision, it stressed that the nuisance was "merely inconvenient or a minor discomfort," and was not an unreasonable threat to health or safety. In the third case, the trial judge awarded both compensatory damages and a permanent injunction that effectively prohibited use of the ninth hole of the defendant's golf course: *Cattell v. Great Plains Leaseholds Ltd.* (2008), 311 Sask. R. 70 (C.A.). The Saskatchewan Court of Appeal upheld the award of damages but found that the trial judge had failed to consider the social benefits associated with the golf course. It accordingly allowed the hole to be used, subject to conditions that better balanced the parties' competing interests.

3. Under the tort of nuisance, an occupier generally is viewed as having merely an *interest*, rather than a *right*, in the reasonable use and enjoyment of the land. The tort of trespass, in contrast, is based on a *right* to uninterrupted possession of land. That difference is reflected in the fact that injunctive relief is available more readily in trespass than in nuisance. The nature of the interest underlying nuisance also explains the balancing exercise that occurred in *Miller*. Nevertheless, if a nuisance creates physical damage, and especially if it does so repeatedly, a court will likely recognize a

nuisance and grant an injunction. This approach was adopted by Lane L.J. in *Miller*, and approved in *Kennaway v. Thompson*, [1980] 3 All E.R. 329 (C.A.). Does the fact that the interference is physical and repeated justify the granting of an injunction, virtually as of right?

4. The impossibility of accurately assessing damages is an argument in favour of injunctive relief. That proposition is illustrated by *Balmain Hotel Group L.P. v. 1547648 Ontario Ltd.* (2009), 60 M.P.L.R. (4th) 262 (Ont. S.C.J.). Late-night noise from the defendant's nightclub violated city by-laws and made it very difficult for guests at the plaintiff's boutique hotel to sleep. Having found that the plaintiff otherwise would suffer an incalculable loss of business, the court enjoined the defendant from creating unreasonable noise between the hours of 11:00 pm and 9:00 am.

SPUR INDUSTRIES INC. v. DEL E. WEBB DEVELOPMENT CO.
494 P.2d 700 (Ariz. S.C. 1972)

[For many years, the appellant operated a cattle feedlot in an exclusively agricultural area. In 1959, the respondent developed plans for a residential community. It purchased 20,000 acres of farmland near the appellant's operations. The price of that land was considerably lower than the price for land in nearby Phoenix. As the development expanded, the respondent discovered that smells and flies originating on the appellant's feedlot made it impossible to use certain plots of land. The respondent therefore sought injunctive relief on the basis of the nuisance allegedly created by the appellant's use of its property.]

CAMERON VICE C.J.: From a judgment permanently enjoining the defendant, Spur Industries, Inc. from operating a cattle feedlot near the plaintiff Del E. Webb Development Company's Sun City, Spur appeals. Webb cross-appeals. Although numerous issues are raised, we feel that it is necessary to answer only two questions. They are:

1. Where the operation of a business, such as a cattle feedlot is lawful in the first instance, but becomes a nuisance by reason of a nearby residential area, may the feedlot operation be enjoined in an action brought by the developer of the residential area?
2. Assuming that the nuisance may be enjoined, may the developer of a completely new town or urban area in a previously agricultural area be required to indemnify the operator of the feedlot who must move or cease operation because of the presence of the residential area created by the developer?

MAY SPUR BE ENJOINED?

The difference between a private nuisance and a public nuisance is generally one of degree. A private nuisance is one affecting a single individual or a definite small number of persons in the enjoyment of private rights not common to the public, while a public nuisance is one affecting the rights enjoyed by citizens as a part of the public. To constitute a public nuisance, the nuisance must affect a considerable number of people or an entire community or neighbourhood. . . .

Where the injury is slight, the remedy for minor inconveniences lies in an action for damages rather than in one for an injunction. . . . Moreover, some courts have held, in the "balancing of inconveniences" cases, that damages may be the sole remedy
. . . .

Thus, it would appear from the admittedly incomplete record as developed in the trial court, that, at most, residents of Youngtown would be entitled to damages rather than injunctive relief.

We have no difficulty, however, in agreeing with the conclusion of the trial court that Spur's operation was an enjoinable public nuisance as far as the people in the southern portion of Del Webb's Sun City were concerned. . . .

Del Webb, having shown a special injury in the loss of sales, had a standing to bring suit to enjoin the nuisance. . . . The judgment of the trial court permanently enjoining the operation of the feedlot is affirmed.

MUST DEL WEBB INDEMNIFY SPUR?

A suit to enjoin a nuisance sounds in equity and the courts have long recognized a special responsibility to the public when acting as a court of equity.

In addition to protecting the public interest, however, courts of equity are concerned with protecting the operator of a lawfully, albeit noxious, business from the result of a knowing and wilful encroachment by others near his business.

In the so-called "coming to the nuisance" cases, the courts have held that the residential landowner may not have relief if he knowingly came into a neighbourhood reserved for industrial or agricultural endeavours and has been damaged thereby:

> Plaintiff chose to live in an area uncontrolled by zoning laws or restrictive covenants and remote from urban development. In such an area plaintiffs cannot complain that legitimate agricultural pursuits are being carried on in the vicinity, nor can plaintiffs, having chosen to build in an agricultural area, complain that the agricultural pursuits carried on in the area depreciate the value of their homes. The area being *primarily agricultural* any opinion reflecting the value of such property must take this factor into account. The standards affecting the value of residence property in an urban setting, subject to zoning controls and controlled planning techniques, cannot be the standards by which agricultural properties are judged.

> People employed in a city who build their homes in suburban areas of the county beyond the limits of a city and zoning regulations do so for a reason. Some do so to avoid the high taxation rate imposed by cities, or to avoid special assessments for street, sewer and water projects. They usually build on improved or hard surface highways, which have been built either at state or county expense and thereby avoid special assessments for these improvements. It may be that they desire to get away from the congestion of traffic, smoke, noise, foul air and the many other annoyances of city life. But with all these advantages in going beyond the area which is zoned and restricted to protect them in their homes, they must be prepared to take the disadvantages. [*Dill v. Excel Packing Company*, 183 Kan. 513, 525, 526 (1958).] . . .

And:

> . . . a party cannot justly call upon the law to make that place suitable for his residence which was not so when he selected it. . . [*Gilbert v. Showerman*, 23 Mich. 448 at 455 (1871)].

Were Webb the only party injured, we would feel justified in holding that the doctrine of "coming to the nuisance" would have been a bar to the relief asked by Webb, and, on the other hand, had Spur located the feedlot near the outskirts of a city and had the city grown toward the feedlot, Spur would have to suffer the cost of abating the nuisance as to those people locating within the growth pattern of the expanding city:

> The case affords, perhaps, an example where a business established at a place remote from population is gradually surrounded and becomes part of a populous center, so that a business which formerly was not an interference with the rights of others has become so by the encroachment of the population. . . . [*City of Ft. Smith v. Western Hide & Fur Co.*, 153 Ark. 99 at 103 (1922)].

We agree, however, with the Massachusetts court that:

> The law of nuisance affords no rigid rule to be applied in all instances. It is elastic. It undertakes to require only that which is fair and reasonable under all the circumstances. In a commonwealth like this, which depends for its material prosperity so largely on the continued growth and enlargement of manufacturing of diverse varieties, "extreme rights" cannot be enforced. . . [*Stevens v. Rockport Granite Co.*, 216 Mass. 486 at 488 (1914).]

There was no indication in the instant case at the time Spur and its predecessors located in Western Maricopa County that a new city would spring up, full-blown, alongside the feeding operation and that the developer of that city would ask the court to order Spur to move because of the new city. Spur is required to move not because of any wrongdoing on the part of Spur, but because of a proper and legitimate regard of the courts for the rights and interests of the public.

Del Webb, on the other hand, is entitled to the relief prayed for (a permanent injunction), not because Webb is blameless, but because of the damage to the people who have been encouraged to purchase homes in Sun City. It does not equitably or legally follow, however, that Webb, being entitled to the injunction, is then free of any liability to Spur if Webb has in fact been the cause of the damage Spur has sustained. It does not seem harsh to require a developer, who has taken advantage of the lesser land values in a rural area as well as the availability of large tracts of land on which to build and develop a new town or city in the area, to indemnify those who are forced to leave as a result.

Having brought people to the nuisance to the foreseeable detriment of Spur, Webb must indemnify Spur for a reasonable amount of the cost of moving or shutting down. It should be noted that this relief to Spur is limited to a case wherein a developer has, with foreseeability, brought into a previously agricultural or industrial area the population which makes necessary the granting of an injunction against a lawful business and for which the business has no adequate relief.

It is therefore the decision of this court that the matter be remanded to the trial court for a hearing upon the damages sustained by the defendant Spur as a reasonable and direct result of the granting of the permanent injunction. Since the result of the appeal may appear novel and both sides have obtained a measure of relief, it is ordered that each side will bear its own costs.

NOTES AND QUESTIONS

1. On its facts, was *Miller v. Jackson* an appropriate case for the unusual remedy adopted in *Spur*?

2. Do you agree with the result in *Spur*? What factors should be considered in adopting this solution in other cases? What would have been the result in *Spur* if the court had found for the defendant?

3. Whatever its merits, the decision in *Spur* to grant a "compensated injunction" has not been followed in subsequent cases. R. Sharpe describes the possibility of indemnification as "mostly theoretical": *Injunctions and Specific Performance*, looseleaf (2007) (consulted December 2014) at para. 4.310.

4. The court in *Spur* gave considerable weight to the interests of the people who had purchased units in the plaintiff's development. Assume that the defendant could not have relocated its feedlot within the same area and that many of its present staff would have lost their jobs if an injunction was granted. Should such considerations be relevant to the court's decision? See *Bottom v. Ont. Leaf Tobacco Co.*, [1935] O.R. 205 (C.A.). See generally Hawkins, "'In and Of Itself': Some Thoughts on the Assignment of Property Rights in Nuisance Cases" (1978) 36 U.T. Fac. L. Rev. 209; and Ogus & Richardson, "Economics and the Environment: A Study of Private Nuisance" [1977] C.L.J. 284. Should the same principles be applied in granting remedies in public and private nuisance? See *Boomer v. Atlantic Cement Co.*, 257 N.E.2d 870 (N.Y. 1970).

5. What role did the doctrine of "coming to the nuisance" play in the judge's analysis in *Spur*? The majority of the American cases do not recognize the fact that the plaintiff "came to the nuisance" as a defence, provided the plaintiff bought the land in good faith and not for the purpose of bringing a claim. Despite Lord Denning's view, the English authorities generally support the same principle.

6. The leading Commonwealth case on the issue of "coming to the nuisance" is *Sturges v. Bridgman* (1879), 11 Ch. D. 852 (C.A.). Frederick Bridgman lived on Wigmore Street. Dr. Octavius Sturges lived on Wimpole Street. Although there were no zoning or planning laws in operation in London at the relevant time, different streets tended to be put to different uses. Wigmore Street contained several premises that contained businesses similar to Bridgman's. Likewise, several physicians lived and worked on Wimpole Street, just like Dr. Sturges. Bridgman had lived in the same house on Wigmore Street for many years. During that time, he had always used his house for both domestic and commercial purposes. Because he was a confectioner, he used his kitchen to prepare his products. Among his equipment was a mortar, which was attached to the rear wall of his kitchen and which was used to grind up ingredients.

Bridgman had used his mortar for many years, with no complaints, before Dr. Sturges moved in. Dr. Sturges established a consulting room, for the purpose of seeing and advising patients, at the back of his house. It was the only room suitable for that purpose. Unfortunately, Wigmore Street and Wimpole Street were located such that Bridgman's house and Dr. Sturges' house shared a common wall. Even more unfortunately, the houses were arranged such that Bridgman's mortar was affixed to the same wall that closed Dr. Sturges' consulting room. The noise from the mortar unreasonably interfered with Dr. Sturges' ability to properly consult with his patients. The parties attempted to negotiate a solution, but those efforts failed.

Dr. Sturges sued for the tort of nuisance and requested an injunction ordering Bridgman to desist from the unreasonable racket. Bridgman's only defence was that he had, over the years, acquired a prescriptive right to operate his mortar. The court rejected that argument and imposed an injunction. In doing so, it recognized that the operative principle might occasionally create hardship. It nevertheless insisted that a contrary rule would lead to even more hardship, and moreover would inhibit the useful development of land. For a discussion of the story behind the case, see Simpson, "The Story of *Sturges v Bridgman*: The Resolution of Land Use Disputes Between Neighbours" in Korngold & Morriss, eds., *Property Stories* (2004) at 9.

The issue of "coming to the nuisance" was revisited in *Coventry v. Lawrence*, [2014] UKSC 13. In 1975, planning permission was granted for the operation of a speedway in a largely unpopulated area. The defendant purchased that property in 2005. The plaintiffs purchased a cottage the next year and brought a claim for nuisance. In defence of the claim, the defendant argued that the plaintiff had come to the nuisance. The Supreme Court of the United Kingdom affirmed the general proposition that the defendant cannot escape liability by pleading that the plaintiff came to the nuisance. Significantly, however, Lord Neuberger contemplated situations in which a defence might be recognized, at para. 56:

> [W]here a claimant builds on, or changes the use of, her land, I would suggest that it may well be wrong to hold that a defendant's pre-existing activity gives rise to a nuisance provided that
>
>> (i) it can only be said to be a nuisance because it affects the senses of those on the claimant's land;
>>
>> (ii) it was not a nuisance before the building or change of use of the claimant's land;
>>
>> (iii) it is and has been a reasonable and otherwise lawful use of the defendant's land;
>>
>> (iv) it is carried out in a reasonable way; and
>>
>> (v) it causes no greater nuisance than when the claimant first carried out the building or changed the use.

Accordingly, "it may well be a defence . . . for a defendant to contend that . . . it is only because the claimant has changed the use of, or built on, her land that the defendant's pre-existing activity is claimed to have become a nuisance": at para. 58. See generally Rogers, *Winfield and Jolowicz on Tort*, 18th ed. (2010) at §14–29.

7. G. Calabresi and D. Melamed provide an interesting analysis of nuisance remedies in "Property Rules, Liability Rules and Inalienability: One View of the Cathedral" (1972) 85 Harv. L. Rev. 1089. The authors suggest that the courts must first decide which party to *entitle* in a nuisance action, and then must decide whether to grant the entitled party *property rule protection* or *liability rule protection*. The authors distinguish between the rules in the following manner at 1092:

> An entitlement is protected by a property rule to the extent that someone who wishes to remove the entitlement from its holder must buy it from him in a voluntary transaction in which the value of the entitlement is agreed upon by the seller. It is the form of entitlement which gives rise to the least amount of state intervention: once the original entitlement is decided upon, the state does not try to decide its value. It lets each of the parties say how much the entitlement is worth to him. . .

Consider *Miller v. Jackson* from the perspective suggested by the authors. Once the court found a nuisance, it had an option. On the one hand, by granting an injunction, the court would entitle the Millers to *property rule protection*. If the cricket club wanted to continue operations, it would be required to offer sufficient consideration in order to induce the Millers into relaxing their rights. For instance, the club might have purchased the Millers' home. On the other hand, by refusing to impose an injunction, and by confining the claimants to compensatory damages, the court provided the Millers with *liability rule protection*. In effect, the club would be entitled to purchase the right to commit a nuisance. It would be permitted to violate the Millers' interests as long as it was prepared to provide compensation. The following chart illustrates the authors' approach in reference to *Miller*.

	Entitle the Homeowner	*Entitle the Cricket Club*
Property Rule	Injunction to enjoin club	Neither injunction nor damages
Liability Rule	Damages for future interference, but no injunction	Allow injunction, but the plaintiff must pay to relocate the club

How do you think the authors would have resolved *Miller* and *Spur*? Can you suggest circumstances in which the property rule would be preferable to the liability rule and vice versa? Will the authors' approach likely produce different results than those produced by the existing doctrine?

See generally Thompson, "Injunction Negotiations: An Economic, Moral and Legal Analysis" (1975) 27 Stan. L. Rev. 1563; Polinsky, "Resolving Nuisance Disputes: The Simple Economics of Injunctive and Damage Remedies" (1980) 32 Stan. L. Rev. 1075; and Prichard, "An Economic Analysis of *Miller v. Jackson*" in McArdle, ed., *The Cambridge Lectures, 1985* (1987) at 71. For an excellent discussion of *Spur*, see Morriss, "Cattle v. Retirees: Sun City and the Battle of *Spur Industries v. Del E. Webb Development Co.*" in Korngold & Morriss, eds., *Property Stories* (2004) at 259.

8. A common law alternative to seeking damages and an injunction is the remedy of *abatement of nuisance*. Like other self-help remedies, abatement can be traced to the early years of the common law. It provided an expedient, informal and inexpensive alternative to legal proceedings. However, it also entailed a potential for violence if the person against whom it was invoked chose to resist. This limitation, common to all self-help remedies, explains the modern trend toward restricting abatement. The case law is quite complex, particularly in regard to rights of entry. J. Wactor has provided a useful summary of the major principles governing abatement. He lists several factors the courts consider in upholding the defence of abatement: (1) Does the nuisance regularly manifest itself and require an immediate remedy? (2) Will the benefit of abatement be lost by waiting for a judicial remedy? (3) Can the abatement be effected without a breach of the peace or unnecessary damage? The defendant may be held civilly, and even criminally, liable for breaching the peace, causing damage, or trespassing without notice: see Wactor, "Self-Help: A Viable Remedy for Nuisance: A Guide for the Common Man's Lawyer" (1982) 24 Ariz. L. Rev. 83 at 98.

REVIEW PROBLEM

Jonathan Bognor is the owner of a farm on which he had raised dairy cattle. When he purchased the farm in 1959, a steel mill owned by the National Steel Corporation, a company 50% owned by the federal government, was already operating on federal land about one mile from the farm. The steel mill is and was a visible source of air pollution because it relies on tall chimneys as a method of dispersing pollutants. This was a common approach to air pollution problems in 1959, but it is one that is no longer used in new plants. Technologies such as electrostatic precipitators now represent the state of the art in stationary source pollution control.

The price that Bognor paid for the farm was several thousand dollars less than the price of comparable properties situated further away from the mill. In the past, however, the pollutants had never had any serious discernible effect on Bognor's farm. The only possible apparent effect had been a slight browning of some grass, and Bognor had never been sure whether this was caused by the mill.

In 1978, dairy prices fell drastically. Foreseeing a difficult period ahead for dairy farmers, Bognor decided to diversify his farming activities in order to obtain greater security against future market fluctuations. After making extensive inquiries, he decided to grow blueberries, strawberries and other fruits.

The results of his first season's crop were disastrous. Most of the fruit was covered with brown speckles. A consultant advised Bognor that the brown speckles had been caused by sulphuric acid which, in turn, was caused by the emissions from the steel mill. The consultant also said that this acid caused the browning of the grass and that Bognor's new crops were much more sensitive to the acid. The consultant's report noted that it had not been known when the steel mill was established that sulphur from the coal fuel could mix with moisture in the atmosphere and produce sulphuric acid. In recent years, however, this connection had been clearly established and had been much discussed in the scientific literature.

Bognor is the only farmer in the area suffering such damage because he is the only one who has switched from dairy farming. It is also clear that the operators at the steel mill have no idea that they are harming Bognor's farming operations.

The steel mill was established by a federal statute which stated that the National Steel Corporation was authorized to erect a steel mill and to use the federal land for this purpose.

Bognor now wants to sue the National Steel Corporation for both damages and an injunction. Advise him.

STRICT AND VICARIOUS LIABILITY

1. Introduction
2. Strict Liability for Escape of Dangerous Substances: *Rylands v. Fletcher*
3. Strict Liability for Animals
4. Products Liability: Negligence or Strict Liability?
5. Vicarious Liability

1. Introduction

As a general rule, liability is imposed in tort law only if the defendant was at "fault." Fault, however, is a broad concept. To this point, we have focussed on situations in which the defendant intentionally or negligently caused the plaintiff's loss. As we saw in Chapter 3, however, "intention" is another frequently misleading term. In the context of the intentional torts, it is enough that the defendant intended to act in a certain way. The plaintiff need not prove that the defendant intended to act unlawfully. Consequently, for example, the "innocent" purchaser of stolen goods may be held liable for conversion. The law is unwilling to grant the defendant leniency for fear of undermining the plaintiff's underlying rights.

Exceptionally, however, liability is imposed even though the defendant was not at "fault," at least in any of the usual ways. In this chapter, we examine two concepts: *strict liability* and *vicarious liability*.

(a) STRICT LIABILITY

Strict liability is triggered simply by the breach of an obligation. The court does not demand proof that the breach was intentional, careless, or unreasonable. It is sufficient that the defendant acted in a prohibited manner. The classic examples address injuries inflicted by dangerous animals and losses falling under the rule in *Rylands v. Fletcher* (1868), L.R. 3 H.L. 330. The basic explanation is the same in each instance: by choosing to engage in a particularly dangerous activity, the defendant assumes responsibility for (almost) all damage that may occur. Consequently, if the defendant owns a dog with a history of aggression, the law bluntly says, "Do not keep a dangerous animal that causes harm." If the dog subsequently bites the plaintiff, liability will be imposed even if, in the circumstances, the defendant neither encouraged the animal to attack nor carelessly failed to control its actions. Likewise, if the defendant chooses to store a large quantity of fireworks in a warehouse, the law imposes a strict obligation that says, "Do not allow this danger to escape your property and injure another person." If the fireworks explode and destroy a neighbouring house, the plaintiff probably will be entitled to relief even if the defendant took every precaution possible.

Because this concept of strict liability sometimes is difficult to understand, it may be useful to draw comparisons with two other areas of private law: *contract* and *unjust enrichment*.

- *Strict Liability in Contract*: The law of contract generally shares tort law's notion of strict liability. Leaving aside exceptional circumstances (*e.g.* frustration), each party is strictly liable to perform its contractual obligations. The law bluntly says, "Perform the agreement." In the event of breach, it is irrelevant that the defendant made every reasonable effort to fulfill the promise.

- *Strict Liability in Unjust Enrichment*: Although unjust enrichment also involves "strict liability," it defines that term much differently than do tort and contract. If the plaintiff mistakenly pays $5,000 to the defendant, the law *prima facie* will demand restitution (*i.e.* the defendant must reverse the transfer by repaying the money). Moreover, that liability is *strict* in the narrowest sense of the word. Once again, there is no question of intentional or careless wrongdoing. Beyond that, however, there is no question of any wrongdoing at all. Breach of an obligation simply never enters into the analysis. Consequently, liability may be imposed even if the defendant was entirely unaware of the transfer (*e.g.* because the plaintiff mistakenly deposited $5,000 into the defendant's bank account while the defendant was on vacation). An unjustified transfer, regardless of culpability or fault, is sufficient to trigger the law of unjust enrichment.

(b) VICARIOUS LIABILITY

Strict liability in tort law occurs when the defendant breaches an obligation, albeit non-intentionally and non-negligently. The concept of *vicarious liability* goes one step further. It allows liability to be imposed on one person as a result of the tortious conduct of another. The most common example occurs in the employment context. If an employee commits a tort, the employer may be held responsible for the damage even though it did nothing wrong and even though it did not itself breach any obligation.

Within a generally fault-based regime of tort law, the concepts of strict liability and vicarious liability are anomalous and hence controversial. As explained in the last section of this chapter, the Supreme Court of Canada has recently provided policy justifications for vicarious liability. Strict liability, in contrast, remains highly contentious. Elsewhere in the Commonwealth, courts have begun to re-interpret areas of strict liability along more orthodox (*i.e.* fault-based) lines. As yet, there is no similar development in Canada.

NOTES AND QUESTIONS

1. Explain the difference between (a) the intention required for liability under the intentional torts, (b) the nature of fault under the strict liability torts, and (c) the nature of strict liability under the action in unjust enrichment.

2. Why is the law of unjust enrichment able to impose liability in the absence of a breach, whereas tort invariably requires proof that the defendant failed to fulfil an obligation? In answering this question, consider the nature of the remedies that are available in each instance. Does restitution (as awarded in unjust enrichment) ever hurt the defendant or help the plaintiff, relative to the *status quo ante*? Do compensation and disgorgement (as awarded in tort) ever hurt the defendant or help the plaintiff, relative to the *status quo ante*? See McInnes, "The Measure of Restitution" (2002) 52 U.T.L.J. 163.

2. Strict Liability for Escape of Dangerous Substances: *Rylands v. Fletcher*

(a) INTRODUCTION

The prime example of strict liability arises under the label of *Rylands v. Fletcher*. The defendants built a reservoir on their property in order to provide a regular supply of water to their mill. Unfortunately, the defendants did not realize that their reservoir was constructed over an abandoned mineshaft that was connected to the plaintiff's property. Water from the reservoir broke through the hidden shaft and flooded the plaintiff's adjoining mine. The House of Lords' decision has generated a large, complex body of law concerning liability for non-natural uses of land. The terms "non-natural use" and "escape" have resisted precise definition, and many of the defences remain somewhat unsettled. The decision and the judicial interpretations of its main elements are considered in this section.

RYLANDS v. FLETCHER
(1868), L.R. 3 H.L. 330

THE LORD CHANCELLOR (Lord Cairns):—My Lords, in this case the plaintiff . . . is the occupier of a mine and works under a close of land. The defendants are the owners of a mill in his neighbourhood; and they proposed to make a reservoir for the purpose of keeping and storing water to be used about their mill upon another close of land, which, for the purposes of this case, may be taken as being adjoining to the close of the plaintiff, although in point of fact some intervening land lay between the two. Underneath the close of land of the defendants on which they proposed to construct their reservoir there were certain old and disused mining passages and works. There were five vertical shafts, and some horizontal shafts communicating with them. The vertical shafts had been filled up with soil and rubbish; and, it does not appear that any person was aware of the existence either of the vertical shafts or of the horizontal works communicating with them. In the course of the working by the plaintiff of his mine, he had gradually worked through the seams of coal underneath the close, and had come into contact with the old and disused works underneath the close of the defendants. In that state of things the reservoir of the defendants was constructed. It was constructed by them through the agency and inspection of an engineer and contractor. Personally the defendants appear to have taken no part in the works, nor to have been aware of any want of security connected with them. As regards the engineer and the contractor, we must take it from the case that they did not exercise, as far as they were concerned, that reasonable care and caution which they might have exercised, taking notice, as they appear to have taken notice, of the vertical shafts filled up in the manner which I have mentioned. However, my Lords, when the reservoir was constructed and filled, or partly filled, with water, the weight of the water, bearing upon the imperfectly filled-up and disused vertical shafts, broke through those shafts. The water passed down them and into the horizontal workings and from the horizontal workings under the close of the defendants, it passed on into the workings under the close of the plaintiff and flooded his mine, causing considerable damage, for which this action was brought. The Court of Exchequer, when the special case stating the facts to which I have referred was argued before them, were of opinion that the plaintiff had established no cause of action. The Court of Exchequer Chamber, before whom an appeal from their judgment was argued, were of a contrary opinion, and unanimously arrived at the conclusion that there was a cause of action, and that the plaintiff was entitled to damages. My Lords, the principles on which this case must be determined appear to me to be extremely simple. The defendants, treating them as owners or occupiers of the close on which the reservoir was constructed, might lawfully have used that close for any purpose for which it might, in the ordinary course of the enjoyment of land, be used; and if in what I may term the natural user of that land there had been any accumulation of water, either on the surface or underground, and if by the operation of the laws of nature that accumulation of water had passed off into the close occupied by the plaintiff, the plaintiff could not have complained that that result had taken place. If he had desired to guard himself against it, it would have lain on him to have done so by leaving or by interposing some barrier between his close and the close of the defendants in order to have prevented that operation of the laws of nature. . . . On the other hand, if the defendants, not stopping at the natural use of their close, had desired to use it for any purpose which I may term a non-natural use, for the purpose of introducing into the close that which, in its natural condition, was not in or upon it — for the purpose of introducing water, either above or below ground, in quantities and in a manner not the result of any work or operation on or under the land; and if in consequence of their doing so, or in consequence of any imperfection in the mode of their doing so, the water came to escape and to pass off into the close of the plaintiff, then it appears to me that that which the defendants were doing they were doing at their own peril; and if in the course of their doing it the evil arose to which I have referred — the evil, namely, of the escape of the water, and its passing away to the close of the plaintiff and injuring the plaintiff — then for the consequence of that, in my opinion, the defendants would be liable. . . . My Lords, these simple principles, if they are well founded, as it appears to me they are, really dispose of this case. The same result is arrived at on the principles referred to by Blackburn, J. in his judgment in the Court of Exchequer Chamber, where he states the opinion of that court as to the law in these words:

> We think that the true rule of law is that the person who, for his own purposes, brings on his land and collects and keeps there anything likely to do mischief, if it escapes must keep it in at his peril, and if he does not do so is *prima facie* answerable for all the damage which is the natural consequence of its escape. He can excuse himself by showing that the escape was owing to the plaintiff's default, or, perhaps, that the escape was the consequence of *vis major* or of the act of God; but, as nothing of this sort exists here, it is unnecessary to inquire what excuse would be sufficient. The general rule as above stated seems on principle just. The person whose grass or corn is eaten down by the escaping cattle of his neighbour, or whose mine is flooded by the water from his neighbour's reservoir, or whose cellar is invaded by the filth of his neighbour's privy, or whose habitation is made unhealthy by the fumes and noisome vapours of his neighbour's alkali works, is damnified without any fault of his own; and it seems but reasonable and just that the neighbour who has brought something on his own property (which was not naturally there), harmless to others so long as it is confined to his own property, but which he knows will be mischievous if it gets on his neighbour's, should be obliged to make good the damage which ensues if he does not succeed in confining it to his own property. But for his act in bringing it there no mischief could have accrued, and it seems but just that he should at his peril keep it there so that no mischief may accrue, or answer for the natural and anticipated

consequence. And upon authority this, we think, is established to be the law, whether the things so brought be beasts, or water, or filth, or stenches.

My Lords, in that opinion, I must say, I entirely concur. Therefore I have to move your Lordships that the judgment of the Court of Exchequer Chamber be affirmed, and that the present appeal be dismissed with costs.

LORD CRANWORTH.—My Lords, I concur with my noble and learned friend in thinking that the rule of law was correctly stated by Mr. Justice Blackburn in delivering the opinion of the Exchequer Chamber. If a person brings or accumulates on his land anything which, if it should escape, may cause damage to his neighbour, he does so at his peril. If it does escape and cause damage, he is responsible, however careful he may have been, and whatever precautions he may have taken to prevent the damage. In considering whether a defendant is liable to a plaintiff for damage which the plaintiff may have sustained, the question in general is, not whether the defendant has acted with due care and caution, but whether his acts have occasioned the damage . . . . And the doctrine is founded on good sense. For when one person in managing his own affairs causes, however innocently, damage to another, it is obviously only just that he should be the party to suffer. He is bound *sic uti suo ut non loedat alienum*.

NOTES AND QUESTIONS

1. What are the elements of an action under the rule in *Rylands v. Fletcher*?

2. In the court below (1866), L.R. 1 Exch. 265, Blackburn J. stated (at 282):

> There does not appear to be any difference in principle, between the extent of the duty cast on him who brings cattle on his land to keep them in, and the extent of the duty imposed on him who brings on his land water, filth, or stenches, or any other thing which will, if it escape, naturally do damage.

Should these two instances of strict liability (*i.e. Rylands v. Fletcher* and animals) be governed by the same principle? See *Read v. J. Lyons & Co.*, [1947] A.C. 156 at 166-67 (H.L.).

3. Other authorities, including Lord Macmillan's *obiter dicta* in *Read v. J. Lyons & Co.*, *supra*, at 173, indicate that *Rylands* applies to personal injuries as well as property damage. See *Shiffman v. Order of St. John*, [1936] 1 All E.R. 557 (K.B.); *Schubert v. Sterling Trusts Corp.*, [1943] 4 D.L.R. 584 (Ont. H.C.); *Aldridge v. Van Patter*, [1952] 4 D.L.R. 93 (Ont. H.C.); *Perry v. Kendricks Transport Ltd.*, [1956] 1 All E.R. 154 (C.A.); and *Gertsen v. Municipality of Metropolitan Toronto* (1973), 41 D.L.R. (3d) 646 (Ont. H.C.). In *Transco plc v. Stockport Metropolitan Borough Council*, [2004] 2 A.C. 1 (H.L.), the House of Lords held that *Rylands v. Fletcher* protects only against property damage. That decision, however, was based on the fact that (as explained below) English law now narrowly views *Rylands* as a particular species of nuisance.

4. What role, if any, does reasonable foreseeability play under *Rylands*? Is it relevant in theory or in practice? Consider the increasingly common case in which dangerous materials were brought on to the defendant's land, seeped into the ground, and escaped to the plaintiff's adjacent property, where they caused contamination and damage. Assume further that those events were not reasonably foreseeable at the time

that they occurred. It was only after the damage had been done that the scientific community recognized the possibility of materials migrating from one property to another. Should liability be imposed? Does a requirement of reasonable foreseeability fit within a regime of strict liability? Is it fair to impose liability for harm that the defendant did not know was even possible? (Are you doing anything today that will be recognized as dangerous a decade or two from now?) Is it fair to withhold recovery from the victim of dangerous materials that escaped the defendant's property?

"There has been mixed acceptance of the reasonable foreseeability requirement in this country": *Huang v. Fraser Hillary's Ltd.*, 2018 ONCA 527 at para. 19, aff'g 2017 ONSC 1500 at para. 62. See also *10565 Nfld. Inc. v. Canada (Attorney General)*, 2017 NLTD (G) 84 at para. 347; *Smith Brothers Excavating Windsor Ltd. v. Camion Equipment & Leasing Inc. (Trustee of)* (1994), 21 C.C.L.T. (2d) 113 (Ont. Gen. Div.); *Windsor v. Canadian Pacific Railway Ltd.*, 2014 ABCA 108; *Smith v. Inco Ltd.*, 2011 ONCA 628 at para. 106-10; and *Cambridge Water Co. v. Eastern Counties Leather plc*, [1994] 2 A.C. 264 (H.L.).

5. Class actions have become far more common in recent years. That development has the potential to significantly affect many areas of law. *Smith v. Inco Ltd.* (2010), 76 C.C.L.T. (3d) 92 (Ont. S.C.J.), rev'd 2011 ONCA 628 was a class action based on *Rylands v. Fletcher*. For many years, the defendant operated a nickel refinery in Port Colborne. The process emitted nickel particles, which drifted on the winds and settled onto neighbouring land. In 2000, the plaintiff commenced a class action representing the owners of approximately 7000 residential properties. The claim was framed in trespass, nuisance and strict liability. The claim in trespass was dismissed, but Henderson J. imposed liability for both nuisance and the tort of *Rylands v. Fletcher*. As to the latter, the court concluded that (1) the defendant brought nickel onto its property, (2) nickel was not a natural part of the atmosphere or the neighbouring land, (3) a nickel refinery was not an ordinary use of land and it constituted a special use that carried new dangers, and (4) although nickel was not dangerous *per se*, its escape adversely affected neighbouring land and caused property values to diminish substantially. Compensatory damages of $36,000,000 were awarded against the defendant, but punitive damages were refused.

The decision was overturned on appeal. Most importantly, the Ontario Court of Appeal rejected the suggestion at trial that "ultra-hazardous" or abnormally dangerous activities necessarily attract a greater burden under *Rylands v. Fletcher*. Rather, it said, in determining whether a given use is "non-natural," one must assess the extent to which that use departs from the ordinary use of such land. The court accordingly stressed that the strict liability tort "aims not at all risks associated with carrying out an activity, but rather with the risk associated with the accidental and unintended consequences of engaging in an activity" (at para. 82). Turning to the facts, it held that a refinery that is operated in "a heavily industrialized part of the city in a manner that was ordinary and usual and did not create risks beyond those incidental to virtually any industrial operation" (at para. 103) was not non-natural.

6. The rule in *Rylands* is popular among proponents of enterprise liability. Although enterprise liability can be supported on loss distribution principles, it is most closely associated with market deterrence. The essential feature of enterprise liability was summarized in Lang, "The Activity-Risk Theory of Tort: Risk, Insurance and Insolvency" (1961) 39 Can. Bar Rev. 530 at 530: "The basic proposition and starting

point is that activity should bear the risks of harm that it produces. Unless the act is sufficiently worthwhile to pay for the increase in risks that accompany it, the act should not be done at all." See generally Calabresi, *The Cost of Accidents* (1970); and Cane, *Atiyah's Accidents, Compensation and the Law*, 7th ed. (2006).

7. One of the most interesting criticisms of enterprise liability is found in Coase, "The Problem of Social Cost" (1960) 3 J.L. & Econ. 1. He suggests that it is difficult to determine which party should be assigned the cost of a particular activity. For example, in *Rylands*, is the damage a cost which ought to be attributed to constructing the reservoir or to maintaining the mine? Presumably, the defendant's conduct would have been harmless if the plaintiffs had not been engaged in an equally "non-natural" use of their land. Since no trespass was committed, should it matter that the water escaped from the defendant's land to the plaintiffs'? Why should the plaintiffs' interest be preferred to that of the defendant, particularly when both are commercial enterprises? See also Morris, "Hazardous Enterprises and Risk-Bearing Capacity" (1951) 61 Yale L.J. 1172; Calabresi, *supra*; Fletcher, "Fairness and Utility in Tort Theory" (1972) 85 Harv. L. Rev. 537; Coleman, "The Morality of Strict Tort Liability" (1976) 18 William & Mary L. Rev. 259; and Schwartz, "The Vitality of Negligence and the Ethics of Strict Liability" (1981) 15 Georgia L. Rev. 963.

8. The same facts, viewed from slightly different perspectives, may support two or more torts. The possibility of "alternative analysis" often applies in connection with the rule in *Rylands v. Fletcher. Blatz v. Impact Energy Inc.* (2009), 478 A.R. 1 (Q.B.) provides an illustration. The defendant was contractually entitled to operate a sour gas well on the plaintiffs' property. In doing so, however, it allowed various materials to enter into the plaintiffs' water supply. The plaintiffs, claiming that they suffered physical injuries and economic losses as a result, sued for nuisance, negligence, and strict liability under *Rylands v. Fletcher*. The court upheld liability for each of these claims and awarded $30,000. On the issue of strict liability, Nation J. explained (at para. 156) that "the plaintiffs have proven that the defendants, in the course of storing drilling mud and drilling the well, kept on the lease site substances that could cause damage if they escaped. . . . The defendants are responsible for the damages which are the natural consequence of this escape." See also *Ivall v. Aguiar* (2007), 86 O.R. (3d) 111 (S.C.J.).

9. The rule in *Rylands* has been the topic of considerable academic attention. See for example Fridman, "The Rise and Fall of *Rylands v. Fletcher*" (1956) 34 Can. Bar Rev. 810; Fleming, "Comment: The Fall of a Crippled Giant" (1995) 3 Tort L. Rev. 56; Husak, "Varieties of Strict Liability" (1995) 8 C.J.L.J. 189; Pardy, "Fault and Cause: Rethinking the Role of Negligent Conduct" (1995) 3 Tort L. Rev. 143; Stanton, "The Legacy of *Rylands v. Fletcher*" in Mullany & Linden, eds., *Torts Tomorrow: A Tribute to John Fleming* (1998) at 84; Shugerman, "The Floodgates of Strict Liability: Bursting Reservoirs and the Adoption of *Fletcher v. Rylands* in the Guilded Age" (2000) 110 Yale L.J. 333; Abraham, "*Rylands v. Fletcher*. Tort Law's Conscience" in Rabin & Sugarman, eds., *Torts Stories* (2003) at 207; Collins & Freitag, "Rescuing Rylands: Strict Liability and Environmental Protection in Canada" (2015) 23 Tort L. Rev. 85; and Wood, "Sticks and Carrots: *Rylands v Fletcher*, CSR, and Accountability for Environmental Harm in Common Law Jurisdictions" (2013) 91 Can. Bar Rev. 275.

(b) ESCAPE

READ v. J. LYONS & CO.
[1947] A.C. 156 (H.L.)

VISCOUNT SIMON L.C.: My Lords, in fulfilment of an agreement dated Jan. 26, 1942, and made between the Ministry of Supply and the respondents, the latter undertook the operation, management and control of the Elstow Ordnance Factory as agents for the Ministry. The respondents carried on in the factory the business of filling shell cases with high explosives. The appellant was an employee of the Ministry, with the duty of inspecting this filling of shell cases, and her work required her (although she would have preferred and had applied for other employment) to be present in the shell filling shop. On Aug. 31, 1942, while the appellant was lawfully in the shell filling shop in discharge of her duty, an explosion occurred which killed a man and injured the appellant and others. No negligence was averred or proved against the respondents. The plea of *volenti non fit injuria*, for whatever it might be worth, has been expressly withdrawn before this House by the Attorney-General on behalf of the respondents, and thus the simple question for decision is whether in these circumstances the respondents are liable, without any proof or inference that they were negligent, to the appellant in damages, which have been assessed at £575 2s. 8d, for her injuries.

. . .

Now, the strict liability recognized by this House to exist in *Rylands v. Fletcher* is conditioned by two elements which I may call the condition of "escape" from the land of something likely to do mischief if it escapes, and the condition of "non-natural use" of the land. This second condition has in some later cases, which did not reach this House, been otherwise expressed, *e.g.*, as "exceptional" user, when such user is not regarded as "natural" and at the same time is likely to produce mischief if there is an "escape". . . . The American Restatement of the Law of Torts, III, s. 519, speaks of "ultra-hazardous activity," but attaches qualifications which would appear in the present instance to exonerate the respondents. It is not necessary to analyse the second condition on the present occasion, for in the case now before us the first essential condition of "escape" does not seem to me to be present at all. "Escape," for the purpose of applying the proposition in *Rylands v. Fletcher* means escape from a place which the defendant has occupation of, or control over to a place which is outside his occupation or control. Blackburn J., several times refers to the defendant's duty as being the duty of "keeping a thing in" at the defendant's peril and by "keeping in" he means, not preventing an explosive substance from exploding, but preventing a thing which may inflict mischief from escaping from the area which the defendant occupies or controls. In two well-known cases the same principle of strict liability for escape was applied to defendants who held a franchise to lay pipes under a highway and to conduct water (or gas) under pressure through them: *Charing Cross Electric Co. v. Hydraulic Power Co.* [[1914] 3 K.B. 772]; *Northwestern Utilities, Ltd. v. London Guarantee, etc., Co.* [[1936] A.C. 108].

In *Howard v. Furness Houlder Argentine Lines, Ltd.* [[1936] 2 All E.R. 781] Lewis, J., had before him a case of injury caused by an escape of steam on board a ship where the plaintiff was working. The judge was, I think, right in refusing to apply the doctrine of *Rylands v. Fletcher* on the ground that the injuries were caused on the premises of the defendants. Apart altogether from the judge's doubt (which I share) whether the owners of the steamship by generating steam therein are making a non-natural use of their steamship, the other condition on which the proposition in *Rylands v. Fletcher* depends was not present, any more than it is in the case with which we have now to deal. Here there is no escape of the relevant kind at all and the appellant's action fails on that ground.

In these circumstances it becomes unnecessary to consider other objections that have been raised, such as the question of whether the doctrine of *Rylands v. Fletcher* applies where the claim is for damages for personal injury as distinguished from damages to property. It may be noted, in passing, that Blackburn, J., himself when referring to the doctrine of *Rylands v. Fletcher* in the later case of *Cattle v. Stockton Waterworks* [(1875), L.R. 10 Q.B. 453] leaves this undealt with. He treats damages under the *Rylands v. Fletcher* principle as covering damages to property, such as workmen's clothes or tools, but says nothing about liability for personal injuries.

. . .

LORD MACMILLAN: . . . The doctrine of *Rylands v. Fletcher*, as I understand it, derives from a conception of the mutual duties of adjoining or neighbouring landowners and its congeners are trespass and nuisance. If its foundation is to be found in the injunction *sic utere tuo ut alienum non laedas*, then it is manifest that it has nothing to do with personal injuries. The duty is to refrain from injuring not *alium* but *alienum*. The two prerequisites of the doctrine are that there must be the escape of something from one man's close to another man's close and that that which escapes must have been brought on the land from which it escapes in consequence of some non-natural use of that land whatever precisely that may mean. Neither of these features exists in the present case. I have already pointed out that nothing escaped from the defendants' premises, and, were it necessary to decide the point, I should hesitate to hold that in these days and in an industrial community it was a non-natural use of land to build a factory on it and conduct there the manufacture of explosives. I could conceive it being said that to carry on the manufacture of explosives in a crowded urban area was evidence of negligence, but there is no such case here and I offer no opinion on the point.

It is noteworthy in *Rylands v. Fletcher* that all the counts in the declaration alleged negligence and that on the same page of the report on which his famous *dictum* is recorded (L.R. 1 Exch. 265, at p. 279), Blackburn J., states that:

the plaintiff . . . must bear the loss, unless he can establish that it was the consequence of some default for which the defendants are responsible.

His decision for the plaintiff would thus logically seem to imply that he found some default on the part of the defendants in bringing on their land and failing to confine there an exceptional quantity of water. Notwithstanding the width of some of the pronouncements, particularly on the part of Lord Cranworth, I think that the doctrine of *Rylands v. Fletcher*, when studied in its setting, is truly a case on the mutual obligations of the owners or occupiers of neighbouring closes and is entirely inapplicable to the present case, which is quite outside its ambit.

. . .

LORD SIMONDS: . . . My Lords, in this branch of the law it is inevitable that reference should be made to what Blackburn, J., said in *Fletcher v. Rylands* and what

Lord Cairns said in *Rylands v. Fletcher*. In doing so I think it is of great importance to remember that the subject-matter of that action was the rights of adjoining landowners and, though the doctrine of strict liability there enforced was illustrated by reference to the responsibility of the man who keeps beasts, yet the defendant was held liable only because he allowed, or did not prevent, the escape from his land onto the land of the plaintiff of something which he had brought onto his own land and which he knew or should have known was liable to do mischief if it escaped from it. I agree with the late Mackinnon, L.J., that this and nothing else is the basis of the celebrated judgment of Blackburn J., and I think it no less the basis of Lord Cairns' opinion. For it is significant that he emphasises that, if the accumulation of water (the very thing which by its escape in that case caused the actionable damage) had arisen by the natural user of the defendant's land, the adjoining owner could not have complained. The decision itself does not justify the broad proposition which the appellant seeks to establish, and I would venture to say that the word "escape" which is used so often in the judgment of Blackburn, J., meant to him escape from the defendant's premises and nothing else. It has been urged that escape means escape from control and that it is irrelevant where damage takes place if there has been such an escape, but, though it is arguable that that ought to be the law, I see no logical necessity for it and much less any judicial authority. For as I have said, somewhere the line must be drawn unless full rein be given to the doctrine that a man acts always at his peril, that "coarse and impolitic idea" as O.W. Holmes somewhere calls it. I speak with all deference of modern American text books and judicial decisions, but I think little guidance can be obtained from the way in which this part of the common law has developed on the other side of the ocean, and I would reject the idea that, if a man carries on a so-called ultra-hazardous activity on his premises, the line must be drawn so as to bring him within the limit of strict liability for its consequences to all men everywhere. On the contrary, I would say that his obligation to those lawfully on his premises is to be ultra-cautious in carrying on his ultra-hazardous activity, but that it will still be the task of the injured person to show that the defendant owed to him a duty of care and did not fulfil it. It may well be that in the discharge of that task he will sometimes be able to call in aid the maxim *res ipsa loquitur*.

My Lords, I have stated a general proposition and indicated that there are exceptions to it. It is clear, for instance, that, if a man brings and keeps a wild beast on his land or a beast known to him to be ferocious of a species generally *mansuetae naturae*, he may be liable for any damage occurring within or without his premises without proof of negligence. Such an exception will serve to illustrate the proposition that the law of torts has grown up historically in separate compartments, and that beasts have travelled in a compartment of their own. So, also, it may be that in regard to certain chattels a similar liability may arise though I accept and would quote with respect to what Lord Macmillan said in *Donoghue v. Stevenson* [[1932] A.C. 562 at 611]:

> I rather regard this type of case as a special instance of negligence where the law exacts a degree of diligence so stringent as to amount practically to a guarantee of safety.

There may be other exceptions. Professor Winfield, to whose "Textbook of the Law of Tort," 3rd edn., 1946, I would acknowledge my indebtedness, is inclined to include certain "dangerous structures" within the rule of strict liability. This may be so. It is sufficient for my purpose to say that, unless a plaintiff can point to a specific rule of law in relation to a specific subject-matter he cannot, in my opinion, bring himself within the exceptions to the general rule that I have stated. I have already expressed my view that there is no rule which imposes on him who carries on the business of making explosives, though the activity may be "ultra-hazardous" and an explosive "a dangerous thing," a strict liability to those who are lawfully on his premises.

. . .

[Lords Porter and Uthwatt delivered separate concurring speeches.]

NOTES AND QUESTIONS

1. What must the plaintiff establish to meet the "escape requirement" that was articulated in *Read*? What are the rationale and purpose for this requirement? Are losses inherently worse if they are suffered off the defendant's land? Are other torts available with respect to losses that occur on the defendant's land?

2. In *Deyo v. Kingston Speedway Ltd.*, [1954] 2 D.L.R. 419 (Ont. C.A.), aff'd [1955] 1 D.L.R. 718 (S.C.C.), two spectators at a stock car race were injured by a racing car that went out of control. A claim based on *Rylands* was dismissed because there had been no escape. In *Aldridge v. Van Patter*, [1952] 4 D.L.R. 93 (Ont. H.C.), a stock car went out of control, crashed through a fence and injured the plaintiff, who was in an adjoining park. One of the bases upon which liability was imposed was the rule in *Rylands*. Can you justify the results in these two cases?

3. Because the escape requirement may defeat otherwise meritorious claims, its judicial interpretation occasionally is difficult to predict. See Fridman *et al.*, *The Law of Torts in Canada*, 3rd ed. (2010) at 216-18.

4. Compare and contrast the rule in *Rylands* with the rules governing occupiers' liability discussed in Chapter 23 and private nuisance discussed in Chapter 24. What are the advantages and disadvantages of each regime? Under what circumstances will the two sets of rules reach different conclusions?

5. An easement exists when a landowner is entitled to exercise some right with respect to a neighbouring property (as when a homeowner is entitled to drive over a neighbour's land in order to reach a highway). For the purposes of *Rylands*, is there an "escape" if a dangerous thing initially located on the defendant's land causes damage to another part of the defendant's land that is subject to an easement in the plaintiff's favour? Is it sufficient that the plaintiff's property interest was damaged, even though the dangerous thing remained on land owned by the defendant? See *Transco plc v. Stockport Metropolitan Borough Council*, [2004] 2 A.C. 1 (H.L.).

6. In *Dokuchia v. Domansch*, [1945] 1 D.L.R. 757 (Ont. C.A.), the plaintiff was injured while pouring the defendant's gasoline into the defendant's truck, which was on a highway. *Rylands* was applied, notwithstanding that there was no connection with either party's land, let alone an escape. Do you agree with this application of *Rylands*? Can you justify a rule that makes the owner of dangerous substances strictly liable for any injuries they cause?

(c) NON-NATURAL USE

GERTSEN v. MUNICIPALITY OF METROPOLITAN TORONTO
(1973), 41 D.L.R. (3d) 646 (Ont. H.C.)

[Two municipalities, Toronto and York, reached an agreement whereby Toronto dumped putrescible organic waste into a landfill site in York. Methane gas seeped from the site, some of which accumulated in the plaintiff's garage and exploded when he started his car. The plaintiff sued both municipalities in nuisance, negligence, and strict liability. The following excerpt is limited to the court's discussion of strict liability.]

LERNER J.: . . . Blackburn, J., in [*Rylands v. Fletcher*], stated the rule which has been sometimes distinguished and sometimes restricted in its application:

We think that the true rule of law is, that the person who for his own purposes brings on his lands and collects and keeps there anything likely to do mischief if it escapes, must keep it in at his peril, and, if he does not do so, is prima facie answerable for all the damage which is the natural consequences of its escape.

This rule, if applicable on the facts of the case, makes liability absolute. The defendants by joint agreement brought putrescible organic matter on the lands of York as a means of disposing of same. This organic matter generated methane gas, admittedly a dangerous substance in itself. The gas escaped onto the plaintiffs' land and caused them damage. *Prima facie* the defendants should be liable without proof of negligence. . . . However, there are sometimes other considerations brought to bear which, if applicable, somewhat restrict the rule.

York argued that the work was under the control of Metro which would relieve it from liability. It has, however, been held that a defendant (York) cannot avail itself of the absence of negligence on its part and even of those over whom it has control. The owner (York) is charged with keeping a dangerous substance at its peril. . . .

Another submission of York is that waste disposal was a natural user of these lands. If the owner uses his land in the exercise of his ordinary rights, he incurs no liability under the rule if he injures his neighbour. . . .

In *Rickards v. Lothian*, [1913] A.C. 263, the Privy Council withdrew a wide range of activities from the ambit of strict liability under this rule on the basis that it applied only to damage due to non-natural use of land. As an incident thereof, since the non-natural user thereof is an essential element of liability, the burden of proving it rests on the plaintiff. . . .

When the use of the element or thing which the law regards as the potential source of mischief is an accepted incident of some ordinary purpose to which land is reasonably applied by the occupier, the *prima facie* rule of absolute responsibility for the consequences of its escape must give way. In applying this qualification, the Courts have looked not only to the thing or activity in isolation, but also to the place and manner in which it is maintained and its relation to its surroundings. Time, place and circumstance, not excluding purpose, are most material. The distinction between natural and non-natural user is both relative and capable of adjustment to the changing patterns of social existence: Fleming, *Law of Torts*, 4th ed. (1971), p. 283.

The distinction between natural and non-natural user has served the function principally of lending the rule in *Rylands v. Fletcher* a desirable degree of flexibility by enabling the courts to infuse notions of social and economic needs prevailing at a given time and place . . . Yet caution should be observed lest the qualification be pushed too far. There is no merit, for example, in occasional suggestions to exempt all activities redounding to the "general benefit of the community", such as nationalized industries or even the manufacture of munitions in time of war. Not only is there no warrant in principle for prejudicing private rights by the facile pleas of overriding public welfare, at least in the absence of statutory authorization, but many are the decisions which have attached strict liability to enterprises engaged in community services such as public utilities and the like.

I must now decide whether this garbage-fill project was natural or non-natural user of the land. I am emboldened by the statement of Lord Porter in *Read v. J. Lyons & Co., Ltd.*, [[1947] A.C. 156 (H.L.)] at p. 176, where he states:

Possibly a further requisite is that to bring the thing to the position in which it is found is to make a non-natural use of that place . . . . Manifestly these requirements must give rise to difficulty in applying the rule in individual cases and necessitate at least a decision as to what can be dangerous and what is a non-natural use . . . For the present I need only say that each seems to be a question of fact subject to a ruling of the judge as to whether the particular object can be dangerous or the particular use can be non-natural, and in deciding this question I think that all the circumstances of the time and place and practice of mankind must be taken into consideration so that what might be regarded as dangerous or non-natural may vary according to those circumstances.

In the same case Viscount Simon stated at pp. 169-70:

I think it not improper to put on record, with all due regard to the admission and dicta in that case, that if the question had hereafter to be decided whether the making of munitions in a factory at the Government's request in time of war for the purpose of helping to defeat the enemy is a "non-natural" use of land, adopted by the occupier "for his own purposes", it would *not seem to me* that the House would be bound by this authority to say that it was.

(The italics are mine.) That statement seems to have been provoked by the opinion of Lord Buckmaster in *Rainham Chemical Works, Ltd. (in Liquidation) et al. v. Belvedere Fish Guano Co., Ltd.*, [1921] 2 A.C. 465 at p. 471. Injuries had been sustained by the inspector in the factory of the defendants who were making munitions when an explosion occurred. Lord Buckmaster stated that the making of munitions was certainly not "the common and ordinary use of the land."

I take judicial notice, supported by the exhibits and all testimony, that this was a relatively small ravine surrounded by heavily populated urban areas. It was originally subdivided apparently for occupation by the citizenry but because of its difficult contours and a stream in the lower areas, it appears to me that it was not practicable for such use. This does not, however, in my view, alter the case and the fact that Metro was seeking garbage and waste disposal areas does not change the situation either. I find that the primary purpose for filling this ravine in this manner was a selfish and self-serving opportunity for Metro who held out a "carrot" to York that if this were permitted York would end up with a level area instead of an "eyesore" and also gain attractive facilities, at no expense. This, in my view, having regard to its location together with the known temporary and permanent problems caused by such a garbage-fill project, cannot be said to be supported by the "overriding public welfare" theory. The initial benefits were to Metro which was responsible for disposing of garbage, etc. and not to the general benefit of the community directly affected by this use, *i.e.*, the owners and occupiers of the surrounding land. They were the community that I must consider. Applying the propositions of time, place and circumstances and not excluding purpose, I find that this was a non-natural user of the land and, therefore, that exception to the rule of strict liability also fails.

. . .

[Both defendants were held liable under the rule in *Rylands*, as well as in nuisance and negligence.]

NOTES AND QUESTIONS

1. In *Rylands*, Lord Cairns suggested that non-natural land use involved the introduction of "that which in its natural condition was not in or upon it." Why was mining considered any less natural a use than milling? In *Richards v. Lothian*, [1913] A.C. 263 at 280 (P.C.), the court said: "There must be some special use bringing with it increased danger to others. . . not merely the ordinary use of the land or such a use as is proper for the general benefit of the community." This latter interpretation of non-natural use was adopted in both *Read* and *Gertsen*. How has the definition of non-natural use changed, and what is the significance of this change? Which interpretation is preferable?

2. The escaping object or substance must be likely to cause harm: it must be a "dangerous thing." This may include both (a) objects that are dangerous in themselves and (b) objects that are likely to escape and thereby pose risks to others. It is difficult to determine which objects and substances would be considered "dangerous things" without resort to the case law. The answer sometimes is surprising. *Rylands* has been applied to water, gas, electricity, sparks from a steam locomotive, strips of metal foil, caravan dwellers, and a car with a full gas tank in a garage.

3. Canadian decisions regarding the classification of substances as non-natural or dangerous are not always easy to reconcile. See *Schenck v. R.; Rokeby v. R.* (1981), 34 O.R. (2d) 595 (H.C.), aff'd [1987] 2 S.C.R. 289 (use of salt on winter highway: no); *Chu v. Dawson* (1984), 18 D.L.R. (4th) 520 (B.C.C.A.) (soil placed on cliff overlooking homes: yes); *John Campbell Law Corp. v. Strata Plan 1350* (2001), 8 C.C.L.T. (3d) 226 (B.C.S.C.) (use of a sewer pipe for domestic water and sewage removal: no); *Mineault v. Kamloops (City)*, 2017 BCSC 316 (lawn irrigation system: no); *Chrysanthis v. Rutkowska*, 2015 ONSC 7236 (use of a boulder in landscaping: no); *Huang v. Fraser Hillary's Ltd.*, 2017 ONSC 1500, aff'd 2018 ONCA 527 (use of chemicals in dry cleaning business: no); *Weenen v. Biadi*, 2015 ONSC 6832, aff'd 2017 ONCA 533 (fill added to residential property: yes); *Alfarano v. Regina*, 2010 ONSC 1538 (cobblestone driveway surface: no); *Deavitt v. Greenly*, 2016 ONSC 1693 (biosolids spread on farmer's field: no); and *Tock v. St. John's Metropolitan Area Board* (1989), 64 D.L.R. (4th) 620 (S.C.C.) (municipal sewer system: no).

4. The early common law held an occupier strictly liable if a fire in his or her control escaped and caused damage to another's property. This common law rule has been supplanted by legislation in all the Canadian provinces that eliminates strict liability for accidental fires. However, it has been held that these statutes do not affect

the rule in *Rylands*. Therefore, the escape of a "non-natural fire," such as that used in an industrial setting, may give rise to strict liability. For examples of fires that constitute a non-natural use see *A.G. Can. v. Diamond Waterproofing Ltd; Pillar Const. v. Defence Const. (1951) Ltd.* (1974), 48 D.L.R. (3d) 353 (Ont. C.A.) (storing highly flammable material near a heater); and *Hudson v. Riverdale Colony of Hutterian Brethren* (1980), 114 D.L.R. (3d) 352 (Man. C.A.) (grass fire started to contain larger fire). For examples of fires that constitute a natural use see *O'Neill v. Esquire Hotels Ltd.* (1972), 30 D.L.R. (3d) 589 (N.B.C.A.) (propane gas used for cooking); *Lickoch v. Madu* (1973), 34 D.L.R. (3d) 569 (Alta. C.A.) (farmer burning trash); *Dudeck v. Brown* (1980), 33 O.R. (2d) 460 (H.C.) (homeowner using wood-burning stove); and *Dahler v. Bruvold*, [1981] 5 W.W.R. 706 (B.C.S.C.) (logger starting fire to clear land pursuant to a provincial permit). But see *Smith v. Widdicombe* (1987), 39 C.C.L.T. 98 (Man. Q.B.), where the court held that a fire used to burn stubble prior to cultivation was a natural use. See also Ogus, "Vagaries in Liability for the Escape of Fire" [1969] C.L.J. 104.

(d) DEFENCES TO THE RULE IN *RYLANDS v. FLETCHER*

As we have seen, the courts have narrowly interpreted and applied *Rylands*. They have further limited its impact by recognizing six defences: consent, common benefit, default of the plaintiff, act of God, act of a stranger, and statutory authority. This situation led J. Fleming, in an earlier edition of his text, to state that "[t]he aggregate effect of these exceptions makes it doubtful whether there is much left of the rationale of strict liability as originally contemplated in 1866": Fleming, *The Law of Torts*, 9th ed. (1998) at 385. See now Sappideen & Vines, eds., *Fleming's The Law of Torts*, 10th ed. (2011) at 394-99.

(i) *Consent*

The defendant who establishes that the plaintiff implicitly or explicitly consented to the presence of the danger enjoys a complete defence to a claim under *Rylands*. The courts may imply consent from the nature of the legal relationship between the parties or from the physical circumstances. For example, a tenant in a lower floor is taken to implicitly consent to the presence of water pipes in the upper floors and cannot invoke *Rylands* if water seeps into his premises causing damage. The tenant's remedy, if any, would lie in negligence. See generally *Peters v. Prince of Wales Theatre (Birmingham) Ltd.*, [1943] 1 K.B. (C.A.); *Holinaty v. Hawkins* (1965), 52 D.L.R. (2d) 289 (Ont. C.A.); *Federic v. Perpetual Investments Ltd.* (1968), 2 D.L.R. (3d) 50 (Ont. H.C.); *Elfassy v. Sylben Invts. Ltd.* (1978), 21 O.R. (2d) 609 (H.C.); and *Pattison v. Prince Edward Region Conservation Authority* (1984), 30 C.C.L.T. 305 (Ont. H.C.).

(ii) *Common Benefit*

If the source of the danger is maintained for the common benefit of both the plaintiff and the defendant, liability will not be imposed under *Rylands*. In the classic case of *Carstairs v. Taylor* (1871), L.R. 6 Exch. 217, rain water was collected in a special box on the roof and flowed through the drains. When a rat made a hole in the box, water flowed into the plaintiff's ground floor premises, damaging his property. The plaintiff's action under *Rylands* was dismissed because the water was collected for the mutual benefit of both the defendant and the plaintiff. Since the defendant had not been careless, the plaintiff's claim in negligence also failed. The common benefit defence sometimes is treated as a form of implied consent. See generally *Danku v. Town of Fort Frances* (1976), 73 D.L.R. (3d) 377 (Ont. Dist. Ct.); and *Gilson v. Kerrier District Council*, [1976] 3 All E.R. 343 (C.A.).

(iii) *Default of the Plaintiff*

A person who voluntarily and unreasonably encounters a known danger cannot recover under *Rylands*. Recovery also will be denied if the plaintiff's wanton, wilful, or reckless misconduct materially increased the probability of injury. Nor will the defendant be held liable for damages which are caused by the abnormal sensitivity of the plaintiff's property. See *Dunn v. Birmingham Canal Co.* (1872), L.R. 8 Q.B. 42 (Ex. Ch.); *Ponting v. Noakes*, [1894] 2 Q.B. 281; and *Hoare v. McAlpine*, [1923] 1 Ch. 167.

(iv) *Act of God*

An act of God is a force of nature that arises without human intervention. To provide a defence, the natural force must be so unexpected that it could not have been reasonably foreseen, and thus its effects could not have been prevented. See *Nichols v. Marsland* (1875), L.R. 10 Exch. 255, aff'd (1876), 2 Ex. D. 1 (C.A.); *Greenock Corp. v. Caledonian Railway Co.*, [1917] A.C. 556 (H.L.); *Smith v. Ont. & Minnesota Power Co.* (1918), 45 D.L.R. 266 (Ont. C.A.); and *Goldman v. Hargrave*, [1967] 1 A.C. 645 (P.C.).

(v) *Act of a Stranger*

The owner of a dangerous thing generally is strictly liable for foreseeable harm caused by third parties. However, liability will not be imposed under *Rylands* if the defendant proves that the escape of the dangerous thing was caused by a stranger's deliberate and unforeseeable act. The onus is on the defendant to show that the escape could not have been prevented through reasonable care. Unfortunately, it is not always clear whether an intermeddler will be considered a stranger (whose deliberate actions may exempt the defendant from responsibility) or someone for whom the defendant may be accountable. That latter category includes the defendant's servants, independent contractors, invitees, licensees, and possibly even family members acting under the defendant's control. Notice that the defence of an act of a stranger introduces into this area concepts commonly associated with negligence. See *Richards v. Lothian*, [1913] A.C. 263 *(P.C.)*; *Northwestern Utilities Ltd. v. London Guarantee & Accident Co.*, [1936] A.C. 108 (P.C.); and *Hale v. Jennings Brothers*, [1938] 1 All E.R. 579 (C.A.). For a discussion of people who are considered to be strangers see *Schubert v. Sterling Trusts Corp.*, [1943] 4 D.L.R. 584 (Ont. H.C.); *Holinaty v. Hawkins* (1965), 52 D.L.R. (2d) 289 (Ont. C.A.); *Saccardo v. Hamilton* (1970), 18 D.L.R. (3d) 271 (Ont. H.C.); *Smith v. Scott*, [1973] Ch. 314; and *Holderness v. Goslin*, [1975] 2 N.Z.L.R. 46 (S.C.).

(vi) *Statutory Authority*

Many of the activities that potentially involve the escape of dangerous substances (such as water, electricity, and sewage) are now managed by public utilities operating under statutory authority. Liability under *Rylands* may be denied if the defendant acted pursuant to statutory authority.

Legislation seldom expressly addresses the issue of tort liability, and the scope of this defence often is a matter of statutory interpretation. If the statutory language is *mandatory* (*i.e.* it imposes an obligation on the defendant to supply the service), then, in the absence of negligence, the defendant will not be held liable for acts done pursuant to that duty. However, if the statutory language is *permissive*, the courts generally will not interpret it as authorizing the defendant to violate the rule in *Rylands*. See *Benning v. Wong* (1969), 43 A.L.J.R. 467 (H.C.A.); *Himmelman v. Nova Const. Co.* (1969), 5 D.L.R. (3d) 56 (N.S.S.C.); *Gertsen v. Municipality of Metropolitan Toronto* (1973), 41 D.L.R. (3d) 646 (Ont. H.C.); *Schenck v. R.; Rokeby v. R.* (1981), 34 O.R. (2d) 595 (H.C.), aff'd [1987] 2 S.C.R. 289; and *Lyon v. Village of Shelburne* (1981), 130 D.L.R. (3d) 307 (Ont. Co. Ct.).

(e) COMPARATIVE PERSPECTIVES ON *RYLANDS v. FLETCHER*

Like all other common law cases, the decision in *Rylands v. Fletcher* was the product of particular legal and historical circumstances. Three factors appear to have been especially important to the outcome. First, as an English landowner who innocently had suffered serious property damage, Fletcher was an ideal plaintiff in the Victorian era. Second, Fletcher was a deserving plaintiff with no obvious legal remedy. When it became clear that Fletcher could not establish a case in negligence, sympathetic Law Lords felt compelled to identify some alternative theory of liability. Third, historical research reveals that the *Rylands* case had been preceded by a number of notorious burst-reservoir disasters. The judges who formulated the strict liability rule appear to have been motivated, in part, by the desire to deter future calamities of this kind. See Simpson, *Leading Cases in the Common Law* (1995) at 194.

Elsewhere in the Commonwealth, however, judges have grown uncomfortable with the doctrine of strict liability underlying *Rylands v. Fletcher*. At least two aspects of that doctrine are problematic. The first is the imprecision of the action's constituent elements. Phrases such as "dangerous substance" and "non-natural use" resist consistent interpretation and application. Second, many judges question the fairness of strict liability and note the anomaly of allowing *Rylands* to operate within a tort regime that generally is premised upon negligent and intentional fault. In recent years, several leading Commonwealth jurists have concluded that *Rylands* is a doctrinal anachronism, a legal principle that has outlived whatever rationale or usefulness that might once have justified its existence. In the 1990s this view hardened and affected appellate judges of England and Australia.

Recent developments in England begin with *Cambridge Water Co. v. Eastern Counties Leather plc*, [1994] 2 A.C. 264 (H.L.). The defendant was a leather manufacturer and the plaintiff was its distant neighbour. Over a 20-year period, 1,000 gallons of chemical solvent seeped from the defendant's property and into the plaintiff's well. When the contamination was discovered and traced, the plaintiff sued in negligence, nuisance, and on the principles established in *Rylands v. Fletcher*. The first two claims failed for lack of reasonable foreseeability. With regard to strict liability, the Law Lords unanimously decided that "knowledge, or at least foreseeability of the risk" is a requirement for even so-called "strict" liability. Since the plaintiff could not prove that the seepage of solvents into his distant well had been foreseeable, the defendant was not liable under the rule in *Rylands v. Fletcher.*

Some commentators interpreted the House of Lords' focus on reasonable foreseeability as proof that *Rylands* had been subsumed within the law of negligence. See Fleming, "The Fall of a Crippled Giant" (1995) 3 Tort L. Rev. 56. Significantly, however, both the English Court of Appeal and House of Lords in *Cambridge Water* had deliberately refrained from overruling *Rylands.*

In *Transco plc v. Stockport Metropolitan Borough Council*, [2004] 2 A.C. 1 (H.L.), the House of Lords once again was invited to abolish the independent doctrine of *Rylands v. Fletcher.* And the court once again declined. Aside from the fact that substantial developments are best left to Parliament, a principle of strict liability was thought to remain important, albeit in relatively few cases. However, the House of Lords did take the opportunity to restate the doctrine. In England, *Rylands* now exists as a species of the tort of private nuisance. As a result, strict liability no longer is available with respect to personal injuries, as opposed to property damage. The court also attempted to refine *Rylands* by restating the conditions of liability. The traditionally troublesome requirements of dangerousness and non-natural use of land now are combined into a single concept that is governed by "ordinary contemporary standards." Unfortunately, the various judges each expressed that focus in different terms: "extraordinary and unusual" (Lord Bingham), "special" (Lord Walker), "non-natural user" (Lord Hoffmann), and "natural" and "ordinary" (Lord Scott). Other aspects of *Transco* were mentioned in earlier notes in this section. For discussion of recent developments in English law, see Nolan, "The Distinctiveness of *Rylands v. Fletcher*" (2005) 121 L.Q.R. 421; Bagshaw, "*Rylands* Confined" (2004) 120 L.Q.R. 388; and Amirthalingam, "*Rylands* Lives" [2004] C.L.J. 273. See also *Hamilton v. Papakura District Council*, [2000] 1 N.Z.L.R. 265 (C.A.).

In *Burnie Port Authority v. General Jones Pty. Ltd.* (1994), 179 C.L.R. 520 (H.C.A.), the High Court of Australia was bolder. The case involved a fire that had spread from part of a building owned by the defendant to part of the same building that the plaintiff rented for cold storage. Prior to the fire, the defendant had brought a large quantity of a highly flammable substance onto its property. The defendant did this with the knowledge that welding would take place in close proximity. After the ensuing fire, the plaintiff sued in both strict liability and negligence.

Writing for five of seven judges, Mason C.J. criticized the notorious "obscurity" and "quite unacceptable uncertainty" of strict liability principles. The Chief Justice further noted that in the hundred years since *Rylands*, tort law had experienced a crucial development: the "emergence of a coherent law of negligence to dominate the territory of tortious liability for unintentional injury." Mason C.J. therefore concluded that the rule in *Rylands* had been "absorbed by the principles of ordinary negligence." The defendant in *Burnie Port Authority* was found liable in negligence for failing to take reasonable care in storing a highly flammable substance, but it was not held strictly liable. In short, *Burnie Port Authority* appears to have expunged strict liability from the common law of Australia.

Canada's highest appellate court has not similarly distanced itself from the rule in *Rylands v. Fletcher.* On the contrary, the Supreme Court of Canada recognized the tort's continued existence in *Tock v. St. John's Metropolitan Area Board* (1989), 64 D.L.R. (4th) 620 (S.C.C.). For that reason, the many cases on "dangerous substances" and "natural use," as well as the common law defences to allegations of strict liability, remain relevant to Canadian lawyers.

NOTES AND QUESTIONS

1. In *Transco*, the House of Lords characterized *Rylands* as a species of nuisance. Do both torts truly operate on the basis of the same rationale? What is the purpose of each tort? Must either or both parties occupy land for the purposes of nuisance? Has the same answer traditionally been given with respect to *Rylands*?

2. In *Transco*, the House of Lords held that since *Rylands* is a species of private nuisance, it cannot redress personal injury. Is the tort of private nuisance confined to property damage in Canadian law?

3. Many of the traditional difficulties associated with *Rylands* stem from the requirements of unusual danger and non-natural use of land. Has the House of Lords overcome those difficulties in *Transco*?

4. In *Das v. George Weston Ltd.*, 2018 ONCA 1053 the Ontario Court of Appeal had occasion to examine *Rylands'* development in India. The case began in 2013 when a building in Savar, Bangladesh collapsed, killing thousands of workers inside. Most of those workers manufactured garments for export. The defendant imported some of that clothing, attached "Joe Fresh" labels, and sold the items in its Loblaws stores. In an attempt to reach deep-pockets overseas, a class action was started, on behalf of the victims, against the defendant in Canada. An assessment of that action required a consideration of *Rylands v. Fletcher* on the sub-continent. The key case was *M.C. Mehta v. Union of India*, which arose in response to the Bhopal gas leak — arguably the worst industrial disaster in history — in 1984: [1987] All Ind. R. 1086 (S.C.). India's Supreme Court observed that *Rylands*, a product of 19th century England, was incapable of producing justice in 20th century India. The law, said Bhagwati C.J., had evolved in response to the greatly increased risks that industry created for surrounding communities. Accordingly, rather than apply a rule of strict liability that was hedged by requirements of "non-natural use" and "escape," Indian law adopted a non-delegable duty and a broad principle of absolute liability for operators of dangerous enterprises.

5. Given the developments elsewhere in the Commonwealth, how should Canadian law treat *Rylands*? Should the doctrine be abolished? Subsumed within the tort of private nuisance? Subsumed within negligence? Does *Rylands* serve any useful purpose that cannot better be served by other means?

3. Strict Liability for Animals

In formulating the rule in *Rylands v. Fletcher*, several members of the House of Lords referred to cases of strict liability involving damage caused by animals. For the purposes of discussion, it is best to subdivide this topic according to whether the instrument of harm was a dangerous animal or "cattle."

(a) DANGEROUS ANIMALS

COWLES v. BALAC
(2005), 29 C.C.L.T. (3d) 284 (Ont. S.C.J.)

[David Balac and Jennifer Cowles were dating in 1996. He worked as an accordion player and studied at Sheridan college; she worked as an exotic dancer. On a warm spring day, they visited African Lion Safari (ALS). ALS offers a unique wildlife experience. In a typical zoo, the animals are enclosed and the customers roam freely from one exhibit to the next. At ALS, the roles are reversed. The animals roam freely within their reserves and it is the customers who are enclosed (in their own vehicles) as they drive through the park.

Tragically, while the attraction of ALS is close contact with wild animals, the couple's encounter was *too* close. Shortly after they had entered the tiger reserve, their car was attacked by the tigers. Although the facts were disputed and unclear, the judge found that the initial attack startled Balac, who accidentally hit a button that rolled down Cowles' window. A Siberian tiger named Paca then lunged through the window and mauled the couple. The injuries were severe. Because of permanent scarring to her scalp and hip, Cowles was unable to continue work as a "featured dancer." David suffered physical injuries that prevented him from playing the accordion and psychological injuries that further limited his employment prospects.]

MACFARLAND J.: . . .

Liability. . .

This case raises the question whether the keeper of a wild vicious animal will be strictly liable for damage caused by that animal regardless of fault and in effect whether the law of strict liability in such circumstances remains a part of law of Ontario today. For the reasons that follow I have concluded that it does.

The learned authors of the tort texts distinguish between the two classes of dangerous animals. The first category is of animals *ferae naturae* such as bears and lions — and quite obviously tigers would be included in this first category and the second category is of animals *mansuetae naturae* like cows, dogs and horses. . . .

In his text, Fridman, G.H.L. *The Law of Torts in Canada*, (2nd edition Carswell), Fridman notes at page 250-1:

> Under the *scienter* doctrine it is very relevant that harm has resulted from the keeping of an animal. The common law developed special rules to deal with the situation where damage was caused by animals, even before the emergence of the modern law of negligence, and quite distinct from the action for cattle-trespass, or under the much later doctrine of *Rylands v. Fletcher*. The *scienter* doctrine was, and remains a form of strict liability, that is to say, liability without proof of negligence. In this respect it is akin to both cattle-trespass and the *Rylands v. Fletcher* doctrine. . . .

and at page 254-255:

> *The Scienter Doctrine*
>
> . . . Where harm is caused by the behaviour of an animal, whether on the property of the defendant or elsewhere, this kind of liability depends upon the type of animal concerned. The law distinguishes between the wild animals, i.e., animals *ferae naturae*,

and tame or domestic animals, i.e., animals *mansuetae naturae* or *domitae naturae*. For damage resulting from the act of a wild animal, the defendant is strictly liable, without proof of negligence or other wrongful conduct, and without the necessity of proving that the defendant was aware of the dangerous character of the particular animal that caused the harm, or of the class of animals to which it belonged. If the animal is mansuetae naturae, that is, one which ordinarily did not cause the kind of harm that is involved, the common law requires that the particular animal concerned have the dangerous or mischievous propensity to commit the harm or damage that it inflicted, and that the defendant knew of such propensity or characteristic of the individual animal. To keep such an animal with knowledge of its potential for causing harm is not in itself negligence, or indeed wrongful in any other way (any more than to keep a wild animal is *per se* unlawful or negligent). Indeed, despite some judicial discussion that appears to introduce elements of negligence into liability for animals, at common law there is no need to prove negligence in the way in which the animal in question was controlled or kept in order to establish liability, as long as the requisite elements of dangerous propensity or character and knowledge are present. Nor will negligence in controlling the animal, so that it is able to escape from the property of the defendant and cause harm, entail liability under the *scienter* doctrine in the absence of knowledge of the dangerous propensity, or if the animal is not normally dangerous. There might be liability based on negligence if other ingredients of such liability, such as a duty of care, exist, as frequently occurs where dogs or cattle escape onto the highway, or get out of control while on the highway, with consequent damage to other road users or adjoining landowners. Such liability, if it arises, is not strict as is the situation where the *scienter* doctrine is applicable: it will depend upon the resolution of the issues of duty, remoteness and causation that are an integral part of the law of negligence.

The underlying rationale for the strict liability of the *scienter* doctrine is that anyone who maintains an animal that is known to be dangerous to humans or other animals or in any other way does so at his peril. He has created a dangerous, or potentially dangerous situation involving risk to others. In the case of the wild animals, such knowledge is irrebutably presumed by the law. Domestic animals are not normally harmful. Therefore, knowledge of the vicious nature of the particular animal must be established. In the days when pleadings in the common law courts were written in Latin, the allegation of the plaintiff was that the defendant knowingly kept (*scienter retinuit*) a dangerous animal which caused harm to the plaintiff. Hence arose the appellation of this kind of liability.

Sometimes it has been suggested that liability is absolute, where the animal is wild or a domestic animal known to be dangerous. This cannot be accurate, because it is clear that there are limits upon the liability of the defendant, for example, contributory negligence on the part of the plaintiff, voluntary assumption of risk or consent, the act of a stranger, or an act of God. Hence, liability although strict in the sense of without proof of negligence, is not absolute, which could mean that it would be imposed whatsoever the circumstances, as long as the animal caused the harm.

and p. 262:

The question of who is the owner or keeper, or the person whose duty it is to exercise control, is a question of fact. The real test of responsibility is not ownership. There may be many circumstances under which a person who is not the owner and indeed one who has not the actual possession of the animal may be under a duty to exercise control and will be responsible if it injures somebody.

What appears to be the crucial factor in liability is the issue of control. Hence, it has been suggested that liability is founded upon the failure of a defendant, who was under a duty to confine or control the offending animal, to maintain a sufficient degree of control to prevent the injury that occurred. Language of this nature carries overtones of negligence, i.e., the failure to exercise reasonable care. However, there is no doubt that, where the *scienter* doctrine applies, the duty is strict. Negligence in controlling the animal does not need to be proved. But reference to control suggests that it is escape from control that is vital to liability. Thus, if an animal is caged, chained or leashed, but nevertheless manages to inflict injury on a plaintiff, it has been held in some cases that the *scienter* doctrine is inapplicable, although some other form of action, such as negligence, might be invoked. In such instances, it is said that for *scienter* to apply, the animal must have escaped from control. In *Maynes v. Galicz*, the plaintiff, aged seven, put her fingers inside a wolf cage constructed of heavy duty two-inch square mesh. The cage was located at the defendant's zoo. The wolf grabbed the child's fingers and pulled her hand into the cage, in the course of which the hand was split. The *scienter* doctrine was held to be inapplicable because the wolf had not escaped from the cage (and the person in charge of the wolf had sufficiently restrained the animal so that injury would not ordinarily happen). A similar view was taken in *Lewis v. Oeming*. There, the tiger which caused the plaintiff's injury was properly housed in a safe enclosure and never did escape from the custody and control of the owner. Moreover, the tiger was segregated into a part of the enclosure off from the main area where the cap, which the plaintiff sought inside the tiger's cage, was lying. For these reasons, Miller J. held that the concept of strict liability, i.e. *scienter*, did not apply.

and p. 263-4:

(vi) *Defences*

(A) *Contributory negligence* If the circumstances justify such a conclusion, a court may find that the injured plaintiff has brought about his injury, in part at least, by his own neglect for his safety. Indeed, the plaintiff may be totally responsible, as in *Dowler v. Bravender*, where the owner of a horse which kicked the plaintiff did not discharge the onus of proving that he lacked knowledge of the horse's dangerous propensity, yet the defendant was not liable because the plaintiff brought the injury on herself by shouting and frightening the horse. Whether a plaintiff is guilty of contributory negligence is a question of fact. Once such conduct is established, its effect in law depends upon the application of common law or statutory principles relevant to the apportionment of liability in consequence of contributory negligence.

(B) *Consent* Where the *scienter* doctrine is invoked, as in other situations, a defendant must plead that the plaintiff consented to the risk of being injured, or voluntarily assumed that risk: *volenti non fit injuria*. Whether a plaintiff has done so is a question of fact that depends on the circumstances. Such a plea was successful in *Young v. Green*, where the plaintiff, an odd-job man working with a traveling show or midway, volunteered to move a sign warning the public not to go near a lion cage. The sign was on top of the cage, from which position the plaintiff had previously retrieved it. On this occasion, while the plaintiff was trying to get hold of the sign, the lion put its paw through the bars and drew the plaintiff's arm into the cage, causing him injury. That plaintiff was denied an action on the ground that he was *volens*. He had consented to run the risk involved in his actions. . . .

Here the defendant ALS suggests that claims such as the one at bar should, in modern times, be resolved "within the modern and flexible parameters of negligence law". . . .

The ALS is a unique game farm experience in Canada and the United States. It is the only such facility to display tigers in an open environment. Tigers roam freely and patrons to the ALS drive in their vehicles among the animals. As it was described in the evidence — the patrons are caged and the animals roam freely — in contrast to the traditional zoo situation. . . .

It remains to consider whether any defence is, on the facts of this case available to the defendant, ALS.

The defendant, ALS relies on three defences, contributory negligence, consent and/ or voluntary assumption of risk and act of stranger.

Contributory Negligence

The defence in this respect relies on the passage in Fridman referenced above at p. 255 of the text more fully discussed by the author at page 263 also set out above.

It seems to me contradictory to hold a defendant strictly liable — i.e. whether negligent or not — and then to consider a plaintiffs "contributory" negligence. If one reads Fridman carefully I don't think he is really speaking of contributory "negligence" per se. He refers to the British Columbia decision of *Dowler v. Bravender* (1968), 67 D.L.R. (2d) 734 (B.C.S.C.). In that decision the court did not find the defendant liable under the scienter doctrine because it was not persuaded that she knew her horse was vicious or mischievous "in the sense that it would kick out purposely at human beings as alleged by the plaintiffs here". He concluded that the female plaintiff had "brought the accident upon herself by doing something that upset the horse with the result that the accident did not flow from any failure to control the animal but from a quite different cause — i.e. the actions of the plaintiff.

In any event, I have found that the injuries to and the damages suffered by both plaintiffs resulted from the unprovoked attack on their vehicle by the tiger Paca. That forceful assault on the vehicle caused Mr. Balac's body to inadvertently come into contact with the window switch resulting in the lowering of the windows on the vehicle which admitted the tiger into the vehicle. There was no conduct, in my view on the part of either David or Jennifer which would constitute contributory negligence on their part even if such defence were available. Their windows were up when they entered the Carnivore Section and were not deliberately put down for any purpose while in that Section before the attack, by either of them.

. . .

Consent/Voluntary Assumption of Risk

There is in my view on the factual findings made no basis for such a defence. Had the plaintiffs rolled their windows down or one of them, there might have been some basis for such a defence. On the facts as I have found them there is not.

It is clear on the evidence that the plaintiffs were aware that tigers are dangerous animals and it would be dangerous to put one's car window down in close proximity to a tiger. That knowledge — absent a finding that the plaintiffs put the window down — does not absolve the defendant ALS of liability. Unlike the situation in *Lewis v. Oeming*, [1983] A.J. No. 734 (Alta. Q.B.) where the plaintiff did something he had no business to do — i.e. enter the tiger's locked cage at night to retrieve his girlfriend's ball cap — these plaintiffs I have found, did nothing they had no business doing. On the contrary, they were, as I have found, merely driving through the compound, in their own vehicle with the windows up stopping occasionally to take photos — just as the owners of ALS contemplated they should do.

In *Crocker v. Sundance*, [[1988] 1 S.C.R. 1186], the Supreme Court of Canada made it clear that the volenti defence will only apply where the plaintiff assumed both the physical risk and the legal risk of his/her activity. The court stated that this defence would rarely be applicable. . . .

By analogy to this case there were but two signs — both just outside the main gate leading to the game reserves — one on each side of the road that are relevant to this argument. They read "All visitors enter the park at their own risk. No responsibility for damage to vehicle or person however caused is accepted". . . . Neither Jennifer nor David recalled seeing the signs and no one from ALS drew their attention to them.

On the brochure probably handed to them when they paid the admit fee it is stated: "All persons entering the reserves do so entirely at their own risk" and "No responsibility is accepted for damage to vehicles or trailers, their car bras, tires, lights or canvas covers, vinyl roofs or other accessories . . .". Neither read the brochure and no one from ALS pointed out the stated limitation to them. Although the employees at the booth were instructed to warn patrons of the possibility of damage to their vehicle, the only evidence on this point came from Jennifer and David who said they received no such warning. ALS called no evidence to contradict them. I accept their evidence on this point and note that employees in any event were only ever instructed to warn about damage to vehicles — nothing was said in relation to any injury to person.

There is simply no evidence — which it was the defence's burden to call — to support the argument that either David or Jennifer assumed any legal risk of their visit into the game reserves that day.

In my view the volenti defence is inapplicable. . . .

[The trial judge awarded $1,701,032 to David Balac and $813,169 to Jennifer Cowles. The Court of Appeal for Ontario upheld that decision: *Cowles v. Balac* (2006), 83 O.R. (3d) 660 (C.A.).]

NOTES AND QUESTIONS

1. As explained in *Cowles*, the common law distinguishes between animals that, by nature of their species, are ordinarily ferocious (*ferae naturae*), and animals that, as a species or by virtue of long domestication, are not usually dangerous (*mansuetae naturae*). A keeper is held strictly liable for injuries caused by *ferae naturae*, but is held strictly liable only for injuries caused by *mansuetae naturae* with *scienter*.

What is the *scienter* requirement? How does it differ from proof of negligence? Is it accurate to state that actions requiring proof of *scienter* involve strict liability?

Liability was claimed under both the tort of negligence and the *scienter* doctrine in *Ross v. Vidnes*, 2012 SKQB 317. The defendant owned a St. Bernard that was enormous, physically aggressive, and difficult to control. The plaintiff was a seven-year-old boy. He had been told to stay away from the defendant's house after he had struck the dog with a metal rod and punched the defendant's son. He nevertheless went to the defendant's door because he wished to retrieve his skateboard, which he had left in the defendant's backyard. The dog, which was indoors at the time, lunged at the boy and tore chunks of flesh from his face. Dawson J. held, on the basis of previous incidents, that the *scienter* doctrine applied. The "defendant knew that her St. Bernard regularly broke free of its restraints, was aggressive and had the propensity to cause harm" (at para. 33). Having caused considerable damage while under the defendant's control, the dog's actions accordingly triggered liability. Likewise, the same result could be reached under the tort of negligence because the defendant, considering all of the circumstances, failed to exercise reasonable care to ensure that her dog did not injure the plaintiff. The plaintiff was awarded non-pecuniary damages of $55,000 and special damages of $6,901.

2. Many of the cases arising from dog bites involve police dogs. In such circumstances, the *scienter* rule may not apply. That was true in *Tataquason v. Saskatoon (City) Board of Police Commissioners*, 2017 SKQB 98, aff'g 2016 SKPC 121. Constable Lalonde and Diego responded to a call regarding a knife robbery. Diego picked up a scent that led him to "engage" the plaintiff by holding her in place until the constable arrived. In the process, the plaintiff suffered a bitten cheek that required three stitches. Innocent of the robbery that initiated the episode, the plaintiff sued for, *inter alia*, the injury inflicted by Diego. In the course of denying liability, Kalmakoff J. explained that police dogs are essentially treated like other weapons or tools that are available to police officers. Consequently, rather than apply the *scienter* doctrine, he directed his "focus [to] the reasonableness of police actions and whether the circumstances under which the dog was deployed, and force was used, fall outside the scope of any statutory immunity or protection": at para. 56. That approach was justified by the unique position of police dogs. They and the officers who handle them receive intensive training. That "includes imprinting of the dogs for police work from the time the dogs are born, having trained dog handlers raise the dogs from the time they are pups, pairing dogs with suitable handling officers, and months of training with the officer before the dog is certified for police service" at para. 59. On the facts, there was no evidence to suggest that Constable Lalonde failed to reasonably handle Diego. See also *Myers v. Graham*, 2005 BCSC 5; *McQuillan v. Wong*, 2008 BCSC 536; *Sam v. Ministry of Public Safety & Solicitor General*, 2005 BCSC 331; *T.L.C. v. Vancouver (City)* (1996), 13 B.C.L.R. (3d) 301 (S.C.); and *Arnault v. Prince Albert (City) Police Commissioners* (1996), 136 Sask. R. 149 (Q.B.).

3. English courts have held that a keeper is strictly liable for any injury caused by a *ferae naturae*, even if the injury is unrelated to the animal's ferocity. However, a keeper is held strictly liable only for injuries attributable to the dangerous propensity of a *mansuetae naturae*. See *Behrens v. Bertram Mills Circus*, [1957] 1 All E.R. 583 (Q.B.); and *Glanville v. Sutton*, [1928] 1 K.B. 571.

4. Traditionally, a keeper was held strictly liable in these actions even if the animal was on the keeper's land and was restrained when it caused the injury. See Sappideen & Vines, eds., *Fleming's The Law of Torts*, 10th ed. (2011) at 412-13; and *McNeill v. Frankenfield* (1963), 44 D.L.R. (2d) 132 (B.C.C.A.). However, as noted in *Cowles*, some courts have held that strict liability applies only if the keeper loses control or custody of the animal. See *Maynes v. Galicz*, [1976] 1 W.W.R. 557 (B.C.S.C.); *Lewis v. Oeming* (1983), 24 C.C.L.T. 81 (Alta. Q.B.); and Irvine, "Annotation" (1983), 24 C.C.L.T. 82.

5. Strict liability generally is divided between *Rylands v. Fletcher* and animals. Both possibilities — plus another — were argued in *George v. Newfoundland &*

Labrador, 2014 NLTD(G) 106, aff'd 2016 NLCA 24. The plaintiffs commenced a class action and alleged that the defendant province, which bore responsibility for both the management of wildlife and the condition of highways, was liable for deaths, injuries, and losses arising from moose-vehicle collisions ("MVCs").

Under *Rylands v. Fletcher*, the plaintiffs pointed to the fact that moose had been deliberately introduced into the province near the end of the 19th century, and argued that the creatures had an unfortunate tendency to wander out of the forest and onto highways, where they present a significant peril. That claim was dismissed on the grounds that (1) "there is nothing unnatural about populating the forests of Newfoundland with an animal whose natural habitat is the forest," (2) moose are not inherently dangerous, and (3) "by moving from one area of Crown land (the forest) to another (the highway), moose are not 'escaping' from the Defendant's property but are simply moving from one place owned by the Defendant to another. Moose are *ferae naturae* and, as such, are wont to roam": at paras. 62, 64.

Under the alternative theory of liability, the plaintiffs argued that the defendant effectively had control over the moose and therefore was strictly liable for the damage that the animals caused. The court rejected that allegation on the ground that while the Crown may briefly have owned the individual animals that it had introduced into the province, moose today wander freely, unconstrained by any human ownership or control.

Finally, the court entertained the possibility of recognizing a new strict liability tort in connection with abnormally dangerous activities, but found that such a principle would not be applicable on the facts. The "presence of moose on our highways is not an act of the Defendant; neither is it so fraught with danger, or so unusual in a given community, that . . . the risk of loss should be shifted from the person injured to the person who merely by engaging in such conduct, created the risk which resulted in harm" (at para. 73). Furthermore, if the plaintiffs' argument was accepted, the defendant "would become a *de facto* insurer for all human-moose interactions in the Province which may result in some form of damage. This would be an untenable result, which would expose the Defendant to a massive and indeterminate amount of strict liability" (at para. 75).

6. Voluntary assumption of risk is the only generally recognized defence to actions involving dangerous animals. It is not clear whether the defendant can raise the plaintiff's contributory negligence. *Cowles* suggests not. See also *Higgins v. William Inglis & Sons Pty. Ltd.*, [1978] 1 N.S.W.L.R. 649 (C.A.). It is also doubtful whether "acts of God" or "acts of a stranger" are applicable defences. See Sappideen & Vines, eds., *Fleming's The Law of Torts*, 10th ed. (2011) at 417-18. See also *McNeill v. Frankenfield, supra; Lewis v. Oeming, supra;* and *Witman v. Johnson* (1990), 5 C.C.L.T. (2d) 102 (Man. Q.B.).

7. A person injured by a wild animal enjoys the option of suing in both strict liability and negligence. In what circumstances would the plaintiff have a remedy in strict liability but not negligence? Are there circumstances in which the reverse is true? See *Fleming v. Atkinson*, [1959] S.C.R. 513; *Morris v. Baily* (1970), 13 D.L.R. (3d) 150 (Ont. C.A.); *Maynes v. Galicz, supra;* and *Moffett v. Downing* (1981), 16 C.C.L.T. 313 (Ont. C.A.).

8. Compensatory relief is the usual remedy. In exceptional cases, however, the plaintiff may also receive aggravated or punitive damages. See *Meloche v. Bezaire*, [2005] O.T.C. 170 (S.C.J.) (confusing aggravated and punitive damages).

9. Many provinces have enacted legislation governing liability for dangerous animals. Some of the statutes simply embody the common law rules, but others operate differently. In Ontario, for example, liability may be imposed, without proof of *scienter*, upon a person whose dog has caused injury: *Dog Owner's Liability Act*, R.S.O. 1990, c. D.16, s. 2. See also *Animal Liability Act*, C.C.S.M. c. A95, s. 2; the *Animal Health and Protection Act*, S.N.L. 2010, c. A-9.1, s. 34; *Halifax Regional Municipality Charter*, S.N.S. 2008, c. 39, s. 197; *Bowles v. Wilton*, 2018 NSSM 55; and *Lofstrom v. Hydamaka*, 2013 MBQB 220.

While the Ontario legislation is based on strict liability, it does state that damages shall be adjusted in proportion to the defendant's degree of fault: *Strom (Litigation Guardian of) v. White* (1994), 21 O.R. (3d) 205 (Gen. Div.). See also *Moretto v. Nicolini-Femia*, 2017 ONSC 3945 (merely patting apparently friendly dog did not constitute contributory negligence).

Ontario's statute was applied in *Kent (Litigation Guardian of) v. Laverdiere*, 2011 ONSC 5411. The defendant, a dog breeder, owned nine French Mastiffs (large and powerful animals). The plaintiff, her eleven-year-old grand-daughter, was brutally mauled while visiting. The statute states:

2(1) The owner of a dog is liable for damages resulting from a bite or attack by the dog on another person or domestic animal. . . .

(3) The liability of the owner does not depend upon knowledge of the propensity of the dog or fault or negligence on the part of the owner, but the court shall reduce the damages awarded in proportion to the degree, if any, to which the fault or negligence of the plaintiff caused or contributed to the damages.

The court consequently was uninterested in evidence showing that the defendant "exerted control over the dogs [which] were obedient" (at para. 108), and that "the dogs had not demonstrated aggressive behaviour with children" previously. Given the legislation, the defendant was "strictly liable for the actions of her dogs" (at para. 109).

Section 2 of Ontario's statute allows a court to impose liability upon the "owner" of a dog that has caused injury. The term "owner" is broadly defined. Section 1 states that an "owner" includes "a person who possesses or harbours the dog." That provision proved crucial in *Wilk v. Arbour*, 2017 ONCA 21. Donna Wilk and Kevin Arbour were in an intimate relationship. She received his permission to take his Great Dane, Zeus, for a walk. During the outing, Zeus had a seizure and stumbled down an embankment into a ditch. When Donna fell into the ditch while trying to retrieve Zeus, he bit off half of her thumb. The ensuing claim under the Act turned on the "ownership" of Zeus. Observing that the Act defines an "owner" as one who "possesses" a dog, the trial judge held that "the word 'possesses' . . . means the exercise of dominion and control similar and in substitution for that which ordinarily would be exerted by its owner (namely the person to whom the dog belongs) over the dog": *Wilk v. Arbour*, 2016 ONSC 1179 at para. 40. Weiler J.A. disagreed. The legislative intention, she found, was to impose responsibility on those who are in the best position to control dogs and thereby prevent injuries. That category includes not only people who "own" dogs in the fullest sense, but also those who "possess" them by controlling them. Since the plaintiff fell within that definition at the time of the incident, she was Zeus' "owner" and consequently did not have a statutory action against her now ex-boyfriend

10. As a result of several well-publicized incidents, Ontario amended its legislation in 2005 to introduce special provisions affecting "pit bulls" (as defined by the statute). The new laws place severe restrictions upon the ownership and control of such animals. Ontario's statute also states that a pit bull that has bitten another dog or a person must be destroyed. The scope of that provision was examined in *R. v. Huggins*, 2010 ONCA 746.

11. Many actions resulting from animal attacks are brought under the common or statutory law of occupiers' liability, as discussed in Chapter 23. What are the advantages and disadvantages of this approach? See *Taller (Guardian ad litem of) v. Goldenshtein*, [1994] 3 W.W.R. 557 (B.C.C.A.). However, where loss or injury is caused by a dog attack on the owner's property, s. 3 of the Ontario *Dog Owner's Liability Act, supra*, states that liability must be resolved under that statute rather than under the *Occupiers' Liability Act*, R.S.O. 1990, c. O.2.

12. Liability for animals is partially governed by statute in England. If the *Animals Act 1971* does not apply, then liability falls to the general action in negligence. If the statute does apply, then liability is strict. The statute applies to dangerous animals. Dangerous animals fall into two categories. The first category includes animals that are not commonly domesticated in the British Isles and are likely to cause severe harm. The second category includes other animals that are known to be dangerous in accordance with a three-part test.: (1) "the damage is of a kind which the animal, unless restrained, was likely to cause or which, if caused by the animal, was likely to be severe" and (2) "the likelihood of the damage or of its being severe was due to characteristics of the animal which are not normally found in animals of the same species or are not normally so found except at particular times or in particular circumstances," and (3) "those characteristics were known to that keeper or were at any time known to a person who at that time had charge of the animal."

While that entire test is opaque, the second element is most contentious. Over the years, it generated two interpretations. The broad view applied strict liability if the relevant risk either was not normal for the species *or* was normal for the species, but only in unusual circumstances. The narrow view applied strict liability only if the relevant risk was abnormal for the species under either normal or abnormal circumstances. The essential difference between the two interpretations pertained to damage caused by animals acting normally in abnormal circumstances (*e.g.* domesticated dogs normally do not bite, but female dogs frequently snap when protecting their young).

The debate was resolved in *Mirvahedy v. Henley*, [2003] 2 A.C. 491 (H.L.). The defendant exercised reasonable control over its horses. Nevertheless, during a thunderstorm, the animals panicked, broke free from their paddock, and ran onto the road. The claimant was injured when his car collided with one of the horses. Although horses seldom panic and stampede under normal conditions, they frequently do so when spooked. The court therefore was required to select from between the broad and narrow interpretations of the statutory provision. By a three-to-two majority, it preferred the broader approach, largely on the belief that it better reflected Parliament's intention. The defendant consequently was strictly liable for the claimant's losses. For discussion, see Howarth, "The House of Lords and the Animals Act: Closing the Stable Door" [2003] C.L.J. 548; and Amirthalingam, "Animal Liability — Equine, Canine and Asinine" (2003) 119 L.Q.R. 563.

(b) CATTLE TRESPASS

ACKER v. KERR
(1973), 42 D.L.R. (3d) 514 (Ont. Co. Ct.)

THOMPSON CO. CT. J.:—This action is brought by the plaintiff as the owner of lot No. 11, Concession 4 in the Township of Proton, in the County of Grey, against the defendant as the owner of adjoining lot No. 12, Concession 4 in the said Township of Proton for damages which the plaintiff alleges were sustained by him as a result of the failure of the defendant to properly confine cattle owned by him and placed by him on his property so that such animals were permitted to stray onto the property of the defendant.

The plaintiff alleges that the straying in question took place in the years 1969, 1970 and 1971 and that as a result of the same, he sustained damages in the sum of $2,650.

Evidence was tendered by both parties which satisfies me that indeed the cattle of the defendant did get onto the property of the plaintiff during the years just mentioned doing some damage to crops of the plaintiff, the extent of which will be more fully referred to later on in my reasons for judgment.

The matter of the liability, if any, of the defendant for the damages in fact sustained by the plaintiff is rather complex and has many ramifications as will be seen.

Counsel for the plaintiff takes the position that once cattle are allowed to stray and damage is done, a trespass has been committed and the injured party is entitled to such damages as he may have sustained regardless of anything done or omitted to be done by such injured party which may have been a contributing factor to the damages so sustained. On the other hand, counsel for the defendant takes the position that the plaintiff was the author of his own misfortune as in essence he failed to keep up and repair a portion of the line fence which existed between the two farms and the cattle were thereby permitted to stray onto his property. Counsel for the plaintiff further contends that whether or not the plaintiff was obliged to maintain the fence and whether or not the fence was in a state of disrepair has nothing whatever to do with the end result and that unless the plaintiff was guilty of some positive act which enabled the defendant's cattle to get onto the plaintiff's land, he could not be held responsible either in whole or in part for the damage resulting from the cattle straying.

. . .

[The judge considered the *Line Fences Act*, R.S.O. 1970, c. 248, s. 2(1), and concluded that it imposed no affirmative duty on the plaintiff to maintain the fence.]

Counsel for the plaintiff cited innumerable authorities for the proposition that the defendant in circumstances as they exist here is liable to the plaintiff for damages for trespass.

I take it from these cases to be the law that the owner of animals *domitae naturae* is bound to keep them under control and is liable if they escape for such damage as it is ordinarily in their nature to commit. The liability is an absolute liability independent of negligence unless the escape or trespass was involuntary or caused by an Act of God or was due to the act or default of the plaintiff or of a third party for whom the defendant is not in law responsible. No case has been referred to me by counsel for the defendant which in any way detracts from this statement of the law.

[The judge then analyzed the *Pounds Act*, R.S.O. 1970, c. 353, s. 2, which, in his view, set out in statute form the requirements of the common law.]

In the cases to which I have made reference there is none which contains exactly the factual situation with which we are confronted here, but none the less I am of the opinion that the principle which I have enunciated is applicable, and on finding as I do, that the escape or trespass was not involuntary or caused by an Act of God or was due to the act or default of the plaintiff or of a third person for whom the defendant is not responsible, liability on the defendant does arise for such escape and subsequent trespass and damages.

As I have indicated, it would be almost impossible to tell just at which part of the fence in question the animals escaped but on the other hand as I have also indicated, it is not necessary for the purposes of my decision to make a finding in that regard because, in my view, it makes no difference whether it was in that portion of the fence which it might be argued was the responsibility of the plaintiff to maintain and repair or that portion of the fence which it might be argued was the responsibility of the defendant to maintain and repair or both. It was the defendant's cattle that escaped and it was the responsibility of the defendant when he put the cattle in the field to see that the fences were kept in such a state of repair as to contain the cattle within such field whether by himself seeing to the necessary work in that connection or by some agreement with the plaintiff which would exonerate the defendant from that responsibility, which agreement I find to be lacking.

NOTES AND QUESTIONS

1. Based on *Acker*, what are the principles governing cattle trespass and its defences? Why was the condition of the plaintiff's fences not considered relevant in determining if there was a defence? In *Singleton v. Williamson* (1861), 158 E.R. 533 (C.A.), the plaintiff's breach of an affirmative obligation to maintain his fence provided the defendant with a defence to cattle trespass. Can you reconcile *Acker* and *Singleton*?

2. The English common law cases provided that an owner of a straying animal was not liable for damages it caused on the highway. See *Searle v. Wallbank*, [1947] A.C. 341 (H.L.). In *Fleming v. Atkinson*, [1959] S.C.R. 513, three judges clearly rejected this principle and held that liability in such cases was governed by negligence. The other two judges for the majority did not find it necessary to reject *Searle*, but they did limit its application to narrow circumstances. The two dissenting judges followed *Searle*. Since *Fleming*, the great majority of Canadian courts have held that liability for straying animals on highways is governed by negligence. See for example *Crosby v. Curry* (1969), 7 D.L.R. (3d) 188 (N.S.S.C.); *MacKinnon v. Ellis* (1978), 20 Nfld. & P.E.I.R. 297 (P.E.I.S.C.); *Windrem v. Hamill* (1978), 95 D.L.R. (3d) 381 (Sask. C.A.); *Rozon v. Patenaude* (1982), 35 O.R. (2d) 619 (Co. Ct.); and *Ruckheim v. Robinson*, [1995] 4 W.W.R. 284 (B.C.C.A.).

3. At common law, if an animal was lawfully on a highway and then escaped onto the plaintiff's land, the case was governed by negligence. See *Goodwyn v. Cheveley* (1859), 157 E.R. 989 (Exch.). However, if the animal escaped from the defendant's land to the highway and then entered the plaintiff's land, strict liability applied. Should the place from where an animal strays affect the owner's liability? See Williams, *Liability for Animals* (1939) at 369-76.

4. Although cattle trespass cases usually involve only property damage, the action can be invoked to recover for personal injuries: see *Wormald v. Cole*, [1954] 1 Q.B. 614 (C.A.).

5. The term "cattle trespass" is misleading. The governing rules apply not only to cattle, but also to other straying animals (*e.g.* goats, pigs, horses, chickens). The same rules do not, however, apply with respect to cats and dogs. What is the rationale for that exception? Most provinces have enacted legislation making the owner of a dog liable for injuries to livestock. In some provinces, the protection extends to any kind of property damage. See, for example, *Animal Health and Protection Act*, S.N.L. 2010, c. A-9.1, s. 34.

6. Most provinces have now enacted legislation to deal with straying animals. In *Acker*, it was held that the *Pounds Act*, R.S.O. 1970, c. 353 (now R.S.O. 1990, c. P. 17) did not alter the common law action for cattle trespass. See also *Stray Animals Act*, R.S.A. 2000, c. S-20.

7. What was the rationale for imposing strict liability in cattle trespass? Can this principle still be justified? Would you favour the adoption of negligence principles for all cases of straying animals?

8. If a cow damaged the plaintiff's property after straying from the defendant's land, could the plaintiff successfully invoke the rule in *Rylands v. Fletcher*?

9. For a detailed discussion of liability for animals see North, *Civil Liability for Animals* (2012); and Sandys-Winsch, *Animal Law* (1984).

4. Products Liability: Negligence or Strict Liability?

In the Canadian common law jurisdictions, the roots of contemporary products liability lie in *Donoghue v. Stevenson*, [1932] A.C. 562 (H.L.). As a general proposition, unless a contract is involved, a consumer injured by a product must sue the manufacturer in negligence. The plaintiff therefore must prove that the manufacturer breached the requisite standard of care in the design, production or distribution of the product, and that the defendant's carelessness caused or contributed to actual harm. The situation is different if the injured party acquired the item under contract. Contractual obligations are strict. Moreover, by virtue of consumer protection legislation (particularly the provincial statutes on the sale of goods), most consumer contracts impose obligations upon vendors to, *inter alia*, provide goods that are "fit for their intended purpose" and of "merchantable quality." If a contractual obligation is breached, and the purchaser consequently suffers injury, the vendor is strictly liable. Notice, however, that the legislation applies only as between contractual parties. That is why May Donoghue was forced to sue in negligence. She received her bottle of ginger beer as a gift from a friend.

In contrast, products liability in Québec and the United States is based on principles of strict liability. A plaintiff need prove only that the product was defective and that the defect caused injury. Considerable effort has been devoted to comparing the relative merits of negligence and strict liability. Manufacturers undoubtedly are held liable more often under principles of strict liability. Advocates of strict liability defend that result. They argue that manufacturers are profit-driven to create risks, that consumers rarely are in a position to evaluate the risks associated with products, and that manufacturers are in the best position to minimize defects and insure against the losses.

Strict liability also has its critics, particularly in the United States. In the 1960s, juries in the United States began making very large general and punitive damage awards in product liability cases, both to generously compensate injured plaintiffs and to punish and deter irresponsible manufacturers. Critics argue that the real beneficiaries were plaintiffs' lawyers, who orchestrated thousands of products liability claims and reaped enormous contingency fees for their efforts. It is often contended that strict liability is a major hindrance to the efficiency and competitiveness of American industry.

In the 1990s, American manufacturers and their insurers lobbied intensively for what they dubbed "tort reform." Essentially, this movement sought legislation to narrow the common law principles of strict liability, limit the discretion of juries, minimize or cap punitive damage awards, and otherwise protect industry from product liability claims. Although some industries were quite successful in restricting their exposure, the tort reform movement has enjoyed only limited success. Needless to say, consumer associations and trial lawyers have vigorously opposed the tort reform efforts.

NOTES AND QUESTIONS

1. There has been relatively little public debate on products liability in Canada. What aspects of Canadian tort law and the legal profession might explain that lack of controversy? What other important differences between Canada and the United States have helped shape their respective products liability laws? For judicial statements of the Canadian position, see: *Cantlie v. Canadian Heating Products Inc.*, 2017 BCSC 286 at para. 272; *Player Estate v. Janssen-Ortho Inc.*, 2014 BCSC 1122 at para. 246; and *Daishowa-Marubeni International Ltd. v. Toshiba International Corp.*, 2010 ABQB 627 at para. 40.

2. Until recently, the Canadian alcohol and tobacco industries have been largely immune to major products liability litigation. Given the deaths, injuries and illnesses attributable to these products, what political and economic factors explain the relative invulnerability of these industries to products liability claims?

3. Many of the most widely publicized products liability claims in Canada have related to breast implants and various aspects of the "tainted-blood scandal": *Hollis v. Dow Corning Inc.* (1995), 129 D.L.R. (4th) 609 (S.C.C.); and *Walker Estate v. York-Finch General Hospital* (2001), 198 D.L.R. (4th) 193 (S.C.C.). What explains the

relative success of this litigation in contrast to the lack of progress in claims against tobacco and alcohol manufacturers?

4. In some cases, the victim of a defective product will enjoy a right of recovery under statute. See for example *Morse v. Cott Beverages West Ltd.* (2001), [2002] 4 W.W.R. 281 (Sask. Q.B.), applying the *Consumer Products Warranties Act*, R.S.S. 1978, c. C-30, s. 2(h)(i). However, consumers must accept some responsibility for their own safety: see *Tudor Inn Reception Hall (1992) Ltd. v. Merzat Industries Ltd.*, 2006 CarswellOnt 5496 (S.C.J.) (WL Can).

5. For a review of the various issues, see Boivin, "Strict Liability Revisited" (1996) 33 Osgoode Hall L.J. 487; "Symposium on Products Liability: Comparative Approaches and Transnational Litigation" in (1999) 34 Tex. Int. L.J.; Waddams, "New Directions in Products Liability" in Mullany and Linden, eds., *Torts Tomorrow: A Tribute to John Fleming* (1998) at 119-29; and Waddams, *Products Liability*, 5th ed. (2011), ch. 11.

5. Vicarious Liability

Under the doctrine of strict liability, the defendant may be held liable without acting intentionally, carelessly, or unreasonably. It is enough that the relevant obligation was breached. The doctrine of vicarious liability goes even further. Liability may be imposed even though the defendant did not breach any obligation at all.

As the following sections indicate, vicarious liability may arise under three headings: (1) *statutory vicarious liability*, (2) *agency*, and (3) *employment* or *master-servant* relationship. Because of a common misperception, however, it is important to identify one other situation that does *not* attract the doctrine. Parents are not vicariously liable for their children's torts. That is true even under "parental responsibility legislation." As explained in Chapter 3, those statutes merely impose a presumption, in some circumstances, that a parent negligently failed to control or supervise the child, and therefore is *personally* liable.

(a) STATUTORY VICARIOUS LIABILITY

A vehicle may be owned by one person, but driven by another, at the time of an accident. Under the common law principles examined below, the vehicle's owner could be held vicariously liable only if the driver was its employee or agent. As a result of legislation, however, the scope of vicarious liability is cast more widely. Unfortunately, the statutes vary somewhat from jurisdiction to jurisdiction. One common approach is exemplified by s. 192 of Ontario's *Highway Traffic Act*, R.S.O. 1990, c. H.8:

> 192. (1) The driver of a motor vehicle or street car is liable for loss or damage sustained by any person by reason of negligence in the operation of the motor vehicle or street car on a highway.
>
> (2) The owner of a motor vehicle or street car is liable for loss or damage sustained by any person by reason of negligence in the operation of the motor vehicle or street car on a highway, unless the motor vehicle or street car was without the owner's consent in the possession of some person other than the owner or the owner's chauffeur.

(3) A lessee of a motor vehicle or street car is liable for loss or damage sustained by any person by reason of negligence in the operation of the motor vehicle or street car on a highway, unless the motor vehicle or street car was without the lessee's consent in the possession of some person other than the lessee or the lessee's chauffeur.

(4) Where a motor vehicle is leased, the consent of the lessee to the operation or possession of the motor vehicle by some person other than the lessee shall, for the purposes of subsection (2), be deemed to be the consent of the owner of the motor vehicle.

Another model appears in Alberta's *Highway Traffic Act*, R.S.A. 2000, c. H.8:

181. In an action for the recovery of loss or damage sustained by a person by reason of a motor vehicle on a highway,

> (a) a person driving the motor vehicle and living with and as a member of the family of the owner of it, and
> (b) a person who is driving the motor vehicle and who is in possession of it with the consent, express or implied, of the owner of it,

is deemed to be the agent or servant of the owner of the motor vehicle and to be employed as such, and is deemed to be driving the motor vehicle in the course of that person's employment, but nothing in this section relieves any person deemed to be the agent or servant of the owner and to be driving the motor vehicle in the course of that person's employment from the liability for the damages.

Similar legislation exists across the country. Whatever form the special rule takes, its rationale is clear. In modern society, vehicles are frequently instruments of harm. Liability insurance is prevalent, but normally it is purchased in connection with the ownership, rather than the operation, of a vehicle. Consequently, if traffic accident victims are to be compensated, they require access to the owner's insurance.

NOTES AND QUESTIONS

1. Explain the difference between the approaches adopted in Ontario and Alberta. Which is more straightforward? Which is more likely to impose liability upon an owner?

2. The concept of statutory vicarious liability applied in *Yeung (Guardian ad litem of) v. Au*, [2007] 3 S.C.R. 371. An action was commenced on behalf of a young woman injured in a car accident. The vehicle was owned by the defendant corporation, leased by a father, and driven by his son. In a one-sentence judgment, McLachlin C.J.C. held that the legislative scheme established by s. 86 of the *Motor Vehicle Act*, R.S.B.C. 1996, c. 318 extended vicarious liability to both the father and the corporation.

3. The legislation imposes vicarious liability if an accident occurs while a vehicle is being driven by a person with the owner's consent. The nature of that consent has proven controversial. *Fernandes v. Araujo*, 2015 ONCA 571 is a leading case. Carlos Almeida owned a farm and an all-terrain vehicle (ATV). He invited two cousins and their respective girlfriends, Eliana and Sara, to visit for the day. Carlos gave the young women permission to use the ATV, but indicated that they must not leave his property. Some time later, the two women rolled the ATV while they were violating that prohibition. Sara, who was riding as the passenger, was injured. In the ensuing

litigation, she argued that Carlos was vicariously liable under s. 192(2) of Ontario's *Highway Traffic Act*, but his insurer sought to escape liability on the ground that the accident occurred while the women were exceeding the scope of his consent. The issue supported contradictory lines of authority. *Finlayson v GMAC Leaseco Ltd.* (2007), 86 O.R. (3d) 481 (C.A.) held that vicarious liability under the Act rested on the owner's consent to *possession*, rather than *operation*. Consequently, as long as the owner permitted the driver to use the vehicle, vicarious liability was possible even if the driver acted in a way that the owner had expressly prohibited. *Newman v. Terdik*, [1953] O.R. 1 (C.A.), in contrast, denied vicarious liability if the accident occurred while the driver was violating a condition imposed by the owner. In *Fernandes v. Araujo*, Sharpe J.A. reviewed the authorities and found *Finlayson* to be preferable. He rejected the idea that rightful possession could transform into wrongful possession merely because the driver ignored the owner's restrictions on the use of the vehicle. Additionally, he found, *Finlayson* better served the purpose of the vicarious liability provision, which is "the protection of the public by insisting that the owner of a vehicle exercise careful management when giving permission to another person to use it. This purpose is achieved by imposing vicariously liability for damages if the vehicle is operated in a negligent fashion": at para. 35. *Newman v. Terdik* was accordingly overruled.

The Alberta Court of Appeal reached the same conclusion in *Mugford v. Weber* (2004), 29 Alta. L.R. (4th) 16 (C.A.). An employer expressly stipulated that a company vehicle was to be used exclusively for business purposes. The plaintiff was injured after an employee, disregarding that prohibition, drunkenly drove a company truck to a friend's house. The employer could not escape vicarious liability by pointing to its own rule. Wittmann J.A. explained that s. 181(1)(b) of Alberta's *Highway Traffic Act* does not accommodate conditional consent to the use of a vehicle.

Those decisions can be contrasted with *Garrioch v. Tessman*, 2017 ABCA 105. A company called Sonex Construction provided an employee named Garrioch with a truck so that he could work at a remote site. Although the company did not know that he lacked a valid driver's license, Garrioch knew that he should not get behind the wheel, so he gave the keys to Tessman. Tessman had previously worked for Sonex, but his employment had been terminated six weeks earlier. Against that backdrop, a difficult question arose after Tessman involved the truck in an accident that injured the plaintiffs. Could it be said that Tessman operated the vehicle with Sonex's consent? The trial judge answered in the affirmative. She reasoned that Sonex's actual consent to Garrioch's possession, and Garrioch's actual consent to Tessman's possession, meant that Sonex also impliedly consented to Tessman's possession: *Garrioch v. Tessman*, 2015 ABQB 480. That was a step too far for the Alberta Court of Appeal. Slatter J.A. accepted "the general rule that consent to possession of the vehicle cannot be given on conditions," (at para. 35) but he also insisted that "[j]ust because the owner consents to one driver having possession of his vehicle does not mean that the owner consents to the whole world having possession": at para. 56. On the contrary, Sonex had a "designated driver" policy that restricted the use of its vehicles to specific employees. The company consequently had not consented to Tessman's use of its truck.

For other examples of the difficulties created by the statutory provisions see *Prentzas v. Rivera*, 2017 ONSC 247; *Ligaj v Ismail*, 2017 ONSC 2056; *MacDonald v. Mitchell* (1969), 10 D.L.R. (3d) 240 (N.B.C.A.); *Deakins v. Aarsen* (1970), 17 D.L.R. (3d) 494 (S.C.C.); *Hayduk v. Pidoborozny* (1971), 19 D.L.R. (3d) 160 (Alta. C.A.);

Daigle v. Theo Couturier Ltd. (1973), 43 D.L.R. (3d) 151 (N.B.C.A.); *Honan v. Gerhold* (1974), 50 D.L.R. (3d) 582 (S.C.C.); *Schroth v. Innes* (1976), 71 D.L.R. (3d) 647 (B.C.C.A.); *Mader v. MacPhee* (1978), 84 D.L.R. (3d) 761 (N.S.C.A.); *Lajeunesse v. Janssens* (1983), 3 D.L.R. (4th) 163 (Ont. H.C.); *Barreiro v. Arana*, [2003] 4 W.W.R. 391 (B.C.C.A.); *Gilbert v. Giffin*, 2010 NSCA 95; and *Pugsley v. Rahbar* (2002), 41 C.C.L.I. (3d) 62 (Ont. S.C.J.). See also *Pawlak v. Doucette*, [1985] 2 W.W.R. 588 (B.C.S.C.), where the test of vicarious liability in motor vehicle cases was applied to the owner of a boat. On the intersection of vicarious liability and the fault provisions in workers' compensation legislation, see *McIver v. McIntyre*, 2018 ABCA 151.

4. For a discussion of the legislation, see Fridman *et al.*, *The Law of Torts in Canada*, 3d ed. (2010) at 266-67. For a discussion of vicarious liability generally, see Atiyah, *Vicarious Liability in the Law of Torts* (1967); Giliker, *Vicarious Liability in Tort: A Comparative Perspective* (2010); and Gray, *Vicarious Liability: Critique and Reform* (2018).

(b) PRINCIPAL-AGENT RELATIONSHIP

In an agency relationship, the principal authorizes the agent to act on its behalf. Quite commonly, for example, a company will empower a person to enter contracts for its benefit. As illustrated in the case extracted below, the principal may be held liable for the agent's torts. It is important to bear in mind, however, that an agent may also be an employee. If so, the doctrine of vicarious liability may arise as a result of that employment relationship. The principles are much the same in either event and, indeed, there may no longer be much need to distinguish between the two situations. See Fridman *et al.*, *The Law of Torts in Canada*, 3d ed. (2010) at 277-78.

T.G. BRIGHT & CO. v. KERR
[1939] 1 D.L.R. 193 (S.C.C.)

[The court considered whether the defendant, a wine dealer, was vicariously liable for the negligence of its motorcycle deliveryman. Although the deliveryman was held to be the defendant's agent, the majority concluded that he was not the defendant's servant or employee because the defendant had no control over the precise manner in which the task was performed. The following excerpt from Duff C.J.C.'s dissenting judgment is limited to the issue of vicarious liability.]

DUFF C.J.C. (dissenting).: . . . It would appear to be necessary to make some reference to the ground upon which the responsibility of a principal for the acts of his agent rests.

Respondant superior is a rule which does not rest upon any notion of imputed guilt or fault. The fallacy that it does was responsible for the difficulty that great lawyers of the last century felt (Bramwell, B., for example) in admitting the liability of a corporation for the fraud of its agents. In *Hern v. Nichols*, 1 Salk. 289, 91 E.R. 256, the point in issue was the responsibility of a merchant for the deceit of his factor beyond the sea. Holt, C.J., states the broad ground of responsibility thus: —

> . . . for seeing somebody must be a loser by this deceit, it is more reason that he that employs and puts a trust and confidence in the deceiver should be a loser, than a stranger . . .

In *Hall v. Smith*, 2 Bing. 156, at p. 160, 130 E.R. 265, Best, C.J., says: —

The maxim of *respondeat superior* is bottomed on this principle, that he who expects to derive advantage from an act which is done by another for him, must answer for any injury which a third person may sustain from it.

The principal having the power of choice has selected the agent to perform in his place a class or classes of acts, and, to adapt the language of Collins, M.R., in *Hamlyn v. Houston & Co.*, [1903] 1 K.B. 81, at pp. 85-6, it is not unjust that he who has selected him and will have the benefit of his services if efficiently performed should bear the risk of his negligence in "matters incidental to the doing of the acts the performance of which has been delegated to him."

The rule has been precisely explained in the House of Lords. . . . In *Percy v. Glasgow Corp.*, [1922] 2 A.C. 299, at pp. 306-7, Viscount Haldane said: —

As was laid down by Story in a passage adopted in an earlier case by Blackburn J. and approved in this House in *Lloyd v. Grace, Smith & Co.* [[1912] A.C. 716 at 737] "the principal is liable to third persons in a civil suit 'for the frauds, deceits, concealments, misrepresentations, torts, negligences, and other malfeasances or misfeasances, and omissions of duty of his agent *in the course of his employment*, although the principal did not authorise, or justify, or participate in, or indeed know of such misconduct, or even if he forbade the acts, or disapproved of them. The limitation is that 'the tort or negligence occurs in the course of the agency. For the principal is not liable for the torts or negligences of his agent in any matters beyond the scope of the agency, unless he has expressly authorised them to be done, or he has subsequently adopted them for his own use and benefit.'"

NOTES AND QUESTIONS

1. According to Duff C.J.C., does the principal's liability arise from its own culpability?

2. A partnership is based on a principle of mutual agency. As a result, if one partner commits a tort, every other partner may be held vicariously liable. See *Blyh v. Fladgate*, [1891] 1 Ch. 377; *McDonic v. Hetherington* (1997), 142 D.L.R. (4th) 648 (Ont. C.A.); and *Partnership Act*, R.S.O. 1990, c. P-5, s. 11

In some situations, however, the traditional rules may now be displaced for the purposes of a *limited liability partnership* (LLP). As the name suggests, such partnerships are unusual insofar as the liability of the individual partners is limited. Sections 11-13 of Alberta's *Partnership Act*, R.S.A. 2000, c. P-3 illustrate the distinction between traditional partnerships and limited liability partnerships:

Liability of partner

11(1) This section is to be applied subject to section 12.
(2) Each partner in a firm is liable jointly with the other partners for debts and obligations of the firm incurred while that partner is a partner. . . .

LLP limited liability

12(1) Subject to subsections (2) and (4), a partner in an Alberta LLP is not individually liable, directly or indirectly by means of indemnification, contribution, assessment or otherwise, for debts, obligations or liabilities of the partnership or another partner that arise from the negligence, wrongful acts or omissions, malpractice or misconduct of

> (a) another partner, or
> (b) an employee, agent or representative of the partnership

that occur in the ordinary course of carrying on practice in an eligible profession within the meaning of section 81 while the partnership is an Alberta LLP.

(2) Subsection (1) does not operate to protect a partner from liability

> (a) where the partner knew of the negligence, wrongful act or omission, malpractice or misconduct at the time it was committed and failed to take reasonable steps to prevent its commission, or
> (b) where

>> (i) the negligence, wrongful act or omission, malpractice or misconduct was committed by an employee, agent or representative of the partnership for whom the partner was directly responsible in a supervisory role, and
>> (ii) the partner failed to provide such adequate and competent supervision as would normally be expected of a partner in those circumstances.

(3) A partner in an Alberta LLP is not a proper party to a proceeding by or against the partnership that claims relief in respect of negligence, wrongful acts or omissions, malpractice or misconduct referred to in subsection (1).

(4) The protection from liability given to a partner under subsection (1) shall not be construed as offering any protection from claims against that partner's interest in the partnership property.

Liability of firm for wrongs

13 When, by a wrongful act or omission of a partner acting in the ordinary course of the business of the firm or with the authority of the partner's co-partners, loss or injury is caused to a person not being a partner in the firm, or a penalty is incurred, the firm is liable for it to the same extent as the partner so acting or omitting to act.

Similar provisions were enacted across the country around the turn of the last century. Can you suggest any explanation for the sudden proliferation of such statutes? Who benefits from the existence of LLPs? Do LLPs adversely affect anyone?

3. A group of people who wish to establish a business generally are free to select from among several models, including partnership and incorporation. For present purposes, there is a significant difference between those two options. Partners normally are vicariously liable for each other's acts. In contrast, the shareholders in a corporation are at risk only to the extent that the company's assets are available to the company's creditors. If those assets are insufficient to satisfy a tort judgment, the claimant is not entitled to extract the shortfall from the shareholders. Likewise, while the courts occasionally "pierce the corporate veil," corporate directors generally are not responsible for a company's debts.

4. Wallbridge is a partnership of lawyers in northern Ontario. Williams Litigation Lawyers is a partnership of lawyers in Ottawa. Faye Brunning was a lawyer who practised "in association" with Williams. Wallbridge sued Brunning in defamation for

making unflattering comments about the firm. Is Williams vicariously liable for any damages that Wallbridge wins against Brunning? What does it mean to say that a lawyer practises "in association" with a firm? Does it matter that Williams allowed Brunning to use its letterhead and its email domain name? Reversing a decision to summarily dismiss the claim of vicarious liability, the Ontario Court of Appeal observed that the operative "question was a novel one. The implications of lawyers 'practicing in association' are potentially far-reaching." It accordingly called for a full airing of the issues: *Wallbridge v Brunning*, 2018 ONCA 363 at para. 26.

5. For a general discussion of vicarious liability in the agency context, see Fridman, *The Law of Agency*, 7th ed. (1996), ch. 13; and Fridman, *Canadian Agency Law*, 3d ed. (2017), ch. 4.

(c) MASTER-SERVANT RELATIONSHIP

Vicarious liability most often arises in a master-servant relationship. That is not to say, however, that the doctrine is uncontroversial or well understood in the employment context. On the contrary, in recent years, appellate courts throughout the Commonwealth have struggled to identify the doctrine's underlying rationale and to establish clear criteria for determining when an employer will be vicariously liable for an employee's torts.

In this country, the governing rules were formulated in a remarkable series of decisions between 1999 and 2010. Beginning with *Bazley v. Curry*, [1999] 2 S.C.R. 534, the Supreme Court of Canada delivered judgments in twelve cases that raised various issues within the doctrine of vicarious liability. An extract from the leading case of *Bazley v. Curry* appears below; the court's other decisions are digested in the notes that follow. Those notes also discuss the extent to which McLachlin J.'s opinion in *Bazley v. Curry* has influenced the law in other jurisdictions. As will be seen, English courts have been particularly impressed with her analysis.

Before turning to the cases, however, it will be useful to observe several aspects of vicarious liability. While the following propositions are presented in the context of employment relationships, the first, second, and fourth ideas govern vicarious liability in other circumstances as well.

- *Alternative Liability*: Vicarious liability does not relieve a tortfeasor of responsibility. Take a simple example. The plaintiff brought a car to a garage for repairs. The vehicle's paint was scratched after one of the garage's employees negligently dropped a tool on it. A court may hold the employer *vicariously* liable and the employee *personally* liable. The doctrine of vicarious liability provides the plaintiff with an alternative source of relief; it does not relieve the employee of responsibility.

- *Right of Indemnification*: The courts traditionally have held that once it satisfies the judgment for vicarious liability, the employer is entitled to *indemnification* by recovering the same amount from its careless employee. See *Lister v. Romford Ice & Cold Storage Co.* (1956), [1957] A.C. 555 (H.L.). As between the two defendants, the primary burden falls on the actual tortfeasor. Especially from the perspective of the employer's insurer (who generally becomes *subrogated* to the employer's right to sue the employee), the ability to shift the loss on to the employee might seem an attractive possibility. Employers, however, seldom exercise their right to indemnification. An employment contract or collective agreement may prevent it from doing so. The employer may decide that pursuing indemnification would be counterproductive if it would damage employee morale, or useless if the wrongdoing employee is impecunious. More broadly, courts and commentators occasionally have questioned an employer's right to receive indemnification from an employee. In a minority opinion in *London Drugs Ltd. v. Kuehne & Nagel International Ltd.*, [1992] 3 S.C.R. 299, for example, LaForest J. suggested that the employee should be liable only in the event of gross negligence. This issue is discussed further in the notes following the next case.

- *Third Party Protection*: The next point involves a slight digression from tort law. If the plaintiff's repair contract with the defendant garage included an exclusion clause that eliminated or reduced the defendant's exposure to liability, the protection of that clause may extend to the defendant's employees as well. As a general rule, of course, the benefit of an agreement is limited to parties that enjoy privity of contract. As a matter of practical justice and commercial reality, however, the Supreme Court of Canada has created an exception in favour of employees. See *London Drugs Ltd.*, *supra*.

- *Vicarious and Personal Liability*: The final point pertains more narrowly to the issue of tort liability. An employer may be held *vicariously* liable for its employee's tort. It is important to remember, however, that an employer also may be held *personally* liable for its own tort. Return to our example and assume that the employee who carelessly dropped the tool onto the plaintiff's vehicle was, because of an intellectual disability, completely ill-suited to working in a garage. The employer itself might have acted negligently in hiring such a person for that job. If so, the plaintiff could sue the employee personally and the employer both vicariously and personally.

BAZLEY v. CURRY
(1999), 174 D.L.R. (4th) 45 (S.C.C.)

[The plaintiff had been sexually assaulted as a young child in a residential care facility for emotionally troubled youths. The Children's Foundation, the non-profit organization that operated the facility, had undertaken a thorough background check of Curry, the perpetrator, prior to hiring him. As soon as Curry's criminal conduct was discovered, the facility fired him.]

MCLACHLIN J.:—. . .

A. May Employers Be Held Vicariously Liable for Their Employees' Sexual Assaults on Clients or Persons Within Their Care?

Both parties agree that the answer to this question is governed by the "Salmond" test, which posits that employers are vicariously liable for (1) employee acts authorized by the employer; or (2) unauthorized acts so connected with authorized acts that they may be regarded as modes (albeit improper modes) of doing an authorized act. Both parties also agree that we are here concerned with the second branch of the test. They diverge, however, on what the second branch of the test means. The Foundation says that its employee's sexual assaults of B. were not "modes" of doing an authorized act. B., on the other hand, submits that the assaults were a mode of performing authorized tasks, and that courts have often found employers vicariously liable for intentional wrongs of employees comparable to sexual assault.

The problem is that it is often difficult to distinguish between an unauthorized "mode" of performing an authorized act that attracts liability, and an entirely independent "act" that does not. Unfortunately, the test provides no criterion on which to make this distinction. In many cases, like the present one, it is possible to characterize the tortious act either as a mode of doing an authorized act (as the respondent would have us do), or as an independent act altogether (as the appellants would suggest). In such cases, how is the judge to decide between the two alternatives?

One answer is to look at decided cases on similar facts. As Salmond and Heuston, [*The Law of Torts*, 19th ed. (1987)], put it, "the principle is easy to state but difficult to apply. All that can be done is to provide illustrations on either side of the line" (p. 438). The problem is that only very close cases may be useful. Fleming observes that "[n]o statistical measurement is possible [of when such torts are properly said to be within the "scope of employment"], and precedents are helpful only when they present a suggestive uniformity on parallel facts" (J.G. Fleming, *The Law of Torts* (9th ed. 1998), at p. 421).

Where decided cases do not help, Salmond and Heuston, *supra*, at p. 522, suggest the impasse may be resolved by the devices of a *prima facie* case and shifting evidentiary burden. If the plaintiff establishes that the employee's act was done on the employer's premises, during working hours, and that it bears a close connection with the work that the employee was authorized to do, then the responsibility shifts to the employer to show that the act is one for which it was not responsible. But this is not so much a test as a default position, and it remains unclear exactly what the employer would need to show to escape responsibility.

Increasingly, courts confronted by issues of vicarious liability where no clear precedent exists are *turning to policy for guidance*, examining the purposes that vicarious liability serves and asking whether imposition of liability in the new case before them would serve those purposes. . . .

This review suggests that the second branch of the Salmond test may usefully be approached in two steps. First, a court should determine whether there are precedents which unambiguously determine on which side of the line between vicarious liability and no liability the case falls. If prior cases do not clearly suggest a solution, the next step is to determine whether vicarious liability should be imposed in light of the broader policy rationales behind strict liability. This Court has an additional duty: to provide guidance for lower tribunals. Accordingly, I will try to proceed from these first two steps to articulate a rule consistent with both the existing cases and the policy reasons for vicarious liability.

1. Previous Cases

This is one of those difficult cases where there is little helpful precedent to guide the Court in determining whether the employee's tortious act should be viewed as an unauthorized mode of an authorized act, or as an altogether independent act. Apart from one recent case in the United Kingdom, the issue before us appears not to have been previously considered in depth by higher tribunals. Nevertheless, it may be useful to review the situations where courts have held employers vicariously liable for the unauthorized torts of employees. At very least, they may suggest recurring concepts and policy considerations that shed light on how the issue should be resolved.

The relevant cases may usefully be grouped into three general categories: (1) cases based on the rationale of "furtherance of the employer's aims"; (2) cases based on the employer's creation of a situation of friction; and (3) the dishonest employee cases. If we can find a common thread among these three categories of cases, it may suggest how the test should be interpreted.

The cases confirming vicarious liability on the basis that the employee was acting in furtherance of the employer's aims rely on the agency rationale implicit in the Salmond test. . . . Because the employee was acting in furtherance of the employer's aims, he or she is said to have "ostensible" or "implied" authority to do the unauthorized act. This rationale works well enough for torts of negligent accident. It does not suffice for intentional torts, however. It is difficult to maintain the fiction that an employee who commits an assault or theft was authorized to do so, even "ostensibly". . . . I would put the line of cases addressing the distinction between a "frolic" and a "detour" in this group.

The cases based on the employer's creation of a situation of friction rest on the idea that if the employer's aims or enterprise incidentally create a situation of friction that may give rise to employees committing tortious acts, an employee's intentional misconduct can be viewed as falling within the scope of the employment and the employer is vicariously liable for ensuing harm. This rationale was used to extend vicarious liability to intentional torts like a provoked bartender's assault on an obnoxious customer. While it does not rest on ostensible or implied authority, it builds on the logic of risk and accident inherent in the cases imposing vicarious liability on the basis that the employee was acting to further the employer's aims. Intentional torts arising from situations of friction are like accidents in that they stem from a risk attendant on carrying out the employer's aims. Like accidents, they occur in circumstances where such incidents can be expected to arise because of the nature of the business and hence their ramifications appropriately form part of the cost of doing business. . . .

Neither furtherance of the employer's aims nor creation of situations of friction, however, suffice to justify vicarious liability for employee theft or fraud, according to cases like *Lloyd v. Grace, Smith & Co.*, [1912] A.C. 716 (H.L.), and *The Queen v. Levy Brothers Co.*, [1961] S.C.R. 189. The language of authority, whether actual or ostensible, is inappropriate for intentional, fraudulent conduct like the theft of a client's property. A bank employee stealing a client's money cannot be said to be furthering the bank's aims. Nor does the logic of a situation of friction apply, unless one believes that any money-handling operation generates an inexorable temptation to steal. Nevertheless, courts considering this type of case have increasingly held employers vicariously liable, even when the employee's conduct is antithetical to the employer's business. . . .

At the heart of the dishonest employee decisions is consideration of fairness and policy. . . . As P.S. Atiyah, *Vicarious Liability in the Law of Torts* (1967), at p. 263, puts it, "certain types of wilful acts, and in particular frauds and thefts, are only too common, and the fact that liability is generally imposed for torts of this kind shows that the courts are not unmindful of considerations of policy." The same logic dictates that where the employee's wrongdoing was a random act wholly unconnected to the nature of the enterprise and the employee's responsibilities, the employer is not vicariously liable. Thus an employer has been held not liable for a vengeful assault by its store clerk: *Warren v. Henlys, Ltd.*, [1948] 2 All E.R. 935 (K.B.D.).

Looking at these three general classes of cases in which employers have been held vicariously liable for employees' unauthorized torts, one sees a progression from accidents, to accident-like intentional torts, to torts that bear no relationship to either agency-like conduct or accident. In search of a unifying principle, one asks what the three classes of cases have in common. At first glance, it may seem little. Yet with the benefit of hindsight it is possible to posit one common feature: in each case it can be said that the employer's enterprise had created the risk that produced the tortious act. The language of "furtherance of the employer's aims" and the employer's creation of "a situation of friction" may be seen as limited formulations of the concept of enterprise risk that underlies the dishonest employee cases. The common theme resides in the idea that where the employee's conduct is closely tied to a risk that the employer's enterprise has placed in the community, the employer may justly be held vicariously liable for the employee's wrong. . . .

2. Policy Considerations

Vicarious liability has always been concerned with policy. . . . The view of early English law that a master was responsible for all the wrongs of his servants (as well as his wife's and his children's) represented a policy choice, however inarticulate, as to who should bear the loss of wrongdoing and how best to deter it. The narrowing of vicarious responsibility with the expansion of commerce and trade and the rise of industrialism also represented a policy choice. Indeed, it represented a compromise between two policies — the social interest in furnishing an innocent tort victim with recourse against a financially responsible defendant, and a concern not to foist undue burdens on business enterprises. . . . The expansion of vicarious liability in the 20th century from authorization-based liability to broader classes of ascription is doubtless driven by yet other policy concerns. "[V]icarious liability cannot parade as a deduction from legalistic premises, but should be frankly recognized as having its basis in a combination of policy considerations" (Fleming, at p. 410).

A focus on policy is not to diminish the importance of legal principle. It is vital that the courts attempt to articulate general legal principles to lend certainty to the law and guide future applications. However, in areas of jurisprudence where changes have been occurring in response to policy considerations, the best route to enduring principle may well lie through policy. The law of vicarious liability is just such a domain.

Recognizing the policy-driven perspective of the law of vicarious liability, LaForest J. in [*London Drugs Ltd. v. Kuehne & Nagel International Ltd.* (1992), 97 D.L.R. (4th) 261 (S.C.C.)] opined that vicarious liability was traditionally considered to rest on one of two logical bases: (1) that the employee's acts are regarded in law as being authorized by the employer and hence as being the employer's acts (the "master's tort theory" or "direct liability theory"); or (2) that the employer was the employee's superior in charge or command of the employee (the "servant's tort theory"). . . . La Forest J., quoting Fridman [*The Law of Torts in Canada* (1990), vol. 2 at 315], went on to note, however, that "neither of the logical bases for vicarious liability succeeds completely in explaining the operation of the doctrine . . . express[ing] 'not so much the true rationale of vicarious liability but an attempt by the law to give some formal, technical explanation of why the law imposes vicarious liability'.". . . Faced with the absence in the existing law of a coherent principle to explain vicarious liability, La Forest J. found its basis in policy. . .: "[T]he vicarious liability regime is best seen as a response to a number of policy concerns. In its traditional domain, these are primarily linked to compensation, deterrence and loss internalization."

Fleming has identified similar policies lying at the heart of vicarious liability. In his view, two fundamental concerns underlie the imposition of vicarious liability: (1) provision of a just and practical remedy for the harm; and (2) deterrence of future harm. While different formulations of the policy interests at stake may be made (for example, loss internalization is a hybrid of the two), I believe that these two ideas usefully embrace the main policy considerations that have been advanced.

First and foremost is the concern to provide a just and practical remedy to people who suffer as a consequence of wrongs perpetrated by an employee. Fleming expresses this succinctly (at p. 410): "a person who employs others to advance his own economic interest should in fairness be placed under a corresponding liability for losses incurred in the course of the enterprise". The idea that the person who introduces a risk incurs a duty to those who may be injured lies at the heart of tort law. As Cardozo C.J. stated in *Palsgraf v. Long Island Ry. Co.*, 162 N.E. 99 (N.Y. 1928), "[t]he risk reasonably to be perceived defines the duty to be obeyed, and risk imports relation; it is risk to another or to others within the range of apprehension." This principle of fairness applies to the employment enterprise and hence to the issue of vicarious liability. While charitable enterprises may not employ people to advance their economic interests, other factors, discussed below, make it fair that they should bear the burden of providing a just and practical remedy for wrongs perpetrated by their employees. This policy interest embraces a number of subsidiary goals. The first is the goal of effective compensation. "One of the most important social goals served by vicarious liability is victim compensation. Vicarious liability improves the chances that the victim can recover the judgment from a solvent defendant." (B. Feldthusen, "Vicarious Liability For Sexual Torts", in *Torts Tomorrow* (1998), 221, at p. 224). Or to quote Fleming, the master is "a more promising source of recompense than his servant who is apt to be a man of straw" (p. 410). . . .

Reviewing the jurisprudence, and considering the policy issues involved, I conclude that in determining whether an employer is vicariously liable for an employee's unauthorized, intentional wrong in cases where precedent is inconclusive, courts should be guided by the following principles:

(1) They should openly confront the question of whether liability should lie against the employer, rather than obscuring the decision beneath semantic discussions of "scope of employment" and "mode of conduct".

(2) The fundamental question is whether the wrongful act is sufficiently related to conduct authorized by the employer to justify the imposition of vicarious liability. Vicarious liability is generally appropriate where there is a significant connection between the creation or enhancement of a risk and the wrong that accrues therefrom, even if unrelated to the employer's desires. Where this is so, vicarious liability will serve the policy considerations of provision of an adequate and just remedy and deterrence. Incidental connections to the employment enterprise, like time and place (without more), will not suffice. Once engaged in a particular business, it is fair that an employer be made to pay the generally foreseeable costs of that business. In contrast, to impose liability for costs unrelated to the risk would effectively make the employer an involuntary insurer.

(3) In determining the sufficiency of the connection between the employer's creation or enhancement of the risk and the wrong complained of, subsidiary factors may be considered. These may vary with the nature of the case. When related to intentional torts, the relevant factors may include, but are not limited to, the following:

    (a)   the opportunity that the enterprise afforded the employee to abuse his or her power;

    (b)   the extent to which the wrongful act may have furthered the employer's aims (and hence be more likely to have been committed by the employee);

    (c)   the extent to which the wrongful act was related to friction, confrontation or intimacy inherent in the employer's enterprise;

    (d)   the extent of power conferred on the employee in relation to the victim;

    (e)   the vulnerability of potential victims to wrongful exercise of the employee's power.

Applying these general considerations to sexual abuse by employees, there must be a strong connection between what the employer was asking the employee to do (the risk created by the employer's enterprise) and the wrongful act. It must be possible to say that the employer significantly increased the risk of the harm by putting the employee in his or her position and requiring him to perform the assigned tasks. The policy considerations that justify imposition of vicarious liability for an employee's sexual misconduct are unlikely to be satisfied by incidental considerations of time and place. For example, an incidental or random attack by an employee that merely happens to take place on the employer's premises during working hours will scarcely justify holding the employer liable. Such an attack is unlikely to be related to the business the employer is conducting or what the employee was asked to do and, hence, to any risk that was created. Nor is the imposition of liability likely to have a significant deterrent effect; short of closing the premises or discharging all employees, little can be done to avoid the random wrong. Nor is foreseeability of harm used in negligence law the test. What is required is a material increase in the risk as a consequence of the employer's enterprise and the duties he entrusted to the employee, mindful of the policies behind vicarious liability. . . .

In summary, the test for vicarious liability for an employee's sexual abuse of a client should focus on whether the employer's enterprise and empowerment of the employee materially increased the risk of the sexual assault and hence the harm. The test must not be applied mechanically, but with a sensitive view to the policy considerations that justify the imposition of vicarious liability — fair and efficient compensation for wrong and deterrence. This requires trial judges to investigate the employee's specific duties and determine whether they gave rise to special opportunities for wrongdoing. Because of the peculiar exercises of power and trust that pervade cases such as child abuse, special attention should be paid to the existence of a power or dependency relationship, which on its own often creates a considerable risk of wrongdoing. . . .

C. Application to the Case at Bar

Applying these considerations to the facts in the case at bar, the Foundation is vicariously liable for the sexual misconduct of Curry. The opportunity for intimate private control and the parental relationship and power required by the terms of employment created the special environment that nurtured and brought to fruition

Curry's sexual abuse. The employer's enterprise created and fostered the risk that led to the ultimate harm. The abuse was not a mere accident of time and place, but the product of the special relationship of intimacy and respect the employer fostered, as well as the special opportunities for exploitation of that relationship it furnished. Indeed, it is difficult to imagine a job with a greater risk for child sexual abuse. This is not to suggest that future cases must rise to the same level to impose vicarious liability. Fairness and the need for deterrence in this critical area of human conduct — the care of vulnerable children — suggest that as between the Foundation that created and managed the risk and the innocent victim, the Foundation should bear the loss.

NOTES AND QUESTIONS

1. In what circumstances will an employer be held vicariously liable for the torts of an employee? Is the employer vicariously responsible for the acts of the employee or for the liability incurred by the employee? Courts originally proceeded under the maxim *qui facit per alium facit per se* ("he who acts through another, acts himself"): *Middleton v. Fowler* (1699), 91 E.R. 247 (Exch.). The fiction underlying that view, however, later convinced courts to hold that it is the employee's liability that is attributed to the employer: *Majrowski v. Guy's & St. Thomas' N.H.S. Trust*, [2007] 1 A.C. 224 (H.L.). Which theory better fits the policies underlying the doctrine of vicarious liability? See Stevens, "Vicarious Liability or Vicarious Action?" (2007) 123 L.Q.R. 30.

The rights-based theory of tort law was introduced in Chapter 1. That theory insists that tortious liability must be rooted in the violation of rights, rather than the instrumental pursuit of policies like loss compensation and deterrence. Vicarious liability consequently poses problems for rights theorists: Cane, "Justice and Justifications for Tort Liability" (1982) 2 O.J.L.S. 30 at 52. The doctrine commonly is understood as a form of parasitic liability. The employer is held responsible not because it has violated the plaintiff's rights, but rather because its employee has done so. But if the employer has not independently breached any duty, how can liability be justified? That question has received several answers. Beever concedes that vicarious liability is "anomalous" but nevertheless maintains that is can be justified. The crucial point, he says, is that rights theory explains the employee's potential liability to the plaintiff. The employer's responsibility, he says, simply builds upon that fact. In that sense, vicarious liability is "external" to tort law and consequently need not be brought within its fundamental structure: Beever, *Rediscovering the Law of Negligence* (2007) at 35-36. Stevens, in contrast, insists that vicarious liability does fit within a rights-based conception of tort law: Stevens, *Torts and Rights* (2007) at 257-74. The key, he says, lies in the fact that it is the employee's *act*, rather than the employee's *liability*, that is attributed to the employer. Consequently, vicarious liability effectively involves the master's tort and not the servant's tort. As a result of the legal doctrine of attribution, the employer is deemed to have done the wrong. The phrase "vicarious liability" therefore is a misnomer because the employer's liability is not parasitic on the employee's breach. Stevens' position, however, is difficult to square with the language of modern cases and it has drawn skepticism: Cane, "Rights in Private Law" in Nolan & Robertson, eds., *Rights and Private Law* (2010) at 57-58.

2. What policy considerations support the imposition of vicarious liability?

3. What is the "Salmond test" of vicarious liability? Is McLachlin J.'s test of vicarious liability any more certain or predictable than Salmond's? How do those two tests differ with respect to unauthorized acts by employees?

4. What impact has *Bazley* likely had on the availability and cost of liability insurance for non-profit organizations that provide free services to children? What impact will it have on the screening procedures for both employees and volunteers of such organizations? Exactly what steps should employers take in their screening processes? Would such measures be subject to possible human rights and problems under the *Canadian Charter of Rights and Freedoms*, Part I of the *Constitution Act, 1982*, being Schedule B to the *Canada Act 1982* (U.K.), 1982, c. 11?

5. Are the tests outlined in *Bazley* limited to cases of childhood sexual abuse or would they apply to any vulnerable population? Would similar principles apply to high school and university students, and nursing and retirement homes? What are the implications of *Bazley* for other types of employers, such as military or the police, that have a clear hierarchical structure?

6. A master's vicarious liability for a servant's tort may arise in countless contexts. Particular circumstances may raise unusual or unique considerations. For instance, doctors at one time were considered to be employees of the patient, and not the hospital. In recent years, however, there has been a trend to extend the scope of a hospital's vicarious liability for doctors and other staff. See *Jaman Estate v. Hussain*, [2002] 11 W.W.R. 241 (Man. C.A.); Magnet, "Liability of a Hospital for the Negligent Acts of Professionals" (1977) 3 C.C.L.T. 135; Picard, *Legal Liability of Doctors and Hospitals in Canada*, 2d ed. (1984) at 313-28; and Fridman *et al.*, *The Law of Torts in Canada*, 3d ed. (2010) at 260-63.

If a player injures an opponent in a way that is not only contrary to the rules of the game, but also tortious, should the offending player's team be vicarious liable? See James & McArdle, "Player Violence or Violent Players? Vicarious Liability for Sports Participants" (2004) 12 Tort L. Rev. 131.

A nightclub employs a doorman to vet guests and remove unruly customers. After becoming involved in an incident with a patron, the doorman leaves the premises, fetches a knife from his apartment, and returns to stab the patron. Is the nightclub vicariously liable for the doorman's actions? Is vicarious liability precluded by the fact that the tort was unauthorized and personally motivated behaviour? See *Mattis v. Pollock*, [2003] 1 W.L.R. 2158 (C.A.); and *Vasey v. Wosk's Ltd*, [1988] B.C.J. No. 2089 (S.C.) (QL). If a taxi driver sexually assaults an intoxicated customer, is the taxi company vicariously liable for the resulting harm? See *Ivic v. Lakovic*, 2017 ONCA 446.

7. Even if a tort is committed by an employee, the employer will not be vicariously liable if, on the facts, the doctrine would not serve the underlying goals of compensation and deterrence. In *Schultz v. Miki* (2006), 264 D.L.R. (4th) 201 (B.C.C.A.), a landlord hired his cousin to make repairs in an apartment. While in the apartment, the cousin sexually assaulted the tenant. The court did not hold the landlord vicariously liable for the tort. Southin J.A. explained that "[t]he policy considerations of fair compensation and deterrence are eliminated in the circumstances of this case. If the appellant's arguments were to succeed, we would be dangerously close to imposing absolute liability on employers for the intentional

torts of their employees." On vicarious liability for criminal conduct, see also *Royal Bank of Canada v. Intercon Security Ltd.*, 2005 C.L.L.C. 210-047 (Ont. S.C.J.); and *Weingerl v. Seo* (2005), 256 D.L.R. (4th) 1 (Ont. C.A.).

8. At common law, the Crown was not vicariously liable for the torts of its agents and servants. That immunity has been abrogated by statute. See for example *Crown Liability and Proceedings Act*, R.S.C. 1985, c. C-50, s. 3(b); and *Proceedings Against the Crown Act*, R.S.A. 2000, c. P-25. Nevertheless, the courts will not lightly visit vicarious liability upon a Minister or Premier. See for example *Tottrup v. Lund* (2000), 186 D.L.R. (4th) 226 (Alta. C.A.); *Decock v. Alberta* (2000), 186 D.L.R. (4th) 265 (Alta. C.A.); *P.(N.I.) v. B.(R.)* (2000), 193 D.L.R (4th) 752 (B.C.S.C.); and *Williams v. Attorney General of Canada* (2005), 257 D.L.R. (4th) 704 (Ont. S.C.J.), rev'd 95 O.R. (3d) 401 (C.A.). See also Fridman *et al.*, *The Law of Torts in Canada*, 3d ed. (2010) at 263-65.

9. Vicarious liability covers compensatory damages, but not punitive relief, where the master is not guilty of "high-handed, malicious, arbitrary or highly reprehensible misconduct that departs to a marked degree from ordinary standards of decent behaviour": *Blackwater v. Plint*, [2005] 3 S.C.R. 3 at 35. A master nevertheless may be vicariously liable for aggravated damages: *T.W.N.A. v. Clarke* (2003), 235 D.L.R. (4th) 13 (B.C.C.A.); and *Weingerl v. Seo*, *supra*. See also *Colistro v. Tbaytel*, 2017 ONSC 2731 (employer vicariously liable for "*Honda*" damages after plaintiff suffered psychological injury as result of outrageous manner of dismissal).

10. Although the doctrine of vicarious liability arose under the common law, it extends, as a matter of logic and principle, to equitable wrongs and statutory wrongs as well: *Majrowski v. Guy's & St. Thomas' N.H.S. Trust*, [2007] 1 A.C. 224 (H.L.); *cf. Nova Scotia (Attorney General) v. Carvery*, 2016 NSCA 21.

11. *Bazley* did not resolve all of the issues arising from vicarious liability of servants. The Supreme Court of Canada consequently has delivered judgment in several other cases since *Bazley*. The Canadian doctrine of vicarious liability can be understood by examining those cases.

The first of those judgments was rendered contemporaneously with *Bazley*. In *Jacobi v. Griffiths*, [1999] 2 S.C.R. 576, a four-to-three majority of the court ruled that the Boys and Girls Club of Vernon was not vicariously liable for the sexual assaults committed by the Club's program director. The majority emphasized that the assaults did not take place at the Club, that the Club offered only recreational activities and occasional outings and not residential services, and that the director was responsible for developing and supervising the recreational programs. In the words of the majority, the director was not placed in a special relationship of trust for the children's "care, protection and nurturing." McLachlin J. wrote a strong dissent.

12. In light of *Griffiths*, how would you respond to the questions raised in notes 4 and 5? For comments arising from *Bazley* and *Griffiths*, see Neyers, "A Theory of Vicarious Liability" (2005) 43 Alta. L. Rev. 287; Cane, "Vicarious Liability for Sexual Abuse" (2000) 116 L.Q.R. 21; Hall, "Responsibility Without Fault" (2000) 79 Can. Bar Rev. 474; Black & Wildeman, "Parsing the Supreme Court's New Pronouncements on Vicarious Liability for Sexual Battery" (1999) 46 C.C.L.T. 126; and Rafferty, "Developments in Contract and Tort Law: The 1998-1999 Term" (1999)

11 S.C.L.R. (2d) 183. See also *H.L. v. Canada* (2002), [2003] 5 W.W.R. 421 (Sask. C.A.), varied on other grounds, [2005] 1 S.C.R. 401. For comments outside of Canada, see Brodie, "Enterprise Liability: Justifying Vicarious Liability" (2007) 27 O.J.L.S. 493; Giliker, "Making the Right Connections: Vicarious Liability and Institutional Responsibility" (2009) 17 Torts L.J. 35; and Glofcheski, "A Frolic in the Law of Tort: Expanding the Scope of Employer's Vicarious Liability" (2004) 12 Tort L. Rev. 18.

13. In 2003, the Supreme Court of Canada rendered three more decisions dealing with vicarious liability: *B.(K.L.) v. British Columbia*, [2003] 2 S.C.R. 403; *B.(M.) v. British Columbia*, [2003] 2 S.C.R. 477; and *G.(E.D.) v. Hammer*, [2003] 2 S.C.R. 459. The general effect was to somewhat reduce the scope of the doctrine. The facts of *B. (K.L.)* and *B.(M.)* were substantially the same. The plaintiffs were sexually, physically and psychologically abused while living in foster homes. Because they had been placed in those homes under the authority of the *Protection of Children Act*, R.S.B.C. 1960, c. 303, they claimed that the provincial government was vicariously liable for the torts. The court held that vicarious liability would be appropriate only if the claimants satisfied two conditions. First, the relationship between the parties had to be sufficiently close or proximate to warrant the doctrine's application. A crucial factor in that respect is the level of control that the master exercised over the servant. Second, the wrongful conduct had to be "sufficiently connected" to the servant's assigned tasks so that the impugned conduct may be regarded as a "materialization of the risks created by the enterprise." The court concluded those conditions were not met on the facts of *B.(K.L.)* and *B.(M.)*. Independence is the essence of the foster home program. The government does not, and practically speaking could not, exercise substantial control over the day-to-day lives of the foster children. Moreover, the court feared that the imposition of vicarious liability might deter the government from placing children in foster homes, rather than less effective institutional settings. Looking ahead to the final sections of this chapter, the court also held that the government had not been subject to a *non-delegable duty of care* to the claimants. In *B.(K.L.)*, however, the court did find that the government had been subject to a standard duty of care in negligence insofar as it was required to exercise care in placing children in foster homes and in supervising their stay. The court also found that the government had breached the standard of care. The defendant nevertheless escaped liability because of the lapse of time under the *Limitations Act*, R.S.B.C. 1996, c. 266, ss. 3(2) and 7(1)(a)(i). See also *Kassian Estate v. Canada (Attorney General)*, 2015 ONCA 544.

G.(E.D.) v. Hammer, the third case in the trilogy, arose in a different context. The plaintiff was sexually assaulted by a janitor at her school. The perpetrator was liable. The plaintiff, however, also alleged that the school board was liable for breach of a non-delegable duty, liable for breach of a fiduciary duty, and vicariously liable for the janitor's torts. The first claim is discussed below. The second claim was dismissed on the ground that, while the school board owed a fiduciary duty to the claimant, the wrongs in question were not of a fiduciary nature. Finally, the claim for vicarious liability was denied at trial and was pursued not on appeal to the Supreme Court of Canada.

In 2010, the court returned to the general context found in *B.(K.L.)* and *B.(M.)*. *Broome v. Prince Edward Island*, [2010] 1 S.C.R. 360 involved allegations of physical and sexual abuse within a privately owned and managed orphanage between 1928 and

1976. Claims were brought against, *inter alia*, the provincial government on the theory of vicarious liability. Cromwell J., writing for a unanimous panel, rejected that allegation. Relying upon the court's earlier decisions, he held that while the province placed children into the orphanage and had legislative authority over the operations, it did not exercise the level of control that would warrant vicarious liability. The province was not involved in the day-to-day management of the orphanage, nor did it act as an employer.

14. The Supreme Court of Canada continued its development of vicarious liability the next year in *John Doe v. Bennett*, [2004] 1 S.C.R. 436. The parish priest in a remote village in Newfoundland committed a series of sexual assaults on several young boys. Although some of the victims complained to the priest's supervising bishops, and to an Archbishop of a neighbouring diocese, nothing was done to stop the attacks. The victims sued many years later. The priest was held personally liable. The local diocese (a corporate body under the authority of local bishops) was directly liable on the basis of the bishops' failure to act. The final question concerned the diocese's vicarious liability for the priest's actions. Because the issue was not settled by precedent, McLachlin C.J.C. examined whether vicarious liability would promote the policy concerns underlying enterprise liability. She found, following *Bazley* and *B.(K.L.)*, that (1) the diocese closely controlled the priest, and (2) the priest's wrongs were closely connected to his assigned tasks. In ultimately siding with the claimants, McLachlin C.J.C. also emphasized the special circumstances of the case. Given the geographical and social context, the priest held enormous authority within the community. The boys (and their parents) regarded the priest as absolute authority and lacked any other role models. By encouraging the community to defer to the priest's wishes, the diocese effectively created a situation ripe for abuse. See also *John Doe v. Fifield* (2007), 53 C.C.L.T. (3d) 261 (N.L.T.D.).

15. Two cases, decided in 2005, involved the abuse of aboriginal students in residential schools. In *B.(E.) v. Order of the Oblates of Mary Immaculate in the Province of British Columbia*, [2005] 3 S.C.R. 45, the claimant was subject to a series of sexual assaults by a lay employee who served the school as a baker, boat driver, and odd-job labourer. The claimant sought damages, on the basis of vicarious liability, against the Catholic Order that operated the school. The claim was dismissed. Binnie J. (writing for the majority) stressed the need for something more than "mere opportunity" to commit a wrongful act. While vicarious liability does not require proof that the tortfeasor was given parent-like authority over the victim, it does presume a "strong connection" between the assigned tasks and the wrongful conduct. On the facts, however, the tortfeasor was neither required, nor permitted, to become involved intimately in the plaintiff's life.

The second case, *Blackwater v. Plint*, [2005] 3 S.C.R. 3, concerned a series of sexual assaults committed by a dormitory supervisor. The assaults occurred within a residential school that was operated by the federal government and the United Church of Canada. Although the plaintiff pursued several claims (including one, discussed below, against the government for breach of a non-delegable duty), the most interesting for present purposes is the allegation that both the government and the church were vicariously liable. The argument alleged that the tortfeasor was employed by both defendants. While the Church was Plint's immediate employer (because, for instance, it nominated the school's principal and hired the staff), the government also was an employer (because, for instance, it hired the principal, selected the students, and funded the program). McLachlin C.J.C. accepted the allegation on two grounds: (1) dual responsibility would further the policy goals underlying the doctrine of vicarious liability, and (2) various members of a partnership may be held vicariously liable for the tort of an employee.

The Chief Justice's reasons were surprisingly thin. They refer to no cases and they do not explore the conceptual difficulties raised by the prospect of dual vicarious liability. Most surprisingly of all, McLachlin C.J.C. failed to mention the fact that there has been a strong presumption, for nearly two centuries, that vicarious liability may be imposed on only one employer: *Laugher v. Pointer* (1826), 108 E.R. 204 (K.B.); and *Mersey Docks and Harbour Board v. Coggins & Griffiths (Liverpool) Ltd.*, [1947] A.C. 1 (H.L.). Nor did she mention the Canadian cases that either accepted or rejected the orthodox view. See for example *McKee v. Dumas* (1977), 12 O.R. (2d) 670 (C.A.); *Hardisty v. 851791 N.W.T. Ltd.* (2004), 26 C.C.L.T. (3d) 305 (N.W.T.S.C.), aff'd (2005), [2006] 4 W.W.R. 199 (C.A.); and *Gemco Equipment Ltd. v. Westen* (1965), 54 W.W.R. 513 (B.C. Co. Ct.). The Supreme Court of Canada's decision therefore compares very poorly with the masterful treatment that the issue received at the hands of May L.J. in *Viasystems (Tyneside) Ltd. v. Thermal Transfer (Northern) Ltd.*, [2006] Q.B. 510 (C.A.). While the English Court of Appeal ultimately arrived at the same conclusion, it did so only after thoroughly canvassing the issues and precedents. Its decision received approval from the Supreme Court of the United Kingdom in *The Catholic Child Welfare Society v. The Institute of the Brothers of the Christian Schools*, [2012] UKSC 56. On the question of "borrowed employees," see Fridman *et al.*, *The Law of Torts in Canada*, 3d ed. (2010) at 269-73; and Sappideen & Vines, eds., *Fleming's The Law of Torts*, 10th ed. (2011) at 447-49.

16. *3464920 Canada Ltd. v. Strother*, [2007] 2 S.C.R. 177 raised the difficult issue of vicarious liability for disgorgement of a benefit acquired through breach of fiduciary duty. A lawyer named Strother committed an equitable wrong by failing to advise a client of the availability of a tax shelter scheme and by directing that information instead to Sentinel, the client's competitor. Damages against Strother were calculated not to compensate the plaintiff's loss, but rather to disgorge the wrongdoer's gain. Part of Strother's fiduciary breach occurred while he was a partner with Davis & Co. Sentinel accordingly paid substantial fees to both the lawyer and the firm. The plaintiff sued the firm both for the fees that it earned itself and, on the theory of vicarious liability, for the fees that Strother earned as a partner. The former claim was disallowed. Since the firm was entirely unaware of the conflict created by Strother's conduct, the fees that it earned were entirely attributable to the services that it provided to Sentinel. In contrast, the vicarious liability claim was successful. As a general rule, equity will not impose vicarious liability in connection with disgorgement. Whereas compensation is aimed at repairing the claimant's loss, disgorgement strips a wrongdoer's gain in order to deter and denounce. It therefore logically is limited to individuals who actually receive improper enrichments. As Binnie J. stressed, however, the claim in *Strother* was purely statutory. The plaintiff relied not upon general equitable principles but rather upon s. 12 of British Columbia's *Partnership Act*, R.S.B.C. 1998, c. 348, which provides:

> If, by any wrongful act or omission of any partner acting in the ordinary course of the business of the firm or with the authority of his or her partners, *loss or injury* is caused

to any person who is not a partner in the firm or any penalty is incurred, the firm is liable for that *loss, injury or penalty* to the same extent as the partner so acting or omitting to act. [Emphasis added]

While the issue of "loss" was debatable, the plaintiff undoubtedly had suffered an "injury" within the meaning of the statute. Moreover, in referring to "loss, injury or penalty" the legislature indicated that the innocent partners were liable not only for the usual remedy of compensatory damages but also for statutory penalties and disgorgement.

17. In *British Columbia (Attorney General) v. Insurance Corporation of British Columbia*, [2008] 1 S.C.R. 21, the Supreme Court of Canada held that if joint and several liability is imposed upon two or more tortfeasors, a party that is vicariously liable for one of the tortfeasors also bears joint and several liability. Constable McBryan of the R.C.M.P. was involved in a high-speed chase with T.B., a 14-year-old who was driving a stolen vehicle. During the chase, T.B. struck and killed Brenda Hohn. The trial judge found that both drivers were negligent, determined that responsibility for Ms Hohn's death was apportioned at 90% for T.B. and 10% for Constable McBryan, and held that the tortfeasors were jointly and severally liable under the *Negligence Act*, R.S.B.C. 1996, c. 333, s. 4(2). The Insurance Corporation of British Columbia (I.C.B.C.) incurred liability on behalf of T.B. because he was uninsured. Under the *Police Act*, R.S.B.C. 1996, c. 367, Constable McBryan was relieved of liability, but the Attorney General was vicariously liability for the officer's negligence. The Attorney General then argued that its vicarious liability was confined to the 10% responsibility that had been assigned to Constable McBryan and that the remaining damages had to be collected from the I.C.B.C. LeBel J., writing for a unanimous panel, rejected that argument. Since the Attorney General was vicariously liable for Constable McBryan, and since the officer was jointly and severally liable for the loss, the victim's estate was entitled to claim the full amount of the damages from the Attorney General. Of course, as between I.C.B.C. and the Attorney General, rights of contribution reflected the original apportionment of liability.

18. *Fullowka v. Royal Oak Ventures Inc.*, [2010] 1 S.C.R. 132 raised important issues regarding a national union's vicarious liability for torts committed by a local union or a union member. Giant Mine, near Yellowknife, was the site of a long and acrimonious strike. The mine owner employed replacement workers and security personnel, and the miners committed various acts of violence and sabotage. Strike actions were coordinated at the local level by Canadian Association of Smelter and Allied Workers Local 4 (CASAW) and at the national level by the National Automobile, Aerospace, Transportation and General Workers Union of Canada (CAW). A miner named Roger Warren sneaked into the facility through an unguarded entrance and planted explosives within the mine. The blast killed nine workers. After Warren was convicted of second-degree murder, the victims' families brought several actions against various parties. By that time, the CASAW (the local union) had been amalgamated with the CAW (the national union). The trial judge awarded $10,700,000 in damages and imposed joint and several liability on a long list of defendants, including Roger Warren, the mine owner, the CAW, the CASAW, the security service, and the territorial government. Two findings are especially important for present purposes. First, the trial judge held that, as a result of the amalgamation, the two unions were a single entity, such that the CAW was directly responsible for the

CASAW's liabilities. Second, he held that the CAW was in control of the local union and hence vicariously liable for the torts committed by the CASAW and its members. The Northwest Territories Court of Appeal, however, disagreed on several points. It denied that the mine owner, the security service, and the government owed duties of care and it accordingly dismissed the claims against them. On the specific points under consideration, it held that the two unions were separate entities and that the CAW was not vicariously liable.

A further appeal came before the Supreme Court of Canada. Writing for a unanimous court, Cromwell J. agreed with the Court of Appeal. On the issue of the CAW's direct liability, he found that the local union was the certified bargaining representative at the relevant time and that it was capable of being sued in its own right. Moreover, notwithstanding the merger, the local and national union's remained separate entities and, on the facts, the CAW had not assumed the CASAW's liabilities. The CAW consequently was not directly liable for anything done at the local level.

Cromwell J. similarly rejected the trial judge's imposition of vicarious liability. Precedent did not, as a general proposition, unambiguously impose vicarious liability upon a union for the torts committed by its members. Moreover, on the test that the court had developed over the previous decade, he concluded that the CAW did not exercise sufficient control over the CASAW or its members. Although the national union had seconded an adviser to the strike prior to the explosion, the terms of that secondment expressly stipulated that the adviser was answerable to the CASAW alone. Furthermore, notwithstanding some superficial similarity, the relationship between union and member is not closely analogous to that of employee and employer, servant and master, or agent and principal. Within the contract that exists between member and union, the member retains a large measure of independence, including an unqualified right to oppose the union's principles and actions. Indeed, on the facts before the court, several members of the local union had crossed the picket lines and attempted to establish a rival organization. The CAW accordingly was not vicariously liable for the torts associated with the explosion.

19. The focus in this area naturally falls on the liability of the employer. As mentioned in the introduction to this section, however, vicarious liability generally is viewed as a basis of alternative liability. It allows the plaintiff to sue the employer as well as the employee. After all, as between the two parties, it was the employee, rather than the employer, who actually committed the tort and caused the loss. For much the same reason, courts have long recognized the employer's right to demand *indemnification* from the employee. Having paid damages to the victim of the tort under the doctrine of vicarious liability, the employer is entitled to receive the same sum from the employee. See *Lister v. Romford Ice & Cold Storage Co.* (1956), [1957] A.C. 555 (H.L.). In practice, as previously explained, employers often refrain from exercising that right. According to one view, however, they generally should not even have the option.

There have long been sceptics of the right to indemnification. An older line of authority held that while "skilled" employees were generally subject to liability, "unskilled" employees could be held liable only in the event of intentional or reckless wrongdoing: *Pearson v. Black* (1922), 22 O.W.N. 20 (S.C.); and *Kleinsasser v. Alexander* (1994), 122 Sask. R. 52 (Q.B.). That distinction, however, was criticized as artificial and unhelpful: *Lister, supra*, at 573:

More recently, some — but by no means all — authorities say that employers should be denied indemnification in cases of simple negligence. The court in *Shamac Country Inns Ltd. v. Sandy's Oilfield Hauling Ltd.*, 2015 ABQB 518 at para. 71 canvassed the literature and offered several justifications for that view:

a. While employees are expected to exercise reasonable care in the course of [their] duties, discipline and dismissal are more useful tools to promote deterrence without the need to impose financial responsibility;

b. The employer is generally in a better position than the employee to internalize the cost of ordinary employee negligence whether as a cost of doing business or acquiring appropriate insurance;

c. Certain types of employment are disproportionately fraught with risk. Minor employee error can result in major equipment malfunction and consequently significant damages. Employment relations would be greatly challenged if an employee were held responsible for a momentary lapse of attention;

d. The employer enjoys the benefit of such work and accordingly, should bear the burden for any attendant losses

e. There is a power imbalance inherent in most employment relationships.

Are you persuaded by the arguments? Is a general prohibition on an employer's right to obtain indemnification from an employee logically necessitated by the doctrine of vicarious liability? Should the courts have the power to redistribute the rights and obligations that traditionally have existed within employment relationships? See also *Kirby v. Amalgamated Income Ltd. Partnership*, 2009 BCSC 1044; *1746646 Alberta Inc. v. Aman Carrier Ltd.*, 2014 ABPC 270; *Cole v. Lockhart* (1998), 205 N.B.R. (2d) 48 (Q.B.); *Douglas v. Kinger (Litigation Guardian of)* (2008), 90 O.R. (3d) 721 (C.A.); Sappideen & Vines, eds., *Fleming's The Law of Torts*, 10th ed. (2011) at 438-39; and Atiyah, *Vicarious Liability in the Law of Torts* (1967) at 426.

20. Notwithstanding the number of Supreme Court of Canada decisions in the area, *Bazley v. Curry* remains the leading authority in this country. Some sense of its significance can be drawn from its impact outside of Canada. For an excellent survey of the law in Canada, England, Australia, and the United States, see Gray, *Vicarious Liability: Critique and Reform* (2018).

The facts in *Lister v. Hesley Hall Ltd.*, [2002] 1 A.C. 215 (H.L.) closely resembled those in *Bazley v. Curry*. The claimant, who lived in a residential home for boys with behavioural difficulties, was sexually abused by the facility's warden. Though they did not necessarily adopt the same policy considerations, several members of the House of Lords endorsed McLachlin J.'s belief that vicarious liability should turn on a "close connection" between the employee's wrongful conduct and that employee's role in the employer's business. Subsequent decisions have similarly drawn upon notions of control and enterprise risk, even as the English courts have sometimes struggled to settle upon a single rationale for all instances of vicarious liability: *Dubai Aluminium Co. Ltd. v. Salaam*, [2003] 2 A.C. 366 (H.L.); *Catholic Child Welfare Society v. Various Claimants*, [2012] UKSC 56; *Mohamud v. Wm. Morris Supermarkets plc*, [2016] UKSC 11; *Cox v. Ministry of Justice*, [2016] UKSC 10; and *Armes v. Nottinghamshire County Council*, [2017] UKSC 60. See Hopkins, "What is the Course of Employment?" [2001] C.L.J. 458; Glofcheski, "A Frolic in the Law of Tort: Expanding the Scope of Employers' Vicarious Liability" (2004) 12 Tort L. Rev. 18; Gilliker, "Rough Justice in an Unjust World" (2002) 65 Mod. L. Rev. 269; Elvin, "The Notion of Vicarious Liability for Sexual Abuse in English Law" (2002) 13 King's College L.J. 97; McBride, "Vicarious Liability in England and Australia" [2003] C.L.J. 255; Giliker, "Analysing Institutional Liability for Child Sexual Abuse in England and Wales and Australia: Vicarious Liability, Non-Delegable Duties and Statutory Intervention" [2018] C.L.J. 506; and Giliker (ed.), *Vicarious Liability in Tort: A Comparative Perspective* (2010).

Unsurprisingly, the views expressed in the Privy Council closely mirror those heard in the House of Lords and the Supreme Court. *Bernard v. Attorney General of Jamaica* is a leading case: [2004] I.R.L.R. 398 (P.C.). A man presenting himself to be a police officer demanded use of a public telephone that the claimant was holding, saying: "I am going to make a long distance call . . . boy leggo this, police." When the claimant refused, the officer pulled out his revolver and shot point blank. In finding the officer's employer vicariously liable, the Privy Council focussed on three facts: (1) the tortfeasor presented himself as a police officer, (2) the tortfeasor subsequently arrested the victim in the hospital, on the grounds of interfering with the administration of justice, and (3) the police department's policy of allowing officers to possess firearms while off-duty.

Australian courts have moved in a different direction. The leading case once again involved abuse committed against children in an educational setting: *New South Wales v. Lepore* (2003), 212 C.L.R. 511 (H.C.A.). However, rather than endorsing the approach taken in *Bazley v. Curry* and *Lister v. Hesley Hall Ltd.*, the High Court of Australia reaffirmed the traditional Salmond test. The court expressed a number of concerns regarding the new Canadian approach: (1) it was too vague to provide certainty and consistency in practice, (2) it potentially cast the net of vicarious liability too widely, and (3) employers' liability could be more sensitively addressed under a generalized action in negligence. See also *Prince Alfred College Inc. v. A.D.C.*, [2016] HCA 37; and *Sweeney v. Boylan Nominees Pty. Ltd.* (2006), 226 C.L.R. 161 (H.C.A.). See Goudkamp, "Vicarious Liability in Australia: On the Move?" (2017) 17 Oxford U. Comm. L.J. 162; Desmond, "From Opportunity to Occasion: Vicarious Liability in The High Court Of Australia" [2017] C.L.J. 14; Hely, "Open All Hours: The Reach of Vicarious Liability in 'Off-duty' Sexual Harassment Complaints" (2008) 36 Federal L. Rev. 173; and White & Orr, "Precarious Liability: The High Court in *Lepore, Samin* and *Rich* on School Responsibility for Assaults by Teachers" (2003) 11 Torts L.J. 101.

(d) INDEPENDENT CONTRACTORS

There are several options open to a person who wants to retain the services of a worker. We already have seen two possibilities: agency and employment. The doctrine of vicarious liability applies to both. Significantly, however, an employer will not be held vicariously liable for torts committed by an "independent contractor." The classification of a worker is therefore critically important. Unfortunately, it often is very difficult as well.

671122 ONTARIO LTD. v. SAGAZ INDUSTRIES CANADA INC.
(2001), 204 D.L.R. (4th) 542 (S.C.C.)

[The plaintiff manufactured synthetic sheepskin car seat covers. It sold its product to Canadian Tire for over thirty years. At the time of the events in question, sales to Canadian Tire accounted for more than half of the plaintiff's annual business.

The defendant also manufactured car seat covers. It hired a marketing company called AIM in an effort to obtain Canadian Tire's business. AIM achieved that goal by bribing the head of Canadian Tire's automotive division.

The loss of Canadian Tire's business devastated the plaintiff. It sued several parties. One of its claims was against the defendant. For present purposes, the key issue was whether the defendant was vicariously liable for the torts (*i.e.* conspiracy and unlawful interference with economic relations) committed by AIM. The resolution of that issue depended upon the classification of AIM as either an employee or an independent contractor.]

MAJOR J.:—

A. Vicarious Liability

(1) Policy Rationale Underlying Vicarious Liability

Vicarious liability is not a distinct tort. It is a theory that holds one person responsible for the misconduct of another because of the relationship between them. Although the categories of relationships in law that attract vicarious liability are neither exhaustively defined nor closed, the most common one to give rise to vicarious liability is the relationship between master and servant, now more commonly called employer and employee.

In general, tort law attempts to hold persons accountable for their wrongful acts and omissions and the direct harm that flows from those wrongs. Vicarious liability, by contrast, is considered to be a species of strict liability because it requires no proof of personal wrongdoing on the part of the person who is subject to it. As such, it is still relatively uncommon in Canadian tort law. What policy considerations govern its discriminate application?

. . .

First, vicarious liability provides a just and practical remedy to people who suffer harm as a consequence of wrongs perpetrated by an employee. Many commentators are suspicious of vicarious liability in principle because it appears to hold parties responsible for harm simply because they have "deep pockets" or an ability to bear the loss even though they are not personally at fault. The "deep pockets" justification on its own does not accord with an inherent sense of what is fair (see also R. Flannigan, "Enterprise Control: The Servant-Independent Contractor Distinction" (1987), 37 U.T.L.J. 25, at p. 29). Besides an ability to bear the loss, it must also seem just to place liability for the wrong on the employer. McLachlin J. addresses this concern in *Bazley* . . . :

> Vicarious liability is arguably fair in this sense. The employer puts in the community an enterprise which carries with it certain risks. When those risks materialize and cause injury to a member of the public despite the employer's reasonable efforts, it is fair that the person or organization that creates the enterprise and hence the risk should bear the loss. This accords with the notion that it is right and just that the person who creates a risk bear the loss when the risk ripens into harm.

Similarly, Fleming stated that "a person who employs others to advance his own economic interest should in fairness be placed under a corresponding liability for losses incurred in the course of the enterprise" [*The Law of Torts*, 9th ed. (1998) 410]. McLachlin J. states that while the fairness of this proposition is capable of standing alone, "it is buttressed by the fact that the employer is often in the best position to spread the losses through mechanisms like insurance and higher prices, thus minimizing the dislocative effect of the tort within society". . . . Finally on this point, it is noteworthy that vicarious liability does not diminish the personal liability of the direct tortfeasor. . . .

The second policy consideration underlying vicarious liability is deterrence of future harm as employers are often in a position to reduce accidents and intentional wrongs by efficient organization and supervision. This policy ground is related to the first policy ground of fair compensation, as "[t]he introduction of the enterprise into the community with its attendant risk, in turn, implies the possibility of managing the risk to minimize the costs of the harm that may flow from it" (*Bazley, supra*).

(2) Employee Versus Independent Contractor

The most common relationship that attracts vicarious liability is that between employer and employee, formerly master and servant. This is distinguished from the relationship of an employer and independent contractor which, subject to certain limited exceptions . . ., typically does not give rise to a claim for vicarious liability. If a worker is determined to be an employee as opposed to an independent contractor such that vicarious liability can attach to the employer, this is not the end of the analysis. The tortious conduct has to be committed by the employee in the course of employment. For the reasons that follow, this second stage of the analysis is not relevant and need not be analysed in the present appeal.

What is the difference between an employee and an independent contractor and why should vicarious liability more likely be imposed in the former case than in the latter? This question has been the subject of much debate. The answer lies with the element of control that the employer has over the direct tortfeasor (the worker). If the employer does not control the activities of the worker, the policy justifications underlying vicarious liability will not be satisfied. See Flannigan, *supra*, at pp. 31-32:

> This basis for vicarious liability discloses a precise limitation on the scope of the doctrine. If the employer does not control the activities of the worker it is clear that vicarious liability should not be imposed, for then insulated risk-taking [by the employer] does not occur. Only the worker, authorized to complete a task, could have affected the probability of loss, for he alone had control in any respect. Thus, because there is no mischief where employer control is absent, no remedy is required.

Explained another way, the main policy concerns justifying vicarious liability are to provide a just and practical remedy for the plaintiffs harm and to encourage the deterrence of future harm. . . . Vicarious liability is fair in principle because the hazards of the business should be borne by the business itself; thus, it does not make sense to anchor liability on an employer for acts of an independent contractor, someone who was in business on his or her own account. In addition, the employer does not have the same control over an independent contractor as over an employee to reduce accidents and intentional wrongs by efficient organization and supervision. Each of these policy justifications is relevant to the ability of the employer to control the activities of the employee, justifications which are generally deficient or missing in the case of an independent contractor. [T]he policy justifications for imposing vicarious liability are relevant where the employer is able to control the activities of the employee but may be deficient in the case of an independent contractor over whom the employer has little control. However, control is not the only factor to consider in determining if a worker is an employee or an independent contractor. For the reasons discussed below, reliance on control alone can be misleading, and there are other relevant factors which should be considered in making this determination.

Various tests have emerged in the case law to help determine if a worker is an employee or an independent contractor. The distinction between an employee and an independent contractor applies not only in vicarious liability, but also to the application of various forms of employment legislation, the availability of an action for wrongful dismissal, the assessment of business and income taxes, the priority taken upon an employer's insolvency and the application of contractual rights. . . . Accordingly, much of the case law on point while not written in the context of vicarious liability is still helpful.

The Federal Court of Appeal thoroughly reviewed the relevant case law in *Wiebe Door Services Ltd. v. M.N.R.*, [1986] 3 F.C. 553. As MacGuigan J.A. noted, the original criterion of the employment relationship was the control test set out by Baron Bramwell in *Regina v. Walker* (1858), 27 L.J.M.C. 207, and adopted by this Court in *Hôpital Notre-Dame de l'Espérance v. Laurent*, [1978] 1 S.C.R. 605. It is expressed as follows: "the essential criterion of employer-employee relations is the right to give orders and instructions to the employee regarding the manner in which to carry out his work" *(Hôpital Notre-Dame de l'Espérance, supra*, at p. 613).

This criterion has been criticized as wearing "an air of deceptive simplicity" [Atiyah, *Vicarious Liability in the Law of Torts*, (1967) 41]. The main problems are set out by MacGuigan J.A. in *Wiebe Door*. . . :

> A principal inadequacy [with the control test] is its apparent dependence on the exact terms in which the task in question is contracted for: where the contract contains detailed specifications and conditions, which would be the normal expectation in a contract with an independent contractor, the control may even be greater than where it is to be exercised by direction on the job, as would be the normal expectation in a contract with a servant, but a literal application of the test might find the actual control to be less. In addition, the test has broken down completely in relation to highly skilled and professional workers, who possess skills far beyond the ability of their employers to direct.

An early attempt to deal with the problems of the control test was the development of a fourfold test known as the "entrepreneur test." It was set out by W. O. Douglas (later Justice) in "Vicarious Liability and Administration of Risk I" (1928-1929), 38 Yale L.J. 584, and applied by Lord Wright in *Montreal v. Montreal Locomotive Works Ltd.*, [1947] 1 D.L.R. 161 (P.C.), at p. 169:

> In earlier cases a single test, such as the presence or absence of control, was often relied on to determine whether the case was one of master and servant, mostly in order to decide issues of tortious liability on the part of the master or superior. In the more complex conditions of modern industry, more complicated tests have often to be applied. It has been suggested that a fourfold test would in some cases be more appropriate, a complex involving (1) control; (2) ownership of the tools; (3) chance of profit; (4) risk of loss. Control in itself is not always conclusive.

As MacGuigan J.A. notes, a similar general test, known as the "organization test" or "integration test" was used by Denning L.J. (as he then was) in *Stevenson Jordan and Harrison, Ltd. v. Macdonald*, [1952] 1 The Times L.R. 101 (C.A.), at p. 111:

One feature which seems to run through the instances is that, under a contract of service, a man is employed as part of the business, and his work is done as an integral part of the business; whereas, under a contract for services, his work, although done for the business, is not integrated into it but is only accessory to it.

This decision imported the language "contract of service" (employee) and "contract for services" (independent contractor) into the analysis. The organization test was approved by this Court in [*Co-operators Insurance Association v. Kearney*, [1965] S.C.R. 106] . . . where Spence J. observed that courts had moved away from the control test under the pressure of novel situations, replacing it instead with a type of organization test in which the important question was whether the alleged servant was part of his employer's organization. . . .

However, as MacGuigan J.A. noted in *Wiebe Door*, the organization test has had "less vogue in other common-law jurisdictions". . ., including England and Australia. For one, it can be a difficult test to apply. If the question is whether the activity or worker is integral to the employer's business, this question can usually be answered affirmatively. For example, the person responsible for cleaning the premises is technically integral to sustaining the business, but such services may be properly contracted out to people in business on their own. . . . As MacGuigan J.A. further noted in *Wiebe Door*, if the main test is to demonstrate that, without the work of the alleged employees the employer would be out of business, a factual relationship of mutual dependency would always meet the organization test of an employee even though this criterion may not accurately reflect the parties' intrinsic relationship. . . .

Despite these criticisms, MacGuigan J.A. acknowledges . . . that the organization test can be of assistance:

> Of course, the organization test of Lord Denning and others produces entirely acceptable results when properly applied, that is, when the question of organization or integration is approached from the persona of the "employee" and not from that of the "employer," because it is always too easy from the superior perspective of the larger enterprise to assume that every contributing cause is so arranged purely for the convenience of the larger entity. We must keep in mind that it was with respect to the business of the employee that Lord Wright [in Montreal] addressed the question "Whose business is it?"

According to MacGuigan J.A., the best synthesis found in the authorities is that of Cooke J. in *Market Investigations, Ltd. v. Minister of Social Security*, [1968] 3 All E.R. 732 (Q.B.D.), at pp. 737-38. . .:

> The observations of LORD WRIGHT, of DENNING, L.J., and of the judges of the Supreme Court in the U.S.A. suggest that the fundamental test to be applied is this: "Is the person who has engaged himself to perform these services performing them as a person in business on his own account?". If the answer to that question is "yes", then the contract is a contract for services. If the answer is "no" then the contract is a contract of service. No exhaustive list has been compiled and perhaps no exhaustive list can be compiled of considerations which are relevant in determining that question, nor can strict rules be laid down as to the relative weight which the various considerations should carry in particular cases. The most that can be said is that control will no doubt always have to be considered, although it can no longer be regarded as the sole determining factor; and that factors, which may be of importance, are such matters as whether the man performing the services provides his own equipment, whether he hires his own helpers, what degree of financial risk he

takes, what degree of responsibility for investment and management he has, and whether and how far he has an opportunity of profiting from sound management in the performance of his task.

Finally, there is a test that has emerged that relates to the enterprise itself. Flannigan, *supra*, sets out the "enterprise test" . . . which provides that the employer should be vicariously liable because (1) he controls the activities of the worker; (2) he is in a position to reduce the risk of loss; (3) he benefits from the activities of the worker; (4) the true cost of a product or service ought to be borne by the enterprise offering it. According to Flannigan, each justification deals with regulating the risk-taking of the employer and, as such, control is always the critical element because the ability to control the enterprise is what enables the employer to take risks. . . .

In my opinion, there is no one conclusive test which can be universally applied to determine whether a person is an employee or an independent contractor. Lord Denning stated in *Stevenson Jordan* . . . that it may be impossible to give a precise definition of the distinction . . . and, similarly, Fleming observed that "no single test seems to yield an invariably clear and acceptable answer to the many variables of ever changing employment relations" (p. 416). Further, I agree with MacGuigan J.A. in *Wiebe Door* . . . that what must always occur is a search for the total relationship of the parties:

> [I]t is exceedingly doubtful whether the search for a formula in the nature of a single test for identifying a contract of service any longer serves a useful purpose. . . . The most that can profitably be done is to examine all the possible factors which have been referred to in these cases as bearing on the nature of the relationship between the parties concerned. Clearly not all of these factors will be relevant in all cases, or have the same weight in all cases. Equally clearly no magic formula can be propounded for determining which factors should, in any given case, be treated as the determining ones.

Although there is no universal test to determine whether a person is an employee or an independent contractor, I agree with MacGuigan J.A. that a persuasive approach to the issue is that taken by Cooke J. in *Market Investigations*. . . . The central question is whether the person who has been engaged to perform the services is performing them as a person in business on his own account. In making this determination, the level of control the employer has over the worker's activities will always be a factor. However, other factors to consider include whether the worker provides his or her own equipment, whether the worker hires his or her own helpers, the degree of financial risk taken by the worker, the degree of responsibility for investment and management held by the worker, and the worker's opportunity for profit in the performance of his or her tasks.

[On the facts, Major J. concluded that AIM was "in business on its own account" — *i.e.* it was an independent contractor, rather than an employee, of the defendant. The defendant consequently was not vicariously liable for AIM's torts. In reaching that decision, Major J. was particularly influenced by a number of factors: (i) AIM had separate offices, (ii) AIM paid all of its own costs, (iii) AIM was free to take on other business, (iv) AIM decided when, where and how to perform the job, and was otherwise generally in control of the project, and (v) AIM was in a position to either suffer a loss or earn a profit, depending upon its performance of the job.]

NOTES AND QUESTIONS

1. In terms of a worker's relationship with an employer, what is the difference between an employee and an independent contractor? Why does that difference affect the availability of vicarious liability? Is it justifiable to draw a sharp distinction between employees on the one hand and non-employees on the other? See Morgan, "Recasting Vicarious Liability" [2012] C.L.J. 615.

2. Do the governing principles sufficiently take into account the plaintiff's interests? How can a potential plaintiff determine whether a particular task is to be performed by an employee, rather than an independent contractor? Are there circumstances in which a potential plaintiff's business decision may be affected by such knowledge? See generally *Johnson v. Canada (Minister of National Revenue)*, 2018 TCC 201.

3. What is the "control test?" What is the "organization test?" What are the deficiencies of each of those tests?

4. The categories concerning vicarious liability are not mutually exclusive. Accordingly, it sometimes is necessary to consider more than one possibility. For instance, a life insurance company may be held vicariously liable for theft by its sales agent, despite the fact that the agent was not an employee: *Thiessen v. Mutual Life Assurance Co. of Canada* (2002), 219 D.L.R. (4th) 98 (B.C.C.A.).

5. *Toshi Enterprises Ltd. v. Coffee Time Donuts Inc.*, 2007 CarswellOnt 8657 (S.C.J.) (WL Can), rev'd (2008), 246 O.A.C. 17 (Div. Ct.) considered the possibility of vicarious liability as between a franchisor and a franchisee. The plaintiff's sports bar suffered damage as a result of a fire that negligently occurred in a neighbouring Coffee Time outlet. The plaintiff sought to hold the defendant franchisor vicariously responsible for the tort committed by the party that operated the franchise in question. The small claims court judge upheld that claim, but on appeal Bellamy J. held that the circumstances did not support that decision. Although a franchisor may be vicariously liable for the torts of a franchisee, the relationship that existed on the facts did not trigger the policy factors underlying that doctrine. See also *Murray v. TDL Group Ltd.*, [2002] O.T.C. 1024 (S.C.J.) (WL Can).

6. As a general rule, torts committed by an independent contractor do not attract the doctrine of vicarious liability. A line of authority nevertheless supports vicarious liability for the acts of an independent contractor committed in the course of an ultra-hazardous activity. That exception applied in *Jans v. Ducks Unlimited Canada* (2008), 314 Sask. R. 12 (C.A.). The defendant retained Sanderson as an independent contractor for the purpose of removing a fence that had been erected around a lake. In the course of doing so, Sanderson negligently started a fire that spread to the plaintiff's property and destroyed approximately 2300 hectares of pasture. Because Sanderson was judgment-proof, the plaintiff argued that the defendant was vicariously liable for the tort. While split on the application of the rule, the Saskatchewan Court of Appeal unanimously agreed that a particularly dangerous activity may trigger vicarious liability in connection with an independent contractor. See also *Honeywill & Stein Ltd. v. Larkin Bros.*, [1934] 1 K.B. 191; *Savage v. Wilby*, [1954] S.C.R. 376; and *Sickel Estate v. Gordy* (2008), 311 Sask. R. 235 (C.A.).

The same issue arose in *Biffa Waste Services Ltd. v. Maschinenfabrik Ernst Hese GmbH*, [2009] Q.B. 725 (C.A.), noted in Tofaris, "Who Pays for the Sub-Contractor's Negligence? Vicarious Liability and Liability for 'Extra-Hazardous Activities' Re-examined" [2010] C.L.J. 13. The plaintiff hired M to design and construct a recycling plant. M sub-contracted the project to H, H contracted with OT to supply and install a particular piece of equipment, and OT sub-contracted the welding on that equipment to P. As a result of P's negligence, the plaintiff's property was damaged by fire. P and H were insolvent. The plaintiff consequently sought to impose liability upon M and OT. For present purposes, the relevant claim consisted of the plaintiff's allegation that OT was vicariously liable for P's tort. That allegation turned on the proposition that a non-delegable duty arises in connection with ultra-hazardous work undertaken by an independent contractor. The Court of Appeal recognized that proposition, but held that the activity in question (welding) was not, in itself, ultra-hazardous. In *obiter dicta*, however, it criticized the doctrine, primarily on the ground that the category of "ultra-hazardous activity" is intolerably vague. See also *Bottomley v. Todmorden Cricket Club*, [2003] EWCA Civ. 1575. The same considerations previously led High Court of Australia to abolish the doctrine altogether: *Stevens v. Brodribb Sawmilling Co. Ltd.* (1986), 160 C.L.R. 16 (H.C.A.).

In *The Catholic Child Welfare Society v. The Institute of the Brothers of the Christian Schools*, [2012] UKSC 56 at para. 36, the Supreme Court of the United Kingdom went even further. While he did not eliminate the distinction between employees and independent contractors, Lord Phillips did recognize that the dividing line may be very difficult to discern in some circumstances:

> In days gone by, when the relationship of employer and employee was correctly portrayed by the phrase "master and servant", the employer was often entitled to direct not merely what the employee should do but the manner in which he should do it. Indeed, this right was taken as the test for differentiating between a contract of employment and a contract for the services of an independent contractor. Today it is not realistic to look for a right to direct how an employee should perform his duties as a necessary element in the relationship between employer and employee. Many employees apply a skill or expertise that is not susceptible to direction by anyone else in the company that employs them. Thus the significance of control today is that the employer can direct what the employee does, not how he does it.

The more important question, the court said, is whether the relationship between the parties was "sufficiently akin to that of employer and employees" (at para. 60). What are the implications of that analysis? See also Morgan, "Vicarious Liability on the Move" (2013) 129 L.Q.R. 139.

(e) NON-DELEGABLE DUTIES

It often is difficult to distinguish between employees and independent contractors. Nevertheless, as *Sagaz* demonstrates, once that threshold issue has been resolved, the general conclusion is straightforward: vicarious liability may attach to the torts of an employee but not to those of an independent contractor. That is not to say, however, that liability is never imposed on a person who retained a contractor's services. McLachlin J. enumerated the exceptions in *Lewis (Guardian ad litem of) v. British Columbia* (1997), 153 D.L.R. (4th) 594 at 614 (S.C.C.):

The general rule at common law is that a person who employs an independent contractor will not be liable for loss flowing from the contractor's negligence. This rule for a long time admitted only three exceptions: (1) where the employer was negligent in hiring the contractor; (2) where the employer was negligent in supervising the contractor; and (3) where the employer hired the independent contractor to do something unlawful. A fourth exception crystallized in *Pickard v. Smith* (1861), 10 C.B. (N.S.) 470, 142 E.R. 535. Lord Blackburn stated the rule as: "a person causing something to be done, the doing of which casts on him a duty, cannot escape from the responsibility attaching on him of seeing that duty performed by delegating it to a contractor" (*Dalton v. Angus* (1881), 6 App. Cas. 740 (H.L.) at p. 829). This exception is referred to as the "non-delegable duty" rule.

Perhaps the most important exception to the employer's general immunity is the last one: *non-delegable duty*. A person subject to such an obligation can delegate its *performance* but not *responsibility*. In other words, despite being entitled to retain an independent contractor to execute the relevant task, the obligee bears the risk of liability if anything goes tortiously wrong. In *Lewis*, for instance, a public authority was statutorily required to maintain a highway in a certain condition. The public authority was free to assign the actual work to an independent contractor. Nevertheless, when the plaintiff was killed as a result of the independent contractor's negligence, the public authority bore responsibility along with the actual tortfeasor.

The primary difficulty with the concept of a non-delegable duty concerns its scope of application. Historically, the courts merely recognized various instances in which a person could not escape responsibility by delegating a task to an independent contractor. The list included cases involving the rule in *Rylands v. Fletcher*, ultra-hazardous activities, the duty to refrain from creating a nuisance, the duty to provide lateral support for adjacent land, and the duty of a bailee for reward to safeguard the bailed goods.

In *Lewis*, the Supreme Court of Canada began the task of extracting a general principal from those discrete circumstances. Cory J. said that:

> . . .a party upon whom the law has imposed a strict statutory duty to do a positive act cannot escape liability simply by delegating the work to an independent contractor. Rather a defendant subject to such a duty will always remain personally liable for the acts or omissions of the contractor to whom it assigned the work.

McLachlin J. continued the analysis in a concurring judgment:

> In essence, a non-delegable duty is a duty not only to take care, but to ensure that care is taken. It is not strict liability, since it requires someone (the independent contractor) to have been negligent. But if it applies, it is no answer for the employer to say, "I was not negligent in hiring or supervising the independent contractor." The employer is liable for the contractor's negligence. The employer already has a personal duty at common law or by statute to take reasonable care. The non-delegable duty doctrine adds another obligation — the duty to ensure that the independent contractor also takes reasonable care.

> While the nature of the exception is clear, when it applies is not. Some courts have held that it applies only in certain categories of cases, such as harm done by inherently dangerous objects or activities, harm done in the course of the exercise of statutory powers and duties, or in the United States, harm caused by failure to

maintain highways and other public places in a reasonably safe condition. . . . The problem with the category approach is that the existing categories have evolved for reasons that may not be acceptable under modern theories of tort liability. . . . Thus Glanville Williams writes that "the courts have extended, seemingly without any reference to considerations of policy, the liability for independent contractors" ("Liability for Independent Contractors," [1956] Cambridge L.J. 180, at p. 180).

Rather than confirm or add to a hodgepodge of categories, we should seek the underlying principles that justify the imposition of a non-delegable duty on a person who hires an independent contractor to have work done. This is the approach that Cory J. takes. Whether a non-delegable duty arises "will depend upon the nature and the extent of the duty owed by the defendant to the plaintiff." . . . "In some circumstances, the duty to take reasonable care may well be discharged by hiring and, if required, supervising a competent contractor to perform the particular work". There is no categorical rule that common law duties arising from the exercise of a statutory power are never non-delegable. Rather, "[w]hether or not there will be liability for the negligence of the acts of the independent contractor will depend to a large extent upon the statutory provisions involved and the circumstances presented by each case". Cory J. goes on to conclude that in this particular case, the wording of the statute, combined with policy considerations, imposes on the Crown, not only a duty to be careful in hiring or supervising independent contractors, but an additional non-delegable duty to ensure that the work of its contractors is done without negligence.

I agree with this analysis. I am not so sure as my colleague that s. 48 of the Ministry of Transportation and Highways Act, R.S.B.C. 1979, c. 280, which provides that the Ministry "shall direct the construction, maintenance and repair" of all highways, demonstrates clearly that the Ministry must "personally direct" and supervise these works in all their aspects. It seems to me that those words are also consistent with a basic direction that works be undertaken. Yet I am satisfied in this case that the circumstances, taken together with the statutory provisions, suffice to establish a non-delegable duty of care on the Ministry with respect to highway maintenance. To determine whether a non-delegable duty should be imposed, the Court should examine the relationship between the parties and ask whether that relationship possesses elements that make it appropriate to hold the defendant liable for the negligence of its independent contractor. In the case at bar, the fact that road maintenance is entirely within the power of the Ministry is an important element to consider. So is the correlative fact that this renders the public, who often have no choice but to use the highway, totally vulnerable as to how, and by whom, road maintenance is performed. Finally, the fact that safety and lives are at issue is of critical importance. Cory J. correctly stresses these factors in concluding that the Ministry cannot discharge its duty in this case merely by proving that it exercised reasonable care in hiring and supervising the contractor. The Ministry must go further and ensure that the contractor's work was carried out without negligence.

NOTES AND QUESTIONS

1. Is the rule governing non-delegable duties an instance of vicarious liability? Sappideen & Vines, eds., *Fleming's The Law of Torts*, 10th ed. (2011) at 467-68 draws a distinction:

[A] non-delegable duty includes responsibility not only for the delegate's failure to perform the duty (for example, to carry out a repair), but also negligence in the course of performing it (for example, injuring a bystander). But it does not extend to "casual" or "collateral" acts of negligence. This limitation provides the most important distinction between a principal's liability for the acts of an independent contractor and the genuinely vicarious liability of a "master" because the latter is accountable for any wrongdoing of the servant, however incidental to the main job, so long as it falls within the course of employment.

2. The Supreme Court of Canada's reasons in *Lewis* were applied in the companion case of *Mochinski v. Trendline Industries Ltd.* (1997), 154 D.L.R. (4th) 212 (S.C.C.). For other discussions of non-delegable duties, see *Kitchener (City of) v. Robe & Clothing Co.*, [1925] S.C.R. 106; *St. John (City) v. Donald*, [1926] S.C.R. 311; *L.R. v. Bromley Estate*, 2013 NLCA 24; *Darling v. Attorney-General*, [1950] 2 All E.R. 793 (H.L.); *Hole v. Sittingbourne & Sheerness Railway Co.* (1861), 158 E.R. 201 (Ch.); *Das v. George Weston Ltd.*, 2018 ONCA 1053; *Woodland v. Swimming Teachers Association*, [2013] UKSC 66; *Kondis v. State Transport Authority* (1984), 154 C.L.R. 672 (H.C.A.); *Burnie Port Authority v. General Jones Pty. Ltd.* (1994) 179 C.L.R. 520 (H.C.A.); and *New South Wales v. Lepore* (2003), 77 A.L.J.R. 558 (H.C.A.).

3. Many commentators initially interpreted *Lewis* as indicating that the Supreme Court of Canada intended to adopt a broad conception of non-delegable duty and thereby substantially increase the incidence of liability. Subsequent decisions, however, have taken a more restricted view of the doctrine. See Rafferty, "Developments in Contract and Tort Law: The 2003-2004 Term" (2004) 26 S.C.L.R. (2d) 147.

The opportunity for reconsideration arose in connection with many of the cases previously discussed in terms of vicarious liability: *B.(K.L.) v. British Columbia*, [2003] 2 S.C.R. 403; *G.(E.D.) v. Hammer*, [2003] 2 S.C.R. 459; and *Blackwater v. Plint*, [2005] 3 S.C.R. 3. In each instance, the plaintiff, who had been sexually assaulted while living in a foster home or a residential school, claimed that the government had breached a non-delegable duty to protect the children. On that theory, the government was entitled to delegate the actual operation of the facilities to other parties, but it remained responsible for any harm that occurred. The court consistently rejected that theory. For instance, in *Blackwater* (at 290) McLachlin C.J.C. examined the *Indian Act*, S.C. 1951, c. 29, and found "that none of 'the general duties gives school boards full responsibility for students' welfare while on school premises, in the way that the statutes in Lewis gave the Ministry full responsibility for overseeing maintenance projects and for ensuring that workers exercised reasonable care.'" Likewise, in *B.(K.L.)* (at 426-27) she found that the *Protection of Children Act*, R.S.B.C. 1960, c. 303:

> offers no basis for imposing on the Superintendent a non-delegable duty to ensure that no harm comes to children through the abuse or negligence of foster parents. Foster parents provide day-to-day care for the children. But the Act does not suggest that the Superintendent is responsible for directing this day-to-day care and for ensuring that no harm comes to the children in the course of this care. . . . Although the Act makes the Superintendent solely responsible for the well-being of a child before placement, it does not suggest that this is work for which the Superintendent retains responsibility after placement. Indeed, if the Superintendent were responsible for all of the wrongs that might befall children in foster care, there would be no need to set out his particular duties with respect to placement and supervision.

4. For discussion of the topic see Dyson & Jarvis, "Taking Two Bites at The Cherry: Vicarious Liability and Non-Delegable Duty" (2018) 134 L.Q.R. 193; Deakin,

"Organisational Torts: Vicarious Liability Versus Non-Delegable Duty" [2018] C.L.J. 15; Giliker, "Analysing Institutional Liability for Child Sexual Abuse in England and Wales and Australia: Vicarious Liability, Non-Delegable Duties and Statutory Intervention" [2018] C.L.J. 506; Young, "Challenges in the Evolution of the Doctrine of Non-delegable Duty" (2018) 25 Tort L. Rev. 143; Morgan, "Fostering, Vicarious Liability, Non-Delegable Duties, and Intentional Torts" (2016) 132 L.Q.R. 399; Tofaris, "Vicarious Liability and Non-Delegable Duty for Child Abuse in Foster Care: A Step Too Far?" (2016) 79 M.L.R. 884; Todd, "Personal Liability, Vicarious Liability, Non-delegable Duties and Protecting Vulnerable People" (2016) 23 Torts L.J. 105; Morgan, "Liability for Independent Contractors in Contract and Tort: Duties to Ensure That Care is Taken" [2015] C.L.J. 109; Stevens, "Non-Delegable Duties and Vicarious Liability" and Murphy, "Juridical Foundations of Common Law Non-Delegable Duties" in Neyers, Chamberlain & Pitel, eds., *Emerging Issues in Tort Law* (2007), chs. 13 and 14; Witting, "Breach of the Non-Delegable Duty: Defending Limited Strict Liability in Tort" (2006) 29 U.N.S.W.L.J. 33; and Murphy, "The Liability Bases of Common Law Non-Delegable Duties — A Reply to Christian Witting" (2007) 30 U.N.S.W. L.J. 86.

REVIEW PROBLEM

Cale owns and operates Scrap and Salvage Inc. (SSI). The business, which occupies a large lot at the edge of an industrial park, accepts derelict vehicles and machinery and sells spare parts and scrap metal. It deals with both private consumers and business customers. The *Business Premises (Valuable Goods) Security Act*, a provincial statute, requires enterprises like SSI to maintain stipulated levels of security in specific circumstances. The legislation became necessary when certain metals, such as copper, escalated in value and attracted thieves.

On the first few occasions when SSI's inventory triggered the operation of the *Business Premises (Valuable Goods) Security Act*, Cale hired Orthrus Protection Ltd., a security firm, to ensure that the premises were properly patrolled as long as the valuable metals were on the site. Each contract was created for a particular purpose and a specified short duration (such as ten days). Orthrus Protection Ltd. was owned by Typhon. Whenever Typhon patrolled SSI's property himself, he brought along his Rottweiler named Cerberus. For the most part, Cerberus' bite was worse than her bark. Despite a fearsome appearance, she was both a security dog and a companion to Typhon's young family. She had bitten in anger only once, several years earlier, after being teased by a letter carrier.

SSI's business grew and the price of metals continued to escalate. The situation eventually reached a point at which the parties recognized that it was no longer convenient or efficient to continue creating a series of short-term contracts. Furthermore, Cale had arranged for several SSI employees, who had undergone the appropriate training, to act as security personnel during business hours. Typhon and Cale accordingly reached a new arrangement that was to operate "on an on-going basis" and "for an indefinite duration." Typhon personally agreed, in exchange for bi-weekly payments based on an hourly rate, to patrol the premises every night between 10:00 p.m. and 7:00 a.m.

The agreement initially worked well. However, an incident occurred two weeks into the "on-going" arrangement. As Typhon's nightly patrol took him past SSI's front gates, Cerberus' attention was drawn to Morley, who was walking across the street. Morley and a few colleagues, all of whom worked as letter carriers, had gone directly to a tavern after work. After drinking for several hours, Morley bid farewell to his friends and began his walk home. Unfortunately, he was both intoxicated and still in uniform. Before Typhon could realize what was happening, Cerberus bolted from his control and attacked Morley.

Morley suffered severe injuries and is unable to work. He therefore wishes to sue in tort. Discuss the various parties' rights and liabilities.

BUSINESS TORTS

1. Introduction
2. Deceit (Fraud)
3. Passing Off
4. Intimidation
5. Conspiracy
6. Interference with Contractual Relations
7. The Unlawful Means Tort

1. Introduction

Tort law plays a significant role in the business world. We already have seen several illustrations. The issues of negligent misrepresentation (Chapter 13) and pure economic loss (Chapter 14) frequently arise in commercial contexts. In some circumstances, business people should be particularly attentive to the rules governing occupiers' liability (Chapter 23) and nuisance (Chapter 24). A store that detains a suspected shoplifter should be concerned about false imprisonment, and a tavern that employs a bouncer should be concerned about battery (Chapter 3). And, of course, the doctrine of vicarious liability (Chapter 25) was designed to extend the scope of liability from an employee to an employer.

In this chapter, we turn our attention to the actions that are often grouped together as the "business torts." Obviously, there is no discrete tort of that name and, as an organizing concept, the phrase is somewhat open-ended. We use the label to focus on six torts: (1) deceit (fraud), (2) passing off, (3) intimidation, (4) conspiracy, (5) interference with contractual relations, and (6) the unlawful means tort. Several related torts, such as injurious falsehood and misappropriation of personality, will be introduced by the accompanying notes.

Before beginning, however, it is important to set the scene by briefly considering tort law's default position. The Canadian economy is based on capitalism, which in turn is based on vigorous, even ruthless, competition. Success in the business world often depends upon an ability to strike a good bargain for oneself — and, by extension, a bad bargain for the other side; upon an ability to hire the most skilful workers — and, by extension, an ability to lure those people away from competitors; and so on. Indeed, the best way to deal with a rival sometimes is to simply get rid of it. Within fairly broad parameters, our legal system condones that strategy.

The common law was previously more protectionist. *Keeble v. Hickeringill* (1707), 103 E.R. 1127 stood for the proposition that "he that hinders another in his trade or livelihood is liable to an action for so hindering him." During the 19th century, however, *laissez-faire* philosophies took hold and the courts began to espouse a much different line. *Allen v. Flood* (1897), [1898] A.C. 1 (H.L.) is the seminal decision. A ship, the *Sam Waller*, was under repair. Woodwork was being done by the plaintiffs, who belonged to a small union. Ironwork was being done by members of a much larger union, which was represented by the defendant. The two unions were not on good terms. The defendant told the company overseeing the repairs that unless the plaintiffs were dismissed, the ironworkers would not perform. The threat was effective and the plaintiffs were replaced with other woodworkers. The House of Lords held that this conduct did not constitute intimidation, conspiracy, or interference with contractual relations, the last of which was precluded by the fact that the plaintiffs had been hired on a day-to-day basis. The court also held that the defendant's malicious motive, in itself, did not render his conduct tortious. As long as he did not achieve his goal by otherwise unlawful means, the defendant was free to deliberately drive the plaintiffs out of business. In the dog-eat-dog world of commerce, the law favours the survival of the fittest. See *JSC BTA Bank v. Khrapunov*, [2018] UKSC 19 at para. 6.

The remainder of this chapter should be read against the backdrop of *Allen v. Flood*. Since that case was decided in 1897, judges repeatedly have revisited the balance that must be struck between competing interests. Consistent with evolving social and economic attitudes, the scope of liability generally expanded during the 20th century. Unfortunately, in the course of developing the law, some of the business torts occasionally have been combined or confused.

2. Deceit (Fraud)

Deceit (or fraud) is a very serious matter, especially in a commercial context. Success in the business world largely depends on facts and choices; deceit skews the decision-making process. It produces errors and miscalculations. The courts consequently are keen to sanction and deter it. At the same time, however, judges appreciate the debilitating stigma that may attach to a finding of deceit. To say that a person has committed fraud is, in the common law, to call that person a liar. And few people are willing to deal with a business person who has a reputation for dishonesty. (In equity, in contrast, the term "fraud" may refer to actual deceit, but it may also refer, in a very broad and misleading way, to almost any failure to act in a prescribed manner.) The following cases illustrate the tension created by the need to both protect the plaintiff from fraud and protect the defendant from unfair stigma.

DERRY v. PEEK
(1889), 14 A.C. 337 (H.L.)

[A company intended to operate a tramway line. The defendants, who were the directors of that company, issued a prospectus stating that they had "the right to use steam or mechanical power instead of horses." If that statement were true, the venture would have had excellent prospects for profitability. In fact, while the defendants honestly believed that government approval of steam or mechanical power was a mere formality, the Board of Trade held a very real discretion, which it ultimately exercised against the defendants. The plaintiff, who had purchased company shares on the strength of the prospectus, sued the defendants for deceit in an effort to recover his lost investment.]

LORD HERSCHELL: . . .

"This action is one which is commonly called an action of deceit, a mere common law action." This is the description of it given by Cotton L.J. in delivering judgment. I think it important that it should be borne in mind that such an action differs essentially from one brought to obtain rescission of a contract on the ground of misrepresentation of a material fact. The principles which govern the two actions differ widely. Where rescission is claimed it is only necessary to prove that there was misrepresentation; then, however honestly it may have been made, however free from blame the person who made it, the contract, having been obtained by misrepresentation, cannot stand. In an action of deceit, on the contrary, it is not enough to establish misrepresentation alone; it is conceded on all hands that something more must be proved to cast liability upon the defendant, though it has been a matter of controversy what additional elements are requisite. I lay stress upon this because observations made by learned judges in actions for rescission have been cited and much relied upon at the bar by counsel for the respondent. Care must obviously be observed in applying the language used in relation to such actions to an action of deceit. Even if the scope of the language used extends beyond the particular action which was being dealt with, it must be remembered that the learned judges were not engaged in determining what is necessary to support an action of deceit, or in discriminating with nicety the elements which enter into it.

There is another class of actions which I must refer to also for the purpose of putting it aside. I mean those cases where a person within whose special province it lay to know a particular fact, has given an erroneous answer to an inquiry made with regard to it by a person desirous of ascertaining the fact for the purpose of determining his course accordingly, and has been held bound to make good the assurance he has given. *Burrowes v. Lock* [10 Ves. 470] may be cited as an example, where a trustee had been asked by an intended lender, upon the security of a trust fund, whether notice of any prior incumbrance upon the fund had been given to him. In cases like this it has been said that the circumstance that the answer was honestly made in the belief that it was true affords no defence to the action. Lord Selborne pointed out in *Brownlie v. Campbell* [5 App. Cas. 935] that these cases were in an altogether different category from actions to recover damages for false representation, such as we are now dealing with.

One other observation I have to make before proceeding to consider the law which has been laid down by the learned judges in the Court of Appeal in the case before your Lordships.

> An action of deceit is a common law action, and must be decided on the same principles, whether it be brought in the Chancery Division or any of the Common Law Divisions, there being, in my opinion, no such thing as an equitable action for deceit.

This was the language of Cotton L.J. in *Arkwright v. Newbould* [17 Ch. D. 320]. It was adopted by Lord Blackburn in *Smith v. Chadwick* [9 App. Cas. 193], and is not, I think, open to dispute.

In the Court below Cotton L.J. said:

> What in my opinion is a correct statement of the law is this, that where a man makes a statement to be acted upon by others which is false, and which is known by him to be false, or is made by him recklessly, or without care whether it is true or false, that is, without any reasonable ground for believing it to be true, he is liable in an action of deceit at the suit of anyone to whom it was addressed or anyone of the class to whom it was addressed and who was materially induced by the misstatement to do an act to his prejudice.

About much that is here stated there cannot, I think, be two opinions. But when the learned Lord Justice speaks of a statement made recklessly or without care whether it is true or false, *that is* without any reasonable ground for believing it to be true, I find myself, with all respect, unable to agree that these are convertible expressions. To make a statement careless whether it be true or false, and therefore without any real belief in its truth, appears to me to be an essentially different thing from making, through want of care, a false statement, which is nevertheless honestly believed to be true. And it is surely conceivable that a man may believe that what he states is the fact, though he has been so wanting in care that the Court may think that there were no sufficient grounds to warrant his belief. I shall have to consider hereafter whether the want of reasonable ground for believing the statement made is sufficient to support an action of deceit. I am only concerned for the moment to point out that it does not follow that it is so, because there is authority for saying that a statement made recklessly, without caring whether it be true or false, affords sufficient foundation for such an action.

. . .

Having now drawn attention, I believe, to all the cases having a material bearing upon the question under consideration, I proceed to state briefly the conclusions to which I have been led. I think the authorities establish the following propositions: First, in order to sustain an action of deceit, there must be proof of fraud, and nothing short of that will suffice. Secondly, fraud is proved when it is shewn that a false representation has been made (1) knowingly, or (2) without belief in its truth, or (3) recklessly, careless whether it be true or false. Although I have treated the second and third as distinct cases, I think the third is but an instance of the second, for one who makes a statement under such circumstances can have no real belief in the truth of what he states. To prevent a false statement being fraudulent, there must, I think, always be an honest belief in its truth. And this probably covers the whole ground, for one who knowingly alleges that which is false, has obviously no such honest belief. Thirdly, if fraud be proved, the motive of the person guilty of it is immaterial. It matters not that there was no intention to cheat or injure the person to whom the statement was made.

. . .

In my opinion making a false statement through want of care falls far short of, and is a very different thing from, fraud, and the same may be said of a false representation honestly believed though on insufficient grounds. Indeed Cotton L.J. himself indicated, in the words I have already quoted, that he should not call it fraud. But the whole current of authorities, with which I have so long detained your Lordships, shews to my mind conclusively that fraud is essential to found an action of deceit, and that it cannot be maintained where the acts proved cannot properly be so termed.

. . .

[Lord Herschell concluded that the plaintiff had failed to establish deceit. Lords Watson, Halsbury, Bramwell, and Fitzgerald delivered separate concurring judgments.]

BRUNO APPLIANCE AND FURNITURE INC. v. HRYNIAK
2014 SCC 8

KARAKATSANIS J.: . . .

[3] Bruno Appliance and Furniture, Inc. is an American corporation, whose principal is Albert Bruno. In late 2001, Bruno met with Robert Cranston, the principal of a Panamanian company, Frontline Investments, Inc. As a result of these meetings, Bruno executed a number of investment documents in favour of Frontline.

[4] In February 2002, Bruno met with Cranston and Gregory Peebles, a corporate-commercial lawyer at the Toronto offices of Cassels Brock and Blackwell. No notes were kept of this meeting, and the recollection of the participants varies. While Robert Hryniak did not attend this meeting, Tropos Financial Corp. (Tropos), a company of which Hryniak was the principal, received and paid a bill for Peebles' attendance.

[5] In early March 2002, Bruno Appliance wired US$1 million to Cassels Brock, who assigned the funds to an account associated with Tropos. Bruno Appliance's funds were then bundled with other funds (totalling US$3.5 million) and paid to Tropos in a bank draft. At the end of April 2002, Tropos paid US$2.5 million to a company called Southern Equity Investors Inc., and in late June 2002 transferred approximately US$550,000 to an individual named Reinhard. By the end of September 2003, Tropos' balance with Cassels Brock had declined to US$19,000.

[6] In short, Bruno Appliance's money was not invested and it never received a return on its investment.

II. Judicial History

A. *Ontario Superior Court of Justice, 2010 ONSC 5490 (CanLII)*

[7] Bruno Appliance [brought] a civil fraud action against Hryniak [and sought summary judgment]. . . .

[8] The motion judge found that Bruno Appliance had established its claim against Hryniak and that there was no issue requiring a trial. He was satisfied that, in spite of Hryniak's absence from an early meeting between Peebles, Cranston and Bruno, Hryniak knew that the meeting was occurring and his company, Tropos, paid for Peebles' attendance. The motion judge further found that Hryniak was aware that US$1 million was placed in Tropos' account on Bruno Appliance's behalf, and that Hryniak gave instructions regarding those funds.

[9] The motion judge found that none of Bruno Appliance's funds were invested. In part, they were used to fund disbursements to another individual, Reinhard, and the remainder was slowly drained.

[10] The motion judge held that the tort of civil fraud was made out and there was no genuine issue requiring a trial. . . .

B. *Court of Appeal for Ontario, 2011 ONCA 764, 108 O.R. (3d) 1*

[14] The Court of Appeal [allowed an appeal on the ground] that the motion judge failed to address the issue of whether Hryniak knowingly made any misrepresentation that induced Bruno Appliance to invest, a necessary element of fraud. The Court of Appeal concluded that there was no compelling evidence that Peebles acted as Hryniak's agent when the relevant representations were made. . . .

III. Analysis . . .

A. *The Tort of Civil Fraud*

[17] The parties disagree as to the elements of the tort of civil fraud, in particular whether proof is required that Hryniak induced Bruno Appliance to part with its funds.

[18] The classic statement of the elements of civil fraud stems from an 1889 decision of the House of Lords, *Derry v. Peek* (1889), 14 App. Cas. 337, where Lord Herschell conducted a thorough review of the history of the tort of deceit and put forward the following three propositions, at p. 374:

> First, in order to sustain an action of deceit, there must be proof of fraud, and nothing short of that will suffice. Secondly, fraud is proved when it is shewn that a false representation has been made (1) knowingly, or (2) without belief in its truth, or (3) recklessly, careless whether it be true or false. . . . Thirdly, if fraud be proved, the motive of the person guilty of it is immaterial. It matters not that there was no intention to cheat or injure the person to whom the statement was made.

[19] This Court adopted Lord Herschell's formulation in *Parna v. G. & S. Properties Ltd.*, [1971] S.C.R. 306, adding that the false statement must "actually [induce the plaintiff] to act upon it". . . . Requiring the plaintiff to prove inducement is consistent with this Court's later recognition in *Snell v. Farrell*, [1990] 2 S.C.R. 311, at pp. 319-20, that tort law requires proof that "but for the tortious conduct of the defendant, the plaintiff would not have sustained the injury complained of".

[20] Finally, this Court has recognized that proof of loss is also required. As Taschereau C.J. held in *Angers v. Mutual Reserve Fund Life Assn.* (1904), 35 S.C.R. 330 "fraud without damage gives . . . no cause of action" (p. 340).

[21] From this jurisprudential history, I summarize the following four elements of the tort of civil fraud: (1) a false representation made by the defendant; (2) some level of knowledge of the falsehood of the representation on the part of the defendant (whether through knowledge or recklessness); (3) the false representation caused the plaintiff to act; and (4) the plaintiff's actions resulted in a loss.

B. *Did the Motion Judge Err in Granting Summary Judgment?*

. . .

[24] [C]ivil fraud requires a finding that Hryniak made a misrepresentation which induced Bruno Appliance to invest. The motion judge neither identified the need for a misrepresentation, nor found that Hryniak made one.

[25] The motion judge found that Tropos did not invest Bruno Appliance's funds and that a misrepresentation had therefore been made to the investors. The point at which a misrepresentation occurred was a meeting between Peebles, Cranston and Bruno Appliance's principal in February 2002. He found: that Hryniak was supposed to be in attendance at this meeting, that Hryniak knew of the purpose of the meeting and that Hryniak's company paid for Peebles' attendance.

[26] However, Hryniak was not present, and he can only be liable for any misrepresentation made by Peebles or Cranston if their statements can be attributed to him. For example, the Court of Appeal considered, and ultimately rejected, the possibility that Peebles or Cranston was acting as Hryniak's agent.

[27] In my view, the motion judge's findings are insufficient to establish that any false statements made at the meeting can be attributed to Hryniak. There was no evidence that Peebles or Cranston were acting on instructions from Hryniak when they met with Bruno. While a principal will generally be vicariously liable "for the torts of her agent committed within the scope of her actual or apparent authority" (P. H. Osborne, *The Law of Torts* (4th ed. 2011), at p. 369), the motion judge did not find Peebles or Cranston to be Hryniak's agent, and there is no indication that the evidence established that Peebles or Cranston was authorized to make representations on behalf of Hryniak and did not do so on their own account. Similarly, there was insufficient evidence to establish that either Peebles or Cranston was acting as Hryniak's unwitting dupe. . . .

[28] While the motion judge found that Hryniak was aware of the falseness of the representation and exercised "full dominion and control" over Bruno Appliance's funds (at para. 169) . . . this finding . . . is not sufficient to establish fraud.

[29] While I agree with the motion judge that the evidence clearly demonstrates that Hryniak was *aware* of the fraud, and may in fact have *benefited* from the fraud, whether Hryniak *perpetrated* the fraud by inducing Bruno Appliance to contribute US$1 million to a non-existent investment scheme is a genuine issue requiring a trial.

[The plaintiff's appeal was dismissed. In the companion case of *Hryniak v. Mauldin*, 2014 SCC 7, in contrast, the Supreme Court of Canada upheld the motion judge's decision to impose liability for civil fraud without the need for a full trial on the merits.]

NOTES AND QUESTIONS

1. On the basis of *Derry v. Peek*, explain the legal significance of the difference between a careless representation and a fraudulent representation. Why did the law traditionally allow damages for the latter but not the former? Do courts continue to deny relief for losses stemming from negligent statements? That question is addressed in Chapter 13.

2. Do the decisions in *Bruno's Appliances* and *Derry v. Peek* formulate the test of fraud in the same terms? If not, identify and explain any differences.

Prior to *Bruno's Appliances*, civil fraud often was said to entail four elements: (1) the defendant must have made *a false statement of fact*, (2) the defendant must have *known* that the statement was false, (3) the defendant must have made the statement with the *intention of misleading* the plaintiff, and (4) the plaintiff must have suffered a loss as a result of *relying* on the statement: Fridman *et al.*, *The Law of Torts*, 3d ed. (2010) at 707-21. The test that Karakatsanis J. articulated in *Bruno's Appliances* appears to depart from that formulation in important respects.

First, while the traditional formulation required proof of the defendant's intention to mislead the plaintiff, Karakatsanis J. required that "the [defendant's] false representation caused the plaintiff to act." Is there a difference between an intention to mislead and a false representation that causes the plaintiff to act? Which formulation better reflects the gist of the action? Is the defendant's intention now irrelevant?

Second, while the traditional test required proof that the plaintiff relied upon the defendant's misrepresentation, Karakatsanis J. required proof that "the plaintiff's actions resulted in a loss." While the third and fourth elements of the test in *Bruno's Appliances* indicate the need for a causal relationship between the defendant's representation and the plaintiff's loss, nothing in the decision expressly requires reliance. Has Canadian law been changed in that respect?

3. The idea of a *false statement of fact* usually is straightforward. In most successful cases, the defendant says or writes something that is positively untrue. That statement is a lie. Occasionally, however, the analysis is more complicated.

First, although the defendant's statement is usually spoken or written, liability may also be imposed on the basis of misleading actions: see *Abel v. McDonald* (1964), 45 D.L.R. (2d) 198 (Ont. C.A.).

Second, although the actionable statement usually consists of a simple lie, liability exceptionally may be imposed in other situations. The defendant may be held responsible for a *half-truth*. For instance, while selling a business, the defendant may present revenue figures so as to suggest that they refer to net profits, rather than gross profits. Liability also may be imposed for a *failure to update information*. For instance, the defendant might refrain from correcting a statement that, while true when stated, has to the defendant's knowledge become untrue.

Third, although mere silence otherwise is not actionable, there are situations in which the law places an obligation on a person to speak up. This is true, for instance, if a person selling a house knows of a hidden defect that renders the premises dangerous or unfit for habitation. See *Sorensen v. Kaye Holdings Ltd.*, [1979] 6 W.W.R. 193 (B.C.C.A.); *C.R.F. Holdings Ltd. v. Fundy Chemical Int. Ltd.* (1981), 19 C.C.L.T. 263 (B.C.C.A.); *Francis v. Dingman* (1983), 43 O.R. (2d) 641 (C.A.); *Canson Enterprises Ltd. v. Boughton & Co.* (1991), 85 D.L.R. (4th) 129 (S.C.C.); and *Freeman v. Perlman* (1999), 169 D.L.R. (4th) 133 (B.C.C.A.).

An issue may arise as to whether a false statement was that of the defendant. In *Derry v. Peek*, for instance, the plaintiff was misled by statements made by a company's directors. In such circumstances, who is the proper defendant: the directors or the company? The question is interesting because company law is based on the fundamental principle that the corporation is a separate entity, even though it acts through human agents (such as its directors). Nevertheless, the House of Lords recently affirmed that, notwithstanding the general rule of corporations, "No one can escape liability for his fraud by saying 'I wish to make it clear that I am committing this fraud on behalf of someone else and I am not to be personally liable'": *Standard Chartered Bank v. Pakistan National Shipping Corp. (Nos. 2 and 4)*, [2003] 1 A.C. 959 at 968 (H.L.). Cf. *Sealand of the Pacific v. Robert C. McHaffie Ltd.* (1974), 51 D.L.R. (3d) 702 (B.C.C.A.) (liability imposed on company, but not human agent, under claim for *negligent* misstatement).

Personal liability was imposed in *1318777 Ontario Ltd. v. 1004847 Ontario Inc.*, 2006 CarswellOnt 2922 (S.C.J.) (WL Can). The plaintiff purchased goods and leased property from a company called "100." Before doing so, it received an affidavit from Karp, the controlling and directing mind of 100, swearing to the fact that that company had no unsecured creditors and only one secured creditor. In fact, Karp had no reason to believe that that information was correct. Some time later, the situation deteriorated and the plaintiff received a judgment against 100 for $30,540. Unfortunately, because of 100's other debt, it was unable to pay the plaintiff. The plaintiff then successfully sued Karp on the basis of his fraudulent affidavit.

4. The plaintiff must prove that the defendant *knew* that the relevant statement was false when it was made. That requirement usually is satisfied by proof of actual

knowledge, but as observed in *Derry v. Peek* and *Bruno's Appliances*, liability may be imposed if the defendant was reckless to the truth or falsity of a statement and therefore had no belief in its accuracy.

5. It generally is said that the defendant must have *intended to deceive* the plaintiff, or have been substantially certain that the statement would deceive the plaintiff. Because of the need for intention, the same statement may trigger liability with respect to one recipient, but not another, if the defendant intended to deceive the former, but not the latter: *Fiorillo v. Krispy Kreme Doughnuts Inc.* (2009), 98 O.R. (3d) 103 (S.C.J.). Curiously, however, the element of intention was not mentioned in *Bruno's Appliances*. Has the Supreme Court of Canada changed the law without discussing the matter?

6. Although *Bruno's Appliances* again was curiously silent on the point, it generally is said that the plaintiff must have suffered a loss as a result of *relying* upon the defendant's statement. The idea of a loss simply demonstrates that deceit is not actionable *per se*. Significantly, however, once the plaintiff has established that the false statement was made with an intention to deceive, the defendant bears the burden of proving that the plaintiff did not actually rely upon it: *Sidhu Estate v. Bains* (1996), 25 B.C.L.R. (3d) 41 (C.A.); but *cf. Smith v. Chadwick* (1884), 9 App. Cas. 187 (H.L.). See generally Handley, "Causation in Misrepresentation" (2015) 131 L.Q.R. 275.

One of the more difficult aspects of the tort of deceit is the requirement of *reliance*. To begin, there is an ongoing debate as to whether simple reliance will suffice or whether liability is premised upon a finding of reasonable reliance. The authorities are divided. Some cases expressly require *reasonable* reliance: *White v. Turner* (1981), 120 D.L.R. (3d) 269 at 286 (Ont. H.C.J.); and *Khaira v. Nelson* 2002 BCSC 1045 at para. 35. In contrast, in *Kelemen v. El-Homeira*, 1999 ABCA 351 the Alberta Court of Appeal held that while the contractual action for fraudulent misrepresentation requires proof of reasonable reliance, the tort of deceit merely requires reliance in fact. See also *Zhou v. Wang*, 2004 BCSC 1073 at para. 74; and Klar & Jefferies, *Tort Law*, 6th ed. (2017) at 811-14. Some academics endorse the subjective approach: Sappideen & Vines, eds., *Fleming's The Law of Torts*, 10th ed. (2011) at 721; and Rogers, *Winfield & Jolowicz on Tort*, 18th ed. (2010) at §11-12. The rationale for the objective standard was provided by *United Services Funds (Trustees of) v. Richard Greenshields of Can. Ltd.*, (1988), 48 D.L.R. (4th) 98 at 111 (B.C.S.C.):

> There may be greater dangers to civilized society than endemic dishonesty. But I can think of nothing which will contribute to dishonesty more than a rule of law which requires us all to be on perpetual guard against rogues lest we be faced with the defence of 'Ha, ha, your own fault. I fool you.' Such a defence should not be countenanced from a rogue.

If the concept of reasonable reliance does apply, then it precludes liability for reliance upon certain types of statements. Because they know that sales people tend to exaggerate, reasonable people do not place stock in empty *puffery*. Because they know that the future is uncertain and unknowable, reasonable people not rely on *predictions*. And because they know that values and perceptions vary, reasonable people are not swayed by personal *opinions*.

Interestingly, liability will be barred with respect to puffery, predictions, and opinions even if the test of reliance is subjective. The explanation for that bar, however, lies not with the element of reliance, but rather with the need for a representation of fact. Puffs, predictions, and opinions are not representations of fact.

7. For a discussion of the elements of deceit and how it differs from mere "sharp" or "hardball" business practices, see *Harland v. Fancsati* (1993), 13 O.R. (3d) 103 (Gen. Div), aff'd (1994), 21 O.R. (3d) 798 (Div. Ct.).

8. Although most deceit actions involve pure economic loss, the action also provides redress for physical harm. In *Graham v. Saville*, [1945] 2 D.L.R. 489 (Ont. C.A.), a married man induced an unmarried woman to believe that he was single and that they had undergone a valid marriage ceremony. That was not true. The woman subsequently gave birth to a child and sued in battery and deceit. The court found for the plaintiff in deceit and awarded her $4,000, which included compensation for the "physical injury, pain, and suffering in consequence of her pregnancy and the birth of a child." See also *Beaulne v. Ricketts* (1979), 96 D.L.R. (3d) 550 (Alta. S.C.).

Likewise, while most deceit actions arise in commercial contexts, the same rules extend to social and family settings. In *Raju v. Kumar* (2006), 265 D.L.R. (4th) 632 (B.C.S.C.), the defendant duped the plaintiff into marrying him. His real goals were (1) to have her pay for his immigration to Canada from Fiji, and (2) to use his marriage status as a basis for legally remaining in this country. In addition to damages for the expenses that the plaintiff incurred in connection with the immigration process and the wedding, the court awarded $10,000 in general damages to reflect the plaintiff's humiliation and lost marriage prospects. Do you agree that the tort of deceit is an appropriate method for resolving such disputes?

People sometimes act dishonestly in sexual matters. The courts, however, have been reluctant to uphold claims in deceit in such circumstances. In *P.(P.) v. D.(D.)*, 2017 ONCA 180, the parties shared a brief sexual relationship. After parting ways, the defendant revealed that she was pregnant and that she intended to raise the child. That news came as a shock, the plaintiff alleged, because he had agreed to unprotected sex only after the defendant had falsely represented that she was taking birth control. The plaintiff sued for deceit and claimed compensation for, *inter alia*, the impending economic burden of child support and the involuntary change in lifestyle. Writing for the Ontario Court of Appeal, Rouleau J.A. upheld the defendant's motion to strike. In dealing with family matters, the law has consistently shied away from notions of fault. Awarding damages to a man who was upset with the consequences of his sexual act would be inconsistent with that trend. Furthermore, while some forms of deceit may vitiate a person's apparent consent to a sexual act, that was not true of a misrepresentation that merely pertained to the likelihood of pregnancy. Do you agree with the court's approach to the issues? Should the tort of deceit ever be available to redress the consequences of dishonesty within sexual relationships?

The High Court of Australia endorsed a similar attitude on different facts in *Magill v. Magill*, [2006] HCA 51. The defendant had three children while she was married to the plaintiff. The parties divorced and the plaintiff paid child support for several years. He then discovered that two of the children had been fathered by another man. The plaintiff sought damages for various expenses (*e.g.* psychiatric counselling) that he incurred upon learning the shocking truth. The action was based on the allegation that, in having the plaintiff sign the two birth certificates, the defendant falsely misrepresented that he was the father and she thereby committed the tort of deceit. The court unanimously dismissed the action. First, it found that, while the plaintiff had acted on the assumption that he was the children's father, he had not relied upon the birth certificates specifically. Second, and much more significantly, a majority of the court held that the tort of deceit was inappropriate on the facts. The individual judges, however, differed on their reasons for that conclusion. Gummow, Kirby and Crennan JJ. said that "conduct which constitutes a breach of promise of sexual fidelity and any consequential false representation about paternity, occurring within a continuing sexual relationship, which is personal, private and intimate, cannot be justly or appropriately assessed by reference to bargaining transactions, with which the tort of deceit is typically associated." In sharp contrast, Heydon J. held that while the claim failed on the facts, there was no reason to exclude the tort from family matters. Gleeson C.J. and Hayne J. fell somewhere between those two extremes. What arguments can be offered for and against the application of the tort of deceit in intimate settings?

See also *S.(F.) v. H.(C.)* (1994), 120 D.L.R. (4th) 432 (Ont. Gen. Div.), aff'd (1994), 133 D.L.R. (4th) 767 (Ont. C.A.) (no duty to disclose; silence not a representation; action was against public policy); *Fleming v. Fleming* (2001), 19 R.F.L. (5th) 274 (Ont. S.C.J.) (no duty to disclose); and *D.(D.R.) v. G.(S.E.)* (2001), 14 R.F.L. (5th) 279 (Ont. S.C.J.) (no duty to disclose; man liable to support child to whom he acted as parent). See also Wiegers, "Fatherhood and Misattributed Genetic Paternity in Family Law" (2011) 36 Queen's L.J. 623.

While the policies that guide Canadian family law may curtail the tort's application, deceit undoubtedly is available to remedy some types of dishonesty that arise within intimate relationships. *Abramowitz v. Lee*, 2018 ONSC 3684 provides an astonishing example. The plaintiff, an exceptionally gifted musician studying at McGill University, applied to do the final two years of his degree at a prestigious conservatory in Los Angeles. Impressed with his credentials, the conservatory sent an email that offered a place in the program, a full scholarship worth $50,000 per year, and an opportunity to be supervised by one of the world's leading clarinetists. The conservatory's graduates routinely enjoyed a fast-track to successful careers. Unfortunately, the plaintiff never even saw the conservatory's email. The defendant, who was his girlfriend at the time, intercepted the message and, posing as the plaintiff, declined the generous offer. She was afraid that their relationship would end if they were apart. The plaintiff learned of that deception only after he had completed his studies at McGill. In the ensuing lawsuit, the court upheld his claim in deceit and awarded $300,000 in general damages (covering loss of reputation, loss of educational opportunity, and two years of lost income potential), as well as $25,000 in aggravated damages (representing "the incompensable personal loss suffered by Mr Abramovitz by having a closely held personal dream snatched from him by a person he trusted"): at para. 36.

A loss of a chance may be recoverable in deceit. In *4 Eng Ltd. v. Harper*, [2009] 1 Ch. 91, the court held that such relief, though historically unprecedented, was appropriate on the facts. The plaintiff purchased Excel Engineering from the defendants. The defendants warranted, within the sales contract, that Excel's financial records were accurate and that they knew of no fact that would deter Mars UK Ltd., the company's principal customer, from providing business in the future. In fact, the defendants had been running a scam with some of Mars' employees under which Excel falsely invoiced Mars for £1,800,000. Once the scheme was discovered, the plaintiff claimed damages under several heads. The defendants uncontroversially were liable for the purchase price and for consequential losses representing the costs associated with the acquisition and the investigation of the fraud. The plaintiff, however, also asked for damages for loss of an opportunity, namely the venture that the plaintiff would have pursued if it had not purchased Excel. David Richards J. conceded that the claim was novel, but saw (at para. 44) no reason for objection: "If damages for loss of a chance are recoverable in negligence, why should they not also be recoverable in deceit?" Issues associated with such damages are discussed in Mitchell, "Loss of a Chance in Deceit" (2009) 125 L.Q.R. 12.

It sometimes is said that the defendant's false statement must have induced the plaintiff to enter into a contract. The actual rule, however, requires proof that the plaintiff was induced to adopt a detrimental course of action. The creation of a contract is just one possible form of reliance: *Catalyst Pulp and Paper Sales Inc. v. Universal Paper Export Co.* (2009), 95 B.C.L.R. (4th) 259 (C.A.).

9. Damages in tort law normally are calculated to provide compensation for the plaintiff's losses. For general discussion of damages in deceit, see *West Coast Finance Ltd. v. Gunderson, Stokes, Walton & Co.* (1974), 44 D.L.R. (3d) 232 (B.C.S.C.), rev'd (1975), 56 D.L.R. (3d) 460 (B.C.C.A.); *Siametis v. Trojan Horse (Burlington) Inc.* (1979), 25 O.R. (2d) 120 (H.C.); *C.R.F. Holdings Ltd. v. Fundy Chemical Int. Ltd.* (1981), 33 B.C.L.R. 291 (C.A.); *Bitton v. Jakovljevic* (1990), 75 O.R. (2d) 143 (H.C.); and *OMV Petrom SA v. Glencore International AG*, [2015] EWCA Civ 778. See also Fridman *et al.*, *The Law of Torts in Canada*, 3d ed. (2010) at 718-21.

Although damages are usually calculated to repair the plaintiff's losses, they may also be assessed by reference to the benefits that the defendant obtained as a result of the tort. Such relief is properly called disgorgement. See *Amertek Inc. v. Canadian Commercial Inc.* (2003), 229 D.L.R. (4th) 419 (Ont. S.C.J.), rev'd on other grounds (2005), 76 O.R. (3d) 241 (C.A.); *Evans v. MacMicking* (1909), 2 Alta L.R. 5 (S.C.); *Lang v. Giraudo*, 40 N.E.2d 707 (Mass. S.C. 1942); and *Janigan v. Taylor*, 344 F.2d 781 (1st Cir. C.A. 1965). English courts, however, have questioned the availability of purely gain-based relief under the tort of deceit: *Halifax Building Society v. Thomas*, [1996] Ch. 217 (C.A.); *Smith New Court Ltd. v. Scrimgeour Vickers*, [1997] A.C. 254 (H.L.); but *cf. Kettlewell v. Refuge Assurance Co.*, [1908] 1 K.B. 545 (C.A.). Suggest a situation in which the plaintiff would prefer disgorgement to compensation.

In appropriate situations, the analysis may be taken one step further. Instead of awarding damages equal in value to the benefit that the defendant obtained, the court may allow the claimant to recover the property itself. Assets (including money) that are acquired by theft or fraud may be impressed with a constructive trust while they are in the wrongdoer's possession. If the wrongdoer transfers the assets to a third party, the trust will persist unless that new party is a *bona fide* purchaser for value. Even in that situation, however, property rights may be available under the rules of *tracing.* While the original asset in the *bona fide* purchaser's hands is untouchable, the claimant can elect to assert a constructive trust over the property that the wrongdoer received under the exchange with the purchaser. For a discussion of the causes of action and remedies that may apply in such situations, see *iTrade Finance Holdings Inc. v. Webworx Inc.*, 2011 SCC 26.

10. In addition to compensation, a successful plaintiff in a case of fraud may also receive punitive damages. As the Supreme Court of Canada stressed in *Performance Industries Ltd. v. Sylvan Lake Golf & Tennis Club Ltd.*, [2002] 1 S.C.R. 678 at 711, fraud

invariably entails "a type of misconduct that to some extent 'offends the court's sense of decency' and which 'represents a marked departure from ordinary standards of decent behaviour,' yet not all fraud cases lead to an award of punitive damages." Consistent with the governing rules, punitive damages are "rational," and hence available, "'if, but only if' compensatory damages do not adequately achieve the objectives of retribution, deterrence and denunciation." See also *Platinum Equity Funding Inc. v. Reingold*, 2010 ONSC 5407. Punitive damages are discussed in detail in Chapter 2.

11. A fraudulent misrepresentation is a tort. It may also provide grounds for the rescission of a transaction, such as a contract. As a general rule, rescission is available if a party's consent to a transaction was improperly induced. Fraud sits alongside duress, undue influence, and unconscionability in that respect. Subject to various limitations, the affected party can elect to either affirm or rescind the transaction. A dramatic example occurred in *Wang v. Shao*, 2018 BCSC 377. After becoming interested in buying a mansion in one of Vancouver's finer neighbourhoods, Feng Yun Shao asked why the vendor was selling. Having been told that the previous owner's daughter had transferred to a school in a different area, Shao agreed to purchase the property for $6,100,000. He ultimately refused to close the deal, however, because he had learned that the previous owner, an alleged leader of a Chinese Triad gang, had been gunned down in front of the home. Shao did not feel that his family would be safe. The court allowed him to rescind the contract, and recover his deposit, on the basis of the deeply misleading answer that he received to his question. The vendor was not positively obligated to disclose the murder to every potential buyer, but having been asked, an accurate response was required.

For a discussion of the circumstances in which the plaintiff is entitled to both rescission of a contract and damages in deceit, see *Roy v. 1216393 Ontario Inc.*, 2014 BCCA 429; *Burrows v. Burke* (1982), 36 O.R. (2d) 737 (H.C.); and *Archer v. Brown*, [1984] 2 All E.R. 267 (Q.B.).

12. Deceit appears to have emerged centuries ago as an independent tort, later becoming associated with contractual warranties. See generally Waddams, *Products Liability*, 4th ed. (2001) at 1-11. This connection was severed by *Pasley v. Freeman* (1789), 100 E.R. 450 (K.B.), which held that the tort of deceit was available against any party who intentionally induced another to act to his or her detriment upon a knowingly false statement.

Deceit remained the major cause of action for recovery of pure economic losses caused by misrepresentations until *Hedley Byrne & Co. v. Heller & Partners Ltd.*, [1964] A.C. 465 (H.L.) created a broad right of recovery within the law of negligence. Furthermore, recent developments in contract law have made it easier to establish that a misrepresentation is part of a contract. See Waddams, *The Law of Contracts*, 6th ed. (2010), ch. 13.

13. As suggested by the high threshold for liability, the issue of fraud is taken very seriously. Another indicium of the legal system's attitude is seen in the fact that an allegation of fraud must be specifically pleaded and proven and that a failure to sustain such an allegation may result in having to pay costs to the other side. Likewise, a discharge from bankruptcy does not release the bankrupt from "any debt or liability

for obtaining property by . . . fraudulent misrepresentation": *Bankruptcy Act*, R.S.C. 1985, c. B-3, s. 178(1).

14. The tort of deceit is not vulnerable to the defence of contributory negligence: *Standard Chartered Bank v. Pakistan National Shipping Corp. (Nos. 2 and 4)*, [2003] 1 A.C. 959 (H.L.). It therefore is irrelevant that, for instance, the plaintiff carelessly failed to verify the information received from the defendant. What is the explanation for denying the defence in such circumstances? See Murphy, "Misleading Appearances in the Tort of Deceit" [2016] C.L.J. 301.

15. See generally Carty, *An Analysis of the Economic Torts* (2011) ch. 9; Burns & Blom, *Economic Interests in Canadian Tort Law*, 2d ed. (2016) ch. 7; Perell, "The Fraud Elements of Deceit and Fraudulent Misrepresentation" (1996) 18 Adv. Q. 23; Hoyano, "Lies, Recklessness and Deception: Disentangling Dishonesty in Civil Fraud" (1996) 75 Can. Bar. Rev. 474; and Fridman *et al.*, *The Law of Torts in Canada*, 3d ed. (2010) at 707-21.

The rights-based theory of tort was introduced in Chapter 1. It has been argued that that theory best explains the nature and operation of the tort of deceit: *Murphy*, *supra*.

3. Passing Off

Reputations, good and bad, play a crucial role in the business world. Consumers favour goods or services that are known (or thought) to be of a high quality, reliable, fashionable, or otherwise desirable. At the same time, they avoid inferior products, at least unless there is a reduction in price. Likewise, personal images can both enhance and diminish sales. Professional athletes may not know a great deal about soft drinks, but their mere association with a company may attract customers.

Reputations are hard won and easily lost. They often are also easily manipulated. An unscrupulous business may take advantage of that fact. It may usurp a competitor's goodwill or exploit a celebrity's image without permission. It may unfairly sully a competitor's name or denigrate its products. Tort law responds to each of those wrongs. The extract that appears below is concerned with the tort of *passing off*. The notes that follow introduce the torts of *misappropriation of personality*, *defamation*, and *injurious falsehood*.

CIBA-GEIGY CANADA LTD. v. APOTEX INC.
(1992), 95 D.L.R. (4th) 385 (S.C.C.)

[Ciba-Geigy, a pharmaceutical company, sold a drug called "metroprolol" under licence. In 1984, Apotex legally began to manufacture and sell the same drug, but in tablets of different size, shape, and colour. In 1986, Apotex changed its marketing strategy and started to market the metroprolol drug in tablets that were virtually identical to the plaintiff's. Ciba-Geigy brought a passing off action against Apotex and another corporate defendant. The lower courts rejected the claim on the basis that the plaintiff had not shown that physicians or pharmacists would be confused by the defendants' actions. The plaintiff appealed to the Supreme Court of Canada.]

GONTHIER J.: . . .

A. *Passing-off action*

(1) *General principles developed by the courts*

The concept of passing-off was developed in 1842 in *Perry v. Truefitt* (1842), 6 Beav. 66, 49 E.R. 749, which seems to have been the first case in which the expression "passing-off" appeared: "A man is not to sell his own goods under the pretence that they are the goods of another man". In *Singer Manufacturing Co. v. Loog* (1880), 18 Ch. D. 395 (C.A.) at pp. 412-13; affirmed 8 App. Cas. 15 (H.L.), James L.J. described passing-off and its origins:

> . . . no man is entitled to represent his goods as being the goods of another man; and no man is permitted to use any mark, sign or symbol, device or other means, whereby, without making a direct false misrepresentation himself to a purchaser who purchases from him, he enables such purchaser to tell a lie or to make a false representation to somebody else who is the ultimate customer . . . he must not, as I said, make directly, or through the medium of another person, a false representation that his goods are the goods of another person.

The House of Lords has set out the requirements for a passing-off action on many occasions. In *Erven Warnink B.V. v. J. Townend & Sons (Hull) Ltd.*, [1980] R.P.C. 31, Lord Diplock identified five conditions. . .: there must be (1) misrepresentation (2) by a trader in the course of trade (3) to prospective customers of his or ultimate customers of goods or services supplied by him, (4) which is calculated to injure the business or goodwill of another trader, and (5) which causes actual damage to the business or goodwill of the trader bringing the action.

More recently, in *Reckitt & Colman Products Ltd. v. Borden Inc.*, [1990] 1 All E.R. 873 (H.L.), Lord Oliver reaffirmed, at p. 880:

> The law of passing off can be summarised in one short general proposition, no man may pass off his goods as those of another. More specifically, it may be expressed in terms of the elements which the plaintiff in such an action has to prove in order to succeed. These are three in number. First, he must establish *a goodwill or reputation attached to the goods or services which he supplies* in the mind of the purchasing public *by association with the identifying "get-up"* (whether it consists simply of a brand name or a trade description, or the individual features of labelling or packaging) under which his particular goods or services are offered to the public, such that the get-up is recognised by the public as distinctive specifically of the plaintiff's goods or services. Second, he must demonstrate *a misrepresentation* by the defendant to the public (whether or not intentional) leading or likely to lead the public to believe that goods or services offered by him are the goods or services of the plaintiff . . . Third, he must demonstrate that he suffers or, in a quia timet action, that he is likely to suffer *damage* by reason of the erroneous belief engendered by the defendant's misrepresentation that the source of the defendant's goods or services is the same as the source of those offered by the plaintiff. (Emphasis added.)

The three necessary components of a passing-off action are thus: the existence of goodwill, deception of the public due to a misrepresentation and actual or potential damage to the plaintiff. . . .

In *Consumers Distributing Co. v. Seiko Time Canada Ltd.* (1984), 10 D.L.R. (4th) 161 at p. 175, this court noted that the requirements of a passing-off action have evolved somewhat in the last 100 years:

> . . . attention should be drawn to the fact that the passing off rule is founded upon the tort of deceit, and while the original requirement of an intent to deceive died out in the mid-1800s there remains the requirement, at the very least, that confusion in the minds of the public be a likely consequence by reason of the sale, or proffering for sale, by the defendant of a product not that of the plaintiff's making, under the guise or implication that it was the plaintiff's product or the equivalent.

A manufacturer must therefore avoid creating confusion in the public mind, whether deliberately or not, by a get-up identical to that of a product which has acquired a secondary meaning by reason of its get-up.

. . .

(2) *Purposes of the passing-off action and target clientele*

In considering those upstream and downstream of the product, two separate aspects must be distinguished. I refer in this regard to the persons who manufacture or market the products, on the one hand ("the manufacturers"), and on the other to those for whom the products are intended, the persons who buy, use or consume them ("the customers").

It is clear that however one looks at the passing-off action, its purpose is to protect all persons affected by the product.

(a) Protection of manufacturers

This corresponds to the third point mentioned by Lord Oliver. The right to be protected against the "pirating" of a brand, trade name or the appearance of a product is linked to a kind of "ownership" which the manufacturer has acquired in that name, brand and appearance by using them.

In *Pinard v. Coderre* [1954] 3 D.L.R. 463 at p. 468, Marchand J.A. of the Québec Court of Appeal noted (translation): "It would seem that the first occupant of this name or these words acquired a right to use them exclusive of all other persons, comparable in many ways to *a true right of ownership*" (emphasis added).

Accordingly, to begin with, from what might be called the individual or manufacturer's standpoint, the passing-off action is intended to protect a form of ownership.

There is also the concept of ownership, protected by the passing-off action in relation to goodwill, a term which must be understood in a very broad sense, taking in not only people who are customers but also the reputation and drawing power of a given business in its market. In *Consumers Distributing Co. v. Seiko Time Canada Ltd.*, *supra*, Estey J., at p. 13 C.P.R., p. 173 D.L.R., cites *Salmond on the Law of Torts*, by R.F.V. Heuston, 17th ed. (London: Sweet & Maxwell, 1977), at pp. 403-4:

> "The courts have wavered between two conceptions of a passing-off action — as a remedy for the invasion of a quasi-proprietary right in a trade name or trade mark, and as a remedy, analogous to the action on the case for deceit, for invasion of the personal right not to be injured by fraudulent competition. The true basis of the action is that *the passing off injures the right of property in the plaintiff*, that right of property being his right to the goodwill of his business.

. . .

"Indeed, it seems that the essence of the tort lies in the misrepresentation that the goods in question are those of another . . .". (Emphasis added.)

It will then be necessary to look at the relationship between the various merchants or manufacturers, and it is at that point that questions of competition have to be considered. As Chenevard says (*Traité de la concurrence déloyale en matière industrielle et commerciale*, vol. 1 (Paris: L.G.D.J., 1914), at pp. 6-7) (translation) "[c]ompetition is the soul of commerce; it requires unceasing effort and as such is the chief factor in economic progress". Drysdale and Silverleaf, *Passing Off: Law and Practice* (London: Butterworths, 1986), are substantially of the same opinion, at p. 1:

> In countries with a free market system the proper functioning of the economy depends upon competition between rival trading enterprises. It is the mechanism of competition which controls the price, quality and availability of goods and services to the public.

. . .

The purpose of the passing-off action is thus also to prevent unfair competition. One does not have to be a fanatical moralist to understand how appropriating another person's work, as that is certainly what is involved, is a breach of good faith.

Finally, another more apparent, more palpable aspect, a consequence of the preceding one, must also be mentioned. The "pirated" manufacturer is very likely to experience a reduction in sales volume and therefore in his turnover because of the breaking up of his market. When such a situation occurs in the ordinary course of business between rival manufacturers, that is what one might call one of the rules of the game, but when the rivalry involves the use of dishonest practices, the law must intervene.

(b) Protection of customers

In the Anglo-Saxon legal systems (translation), "the person chiefly concerned is the competitor affected by the unfair act": Louis Mermillod, *Essai sur la notion de concurrence déloyale en France et aux États-Unis* (Paris: Pichon & Durand-Auzias, 1954), at p. 176. He is frequently in fact the first party affected by the practice or aware of it.

However, "[i]t should never be overlooked that . . . unfair competition cases are affected with a public interest. A dealer's good will is protected, not merely for his profit, but in order that the purchasing public may not be enticed into buying A.'s product when it wants B.'s product": *General Baking Co. v. Gorman*, 3 F. 2d 891 (1st Cir., 1925). Accordingly (translation), "the power of the court in such cases is exercised, not only to do individual justice, but to safeguard the interests of the public": *Scandinavia Belting Co. v. Asbestos & Rubber Works of America, Inc.*, 257 F. 937 (2d Cir., 1919) at p. 941. The ordinary customer, the consumer, is at the heart of the matter here. According to the civilian lawyer Chenevard, *op. cit.*, at p. 20, in a case of unfair competition it is (translation) "the buyer who is the first to be injured".

The customer expects to receive a given product when he asks for it and should not be deceived. It often happens that products are interchangeable and that a substitution will have little effect. However, the customer may count on having a specific product. There are many reasons for such a choice: habit, satisfaction, another person's recommendation, the desire for change, and so on. I have no hesitation in using the classic saying, taken from popular imagery: "the customer is always right". Merchants must respect his wishes, choices and preferences as far as possible. Where this is simply not possible, no substitution must be made *without his knowledge*. That is the minimum degree of respect which manufacturers and merchants, who we should remember depend on their customers, should show.

There is no shortage of fraudulent or simply misleading practices: one may think, for example, of products having a similar get-up, the use of similar labelling, use of the same trade name, counterfeiting, imitation of packaging. These are all possible ways of attempting, deliberately or otherwise, to mislead the public. The courts and authors have unanimously concluded that the facts must be weighed in relation to an "ordinary" public, "average" customers: ". . . you must deal with the ordinary man and woman who would take ordinary care in purchasing what goods they require, and, if desiring a particular brand, would take ordinary precautions to see that they get it" (Neville J. in *Henry Thorne & Co. v. Sandow* (1912), 29 R.P.C. 440 (Ch. D.) at p. 453.)

The average customer will not be the same for different products, however, and will not have the same attitude at the time of purchase. Moreover, the attention and care taken by the same person may vary depending on the product he is buying: someone will probably not exercise the same care in selecting goods from a supermarket shelf and in choosing a luxury item. In the first case, the misrepresentation is likely to "catch" more readily.

. . .

[Gonthier J. allowed the appeals and held that the plaintiff was required to show only that the defendants' actions were likely to confuse physicians, pharmacists or patients and customers]

NOTES AND QUESTIONS

1. In *Ciba-Geigy*, Gonthier J. said that the cause of action requires proof of "actual or *potential* damage to the plaintiff." Notice that the plaintiff is not required to prove that it actually suffered any loss as a result of the defendant's deception. Suggest an explanation for that rule. In doing so, consider the evidentiary difficulties that the plaintiff would face if required to prove actual loss.

Where must the potential damage occur? Must the claimant have actual customers in the jurisdiction where the claim is made? Or is it enough to enjoy a favourable reputation within that jurisdiction? Those questions arose in *Starbucks (H.K.) Ltd. v. British Sky Broadcasting Group Plc*, [2015] UKSC 31. The claimant had a very successful Internet enterprise in Hong Kong that provided subscribers with video content. That service operated under the name of NOW TV. In 2012, the defendant launched a similar service, under the same name, in the United Kingdom. In support of its action for passing off, the claimant argued that while it did not have any subscribers in the U.K., a small but significant number of Chinese people in the U.K. were aware of its operations in Hong Kong. The defendant countered by pointing to a line of authority that required proof that the claimant had actual customers in the jurisdiction. The comparative opinion was divided. The law in Australia and South Africa favoured the defendant; the law in Singapore favoured the claimant. The Canadian position was found to be unclear; *cf. Orkin Exterminating Co. Inc. v. Pestco*

Co. of Canada Ltd. (1985), 19 D.L.R. (4th) 90 (Ont. C.A.). Against that backdrop, Lord Neuberger held (at paras. 61, 62) that the tort of passing off entails:

> a compromise between two conflicting objectives, on the one hand the public interest in free competition, on the other the protection of a trader against unfair competition by others. . . . If it was enough for a claimant merely to establish reputation within the jurisdiction to maintain a passing off action, it appears to me that it would tip the balance too much in favour of protection. It would mean that, without having any business or any consumers for its product or service in this jurisdiction, a claimant could prevent another person using a mark, such as an ordinary English word, "now", for a potentially indefinite period in relation to a similar product or service.

Liability consequently was denied. See Davis "The Continuing Importance of Local Goodwill in Passing Off" [2015] C.L.J. 419. More recent Canadian cases, however, question the view expressed in *Starbucks (H.K.) Ltd. v. British Sky Broadcasting Group Plc.* See *Sadhu Singh Hamdard Trust v. Navsun Holdings Ltd.*, 2016 FCA 69 at para. 25, rev'g 2014 FC 1139.

If the defendant intended to deceive the public, the court readily will assume that deception took place. Otherwise, the plaintiff bears the onus of proving that the defendant's practices were likely to mislead. In that regard, the courts recognize that consumers do not always carefully inspect products before using them. As Lord Macnaghten said, "Thirsty folk want beer, not explanations": *Montgomery v. Thompson*, [1891] A.C. 217 at 225 (H.L.). The question, therefore, is whether or not the reasonable customer might have been misled: *San Miguel Brewing International Ltd. v. Molson Canada 2005*, 2013 FC 156; and *Teavana Corp. v. Teayama Inc.*, 2014 FC 372.

2. The Supreme Court of Canada revisited the tort of passing off in *Kirkbi AG v. Ritvik Holdings Inc.*, [2005] 3 S.C.R. 302. The patent protecting the plaintiff's Lego building blocks expired. The defendant company therefore began manufacturing Mega Bloks, with essentially the same design as Lego products (*i.e.* each piece was topped by raised studs that allowed pieces to be joined together). The plaintiff sued (1) under statute for trademark infringement, and (2) at common law for the tort of passing off. Both claims failed.

Trademark laws exist to protect distinctive guises or appearances, not to create monopolies over utilitarian features. The court held that the raised studs traditionally used for Lego blocks fell into the latter category and therefore were not protected. The plaintiff previously had enjoyed such protection under the *Patent Act*, R.S.C. 1985, c. P-4, but that protection had expired. Patent legislation strikes a balance between competing interests. In exchange for disclosing the relevant secret, an inventor is entitled to exclude competitors for 20 years. After that time, however, everyone is free to use the new process.

The court affirmed that the tort of passing off consists of three elements: (1) goodwill attached to a distinctive product belonging to the plaintiff, (2) deception of the public, either deliberately or carelessly, by the defendant, and (3) actual or potential damage to the claimant. On the facts of *Kirkbi*, the tort claim, like the trademark claim, was defeated by the doctrine of *functionality*. LeBel J. explained:

> The alleged distinctiveness of the product consisted precisely of the process and techniques which were now common to the trade. Again, Kirkbi could not overcome another form of the functionality problem. Granting such a claim in these circumstances would amount to recreating a monopoly contrary to basic policies of

the laws and legal principles which inform the various forms of intellectual property in our legal system. The appellant is no longer entitled to protection against competition in respect of its product. It must now face the rigours of a free market and its process of creative destruction.

Do you agree with the court's decision? Do you have any experience with Lego blocks and Mega Bloks? Are the two products essentially interchangeable or is one noticeably better than the other? If one is superior, should the law protect consumers against the risk of confusion?

3. As in *Kirkbi AG v. Ritvik Holdings Inc.*, a plaintiff may claim both violation of trademark and passing off on the same facts. The concepts of passing off and trademarks are, in fact, closely related. Under the *Trademarks Act*, R.S.C. 1985, c. T-13, registration entitles the owner to exclusive use of a trademark throughout Canada. Registration also provides a complete defence to the common law claim of passing off: *Molson Canada v. Oland Breweries Ltd.* (2002), 59 O.R. (3d) 607 (C.A.). The tort of passing off, however, operates more broadly than the trademark legislation. It applies not only to unregistered trademarks but also to other "identifiers" of a product.

The interplay between registered trademarks and the tort of passing off is illustrated by *Remo Imports Ltd. v. Jaguar Cars Ltd.*, [2008] 2 F.C.R. 132 (C.A.). The plaintiff company had sold Jaguar vehicles in Canada since 1936. Its brand is internationally famous. The defendant manufactured luggage and related goods (such as address books and wallets). In 1980, it registered a Jaguar trademark and sold its wares under that identifier. The defendant was accused of passing off its goods as though they had been manufactured by the plaintiff. The Federal Court of Appeal agreed that luggage was a "natural zone of expansion" for a manufacturer of luxury vehicles and found that the defendant had traded on the plaintiff's reputation. The defendant's registration of the Jaguar trademark consequently was expunged. Nevertheless, the court also held that because the defendant's trademark was not expunged retroactively *ab initio*, registration constituted a defence to the tort of passing off for the period during which the registered trademark actually existed. Damages for past losses were limited accordingly. On the difference between trademark protection and the tort of passing off, see also *Mattel Inc. v. 3894207 Canada Inc.*, [2006] 1 S.C.R. 772 (manufacturer of Barbie dolls opposing trademark application by chain of Montreal restaurants using the name "Barbie").

4. The tort of passing off is frequently litigated. Many of the cases arise in the context of sports and entertainment industries. See for example *Paramount Pictures Corp. v. Howley* (1991), 5 O.R. (3d) 573 (Gen. Div.); *National Hockey League v. Pepsi Cola Ltd.* (1992), 70 B.C.L.R. (2d) 27 (S.C.), aff'd (1995), 2 B.C.L.R. (3d) 3 (C.A.); *Walt Disney Productions v. Triple Five Corp.* (1994), 149 A.R. 112 (C.A.); and *Walt Disney Productions v. Fantasyland Hotel Inc.* (1996), 184 A.R. 110 (C.A.).

The passing off tort can also be used against cyber-squatters who cynically register domain names that consumers are apt to believe are associated with well-known companies or products: *Dentec Safety Specialists Inc. v. Degil Safety Products (1989) Inc.*, 2012 ONSC 4721; *Law Society (British Columbia) v. Canada Domain Name Exchange Corp.*, 2002 BCSC 1249, aff'd 2005 BCCA 535; *British Columbia Automobile Assn. v. O.P.E.I.U. Local 378*, 2001 BCSC 156; *British Columbia Recreation and Parks Assn. v. Zakharia*, 2015 BCSC 1650; *British Telecommunications Plc. v. One in a Million Ltd.*, [1998] 4 All E.R. 476 (C.A.); *Brookfield Communications Inc. v. West Coast*

Entertainment Corp., 174 F.3d 1036 (C.A., 9th Cir., 1999); and *Jews for Jesus v. Brodsky*, 993 F. Supp. 282 (D.C.N.J., 1988), aff'd 159 F.3d 1351 (C.A., 3rd Cir., 1998). *Cf. Queen's University at Kingston v. Oliver Twist Domains Inc.*, 2017 LNCIRA 23 (domain name: < queensunivettisty.ca >).

For other examples, see *Wenger SA v. Travel Way Group International Inc.*, 2017 FCA 215; *United Airlines Inc. v. Cooperstock*, 2017 FC 616; *Dairy Queen Canada Inc. v. M.Y. Sundae Inc. (c.o.b. DQ Grill and Chill)*, 2017 BCCA 442; *Vancouver Community College v. Vancouver Career College (Burnaby) Inc. (c.o.b. Vancouver C.C.)*, 2015 BCSC 1470, aff'd 2017 BCCA 41; *Eli Lilly & Co. v. Novopharm Ltd.* (2000), 195 D.L.R. (4th) 547 (Fed. C.A.); *Inform Cycle Ltd. v. Rebound Inc.* (2008), 93 Alta. L.R. (4th) 312 (Q.B.); and *Campomar v. Nike* (2000), 169 A.L.R. 677 (H.C.A.).

5. In a typical passing off case, the defendant misrepresents its goods as having been produced by the plaintiff. However, the tort extends to other situations as well. For instance, a business cannot usurp goodwill by falsely suggesting that its product was produced in a geographical region known for particularly high quality. Champagne comes from a particular region of France, not from Spain, just as Advocaat comes from the Netherlands, not England. See *Bollinger v. Costa Brava Wine Co.*, [1960] Ch. 262 (Ch. Div.); and *E.W.B. Venootschap. v. J. Townend & Sons (Hull) Ltd.*, [1979] A.C. 731 (H.L.).

6. The courts generally have been reluctant to extend the economic torts beyond the commercial law contexts in which they were first recognized: see *Polsinelli v. Marzilli* (1987), 42 C.C.L.T. 46 (Ont. H.C.).

7. See generally MacInnis, "Commercial Morality and Passing Off: A Model for a Modern Tort" (1998) 30 C.B.L.J. 415; Crowne & Nassabi, "Parsing Off the Elements of Passing Off" (2012) 39 Adv. Q. 452; Carty, *An Analysis of the Economic Torts* (2011), ch. 11; and Burns & Blom, *Economic Interests in Canadian Tort Law*, 2d ed. (2016), ch. 9.

8. Monetary relief may be calculated in various ways. Most commonly, of course, the defendant is compelled to pay compensatory damages in reparation of the plaintiff's loss. Egregious misconduct may additionally attract punitive damages: *Dentec Safety Specialists Inc. v. Degil Safety Products (1989) Inc.*, 2014 ONSC 2449 (Div. Ct.). Because passing off typically is committed with a view to financial gain, disgorgement (or "restitutionary" damages) may be used to strip away the defendant's improper enrichment: *Draper v. Trist* (1939), 56 R.P.C. 429 (C.A.); and *Procea Products Ltd. v. Evans & Sons Ltd.* (1951), 68 R.P.C. 210 (Ch. D.). In *My Kinda Town Ltd. v. Soll*, [1982] F.S.R. 147, rev'd as to liability [1983] R.P.C. 407 (C.A.), the defendant passed off its restaurant ("Chicago Pizza Company") as the plaintiff's ("The Chicago Pizza Pie Factory"). Slade J. ordered the defendant to give up *all* of its wrongful profits and not merely those that otherwise would have been earned by the plaintiff.

The tort of passing off also supports non-monetary relief. A declaration may recognize the rights that exist between the parties. Going further, injunctive relief may compel the defendant to honour its obligations in the future: *Pick v. 1180475 Alberta Ltd. (c.o.b. Queen of Tarts)*, 2011 FC 1008. So too, while the threshold is relatively high, an interlocutory injunction may be granted to prevent the defendant from continuing to harm the plaintiff prior to trial: *Wildman (c.o.b. Weight Loss Forever Consulting) v.*

Kulyk, 2013 SKCA 55; *BGM Holdings Ltd. (c.o.b. Birchwood Chevrolet Buick GMC) v. Jim Gauthier Chev Cadillac Ltd. (c.o.b. Jim Gauthier Chevrolet Cadillac)*, 2010 MBQB 213; and *Jamieson Laboratories Ltd. v. Reckitt Benckiser LLC*, 2015 FCA 104.

Going further still, a court may take steps to ensure that the tortfeasor no longer has possession of anything that would violate the plaintiff's rights. *Diageo Canada Inc. v. Heaven Hill Distilleries Inc.*, 2017 FC 571 arose after the defendant began marketing its "Admiral Nelson" rum outside of its original home in Alberta. The plaintiff, which began marketing Captain Morgan rum throughout Canada in the 1980s, sued. Its product was supported by an enormously successful advertising campaign that featured a flamboyant "Captain Morgan" character, outfitted with a strap across his chest, a sword, a cape, long hair and moustache, and an eye-catching hat. The defendant employed an "Admiral Nelson" character of very similar appearance. A consumer survey indicated a confusion rate between 11 and 28%, which was considered high by legal standards. Having found the defendant liable, the court awarded several remedies including an injunction prohibiting future violations and an order requiring the defendant, at the plaintiff's election, to either deliver up offending materials or swear an oath that those materials had been destroyed.

9. The tort of passing off is concerned with goods and services. The tort of *misappropriation of personality* is available if the defendant made unauthorized use of the plaintiff's image. Consequently, a company will be held liable if it attempts to increase sales through the use of a famous athlete's photograph: *Athans v. Canadian Adventure Camps Ltd.* (1977), 80 D.L.R. (3d) 583 (Ont. H.C.). See also *Krouse v. Chrysler Canada Ltd.* (1973), 1 O.R. (2d) 225 (C.A.); *Racine v. C.J.R.C. Radio Capitale Ltée* (1977), 17 O.R. (2d) 370 (Co. Ct.); and *Horton v. Tim Donut Ltd.* (1997), 45 B.L.R. (2d) 7 (Ont. Gen. Div.). Protection also is provided by privacy statutes in British Columbia, Manitoba, Newfoundland, Nova Scotia and Saskatchewan: see *Poirier v. Wal-Mart Canada Corp.*, 2006 BCSC 1138.

10. The torts of misappropriation of personality and passing off generally involve situations in which the defendant seeks to take advantage of the plaintiff's reputation and goodwill. The torts of defamation and injurious falsehood are available if, to the contrary, the defendant acts in a way that could be harmful to the plaintiff's reputation.

Defamation occurs when the defendant makes a false statement to a third party that could lead a reasonable person to have a lower opinion of the plaintiff. Defamation is discussed in Chapter 27.

Whereas defamation protects a person's reputation, *injurious falsehood* (sometimes called *slander of goods* or *slander of title*) protects a person's business or commercial interests. The plaintiff must prove four elements: (1) the defendant made a disparaging statement to a third party regarding the plaintiff's land, goods, services or business, (2) the statement was false, (3) the defendant acted out of "malice," and (4) the plaintiff suffered a loss as a result.

British Columbia Recreation and Parks Assn. v. Zakharia, 2015 BCSC 1650 provides an example. The plaintiff was a not-for-profit organization that ran a program to certify fitness trainers. Suzanne Strutt was its Chief Executive Officer. Feeling aggrieved because the organization refused to reduce or waive an annual fee, the defendant began a campaign of online abuse. He accused the CEO personally of victimizing him on account of a visual impairment; he accused the organization of bullying, extortion, and abuse of power. The court awarded damages to both the CEO ($115,000) and the organization ($106,000). The bulk of the damages arose from defamation, but because the court wanted to demonstrate a basis for additionally imposing injunctive relief to prevent future wrongs, it also made a point of imposing liability for, *inter alia*, injurious falsehood. As Funt J. explained, "None of the attacks had a skerrick of truth": at para. 1. The "injurious falsehoods were made with actual malice, [they] reflected adversely on [the organization's] business [and] there was pecuniary loss resulting from [them]": at paras. 114, 115.

See also *Windsor Energy Inc. v. Northrup*, 2017 NBCA 37; *John A. Ford & Associates Inc. (c.o.b. Training Services) v. Keegan*, 2014 ONSC 4989 (no liability without false statement); *Sankreacha v. Cameron J. and Beach Sales Ltd.*, 2018 ONSC 7216 at para. 200 (no liability without malice); *Myers v. Blackman*, 2014 ONSC 5226 (no liability without loss); and *Cana International Distributing Inc. (c.o.b. Sexy Living) v. Standard Innovation Corp.*, 2016 ONSC 7197, varied on other grounds 2018 ONCA 145. For discussion, see Fridman *et al.*, *The Law of Torts in Canada*, 3d ed. (2010) at 777-90; Sappideen & Vines, eds., *Fleming's The Law of Torts*, 10th ed. (2011) at 795-98; and Osborne, *The Law of Torts*, 5th ed. (2015) at 334-35.

4. Intimidation

If (1) the defendant threatened to commit an unlawful act, such as a crime, a tort or, in some circumstances, a breach of contract, (2) that threat caused someone to act in particular way, and (3) the plaintiff consequently suffered a loss, then a court may impose liability for the tort of intimidation. Notice that the plaintiff does not have to prove that the threat was carried out, though if the unlawful act was committed, action may be taken against the defendant on that basis as well. The gist of the action lies instead in the fact that the defendant's threat induced someone — either the plaintiff or a third party — to act in a way that adversely affected the claimant. See *Robin Hood Management Ltd. (c.o.b. Merriman & Co.) v. Gelmich*, 2016 SKQB 279 at para. 23.

The fact that the defendant's threat may have been made against either the plaintiff or some third party reveals that the tort of intimidation has two forms: *two-party intimidation* and *three-party intimidation*.

- *Two-party intimidation* occurs when the defendant coerces the plaintiff into a course of action that entails a loss. That was true in *Mintuck v. Valley River Band No. 63A* (1977), 75 D.L.R. (3d) 589 (Man. C.A.). The plaintiff, an experienced farmer, obtained a ten-year lease on a large plot of land. The only road to the property was located on the Valley River Band Reserve. Shortly after the lease was granted, the defendants began a pattern of concerted harassment and coercion. Their trucks blocked the road, they allowed stray cattle to trample the claimant's crops, they drove over the farmland under the pretext of hunting, and they intimidated the plaintiff and his family with their firearms. Those efforts had the intended effect of driving the plaintiff from the land. Manitoba's Court of Appeal upheld the trial judge's decision to award $10,000 in damages under the tort of two-party intimidation. See also *Red Chris Development Co. v. Quock*, 2014 BCSC 2399; and *Metropolitan Conference Centre Inc. v. Hunter*, 2016 ABCA 83.

- *Three-party intimidation* occurs when the defendant's threats induce a third party to act in a way that hurts the claimant. That was true in the leading case of *Rookes v. Barnard*, [1964] A.C. 1129 (H.L.). The plaintiff was a member of the defendant union and an employee of an airline called B.O.A.C. As a result of a dispute with the union, the plaintiff resigned his union membership but remained with the airline. The union then threatened to withdraw all of its services from B.O.A.C. unless the airline terminated the plaintiff's employment. That threat was unlawful because it arose from a conspiracy between various members of the union. B.O.A.C. succumbed to the pressure and fired the plaintiff. Notice the vulnerability of the plaintiff's position. Because the defendant's threatened breach of contract was directed toward the third party rather than the claimant, there was no way for him to directly combat it. Furthermore, while B.O.A.C. terminated the plaintiff's contract without cause, it had also given him payment in lieu of notice. It therefore could not be held further liable for breach of contract. Fortunately for the plaintiff, he enjoyed one source of protection. He held a good claim in intimidation against the union.

As illustrated by the extract that appears below, both species of intimidation are governed by the same general principles, but some of the specific rules vary.

CENTRAL CAN. POTASH v. GOVT. OF SASK.
(1979), 88 D.L.R. (3d) 609 (S.C.C.)

MARTLAND J.: . . . Pursuant to the *Mineral Resources Act*, a scheme for the control of production of potash in Saskatchewan had been put into effect. The appellant, as a potash producer, was prohibited from producing potash in excess of the amounts prescribed by the licences issued to it. It was required after receiving a licence to submit a production schedule, showing monthly production during the 12-month term of the licence not exceeding the total production authorized.

The appellant, being understandably unhappy with the quota allotted to it, endeavoured to persuade the Minister to increase its allocation, but without success. It sought to compel such an increase by *mandamus*, again without success. It failed to submit a proper production schedule within 30 days of the receipt of its licence for the 1972-73 year. It continued its production upon a scale beyond that which was contemplated by its licence.

This was the situation in which the Deputy Minister wrote the letter of September 20, 1972, calling on the appellant to reduce its production or to face the possibility of a cancellation of its mineral lease. That lease, as has been noted, included a requirement that the appellant, as lessee, would observe, perform and abide by all obligations imposed upon holders of mineral leases by the Act or Regulations thereunder in effect from time to time.

In the present case, the threat by the Deputy Minister was the possible exercise by the Minister of powers which he had reasonable grounds for believing the Minister possessed. In *Rookes* the threat was to pursue a course of action which the defendants knew would be a breach of the collective agreement between the union and B.O.A.C.

In the present case, the Deputy Minister sought to induce the appellant to limit the amount of its production to conform with the prorationing scheme which had been established. In the *Rookes* case, the object of the threat was to compel B.O.A.C. to discharge the plaintiff, an action which, except for the pressure, it did not wish to take and which it was under no legal obligation to take.

In the *Rookes* case, the threat was not made to the plaintiff. It was made to a third party, B.O.A.C., with a view to compel it to take a course of action detrimental to the plaintiff. In the present case, the threat was made directly to the appellant and no third party was involved.

I will deal with this distinction now, and will revert to the other distinctions later. It is significant because the plaintiff, in the *Rookes* case, was not in a position to claim a breach of contract by his employer when he was dismissed. The only recourse he could seek was against the defendants who had threatened a breach of the collective agreement between the union and the employer as a means to compel the employer to discharge Rookes. Here the appellant is a party to the contract which it says was threatened to be breached, *i.e.*, the lease, and would have been entitled to pursue its contractual remedies had that contract been illegally breached.

On this point, I am in agreement with the view expressed by the author of *Winfield and Jolowicz on Tort*, 10th ed., p. 458, as follows:

> It is submitted, therefore, that the two-party situation is properly distinguishable from the three-party situation and that it does not necessarily follow from *Rookes v. Barnard* that whenever A threatens B with an unlawful act, including a breach of his contract with B, he thereby commits the tort of intimidation. In fact the balance of advantage seems to lie in holding that where A threatens B with a breach of his contract with B, B should be restricted to his contractual remedies. The law should not encourage B to yield to the threat but should seek to persuade him to resist it. If he suffers damage in consequence he will be adequately compensated by his remedy in damages for breach of contract, as his damage can scarcely be other than financial. Where, however, what is threatened is tort, and especially if the threat is of violence, it is both unrealistic to insist that proceedings for a *quia timet* injunction afford him adequate protection against the consequences of resistance and unreasonable to insist that if violence is actually inflicted upon him he is adequately compensated by an award of damages thereafter. The view is preferred, therefore, that although A commits the tort of intimidation against B where he threatens B with violence or perhaps with any other tort, no independent tort is committed when all that is threatened is a breach of contract.

In my opinion the tort of intimidation is not committed if a party to a contract asserts what he reasonably considers to be his contractual right and that other party, rather than electing to contest that right, follows a course of conduct on the assumption that the assertion of right can be maintained.

I am also of the view that if the course of conduct which the person making the threat seeks to induce is that which the person threatened is obligated to follow, the tort of intimidation does not arise. If, in the *Rookes* case, the collective agreement between the union and B.O.A.C. had contained a closed shop provision so as to require B.O.A.C. to discharge the plaintiff upon his ceasing to be a member of the union, the plaintiff could not have succeeded in his suit because of the threat of a strike, even though the agreement provided that there should be no strikes.

In the present case the *Potash Conservation Regulations, 1969* made under the *Mineral Resources Act* prohibited the appellant from exceeding a specified production of potash. By conforming to the requirements of the Regulations, the appellant would not suffer damage and, therefore, the claim for intimidation is not well founded.

What, then, is the position if, subsequently, it is found that the Regulations were *ultra vires*? Does that finding then mean that there has been intimidation?

In my opinion it does not. The conduct of the Deputy Minister in relation to the tort of intimidation must be considered in relation to the circumstances existing at the time the alleged threat was made. The Deputy Minister was then seeking to induce conformity with the prorationing plan which had been created by legislation which it was his duty to enforce. At the time the threat was made, the legislation stood unchallenged.

. . .

In my opinion it would be unfortunate, in a federal state such as Canada, if it were to be held that a government official, charged with the enforcement of legislation, could be held to be guilty of intimidation because of his enforcement of the statute whenever a statute whose provisions he is under a duty to enforce is subsequently held to be *ultra vires*.

This brings me to the latter portion of the definition of intimidation from Clerk & Lindsell which I have adopted. "The tort is one of intention and the plaintiff, whether it be B or C, must be a person whom A intended to injure." The authority for this statement is found by the authors in the judgments of Lord Devlin and Lord Evershed in the *Rookes* case, and I am in agreement with it. There is no evidence that the Deputy Minister intended to injure the appellant. The correspondence, and particularly the letter of September 20, 1972, make it clear that his purpose was to induce compliance with an existing legislative scheme.

. . .

I would dismiss the appellant's claims for damages.

NOTES AND QUESTIONS

1. For an interesting forerunner to *Rookes*, see *Int. Brotherhood of Teamsters v. Therien*, [1960] S.C.R. 265, in which the same principles were applied without specific reference to the tort of intimidation. See also *J.T. Stratford & Son v. Lindley*, [1965] A.C. 307 (H.L.); and *Selig v. Mansfield* (1982), 53 N.S.R. (2d) 246 (C.A.).

2. *Allen v. Flood*, [1898] A.C. 1 (H.L.) was discussed in the introduction to this chapter. Why was the plaintiff in that case unable to succeed in intimidation?

3. In terms of the governing rules, what is the difference between two-party intimidation and three-party intimidation? Is there a difference if the defendant threatens to commit a crime or a tort? What if the defendant threatens to breach a contract?

4. An interesting application of three-party intimidation occurred in the Australian case of *Uber BV v. Howarth*, [2017] NSWSC 54. Unhappy that Uber had begun operating in his city, the defendant took action by purporting to make "citizen's arrests" of Uber's drivers. Since it was not authorized by law, that behaviour constituted actual and threatened torts of assault, battery, and false imprisonment. And since his actions against the drivers had the desired effect of causing the company to lose workers, the defendant was liable to Uber under the tort of intimidation.

5. Do you agree with Martland J.'s finding in *Central Can. Potash* that the defendant did not intend to injure the plaintiff? Was the injury a necessary consequence of the defendant's conduct? Should the defendant's motive be relevant in intimidation? Is there something special about this case that justifies the concern with motive?

6. The issues of intent, motive, and justification are further complicated by Martland J.'s statement in *Central Can. Potash* that:

> In my opinion the tort of intimidation is not committed if a party to a contract asserts what he reasonably considers to be his contractual right and that other party, rather than electing to contest that right, follows a course of conduct on the assumption that the assertion of the right can be maintained.

According to Martland J., does the defendant's mistaken belief that the threat is lawful preclude liability in intimidation? In the alternative, must both the defendant and the plaintiff mistakenly believe that the threat is lawful? See *Roehl v. Houlahan* (1990), 74 D.L.R. (4th) 562 (Ont. C.A.); and *Roth v. Roth* (1991), 4 O.R. (3d) 740 (Gen. Div.).

In *J.C. Kerkhoff & Sons Contracting Ltd. v. XL Ironworks Co.* (1983), 26 C.C.L.T. 1 (B.C.S.C.), this principle was applied in a situation involving three-party intimidation. Even though the threat was unlawful, the defendant was absolved of liability because it reasonably believed that the threat was lawful. Should this principle apply in three-party intimidation cases, given the different relationships that exist in the two types of intimidation actions?

7. Several points should be noted regarding the nature of the threat underlying a claim in intimidation. It may be implicit or explicit. It may consist of a threat or a warning — the courts generally do not distinguish those two concepts. It must pertain to an unlawful act. Some issues, however, remain controversial. A threat to commit a crime or a tort is clearly unlawful, but "beyond that, the approach has been casuistic, without any evident rationale related to policy ends, and suffering from some inexplicable inconsistencies": Sappideen & Vines, eds., *Fleming's The Law of Torts*, 10th ed. (2011) at 784. In *Rookes v. Barnard*, [1964] A.C. 1129, the House of Lords established that, at least in regard to three-party intimidation, a threatened breach of contract is an unlawful threat. This principle has been criticized. Can you suggest why? Should this principle apply to two-party intimidation cases?

8. Damages in tort law are usually calculated to provide compensation. Intimidation, however, is one of the torts that allows the successful claimant to choose between compensation and disgorgement. Whereas compensation is measured by the plaintiff's loss, disgorgement is measured by reference to the benefits that the defendant obtained by virtue of the wrong. See *Rookes v. Barnard*, [1964] A.C. 1129 at 1232 (H.L.); and *Universe Tankship Inc. of Monrovia v. I.T.W.F.*, [1983] 1 A.C. 366 (H.L.) (transfer between the parties reversed on the basis of the independent action in unjust enrichment). Suggest a situation in which it would be preferable to receive disgorgement rather than compensation.

In *Rookes v. Barnard*, the House of Lords held that punitive damages were confined to three categories: (1) cases involving "oppressive, arbitrary or unconstitutional action by the servants of the government," (2) cases in which "the defendant's conduct has been calculated by him to make a profit for himself which may well exceed the compensation payable to the plaintiff," and (3) situations in which "exemplary damages are expressly authorized by statute": *Rookes v. Barnard*, [1964] A.C. 1129 at 1225-27; cf. *Kuddus v. Chief Constable of Leicestershire Constabulary*, [2002] 2 A.C. 2122 (H.L.). That category approach, however, became discredited over time and Canadian courts are now prepared to award punitive damages in appropriate cases of intimidation: *Whiten v. Pilot Insurance Co.*, 2002 SCC 18; *Gershman v. Manitoba (Vegetable Producers' Marketing Board)* (1976), 69 D.L.R. (3d) 114 (Man. C.A.); *Boychuk v. Northwest Territories Housing Corp.*, [1985] N.W.T.R. 159 (N.W.T. S.C.).

9. For a general discussion of the tort of intimidation, see Fridman *et al.*, *The Law of Torts in Canada*, 3d ed. (2010) at 739-50; Carty, *An Analysis of the Economic Torts* (2011), ch. 5; Burns & Blom, *Economic Interests in Canadian Tort Law*, 2d ed. (2016), ch. 5; Osborne, *The Law of Torts*, 5th ed. (2015) at 345-46; Murphy, "Understanding Intimidation" (2014) 77 M.L.R. 33; Tamblyn, "The Tort of Intimidation and Breach of Contract" (2015), 23 Tort L.R. 164; and Burns, "Tort Injury to Economic Interests: Some Facets of Legal Response" (1980) 58 Can. Bar Rev. 103 at 126-40.

5. Conspiracy

Despite being frequently litigated, the tort of conspiracy remains something of a puzzle. As we saw in the introduction to this chapter, *Allen v. Flood* (1897), [1898] A.C. 1 (H.L.) stands for the general proposition that, so long as otherwise lawful means are used, it is not tortious to deliberately destroy someone's business. And yet, if two or more people act together for the same purpose, they may be held liable under the tort of conspiracy.

That "magic of combination" remains a mystery. It sometimes is said that there is an inherent moral difference between being victimized by several conspirators, rather than by a single competitor. On that view, the common law condones aggressive competition, but its sense of fair play is offended when several people "gang up" on someone. Particularly in modern times, however, that explanation leaves something to be desired. As a matter of both moral intuition and sheer brute force, a large multinational corporation often poses much more of a threat than two local enterprises that temporarily have banded together.

Tort law recognizes two species of conspiracy: *Pro-Sys Consultants Ltd. v. Microsoft Corporation*, 2013 SCC 57 at para. 73; and *Canada Cement LaFarge Ltd. v. B.C. Lightweight Aggregate Ltd.* (1983), 145 D.L.R. (3d) 385 (S.C.C.):

- *Predominant Purpose Conspiracy*: If the conspirators agreed to execute an otherwise *lawful act*, then they may be held liable only if their *predominant purpose* was to hurt the plaintiff. That burden often is difficult to discharge. The defendants in *Daishowa Inc. v. Friends of the Lubicon* (1998), 158 D.L.R. (4th) 699 (Ont. Gen. Div.) organized a consumer boycott of the plaintiff's paper products in order to draw attention to Aboriginal land claim issues. The plaintiff lost a great deal of money because many of its usual customers purchased elsewhere. The action in conspiracy nevertheless failed because the defendants' primary purpose was not to hurt the plaintiff, but rather to raise public awareness of a political agenda.

- *Unlawful Means Conspiracy*: In contrast, if the conspirators agreed to execute an otherwise *unlawful act* (*e.g.* a tort, a crime, a breach of contract, or a statutory violation), they may be held liable as long as (1) their scheme was *directed toward* the plaintiff, and (2) they *should have known* that they might thereby hurt the plaintiff. Of course, those elements constitute minimum standards. Liability also may be imposed if the defendants' predominant purpose was to hurt the plaintiff, or if they actually knew that their scheme would do so.

POSLUNS v. TORONTO STOCK EXCHANGE
(1964), 46 D.L.R. (2d) 210 (Ont. H.C.)

[Employees of firms in the Toronto Stock Exchange ("TSE") required approval from the TSE before participating in various trading activities. The TSE formed the opinion that Posluns had engaged in such activities without approval. It then informed Posluns' employer, Daly Co., that he no longer was entitled to act in any capacity for any firm in the TSE. Daly Co. promptly fired Posluns. Posluns subsequently sued the TSE for both conspiracy and interference with contractual relations. The first claim is considered in this excerpt. The second claim is addressed later in this chapter.]

GALE J.: . . . While his counsel did not exhibit much confidence in the plaintiff's alleged cause of action for damages for conspiracy, it was not abandoned and I must therefore give attention to it.

It was pleaded that the defendant George Gardiner along with the other members of the Board who participated in the events of February 28th and March 2nd and the Exchange itself, all combined together to unlawfully injure the plaintiff by sending out the notice, ex. 33, which probably had the result, not only of bringing about his dismissal as an employee and his removal as a director and shareholder, but also of precluding him from obtaining immediate employment with any other member or member corporation of the Exchange, and of damaging his reputation to some extent. Both compensatory and punitive damages were asked for on this branch of the case, and it will be observed, as stated above, that the complaint was not confined to interference with the plaintiff's contract of employment only.

It need hardly be said that a conspiracy consists of an agreement of two or more to do an unlawful act or to do a lawful act by unlawful means. Thus, the tort of conspiracy is committed if a person is damaged by a combination which is formed for the purpose of harming him in his trade, business or other interests, whether or not a breach of contract is the result, or if that damage is caused by an unlawful act on the part of those acting in concert.

. . .

In my opinion, the claim based upon a supposed conspiracy fails for several reasons. To begin with, there was not any agreement to injure the plaintiff or any agreement to do something the doing of which would harm him. All the governors did was to vote in the same way, but, because they had agreed upon nothing before voting, and were not at any time actuated by malice or any other improper motive, they did not merely, by so voting, enter into an agreement, express or implied, to do something which had not yet been done, the requisite of any conspiracy. As Mr. Arnup said, the directors of a corporation do not make an "agreement" in the conspiracy sense by voting the same way. They individually make the same decision. In the popular sense they are "in agreement", but in the sense in which the law of conspiracy uses "agree" they were not. Each simply expressed an individual opinion and the majority opinion prevailed. A contrary view would bring extraordinary consequences. One of its implications would be that each time the majority of a Board of Directors voted to have the corporation pursue a course of action which ultimately turned out to be illegal, those who were in favour of having the corporation act as it did would be conspirators by reason solely of having so voted.

The proposition that the mere taking of a decision by directors or others at a meeting cannot constitute an agreement to conspire unless some of them have entered into a compact in advance of the meeting to induce others to cause the organization on whose behalf they are acting to do something which is wrong, is supported by authority. In *De Jetley Marks v. Greenwood (Lord) et al.*, [1936] 1 All E.R. 863, Porter, J., as he then was, observed at p. 872:

> ... I think it is true that directors in a board meeting could not induce or conspire to induce that meeting to break a contract — at any rate, not without malice.

That language does not substantiate Mr. Williston's suggestion that there is a difference between a vote to have a company break one of its own contracts and a vote to wrongfully procure the breach of a contract between others. I should add that Porter, J., was careful to qualify the quoted statement by pointing out that some or all of the directors could conspire before the meeting to cause the Board to wrongfully break a contract.

. . .

[Gale J. dismissed the claim in conspiracy.]

NOTES AND QUESTIONS

1. Why did the conspiracy action fail in *Posluns*? Was Gale J. suggesting that corporate directors could only be liable in conspiracy if they agreed to a course of conduct in advance of a board meeting?

2. "[I]n Canada, two types of actionable conspiracy remain available under tort law: predominant purpose conspiracy and unlawful means conspiracy": *Pro-Sys Consultants Ltd. v. Microsoft Corporation*, 2013 SCC 57 at para. 73. The same distinction is sometimes phrased in terms of "lawful means conspiracy" and "unlawful means conspiracy": *JSC BTA Bank v. Khrapunov*, [2018] UKSC 19 at para. 8. That formulation is slightly misleading, however, insofar as predominant purpose conspiracies may be built upon either lawful or unlawful acts.

However it is expressed, the distinction occasionally causes difficulties. Canadian judges sometimes conflate the two: *McLean v. Law Society of British Columbia*, 2015 BCSC 1431 at para. 57; and *Kamloops-Cariboo Regional Immigrants Society v. Herman*, 2015 BCSC 886 at para. 161.

3. As observed in the introduction to this section, lawyers and judges have long struggled to explain the precise rationale for the tort of conspiracy. Lord Sumption and Lord Lloyd-Jones offered an answer in *JSC BTA Bank v. Khrapunov*, [2018] UKSC 19 at para. 10.

> What is it that makes the conspiracy actionable as such? To say that a predominant purpose of injuring the claimant in the one case and the use of unlawful means in the other supply the element of unlawfulness required to make a conspiracy tortious simply restates the proposition in other words. A more useful concept is the absence of just cause or excuse. A person has a right to advance his own interests by lawful means even if the foreseeable consequence is to damage the interests of others. The existence of that right affords a just cause or excuse. Where, on the other hand, he seeks to advance his interests by unlawful means he has no such right. The position is

the same where the means used are lawful but the predominant intention of the defendant was to injure the claimant rather than to further some legitimate interest of his own. This is because in that case it cannot be an answer to say that he was simply exercising a legal right. He had no interest recognised by the law in exercising his legal right for the predominant purpose not of advancing his own interests but of injuring the claimant. In either case, there is no just cause or excuse for the combination.

Are you persuaded by that explanation?

4. Whichever species of civil conspiracy is invoked, the plaintiff must establish the existence of an *agreement* between the conspirators: *Weaver v. Corcoran*, 2017 BCCA 160; and *Kent v. Martin*, 2013 ABQB 436. There is no possibility of liability if the defendant merely knew of, or acquiesced in, a plan concocted by others: *Western Ontario Natural Gas Co. Ltd. v. Aikens*, [1946] O.R. 661 (H.C.). Nor is a tort committed if the defendant and another party independently acted with the same idea in mind. An agreement exists only if two or more minds join together on a project. Likewise, a conspiracy exists only insofar as two or more parties agreed upon a plan. If one party acts in excess of the agreed upon plan, liability may be denied. Accordingly, if A and B agree to commit one unlawful act, but the plaintiff's injury is attributable to some *other* unlawful act that A committed alone, B will not be liable for conspiracy: *Golden Capital Securities Ltd. v. Holmes*, 2004 BCCA 565.

While conspiracy requires an agreement between two or more parties, the persons involved may be natural or legal. Indeed, because the tort of conspiracy most often arises in the business world, the idea of a legal person is particularly important. Because a corporation is regarded as a legal person, a tort may be committed if a company enters into an agreement with one of its directors: *Hall-Chem Inc. v. Vulcan Packaging Inc.* (1994), 12 B.L.R. (2d) 274 (Ont. Gen. Div.). The tort may also be possible if a parent company enters into an agreement with one of its subsidiaries: *Pro-Sys Consultants Ltd. v. Microsoft Corporation*, 2013 SCC 57 at para. 79; and *Smith v. National Money Mart Co.* (2006), 80 O.R. (3d) 81 (C.A.) at para. 19.

The requisite agreement need not take any particular form (*e.g.* it need not be written) and it does not have to rise to the level of an enforceable contract. It may be express or its existence may be inferred from the circumstances: *XY, LLC v. Canadian Topsires Selection Inc.*, 2016 BCSC 1095 at para. 247; *Golden Capital Securities Ltd. v. Holmes*, 2004 BCCA 565 at para. 46; and *Sweeney v. Coote*, [1907] A.C. 221 at 222.

5. Commercial activities are increasingly multi-jurisdictional. If the requisite agreement is created outside of Canada, when, if ever, can a Canadian court entertain a claim for conspiracy and apply its own laws? The Supreme Court of Canada was open to the possibility in *Sun Rype Products Ltd. v. Archer Daniels Midland Company*, 2013 SCC 58 at para. 46 ("There is at least some suggestion in the case law that where defendants conduct business in Canada, make sales in Canada and conspire to fix prices on products sold in Canada, Canadian courts have jurisdiction"). See also *VitaPharm Canada Ltd. v. F. Hoffmann-LaRoche Ltd.* (2002), 20 C.P.C. (5th) 351 (Ont. S.C.J.) at para. 58 ("It is arguable that a conspiracy that injures Canadians gives rise to liability in Canada, even if the conspiracy was formed abroad"); *Fairhurst v. Anglo American PLC*, 2012 BCCA 257 at para. 32; and *British Columbia v. Imperial Tobacco Canada Ltd.*, 2006 BCCA 398 at para. 41 ("A conspiracy occurs in British Columbia if the harm is suffered here, regardless of where the 'wrongful conduct' occurred. On

that basis, the court has jurisdiction over the *ex juris* defendants who are alleged to be parties to the conspiracy").

6. The first species of the tort is called *predominant purpose conspiracy* (or *lawful means conspiracy*). That version of the tort is marked by two characteristics.

First, as the name indicates, the court must be satisfied that the defendant subjectively acted with the sole or predominant purpose of harming the plaintiff. That is a high threshold and it is not easily met: *Driskell v. Dangerfield*, 2007 MBQB 142. Liability will not be imposed merely because the defendant knew, or ought to have known, that the planned project was likely to hurt the plaintiff: *Daishowa Inc. v. Friends of the Lubicon* (1998), 158 D.L.R. (4th) 699 (Ont. Gen. Div.). That proposition proves fatal for the plaintiff's claim if — even though the plaintiff's ruin may have been a happy side effect of the venture — the defendant acted primarily with a view to protecting or advancing its own interests. Of course, in a competitive business world, loss and gain often are two sides of the same coin, such that one cannot occur without the other. It nevertheless is true that allegations of conspiracy frequently fail on this basis: *D'Agnone v. D'Agnone*, 2017 ABCA 35; *790668 Ontario Inc. v. D'Andrea Management Inc.*, 2017 ONCA 1019; *Keyland Development Corp. v. Rocky View (Municipal District No. 44)*, 2016 ABQB 735; *Harris v. GlaxoSmithKline Inc.*, 2010 ONCA 872; and *Liu v. Sung* (1997), 37 B.C.L.R. (3d) 158 (C.A.).

Second, as long as the defendant's predominant purpose was to injure the plaintiff, liability may be imposed whether the agreed upon course of action, in itself, was lawful or unlawful. In other words, the primary intention of hurting the plaintiff may transform otherwise lawful behaviour into unlawful behaviour. In one sense, at least, that is a remarkable proposition. This chapter opened with a discussion of *Allen v. Flood*, [1898] A.C. 1 (H.L.), in which the House of Lords held that a malicious motive is not actionable. The defendant generally is entitled to destroy the plaintiff's business as long as the means to the end are not themselves tortious. The first form of conspiracy, however, constitutes an exception to that rule. If you slash your prices for the sole purpose of driving me to ruin and eliminating me from the marketplace, I have no cause for legal complaint. If you and another party combine for precisely the same purpose, you both may be liable to me in tort.

7. At first glance, liability for predominant purpose conspiracy appears to be irreconcilable with the rights-based theory that was introduced in Chapter 1. That theory conceives of torts in terms of the violation of rights. The defendant is liable if, but only if, there has been a breach of an obligation owed to the plaintiff. In contrast, liability can never be justified purely on policy grounds. The social desirability of deterring cooperative efforts that are aimed at causing harm cannot properly explain an award of damages. The first species of the tort of conspiracy accordingly seems illegitimate. The intentional infliction of economic harm by a single individual is not actionable because it does not involve the violation of any right. The same ought to be true even if the defendant joins together with another party for the same end.

Neyers nevertheless argues that lawful means conspiracy is reconcilable with a rights-based theory of tort: Neyers, "Explaining the Inexplicable: Four Manifestations of Abuse of Rights in English Law" in Nolan & Robertson, eds., *Rights and Private Law* (2010), ch. 11. The key, he holds, lies in the fact that one who claims rights must equally recognize the rights of others. Rights must be exercised in a manner consonant with the ability of others to do the same. The pursuit of self-interest is legitimate; the deliberate frustration of another's projects is not. Neyers accordingly concludes that a court may justifiably impose liability if the defendants acted for the purpose of gratuitously injuring the plaintiff. The abuse of rights, he says, is appropriately actionable. Should the same analysis apply if only one person, using otherwise lawful means, deliberately frustrates another's projects?

8. The second species of the tort is called unlawful means conspiracy. Once again, two features mark the tort.

First, the court need not be satisfied that the defendant acted with the predominant purpose of hurting the plaintiff. It is enough that the agreed upon course of "conduct is *directed* towards the plaintiff (alone or together with others), and the defendants *should know* in the circumstances that injury to the plaintiff is likely to and does result": *Canada Cement LeFarge Ltd. v. B.C. Light Weight Aggregate Ltd.*, [1983] 1 S.C.R. 452 at 471-72 (emphasis added). Accordingly, in contrast to the first form of conspiracy, the mental component of the tort is somewhat diminished. As Estey J. explained in *Canada Cement LaForge*, "it is not necessary that the predominant purpose of the defendants' conduct be to cause injury to the plaintiff," as long as "a constructive intent [can be] derived from the fact that the defendants should have known that injury to the plaintiff would ensue." The precise nature of that requirement, however, is difficult to formulate. Mere reasonable foreseeability, of the type that would suffice in a claim for negligence, is insufficient: *Mraiche Investment Corp. v. McLennan Ross LLP*, 2012 ABCA 95 at para. 10. The defendant must have possessed a "clear expectation" — "greater than a 50% chance" — that damage would ensue: *Golden Capital Securities Ltd. v. Holmes*, 2004 BCCA 565 at para. 56.

The second essential element of this species of conspiracy pertains to the nature of the agreed upon act. The conspirators must have combined to act *unlawfully*: *Berry v. Pulley*, 2015 ONCA 449. Unlawfulness may take a variety of forms. Crime is an obvious example, but so too, the unlawful act may consist of a breach of contract or a tort of inducing breach of contract: *Culzean Inventions Ltd. v. Midwestern Broom Co.* (1984), 31 Sask. R. 180 (Q.B.); and *Le Soleil Hospitality Inc. v. Louie*, 2010 BCSC 1183, aff'd 2011 BCCA 305. It may involve the payment of a bribe or the breach of a fiduciary duty: *671122 Ontario Ltd. v. Sagaz Industries Canada Inc.* (1998), 40 O.R. (3d) 229 (Gen. Div.); and *Prim8 Group Inc. v. Tisi*, 2016 ONSC 5662. A conspiracy based on breach of contract, however, requires that all of the conspirators commit the contractual wrong. That is not possible if only one alleged conspirator was contractually bound at the relevant time: *Agribrands Purina Canada Inc. v. Kasamekas*, 2011 ONCA 460; and *Bank of Montreal v. Tortora*, 2010 BCCA 139. Alternatively, the unlawful act may arise from a contravention of a statute: *Westfair Foods Ltd. v. Lippens Inc.* (1989), 64 D.L.R. (4th) 335 (Man. C.A.) (*Competition Act*); and *Canada Cement LeFarge Ltd.*, *supra* (*Combines Investigation Act*).

The breadth of the unlawfulness element is illustrated by *JSC BTA Bank v. Khrapunov*, [2018] UKSC 19. Mukhtar Ablyazov was the chairman of the claimant bank in Kazakhstan until the bank was nationalized in 2009. After Ablyazov fled to the United Kingdom, the bank claimed that he had stolen US$6 billion. English courts issued two orders, requiring Ablyazov to disclose the money's whereabouts and preventing him from dealing with the funds, and appointed a receiver to take control of the assets. Unfortunately, by the time that the bank had obtained default judgment and an order for contempt of court, "the bird had flown": at para. 3. And since he had disappeared along with the bulk of the money, Ablyazov was not available to either satisfy the judgment for US$4.6 billion nor serve his 22-month sentence.

Seeking another source of relief, the claimant then alleged Ablyazov and the defendant, Ablyazov's son-in-law, had entered into a "combination" to dissipate and conceal the funds. The crucial question was whether contempt of court constituted an "unlawful" act for the purposes of the tort of conspiracy. All three levels of court answered in the affirmative. The defendant was liable because he and Ablyazov had executed an agreement to frustrate the original court orders.

Some decisions regarding the unlawfulness element are more controversial. The court arguably went too far in *Canadian Training and Development Group v. Air Canada* (1986), 57 O.R. (2d) 659 (Div. Ct.). The defendant was a member of an air traffic controllers' union. In an attempt to pressure his employer, he falsely called in sick and thereby breached the collective agreement and the provisions of the *Public Service Staff Relations Act*, R.S.C. 1970, c. P-35. The court accordingly held that the defendant had conspired with other air traffic controllers in an *unlawful* act. It further held that the defendant *prima facie* was liable for the losses suffered by the plaintiffs, who were passengers on flights that had been affected by the industrial action. The claim ultimately failed only because of an immunity provided by the *Rights of Labour Act*, R.S.O. 1980, c. 456.

Despite the general breadth of the unlawfulness requirement, one important restriction must be kept in mind. While a tortious act certainly is unlawful, an allegation of conspiracy may be superfluous if the plaintiff can successfully sue the defendant on the basis of that underlying tort. As Lord Denning explained in *Ward v. Lewis*, [1955] 1 All E.R. 55 at para. 56 (C.A.): "when a tort has been committed by two or more persons, an allegation of a prior conspiracy to commit the tort means nothing. The prior agreement merges in the tort." See also *Hunt v. Carey Canada Inc.*, [1990] 2 S.C.R. 959; *Normart Management Ltd. v. West Hill Redevelopment Co.* (1998), 37 O.R. (3d) 97 at para. 28 (C.A.); *Waters v. Michie*, 2011 BCCA 364; *Perth Insurance Co. v. Osler Rehabilitation Centre Inc.*, 2013 ONSC 7033; *Wolf v. Ontario (Attorney General)*, 2012 ONSC 72; *Economical Insurance Co. v. Fairview Assessment Centre Inc.*, 2011 ONSC 7535; *Jevco Insurance Co. v. Pacific Assessment Centre Inc.*, 2015 ONSC 7751; and *Catalyst Capital Group Inc. v. Veritas Investment Research Corp.*, 2016 ONSC 23, rev'd on other grounds 2017 ONCA 75. In contrast, if the merger doctrine is not applicable, an agreement to commit a tort undoubtedly may provide the basis for an unlawful means conspiracy: *Hammer v. Kemmis* (1956), 7 D.L.R. (2d) 684 (B.C.C.A.) (nuisance); *Elliott v. Canadian Broadcasting Corp.* (1993), 108 D.L.R. (4th) 385 (Ont. Gen. Div.) (defamation); *Royal Bank v. Holoboff*, 1998 ABQB 288; and *HSBC Bank Canada v. 1100336 Alberta Ltd. (c.o.b. Incredible Electronics Wholesale)*, 2011 ABQB 748, aff'd 2013 ABCA 235 (fraud).

Finally, it is helpful to consider how English courts have treated the issue of unlawfulness. As discussed later in this chapter, the House of Lords has held that the tort of interference with economic relations by unlawful means — or the "unlawful means tort" as it is now known — requires proof of an act that is "unlawful" insofar as it is privately actionable: *OBG Ltd. v. Allan*, [2008] 1 A.C. 1 (H.L.). Liability accordingly cannot be imposed if the underlying act is unlawful as a matter of, say, criminal law, rather than civil law. Many criminal acts can alternatively be analyzed as torts, but some (like perjury) cannot. The question for the court in *Total Network SL v. Revenue and Customs Commissioners*, [2008] 1 A.C. 1174 (H.L.) was whether the same definition of "unlawful" restricts the scope of the tort of conspiracy. The case arose from a "missing trader" fraud. Paperwork was generated to purportedly show that mobile phones (likely non-existent) were imported into England, sold several times, and exported from England, all in a single day. Tax legislation entitled a seller within a chain of transactions to a refund; a corresponding tax liability was imposed upon a buyer within the same chain. Of course, given the fraudulent nature of the exercise, the seller extracted payment from the tax authorities, but the buyer disappeared without paying the tax. When the scam came to light, the claimant sought damages on behalf of Her Majesty's government. The action was framed in terms of the second species of civil conspiracy. Significantly, however, the underlying acts that the claimant relied upon were criminal, but not civilly actionable. Liability nevertheless was imposed. Notwithstanding the contrary position adopted in *OBG*, the House of Lords held that, for the purposes of the tort of conspiracy, an act may be "unlawful" even though it is not civilly actionable. The court's reasoning is largely pragmatic. The suggestion that two or more people could be immune in tort law despite conspiring to carry out a criminal scheme with the intention of harming a party was, Lord Scott found (at para. 56), simply "unacceptable." See also *JSC BTA Bank v. Khrapunov, supra.* And see Edmundson, "Conspiracy by Unlawful Means: Keeping the Tort Untangled" (2008) 16 Torts L.J. 189; and O'Sullivan, "Unlawful Means Conspiracy in the House of Lords" [2008] C.L.J. 459.

9. "The gist of the cause of action [for conspiracy] is damage to the plaintiff; so long as it remains unexecuted, the agreement, which alone constitutes the crime of conspiracy, causes no damage; it is only acts done in execution of the agreement that are capable of doing that. So the tort, unlike the crime, consists not of an agreement but of concerted action taken pursuant to agreement": *Lonrho Ltd. v. Shell Petroleum Co. (No. 2)*, [1982] A.C. 173 at 188 (H.L.). See also *Canada Cement LeFarge Ltd., supra*; and *Berry v. Pulley*, 2015 ONCA 449.

Because loss is the gist of the action, damages are usually compensatory in nature. The defendant is required to monetarily repair the plaintiff's loss. The analysis becomes complicated if the alleged loss consists of the loss of a chance to avoid a burden or obtain a benefit. In that event, if the court determines that the lost chance was "sufficiently real and significant," it must discount the total damages to reflect the relevant probability: *Berry v. Pulley, supra.*

While conspiracy generally is said to be actionable only upon proof of loss, an exception of sorts may exist. The precise nature of that exception, however, is unclear. Klar reads the cases to say that while pecuniary loss must be proven if the plaintiff complains of interference with business interests, it is otherwise if the conspiracy entailed a violation of the claimant's "legal rights": Klar & Jefferies, *Tort Law*, 6th ed. (2017) at 846. Fridman, in contrast, maintains that if a distinction is to be drawn, it should reflect the nature of the tort. A conspiracy to injure "may require proof of pecuniary loss," but a conspiracy to act by unlawful means "may need nothing more than proof of an intention to act unlawfully": Fridman *et al., The Law of Torts in Canada*, 3d ed. (2010) at 735. See also *Shaw v. Lewis*, [1948] 2 D.L.R. 189 (B.C.C.A.); and *Valley Salvage Ltd. v. Molson Brewery B.C. Ltd.* (1976), 64 D.L.R. (3d) 734 (B.C.S.C.).

Although compensation is the usual remedy for conspiracy, other responses are available as well. Injunctive relief may be granted to prevent a threatened conspiracy from taking effect: *Garry v. St. Eloi* (1989), 77 Sask. R. 187 (Q.B.) (relief denied on facts). Punitive damages will be awarded if the defendant's conduct is particularly reprehensible: *Claiborne Industries v. National Bank of Canada* (1989), 59 D.L.R. (4th) 533 (Ont. C.A.); and *321665 Alberta Ltd. v. Mobil Oil Canada Ltd.*, 2011 ABQB 292, rev'd 2013 ABCA 221.

10. It sometimes is said that an allegation of conspiracy may be defeated by the defence of *justification*. That proposition, however, is qualified. To begin, there can be no justification if the plaintiff has established the tort of conspiracy to act by unlawful means. Unlawful acts, by definition, are not justifiable. In contrast, if the tort takes the form of a conspiracy to injure, justification may preclude liability. That point was discussed previously. A conspiracy to injure requires proof that the defendant acted with the predominant purpose of hurting the claimant. That requirement cannot be met if, in fact, the defendant acted primarily with a view to advancing its own self-interests. There are many illustrations of that rule. *Mogul S.S. Co. v. McGregor, Gow & Co.*, [1892] A.C. 25 (H.L.), provides one illustration. Although the defendants conspired together in an effort to cut prices and thereby drove the plaintiff out of business, their scheme was not actionable because they acted out of self-interest. See also *Crofter Hand Woven Harris Tweed Co. v. Veitch*, [1942] A.C. 435 (H.L.). The question at this point, however, asks whether justification is a *defence*. A defence, properly speaking, must be proven by the defendant. Canadian courts, however, generally hold that it is for the plaintiff to negate the existence of a justification by positively establishing that the defendant primarily intended to cause injury: *Liu v. Sung* (1997), 37 B.C.L.R. (3d) 158 at para. 14 (C.A.). See also Haydon, "The Defence of Justification in Cases of Intentionally Caused Economic Harm" (1970) 20 U.T.L.J. 139 at 150.

In appropriate circumstances, the defendant may also enjoy a statutory defence. Several provinces protect trade union members. For example, s. 3(1) of Ontario's *Rights of Labour Act*, R.S.O. 1990, c. R.33, states that "Any act done by two or more members of a trade union, if done in contemplation or furtherance of a trade dispute, is not actionable unless the act would be actionable if done without any agreement or combination." A simple labour grievance cannot, by the simple expedient of linking some of the actors involved, be dressed up as conspiracy claims: *Lapchuk v. Saskatchewan*, 2017 SKCA 68. So too, an allegation of conspiracy may fail if the underlying acts are non-justiciable as a matter of public policy. Accordingly, an erstwhile Member of Parliament's claim that the Prime Minister and others conspired to remove her as a Minister of the Crown failed on the ground that the matter was wholly protected by the doctrine of Crown prerogative: *Guergis v. Novak*, 2012 ONSC 4579, aff'd 2013 ONCA 449.

11. Although the tort of conspiracy most often arises in the business world, it may also arise in social or family settings. In *Helmy v. Helmy* (2000), 36 E.T.R. (2d) 100 (Ont. S.C.J.), a husband won $2,500,000 in a lottery. He did not tell his wife, from whom he separated a short time later. With the help of several family members, he continued to hide the winnings from his estranged wife while she was seeking a division of the matrimonial assets. The wife did not discover the truth until after those proceedings were closed. She then commenced several claims, including one in conspiracy against her husband and the relatives who had participated in his scheme. The court held that the wife was entitled to (1) a half-interest in the lottery winnings and their traceable proceeds, (2) compensatory damages under the tort of conspiracy

against her husband and his complicit relatives, to the extent that she was otherwise unable to actually recover her share of the lottery winnings, and (3) punitive damages of $50,000 against her husband and his complicit relatives.

The tort of conspiracy nevertheless is inappropriate in some family contexts. In *Frame v. Smith*, [1987] 2 S.C.R. 99, the Supreme Court of Canada held that it would be contrary to the interests of children to allow parents to use the tort in connection with issues like custody and access.

12. For further discussion of the tort of conspiracy, see Witting, "Intra-Corporate Conspiracy: An Intriguing Prospect" [2013] C.L.J. 178; Guy & Del Gobbo, "Understanding the Anomalous: The Tort of Conspiracy" (2013) 42 Adv. Q. 143; Davies & Sales, "Intentional Harm, Conspiracies and Accessories" (2018) 134 L.Q.R. 69; Ross, "The Evolving Tort of Conspiracy to Restrain Trade Under Canadian Common Law" (1996) 75 Can. Bar Rev. 193; Burns, "Civil Conspiracy: An Unwieldy Vessel Rides a Judicial Tempest" (1982) 16 U.B.C.L. Rev. 229; Carty, *An Analysis of the Economic Torts* (2011), ch. 6; and Burns & Blom, *Economic Interests in Canadian Tort Law* (2016), ch. 6.

13. The tort of conspiracy must be distinguished from the crime of conspiracy. Section 465 of the *Criminal Code*, R.S.C. 1985, c. C-46, states:

465. (1) Except where otherwise expressly provided by law, the following provisions apply in respect of conspiracy:

(a) every one who conspires with any one to commit murder or to cause another person to be murdered, whether in Canada or not, is guilty of an indictable offence and liable to a maximum term of imprisonment for life;

(b) every one who conspires with any one to prosecute a person for an alleged offence, knowing that he did not commit that offence, is guilty of an indictable offence and liable

(i) to imprisonment for a term not exceeding ten years, if the alleged offence is one for which, on conviction, that person would be liable to be sentenced to imprisonment for life or for a term not exceeding fourteen years, or

(ii) to imprisonment for a term not exceeding five years, if the alleged offence is one for which, on conviction, that person would be liable to imprisonment for less than fourteen years;

(c) every one who conspires with any one to commit an indictable offence not provided for in paragraph (a) or (b) is guilty of an indictable offence and liable to the same punishment as that to which an accused who is guilty of that offence would, on conviction, be liable; and

(d) every one who conspires with any one to commit an offence punishable on summary conviction is guilty of an offence punishable on summary conviction

14. Conspiracy is an offence under section 45 of the *Competition Act*, R.S.C. 1985, c. C-34. The main provisions state:

45. (1) Every person commits an offence who, with a competitor of that person with respect to a product, conspires, agrees or arranges

(a) to fix, maintain, increase or control the price for the supply of the product;

(b) to allocate sales, territories, customers or markets for the production or supply of the product; or

(c) to fix, maintain, control, prevent, lessen or eliminate the production or supply of the product.

(2) Every person who commits an offence under subsection (1) is guilty of an indictable offence and liable on conviction to imprisonment for a term not exceeding 14 years or to a fine not exceeding $25 million, or to both.

Although private actions occasionally are available under the *Competition Act*, they are narrowly confined and relatively infrequent. The statutory claim for conspiracy does not, however, displace the tort of conspiracy: *Watson v. Bank of America Corp.*, 2015 BCCA 362. See generally Pitel, ed., *Litigating Conspiracy* (2006).

6. Interference with Contractual Relations

Contracts are the lifeblood of commerce. They are used to secure supplies of raw materials and labour, and to sell finished products and services. A breach of contract consequently can be very disruptive to a business. Contractual remedies are available, but often they are inadequate. Specific enforcement is limited to exceptional circumstances and, whatever the position in theory, monetary damages frequently are a poor substitute for actual performance. As a result, there is a strong temptation for an unscrupulous business person, searching for a competitive advantage, to target the agreements that a rival has created with third parties (*e.g.* suppliers, employees, and customers). See generally Chsherbinin, *The Law of Inducement in Canadian Employment Law* (2012).

To effectively deal with such situations, our legal system offers two avenues of relief: (1) an action for *breach of contract* against the part that actually failed to perform as promised, and (2) an action for *accessory liability* against the party that induced or assisted that breach of contract. The concept of accessory liability is well known in criminal law. Most lawyers recognize the possibility of being held responsible for aiding or abetting a criminal act. See for example *Criminal Code*, R.S.C. 1985, c. C-46, s. 21(1). Although less familiar, a similar principle occasionally applies in private law. Equity has developed a general principle of accessory liability that applies if, for instance, a stranger knowingly assists in a trustee's breach of trust: *Air Canada v. M & L Travel Ltd.* (1993), 108 D.L.R. (4th) 592 (S.C.C.). Law, in contrast, traditionally has been more reluctant to impose liability on accessories. See generally Sales, "The Tort of Conspiracy and Civil Secondary Liability" [1990] C.L.J. 491. It nevertheless does offer a tort of *interference with contractual relations* (often known as *inducing breach of contract*).

The tort of interference with contractual relations consists of four elements:

- *Defendant's Knowledge*: The defendant must have known about the contract between the plaintiff and the third party, though not necessarily about all of its details.

- *Defendant's Intention*: The defendant must have intended the third party to break its agreement with the plaintiff, though the defendant need not have been motivated by a malicious desire to hurt the plaintiff.

- *Causation of Breach*: The defendant in fact must have caused the third party to break its contract with the plaintiff. In that respect, an important, though controversial, distinction sometimes is drawn between actually encouraging a breach of contract and merely providing information regarding the possible benefits of breach. On that view, liability is possible in the former case, but not the latter. The operative line, however, is notoriously difficult to draw and it may be better to recognize the possibility of liability in either event. As always, however, there is no question of upholding a claim if, for instance, the defendant's actions lacked the requisite intention or were not actually a cause of the subsequent breach.

- *Plaintiff's Loss*: The plaintiff must have suffered a loss as a result of the third party's breach, though mere lack of contractual performance normally is sufficient.

Until recently, the tort of interference with contractual relations was thought to have two branches: *direct interference* and *indirect interference*. The central difference pertained to the nature of the defendant's acts.

- *Direct Interference*: The tort's first branch applied if the defendant *directly* interfered with the plaintiff's contractual relationship with a third party. That was true, for instance, if the defendant used a promise of more money to persuade the plaintiff's employee to leave that position. Because the interference was direct, liability was possible even if, aside from the tort itself, the defendant's acts were entirely lawful. Offering a higher salary is not inherently wrongful.

- *Indirect Interference*: The tort's second branch applied if the defendant *indirectly* interfered in a contract between the plaintiff and a third party. That was true, for instance, if, by stealing a worker's tools and equipment, the defendant prevented that person from performing an agreement with the plaintiff. Regardless of the tort, the theft of goods is wrongful in itself.

As explained in the notes that follow, those two situations are no longer bundled together under a single, generalized claim. They raise different concerns and they must be addressed by different rules. Accordingly, while direct acts continue to be addressed through the tort of interference with contractual relations, the *unlawful means tort* now governs if the defendant indirectly meddled in the plaintiff's third-party contract. That first possibility is examined here; the second is discussed in the final section of this chapter.

The following extract is taken from the leading case in this area.

LUMLEY v. GYE
(1853), 118 E.R. 749 (Q.B.)

[An opera singer named Johanna Wagner agreed to sing for one season with the plaintiff's company, Her Majesty's Theatre. The defendant subsequently induced Ms Wagner to break that contract by offering to pay her a higher fee to sing with his company, the Royal Italian Opera. The plaintiff suffered a financial loss as a result of losing the diva's services. He therefore sued the defendant for inducing breach of contract.]

EYRE J.:

The question raised upon this demurrer is whether an action will lie by the proprietor of a theatre against a person who maliciously procures an entire abandonment of a contract to perform exclusively at that theatre for a certain time, whereby damage was sustained? It seems to me that it will. The authorities are numerous and uniform that an action will lie by a master against a person who procures that a servant should unlawfully leave his service. . . .

If it is objected that this class of actions for procuring a breach of contract of hiring rests upon no principle and ought not to be extended beyond the cases heretofore decided, and that, as those have related to contracts respecting trade, manufactures, or household service, and not to performance at a theatre, therefore, they are no authority for an action in respect of a contract for such performance, the answer appears to me to be that the class of cases referred to rests upon the principle that the procurement of the violation of the right is a cause of action, and that when this principle is applied to a violation of a right arising upon a contract of hiring, the nature of the service contracted for is immaterial. It is clear that the procurement of the violation of a right is a cause of action in all instances where the violation is an actionable wrong, as in violations of a right to property, whether real or personal, or to personal security. He who procures the wrong is a joint wrongdoer, and may be sued, either alone or jointly with the agent, in the appropriate action for the wrong complained of. Where a right to the performance of a contract has been violated by a breach thereof, the remedy is upon the contract against the contracting party. If he is made to indemnify for such breach, no further recourse is allowed, and, as in case of the procurement of a breach of contract the action is for a wrong and cannot be joined with the action on the contract, and as the act itself is not likely to be of frequent occurrence nor easy of proof, therefore, the action for this wrong, in respect of other contracts than those of hiring, are not numerous, but still they seem to me sufficient to show that the principle has been recognised. . . .

This principle is supported by good reason. He who maliciously procures a damage to another by violation of his right ought to be made to indemnify, and that whether he procures an actionable wrong or a breach of contract. He who procures the non-delivery of goods according to contract may inflict an injury, the same as he who procures the abstraction of goods after delivery, and both ought on the same ground to be made responsible. The remedy on the contract may be inadequate, as where the measures of damages is restricted; or in the case of nonpayment of a debt where the damage may be bankruptcy to the creditor who is disappointed, but the measure of damages against the debtor is interest only; or, in the case of the non-delivery of the goods, the disappointment may lead to a heavy forfeiture under a contract to complete a work within a time, but the measure of damages against the vendor of the goods for non-delivery may be only the difference between the contract price and the market value of the goods in question at the time of the breach. In such cases, he who procures the damage maliciously might justly be made responsible beyond the liability of the contractor.

[The Court of Queen's Bench held that the plaintiff, upon proving the relevant facts, would be entitled to recover in tort.]

NOTES AND QUESTIONS

1. Most discussions of *Lumley v. Gye* end where the above extract does. In truth, however, the extracted decision merely dealt with a demurrer, which required the plaintiff to show that the pleaded action was good in law. Once the court held that liability was possible in principle, another round of litigation dealt with the facts. And at that stage, the defendant escaped liability by proving that he honestly, though mistakenly, believed that Ms Lumley was entitled to discharge her contract with the plaintiff because she had not received a particular payment. See Waddams, "Johanna Lumley and the Rival Opera Houses" (2001) 117 L.Q.R. 431. See also Howarth, "Against Lumley v. Gye" (2005) 68 M.L.R. 195.

Although the plaintiff was not able to recover from the defendant in tort, he did obtain an injunction that restrained Ms Lumley from singing for the defendant's company: *Lumley v. Wagner* (1852), 42 E.R. 687 (Ch.).

2. State the rule that emerges from *Lumley v. Gye*. What precisely is the basis upon which a defendant may be held liable for interfering with contractual relations? To what extent does the law protect rights that are held under a contract? Does, or should, the tort protect other sorts of rights? Consider, for example, the manner in which tort law protects rights to real property (trespass to land), personal property (conversion, detinue and trespass), reputation (defamation), and bodily integrity (battery). Do contractual rights receive relatively more or relatively less protection? What is the explanation for your answer to that question? For discussion of the manner in which tort law protects property rights in contracts, see Lee, "Inducing Breach of Contract, Conversion and Contract as Property" (2009) 29 O.J.L.S. 511.

3. In *Lumley v. Gye*, liability initially was said to require proof that the defendant acted *maliciously*. It soon was accepted, however, that the real standard is *intention*: *Allen v. Flood*, [1898] A.C. 1 (H.L.); and *Quinn v. Leathem*, [1901] A.C. 495 (H.L.). See also *1670002 Ontario Ltd. (c.o.b. Canadian Professional Recruiters) v. Redtree Contract Carriers Ltd.*, 2014 ONCA 501. That point was raised in *Posluns v. Toronto Stock Exchange* (1964), 46 D.L.R. (2d) 210 at 261 (Ont. H.C.). Gale J. said that the "wrong does not rest upon the fact that the intervenor has acted in order to harm his victim, for a bad motive does not *per se* convert an otherwise lawful act into an unlawful one, but rather because there has been an unlawful invasion of legal relations existing between others." It accordingly is sufficient that the defendant intended to procure the breach or acted with a substantial certainty that its course of action would lead to that result: *Drouillard v. Cogeco Cable Inc.*, 2007 ONCA 322. Furthermore, the "intention to bring about a breach of contract need not be the *primary* object; it is sufficient if the interference is necessarily incidental to attaining the defendant's primary objective: *369413 Alberta Ltd. v. Pocklington*, 2000 ABCA 307 at para. 40, citing *Fraser v. Board of Trustees of Central United Church* (1983), 38 O.R. (2d) 97 at 103 (H.C.J.); and *Bank of Nova Scotia v. Gaudreau* (1985), 48 O.R. (2d) 478 (H.C.J.).

The issue of intention was determinative of the dispute in *Sar Petroleum Inc. v. Peace Hills Trust Co.*, 2010 NBCA 22. The plaintiff created a contract to build a gas station for the owner of certain land. That building contract required periodic payments to be made without any "holdback" (*i.e.* a special fund created for the purpose of discharging any liens that may arise). The owner financed the project by obtaining a loan from the defendant. When the time for payment arrived, the defendant bank consulted with its lawyer and decided to advance funds subject to a

15% holdback. Because it did not immediately receive full payment, the plaintiff was unable to pay its suppliers and it consequently was forced into receivership. It then sued the defendant for inducing the owner to commit a breach of contract. Although the defendant undoubtedly knew that its actions would prevent the owner from honouring its obligation under the construction agreement (*i.e.* the obligation to make payment without any holdback), the plaintiff's claim was dismissed for lack of the requisite intention. The defendant intended only to protect itself by acting pursuant to a right that it believed that it enjoyed under the loan agreement.

Moreover, it often is said that the plaintiff must prove that "the intentional acts [were] directed, at least in part, against the complaining party." That requirement is not satisfied if "the wrongful conduct . . . was not deliberately targeted against the complaining party but, rather, was simply an incidental or foreseeable result of the defendant's wrongful conduct. The purpose of the . . . conduct must be to inflict injury *on the complaining party*, that is, the plaintiff": *Print N' Promotion (Canada) Ltd. v. Kovachis*, 2011 ONCA 23 at paras. 23-24. And, of course, the plaintiff must identify the particular defendant who purportedly possessed the relevant intention: *Lysko v. Braley* (2006), 79 O.R. (3d) 721 (C.A.), and show that person was aware of the relevant contract: *Super-Save Enterprises Ltd. v. 249513 B.C. Ltd. (c.o.b. Mike's Auto Towing)* (2004), 43 B.L.R. (3d) 23 (B.C.C.A.).

4. It sometimes is suggested that the standard should be lowered further so as to support liability as long as the defendant should have known that its course of conduct would interfere with the contractual rights that the plaintiff held against the third party. The tort, in other words, should be triggered by negligence or carelessness rather than intention: *Nicholls v. Richmond (Township)* (1983), 43 B.C.L.R. 162 (C.A.); and *Yellow Submarine Deli Inc. v. A.G.F. Hospitality Associates Inc.* (1998), 118 Man. R. (2d) 270 (C.A.). As previously observed, the courts in *Lumley v. Gye* ultimately denied liability because the defendant honestly, though perhaps unreasonably, believed that the diva was entitled to terminate her agreement with the plaintiff. And indeed, the better view is that the tort ought to remain based on intention. As evidenced by the relatively late development of the law in *Hedley Byrne & Co. v. Heller & Partners Ltd.*, [1964] A.C. 465 (H.L.), courts generally have been reluctant to impose liability for negligently caused economic loss. It arguably would be undesirable to weaken the restrictions that currently exist under the intentional torts. See *Brae Centre Ltd. v. 1044807 Alberta Ltd.* (2008), 99 Alta. L.R. (4th) 41 (C.A.); *Correia v. Canac Kitchens* (2008), 91 O.R. (3d) 353 (C.A.); and Danforth, "Tortious Interference with Contract: A Reassertion of Society's Interest in Commercial Stability and Contractual Integrity" (1981) 81 Colum. L. Rev. 1491.

5. The fact that interference with contractual relations presumes the existence of a valid contract generally is non-problematic. Difficulties nevertheless occasionally arise. In *Unident v. DeLong* (1981), 50 N.S.R. (2d) 1 (T.D.), the plaintiff was awarded damages even though the contract was unenforceable because it violated the *Sale of Goods Act*, R.S.N.S. 1967, c. 274, s. 6(1). The judge emphasized that the contract was valid in substance and only unenforceable due to a technical defect. In *Royal Bank v. Wilton*, (1995), 165 A.R. 261 (C.A.), liability was imposed for interference with a sale contract that was subject to a true condition precedent, even though the condition was never satisfied. See also *Persaud v. Telus Corp.*, 2017 ONCA 479; and *410784 Ontario Ltd. v. Little Zinger Inc. (c.o.b. Corktown Esso)*, 2016 ONCA 90. Should liability be

imposed if the defendant persuaded a third party to dismiss the plaintiff from a *volunteer* position? See *Potter v. Rowe*, [1990] B.C.J. No. 2912 (S.C.) (QL).

6. As previously observed, a distinction was previously drawn between *direct interference* and *indirect interference* with contractual relations: *DC Thomson & Co. Ltd. v. Deakin*, [1952] Ch. 646; and *GWK Ltd. v. Dunlop Rubber Co. Ltd.* (1926), 42 T.L.R. 376. Direct interference occurred if the defendant persuaded a third party to breach its agreement with the defendant. In that event, the defendant's actions did not have to be wrongful in addition to inducing the breach of contract. In contrast, indirect interference occurred if the defendant made it impossible for a third party to perform its agreement with the plaintiff. In that event, the defendant's actions had to be wrongful even from the fact that they entailed a contractual breach.

The House of Lords abandoned the idea of *indirect* interference with contractual relations in *OBG Ltd. v. Allan*, [2008] 1 A.C. 1 (H.L.). As a result, there is now only one species of interference with contractual relations. As was alleged in *Lumley v. Gye*, the defendant must have directly induced a breach of contract. That tort entails a form of accessory liability. The party in breach of the contract is primarily liable; the defendant in tort is secondarily liable as a result of its participation in the underlying wrong.

In contrast, according to *OBG*, situations that previously might have been redressed through the tort of indirect interference with contractual relations ought to be analyzed in terms of the distinct *unlawful means tort*. That tort is discussed in the next section of this chapter. Consider, for instance, a case in which the defendant intentionally causes the plaintiff harm by stealing tools that belong to the plaintiff's employees. The employees obviously may have rights against the defendant. More importantly for present purposes, the defendant incurs a form of *primary* liability to the plaintiff as a result of acting in an unlawful manner against the third party employees.

As Lord Hoffmann observed in *OBG*, those two forms of liability — direct and indirect — historically evolved along different lines, but were bound together, during the 20th century, under a single "unified" tort of interference with contractual relations. The explanation largely lies in the fact that courts lost sight of the *unlawful means tort* as an independent head of liability. That was true even though it served different interests and operated according to different rationale.

By 2007, the mis-step had become clear and it was possible for the House of Lords to make a clear break. In *OBG* (at paras. 8, 32), Lord Hoffmann distinguished between the unlawful means tort and "*Lumley v. Gye*" (as he referred to the tort of direct interference with contractual relations) and identified four crucial differences.

> First, unlawful means is a tort of primary liability, not requiring a wrongful act by anyone else, while *Lumley v Gye* created accessory liability, dependent upon the primary wrongful act of the contracting party. Secondly, unlawful means requires the use of means which are unlawful under some other rule ("independently unlawful") whereas liability under *Lumley v Gye* . . . requires only the degree of participation in the breach of contract which satisfies the general requirements of accessory liability for the wrongful act of another person. . . . Thirdly, liability for unlawful means does not depend upon the existence of contractual relations. It is sufficient that the intended consequence of the wrongful act is damage in any form; for example, to the claimant's economic expectations. . . . Fourthly, although both are described as torts of intention . . . the *results* which the defendant must have intended are different. In

unlawful means the defendant must have intended to cause damage to the claimant (although usually this will be . . . a means of enhancing his own economic position). Because damage to economic expectations is sufficient to found a claim, there need not have been any intention to cause a breach of contract or interfere with contractual rights. Under *Lumley v Gye*, on the other hand, an intention to cause a breach of contract is both necessary and sufficient. Necessary, because this is essential for liability as accessory to the breach. Sufficient, because the fact that the defendant did not intend to cause damage, or even thought that the breach of contract would make the claimant better off, is irrelevant.

Lumley v Gye was founded on a different principle of liability than the intentional harm tort. It treats contractual rights as a species of property which deserve special protection, not only by giving a right of action against the party who breaks his contract but by imposing secondary liability on a person who procures him to do so. In this respect it is quite distinct from the unlawful means principle, which is concerned only with intention and wrongfulness and is indifferent as to the nature of the interest which is damaged.

As will be seen in the next section of this chapter, Canadian courts have largely adopted the unlawful means tort that was formulated in *OBG*: *A.I. Enterprises Ltd. v. Bram Enterprises Ltd.*, 2014 SCC 12; *Correia v. Canac Kitchens* (2008), 91 O.R. (3d) 353 (C.A.); and *Alleslev-Krofchak v. Valcom Ltd.* (2010), 322 D.L.R. (4th) 193 (Ont. C.A.). The logic of Lord Hoffmann's analysis, of course, means that courts in this country similarly should abandon the idea of *indirect* interference with contractual relations by unlawful means.

7. The tort recognized in *Lumley v. Gye* often is discussed in terms of "inducing breach of contract." It occasionally has been held, however, that liability should be possible if the defendant *interferes* with an agreement between the plaintiff and a third party, but does not actually go so far as to induce a breach. See *Stratford (J.T.) & Son Ltd. v. Lindley*, [1965] A.C. 269 (H.L.); *Emerald Const. Co. v. Lowthian*, [1966] 1 All E.R. 1013 (C.A.); *Merkur Island Shipping Corp. v. Laughton*, [1983] 2 A.C. 570 (H.L.); *Potechin v. Yashin* (2000), 186 D.L.R. (4th) 757 (Ont. S.C.J.); *College of Dental Surgeons (Saskatchewan) v. Thorvaldson* (1991), 93 Sask. R. 22 (C.A.); *Mark Fishing Company Ltd. v. United Fishermen and Allied Workers Union* (1972), 24 D.L.R. (3d) 585 (B.C.C.A.); *Saskatchewan v. Eacom Timber Corp.*, 2012 SKQB 226; *Moulton Contracting Ltd. v. British Columbia*, 2013 BCSC 2348; and *Garry v. Sherritt Gordon Mines Ltd.* (1987), 59 Sask. R. 104 (C.A.). *Torquay Hotel Co. v. Cousins*, [1969] 1 All E.R. 522 at 530 (C.A.), provides an illustration. Esso Petroleum Co. had a contractual obligation to provide oil to the plaintiff hotel. After the plaintiff became embroiled in an ugly labour dispute, the defendant union executive contacted Esso and advised it that it should not cross a picket line in order to deliver oil to the plaintiff. Esso complied and the plaintiff had difficulty securing a supply from other sources. When the dust settled, the plaintiff sued the defendant for interference with contractual relations. Significantly, however, the defendant had not caused Esso to *breach* its agreement with the plaintiff. That agreement contained a *force majeure* clause that exempted Esso from liability with respect to losses arising from labour disputes. Lord Denning nevertheless held the defendant responsible in tort. The tort, he said, extended to any situation in which the defendant "prevents or hinders one party from performing his contract, even though it be not a breach."

That extension of the tort attracted criticism. See Burns, "Tort Injury to Economic Interests: Some Facets of Legal Response" (1980) 58 Can. Bar Rev. 103 at 114-25; Richardson, "Interference with Contractual Relations: Is *Torquay Hotel* the Law in Canada?" (1983) 41 U.T. Fac. L. Rev. 1; and Carty, "Unlawful Interference with Trade" (1983) 3 J. Legal Stud. 193. In *OBG, supra*, the House of Lords agreed that Lord Denning had indeed gone too far. While acts falling short of inducing a breach of contract may be actionable under the *unlawful means tort*, they logically are irrelevant to the action that was formulated in *Lumley v. Gye*. Lord Hoffmann explained (at para. 44) that "one cannot be liable for inducing a breach unless there has been a breach. No secondary liability without primary liability." Canadian courts have not yet resolved the issue.

8. Certain circumstances frequently generate liability under the tort of interference with contractual relations. An employee who leaves a company to develop a new business invites trouble by pressuring former colleagues to join the new venture: *Prim8 Group Inc. v. Tisi*, 2016 ONSC 5662. In addition, the tort often places certain types of people in precarious positions. Lawyers occasionally are asked for advice as to whether a contract ought to be performed. If the lawyer responds in a way that is interpreted as an inducement to breach, liability might be imposed. Likewise, a corporate director might form the opinion that it would not be in the company's best interest to perform a contract. In recognition of those potential dilemmas, courts generally refrain from imposing liability for advice or decisions taken in good faith. See *369413 Alberta Ltd. v. Pocklington*, 2007 ABCA 307; *Bank of Nova Scotia v. Black River Logging Inc.*, 2011 ONSC 6165; *Spectra Architectural Group Ltd. v. Eldred Sollows Consulting Ltd.* (1991), 7 C.C.L.T. (2d) 169 (Alta. Master); *Brae Centre Ltd. v. 1044807 Alberta Ltd., supra*; and Welling, "Individual Liability for Corporate Acts: The Defence of Hobson's Choice" (2000) 12 S.C.L.R. (2d) 55. The issue arose in *Heydary Hamilton PC v. Muhammad*, 2013 ONSC 4938, appeal dismissed as abandoned 2014 ONCA 84. The defendant law firm provided advice to a client who was disputing a bill received from the plaintiff law firm. Morgan J. denied the possibility of relief by saying that "[s]ince there is nothing unlawful about advising a client to assess its former law firm's fees and to challenge the enforceability of its retainer agreement, there can be no tort of inducing breach of contract or interference with economic relations" (at para. 24).

9. Liability may be defeated by the defence of *justification*. Not surprisingly, however, the courts are reluctant to accept an argument that the defendant was justified in inducing a third party to break a contract with the plaintiff. Consequently, the defence seldom succeeds. Although they have not devised any clear tests, the courts generally consider several factors, including the nature of the breached contract, the nature of the breach, the relationship between the various parties, the defendant's motivation, and the means by which the breach was procured: *Glamorgan Coal Co. v. South Wales Miner's Federation*, [1903] 2 K.B. 545 at 573-74 (C.A.), aff'd [1905] A.C. 239 (H.L.). The cases fall into two groups, depending upon the nature of the purported justification.

Self-interest can provide a justification only if the defendant's own rights were in jeopardy. Liability was denied, for instance, after a waste management company persuaded a customer to renew its existing contract rather than honour an agreement to provide business to a competitor: *Johnson v. BFI Canada Inc.* (2010), 78 C.C.L.T.

(3d) 66 (Man. C.A.). See also *Franklin Supply Co. v. Midco Supply Co.* (1995), 33 Alta. L.R. (3d) 362 (Q.B.); and *Rogers Cable TV Ltd. v. 373041 Ontario Ltd.* (1996), 69 C.P.R. (3d) 85 (Ont. Gen. Div.). Self-interest will not provide a defence, however, if the defendant simply acted in pursuit of some general *interest* (as when a person steals away an employee from a competitor and claims that the deed was done in the name of "freedom of contract").

Public interest and morality may provide a justification for otherwise tortious conduct. Liability therefore may be denied if the defendant's purpose in persuading a third party to breach a contract with the plaintiff was to draw attention to environmental destruction or exploitation of migrant workers, for example. So too if a government agency intervenes to prevent performance of a contract that would violate a statute or regulation: *Atcheson v. College of Physicians and Surgeons (Alta.)* (1994), 148 A.R. 395 (Q.B.). More intimately, it previously was suggested that a father would be justified in persuading his daughter to break off her engagement to a cad: *Crofter Hand Woven Harris Tweed Co. v. Veitch*, [1942] A.C. 435 (H.L.). In such circumstances, however, the court may deny the defence if the same objectives could have been pursued or secured through lawful means. See generally *Brimelow v. Casson*, [1924] 1 Ch. 302; and *Verchere v. Greenpeace Canada Ltd., supra.* For a discussion of the relationship between intent and justification, see *Babcock v. Carr; Babcock v. Archibald* (1981), 34 O.R. (2d) 65 (H.C.); *Thermo King Corp. v. Provincial. Bank of Can.* (1981), 34 O.R. (2d) 369 (C.A.); and *Bank of N.S. v. Gaudreau* (1984), 48 O.R. (2d) 478 (H.C.).

A final form of protection appears in *Mainstream Properties Limited (Appellants) v. Young*, [2008] 1 A.C. 1 (H.L.), which was included in the House of Lords' judgment in *OBG Ltd. v. Allen.* Two directors of a company approached the defendant seeking funds for a new business venture. The defendant asked whether that venture would place the directors into a conflict of interest by requiring them to breach their contracts of employment. They untruthfully told him that their employer already had declined the opportunity to pursue the venture and that there consequently was no problem. The defendant financed the new venture but was later sued by the employer. The House of Lords held that he was not liable. Even if his belief in the directors' assertions had been "muddle-headed and illogical," it was honest. An honest belief in the legality of a venture is sufficient to preclude liability.

10. For an interesting contrast between the alleged tortious interference of governmental and private sector actors, see *Cheticamp Fisheries Co-operative Ltd. v. Canada* (1994), 134 N.S.R. (2d) 13 (T.D.), rev'd (1995), 139 N.S.R. (2d) 224 (C.A.); and *A. & B. Sound Ltd. v. Future Shop Ltd.* (1995), 25 C.C.L.T. (2d) 1 (B.C.S.C.).

11. The tort of interference with contractual relations is actionable only upon proof of loss. It logically follows that relief usually consists of compensatory damages. See for example *Grand Financial Management Inc. v. Solemio Transportation Inc.*, 2016 ONCA 175; and *Colborne Capital Corp. v. 542775 Alberta Ltd.*, [1999] 8 W.W.R. 222 (Alta. C.A.). Of course, while the plaintiff also is free to bring a contractual claim against the party that actually breached the agreement, double recovery is impermissible. The availability of the tort action nevertheless may be significant in a variety of circumstances. The contractual counterparty may be insolvent, absent, protected by a limitation clause, or otherwise unable to be sued. So too, in certain situations, compensation may be assessed more generously in tort than in contract:

Vale v. International Longshoremen's and Warehousemen's Union Local 508 (1979), 12 B.C.L.R. 249 (C.A.).

The option of suing for the tort may also be significant if the plaintiff seeks punitive damages. While such relief is available in both tort and contract, additional hurdles must be cleared if the plaintiff sues for breach of contract: *Whiten v. Pilot Insurance Co.*, 2002 SCC 18.

Similarly, while disgorgement theoretically is possible in both categories of claim, it generally enjoys broader scope in tort than in contract: *Blake v. Attorney General*, [2001] 1 A.C. 268 (H.L.). Moreover, while precedent is sparse, there is positive authority for allowing purely gain-based relief under the tort of interfering with contractual relations: *Federal Sugar Refining Co. v. United States Sugar Equalization Bd.*, 268 F. 575 (S.D. N.Y. 1920). Suggest a situation in which the plaintiff would prefer disgorgement to compensation.

12. Quite often, the same facts will support various claims by the same plaintiff. See for example *Daishowa Inc. v. Friends of the Lubicon* (1998), 39 O.R. (3d) 620 (Gen. Div.) which involved allegations of interference with contractual relations, interference with economic relations, intimidation, conspiracy, and defamation. As a general rule, the plaintiff is, of course, entitled to plead in the alternative: *Enviro-Tex Products Ltd. v. Fibrex Insulations Inc.* (2006), 80 O.R. (3d) 641 (C.A.). See also *Roman Corp. v. Hudson's Bay Oil & Gas Co.*, [1973] S.C.R. 820; and *Lysko v. Braley* (2006), 79 O.R. (3d) 721 (C.A.).

13. See generally Herschorn, "Some Recent Decisions on the Element of Unlawfulness in Intentional Torts" (2011) 90 Can. Bar Rev. 645; MacKenzie, "Shifting Blame: Reassessing the Tort of Inducing Breach of Contract Following *A.I. Enterprises v. Bram*" [2016] Ann. Rev. Civ. Lit. 245; Carty, *An Analysis of the Economic Torts* (2011), ch. 3; and Burns & Blom, *Economic Interests in Canadian Tort Law*, 2d ed. (2016), ch. 3.

7. The Unlawful Means Tort

As observed in the preceding section, much of the confusion regarding the scope of the tort of interference with contractual relations (or "inducing breach of contract" as it commonly is called) has now been eliminated. In *OBG Ltd. v. Allan*, [2008] 1 A.C. 1 (H.L.), Lord Hoffmann held that that tort contains one branch, not two. The tort in *Lumley v. Gye* (1853), 118 E.R. 749 (Q.B.) occurs when the defendant *directly* induces a third party to breach a contractual obligation owed to the plaintiff. In contrast, Lord Hoffmann insisted that *Lumley v. Gye* is inapplicable if the defendant does something that *indirectly* causes a third party to breach its contract with the plaintiff (as when the defendant steals tools used by the plaintiff's employees and thereby prevents them from performing their job). Such situations, he explained, must be addressed instead by the *unlawful means tort*.

Until recently, the unlawful means tort was not clearly isolated and identified, and even today, it is not well understood. The roots of the tort reach back hundreds of years, but it was only at the turn of the twenty-first century that lower courts began the difficult task of explaining the concept. In England, that problem was overcome by Lord Hoffmann's masterful judgment in *OBG*, which elucidated the tort's rationale and authoritatively stated its elements. Cromwell J. provided a similar service for Canadian law in *A.I. Enterprises Ltd. v. Bram Enterprises Ltd.*

A.I. ENTERPRISES LTD. v. BRAM ENTERPRISES LTD.
2014 SCC 12

[An apartment building was owned by a company called Joyce Avenue Apartments Ltd. ("Joyce Ltd."). Joyce Ltd. was owned, through corporate entities, by Lillian Schelew and her four sons: Jeffrey, Michael, Bernard, and Allan. More precisely, 40% of Joyce Ltd. was owned by Bram Enterprises Ltd.; another 40% was owned by Jamb Enterprises Ltd.; and the remaining 20% was owned by A.I. Enterprises Ltd. All five family members owned shares in Bram and Jamb, but Allan alone served as shareholder and director of A.I.]

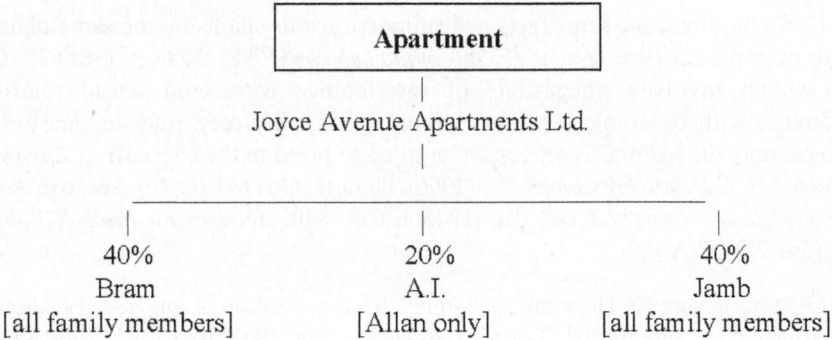

Joyce Ltd., Bram, Jamb, and A.I. entered into a Syndication Agreement. That contract stated that the apartment building could be sold if a majority of the interests in Bram, Jamb, and A.I. wished to do so, but the agreement gave a dissenting party the right of first refusal at fair market value.

A family squabble erupted in 2000. All of the parties, except A.I. and Allan, wished to sell the property. A.I. and Allan were given the opportunity to buy at the appraised price, but they declined to do so. The other parties accordingly brought the property onto the open market. Over the next sixteen months, four potential buyers came forward, but none actually agreed to buy. A.I. finally purchased the apartment for $2.2M.

The other parties then sued A.I. and Allan. The gist of the claim was that A.I. and Allan had engaged in a course of unlawful conduct that prevented the property from being sold to any of the prospective outside purchasers. The plaintiffs argued that they lost approximately $400,000 in sale proceeds as a result.

The trial judge (2010 NBQB 245) held that the plaintiffs had established the tort of "interference by unlawful means" because the defendants had (1) mis-used an arbitration clause contained in the Syndication Agreement in order to delay an outside sale, (2) asserted groundless defences in connection with a Notice of Right of First Refusal that they registered against the property, (3) filed a baseless Certificate of Pending Litigation against the property, and (4) barred prospective purchasers from entering the premises. The defendants' acts were unlawful, the trial judge held, because they were performed without legal justification. In the alternative, the trial judge held, Allan's actions constituted a breach of the fiduciary duty that he owed as a director of Bram and Jamb.

The New Brunswick Court of Appeal (2012 NBCA 33) dismissed the defendants' appeal, but adopted a different model of the "unlawful means tort" as a result of its reading of *OBG*. As Robertson J.A. explained, there are two views of "unlawful means." The broad view encompasses, *inter alia*, common law torts, statutory torts, crimes, breaches of contract, breaches of trust and other equitable obligations, and breaches of confidence. The narrow view, as championed by Lord Hoffmann in *OBG*, is confined to instances in which the defendant breaches a civil obligation (as in tort or contract) owed to a third party, such that the third party would enjoy a right of action against the defendant (or at least would do so if it suffered a loss as a result of the defendant's actions). Robertson J.A. preferred the narrow approach as a matter of law, but held that it could not be satisfied on the facts because the defendants had not done anything that would support a right of action by the prospective purchasers. He nevertheless imposed liability on the basis of a "principled exception" to the general test of unlawful means. By analogy to the tort of abuse of process, that exception applies if the defendant deliberately acts contrary to the plaintiff's interests by fabricating legal arguments.

The defendants further appealed the matter to the Supreme Court of Canada.]

CROMWELL J.: . . .

[2] While this tort is far from new, its scope is unsettled and needs clarification. There is not even any generally accepted nomenclature for the tort. It is variously referred to as "unlawful interference with economic relations", "interference with a trade or business by unlawful means", "intentional interference with economic relations", or simply "causing loss by unlawful means". I will refer to it by either the latter name or simply as the "unlawful means" tort. . . .

A. What Is the Scope of Liability for the Tort of Causing Loss by Unlawful Means?

What Sorts of Conduct Are Considered "Unlawful" for the Purposes of This Tort?

[23] The unlawful means tort creates a type of "parasitic" liability in a three-party situation: it allows a plaintiff to sue a defendant for economic loss resulting from the defendant's unlawful act against a third party. Liability to the plaintiff is based on (or parasitic upon) the defendant's unlawful act against the third party. While the elements of the tort have been described in a number of ways, its core captures the intentional infliction of economic injury on C (the plaintiff) by A (the defendant)'s use of unlawful means against B (the third party). . . . There is no dispute here that this is an intentional tort; the focus of the dispute in this case is on the unlawful means element.

[24] An old case will serve as an example. The defendant, the master of a trading ship, fired its cannons at a canoe that was attempting to trade with its competitor, the plaintiffs' trading ship, in order to prevent it from doing so. The defendant was held liable, Lord Kenyon being of the opinion that these facts supported an action: *Tarleton v. M'Gawley* (1793) 170 E.R. 153. The plaintiffs were able to recover damages for the economic injury resulting from the defendant's wrongful conduct toward third parties (the occupants of the canoe) which had been committed with the intention of inflicting economic injury on the plaintiffs.

[25] The question of what sort of conduct constitutes the necessary unlawful means is important. It has been described as the most important question concerning this tort. . . . Giving the concept of "unlawful means" a "sound, economically relevant and judicially supported interpretation" is "[t]he key to keeping the economic torts in

harmony with contemporary legal values": *No. 1 Collision Repair & Painting (1982) Ltd. v. Insurance Corp. of British Columbia* 2000 BCCA 463 at para. 19. . . .

[26] The scope of the unlawful means tort depends on the answers to three questions. First, does the unlawful conduct have to be actionable by the person at whom it is immediately directed? In my view, the conduct must be an actionable civil wrong or conduct that would be actionable if it had caused loss to the person at whom it was directed. Second, is there a requirement that the unlawful means not be otherwise actionable by the plaintiff? I propose to answer this question "no". Third, should the definition of "unlawful means" be subject to principled exceptions? I would also answer this question in the negative. While the approach outlined by these answers leaves only a narrow scope for liability, my view is that it is most consistent with the history and rationale of the tort as well as with its place in the modern scheme of liability for causing economic harm.

[27] I will turn first to my understanding of these broader concerns and a review of the relevant law before returning to the reasons for my conclusions.

(a) The Economic Torts and the Common Law

. . .

[29] The scope of the unlawful means tort should be understood in the context of the broad outlines of tort law's approach to regulating economic and competitive activity. Several aspects of that approach support adopting a narrow scope for the unlawful means tort: the common law accords less protection to purely economic interests; it is reluctant to develop rules to enforce fair competition; it is concerned not to undermine certainty in commercial affairs; and the history of the common law shows that tort liability, if unduly expanded, may undermine fundamental rights.. . .

(b) Rationale of the Unlawful Means Tort

[36] As Hazel Carty wisely said, "the scope of this tort can only be established by clarifying its rationale so that there is a principled definition of unlawful means": *An Analysis of the Economic Torts* (2nd ed.), at p. 102. Unfortunately, there is no consensus about what that rationale is or should be. . . . But, although there may be no clear rationale as a matter of historical fact, we can consider what rationale best reflects the modern role that the tort should play in the broader scheme of civil liability.

[37] There are several possible rationales for the tort but they are mostly variations on two themes. . . . The first — what I will call the "intentional harm" rationale — focuses on the fact that harm has been intentionally inflicted. This rationale supports the creation of new tort liabilities in order to reach clearly excessive and unacceptable intentional conduct. . . . The second, and in my view the preferred rationale, focuses on extending an existing right to sue from the immediate victim of the unlawful act to another party whom the defendant intended to target with the unlawful conduct. I will call this the "liability stretching" rationale. The focus of the tort on this understanding is not on enlarging the basis of civil liability, but on allowing those intentionally targeted by already actionable wrongs to sue for the resulting harm. On either rationale, the tort is, at its core, a tort of intention. The main difference is that on the "intentional harm" rationale, the intention requirement is seen as the main limitation on the potential scope of liability, whereas in the "liability stretching" rationale, the potential scope of liability is limited by both the intention

requirement and the more restrictive definition of the conduct which will support liability. . . .

[40] The intentional harm rationale supports a broader understanding of the unlawful means requirement. Under this rationale, the tortfeasor's conduct must rise to a level of wrongfulness that amounts to cheating or upsetting the fundamental rules of market competition. Such conduct clearly encompasses torts and crimes but not conduct that is simply *ultra vires* or morally objectionable. . . . The unlawfulness requirement exists mainly to provide some broad outer limit for the judicial discretion to impose liability.

[41] This understanding of the tort is attractive because it provides a principled explanation for why liability should be imposed and one that accords with widely held views of commercial morality. While no person has a common law right to trade *per se*, a person does have a general freedom to participate in the commercial and labour market and a legitimate expectation that the basic rules of the game will be respected. To the extent that the defendant intentionally inflicts economic loss on the plaintiff through unlawful means which are clearly off-side those basic rules, the defendant gains an illegitimate advantage and causes the plaintiff to suffer an unfair disadvantage.

[42] However, for several reasons, I do not accept . . . the intentional harm rationale [which] would lead to an unwieldy concept of "unlawful means" and thus to undue uncertainty in commercial affairs. . . .

[43] This brings me to the rationale I prefer. The liability stretching rationale sees the tort as extending civil liability without creating new actionable wrongs. It thereby closes a perceived liability gap where the wrongdoer's acts in relation to a third party, which are in breach of established legal obligations to that third party, intentionally target the injured plaintiff: . . . . The liability stretching rationale underlies Lord Hoffmann's speech on behalf of the majority in *OBG* [and] commands considerable (although far from unanimous) support among commentators. . . .

[44] Why do I favour the liability stretching rationale? It provides a rational explanation for the expansion of tort liability which rests on pre-existing causes of action. This type of expansion provides certainty because it establishes a clear "control mechanism" on liability in this area of the law, consistent with tort law's reticence to intrude too far into the realm of competitive economic activity. . . .

[45] This rationale of the tort supports a narrow definition of "unlawful means": the tort does not seek to create new actionable wrongs but simply to expand the range of persons who may sue for harm intentionally caused by existing actionable wrongs to a third party. Thus, criminal offences and breaches of statute would not be *per se* actionable under the unlawful means tort, but the tort would be available if, under common law principles, those acts also give rise to a civil action by the third party and interfered with the plaintiff's economic activity. For example, crimes such as assault and theft would be actionable by a third party in the torts of trespass to the person and conversion. But other breaches of criminal or regulatory law will not give rise to a civil action and there will be therefore no potential liability under the unlawful means tort. This approach avoids "tortifying" the criminal and regulatory law by imposing civil liability where there would not otherwise be any. . . . The two core components of the unlawful means tort are thus that the defendant must use unlawful means, in the narrow sense, and that the defendant must intend to harm the plaintiff through the use of the unlawful means. . . .

(c) Review of the Jurisprudence

[50] The case law does not form a tidy package of consistent approaches. But on balance it favours a narrow approach to the unlawful means requirement.

(i) England and Wales

[51] The leading case on the unlawful means tort in England is the decision of the House of Lords in *OBG*. Lord Hoffmann, for the majority, adopted a narrow definition of "unlawful means". The plaintiff will have a claim only where the wrong to the third party would have been actionable at the instance of that third party. . . . The only exception identified by Lord Hoffmann to this narrow view was that the defendant would still be liable if the third party would have had an action but for the fact that he or she had suffered no loss. This exception is tailored to capture facts where the loss is suffered by the plaintiff rather than the third party, as where, for example, the defendant intimidates the third party into acting to the detriment of the plaintiff. Lord Hoffmann added a further requirement to his definition of "unlawful means": the unlawful means must interfere with the third party's "freedom to deal with the claimant": para. 51. The plaintiff must therefore have an economic interest at stake in the interference by the defendant with the third party.

[52] The majority in *OBG* rejected the much broader view of unlawful means adopted by Lord Nicholls. On that wider view, "unlawful means" comprise "all acts which a person is not permitted to do. The distinction is between 'doing what you have a legal right to do and doing what you have no legal right to do'": para. 150.. . . "Unlawful means" include common law torts, statutory torts, crimes, breaches of contract, breaches of trust and equitable obligations, breaches of confidence, and so on: para. 150. To this broad definition of "unlawful means", Lord Nicholls added the requirement that the plaintiff must be harmed through the "instrumentality" of the third party: paras. 159-60. . . .

(iv) United States

[56] The approach in several states of the United States departs markedly from the commonwealth jurisprudence. In many states, liability is imposed where the defendant's conduct is "improper". In the several states that follow the *Restatement of the Law, Second: Torts 2d* (1989), this is determined by reference to a combination of factors including the defendant's motive, the nature of the plaintiff's interest, and the social value of the defendant's conduct. . . . The lack of an "unlawful means" requirement in most U.S. states has been criticized as creating commercial uncertainty . . . . Given the fundamentally different paths which Anglo-Canadian and American tort law have taken on this subject, there is no need to examine the American jurisprudence in greater detail here. It is sufficient to note that the feared dangers associated with a broad approach to this tort appear to have materialized.

(v) Canada

. . .

[68] While the economic torts may sometimes develop along parallel lines, they have distinct historical roots and roles to play in the regulation of the modern marketplace. So, for example, this Court in *Central Canada Potash* accepted the proposition that a narrower definition of "unlawful means" applies in the two-party intimidation tort than in the three-party intimidation tort. This suggests that there is

no general requirement of consistency in the elements of the economic torts. Similarly, the House of Lords accepted the need for different definitions of "unlawful means" for the unlawful means and conspiracy torts in *Total Network*. As Lord Mance put it, "the two torts are different in their nature, and the interests of justice may require their development on somewhat different bases": at para. 123. . . . Moreover, it may well be that the presence of an agreement in the tort of conspiracy justifies a different and broader definition of "unlawful means" for the tort of "unlawful means" conspiracy than is appropriate for the unlawful means tort. This is illustrated by the Court's retention, although as an anomaly, of the so-called predominant purpose conspiracy tort on the basis that the fact of agreement between conspirators (or "combination") could itself justify imposing liability.. . .

[71]   The unlawful means tort has been addressed by many appellate courts across the country. . . . In decisions that address the unlawful means component, there has been a general trend towards a narrower understanding of it. Earlier cases such as *Reach M.D. Inc. v. Pharmaceutical Manufacturers Association of Canada* (2003), 65 O.R. (3d) 30 (C.A.), had advanced a broad definition of "unlawful means" that included any act the defendant "is not at liberty to commit. . . . However, *Reach* has been narrowed by subsequent decisions: *Drouillard v. Cogeco Cable Inc.*, 2007 ONCA 322 . . .; *Correia v. Canac Kitchens*, 2008 ONCA 506. . . . The Ontario Court of Appeal has confirmed that it "has now opted for the Lord Hoffmann side of the debate" in *OBG* and adopted the narrow definition of "unlawful means": see *Alleslev-Krofchak v. Valcom Ltd.*, 2010 ONCA 557 at paras. 57 and 63. . . .

Is the Tort Available Only if There Is no Other Cause of Action Available to the Plaintiff Against the Defendant in Relation to the Alleged Misconduct?

[77]   The appellants urge us to hold that the unlawful means tort, because it has a gap-filling function, should only be available where the defendant's conduct does not provide the plaintiff with any other cause of action against the defendant. This was the view of the Court of Appeal in this case and this view has also been adopted by the Ontario Court of Appeal and followed by other Canadian courts. . . . The question is whether we should accept this limitation on the scope of the unlawful means tort. My view is that, for several reasons, we should not.

[78]   This limitation seems to me to be wrong in principle. The gist of the tort is the targeting of the plaintiff by the defendant through the instrumentality of unlawful acts against a third party. It is that conduct by the defendant which gives rise to liability quite apart from conduct that may be otherwise actionable by the plaintiff. Moreover, general principles of tort liability accept concurrent liability and overlapping causes of action for distinct wrongs suffered by the plaintiff in respect of the same incident. . . .

Should the "Unlawfulness" Requirement Be Subject to Principled Exceptions?

[83]   The Court of Appeal, while adopting a narrow view of the unlawful means requirement, held that it must be subject to principled exceptions. The court found that this case falls within such an exception because the appellants' conduct was akin to the tort of abuse of process. As Robertson J.A. put it for the court, "the intentional erection of legal barriers, some of which are enforceable through statutory processes not subject to prior judicial authorization, in circumstances where those barriers rest on rights fabricated with arguments of sand" falls within the ambit of the unlawful means tort: para. 82. This approach was intended to provide judges with some "wiggle

room" to respond "adequately" to unanticipated factual scenarios or changing circumstances: para. 81.

[84] I respectfully disagree with this approach and would hold that there are no exceptions to the scope of liability which I propose for the unlawful means tort.

[85] My difficulty with the "principled exception" approach is that I cannot, with respect, find any principle on which it is based. Providing trial judges with "wiggle room" to deal "adequately" with cases that do not fall within the scope of the tort's liability simply confers an unstructured judicial discretion to do what appears to the particular judge to be just in the particular circumstances. [I]t would largely undercut the efforts to give a certain and narrow ambit to the tort. Allowing for exceptions without clearly outlining the principles to guide the development of the law invites the danger of *ad hoc* decisions tailored to achieve a vision of commercial morality — precisely the danger which the unlawful means requirement is meant to avoid.

[86] I conclude that for the purposes of the unlawful means tort, the defendant's means are "unlawful" if they support a civil action for damages or compensation by the third party, or would do so except for the fact that the third party did not suffer any loss as a result of the defendant's acts. . . .

Application to This Case

[88] The Court of Appeal concluded that there was no wrong that would be actionable by the third party (the prospective purchasers) against the appellants, and the respondents do not point to one: at paras. 79 and 83.

[89] Accordingly, I conclude that the appellants cannot be found liable to the respondents on the basis of the unlawful means tort.

B. Did the Court of Appeal Err in Finding That the Defendants Had the Required Knowledge for the Unlawful Means Tort?

[90] The trial judge found that the appellants had unlawfully interfered with the sale of the property in various ways. The appellants contend, however, that none of this activity can sustain liability because there was no proof that they had appropriate knowledge of the existence of any business relationship between the respondents and prospective purchasers. The appellants submit that they must be shown to have had actual knowledge of the relationship between prospective purchasers . . . and the respondents and that the record does not support such a finding.. . .

[92] In my opinion, the appellants' submission is premised on a faulty view of the elements of the unlawful means tort.

[93] I do not agree with the Court of Appeal that the existence of a valid business relationship between the plaintiff and the third party and the defendant's knowledge of that relationship are essential elements of the unlawful means tort. The inclusion of these elements in my view flows from confusion between the unlawful means tort and the tort of inducing breach of contract. It is now commonly accepted that for the latter, the plaintiff must prove that the defendant actually understood that he or she was procuring a breach of contract. . . . The position is different, however, in the unlawful means tort, the focus of which is unlawful conduct that intentionally harms the plaintiff's economic interests. There need be no contract or even other formal dealings between the plaintiff and the third party so long as the defendant's conduct is unlawful and it intentionally harms the plaintiff's economic interests. In this case, it was more than sufficient that the appellants were shown to know that "various persons were negotiating with the majority of investors" for the purchase of the

premises and that the allegedly unlawful acts were committed with the intention to cause economic harm to the respondents. . . .

[95] . . . It is the intentional targeting of the plaintiff by the defendant that justifies stretching the defendant's liability so as to afford the plaintiff a cause of action. It is not sufficient that the harm to the plaintiff be an incidental consequence of the defendant's conduct, even where the defendant realizes that it is extremely likely that harm to the plaintiff may result. Such incidental economic harm is an accepted part of market competition. . . .

[97] In my view, this narrow approach to intention is consistent both with the policy concerns relevant to this area of law as well as the underlying "liability stretching" rationale for the tort. It is an important safeguard against attaching liability to vigorous but lawful competitive behaviour. Economic harm to a competitor is often a foreseeable consequence of such behaviour. Mere foreseeability of such harm does not meet the requirement for intention in the unlawful means tort.

[Liability under the unlawful means tort was not supported by the facts. Cromwell J., however, did find that Allan was liable for breach of the fiduciary duty that he owed as a director of Bram and Jamb. He also found that A.I. was liable under the equitable actions for knowing assistance and knowing receipt insofar as it participated in Allan's fiduciary breach and received the benefit of that wrong.]

NOTES AND QUESTIONS

1. Old habits die hard. Despite the Supreme Court of Canada's excellent judgment, many lower courts continue to refer to the tort of "intentional interference with economic relations," either alongside references to the "unlawful means tort" or in disregard of the preferred phrase. Aside from complicating the search for relevant cases, that practice militates against the development of clear and consistent principles. See *Correct Building Corp. v. Lehman*, 2018 ONCA 462; *Low v. Pfizer Canada Inc.*, 2015 BCCA 506; *Grand Financial Management Inc. v. Solemio Transportation Inc.*, 2016 ONCA 175; and *First Choice Outfitters Ltd. v. Neilly*, 2014 SKCA 55.

2. Cromwell J. described the unlawful means tort as a "type of 'parasitic' liability in a three-party situation." How did the plaintiffs believe that the tort applied on the facts of *Bram Enterprises*? Identify the participants in the "three-party situation." In what sense is liability "parasitic"? If the defendant's wrong is against the plaintiff, rather than the third party, the unlawful means tort obviously is unavailable: *Kaptor Financial Inc. v. Alexander*, 2014 ONSC 2185; and *Szecsodi v. MGM Resorts International*, 2014 ONSC 1323.

3. Describe the two rationales that Cromwell J. considered in connection with the unlawful means test. Which rationale did he adopt? What explanation did he provide for that decision?

4. For the purposes of the unlawful means tort, how did Lord Hoffmann and Lord Nicholls define the concept of "unlawful" in *OBG*? What definition did Cromwell J. adopt in *Bram Enterprises*? What did Cromwell J. mean when he warned

against the dangers of "tortifying" criminal and regulatory rules? Did the facts of *Bram Enterprises* involve unlawful conduct?

As Cromwell J. mentioned, prior to *Bram Enterprises* Canadian courts struggled with the scope of the concept of unlawfulness. One of the most significant decisions at the turn of the century was *Reach MD Inc. v. Pharmaceutical Manufacturers Association of Canada* (2003), 227 D.L.R. (4th) 458 (Ont. C.A.). The plaintiff sold calendars, which featured the cartoon character Herman, to health care professionals. The venture was remarkably successful, largely because the calendars also contained advertisements that had been purchased by drug companies. The plaintiff's business suffered a devastating blow, however, when its calendars caught the defendant's attention. The defendant was an organization of companies involved in the drug industry. It told its members that the advertisements contravened its Code of Conduct. In fact, that was not true. While the defendant *could* have prohibited its members from purchasing advertising space in the plaintiff's calendars, its Code of Conduct did not actually do so. The Ontario Court of Appeal held that the defendant was liable for the tort of "unlawfully interfering with the plaintiff's economic relations." "Unlawful" was defined, very broadly, to encompass any situation in which the defendant did something that it was not entitled to do. Since the Code of Conduct did not actually prohibit the purchase of advertising space on the calendars, the defendant did not have the authority to tell its members to stop advertising. See also *Barber v. Vrozos*, 2010 ONCA 570; *U.F.C.W., Local 1252 v. Cashin*, 2002 NFCA 48; *Tran v. Financial Debt Recovery Ltd.* (2000), 193 D.L.R. (4th) 168 (Ont. S.C.J.), set aside on other grounds (2001), 40 C.C.L.T. (3d) 106 (Ont. Div. Ct.); and *A. & B. Sound Ltd. v. Future Shop Ltd.* (1995), 25 C.C.L.T. (2d) 1 (B.C.S.C.).

The breadth of *Reach MD*, however, subsequently was cut back in other decisions of the same court. In *Alleslev-Krofchak v. Valcom Ltd.*, 2010 ONCA 557, for instance, the Ontario Court of Appeal held that the element of unlawfulness required proof that the defendant committed a civilly actionable wrong against a third party. See also *Drouillard v. Cogeco Cable*, 2007 ONCA 322. Would the defendant in *Reach MD* be liable under the test that was formulated in *Bram Enterprises*? What is the relationship between the test in *Bram Enterprises* and the test in *Alleslev-Krofchak*?

Is the test in *Bram Enterprises* satisfied if the defendant breached a contractual obligation owed to a third party or merely threatened to do so? See *Gaur v. Datta*, 2015 ONCA 151. What if the third party enjoys a statutory right of action against the defendant? See *Low v. Pfizer Canada Inc.*, 2015 BCCA 506 at para. 85 (defendant's conduct "must be actionable outside the context of the statute itself"). Can the unlawful means tort be built upon the defendant's violation of a third party's rights under the *Competition Act*? See *Godfrey v. Sony Corp.*, 2017 BCCA 302, leave to appeal granted [2017] SCCA No. 404 (matter settled before hearing); and *Watson v. Bank of America Corporation*, 2015 BCCA 362. See also *International Sausage House Ltd. v. Hammer Estate*, 2015 BCSC 1155 (slander of title arising from improper filing of caveat and certificate pending litigation against third party's land).

5. Identify and explain the "two core components of the unlawful means tort" as identified by Cromwell J.

Both elements were discussed in *Siksika Nation v. Crowchief*, 2016 ABQB 596. After many homes on the applicant's land were damaged by floods, a contractor was retained to rebuild the houses. That work was opposed by some members of the Siksika Nation, including the respondent. Together with a number of unknown associates, he created a "peaceful blockade protestion" that resulted in the contractor's employees being threatened with physical violence if they attended the worksite. Against that backdrop, the court found ample evidence that the respondent had (1) committed the torts of intimidation and inducing breach of contract against the contractor, and (2) acted with the intention of causing the applicant to suffer economic harm. She accordingly was persuaded to grant an injunction restraining the respondent from continuing his "peaceful" protest.

The unlawful means tort requires the plaintiff to prove that the defendant committed an actionable wrong against a third party. Who qualifies as a third party? Can a corporate claimant rely on wrongs that were committed against one of its own principals by the defendant? See *Rain Coast Water Corp. v. British Columbia*, 2016 BCSC 845 at para. 130.

6. Is the concept of "unlawful" defined in the same manner for the purposes of the various business torts? In that respect, is there a material difference between the unlawful means tort and the tort of conspiracy?

The House of Lords addressed that question in *Total Network SL v. Revenue and Customs Commissioners*, [2008] 1 A.C. 1174 (H.L.). Despite accepting that the concept of unlawfulness must be narrowly construed for the purposes of the unlawful means tort, the court recognized a broader conception of unlawfulness for the purposes of conspiracy. The unlawful means tort, it explained, is a form of parasitic liability. In effect, the plaintiff piggybacks on the third party's right of action against the defendant. In contrast, "a conspiracy is tortious if an intention of the conspirators was to harm the claimant by using unlawful means to persuade him to act to his own detriment, even if those means were not in themselves tortious" (at para. 44). Consequently, for example, "criminal conduct engaged in by conspirators as a means of inflicting harm on the claimant is actionable as the tort of conspiracy, whether or not that conduct, on the part of a single individual, would be actionable as some other tort. To hold otherwise would, as has often been pointed out, deprive the tort of conspiracy of any real content, since the conspirators would be joint tortfeasors in any event" (at para. 94).

7. Explain Cromwell J.'s response to the argument that the unlawful means tort is available only if the plaintiff has no other cause of action against the defendant. Is the unlawful means tort a "gap-filling" doctrine? See also *Swift Current (City) v. Saskatchewan Power Corp.* (2007), 293 Sask. R. 6 (C.A.); and *Resolute Forest Products Inc. v. 2471256 Canada Inc. (c.o.b. Greenpeace Canada)*, 2014 ONSC 3996. See also Lee, "The Unlawful Means Tort in Canada" (2014) 130 L.Q.R. 559.

8. Is the general test for the unlawful means tort subject to any "principled exceptions"? On that question, explain the difference between the views expressed in *Bram Enterprises* by Robertson J.A. and Cromwell J.

9. Explain the intent element of the unlawful means tort. Is liability possible if the defendant realized that the plaintiff's injury was a likely, but incidental, consequence of its unlawful act? Is it still accurate to say, as a matter of law, that incidental harm is an inevitable and non-actionable aspect of market competition? See generally *Frank v. Legate*, 2015 ONCA 631.

How should the following cases be decided in light of the intention requirement that was established in *Bram Enterprises*? In *Culhane v. ATP Aero Training Products*

Ltd., 2004 FC 535, aff'd 2005 FCA 129 both parties sold flight training manuals and examinations. The defendant began to offer its examinations free of charge over the Internet. It realized at the outset that it would lose profits from the sale of examinations, but it had acted with a view to increasing traffic to its website, which offered other items for sale. Unfortunately, when the defendant's examinations became available free of charge online, the plaintiff experienced a substantial loss of business. Will the plaintiff be successful under the unlawful means tort if it argues that the defendant's conduct constituted "predatory pricing" aimed at driving him out of business? In *People Recycling Inc. v. Vancouver (City)* (2002), 13 C.C.L.T. (3d) 312 (B.C.S.C.), a municipality, acting in good faith and *intra vires*, created a mandatory recycling program that it knew was almost certain to devastate the business of a private firm. Was the municipality liable under the unlawful means tort? See also *Correia v. Canac Kitchens*, 2008 ONCA 506; and *Pembina County Water Resource District v. Manitoba* (2008), 58 C.C.L.T. (3d) 137 (F.C.).

10. Will a court require proof that the defendant knew of the relationship that existed between the plaintiff and the third party? See *Geophysical Service Inc. v. Canada (Attorney General)*, 2014 NSCA 14. On that point, compare the requirements for the unlawful means tort and the tort of inducing breach of contract.

In *OBG*, Lord Hoffmann identified an additional requirement for the tort: the unlawful means employed must interfere with the third party's freedom to deal with the plaintiff. Without that element, he believed, "there is a danger that it will provide a cause of action based on acts which are wrongful only in the irrelevant sense that a third party has a right to complain if he chooses to do so" (at para. 56). In *Bram Enterprises*, however, Cromwell J. thought differently. "This requirement," he said, "is not supported either by the authorities or by the rationale for imposing liability. Whether the unlawful means interfere with the plaintiff's right to deal with the injured third party or with some other party, the fact that the defendant aims at the plaintiff provides a sufficient nexus between the unlawful means and the interests of the plaintiff to justify imposing liability. Rather than resort to this additional 'freedom to deal' qualification, I prefer to limit the scope of the unlawful means tort through a narrow approach to both the unlawful means component. . . and the intention component" (at para. 87).

11. Which defences are available in this context? Should justification defeat liability, as it does in the context of interference with contractual relations?

12. For further discussion of the unlawful means tort see Iacono, "By All Unlawful Means: An Inquiry into the Scope of the Unlawful Means Tort" (2018) 26 Dal. J. of Leg. Stud. 137; Kain & Alexander, "The Unlawful Means Element of the Economic Torts: Does a Coherent Approach Lie Beyond Reach?" in Archibald & Echlin, eds., *Annual Review of Civil Litigation* (2010) at 33; Effendi, Pessione & Nguyen, "*A.I. Enterprises Ltd. v. Bram Enterprises Ltd.*: A Clearer Approach for the Tort of Unlawful Means in Canada?" (2014) 42 Adv. Q. 470; Carty, "The Modern Functions of the Economic Torts: Reviewing the English, Canadian, Australian, and New Zealand Positions" [2015] C.L.J. 261; Carty, "The Economic Torts in the 21 Century" (2008) 124 L.Q.R. 641; Deakin & Randall, "Rethinking the Economic Torts" (2009) 72 M.L.R. 519; Lee, "Causing Loss by Unlawful Means" [2011]

Singapore J.L.S. 330; and Neyers, "Rights-Based Justifications for the Tort of Unlawful Interference with Economic Relations" (2008) 28 L.S. 215.

REVIEW PROBLEM

Import Company purchased 50 mink coats and contracted to supply them to its best customer, Bridget Furs. The wholesale price of the furs was so low that Bridget advertised them at 25% below the regular price in a brochure that it mailed to 250 preferred customers. It offered to sell the coats to the first 50 customers who presented preferred customer cards on January 20.

Retail Union represented the employees of Bridget and was engaged in a lawful strike at the time. The strike was proving ineffective because customers were ignoring the picket lines around the store. Consequently, Retail Union set up "secondary picket" lines around suppliers of Bridget, including Import. Secondary picketing is not referred to in any relevant legislation. The employees of Import, members of another union, refused to cross the picket line, thereby preventing the delivery of the mink coats to Bridget.

Steven, an independent trucker, telephoned Import and volunteered to deliver the coats for a fee. Import's management doubted that Steven would be able to do so, but indicated that it would agree if he could enter its premises. Import's guess proved correct as Steven was turned back at the gates by an angry mob of picketers.

Import's management then met with Retail Union, which agreed to remove the picket line if Import returned the furs to the American supplier. Import agreed on January 19. As a result, Bridget was forced to turn away 100 preferred customers, who had lined up at the store on January 20 for the sale.

Discuss the possible economic torts arising from this incident.

DEFAMATION

1. Introduction
2. Elements of a Defamation Action
3. Defences
4. Remedies

1. Introduction

The torts discussed in the preceding chapters involve the protection of one's person, property and financial interests. The tort of defamation is unique in protecting one's reputation from unjustified attacks. While chattels can be replaced, and many physical injuries will heal, damage to one's reputation can often be irremediable. Thus, the damages awarded for defamation are aimed not only at compensating the plaintiff for damage to his or her personal or professional reputation, but also at vindicating the plaintiff's reputation and deterring future defamatory publications.

Nevertheless, the protection of reputation has to be balanced against another fundamental legal principle: the freedom of expression, enshrined in s. 2(b) of the *Canadian Charter of Rights and Freedoms*, Part I of the *Constitution Act, 1982*, being Schedule B to the *Canada Act 1982* (U.K.), 1982, c. 11. While the *Charter* does not apply directly to the common law tort of defamation, the Supreme Court of Canada affirmed in *Hill v. Church of Scientology*, [1995] 2 S.C.R. 1130, that the law of defamation should develop in light of *Charter* values. Further, as explained by LeBel J. in *Gilles E. Néron Communication Marketing Inc. v. Chambre des notaires du Québec*, [2004] 3 S.C.R. 95, freedom of expression predates the *Charter* and lies at the heart of our democratic institutions.

The tort of defamation recognizes the competing values of reputation and freedom of expression. This is reflected in the fact that, while it is relatively easy for a plaintiff to prove a *prima facie* case of defamation, there are also numerous defences available. Indeed, most of the law on the tort of defamation involves the applicability of the various defences. The defences signal that, in some situations, the value of free and uninhibited speech outweighs the need to protect a person's reputation. At the same time, however, a defendant who speaks falsely and maliciously will often lose the benefit of the defences. As you proceed through this chapter, ask yourself whether the current law strikes the appropriate balance between protecting reputation and freedom of expression.

Many of the principles underlying the law of defamation stem from older English case law. For example, the common law historically distinguished between slander (spoken defamation) and libel (written defamation, films, pictures, or other concrete forms of expression). Because slander is transitory, it was considered to be less damaging than libel and was actionable only in certain situations or on proof of special damages. The types of slander that were historically actionable *per se* were imputations of the commission of a crime, a loathsome disease, a lack of chastity (women only), and unfitness to practice one's trade or profession. On the other hand, damage is presumed in cases of libel. However, several Canadian jurisdictions have removed the distinction between libel and slander, replacing them with the broader notion of "defamation."

All Canadian jurisdictions have introduced some legislation regarding defamation. The legislation varies from province to province, but often contains provisions specific to the media and guidelines on the applicability of certain defences. Nevertheless, the common law principles are still predominant, and are the main focus of this chapter.

The tort of defamation is somewhat unusual in that it continues to involve the use of civil juries. Some jurisdictions provide an absolute right to a jury trial for defamation claims. The reasons for this are twofold. First, particularly in cases where the defendant has spoken out against a public official, it is believed that a jury provides protection from indirect censorship by the state. Second, as will be seen throughout this chapter, many of the issues in a defamation claim refer to community standards. For instance, "how would a reasonable person understand the defendant's remarks?" or "would this damage the plaintiff's reputation in the eyes of a reasonable person?" It can be argued that using a jury is the best way to apply such community standards.

Finally, the advent of the internet and electronic communications has had, and will continue to have, a significant effect on the law of defamation. The internet provides the opportunity to publish defamatory statements instantly to a worldwide audience, and the author of the statements is often permitted to use a pseudonym. It also raises questions with respect to jurisdiction (*e.g.*, where is an electronic communication "published?"); and with respect to those responsible for the publication (*e.g.*, should an internet service provider or the host of a chat room be liable for defamatory statements published there?). If the defamatory statements are "published" in a foreign jurisdiction, a plaintiff might have difficulty, as a practical matter, obtaining compensation or having the defamatory remarks removed from the website. All of these issues will need to be addressed as the law of defamation enters the information age.

NOTES AND QUESTIONS

1. For general texts on the law of defamation, see Brown, *Brown on Defamation (Canada, United Kingdom, Australia, New Zealand, United States)*, 2d ed., looseleaf (1994) (consulted January 2019); McConchie & Potts, *Canadian Libel and Slander Actions* (2004); Milmo & Rogers, eds., *Gatley on Libel and Slander*, 12th ed. (2013); and Price, Duodu & Cain, *Defamation Law, Procedure & Practice*, 4th ed. (2010). For an historical review of the competing values in this area of the law, see Jones, *Insult to Injury: Libel, Slander, and Invasions of Privacy* (2003).

2. The United States Supreme Court has attempted to balance free speech against the protection of reputation in a different way. In *New York Times Co. v. Sullivan*, 376 U.S. 254 (Ala. 1964), the court decided that the existing common law of defamation violated freedom of speech and unduly prevented the press from speaking out against public officials. The court ruled that, where the plaintiff is a public figure, he or she must establish that the defendant knew the statements were false or was reckless as to whether they were false at the time they were made. This has come to be known as the "actual malice" rule.

In *Hill v. Church of Scientology*, [1995] 2 S.C.R. 1130, the Supreme Court of Canada considered and rejected the approach in *Sullivan*, finding that the existing law of defamation struck the appropriate balance between competing values. Thus, in Canada, once the plaintiff proves that the defendant's statements were defamatory, they are presumed to be false and the burden is on the defendant to prove otherwise.

Do you prefer the approach in *Sullivan* or in *Hill*? At least one author has criticized the Supreme Court of Canada for not adopting *New York Times Co. v. Sullivan*. See Boivin, "Accommodating Freedom of Expression and Reputation in the Common Law of Defamation" (1997) 22 Queen's L.J. 229. See also Tingley, "Reputation, Freedom of Expression and the Tort of Defamation in the United States and Canada: A Deceptive Polarity" (1999) 37 Alta. L. Rev. 620; and Tarantino, "Chasing Reputation: The Argument for Differential Treatment of 'Public Figures' in Canadian Defamation Law" (2010) 48 Osgoode Hall L.J. 595.

For criticism of the actual malice rule, see Lewis, "*New York Times v. Sullivan* Reconsidered: Time to Return to 'The Central Meaning of the First Amendment'" (1983) 83 Col. L. Rev. 603; Epstein, "Was *New York Times v. Sullivan* Wrong?" (1986) 53 U. Chi. L. Rev. 782; and Levai, "The No-Money, No-Fault Libel Suit: Keeping *Sullivan* in its Proper Place" (1988) 101 Harv. L. Rev. 1287. See also Tushnet, "*New York Times v. Sullivan* around the world" (2014) 66 Ala. L. Rev. 337. It has been argued that the decision in *Sullivan* actually increased the number of defamation actions, and has also made them longer and more expensive to litigate.

3. It is generally accepted that governments and public institutions cannot sue in defamation. What is the rationale for such a prohibition? How broadly should it apply? See Young, "Public Institutions as Defamation Plaintiffs" (2016) 39:1 Dal. L.J. 249.

4. For articles discussing the actual or desired impact of the *Charter* on defamation actions, see Ross, "The Common Law of Defamation Fails to Enter the Age of the *Charter*" (1996) 35 Alta. L. Rev. 117; Boivin, *supra*; Schabas, "The Constitutionalization of Libel Law and Other Long-Overdue Developments in Freedom of the Press" (2009) 25 N.J.C.L. 133; and Cameron, "Does Section 2(b) Really Make a Difference? Part 1: Freedom of Expression, Defamation Law and the Journalist-Source Privilege" (2010) 51 S.C.L.R. (2d) 133. The authors suggest that the current common law of defamation does not adequately protect freedom of expression, citing the Supreme Court of Canada's rejection of *Sullivan* as an example. They also suggest that the value of a good reputation is outdated and ought not to be protected as fiercely in modern society. Do you agree?

There have been similar struggles to balance freedom of expression against reputation in the United Kingdom. While the courts seemed to prioritize expression in the 1990s and early 2000s, their position changed in the early 2000s. See Mullis & Scott, "The Swing of the Pendulum: Reputation, Expression and the Recentering of English Libel Law" (2012) 63 N.I.L.Q. 27. The courts' apparent favouritism toward plaintiffs gave rise to a trend of so-called "libel tourism," which Parliament hoped to curb through the *Defamation Act 2013* (UK), c. 26. Among other things, the statute requires a plaintiff to show "serious harm" to reputation in order to bring a successful claim.

5. The importance of free expression has risen to prominence in debates about so-called SLAPPs (strategic litigation against public litigation). It has been argued that certain public figures or corporations use defamation proceedings to intimidate their critics, drain their resources, and deter them and others from participating in debates on matters of public interest. To reduce such abusive litigation, some jurisdictions have introduced special rules to, *inter alia*, expedite procedures to dismiss SLAPPs and provide for enhanced costs against plaintiffs. Such laws exist in many American states. British Columbia enacted anti-SLAPP legislation in 2001 (see *Protection of Public Participation Act*, S.B.C. 2001, c. 19) but it was repealed later the same year following a provincial election.

See also Uniform Law Conference of Canada, *Strategic Lawsuits Against Public Participation (SLAPPs) (and Other Abusive Lawsuits)* (2008); and Anti-SLAPP Advisory Panel, *Report to the Attorney General of Ontario* (2010), which inspired the introduction of the *Protection of Public Participation Act*, 2015, S.O. 2015, c. 23. For guidance on the interpretation and application of that legislation, see *1704604 Ontario Ltd. v. Pointes Protection Association*, 2018 ONCA 685. In that case, the court described the "heart of the legislation" as an evaluation of whether the harm suffered by the plaintiff is sufficiently serious as to outweigh the public interest in protecting freedom of expression.

Even in the absence of legislation, some courts have awarded enhanced costs against plaintiffs who use defamation claims as a means of limiting participation in debates on matters of public interest. See for example *Scory v. Krannitz*, 2011 BCSC 1344; and *Morris v. Johnson*, 2012 ONSC 5824. But see *Northwest Organics v. Maguire*, 2013 BCSC 1328, aff'd 2014 BCCA 454.

See generally Tollefson, "Strategic Lawsuits against Public Participation: Developing a Canadian Response" (1994) 73 Can. Bar. Rev. 200; Pring & Canon, *SLAPPs: Getting Sued for Speaking Out* (1996); Public Interest Advocacy Centre, *Corporate Retaliation Against Consumers: The Status of Strategic Lawsuits Against Public Participation (SLAPPs) in Canada* (2004); Johnson & Duran, "A View From the First Amendment Trenches: Washington State's New Protections for Public Discourse and Democracy" (2012) 87 Wash. L. Rev. 495; Kelly, "Election SLAPPs: Effective at Suppressing Political Participation and Giving Anti-SLAPP Statutes the Slip" (2013) 66 Me. L. Rev. 191; Sheldrick, *Blocking Public Participation: The Use of Strategic Litigation to Silence Political Expression* (2014); and Young, "Responsible Communication and Protection of Public Participation: Assessing Canada's Newest Public Interest Speech Protections" (2018) 47:2 Sw. L. Rev. 385.

6. For examples of provincial legislation regarding defamation, see *Libel and Slander Act*, R.S.B.C. 1996, c. 263; *Libel and Slander Act*, R.S.O. 1990, c. L.12; *Defamation Act*, R.S.N.S. 1989, c. 122; and *Defamation Act*, R.S.A. 2000, c. D-7.

7. Since a web article that is viewed once in a jurisdiction could be considered "published" in that jurisdiction, there is a risk that plaintiffs will seek out the jurisdiction whose defamation law is most favourable to their cases. The Supreme Court of Canada addressed this issue of "libel tourism" in *Haaretz.com v. Goldhar*, 2018 SCC 28, in which the plaintiff, who lived and operated his business in Ontario, sued an Israeli newspaper for an allegedly defamatory article about his management of an Israeli soccer team. While the majority explained that the traditional *lex loci delicti* rule ("the place where the tort occurred"), *i.e.*, publication to an Ontario

audience, was a presumptive connecting factor, it ultimately concluded that Israel was the more appropriate forum on account of the comparative inconvenience and expense, and potential unfairness to the defendant if the trial were held in Ontario. The concurring judges argued that the *lex loci delecti* rule should be discarded in internet defamation cases in favour of a rule focused on where the most substantial harm to the plaintiff's reputation occurred.

For an examination of the jurisdictional issues implicated in actions for defamation via the internet, see Martin, "*Tolofson* and Flames in Cyberspace: The Changing Landscape of Multistate Defamation" (1997) 31 U.B.C.L. Rev. 127. See also Kohl, "Defamation on the Internet: Nice Decision, Shame about the Reasoning: *Dow Jones & Co Inc v Gutnick*" (2003) 52 I.C.L.Q. 1049; Scassa, "Journalistic Purposes and Private Sector Data Protection Legislation: Blogs, Tweets and Information Maps" (2010) 35 Queen's L.J. 733; Collins, *The Law of Defamation and the Internet*, 3d ed (2011); Castel, "Jurisdiction and Choice of Law Issues in Multistate Defamation on the Internet" (2013) 51 Alta. L. Rev. 153; and Auda, "A proposed solution to the problem of libel tourism" (2016) 12:1 J. Priv. Intl. L. 106.

2. Elements of a Defamation Action

In order to succeed in a defamation action, the plaintiff must prove on the balance of probabilities that the impugned statements (i) were defamatory, (ii) made reference to the plaintiff, and (iii) were published or disseminated.

(a) DEFAMATORY MATERIAL

It is relatively easy for a plaintiff to establish that statements are defamatory, and few cases are dismissed at this stage. A plaintiff may allege that the statements were defamatory in the plain and ordinary sense (sometimes referred to as their "literal" meaning). However, even if the plain and ordinary meaning of the words seems innocent, the plaintiff may establish defamatory meaning in two other ways. First, if there are facts or circumstances extraneous to the publication that are known to those receiving the publication and would give the publication a defamatory meaning, the plaintiff may succeed on the basis of "legal innuendo" or "true innuendo." For example, a photo caption describing a man and his "girlfriend" seems innocent enough on its face. Nevertheless, if extraneous materials prove that the man was married, there is an innuendo that the man is having an illicit affair, and the publication could be considered defamatory. See the similar circumstances in *Duval v. O'Beirne* (1912), 20 O.W.R. 884 (H.C.); and *Cairns v. John Fairfax & Sons Ltd.*, [1983] 2 N.S.W.L.R. 708 (C.A.). Legal innuendo may also arise if the statements make use of slang or technical language that would be known to the particular audience. The plaintiff has the burden of proving the extraneous facts or circumstances necessary to support the plea of innuendo.

Second, if the plaintiff can establish that an ordinary person would infer something defamatory from apparently innocent remarks, even without special knowledge of the plaintiff or the circumstances, then the plaintiff may succeed on the basis of "false innuendo" or "popular innuendo." This is not an independent pleading: a plaintiff arguing false innuendo is essentially arguing that a reasonable person would understand the "plain and ordinary" meaning of the statements to be something more than their literal meaning. In other words, the plain and ordinary meaning of a statement includes those things that a reasonable person would infer from them. The plaintiff raised false innuendo in the case below.

SIM v. STRETCH
[1936] 2 All E.R. 1237 (H.L.)

[A housemaid, Edith, worked for the defendant and then for the plaintiff. She later returned to her employment with the defendant, who sent the following telegram to the plaintiff: "Edith has resumed her service with us to-day. Please send her possessions and the money you borrowed, also her wages to Old Barton.—Sim." Old Barton was the defendant's home.]

LORD ATKIN:—. . . Before dealing with the appeal it is necessary to explain the reference in the telegram to "money borrowed." It appears that at the end of March, "a week just before Easter," which that year fell on Apr. 1, Mrs. Sim had been away for a week. She had left money with Edith to pay the books, but had arranged on Edith's suggestion that anything over Edith should pay out of her own money. Apparently Edith paid two small items amounting to 14s., which sum was outstanding on Apr. 12, and was in fact paid on Apr. 15.

The statement of claim, after alleging publication of the words of the telegram to the officials of the post office whose duty it was to transmit and deal with the telegram, alleged in para 7:

By the said words the defendant meant and was understood to mean that the plaintiff was in pecuniary difficulties, that by reason thereof he had been compelled to borrow and had in fact borrowed money from the said housemaid, that he had failed to pay the said housemaid her wages and that he was a person to whom no one ought to give any credit.

At the close of the plaintiff's case counsel for the defendant submitted that the words were incapable either of the meaning alleged in the innuendo or of any defamatory meaning. The learned judge rejected the submission, and counsel for the plaintiff urged the innuendo before the jury as he has done both in the Court of Appeal and in your Lordships' House. My Lords, it appears to me that the alleged innuendo is fantastic and that the words used are in their ordinary meaning incapable of being understood by reasonable persons as conveying an imputation upon the plaintiff's financial credit. It was, in my opinion, the duty of the judge so to hold, and to withdraw the count alleging the innuendo from the jury. . . .

. . .

The question, then, is whether the words in their ordinary signification are capable of being defamatory. Judges and textbook writers alike have found difficulty in defining with precision the word "defamatory." The conventional phrase exposing the plaintiff to hatred, ridicule and contempt is probably too narrow. The question is complicated by having to consider the person or class of persons whose reaction to the publication is the test of the wrongful character of the words used. I do not intend to ask your Lordships to lay down a formal definition, but after collating the opinions of many authorities I propose in the present case the test: would the words tend to lower the plaintiff in the estimation of right-thinking members of society generally? Assuming such to be the test of whether words are defamatory or not there is no dispute as to the relative functions of judge and jury, of law and fact. It is well settled that the judge must decide whether the words are capable of a defamatory meaning. That is a question of law: is there evidence of a tort? If they are capable, then the jury is to decide whether they are in fact defamatory. Now, in the present case it is material to notice that there is no evidence that the words were published to anyone who had any knowledge at all of any of the facts that I have narrated above. There is no direct evidence that they were published to anyone who had ever heard of the plaintiff. The post office officials at Maidenhead would not be presumed to know him, and we are left without any information as to the officials at Cookham Dean. The plaintiff and his wife dealt at the shop at which was the sub-post office, but there is no evidence that the shopkeeper was the telegraph clerk; the probability is that he was not. It might, however, be inferred that the publication of the telegram at Cookham Dean was to someone who knew the plaintiff. What would he or she learn by reading the telegram? That Edith Saville had been in the plaintiff's employment; that she had that day entered the defendant's employment; and that the former employer was requested to send on to the new place of employment the servant's possessions together with the money due to her for money borrowed and for wages. How could perusal of that communication tend to lower the plaintiff in the estimation of the right-thinking peruser who knows nothing of the circumstances but what he or she derives from the telegram itself. The defamatory imputation is said to be in the words "the money you borrowed," coupled with the request for the return of it sent in a telegram. It was said by the learned judge at the trial and accepted by the two members of the Court of Appeal who affirmed the judgment that the words were capable of conveying to anybody that the plaintiff had acted in a mean way borrowing money from his own maid and not paying her as he was required to and required to by telegram and also withholding her wages. With the greatest respect, that is imputing to the words a suggestion of meanness both in borrowing and in not repaying which I find it impossible to extract from their ordinary meaning. The sting is said to be in the borrowing. It happens that the phrase is substantially true. I myself have no doubt that if we were merely regarding legal technicalities the transaction which I have described as to the 14s. which was still unpaid could be covered by an indebitatus count for money lent as well as for money paid. In substance and in fact a justification of money borrowed would have been made out. But I am at a loss to understand why a person's character should be lowered in anyone's estimation if he or she has borrowed from a domestic servant. I should have thought it such a usual domestic occurrence for small sums to be advanced in such circumstances as the present, and with the assent of everyone concerned to be left outstanding for some days that the mere fact of borrowing from a servant bears not the slightest tinge of "meanness." Of course there may be special circumstances, and so large an amount may be borrowed or left so long unpaid that the facts when known would reflect on the character of the master. But to make an imputation which is based upon the existence of facts unknown and not to be inferred from the words attacked is surely exactly to come under the ban of Lord Esher [then Brett L.J.] cited in *Nevill v. Fine Art & General Insurance Co*, [[1897] A.C. 68 (C.A.)] at p 73:

> It seems to me unreasonable that, when there are a number of good interpretations, the only bad one should be seized upon to give a defamatory sense to the document.

It is not a case where there is only the choice between two reasonable meanings, one harmless and one defamatory. It is a case where there is only one reasonable meaning which is harmless, and where the defamatory meaning can only be given by inventing a state of facts which are not disclosed, and are in fact non-existent. . . .

[Lord Atkin discussed several cases cited by counsel which he found to be unhelpful.]

I only cite *Clay v. Roberts* [(1863), 8 L.T. 397] because of its reference to social conditions 70 years ago. It was held that it could not be defamatory to say of a physician that he met homopathists in consultation.

Would it be libellous, asked Pollock, C.B., at p. 398, to write of a lady of fashion that she had been seen on the top of an omnibus; or of a nobleman, that he was in the habit of burning tallow-candles? There is a distinction between imputing what is merely a breach of conventional etiquette, and what is illegal, mischievous, or sinful.

I think that no importance can be attached to the words being published by a telegram. The defendant who had acted quite unjustifiably repaired his wrong to some extent by giving immediate notice as to what had happened to the maid. It was quite natural and proper that he should ask for the maid's possessions to be sent to a named address and natural that he should in the same communication ask that the money, which in fact was due to her, should be sent to the same place. The truth of this case is that the whole matter is a trumpery affair and that the alleged libel would probably never have been heard of but for the wounded feelings caused by the improper enticement. That juries should be free to award damages for injuries to reputation is one of the safeguards of liberty. But the protection is undermined when exhibitions of bad manners or discourtesy are placed on the same level as attacks on character; and are treated as actionable wrongs. In the present case I find myself in complete agreement with the judgment of Slesser LJ. Being of opinion with him that the words complained of are incapable of a defamatory meaning, I am of opinion that the appeal should be allowed. The order of the Court of Appeal should be set aside and the verdict and judgment at the trial on the issue of libel should be set aside and judgment entered for the defendant. . . . I move your Lordships accordingly.

[Lord Macmillan and Lord Russell of Killowen agreed.]

NOTES AND QUESTIONS

1. How does Lord Atkin identify "defamatory" statements? Is the test objective or subjective? Is there a difference between statements that harm the plaintiff's reputation and statements that merely hurt the plaintiff's feelings? See Young, "But Names Won't Necessarily Hurt Me: Considering the Effect of Disparaging Statements on Reputation" (2011) 37 Queen's L.J. 1.

2. The courts have gone to considerable lengths to define an "ordinary" or "right thinking" person. For instance, in *Lewis v. Daily Telegraph*, [1964] A.C. 234 at 259-60 (H.L.), Lord Reid remarked,

Ordinary men and women have different temperaments and outlooks. Some are unusually suspicious and some are unusually naive. One must try to envisage people between these two extremes and see what is the most damaging meaning that they would put on the words in question. . .

What the ordinary man, not avid for scandal, would read into the words complained of must be a matter of impression.

Similarly, in *Saunders v. Randolph Hotel Co. Ltd.*, [1945] O.R. 600 at 604 (C.A.), Laidlaw J.A. warned against assuming the position of someone "of prejudice, bias or evil mind" or someone "of low mentality and intellect." See also *Macdonald v. Mail Printing Co.* (1900), 32 O.R. 163 (H.C.J.), rev'd on other grounds (1901), 2 O.L.R. 278 (C.A.); *W. v. A.* (1908), 13 B.C.R. 333 (C.A.); *I.W. Holdsworth Ltd. v. Assoc. Newspapers Ltd.* (1937), 53 T.L.R. 1029 (C.A.); *Botiuk v. Toronto Free Press Publications Ltd.*, [1995] 3 S.C.R. 3; *Color Your World Corp. v. Canadian Broadcasting Corp.* (1998), 38 O.R. (3d) 97 (C.A.); *Hodgson v. Canadian Newspapers Co.* (1998), 39 O.R. (3d) 235 (Gen. Div.), varied with respect to damages (2000), 49 O.R. (3d) 161 (C.A.); and *Mantini v. Smyth Lyons LLP (No. 2)* (2003), 64 O.R. (3d) 516 (C.A.).

3. Is there a difference between an ordinary person and a right thinking person? Should a plaintiff be allowed to succeed in a defamation action if the statements would lower his or her reputation in only part of the community? For example in *Mawe v. Pigott* (1869), I.R. 4 C.L. 54, an Irish priest claimed that he had been defamed by accusations that he was an informer against Irish criminals. He argued that a certain class of Irishmen would therefore think ill of him. The court found that "right thinking" men would likely think better of the priest as a result of the accusations, so they could not be defamatory just because they might cause a smaller class of persons to think less of him.

The test of "right thinking" persons has been criticized as impractical in modern pluralistic society: Deakin, Johnston & Markesinis, *Markesinis and Deakin's Tort Law*, 7th ed. (2013) at 634-36. For example, it has historically been considered defamatory to call someone a homosexual, and some people might still consider it to be so. However, given changing attitudes and recent equality jurisprudence, it may be difficult to maintain that "right thinking" members of society continue to find this defamatory. Moreover, the conclusion that it is defamatory may be seen as complicit in suggesting that homosexuals are somehow "less than" heterosexuals. See also Baker, "Defamation and the Moral Community" (2008) 13 Deakin L Rev. 1; and Bennett, "Not So Straight-Talking: How Defamation Law Should Treat Imputations of Homosexuality" (2016) 35:2 U. Queensland L.J. 313.

Courts will consider community standards when deciding whether a statement would be understood as defamatory. For example the label of "papist" has been considered defamatory at different times during the history of England (see for example *Walden v. Mitchell* (1692), 86 E.R. 431 (K.B.)) and the label of "freemason" was considered actionable by a candidate running for office in a Catholic community of Québec (*Lareau v. La Compagnie d'Imprimerie de la Minerve* (1883), 27 L.C. Jur. 336 (S.C.)). See also *Khalil v. Barakat*, [2013] EWHC 85 (Q.B.), in which the judge suggested it may be defamatory to suggest that a practising Muslim had lost her virginity prior to marriage. But see *Best v. Weatherall* (2010), 3 B.C.L.R. (5th) 388 (C.A.), where the presence of a "robust" community debate did not diminish the defamatory sting of the defendant's statements.

Which community standards should apply to statements made on social media? See Mills, "The law applicable to cross-border defamation on social media: whose law governs free speech in 'Facebookistan'?" (2015) 7:1 J. Media Law 1. See also *Stocker v. Stocker*, 2019 UKSC 17, where the court considered the Facebook context when concluding that the defendant's statement, "He tried to strangle me" about her ex-husband should be read as a statement that he had grabbed her by the throat, not that he had tried to murder her. She was therefore successful in her defence of justification.

4. In determining whether something is defamatory, one must examine both the context of the words and the mode of publication. The courts will generally view the publication as a whole, rather than focus on isolated passages, because that is how the ordinary reader would understand it. This includes headlines, pictures and illustrations. See *Slim v. Daily Telegraph Ltd.*, [1968] 2 Q.B. 157 (C.A.). See also *Weaver v. Ball*, 2018 BCSC 205, where the court found that a poorly-written article which lacked credibility did not genuinely threaten the plaintiff's reputation in the minds of reasonable, thoughtful readers.

If the allegedly defamatory remarks are made during a radio or television broadcast, the court should consider gestures, facial expressions, and tone of voice. Esson J. wrote in *Vogel v. Canadian Broadcasting Corporation*, [1982] 3 W.W.R. 97 (B.C.S.C.):

> [T]elevision programs. . . by reason of their transitory nature, tend to leave the audience with an impression rather than a firm understanding of what was said. Images, facial expressions, tones of voice, symbols and the dramatic effect which can be achieved by juxtaposition of segments may be more important than the meaning derived from careful reading of the words of the script.

See also *Lougheed v. Canadian Broadcasting Corporation*, [1979] 3 W.W.R. 334 (Alta. C.A.); *Color Your World, supra*; *Pressler v. Lethbridge* (2000), 86 B.C.L.R. (3d) 257 (C.A.); and *Marcotte c. Société TVA Inc.*, 2013 QCCS 5110.

In the era of social media, an emoji, hashtag or similar item may contribute to the defamatory context of a comment. For example, in *McAlpine v. Bercow*, [2013] EWHC 1342 (Q.B.), the court concluded that the defendant's addition of "*innocent face*" at the end of a tweet reading, "Why is Lord McAlpine trending?" suggested to her followers that Lord McAlpine was the previously unidentified Thatcher-era politician who had been accused of child molestation in news broadcasts. See also *AvePoint Inc. v. Power Tools Inc.*, 981 F.Supp.2d 496 (WD Va 2013) (involving liability for using the hashtag #MadeinCHINA in reference to the plaintiff's product). See also Pelletier, "The Emoji that Cost $20,000: Triggering Liability for Defamation on Social Media" (2016) 52:1 Wash U.J.L. & Pol'y 227.

5. In *Baglow v. Smith*, 2015 ONSC 1175, Polowin J. found that it was defamatory to refer to the plaintiff as "one of the Taliban's more vocal supporters" on a highly-charged political blog, even though such derogatory language is not uncommon in online debates. Nevertheless, the judge applied the test from *WIC Radio v. Simpson*, [2008] 2 S.C.R. 420, excerpted later in this chapter, and concluded that the defendants had a valid defence of fair comment. Given the to and fro of vitriolic language in online commentary, how should a court determine when one of the participants has crossed the line into defamation?

6. In the context of a live debate, the court may consider the plaintiff's opportunity to respond and, thus, remove the defamatory "sting" of the defendant's comments. For example, in *Marley v. Kains*, 2011 BCSC 1306, the court found that the plaintiff was not defamed by a question posed by the defendant at a candidates' forum

for a provincial election. The plaintiff gave a calm and persuasive answer to the question and, given his longstanding political reputation, there was no evidence that those in the audience thought less of him as a result of the question. See also *Austin v. Lynch*, 2016 BCSC 1344.

7. If the court concludes that ordinary people would find a statement to be defamatory, it is not a defence to argue that the defendant did not intend the statement to be defamatory (*E. Hulton & Co. v. Jones*, [1910] A.C. 21 (H.L.)) or that the defendant had a commendable motive (*Dennis v. Southam Co.* (1954), 13 W.W.R. (N.S.) 494 (Man. C.A.)).

8. The types of allegations that have been considered defamatory are legion, and are limited only by the human imagination. The allegations in the following cases have been found to be defamatory: *Mychajluk v. Kolisnyk*, [1923] 4 D.L.R. 724 (Man. K.B.) (corruption); *Lawrence v. Finch* (1930), 66 O.L.R. 451 (C.A.) (dishonesty); *Patching v. Howarth* (1930), 43 B.C.R. 108 (C.A.) (sexual immorality); *Houseman v. Coulson*, [1948] 2 D.L.R. 62 (Sask. K.B.) (having a venereal disease); *Warren v. Green* (1958), 25 W.W.R. 563 (Alta. S.C.) (doctor referred to as a "quack"); *Theater v. Richardson*, [1962] 1 W.L.R. 151 (C.A.) (prostitution); *Wheeler v. Somerfield*, [1966] 2 Q.B. 94 (C.A.) (glibness); *Bonham v. Pure Water Association* (1970), 74 W.W.R. 617 (B.C.S.C.) (hypocrisy); *Murphy v. LaMarsh*, [1971] 2 W.W.R. 196 (B.C.C.A.) (being detested by others); *Loan v. MacLean* (1975), 58 D.L.R. (3d) 228 (B.C.S.C.) (stupidity); *Cherneskey v. Armadale Publishers Ltd.*, [1979] 1 S.C.R. 1067 (racism); *Bennett v. Stupich* (1981), 30 B.C.L.R. 57 (S.C.) (habitual drunkenness of politician); *Moores v. Salter* (1982), 37 Nfld. & P.E.I.R. 128 (Nfld. Dist. Ct.) (profanity); *Planned Parenthood Newfoundland/ Labrador v. Fedorik* (1982), 135 D.L.R. (3d) 714 (Nfld. S.C.) (causing a rise in illegitimacy and abortion rates); *Berkoff v. Burchill*, [1996] 4 All E.R. 1008 (C.A.) (ugliness); *Seraphim v. Sterling Newspapers Ltd.*, 2001 CarswellBC 2107 (S.C.) (WLCan) (criminal conviction); *Newman v. Halstead*, 2006 CarswellBC 52 (S.C.) (WL Can) (suggesting that teachers were bullies and associated with pedophiles); *Puddister v. Wells* (2007), 265 Nfld. & P.E.I.R. 174 (N.L.C.A.) (city councillors a "bunch of shysters"); and *Durakovic v. Guzman*, 2014 ONSC 4678 (estranged husband had connections to the Taliban and Al Qaida).

The allegations in the following cases have been found not to be defamatory: *Simms v. Foyer Wales Home* (2009), 71 C.C.E.L. (3d) 67 (Que. S.C.) (not being bilingual); *Hagan v. Drover* (2009), 291 Nlfd. & P.E.I.R. 193 (N.L.S.C.) (defendant swearing at plaintiff in front of another employee); *Lund v. Black Press Group Ltd.*, 2009 CarswellBC 1809 (S.C.) (WL Can) (local politician accused of exerting influence over land-use planning decisions); *Dee v. Telegraph Media Group Ltd.*, [2010] EWHC 924 (Q.B.) (plaintiff the "worst professional tennis player in the world"); and *Bernstein v. Poon*, 2015 ONSC 155 (calling the plaintiff's diet program a "very low calorie diet" rather than a "reduced calorie diet"). In *Lund*, the judge explained that strong criticism of a public figure, even if it is derogatory or causes offence, is not sufficient to amount to defamation.

For a more complete catalogue, see Brown, *Brown on Defamation (Canada, United Kingdom, Australia, New Zealand, United States)*, 2d ed., looseleaf (1994) (consulted January 2019), ch. 4. However, Brown warns that precedents on what constitutes defamation do not carry as much weight as precedents in other area of tort law, due to changes in social conditions and the meaning of language, as well as the context and circumstances of any given case.

(b) REFERENCE TO THE PLAINTIFF

The plaintiff in a defamation action has the burden of showing, on a balance of probabilities, that the defamatory statement made reference to the plaintiff. This requirement has historically been known as "colloquium." The case is simple if the defamatory statement refers to the plaintiff by name. However, the requirement can also be satisfied in the absence of express reference, as explained in the case below.

KNUPPFER v. LONDON EXPRESS NEWSPAPER, LTD.
[1944] A.C. 116 (H.L.)

[The defendants published an article regarding a group known as "Young Russia." The article claimed that the members of this group were pro-Hitler and expected that one of them would be selected as a "puppet fuehrer" by Hitler to head up a fascist Russian state. The plaintiff was the leader of the British branch of Young Russia, but was not named in the article. At trial, he called four witnesses who were asked, "To whom did your mind go when you read that article?" Each one indicated the plaintiff. The plaintiff was awarded £3,500 at trial, but this was reversed by the Court of Appeal. The plaintiff appealed to the House of Lords.]

VISCOUNT SIMON L.C.:—My Lords, it is an essential element of the cause of action for defamation that the words complained of should be published "of the plaintiff." If the words are not so published, the plaintiff is not defamed and cannot have any right to ask that the defendant should be held responsible to him in respect of them.

In the words complained of in this case there is no specific mention of the appellant from beginning to end, and the only countries in which it is stated that this group of emigrés is established are France and the United States. Evidence was given at the trial that the appellant had joined the Young Russia Party in 1928, that in 1935 he became assistant representative of the Young Russia movement in Great Britain, and that in 1938 he was appointed representative of the movement in Great Britain and head of the British branch of the movement. The headquarters of the movement were in Paris until June, 1940, when they were removed to America.

These facts, standing alone, however, do not justify the conclusion that the words complained of are capable of being read as a defamation of the appellant. The words make allegations of a defamatory character about a body of persons — some thousands in number — who belong to a society whose members are to be found in many countries.

. . .

There are two questions involved in the attempt to identify the appellant as the person defamed. The first question is a question of law — can the article, having regard to its language, be regarded as capable of referring to the appellant? The second question is a question of fact — Does the article, in fact, lead reasonable people, who know the appellant, to the conclusion that it does refer to him? Unless the first question can be answered in favour of the appellant, the second question does not arise, and where the trial judge went wrong was in treating evidence to support the identification in fact as governing the matter, when the first question is necessarily, as a matter of law, to be answered in the negative. I move that this appeal be dismissed.

NOTES AND QUESTIONS

1. What error in the trial judge's reasoning did Viscount Simon L.C. identify?

2. The test in *Knuppfer* has been affirmed in Canada. See for example *Arnott v. College of Physicians and Surgeons (Sask)*, [1954] S.C.R. 538; *Booth v. B.C.T.V. Broadcasting Systems* (1982), 139 D.L.R. (3d) 88 (B.C.C.A.); and *Butler v. Southam Inc.* (2001), 197 N.S.R. (2d) 97 (C.A.).

3. There are many ways that a plaintiff can be identified without being specifically named. See for example *Barnes v. Carter* (1910), 16 O.W.R. 911 (H.C.J.) (obituary indicating that plaintiff's mother was an unmarried woman, leading to the inference that the plaintiff was conceived out of wedlock); *Byrne v. Deane*, [1937] 1 K.B. 818 (C.A.) (play-on-words involving the plaintiff's name); *Jozwiak v. Sadek*, [1954] 1 W.L.R. 275 (Q.B.) (allegedly fictional character closely resembled the plaintiff); *Scelfo v. Rutgers University*, 282 A.2d 445 (N.J. 1971) (photograph of plaintiff accompanying article); *E.W. Scripps Co. v. Cholmondelay*, 569 S.W.2d 700 (Ky. App. 1978) (news article identified one party to a fight but not the plaintiff); and *Hayward v. Thompson*, [1981] 3 W.L.R. 470 (C.A.) (reference to political donations for which plaintiff had gained notoriety).

4. *Knuppfer* also addresses the more specific issue of when a plaintiff can be considered "identifiable" through membership in a group that has been defamed. The general rule is that the individual members of a large group cannot succeed in an action for defamation unless there is something in the statement that identifies a particular member: *Abraham v. The Advocate Co.*, [1946] 2 W.W.R. 181 (P.C.); and *Elliott v. Canadian Broadcasting Corp.* (1993), 108 D.L.R. (4th) 385 (Ont. Gen. Div.), aff'd on other grounds (1995), 25 O.R. (3d) 302 (C.A.). But see *A.U.P.E. v. Edmonton Sun* (1986), 75 A.R. 253 (Q.B.), where the court found that a group of nearly 200 officers employed at a Correction Centre were defamed by an editorial that described officers at the centre as "goons" and a "gang of bumbling yo-yos." The writer had not taken care to restrict his comments to the individuals involved in a recent incident with a photographer, and a reasonable person who knew one of the plaintiffs or identified the plaintiffs through their distinctive uniforms would be of the opinion that the comments referred to the plaintiffs.

See also *Bou Malhab v. Diffusion Metromedia CMR Inc.*, 2011 SCC 9, where the court dismissed a class action by Montreal taxi drivers whose mother tongue is Arabic or Creole against a radio host who accused them of being unclean, incompetent, corrupt, and unable to speak Canada's official languages. Deschamps J., for the majority, found that the size and heterogeneity of the class (some 1,100 drivers) meant that ordinary listeners would not find the defendant's sweeping generalizations to be plausible allegations of fact. Accordingly, no individual taxi driver's reputation was harmed. The majority compared the defendant's statements to allegations that "all lawyers are thieves" or "all police officers are racists," which are so broad and unfounded that the ordinary person would not think less of any given taxi driver, lawyer, or police officer, as the case may be. See also *Gauthier v. Toronto Star*

Newspapers Ltd. (2003), 228 D.L.R. (4th) 748 (Ont. S.C.J.); and *Djoufo c. Mailloux*, 2013 QCCS 4147.

Where the group in question is small and the statement refers to the entire group, *Knupffer* indicates that each member may have an action for defamation.

Some jurisdictions have enacted legislation allowing members of religious or racial groups that have been defamed by racist comments to sue for an injunction to end such remarks. See for example *Defamation Act*, C.C.S.M. c. D20, s. 19(1).

5. In *Trkulja v. Google LLC*, [2018] HCA 25, the High Court of Australia refused to set aside a defamation claim against Google for the way that its autocomplete functions and "images" tab associated the plaintiff with the criminal underworld in Melbourne. Among other things, the plaintiff's picture appeared when users searched for "Melbourne criminal underworld" and "Melbourne underworld killings." The Court concluded that this may be capable of defamatory imputation in the eyes of a reasonable person. How could Google avoid liability in claims such as this?

6. If a plaintiff satisfies the colloquium requirement, it is not a defence to argue that the defendant did not intend to identify the plaintiff. Nor can the defendant argue that he or she did not know the plaintiff existed. The test is not what the defendant meant, but how the defendant's statement would be understood by a reasonable person to whom it was published: *Clarke v. Stewart* (1916), 10 Alta. L.R. 393 (C.A.). In making this determination, the court will consider the surrounding circumstances (*e.g.*, who the speaker was, the knowledge the speaker would be presumed to have, and the likely audience). See *Booth, supra.*

However, it is not sufficient if only the *plaintiff* believed that the statements made reference to him or her. The plaintiff must show that the reasonable person to whom the statements were published would understand them to be referring to the plaintiff. See *Willows v. Williams* (1950), 2 W.W.R. (N.S.) 657 (Alta. S.C.); and *Risk v. Zeller's Ltd.* (1977), 27 N.S.R. (2d) 532 (S.C. (T.D.)). Furthermore, it is likely not sufficient for the plaintiff to call his or her relations or close friends to testify as to how they understood the statement: *Halprin v. The Sun Publishing Company Ltd.*, [1978] 4 W.W.R. 685 (B.C.S.C.); and *Dale's Trad'N Post v. Rhodes* (1987), 19 B.C.L.R. (2d) 73 (S.C.).

(c) PUBLICATION

Since the essence of this tort is injury to reputation, defamatory remarks are not actionable unless they are communicated to someone other than the plaintiff. This element of the tort is known as "publication," and will be satisfied as long as the statement is communicated, in any way, to a third party who understands the statement. Accordingly, there is no liability if the defendant made a remark to an empty room, or to a person who did not hear it or understand the language, or to the plaintiff alone.

As a general rule, every repetition of a defamatory statement is considered a new publication that is independently actionable: *Lambert v. Thomson*, [1937] O.R. 341 (C.A.), rev'd on other grounds [1938] S.C.R. 253. Thus, someone who repeats a statement that originated with someone else may be held liable in defamation, even if he or she believed the statement to be true, specifically named the source of the statement, or did not adopt the defamatory remark. As Grimmer J. noted in *Trafton v.*

Deschene (1917), 44 N.B.R. 552 at 559 (S.C. (A.D.)), "Tale bearers are as bad as tale makers."

Further, any party who had a part in communicating the defamatory statements may be subject to liability. Thus, a defendant may be liable not only for originating the statement, but also for repeating it, printing it, or allowing it to be posted on premises over which the defendant has control. Similarly, an employer may be liable for defamatory remarks made by an employee acting within the scope of employment. Nevertheless, the person who originated the defamatory remarks will not be liable for their repetition by others unless (i) he or she has given express or implied authority for the remarks to be republished, (ii) he or she made the remarks to someone who had a moral, legal or social duty to republish those remarks, or (iii) the republication is a natural and probable consequence of the original publication.

NOTES AND QUESTIONS

1. Publication can occur orally, in writing, by posters, signs or cartoons, by gestures, or any other form of communication. In some, but not all, American states, publication has even been found to occur when a will is probated. Thus, the estate may be liable if the testator made defamatory remarks when explaining why certain distributions were made: see for example *Harris v. Nashville Trust Co.*, 128 Tenn. 573 (1914); and *Brown v. Mack*, 56 N.Y.S.2d 910 (1945).

2. Publication does not occur when a person makes a defamatory remark about the plaintiff to his or her own spouse. See *Wennhak v. Morgan* (1888), 20 Q.B.D. 635; and *Huth v. Huth*, [1915] 3 K.B. 32 (C.A.). What do you think is the reason for the special treatment of conversation between spouses? Is it justifiable? Should it apply to other relationships?

3. A defendant may not be liable if a defamatory remark is overheard entirely by accident: *McNichol v. Grandy*, [1931] S.C.R. 696. Similarly, if the statement is read by someone for whom it was not intended, and the defendant had no reason to believe that it would be read by such a person, the defendant may avoid liability. For instance, in *Huth*, *supra*, the defendant wrote a letter to his wife which was opened and read, out of curiosity, by the wife's servant. This was found not to be "publication" to the servant, since the husband had no reason to believe that the letter would be opened by the servant. However, if a writer knows that the addressee's mail is normally opened and screened by someone else, then the writer may be considered to have "published" the statement to that person: see *Delacroix v. Thevenot* (1817), 171 E.R. 573 (K.B.). See also *O'Malley v. O'Callaghan* (1992), 128 A.R. 28 (Q.B.).

4. It is not publication for the defendant to send a letter to the plaintiff's lawyer in connection with a legal action. Because the lawyer must keep the letter confidential, writing to the plaintiff's lawyer is equivalent to writing the plaintiff directly. See *Grimmer v. Carleton Road Industries Assn.* (2009), 282 N.S.R. (2d) 159 (S.C.), where the defendant's letter to the plaintiff's lawyer was alternatively governed by the defence of consent. See also *Heydary Hamilton P.C. v. Muhammad*, 2013 ONSC 4938, appeal dismissed as abandoned 2014 ONCA 84.

5. Where defamatory material is contained in a newspaper, magazine or book, the plaintiff may sue anyone who takes part in its publication, including the author,

editor, proprietor and printer: see *Popovich v. Lobay (No. 2)* (1937), 45 Man. R. 327 (C.A.). These parties should be sued as joint tortfeasors in a single cause of action: *Thomson v. Lambert*, [1938] S.C.R. 253. It is no defence to claim that the defendant was not aware of the defamatory remarks. However, those playing a subordinate role in the distribution of such material (*e.g.* vendors, newspaper carriers, or librarians) are not liable unless they know or ought to suspect that the material is defamatory. See *Vizetelly v. Mudie's Select Library Ltd.*, [1900] 2 Q.B. 170 (C.A.). See also *Kent v. Postmedia Network Inc.*, 2015 ABQB 461 (officers and directors of a news corporation not automatically liable for materials posted on the corporation's news websites).

In *Menear v. Miguna* (1996), 30 O.R. (3d) 602 (Gen. Div.), rev'd (1997), 33 O.R. (3d) 223 (C.A.), on a motion for summary judgment the judge had concluded that a printing company played a subordinate role in the publication of defamatory material and could succeed on a defence of "innocent dissemination." The judge relied on evidence that modern technology does not require a printer to read or edit the material that is being printed. The Court of Appeal reversed the granting of summary judgment on the grounds that the argument ought to be examined more fully at trial. Do you think that printers should be considered subordinate players, or should they be liable as joint tortfeasors even if they are unaware of defamatory content?

6. *Botiuk v. Toronto Free Press Publications Ltd.*, [1995] 3 S.C.R. 3, examined the issue of joint liability for defamation. The plaintiff, a lawyer, had performed substantial legal services on behalf of the Ukranian-Canadian Committee (UCC) during a public inquiry. He did not expect to be paid for his services because the UCC did not have sufficient funds for this purpose. However, the UCC received an award of costs and the plaintiff then submitted a bill for his services. The first defendant, Maksymec, submitted a report to the UCC complaining about the plaintiff's fees, and the report was later reprinted in a Ukranian-Canadian newspaper. Maksymec alleged that, in accordance with his agreement to provide services pro bono, the plaintiff should not receive any payment. Maksymec then wrote and published a declaration signed by the second defendants, a group of Ukranian lawyers who had provided very minimal services at the inquiry and suggested that there was an understanding that the work was to be performed pro bono. Maksymec later wrote another article on the subject that was reproduced in a Ukranian-Canadian publication, making reference to the declaration signed by the second defendants.

The plaintiff claimed in defamation for the damage done to his personal and professional reputation by all three publications, and was successful at trial and on appeal. Before the Supreme Court of Canada, the second defendants argued that they should not be held liable for the full defamatory effect of all three publications, since they had only participated in one of them. However, a majority of the Supreme Court of Canada affirmed that the second defendants were liable as joint tortfeasors for the consequences of all three publications. In doing so, the court relied on the notion of conspiracy, suggesting that the second defendants acted with Maksymec for a common intention and purpose, and knew that he would make extensive use of their declaration.

Is there any way that the second defendants could have avoided such liability? Is *Botiuk* consistent with the principle that each publication is a separate incidence of defamation? In a concurring opinion, Major J. doubted whether a common intention existed on the facts, and suggested that similar cases might be treated as separate instances of defamation in the future.

See also *Rutman v. Rabinowitz*, 2018 ONCA 80, where the court confirmed that a defendant could be held jointly liable for defamation even if he was not actively involved in publication and did not publicly approve of it. One of the defendants, Bergman, was aware that his business partner was conducting a calculated defamation campaign against the plaintiff, in part to pressure him to settle a contentious business transaction with them. Bergman had also authorized the use of company equipment and personnel to carry out the defamation, jointly authorized a lawyer to effectively extort the plaintiff, and had deleted relevant emails in violation of a court order.

7. *Carter v. B.C. Federation of Foster Parents Assn.* (2005), 257 D.L.R. (4th) 133 (B.C.C.A.) examined the liability of those who host internet chat rooms for defamatory statements that are posted by subscribers. The defendant had a website with a chat room. One subscriber posted statements in the chat room that defamed the plaintiff. The plaintiff complained to the defendant, a representative of which undertook to remove the defamatory remarks. Two years later, however, the remarks remained on the website. The defendant's argument of "innocent dissemination" was rejected by the British Columbia Court of Appeal because the defamatory statements were brought to the defendant's attention and the defendant was clearly negligent. See also *Defamation Act 2013* (U.K.), c. 26, s. 5, which deals with the liability of website operators and provides procedures by which individuals can seek to have defamatory material removed from a website.

Can you think of situations where a defence of innocent dissemination might be successful by the host of an internet chat room? How closely should such sites be monitored? How soon after a defamatory comment is posted should the host be expected to remove it?

8. In *Crookes v. Wikimedia Foundation Inc.* (2009), 96 B.C.L.R. (4th) 315 (C.A.), aff'd 2011 SCC 47, the court found that including hyperlinks to other websites that contained defamatory comments was not "publication" capable of supporting a claim in defamation. Do you agree? How is the deliberate creation of a hyperlink distinguishable from hosting a chat room in which other people make defamatory comments? The trial judge in *Crookes* compared the creation of a hyperlink to the provision of a footnote in an article, in that both merely provide a reference to another source, without encouraging or recommending to readers that they consult that source. However, the British Columbia Court of Appeal expressed some scepticism with regard to the comparison. But see *McGrath v. Dawkins*, [2012] EWHC B3 (Q.B.), in which the court distinguished hyperlinks from a "home" button that linked two similar but distinctly-operated websites.

What is the role of internet service providers, search engines, and social media platforms in circulating defamatory statements? See Gosnell, "Hate Speech on the Internet: A Question of Context" (1998) 23 Queen's L.J. 369; Savage, "Between a Rock and a Hard Place: Defamation and Internet Service Providers" (2002) 2 Asper Rev. of Int'l Bus. and Trade Law 107; Fischer & Lazier, "*Crookes v. Newton*: The Supreme Court of Canada Brings Libel Law into the Internet Age" (2012) 50 Alta. L. Rev. 205; Turner, "Internet Defamation Law and Publication by Omission: A Multi-Jurisdictional Analysis" (2014) 37:1 U.N.S.W.L.J. 34; Law Commission of Ontario, *Defamation Law in the Internet Age, Consultation Paper* (2017); and Lavi, "Taking Out of Context" (2017) 31:1 Harv. J. Law Technol. 145. See also *Niemela v. Malamas*, 2015 BCSC 1024; and *Google Inc. v. Duffy*, [2017] SASCFC 130.

3. Defences

As with other torts, the defendant has the burden of proving any defence on a balance of probabilities. Since it is relatively easy for plaintiffs to make out a *prima facie* case of defamation, most of the litigation about this tort is focused on the various defences that can be raised. The first defence, justification, applies if the defendant can prove that the allegedly defamatory statements were true. The next four defences — absolute privilege, qualified privilege, fair comment, and responsible communication on matters of public interest — do not rely on the truth of the statements but on the types of circumstances in which the statements were published. In these circumstances, the importance of free and open communication takes precedence over the damage to reputation that the plaintiff may suffer. The final defence, consent, rests on the principle that a person who has agreed to the publication of certain information cannot thereafter complain that it is defamatory.

In addition to these defences, of course, the defendant may argue that the impugned statements were not defamatory, did not refer to the plaintiff, or were not published.

(a) JUSTIFICATION

Once the plaintiff has proven that the statements made by the defendant were defamatory, the court will presume that those statements were false. Thus, it falls to the defendant to prove that the statements, though defamatory, were true. This defence is known as "justification." Justification is a complete defence to defamation: if the defendant proves that the statements were true, then the plaintiff's claim will be dismissed. A variety of reasons are typically offered for this result. In *McPherson v. Daniels* (1829), 109 E.R. 448 at 451 (K.B.), Littledale J. defended justification on the grounds that "the law will not permit a man to recover damages in respect of an injury to a character which he either does not, or ought not to possess." It has also been said that "What is true cannot be defamatory": *Courchene v. Marlborough Hotel Co.* (1971), 20 D.L.R. (3d) 109 (Man. Q.B.), aff'd [1972] 1 W.W.R. 149 (C.A.). Finally, as a matter of policy, the common law refuses to restrict free speech to the point that the truth is actionable. Thus, even though the plaintiff may be embarrassed by the revelation of certain facts about his or her life, and even though the revelation of those facts is of no benefit to the public interest, the plaintiff's claim will be defeated if those facts turn out to be true. A defendant can even succeed on a defence of justification if the statements were made maliciously.

A defendant pleading justification must show that "the whole of the defamatory matter is substantially true": *Meier v. Klotz* (1928), 22 Sask. L.R. 385 at 388 (C.A.). It is not sufficient for the defendant to show that he or she believed the statements to be true or relied on information provided by a third party. Nevertheless, the defendant need not prove the literal truth nor the truth of every single fact in the allegation. Generally speaking, the defendant needs to prove the truth of the statements that comprise the "sting" of the defamation. As discussed below in *Williams v. Reason* (1983), [1988] 1 All E.R. 262 (C.A.), a defamatory statement that is general in character may be justified by proving the truth of specific instances that support the general imputation. However, a single instance will not suffice. For example, in *Wakley v. Cooke* (1849), 154 E.R. 1316 (Exch.), the statement that the plaintiff was a "libellous journalist" was not justified by proving that the plaintiff had published one libellous story.

There is a disincentive to bringing a plea of justification: the defence is considered a re-publication of the impugned statements and, if the defence fails, the defendant will be liable for a separate instance of defamation. This may serve to aggravate damages, as discussed later in this chapter. Indeed, Idington J. warned in *Price v. Chicoutimi Pulp Co.* (1915), 51 S.C.R. 179 at 193-94, "A defence of justification involving the truth in substance and in fact of an alleged libel is often a perilous sort of proceeding."

WILLIAMS v. REASON
(1983), [1988] 1 All E.R. 262 (C.A.)

[The plaintiff was an amateur rugby player. The defendant was a sports correspondent for a national newspaper. The defendant wrote two articles accusing the plaintiff of "shamateurism" (*i.e.*, playing amateur rugby while accepting money from outside sources). The articles specifically referred to money that the plaintiff had received for writing a book about his rugby career. The plaintiff was successful at trial, but on appeal the defendant requested a new trial and sought to introduce new evidence that the plaintiff had received "boot money" from Adidas. The excerpts below discuss whether such evidence would be relevant to the defendant's plea of justification.]

STEPHENSON L.J.:—. . . In support of his submission that the evidence is admissible and leave to amend should be granted, counsel for the defendants cites, and I think is content to adopt, Duncan and Neill *Defamation* (1978) p 58, para 11.12 as an accurate statement of a difficult and developing branch of the law; cf *Gatley on Libel and Slander* (8th edn, 1981) pp 151-152, para 354. The former paragraph reads:

'In some cases the defendant may wish to contend that the words bear a less defamatory meaning than that alleged by the plaintiff and that in the less defamatory sense they are true. On the other hand, a defendant, with a view perhaps to introducing evidence of "similar facts", may wish to contend that the words, which ex facie relate to a specific incident, would be understood in a wider sense, for example, as conveying a general charge of dishonesty. The law on this matter appears to be at a stage of development. If the plaintiff himself pleads an inferential meaning to the effect that the words meant, for example, that he was a dishonest man or unfit to be a director, the defendant will then be free to introduce evidence of other incidents which are relevant to prove the truth of the inferential meaning. But where the plaintiff, exercising perhaps a wise discretion, does not allege that the words impute, for example, general dishonesty, the position is less clear. It is submitted, however, that the scope of the defence of justification should not depend upon the way in which the plaintiff pleads his case but on the meaning which the words are found to bear. It is submitted therefore that the defendant is entitled to put before the jury evidence of any facts which are relevant to justify the words in any meaning which they are capable of bearing.'

. . .

None of the authorities comes very near the present case, and I have not found it easy to decide whether the evidence of boot money is relevant to the words which Mr Reason wrote of the plaintiff, understood in any meaning which they are reasonably capable of bearing. But I conclude that counsel for the defendants is right in contending that the sting of the libel here is 'shamateurism', the charge, still tied to his book but nevertheless carrying with it a charge of hypocrisy and deviousness, that the plaintiff was a professional while claiming to be an amateur, that the evidence which alleges that he regularly took boot money, if accepted, would prove that he had by reason of [the regulations governing amateur rugby] no amateur status to infringe or lose at the time he wrote the book because he had already lost it by taking boot money and that a jury which heard evidence that he had accepted boot money might have been influenced into finding that he had, on any interpretation of the regulations, infringed them by writing a book for money which he never intended to give to charity until the publication of the first of Mr Reason's articles in the Daily Telegraph.

A jury might think that to take comparatively small sums of boot money was much less serious than to get thousands of pounds for writing a book, even for one who put a high value on amateur status in Rugby Union football. They might consider the distinction between 'gentlemen' and 'players' long since dead and buried, not only on the cricket field, and, to give a new meaning to the words which Shakespeare's Jacques spoke in a theatrical context (*As You Like It* II. vii. 140), in every field of sport nowadays 'all the men and women merely players'. But a jury might take a more serious view of boot money and consider that by undermining the plaintiff's claim to amateur status its acceptance would provide justification for the more general allegation of 'shamateurism' which the defendants' articles might reasonably be understood to make. Accordingly, I cannot say that evidence of taking boot money would be irrelevant to the sting of the libel, and therefore inadmissible if this court allows the defendants' amendment.

The first trial was conducted on the basis that the sting of the libel was shamateurism and hypocrisy. . . . The trial developed, as counsel for the plaintiff described it, into 'a slanging match' between the plaintiff and the defendant Mr Reason, the only two witnesses called. In a comprehensive cross-examination, counsel for the defendants had taken the plaintiff through a number of documents which seemed on their face to require explanation if they were to be consistent with the plaintiff's evidence that he never intended to make anything out of his book but always intended to give what he or his agents received for it to a charity. Before the plaintiff left the witness-box counsel for the defendants was rightly compelled by the judge to admit that he was challenging the plaintiff's honesty and the truth of his evidence that he decided to donate the proceeds of the book to charity at the very outset. The defendants were calling him a liar and that was made doubly sure by Mr Reason in his cross-examination. Mr Reason not merely disagreed with the opinion of the Welsh Rugby Union that the plaintiff had not lost his amateur status when he contracted to write the book but went further. The judge asked him:

> Q. Worse than that, Mr Reason, you think he is a shamateur because he is professing to be an amateur when in reality he is a professional?
>
> A. He was for a period of time, yes.
>
> Q. And a shamateur is a hypocrite?
>
> A. That is right.

The jury can have been left in no doubt how serious was the charge Mr Reason was making against the plaintiff's character in court. Though it was not for Mr Reason to say what his articles meant but for the judge to rule what they were capable of meaning and for the jury to say what they meant, they were in my judgment capable of meaning what the judge suggested to the jury they meant: that the plaintiff was a shamateur; that his evidence that he always genuinely intended to give the proceeds of his book to charity was a lie, his conduct in relation to the book devious, his claim to amateur status sheer hypocrisy. Since that was a meaning which the articles, or at any rate the second article, could reasonably bear, evidence that he had earlier lost his amateur status by being paid like a professional such remuneration as boot money seems to me admissible to justify the allegation of shamateurism, on the authority of those cases to which I have referred.

[O'Connor and Purchas LLJ. rendered concurring judgments. The appeal was allowed and a new trial ordered.]

NOTES AND QUESTIONS

1. How does Stephenson L.J. define the scope of the justification defence? What is the relevance of the plaintiff's pleadings? What meaning of the defamatory statements is the defendant required (or permitted) to justify? See also *Hare & Grolier Society v. Better Business Bureau* (1946), [1947] 1 D.L.R. 280 (B.C.C.A.); *Polly Peck (Holdings) plc v. Trelford*, [1986] 2 All E.R. 84 (C.A.); and *Pizza Pizza Ltd. v. Toronto Star Newspapers Ltd.* (1998), 42 O.R. (3d) 36 (Div. Ct.), aff'd (2000), 49 O.R. (3d) 254 (C.A.).

2. A defendant cannot justify a defamatory allegation by proving that the plaintiff engaged in other reprehensible behaviour. See *London Computer Operators Training Ltd. v. British Broadcasting Corporation*, [1973] 1 W.L.R. 424 (C.A.). See also *Nazerali v. Mitchell*, 2018 BCCA 104, where the British Columbia Court of Appeal rejected the defendants' contention that they had established the defence of justification by their cross-examination of the plaintiff, which showed him to be "a fraud artist," "dishonest" and "not to be trusted." This did not, in the court's view, amount to proving the truth of defamatory statements that the plaintiff had run stock scams, was an arms dealer, and had ties to the mafia.

3. A defendant cannot succeed by showing that the defamatory statements were literally true if they were expressed in a way to create an overall false impression. See *Dunlap v. Philadelphia Newspapers Inc.*, 301 Pa. Super. 475 (1982); and *Bank of British Columbia v. Canadian Broadcasting Corporation* (1995), 126 D.L.R. (4th) 644 (B.C.C.A.).

4. A discrepancy in material facts will normally defeat a claim of justification: *Green v. Minnes* (1892), 22 O.R. 177 (Q.B.). The difficulty lies in determining whether something is a material fact or an insignificant detail. Generally, the court should consider whether the discrepancy would change the overall impression in the minds of the reader or listener: *Thomson v. Herman* (1931), 39 O.W.N. 375 (H.C.). See also *Casses v. Canadian Broadcasting Corporation*, 2015 BCSC 2150; and *Sandu v. Fairmont Hotels Inc.*, 2017 ONSC 3472.

5. Where the defendant has stated that the plaintiff is guilty of a criminal offence, proof that the plaintiff was convicted of the offence is sufficient: see *York v. Okanagan Broadcasters Ltd.*, [1976] 6 W.W.R. 40 (B.C.S.C.). Historically, however, the defendant had to meet the criminal burden of proof, *i.e.*, beyond a reasonable doubt: *Meier v. Klotz* (1928), 22 Sask. L.R. 385 (C.A.).

In England, this issue is resolved by the *Civil Evidence Act, 1968* (U.K.), c. 64, s. 13, which states that proof of the plaintiff's conviction for a criminal offence is conclusive evidence that the plaintiff committed the offence.

6. Where the plaintiff claims for multiple defamatory statements, a defendant can bring a defence of partial justification at common law to justify one or more of the defamatory imputations. The defendant will remain liable for any statements that have not been justified. However, the court may consider the partial justification in assessing damages for the unjustified statements. For example in *Makow v. Winnipeg Sun* (2003), 172 Man. R. (2d) 213 (Q.B.), aff'd (2004), 184 Man. R. (2d) 97 (C.A.), the defendants justified only 3 of 12 statements made about the plaintiff. The trial judge considered this in assessing damages for lost reputation, stating that "the plaintiff should not be viewed as a university lecturer of unimpeachable character, but one whose reputation has been partially blemished" (at para. 146). Thus, the award reflected that the plaintiff's reputation was not impeccable at the time the libel was published.

Ontario's *Libel and Slander Act*, R.S.O. 1990, c. L.12, s. 22, provides as follows with respect to the defence of partial justification: "In an action for libel or slander for words containing two or more distinct charges against the plaintiff, a defence of justification shall not fail by reason only that the truth of every charge is not proved if the words not proved to be true do not materially injure the plaintiff's reputation having regard to the truth of the remaining charges."

7. Should a defendant succeed on a plea of justification even if the defendant acted maliciously and there was no public interest at stake? Should those who wish to air others' dirty laundry in public be protected from liability? See Wright, "Note" (1939) 17 Can. Bar Rev. 276; Thayer, "The Changing Libel Scene" [1943] Wise. L. Rev. 331; and Harnett & Thornton, "The Truth Hurts: A Critique of a Defense to Defamation" (1949) 35 Va. L. Rev. 425.

Should justification be limited to situations involving matters of public interest? Are there other avenues of redress for a plaintiff whose indiscretions have been made a matter of public knowledge by a malicious defendant? Is this an area where the evolving tort of invasion of privacy might have a role?

(b) ABSOLUTE PRIVILEGE

As its name suggests, absolute privilege provides complete immunity in tort for statements falling within the privilege. There are three categories of communication attracting absolute privilege: statements by executive officers relating to affairs of the state, statements made during Parliamentary proceedings, and statements made in the course of judicial or quasi-judicial proceedings. In all of these situations, immunity from defamation claims is thought necessary to maintain the independence of those involved and to promote honest and candid speech in the public interest.

(i) *Executive Officers*

DOWSON v. THE QUEEN
(1981), 124 D.L.R. (3d) 260 (F.C.A.)

[A member of the Ontario Legislative Assembly requested, during a session of the Assembly, that the Attorney-General seek information about an alleged RCMP investigation into certain members of the New Democratic Party. The Attorney-General agreed to the request and wrote a letter to the Solicitor-General to ask for the information. The Solicitor-General then asked Sexsmith, the Deputy Director General, Operations, of the RCMP, to provide the requested information. Sexsmith, in turn, asked Chief Superintendent Vaughan to make the inquiries and prepare a report. Vaughan submitted the report to the Solicitor-General. Sexsmith then met with the Acting Assistant Deputy Attorney-General of Ontario, McLeod, to discuss the findings. It was during this meeting that the defamatory statements about the plaintiff were made. In particular, the statements suggested that some members of the NDP might support change "by violent and undemocratic means." The excerpt below addresses whether Sexsmith and Vaughan were entitled to assert absolute privilege with respect to the statements.]

The judgment of the Court was delivered by

LE DAIN J:—. . .The respondent's defence of absolute privilege is based on two categories of privileged occasion recognized by the authorities: communications between officers of state in relation to state affairs, and proceedings in Parliament or the Legislature. The learned trial Judge held that there was absolute privilege in the present case on the basis of both of these categories of privileged occasion.

The law with respect to the first category of privileged occasion is stated in 28 Hals., 4th ed., p. 54, para. 107, as follows: "An official communication relating to state affairs, including commercial matters, made by one officer of state to another in the course of his official duty is absolutely privileged." The authority cited for that proposition is *Chatterton v. Secretary of State for India in Council*, [1895] 2 Q.B. 189 (C.A.). That was a case of an action for libel that was dismissed as vexatious on the ground that the statement complained of was protected by absolute privilege. The statement was made by the Secretary of State for India to the Parliamentary Under-Secretary for India to enable the latter to answer a question in the House of Commons concerning the treatment of the plaintiff as an officer in the Indian Army by the Indian military authorities and Government. Lord Esher M.R. said at pp. 190-1:

> The substance of the case is that it is an action brought against him in respect of a communication in writing made by him as Secretary of State, and, therefore, a high official of the state, to an Under-Secretary of State in the course of the performance of his official duty. The master, the judge at chambers, and the Divisional Court have all come to the conclusion that the action is one which cannot by any possibility be maintained; that it is not competent to a civil Court to entertain a suit in respect of the action of an official of state in making such a communication to another official in the course of his official duty, or to inquire whether or not he acted maliciously in making it. I think that conclusion was correct.

And after referring to the authorities, he concluded at pp. 191-2:

In my opinion, the statement of which the plaintiff complains, being a communication relating to a state matter made by one state official to another, was absolutely privileged.

I conclude from what was said in the *Chatterton* case that there are three conditions for this category of absolute privilege: (a) the statement must have been made by one officer of state to another officer of state; (b) it must relate to state matters; and (c) it must be made by an officer of state in the course of his official duty.

The issue with respect to the first condition is whether the statement that was made by Chief Superintendent Vaughan to Acting Assistant Deputy Attorney-General McLeod at the meeting that was also attended by Assistant Commissioner Sexsmith can be said to have been made by one officer of state to another officer of state within the meaning of the principle affirmed in the *Chatterton* case.

In some judicial expressions of this category or occasion of absolute privilege the expression used has been "high officer of state". . . . In *Chatterton*, Lord Esher M.R., after referring to the Secretary of State for India as a "high official of state", used the unqualified expressions "official of state", "officer of state" and "state official" in referring to this occasion of absolute privilege. On the other hand, the passage from *Fraser on the Law of Libel and Slander*, 6th ed., which was adopted by the Court as correctly stating the law, gave as an example of this case of absolute privilege "every communication relating to state matters made by one minister to another, or to the Crown", and the statement in the *Chatterton* case was made by a Minister of the Crown. The case is not clear authority as to the other officers of state who should, on grounds of public policy, enjoy the protection of absolute privilege.

[Le Dain J. surveyed other Commonwealth authorities on the types of officials permitted to claim absolute privilege, ending with a quotation from Denning M.R. that reviewed the state of the law]:

> The authorities do show that a report by a very senior military or naval officer to his superior is absolutely privileged; but nothing else is settled. It is doubtful whether reports by the middle or lower ranks of the army and navy are absolutely privileged. The middle ranks of the police do not appear to be absolutely privileged. It has been held by the High Court of Australia that a report made by an inspector of police to his superior officer is not absolutely privileged; see *Gibbons v. Duffell* [(1932), 47 C.L.R. 520 (H.C.A.)]. It is a nice question whether the secret service should be treated like the police force or like the army or navy. Apart from these difficulties about our own English forces in this country, it is very difficult to say how far this absolute privilege applies to the visiting forces of a friendly foreign power. In *Szalatnay-Stacho v. Fink* [[1946] 2 All E.R. 231] a letter written in England by a senior Czecho-Slovakian officer to his government was held not to be the subject of absolute privilege.

The appellant relied particularly on this passage in his contention that it was arguable whether a statement by a chief superintendent of the R.C.M.P. should be subject to absolute privilege. I would certainly agree, if the statement made by Chief Superintendent Vaughan is to be regarded as his own statement, made on his own behalf and on his own initiative. But it is clear in my opinion that it cannot be so regarded in the light of the facts which must be taken as established. It was a statement that was made for and on behalf of the Solicitor-General of Canada and pursuant to his instructions. The request for information was addressed by the Attorney-General of Ontario to the Solicitor-General. The Solicitor-General replied by letter on

November 30, 1977, setting out the substance of his reply to the Attorney-General's question in two sentences and indicating that he had instructed Assistant Commissioner Sexsmith to provide any further information that the Attorney-General might require at a meeting to be arranged at his convenience. The statement made by Vaughan under Sexsmith's direction at the meeting with McLeod was thus simply an elaboration of the Solicitor-General's reply to the Attorney-General. Vaughan should therefore be likened to a person who makes a statement as the agent of another, and as such should be regarded as having the benefit of the absolute privilege that would clearly apply, on the authority of the Chatterton case, to a statement in relation to a state matter made by the Solicitor-General in the course of his official duty. This principle — that an agent who makes a statement takes the benefit of the privilege that would attach to the statement if made by the person on whose behalf it is made — has been recognized in cases of qualified privilege. . .and I can see no reason why it should not apply to the occasion of absolute privilege created by the statement of a Minister of the Crown in relation to a matter of state, particularly, in view of the necessary delegation that is involved in the exercise of that office: cf. Powell, *The Law of Agency*, 2nd ed. (1961), pp. 279-80.

By the same reasoning the statement must be taken to have been made to Mr. McLeod as an officer acting for and on behalf of the Attorney-General of Ontario and thus to have been made to the Attorney-General, who, like the Solicitor-General of Canada, is clearly an officer of state within the principle in *Chatterton*.

As for the other two conditions for this occasion of absolute privilege, there can be no doubt, in my view, that the statement complained of related to state affairs and that it was made in the course of official duty. It was concerned with surveillance by the R.C.M.P. for security purposes, and it was made in response to a question in the Legislature of Ontario and a formal request for information addressed by the Attorney-General of Ontario to the Solicitor-General of Canada. Because of his responsibility for the R.C.M.P. the Solicitor-General and those acting under his instructions were in the exercise of their official duty in making the statement.

It was the appellant's contention that whether or not the officers of the R.C.M.P. who engaged in the preparation and communication of the report were in the exercise of their official duty was a question of fact that should be allowed to go to trial. It was his contention that the pleadings alleged in effect that the R.C.M.P. had seized an occasion of absolute privilege to pursue an object other than a response to the request for information by the provincial Attorney-General. He argued that on its face the statement complained of did not address the questions raised by the request, but evaded them in the pursuit of some other purpose. It is necessary not to confuse the question whether the statement was made in the exercise of official duty with the question of the intention or motive with which it might have been made — that is, the question of malice, which is irrelevant in a case of absolute privilege. Whether the statement was an adequate answer to the request for information from the Attorney-General or whether it was intended to serve some other purpose at the same time is, in my opinion, beside the point. It purported to be an answer to that request and it was acted on as such.

For these reasons I am of the opinion that the statement made by Chief Superintendent Vaughan to Mr. McLeod was clearly made on an occasion of absolute privilege, and that accordingly the action cannot possibly succeed in so far as it is based on the statement having been made on this occasion. The learned trial Judge was therefore right in striking out the statement of claim and dismissing the action for so much as he did, and accordingly the appeal should be dismissed.

(ii) *Parliamentary Privilege*

Parliamentary privilege provides immunity for defamatory statements made during parliamentary proceedings. Such statements are protected as a matter of policy: legislators should be encouraged to speak freely for the public interest and ought not to be inhibited by fear of actions for defamation. The privilege extends to parliamentary proceedings, including testimony before committees, parliamentary reports and papers. However, it does not protect a member who makes or repeats defamatory statements outside of the assembly.

(iii) *Judicial Proceedings*

There is absolute privilege for statements made in the course of judicial or quasi-judicial proceedings: *Stark v. Auerbach*, [1979] 3 W.W.R. 563 (B.C.S.C.). The rationale for this privilege is that participants in such proceedings should be encouraged to speak honestly and candidly. The privilege also seeks to avoid a multiplicity of proceedings, as when a litigant who is unsuccessful in one proceeding goes on to bring a defamation action against witnesses who testified during that proceeding: *Cinapri v. Guettler* (1997), 33 B.L.R. (2d) 289 (Ont. Gen. Div.). The privilege extends to anyone involved in a judicial or quasi-judicial proceeding, including the judge, jury, counsel, parties and witnesses. It includes not only the trial proper, but also any proceedings leading up to the trial (*e.g.* pleadings, preliminary motions, discovery, written submissions) or following it (motions for a new trial, the assessment of costs, and the satisfaction of judgments). Moreover, the privilege applies even if the statements were made maliciously and without justification: *Royal Aquarium and Summer & Winter Garden Society Ltd. v. Parkinson*, [1892] 1 Q.B. 431 (C.A.).

HUNG v. GARDINER
(2003), 227 D.L.R. (4th) 282 (B.C.C.A.)

The judgment of the court was delivered by

LEVINE J.A.: —

Introduction

At issue in this appeal is whether a person who provides information to a professional disciplinary body about the conduct of one of its members is liable in an action brought by that member. The clear answer is that the communication of the information is subject to absolute privilege, which provides a defence to all claims.

The appellant, Christine Hung, is a member of the Law Society of British Columbia and the Certified General Accountants Association of British Columbia (the "CGA Association"). Actions taken by her while she was employed by a firm of chartered accountants resulted in an investigation and reprimand of her supervisor by the Professional Conduct Enquiry Committee (the "PCEC") of the respondent, the Institute of Chartered Accountants of British Columbia (the "ICABC"). The members of the PCEC. . . decided that the Law Society and the CGA Association should be informed of the appellant's conduct. The respondent, Brian Gardiner, the Director of

Ethics for the ICABC, forwarded to those professional bodies the report of the investigator, the respondent, Wayne McIlroy. Both professional bodies declined to investigate further or to take any disciplinary action against the appellant.

The appellant brought an action for damages for defamation, malicious prosecution, negligence, breach of confidentiality under the *Freedom of Information and Protection of Privacy Act*, R.S.B.C. 1996, c. 165, breach of the *Accountants (Chartered) Act*, R.S.B.C. 1996, c. 3, and bylaws, misfeasance in public office, breach of the *Privacy Act*, R.S.B.C. 1996, c. 373, invasion of privacy and conspiracy.

Mr. Justice Joyce, after a summary trial under Rule 18A of the Supreme Court Rules, dismissed all of the appellant's claims, finding that they were barred by the absolute privilege that surrounded the act of providing the report to the professional bodies. . . .

. . .

Absolute Privilege

The trial judge began his discussion of the application of the defence of absolute privilege by quoting the decision of Smith J. in *Sussman v. Eales* (1985), 33 C.C.L.T. 156 (Ont. H.C.J.) at 157, appeal allowed in part (1986), 25 C.P.C. (2d) 7 (Ont. C.A.).

. . .

Smith J. explained the rationale for the immunity [regarding complaints to professional bodies] (at pp. 159-60):

> The principle is the same. It is a question of balancing two interests. The public interest should outweigh that of the individual for at least two reasons. Firstly the immunity will only be conferred upon a citizen complaining in a confidential way to a body created by statute. A communication of that kind can hardly be said to be a publication of the kind that is apt to harm one's reputation in the community to a degree sufficient to attract an award of compensation.

> Secondly, the right to engage in professional activities must be the subject of rules governing them. These rules cannot be enforced without a corresponding right in the members of the public to complain uninhibited and without fear of being found wrong and as a result being subject to actions in defamation. Surely it is a small price for a professional person to pay.

The Court of Appeal agreed that the doctrine of immunity applied to statements made to a disciplinary body [p. 8]:

> In our view, the doctrine of immunity by reason of absolute privilege with respect to statements made in the course of proceedings before a statutory body, exercising disciplinary powers over a member with respect to unprofessional conduct, applies to statements made in a letter of complaint addressed to the Registrar of the Royal College of Dental Surgeons. It is a document incidental to the initiation of quasi-judicial proceedings, and it matters not that the Complaints Committee has investigatory powers which may or may not lead to a direction that the matter be referred to the Discipline Committee. A complainant in the respondent Eales' position should not be deterred by the fear of proceedings and "the vexation of defending actions". (*Lincoln v. Daniels*, [1962] 1 Q.B. 237, [1961] 3 All E.R. 740 at 748 (C.A.).)

In *Sussman*, the issue was whether the body to which the complaint was sent was quasi-judicial or whether it was merely administrative in nature.

That is not an issue on this appeal. The trial judge found, and the appellant does not dispute that both the Law Society and the CGA Association are quasi-judicial bodies, empowered by statute, and each having a duty, to investigate complaints and hold disciplinary proceedings. The trial judge concluded that the act of sending the report to the Law Society and the CGA Association was the necessary first step in quasi-judicial proceedings, and was sufficiently proximate to potential disciplinary proceedings to be protected by absolute privilege.

The appellant claims that the trial judge erred in finding that the respondents enjoyed absolute privilege where neither the Law Society nor the CGA Association commenced disciplinary proceedings against her. She argues that absolute privilege extends to a complaint submitted to a quasi-judicial body only if proceedings ensue.

[Levine J.A. reviewed similar arguments in other cases.]

In support of her argument that neither the Law Society nor the CGA Association exercised any quasi-judicial functions when they decided not to proceed with disciplinary action, the appellant relies on *Lincoln v. Daniels*, [1962] 1 Q.B. 237 (C.A.); *Rajkhowa v. Watson* (1998), 167 N.S.R. (2d) 108 (S.C.); and *O'Connor v. Waldron*, [1935] A.C. 76, [1935] 1 D.L.R. 260 (P.C.), reversing [1932] S.C.R. 183, [1932] 1 D.L.R. 166.

[The discussion of *Lincoln v. Daniels* is omitted.]

In *Rajkhowa*, the defendant investigated and audited claims submitted by doctors under the Medical Services Insurance Plan. He gave information to the police concerning the plaintiff's billing practices, so that they could conduct a criminal investigation. No charges were laid and the investigation came to an end.

Hood J., citing from *Sussman*, set out the test to determine whether the information was protected by absolute privilege (at para. 36):

> The proper question to be asked in this case is that set out by Smith, J. in Sussman: "whether the body to which the complaint . . . was sent is quasi-judicial or whether it is merely administrative in nature."

Citing from *Boyachyk v. Dukes* (1982), 136 D.L.R. (3d) 28 (Alta. Q.B.), he applied the test as follows (at para. 46):

> If the question is asked: Do the police exercise quasi-judicial or administrative functions? to ask the question is to answer it. The police investigate, they do not adjudicate. Or to paraphrase Adams, J. in *Boyachyk*: they do not have the duty and authority to determine guilt or innocence nor the disciplinary powers to enforce sanctions. The police are therefore in a position similar to that of the Bar Council in the *Lincoln* case: they do not exercise judicial or quasi-judicial functions.

It is noteworthy that in *Boyachyk*, the court found that a complaint to the chief of police concerning the conduct of a police officer was subject to absolute privilege, because:

> Unlike the commissioner in the *O'Connor* case and the bar council in the *Lincoln* case, the chief of police in the present case had not only the authority but the duty to determine the guilt or innocence of the plaintiff and the disciplinary powers to enforce sanctions.

The appellant also relies on *O'Connor*, arguing that it settled the law on absolute privilege in Canada. The *O'Connor* case concerned words uttered by a commissioner appointed under the *Combines Investigation Act*, R.S.C. 1927, c. 26, alleging misconduct by the plaintiff, who was a barrister, during proceedings under the Act. In his defence, the commissioner claimed he uttered the words on an occasion of absolute privilege. In determining the issue, Lord Atkin, writing for the Privy Council, stated (at p. 81):

> The question therefore in every case is whether the tribunal in question has similar attributes to a court of justice or acts in a manner similar to that in which courts act?

He applied the test to the facts of the case as follows:

> Has then a commissioner appointed under the Combines Investigation Act attributes similar to those of a court of justice; or does he act in a manner similar to that in which such courts act? In their Lordships' opinion the answer must be in the negative.

He explained (at p. 82):

> It is only necessary to remember that the commissioner by the Act is empowered to enter premises and examine the books, papers and records of suspected persons to see how far his functions differ from those of a judge. His conclusion is expressed in a report; it determines no rights, nor the guilt or innocence of any one. It does not even initiate any proceedings, which have to be left to the ordinary criminal procedure.

In the result, the Privy Council reversed the decision of the Supreme Court of Canada and adopted the dissenting reasons of Hodgins J.A., of the Appellate Division of the Supreme Court of Ontario ([1931] O.R. 608, [1931] 4 D.L.R. 147). In reaching the conclusion that absolute privilege did not apply, Hodgins J.A. (at pp. 614-5) cited the following passage from *Odgers on Libel and Slander*, 6th ed. (1929), at p. 195:

> An absolute privilege also attaches to all proceedings of, and to all evidence given before, any tribunal which by law, though not expressly a Court, exercises judicial functions — that is to say has power to determine the legal rights and to effect (*sic*) the status of the parties who appear before it.

On close reading, the authorities cited by the appellant are consistent with those relied on by the trial judge. He applied the proper test to determine whether the report was sent on an occasion of absolute privilege. The test is whether the Law Society and the CGA Association, exercising their disciplinary powers, have attributes similar to a court of justice or act in a manner similar to that in which such courts act. There is no real question that they do.

The Law Society and the CGA Association are quasi-judicial bodies and are not merely administrative in nature. They have the power to determine the legal rights and to affect the status of their members. Thus, a complaint made to them in a confidential way concerning a member's conduct is absolutely privileged.

There are important public policy reasons for this finding. Absolute privilege allows a member of the public to raise a concern about the conduct of a professional person, without fear of reprisal. In this way, the immunity afforded by absolute privilege protects both professionals and the public.

The purpose of the immunity would be undermined if absolute privilege only applied where the complaint leads to proceedings, as contended by the appellant. Nor is the defence of absolute privilege affected by the fact that the Law Society and the CGA Association declined to pursue the matter further.

Thus, the trial judge was correct in finding that the respondents sent the report to the Law Society and the CGA Association on an occasion of absolute privilege.

The trial judge was also correct in concluding that the absolute privilege applies to all causes of action arising from that act. That is clear from the reasons for judgment of Sellers L.J., concurred in by Willmer and Diplock L.JJ., in *Marrinan v. Vibart*, [1962] 3 All E.R. 380 (C.A.) where, after citing the Court's decision in *Lincoln*, he said (at p. 383):

> Whatever form of action is sought to be derived from what was said or done in the course of judicial proceedings must suffer the same fate of being barred by the rule which protects witnesses in their evidence before the court and in the preparation of the evidence which is to be so given. . . .

Sellers L.J. quoted further from *Royal Aquarium [and Summer and Winter Garden Society v. Parkinson*, [1892] 1 Q.B. 431 (C.A.)], as follows:

> But it does not matter whether the action is framed as an action for defamation or as an action analogous to an action for malicious prosecution or for deceit or, as in this instance, for combining or conspiring together for the purpose of injuring another: the rule of law is that no action lies against witnesses in respect of evidence prepared (*Watson v. M'Ewan, Watson v. Jones* [[1905] A.C. 480], given, adduced or procured by them in the course of legal proceedings. The law protects witnesses and others, not for their benefit, but for a higher interest, namely, the advancement of public justice.

. . .

The appellant's action against the respondents cannot be maintained. All of the respondents are entitled to claim absolute privilege and are immune from liability for their actions in sending information to the Law Society and the CGA Association concerning the appellant's professional conduct.

NOTES AND QUESTIONS

1. Based on the authorities cited in *Hung v. Gardiner*, how is a quasi-judicial body identified for the purposes of absolute privilege? The following bodies have been found to be quasi-judicial: a board of review under the *Workers Compensation Act* (*Stark v. Auerbach* (1979), 11 B.C.L.R. 355 (S.C.)); the registrar of the Royal College of Dental Surgeons initiating a complaint against a dentist (*Sussman v. Eales* (1985), 33 C.C.L.T. 156 (Ont. H.C.), rev'd on other grounds (1986), 25 C.P.C. (2d) 7 (Ont. C.A.); the Ontario New Home Warranty Plan when receiving complaints against builders (*Gala Homes Inc. v. Flisar* (2000), 48 O.R. (3d) 470 (S.C.J.), aff'd on other grounds 2000 CarswellOnt 3584 (C.A.) (WL Can)); arbitration proceedings under residential tenancy legislation (*Zanetti v. Bonniehon Enterprises Ltd.*, 2002 CarswellBC 1945 (S.C.) (WL Can), aff'd 2003 CarswellBC 1278 (C.A.) (WL Can); and a hospital board cancelling a doctor's hospital privileges under a statutory regime (*Cimolai v. Hall* (2004), 25 B.C.L.R. (4th) 117 (S.C.)). See also *Trapp v. Mackie*, [1979] 1 W.L.R. 377 (H.L.), where Lord Diplock summarized the criteria identifying a quasi-judicial body.

2. An important factor to consider when determining whether a body's proceedings attract absolute privilege is whether such privilege is necessary in order to protect the public interest. In other words, would a lack of absolute privilege impede the body's search for truth and justice? Given that absolute privilege provides immunity for defamatory statements, it should not be extended without clear justification. See *Mann v. O'Neill*, [1997] HCA 28; *Elliott v. Insurance Crime Prevention Bureau*, 2005 NSCA 115; *Wilson v. Williams*, 2013 BCCA 471; *Amato v. Walsh*, 2013 ONCA 258; and *Gutowski v. Clayton*, 2014 ONCA 921.

3. Although statements made by witnesses in court are generally protected by absolute privilege, it is doubtful whether this protects statements that are completely irrelevant to the proceedings. Thus, a witness cannot use the courtroom as an opportunity to utter gratuitous defamatory statements: see *Duke v. Puts* (2004), 241 Sask. R. 187 (C.A.); and *Liboiron v. Majola* (2007), 72 Alta. L.R. (4th) 222 (C.A.). Nevertheless, the threshold for relevancy is low: a statement will be relevant if it has some nexus or connection to the proceedings. For instance, in *Rybachuk v. Dyrland* (2007), 222 Man. R. (2d) 131 (Master), the defendant alleged in an affidavit to an assessor during child custody proceedings that the plaintiff (the father) was involved in organized crime and drug trafficking and was a "dangerous person." These statements were protected by absolute privilege.

4. Absolute privilege may also apply to defamatory statements that are made prior to the official commencement of judicial proceedings, such as communications by a solicitor, as long as they are directly concerned with actual contemplated proceedings. In deciding whether absolute privilege applies to such statements, the courts will consider whether: steps had been taken to prepare for litigation; the decision to litigate had already been made; the defendant commenced legal action shortly after publication of the statements; the statements were made for the purpose of obtaining evidence; and the statements were made during a solicitor's investigation of a client's case. See *Moseley-Williams v. Hansler Industries Ltd.* (2004), 32 C.C.L.T. (3d) 266 (Ont. S.C.J.); *Peak Innovations Inc. v. Pacific Rim Brackets Ltd.* (2009), 99 B.C.L.R. (4th) 388 (S.C.); and *1522491 Ontario Inc. v. Stewart, Esten Professional Corporation* (2010), 100 O.R. (3d) 596 (Div. Ct.). But see *Rubin v. Ross*, 2013 SKCA 21, in which the court found that absolute privilege did not extend to publicly posting a grievance report in order to find corroborating witnesses.

The defence is not defeated by the defendant's malice or bad faith. It seems, however, that Ontario extends the pre-litigation period further back than other jurisdictions. See *Lincoln v. Daniels*, [1961] 3 W.L.R. 866 (C.A.).

See generally Hill, "The Litigation Privilege: Its Place in Contemporary Jurisprudence" (2015) 44:2 Hofstra L. Rev. 401.

5. According to *Dowson*, what officials qualify for executive privilege? Is there good reason to restrict such privilege to "high officials?" See *Gibbons v. Duffell* (1932), 47 C.L.R. 520 (H.C.A.); *Merricks v. Nott-Bower* (1964), [1965] 1 Q.B. 57 (C.A.); and Williams, "Absolute Privilege for Licensing Justices" (1909) 25 L.Q.R. 188. See also *Guergis v. Novak*, 2013 ONCA 449, in which a member of a cabinet minister's staff had absolute privilege in reporting to the Prime Minister's Chief of Staff that the plaintiff (a Member of Parliament) had been seen using cocaine.

6. For the law on parliamentary privilege, see generally Veeder, "Absolute Immunity in Defamation: Legislative and Executive Proceedings" (1910) 10 Col. L.R. 131.

(c) QUALIFIED PRIVILEGE

Qualified privilege protects defamatory materials that are communicated on certain occasions. It applies even if the statements are untrue. Unlike absolute privilege, however, it does not apply if the plaintiff can establish that the statements were made maliciously. Moreover, there are no clear rules as to the occasions attracting qualified privilege. Generally speaking, it applies in situations where the speaker has an interest or duty (legal, social or moral) to make the statement, and the recipient has a reciprocal interest to receive the statement: see *Toogood v. Spryring* (1834), 149 E.R. 1044 (Exch.). Qualified privilege also applies to statements made in protection of one's own interests. The types of occasions attracting qualified privilege can be roughly (and non-exhaustively) categorized as follows.

First, qualified privilege applies to statements made by the defendant in protection of his or her own interests. Thus, a person who is being subjected to an attack on his or her character is permitted to utter statements to defend him or herself. Such statements will be protected by qualified privilege unless they are excessive or irrelevant to the original attack. The occasion cannot be used as an opportunity to launch gratuitous insults. At the same time, the courts will not be overly critical of statements uttered in self-defence. Lord Atkinson wrote in *Adam v. Ward*, [1917] A.C. 309 at 334 (H.L.) that the defendant will be protected "even though his language should be violent or excessively strong, if, having regard to all the circumstances of the case, he might have honestly and on reasonable grounds believed that what he wrote or said was true and necessary for the purpose of his vindication, though in fact it was not so." See also *Davies & Davies Ltd. v. Kott*, [1979] 2 S.C.R. 686; and *Harbour Radio Pty Ltd. v. Trad*, [2012] HCA 44.

Second, qualified privilege applies in situations where the defendant publishes the relevant statements in order to protect the interests of another person. The defendant must show that he or she had a legal, social or moral duty to communicate the information. It typically applies in situations where, for example, credit or character references are provided with respect to the plaintiff. It may also apply if the defendant has a legal obligation to report matters like suspected child abuse: *Rolon v. Bell*, 2015 ONSC 6042. It is less clear what situations will qualify as creating a "moral duty" to communicate information. A leading English case, *Watson v. Longsdon*, [1930] 1 K.B. 130 (C.A.), decided that qualified privilege did not apply when a friend of the plaintiff's wife informed the wife of the plaintiff's alleged infidelity. More recently, the Ontario Court of Appeal refused to extend qualified privilege when the defendants reported their suspicions of immoral behaviour to the plaintiff's priest: *D'Addario v. Smith*, 2018 ONCA 163.

Third, communications made in the furtherance of a common interest may be protected by qualified privilege, as long as there is a reciprocity of interests. For instance, in *McLoughlin v. Kutasy*, [1979] 2 S.C.R. 311, the defendant was a physician who was hired to examine prospective employees for a hazardous construction project and make reports about the candidates to the Ontario Ministry of Labour, Construction Safety Branch. The plaintiff was denied employment as a result of the doctor's report, which suggested the plaintiff had a psychopathic personality and "would be dangerous" to the safety of the project. The defendant successfully argued that the statements were protected by qualified privilege, since he had a duty to make the report to the government and the government had a duty to receive it. See also *Wang v. British Columbia Medical Association*, 2014 BCCA 162.

Finally, qualified privilege will attach to statements that are made in the protection of the public interest. This category covers a broad spectrum of occasions, including some political speech, as well as communications among public officials over matters of public interest, health or safety. It also applies to speech in municipal politics: *Prud'homme v. Prud'homme*, [2002] 4 S.C.R. 663; *Wells v. Sears*, 264 Nfld. & P.E.I.R. 171 (N.L.C.A.); and *Gutowski v. Clayton*, 2014 ONCA 921. Again, it is generally necessary that the speaker have a duty to publish the information and the recipient have a reciprocal interest to receive it. For this reason, defamatory statements made by the media are not generally covered under the rubric of public interest: there is no *duty* for the media to report matters of public interest. See *Globe & Mail Ltd. v. Boland*, [1960] S.C.R. 203; and *Banks v. Globe & Mail Ltd.*, [1961] S.C.R. 474. However, media defendants may now take advantage of the "responsible communication on matters of public interest" defence established in *Grant v. Torstar Corp.*, [2009] 3 S.C.R. 640, which is excerpted later in this chapter.

The qualified privilege with respect to public interest was extended in *Campbell v. Jones* (2002), 209 N.S.R. (2d) 81 (C.A.). During an investigation into a theft at a school, the plaintiff police officer conducted a strip search of three female students, in view of each other and an open window facing a hallway. The plaintiff conceded that she had violated the students' *Charter* rights to be free from arbitrary detention and unreasonable search. The lawyers representing the students then held a press conference in which they suggested that the searches would not have occurred if the students had not been black and poor. A majority of the Nova Scotia Court of Appeal held that the statements at the press conference were protected by qualified privilege. The majority reasoned at para. 58 that "lawyers, by virtue of their role as officers of the court with a specific duty to improve the administration of justice and uphold the law, have a special relationship with and responsibility to the public to speak out when those involved in enforcing our laws violate the fundamental rights of citizens." Thus, the public interest in receiving the information about the officer's conduct was more important than the plaintiff's right not to be defamed to "the world at large." For commentary see Duckworth, "The Impact of 'Charter Values' and Campbell v. Jones: Is It Now Easier to Establish Qualified Privilege Against Defamation?" (2006) 29 Dal. L.J. 277.

A separate form of qualified privilege is that of "fair and accurate reporting." This applies to reports of proceedings that are open to the public, such as judicial proceedings, legislative proceedings, public meetings and public documents. This privilege is available at common law as long as the reporting is fair and accurate, and not blasphemous, indecent, seditious or malicious. Fair and accurate reporting is also covered by legislation in some jurisdictions. For example, ss. 3-4 of the Ontario *Libel and Slander Act*, R.S.O. 1990, c. L.12, define the qualified privilege afforded to the media for fair and accurate reporting.

The common law privilege for fair and accurate reporting of a judicial proceeding was discussed in *Hill v. Church of Scientology*, [1995] 2 S.C.R. 1130. In particular, the court had to determine whether the privilege applied to a report about court documents that had not yet been filed.

HILL v. CHURCH OF SCIENTOLOGY
[1995] 2 S.C.R. 1130

[The plaintiff, Casey Hill, was a Crown attorney working in Toronto. The first defendant, the Church of Scientology, intended to initiate contempt of court proceedings against the plaintiff, alleging that he had misled a judge and opened sealed documents pertaining to the defendant. Before filing the notice of motion, the defendants organized a press conference on the steps of Osgoode Hall. The second defendant, Morris Manning, represented the Church of Scientology and appeared at the press conference wearing his barrister's gown. Manning read out the notice of motion at the press conference, including the accusations against the plaintiff and the desired sanction of fine or imprisonment. Copies of the notice of motion were also distributed to the reporters in attendance. The plaintiff was exonerated at the contempt proceedings and then brought a defamation claim against the defendants. The following excerpt deals with the defendants' argument that their statements were covered by qualified privilege, *i.e.*, that they constituted a report on court proceedings.]

CORY J.:—. . .Qualified privilege attaches to the occasion upon which the communication is made, and not to the communication itself. As Lord Atkinson explained in *Adam v. Ward*, [1917] A.C. 309 (H.L.), at p. 334:

> . . . a privileged occasion is . . . an occasion where the person who makes a communication has an interest or a duty, legal, social, or moral, to make it to the person to whom it is made, and the person to whom it is so made has a corresponding interest or duty to receive it. This reciprocity is essential.

This passage was quoted with approval in *McLoughlin v. Kutasy*, [1979] 2 S.C.R. 311, at p. 321.

The legal effect of the defence of qualified privilege is to rebut the inference, which normally arises from the publication of defamatory words, that they were spoken with malice. Where the occasion is shown to be privileged, the *bona fides* of the defendant is presumed and the defendant is free to publish, with impunity, remarks which may be defamatory and untrue about the plaintiff. However, the privilege is not absolute and can be defeated if the dominant motive for publishing the statement is actual or express malice. See *Horrocks v. Lowe*, [1975] A.C. 135 (H.L.), at p. 149.

Malice is commonly understood, in the popular sense, as spite or ill-will. However, it also includes, as Dickson J. (as he then was) pointed out in dissent in *Cherneskey* [*v. Armadale Publishers*, [1979] 1 S.C.R. 1067] at p. 1099, "any indirect motive or ulterior purpose" that conflicts with the sense of duty or the mutual interest which the occasion created. See, also, *Taylor v. Despard*, [1956] O.R. 963 (C.A.). Malice may also be established by showing that the defendant spoke dishonestly, or in knowing or reckless disregard for the truth. See *McLoughlin, supra*, at pp. 323-24, and *Netupsky v. Craig*, [1973] S.C.R. 55, at pp. 61-62.

Qualified privilege may also be defeated when the limits of the duty or interest have been exceeded. . . .. As Loreburn E. stated at pp. 320-21 in *Adam v. Ward, supra*:

. . . the fact that an occasion is privileged does not necessarily protect all that is said or written on that occasion. Anything that is not relevant and pertinent to the discharge of the duty or the exercise of the right or the safeguarding of the interest which creates the privilege will not be protected.

In other words, the information communicated must be reasonably appropriate in the context of the circumstances existing on the occasion when that information was given. For example, in *Douglas v. Tucker*, [1952] 1 S.C.R. 275, the defendant, during an election campaign, stated that the plaintiff, who was the officer of an investment company, had charged a farmer and his wife an exorbitant rate of interest causing them to lose their property. The plaintiff maintained that the allegation was without foundation. In response, the defendant asserted that the plaintiff was facing a charge of fraud which had been adjourned until after the election. This Court held that the defendant had an interest in responding to the plaintiff's denial, thereby giving rise to an occasion of qualified privilege. However, it ruled that the occasion was exceeded because the defendant's comments went beyond what was "germane and reasonably appropriate" (p. 286).

In *Sun Life Assurance Co. of Canada v. Dalrymple*, [1965] S.C.R. 302, the district manager of the defendant insurance company threatened to resign and take the district agents with him. This Court held that it fell within the scope of the privilege for the company to make certain defamatory comments about the plaintiff in order to dissuade its agents from leaving.

The principal question to be answered in this appeal is whether the recitation of the contents of the notice of motion by Morris Manning took place on an occasion of qualified privilege. If so, it remains to be determined whether or not that privilege was exceeded and thereby defeated.

The traditional common law rule with respect to reports on documents relating to judicial proceedings is set out in *Gatley on Libel and Slander* (8th ed. 1981), at p. 252, in these words:

> The rule of law is that, where there are judicial proceedings before a properly constituted judicial tribunal exercising its jurisdiction in open court, then the publication without malice of a fair and accurate report of what takes place before that tribunal is privileged.

. . .

The rationale behind this rule is that the public has a right to be informed about all aspects of proceedings to which it has the right of access. This is why a news report referring to the contents of any document filed as an exhibit, or admitted as evidence during the course of the proceedings, is privileged. However, the common law immunity was not extended to a report on pleadings or other documents which had not been filed with the court or referred to in open court. Duff C.J. explained the reasoning for this in *Gazette Printing Co. v. Shallow* (1909), 41 S.C.R. 339, at p. 360:

> The publicity of proceedings involving the conduct of a judicial authority serves the important purposes of impressing those concerned in the administration of justice with a sense of public responsibility, and of affording every member of the community an opportunity of observing for himself the mode in which the business of the public tribunals is carried on; but no such object would appear to be generally served by applying the privilege to the publication of preliminary statements of claims and

defence relating only to private transactions; formulated by the parties themselves; in respect of which no judicial action has been taken, and upon which judicial action may never be invoked. It is only when such preliminary statements or the claims or defences embodied in them form the basis or the subject of some hearing before, or some action by, a court or a judicial officer, that their contents can become the object of any real public concern as touching the public administration of justice.

In *Edmonton Journal* [*v. Alberta (Attorney General)*, [1989] 2 S.C.R. 1326] at pp. 1338-40, I noted that the public scrutiny of our courts by the press was fundamentally important in our democratic society and that s. 2*(b)* protected not only speakers, but listeners as well. This right to report on court proceedings extended to pleadings and court documents filed before trial, since access to these documents served the same societal needs as reporting on trials. Even in private actions, such as those for wrongful dismissal or for personal damages, the public may well have an interest in knowing the kinds of submissions which can be put forward.

Both societal standards and the legislation have changed with regard to access to court documents. When the qualified privilege rule was set out in *Shallow, supra*, court documents were not open to the public. Today, the right of access is guaranteed by legislative provision, in this case s. 137(1) of the *Courts of Justice Act*, R.S.O. 1990, c. C.43. As well, s. 2*(b)* of the *Charter* may in some circumstances provide a basis for gaining access to some court documents. However, just as s. 137(1) provides for limitations on the right of access to court documents, so too is the s. 2*(b)* guarantee subject to reasonable limits that can be demonstrably justified in a free and democratic society. This Court's reasons in *Canadian Newspapers Co. v. Canada (Attorney General)*, [1988] 2 S.C.R. 122, provide an illustration of the kind of restriction that has been upheld in relation to information flowing from court proceedings. In that case, the constitutionality of s. 442(3) of the *Criminal Code* was upheld. It imposed a publication ban on the identity of a complainant in sexual assault cases (or any information that might disclose her identity) upon the request of that complainant. There is no need to elaborate further on the scope of access, however, since it does not arise on the facts of this case. It is sufficient to observe that, in appropriate circumstances, s. 2*(b)* may provide the means to gain access to court documents. It follows that the concept of qualified privilege should be modified accordingly.

The public interest in documents filed with the court is too important to be defeated by the kind of technicality which arose in this case. The record demonstrates that, prior to holding the press conference, Morris Manning had every intention of initiating the contempt action in accordance with the prevailing rules, and had given instructions to this effect. In fact, the proper documents were served and filed the very next morning. The fact that, by some misadventure, the strict procedural requirement of filing the documents had not been fulfilled at the time of the press conference should not defeat the qualified privilege which attached to this occasion.

This said, it is my conclusion that Morris Manning's conduct far exceeded the legitimate purposes of the occasion. The circumstances of this case called for great restraint in the communication of information concerning the proceedings launched against Casey Hill. As an experienced lawyer, Manning ought to have taken steps to confirm the allegations that were being made. This is particularly true since he should have been aware of the Scientology investigation pertaining to access to the sealed documents. In those circumstances he was duty bound to wait until the investigation was completed before launching such a serious attack on Hill's professional integrity.

Manning failed to take either of these reasonable steps. As a result of this failure, the permissible scope of his comments was limited and the qualified privilege which attached to his remarks was defeated.

The press conference was held on the steps of Osgoode Hall in the presence of representatives from several media organizations. This constituted the widest possible dissemination of grievous allegations of professional misconduct that were yet to be tested in a court of law. His comments were made in language that portrayed Hill in the worst possible light. This was neither necessary nor appropriate in the existing circumstances. While it is not necessary to characterize Manning's conduct as amounting to actual malice, it was certainly high-handed and careless. It exceeded any legitimate purpose the press conference may have served. His conduct, therefore, defeated the qualified privilege that attached to the occasion.

[La Forest, Gonthier, McLachlin, Iacobucci and Major JJ. concurred with Cory J.]

L'HEUREUX-DUBÉ J.:—I have had the advantage of reading the reasons of my colleague Justice Cory and, except on one point, generally agree with them as well as with his disposition of this appeal.

. . .

. . . the one issue on which I part company with my colleague concerns the scope of the defence of qualified privilege. Traditionally, this Court has held that the defence of qualified privilege is available with respect to reports of judicial proceedings, but not with respect to reports of pleadings in purely private litigation upon which no judicial action has yet been taken: *Gazette Printing Co. v. Shallow* (1909), 41 S.C.R. 339. The appellants, however, argue that *Shallow* is no longer good law as it had been overtaken by this Court's more recent decision in *Edmonton Journal v. Alberta (Attorney General)*, [1989] 2 S.C.R. 1326. My colleague appears to accept this argument. Accordingly, he broadens the scope of the defence of qualified privilege, making it available with respect to reports of pleadings upon which no judicial action has yet been taken. I disagree. In my view, *Shallow* and *Edmonton Journal* are entirely consistent. In this respect, I adopt the following statement from the judgment of the Court of Appeal in the case at hand ((1994), 18 O.R. (3d) 385, at p. 427):

> We were urged to extrapolate from *Edmonton Journal* the proposition that the common law of defamation should respect such constitutional forms of expression as the reporting of information pertaining to intended court proceedings by conferring qualified privilege on the occasion of the publication of such reports. With respect, we do not agree. *Edmonton Journal* struck down, in the name of freedom of expression, statutory provisions which sought to inhibit the publication of the details of pending matrimonial and other civil actions. But it by no means follows that the publication of such details should be accorded the mantle of qualified privilege if they are defamatory.

> *Edmonton Journal* and *Gazette Printing* stand together without conflict: there is a right to publish details of judicial proceedings before they are heard in open court, but such publication does not enjoy the protection of qualified privilege if it is defamatory. As Duff J. noted in the extract from p. 364 of *Gazette Printing* set out above, no such privilege is necessary if the statements published are true, and no such privilege is desirable if they are not true.

Subject to the above, I would dispose of this appeal as does my colleague Cory J.

[The appeal was dismissed. The portions of the judgment pertaining to damages are reproduced later in this chapter.]

NOTES AND QUESTIONS

1. What does Cory J. mean when he says that qualified privilege "attaches to the occasion upon which the communication is made, and not to the communication itself?"

2. What is the *ratio decidendi* of the majority's decision on the issue of qualified privilege?

3. How does L'Heureux-Dubé J. reconcile *Edmonton Journal* and *Gazette Printing*? If statements are defamatory, how can they be considered "fair and accurate reporting?"

4. It is not necessary for the media to consult all the parties mentioned in a judgment or to review court files before publishing a report on a judicial decision. The defence only requires that the media report be fair and accurate. Further, the defence is not invalidated simply because the judge's decision is later reversed by a higher court. See *Chidley-Hill v. Daw*, 2010 CarswellOnt 9536 (C.A.) (WL Can).

5. The defence of qualified privilege will be defeated if the defendant acted with actual or express malice. See *Botiuk v. Toronto Free Press Publications Ltd.*, [1995] 3 S.C.R. 3. Malice includes spite and ill-will, but also includes situations where the defendant publishes a comment knowing or being recklessly indifferent as to whether it is false, or for a dominant purpose unrelated to the privileged occasion. See *Smith v. Cross* (2009), 99 B.C.L.R. (4th) 214 (C.A.).

6. The defence of qualified privilege will also be lost by "over-publication": publishing more information than is necessary or to parties who have no duty or interest to receive the information. See *Teamsters Local Union 987 v. O'Holloran* (2005), 371 A.R. 137 (C.A.); *Vanderkooy v. Vanderkooy*, 2013 ONSC 4796; and *A.J.W. v. B.W.*, 2016 ONCA 581. In *McGarrigle v. Dalhousie University* (2007), 252 N.S.R. (2d) 280 (S.C.), the defendant athletic director sent a self-disclosure letter to Canadian Interuniversity Sports indicating that a basketball player had played several games while ineligible. It was essentially conceded that this was covered by qualified privilege. However, the plaintiff basketball coach argued that qualified privilege was lost because the self-disclosure letter was also shown to certain university employees and was copied to Atlantic University Sport (AUS), which runs the regional basketball league. The court acknowledged that it would have been more prudent to send AUS a more limited communication indicating that some games might have to be forfeited or rescheduled. Nevertheless, the court explained that there should be a broad interpretation of which parties have an "interest" in receiving the information, and concluded that the communications to AUS were indeed covered by qualified privilege.

7. Because of the general need for reciprocity of interests, the defence of qualified privilege will typically fail if the defamatory statements are made "to the world." See *Jones v. Bennett*, [1969] SCR 277. In *Angle v. LaPierre* (2008), 89 Alta. L.R. (4th) 56

(C.A.), the defendants criticized the education system, including allegations of dishonesty and abuse of position against various principals and teachers. While the court acknowledged that there was a public interest in the education system, qualified privilege only applied to statements or complaints made to proper authorities, such as school boards or teacher licensing bodies. Qualified privilege did not apply to statements posted on a public website. See also *Gibbs v. Jalbert* (1996), 18 B.C.L.R. (3d) 351 (C.A.); *Rubin v. Ross*, 2013 SKCA 21; and *Elkow v. Sana*, 2015 ABQB 803. But see *Shavluk v. Green Party of Canada*, 2010 BCSC 804, aff'd 2011 BCCA 286, in which the defence of qualified privilege applied to a press release by the Green Party in which it withdrew its endorsement of the plaintiff's electoral candidacy as a result of his apparently anti-Semitic beliefs. The court found that, given that a federal election was imminent, the public at large had an interest in learning that the Green Party no longer endorsed the candidate.

8. In some instances, the defence of qualified privilege may be circumvented by bringing a claim in negligence rather than defamation. In *Young v. Bella*, [2006] 1 S.C.R. 108, the plaintiff was studying to become a social worker. She submitted a term paper that failed to acknowledge the source of a case study. As a result, her professor suspected that the study might be a personal confession that the plaintiff had abused children. The professor and director of the school reported this suspicion to Child Protection Services, and the report was subsequently circulated to police and several social workers, effectively ruining the plaintiff's intended career. The plaintiff's negligence claim was successful because the professor had acted out of mere speculation and conjecture. The trial judge withdrew the parallel claim of defamation from the jury. Would the professor's statements in the case have been governed by qualified privilege? See also *Spring v. Guardian Assurance plc*, [1994] 3 All E.R. 129 (H.L.), where the House of Lords allowed the plaintiff's claim that his employer's negligent reference letter had prevented him from obtaining subsequent employment. The House of Lords seemed determined to bypass the effects of qualified privilege, which would have defeated the plaintiff's claim in defamation. See Mitchell, "Negligent Misstatement in Canada: *Young v Bella*" (2006) 17 K.C.L.J. 341; and Descheemaeker, "Protecting Reputation: Defamation and Negligence" (2009) 29 O.J.L.S. 603.

(d) FAIR COMMENT

The defence of fair comment reflects the importance of free speech in Canada. As its name suggests, it provides a defence to those who comment fairly on matters of public interest. In order to establish the defence, the defendant must show that the material in question was (a) a comment, as opposed to an accusation or allegation of fact, (b) which any person could honestly express, (c) based on facts that are true, and (d) pertaining to a matter of public interest. The defence will fail if it is shown that the comments were made maliciously. However, there is generally no need for the defendant to show that the comments were "fair," so the name of this defence is slightly misleading. As Diplock J. (as he then was) famously remarked to the jury in *Silkin v. Beaverbrook Newspapers Ltd.*, [1958] 1 W.L.R. 743 (Q.B.) at 747:

People are entitled to hold and to express freely on matters of public interest strong views, views which some of you, or indeed all of you, may think are exaggerated, obstinate or prejudiced, provided — and this is the important thing — that they are views which they honestly hold. The basis of our public life is that the crank, the enthusiast, may say what he honestly thinks just as much as the reasonable man or woman who sits on a jury, and it would be a sad day for freedom of speech in this country if a jury were to apply the test of whether it agrees with the comment instead of applying the true test: was this an opinion, however exaggerated, obstinate or prejudiced, which was honestly held by the writer?

Indeed, the United Kingdom Supreme Court re-named the defence "honest comment" in *Spiller v. Joseph*, [2010] UKSC 53. This was later changed to "honest opinion" in the *Defamation Act 2013* (U.K.), c. 26, s. 3.

In *WIC Radio Ltd. v. Simpson*, [2008] 2 S.C.R. 420, excerpted below, the Supreme Court of Canada reviewed the law of fair comment, including its incorporation of *Charter* values. The decision focused primarily on the distinction between fact and comment and on the requirement of honest belief. In the course of his judgment, Binnie J. overturned *Cherneskey v. Armadale Publishers, Ltd.*, [1979] 1 S.C.R. 1067, where the majority had insisted that, to successfully plead the defence of fair comment, the defendant had to have a subjectively honest belief in the defamatory statements.

WIC RADIO LTD. v. SIMPSON
[2008] 2 S.C.R. 420

The judgment of McLachlin C.J. and Bastarache, Binnie, Deschamps, Fish, Abella and Charron JJ. was delivered by

[1] BINNIE J.:—This appeal requires the Court to re-examine the defence of fair comment which helps hold the balance in the law of defamation between two fundamental values, namely the respect for individuals and protection of their reputation from unjustified harm on the one hand, and on the other hand, the freedom of expression and debate that is said to be the "very life blood of our freedom and free institutions": *Price v. Chicoutimi Pulp Co.* (1915), 51 S.C.R. 179, at p. 194. Under the present law, if a plaintiff shows the defendant published something harmful to his or her reputation, then both falsity and damage are presumed, and the onus shifts to the defendants to establish an applicable defence, including the defence of fair comment. In *Cherneskey v. Armadale Publishers Ltd.*, [1979] 1 S.C.R. 1067, Dickson J., in dissent, identified the elements of the "fair comment" defence as follows:

(a) the comment must be on a matter of public interest;
(b) the comment must be based on fact;
(c) the comment, though it can include inferences of fact, must be recognisable as comment;
(d) the comment must satisfy the following objective test: could any man honestly express that opinion on the proved facts?
(e) even though the comment satisfies the objective test the defence can be defeated if the plaintiff proves that the defendant was actuated by express malice.
[Emphasis in original deleted; pp. 1099-1100.]
(citing *Duncan and Neill on Defamation* (1978), at p. 62)

Although on that occasion a majority of the Court insisted on framing the honest belief requirement in subjective terms (the comment must express an opinion honestly held by the speaker), I believe experience has shown that Dickson J.'s "objective" formulation of the "honest belief" test better conforms to the requirements of free expression endorsed as a fundamental value of our society by s. 2*(b)* of the *Canadian Charter of Rights and Freedoms*. Of course, even if the elements of the "fair comment" defence are established, the plaintiff can still succeed by proving that the defendant was actuated by malice, i.e. for an indirect or improper motive not connected with the purpose for which the defence exists (*Sun Life Assurance Co. of Canada v. Dalrymple*, [1965] S.C.R. 302, at p. 309).

[2] This is a private law case that is not governed directly by the *Charter*. Yet it was common ground in the argument before us that the evolution of the common law is to be informed and guided by *Charter* values. Particular emphasis was placed on the importance of ensuring that the law of fair comment is developed in a manner consistent with the values underlying freedom of expression. However, the worth and dignity of each individual, including reputation, is an important value underlying the *Charter* and is to be weighed in the balance with freedom of expression, including freedom of the media. The Court's task is not to prefer one over the other by ordering a "hierarchy" of rights (*Dagenais v. Canadian Broadcasting Corp.*, [1994] 3 S.C.R. 835), but to attempt a reconciliation. An individual's reputation is not to be treated as regrettable but unavoidable road kill on the highway of public controversy, but nor should an overly solicitous regard for personal reputation be permitted to "chill" freewheeling debate on matters of public interest. As it was put by counsel for the intervener Media Coalition, "No one will really notice if some [media] are silenced; others speaking on safer and more mundane subjects will fill the gap" (Factum, at para. 14).

[3] The issue of balance is raised here in the context of a "shock jock" radio talk show hosted by the appellant Rafe Mair, a well-known and sometimes controversial commentator on matters of public interest in British Columbia. The target of his "editorial" on October 25, 1999 was the respondent Kari Simpson, a widely known social activist. The context was public debate over the introduction of materials dealing with homosexuality into public schools. Mair and Simpson took opposing sides in the debate about whether the purpose of this initiative was to teach tolerance of homosexuality or to promote a homosexual lifestyle. Simpson was a leading public figure in the debate, and the trial judge found that she had a public reputation as a leader of those opposed to any positive portrayal of a gay lifestyle. The nub of Simpson's complaint is the following portion of the Rafe Mair editorial broadcast on October 25, 1999:

> Before Kari was on my colleague Bill Good's show last Friday I listened to the tape of the parents' meeting the night before where Kari harangued the crowd. It took me back to my childhood when with my parents we would listen to bigots who with increasing shrillness would harangue the crowds. For Kari's homosexual one could easily substitute Jew. I could see Governor Wallace — in my mind's eye I could see Governor Wallace of Alabama standing on the steps of a schoolhouse shouting to the crowds that no Negroes would get into Alabama schools as long as he was governor. It could have been blacks last Thursday night just as easily as gays. Now I'm not suggesting that Kari was proposing or supporting any kind of holocaust or violence but neither really — in the speeches, when you think about it and look back — neither did Hitler or Governor Wallace or [Orval Faubus] or Ross Barnett. They were simply declaring their hostility to a minority. Let the mob do as they wished.

. . .

[4] The courts in British Columbia were divided on the legal outcome. The trial judge dismissed the action on the basis that, while statements complained of in the editorial (in particular the imputation that Simpson "would condone violence toward gay people") were defamatory, nevertheless, the defence of fair comment applied and provided a complete defence ((2004), 31 B.C.L.R. (4th) 285, 2004 BCSC 754, at para. 6). The Court of Appeal reversed ((2006), 55 B.C.L.R. (4th) 30, 2006 BCCA 287). In its view, the defence of fair comment was not available because there was no evidentiary foundation for the imputation that Simpson would condone violence; nor had Mair testified that he had an honest belief that Simpson would condone violence. In my view, with respect, the Court of Appeal unduly favoured protection of Kari Simpson's reputation in a rancourous public debate in which she had involved herself as a major protagonist. The factual basis of the editorial was Simpson's speech. Mair stated in the editorial that he had listened "to the tape of the parents' meeting the night before where Kari harangued the crowd". Simpson had been making speeches in a similar vein for some time. Whatever view one may take of Mair's commentary, the factual basis of the controversy was indicated in the editorial and widely known to his listeners. In the absence of demonstrated malice on his part (which the trial judge concluded was not a dominant motive), his expression of opinion, however exaggerated, was protected by the law. We live in a free country where people have as much right to express outrageous and ridiculous opinions as moderate ones. I would therefore allow the appeal.

. . .

III. Analysis

[14] In the almost 30 years since *Cherneskey*, courts across the common law world have re-examined the balance between freedom of expression and the protection of private reputation.

[15] The function of the tort of defamation is to vindicate reputation, but many courts have concluded that the traditional elements of that tort may require modification to provide broader accommodation to the value of freedom of expression. There is concern that matters of public interest go unreported because publishers fear the ballooning cost and disruption of defending a defamation action. Investigative reports get "spiked", the Media Coalition contends, because, while true, they are based on facts that are difficult to establish according to rules of evidence. When controversies erupt, statements of claim often follow as night follows day, not only in serious claims (as here) but in actions launched simply for the purpose of intimidation. Of course "chilling" false and defamatory speech is not a bad thing in itself, but chilling debate on matters of legitimate public interest raises issues of inappropriate censorship and self-censorship. Public controversy can be a rough trade, and the law needs to accommodate its requirements.

. . .

B. *Distinguishing Fact From Comment*

[26] The pleaded innuendo that Simpson was so "hostile toward gay people to the point that she *would* condone violence toward gay people" (emphasis added) is framed as an inference ("would condone violence") from a factual premise, (i.e. was so "hostile toward gay people"). In *Ross v. New Brunswick Teachers' Assn.* (2001), 201 D.L.R. (4th) 75, 2001 NBCA 62, at para. 56, the New Brunswick Court of Appeal correctly took the view that "comment" includes a "deduction, inference, conclusion,

criticism, judgment, remark or observation which is generally incapable of proof. Brown's *The Law of Defamation in Canada* (2nd ed. (loose-leaf)) cites ample authority for the proposition that words that may appear to be statements of fact may, in pith and substance, be properly construed as comment. This is particularly so in an editorial context where loose, figurative or hyperbolic language is used (Brown, vol. 4, at p. 27-317) in the context of political debate, commentary, media campaigns and public discourse. . . .

[27] The respondent on this appeal did not challenge the view that Mair's imputation, that Simpson "would condone violence toward gay people", was a comment not an imputation of fact (Factum, at para. 40). I agree that the "sting" of the libel was a comment and it would have been understood as such by Mair's listeners. "What is comment and what is fact must be determined from the perspective of a 'reasonable viewer or reader'" (*Ross*, per Daigle C.J.N.B., at para. 62). Mair was a radio personality with opinions on everything, not a reporter of the facts. The applicable defence was fair comment. On that point, I agree with the trial judge.

C. *The Test for Fair Comment*

[28] [Binnie J. repeated the test set out by Dickson J., dissenting, in *Cherneskey*.] I note, parenthetically, that *Duncan and Neill* subsequently reformulated proposition (d) to say: "[C]ould any *fair-minded* man honestly express that opinion on the proved facts?" [reference omitted]. In my respectful view, the addition of a qualitative standard such as "fair minded" should be resisted. "Fair-mindedness" often lies in the eye of the beholder. Political partisans are constantly astonished at the sheer "unfairness" of criticisms made by their opponents. Trenchant criticism which otherwise meets the "honest belief" criterion ought not to be actionable because, in the opinion of a court, it crosses some ill-defined line of "fair-mindedness". The trier of fact is not required to assess whether the comment is a reasonable and proportional response to the stated or understood facts.

. . .

E. *Existence of a Factual Foundation*

[31] It is true that "[t]he comment must explicitly or implicitly indicate, at least in general terms, what are the facts on which the comment is being made" [references omitted]. What is important is that the facts be sufficiently stated or otherwise be known to the listeners that listeners are able to make up their own minds on the merits of Mair's editorial comment. If the factual foundation is unstated or unknown, or turns out to be false, the fair comment defence is not available (*Chicoutimi Pulp*, at p. 194).

. . .

[34] I agree with Southin J.A. that a properly disclosed or sufficiently indicated (or so notorious as to be already understood by the audience) factual foundation is an important objective limit to the fair comment defence, but the general facts giving rise to the dispute between Mair and Simpson were well known to Mair's listening audience, and were referred to in part in the editorial itself. Simpson's involvement in the *Declaration of Family Values* was familiar to Mair's audience. Her repeated invitations to her followers to pick up the phone and call talk shows and politicians assured her views a measure of notoriety (*Barltrop v. Canadian Broadcasting Corp.*

(1978), 25 N.S.R. (2d) 637 (C.A.)). The respondent has offered no persuasive reason to justify the Court of Appeal's interference with the trial judge's conclusion that

> the defence has established that every element of the factual foundation was either stated or publicly known; that Mair was aware of them all; and that they were all substantially true in the sense that they were true in so far as they go to the pith and substance of the opinion Mair expressed, [para. 61]

This provides a sufficient launching pad for the defence of fair comment.

F. *The Honest Belief Requirement*

[35] The respondent Simpson relies on this Court's judgment in *Cherneskey*, for the proposition, as stated by Ritchie J., at p. 1081, that

> it is an essential ingredient to the defence of fair comment that it must be the honest expression of the writer's opinion . . . .

Simpson's argument on this point therefore runs as follows. Although the trial judge found Mair had an honest belief in the comment Mair subjectively thought he was making (that Simpson is a bigot), there was no evidence that he honestly believed the innuendo imputed to his words by the trial judge (that Simpson "would condone violence toward gay people"). On this view, if Mair had simply sworn that he honestly believed that Simpson condoned violence (leaving aside the debate about the ambiguity of the word "condoned"), he would have had a good defence. However, Mair undermined his own legal position (so goes the argument) by persisting at trial in talking about Simpson's alleged bigotry and intolerance with the result that he was never asked in chief or cross-examination about his honest belief in the pleaded innuendo that Simpson condoned violence. He stuck to his belief that "Kari Simpson is not a violent person". It seems to me that defamation proceedings will have reached a troubling level of technicality if the protection afforded by the defence of fair comment to freedom of expression ("the very lifeblood of our freedom") is made to depend on whether or not the speaker is prepared to swear to an honest belief in something he does not believe he ever said.

(1) Is There Still a Role for Honest Belief?

[36] Concern about the obvious anomalies in such a requirement has prompted the intervener [Canadian Civil Liberties Association] to urge that "the honest belief requirement be eliminated" altogether (Factum, at para. 7), despite the description in *Cherneskey*, at p. 1082, of honesty of belief as the "cardinal test" of the defence of fair comment [reference omitted]. I do not think abolition of the requirement of honest belief, however formulated, would be "incremental". . . . Nor does the desire to evolve the common law to reflect *Charter* values require such a fundamental shift, in my opinion.

[37] The common law judges long ago decided that the gravamen of the defence of fair comment would not be the reasonableness or proportionality of the comment in relation to the facts (which would, of course, create stronger protection for the person defamed, but would depend in its application on the mental yardstick employed by a particular court) but whether the comment reflected honest belief. The intervener Media Coalition would substitute for honest belief the requirement that the relationship of the comment to the facts merely "be one of relevancy". . . . However,

there is a world of difference between an attack made without honest belief and an attack whose relevance to the underlying facts may be disputed.

. . .

[39] Of course it is true that the comment must have "a basis" in the facts, but a requirement that the comment be "supported by the facts", read strictly, might be thought to set the bar so high as to create the potential for judicial censorship of public opinion. Even the assessment of "relevance" has in the past misled courts into asking whether the facts "warranted" the comment, or whether the comment "fairly" arose out of the facts (*Vander Zalm*), or other such judgmental evaluations. Insistence on a court's view of reasonableness and proportionality was thought to represent too great a curb on free expression, but it was not too much to ask a defamer to profess an honest belief in his or her defamatory comment. If the speaker, however misguided, spoke with integrity, the law would give effect to freedom of expression on matters of public interest.

[40] "Honest belief, of course, requires the existence of a nexus or relationship between the comment and the underlying facts. Dickson J. himself stated the test in *Cherneskey* as "could any man honestly express that opinion *on the proved facts*" (p. 1100 (emphasis added)). His various characterizations of "any man" show the intended broadness of the test, i.e. "however prejudiced he may be, however exaggerated or obstinate his views" (p. 1103, citing *Merivale v. Carson* (1887), 20 Q.B.D. 275 (C.A.), at p. 281). Dickson J. also agreed with the comment in an earlier case that the operative concept was "'honest' rather than 'fair' lest some suggestion of reasonableness instead of honesty should be read in" (p. 1104).

[41] There is a further practical objection to the proposal of the CCLA and the Media Coalition to eliminate altogether the honest belief requirement. By way of explanation to a jury of what is meant by the test of whether the comment is based on relevant or true facts, the court would have to warn the jury not to embark on a reasonableness inquiry. An effective way of explaining to the jury how the necessary connection between the comment and the facts is to be established would be to tell them to ask themselves the question: Could any person honestly express that opinion on the proved facts? We would therefore be back at the point of departure.

(2) The *Cherneskey* Case

[42] Curiously, *Cherneskey* also involved a strange debate over the role and function of "honest belief." In that case, a couple of law students had written a provocative letter to the editor of the Saskatoon *Star-Phoenix* which was found to have libelled a city alderman as a racist. The newspaper published the letter but its publisher testified at trial that he did not agree with its contents. The letter writers were not called to testify. In the absence of any evidence from anybody associated with its publication that the letter represented his, her or its "honest belief", it was held in this Court by a 6-3 majority that the defence of fair comment was not available because the newspaper offered no proof that the defamatory opinions were "honestly held" by the actual writers. Dickson J., dissenting, pointed out with justice that

> Newspapers will not be able to provide a forum for dissemination of ideas if they are limited to publishing opinions with which they agree. . . . The integrity of a newspaper rests not on the publication of letters with which it is in agreement, but rather on the publication of letters expressing ideas to which it is violently opposed. [p. 1097]

[43] The Dickson J. test may be thought to marginalize the "honest belief" requirement, as it is possible to imagine most silly or ridiculous opinions finding a home somewhere in the minds of silly or ridiculous people. However, his dissent was really driven by an appreciation that the originator and the publisher of a defamatory comment play different roles. Nobody expects the newspaper publisher personally to have an honest belief in all of the contradictory opinions expressed on a "letters to the editor" page, much of it inspired by disagreement with something the newspaper itself has said in an editorial. Dickson J. was responding to the need to protect free expression on matters of public interest in a democratic society.

[44] Nevertheless, it remains true that an effective way to establish that somebody could "honestly express that opinion on the proved facts" is to call the defamer (if available) to establish that he or she did indeed express an honest belief. As the philosopher Bertrand Russell once observed with suitable gravity, the existence of a thing is absolute proof of its possibility.

. . .

(3) The Test Is Whether Anyone Could Honestly Have Expressed the Defamatory Comment on the Proven Facts

[49] The test represents a balance between free expression on matters of public interest and the appropriate protection of reputation against damage that exceeds what is required to fulfill free expression requirements. The objective test is now widely used in common law jurisdictions as the "honest belief" component of fair comment, including the United Kingdom: *Telnikoff v. Matusevitch*, [1991] 3 W.L.R. 952 (H.L.), quoting with approval Dickson J.'s dissent, at p. 959. In Australia, the High Court recently affirmed a similar approach; see the observation of Gleeson C.J.:

> The protection from actionability which the common law gives to fair and honest comment on matters of public interest is an important aspect of freedom of speech. In this context, "fair" does not mean objectively reasonable. The defence protects obstinate, or foolish, or offensive statements of opinion, or inference, or judgment, provided certain conditions are satisfied. *The word "fair" refers to limits to what any honest person, however opinionated or prejudiced, would express upon the basis of the relevant facts.* (*Channel Seven Adelaide Pty. Ltd. v. Manock* (2007), 241 A.L.R. 468, [2007] HCA 60, at para. 3 (emphasis added))

. . .

[50] Admittedly, the "objective" test is not a high threshold for the defendants to meet, but nor is it in the public interest to deny the defence to a piece of devil's advocacy that the writer may have doubts about (but is quite capable of honest belief) which contributes to the debate on a matter of public interest.

[51] Of course, even the latitude allowed by the "objective" honest belief test may be exceeded. "Comment must be relevant to the facts to which it is addressed. It cannot be used as a cloak for mere invective"; [*Reynolds v. Times Newspapers Ltd.*, [1999] 4 All E.R. 609], at p. 615.

(4) "Malice" Does Not Provide an Adequate Substitute for the Honest Belief Component of the Fair Comment Defence

[52] As usual, the debate is about onus:

> It is difficult to know whether malice is an element to be considered independently of the issue of fairness, and thus a matter which the plaintiff must prove to defeat the defence of fair comment, or to be treated as part of the issue of fairness, which the defendant must prove in order to establish that element of the defence. . . . [I]f the issue is treated as one which goes to the question of fairness, the defendant has the burden of showing it was fair. This latter position appears to have gained some acceptance in Ontario. (Brown, at p. 15-101)

At this point in the analysis, the comment will have been found to be defamatory and the defendant is scrambling for a defence. Interveners supporting the media suggested that "honest belief", however formulated, should be pushed into the analysis of malice, where the plaintiff bears the onus of proof. Such an approach would disproportionately favour the media, in my view. Proof of malice on the part of the media is generally very difficult. The media are well-resourced, secretive about their inner workings and highly protective of their confidential sources. At the same time, as many in the U.S. media have come to learn since *New York Times Co. v. Sullivan*, 376 U.S. 254 (1964), putting the judicial spotlight on journalistic operations in a malice enquiry (that is now the fulcrum of a libel case against a public figure) may not be in anyone's interest. I would therefore affirm the present allocation of proof whereby the defendant must prove the elements of the fair comment defence (including the objective honest belief requirement) before the onus switches back to the plaintiff to defeat the defence by establishing, if it can, malice on the part of the defendant(s).

[53] Some commentators have suggested that proof of honest belief negates the possibility of a finding of malice. This is not necessarily true. If a defendant relies on objective honest belief the defence can still be defeated by proof that subjective malice was the dominant motive of the particular comment.

G. *Applying the Law of Fair Comment to the Facts of This Case*

[54] In a lengthy and careful judgment, the trial judge dealt with the issues in an appropriate sequence:

(1) What Is the Defamatory Meaning of the Words Complained of, in Their Full Context?

[55] At common law, the judge is to make a legal determination "whether there is a case or an issue to go to the jury" by deciding if the words are "capable of being a statement of a fact or facts". It is then "for the jury to decide as to what is fact and what is comment" [references omitted]. As pointed out by the intervener British Columbia Civil Liberties Association, "the judge's role in that test is a response to concerns about freedom of expression" (Factum, at para. 34).

[56] The "full context" is important. While argument in this Court largely focussed on the innuendo that Simpson "would condone violence toward gay people", the broader analysis of the trial judge left no doubt about her view of the "[u]nwholesome virulence" (para. 78) of the editorial taken as a whole. The appellants argue that in assessing meaning, the Court is to consider what reasonable and right-thinking listeners would understand. The Court is to avoid putting the worst possible meaning on the words: *Color Your World Corp. v. Canadian Broadcasting Corp.* (1998), 38 O.R. (3d) 97 (C.A.), at pp. 106-7, and *Scott v. Fulton* (2000), 73 B.C.L.R. (3d) 392, 2000 BCCA 124, at paras. 13-15. However, both courts below found that Mair's

editorial about Simpson was defamatory. This is a mixed question of law and fact. There is no reason to interfere with that conclusion. It is plainly correct.

(2) Do the Words Complained of Relate to a Matter of Public Interest?

[57] The public debate about the inclusion in schools of educational material on homosexuality clearly engages the public interest. As the Ontario Court of Appeal recognized over a century ago in words that apply equally to the case on appeal, "[w]hoever seeks notoriety, or invites public attention, is said to challenge public criticism; and [s]he cannot resort to the law courts, if that criticism be less favorable than [s]he anticipated" (*Macdonell v. Robinson* (1885), 12 O.A.R. 270, at p. 272).

(3) Are the Words and the Defamatory Meaning More Likely to Be Understood, in Context, as Comment Rather Than Fact?

[58] The trial judge, after reviewing the editorial as a whole, concluded:

The facts in those statements which are clearly facts are: 1) that Kari was on Bill Good's show last Friday; and 2) that she did speak to a rally the night before. These facts were true. *There is no other sentence or statement or phrase which would be understood to be a matter of fact*, and the language in which it is couched is such that it is clearly opinion. [Emphasis added; para. 44.]

For reasons stated earlier, I agree with this conclusion.

(4) Are the Facts Relating to the Comment Substantially True or Privileged?

[59] The law requires the comment be based on a sufficient substratum of facts to anchor the defamatory comment: [references omitted]. This is another mechanism to prevent tenuous facts serving as a springboard for defamatory comment, which, in my view, would be the danger of the "relevance" test proposed by the CCLA. Simpson does not dispute the contents or tone of her speeches in the court record. In my view, as in the view of the trial judge, the factual substratum exists

(5) Did the Defendants Mair and WIC Radio Ltd. Satisfy the Honest Belief Requirement?

[60] Mair testified as to his subjective honest belief in what he intended to say, but acknowledged that he did not honestly believe that Simpson would condone violence. Notwithstanding the absence of a subjective honest belief that Simpson would condone violence, Mair and WIC Radio, like the newspaper publisher in *Cherneskey*, were entitled to rely on the objective test, i.e. could any person honestly have expressed the innuendo that Simpson would condone violence toward gay people on the proven facts? As mentioned earlier, Simpson's public speeches were full of references to "war . . . [where] the spoils turn out to be our children", "militant homosexuals", "[w]ar, you shoot, they shoot" and so on. Simpson's use of violent images could support an honest belief on the part of at least some of her listeners that she "would condone violence toward gay people", even though Mair denied that he intended to impute any such meaning.

. . .

[62] The trial judge concluded that Mair honestly believed what he thought he had said:

I consider that Mair was on a "campaign" to expose what Mair believed were Simpson's "irresponsible" statements and speeches against the teaching of tolerance of a homosexual lifestyle in public schools. This, together with the overall content of the defamatory editorial, is evidence supporting a finding that *the dominant motive for publishing the editorial was Mair's honestly held opinion*. [Emphasis added; para. 84.]

The trial judge did not explicitly apply the "objective honest belief" test to the imputation that Simpson "would condone violence". In my view, however, having regard to the trial judge's reasons as a whole, and considering both the content of some of Simpson's speeches already mentioned, and the broad latitude allowed by the defence of fair comment, the defamatory imputation that while Simpson would not engage in violence herself she "would condone violence" by others, is an opinion that could honestly have been expressed on the proved facts by a person "prejudiced . . . exaggerated or obstinate [in] his views". That is all that the law requires.

(6) Has the Respondent Proven Sufficient Malice on the Appellants' Part to Defeat the Defence?

[63] The defence is defeated if the commentary was actuated by malice in the sense of improper motive, proof of which lay on the plaintiff. Simpson does not appeal against the trial judge's conclusion that Mair's fair comment defence was not vitiated by malice.

IV. Conclusion

[64] Applying the elements of the fair comment defence set out above, I conclude that the trial judge was correct to allow the defence.

[LeBel J. wrote a concurring judgment in which he found that the Mair's statements were not defamatory, given both the context of the ongoing debate regarding the teaching of homosexuality and Mair's known reputation as a controversial radio host. Further, LeBel J. would have dispensed with the honest belief requirement for the defence of fair comment, requiring only that a statement (a) be comment, (b) with a basis in true facts, (c) on a matter of public interest. In a separate concurring judgment, Rothstein J. agreed with Binnie J. that the impugned statements were defamatory, but adopted LeBel J.'s rejection of the honest belief requirement for the fair comment defence. The appeal was allowed and the trial judgment was restored.]

NOTES AND QUESTIONS

1. Binnie J. defined the test of honest belief as whether "any person" could have honestly made the comment. Can you think of a situation where such a test would not be satisfied? See Frankel, Case Comment on *WIC Radio v. Simpson* (2009) 67 U. Toronto Fac. L. Rev. 93.

2. Explain the relationship between the newly-stated honest belief requirement and the element of malice. If the defendant does not subjectively have an honest belief in his or her comments, what is the motivation for making such comments?

3. In *Cherneskey v. Armadale Publishers, Ltd.*, [1979] 1 S.C.R. 1067, the majority applied a subjective test of honest belief. The defendant newspaper was found liable for publishing a defamatory letter to the editor with which it did not agree. How would this test affect the ability of newspapers to act as a forum for public debate? The

decision in *Cherneskey* was severely criticized and was addressed by legislation in most provinces. See for example *Defamation Act*, R.S.A. 2000, c. D-7, s. 9(1); *Defamation Act*, R.S.O. 1990, c. L.12, s. 24; and *Defamation Act*, C.C.S.M. c. 20, s. 9(1). Although the provisions are slightly different, they essentially provide that the defence of fair comment will not fail simply because the defendant did not share the defamatory opinion expressed by another person. In most jurisdictions, however, the defence will fail if the defendant knew that the *original* opinion was dishonestly expressed. How, if at all, does the decision in *WIC Radio* affect the interpretation of these statutory provisions?

4. It is important to distinguish between comment and allegations of fact. The defence of fair comment protects freedom of discussion; it does not provide licence to make unsubstantiated accusations against those in the public eye. Thus, to suggest that a politician has taken bribes is an allegation of fact that is not protected by the defence of fair comment. However, fair comment may apply if a politician has been found guilty of taking bribes, and the defendant has commented that such conduct is disgraceful or dishonourable. These latter comments are subjective statements of opinion and, as long as they are honestly expressed, can be defended as fair comment.

Nevertheless, it is often difficult to distinguish between comments and statements of fact. The burden is on the defendant to show that the impugned statements were comments, and the test is whether they would "be recognizable to the ordinary reasonable man as a comment upon true facts, and not as a bare statement of fact": *Vander Zalm v. Times Publishers* (1980), 18 B.C.L.R. 210 at 213 (C.A.). Generally, facts are statements that are susceptible to proof: their truth or falsity can be determined. For instance, witnesses can testify whether a politician has, in fact, taken bribes. Conversely, comments are subjective opinions that cannot be proved or disproved.

It must be clear to the reader or listener that the impugned statements were comments rather than facts. If the facts and commentary are so intermingled as to be indistinguishable, the defence of fair comment will not apply. See *Jones v. Bennett*, [1969] S.C.R. 277; *Mitchell v. Times Printing and Publishing Company Limited (No. 2)*, [1944] 1 W.W.R. 400 (B.C.S.C.); and *John v. Kim* (2007), 52 C.C.L.T. (3d) 123 (B.C.S.C.).

If the defendant fails to establish that the impugned statements were comments, they will be treated as facts and will only be protected if the defendant can satisfy the defence of justification (*i.e.*, if the defendant can prove the truth of those facts) or some other privilege. See *Murphy v. LaMarsh* (1970), 73 W.W.R. 114 (B.C.S.C.), aff'd (1970), [1971] 2 W.W.R. 196 (B.C.C.A.).

5. A defendant raising the defence of fair comment must prove that the facts underlying its opinion are true. The defence is not available if the underlying facts are unproven or misstated: *Holt v. Sun Publishing Co. Ltd.* (1979), 100 D.L.R. (3d) 447 (B.C.C.A.); *Hodgson v. Canadian Newspapers Co.* (1998), 39 O.R. (3d) 235 (Gen. Div.), aff'd (2000), 49 O.R. (3d) 161 (C.A.); *Rogacki v. Belz* (2004), 243 D.L.R. (4th) 585 (Ont. C.A.); and *Awan v. Levant*, 2014 ONSC 6890, aff'd 2016 ONCA 970. Nor is it available if the facts are fabricated or twisted: *Price v. Chicoutimi Pulp Co.* (1915), 51 S.C.R. 179; *Leenen v. Canadian Broadcasting Corporation* (2000), 48 O.R. (3d) 656 (S.C.J.), aff'd (2001), 54 O.R. (3d) 612 (C.A.); and *Myers v. Canadian Broadcasting Corp.* (1999), 47 C.C.L.T. (2d) 272 (Ont. S.C.J.), aff'd (2001), 54 O.R. (3d) 626 (C.A.). However, the defendant need not set out all the facts relevant to the matter. A

defendant is entitled to omit relevant facts, as long as doing so does not provide a false or twisted account: *Creative Salmon Company Ltd. v. Staniford* (2009), 90 B.C.L.R. (4th) 328 (C.A.).

If facts are sufficiently notorious to have become public knowledge, they do not need to be provided as long as they are clearly identifiable. For instance, political cartoons do not necessarily need to set out the facts upon which they are based. See *Ross v. New Brunswick Teachers' Association* (2001), 238 N.B.R. (2d) 112 (C.A.). However, mere rumour is not sufficient to be "fact" for the purposes of fair comment: *Pressler v. Lethbridge* (2000), 86 B.C.L.R. (3d) 257 (C.A.). Moreover, if the facts on which the comment is based are not notorious or part of the public domain, the defendant "must explicitly or implicitly indicate, at least in general terms, the facts on which it is based": *Spiller v. Joseph*, [2010] UKSC 53 at para. 105. This is required so that the audience can understand what has led the commentator to make the comment. See also *Channel Seven Adelaide Pty Ltd v. Manock* (2007), 232 C.L.R. 245 (H.C.A.), which applied an even stricter test. In the absence of an identifiable factual basis, the statement is "bare comment," which can only be excused by the defence of justification.

Although the defendant must show that the facts underlying the comment are true, there is no need to show that the comment itself is true. There is no need to show that the defendant made a correct inference on the facts. Indeed, evidence regarding the falsity of the comment is inadmissible. See *Leech v. Leader Publishing Co.* (1926), 20 Sask. L.R. 337 (C.A.); and *Boys v. Star Printing and Publishing Co.* (1927), 60 O.L.R. 592 (C.A.).

6. The defence of fair comment is only available for subjects that are matters of public interest. The public interest may be satisfied by the importance of the person about whom the comments are made, or by the event or occasion giving rise to the comment. A person may be the legitimate target of fair comment if he or she is a public figure or official (*e.g. Boland v. Globe and Mail Ltd.*, [1961] O.R. 712 (C.A.)); or has sought out the public spotlight (*e.g. Pound v. Scott*, [1973] 4 W.W.R. 403 (B.C.S.C.)). However, the defence of fair comment is not available for defamatory statements about the private life of a public official (*Vander Zalm, supra*) or personal attacks (see *Chélin c. Gill*, 2013 QCCS 2377). Is the private conduct of a public official ever a matter of public importance? See *Coleman v. MacLennan*, 78 Kan. 711 (1908).

The types of events and occasions capable of giving rise to fair comment are numerous. They include, not surprisingly, governmental affairs and the administration of justice, political elections, and public health. They also include criticism of literary or artistic exploits, sporting events and coaching decisions, and restaurant cuisine.

In *Wood v. Jaffer*, 2018 BCSC 85, the defence of fair comment was denied when the defendant sent a seven-page statement to the Better Business Bureau accusing the plaintiff builder of criminal fraud. The matter dealt with a private contract and was, thus, not a matter of public interest. But see *Walsh Energy Inc. v. Better Business Bureau of Ottawa-Hull Incorporated*, 2018 ONCA 383, where the defence of fair comment was established by the Bureau in defence to the D- rating it had assigned to the plaintiff on its website.

The requirement of public interest has been removed from the statutory defence of "honest opinion" in the *Defamation Act 2013* (U.K.), c. 26, s. 3.

7. The defence of fair comment will fail if the plaintiff can prove on a balance of probabilities that the comments were made maliciously. Thus, even if a defendant honestly believes a statement, the defence is not available if it can be shown that the statement was published for an improper reason or motive. See *Christie v. Westcom Radio Group Ltd.* (1990), 75 D.L.R. (4th) 546 (B.C.C.A.). Media defendants may be tainted by malice if their primary motives are to enhance their own reputations through sensational programming rather than to serve the public interest: *Vogel v. Canadian Broadcasting Corporation*, [1982] 3 W.W.R. 97 (B.C.S.C.). Moreover, media defendants who do not provide an opportunity for the subject of a story to respond to the allegations made therein may be tainted by malice: *Munro v. Toronto Sun Publishing Corp.* (1982), 39 O.R. (2d) 100 (H.C.J.). See also *Tse Wai Chun Paul v. Albert Cheng*, [2001] E.M.L.R. 777 (Court of Final Appeal of Hong Kong).

In *WeGo Kayaking Ltd. v. Sewid*, 2007 CarswellBC 71 (S.C.) (WL Can), the plaintiffs and defendant were commercial rivals competing for eco-tourism business in the Broughton Archipelago and Johnstone Strait of Vancouver Island. The defendant posted defamatory material on his website regarding the plaintiffs' businesses. Among other things, he alleged that guests on tours operated by the plaintiffs would have to stay in soggy, wet, dirty tents, that their tours had environmental concerns, and that they took advantage of "token Indians." The defence of fair comment was defeated, in part, due to the malicious nature of the publication. In particular, the defendant had the improper motive of trying to injure the plaintiffs' businesses and gain economic advantage.

8. Special rules apply if the defendant has imputed "corrupt or dishonourable motives" to the plaintiff. Such comments will only be protected if the imputations were warranted on the facts, *i.e.*, that the conclusion is one that a fair-minded person might make in the circumstances. See *Masters v. Fox* (1978), 85 D.L.R. (3d) 64 (B.C.S.C.). The rules apparently originated in *Campbell v. Spottiswoode* (1863), 122 E.R. 288 (Q.B.), where Cockburn C.J. feared that lesser treatment might discourage persons of honour and integrity from enlisting in public affairs. These rules have been criticized, but have so far been upheld in the Canadian courts. See *Vogel, supra*, *Hodgson v. Canadian Newspapers Co.* (1998), 39 O.R. (3d) 235 (Gen. Div.), aff'd without comment on point (2000), 49 O.R. (3d) 161 (C.A.); and *Leenen, supra*.

(e) RESPONSIBLE COMMUNICATION ON MATTERS OF PUBLIC INTEREST

In *Grant v. Torstar Corp.*, [2009] 3 S.C.R. 640, excerpted below, the Supreme Court of Canada recognized a new defence to defamation called responsible communication on matters of public interest. This defence addressed a gap in defamation law that existed when a defendant published statements of fact on a matter of public interest that defamed the plaintiff. The defence of justification would fail if the defendant could not prove on a balance of probabilities that the statements were true. The defence of fair comment would be unavailable because the statements were allegations of fact, rather than comment or opinion. Finally, the defence of qualified privilege would likely fail because there is generally no "duty" to publish information to the world at large. It was argued that, in some circumstances, this gap in the law of defamation would inhibit freedom of expression on matters of a public interest.

GRANT v. TORSTAR CORP.
[2009] 3 S.C.R. 640

The judgment of McLachlin C.J. and Binnie, LeBel, Deschamps, Fish, Charron, Rothstein and Cromwell JJ. was delivered by

McLACHLIN C.J.: —

I. Introduction

[1] Freedom of expression is guaranteed by s. 2*(b)* of the *Canadian Charter of Rights and Freedoms.* It is essential to the functioning of our democracy, to seeking the truth in diverse fields of inquiry, and to our capacity for self-expression and individual realization.

[2] But freedom of expression is not absolute. One limitation on free expression is the law of defamation, which protects a person's reputation from unjustified assault. The law of defamation does not forbid people from expressing themselves. It merely provides that if a person defames another, that person may be required to pay damages to the other for the harm caused to the other's reputation. However, if the defences available to a publisher are too narrowly defined, the result may be "libel chill", undermining freedom of expression and of the press.

[3] Two conflicting values are at stake — on the one hand freedom of expression and on the other the protection of reputation. While freedom of expression is a fundamental freedom protected by s. 2*(b)* of the *Charter,* courts have long recognized that protection of reputation is also worthy of legal recognition. The challenge of courts has been to strike an appropriate balance between them in articulating the common law of defamation. In this case, we are asked to consider, once again, whether this balance requires further adjustment.

[4] Peter Grant and his company Grant Forest Products Inc. ("GFP") sued the Toronto Star in defamation for an article the newspaper published on June 23, 2001, concerning a proposed private golf course development on Grant's lakefront estate. The story aired the views of local residents who were critical of the development's environmental impact and suspicious that Grant was exercising political influence behind the scenes to secure government approval for the new golf course. The reporter, an experienced journalist named Bill Schiller, attempted to verify the allegations in the article, including asking Grant for comment, which Grant chose not to provide. The article was published, and Grant brought this libel action.

[5] The trial proceeded with judge and jury. The jury found the respondents (the "Star defendants") liable and awarded general, aggravated and punitive damages totalling $1.475 million.

[6] The Star defendants argue that what happened in this trial shows that something is wrong with the traditional law of libel: a journalist or publisher who diligently tries to verify a story on a matter of public interest before publishing it can still be held liable in defamation for massive damages, simply because the journalist cannot prove to the court that all of the story was true or bring it within one of the "privileged" categories exempted from the need to prove truth. This state of the law, they argue, unduly curbs free expression and chills reporting on matters of public interest, depriving the public of information it should have. The Star defendants ask this Court to revise the defences available to journalists to address these criticisms, following the lead of courts in the United States and England. Mr. Grant and his

corporation, for their part, argue that the common law now strikes the proper balance and should not be changed.

[7] For the reasons that follow, I conclude that the common law should be modified to recognize a defence of responsible communication on matters of public interest. In view of this new defence, as well as errors in the jury instruction on fair comment, anew trial should be ordered.

. . .

(1) The Current Law

. . .

[32] Where statements of fact are at issue, usually only two defences are available: the defence that the statement was substantially true (justification); and the defence that the statement was made in a protected context (privilege). The issue in this case is whether the defences to actions for defamatory statements of fact should be expanded, as has been done for statements of opinion, in recognition of the importance of freedom of expression in a free society.

[33] To succeed on the defence of justification, a defendant must adduce evidence showing that the statement was substantially true. This may be difficult to do. A journalist who has checked sources and is satisfied that a statement is substantially true may nevertheless have difficulty proving this in court, perhaps years after the event. The practical result of the gap between responsible verification and the ability to prove truth in a court of law on some date far in the future, is that the defence of justification is often of little utility to journalists and those who publish their stories.

[34] If the defence of justification fails, generally the only way a publisher can escape liability for an untrue defamatory statement of fact is by establishing that the statement was made on a privileged occasion. However, the defence of qualified privilege has seldom assisted media organizations. One reason is that qualified privilege has traditionally been grounded in special relationships characterized by a "duty" to communicate the information and a reciprocal "interest" in receiving it. The press communicates information not to identified individuals with whom it has a personal relationship, but to the public at large. Another reason is the conservative stance of early decisions, which struck a balance that preferred reputation over freedom of expression. . . .

[35] In recent decades, courts have begun to moderate the strictures of qualified privilege, albeit in an *ad hoc* and incremental way. When a strong duty and interest seemed to warrant it, they have on occasion applied the privilege to publications to the world at large. For example, in suits against politicians expressing concerns to the electorate about the conduct of other public figures, courts have sometimes recognized that a politician's "duty to ventilate" matters of concern to the public could give rise to qualified privilege: *Parlett v. Robinson* (1986), 5 B.C.L.R. (2d) 26 (C.A.), at p. 39.

[36] In the last decade, this recognition has sometimes been extended to media defendants. For example, in *Grenier v. Southam Inc.*, [1997] O.J. No. 2193 (QL), the Ontario Court of Appeal (in a brief endorsement) upheld a trial judge's finding that the defendant media corporation had a "social and moral duty" to publish the article in question. Other cases have adopted the view that qualified privilege is available to media defendants, provided that they can show a social or moral duty to publish the information and a corresponding public interest in receiving it: *Leenen v. Canadian Broadcasting Corp.* (2000), 48 O.R. (3d) 656 (S.C.J.), at p. 695, aff'd (2001), 54 O.R.

(3d) 612 (C.A.), and *Young v. Toronto Star Newspapers Ltd.* (2003), 66 O.R. (3d) 170 (S.C.J.), aff'd (2005), 77 O.R. (3d) 680 (C.A.).

[37] Despite these tentative forays, the threshold for privilege remains high and the criteria for reciprocal duty and interest required to establish it unclear. It remains uncertain when, if ever, a media outlet can avail itself of the defence of qualified privilege.

(2) The Case for Changing the Law

[38] Two related arguments are presented in support of broadening the defences available to public communicators, such as the press, in reporting matters of fact.

. . .

(a) *The Argument From Principle*

[41] The fundamental question of principle is whether the traditional defences for defamatory statements of fact curtail freedom of expression in a way that is inconsistent with Canadian constitutional values. Does the existing law strike an appropriate balance between two values vital to Canadian society — freedom of expression on the one hand, and the protection of individuals' reputations on the other? . . .

. . .

[47] The guarantee of free expression in s. 2(b) of the *Charter* has three core rationales, or purposes: (1) democratic discourse; (2) truth-finding; and (3) self-fulfillment: *Irwin Toy Ltd. v. Québec (Attorney General)*, [1989] 1 S.C.R. 927, at p. 976. These purposes inform the content of s. 2*(b)* and assist in determining what limits on free expression can be justified under s. 1.

[48] First and foremost, free expression is essential to the proper functioning of democratic governance. As Rand J. put it, "government by the free public opinion of an open society . . . demands the condition of a virtually unobstructed access to and diffusion of ideas": *Switzman,* at p. 306.

[49] Second, the free exchange of ideas is an "essential precondition of the search for truth": *R. v. Keegstra*, [1990] 3 S.C.R. 697, at p. 803, per McLachlin J. This rationale, sometimes known as the "marketplace of ideas", extends beyond the political domain to any area of debate where truth is sought through the exchange of information and ideas. Information is disseminated and propositions debated. In the course of debate, misconceptions and errors are exposed. What withstands testing emerges as truth.

[50] Third, free expression has intrinsic value as an aspect of self-realization for both speakers and listeners. As the majority observed in *Irwin Toy*, at p. 976, "the diversity in forms of individual self-fulfillment and human flourishing ought to be cultivated in an essentially tolerant, indeed welcoming, environment not only for the sake of those who convey a meaning, but also for the sake of those to whom it is conveyed".

[51] Of the three rationales for the constitutional protection of free expression, only the third, self-fulfillment, is of dubious relevance to defamatory communications on matters of public interest. This is because the plaintiff's interest in reputation may be just as worthy of protection as the defendant's interest in self-realization through unfettered expression. . . .

[52] By contrast, the first two rationales for free expression squarely apply to communications on matters of public interest, even those which contain false imputations. The first rationale, the proper functioning of democratic governance, has profound resonance in this context. As held in *WIC Radio*, freewheeling debate on matters of public interest is to be encouraged, and must not be thwarted by "overly solicitous regard for personal reputation" (para. 2). Productive debate is dependent on the free flow of information. The vital role of the communications media in providing a vehicle for such debate is explicitly recognized in the text of s. 2*(b)* itself: "freedom of thought, belief, opinion and expression, including freedom of the press and other media of communication".

[53] Freedom does not negate responsibility. It is vital that the media act responsibly in reporting facts on matters of public concern, holding themselves to the highest journalistic standards. But to insist on court-established certainty in reporting on matters of public interest may have the effect of preventing communication of facts which a reasonable person would accept as reliable and which are relevant and important to public debate. The existing common law rules mean, in effect, that the publisher must be certain before publication that it can prove the statement to be true in a court of law, should a suit be filed. Verification of the facts and reliability of the sources may lead a publisher to a reasonable certainty of their truth, but that is different from knowing that one will be able to prove their truth in a court of law, perhaps years later. This, in turn, may have a chilling effect on what is published. Information that is reliable and in the public's interest to know may never see the light of day.

[54] The second rationale — getting at the truth — is also engaged by the debate before us. Fear of being sued for libel may prevent the publication of information about matters of public interest. The public may never learn the full truth on the matter at hand.

. . .

[57] I conclude that media reporting on matters of public interest engages the first and second rationales of the freedom of expression guarantee in the *Charter*. The statement in *Hill* (at para. 106) that "defamatory statements are very tenuously related to the core values which underlie s. 2*(b)*" must be read in the context of that case. It is simply beyond debate that the limited defences available to press-related defendants may have the effect of inhibiting political discourse and debate on matters of public importance, and impeding the cut and thrust of discussion necessary to discovery of the truth.

[58] This brings me to the competing value: protection of reputation. Canadian law recognizes that the right to free expression does not confer a licence to ruin reputations. In assessing the constitutionality of the *Criminal Code*'s defamatory libel provisions, for example, the Court has affirmed that "[t]he protection of an individual's reputation from wilful and false attack recognizes both the innate dignity of the individual and the integral link between reputation and the fruitful participation of an individual in Canadian society": *R. v. Lucas*, [1998] 1 S.C.R. 439, at para. 48, per Cory J. This applies both to private citizens and to people in public life. People who enter public life cannot reasonably expect to be immune from criticism, some of it harsh and undeserved. But nor does participation in public life amount to open season on reputation.

. . .

[62] The protection offered by a new defence based on conduct is meaningful for both the publisher and those whose reputations are at stake. If the publisher fails to take appropriate steps having regard to all the circumstances, it will be liable. The press and others engaged in public communication on matters of public interest, like bloggers, must act carefully, having regard to the injury to reputation that a false statement can cause. A defence based on responsible conduct reflects the social concern that the media should be held accountable through the law of defamation. As Kirby P. stated in *Ballina Shire Council v. Ringland* (1994), 33 N.S.W.L.R. 680 (C.A.), at p. 700: "The law of defamation is one of the comparatively few checks upon [the media's] great power." The requirement that the publisher of defamatory material act responsibly provides accountability and comports with the reasonable expectations of those whose conduct brings them within the sphere of public interest. People in public life are entitled to expect that the media and other reporters will act responsibly in protecting them from false accusations and innuendo. They are not, however, entitled to demand perfection and the inevitable silencing of critical comment that a standard of perfection would impose.

. . .

[65] Having considered the arguments on both sides of the debate from the perspective of principle, I conclude that the current law with respect to statements that are reliable and important to public debate does not give adequate weight to the constitutional value of free expression. While the law must protect reputation, the level of protection currently accorded by the law — in effect a regime of strict liability — is not justifiable. The law of defamation currently accords no protection for statements on matters of public interest published to the world at large if they cannot, for whatever reason, be proven to be true. But such communications advance both free expression rationales mentioned above — democratic discourse and truth-finding — and therefore require some protection within the law of defamation. When proper weight is given to the constitutional value of free expression on matters of public interest, the balance tips in favour of broadening the defences available to those who communicate facts it is in the public's interest to know.

[McLachlin C.J.C. then considered "The Argument on the Jurisprudence," reviewing the approaches of other common law democracies to defamatory statements of fact on matters of public interest. She went on to consider how the new defence should be formulated in Canada.]

[96] A second preliminary question is what the new defence should be called. In arguments before us, the defence was referred to as the responsible journalism test. This has the value of capturing the essence of the defence in succinct style. However, the traditional media are rapidly being complemented by new ways of communicating on matters of public interest, many of them online, which do not involve journalists. These new disseminators of news and information should, absent good reasons for exclusion, be subject to the same laws as established media outlets. I agree with Lord Hoffmann that the new defence is "available to anyone who publishes material of public interest in any medium": *Jameel*, at para. 54.

[97] A review of recent defamation case law suggests that many actions now concern blog postings and other online media which are potentially both more ephemeral and more ubiquitous than traditional print media. While established journalistic standards provide a useful guide by which to evaluate the conduct of journalists and non-journalists alike, the applicable standards will necessarily evolve

to keep pace with the norms of new communications media. For this reason, it is more accurate to refer to the new defence as responsible communication on matters of public interest.

(2) Formulating the Defence of Responsible Communication on Matters of Public Interest

[98] This brings us to the substance of the test for responsible communication. In *Quan*, Sharpe J.A. held that the defence has two essential elements: public interest and responsibility. I agree, and would formulate the test as follows. First, the publication must be on a matter of public interest. Second, the defendant must show that publication was responsible, in that he or she was diligent in trying to verify the allegation(s), having regard to all the relevant circumstances.

(a) *Was the Publication on a Matter of Public Interest?*

. . .

[101] In determining whether a publication is on a matter of public interest, the judge must consider the subject matter of the publication as a whole. The defamatory statement should not be scrutinized in isolation. The judge's role at this point is to determine whether the subject matter of the communication as a whole is one of public interest. If it is, and if the evidence is legally capable of supporting the defence, as I will explain below, the judge should put the case to the jury for the ultimate determination of responsibility.

[102] How is "public interest" in the subject matter established? First, and most fundamentally, the public interest is not synonymous with what interests the public. The public's appetite for information on a given subject — say, the private lives of well-known people — is not on its own sufficient to render an essentially private matter public for the purposes of defamation law. An individual's reasonable expectation of privacy must be respected in this determination. Conversely, the fact that much of the public would be less than riveted by a given subject matter does not remove the subject from the public interest. It is enough that some segment of the community would have a genuine interest in receiving information on the subject.

. . .

[104] In *London Artists, Ltd. v. Littler*, [1969] 2 All E.R. 193 (C.A.), speaking of the defence of fair comment, Lord Denning, M.R., described public interest broadly in terms of matters that may legitimately concern or interest people:

> There is no definition in the books as to what is a matter of public interest. All we are given is a list of examples, coupled with the statement that it is for the judge and not for the jury. I would not myself confine it within narrow limits. Whenever a matter is such as to affect people at large, so that they may be legitimately interested in, or concerned at, what is going on; or what may happen to them or to others; then it is a matter of public interest on which every-one is entitled to make fair comment. [p. 198]

[105] To be of public interest, the subject matter "must be shown to be one inviting public attention, or about which the public has some substantial concern because it affects the welfare of citizens, or one to which considerable public notoriety or controversy has attached": Brown, vol. 2, at pp. 15-137 and 15-138. The case law on fair comment "is replete with successful fair comment defences on matters ranging

from politics to restaurant and book reviews": *Simpson v. Mair*, 2004 BCSC 754, 31 B.C.L.R. (4th) 285, at para. 63, per Koenigsberg J. Public interest may be a function of the prominence of the person referred to in the communication, but mere curiosity or prurient interest is not enough. Some segment of the public must have a genuine stake in knowing about the matter published.

[106] Public interest is not confined to publications on government and political matters, as it is in Australia and New Zealand. Nor is it necessary that the plaintiff be a "public figure", as in the American jurisprudence since *Sullivan*. Both qualifications cast the public interest too narrowly. The public has a genuine stake in knowing about many matters, ranging from science and the arts to the environment, religion and morality. The democratic interest in such wide-ranging public debate must be reflected in the jurisprudence.

. . .

(b) *Was Publication of the Defamatory Communication Responsible?*

[110] Against this background, I turn to some relevant factors that may aid in determining whether a defamatory communication on a matter of public interest was responsibly made.

(i) *The Seriousness of the Allegation*

[111] The logic of proportionality dictates that the degree of diligence required in verifying the allegation should increase in proportion to the seriousness of its potential effects on the person defamed. This factor recognizes that not all defamatory imputations carry equal weight. The defamatory "sting" of a statement can range from a passing irritant to a blow that devastates the target's reputation and career. The apprehended harm to the plaintiff's dignity and reputation increases in relation to the seriousness of the defamatory sting. The degree to which the defamatory communication intrudes upon the plaintiff's privacy is one way in which the seriousness of the sting may be measured. Publication of the kinds of allegations traditionally considered the most serious — for example, corruption or other criminality on the part of a public official — demand more thorough efforts at verification than will suggestions of lesser mischief. So too will those which impinge substantially on the plaintiff's reasonable expectation of privacy.

(ii) *The Public Importance of the Matter*

[112] Inherent in the logic of proportionality is the degree of the public importance of the communication's subject matter. The subject matter will, however, already have been deemed by the trial judge to be a matter of public interest. However, not all matters of public interest are of equal importance. Communications on grave matters of national security, for example, invoke different concerns from those on the prosaic business of everyday politics. What constitutes reasonable diligence with respect to one may fall short with respect to the other. Where the public importance in a subject matter is especially high, the jury may conclude that this factor tends to show that publication was responsible in the circumstances. In many cases, the public importance of the matter may be inseparable from its urgency.

(iii) *The Urgency of the Matter*

[113] As Lord Nicholls observed in *Reynolds*, news is often a perishable commodity. The legal requirement to verify accuracy should not unduly hamstring the

timely reporting of important news. But nor should a journalist's (or blogger's) desire to get a "scoop" provide an excuse for irresponsible reporting of defamatory allegations. The question is whether the public's need to know required the defendant to publish when it did. As with the other factors, this is considered in light of what the defendant knew or ought to have known at the time of publication. If a reasonable delay could have assisted the defendant in finding out the truth and correcting any defamatory falsity without compromising the story's timeliness, this factor will weigh in the plaintiff's favour.

(iv) *The Status and Reliability of the Source*

[114] Some sources of information are more worthy of belief than others. The less trustworthy the source, the greater the need to use other sources to verify the allegations. This applies as much to documentary sources as to people; for example, an "interim progress report" of an internal inquiry has been found to be an insufficiently authoritative source in the circumstances: *Miller v. Associated Newspapers Ltd.*, [2005] EWHC 557 (QB) (BAILII). Consistent with the logic of the repetition rule, the fact that someone has already published a defamatory statement does not give another person licence to repeat it. As already explained, this principle is especially vital when defamatory statements can be reproduced electronically with the speed of a few keystrokes. At the same time, the fact that the defendant's source had an axe to grind does not necessarily deprive the defendant of protection, provided other reasonable steps were taken.

[115] It may be responsible to rely on confidential sources, depending on the circumstances; a defendant may properly be unwilling or unable to reveal a source in order to advance the defence. On the other hand, it is not difficult to see how publishing slurs from unidentified "sources" could, depending on the circumstances, be irresponsible.

(v) *Whether the Plaintiff's Side of the Story Was Sought and Accurately Reported*

[116] It has been said that this is "perhaps the core *Reynolds* factor" (Gatley, at p. 535) because it speaks to the essential sense of fairness the defence is intended to promote, as well as thoroughness. In most cases, it is inherently unfair to publish defamatory allegations of fact without giving the target an opportunity to respond: see, e.g., *Galloway v. Telegraph Group Ltd.*, [2004] EWHC 2786 (QB) (BAILII), at paras. 166-67, per Eady J. Failure to do so also heightens the risk of inaccuracy, since the target of the allegations may well be able to offer relevant information beyond a bare denial.

[117] The importance of this factor varies with the degree to which fulfilling its dictates would actually have bolstered the fairness and accuracy of the report. For example, if the target of the allegations could have no special knowledge of them, this factor will be of little importance: see *Jameel*, at paras. 35, and 83-85, where the House of Lords held that the plaintiff (whose group of companies had been put on a terrorism monitoring list) could not realistically have added anything material to the story because the relevant actions of the Saudi and U.S. governments were secret and entirely beyond his control.

(vi) *Whether Inclusion of the Defamatory Statement Was Justifiable*

[118] As discussed earlier (paras. 108-9), it is for the jury to determine whether inclusion of a defamatory statement was necessary to communicating on a matter of

public interest. Its view of the need to include a particular statement may be taken into account in deciding whether the communicator acted responsibly. In applying this factor, the jury should take into account that the decision to include a particular statement may involve a variety of considerations and engage editorial choice, which should be granted generous scope.

(vii) *Whether the Defamatory Statement's Public Interest Lay in the Fact That It Was Made Rather Than Its Truth ("Reportage")*

[119] The "repetition rule" holds that repeating a libel has the same legal consequences as originating it. This rule reflects the law's concern that one should not be able to freely publish a scurrilous libel simply by purporting to attribute the allegation to someone else. The law will not protect a defendant who is "willing to wound, and yet afraid to strike": *"Truth" (N.Z.) Ltd. v. Holloway*, [1960] 1 W.L.R. 997 (P.C.), at p. 1001, per Lord Denning. In sum, the repetition rule preserves the accountability of media and other reporting on matters of public interest. The "bald retailing of libels" is not in the public interest: *Charman*, at para. 91, per Sedley L.J. Maintaining the repetition rule is particularly important in the age of the Internet, when defamatory material can spread from one website to another at great speed.

[120] However, the repetition rule does not apply to fairly reported statements whose public interest lies in the fact that they were made rather than in their truth or falsity. This exception to the repetition rule is known as reportage. If a dispute is itself a matter of public interest and the allegations are fairly reported, the publisher should incur no liability even if some of the statements made may be defamatory and untrue, provided: (1) the report attributes the statement to a person, preferably identified, thereby avoiding total unaccountability; (2) the report indicates, expressly or implicitly, that its truth has not been verified; (3) the report sets out both sides of the dispute fairly; and (4) the report provides the context in which the statements were made [references omitted].

[121] Where the defendant claims that the impugned publication (in whole or in part) constitutes reportage, i.e. that the dominant public interest lies in reporting what was said in the context of a dispute, the judge should instruct the jury on the repetition rule and the reportage exception to the rule. If the jury is satisfied that the statements in question are reportage, it may conclude that publication was responsible, having regard to the four criteria set out above. As always, the ultimate question is whether publication was responsible in the circumstances.

(viii) *Other Considerations*

[122] As noted, the factors serve as non-exhaustive but illustrative guides. Ultimately, all matters relevant to whether the defendant communicated responsibly can be considered.

[123] Not all factors are of equal value in assessing responsibility in a given case. For example, the "tone" of the article (mentioned in *Reynolds*) may not always be relevant to responsibility. While distortion or sensationalism in the manner of presentation will undercut the extent to which a defendant can plausibly claim to have been communicating responsibly in the public interest, the defence of responsible communication ought not to hold writers to a standard of stylistic blandness: see *Roberts*, at para. 74, per Sedley L.J. Neither should the law encourage the fiction that fairness and responsibility lie in disavowing or concealing one's point of view. The best investigative reporting often takes a trenchant or adversarial position on pressing

issues of the day. An otherwise responsible article should not be denied the protection of the defence simply because of its critical tone.

[McLachlin C.J.C. ordered a new trial, where the defence of responsible communication on matters of public interest should be considered. Based on the evidence presented at the first trial, McLachlin C.J.C. held that the matter was one of public interest. She explained that the jury should be instructed to determine whether the publication was responsible in the circumstances. Abella J. gave a concurring opinion, arguing that the issue of whether the communication was responsible was a matter of law to be decided by the judge, rather than the jury. The appeal was dismissed.]

NOTES AND QUESTIONS

1. Part of the rationale for the new defence of responsible communication is that it may be difficult for defendants to establish the truth of their statements on a balance of probabilities in court, as required for the defence of justification. Is this a legitimate concern? If the defendant cannot prove the truth of the statements to a civil standard, is it "responsible" to publish them in the first place?

2. How does McLachlin C.J.C. define the public interest? Can you think of examples of media stories that do or do not qualify as being in the public interest? See generally *Quan v. Cusson*, [2009] 3 S.C.R. 712, which was released concurrently with *Grant v. Torstar Corp.*

3. In England, the defence of "responsible journalism" was characterized as a branch of qualified privilege. See *Reynolds v. Times Newspapers Ltd.*, [1999] 4 All E.R. 609 (H.L.); *Jameel v. Wall Street Journal Europe SPRL* (2006), [2007] 1 A.C. 359 (H.L.); and *Flood v. Times Newspapers Ltd.*, [2012] UKSC 11. What are the reasons for characterizing it this way? Is it preferable to create a new defence altogether, as the court did in *Grant v. Torstar Corp.*? How would each defence be affected by a finding that the defendant was motivated by malice? See Lim, "Malice, Qualified Privilege, and the New Responsible Communication Defence to Defamation: Which Way Forward for Investigative Journalism in Canada?" (2012) 45 U.B.C.L. Rev. 223.

The so-called "*Reynolds* privilege" in England was abolished by the *Defamation Act 2013* (U.K.), c. 26, s. 4, and was replaced with a broader and simpler defence of publication on a matter of public interest. The new defence applies to both statements of fact and opinion and requires the court to take into account "editorial judgement." For analysis, see Descheemaeker, "'A Man Must Take Care not to Defame his Neighbour': The Origins and Significance of the Defence of Responsible Publication" (2015) 34:2 Queensland L.J. 239, where the author notes how this defence brings the tort of defamation closer in line to the tort of negligence, with "unreasonableness" being the standard of fault.

See also *Economou v. De Freitas*, [2018] EWCA Civ 2591, in which the court applied the statutory defence to the case of a citizen who made defamatory statements about the plaintiff in two press releases, which then formed the bases of reports in the mainstream media. The court acknowledged that the defendant had not observed the standards of responsible journalism; however, as a mere "contributor" of information, it was not his responsibility to verify the relevant information or get the plaintiff's side of the story. He could rely on the journalists to perform these tasks before reporting the story. Do you agree with this analysis? Does it create a form of "contributor immunity"? Will it always be clear which party has the burden of performing due diligence before information is published?

4. The responsible communication defence was unsuccessful in *Reaburn v. Langen* (2009), 100 B.C.L.R. (4th) 1 (C.A.), where the defendant published a story alleging that police had used excessive force on a suspect. The Court of Appeal upheld the trial judge's decision that the defendant had not acted responsibly. The defendant effectively accepted the suspect's story as true and, when the police refused to comment, he failed to contact other potential witnesses. In addition, he used inflammatory language and omitted facts that might have presented a more balanced account. Finally, the Court of Appeal held that the repeated use of the term "alleged" did not assist the defendant when the thrust of the article was written as fact. See also *Vigna v. Levant*, 2010 CarswellOnt 10295 (S.C.J.) (WL Can); *Hunter v. Chandler*, 2010 CarswellBC 1306 (S.C.) (WL Can); *Hansen v. Tilley* (2010), 11 B.C.L.R. (5th) 67 (C.A.); *Vellacott v. Saskatoon Starphoenix Group Inc.*, 2012 SKQB 359; and *Graham v. Purdy*, 2017 SKQB 42.

(f) CONSENT

The defence of consent is based on the maxim *volenti non fit injuria*. It applies when statements have been put into circulation by the plaintiff him or herself, or by someone acting on the plaintiff's behalf. It also applies to statements that have been invited or elicited from the defendant at the plaintiff's instigation in situations where it is reasonable to conclude that the plaintiff consents to their publication. For instance, if the plaintiff asks the defendant a question in which a defamatory remark is invited or anticipated, the defendant will have a good defence of consent.

The plaintiff's consent can be express or implied, but is typically construed narrowly and applies only to statements that the plaintiff could reasonably have anticipated. Further, as with the defence of consent more generally, a defendant who exceeds the scope of the plaintiff's consent will not be permitted to rely on the defence.

JONES v. BROOKS
(1974), 45 D.L.R. (3d) 413 (Sask. Q.B.)

[The plaintiff, a lawyer, provided services to a municipality with respect to a development project. He was removed from the project when it was learned that he had a financial conflict of interest. The plaintiff's legal practice soon began to suffer, and the plaintiff suspected that the defendants, Mayor Brooks and Councillor Bracken, were circulating defamatory remarks about him. He hired Flaman and Poley, who were private detectives, to elicit and secretly record defamatory statements from the defendants.]

MACPHERSON J:—[The judge reviewed the background facts and continued.] Each detective had a cover story. He was investigating the plaintiff on behalf of national corporations who proposed to invest in West Bay, that the inquiry was confidential and the source would not be reported to anyone. In his interview with Flaman, Brooks said of the plaintiff that he was unethical, that he had no character, that he was a shyster, that he had no scruples. To Poley, Brooks referred to the plaintiff as a crooked son-of-a-bitch and as a real shyster. Flaman and Brooks drove to West Bay and picked up Bracken on the way. Bracken said, according to Flaman, that Jones had used his influence as town solicitor to get land for his companies. This is the only allegation of slander against Bracken. It is denied by Bracken and not mentioned by any other witness. Kondra said to Poley that he thought the plaintiff was about the most corrupt lawyer there is, that he had the legal know-how to shaft anyone and that he was a manipulator.

I have no difficulty in finding as a fact that the defendants Brooks and Kondra did say the words identified to their voices on the tapes by the two detectives and appearing in the transcripts of the tapes filed. Neither defendant when testifying made any effort to deny them. But I comment, too, that much of what was said of a defamatory nature by Brooks and Kondra to the detectives was provoked and cajoled and indeed invited by the words and manner of the detectives, particularly Poley.

. . .

[MacPherson J. reviewed the Canadian authorities and found them unhelpful.] Whereas our law seems to have atrophied, there has been considerable judicial debate in the United States. There the leading case is *Teichner v. Bellan*, (1959) 181 N.Y.S.2d 842, a decision of the appellate division of the Supreme Court of the State of New York. Justice Halpern for the Court of five said at p. 845:

> There are decisions in some States that a communication of defamatory matter to an agent of the person defamed in response to an inquiry does not constitute a publication to a third person . . .

> But the better view seems to us to be that taken in another line of cases, holding that the communication to the plaintiff's agent is a publication, even though the plaintiff's action may ultimately be defeated for other reasons. The agent is, in fact, a different entity from the principal; the communication to the agent is, in fact, a publication to a third person . . .

> Consent is a bar to a recovery for defamation under the general principle of *volenti non fit injuria* or, as it is sometimes put, the plaintiff's consent to the publication of the defamation confers an absolute immunity or an absolute privilege upon the defendant . . . However, a plaintiff who had authorized an agent to make an inquiry on his behalf is not to be charged with consent to a defamatory statement made in reply to the inquiry, unless he had reason to anticipate that the response might be a defamatory one . . . Only in such a case can it be said that he had impliedly agreed to assume the risk of a defamatory communication to his agent . . .

I have omitted only the learned Judge's authorities.

I think that this passage represents a fair statement of the law to be applied to the present case insofar as it concerns the defences of no publication and *volenti*. . .

It follows. . . that what was said by the defendants to the detectives constituted publication notwithstanding that they were agents for the plaintiff.

. . .

The detectives were experienced investigators and they were paid by the plaintiff. Each had a tape recorder and a cover story and was told by the plaintiff what to ask. Flaman was told to talk to Brooks. Poley was told to talk to all three defendants and the former defendant Miller. The whole purpose of each detective was to get the defendants to make slanderous remarks about the plaintiff and to record them on tape as evidence for this action which the plaintiff then had in contemplation.

Unquestionably the plaintiff knew when he dispatched the detectives that he had been defamed. The plaintiff testified that he instructed Flaman to learn the nature of the statements Brooks was making about him. Flaman said that the plaintiff felt he was being slandered and he was to find out what was being said. Poley said that his purpose was "to check out the slanders". When the plaintiff instructed Poley the plaintiff knew what Brooks had said to Flaman. He knew also the Mittelstadt evidence which I shall discuss presently. The plaintiff knew the nature of his difficulties with the town council.

The plaintiff therefore had good reason when he sent the detectives to anticipate that the response by the defendants to the inquiries might be defamatory.

This is the very essence of *volenti non fit injuria* — the knowing consent of the plaintiff to the defendant's wrong which the plaintiff expected. . .

. . .

In my view, the defendants have successfully met the burden and with respect to the evidence of the detectives concerning all three defendants the defence of *volenti* succeeds.

When *volenti* applies the issues of privilege and malice become redundant. Because he had assumed the risk of being slandered the plaintiff cannot now be heard to say that a defendant exceeded his privilege or was malicious. The defendants have, as Justice Halpern said above, an absolute privilege.

NOTES AND QUESTIONS

1. As indicated above, the defence of consent will fail if the defendant has exceeded the scope of the plaintiff's consent. For example, in *Syms v. Warren* (1976), 71 D.L.R. (3d) 558 (Man. Q.B.), the plaintiff had agreed to participate in a radio show to explain defamatory comments that had been made about him. The court found that he had given implied consent for the republication of those statements in order that he might clarify them. However, after the plaintiff went off the air, a caller to the show repeated the rumours circulating about him. The court held that the plaintiff's consent was thereby exceeded and the radio station was held liable. The court stressed that the defence of consent must be construed narrowly, or else "consent to the merest publication would open the door to wide dissemination that might be very damaging and never intended to be authorized by the person giving the initial consent" (at 563).

2. The defence of consent has been criticized in situations, like *Jones*, where the plaintiff elicits defamatory remarks in an effort to provide evidence of remarks that the defendant has already made. In England, the law appears to favour the plaintiff who thereby seeks to "trap" or "challenge" the defendant into repeating defamatory remarks. See Milmo & Rogers, eds., *Gatley on Libel and Slander*, 12th ed. (2013) at §19-12.

3. In *Grimmer v. Carleton Road Industries Assn.* (2009), 282 N.S.R. (2d) 159 (S.C.), the plaintiff retained a lawyer with respect to a dispute with his employer. He requested that the employer write a letter detailing the allegations against him and direct it to his lawyer, which the employer did. The plaintiff later sued for allegedly defamatory statements contained in the employer's letter. The court found that the letter was not a "publication" because confidential communications to the plaintiff's legal counsel were equivalent to direct communications with the plaintiff.

Alternatively, the court found that the letter was governed by the defence of consent, even though the plaintiff may not have anticipated all the allegations it contained. Which of these approaches is preferable?

Should the defence of consent apply when job candidates request that previous employers act as a references? If so, what is the scope of the candidate's consent? Is another defence, such as qualified privilege, preferable? See Long, "The Forgotten Role of Consent in Defamation and Employment Reference Cases" (2014) 66:2 Fla. L. Rev. 719.

4. A plaintiff who knows that potentially defamatory statements have been made about him or her on a website, and who indicates that he or she does not care whether the statements are withdrawn, may be found to have consented to their publication. This may alternatively be framed as a type of acquiescence, waiver or estoppel. See *Carrie v. Tolkien*, [2009] EWHC 29 (Q.B.); and *Flood v. Times Newspapers Ltd.*, [2010] EWCA Civ 804.

4. Remedies

(a) INJUNCTION

A plaintiff claiming in defamation may seek an injunction prior to trial to enjoin further publication of the allegedly defamatory statements. However, the courts are quite reluctant to grant such injunctions. A plaintiff will not be granted an injunction unless (i) the statements are clearly defamatory, and (ii) either the defendant does not plead justification or it is impossible for the defence of justification to succeed: *Canada Metal Co. Ltd. v. Canadian Broadcasting Corporation* (1975), 55 D.L.R. (3d) 42 (Ont. Div. Ct.). Further, as with interlocutory injunctions more generally, an injunction will not be granted if the continued publication of the defamatory material could be adequately compensated by damages at trial.

If there is any doubt over whether the statements are defamatory or whether a successful defence could be raised, then the court will not award an injunction prior to trial. It is feared that awarding injunctions too readily would have a chilling effect on democratic dialogue and freedom of the press. Thus, they are limited to situations where the impugned statements are clearly defamatory and false.

Of course, this issue will only arise in situations where the defendant threatens to continue publishing the allegedly defamatory statements. For instance, if the defendant refuses to remove the impugned material from a website, refuses to take down an allegedly defamatory poster, or continues to broadcast an allegedly defamatory advertisement, the plaintiff may wish to seek an injunction.

A permanent injunction may be granted if it is likely that the defendant will continue to publish defamatory statements or if it is unlikely that the plaintiff will be able to obtain enforcement of any damage award from the defendant. A pre-emptive restraint on freedom of expression should not be ordered lightly. See *Barrick Gold Corp. v. Lopehandia*, (2004), 71 O.R. (3d) 416 (C.A.); *Astley v. Verdun*, 2011 ONSC 3651; *St. Lewis v. Rancourt*, 2015 ONCA 513; and *Zall v. Zall*, 2016 BCSC 1730.

Recall that each publication of defamatory material is a new instance of defamation for which the defendant may be held liable. Thus, even if no injunction is sought, it may be advisable for a defendant to refrain from republishing allegedly defamatory statements to prevent an increase in damages if the defendant is ultimately found liable.

(b) DAMAGES

HILL v. CHURCH OF SCIENTOLOGY
[1995] 2 S.C.R. 1130

[The facts in *Hill* were explained in the earlier section on qualified privilege. At trial, the jury awarded $300,000 in general damages against Morris Manning and the Church of Scientology jointly. The jury also awarded $500,000 in aggravated damages and $800,000 in punitive damages against the Church of Scientology alone. These awards were upheld by the Court of Appeal for Ontario. The Supreme Court of Canada's decision on damages is below.]

Cory J.: —

(1) *The Standard of Appellate Review*

The appellants do not contend that the trial judge made any substantive error in his careful directions to the jury. Thus, there is no question of misdirection of the jury or of its acting upon an improper basis or of any jury consideration given to wrongfully admitted or excluded evidence. The sole issue is whether the quantum of the jury's award can stand.

Jurors are drawn from the community and speak for their community. When properly instructed, they are uniquely qualified to assess the damages suffered by the plaintiff, who is also a member of their community. This is why, as Robins J.A. noted in *Walker v. CFTO Ltd.* (1987), 59 O.R. (2d) 104 (C.A.), at p. 110, it is often said that the assessment of damages is "peculiarly the province of the jury". Therefore, an appellate court is not entitled to substitute its own judgment as to the proper award for that of the jury merely because it would have arrived at a different figure.

The basis upon which an appellate court can act was very clearly enunciated by Robins J.A. in *Walker, supra*. He stated at p. 110 that the court should consider:

> . . . whether the verdict is so inordinately large as obviously to exceed the maximum limit of a reasonable range within which the jury may properly operate or, put another way, whether the verdict is so exorbitant or so grossly out of proportion to the libel as to shock the court's conscience and sense of justice.

The history of this action emphasizes the reasonableness of the jury's verdict. It was the [Church of Scientology] who had always insisted upon the jury assessing damages for the libel. . . .

. . .

If guidelines are to be provided to juries, then clearly this is a matter for legislation. In its absence, the standard which must be applied remains that the jury's assessment should not be varied unless it shocks the conscience of the court. With this in mind, let us first consider the jury's assessment of damages.

(2) *General Damages*

It has long been held that general damages in defamation cases are presumed from the very publication of the false statement and are awarded at large. See *Ley v.*

Hamilton (1935), 153 L.T. 384 (H.L.), at p. 386. They are, as stated, peculiarly within the province of the jury. These are sound principles that should be followed.

The consequences which flow from the publication of an injurious false statement are invidious. The television report of the news conference on the steps of Osgoode Hall must have had a lasting and significant effect on all who saw it. They witnessed a prominent lawyer accusing another lawyer of criminal contempt in a setting synonymous with legal affairs and the courts of the province. It will be extremely difficult to correct the impression left with viewers that Casey Hill must have been guilty of unethical and illegal conduct.

The written words emanating from the news conference must have had an equally devastating impact. All who read the news reports would be left with a lasting impression that Casey Hill has been guilty of misconduct. It would be hard to imagine a more difficult situation for the defamed person to overcome. Every time that person goes to the convenience store, or shopping centre, he will imagine that the people around him still retain the erroneous impression that the false statement is correct. A defamatory statement can seep into the crevasses of the subconscious and lurk there ever ready to spring forth and spread its cancerous evil. The unfortunate impression left by a libel may last a lifetime. Seldom does the defamed person have the opportunity of replying and correcting the record in a manner that will truly remedy the situation. It is members of the community in which the defamed person lives who will be best able to assess the damages. The jury as representative of that community should be free to make an assessment of damages which will provide the plaintiff with a sum of money that clearly demonstrates to the community the vindication of the plaintiff's reputation.

(a) *Should a Cap be Imposed on Damages in Defamation Cases?*

The appellants contend that there should be a cap placed on general damages in defamation cases just as was done in the personal injury context. In the so-called "trilogy" of *Andrews v. Grand & Toy Alberta Ltd.*, [1978] 2 S.C.R. 229, *Arnold v. Teno*, [1978] 2 S.C.R. 287, and *Thornton v. Board of School Trustees of School District No. 57 (Prince George)*, [1978] 2 S.C.R. 267, it was held that a plaintiff claiming non-pecuniary damages for personal injuries should not recover more than $100,000.

In my view, there should not be a cap placed on damages for defamation. First, the injury suffered by a plaintiff as a result of injurious false statements is entirely different from the non-pecuniary damages suffered by a plaintiff in a personal injury case. In the latter case, the plaintiff is compensated for every aspect of the injury suffered: past loss of income and estimated future loss of income, past medical care and estimated cost of future medical care, as well as non-pecuniary damages. Second, at the time the cap was placed on non-pecuniary damages, their assessment had become a very real problem for the courts and for society as a whole. The damages awarded were varying tremendously not only between the provinces but also between different districts of a province. Perhaps as a result of motor vehicle accidents, the problem arose in the courts every day of every week. The size and disparity of assessments was affecting insurance rates and, thus, the cost of operating motor vehicles and, indeed, businesses of all kinds throughout the land. In those circumstances, for that *one* aspect of recovery, it was appropriate to set a cap.

A very different situation is presented with respect to libel actions. In these cases, special damages for pecuniary loss are rarely claimed and often exceedingly difficult to prove. Rather, the whole basis for recovery for loss of reputation usually lies in the general damages award. Further, a review of the damage awards over the past nine years reveals no pressing social concern similar to that which confronted the courts at the time the trilogy was decided. From 1987 to 1991, there were only 27 reported libel judgments in Canada, with an average award of $30,000. Subsequent to the decision in this case, from 1992 to 1995, there have been 24 reported libel judgments, with an average award of less than $20,000. This later figure does not include the award in *Jill Fishing Ltd. v. Koranda Management Inc.*, [1993] B.C.J. No. 1861 (S.C.), which involved the assessment of damages for a number of different causes of action. Therefore, there is no indication that a cap is required in libel cases.

There is a great difference in the nature of the tort of defamation and that of negligence. Defamation is the *intentional* publication of an injurious false statement. While it is true that an actual intention to defame is not necessary to impose liability on a defendant, the intention to do so is nevertheless inferred from the publication of the defamatory statement. This gives rise to the presumption of malice which may be displaced by the existence of a qualified privilege. Personal injury, on the other hand, results from negligence which does not usually arise from any desire to injure the plaintiff. Thus, if it were known in advance what amount the defamer would be required to pay in damages (as in the personal injury context), a defendant might look upon that sum as the maximum cost of a licence to defame. A cap would operate in a manner that would change the whole character and function of the law of defamation. It would amount to a radical change in policy and direction for the courts.

[Cory J. reviewed the issue of placing a cap on awards for defamation in other Commonwealth jurisdictions.]

In any event, I would observe that, if the trilogy were to be applied, the value of the cap in 1991 would be approximately $250,000. It follows that even if the appellants' contention on this issue was accepted, the general damages of $300,000 assessed by the jury would come very close to the range said to be reasonable by the appellants.

(b) *Joint Liability for General Damages*

Manning complains that the judge erred in refusing to accept his request that the verdict in general damages be rendered separately. He argues that his liability should be limited to the statement he made at the press conference and should not extend to the subsequent circulation of the notice of motion. The trial judge's error, he argues, contributed to the very high award by the jury. This position cannot be accepted.

It must be remembered that at trial: a) it was the position of Manning's counsel that Manning and Scientology should be jointly and severally liable for general damages in respect of each of the defamatory statements published by them; b) Scientology admitted that it published each of the defamatory statements at issue in the action; c) Manning admitted that he published each of the defamatory statements with the exception of the notice of motion; and d) the jury specifically found that Manning published the notice of motion.

Thus, both Manning and Scientology published the notice of motion. It is a well-established principle that all persons who are involved in the commission of a joint tort are jointly and severally liable for the damages caused by that tort. If one person writes a libel, another repeats it, and a third approves what is written, they all have made the defamatory libel. Both the person who originally utters the defamatory statement, and the individual who expresses agreement with it, are liable for the injury. It would thus be inappropriate and wrong in law to have a jury attempt to apportion liability either for general or for special damages between the joint tortfeasors Manning and Scientology. See *Lawson v. Burns*, [1976] 6 W.W.R. 362 (B.C.S.C.), at pp. 368-69; *Gatley on Libel and Slander* (8th ed.). . . at p. 600. However, this comment does not apply to aggravated damages, which are assessed on the basis of the particular malice of each joint tortfeasor.

(c) *Application of Principles to the Facts Established in this Case*

It cannot be forgotten that at the time the libellous statement was made, Casey Hill was a young lawyer in the Crown Law office working in the litigation field. For all lawyers their reputation is of paramount importance. Clients depend on the integrity of lawyers, as do colleagues. Judges rely upon commitments and undertakings given to them by counsel. Our whole system of administration of justice depends upon counsel's reputation for integrity. Anything that leads to the tarnishing of a professional reputation can be disastrous for a lawyer. It matters not that subsequent to the publication of the libel, Casey Hill received promotions, was elected a bencher and eventually appointed a trial judge in the General Division of the Court of Ontario. As a lawyer, Hill would have no way of knowing what members of the public, colleagues, other lawyers and judges may have been affected by the dramatic presentation of the allegation that he had been instrumental in breaching an order of the court and that he was guilty of criminal contempt.

This nagging doubt and sense of hurt must have affected him in every telephone call he made and received in the course of his daily work, in every letter that he sent and received and in every appearance that he made before the courts of the province of Ontario. He would never know who, as a result of the libellous statement, had some lingering suspicion that he was guilty of misconduct which was criminal in nature. He would never know who might have believed that he was a person without integrity who would act criminally in the performance of his duties as a Crown counsel. He could never be certain who would accept the allegation that he was guilty of a criminal breach of trust which was the essential thrust of the libel.

The publication of the libellous statement was very carefully orchestrated. Members of the press and the television media attended at Osgoode Hall in Toronto to meet two prominent lawyers, Morris Manning and Clayton Ruby. Osgoode Hall is the seat of the Court of Appeal and the permanent residence of the Law Society. The building is used as the background in a great many news reports dealing with important cases emanating from the Court of Appeal. In the minds of the public, it is associated with the law, with the courts and with the justice system. Manning went far beyond a simple explanation of the nature of the notice of motion. He took these very public steps without investigating in any way whether the allegations made were true.

At the time this press conference was called, Scientology members had been working with the sealed documents for some time and they had not yet discovered any of the sealed documents to have been opened. Yet, Scientology persisted in the publication of this libel against Hill, who was listed in their files as an "enemy".

Hill movingly described the effect the reading of the press reports of the press conference had upon him and of viewing the television broadcast. He put it in this way:

I was sick. I was shocked. I understood from reading it that it related to access to the documents. The type of thing that Mr. Ruby and I had been dealing with over many months, and I was just incredulous.

. . .

I was horrified when I saw it. I had had a long history of dealing with counsel for the Church of Scientology. Small problems, medium-sized problems and very serious problems had been raised between us.

Every effort was made to answer those issues as they came up. When I saw the newscast, I realized that there was really nothing I could do to stop the information from getting out. I thought it was false. I thought it was a very dramatic representation. A well-known lawyer as Mr. Manning was — and he was gowned.

. . .

And he was standing before the High Court. The indication that I had been involved in opening sealed documents and giving permission was totally false. For me, in seeing it, it was equivalent to saying I was a cheat and that I had obstructed the course of justice. It was an attack on my professional reputation and I had no way of stopping it.

. . .

I also have no way of knowing whether there are people in the community who would be in a position to place some reliance on the fact that regardless of the outcome of the criminal case, Manning, a prominent lawyer, and the Church of Scientology of Toronto, had still expressed a view on September 17th.

The factors which should be taken into account in assessing general damages are clearly and concisely set out in *Gatley on Libel and Slander* (8th ed.). . . at pp. 592-93, in these words:

Section 1. Assessment of Damages

1451. Province of the jury. In an action of libel "the assessment of damages does not depend on any legal rule." The amount of damages is "peculiarly the province of the jury," who in assessing them will naturally be governed by all the circumstances of the particular case. They are entitled to take into their consideration the conduct of the plaintiff, his position and standing, the nature of the libel, the mode and extent of publication, the absence or refusal of any retraction or apology, and "the whole conduct of the defendant from the time when the libel was published down to the very moment of their verdict. They may take into consideration the conduct of the defendant before action, after action, and in court at the trial of the action," and also, it is submitted, the conduct of his counsel, who cannot shelter his client by taking responsibility for the conduct of the case. They should allow "for the sad truth that no apology, retraction or withdrawal can ever be guaranteed completely to undo the harm it has done or the hurt it has caused." They should also take into account the evidence led in aggravation or mitigation of the damages.

There will of necessity be some overlapping of the factors to be considered when aggravated damages are assessed. This can be seen from a further reference to the Gatley text at pp. 593-94 where this appears:

1452. Aggravated damages. The conduct of the defendant, his conduct of the case, and his state of mind are thus all matters which the plaintiff may rely on as aggravating the damages. "Moreover, it is very well established that in cases where the damages are at large the jury (or the judge if the award is left to him) can take into account the motives and conduct of the defendant where they aggravate the injury done to the plaintiff. There may be malevolence or spite or the manner of committing the wrong may be such as to injure the plaintiff's proper feelings of dignity and pride. These are matters which the jury can take into account in assessing the appropriate compensation." "In awarding 'aggravated damages' the natural indignation of the court at the injury inflicted on the plaintiff is a perfectly legitimate motive in making a generous, rather than a more moderate award to provide an adequate *solatium*. . . that is because the injury to the plaintiff is actually greater, and, as the result of the conduct exciting the indignation, demands a more generous solatium."

In considering and applying the factors pertaining to general damages in this case it will be remembered that the reports in the press were widely circulated and the television broadcast had a wide coverage. The setting and the persons involved gave the coverage an aura of credibility and significance that must have influenced all who saw and read the accounts. The insidious harm of the orchestrated libel was indeed spread widely throughout the community.

The misconduct of the appellants continued after the first publication. Prior to the commencement of the hearing of the contempt motion before Cromarty J., Scientology was aware that the allegations it was making against Casey Hill were false. Yet, it persisted with the contempt hearings as did Morris Manning. At the conclusion of the contempt hearing, both appellants were aware of the falsity of the allegations. Nonetheless, when the libel action was instituted, the defence of justification was put forward by both of them. The statement of defence alleging justification or truth of the allegation was open for all the public to see. Despite their knowledge of its falsity, the appellants continued to publish the libel. Although Manning withdrew the plea of justification, this was only done in the week prior to the commencement of the trial itself. For its part, Scientology did not withdraw its plea of justification until the hearing of the appeal. Finally, the manner in which Hill was cross-examined by the appellants, coupled with the manner in which they presented their position to the jury, in light of their knowledge of the falsity of their allegations, are further aggravating factors to be taken into account.

When all these facts are taken into account there is no question that the award of $300,000 by way of general damages was justified in this case.

(d) *Comparison with Other Libel Cases*

At the outset, I should state that I agree completely with the Court of Appeal that each libel case is unique and that this particular case is in a "class by itself." The assessment of damages in a libel case flows from a particular confluence of the following elements: the nature and circumstances of the publication of the libel, the nature and position of the victim of the libel, the possible effects of the libel statement upon the life of the plaintiff, and the actions and motivations of the defendants. It follows that there is little to be gained from a detailed comparison of libel awards.

(3) *Aggravated Damages*

(a) *General Principles*

Aggravated damages may be awarded in circumstances where the defendants' conduct has been particularly high-handed or oppressive, thereby increasing the plaintiff's humiliation and anxiety arising from the libellous statement. The nature of these damages was aptly described by Robins J.A. in *Walker v. CFTO Ltd., supra,* in these words at p. 111:

> Where the defendant is guilty of insulting, high-handed, spiteful, malicious or oppressive conduct which increases the mental distress — the humiliation, indignation, anxiety, grief, fear and the like — suffered by the plaintiff as a result of being defamed, the plaintiff may be entitled to what has come to be known as "aggravated damages".

These damages take into account the additional harm caused to the plaintiff's feelings by the defendant's outrageous and malicious conduct. Like general or special damages, they are compensatory in nature. Their assessment requires consideration by the jury of the entire conduct of the defendant prior to the publication of the libel and continuing through to the conclusion of the trial. They represent the expression of natural indignation of right-thinking people arising from the malicious conduct of the defendant.

If aggravated damages are to be awarded, there must be a finding that the defendant was motivated by actual malice, which increased the injury to the plaintiff, either by spreading further afield the damage to the reputation of the plaintiff, or by increasing the mental distress and humiliation of the plaintiff. [Examples omitted.] The malice may be established by intrinsic evidence derived from the libellous statement itself and the circumstances of its publication, or by extrinsic evidence pertaining to the surrounding circumstances which demonstrate that the defendant was motivated by an unjustifiable intention to injure the plaintiff. . . .

There are a number of factors that a jury may properly take into account in assessing aggravated damages. For example, was there a withdrawal of the libellous statement made by the defendants and an apology tendered? If there was, this may go far to establishing that there was no malicious conduct on the part of the defendant warranting an award of aggravated damages. The jury may also consider whether there was a repetition of the libel, conduct that was calculated to deter the plaintiff from proceeding with the libel action, a prolonged and hostile cross-examination of the plaintiff or a plea of justification which the defendant knew was bound to fail. The general manner in which the defendant presented its case is also relevant. Further, it is appropriate for a jury to consider the conduct of the defendant at the time of the publication of the libel. For example, was it clearly aimed at obtaining the widest possible publicity in circumstances that were the most adverse possible to the plaintiff?

(b) *The Application to the Facts of this Case*

In this case, there was ample evidence upon which the jury could properly base their finding of aggravated damages. The existence of the file on Casey Hill under the designation "Enemy Canada" was evidence of the malicious intention of Scientology to "neutralize" him. The press conference was organized in such a manner as to ensure the widest possible dissemination of the libel. Scientology continued with the contempt proceedings although it knew its allegations were false. In its motion to remove Hill from the search warrant proceedings, it implied that he was not trustworthy and might act in those proceedings in a manner that would benefit him in his libel action. It pleaded justification or truth of its statement when it knew it to be false. It subjected Hill to a demeaning cross-examination and, in its address to the jury, depicted Hill as a manipulative actor.

It is, as well, appropriate for an appellate court to consider the post-trial actions of the defendant. It will be recalled that Scientology, immediately after the verdict of the jury, repeated the libel, thus forcing the plaintiff to seek and obtain an injunction restraining Scientology from repeating the libel. It did not withdraw its plea of justification until the hearing of the appeal. All this indicates that the award of aggravated damages was strongly supported by the subsequent actions of Scientology.

In summary, every aspect of this case demonstrates the very real and persistent malice of Scientology. Their actions preceding the publication of the libel, the circumstances of its publication and their subsequent actions in relation to both the search warrant proceedings and this action amply confirm and emphasize the insidious malice of Scientology. Much was made of their apology tendered at the time of the hearing in the Court of Appeal. There is a hollow ring to that submission when it is remembered that it was not until the fifth day of oral argument before the Court of Appeal that the apology was tendered. Scientology can gain little comfort from such a late and meaningless apology.

These damages were awarded solely against Scientology and are based upon the misconduct of that appellant. There is no question of Manning being in any way responsible for these damages. Indeed, there cannot be joint and several responsibility for either aggravated or punitive damages since they arise from the misconduct of the particular defendant against whom they are awarded. . . . Scientology's behaviour throughout can only be characterized as recklessly high-handed, supremely arrogant and contumacious. There seems to have been a continuing conscious effort on Scientology's part to intensify and perpetuate its attack on Casey Hill without any regard for the truth of its allegations.

(4) *Punitive Damages*

(a) *General Principles*

Punitive damages may be awarded in situations where the defendant's misconduct is so malicious, oppressive and high-handed that it offends the court's sense of decency. Punitive damages bear no relation to what the plaintiff should receive by way of compensation. Their aim is not to compensate the plaintiff, but rather to punish the defendant. It is the means by which the jury or judge expresses its outrage at the egregious conduct of the defendant. They are in the nature of a fine which is meant to act as a deterrent to the defendant and to others from acting in this manner. It is important to emphasize that punitive damages should only be awarded in those circumstances where the combined award of general and aggravated damages would be insufficient to achieve the goal of punishment and deterrence.

Unlike compensatory damages, punitive damages are not at large. Consequently, courts have a much greater scope and discretion on appeal. The appellate review should be based upon the court's estimation as to whether the punitive damages serve a rational purpose. In other words, was the misconduct of the defendant so outrageous that punitive damages were rationally required to act as deterrence?

This was the test formulated by Robins J.A. in *Walker v. CFTO Ltd., supra*. In that case, he found that the general damages award of $908,000 was obviously sufficient to satisfy whatever need there was for punishment and deterrence. He found that, in those circumstances, the $50,000 punitive damage award served no rational purpose. The Court of Appeal, in the case at bar, applied the same reasoning and upheld the award of punitive damages.

Punitive damages can and do serve a useful purpose. But for them, it would be all too easy for the large, wealthy and powerful to persist in libelling vulnerable victims. Awards of general and aggravated damages alone might simply be regarded as a licence fee for continuing a character assassination. The protection of a person's reputation arising from the publication of false and injurious statements must be effective. The most effective means of protection will be supplied by the knowledge that fines in the form of punitive damages may be awarded in cases where the defendant's conduct is truly outrageous.

(b) *The Application to the Facts of this Case*

There can be no doubt that the conduct of Scientology in the publication of the injurious false statement pertaining to its "enemy" was malicious. Its publication was carefully planned and carried out in a manner which ensured its widest possible dissemination in the most damaging manner imaginable. The allegation made against Hill was devastating. It was said that he had been guilty of breach of trust, breach of a court order and that his conduct and behaviour was criminal. Scientology's actions from the time of publication, throughout the trial, and after the trial decision was rendered constituted a continuing attempt at character assassination by means of a statement which it knew to be false. It was such outrageous conduct that it cried out for the imposition of punitive damages.

There might have been some concern that, in light of the award of general and aggravated damages totalling $800,000, there might not be a rational basis for punitive damages. However any lingering doubt on that score is resolved when Scientology's persistent misconduct subsequent to the trial is considered. On the very next day following the verdict, Scientology republished the libel in a press release delivered to the media. It then brought a motion to adduce fresh evidence which it stated would have a bearing "on the credibility and reputation of the plaintiff S. Casey Hill" which, if presented at trial, "would probably have changed the result". Its actions were such that Hill was forced to bring an application for an injunction enjoining Scientology from republishing the libel. In his reasons for granting the injunction, Carruthers J. stated that he was forced to take that action because "no amount awarded on account of punitive damages would have prevented or will prevent the Church of Scientology from publishing defamatory statements about the plaintiff. Even the injunction did not deter Scientology which moved to set it aside. Further, in its notice of appeal of the libel judgment, Scientology alleged that the trial judge had erred in ruling the decision of Cromarty J. in the contempt proceedings was *res judicata* of the issues raised in the libel trial.

During the appeal, it was conceded and the evidence and events confirmed that in all likelihood, no amount of general or aggravated damages would have deterred Scientology. Clearly then, this was an appropriate case for an award of punitive damages. Scientology did not withdraw its plea of justification until the first day of the oral argument in the Court of Appeal. Nor was any apology tendered by Scientology until the fifth day of oral argument before the Court of Appeal.

The award of punitive damages, therefore, served a rational purpose in this case. Further, the circumstances presented in this exceptional case demonstrate that there was such insidious, pernicious and persistent malice that the award for punitive damages cannot be said to be excessive. Scientology has alleged that the size of the award of punitive damages had a chilling effect on its right to freedom of expression. However as stated earlier, in spite of the slow and methodical progress of this case to trial and appeal, and despite the motion brought six years before the trial which drew attention to the need for evidence, Scientology adduced no evidence as to the chilling effect of the award. In its absence, this argument should not be considered. It may be that different factors will have to be taken into consideration where evidence is adduced and where a member of the media is a party to the action. However, those are considerations for another case on another day.

[The court upheld the damages awarded by the jury and dismissed the appeal with costs.]

NOTES AND QUESTIONS

1. Why is it important for the jury to assess damages for defamation? What does Cory J. mean when he says that damages in a defamation case are "at large?" See *Farrell v. Canadian Broadcasting Corporation* (1987), 66 Nfld. & P.E.I.R. 145 (Nfld. C.A.).

2. Why did Cory J. decide that a cap on defamation awards was not warranted, as compared to personal injury awards? Are his reasons convincing? Awards may be particularly high in cases involving corporate plaintiffs if the courts conclude that this is necessary to vindicate the plaintiffs' business reputations. This may even occur in cases where there is no evidence of proof of loss. See for example *Barrick Gold Corp. v. Lopenhandia* (2004), 71 O.R. (3d) 416 (C.A.); and *Second Cup Ltd. v. Eftoda* (2006), 41 C.C.L.T. (3d) 111 (Ont. S.C.J.). See generally Young, "Rethinking Canadian Defamation Law as Applied to Corporate Plaintiffs" (2013) 46 U.B.C.L. Rev. 529; and Young, "The Canadian Defamation Action: An Empirical Study" (2017) 95 Can. Bar Rev. 591. The latter study found that punitive damages were awarded more often to corporate plaintiffs than to human plaintiffs, and in higher amounts.

3. According to *Hill*, what factors are to be considered when assessing aggravated damages in defamation? How are these different from the factors considered when assessing punitive damages? See *Mudford v. Smith*, 2009 CarswellOnt 6326 (S.C.J.) (WL Can), aff'd 2010 CarswellOnt 3615 (C.A.) (WL Can); *Tremblay v. Campbell*, 2010 CarswellNfld 301 (C.A.) (WL Can); *Sagman v. Politi*, 2014 ONSC 4183; and *Zall v. Zall*, 2016 BCSC 1730.

4. What mitigating factors might serve to lower an award in a defamation case? Most provincial legislation permits the defendant to argue mitigation if the defendant has provided a written apology or, in the case of broadcast libel, broadcast a full apology at the earliest opportunity. See for example *Libel and Slander Act*, R.S.O. 1990, c. L. 12, ss. 9 and 20; *Libel and Slander Act*, R.S.B.C. 1996, c. 263, s. 10; and *Defamation Act*, R.S.N.S. 1989, c. 122, s. 5. See *Second Cup Ltd. v. Eftoda, supra*, in

which damages were increased because the defendant refused to apologize; and *Awan v. Levant*, 2014 ONSC 6890, aff'd 2016 ONCA 970, in which aggravated damages were awarded because the defendant refused to correct errors in his blog.

5. Why was the defendants' plea of justification relevant to the award of damages in *Hill?*

REVIEW PROBLEM

Heidi is the host of a local radio call-in show. Since there have recently been several complaints against the local police for excessive use of force, Heidi decided to produce a show on that topic. As background research, Heidi read a few local news stories and editorial columns. She learned that one officer, John Fraser, was implicated in several of the complaints. However, the investigation into the complaints was ongoing, and there had not yet been any criminal charges or disciplinary action taken.

On the day of the show, Heidi began her broadcast by describing the complaints according to the information she had read in the local papers. She then quoted directly from an editorial in the Daily Dirt, which read, "It seems like the police in this area have let power go to their heads. It is time for heads to roll." Heidi continued by adding her own comments, saying, "John Fraser is at the centre of these complaints. He is willing to beat up anyone who gets in his way. It is an outrage when officers of the law turn into criminals."

Heidi then turned to the call-in portion of the show. Her assistant, whose job it is to screen callers, informed her that one of the complainants was on the line. Heidi was thrilled and told her assistant to put the caller on. The caller, who refused to be identified for fear of further police brutality, described in detail her complaint of excessive force against John Fraser. She ended her call by saying "I've heard that he cheated on his wife, too. I don't know if that's true, but I wouldn't put it past him." Heidi did not comment on this last accusation, and immediately took a commercial break.

Some officers at the police station were listening to Heidi's show and heard the accusations against Fraser and the rest of the force. A senior officer decided he wanted to call into the show to set the record straight. However, Heidi's assistant refused to put him on the air. When he protested, she told him he could write the manager of the radio station to complain.

The local police and John Fraser have come to you for advice on their potential claims in defamation.

TORT LAW: THEORIES, CRITICISMS AND ALTERNATIVES

1. Introduction
2. Theoretical Criticism of Tort Law
3. The No-Fault Alternatives

1. Introduction

Why do we have tort law? Does it do what it purports to be doing? Does it do what it should be doing? Are there any preferable alternatives? There is a great deal of academic literature devoted to tort law's theoretical bases and its role in modern society. It is not possible in this chapter to consider that literature in any great depth. Our aim, instead, is to provide an overview and, hopefully, to spur further thought. The discussion is divided into two parts. The first reviews some of the more important theories of tort law and highlights the debates they have generated. The second examines the concept of "no-fault" recovery. As we shall see, tort law provides only one means by which losses can be redressed. Some commentators believe that tort law has outlived its usefulness.

2. Theoretical Criticism of Tort Law

(a) INTRODUCTION

Theoretical criticism of tort law falls into two general categories: analytical and normative. Analytical criticism is concerned with the basic concepts of tort law. In particular, analytical critics identify and evaluate both the supposed functions of tort law and foundational tort concepts, such as intent, consent, duty of care and fault. The work of analytical critics can be either empirical (*i.e.* observational investigations of the actual operation of tort systems) or more philosophical (*i.e.* rigorous investigations of the internal logic of concepts).

The second category of tort criticism involves the use of normative theory. Normative critics engage in the moral evaluation of tort concepts and systems. These critics are interested in the degree to which tort principles and outcomes conform to concepts of "justice." While some normative theorists analyze the morality of particular tort decisions or doctrines in terms of their consequences, others are more interested in the inherent moral qualities and defects of the law.

The first two parts of this section concern the analytical theory of two purported functions of tort law: deterrence and compensation. The third part investigates some recent normative criticisms of tort law.

NOTES

1. See generally Owen, ed., *Philosophical Foundations of Tort Law* (1995); Cane, *The Anatomy of Tort Law* (1997); Deakin, "The Evolution of Tort" (1999) 19 O.J.L.S. 537; Goldberg, "Twentieth-Century Tort Theory" (2003) 91 Geo. L.J. 513; Madden, ed., *Exploring Tort Law* (2005); Lucy, *Philosophy of Private Law* (2007); Geistfeld, "The Coherence of the Compensation-Deterrence Theory in Tort Law" (2012) 61 DePaul L. Rev. 383; Oberdiek, ed., *Philosophical Foundations of the Law of Torts* (2014); Ripstein, *Private Wrongs* (2016); and Beever, *A Theory of Tort Liability* (2016).

2. Before reading this chapter, it may be helpful to review sections 6 and 7 of Chapter 1.

(b) DETERRENCE

Many authors suggest that one of the primary goals of tort law is, or should be, the deterrence of intentional and negligent wrongdoing. In this section, we will examine some of the limits on the effectiveness of tort law as a deterrent and the contributions that economists have made to deterrence theories.

The object of deterrence is to prevent undesirable conduct. Tort liability has the potential to deter both particular defendants (specific deterrence) and other members of the public (general deterrence). The level of deterrence is often defined as the product of the swiftness, certainty and severity of an action's consequences. Moreover, effective deterrence requires a precise definition of the objectionable conduct, and a sanction that discourages such conduct without inhibiting desirable conduct.

There are several inherent limitations on the deterrent impact of tort law. Much of the conduct giving rise to tort liability involves spontaneous, careless behaviour, which is not particularly amenable to deterrence. For example, drivers do not contemplate liability when making the complex, split-second decisions that are part of driving. The available empirical evidence suggests that individuals who are risk-takers are greatly over-represented in car and other types of accidents and that they are not easily deterred. If dangerous drivers are not deterred by the risk of death or injury to themselves and others, the risk of criminal prosecution and licensing sanctions, or the risk of higher insurance costs, it is questionable whether the risk of a tort claim will deter them in any significant way.

Tort law probably has its greatest impact on planned decision-making in business. For example, profit-maximizing industrial managers would presumably weigh potential liability costs against the costs of safety precautions, and take cost-justified measures of accident avoidance. In Chapter 15, we saw that R. Posner explains the standard of reasonable care in this manner. However, if this theory is to create efficient levels of accident prevention, it must assume that defendants will actually incur liability for losses caused by their unreasonable conduct. In reality, many legitimate tort claims are not pursued, and damage awards rarely reflect all of the personal and social losses that are suffered. In this sense, tort law may encourage careless conduct.

The deterrent impact of tort law is also affected by an individual's perception of the likelihood of both litigation and a finding of liability. The typically long delay between the tortious conduct and the imposition of liability lessens the law's deterrent effect. In addition, the contingencies of litigation and deficiencies in evidence mean that some tortfeasors may not be found liable in court, and others will settle for amounts far less than the damages they cause. Finally, the fact that almost all drivers, businesses and industries carry some form of liability insurance further reduces tort law's deterrent impact: even if found liable, the actors responsible for tortious harms may not bear the financial consequences of their actions. As J. Fleming famously remarked in "The Role of Negligence in Modern Tort Law" (1967) 53 Va. L. Rev. 815 at 823: "the deterrent function of the law of torts was severely, perhaps fatally, undermined by the advent of liability insurance."

Deterrence theory in tort law has been heavily influenced by legal economists. They suggest that tort law can operate as an efficient deterrent in two ways. First, tort rules may address the problem of "externalities" by allocating accident costs to the activities that generate them. Second, tort rules can lower the cost of accidents by allocating these costs to the party who is able to avoid them at the lowest possible cost.

The basic premise of economic analysis is that society chooses how much of a good, service or activity its members want through the price system. Other things being equal, demand will fall as prices rise. Provided prices accurately reflect the cost of the activity in question, the price system will produce an efficient allocation of resources. Given the existing distribution of wealth, society is obtaining the optimum mixture of the goods and services that it wants, based on its members' willingness to pay.

Since perfect market conditions rarely exist, our economy does not automatically produce an efficient allocation of resources. One major problem is that prices will not accurately reflect costs if a portion of those costs have been externalized. Economists have recognized that legal rules can be important in preventing the externalization of such costs. For example, if motorists are required to have liability insurance, they must take this cost into account in deciding whether to drive. The law internalizes the cost of accidents and ensures that it is reflected in the price of driving.

If the law were changed so that liability insurance was paid for out of general tax revenue, the cost of accidents would be externalized from the activity of driving in two ways. First, some of the costs of accidents would be paid by taxpayers who do not drive. More importantly, drivers would not have to consider the cost of accidents in deciding whether to drive; they would have to pay the tax regardless. Consequently, some people who would not have driven because of the insurance costs would now choose to drive, thereby increasing the number of cars on the roads and the number of accidents. By externalizing part of the insurance costs of driving, the law would have produced an inefficiently high number of automobile accidents.

Once costs have been internalized, tort law may play a role in determining who should bear them. For example, should the costs of defective brakes be borne by automobile owners or manufacturers? If tort law held owners liable, they would incur the personal and third-party accident costs. In response, they might attempt to reduce their liability by arranging for inspections, repairs or modifications. If manufacturers were held liable, they would either pay damage awards or minimize these costs by designing a safer braking system. An economist would argue that tort law should impose liability on the party who is able to minimize these accidents at the lowest cost and that the law should provide that party with an incentive to adopt the lowest cost solution. Thus, if manufacturers are the cheapest cost-avoiders, liability should be imposed on them. Such a rule would encourage manufacturers to install safe braking systems, rather than risk incurring liability costs.

In summary, according to economic theory, tort law can serve as a deterrent in two ways. First, it can internalize costs, which allows the price system to determine the level of accidents for which society is willing to pay. Second, tort law can reduce total accident costs by allocating liability to the cheapest cost-avoider.

NOTES AND QUESTIONS

1. There are many rules of tort law that are not predicated on deterrence. For example, does the defence of private necessity serve to deter the relevant conduct? Can the rules of tort law governing duress be explained in terms of deterrence?

2. For a comprehensive critique of the deterrent aspects of tort law, see Sugarman, "Doing Away with Tort Law" (1985) 73 Cal. L. Rev. 555. For the opposing view, see Popper, "In Defense of Deterrence" (2011) 75 Alb. L. Rev. 181.

3. Empirical studies suggest that the potential for tort liability has little effect on individuals' willingness to engage in risky behavior and that it may have only a weak effect on corporate behaviour. See for example, Brennan, "Environmental Torts" (1993) 46 Vand. L. Rev. 1; and Cardi, Penfield & Yoon, "Does Tort Law Deter Individuals? A Behavioral Science Study" (2012) 9 J. Empirical Leg. Stud. 567.

4. Several studies suggest that tort liability has little deterrent impact on driving. See for example Brown, "Deterrence in Tort and No-Fault: The New Zealand Experience" (1985) 73 Cal. L. Rev. 976; and Osborne, *Report of Inquiry Into Motor Vehicle Accident Compensation in Ontario* (1988). But see Dewee, Duff & Trebilcock, *Exploring the Domain of Accident Law* (1995) at 21-22, who conclude that "several features of the current automobile liability system comport relatively well with the ideal deterrence model." See also Cummins, Phillips & Weiss, "The Incentive Effects of No-Fault Automobile Insurance" (2001) 44 J.L. & Econ. 427; and Cohen & Dehejia, "The Effects of Automobile Insurance and Accident Liability Laws on Traffic Fatalities" (2004) 47 J.L. & Econ. 357.

In Lemann, "Coercive Insurance and the Soul of Tort Law" (2016) 105 Geo. L.J. 55, the author discusses new telematics devices that can collect data about individual driving patterns (*e.g.* rapid acceleration and deceleration) and thus allow insurance companies to penalize risky practices in real time. These features may make insurance a more efficient system of deterrence than tort law.

5. Deterrence is undermined by the doctrine of vicarious liability, which makes employers liable for the torts committed by employees in the course of their work. As a practical matter, few employers go on to seek contribution from their employees for the amounts they have had to pay to injured plaintiffs. This means that many employees who make loss-creating decisions will not bear the financial consequences of their actions, and will not feel the deterrent impact of the law. See Sykes, "The Economics of Vicarious Liability" (1984) 93 Yale L.J. 1231.

6. R. Posner has argued that tort damages are awarded to induce plaintiffs to initiate legal proceedings, thereby maintaining a private system of deterrence: "A Theory of Negligence" (1972) 1 J. Legal Stud. 29. See also Holmes, *The Common Law* (1881) at 95-96; White, "Risk-Utility Analysis and the Learned Hand Formula: A Hand that Helps or a Hand that Hides?" (1990) 32 Ariz. L. Rev. 77; and England,

"Law and Economics in American Tort Cases: A Critical Assessment of the Theory's Impact on Courts" (1991) 41 U.T.L.J. 359. However, the current system still appears to have a problem of "under-enforcement" which weakens the deterrent effects of tort law. See Perry, "Re-Torts" (2008) 59 Ala. L. Rev. 987.

7. For an explanation of the role of tort law in internalizing the costs of accidents, see Calabresi, *The Cost of Accidents* (1970). Calabresi's thesis is reassessed by Attanasio in "The Calabresian Approach to Products Liability" in Owen, ed., *Philosophical Foundations of Tort Law* (1995) 299. See also Goldberg & Zipursky, "Accidents of the Great Society" (2005) 64 Md. L. Rev. 364.

8. In contrast to Calabresi's thesis, the 1967 *Report of the Royal Commission of Inquiry on Compensation for Personal Injury in New Zealand* expressly rejected economic efficiency as an appropriate social goal (at 177-88). The Commission favoured a general pooling of all risks on the theory that activities are interdependent. Calabresi's analysis suggests that the Commission's approach distorts efficient consumption choices, creating more dangerous activities and fewer safe ones than would be the case if costs were assigned properly.

9. The main thrust of the law and economics approach to tort law is that compensatory damages represent the cost of accidents and, if a tortfeasor prefers to pay damages rather than take precautions to prevent the harm, it is efficient to allow the harm. Even assuming the tort system worked perfectly to achieve such efficiency, is this a sound or desirable premise? Are some accidents "worth having?" See Schwartz, "The Myth of the Ford Pinto Case" (1991) 43 Rutgers L. Rev. 1013.

10. What role should punitive damages play in deterring actors from choosing to sacrifice human safety in the name of economic efficiency? See Cooter, "Punitive Damages for Deterrence: When and How Much?" (1989) 40 Ala. L. Rev. 1143; Polinsky & Shavell, "Punitive Damages: An Economic Analysis" (1998) 111 Harv. L. Rev. 869; Calabresi, "The Complexity of Torts — The Case of Punitive Damages" in Madden, ed., *Exploring Tort Law* (2005) 333; and Rhee, "A Financial Economic Theory of Punitive Damages" (2012) 111 Mich. L. Rev. 33. See also Steinzor, "(Still) 'Unsafe at Any Speed': Why Not Jail for Auto Executives?" (2015) 9 Harv. L. & Pol'y Rev. 443.

11. Under perfect market conditions, society would always find the lowest cost solution, regardless of how the law allocated responsibility. For example, assume that the law did not hold a manufacturer liable for injuries caused by defective brakes. If the lowest cost solution was to have manufacturers design and install an improved braking system, owners and accident victims would be better off to pay manufacturers to develop such a system than to incur the accident costs themselves. However, the transaction costs of getting these people together, allocating a fair share to each driver and enforcing this system are far too great to make it practical. Thus, in the real world, the proper choice of the liability rule is essential to ensure the lowest cost solution. See Coase, "The Problem of Social Cost" (1960) 3 J.L. & Econ. 1.

12. Some have argued that the threat of tort liability actually over-deters and discourages socially desirable behaviour. For instance, the risk of malpractice claims and rising insurance costs may discourage doctors from entering certain specialist

fields that have high rates of lawsuits (*e.g.* obstetrics). See Domin, "Where Have All the Baby-Doctors Gone? Women's Access to Healthcare in Jeopardy: Obstetrics and the Medical Malpractice Insurance Crisis" (2004) 53 Cath. U.L. Rev. 499; and Klick & Stratmann, "Medical Malpractice Reform and Physicians in High-Risk Specialties" (2007) 36 J. Leg. Stud. S121. Other doctors may engage in defensive medicine, ordering unnecessary tests and making compendious records to protect them in the event of litigation, leading to an inefficient level of medical costs. But see Hyman & Silver, "The Poor State of Health Care Quality in the U.S.: Is Malpractice Liability Part of the Problem or Part of the Solution?" (2005) 90 Cornell L. Rev. 893; Shepherd, "Tort Reforms' Winners and Losers — The Competing Effects of Care and Activity Levels" (2008) 55 U.C.L.A.L. Rev. 905; Frank & Shadle, "Is There Empirical Evidence for 'Defensive Medicine'?" (2009) 28 J. Health Econ. 481; Frakes & Jena, "Does medical malpractice law improve health care quality?" (2016) 143 J. Public Econ. 152; and Safrin, "The C-Section Epidemic: What's Tort Reform Got to Do with It?" (2018) 2 Ill. L. Rev. 747.

13. Economic analysis is also implicated in the decision to immunize certain activities from tort liability. See for example Horwitz & Mead, "Letting Good Deeds Go Unpunished: Volunteer Immunity Laws and Tort Deterrence" (2009) 6 J. Empirical Legal Stud. 585.

14. For a comprehensive survey of the ways that economic analysis can be applied to tort law, see Faure, ed., *Tort Law and Economics* (2009). It examines specific doctrines like causation and multiple tortfeasors, contributory negligence, vicarious liability and damages; analyzes specific industries like products liability, environmental harm and medical malpractice; and debates the values of the tort law system in comparison to no-fault or insurance-based alternatives.

(c) COMPENSATION

Accident compensation is widely regarded as one of the most important functions of tort law, particularly in negligence. As noted in Chapter 1, compensation serves important social goals and acts as the major motivating factor for individual plaintiffs. However, the present tort system is increasingly difficult to justify as a rational compensation scheme. For example, in *The Damages Lottery* (1997), P.S. Atiyah provides a scathing criticism of the tort system as a coherent and predictable means of compensating accident victims. He contends that the current tort regimes fail miserably at their principal task: providing speedy and adequate reparations to the injured. The complexity of the law, its clumsy procedures, and its arcane doctrines of fault, causation, proof and damages generally conspire against the plaintiff. While a handful of tort victims receive generous, even over-generous, compensation from the tortfeasor's insurer, most victims get nothing at all. To make matters worse, corporate retailers and purchasers of insurance pass on the costs of this system to consumers. Atiyah advocates replacing the tort system with a comprehensive accident insurance system that will end tort litigation while guaranteeing a measure of compensation to all accident victims.

Many potential defendants carry liability insurance, and many potential plaintiffs are eligible for some public and private first party insurance benefits. Most of these collateral compensation systems were created independently of tort law. The overlap among and *ad hoc* development of collateral sources have created a very complicated system of accident compensation, only tangentially related to tort law. Critics argue that tort law has become largely irrelevant in accident compensation. They favour a comprehensive and rationalized approach to accident compensation, free from the historical fetters of tort law.

There is overwhelming evidence that tort law performs poorly in terms of accident compensation. For example, The Ontario Law Reform Commission stated in its *Report on Motor Vehicle Accident Compensation* (1973) at 48 that:

> All the studies demonstrate that the tort system pays only about one-third of the total pecuniary losses (called "economic losses" in the studies) and further that the money paid out is distributed very unevenly among the victims. Less than half the people who suffer losses receive compensation through the tort regime. More important, perhaps, is the consistent finding in all studies that the more serious the accident, and therefore, generally speaking, the greater the loss, the lower the recovery percentage. Even with non-tort sources added, a large fraction of pecuniary losses remain uncompensated and the pattern of maldistribution does not improve.

Furthermore, the administrative costs of the tort law system are remarkably high relative to the amount of compensation actually paid. It has been estimated that the administrative expenses of the tort system amount to approximately 85% of the sums paid out, *i.e.*, for every dollar paid in compensation, 85 cents are spent on administrative costs. P. Cane explains the reasons for these costs in *Atiyah's Accidents, Compensation and the Law*, 7th ed. (2006) at 397-98:

> First, it is necessary (in theory, at least) to ascertain in every case who, if anyone, was at fault and whether that fault caused the plaintiff's injuries. These are very difficult questions to answer in many cases, and the process of investigation may be time-consuming (and time is money); it requires expertise (which costs money); and it may require the interviewing of witnesses, the taking of statements, the commissioning of technical or medical experts to analyse the evidence, and so on. . . . Secondly, the compensation payable in a tort case depends on the medical condition and other circumstances of the particular plaintiff; there are no rigid tariffs or formulae for assessing tort compensation: every case is different. Thirdly, because of the adversarial nature of the tort process, both parties will employ advisers to make the same inquiries about the causes and consequences of the accident. This duplication itself accounts for a considerable portion of the total cost.

It quickly becomes clear why the tort system is so expensive to operate. This can be contrasted to the social welfare system, where administrative costs run at only 12% of the sums paid out. Thus, tort law not only fails to adequately compensate a large proportion of accident victims, but does so on a very uneconomical basis.

It is perhaps unfair to criticize tort law as an accident compensation scheme. Indeed, there is no historical evidence to indicate that tort law was ever intended to operate solely as an accident compensation plan. The tort law system is a means of empowering private individuals to seek redress for the civil wrongs they have suffered, and compensation is only one component of the overall scheme. Even staunch supporters of the current tort system would admit that it is hardly comprehensive in the compensation it offers, and that no society should rely solely on tort law to compensate injured parties. It is not, therefore, surprising that most countries have found it necessary to supplement tort law with alternative accident compensation programs.

NOTES AND QUESTIONS

1. Is the goal of compensation compatible with the other goals of tort law like deterrence and punishment? P.S. Atiyah observed that the more we limit liability to morally blameworthy conduct, the less likely we are to achieve adequate compensation for accident victims. On the other hand, if the compensation objective is treated as paramount, defendants may be held liable in the absence of subjective fault. See Atiyah, *Accidents, Compensation and the Law* (1970) at 456.

2. Judicial disagreements on breach of the standard of care often reflect the incompatibility of the goals of deterrence and compensation. To hold a defendant who has taken cost-justified precautions liable in negligence secures compensation for the victim at the expense of discouraging efficient conduct. To encourage "efficient" safety measures may leave many accident victims uncompensated. For example, contrast the views of Spence J. and de Grandpré J. on the issue of the mother's negligence in *Arnold v. Teno*, [1978] 2 S.C.R. 287. See also Laskin C.J.C. and de Grandpré J. on the liability issue in *Wade v. C.N.R.*, [1978] 1 S.C.R. 1064. This case involved a young child who, as the result of a dare, jumped aboard a moving train. Can you think of other examples? Is it realistic to expect tort law to achieve all of the goals that have been set for it?

3. Several scholars have criticized compensation under the tort system as being arbitrary, in that it depends on the "good fortune" of someone else being at fault for an accident. Leading examples are Ison, *The Forensic Lottery* (1967); and Atiyah, *supra*. Injured persons who are equally in need of compensation, but cannot prove that the accident was caused by the fault of another, receive nothing from the tort system. See also Stapleton, *Disease and the Compensation Debate* (1986) which critically analyzes tort law's focus on traumatic accidents and its corresponding neglect of other sources of disability.

4. In the *Report of the Royal Commission on Compensation for Personal Injury in New Zealand* (1967) at 39-41, the Commissioner identified the following as objectives of a compensation scheme: community responsibility, comprehensive entitlement, complete rehabilitation, real compensation, and administrative efficiency. Are these the proper goals of a compensation scheme? Does the present tort system adequately serve these goals?

5. The New Zealand Royal Commission Report was very critical of tort law's performance in providing accident compensation. Other critical studies include Ison, *supra;* Elliott & Street, *Road Accidents* (1968); McLaren, "The Theoretical and Policy Challenges in Canadian Compensation Law" (1985) 23 Osgoode Hall L.J. 609; Sugarman, "Doing Away With Tort Law" (1985) 73 Cal. L. Rev. 555; Dewees & Trebilcock, "The Efficacy of the Tort System and Its Alternatives : A Review of Empirical Evidence" (1992) 30 Osgoode Hall L.J. 57; and Abel, "A Critique of Torts" (1994) 2 Tort L. Rev. 99.

6. One of the chief obstacles in the way of an improved understanding of tort systems is the lack of systematic empirical data. See generally Saks, "Do We Really Know Anything about the Behavior of the Tort Litigation System — and Why Not?" (1992) 140 U. Pa. L. Rev. 1147; and van Velthoven, "Empirics of tort" in Faure, ed., *Tort Law and Economics* (2009) 453.

7. Even if the tort law system provides inadequate compensation at high administrative costs, does it serve other useful purposes? Is there value in having one's "day in court" and seeing a wrongdoer held liable? This notion of responsibility was cited in the report of the British *Royal Commission on Civil Liability and Compensation for Personal Injury* (1978) as one reason to maintain the tort law system in preference over a no-fault compensation scheme. See also Fleming, "The Pearson Report: Its 'Strategy'" (1979) 42 M.L.R. 249; and Hershovitz, "Treating Wrongs as Wrongs: An Expressive Argument for Tort Law" (2018) 10:2 J. Tort Law 405. The goal of vindication may be particularly important to plaintiffs suing large corporations or government entities. See Koenig & Rustad, *In Defense of Tort Law* (2001); and Varuhas, "The Concept of 'Vindication' in the Law of Torts: Rights, Interests and Damages" (2014) 34:2 O.J.L.S. 253.

(d) THEORIES OF TORT LAW BASED ON CONCEPTS OF JUSTICE

To this point, we have discussed several goal-based (sometimes called "instrumentalist") theories of tort law, namely those that focus on deterrence, efficiency and accident compensation. In this subsection, we examine those theories that evaluate the principles of tort according to notions of "justice." The various concepts of justice underlying these theories are purportedly derived independently of desirable social consequences. It is important to distinguish these "pure theories" of justice from those that assert that a principle of tort law is "just" because it promotes a desirable goal, such as accident compensation. The most provocative articles concerning the concepts of justice in tort law have been written in the past 40 years, largely in response to the literature claiming that tort law is based on principles of economic efficiency.

Corrective and Distributive Justice: The concepts of corrective and distributive justice are typically traced back to Aristotle's account of justice in Book V of his *Nicomachean Ethics*:

> [p]articular justice on the other hand, and that which is just in the sense corresponding to it, is divided into two kinds. One kind is exercised in the distribution of honour, wealth, and the other divisible assets of the community, which may be allotted among its members in equal or unequal shares. The other kind is that which supplies a corrective principle in private transactions.

Distributive justice seeks to effect the just distribution of a particular benefit or burden based on some measure of merit or desert, and theories of distributive justice are accordingly concerned with the appropriateness of the distribution of wealth and entitlements in society. There are many different views, most based on concepts of natural rights or equality. It is generally conceded that tort law plays a relatively minor role in achieving distributive justice. However, some tort rules and decisions have explicit distributional aims, such as those involving the "deep pocket" approach to loss allocation, or rules that apportion liability among defendants based on their market share.

Most tort rules have distributional consequences, although these are often subtle and perhaps unintended. For example, it can be demonstrated that, in theory, strict liability and negligence promote precisely the same level of deterrence. But by adopting principles of negligence rather than strict liability, society imposes the costs of "unavoidable" injuries on accident victims and not on those who cause accidents. Moreover, compensatory damage awards usually protect the pre-existing distribution of wealth. For instance, the damages awarded for loss of income to an unemployed labourer will be significantly lower than those awarded to an established accountant. However, the liability insurance premiums paid by the labourer guard against his or her potential liability to higher income earners.

Over the last few decades, tort theory has been largely dominated by the concept of corrective justice. The basic premise of corrective justice is that when one party has committed and another has suffered a wrong, the law should rectify or "correct" the wrong and return the parties to their initial positions. In tort law, this corrective principle is manifested in the objective of *restitutio in integrum*, according to which the remedy ordered by the court seeks to restore the plaintiff to the position he or she would have enjoyed, had the defendant not committed the tort.

Many scholars have propounded theories of corrective justice, and they cannot all be surveyed here. The flavour of the debate can be captured by noting the positions of two leading corrective justice theorists: J. Coleman and E. Weinrib. In his influential book, *Risks and Wrongs* (1992), Coleman argues that tort law is concerned with the rectification of wrongful losses. The plaintiff has suffered a loss through no fault of his or her own. If the plaintiff wishes to shift that loss to the defendant, the plaintiff must prove that the defendant (i) committed a wrong and (ii) caused the plaintiff's loss. It is the fact that the plaintiff's wrongful loss came through the agency of the defendant that permits corrective justice to shift the loss to the defendant.

Weinrib, however, argues that corrective justice is aimed at rectifying not wrongful losses, but the wrongs themselves. It is not sufficient that the defendant has committed a wrong and caused loss to the plaintiff; rather, the factors that made the defendant's conduct wrongful toward the plaintiff must be the same factors that caused the plaintiff's loss. In his book, *The Idea of Private Law* (1995), Weinrib illustrates his theory by reference to Justice Cardozo's famous opinion in *Palsgraf v. Long Island Ry. Co.*, 248 N.Y. 339 (1928), excerpted in Chapter 10. In that case, the railroad employee committed a wrong by carelessly pushing a running passenger onto the train, causing him to drop his package of explosives. The plaintiff, who was standing further down the platform, suffered a loss when the explosion caused a set of scales to fall on her. However, Cardozo J. dismissed the plaintiff's claim because the plaintiff did not fall within the scope of the risk created by the defendant's careless conduct, *i.e.*, he had not been negligent *toward her*. Although the defendant had committed a wrong, it was not a wrong with respect to the plaintiff.

Thus, Weinrib's account of corrective justice stresses the notion of correlative rights and duties. He explains in "Corrective Justice in a Nutshell" (2002) 52 U.T.L.J. 349 at 352-53:

> The injustice that liability rectifies consists in the defendant's having something or having done something that is incompatible with a right of the plaintiff. Right and

duty are correlated when the plaintiff's right is the basis of the defendant's duty and, conversely, when the scope of that duty includes avoiding the kind of right-infringement that the plaintiff suffered. Under those circumstances the reasons that justify the protection of the plaintiff's right are the same as the reasons that justify the existence of the defendant's duty.

. . . Then correlativity obtains because the parties are the doer and sufferer of the same injustice, and the reason for the plaintiff's entitlement to win the lawsuit would be the same as the reason for the defendant's liability to lose it.

Weinrib's account thus explains the structure of modern tort law: the defendant's wrongful infringement of the plaintiff's right explains why the defendant (and no one else) has an obligation to compensate the plaintiff. And the plaintiff's suffering of a correlative loss explains why the plaintiff (and no one else) can demand that the defendant pay compensation. Corrective justice links the doer and sufferer of the harm in a single normative unit.

Corrective justice is oblivious to the "justice" of the initial distribution of wealth between the parties. As Aristotle wrote, "it makes no difference whether a good man has defrauded a bad man or a bad one a good one. . . the law looks only at the nature of the damage, treating the parties as equal, and merely asking whether one has done and the other suffered injustice, whether one inflicted and the other has sustained damage." For instance, assume that the plaintiff is incredibly wealthy, not because of his or her own merit, but only through a privileged birth. The defendant, by contrast, is hopelessly poor due to a disadvantaged birth. If the defendant carelessly injures the plaintiff, and the plaintiff has to spend money on medical treatment, the situation is arguably better from the perspective of distributive justice: the plaintiff now has less undeserved wealth than before. But this is irrelevant to the notion of corrective justice, which requires the defendant to compensate the plaintiff for the loss irrespective of the apparent inequality of their initial positions.

Corrective justice provides a formalist or procedural account of tort law, but not necessarily a substantive one. Theories of corrective justice seek to explain how tort law works, and seldom ask whether this is fair or whether the tort system, itself, is justifiable. As Weinrib writes in *The Idea of Private Law*, *supra*, at 8: "the sole purpose of private law is to be private law." Further, while corrective justice theories generally invoke some concept of wrongdoing, they typically avoid defining what a "wrong" is. Thus, while it can provide a stimulating intellectual debate and help to make the operation of tort law more intelligible, corrective justice theory does not necessarily explain why tort law is an important aspect of the modern legal system or overall compensation scheme.

Rights-based Theory: a variation on corrective justice theory, the so-called "rights-based" approach to tort law also insists on a bilateral relationship between the plaintiff and defendant, and stresses that a plaintiff can only bring a claim if the defendant has violated his or her rights. As R. Stevens explains in *Torts and Rights* (2007) at 2: "The infringement of rights, not the infliction of loss, is the gist of the law of torts." Similarly, A. Beever opines in *Rediscovering the Law of Negligence* (2007) at 218: "The law is not interested in loss *per se,* but only in losses that flow from a violation of the claimant's primary legal rights." Among other things, rights-theorists argue that their approach helps to explain why there is generally no liability in tort for pure omissions (because there is no "right" against the world to compel others to come to one's assistance) and relational economic loss (because the plaintiff has no primary right against the wrongdoer in the circumstances). Like corrective justice theory, the rights-based approach is more of a formalist approach to tort law than a substantive one: rights-theorists tend to be elusive about the sources of primary rights. They do, however, tend to eschew arguments that tort law should serve social or other goals. These are matters of "policy" which the courts lack the political and technical competence to assess.

Civil Recourse: American torts theorists J. Goldberg and B. Zipursky have developed a "civil recourse" theory of tort law, which shares some features with the corrective justice and rights-based approaches. The basis of civil recourse theory is that tort law provides the institutional mechanism by which private individuals who have suffered harm may seek redress against those who were responsible for it. Tort law is thus a civil substitute for more primal modes of retribution: the state, through the courts, provides the opportunity for plaintiffs to seek compensation. Like the corrective justice and rights-based approaches, civil recourse theory stresses the relational structure of tort law. A plaintiff can only use the machinery of the state to obtain damages from the defendant if the defendant has interfered with the plaintiff's rights: committing a wrong against a third party will not do. So, for example, a woman cannot sue in defamation merely because her husband was falsely accused of irresponsible conduct. Although the woman might have suffered some loss as a consequence of the false accusation, her claim must fail because none of *her* rights has been infringed. This aspect of civil recourse theory is sometimes referred to as the principle of "substantive standing," that is, the violation of rights determines which plaintiff(s) are able to sue the defendant for their losses.

Retributive Justice: A tort system based on retributive justice would impose liability on blameworthy actors to penalize, punish or nullify their moral fault. A "pure" theory of retribution is solely concerned with ensuring that wrongful acts are appropriately punished. In contrast, retribution could be imposed not because it is just, but rather as a means of appeasing the plaintiff and society by having the wrongdoer's conduct judged and condemned.

There are two criticisms of retributive theories of modern tort law. First, some authors argue that society should not provide an institutionalized vehicle for retribution. Even if retribution is an appropriate social concern, many feel it should be a matter for the criminal law. These concerns are reflected in the debates over punitive damages, the area of tort law in which concepts of retributive justice most obviously arise.

Second, most tort actions, and in particular negligence cases, rarely involve morally reprehensible conduct that would warrant retribution. Thus, it has been argued that modern tort law cannot be explained or justified on the basis of retributive justice. However, retribution is a powerful notion both on an individual and societal level. The belief that tort law serves a retributive purpose may explain much of the support for the continued existence of the present tort system.

NOTES AND QUESTIONS

1. The most influential modern work on distributive justice is Rawls, *A Theory of Justice* (1971). From his famous starting point of the "veil of ignorance," Rawls derives, *inter alia*, his "Difference Principle," which posits that inequalities can only be justified to the extent that they benefit the least advantaged members of society. Rawls is often contrasted with Nozick's *Anarchy, State and Utopia* (1974), a libertarian work

which argues that the role of the state should be limited to protection against force, theft or fraud. For recent analysis of Rawlsian principles and private law, see Scheffler, "Distributive Justice, the Basic Structure and the Place of Private Law" (2015) 35:2 O.J.L.S. 213.

2. Libertarian theories of tort law rest on notions of ownership and the belief that individuals have complete dominion over themselves and the activities they undertake. If those activities cause losses to others, then those losses are as much the "property" of the actors as any benefits of the activity would be. Thus, libertarian theories of tort law tend to focus on causation and favour strict liability for the consequences of one's activities. See Coleman & Ripstein, "Mischief and Misfortune" (1995) 41 McGill L.J. 91.

3. Cases on "gendered earnings" provide an example of how tort law can serve the interests of distributive justice. For an overview and criticism, see McInnes, "The Gendered Earnings Proposal in Tort Law" (1988) 77 Can. Bar Rev. 152. Can you think of other ways that tort law can foster distributive justice? Is this a legitimate goal for tort law? See Keren-Paz, "An Inquiry into the Merits of Distribution Through Tort Law: Rejecting the Claim of Randomness" (2003) 16 C.J.L.J. 91. Further, in *Torts, Egalitarianism and Distributive Justice* (2007), T. Keren-Paz argues that tort compensation should be awarded at average income levels, rather than on the basis of *restitutio in integrum*, in order to reduce the gap between rich and poor. Given the relatively small number and randomness of tort claims, would this proposal make any noticeable difference in rectifying societal wealth inequality? See also Gardner, "What is Tort Law For? Part 2. The Place of Distributive Justice" in Oberdiek, ed., *Philosophical Foundations of the Law of Torts* (2014) 335.

4. Distributive justice theories can also be applied to tort doctrine itself. That is, rather than examining the distribution of benefits and burdens within society generally, they can be used to examine the distribution of the benefits and burdens of risky, but valuable activities. See Keating, "Distributive and Corrective Justice in the Tort Law of Accidents" (2000) 74 S. Cal. L. Rev. 193.

5. The correlativity aspect of corrective justice theory stresses that tort law is aimed at putting matters right between two parties. Even though wrongful acts could be addressed through criminal or regulatory law, and wrongful losses could be compensated through alternative compensation schemes, only tort law combines the retribution for wrongs and compensation for losses in a unitary whole. Do you think that an element of "justice" would be sacrificed if litigation between the parties were not permitted?

6. As indicated, corrective justice is a popular topic for tort theorists and the literature is vast. For a selection of arguments both for and against corrective justice theory, see Fletcher, "Fairness and Utility in Tort Theory" (1972) 85 Harv. L. Rev. 537; Perry, "The Moral Foundations of Tort Law" (1992) 77 Iowa L. Rev. 449; Keating, "Reasonableness and Rationality in Negligence Theory" (1996) 48 Stan. L. Rev. 311; Perry, "The Distributive Turn: Mischief, Misfortune and Tort Law" in Bix, ed., *Analyzing Law: New Essays in Legal Theory* (1998) 141; Ripstein, *Equality, Responsibility, and the Law* (1999); Coleman, *The Practice of Principle: In Defence of a Pragmatist Approach to Legal Theory* (2001); Walt, "Eliminating Corrective Justice"

(2006) 92 Va. L. Rev. 1311; Gardner, "What is Tort Law For? Part 1: The Place of Corrective Justice" (2011) 30 J.L. & Phil. 1; Weinrib, *Corrective Justice* (2012); Steel, "Private Law and Justice" (2013) 33 O.J.L.S. 607; Dorfman, "Private Law Exceptionalism? Part I: A Basic Difficulty with the Structural Arguments from Bipolarity and Civil Recourse" (2016) 35 Law and Philosophy 165; and Shaunessy, "A Matter of Choice: Rethinking Legal Formalism's Account of Private Law Rights" (2017) 37:1 O.J.L.S. 163.

7. The body of literature on the rights-based approach to tort law has grown extensively in recent years. See for example Stevens, *Torts and Rights* (2007); Beever, *Rediscovering the Law of Negligence* (2007); Neyers, "Rights-based justifications for the tort of unlawful interference with economic relations" (2008) 28 L.S. 215; Ripstein, "As If It Never Happened" (2007) 48 William and Mary L. Rev. 1957; Perry, "The Role of Duty of Care in a Rights-Based Theory of Negligence Law" in Robertson & Tang, eds., *The Goals of Private Law* (2009) 79; Neyers, "The Economic Torts as Corrective Justice" (2009) 17 Torts L.J. 162; and Nolan & Robertson, eds., *Rights and Private Law* (2012).

There is an equally extensive body of criticism of the rights-based approach. These criticisms suggest, for instance, that the rights-based approach does not accurately reflect how judges actually decide cases, that it provides no principled explanation for why some rights are protected by tort law and not others, and that it seeks only to protect the existing distribution of wealth. See for example Cane, "Corrective Justice and Correlativity in Private Law" (1996) 16 O.J.L.S. 471; Murphy, "Rights, Reductionism and Tort Law" (2008) 28 O.J.L.S. 393; Dagan, "The Limited Autonomy of Private Law" (2008) 56 Am. J. Comp. L. 809; Witting, "The House that Dr Beever Built: Corrective Justice, Principle and the Law of Negligence" (2008) 71 Mod. L. Rev. 621; Bagshaw, "Tort Law, Concepts and What Really Matters" in Robertson & Tang, *supra* at 239; Priel, "That Can't Be Rights: Review of Robert Stevens's *Torts and Rights*" (2011) 2 Jurisprudence 227; Priel, "Torts, Rights, and Right-Wing Ideology" (2011) 19 Torts L.J. 1; and Cornford, "Public Authority Liability and the Heteronomy of Tort Law" (2013) 21 Torts L.J. 16.

Another group of scholars argues not against the rights-based approach, but rather that the rights-based approach does not provide a full explanation of tort law in theory or practice. See Hedley, "Looking Outward or Looking Inward? Obligations Scholarship in the Early 21st Century" in Robertson & Tang, *supra*; Robertson, "Rights, Pluralism and the Duty of Care" in Nolan & Robertson, *supra*; McBride, "Rights and the Basis of Tort Law" in Nolan & Robertson, *supra*; and Shmueli, "Legal Pluralism in Tort Law Theory: Balancing Instrumental Theories and Corrective Justice" (2015) 48:3 U. Mich. J. L. Reform 745. See also Robinette, "Can There Be a Unified Theory of Torts? A Pluralist Suggestion from History and Doctrine" (2005) 43 Brandeis L.J. 369.

8. Civil recourse theory was and remains the brainchild of J. Goldberg and B. Zipursky. See Zipursky, "Rights, Wrongs, and Recourse in the Law of Torts" (1998) 51 Vand. L. Rev. 1; Zipursky, "Civil Recourse, Not Corrective Justice" (2003) 91 Geo. L.J. 695; Goldberg & Zipursky, "Civil Recourse Revisited" (2011) 39 Fla. St. U.L. Rev. 341; Goldberg & Zipursky, "Rights and Responsibility in the Law of Torts" in Nolan & Robertson, *supra*; Goldberg & Zipursky, "Civil Recourse Defended: A Reply to Posner, Calabresi, Rustad, Chamallas, and Robinette" (2013) 88 Ind. L.J.

569. See also Gold, "The Taxonomy of Civil Recourse" (2011) 39 Fla. St. U.L. Rev. 65; Oman, "The Honor of Private Law" (2011) 80 Fordham L. Rev. 31; Hershovitz, "Corrective Justice for Civil Recourse Theorists" (2011) 39 Fla. St. U.L. Rev. 107; and Oberdiek, "Method and Morality in the New Private Law of Torts" (2012) 125 Harv. L. Rev. F. 189.

For criticisms of civil recourse theory, see Stapleton, "Evaluating Goldman and Zipursky's Civil Recourse Theory" (2006) 75 Fordham L. Rev. 1529; Robinette, "Why Civil Recourse Theory is Incomplete" (2010) 78 Tenn. L. Rev. 431; Hylton, "New Private Law Theory and Tort Law: A Comment" (2011) 125 Harv. L. Rev. F. 173; Calnan, "The Distorted Reality of Civil Recourse Theory" (2012) 60 Clev. St. L. Rev. 159; Posner, "Instrumental and Noninstrumental Theories of Tort Law" (2013) 88 Ind. L.J. 469; Calabresi, "Civil Recourse Theory's Reductionism" (2013) 88 Ind. L.J. 449; and Chamallas, "Beneath the Surface of Civil Recourse Theory" (2013) 88 Ind. L.J. 527.

9. Can any single theory truly capture the goals and structure of a heterogeneous body of law like torts? How well do you think any of the above theories reflects the way that judges decide cases? See Hedley, "Is Private Law Meaningless?" (2011) 64 Current Leg. Probs. 89; Goudkamp & Murphy, "The Failure of Universal Theories of Tort Law" (2015) 21:2 Legal Theory 47; and Hershovitz, "The Search for a Grand Unified Theory of Tort Law" (2016) 130 Harv. L. Rev. 942.

10. As indicated, tort law's most obvious vehicle for retributive justice is punitive damages. However, in the last decade, tort reforms in the United States have sought to reduce or cap punitive damage awards to halt what is perceived as a litigation crisis. See generally Daniels & Martin, "The Strange Success of Tort Reform" (2004) 53 Emory L.J. 1225; Carlson, "Tort Reform: Redefining the Role of the Court and the Jury" (2005) 47 S. Tex. L. Rev. 245; and Galligan, "U.S. Supreme Court Tort Reform: Limiting State Power to Articulate and Develop Tort Law — Defamation, Preemption, and Punitive Damages" (2006) 74 U. Cin. L. Rev. 1189. But see Hemphill, "Smoke Screens and Mirrors; Don't be Fooled Get the Economic Facts Behind Tort Reform and Punitive Damages Limitations" (1997) 23 T. Marshall L. Rev. 143; and Boulton, "The Farmer's Retort to Tort Reform: Why Legislation to Limit or Eliminate Punitive Damages Hurts the Agricultural Sector" (2004) 9 Drake J. Agric. L. 415.

Australian legislatures have similarly limited the availability of punitive or "exemplary" damage awards. In particular, punitive damages are now prohibited in negligence claims for personal injury. See *Civil Liability Act 2002* (N.S.W.), s. 21; and *Civil Liability Act 2003* (Qld.), s. 52. See also Commonwealth of Australia, *Review of the Law of Negligence: Final Report* (2002) at 224-227, which recommends abolishing both punitive and aggravated damages.

11. Some authors have argued for an increased role for punitive damages in tort law. For example, I. Englard argues that, given the deplorable state of public enforcement, the self-initiated private action for punitive damages has an important role to play in achieving society's penal goals: "The System Builders: A Critical Appraisal of Modern American Tort Theory" (1980) 9 J. Legal Stud. 27. See also Galanter & Luban, "Poetic Justice: Punitive Damages and Legal Pluralism" (1993) 42 Am. U.L. Rev. 1393; Markel, "Retributive Damages: A Theory of Punitive Damages

as Intermediate Sanction" (2009) 94 Cornell L. Rev. 239; Zipursky, "*Palsgraf,* Punitive Damages, and Preemption" (2012) 125 Harv. L. Rev. 1757; Sebok, "Normative Theories of Punitive Damages: The Case of Deterrence" in Oberdiek, *supra*; and Sommers, "The Psychology of Punishment and the Puzzle of Why Tortfeasor Death Defeats Liability for Punitive Damages" (2015) 124:4 Yale L.J. 1294.

(e) FEMINIST PERSPECTIVES

Tort law has not received as much attention from feminist legal scholars as areas where women's concerns are more obvious (*e.g.* family law, human rights, employment law). Nevertheless, feminist torts scholarship has increased in recent years and addresses a wide range of issues. A useful summary can be found in Bender, "An Overview of Feminist Torts Scholarship" (1993) 78 Cornell L. Rev. 575.

First, some feminist scholars examine existing issues in tort law that are of particular concern to women. For example, claims for wrongful conception and birth have a disproportionate effect on women, and the issue of liability for injuries suffered *in utero* has particular implications for the autonomy of pregnant women. Further, the litigation surrounding pharmaceutical products like DES and Dalkon Shield necessarily raises issues about women's reproductive health.

Second, feminist scholars have begun to create what they describe as a "woman-centred" perspective on the law of torts. The major premise of this work is that the body of judge-made law and critical commentary on torts has assumed a false posture of inclusiveness and neutrality. It is asserted that the common law of torts has, at best, ignored the unique concerns of women and, at worst, contributed to their position of social inequality.

Feminist criticism of tort law has both analytical and normative aims. One strand addresses the "gendered" nature of specific legal concepts and standards. For example, it is argued that tort law concepts like "injury" and "harm" are determined on a patriarchal basis: there is greater concern for losses traditionally claimed by men (property damage, economic loss) than for those traditionally claimed by women (sexual abuse, harassment, emotional distress). Indeed, claims for domestic abuse were historically barred by the doctrine of spousal immunity and, even where this bar was removed, were sometimes seen as non-tortious or distasteful to litigate.

Another important task is the critical evaluation of tort concepts such as the "reasonable man" standard of prudent action. In "A Lawyer's Primer on Feminist Theory and Tort" (1988) 38 J. Legal Educ. 3, L. Bender argues that "reasonableness" is a concept which has disguised and suppressed the seemingly divergent standards by which men and women evaluate conduct. The re-naming of the reasonable man as the reasonable person, Bender further asserts, should not be taken to indicate that the courts have come to accept a less male-centred view of the negligent blameworthiness (or not) of particular actions.

In a similar line of discourse, some feminist scholars have advocated a "reasonable woman" standard for certain types of claims, especially workplace sexual harassment: the level of workplace sexual innuendo acceptable to a reasonable man might not be acceptable to a reasonable woman. Other scholars suggest that, if the reasonable person test drew more heavily on feminine values like care, compassion and responsibility, the current cost-benefits calculus could be replaced by a more humane standard of care.

At the same time, feminist tort scholars are also interested in the larger social and moral implications of the tort system for women. Common points of concern include the undervaluation of women's work, as reflected in damage awards for lost earning capacity, and the minimization of the psychological harms suffered by women in cases of sexual battery, workplace harassment, or the loss of a loved one. Finally, on a more pragmatic basis, some scholars have lamented the difficulties encountered by female plaintiffs in persuading the largely male-dominated judiciary of the harms they have suffered.

NOTES AND QUESTIONS

1. Feminist legal historians have described the role of gender ideology in historical tort doctrines, particularly in the reluctance to award damages for so-called "nervous shock." See Chamallas & Kerber, "Women, Mothers, and the Law of Fright: A History" (1990) 88 Mich. L. Rev. 814; Welke, *Recasting American Liberty* (2001); Vines, San Roque & Rumble, "Is 'nervous shock' still a feminist issue? The duty of care and psychiatric injury in Australia" (2010) 18 Tort L. Rev. 9; Bitton, "Liability of Bias: A Comparative Study of Gender-Related Interests in Negligence Law" (2010) 16 Ann. Surv. Int. & Comp. L. 63; and van Rijswijk, "Neighbourly Injuries: Proximity in Tort Law and Virginia Woolf's Theory of Suffering" (2012) 20 Fem. Leg. Stud. 39. On the difficulties of claiming damages for emotional distress within intimate relationships, see Nicola, "Intimate Liability: Emotional Harm, Family Law, and Stereotyped Narratives in Interspousal Torts" (2013) 19 Wm. & Mary J. Women & L. 445.

2. For an illustration of the difficulties faced by women making sex-based complaints in the tort system, see *Waters v. Metropolitan Police Commissioner*, [2000] 1 W.L.R. 1607 (H.L.). The plaintiff, a female police officer, alleged that she had been raped by a fellow officer while off duty. She filed a complaint with senior officers, but the ensuing investigation did not lead to charges. On account of her complaint, the plaintiff's coworkers subjected her to continued bullying, aggression, offensive or pornographic literature, and job-related sabotage. The plaintiff claimed, *inter alia*, in negligence against the Police Commissioner for breaching his duty, as employer, to not cause foreseeable injury to her. After a lengthy court battle in which her claims were struck out as "doomed to fail" by an Industrial Tribunal, the High Court and the Court of Appeal, the House of Lords finally allowed the plaintiff's claim to proceed. See the analysis of *Waters* in Conaghan, "Law, Harm and Redress: a Feminist Perspective" (2002) 22 L.S.319.

3. Some feminist scholars have argued that a woman-centred tort law would be more likely to adopt a duty to rescue, due to a preference for values like interconnectedness, responsibility and safety over the "masculine" values of autonomy, profit and efficiency. Do you agree? See Bender, "A Lawyer's Primer on Feminist Theory and Tort" (1988) 38 J. Legal Educ. 3 at 33-36; and Steele, "Duty of Care and Ethic of Care: Irreconcilable Difference?" in Richardson & Rackley, eds., *Feminist Perspectives on Tort* (2012) 14. But see Posner, "Conservative Feminism"

[1989] U. Chicago Legal F. 191 at 213-14; and McClain, "'Atomistic Man' Revisited: Liberalism, Connection, and Feminist Jurisprudence" (1992) 65 S. Cal. L. Rev. 1171.

4. On the application of the "reasonable woman" standard in sexual harassment litigation, see Conaghan, "Tort Law and the Feminist Critique of Reason" in Bottomley, ed., *Feminist Perspectives on the Foundational Subjects of Law* (1996) 47. But see McGinley, "Reasonable Men?" (2012) 45 Conn. L. Rev. 1 which argues for a more universal standard that takes into account not only the victim's identity but also the workplace and social context in which the alleged harassment occurs. See also Agostino, "The Reasonable Woman Standard's Creation of the Reasonable Man Standard: The Ethical and Practical Implications of the Two Standards and Why they Should be Abandoned" (2017) 41:2 J. Legal Prof. 339.

5. Is there such a thing as a universal standard of reasonable behaviour, whether male or female? Is it preferable to recognize diversity in outlook and experience, and to adapt the standard of care depending on the particular context? See Moran, *Rethinking the Reasonable Person: an Egalitarian Reconstruction of the Objective Standard* (2003); and Moran, "The Reasonable Person: A Conceptual Biography in Comparative Perspective" (2010) 14 Lewis & Clark L. Rev. 1233. See also Miller & Perry, "The Reasonable Person" (2012) 87 N.Y.U.L. Rev. 323.

6. What aspects of the damages calculation are potentially unfair to women? See Cassels, "Damages for Lost Earning Capacity: Women and Children Last!" (1992) 71 Can. Bar. Rev. 445; Adjin-Tettey, "The Marginalizing Effect of Deductibility of Past Welfare Benefits from Compensation for Personal Injury" in Rodgers, Ruparelia & Bélanger-Hardy, eds., *Critical Torts* (2009) 37; Graycar, "Damaging Stereotypes: the Return of 'Hoovering as a Hobby'" in Richardson & Rackley, *supra*; and Grant, "Judging gender in tort thresholds" (2016) 25:1 Griffith L. Rev. 104. This issue is discussed in Chapter 18.

7. See generally Chamallas & Wriggins, *The Measure of Injury: Race, Gender and Tort Law* (2010), which examines various tort doctrines and practices that adversely affect women and racial minorities. These include the failure to recognize certain gender-related injuries, such as reproductive injury and sexual exploitation, and limited non-pecuniary damages for pain and suffering or emotional harm. The authors also critique the general lack of liability insurance coverage for violent intentional torts, which ultimately disadvantages women who seek to claim for domestic or other gender-related violence. See also Bitton, "Transformative Feminist Approach to Tort Law: Exposing, Changing, Expanding — The Israeli Case" (2014) 25 Hastings Women's L.J. 221; and Chamallas, "Feminist Theory and Tort Law" in West & Bowman, eds., *Research Handbook on Feminist Jurisprudence* (2019).

8. There is a growing literature on the discriminatory effects of tort law's treatment of interferences with reproductive freedom. For more recent discussion, see Priaulx, *The Harm Paradox: Tort Law and the Unwanted Child in an Era of Choice* (2007); Adjin-Tettey, "Claims of Involuntary Parenthood: Why the Resistance?" in Neyers, Chamberlain & Pitel, eds., *Emerging Issues in Tort Law* (2007) 85; Rodgers, "A Mother's Loss is the Price of Parenthood: The Failure of Tort Law to Recognize Birth as Compensable Reproductive Injury" in Rodgers, Ruparelia & Bélanger-Hardy, eds., *Critical Torts* (2009) 161; and Abrams, "Distorted and Diminished Tort

Claims for Women" (2013) 34 Cardozo L. Rev. 1955. See also the opinion of Lady Justice Hale in *Parkinson v. St. James and Seacroft University Hospital NHS Trust*, [2001] EWCA Civ 530 at paras. 63-71, in which she personally recounts the physical and psychological effects of pregnancy and childbirth, including the restrictions on personal autonomy it entails.

3. The No-Fault Alternatives

(a) INTRODUCTION

No-fault accident compensation plans are designed to compensate victims of accidents. These schemes are usually a form of first-party insurance under which victims are compensated by their own insurers for their own losses. In contrast, liability insurance covers insured individuals for liability they incur to others. The term "no-fault" indicates only that the victim need not prove fault of another to obtain compensation, and that the victim's compensation does not depend generally on his or her own conduct having been blameless. Moreover, no-fault compensation has no impact on the significance of the parties' fault for other purposes. For example, a reckless or impaired driver may still be subject to criminal prosecution.

It is misleading to describe no-fault insurance as an alternative to tort law. Tort law purports to achieve other goals than accident compensation. No-fault is premised on isolating compensation from other goals, such as deterrence or punishment. Typically, the compensatory goals of tort law are different from those under no-fault schemes. The purpose of no-fault is to make compensation more widely and swiftly available to all victims of accidents.

In theory, tort law could co-exist unmodified with no-fault plans, much as it coexists with other forms of first-party insurance. In practice, the broader coverage of no-fault tends to be funded in part from restrictions on traditional tort rights. This is usually done by restricting the right to sue to the victims of relatively serious injuries and by curtailing the right to recover for non-pecuniary loss.

There is no such thing as a typical no-fault insurance plan. The activities covered by the schemes vary from jurisdiction to jurisdiction. The degree to which they replace the victim's right to maintain a common law tort action also differs. Some are administered by government agencies and others by private insurers. The schemes may be funded by general tax revenue or by levies on the participants in the plan. These categories are not mutually exclusive.

Comprehensive no-fault plans, which provide compensation for all accident losses, are relatively rare. Activity-specific compensation plans are far more common, such as those that deal exclusively with employment or automobile accidents.

A "pure" no-fault plan abolishes all tort actions for personal injuries within the scope of the plan. Victims of accidents are paid compensation entirely from the plan. This is the basis upon which most workers' compensation systems operate. It is also an essential feature of Quebec's government-run compensation program for personal injuries caused by automobile accidents.

Many no-fault plans are what J. O'Connell and R. Henderson describe in *Tort Law, No-Fault and Beyond* (1975) as either "add-on" or "modified" plans. The add-on plans provide some no-fault coverage without eroding the right to sue in negligence. Injured persons are entitled to compensation up to the no-fault policy limit for pecuniary loss, regardless of their own fault or ability to sue another party. The injured persons may also sue in tort, subject to provisions to prevent double recovery. In some American states, no-fault automobile insurers have a right to reimbursement if the injured person collects from the defendant. In most Canadian provinces, the no-fault fund is the primary source, in that amounts received through the no-fault scheme are deducted from the tortfeasor's liability.

"Modified" plans are similar, but they impose some limitations upon the victim's right to maintain a tort action. In some instances, the right to sue for pecuniary damages is retained, while the right to sue for non-pecuniary damages is severely restricted. For example, the right to sue for pain and suffering might be limited to individuals who have suffered at least $1,000 in medical expenses. The point at which this threshold is placed has been a source of concern. It is argued that such fixed criteria provide an incentive to increase medical bills. Thresholds limiting the right to sue to certain types of injuries or to injuries that necessitate missing work for a specified number of days are also common. Other modified plans abolish not only the right to sue for pain and suffering, but also the right to sue for pecuniary losses that are provided for by the no-fault coverage.

These various plans can be administered either by a government agency or by private insurance companies. Whether public or private, the schemes can be compulsory or voluntary. There are a number of possible funding mechanisms for no-fault plans, and each funding alternative would have different deterrent and loss allocation effects. Although a no-fault scheme can incorporate whatever compensatory principles are desired, most set modest compensatory goals. Proponents of comprehensive no-fault schemes prefer rapid and adequate compensation for all accident victims, rather than "full" compensation for the more limited class of successful plaintiffs.

(b) NO-FAULT ACCIDENT COMPENSATION IN NEW ZEALAND

In 1974, New Zealand abolished all statutory and common law damage claims arising out of accidental death and personal injury. In their place, the government created a comprehensive no-fault accident compensation scheme. The scheme, administered by a Crown Corporation, was designed to provide compensation for all injuries except those that were deliberately self-inflicted. The legislation is lengthy and complicated and the following is a brief summary.

The scheme was comprehensive, governing all accidental injuries, regardless of how or where the accident occurred. Although the injured party simply applied to the Crown Corporation, for internal purposes the payment was drawn from one of three separate funds. The Earner's Fund covered both employees and self-employed persons, and was financed by levies against employers and the self-employed. The Motor Vehicle Fund covered all victims of automobile accidents, and was financed by levies on owners and drivers of motor vehicles. The Supplementary Fund, which was financed by general taxation, covered all other cases, such as non-earners injured otherwise than by motor vehicles. The Corporation was empowered to vary the levies against employers or drivers according to the individual's safety record, but this power was seldom used. Claims were assessed by agents of the Corporation. There were numerous provisions for appeal, first within the Corporation, then to an independent agency, and ultimately to the courts in some cases.

Since its inception in 1974, both the boundaries and the costs of New Zealand's Accident Compensation Scheme have grown steadily. As a consequence, there have been at least 13 major reviews of the plan. In 1992, the New Zealand government substantially amended the original legislation. The main aim of the reform was to create a more tightly controlled and cost efficient system that respected the objectives of the 1974 plan. This was to be achieved by a combination of measures, including narrower definitions of compensable injury and the elimination of lump sum compensation for non-economic loss. In 2001, the government introduced the *Injury Prevention, Rehabilitation and Compensation Act*, which again redefined personal injury and, in an effort to curb claims arising from alleged medical malpractice, provided a limited definition of the "medical misadventure" for which victims could claim through the fund. This definition was again reformed in 2005, substituting the term "treatment injury" and providing more detailed criteria about which injuries arising from medical care would be covered. The 2005 reforms were aimed at improving patient care by encouraging the reporting of treatment injuries and downplaying any notions of "fault" by healthcare providers. The result has been an increase in the number of claims for less severe treatment injuries, but an improvement in the efficiency with which those claims are processed. A helpful review of the reforms is provided in Oliphant, "Beyond Misadventure: Compensation for Medical Injuries in New Zealand" (2007) 15 Med. L. Rev. 357.

The reforms of the last two decades appear to have increased certainty in the scope and cost of the scheme. However, the internal consistency and adequacy of accident compensation, especially for very seriously injured claimants, continues to be debated. To some extent, the reforms are driven by the political and financial climate of the day and the pressure of various stakeholders. Nevertheless, New Zealand apparently remains committed to the principles of "community responsibility" and "comprehensive entitlement" upon which the compensation scheme was originally founded.

NOTES AND QUESTIONS

1. For an assessment of the New Zealand Accident Compensation Scheme, see Keith, "Compensation in New Zealand 1974-1991," in Wall, ed., *Proceedings of the Medical Defence Union Conference* (1991); Palmer, "New Zealand's Accident Compensation Scheme: Twenty Years On" (1994) 44 U.T.L.J. 223; McLay, ed., *The Future of Accident Compensation* (2004); and Todd, "Forty Years of Accident Compensation in New Zealand" (2011) 28 T.M. Cooley L. Rev. 189. See also the papers from an "Accident Compensation Symposium" collected in [2008] N.Z.L. Rev. 3-140.

2. Several notable exceptions to New Zealand's plan are exemplary (punitive) damages, damages for secondary trauma (*i.e.* psychiatric harm suffered by witnesses to an accident), and injuries caused by gradual processes unrelated to work. Due to the limited definitions of "personal injury" and "accident," other potential exclusions include: psychiatric harm arising from a "near miss" (not actual impact); certain negligently caused diseases (*e.g.* infecting one's partner with HIV); heart attacks and strokes caused by negligent or intentional conduct outside the spheres of employment

or medical misadventure; and chronic pain syndrome. Further, the common law of tort survives for the protection of other interests (*e.g.* defamation, wrongful imprisonment, damage to property and economic interests). Thus, it is misleading to suggest that the New Zealand accident compensation scheme has "eliminated" tort actions in that country. See generally Cheer *et al.*, *The Law of Torts in New Zealand*, 7th ed. (2016).

For an explanation of the Accident Compensation Scheme's relationship to the common law in cases of injuries related to medical treatment, including claims based on the failure to obtain informed consent, see Todd, "Treatment Injury in New Zealand" (2011) 86 Chi.-Kent L. Rev. 1169. In *Allenby v. H*, [2012] NZSC 33 the New Zealand Supreme Court concluded, contrary to previous case law, that unwanted pregnancy resulting from a failed sterilization procedure qualified as a "physical injury" that could be compensated under the Accident Compensation Scheme.

3. J. O'Connell states in "Elective No-Fault Liability Insurance for All Kinds of Accidents: A Proposal" [1973] Ins. L.J. 495 at 497-98: "Much more than half — 56 cents — of every auto insurance premium dollar is chewed up in administrative and legal costs. This is in contrast to administrative and legal expenses of 3 cents for Social Security, 7 cents for Blue Cross, and 17 cents for Health and Accident plans." The administrative cost of the New Zealand plan is 10-12% of the total amount paid into it. Can you explain or justify the marked differences in the costs of operating these plans? What are the implications of these data? Unfortunately, these data have not been comprehensively updated since the no-fault debate reached its peak in the 1970s. Nevertheless, some American data suggest that the administrative costs of the tort system have not changed significantly. See Council of Economic Advisers, *Who Pays for Tort Liability Claims? An Economic Analysis of the U.S. Tort Liability System* (2002). See also Cane, *Atiyah's Accidents, Compensation and the Law*, 7th ed. (2006) at 397.

4. What was the rationale for the three separate compensation funds in the New Zealand plan? How does this compare to a wholly tax-funded system? Why did the legislature provide for differential levies against certain industries, employers and drivers?

5. What are the advantages and disadvantages of having a fixed schedule and statutory maximums for lost earnings and non-pecuniary damage awards? Which groups benefit the most from the principles that govern the common law assessment of damages?

6. Liability insurance is compulsory for Canadian automobile owners and is commonly carried by all persons likely to be exposed to negligence liability. Compared to the New Zealand plan, how efficient is liability insurance at spreading losses and ensuring that funds will be available? Would you favour making liability insurance compulsory for activities other than driving? What effect might such compulsory liability insurance and/or comprehensive no-fault accident compensation plan have on the notion of the personal responsibility of individuals? See Solender, "New Zealand's No-Fault Accident Compensation Scheme Has Some Unintended Consequences: A Caution to U.S. Reformers" (1993) 27 Int'l Law. 91.

7. The most common activity-specific schemes are the Workers' Compensation and no-fault automobile insurance plans, which are discussed below. Another activity-specific no-fault scheme was recommended for Canadian victims of medical malpractice in Prichard (Chair), *Liability and Compensation in Health Care* (1990). The report stated that over $200 million were paid out each year on direct insurance costs, but that only 250 victims, fewer than 10% of the total number of malpractice victims, received any compensation from the tort system. The report nevertheless called for retention of the tort system for the purpose of deterrence. See also Weiler, "The Case for No-Fault Medical Liability" (1993) 52 Md. L. Rev. 908; Brown, "Eight Questions About No-Fault Compensation for Blood-Product Harm" (2000) 18 Windsor Y.B. Access Just. 217; Tappan, "Medical-Malpractice Reform: Is Enterprise Liability or No-Fault a Better Reform" (2005) 46 B.C.L. Rev. 1095; Hitzhusen, "Crisis and Reform: Is New Zealand's No-Fault Compensation System a Reasonable Alternative to the Medical Malpractice Crisis in the United States?" (2005) 22 Ariz. J. IntT & Comp. L. 649; Barringer *et al.*, "Administrative Compensation of Medical Injuries: A Hardy Perennial Blooms Again" (2008) 33 J. Health Pol. 725; Scottish Government, *Consultation on Recommendations for No-Fault Compensation in Scotland Resulting from Clinical Treatment* (2012); Farrell, "No-Fault Compensation for Medical Injury: Principles, Practice and Prospects for Reform" in Ferguson & Laurie, eds., *Inspiring a Medico-Legal Revolution: Essays in Honour of Sheila McLean* (2014); Barbot, Parizot & Winance, "'No-fault' compensation for victims of medical injuries. Ten years of implementing the French model" (2014) 114 Health Policy 236; and Gibson, "Is it Time to Adopt a No-Fault Scheme to Compensate Injured Patients?" (2016) 47:2 Ottawa L. Rev. 307.

8. While common law jurisdictions have been reluctant to implement a no-fault compensation system for medical malpractice generally, some have adopted limited compensation systems for particular types of injury, such as vaccine-related injury. For discussion, see Murray, "DTP Vaccine Related Injury: An examination of proposed Vaccine Injury Compensation Legislation" (1997) 3 J. Contemp. Health L. & Pol'y 233; Manitoba Law Reform Commission, *Compensation of Vaccine-Damaged Children* (2000); Law Reform Commission of Saskatchewan, *Consultation Paper: Vaccination and the Law* (2007); Henson, "Inoculated Against Recovery: A Comparative Analysis of Vaccine Injury Compensation in the United States and Great Britain" (2007) 5 Tul. J. Comp. & Int'l L. 61; Moreland, "National Vaccine Injury Compensation Program: The Potential Impact of Cedillo for Vaccine Related Autism Cases" (2008) 29 J. Legal Med. 363; Looker & Kelly, "No-fault compensation following adverse events attributed to vaccination: a review of international programmes" (2011) 89 Bull. World Health Organ. 371; and Holland, "Liability for Vaccine Injury: The United States, the European Union, and the Developing World" (2018) 67:3 Emory L.J. 415. No-fault compensation has also been suggested for those injured through medical research: Pike, "Recovering from Research: A No-Fault Proposal to Compensate Injured Research Participants" (2012) 38 Am. J. Law & Med. 7; and Henry, "Moral Gridlock: Conceptual Barriers to No-Fault Compensation for Injured Research Subjects" (2013) 41 J.L. Med. & Ethics 411.

9. It has also been proposed to treat domestic and sexual abuse through a no-fault system. See Brown & Randall, "Compensating the Harms of Sexual and Domestic Violence: Tort Law, Insurance and the Role of the State" (2004) 30 Queen's

L.J. 311. See also Brown, "School Board Liability, the Insurance Crisis and Accident Compensation" (2003) 12 E.L.J. 273.

(c) WORKERS' COMPENSATION

Although no-fault insurance received a great deal of attention toward the end of the last century, the idea is by no means new. Most jurisdictions had no-fault compensation schemes for work-related injuries by the early 20th century. Germany was the first country to establish a comprehensive workers' compensation system, including medical treatment and sick benefits. England established a more modest plan in 1897, and all but six American states had workers' compensation systems by 1920.

British Columbia established a compensation scheme based on the English model in 1902, and most of the other provinces followed suit shortly thereafter. In 1914, Ontario introduced the first Canadian workers' compensation scheme administered by an independent government agency. Similar agencies have since been created in every Canadian jurisdiction.

Workers' compensation boards are public bodies created by statute. Employers and employees governed by the scheme are required to participate. As the title suggests, workers' compensation is an activity-specific scheme which provides compensation for personal injuries that occur in the course of employment. Minor injuries are excluded from most schemes by a requirement that the employee must be disabled beyond the day of the accident to make a claim. In part, the Canadian schemes are "pure" no-fault, because the legislation prohibits employees from suing their employers in tort for personal injuries suffered at work. However, employees have the option of claiming from the fund or bringing a tort action against persons other than their employers. Nevertheless, the vast majority of work-related accident claims are dealt with by workers' compensation boards and not courts.

The damages payable under workers' compensation schemes differ significantly from those awarded in negligence. For example, there is no recovery for pain and suffering or loss of amenities. The statutes classify the worker's injury as "temporary total disability," "temporary partial disability," "permanent total disability," or "permanent partial disability." Statutory guidelines are provided for assessing compensation in each category. For example, workers with a temporary total disability are entitled to 75% of their average weekly earnings, subject to statutory minimums and maximums.

The legislation provides compensation for other special medical expenses, such as the cost of medical attendants and equipment. The board has discretion to authorize expenditures that it deems necessary for a worker's expedient re-entry into the work force. The schemes also provide for benefits in the case of fatal accidents.

NOTES AND QUESTIONS

1. R.C.B. Risk suggests several reasons why workers' compensation plans were initially introduced. First, he indicates that litigation was generally regarded as a nuisance. Second, the notion that every accident involved individual responsibility on the part of either the actor or victim was falling into disfavour. Finally, there was increased social concern with the plight of accident victims. He goes on to provide an

interesting analysis of why employment injuries were singled out for special treatment. See Risk, "This Nuisance of Litigation: The Origins of Workers' Compensation in Ontario" in Flaherty, ed., *Essays in the History of Canadian Law*, vol. 2 (1983) 418. For a historical analysis of workers' compensation in the United States, see Witt, *The Accidental Republic* (2004); and Fishback & Kantor, *A Prelude to the Welfare State: The Origins of Workers' Compensation* (2006).

2. Given the positive experience with workers' compensation, why have the provinces not introduced more comprehensive no-fault insurance programs?

3. Workers may be denied recovery if their injuries are attributable solely to their own serious and wilful misconduct. What is the purpose of this rule? Is it consistent with the overall objectives of the legislation? How does it compare to the provisions of New Zealand's plan?

4. A contentious issue over the last few decades was whether workers' compensation schemes should provide compensation for mental stress arising out of employment. See for example Troost, "Workers' Compensation and Gradual Stress in the Workplace" (1985) 133 U. Pa. L. Rev. 847; Cook, "Workers' Compensation and Stress Claims: Remedial and Restrictive Application" (1987) 62 Notre Dame L. Rev. 879; Noble, "Workers' Compensation Stress Claims: Is it Really a Brave New World?" (1994) 10 J.L. & Soc. Pol'y 71; Nisbet, "Workers' Compensation and Teacher Stress" (1999) 28 J.L. & Educ. 531; and Lippel & Sikka, "Access to Workers' Compensation Benefits and Other Legal Protections for Work-related Mental Health Problems: A Canadian Overview" (2010) 101 (Suppl 1) CJ.P.H. 516. Are there good reasons to include or exclude such claims from the workers' compensation system?

In 2012, British Columbia amended its *Workers' Compensation Act*, R.S.B.C. 1996, c. 492, s. 5.1 to include compensation for mental disorder caused by traumatic events or significant work-related stressors, provided the disorder is diagnosed by a psychiatrist or psychologist and is not caused by the employer's decision to change the employee's working conditions or to discipline or terminate the employee. Similar provisions were introduced in Ontario in 2017: *Workplace Safety and Insurance Act*, 1997, S.O. 1997, c. 16, Sched. A, s. 13(4).

5. Depending on the industry involved, employers may be required to either contribute to the general workers' compensation fund or provide equal or greater benefits to their workers through private insurance. See for example *Workplace Safety and Insurance Act*, S.O. 1997, c. 16 and its associated regulations: O. Reg. 175/98, Schedules 1 and 2.

(d) NO-FAULT AUTOMOBILE INSURANCE IN CANADA

Apart from workers' compensation, no-fault insurance has had its greatest impact in Canada in the field of automobile accidents. The majority of academic writing about no-fault insurance has focused on automobile accidents, reflecting the importance of the automobile in our society, the staggering number of deaths and injuries which occur on the nation's highways, and the potentially huge number of legal proceedings that automobile crashes could engender.

Saskatchewan introduced the first no-fault automobile accident insurance plan in the English-speaking world in 1946. Similar plans have since been adopted in many other jurisdictions. No-fault automobile accident benefits are now available in every Canadian province, but the plans vary considerably. Coverage for no-fault accident benefits is compulsory in most jurisdictions. The maximum amounts and the duration of the payments differ considerably from province to province. These no-fault benefits are provided by private insurers in most provinces. Only Québec and Manitoba provide something resembling a "pure" no-fault plan. Most of the other provinces have add-on plans that give rise to problems of overlapping compensation. Generally, the no-fault benefits are intended to be the primary source of compensation; plaintiffs can only seek damages in tort if their losses exceed the no-fault benefits.

In 1990, Ontario adopted a modified threshold scheme, administered by private insurers. The legislation was designed to preserve common law tort actions for the comparatively small group of persons who were killed, seriously disfigured or permanently and significantly disabled in car accidents. During the 1990s, successive governments submitted the original no-fault scheme to significant reforms. This tinkering generated extensive litigation regarding the original and reformulated thresholds of private tort actions. Despite these skirmishes over the boundaries of the no-fault scheme, Ontario continues to have a relatively comprehensive no-fault compensation system for automobile accidents.

Saskatchewan's automobile insurance plan is unique: it provides residents with the option of being subject to either the no-fault scheme or the tort law system. By default, everyone is subject to the no-fault plan, which provides comprehensive benefits in the case of a collision, but severely limits claims for pain and suffering. Those wishing to choose the tort system must file a written declaration indicating this desire. Although those subject to tort coverage still receive a basic package of benefits, they are required to sue if they wish to recover additional expenses or pain and suffering. Whatever coverage is in effect at the time of the accident will govern the parties' rights. However, it is the plaintiff's coverage that is potentially the most crucial. For example, even if the at-fault driver has chosen no-fault coverage (and will thus have his or her own injuries covered by the no-fault plan), the at-fault driver can still be sued in tort if the plaintiff has elected for the tort law system.

NOTES AND QUESTIONS

1. Typical no-fault auto schemes do not deal with property damage on a no-fault basis. Does this make sense?

2. For reviews of the no-fault automobile legislation in Ontario, see Brown, "No-Fault Automobile Insurance in Ontario: A Long and Complicated Story" (1998) 66 Assurances 399; and Feldthusen, "Have the Politics of Rate Regulation Produced a Better No-Fault Regime for Ontario" (1998) 39 C. de D. 473. For a national overview, see Solomon *et al.*, "Automobile Insurance, Impaired Driving and Victim Compensation Across Canada" (2005) 12 M.V.R. (5th) 22. See also Kelly, Kleffner & Tomlinson, "First-Party Versus Third-Party Compensation for Automobile Accidents: Evidence from Canada" (2010) 13 Risk Management and Insurance Review 21, which concludes that no-fault automobile insurance systems tend to run at lower cost than fault-based systems, with higher compensation levels for injured drivers.

3. In 1978, Québec abolished entirely the right of traffic accident victims to sue for bodily injury damages. Victims are entitled to recover no-fault compensation from the Regie de l'assurance automobile du Québec, a public carrier. The plan is funded by fees paid by registered owners and drivers of motor vehicles. Benefits are indexed to the consumer price index. Employed workers may recover wage replacement to a maximum gross income of approximately $73,500. There are provisions to address lost earning potential and special provisions for homemakers, the unemployed and students. Limited lump-sum awards for non-pecuniary loss are paid. The Regie operates extensive rehabilitation programs. In 1989, the legislation was amended to allow reduced income replacement for victims detained under a judicial process for an indictable offence committed while driving a motor vehicle. See *Automobile Insurance Act*, R.S.Q. 1989, c. A-25, s. 83.30.

4. Reports on Québec's no-fault system indicate that it provides benefits in a timely and cost-efficient manner. For instance, a 2001 report from SAAQ, the body that administers the no-fault system in Québec, indicated that the first income compensation cheques are issued to accident victims on average 22 days after the receipt of a claim. Moreover, 88 cents out of every dollar are paid toward compensation: SAAQ, *Québec's Automobile Insurance Plan* (2001). See also Kelly, Kleffner & Tomlinson, *supra*.

5. Manitoba's no-fault plan came into force in 1994. The plan is administered by the government-owned Manitoba Public Insurance Corporation. It provides compensation for any bodily injury (including death) caused by an automobile, irrespective of fault. Apart from some limited exceptions regarding non-residents, the right to sue for bodily injury caused by automobiles has been abolished in the province. Motorists can also sue each other to recover any "deductible" amounts. For a review of the legislation, see Schnoor, "No-Fault Automobile Insurance in Manitoba: An Overview" (1998) C. de D. 27. See also *McMillan v. Rural Municipality of Thompson* (1997), 115 Man. R. (2d) 2 (C.A.), where the plaintiffs unsuccessfully alleged that a crash caused by a gap in the road was not "caused by" an automobile and could be the subject of a tort claim against the municipality. A decision in the plaintiff's favour would have seriously undermined the efficiency of the no-fault system, effectively requiring a judicial determination of the proximate cause of every accident.

6. For an academic proposal to allow motorists to select either no-fault or tort coverage, see O'Connell & Joost, "Giving Motorists a Choice Between Fault and No-Fault Insurance" (1986) 72 Va. L. Rev. 61. Should motorists be required to elect their coverage prior to the accident (as in Saskatchewan) or should they be allowed to choose the most beneficial system after the accident? See Brown, "A Choice of Choice: Adding Postaccident Choice to the Menu of Non-fault Models" (1989) 26 San Diego L. Rev. 1095.

7. When assessing the income replacement provisions of the no-fault plans, keep in mind that they are usually based on gross income and that the no-fault benefits themselves are tax free.

8. Based on the earlier discussion of the different types of no-fault schemes, categorize the no-fault automobile plan in your province.

9. Automobile liability insurance has been common, if not compulsory, throughout Canada for some time. Thus, even before the introduction of no-fault plans, there was more comprehensive accident compensation in this area than in most others.

10. Given that most employment accidents and an increasing number of automobile accidents are now dealt with by no-fault insurance, what is the rationale for treating other accident victims differently? What is the rationale for treating accident victims differently from victims of serious illness and disease? See Stapleton, *Disease and the Compensation Debate* (1986).

11. Although Ontario's no-fault auto scheme reduces litigation, legal counsel may still be needed given the three concurrently operating auto injury compensation systems and the disparities in bargaining power between the insurers and injured claimants. See generally Lackman & Firestone, "Ontario Lawyers Still Needed to Negotiate Complex Benefits Web in No-Fault Auto Insurance Scheme" *The Lawyers Weekly* (31 March 1995) 9. See also Sachs, "Dispute Resolution in a Statutory Accident Benefits Compensation Scheme: The Ontario Model" (1994) 16 Adv. Q. 218.

12. A continuing debate regarding no-fault automobile insurance is whether it reduces incentives to drive safely. See for example Kochanowski & Young, "Deterrent Aspects of No-Fault Automobile Insurance: Some Empirical Findings" (1985) 52 J. Risk and Ins. 269; Brown, "Deterrence and No-Fault: The New Zealand Experience" (1985) 73 Cal. L. Rev. 976; Schwartz, "Auto No-Fault and First-Party Insurance: Advantages and Problems" (2000) 73 S. Cal. L. Rev. 611; Cummins, Phillips & Weiss, "The Incentive Effects of No-Fault Automobile Insurance" (2001) 44 J.L. & Econ. 427; and Loughran, *The Effect of No-Fault Auto Insurance on Driver Behavior and Auto Accidents in the United States* (2001). A similar issue is whether no-fault plans increase the number of claims for medical care: Lemstra & Olszynski, "The influence of motor vehicle legislation on injury claim incidence" (2005) 96 C.J.P.H. 65; and Ebrahim *et al.*, "Managing moral hazard in motor vehicle accident insurance claims" (2013) 34 J. Pub. Health Pol'y 320.

13. Given the high degree of government involvement in many Canadian automobile insurance schemes, should disputes about claims and coverage be interpreted with public, rather than private, goals in mind? See Knutsen, "Auto Insurance as a Social Contract: Solving Automobile Insurance Coverage Disputes Through a Public Regulatory Framework" (2011) 48 Alta. L. Rev. 715.

14. The advent of autonomous vehicles raises new problems for liability, including, who is the at-fault party if an autonomous vehicle causes a crash? Is it the manufacturer, the programmer, or someone else? What standard of care should apply? Are these questions better addressed through a tort-based system, or through a no-fault system? See Thomas, "Putting Programmers in the Driver's Seat: State Tort Systems Applied to Autonomous Automobiles" (2016) 93:3 U Det. Mercy L. Rev. 553; and Blunt, "Highway to a Headache: Is Tort-Based Automotive Insurance on a Collision Course with Autonomous Vehicles?" (2017) 53:2 Williamette L. Rev. 107.

REVIEW PROBLEM

Iris earns $1,000 a week (gross) as a graphic artist. She is extremely talented and much sought after in the industry. She is also independently wealthy and notoriously indifferent to her work. This is her first job in two years. Otherwise, she sketches at home, but does not sell her work. She has told co-workers she plans to quit within the year. Her absentee rate is unusually high and she has been cautioned about this by her employer. She was struck by an automobile while crossing the street. It is agreed she will be unable to work for 52 weeks and will be completely recovered thereafter. Under an employee benefit plan, she is entitled to $400 a week in disability benefits to replace lost wages.

Compare how Iris would fare in receiving compensation for loss of income under the no-fault scheme in Ontario and Québec to how she would fare under the scheme in effect in your province. How do these outcomes compare to how she would fare under the lost earning capacity head under a pure tort system? Make the same assessments of how you would fare if you suffered the same injuries as Iris.